W9-BSQ-674

The American Heritage®

Encyclopedia *of* American History

The
AmericanHeritage®

Encyclopedia
of American
History

General Editor
John Mack Faragher

HENRY HOLT AND COMPANY
NEW YORK

Henry Holt and Company, Inc.
Publishers since 1866
115 West 18th Street
New York, NY 10011

Henry Holt® is a registered trademark of
Henry Holt and Company, Inc.

Library of Congress Cataloging-in-Publication Data
The American Heritage encyclopedia of American history / edited by
    John Mack Faragher.
        p.   cm.
    Includes bibliographical references and index.
    ISBN 0-8050-4438-8 (alk. paper)
    1. United States–History–Encyclopedias,   I. Faragher, John
    Mack, 1945-
    E174.A535   1997   97-19097
    973' .003–dc21   CIP

Henry Holt books are available for special promotions and premiums.
For details contact: Director, Special Markets.

First Edition 1998

Designed by Kirchoff/Wohlberg, Inc.

Prepared for Henry Holt and Company, Inc., by Sachem Publishing Associates, Inc.,
P.O. Box 412, Guilford, CT 06437, Stephen P. Elliott, President

Printed in the United States of America
All first editions are printed on acid-free paper. ∞

10 9 8 7 6 5 4 3 2 1

■ CONTENTS

CONTRIBUTORS

Kathryn A. Abbott
Western Kentucky University

Catherine Allgor
Yale University

Stephen Aron
University of California at Los Angeles

Tim Ashwell
Iowa State University

Matthew E. Babcock
Yale University

Lewis V. Baldwin
Vanderbilt University

Hal S. Barron
Harvey Mudd College

Roger Beaumont
Texas A&M University

Daniel R. Beaver
University of Cincinnati

Doron Ben-Atar
Fordham University

Edward Berkowitz
George Washington University

James C. Bradford
Texas A&M University

H. W. Brands
Texas A&M University

T. R. Brereton
Texas A&M University

Lloyd L. Brown
Independent Scholar

Robert V. Bruce
Boston University

W. Fitzhugh Brundage
Queen's University, Ontario

Paul Buhle
Brown University

Jon Butler
Yale University

Robert Campbell
Yale University

Andrew Cayton
Miami University, Ohio

Eileen Ka-May Cheng
Yale University

Robert H. Churchill
Rutgers University

Annie Gilbert Coleman
Quinnipiac College

Kathy J. Cooke
Quinnipiac College

Graham A. Cosmas
U.S. Army Center for Military History

Edward Countryman
Southern Methodist University

John Stuart Cox
Independent Scholar

Donald T. Critchlow
St. Louis University

Barry A. Crouch
Gallaudet University

Laurie Crumpacker
Susquehanna University

Thomas W. Cutrer
Arizona State University

David B. Danbom
North Dakota State University

Darrell Donnell Darrisaw
University of California at Los Angeles

Joseph G. Dawson III
Texas A&M University

Paul Dover
Yale University

R. David Edmunds
Indiana University

Carl J. Ekberg
Illinois State University

Joseph J. Ellis
Mount Holyoke College

Melvin Patrick Ely
College of William and Mary

Leonard W. Engel
Quinnipiac College

Dean Fafoutis
Salisbury State University

John Mack Faragher
Yale University

Michael Fellman
Simon Fraser University

Donald L. Fixico
Western Michigan University

Robert S. Fogarty
Antioch College

Robert P. Forbes
Yale University

Edwin S. Gaustad
University of California at Riverside

James N. Giglio
Southwest Missouri State University

Jay Gitlin
Yale University

Nancy M. Godleski
Yale University

Robert Alan Goldberg
University of Utah

Michael A. Gomez
Spelman College

Sarah H. Gordon
Quinnipiac College

H. Roger Grant
Clemson University

John Robert Greene
Cazenovia College

Louis Haas
Duquesne University

Robert Halasz
Independent Scholar

M. Jeff Hardwick
Yale University

Catherine A. Haulman
Cornell University

Bryan Masaru Hayashi
Yale University

Donald R. Hickey
Wayne State College

Peter Hinks
Yale University

Jesse Hoffnung-Garskof
Princeton University

Albert L. Hurtado
Arizona State University

Ann F. Hyde
Colorado College

Paul Israel
Thomas A. Edison Papers, Rutgers University

Karl Jacoby
Oberlin College

Francis Jennings
Newberry Library, Emeritus

Mark Johnston
Quinnipiac College

John P. Kaminski
Center for the Study of the American
Constitution, University of Wisconsin

James Kessenides
Yale University

Robert C. Khayat
University of Mississippi

Martha J. King
Nathanael Greene Papers, Rhode Island
Historical Society

Denis Kozlov
University of Connecticut

Richard Leffler
Center for the Study of the American
Constitution, University of Wisconsin

David Rich Lewis
Utah State University

Brian McAllister Linn
Texas A&M University

■ INTRODUCTION

The nearly three thousand entries in the AMERICAN HERITAGE **Encyclopedia of American History** comprehensively survey the people and events of America's complex past. This is the first one-volume readers' encyclopedia to give full weight to social history — the most important development in the practice of American history in the past three decades — while retaining detailed coverage of political topics. Readers will find entries on the history of government, law, science, and education; on economic history, immigration, and the labor movement; on the history of the frontier, exploration, and warfare; on religion, art, literature, and many forms of popular cultural expression. There are entries on community and urban history, family life, gender, and popular culture, as well as expansive coverage of ethnic history. Within these pages are biographical sketches of more than a thousand Americans, including hundreds of women, African Americans, and Indians, far more than have ever been included in a one-volume encyclopedia of American history. There are brief biographies of every Supreme Court justice, with entries on the Court's most fundamental rulings. Moreover, this volume is continental in its scope, departing from an Atlantic coastal perspective to include the history of the South and West. Leading historians at the country's top colleges and universities lent their talents to this project, contributing entries that are grounded in the best contemporary historical scholarship.

The AMERICAN HERITAGE **Encyclopedia of American History** has been designed for ease of reference, with entries listed alphabetically. But readers may also use it for deeper exploration and study. Entries are cross-referenced with **See Also** citations at their conclusion. The Bibliographies accompanying longer entries offer a guide to the most recent scholarship. There are several appendixes, including the full text of the Declaration of Independence and the Constitution, and a **Time Line** of American history. And there is an extensive index.

Readers thus may use this book to find not only the answers to particular queries about the nation's history, but as a way of sampling the best of today's thinking about the American past.

John Mack Faragher
Yale University

A

■ **AARON, HENRY ("HANK") (1934-),** baseball player. Born in Mobile, Alabama, Aaron became king of the home-run hitters when he hit his 715th on Apr. 18, 1974, breaking Babe Ruth's record. He spent his entire major-league career with the Braves, first in Milwaukee (1954-65) and then in Atlanta (1966-76), amassing 755 total career home runs. Aaron set more major-league career records than any other player and was inducted into the Baseball Hall of Fame in 1982. He subsequently became an executive with the Braves.
See Also: African Americans; Sports.

■ **ABDUL-JABBAR, KAREEM (1947-),** basketball player. Born Lew Alcindor in New York City, Kareem Abdul-Jabbar played center on the National Collegiate Athletic Association (NCAA) 1967-69 championship teams of the University of California, Los Angeles. He then joined the National Basketball Association (NBA) with the Milwaukee Bucks, earning the Rookie of the Year award for 1969-70. The following year, he was named the league's Most Valuable Player (MVP) and led the Bucks to the championship. After being traded in 1975 to the Los Angeles Lakers, with whom he would win five championships, he converted to Islam and took the name Kareem Abdul-Jabbar, meaning "powerful servant." With his devastating skyhook, he dominated the court, and by the time of his retirement in 1989, Abdul-Jabbar had become the NBA's all-time leading scorer with 38,387 points.
See Also: African Americans; Sports.

■ **ABERNATHY, RALPH DAVID (1926-90),** civil rights leader. He was born in Linden, Alabama. In 1957 Abernathy helped found the Southern Christian Leadership Conference (SCLC) with Martin Luther King, Jr. Following King's assassination in 1968, Abernathy became president of the SCLC and held that position until 1977. After an unsuccessful bid for Congress, he returned to the ministry and the lecture circuit.

Hank Aaron hit his 715th home run on Apr. 8, 1974, breaking Babe Ruth's 1935 record. Aaron's major league career lasted 23 seasons, and in 1982 he was elected to the Baseball Hall of Fame.

See Also: Civil Rights Movement; King, Martin Luther, Jr.; Southern Christian Leadership Conference.

■ **ABNAKI INDIANS.** *See:* Algonquian.

■ **ABOLITIONISM.** *See:* Antislavery Movement.

■ **ABORTION,** practice of terminating a pregnancy. Legal under both colonial and American common law, abortion was tolerated and practiced widely through the mid-19th century. During the middle decades of that century, however, it came under attack. Some lawmakers feared for the safety of women, while some Americans sought to curb what they considered indecent abortion advertising. The most powerful coalition for legal change was the American Medical Association (AMA), which sought to expand its legitimacy and influence through the abortion issue.

Antiabortion laws that were passed during the second half of the 19th century, however, failed to end the practice of abortion. Indeed, abortion remained widespread through the 1930s, although its underground practice put the health of women in danger. Informed by new medical research, many Americans in the late 1950s began to seek a repeal of regulations that outlawed abortion. This in turn spurred a profound shift in the political role of women, as many became publicly vocal about abortion politics in the 1960s. Almost 90 percent of doctors favored the reversal of antiabortion laws, while defenders of antiabortion legislation, for example Christian fundamentalists and Roman Catholics, became more resolute.

The 1973 Supreme Court decision in *Roe v. Wade* determined that a woman had the legal right to terminate her pregnancy before the point when a fetus could live outside the womb. *Roe* initiated an emotional, contentious, and sometimes violent public debate about abortion that cut across political, class, gender, and racial lines and that has continued at all levels of politics to this day. On one side were those who saw abortion as murder, on the other were those who favored a woman's right to control her own reproductive processes.

—GUY NELSON

See Also: Women in American History.
BIBLIOGRAPHY: Brodie, Janet Farrel, *Contraception and Abortion in Nineteenth-Century America* (Cornell Univ. Press 1994); Luker, Kristin, *Abortion and the Politics of Motherhood* (Univ. of California Press 1984).

■ **ABRAMS, CREIGHTON (1914-74),** U.S. Army officer, born in Springfield, Massachusetts. He commanded the 37th Tank Battalion in World War II and was instrumental in relieving Allied forces at Bastogne during the Battle of the Bulge (1944-45). He served as the U.S. commander in Vietnam (1968-72) and Army chief of staff (1972-74).

■ ***ABRAMS* V. *UNITED STATES* (1919),** U.S. Supreme Court case in which the Court upheld (7-2) the sedition conviction of anarchists who published an antiwar pamphlet during World War I. *Abrams* is notable for the dissenting opinion by Justice Oliver Wendell Holmes. Retreating from the "clear and present danger" test he had suggested in *Schenck* v. *United States* (1919), Holmes argued for fewer limits on free speech. Speech, he said, should be restricted only if it posed a "clear and imminent" threat of "substantive evils."

See Also: Holmes, Oliver Wendell, Jr.; Schenck v. United States; Supreme Court.

■ **ACADEMY AWARDS,** annual film honors presented by the Academy of Motion Picture Arts and Sciences. First presented in 1928, the awards have often caused controversy among fans and critics while allowing the industry to promote the movie business and its stars. *Wings*, a World War I air drama, won the first best picture prize. The gold-plated, eight-and-a-half-pound statuettes presented to the winners, known since the early 1930s as "Oscars," were designed by Cedric Gibbons, an art director at Metro-Goldwyn-Mayer and founding member of the Academy who subsequently won 11 Oscars for his work. The Academy has over the years expanded the awards, presenting lifetime achievement and public service Oscars as well as prizes for the past year's films. The presentation ceremonies in Los Angeles, California, were broadcast on network radio (1945-69) and since 1952 have attracted huge audiences on television.

BIBLIOGRAPHY: Osborne, Robert A., *65 Years of the Oscar: The Official History of the Academy Awards* (Abbeville Press 1994).

■ **ACADIANS,** emigrating from the Languedoc region of France in the 17th century, established a culturally distinct society from Cape Breton to northern Maine. Tapping the rich resources of the region, Acadians fished cod on the Grand Banks, lumbered the huge forests covering the peninsula, and farmed the alluvial land along the shoreline. To maximize tillable land, Acadians constructed an elaborate system of dykes that allowed fresh water to flow out of the tidal marshes while preventing sea water from reclaiming cultivated fields. With its tiny population and relatively small importance in French imperial interests, Acadia was nevertheless a strategic prize that passed into British control through the Treaty of Utrecht (Apr. 11, 1713). Four decades later British authorities, convinced that the French Acadians could not be trusted, decided to deport them (1755). The diaspora, commemorated by Longfellow's *Evangeline* (1847), resulted in pockets of Acadian settlement all over North America. The Cajuns of southern Louisiana's bayou are descendants of the 1,000 Acadians who settled there between 1757 and 1779.

■ **ACCULTURATION,** the process of groups or individuals adopting the cultural traits or social patterns of other groups. It is a concept at the heart of American history, which in many ways is the story of the encounter of many diverse peoples. Although they have called it by different terms, Americans have never ceased arguing over the implications of acculturation. Fearing that European immigrants to the United States would "warp and bias" the development of the country, Thomas Jefferson, like most of the leaders of the new nation, insisted on their adoption of Anglo-American cultural patterns. In the early 20th century, with immigration running at high tide, similar concerns about "assimilation" stimulated movements to "Americanize" the foreign born.

Other Americans, however, have expressed themselves in favor of a two-way process of acculturation, with groups learning from each other. "What is the American, this new man?" asked French immigrant Michel Crèvecoeur in 1782. "A strange mixture of blood which you will find in no other country"; in America, "individuals of all nations are melted into a new race of men." For a century or more Americans with these views argued for "the melting pot," but in the late 20th century, this old metaphor has given way to the "mosaic." A number of historians and sociologists point to the fact that, while participating in the common civic life of the nation, ethnic groups have retained much of their distinctive cultural tradition. The optimism of these "cultural pluralists" contrasts with the warnings of conservatives who worry that high levels of Asian and Latino immigration threaten to overwhelm the common culture. Arguments over acculturation are part of the American heritage of diversity.

See Also: Assimilation; Ethnic Groups; Immigration.

BIBLIOGRAPHY: Gordon, Milton M., *Assimilation in American Life* (Oxford Univ. Press 1964).

■ **ACHESON, DEAN (1893-1971),** U.S. secretary of state (1949-53). He was born in Middletown, Connecticut, and graduated from Yale (1915) and Harvard Law School (1918). He served as law secretary (1919-21) to Supreme Court Justice Brandeis and then successfully practiced law in Washington, D.C. Having been appointed undersecretary of the treasury in 1933, he resigned several months later, disagreeing with President Roosevelt's intention to devalue the dollar. At the state department, he served as assistant secretary

In 1947, Dean Acheson warned Congress that if Greece and Turkey were absorbed into the Soviet sphere, then the Middle East, northern Africa, and southern Europe would become Communist "like apples in a barrel infected one by rotten one."

(1941-45) and undersecretary of state (1945-47) before becoming secretary of state in 1949. Acheson played a major role in the elaboration of the Truman Doctrine (1947), a political course aimed at the "containment" of communism within its existing territorial limits. Acheson urged the United States to increase aid to the countries bordering the Communist bloc. He was also instrumental in devising the Marshall Plan to help non-Communist Europe to rebuild after the war, as well as in the creation of the North Atlantic Treaty Organization (1949).

See Also: Cold War; Marshall Plan; North Atlantic Treaty Organization (NATO); Truman Doctrine.

■ **ACID RAIN,** polluted rain harmful to forests and aquatic life. The result of air pollution from vehicles and industries, acid rain was targeted by U.S. environmentalists supporting federal clean air laws in the 1970s.

■ **ACQUIRED IMMUNE DEFICIENCY SYNDROME.** *See: AIDS.*

■ **ACTORS STUDIO,** influential New York City theater school. Lee Strasberg led classes in the Stanislavsky Method, a style of acting that seeks to develop a wide emotional range through empathetic observation, which began in 1948 and inspired a new wave of stage and film realism among young actors.

■ ***ADAIR V. UNITED STATES* (1908),** U.S. Supreme Court case that struck down federal safeguards for organized labor. The Erdman Act (1898) barred employers from firing workers for joining unions. The Court ruled (7-2) that workers and employers were legal equals and that the act interfered with the right of contract. Also the Court declared unions were not engaged in interstate commerce and could not be regulated by Congress. *Adair* was used to overturn state and federal labor legislation until the 1930s.

See Also: Supreme Court.

■ **ADAMS, ABIGAIL SMITH (1744-1818),** wife of the president of the United States. Born in Weymouth, Massachusetts, she married John Adams in 1764. She raised their five children and skillfully

"In the new code of laws which I suppose it will be necessary for you to make," wrote Abigail Adams to her husband, John, in 1776, "I desire you would remember the ladies, and be more generous and favourable to them than your ancestors."

managed their farm while her husband became a successful statesman. Although embarrassed by her lack of formal education, Abigail was a tireless letter writer and an astute thinker whose ideas deeply influenced the political life of the country.

See Also: Adams, John; Women in American History.

■ **ADAMS, ANSEL (1902-84),** photographer of the American West and conservationist. Adams was born in San Francisco, California. In 1916 he took his first trip to Yosemite National Park, a landscape that would inspire many of his later photographs and portfolios and would eventually become his home. In 1932 he helped form the loose association of photographers known as Group f/64, who advocated what they called "straight photography" as an art form. Adams developed the "zone system" for black and white photography, dividing tone values into ten groupings in order to best depict variations in his subjects. He continued to champion photography as a fine art, helping to establish the department of photography at the Museum of Modern Art in New York City in 1940 and starting the first academic department in photography at the California School of Fine Arts in San Francisco in 1946. Adams's love for the natural landscape, and its expression in his photography, led to his 50-year association with the Sierra Club; he received the John Muir Award for work in conservation in 1963.

■ **ADAMS, HANNAH (1755-1831),** self-taught writer and historian, the first American woman to attempt to earn a living from her scholarship. Born in Medford, Massachusetts, she was a religious liberal and published a number of works on religion as well as *A Summary History of New England* (1799).

■ **ADAMS, JOHN (1735-1826),** Revolutionary War leader, vice president (1789-97), and second president of the United States (1797-1801). Adams, born in Braintree, Massachusetts, graduated from Harvard and practiced law in Boston. Although initially a reluctant revolutionary, he opposed the Stamp Act in 1765 but tried to maintain a generally moderate stance. Following the Boston Massacre in 1770, Adams defended the British officers accused of murder. The Boston Tea Party and the Coercive Acts of 1774, however, convinced Adams to openly support independence.

Adams became one of the most active political leaders of the Revolution. He served in both the First and Second Continental Congresses, acted as the U.S. foreign diplomat to raise money for Congress, and, with Benjamin Franklin and John Jay, negotiated the Treaty of Paris in 1783, which ended the conflict with Britain. A political conservative, Adams vigorously favored ratification of the Constitution and became a Federalist.

In 1789, Adams became the nation's first vice president, serving under George Washington for nearly eight years. After ascending to the presidency in 1797, Adams fell from public grace when he signed the Alien and Sedition Acts (1798) and failed to declare war on France after the XYZ Affair (1797-98). He suffered defeat at the hands of Thomas Jefferson in the presidential election of 1800. Embittered and resentful, Adams retired from political life.

Adams published numerous political tracts, but among his best-known writings are his personal correspondence with his wife Abigail during the Revolution and his letters to Thomas Jefferson after their reconciliation in 1812. He and Jefferson died on the same day, the 50th anniversary of the Declaration of Independence. His son John Quincy Adams was the sixth U.S. president.

—GUY NELSON

See Also: *Adams, Abigail Smith; Adams, John Quincy; Adams Family; Alien and Sedition Acts; Declaration of Independence; President of the United States; Revolution, American; Treaty of Paris (1783); Washington, George; XYZ Affair.*

BIBLIOGRAPHY: Ellis, Joseph J., *Passionate Sage: The Character and Legacy of John Adams* (Norton 1993); Ferling, John E., *John Adams: A Life* (Univ. of Tennessee Press 1992).

John Adams, an outspoken leader of the Revolution, became George Washington's vice president and served one term as president (1797-1801).

■ **ADAMS, JOHN QUINCY (1767-1848),** sixth president of the United States (1825-29). He was born in Braintree, Massachusetts, the eldest child

After losing the 1828 presidential election, John Quincy Adams returned to Congress, where his persistent opposition to the "gag rule" and his vindication of the *Amistad* slave captives identified him with the growing antislavery cause.

of Abigail and John Adams. Bred from the cradle to a life of public service, Adams embarked on his first government mission at age 14, as private secretary to Francis Dana, the U.S. representative at the Russian court. He returned to Massachusetts in 1785 and graduated from Harvard College. While in England on a diplomatic mission, Adams married Louisa Catherine Johnson in 1797. Adams was elected to the U.S. Senate as a Federalist (1803) but broke with the Federalists by supporting Thomas Jefferson's embargo. He was ambassador to Russia (1809-14), helped negotiate the Treaty of Ghent (1814) that ended the War of 1812, and was ambassador to Britain (1815-17).

Adams served Pres. James Monroe as secretary of state (1817-25) and excelled in the post. He was responsible for the Adams-Onis Treaty with Spain (1819) that acquired Florida and set the stage for further western expansion, and he played a decisive role in drafting the Monroe Doctrine (1823).

Adams's presidency, however, proved disappointing. He was elected by the House of Representatives after no candidate received an electoral college majority. When he appointed Speaker of the House Henry Clay secretary of state, supporters of Andrew Jackson charged, falsely, that Adams had been elected as a result of a "corrupt bargain" with Clay. Adams lacked popular appeal. His prophetic inaugural address, which envisioned an active federal government, was unpopular with most Americans, and his term consisted of one frustration after another. Like his father, John Quincy Adams was defeated for reelection.

In 1831 he returned to Congress as a representative from Massachusetts and served until his death, gaining great respect for his integrity. Although not an abolitionist, he fought doggedly against the "gag rule" on antislavery petitions, obtaining its repeal in 1844. "Old Man Eloquent" died in the Capitol after suffering a stroke in the House.

—CATHERINE ALLGOR

See Also: Adams-Onis Treaty; Embargo Act; Gag Rule; Ghent, Treaty of; Monroe Doctrine.

BIBLIOGRAPHY: Miller, William Lee, *Arguing about Slavery: The Great Battle in the United States Congress* (Knopf 1996); Nagel, Paul C., *John Quincy Adams: A Public Life, A Private Life* (Knopf 1997).

■ **ADAMS, SAMUEL (1722-1803),** patriot leader during the American Revolution era, born in Boston. He became tax collector in Boston in 1756. In 1765, he was elected to the Massachusetts House of Representatives and became its clerk in 1766. Throughout his career, Adams adhered to an ascetic ideal of virtue that reflected both his Puritan heritage and his republican principles. He mobilized popular opinion against Britain through his mastery of propaganda techniques and his use of the press. Equally important was his participation in political organizations such as the Sons of Liberty. Adams was especially active in securing the passage of the 1768 Massachusetts Circular Letter, which denounced the Townshend Acts (1767). In 1772, he established the Boston Committee of Correspondence, which served as a model for the other colonies.

Adams presided over the mass meeting that preceded the Boston Tea Party in 1773. He has been credited with giving the signal that instigated the tea's destruction, although his exact role in this event remains unclear. Elected to the Continental Congress in 1774, Adams continued to be active in revolutionary politics. His revolutionary fervor coexisted with a firm belief in social order, which became especially evident after the Revolution. Thus, he supported the suppression of Shays's Rebellion in 1786. After his tenure as lieutenant governor of Massachusetts (1789-93), he served as its governor until 1797.

—EILEEN KA-MAY CHENG

See Also: Boston Tea Party; Committees of Correspondence; Declaration of Independence; Revolution, American; Shays's Rebellion; Sons and Daughters of Liberty; Townshend Acts.

BIBLIOGRAPHY: Maier, Pauline, *The Old Revolutionaries: Political Lives in the Age of Samuel Adams* (Knopf 1980); Miller, John C., *Sam Adams: Pioneer in Propaganda* (Stanford Univ. Press 1936).

By mobilizing professionals, craftsmen, and working-men against British taxation policy, Samuel Adams united Boston's social classes into an anti-British alliance. He also helped organize the Sons of Liberty in 1765 and the Boston Tea Party in 1773.

ADAMS FAMILY, one of the most distinguished families in American history, whose members include two presidents, writers, historians, lawyers, and politicians. The family first achieved prominence during the Revolutionary era, when John Adams (1735-1826) became an active leader in virtually every phase of the Revolution and second president of the United States (1797-1801). Abigail Adams (1744-1818), John's wife, wrote letters to her husband, children, and friends for more than four decades, leaving volumes of insightful correspondence. Abigail and John's eldest and most able son, John Quincy (1767-1848), was sixth president of the United States (1825-29).

The Adams line descended from John Quincy to his son Charles Francis (1807-86), who like his father and grandfather, served as minister to Britain. He also wrote history and published the papers of John Adams and the correspondence of Abigail Adams. Charles Francis and his wife Abigail (1808-89) had three daughters and four sons, each of whom became nationally prominent. The second Charles Francis (1835-1915) was active in railroad reform, while his brother John Quincy (1833-94) became a Massachusetts politician. Henry (1838-1918) and Brooks (1848-1927) were each prolific and influential authors and historians. The Adamses left a significant imprint on American history through extraordinary accomplishments in politics, literature, and diplomacy.

See Also: Adams, John; Adams, John Quincy; Revolution, American.

BIBLIOGRAPHY: Nagel, Paul C., *Descent from Glory: Four Generations of the John Adams Family* (Oxford Univ. Press 1983); Shepard, Jack, *The Adams Chronicles: Four Generations of Greatness* (Little, Brown 1975).

ADAMSON ACT (1916), congressional act that averted a nationwide rail strike by granting railroad workers an eight-hour day. The act, opposed by rail owners, had the backing of Pres. Woodrow Wilson, who was then running for his second term.

See Also: Eight-Hour Day.

ADAMS-ONIS TREATY (1819), agreement (known also as the Transcontinental Treaty) between the United States and Spain through which Spain sold Florida to the United States.

The Spanish empire in South and Central America crumbled in the second decade of the 19th century. Spain's ability to resist American incursion into Florida depended on support from Britain. As long as Britain was at odds with the United States, it was unlikely to accept American territorial expansion into Florida. However, in the aftermath of the Treaty of Ghent (1814) Britain's foreign minister, Lord Castlereagh, moved toward closer ties with the United States. The two countries signed a series of treaties that formalized the new rapprochement.

Meanwhile, Pres. James Monroe appointed Gen. Andrew Jackson to head the campaign against the Seminole Indians of northern Florida, who fought to block the advancing Euro-American settlements. In 1818 Jackson invaded Florida, defeated the Seminoles, and captured two Spanish fortresses. Jackson then court-martialed and executed (without waiting for approval from Washington) two British veterans of the war against Napoleon who were advising the Seminole.

Monroe's cabinet refused to disavow Jackson's defiance of both military and international law. And Castlereagh did not even file a protest over the executions. The affair demonstrated to Spain that the United States could take Florida at almost no cost whenever it decided to do so and that Britain was not going to stand in its way. Jolted into action, Spain's minister to the United States, Luis de Onis, signed a treaty with Sec. of State John Quincy Adams, selling Florida as well as Spain's claims to the Pacific Northwest.

—DORON BEN-ATAR

See Also: Adams, John Quincy; Florida; Frontier in American History.

BIBLIOGRAPHY: Perkins, Bradford, *Castlereagh and Adams* (Univ. of California Press 1964); Russell, Greg, *John Quincy Adams and the Public Virtues of Diplomacy* (Univ. of Missouri Press 1995); Weeks, William Earl, *John Quincy Adams & American Global Empire* (Univ. Press of Kentucky 1992).

■ **ADDAMS, JANE (1869-1935),** settlement house founder, social reformer, suffragist, and peace activist. She was born in Cedarville, Illinois. The youngest of five children who survived infancy, Addams attended Rockford Female Seminary in the tradition of her female siblings. Her father refused to allow her to attend Smith Col-

Social reformer Jane Addams cofounded Chicago's Hull House in 1889, where she worked to improve the surrounding immigrant neighborhood.

lege, but she completed one year of medical studies at the Pennsylvania Woman's Medical College in Philadelphia. Addams visited Toynbee Hall in London during a European trip in 1888 and claimed that the experience helped her create the vision for the reform centers, or settlement houses, she later established in Chicago. Addams believed such institutions could help correct the inequities that had been created in American society as the result of industrialization and immigration. With the help of Ellen Gates Starr, Florence Kelley, Mary Rozet Smith, Grace Abbott, and other settlement workers, she set about improving the physical and mental health of the urban working-class population. The settlement movement under Addams also called for a role for government in the furthering of public health and welfare. Hull House, the first settlement house Addams established in 1889, provided English language and U.S. civics classes, recreational and cultural activities, and child care. Hull House became a magnet for intellectuals and a discussion ground for those interested in social work, sociology, and socialism. Addams, who never married, espoused the public sphere of activism for women, thereby expanding rather than breaking from the domestic roles typically embraced by women. Between 1902 and 1930 Addams wrote a dozen books drawn chiefly from her national lectures. Her autobiographical recollections and motivations for the creation of settlement houses, *Twenty Years at Hull House*, was published in 1910 and updated in 1920 in *The Second Twenty Years at Hull House*. Addams was vice president of the National American Woman Suffrage Association from 1911 to 1914. She was outspoken in the leadership of the peace movement during World War I (1914-18) and in 1919 was elected president of the Women's International League for Peace and Freedom. In 1920 Addams became a founder of the American Civil Liberties Union. In 1931 she was the joint recipient of the Nobel Peace Prize with educator Nicholas Murray Butler.

—MARTHA J. KING

See Also: American Civil Liberties Union; Hull House; Women in American History.

BIBLIOGRAPHY: Addams, Jane, *Twenty Years at Hull House with Autobiographical Notes* (Signet 1910); Bryan, Mary Lynn McCree et al., eds., *The Jane Addams Papers: A Comprehensive Guide* (Indiana Univ. Press 1996); Davis, Allen F., *American Heroine: The Life and Legend of Jane Addams* (Oxford Univ. Press 1973); Linn, James Weber, *Jane Addams: A Biography* (Appleton Century 1935).

■ **ADENA (c. 1000 B.C.-A.D. 400),** thought to be the earliest farming society in eastern North America. Best known for their elaborate burial mounds,

including the Serpent Mound in southern Ohio, they lived in permanent villages. The Adena people were cultivators as well as hunters and gatherers and used a variety of stone, wood, bone, and copper tools to produce pottery and woven cloth.

See Also: Indians of North America; Serpent Mound.

■ **ADIRONDACK MOUNTAINS,** mountain range of northern New York State. The mountains extend south from the St. Lawrence River valley and Lake Champlain to the Mohawk River valley. French explorer Samuel de Champlain entered the mountains in 1609, but the area remained thinly settled by Europeans until the 19th century. The eastern edge of the Adirondacks formed by Lake Champlain and Lake George was an important trade and war route predating European arrival and extending through the War of 1812. New York State created the Forest Preserve of the Adirondacks in 1885 and in 1892 the Adirondack Park, protected in the state constitution as "forever...wild." Both were among the earliest conservation efforts by government.

■ ***ADKINS* V. *CHILDREN'S HOSPITAL* (1923),** U.S. Supreme Court case that invalidated a minimum wage law as improper government interference in the marketplace. In 1918 the federal government established a minimum wage for women workers to protect their health and welfare. Children's Hospital in the District of Columbia sued, claiming the law illegally fixed the price of labor and interfered with the hospital's right to negotiate contracts with individual workers. The Court decided (5-3) that the law was an unconstitutional violation of the Fifth Amendment's due process clause.

Adkins reflected the Supreme Court's strict adherence to laissez-faire economic policies that had come to the forefront in the late 19th century. Justice George Sutherland wrote for the majority that the government could only interfere with freedom of contract in rare circumstances and that wage levels should be determined by the market, not by government fiat. *Adkins* served as a basis for similar decisions striking down minimum wage laws until 1937. Then, in light of the Great Depression and the political success of Pres. Franklin D. Roosevelt's New Deal, the Court in

The tallest peaks in the Adirondack Mountains rise above Heart Lake. In 1892, New York state created the Adirondack Park, which includes both public and private holdings.

West Coast Hotel v. *Parrish* upheld a similar Washington State minimum wage law for women and children on the grounds that government could regulate wages and working conditions under its constitutional police powers.

—TIM ASHWELL

See Also: *Supreme Court.*

BIBLIOGRAPHY: McCraw, Thomas, *Prophets of Regulation: Charles Francis Adams, Louis D. Brandeis, James M. Landis, Alfred E. Kahn* (Belknap Press of Harvard Univ. Press 1984).

■ **ADMIRALTY COURTS,** regular system of courts created by Britain's Privy Council in 1697 to hear maritime cases. Under the council's direction, colonial governors appointed the judges, subject to the approval of the Admiralty in England. Developed to deal with a well-developed network of smugglers, privateers, and pirates in the colonies, American admiralty courts heard cases and punished offenders without benefit of local juries or judges.

■ **ADULT EDUCATION,** school programs for adults. Massachusetts established the first statewide program (1847) to teach reading, writing, and arithmetic to undereducated adults. Similar efforts quickly developed in urban areas across the country to give adults the skills they needed to work in industrial settings. The programs were also aimed at "Americanizing" the immigrant population. By 1900, 165 American cities operated evening schools for adults. While many current programs continue to focus on basic literacy and language skills for immigrants and the undereducated, most also offer job-skills training. The decline of traditional heavy industry and the rise of a high-technology, information-driven economy has caused a boom in adult education. Since 1970 colleges and universities have assumed a leading role, offering both part-time degree programs and enrichment courses to older students.

BIBLIOGRAPHY: Knowles, Malcolm S., *The Adult Education Movement in the United States* (Holt 1962).

■ **ADVENTISTS (MILLERITES),** followers of William Miller (1782-1849), a Baptist lay preacher who predicted through study of the prophecies of Daniel that at Christ's second coming fire would cleanse the earth. In 1831, Miller first presented his findings and later established March 21, 1843, to March 21, 1844, as the period of the Advent. Through Miller's skilled public lectures, papers, tracts, books, camp meetings, and citywide campaigns, the message spread. When the world did not end in 1844, the group disintegrated, but several adventist churches, including the Seventh-Day Adventists, formed.

See Also: Religion.

■ **AFFIRMATIVE ACTION,** a legal and philosophical principle favoring preferential treatment for women and minority groups to counteract the results of past prejudicial legal and social standards. It was perhaps first articulated by Martin Luther King, Jr., when he argued for the creation of a "program by the government of special compensatory measures," modeled on the GI Bill, that would ameliorate the impediments African Americans "had inherited from the past." Drawing upon Title VII of the Civil Rights Act of 1964, which established federal judicial authority to correct discriminatory employment practices, the Supreme Court broadened its definition of discrimination to include not only disparate treatment of an individual but the disparate impact of policies prejudicial to racial minorities and other groups. Affirmative action policies have been applied to private and public employment and to access to housing, education, and public services. In many fields these rulings have sought to correct imbalance as they have encouraged diversity.

Affirmative action is highly controversial. Some opponents claim it amounts to reverse discrimination. Although reaffirmed in the Civil Rights Act of 1991, the issue returned to the courts when California voters passed (1996) an initiative eliminating affirmative action from all state government practices.

—JOHN R. NEFF

See Also: African Americans; Civil Rights Movement.
BIBLIOGRAPHY: Belz, Herman, *Equality Transformed* (Transaction Books 1991); King, Martin Luther, Jr., *Why We Can't Wait* (Penguin 1964).

■ **AFL-CIO,** the American Federation of Labor and the Congress of Industrial Organizations. Founded in 1955 when the American Federation of Labor merged with its former rival the Congress of Industrial Organizations, it is an organization of autonomous trade unions that represents about 14 million of the 20 million U.S.

In December 1955, the American Federation of Labor (AFL) merged with the Congress of Industrial Organizations (CIO). The new organization—AFL-CIO—represented more than 15 million workers.

union workers. It seeks to improve wages and work conditions, secure pro-labor legislation, and extend union representation to the unorganized. The AFL, formed in 1886, was made up of unions representing skilled workers. The CIO formed in 1935 when eight unions broke away from the AFL as they sought to organize semi- or unskilled industrial workers. The two merged under AFL president George Meany, who served as the AFL-CIO president for its first 25 years. Since then, its numbers have declined with the decrease in industry and an increase in antiunion sentiment. In 1955, the AFL-CIO represented over 30 percent of the American workforce; by the mid-1990s, that number had dropped to less than 16 percent.

See Also: American Federation of Labor (AFL); Congress of Industrial Organizations (CIO); Labor Movement; Meany, George.

■ **AFRICAN-AMERICAN RELIGION,** ways in which people of African ancestry in the United States perceive and relate to the realm of the supernatural. It resulted from an amalgam of

African religious traditions, Euro-American Christian elements, and the experience of oppression and victimization.

African-American religion predated the African-American church in America. It began in the early 17th century as enslaved Africans struggled to understand their world, ultimate reality, and God. European missionary efforts among the slaves added a veneer of Christianity to what had previously been a network of African beliefs and practices.

By the mid-18th century the first African-American churches had been organized. Baptist and Methodist churches dominated, with sprinklings of Episcopal, Presbyterian, and Catholic churches. These developments carried through the 19th century as Richard Allen, Peter Spencer, James Varick, and numerous other African-American clergy and laity walked out of predominantly white churches in search of spiritual freedom and ecclesiastical independence. This process largely occurred in the American South through the "Invisible Institution," secret meetings held by slaves in the absence of whites.

The early years of the 20th century witnessed the diversification of African-American religion on an unprecedented scale. African-American Holiness-Pentecostal churches, African-American spiritual churches, the Father Divine Peace Mission movement, the Black Muslims, African-American Hebrew-Jewish groups, and a host of other churches, cults, and sects emerged. Predominantly African-American leadership and membership and a cultural experience shaped in the context of oppression became the unifying feature of these various expressions.

The distinctiveness of African-American religion has been evident historically in its connections with the struggle for equal rights and social justice. From the preacher-led slave revolts and the abolitionism of early African-American churches to the more recent struggles for civil rights, political power, and economic justice, religion has remained a central force in the lives of African Americans.

Since the 1960s African-American religion has developed as a field of teaching and research. Building on the work of W. E. B. Du Bois, Carter G. Woodson, E. Franklin Frazier, and others, scholars such as Gayraud S. Wilmore, Milton C. Sernett, and Albert J. Raboteau investigated and analyzed a wide variety of data related to the religions of people of African descent in the United States. African-American church studies programs developed in colleges, universities, and seminaries.

The study of African-American religion is being reinvigorated with the introduction of womanist and Afrocentric literature. Womanist scholars like Delores S. Williams and Katie G. Cannon and Afrocentrists such as Molefi Kete Asante are forcing a more critical reinterpretation of the traditions of the African-American church and African-American religion.

—LEWIS V. BALDWIN

See Also: *African Americans; Black Muslims; Civil Rights Movement; Divine, Father; Religion; Slavery.*

BIBLIOGRAPHY: Du Bois, W.E.B., *The Negro Church: A Social Study Done under the Direction of Atlanta University* (Atlanta Univ. Press 1903); Raboteau, Albert J., *Slave Religion: The "Invisible Institution" in the Antebellum South* (Oxford Univ. Press 1978); Wilmore, Gayraud S., ed., *African American Religious Studies: An Interdisciplinary Anthology* (Duke Univ. Press 1989).

■ **AFRICAN AMERICANS,** people descended from those transported to the New World as slaves, from the western regions of sub-Saharan Africa. A succession of vast, wealthy, and culturally advanced empires rose and fell in West Africa during the medieval and early modern eras. Portuguese mariners who sailed down the African coast in the 15th century encountered a variety of African nations, a number of which were politically and materially sophisticated. Europeans went on to trade actively with these peoples, and some settled along the West African seaboard or on offshore islands.

Early Slavery in the Americas. Africans and people of mixed African and European heritage took part in the great voyages of discovery to the New World. In the 1500s, Africans began to reach the Americas in large numbers, but under much different circumstances, having been captured and sold by other Africans responding to the growing demand of European slave traders. Over the next three centuries, European ships carried some 10 million human beings, in conditions of appalling brutality, from their African homelands to the plantations of the Americas, while uncounted others died before reaching that destination.

Residents of Virginia, the first permanent English colony in North America, began purchasing Africans by 1620. In the colony's early decades, relatively few Africans arrived, and some of those were indentured servants who were eventually freed. But gradually, and then rapidly from the late 1600s, law and custom consigned most blacks to slavery, a permanent condition from which all whites were exempt.

Ultimately, all the Anglo-American colonies accepted or avidly adopted racial slavery. The system became most deeply entrenched, however, in the colonies that lay south of Pennsylvania. In the 18th century, the importation of Africans into British North America accelerated dramatically; by the American Revolution, 40 percent of Virginia's inhabitants and 60 percent of South Carolina's inhabitants were enslaved blacks.

African-American Cultural Beginnings. The uprooting of Africans through enslavement caused much of their original culture to be lost, but they brought some elements of their heritage with them. Some Africans' experience in their homelands with rice cultivation and free-range cattle herding, for example, seems to have helped establish those pursuits in South Carolina. Over the years, the culture of each race, ranging from speech and cookery to understandings of the supernatural, profoundly affected that of the other. More than half the Africans imported into colonial America during the period of the slave trade arrived between the 1720s and the Revolutionary War, but these newcomers were absorbed into a veteran black population that had already become "African American."

Baptist and Methodist preachers during the late 18th and early 19th centuries attracted both

In July 1862, African-American troops, including several former slaves, began service in the Union's segregated First Carolina Regiment. Not until 1948 were the armed forces racially integrated.

black and white believers to demonstrative, emotional worship services that were deeply influenced by the style of the black congregants. African Americans sometimes preached to attentive white listeners. In the Upper South, revolutionary and evangelical ideals led some slave holders to manumit (liberate) slaves before about 1800. In the 19th century, however, southern states passed laws making manumission difficult or impossible. At all times, free blacks across the South were denied many rights, but some free African Americans prospered.

Post-Revolutionary America. After the Revolutionary War, in which black Americans fought on both sides, the northern states gradually put an end to slavery. Yet, white racism in the North deepened, and African Americans in northern cities were founding churches and other community organizations of their own by the last years of the 18th century. During the several decades that followed, as democracy expanded for white men, laws denying African Americans such basic rights as voting and jury service became more widespread in the North. Urban antiblack race riots and racial segregation of public facilities came to typify northern society.

During the 60 years preceding the Civil War, the slave population of the United States grew at a rapid rate through natural increase, quadrupling to nearly 4 million, alongside 27 million whites. As slaveholders and slaves settled new territories west of the southern seaboard states, cotton became the dominant crop. In the Upper South, meanwhile, slavery proved adaptable to grain production and even to industry.

Living in Slavery. The southern farm and plantation were scenes both of exploitation and of black adjustment, creativity, and resistance. Slaves often managed to moderate the pace of labor somewhat, winning a measure of relief from the onerous dawn-to-dark workday. Evangelical churches in the South, though still biracial, came increasingly to be dominated by white members, and many white clergy justified slavery on scriptural grounds. African Americans responded by worshiping not only in church but on their own as well, with or without their masters' acquiescence. Slaves frequently ran away. Some resisted masters or overseers physically, and a few attempted to or-

ganize large-scale revolts. The most sensational rebellion was led by Nat Turner, a Baptist lay preacher, in Virginia in 1831; some 60 whites and scores of blacks were killed.

The master depended on his slaves' labor, and he therefore found it in his interest to accommodate at least some of their desires. Most slave owners, for example, permitted slaves to choose and live with, or at least visit, their own spouses. These limited concessions and African Americans' own determination enabled many slaves to sustain family life even in a system where the master's death, economic reverses, or simple callousness frequently led to the separation of family members. Similarly, the master had nothing to gain by attempting to control the folk life of the slave quarters. It was in this realm of black autonomy within slavery that the African-American culture born in the 18th century flowered in the 19th; the music, dance, humor, and oratory that developed among slaves would later take America and the world by storm.

Civil War and Emancipation. In the 1830s, a biracial abolitionist movement arose in the North seeking to end slavery throughout the nation. Abolitionists also attacked the colonization movement, which linked the freeing of slaves to their resettlement outside the United States. African Americans organized conventions of their own to oppose slavery and racial discrimination, and they furnished some of the more eloquent and influential abolitionist leaders, including Frederick Douglass.

Conflict over slavery and its extension into western territories led the United States into the Civil War in 1861. The federal government at first excluded blacks from its armies and disavowed any intention to abolish slavery, proclaiming that it sought only to restore the Union and prevent slavery's expansion. African-American and white abolitionists, however, strove to ensure that the conflict destroyed slavery through a victory achieved in part by black soldiers.

Pres. Abraham Lincoln's Emancipation Proclamation of Jan. 1, 1863, meant that a Union victory would indeed put an end to slavery. The document also opened the door to the enlistment of some 180,000 black Union soldiers, plus the use of civilian African-American laborers. A large majority of these African Americans were ex-slaves.

When freedom came through the Union victory and the 13th Amendment in 1865, black Southerners responded in myriad ways. Simply moving about, seeking better conditions of employment, reuniting families divided by slavery, formalizing marriages and family names, organizing politically, even choosing to stay put and work for wages on the old home place; all these were means through which blacks exercised their newly won freedom.

Reconstruction. Provisional governments set up in the vanquished ex-Confederate states endorsed slavery's abolition, but they also passed Black Codes, laws whose purpose was to ensure that the former slaves remained a subservient, mostly agricultural, work force with no say in their governments. In 1867, an overwhelmingly Republican Congress took control of southern Reconstruction and dissolved the state governments that had passed the Black Codes. Congress also took the revolutionary step of requiring 10 ex-Confederate states to choose delegates to constitutional conventions through elections in which the black freedmen were allowed to vote.

In two states, blacks constituted a majority of the population. Some southern white men were temporarily denied the vote because of their roles in the Confederacy, and for a time this produced black majorities in an additional three states. Two state conventions contained black majorities. All 10 produced state constitutions that made African Americans full citizens.

The voters of the former Confederate states proceeded to elect state legislatures that included black men, but African Americans won a majority of legislative seats only in South Carolina. Some blacks held high state office during Reconstruction, and the South sent nearly two dozen to Congress by 1900. Republican governors and lawmakers inaugurated numerous reforms that benefited both freed people and whites of modest means, including the South's first extensive public school systems, which served all children in segregated facilities.

Late-19th-Century America. The Republican party in the South was an unstable coalition, encompassing whites and blacks, recent arrivals from the North and native Southerners, and wealthy and poor people. White conservatives strove to win away the Republicans' native white constituency, often by means of racist appeals. They also resorted to election fraud, economic pressure on impoverished freed people, and violence against political enemies. Conservatives, who ultimately adopted the Democratic party label, gained control of all the southern states by 1877.

Even so, public schooling survived for both blacks and whites, although the Democrats failed to fund schools adequately for either race. In southern localities that were heavily populated by blacks, African-American men continued to win election to office as late as the 1890s. By 1880, one in seven blacks employed in southern agriculture had managed to purchase land. Other black Southerners, and more than a few whites, became sharecroppers or tenant farmers during the latter decades of the 19th century. Sharecropping offered blacks a measure of control over their lives that had been missing under slavery, but landlords, legally, often ensnared sharecroppers in a web of unending debt and poverty.

Occasionally, blacks and disaffected whites banded together to challenge conservative Democratic rule, as in the reformist Readjuster party that took power in Virginia for four years around 1880, and in certain phases of the Populist party revolt of the 1890s. After 1890, however, Democrat-dominated southern states adopted laws and constitutions that deprived most black men of the right to vote. Southern states and localities also codified racial segregation and extended it into virtually every area of life. Lynching became a hallmark of southern society, with scores of African Americans dying annually at the hands of mobs.

Meanwhile, black teachers worked faithfully in grammar schools across the South, and several dozen colleges for African-American men and women opened their doors. Booker T. Washington, founder of Tuskegee Institute in Alabama, concluded by 1895 that blacks had no choice but to defer aspirations for political and social equality. Washington called on southern whites, in return, to give African Americans a fair chance at economic advancement based in significant part on vocational or "industrial" training. W. E. B.

Du Bois, an activist leader, supported industrial education but also championed the right of African Americans to pursue higher learning and exhorted the race as a whole to struggle militantly for full equality.

Most blacks had left the white-dominated southern Protestant churches during Reconstruction, forming new congregations. These churches became crucial centers of southern black communal life and culture. The membership and influence of African-American fraternal organizations and mutual benefit societies expanded rapidly in the South. A growing number of blacks opened small businesses from the late 19th century. Some Afro-Southerners sought greater opportunity by moving to cities in their native region or to the North, where blacks had gained full citizenship through the Reconstruction-era 14th and 15th Amendments. Others migrated west to states or territories such as Kansas and Oklahoma, sometimes founding all-black towns.

Building Community in the New Century. By the beginning of the 20th century, white racism helped convince a new generation of African-American leadership in the urban North that blacks should concentrate on building community institutions of their own. This process accelerated during World War I with the migration of thousands of blacks into northern cities, where the wartime economy had opened up jobs that could be filled by African Americans. About 1.5 million blacks moved north between 1910 and 1940; a further 1.5 million left the South each decade from 1940 to 1970.

A black populace that historically had been almost entirely southern eventually found nearly half its members living outside the South. Many African-American men served in the segregated U.S. Army during World War I. They returned home to a series of race riots in which whites hunted down blacks in the streets of cities. Blacks, however, were beginning to fight back aggressively, and the death toll now included whites as well as African Americans. A more positive development of the decade following World War I was a "renaissance" of African-American music, art, and literature in Harlem, New York City's principal black district, and in other cities.

For some African Americans, the view of Ja-

maican-born leader Marcus Garvey that white America would never accept blacks into the mainstream held appeal. Garvey forswore integration, advocating instead the liberation of Africa from European colonial rule and the building there of a spiritual center and physical haven for the black people. During the late 1910s and early 1920s, Garvey built his largely urban, working-class following into the first true mass movement of African Americans.

Emigrationism never supplanted the black struggle for advancement at home, however. African-American migration into residentially segregated northern cities, where blacks could still vote, was producing black-majority electoral districts. African Americans in the North had won office as legislators and city councilmen as early as the 1910s. Urban political machines now courted black voters, and Chicago elected America's first black congressman of the 20th century in 1928. The National Association for the Advancement of Colored People (NAACP), a biracial civil rights organization founded before World War I by Du Bois and others, fought discrimination in the courts.

Depression and War. The Great Depression brought Franklin D. Roosevelt and the Democrats to power in 1933. FDR never crusaded for racial equality, and many of his New Deal programs aided blacks less than other citizens, yet the weaving of a social safety net did benefit African Americans. His wife, Eleanor, and some of his advisers supported black advancement, and FDR appointed more African Americans to high federal office than any previous president. Much of the black vote, Republican since Reconstruction, now shifted to the Democrats.

As America moved toward involvement in World War II, the threat of black labor leader A. Philip Randolph to stage an African-American march on Washington led Roosevelt to take some preliminary but symbolically important steps to eliminate racial discrimination in defense industries. When the United States entered the war, black men, and this time women as well, again donned American uniforms, and again they did so in a racially segregated American military. Still, the creation of some elite black units in the army, the stationing of black servicemen around the globe, and the wartime economic boom brought novel experiences and opportunities to many African Americans, fortifying both their impatience with old ways and their hope for a better future. By the 1950s, blacks in the South and elsewhere were demanding an end to segregation and discrimination.

The Civil Rights Movement. Pres. Harry Truman's decision to desegregate the armed forces in 1948 and the Supreme Court's *Brown* v. *Board of Education of Topeka* decision of 1954 prohibiting school segregation encouraged blacks in their struggle. Blacks in Montgomery, Alabama, displayed great fortitude in 1955-56; an entire community of some 50,000 African Americans mobilized for a disciplined, year-long boycott of segregated buses and made Martin Luther King, Jr., into a national figure. In 1960, "sit-ins" by black students demanding service at white-only lunch counters in Greensboro, North Carolina, rapidly spread across the South. Members of the Student Nonviolent Coordinating Committee (SNCC) and other young people withstood intimidation and violent white resistance as they worked to register African-American voters in the rural and small-town South. For the first time in nearly a century, Congress passed strong civil rights acts in 1964 and 1965, and Pres. Lyndon B. Johnson signed them into law.

Diverse Voices and Unrest. Yet, it became clear by the mid-1960s that the problems of black poverty and institutional racism extended far beyond the South. Malcolm X gained national attention as an angry, eloquent spokesman for urban Afro-America until his assassination in 1965. Inner cities from the Watts area in Los Angeles to Newark, New Jersey, exploded in deadly riots, quelled by police and National Guard troops, during the summers of 1964 through 1968, and occasionally thereafter.

By 1965, the civil rights coalition was beginning to splinter over both tactics and ideology. "Black Power" became a popular slogan. To some, the term meant simply that blacks should register to vote and then make the American system serve all its citizens. Others, alienated from white liberals and from "mainstream" black leaders such as King, urged blacks to reject integration and "white middle-class" values altogether,

seeking instead to gain control of black communities for African Americans themselves.

The concentration of the African-American population in urban areas helped black politicians win mayorships in Cleveland and in Gary, Indiana, in the late 1960s, an achievement eventually matched in many other major cities. The Voting Rights Act of 1965 had put suffrage in the South under federal supervision, and by 1992 there were 40 blacks serving in the U.S. Congress. Meanwhile, Jesse Jackson combined black votes with those of whites from the Democratic left wing in the 1980s to make himself a force in the national party. During the years that followed, African Americans such as Virginia's Gov. L. Douglas Wilder and Seattle's Mayor Norm Rice proved that black candidates could win in heavily white constituencies.

Much of what the world had come to revere by that time as "American culture" had been created or inspired by blacks. Popular musical genres such as spirituals, ragtime, jazz, blues, gospel, rock and roll, soul, and rap had covered the globe, and so had the styles associated with them; African Americans had become the world's most culturally imitated people. This triumph that spanned a century occurred alongside equally striking achievements by African-American poets and authors and by black artists who performed mainly within European traditions, ranging from the 19th-century Shakespearean actor Ira Aldridge to opera stars such as Leontyne Price and Jessye Norman.

As the 21st century approached, decades of black struggle had lowered many racial barriers. Of the one in eight Americans who were of African descent, one-third had become firmly middle-class and upwardly mobile. Another third, however, lived in poverty, physically separated and often psychologically alienated from the rest of the society. The remaining third found itself somewhere in between. Affirmative action, introduced under the Johnson administration, had provided few benefits to those mired in deep poverty. Even blacks who had succeeded bristled at racial obstacles and slights.

Toward the Future. Nonetheless, commentators who glibly declared that white and black Americans were more alienated from one another than they had ever been before revealed their own ignorance of history. Rather, the very successes of the black struggle for equality had brought people into contact who in earlier years would never have heard each other's sometimes angry voices. Those same advances, like every social reform, had left some problems unsolved and given rise to new dilemmas.

Progress for African Americans in the 21st century would depend partly on the readiness of all citizens to learn from their country's history. A knowledge of the victories that black courage and perseverance had won could help arm African Americans for the struggles that still lay ahead. And an understanding of the enormous obstacles blacks had faced, and of the challenges they still confronted, might help Americans who were not black to understand that the nation's ledger with its African-American citizens had yet to be balanced.

—MELVIN PATRICK ELY

See Also: Affirmative Action; African-American Religion; Civil Rights Movement; Desegregation; Race and Racism; Slavery; individual biographies.

BIBLIOGRAPHY: Franklin, John Hope, and Alfred A. Moss, Jr., *From Slavery to Freedom: A History of African Americans,* 7th ed. (Knopf 1994); Hughes, Langston, *A Pictorial History of African Americans,* 6th ed. (Random House 1995); Stuckey, Sterling, *Going Through the Storm: The Influence of African American Art in History* (Oxford Univ. Press 1994).

■ **AGASSIZ, LOUIS (1807-73),** naturalist, geologist, and supporter of American science. Born in Môtiers-en-Vuly, Switzerland, Agassiz studied at the Universities of Zürich, Heidelberg, and Munich (1824-30), wrote a monograph on the fish of Brazil (1829), and studied in France with naturalist George Cuvier (1830-32). While professor at Neuchâtel, Switzerland (1832-46), he published a pathbreaking multivolume study of Europe's fossil fish and wrote three works explaining his study of glaciers, introducing the concept of an Ice Age in the recent geological past that left its mark in the form of geological formations and land contours. He came to the United States in 1846 on a lecture tour and became professor of natural history at Harvard (1847-73), during which time he published the four-volume *Contri-*butions to the Natural History of the United States and became a vocal opponent of Darwin's theory of evolution. His prestige, enthusiasm, and teaching methods greatly improved the study of natural history in America. Agassiz founded Harvard's Museum of Comparative Zoology (1859) and the Anderson School of Natural History (1873) and helped found the National Academy of Sciences (1863).

See Also: Science.

■ **AGNEW, SPIRO T. (1918-97),** U.S. vice president (1969-73). Born in Baltimore, Maryland, he was elected governor of Maryland as a Republican (1966) after serving in local government. In 1968 and 1972 he ran successfully for vice president with Richard M. Nixon. Virtually unknown on the national scene when he took office, Agnew doggedly defended Nixon against his critics and regularly attacked liberals in the media as being out of touch with the silent majority of Americans. In 1973, as controversy over White House involvement in the cover-up of the 1972 Watergate break-in intensified, Agnew was charged with tax evasion for accepting bribes while a Maryland official. Although he maintained he wanted to fight the charges, he pleaded no contest in federal court and resigned. He was replaced as vice president by Rep. Gerald Ford who became president when Nixon resigned in 1974.

See Also: Vice President of the United States.

BIBLIOGRAPHY: Agnew, Spiro T., *Go Quietly...Or Else* (Morrow 1980); Cohen, Richard, and Jules Witcover, *A Heartbeat Away* (Viking 1974).

■ **AGRICULTURAL ADJUSTMENT ACT (1933),** federal law that provided immediate relief for the nation's farmers, instituted several lasting recovery programs, and established the Agricultural Adjustment Administration (AAA). Major problems of overproduction and depressed prices had plagued farmers since the late 19th century. As these difficulties became acute during the 1920s, farmers and politicians sought a variety of unsuccessful solutions, such as monetary inflation and land retirements.

With the situation growing dire for many farmers, Pres. Franklin D. Roosevelt and Congress enacted the Agricultural Adjustment Act in May

1933. This expansive bill increased agricultural purchasing power by establishing parity prices for seven basic farm commodities, an action that was found unconstitutional by the Supreme Court in 1936. A more lasting component of the bill was the creation of farm subsidies, the funding for which came from taxes on food processing. Farmers received subsidies—compensatory payments—from the government in return for reducing productive acreage or limiting production. The act also gave the president virtual carte blanche to inflate the money supply.

Under the implementation of the Agricultural Adjustment Administration, the act effectively raised total farm income and increased the prices of wheat, cotton, and corn. But the legislation was not without its flaws. Some landlords refused to share their AAA payments with their tenant farmers, particularly African Americans. In addition, many people resented the destruction of farm products at a time when millions were starving.

See Also: New Deal.

BIBLIOGRAPHY: Perkins, Van L., *Crisis in Agriculture: The Agriculture Adjustment Administration and the New Deal 1933* (Univ. of California Press 1969).

■ **AGRICULTURAL FAIRS,** American rural institution that evolved in the early 1800s from traditional European market fairs and elite Anglo-American livestock shows. The institution endures today, as demonstrated by the 2,600 fairs that draw more than 125 million Americans each year. Sponsored by local, county, state, or other agricultural organizations, these annual harvest-time celebrations always attract people by their social, recreational, and commercial opportunities as well as by the superior farm animals, products, and domestic or artistic productions that are exhibited and compete for well-publicized prizes. Elkanah Watson (1758-1842) is generally considered the father of the American agricultural fair. He organized the Berkshire County Agricultural Society and its Pittsfield Fair in western Massachusetts in 1810-11 and widely promoted his ideas on agricultural improvement, education, and social and moral reform. Watson, however, drew heavily from preexisting elite urban agricultural associations as well as from previously held exhibitions in New York, the New England states, and the Washington, D.C., area.

BIBLIOGRAPHY: Neely, Wayne Caldwell, *The Agricultural Fair* (Columbia Univ. Press 1935).

■ **AGRICULTURE,** the cultivation of land and the raising of livestock, the success of which sustained the American colonies and the early republic and formed the basis for the nation's prosperity. While agriculture provided employment to proportionately fewer Americans and composed a steadily shrinking portion of the gross domestic product in the 125 years after the Civil War, its social significance to the United States continues.

European colonists found a Native American agricultural system in operation along the Atlantic seaboard. Eastern woodlands Indians cleared land by girdling trees and burning. Their cultivated crops, especially corn, beans, and squash, provided about 80 percent of the caloric intake for most groups.

The colonists adopted some native crops, especially corn, and they frequently used girdling and fire to clear lands. In general, however, they followed the methodology of European agriculture. Their agricultural system introduced a market economy and European property practices to the New World. They used advanced technologies, including plows, harrows, and wind- or water-powered mills, to produce and process imported crops such as small grains. European livestock—swine, cattle, horses, and sheep—also arrived in significant numbers, providing the colonists with renewable resources of food, clothing, and power.

After an early period of experimentation, the colonists developed regionally differentiated agricultural regimes. Farmers in the middle colonies and New England produced foodstuffs for home consumption and for export, especially to the West Indian sugar islands. Of these colonies, Pennsylvania was the most productive and the most prosperous.

Farmers in the Chesapeake region and farther south produced export crops for the European market, especially tobacco, rice, and indigo. These crops were "enumerated," meaning that by law they had to be marketed through England.

The high profitability of these labor-intensive southern crops induced commercial planters to import labor. In the 17th century, most imported laborers were indentured servants from the British Isles, but as the 18th century proceeded, planters turned increasingly to the importation of African slaves. By the time of the American Revolution, about 40 percent of Virginians and 60 percent of South Carolinians were slaves of African birth or descent.

Agriculture in the Young Republic. The productivity of their lands and their labor resulted in Americans being the best fed and perhaps the most prosperous people in the world at the time that they declared their independence from Great Britain. Mindful of the centrality of agriculture in the national economy, government in the new United States moved quickly to assure a bright future for farming. The government sought to assure ample lands for farmers, both through physical expansion, as in the Louisiana Purchase (1803), and through the extinguishment of Indian claims on lands controlled by the United States. The United States developed a land policy, beginning with the Basic Land Ordinance in 1785, which became increasingly permissive until finally, in 1862, the Homestead Act allowed a farmer to acquire 160 acres virtually for nothing. The government encouraged agricultural trade and undertook internal improvements to facilitate commerce in crops and livestock. Finally, the government began the systematic encouragement of agricultural science. In 1862, Congress made the U.S. Department of Agriculture (USDA) an independent scientific agency and passed the Morrill Land-Grant College Act, encouraging the states to create agricultural colleges. In 1887, the Hatch Act provided funds for scientific investigation in agricultural experiment stations, and the Smith-Lever Act (1914) created an extension system to carry technical information to farmers.

Agriculture dominated the economy of the young republic. Farming rapidly overspread the region between the Appalachian Mountains and the Mississippi River, and farm products composed the bulk of exports. Cotton, which expanded rapidly after Eli Whitney's invention of the gin in 1793, alone accounted for over half of the value of all exports by 1860. Moreover, most other economic enterprises were dependent on agriculture, either directly, as in the case of the implement, milling, and meat-packing industries, or indirectly, as in the case of most manufacturers and merchants who sold to farmers or handled their products. Agriculture allowed the generation and accretion of capital and freed the labor on which the entire economy depended, becoming a key facilitator of industrial development.

The Perils and Pleasures of Commercial Farming. The Civil War (1861-65) resulted in the end of slavery and the extension of the free labor system to commercial production in the south. It did not reverse the trend toward greater market participation on the part of American farmers. Indeed, late-19th-century farmers became increasingly commercial, aided by such machines as reapers and steam threshers for grain, in response to expanding market opportunities in the United States and in Europe.

Farmers participated more fully in the market in order to improve their living standards, but by so doing they also increased their economic risks. Market fluctuations, the depredations of middlemen, and high real interest rates induced farmers to join the Grange and the Farmers Alliance and to support the Populist party in the late 19th century. None of these movements succeeded, but they initiated a pattern of agrarian insurgency that continued periodically through the early 1890s.

Many observers of agriculture from outside of farming believed that farmers' problems derived from their own shortcomings. The Country Life Movement, which thrived between 1900 and 1920, aimed to get at rural problems by improving schools, churches, and family life, and by making farmers more skilled producers and sophisticated businessmen.

During the Great Depression of the 1930s, Pres. Franklin D. Roosevelt's New Deal administration took steps to reduce the economic risks confronting some commercial producers. Crop loan programs created a floor under basic commodity prices, and subsidies raised farm incomes. The effect of income-support programs was uneven. Only basic commodities, such as wheat, corn, and cotton, were covered, and the largest, most commercial producers of these derived most of the benefits. At the same time, the Rural Electrification Administration facilitated electrification of farms, dramatically improving rural material life, and the Federal Crop Insurance Corporation protected farmers against natural risk.

The 1930s also witnessed the beginning of government concern with the relationship between agriculture and the environment. The Great Plains drought and related Dust Bowl phenomenon resulted in the creation of government programs to fight erosion and conserve soil resources.

The Productivity Revolution. The years following World War II witnessed a dramatic upsurge in agricultural productivity, rooted in mechanization, chemicalization, and improved crops and animal breeds. By 1970, American agriculture had become so productive that one farmer could feed 90 people.

Crucial to American agriculture has been the gasoline-powered tractor. The tractor was introduced prior to World War I, but as late as 1945, only two in five farmers had them; by 1960, they were so universal that the USDA stopped counting farm horses and mules. Self-propelled machines to harvest such crops as small grains, corn, and cotton further increased agricultural productivity.

A new generation of farm chemicals appeared in the years around World War II. The widespread availability and use of insecticides (including DDT, which was banned in 1973), herbicides, and fertilizers for crops, and a range of antibiotics and growth hormones for animals, all added significantly to agricultural productivity in the United States.

New crop varieties and improved animal breeds, most of them in development for decades, also appeared beginning in the 1940s. New varieties and breeds helped revolutionize the production of such products as cotton, tomatoes, and chickens.

The possibility of greater individual productivity conjoined with government programs and shrinking unit profit margins to alter the scale of agriculture dramatically. In 1940, there were about 6 million farms in the United States. Fifty years later, there were fewer than 2 million. Of these, half produced less than $10,000 in marketable produce per year. Agricultural economists denominated only 40,000 farms, those marketing crops and animals worth more than $250,000 per year, as economically significant. Farmers shrank into demographic and economic insignificance as the productivity revolution proceeded. By 1990, less than 2 percent of the American population lived on farms. In that year, production agricul-ture, once the republic's lifeblood, contributed 2 percent of the gross domestic product.

The shrinkage of agriculture hardly diminished public concern with it. Indeed, the 1970s witnessed the development of intense interest in agriculture by environmentalists, consumer advocates, champions of organic farming, rural poverty reformers, and others. Moreover, farming remained an enterprise close to the hearts of many Americans. From Thomas Jefferson on, Americans have seen farming as an especially valuable endeavor. The endurance of that positive attitude has ensured public interest in agriculture, the shrinking number and economic importance of farmers notwithstanding.

—DAVID B. DANBOM

See Also: Food in American History; Granger Movement; New World Crops; Populism; Rural Life; Tenant Farming.

BIBLIOGRAPHY: Danbom, David, *Born in the Country: A History of Rural America* (Johns Hopkins Univ. Press 1995); Hurt, R. Douglas, *American Agriculture: A Brief History* (Iowa State Univ. Press 1994); Schlebecker, John T., *Whereby We Thrive: A History of American Farming, 1607-1972* (Iowa State Univ. Press 1975).

■ **AGRICULTURE, DEPARTMENT OF,** cabinet department of the U.S. government that administers farm policies. Created by Congress as a commission (1862) and later elevated to cabinet status (1889), the Department of Agriculture promotes the farm economy and regulates the food industry by sponsoring research, encouraging modern production and processing methods, and publicizing consumer information. The department also administers the government's farm subsidy and loan programs and runs conservation projects.

See Also: Agriculture.

■ **AGUINALDO, EMILIO (1869-1964),** Filipino revolutionary who led insurrections against both Spanish and American rule in the Philippines. In 1896 Aguinaldo went into exile after campaigning against the Spanish. He returned to the Philippines in 1898 shortly after U.S. forces seized the islands. Aguinaldo became the nominal president of a republic, but he resumed a bloody guerrilla war between 1899 and 1901, when it became clear that the American presence in the Philippines was permanent.

See Also: Philippines; Philippine War.

■ **AIDS,** acronym for acquired immune deficiency syndrome, a disease that cripples the body's immune system. Caused by the human immunodeficiency virus infection (HIV), AIDS was first identified in the early 1980s. Researchers suspect that it originated in sub-Saharan Africa and spread throughout the world, although more than 60 percent of all cases worldwide are still found in Africa. The disease enters the body through the bloodstream and may be contracted through sexual contact that exchanges body fluids, intravenous use of contaminated needles, and transfusion using contaminated blood.

Initially, AIDS in the United States seemed largely confined to gay men and intravenous drug users. Yet, while mortality rates remained highest among those two groups, the disease spread during the 1980s and 1990s throughout the American population and became one of the dozen leading killers. Mortality rates became especially high among Americans between the ages of 25 and 34. By 1997 the number of HIV-infected people worldwide had grown to almost 22 million, of which 42 percent were women.

The onset of the AIDS epidemic in the early 1980s spurred antihomosexual rhetoric and stimulated greater organization in the gay and lesbian communities. Political organization by local and national gay civil rights groups sought to provide services to those infected and to press the federal government to increase funding for research and education and to commit itself to finding a cure. A politically divisive issue, AIDS has caused immense personal and social tragedy and has exposed the limitations of medical science. Although progress was made in treating the symptoms of the disease, a vaccine to prevent AIDS had still not been developed by the late 1990s.

BIBLIOGRAPHY: Berridge, Virginia, and Philip Strong, eds., *AIDS and Contemporary History* (Cambridge Univ. Press 1993); Fee, Elizabeth, and Daniel M. Fox, eds., *AIDS: The Burdens of History* (Univ. of California Press 1988).

■ **AILEY, ALVIN (1931-89),** dancer and choreographer. Born in Rogers, Texas, Ailey became one of the preeminent dance talents of the 20th century. He began dancing with the Lester Horton Company in 1950 and in 1958 founded the American Dance Theater. Ailey's choreography won international acclaim. His compositions were a unique blend of ballet, jazz, and African and Caribbean influences.

See Also: African Americans.

■ **AIR FORCE,** branch of the U.S. military dedicated to aviation and air warfare. In 1907 the U.S. Army created an aeronautical division, which by World War I had only 35 pilots. Congressional and public support for military aviation waned during the interwar years. With the specter of U.S. involvement in World War II looming, however, the government created the Army Air Corps in 1941. Six years later, it became a separate service, the U.S. Air Force, under the National Security Act of 1947.

During World War II, the Army Air Force offered a seemingly effective alternative to the costly stalemates associated with ground fighting. Strategic bombing of enemy military installations and more general bombing of urban centers weakened both Germany and Japan, but the effectiveness of bombing in the defeat of the Axis is still debated. The public and the military favored bombing, especially against enemies who had resorted as well to widespread and indiscriminate bombings of urban areas.

The atomic bombing of Hiroshima and Nagasaki, Japan, in 1945 and the ensuing nuclear age made the air force a central aspect of national security policy. The unconventional military character of both the Vietnam and Gulf Wars rendered the air force even more important, as the United States relied heavily on strategic bombing to advance its military and political goals. In 1990, the active-duty enlistment was more than 600,000.

See Also: Army; Marine Corps; Navy.

BIBLIOGRAPHY: Boyne, Walter J., *Beyond the Wild Blue: A History of the United States Air Force, 1947-1997* (St. Martin's Press 1997).

■ **AIR FORCE ACADEMY,** military school in Colorado Springs, Colorado. It was initially authorized by Congress in 1954 to train young

BRING ME MEN

Modeled after West Point and Annapolis, the Air Force Academy was established in 1955 to train and cultivate military leadership.

men (and later women) to be officers in the U.S. Air Force. The first campus was established at Lowry Air Force Base in Denver the following year. The Colorado Springs site opened in 1958. Students are nominated by the president, vice president, members of Congress, and other public officials and from among children of military personnel.

See Also: Air Force.

■ *AKE V. OKLAHOMA* **(1985),** U.S. Supreme Court case concerning court-provided psychiatric assistance to impoverished criminal defendants. Ake, an accused murderer, pleaded not guilty by reason of insanity but could not afford to hire a psychiatrist. The Oklahoma court refused to provide one, and Ake was convicted and sentenced to death. The Court threw out the conviction (8-

1), ruling the state had denied Ake the assistance needed for a fair trial.

See Also: Supreme Court.

■ **ALABAMA,** the first home of the Confederacy and known as "the Heart of Dixie." The state is bounded on the north by Tennessee, on the east by Georgia, on the south by Florida and the Gulf of Mexico, and on the west by Mississippi. Mobile is a major port of the Gulf of Mexico. The main industrial products are steel and other fabricated metal goods, petroleum products, and apparel and textiles; the main farm products, soybeans and peanuts.

Alabama became a state in 1819. Slaves made up almost half the population just before the Civil War. Montgomery was the first capital of the Confederate States of America. Nearly a century later, the Montgomery bus boycott organized by the Rev. Martin Luther King, Jr., touched off the modern civil rights movement. Further protests by African Americans in the early 1960s, and the sometimes violent reactions against them, led to major civil rights legislation.

Capital: Montgomery. Area: 51,718 square miles. Population (1995 est.): 4,253,000.

See Also: Davis, Jefferson; De Soto, Hernando; Horseshoe Bend, Battle of; Mobile Bay, Battle of; Wallace, George C.; Washington, Booker Taliaferro; Wilkinson, James.

■ **ALABAMA CLAIMS,** demands for reparations made by the United States against Britain for damages to U.S. shipping during the Civil War. Britain had permitted the construction in British ports of 11 Confederate warships. These, especially C.S.S. *Alabama* and *Florida*, had successfully attacked Union vessels. The United States claimed the British violated international law by allowing the ships to be built and demanded more than $19 million in damages.

The issue became a highly charged one in American politics and was caught up in the antagonism between Congress and Pres. Andrew Johnson. Some Americans, including Sen. Charles Sumner of Massachusetts, tried to use it to force Britain to cede Canada. An agreement was negotiated but Congress rejected it in 1869. Finally Sec. of State Hamilton Fish and British Foreign Minister Lord Granville reached an acceptable settlement in which Britain expressed regret and, following international arbitration in 1872, agreed to pay $15.5 million.

See Also: Civil War; Fish, Hamilton; Sumner, Charles.

■ **ALAMO,** site of a battle during the Texas War for Independence, originally a Spanish mission in San Antonio established in 1718. In 1835 the Alamo was captured by Texan rebels from the Mexican army. The following year 187 Texans fought a 5,000-man Mexican force led by Pres. Antonio López de Santa Anna for two weeks before being overwhelmed. All defenders, which included Davy Crockett, William Travis, and Jim Bowie, were eventually killed. "Remember the Alamo" became a rallying cry for the Texans.

■ **ALASKA,** the largest of the 50 states and, except for Wyoming and Vermont, the least populated. Separated by Canada to the east from the other 48 mainland states, it is the northwesternmost part of the North American continent. It is bounded on the north by the Arctic Ocean and on the south by bays and inlets of the Pacific Ocean. The 40-mile-long Bering Strait separates it from Russia to the west. The 11 highest U.S. mountains are in the state, including the highest in North America, Mount McKinley.

Once part of the Russian Empire, Alaska was sold to the United States in 1867. It did not become a state until 1959. Discovery of a major oilfield on the Arctic North Slope in 1968 transformed its economy. Alaska leads all states in income from fishing and all but Texas in oil production.

Capital: Juneau. Area: 587,875 square miles. Population (1995 est.): 604,000.

See Also: Klondike; Seward, William Henry; Seward's Folly.

■ **ALASKA NATIVE CLAIMS SETTLEMENT ACT (1971),** legislation that extinguished all native Alaskans' claims to the state's fish and game in exchange for 44 million acres and nearly $1 billion divided among 13 regional and 200 village corporations. All native Alaskan Indians, Inuits, and Aleuts who could prove a quarter-blood quantum received stock in native corporations. However, while some of these native corporations fared extremely well, others floundered, leaving many Alaskan natives impoverished.

See Also: Alaska; Indian Policy; Indians of North America.

■ **ALBANY CONGRESS (1754),** meeting in Albany, New York, of representatives from the various English colonies in response to the impending war between France and Britain. The delegates

In the winter of 1836, Gen. Antonio López de Santa Anna's 5,000 Mexican troops laid siege upon the Alamo mission fortress in San Antonio, Texas. All 187 rebels who held the mission were killed.

hoped both to form a plan for the defense of the colonies and to enlist the support of the Iroquois Confederacy. In addition, a scheme for intercolonial government was debated. The chief authors of the Albany Plan, Benjamin Franklin and Thomas Hutchinson, proposed that an elected assembly joined by agents of the British Crown would plan for common defense paid for with taxes levied by the congress. Despite an initial enthusiasm, individual colonial assemblies were not willing to share their power to tax with any other entity. Likewise, Parliament understood that the creation of a centralized assembly with such powers had the potential to supplant English control over its colonies.

See Also: *Franklin, Benjamin; Hutchinson, Thomas.*

■ **ALBEE, EDWARD (1928-),** playwright known for his frank portrayals of men and women confronting modern life. Born in Washington, D.C., he won a Pulitzer Prize for *Who's Afraid of Virginia Woolf?* (1962).

■ **ALBRIGHT, MADELEINE (1937-),** diplomat and U.S. secretary of state (1997-). With her appointment by Pres. Bill Clinton, Albright became the first female secretary of state and the highest-ranking female government official in U.S. history. Born in Czechoslovakia, Albright fled the communist takeover with her family in 1948 and immigrated to the United States. She earned her doctorate in political science at Columbia University and entered government as a senatorial legislative assistant. After an academic career she became (1993) U.S. ambassador to the United Nations before assuming leadership of the State Department.

■ **ALCOHOL,** intoxicating and addictive substance that has created social, economic, political, and judicial problems throughout the history of the United States. The American people have held two competing views of alcohol over the course of the nation's history: they have seen it as a tonic that heals and gives energy and as a poison that destroys bodies and morals. In the several decades after the American Revolution alcohol consumption, mostly in the form of distilled spirits, soared: by the 1830s it reached an annual level of 7.1 gallons of alcohol per person

over the age of 15. The perception that alcohol use was out of control and that it was destroying families and threatening economic productivity spurred a temperance movement that succeeded in lowering per-capita consumption to about 2 gallons per year. By 1855 about a third of Americans lived under state prohibition. This "dry" movement lost momentum as problems associated with enforcement and lack of broad public support combined with the need for alcohol revenue to finance the Civil War of 1861-65.

The second period of political agitation to control alcohol began in the 1870s and derived its initial impetus from women activists who founded the Woman's Christian Temperance Union in 1874. Later, the Anti-Saloon League, founded in 1895, led the cause to victory in the form of the 18th Amendment to the Constitution, which in January 1920 banned beverage alcohol except for medicinal and sacramental purposes. Although per-capita alcohol consumption fell to an all-time low in the 1920s, this so-called Prohibition Era elicited such strong opposition that the amendment was repealed in 1933.

Thereafter, per-capita alcohol consumption slowly climbed to about 2.8 gallons in 1980. Since then consumption has declined by about a sixth as a renewed perception of alcohol's dangers—ranging from drunk driving to fetal alcohol syndrome—has reduced its appeal. Grass-roots organizations, such as Mothers Against Drunk Driving (MADD), founded in 1980, have lobbied successfully for increased penalties for those who drink and drive. The federal government mandated warning labels on all alcohol beverages in 1989.

It is estimated that 5 percent of adult Americans are seriously dependent on alcohol; this population is the most affected by liver cirrhosis, brain damage, high blood pressure, and serious accidents. Many more Americans are at risk for such alcohol-related problems. On the other hand, recent research suggests that a small amount of alcohol, about one average drink a day, may exert a protective effect against heart and vascular diseases.

—DAVID F. MUSTO

BIBLIOGRAPHY: Burnham, John C., *Bad Habits* (New York Univ. Press 1993); Clarke, Norman H., *Deliver Us From Evil: An Interpretation of American Pro-*

hibition (Norton 1976); Lender, Mark E., and James K. Martin, *Drinking in America: A History* (Free Press 1987); Musto, David F., "Alcohol in American History," *Scientific American* (Apr. 1996); Rorabaugh, W. J., *The Alcoholic Republic: An American Tradition* (Oxford Univ. Press 1979).

■ **ALCOTT, AMOS BRONSON (1799-1888),** American educator and transcendental philosopher. Born in Wolcott, Connecticut, he was a self-taught peddler-turned-teacher. He became superintendent of schools in Concord, Massachusetts, in 1859 and founded the Concord Summer School of Philosophy and Literature in 1879. Alcott was a friend and neighbor of Ralph Waldo Emerson, Nathaniel Hawthorne, and Henry David Thoreau and father of Louisa May Alcott, author of *Little Women* (1868).

See Also: Alcott, Louisa May; Emerson, Ralph Waldo; Hawthorne, Nathaniel; Thoreau, Henry David.

■ **ALCOTT, LOUISA MAY (1832-88),** author of children's books. Born in Germantown, Pennsylvania, the daughter of transcendentalist educa-

Louisa May Alcott's childhood provided her with the subject matter of her most popular book, *Little Women,* published in 1868.

tional reformer Amos Bronson Alcott, she had her greatest success in a series of semiautobiographical novels about the adolescent adventures of an independent and creative girl named Jo March. *Little Women* (1868), the first of these, is one of the most widely read children's books ever written.

See Also: Alcott, Amos Bronson; Women in American History.

■ **ALDEN, PRISCILLA MULLINS (b. 1602?),** passenger on the *Mayflower,* folk heroine of the Pilgrim story, born in Dorking, Surrey, England. Her 1623 marriage to John Alden, one of the first weddings in the Plymouth Colony, became part of American folklore as a subject of Henry Wadsworth Longfellow's poem, "The Courtship of Miles Standish" (1858).

See Also: Women in American History.

■ **ALDRICH, NELSON WILMARTH (1841-1915),** U.S. senator. He was born in Foster, Rhode Island, fought in the Civil War, and worked his way up from a wholesale grocery business to become a prominent and wealthy businessman in Providence before entering politics in 1869. Elected to the U.S. Senate in 1881, Aldrich for the next 30 years was one of the reigning conservative and probusiness leaders of the Republican party. A chief architect of the Payne-Aldrich Tariff Act (1909), he also cosponsored the Platt Amendment (1901), which gave the United States full control over Cuba.

See Also: Payne-Aldrich Tariff Act; Platt Amendment.

■ **ALDRICH-VREELAND CURRENCY ACT (1908),** legislation passed in response to the Panic of 1907. This act made the nation's money supply more flexible by allowing national banks to issue notes based on securities other than federal bonds. It also created the National Monetary Commission to control the money supply.

See Also: Banks and Banking.

■ **ALEUTS,** indigenous people of the Aleutian islands and western Alaska. They came relatively late to North America, migrating in boats across the Bering Strait around 3000 B.C. They adapted remarkably well to the harsh northern climate, fishing and hunting sea mammals and caribou. They utilized all parts of the animals for clothing, housing, tools, weapons, transportation (boats and sleds), and ceremonial purposes. Dogs, used to pull sleds and track animals, were an important part of Aleut culture. The first Aleut contact with Europeans was with the Russians in the early 1700s; between 1750 and 1780, some 90 percent of the Aleut population died from smallpox, which they contracted from the Europeans. During the 20th century, many Aleuts have continued their subsistence lifeways, supplementing their seasonal activities with paid labor.

See Also: Indians of North America.

■ **ALEXANDER, MARY PROVOOST (1693-1760),** wealthy colonial merchant. From a well-to-do Dutch family, she skillfully invested her inheritance and became a prominent figure in New York commerce. In 1721 she wed James Alexander, a leading lawyer and politician.

■ **ALEXANDERSON, ERNST (1878-1975),** electrical engineer, inventor. Born in Uppsala, Sweden, Alexanderson came to the United States in 1901 and worked with Charles Steinmetz at the General Electric Company. He invented motors adopted by electric railroads but is best known for his high-frequency alternator for radio, which he developed in 1906 and continued to improve. Alexanderson alternators enabled the world's first long-range broadcast of voice and music in 1906 and the first transatlantic radio transmission in 1911; they were soon installed all over the world. After a stint as the Radio Corporation of America's chief engineer (1919-25), Alexanderson returned to General Electric (1925-48) and continued to work on radio transmission and reception. He invented the multiple-tuned antenna, a high-frequency transmitter, and a system to transmit visual images via radio waves. Alexanderson demonstrated home television reception in 1927, transmitted pictures across the country in 1928, and continued to work past retirement into his nineties. He held more than 300 U.S. patents and earned international recognition for his pioneering work in radio and television engineering.

See Also: Invention.

■ **ALGER, HORATIO (1832-89),** novelist and popularizer of rags-to-riches tales. Alger was born in Revere, Massachusetts, and graduated from Harvard in 1852. He became a Unitarian minister and incorporated his sense of moralism into his writings. Alger wrote more than 100 books, geared primarily to young boys, that usually charted the rise of the main character through hard work and determination. Among his best-known novels are *Ragged Dick* (1867), *Luck and Pluck* (1869), and *Tattered Tom* (1871).

■ **ALGONQUIAN,** Indians of the Northeast, speakers of a family of languages seemingly evolved from one proto-Algonquian ancestor. Their ancestral bands migrated from Siberia through the former subcontinent of Beringia, or along its coast at disputed times some 15,000-40,000 years ago.

The migrants' "paleo-Indian" cultures diverged as they marched eastward around the Great Lakes to the Atlantic Coast. Tribal traditions took the Ojibwa to the coast and back to the Great Lakes, but the Delaware and related peoples stayed in the east. The Shawnee and the Illinois drifted southward to the Ohio Valley. The far north became home to the hunter tribes of Cree, Montagnais, and Algonquin. From the mouth of the St. Lawrence River southward along the Atlantic Coast were the Micmac, Abenaki, Penobscot, Massachuset, Wampanoag, Narragansett, Pequot, and Montauk. Along the Hudson River lived the Esopus and the Mahican. Along the Delaware River were the Minisink and the Delaware.

All factions of the broad Algonquian group hunted and fished, and those who lived in temperate climates became planters also, although they did not domesticate animals for labor, meat, and dairy products. Men hunted, fished, and prepared the soil for planting. Women seeded and cultivated crops (typically maize, beans, and squash) and had charge of dwellings and the children of extended families. Women also dressed the skins delivered by hunters. Villages moved cyclically to family hunting territories, to fishing and shellfishing spots, and back to the village farmland.

Before European contact, political structures typically formed around kinship, with village councils and clan chiefs whose duties and privileges were prescribed by customary law. The office of chief, "sachem," or "sagamore" was semihereditary, descending to one of the sons of the old sachem's sister. Two "squaw sachems" appear in New England's records.

The Delaware were ceremonially deferred to as "grandfathers" because of ascribed seniority; as such, they had a function for making peace between hostile Iroquois and Algonquian, a function so widely accepted that their scattered habitations, although surrounded by warlike neighbors, were not stockaded and were not attacked.

Indians and Europeans accommodated each other through the exchange of trade goods (especially wool cloth, firearms, and rum or brandy) for pelts and lands. New stress on hunting for markets transformed subsistence to commercial activity and revolutionized Algonquian cultures. In this process the Indians, because of the universal cultural stress on redistribution of wealth, never amassed capital.

Semipermanent trading relationships made particular tribes into clients of particular colonial patrons. Dependence required clients to engage in the wars of their patrons for the patrons' goals, with battlefield Algonquian population loss added to the dire mortality from European diseases.

Missions were an ambiguous institution for accommodation. Indians who joined a mission were preserved from attack by the mission's sponsors, but they were also reduced to the role of warrior clients. New England had three Puritan missions in the colonial era: John Eliot's to the Massachusett and Nipmuck on the mainland, Richard Bourne's to the Wampanoag on Cape Cod, and Thomas Mayhew's to the Wampanoag on Martha's Vineyard.

Northern Indians generally preferred the colonials of New France to the English colonials because Frenchmen mixed readily among the Indians, as opposed to English segregationism—and because smaller French populations made fewer demands for land. The French also missionized more extensively. When Britain conquered New France, the Algonquian became wholly dependent on the British for arms and trade goods. Many rose in the liberation conflict called Pontiac's War. Defeated in that, dispossessed easterners joined Tecumseh's Shawnee in futile uprising, after which the tribes scattered in

diasporas across the continent. Some remnants still remain in the east, notably the Mashantucket Pequot in Connecticut and the Wampanoag and Mashpee in Massachusetts. Except for the far northern hunters, who still hold to many traditional ways, peoples of Algonquian heritage have largely assimilated to the dominant culture of their surroundings, but they securely retain tribal identities and awareness of kinship.

—FRANCIS JENNINGS

See Also: Indians of North America.

BIBLIOGRAPHY: Axtell, James, *The European and the Indian* (Oxford Univ. Press 1981); Fitzhugh, William W., and Aron Crowell, eds., *Crossroads of Continents: Cultures of Siberia and Alaska* (Smithsonian Inst. Press 1988); Jennings, Francis, *The Founders of America* (Norton 1993); Salisbury, Neal, *Manitou and Providence* (Oxford Univ. Press 1984); Simmons, William S., *Spirit of the New England Tribes: Indian History and Folklore, 1620-1984* (Univ. Press of New England 1986); Trigger, Bruce G., ed., *Handbook of North American Indians, Vol. 15: Northeast* (Smithsonian Inst. Press 1978).

■ **ALI, MUHAMMAD (1942-),** champion boxer. Born Cassius Clay in Lexington, Kentucky, Ali first seized the attention of the world at the 1960 Olympic Games in Rome, where he won the heavyweight boxing gold medal. Styling himself "The Greatest," Ali went on to prove that he indeed was, becoming world heavyweight champion by defeating Sonny Liston in 1964. That year he converted to Islam and changed his name. In 1967 Ali was stripped of his title for refusing military service, which he opposed on religious grounds. In 1970 the Supreme Court overturned that ruling and Ali returned to boxing. Ahead lay his greatest contests, the legendary battles with Joe Frazier, Ken Norton, and George Foreman. The only man to win the heavyweight title three times, Ali retired in 1981 with a career record of 56 wins and 5 losses. He suffers from Parkinson's disease and remains one of the most widely recognized and respected figures in public life.

See Also: African Americans; Sports.

■ **ALIEN AND SEDITION ACTS,** term for four laws passed by Congress under the control of the Federalist party in June and July 1798. They were enacted amid bitter domestic political conflict and during a period of tension with France that resulted in a quasi-war (1798-1800). The laws were directed at the many politically active anti-Federalist foreigners who had recently come to America from Europe, and they were intended to stifle criticism of the administration of John Adams.

The Naturalization Act increased the citizenship residency requirement from 5 to 14 years, required immigrants to declare their intention to seek citizenship 5 years in advance, and made immigrants from "enemy" nations ineligible for citizenship. The Alien and Alien Enemy Acts empowered the president to deport any noncitizen he deemed dangerous and to deport or incarcerate foreigners during wartime. The Sedition Act made it a crime punishable by fine or imprisonment to defame the president—not the vice president, who was then Thomas Jefferson, leader of the Federalists' Republican opponents—or the U.S. government. Both the Alien law and the Sedition law were to expire after the 1800 election.

President Adams deported nobody, although several aliens did leave the country voluntarily. Many government critics, all Republicans, were prosecuted under the Sedition Act, however. At least one, Matthew Lyon of Vermont, a Republican congressman, won his 1799 reelection campaign from a jail cell.

Jefferson and his ally James Madison, considering the Alien and Sedition Acts unconstitutional, wrote the Kentucky and Virginia Resolutions to protest them. Overall the acts proved widely unpopular and contributed to the eclipse of the Federalists and the sweeping victory of Jefferson and the Republicans in the 1800 election. President Jefferson pardoned those convicted under the Sedition Act and remitted their fines.

—CATHERINE ALLGOR

See Also: *Federalism.*

BIBLIOGRAPHY: Miller, John C., *Crisis of Freedom: The Alien and Sedition Acts* (Little, Brown 1951); Smith, James Morton, *Freedom's Fetters: The Alien and Sedition Laws and American Civil Liberties* (Cornell Univ. Press 1956).

■ **ALLEN, ETHAN (1738-89),** Revolutionary War hero, soldier, and political leader. Born in Litchfield, Connecticut, Allen fought in both the

Ethan Allen and his Green Mountain Boys captured strategically important Fort Ticonderoga from the British in May 1775.

French and Indian Wars and the Revolution. He was best known for his efforts with the Green Mountain Boys to gain either independence or statehood for Vermont. Disputed land claims by neighboring states precipitated Allen's movement, which also fought against Britain during the Revolution. Allen later worked to preserve Vermont as a political entity. Statehood was not achieved until two years after his death.

See Also: *Green Mountain Boys; Revolution, American.*

■ **ALLIANCE FOR PROGRESS,** U.S. commitment initiated by Pres. John F. Kennedy in 1961. Its objectives were long-term economic assistance to Latin American states in order to support economic growth, social modernization, and political democratization. The program gradually died in the 1970s.

See Also: *Cold War.*

■ **ALLOTMENT,** policy of breaking up tribally held lands practiced from the early 19th century to 1934. Allotment first occurred in the early 1800s as part of the policy of Indian Removal. In 1832 the Creeks of Alabama signed a treaty agreeing to cede their lands east of the Mississippi River in exchange for lands west of it. The treaty stipulated that the Creeks could choose allotments—individual parcels of land given to heads of households—on the eastern lands if they did not choose to remove. The Creeks, who chose allotments, however, were subject to the harassment of local white Alabamians and the state government.

With the development of the reservation system in the 1850s, allotment plans were laid out in detail. Early treaties with so-called "friendly" Indians often provided for allotment of some of the ceded tribal lands. By 1887, when allotment became the official federal policy under the terms of the General Allotment Act, several reservations had already been divided. The philosophy behind the idea was that the individual ownership of property would instill in Indian people the desire to be like their white neighbors, to farm a homestead, develop market values, adopt Christianity, and become educated in American schools. Allotment, then, lay at the heart of the assimilation program.

The allotment policy itself was disastrous. Most of the allotted lands were of poor quality, and most of the men had no experience with farming. Further, white pressure for lands and natural resources that belonged to Indian reservations led to a demand that the federal government release the allotments from a 25-year trust period established under the General Allotment Act. As a result, during the official years of allotment policy, two-thirds of Indian lands in the United States moved out of their ownership. Allotment as a policy was officially abandoned in 1934 under the terms of the Indian Reorganization Act.

—KATHRYN A. ABBOTT

See Also: General Allotment Act (Dawes Act); Indian Policy; Indian Removal; Indian Reorganization Act; Indians of North America; Wounded Knee, Occupation of.
BIBLIOGRAPHY: Prucha, Francis Paul, *The Great Father: The United States Government and the American Indians,* 2 vols. (Univ. of Nebraska Press 1984).

■ **ALLSTON, WASHINGTON (1779-1843),** influential history painter. Allston was born in Waccamaw, South Carolina, and, after graduating from Harvard College in 1800, went to England to study painting with, among others, Benjamin West. Allston, who was to be influenced by European art to the end of his career, achieved recognition in Europe as a painter of religious and historic scenes before returning permanently to the United States in 1818. He is best known for an unfinished work, *Belshazzar's Feast,* which he began in 1817.

See Also: West, Benjamin.

■ **ALPHABET AGENCIES,** group of influential New Deal government agencies designed by Pres. Franklin D. Roosevelt and his advisers to restore confidence and stability to the country during the Great Depression. Shortly after his inauguration in March 1933, Roosevelt called for a special session of Congress to deal with the bank crisis, farm relief, and rising unemployment. During the ensuing "Hundred Days" he pushed through a series of acts that established the first of the commissions known for their acronyms as the "Alphabet Agencies."

Among these agencies were the Civilian Conservation Corps (CCC), the Agricultural Adjustment Administration (AAA), the Tennessee Valley Authority (TVA), the Federal Emergency Relief Administration (FERA), the National Recovery Administration (NRA), and the Public Works Administration (PWA). Although they all made significant contributions in easing the problems caused by the Depression, these often controversial agencies were not part of a unified program.

During the "Second Hundred Days," in spring 1935, Roosevelt advocated more progressive social reforms. This more radical phase of the New Deal saw the creation of new agencies such as the Works Progress (later, Projects) Administration (WPA), the National Labor Relations Board (NLRB), and the Resettlement Administration (RA). Taken together, the Alphabet Agencies helped to establish the federal government as a primary vehicle for social and economic change.

See Also: Civilian Conservation Corps (CCC); Hundred Days; National Recovery Administration (NRA); New Deal; Tennessee Valley Authority; Works Projects Administration (WPA).

BIBLIOGRAPHY: Conkin, Paul K., *The New Deal*, 2nd ed. (Harlan Davidson 1975).

■ **ALTGELD, JOHN PETER (1847-1902),** governor of Illinois. Born in Germany, he immigrated with his parents to the United States as a baby. He served two years in the Union army (1864-65) during the American Civil War, and then became a lawyer and was active in penal reform. In 1884 he published *Our Penal Machinery and Its Victims*. Active in Democratic state politics, he was elected Superior Court judge for Cook County, Illinois, in 1886. In 1893 he was elected governor of Illinois, holding that office for four years. His actions as governor were criticized within Illinois and nationally as dangerously radical. In his first year in office, he pardoned the three surviving 1886 Haymarket Riot anarchists, claiming they had not received a fair trial. When Pres. Grover Cleveland sent U.S. troops to Chicago in 1894 to quell riots associated with the bitter Pullman strike, Altgeld publicly protested the president's action as an unnecessary use of federal power.

See Also: Cleveland, Grover; Gilded Age; Haymarket Incident; Pullman Strike.

BIBLIOGRAPHY: Barnard, Henry, *Eagle Forgotten* (Bobbs-Merrill 1938); Ginger, Ray, *Altgeld's America* (Quadrangle Books 1965).

■ **AMANA SOCIETY,** Pietist sect formed in 1714 in Hesse, Germany. The movement revived in the early 19th century, and 600 members immigrated to New York in 1842. Between 1855 and 1864, members moved to Iowa to escape urban "corruption." Under the leadership of Christian Metz and Barbara Heinemann Landmann, they established seven cooperative villages, the Amana colonies. In 1932, the society reorganized as an independent church and a separate joint stock company.

See Also: Religion.

■ **AMERICA, NAMING OF,** the result of European recognition that the Americas were new continents. Despite the acknowledged "discovery" of the New World by Christopher Columbus, the new continents were named for Amerigo Vespucci, a Florentine merchant and explorer who traveled to South America in 1501. Vespucci's discovery of Guiana convinced him that the new land lay between Europe and China, while Columbus continued to claim that he had reached China. Vespucci published his observations, including his contention that the newly discovered land was distinct from Asia. Widely circulated, Vespucci's account was accepted by German cartographers who assigned the name "America" to their sketchy maps of the new continents. The validity of Vespucci's claim was confirmed when Magellan sailed around the tip of South America and across the Pacific less than 20 years later (1519-22).

■ **AMERICAN ANTI-SLAVERY SOCIETY,** national abolitionist organization, established in 1833. Modeled after William Lloyd Garrison's New England Anti-Slavery Society, it provided a national medium for communication and coordination among local and regional abolitionist groups. Centered in New York City, the more conservative American Anti-Slavery Society distanced itself from Garrison's radicalism, although he remained a member. Other prominent members included Arthur and Lewis Tappan, Theodore Weld, and James G. Birney. Additionally George B. Vashon, James McCrummell, and three other African Americans sat on the first board of managers. The society published pamphlets documenting the crimes of slavery, such as *Human Rights and Anti-Slavery Record*. In 1839, Garrisonians took control of the society. Dedicated to the same goals but differing on methods, a New York group then formed out of the schism, the American and Foreign Anti-Slavery Society.

See Also: Abolitionism; Garrison, William Lloyd; Weld, Theodore.

■ **AMERICAN BOARD OF CUSTOMS COMMISSIONERS,** colonial tax collecting agency. In 1767, in the wake of the Stamp Act crisis, British chancellor of the exchequer Charles Townshend imposed a host of external taxes on the colonies. To enforce the collection of these duties on items imported from England, Townshend established the American Board of Customs Commissioners in Boston. Many colonists responded to this British-controlled agency with scornful pamphlet literature and demonstrations.

See Also: Townshend Acts.

■ **AMERICAN CIVIL LIBERTIES UNION (ACLU),**
legal aid and lobbying organization. Founded in
1920 in response to the U.S. government's prosecution of antiwar activists during World War I
and the postwar "red scare" led by U.S. Attorney
General Mitchell Palmer, the ACLU is devoted to
protecting the civil liberties guaranteed every
citizen by the Bill of Rights. Often associated
with liberal and progressive causes and attacked
by conservatives, the ACLU expelled Communist
members at the start of World War II but has
rarely shied from controversy. ACLU attorneys
participated in the defense of John Scopes
(1925), Sacco and Vanzetti (1927), and the
Scottsboro Boys (1931). The organization has
also defended scores of unpopular defendants in
free speech cases, including American Nazi
party members and publishers of "adult" books,
films, and magazines.

   *See Also: Bill of Rights; Red Scare; Sacco-Vanzetti
Case; Scopes Trial; Scottsboro Case.*

BIBLIOGRAPHY: Walker, Samuel, *In Defense of American Liberties: A History of the ACLU* (Oxford Univ.
Press 1990).

■ **AMERICAN COLONIZATION SOCIETY,** (founded
1816-17), organization that sought to resettle freed
black slaves in Africa. Although abolitionists and
most free blacks opposed relocation, the society raised
enough money to transport some 12,000 blacks to
Liberia. The organization declined after 1840.

   See Also: Slavery.

■ **AMERICAN EQUAL RIGHTS ASSOCIATION
(AERA),** civil rights lobbying group founded in
1866 by Elizabeth Cady Stanton, Susan B. Anthony, and Lucy Stone. The women of the AERA,
mostly Northern whites, published essays and lectured against the disfranchisement of black
Americans and women. The Association broke up
in 1869 when two factions, one led by Stanton
and Anthony, the other by the more conservative
Stone, split as a result of political and personal
differences. They were eventually reunited in
1890 with the formation of the National American
Woman Suffrage Association.

   *See Also: American Woman Suffrage Association; An-
thony, Susan B.; Stanton, Elizabeth Cady; Stone, Lucy;
Women in American History; Women's Movement.*

■ **AMERICAN EXPEDITIONARY FORCE (AEF),**
U.S. force sent to Europe in World War I. Under
the leadership of Gen. John J. Pershing, the AEF,
which numbered over 2 million men by the war's
end, participated in the final battles that defeated
Imperial Germany. Pershing committed himself
to the construction of an independent American
army in France, doggedly resisting amalgama-
tion into the Allied forces. Although beset by
shortages of skilled and experienced officers, epic
logistical difficulties, uneven levels of discipline
within the army, and a prickly relationship with
the U.S. War Department, the AEF made a crucial
contribution to the Allied victory.

   See Also: Pershing, John Joseph; World War I.

■ **AMERICAN FEDERATION OF LABOR (AFL),**
the largest and longest-lived union federation in
American history. The AFL was established in
1886 by skilled tradesmen who rejected the
sweeping reformism, inclusive membership policies, and industry-based organization of the
Knights of Labor. Under the leadership of Samuel
Gompers, who served as the AFL's president until
1924, the AFL followed a course of neutrality in
politics, discrimination in membership, and trade
autonomy in organization. Although such policies proved successful in sustaining the fledgling
federation through its first decades, they also left
increasing numbers of working women, racial
minorities, and the unskilled outside of the labor
movement.

   By 1902, the AFL had over a million members,
a total that would double by World War I and
double again by 1920. During this era, some AFL
unions, particularly in the building trades, won
great advances in hours and wages and even assumed control over hiring policies. Other AFL af-
filiates, most notably steel workers, meat packers,
machinists, and miners, were severely weakened
by coordinated employer "open shop" campaigns
to include nonunion labor among their employees and court injunctions that limited workers'
rights of assembly and free speech. Gompers
forged a tactical alliance with the Democratic
party in an attempt to curtail such injunctions,
but the AFL's support for Pres. Woodrow Wilson,
and even for American entry into World War I,
brought only symbolic changes in labor law.

In contrast to the AFL's rapid rise prior to World War I, during the 1920s automation steadily eroded skilled workers' control over production, corporate welfare practices made unions less attractive, and the continuing eagerness of courts to issue injunctions combined to shrink the AFL's ranks. In response the AFL dabbled in third party politics by supporting Sen. Robert La Follette's presidential bid in 1924. Gompers died later that year, and his replacement by the conservative William Green indicated that the AFL was institutionally unable to adapt itself to the changing social and industrial face of America.

When the Great Depression of the 1930s evoked a new forceful movement of mass-production workers, the steadfast AFL leadership refused to organize them, precipitating a bitter split and the birth of the Congress of Industrial Organizations (CIO). Although initially at opposite poles, the rival labor federations were pulled toward the political center by the New Deal's sweeping reform of labor law, their partnership in the Democratic party, and the onset of the Cold War. In 1955, they merged as the AFL-CIO, which remained the primary representative of working people at the end of the 20th century.

—TIMOTHY MESSER-KRUSE

See Also: Congress of Industrial Organizations (CIO); Gompers, Samuel; Knights of Labor; Labor Movement; La Follette, Robert; Open Shop; Trade Unions.

BIBLIOGRAPHY: Gompers, Samuel, *Seventy Years of Life and Labor* (E.P. Dutton 1925); Montgomery, David, *The Fall of the House of Labor* (Cambridge Univ. Press 1987); Taft, Phillip, *The A.F.L. from the Death of Gompers to the Merger* (Harper 1959).

■ **AMERICAN FUR COMPANY,** organization founded to compete with Canadian fur-trading companies. John Jacob Astor founded it in 1808 to bypass Canadian and British traders and more directly control the marketing of furs between the Pacific Northwest, the East Coast, and China. Strengthening his market share by expansion, political maneuvers, and economic alliance, Astor founded the Pacific Fur Company in 1810, took over the Southwest Company by 1817, and controlled the Indian agents of the Old Northwest by 1818. In 1822, the American Fur Company formed the Western Department to control the upper Missouri River trade, buying out Bernard Pratte and Company in 1826 and allying with the Columbia Fur Company in 1827. Building Fort McKenzie at the Marias River in 1830, Astor controlled perhaps three-fourths of American fur exports by 1834. Foreseeing the decline of the fur business, Astor sold off his holdings, but remained in the profitable trading-post trade, finally selling out to the Northwest Fur Company in 1864.

See Also: Frontier in American History.

■ **AMERICAN INDIAN CIVIL RIGHTS ACT (ICRA) (1968),** legislation that required Indian nations to incorporate the First and Fourth through Eighth Amendments of the U.S. Constitution into their governing systems, but excluded the section of the First Amendment regarding the establishment of religion. Originally intended as a way of ensuring the rights of individual Indians against the arbitrary and discriminatory control of state and local non-Indian courts, the ICRA was seen by many Indians as a threat to their sovereignty, because it allowed individuals to sue their tribes in federal courts.

See Also: Indian Policy; Indians of North America.

■ **AMERICAN INDIAN MOVEMENT (AIM),** activist organization for Indian civil rights. Founded in Minneapolis in 1968, AIM's original concerns were jobs, housing, and education for Indians, as well as protection from police abuse. Many young Indians were drawn to AIM, and AIM chapters began in many urban areas. In 1972 AIM organized the "Trail of Broken Treaties," three auto caravans that converged on Washington, D.C., to present to U.S. leaders a 20-point plan for Indian policy reform. Finding that promised housing was wholly inadequate, AIM activists barricaded themselves in the Bureau of Indian Affairs building, occupying it for three days. After the occupation, the FBI classified AIM as an extremist organization.

AIM formed an alliance with traditional Sioux at Pine Ridge Reservation in South Dakota. This led to the Wounded Knee occupation of 1973, which lasted 71 days and left two AIM supporters dead. In the aftermath, the reservation police, directed by tribal chairman Richard Wilson, instituted tight controls on the reservation. Some people believe that at least 100 Sioux died in the three years following the occupation. Throughout the country, AIM was a target of the FBI and the state police. In 1975 two FBI agents were killed on the Pine Ridge Reservation. Several men were tried for these killings, and one was convicted and sentenced to two life sentences. In 1996 there were two chapters of AIM still in existence, one in Colorado and one in Minnesota.

See Also: Indians of North America; Wounded Knee, Occupation of.

■ **AMERICAN INDIAN POLICY REVIEW COMMISSION (1975),** a group established by the U.S. Congress to interpret the relationship between the United States and Indian nations. Consisting of three senators, three representatives, and five Indians, the commission reviews trust responsibilities, tribal governments, Indian affairs, jurisdiction, education and health, reservation development and protection, and nonreservation Indians. In 1977 the commission concluded that the relationship was a "continually evolving concept."

See Also: Indian Policy; Indians of North America.

■ **AMERICAN INDIAN RELIGIOUS FREEDOM ACT (1978),** legislation that affirmed the right of native peoples in the United States to practice their traditional religions. The act promised to "protect and preserve their inherent right of freedom to believe, express, and exercise the traditional religions of the American Indian, Eskimo, Aleut, and Native Hawaiians." Largely ineffective, the bill was replaced in 1993 by the Native American Free Exercise of Religion Act, which protected Indian freedom of religion more explicitly.

See Also: Indian Policy; Indians of North America.

■ **AMERICANISM,** has had two different but interconnected meanings in American history. Linguistically it has referred to a distinctive use of a term or a figure of speech. In 1781 John Witherspoon of Philadelphia defined an Americanism as the "use of phrases or terms, or a construction of sentences, even among persons of rank and education, different from the use of the same terms or phrases, or the construction of similar sentences, in Great Britain." In 1849 the scholar John Russell Bartlett published *The Dictionary of Ameri-*

canisms, the first attempt to make a catalog of such Americanisms. In its second but related meaning, Americanism referred to attachment and loyalty to the United States as a distinctive and unique culture, as when Thomas Jefferson in 1797 referred to "the dictates of reason and pure Americanism." This notion frequently intermixed with a sense of "American exceptionalism," the belief that the United States was, alone among nations, the exemplar of liberty, freedom, and enterprise, selected by God as a "chosen people." In this version Americanism was frequently allied with "nativism," the distrust and suspicion of immigrants. Americanism thus has meant the traits of speech and culture that have made the United States a distinctive culture, as well as the belief that it was the world's most superior culture.

See Also: Immigration.

■ **AMERICANIZATION,** process and movement that sought to impose the values and behaviors of the dominant white Anglo-Saxon Protestant culture on immigrants. With the explosion of European immigration after 1830, members of the dominant culture emphasized conformity in language, religion, and manners.

These sentiments became more codified when an Americanization movement developed in the first two decades of the 20th century. This organized campaign to guarantee political loyalty and cultural assimilation was promoted by settlement-house workers, advocates of the social gospel, and other progressive reformers.

A more aggressive phase of the movement began in about 1915, when, in the shadow of World War I, immigrants were perceived as potentially disloyal. Although no federal legislation was enacted, states and cities across the country adopted Americanization measures, often with the assistance of the National Americanization Committee. Legislation included English language and civics classes for immigrants and programs to teach immigrants "proper hygiene."

The immediate postwar years, which coincided with the "red scare," saw the most intense phase of the Americanization movement, as measures became more severe. The movement, however, lost credibility with many white Americans because of its vehement nativistic associations and its affiliation with groups such as the Ku Klux Klan.

See Also: Assimilation; Ethnic Groups; Immigration; Nativism; Red Scare.

■ **AMERICAN PROTECTIVE ASSOCIATION,** secret, anti-Catholic organization founded in 1886. This association arose amid the intense nationalistic and xenophobic atmosphere of post-Civil War America, a time in which some Americans feared that a Catholic conspiracy with the pope would threaten American institutions.

See Also: Immigration.

■ **AMERICAN REVOLUTION.** *See:* Revolution, American.

■ **AMERICAN SCHOOL OF ANTHROPOLOGY,** group of early-20th-century American anthropologists. The term refers to an informal group of turn-of-the-century anthropologists, including Franz Boas and his students Alfred Kroeber and Robert Lowie, who focused on describing Indian cultures from the inside. The growth of American anthropology was linked to the destruction of Indian tribes by white Americans in the late 19th century. The historic disaster prompted anthropologists to attempt to collect, record, and document information about Indian cultures. The most prolific and important anthropologist of the group was Franz Boas. Working out of Columbia University and the American Museum of Natural History, Boas undertook detailed studies of Indians living in the Pacific Northwest, especially the Kwakiutl tribe. Boas's approach emphasized detailed fieldwork and attempted to describe the internal complexities of Indian culture. Boas was, in addition, a great teacher who trained the leading anthropologists of the next generation, including Margaret Mead, Ruth Benedict, Melville Herskovits, and Edward Sapir. In the 1950s and 1960s Boas and the American School were criticized by anthropologists more interested in systematic descriptions of culture.

See Also: Anthropology and Ethnology; Boas, Franz.

■ **AMERICAN SYSTEM,** program put forth by Henry Clay to unite and develop the country's economy through a national bank, a protective tariff, and internal improvements. That Democratic-Republican Presidents Madison and Monroe supported such a Federalist vision of economic growth testified to the changing politics and prevalent nationalism during the "Era of Good Feelings." Congress funded the National Road, it chartered the Second Bank of the United States for 20 years in 1816, and it passed the first substantial protective tariff the same year. Clay pushed for the American System as a presidential candidate in 1824 and 1832, but sectional politics quickly surrounded each part of his program with contention. Fears over the power of the national bank prompted President Jackson's war against the bank and the rise of the Whig party. South Carolina introduced the doctrine of nullification in response to the 1828 "Tariff of Abominations" and threatened to secede from the Union. Internal improvements including roads, canals, and railroads united the country, but the extent to which the federal government should support them remained contested. The Whig party became largely associated with Clay and his policies, and they won the election of 1840 with William Henry Harrison, but Presidents Tyler and Polk thwarted American System policies. Aspects of Clay's program continued to raise sectional controversy and reappeared in the Republican party platform of 1860.

See Also: Banks of the United States, First and Second; Clay, Henry; Mass Production; Nullification; Whig Party.

BIBLIOGRAPHY: Baxter, Maurice G., *Henry Clay and the American System* (Univ. Press of Kentucky 1995).

■ **AMERICAN WOMAN SUFFRAGE ASSOCIATION (AWSA),** founded by Lucy Stone and Julia Ward Howe in 1869, one of two national suffrage organizations created by the breakup of the American Equal Rights Association. Stone and Howe's opposition to the more scandalous progressive causes, such as unionism and divorce, and their commitment to working for universal suffrage through local campaigns in state legislatures, not in Congress, distinguished AWSA from its rival, the National Woman Suffrage Association. The two groups united as the National American Woman Suffrage Association in 1890.

See Also: American Equal Rights Association (AERA); Howe, Julia Ward; National Woman Suffrage Association; Stone, Lucy; Women's Movement.

■ **AMISH,** followers of Jakob Amman, who separated from orthodox Mennonites in Switzerland in the late 17th century. Amish families began immigrating to America sometime after 1710. They believe in baptism for believers only, refuse to take oaths and bear arms, and avoid worldly concerns. Their conservatism has held them in tight communities and is evident in their clothing and speech, forbiddance of the use of electricity, avoidance of farming machinery, and maintenance of their own elementary schools. Today the Old Order Amish are concentrated in Pennsylvania, Ohio, and northern Indiana.

See Also: Religion.

■ **AMISTAD CASE,** U.S. Supreme Court case (1841) stemming from a slave revolt. In 1839 the American navy captured the Spanish schooner *Amistad* off Montauk Point, New York. On board were 54 enslaved Africans and 2 Spanish prisoners, who had surreptitiously navigated the ship far off course. The slaves, led by Joseph Cinque, had seized the ship as it had sailed from Cuba, a Spanish colony, killing the captain and a crewman. Abolitionist groups provided legal defense counsel for the Africans when they were charged with murder and piracy. The Africans claimed that they could not be legally recognized as slaves since Spain had outlawed slavery in 1820 and that their acts of violence were in self-defense of their lives and liberty. The case eventually reached the Supreme Court, where former president John Quincy Adams successfully argued for the Africans. Private donations made it possible for the defendants to return to Africa after their acquittal.

See Also: Slavery.

■ **AMNESTY ACT (1872),** congressional legislation that restored full political rights to all but the most prominent former Confederates. In the aftermath of the Civil War, Radical Republicans in Congress had enacted legislation that barred former Confederates from voting and holding office. By the early 1870s, however, sentiment for forgiveness and national reconciliation was increasing in the North. Carl Schurz and Horace Greeley were in the forefront of this movement.

In the 1872 presidential election, amnesty for Confederates became a prime issue of the liberal Republican faction that was unwilling to support Pres. Ulysses S. Grant for a second term and backed instead Greeley, who had been nominated by the Democrats. To counter them, regular Republicans in Congress pushed through the Amnesty Act in May.

See Also: Amnesty Proclamations; Greeley, Horace; Reconstruction; Schurz, Carl.

■ **AMNESTY PROCLAMATIONS,** attempts to end the Civil War and restore the Confederate states to the Union. All the amnesty plans were designed to conciliate white Southerners who supported or had supported rebellion against the United States. In fall 1863, Pres. Abraham Lincoln issued a proclamation offering a pardon and amnesty to Confederates who took an oath of allegiance to the United States, to its laws, and to established policies regarding slavery. This was the so-called "10 percent plan," stating that a Confederate state could rejoin the Union and hold elections when 10 percent of the number of voters in the 1860 election had taken the loyalty oath. In 1866 Pres. Andrew Johnson advocated allowing former Confederates officeholding privileges, a proposal that was rejected by Congress. Finally in 1872 Congress passed the Amnesty Act, which restored voting and officeholding privileges to all but a few hundred former Confederates.

See Also: Amnesty Acts; Reconstruction.

■ **AMOS 'N' ANDY,** popular radio (1926-60) and television (1951-53) serial that parodied urban black society. Created and performed by two Southern whites, Freeman Gosden ("Amos") and Charles Correll ("Andy"), the show debuted on network radio in 1929 and became the most popular program of the early 1930s. The television version featured an African-American cast and was condemned in the 1960s for promoting racist stereotypes.

■ **ANABAPTISTS,** from the Greek word *anabaptizin,* meaning "to rebaptize." Originating in the 16th-century reform movement in Europe, Anabaptists were neither Catholic nor Protestant. They were absolute pacifists who condemned oaths, believed in a separation of church and state, and obeyed no laws that conflicted with their consciences. Membership was for adult believers only. In North America there are 20 organized church bodies in the Anabaptist tradition, including the Mennonites, Amish, and Hutterites.

See Also: Religion.

■ **ANACONDA PLAN,** Civil War plan of the Union's Gen. Winfield Scott. In spring 1861 Scott devised a strategy for a limited war, based on a blockade of Confederate seaports and a fleet of gunboats controlling the Mississippi River. The U.S. Navy did not then have enough ships to make the blockade effective, and critics argued that Scott was reluctant to attack his home state of Virginia. Scott, however, thought the Union Army was unprepared for battle. Ultimately the sea strategy was adopted, even as the land war intensified.

See Also: Civil War; Scott, Winfield.

■ **ANARCHISM,** political theory that opposes all forms of government. It had its philosophical origins in Europe, and immigrants brought its concept to the United States, where the movement reached its height in May 1886 when the Haymarket Square Riot caused widespread antiradical reaction. In 1901 Pres. William McKinley was assassinated by anarchist Leon Czolgosz. The theory of anarchism also influenced the principles of the Industrial Workers of the World. The so-called Palmer Raids (1919-20) during the "red scare" after World War I represented perhaps the most dramatic federal attempt to rid the country of anarchists, who collectively received a great deal of attention, mostly negative, during the controversial Sacco and Vanzetti trial of the 1920s.

See Also: Haymarket Incident; Industrial Workers of the World; Palmer Raids; Sacco-Vanzetti Case.

■ **ANASAZI,** native people who were centered in the present-day Four Corners region of the Southwest, where the states of New Mexico, Arizona, Utah, and Colorado meet. The culture took shape during the 1st century A.D. In the 8th century, a shift to a drier climate led the Anasazi to intensify their farming. In irrigated, terraced fields, they grew high-yield varieties of maize, supplementing their diet with hunting. The Anasazi produced basketry and painted pottery, but they are best known for their urban architecture. They lived in multistoried apartments clustered about central plazas, with underground kivas for storage and religious ceremonies. The village of Pueblo Bonito, completed in the 12th century, contained over 650 interconnected rooms. Hundreds of miles of roads connecting thousands of community sites were used to distribute food and other resources through a region prone to drought. During the 13th century, conditions in the Southwest worsened, and a long-term drought extending from 1276 to 1293 resulted in repeated crop failures and eventual famine. Gradually the Anasazi abandoned the Four Corners. They are

Singer Marian Anderson, who entertained the troops during World War II, in 1955 became the first African American asked to join the Metropolitan Opera Company as a permanent member.

thought to be the ancestors of the Rio Grande Pueblo in northern New Mexico.

See Also: Indians of North America.

■ **ANDERSON, MARIAN (1897-1993),** opera singer. Born in Philadelphia, Pennsylvania, she was at first a gospel singer in the African-American churches of Philadelphia but began a solo concert career in 1924. She was endowed with a rich contralto voice and a rare talent. When the Daughters of the American Revolution refused to let her perform in Washington's Constitution Hall in 1939 because of her race, she performed at the Lincoln Memorial instead. Anderson became the first African-American member of the permanent company at the Metropolitan Opera, where she debuted in 1955. In 1963, she received the Presidential Medal of Freedom.

See Also: African Americans; Gospel Music; Opera; Women in American History.

■ **ANDERSON, SHERWOOD (1876-1941),** regional novelist and story writer. Originally from Camden, Ohio, Anderson served in the army during the Spanish-American War and spent time in Chicago. Anderson used his native Midwestern small towns as the setting for many of his works,

such as his first novel, *Windy McPherson's Son* (1916), and the volume of poetry *Mid-American Chants* (1918). These were followed by his classic *Winesburg, Ohio* (1919), a collection of interwoven character studies in the realist mode.

■ **ANDERSONVILLE PRISON,** Confederate prisoner-of-war camp. Commanded by Capt. Henry Wirz, Andersonville was constructed (1864) in Georgia when military prisoners in Richmond became so numerous that they presented a strategic hazard to the Confederacy. It earned the reputation as a disease-ridden death camp because of its poor sanitation, overcrowding, and inadequate food. Today there are 12,912 graves in Andersonville cemetery, but many historians believe that the death toll was actually much higher. Wirz was the only Confederate officer executed for treason at the end of the Civil War.

See Also: Civil War.

■ **ANDROS, EDMUND (1637-1714),** governor of New York (1674-81), Dominion of New England (1686-88), and Virginia (1692-97). Born on the island of Guernsey, England, to a wealthy aristocratic family, Andros was first a military officer and then an administrator. As a junior offi-

Poor rations, abominable conditions, and lack of medical attention distinguished Andersonville as the most notorious of Civil War prisons. Its Confederate commander from February 1864 to April 1865, Capt. Henry Wirz, was hanged for war crimes in November 1865.

cer, Andros went to the West Indies in 1666. By 1674 he was royal governor of New York. In 1686 the Crown appointed Andros governor of the Dominion of New England. An Anglican, Andros proceeded to antagonize Puritan leaders of Massachusetts by authorizing Anglican services in Boston. In addition, he levied new taxes, stripped the General Court of legislative power, imposed quitrents, and questioned the validity of land grants bestowed by the court. This last affected every freeholder in the colony because land title passed from the General Court through the towns to the individual owners. When William and Mary ascended the throne in 1688 the angry citizens of Boston seized and deported Andros. In 1692 Andros left England with a royal commission, this time to Virginia, where he remained until 1697.

ANGELOU, MAYA (1928-), author, performer, and civil rights activist. Born in St. Louis, Missouri, she was a nightclub singer and actress in Harlem during the 1950s and was active in the civil rights movement during the 1960s. Best known for her five popular autobiographies, beginning with *I Know Why the Caged Bird Sings* (1970), she captured national attention when she read her poem "On the Pulse of the Morning" as the keynote of the 1993 inauguration of Pres. Bill Clinton.

See Also: African Americans; Civil Rights Movement; Women in American History.

ANGLO-DUTCH WARS (1652-54, 1664-67), naval wars prompted by overseas commercial rivalries. England was victorious in the first war. The second war arose over competition for the slave trade and East Indies commerce and conflicting ambitions in North America. King Charles II had allowed the English fleet to decline, and the Dutch won victories that forced the English to make concessions in the Treaty of Breda (1667). But England retained the captured Dutch colonies of New Netherland (later New York) and Delaware.

See Also: Dutch Colonies.

ANNAPOLIS CONVENTION (1786), meeting of delegates from five states to discuss interstate commerce. With the country reeling from inter-

nal unrest and financial troubles, Virginia proposed a meeting to consider uniform trade regulations. When the meeting commenced, the delegates found that the necessary reforms were beyond their powers to implement. Led by the Virginia delegation and Alexander Hamilton, they drafted a report calling for a general convention in 1787 in Philadelphia. That meeting became the Constitutional Convention.

See Also: Constitutional Convention; Constitution of the United States.

ANTHONY, SUSAN B. (1820-1906), women's rights leader, social reformer, and politician. The preeminent organizer of the U.S. women's suffrage movement, Anthony devoted her life to social reform, serving as the figure around which the women's movement coalesced. Born in Adams, Massachusetts, she was well educated and worked as a teacher when her family suffered economic reverses.

In the 1850s Anthony became a reformer, active in the temperance, abolition, and women's labor movements. In 1851 she began a 50-year collaboration with Elizabeth Cady Stanton, organizer of the Seneca Falls Convention. Barred by men from speaking at temperance meetings, the two women founded the New York Women's State Temperance Society in 1852. Radicalized by Cady Stanton, Anthony devoted increasing amounts of energy to women's issues. Her talents lay in her ability to educate women about political equality, to organize them, and to push legislation.

During the Civil War Anthony and Cady Stanton founded the National Women's Loyal League, which demanded the constitutional abolition of slavery and the emancipation of women. After the war Anthony and Cady Stanton felt betrayed when the 14th and 15th amendments failed to grant women the vote; in response they formed in 1869 the National Woman Suffrage Association (NWSA). More conservative reformers, willing to make African-American suffrage their priority, responded by creating the American Woman Suffrage Association (AWSA). In spite of their abolitionist backgrounds, Anthony and Cady Stanton even appealed to white racism to further the cause of white female suffrage.

With Anthony as organizer and Cady Stanton

Cofounder of the National Woman Suffrage Association (NWSA) in 1869 and president of the National American Woman Suffrage Association (NAWSA) from 1892 to 1900, Susan B. Anthony played a leading role in winning the right to vote for women.

as writer, the two women began the periodical *The Revolution* (1868-70) and also traveled west campaigning for suffrage. Anthony was burned in effigy and ridiculed by the press. During the presidential election of 1872 she was arrested for voting in Rochester, New York, and fined $100, which she refused to pay.

The post–Civil War years saw a marked divergence between the goals of Anthony and the more radical and secular Cady Stanton. Anthony's plan was to organize diverse groups of women around the single cause of suffrage, joining forces with the charismatic Frances Willard, head of the influential Women's Christian Temperance Union. Beginning in 1865, Anthony annually petitioned Congress, becoming a savvy lobbyist.

In 1890 the NWSA and AWSA united, forming the National American Woman Suffrage Association. Anthony served as its president from 1892 until her retirement in 1900. Although she did not live to see the passage of the 19th Amend-

ment (sometimes called the "Anthony Amendment"), she is the suffrage leader most remembered. In 1979, Anthony became the first woman to have her likeness appear on U.S. currency, the dollar coin.

—CATHERINE ALLGOR

See Also: *Gilded Age; National Woman Suffrage Association; Stanton, Elizabeth Cady; Suffrage; Willard, Frances; Women in American History; Women's Movement.*

BIBLIOGRAPHY: Barry, Kathleen, *Susan B. Anthony* (New York Univ. Press 1988); DuBois, Ellen Carol, ed., *Elizabeth Cady Stanton-Susan B. Anthony: Correspondence, Writings, Speeches* (Schocken 1981).

■ **ANTHROPOLOGY AND ETHNOLOGY,** social science disciplines. These terms frequently overlap in both methodologies and results in that both disciplines focus on different cultures and the detailed descriptions of those cultures. Ethnology is widely used as a synonym for anthropology. For the British, anthropology and ethnology are interchangeable. For Americans, anthropology also includes archaeology and physical anthropology. Both anthropology and ethnology focus on the comparative and historical study of people's cultures without a bias toward their beliefs or practices. The written descriptions of these other cultures, called ethnography, attempt to convey a people's culture from an insider's point of view. Topics traditionally covered in ethnographic writings include kinship, religion, political organization, speech, warfare, material culture, or foodways. One classic in anthropology is Margaret Mead's *Coming of Age in Samoa* (1928), which details the parent-child socialization process of Samoans. Ethnology came under criticism for romanticizing other cultures in order to implicitly critique the growth of capitalism in the West and for not acknowledging the anthropologist's role in the recording, editing, and writing about other cultures. In response, ethnographic writing has become more self-reflexive and more prone to blur the traditional topics of ethnography. For instance, Clifford Geertz's influential "Deep Play: Notes on A Balinese Cockfight" (1972) focuses on the cockfight as a symbolic act that reveals the internal interpretations of Balinese culture. Other more recent ethnographic writing has also probed the various meanings of attempting to write about another culture as its subject.

—JEFF HARDWICK

BIBLIOGRAPHY: Geertz, Clifford, *The Interpretation of Cultures* (Basic Books 1972); Mead, Margaret, *Coming of Age in Samoa* (William Morrow 1928).

■ **ANTICOMMUNISM,** U.S. policy of opposing communist regimes, complemented by fear of communist influence in the United States. For almost six decades following the Bolshevik Revolution of 1917 an unofficial cold war existed between the United States and the Union of Soviet Socialist Republics. This international tension strongly influenced U.S. foreign policy during this period. At the same time, many Americans, fearful that they might be losing the war, lashed out at suspected domestic sympathizers. This resulted in one of the most sustained attacks on civil liberties in American history.

The Bolsheviks' success in 1917 produced immediate repercussions in the United States. The administration of Pres. Woodrow Wilson reacted harshly, eventually supporting the White Russian counterrevolution with an American expeditionary force. Meanwhile Wilson's attorney general, A. Mitchell Palmer, prompted by his young subordinate J. Edgar Hoover, initiated a series of raids on suspected domestic communists, jailing and deporting a few and in the process chilling or enraging many liberals.

The American Communist party was not then or later a threat to national security, not even in its heyday of the 1930s, when European Popular Front governments including Communists tried to stop the rise of fascism, thereby gaining sympathy and new American adherents. However, "red scare" did not entirely die down, notwithstanding U.S. recognition of the USSR in Pres. Franklin D. Roosevelt's first administration, and with disclosure of the Nazi-Soviet Pact of 1939 it returned with a vengeance. The United States and its allies welcomed the Soviet Union as a partner against the Axis in World War II only reluctantly, and several scholars have suggested that the Allies delayed opening a second front in Europe—the D-Day invasion—in hopes of playing off the Russians against the Germans.

In the years immediately after World War II fear of domestic communism became a part of mainstream political life, and it was used by reigning Republicans to tar New Deal Democrats with the taint of treason. In self-defense, Pres. Harry S. Truman created loyalty boards designed to keep individuals with suspected communist ties out of government jobs, and the Republican-controlled Congress gave additional power to the House Un-American Activities Committee (HUAC) to hunt down and discredit alleged subversives.

Public opinion split, however, over Sen. Joseph R. McCarthy's orgy of unfounded accusations that prominent Americans including Sec. of State Dean Acheson were Communist sympathizers. Right-wing Republicans and conservatives supported both the senator's charges and his unfair investigative practices, but most Democrats and some moderate Republicans joined together to censure the senator in 1954, bringing to an end the red hunts of the 1950s.

At the same time, however, anticommunism was the cornerstone of U.S. foreign policy, which relied on domestic anticommunism to assure public support for the Cold War. The Korean War, CIA-sparked coups against suspected communist governments in Latin America, military (and economic) measures taken against Castro's Cuba, the Vietnam War, and Pres. Ronald Reagan's clandestine war against Nicaraguan Sandanistas were all attempts to destroy communist regimes before they could spread to other underdeveloped nations—a hypothesis of American policy planners popularly known as the Domino Theory. Only after the disintegration of the Soviet empire itself in 1989 did anticommunism cease to be pivotal in American affairs.

—JOHN ROBERT GREENE

See Also: *Cold War; Communist Party; D-Day; Korean War; McCarthy, Joseph; Nicaraguan Interventions; Palmer Raids; Red Scare; Roosevelt, Franklin Delano; Truman, Harry S.; Un-American Activities, House Committee on (HUAC); Vietnam War; Wilson, (Thomas) Woodrow.*

BIBLIOGRAPHY: Bennett, David, *The Party of Fear: From Nativist Movements to the New Right in American History* (Univ. of North Carolina Press 1988); Caute, David, *The Great Fear: The Anti-Communist Purge Under Truman and Eisenhower* (Simon & Schuster 1978).

Battle of Antietam, on Sept. 17, 1862, was the bloodiest day of the Civil War, with 5,000 dead and 19,000 wounded, and effectively ended in a stalemate.

ANTIETAM (OR SHARPSBURG), BATTLE OF

(1862), the bloodiest single-day battle of the Civil War, pitting the forces of Confederate Gen. Robert E. Lee against Union Gen. George B. McClellan. Having invaded Maryland, Lee's army assumed a defensive position behind Antietam Creek. On September 17 ill-coordinated Union attacks hit first the Confederate left, then the center and right. McClellan failed to take advantage of large gaps in the Southern line. The result was a tactical victory for the Confederates, who retreated from Maryland unpursued, but a strategic one for the Union, emboldening Pres. Abraham Lincoln to announce the Emancipation Proclamation.

See Also: *Civil War; Lee, Robert E.; McClellan, George.*

ANTIFEDERALISM, loose alliance of politicians

and citizens, and a localist political philosophy promoted by opponents of ratification of the Constitution. Originating as a political force during the Revolution, Antifederalism represented the belief in a voluntary attachment by the people to the government and its laws, a fundamental responsibility of the government to the people, and the necessity of a citizenry that maintains republi-

can ideals. Though Antifederalists repudiated the Constitution, they did not oppose a federal form of government. Instead, they objected to the Constitution on the grounds that it was attempting to replace true federalism with centralization. Antifederalists feared that the Constitution would concentrate power in the national government, subvert the authority of individual states, and lead inevitably to an aristocracy.

The Antifederalists, unlike the Federalists, did not produce a coherent body of philosophical positions and political tracts. Indeed, from their scattered writings in pamphlets, letters, newspapers, and debate records, it is evident that they often held inherently contradictory positions. While supporting a great republic, they also strongly favored small, self-governing communities. Their leaders included George Mason and Patrick Henry.

Although the Antifederalists failed to stop ratification, they were largely responsible for the quick adoption of the Bill of Rights by 1791. The Antifederalists did not outlast the Constitutional debates, but their concern with centralized authority and infringement on personal freedoms had persisted as a topic of political debate throughout American history.

See Also: Constitution of the United States; Federalism; Henry, Patrick; Mason, George.

BIBLIOGRAPHY: Main, Jackson Turner, *The Antifederalists: Critics of the Constitution, 1781-1788* (Univ. of North Carolina Press 1961); Storing, Herbert, *What the Anti-Federalists Were For* (Univ. of Chicago Press 1981).

■ **ANTI-MASONRY,** movement begun in upstate New York in the 1820s against the Order of Freemasons and other secret societies. Anti-Masonry highlighted tensions over industrialization and the economic elite. In 1830 the Anti-Masons created the nation's first third party. Running William Wirt against National Republican Henry Clay and Democrat Andrew Jackson in the 1832 presidential election, the Anti-Masons were the first to hold a national convention and the first to announce a platform.

■ **ANTIN, MARY (1881-1949),** Russian-born, Jewish author who wrote and lectured about the immigrant experience in America. She was a staunch opponent of restrictive immigration policies and defended progressive measures such as public schools and civic education. She wrote *The Promised Land* (1912).

■ **ANTI-PRICE DISCRIMINATION.** *See: Robinson-Patman Act.*

■ **ANTISLAVERY MOVEMENT,** in U.S. history, a diverse movement that sought to emancipate the millions of African Americans held in involuntary servitude. In colonial-era North America the Society of Friends almost alone condemned slaveholding as immoral. The ideological ferment of the Age of Enlightenment followed by the American Revolution, however, led many Americans to equate the slaves' right to freedom with the colonists' demand for independence. Consequently, northern states began the gradual emancipation of their slaves. Although the federal government prohibited slavery in the Northwest Territory in 1787 and banned the transatlantic slave trade in 1808, southern slavery's increasing profitability produced a general reduction of abolitionist agitation by the early 19th century. What remained of antislavery sentiment became channeled through the African Colonization Society, begun in 1816, which was created to return African Americans to their home continent.

Abolitionism in the 1830s. During the 1830s the modern abolition campaign in the United States emerged as a by-product of the upsurge of religious revivalism popularly known as the Second Great Awakening. Revivalistic assumptions led abolitionists to regard slavery as the product of personal sin and to demand emancipation as the cost of repentance. Abolitionists also recognized that slavery received moral support from racial prejudice, and they lobbied to overturn their many discriminatory practices against African Americans.

During the 1830s the abolitionists attempted to reach and convert a mass audience. By means of lecturing agents, petition drives, and a wide variety of printed materials, the abolitionists' American Anti-Slavery Society (AASS), founded in 1833, attracted tens of thousands of members. Throughout the same period, however, the targets of abolitionist efforts, the individual slaveholders and the national religious institutions, rejected antislavery appeals. In addition, the early abolitionists endured attempts to silence antislavery agitation by mob violence and by legal and ecclesiastical enactments.

Women and African Americans in the Abolitionist Movement. Thousands of women braved public disapproval to participate in the antislavery movement. Often veterans of moral reform causes, these women were inspired by a blend of religious principles and republican ideology to call for an immediate end to slavery. Although a few women attended its founding convention in 1833, the AASS at first barred female members. Abolitionist women instead formed their own local organizations, which held national conventions in 1837 and 1838, and raised considerable money for the antislavery movement through sponsoring events such as picnics and bazaars.

Another significant element in the new immediate abolitionist movement were African-American activists. Some had long records of public opposition to the colonization movement and the

North's pervasive racial discrimination. Fugitive slaves such as Frederick Douglass and William Wells Brown provided compelling antislavery testimony. African-American abolitionists sometimes encountered patronizing attitudes from their white counterparts, and many shifted their labors to self-help and civil rights efforts while a few concentrated on separatist projects such as African emigration.

Garrison and His Opponents. The rejection of the emancipation and antiracial-discrimination programs by every major American religious body in the 1830s forced abolitionists to reconsider their original church-oriented strategy. Many followed the lead of the Boston abolitionist William Lloyd Garrison and abandoned the churches, which they considered hopelessly corrupted by slavery. These Garrisonians also adopted pacifist or "nonresistant" political practices and counseled northerners to withhold their sanction from what they regarded as the proslavery U.S. Constitution by refusing to vote. The Garrisonians championed the right of women to participate in every part of the movement. After gaining the right to vote in the AASS's annual meeting in 1839, women provided the Garrisonians with the strength to win control of the society the following year, when their opponents quit to protest the election of a female officer.

Many non-Garrisonian abolitionists regrouped in a new organization, the American and Foreign Anti-Slavery Society (AFASS). In their lecturing and writing, AFASS abolitionists concentrated on inducing the churches to take stronger antislavery stands. The AFASS gained valuable allies in the early 1840s in the form of well-organized Methodist, Baptist, and Presbyterian denominational antislavery movements. This agitation helped foment the sectional schisms of the Methodist and Baptist churches in the mid-1840s and the New School Presbyterians in 1857. Even after those divisions, however, abolitionists continued to protest that the northern church branches still tolerated thousands of border state slave owners in their fellowship.

While some non-Garrisonian abolitionists focused on reforming the churches, others shifted their energies to political antislavery reform. Beginning in the mid-1830s, abolitionists had petitioned legislatures and interrogated political candidates on slavery-related issues. When no candidate expressed antislavery sentiments, abolitionists often protested by "scattering" their ballots among write-in candidates. When the federal government failed to respond to their petitioning or lobbying, these politically minded abolitionists formed an independent antislavery party in 1840.

Abolitionism and Politics in the 1840s. The new Liberty party was launched to allow the advancement of the immediate emancipation program through partisan politics. Although some political abolitionists made efforts to introduce economic considerations into their party's arguments against slavery, the Liberty platform in the 1840 and 1844 presidential elections differed little from those of the old antislavery societies. It called for an immediate abolition of slavery wherever constitutionally possible and for the repeal of all racially discriminatory legislation as a religious as well as a political duty.

In the early 1840s abolitionists were deeply divided about the fledgling Liberty party. Most Garrisonians condemned all political activity, including that of the Liberty party, as an implied endorsement of the legality of slavery. Many non-Garrisonian abolitionists were reluctant to support the Liberty party because of their strong allegiances to the Whig party. The Whig's moralistic rhetoric and occasional support of Sabbatarian practices and prohibition were highly attractive to the same evangelical voters who were most inclined to abolitionism. By bringing a new ethically defined issue into politics, the Liberty party challenged the Whig hold on evangelical voters. The support for the Liberty party presidential candidate James G. Birney—7,000 votes (0.29 percent) in 1840 and 62,000 (2.31 percent) in 1844—however, showed that the single issue of slavery was not yet strong enough to turn many voters, evangelical or not, away from the Whigs.

Free Soil and Kansas-Nebraska. Events in the 1840s fostered the growth of northern political antislavery sentiment. Public controversy over such issues as the congressional "gag rule" against antislavery petitions, the annexation of Texas (1845) as a new slaveholding state, and the disposition of territory won in the Mexican War

(1846-48) made opposition to the "Slave Power" more respectable in northern circles. A Liberty party faction led by Salmon P. Chase, Gamaliel Bailey, and Henry B. Stanton advocated electoral cooperation in the 1848 election with groups in the major parties who were opposed to slavery's extension into the new western states. In a complicated series of intraparty battles the procoalition forces outmaneuvered all opponents and merged the Liberty party with antiextensionist Whigs and Democrats, creating a new Free Soil party. Unlike the Liberty party, the Free Soilers gave no endorsements for immediate abolition or equal rights for African Americans.

The 1848 Free Soil ticket of Martin Van Buren and Charles Francis Adams received 290,000 votes. The passage of the Compromise of 1850, however, temporarily depressed northern antislavery sentiment and the party received only 156,000 votes in 1852.

This trend was reversed with passage in 1854 of the controversial Kansas-Nebraska Act, which repealed the 1820 Missouri Compromise ban on slavery in western territories north of 36° 30'. The simultaneous rise of nativism in the early 1850s as a political issue weakened traditional party allegiances. No longer able to satisfy either northern or southern militants, the Whig party performed poorly in the 1852 election and disintegrated amid the turmoil accompanying the Kansas-Nebraska Act. At the same time, Free Soilers merged with recent converts to antiextensionism from the Whigs and Democrats to form (1854) the Republican party. The new party attracted a broad range of voters, including many who were more concerned with economic development and freedom from competition with African-American labor than with ending slavery.

Abolitionists and Republicans. The large majority of political abolitionists were content to work with more moderate antislavery northerners inside the Republican party. Chase, Bailey, and other former Liberty party leaders joined forces with "radical" antislavery defectors from the major parties, such as Joshua Giddings, Charles Sumner, and John P. Hale, to resist efforts by conservative or racist elements in the Republican coalitions to shift those parties' focus away from moral opposition to slavery's expansion. These efforts were so successful that by 1860 nearly all political abolitionists and even some Garrisonians endorsed the election of Abraham Lincoln as a principled means of battling slavery.

During the Civil War the abolitionists pressed Lincoln until he adopted emancipation as a war goal. In the postwar era surviving abolitionists continued to lobby the federal government to act to protect the rights of the newly freed African Americans. As dedicated agitators for more than 30 years, the abolitionists contributed significantly to moving the political system to act against slavery and racism.

—JOHN R. MCKIVIGAN

See Also: *Free Soil Party; Garrison, William Lloyd; Kansas-Nebraska Act; Liberty Party; Republican Party; Slavery.*

BIBLIOGRAPHY: Dillon, Merton L., *The Abolitionists: The Growth of a Dissenting Minority* (Northern Illinois Univ. Press 1974); Sewell, Richard, *Ballots for Freedom: Antislavery Politics in the United States, 1837-1860* (Oxford Univ. Press 1976); Stewart, James B., *Holy Warriors: The Abolitionists and American Slavery* (Hill & Wang 1976).

■ **ANTITRUST CASES (1895-1911)**, series of U.S. Supreme Court cases that clarified the meaning and scope of the Sherman Antitrust Act. In response to the public outcry over the proliferation of corporate combinations and monopolies, Congress passed the Sherman Antitrust Act in 1890. The statute outlawed any business practice that acted "in restraint of trade or commerce among the several states." The commerce clause of the Constitution gave Congress authority to regulate commerce. It fell to the Supreme Court, however, to construe exactly what "commerce" meant and thus to determine the scope of congressional regulatory authority. Initially, as in *United States* v. *E. C. Knight* (1895), the Court held that there was a crucial distinction between commerce and manufacturing. In *Knight* the Court determined that the activity in question, sugar refining, was essentially a manufacturing enterprise that was only *indirectly* implicated in commerce and so was outside the scope of the Sherman Act. Over the next 10 years, even under this stricter requirement of a finding of a *direct* impact on commerce, a handful of cases, *Addyston Pipe and Steel Co.* v. *United States*

(1899) among them, came before the Supreme Court. Beginning in 1904 with *Northern Securities Co. v. United States* and, a year later, with *Swift & Co. v. United States*, the Court significantly broadened its definition of commerce. In *Swift* the "stream of commerce" doctrine introduced a rationale for implicating what were essentially manufacturing enterprises, slaughterhouses, in a nexus of interstate commerce. The Court determined in 1911, however, that such an implication in interstate commerce was not a prima facie violation of the Sherman Act. In *Standard Oil Company of New Jersey v. United States* (1911), Chief Justice Edward White presented his "rule of reason" test. Only where trusts *unreasonably* limited competition, White announced, did the Sherman Act apply. Whether or not Congress had intended such a standard, the "rule of reason" thenceforth became established as the basic test for determining the legality of a trust or monopoly.

—MATTHEW E. BABCOCK

See Also: Sherman Antitrust Act; Supreme Court.
BIBLIOGRAPHY: Letwin, William, *Law and Economic Policy in America: The Evolution of the Sherman Antitrust Act* (Random House 1965); McCurdy, Charles W., "The Knight Sugar Decision of 1895 and the Modernization of American Corporate Law, 1869-1903," *Business History Review* (August 1979).

■ **ANTITRUST LEGISLATION,** series of federal laws passed in the late 19th century that sought to curb the economic abuses of trusts. In the final decades of the 1800s, certain corporations came to dominate their industries by combining in ways that reduced or eliminated competition. Unclear and inefficient legal guidelines failed to curb illegal or unethical practices of these trusts. The first major piece of legislation was the Interstate Commerce Act of 1887, which created the Interstate Commerce Commission (ICC). In 1890, Congress confronted the problem of trusts directly with the passage of the Sherman Antitrust Act. Although the law proscribed trusts or any conspiracies that restrained trade or commerce, it was a vague and inefficient reform measure and was essentially left idle by unresponsive administrations and the court system. Not until the administrations of Pres. Theodore Roosevelt (1901-09) and Pres.

William Howard Taft (1909-13) were many prosecutions instituted under the 1890 law.

A turning point in antitrust legislation occurred during Pres. Woodrow Wilson's administration (1913-21). Seeking clearer and more effective legislation, Wilson pushed through Congress the Federal Trade Commission Act of 1913 and the Clayton Antitrust Act of 1914, which expanded the Sherman bill. Despite good intent, these bills remained more show than substance, as the courts again failed to implement them rigorously.

Support for antitrust legislation grew during the late New Deal of the 1930s. But with some notable exceptions, such as the federal suit against American Telephone and Telegraph (AT&T), which resulted in its dismemberment in 1981, antitrust legislation in the post–World War II period has mostly been honored in the breech.

See Also: Clayton Antitrust Act; Interstate Commerce Commission (ICC); Sherman Antitrust Act.
BIBLIOGRAPHY: Dewey, Donald J., *The Antitrust Experiment in America* (Columbia Univ. Press 1990); Peritz, Rudolph J. R., *Competition Policy in America, 1888-1992: History, Rhetoric, Law* (Oxford Univ. Press 1996).

■ **ANZA, JUAN BAUTISTA DE (1735-88),** Spanish soldier and explorer of the American Southwest, born in Fronteras, Mexico. In 1774 Anza, then captain of the Sonoran presidio of Tubac (south of present-day Tucson, Arizona), established, with the help of a Cochimí guide, a route across the Sonoran Desert into the Los Angeles Basin to Monterey. Anza led a second expedition that founded San Francisco in 1776. He served as governor of New Mexico from 1778 to 1787.

See Also: Exploration and Discovery.

■ **ANZIO LANDING (1944),** World War II British-American amphibious operation. With the Allied advance up the Italian peninsula toward Rome stalled at the German Gustav Line, the Allied VI Corps under Gen. John Lucas was landed on Jan. 22, 1944, at Anzio, 30 miles south of Rome and 60 miles behind German lines. Although virtually unopposed, Lucas moved overcautiously (he was later relieved), and German Field Marshal Albert Kesselring rushed in reinforcements who pinned the Allied force on the beachhead where they remained until May, when reinforcements enabled them to break out.

See Also: World War II.

■ **APACHE,** Indian tribe that, along with the Navahos, forms the southernmost extension of the Na-Dene language family. Modern anthropologists and linguists differentiate "Eastern" and "Western" Apache. Western Apache are those descended from bands holding reservations within the present-day state of Arizona. Eastern Apache are all the others, who have lands in New Mexico and Oklahoma. Linguistic experts have placed the Apache movement from Arctic regions of western Canada to the southwestern desert sometime between the 13th and 16th centuries. Until the arrival of the Spanish, the Apache subsisted by combining hunting, gathering, small-scale agriculture, trading, and some raiding. The arrival with the Spanish of the horse in the 16th century made a nomadic lifestyle even more attractive, and the Apache expertly adapted the horse to their cultural pattern. The Apache and Navaho began to diverge at the end of the 17th century. The Apache retained more of their earlier cultural emphasis on mobility. They lived in quickly constructed thatch huts called "wickiups" rather than in the larger hogans of the Navaho.

After the Civil War, the U.S. government set about realizing the goal of Manifest Destiny by establishing control of all the land in the West. This required subjugating all the Indians within the nation's borders including, of course, the Apache. Because these people were not dependent upon fields and flocks, the United States could not simply conquer them by destroying farms and livestock. The mobility of the Apache, their expertise with horses, and their familiarity with the desert terrain made them formidable opponents despite their small numbers.

Campaigns Against the Apaches. Eventually, only negotiations could bring all the Apache under the American mantle. Five reservations were marked out for them, lands supposedly remote from white settlements and resources, and band by band the Apache were cajoled into moving onto the reservations. By late 1872 enough had been lured by the promises of peace and rations that a campaign could be mounted under Gen. George Crook to secure the remaining Apache by arms. Crook was able to capture Apache only by using Apache scouts from friendly bands to lead soldiers to resisting bands, who then were either killed or dragged to a reservation.

The Chiricahua band led by the dynamic shaman, Goyalke, known to the white men as Geronimo, was one of the last to surrender. On several occasions the Chiricahua surrendered and accepted reservations, but time after time they found that promises were not kept and that reser-

The Apache, known as tireless and fierce opponents of American expansion, resisted the army until the 1880s.

vation life was too stifling. At one time in 1885 nearly 5,000 troops were engaged to hunt Geronimo's band of 400 Apaches. Geronimo finally surrendered on Sept. 4, 1887, and promised to stay on a reservation in Arizona. However, the army broke the agreement under pressure from Arizona ranchers. Rather than allowed to live in Arizona, the Chiricahua were taken as prisoners of war to Florida until 1894, then removed to Oklahoma, and not permitted to choose their place of habitation until 1913. Geronimo would become a legend in his own time and even participated in Pres. Theodore Roosevelt's inaugural parade in 1905. A few Apache groups were never subjugated and were hunted and raided in the mountains of northern Sonora in Mexico through the 1930s.

—RYAN MADDEN

See Also: Geronimo; Indians of North America; Navaho.

BIBLIOGRAPHY: Ballantine, Betty and Ian, eds., *The Native Americans* (Turner 1993); Spicer, Edward, *The Impact of Spain, Mexico, and the U.S. on the Indians of the Southwest* (Univ. of Arizona Press 1962).

■ **APPALACHIA,** region of eastern North America containing the Appalachian Mountains, a system stretching some 2,000 miles from Maine to Alabama. The northern section encompasses mountains from Maine to Maryland, but it is in the southern region from West Virginia to Georgia that the most rugged terrain is found and to which the term *Appalachia* usually refers. Scots-Irish, German, and English immigrants settled in Appalachia in the early 19th century after the American Revolution, when the native inhabitants—the Iroquois in the north and the Cherokee in the south—had been decimated by disease and war and removed to reservations in the west. During the Civil War (1861-65) the Appalachian region experienced bitter guerrilla warfare because its people were divided between Confederate and Union loyalists. Out of that conflict, the state of West Virginia was created in 1863, the only state located entirely in the Appalachian region. After the war Southern Appalachia began to acquire its reputation as a folk culture characterized by backwardness and brutality. Other parts of the country perceived Appalachians romantically as "our contemporary ancestors" or as a collection of feuding clans, the most notorious of which were the Hatfields and McCoys, whose famous feud took place between 1878 and 1890. Between 1890 and 1920 the region became the greatest coal-producing area in the country, but poverty among mountain people increased. Despite the attempts of the presidential administrations of Franklin D. Roosevelt in the 1930s and John F. Kennedy and Lyndon B. Johnson in the 1960s to alleviate hunger and destitution with welfare programs, the southern Appalachians remain one of the most impoverished regions of the country.

—ALTINA L. WALLER

BIBLIOGRAPHY: Shapiro, Henry, *Appalachia On Our Mind: The Southern Mountains and Mountaineers in the American Consciousness* (Univ. of North Carolina Press 1978); Salstrom, Paul, *Appalachia's Path To Dependency: Rethinking a Region's Economic History 1730-1940* (Univ. Press of Kentucky 1994).

■ **APPALACHIAN MOUNTAINS,** mountain system of eastern North America, running some 2,000 miles from Newfoundland, Canada, southwest to central Alabama. The Appalachian range includes all of the major mountains of the eastern United States, including the White Mountains, the Green Mountains, the Berkshires, the Catskills, the Blue Ridge, the Great Smoky Mountains, and the Cumberland Mountains. During the colonial period, the mountain system formed a natural barrier to westward settlement and represented the first American frontier. The Appalachians are rich with minerals. In Pennsylvania, West Virginia, and Kentucky large coal deposits have been mined since the late 19th century. The closing of coal mines in the post–World War II period left many people in the area without jobs. The region became a symbol for Pres. Lyndon B. Johnson's War on Poverty during the 1960s and received much federal money in an attempt to improve housing, health, and education. The Appalachians contain many national parks and are a popular tourist attraction. The 2,100-mile Appalachian Trail was constructed between 1922 and 1937, and in 1968 Congress made it one of the initial parts of the National Trail System.

See Also: Blue Ridge; Catskill Mountains; Cumberland Gap; Great Smoky Mountains; Green Mountains; White Mountains.

■ **APPLESEED, JOHNNY (1774-1845),** nickname of John Chapman, a horticulturist in the Pennsylvania and Ohio region and a prominent figure in early American folklore. Contrary to legend, Chapman, who was born in Massachusetts, was not the first to bring apple trees to the Midwest. Many settlers carried seeds with them. He was, however, surely the most peripatetic, with nurseries scattered along the Allegheny and Ohio river valleys. In his travels among the region's far-flung settlements, Chapman distributed news and Bible tracts along with his seeds and saplings, giving rise to tales about "Johnny Appleseed," a kindly, eccentric wanderer.

BIBLIOGRAPHY: Price, Robert, *Johnny Appleseed: Man and Myth* (Indiana Univ. Press 1954).

■ **APPOMATTOX COURTHOUSE,** Virginia town where in the Civil War Confederate Gen. Robert E. Lee surrendered to Union Gen. Ulysses S. Grant on Apr. 9, 1865. Grant's surrender terms were generous. Lee's capitulation is often regarded as the end of the war, although other Confederate armies remained in the field.

See Also: *Civil War; Lee, Robert Edward.*

■ **APTHEKER V. SECRETARY OF STATE (1964),** U.S. Supreme Court case that limited the government's ability to forbid international travel by U.S. citizens. At the height of the Cold War, the U.S. government refused to grant passports to members of the Communist party and other alleged subversives who wished to travel overseas. Enforcement of the policy was a source of controversy, and the Supreme Court ruled in *Kent* v. *Dulles* (1958) that the State Department was not empowered to deny passports to U.S. citizens. The State Department then attempted to invoke sections of the Internal Security Act of 1950 (the McCarran Act) that required members of subversive organizations to register with the government and allowed the government to deny them

The Union's Gen. Ulysses S. Grant (*seated, center right*) accepted the surrender of Gen. Robert E. Lee at Appomattox Courthouse, Virginia, on Apr. 9, 1865.

passports needed for international travel. The law's registration requirements were upheld in *Communist Party* v. *Subversive Activities Control Board* (1961), but in *Aptheker*, the Court ruled (6-3) that the McCarran Act's travel restrictions were too broad. While citizens do not enjoy an absolute right to travel, the Court determined, the McCarran Act blanket ban did not allow for adequate consideration of an individual's circumstances. The Court in *Zemel* v. *Rusk* (1963) did uphold the government's right to restrict travel to specific places.

—TIM ASHWELL

See Also: *Communist Party; Supreme Court.*
BIBLIOGRAPHY: Caute, David, *The Great Fear: The Anti-Communist Purge under Truman and Eisenhower* (Simon & Schuster 1978).

■ **ARAPAHO INDIANS.** *See: Great Plains Indians.*

■ **ARCHITECTURE.** Architecture in America begins with the varied Indian construction styles. In addition to small wigwams and teepees—frames of poles covered with animal skins or bark—there were large structures that never failed to impress European explorers and traders: rectangular, barrel-roofed longhouses in the Northeast; wattle and daub, thatched-roof houses in the Southeast; dome-shaped earthlodges in the river valleys of the Great Plains; large plank houses along the coast of the Pacific Northwest; and flat-roofed, multistoried apartment dwellings in the Southwest. In the Ohio and Mississippi valleys Indians constructed monumental earthworks such as Snake Mound or the great temple mound at Cahokia.

European colonial architecture was little influenced by these Indian traditions, except perhaps in the Southwest, where the Spanish colonists, building with adobe bricks, incorporated some of the stylistic features of Pueblo architecture into their homes and public buildings, evident in extant structures such as the Palace of Governors (c. 1610) in Santa Fe, New Mexico. Elsewhere, European styles were modified by American conditions if not by American styles. Early modern England had experienced a shortage of wood, resulting in the development of the "half-timbered" style of construction, and the extensive use of stone as a building material; but in the eastern part of North America wood was abundant, and the vast majority of domestic structures and public buildings in the English colonies were built of massive timber frames, sheathed against the weather with wooden clapboards, and roofed with wooden shingles. Scandinavian colonists in the Delaware valley introduced the techniques of log construction in the 17th century, and within a generation that rough-and-ready style had become common on all the colonial frontiers, not only among European settlers, but among Indians as well, who quickly adopted metal tools such as the ax and began constructing their homes and council houses out of dovetailed logs.

Among the colonial elites of the 18th century, architecture followed the conventions of England, often copying plans and designs directly from architectural style books. The great mansion houses of the southern planter elite were frequently built in the British period style known as Georgian (from the accession of George I in 1714 to the death of George IV in 1830), which emphasized symmetry and proportion. Drayton Hall (1742), near Charleston, which still stands, is classically proportioned, with hand-carved interior moldings of imported Caribbean mahogany. (Nearby, but a world apart, the rough wooden cabins of the slave quarters featured steep ascending roofs, an African architectural feature that allowed heat to rise and dissipate in the rafters.) Symmetry was also a feature of construction in the 18th-century North; windows were set in balance to central entranceways, often framed by classical columns. In Rhode Island the merchant Peter Harrison designed a number of Georgian buildings, including the Redwood Library (1749) in Newport, the first building to pattern itself self-consciously on the Palladian style (from Andrea Palladio, a 16th-century Italian architect) so popular in England at the time.

After the American Revolution architects of the new nation were attracted to the classical styles of Greece and Rome. Thomas Jefferson's Virginia State House (1785) copied a Roman temple he had seen in Europe, and his library building at the University of Virginia (1821) was a scaled-down copy of the Pantheon of Rome. In 1801, Jefferson appointed architect Benjamin Latrobe to supervise the construction of federal buildings in the new capital city of Washington. Latrobe's Bank of Philadelphia (1799) was the first bank built in the form of a Roman temple and established a long precedent. He brought the classic style to Washington with his design for the Capitol building (1816), which he rebuilt after the British burned the city during the War of 1812. Latrobe was succeeded as capital architect by Bostonian Charles Bulfinch, whose Boston State House (1798) was distinguished by an impressive classical dome. The homes and public buildings of Latrobe, Bulfinch, and other architects of the day are sometimes characterized as in the "Federal Style." It was disseminated and popularized in building manuals such as the *Country Builder's Assistant* (1797) by New England architect Asher Benjamin. Although incorporating architectural details from current styles, domestic house construction remained conservative in the United States, at least in rural areas.

The dependence on European models for more sophisticated architects continued in a series of 19th-century "revival" styles. The first, Greek Revival, relied on Greek rather than Roman models. Notable examples include William Strickland's Second Bank of the United States (1819) in Philadelphia, and Thomas Ustick Walter's transformation of the country home of the Bank's director Nicholas Biddle into a Greek temple (1832). The most traditional building styles often incorporated a classical detail to bring them up to date: pillasters framing the door on a Cape Cod cottage, or Ionic columns supporting an overhanging pediment on a southern mansion. The Gothic Revival followed in the years before the Civil War. James Renwick's design for the Smithsonian Institution (1847) included moats and turrets, and his St. Patrick's Cathedral (1858-79) in New York City was a magnificent reinterpretation of the French medieval cathedrals. The most prominent stylist of the gothic was Alexander Jackson Davis, a founder of the American Institute of Architects (1857).

Before the middle of the century a few American architects attended English or European academies, but most were self-taught. The first American school of architecture was opened at the Massachusetts Institute of Technology (1866), followed by Yale (1869), Illinois (1870), and Cor-

nell (1871). The premier architects of the late 19th century showed the influence of academic training and transformed the stylistic traditions of American architecture. Of first importance was H. H. Richardson, who developed a domestic "shingle style"—elegant two- and three-story homes clad in wood shingles—that was widely imitated by architects of far less skill. Richardson also built heavy, solid, monumental public buildings, structures full of integrity, like Trinity Church (1877) in Boston. His Marshall Field building (1885) in Chicago pointed the way to architectural "modernism" by conveying, through the classical proportions of the design, a sense of the building's construction. The partners of the architectural firm of McKim, Mead, and White had worked with Richardson, but took his work in the direction of a renewed classicism in such commissions as the Boston Public Library (1888), which faced Richardson's Trinity Church across Copley Square. At the end of the century McKim, Mead, and White was the most influential force in American architecture.

Pointing with Richardson toward modernism, however, was Louis Sullivan, who professed the belief that a building's style should reflect the principles of its construction, or that "form follows function." His Wainwright Building (1890) in St. Louis, one of the country's first "skyscrapers," was one of the first steel-frame buildings; although classically proportioned, the building soared 10 stories high. Daniel H. Burnham's Flatiron Building (1910) in New York City is an elegant example of the early modernist style in skyscraper construction. Sullivan's most important student was Frank Lloyd Wright, who probably did more than any other architect in American history to develop a truly indigenous, American style.

The principles of Sullivan and Wright reached their apogee in the modernist International Style, developed by Europeans such as Ludwig Mies van der Rohe, who immigrated to the United States before World War I after directing the famous Bauhaus School. Mies collaborated with architect Philip Johnson on the Seagram Building (1958) in New York City; a similar example is Lever House (1952) in New York, built by the firm of Skidmore, Owings, and Merrill. These two buildings are often considered the finest examples of the modernist "glass sheath" skyscraper, establishing the precedent for hundreds of buildings built in cities throughout America during the last third of the 20th century.

> **See Also:** *Benjamin, Asher; Bulfinch, Charles; Burnham, Daniel; Davis, Alexander Jackson; Jefferson, Thomas; Johnson, Philip Cortelyou; Kahn, Louis Isadore; Latrobe, Benjamin; McKim, Mead, and White; Mies van der Rohe, Ludwig; Pei, Ieoh Ming; Renwick, James; Richardson, Henry Hobson; Root, John W.; Saarinen, Eero; Saarinen, Eliel; Skidmore, Owings, and Merrill; Strickland, William; Sullivan, Louis; Venturi, Robert; Walter, Thomas Ustick; Wright, Frank Lloyd.*

BIBLIOGRAPHY: Carley, Rachel, *The Visual Dictionary of American Domestic Architecture* (Henry Holt 1994); Hunt, William Dudley, *Encyclopedia of American Architecture* (McGraw Hill 1980); Whiffen, Marcus, *Whiffen's American Architecture Since 1780: A Guide to the Styles* (MIT Press 1992).

■ **ARDENNES, BATTLE OF.** *See: Bulge (Ardennes), Battle of the.*

■ **ARIKARA INDIANS.** *See: Great Plains Indians.*

■ **ARIZONA,** the most populous of the Rocky Mountain states. It is bounded on the north by Utah, on the west by California and Nevada, on the west and south by Mexico, and on the east by New Mexico. The Colorado River, which forms most of its western border, also runs through much of the northern part of the state, including the spectacular Grand Canyon. The Painted Desert and Petrified Forest also lie in this plateau region. The Sonoran, or Gila, Desert lies in southwestern Arizona. Dams on the Colorado River have created many large lakes.

Arizona was under first Spanish, then Mexican, rule before passing to the United States in 1848 as a result of the Mexican War. It did not become a state, however, until 1912. With 22 reservations, Arizona has more Indian lands than any other state. Manufacturing and tourism have replaced farming and mining as the mainstays of the economy. Its warm, dry climate has attracted large numbers of retirees, and its population growth is one of the highest in the nation.

Capital: Phoenix. Area: 114,006 square miles. Population (1995 est.): 4,218,000.

> **See Also:** *Coronado, Francisco Vásquez de; Earp, Wyatt; Gadsden Purchase; Geronimo; Grand Canyon; Hopi; Kino, Eusebio Francisco; Mexican War.*

■ **ARKANSAS,** the smallest in population of the 11 states of the old Confederacy. It is bounded on the north by Missouri, on the west by Oklahoma, on the west and south by Texas, on the south by Louisiana, and on the east by Tennessee and Mississippi. The Mississippi River forms its eastern border. The Arkansas River flows through the center of the state before emptying into the Mississippi. Eastern Arkansas is fertile farming country, while much of the north and west has low but rugged and heavily wooded mountains. The economy is characterized by diversified farming and industry. Always one of the poorest states, Arkansas ranked next to last in per-capita personal income in 1990.

Arkansas was part of the Louisiana Territory sold to the United States by France in 1803. There was little fighting in the state during the Civil War, but the economy was slow to recover and advance. National and even world attention turned to Little Rock in 1957, when federal troops were needed to enforce a court order integrating Central High School. Arkansas came into the spotlight again with the election to the presidency of Gov. William Jefferson (Bill) Clinton in 1992.

Capital: Little Rock. Area: 53,182 square miles. Population (1995 est.): 2,484,000.

> **See Also:** *Clinton, William Jefferson Blythe (Bill); Desegregation; De Soto, Hernando; Five Civilized Tribes.*

■ **ARMINIANISM,** a doctrine of the followers of Dutch theologian Jacobus Arminius (1560-1609), who opposed the absolute predestinarianism of John Calvin. Arminians believed that all believers, not only the elect, were assured of salvation. Methodism and Unitarianism are rooted in Arminianism.

> **See Also:** *Methodist Church; Religion; Unitarians.*

■ **ARMORY SHOW,** popular name for a watershed event in American art, the International Exhibition of Modern Art held in New York City from February to March 1913 at the 69th Regiment Armory at Lexington Avenue and 26th

Street. The Armory Show assembled under one roof some 1,600 paintings and sculptures by more than 300 artists, one-third of whom were not American. Although many well-established American artists of traditional or progressive sympathies were represented at the exhibition, the greatest notice in the press and by the public went to the European modernists such as Constantin Brancusi, Georges Braque, Paul Cezanne, Marcel Duchamp, Paul Gauguin, Henri Matisse, and Pablo Picasso, and to their lesser-known American followers, avant-garde artists such as Stuart Davis, Marsden Hartley, John Marin, Charles Sheeler, and Joseph Stella. Duchamp's Cubist painting *Nude Descending a Staircase* (1912), ridiculed as an "explosion in a shingle factory," was a popular sensation, caricatured across the land. During the brief time the show was in New York, more than 70,000 modern art lovers, haters, and curiosity-seekers waited in lines for admission; by the time a compact version of the show traveled to Chicago, its notoriety was such that attendance approached 190,000. In Boston, the final venue of the exhibition, the show was greeted with storms of protest. Controversial to the last, the Armory Show introduced and permanently established the presence of modern art in the United States.

—DAVID M. LUBIN

See Also: *Painting.*

BIBLIOGRAPHY: Brown, Milton W., *American Painting from the Armory Show to the Depression* (Princeton Univ. Press 1970).

■ **ARMOUR, PHILIP (1832-1901),** meat packer. Born in Stockbridge, New York, Armour entered the grain-dealing and meat-packing business with John Plankinton in 1863, speculating in pork at the end of the Civil War and netting $2 million. He invested in his brother's grain business, which added a pork-packaging plant in 1868 and took the name Armour & Co., and moved to Chicago to head the firm in 1875. Armour's innovations expanded his business, helped make Chicago the U.S. meat-packing center, and changed the industry. He brought live hogs to Chicago for slaughtering, used waste materials in numerous by-products, and, along with Gustavus Swift, canned meat for export to Eu-

rope. With the introduction of refrigeration, Armour bought his own refrigerated railroad cars and, like Swift, established distributing plants in eastern cities. Increasingly wealthy and powerful, Armour participated actively in the stock exchange, but the "embalmed beef" scandals of 1898-99 damaged the reputation of his packing house and of the business in general. Armour defended the quality of his product but never recovered from the shock of such inquiries. He died leaving a fortune of $50 million.

See Also: *Industrial Revolution.*

■ **ARMSTRONG, EDWIN (1890-1954),** electrical engineer, inventor of three of the basic electronic circuits essential to radar, radio, and television. Born in New York City, Armstrong made his first invention while attending Columbia. It consisted of a new regenerative circuit (1912) that yielded the first radio amplifier and the key to the continuous-wave transmitter that is the base of all radio operations. While in the U.S. Army Signal Corps during World War I, he built a superheterodyne circuit that amplified weak signals and became the basic circuit used in radio and television receivers. Armstrong became embroiled in a corporate battle over one of his patents but continued his work at Columbia (1935-54) and announced a third important invention in 1939. His wideband frequency modulation (FM) system eliminated radio static and offered the highest fidelity sound. It required basic changes in all receivers and transmitters, however, and the Depression, World War II, the Federal Communications Commission (FCC), and competing corporations all contributed to the delay in the expansion of FM broadcasting. Ill and facing another long legal battle, he committed suicide in 1954 and did not see FM dominate radio, microwave, and space communication.

See Also: *Invention; Science; Television and Radio.*

■ **ARMSTRONG, LOUIS DANIEL ("SATCHMO") (1900-71),** jazz musician. Born in New Orleans, Louisiana, Armstrong grew up singing on street corners and began playing the cornet and trumpet at the age of 13. Befriended by musician James "King" Oliver, Armstrong traveled with him to Chicago, then the heartland of American

Louis Armstrong transformed jazz music by introducing solo virtuosity into the jazz ensemble and by inventing "scat" instrument-like vocals. Armstrong became a band leader in the 1920s.

jazz. He played in a multitude of groups and in the late 1920s made his first recordings with his own Hot Five and Hot Seven. Popular at first only among African-American audiences, Armstrong's talent soon became nationally recognized. His beautiful tone, marvelous rhythm, and stunning virtuosity altered jazz forever and influenced many other instrumentalists and singers as well. A gravel-voiced, highly innovative singer as well as a trumpet player and band leader, Armstrong toured the world, becoming an international goodwill ambassador of American culture. Such was his gift that he is considered one of America's most significant cultural figures. He also appeared in several movies.

See Also: *African Americans; Jazz.*
BIBLIOGRAPHY: Jones, Max, and John Chilton, *Louis: The Louis Armstrong Story* (Little, Brown 1972).

■ **ARMY,** branch of the U.S. military system, which defends the nation and its interest overseas according to policies set by the president and Congress. The U.S. Army traces its roots to the American Revolution when in 1775 the Continen-

tal Congress named George Washington to command the militia gathered to fight the British. Washington decided that, in order to win independence, America needed its own regular (professional) army on the British model. American regulars employed conventional European tactics and gained respect from the British. After the Revolution many Americans believed that a standing army could threaten the republic. Washington, however, concluded that the regulars' invaluable role in winning the Revolution justified their ongoing availability for the nation's defense.

From 1789 to 1914 Americans tolerated a standing army that was small in relation to the size of the country. A few thousand regulars fulfilled constabulary duties such as guarding the borders, exploring the continent, protecting settlers, and fighting Indians. During wartime citizen-soldier volunteers supplemented the regulars; conscription (the draft) was used only once in the 19th century—during the Civil War. The U.S. Military Academy (founded in 1802) and state military colleges provided most of the officers. Despite some defeats or disappointments, especially during the War of 1812 and the first year of the Civil War (1861), the regular army guarded the nation in peacetime and provided the nucleus of a larger force in wartime. However, foreign observers noted the uneven qualities of American officers, equipment, and weapons, subjects that generated domestic controversies during and after all U.S. wars. Americans touted their army's victories, such as defeating the British at New Orleans in 1815 and capturing Mexico City in 1847. Americans believed that the Union and Confederate armies were remarkable, but few foreigners ranked them equal to Europe's best. Even after America's army and navy defeated Spain in 1898, few Europeans changed their opinions. In 1903 Sec. of War Elihu Root's reforms—calling for improvements in officer training, weapons procurement, the National Guard, and army administration—helped to modernize the army.

The U.S. Army stood at 99,000 soldiers in 1914. It had grown to 400,000 when America entered World War I in 1917, but German leaders dismissed it as not being of much importance. Relying on volunteers and a congressional draft law, America raised 2 million more soldiers, more than half of whom served in France by the armistice of 1918. Americans carried improved weapons, conducted sophisticated officer training, and fought well in several battles. Despite noting improvements, some Europeans contended that the U.S. Army had not made a significant contribution to the Allied victory.

From 1941 to 1945 more than 8 million men and women served in the U.S. Army's ground and air forces around the world. Reserve Officer Training Corps programs at universities and officer candidate schools provided more officers than West Point. Respect came grudgingly from both allies and enemies. But critics could not overlook America's logistical accomplishments and combat victories over Axis armies. By 1945 the U.S. Army was the best supplied and one of the most powerful in the world, but rapid demobilization mirrored previous American postwar reductions.

The Cold War from the 1950s to the 1980s marked a major departure for the army. Congress continued conscription from 1950 to 1973, and after the Korean War (1950-53), the army maintained unusually large regular forces facing the apparent threat of Communism in Europe and Asia. In Indochina, Vietnamese Communists used a combination of guerrilla and conventional tactics to defeat U.S. forces. After 1973 the U.S. Army instituted numerous reforms in conventional training and weapons and returned to an all-volunteer status. During the 1991 Persian Gulf War America's regular forces took only six weeks to defeat Iraq, which had invaded Kuwait and threatened Saudi Arabia. The Gulf War demonstrated the army's excellence in technology, logistics, military personnel, and employing combat power.

The modern U.S. Army is noted for its pursuit of equitable policies toward women and minorities. African Americans served in small numbers during the Revolution and comprised 10 percent of the Union's army during the Civil War, but after 1866 they were recruited into regular (but segregated) units. Pres. Harry S. Truman abolished racial segregation in the armed forces in 1948. Women were not permitted to serve until the world wars of the 20th century. Since 1965 increasing numbers of minorities and women have sought careers in the army.

—JOSEPH G. DAWSON III

See Also: *Women in the Armed Forces.*
BIBLIOGRAPHY: Heller, Charles E., and William A. Stofft, *America's First Battles* (Univ. Press of Kansas 1986); Weigley, Russell F., *History of the United States Army*, rev. ed. (Indiana Univ. Press 1984).

■ **ARMY-MCCARTHY HEARINGS,** 1954 U.S. Senate hearings on subversion in the army. On June 9 a clash between Sen. Joseph McCarthy and Army counsel Joseph Welch helped turn public opinion against the Wisconsin Republican senator.

See Also: *Cold War; McCarthy, Joseph; McCarthyism.*

■ **ARNOLD, BENEDICT (1741-1801),** Revolutionary War military leader. A volatile and reckless military commander, but a brilliant tactician, Arnold remains synonymous in American history with treason because of his plot to turn West Point over to the British. He was born in Norwich, Connecticut, sold into apprenticeship by his parents, and was active in the French and Indian War at the age of 16. He was a well-to-do merchant before entering the Connecticut militia as a captain in 1774.

Although Arnold participated in the capture of Fort Ticonderoga in 1775, he first received adulation when he bravely led his men in an attack on Quebec in 1776. Wounded in the battle, Arnold was promoted to brigadier general and later performed heroically in the Battle of Bemis Heights.

After the British evacuation of Philadelphia in 1778, Arnold took command of the city. Contentious and duplicitous, Arnold alienated his commanders and faced a court-martial for corruption. Although cleared of most charges, he received a reprimand from Gen. George Washington.

An embittered Arnold plotted with the British to betray West Point, a fort over which he took command in 1780. British Gen. Henry Clinton agreed to pay Arnold a large sum for facilitating the capture of West Point. The plot was exposed, however, when American soldiers seized correspondence between Arnold and Clinton from British spy John André. André was hanged but Arnold escaped behind British lines and fought against the Americans in Virginia and Connecticut before traveling to England in 1781. He spent the remainder of his life in England and Canada.

See Also: *Revolution, American.*

BIBLIOGRAPHY: Brandt, Clare, *The Man in the Mirror: A Life of Benedict Arnold* (Random House 1994); Randall, Willard Sterne, *Benedict Arnold: Patriot and Traitor* (Morrow 1990).

■ **ARNOLD, HENRY HARLEY ("HAP") (1886-1950),** chief of the U.S. Army air forces in World War II. Born in Gladwyne, Pennsylvania, Arnold led the air force through a massive build-up during the war years and advocated total independence from the army, which was achieved in 1947.

See Also: World War II.

■ **AROOSTOOK WAR (1839),** U.S.-British conflict over the Aroostook region disputed by New Brunswick, Canada, and Maine. The region was repeatedly entered by Canadian lumberjacks, who seized the American agent appointed to expel them. Maine and New Brunswick called out their militias, but U.S. Gen. Winfield Scott managed to reconcile the parties.

See Also: Frontier in American History; Scott, Winfield.

■ **ART.** *See: Architecture; Museums; Painting; Photography; Sculpture; individual biographies.*

■ **ARTHUR, CHESTER ALAN (1830-86),** 21st president of the United States (1881-85). Born on Oct. 5, 1830, in Fairfield, Vermont, Arthur was admitted to the New York bar in 1854. In the years leading up to the Civil War, he defended runaway slaves through his New York City law practice and was an early leader in the newly formed Republican party. During the war, he served with honesty and efficiency as quartermaster general for New York State, supplying the state's thousands of volunteers. He became collector of the port of New York in 1871, through the patronage of New York Republican Sen. Roscoe Conkling, but was removed from office by Pres. Rutherford B. Hayes seven years later because of his association with the Conkling machine and with the state Republican party's "Stalwart" faction.

Elected vice president in 1880, Arthur became president after the assassination of James A. Garfield in 1881. As president, he employed the same quietly efficient and honest methods he had demonstrated throughout his public career. While

Chester A. Arthur became the nation's president upon the assassination of James A. Garfield on Sept. 19, 1881.

he did not actively support it, Arthur signed into law the Pendleton Act (1883), the first move toward federal civil service reform. He vetoed the first Chinese Exclusion Act but in 1882 signed one that barred Chinese laborers from immigrating for 10 years. Keeping his kidney failure a secret, Arthur made only halfhearted attempts in 1884 to seek his party's nomination for another term.

—KATHLEEN BANKS NUTTER

See Also: Gilded Age.

BIBLIOGRAPHY: Doenecke, Justus D., *The Presidencies of James A. Garfield and Chester A. Arthur* (Regents Press of Kansas 1981); Reeves, Thomas C., *Gentlemen Boss: The Life of Chester Alan Arthur* (Knopf 1975).

■ **ARTICLES OF CONFEDERATION,** first national constitution of the independent United States, drawn up in 1776, adopted in 1781, and replaced by the present federal Constitution in 1789. The motion for independence approved at the meeting of the Second Continental Congress (June 7,

1776) also included a directive that a committee prepare a plan of national confederation. The committee submitted draft articles on July 12.

In the subsequent debate in Congress, continuing from July 1776 until late in 1777, delegates favoring a loose union of autonomous states outnumbered those who wanted a strong national government. Key issues included representation and the manner of voting, the apportionment of expenses, and the disposition of western lands. The question of allocating power between the states and the national government was also controversial, given the widespread hostility toward central authority provoked by British policy during the previous decade. Fears that the national government would take all powers not enumerated led to the adoption of an amendment that reserved those powers to the states. In November 1777, the Articles of Confederation were formally adopted by the Continental Congress and sent to the states for ratification.

The articles created a national assembly, called the Congress, in which each state had a single vote. Delegates were to be selected annually in a manner determined by the individual state legislatures. These arrangements preserved the operating procedures of the Continental Congress. Delegates were subjected to term limits, prohibited from serving in more than three years out of any six-year period. Similarly, a presiding president, elected annually by Congress, was eligible to serve no more than one year out of any given three. Votes would be decided by a simple majority of the states, but major questions would require the agreement of nine states.

Congress was granted national authority in the conduct of foreign affairs, matters of war and peace, and maintenance of the armed forces. It could raise loans, issue bills of credit, establish a coinage, and regulate trade with Native-American peoples, and it was to be the final authority in jurisdictional disputes between states. It was charged with establishing a national postal system as well as a common standard of weights and measures. Lacking the power to tax citizens directly, however, the national government was to apportion its financial burdens among the states according to the extent of their surveyed land. The articles explicitly guaranteed the sover-

eignty of the individual states, reserving to them all powers not "expressly delegated" to Congress. Ratification or amendment required the agreement of all 13 states. This constitution thus created a national government of specific, yet sharply circumscribed, powers.

Problems and Weaknesses. The legislatures of 12 states soon voted in favor of the articles, but final ratification was held up for over three years by Maryland. Representing the interests of states without claims to lands west of the Appalachians, Maryland demanded that states cede to Congress their western claims, the new nation's most valuable resource, for "the good of the whole." Excepted, however, would be the colonial grants made to land companies. The eight states with western claims were reluctant to give them up, and the remaining states included powerful land speculators among their most influential citizens. While the stalemate over western lands continued, Congress remained an extralegal body, but it agreed to work under the terms of the unratified document. It was 1781 before all eight states with western claims voted to cede them. Maryland then agreed to ratification, and in March, the Articles of Confederation took effect.

The Confederation Congress was successful in waging the war of the American Revolution, concluding the peace, reorganizing national finances, and drawing up fundamental ordinances for the western lands, principally the Northwest Ordinance of 1787. But despite these successes Congress came under severe criticism during the 1780s for its inadequate handling of foreign affairs and interstate commerce, for its lack of direct taxing power, for its inability to enforce its measures, and for the stringent conditions that made amendment all but impossible. These discontents coalesced in 1786–87, following the failure of several attempts to provide Congress with limited powers to raise revenues and regulate commerce. Nationalist critics abandoned the amendment process and turned to the organization of a new Constitutional Convention, which in 1787 drew up the new document that replaced the articles.

—JOHN MACK FARAGHER

See Also: *Confederation Congress; Constitutional Convention; Northwest Ordinance; Revolution, American.*

BIBLIOGRAPHY: Hoffert, Robert W., *A Politics of Tensions: The Articles of Confederation and American Political Ideas* (Univ. Press of Colorado 1992); Jensen, Merrill, *The Articles of Confederation: An Interpretation of the Social-Constitutional History of the American Revolution* (Univ. of Wisconsin Press 1970).

■ **ASHWANDER V. TENNESSEE VALLEY AUTHORITY (1936),** U.S. Supreme Court case that upheld the constitutionality of the Tennessee Valley Authority (TVA), a major New Deal initiative. The Court ruled (8-1) that Congress had the power to authorize dams, flood control, and navigation projects that aided interstate commerce. Sale of hydroelectric energy produced by the dams was also allowed because the Constitution allows the government to sell property it lawfully acquires. Although *Ashwander* marked a political victory for the New Deal, the case is most notable for the "Ashwander rules," a call for judicial restraint by Justice Louis Brandeis. Noting that the case was fundamentally a dispute among stockholders of a private utility that had contracted to buy electricity from the TVA, Brandeis said the Court should not pass on the validity of laws unless the plaintiff had suffered actual injury and, in any case, should rule as narrowly as possible, avoiding broad constitutional statements.

See Also: New Deal; Supreme Court; Tennessee Valley Authority.

■ **ASSIMILATION,** the model of acculturation favored by Americans who have insisted that Anglo-American culture is the true foundation of American values and institutions. John Quincy Adams argued that immigrants "must cast off the European skin, never to resume it." If they could not "accommodate themselves to the character—moral, political, and physical—of this country," he insisted, "the Atlantic is always open to them to return to the land of their nativity and their fathers."

Assimilation sentiment was strongest from the 1880s to the 1920s, the heyday of "Americanization" programs. "Our task is to break up these groups or settlements," wrote one advocate, "to assimilate and amalgamate these people as a part of our American race, and to implant in their children, so far as can be done, the Anglo-Saxon conceptions of righteousness, law and order, and popular government." Similar thinking motivated Congress to bar the immigration of Asians and other ethnic groups into the country, and to force assimilation on Native Americans by denying them the freedom to practice their religions or even speak their own languages. Alternative views of acculturation have often been argued through the metaphors of "the melting pot," in which America's peoples blend together to form a composite nationality, or the "mosaic," in which ethnic differences are preserved, but unite to form a diverse but common civic culture.

See Also: Acculturation; Ethnic Groups; Immigration.

BIBLIOGRAPHY: Gordon, Milton M., *Assimilation in American Life* (Oxford Univ. Press 1964).

■ **ASSINIBOINE INDIANS.** *See: Great Plains Indians.*

■ **ASTAIRE, FRED (1899-1987),** dancer, singer, and actor. Born in Omaha, Nebraska, he danced on stage with his sister Adele before starring in films such as *Top Hat* (1935) with Ginger Rogers, *Holiday Inn* (1942), and *Funny Face* (1957). A master of tap, jazz, and elegant ballroom dancing, he insisted that his dance sequences be filmed without editing in a single, full-body tracking shot. Astaire was also a deft interpreter of popular songs.

■ **ASTOR, JOHN JACOB (1763-1848),** merchant and investor who made a large fortune by dominating the American fur trade and investing wisely in New York City real estate. Born in Waldorf, Germany, the son of a butcher, he immigrated to New York in 1784. Following a short apprenticeship with a fur trader, Astor went into business for himself, and by 1800 was the leading fur trader in America with a fortune of $250,000.

Astor put his profits into Manhattan real estate and expanded his fur business to the West Coast and China. With profits from his American Fur Company soaring, he made a large loan to the U.S. government during the War of 1812. He sold out his interests in the company in 1834 to devote himself to speculating in New York real estate. Astor left most of his $40 million fortune to his son William.

See Also: American Fur Company; Fur Trade; Industrial Revolution.

■ **ASTOR PLACE RIOT (May 10, 1849),** a deadly scene of public unrest in New York City, sparked by the longstanding dispute between American actor Edwin Forrest and English actor William Charles Macready. Pro-Forrest protestors gathered outside the Astor Place Opera House, where Macready was playing the title role in *Macbeth*. When the protestors refused to disperse, the militia killed 22 people and wounded 36. This riot exhibited both anti-British sentiments and class tensions in New York City.

■ **ATHERTON, GERTRUDE (1857-1948),** author of historical fiction. She was born in San Francisco, California. Widowed in 1887, Atherton took advantage of her freedom, traveling extensively and writing numerous meticulously researched works of historical fiction. *The Conqueror* (1902), her fictional biography of Alexander Hamilton, sold nearly a million copies. In 1923 she wrote *Black Oxen*, a best-selling novel about an aging woman who regains her youth through glandular therapy.

See Also: Women in American History.

■ **ATLANTA,** city, capital of Georgia, located in the southern foothills of the Appalachian Mountains. Before white settlers arrived permanently during the War of 1812, the Creek tribe lived on the site of what is now Atlanta in a settlement called Standing Peachtree. By 1845 Atlanta had become a major rail and commercial center of the South. During the Civil War (1861-65) the city became a crucial Confederate communication and supply center. In 1864, Union Gen. William Tecumseh Sherman captured Atlanta after a long siege and then burned it before embarking on his march to the sea. Only 400 of the city's 4,500 buildings were left standing. Rising from the ashes of the Civil War, Atlanta became the transportation, financial, and cultural center of the South. Martin Luther King, Jr., led the civil rights movement of the 1950s and 1960s from Atlanta. With a huge international airport, a new convention center, major hotels, and the 1996 Summer Olympics, Atlanta has become the symbol of the economically booming New South. Population (1994): 396,052.

See Also: City in American History; Sherman, William Tecumseh.

■ **ATLANTIC CABLE (1858),** underwater telegraph cable across the Atlantic Ocean, joining Valentia, Ireland, and Trinity Bay, Newfoundland. Financier Cyrus W. Field promoted the idea and raised $1.5 million for the project. Using vessels borrowed from Great Britain and the United States and overcoming two failed attempts, Field completed the cable laying on Aug. 5, 1858. Pres. James Buchanan and Queen Victoria exchanged the first transatlantic message on August 16, but the cable stopped working soon after. Field was temporarily discredited but managed to lay an improved cable in 1866 that assured a permanent transatlantic link.

See Also: Field, Cyrus West.

■ **ATLANTIC CHARTER,** term used to designate the Allied powers' peace aims during World War II. The Atlantic Charter emerged from the first wartime meeting between British Prime Minister Winston Churchill and U.S. Pres. Franklin D. Roosevelt. The meeting took place on two warships, the British battleship *Prince of Wales* and the U.S. cruiser *Augusta*, in Placentia Bay, Newfoundland, Aug. 9-12, 1941.

The two leaders issued a statement on August 14 that outlined their ideals and goals for the postwar world. Similar in many respects to Woodrow Wilson's Fourteen Points, the Atlantic Charter proclaimed the "four freedoms" they hoped to secure after the war: freedom of speech, freedom of religion, freedom from want, and freedom from fear. They declared that their nations would seek neither new territory nor territorial changes contrary to the will of the peoples affected and pledged to respect the right of national self-determination and to restore it to countries occupied by the Nazis. They expressed their aim to create a global marketplace, with equality of access to trade and resources for all countries and international cooperation to address questions of working conditions, economic development, and social welfare. In the postwar world people would enjoy freedom of the seas, and nations would abandon force. These principles established the basis for the United Nations Declaration, signed by the United States, Britain, China, and the Soviet Union on Jan. 1, 1942, and eventually by 22 other countries.

The Atlantic Charter did not eliminate tensions between the United States and Britain over imperial and economic questions, nor would it thwart Soviet leader Joseph Stalin's ambitions to control east-central Europe as the war came to an end. But it did enshrine democratic principles and individual freedoms as goals worth fighting for, after a decade in which many Americans and Britons had proven willing to accommodate and, in some cases, admire the dictators who now were destroying Europe. It also marked a further step toward an Anglo-American alliance; although the United States essentially had declared economic war on the Axis powers with the passage of the Lend-Lease Act in March 1941, it did not become a belligerent power until after Japan attacked Pearl Harbor on Dec. 7, 1941. The "four freedoms" became an important theme in American wartime propaganda, most famously in a series of Norman Rockwell posters.

—MAARTEN L. PEREBOOM

See Also: *Fourteen Points; Lend-Lease; World War II.*
BIBLIOGRAPHY: Reynolds, David, *The Creation of the Anglo-American Alliance* (Univ. of North Carolina Press 1982); Wilson, Theodore A., *The First Summit: Roosevelt and Churchill at Placentia Bay, 1941* rev. ed. (Univ. Press of Kansas 1991).

■ **ATTUCKS, CRISPUS (c. 1723-70),** American patriot. Little is certain about Attucks's early life. Possibly a runaway slave from Framingham, Massachusetts, possibly a descendant of both African and Indian ancestors, he seems to have spent more than 20 years working on ships sailing from Boston. Attucks and four other men were killed in the encounter between a crowd and British soldiers known as the Boston Massacre (Mar. 5, 1770). In the front ranks, Attucks was one of the first deaths in the American Revolution. His own uncertain claim to individual liberty makes his sacrifice all the more poignant.

See Also: *African Americans; Boston Massacre.*

■ **AUDUBON, JOHN JAMES (1785-1851),** artist and ornithologist. Audubon was born in Santo Domingo but, after living in Paris, moved to the United States in 1803. Settling first near Philadelphia and later in Louisville, Kentucky, he tried unsuccessfully to become a merchant. His bankruptcy in 1819 freed Audubon to explore the growing nation and, while on a trip down the Mis-

sissippi River, he began recording and painting birds. He worked as a tutor and drawing teacher in New Orleans while finishing his first book and then went to England to secure a publisher for it in 1826. *Birds of America* was published in four volumes between 1827 and 1838 and included 435 hand-colored aquatints depicting 1,065 birds of 489 species. This lengthy portfolio was followed by the *Ornithological Biography* (1839) and the *Synopsis of the Birds of North America* (1839), on which he worked with William Macgillivray. Audubon settled in New York in 1841 and was working on *The Viviparous Quadrupeds* of North America at the time of his death.

See Also: *Painting.*

■ **AUGUSTA, TREATY OF (1773),** agreement made with the Creek and Cherokee nations by Gov. James Wright of Georgia and John Stuart, superintendent of Indian affairs in the Southern District. The treaty conveyed 2.1 million acres of Indian land to Georgia for white settlement.

■ **AUSTIN, MARY (1868-1934),** eccentric author and lecturer born in Carlinville, Illinois. She was associated with the group of Bohemian authors that included Jack London and was also a companion of writers Willa Cather and Mabel Dodge. She wrote a number of classic narratives set in the desert Southwest, including *The Land of Little Rain* (1903) and *The Basket Woman* (1904). Fascinated by Indian songs, she lectured on her theory of native rhythmic poetry at Yale University and published *The American Rhythm* (1923).

See Also: *Cather, Willa; London, Jack; Women in American History.*

■ **AUSTIN, STEPHEN FULLER (1793-1836),** leader of colonization in Texas. Born in Virginia, Austin moved to Missouri and managed his father's lead mine, served in the militia, and in the Missouri territorial legislature from 1814 to 1820. When his father died before establishing a colony of immigrants on a Spanish land grant in Texas, Austin took over. Colonists arrived at Austin's site on the Colorado and Brazos rivers in 1821. When Mexican authorities refused to acknowledge the Spanish grant, Austin's skillful diplomacy in

Mexico City led to the empresario system. By 1832, some 8,000 people lived in Austin's colony, even after Mexico passed an anti-Anglo immigration law in 1830. At the San Felipe Convention of 1833, Texans instructed Austin to ask Mexico for independence for Texas. President Santa Anna refused the request, but repealed the 1830 law, although Austin was imprisoned in Mexico in August 1835 for treason. When the war for Texas independence started at Gonzales, Texas, on Oct. 1, 1835, Austin was placed in command. Austin lost his campaign for president of the Republic of Texas to Sam Houston, but served as secretary of state until his death.

See Also: Frontier in American History; Texas Rebellion.

■ **AUSTRALIAN BALLOT,** or secret ballot, a means of assuring a secret vote. Adopted by almost all the states during the 1890s in an attempt to curb election fraud, the Australian ballot stipulated that the government, and not political parties, print and distribute ballots and oversee elections.

See Also: Gilded Age.

■ **AUTOMATION,** an industrial technique developed in the 1950s by which self-regulating machines put large parts of the industrial system under automatic control. Electronic computers could count, memorize, and correct the operations they controlled through feedback devices, streamlining production and fundamentally altering industrial labor. Railroad employment dropped from 1.4 million in 1947 to 730,000 in 1961; employment in steel dropped 28 percent from 1951 to 1962; the automobile industry produced a million more cars and trucks in 1963 than in 1953 with 20 percent fewer workers; and in 1964, 125,000 coal miners dug as much coal as 293,000 had in the mid-1950s.

Trade unionism seemed utterly unable to deal with these structural changes in the labor force. A rash of wildcat strikes in the mid-1950s led intellectuals to address the alienation of workers in books such as Daniel Bell's *The End of Ideology* (1960) and Robert Blauner's *Alienation and Freedom* (1964). By the end of the 1960s "blue-collar blues" had become an obsession in management circles, and there was widespread popular anxiety over the impact of automation. At the same time automation phased out many manufacturing jobs, it boosted white-collar jobs and turned the electronic/computer industry into a billion-dollar business by 1960. Automation led the United States into a postindustrial economy where high-tech industries have replaced manufacturing and brought with them a new society and culture.

See Also: Industrial Revolution; Labor Movement.
BIBLIOGRAPHY: Hall, George M., *The Age of Automation: Technical Genius, Social Dilemma* (Praeger 1995).

■ **AZTECS,** Indian people whose "chichimec" ("barbarian") origins are obscure. Early in the 12th century, two related banks of migrants came from the north around the east and west shores of Lake Texcoco in the Basin of Mexico. The easterners founded the city of Texcoco; the westerners, who became the Aztecs proper, were rebuffed by preestablished urbanites and were compelled to settle on an island in the lake. Here, by immense effort, they raised the cities of militaristic Tenochtitlán and commercial Tlatelolco. These grew together and, about 1473, Tenochtitlán conquered its neighbor.

Apparently a congeries of tribes was linked primarily by worship of the war god Huitzilopochtli, whose priests sacrificed slaves and captives to satisfy the god's insatiable thirst for blood. The cities were built on a rectangular grid unlike Europe's winding streets, and each tribe occupied a *calpul* (ward). They were highly organized under government by councils of kin-related nobles who chose one of their number to be the ruling *tlatoani*. A ruse devised by Texcoco's King Nezahualcóyotl linked that city in alliance. With that extra power, Tenochtitlán acquired a populous empire in central Mexico estimated at 25 million persons. Through networks of trade, its influence spread through the Gulf of Mexico and the peoples of the Gulf shores, but Aztec soldiers were amateurs recruited for particular campaigns and then discharged. Their empire could not replicate ancient Rome's, which had controlled distant peoples with professional full-time legions.

Aztec cities were immensely greater than Europe's in the 15th century. At maximum, 250,000 persons were supported by horticultural products, especially maize, producing three crops a year and carried in organized trade and tribute from great distances. The Aztecs assimilated the high culture of the Toltecs of the abandoned cities of Teotihuacán and Tula. Trade was brought from Lake Texcoco's shores over carefully engineered causeways and by canoe through the lake. A dike guaranteed sweet drinking water by blocking salinity from the rest of the lake. Although all the high-culture people of Mexico spoke the same Nahuatl language (still current today), its unifying influence was offset by exorbitant imperial demands for tribute and sacrificial victims.

Thus, when Hernando Cortés and his Spanish conquistadors launched their conquest in 1519, they could and did appeal for help from exploited peoples, especially the city of Tlaxcala. As historian Benjamin Keen has remarked, "The handful of Spaniards owed their victory . . . to the aid of masses of Indians eager to throw off the Aztec yoke." Much Aztec history is uncertain because the picture books of record were ordered burned by *tlatoani* Itzcotl, but the missionary Father Bernardino de Sahagún created new evidence with questionnaires to his student converts.

—FRANCIS JENNINGS

See Also: *Indians in North America.*

BIBLIOGRAPHY: Coe, Michael D., *Mexico,* 3d ed. (Thomas & Hudson 1984); Davies, Nigel, *The Aztecs: A History* (Univ. of Oklahoma Press 1986); Duran, Fray Diego, *The Aztecs: The History of the Indies of New Spain 1581,* tr. and ed. by Doris Heyden and Fernando Horcasitas (Orion Press 1964); Jennings, Francis, *The Founders of America* (Norton 1993); Sahagún, Bernardino de Florentine, *Codex: General History of the Things of New Spain,* tr. and ed. by Doris Heyden and Fernando Horcasitas (Orion Press 1964).

B

BACKUS, ISAAC (1724-1806), Baptist minister, born in Norwich, Connecticut. Although born a Puritan, he became an itinerant evangelical preacher after his "rebirth" during the Great Awakening of the 1740s and eventually accepted Baptist beliefs. Backus was a proponent of religious freedom and separation of church and state. In 1773, he wrote his most important tract, *An Appeal to the Public for Religious Liberty Against the Oppression of the Present Day.*

See Also: Baptist Church; Great Awakening; Religion.

BACON'S REBELLION (1676), conflict between planters on Virginia's frontier and Gov. Sir William Berkeley. An escalation of Indian raids and English retaliation along the western settlements in the early 1670s made life there dangerous. Frontier planters demanded that Governor Berkeley allow them to eliminate the Indian threat. To Berkeley, such a policy would disrupt the fur trade partnership between his administration and peaceful Indians. Instead, he attempted to craft policy that would restore peace and protect the Indians. The frontiersmen countered with an illegal militia bent on killing all Indians.

Nathaniel Bacon, ambitious and eager, rose to leadership among the "rebels." After several forays against southwestern Indian towns, Bacon's force turned and marched on Jamestown, demanding official sanction for their extermination raids. Outnumbered by the rebel force, Berkeley's administration awarded Bacon a commission to wage war against the Indians. Emboldened, Bacon decided to push the political stakes higher. He attempted to arrest Berkeley and take control of Virginia's assembly, but Berkeley's position, based on imperial power, was entrenched. In the end, Bacon's Rebellion failed to overpower the status quo in Virginia. Fatally ill from his time in the swamps of Virginia, Bacon died even as his rebellion collapsed.

See Also: Berkeley, Sir William; Virginia.

BIBLIOGRAPHY: Morgan, Edmond S., *American Slavery, American Freedom* (Norton 1975).

BADLANDS, area of South Dakota. The Badlands Park, established by Congress in 1978, is located between the White and Cheyenne rivers and contains spectacular formations of clay and sandstone. In the 19th century geologists frequently compared the perpendicular structures to ruins of ancient cities. The area is extraordinarily rich in fossil remains, for example, saber-toothed tigers, three-toed horses, and ancestors of the rhinoceros, camel, and hog.

See Also: South Dakota.

BAEKELAND, LEO (1863-1944), chemist, inventor of Velox paper and Bakelite. Born near Ghent, Belgium, Baekeland earned a Ph.D. from the University of Ghent (1884) and obtained a Belgian patent on a photographic dry plate he invented (1887) that carried its own developer in inactive form. Seeking work in the photographic industry, he came to New York City in 1890 and set up his own consulting business in 1893. Baekeland went on to invent a photographic print paper with silver chloride that could be developed by artificial light. He called it Velox and formed a company to manufacture it. After selling the company to George Eastman in 1899, Baekeland then began experimenting with the reaction of phenol and formaldehyde to produce synthetic resins. In 1907 he developed a resin that, unlike celluloid and others, became permanently solid when heated. He named the product Bakelite, and it became a success as an electrical insulator because of its vast versatility. After exploring its applicability in at least 40 industries, Baekeland formed the General Bakelite Company (1910) for its production and sale. This product began the modern age of plastics.

See Also: Invention; Science.

■ **BAEZ, JOAN (1941-)**, folk singer and human rights activist. Born in New York City, she began her career singing traditional folk songs and spirituals in coffee houses in Cambridge, Massachusetts. She became one of the most influential performers in the revitalized folk movement of the 1960s. Her clear voice, remarkable range, and outspoken support of progressive political causes made her a favorite of students in the antiwar and civil rights movements. She performed at the Newport Folk Festival in 1959 and at Woodstock in 1969.

See Also: *Women in American History; Woodstock.*

■ **BAGLEY, SARAH (fl. 1835-47)**, labor leader in the textile mills of New England. Born in Candia, New Hampshire, she was a central figure in the 10-hour-day movement. In 1844 she founded a union for women working in a mill in Lowell, Massachusetts. The union quickly spread to other mills in nearby towns.

■ *BAILEY* V. *DREXEL FURNITURE CO.* **(1922)**, U.S. Supreme Court case that overturned the federal Child Labor Tax Act (1919). After the Court invalidated the federal Keating-Owen anti-child labor law (1916) in *Hammer* v. *Dagenhart* (1918), Congress sought another means to bar child labor. The Keating-Owen Act had relied on the commerce clause, which authorizes Congress to regulate interstate trade. In the 1919 law Congress utilized its taxing powers and imposed a new tax on products made with child labor. The Court ruled (8-1) that the tax was in fact an attempt by Congress to ban child labor across the country. Chief Justice William Howard Taft, a defender of laissez-faire economics, wrote for the Court that Congress could use its taxing authority to regulate but not prohibit interstate commerce. Although the legal distinction between "regulation" and "prohibition" was not clear, Congress subsequently relied on the commerce clause as a constitutional basis for social legislation.

See Also: *Child Labor; Supreme Court.*

■ **BAKER, ELLA JOSEPHINE (1903-86)**, civil rights leader. Born in Norfolk, Virginia, she was a founder and primary organizer of the Southern Christian Leadership Conference (SCLC). She favored a democratically organized civil rights movement with an expanded role for women in the leadership. In 1960 she left SCLC to help student activists create the Student Nonviolent Coordinating Committee (SNCC), modeled on this more democratic vision. Also dedicated to grassroots education and citizenship efforts, she helped create the Voter Education Project in Mississippi in 1964 and the Mississippi Freedom Democratic party in 1965.

See Also: *Civil Rights Movement; Southern Christian Leadership Conference (SCLC); Student Nonviolent Coordinating Committee (SNCC); Women in American History; Women's Movement.*

■ **BAKER, GEORGE.** *See: Divine, Father.*

■ *BAKER* V. *CARR* **(1962)**, U.S. Supreme Court case that directed states to create legislative districts of similar size. Although *Baker* itself was a limited opinion, it set the stage for subsequent "one person, one vote" decisions such as *Gray* v. *Sanders* (1963), which ended the representation advantage rural areas historically had in Congress and many state legislatures.

The case originated in Tennessee, where urban interests charged the state failed to follow a law requiring the General Assembly to be reapportioned every 10 years to reflect population changes. Plaintiffs from Knoxville, Memphis, and Nashville argued the cities were underrepresented and brought suit to force Joseph Carr, the Tennessee secretary of state, to obey the law. Lower courts ruled such disputes did not fall under the jurisdiction of the federal courts, but the Supreme Court ruled (6-2) that the allegations, if true, represented a violation of the 14th Amendment's equal protection clause and were therefore appropriate matters for the federal courts to settle.

By questioning the way most state legislatures had conducted business for generations, *Baker* triggered similar suits in three dozen states. The Supreme Court in a series of related cases ruled that only legislative districts of equal population met the standards of the equal protection clause.

—TIM ASHWELL

See Also: *Equal Protection; Supreme Court.*
BIBLIOGRAPHY: Rush, Mark, *Does Redistricting Make a Difference?: Partisan Representation and Electoral Behavior* (Johns Hopkins Univ. Press 1993).

Russian-born choreographer George Balanchine worked in France before coming to the United States, where he founded the New York City Ballet in 1948.

■ **BALANCHINE, GEORGE (1904-83),** choreographer and founder of the New York City Ballet (1948). Born in St. Petersburg, Russia, he emigrated in 1924 and settled in the United States in 1934. He trained many of the leading female dancers of the era. Balanchine's dances, performed by companies around the world, fused modernism with classical techniques. His *Nutcracker* (1954) became a holiday tradition.

■ **BALBOA, VASCO NÚÑEZ DE (1475-1519),** Spanish conquistador and first European to reach the eastern Pacific Ocean. In 1513 Balboa crossed the Isthmus of Panama, reaching the Pacific on Sept. 25 and claimed the coast for Spain. His discovery opened the way for Spanish expansion on the western coast of the Americas. After settling Acla on the Pacific coast, Balboa was accused of treason and beheaded in 1519.

See Also: Exploration and Discovery.

■ **BALCH, EMILY GREEN (1867-1961),** economist and sociologist, international peace activist. Born in Jamaica Plain, Massachusetts, she taught in the Economics and Sociology department at Wellesley College (1896-1919) and wrote a number of scholarly works. In 1919 she was fired from Wellesley because of her opposition to World War I. After the war she became secretary of the Women's International League for Peace and Freedom, and, during World War II, was an outspoken antifascist. She was awarded the Nobel Peace Prize in 1946.

See Also: Women's Movement.

■ **BALDWIN, HENRY (1780-1844),** U.S. representative (1817-22) and associate justice of the U.S. Supreme Court (1833-40). A New Haven, Connecticut, native, Baldwin supported slavery and states rights. He distanced himself from the ascendant judicial nationalism of Chief Justice John Marshall.

See Also: Supreme Court.

On Sept. 25, 1513, after marching across the Isthmus of Panama, the Spaniard Vasco Núñez de Balboa stopped and stood "silent, upon a peak in Darien." He was the first European to view the Pacific Ocean.

■ **BALDWIN, JAMES (1924-87),** writer and social critic. He was born and raised in the Harlem section of New York City. As a young teenager he developed strong Christian values, becoming a junior minister at age 14. Although he eventually strayed from the church, he retained a belief in some tenets of Christianity. While living in Greenwich Village, Baldwin began publishing reviews and articles in such periodicals as the *Nation* and *Commentary*.

In 1948, seeking greater creative and personal freedom, Baldwin moved to Paris, where he wrote his first novel, *Go Tell It on the Mountain* (1953). Largely autobiographical, this book described the travails of an African-American boy in Harlem and the troubles with his stepfather. His first collection of essays, *Notes of a Native Son* (1955), recounted Baldwin's strong views about racism, while his novel *Giovanni's Room* (1956) dealt skillfully with homosexuality.

Baldwin's return to the United States in 1956 influenced some of his most well-known work. The civil rights movement and southern race relations informed his highly acclaimed collection of essays, *The Fire Next Time* (1963). Like many of Baldwin's other works, *Another Country* (1961) explored relationships of love and sexuality. The debut of the play *Blues for Mister Charlie* (1964) on Broadway marked the beginning of Baldwin's moderately successful attempt at writing drama. He continued writing into the 1980s but is perhaps best known for his earlier work, especially his stirring essays about the consequences of segregation and racial violence.

See Also: African Americans; Novel.

BIBLIOGRAPHY: Campbell, James, *Talking at the Gates: A Life of James Baldwin* (Viking 1991); Leeming, David A., *James Baldwin: A Biography* (Knopf 1994).

The perceptive essays published as *The Fire Next Time* (1963) brought recognition to author James Baldwin as a spokesman for the feelings and attitudes of African Americans. He wrote essays, books, and plays describing the effects of racial strife and prejudice against homosexuality.

■ **BALL, LUCILLE (1911-89),** comedienne. Born in Celoron, New York, she became a television star in the comedy series "I Love Lucy" (1951-57) with her then-husband Desi Arnaz. Ball retired from weekly television in 1974.

■ **BALLINGER-PINCHOT CONTROVERSY (1910),** political controversy that arose when U.S. chief forester Gifford Pinchot publicly charged Sec. of the Interior Richard A. Ballinger with conspiring to sell public coal reserves in Alaska to a private concern.

See Also: Pinchot, Gifford.

■ **BALTIMORE,** largest city in Maryland, located on the northern end of Chesapeake Bay. Founded in 1729 by the provincial assembly, the town was named for the colonial proprietors, the English Lords Baltimore. During the 18th century Baltimore grew as a shipping center for agricultural products, especially tobacco. In 1790 the first Roman Catholic diocese in the United States was established in Baltimore. During the early 19th century European immigrants flocked to the city, and by 1860 the population had swelled to 212,000, making it the third largest city in America. Pro-Confederate sentiment in Baltimore during the Civil War (1861-65) led to Union occupation of the city.

After 1900 many southern blacks and Appalachian whites moved to Baltimore seeking employment in manufacturing and shipping. The city continued to grow throughout the early 20th century, reaching a population of 950,000 by 1950. Since that time, whites have left the central city for surrounding suburbs. In the 1960s and 1970s extensive urban renewal programs were undertaken in an effort to revive the city. A massive restoration of Baltimore's waterfront, called the Inner Harbor, was completed in 1980 and has become a major tourist magnet that features an aquarium, shopping mall, and other attractions. Population (1994): 702,979.

See Also: Baltimore, Lords; Maryland.

■ **BALTIMORE, LORDS,** Irish peerage bestowed on members of the Calvert family commencing with George Calvert (1580-1632), who received the title from Charles I, and ending with Frederick Calvert (1732-71), the last Lord Baltimore. George Calvert, first Lord Baltimore, played a significant role in the founding of the Calvert family's most valuable possession, colonial Maryland. After a brief experience in colonizing the frigid coast of Newfoundland, Calvert redirected his efforts to the Chesapeake region and shortly before his death obtained a charter for a colony. Cecilius Calvert, second Baron Baltimore, inherited his father's proprietary interests in the colony and took advantage of the absolute power granted to him. The palatine rights over Maryland's administration passed out of the family's hands (1692) during the lifetime of the third baron, Charles Calvert, but the Calverts retained considerable property rights in land and tax revenues down to Frederick Calvert, the last baron.

See Also: Baltimore; Maryland.

■ **BANCROFT, GEORGE (1800-91),** historian and public official. A native of Worcester, Massachusetts, Bancroft was a school teacher from 1822 to 1831. The first volume of his *History of the United States* was published in 1834; the work grew to 10 volumes, the last of which was published in 1874. Beyond work as a writer, Bancroft served as secretary of the navy (1845-46), helped to establish the Naval Academy at Annapolis, Maryland, and was the U.S. minister to Germany (1867-74).

See Also: History.

■ **BANKHEAD-JONES FARM TENANT ACT (1937),** federal legislation authorizing low-interest, long-term government loans to tenant farmers. The act was intended to end sharecropping in the South and establish family-owned farms.

See Also: New Deal.

■ **BANK HOLIDAY (Mar. 6-9, 1933),** a four-day shutdown of the nation's banks ordered by Pres. Franklin D. Roosevelt one day after his inauguration. The deepening Depression had led to thousands of bank failures. This caused customers to lose confidence in the remaining banks and to withdraw their funds, compounding the crisis. On Mar. 9, 1933, Roosevelt sent an Emergency Banking Act to Congress requiring banks to prove their financial stability before reopening, restricting currency transactions, strengthening the Federal Reserve system, and insuring deposits. The legislation was passed by Congress and signed into law by the end of the day. By mid-March banks holding more than 90 percent of the nation's deposits had reopened, and the crisis had passed. The bank holiday marked the start of the "Hundred Days" that saw Congress pass dozens of important measures to launch Roosevelt's New Deal.

See Also: Hundred Days; New Deal; Roosevelt, Franklin Delano.

BIBLIOGRAPHY: Schlesinger, Arthur M., Jr., *The Age of Roosevelt: The Coming of the New Deal* (Houghton Mifflin 1959).

■ ***BANK OF AUGUSTA V. EARLE (1839),*** U.S. Supreme Court case that was a landmark in early American corporate law. Earle, an Alabama merchant, had refused to honor a bill of exchange when the Bank of Augusta sought to redeem it. He argued that the Georgia-chartered bank had no legal status in Alabama. At issue was the discretionary power of a state not to recognize a corporation chartered by another state. Writing for the Court, Chief Justice Roger Taney held that one state could not unilaterally ignore the legal existence of an out-of-state corporation doing business within its borders. Taney made clear, however, that the states retained considerable power to regulate internal corporate activity. The decision helped to clear the way constitutionally for the formation of national corporations.

See Also: *Supreme Court; Taney, Roger Brooke.*

■ **BANK OF NORTH AMERICA (1781),** first private commercial bank in the United States and the first bank incorporated by the government. This bank emerged out of the financial chaos created by the American Revolution. The Continental Congress lacked the ability to tax and, despite subsidies and loans from Spain and France, faced financial collapse after 1779. Congress had tried to finance the war by issuing bills of credit that circulated as paper money (Continentals) and had issued $191.5 million by 1780. By that time their value had already depreciated to 40 to 1 in relation to specie. Continentals became virtually worthless despite Congressional efforts. In response to the crisis, Congress appointed Robert Morris superintendent of a new department of finance in early 1781. He called for a national bank to restore the nation's credit, and the Bank of North America opened in Philadelphia in January 1782, issuing notes redeemable in specie and establishing a stable national currency. This bank sparked the incorporation of other commercial banks, funded Washington's army and the government through the end of the Revolution, and instilled enough confidence abroad to attract loans from France and Holland that turned the war in favor of the Americans.

See Also: *Banks and Banking; Morris, Robert.*

■ **BANKS AND BANKING.** The first private commercial bank in the United States, the Bank of North America, organized by Robert Morris, opened for business in Philadelphia in 1781. Morris, who had been appointed by Congress as the nation's superintendent of finance, used his bank as the de facto depository for government funds.

In 1791, two years after the ratification of the Constitution, Treasury Sec. Alexander Hamilton proposed the establishment of a central bank for the new nation. Opponents, led by Thomas Jefferson, argued that a central bank was unconstitutional, that it would drain scarce investment funds away from farming toward the emerging industrial sector, and that it would provide too much influence for wealthy men. In a close sec-

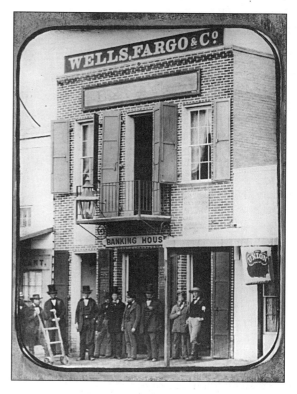

Wells, Fargo & Co. started as a banking and shipping company during the California Gold Rush.

tional vote, Congress chartered the First Bank of the United States for a 20-year term. The bank became the official agent of the federal government's financial business and the depository of federal revenues. Its eight branches, located in the principal cities, provided commercial credit and acted as lenders-of-last-resort to state banks. Its conservative management also acted as a moderating influence on speculation.

In 1811, however, a coalition of Jeffersonians and state bankers who wanted the freedom to pursue their own course persuaded Congress not to renew the bank's charter. In the banking boom that followed the demise of the First Bank of the United States, 120 new banks were chartered, many with limited regulation, and they recklessly extended credit beyond their financial reserves. As a result, many of the new banks failed.

Surveying the financial chaos that had followed the end of the first central bank, Congress in 1816 chartered the Second Bank of the United States, which was to function in the same manner as its predecessor. Unfortunately, the bank's first director mismanaged its affairs, helping to bring on the Panic of 1819. But under the leadership of its subsequent director, Nicholas Biddle, the bank was restored to a sound condition and its operations expanded. It continued to have many opponents, however, including those who had suffered financial losses in 1819, state bankers who sought federal deposits, and Jeffersonians for whom a central bank violated constitutional scruples. During his first term (1829-33), Pres. Andrew Jackson made it clear he intended to oppose the bank. When the bank's supporters in Congress passed early recharter legislation in 1832, Jackson vetoed the bill, and the matter became one of the principal issues of his reelection campaign that same year. After his victory, the president withdrew federal funds from the bank and deposited them in a number of state banks (called "pet banks" by his opponents). There followed another period of "wildcat" banking, with excesses of speculation and an overextension of credit that led directly to the Panic of 1837.

In response, Pres. Martin Van Buren proposed, and Congress in 1840 passed, the Independent Treasury Act, which entrusted the federal government with the care of its own funds. The act created a system of "subtreasuries" in the nation's principal cities to provide credit and currency. The Whigs, who won control of Congress in the elections of 1840, repealed the law in 1841 but failed to win approval of a new national bank; when the Democrats regained control of Congress in 1845, they reenacted the bill. This structure served as the basis of the U.S. fiscal system for the next 67 years. There were some controls on banking. A few states, notably New York and Massachusetts, required banks to maintain specie reserves to back their credit; and during the Civil War (1861-65), Congress passed legislation in 1863 and 1864 requiring national banks to maintain a third of their assets in government securities. But unlike the nations of Europe, all of which had central banks that operated to stabilize the financial system, the banking system of the United States was characterized by laissez-faire.

The financial history of the post–Civil War years was dominated by the great investment banking houses such as Jay Cooke's and J. P. Morgan's. These institutions provided ample capital for economic expansion but also encouraged rampant speculation and financial uncertainty. Commercial banking prospered as well, but without a central bank to act as a lender-of-last-resort, a large percentage of banks failed, especially in the crisis years of 1873, 1893, and 1908.

20th-Century Banking. Gradually the nation's financial and political elite came to a consensus that the nation required a central banking system to add ballast to the economy. In 1913, Pres. Woodrow Wilson proposed, and Congress passed, legislation creating the Federal Reserve System, which fundamentally restructured the nation's banking and currency system. It created 12 Federal Reserve banks, regulated by a presidentially appointed central board in Washington. Member banks were required to keep a portion of their cash reserves in the Federal Reserve Bank of their district. By raising or lowering the percentage required in reserve, "the Fed" could discourage or encourage credit expansion by member banks. Varying the interest rate charged on loans and advances by federal reserve banks to member banks also helped regulate both the quantity and cost of money circulating in the national economy. The Federal Reserve also served to diminish the power of large private banks.

The banking system was strengthened, but it failed to withstand the shock of the Great Depression. From 1929 to 1933 a third of all banks suspended payments and locked their doors. Between election day in November 1932 and the inauguration of Pres. Franklin D. Roosevelt on Mar. 4, 1933, the country's banking system nearly collapsed. Roosevelt's first official act was to issue an executive order calling for a four-day "bank holiday." Congress immediately passed the Emergency Banking Relief Act, providing the president with broad discretionary powers over all banking transactions, authorizing healthy banks to reopen only under licenses from the Treasury Department, and providing for greater federal authority in the management of the affairs of failed banks. A few months later, the Banking Act created the Federal Deposit Insurance Corporation, which guaranteed individual bank deposits up to $5,000, and subsequent legislation similarly guaranteed individual accounts in savings banks ("thrifts"). The New Deal legislation offered federal guarantees in exchange for regulation, and as a result, public confidence in the banking system was restored.

The structure created during the New Deal prevailed mostly unchanged until 1980, when Congress passed legislation removing some banking regulations and loosening others. During the subsequent decade, rapid changes had taken place in finance, with securities firms offering "money market" accounts and thrifts offering checking services that made them both more like commercial banks, but without the same regulation. Rather than reign in these practices, Congress elected to deregulate much of the banking system. Whatever the advantages of deregulation in the long term, it produced an orgy of speculation over the next few years, and when the inevitable contraction came after a stock market crash in 1987, many thrifts and banks failed. The formula had become deregulation plus protection, and taxpayers were forced to bail out the banking system at a cost of several hundred billion dollars.

—JOHN MACK FARAGHER

See Also: Bank Holiday; Bank of North America; Banks of the United States, First and Second; Bank War; Emergency Banking Relief Act; Federal Reserve System; National Banking System.

BIBLIOGRAPHY: Hammond, Bray, *Banks and Politics in America: From the Revolution to the Civil War* (Princeton Univ. Press 1991); Hooks, Linda M., *Bank Failures and Deregulation in the 1980s* (Garland 1994); Timberlake, Richard H., Jr., *The Origins of Central Banking in the United States* (Harvard Univ. Press 1978).

■ **BANKS OF THE UNITED STATES, FIRST AND SECOND,** federally chartered corporations funded by private capital and designed to serve as depositors of federal funds. In 1790, Sec. of the Treasury Alexander Hamilton proposed the establishment of the national bank as a primary component of his ambitious but controversial fiscal plan to stabilize and stimulate the economy. Following a lively debate between Hamilton and Thomas Jefferson over the constitutionality of a federal bank, Pres. George Washington signed the bank bill into law. The First Bank of the United States began operations in 1791 with a 20-year charter

and capital reserves of $10 million. The federal government owned one-fifth of the bank's stock, with the remainder in the hands of private business. The notes of the bank became the most important circulating currency in the growing economy. Despite the bank's advantages, its Congressional opponents allowed the charter to expire in 1811 because of fears of concentrated economic power in the bank.

After five years of unstable and unsatisfactory state banking, Congress chartered the Second Bank of the United States in 1816. Like its predecessor, the bank stabilized the circulation of the currency, stimulated the economy, and exercised control over state banks. Although the national bank had many supporters, its detractors grew in numbers as the bank increasingly wielded its power over the state banks. Many farmers, urban workers, and western land speculators feared the consolidation of economic power in the bank and the elites who controlled it. The clash of interests surfaced in a volatile struggle between the bank's director, Nicholas Biddle, and Pres. Andrew Jackson, who in 1832 vetoed the bill to renew the bank's charter, and it ceased to function in 1836.

See Also: Biddle, Nicholas; Jackson, Andrew.

BIBLIOGRAPHY: Holdsworth, John T., and Davis R. Dewey, *The First and Second Banks of the United States* (Government Printing Office 1910); Remini, Robert V., *Andrew Jackson and the Bank War: A Study in the Growth of Presidential Power* (Norton 1967).

■ **BANK WAR (1832),** conflict over the Bank of the United States. The Second Bank of the United States was chartered in 1816 during the administration of Pres. James Madison in the hopes of providing a stable economy to encourage investments while paying off the debts incurred during the War of 1812. Madison's successor, James Monroe, appointed Philadelphia financier Nicholas Biddle to head the Bank of the United States in 1819. Under Biddle, the bank produced a sound national currency and a controlled credit system.

When he became president in 1829, Andrew Jackson attacked the bank as unconstitutional and sought to distribute the bank's assets to state banks throughout the United States. Jackson warned Congress that he intended to fight the Bank of the United States when its charter ex-

Pres. Andrew Jackson vetoed Congress's 1832 bill renewing the charter of the Second Bank of the United States, due to expire in 1836. This cartoon depicts Jackson plagued by a nightmare in which his veto power is "broken" and things turn out differently.

pired. To head off Jackson's attacks on the bank, Biddle applied to Congress in 1832 for an extension of the bank's charter, four years earlier than necessary. Congress approved the charter, but Jackson vetoed it and Congress could not override the veto. In his veto message, Jackson wrote: "The rich and powerful too often bend the acts of government to their selfish purposes. . . . Many of our rich men have not been content with equal protection and benefits, but have besought to us to make them richer by act of Congress."

In 1836 state banks received the surplus from the national bank and began to issue paper money to encourage investment. A wave of speculation in western lands and state internal improvements ensued, leading to runaway inflation and worthless paper money, prompting Jackson to issue the Specie Circular of 1836, requiring government land offices to accept only gold and

silver coin as payment. The result was the Panic of 1837, which led the country into a seven-year economic depression.

—KATHRYN A. ABBOTT

See Also: *Banks of the United States, First and Second; Jackson, Andrew; Specie Circular.*

BIBLIOGRAPHY: Sellers, Charles G., *The Market Revolution: Jacksonian America, 1815-1846* (Oxford Univ. Press 1991).

■ **BANNEKER, BENJAMIN (1731-1806),** author and mathematician. Born in Ellicott, Maryland, Banneker had little formal education but was a prodigy with all things mechanical. Blessed with an inquisitive mind and great talent, he accurately predicted the solar eclipse of 1789. He published the *Almanac* from 1791 to 1802, the first scientific publication by an African American. Banneker corresponded frequently with Thomas

Jefferson and assisted Pierre L'Enfant and George Ellicott in the surveying of Washington, D.C.

See Also: African Americans.

■ **BANNOCK INDIANS.** *See: Great Basin and Rocky Mountain Indians.*

■ **BAPTIST CHURCH,** the largest Protestant denomination in America, originating in English Puritanism. Puritans believed that the Church of England was no longer the true church of Christ and that congregations should be comprised of saints, people who could testify to the grace of God in their lives. But Baptists were more radical. They believed that children of believers should be denied baptism until they were old enough to testify; hence, the name Baptist. Unlike the Puritans, they argued for the separation of church and state.

Roger Williams has been credited with the founding of American Baptism. After he was banished from Massachusetts Bay Colony in 1639, he established the first Baptist church in Providence, Rhode Island. But Baptists had greater success in the Middle Colonies. Five churches united in 1707 to form the Philadelphia Baptist Association and launched missionary efforts. During the Great Awakening the Baptists, led by uneducated farmer-preachers, grew in great numbers in the South and on the frontiers.

Today there are more than 50 distinct Baptist bodies, the largest being the Southern Baptist Convention, followed by the African-American Conventions: National Baptist Convention, U.S.A. and the National Baptist Convention of America. The variety of Baptist groups is the result of developments and schisms. From the beginning, Baptists were divided theologically between Calvinists and Arminians. As early as 1773 in Silver Bluff, Georgia, African Americans began to organize independent Baptist organizations. In the 1820s and 1830s Baptists split over missionary issues. (Primitive Baptists resisted missions because they were without biblical precedent.) In 1845, Baptists divided over the slavery controversy into Northern and Southern factions. And in the 20th century they split over denominational structure issues and liberalism.

—NANCY M. GODLESKI

See Also: Puritans; Religion; Williams, Roger.

BIBLIOGRAPHY: Brackney, William Henry, *The Baptists* (Greenwood 1988); McBeth, H. Leon, *The Baptist* (Heritage Broadman 1987).

■ **BARBARY COAST WARS (1801-05, 1815),** a series of military clashes between the United States and the "Barbary States" (Algiers, Morocco, Tripoli, and Tunis) over tributes customarily paid by U.S. traders to these states. In 1801, Tripoli increased demands for tribute and declared war against the United States. A successful naval expedition under Commodore Edward Preble (1804) ended the conflict. In 1815, Capt. Stephen Decatur effectively defeated the Algerine fleet, exacting guarantees from Algiers, Tunis, and Tripoli to renounce molestation of U.S. commerce.

See Also: Decatur, Stephen.

■ **BARBED WIRE,** twisted wire with barbs on sharp points. It was patented by Joseph Farwell Glidden in 1873. Barbed wire solved the problem of economical fencing of crops to exclude wildlife and open-range cattle from farms on the treeless Great Plains.

See Also: Frontier in American History.

■ **BARBER, SAMUEL (1910-81),** composer. Born in West Chester, Pennsylvania, he was a graduate of Philadelphia's Curtis Institute (1932). Barber composed symphonic, chamber, and vocal works marked by their lyrical melodies. His 1936 *String Quartet* introduced the popular *Adagio for Strings*, which Barber later reworked for string orchestra. *Vanessa*, an opera with libretto by Gian Carlo Menotti, won the 1958 Pulitzer Prize.

■ **BARBOUR, PHILIP PENDLETON (1783-1841),** U.S. representative (1814-25, 1827-30) and associate justice of the U.S. Supreme Court (1836-41). An Orange County, Virginia, native, Barbour had been speaker of the House before joining the Court. His previously strong support of states' rights softened somewhat during his tenure on the Court.

See Also: Supreme Court.

■ **BARKLEY, ALBEN (1877-1956),** vice president of the United States (1949-53). Born in Lowes, Kentucky, he was a stalwart in Kentucky Democratic politics. Elected to the U.S. House of Representatives in 1912 and the U.S. Senate in

1926, he served as majority leader (1937-47). He was elected vice president with Pres. Harry S. Truman in 1948. After leaving office, Barkley ran again for the Senate and was reelected in 1954.

See Also: Vice President of the United States.

■ **BARNARD, HENRY (1811-1900),** public school administrator and reformer. Born in Hartford, Connecticut, he helped create Connecticut's public school system while a state legislator (1837-39). Barnard served as education commissioner in Rhode Island (1843-49) and Connecticut (1850-54), chancellor of the University of Wisconsin (1858-60) and first U.S. commissioner of education (1867-70). From 1855 to 1882 Barnard edited the influential *American Journal of Education.*

■ **BARNBURNERS (1840s),** New York Democratic supporters of Martin Van Buren for president in 1844 who opposed the extension of slavery. Many abandoned the Democrats for the Free Soil party in 1848 but returned as Free Democrats in 1852.

See Also: Civil War; Free Soil Party.

■ **BARNUM, PHINEAS T. (1810-91),** entrepreneur and showman. A masterful self-promoter, Barnum was born in Bethel, Connecticut. After a few failed business ventures in New York City, he succeeded with a touring show featuring Joice Heth, an African American who claimed to be George Washington's 160-year-old nurse. This began Barnum's long career of presenting acts that exceeded the bounds of truth and credulity.

In 1842, Barnum opened a museum in New York City featuring "freaks of nature," fossils, historical objects, and live shows. He followed with touring shows in Europe and the United States that featured the Swedish singer Jenny Lind and the midget Tom Thumb. In large part, the success of these ventures lay in Barnum's use of advertising and publicity stunts. Barnum's most lasting contribution to mass amusement was his traveling three-ring circus, "The Greatest Show on Earth," founded in 1871. He combined the circus with James A. Bailey's in 1881 to form the noted Barnum and Bailey Circus. A year later, they introduced the famous elephant, Jumbo.

As in his businesses, Barnum regularly reinvented himself in his autobiography, which was first published in 1855 and updated and modified every few years until 1888. Despite his success and contrary to his claims, Barnum did not invent many of the attractions and shows he made popular. Instead, he accumulated great wealth and fame by presenting a compelling combination of fraud, reality, and myth.

See Also: Circuses.

BIBLIOGRAPHY: Saxon, A. H., *P. T. Barnum: The Legend and the Man* (Columbia Univ. Press 1989).

■ ***BARRON V. BALTIMORE* (1833),** U.S. Supreme Court case that considered whether the Fifth Amendment extended to suits against the states. The controversy arose when the city of Baltimore made changes to its harbor. A local wharf owner sued the city, claiming that the changes had diminished the economic value of his property. After Maryland courts dismissed the case, the plaintiff sought relief from the Supreme Court, arguing that under the Fifth Amendment, his property had been "taken" unconstitutionally, without compensation. Writing for a unanimous Court, Chief Justice John Marshall held that constitutional rights such as those found in the Fifth Amendment protected citizens against only the federal government and not against state governments. Marshall's opinion in this case stands as his last in a long line of historic constitutional decisions. An ironic coda to a career dedicated to strengthening federal authority, *Barron* set a precedent that limited rather than expanded federal power.

See Also: Marshall, John; Supreme Court.

■ **BARRYMORE FAMILY,** stage and screen actors. Beginning with British actor Maurice (1847-1905) and his American wife Georgiana (1854-93), the daughter of actor John Drew, the Barrymores were the leading family of the American theater for more than half a century. The Barrymore's three children followed their parents to the stage and subsequently enjoyed success in films. Lionel (1878-1954) and Ethel (1879-1959) had long careers in leading roles and later as character actors. Lionel's portrayal of Scrooge in *A Christmas Carol* became a radio tradition in the 1940s. The handsome and self-destructive John (1882-1942), known as "the Great Profile," won

Lionel, Ethel, and John Barrymore all gained fame as actors—the latter two on both stage and screen, the former primarily in film. The three siblings co-starred only once, in the 1932 film, *Rasputin and the Empress.*

critical acclaim for his *Richard III* (1920) and *Hamlet* (1922) on stage and for leading roles on screen, including *Dr. Jekyll and Mr. Hyde* (1920), *Grand Hotel* (1932), and *Dinner at Eight* (1933).

BIBLIOGRAPHY: Alpert, Hollis, *The Barrymores* (Dial Press 1964); Peters, Margot, *The House of Barrymore* (Knopf 1990).

■ **BARTER,** trade in kind, used in place of money. Colonists had limited access to local or foreign coins, bills of exchange from merchants, and paper money (first printed by Massachusetts in 1690), and so relied on barter to obtain goods they did not produce themselves. Merchants accepted farm produce, animals, home manufactures, or even promises of labor in exchange for goods. Commodities, including Indian wampum and receipts for tobacco or sugar, became common mediums of exchange, but the lack of ready money prevented merchants from expanding and limited colonial economic development. After the American Revolution an early banking system and the rapid growth of urban centers made barter less necessary. Even after the Revolution, however, barter continued to characterize trade in isolated communities as well as with and among Indian peoples. Indian trade established military alliances as well as economic ties, and during the 17th and 18th centuries many tribes

played French, English, and later American traders off one another, exercising significant power by forcing Europeans to compete through barter for their trade and allegiance.

See Also: *Fur Trade; Money and Currency.*

BIBLIOGRAPHY: Clark, Christopher, *The Roots of Rural Capitalism* (Cornell Univ. Press 1990); Usner, Daniel H., Jr., *Indians, Settlers, and Slaves in a Frontier Exchange Economy* (Univ. of North Carolina Press 1992); White, Richard, *Middle Ground: Indians, Empires, and Republics in the Great Lakes Region, 1650-1815* (Cambridge Univ. Press 1991).

■ **BARTLETT, JOSIAH (1729-95),** statesman and Revolutionary War leader. Born in Amesbury, Massachusetts, Bartlett was a physician who resided in New Hampshire. He later served as a member of the Continental Congress, signed the Declaration of Independence, and became New Hampshire's first governor in 1793.

See Also: *Declaration of Independence.*

■ **BARTON, CLARISSA HARLOWE (CLARA) (1821-1912),** founder of the American National Red Cross, born in North Oxford, Massachusetts. During the American Civil War, she collected and carried much needed medical supplies to field hospitals, where she was known as "the angel of the battlefield." In 1870 she worked with the newly created International Red Cross in Europe. On returning to the United States, she dedicated herself to persuading the U.S government to ratify the Geneva Treaty. In 1881, she founded the American Association of the Red Cross and served as its president until 1904.

See Also: Civil War; Red Cross, American National; Women in American History.

■ **BARTRAM, JOHN (1699-1777)** and **BARTRAM, WILLIAM (1739-1823),** early American botanists and explorers. Born to a Quaker family in Pennsylvania, John was self-educated in botanical science. In 1728 he established a botanical garden near Philadelphia where he began the first American experiments in hybridization. The garden became internationally famous. Linnaeus called Bartram "the greatest natural botanist in the world," and a number of notable English scientists agreed to finance his further research. In trips ranging from Canada to Florida, often accompanied by his son William, he gathered specimens and established classifications for American flora. His findings were published in a celebrated series of books, which won him appointment in 1765 as royal botanist to King George III. William contin-

ued his father's efforts and achieved comparable fame, not only for his botanical studies but his ornithology, having compiled the first extensive list of American birds. Both men inspired important literary works. J. Hector de Crèvecoeur idealized John as the archetype of the American farmer, and Samuel Coleridge incorporated William's descriptions into the landscapes of his poem "Kubla Khan."

See Also: Science.

BIBLIOGRAPHY: Slaughter, Thomas P., *The Natures of John and William Bartram* (Knopf 1996).

■ **BARUCH, BERNARD MANNES (1870-1965),** wealthy American investor and economic and foreign policy adviser to government leaders. Born in Camden, South Carolina, he made a fortune by 1900 through shrewd stock speculations. A superb publicist who believed that government should provide a stable environment for business, he was active in politics and public policy for more than 60 years. Baruch was named chairman of the powerful War Industries Board (1918) by Pres. Woodrow Wilson, and he advised the U.S. delegation to the Versailles peace talks on economic matters following World War I. An ad-

After joining in the relief efforts of the International Committee of the Red Cross during the Franco-Prussian War (1870-71), Clara Barton returned to the United States to spearhead the establishment of an American branch of the Red Cross.

vocate of military preparedness in the late 1930s, Baruch was influential with Democratic members of Congress, persuading conservatives to support Pres. Franklin D. Roosevelt's New Deal legislation. As U.S. representative to the United Nations Atomic Energy Commission (1946), he proposed the "Baruch Plan" for international control of atomic power.

See Also: New Deal.

BIBLIOGRAPHY: Schwarz, Jordan A., *The Speculator: Bernard M. Baruch in Washington, 1917-1965* (Univ. of North Carolina Press 1981).

◼ **BASEBALL,** the national game of the United States. The game emerged from bat-and-ball folk games in 1845 when Alexander Cartwright, a New York City bank clerk, drew up the sport's first formal rules for the Knickerbocker Base Ball Club. Baseball spread rapidly among urban men's clubs, and the first governing body, the National Association of Base Ball Players, was organized in 1858. The first professional club, the Cincinnati Red Stockings, was formed in 1869 and demonstrated baseball's potential as a spectator sport. Amateur ball continued to thrive, but many of the best players joined the National Association of Professional Base Ball Players (1871-75). In 1876 the business of baseball was firmly established when teams in eight cities formed the National League of Professional Base Ball Clubs. The owners crushed the Brotherhood of Professional Base Ball Players (1885-90), absorbed the rival American Association (1891), and in 1903 signed a National Agreement with the new American League to create the "major league" structure that still exists.

The scandal that resulted when eight Chicago White Sox players took bribes to fix the 1919 World Series did not reduce the popularity of the game. Baseball's low-scoring "dead ball" era ended as a new age, dominated by home run hitters such as Babe Ruth and promoted by newspapers, radio, and, after World War II, television, made baseball the nation's most popular spectator sport. In 1947, Jackie Robinson became the first African American to play in the major leagues since the 1890s. During the 1950s a number of major league franchises (previously confined to the eastern half of the United States) moved westward and finally reached the West Coast when the Brooklyn Dodgers and New York Giants relocated to California (1958).

The major leagues expanded from 16 to 28 teams between 1961 and 1996. The sport was shaken in 1975 when the courts struck down the reserve clause, which had bound players to one club, and instead allowed them to become free agents. Player strikes and lockouts hobbled the game in the 1980s and 1990s, creating a backlash by fans who noticed, a hundred years after the fact, that baseball was a business.

—TIM ASHWELL

See Also: Black Sox Scandal; Robinson, Jackie (Jack Roosevelt); Ruth, George Herman (Babe); Sports.

BIBLIOGRAPHY: Seymour, Harold, *Baseball*, 3 vols. (Oxford Univ. Press 1989); Ward, Geoffrey, *Baseball: An Illustrated History* (Knopf 1994).

◼ **BASIE, WILLIAM "COUNT" (1904-84),** jazz pianist, composer, and bandleader. Born in Red Bank, New Jersey, Basie started his career in

Bandleader William Basie needed a clever title to match those of Duke Ellington and other musical celebrities of the 1930s, so one evening a Kansas City radio announcer dubbed him "Count Basie." His own compositions include "One O'Clock Jump."

vaudeville. After playing in small groups, he formed his own big band in 1935. Basie's understated, lilting style on the piano and his big band's rhythmic sound made him a dominant force in American jazz for decades. In 1957 his band became the first American group to give a command performance for the Queen of England.

See Also: *African Americans; Jazz; New Deal.*

■ **BASKETBALL,** sport devised by James Naismith at the Young Men's Christian Association (YMCA) training school in Springfield, Massachusetts (1891). The game spread to YMCAs, colleges, and schools across the country and around the world and soon became a favorite for both men and women. The men's game has long been played with five men to a side, but women often played six to a side with three players on each team confined to each end of the court until the 1960s. U.S. high school and college seasons traditionally end with championship tournaments, which have become major sporting spectacles. The National Collegiate Athletic Association men's and women's Division I tournaments are televised nationally and attract huge audiences. Television has also helped boost the popularity of the professional National Basketball Association (NBA). Founded in 1949, the NBA struggled through its early years and did not become a major attraction until the 1960s. Thanks to television, players such as Larry Bird, Magic Johnson, and Michael Jordan made the NBA a worldwide entertainment success. Professional leagues have blossomed around the world, often featuring a few U.S. stars as well as native players, and international players have played in the NBA.

—Tim Ashwell

See Also: *Abdul-Jabbar, Kareem; Bird, Larry; Johnson, Earvin, Jr. ("Magic"); Jordan, Michael; Sports.*

BIBLIOGRAPHY: Isaacs, Neil, *All the Moves: A History of College Basketball* (Harper & Row 1984); Peterson, Robert, *Cages to Jump Shots: Pro Basketball's Early Years* (Oxford Univ. Press 1990).

■ **BASS, SAM (1851-78),** outlaw. Bass was born in Mitchell, Indiana, and achieved notoriety by robbing a Union Pacific Train of $60,000 in gold at Big Springs, Nebraska, in 1877. At a bank robbery in Round Rock, Texas, on July 21, 1878, Bass was mortally wounded and eventually captured

outside of town by Texas Rangers who had been tipped off by Bass's companion, Jim Murphy. Despite an inconsequential criminal career, Bass became a legend in death.

See Also: *Frontier in American History.*

■ **BATAAN AND CORREGIDOR,** in World War II, the last stronghold of American power in the Philippines after the Japanese bombed Pearl Harbor and seized Guam and Wake Island in December 1941. American forces staged a valiant defense down the Bataan peninsula until Apr. 9, 1942, then moved to Corregidor, a fortified island in Manila Bay. With no prospects of reinforcement and a garrison suffering from disease and lack of supplies, Gen. Jonathan Wainwright surrendered the U.S. forces on May 6, 1942.

See Also: *World War II.*

■ **BAY PSALM BOOK (1640),** Puritan hymnal. The *Bay Psalm Book* was created by New England ministers, including Richard Mather and John Eliot. The first bound book printed in the American colonies, it was published by Stephen Daye in Cambridge, Massachusetts.

See Also: *Eliot, John.*

■ **BEACH, AMY CHENEY (1867-1944),** pianist and the first American woman to gain popularity as a composer of classical music. She was born in Henniker, New Hampshire. Her compositions, marked by broad melodic lines, altered chords, and enharmonic modulations, are often grouped with the work of Arthur Foote and the Boston classicists.

See Also: *Women in American History.*

■ **BEARD, CHARLES AUSTIN (1874-1948),** historian and social activist. A passionate and controversial social critic, Beard was born and raised in Indiana. After graduating from DePauw University, where he met his future wife and collaborator, Mary Ritter Beard, he spent a year at Oxford University. He received his Ph.D. in political science from Columbia University in 1904, where he became a faculty member that same year.

Influenced by the stimulating scholars in the social sciences at Columbia, Beard challenged well-established scholarship on the American Revolution with *An Economic Interpretation of the Constitution* (1913), which argued that economic, not ideological, interests motivated colonial elites to rebel. A vocal proponent of free speech, Beard resigned from Columbia in 1917 after university officials refused to hire scholars who opposed U.S. participation in World War I. Although he never again held a full-time faculty position, Beard remained active in the historical profession, holding numerous positions in historical organizations. He and his wife coauthored several influential historical volumes, including *The Rise of American Civilization* (2 vols., 1927) and *America in Midpassage* (1939).

Beard's opposition to U.S. involvement in World War II was reflected in two highly criticized works: *American Foreign Policy in the Making, 1932-1940* (1946) and *President Roosevelt and the Coming of War, 1941* (1948). Although vilified at the end of his life for his views about the war, Beard is remembered as a distinguished historian, who established a non-Marxian economic interpretation of American history and advocated scholarly engagement in politics and society.

See Also: History.

BIBLIOGRAPHY: Hofstadter, Richard, *The Progressive Historians: Turner, Beard, Parrington* (Knopf 1968); Nore, Ellen, *Charles A. Beard: An Intellectual Biography* (Southern Illinois Univ. Press 1983).

▨ **BEARDEN, ROMARE (1914-88),** painter and collagist. Born in Charlotte, North Carolina, Bearden migrated to New York City's Harlem. His art grew to reflect the central tensions of African-American life and cultural striving in urban environments.

See Also: African Americans; Painting.

▨ **BEAR FLAG REVOLT,** uprising of American settlers in California's Sacramento Valley on June 14, 1846, during the war with Mexico. The uprising followed a period of tension among the settlers, who feared that Mexican authorities were about to expel them from the region. On June 10 a group of Americans, encouraged by Capt. John C. Frémont, recently arrived at the head of an official U.S. Army exploring party, seized the town of Sonoma, arrested retired Mexican colonel Mariano Vallejo, and proclaimed the independence of the province under the standard of the Republic of California, a flag showing a grizzly bear facing a red star. It was an inauspicious sign for the Mexican Californios, for the cattle-thieving bear was to them a symbol of piracy. The Americans played the part expected of them. They imprisoned and insulted Vallejo and other important Californians, plundered homes, and killed civilians, unnecessarily embittering relations between Americans and Californios. The new government lasted only until early July, when U.S. forces occupied California and replaced the bear and red star with the American flag.

See Also: California; Frontier in American History; Mexican War.

▨ **BEATS, THE,** a social and literary counterculture of the post–World War II era. The Beat Generation was characterized by an emphasis on individualism and freedom from social confines, but at the same time it became a recognizable community in areas such as New York's Greenwich Village and San Francisco's North Beach. The philosophy and lives of the Beats are remembered through the literature of members of these communities, most notably poetry by Allen Ginsberg and novels by William Burroughs and Jack Kerouac.

See Also: Burroughs, William; Ginsberg, Allen; Kerouac, Jack.

▨ **BEAUMONT, WILLIAM (1785-1853,),** physician who discovered how the digestive system works. Born in Lebanon, Connecticut, Beaumont apprenticed to a doctor in Vermont and became an army surgeon (1812-15, 1820-40). He served in the War of 1812, established a practice in Plattsburg, New York, reenlisted, and became the post surgeon at Fort Mackinac, Michigan. There he met a young Canadian trapper named Alexis St. Martin who had suffered a gunshot wound to the stomach. The wound healed only partially, developing a permanent opening to the stomach and giving Beaumont the opportunity to study the nature of digestion. His research (1825) overthrew many prevalent theories on the subject, but it wore on St. Martin, who ran away. Beaumont found him in 1829 and continued his research until St. Martin returned to Canada in 1834 and refused to come back. After 238 experiments, Beaumont established the relative digestibility of many foods, identified (with chemists' help) hydrochloric acid and a second digestive factor that turned out to be pepsin, published his findings (1833), and started a new era in the study of the stomach and digestion.

See Also: Medicine; Science.

■ BEAUREGARD, PIERRE GUSTAVE TOUTANT

(1818-93), American army officer and Confederate general. Born in Saint Bernard parish, Louisiana, he graduated from the U.S. Military Academy at West Point in 1838, served on the staff of Gen. Winfield Scott during the Mexican War (1846-48), and wrote military texts. Just before the onset of the Civil War, Beauregard resigned his position as superintendent of West Point to join the Confederacy. His capture of Fort Sumter (Apr. 14, 1861) and contribution to the victory at Manassas (July 21, 1861) made him the South's first hero of the war. At the Battle of

On Apr. 12, 1861, Gen. P.G.T. Beauregard commanded the Confederate attack on Fort Sumter, South Carolina, the opening engagement of the Civil War.

Shiloh (Apr. 6-7, 1862), he succeeded to command following the death of Gen. Albert Sidney Johnston and halted the Confederate attack, a move that remains controversial. Although Beauregard failed as a field commander during subsequent campaigns, thereby earning the enmity of Confederate Pres. Jefferson Davis, he rendered invaluable service from 1863 to 1864 commanding the Atlantic coastal fortifications, and he helped save Richmond, Virginia, in May 1864 by his defense of nearby Petersburg. Following the war, Beauregard devoted himself to politics and railroad interests in Louisiana.

—WILLIAM GARRETT PISTON

See Also: Civil War; Shiloh, Battle of.

BIBLIOGRAPHY: Williams, T. Harry, *P.G.T. Beauregard: Napoleon in Gray* (Lousiana State Univ. Press 1955).

■ BEAUX, CECILLA (1855-1942),

portrait artist born in Philadelphia. A painter of international renown, she displayed her work in the Paris Salon in 1896. Her style is often compared with that of her contemporary John Singer Sargent. Her 1925 self-portrait, commissioned by the Italian government, hangs in the Uffizi Gallery in Florence.

■ BEAVER WARS,

North American intertribal wars for control of trade between Indians and New France and/or New Netherland through the 17th century. Access to hunting territory and trading centers, and secure transportation were at first advantageous to the Huron trading with Quebec. The Dutch armed Iroquois tribes in order to divert trade to Fort Orange/Rensselaerville (Albany, after English conquest). For several years, the Iroquois raided Huron paddling to Quebec, but the founding of Montreal in 1642 protected Huron transportation.

The Iroquois turned to raids against Huron home communities, and in 1649, the Iroquois, Mohawk, and Seneca mounted a long-range winter attack armed with 400 Dutch guns. Because the French had allowed only Catholic converts to obtain guns, the Huron faced overwhelmingly superior Iroquois firepower and fled.

The Iroquois then attacked and dispersed tribes of the former Huron trading circuit. Successful until 1655, the Iroquois turned south to attack the Susquehannock, but met determined resistance and some defeats by Indians armed as well as themselves.

The Mohawk finally won complete control over access to trade at the Hudson River. The Seneca adopted and assimilated enough captives to outnumber all other Iroquois combined. Merchants of the St. Lawrence and Hudson centers agreed to smuggle northern furs in exchange for trade goods from the Hudson Valley. Indian tactical victories were offset by disastrous casualties.

—FRANCIS JENNINGS

See Also: French Colonies; Fur Trade; Indians of North America.

BIBLIOGRAPHY: Jennings, Francis, *The Ambiguous Iroquois Empire* (Norton 1984); Trigger, Bruce G., *The Children of Aataentsic: A History of the Huron People to 1660,* 2 vols. (McGill-Queen's Univ. Press 1976); Trudel, Marcel, *The Beginnings of New France, 1524-1663* (McClelland & Stewart 1973).

■ **BE-BOP,** a driving, up-tempo form of jazz that developed in the 1940s. Originated by younger African-American musicians such as alto saxophonist Charlie Parker and trumpeter Dizzy Gillespie in after-hours jam sessions around New York City, be-bop improvisations were often based on new melodies created from the chord progressions of popular songs. Many of the leaders of the be-bop movement performed in popular swing bands and saw their new music as a means of artistic expression that could not be displayed at dances and concerts where audiences demanded familiar melodies with predictable rhythms. In the 1950s, the be-bop style itself fragmented; blues-influenced bands, led by musicians such as bassist Charles Mingus, vied for fans with the cool and cerebral Modern Jazz Quartet, and innovators such as tenor saxophonist John Coltrane took jazz to new levels of exploratory improvisation.

See Also: Gillespie, Dizzy.

BIBLIOGRAPHY: Owens, Thomas, *Bebop: The Music and its Players* (Oxford Univ. Press 1995).

■ **BECKWOURTH, JIM (1798-1867?),** legendary frontiersman and guide. The son of a white man and a mulatto slave woman in Virginia, he was born a slave but was freed after his father took him to Missouri. Beckwourth was on Gen.

William Ashley's trade venture in 1824 that became the Green River Rendezvous. Beckwourth wintered with Jedediah Smith in 1825-26 and lived with the Crow Indians for six years after. Beckwourth fought as a mule driver in the Florida Seminole War and was in California during the 1848 gold rush. He was a scout for the Second Colorado Infantry at the Sand Creek Massacre of 1864. Beckwourth is reported to have died on a hunting trip with the Crow.

See Also: Frontier in American History.

■ **BEECHER, CATHARINE (1800-78),** educator and author dedicated to the cause of women's education. She was born in East Hampton, New York. In 1852 she organized the American Women's Educational Association with the goal of establishing women's colleges in the West. She was the older sister of author Harriet Beecher Stowe.

See Also: Beecher Family; Women in American History; Women's Movement.

■ **BEECHER, HENRY WARD (1813-87),** Congregational minister and social reformer. He was born in Litchfield, Connecticut, the son of Lyman Beecher, a leading revivalist in the West. The younger Beecher was an itinerant preacher in Indiana before serving 40 years (1847-87) as the pastor of Plymouth Church in Brooklyn Heights, where his oratorical skills drew weekly audiences of 2,500. Beecher believed that theology should meet the needs of contemporary society. He preached often on social concerns of the day, including political corruption, slavery, and women's rights. During the Kansas-Nebraska dispute in the 1850s, he raised funds to supply Northern settlers with rifles ("Beecher's Bibles"). After the Civil War, Beecher called for a moderate policy toward the South, supported Grover Cleveland in the 1884 presidential race, and advocated voting rights for women, Darwinism, and scientific biblical criticism. He influenced many outside of his own church as the editor of two popular journals, *The Independent* (1861-63) and *The Christian Union* (1870-81). In the 1870s, Beecher survived a public scandal. Theodore Tilton (1835-1907), a New York journalist and former friend, sued Beecher for adultery with his wife. Beecher was exonerated in the church hearings, but the civil jury was divided. He endured and remained influential until his death.

See Also: Beecher Family; Religion.

■ **BEECHER FAMILY,** prominent American family of the 19th century. The patriarch of the famous Beecher family was Lyman Beecher (1775-1863), a Presbyterian minister born in New Haven, Connecticut. Beecher was a proponent of the new school of Calvinism that stressed free will. Among his 13 children was the Rev. Henry Ward Beecher (1813-87), born in Litchfield, Connecticut, who became an influential voice against slavery and an outspoken advocate of women's suffrage. Another child was Catharine Beecher (1800-78), born in East Hampton, New York, who was a proponent of women's higher education but who was strongly antisuffrage and advocated that women remain at home raising children and caring for their husbands. Harriet Beecher Stowe (1811-96), born in Litchfield, is perhaps the most famous of Lyman Beecher's offspring. During her residence in Cincinnati, where her father headed the Lane Theological Seminary for 18 years, Har-

riet became a staunch abolitionist. She wrote the novel *Uncle Tom's Cabin, or Life Among the Lowly*, published in 1852. Based in part on actual slave accounts, *Uncle Tom's Cabin* became a rallying cry for Northern antislavery sentiments.

See Also: Beecher, Catharine; Beecher, Henry Ward; Stowe, Harriet Beecher.

■ **BEISSEL, JOHANN CONRAD (1690-1768),** religious leader and composer. He emigrated from Eberbach, Germany to Pennsylvania (1720), founded Economy, a cloister at Ephrata near Lancaster (1728), and from there led the Seventh-Day Baptists, an offshoot of the Dunkards known for their music. Beissel is said to have written more than 1,000 hymns. He compiled the first Pennsylvania-German hymnal, published by Benjamin Franklin in 1730, and *The Turtle Dove* (1747).

■ **BELL, ALEXANDER GRAHAM (1847-1922),** inventor of the telephone and crusader for the teaching of speech to the deaf. Born in Edinburgh, Scotland, the son and grandson of speech teachers, he immigrated with his parents to On-

Alexander Graham Bell's work for the deaf and interest in acoustics inspired him, between 1874 and 1876, to develop the "electric speaking telegraph," otherwise known as the telephone. Bell also invented the wax cylinder phonograph and the tetrahedral kite.

tario, Canada, in 1870 and in the following year began teaching speech to the deaf in several New England schools, using his father's system of speech notation. From 1873 to 1877 he served as professor of speech and vocal physiology at Boston University. Meanwhile he developed a device to send several telegraphic messages simultaneously at different frequencies over a single wire and also, for the sake of his deaf pupils, experimented with a device for the graphic recording of sound waves impinging on diaphragms. In the summer of 1874 he fused the two lines of thought into the basic principle of the telephone. At Boston on June 2, 1875, he transmitted vocal sounds, although not yet intelligible speech, and on Mar. 7, 1876, received a patent for the perfected telephone. Later on the same day Elisha Gray, an electrical inventor, recorded a similar but untested conception and subsequently became the best known of many others who for two decades unsuccessfully contested Bell's patent, although Gray dated his own conception more than a year later than Bell's first documented statement of it.

After the early 1880s Bell ceased work in telephony but produced other inventions. His "photophone" transmitted speech without wires by varying a beam of light. He pioneered in space frame construction and helped make Edison's phonograph commercially feasible, improve hydrofoil boats, and develop aeronautics. He also contributed to the study of inheritance in deafness and longevity. He guided the National Geographic Society and its magazine in its early years. For half a century he promoted integration of the deaf into society through lipreading and speech. All his life Bell struggled to overcome his own tendency toward solitude. Indeed, through all his varied activities ran the theme of promoting communication.

—ROBERT V. BRUCE

See Also: Industrial Revolution; Science; Telephone.
BIBLIOGRAPHY: Bruce, Robert V., *Bell: Alexander Graham Bell and the Conquest of Solitude* (Cornell Univ. Press 1990).

■ **BELLAMY, EDWARD (1850-98),** author and social critic. Born in Chicopee Falls, Massachusetts, he attended Union College and briefly prac-

ticed law before turning to journalism. He published his first short story in 1875 and his first of six novels three years later. He is best known for his utopian socialist novel *Looking Backward, 2000-1887* (1888), in which he depicts the ideal society as realized in Boston after a peaceful revolution. The novel inspired the formation of the Nationalist movement, which had clubs across the country throughout the 1890s; thousands of discontented middle- and working-class radicals considered themselves Bellamites. Bellamy's other novels include *Equality* (1897), an even more radical sequel to *Looking Backward*, and *The Duke of Stockbridge* (1879), a sympathetic account of Daniel Shays's Rebellion (1786).

See Also: Gilded Age; Shays's Rebellion.
BIBLIOGRAPHY: Bowman, Sylvia, et al., *Edward Bellamy Abroad* (Twayne 1962); Morgan, Arthur E., *Edward Bellamy* (Columbia Univ. Press 1944); Patai, Daphne, ed., *Looking Backward 1988-1888: Essays on Edward Bellamy* (Univ. of Massachusetts Press 1988); Rosemont, Franklin, ed., *Apparitions of Things to Come* (Charles H. Kerr 1989).

■ **BELLEAU WOOD, BATTLE OF (1918),** World War I battle. In May 1918, in response to urgent French pleas, U.S. commander in chief Gen. John Pershing sent the Second Division to occupy nine kilometers of front near the town of Chateau-Thierry to prevent the Germans from advancing on Paris. On June 5 this force, spearheaded by the Fourth Marine Brigade, moved forward to seize Belleau Wood from the Germans. For 20 "Days of Hell" the battle raged in the wood before it fell to the Americans. After the war the French renamed the wood after the Marine brigade, which had suffered 50 percent loss there.

See Also: Pershing, John Joseph; World War I.

■ **BELLOW, SAUL (1915-),** novelist. Bellow was born in Montreal, Canada, but was raised in Chicago. He attended the University of Chicago and Northwestern University. Bellow's first novel, *Dangling Man*, was published in 1944 and was followed in 1947 by *The Victim*. In 1948 Bellow won a Guggenheim Fellowship, which allowed him to spend two years in Paris. On returning to the United States in 1950, he settled in New York City. In 1953 Bellow published *The Adventures of Augie*

March, which won the National Book Award, and followed in 1956 with *Seize the Day*, one of his best-known works. Bellow's novels usually concentrate on the experience of one central figure, often a Jewish character, facing the complexities of life in the 20th century. He won the National Book Award two additional times, for *Herzog* (1964) and *Mr. Sammler's Planet* (1970). After publishing in 1975 *Humboldt's Gift*, an exploration of a writer's life in the urban United States, Bellow won both the Pulitzer Prize (1975) and the Nobel Prize for Literature (1976).

See Also: Novel.

■ **BELLOWS, GEORGE (1882-1925),** realist painter. Bellows was born in Columbus, Ohio, and, after attending Ohio State University, moved to New York City in 1904. He studied painting at the New York School of Art with Robert Henri and, along with his fellow students, concentrated primarily on capturing urban life in such paintings as *Steaming Streets* (1908). He was one of The Eight, a group of artists known more popularly as "the ashcan school," who focused on portraying contemporary urban reality. He often depicted sporting events, ranging from boxing pictures such as *Stag at Sharkey's* (1902) to outdoor recreation scenes such as *Tennis at Newport* (1920). Bellows was concerned both with the spectacle of middle-class life in the city and the struggles of the working class, as depicted in *Cliff Dwellers* (1913); from 1912 to 1917 he also worked with John French Sloan on the art staff of *The Masses*, a radical magazine. During World War I Bellows's social concern was translated into a series of paintings and prints depicting the horrors of the war, including *The Murder of Edith Cavell* of 1918.

See Also: Henri, Robert; Painting; Sloan, John French.

■ **BENEDICT, RUTH FULTON (1887-1948),** anthropologist. Born in New York City, she studied and taught anthropology at Columbia University. Her books—such as *Patterns of Culture* (1934), *Zuni Mythology* (1935), and *Race: Science and Politics* (1946)—challenged many popular racist and ethnocentric views and contributed much to the understanding of the broader theoretical constructs of race, culture, and national identity.

See Also: Women in American History.

■ **BENJAMIN, ASHER (1773-1845),** influential architectural writer. Born in Greenfield, Massachusetts, Benjamin had established an architect's office in Boston by 1803. Best-known for his books on architecture and building, including *The Country Builder's Assistant* (1797), *The American Builder's Companion* (1806), and *Elements of Architecture* (1843), Benjamin also had a busy practice, designing churches and houses in New England towns, including Boston's Charles Street Church (1807).

■ **BENJAMIN, JUDAH P. (1811-84),** Confederate cabinet member. Born to Jewish parents in the West Indies, Benjamin practiced law in New Orleans and became a planter. He served in the Louisiana legislature in the 1840s and in the U.S. Senate from 1853 to 1861. Confederate Pres. Jefferson Davis first named him attorney general, then later secretary of war, and finally, secretary of state in 1862. Benjamin negotiated European loans to the Confederacy but failed to achieve recognition of its independence. At war's end he fled to England, where he practiced law until 1882.

See Also: Civil War; Confederate States of America; Davis, Jefferson.

■ **BENNETT, JAMES GORDON (1841-1918),** newspaper editor. Born in New York City, Bennett succeeded his father as editor of the *New York Herald* in 1867. He financed several major expeditions, including Henry Morton Stanley's journey to Africa to find David Livingstone (1869-71) and George W. DeLong's trip to the Arctic (1879-81). In 1887 Bennett founded the Paris edition of the *Herald*. He also was involved with the Commercial Cable Company, which laid a transatlantic cable.

■ **BENNINGTON, BATTLE OF (1777),** Revolutionary War battle fought near Bennington, Vermont. On Aug. 16, 1777, American militia under Gen. John Stark defeated a Brunswicker detachment from British Gen. John Burgoyne's army, which was descending the Hudson River Valley. The defeat greatly weakened Burgoyne's force and helped lead to his surrender two months later.

See Also: Revolution, American.

■ **BENTON, THOMAS HART (1889-1975),** muralist and painter of the American scene. Benton was born in Neosho, Missouri, to a prominent political family of the Midwest. He studied at the Chicago Art Institute (1906-07) and at the Académie Julian in Paris from 1908 to 1911. Benton's stint as a draftsman in the architectural service during World War I led him to observe the national characteristics and types he captured in paintings such as *Cotton Pickers* (1928-29); he became an exponent of American scene painting. He completed murals on both contemporary and historical subjects, such as *America Today* for the New School of Social Research in 1930 and *The Arts of Life in America* for the Whitney Museum of American Art in New York in 1932. He also represented state histories for the Indiana building at the 1933 Century of Progress Exposition in Chicago and for the Missouri State House in Jefferson City in 1935. Works such as these revived interest in murals and led to federal support for them under the Federal Arts Project of the New Deal.

See Also: Federal Arts Project; Painting.

■ **BENT'S FORT,** trading post in present-day Colorado. Also known as Fort William, it was built by Ceran St. Vrain and the brothers Charles and William Bent in 1833. As a terminus for the mountain branch of the Santa Fe Trail, the fort was on the north bank of the Arkansas River. Dominating the fur and Indian trade for decades, Bent's Fort was reconstructed miles to the south in 1853 and finally leased to the U.S. government in 1860. A replica of the fort still stands today as a national historic site.

See Also: Frontier in American History.

■ **BERGER, VICTOR LOUIS (1860-1929),** American Socialist politican. He was born in Nieder-Rehbach, Transylvania (now Romania) and was educated in Hungary and Austria before immigrating to Milwaukee, Wisconsin, in 1878. He soon entered local politics and built a powerful Socialist machine. In 1910 Berger became the first Socialist elected to the U.S. House of Representatives but served only one term. Reelected in 1918 as an opponent of World War I, he was found guilty of sedition for violating the Espionage Act, sentenced to 20 years in prison, and denied his seat in Congress. In 1921 the U.S. Supreme Court reversed his conviction, and Berger was once again elected to the House, where he served three more terms (1923-29).

See Also: Espionage Act; Progressivism.

■ **BERING, VITUS JONASSEN (1681-1741),** Danish navigator and European discoverer of Alaska. Sailing on behalf of Russia in 1741, Bering crossed the North Pacific and explored Alaska's southwest coast and the Aleutian Islands. On his return Bering shipwrecked and later died on islands off Siberia's Kamchatka Peninsula. Survivors reaching Russia told of their discoveries and opened the way for Russian settlement of Alaska. The Bering Strait and Bering Sea, separating Alaska and Siberia, are named for him.

See Also: Exploration and Discovery.

■ **BERING STRAIT MIGRATION.** No trace of prehuman hominids has ever been discovered in the Americas. Until recently, scholars thought that the ancestors of American Indians must have migrated from Siberia across an ancient land bridge to Alaska at about the latitude of Nome. Thereafter, the thesis went, glacier melt raised the sea level to divide the continents with the strait named for explorer Vitus Bering. It was vaguely thought that migration probably occurred only once; the open questions were when it happened and what route was followed later in North America.

This view has changed. Archaeologists have discovered evidence of humans in South America dating back 30,000 years. These humans could not have crossed at Nome's latitude because no humans lived in northern Siberia before 20,000 years ago. Now it is realized that glaciers locked up so much water that sea level was 300 feet below its present elevation, so that an enormous subcontinent (called Beringia) was exposed. This permitted multiple migrations either by land or along Beringia's southern coast so that very early journeys could have come from Asia's populous Amur basin, following the Kurile Islands, the Kamchatka Peninsula, and the Aleutian Islands. All traces were lost when the glaciers melted 20,000 years ago and drowned the evidence.

Although some tribal natives insist that their ancestors "jumped out of this very ground," much evidence has emerged of likeness between Siberian and Northwest American Indians cultures. Some Alaskan natives still visit relatives in Siberia when the strait is frozen over in winter. It is now thought that some Asian people followed the west coast to South America while others fanned out south of the glaciers into present-day United States. Chronological estimates range from 25,000 to 70,000 years ago, with general acceptance of about 40,000 years ago.

—FRANCIS JENNINGS

See Also: Exploration and Discovery; Indians of North America.

BIBLIOGRAPHY: Coe, Michael, et al., eds., *Atlas of Ancient America* (Facts on File 1986); Dikov, Nikolai, "On the Road to America," *Natural History* (Jan. 1988); Fitzhugh, William W., and Aron Crowell, eds., *Crossroads of Continents: Cultures of Siberia and Alaska* (Smithsonian Inst. Press 1988); Fladmark, Knut R., "Getting One's Berings," *Natural History* (Nov. 1986).

■ **BERKELEY, GEORGE (1685-1753),** Anglo-Irish philosopher and minister. Born in Kilkenny, Ireland, Berkeley was educated at Trinity College, Dublin. After publishing a number of important philosophy books, he made plans to convert Native Americans to Christianity at a college to be founded in Bermuda. Berkeley arrived in Newport, Rhode Island, in January 1729 and then bought a farm he named Whitehall. With government support not forthcoming for the college in Bermuda, Berkeley left Boston in September, 1731, to return to England. Berkeley donated his farm and a valuable collection of books to Yale College before he left.

■ **BERKELEY, LADY FRANCIS (1634-post-1695),** key political figure in Virginia during Bacon's Rebellion (1676), which challenged the authority of Virginia's governor, Lady Francis's second husband, Sir William Berkeley. During the rebellion, Lady Francis used her influence to defend the interests of her husband and to put in place his chosen successor, Thomas, Lord Culpeper. She was also married to Samuel Stephens and Philip Ludwell, both governors of North Carolina.

See Also: Bacon's Rebellion.

■ **BERKELEY, SIR WILLIAM (1606-77),** colonial governor of Virginia (1642-76) and staunch royalist. Born in London, England, Berkeley began his colonial career as commissioner of Canadian affairs. He did not live in the colonies until 1642, when he became governor of Virginia. As a leader, Berkeley promoted Virginia's economic growth through crop diversification and the fur trade. However, his Indian policy frequently clashed with the interests of frontier planters, as in Bacon's Rebellion (1676).

See Also: Bacon's Rebellion.

■ **BERLE, ADOLF AUGUSTUS, JR. (1895-1971),** American economist and government official. A member of the faculty at Columbia University in New York City (1927-63), he was a member of Pres. Franklin D. Roosevelt's "Brain Trust," an informal group of academics who played an important role in forming New Deal policies. Berle co-authored with Gardiner C. Means *The Modern Corporation and Private Property* (1932), which argued that due to diversified stock ownership and modern management techniques, ownership and operation of business had been separated. Therefore, industrial policy could be directed by democratic government agencies for the common good without sacrificing private ownership. Berle served as assistant secretary of state (1938-44) and U.S. ambassador to Brazil (1945-46) before returning to Columbia. From 1951 until 1971 Berle chaired the Twentieth Century Fund.

See Also: New Deal.

BIBLIOGRAPHY: Schwarz, Jordan A., *Liberal: Adolf A. Berle and the Vision of an American Era* (Free Press 1987).

■ **BERLE, MILTON (1908-),** film comedian. Known as "Mr. Television," he was one of the medium's first major stars. Berle was born in New York City and starred in a weekly variety show (1948-56) featuring his slapstick comedy.

■ **BERLIN, IRVING (1888-1989),** composer of popular songs who throughout his long career displayed a gift for combining memorable lyrics with catchy tunes. Born in Tyuman, Russia, he came to New York City with his family in 1893. He worked as a singing waiter and song plugger before publishing the first of his more than 1,500 songs in 1907. His "Alexander's Ragtime Band," "Easter Parade," and "Oh, How I Hate to Get Up in the Morning" highlighted Broadway revues, including

Irving Berlin wrote many of modern America's most memorable songs, including "God Bless America," "White Christmas," and "Alexander's Ragtime Band."

several editions of the *Ziegfeld Follies, As Thousands Cheered* (1933), and *This is the Army* (1942). He also composed scores for films such as *Top Hat* (1935) and *Holiday Inn* (1942), which featured "White Christmas," and for stage musical comedies, including *Annie Get Your Gun* (1946). Berlin was so prolific that some of his songs went unheard for decades. He did not publish "God Bless America," a patriotic anthem originally written for a 1918 revue, until 1939.

See Also: Broadway.

BIBLIOGRAPHY: Bergreen, Laurence, *As Thousands Cheer* (Viking 1990); Hyland, William G., *The Song Is Ended: Songwriters and American Music 1900-1950* (Oxford Univ. Press 1995).

■ **BERLIN AIRLIFT (1948-49),** an operation started by Western Powers on June 2, 1948, to support the 2 million inhabitants of the western sectors of Berlin blockaded by the Soviet and East German forces. Overall, the West delivered 2.3 million tons of food, coal, and other supplies in more than 275,000 flights. The airlift proved highly successful, which finally made the Soviets and East Germans pull back from plans to control West Berlin. The blockade was lifted on May 12, 1949.

See Also: Cold War.

■ **BERLIN WALL,** wall dividing East and West Berlin. It was erected by the Soviets in 1961 to prevent the escape of East Germans to West Berlin. The wall became a symbolic border between the two worlds. In November 1990, during the reunification of Germany, it was almost totally destroyed.

See Also: Cold War.

■ **BERNSTEIN, LEONARD (1918-90),** pianist, conductor, and composer. Born in Lawrence, Massachusetts, and educated at Harvard, he studied conducting under Boston Symphony Orchestra music director Serge Koussevitzky (1940-41) and debuted as conductor of the New York Philharmonic (1943). Bernstein's exuberant personality made him a star on the podium as music director of the New York Philharmonic (1958-69). He specialized in Romantic works, notably those of Gustav Mahler, and often performed works by American composers such as Aaron Copland. Thanks largely to televised "Young People's Concerts," he was the nation's best-known conductor. As a composer, he worked successfully in both the classical and popular fields. Bernstein wrote three symphonies, two operas, a Mass, and other classical works—as well as the music for the ballet *Fancy Free* (1944) and the Broadway classic *West Side Story* (1957).

See Also: Broadway.

BIBLIOGRAPHY: Peyser, Joan, *Bernstein: A Biography* (Beech Tree Books 1987).

■ **BERRY, CHARLES EDWARD ANDERSON ("CHUCK") (1926-),** musician, singer, and songwriter. Born in St. Louis, Missouri, Berry, with his signature duckwalk, became a rock-and-roll pioneer. His numerous singles, including his first hit "Maybellene" (1955), as well as "Johnny B. Goode," and "Sweet Little Sixteen," influenced an entire generation of rising performers. Berry was awarded a lifetime achievement Grammy in 1984 and inducted into the Rock and Roll Hall of Fame in 1986.

See Also: African Americans; Rock and Roll.

■ **BESSEMER STEEL PROCESS,** method to produce steel by shooting a blast of air through a huge vessel of molten iron in order to burn off carbon and impurities. Invented in Europe by Sir Henry Bessemer around 1872, this process underpinned America's industrialization during the 1880s and 1890s. It allowed for the mass production of steel by ever-larger corporations such as Carnegie Steel, led to the formation of industrial mill towns such as Homestead, Pennsylvania, enabled the growth of the railroad industry, and reduced the need for the skilled workers who had controlled the production of the iron industry.

See Also: Carnegie, Andrew; Industrial Revolution.

■ **BETHUNE, MARY MCLEOD (1875-1955),** educator and civil rights leader. Born in Mayesville, South Carolina, she was the daughter of freed slaves. Believing that the education of African-American children was the key to the advancement of the race, she established a school for them in Daytona, Florida. She served as president of the National Association of Colored Women and vice president of the National Urban League. She was also an adviser to the National Child Welfare Commission under both Presidents Calvin Coolidge and Herbert Hoover.

See Also: Civil Rights Movement; National Association of Colored Women; Women's Movement.

■ **BEVERIDGE, ALBERT JEREMIAH (1862-1927),** American politician and writer. He was born in Highland County, Ohio, and attended DePauw University in Greencastle, Indiana, after which he settled in Indianapolis, where he practiced law. Elected to the U.S. Senate as a Republican in 1899, Beveridge became one of the most ardent advocates for U.S. imperialism abroad. Reelected in 1906, he aligned himself with the insurgent Progressives, supporting such reforms as the Pure Food and Drug Act (1906) and the Meat Inspection Act (1906). That alliance cost him the support of more conservative Republicans and he lost his Senate seat in 1912. Beveridge then turned to writing, producing the Pulitzer Prize–winning four-volume biography *Life of John Marshall* (1916-19) and a posthumously published two-volume work on Abraham Lincoln (1928).

See Also: Progressivism.

■ **BIBLE BELT,** term coined by H. L. Mencken in the 1920s to describe areas of the United States, especially the South, where Protestant fundamentalism is the dominant belief.

See Also: Religion.

■ **BIDDLE, NICHOLAS (1786-1844),** American financier and scholar. Born in Philadelphia, he supported Pres. James Madison's chartering the Second Bank of the United States in 1816. In 1819 Pres. James Monroe appointed Biddle director of the bank and, in 1827, Biddle became its president. In his 1832 reelection campaign, Pres. Andrew Jackson attacked the Bank of the United States, arguing that the bank was unconstitutional, that it took power away from the states and protected the "moneyed interests" to the exclusion of the "great body of people." Jackson urged Congress to abolish the bank and distribute its resources to state banks. Biddle worked to save the bank, using bank funds to retain attorneys and urging friends to write editorials supporting the bank. To head off Jackson's attacks on the bank, Biddle applied to Congress in 1832 for an extension of the bank's national charter, four years earlier than necessary. Congress approved the charter, but Jackson vetoed it, and, in 1836, the Bank of the United States obtained a state charter and became "The Bank of the United States of Pennsylvania." Biddle retired as its president in 1839.

See Also: Banks of the United States, First and Second; Jackson, Andrew.

BIBLIOGRAPHY: Schlesinger, Arthur M., Jr., *The Age of Jackson* (Little, Brown 1945); Sellers, Charles G., *The Market Revolution: Jacksonian America 1815-1846* (Oxford Univ. Press 1991).

■ **BIERSTADT, ALBERT (1830-1902),** painter of the American western landscape. Bierstadt was born in Solingen, Germany, but came to the United States with his family as a small boy; they settled in New Bedford, Massachusetts. From 1853 to 1857, Bierstadt studied painting in Düsseldorf, Germany, and in Rome, Italy. Bierstadt made two trips to the American West (1858; 1863) and thereafter transferred the landscape he saw there to canvas. He was fascinated with mountains, which are frequently a subject for his landscape paintings, in *The Rocky Mountains* (1863) and *Storm in the Rocky Mountains* (1866). Bierstadt often worked on a monumental scale in his efforts to replicate the landscape that so inspired him. Bierstadt also did historical paintings, such as *Discovery of the Hudson River* (1875) and *Landing of Columbus*, done for the World's Columbian Exposition in Chicago in 1893.

See Also: Painting.

■ **BIG BANDS,** popular orchestras of the 1930s-40s. Jazz-influenced "swing," or "hot," bands and "sweet" dance bands dominated the music scene. Leaders included Duke Ellington, Benny Goodman, Tommy Dorsey, and Glenn Miller.

See Also: Jazz.

■ **BILLINGS, WILLIAM (1746-1800),** the first professional musician in the United States. Born in Boston, Massachusetts, he wrote hymns and songs, often using a rough fugue style, and encouraged enthusiastic singing by church congregations. "Chester," a setting of psalms written during the American Revolutionary War, enlisted God in the patriot cause. Billings published *The New England Psalm Singer* (1770) and *The Continental Harmony* (1794).

■ **BILL OF RIGHTS,** first 10 amendments to the U.S. Constitution, adopted during the first session of the new federal Congress but first proposed during the debates over ratification. The delegates to the Constitutional Convention had initially considered adding to the document a Bill of Rights, patterned on the declarations of rights in several of the state constitutions; but finally they rejected it as superfluous, agreeing with James Madison that the federal government would exercise only those powers expressly delegated to it. George Mason of Virginia, however, author of the Virginia Declaration of Rights, refused to sign the Constitution because it failed to contain similar provisions. Speaking for a large body of moderate Antifederalist opinion, Mason played an important role in getting the Virginia ratifying convention to endorse a set of constitutional amendments. Campaigning for a seat in the new Congress, Madison was pressed to affirm his willingness to propose and support a set of amendments guaranteeing "essential rights."

Various state ratification conventions proposed a grab bag of over 200 potential amendments for such a Bill of Rights. Madison set about

transforming these into a series that he introduced into the new Congress on June 8, 1789. Congress passed 12 and sent them to the states, and 10 survived the ratification process to become the Bill of Rights adopted in 1791. The First Amendment prohibited Congress from establishing an official religion and provided for the freedoms of assembly, speech, and the press and the right of petition. The other amendments guaranteed the right to bear arms, limited the government's power to quarter troops in private homes, and restrained the government from unreasonable searches or seizures; they assured the people their legal rights under the common law, including the prohibition of double jeopardy, the right not to be compelled to testify against oneself, and due process of law before life, liberty, or property can be taken. Finally, the unenumerated rights of the people were protected, and those powers not delegated to the federal government were reserved to the states.

The first 10 amendments to the Constitution have been a restraining influence on the growth of government power over American citizens. Throughout the world their provisions are one of the most admired aspects of the American political tradition. The Bill of Rights is the most important constitutional legacy of the Antifederalists.

See Also: Constitution of the United States; Supreme Court.

BIBLIOGRAPHY: Rutland, Robert Allen, *The Birth of the Bill of Rights, 1776-1791* (Univ. of North Carolina Press 1955); Schwartz, Bernard, *The Great Rights of Mankind: A History of the American Bill of Rights* (Madison House 1992); Veit, Helen E., Kenneth R. Bowling, and Charlene Bangs Bickford, eds., *Creating the Bill of Rights: The Documentary Record from the First Federal Congress* (Johns Hopkins Univ. Press 1991).

■ **BILLY THE KID (1859?-81),** criminal and gunman. Known also as William H. Bonney and Henry McCarty, Billy the Kid spent his childhood in Indiana, Kansas, and New Mexico. Although he was a rather inconsequential thief and hired gunman during his short life, he attained mythical status in the popular press and in fictional portrayals after his death. He first ran afoul of the law in 1874 but escaped from jail and fled to Ari-

Billy the Kid embarked on his career as a New Mexico cattle thief and outlaw when still in his teens. He was shot to death at age 21 by Sheriff Pat Garrett.

zona, eventually making his way to Lincoln County, New Mexico, in 1877. Billy the Kid joined the Tunstall-McSween faction, who engaged in the Lincoln County War of 1878 with their rivals Murphy and Dolan. As a hired gunman, he killed several men, including the local sheriff. After the conflict ended, Billy the Kid and his small gang stole cattle to recover unpaid wages. His fate was sealed, however, when he was convicted of murder in Lincoln County. He was killed at age 21 by the new sheriff, Pat Garrett.

See Also: Frontier in American History.

◼ **BINGHAM, GEORGE CALEB (1811-79),** genre painter. Bingham was born in Augusta County, Virginia, but he was raised in Franklin, Missouri,

the Midwestern site that became the subject of much of his artwork. Bingham began his career as a portraitist, studying in Philadelphia at the Pennsylvania Academy of Fine Arts and opening a studio in Washington, D.C., from 1840 to 1844. He then returned to the Midwest, where he found his best-known subjects in the landscape and culture of the Missouri and Mississippi rivers and the city of St. Louis. *Fur Traders Descending the Missouri* (1845) and *The Jolly Flatboatmen* (1846) typify this period of Bingham's work. The latter was so popular that he continued to paint new versions of it for several years thereafter. Engravings of Bingham's paintings were also popular and were distributed through the American Art Union, an organization founded to promote American art by purchasing, exhibiting, and distributing works by American artists. Bingham's work also had political overtones, as in his comment on universal male suffrage in *The County Election* (1852), which celebrates workings of democracy in a free society.

See Also: Painting.

◼ **BIRD, LARRY (1957-   ),** basketball player. Born in French Lick, Indiana, Bird, a deadly shooter and creative passer, starred at Indiana State University from 1975 to 1979 and then led the Boston Celtics to three professional titles in 1981, 1984, and 1986. In 1997 he became head coach of the Indiana Pacers.

See Also: Sports.

◼ **BIRNEY, JAMES GILLESPIE (1792-1857),** antislavery activist. Born in Danville, Kentucky, he was the son of a wealthy slaveholder. Birney graduated from the College of New Jersey (now Princeton) in 1816. In 1832 he became an agent for the American Colonization Society, which favored returning African-American slaves to Africa. In 1834 he emancipated his slaves and resigned from his position at the Colonization Society. Henceforth Birney advocated a strong antislavery position, although his political approach was shunned by the abolitionist followers of William Lloyd Garrison. In 1840 and 1844, Birney ran as the Liberty party's candidate for president.

See Also: American Colonization Society; Antislavery Movement; Garrison, William Lloyd.

■ **BIRTH CONTROL,** term coined by American reformer Margaret Sanger in 1913 to describe the variety of means that women might choose to limit their childbearing. Women have always sought to control their reproductive lives. In traditional societies women understood that prolonged periods of breast feeding, which has the effect of inhibiting ovulation, helped prevent conception; and frequently there were cultural rules requiring sexual abstinence during particular periods in the lives of women and men. But the extremely high birthrate in colonial America, an average of seven live births for each woman of childbearing age, indicates that family limitation was little practiced.

During the 19th century, however, the birthrate fell steadily and dramatically, reaching an average of only four births per woman in 1900. This decline began before the wide availability of mechanical forms of contraception. Condoms were available, but few people used them, partly because they were difficult to obtain, partly because their use was associated with prostitution and the prevention of venereal disease rather than family limitation. The principal forms of birth control in the 19th century were coitus interruptus, abstinence, and abortion. Rates of abortion rose dramatically during the first half of the 19th century, the procedure becoming as common by 1850 as it would be in 1990.

The falling birthrate and the increase in abortion led to a movement to restrict access to birth control. In 1827, Illinois became the first state to pass an anti-abortion law, and by the 1880s similar statutes had been enacted in all the states. Historians who have examined the writings of the 19th-century anti-abortion movement have argued that the campaign was part of a backlash against the women's rights movement. There was also a movement against the dissemination of birth-control information. By the 1860s, there were scores of medical manuals available to ordinary Americans with information on the rhythm method of contraception, with recipes for home-brewed abortifacients, or with information on condoms. In 1873, Congress passed the so-called "Comstock Act," named for its crusading author, Anthony Comstock, which defined all discussion of birth control as obscene, and barred it from in-terstate commerce and the mails. This law made it much more difficult for women and couples to obtain birth-control information, but the birthrate continued to fall nonetheless. Conservatives decried the trend, especially the much lower rates among whites than among African Americans and other minorities, and they worried over the prospects for what was termed "race suicide."

The 20th Century. This was the background for the development of the birth-control movement in the early 20th century, led by feminists such as Margaret Sanger and socialists such as Emma Goldman. In 1914, postal inspectors confiscated a pamphlet in which Sanger discussed the use of the vaginal diaphragm, which was popular in Europe. Two years later, she was arrested and jailed for distributing devices and information at her birth-control clinic in Brooklyn. Sanger became a hero to many women, and within a few years other activist women had opened clinics in every major American city and most large towns. After World War I, Sanger worked to legalize the dissemination of contraception devices and information by physicians. The birthrate continued to fall, reaching just two births per woman in the 1930s.

The Comstock Law was finally overturned by a federal court in 1938, but the public discussion of contraception remained illegal in many states. Not until *Griswold* v. *Connecticut* (1965) did the Supreme Court rule that such laws were unconstitutional on the ground that they interfered with marital privacy. Another landmark came with the 1967 revision of the Social Security Act, in which Congress required federal and state welfare agencies to provide contraception to recipients without regard to marital status or age.

The birth-control pill—measured doses of hormones to prevent ovulation—was introduced in 1960; within a year it had been adopted by a million women, and soon it had become the most popular method of birth control. "The pill" for the first time made it possible for women to engage in sexual intercourse without fear of pregnancy, and it reshaped the landscape of sex and gender in the late 20th century. Other forms of birth control, such as interuterine devices (IUDs), soon followed. Concerns about the dangers of illegal abortion and the possibility of fetal deformities prompted a campaign for legal abortion among doctors, civil libertarians, and feminists in the 1960s. In *Roe v. Wade* (1973) the Supreme Court ruled that Congress and the states could make no law restricting abortion during the first trimester of a pregnancy and could place restrictions in the second trimester only to protect women's health, leaving the decision on an abortion to the discretion of women and their physicians. But the decision led to a growing controversy between proponents and opponents of abortion. In the 1980s, the discovery of reliable abortifacients (notably the drug RU-486, popularly known as "the morning-after pill") and their introduction into the United States in the 1990s offered the prospect of reshaping the landscape of birth control once again.

—JOHN MACK FARAGHER

See Also: Abortion; Griswold v. Connecticut; Goldman, Emma; Roe v. Wade; Sanger, Margaret; Women in American History.

BIBLIOGRAPHY: Brodie, Janet Farrel, *Contraception and Abortion in Nineteenth-Century America* (Cornell Univ. Press 1994); Critchlow, Donald T., *The Politics of Abortion and Birth Control in Historical Perspective* (Pennsylvania State Univ. Press 1996); Gordon, Linda, *Woman's Body, Woman's Right: A Social History of Birth Control in America* (Grossman 1976); McCann, Carole R., *Birth Control Politics in the United States, 1916-1945* (Cornell Univ. Press 1994).

■ **BLACK, HUGO LAFAYETTE (1886-1971),** political leader and associate justice of the U.S. Supreme Court (1937-71). A powerful and influential Supreme Court justice, Black was born and reared in Harlan, Alabama. After graduating from law school at the University of Alabama in 1906, Black practiced law and served as a police court judge in Birmingham. Briefly a member of the Ku Klux Klan, he was elected as a Democrat to the U.S. Senate in 1926. During his decade in the Senate, Black became a crusader against social injustice and a supporter of Pres. Franklin D. Roosevelt and New Deal legislation.

In 1937, President Roosevelt appointed Black to the Supreme Court. During his long tenure, he sought to use the 14th Amendment to achieve federal enforcement of the Bill of Rights against the states and to adhere to a literal interpretation of specific provisions of the Constitution, especially with regard to the freedom of speech. Throughout his years on the bench, he tenaciously tried to protect civil liberties, with varying degrees of success. His critics contended that his defense of personal rights meant that he used the Constitution as a tool of social and economic reform. Black, however, was one of the Court's greatest literal interpreters of the Constitution. Two of his many influential opinions were presented in *Engle v. Vitale* (1962) and *Gideon v. Wainwright* (1963). The latter required states to provide counsel to anyone accused of a felony who could not afford a lawyer.

See Also: Engel v. Vitale; Gideon v. Wainwright; Supreme Court.

BIBLIOGRAPHY: Ball, Howard, *Hugo Black: Cold Steel Warrior* (Oxford Univ. Press 1996); Newman, Robert K., *Hugo Black: A Biography* (Pantheon Books 1994).

■ **BLACK, SHIRLEY TEMPLE.** *See:* Temple, Shirley.

■ **BLACK BELT,** term applied to fertile agricultural region that extends across central Alabama, northeast Mississippi, and into Tennessee. During the 19th century the region's black soil was especially suited for cotton cultivation done by slave labor. Cotton was raised by white or black tenant farmers until the early 20th century, when boll weevil infestations and soil depletion destroyed the crop. James Agee and Walker Evans's *Let Us Now Praise Famous Men* (1941) described the difficult lives of white tenant farmers in this region.

■ **BLACK CODES,** body of legal restrictions on former slaves created in most Southern states following the Civil War. Although the codes varied from state to state, their general intent was to reduce free African-American citizens to a tractable labor force under conditions as close to slavery as possible. Restrictions were imposed on numerous rights, among them the rights to travel, congregate, and barter for better wages among different employers. Harsh employment requirements meant the separation of families through involuntary apprenticeships and the forced field labor of women, both of which were noxiously reminiscent of slavery. The 1866 Civil Rights Act and the 14th

Amendment (1868) to the Constitution largely eliminated the black codes but could not halt the further spread of social inequity in other guises.

See Also: African Americans; Civil Rights Acts.

BIBLIOGRAPHY: Foner, Eric, *Reconstruction* (Harper & Row 1988); Franklin, John H., *Reconstruction after the Civil War* (Univ. of Chicago Press 1961).

■ **BLACK ELK (1863-1950),** Oglala Sioux medicine man. Born on the Powder River in present-day Wyoming, Black Elk experienced a series of visions beginning when he was five years old. Black Elk's family supported the resistance of Crazy Horse in 1876 and traveled with him after the Battle of Little Bighorn. Later, they went into exile in Canada with Sitting Bull. Because of his visions, Black Elk became revered as a medicine man and spiritual leader among the Oglala. In the late 1880s, he traveled with Buffalo Bill's Wild West show throughout the United States and Europe. However, he grew homesick in Europe, and William Cody ("Buffalo Bill") gave him the money to return home. Black Elk witnessed the aftermath of the Wounded Knee massacre in December 1890, precipitated by the white Indian agents' fear of the Ghost Dance religion. In the 1930s, the poet John Neihardt interviewed Black Elk, publishing his life story in 1932.

See Also: Cody, William ("Buffalo Bill"); Crazy Horse; Frontier in American History; Indians of North America; Little Bighorn, Battle of; Sitting Bull.

■ **BLACKFEET INDIANS,** Algonquian-speaking tribe of the northern Great Plains. The Blackfeet were nomadic buffalo hunters between the upper Missouri River and the Saskatchewan River in the 18th and 19th centuries, known for their abilities as horse breeders. Recurrent hostilities between the Blackfeet and the United States began in 1806, when a Blackfoot was killed by a member of the Lewis and Clark expedition. Throughout the early 19th century, the Blackfeet drove trappers and missionaries from their country before signing a peace treaty in 1855. In the 1860s, as U.S. administrators failed to keep miners and settlers off the Blackfoot reservation in northern Montana Territory, many Blackfeet resumed guerrilla attacks. In January 1870 federal troops killed some 170 Blackfeet in the Massacre of the

Marias. In 1877 the majority of Blackfeet settled permanently in Canada. Of those who remained in the United States, many starved to death in 1883-84 because of crop failures, the disappearance of the buffalo, and insufficient federal aid. The 2,000 survivors were confined on a small reservation in northeastern Montana, where some of them became self-sufficient, primarily as ranchers.

See Also: Indians of North America; Lewis and Clark Expedition.

■ **BLACK HAWK WAR (1832),** military conflict between one band of the Sac and Fox and the United States. In 1804, Sac and Fox leaders ceded tribal lands in northwestern Illinois to the United States but continued to occupy the region until 1830, when pressure by white settlers forced most of the Sac and Fox people into Iowa. About 1,200 tribespeople, led by Black Hawk, remained in Illinois until 1831, when they too were forced across the Mississippi. Short of food, in April 1832, Black Hawk led approximately 1,000 Indians, including 600 women and children, back to Illinois to harvest corn in tribal fields near Rock Island.

Black Hawk's return panicked American settlers, and when Potawatomi and Winnebago tribesmen refused to assist him, he attempted on May 14 to surrender to the Illinois militia. Tragically, the ill-disciplined militia opened fire, and the resulting Battle of Stillman's Run was an Indian victory, but it ended any chance for a peaceful settlement.

Fleeing north into Wisconsin, the Indians fought a series of rearguard actions, then turned westward, trying to reach Iowa. On August 1, closely pursued by regulars and militia, they reached the Mississippi, where they again attempted to surrender. The Sac and Fox again were attacked by the Americans, and as they sought refuge on islands in the river, the Indians were shelled by a federal gunboat. Several hundred Indians were killed in the resulting Battle of the Bad Axe. Black Hawk was captured, imprisoned, and then taken to Washington, D.C., where he met with Andrew Jackson. He then returned to Iowa, where he died in 1837.

—R. DAVID EDMUNDS

See Also: Indians of North America.

BIBLIOGRAPHY: Hagan, William T., *The Sac and Fox Indians* (Univ. of Oklahoma Press 1958); Nichols, Roger, *Black Hawk and the Warriors' Path* (Harlan Davidson 1992).

■ **BLACK HILLS,** rugged mountains located in western South Dakota. This fertile area of hills and grasslands stretches some 120 miles from north to south and covers about 6,000 square miles. Because of their rich timber and game, the Black Hills were important to a number of Indian groups, including the Kiowa, Sioux (Lakota), Cheyenne, and Arapaho. In 1867 the Sioux signed a treaty with the United States under which they agreed to resettle by 1876 to a reservation that included the Black Hills territory. In 1874, however, gold was discovered in the hills by an expedition led by Col. George Armstrong Custer. The resulting gold rush drove out the Indians and led to bloody clashes, the most famous of which was the Battle of Little Big Horn in 1876, in which Custer and his forces were annihilated by the Sioux led by Crazy Horse and Sitting Bull. Under an 1876 agreement with the United States, the Sioux ceded all claims to the Black Hills. In 1903 Pres. Theodore Roosevelt designated some 28,000 acres of limestone caverns in the Black Hills as Wind Cave National Park. Other portions of the hills, which are a favorite tourist spot in the northern Plains, are included in the Jewel Cave National Monument and the famous Mt. Rushmore National Memorial (1927), which contains the monumental mountainside carvings of the faces of Washington, Jefferson, Lincoln, and Theodore Roosevelt.

See Also: Mount Rushmore National Memorial; National Parks; Sioux; South Dakota.

■ **BLACK KETTLE (c. 1803-68),** Cheyenne leader. He was born Moketavato in present-day South Dakota. In 1864, when conflict erupted on the Great Plains, Black Kettle voluntarily moved his band to Fort Lyon, Colorado, where they set up camp along Sand Creek. On Nov. 28, 1864, the group was attacked by the Colorado militia, who killed some 150 Cheyenne, three-fourths of them women and children. Black Kettle survived the Sand Creek Massacre but was killed four years later at Washita Creek, in present-day Oklahoma, during another attack by the U.S. cavalry.

See Also: Frontier in American History; Indians of North America; Sand Creek Massacre.

■ **BLACK LEGEND OF SPANISH COLONIZATION,** collective accounts emphasizing the oppression of Indians by the Spanish conquerors, provided important ideological justification for the colonial enterprises of competing nations in the 16th century. After the violent Spanish conquest of the Caribbean, Mexico, Central America, and Peru, a controversy erupted within Spain over the justice and morality of what had taken place. The single most important figure in this debate was Bartolomé de Las Casas, a Dominican witness to the horrors of the conquest in the Caribbean, whose infamous 1552 text *Brief Relation of the Destruction of the Indies* provided a detailed account of Spanish atrocities and claimed that the conquest had caused the deaths of millions of Native Americans. Widely reissued throughout Europe and translated into English in 1583, Las Casas's account (along with other histories of the conquest) added considerable fuel to the anti-Catholic and anti-Spanish passions of English nationalists and Protestants.

After the nationalist passions of the colonial period had passed, historians tended to dismiss Las Casas's claims as exaggerated. More recently, however, many have been substantiated. The indigenous 8 million inhabitants of Hispaniola, for example, had disappeared by 1550, although more as a result of disease than warfare. What is certain from the Black Legend, however, is the fact that in both the New World and Spain there were moral critics such as Las Casas who fervently fought against the cruelties of conquest and laid the groundwork for concepts of universal justice and international law. Moreover, the English, who argued that theirs would be an example of "moral" colonization, practiced many of the same "Spanish" cruelties on the Indians of North America.

See Also: Spanish Colonies.

BIBLIOGRAPHY: Hanke, Lewis, *The Spanish Struggle for Justice in the Conquest of America* (Univ. Presses of Florida 1949).

■ **BLACKLIST,** originally a list of men who were known to belong to unions, used by anti-union businesses and corporations to prevent the employment of union members. Such blacklists were outlawed by federal legislation in 1935. During the anticommunism crusade of the 1950s, blacklists were used widely to prevent the employment of alleged or known members of the Communist party or persons sympathetic to left-wing causes. The most famous of the blacklists were the ones used within the entertainment industry, which resulted in the loss of careers by hundreds of actors, writers, directors, and other professionals.

See Also: *Anticommunism; Cold War.*

■ **BLACKMUN, HARRY ANDREW (1908-),** associate justice of the U.S. Supreme Court (1971-94). He was born in Nashville, Illinois, and raised in St. Paul, Minnesota, where his father owned a store. Blackmun attended Harvard University and Harvard Law School, practiced law in Minnesota, and was appointed to the U.S. Eighth Circuit Court of Appeals in 1959. In 1971, after the Senate rejected nominees Clement Haynesworth and G. Harrold Carswell, Pres. Richard M. Nixon chose the little-known Blackmun to fill a vacancy on the Supreme Court. Appointed as a reliable conservative ally for Chief Justice Warren E. Burger, a fellow Minnesotan, Blackmun soon shifted toward the left and proved himself a liberal counterweight to the emerging conservative majority on the Court. He was especially outspoken in his defense of women's reproductive rights and resisted attempts to limit legal access to abortion. After his retirement from the Court, he declared himself opposed to the death penalty, which he had sanctioned in *Gregg* v. *Georgia* (1976).

See Also: *Supreme Court.*

■ **BLACK MUSLIMS (NATION OF ISLAM),** African-American religious sect and protest movement. It began in the ghetto of Detroit in 1930 when Wallace D. Farrad Muhammad, a mysterious silk peddler who claimed to be from the holy city of Mecca, introduced his black clients to teachings concerning their "true identity" and religion. Denouncing the word "Negro," he insisted that blacks in America were descendants of "Asiatics" who were taken from the Afro-Asian continent and enslaved by white Christians. He characterized whites as "blue-eyed devils" and blacks as the personification of divine.

In 1933 Farrad Muhammad mysteriously disappeared and was succeeded by his student Elijah Poole, who adopted the name Elijah Muhammad (1897-1975). The son of a Baptist preacher, Muhammad moved the Black Muslims' headquarters from Detroit to Chicago in 1934. The movement's membership grew steadily and reached some 10,000 during Muhammad's imprisonment for draft evasion (1942-46). After his release the Nation blossomed into a movement that affirmed black supremacy, racial separatism, black self-help, and the moral elevation of the race.

Malcolm X joined the Nation in 1949 while in prison. After his release in 1952 he became its most dynamic and successful minister. Malcolm organized numerous temples, introduced millions to the Nation through his lectures at universities and his interviews on radio and television, and sought to bring the Muslims into dialogue with Martin Luther King, Jr. and the more moderate wing of the African-American freedom movement. The Nation grew from 16 temples in 1955 to 75 in 1963 and from 12,000 to roughly 200,000 members. A dispute with Muhammad forced Malcolm out of the Black Muslims in December 1963 and led to his assassination.

The death of Elijah Muhammad in 1975 brought other changes. His son Wallace D. Muhammad emerged as his successor, and tensions developed as the new leader transformed the Nation and brought it into conformity with orthodox Islam. Orthodox teachings were embraced, the focus on race and black nationalism was abandoned, and whites were accepted into the movement. Devoted to the old brand of Black Muslimism, Louis Farrakhan defected in the late 1970s and continued the teachings of Elijah Muhammad with about 12,000 followers. Other splits have occurred since then within the movement, resulting in contemporary communities such as the Hanafis and the Five Percenters.

—LEWIS V. BALDWIN

See Also: *African-American Religion; Civil Rights Movement; Farrakhan, Louis; Malcolm X.*

BIBLIOGRAPHY: Lincoln, C. Eric, *The Black Muslims in America* (World Press 1994); McLoud, Aminah B., *African American Islam* (Routledge 1995); Malcolm X (with Alex Haley), *The Autobiography of Malcolm X* (Grove 1965).

■ **BLACK PANTHERS,** group advocating black power and grass-roots militancy. It was founded in Oakland, California, in October 1966 by Huey P. Newton and Bobby G. Seale, who were inspired by the rhetoric of Malcolm X. The Black Panthers promoted demands that included full employment, decent housing, land, education, food and clothing, the exclusion of African-American men from the military, and freedom for all African Americans in America's jails. They also insisted on the right of African Americans to carry weapons and to defend themselves.

The Panthers grew rapidly, recruiting young urban African Americans with working-class roots. Bobby Hutton, David Hilliard, and Eldridge Cleaver were among the earliest recruits, and dozens joined the group when it became more popular and visible outside the Bay Area. By 1968 it claimed 13 chapters and nearly 2,000 members. In 1969 *The Black Panther*, the group's newspaper, had a national circulation of more than 100,000.

Explosive rhetoric and confrontations with police created a frightening public image of the Black Panthers. The Panthers achieved little success in establishing alliances with other African-American groups. Their harsh criticisms of African-American churches, the Southern Christian Leadership Conference, the National Association for the Advancement of Colored People, and other organizations alienated them from the mainstream civil rights movement. Haunted by unfavorable public opinion and targeted by the police, the Panthers declined. With the arrests and trials of their leaders, as well as the killing of Fred Hampton, Mark Clark, and other Panthers by police, the Panthers ceased being a vital presence in black America by the early 1970s.

—LEWIS V. BALDWIN

See Also: Civil Rights Movement; Malcolm X; Student Nonviolent Coordinating Committee (SNCC).
BIBLIOGRAPHY: Foner, Philip S., ed., *The Black Panthers Speak* (Da Capo Press 1995); Haines, Herbert H., *Black Radicals and the Civil Rights Mainstream, 1954-1970* (Univ. of Tennessee Press 1988); Marine, Gene, *The Black Panthers* (New American Library 1969).

■ **BLACK SOX SCANDAL (1919-21),** scandal in major league baseball involving serious ethical infractions in the playing of the 1919 World Series. Seven players from the Chicago White Sox were accused of accepting bribes from professional gamblers in exchange for purposefully losing to the Cincinnati Reds in the series. An eighth player who knew of the scheme was also implicated. To deal with the crisis, Kennesaw Mountain Landis, a federal judge and former semiprofessional baseball player, was appointed the game's first commissioner in 1920. All eight players were tried in court in 1921 and all were banned from baseball. Since then, many have questioned the fairness of the trial and the verdict.
See Also: Baseball.

■ **BLACK STAR LINE,** steamship line created by black nationalist Marcus Garvey in 1919 as the foundation of a black-owned economic empire. Although successful at stimulating racial pride, the company went out of business in 1922 because of poor management and dilapidated equipment.
See Also: Garvey, Marcus Mosiah.

■ **BLACKWELL FAMILY,** the children and grandchildren of Samuel and Hannah Blackwell, remembered for their contributions to the American women's movement. The family emigrated from England in 1832. The most prominent of the siblings was Elizabeth Blackwell (1821-1910), who overcame opposition and ridicule to become in 1849 the first American woman to receive a medical degree. She and her sister Emily Blackwell (1826-1910), also a doctor, founded the New York Infirmary for Women and Children and the Women's Medical College. Elizabeth published controversial books on education and sex. Brother Henry Brown Blackwell (1825-1909) married the feminist leader Lucy Stone. Their daughter Alice Stone Blackwell (1857-1950) helped mend the rift between her mother and rival leader Susan B. Anthony. After her mother's death in 1893, Alice became increasingly radical, supporting the labor and civil rights movements. Louisa Antoinette Brown Blackwell (1825-1921) married Samuel Blackwell, Elizabeth and Henry's brother. In 1853, she became the first woman to be ordained as a minister in the United States. She wrote about conditions in prisons and tenements and criticized Charles Darwin for ignoring the role of women in natural history.

See Also: Women's Movement.

BIBLIOGRAPHY: Sahli, Nancy Ann, *Elizabeth Blackwell, M.D.: A Biography* (Arno Press 1982).

■ **BLADENSBURG, BATTLE OF (1814),** battle in Maryland during the War of 1812. Soldiers from a British fleet anchored in Maryland's Patuxent River on August 24 and marched toward Washington, D.C. A makeshift force of American soldiers positioned themselves at Bladensburg in the path of the advancing British. In the ensuing battle the Americans were routed; many ran away when the fighting began. The victory cleared the British way to Washington, which they burned.

See Also: War of 1812.

■ **BLAINE, JAMES GILLESPIE (1830-93),** U.S. secretary of state (1881, 1889-92). Born in West Brownsville, Pennsylvania, he graduated from Washington and Jefferson College in 1847. First appointed secretary of state by Pres. James A. Garfield, Blaine left office after Garfield's assassination (1881). His second term as secretary of state was under Pres. Benjamin Harrison. Blaine was a staunch nationalist, believing in the great-power destiny of the United States and in U.S. domination of the Western Hemisphere.

See Also: Garfield, James Abram; Harrison, Benjamin.

■ **BLAIR, JOHN (1732-1800),** associate justice of the U.S. Supreme Court (1789-96). A Virginia native, Blair was appointed to the Court by Pres. George Washington. Committed to the principle of the separation of powers, Blair often argued forcefully that the Court should refrain from meddling in the spheres of the other branches.

See Also: Supreme Court.

■ **BLALOCK, ALFRED (1899-1964),** surgeon and educator. Born in Colloden, Georgia, Blalock earned his M.D. from Johns Hopkins (1924) and became chief resident in surgery at Vanderbilt University's school of medicine (1925-41). There he began researching "shock" and established that the condition was caused by a decrease in blood volume. During World War II his recognition of the need for blood volume replacement was corroborated, and

many lives were saved by the use of blood, plasma, and blood substitutes. Blalock became chairman of the department of surgery at Johns Hopkins and surgeon in chief at Johns Hopkins Hospital in 1941. There he collaborated with others in completely removing the thymus gland for the first time from patients with myasthenia gravis. The surgery is still used as treatment for this rare chronic disease characterized by muscle weakness. He also devised an operation for improving pulmonary circulation in children with pulmonic stenosis, called subclavian pulmonary artery anastomosis. He performed this procedure for the first time on a patient with "blue baby" syndrome in 1944. This achievement brought fame to him and to Helen B. Taussig, a pediatric cardiologist who had suggested the procedure.

See Also: Medicine; Science.

■ **BLAND, JAMES (1854-1911),** songwriter. Born in Flushing, New York, he became a member of the Original Georgia Minstrels after studying music at Howard University. He went on to write more than 600 songs. Among the best known are "Oh, Dem Golden Slippers" and "Carry Me Back to Old Virginny," which was adopted as the official state song of Virginia in 1940.

See Also: African Americans.

■ **BLAND-ALLISON ACT (1878),** a congressional act designed to expand currency through the increase of silver coinage. The act ordered the Treasury to coin $2 million to $4 million worth of silver a month. "Free-silver" Democrats argued this was necessary to relieve the ongoing depression, which had begun in 1873.

■ **BLATCH, HARRIOT STANTON (1856-1940),** leader of the women's movement, daughter of woman suffrage leader Elizabeth Cady Stanton. Born in Seneca Falls, New York, she was an organizer and lobbyist for women's suffrage. She was also active in women's labor unions and campaigned for the Equal Rights Amendment.

See Also: Stanton, Elizabeth Cady; Women's Movement.

■ **BLATCHFORD, SAMUEL MILFORD (1820-93),** associate justice of the U.S. Supreme Court (1882-93). A New York City native, Blatchford was placed on the Court by Pres. Chester A. Arthur. Blatchford influenced the Court's position in the areas of commercial law and the Fifth Amendment's protection for self-incrimination.

See Also: Supreme Court.

■ **BLAVATSKY, HELENA PETRIVBA (1831-91),** spiritualist. Born in Russia, she went to New York City in 1873 where, in 1875, she founded the Theosophical Society. She left the United States in 1878, but despite allegations that her psychic powers were fraudulent, she became an influential interpreter of the occult, recruiting followers in America, Europe, and India.

■ **BLEEDING KANSAS (1855-56),** term for Kansas following the Kansas-Nebraska Act (1854), which allowed local voters to decide whether Kansas would be a slave or free state. Pro- and antislavery agitators flocked into Kansas, setting up separate governments and fighting a war over the slavery issue.

See Also: Civil War; Kansas-Nebraska Act.

■ **BLOODY SHIRT,** provocative expression, in full, "waving the bloody shirt." It referred to the post–Civil War Republican campaign tactic of linking Democratic opponents with secession and treason. The phrase originated earlier, in the British Isles during the Scottish rebellions of the 17th and 18th centuries, when widows were said to have waved the blood-stained shirts of their dead husbands to provoke a spirit of vengeance among the Scots.

See Also: Civil War.

■ **BLOOMER, AMELIA JENKS (1818-94),** editor, lecturer, and proponent of women's rights. She was born in Homer, New York. In 1849 she began publishing *Lily*, a temperance journal that soon included feminist writings. Her ardent defense of the controversial new dress outfit, full pantalettes worn with short skirts, that Elizabeth Cady Stanton and other suffragists adopted led to its being called the "Bloomer costume."

See Also: Stanton, Elizabeth Cady; Women's Movement.

■ **BLUE LAWS,** laws that govern public and personal conduct. Blue laws first appeared in Virginia in 1624 and spread throughout the colonies, especially those under the influence of

Armed conflict erupted in 1856 between supporters and opponents of allowing slavery in Kansas, which led to the nickname "Bleeding Kansas."

the Puritans. Colonial blue laws, named for the color of paper on which they were issued by New Haven Colony, primarily enforced observance of the Sabbath. During the 19th century, such laws were generally not enforced until the growth of the Prohibition movement. In some communities today, blue laws continue to prohibit store openings on Sundays.

See Also: Prohibition.

■ **BLUE RIDGE,** eastern range of the Appalachian Mountains. It runs some 1,500 miles from southern Pennsylvania in the north through Maryland, Virginia, North Carolina, South Carolina, and into northern Georgia. In colonial times the mountains formed a natural barrier between the European settlements in the east and Indians to the west. English and German settlers moved into the area during the late 1700s. In 1936 the National Park Service built a scenic parkway (the Blue Ridge Parkway) along the mountain's ridge.

See Also: Appalachian Mountains.

■ **BLUES,** musical genre of African-American culture that emerged from the tradition of work songs and street vendors' cries in the South during the 19th century. Blues lyrics typically comment on the trials of everyday life in a simple 12-bar pattern of call-and-response, with solo improvisation echoing the vocalist. The music itself is based on the "blues scale," in which the third and seventh note of the diatonic scale are "bent," or flattened, a form that derives from African influences. Blue notes can be achieved through vocal effects, or by stretching the strings of a guitar, which became the characteristic instrument of the blues.

The first published blues was composed by W. C. Handy of Memphis in 1911. The first commercial recordings were made in the 1920s by performers such as Bessie Smith, Ethel Waters, and Gertrude "Ma" Rainey. Blues tunes and blues sensibility became part of the jazz music tradition through the influence of Louis Armstrong and the big-band leader Count Basie.

In the 1930s, folklorists discovered the vital tradition of blues being played by itinerant guitarists in the rural South. One of them, Muddy Waters, was recorded on a plantation in Mississippi before he migrated to Chicago during World War II. As a performer in the bars and clubs of the city's predominantly African-American Southside, Waters became one of the first blues musicians to use the electric guitar, so that he could be heard over the din of the crowd. "Urban blues," as this variant was known, spawned a new musical tradition, known as rhythm and blues, and was also the progenitor of rock and roll.

See Also: Armstrong, Louis Daniel ("Satchmo"); Basie, William "Count"; Big Bands; Handy, W.C. (William Christopher); Jazz; Rainey, Gertrude (Ma); Rhythm and Blues; Rock and Roll; Smith, Bessie; Waters, Ethel; Waters, Muddy (McKinley Morganfield).

BIBLIOGRAPHY: Lomax, Alan, *The Land Where the Blues Began* (Pantheon 1993); Oliver, Paul, *The Meaning of the Blues* (Collier 1963); Palmer, Robert, *Deep Blues* (Viking 1981).

■ **BOARD OF TRADE (1696-1782),** permanent agency created to advise English political leaders on colonial economic issues. The Board of Trade was assembled in response to a lack of imperial control over provincial economic activities and markets. Adopting a fundamentally mercantilist approach, the Board of Trade was principally focused on crafting parliamentary legislation that would restrain colonial manufactures, especially those that competed with goods produced in England. At the same time, the Board of Trade encouraged the production of resources needed in England, such as raw iron. In addition, the Board of Trade shaped policies that reserved colonial markets for English manufactured goods.

■ **BOAS, FRANZ (1858-1942),** anthropologist and ethnographer. Boas was born in Westphalia, Germany. He taught anthropology at Columbia University in New York City, becoming a full professor in 1899. Boas served as curator of anthropology at the American Museum of Natural History in New York from 1901 to 1905 and had a particular interest in the linguistics of American Indian groups. Among his many writings are *The Mind of Primitive Man* (1911) and *Anthropology and Modern Life* (1928).

See Also: Anthropology and Ethnology.

Franz Boas challenged evolutionism and theories of racial superiority that dominated Anglo-American anthropology. Boas, who became professor of anthropology at Columbia University in 1899, is pictured here in a photograph taken in the 1930s.

■ **BODMER, KARL (1809-93),** artist and visitor to the American West. Born in Switzerland, Bodmer was in the United States between 1832 and 1834 as a documentary artist for a scientific expedition on the Missouri River. The watercolors he executed on this trip were reproduced as aquatint engravings in the account of the expedition, published between 1839 and 1841. They were among the earliest widely distributed images of the landscape and Indians of the Great Plains.
See Also: Painting.

■ **BOGART, HUMPHREY (1899-1957),** film actor. Born in New York City, he appeared on stage and in supporting film roles before achieving stardom as a gangster in *The Petrified Forest* (1936). In memorable films such as *The Maltese Falcon* (1941), *Casablanca* (1942), *To Have and Have Not* (1944), *The Treasure of the Sierra Madre* (1948), and *The African Queen* (1952), Bogart played cynical outsiders who reveal unexpected complexity and depth.
See Also: Motion Pictures.

■ **BOND, CARRIE JACOBS (1862-1946),** composer and songwriter of American popular music, born in Janesville, Wisconsin. Author of more than 400 songs including "I Love You Truly " and "Just a Wearyin' for You," she achieved her greatest popularity between 1910 and 1920.

■ **BOND, HORACE MANN (1904-72),** educator. Born in Nashville, Tennessee, Bond became a lifelong teacher and administrator. His career was spent improving educational opportunity for African Americans. Bond's landmark studies, *The Education of the Negro in the American Social Order* (1934) and *Negro Education in Alabama* (1939), eloquently documented educational inequality in the South. He was among the first to criticize the inherent bias in intelligence testing.
See Also: African Americans.

■ **BOND, JULIAN (1940-),** civil rights activist. Born in Nashville, Tennessee, Bond was a founder (1960) and communications director (1960-65) of the Student Nonviolent Coordinating Committee (SNCC). He was elected to the Georgia state legislature in 1965 but was barred from serving because of anti–Vietnam War statements. The U.S. Supreme Court upheld (1966) his right to hold office, and Bond served in the legislature until 1986. He was president of the board of directors (1974-89) of the National Association for the Advancement of Colored People (NAACP) and became professor of history at the University of Virginia.
See Also: Civil Rights Movement; Student Nonviolent Coordinating Committee (SNCC).

■ **BONNIN, GERTRUDE SIMMONS (1876-1938),** American Indian leader. Born Zitkala-Sa, at the Yankton Sioux agency in South Dakota, she was educated in a Quaker missionary school. She was a proponent of full citizenship for Indians, improved health care and education, conservation of natural resources, and preservation of the Indian cultural heritage. In 1921, she helped to create the Indian Welfare Committee of the General Federation of Women's Clubs. She was the president of the National Council of American Indians from 1926 to 1938.

See Also: Frontier in American History; General Federation of Women's Clubs (GFWC); Women in American History.

■ **BONUS ARMY (1932),** alliance of 20,000 World War I veterans and their families who assembled in Washington, D.C., from May to July 1932 to demand immediate payment of promised benefits. In 1924 Congress had voted in favor of a veteran's bonus program, payable in 1945. As the Depression deepened, jobless veterans poured into Washington from around the country to lobby Congress and Pres. Herbert Hoover for early payment of the promised funds. The so-called Bonus Army set up tents and held rallies and marches on Capitol Hill. Despite Hoover's opposition, the House of Representatives voted for early payment. The Senate, however, refused to act and adjourned in July.

Most of the bonus marchers then left Washington, but about 2,000 remained behind in a camp in the Anacostia Flats section of the city. On July 28, after two veterans and two policemen had been killed in a skirmish, Sec. of War Patrick J. Hurley ordered Gen. Douglas MacArthur to use the army to remove the protesters. Four troops of cavalry with drawn sabers supported by tanks and infantry with fixed bayonets swept through Anacostia, burning the camp to the ground and dispersing the veterans. This rout of jobless war veterans and their families by U.S. troops symbolized both the social tragedy of the Depression and Hoover's apparent inability to end the crisis.

—TIM ASHWELL

See Also: Great Depression; Hoover, Herbert Clark; MacArthur, Douglas.

BIBLIOGRAPHY: Lisio, Donald J., *The President and Protest: Hoover, MacArthur, and the Bonus Riot,* 2nd ed. (Fordham Univ. Press 1994).

■ **BOONE, DANIEL (1734-1820),** legendary pioneer and hero of the American Revolution in the West. He was born near present-day Reading, Pennsylvania. After a boyhood in the Pennsylvania woods, learning woodscraft from white and Indian hunters, his family moved south in 1750 and settled in the backcountry of North Carolina. There, in 1756, young Boone married Rebecca Bryan; their marriage lasted until her death in 1813 and produced 10 children. Hunting and trapping was Boone's livelihood, and in pursuit of game in 1769 he became one of the first Americans to cross the Appalachians to the fabled land of Kentucky.

In 1773, Boone attempted to lead a party of family and friends over the mountains to settle, but they were turned back by an Indian attack that killed his eldest son. During the subsequent Lord Dunmore's War he was sent by Virginia authorities to Kentucky to warn surveyors there. In 1774, employed by a land speculator, he led the party that cut the Wilderness Road across the Cumberland Gap into Kentucky; later that year he helped found the settlement of Boonesborough, to which he moved his family.

During the years of the American Revolution, Boone was a leader of the Kentucky forces fighting the western Indian allies of the British. In 1776 he led the rescue of three girls (including his daughter Jemima) kidnapped by Shawnees, and the next year was wounded during an attack on Boonesborough. In 1778 he and a party of men were captured by Shawnees; Boone later escaped, but he fell under suspicion of being too friendly with his captors. He won the support of his fellow settlers, however, by directing the successful defense of Boonesborough during a prolonged siege later that year. In 1784 writer John Filson published "The Adventures of Col. Daniel Boon," which brought Boone to national attention. Filson's Boone was the prototype for dozens of subsequent American western heroes. Adding to Boone's legend was his failure as a land speculator and his troubles with the law, leading to his immigration to Missouri (then under Spanish control) in 1798. Thousands of pioneers saw their own experience embodied in Boone's story. Boone spent the last 20 years of his life working as a hunter and trapper in Missouri, where he was surrounded by his large extended family.

—JOHN MACK FARAGHER

See Also: Cumberland Gap; Exploration and Discovery; Frontier in American History; Revolution, American; Wilderness Road.

BIBLIOGRAPHY: Faragher, John Mack, *Daniel Boone: The Life and Legend of an American Pioneer* (Henry Holt 1992).

■ **BOOTH, JOHN WILKES (1838-65),** assassin of Pres. Abraham Lincoln. Born near Bel Air, Maryland, Booth was an actor before the Civil War. Fanatically pro-Southern, he joined the Virginia militia in 1859 and assisted in capturing John Brown. On Apr. 14, 1865, after planning with others the assassination of several Union leaders, Booth went to Ford's Theater in Washington,

During an Apr. 14, 1865, performance at Ford's Theater in Washington, D.C., actor John Wilkes Booth fatally shot Pres. Abraham Lincoln at point-blank range. Booth broke a leg in escaping from the theater and was later killed when he refused to surrender.

where Lincoln was attending a play, and shot him. Booth was trapped on April 26 in a barn near Bowling Green, Virginia, and killed.

See Also: Civil War; Lincoln, Abraham.

■ **BOOTH FAMILY,** 19th-century family of actors established by Junius Brutus Booth (1796-1852) and notoriously remembered because his son John Wilkes Booth (1838-65) shot and killed Pres. Abraham Lincoln (Apr. 14, 1865). Two weeks later, John Wilkes Booth was hunted down by federal troops and killed in Bowling Green, Virginia. After gaining stage success in his native London, the elder Booth moved to the United States in 1821 and organized a theater company specializing in Shakespearean plays. Despite bouts of mental illness aggravated by excessive drinking, he remained one of the leading actors of his time. His sons, Junius Brutus (1821-83), Edwin (1833-93), and John Wilkes, continued the family's theatrical tradition. Edwin, the most successful, was known as the greatest Hamlet of his day. He made his stage debut in 1849, toured the United States and Australia (1852-55), opened his own theater in New York City (1869), and toured Europe (1880-82).

See Also: Theater.

BIBLIOGRAPHY: Smith, Gene, *American Gothic: The Story of America's Legendary Theatrical Family* (Simon & Schuster 1992).

■ **BOOTLEGGING,** the transport or sale of illegal liquor, a flourishing trade in the United States during the Prohibition era of the 1920s. The passage of the liquor-banning Volstead Act in 1920 did not end American demand for alcoholic beverages. Rather it spawned an illegal industry worth millions of dollars, which ultimately cost thousands of lives—due not only to gang-related killings (which were common), but also to the consumption of the often lethal bootleg liquor itself.

Gangsters such as Al Capone operated criminal organizations that shipped and sold liquor smuggled across the Canadian border or landed at various spots on both the East and West coasts. Underfunded law enforcement agencies were hard-pressed to stem the tide. Alcohol produced within the United States was often deadly, relying on potentially poisonous ingredients such as iodine or gasoline. It is thought that the term "bootlegging" originated during the Civil War when soldiers hid their whiskey in the legs of their boots (or "bootlegs").

See Also: Capone, Al; National Prohibition Enforcement Act.

BIBLIOGRAPHY: Allsop, Kenneth, *The Bootleggers: The Story of Chicago's Prohibition Era* (Arlington House 1968).

■ **BORAH, WILLIAM EDGAR (1865-1940),** U.S. senator from Idaho (1907-40). Born in Fairfield, Illinois, he studied law in Kansas. He moved to Boise, Idaho, where he practiced law and became active in Republican party politics. Known as "the Lion of Idaho," Borah was a noted orator whose reputation for independence disguised an often contradictory record. A supporter of U.S. participation in World War I, he then opposed ratification of the Versailles treaty and membership in the League of Nations. He was a staunch isolationist in the late 1930s, predicting there would be no second war in Europe. On most domestic issues, Borah was considered a progressive. He was suspicious of corporate power unless it directly benefited Idaho's economy, and he crossed party lines to support most New Deal legislation. However, he became increasingly critical of government agencies that he feared threatened individual liberty.

See Also: New Deal.

BIBLIOGRAPHY: Johnson, Claudius O., *Borah of Idaho 1936;* reprint (Univ. of Washington Press 1967).

■ **BORDER STATES,** the slave states adjacent to the northern states in the years preceding and during the Civil War: Delaware, Maryland, Virginia, Kentucky, and Missouri. All of them considered themselves "southern," but included groups with strong antislavery sentiments. Virginia was the only border state to secede, which resulted in antislavery forces in the western part of the state breaking away in 1861 to form the new state of West Virginia, which remained in the Union and was admitted as a separate state in 1863. Once the war began, one of Pres. Abraham Lincoln's primary goals was to prevent the secession of the other border states; the Emancipation Proclamation (1863), for example, explicitly excluded the Border States. A rump government in Missouri attempted to join the Confederacy but was prevented by harsh military action. Men from the Border States served in both armies.

See Also: Civil War.

■ **BORLAUG, NORMAN E. (1914-),** agronomist who developed new strains of wheat that brought on the "green revolution." Born in Cresco, Iowa, Borlaug earned his Ph.D. from the University of Minnesota (1941) and then went to Mexico City with a team of scientists from the Rockefeller Foundation to help bring agricultural technology to underdeveloped nations (1944-66). There, Borlaug introduced a disease-free strain of wheat he had developed that remedied Mexico's crop failures. He also developed new, high-yield, adaptable dwarf wheats, which were introduced in 1961. With his wheat, Borlaug brought the "green revolution" to many nations, including India, Pakistan, Tunisia, and Morocco, tremendously increasing the world's cereal supply during a time of great population growth. He was awarded the Nobel Peace Prize in 1970 for "help[ing] to provide bread for a hungry world." Borlaug supported the use of fertilizers, pesticides, and other technical means to help grain-importing economies become self-sufficient. He became head of the International Maize and Wheat Improvement Center in Mexico City (1966) and a consultant there (1981) before accepting a professorship at Texas A & M (1984) and directing the Global 2000 Agricultural Programs in Africa (1988).

See Also: Agriculture; Science.

■ **BOSOMWORTH, MARY MUSGROVE (c. 1700-c. 1763; fl. 1716-50),** biracial American Indian leader, born along the Chattahoochee River in Alabama, possibly the niece of Creek chief "Old Brim." As James Oglethorpe's primary ambassador, she maintained an alliance between the Georgia colonists and the Creek, who were a crucial buffer between British Georgia and Spanish Florida.

■ **BOSTON,** capital city of Massachusetts and for the last 300 years the largest city in New England. The peninsula between the Charles River and Boston Harbor was called Shawmut by the Indi-

The port of Boston is shown in an English print of the mid-18th century. The capital of the Massachusetts colony, it became the center of the growing opposition to British authority, site of the Boston Massacre and the Boston Tea Party.

ans who lived in the area. In the 1620s the Rev. William Blackstone settled there, and in 1630 he helped the Rev. John Winthrop and 800 Puritans to move from Charlestown to settle on the land as the main colony of the Massachusetts Bay Company. Boston was the hub of New England cultural and economic life throughout the 18th century. The city was a vital center of the American Revolution and was the site of the Boston Massacre (Mar. 5, 1770), the Boston Tea Party (Dec. 16, 1773), and the battles of Lexington and Concord (April 1775). European immigrants, especially Irish and Italian, moved into the city during the 19th century, and the construction of new suburbs expanded the city's surrounding towns. Throughout the 20th century Boston has remained the most important urban center in New England. Population (1994): 547,725.

See Also: Boston Massacre; Boston Tea Party.

■ **BOSTON ASSOCIATES,** a group of Boston merchants, led by Francis Cabot Lowell and including Patrick Tracy Jackson, Nathan Appleton, and Israel Thorndike, who invested in the Boston Manufacturing Company in Waltham, Massachusetts (1813), and established the Waltham factory system. The corporations these men formed represented a new, more efficient financial organization for private business, allowing them to sell stock and finance larger factories than ever before. After building the Waltham factory, the Boston Associates expanded to a site along the Merrimack River, establishing the Locks and Canals Company to construct a factory to manufacture textile machinery, to build and own a system of locks and canals to develop the property's water power, and to lay out sites for new textile mills. The investors retained control of the Locks and Canal Company and incorporated separate firms such as the Merrimack Manufacturing Company to build mills on the developed sites. Their success at Waltham and their reputations as merchants gave these men access to most of the capital in Boston, allowing them to finance new companies and then sell them to friends and colleagues, who in turn let them choose factory management and thereby retain control over each business. The Boston Associates' financial methods enabled them to expand their industrial development along the Merrimack and Connecticut rivers. Other New England capitalists adopted similar methods to develop factories in Massachusetts, New Hampshire, and Maine.

See Also: Industrial Revolution; Waltham System.
BIBLIOGRAPHY: Vernon-Wortzel, Heidi, *Lowell: The Corporations and the City* (Garland 1992).

■ **BOSTON MASSACRE (1770),** killing of five colonists, including Crispus Attucks, by British soldiers in Boston. British redcoats were sent to Boston in 1768 to keep order after colonial protests, but the standing army only exacerbated tensions. On Mar. 5, 1770, the prolonged contention between townspeople and the soldiers erupted violently, as panicked troops fired on a taunting crowd. This bloody incident, which became a rallying point of the Revolution, brought the removal of the troops, only two of whom were found guilty.

See Also: Attucks, Crispus; Revolution, American.

■ **BOSTON TEA PARTY (1773),** colonial protest against the Tea Act of 1773. On the night of December 16, a group of 60 men organized by Samuel Adams and disguised as Indians boarded three British ships in Boston harbor and emptied hundreds of chests of tea into the harbor. The Boston Tea Party was one of the main events leading to the American Revolution.

See Also: Adams, Samuel; Revolution, American; Tea Act.

■ **BOUDINOT, ELIAS (c. 1803-39),** Cherokee publisher and leader. Born Galegina near Rome, Georgia, he was educated in Connecticut. Boudinot advocated adoption of American values combined with Cherokee nationalism. He founded the bilingual *Cherokee Phoenix*, the first Indian newspaper in North America. Boudinot initially led Cherokee resistance to removal west of the Mississippi, but by 1835 he had decided that removal was the only way to save the Cherokees, and he signed the Treaty of New Echota, which was opposed by the vast majority of the Cherokee nation. He was killed in Indian Territory in 1839 by Cherokee opponents of removal.

See Also: Cherokee; Indians of North America.

■ **BOURKE-WHITE, MARGARET (1907-70),** photojournalist. Born in New York City, she worked for news magazines, including *Life* and *Time*. She is best known for her photographs of the liberation of German concentration camps during World War II. Other photographs, dealing with depression in the rural South, American factories, World War II, and the war in Korea, are published in *Have You Seen Their Faces* (1937), *Purple Heart Valley* (1944), and other collections.

See Also: New Deal; Photography; Women in American History.

■ **BOURNE, RANDOLPH (1886-1918),** essayist. A native of Bloomfield, New Jersey, Bourne suffered an accident early in his life that left him disabled. He attended Columbia University and also studied in Europe. Bourne held radical ideals about education and politics, which he expressed in acerbic prose for the journal the *New Republic*. He died of influenza during the epidemic of 1918. Bourne's collected essays included *Youth and Life* (1913), *Education and Living* (1917), and the posthumous works *Untimely Papers* (1919) and *The History of a Literary Radical* (1920).

■ **BOWDITCH, NATHANIEL (1773-1838),** astronomer and mathematician. Born in Salem, Massachusetts, Bowditch took his first sea voyage in 1795 and traveled all over the world for the next eight years, studying languages, mathematics, science, and navigation along the way. In 1799, he edited J. H. Moore's *The Practical Navigator*, revising and publishing it under his own name in 1802 as *The New American Practical Navigator*. Sixty-five editions have been published since. Bowditch became president of the Essex Fire and Marine Insurance Company (1804-23) and actuary for the Massachusetts Hospital Life Insurance Company (1823-38), jobs that gave him ample time to pursue his interests in science. He wrote a series of 23 papers that were published by the American Academy of Arts and Sciences (1804-20) and became one of the first men in the United States to understand continental mathematics, which were far more advanced at the time than English mathematics. His translation and elucidation of Laplace's *Mechanique celeste* (1829-39) introduced and explained the latest mathematical thought to the English-speaking world. Despite being completely self-taught, Bowditch was accepted in the highest circles as a scientist of the first rank.

See Also: Science.

■ **BOWERS V. HARDWICK (1986),** U.S. Supreme Court case that upheld a Georgia state law banning sodomy. Hardwick, a Georgia man, had been discovered by police engaging in consensual homosexual acts with another adult in his home. Although he was never prosecuted, he sued to overturn the law making such acts a felony. Writing for the narrow Court majority (5-4), Justice Byron White said that the constitutional right to privacy established in cases such as *Griswold* v. *Connecticut* (1965) pertained to issues of family and procreation. Laws against homosexual conduct, he argued, reflected widespread public attitudes and were not covered by the privacy precedent. Justice Harry Blackmun in dissent argued that the Court was not being asked to establish a legal right to engage in homosexuality but to affirm an individual's "right to be let alone" in his own home. The case was complicated by Georgia's refusal to prosecute Hardwick. Justice Lewis Powell, who voted with the majority, said since the plaintiff had not been brought to trial, Eighth Amendment protections against cruel and unusual punishment did not apply.

See Also: Griswold v. *Connecticut; Supreme Court.*

■ **BOWIE, JIM (JAMES) (1795-1836),** hero of the revolution in Texas in the 1830s. Born in Elliott Spring, Tennessee, Bowie moved to Texas in 1828, where he converted to Catholicism and married Ursula Maria, the daughter of the vice governor, Juan Martin Veramundi. A colonel in the Texas Rangers by 1830, Bowie fought in several skirmishes in the war for Texas's independence from Mexico. Best known for fighting at the Battle of the Alamo (Mar. 6, 1836), Bowie either fought with exemplary bravery and died a hero or was too sick with pneumonia to move from his bed, depending on which account one believes.

Bowie alleged to have invented the bowie knife, but there are different stories as to its origin.

See Also: Alamo; Frontier in American History.

■ **BOXER REBELLION (1900),** a popular uprising in China directed against European influence in the country. The rebels known as Boxers directed their hatred against all foreigners. In the summer of 1900, the rebellion inflamed northeastern China and spread to Beijing. World powers, including Russia, Japan, Germany, France, Great Britain, and the United States, responded by sending military forces to Beijing. The punitive expedition launched under the command of a German general, Count von Waldersee, succeeded in quelling the rebellion.

See Also: Open Door Policy.

■ **BOXING,** a violent sport of enduring popularity and controversy. Boxing became established in the United States in the early 19th century, but the sport's following was limited by associations with gambling, vice, and corruption. It became a major spectator sport in the late 19th century, thanks in large part to John L. Sullivan (1858-1918), a Boston Irishman who held the heavyweight championship from 1882 to 1892. The sporting press turned Sullivan into a national hero. Ethnic and national pride and rivalries have long been part of the sport. Leading boxers are seen quite literally as champions, representing millions in single combat. European immigrants, African Americans, Hispanics, and occasionally the entire nation have rallied behind their fighters. When Joe Louis defeated Germany's Max Schmeling in 1938, his victory was hailed as a triumph over Nazism, and the championship of Muhammad Ali was a point of pride for the civil rights movement of the 1960s.

See Also: Sports.

BIBLIOGRAPHY: Liebling, A. J., *The Sweet Science* (Viking 1956); Sugar, Bert Randolph, *100 Years of Boxing* (Routledge 1986).

■ **BOY SCOUTS OF AMERICA,** youth organization incorporated in the United States in 1910, based on the movement founded in England two years earlier by Sir Robert Baden-Powell. Established to encourage character development in

The Boy Scouts of America, chartered in 1910, was modeled on a British group of the same name organized by Sir Robert Baden-Powell. James E. West (*shown with scouts*) served as chief scout executive from that year until 1943.

boys and young men, scouting emphasized outdoor activities at a time when the nation was becoming increasingly urban. The Boy Scouts, whose motto is "Be Prepared," still combine the learning of camping skills with participation in community service.

■ **BRADDOCK, EDWARD (1695-1755),** British general. Braddock, a Scot, was sent to America to fight in the French and Indian War. He became infamous among Indian allies and his soldiers, including his aide, Lt. Col. George Washington, for his arrogant and tempestuous leadership. In 1755, near Fort Duquesne (present-day Pittsburgh), an outnumbered force of French and Indians routed Braddock's disorganized troops in the Battle of the Wilderness. Braddock was killed in the battle, and his body buried hastily by a retreating Washington.

See Also: French and Indian War.

■ **BRADFORD, CORNELIA SMITH (d. 1755),** one of the few female printers and journalists in colonial America, she was born in New York City. She took over her husband's Philadelphia print shop after his death in 1742 and was editor and publisher of the *American Weekly Mercury* from 1744 to 1746.

■ **BRADFORD, WILLIAM (1589-1657),** governor of Plymouth Colony (1622-32, 1635, 1637, 1639-43, 1645-56) and author of *History of Plimoth Plantation*. Born in Yorkshire, England, Bradford became a member of the Separatist congregation at Scrooby, England, and moved with its members to Leyden, Holland (1609). He arrived in America on the *Mayflower* (1620). As the governor of Plymouth, Bradford held wide political and religious powers in the colony. He also accepted great responsibility, drafting a body of laws for the colony (1636), and assuming (with a group of other leaders) the colony's debt with its London investors. Throughout his tenure as Plymouth's predominant leader, Bradford assiduously guarded the colony's autonomy even as he participated regularly in pan-colonial efforts such as the Pequot War (1637) and the New England Confederation (1643).

■ **BRADLEY, BILL (1943-),** U.S. senator (1979-97) and basketball star. Born in Crystal City, Missouri, he was an All-America basketball player at Princeton (1962-65), Rhodes scholar at Oxford (1966), and star forward for the professional New York Knicks (1967-77). Bradley was elected to the Senate as a Democrat from New Jersey in 1978 in his first bid for elective office.

Twice reelected, he announced in 1995 he would not run for a fourth term.

See Also: Senate of the United States; Sports.

■ **BRADLEY, JOSEPH P. (1813-92),** associate justice of the U.S. Supreme Court (1870-92). A Berne, New York, native, Bradley broke with the majority in the *Slaughterhouse Cases* (1873), contending that the Court had interpreted too narrowly the rights of national citizenship protected by the 14th Amendment. Nonetheless, a decade later, he joined the majority in the Civil Rights Cases, arguing that the 14th Amendment did not permit the federal government to prohibit private racial discrimination.

See Also: Civil Rights Cases; Slaughterhouse Cases; Supreme Court.

■ **BRADLEY, OMAR NELSON (1893-1981),** World War II general who commanded the largest U.S. army group in history and was the last general elevated to five-star rank. Born in Clark, Missouri, Bradley graduated from West Point but failed to get a combat assignment during World War I. In the postwar years he was assigned as an instructor at West Point and then at Fort Benning's Infantry School. By the start of World War II, Bradley had attained the rank of brigadier general and was in charge of the Infantry School. He commanded troops in North Africa and Sicily and when the invasion of Normandy commenced in June 1944 was put in command of the huge 12th Army Group. Bradley led the group through to the eventual defeat of Nazi Germany. After the war he reorganized the Veterans Administration and became chairman of the Joint Chiefs of Staff, among other posts. Bradley died in New York City on Apr. 8, 1981.

See Also: Korean War; World War II.
BIBLIOGRAPHY: Bradley, Omar N., *A General's Life* (Simon & Schuster 1983); Bradley, Omar N., *A Soldier's Story* (Henry Holt 1951).

■ **BRADLEY, TOM (1917-),** politician and mayor of Los Angeles, California. Born in Calvert, Texas, Bradley began his career in public service as a Los Angeles police officer in 1940. Retiring from the force in 1962, he practiced law from 1961 to 1963. Following a decade of service as a member of the city council, Bradley was elected as the first black mayor of Los Angeles in 1973, a post he held for 20 years. He was the unsuccessful Democratic candidate for governor of California in 1982 and 1986.

See Also: Civil Rights Movement; Los Angeles.

■ **BRADSTREET, ANNE (c. 1612-72),** colonial author. Born in Northampton, England, she immigrated to Massachusetts in 1630 with her father, Thomas Dudley, and her husband, John Bradstreet. There, she raised eight children and wrote simple, deeply spiritual poetry. Without her consent, her brother-in-law published a collection of her poems in London in 1650, making her the first published American poet. Her most important work, "Contemplations," appeared in the posthumous volume *Several Poems* (1678).

See Also: Women in American History.

■ **BRADY, MATHEW B. (1823-96),** Civil War photographer. Brady was born in Warren County, New York. He moved to New York City in 1839, where he learned photography from Samuel F. B. Morse. Brady opened a daguerreotype gallery in 1844: he won both the first gold medal for daguerreotypes given by the American Institute in 1849 and a medal at the 1851 Crystal Palace Exhibition in London, England. Brady created a collection of daguerreotype portraits of eminent Americans of his day, including presidents, scientists, writers, and actors—a project that was largely carried out in the Washington, D.C., studio that he opened in 1847. In 1850 he published a selection of these images in *The Gallery of Illustrious Americans.* When the Civil War began, Brady received permission to travel with the Union Army; he recorded the first Battle of Bull Run on July 21, 1861. From 1861 to 1865, he documented the battles of the Civil War. Using the wet-plate technique, he photographed in the field and developed his plates in wagons set up as darkrooms. Brady employed other photographers—including Timothy O'Sullivan and Alexander Gardner—to help him in this endeavor.

See Also: Civil War; Morse, Samuel Finley Breese; Photography.

■ **BRAIN TRUST,** the group of advisers to Franklin D. Roosevelt, formed in 1932 while he was still governor of New York, to develop a strategy to overcome the Great Depression and win the campaign for the presidency. The group included specialists in law, economics, and welfare policy, including Frances Perkins, Rexford G. Tugwell, Raymond Moley, and A. A. Berle, Jr.

See Also: New Deal.

■ **BRANDEIS, LOUIS DEMBITZ (1856-1941),** reformer and associate justice of the U.S. Supreme Court (1916-39). A conscientious defender of a liberal progressive society, Brandeis was born in Louisville, Kentucky. After graduating from Harvard Law School in 1877, he established a law practice in Boston. He soon came to believe that in that era of intense industrialization the law must be used as a corrective to regulate political corruption and the excesses of big business. Turning his energies toward reform, Brandeis became known as the "people's attorney" for providing free defense for public causes. In 1907, he created a system of affordable life insurance for workers through savings banks. In his landmark defense in *Muller* v. *Oregon* (1908), his use of economic and sociological evidence instead of legal precedents became known as the "Brandeis brief."

A shrewd, progressive reformer, Brandeis assisted Woodrow Wilson in formulating the New Freedom during the presidential campaign of 1912. Four years later, President Wilson appointed Brandeis to the U.S. Supreme Court, where the justice continued to advocate the primacy of social and economic factors over legal theory. Although often a voice of liberal dissent in a conservative Court, Brandeis was one of the greatest legal minds of his time. Among other contributions, he worked to uphold the Bill of Rights and the right to privacy. As a prominent member of the Jewish community, Brandeis was active in the American Zionist movement.

See Also: Muller v. *Oregon; Supreme Court.*

BIBLIOGRAPHY: Mason, Alpheus Thomas, *Brandeis: A Free Man's Life* (Viking 1949); Strum, Philippa, *Louis D. Brandeis: Justice for the People* (Harvard Univ. Press 1984).

The "people's attorney," Louis Brandeis made a career of advocating public causes. In 1916, Brandeis was appointed associate justice of the U.S. Supreme Court and served until 1939.

■ **BRANDO, MARLON (1924-),** stage and film actor, born in Omaha, Nebraska. Brando's raw emotional realism and physical presence caused a sensation on Broadway in *A Streetcar Named Desire* (1947). Successes in the film version of *Streetcar* (1951), *The Wild One* (1953), and *On the Waterfront* (1954) were followed by an uneven career, but Brando silenced his critics with a bravura performance in *The Godfather* (1972).

■ **BRANDYWINE CREEK, BATTLE OF (1777),** Revolutionary War battle. American Gen. George Washington, who sought to halt British Gen. William Howe's advance toward Philadelphia, took up a strong defensive position behind Brandywine Creek. On September 11, while a British force demonstrated in the American center, Howe outflanked the American right with troops landed upstream. Outmaneuvered, the Americans retreated toward Philadelphia, which, after a number of sharp small-scale fights, fell to Howe on September 26.

See Also: Howe, Sir William; Revolution, American; Washington, George.

■ **BRANT, JOSEPH (1742-1809),** Mohawk leader. Born Thayendanega in Ohio, Brant was an early sympathizer with the British. In 1777, he called for a council of the Iroquois Six Nations Confederacy to discuss support for the British during the American Revolution but could not achieve consensus; the leaders of the Mohawk, Seneca, Cayuga, and Onondaga nations agreed to meet at the British post of Oswego, while the Oneida and Tuscarora nations supported the American colonists. For the first time in the colonial era, the Iroquois alliance was broken. After the Revolution, Brant fled to Canada.

See Also: Indians of North America; Iroquois Confederacy; Revolution, American.

■ **BRANT, MARY (MOLLY) (c. 1736-96),** common-law wife of Sir William Johnson, superintendent of Indian affairs for the Northern Colonies. She was probably born in the Mohawk Valley in New York. Of Mohawk descent, she used her influence among Indian leaders to aid the British during the Revolutionary War.

See Also: Frontier in American History; Women in American History.

■ **BRAXTON, CARTER (1736-97),** statesman and Revolutionary War leader. A signer of the Declaration of Independence, Braxton was born to a prominent Virginia family. He served in the House of Burgesses, participated in the Second Continental Congress, and helped draft Virginia's constitution.

See Also: Declaration of Independence.

■ **BRECKINRIDGE, JOHN C. (1821-75),** vice president of the United States (1857-61) and Confederate general and cabinet member. Born near Lexington, Kentucky, Breckinridge served in the House of Representatives (1851-55) and then became the youngest vice president in U.S. history. He ran unsuccessfully for the presidency (1860) as the pro-South Democratic candidate. Breckinridge became a general in the Confederate army and

fought in the battles of Shiloh (1962) and Stones River (1862-63). In February 1865, Breckinridge became the Confederacy's last secretary of war. At war's end he escaped to Cuba and traveled in Europe before returning to Lexington (1868).

See Also: Civil War; Presidential Elections; Vice President of the United States.

■ **BRENNAN, WILLIAM JOSEPH, JR. (1906-97),** associate justice of the U.S. Supreme Court (1956-90). He was born in Newark, New Jersey, attended the University of Pennsylvania's Wharton School and Harvard Law School, and was a New Jersey state supreme court justice when nominated to the Supreme Court by Pres. Dwight D. Eisenhower. A steadfast liberal who believed the Constitution should be broadly interpreted to protect individual rights, Brennan became an influential leader of the Court and close confidant of Chief Justice Earl Warren. He was able to balance competing interests, build majorities, and express the Court's consensus in authoritative opinions. He was especially supportive of 1st and 14th Amendment liberties and was an implacable foe of the death penalty. Brennan was criticized by conservatives for being too willing to overturn laws that, they said, represented the will of the people. He responded that it was the duty of the Court to protect the fundamental rights of the people against transient political majorities.

See Also: Supreme Court.

BIBLIOGRAPHY: Eisler, Kim I., *William J. Brennan, Jr., and the Decisions that Transformed America* (Simon & Schuster 1993).

■ **BRENT, MARGARET (c. 1601-71),** colonial businesswoman. Born in Gloucester, England, she immigrated to colonial Maryland in 1638, where she became the first woman to own property in that colony. By 1647 Brent was among the wealthiest landowners in Maryland and was the executor of the estate of Lord Leonard Calvert. On these grounds, she demanded a seat in the Maryland Assembly in 1648 but was denied it because she was a woman.

See Also: Women in American History.

■ **BRETTON WOODS CONFERENCE (1944),** an international forum at Bretton Woods, New

Hampshire, that established the post–World War II international economic order. A U.S.-dominated world economic system was designed, its fundamental principles being free flow of goods and monetary stability based on fixed exchange rates. Three new institutions were founded: The International Bank for Reconstruction and Development (World Bank), the International Monetary Fund (IMF), and the International Trade Organization, although the latter did not come into existence.

See Also: United Nations (UN); World War II.

■ **BREWER, DAVIS JOSIAH (1830-1910),** associate justice of the U.S. Supreme Court (1889-1910). Born in Smyrna, Turkey, where his parents were missionaries, Brewer was never comfortable with the growing power of the national government. He significantly influenced how the Court read the Constitution concerning federal regulatory authority over economic activities.

See Also: Supreme Court.

■ **BREYER, STEPHEN GERALD (1938-),** associate justice of the U.S. Supreme Court (1994-). Born in San Francisco, California, he attended Stanford University and Harvard Law School. Before joining the U.S. First Circuit Court of Appeals (1980), he combined teaching at Harvard (1967-80) with government service. Breyer served in the Justice Department (1965-67), as an assistant Watergate prosecutor (1973), and as counsel to the U.S. Senate Labor Committee (1974-75). An expert in federal administrative law, he is considered a member of the Court's liberal wing.

See Also: Supreme Court.

■ **BRIDGER, JIM (JAMES) (1804-81),** fur trader and mountain man. He was born in Richmond, Virginia, and raised near St. Louis, Missouri. Bridger accompanied Gen. William Ashley to the Rocky Mountains in 1822 and later worked for Jedediah Smith. He trapped for the Rocky Mountain Fur Company in the 1830s and worked for the American Fur Company after 1838. With his partner, Luis Vasquez, he built Fort Bridger in 1843, an important trading post that he was forced to give up by the Mormons. After several more years guiding western expeditions, Bridger

retired to Westport, Missouri, in 1868.

See Also: Frontier in American History.

■ **BROADWAY,** the main thoroughfare of New York City, which has become synonymous with theater and urban night life. Running the length of Manhattan, Broadway became by the mid-19th century the city's primary business avenue. Theaters, restaurants, and night clubs opened in its vicinity and clustered around Times Square after World War I. Broadway theaters became the nation's most famous and the top of the show business ladder for young actors and musicians. The entertainment industry, its audience, and colorful hangers-on fascinated the nation as symbols of both the attraction and dangers of the modern city. New York journalists, such as Damon Runyon and Walter Winchell, chronicled the glamour and gossip of the guys and dolls of Broadway, known as the Great White Way. Despite urban decline and competition from television in the 1950s and 1960s, Broadway continues as the hub of the nation's theater industry.

See Also: Theater.

BIBLIOGRAPHY: Breslin, Jimmy, *Damon Runyon* (Ticknor & Fields 1991); Dunlap, David W., *On Broadway* (Rizzoli 1990).

■ **BROOK FARM,** a utopian community in Concord, Massachusetts, that sought to integrate "high thinking" with "manual labor." Founded in 1841 by Bronson Alcott (father of Louisa May Alcott) and George Ripley, Brook Farm housed a number of prominent residents at times, including Ralph Waldo Emerson, Margaret Fuller, and Nathaniel Hawthorne. Residents worked in the fields and engaged in intellectual pursuits. In 1846, after a fire destroyed a communal building, the commune collapsed. Hawthorne wrote an 1852 novel, *The Blithedale Romance*, that criticized the utopian optimism of Brook Farm.

See Also: Alcott, Amos Bronson; Ripley, George; Utopian Communities.

■ **BROOKS, GWENDOLYN (1917-),** poet and activist. She was born in Topeka, Kansas. In her poetry, she often deals with the experiences of working-class African-American women, sometimes writing in the local dialect of Chicago's African-American neighborhoods. She was appointed to the National Institute of Arts and Letters and, in 1950, was the first African-American poet to win the Pulitzer Prize, awarded for *Annie Allen* (1949). Other works include *A Street in Bronzeville* (1945) and *Riot* (1970).

See Also: African Americans; Women in American History.

■ **BROOKS, PHILLIPS (1835-93),** Episcopal minister and bishop. Born in Boston, Massachusetts, Brooks believed that "preaching is the bringing of truth through personality." Aided by his size (six feet, four inches and 300 pounds) and rapid speech delivery, Brooks earned a reputation as an eloquent preacher at pulpits in Philadelphia and Boston. He is best known for his composition, "O Little Town of Bethlehem," a Christmas carol for his Sunday School.

See Also: Religion.

■ **BROWN, CHARLES BROCKDEN (1771-1810),** American novelist. Brown was born in Philadelphia, Pennsylvania. After studying law, he devoted himself to writing as a profession, one of the earliest American authors to do so, although he took over his father's importing business later in life. Brown submitted his early writings to *Columbian Magazine* and later edited a succession of his own literary magazines. Among Brown's novels are *Wieland* (1798), *Ormond* (1799), and *Arthur Mervyn* (1799-1800).

■ **BROWN, CHARLES FARRAR.** *See: Ward, Artemus.*

■ **BROWN, HENRY BILLINGS (1836-1913),** associate justice of the U.S. Supreme Court (1890-1906). Born in South Lee, Massachusetts, Brown often functioned as a referee among his more extreme colleagues. He authored the Court's opinion in *Plessy* v. *Ferguson* (1898), upholding the constitutionality of the segregationist "separate but equal" doctrine.

See Also: Plessy v. *Ferguson; Supreme Court.*

■ **BROWN, JIM (1936-),** football player and actor. He was born in St. Simons Island, Georgia. Brown played for the Cleveland Browns (1957-65) and is considered one of the greatest fullbacks in the history of the sport. He was inducted into the

Football Hall of Fame in 1971. Brown's acting roles include the movies *The Dirty Dozen* and *Ice Station Zebra*. He is the founder and president of the Amer-I-can Foundation, an organization dedicated to helping young urban black men find a future outside of poverty and violence.

See Also: African Americans; Football; Sports.

■ **BROWN, JOHN (1800-59),** abolitionist fanatic, who became a hero to Northern antislavery people after his execution following his seizure of the federal armory at Harpers Ferry, Virginia. Brown was born in Torrington, Connecticut, the son of abolitionist and "underground railway" agent Owen Brown and a mother who died in-

After seizing the Harpers Ferry armory in 1859 in an effort to incite a slave insurrection, John Brown was hanged for treason and became a martyr to antislavery forces. Sympathetic responses in the North to Brown's actions inflamed the South.

sane. He had failed at several occupations, including tanner, land speculator, and shepherd in 10 locations before moving in 1856 to the free-soil colony of Ossawatomie in the Kansas Territory. Soon captain of the local militia company, he became convinced of his messianic destiny to destroy slavery.

Believing that the institution had to be overthrown by force, Brown and a small group, including four of his sons, planned and carried out the massacre of five proslavery men on May 24, 1856. Retaliatory attacks against the colony soon forced Brown to leave Kansas and go back east.

There Brown enlisted the financial aid of several leading New York and New England abolitionists in his scheme to incite a slave revolt in the South. His plan was to establish a free state in the southern Appalachian Mountains from where the slave rebellion could spread southward. On Oct. 16, 1859, he and 18 men, 5 of them African Americans, seized the arsenal, armory, and bridges in Harpers Ferry, along with several civilian hostages. But no slaves rose up to join him, and the plan to inflame the countryside ingloriously collapsed. What remained of Brown's little band—several had been killed—was forced to surrender after a two-day battle to a U.S. Army detachment under Col. Robert E. Lee. Brown was quickly tried in Virginia's courts for treason against the state and criminal conspiracy, found guilty, and hanged.

His dignity and demeanor during his imprisonment and trial inspired the North, but his abortive plan struck terror in the South, which not only blamed the abolitionists, but also the "Black Republican" party. In the end, Brown's raid only further embittered the sections and hastened the coming of the Civil War. Brown's exploits inspired the most famous song of the Civil War era: "The Battle Hymn of the Republic."

—THOMAS E. SCHOTT

See Also: *Antislavery Movement; Bleeding Kansas; Civil War.*

BIBLIOGRAPHY: Oates, Stephen B., *To Purge This Land with Blood: A Biography of John Brown* (Harper & Row 1970).

■ **BROWN, OLYMPIA (1835-1926),** the first American woman to become a fully ordained minister. She was born in Prairie Ronde, Michigan. Also an activist in the woman suffrage movement, she served as president of the Federal Suffrage Association from 1903 to 1920 and was on the advisory council of the more militant Congressional Union after 1913.

■ ***BROWN V. BOARD OF EDUCATION OF TOPEKA (1954),*** landmark Supreme Court case that ended legalized racial segregation in the United States. Beginning in the mid-1930s, the National Association for the Advancement of Colored People (NAACP) challenged, in federal and state courts, the constitutionality of Jim Crow laws that legalized racial segregation in public facilities, including schools. The primary target of the NAACP was *Plessy* v. *Ferguson* (1896), in which the Supreme Court upheld the legality of racial segregation in public accommodations. The NAACP cases resulted ultimately in a series of rulings in which the Court required segregated schools to make all facilities equal.

When *Brown* was first argued in 1952, the Court did not debate the merits of ending school segregation but the pace. In the summer of 1953, Earl Warren became chief justice and ordered the Court to make two rulings on the *Brown* case. A year later, in his short and clear opinion of the unanimous decision, Warren stated that segregated educational facilities violated the equal protection clause of the 14th Amendment. In 1955 the Court established guidelines for federal district courts to monitor school desegregation but equivocated on the pace of change.

Because of *Brown's* ineffectual language regarding the rate of desegregation, change came slowly and was met with resistance. Yet the decision eventually became an enormous catalyst for social change and a symbol of the civil rights struggle in America.

See Also: *Civil Rights Movement; Marshall, Thurgood; Plessy v. Ferguson; Supreme Court.*

BIBLIOGRAPHY: Kluger, Richard, *Simple Justice: The History of Brown v. Board of Education and Black America's Struggle for Equality* (Vintage Books 1977); Sarat, Austin, ed., *Race, Law, and Culture: Reflections on Brown v. Board of Education* (Oxford Univ. Press 1997).

■ **BROWNSVILLE AFFAIR,** incident of racial injustice. In 1906 Companies B, C, and D of the 1st

Battalion, 25th Infantry (Colored), U.S. Army, were assigned to Fort Brown, Texas. Citizens of nearby Brownsville resented the presence of the African-American troops, and racial tensions were high. Two weeks later, on the night of August 13, numerous shots were fired in town, killing a white bartender and injuring a white police officer. Shell casings from the army's Springfield rifles suggested the involvement of nearby troops. Despite evidence of the black companies' soldiers' innocence, Pres. Theodore Roosevelt ordered that the soldiers identify the guilty individuals. When they did not comply, he ordered the dishonorable discharge of all three companies, without due process. In 1971, Congress reopened the investigation and found reason to believe the soldiers had been framed for the violence, and the dishonorable discharges were rescinded.

BIBLIOGRAPHY: Weaver, John D., *The Brownsville Raid* (Norton 1970).

■ BRYAN, WILLIAM JENNINGS (1860-1925),

politician, presidential candidate, and secretary of state. He was born in Salem, Illinois. After graduating from Illinois College in 1881, Bryan studied for two years at Union College of Law in Chicago. On admission to the bar, he practiced law in Jacksonville, Illinois. In 1887 he moved to Lincoln, Nebraska, where he immediately entered politics and rose to prominence in the state Democratic party. Elected to Congress in 1890, he served two terms. Defending farmers who were beset by falling prices and rising debts, Bryan asserted that deflation could be curbed if the country returned to a bimetalic standard, where silver would be coined at a ratio of 16:1 to gold. At the 1896 Democratic National Convention in Chicago, the 36-year-old Bryan gave a rousing address, concluding with the memorable exhortation, "You shall not crucify mankind upon a cross of gold." The electrified crowd promptly nominated him for president and in effect co-opted the Populists, a third party that pressed for the unlimited coinage of silver. Dubbed the "Boy Orator," Bryan traveled throughout the country, attracting large crowds eager to hear the most charismatic speaker of the day. But his evangelical style and opposition to the gold standard, a symbol of economic stability, alienated many voters, and the

Republican candidate, William McKinley, won the pivotal election. Bryan retained a large following and ran unsuccessfully for president again in 1900 and 1908. Known as the "Great Commoner," he championed progressive reforms such as a federal income tax, the eight-hour-workday, and women's suffrage. Named secretary of state by Pres. Woodrow Wilson in 1913, Bryan, who proved most effective in domestic politics, was out of his element in foreign affairs. He helped engineer passage of the Federal Reserve Act (1913), but his refusal, as a teetotaler, to serve alcoholic beverages at state functions met public criticism. Committed to neutrality during World War I, he resigned in 1915 in protest against Wilson's policies toward Germany. In his final decade Bryan served as spokesman for the Fundamentalist movement, a conservative religious reaction to modernism in American life. He assisted the pros-

"You shall not press down upon the brow of labor this crown of thorns," William Jennings Bryan vowed at the 1896 Democratic party convention where he argued in favor of the free coinage of silver. "You shall not crucify mankind upon a cross of gold."

ecution in the Scopes trial (July 1925), in which the state of Tennessee prosecuted a biology teacher for teaching evolution. Under intense questioning from defense attorney Clarence Darrow, Bryan's literal interpretation of the Bible and ignorance of modern science were exposed to ridicule. It was his last public act, for he died less than a week later.

—MARTHA J. KING

See Also: Gilded Age; Progressivism; Scopes Trial.

BIBLIOGRAPHY: Cherny, Robert W., *Righteous Case: The Life of William Jennings Bryan* (Little, Brown 1985); Garraty, John, "Bryan: The Progressives, Part I" *American Heritage* (Dec. 1961); Levine, Lawrence W., *Defender of the Faith: William Jennings Bryan: The Last Decade, 1915-1925* (Oxford Univ. Press 1965); Long, J. C., *Bryan: The Great Commoner* (Appleton 1928); Springen, Donald K., *William Jennings Bryan, Orator of Small-Town America* (Greenwood 1991).

■ **BRYANT, WILLIAM CULLEN (1794-1878),** editor and Romantic poet. Born in Cummington, Massachusetts, Bryant attended Williams College and practiced law in Great Barrington, Massachusetts, from 1815 to 1825. During this time he began publishing poetry in the Romantic tradition, including "Thanatopsis" and "To a Waterfowl," both published in the *North American Review* in 1817. In 1829 Bryant became the co-owner and coeditor of the *New York Evening Post*, a position he held until the year of his death.

■ **BUCHANAN, JAMES (1791-1868),** 15th president of the United States (1857-61). Born near Mercersburg, Pennsylvania, Buchanan became a lawyer. He began his political career as a Federalist but in the 1820s became a Jackson Democrat. Buchanan had an extensive career in national government service before becoming president. He was a congressman (1821-31), ambassador to Russia (1831-33), U.S. senator (1834-45), secretary of state under Pres. James K. Polk (1845-49), and ambassador to Britain (1854-56).

Buchanan was elected president with the support of the South. In the worsening sectional conflict over slavery, he invariably sided with the proslavery forces. In Kansas, for example, he was willing to accept the Lecompton constitution.

James Buchanan, who won the presidential election in 1856, with the support of the South, generally supported the southern cause during his term and left office in 1861 with the nation on the verge of civil war.

During the secession crisis at the end of his term, Buchanan said states had no constitutional right to secede but at the same time maintained the president had no power to do anything about it.

See Also: Lecompton Constitution; President of the United States; Secession.

■ **BUCK, PEARL (1892-1973),** author. Born in Hillsborough, West Virginia, the daughter of Presbyterian missionaries, she grew up in China and taught at the University of Nanking in the 1920s. Her experiences in rural northern China became the basis of her prolific body of fiction. *The Good Earth* won the Pulitzer Prize in 1931. She then won the 1938 Nobel Prize for Literature for her translation of *All Men Are Brothers* (1937). In the 1940s and 1950s, she published *Asia*, a magazine that was the primary source of information on Asian culture and politics for many Americans.

See Also: Novel; Women in American History.

■ **BUENA VISTA, BATTLE OF (1847),** American victory during the Mexican War. With an American force of fewer than 5,000 led by General Zachary Taylor threatening northeastern Mexico, Mexican President Antonio López de Santa Anna raised an army of almost 20,000. The two armies clashed in February near the hacienda of Buena Vista, west of Monterey. From his excellent defensive positions, Taylor repelled most of the Mexican attacks. Although the battle was a tactical stalemate, Santa Anna eventually opted to retreat to Mexico City, thus surrendering northern Mexico.

See Also: Mexican War; Taylor, Zachary.

■ **BUENOS AIRES CONFERENCE (1936),** an inter-American forum. Opened by Pres. Franklin D. Roosevelt of the United States, it proposed consultations between American states in case of external threat. Additionally, a program was adopted for exchange of graduate students and teachers between the United States and other American nations.

■ **BUFFALO,** misnomer for the North American wild bison (*Bison bison*), unrelated to the true buffalo of Asia. Measuring up to 7 feet at the shoulders, 12 feet from head to tail, and weighing nearly a ton, this massive bovine filled the Great Plains and migrated as far east as the Virginia tidewater, probably numbering some 40 million at their peak. Indian adoption of the horse in the 17th and 18th centuries made buffalo hunting extremely efficient and allowed the development of complex high cultures among the Great Plains Indians. Despite such hunting, the size of the buffalo population remained relatively constant until the Overland Trail migration of the 1840s and 1850s divided them into separate northern and southern herds. Disaster struck in the 1870s and 1880s as American hunters of meat and hides practically exterminated the herds and as buffalo grazing lands were taken over by farms and cattle ranches. Protected by the Canadian and U.S. governments, a few small herds exist today in national parks.

See Also: Frontier in American History; Indians of North America.

BIBLIOGRAPHY: Barsness, Larry, *Heads, Hides, and Horns: The Compleat Buffalo Book* (Texas Christian Univ. Press 1985).

■ **BUFFALO BILL.** *See:* Cody, William ("Buffalo Bill").

■ **BUFFALO SOLDIERS,** African-American U.S. Cavalry soldiers who served throughout the Southwest after the end (1865) of the Civil War. The name, adopted by the 9th Cavalry, an all-black unit, is said to have been given to the soldiers by American Indians. During the Spanish-American War (1898), the 9th, along with another all-black unit, the 10th Cavalry, was credited by many with ensuring the survival and victory of the fabled Rough Riders at the Battle of Las Guasimas in Cuba.

See Also: African Americans; Frontier in American History.

Very few buffalo survived the war waged by hide hunters after the Civil War. By the 1880s they were on the verge of extinction.

In 1866, Congress authorized the organization of African-American troops into the 9th and 10th Cavalries. Known as the Buffalo Soldiers, they fought in the Apache wars until Geronimo's capture in 1886.

BULFINCH, CHARLES (1763-1844), prominent Federal-period architect. Bulfinch was born in Boston, Massachusetts, where he practiced architecture and served in civic positions for much of his life. He was one of the first American architects to use a thorough series of drawings as a plan for construction and thus contributed to the early professionalization of architecture. Bulfinch helped shape the character of Boston's urban landscape with designs for the Federal Street Theater (1794), Tontine Crescent (1794), Massachusetts State House (1798), and Massachusetts General Hospital (1820), as well as for five churches and numerous houses. Examples of buildings designed outside of Boston are the Connecticut State House in Hartford (1796) and the Maine State House in Augusta (1829). In 1817 President James Monroe appointed Bulfinch to replace Benjamin Henry Latrobe as architect in charge of rebuilding the U.S. Capitol,

which had been burned in the War of 1812; Bulfinch worked in Washington, D.C., until 1830, when he returned to Boston.

See Also: Architecture; Capitol; Latrobe, Benjamin.

BULGE (ARDENNES), BATTLE OF THE (1944-45), last major German offensive of World War II. Using elaborate deception (including a commando unit disguised as U.S. troops), the Germans attacked the U.S. First Army in the Ardennes forest on Dec. 16, 1944, seeking to divide the Allied armies and retake Antwerp. The surprised Americans were driven back 50 miles, but their ferocious defense at St. Vith and Batogne slowed the German advance, which, by Christmas, had all but stopped. Counterattacks recaptured the "bulge" in the Allied line by the end of January 1945.

See Also: World War II.

BULL MOOSE PARTY, the familiar name for the first of three 20th-century Progressive parties, grown out of the intense factionalism within the Republican party in 1912. Denied the presidential nomination of his party, which went to the more conservative incumbent, William Howard Taft, former president Theodore Roosevelt formed his own third party. Soon nicknamed the Bull Moose party, its platform was based on Progressive demands such as restriction of child labor, direct primaries, and women's suffrage. While Roosevelt received far more votes than Taft, the election went to the Democrat, Woodrow Wilson. Most of Roosevelt's supporters soon returned to the Republican party, and the Bull Moose party ceased to exist by 1917.

See Also: Political Parties; Presidential Elections; Progressive Party; Roosevelt, Theodore.

BULL RUN, BATTLES OF (1861, 1862), two Civil War battles fought near the Virginia railway junction at Manassas. The first (July 21, 1861) was the war's first large-scale engagement. In a disorganized fight between untested soldiers, a strong Confederate counterattack and headlong Union retreat dispelled Northern hopes that the war could be quickly won, while Southern confidence soared. In the second battle, frontal attacks by the Union army on Aug. 29, 1862, failed to carry the Confederate positions. The next day an attack on the Union left flank almost routed the Union forces, which retreated toward Washington, enabling Confederate Gen. Robert E. Lee to invade Maryland.

See Also: Civil War.

■ **BUNCHE, RALPH JOHNSON (1904-71),** diplomat. He was born in Detroit, Michigan. After a professorship at Howard University (1928-41), Bunche served in the Office of Special Services (OSS) (1941-44) and the State Department (1944-47). He was appointed to the United Nations in 1946 as the head of the Trusteeship Division. Bunche's skills as a negotiator were invaluable during crises in the Suez (1956), the Congo (1960), Yemen (1963), and Cyprus (1964). In 1950, he was awarded the Nobel Peace Prize for his efforts to help settle Arab-Israeli disputes in the Middle East.

See Also: Civil Rights Movement.

■ **BUNDLING,** courtship custom that allowed engaged couples, fully clothed, to sleep in the same bed. While it is believed that the practice originated in Wales, it was also common in New England during the 18th century.

■ **BUNKER HILL, BATTLE OF (1775),** the first major battle of the Revolutionary War, fought on June 17. The battle actually took place on Breed's Hill in Charlestown, Massachusetts. The Americans, ensconced behind earthworks at the crest of the hill, were ordered not to fire at the British until they could see "the whites of their eyes" and repulsed two attacks before being dislodged. The British suffered nearly three times as many casualties as the Americans.

See Also: Revolution, American.

It took three assaults for Gen. William Howe and British forces to seize the heights from the Americans in the Battle of Bunker Hill on June 17, 1775. John Trumbull's 1786 painting of the battle shows the Americans defending the crest of the hill.

BUNYAN, PAUL, mythic American lumberjack. Paul Bunyan is legendary for chopping down whole forests in a day, while his blue ox, Babe, made lakes with his hoofprints. Bunyan first appeared as a fictional character in the *Detroit News Tribune* in 1910. In 1914, W. B. Laughead made Bunyan the hero of a promotional pamphlet for the Red River Lumber Company and furthered Bunyan's glory in *The Marvelous Exploits of Paul Bunyan* in 1922. James Stevens secured Bunyan's fame with *Paul Bunyan* (1925) and *The Saginaw Paul Bunyan* (1932).

BURGER, WARREN EARL (1907-95), 15th chief justice of the United States (1969-86). Burger attended the University of Minnesota and in 1931 received his law degree from the St. Paul College of Law. In his native St. Paul, Burger practiced law until 1953, specializing in real estate and corporate work. A long-time supporter of Minnesota politician Harold Stassen, Burger, a Republican, received attention from party leaders for his work during the 1948 and 1952 presidential campaigns. In 1955 Pres. Dwight D. Eisenhower appointed Burger to the U.S. Court of Appeals for the District of Columbia. During his years on that court, Burger became a critic of the liberal Earl Warren Supreme Court. In particular, he tended to oppose decisions that expanded the rights of accused persons, as in *Miranda* v. *Arizona* (1966).

Seeking to appoint a conservative and strict constructionist as the replacement for Chief Justice Earl Warren, Pres. Richard Nixon named Burger to head the Supreme Court in 1969. During his 17 years as chief justice, Burger proved to be a centrist conservative who did not seek to reverse any of the Warren Court's major rulings. Although the Burger Court was on the whole more restrained than the Warren Court, it also enacted important liberal decisions, such as *Roe* v. *Wade* (1973), which made abortion legal. Perhaps Burger's most important legacy was his impact on court reform and on the modernization of the Supreme Court's administration.

See Also: Roe v. Wade; Supreme Court.
BIBLIOGRAPHY: Schwartz, Herman, ed., *The Burger Years: Rights and Wrongs in the Supreme Court, 1969-1986* (Viking 1987).

BURLESQUE, a popular form of bawdy stage entertainment. Burlesque gained a foothold in the United States with *The Black Crook* (1866), a melodrama featuring the British Blondes, the first female troupe to wear tights on stage. In later years, burlesque became identified with lewd humor, striptease dancers, and general immorality and was a frequent target of censorship campaigns. New York City denied new licenses to its burlesque houses in 1937.

BURLINGAME TREATY (1868), agreement between the United States and China. It established free immigration between the countries; guaranteed the right of travel, residence, and education to citizens of either country; and pledged U.S. noninterference in Chinese internal affairs. The immigration clause was later abbrogated by the Chinese Exclusion Act of 1882, and the U.S. directly intervened in Chinese domestic affairs by sending troops to Beijing during the Boxer Rebellion of 1900.

See Also: Boxer Rebellion; Chinese Exclusion Act; Immigration.

BURMA CAMPAIGN, American-Anglo effort in World War II to recapture Burma from the Japanese. In spring 1942 the Japanese had gained control by cutting off the "Burma Road" between India and China. Resupply of Chinese forces could only be realized by a tremendous air effort to overfly the Himalayas, a route known as the "hump." Allied land offenses were repeatedly repulsed by Japanese counteroffensives until Burma's capital, Rangoon, fell to Allied troops in May 1945.

See Also: World War II.

BURNHAM, DANIEL (1846-1912), architect and urban planner. Burnham was born in Henderson, New York, but settled in Chicago. Designer of the Flatiron building in New York City (1903) and Union Station in Washington, D.C. (1907-10), Burnham served as the chief of construction for the World's Columbian Exposition in Chicago in 1893. After that success he served as chair of the committee to oversee the development of Washington, D.C., in 1901, and consulted on the planning of San Francisco and Chicago.

See Also: Architecture.

■ **BURR, AARON (1756-1836),** politician and vice president of the United States (1801-05). Born to an austere Protestant family in Newark, New Jersey, Burr, a descendant of Jonathan Edwards, attended the College of New Jersey (now Princeton). During the American Revolution he participated in the invasion of Canada and was an officer on George Washington's staff. Burr resigned his commission as lieutenant colonel in 1779 to complete his law studies.

After practicing law in New York City, Burr served in the state assembly, was state attorney general, and was elected to the U.S. Senate in 1791. With growing political ambition, Burr strengthened the organization of the state Republican Party and helped secure a surprise victory over the Federalists in the 1800 election. It was the intent of the party leaders to make Jefferson president and Burr vice president, but confusion in the electoral college led to a tie vote. The election was thrown into the House of Representatives, where the Federalist Alexander Hamilton helped secure the victory of Jefferson, whom he regarded as the lesser of two evils. Burr was named vice president on the 36th ballot.

Burr ran for governor of New York in 1804, and once again, Hamilton played a role in denying him victory. Stung by Hamilton's slurs, Burr challenged him to a duel, and on July 11, 1804, Hamilton was fatally shot by Burr in Weehawken, New Jersey.

Burr resurfaced from a self-imposed exile in an apparent attempt, with Gen. James Wilkinson, to wrest Mexico away from Spain and the western territories from the United States. Arrested on charges of treason, Burr was acquitted at the conclusion of a landmark trial in 1807, and his role in the affair remains a mystery. Scorned for his schemes and reviled as Hamilton's killer, Burr moved to Europe, only to return in 1812 to resurrect his New York law practice. He remained out of politics for the rest of his life.

—GUY NELSON

See Also: Hamilton, Alexander; Presidential Elections; Vice President of the United States.
BIBLIOGRAPHY: Lomask, Milton, *Aaron Burr,* 2 vols. (Farrar, Straus, & Giroux 1979, 1982).

■ **BURROUGHS, WILLIAM (1914-97),** writer and inspiration to the Beat Generation. Burroughs was born in St. Louis, Missouri, and attended Harvard University. Discharged from the U.S. Army for psychiatric reasons during World War II, Burroughs was unrooted, both geographically and emotionally. His first book, *Junkie: Confessions of an Unredeemed Drug Addict* (1953), described this phase of his life. Burroughs's best-known work, *Naked Lunch* (1959), was an autobiographical nonnarrative novel.

See Also: Beats, The.

■ **BURTON, HAROLD HITZ (1888-1964),** associate justice of the Supreme Court (1945-58). Born in Jamaica Plains, Massachusetts, he received his law degree from Harvard Law School (1912), then practiced law in Cleveland, Ohio, and other cities before serving in World War I. He returned to practice law in Cleveland and became active in local politics, serving three terms as mayor before his election to the U.S. Senate in 1940 as a Democrat. In 1945 he was appointed to the Supreme Court by Pres. Harry

Thomas Jefferson's vice president, Aaron Burr, became a fugitive in 1804 after he killed his arch political enemy, Alexander Hamilton, in a pistol duel.

S. Truman. Known as a strict constructionist and as an anticommunist, Burton voted to uphold loyalty-oath legislation and, in *Dennis* v. *United States* (1951), the conviction of Communist party leaders. In racial segregation cases that reached the Supreme Court, he gradually became more liberal, culminating in his vote to overturn school segregation in *Brown* v. *Board of Education of Topeka* in 1954. He retired from the Court in 1958.

See Also: *Brown v. Board of Education of Topeka; Supreme Court.*

■ **BUSH, GEORGE H. W. (1924-),** 41st president of the United States (1989-93). Born in Milton, Massachusetts, Bush served as a navy aviator during World War II. In September 1944, he was shot down over the Pacific, losing several members of his command. After the war, he graduated from Yale University and entered the oil business in Texas. He ran unsuccessfully as a Republican for the Senate in 1964, but in 1966 he won a seat in the House, where he served two terms before losing the 1970 Senate race to Democrat Lloyd Bentsen. Bush then entered a decade of service in a series of appointive positions, including ambassador to the United Nations and director of the Central Intelligence Agency. In 1980, Bush ran for the Republican nomination for president but lost to Ronald Reagan, who chose him as his running mate.

Bush's eight years as vice president (1981-89) were highlighted by an unswerving loyalty. Although consequently branded a lightweight without an agenda of his own, a determined Bush nevertheless captured the 1988 Republican nomination for president. Behind at one point by 20 points in the polls, Bush was uncharacteristically brutal in the presidential campaign. Despite a pledge in his acceptance speech to seek a "kinder, gentler nation," Bush savaged his Democratic opponent, Gov. Michael Dukakis, as being soft on crime and unpatriotic, and this negative campaign led to Bush's convincing victory in November.

Presidency. On the domestic front, Bush had a mixed record as president. He had to renege his promise not to raise taxes in order to lower the federal deficit, but this decision had produced results by 1992. He encountered public resentment over the dissolution of many of the nation's savings and loan banks, but his Office of Thrift Supervision began the process of repairing that industry. In foreign policy, however, most contemporary observers considered as successes his handling of the fall of the Soviet empire in 1989, the U.S. incursion in Panama later that year, and the brief Persian Gulf War of 1990-91.

Nevertheless, Bush was constantly criticized for not having a vision for the country. His defeat in his bid for reelection in 1992 at the hands of Gov. Bill Clinton of Arkansas was caused in equal measure by this lack of vision, a sharp economic downturn, Clinton's skill before the cameras, public distrust with politicians (which fed into the debilitating third-party candidacy of H. Ross Perot), and Bush's lethargic campaign.

—JOHN ROBERT GREENE

See Also: *Clinton, William Jefferson Blythe (Bill); Cold War; Panama Invasion; Persian Gulf War; Presidential Elections; President of the United States; Reagan, Ronald Wilson.*

After serving two terms as Ronald Reagan's vice president, George Bush became president in 1989. His popularity peaked during the 1991 Persian Gulf War, but Bush lost his reelection bid in 1992 to the politically centrist Democrat, Bill Clinton.

BIBLIOGRAPHY: Barilleaux, Ryan J., and Mary E. Stuckey, *Leadership and the Bush Presidency* (Praeger 1992); Merwin, David, *Presidency* (St. Martins 1996).

■ **BUSINESS REGULATION** was common during the colonial period, when the British government regulated both trade and industry and the colonies supervised business within their borders. The American Revolution swept away British legislation, but regulation continued. In the early republic, states used their power to charter corporations in order to regulate the service, safety, and rates of companies, as well as subsidizing economic activities considered in the public interest (such as transportation). The federal government, however, was limited to the supervision of foreign commerce and the regulation of interstate steamboat operations.

The federal government began to play a larger role in the late 19th century. In 1886, the U.S. Supreme Court ruled that states lacked the power to regulate interstate railroads, and Congress responded by passing the Interstate Commerce Act (1887). Enforcement was vested in the Interstate Commerce Commission (ICC), to which presidents appointed railroad men, thus rendering regulation ineffective. Similarly, the Sherman Antitrust Act (1890), passed to mollify farmers and small businessmen horrified at the growth of huge corporate power, was stripped of its potency when in 1895 the Supreme Court ruled that the sugar trust, which controlled 98 percent of the business, was not operating in restraint of trade.

The first effective federal regulation came during the presidency of Theodore Roosevelt (1901-09). In 1903, his administration sought and won the power to establish a Bureau of Corporations. Its investigations led to dozens of successful antitrust suits over the next two decades. Roosevelt pushed Congress to strengthen the independence of the ICC, and also won passage of the Pure Food and Drug Act and the Meat Inspection Act in 1906. The subsequent administration of Pres. Woodrow Wilson (1913-21) secured the passage of several substantial regulatory measures, including the Federal Reserve Act (1913), the Federal Trade Commission Act (1914), and the Clayton Antitrust Act (1914), which strengthened the Sherman Act. The most impressive period of regulation, however, came during World War I, when the War Industries Board essentially took over management of the entire economy.

The economy was liberated from federal control after the war, but the wartime experience provided something of a model for Pres. Franklin D. Roosevelt's New Deal, which assumed power at the nadir of the Great Depression in 1933. The first of Roosevelt's acts to spur economic recovery was the National Industrial Recovery Act (1933), which empowered the president to set up codes of fair competition within dozens of industries, with overall regulatory authority vested in a National Recovery Administration (NRA). The NRA ended in 1935 when it was declared unconstitutional by the Supreme Court. Other measures had more lasting effect. The Emergency Banking Act (1933) established the Federal Deposit Insurance Corporation (FDIC), which provided a measured federal guarantee of individual bank accounts, and the Securities Exchange Act (1934) created the Securities and Exchange Commission, which regulated the nation's stock exchanges and protected investors from insider trading and broker misrepresentation. The Agricultural Adjustment Act (1933) represented a major manipulation of agricultural markets, making the federal government a guarantor of "parity prices" for agricultural commodities. The National Labor Relations Act (1935) protected the right of workers to organize unions, and the Fair Labor Standards Act (1938) set minimum wages and maximum working hours. During World War II, the federal government again assumed control of the entire economy, this time through the War Production Board, but in 1945 these regulations were lifted.

Many of the New Deal measures continued as permanent structural features of the economy. Perhaps the most dramatic economic intervention of the postwar period was the imposition of wage and price controls by Pres. Richard Nixon in 1971, but this experiment was short-lived. The main trend of the last three decades of the 20th century has been a turn away from federal regulation, first under the administration of Pres. Jimmy Carter (1977-81), then accelerating during the presidencies of Ronald Reagan (1981-89) and George Bush (1989-93). The deregulation of the savings and loan industry led to massive speculation and institutional collapses that cost taxpayers billions of dollars. The Democratic opposition criticized the extent of the federal pullback, but the trend to deregulate continued during the term of Pres. Bill Clinton (1993-). Yet the main governmental power over business remained unchanged, as did the enormous spending that makes the federal government the nation's leading consumer. Government decisions continue to determine the economic health of the American economy.

—JOHN MACK FARAGHER

See Also: Antitrust Cases; Antitrust Legislation; New Deal; Roosevelt, Theodore.

BIBLIOGRAPHY: Freyer, Tony, *Regulating Big Business: Antitrust in Great Britain and America, 1880 to 1990* (Cambridge Univ. Press 1992); Goldin, Claudia, and Gary D. Libecap, eds., *The Regulated Economy: A Historical Approach to Political Economy* (Univ. of Chicago Press 1994); Kolko, Gabriel, *Railroads and Regulation: 1877-1916* (Princeton Univ. Press 1965); McCraw, Thomas K., *Prophets of Regulation: Charles Francis Adams, Louis D. Brandeis, James M. Landis, Alfred E. Kahn* (Harvard Univ. Press 1984).

■ **BUTKUS, DICK (1942-),** football player. A middle linebacker, he was born in Chicago, earned All-America honors at the University of Illinois, and starred for the National Football League's Chicago Bears (1965-73).

See Also: Football; Sports.

■ **BUTLER, BENJAMIN FRANKLIN (1818-93),** Union general and politician. Born in Deerfield, New Hampshire, Butler was active as a Democrat. Made a Union general in the Civil War for political reasons, Butler became the military commander of New Orleans (1862), where his authoritarianism alienated many. Later Butler unsuccessfully commanded in southern Virginia. He served as an influential congressman from Massachusetts (1867-75, 1877-79) and governor (1882-84) and was the presidential candidate of the Greenback and Anti-Monopoly parties (1884).

See Also: Civil War; Presidential Elections.

■ **BUTLER, NICHOLAS MURRAY (1862-1947),** president of Columbia University in New York City (1901-45). Born in Elizabeth, New Jersey, he graduated from Columbia (1882), joined the faculty (1885), and helped found Columbia's Teachers College (1888) before becoming the university's president. A social as well as educational activist, Butler was president of the Carnegie Endowment for International Peace (1925-45) and in 1931 shared the Nobel Peace Prize with urban reformer Jane Addams.

■ **BUTLER, PIERCE (1866-1939),** associate justice of the U.S. Supreme Court (1923-39). Born in Pine Bend, Minnesota, he practiced law in St. Paul, representing railroads such as James J. Hill's Great Northern and making a reputation by attacking "radical" professors at the University of Minnesota. A conservative Democrat, Butler was one of the "Four Horsemen" on the Court in the 1930s, implacable foes of Pres. Franklin D. Roosevelt's New Deal initiatives.

See Also: New Deal; Supreme Court.

■ **BYRD, RICHARD EVELYN (1888-1957),** American polar explorer. Born in Winchester, Virginia, he attended the U.S. Naval Academy and became a navy pilot. Commander Byrd and Floyd Bennett claimed to be the first to fly over the North Pole on May 9, 1926. This feat was disputed on the basis of weather conditions and the speed of the plane. Byrd went on to lead five Antarctic expeditions between 1928 and 1956. His scientific base, Little America, provided support for his flight to the South Pole and back on Nov. 29, 1929.

See Also: Exploration and Discovery.

■ **BYRD, WILLIAM (1652-1704),** English planter and trader in Virginia. Born in London, England, Byrd inherited his American estate from a maternal uncle, Thomas Stegge, Jr. At 18, he traveled to Virginia, acquired his uncle's fortune, married a young widow, and began a family. Remote and vulnerable to native attacks, the 1,800 acres of Byrd's plantation were operated by a combination of slaves and indentured servants, some of whom died in the Indian raids of 1675-76. A frontier planter, Byrd rode with Nathaniel Bacon in his unauthorized reprisals against the Indians (1676) but did not become embroiled in the recriminations after the failure of the rebellion. Instead, he turned proximity to the Indians to his advantage by developing trade relationships that made him a leading trader in the Virginia colony. Coupled with the production of tobacco on his plantation, Byrd's trade business gave him the economic and political power to rise to the top of Virginia society. The family remained influential in Virginia through the 20th century.

See Also: *Virginia.*

■ **BYRNES, JAMES FRANCIS (1879-1972),** associate justice of the U.S. Supreme Court (1941-42) and secretary of state (1945-47). Born in Charleston, South Carolina, he represented South Carolina in the House (1911-25) and Senate (1931-41). A powerful legislative ally of Pres. Franklin D. Roosevelt, Byrnes was rewarded with a Supreme Court appointment but resigned to become director of economic stabilization (1942-43) and subsequently director of war mobilization (1943-45). He served as governor of South Carolina (1951-55).

See Also: *Supreme Court.*

C

CABEZA DE VACA, ÁLVAR NÚÑEZ (c. 1490-c. 1560), Spanish explorer. During the Narváez expedition to Florida in 1527-28, a party of 300 soldiers, including second-in-command Cabeza de Vaca, became separated from their support ships. The large party built makeshift vessels and attempted to return to New Spain (Mexico) but was shipwrecked at Galveston Island, Texas. Reduced by disease, starvation, and Indian attack, the stragglers were enslaved by the local Karankawas. In 1534 the remnant, including Cabeza de Vaca, a Moorish slave named Estavanico, and two other Spaniards, set out overland to reach New Spain. Cabeza de Vaca earned his small party assistance by acting as medicine man to local Indians during a two-year odyssey. Escorted by Indians, Cabeza de Vaca encountered a Spanish slave-raiding party in northern Mexico in 1536. Stories told by Cabeza de Vaca helped generate the tale of the gold-rich Seven Cities of Cíbola, spurring interest in the North American interior.

See Also: Estavanico; Exploration and Discovery.
BIBLIOGRAPHY: Bannon, John Francis, *The Spanish Borderlands Frontier, 1513-1821* (Univ. of New Mexico Press 1974).

CABINET, advisory council to the president, whose members are the secretaries of the executive departments and must be confirmed by the Senate. Although the Constitution only alluded to presidential advisers, George Washington created a functioning cabinet during his first administration. With Alexander Hamilton as the dominant member, the cabinet was officially forged in 1793 when Washington sought extensive counsel from the department heads during a series of foreign and domestic controversies.

Although every subsequent president has formed and used a cabinet, the effectiveness of the institution and its members has varied greatly. During the 19th century, presidents such as Monroe and Polk placed great importance on the cabinet, while Jackson undermined his cabinet by convening it only 16 times in 8 years. In addition, members increasingly represented political factions, often resulting in inter-cabinet conflict. Some presidents responded to this discord by using their own personal advisers, as did Grover Cleveland with his "Fishing Cabinet."

During the first two decades of the 20th century, presidents responded to the increasing complexity of domestic and foreign policy issues by expanding the cabinet. Franklin D. Roosevelt appointed the first woman and used his cabinet as a political instrument. During the postwar years the importance of the cabinet fluctuated, while Senate confirmations of cabinet members became battlegrounds of partisan politics. Apart from responsibility to the president, cabinet members answer to Congress and political interest groups, as well as administering the bureaucracy of their departments.

BIBLIOGRAPHY: Fenno, Richard F., Jr., *The President's Cabinet: An Analysis in the Period from Wilson to Eisenhower* (Harvard Univ. Press 1959).

CABLE, GEORGE WASHINGTON (1844-1925), local color writer. Originally from New Orleans, Louisiana, Cable served in the Confederate army during the Civil War. In 1879 he published his first book, *Old Creole Days*, a collection of stories including "Sieur George" and "Belles Damoiselles Plantation." He then wrote several novels, including *The Grandissimes* (1880) and *Dr. Sevier* (1884). Cable's support of civil rights for African Americans was controversial in the South during the Reconstruction era, and he moved to Northampton, Massachusetts, in 1884.

CABOT, JOHN (c. 1450-c. 1499) and **CABOT, SEBASTIAN (c. 1483-1557),** navigators and explorers. John Cabot, born in Genoa, sailed from Bristol, England, with the backing of King Henry VII in 1497. He most likely landed at Newfoundland on June 24. His landing formed the basis for

English claims to North America. Cabot believed he had reached the Asian coast. He sailed across the Atlantic on a second voyage in 1498 but was lost at sea. His son, Sebastian, carried on his father's efforts to secure a Northwest Passage to Asia. In 1509 the expedition with which he sailed may have reached Hudson Bay. Sebastian explored the Río de la Plata, Brazil, in 1526-30 for Spain. Returning to England in 1548, he served as governor of the Muscovy Company, opening trade with Russia. Cabot, a skilled cartographer, continued to push for a northern sea route to the Orient and aided others in their search for a Northwest Passage.

See Also: Exploration and Discovery; Northwest Passage.

BIBLIOGRAPHY: Morison, Samuel Eliot, *The Great Explorers: The European Discovery of America* (Oxford Univ. Press 1978).

■ **CABRILLO, JUAN RODRIGUEZ DE (1495-1543),** first European explorer of the Pacific coast of North America. Born in Portugal, he arrived in Mexico in 1520 and accompanied Cortés in the conquest of the Aztecs. In 1542, he was placed in command of two ships and sent north along the Pacific coast and instructed to find the western mouth of the Northwest Passage that European powers had long been seeking. He entered the bay of San Diego, sailed up the Santa Barbara Channel, and continued north as far as Point Reyes, although he missed the entrances to Monterey and San Francisco harbors. Contracting an infection, Cabrillo died on board ship. The expedition continued north to the Oregon coast before returning to New Spain.

See Also: Exploration and Discovery.

■ **CADILLAC, ANTOINE DE LA MOTHE (1658-1730),** French explorer and colonial governor in North America. He commanded (1694-97) the key fur trade post at Michilimackinac, near the convergence of Lakes Superior, Michigan, and Huron. Ostensibly to protect the valuable fur trade from the British, Cadillac received permission to found a fort at what became Detroit, Michigan, in 1701, remaining there until 1710 and enriching himself smuggling to the English. In 1710 French officials appointed him governor of Louisiana. He was recalled in 1717.

See Also: Exploration and Discovery; French Colonies; Fur Trade.

■ **CAGE, JOHN (1912-92),** avant-garde composer and performer. Born in Los Angeles, California, he studied composition in the United States and Europe. His works shattered both popular and scholarly conceptions of music, incorporating ambient sound and altered instruments. His *4'33"* (1952) consisted of a performer sitting silently on stage for 4 minutes and 33 seconds. Cage often worked with choreographer Merce Cunningham.

See Also: Cunningham, Merce.

■ **CAGNEY, JAMES (1904-86),** film actor. Born in New York City, he starred in gangster classics such as *The Public Enemy* (1931) and *White Heat* (1949) and portrayed George M. Cohan in *Yankee Doodle Dandy* (1942).

■ **CAHAN, ABRAHAM (1860-1951),** journalist and politician. Born in Vilna, Lithuania, he immigrated to New York City and in 1897 founded the *Jewish Daily Forward*, a Yiddish-language newspaper that he edited until his death. Cahan was a founder of the Social Democratic party (1898). He wrote a five-volume autobiography (1916-36) and several novels, most notably *The Rise of David Levinsky* (1917), describing the immigrant experience.

■ **CAHOKIA (c. 900-1300),** largest city and temple mound in pre-Columbian North America, site of a Mississippian Indian society. At its height, Cahokia had some 30,000 inhabitants and stretched 6 miles along the Mississippi River across from present-day St. Louis. Monk's Mound, the central temple, was an earthwork pyramid, 15 acres at its base and as high as a 10-story building. Also at Cahokia was a structure of wooden columns dubbed "Woodhenge," part of an astronomical device to determine times for planting and harvest.

See Also: Indians of North America; Mississippian Culture.

■ **CAJUNS,** popular term for the Acadian settlers in Louisiana who migrated there after being expelled from Nova Scotia in 1755 by the English. (Acadia, the Micmac Indian word for plenty, was the original name for Nova Scotia.) More than

6,000 French colonists were expelled between 1755 and 1758 during the imperial conflict between France and England. Although many resettled in the English colonies, French Louisiana became home to some 4,000 Cajuns (a corruption of the word *Acadians*).

Cajuns successfully adapted to various governments, as Louisiana was controlled at different times by France, Spain, and the United States. They were, however, displaced by Americans and spread across southern Louisiana during the first half of the 19th century. Possessing one of the most resilient and distinctive folk cultures in the United States, Cajuns have heavily influenced Louisiana, particularly through their cuisine and music.

See Also: *Ethnic Groups.*

■ **CALAMITY JANE (1852-1903),** nickname of Martha Jane Canary, archetypal western hero.

Martha Jane Canary, a prostitute who dressed in men's clothing and worked for a time as a teamster for the frontier army, was transformed by dime novelists into the heroine Calamity Jane, who captured the public imagination by demanding equal rights in a man's world.

Born near Princeton, Missouri, she was a camp-follower and prostitute in the mining towns of Montana and South Dakota. Late in life, she boastfully cultivated fictional accounts of her exploits. There is no reliable evidence for legends that she was James (Wild Bill) Hickok's clandestine wife, a uniformed scout in General Custer's army, a railroad construction worker, or a teamster in the mining towns of the Dakotas.

See Also: *Frontier in American History; Hickok, Wild Bill (James Butler); Women in American History.*

■ **CALDER, ALEXANDER (1898-1976),** innovative sculptor and creator of mobiles and stabiles. Calder was born in Philadelphia, Pennsylvania. He graduated from Stevens Institute of Technology in 1919 with a degree in mechanical engineering. After working a few years, Calder moved to New York City in 1923, where he took classes at the Art Students League, studying with John French Sloan. Calder's early line drawings of animals were a precursor to his early wire sculpture—such as *The Brass Family* (1928)—in which one wire, bent and twisted, would define a form. Calder spent from 1926 to 1933 in Paris, gaining acclaim for his abstract constructions, known as stabiles, and his motorized or wind-driven mobiles. Calder was equally praised when he returned to the United States; he continued to create stabiles, such as *Whale* (1937), and mobiles, such as *Universe* (1938), that were conceptually related to modern art movements in painting. Later in his career Calder enlarged the scale of his work to produce public art commissioned by clients ranging from the federal government to private corporations.

See Also: *Painting; Sloan, John French.*

■ **CALDWELL, SARAH (1924-),** opera conductor, director, and producer. Born in Maryville, Missouri, she founded the Opera Company of Boston in 1957. She has conducted the American Symphony Orchestra and has directed and conducted performances at the Metropolitan Opera.

■ **CALENDARS, JULIAN AND GREGORIAN,** two systems of reckoning time. Established by Julius Caesar (46 B.C.), the Julian, or "Old Style," calendar was subsequently adopted throughout Western Europe and remained the accepted English calendrical system during the first century of English settlement in North America. The Gregorian, or "New Style," calendar, introduced by Pope Gregory XIII in 1582, slightly modified the Julian calendar and was adopted by England and its American colonies in 1752.

CALHOUN, JOHN CALDWELL (1782-1850),

politician and defender of states' rights and Southern interests. He was born near Abbeville, South Carolina, and was educated at Moses Waddell's Willington Academy, Yale College, and Tapping Reeve's law school in Litchfield, Connecticut. Calhoun served as a U.S. representative (1811-17), secretary of war (1817-25), secretary of state (1844-45), and as a U.S. senator (1832-43; 1845-50). He remains the only person to serve as vice president under two different presidents: John Quincy Adams (1825-29) and Andrew Jackson (1829-32).

As a South Carolina congressman, Calhoun championed a large and active federal government, supporting federally funded internal improvements, a national bank, and the protective tariff of 1816. Largely reacting against the rising tide of antislavery sentiment in the North, Calhoun soon became the nation's foremost champion of states' rights and limited federal powers. His "South Carolina Exposition and Protests" (1828) together with his posthumous *Discourse on the Constitution and Government of the United States* (1851) present his philosophy of government, federalism, and state sovereignty. According to Calhoun, sovereignty resided with the people of individual states. Ratification of the Constitution was an act of sovereignty, not a surrender of it. The federal government, therefore, acted as an agent of the united but sovereign capacity, reserved the right and the authority to review every act of the federal government, and could decide for themselves its constitutionality. Calhoun insisted that states could nullify any federal law they believed unconstitutional, and that the law in question would automatically become null and void within an aggrieved state unless and until three-quarters of all states ratified a constitutional amendment that would clearly allow the federal government to act in the matter. Even then the protesting state or states could continue to resist by invoking their sovereignty to repeal ratification of the Constitution and secede.

—ERIC H. WALTHER

See Also: Nullification; Vice President of the United States.

BIBLIOGRAPHY: Bartlett, Irving, *John C. Calhoun: A Biography* (Norton 1993); Niven, John, *John C. Calhoun and the Price of Union* (Louisiana State Univ. Press 1988); Wilson, Clyde, et al., eds., *The Papers of John C. Calhoun,* 26 vols. to date (Univ. of South Carolina Press 1959-); Wiltse, Charles M., *John C. Calhoun,* 3 vols. (Bobbs 1944-51).

Responding to attacks by Northern abolitionists, Sen. John C. Calhoun of South Carolina declared, "I am a southern man and a slaveholder; a kind and merciful one, I trust—and none the worse for being a slaveholder."

CALIFORNIA, the nation's most populous state

and the third largest. It is bounded on the north by Oregon, on the west by the Pacific Ocean, on the south by Mexico, on the south and east by Arizona, and on the east by Nevada. The Colorado River forms its border with Arizona. Its coastline is longer than any state's but Alaska's. Extremely diverse in geography, California has 41 mountains exceeding 10,000 feet, including Mount Whitney, the highest point in the contiguous 48 states. By contrast, the state's Death Valley falls to the lowest point in the Americas. The economy is equally diverse; California leads all states in agriculture, manufacturing, and retail trade.

California was first under Spanish, then Mexican rule until ceded to the United States in 1848, at the conclusion of the Mexican War. It became a state in 1850. Immigration from all parts of the world made first San Francisco, then Los Angeles, major cities. California passed New York in population in 1962.

Capital: Sacramento. Area: 158,647 square miles. Population (1995 est.): 31,589,000.

See Also: Drake, Sir Francis; Forty-Niners; Mexican War; Nixon, Richard Milhous; Reagan, Ronald Wilson; San Francisco; Serra, Junipero.

■ **CALIFORNIA GOLD RUSH (1849),** the massive movement of people to California following the discovery of gold there. In 1848, men building a sawmill in the American River discovered gold nuggets in the mill race. Their employer, John A. Sutter, founder of Sutter's Fort (near present-day Sacramento), tried unsuccessfully to keep the discovery secret so that he could monopolize the lode himself. A worldwide rush brought hundreds of thousands of inexperienced but hopeful miners to California. The gold deposits proved to be extensive and included the western slope of the Sierra Nevada Mountains as well as less rich diggings in northeastern California. Despite the magnitude of the discovery, few miners got rich digging for gold. The first miners used the simple techniques of placer mining, skimming the easy pickings with gold pans and shovels. Soon the technical problems of getting comparatively

In mid-November 1848, an army courier from California arrived in Washington, D.C., with a tea caddy full of gold dust and nuggets, confirming that gold had been discovered. Thousands upon thousands of "forty-niners" then flocked to California, hoping to make a fortune.

small amounts of gold from huge volumes of gravel and solid granite were beyond the ability of individual miners to solve. In the 1850s and 1860s, Californians organized sufficient capital and developed technical means of getting gold ore and refining it. Some of the technical developments proved to be environmentally costly. Huge piles of worthless mine tailings and badly damaged rivers are some of the monuments of the gold rush that remain today.

Nevertheless, Californians have romanticized the gold rush, portraying it as a time of unbridled frontier spirit and adventure. At the first hint of a new strike, prospectors quickly built mining camps; they disappeared just as rapidly when the gold played out. Social life was characterized by gambling, prostitution, reckless land speculation, violence, and vigilantism, which was supposed to provide security for honest citizens until regular peace officers and courts could establish justice. Vigilante mobs in the mines often focused their attention on Mexican and Latino miners and punished them whether they were guilty or not. The more carefully organized and business-dominated vigilance committees in San Francisco pledged to cleanse the city of crime, but attacked the Irish Democratic machine.

The gold rush rapidly populated California with white citizens, but at the expense of Indians who unluckily lived in the mining districts. Miners and state militia killed Indians without regard for age, sex, or condition and drove out most of the survivors. California's Indian population fell from about 175,000 to 30,000 between 1848 and 1860.

The gold rush ushered in the era of industrial mining in the West and was a model for subsequent mineral rushes throughout the region. California entrepreneurs developed the economic and technical means to mine precious metals. Their experience was reflected in the boisterous mining camp life and the laws that governed the western mining industry.

—ALBERT L. HURTADO

See Also: California; Forty-Niners; Frontier in American History; Mining Rushes; Sutter, John Augustus.

BIBLIOGRAPHY: Dasmann, Raymond F., *The Destruction of California* (Collier Macmillan 1965); Holliday, J. S., *The World Rushed In: The California Gold Rush Experience* (Simon & Schuster 1981); Hurtado, Albert L., *Indian Survival on the California Frontier* (Yale Univ. Press 1988); Starr, Kevin, *Americans and the California Dream, 1850-1915* (Oxford Univ. Press 1973).

■ **CALIFORNIA INDIANS,** Indians native to the California area, among the most culturally diverse native peoples within the present boundaries of the United States. Although the diversities are many, some generalizations are possible. California Indians were primarily hunters, fishers, and food collectors. Anthropologists postulate that the salubrious climate and environmental abundance of the region made farming unnecessary, except along the Colorado River, where the Quechan took advantage of the annual flooding of the surrounding plains. Elsewhere, women gathered plant foods, especially acorns, which they made into a nutritious mush that was a California staple. Men supplemented the food stores with meat and fish. California Indians spoke more than 100 distinct languages, some of which were as different as French and German. There was also notable religious diversity, although there were major religious complexes that dominated particular locales. Californians lived in many small communities—sometimes called "rancherias"—from several hundred to more than a thousand inhabitants. The rancheria, or at most a cluster of nearby rancherias, was the center of Indian life. Before the arrival of Europeans, there were probably more than 300,000 Indians within the present state's boundaries.

Indian diversity made it impossible to maintain a united front when Spaniards began to colonize California in 1769. Working in consort with the Spanish government, Catholic missionaries established 21 missions along the California coast. These institutions attracted thousands of Indian converts while simultaneously disrupting the California environment on which nonmission Indians depended. In 1821 Mexico declared its independence from Spain and began to dismantle the missions. Former mission Indians then became workers on private "ranchos" or retired beyond the reach of Mexican settlements. Thus, in the missions and on private ranchos, Indians were the first farm workers in California. Spanish and Mexican colonization brought new diseases to which Indians had little resistance. Consequently, the Indian population declined to about 175,000 by 1848, when the United States acquired California as a result of the Mexican War.

U.S. sovereignty was not a boon for California Indians. The discovery of gold in 1848 brought hundreds of thousands of miners from all over the world to California. Most of them went to areas with large Indian populations that had not been directly affected by the missions and ranchos. Miners, with no regard for any rights that Indians held under U.S. law, were determined to drive most Indians out of the mining districts. They did so with the help of state militias. By 1860 the native population had been reduced to about 30,000. The federal government at first negotiated treaties with the Indians, but in 1852 the Senate refused to ratify them. During the 1850s the federal government set up a few "temporary" reservations, and declined to interfere directly with state militia and independent expeditions that killed Indians without regard to age, sex, or condition. Eventually the federal government established three reservations, but most Indians were left to survive on their own as best they could.

At the end of the 19th century the condition of California Indians began to arouse humanitarian interest around the nation. Helen Hunt Jackson wrote a romantic novel, *Ramona*, and factual reports about southern California Indians that fixed attention on their condition. Consequently, Congress appropriated funds to purchase many small parcels for California's landless Indians.

In the 20th century California Indians began to organize to assert their rights. A series of court decisions provided compensation for lands the federal government had promised during treaty negotiations but never delivered and for other indemnities, but the awards were distributed on a per capita basis and only amounted to a few hundred dollars each. In 1969 California and other Indians occupied Alcatraz Island to publicize their situation. The occupation stimulated political activism among the state's Indians. Today, California Indians are a political force to be reckoned with, although they remain among the poorest of the state's citizens.

—ALBERT L. HURTADO

See Also: Indians of North America; Jackson, Helen Hunt; Militia and National Guard; Mining and Mining Rushes.

BIBLIOGRAPHY: Cook, Sherburne F., *The Conflict Between the California Indian and White Civilization* (Univ. of California Press 1976); Costo, Rupert, and Jeannette Henry Costo, *Natives of the Golden State: The California Indians* (Indian Historian Press 1995); Heizer, Robert F., ed., *Handbook of North American Indians*, vol. 8 (California Smithsonian Inst. 1979); Hurtado, Albert L., *Indian Survival on the California Frontier* (Yale Univ. Press 1988); Phillips, George H., *The Enduring Struggle: Indians in California History* (Boyd & Fraser 1981).

■ **CALVINISM,** religious doctrines of French-born Swiss Protestant theologian John Calvin (1509-1564), who believed in a rigid doctrine of predestination. Salvation is for God's elect only, not through a person's good works. Predestination became the doctrine of "Reformed" churches (Huguenot, Presbyterian, and Puritan).

See Also: Presbyterian Church; Puritans; Religion.

■ **CAMBRIDGE PLATFORM (1648),** document drawn by a synod of ministers from Massachusetts, Connecticut, and New Hampshire. Drafted by Richard Mather, it described the practices ("Congregational Way") of local, independent New England churches in which church government was shared by church officers and members.

See Also: Religion.

■ **CAMDEN, BATTLE OF (1780),** British victory in the American Revolution. At Camden, South Carolina, on Aug. 16, 1780, Gen. Horatio Gates led an ill-provisioned and poorly trained American force of some 3,000 soldiers against effective British troops led by General Cornwallis. Gates's unwise decisions during the battle facilitated a swift British victory. This major defeat closely followed the British capture of Charleston and marked the nadir of the war in the South for the Americans.

See Also: Revolution, American.

■ **CAMPANELLA, ROY (1921-93),** baseball catcher. Born in Philadelphia, he began his baseball career in the Negro Leagues. His reputation for durability and defense drew the attention of the Brooklyn Dodgers. Campanella played in the major leagues for 10 extraordinary seasons during the 1940s and 1950s, garnering three Most Valuable Player (MVP) awards. Although an accident and paralysis in 1958 cut short his baseball career, he remained a stalwart ambassador of the game. He was elected to the Baseball Hall of Fame in 1969.

See Also: *African Americans; Baseball.*

■ **CAMPBELL, JOHN, 4TH EARL OF LOUDOUN (1705-1782),** British general. He was born in Ayrshire, Scotland, and joined the army at the age of 22. In 1756, he was sent to America as commander in chief of all the British mainland colonies, having also title as governor of Virginia. His overt assignment was to conquer New France, but he spent more effort quarreling with colonial assemblies to make them accept rule by royal prerogative. When he met resistance, he threatened to quarter troops (and sometimes did) to enforce his decrees. Thus Loudoun's administration is remembered in the Declaration of Independence's clauses denouncing royal establishment of the military "superior to the Civil Power" and quartering troops on the people. Loudoun was a politician-soldier, incompetent for battle. After organizing an immense assault on French Fort Louisbourg, he withdrew without firing a shot. British Prime Minister William Pitt condemned and replaced him.

See Also: *French and Indian War.*
BIBLIOGRAPHY: Jennings, Francis, *Empire of Fortune* (Norton 1988).

■ **CAMPBELL, JOHN ARCHIBALD (1811-89),** associate justice of the U.S. Supreme Court (1853-61). He was born in Washington, Georgia. Campbell's opinions reflected a desire to curb the growth of federal power. He joined the majority in the Dred Scott decision (1857) and later left the Court to serve the Confederacy.

See Also: *Dred Scott v. Sandford; Supreme Court.*

■ **CAMP DAVID ACCORDS (1978),** two agreements signed by Egyptian Pres. Anwar Sadat and Israeli Prime Minister Menachem Begin at Camp David, Maryland, on Sept. 17, 1978. The 13-day negotiations preceding the agreements were under the personal mediation of Pres. Jimmy Carter. The first agreement provided for a transitional period of not more than five months for Egypt, Israel, Jordan, and the Palestinian representatives to determine the legal status of the West Bank of the Jordan River and the Gaza Strip. The second agreement stipulated that a peace treaty be signed between Egypt and Israel within three months of the Camp David Accords. Within three years, Israeli troops were to be withdrawn from the Sinai Peninsula, and Israeli settlements and air bases in the Sinai were to be dismantled. The symbolic meaning of the Camp David Accords was perhaps more important than the practical one; they were the first major diplomatic success in the hostilities between Israel and Arab states.

See Also: *Carter, James Earl, Jr. (Jimmy); Cold War.*

■ **CAMP MEETINGS,** 19th-century outdoor revival meetings, initially interdenominational and usually in the trans-Allegheny West. Although outdoor services were part of the Great Awakening and early Methodism in the 17th century, the camp meeting became popular in Kentucky with the Presbyterian revivalists. James McGready (c. 1760-1817) led the first typical camp meetings between 1799 and 1801 in Logan County, Kentucky. The most famous one soon followed in Cane Ridge, Bourbon County (August 1801), led by Baron W. Stone. Some participants traveled 30 to 40 miles to the site and were prepared to encamp for several days. In a forest clearing, revivalists constructed log benches and a preaching platform, which would be in continuous use for three or four days. Some meetings were reported to attract as many as 10,000 to 20,000 people. They came for many reasons: simple curiosity, social contact, and religious worship. The preaching, prayer meetings, hymn singing, weddings, and baptisms combined to create an emotionally charged event. Many participants were overcome with a sudden conversion experience. By the 1840s, Baptists and Presbyterians preferred indoor church revivals, while Methodists organized the camp meetings and built permanent sites. The camp meeting regained popularity in the Holiness movement of the late 19th century.

See Also: *Religion.*

■ **CANADA, BORDER DISPUTES WITH,** British, Canadians, and American boundary questions that persisted until the early 20th century. There was some initial bad feeling on both sides of the border: Loyalists fled the American Revolution to Ontario and the Maritime Provinces, and British agents in Canada urged Indians to attack U.S. settlers in the Ohio Valley. British and Canadian soldiers turned back an attempted American invasion of Ontario in 1812.

U.S.-Canadian relations after the end of the War of 1812 (1815) continued to be poor. Americans viewed an 1837 rebellion in eastern Canada as a chance for expansion: many aided Canadian rebels, and armed New Yorkers swarmed across the border to attack British soldiers. Canadian forces crossed into New York, killed a rebel, and burned the American ship *Caroline*. Simultaneous feuds between U.S. and Canadian lumbermen and farmers along the Maine-New Brunswick border were finally resolved in the Webster-Ashburton Treaty (1842). At the same time disputes over the border in the Northwest continued; however, despite President Polk's campaign plank of "50°40' or Fight!," the United States accepted a compromise border at the 49th parallel.

Canada has played odd roles in internal American affairs: Confederates used Canada's eastern coast as a raiding base against Union shipping during the Civil War (1861-65). Moreover, Irish nationalism spurred the Fenian Brotherhood to effect several attacks on Canada, which both the Canadian and American navies blocked (1866-70). The main 20th-century disagreement centered on the Alaskan border (1903). Pres. Theodore Roosevelt, threatening to "send a brigade of American regulars," stacked a joint international committee that finally voted in favor of the United States. Growing U.S.-Canadian agreement over matters such as trade and fishing rights underscores the modern consensus that commerce makes peace easier.

—WILLIAM EUGENE SCARING

See Also: Caroline Affair; Webster-Ashburton Treaty.
BIBLIOGRAPHY: Stacey, C. P., *Canada and the Age of Conflict* (Macmillan 1977); Stuart, R. C., *United States Expansionism and British North America, 1775-1870* (Univ. of North Carolina Press 1988).

■ **CANADIAN IMMIGRANTS,** the peaceful relationship long enjoyed between Canada and the United States has facilitated fluid movement across the border. Despite the relative similarity of the dominant cultures, Canadians, especially in the 20th century, have made important social and cultural contributions to the United States.

Significant Canadian immigration into the United States coincided with the large-scale European immigration into the United States and Canada during the first half of the 19th century. Several hundred thousand unskilled European-born laborers came to the United States after passing through Canada. Other 19th-century Canadian immigrants were French-speaking Catholics, who altered the ethnic and cultural composition of many towns in New England and New York. Although these patterns of immigration persisted, by the mid-20th century many Canadian immigrants moved beyond the northeast for destinations as far away as Florida and California. After 1960 Canadian immigration to the United States waned to about 25,000 annually, many of whom were professionals and their families.

See Also: Ethnic Groups.

■ **CANALS,** premier transportation of the early American industrial revolution, before the advent of the railroad. The first important transportation canals were constructed in the late 18th century, around the falls of rivers; on the Connecticut River, for example, a canal built in 1790 circumvented the falls and rapids at the town of South Hadley. But the enthusiasm for building large-scale canal systems dates from the construction of the Erie Canal in New York, begun in 1817 and opened in 1825. It extended 363 miles from the port of Buffalo on Lake Erie, to Albany on the Hudson River, thus allowing access from the Great Lakes to New York City, on the lower Hudson. Its cost of more than $7 million, financed by the state of New York, was justified by its success. Because New York City was now the gateway to the Great Lakes and the Ohio Valley, the bulk of agricultural trade shifted from the rival port of New Orleans.

The Erie Canal initiated a frenzy of canal building. Between 1820 and 1840 more than

$200 million ($3 billion in 1990 values) was invested in canal construction, three-quarters of it provided by state governments. By 1840, there were more than 3,000 miles of canals in the United States. The Blackstone Canal linked Worcester, Massachusetts, with Providence, Rhode Island; the Pennsylvania Main Line Canal ran all the way from Philadelphia to Pittsburgh; the Chesapeake and Ohio Canal tied Baltimore to the farms of the Ohio Valley; and the Illinois and Michigan Canal connected the new port of Chicago to the Mississippi River.

None of these waterways, however, achieved the success of the Erie Canal, and most states failed to raise revenues sufficient to pay off the bonds they had issued to finance canal construction. Most canals were hastily built and were often not adequately maintained. The railroad construction boom, which began in the 1840s, ended the short period of canal transportation in the United States. Most of the canals were abandoned, although the Erie Canal continued commercial operations through the 19th and 20th centuries.

The interest in canal building revived in the 1850s, when both the United States and Great Britain began to consider the possibilities of a canal across Central America that would provide easy access to the Pacific. The Panama Canal was finally constructed by the United States from 1904 to 1914.

See Also: *Erie Canal; Panama Canal; Transportation.*
BIBLIOGRAPHY: Goodrich, Carter, *Government Promotion of American Canals and Railroads, 1800-1890* (Columbia Univ. Press 1960); Shaw, Ronald E., *Canals for a Nation: The Canal Era in the United States, 1790-1860* (Univ. Press of Kentucky 1990); Taylor, George Rogers, *The Transportation Revolution, 1815-1860* (Rinehart 1951).

■ **CANNON, JOSEPH GURNEY (1836-1926),** U.S. congressman and Speaker of the House. He was born in Guilford County, North Carolina, was educated at the Cincinnati Law School, and became an Illinois lawyer. In 1873, he was elected to the House of Representatives as a conservative Republican, where he remained until 1923, losing his seat only twice, in 1890 and 1912. Known as "Uncle Joe," Cannon was Speaker of the House from 1903 to 1911. He wielded such partisan

power, effectively blocking much progressive reform, that in 1910 Congress passed a resolution that reduced the powers of future speakers.
See Also: *House of Representatives.*

■ **CANONCHET (c. 1630-76),** Narragansett leader. Canonchet joined the Wampanoag leader Metacomet in fighting the British colonists in New England during King Philip's War (1675-76). Canonchet suffered a severe defeat during the Great Swamp Fight (Dec. 9, 1675), in which the colonists and their Mohegan allies attacked the central Narragansett village near present-day Kingston, Rhode Island. Canonchet escaped, but was captured in April 1676. Refusing to end his resistance by advocating peace, he was shot and beheaded by the colonists.
See Also: *Great Swamp Fight; Indians of North America; Metacomet.*

■ **CANONICUS (c. 1565-1647),** Narragansett leader. Canonicus established friendly relations with the Pilgrims shortly after their arrival at Plymouth in 1620. He later befriended banished Massachusetts Bay colonist Roger Williams. Canonicus and the Narragansett remained neutral during the Pequot War of 1636-37. After his nephew Miantonomo's death on the order of the colonists in 1643, however, Canonicus denounced the whites.
See Also: *Indians of North America; Miantonomo; Pequot War; Williams, Roger.*

■ **CANTIGNY, BATTLE OF (1918),** the first offensive action by U.S. land forces in World War I. On May 28, following an artillery barrage, the 28th Regiment, First Division, left the trenches to assault the French village of Cantigny, the point of farthest advance of the March German offensive. American infantry and French tanks drove the German defenders from the village and then withstood at least six counterattacks. While only a minor success, the victory boosted American confidence.
See Also: *World War I.*

■ **CAPITOL,** home of the legislative branch of the U.S. government in Washington, D.C. Construction for the Capitol, designed by William Thornton, began in 1793. After it was burned in the War of 1812, the building was enlarged, resulting in the current plan with two wings that flank a central dome.

■ **CAPONE, AL (1899-1947),** American gangster. Born in Naples, Italy, he grew up in Brooklyn, New York. He only briefly attended school before joining a Brooklyn gang and receiving the cut on his face for which he earned the nickname "Scarface." In the 1920s, Capone moved to Chicago, challenging local mobster Johnny Torrio for control of an organization whose illegal activities included bootlegging, prostitution, and illegal gambling. Capone sought total control of Chicago's vast criminal enterprises during Prohibition through bloody gang wars, ending with the Saint Valentine's Massacre in 1929. He evaded the law until 1931 when he was sentenced to 11 years in federal prison for tax evasion.

See Also: Prohibition.

■ **CAPOTE, TRUMAN (1924-84),** novelist and journalist. Capote was born in New Orleans, Louisiana, and began his literary career on the staff of the *New Yorker*. His short novel *Other Voices, Other Rooms* (1948) garnered attention and was followed by the collection *A Tree of Night and Other Stories* (1949). In 1958 Capote published *Breakfast at Tiffany's*, a snapshot of life in New York City. Later Capote turned to nonfiction writing, including the novelistic *In Cold Blood* (1965) about a Kansas murder.

See Also: Novel.

■ **CAPRA, FRANK (1897-1991),** film director known for his celebrations of the common man. He was born in Palermo, Italy. Capra's best-known films, notably *Mr. Deeds Goes to Town* (1936), *Mr. Smith Goes to Washington* (1939), and *It's a Wonderful Life* (1946), display a sentimental view of American virtues that Capra himself described as "Capra-corn." During World War II he directed *Why We Fight* (1942-45), a film series on the nation's war goals.

See Also: Motion Pictures.

■ **CAPTIVITY, INDIAN,** in the colonies and the United States, both a tactic of warfare and a literary genre. As a tactic of warfare, captivity was used by one tribal enemy against another and was common practice in many areas of North, South, and Central America. In the northeast, especially among the Iroquois and Huron nations, adoption was often the fate of females, children, and young males who were able to pass the physical and psychological tests of adaptation. This Indian way of war was also used against Europeans, of whom more than 1,500 men, women, and children were taken captive between 1675 and 1763.

But Indians were not alone in using capture as a tactic in war and invasion. Columbus in the Caribbean, Cartier in eastern Canada (1534-35), Nuñno de Guzman in Mexico (1530s), and the early British in Roanoke (1585-87) all took captives. After the Pequot War in Connecticut (1637), 48 Pequot women and children were enslaved in Massachusetts Bay Colony, and Pequot men were exchanged for African slaves in the West Indies. Similar stories could be told of King Philip's War in New England (1675-76), Bacon's Rebellion in Virginia (1675), and wars in the Carolinas.

But, despite this, European and Anglo-American circles reported mainly stories of whites captured by Indians, thus creating the captivity narrative. The two earliest and most compelling of these narratives were by English Puritans Mary White Rowlandson and John Williams. Rowlandson was taken captive in a frontier attack on Lancaster, Massachusetts, at the opening of King Philip's War on Feb. 10, 1675. Her narrative, *The Sovereignty and Goodness of God* (1682), was published in Boston and London and republished in many editions. Williams's account, *Redeemed Captive, Returning to Zion* (1707), bemoans the assault of a party of Abenaki, Caughnawaga, and some Frenchmen on Deerfield, Massachusetts, in February 1704, near the beginning of Queen Anne's War. Williams's wife and two of his children were among 38 parishioners who died as a result of the assault. He and most of the rest of his children were taken prisoner and marched to Canada with approximately 100 others. His seven-year-old daughter, Eunice, never returned to New England but chose to stay in Caughnawaga country.

These and other dramatic stories of suffering, loss, and vulnerability among a "savage" foe became popular religious, national, and moral tales. They often were filled with hatred for Indians and thus offered justification for the appropriation of Indian lands. But some, like *A Narrative of the Life of Mrs. Mary Jemison* (1824), were more sympathetic toward Indian peoples and gave insight into their way of life. Captivity narratives became prototypes for vast numbers of historical narratives, 18th- and 19th-century sentimental novels, late-19th-century dime novels, and 20th-century films, such as *The Searchers*, in which John Wayne portrays a man obsessed with finding two nieces captured by Comanches.

—JUNE NAMIAS

See Also: Indians of North America.

BIBLIOGRAPHY: Axtell, James, *Beyond 1492: Encounters in Colonial North America* (Oxford Univ. Press 1992); Namias, June, *White Captives: Gender and Ethnicity on the American Frontier* (Univ. of North Carolina Press 1993); Vaughan, Alden T., and Edward W. Clark, eds., *Puritans among the Indians: Accounts of Captivity and Redemption, 1676-1724* (Harvard Univ. Press 1981).

■ **CARDOZO, BENJAMIN NATHAN (1870-1938),** associate justice of the U.S. Supreme Court (1932-38). Born in New York City, he was elected to the New York State Supreme Court (1913-17) and Court of Appeals (1917-32) before being elevated to the Supreme Court. Cardozo was a noted legal theorist and elegant writer whose *The Nature of the Judicial Process* (1921) argued that legal precedents must be viewed in light of changing social trends.

See Also: Supreme Court.

■ **CARLISLE INDIAN SCHOOL,** the first of the boarding schools for Indians established by the government, located in Carlisle, Pennsylvania, and founded (1879) by Lt. Richard Pratt. At Carlisle, Indian children were separated from their families and reservations; for part of the year, they were even separated from other Indian children while they were boarded with American families in an effort to immerse them in white culture. Carlisle gave training in both academic subjects and industrial arts.

See Also: Indian Policy; Indians of North America.

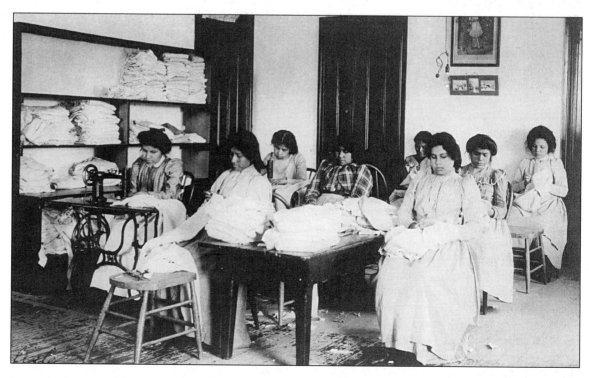

Instruction in manual labor was the first priority at the Carlisle Indian School, founded in 1879 in Carlisle, Pennsylvania.

■ **CARLSON, CHESTER (1906-68),** inventor who created the Xerox machine. Born in Seattle, Washington, Carlson earned a degree in physics from the California Institute of Technology (1930) and a law degree from New York Law School (1939). He developed the basic concept of electrophotography or xerography by 1937, built a partially successful automatic machine in 1940, and patented it in 1942. The Haloid Company (later the Xerox Company) of Rochester, New York, manufactured the first commercial copier in 1950 and introduced a simple, convenient office copier, the Xerox 914, in 1959. Proceeds from his licensing agreements allowed Carlson to retire in 1945 and eventually made him a multimillionaire.

See Also: Science.

■ **CARMICHAEL, STOKELY (KWAME TOURÉ) (1941-),** civil rights activist. He was born in Port of Spain, Trinidad and Tobago. An activist at Howard University, Carmichael joined (1966) the Student Nonviolent Coordinating Committee (SNCC) and served as its chairman from 1966 until 1967. An outspoken proponent of black power, he urged African Americans to reject white values and control their own destinies. He was associated with the Black Panthers but in 1969 moved to Guinea, Africa, where he changed his name to Kwame Touré.

See Also: Civil Rights Movement.

■ **CARNEGIE, ANDREW (1835-1919),** industrialist and philanthropist. A paradoxical figure, Carnegie was at once a ruthless captain of enterprise and a benevolent advocate of social justice. At the age of 12, Carnegie emigrated with his family to Pennsylvania from his native Scotland. He began work for Pennsylvania Railroad in 1853 as a telegraph operator and by 1859 was western superintendent of the railroad. By the mid-1860s, Carnegie had become a wealthy investor and entrepreneur.

During the depression of 1873, Carnegie shrewdly invested all his resources and energy into producing steel. He adopted the best technology, including the Bessemer process, and hired the most experienced people in the steel industry. Carnegie Steel rapidly came to dominate the industry by maintaining competitive prices and low wages and often operating at maximum capac-

ity. Such practices achieved financial success for the company but led to a violent labor dispute at the steel plant in Homestead, Pennsylvania, in 1894 that Carnegie ended with the use of Pinkerton detectives and the state militia. In 1901, Carnegie sold his interests to the United States Steel Corporation for $250 million.

Now one of the world's richest individuals, Carnegie turned his attention to philanthropy, creating several trusts and foundations, and financing universities, building projects, and public libraries. In an 1889 article, "The Gospel of Wealth," Carnegie articulated his philosophy that accumulation of capital made possible social progress through charitable giving.

—GUY NELSON

See Also: Homestead Strike; Industrial Revolution.

BIBLIOGRAPHY: Meltzer, Milton, *The Many Lives of Andrew Carnegie* (Franklin Watts 1997); Wall, Joseph Frazier, *Andrew Carnegie* (Oxford Univ. Press 1970).

In 1901, Andrew Carnegie sold his steel empire to J. P. Morgan for $250 million. The "richest man in the world" then retired and devoted the rest of his life to philanthropy, preaching the "Gospel of Wealth," his formula for "genuine, praiseworthy success in life."

■ **CAROLINE AFFAIR (1837),** incident in which Canadian forces entered the United States and took deadly action against an American ship that was carrying supplies to a group of Canadian rebels. In November 1837 Canadian insurrectionist William Lyon Mackenzie launched an unsuccessful rebellion in Upper Canada. He and his hundreds of followers were driven south to the Niagara River, where American sympathizers supplied them with food, arms, and men, using the American steamer *Caroline*. On December 29 Canadian troops crossed over the boundary of the United States and seized the boat, killing an American in the process. Afterward, the Canadians towed the steamer into the river and set it on fire. Pres. Martin Van Buren protested to the British government, which ignored him, and for a time there was fear that British Canada would invade the United States. American newspapers fueled anti-British sentiment with cartoons of the flaming ship, with dozens of screaming civilians aboard, going over Niagara Falls. A Canadian sheriff was arrested for the murder of the American on board the *Caroline*, and he was tried and found guilty in a New York court. Threatened with invasion if he was executed, the Americans eventually freed him. In 1842, as part of the Webster-Ashburton Treaty, the British formally apologized for the Caroline affair.

■ **CAROTHERS, WALLACE (1896-1937),** chemist who invented neoprene and nylon. Born in Burlington, Iowa, Carothers earned his Ph.D. in organic chemistry at the University of Illinois (1924) and was an instructor at Illinois and Harvard before becoming director of organic chemistry research for the E. I. Du Pont de Nemours Company in Wilmington, Delaware (1928). He and his associates invented neoprene "rubber" by synthesizing hydrogen chloride and an acetylene compound, invented nylon fiber, and laid the groundwork for most of today's synthetic fibers such as Orlon and Dacron. An intense, perhaps compulsive worker, Carothers suffered from increasingly severe depression, nervous illness, and failing health; he committed suicide in 1937.
See Also: Science.

■ **CARPETBAGGERS (1865-76),** derogatory term given by southerners to northerners who came to the South after the Civil War to participate in Reconstruction. The "carpetbag" was a cheap cloth suitcase, indicating that southern opponents considered the northerners to be lower class.
See Also: Reconstruction.

■ **CARRIER, WILLIS HAVILAND (1876-1950),** mechanical engineer and inventor. Born near Angola, New York, Carrier graduated with a degree in engineering from Cornell University in 1901 and soon designed the centrifugal compressor, a new kind of refrigerating machine from which he developed modern air conditioners. He started the Carrier Engineering Corporation in 1915. By 1930, his air conditioners cooled more than 300 theaters, and in 1939 he developed a practical air-conditioning system for skyscrapers. When he retired from the Carrier Corporation in 1948, he held more than 80 patents.
See Also: Invention.

■ **CARROLL, CHARLES ("OF CARROLLTON") (1737-1832),** revolutionary statesman. Born in Annapolis, Maryland, Carroll was elected to the Continental Congress in 1776, where he signed the Declaration of Independence on Aug. 2, 1776. Carroll was the only Roman Catholic to sign the Declaration and its last surviving signer.
See Also: Declaration of Independence; Revolution, American.

■ **CARSON, KIT (CHRISTOPHER HOUSTON CARSON) (1809-68),** frontier guide and Indian agent. Born near Richmond, Kentucky, Carson grew up on a Missouri farm, ran away to New Mexico, and traveled with trapper Ewing Young from 1828 to 1831. Carson killed a man in a duel at the Green River Rendezvous of 1835, and later married two successive Indian wives. From 1842 to 1846 Carson was a scout for three of John C. Frémont's expeditions to the West. In the Mexican War (1846-48), Carson guided Gen. Stephen Kearny's army from New Mexico to California. Carson returned to Rayado, New Mexico, after the war and took up ranching. Carson served as an Indian agent in New Mexico from 1853 to 1861. As a colonel in the First New Mexico Volunteer Infantry, Carson saw action at the Civil War battle of Valverde on Feb. 21, 1862, before suppressing the Mescalero Apache

In 1842, Kit Carson was John C. Frémont's guide on his government-sponsored expeditions of the West. As Indian-fighter, trailblazer, messenger, and Civil War colonel, Carson acquired folk-hero renown in the United States.

near Fort Stanton in 1862-63. Carson forced some 8,000 Navaho to surrender after a fierce battle at Canyon de Chelly in 1864, destroying crops and livestock. Resettling his family near Boggsville, Colorado, after the war, Carson died in 1868 and was interred eventually in Taos, New Mexico.

See Also: Frontier in American History.

■ **CARSON, RACHEL (1907-64),** zoologist, author, and environmentalist. She was born in Springdale, Pennsylvania. From 1936 to 1952, while working for the U.S. Fish and Wildlife Service, she published remarkably poetic and accessible scientific writings in the *New Yorker* and other magazines. *The Sea Around Us* (1951) was immensely popular and won the National Book Award. *Silent Spring* (1962), an exposé of damage to the natural environment from pesticides, fundamentally changed American thought about environmental issues.

See Also: Women in American History.

■ **CARTER, JAMES EARL, JR. (JIMMY) (1924-),** 39th president of the United States (1977-81). He was born in Plains, Georgia, and graduated from the U.S. Naval Academy in 1946 and served until 1953, when he returned home to run the family peanut business. In 1970 he was elected Democratic governor of Georgia, drawing national attention when he called for racial reconciliation after years of segregationist leadership. Carter ran for president in 1976, won all the early primaries, and took the Democratic nomination on the first ballot—one of the great "dark horse" success stories of modern American politics. With running mate Walter Mondale, he narrowly defeated Republican incumbent Gerald Ford.

"I will not lie to you," pledged Democrat Jimmy Carter to American voters in 1976. Campaigning as an anti-politician and outsider, the former governor of Georgia won the presidency with just under 50 percent of the popular vote.

President Carter reorganized the federal bureaucracy by consolidating agencies and offices and by establishing new cabinet-level departments of energy, education, and health and human services. In foreign policy he imposed human rights guidelines for foreign and military aid; negotiated the 1978 Camp David Accords between Egypt and Israel; and led the ratification of the Panama Canal Treaty, which provided for eventual Panamanian control of the canal. In 1979 he restored full diplomatic relations with China and negotiated an arms control agreement with the Soviet Union. Carter's wife, Rosalynn, his outspoken champion, traveled worldwide in support of his programs, the most politically active first lady since Eleanor Roosevelt.

Carter's presidency, however, was marked by significant failures. Annual inflation rates reached 13 percent in 1979, fueled in part by dramatic oil-price increases, and interest rates rose to a historic high of 20 percent. Carter's appeal to Americans to accept a new age of limits during this "energy crisis" was extremely unpopular. His response to the Soviet invasion of Afghanistan in early 1980, a boycott of the summer Olympic games in Moscow and cancellation of planned wheat sales, seemed ineffective. Most disastrous was the Iranian hostage crisis, which practically destroyed Carter's political credibility.

In assessing Carter, historians tend to divide along partisan lines. His foreign policy is praised by some as an affirmation of the importance of morality, condemned by others as dangerous idealism. Some blame the economic crisis on his mismanagement, but others suggest it was beyond the control of any president and argue that his emphasis on limits was essentially correct, if politically foolish. His handling of the Iranian crisis may look somewhat better when one considers the inability of his successors to gain the release of hostages taken during their terms.

A challenge for the 1980 presidential nomination from Sen. Edward Kennedy revealed Carter's weak support among members of his own party, many of whom condemned him as the most conservative Democratic president since Grover Cleveland. Republican Ronald Reagan defeated Carter in a landslide victory. After leaving office, Carter lectured and established an institute at Emory University in Atlanta, but he had little impact on national party politics. Carter recounted his experiences in *Keeping Faith* (1983).

See Also: Camp David Accords; Cold War; Mondale, Walter; Presidential Elections; President of the United States.

BIBLIOGRAPHY: Hargrove, Erwin C., *Jimmy Carter as President: Leadership and the Politics of the Public Good* (Louisiana State Univ. Press 1988); Smith, Gaddis, *Morality, Reason, and Power: American Diplomacy in the Carter Years* (Hill & Wang 1986).

■ **CARTERET FAMILY,** adventurers and royal administrators native to the Isle of Jersey, England. Sir George Carteret (c.1610-80), privateer and sometime pirate, was knighted by Charles II. Granted an island off Virginia for services to the king, Carteret eventually became a proprietor of New Jersey and the Carolinas. His son, Philip Carteret (1639-82), served as the first governor of New Jersey Colony (1664-76) and, after its division, of East New Jersey (1676-82). Embroiled in controversy concerning the collection of perpetual quitrents in New Jersey, Philip Carteret finally resigned (1682) over a customs duty dispute with New York.

■ **CARTIER, JACQUES (1491-1557),** French explorer of Canada. Cartier, born in St. Malo, Brittany, led three expeditions to North America between 1534 and 1542. During his initial foray Cartier discovered the entrance to the St. Lawrence River and sailed inland as far as the first rapids. This venture formed the basis for French claims to the St. Lawrence hinterland. On a second voyage in 1535-36 Cartier penetrated as far as the site of modern Montreal. Sufficiently impressed by the region's resources, Cartier founded a settlement near the site of present-day Quebec and prospected for diamonds and gold. When these potential riches proved to be quartz and fool's gold (iron pyrite), the colonists abandoned New France's first colony. Cartier's written accounts of his Canadian exploits endured, firing the imaginations of the next generation of French voyageurs and missionaries.

See Also: Exploration and Discovery.

BIBLIOGRAPHY: Morison, Samuel Eliot, *The Great Explorers: The European Discovery of America* (Oxford Univ. Press 1978).

■ **CARTWRIGHT, PETER (1785-1872),** Methodist circuit rider. Born in Amherst County, Virginia, he moved with his family to Kentucky in 1790. After a camp meeting conversion in 1801, he joined the Methodist Episcopal Church and became a traveling preacher at age 17. He was a deacon at 20 and a presiding elder at 22. Cartwright's extemporaneous, hell-fire sermons and colorful exploits made "God's plowman," as he called himself, well known throughout his 50 years on the midwestern frontier circuit. Running for Congress as the Democratic candidate from Illinois in 1846, he was defeated by Abraham Lincoln.

See Also: Methodist Church; Religion.

■ **CARVER, GEORGE WASHINGTON (1864-1943),** agricultural scientist. Born in slavery near Diamond Grove, Missouri, Carver's education was limited but he finally earned a master's degree in 1894 from Iowa State Agricultural College. Soon after, Carver accepted an invitation from Booker T. Washington to direct agricultural research at the

A son of slave parents, George Washington Carver was illiterate until he was almost 20 years old. In 1896, at the age of 32, Carver became director of Tuskegee Institute's agricultural research department, where he promoted crop diversification, particularly with peanuts.

Tuskegee Institute. He became an ardent advocate of crop diversification. Soils impoverished by cotton could be rejuvenated by planting nitrogen-fixing crops of legumes such as soybeans. He developed hundreds of derivative applications for peanuts and sweet potatoes to improve their commercial appeal. Throughout his career Carver patented few of his discoveries, preferring to contribute to knowledge rather than profit from it.

See Also: Agriculture; Washington, Booker Taliaferro.

BIBLIOGRAPHY: Kremer, Garry R., *George Washington Carver in His Own Words* (Univ. of Missouri Press 1987); McMurry, Linda O., *George Washington Carver* (Oxford Univ. Press 1981).

■ **CASABLANCA CONFERENCE (1943),** World War II meeting in Morocco between U.S. Pres. Franklin D. Roosevelt and British Prime Minister Winston Churchill in January to discuss the conduct of the war. Instead of an immediate cross-channel invasion of Europe, the Allies decided to attack the "soft underbelly of the Axis," through Sicily and Italy. In a controversial statement to appease Soviet leader Joseph Stalin, Roosevelt and Churchill demanded the "unconditional surrender" of all enemy nations.

See Also: World War II.

■ **CASCADES,** mountain chain extending some 700 miles from British Columbia in Canada through Oregon and Washington into northern California. It forms a barrier between the moist Pacific coastal region and the arid interior. Much of the eastern watershed of the Cascades acts as the tributary of the Columbia River. The northern Cascades is one of the wettest places in the lower 48 states, with an average of more than 100 inches of rain each year.

■ **CASS, LEWIS (1782-1866),** American politician. Born in Exeter, New Hampshire, he served as a general during the War of 1812. In 1813 Cass became the governor of Michigan Territory, a position he held until 1831. He was responsible for negotiating with the various Indian tribes in Michigan in order to open up land for American settlement. Cass advocated American expansion and the doctrine of Manifest Destiny, arguing that the West represented not only economic opportunity but also political stability for the American nation. As Pres. Andrew Jackson's secretary of war (1831-36), he oversaw the removal of many of the eastern tribes west of the Mississippi River. As a U.S. senator from Michigan (1845-48), Cass proposed the concept of "popular sovereignty" to settle the question of slavery within the territories acquired during the Mexican War (1846-48). Cass was the Democratic candidate for president in 1848, but he lost to Zachary Taylor, largely because of his position on popular sovereignty.

See Also: Popular Sovereignty.

■ **CASSATT, MARY (1844-1926),** impressionist painter known for her skillful use of color. Born in Allegheny City, Pennsylvania, she moved to France in 1866. Befriended by painter Edgar Degas, she became part of the Impressionist circle, exhibiting with them in Paris until 1882. Exhibits of her work and her advice to American collectors helped build interest in Impressionism in America. Her *Mother and Child* hangs in the Metropolitan Museum of Art in New York City.

See Also: Painting; Women in American History.

■ **CASTLE, VERNON (1887-1918)** and **CASTLE, IRENE (1893-1969),** ballroom dancers. Vernon, a British-born vaudevillian, created such dances as the one-step, turkey trot, and the Castle walk. He married Irene Foote in 1911, and their elegant performances and book, *Modern Dancing* (1914), sparked a ballroom dancing craze. Irene's bobbed hair created a fashion fad. Vernon, who enlisted in Britain's Royal Flying Corps in 1916, died in a 1918 crash.

■ **CATHER, WILLA (1873-1947),** author. Born in Back Creek Valley, Virginia, she grew up in Nebraska but finally settled in Greenwich Village in New York City, where she edited and managed *McClure's* from 1908 to 1912. She then turned to writing fiction. *Oh Pioneers!* (1913) captures the texture of the frontier immigrant experience, and *A Lost Lady* (1923) shows the struggle to escape the stifling atmosphere of small-town life. *One of Ours* (1922) won the Pulitzer Prize in 1923.

See Also: Novel; Women in American History.

■ **CATLIN, GEORGE (1796-1872),** painter of Indians. Catlin was born in Wilkes-Barre, Pennsylvania. He practiced law before turning to art as a profession in 1823. At first Catlin painted portraits and miniatures in Philadelphia, Pennsylvania, and Washington, D.C, but when he saw a delegation of Plains Indians traveling between those two cities in 1824, he became fascinated with the rapidly changing Indian way of life. In 1832 he set out traveling, returning to the East Coast six years later with hundreds of paintings—portraits and scenes of Indian life that depicted close to 50 different tribes. Catlin painted Indians both in their camps and when traveling, for example, on buffalo hunts. Catlin exhibited these works, known as the Indian Gallery, in the United States and in Europe. In the 1840s he began publishing selections of the works, contributing to the popular image of the Indians in the American West. In 1867 he wrote *Life Among the Indians,* his account of his experiences in the West.

See Also: Painting.

■ **CATRON, JOHN (c. 1786-1865),** associate justice of the U.S. Supreme Court (1837-65). Thought to have been born in Pennsylvania, Catron exercised probably his greatest judicial influence in drafting the majority opinion in the Dred Scott decision (1857), which held that a slave could not be a citizen.

See Also: Dred Scott v. Sandford; Supreme Court.

■ **CATSKILL MOUNTAINS,** in southeastern New York, part of the Appalachian mountain system. The Catskills became immortalized in the 1830s and 1840s through Washington Irving's short story about Rip Van Winkle and Thomas Cole's romantic landscape paintings. The mountains became a favorite vacation spot for wealthy New Yorkers in the middle of the 19th century and are still a popular summer and winter resort. Catskill reservoirs supply New York City with much of its drinking water.

See Also: Appalachian Mountains; Cole, Thomas; Irving, Washington.

■ **CATT, CARRIE CLINTON CHAPMAN (1859-1947),** woman suffrage leader. She was born near Ripon, Wisconsin. In 1900, she replaced Susan B. Anthony as president of the National

American Woman Suffrage Association. Two years later, she assumed the presidency of the newly formed International Woman Suffrage Alliance. A precise administrator and an imaginative, hard-working organizer, she successfully led the American suffrage movement in its campaign to gain the franchise through a constitutional amendment. In 1920 she was instrumental in the creation of the League of Women Voters.

See Also: League of Women Voters; Woman Suffrage Movement; Women's Movement.

■ **CATTLE,** domesticated animal of Old World origin, valued as a source of meat and dairy products. Although early immigrants from Great Britain and Africa both had established cattle-herding traditions, the prototype for the American cattle ranch came from the Spanish, who introduced steers into the Southwest in the early 17th century. With the breakup of the Spanish mission system in the 1800s, many of these animals became feral, multiplying rapidly as they took the place of the exterminated buffalo. These wild steers, in turn, provided the raw material for the celebrated cattle drives of the 1870s and 1880s, in which cowboys (much of their equipment adopted from Mexican *vaqueros*) rounded up free-roaming cattle and herded them to the nearest rail head for shipment to slaughterhouses in Chicago and, ultimately, the tables of urban consumers. With the adoption of barbed wire (invented in 1873) and the rise of a federal conservation policy for the public lands, however, open-range grazing gave way to fenced ranches and, eventually, the modern-day feedlot.

See Also: Agriculture.

■ **CAUCUS, POLITICAL (1796-1824),** controversial nominating process in which Congress possessed the nearly exclusive privilege of selecting presidential candidates. The political caucus was a critical feature in the development of America's two-party system. Within the U.S. Congress, party members met to determine their position on legislation, so that they might vote in unison, and to nominate candidates for House and Senate offices. The party caucuses in Congress between 1796 and 1824 also nominated the candidates for president and vice president, since the Constitution made no provision for presidential nominations. In 1796 the Federalists met in secret and agreed to support John Adams as president. Afterwards, caucuses determined the presidential nominees until 1824. This system was extremely unpopular, as many people thought that it was contrary to the Constitution, since it ensured that members of Congress would choose the president. It was denounced loudly by Andrew Jackson and his supporters, and by 1824 the caucus was in decline. In that year only about one-fourth of congressional members attended the nominating caucus. The nominating caucus was replaced in the 1830s by national conventions.

See Also: Conventions, Political.

■ **CENSORSHIP,** suppression or removal from the public of anything the government considers objectionable. Censorship was practiced as early as the Roman republic, where the office of the censor inspected and corrected moral conduct under the laws of the state. Censorship can involve anything from punishments for authors or consumers of censored material, or it can involve "prior restraint," which is the suppression of expression before it is made public.

The U.S. Supreme Court has consistently found prior restraint to be unconstitutional. The First Amendment to the Constitution appears to prohibit censorship and protect all speech, but these rights must be balanced against other government interests. For example, libel, personal threats, seditious conspiracy, and obscenity are not considered protected speech, while speech concerning political or social issues and even some kinds of pornography are protected. A major constitutional problem is how to decide which kinds of speech fall into the protected or unprotected categories.

Justice Oliver Wendell Holmes in 1919 argued that government may not restrict or punish speech unless it is shown to be "a clear and present danger" to national security. Despite a brief period in the 1950s when Communists were punished, the Supreme Court has consistently protected even symbolic political speech, including controversial acts such as flag burning, wearing Nazi insignias, or cross burning.

Although some forms of pornography have been protected, the Court has struggled to define "obscenity." In 1973 the Court developed a definition of obscenity as material that an average person, using community standards, would find appeals to prurient interest, graphically depicts sexual activity, and has no serious political, social, or educational value.

In the 1990s, courts have let stand certain legislative restrictions on so-called hate speech. In *R.A.V.* v. *City of St. Paul* (1992), Justice Antonin Scalia argued that states may punish hate speech but only by increasing the penalties for crimes that can be shown to have hatred of a specific group as a motive.

—Scott L. McLean

See Also: *Bill of Rights; Constitution of the United States.*

BIBLIOGRAPHY: American Civil Liberties Union, *Freedom of Expression* (American Civil Liberties Union 1991); Demac, Donna, *Liberty Denied: The Current Rise of Censorship in America* (PEN Center 1988); Downs, Alexander, *The New Politics of Pornography* (Univ. of Chicago Press 1989); Ehrlich, Howard, *Campus Ethnoviolence and the Policy Options* (National Institute Against Prejudice and Violence 1990).

■ **CENSUS,** federal government enumeration of the U.S. population required by Article I, Section 2, of the Constitution. The size of each state's delegation in the House of Representatives is determined by population, and the Constitution required an official count to be taken within 3 years of its ratification and every 10 years thereafter. The first census was conducted in 1790. As directed by the Constitution, Indians were not included, and African-American slaves were counted as three-fifths of a white person. Congress created an independent superintendent of the census in 1880 and a permanent Census Bureau in 1902. The bureau became part of the Commerce Department in 1913. Over time the census, in addition to counting heads, began collecting a range of social and economic information that helped shape federal policies. Now largely conducted by mail, the census has become controversial.

Some cities and states claim poor people are often not counted, while libertarians maintain the surveys are too intrusive.

BIBLIOGRAPHY: Halacy, D. S., *Census: 190 Years of Counting America* (Elsevier/Nelson Books 1980).

■ **CENTENNIAL EXPOSITION,** celebration of America's first 100 years as a nation that opened in Philadelphia in 1876. While it acknowledged America's past, most of the exhibits focused on recent inventions and discoveries that would shape its future. Over six months, almost 10 million visitors saw demonstrations of the telephone, the typewriter, the telegraph, and the incredible 2,500-horsepower Corliss engine.

See Also: *Gilded Age.*

■ **CENTRAL INTELLIGENCE AGENCY (CIA),** U.S. government intelligence and espionage agency. Established by Congress at the beginning of the Cold War (1947), the agency was the successor of World War II's Office of Strategic Services. It is responsible for intelligence gathering and analysis as well as counterespionage and covert political activities overseas. The agency's budget and the details of many of its operations are protected by law from both public and congressional scrutiny. Supporters of CIA activities argued that the perils of the Cold War required the United States to protect its national security through secret and sometimes distasteful operations. Critics often attack the CIA as a rogue agency that in the long run damages U.S. interests. Congressional hearings in the 1970s and 1980s that publicized failed and illegal CIA operations, and the collapse of the Soviet bloc in the early 1990s, harmed the agency's image and left its mission in question.

BIBLIOGRAPHY: Thomas, Evan, *The Very Best Men: Four Who Dared: The Early Years of the CIA* (Simon & Schuster 1995).

■ **CERRO GORDO, BATTLE OF (1847),** Mexican War engagement between Gen. Winfield Scott's force advancing toward Mexico City and Mexican troops under Gen. Antonio López de Santa Anna. On April 17 the Americans failed to cut the Mexican supply line, but on April 18, U.S. flanking movements dislodged the Mexicans from their fortifications, Santa Anna's army was routed, and Scott continued his advance.

See Also: Mexican War.

■ CHAMBERLAIN, WILTON NORMAN ("WILT") (1936-), basketball center.

He was born in Philadelphia, Pennsylvania. In his 14 seasons in the National Basketball Association (NBA), Chamberlain's athleticism and legendary scoring and rebounding earned him acclaim as one of the greatest players in the history of the game. He is the only NBA player to score 100 points in a game.

See Also: African Americans; Sports.

■ CHAMPION V. AMES (1903),

U.S. Supreme Court case concerning expanding the federal government's power to regulate and police interstate commerce. Known as "the lottery case," *Champion* challenged an 1895 federal law restricting interstate lotteries. The Court ruled (5-4) that lottery tickets were objects of trade, which could be regulated by Congress under the commerce clause and that Congress could establish mechanisms to enforce those regulations. The decision cleared the way for additional Progressive Era protective legislation.

See Also: Lotteries; Supreme Court.

■ CHAMPLAIN, SAMUEL DE (1567?-1635),

French explorer and founder of Quebec. Under the rule of King Henri IV of France, Champlain began his explorations along the northeast coast of North America at the turn of the 17th century. After spending a summer at Tadoussac, a seasonal fishing and fur-trading outpost located on the St. Lawrence estuary, he served as cartographer on the 1604 expedition led by Pierre Du Gua, the Sieur de Monts. De Monts established the colony of Port Royal on the coast of Acadia (Nova Scotia), which was destroyed by the English in 1613.

In July 1608 Champlain established a base on the north shore of the St. Lawrence River 130 miles upriver from Tadoussac. This base, located at a narrows on the river, was named Quebec,

This illustration, from Samuel de Champlain's account of his adventures in New France, shows him joining a Huron attack on Iroquois warriors in 1609. The alliance Champlain established between the French and the Hurons forced the Iroquois to seek European allies of their own.

which was destined to become the first permanent French settlement in North America. At the time of its founding, the Iroquois had abandoned the St. Lawrence Valley and no European competitors were active in the region. As Champlain and his 27 men would soon discover, the climate was bitter and the terrain inhospitable. By the end of their first winter in Quebec, 20 of these men had died.

With the murder of Henri IV in 1610 France sank into the morass of Marie de Medici's regency government. Champlain's tenacity and bravery obviously had much to do with Quebec's survival during the settlement's first two decades of existence, when generally fewer than 100 Frenchmen were in residence. For security and trade, he established alliances with the Huron and Algonquian, traditional enemies of the Iroquois. These alliances led to conflict with the Iroquois, who became the enduring enemies of French settlements in the St. Lawrence Valley.

Champlain was forced to surrender Quebec to an Anglo-Scottish force in 1629, but after much haggling France retained possession of the St. Lawrence Valley. Champlain, commissioned Lieutenant of New France, returned to Quebec in 1633 with three shiploads of supplies and a group of new colonists, including some women and children. Trois Rivières was established 80 miles from Quebec in 1634, and when Champlain died a year later, he left his colony on a small but secure footing; agriculture had begun, the fur trade was flourishing, and Recollect and Jesuit missionaries were spreading the Roman Catholic faith. Champlain was buried at Quebec.

—CARL J. EKBERG

See Also: *Exploration and Discovery.*

BIBLIOGRAPHY: Eccles, W. J., *The Canadian Frontier, 1534-1760* (Holt, Rinehart & Winston 1969; reprint Univ. of New Mexico Press 1986); Morris, Bishop, *Champlain, the Life of Fortitude* (Knopf 1948); Trudel, Marcel, *The Beginnings of New France* (Univ. of Toronto Press 1973).

■ **CHAMPLAIN, LAKE,** 125-mile-long lake that lies in a broad valley between the Adirondack and Green mountains. The lake, which forms part of the border between New York and Vermont and extends northward into Canada, was explored in 1609 by Samuel de Champlain, who provided the French a foothold in the area that lasted 150 years. Early settlers and Indians used the lake to travel back and forth between French Canada and the English colonies. Numerous battles were fought over possession of the area during the French and Indian Wars, the American Revolution, and the War of 1812.

■ **CHANCELLORSVILLE, BATTLE OF (May 1-4, 1863),** Civil War battle near Chancellorsville, Virginia, in which the outnumbered army of Confederate Gen. Robert E. Lee defeated the Union forces of Gen. Joseph Hooker. After a long flank march, Confederate Gen. Thomas J. (Stonewall) Jackson's corps struck the Union right on May 2. Hooker was gradually driven back and withdrew his army across the Rappahannock River on May 5-6. Meanwhile, on May 4, Lee defeated a separate Union force arriving from Fredericksburg. The crushing Confederate victory was tainted by the death of Jackson, killed by friendly fire.

See Also: *Civil War; Jackson, Thomas J. "Stonewall"; Lee, Robert Edward.*

■ **CHANDLER, RAYMOND (1888-1959),** novelist and screenwriter. A master of the moody mystery novel, the Chicago-born Chandler created the cynical private investigator Philip Marlowe in a series including *The Big Sleep* (1939), *Farewell My Lovely* (1940), and *The Long Goodbye* (1953). The books became popular films featuring Humphrey Bogart, Dick Powell, and Robert Mitchum as Marlowe. Chandler also wrote screenplays, most notably *Double Indemnity* (1944).

See Also: *Novel.*

■ **CHANNING, WILLIAM ELLERY (1780-1842),** Unitarian minister and theologian. Born in Newport, Rhode Island, he became the lifelong minister at Federal Street Church in Boston in 1803. Channing defined the liberal movement in New England Congregationalism. With famous sermons such as "Unitarian Christianity" (1819) and "The Moral Argument Against Calvinism" (1820), he became the leading spokesman for Unitarianism. Channing rejected orthodox Calvinism. He explained that human potential aspired toward a benevolent God and was the opposite of the human depravity in Calvinism. Channing also believed in the perfectibility of human beings and wrote about pacifism, prison reform, education, the abolition of slavery, and child labor. Channing's eloquence and literary essays influenced many American authors, particularly Ralph Waldo Emerson and other transcendentalists.

See Also: Religion; Unitarians.

■ **CHAPLIN, CHARLIE (1889-1977),** film actor, director, and producer who was among the biggest stars of the silent screen. Born into poverty in London, England, he first appeared in films in 1914. Chaplin starred in scores of films as the little tramp, blending graceful physical comedy and sentimental stories into a string of box office hits highlighted by *The Gold Rush* (1925), a feature-length comedy that transported the tramp to the Klondike. Chaplin was slow to adapt to sound. *City Lights* (1931) and *Modern Times* (1936), the last film in which he appeared as the

Charlie Chaplin had established himself as the leading comic film actor by the time of *The Kid* (1921), with Jackie Coogan.

little tramp, contained no dialogue. *Limelight* (1952), a bitter tale of an aging entertainer, was his last major film. His popularity declined in later years, due in part to his leftist politics, and he lived in Switzerland after 1952. He returned to the United States to accept an Academy Award in 1972 and was knighted in 1975.

See Also: Motion Pictures.

BIBLIOGRAPHY: Robinson, David, *Chaplin: His Life and Art* (HarperCollins 1992).

■ **CHAPULTEPEC, BATTLE OF (1847),** final battle of the Mexican War. With Mexican Pres. Antonio López de Santa Anna's forces decimated, U.S. Gen. Winfield Scott on September 13 attacked the only fortified position remaining in Mexico City—Chapultepec Castle. A formidable defensive post, the castle was manned by about 1,000 troops and cadets from Mexico's military academy. After an artillery barrage failed, Scott ordered his troops to scale the walls and engage in hand-to-hand combat. A group of Mexican cadets—the Niños Héroes—leapt to their deaths rather than surrender.

See Also: Mexican War; Scott, Winfield.

■ **CHARLES, RAY (1930-),** singer, songwriter, and musician. He was born Ray Charles Robinson in Albany, Georgia. Although blinded as a child, he developed an early interest in the piano. By the time he was 15 he was on tour with dance bands. At 24, Charles began a lifelong career as a recording artist, singing rhythm and blues to the accompaniment of his piano and orchestra and eventually earning 10 Grammy Awards. In 1986, he was awarded the Kennedy Center Honors Medal and inducted into the Rock and Roll Hall of Fame.

See Also: African Americans.

■ *CHARLES RIVER BRIDGE* **V.** *WARREN BRIDGE* **(1837),** U.S. Supreme Court case that transformed the constitutional protection of private property rights. Under a 1785 charter, the Charles River Bridge Company had built and maintained a toll bridge connecting Cambridge and Boston. Many members of the Boston establishment were stockholders in the company and profited handsomely over the years, as the bridge remained the only span across the river. Then in 1828 the

Massachusetts state legislature chartered the Warren Bridge Company, which was intended to compete with and break the monopoly of the first bridge. The Charles River Bridge Company and its investors cried foul, claiming that their original charter implied an exclusive right to handle all bridge traffic. The suit pitted against each other two very different notions of property rights. One, represented by the Charles River Bridge Company, was that private property was an absolute right in perpetuity. The other, represented by the Warren Bridge Company and the legislature, was that rights to private property were not absolute and must yield where necessary to the interests of the larger community. In a 4-3 decision, the Supreme Court ruled that it fell within the police power of the state of Massachusetts to charter a second bridge. Writing for the Court, Chief Justice Roger Taney broke with his predecessor, John Marshall, and declared that the states had the authority to regulate private property, especially where economic competition promised to benefit the community at large. Associate Justice Joseph Story, one of the dissenters, sharply criticized this infringement on absolute private property rights. Whereas Story believed that the law should ensure economic security, even if that meant the existence of monopolies, Taney believed that the law should ensure economic opportunity, even if that meant private property rights would be less than absolute.

—MATTHEW E. BABCOCK

See Also: Supreme Court; Taney, Roger Brooke.
BIBLIOGRAPHY: Horwitz, Morton J., "The Transformation in the Conception of Property in American Law, 1780-1860," *Univ. of Chicago Law Review 40* (1973); Kutler, Stanley I., *Privilege and Creative Destruction: The Charles River Bridge Case* (Lippincott 1971).

■ **CHARLESTON,** city in southeastern Carolina, on a peninsula between the Ashley and Cooper rivers. One of the earliest southern settlements and easily the most prosperous, Charleston was founded in 1670. During colonial times Charleston served as a port for the sale and shipment of agricultural products (especially rice and indigo) and for the importation and sale of African slaves for work on nearby plantations. The low-country plantations of the surrounding area brought prosperity to a small group of whites, who often maintained residences in Charleston. The city quickly became a center of wealth and culture. By 1750 Charleston was the fourth largest city in the colonies and the largest in the South, with 7,000 residents, about half white and half black. South Carolina was the first state to secede from the United States (1860) and the first shot of the Civil War was fired at Fort Sumter, which surrendered to Confederate forces on Apr. 14, 1861. The city never regained its economic or cultural importance after the Civil War. Tourism has become extremely important to Charleston's current economy, and the city now cultivates and sells its historical importance to visitors. Population (1990): 79,925.

See Also: South Carolina; Sumter, Battle of Fort.

■ **CHARTER OF PRIVILEGES (1701),** granted by William Penn to Pennsylvania (Oct. 28, 1701). The charter guaranteed freedom of worship, made all Christians eligible for public office, and established a unicameral legislature that superseded the original proprietary council.

See Also: Penn, William.

■ **CHASE, SALMON PORTLAND (1808-73),** sixth chief justice of the United States (1864-73). An active and influential politician and jurist during a tumultuous period in U.S. history, Chase was born in Cornish, New Hampshire. After studying law in Washington, D.C., he moved to Cincinnati in 1830 and embarked on a crusading political career. An abolitionist, Chase defended fugitive slaves, became active in the Free Soil party, and was elected to the U.S. Senate in 1848. He continued his opposition to slavery during his two terms as governor of Ohio (1855-60). Chase again served briefly in the U.S. Senate (1860-61) before becoming secretary of the treasury under Pres. Abraham Lincoln.

During the Civil War, Chase worked primarily to bolster the financial strength of the Union, establishing the national banking system in 1863. Loyal to his radical views, Chase opposed moderate policies and politicians and was often at odds with Lincoln. Throughout his political life Chase never lost his ambition to be president, but shortly after he resigned his cabinet post in 1864, he was appointed chief justice by Lincoln. Chase presided over the Court during the volatile political atmosphere of Reconstruction. He supported civil rights for the freed slaves and dissented on such important decisions as the Legal Tender Case of 1870 and the Slaughterhouse Cases of 1873, which interpreted the 14th Amendment narrowly as applying only to federal, not state, citizenship. Chase also presided over the trial of Jefferson Davis in 1868 and the impeachment proceedings of Pres. Andrew Johnson that same year.

See Also: Johnson, Andrew; Slaughterhouse Cases; Supreme Court.

BIBLIOGRAPHY: Blue, Frederick J., *Salmon P. Chase: A Life in Politics* (Kent State Univ. Press 1987); Niven, John, *Salmon P. Chase: A Biography* (Oxford Univ. Press 1995).

CHASE, SAMUEL (1741-1811), associate justice of the U.S. Supreme Court (1796-1811). A Somerset County, Maryland, native and signatory of the Declaration of Independence, Chase had also been a delegate both to the Continental Congress and to Maryland's Constitutional Ratification Convention. He was an outspoken Federalist on the bench, and the Jeffersonians brought impeachment proceedings against him (1804). The Senate, however, failed to convict him.

See Also: Declaration of Independence; Supreme Court.

CHATTANOOGA, BATTLE OF (1863), Civil War battle in which Union Gen. Ulysses S. Grant sought to drive Confederate Gen. Braxton Bragg's forces from their positions on the heights overlooking Chattanooga, Tennessee. On November 24, Union Gen. Joseph Hooker's corps seized Lookout Mountain in the "Battle Above the Clouds." The following day, when attacks on the northern and southern ends of Missionary Ridge stalled, Grant sent Gen. George Thomas's divisions straight up the steep slope in the ridge's center. The unlikely result was a rout of Bragg's forces, leaving the Union army free to press on into Georgia.

See Also: Civil War; Grant, Ulysses Simpson.

CHAUTAUQUA MOVEMENT, an adult education and lecture program founded in southwestern New York in 1874 as an offshoot of a Methodist summer camp. The Chautauqua Assembly originally offered courses in the sciences and humanities. It soon expanded to operate a home reading program and began attracting renowned lecturers to its summer session. Before long, "Chautauqua" became synonymous with any lecture series featuring guest speakers.

CHÁVEZ, CÉSAR (1927-93), labor leader. The son of Mexican immigrants, Chávez was born in Yuma, Arizona. When the family moved to California in 1939 to seek employment in the agricultural fields, they became part of a growing population of migrant laborers. After more than a decade in the fields, Chávez joined the Community Service Organization in 1952. He rose to national director but resigned in 1962 to dedicate himself to unionizing farm workers.

Chávez moved to Delano, California, and founded the National Farm Workers Association (later renamed the United Farm Workers). In 1965 the United Farm Workers called for a national boycott of table grapes as part of its campaign for union recognition. After 5 years of struggle, 26 grape growers signed contracts recognizing the United Farm Workers.

The Teamsters union, however, challenged Chávez's success by also signing contracts with farm workers. The ensuing four-year struggle ended when the UFW and the Teamsters signed an agreement. In 1974, Chávez's advocacy resulted in California's adoption of the Agricultural Labor Relations Act, a landmark piece of legislation that established collective bargaining for the state's farm workers. These victories, however, were undercut by antiunion politicians during the 1980s. Although Chávez never achieved the widespread social change he sought, his unstinting work raised wages and improved the working conditions for farm workers throughout the Southwest.

See Also: Labor Movement.

BIBLIOGRAPHY: del Castillo, Richard Griswold, and Richard A. Garcia, *César Chávez: A Triumph of Spirit* (Univ. of Oklahoma Press 1995); Ferriss, Susan, and Ricardo Sandoval, *The Fight in the Fields: César Chávez and the Farm Workers Movement* (Harcourt Brace 1997).

■ **CHECKS AND BALANCES,** phrase that describes how the federal government created by the U.S. Constitution in 1787 prevents concentrations of power through a system of separate institutions that share power. The concept has a long history in constitutional theory. Nevertheless, checks and balances did not play a role in the Articles of Confederation of 1777. Government under the Articles was designed to be weak and merely represented the states. Shays's Rebellion in Massachusetts (1786-87), however, demonstrated the dangers of a weak central government and increased support for the ratification of the new Constitution.

The framers agreed on the need for a stronger government to control the governed, but they also wanted government to be able to control itself. While there was some interest in creating a British-style constitution based on socioeconomic class, the framers feared that such a system would leave the wealthy at the mercy of the many who could gain control of the legislative branch. Hence, checks were created based solely on institutional interests. In addition, Congress was divided and could pass laws only if both the House of Representatives and the Senate agreed.

Another check was the power of the president to veto an act of Congress and to appoint justices to the Supreme Court. In turn, the Congress may override the president's veto with a two-thirds majority vote in both houses and may remove presidents or judges from office through the process of impeachment.

The powers of the Supreme Court are not clearly spelled out in the Constitution. Congress defines the number of justices who may sit on the Supreme Court and is in charge of organizing the federal judicial system throughout the country. Judicial review, or the judiciary's power to declare laws unconstitutional, emerged from the words of some of the framers, but mainly from the precedent set by the landmark case *Marbury* v. *Madison* in 1803.

—SCOTT L. MCLEAN

See Also: Constitution of the United States; Marbury v. Madison; Separation of Powers; Shays's Rebellion.

BIBLIOGRAPHY: Bailyn, Bernard, *Ideological Origins of the American Revolution* (Harvard Univ. Press 1967); Hamilton, Alexander, John Jay, and James Madison, *The Federalist Papers* (Bantam 1982); McDonald, Forrest, *Novus Ordo Seclorum* (Univ. Press of Kansas 1985); Wood, Gordon, *The Creation of the American Republic, 1776-1787* (Univ. of North Carolina Press 1969).

■ **CHEROKEE,** Indians who originally lived in what is now the southeastern United States. They were one of the so-called Five Civilized Tribes. Most Cherokees were relocated in the 1830s to the Oklahoma Territory. Today they maintain reservations in North Carolina and Oklahoma.

At the time of European contact the Cherokees controlled part of eight present-day states, an area of approximately 40,000 square miles. They lived in small villages, each with a seven-sided council house that represented the seven Cherokee clans. Each community chose two chiefs: a peace chief who governed in peacetime and a war chief who ruled in periods of hostilities. The Cherokees recognized lineage through the mother's family, and children belonged to the mother's clan. Marriages took place only between people of different clans. The cultivation of corn was a primary activity. One of the most important observances was the "busk" ceremony, celebrated when the new crop of corn was harvested each autumn. Games were also important in Cherokee culture. The modern sport of lacrosse is a version of the traditional southeastern Indian ball game.

In the early 1800s the Cherokees organized themselves into a single nation with a democratic government headed by a chief, vice chief, and 32-man council. A constitution and law code were adopted. The chief Sequoya devised a written alphabet for the Cherokee language.

The Cherokees ceded their last remaining territory east of the Mississippi River in the December 1835 Treaty of New Echota. In exchange they received most of what is now northeastern Oklahoma. The removal to Oklahoma in the winters of 1838 and 1839 is called the "Trail of Tears" by the Cherokees and the other Indians involved. During the 1,000-mile journey many died from disease, poor food, and lack of shelter. U.S. soldiers drove the Indians at a cruel pace, and about 4,000 died, nearly a quarter of their total population. The removal is now considered one of the most shameful acts in American history.

Today Cherokee communities maintain many of their traditional cultural practices. The Cherokee language is still widely spoken among them.

—RYAN MADDEN

See Also: Five Civilized Tribes; Indians of North America; Sequoya; Trail of Tears.

BIBLIOGRAPHY: Satz, Ronald, *American Indian Policy in the Jacksonian Era* (Univ. of Nebraska Press 1975); Wilkins, Thurman, *Cherokee Tragedy* (Macmillan 1970).

■ **CHEROKEE NATION CASES (1831-32),** two U.S. Supreme Court cases concerning legal control of tribal lands. As white settlement of the Southeast expanded in the early 19th century, both state and federal governments sought to remove Indian tribes from lands that had been ceded by treaty. When gold was discovered on Cherokee tribal land in 1829, thousands of white settlers went there. The state of Georgia refused to protect tribal claims and passed a law forbidding Cherokee from mining gold. The Cherokee sued the state. In *Cherokee Nation v. Georgia* (1831), the Supreme Court ruled (4-2) that the tribe was a "domestic, dependent nation" under the guardianship of the federal government and not subject to state jurisdiction. In *Worcester v. Georgia* (1832) the Court ruled (5-1) to expand the Cherokee nation's autonomy. The nation, wrote Chief Justice John Marshall, was a distinct political unit with the right to administer its own affairs. Pres. Andrew Jackson, an advocate of tribal removal to pave the way for new white settlement, refused to support the Court's decision. The government ordered the Cherokee Nation to relocate to the Indian Territory in 1838, and thousands died along the "Trail of Tears" to what is now Oklahoma.

See Also: Cherokee; Supreme Court; Trail of Tears.

BIBLIOGRAPHY: Wallace, Anthony F. C., *The Long, Bitter Trail: Andrew Jackson and the Indians* (Hill & Wang 1993).

■ **CHERRY VALLEY MASSACRE (1778),** British attack in frontier New York during the American Revolution. In response to American attacks on British-allied Iroquois, a force of British regulars, Indians, and Loyalists raided and destroyed Cherry Valley, a community of about 300 in central New York. Led by British Capt. Walter Butler and Mohawk leader Joseph Brant, the 300 invaders killed 30 residents, most of them women and children. This frontier atrocity outraged Americans and led to more raids on Iroquois villages.

See Also: Brant, Joseph; Revolution, American.

■ **CHESAPEAKE AND LEOPARD AFFAIR (1807),** maritime incident that helped to intensify anti-British sentiments among Americans. On June 22, 1807, the British warship *Leopard* stopped the American frigate *Chesapeake* off the Virginia coast. Claiming that four of the American seaman aboard the *Chesapeake* were British deserters, the *Leopard* commander demanded their surrender. When the American commander refused, the British opened fire, killing three Americans. News of the hostility provoked U.S. anger, but when Pres. Thomas Jefferson attempted to force the British to make reparations, they refused, further increasing British-American tensions and drawing the two countries closer to open warfare. Finally, on Nov. 1, 1811, the British offered a settlement regarding the *Chesapeake* incident and Sec. of State James Monroe accepted it, but by then the stage for war was well set, and within eight months the War of 1812 began.

■ **CHESNUT, MARY BOYKIN (1823-86),** American Civil War diarist. Born in Pleasant Hill, South Carolina, she married James Chesnut, Jr., in 1840. He became a prominent political figure in South Carolina. Mary Chesnut's 400,000-word diary, published in part after her death as *A Diary from Dixie* (1905), perceptively depicts the Southern aristocracy among whom she lived. Although she was opposed to slavery, she remained fiercely loyal to the Confederacy.

See Also: Women in American History.

■ **CHEYENNE INDIANS.** *See:* Great Plains Indians.

■ **CHICAGO,** the third largest city in the United States and the Midwest's center of commerce and culture, located in Illinois on the southwestern shore of Lake Michigan. The first European settlement occurred when Jean Baptiste du Sable, a black New Orleans fur trader, established a trading post at the Chicago River's mouth about

1770. The town incorporated as a city in 1833 with a population of 150. After the opening of the Erie Canal in New York in 1825 Chicago became the focus of westward expansion. With the completion of the railroad in 1852 the city became the busiest rail center in the world and the Midwestern center for trading in livestock, grain, lumber, and manufactured goods. The population exploded to 300,000 by 1870. With industry came urban problems and labor unrest. In 1886 the Haymarket Square Riot resulted when police stormed a group of workers listening to speeches about workers' rights. In 1889 the social reformers Jane Addams and Ellen Starr founded Hull House to alleviate some of the working-class hardships and to train ethnic whites in the mores of the middle class. After the turn of the century many Southern African Americans moved to Chicago in an attempt to find better living conditions and economic opportunities. Population (1994): 2,731,743.

See Also: City in American History; Erie Canal; Haymarket Incident; Hull House; Skyscrapers.

■ **CHICKAMAUGA, BATTLE OF (1863),** Civil War engagement in northern Georgia between the forces of Union Gen. William Rosecrans and Confederate Gen. Braxton Bragg. On September 19, day-long frontal fighting was indecisive. On the 20th, Bragg failed to turn the Union left, but the corps of Gen. James Longstreet rushed through a large gap in the Union right, the result of a blunder by Rosecrans. Only the stand of Union Gen. George Thomas, the "Rock of Chickamauga," saved the Union army from annihilation. After the battle, the Union army fell back to Chattanooga.

See Also: Civil War.

■ **CHICKASAW,** Muskogeean-speaking tribe originally inhabiting the area of present-day western Tennessee and Kentucky and northern Mississippi and Alabama. They lived in villages, farming the fertile fields and hunting and gathering wild foods. In the 1540s, they successfully fought off the invasion of Spanish soldiers under Hernando de Soto, but the encounter took its toll, as many Chickasaws died from Virgin Soil Epidemics introduced by the invaders. By the time the British and French arrived in the late 17th century, the Chickasaws had re-

grouped. During the colonial era, they engaged in an active trade with both the French and the British. However, after the American Revolution, the Chickasaws came increasingly under the dominion of the United States, and despite their support of the Americans during the Creek War of 1813-14, they were forced to sell most of their lands in 1818. In 1832, they ceded the remainder of their lands east of the Mississippi in exchange for lands in Indian Territory and in 1838 were removed there.

See Also: Creek; De Soto, Hernando; Indian Removal; Indians of North America.

■ **CHILD, LYDIA MARIA (1802-80),** author and reformer. She was born in Medford, Massachusetts. She published America's first children's magazine, *Juvenile Miscellany* (1826). In 1833, she wrote *An Appeal in Favor of That Class of Americans Called Africans*, an abolitionist tract that damaged her popularity and social standing. Nevertheless, she continued to work for abolition. Child moved to New York City in 1841 to edit *National Anti-Slavery Standard*, the weekly newspaper of the American Anti-Slavery Society.

See Also: Antislavery Movement; Women in American History.

Prolific author and ardent abolitionist, Lydia Maria Child was ostracized from her community after denouncing racial inequality of education and employment in her 1833 book, *An Appeal in Favor of That Class of Americans Called Africans.*

CHILD LABOR, often exploitative work that became widespread during the industrialization of the 19th century and was subsequently contested by social reform movements. During the 17th and 18th centuries, child labor was common in the family and farm economies and in the trades. Patterns of child labor changed, however, with the rise in factory production in the early 19th century when children were seen as pliant workers who could be paid low wages. Reformers challenged this system, advocating education requirements and initiating legal changes. The surge in immigration into the United States after 1840, however, provided a new pool of child labor and undermined reform efforts.

The expansion of American industry in the last decades of the 19th century resulted in increased abuses of child laborers and prompted Progressive reformers into action. Between 1900 and 1930, child-labor organizations pushed many protective laws through state legislatures and Congress but experienced as many setbacks at the hands of conservative opponents. Child-labor reform benefited from the New Deal of the 1930s. The National Industrial Recovery Act (1933) reduced child labor, while the Fair Standards of Act (1938) set minimum wages and maximum hours for child workers. Apart from social and political changes, child labor declined with increased mechanization in factories, a greater skill level required of much industrial work, and a lengthening of the school day and year. At the end of the 20th century, child labor in America could be found primarily among illegal immigrants in urban textile factories and in agricultural fields.

See Also: Fair Labor Standards Act; Labor Movement.

BIBLIOGRAPHY: Trattner, Walter I., *Crusade for the Children: A History of the National Child Labor Committee and Child Labor Reform in America* (Quadrangle Books 1970).

CHILD REARING, method of raising children that differs among cultures and periods in American history. The history of child rearing reveals important information about parental, gender, and economic roles within families.

Approaches to raising children have changed from the colonial period to the present. The shared labor and economy of whites inhabiting rural colonial households resulted in shared parenting, as mothers guided daughters and fathers directed sons. As the birthrate declined in the 19th century, so did white women's economic contributions to the family economy. With increasing urbanization and industrialization came the division of gendered "spheres." Middle- and upper-class women controlled the domestic realm, while men inhabited the public world of work. Fathers spent less time with their children, and the role of the mother as moral instructor for children of both sexes gained importance.

Although certain gender divisions within relatively isolated nuclear families were standard in white society, not all cultures in America followed similar patterns. African Americans, for example, adopted a more communal approach to raising children, since many African-American women were employed outside the home.

Today, mothers and fathers of many ethnicities in America work, as two-income families are the norm. Spouses must share child-care responsibilities, although men are often reluctant to assume what are often regarded as traditional "female" roles. Additional child care is often needed, and many companies have programs to make occupations and workplaces more "family friendly."

—CATHERINE A. HAULMAN

See Also: Women in American History.

BIBLIOGRAPHY: Jones, Jacqueline, *Labor of Love, Labor of Sorrow: Black Women, Work and the Family from Slavery to the Present* (Basic Books 1985); Mintz, Steven, and Susan Kellogg, *Domestic Revolutions: A Social History of American Family Life* (Free Press 1987).

CHINESE EXCLUSION ACT (1882), first law to prohibit the immigration of a specific ethnic group to the United States. Originally designed to prevent the entry of Chinese laborers, who were thought to be an economic threat to white workers, the act was revised in 1888 to include all Chinese, with some exceptions.

See Also: Chinese Immigration; Immigration.

CHINESE IMMIGRATION, the arrival of Chinese immigrants to the United States, which occurred in two great movements. Between 1852 and 1875, about 200,000 Chinese workers were brought to

A Chinese immigrant displays his queue for the camera. Congress passed the Chinese Exclusion Act in 1882, and extensions of the act barred Chinese immigration until 1943, after which 105 were admitted annually.

California from Kwangtung Province in southern China. These early immigrants were mostly men and worked mainly in agriculture, mining, and railroad construction. During the economic depression of the 1870s, American labor organizations blamed Chinese immigrants for taking jobs from white workers. In 1882, these groups succeeded in lobbying Congress to pass the first of a series of exclusion laws, which effectively closed the door on further Chinese immigration until the Immigration Reform Act of 1965 ended quotas. Between 1965 and 1990, more than 700,000 Chinese, many from professional classes, immigrated to the United States from Hong Kong, Taiwan, and China. The 1990 census counted about 1,645,000 Chinese Americans. About half of this population resides in California and Hawaii.

See Also: Chinese Exclusion Act; Ethnic Groups; Immigration.

BIBLIOGRAPHY: Ong Hing, Bill, *Making and Remaking Asian America Through Immigration Policy, 1850-1990* (Stanford Univ. Press 1992); Takaki, Ronald, *Strangers from a Different Shore: A History of Asian Americans* (Penguin Books 1989).

■ **CHINOOK INDIANS.** *See:* Northwest Coast Indians.

■ **CHIPEWYAN INDIANS.** *See:* Subarctic Indians.

■ **CHIPPEWA INDIANS.** *See:* Ojibwa (Chippewa) Indians.

■ **CHISHOLM, SHIRLEY (1924-),** educator and Democratic politician. Born in Brooklyn, New York, she taught and built day-care centers in low-income neighborhoods in New York City. From 1959 to 1964, she was an adviser to New York City's Bureau of Child Welfare. The first African-American woman elected to Congress, she served there from 1968 to 1982 and was an outspoken opponent of the Vietnam War, a leader of the Congressional Black Caucus, and a fierce advocate for the poor.

See Also: African Americans; Women in American History; Women's Movement.

■ *CHISHOLM V. GEORGIA (1793),* U.S. Supreme Court case, one of its earliest, that considered the right of citizens of one state to bring suit in another state. The South Carolina estate of a one-time Georgia resident, Alexander Chisholm, sued the state of Georgia to recover bonds belonging to Chisholm. The bonds had been seized by Georgia during the Revolution. Georgia maintained that its sovereign status shielded it from the heirs' claims, since those claims now originated from out of state. By a vote of 4-1, with Justice James Iredell dissenting, the Supreme Court rejected that argument. Writing for the Court, Chief Justice John Jay grounded his holding in Article III, Section 2, of the Constitution. Justice James Wilson's opinion remains the most notable, however, for its declaration of a national popular sovereignty. Wilson dismissed, out-of-hand, the claim that any state enjoyed anything like a sovereign status vis-à-vis the federal government. Sovereignty, explained Wilson, was located in the people of the United States. At no time during the creation of the new nation had the American people entrusted any of their sovereignty to the states. But Wilson's opinion was so unpopular that within five years the 11th Amendment was ratified, guaranteeing all states immunity from suits brought by a citizen of another state.

—MATTHEW E. BABCOCK

See Also: Supreme Court.

BIBLIOGRAPHY: Jacobs, Clyde E., "Prelude to Amendment: The States Before the Court," *American Journal of Legal History 12* (1968); Mathis, D., "Chisholm v. Georgia: Background and Settlement," *Journal of American History 54* (1967).

■ **CHOCTAW INDIANS,** Muskogeean-speaking tribe originally from southeastern North America. The Choctaws lived in towns in the present-day states of Mississippi, Arkansas, and Alabama, subsisting through farming and hunting. Because the Choctaws were in the last stages of mound-building in the 16th century, many anthropologists believe they are descendants of the Mississippians. In the 18th century, the Choctaws were formally allied with the French, although many Choctaw villages traded with the British. They sided with the colonists during the American Revolution, but, despite their support, they were forced to sign a removal treaty in 1830. In that year the Choctaws were the first of the so-called Five Civilized Tribes to move west of the Mississippi River into Indian Territory. Today some Choctaws still live in Mississippi and Alabama, while another group resides in Oklahoma.

See Also: Five Civilized Tribes; Indians of North America; Mississippian Culture.

■ **CHOPIN, KATE (1851-1904),** author. Born in St. Louis, Missouri, she wrote more than 100 stories drawing on her Creole background and her experiences living in Louisiana. A number of these stories were collected in *Bayou Folk* (1894) and *A Night in Acadie* (1897). She shocked her contemporaries with *The Awakening* (1899), a frank and psychologically complex novel about a young married woman's sexual and artistic self-discovery.

See Also: Women in American History.

■ **CHOUTEAU FAMILY,** founding family of St. Louis whose business partnerships dominated the fur trade of the Missouri River until the Civil War. The family matriarch, Marie Thérèse Bourgeois Chouteau (1733-1814), was born in New Orleans and married René Chouteau in 1748. Abandoned by her husband, she later settled in St. Louis, a new town founded in 1764 by her son Auguste (1749-1829) and Pierre de Laclède Liguest (1729-78). Laclède had become Marie Chouteau's true partner and the father of her four younger children. (All her children kept the Chouteau name.) Auguste and his half-brother Jean Pierre (1758-1849) both prospered in the fur trade and became large landholders. They helped negotiate treaties with a variety of Indian tribes and also hosted and provided credit for the Lewis and Clark expedition in the early 1800s. The next generation of Chouteaus continued to build the wealth and power of this dynasty. Pierre Chouteau, Jr. (1789-1865), the second son of Jean Pierre, formed a series of family partnerships, one of which purchased the Western Department of the American Fur Company from John Jacob Astor in 1834. Under Pierre's leadership, the company pioneered the use of steamboats in the Missouri fur trade and built or acquired strategic trading posts in the West such as Fort Union, Fort Laramie, and Fort Benton. The family company held sway over a vast region and arguably had more influence and greater resources in the Far West than the federal government in the pre–Civil War period. In his later years, Pierre, Jr., became increasingly involved with iron mines, rolling mills, and railroad bonds. Through such activities and real estate holdings in Missouri and a variety of western places, Pierre and other family members increased their wealth despite the decline of the fur trade.

—JAY GITLIN

See Also: Frontier in American History; Fur Trade.

BIBLIOGRAPHY: Foley, William E., and C. David Rice, *The First Chouteaus* (Univ. of Illinois Press 1983).

■ **CHRISTIAN SCIENCE,** indigenous American religion founded in 1879 by Mary Baker Eddy and based on principles of divine healing. Eddy suffered from poor health and tried various remedies before studying with Phineas Pankhurst Quimby, a mental healer. She discovered divine healing when she recovered from an illness in 1866 after reading an account of healing by Jesus in the

New Testament. Eddy believed that illness and death are an illusion and that mind and spirit are the only reality. From 1870 to 1880, she taught her beliefs in Lynn, Massachusetts. In 1875 she published a textbook on Christian Science, *Science and Health*, which was published in a revised edition in 1883 as *Science and Health, with Key to the Scriptures*. Eddy and 26 followers founded the Church of Christ, Scientist. They moved the headquarters to Boston in 1892 and founded the First Church of Christ, Scientist, of Boston ("the Mother Church"). In 1898, the movement established the Christian Science Publishing Society to support worldwide evangelism. The *Christian Science Monitor*, founded in 1908, is today an international newspaper noted for its accurate reporting. Currently, there about 3,000 Christian Science churches worldwide. Services are led by two readers, one citing the Scripture and the other reading from *Science and Health*. Controversies about the healing practices still bring followers public attention and at times legal challenges.

See Also: Eddy, Mary Baker; Religion.

■ **CHURUBUSCO, BATTLE OF (1847),** battle during the Mexican War. After taking the city of Puebla, Gen. Winfield Scott's army moved on Mexico City. Although the Americans held the advantage in leadership, armament, and tactics, the outnumbered Mexican force at Churubusco, outside Mexico City, halted Scott's army on August 20 and fought bravely before being overwhelmed. The American victory opened the door to Mexico City and led to the ultimate defeat of Mexico.

See Also: Mexican War; Scott, Winfield.

■ **CINCINNATI, SOCIETY OF,** the first veterans' group in the United States. Established in 1783 by officers of the American Continental Army at the urging of Gen. Henry Knox, the society worked to retain the bonds forged during the American Revolution and to press for the payment of war salaries that were in arrears. Its first president-general was George Washington. The society established a fund for war widows and indigent soldiers and sought to perpetuate the society by making membership hereditary, arousing charges of elitism.

See Also: Knox, Henry.

■ **CIRCUIT RIDERS,** traveling Methodist preachers of the frontier regions of early America. Robert Strawbridge, who arrived about 1764, was the first of many men who with a horse and saddlebags served as many as 30 communities. The best known, Peter Cartwright, traveled Tennessee, Kentucky, Ohio, Indiana, and Illinois throughout the first half of the 19th century.

See Also: Methodist Church; Religion.

■ **CIRCUSES,** form of entertainment often in rings and usually featuring trained animals, feats of horsemanship, and performances by clowns, acrobats, and aerialists. Philip Astley developed the first modern circus in 1768 in London, when he organized a series of equestrian and acrobatic performances. John Williams Ricketts founded the first American circus, closely modeled on the English version, in Philadelphia in 1793. This and other early American circuses were primarily shows of horsemanship that were performed in semipermanent structures and that moved infrequently. With the appearance of the first elephant in an American show, the traveling menagerie developed independently. By about 1825, however, the menagerie and the circus merged to become one of the most famous forms of popular entertainment.

During the 19th century, circuses traveled continuously to cities and towns throughout America with much fanfare. A typical circus consisted of dozens of horses and wagons, two or three large tents, and a cast of performers and trained animals. Wild animal acts were first introduced in the 1820s and steam calliopes in 1857.

A pioneer in mass entertainment, Phineas T. Barnum created his circus in 1871 and combined it with James A. Bailey's in 1881. Barnum & Bailey's Circus eventually merged with the Ringling Brothers to form the largest and most successful circus in American history. During the 1950s and 1960s, most circuses went indoors, but their popularity remained unabated at the close of the 20th century.

BIBLIOGRAPHY: Albrecht, Ernest, *The New American Circus* (Univ. of Florida Press 1995); May, Earl Chapin, *The Circus from Rome to Ringling* (Dover 1963).

■ **CITIZEN GENÊT AFFAIR (1793),** incident in which the French minister to the United States contrived actions infringing on American sover-

Circuses in the 19th century emphasized the exotic—women in unconventional roles and wild animals such as leopards, tigers, and elephants. This emphasis helped establish the circus as a popular form of entertainment.

eignty. At the height of the radical phase of the French Revolution, Minister Edmond Genêt traveled to the United States to garner support for France. Upon arriving in April 1793, Genêt began to commission U.S. mercenaries for service against British shipping in the Caribbean and against the Spanish in Florida. Enormous crowds greeted Genêt wherever he went, but when he urged the U.S. Congress to reject Pres. George Washington's neutrality proclamation and to pass instead a resolution favoring France, Washington demanded, with the support of Congress, that he be removed from his ministerial office. As strongly as Washington felt about Genêt's inappropriate conduct, the president refused in 1794 to turn Genêt over to the new Jacobin government in France, which sought to arrest (and likely kill) the former minister. Genêt, who remained in the United States, married the daughter of New York Gov. George Clinton and became a U.S. citizen.

■ **CITIZENSHIP,** membership in a nation, with rights and obligations that inform political participation. In the United States, citizenship and equal protection of the laws are guaranteed by the 14th Amendment, which was adopted in 1868. Prior to 1868, birthright citizenship was not secure for freed African-American slaves, Asian workers, women, and Indians, mainly because the framers left citizen status undefined in the Constitution.

Birthright citizenship is rare. Most modern nations, including Germany and Japan, base citizenship on descent or ethnicity (*jus sanguinis*). Birthright citizenship, however, is common in countries that are culturally diverse or built on immigration, such as the United States, France, Canada, and India.

Birthright citizenship has always worried some Americans, who have argued that it violates the idea that citizens must show openly that they freely consent to their government. Efforts to exclude some individuals from equal protection and privileges because of race, language, national origin, political views, religion, and sexual preference occasionally succeed in spite of the 14th Amendment. Throughout U.S. history, witch hunts have emerged seeking to root out "un-American" citizens or calling for loyalty oaths. More recently, some have called for limits on non-European immigration in order to preserve territorial integrity and national culture.

—SCOTT L. MCLEAN

See Also: Constitution of the United States; Immigration.

BIBLIOGRAPHY: Jacobsen, David, *Rights Across Borders: Immigration and the Decline of Citizenship* (Johns Hopkins Univ. Press 1996); Schuck, Peter, and Rogers Smith, *Citizenship Without Consent: Immigrants in the American Polity* (Yale Univ. Press 1985); Shklar, Judith, *American Citizenship: The Quest for Inclusion* (Harvard Univ. Press 1991).

■ **CITY IN AMERICAN HISTORY.** Colonial America was overwhelmingly rural, and its few urban centers were small by European standards. The first federal census of 1790 counted only five cities with more than 10,000 inhabitants: New York City (33,000), Boston (18,000), Philadelphia (16,000), Charleston (16,000), and Baltimore (13,000). Their combined population amounted to less than 3 percent of the nation's population. Yet, colonial cities had a profound impact on the development of colonial society. Especially in the North, port towns were the center of colonial economic and political life. The cities were the gateways to the colonies, the point of entry for immigrants and imports as well as the collection centers for the export of raw materials. In the 18th century, Boston, New York, and Philadelphia grew into bustling ports with large shipping and ship-building industries employing growing numbers of seamen, longshoremen, artisans, and laborers. The social structure of these colonial cities was dominated by the merchants, for they provided the key links in the colonial economic system.

The colonial South did not develop dynamic cities of this type. Even in large cities such as Charleston and Baltimore, the merchants were largely subservient to the operations of northern or British companies, and there was relatively little local industry or enterprise. The subordination of cities to the slave economy was a dominant feature of the South.

19th Century. From 1800 to 1860 the urban population of America grew at a greater rate than at any other time in the nation's history. The rise of the factory system and the development of efficient forms of transportation (especially the railroad), both aspects of the industrial revolution, worked to concentrate the growing manufacturing labor force in urban centers. By the eve of the Civil War, 12 percent of the nation's population lived in cities with 25,000 or more inhabitants. Greater New York City had more than 1 million residents by 1860, Philadelphia had more than 500,000, and the populations of Boston and Baltimore were each about 200,000. All of these cities had become industrial as well as commercial centers, with large populations of immigrants.

One of the most significant developments was the appearance of great new cities to the west. Westward expansion was accompanied by the development of regional trading centers. By 1860, Cincinnati, St. Louis, Chicago, and New Orleans all had populations of more than 100,000. These cities dominated the trade of large rural "hinterlands." Cincinnati, for example, specialized in the slaughter and packing of hogs and on this economic base rose to become the premier industrial city of the mid-19th-century West. Chicago became a railroad center for lines stretching east and west, the go-between linking the settlements and resources of the West with the cities, factories, and commercial networks of the Northeast. By the 1880s, Chicago had become the nation's "second city," with a powerful industrial economy and a booming population of migrants from the American countryside and immigrants from eastern and southern Europe.

During the second half of the 19th century, important cities also developed in the Far West. San Francisco was built with the fabulous wealth of the California Gold Rush, and Denver rose as a center for processing the ores produced by the mines of the Rocky Mountains. After the railroad linked southern California to the national rail system in the 1880s, Los Angeles became the commercial center for orchard and row-crop agribusiness. Lacking a good harbor and a sufficient water supply, the city's leaders persuaded the federal government to invest millions in the construction of a port and waged a successful campaign to divert mountain water hundreds of miles to quench the thirst of the growing city. By 1900, a higher proportion of people lived in the cities of the West than in any other region of the country except the Northeast. In the nation as a whole, 26 percent of the population lived in cities of 25,000 inhabitants or greater.

20th Century. At the turn of the century, industrial urbanization in America entered its second phase, characterized by the wide availability of electricity for both home and industry, the adoption of the telephone, the spread of rapid transit, and, most significantly, by the appearance of the automobile. All these factors encouraged the decentralization of both production and residential patterns, with urban areas spreading across much greater areas. The history of Houston, Texas, is an example of these kinds of changes. Developing in the late 19th century as a marketing center for lumber and cotton, Houston had a population of about 75,000 in 1910. Then, the discovery of vast petroleum reserves along the Gulf coast transformed the city into a busy refining center. Abundant land surrounding the city center combined with the availability of the automobile determined a pattern of urban sprawl. Houston became a decentralized, low-density city, spreading dozens of miles in all directions from the downtown center. Suburbs were part of this urban sprawl, which became the dominant pattern of American urban development in the 20th century.

The federal census for 1920 showed that for the first time in American history the urban outnumbered the rural population, but since the census bureau's definition of an urban place was one with a population of at least 2,500 residents this statistic was not particularly revealing. More so was the fact that 36 percent of Americans lived in 752 cities of 25,000 residents or more. By 1990 that proportion had topped 50 percent. The combination of growing urban populations and sprawling cities led to the phenomenon known as "conurbation": the convergence of the peripheral zones of several cities. Best known is the urban region sometimes dubbed "Boswash," the chain of continuous cities along the northeastern seaboard that stretches from Boston to Washington, D.C. Other similar areas include the Buffalo-Pittsburgh-Cleveland corridor and the greater Milwaukee-Chicago-Gary region. Eventually these conurbations will likely all come together to form a huge urban region covering much of the Northeast. Such total urbanization already characterizes most of southern California. As important as the city has been in American history, there were indications at the end of the 20th century that the next era would be dominated by the "megalopolis."

—JOHN MACK FARAGHER

See Also: *Atlanta; Baltimore; Boston; Chicago; Kansas City; Las Vegas; Los Angeles; Miami; New Orleans; New York City; Philadelphia; Pittsburgh; San Francisco; St. Louis; Suburbanization; Urbanism.*

BIBLIOGRAPHY: Chudacoff, Howard P., *The Evolution of American Urban Society* (Prentice-Hall 1975); Monkkonen, Eric H., *America Becomes Urban: The Development of U.S. Cities and Towns, 1780-1980* (Univ. of California Press 1988); Teaford, Jon C., *The Twentieth-Century American City* (Johns Hopkins Univ. Press 1993).

■ **CIVILIAN CONSERVATION CORPS (CCC),** New Deal public-works project. Created in 1933 to provide both worthwhile employment and a wholesome environment for young men during the Depression, the CCC operated some 1,500 camps across the country and left a lasting mark on the nation. Workers received room and board plus $30 a month while working on conservation-related projects such as roads, bridges, and dams. They created or renovated national and state parks, campgrounds, and recreation areas, many of which are still in use. In addition to its public-works aspect, the CCC served another purpose. By relocating jobless urban youth to rural areas and requiring them to send a portion of their monthly stipend home, it helped ease social tension in the cities while providing some economic relief for low-income families. More than 2.5 million youths took part in the CCC before it was phased out at the start of World War II.

See Also: *New Deal.*

BIBLIOGRAPHY: Lacy, Leslie A., *The Soil Soldiers: The Civilian Conservation Corps in the Great Depression* (Chilton 1976).

■ **CIVIL LIBERTIES,** basic rights guaranteed to all citizens under the Bill of Rights. Although civil liberties are institutionalized in the Constitution's first 10 amendments, they have often been denied to minorities and women.

The Constitution outlined several civil liberties, including the jury trial and habeas corpus. The Bill of Rights expanded them, by guaranteeing freedom of speech, religion, and assembly, among others. Federal enforcement of civil liberties was dramatically strengthened with the adoption of the 13th, 14th, and 15th Amendments during the Civil War era and with five general civil rights acts between 1866 and 1876.

Despite the amendments and the legislation, however, African Americans were denied civil liberties, even at the federal level. *Plessy* v. *Ferguson* (1896), for example, legalized racial segregation in public accommodations. It was not until the civil rights movement of the 1950s and 1960s that significant reversals resulted in such institutionalized abuses of civil liberties.

Although African Americans and women had been central in the efforts to extend individual civil liberties, Hispanics, Indians, Asian Americans, and others have also been victims of denied rights as well as facilitators of change. Although the framers ensured basic civil liberties, history has shown the necessity for individual and collective action in changing laws and influencing judicial decisions that serve to expand and protect these liberties.

See Also: Civil Rights Movement; Constitution of the United States.

BIBLIOGRAPHY: Abraham, Henry J., *Freedom and the Court: Civil Rights and Liberties in the United States* (Oxford Univ. Press 1994); Hall, Kermit L., ed., *Civil Liberties in American History: Major Historical Interpretators* (Garland Press 1987).

■ **CIVIL RIGHTS ACTS.** Under pressure from a resurgent civil rights movement, Congress ended almost a century of inaction on civil rights, passing six civil rights laws between 1957 and 1972. Restrained by a coalition of southern Democrats and conservative Republicans, it initially acted cautiously, passing weak laws in 1957 and 1960. The Civil Rights Act of 1957 established a Commission on Civil Rights to investigate discrimination in voting, made it a federal offense to interfere with the right to vote, and gave the attorney general authority to prosecute violations. The Civil Rights Act of 1960 added modestly to these provisions, requiring state officials to preserve election records for at least two years, authorizing federal judges to appoint federal referees to supervise voter registration when they found local officials guilty of discrimination, and establishing penalties for anyone found guilty of obstructing federal court orders or crossing state lines to participate in bombings or arson.

Landmark Acts of the 1960s. The crescendo of civil rights protest in the early 1960s, coupled with support for tough new legislation from Presidents John F. Kennedy and Lyndon B. Johnson, resulted in two landmark laws. The Civil Rights Act of 1964 struck a powerful blow against discrimination on the basis of race, religion, or national origin. It banned such discrimination in all public accommodations that affected interstate commerce, authorized the attorney general to bring lawsuits to end discrimination in schools or other public facilities, and provided for ending federal financial support for any program found guilty of discrimination. It also attacked employment discrimination, making it illegal for most employers to discriminate on the basis of race, religion, national origin, or sex and establishing a federal agency, the Equal Employment Opportunity Commission (EEOC), to monitor compliance. A year later, Congress adopted the Voting Rights Act of 1965. The act banned the use of literacy tests (historically the most notorious disfranchising tool) in states and counties with a history of discrimination, required those jurisdictions to obtain approval from the Justice Department or the federal courts before implementing any new voting regulations, and authorized the Justice Department to appoint federal officers to register voters in counties where there was evidence of continued discrimination. Landmark pieces of legislation containing effective means of enforcement, these laws quickly brought to an end the system of segregation and disfranchisement that had taken root in the South in the 1890s.

Although civil rights advocates pressed for additional legislation, the white backlash of the late 1960s and the nation's increasingly conservative mood made progress difficult. The Civil Rights Act of 1968 clarified federally protected civil rights, gave the attorney general broad authority to prosecute persons who interfered with those rights, and banned discrimination on account of race, religion, or national origin in the sale or rental of real estate. However, the provisions for enforcing the open-housing guarantee lacked teeth. In 1972, Congress passed the Equal Employment Opportunity Act, which modestly expanded the 1964 act's ban on discrimination in employment, extending its coverage to state and local government, and gave the EEOC authority to sue employers who refused to end discriminatory practices.

Later Acts. Action on the legislative front continued in the 1970s and 1980s, although with diminished returns. In 1970, 1975, and 1982, civil rights advocates prodded Congress to extend the life of the Voting Rights Act and to add language to ensure creation of more predominantly minority electoral districts. In 1991, civil rights leaders secured passage of the Civil Rights Restoration Act, which reversed a series of 1989 Supreme Court decisions that had significantly weakened legal remedies against employment discrimination.

—DONALD G. NIEMAN

See Also: Civil Rights Movement; Supreme Court.
BIBLIOGRAPHY: Graham, Hugh Davis, *Civil Rights and the Presidency: Race and Gender in American Politics, 1960-1972* (Oxford Univ. Press 1992); Nieman, Donald G., *Promises to Keep: African Americans and the Constitutional Order, 1776 to the Present* (Oxford Univ. Press 1991).

■ **CIVIL RIGHTS CASES (1883),** group of U.S. Supreme Court cases that concerned the constitutionality of the 1875 Civil Rights Act and, specifically, the scope of the 14th Amendment as it applied to public accommodations. With the 1875 Civil Rights Act, Congress had sought to establish that the antidiscrimination guarantees of the 14th Amendment's equal protection clause extended not only to racial discrimination practiced by the states but also to discrimination in

privately owned public accommodations. The Supreme Court rejected this construction of the amendment and ruled the 1875 statute unconstitutional. Writing for the majority, Justice Joseph Bradley argued that Congress had overstepped the limited intention of the 14th Amendment. In the lone dissent, Justice John Harlan accused the Court of effectively emasculating the 14th Amendment. The 1883 decision represented a turning point in the history of legal struggles to eliminate racial discrimination. It would be 80 years before another set of federal laws was enacted to protect civil rights.

See Also: Civil Rights Acts; Harlan, John Marshal (1833-1911); Reconstruction.

■ **CIVIL RIGHTS MOVEMENT,** social and cultural activism intent upon dismantling the barriers of racism present in American life and institutions. Although the movement has deep roots in American history, the name refers most often to the period of activity from the end of World War II in 1945 to the late 1960s.

During the war, discrimination in the war industries was targeted by labor and civil rights leader A. Philip Randolph, who threatened a "thundering" all-black march of 10,000 on Washington, D.C., to "shake up white America" if discrimination did not end. His emphasis on the need for thousands of ordinary blacks to play a direct role in their own liberation figured in Pres. Franklin Roosevelt's issuance of Executive Order 8802, which created the Fair Employment Practices Committee.

The United States and the Soviet Union emerged from the war locked in competition for the minds of the "uncommitted peoples" of the world. Since the United States championed the "free world," the continued oppression of black Americans, according to singer and actor Paul Robeson, was evidence of hypocrisy. Such was Robeson's stature that when blacks were appointed to high posts, federal officials asserted that such appointments were "an answer to Paul Robeson."

In a brilliant victory for the National Association for the Advancement of Colored People (NAACP) lawyers, the Supreme Court declared in *Brown v. Board of Education of Topeka* (1954) that segregation "is inherently unequal," which helped set the stage for broad challenges to segregation in American public life. The next year, seamstress Rosa Parks refused to give her seat to a white man in a Montgomery bus and was jailed. A young minister, Martin Luther King, Jr., led Montgomery African Americans in a boycott of the buses that lasted a year before victory was achieved. Committed to nonviolent, direct action, King and his associates were harnessing the energy of the thousands to whom Randolph had directed attention. In 1957 at Little Rock, Arkansas, a courageous group of black school children, testing the *Brown* decision, faced a mob of whites enraged that they would attempt to desegregate Central High School. More than that, their entry was blocked by national guardsmen with fixed bayonets. President Eisenhower finally ordered out a U.S. airborne unit to protect the students and uphold the Constitution.

Protests in the Early 1960s. Still greater attention was focused on racism in February 1960, in Greensboro, North Carolina, when four black college students sat in at a "whites only" lunch counter and were beaten and jailed. Their example of nonviolent resistance was followed by sit-ins across the South that were widely publicized. Yet another dimension of the struggle was revealed when middle-class black adults joined students in boycotts of department stores, in cities such as Atlanta and Nashville, that denied blacks courteous service.

Music was drawn on by thousands of activists in and out of jail, and it remained vital to the movement, helping them absorb psychological and even physical abuse, contributing to a renewal of the spirit. That the music sung was mostly created by the slave ancestors of activists, at times with only slight changes of the words, indicates the continuity of the struggle. The song that became symbolic of the movement was "We Shall Overcome," key lines of which were very widely known: "We Shall Overcome, We Shall Overcome, We Shall Overcome Some Day/ Oh, Deep in My Heart, I Do Believe, We Shall Overcome Someday."

The Student Nonviolent Coordinating Committee (SNCC), founded in the spring of 1960, began directing student efforts. SNCC joined the Southern Christian Leadership Conference (SCLC), formed in 1957 out of the Montgomery Move-

Martin Luther King, Jr., confers with integration pioneer James Meredith (*to King's left*) while leading a civil rights march to Tougaloo College, Mississippi, in June 1960.

ment, as the new force in the civil rights movement. In 1961, the Congress of Racial Equality (CORE), which had a history of nonviolent action dating back to the early 1940s, challenged segregation in interstate travel by sending white and black "freedom riders" South to oppose seating arrangements at lunch counters in bus terminals.

When CORE, at the urging of President Kennedy's administration, called off the "freedom rides," which were met with brutal opposition, a group of freedom riders led by Diane Nash continued the rides to prevent fear of violence from defeating the movement.

The continued jailing and harassing of blacks heightened northern concern about the movement dating from Montgomery days. Such concern was a factor in the Justice Department urging the Interstate Commerce Commission to issue, on Nov. 1, 1961, a regulation prohibiting separate facilities for whites and blacks in bus and train terminals.

SNCC organizer Robert Moses, in the summer of 1961, mounted a voter registration campaign in McComb, Mississippi, building on indigenous leadership while attracting more seasoned SNCC organizers to McComb. In the process, he deepened and broadened the youth movement that had been growing since Montgomery. Also working with SNCC in voter registration was ex-sharecropper Fannie Lou Hamer. Her quality of courage was especially needed in Mississippi, where there was sweltering hatred of blacks by whites, including sheriffs, who were willing to shield as well as join in the murderous activities of the Ku Klux Klan.

March on Washington. The use of fire hoses and dogs against blacks demonstrating for desegregation in Birmingham, Alabama, in the spring of 1963 confirmed its reputation as the most segregated city in America. But vicious attacks did not dishearten the blacks of Birmingham. Partly because of the marchers' courageous spirit, a March on Washington for Jobs and Freedom occurred on Aug. 23, 1963, with more than 250,000 blacks and whites participating. During the speeches, it was announced that the previous day, in Ghana, W. E. B. Du Bois, the century's leading theorist of black liberation and a founder of the NAACP, had died at the age of 95.

Responding to the march, President Kennedy's proposed civil rights legislation, following his assassination, was steered through Congress by Pres. Lyndon B. Johnson. Thus, the Civil Rights Act of 1964 ended segregation in public accommodations and provided long-denied opportunities in employment and education for minorities and women. This legislation had resulted from such mounting protest that some observers had begun referring to the civil rights movement as the "Negro Revolution."

The Movement in the Mid-1960s. SNCC tested the willingness of the federal government to protect civil rights workers by inviting hundreds of white college students to participate in the Mississippi Summer Project of 1964. Within days, three young workers, two white and one black, were murdered by Klansmen with the complicity of Mississippi law enforcement officials. Widely covered by the media, their deaths highlighted the danger of blacks fighting for elementary rights in Mississippi. While the project had stressed the importance of the vote, the vote did not come to most southern African Americans until voting rights legislation was passed by Congress in 1965

Spreading civil rights demonstrations in the first half of 1963 set the stage for the enormously successful March on Washington in August of that year, in which over 250,000 Americans participated.

following the Selma, Alabama, campaign for the vote that culminated in a march of 25,000 to Montgomery, the state capital.

During a march on Jackson, Mississippi, in the summer of 1966 to protest the shooting of Medgar Evers, SNCC activists shouted "black power!" The thought behind the slogan, not universally supported by movement leaders, was that despite having the ballot and desegregated facilities, without economic power blacks had gained relatively little. Meanwhile, SNCC and SCLC, looking for new fields of civil rights work, faltered in the North. SCLC used nonviolent protests to oppose entrenched political injustice in Chicago and found racism there as ugly as anything seen in Mississippi or Alabama. The use of money once earmarked for fighting poverty to help finance the war in Vietnam compounded problems in inner cities, affecting huge numbers of people, including those once appealed to by the Black Panther party. SNCC's alliance with the Panthers, composed of young blacks favoring the gun to protect black communities from police violence, came apart with the discovery by both of how little, in methods and temperament, they had in common.

Martin Luther King, Jr.'s, opposition to the Vietnam War and his increasing attention to the plight of the poor are thought by many to have been related to his death. With a Poor People's March on Washington being planned while aiding garbage workers in Memphis, King was assassinated in April 1968 following a long and hateful campaign against him and other black leaders by J. Edgar Hoover of the FBI. But the very success of the movement in achieving the goals of the early 1960s was largely responsible for it not being able to hold itself together. Economic power, as poverty persisted in black and other minority communities, remained the most elusive of civil rights goals.

—STERLING STUCKEY

See Also: African Americans; Black Panthers; Congress of Racial Equality (CORE); Freedom Riders; March on Washington; National Association for the Advancement of Colored People (NAACP); Southern Christian Leadership Conference (SCLC); Student Nonviolent Coordinating Committee (SNCC); individual biographies.

BIBLIOGRAPHY: Bates, Daisy, *The Long Shadow of Little Rock* (David McKay 1962); Branch, Taylor, *Parting the Waters* (Simon & Schuster 1988); Du Bois, W. E. B., *Souls of Black Folk,* reprint (New American Library 1982); King, Martin Luther, Jr., *Why We Can't Wait* (New American Library 1964); Raines, Howell, *My Soul is Rested* (Viking 1983); Stuckey, Sterling, *Going Through the Storm* (Oxford Univ. Press 1995); Thelwell, Michael, *Duties, Pleasures, and Conflicts* (Univ. of Massachusetts 1987).

■ **CIVIL SERVICE,** collective term for all nonelected, nonmilitary employees of the federal government. Responsible for all government-administered bodies, from the postal service to the prison system, the civil service grew during the first decades of the republic. During Andrew Jackson's administration in the 1830s, the civil service became dominated by the spoils system, the policy of filling government posts with supporters of the victorious political party. Until the Civil War, the spoils system flourished and the civil servants rotated frequently in and out of office, diminishing the efficiency of the civil service. Protests for reform mounted during the Civil War, as the civil service expanded. Support for reform reached its zenith after the 1881 assassination of Pres. James A. Garfield. His death created the political climate for the passage of the Pendleton Act of 1883, which created the Civil Service Commission to administer the new merit system. The act profoundly altered the civil service and affected the organization of the political parties.

By 1900 civil servants were becoming better educated, professionalized, and depoliticized. The New Deal, however, temporarily replaced the merit system with independent appointments made by the numerous new agencies. During the postwar era, reforming the civil service remained a preoccupation. Pres. Jimmy Carter's Civil Service Reform Act of 1978 abolished the Civil Service Commission and divided its functions among three new agencies.

—GUY NELSON

See Also: Pendleton Act.

BIBLIOGRAPHY: Maranto, Robert, and David Schultz, *A Short History of the United States Civil Service* (Univ. Press of America 1991); Van Riper, Paul P., *History of the United States Civil Service* (Row, Peterson 1958).

■ **CIVIL SERVICE REFORM ACT (1871),** an act that allowed Pres. Ulysses S. Grant to appoint the first Civil Service Commission. However, before the commission could establish any procedures or guidelines for federal employment, Congress stopped funding in 1873. Not until passage of the Pendleton Act in 1883 would there be meaningful reform of the civil service system.

See Also: Pendleton Act.

■ **CIVIL WAR (1861-1865),** conflict fought between the North and the South over disputes concerning slavery and states' rights, a watershed event in American history.

Origins of the War. Southern political leaders, wanting to protect state prerogatives from federal infringement, employed the phrase "states' rights" to imply that each state should decide such matters as chartering banks and railroads; establishing colleges; funding construction projects such as road building, river dredging, and harbor clearing; and setting state residency requirements for voting. Plainly, however, the most important and controversial "state right" was to decide if a state would legally authorize slavery.

Differences over slavery in the 1850s led to violence between congressmen in Washington, D.C., and fighting in Kansas Territory. Americans debated how slavery would expand into the national territories and the status of slavery in the nation's future. Sectional disagreements culminated in the presidential election of 1860. Democrats divided into Northern and Southern factions. Abraham Lincoln, nominee of the new Republican party and opposed to slavery's expansion, won the election, sparking the secession of several Southern states. Concerned that the federal government would act against slavery, Southern leaders met to create the Confederate States of America. Stars in the Confederate flag represented South Carolina, Mississippi, Florida, Georgia, Alabama, Louisiana, Texas, Virginia, Arkansas, Tennessee, North Carolina, Missouri, and Kentucky, although the last two states did not officially secede and were also counted as Union states. According to Confederate Vice Pres. Alexander Stephens's "Cornerstone Speech" in March 1861, Southerners formed the Confederacy to defend slavery and states' rights—the economic, social, and political structure of the South.

Political and Strategic Goals. Both sides announced political goals for the war. President Lincoln stated that the North fought to preserve the Union or, in other words, reunite the nation. Pres. Jefferson Davis of the Confederacy sought Southern independence. These clear goals could not be compromised. To everyone's amazement, the conflict lasted four desperate years, approaching the level of a total war and displaying many features of modern war, including impact on civilians, mass armies, armored warships, government in-

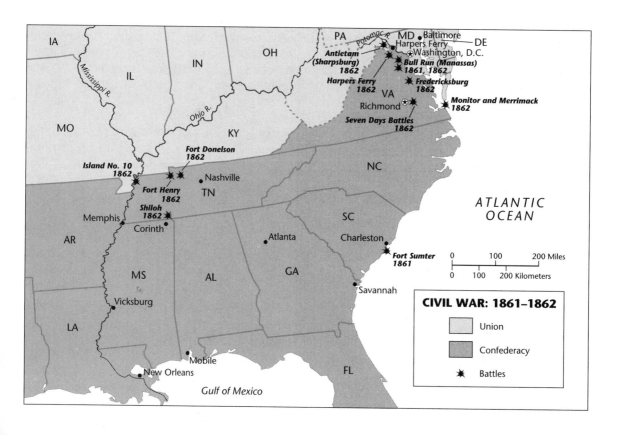

trusions into the economy, and widespread use of telegraph and railroads. Although both sides set out to conserve their ways of life, the unpredictable war changed much about the country.

Opposing leaders selected military strategies to achieve their political goals. Davis announced a defensive strategy for the Confederacy. He wanted Southern armies to block Union thrusts into the South in order to maintain the claim of Confederate independence. President Lincoln chose an offensive strategy. In his "Anaconda Plan" (named for the snake that chokes its prey) the commanding general of the U.S. Army, Winfield Scott, suggested implementing a naval blockade of the Southern coast and controlling the Mississippi River. Approving Scott's suggestions, Lincoln also ordered multiple Union armies into the rebellious states to reassert federal authority.

To win independence, the Confederacy did not have to win all the battles or invade the North.

Both the North and the South relied primarily on volunteers to fight the Civil War, and recruiting posters offered a bonus to those who signed up.

Over a period of many months, Southerners needed to undermine Northern will to prosecute the war. If Southern resistance to reunion convinced Northerners that preserving the United States was not worth their tremendous effort, then the Confederacy could be established. If the South won independence in a year or two, then it would have attained its goal before the full weight of the North's warmaking potential could be brought to bear.

Ironically, both sections looked for inspiration to the American Revolution. Both wanted to advance the "Spirit of '76" from the war against the British, guard liberty, and protect representative government as described in the U.S. Constitution. Crucial to the conflict was whether Northerners would make sacrifices for the concept of the United States, saving in one nation the American experiment in democracy.

Organizing for War. Americans organized for war, marshaling industries and populations to an extraordinary extent. For both sides, the war unexpectedly spawned national paper currencies and military draft laws. The North took unprecedented steps for government to cooperate with businesses and supervise industries and railroads. In the South, Davis carried out similar measures, contradicting the tenets of states' rights. Thousands of men served in uniform and thousands of other men and women toiled in factories and fields to produce the goods and food to sustain each section's war effort.

The Union possessed tremendous material advantages, including more railroads, heavy industries, wheat production, ships, and shipyards. Also, they had the considerable advantage of a functioning government recognized by European nations. The population of the Union states totaled 20 million to the Confederacy's 9.5 million (of whom more than 3.5 million were slaves). The Confederacy achieved remarkable levels of mobilization, especially during 1861 and 1862. Southern industries and imports through the Union blockade supplied thousands of enlisted in Confederate armies. Perhaps some 750,000 Southerners served in Confederate gray during the war. In the Confederate capital of Richmond, Virginia, a congress assembled and government offices opened. Southern diplomats sailed overseas and a few warships were commissioned. To all appearances, the Confederacy was a nation. In the North, factories churned out much of what the Union needed to fight the war and its excellent railroad system delivered the goods and troops where they were needed. Eventually, more than 2 million soldiers served in Union blue. The U.S. Navy grew from a handful of ships to more than 50,000 sailors in more than 600 vessels, dwarfing the tiny Confederate navy. Skilled U.S. diplomats offset the enthusiasm of Southerners overseas.

Early War Years. No Americans were prepared for the war's casualties, and the opening engagements gave no indication of the slaughters to come. Early salvos on Apr. 12, 1861, at Fort Sumter at Charleston, South Carolina, produced no combat deaths. In the first big battle, near Manassas, Virginia, along Bull Run (July 21, 1861), two armies, each with about 30,000 soldiers, suffered some 5,000 total casualties. Stakes went higher at the Battle of Shiloh (Apr. 6-7, 1862) in Tennessee. There two armies, each deploying more than 35,000 soldiers, suffered combined casualties of 20,000. Worse lay ahead.

During the first two years of the war, the Union gained the upper hand in the western theater (Kentucky, Tennessee, Mississippi, Alabama, and western Georgia) while the Confederacy fulfilled its strategy effectively in the eastern theater (Virginia, Maryland, the Carolinas, and the Atlantic coast). Under the command of Gen. Robert E. Lee, Confederate forces defended Richmond in the spring of 1862 against a Union army led by Gen. George B. McClellan. Applying pressure on the North, Davis authorized Lee to take the offensive. Lee's forces penetrated into Kentucky but retreated after heavy fighting. Then came a significant turning point, the Battle of Antietam, at Sharpsburg, Maryland. On Sept. 17, 1862, 25,000 men fell killed and wounded. The combined casualties on both sides at Antietam more than doubled the total American combat deaths of the American Revolution, War of 1812, and Mexican War. Americans realized they were in a titanic struggle. It intensified in the months to come.

Antietam assumed unusual significance. McClellan's army blocked Lee's incursion into the North and prompted a Confederate retreat. This outcome forestalled European diplomatic recognition of the Confederacy. Moreover, Lincoln understood that slave labor helped the Confederate war effort and recognized the thorn of slavery would

Pres. Abraham Lincoln meets with Gen. George McClellan (*facing Lincoln*) and senior officers of the Army of the Potomac on Oct. 1, 1862, soon after the Battle of Antietam.

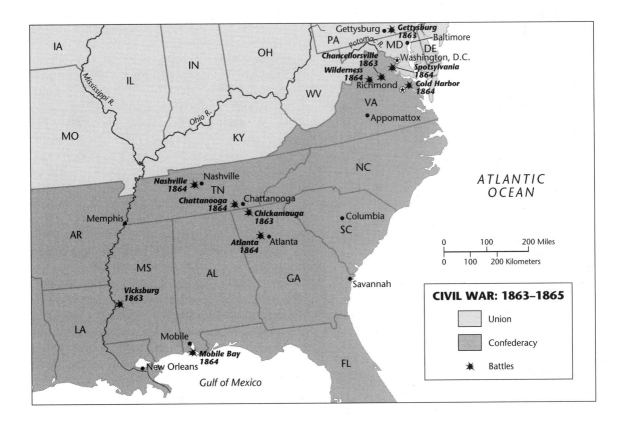

constantly aggravate Americans in the future. On Sept. 22, 1862, he issued his preliminary Emancipation Proclamation, stating that unless the insurrection ended, all slaves in states still in rebellion as of Jan. 1, 1863, would be considered free. Radical Republicans protested that Lincoln's proclamation did not go far enough: it neither included slaves in the loyal border slave states, such as Maryland or Delaware, or in southern states mostly under federal control, such as Louisiana, Arkansas, and Tennessee. By his proclamation, Lincoln added abolishing slavery to his primary war aim of preserving the Union. If slavery were destroyed in the Deep South states that had claimed to secede, it could not exist in border states after the war. The Emancipation Proclamation heralded the eventual end of slavery if federal forces reunited the country, but soon questions rose about the status of former slaves after emancipation.

By mid-summer 1863 the Union navy had tightened its blockade of the Southern coast, and federal armies had earned victories at two turn-

ing points. Guided by the great tactician, Gen. Thomas "Stonewall" Jackson, Lee's Confederates won the Battle of Chancellorsville, Virginia (May 1-4). It was offset by the dramatic Battle of Gettysburg, Pennsylvania (July 1-3), where 90,000 Federals defeated Lee's 75,000 men in their second incursion into the North. To the west, on July 4, Gen. Ulysses S. Grant's army captured Vicksburg, Mississippi, after a long campaign, putting most of the Mississippi River under Union control. The longer the war lasted, the more the North's agricultural, industrial, diplomatic, and population advantages tipped the balance to the Union.

That summer, however, enlistments for the Union army declined, leading Lincoln to authorize the use of black soldiers. Recruiting depots opened in many states, including Louisiana and Tennessee. Ironically, each of those Southern states contributed thousands of black soldiers to the Union war effort. At first, blacks received lower pay than whites, but pay was equalized in 1864. By the end of the war nearly 180,000 blacks had served in the Union army; about 10 percent of Union soldiers and 25 percent of U.S. Navy sailors were black, helping to provide the margin of victory.

The War's Last Years. By January 1864 it was obvious that the war had gone badly for the Confederacy. During three years of conflict, Union forces had won in Kentucky and Missouri; reasserted federal authority over most of Tennessee, Arkansas, and Louisiana; captured New Orleans (the South's largest city containing its busiest port, biggest banks, and significant industries); cut off Texas and the trans-Mississippi theater from the East by controlling the Mississippi River; established Union naval bases along the Atlantic coast; and tightened the blockade from Virginia to Texas. Yet, Davis, Lee, and other Confederates continued to fight. If they eroded Northern will during 1864, Lincoln could lose his bid for reelection, creating the possibility of ending the war and giving the South its independence.

To the dismay of Confederates, several federal military victories contributed to Northern support for Lincoln in the 1864 election. Adm. David Farragut's squadron won the naval battle in Alabama at Mobile Bay (August 5), Gen. William T. Sherman's army captured Atlanta, Georgia (September 1), Gen. Philip H. Sheridan's army devastated the "Confederate Breadbasket" of Virginia's Shenandoah Valley (September-October), and Grant's army locked Lee in a siege at Richmond. Lincoln won reelection in November over his former general, George McClellan, nominee of the Democrats. Across the map, few bright spots flickered for the Confederacy.

After Lincoln's reelection, the Northern juggernaut ended the war. Sherman's "March to the Sea" across Georgia to Savannah (November-December 1864) and another federal army's crushing defeats of Southerners in Tennessee at the battles of Franklin (November 30) and Nashville (December 15-16) foretold Confederate doom. Sherman next campaigned through the Carolinas (January-March 1865). Lee attempted desperate maneuvers in Virginia but was cornered at Appomattox, where he surrendered to Grant on Apr. 9, 1865. On April 14, the assassination of Lincoln shocked the country; he died the next day. Lee's

example at Appomattox persuaded other Confederate generals to surrender their armies.

While estimates vary, more than 1 million Union and Confederate soldiers died or were wounded in the Civil War. The North suffered about 640,000 military casualties: 112,000 were killed or died of wounds, plus 250,000 died of diseases and other causes and 278,000 were wounded. For the South, about 455,000 men became casualties, including 94,000 combat dead or succumbed to wounds, 167,000 who died of diseases and other causes, and 194,000 wounded. Almost 25 percent of white Southern men of military age were casualties during the war. Deaths of military personnel in the Civil War nearly equal the combined military deaths in all other American wars. It is no wonder that the war left a bitter legacy on both sides.

Legacy of the War. By 1865, Confederates had failed in their drive for independence and were in no position to negotiate terms for a Southern nation. To his credit, Jefferson Davis sought and used greater governmental authority, but his actions only galvanized critics who exploited states' rights to hinder the Confederate

Gen. William T. Sherman led Union forces in the capture of Atlanta in September 1864. His famous "March to the Sea" followed, with the capture of Savannah in December.

war effort. Under stress of war, the Confederate government crumbled, the South's economy collapsed, and slavery was destroyed.

In contrast, and pointing toward the future, during the war the North's economy and society thrived and grew. The U.S. Congress passed the Morrill Land Grant College Act to aid state agricultural and mechanical colleges, the Homestead Act to assist western settlers, the Transcontinental Railroad Act to build a rail line across the nation, and higher tariffs to protect American industries. Abraham Lincoln became the model of a modern president, far surpassing Jefferson Davis. After a faltering start, Union generals, led by Grant, proved to be better military managers than Confederate commanders.

The outcome of the Civil War invalidated secession, preserved the Union, and abolished slavery, which was ended completely in December 1865 by the 13th Amendment to the Constitution. The 14th Amendment (1868) specified that former slaves were U.S. citizens and the 15th Amendment (1870) gave African-American men the right to vote. The Civil War put the United States on the path to modernity and renewed its experiment in representative democracy and individual freedom.

—JOSEPH G. DAWSON III

See Also: Appomattox Courthouse; Confederate States of America; Emancipation Proclamation; Kansas-Nebraska Act; Reconstruction; Secession; individual battles and biographies.

BIBLIOGRAPHY: Donald, David H., *Why the North Won the Civil War* (Louisiana State Univ. Press 1960); Hattaway, Herman, and Archer Jones, *How the North Won* (Univ. of Illinois Press 1983); McPherson, James M., *Battle Cry of Freedom* (Oxford Univ. Press 1988); Thomas, Emory, *The Confederate Nation* (Harper & Row 1979); Williams, T. Harry, *Lincoln and His Generals* (Knopf 1952); Woodworth, Steven E., *Jefferson Davis and His Generals* (Univ. Press of Kansas 1990).

■ **CIVIL WORKS ADMINISTRATION,** an emergency unemployment relief agency established in 1933 as part of Pres. Franklin D. Roosevelt's New Deal. It distributed funding for federal, state, and local public works projects.

See Also: New Deal.

■ **CLAFLIN, TENNESSEE CELESTE (1845-1923),** sister and partner of Victoria Claflin Woodhull. Once occultists and performers in traveling medicine shows, the sisters—both born in Homer, Ohio—later established themselves as Wall Street investors and radical political reformers. Their journal, *Woodhull and Claflin Weekly*, issued the first American publication of Karl Marx and Friedrich Engels's *Communist Manifesto*.

See Also: Women's Movement.

■ **CLAPP, LOUISE A. K. S. (1819-1906),** writer. She was born in Elizabeth, New Jersey. She artfully described the colorful and chaotic life of the Gold Rush in a series of letters written while living with her husband in a remote mining settlement in California (1851-52). The letters, later used by many authors, including Bret Harte, were published in 1854 and 1855 in *The Pioneer: or California Monthly Magazine* under the name Dame Shirley.

See Also: Women in American History.

■ **CLARK, ABRAHAM (1726-94),** lawyer and politician. Born in Elizabethtown, New Jersey, Clark enjoyed an influential political career during the American Revolution. After holding provincial offices in New Jersey, he became a delegate to the Second Continental Congress and signed the Declaration of Independence.

See Also: Declaration of Independence.

■ **CLARK, GEORGE ROGERS (1752-1818),** frontiersman. Born near Charlottesville, Virginia, Clark fought against Indians in Lord Dunmore's War in 1774. Spying on the British in 1777, Clark persuaded Gov. Patrick Henry of Virginia to let him launch a surprise attack. With only 175 men, Clark took Fort Massaac near the Tennessee River on July 4, 1778. The British then moved from Detroit down to Vincennes in October 1778, renaming Fort Patrick Henry as Fort Sackville. With only 130 American and French troops, Clark received the British surrender of Fort Hamilton on Feb. 24, 1779. Clark continued to raid Indian villages on the Ohio and speculate in land. Later, as Virginia and the confederation failed to honor financial obligations from the Northwest campaign and discredited by corruption in his administration as Indian commissioner, Clark failed in his attempts to colonize the upper Mississippi valley with the French and Spanish settlers. Clark lived near Clarksville, in the Northwest Territory, from 1794 to 1815, and saw his younger brother William rise to fame on the Lewis and Clark expedition. A poorly executed amputation of Clark's leg in 1808 left him partially paralyzed until his death.

See Also: Frontier in American History.

■ **CLARK, TOM CAMPBELL (1899-1977),** U.S. attorney general (1945-49) and associate justice of the U.S. Supreme Court (1949-67). Born in Dallas, Texas, he joined the U.S. Justice Department in 1937 and served as attorney general under Pres. Harry S. Truman. Clark oversaw the administration's loyalty and security programs. On the Supreme Court he was regarded as a liberal and resigned to avoid potential conflicts of interest when his son, Ramsey Clark, was named U.S. attorney general by Pres. Lyndon B. Johnson.

See Also: Supreme Court.

■ **CLARK, WILLIAM (1770-1838),** explorer and military figure. Younger brother of American Revolutionary War hero George Rogers Clark, William Clark was born in Caroline County, Virginia. He was commissioned a lieutenant in March 1792 and fought at the Battle of Fallen Timbers under Gen. Anthony Wayne in 1794. Resigning, Clark returned home and managed his family's plantation near Louisville, Kentucky, from 1796 to 1803. A close friend, Meriwether Lewis, offered Clark a position as coleader of an expedition to explore the West (1803-06). Instrumental in the Lewis and Clark expedition's final preparations at Camp Wood River, Illinois, Clark was the principal mapmaker on the exploration as well as the better negotiator with Indians. After the expedition, Clark was principal Indian agent and brigadier general of the militia for Louisiana Territory from 1807 to 1813. Serving as governor of Missouri Territory from 1813 to 1820, Clark lost his bid for Missouri state governor in 1820. In 1822, Clark became the superintendent of Indian Affairs in St. Louis, administering Indian policy on the Missouri and upper Mississippi until his death in 1838.

See Also: Frontier in American History.

■ **CLARKE, JOHN HESSIN (1857-1942),** associate justice of the U.S. Supreme Court (1916-22). Born in New Lisbon, Ohio, he practiced corporate law in Cleveland and was a political ally of the progressive mayor Tom Johnson. He was appointed to the federal district court for northern Ohio in 1914 and to the Supreme Court two years later, when Charles Evans Hughes resigned to run for president. Clarke resigned unexpectedly in 1922 to campaign for U.S. entry into the League of Nations.

See Also: Supreme Court.

■ **CLAY, HENRY (1777-1852),** American politician and statesman. Born in Virginia, Clay studied law in Richmond and in 1797 began his practice in the frontier town of Lexington, Kentucky. After serving in the state legislature (1803-06, 1807-09) and filling two unexpired terms in the U. S. Senate (1806-07, 1809-10), he won election to the House of Representatives, where (in an age before seniority ruled Congress) he was immediately chosen as Speaker. Clay gained national attention as one of the "War Hawks," the group of

During the War of 1812, Henry Clay allied himself with other War Hawks who sought to eliminate the British presence in North America. Later in his career he became known as the "Great Pacificator" for his attempt to avoid sectional conflict.

militant congressmen who pressed Pres. James Madison into war with Great Britain in 1812. After the war, Clay served on the commission that negotiated the Treaty of Ghent (1814), then was elected again to the House and chosen again as its Speaker. Clay was instrumental in arranging the Missouri Compromise of 1820, which gained him the reputation as the "Great Pacificator."

Clay first ran for president in 1824, putting forth his conservative "American System," a program of protective tariffs to stimulate industry, a national bank to facilitate credit and exchange, and federally funded internal improvements (roads and canals) to aid trade and commerce. Clay thus positioned himself as the friend of business and industry, the successor to Alexander Hamilton and the defunct Federalist party. In the election he came in a poor fourth, but when the Electoral College failed to form a majority for any of the candidates, throwing the election into the House, Clay used his influence to throw the victory to John Quincy Adams. Adams rewarded Clay by appointing him secretary of state, which drew charges of a "corrupt bargain" from the supporters of Andrew Jackson, who had won the largest proportion of the popular vote. Clay and Jackson would remain the dominant political opponents of their age.

With Jackson's election as president in 1828, Clay threatened to retire altogether from politics, but in 1831, Kentucky sent him to the Senate. The Senate became the platform from which he ran against Jackson for president in 1832, coalescing about him the forces that would soon become the Whig party. Clay was badly beaten by the overwhelmingly popular Jackson. Although Clay made his availability clear, the Whigs chose William Henry Harrison as their candidate in 1836. Harrison lost to Martin Van Buren in 1836 but was elected in 1840, the first Whig presidential victory. But Harrison died in 1841 and was succeeded by Vice Pres. John Tyler, who so frustrated the Whig congressional initiatives that Clay resigned from the Senate in protest in 1842.

Clay ran for president again in 1844 but was crushed by Democrat James K. Polk. Returned to the Senate in 1849 for what would prove to be his final years, Clay was instrumental in proposing the Compromise of 1850, another futile effort to solve the slavery controversy. Clay's oratory in defense of the Union was nationally celebrated. It was his final act. His death in 1852 spared him from witnessing the quick return to sectional controversy over slavery that would devolve into the Civil War.

Renowned in his final days as the champion of reconciliation, Clay has been noticed by historians as the originator of the "American System," a strategist of the Whig party, and a perennial presidential candidate. He is often remembered most for his declaration that he would "rather be right than be president."

—JOHN MACK FARAGHER

See Also: Compromise of 1850; Missouri Compromise; War Hawks; Whig Party.

BIBLIOGRAPHY: Baxter, Maurice G., *Henry Clay and the American System* (Univ. Press of Kentucky 1995); Remini, Robert V., *Henry Clay: Statesman for the Union* (Norton 1991).

■ **CLAYTON ANTITRUST ACT (1914),** legislation passed by Congress as an amendment to the Sherman Antitrust Act (1890). The Clayton Antitrust Act contains certain prohibitions on monopolies, particularly making clear that labor unions were not to be restricted by antitrust laws.

See Also: Sherman Antitrust Act.

■ **CLAYTON-BULWER TREATY (1850),** agreement between Great Britain and the United States to control jointly a canal on the Central American isthmus. Critics in the United States argued that it violated the Monroe Doctrine. No canal was built, and the Clayton-Bulwer Treaty was superseded in 1901 by the Hay-Pauncefote Treaty.

See Also: Hay-Pauncefote Treaty; Monroe Doctrine.

■ **CLEAR AND PRESENT DANGER,** legal test first formulated by U.S. Supreme Court Justice Oliver Wendell Holmes as a way to determine whether speech is protected under the First Amendment. In *Schenck* v. *United States* (1919) Holmes upheld the Espionage Act (1917) on the grounds that distributing antiwar literature to draftees posed "a clear and present danger" of evils Congress was empowered to prevent. Both Holmes and Justice Louis Brandeis further developed the test in cases such as *Abrams* v. *United States* (1919) and *Gitlow* v. *New York* (1925) to offer greater protection to unpopular political speech and make it clear that any danger must be immediate. The Court revised the Holmes-Brandeis standard of immediacy in *Dennis v. United States* (1951) when it upheld the conviction of 11 Communist party officials. In *Dennis*, the Court held that the government should consider both the gravity and the immediacy of the threat. Since then the Court has largely ignored the clear and present danger test.

See Also: Brandeis, Louis Dembitz; Holmes, Oliver Wendell, Jr.; Schenck v. United States; Supreme Court.

BIBLIOGRAPHY: Hentoff, Nat, *The First Freedom: A Tumultuous History of Free Speech in America* (Delacorte Press 1980).

■ **CLEMENS, SAMUEL.** *See: Twain, Mark.*

■ **CLEVELAND, GROVER (1837-1908),** 22nd and 24th president of the United States (1885-89; 1893-97). The only president to serve two nonconsecutive terms, Stephen Grover Cleveland was born in Caldwell, New Jersey. Although he never graduated from college, he earned a law degree and practiced in Buffalo, New York, before becoming active in Democratic politics. Cleveland's ascent to the White House was rapid. As mayor of Buffalo (1881-82) he won support as a conservative reformer and during his governorship of New York (1882-84), he received praise for his opposition to Tammany Hall.

Honest, pugnacious, and politically conservative, Cleveland united a fractious Democratic party, narrowly defeating James G. Blaine for the presidency in 1884. Upon taking office, Cleveland espoused the virtues of tariff reduction and became enmeshed in the administrative details of government. He developed no major legislation but signed into law the Dawes Act of 1887 and the Interstate Commerce Act of 1887. Cleveland won the popular vote but lost his reelection bid in 1888 in the electoral college to Benjamin Harrison. In 1892, Cleveland returned to defeat Harrison decisively for a second term.

Unlike his first term, however, Cleveland's second was disastrous. The economic and social realities of the depression-plagued 1890s called for more than Cleveland's policy of efficient and honest government. He alienated westerners and farmers by persuading Congress to repeal the Sherman

Grover Cleveland served two nonconsecutive terms as president, from 1885 to 1889 and from 1893 to 1897.

Silver Purchase Act of 1890 and by supporting the gold standard. He also enraged labor by backing the railroads during the Pullman Strike of 1894. When Cleveland left office, he was unpopular and the Democratic party was deeply divided.

See Also: Harrison, Benjamin; Presidential Elections; President of the United States; Pullman Strike.

BIBLIOGRAPHY: Nevins, Allan, *Grover Cleveland: A Study in Courage* (Dodd, Mead & Co. 1932); Welch, Richard E., *The Presidencies of Grover Cleveland* (Univ. of Kansas Press 1988).

■ **CLIFFORD, NATHAN (1803-81),** U.S. representative (1839-43) and associate justice of the U.S. Supreme Court (1858-81). A Romney, New Hampshire, native, Clifford sided with the majority in *Ex parte Milligan* (1866), which held that the president could not impose martial law in the absence of an open insurrection.

See Also: Ex parte Milligan; Supreme Court.

■ **CLINTON, DEWITT (1769-1828),** American politician and principal supporter of the Erie Canal project. A member of a prominent political family, Clinton was born in Little Britain, New York. He served in the New York legislature (1798-1802) and in the U.S. Senate (1802-03), but Clinton's major political position was as the mayor of New York City (1803-15). He ran as the Federalist candidate for U.S. president in 1812 but was defeated by the incumbent James Madison. Clinton served as governor of New York (1817-23; 1825-28), an office his uncle, George Clinton, had held. DeWitt Clinton's greatest personal success was achieved on Oct. 26, 1825, when the Erie Canal was opened, facilitating upper New York State commerce to New York City.

See Also: Erie Canal.

■ **CLINTON, GEORGE (1739-1812),** Revolutionary War soldier and vice president of the United States (1805-12). He was born in Little Britain, New York. Clinton served in the French and Indian War and later joined the fight for American independence, attaining the rank of brigadier general in New York's militia (1775) and in the continental army (1777). He was a member of the New York provincial assembly (1768-75) and governor of New York (1777-95; 1801-04). He opposed the Federalist policies of Alexander Hamilton and the ratification of the U.S. Constitution. In 1804 Clinton became the first person nominated for the office of U.S. vice president (previously, the second-best vote-getter in the presidential race became vice president). Twice elected, he held the office during Pres. Thomas Jefferson's second term and Pres. James Madison's first term. Clinton died in office.

See Also: Vice President of the United States.

■ **CLINTON, (SIR) HENRY (1738-95),** British commander in chief (1778-82) during the latter part of the American Revolution. He had served as a general under Thomas Gage (1775) and Sir William Howe (1775-78). Clinton planned an initially successful strategy to conquer the U.S. South (1778-81), but his failure to relieve the army of Lord Cornwallis, the British commander at Yorktown, in 1781 was instrumental in Britain's defeat.

See Also: Revolution, American; Yorktown, Seige of.

George Clinton served seven terms as New York's governor between 1777 and 1804. He was leader of the New York antifederalists and spoke out against the ratification of the Constitution.

■ **CLINTON, HILLARY RODHAM (1947-),** lawyer, child advocate with the Children's Defense Fund, and first lady of the United States. Born in Park Ridge, Illinois, she married Bill Clinton in 1975. As first lady, she led an unsuccessful drive for national health care reform and authored *It Takes a Village* (1996).

See Also: Women in American History.

■ **CLINTON, WILLIAM JEFFERSON BLYTHE (BILL) (1946-),** 42nd president of the United States (1993-). Born in Hope, Arkansas, Clinton attended Georgetown University, was a Rhodes scholar at Oxford University in England from 1969 to 1970, and graduated from Yale Law School in 1973.

Early Political Career. A staunch Democrat, Clinton lost his first bid for the Arkansas legislature in 1974, only to be elected the state's youngest attorney general in 1976. In 1978, he was elected governor, but his first term was marred by a series of clashes with the state legislature. After a defeat in 1980, Clinton modified his style and went on to win four straight terms in the statehouse (1982-92).

His success as governor brought Clinton national attention and leadership roles with the Democrats. He announced his candidacy for president in late 1991 and after tough state primary battles won the nomination. During his 1992 presidential campaign Clinton called for an increase in social justice and welfare reform, as well as for a tax break for the middle class. His relaxed manner in front of the television camera was of critical importance to the campaign. Despite accusations concerning Clinton's personal life, his polished style, plus an economic downturn toward the

end of the campaign, combined to give him a victory over Republican incumbent Pres. George Bush and third-party challenger H. Ross Perot.

Presidency. Clinton began his presidency with a high popularity rating, only to see it plummet after he reversed his stand on several issues, most notably his promised tax cut. His health care initiative, in which his wife, Hillary Rodham Clinton, played an important role, was defeated on Capitol Hill, and he seemed anything but experienced in foreign affairs. In the off-year elections of 1994, Clinton's sagging popularity was a major factor in the Republican landslide, giving them control of both houses of Congress. Yet, Clinton's first term was not without its victories, especially the narrow passage of the North American Free Trade Agreement.

The later months of the term were dominated less with policy issues than with news of alleged illegal real-estate dealings and campaign donations while he was governor of Arkansas, all lumped under the sobriquet of the Whitewater Scandal.

Despite such negative press, Clinton remained well ahead of his opponents going into the 1996 presidential race, testimony to his political acumen and a healthy national economy. Easily renominated by the Democrats, Clinton faced Republican challenger Bob Dole, former U.S. senator from Kansas, who could not convey a clear message to voters, and independent H. Ross Perot. Clinton won a second term handily. His early second term was marked by the country's continued economic buoyancy and by allegations of Clinton's sexual misconduct and the continuation of Whitewater.

—JOHN ROBERT GREENE

See Also: *Bush, George H. W.; North American Free Trade Agreement; Presidential Elections; President of the United States.*

BIBLIOGRAPHY: Cohen, Richard, *Changing Course in Washington: Clinton and the New Congress* (Macmillan 1994); Maraniss, David, *First in his Class: A Biography of Bill Clinton* (Simon & Schuster 1995).

Bill Clinton was governor of Arkansas when he was elected president in 1992. His wife, Hillary Rodham Clinton, has played an important, if largely unofficial, role in his administration.

■ **CLIPPER SHIPS,** large wooden sailing ships built between 1830 and 1860. They were developed in response to the extraordinary demands for speed brought on by the New York-China tea trade and by the discovery of gold in California and Australia. Built mainly in Baltimore and New England, clipper ships had long, narrow lines, hollow bows, high masts, and enormous sail area. No other vessel of the time matched them in speed or beauty. Their style and design allowed them to set new records. In 1850, the *Sea Witch* sailed from New York around Cape Horn to San Francisco in 97 days, instead of the normal 159, and was beaten four years later by Donald McKay's *Flying Cloud*, which made the trip in a record of 89 days that still stands. The *Oriental* sailed from Hong Kong to London in a celebrated 97 days and McKay's *Lightning* set a one-day record of 436 nautical miles. Despite their impressive style, clipper ships grew less useful as the demand for speed dwindled and steamboats grew more advanced. By the 1840s, steamers were crossing the Atlantic. By the 1880s, twin-screw propulsion, new engines, and steel hulls had established the dominance of steamships.

See Also: Shipping.

■ **CLOSED SHOP,** a term applying to a place of work that employs only workers who are already members of an established union. This contrasts with an Open Shop and differs from a "Union Shop," where workers must join a union within a fixed period of time.

See Also: Labor Movement; Open Shop.

■ **CLOTURE,** parliamentary rules to limit further debate prior to a vote. In the U.S. Senate debate can be limited and a vote forced if two-thirds of the members present vote for cloture. Senators sometimes vote against cloture to avoid a recorded vote on a controversial issue.

■ **CLOVIS CULTURE (14,000-12,000 B.C.),** precontact North American culture, named after the site where their artifacts were first discovered, near Clovis, New Mexico. Beginning about 14,000 B.C., the indigenous peoples of North America developed a unique, sophisticated style of toolmaking unlike anything found in the Old World. Archaeologists have unearthed artifacts in the Clovis traditions at sites from Montana to Mexico, Nova Scotia to Arizona, suggesting that Clovis culture spread quickly throughout North America. In order to feed the expanding population, commu-

nities found a more efficient way to hunt. Clovis bands, which were mobile communities containing several interrelated families, returned to the same hunting camps annually, pursuing seasonal migration within territories of several hundred square miles. Clovis sites were situated on elevations overlooking watering places that attracted game. Clovis blades have been found amid the remains of mammoth, camel, horse, giant armadillo, and sloth, which were apparently driven into shallow bogs and killed with spears.

See Also: Indians of North America.

■ **CLYMER, GEORGE (1739-1813),** statesman and Revolutionary War leader. A resident of Philadelphia, Clymer entered the struggle against Britain in the early 1770s on the local level. He later served in the Second Continental Congress, signed the Declaration of Independence, was a member of the Constitutional Convention, and served in the first U.S. Congress (1789-91).

See Also: Declaration of Independence.

■ **COAL,** fossil fuel first mined at the Virginia Coal Mine on the James River in 1750 and the main energy source of industry after the Civil War. Hard coal (anthracite) had become an important industrial and domestic heating fuel by 1800. Coal, which yielded a more intense and controllable level of heat than wood, helped increase the speed and scale of production and supported the industrial revolution. Soft (bituminous) coal became important in the manufacture of coke for the production of iron and steel. The mining of coal, however, proved dangerous, and disasters such as the one in Monongah, West Virginia, that killed 361 people in 1907 led to the enactment of safety laws. The United Mine Workers (1890) helped coal miners strike for higher wages in the 1902 anthracite strike and in later work stoppages, but relations between labor and management remained hostile. The coal industry lost markets to oil and natural gas after 1920, which expanded to fill the need for electric power. Strip mining helped coal stay competitive, but it raised serious health, safety, and environmental concerns.

■ **COAST GUARD,** one of the five military services of the United States and the primary federal agency for maritime safety and law enforcement. Established by Congress on Jan. 28, 1915, the modern U.S. Coast Guard was formed by combining the Revenue Cutter Service (established in 1790), whose ships enforced customs laws, and the Life-Saving Service (established 1848), designed to conduct search and rescue operations along America's vast coastline. In 1939 the Coast Guard took on another key mission: maintaining lighthouses, buoys, and other navigational devices to ensure safety on the seas. Under a 1966 reorganization, jurisdiction was shifted from the Treasury Department to the Transportation Department. In wartime control of the Coast Guard is transferred to the U.S. Navy. Coast Guard personnel have served in many military operations, dating back to the quasi-war against France in the 1790s. In both world wars Coast Guard ships protected Allied convoys. In World War II Coast Guard personnel often served in amphibious operations. During the Vietnam War the service was active in interdicting the flow of arms into South Vietnam. Today's Coast Guard conducts search and rescue missions, collects meteorological and oceanographic data, and enforces U.S. laws on the seas, including environmental law, among other duties.

BIBLIOGRAPHY: Johnson, Robert E., *Guardians of the Sea: History of the United States Coast Guard, 1915 to the Present* (Naval Institute Press 1987).

◾ **COBB, TY (1886-1961),** baseball player. Born in Narrows, Georgia, and known as "the Georgia Peach," Cobb was the game's greatest hitter. An outfielder for the Detroit Tigers (1905-26) and Philadelphia Athletics (1927-28), he batted over .400 three times, led the league in hitting 12 times between 1907 and 1919, and retired with a record .367 career average. He was disliked by teammates and opponents alike for his intense competitive manner. He died a millionaire thanks to early investments in Coca Cola and General Motors.

See Also: Baseball; Sports.

◾ **COBBETT, WILLIAM (1763-1835),** journalist and reformer, born in Farnham, Surrey, England, known in the United States as "Peter Porcupine." Cobbett resigned from the British army in 1791 and fled to France. In 1792 he immigrated to the United States, eventually opening a bookstore in Philadelphia and publishing the vitriolic *Porcupine's Gazette* (1795-97), which attacked Thomas Jefferson and other Republican supporters of the French Revolution. Cobbett closed his newspaper after losing a libel case, returned to England, and was later elected to Parliament, where he fought for reform.

◾ **COCHISE (c. 1812-74),** Chiricahua Apache chief. Originally friendly to the Americans, Cochise became embroiled in American attempts to subdue the Indian peoples of the Southwest. In 1861, American authorities called for a meeting to discuss the kidnapping of a 12-year-old boy by the Coyotero Apaches, with army authorities threatening to take Cochise's family hostage until the boy was returned. Reacting to this threat, Cochise pulled a knife, cut a hole through the wall of the tent where the meeting was being held, and then charged through a line of American soldiers. Cochise made several attempts to negotiate his family's release, but the Americans would not release them until the captive was returned. Cochise seized several Mexican hostages whom he murdered in the belief that the Americans would kill his relatives. When the Americans found the bodies of the victims, they hanged six male kinsmen of Cochise. He then fought against Americans until his surrender in 1871, briefly rebelling again in 1872.

See Also: Apache; Frontier in American History; Indians of North America.

◾ **CODE TALKERS (1941-45),** a select group of Navahos specially trained as communications specialists for the U.S. Marines during World War II. The Navahos sent messages in their native language—one of the most complicated in the world. Without losing any time in encoding and decoding, they were thus able to deliver and receive messages that the Japanese were never able to decipher.

See Also: Navaho.

◾ **CODY, WILLIAM ("BUFFALO BILL") (1846-1917),** western hunter, scout, and showman. He was born in Iowa and relocated with his family to Kansas in 1854, where they were caught up in the border violence between slavery and antislavery forces. His father was stabbed while giving a free-soil speech and died of his wound in 1857. Only 12 years old, young Cody went to work as a mounted messenger for the freighting firm of Majors & Russell and three years later became a rider for the legendary Pony Express. During the Civil War (1861-65), he rode with the "jayhawkers," the marauding pro-Union irregular militia. In 1864, Cody enlisted as a private in the Seventh Kansas Volunteer Cavalry, where he served in several campaigns.

In 1866, Cody married Louisa Frederici of St. Louis, but, unable to make a living as a hotel keeper, he returned to the plains, where he found work as a buffalo hunter for railroad construction crews, earning the nickname "Buffalo Bill." From 1868 to 1872, he was employed as a civilian scout by the 5th Cavalry, participating in numerous Indian campaigns and winning the accolades of his superiors, including Gen. Philip Sheridan.

The turning point in Cody's life, however, came in 1869, when he met the dime novel writer Edward Judson, whose pen name was Ned Buntline. Buntline made Cody the hero of a dime novel, which he then brought to the stage as a melodrama. "Buffalo Bill" became a national sensation, and over the next several decades he was portrayed as a hero in hundreds of books, dime novels, and stories. In 1872, Buntline convinced Cody to play himself on the Chicago stage, and although the two men soon fell out, Cody fell in love with show business. For the next 11 years he worked as an actor during the theatrical season, returning to the plains as a scout or guide during the summer. After the defeat and death of George Armstrong Custer in 1876, Cody took part briefly in Indian fighting in which he claimed to have killed a Cheyenne chief; on the stage later that year he displayed what he said was the man's scalp as part of his act. Cody's theatrical genius was his ability to combine authenticity and fantasy.

In 1883, Cody organized Buffalo Bill's Wild West Show, an exhibition dramatizing western characters and events. For the next 30 years he and his troupe—which included Buck Taylor ("King of the Cowboys"), Annie Oakley, and (for one season) Sitting Bull—traveled all over the country as well as to England and the European continent. In addition to demonstrations of shooting, roping, bronco riding, and Indian dancing, Cody staged reenactments of historic

William "Buffalo Bill" Cody, shown in a publicity shot taken in 1872 during his first tour as a performer, organized his Wild West extravaganza in 1883, recruiting former cowboys and Indians to reenact famous incidents of western history for his audiences.

western events, including the ride of the Pony Express, the attack on the Deadwood stagecoach, and Custer's last stand. Cody helped fix an image of the "Wild West" in the public mind that remains to this day.

See Also: *Wild West Shows.*

BIBLIOGRAPHY: Rosa, Joseph G., and Robin May, *Buffalo Bill and His Wild West: A Pictorial Biography* (Univ. of Kansas Press 1989); Russell, Don, *The Lives and Legends of Buffalo Bill* (Univ. of Oklahoma Press 1960).

■ **COHAN, GEORGE M. (1878-1942),** entertainer, songwriter, and theatrical producer. Born in Providence, Rhode Island, on the 3rd, not as he later claimed the 4th, of July, he made his stage debut when he was carried on stage by his father as an infant. The family vaudeville act, The Four Cohans, was by 1900 among the most popular in the United States. He formed a partnership with producer Sam Harris (1904), and together they produced a string of flag-waving musical hits showcasing Cohan's energetic singing and dancing and his ability to write such memorable tunes as "Give My Regards to Broadway," "Yankee Doodle Boy," "You're a Grand Old Flag," and "Over There." Later in his career, Cohan starred in Eugene O'Neill's *Ah, Wilderness!* (1933) and portrayed Pres. Franklin D. Roosevelt in the musical comedy *I'd Rather Be Right* (1937). A statue of Cohan was erected on Broadway in New York City's theater district after his death.

See Also: Theater.
BIBLIOGRAPHY: McCabe, John, *George M. Cohan: The Man Who Owned Broadway* (Doubleday 1973).

■ *COHENS V. VIRGINIA* **(1821),** U.S. Supreme Court case that established the power of the Court to review state court decisions alleged to be unconstitutional. Two brothers appealed to the Supreme Court to throw out their Virginia conviction for illegally selling District of Columbia lottery tickets in Virginia. They claimed the District's lottery, as an act of Congress, constitutionally could not be subject to state laws or prohibitions. Over the objections of Virginia, the Court asserted its appellate jurisdiction to review the case. In the end, the Court upheld the original convictions handed down by the state court. Chief Justice John Marshall's majority opinion in this case reinforced the Court's decision in *Martin* v. *Hunter's Lessee* (1816), a case from which Marshall had recused himself, and laid to rest any lingering doubts about the appellate jurisdiction of the Supreme Court over state courts.

See Also: Martin v. Hunter's Lessee; Supreme Court.

■ **COHN, EDWIN (1892-1953),** biochemist and pioneer in protein chemistry. Born in New York City, Cohn earned his Ph.D. from the University of Chicago (1917). During World War I, he examined the physical chemistry of making bread from potatoes and other nongrain sources. He studied abroad (1919-20) and then joined the new department of physical chemistry at Harvard Medical School (1920-53). Cohn worked to purify vitamin B-12 and studied the correlation between structures of amino acids and peptides and different physical properties (1930-38). As World War II grew increasingly imminent, Cohn concentrated on separating the different proteins of blood plasma, gathering a number of biochemists to work with him. In 1942, they obtained serum albumin, used for transfusion in treatment of shock, and produced more than 2 million units before the war ended. They also produced gamma globulin, used for immunization against measles and hepatitis, and fibrin foam and film, for neurosurgery. Cohn continued to develop new techniques for fractioning blood plasma, preserving red cells for transfusion, and studying other constituents of blood. He established the Protein Foundation (now the Center for Blood Research) the year he died.

See Also: Science.

■ **COINAGE ACT OF 1792,** legislation that set the value of U.S. currency at specific weights of silver and gold in a ratio of 15 to 1. It allowed for the free and unlimited coinage of silver and gold, but few coins were actually minted, and the country experienced a chronic shortage of hard currency.

■ **COINAGE ACT OF 1873,** legislation also known as the "Crime of 1873" and the Demonetization Act. This bill removed the silver dollar from circulation, ostensibly helping eastern financiers limit the money supply and enraging those who sought the increased production of silver and the inflation of falling farm prices.

■ **COLDEN, CADWALLADER (1688-1776),** scientist, author, and lieutenant governor of New York (1761-75). Born in Dunse, Scotland, and educated at the University of Edinburgh, Colden immigrated to Philadelphia, in 1710 and practiced medicine there until 1715. Resettling in New York, he became its first surveyor general (1719). An author, Colden published a variety of scientific works and *The History of the Five Indian Nations*, a substantial colonial treatise on the Iroquois.

■ **COLD HARBOR, BATTLE OF (1864),** Civil War engagement between the forces of Confederate Gen. Robert E. Lee and Union Gen. Ulysses S. Grant 10 miles northeast of Richmond, Virginia. The battle consisted of little more than disastrous frontal assaults by Union forces against heavily fortified Confederate entrenchments. The Union attackers, many of whom pinned their names to their uniforms in expectation of death, made no progress. "I regret this assault more than any one I have ever ordered," said Grant.

See Also: Civil War; Grant, Ulysses Simpson; Lee, Robert Edward.

■ **COLD WAR,** period of armed hostility between the United States and the former Soviet Union, together with their respective allies, that lasted from the waning days of World War II until the Soviet collapse in 1991. The two blocs never fought a major war, although they came close on several occasions, but the rivalry produced numerous smaller conflicts. It was made the more dangerous because both sides developed nuclear arsenals of unprecedented destructiveness.

The Soviet Union originated with the Communist revolution in Russia in 1917. The United States did not recognize the new regime until 1933, and even after that, relations were never cordial. Following the German invasion of the Soviet Union in June 1941, however, and especially after the United States became an ally in the war, Pres. Franklin D. Roosevelt tried to forge a genuine partnership with Soviet leader Joseph Stalin. Roosevelt believed that a coalition of the allied powers would have to continue after the war to maintain a lasting peace.

Despite Roosevelt's efforts, relations became increasingly strained during the weeks after the Yalta Conference (Feb. 4-11, 1945). American and British officials grew alarmed at what they perceived to be deliberate Soviet violations of agreements made at Yalta, especially with regard to Eastern Europe. By the time of his death (Apr. 12, 1945), Roosevelt clearly was moving toward a "tougher" approach. His successor, Pres. Harry S. Truman, came to believe that he could work with Stalin by being friendly but firm. Friction continued to develop, however, especially after Japan surrendered in August 1945. The inability to reach agreement on control of atomic energy, over which the United States had a monopoly at the time, cast a pall over all other issues.

Early Crises. During the first few years after World War II, relations hardened to the point where some believed war was inevitable. As British statesman Winston Churchill put it, the Soviets constructed an "iron curtain" across Europe. Millions were affected as what were intended as temporary divisions of nations such as Germany and Korea evolved into separate entities that themselves became participants in the Cold War.

The United States in 1947 adopted what became known as the "containment policy." This strategy was based on the assumption that for historical and ideological reasons the Soviet Union was inherently expansionist and would seek to extend its hegemony wherever possible through any means short of all-out war. The proper response for the United States and its allies would therefore be to prevent such expansion through the measured application of pressure, even military force if necessary. According to this line of thought, if contained for a sufficient period, the Soviet Union would eventually either mellow or collapse entirely because of the internal contradictions of Communism. The Truman Doctrine (1947), the Marshall Plan (1948), and the North Atlantic Treaty Organization (1949) were early examples of containment. Although the word "containment" was abandoned for political reasons, the policy was followed for decades.

Events such as the Berlin blockade (1948), the communist victory in China (1949), the Soviet explosion of an atomic bomb (1949), and the outbreak of the Korean War in 1950 heightened tensions. The North Korean invasion of South Korea was widely thought to be a Soviet probe of Western intentions. If the United States and its allies failed to respond forcefully, American officials believed, the Soviets would be emboldened to commit aggression elsewhere, just as Adolf Hitler had done earlier.

By the 1950s the Cold War colored many Americans' views of developments throughout the world, which they thought was involved in a global struggle between the "Free World" and the forces of Communism, bent upon world conquest. The threat, they thought, came not only from the

Soviet Union and its allies abroad, but from subversive elements within the United States. The era witnessed a massive military buildup in the United States, the use of clandestine organizations such as the Central Intelligence Agency, and political repression at home against those suspected of being Communists or their sympathizers.

1960s and 1970s. In the 1960s the Cold War was waged around the world as the Soviet and U.S. blocs jockeyed for advantage by providing client states with military and economic assistance and by trying to woo neutrals into their camp. Confrontations erupted with dismaying frequency in the Middle East, Africa, and Latin America, as well as in Europe. The Cuban missile crisis (1962) probably brought the two superpowers closer to nuclear war than ever before or after.

The arms race took on a life of its own as technological advances vastly increased the power of nuclear weapons and improved the means to deliver them. The destructiveness of hydrogen bombs dwarfed that of earlier atomic weapons, and a vast array of missiles augmented the use of manned bombers. Agreements to suspend nuclear tests and to limit the development of certain kinds of missiles slowed the arms race but never stopped it. The temptation to build more sophisticated and deadly missile systems was all but irresistible because of the arguments advanced by both sides that "if we don't, they will." Some people speculated that a total nuclear war might make the planet uninhabitable.

A widely held belief was that the Soviet Union orchestrated Communist activity everywhere. Such a world view led the United States to intervene overtly or covertly against governments that were thought to be under Moscow's influence and to prop up others threatened by Communist insurgents. The most notable example was Vietnam. Pres. Dwight D. Eisenhower provided economic and military assistance to the embattled South Vietnamese government (1961), Pres. John F. Kennedy introduced American ground units (1962), and Pres. Lyndon B. Johnson presided over an escalation of the conflict that cost more than 50,000 American lives. Pres. Richard M. Nixon eventually withdrew American forces, but many lives were lost in the process, and the Communists took over in 1975.

Nixon's presidency (1969-74) significantly lessened tensions between the two superpowers. He and National Security Adviser (later Sec. of State) Henry Kissinger took advantage of the rivalry between the Soviet Union and the People's Republic of China to begin negotiating with the latter. This "opening to China" (which previously had been regarded by many as little more than a Russian client state) in turn caused the Soviets to become more accommodating toward the United States. In 1972 Nixon and Soviet leader Leonid Brezhnev signed both an agreement on principles that contributed to the normalization of relations and two treaties that limited the development of strategic nuclear weapons.

The thaw did not last much beyond Nixon's resignation in 1974, since Soviet actions in Africa and elsewhere appeared to be blatant violations of the Nixon-Brezhnev accords. The Soviet invasion of Afghanistan in 1979 led Pres. Jimmy Carter to shelve a new treaty on nuclear weapons, embargo grain shipments to the Soviet Union, and boycott the 1980 Olympic Games that were held in Moscow.

Pres. Ronald Reagan's election in 1980 heralded a return to the confrontational relationship of the past. Reagan, who referred to the Soviet Union as an "evil empire," embarked on a massive military buildup that included an incredibly complex space-based antimissile system critics referred to as "Star Wars." He also showed willingness to send American troops to trouble spots from the Middle East to Latin America as a way of informing Moscow that the United States was taking the initiative in the Cold War.

End of the Cold War. The situation changed rapidly following Mikhail Gorbachev's rise to power in the Soviet Union in 1985. Aware that the Soviet system was heading toward collapse, Gorbachev sought reform, partly by reducing the terrible economic strains imposed by an enormous military budget. He eagerly sought arms control agreements, wound down the war in Afghanistan, and began withdrawing Soviet troops from Eastern Europe.

Against the advice of some advisers, Reagan cooperated with Gorbachev on arms control and did not seek to exploit the subsequent overthrow of Communist regimes in Eastern Europe in 1987 and 1988. Soon, some non-Russian republics within the Soviet Union began to demand independence. Soviet reactionaries staged a coup against Gorbachev in August 1991. It was put down, but the system was in disarray and the republics pronounced the Soviet Union dissolved in December of that year. The Cold War was over.

Responsibility for the Cold War continues to be debated. During its early years, most American scholars believed that the United States and its allies acted appropriately in the face of Soviet aggression. From the 1960s on, however, "revisionists" have argued the reverse: that American bullying and "atomic diplomacy" caused an essentially conservative Stalin to react defensively to protect Soviet security. Others have sought to combine various aspects of both positions. Documents being released from former Soviet archives have greatly discredited the revisionist view.

—ROBERT JAMES MADDOX

See Also: *Containment; Cuban Missile Crisis; Iron Curtain; McCarthyism; Marshall Plan; North Atlantic Treaty Organization (NATO); Truman Doctrine; individual biographies.*

BIBLIOGRAPHY: Crockett, Richard, *The Fifty Years War: The United States and the Soviet Union in World Politics, 1941-1991* (Routledge 1995); Frankel, Benjamin, ed., *The Cold War, 1945-1991,* 3 vols. (Gale 1992); Gaddis, John Lewis, *The United States and the End of the Cold War: Implications, Reconsiderations, Provocations* (Oxford Univ. Press 1992).

■ **COLE, NAT "KING" (1919-65),** pianist and singer. Born Nathaniel Adams Coles in Montgomery, Alabama, Cole began his career as an instrumentalist, playing brilliant jazz piano with small bands, then his own King Cole Trio. In 1943, he made his first vocal recording and soon vaulted to the top of the industry. Cole's silken renditions of songs like "Mona Lisa" and "Embraceable You" have become classics.

See Also: *African Americans.*

■ **COLE, THOMAS (1801-48),** leading Hudson River School painter. Cole was born in Lancashire, England, and started learning the techniques of engraving at the age of 14. He emigrated with his family to the United States in 1819. After working and studying in Philadel-phia, he moved in 1825 to New York City, where he met a number of leading American painters, such as John Trumbull and Asher B. Durand. In 1825, he also took his first sketching trips to the Hudson River Valley; he eventually settled in Catskill, New York. In the natural landscape of this region—into which he often incorporated a moral or philosophical spirit—he found the primary inspiration for such paintings as *Lake with Dead Trees* (1825), *Expulsion from the Garden of Eden* (1827-28), and *The Oxbow* (1836). In the 1830s, Cole's fascination with panoramas led him to execute series of paintings that, when viewed together, added the factor of time to his depiction of the landscape. These series include *The Course of Empire* (1836), *The Past and The Present* (1838), and *The Voyage of Life* (1840).

See Also: *Durand, Asher B.; Hudson River School; Painting; Trumbull, John.*

■ **COLFAX, SCHUYLER (1823-85),** vice president of the United States (1869-73). Born in New York City, he was an influential Whig and newspaper editor in Indiana, before becoming a Republican congressman from that state in 1854. He served seven terms, three as Speaker of the House. Elected in 1868 as Pres. Ulysses S. Grant's running mate, he was not chosen for a second term in 1872. A year later he was linked to the Credit Mobilier scandal.

See Also: *Credit Mobilier of America; Grant, Ulysses Simpson; Vice President of the United States.*

■ **COLLIER, JOHN (1884-1968),** activist for Indian causes and commissioner of Indian Affairs (1934-45). Collier was born in Atlanta, Georgia, the son of a prominent lawyer and businessman. In 1902, Collier entered Columbia College in New York, where he quickly focused his energies on contemporary social problems, especially the impact of industrialization and urbanization. In 1907 Collier went to work for the People's Institute in New York City, a group founded to help immigrants. The institute held evening classes for adults and offered lectures on history, literature, and the social sciences. Collier was an advocate of Eastern European communalism until a 1920 visit to Taos Pueblo in New Mexico. There, Collier experienced an epiphany and formulated the idea of merging the communal life of the Pueblos with the urban/industrial world to create a perfect society. Collier founded the American Indian Defense Association (AIDA) in 1923 to fight for Pueblo land rights in New Mexico. The AIDA later sought to preserve Indian cultural integrity and autonomy and to restore and strengthen the power of tribal government.

As commissioner of Indian affairs, Collier was the principal architect of the 1934 Wheeler-Howard Act, also known as the Indian Reorganization Act (IRA). The IRA ended the disastrous allotment policy and put in place the means for tribes to reorganize as corporations, borrow money, and adopt constitutions. Despite his admiration for Pueblo communalism, Collier apparently stopped short of embracing traditional Pueblo governments as an ideal. Rather, the IRA was based on the U.S. Constitution and on corporatism. The entire breadth of policy toward Indians under Collier is known as the Indian New Deal. Although many of his programs never reached their full potential because of lack of funding from Congress, Collier laid the foundation for internal sovereignty and self-determination by Indians in future generations.

—KATHRYN A. ABBOTT

See Also: Allotment; Indian Self-Determination; Indians of North America; Pueblo; Wounded Knee, Occupation of.

BIBLIOGRAPHY: Vine, Deloria, Jr., and Clifford Lytle, *The Nations Within: The Past and Future of American Indian Sovereignty* (Pantheon 1984); Olson, James Stuart, and Raymond Wilson, *Native Americans in the Twentieth Century* (Univ. of Illinois Press 1984); Philip, Kenneth R., *John Collier's Crusade for Indian Reform, 1920-1954* (Univ. of Arizona Press 1977).

■ **COLONIAL AMERICA.** *See: Colonial Government; Glorious Revolution in America; Jamestown Settlement; Maritime Colonies; Mayflower Compact; Plymouth Settlement; Thirteen Colonies.*

■ **COLONIAL GOVERNMENT.** European governments administered their colonial holdings in the Americas in a variety of ways. The administration of both the Spanish and French American colonies was highly centralized. New France was ruled by a superior council including the royal governor and intendant, as well as the bishop of Quebec. In New Spain, the Council of the Indies and the royal viceroy had direct executive authority over all political affairs. Thus, the far-flung communities of the French and Spanish empires developed few representative institutions of self-government. In the English colonies, however, colonial government took a very different form.

English Colonies in the 1600s. Almost from their founding, the English colonies were distinguished by the weakness of central administrative authority. In 1624, Virginia was declared a royal colony, with an appointed governor, but his power was consistently countered by the House of Burgesses, whose members were elected by the planter elite. Maryland was a proprietary colony controlled by a single family, the Calverts, but the House of Delegates gained the right to legislate and in mid-century repudiated Calvert rule. Proprietary control was reestablished only with difficulty. In New England the Pilgrims instituted their own system of governance with the Mayflower Compact. The officers of the Massachusetts Bay Company, taking advantage of a loophole in their charter, transferred their operations to New England and established the first self-governing commonwealth in America. That model of government was repeated in Connecticut and Rhode Island.

In the mid-1670s there were rebellions against central governmental authority in Virginia and Carolina (Bacon's Rebellion, 1676, and Culpeper's Rebellion, 1677) and during the so-called Glorious Revolution of 1689 in Massachusetts, Maryland, and New York (Leisler's Rebellion). These uprisings were triggered by events unique to each colony, but they also represented a tradition of challenge against central authority. William Penn's charters for Pennsylvania and Delaware granted him total governance, stipulating only that legislation be approved by an assembly. But Penn faced an unruly legislature that in 1696 gained from him the power to initiate legislation, and in 1701 a new Frame of Government created representative governments for both colonies. Penn spent the last two decades of his life trying to resolve disputes with the assembly.

Colonial Policy in the 1700s. The English government sought to control the colonies through the Lords of Trade (1660-95) and the Board of Trade (after 1696) and by converting most of the settlements to royal colonies. Royal government was also established in South Carolina and Georgia in the early 18th century. But throughout the colonies royal governors and imperial officials fostered a scorn for English authority and accentuated the importance of the assemblies for the furtherance of local interests. The colonial assemblies established and controlled the power to raise local revenues, and the dependence of colonial officials upon those revenues was an important aspect of local control.

During the early 18th century the British government of Prime Minister Robert Walpole worked on the assumption that a decentralized administration would best accomplish the nation's economic goals. Contented colonies, Walpole argued, would present far fewer problems. "One would not strain any point where it can be of no service to our King or country," a British official advised the governor of South Carolina in 1722; "the government should be as easy and mild as possible." This governing principal has become known as "salutary neglect." The Board of Trade, empowered by Parliament to manage the colonies, played a coordinating rather than an executive function. Armed with royal charters guaranteeing a measure of independence and self-government, the British colonies acted like separate provinces. They argued and contested with each other as well as with the mother country.

Colonial Self-Government. Each of the British colonies was administered by royally appointed governors and constituent assemblies. Because property holding became relatively widespread in the 18th century, the proportion of adult white men enjoying the right to vote for representatives to the assembly was 50 percent or higher in all the British colonies. By proportion, this was the largest electorate in the world. In contrast, because of restrictions on the franchise, two-thirds of the political boroughs of 18th-century England, each with populations in the tens of thousands, had electorates of 500 or fewer voters.

A large electorate, however, did not mean that colonial politics was democratic. The world view of the British was founded on the principle of deference to authority. The well-ordered family, in which children were to be strictly governed by their parents and wives by their husbands, was the model for civil order. The occupant of each rung on the social ladder was entitled to the deference of those below. Members of subordinate groups, which in some colonies amounted to 9 of every 10 adults in the population, were denied the right to vote and hold public office. This was a world of hierarchies, of lesser born and better born, slaves and servants, as well as racial and ethnic ranks in which Africans, Indians, and other groups were considered social inferiors to Englishmen.

This ideology of deference demanded that leadership be entrusted to men of merit, a quality closely associated with social position and wealth. Thus, at all levels British colonial government was dominated by an elite. In New England towns, John Adams remembered after the Revolution, "you will find that the office of justice of the peace, and even the place of representative, which has ever depended only on the freest election of the people, have generally descended from generation to generation, in three or four families at most." Likewise, large landowners and planters were most likely to be elected to serve on the county court, the most important institution of local government outside of New England. Provincial councils and assemblies were also controlled by the elite of planters, merchants, and professionals.

Early Moves Toward Independence. The important political developments in 18th-century British North America, then, had little to do with democracy. To educated British colonists, the word democracy implied rule by the mob, the normal order of the world turned upside down. Over the century, however, there was an important movement toward stronger institutions of representative government. By mid-century most colonial assemblies had achieved considerable power over provincial affairs and enjoyed parity with governors and imperial authorities. They collected local revenues and allocated funds for government programs, asserted the right to audit the accounts of public officers, and in some cases even acquired the power to approve the appointment of provincial officials. Royal governors sometimes balked at such claims of power, but because the assemblies controlled the purse strings, most governors were unable to resist this trend.

The potential power of the assemblies was compromised somewhat by competition among elite families for patronage and government contracts.

The royal governors who were most successful at realizing their agendas were those who became adept at playing off one provincial faction against another. Nevertheless, all this conflict had the important effect of schooling the colonial elite in the art of politics. It was not democratic politics, but it nevertheless held important implications for the development of American institutions.

Those implications were realized during the 1760s, when the British abandoned mild controls and governed the colonies more closely to raise revenues to pay for their expensive empire. The representative bodies of the colonies responded by denouncing and ultimately attempting to circumvent imperial authority. During the crisis over the Stamp Act, delegates from nine colonies met in New York City at the Stamp Act Congress (1765) and passed a set of resolutions denying Parliament's right to tax the colonies, since there could be "no taxation without representation." During the early 1770s resistance continued to grow, culminating in the meeting of the First Continental Congress (1774), which declared British regulations (the Intolerable Acts, 1774) unconstitutional. The demise of colonial government over the next two years was followed by the adoption of state constitutions and the Articles of Confederation.

—JOHN MACK FARAGHER

See Also: *French Colonies; Mayflower Compact; Spanish Colonies; Thirteen Colonies.*

BIBLIOGRAPHY: Andrews, Charles M., *The Colonial Background of the American Revolution* (Yale Univ. Press 1931); Bailyn, Bernard, *The Origins of American Politics* (Knopf 1968); Christie, Ian R., and Benjamin W. Labaree, *Empire of Independence, 1760-1776* (Norton 1976); Greene, Jack P., *Peripheries and Center: Constitutional Development in the Extended Politics of the British Empire and the United States, 1607-1788* (Univ. of Georgia Press 1986).

■ **COLORADO,** the second most populous of the Rocky Mountain states and, along with Wyoming, the only perfectly rectangular state. It is bounded on the north by Wyoming, on the north and east by Nebraska, on the east by Kansas, on the south by Oklahoma and New Mexico, and on the west by Utah. With an average elevation of about 6,800 feet above sea level, Colorado is the highest of all the states. Fifty-four of its Rocky Mountain peaks are 14,000 feet or higher. But the eastern third of the state is a high plateau, part of the Great Plains. Colorado has farms, ranches, mines, and an industrial base characterized by the processing of raw materials. Denver, its largest city, is a financial center. Tourism is also important, and the state has many ski resorts.

The first Europeans to explore Colorado were Spanish and French, but all of the area had passed to the United States by the end of the Mexican War in 1848. Colorado became a state in 1876.

Capital: Denver. Area: 104,100 square miles. Population (1995 est.): 3,747,000.

See Also: *Air Force Academy; Anasazi; Guadalupe-Hidalgo, Treaty of; Pike, Zebulon; Pueblo; Sand Creek Massacre.*

■ **COLORADO RIVER,** river running some 1,450 miles southwest from Colorado to the Gulf of California in Mexico. The Colorado rises in the northwestern Colorado Rockies and runs a circuitous route through Colorado, Utah, Arizona, and California and into Mexico. Pueblo Indians first occupied the area near the river in southwestern Colorado in 1100-1300. Two different parties of the Spanish explorer Francisco de Coronado's expedition explored the river in 1539 and 1540. Throughout the 17th and 18th centuries numerous Spanish priests traveled in the area. The most famous expedition on the Colorado was John Wesley Powell's trips in 1869, 1871, and 1872, which were financed by the Smithsonian Institution. In 1908 Congress established the Grand Canyon National Park, undoubtedly the river's most spectacular part. The Colorado's water has been heatedly fought over for years. In 1928 Congress passed laws regulating water rights among seven southwestern states. Other compacts and treaties regulate the river's use with Mexico. During the 20th century the Colorado has been the most heavily dammed river in America, with Hoover Dam (1947) and other facilities providing water and electricity for millions of people. In many ways the river has been the machine behind the growth of the Southwest, especially of cities like Phoenix, Albuquerque, and Los Angeles, and fertile agricultural areas like California's Imperial Valley.

See Also: *Grand Canyon; Powell, John Wesley.*

■ **COLT, SAMUEL (1814-62),** inventor and manufacturer. Born in Hartford, Connecticut, Colt worked at his father's textile factory and spent a year at sea, where he made a wooden model of an automatically revolving breech pistol (1831). Upon returning, he made metal models of the pistol and received patents in England, France, and the United States by 1836. His factory in Paterson, New Jersey, used new mass-production techniques, including assembly lines, completely interchangeable parts, and final inspections. Although his "six shooter" caught on with individuals and in Texas, Colt could not get the business of the U.S. Army, and as a result his company failed in 1842. Colt then turned to developing underwater mines and telegraph cable. With the outbreak of the Mexican War (1846), however, the army placed an order for 1,000 revolvers. Colt had to subcontract the work to Eli Whitney's factory until 1848, when he opened his own factory and utopian industrial community along the banks of the Connecticut River in Hartford. There, he manufactured his famous .44, the major development in 19th-century weaponry, and ran Colt's Patent Fire Arms Manufacturing Company until he died.

See Also: *Industrial Revolution.*

■ **COLTRANE, JOHN (1926-67),** jazz musician. Born in Hamlet, North Carolina, Coltrane began playing the tenor saxophone while in his teens. His spectacular technique and gift for composition added new dimensions of sound to the experimentation that was the hallmark of avant-garde jazz in the 1950s. Through dissonance and his "sheets of sound," in songs like "Equinox" and "Impressions," he blazed new trails for future performers, both alone and in company with Miles Davis, Dizzy Gillespie, and Thelonius Monk.

See Also: *African Americans; Jazz.*

■ **COLUMBIA RIVER,** longest river in the Northwest, running some 1,210 miles from British Columbia in Canada to the Pacific Ocean on the border between Washington and Oregon in the United States. It is second only to the Mississippi River in volume of water carried. The area was densely settled by Indians, with the Chinook, Willamette, and Tillamook located largely along the Columbia. In 1805 Lewis and Clark descended the river in dugout canoes to the Pacific Ocean. In 1811 John Jacob Astor's Pacific Fur Company established a fur-trading post on the Columbia. By 1836 Presbyterians had founded four missions on the Columbia's tributaries. Travelers on the Oregon Trail ended their trip from St. Louis at The Dalles, a town on the river that was the terminus of the trail. The gigantic Grand Coulee Dam in northern Washington was completed in 1942 as the key unit of the Columbia Basin Project. The system of dams on the Columbia provides electricity and irrigated land to the area, but they have also come close to stopping the annual salmon runs for which the river is famous.

See Also: *Lewis and Clark Expedition.*

■ **COLUMBUS, CHRISTOPHER (1451-1506),** explorer who sailed for the Spanish Crown. Born in Genoa, Italy, the son of a woolen weaver, Columbus went to sea as a youth. After being shipwrecked in 1476 off the coast of Portugal, he made his way to Lisbon, where he joined his brother. The Portuguese were the most accomplished sailors in Europe, and over the next decade Columbus worked as a merchant seaman for Portuguese contractors, visiting ports from Iceland to the Gold Coast of Africa. He married and settled on the Portuguese island colony of Madeira in the Atlantic, and it was there that he developed the idea of opening a new route to "the Indies" of the Far East by sailing west. Rejected by the advisers of several European monarchs, Columbus finally sold his idea to Isabella and Ferdinand, monarchs of the newly consolidated kingdom of Spain. Eager for new lands to conquer and observing the successful explorations of the Portuguese, they were interested in opening lucrative trade routes of their own with Asia. Columbus's name for his undertaking, "the Enterprise of the Indies," suggests its commercial nature.

Voyages of Discovery. The small fleet of three caravels, the *Niña*, *Pinta*, and *Santa Maria*, embarked from the port of Palos on Aug. 3, 1492. By early October flocks of birds and bits of driftwood announced the approach of land, which was sighted on October 12. Although scholars disagree on the precise location, many believe it to be a spot now known as Samana Cay, in the Bahamas.

QVI RATE VELIVOLA OCCIDVOS PENETRAVIT AT IDOS
PRIMVS ET AMERICAM NOBILITAVIT HVMVM

CHRISTOPHORVS COLVMBVS LIGVR INDIARV PRIM INVET

ASTRORVM CONSVLT ET IPSO NOBILIS AVSV
CHRISTOPHOR TALI FRONTE COLVMB ERAT

No images were produced of Christopher Columbus during his lifetime. This engraving, published in 1571, is among the earliest.

Columbus, however, believed he was somewhere near the Asian mainland. He explored the northern island coasts of Cuba and Hispaniola (now Haiti and the Dominican Republic), and leaving a small force of men behind to explore for gold, he headed home, fortuitously catching the westerly winds that blow from the American coast toward Europe north of the tropics. One of Columbus's most important discoveries was the clockwise circulation of Atlantic winds and currents that ultimately carried thousands of ships back and forth between Europe and America.

Columbus was greeted as a hero by the Spanish court. With him were a number of kidnapped Taino Indians. "Should your majesties command it," Columbus wrote in his famous "Letter" that announced his successful voyage, "all the inhabitants could be made slaves." He also reported the discovery of "great mines of gold." In fact, there were only small quantities of the precious metal on the Caribbean islands, but the sight of Indians wearing little gold ornaments had infected Columbus with a bad case of gold fever. The

monarchs financed a convoy of 17 ships and 1,500 men to return to the Indies, and Columbus departed on his second voyage in September 1493. He expected to force the Tainos into laboring for him, but he found that they had killed all the Europeans he had left behind. Columbus destroyed several nearby villages, enslaved hundreds of Tainos, and demanded tribute from them in gold. When the supply of gold ran out, Columbus was recalled to Spain.

For the rest of his career, Columbus struggled to regain the confidence of the monarchs. He made a third voyage to the Caribbean in 1498, making landfall on the island of Trinidad and exploring the mouth of the great Orinoco River on the northern coast of South America. But dissatisfaction with his leadership grew so intense that the monarch ordered Columbus home in leg irons in 1500. He made a fourth and final voyage in 1502, along the eastern coast of Central America, that was characterized by the same violent slave raiding and obsessive searching for gold. Returning to Spain, he died there in 1506, still convinced that he had opened the way to Asia, a belief that persisted among many Europeans for several decades.

—JOHN MACK FARAGHER

See Also: *Exploration and Discovery.*

BIBLIOGRAPHY: Koning, Hans, *Columbus: His Enterprise* (Monthly Review Press 1991); Morison, Samuel Eliot, *Admiral of the Ocean Sea: A Life of Christopher Columbus* (Little, Brown 1942); Sale, Kirkpatrick, *The Conquest of Paradise: Christopher Columbus and the Columbian Legacy* (Knopf 1990).

■ **COMANCHE INDIANS.** *See: Great Plains Indians.*

■ **COMEDY,** popular humor that reflects American society and its constantly changing character. American comedy has taken on numerous forms, including political cartoons, bawdy jokes, minstrel acts, television sit-coms, racist propaganda, and satirical literature. Early comedy consisted of African-American storytelling, the literary humor of New England almanacs, and political satires. Each drew heavily from old traditions but reflected new experiences as well.

During the early 19th century, political humor and local legend became central components of American comedy. After the Civil War, Mark

Twain helped bridge the gap between rural, folk comedy and cosmopolitan humor by developing the genre of literary satire. A transformation in American comedy occurred around the turn of the 20th century. As southern African Americans and European immigrants moved into northern cities, a new, more belligerent strain of comedy arose, one that expressed racial, ethnic, religious, and sexual sentiments of white Americans. The new arrivals, too, affected change in humor. Jews and African Americans, especially, developed forms of comedy in response to their economic and social suppression.

Perhaps the greatest transformations in American comedy have accompanied technological innovations. Radio, motion pictures, and television have brought a larger variety of comedy to more people than was previously possible and have helped to make comedians like Bill Cosby and Bob Hope international celebrities.

BIBLIOGRAPHY: Bier, Jesse, *The Rise and Fall of American Humor* (Holt, Rinehart & Winston 1968); Walker, Nancy A., *A Very Serious Thing: Women's Humor and American Culture* (Univ. of Minnesota Press 1988).

■ **COMICS,** cartoons that depict the same characters in an ongoing series. They first became popular in the 1890s. From the time of Felton Oucault's "The Yellow Kid" (1896), the subject of a bidding war between publishers Joseph Pulitzer and William Randolph Hearst, comic strips have been used by U.S. newspapers to attract readers. Some, such as Chester Gould's "Dick Tracy," featured continuing story lines; others, such as Walt Kelly's "Pogo," offered humorous observations on the passing scene or the human condition. A few, such as George Herriman's "Krazy Kat," created worlds of their own. The development of color presses led in the 1910s to the growth of Sunday comic sections and in the 1930s to comic books, which were often blamed for distracting the nation's youth from more serious reading. A new genre of adult "comix" blossomed in the 1960s, and some newspaper comic strips, such as "Doonesbury" by Garry Trudeau, have since addressed current events with a sharper edge.

BIBLIOGRAPHY: Feiffer, Jules, ed., *The Great Comic Book Heroes* (Dial Press 1965).

■ **COMMERCE, DEPARTMENT OF,** cabinet department of the U.S. government established by Congress (1913) during Pres. Woodrow Wilson's administration to promote business and trade. Originally created as part of the Department of Commerce and Labor (1903), the Commerce Department administers the Census Bureau and the Patent Office, regulates weights and measures, forecasts the weather, produces detailed maps and statistical studies of the nation, and promotes the sale of U.S. products in international markets.

See Also: Census; Patent Office.

■ **COMMITTEE ON PUBLIC INFORMATION,** U.S. government propaganda agency. Created in 1917 and led by George Creel, it produced anti-German propaganda during World War I. Most of the group's themes mirrored British images of the Germans as barbarians or "Huns."

See Also: World War I.

■ **COMMITTEES OF CORRESPONDENCE,** colonial bodies formed to disseminate information about British actions that appeared to violate colonial rights. In response to the *Gaspée* Incident (1772) and the increasing financial independence of royal officials from the colonists, Samuel Adams called for a committee of correspondence at a Boston town meeting in November 1772. The purpose of this committee was to draft a list of colonial rights, document British violations, submit this information to other towns throughout the colonies, and encourage the formation of other committees. The activities of Boston radicals and the long list of violations of the colonists' common law rights spurred the Virginia House of Burgesses to also establish a committee, and by early 1774 every colony but Pennsylvania had a standing committee. Prior to the First Continental Congress in 1774, committees of correspondence became the primary means of sharing information, influencing public opinion, and establishing intercolonial cooperation.

See Also: Gaspée Incident; Revolution, American.

BIBLIOGRAPHY: Countryman, Edward, *The American Revolution* (Hill & Wang 1985); Morgan, Edmund S., *The Birth of the Republic: 1763-1789* (Univ. of Chicago Press 1992).

■ **COMMITTEES OF SAFETY,** political bodies designed to govern local Revolutionary War efforts. Seeking a way to enforce economic sanctions against British violations of the colonists' rights, the delegates to the First Continental Congress in 1774 urged that every county, city, and town form a committee of safety. Democratically elected, these committees soon eclipsed their original intended purpose and became de facto local governments. They organized and called out the militia, established extralegal courts, and formed provincial congresses. Also coercive, they suppressed Loyalist sentiments and closely monitored the activities of all citizens. The first committee of safety was formed in October 1774 by the Massachusetts legislature, and soon thereafter the other colonies followed suit. The committees' effectiveness was so widespread that important connections developed between the cities and the countryside. Committees of safety functioned throughout the Revolution, but they eventually disbanded with the adoption of state constitutions.

See Also: Revolution, American.

■ **COMMODITY CREDIT CORPORATION,** federal agency established by the Agricultural Adjustment Act (1933) to support farm prices. It bought and sold farm commodities in hopes of keeping prices high and ensuring economic stability to farmers.

See Also: Agricultural Adjustment Act; New Deal.

■ **COMMON LAW,** system of law made by courts and judges, rather than by legislatures. Originating in medieval England, common law is contrasted with civil or code-based legal systems that descend from continental Europe and Roman law. Common law is considered to be natural or universal and emerges through litigation and legal decisions about actual controversies.

Common law traditions accompanied English settlers to the American colonies. During the American Revolution, Americans adhered to the system, particularly the notion that common law principles controlled government. First articulated in the Declaration of Independence as "certain unalienable rights," the system of common law took shape in the Constitution. Article III and the Seventh Amendment implicitly recognized the Supreme Court as a common law court. Both state and federal constitutions and their bills of rights are composed of statements of common-law rights and of methods to protect them.

Common law has constantly evolved in the state and federal courts. In the cases where states have codified common law, the codes are largely derived from common-law doctrines established in the courts. The sole exception to common law as the basic legal system in the United States is the Code Napoleon, which originated in France and serves as the legal order for Louisiana.

See Also: Supreme Court.

BIBLIOGRAPHY: Friedman, Lawrence M., *A History of American Law* (Simon & Schuster 1985); Nelson, William Edward, *Americanization of the Common Law: The Impact of Legal Change on Massachusetts Society, 1760-1830* (Harvard Univ. Press 1975).

■ *COMMON SENSE* **(1776),** political pamphlet advocating American independence from England, written by Thomas Paine. First published in January 1776, it achieved instant success, selling 120,000 copies within three months. *Common Sense* appeared at a stage when Americans had begun to despair of reconciliation with Britain but had not yet seriously broached the idea of independence. Although many of the ideas did not originate with Paine, he combined them in a distinctive way. The result was a compelling argument that crystallized American sentiment for independence. Paine made his arguments widely accessible by writing in a plain and straightforward style that used biblical imagery in combination with language familiar to most Americans. Through his scathing attack on King George III and on the whole idea of monarchy, Paine cut the last tie binding Americans to Britain. He also appealed to a utopian vision of America's mission to be a bastion of freedom for the rest of the world.

See Also: Paine, Thomas; Revolution, American.

BIBLIOGRAPHY: Foner, Eric, *Tom Paine and Revolutionary America* (Oxford Univ. Press 1976); Paine, Thomas, *Common Sense,* ed. Isaac Kramnick (Penguin Books 1976).

■ **COMMUNICATIONS ACT OF 1934,** law creating the Federal Communications Commission.

Based on the Radio Act of 1927, it required broadcasters to be licensed to serve the public interest, convenience, and necessity.

See Also: Television and Radio.

■ ***COMMUNICATION WORKERS V. BECK* (1988),** U.S. Supreme Court case that limited labor unions' use of dues for political purposes. The National Labor Relations Act (1935) allows unions to collect agency fees from workers who benefit from union contracts but choose not to join the organization. Beck, a worker, refused to pay a portion of the fee that the union used for lobbying and political action. The Court ruled (8-0) that agency fees must cover only the union's collective bargaining costs.

See Also: Supreme Court.

■ **COMMUNIST CONTROL ACT (1954),** law stating the U.S. Communist party was conspiring to overthrow the government. Party members were denied federal jobs and passports and were required to register with the government.

See Also: Cold War.

■ **COMMUNIST PARTY,** American representative of the world communist movement. At times the Communist party was a foremost element in struggles for racial equality and workers' rights and against fascism. Often, however, it was a tool of the foreign policy of the Soviet Union, which usually dictated the party's positions.

Prompted by the Russian Revolution and the formation in Moscow of a Communist International, representatives of nearly 100,000 socialists formed several competing U.S. communist parties in 1919. Government repression nearly eliminated the movement, which re-emerged as a single party in 1922. Through the 1920s the party supported the struggles of unskilled workers while exhausting itself in factional quarrels. It was far from democratic in its internal life.

The Depression revived Communist expectations of imminent revolution and spawned Communist involvement in a multiplicity of campaigns. In a mid-1930s strategic shift known as the Popular Front, the Communist party increased its influence by supporting Franklin Roosevelt's New Deal. Its membership scarcely reached 100,000, but its following, through labor and cultural and fraternal groups, numbered perhaps 1 million. In Hollywood, where many screenwriters were party members, and Washington, where some New Deal intellectuals followed Communist positions, the Communist party counted as an important left-liberal organization.

The 1939 Hitler-Stalin Pact caught the party by surprise. After Germany invaded the Soviet Union in 1941, however, Communists enjoyed one last moment of prestige and influence as a leading antifascist force.

The party dominated the losing presidential campaign of Progressive party candidate Henry Wallace in 1948. During the Cold War a massive "red hunt" in government, labor, and business helped destroy its already waning influence. In the 1950s revelations of Soviet anti-Semitism and Stalin's brutality reduced the U.S. Communist party to a small and uninfluential group that played little part in national events.

—PAUL BUHLE

See Also: Labor Movement; Political Parties; Wallace, Henry A.

BIBLIOGRAPHY: Draper, Theodore, *Roots of American Communism* (Viking Press 1957).

■ **COMPROMISE OF 1850,** collective name given to five bills passed by Congress between Sept. 9 and Sept. 20, 1850, that addressed all outstanding differences between North and South on the slavery question. Originally proposed as a set of resolutions by Sen. Henry Clay in January 1850, the measures prompted a storm of debate in Congress. Clay's "Omnibus Bill" failed to pass, partly as a result of Pres. Zachary Taylor's opposition and partly because of implacable opposition by extreme elements in both sections and parties. Taylor's death on July 9 elevated pro-Compromise Millard Fillmore to the presidency. This, along with growing Union sentiment in the nation and the division of the compromise measures into separate bills, ensured their passage.

The Compromise measures and the date of final House passage—the bills had passed the Senate in August—were as follows: (1) the admission of California as a free state (September 7); (2) the Texas and New Mexico Act, which adjusted the boundary between the two and applied the "popular sovereignty" principle to slavery in the territory of New Mexico (September 9); (3) the Utah Act, which established territorial government with the same provisions (September 9); (4) the Fugitive Slave Act, which placed the capture of fugitives under federal jurisdiction and applied stringent penalties for obstructing the law (September 12); (5) the prohibition of the slave trade in the District of Columbia (September 19).

—THOMAS E. SCHOTT

See Also: Civil War; Clay, Henry; Popular Sovereignty.
BIBLIOGRAPHY: Foner, Eric, *Free Soil, Free Labor, Free Men: The Ideology of the Republican Party before the Civil War* (Oxford Univ. Press 1995); Hamilton, Holman, *Prologue to Conflict: The Crisis and Compromise of 1850* (Univ. of Kentucky Press 1964); McPherson, James M., *Battle Cry of Freedom: The Civil War Era* (Ballantine 1988).

■ **COMPROMISE OF 1877,** agreement between Republicans and Democrats in Congress to end Reconstruction and elect Rutherford B. Hayes president. The Compromise of 1877 marked the end of the attempt to guarantee African Americans in the South full political and civil rights.

In the 1876 election Democrat Samuel B. Tilden won a popular majority over the Republican Hayes. The electoral votes of Florida, South Carolina, Louisiana, and Oregon were disputed. Without them Tilden lacked an electoral majority. The three southern states were still occupied by federal troops. A special committee set up by Congress narrowly voted to settle the dispute by awarding all the votes in question to Hayes, giving him an electoral majority of one.

Democrats in Congress agreed to accept this outcome when Republicans promised to withdraw the remaining troops, make economic concessions to the South, and in general allow the southern states, now mainly ruled by conservative Democrats, to go their own way.

See Also: Hayes, Rutherford Birchard; Reconstruction; Tilden, Samuel Jones.

■ **COMPTON, ARTHUR H. (1892-1962),** physicist. Born in Wooster, Ohio, Compton studied X rays at the College of Wooster (B.S., 1913) and Princeton (Ph.D., 1916). While at Washington University (1920-23), he discovered the Compton Ef-

fect, which demonstrated that X rays displayed particle-like as well as wave behavior. The Compton Effect offered the first experimental proof of Einstein's light quantum hypothesis of 1905, and it won Compton the 1927 Nobel Prize in Physics. He taught at the University of Chicago (1923-45) and worked on the Manhattan Project (1942-45) before returning to Washington University (1945-61).

See Also: Science.

■ **COMPUTERS,** machines using digital technology to perform various tasks. Computers have altered the lives of Americans in the latter half of the 20th century in many ways. In this respect they are comparable to the automobiles, electric lights, and communication technologies that so transformed American life in the first half of the century. In other respects, however, computers represent new developments in science and technology that first became apparent during and after World War II, when they originated. Mechanical computers played a part in business and in government prior to the war, when punched-card machines transformed the enumeration of the census and came into increasing use in banking, insurance, and other businesses that handled large amounts of data. These machines were, however, very slow, and with few exceptions they found little use in education, research, and the home.

The First Electronic Computers. The advent of the much faster and much larger electronic digital computers did not immediately change this situation. Nevertheless although scientists in the new government laboratories spawned by the war and in some universities did take advantage of early electronic machines, so did the military, which footed the bill for machines like the Electronic Numerical Integrator and Computer (ENIAC), developed by the Moore School at the University of Pennsylvania for the U.S. Army in 1943-45. Although ENIAC was completed too late to be of use in the war, it was used for calculations of the behavior of thermonuclear fusion and postwar work at the Aberdeen Proving Grounds. Other special-purpose electronic computers were developed in Britain and the United States during the war to break enemy codes. The most famous of these were the Colossus computers developed in Britain by A. M. Turing, who became famous for his contributions to computer logic and artificial intelligence.

Turing's counterpart in the United States, John von Neumann, devised the logic for early computers as a result of his studies of ENIAC. Von Neumann-type machines became the basis for the development of mainframe computers throughout the world, including the electronic computers built by IBM. The IBM machines came to dominate the industry that smaller firms, like the Eckert and Mauchly Company, Engineering Research Associates, and their successor, UNIVAC (now Unisys), had opened up in the United States.

In Britain Maurice Wilkes at Cambridge University and the University of Manchester built the first machines of von Neumann's design and the Leo Computer, developed by J. Lyons & Company, became the first commercial electronic computer. Despite this early British start, however, massive government investment in electronic digital computers for nuclear science and military applications made the United States preeminent in computer development by the 1950s. For example, the Whirlwind Project at M.I.T. was developed for the Air Force Strategic Air Command's Semi-Automatic Ground Environment (SAGE) air defense system in the 1950s by IBM, the RAND Corporation, and its spin-off, the Systems Development Corporation. It spawned many of the technologies that would later be used in commercial computers.

Minicomputers and Personal Computers. One significant spin-off were the minicomputers, built by Digital Equipment Corporation in the 1960s. These powerful yet comparatively less expensive machines found widespread applications in business and industry. They also made it possible for many universities and colleges to acquire computer technology and to train people for the growing industry. The advent of computer languages like FORTRAN for scientific and engineering calculations, COBOL for business applications, and BASIC for educational programming, together with the development of time-sharing, which allowed many more people to work with a computer simultaneously and in real time, accelerated computer education and innovation. The contractor laboratories of the Atomic Energy Commission (later the Department of Energy) proved demanding customers for these and for high-performance computers such as the UNIVAC LARC, IBM Stretch, Control Data Corporation's 6600 and 7600, and the Cray supercomputers. These machines advanced the art of scientific calculation in weapons design, fluid dynamics, and other simulations.

The Defense Advanced Research Projects Agency was another significant government patron of advanced computers and introduced the ARPANET, a computer network that grew to form the Internet. Techniques of computer graphics and user interfaces developed under its patronage were fundamental to the development of the personal computer, which Steve Jobs and Steve Wozniak popularized with their Apple II computer. IBM and many other companies quickly entered the personal computer (PC) market, which expanded rapidly in the 1980s. By the 1990s PCs had become commonplace in both offices and homes, and links to the "Internet" via telephone lines offered unparalleled opportunities for retrieving information.

—ROBERT W. SEIDEL

See Also: Science; Von Neumann, John.

BIBLIOGRAPHY: Aspray, William, *John von Neumann and the Origins of Scientific Computing* (MIT Press 1990); Ceruzzi, Paul, "The Reckoners: The Prehistory of the Digital Computer," from *Relays to the Stored Program Concept, 19* (Greenwood Press 1983); Cortada, James, *The Computer in the United States: From Laboratory to Market, 1930-1960* (M. E. Sharpe 1993); Edwards, Paul, *The Closed World: Computers and the Politics of Discourse in Cold War America* (MIT Press 1996).

■ **COMSTOCK LAW (1873),** federal statute that outlawed the transmission of obscene material through the U.S. mail. The law was named for its sponsor, Anthony Comstock (1844-1915). As a young man from New England, Comstock was disturbed by what he saw as immorality in his new home, New York City. He founded the New York Society for the Prevention of Vice in 1873, the same year he convinced the U.S. Congress to pass the law, which outlawed a vast amount of material broadly defined as obscene. Well into the 20th century, the Comstock law, which opponents saw as biased in terms of class and gender, was used to block the dissemination of birth-control devices and informational tracts. Radicals and birth-control advocates, such as Emma Goldman and Margaret Sanger, risked imprisonment in their deliberate challenges to what they saw as an unclear and discriminatory law.

See Also: Goldman, Emma; Sanger, Margaret.

COMSTOCK LODE, greatest silver mine in American history, discovered in Nevada by prospector Henry Comstock in 1859. He soon sold his claim for a mere $11,000, but over the next two decades more than $300 million in silver was taken from the lode, feeding the fortunes of a small group of San Franciscans like George Hearst, father of the newspaper baron, and the "Silver Kings," four Irish immigrants who became the wealthiest men in the city. The operation involved deep tunneling, and in the lower shafts temperatures rose as high as 150 degrees and men sometimes dropped dead from the heat. During the 1870s engineer Adolph Sutro designed and built a massive three-mile tunnel to provide ventilation and drainage. It was one of the greatest engineering feats of the 19th century. In 1864 the miners of the Comstock Lode organized the first successful labor union in the West, when they struck successfully to maintain the $4 daily wage.

See Also: Frontier in American History; Mining and Mining Rushes.

BIBLIOGRAPHY: Lewis, Oscar, *Silver Kings: The Lives and Times of Mackay, Fair, Flood, and O'Brien, Lords of the Nevada Comstock* (Knopf 1947); Paul, Rodman W., *Mining Frontiers of the Far West, 1848-1880* (Univ. of New Mexico Press 1974).

CONANT, JAMES BRYANT (1893-1978), chemist and education reformer. Born in Dorchester, Massachusetts, Conant earned his Ph.D. from Harvard (1916), taught organic chemistry there (1916-33), and researched hemoglobin and chlorophyll. During World War I, he worked for the Chemical Warfare Service. As president of Harvard (1933-53) he instituted many reforms, including revising the promotion process, strengthening the professional schools, opening the university to women, and reforming the curriculum. He became chairman of the National Defense Research Committee during World War II, supporting the feasibility of the Manhattan Project and later serving on the scientific advisory committee of the Atomic Energy Commission. One of his last

government posts was U.S. ambassador to West Germany (1955-57). Always interested in education reform, Conant wrote *The American High School Today* (1959), which stressed higher intellectual standards for teachers and students. In 1970, he published his appropriately titled autobiography, *My Several Lives: Memoirs of a Social Inventor.*

See Also: Science.

CONFEDERATE STATES OF AMERICA (1861-65), the nation composed of the 11 Southern states that seceded from the United States in 1861. The Confederacy came into being on Feb. 8, 1861, at a convention of the seceded states in Montgomery, Alabama. Delegates from seven Deep South states—South Carolina, Georgia, Florida, Alabama, Mississippi, Louisiana, and Texas—drew up a constitution and set up a provisional government. The Confederate Constitution closely mirrored that of the United States but contained special provisions protecting slavery and the rights of individual states. Two days later, delegates selected a provisional president, Jef-

The Confederate States of America was led by Jefferson Davis throughout the Civil War.

ferson Davis, and vice president, Alexander H. Stephens, choices that were ratified at a general election in November.

The Confederacy's attempt on Apr. 12, 1861, to seize Fort Sumter in Charleston, South Carolina, precipitated war with the United States. U.S. Pres. Abraham Lincoln's subsequent call for 75,000 volunteers to quell "rebellion" caused four more states—Virginia, North Carolina, Tennessee, and Arkansas—to leave the Union and join the Confederacy.

The Southern nation survived for four years, but ultimately it could not maintain its independence against the greatly superior population, industrial capacity, and economic might of the North. A Union naval blockade of the Southern coastline gradually choked off all outside sources of supply. The South's largest port city, New Orleans, was in Union hands by April 1862; its last remaining port, Wilmington, North Carolina,

was closed in February 1865.

Despite some early military successes on land under such generals as Robert E. Lee and Thomas J. "Stonewall" Jackson, Confederate armies were eventually forced into costly campaigns of attrition. The loss of the battle of Gettysburg, Pennsylvania (July 1-3, 1863), and Vicksburg, Mississippi (July 4, 1863), the last Confederate bastion on the Mississippi River, proved to be turning points in both the eastern and western theaters of the war.

The key railroad terminus of Atlanta, Georgia, fell in early September 1864, and in the following weeks Gen. William T. Sherman's victorious Union army ravaged its way to Savannah and the sea. After a bloody campaign of maneuver in Virginia, Gen. Ulysses S. Grant pinned Lee's army to the defense of Petersburg, Virginia, the last rail link with the Confederate capital at Richmond. Both cities fell on Apr. 2, 1865. By the end of April the two main Confederate armies, Lee's and Gen.

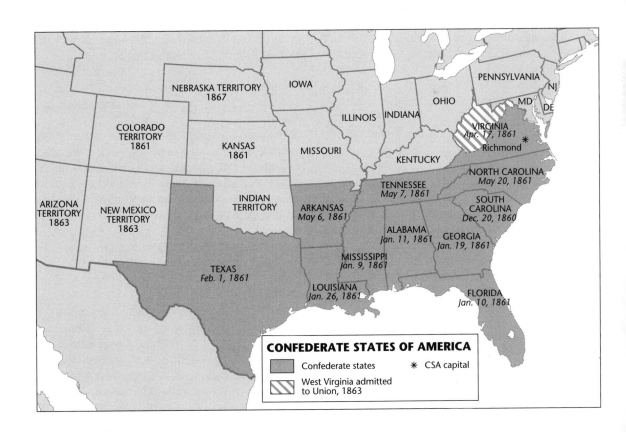

CONFEDERATE STATES OF AMERICA

■ Confederate states   ✳ CSA capital

▧ West Virginia admitted to Union, 1863

Joseph E. Johnston's in North Carolina, had been forced to surrender.

Internal divisions increasingly plagued the Confederacy as the government attempted to cope with the war's toll of blood and treasure. War measures such as conscription, suspension of the writ of habeas corpus, and impressment of goods and services grew intensely unpopular and aroused outright defiance from states' rights governors and politicians. As the South's military prospects waned, many of these same states' rights leaders melded their opposition to the Davis administration into a burgeoning peace movement that further divided the country.

Reluctant to tax the populace, the Confederate Congress authorized ever-larger issues of paper money to finance the war. The horrendous resulting inflation only made the shortage of hundreds of basic items, from flour to shoes to nails, even more burdensome. By war's end, it took 60 Confederate dollars to buy a single gold one.

The Confederacy was no more successful diplomatically. It had counted on the economic power of its cotton to hasten recognition and support by European countries. But effective U.S. diplomacy, the stigma of slavery, and the South's failure to achieve sustained battlefield success kept the Confederacy isolated.

Not until well into the 20th century did the South recover from the devastation the defeat of the Confederacy had brought.

—THOMAS E. SCHOTT

See Also: *Civil War; Davis, Jefferson; Stephens, Alexander H.*

BIBLIOGRAPHY: Boritt, Gabor S., *Why the Confederacy Lost* (Oxford Univ. Press 1992); Coulter, E. Merton, *The Confederate States of America, 1861-1865* (LSU Press 1950); Thomas, Emory M., *The Confederate Nation, 1861-1865* (Harper & Row 1979).

■ **CONFEDERATION CONGRESS (1781-89),** the national legislature of the United States under the Articles of Confederation. The Confederation Congress superseded the Second Continental Congress when the last state, Maryland, ratified the Articles on Mar. 1, 1781. In the Confederation Congress each state possessed one vote. The Congress comprised the only branch of the Confederation government. A handful of officials served at the discretion of Congress.

Congress managed foreign and Indian affairs, ran the post office, borrowed money, and appointed military officers. The requirement that many decisions needed the approval of nine states hamstrung the government, however. Moreover, Congress could not tax, raise troops directly, or regulate commerce. As a result the Confederation racked up huge debts, proved unable to suppress insurrections like Shays's Rebellion (1787), and earned the scorn of foreign governments.

As the Articles could not be amended without the approval of all the states, critics like James Madison sought to replace them. Their efforts culminated in the Constitutional Convention of 1787, which wrote the U.S. Constitution that is still in effect. The new government under the Constitution took office in April 1789.

Despite its weaknesses, the Confederation Congress had three notable achievements. It concluded the American Revolution with a treaty favorable to the United States; its Land Ordinance of 1785 established procedures for selling western lands to private citizens; and finally, Congress's Northwest Ordinance of 1787 created a procedure for enabling territories to become states after meeting certain basic requirements.

—RICKY EARL NEWPORT

See Also: *Articles of Confederation; Constitution of the United States; Northwest Ordinance; Revolution, American.*

BIBLIOGRAPHY: Jensen, Merrill, *The New Nation: A History of the United States during the Confederation, 1781-1789* (Knopf 1950); Morris, Richard B., *The Forging of the Union, 1781-1789* (Harper & Row 1987); Onuf, Peter S., *Statehood and Union: A History of the Northwest Ordinance* (Indiana Univ. Press 1987).

■ **CONFISCATION ACTS,** legislation passed by Congress (1861, 1863) during the Civil War. The laws were intended to deprive the South of the economic benefits of slavery. They provided that African Americans used in the Confederate war effort be confiscated and freed. Slaves in areas of the South liberated by Union troops were also freed. Questions of the constitutionality of the legislation led to the issuance by President Lincoln of the Emancipation Proclamation (January 1863).

See Also: *Emancipation Proclamation; Reconstruction.*

■ **CONGREGATIONALISTS,** followers of the system of church government that grants autonomy to local congregations, in which polity is shared by clergy and members. Congregationalism falls between episcopal and presbyterian government. Today, this type of polity can be found in many denominations in America, especially in Baptist and independent churches.

Congregationalism is an offspring of Puritanism. A synod of ministers from Massachusetts, Connecticut, and New Hampshire explained "Congregational Way" in the Cambridge Platform (1648). As Puritans immigrated, Congregationalism expanded. Harvard College (1636) and Yale College (1701) were established to meet the need for an educated Congregational ministry. The Halfway Covenant (1662), which allowed for halfway church membership, also increased the numbers. The Great Awakening of the 1730s and 1740s drew members but split many congregations over doctrinal issues. Congregationalism had difficulty spreading to the frontiers. So in 1801 a Plan of Union with the Presbyterians was drawn, and the two united their frontier churches. In 1852, Congregationalists withdrew and formed the American Congregational Union, their first national organization.

Congregationalists are noted for their missionary work and emphasis on education. They formed the first foreign mission society in 1810 and the American Home Missionary Society in 1826. The American Missionary Association worked in the post–Civil War South. Congregationalists have founded some of the finest American colleges, including Amherst, Carleton, Grinnell, Oberlin, and Williams.

In 1957, Congregational churches joined with the Evangelical and Reformed Church to form the United Church of Christ. This was the first time in the United States that churches of differing governing structures and historical backgrounds united.

—NANCY M. GODLESKI

See Also: Great Awakening; Puritans; Religion.
BIBLIOGRAPHY: Hodgkins, Harold, *The Congregational Way: Apostolic Legacy, Ministry, Unity, Freedom* (Congregational Federation 1982); Starkey, Marion Lena, *The Congregational Way* (Doubleday 1966).

■ **CONGRESS OF INDUSTRIAL ORGANIZATIONS (CIO),** labor organization founded in 1938 to unionize mass-production workers. The American Federation of Labor (AFL) and its leader Samuel Gompers succeeded in organizing skilled trade and crafts workers during the late 19th and early 20th centuries. They failed, however, to organize unskilled workers in mass production industries. At the AFL convention in 1934 a group led by John L. Lewis, president of the United Mine Workers (UMW), called on AFL membership to organize mass-production workers, both skilled and unskilled. The measure failed, receiving only 30 percent of the votes. After a similar response in 1935, Lewis and leaders from the Amalgamated Clothing Workers, International Ladies' Garment Workers, and other unions formed the Committee for Industrial Organization. Following suspension from the AFL, 10 of the participating unions formed the Congress of Industrial Organizations (CIO) in 1938.

With New Deal legislation protecting union activity, the CIO became a force in the American economy and contributed heavily to political campaigns. Massive sit-down strikes forced companies, such as General Motors, to recognize CIO unions and to meet their demands. CIO membership expanded rapidly, exceeding 2.5 million by 1940 and continuing to grow during the post–World War II years. John L. Lewis served as president until 1940, when his former assistant Philip Murray assumed control. In 1955, the AFL and CIO merged, forming America's largest and most powerful labor organization.

See Also: AFL-CIO; Labor Movement; Lewis, John L..
BIBLIOGRAPHY: Zeiger, Robert H., *The CIO, 1935-1955* (Univ. of North Carolina Press 1995).

■ **CONGRESS OF RACIAL EQUALITY (CORE),** civil rights organization. Founded by members of the Fellowship of Reconciliation in 1942, CORE was committed to interracial organization and nonviolent direct action in the struggle for civil rights. George Houser and James Farmer were early leaders. CORE pioneered the use of sit-ins and its "Journey of Reconciliation" (1947) attempted the desegregation of bus lines. After surviving organizational difficulties and the national anticommunist temper of the 1950s, CORE turned toward the Deep South with new energy. It provided training for the sit-in protesters of 1960 and helped pioneer the "jail–no bail" tactic that clogged jails and brought publicity to the cause. In 1961, with volunteers from the Student Nonviolent Coordinating Committee (SNCC), CORE organized the Freedom Rides. Over the next few years CORE worked alongside other groups in voter registration projects and other activities.

Facing internal tension over white activism and the commitment to nonviolence, CORE officially endorsed "black power" in 1966 and eventually adopted a more radical position of black separatism. After 1968 CORE's dramatic shifts in policy resulted in equally dramatic shifts in membership, so that today CORE resembles its former incarnation largely in name only.

See Also: Civil Rights Movement; Desegregation; Farmer, James; Freedom Riders.

BIBLIOGRAPHY: Meier, August, and Elliott Rudwick, *CORE: A Study in the Civil Rights Movement* (Univ. of Illinois Press 1975).

■ **CONKLING, ROSCOE (1829-88),** politician and lawyer. Born in Albany, New York, he served three terms as a Republican congressman from New York (1859-63, 1865-67) until he was elected to the U.S. Senate (1867-81), where he led the "Stalwart" faction. He led the New York state Republican party through the use of political patronage. In 1876 he failed to secure the Republican nomination for president and then opposed the successful nominee, Pres. Rutherford B. Hayes, particularly with regard to civil service reform.

See Also: Hayes, Rutherford Birchard; Stalwarts and Half-Breeds.

■ **CONNECTICUT,** the southernmost of the New England states. Except for Delaware and neighboring Rhode Island, it is the smallest state. It is bounded by Massachusetts to the north and east, Rhode Island to the east, the Long Island Sound to the south, and New York to the west. The Connecticut River, New England's longest, runs southward through the center of the state, emptying into Long Island Sound.

Settled by English Puritans in the 1620s, Connecticut became one of the original 13 colonies and states. Abundant waterpower enabled industry to flourish. Still highly industrialized but with an economy also relying heavily on the finance, insurance, and real estate sectors, Connecticut had higher per-capita income than any other state in the early 1990s, partly because of the wealthy suburbs adjoining New York City where many large corporations have relocated their headquarters.

Capital: Hartford. Area: 5,026 square miles. Population (1995 est.): 3,275,000.

See Also: Connecticut River; Puritan.

■ **CONNECTICUT COMPROMISE (1787),** compromise at the Constitutional Convention that broke the impasse on the issue of legislative representation. Six of the largest states wanted representation in the legislature proportional to population (the Virginia Plan), a proposal opposed by five other states, which favored a one-house legislature with equal representation (the New Jersey Plan). The issue was resolved by creating an upper house (the Senate) based on equal representation and a lower house (the House of Representatives) based on population.

See Also: Constitutional Convention; Constitution of the United States; New Jersey Plan; Virginia Plan.

■ **CONNECTICUT RIVER,** longest river in the New England states. Beginning in northeastern Vermont, the Great River (as it was called in colonial days) flows south some 407 miles to form the Vermont–New Hampshire boundary before entering Massachusetts and Connecticut and emptying into Long Island Sound. During the 17th century the Englishman William Pynchon obtained an exclusive right to trade with the Pequot Indians living along the river. White settlers moving into the area decimated the Pequots during the Pequot War of 1637. The river was an extremely important transportation route during colonial times, carrying tobacco, timber, and manufactured goods. In the 1800s the river's numerous rapids and falls were used to create power, thus spurring the growth of manufacturing cities like Holyoke and Springfield. The Connecticut is the site of numerous modern hydroelectric plants.

See Also: Pequot War; Pynchon, William.

■ **CONQUISTADORS,** properly *conquistadores*, the common name for Spanish conquerors and explorers of North, Central, and South America in the 16th century. Spanish subjugation of the New World had been preceded by *reconquista*, the armed liberation of Spain and Portugal from the Moors (718-1492). Almost eight centuries of frontier life and recurrent warfare with the "infidels" at home had shaped the minds of generations of Spanish *hidalgos* (mostly small nobility), accustoming them to earn their bread with swords, as well as to being constantly on a crusade, enforcing Christendom upon the heathens. In America, the conquistadors ruthlessly destroyed native cultures, such as those of the Aztecs, the Mayas, and the Incas, often not stopping at vandalism and atrocity. Their actions, however, came not only from brutality, which was routine all over 16th-century Europe, but also from religious fervor. Mostly devout Catholics, the conquistadors regarded indigenous cultures as the epitome of Satan that had to be crushed. What enticed the conquistadors to America was gold. Few of them, however, ended their lives in opulence. More often they died in oblivion, like Hernán Cortés (1485-1547), or, more frequently, they perished in the lands they discovered, like Hernando de Córdoba (1475-1526), Pedro de Valdivia (c. 1500-53), Francisco Pizarro (c. 1470-1541), or Hernando de Soto (c. 1500-42). Having vanquished immense territories for the Spanish Crown and the Roman Catholic Church, the conquistadors got little for it.

See Also: Aztecs; Spanish Colonies.

BIBLIOGRAPHY: Descola, Jean, *The Conquistadors* (Allen & Unwin 1957); Madariaga, Salvador de, *Hernán Cortés* (Univ. of Miami Press 1942); Prescott, William H., *History of the Conquest of Mexico and History of the Conquest of Peru* (Random House 1936).

■ **CONSCRIPTION ACT (1863),** act passed by Congress in March 1863 to meet a growing manpower shortage in the Union armies. It stipulated that every congressional district provide a quota of draftees, to be chosen by lot. The first draft occurred in July 1863.

See Also: Civil War.

■ **CONSERVATION AND ENVIRONMENTAL MOVEMENTS,** two conceptions of nature protection in the United States. Both evolved from the general anxiety that industrial capitalism, while turning trees, minerals, and soils into affluence for the present generation, was leaving desolation for those to come.

Origins of the Conservation Movement. That nature needed protection of any kind was not obvious to most Americans before the middle of the 20th century. Since the founding of the first colonies on the Atlantic coast, European settlers and their descendants considered the continent a fearsome wilderness and an abounding prize. Neither conception beheld the environment as vulnerable or finite.

But by the 1890s the foundations of what would become conservation had already been established. George Perkins Marsh of Vermont authored the first work of conservationist literature in 1864, while serving as an ambassador to Italy. In *Man and Nature* he detailed forests cut, soils washed, and rivers silted. He concluded that because people have changed Earth they have an enduring responsibility to take care of it. Marsh's insights led Lewis Mumford to call *Man and Nature* "the fountainhead of the conservation movement."

Yet Marsh had little to say about animals and their habitats—the inspiration behind the first generation of American conservationists. Wealthy hunters like Theodore Roosevelt, Gifford Pinchot, and George Bird Grinnell in the 1890s decried the taking of buffalo and other big-game species for profit. Through the Boone and Crockett Club and Grinnell's *Forest and Stream* magazine, elite hunters and weekend anglers asserted the first programs for wildlife preservation in the United States.

Around this time Congress created the first national parks: Yellowstone (1872), Yosemite (1890), and Grand Canyon (1919). In 1871 the photographer William Henry Jackson and the painter Thomas Moran accompanied a mapping expedition and created images of Yellowstone's strange formations, hot-water geysers, and giant granite gorges that captivated eastern audiences. Yellowstone would enshrine the monumental landscape of the United States; it would bear the nation's natural heritage. But no protection had been granted that could not be taken away. The parks had not been given absolute refuge from logging, agriculture, grazing, and mining.

The equivocal status of the parks fit the conservation doctrine as that idea evolved during the last decades of the 19th century. Conservation proposed to hold from exploitation "natural resources" considered vital to the future wealth and security of the United States. The idea was not to halt that exploitation but to regulate it, to manage the wealth of nature for future use.

Conservation entered its first decade of governmental activism when Theodore Roosevelt became president in 1901. Roosevelt depended on his friend and adviser Gifford Pinchot to make conservation policy. Pinchot founded the Yale School of Forestry to educate conservation professionals who would then work for government and manage the public lands. In 1905 Congress created the U.S. Forest Service within the Department of Agriculture, with Pinchot as the first U.S. chief forester. Roosevelt and Pinchot increased federal protection of the public lands to 172 million acres in 21 states, and they hosted a White House Governors Conference in 1907 to consider utilitarian conservation.

The Preservationists. But the Governors Conference excluded other supporters of conservation who valued nature for its spiritual power and aesthetic value. This view, stressing preservation over use, took inspiration from the work of writers and artists who located ultimate meaning in nature. Associated with transcendentalism in the United States and with European romanticism more broadly, it included the poetry of William Wordsworth (*The Prelude*), the essays of Ralph Waldo Emerson (*Nature*) and Henry David Thoreau (*Walden*), and the paintings of J. M. W. Turner and Thomas Cole.

Romantic preservation found a public voice in the person of a Scottish immigrant with a love for lonely places. In 1868 John Muir saw the Yosemite Valley for the first time and discovered there a purpose and a career. He spent the next 25 years in the Sierra Nevada and founded the Sierra Club in 1892 to take city people to the mountains, where he expected them to feel his ecstatic wonderment, his exultation for Earth.

Preservationists and Conservationists Clash. Not all of them did. In 1901 an issue arose that caused the nation's first environmental conflict and absorbed Muir's energy till his death in 1914. It concerned drinking water for San Francisco and a sheer granite river valley within

Yosemite National Park called the Hetch Hetchy. Muir compared the site in its beauty to Yosemite Valley itself. He had insisted that the Hetch Hetchy be included in the 1890 act that created the park. Now San Francisco proposed a dam across the Tuolumne River at the southern end of the Hetch Hetchy to create a reservoir and appealed to the federal government for permission. The Sierra Club protested, and a political battle began that only ended in 1913 when Congress finally sided with the utilitarian conservationists and dedicated the valley to the city for its continued growth.

The Hetch Hetchy conflict had enormous consequences for the future of environmental politics. Congress had abandoned portions of a previously protected area in the name of the greatest good for the greatest number, while the Sierra Club failed to sway public opinion to its view that the valley should be made a monument for all time. The fight showed that two views had emerged over the previous 30 years: one that recognized transcendent values in wild places and another that considered protection a means of storage across difficult times for eventual use. The image of a flooded Hetch Hetchy, its trees stripped by loggers before the inundation, haunted preservationists for the next half century.

In the meantime, Franklin Roosevelt's New Deal made conservation a cornerstone of its program to bring the United States out of the Great Depression in the 1930s. Young men fought fires and soil erosion as members of the Civilian Conservation Corps, and the Works Project Administration built a series of dams in the Tennessee Valley and all over the West. The National Park Service, founded in 1916, made the parks easy and pleasant to visit and dedicated itself to the education, pleasure, and convenience of visitors. The parks became off limits to hunting and grazing and accessible by railroad and automobile. They featured restaurants and hotels and rangers as tour guides.

Then in the 1940s a group of elite wilderness advocates began to call for "primitive areas," or protected regions without roads or facilities. The most important of their organizations was the Wilderness Society (1935). Aldo Leopold, one of its leaders, emerged in the 1940s as a philosopher of wilderness. His "land ethic" and posthumous *Sand County Almanac* defined humans as part of a larger biological community in which they enjoyed no favored position. Leopold's essays lent strength to wilderness advocates searching for ideas to move the nation beyond the national parks and the Pinchot tradition.

Preservation and conservation clashed again in the 1950s over a question that finally caused the formation of a new nature politics. When the federal Bureau of Reclamation announced a project to build a series of dams on the Colorado River in the Grand Canyon, including one in Echo Park that would flood Dinosaur National Monument, the Sierra Club vowed to stop it. The club published books and advertised in newspapers to gather public support for its position that Dinosaur must be saved from the waters. It argued the project would not accomplish the Reclamation Service's stated goals and offered Glen Canyon (also part of the Grand Canyon) as an alternative site and nuclear power as an alternative source of energy to hydroelectric. Congress agreed to remove Dinosaur from the bill in 1955.

Environmentalism. The victory added nothing to the protected lands of the United States; it only maintained the protected status of an existing unit of the national park system. It also upheld the idea of protection. The battle drove a final wedge between conservationists and preservationists and began to shape a new movement, environmentalism, that opposed economic development, questioned consumption and the American way of life, and fought government and business for wilderness protection and species preservation.

Rachel Carson's *Silent Spring* (1962) depended on many of the same ideas. The book told Americans that trusted chemicals used to control insects, like DDT, acted as biocides in the environment, killing birds and fish and infiltrating the human body in ways that no one had anticipated. An aroused public caused the banning of DDT in 1972, the first mass demonstration against a product in the name of the environment.

Environmentalism made conspicuous gains during the 1960s and 1970s. National leaders including Lady Bird Johnson and Stewart Udall supported a national beautification campaign aimed at cleaning up roadsides and neighborhoods. Congress passed a series of unprecedented laws, including the Clean Air Act (1970), the Federal Water Pollution Control Act (1972), the Endangered Species Act (1970), and the National Environmental Policy Act (NEPA; 1970), that Pres. Richard M. Nixon signed into law. The NEPA created the Environmental Protection Agency from a collection of scattered government bureaus. The first Earth Day in 1970 brought thousands of young people to environmentalism. No longer an elite concern, environmentalism had become a popular cause and a political issue.

Yet with the election of Ronald Reagan in 1980, environmentalism faced its first hostile president. Under Reagan's secretary of the interior, James Watt, the government sought to turn over portions of the public lands to private interests. The "Sage-Brush Rebellion," centered in the western states, became a key event in the founding of a countermovement to environmentalism. Advocates of "wise-use" enjoyed the support of conservative Joseph Coors and his Mountain States Legal Foundation (which once employed Watt).

In reaction to Reagan's policies, Dave Foreman founded Earth First! to fight conservative forces as well as Pinchot-style conservation itself. Informed by a series of ideas called Deep Ecology, Earth First! accepted no compromise that resulted in the cutting of trees.

Environmental issues continued to be of national concern. During George Bush's presidency a controversy over logging old-growth trees in the Pacific Northwest erupted. Loss of the trees, some of them thousands of years old, threatened an entire ecosystem and the northern spotted owl with extinction. When environmental organizations used the Endangered Species Act to protect the owl and stop the logging, lumber companies sued for the right to continue. In 1993 Al Gore became the first vice president with environmentalist credentials.

Nature has become part of what we argue about as a nation. Although most Americans now consider themselves environmentalists, their willingness to spend tax dollars to protect ecosystems and species remains in question. A great regulatory structure has been put into place, but it remains only as strong as public support for it.

—STEVEN STOLL

See Also: Muir, John; National Parks; New Deal; Pinchot, Gifford.

BIBLIOGRAPHY: Carson, Rachel, *Silent Spring* (Houghton Mifflin 1962); Fox, Stephen, *The American Conservation Movement: John Muir and His Legacy* (Univ. of Wisconsin Press 1986); Hays, Samuel, *Conservation and the Gospel of Efficiency* (Harvard Univ. Press 1959); Runte, Alfred, *National Parks: The American Experience* (Univ. of Nebraska Press 1979).

■ **CONSERVATISM,** a political philosophy that resists change and exalts the established institutions of society. A distinctly American form of conservatism developed during the era of the American Revolution. Fearful of the economic and political egalitarianism unleashed by the break from Britain, wealthy and landed white men responded by attempting to retain their status and power. In this sense the Federalists were more "conservative" than the Antifederalists, who were proponents of a more local form of democracy.

During the 19th century the term *conservative* acquired different meanings. The ideology of Social Darwinism, the institution of the courts, and the Americanization movement became some of the purveyors of a kind of social conservatism. By the early 20th century, conservatism became associated with Protestantism, nativism, and self-regulation. The Great Depression and the New Deal of the 1930s marked the low point of American conservatism, as government grew and federal social programs attempted to respond to the plight of the poor. The post–World War II years saw conservatives unleash their frustration, first in the paranoia of McCarthyism and then with the artificial and imposed tranquillity of the Eisenhower years (1953-61). Modern political conservatism emerged in the 1960s and achieved its high-water mark during the Reagan-Bush years (1981-93).

Never a fixed category, conservatism has had varying and often disunited social and economic agendas. Both major parties have historically had many conservatives, but since the 1920s the Republican party has been the bastion of American political conservatism.

See Also: Americanization; Political Parties.

BIBLIOGRAPHY: Himmelstein, Jerome L., *To the Right: The Transformation of American Conservatism* (Univ. of California Press 1990); Nisbet, Robert, *Conservatism: Dream and Reality* (Univ. of Minnesota Press 1986).

■ **CONSTITUTIONAL AMENDMENTS,** changes to the Constitution since it was ratified in 1788. The Constitution currently has 27 amendments. They have been added over the years to adapt the Constitution to changing times and to address new issues that were not considered by the framers. The Constitution can be amended in two ways, as set forth in Article V. The Congress of the United States can propose an amendment by a two-thirds vote of both houses. The amendment must then be ratified by three-fourths of the states in state legislatures or by ratifying conventions. Two-thirds of the state legislatures may also call for a convention to propose an amendment and any amendment created by this method must also be ratified by three-fourths of the state legislatures or by ratifying conventions. There has never been a convention called by the states to propose amendments.

Bill of Rights. The first 10 amendments were ratified by Dec. 15, 1791, and are known collectively as the Bill of Rights. When the Constitution was sent to the states for ratification, Virginia, New York, and Massachusetts were concerned about the lack of explicit individual rights. Those states discussed rejecting the Constitution until a list of rights was included. Advocates of the Constitution persuaded the states that such rights had never been given up and did not need to be included in the new document. The new government had only the powers specifically set forth in the Constitution, and the people and the states retained all other rights. To gain approval by Virginia, however, James Madison agreed to propose a Bill of Rights in the first Congress.

The first Congress approved 12 amendments to send to the states for ratification, and 10 of them were approved. The Bill of Rights does not provide rights to individuals but instead puts limits on the federal government's ability to restrict individual rights. The First Amendment prevents the Congress from passing laws establishing a religion, prohibiting the free exercise of religion, abridging the freedom of the press or of speech, or abridging the right of the people to assemble peaceably and to petition the government for a redress of grievances. The Second Amendment recognizes the need for state militias and prevents the federal government from infringing on the right of the people to bear arms. The Third Amendment prevents the quartering, or housing, of soldiers in civilian homes.

The Fourth through Eighth Amendments are mainly concerned with the rights of those accused of crimes. However, the Fourth Amendment protects the "right of the people to be secure in their persons, houses, papers and effects" from unreasonable searches and seizures and has been read by later courts as recognizing a right of privacy. For those accused of crimes, the amendments require warrants with probable cause for searches and seizures, indictment by a grand jury, a prohibition against double jeopardy, a speedy and public trial, the right not to testify against oneself, to be confronted with adverse witnesses, to be informed about the charges, and to have the assistance of counsel. The Seventh Amendment gives one the right to have a jury in a federal civil trial. The Eighth Amendment prohibits excessive bail and cruel and unusual punishment.

The Ninth Amendment was added to address the fears of those who believed the enumeration of specific rights would imply that these were the only rights that people had. The Ninth Amendment specifically states that the enumeration of certain rights shall not be construed to deny other rights retained by the people.

The 10th Amendment reiterates the fact that the Constitution creates a government of enumerated powers. It provides that any powers not delegated to the federal government or not prohibited to the states remain with the states or with the people. When the Constitution was adopted many people were concerned about giving the federal government too much power. The 10th Amendment carefully sets forth the idea that the government is limited and exists at the sufferance of the people, with only those powers specifically delegated to it.

The 11th Amendment limits the judicial power of the United States set forth in Article III. It takes out of federal jurisdiction cases against a state by citizens of another state or foreign government.

Voting Rights. The 13th, 14th, and 15th Amendments, the so-called Civil War Amendments, extend democratic principles to those previously excluded. The 13th Amendment (1865) abolishes slavery. The 15th Amendment (1870), which provides that the right to vote cannot be denied on account of race, color, or previous condition of servitude, was designed to give the right to vote to African-American men. Voting rights were extended to women with the 19th Amendment (1920) and to 18-year-olds with the 26th Amendment (1971). The right to elect presidential electors is given to citizens of the District of Columbia in the 23rd Amendment (1961). The 24th Amendment (1964) prohibits denying the right to vote to anyone for failure to pay a poll tax or other state tax.

The 14th Amendment. The 14th Amendment (1868) has become one of the most important amendments to the Constitution. It provides that "all persons born or naturalized in the United States, and subject to the jurisdiction thereof" are citizens of the United States and of the states in which they reside. This was to recognize former slaves as citizens. The amendment prohibits any state from depriving "any person of life, liberty, or property, without due process of law," or denying to any person "the equal protection of the laws." The due process and the equal protection clauses have been used by the Supreme Court to advance most of the individual rights found in the Bill of Rights against opposition at the state level. Over many rulings, the Court has involved the 14th Amendment to prohibit states from denying people the same rights that the federal government cannot deny under the Bill of Rights.

Miscellaneous Amendments. The 16th Amendment (1913) allows Congress to pass an income tax. The 17th Amendment (1913) changes the way that U.S. senators are elected, from election by the state legislatures to direct election by the people.

The 18th and 21st Amendments are related. The 18th Amendment (1919) prohibited the sale, manufacture, or importation of intoxicating liquors in the United States. It is the only amendment that was later repealed, in 1933, by the 21st Amendment. The 21st Amendment was the only one ratified by state ratifying conventions.

Presidential Amendments. The 12th, 20th, 22nd, and 25th Amendments all concern the presidency. The 12th Amendment (1804) addresses a specific problem that arose during the 1800 presidential election. Thomas Jefferson and Aaron Burr received the same number of electoral votes. The Constitution stated that the person with the greatest number of electoral votes was president, and the person with the second greatest number of electoral votes was vice president. The 12th Amendment required that the electors cast votes specifically for president and vice president.

The 20th Amendment (1933) changed the date of the presidential and vice-presidential inauguration from March 4 to January 20. The original date was adopted when transportation and communication systems required months to notify people of election results. The 20th Amendment recognized the almost instantaneous election results and reduced the time of a lame-duck president. The 22nd Amendment (1951) stated that no one could be elected president more than two times. This amendment was adopted after Franklin D. Roosevelt had been elected four times, thus changing the tradition set by George Washington of only serving two terms. The 25th Amendment (1967) addressed the issues of presidential incapacitation and vacancies in the vice presidency. Until 1967, a vacancy in the office of vice president, whether resulting from the death of the incumbent or his succession to the presidency, remained until the next presidential election. Following the assassination of Pres. John F. Kennedy in 1963 and the succession of Lyndon B. Johnson, the vice-presidential office was vacant until 1965. The 25th Amendment allowed the president to appoint a new vice president subject to confirmation by both houses of Congress. It also provided procedures for temporary transfer of power should the president become incapacitated.

The 27th Amendment was adopted in 1992 but had been approved by the Congress and sent to the states in 1789 as one of the first twelve amendments. Because it did not have a time limit on it, the amendment was finally passed by three-fourths of the states in 1992. It requires that the compensation for senators and representatives cannot be increased until another election has passed. Since the 18th Amendment in 1919, most amendments have had time periods by which three-fourths of the states must pass them, or they expire.

Twenty-seven amendments in more than 200 years are relatively few changes to a major document that established the U.S. government. The amendment process allows changes to be made but only after much discourse by the Congress and the states.

—JILL E. MARTIN

See Also: Bill of Rights; Constitution of the United States.

BIBLIOGRAPHY: Currie, David P., *The Constitution of the United States* (Univ. of Chicago Press 1988); Lieberman, Jethro K., *The Enduring Constitution: A Bicentennial Perspective* (West 1987).

■ **CONSTITUTIONAL CONVENTION (1787),** convention that wrote the Constitution of the United States. Called by the Annapolis Convention in September 1786 and the Articles of Confederation Congress in February, the convention met in Philadelphia from May 25 to Sept. 17, 1787. Fifty-five delegates from 12 states attended at one time or another. Only Rhode Island refused to send a delegation. Some of the most prominent men in America attended, among them George Washington, Benjamin Franklin, and James Madison; others of eminence did not. John Adams and Thomas Jefferson were serving as diplomats in Europe, while Patrick Henry and Richard Henry Lee refused appointments. Only two sitting governors attended.

The convention immediately elected Washington as its president, although many of its debates until June 19 took place in Committee of the Whole with Nathaniel Gorham of Massachusetts presiding. Although William Jackson of Pennsylvania served as the convention's secretary, the most detailed notes that remain were those studiously taken by James Madison. The convention adopted rules providing that its sessions be kept secret, that each state delegation had to have a minimum of two delegates to be properly represented, that each state had one vote, and that any issue once decided could be brought up for reconsideration.

In calling the convention, Congress resolved that the delegates should revise and amend the Articles of Confederation. Some delegates, however, especially those from the large states of Virginia, Massachusetts, and Pennsylvania, wanted to abandon the articles and to replace the equal representation of the states in the Confederation Congress with a system of proportional representation.

The Virginia Plan, reflecting these views and based on a draft by James Madison, was submitted to the convention on May 29 and set the agenda for the convention. Other delegates, who wanted merely to revise the articles and augment Congress's power, submitted the New Jersey Plan, which was defeated in mid-June. During July the convention came to accept the Connecticut Compromise, which balanced the Virginia and New Jersey plans by creating a lower chamber with proportional representation and an upper chamber in which each state would have an equal voice.

In late July the Convention recessed for 10 days while a five-member Committee of Detail incorporated all of the provisions already approved into a draft constitution. The convention reassembled on August 6. On September 8 it appointed a five-member Committee of Style that wrote the final version of the Constitution. Gouverneur Morris of New York is credited with crafting much of the final language of the Constitution. Between September 12 and 15 the convention debated and rejected motions to appoint a committee to consider a bill of rights and to call a second convention to consider amendments.

The Constitution proposed by the convention completely changed the structure of the federal government and its relationship with the states and the people. Many powers were transferred from the states to the central government. The convention ignored the amendment procedure in the Articles of Confederation, providing instead that its ratification by nine state conventions would be sufficient to establish the Constitution among the ratifying states.

A four-page version of the Constitution was then prepared on parchment. Thirty-nine delegates signed the Constitution on September 17. Only three delegates in attendance on the last day refused to sign: Edmund Randolph and George Mason of Virginia and Elbridge Gerry of Massachusetts. The convention then sent the signed copy to Congress, and printed copies were given to the delegates to take home to their states.

—JOHN P. KAMINSKI

See Also: Annapolis Convention; Articles of Confederation; Connecticut Compromise; Constitution of the United States; Madison, James; New Jersey Plan; Virginia Plan.

BIBLIOGRAPHY: Collier, Christopher, and James Lincoln Collier, *Decision in Philadelphia: The Constitutional Convention of 1787* (Random House 1986); Farrand, Max, ed., *The Records of the Federal Convention of 1787*, 3 vols. (Yale Univ. Press 1911; reprint 1966); Rossiter, Clinton, *1787: The Grand Convention* (Macmillan 1966).

■ **CONSTITUTION OF THE UNITED STATES,** document creating the U.S. form of government and defining the rights and liberties of the American people. The Constitution was drafted in 1787 to replace the Articles of Confederation, the first governing document of the United States. The articles established a unicameral legislature in which each state had one vote, and all actions needed approval of 9 of the 13 states to pass. Additionally, the legislature did not have the power to raise money; it could only ask the states for voluntary payments.

Recognizing that the articles did not provide a workable government, the states sent delegates to Philadelphia to review them and recommend changes. Meeting in closed sessions, the delegates instead drafted a new document: the Constitution. It took more than four months to draft and included many compromises.

The Constitution was sent to the states, and a public relations campaign began to press for adoption of the new form of government. The *Federalist Papers*, a series of 85 newspaper essays written in 1787-88 by Alexander Hamilton, James Madison, and John Jay under the pseudonym of Publius, set forth the philosophical and practical reasons for adopting the Constitution. Nine states were necessary for the Constitution to be adopted, and ratification occurred in June 1788. Some of the states approved the Constitution only after being assured that a bill of rights would be added. The final Bill of Rights, the first 10 amendments to the Constitution, was adopted during the first Congress and approved by the required three-fourths of the states in 1791.

The preamble of the Constitution sets forth the reasons why the people are establishing a constitution. It is significant that the Constitution begins, "We the people of the United States . . ." The Constitution does not come from the state but from the people, the individual citizens of the

United States. The purposes set forth in the preamble are both practical and noble. The Constitution was created "in order to form a more perfect Union, establish justice, insure domestic tranquillity, provide for the common defense, promote the general welfare, and secure the blessings of liberty to ourselves and our posterity." The preamble has been viewed by some as mere rhetorical flourishes but by others as the true foundation of the new democracy.

The Constitution has seven articles. The first three articles create the legislative, executive, and judicial branches of government.

The Legislative Branch. Article I creates the legislative branch of the national government and establishes a bicameral legislature consisting of a Senate and a House of Representatives. This arrangement was the result of a compromise made between the smaller, less-populated states such as Rhode Island and Delaware and the larger, more-populated states, such as Virginia. The smaller states were afraid that if the legislature were apportioned on the basis of population, they would effectively be excluded from policy making. The larger states, on the other hand, were concerned about the ability of a smaller state to prevent the legislature from acting, as was the case under the Articles of Confederation's requirement for a super-majority vote.

The compromise, proposed by Roger Sherman of Connecticut, established a two-house Congress. The Senate, the upper house, had equal representation from all the states. The House of Representatives was elected on the basis of population, with each state having at least one representative. The House and Senate were also elected differently. Senators were elected by the state legislatures of each state. This was later changed by the 17th Amendment (1913), which allowed election by popular vote. Representatives in the House were elected directly by the people. The House was also given the power to propose all revenue measures.

The Constitution required the two houses to work together in order to pass laws. All laws had to pass both houses by a simple majority vote before being sent to the executive for approval.

Article I also sets forth the enumerated powers of Congress, including the power to pass laws necessary to carry out its enumerated powers—otherwise known as the necessary and proper clause. The necessary and proper clause allows Congress to determine how it will execute its powers, and any means that are reasonable will generally be found constitutional.

Congress has only those powers specifically delegated to it in the Constitution and those powers necessary to carry out the delegated powers. Article I also prohibits Congress from acting in certain ways, such as passing bills of attainder or granting titles of nobility. A bill of attainder is a special act of the legislature to inflict punishment upon a specific individual. Congress cannot pass ex post facto laws, which would make something done in the past illegal, nor can it pass laws that increase the punishment for something done in the past. Congress may not suspend the writ of habeas corpus, which allows someone in the custody of the state to go before a judge to determine if his or her incarceration is legal. All these limitations on Congress were designed to protect individuals from abuse of power by the government.

Article I attempted to resolve another controversy that had almost prevented the creation of a new Constitution. The states that depended on slave economy, mostly those states in the South, wanted slavery to be legalized in the Constitution. Other states believed slavery was a contradiction to democracy.

The compromise appeared in two forms. Congress would not prohibit the importation of slaves until 1808 but would instead impose an import tax not to exceed $10 per slave. Additionally, slaves would be counted as three-fifths of a person, rather than as full persons, for apportionment purposes. Slavery was later abolished by the 13th Amendment (1865).

The Executive Branch. The executive branch of government was also the subject of controversy during the constitutional convention. The framers were concerned about giving one person too much power and were aware of the excesses of monarchy in Europe. So they created the office of president and limited the term to four years. The president was not originally to be chosen by direct election but selected instead by the electoral college. Each state appointed electors equal to its number of senators and representatives and these electors met and voted for the president. If no person receives a majority of all the electoral votes, the House of Representatives chooses the president from among the top three contenders. When the House selects the president, each state has one vote.

The framers believed that other than someone like George Washington, no one person would be able to get a majority of votes because so few had the national stature of the great leader. They expected that the House of Representatives would elect the president in most cases. In fact, this only happened in three cases: in 1800 with Thomas Jefferson, in 1824 with John Quincy Adams, and in 1876 when Rutherford B. Hayes was selected by a commission appointed by the House. Today, with television and national exposure, it seems unlikely that the election would go to the House, unless a strong third party comes into existence. And although the electoral college still exists, the electors are chosen by the voters, thereby in effect subjecting the presidency to direct election.

The president is given the power to sign or veto bills sent to him by Congress. If he vetoes a bill, it is sent back to Congress and must be approved by each house by a two-thirds vote in order to override the veto. This provision is an example of the checks and balances that the framers built into the Constitution. Both houses of Congress and the president are necessary to make new laws. Neither the executive nor legislative branch can change laws on its own. Although a somewhat cumbersome process, it avoids the threat of absolute power and tyranny.

The president is the commander in chief of the armed forces and has the power to make treaties with the advice and consent of the Senate. He can appoint ambassadors, justices of the Supreme Court, and other officers of the United States, subject to the advice and consent of the Senate. The confirmation process allows the Senate to check the power of the president.

The Judicial Branch. Article III sets forth the judicial power of the United States, extending it to all cases and controversies arising under the Constitution and laws and treaties of the United States. The federal courts also have the power to hear admiralty and maritime cases and cases between citizens of different states.

The Supreme Court is established by the Constitution, but Congress has the power to create lower federal courts. Decisions regarding the number of justices, and the details of the lower courts, are left to Congress. The Supreme Court is given original jurisdiction in cases affecting ambassadors, public ministers, and in those in which a state is a party. In all other cases where the federal courts have jurisdiction, the Supreme Court has appellate jurisdiction. Most cases come to the Supreme Court on appellate jurisdiction.

Articles IV, V, VI, and VII. Article IV concerns relations between the states. It contains provisions for admitting new states to the Union on an equal basis with the original states. Article V provides the means to amend the Constitution, which has been done 27 times.

The supremacy of the United States is set forth in Article VI. The Constitution and the laws of the United States and all treaties are the supreme law of the land. Judges in every state are bound by the federal Constitution, even if the state laws disagree. The Constitution is the one law that applies throughout all the states, binding the states together as one nation.

Article VII provides for the approval of the Constitution as a new form of government by state ratifying conventions.

Principles of Democracy. The Constitution is the oldest living written constitution in the world. It embodies a number of principles for governance, among them the separation of powers and checks and balances. The framers were concerned about the abuse of power and about the concentration of power in any one person or unit of government. They therefore required both houses of Congress to pass a bill and the executive branch to sign it before it becomes a law. The landmark case of *Marbury* v. *Madison* (1803) established the principle of the Supreme Court ruling on the constitutionality of all laws.

Another principle embodied in the Constitution is that of federalism. The Constitution created a strong federal government that was not formed by the states but by the people of the United States. The states were concerned that a national government would absorb or subsume the state governments. But the state and federal governments coexist and govern in different spheres. The federal government has only those powers delegated to it, although in the 20th century this distinction blurred significantly as the national government assumed greater powers.

The Constitution has been amended 27 times since its adoption. The first 10 amendments, known as the Bill of Rights, were ratified in 1791, following the adoption of the Constitution. The Bill of Rights sets forth rights of individuals that the government cannot limit or interfere with. Once again, they are limitations on the power of the federal government.

Interpretations. Since the founding of the nation there have been disagreements as to how the Constitution should be interpreted. Some scholars argue for the concept of original intent. Under this interpretation, the Court looks only to what was originally intended by the wording of the Constitution and applies that intent to the case before it. This is a literal reading, or strict construction, of the Constitution. If the rights or powers are not specifically set forth in the words of the document, then they do not exist.

Other scholars argue that the Constitution is a living document and has to be adapted to changing circumstances. These scholars argue for a liberal interpretation, or loose construction, looking at the Constitution in terms of such broad principles as democracy, individual freedom, and limited government and applying those principles in a contemporary context.

These various interpretations have been prevalent at different times in the nation's history and with different justices and scholars. The Constitution itself does not tell us how it should be interpreted. This in fact is one of its strengths. It is a document that has proved adaptable to new issues, new challenges, and new problems, and one that has contributed to the stability of the government it established over 200 years ago.

—JILL E. MARTIN

See Also: Bill of Rights; Checks and Balances; Constitutional Amendments; Constitutional Convention; President of the United States; Separation of Powers; Supreme Court.

BIBLIOGRAPHY: Cox, Archibald, *The Court and the Constitution* (Houghton Mifflin 1987); Currie, David P., *The Constitution of the United States* (Univ. of Chicago Press 1988); Lieberman, Jethro K., *The Enduring Constitution: A Bicentennial Perspective* (West 1987).

■ **CONTAINMENT,** U.S. policy toward the Soviet Union adopted in 1947. The author of the principle was George F. Kennan, a distinguished diplomat and specialist in Russian affairs, who in 1947 was placed in charge of long-term policy planning by Sec. of State George C. Marshall. In July 1947, under the pseudonym 'X,' Kennan explained his rationale in *Foreign Affairs*. His idea was to contain the alleged Russian expansion after the end of World War II to the territories already under Soviet control. He asserted that it was possible to deter the U.S.S.R. from future expansion by resolute countermeasures aimed at preserving the status quo. Containment had to be "patient but firm and vigilant." The result, Kennan thought, would be not only a halt on Russian "expansion" but also changes within the Soviet Union, which might rearrange its internal policy along more liberal lines. The Marshall Plan of 1947, together with the creation of the North Atlantic Treaty Organization in 1949 and U.S. intervention in Korea in 1950, represented the economic and military dimensions of containment. Rational as it was, the idea of containment succeeded mainly because of the practical absence of expansion itself, not because of the sophistication of measures against Soviet expansion. Besides, despite much praise given to it, containment was hardly a precipitant of democratic changes in the U.S.S.R., which were prompted by internal rather than external circumstances.

See Also: Cold War; Kennan, George Frost; Marshall Plan; North Atlantic Treaty Organization (NATO).

BIBLIOGRAPHY: Deibel, Terry L., and John L. Gaddis, eds., *Containing the Soviet Union: A Critique of U. S. Policy* (Pergamon 1987); Kennan, George F., *American Diplomacy* (Univ. of Chicago Press 1984).

■ **CONTINENTAL ASSOCIATION (1774),** economic boycott by the American colonies in response to Parliament's Coercive Acts of 1774. Passed by the Continental Congress, the association sought to pressure Parliament and British merchants to support the repeal of the repressive legislation through nonimportation.

See Also: Revolution, American.

■ **CONTINENTAL CONGRESSES (1774-81),** legislative assemblies during the American Revolution. The First Continental Congress (Sept. 5-Oct.

26, 1774) met specifically to protest Britain's Intolerable Acts (1774). The Second Continental Congress (May 10, 1775-Mar. 1, 1781) developed into an ad hoc national government.

The First Continental Congress convened with 12 colonies represented. (Georgia sent no delegates.) Each colony had one vote, a practice that would continue in the Second Continental Congress. Congress urged the colonies to organize militias, formed the Continental Association to boycott British goods, and voted to reconvene the following spring if Britain did not redress American grievances.

By the time the Second Continental Congress (with Georgia in attendance) met, war had begun. Congress rapidly evolved into the government of the United States. It formed a Continental army with George Washington in command and authorized negotiations for an alliance with France. Congress approved American independence on July 2, 1776, and endorsed the Declaration of Independence two days later.

The Second Continental Congress, with many changes in delegates, continued to operate as the U.S. national government until ratification of the Articles of Confederation in 1781. The Confederation Congress (1781-89) retained its procedures.

The Second Continental Congress muddled its way through the Revolution. Its depreciated currency wreaked financial havoc. Congressmen squabbled, profiteered, and berated Washington unmercifully. Nevertheless, the two Continental Congresses deserve credit for creating the United States.

—RICKY EARL NEWPORT

See Also: Articles of Confederation; Confederation Congress; Declaration of Independence; Revolution, American.

BIBLIOGRAPHY: Burnett, Edmund Cody, *The Continental Congress* (Macmillan 1941); Rakove, Jack N., *The Beginnings of National Politics: An Interpretive History of the Continental Congress* (Knopf 1979).

CONTINENTAL DIVIDE, ridge of the Rocky Mountains that divides waters flowing east or west. The divide runs north to south from British Columbia, Canada, through Montana, Wyoming, Colorado, and New Mexico to Chihuahua and Sonora, Mexico. The waters flowing eastward empty into Hudson Bay or the Mississippi River, while those flowing westward run to the Pacific Ocean. Westward travelers on the Oregon Trail in the 19th century traveled over the divide at South Pass in Wyoming.

See Also: South Pass.

CONTRACT LABOR ACT (1885), law prohibiting employers from indenturing a worker for a set period of time (normally seven years) in exchange for paying for that worker's transportation to the United States. Among the act's leading supporters were U.S. labor unions, worried that foreign contract laborers would drive down wages.

See Also: Immigration.

CONVENTIONS, POLITICAL, meetings of the delegates of a political party to select candidates for office, elect governing committees, and decide on party policy. During the first four decades of the American republic, the candidates for president and vice president were selected by caucuses of congressional leaders. The first national nominating convention of a major party was held by the National Republicans in December 1831 at Baltimore, where the delegates nominated Henry Clay for president. The Democrats followed suit the next May, renominating Pres. Andrew Jackson for a second term. The convention system was intended to open up the decision-making process, making it more democratic and less susceptible to manipulation by powerful men. But through most of their history, the real work of conventions went on in "smoke-filled rooms" behind the scenes among party bosses. In 1844, for example, the Democratic convention deadlocked. Party leaders caucused, and on the eighth ballot placed in nomination the name of a little-known former congressman from Tennessee, James K. Polk.

In the majority of cases, conventions nominated candidates on the first or second ballot, but there were some memorable exceptions. It took 46 ballots before the Democrats selected Woodrow Wilson as their nominee in 1912, and a total of 103 ballots (the record) for them to nominate John W. Davis in 1924. Before the modern era of the presidential primary, most state delegations came to the national convention uncommitted to a particular candidate, or pledged to vote for a "favorite son," often the governor or one of the senators who led the state party. Fa-

Every four years, delegates of the Republican and Democratic parties gather in national conventions to nominate presidential and vice-presidential candidates and to approve a party platform. Here, the Democrats assemble in Miami Beach, Florida, in 1972 to nominate George McGovern.

vorite sons made it possible for delegates to be swept up in the enthusiasm for particular candidates at the convention. Perhaps the most famous example was the Democratic convention of 1896, where young William Jennings Bryan so mesmerized the delegates with his famous "Cross of Gold" speech that it won him the nomination.

The increasing popularity of presidential primaries in the second half of the 20th century eventually limited conventions to simply ratifying the candidate selected by the voters of the various states. Conventions remain important as an occasion for the party faithful to come together, gathering their strength for the coming election. Conventions also frequently provide a focus for protests, most famously at the Democratic Convention in Chicago in 1968, when hundreds of antiwar activists were beaten by police. On the floor of the modern political convention, candidates continue to be nominated in long, windy speeches followed by demonstrations. The roll call of states is still held, but it has become a mere noisy ritual. Broadcast by television, modern conventions are political extravaganzas,

stage managed for a national audience.

See Also: *Political Parties; Primaries.*
BIBLIOGRAPHY: *National Party Conventions, 1831-1992* (Congressional Quarterly 1995).

■ **COOK, JAMES (1728-79),** English naval officer, explorer, and surveyor. Born to a poor family, he entered the Royal Navy as an able seaman at the late age of 27 but rose quickly through the ranks and was appointed first lord of the admiralty in 1775. He participated in the naval operations of the Seven Years' War in North America and charted the St. Lawrence River, making possible the British amphibious assault on Quebec. From 1771 to 1779, Cook engaged in three historic voyages around the world in search of a great southern continent. He was the first European to explore and chart the coasts of Australia, New Zealand, and many of the Pacific islands. In the last of these voyages, in search of the Northwest Passage, Cook charted the northwest coast of North America, the Bering Strait, and the Hawaiian Islands, where he was killed in a fight with the inhabitants.

See Also: *Exploration and Discovery.*

■ **COOKE, JAY (1821-1905),** investment banker. Born in Sandusky, Ohio, he left school at 14 to work as a store clerk. In 1839 he moved to Philadelphia where he went to work for a bank, becoming a junior partner three years later. In 1861 he opened his own bank and, with the outbreak of the Civil War, was appointed the primary government agent to sell war bonds. He raised millions of dollars for the Union cause. After the war, Cooke, like much of the nation, turned his attention to railroad expansion. He raised $100 million for the construction of the Northern Pacific Railroad, which was to run from Minnesota to Washington state. Overinflated stock and construction mismanagement put the railroad and Cooke's investment firm into bankruptcy, bringing on the devastating Panic of 1873, a depression that lasted several years. By 1876 Cooke was investing in mining interests in Utah, recovering much of his earlier vast wealth.

See Also: *Panics, Financial.*

BIBLIOGRAPHY: Larson, Henrietta M., *Jay Cooke, Private Banker* (Greenwood Press 1968).

■ **COOLEY, THOMAS (1824-98),** legal scholar, jurist, and first chairman of the U.S. Interstate Commerce Commission (1887-91). A professor at the University of Michigan (1859-98) and justice of the Michigan State Supreme Court (1864-85), Cooley defended laissez-faire economics and limited government that deferred to individual rights and responsibilities. His *Treatise on Constitutional Limitations* (1868) was among the most influential legal commentaries of the time.

■ **COOLIDGE, (JOHN) CALVIN (1872-1933),** 30th president of the United States (1923-29). He was born on July 4, 1872, on the Plymouth, Vermont, farm that had been in his family for five generations. After graduating from Amherst College in 1895, he studied law, opened a law practice in Northampton, Massachusetts, and soon became involved in local Republican politics. He was elected lieutenant governor in 1916 but did not enter the national scene until his term as governor (1919-20), when he squashed the Boston police strike of 1919, stating that "there is no right to strike against the public safety by anybody, anytime, anywhere." In 1920, he was elected U.S. vice president with Republican Pres. Warren G. Harding. On Harding's death in 1923, Coolidge assumed office and was elected in his own right in 1924.

Known as "Silent Cal" for his taciturn nature, Coolidge's puritan ethics seemed a welcome relief following the corruption of the Harding presidency. Asserting that "the business of America is business," he allowed Sec. of the Treasury Andrew Mellon, one of the country's wealthiest men, to direct his pro-business administration, adopting policies that set the stage for the stock market crash of 1929 and the resulting Great Depression. By then, however, Coolidge had retired

Pres. Calvin Coolidge and his wife *(left)* pose in Washington with cowboy star Tom Mix and his wife in 1927.

from office and returned to Northampton, where he died in 1933.

—KATHLEEN BANKS NUTTER

See Also: Harding, Warren Gamaliel; Presidential Elections; President of the United States.

BIBLIOGRAPHY: McCoy, Donald R., *Calvin Coolidge: The Quiet President* (Macmillan 1967); Murray, Robert K., *The Politics of Normalcy: Governmental Theory and Practice in the Harding-Coolidge Era* (Norton 1973).

■ **COOPER, GARY (1901-61),** film actor. A laconic leading man born in Helena, Montana, he played the hero in films such as *The Virginian* (1929), *Meet John Doe* (1941), *Sergeant York* (1941), and *High Noon* (1951).

■ **COOPER, JAMES FENIMORE (1789-1851),** author. Born in Burlington, New Jersey, and reared between 1790 and 1800 in the village founded by his father, Cooperstown, New York, James Fenimore Cooper published his first novel, an unremarkable effort, in 1820. The next year, however, witnessed the international success of Cooper's *The Spy*, prompting his move to New York City in 1822 to further his career. *The Pioneers* (1823) inaugurated Cooper's Leatherstocking Tales and introduced the memorable character of Natty Bumppo. Four Leatherstocking novels followed: *The Last of the Mohicans* (1826), *The Prairie* (1827), *The Pathfinder* (1840), and *The Deerslayer* (1841). In 1833, Cooper returned from a seven-year stay in Europe, after which he lost favor with much of his reading public, largely due to the controversial judgments of American culture contained in such works as *A Letter to His Countrymen* (1834) and *The American Democrat* (1838). Cooper repaid the hostility he aroused in his critics with a series of mostly successful libel actions from 1837 to 1842. He had settled in Cooperstown in 1834 and lived until his death, while producing several more works, including his scholarly *The History of the Navy of the United States of America* (1839). Over the course of his 30-year career as a writer, Cooper exerted a significant influence upon Americans' sense of their nation and its history, perhaps most especially upon their ideas of the wilderness and the American West.

See Also: Novel; Westerns.

Author James Fenimore Cooper first introduced the character of Natty Bumppo, the old hunter, in the initial volume of his Leatherstocking Tales, *The Pioneers,* published in 1823.

BIBLIOGRAPHY: McWilliams, John P., Jr., *Political Justice in a Republic: James Fenimore Cooper's America* (Univ. of California Press 1972).

■ **COOPER, PETER (1791-1883),** inventor, industrialist, and philanthropist. Born in New York City, Cooper had almost no formal education but became one of the leading businessmen of the 19th century. He apprenticed to a coach maker at age 17 and invented a machine for mortising the hubs of carriages. After a stint in the cloth-shearing business, he bought a glue and isinglass factory that soon dominated the industry in America. Cooper then established the Canton Iron Works in Baltimore (1828) and built Tom Thumb, the first steam locomotive in the United States. He sold the iron works in 1836 for Baltimore and Ohio Railroad stock, profits from which he used to begin a wire factory, blast furnaces, a rolling mill, foundries, and iron mines. In 1854, he produced the first iron beams for structural use and his furnaces initiated the Bessemer process in America in 1856. Despite his wealth, he identified himself as "a mechanic of New York" and became a philanthropic example to Andrew Carnegie, founding the Cooper Union (1857-59), a free educational institution with a museum, library, and lecture series. He served as a New York City alderman and ran unsuccessfully for president on the Greenback ticket in 1876.

See Also: *Science.*

■ **COPLAND, AARON (1900-90),** composer best known for orchestral works drawing on American folk themes. Born in Brooklyn, New York, he studied composition in Paris (1921-24) and advocated making classical music popular with the mainstream audience by incorporating into it the themes and rhythms of popular music. Copland's most performed works were premiered during World War II, including the brief but inspiring "Fanfare for the Common Man," ballet scores such as *Rodeo* (1942) and *Appalachian Spring* (1943), and *A Lincoln Portrait* (1942) for orchestra and narrator. After 1950 Copland turned in new directions, and his compositions reflected modernist trends such as 12-tone scales. Copland was also a noted writer and teacher, particularly at the Berkshire Music Center at Tanglewood in Massachusetts (1940-65). There, he influenced a generation of younger composers including Leonard Bernstein and Lukas Foss.

BIBLIOGRAPHY: Dobrin, Arnold, *Aaron Copland, His Life and Times* (Crowell 1967).

■ **COPLEY, JOHN SINGLETON (1738-1815),** history painter and portraitist. Born in Boston, Massachusetts, Copley began studying painting and engraving at an early age with his stepfather, Peter Pelham. Although Copley had set his sights on history painting, considered to be the most prestigious artistic genre, he relied on portraiture in order to earn a living when he set up a studio in Boston in 1757. Portraits such as *Paul Revere* (1765-70), which captured the silversmith at work, won acclaim. His *Boy with Squirrel* (1765) was exhibited in London, where it drew the attention of the painter Benjamin West, who encouraged Copley to join him in England. Copley remained in Boston until just before the Revolutionary War, when his portrait practice waned considerably; he then traveled in Europe before settling in London (1775). In England, Copley

adopted a more academic style for his portraits, but he also started to complete large history paintings. His *Watson and the Shark* (1778) and *The Death of the Earl of Chatham* (1779-80) were particularly well received.

See Also: *Painting; West, Benjamin.*

■ **COPPERHEADS,** Northern antiwar Democrats during the Civil War. They opposed a total war aimed at destroying the Old South. Copperheads maintained a strong antidraft and antiwar voice and in the 1864 presidential election nominated former general George McClellan to oppose Abraham Lincoln.

See Also: *Civil War; Democratic Party.*

■ **COPYRIGHT LAWS,** legislation intended to regulate the use of literary, artistic, and musical creations. A copyright gives the author of a book, song, drawing, computer program, or other original intellectual creation control over how the work is reproduced, displayed, or used. In practice that means no one can sell or otherwise profit from the author's creation without the author's permission. The U.S. Constitution recognized that copyright was essential to encourage and reward creative work and directed Congress (Article II, Section 7) "to promote the progress of science and useful arts" by "securing for limited times" an author's "exclusive right" to his or her creation. The first federal copyright law, modeled after existing British statutes that protected books and maps, was passed in 1790. International copyright protection for creative works was formalized by the Berne Convention (1886).

Copyright protection has been expanded to keep pace with new technology such as photography, sound recordings, motion pictures, and computers that allows new forms of creativity and also enables original works to be widely and quickly distributed. Current U.S. copyright law (1976, 1988) protects "original works" that are "fixed in tangible form," typically for the lifetime of the author or authors plus 50 years.

BIBLIOGRAPHY: Rose, Mark, *Authors and Owners: The Invention of Copyright* (Harvard Univ. Press 1993).

■ **CORAL SEA, BATTLE OF THE (1942),** early World War II naval battle between U.S. and

Japanese aircraft carrier forces that prevented the Japanese from invading Australia. On May 7-8 the U.S. carrier *Lexington* was sunk and the carrier *Yorktown* badly damaged, but the Japanese lost more planes and men, and their troop transports, bound for Port Moresby, New Guinea, were forced to abandon their objective.

See Also: World War II.

■ **CORBIN, MARGARET COCHRAN (1751-c. 1800),** known as the first woman to "take a soldier's part" in the American Revolution. Born in Franklin County, Pennsylvania, she became a combatant in the Battle of Fort Washington when her husband was killed in battle (Nov. 16, 1776). She assumed his post and defended it until she herself was disabled by enemy fire.

■ **CORN,** cereal grain domesticated by the Indian peoples of central Mexico between 6000 and 5000 B.C. Typically grown on plots together with squash and beans, corn (or maize) became the staple crop of Indians, spreading beyond Mesoamerica to agricultural tribes as far north as present-day Canada.

Because of corn's productivity, it can grow in a wide range of climates. Although it has a shorter growing season, corn yields twice as much grain per acre as wheat. It was one of the first Indian crops adopted by European colonists.

Parts of the maize plant were used for everything from medicine to animal feed to whiskey, while the early American diet, with its many corn-based dishes—pone, hoe-cakes, slapjacks, dodgers, mush, and the like—was in large part a hybrid of European culinary practices and the varied techniques that Indians had long possessed for preparing corn.

Maize also won rapid acceptance in the Old World, where its hardiness helped to bring previously marginal agricultural areas into production, spurring population growth and, ultimately, increased immigration to the Americas.

Today, the United States is the largest cultivator of corn in the world, producing some 200 million tons annually. Corn is used in foodstuffs ranging from tortilla chips to chewing gum to soft drinks, but the bulk of the crop—some 85 percent—enters the U.S. diet indirectly, as feed for livestock.

See Also: Agriculture.

BIBLIOGRAPHY: Crosby, Alfred W., Jr., *The Columbian Exchange: Biological and Cultural Consequences of 1492* (Greenwood Press 1972); Fussell, Betty, *The Story of Corn* (Knopf 1992).

■ **CORNPLANTER (c. 1735-1836),** Seneca leader. Born Galant-wa'ka along the Genesee River in present-day New York, Cornplanter was among those Iroquois who invited Quaker missionaries to settle among them after the American Revolution, telling them that the Iroquois were "determined to try to learn your ways." Among the Iroquois, he led the faction of "progressives," who believed that their people's future depended on learning the ways of the whites, including rearrangement of gender roles and adoption of American farming methods.

See Also: Indians of North America.

■ **CORNSTALK (c. 1720-77),** Shawnee leader. When Lord Dunmore's War broke out in spring 1774, Cornstalk assured the British of his good intentions, but British colonists along the Ohio had already begun killing Shawnee. On October 10, Cornstalk and 300 warriors were defeated by colonial militia at Point Pleasant on the Ohio River. Cornstalk and other chiefs eventually yielded Shawnee hunting rights south of the Ohio River in exchange for British promises to keep colonists out of the northern Ohio Valley. In 1777, Cornstalk was killed by American militia.

See Also: Indians of North America; Lord Dunmore's War.

■ **CORNWALLIS, CHARLES (1738-1805),** 2nd Earl (1762) and 1st Marquess (1792), British general during the American Revolution. Born in London, Cornwallis contributed to British victories in the North, including the capture of New York in 1776. He helped force the surrender of Charleston in 1780 and assumed command of British forces in the South. Cornwallis made the fatal mistake, however, of overextending his troops and soon suffered several defeats. The war effectively ended when he retreated to Yorktown, Virginia, and surrendered to American forces in October 1781.

See Also: Revolution, American; Yorktown, Siege of.

■ CORONADO, FRANCISCO VÁSQUEZ DE (1510-54),

Spanish conquistador and explorer of North America. Born in Salamanca, Spain, he sailed to America in 1535 with Antonio de Mendoza, newly appointed viceroy of Mexico. Mendoza's protégé, Coronado quickly rose to eminence in Mexico. In 1537 he quelled a rebellion of black miners in Amatepeque and was appointed to the Mexico City council (1538-54). In 1539 he became governor of New Galicia and on Feb. 23, 1540, led an expedition of conquest and exploration from Compostela, Mexico, to the north. The aim was to find the legendary Seven Cities of Cibola, reputed to be fabulously rich. With about 300 Spaniards and 700 Indians, Coronado moved northeast and in 1540 explored today's Arizona and New Mexico, while Hernando de Alarcon with three vessels sailed up the Gulf of California and reached the mouth of the Colorado River. One of Coronado's lieutenants, Garcia López de Cárdenas, sighted the Grand Canyon (1540). In 1541, Coronado pushed northeast to the land of Quivira (Kansas), which turned out to be as poor as any other seen by the expedition. Having found no fabulous riches, Coronado turned back in April 1542 and by summer had returned to Mexico. He was vigorously attacked by many, including Hernán Cortés, for mismanagement of his expedition, underwent a trial (1543-45), and was fined. He died in Mexico.

See Also: Exploration and Discovery; Spanish Colonies.

BIBLIOGRAPHY: Day, A. Grove, *Coronado's Quest: The Discovery of the American Southwest* (Greenwood Press 1986); Hammond, George P., and Agapito Rey, eds., *Narratives of the Coronado Expedition, 1540-1542* (Univ. of New Mexico Press 1940; reprint AMS Press 1977).

■ CORRUPT BARGAIN (1825),

the term given to the election of Pres. John Quincy Adams by the U.S. House of Representatives. In the 1824 election none of the four presidential candidates received an electoral majority. Andrew Jackson received the most electoral votes (99) while also receiving a plurality of the popular vote, with 42.15 percent. Adams was second, with 84 electoral votes and 31.89 percent of the popular vote. Third, and well behind Adams, was Treasury Sec. William H. Crawford. Under the terms of the Constitution, the House of Representatives would choose among the top three candidates. The fourth candidate, Henry Clay, was the Speaker of the House, and hence presided over the election of the new president. Clay hated Jackson and threw his support to Adams, who was elected on the first ballot.

A few days later Adams nominated Henry Clay as his secretary of state, a post that had led three previous holders to the presidency. There was a public outcry among Jackson's supporters who charged that a "corrupt bargain" had been made by Adams and Clay. Clay would likely have supported Adams without the cabinet post, but the popular view was that Adams had bought the election. In the 1828 election Jackson easily defeated Adams.

See Also: Adams, John Quincy; Clay, Henry; Jackson, Andrew.

BIBLIOGRAPHY: Sellers, Charles G., *The Market Revolution: Jacksonian America 1815-1846* (Oxford Univ. Press 1991).

■ CORRUPT PRACTICES ACTS,

state and federal laws passed from time to time to clean up political campaigns and elections. The first state corrupt practices law was enacted in New York (1890) as a reaction to alleged bribery and voting fraud by political bosses. Congress passed the first federal campaign reform law in 1925, limiting corporate contributions to officeholders and candidates and banning secret political donations.

■ CORTÉS, HERNÁN (1485-1547),

Spanish conqueror of the Aztec empire in Mexico (1519-21). He was born in Medellin, Estremadura, and at the age of 14 was sent to the University of Salamanca but quit after two years. In 1504 he sailed to the New World and in 1511 took part in Diego Velasquez's conquest of Cuba. In 1518 Cortés was given command of an expedition to the mainland. With 508 soldiers he sailed in February 1519, coasted along Yucatán, and founded Veracruz on the Mexican coast. On his march inland he made an alliance with the nation of Tlascalans against the Aztecs (August-September 1519). On Nov. 8, 1519, Cortés entered Tenochtitlán, the Aztec capital. He managed to capture Montezuma, the Aztec ruler, and held him hostage. In

May 1520 he marched to the coast, captured Pánfilo de Narváez who had been sent to arrest him, and returned to Tenochtitlán. The Aztec uprising and Montezuma's death forced him to evacuate the city in early July 1520 after severe fighting. Cortés recaptured Tenochtitlán in August 1521, in 1523 became governor, and in 1528 was appointed captain-general of New Spain (the name for the conquered territories). Bickering with other royal officials in Mexico led him repeatedly to seek justice at the king's court in Spain. Initially receptive, the king later turned against Cortés, who died in 1547 near Seville. An excellent fighter and penetrating strategist, Cortés was a suave, charismatic leader who commanded respect and obedience. His statesmanlike approach and relative indifference to personal enrichment distinguished him from many other conquistadors.

—DENIS KOZLOV

See Also: Aztecs; Conquistadors; Exploration and Discovery.

BIBLIOGRAPHY: Helps, Arthur, *The Life of Hernando Cortes,* 2 vols. (George Bell & Sons 1894); Johnston, William W., *Cortés* (Little, Brown 1975); Madariaga, Salvador de, *Hernán Cortés: Conqueror of Mexico* (Univ. of Miami Press 1942); Marks, Richard L., *Cortés: The Great Adventurer and the Fate of Aztec Mexico* (Knopf 1993).

■ **COSBY, WILLIAM H. ("BILL") (1937-),** comedian and television performer. Born in Germantown, Pennsylvania, Cosby is a popular entertainer as well as an educator and philanthropist. He was the first African American to star in a major dramatic series on television ("I Spy"). His other series, "The Bill Cosby Show" and "The Cosby Show," have enjoyed wide popularity, and during his career he has earned eight Grammy awards and four Emmys. Cosby has shown a keen interest in education and promoted strengthening of the family. He holds a doctorate in education from the University of Massachusetts and has written several books about his life.

See Also: African Americans.

■ **COTTON, JOHN (1584-1652),** minister and author. Born in Derby, England, Cotton attended Trinity College, Cambridge, where he embraced Puritan theology. As minister at Boston, in Lincolnshire, England, Cotton preached Puritan doctrine until he and his loyal parishioners were forced to leave for New England. On arriving in Boston, Massachusetts, in 1633, Cotton immediately began teaching at the Boston Church. A scholar as well as a minister, Cotton published many sermons and religious tracts.

See Also: Religion.

■ **COTTON,** principal American export during the 19th century and a staple of the Southern slave system. Cotton was cultivated by Indians and European settlers alike during the colonial era, but it remained a limited cash crop until the late 18th century, when a number of factors converged to create the "King Cotton" of Southern legend. At that time, mechanization of cloth production, first in Great Britain and, beginning in 1790, in New England, heightened demand for cotton fiber. Then, in 1793, Eli Whitney invented the cotton gin, which sped up the once-laborious process of separating cotton seeds from the raw fiber. These two events combined to produce a vast cotton belt that stretched from South Carolina to Texas, dominated by plantations that used gangs of African-American slaves to cultivate cotton for export.

After the Civil War ended (1865), Southern planters experimented with a number of alternatives to slave labor, the most common being sharecropping. This system endured until the 1930s, when the planting and then the picking of cotton was mechanized, and the cultivation of cotton shifted to the irrigated farmlands of California, Arizona, and New Mexico, where most of today's cotton is now grown.

See Also: Agriculture; Slavery; Tenant Farming; Whitney, Eli.

BIBLIOGRAPHY: Danbom, David, *Born in the Country: A History of Rural America* (Johns Hopkins Univ. Press 1995); Hobhouse, Henry, *Seeds of Change* (Harper & Row 1985).

■ **COTTON GIN (1793),** machine invented by Eli Whitney to remove seeds from short-staple cotton. Americans planted Sea Island, or long-staple, cotton along the Carolina coast as early as 1767. The growth of the English textile industry boosted cotton prices in the late 18th century and encouraged planting inland, where only short-staple, or greenseed, cotton would grow. Despite its heavy demand this cotton was unprofitable because it required arduous manual labor to remove the tiny seeds that stuck to the fibers. Eli Whitney's invention removed the seeds mechanically and made it possible for one slave to process 50 pounds of cotton a day where previously only 1 pound had been possible. The cotton gin, which others imitated and Whitney patented in 1794, altered the course of southern agriculture and expansion by making it profitable to grow short-staple cotton. The plantation system, which appeared to be declining, was revived, with concentrations of large numbers of slaves in the hands of a few owners. Cotton exports rose from 9,840 pounds in 1789-90 to 8 million pounds in 1800-01. Production spread into the Piedmont, through the southeast, and west into Texas by 1860. By the 1820s the United States was the dominant world supplier of cotton, largely because of the invention of the cotton gin.

See Also: Agriculture; Cotton; Industrial Revolution; Tenant Farming; Whitney, Eli.

■ **COUGHLIN, CHARLES EDWARD (1891-1979),** Roman Catholic priest and political activist known as the "Radio Priest." Born in Hamilton, Ontario, Coughlin served as pastor of the Shrine of the Little Flower in Royal Oaks, Michigan (1926-66). He first broadcast church services for shut-ins on a Detroit radio station in the late 1920s and developed a loyal audience. After 1930 his broadcasts became increasingly political and were soon heard on a network of stations across the country. After initially backing Pres. Franklin D. Roosevelt, Coughlin turned against the New Deal, blaming the Depression on a conspiracy of financiers and government leaders. He formed the National Union for Social Justice (1935) and, both on radio and in the organization's newspaper, began expressing anti-Semitic and profascist opinions. By 1940 his views had alienated many of his former supporters, and he was ordered by the church in 1942 to end all political activities.

See Also: New Deal.

BIBLIOGRAPHY: Warren, Donald I., *Radio Priest: Charles Coughlin, the Father of Hate Radio* (Free Press 1996).

■ **COUNTRY AND WESTERN MUSIC,** commercial music genre that began with the first recordings of country folk music artists in the 1920s. In 1924, Okeh records issued a catalog listing "Old Southern Songs," "Mountain Ballads," and "Hill Country Music," most of these field recordings. The first commercially successful recordings, done by the Carter Family and Jimmie Rodgers in 1927, represented the currents of tradition and innovation that would shape the genre. The Carters played "mountain music" featuring church-based vocal harmonies, autoharp, and acoustic guitar. Rodgers combined country yodeling with 12-bar blues and was backed up by jazz artists such as Louis Armstrong. The "western" component entered in the early 1930s with the "singing cowboys" of matinee western movies, including Tex Ritter, Roy Rogers, and, most famously, Gene Autry. Cowboy costumes became the norm for the country music performer.

In 1924, station WLS in Chicago began broadcasting the "National Barn Dance," and the next year station WSM in Nashville began production of the "Grand Ole Opry." Widely heard throughout the Midwest and South, these stations propelled the music to regional commercial dominance by World War II. Indeed, the fabulous success of the "Opry" made Nashville into the center of country music publishing and recording.

Country and western music went national with the meteoric rise to stardom of singer-songwriter Hank Williams in 1949. His hits, including "Hey, Good Lookin'" and "Cold, Cold Heart," were "covered" by mainstream artists and his own recordings "crossed over" from the country to the pop music chart, pioneering the way for a new generation of country performers. In 1958, major players in the business formed the Country Music Foundation to promote and market the music; in 1967 this group opened the Country Music Hall of Fame in Nashville.

The winning formula of music innovation combined with the authenticity of rural musical roots has provided country and western music with a dynamism lacking in late-20th-century pop music generally and rock and roll in particular. In the final decades of the century, country music benefited from the growing popularity of country "line dancing" and "two-stepping." A connection to social dancing has always been the most powerful force in the success of commercial music.

See Also: Folk Music; Williams, Hank.

BIBLIOGRAPHY: Country Music Foundation, *Country: The Music and the Musicians* (Abbeville Press 1988); Malone, Bill C., *Country Music U.S.A.* (Univ. of Texas Press 1985).

■ **COUREURS DE BOIS,** fur traders (whose name in French means "runners in the woods") of New France operating in native areas without official permission. In the decades following the founding of Quebec in 1608, young Frenchmen were sent to live in Indian communities to learn native languages, establish friendly relations, explore the country, and encourage the beaver trade. They linked the interests of the colony and the native "residents of the woods" (*sauvages*) and proved invaluable to the economic survival of New France at a time when the Iroquois attacked the colony's Indian allies (1647-67) and disrupted normal patterns of trade. A temporary peace led to a flood of idle soldiers and other colonists into the animal-rich Great Lakes basin. One official put the number of illegal traders at 800 in 1680, a substantial number in a colony with fewer than 11,000 people. Attempts to control this diffusion of manpower by the annual issuance of permits (*congés*) proved futile. This policy, begun in 1681, did lead to a restructuring and consolidation of the fur trade. After this, traders under contract and hired men (*voyageurs, engagés*) would be distinguished from their illegal counterparts. Despite their status, *coureurs de bois* continued to serve French interests by establishing relations and trading communities in the Great Lakes basin and the Illinois country. The pipe-smoking *coureur de bois* or *voyageur,* with his buckskin leggings (*mitasses*), moccasins, and tasseled cap (*tuque*), singing his songs while paddling his canoe, has become a romantic figure in popular accounts of the frontier.

—JAY GITLIN

See Also: French Colonies; Frontier in American History; Fur Trade.

BIBLIOGRAPHY: Eccles, W. J., *The Canadian Frontier, 1534-1760,* rev. ed. (Univ. of New Mexico Press 1983).

■ **COURT PACKING,** unsuccessful attempt by Pres. Franklin D. Roosevelt to place more justices favorable to the New Deal on the Supreme Court. In

1936 Roosevelt became increasingly frustrated with Supreme Court decisions that declared New Deal legislation, such as the National Recovery Administration and the Agricultural Adjustment Administration, unconstitutional.

After exploring other options, Roosevelt and his advisers decided in February 1937 to ask Congress for legislation that would expand the high court from 9 to 15 justices. This legislation would also empower the president to appoint a new justice any time an incumbent failed to retire at age 70. The intentions of this "court-packing" bill were so thinly veiled, however, that once it was announced, conservative legislators and the media launched scathing attacks. Much of the controversy centered on the balance of power. Opponents argued that Roosevelt was attempting to tip the balance in his favor, while the president maintained that his purpose was to restore a balance.

As the battle continued, Roosevelt's position weakened, until a conservative justice (Willis Van Devanter) announced his intention to retire. The Supreme Court also made rulings upholding several crucial pieces of New Deal legislation, including the National Labor Relations Act. Roosevelt

When his New Deal legislation encountered Supreme Court opposition, Pres. Franklin D. Roosevelt unsuccessfully attempted in 1937 to pack the Court, intending to appoint additional justices who would tip opinion in his favor, an attempt ridiculed in this cartoon.

eventually backed down from his position and accepted a compromise that reformed lower court procedures but did nothing about the Supreme Court. The president had succeeded in gaining a more responsive Court but weakened his political influence in Congress.

See Also: New Deal; Roosevelt, Franklin Delano; Supreme Court.

BIBLIOGRAPHY: Baker, Leonard, *Back to Back: The Duel Between FDR and the Supreme Court* (Macmillan 1967).

■ **COVERTURE,** a legal convention, derived from English common law, denying married women the rights to own property, sign contracts, or sue in court. Under coverture, unmarried women—*feme sol*—were allowed a degree of economic independence. But married women—*feme covert*—forfeited their rights of participation in the economy, their property, and their wages to their husbands. Coverture existed in the United States until the passage of the Married Women's Property Acts (1848-70 by states, 1875 by Congress).

See Also: Married Women's Property Acts; Women in American History.

■ **COWBOYS,** men who worked the ranches and drove the cattle in the West. An American folk hero, the cowboy can trace his historical roots from Mongolian pastoralists to the Moorish invasion of Spain and the conquest of Mexico. In Texas, African-American cattle-raising met Spanish ranching, and the cowboy's dashing dress developed from earlier origins. The large brimmed hats started in Mongolia and were worn in Mexico but were perfected by Philadelphia hat-maker John B. Stetson in the late 19th century. High-heeled boots, worn by Mongolians, found their way to Texas as protection against a foot slipping through a stirrup. Chaps, from the Spanish *chaparejos*, were leather leggings worn over the pants to protect against brush, and rawhide *la reatas* became grass rope lariats, used to *dar la vuelta*, or dally, around the saddle horn in catching and working cattle from horseback. As distinct from ranchers and cattlemen, who have a capital investment in the cattle being worked, cowboys were wage earners, usually young men, who worked at the profession an average of seven years, for wages of about $30 to $40 a month.

Great Cattle Drives. There were early drives of cattle to market in Mexico and across the Alleghenies in the 18th century, and several drives from New Mexico to the California Gold Rush in the 1850s. But it was after the end of the Civil War in 1865 that cattle-rich, but cash-poor, Texans drove their herds to railhead markets in

Cowboys of the 19th-century American West came from diverse backgrounds. Many were Mexican, African-American, and Indian.

Kansas at Abilene and Dodge City in what has become the classic image of the great cattle drive. The containment of Indians in Montana and Wyoming also saw cattle herds make their way north to take advantage of the abundant grass. Working outfits of 10-20 men drove 1,000 to 3,000 head of cattle in a bunch, traveling 12 to 15 miles a day. The work was hot and dusty, or cold and wet, and the hours long, with 14- and 16-hour days common. The occasional stampede or roping accident was dangerous and sometimes fatal, but the biggest problem was simple exhaustion and boredom from long hours in the saddle. Cowboys were assigned several horses, which became a working tool as much as a saddle or rope, on which cowboys depended for their very lives.

Working on ranches, cowboys saw to the well-being of the animals, assisted in calving, and rode the boundaries of the home-outfit's open range, driving the cattle back. Usually twice a year, cattle were rounded up and sorted, in the spring for castration and branding and in the fall for shipping to market. By the catastrophic winter of 1886-87, overgrazing, drought, and falling market prices, along with homestead fences and population increase in the West, brought an end to the golden era of the cowboy.

Modern Cowboy Images. Tens of thousands of men and women make their living on horseback today across the West, although work is often done with pickups and horse trailers, and barbed wire fence has replaced many a cowboy. And although the historical reality of the cowboy is essential to understanding the West, so is the mythical cowboy. Owen Wister's *The Virginian* (1902) as well as Frederic Remington's and Charles Russell's paintings firmly established the cowboy as a national hero that had begun in the dime novels of the 19th century. Cowboy stars of the motion pictures, from Bronco Billy Anderson and Tom Mix of the 1910s and 1920s to the singing cowboys, Gene Autry and Roy Rogers, of the 1930s, 1940s, and 1950s, furthered the myth of the cowboy. And if Clint Eastwood is the most popular western star of today, no one can ever replace John Wayne, whose career spanned nearly half a century on the screen. As the rodeo and the ranch continue into the 21st century, the cowboy is still alive and well, if struggling a bit to find his place in the modern world.

—J. C. MUTCHLER

See Also: Frontier in American History.
BIBLIOGRAPHY: Dary, David, *Cowboy Culture: A Saga of Five Centuries* (Knopf 1981); Slatta, Richard W., *Cowboys of the Americas* (Yale Univ. Press 1990).

■ **COWPENS, BATTLE OF (1781),** major American victory in the American Revolution. On Jan. 17, 1781, American Gen. Daniel Morgan positioned his troops in South Carolina near the cowpens of Loyalist Hiram Saunders to await an approaching British force commanded by Banastre Tarleton. In less than an hour, Morgan's masterful tactics guided his soldiers to a pivotal victory over the British regiment. The battle provided momentum that culminated in the American victory at Yorktown.

See Also: Revolution, American.

■ **COX, JAMES MIDDLETON (1870-1957),** American newspaper publisher and politician. He was born in Jacksonburg, Ohio. After working as a schoolteacher and a newspaper reporter, he bought his first newspaper, the *Dayton Daily News*, in 1898. Ten years later he was elected to Congress, serving until 1913. Cox then went on to be governor of Ohio (1913-15, 1917-21). In 1920 he was the unsuccessful presidential candidate of the Democratic party, along with vice-presidential candidate Franklin Delano Roosevelt.

■ **COXEY'S ARMY,** officially known as the Commonweal for Christ, a band of men who marched to Washington, D.C., in 1894 to demand a national public works program. The army symbolized the frustration of millions of unemployed American workers after the panic of 1893 stretched into 1894, leaving perhaps one-quarter of the U.S. work force out of work. Jacob S. Coxey, a successful businessman from the Midwest, proposed that Congress institute a national public works program, financed by the issuance of legal tender notes, thus putting the unemployed back to work. On Mar. 25, 1894, 100 men left Coxey's hometown of Massillon, Ohio, to deliver to the nation's capital what Coxey called a "petition in boots." By the time Coxey's Army reached Washington, D.C., it had grown to over 500 men. On May 1 some 15,000 to 20,000 spectators waited at the Capitol Building as Coxey's Army approached. Once on the Capitol grounds, Coxey and two other leaders of the march were arrested for trespassing and sentenced to 20 days in jail. The actual text of their petition was never presented to Congress. Part of a long tradition of demands for public work during times of economic crisis, the demands of Coxey's Army of 1894 would only be answered on the national level 40 years later as part of the New Deal.

—KATHLEEN BANKS NUTTER

See Also: Labor Movement; Panics, Financial.
BIBLIOGRAPHY: Folsom, Franklin, *Impatient Armies of the Poor: The Story of Collective Action of the Unemployed, 1808-1942* (Univ. Press of Colorado 1991); Schwantes, Carlos A., *Coxey's Army: An American Odyssey* (Univ. of Nebraska Press 1985).

■ **CRAIG V. MISSOURI (1830),** U.S. Supreme Court case that considered the authority of state governments to issue their own securities. The state of Missouri was sued after passage of a state law that permitted state loan certificates to circulate. The Court ruled (4-3) that these state-backed financial instruments were unconstitutional tender. Writing for the Court, Chief Justice John Marshall held that the loan certificates amounted to bills of credit and that the Constitution had reserved to the federal government the authority to issue government-backed paper.

See Also: Marshall, John; Supreme Court.

■ **CRANE, HART (1899-1932),** modernist poet. Crane was born in Garrettsville, Ohio, the son of a candy manufacturer. Resisting pressure to enter the family business, Crane dropped out of school to pursue his love of poetry. In his early 20s, Crane moved to New York City, and he published his first volume of poems, *White Buildings*, in 1926. After traveling in Europe, he returned to New York, where he finished the collection *The Bridge* (1930), for which he is best known. Crane committed suicide.

■ **CRANE, STEPHEN (1871-1900),** writer of naturalism. Crane was born in Newark, New Jersey. After studying briefly at Lafayette College and Syracuse University, he worked as a freelance

writer in New York City from 1890 to 1895. Using his own close observations and others' accounts of life in New York City tenements, Crane wrote his first novel, *Maggie: A Girl of the Streets* (1893). He financed the publication of *Maggie* himself because its vivid descriptions of the underside of urban life were so controversial in their day. Crane achieved much more success with *The Red Badge of Courage*, which was published in book form in 1895. For his journalistic work Crane traveled in the American West, Mexico, and Florida; his experience with a gun-running crew to Cuba became the basis for one of his best-known short stories, "The Open Boat." In 1897 he settled in England, where he became acquainted with Henry James. Crane returned to Cuba as a correspondent for the *New York World* during the Spanish-American War. He returned to England in 1899, ill with tuberculosis, and died at the age of 28.

See Also: James, Henry; Novel.

■ **CRATER, BATTLE OF THE (1864),** Civil War battle near Petersburg, Virginia, also known as the Petersburg Mine Assault. The Union army blew up the Confederate earthworks near Petersburg on July 30 and then attacked. African-American troops had been specially trained to carry out the assault but were called back because Gen. George G. Meade feared that if the mission failed the Union would be accused of callously disregarding their lives. The explosion created a crater 170 feet long and 70 feet wide and killed at least 278 Confederate soldiers. But 15,000 Union troops became trapped in the maze of trenches and pits created by the blast. The North sustained 3,748 casualties in the disastrous assault.

See Also: Civil War; Petersburg, Battle of.

■ **CRAZY HORSE (c. 1841-77),** military leader of the Oglala Sioux (Lakota). He was born Tashunca Witco in present-day South Dakota. After the Black Hills gold rush of the 1870s, Crazy Horse's village became a haven for nontreaty Lakota and Cheyenne bands. On June 25, 1876, at the Battle of Little Bighorn, Crazy Horse joined Sitting Bull and his followers in fighting off an unprovoked attack by Lt. Col. George Armstrong Custer and his cavalry. In May 1877, Crazy Horse surrendered to Brig. Gen. George Crook and was detained at the government's Red Cloud Agency in Nebraska. On Sept. 5, 1877, after having left the agency without authorization, he was killed by a soldier as he was being led to a guardhouse.

See Also: Indians of North America; Little Bighorn, Battle of.

■ **CREDIT MOBILIER OF AMERICA,** dummy construction company formed in 1864 by prominent stockholders in the Union Pacific Railroad, a symbol of the corruption of the administration of Pres. Ulysses S. Grant. By awarding the contract to complete construction of the transcontinental railroad to their own dummy construction company, these stockholders were able to reap the incredible profits by inflating construction costs, much of it financed through government loans. While building the transcontinental railroad actually cost about $44 million, Credit Mobilier charged more than $84 million, earning its stockholders a 500 percent profit in 1867-68.

As word began to spread of the dubious connection between the railroad and its construction company, Rep. Oakes Ames of Massachusetts, a major Union Pacific stockholder and an organizer of Credit Mobilier, sought to block a congressional investigation by offering Credit Mobilier stock cheaply to his fellow congressmen, earning those who accepted the offer a $33 million profit. In 1872, the *New York Sun* published a list of those involved, including several congressmen and Vice Pres. Schuyler Colfax. Although a full investigation was never completed, the revelations made Americans increasingly aware of the depth of government and corporate corruption, thus leading to an increased demand for reform.

See Also: Railroads.

BIBLIOGRAPHY: Crawford, Jay Boyd, *The Credit Mobilier of America 1880* (Greenwood Press 1969).

■ **CREE INDIANS.** *See: Subarctic Indians.*

■ **CREEK,** Indian group originally occupying the coastal plain of what is now Georgia and Alabama, from the Savannah River westward to the Alabama River. English colonists referred to them as "the people of the Creeks," later shortened simply to "Creeks." They called themselves the Muskogees.

The Muskogees shared a common language, but before European invasion there was no tribal unity among them. They lived in dozens of autonomous towns spread along the river lowlands, practicing a mixed economy of farming and hunting. After the establishment of the colony of South Carolina in the late 17th century, the Muskogees became economic and political allies of the British, as hunters and traders of deer skins (one of the most important exports of the colony) and as warriors in the wars against the Spanish missions and settlements in Florida. Over the next century the Muskogees combined into a powerful multivillage confederacy with two principal centers, the Lower Towns along the lower Chattahoochee River and the Upper Towns on the Alabama River in the upriver piedmont country. By the mid-18th century the Creek Confederation had become the most powerful Indian nation in the Southeast. Epidemic disease ravaged many Muskogee communities, but the towns maintained their population by the incorporation of other native peoples through conquest.

The Creek Confederation sided with the British during the American Revolution, considering American frontiersmen their primary enemies. Invading patriot forces destroyed many towns, and the Muskogees were further weakened by a devastating epidemic of smallpox. After the war, the brilliant mixed-ancestry Muskogee leader Alexander McGillivray negotiated the Treaty of New York (1790); in exchange for Creek acknowledgment of U.S. sovereignty over foreign affairs, they received a federal pledge to protect the confederation from the invasion of squatters and settlers. A large number of Muskogees took up plantation agriculture, and many villages saw a return to moderate prosperity, but the inability of federal authorities to prevent continuing encroachments of Muskogee lands led to rising anger. During the War of 1812 warriors of the Upper Towns took up "the red stick," the symbol of warfare, while the Lower Towns—where commercial farming was more firmly established— sided with the Americans. The Muskogees remember this as their civil war. At the Battle of Horseshoe Bend (1814) American general Andrew Jackson, in command of a mixed force of American militia and Muskogees from the Lower

Towns, crushed the Red Sticks. The Creek Confederacy emerged from the War of 1812 in a greatly weakened condition.

In 1832, during the period of Indian Removal, the United States forced the Creek Confederation to give up their traditional homelands and relocate to Indian Territory. Many Muskogees died on the move westward over the winter of 1834-35, but most communities were able to reestablish their towns in the West. Soon thereafter, the confederation was officially renamed the Muskogee Nation. But during the Civil War (1861-65) the nation split into Confederate and Union factions, and the Muskogee were ravaged by the fighting. The nation reunited once again but faced a final assault by the allotment of Muskogee lands at the turn of the century. The nation lost its land base, and tribal government was abolished. The Muskogee Nation was revived after the Indian Reorganization Act of the New Deal, but it was not until 1972 that the Muskogees elected a principal chief to lead the nation. Today the Muskogee Nation, with its capital at Okmulgee, Oklahoma, boasts a revised constitution, health-care and education systems, and housing for low-income tribal members.

See Also: Indian Removal; Indians of North America.
BIBLIOGRAPHY: Debo, Angie, *The Road to Disappearance: A History of the Creek Indians* (Univ. of Oklahoma Press 1941); Martin, Joel W., *Sacred Revolt: The Muskogees' Struggle for a New World* (Beacon Press 1991).

■ **CREOLES,** ethnic term that has had various meanings in the history of the Americas. Some historians believe the term was first used by South American slaves to refer to children born in America as distinguished from the African-born. By the 16th century it was used by the Spanish to refer to anyone born in the New World. The term Creole eventually evolved to mean the cultures of non-native peoples of mixed ancestry born in the Americas. With this expanded definition, Creoles began to identify themselves as separate ethnic groups. In this context, Creole cultures were characterized by distinctive languages, cuisines, and music.

The largest self-defined Creole population in the United States is in Louisiana. There are both white and black Louisiana Creoles. The whites distinguish themselves from the Acadian immigrants of the late 18th century, known as the Cajuns. The colonial French residents around St. Louis, Missouri, were also known as Creoles, as were the mixed-ancestry offspring of Russians and Indians in Alaska.

See Also: Cajuns; Ethnic Groups.

■ **CRÈVECOEUR, J. HECTOR ST. JOHN DE (1735-1813),** writer and observer of early American culture. Crèvecoeur was born near Caen, in Normandy, France. After serving with the French colonial militia in America during the French and Indian War, he went to New York in 1759. Crèvecoeur traveled extensively in the British American colonies while working as a surveyor and trader. He became a naturalized citizen of New York in 1765. In 1769 he married, purchased a farm northeast of New York City, and, witnessing what became the transformation of the British colonies into the United States, began writing a series of essays in which he adopted the persona of a farmer and explained the culture of the new country. As a sympathizer with the British, Crèvecoeur sought to return to Europe during the American Revolution but could not leave America until 1780. Stopping in England on his way to his native France, Crèvecoeur secured a publisher, and in 1782 he published *Letters from an American Farmer.* He returned to the United States as a French diplomat in 1783 to great acclaim.

■ **CROCKETT, DAVY (DAVID) (1786-1836),** frontiersman, soldier, and politician. Born in Green County, Tennessee, Crockett worked as a laborer, marrying Polly Finley in 1806. In 1811, he joined the militia in the war against the Creeks but missed the battle of Horseshoe Bend. Crockett later joined Major Russell's "Separate Battalion of Tennessee Mounted Gunmen" but was too late for the fight at Fort Barancas. As a widower, Crockett married Elizabeth Patton, a widow, in 1816. In 1817, Crockett became a justice of the peace and was elected to the Tennessee legislature in 1820, where he outspokenly favored easier land grants for settlers. Crockett earned the enmity of the Jacksonians after his reelection in 1823 by favoring the Bank of the United States. Crockett was defeated for U.S. Congress in 1825, elected to Congress in 1827, reelected in 1829, defeated in 1831, reelected in 1833, and finally defeated in 1835. Venturing to Texas,

I leave this rule, for others when I am dead
Be always sure, you are right, then go, a head

David Crockett

"You can go to hell," Davy Crockett reportedly told his constituents after being defeated for a fourth term in Congress in 1835. "I'm going to Texas." He died at the battle of the Alamo.

Crockett was killed at the Alamo on the fateful day of Mar. 6, 1836, when the Texans were defeated by Santa Anna.

See Also: Alamo; Frontier in American History; Texas Rebellion.

■ **CROGHAN, GEORGE (c. 1720-82),** land speculator and Indian agent. Born near Dublin, Ireland, Croghan immigrated to Pennsylvania in 1741. A frontier trader, he traveled the Ohio Valley and learned various Indian dialects, including Delaware and Iroquois. When the French began to press their Ohio Valley claims in the 1750s, Croghan's trade network collapsed. In 1756, Croghan became deputy superintendent of Indian affairs. In this capacity, Croghan played a pivotal role in the negotiations ending Pontiac's War (1765).

■ **CROLY, HERBERT (1869-1930),** editor and political writer. Croly was born in New York City. He entered Harvard University in 1886 but left and returned several times, not finally receiving his degree until 1910. At Harvard he studied philosophy with Josiah Royce, William James, and George Santayana. In 1909 Croly published his first book, *The Promise of American Life,* which was highly influential in American progressive political thought. Croly was the founding editor of the *New Republic* in 1914.

■ **CRONKITE, WALTER (1916-),** radio and television journalist. Born in St. Joseph, Missouri, he covered World War II for the United Press and joined the Columbia Broadcasting System (CBS) as a radio and television correspondent in 1950. Cronkite anchored the nightly "CBS Evening

News" (1962-81) as well as the network's news specials during the Vietnam and Watergate eras, earning a reputation as the most trusted reporter on television.

■ CROSBY, BING (HARRY LILLIS) (1904-77),

popular singer, radio, and film star. Born in Tacoma, Washington, he joined Paul Whiteman's orchestra as a member of the Rhythm Boys vocal trio (1927) then launched a solo career. Crosby's smooth baritone voice and relaxed crooner's style sold millions of records, notably Irving Berlin's "White Christmas," and won him film stardom in *Holiday Inn* (1942), *Going My Way* (1944), and six *Road* comedies costarring Bob Hope (1940-52).

See Also: Hope, Bob.

■ CROW INDIANS, Indian tribe of the Great Plains.

The Siouan-speaking Crows are thought to be distantly related to the agricultural Hidatsas. However, the Crows separated, eventually adopting the horse and becoming nomadic buffalo hunters. Located in present-day Wyoming, the Crows came to occupy a prosperous position in the fur trade of the 18th and 19th centuries. In the mid-1800s, threatened by growing conflicts with the more numerous Lakota Sioux to the east, the Crow allied themselves with the United States. Crow warriors served as scouts for the U.S. Army during the Sioux Wars of the 1860s and 1870s. In the late 19th and early 20th centuries, the U.S. government pressured the Crows to abandon their migratory lifestyle and take up farming on individual allotments of land on their Montana reservation. Unalloted lands were opened to American settlement, resulting in a substantial loss of Crow land within the reservation boundaries. Today, the Crows' tribal council is active in developing the tribe's resources, including coal, but poverty is a continuing problem on the reservation.

See Also: Allotment; Fur Trade; Indians of North America; Sioux.

■ CRUZAN V. DIRECTOR, MISSOURI DEPARTMENT OF HEALTH (1990), U.S. Supreme Court case that

upheld a state's authority to regulate the "right to die." Nancy Cruzan, brain-injured in an auto accident, was in an irreversible coma when her parents sued to force the state hospital to turn off life support systems. Their daughter, they said, had indicated she did not want to be kept alive in a permanent vegetative state. The Court ruled (5-4) that Missouri had the right to regulate life-and-death decisions made on behalf of incompetent patients and could require clear and convincing evidence of an incompetent patient's wishes. While *Cruzan* highlighted the ethical, personal, and legal dilemmas society faces as medical technology advances, and it was interpreted to encourage "living wills" describing desired limits on medical care, the decision allowed individual states great latitude in establishing regulations. Most states continue to allow legal guardians to make medical decisions for incompetent patients.

See Also: Supreme Court.

■ CUBA, island country of the West Indies. It is located 90 miles south of the Florida peninsula and is situated between the Caribbean Sea, the Atlantic Ocean, and the entrance to the Gulf of Mexico. Before Spanish conquest the native population of Arawak numbered about 112,000. In 1492 Christopher Columbus claimed the island for Spain. In 1511 Diego de Velázquez founded the first permanent European settlement at Baracoa. Up to the 17th century Indian laborers worked large estates for the Spanish under a tributary labor system known as *encomienda*. During the 18th and 19th centuries Cuba prospered by using African slave labor to work large sugar plantations. After two wars for independence, Cuba overthrew Spanish rule in 1898 during the Spanish-American War, although the United States occupied the island until 1902. In 1959 Fidel Castro overthrew the dictator Fulgencio Batista and established the first communist regime in the Western Hemisphere. Castro abolished capitalism, nationalized industries, and aligned Cuba with the Soviet Union. Because of the Cold War, political relations with the United States deteriorated. The United States supported a failed attempt by anti-Castro Cuban exiles to invade Cuba in 1961 at the Bay of Pigs on the southern coast. In 1962 the Soviet Union began to install nuclear missiles in Cuba. The resulting crisis with the United States brought the world close to war until the Soviets withdrew the weapons. Relations with the United States remained hostile well into the 1990s.

See Also: Cuban Missile Crisis.

■ **CUBAN IMMIGRANTS.** Most Cuban immigrants arrived in the United States after the Cuban revolution of 1959. A significant number, however, immigrated during the late-19th and early-20th centuries. In 1868, for example, political exiles fled war in Cuba for Key West, establishing South Florida as the primary destination for Cuban immigrants.

After Fidel Castro ascended to power in 1959 and imposed a communist government, many upper- and middle-class Cubans sought political exile in the United States, especially in Miami. They were followed over the years by Cubans of all classes, including those of the controversial Mariel boatlift of 1980, when Castro emptied many of his jails and allowed a large number of people to go to the United States. In all, the exodus between 1959 and 1980 brought some 800,000 Cubans to the United States.

Politically powerful and economically prosperous, Florida's Cuban community has made a significant impact on the politics and culture of South Florida.

See Also: *Ethnic Groups; Immigration.*

■ **CUBAN MISSILE CRISIS (1962),** the most serious crisis of the Cold War. In October 1962 the United States and the Soviet Union came "eyeball to eyeball," as then Sec. of State Dean Rusk put it. The crisis resulted from the placement in Cuba of surface-to-surface missiles capable of launching a nuclear strike against the United States. Soviet Premier Nikita S. Khrushchev was seeking to regain the strategic initiative in the Cold War after the United States stationed Jupiter missiles in Turkey; to show resolve in the Soviet dispute with Communist China; and to strengthen Cuban leader Fidel Castro, whom the United States hoped to remove from power.

The missiles were discovered by a U-2 reconnaissance plane on a routine flight in August over Cuban airspace, and their presence led, with barely three weeks before congressional elections, to calls within the national security bureaucracy for Pres. John F. Kennedy to respond militarily to the apparent provocation. The president assembled an advisory group known as ExComm (Executive Committee). Under-Sec. of State George Ball, supported by Atty. Gen. Robert F. Kennedy,

Pres. John F. Kennedy meets with military advisers, including Gen. Curt LeMay (*far right on couch*), during the Cuban Missile Crisis.

counseled caution. President Kennedy decided to impose a blockade to prevent the introduction of further offensive weapons into Cuba. He also publicly urged Khrushchev to remove, under UN supervision, missiles already in place.

The Soviet premier complied with Kennedy's demand but not until after he sent the president two letters. The first, dated October 26, elicited a response that would end the crisis: the United States promised not to invade Cuba. The other letter, to which the White House did not directly respond, demanded the removal of Jupiter missiles from Turkey. A private accord resulted in a U.S. promise to remove the missiles at a later date.

Resolution of the crisis helped the cause of arms control and further strained the Sino-Soviet relationship. It also contributed to Khrushchev's fall from power in October 1964. A remarkable series of meetings convened in the late 1980s, which brought together surviving participants of the crisis, bore out former Sec. of Defense Robert S. McNamara's warnings about the hazards of nuclear crisis management.

—WILLIAM O. WALKER III

See Also: *Cold War; Kennedy, John Fitzgerald; McNamara, Robert.*

BIBLIOGRAPHY: Blight, James G., and David A. Welch, *On the Brink: Americans and Soviets Reexamine the Cuban Missile Crisis* (Hill & Wang 1989); Nathan, James A., ed., *The Cuban Missile Crisis Revisited* (St. Martin's 1992).

■ **CUFFEE, PAUL (1759-1818),** shipping merchant. Born in Massachusetts, Cuffee opened his own shipping company in 1780. He attracted attention when he and his brother refused to pay taxes because, as blacks, they were denied the right to vote. As a result of his efforts, Massachusetts extended the franchise in 1783 to all free black men who were liable for taxes. Long a proponent of recolonization, Cuffee transported 38 blacks to Africa at his own expense in 1815.

See Also: *African Americans.*

■ **CULLEN, COUNTEE (1903-46),** poet, born Countee Porter in New York City. While still in college, Cullen published his first poetry collection, *Color* (1925). After receiving a degree from Harvard, he taught in the New York public school

system. Cullen wrote numerous works of poetry and fiction, the most noteworthy being *The Ballad of the Brown Girl* (1926), *One Way to Heaven* (1932), and *My Lives and How I Lost Them* (1942). Cullen's lyrical verse made him a leading voice in the New Negro Movement (Harlem Renaissance).

See Also: *African Americans; Harlem Renaissance.*

■ **CULTURAL PLURALISM,** term coined by the American philosopher Horace Kallen in 1924 to stand for his ideal of the United States as a "cooperation of cultural diversities, as a federation or commonwealth of national cultures." This has proved to be one of the most powerful and controversial ideas about the nature of American society. Traditionally, the more common ideal was that of assimilation, a model of acculturation that insisted on Anglo-American culture as the foundation of American values and institutions to which immigrants had to conform, giving up their old languages and customs. In the early 20th century, however, liberal thinkers began to argue for an appreciation of the positive contributions of cultural diversity to American life. Among the first advocates of cultural pluralism were the workers in the urban settlement houses, women such as Jane Addams, who took a stand against Americanization programs. The educator John Dewey was among the first to suggest that the teaching of American history "should take more account of the great waves of migration by which our land for over three centuries has been continuously built up."

Critics have argued that the concept of cultural pluralism—or its more contemporary articulation as "multiculturalism"—while contributing to a more accurate accounting of the diverse backgrounds of Americans, tends to undervalue those things Americans hold in common. The problem, writes Arthur M. Schlesinger, Jr., is "how to vindicate cherished cultures and traditions without breaking the bonds of cohesion—common ideals, common political institutions, common language, common culture, common fate—that hold the republic together."

See Also: *Acculturation; Assimilation; Ethnic Groups; Immigration; Melting Pot.*

BIBLIOGRAPHY: Gordon, Milton M., *Assimilation in American Life* (Oxford Univ. Press 1964);

Schlesinger, Arthur M., Jr., *The Disuniting of America* (Norton 1992).

■ **CULTURAL RELATIVISM,** anthropological theory, a central premise of anthropology that suggests that each culture possesses its own internal rationality and coherence in beliefs, practices, and customs. Its emphasis on inclusiveness and each individual culture's inherent complexity has also been used to counter proponents of racial superiority. Also referred to as cultural determinism, this fundamental theory was most clearly outlined by Franz Boas in *The Mind of Primitive Man* (1911). In this work he argued that primitive speech, language, and music, while different from Western European traditions, have their own complexities that are often misinterpreted by Western anthropologists. Boas formulated his ideas in response to 19th-century anthropologists, for example, Lucien Levy-Bruhl and James Frazer, who made universal claims about cultural traits that were frequently based on racist or culturally superior assumptions. Boas emphasized the differences, particularities, and context of each culture in relation to its specific historical circumstances. Later ethnographic writing took cultural relativism as a basic tenet in its attempts to catalog and convey non-Western cultures from an insider's (or emic) conceptualization. For example, Bronislaw Malinowski's *Argonauts of the Western Pacific* (1922) and *The Sexual Life of Savages* (1929) strived to reproduce "the native point of view" in order to make it accessible to the West. Cultural relativism has been criticized because its emphasis on one culture's particularity prevents cross-cultural comparisons and because it implies an inability to form moral or ethical positions about a culture's practices. Nevertheless, cultural relativism has remained a key principle of anthropological descriptions of a people's rituals, values, and symbols.

—M. JEFF HARDWICK

See Also: Boas, Franz.

BIBLIOGRAPHY: Boas, Franz, *The Mind of Primitive Man* (Macmillan 1911); Malinowski, Bronislaw, *The Sexual Life of Savages: An Ethnographic Account of Courtship, Marriage, and Family Life among the Natives of the Trobriand Islands, British New Guinea* (Harcourt Brace & World 1929); Torgovnick, Marianna, *Gone Primitive: Savage Intellects, Modern Lives* (Univ. of Chicago Press 1990).

■ **CUMBERLAND GAP,** natural pass through the western Appalachian Mountains. Located near the intersection of Kentucky, Virginia, and Tennessee, the 1,640-foot-high pass was cut into the mountains by a former stream. In 1750 the Englishman Thomas Walker explored the pass, and in 1769 Daniel Boone, with a group of five men, followed the trail of other hunters through the gap. During the 18th and 19th centuries the passage became the main thoroughfare of trans-Allegheny migration for trappers and farmers moving west. This westward migration extended the boundary of the original 13 colonies west to the Mississippi River. The gap was also of strategic importance during the Civil War and was alternately held by Union and Confederate troops. In 1940 some 20,000 acres of land surrounding the pass were established as the Cumberland Gap National Historical Park. Today U.S. route 58, known as the Boone Heritage Trail, runs through the pass.

See Also: Appalachian Mountains.

■ **CUMMINGS, E. E. (1894-1962),** modernist poet. Cummings was born in Cambridge, Massachusetts, and received his A.B. (1915) and M.A. (1916) from Harvard University. After spending time in Europe during and after World War I, he published his first volume of poetry, *Tulips and Chimneys*, in 1923. Cummings's poems are noted for their individualistic choices in matters usually considered fixed, such as spelling, grammar, and spacing, but often touch on traditional themes such as the importance of nature, beauty, and love.

See Also: Poetry.

■ **CUNNINGHAM, KATE O'HARE (1877-1948),** socialist organizer and lecturer, influential in the prison reform movement of the 1920s. She was born near Ada, Kansas. After being jailed in 1919 for her opposition to World War I, she published *In Prison* (1920) and conducted a national survey of prison labor (1924).

■ **CUNNINGHAM, MERCE (1922-),** dancer and choreographer. Born in Centralia, Washington, he was a member of Martha Graham's modern dance troupe (1940-45) before launching a solo career and starting his own dance company in 1955.

Known for his avant-garde works, which incorporated all forms of movement into dance, Cunningham often collaborated with composer John Cage and artist Robert Rauschenberg, who was the company's set and lighting director (1955-64).

■ **CURRENCY ACT (1764),** law passed by Parliament prohibiting the issuance of paper money in the American colonies. The act was designed to control rapid, intercolony inflation and to reduce a massive provincial debt in Virginia accrued during the French and Indian Wars (1754-63).

See Also: Revolution, American.

■ **CURRENCY ACT (1900),** legislation also known as the Gold Standard Act of 1900. It ended the monetary debate of the 1890s by making the gold dollar the monetary standard, setting its value at 25.8 grains of nine-tenths fine gold and setting up a $150 million gold reserve. The gold standard lasted until 1933.

■ **CURRIER AND IVES,** printmakers whose lithographs recorded 19th-century American scenes. Nathaniel Currier (1813-88), born in Roxbury, Massachusetts, founded a printmaking company in New York in 1835, and James Ives (1824-95), born in New York City, joined him in 1850. The Currier and Ives brand first appeared in 1857, and the company sold millions of colored lithographs featuring sentimental, idealized depictions of social, political, and sporting scenes.

■ **CURTIS, BENJAMIN ROBBINS (1809-74),** associate justice of the U.S. Supreme Court (1851-57). A Watertown, Massachusetts, native and abolitionist, Curtis dissented in the Dred Scott decision (1857), after which he resigned from the Court. Curtis represented Pres. Andrew Johnson during his impeachment trial (1867).

See Also: Dred Scott v. Sandford; Johnson, Andrew; Supreme Court.

■ **CURTIS, CHARLES BRENT (1860-1936),** vice president of the United States (1929-33). He was born in Topeka, Kansas, a descendant of Kansa-Kaw Indian people, attended local public schools, studied law, and began work as an attorney in 1881. In 1893 he was elected to the House of Representatives as a Republican, serving there until 1907, when he was appointed to a vacant seat in the U.S. Senate. Reelected for three full terms, Curtis left the Senate in 1928 when he was elected vice president under Herbert Hoover. Renominated by their party in 1932, both men were defeated in that year's presidential election.

See Also: Hoover, Herbert Clark; Vice President of the United States.

In 1850, Nathaniel Currier and James M. Ives became partners. Their lithography business did extremely well, selling prints of 19th-century American scenes.

CUSHING, CALEB (1800-79), American lawyer and diplomat. Born in Salisbury, Massachusetts, to a prominent family, he became a lawyer in Newburyport, Massachusetts. Cushing served (1835-43) in the U.S. House of Representatives, where, during early controversies over slavery, he upheld the established order, believing that the North had no constitutional right to interfere with slavery in the South. While he was U.S. envoy to China (1843-45), he negotiated the Treaty of Wanghia, which opened five Chinese ports to American trade. In 1860, after Abraham Lincoln's election, Cushing advocated making concessions to the South to save the Union. When Pres. Ulysses S. Grant nominated Cushing as chief justice of the United States in 1873, the nomination was defeated in the Senate. Grant then appointed him U.S. minister to Spain (1874-77).

CUSHING, HARVEY WILLIAMS (1869-1939), neurosurgeon. Born in Cleveland, Ohio, Cushing graduated from Harvard Medical School (1895), and earned a national reputation as a brilliant neurosurgeon while at Johns Hopkins (1901-1911). While surgeon in chief at Peter Bent Brigham Hospital in Boston and professor of surgery at Harvard Medical School (1912-32), he studied the pituitary gland and wartime brain injuries, discovered Cushing's disease (a disorder of the adrenal system), and won the Pulitzer Prize for his book on Dr. William Osler (1925). Cushing became a professor of neurology at Yale in 1933 and directed the history of medicine program.
See Also: Medicine.

CUSHING, WILLIAM (1732-1810), associate justice of the U.S. Supreme Court (1789-1810). A Scituate, Massachusetts, native, Justice Cushing was Pres. George Washington's first nominee to be associate justice. Cushing joined the majority in *Ware v. Hylton* (1796), which held that state statutes were constitutionally inferior to international treaties.
See Also: Supreme Court.

CUSHMAN, CHARLOTTE (1816-76), actress famed for her portrayals of Lady Macbeth. She was also noted for her frequent portrayal of male characters. Born in Boston, Massachusetts, she

moved from New York to England in 1844, where she was prima donna of the London stage until she retired in 1852.

CUSTER, GEORGE ARMSTRONG (1839-76), cavalry commander who led his troops to destruction and became one of the most admired—and despised—characters in American history. A rambunctious youth from a close Ohio family, Custer entered West Point in 1857 and graduated in 1861 at the bottom of his class. He was assigned to the Union cavalry and to the surprise of nearly everyone compiled one of the most impressive arrays of battle victories of the Civil War and was promoted brevet general at the age of 23. Although his men suffered enormous casualties, Custer inspired them with his daring and bravado. Making war was the first love of his life. "So far as my country is concerned, I of course must wish for peace," he wrote home in 1862,

A general in the Civil War, George Armstrong Custer later fought the Indians on the frontier. Confident enough to invite reporters along on his 1876 advance into Sioux territory, Custer proved no match for the thousands of Indian warriors at the Battle of Little Bighorn.

"but if I answer for myself alone, I must say that I shall regret to see the war end. I would be willing, yes glad, to see a battle every day during my life."

At the war's conclusion, Custer was assigned to the Seventh Cavalry as a lieutenant colonel. He was sent to the frontier, where indecisive engagements with elusive Indian enemies brought frustrations that led him to abuse his men and disobey his superiors. In 1867 he was court-martialed, convicted, and suspended for leaving his post to visit his wife, Elizabeth Bacon Custer, the second love of his life. When he was returned to service the following year, at the request of Gen. Philip Sheridan, Custer knew that only a decisive victory would clear his name. At the Washita River in Indian Territory (present-day Oklahoma) in November 1868, Custer got what he wanted: a victorious cavalry charge through a sleeping Cheyenne village that left 103 Indians dead, only 11 of them warriors, the rest "noncombatants." But most Americans applauded. Custer was once again a hero.

In 1874, Custer led a military expedition into the Black Hills of Dakota Territory. His announcement of a gold discovery there led to a mining rush that sparked a military confrontation with the Sioux, who had been guaranteed possession of the region by treaty. Two years later, in June 1876, as part of the military campaign against the Sioux and their Cheyenne allies, Custer led his Seventh Cavalry in an attack against a large encampment. In a fatal mistake, he divided his forces, only to be met by angry warriors who outnumbered the cavalrymen by 15 to 1. In the most famous military engagement in American history, Custer and his men were annihilated in the Battle of Little Bighorn. The national shock at the fact that white soldiers could be overwhelmed by Indians led to the myth of "the Last Stand." Elizabeth Custer, who outlived her husband by 57 years, was one of the primary mythmakers, retelling his story in three immensely popular books of reminiscence.

See Also: *Frontier in American History; Little Bighorn, Battle of.*

BIBLIOGRAPHY: Barnett, Louise, *Touched by Fire: The Life, Death, and Mythic Afterlife of George Armstrong Custer* (Henry Holt 1996); Connell, Evan S., *Son of the Morning Star* (North Point Press 1984).

D

DALL, CAROLINE HEALY (1822-1912), author and social reformer born in Boston, Massachusetts. An outspoken proponent of women's rights, she wrote *The College, the Market, and the Court; or Woman's Relation to Education, Labor, and Law* (1867).

DALLAS, GEORGE MIFFLIN (1792-1864), American diplomat and vice president of the United States (1845-49). Born into a prominent Philadelphia family, he was educated in law at Princeton University. He was counsel to the Second Bank of the United States (1815-17), a position that caused him some difficulty because of his support for bank opponent Andrew Jackson. Soon a prominent Democrat, Dallas served in the U.S. Senate (1831-33) and as Pres. Martin Van Buren's minister to Russia (1837-39). In 1845 Dallas was elected as James Polk's vice president. He then served as minister to Great Britain (1856-61) under Presidents Franklin Pierce and James Buchanan. His public career, as a northern Democrat, ended with the Civil War. The city of Dallas, Texas, is named for him.

DALLAS, city in northeastern Texas, on the Trinity River. Dallas began when John Neele Bryan settled in the 1840s on the banks of the Trinity River to begin trading with the people of the native Caddo tribe. In the early 1870s, when two railroads arrived, Dallas began to grow as a commercial center and was incorporated as a city in 1871. By 1890 Dallas surpassed Galveston as the largest city in Texas, with 38,000 residents. The city's trade focused on cotton, wheat, wool, sheep, and cattle. The East Texas oil boom of the 1920s and 1930s boosted Dallas's economy immensely. Between 1940 and 1970 the city's economic base expanded and diversified rapidly, especially in defense-related industries. By the early 1970s the Dallas metropolitan area had a population of more than 1.5 million. On Nov. 22, 1963, the city acquired unwanted notoriety when Pres. John F. Kennedy was assassinated there while riding in a motorcade. During the 1970s and 1980s, the Dallas-Ft. Worth area continued to grow by leaps and bounds and came to epitomize many of Americans' fantasies about wealth and prosperity, an image reinforced by the extremely popular 1980s television series "Dallas". Population (1994): 1,022,830.

See Also: City in American History; Texas.

DANA, CHARLES A. (1819-97), editor. Dana was born in Hinsdale, New Hampshire. From 1841 to 1846 he lived at the Brook Farm community with Nathaniel Hawthorne and Margaret Fuller. Dana did editorial work for the *New York Tribune* from 1847 to 1862 and during this time also edited the *New American Cyclopedia* (16 vols., 1858-63) with George Ripley. He served as assistant secretary of war during the last years of the Civil War (1864-65). From 1868 until his death in 1897, Dana owned and edited the *New York Sun*.

DANA, RICHARD HENRY (1815-82), naval adventure writer. A native of Cambridge, Massachusetts, Dana began his adult life as a sailor. He left Boston in 1834 on a brig and sailed around Cape Horn to California. He recounted his experiences on the voyage in *Two Years before the Mast*, a popular adventure novel published in 1840. That same year Dana was admitted to the bar and began practicing, often representing sailors. Dana wrote *The Seaman's Friend* (1841), a treatise advocating sailors' rights.

DANIEL, PETER VIVIAN (1784-1860), associate justice of the U.S. Supreme Court (1841-60). A Virginia native, Daniel consistently opposed what he viewed as the runaway expansion of federal power. He joined the Court's majority in the *Dred Scott* decision (1857).

See Also: Dred Scott v. *Sandford, Supreme Court.*

■ **DARE, VIRGINIA (b. 1587),** born in Roanoke, Virginia, the first child born to British colonists in the New World. Her grandfather Gov. John White sailed to England three days after Dare's birth. When he returned in 1590, she and the other settlers on Roanoke Island had mysteriously disappeared.

See Also: *Frontier in American History.*

■ **DARRAGH, LYDIA BARRINGTON (1729-89),** nurse and midwife, folk-heroine of the American Revolutionary War. She was born in Ireland and immigrated to Philadelphia after her marriage in 1753. According to legend, after overhearing British officers planning an attack, she risked her life on Dec. 4, 1777, to cross British lines and warn American troops camped outside Philadelphia.

■ **DARROW, CLARENCE (1857-1938),** lawyer and reformer. A skilled and passionate trial lawyer, Darrow was born in Kinsman, Ohio, and educated at Allegheny College and the University of Michigan Law School. After passing the bar in 1878, he practiced law in Ohio and in 1887

Clarence Darrow's most famous courtroom moments occurred during the Scopes Trial in 1925, while he cross-examined the legendary William Jennings Bryan as an expert on the Bible.

moved to Chicago. While representing the Chicago and North West Railroad against the striking American Railway Union and its leader Eugene V. Debs in 1894, Darrow came to sympathize with the labor movement and quit his job to represent Debs. He became a staunch advocate of the less fortunate, especially in cases of labor versus big business. Darrow fell out of favor with labor unions and socialists, however, when in 1911 he entered a plea of guilty for two labor leaders who were charged with bombing the offices of the *Los Angeles Times.*

Upon returning to Chicago, Darrow became a national figure for his work in spectacular criminal trials. In 1924, he defended Nathan Leopold and Richard Loeb for the murder of young Bobbie Franks. His introduction of psychiatric evidence and a stirring plea for mercy won the defendants life in prison instead of the death penalty. A year later, in the famous Scopes "monkey" trial, Darrow defended a Tennessee school teacher who had violated a ban on teaching evolution. Late in life Darrow turned to lecturing and writing about legal and social issues, but to the end he remained an equivocal skeptic.

See Also: *Debs, Eugene V.; Scopes Trial.*
BIBLIOGRAPHY: Livingston, John Charles, *Clarence Darrow: The Mind of a Sentimental* (Garland 1979); Tierney, Kevin, *Darrow: A Biography* (Crowell 1979).

■ **DARTMOUTH, LORD (1731-1801),** British politician. Born in London, Dartmouth, the stepbrother of Lord North, the British prime minister, served as secretary of state to the American colonies (1772-75), consistently upholding parliamentary authority during his tenure. Shortly after the outbreak of the American Revolution he returned to England and became lord privy seal.

See Also: *Revolution, American.*

■ **DARTMOUTH COLLEGE CASE (1819),** U.S. Supreme Court case and a watershed moment in the history of American corporate and property law. In 1816 the New Hampshire state legislature had canceled Dartmouth College's colonial charter, adopting a new charter and installing a new board of trustees. Taking their case to the Supreme Court, the school's original trustees sued, seeking the restoration of the original board and the original charter. Daniel Webster represented the original trustees of his beloved alma mater before the Court. In a 5-1 decision, the Court sided with Webster and the original trustees. Writing for the majority, Chief Justice John Marshall held that under the Constitution's contract clause, the original charter was as binding on the state of New Hampshire as it previously had been on colonial authorities. According to this reasoning, a corporation originally might owe its existence to a legislative charter, a public act, but once that charter was granted, it became tantamount to a private contract and the corporation was shielded from public interference. In dissolving the old board and voiding the old charter, New Hampshire had acted unconstitutionally, for it had broken its contract, albeit an inherited contract, with the original trustees of the college. By this decision the contract clause entered American jurisprudence as the ultimate constitutional safeguard of private property rights.

—MATTHEW E. BABCOCK

See Also: *Marshall, John; Supreme Court; Webster, Daniel.*

BIBLIOGRAPHY: Sites, Francis N., *Private Interests and Public Gain: The Dartmouth College Case, 1819* (Univ. of Massachusetts Press 1972).

▪ **DARWINISM,** concept of evolution developed by Charles Darwin in the 19th century. Darwinism describes the theory of natural selection, or the view that in nature there is inherent competition that leads to evolutionary change. Darwinism, while not technically synonymous with evolution, describes a mechanism for the process of evolution. It has had extensive effects on American science, American society, and Christianity in America.

When Englishman Charles Darwin published his theory of natural selection *On the Origin of Species* in 1859, Americans were distracted by the growing division between North and South and the likelihood of civil war. Nonetheless, some of the country's foremost scholars, in particular Harvard botanist Asa Gray and Harvard zoologist Louis Agassiz, read the work and realized that intellectual conflict likely would follow. These two men became the most visible example of the struggle over Darwinism in America, Gray as the supporter of Darwinism and Agassiz as its opponent. Gray and Darwinians credited the theory's explanatory force, but others, including Agassiz, believed it had minimal value, leaving many questions unanswered while at the same time raising a serious threat to traditional Christianity.

As a scientific theory, Darwinism has not always been received favorably by American scientists, as Agassiz's reservations in the late 19th century demonstrate. During the early 20th century, several other hypotheses about the mechanisms of evolution gained influence, and the fortunes of Darwinism waned. However, by about 1920, thanks in large part to Columbia University scientist Thomas Hunt Morgan and his colleagues who proved the existence of genetic material in the form of chromosomes, Darwinism gained greater acceptance in the scientific community. The existence of genes bolstered Darwin's theory by helping to illustrate that traits of living beings were inherited by way of hereditary material. As scientists developed a complex understanding of the way genes interact and realized that many genes contributed to the development of one trait, they realized that much of the diversity of the natural world could be accounted for by way of Darwinian natural selection.

Impact on Religion. One of the most far-reaching effects of Darwinism in America has been its impact on religion. For many, Darwinism threatened the traditional vision of the world under the direction of a caring and involved God, since nature and natural processes, seemingly acting at random, controlled the development of the earth. This interpretation led some to modernize their religious views to account for evolution, while others rejected evolutionary theory in general and Darwin specifically. In the early 20th century this reaction culminated in the development of Christian fundamentalism. The clash between "fundamentalists" and "modernists" reached its apex in the Scopes trial in 1925, in which biology teacher John Scopes was prosecuted for violating Tennessee's law against teaching that man had developed from another animal. The "great monkey trial" was for many a mockery of traditional religion and seemingly aided the success of Darwinism and lowered the fortunes of fundamental Christianity in America.

Still, since the Scopes trial, other states, including Arkansas and Louisiana, have continued to pass laws restricting the teaching of evolution within state schools.

Social Darwinism. Social Darwinism also developed in the wake of the publication of the theory of natural selection. Widely publicized by the British philosopher Herbert Spencer, who coined the phrase "the survival of the fittest," social Darwinism advocated social and economic struggle as the means to the best and most efficient society and economy. This mind-set contributed to an often brutal form of laissez-faire views of social and economic life in the increasingly industrial and urban America of the late 19th and early 20th centuries.

—KATHY J. COOKE

See Also: *Religion; Science; Scopes Trial.*

BIBLIOGRAPHY: Bowler, Peter J., *Darwinism* (Twayne 1993); Himmelfarb, Gertrude, *Darwin and the Darwinian Revolution* (Norton 1962); Hofstadter, Richard, *Social Darwinism in American Thought* (Beacon Press 1955); Russett, Cynthia Eagle, *Darwin in America: The Intellectual Response, 1865-1912* (Freeman 1976).

■ **DAUGHTERS OF THE AMERICAN REVOLUTION,** a patriotic society founded in Washington, D.C., in 1890. Membership is open only to females who are direct descendants of those who fought in the American Revolution.

■ **DAVIS, ALEXANDER JACKSON (1803-92),** architect of public buildings, most famous for the "carpenter Gothic" rural house design he helped to establish. Davis was born in New York City. In 1829 he started the architectural firm of Town and Davis with Ithiel Town; the pair designed the Indiana state capitol (1831-35) and the Illinois state capitol (1837-41). In 1843 Davis established his own firm; notable buildings built by this firm include the Assembly Hall at the University of North Carolina at Chapel Hill (1844) and buildings for the Virginia Military Institute in Lexington (1852-59).

See Also: *Architecture.*

■ **DAVIS, ANGELA (1944-),** intellectual and political activist. Born in Birmingham, Alabama, she became known for her commitment to Marxism, feminism, and African-American liberation. She authored *Women, Race, and Class* (1981) and was the vice presidential candidate for the American Communist party in 1980.

■ **DAVIS, BENJAMIN OLIVER, JR. (1912-),** military officer, the first African American to achieve (1954) the rank of general in the U.S. Air Force. Born in Washington, D.C., he graduated from West Point in 1936. In 1941, he joined the Tuskegee Airmen, a group of African-American pilots that became (1942) the 99th Pursuit Squadron with Davis as its leader. After World War II he commanded Lockbourne Army Air Base, where he became noted for his programs that successfully combated racial discrimination. Davis served as deputy commander of Strike Force before retiring as a lieutenant general in 1970.

■ **DAVIS, DAVID (1815-86),** associate justice of the U.S. Supreme Court (1862-77) and U.S. senator (1877-83). A Cecil County, Maryland, native, Davis distinguished himself on the Court as a fierce defender of civil liberties, notably in his *Ex parte Milligan* opinion (1866), which held that the imposition of martial law was unconstitutional unless open insurrection existed. Where economic regulation was

Lt. Col. Benjamin O. Davis, Jr., the son of an army general, briefs pilots before a mission in Italy in World War II. He rose to the rank of lieutenant general.

concerned, Davis was considerably less leery of a strong federal government. He ran for president as the Labor Reform party's candidate in 1872 and served one term in the Senate as a Democrat.

See Also: Ex parte Milligan; Supreme Court.

■ **DAVIS, JEFFERSON (1808-89),** U.S. congressman and senator, secretary of war, and only president of the Confederate States of America. Born in Todd County, Kentucky, only about 30 miles from the birthplace of Abraham Lincoln, Davis was educated as a soldier. He graduated from West Point in 1828 and served in the Black Hawk War four years later. He resigned his commission in 1835 to marry Zachary Taylor's daughter, who died within months of their wedding.

Distraught, Davis retired to his Mississippi plantation and assumed the life of a gentleman planter. His marriage to Varina Howell in 1845 heralded his entry into public life as a Democratic congressman. He left Congress in 1846 to command a Mississippi regiment in the Mexican War, where he was wounded at Buena Vista. His two terms as U.S. senator (1847-51; 1857-61) were both cut short. In 1851, he resigned to run for governor of Mississippi and was narrowly defeated by Henry S. Foote. He then served as secretary of war in Pres. Franklin Pierce's cabinet (1853-57) before returning to the Senate to become one of the foremost advocates of slavery and Southern rights.

Confederate President. He again resigned from the Senate when Mississippi seceded from the Union. Elected provisional president of the newly formed Confederacy by the convention of Southern states in Montgomery, Alabama, in February 1861, he was popularly elected the following November and inaugurated in Richmond, Virginia, for a full six-year term on Feb. 22, 1862. He presided over a nation at war throughout its existence, and he solved few of its many financial, military, diplomatic, and internal political problems. After the South's defeat at Gettysburg in July 1863, Davis had to contend with a growing host of Confederate critics and peace advocates.

Captured by Union troops near Irwinville, Georgia, in May 1865 after fleeing Richmond, Davis spent the next two years in prison at Fortress Monroe, Virginia. Although he was indicted for treason, the federal government never

As a "cotton nabob," or newly rich slaveholder in Mississippi, Jefferson Davis was not embraced by the South's older plantation aristocracy. His social position, as well as his autocratic methods, hindered Davis's ability to lead and hold the Confederacy together.

brought him to trial.

Davis spent the remaining years of his life at his Beauvoir estate near Biloxi, Mississippi, where he wrote *The Rise and Fall of the Confederate Government* (1878-81) and steadily rose to demigod status in Southern esteem.

—THOMAS E. SCHOTT

See Also: Civil War; Confederate States of America; Stephens, Alexander H.

BIBLIOGRAPHY: Davis, William C., *Jefferson Davis: The Man and His Hour* (HarperCollins 1991).

■ **DAVIS, MILES DEWEY, III (1926-91),** jazz trumpeter. Born in Alton, Illinois, Davis was presented a trumpet by his father at the age of 13. He excelled at music and began sitting in with professional bands like Billy Eckstein's as they passed through town. In 1945 he attended the

Juilliard School of Music in New York City and while there cemented relationships with the musical notables of his day. Davis sat with various bands and in 1949 created a studio group of his own. In these sessions Davis's subtle and quiet performances introduced the "cool" style of jazz, a departure from the more boisterous be-bop. Davis continued to innovate, first with modal improvisation and orchestral works in the 1960s and then in the 1970s with a shift to electric and edgy, rhythmically intensive compositions. Although at times confusing to his critics, Davis never stopped reaching beyond what was successful to find new directions in music.

See Also: African Americans; Jazz.

BIBLIOGRAPHY: Carr, Ian, *Miles Davis: A Critical Biography* (Quartet Books 1982); Feather, Leonard, *The Encyclopedia of Jazz* (Horizon Press 1960).

■ **DAVISSON, CLINTON (1881-1958),** physicist. Born in Bloomington, Illinois, Davisson studied at the University of Chicago and Princeton (Ph.D., 1908), taught at the Carnegie Institute of Technology (1911-17), and worked at the Bell Telephone Laboratories in New York City (1917-46). Davisson discovered (1927) that electrons could behave as waves as well as particles. For this, he shared the 1937 Nobel Prize in Physics with George P. Thompson. As a professor at the University of Virginia (1946-54), he continued research on electron optics, thereby contributing to the development of the electron microscope.

See Also: Science.

■ **DAWES, CHARLES GATES (1865-1951),** vice president of the United States (1925-29). He was born in Marietta, Ohio. He attended college there and then went on to the Cincinnati Law School. He had a law practice in Nebraska before moving in 1894 to Evanston, Illinois, where he went into banking. He was comptroller of the currency in the U.S. Treasury Department from 1897 to 1901. After leaving the Treasury, Dawes founded and served as president of the Central Trust Company of Illinois, based in Chicago. When the United States entered World War I, he became chief of supply procurement for the American Expeditionary Force, retiring with the rank of brigadier general. Appointed chairman of the Allied Repa-rations Commission (1923-24), he coauthored the Dawes Plan, which established the reparations that Germany was to pay to the Allies. In 1924 Dawes was elected vice president under Republican Calvin Coolidge.

See Also: Vice President of the United States; World War I.

BIBLIOGRAPHY: Timmons, Bascom N., *Portrait of an American: Charles G. Dawes* (Holt 1953).

■ **DAWES ACT.** *See: General Allotment Act (Dawes Act).*

■ **DAWES PLAN (1924),** proposition to settle the post–World War I European reparations question. The plan designed by Chicago banker Charles G. Dawes reorganized the German Reichsbank under Allied supervision in order to stabilize German currency. Germany also received a $200-million loan from American and European investors. Germany was to pay its reparations to the Allies gradually, starting from $250 million in 1925; later, the quota of payments would increase as the country's economy improved.

See Also: World War I.

■ **DAY, WILLIAM RUFUS (1849-1923),** jurist and diplomat. Born in Ravenna, Ohio, he was secretary of state (1898) and led the U.S. delegation in peace talks with Spain (1898-99) to end the Spanish-American War. Day later became an associate justice of the Supreme Court (1903-22).

See Also: Supreme Court.

■ **D-DAY (June 6, 1944),** term for the Allied invasion of Normandy in German-occupied France during World War II. Plans for an invasion of Europe had been discussed by the Allies since 1942, but because of logistical difficulties and the sheer magnitude of the undertaking, which was called Operation Overlord, the projected invasion was repeatedly delayed. Gen. Dwight D. Eisenhower was chosen to command Overlord, and from his headquarters in London he assembled a titanic armada. Because of the severe tides in the landing area and the unpredictability of the weather, the landings could only be made on a few days out of the year. The invasion was scheduled to go off on June 5, but an unexpected storm moving into the

Under the command of Gen. Dwight Eisenhower, Allied forces invaded Normandy in France on June 6, 1944. The World War II assault, given the code word D-Day, was history's largest amphibious action.

English Channel caused it to be postponed for one day. Airborne forces were dropped that night, followed by the amphibious landings early on the morning of June 6. American troops were to seize Utah Beach, which was relatively lightly defended, and Omaha Beach, where they met fierce German resistance. British troops had the somewhat less difficult targets of Gold, Juno, and Sword beaches. The daring assault succeeded in no small part because of German bungling at the command level, and by June 12, the Allied beachheads were consolidated. Although the war would continue for nearly another year, the successful landings on D-Day spelled doom for the Nazi empire.

—STEVE O'BRIEN

See Also: World War II.

BIBLIOGRAPHY: Ambrose, Stephen E., *D-Day June 6, 1944: The Climactic Battle of World War II* (Simon & Schuster 1994); Morrison, Samuel Eliot, *The Invasion of France and Germany, 1944-1945* (Little, Brown 1959); Ryan, Cornelius, *The Longest Day: The Classic Epic of D-Day, June 6, 1944* (Simon & Schuster 1959).

■ **DEANE, SILAS (1737-89),** Revolutionary War diplomat and politician. An early supporter of the Revolution and a colonial political leader, Deane was born in Groton, Connecticut. In 1776 he became America's first foreign diplomat and helped orchestrate a treaty of alliance with France in 1778. He was recalled, however, after suspicions arose about his involvement with a British spy.

Deane responded by denouncing the war in letters to British friends and fled the country after they were published in a colonial newspaper.

See Also: Revolution, American.

■ **DEATH VALLEY,** deep, arid depression of land in southeastern California. East of the Sierra Nevada Mountains, this desert is some 140 miles long and from 5 to 15 miles wide and forms the southwestern part of the Great Basin. As the hottest and driest part of North America, Death Valley presented a significant and often lethal barrier to settlers traveling west. In 1933 the land was declared a national monument. Despite its extreme environment (up to 134 degrees Fahrenheit in summer) it still attracts many tourists.

See Also: Great Basin.

■ **DEBS, EUGENE V. (1855-1926),** revered socialist and frequent presidential candidate, the preeminent social activist of the late 19th and early 20th centuries.

Named after novelists Victor Hugo and Eugene Sue, Debs was born to French parents in Terre Haute, Indiana, where his father operated a small grocery store. He left school to become a railwayman and joined the Brotherhood of Locomotive Firemen. Rising to editor of the brotherhood's national journal, he responded at first to the transformation of the work atmosphere by urging more cooperation between labor and capital. The increasingly autocratic behavior of corporations and the intense suffering of the impoverished during the 1890s depression turned Debs toward appealing for the solidarity of all working people. Denounced in the press as "King Debs," he led the Pullman Strike, a nationwide action in 1894 by the new American Railway Union in defense of locomotive workers in company-owned Pullman, Illinois. Jailed for his efforts, Debs emerged from prison a socialist.

At the turn of the century, Debs became a founder of the new Socialist party of America. He toured the nation incessantly for lecture engagements and meetings. In 1905 he became one of the leaders of the new Industrial Workers of the World. In the 1912 presidential campaign, Debs won nearly 1 million votes (many more, it was said, were "counted out") and promised a dawn of universal brotherhood.

The approach of World War I ended his upward climb. Declared an enemy of the state by the U.S. government, Debs was arrested and imprisoned in 1918 for speaking against U.S. participation in a European conflict. While in the Atlanta Penitentiary, he received more than 900,000 votes for president in 1920. In 1921 he emerged from

After spending six months in jail for his involvement in the 1894 Pullman Strike, labor leader Eugene V. Debs became a convert to socialism and founded the Social Democratic party.

jail a physically broken man, unable to piece back together a fragmented radical movement.

—PAUL BUHLE

See Also: *Labor Movement; Pullman Strike; Socialist Party.*

BIBLIOGRAPHY: Ginger, Ray, *The Bending Cross: A Biography of Eugene Victor Debs* (Rutgers Univ. Press 1949); Salvatore, Nick, *Eugene V. Debs: Citizen and Socialist* (Univ. of Illinois Press 1982).

■ **DECATUR, STEPHEN (1779-1820),** U.S. naval officer. Born in Sinepuxent, Maryland, to a naval family, Decatur was commissioned in 1798. He acquired a reputation for foolhardy bravery by sneaking into the harbor of Tripoli and destroying the captured U.S. frigate *Philadelphia* (1804). A successful captain in the War of 1812, Decatur returned to North Africa in 1815 to force the submission of the hostile ruler of Algiers. His particular brand of patriotism is recalled by his frequent toast, "Our country, right or wrong!"

See Also: *War of 1812.*

■ **DECLARATION OF INDEPENDENCE (1776),** document embodying the American colonists' proclamation of independence from English rule. Only the U.S. Constitution (1787) and Abraham Lincoln's Gettysburg Address (1863) rival the Declaration of Independence as revered American documents. Yet the Declaration was profoundly ambiguous at the time of its production. It remains so now.

Four others joined Thomas Jefferson of Virginia on the committee that the Continental Congress appointed on June 11, 1776, to prepare a declaration separating the 13 American colonies from Britain. They were John Adams (Massachusetts), Roger Sherman (Connecticut), Robert R. Livingston (New York), and Benjamin Franklin (Pennsylvania). Adams and Sherman betokened the centrality of New England in the whole confrontation with Britain. Franklin and especially Livingston showed Congress's need to address the doubts felt in the "middle" colonies. Jefferson stood for white Virginia's role as New England's prime ally. All agreed with Adams's aesthetic judgment that, among them, Jefferson wrote best, and with Adams's political judgment that "a Virginian ought to be at the head of this business."

Strictly, the Declaration explains American independence rather than establishes it. That task was done by a simple resolution "that these United Colonies are and of right ought to be free and independent states," which Richard Henry Lee of Virginia proposed on June 7, 1776. Congress accepted the resolution on July 2. On what date Jefferson submitted his draft to the committee is unknown, but the committee turned in its revised text to Congress on June 28. In principle, then, three separate versions of the Declaration need understanding: what Jefferson wrote, how the committee revised it, and what Congress finally adopted on July 4. Signing took the rest of the summer.

All the versions break into several parts. In the final version, the first sentence asserts that Americans have become "one people" who find it necessary "to separate the political bonds that have connected them with another." A long debate had taken place about the terms of being British in America. Now the debate was over: the Americans were British no more, and the difficulties British identity had posed no longer applied.

Next comes a general statement of the right of revolution, if extreme need provokes it. What the declaration considers to be the causes of the American Revolution follow. They take the form of an extended bill of indictment against King George III. Together, the Declaration argues, the charges show his "history of abuses and usurpations, all having in direct object the establishment of an absolute tyranny over these states," as a "candid world" could see. Then comes the statement of separation, which follows Lee's original motion, with the additional assertion that "these states" could undertake all actions "which Independent States may of right do." That may be read as saying that each state acquired separate independence. But the preamble's assertion that "one people" was at work suggests that the whole United States was assuming "among the powers of the earth, the separate and equal station to which the Laws of Nature and of Nature's God entitle them."

Philosophy of the Declaration. What Jefferson wrote, what the committee presented, and what Congress adopted differ in many respects. One difference may be philosophical. Scholars have long accepted that the Declaration is a statement of the political theory of the 17th-century English writer John Locke. Locke's "life, liberty, and property" turned into the Declaration's "life, liberty, and the pursuit of happiness." Locke's emphasis on the primacy of individuals, rather than of society, runs through the whole process of writing and revising the document. Yet historian Garry Wills sees it otherwise. Whatever Congress adopted, he writes, Jefferson's declaration drew not on Locke but on the Scottish Enlightenment, whose thinkers emphasized the primacy of communities acting together rather than those of individuals acting separately.

To late-20th-century eyes, the most striking change between Jefferson's draft and the final version comes at the end of the charges against the king. Jefferson had no absolute proof of the king's evil intent, so like a good prosecutor, he constructed his case from many pieces of evidence. In Jefferson's phrasing, the longest of these charges accused the king of foisting slavery on unwilling colonists, frustrating their efforts to end the African slave trade, and then encouraging the slaves to revolt. Among these counts, the second and the third did ring true. But to blame slavery on King George was silly, and colonial efforts to choke the African trade had been made in slave owners' self-interest. The Declaration recognized that slavery was becoming a moral and political problem, but the recognition was steeped in uncertainty. Throughout the passage, Jefferson's normal cool prose yielded to heated rhetoric and typographical tricks: the king "has waged cruel war against . . . the persons of a distant people who never offended him . . . [he has been] *determined to keep open a market where MEN should be bought and sold* . . . he is now exciting those very people . . . to purchase that liberty of which he has deprived them, by murdering the people upon whom he has also obtruded them." In effect, as Wills notes, the charge came down to the king encouraging the slaves to find their own freedom by siding with him against the white American rebels. Congress dropped the whole passage, except for one faint allusion. Even that drew scathing British criticism.

Did the charges form a true bill? If so, the king deserved to be dismissed. If not, loyalism was appropriate, and many colonials chose it. In the summer of 1776 prominent people and obscure ones debated the question. Communities, friendships, and even marriages came apart because of differing views. Behind this problem lurked other issues. Jefferson, the committee, and Congress all accepted the essential premise, which was that Americans and Britons were not one people. Their connection to Britain had been only their common allegiance to a Crown that each separate polity accepted on its own terms. That is why after a decade of intense legalistic argument about what powers Parliament might wield over the colonies, the Declaration does not mention Parliament at all and blames the entire crisis on the king.

The Declaration was addressed to powerful readers overseas as well as to Americans. When Congress appointed the drafting committee, it also authorized exploring relations with possible European allies, especially France. Clandestine support already was flowing, based on no more than French resentment of the great defeat at British hands in 1763 that ended the colonial-era wars. Courting the French was why the Declaration went no further than asserting the perfidy of "the present king of Great Britain." It did not condemn monarchy itself, lest it offend King Louis XVI.

Yet there was no question of continuing monarchy within the United States, as the British had done when they replaced James II with William and Mary in 1688. However restrained the Declaration on the subject of monarchy, the other great American statement of 1776 was Thomas Paine's January pamphlet, *Common Sense*, which stridently asserted that monarchy was the root of public evil and that republicanism was the only desirable form of government. Paine's point agreed with Jefferson's personal thought: even if monarchy did exist, its justification only could be the "people's" choice to have it. This had been Jefferson's position since his *Summary View of the Rights of British America* in 1774. By 1776 Congress agreed. As early as May, it authorized the suppression of all government emanating from the king, to be replaced by authority derived from general consent.

Sovereignty of the People. Unspoken, then, but powerful in its silence, lay the Declaration's fundamental change. Sovereignty, the ultimate, unchallengeable authority, did not hover over a people who were subject to it, personified in a king who could do no wrong. Instead, sovereignty belonged to citizens, who somehow could cohere, know their collective mind, and act in their own interests. It was not a new idea: republicanism had more than two millennia of history by 1776, although much of that history seemed to discredit the whole idea, as self-rule turned into chaos and military tyrants took control. Jefferson himself thought only that he was summing up what most of his fellows had come to think after more than a decade of British policies that worked against American self-control and well-being. But he and Congress did assert the "self-evident" truth that "all men are created equal, that they are endowed by their Creator with certain unalienable rights [and] that among these are life, liberty, and the pursuit of happiness."

Virtually nobody in white Colonial America had assumed any such truth. On the contrary, they had ordered their lives and made sense of themselves around the assumption that humans are not inherently equal at all. Precisely what the Declaration's authors meant by their assertion remains unclear. Perhaps it was no more than the collective equality of Americans, as a people, with Britons, who were a separate people with no claim to rule over them.

Yet the Declaration's actual language of liberty and equality remained open, and anybody at all could claim it, even then. That may be why it has been honored by imitation ever since.

—EDWARD COUNTRYMAN

See Also: *Colonial Government; Continental Congresses; Jefferson, Thomas; Revolution, American; Thirteen Colonies.*

BIBLIOGRAPHY: Becker, Carl, *The Declaration of Independence: A Study in the History of Political Ideas* (Knopf 1922); Bridenbaugh, Carl, *The Spirit of '76: The Growth of American Patriotism Before Independence* (Oxford Univ. Press 1975); Maier, Pauline, *Making the Declaration of Independence* (Knopf 1997); Wills, Garry, *Inventing America: Jefferson's Declaration of Independence* (Random House 1978).

■ **DECLARATION OF RIGHTS (1776),** statement passed by the Virginia Convention at the outset of the American Revolution declaring individual liberty for Americans. The declaration, drafted mainly by George Mason as tensions with Britain mounted, influenced other state constitutions and the U.S. Bill of Rights.

See Also: Revolution, American.

■ **DECLARATION OF RIGHTS AND GRIEVANCES (1765),** colonial proclamation that denounced the Stamp Act passed by Parliament as unconstitutional. Drafted primarily by John Dickinson and passed by the Stamp Act Congress, the declaration argued that the American colonists had the same rights as the king's subjects in England and therefore deserved equal representation.

See Also: Revolution, American; Stamp Act.

■ **DECLARATORY ACT (1766),** law enacted by Parliament in response to colonial opposition in America to taxation. It repealed the Stamp Act (1765) but asserted Parliament's right to make laws and statutes binding in the colonies "in all cases whatsoever."

See Also: Revolution, American; Stamp Act.

■ **DEERE, JOHN (1804-1886),** inventor and manufacturer of the steel plow. Born in Rutland, Vermont, Deere worked as a blacksmith and moved to Illinois in 1837. Iron and wood plows from the east worked poorly in the tough, sticky prairie soil; Deere designed a steel plow that cut and turned the soil much more easily. He started to manufacture them in the 1840s and by 1857 was producing 10,000 plows a year. This plow, part of the first American agricultural revolution, opened the prairie and the Great Plains to cultivation. In 1868, Deere incorporated and produced farming implements until he died.

See Also: Agriculture; Industrial Revolution.

■ **DEFENSE, DEPARTMENT OF,** cabinet department of the U.S. government in charge of the military. Established by Congress (1947) as the National Military Establishment and renamed the Department of Defense (1949), it was created to coordinate the activities of the armed forces. Headquartered in the immense Pentagon building, across the Potomac River from Washington, D.C., the Defense Department absorbed the War Department, created in 1789, the Navy Department, created in 1798, and the Air Force, created

as an independent service in 1947. The agency was established in response to long-standing interservice rivalries that had flared anew during World War II and to coordinate U.S. military activities in light of the development of atomic weapons and the emerging Cold War with the Soviet Union. Thanks to the postwar military buildup, the department quickly became the largest and most expensive government agency and the focus of what Pres. Dwight D. Eisenhower in 1961 called "the military-industrial complex."

See Also: Cabinet; War, Department of.

■ **DE FOREST, LEE (1873-1961),** inventor, frequently called the "father of radio." Born in Council Bluffs, Iowa, he studied at Yale (Ph.D., 1899) and invented a responder to transmit radio waves (1902) while working for the Western Electric Company in Chicago. He formed the De Forest Wireless Telegraph Company (1902) but proved a better inventor than businessman. Fired by the directors in 1905, De Forest went on to invent the audion, or triode vacuum tube, the next year. Although he never realized its significance, the triode proved essential to radio and the electronics industry. De Forest used it to build a radio transmitter in 1912 that made international telephony possible, selling long-distance telephony rights to the American Telephone and Telegraph Company in 1913 and radio signaling rights for the triode in 1914. He then turned to motion pictures and developed the first commercial talking picture in 1923. De Forest's prickly personality led him frequently to patent litigation, and he decided late in life to concentrate on invention and let others develop the commercial potential of his inventions. His triode tube was one of the most important inventions of the 20th century. De Forest's autobiography is called *The Father of Radio* (1950).

See Also: Invention; Science; Television and Radio.

■ **DEISM,** rationalistic religious belief that describes the world in terms of reason, prevalent during the Enlightenment of the 18th century. Voltaire and Rousseau were leading European deists of the time. Deists believed that men are rational creatures and that reason can guide their lives. Man knows God through reason and in nature and not through Jesus Christ, the Holy Spirit,

Scriptures, or traditional religious practices. Deism influenced American thought and became popular among upper-class intellectuals, especially during the Revolutionary era. Deistic views are evident in the thoughts of Ethan Allen (*Reason the Only Oracle of Man*, 1784) and Thomas Paine (*Age of Reason*, 1794-96). Each called for the abolition of traditional religion in favor of deism. Also deists, but much less militant, were Thomas Jefferson and Benjamin Franklin, who applied deistic thought to democracy and political liberalism. Deism lost its popularity in the early-19th century with the beginnings of the Second Great Awakening.

See Also: Religion.

■ **DEKANAWIDAH (c. 1500s),** legendary cofounder of the Iroquois Five Nations Confederacy. According to one story, Hiawatha, a Mohawk, saw Dekanawidah's face in a cooking pot urging him to form the confederacy in order to stop the feuding among the Five Nations. In this story, Dekanawidah is a god sent to Hiawatha. In another version, Dekanawidah is depicted as a Huron visionary, who, because of a speech impediment, required Hiawatha as his spokesman.

See Also: Hiawatha; Indians of North America; Iroquois Confederacy.

■ **DE KOONING, WILLEM (1904-97),** abstract expressionist painter. De Kooning was born in Rotterdam, the Netherlands, where he apprenticed with commercial artists and designers Jan and Jaap Gidding, who took him under their wing and provided artistic training. De Kooning came to the United States in 1926, settling for a year in a Dutch community in Hoboken, New Jersey, before moving to New York City. He supported himself with lettering and sign painting until he started producing murals and easel paintings in 1935. He met other artists, particularly Arshile Gorky, with whom he began sharing a studio in 1937. In 1942 he exhibited with Jackson Pollock and began to form the group of artists known as the abstract expressionists, or the New York School, who were noted for the active quality of their painting. De Kooning's work shifted back and forth between more abstract and more representational styles; he is best known for several series of abstracted figures of women.

See Also: Pollock, Jackson.

■ **DELANY, MARTIN ROBINSON (1812-85),** author, physician, and soldier. He was born to free parents in Charles Town, Virginia. After studying medicine at Harvard, Delany turned his talents to the issues of race in America. He coedited Frederick Douglass's *The North Star*, explored the Niger Valley in Africa in 1854 with an eye toward the recolonization of African-American blacks, and was a pioneer in ethnology and social science. During the Civil War, as a major, he was the first black officer commissioned by the U.S. Army.

See Also: African Americans; Civil War.

■ **DELAWARE,** the nation's second smallest state and the fourth lowest in population. It is bounded on the north by Pennsylvania, on the west and south by Maryland, and on the east by the Delaware River, which separates it from New Jersey, Delaware Bay, and the Atlantic Ocean. Its average elevation of only 60 feet above sea level is the lowest among states. Delaware was first settled by Swedes in 1638, then controlled by the Dutch from 1655 to 1664, when it was seized by the English. It was part of Pennsylvania until 1704 when it became a separate colony. In 1787 Delaware became the first state to ratify the U.S. Constitution. Delaware is best known for the Wilmington headquarters of the chemical giant E.I. du Pont de Nemours and Company and for its incentives to companies to be incorporated and chartered in the state.

Capital: Wilmington. Area: 2,026 square miles. Population (1995 est.): 717,000.

See Also: Stuyvesant, Peter.

■ **DELAWARE INDIANS,** members of an Indian tribe known also as the Lenni-Lenape, which translates roughly to "the real people." Their status of ceremonial deference made them the "grandfathers" of Algonquian speakers. Legends of the Delaware's origins place them in northwestern North America, whence they migrated eastward to the Atlantic coast, settling in decentralized bands in New Jersey and eastern Pennsylvania. They lived in scattered open villages, notably without stockades, along river valleys. This pattern of settlement indicates that the Delawares did not fear attack from surrounding militaristic tribes, apparently because they were accepted as peacemakers. The Delawares followed an annual cycle including horticulture in settled villages in summer and dispersion to family hunting grounds in winter, with seasonal visits to fishing and shellfishing spots.

The tribe's earliest European contacts were with the Dutch and Swedes, who began to explore and trade for furs on the Delaware River in 1624. Trade rivalry caused war between the Delawares and their Susquehannock neighbors, but this ceased when the Delawares withdrew to avoid obstructing Susquehannock trade. The English began settling in New Jersey in the 1670s, and William Penn founded Pennsylvania in 1681, initiating extensive immigration from Britain and Germany, for whose use he bought lands from the Delawares. It was he who first called the Lenni-Lenape the "Delaware," referring to the English name for their river, which honored the British colonial governor Lord De La Warr.

The terms of Penn's land treaties failed to outline the extent of lands purchased, and he died before he could properly compensate the Delawares. Thereafter his profligate and unscrupulous sons cheated the tribe, especially by manipulating the "Walking Purchase" of 1700, an agreement through which William Penn acquired land from Delaware chief Mechkiliki-Shii that equaled a common day's journey along the Delaware River. John and Thomas Penn hired Iroquois to dispossess Delaware claimants.

Some of the Delawares remained in the United Brethren (Moravian) mission. These converts embraced pacifism and were attacked by pagan kinsmen on the one side and Scots-Irish Calvinists on the other. Many Moravian converts were massacred unresistingly in Pennsylvania and others after immigrating into Ohio. Those Delawares inclined to fight back took revenge in the Seven Years' War, but this faction made peace at the 1758 Treaty of Easton after being promised a boundary between themselves and the English, a promise honored in the breach. Renewed hostilities prompted the Royal Proclamation of 1763, which forbade colonists to expand further westward into tribal lands.

Constant population pressure drove the Delawares westward in a diaspora through Ohio and Indiana. Some went to Canada. Others eventually settled in a community at Dewey, Oklahoma, where they have federal recognition under Cherokee spokesmen. Remnants still live unobtrusively assimilated in their eastern homeland and in the Muskingum Valley of Ohio.

—FRANCIS JENNINGS

See Also: Indians of North America; Penn, William.
BIBLIOGRAPHY: Heckewelder, John, *An Account of the History, Manners, and Customs of the Indian Nations Who Once Inhabited Pennsylvania* (Hist. Soc. Of Pennsylvania 1876); Jennings, Francis, *The Ambiguous Iroquois Empire* (Norton 1984); Jennings, Francis, *Empire of Fortune* (Norton 1988); Wallace, Anthony F. C., *King of the Delawares: Teedyuscung, 1706-1763* (Univ. of Pennsylvania Press 1949); Weslager, C. A., *The Delaware Indians: A History* (Rutgers Univ. Press 1972).

■ **DELAWARE RIVER,** 280-mile-long river on the eastern seaboard that empties into Delaware Bay. Formed in New York's Catskill Mountains, the Delaware flows in a generally southern direction through New York, Pennsylvania, New Jersey, and Delaware. The Delaware was first explored by Henry Hudson in 1609. The first European settlements along the river were the Dutch Fort Nassau (1623), near present-day Gloucester, New Jersey, and the Swedish Fort Christina (1638), at present-day Wilmington, Delaware. The British gained control of the area in 1664 and a wide variety of Europeans moved into the Delaware Valley, including English Quakers, Germans, Welsh, Scottish, and French Huguenots. During the American Revolution battles were fought along the Delaware at Princeton, Trenton, Brandywine, Germantown, and Monmouth. German artist Emmanuel Leutze immortalized the river in his popular 1851 painting *Washington Crossing the Delaware*. During the 19th century the Delaware was the site of major industrial plants, including Robert Fulton's shipyards, du Pont's powder mills, and Roebling's iron works. During the 20th century the Delaware Valley has remained an important industrial site and a source of drinking water for New York City, Trenton, Philadelphia, and Wilmington.

■ **DE LEON, DANIEL (1852-1914),** socialist leader, born on the Caribbean island of Curaçao to Dutch-Jewish parents. He came to the United States in the early 1870s and graduated with honors from Columbia Law School. Joining the Socialist Labor party in 1891, he went on to form the Socialist Trades and Labor Alliance in 1895. A combative man, as well as a powerful speaker and writer, he caused much of the factionalism within radical politics during his lifetime. Yet his theoretical contributions, including the "Preamble to the Industrial Workers of the World" (1905), were unmatched.

See Also: Labor Movement.

■ **DE LÔME LETTER (1898),** a letter written by the Spanish minister to the United States, Enrique Dupuy de Lôme, to a friend in Havana deriding U.S. Pres. William McKinley. The letter was intercepted, and its publication on Feb. 9, 1898, strengthened American opinion in favor of intervention against Spain in Cuba.

See Also: Spanish-American War.

■ **DE MILLE, AGNES (1909-93),** dancer and choreographer, born in New York City. Through her performances and lectures, she was the ambassador of dance as an art form in the United States. In *Oklahoma!* (1943), *Carousel* (1945), and other Broadway productions, she pioneered the use of ballet choreography in musical comedy. In 1973, she founded the Heritage Dance Company. Some of her most famous dances are *Rodeo* (1942) and *Fall River Legend* (1948).

See Also: Women in American History.

■ **DE MILLE, CECIL B. (1881-1959),** film director born in Ashfield, Massachusetts, and famed for his lavish productions. From his first film, *The Squaw Man* (1913), to his last, *The Ten Commandments* (1956), De Mille's films gave meaning to the term "Hollywood spectacular." A moralist and a sentimentalist who often favored historical or biblical themes, he frequently titillated the audience with sex and violence, but wrongdoers were always punished.

■ **DEMOCRATIC PARTY,** one of the two major 20th-century political parties in the United States and the oldest, tracing its antecedents to the Democratic-Republicans of the late 18th century. The party first developed as a political faction opposed to the policies of Sec. of the Treasury Alexander Hamilton in the first George Washington administration, particularly to his promotion of a powerful central government and his pro-British and anti-French foreign policy. The quasi-party contested the presidential election of 1796, pitting "Democratic-Republican" Thomas Jefferson against "Federalist" John Adams; it lost that contest but prevailed in the rematch in 1800. The Federalists evaporated as a national party during Jefferson's administration (1801-09), but by the end of James Madison's presidency in 1817 the Democratic-Republicans had come to accept the Hamiltonian program of tariff protection and central banking. The so-called "Era of Good Feelings," roughly 1815 to 1825, was really a disintegration of party cohesion in favor of elite rule managed by congressional caucus.

The party was reborn after the presidential election of 1824, when the four candidates—all Democratic-Republicans—divided on issues and by sections. When none of them won a majority in the electoral college, the contest was thrown into the House of Representatives, which elected John Quincy Adams. The outraged supporters of Andrew Jackson, who had claimed the largest proportion of the popular vote, spent the next four years organizing for the campaign of 1828, which was the most democratic in the nation to that time. The "Democratic party" was created by the Jackson victory in 1828.

The subsequent political polarization between Democrats and the opposition—known as Whigs after 1834—focused on the personality of Jackson but also contested such issues as the national bank, the tariff, internal improvements, the sale of public lands, territorial acquisition, and Indian removal. The Jacksonian Democratic party was a national coalition, uniting western farmers, Southern planters, and urban workers—including Roman Catholic Irish and German immigrants. Because it linked voters in the North and the South, the coalition was premised on avoiding the divisive topic of slavery. After the conquests of the Mexican War, however, the question of the extension of slavery to the West became the dominating public issue. The Democrats found themselves unable to hold the center, and the subsequent breakdown of party unity was one of the factors leading to the Civil War.

After the war the Democrats were burdened with the stigma of disloyalty, characterized as late as 1884 as the party of "rum, romanism, and rebellion." For 75 years the Democrats were a minority national party, with only two presidential candidates—Grover Cleveland and Woodrow Wilson—able to capture the White House between the elections of 1860 and 1932.

It took the Great Depression to achieve a new Democratic ascendancy. Al Smith's urban ethnic support in 1928 foreshadowed Franklin Roosevelt's victory of 1932. The New Deal abandoned (except in the South) the states-rights and small government philosophy. The Democrats survived the Dixiecrat and Progressive defections of 1948, and from the perspective of the mid-1960s even the Eisenhower presidency of 1953-61 seemed but a Republican interlude in a Democratic era. But the loss of the "Solid South" in 1964 and 1968 was the first indication that the New Deal coalition had broken apart. The presidential victories of Ronald Reagan in 1980 and 1984, and the Republican seizure of Congress in 1994 confirmed that the Republicans had once again become the majority party.

—JOHN MACK FARAGHER

See Also: Conventions, Political; Political Parties; Presidential Elections.

BIBLIOGRAPHY: Goldman, Ralph M., *Search for Consensus: The Story of the Democratic Party* (Temple Univ. Press 1979); Kovler, Peter B., ed., *Democrats and the American Idea* (Center for National Policy Press 1992).

■ **DEMOCRATIC-REPUBLICANS,** the first opposition political party in the United States. In the 1790s no political parties existed. The founders initially considered politically motivated groups as "factions" dangerous to the public good. During the 1790s, however, differences over domestic and, especially, foreign policies led to the growth of proto-parties that contested the election of 1796.

The followers of John Adams and Alexander Hamilton identified themselves as "Federalists," using the name previously employed by supporters of the new Constitution; tied to commercial interests and Anglophilic, they believed in a strong federal government run by elites. The more agrarian, Francophilic opposition group, which also included town workers, was led by Thomas Jefferson and chose the name "Republicans" to emphasize that their commitment to states' rights and individual liberties hearkened back to the virtuous ideals of ancient republics. The appellation "Democrat" was used pejoratively by the Federalists to portray the Republicans as anarchists. In the 1790s only a few state parties identified themselves as "Democratic-Republicans."

The election of 1800 swept Jefferson and other Republican candidates into power. From 1801 to 1825 a Republican dynasty of the Virginians Jefferson, James Madison, and James Monroe held the White House. During the War of 1812 talk of secession by New England Federalists effectively destroyed the Federalist party.

With no strong opposition, the Republican party splintered during the 1820s. In the election of 1824 several Republicans vied for the presidency; the winner, John Quincy Adams, proved an ineffective leader. The election of Andrew Jackson in 1828 led to a restructuring of the party system. The Democratic-Republicans split into the anti-Jackson National Republicans (later Whigs) and the Democrats.

—CATHERINE ALLGOR

See Also: Democratic Party; Federalism; Political Parties.

BIBLIOGRAPHY: Schlesinger, Arthur M., Jr., *History of U.S. Political Parties, 1789-1860: From Factions to Parties* (Chelsea House 1973); Smelser, Marshall, *The Democratic Republic, 1801-1815* (Harper & Row 1968).

■ **DEMOGRAPHY, HISTORICAL,** the identification and analysis of a population's fertility, mortality, marital, and migration rates over time. Historical demographers use a vast array of social science methodologies, but most of their source materials come from vital statistic records and censuses.

Serious historical study of past populations did not begin until after World War II when concern about the population boom led demographers to study past societies with high fertility rates to find out both the effects of these rates and the means to control them. Their study was aided at that time by the growing use of quantitative techniques and computers in the social sciences. This was evident in the demographic work done in Great Britain and France. Moreover, in the 1960s, a new methodology, family reconstitution, greatly increased the accuracy and sophistication of historical demography. This methodology linked local genealogies with local vital statistics from the area (usually listed in the local parish registers) to find the general patterns in an area's births, marriages, and deaths. Local studies proliferated.

Historical demographers have fairly well mapped out the ebb and flow of the world's populations, developing many interesting hypotheses to explain them. One essential feature of this ebb and flow is the existence of a demographic transition, the point at which a population's high birth rates and mortality rates decrease dramatically.

Prompted by the European developments in the field of historical demography and by the concerns and findings of the new social history and the new urban history, American historians in the 1960s increasingly turned their attention to the study of the American population. Coupled with the computer, the U.S. Census gave these historians a marvelous tool with which to study that population. In America, unlike other countries, migration—both internal and external—has been the most significant factor in population changes over time. In addition to analyzing demographic transition and migration rates, American historical demographers also focus on the population shifts from country to city and from one geographic area to another. Population changes for particular races, ethnic groups, and social classes are other focal areas for study. Although historical demographers have done much to explain how and why the American population grew from 3.9 million in 1790 to 250 million in 1990, the increased use of quantitative analysis and social science terminology have, unfortunately, made for some boring and almost inaccessible reading. Something that deals with sex and death should be more interesting.

—LOUIS HAAS

See Also: Population.

BIBLIOGRAPHY: Glass, D. V., and D. E. C. Eversley, eds., *Population in History: Essays in Historical Demography* (Aldine 1965); Hareven, Tamara, and Maris Vinovskis, eds., *Family and Population in Nineteenth-Century America* (Princeton Univ. Press 1978); McClelland, Peter, and Richard Zeckhauser, *Demographic Dimensions of the New Republic* (Cambridge Univ. Press 1982); Wells, Robert, *Uncle Sam's Family: Issues and Perspectives on American Demographic History* (State Univ. of New York Press 1985).

■ **DEMPSEY, JACK (1895-1983),** boxer. Born in Manassa, Colorado, and dubbed "the Manassa Mauler," he turned professional in 1915 and won the heavyweight championship in 1919. A leading figure of the so-called Golden Age of Sports in the 1920s, "Tiger Jack" lost the belt to Gene Tunney in 1927. His title bouts promoted by Tex Rickard were the first "million dollar gates" and starting in 1921, the first to be broadcast on radio.

See Also: Sports.

■ ***DENNIS V. UNITED STATES* (1951),** U.S. Supreme Court case that upheld the constitutionality of the Smith Alien Registration Act (1940) and the conviction under it of 11 Communist party leaders. As the Cold War between the United States and the U.S.S.R intensified, members of the Communist party were tried and convicted (1949) of violating the Smith Act by conspiring to advocate the violent overthrow of the U.S. government. Chief Justice Fred Vinson argued that communism represented a significant threat to the United States and the government must be empowered to defend itself against its enemies. Free speech, he wrote, may be limited if it posed a grave and probable danger to the state.

Although the Court affirmed (6-2) the convictions, only three other justices endorsed Vinson's opinion. Justices Hugo Black and William O. Douglas dissented, arguing the decision represented an unwarranted attack on political speech. *Dennis* marked a significant departure from the "clear and present danger" test the Court had first established in *Schenck* v. *United States* (1919).

See Also: Schenck v. United States; Supreme Court.

■ **DENVER,** capital city of Colorado, located in the eastern foothills of the Rocky Mountains. Denver was founded in 1858 by gold miners, and gold mining remained a crucial element in the town's early history. The city followed a boom and bust cycle typical of many early Western towns. Silver mining became increasingly important, but a silver boom in the 1880s and

1890s ended abruptly with the adoption of the gold standard in 1893. Another boom boosted the economy, however, when gold was discovered at Cripple Creek in the 1890s. During the late 19th century tourism started to gain economic significance as tourists attracted by the dry climate and mountain views traveled by railroad to the area's numerous spas and hotels. Denver's economy slowed through the Depression of the 1930s, only to soar during World War II (1941-45) as federal employees and defense industries moved to the city. At the same time oil discoveries in the Dakotas and southern Canada attracted laborers, researchers, and managers to Denver. Recently the region's vast tourist trade, especially for winter skiing, has become crucial to the city's economy and is best symbolized by the opening of the new Denver International Airport on Feb. 28, 1995. Population (1994): 493,559.

See Also: *City in American History; Colorado.*

■ **DEPRESSIONS AND RECESSIONS,** the major and minor business crises that have occurred periodically in American history and have slowed the pace of economic development. The term depression usually denotes a major decline in economic activity, accompanied by bankruptcies and unemployment, while recession describes a similar but short-term and less severe slowing of economic activity.

While economic crises marked certain periods of colonial history, particularly just before and during the era (1640-60) of the English Civil War, a cyclical pattern of "boom and bust" emerged with the rapid expansion of industry and trade after the American Revolution. In boom periods, the level of manufacturing, trade, and profit has been high. Historically, each boom has been followed by a bust, a sudden crisis small or large that interrupted the flow of exchange, rapidly lowered the level of economic activity, and spread through many sectors of the business economy. In the severest depressions, business remained slow for a period of years.

Pre–Civil War Depressions. Before the American Civil War, the most significant such depressions in business activity, then known as panics, occurred from 1815 to 1820, 1837 to 1842, and

1856 to 1860. The historical circumstances that caused these crises differed in each case, but all three depressions were preceded by overspeculation. This took the form of investors going into debt making purchases on credit and then, for reasons that differed from one depression to another, not having sufficient means to repay these debts.

In 1815, at least three factors stimulated a collapse of business. In 1811, the charter for the First Bank of the United States expired, leading to chaotic and decentralized bank policies. In 1814, many American banks decided to suspend the circulation of gold or silver coin and to substitute paper money instead. Since paper money has never been valued as highly as precious metals, price inflation resulted, followed by a shortage overall in the amount of money needed to pay debts at their full value. Almost simultaneously, the end of the War of 1812 in 1815 brought with it a resumption of trade with Europe. European goods flooded the American market and drastically reduced the profits needed by American manufacturers to sustain their businesses. Factories throughout New England and elsewhere closed or struggled for survival until the early 1820s. The chartering of the Second Bank of the United States in 1816, the passage of a protective tariff in 1816, and the resumption in use of specie in 1817 marked the beginning of a slow business recovery.

The Panic of 1837 had its roots in the monetary policies of Andrew Jackson, who opposed the Second Bank of the United States as elitist, and therefore removed money from this bank and placed it in state banks of his own choosing. In the short term, these state banks were able to loan out the money to investors and speculators in an unregulated way. This bubble of activity burst in 1836, however, when Jackson was succeeded as president by the more fiscally conservative Martin Van Buren. This, combined with the recognition that many investors in both domestic and foreign trade had borrowed far beyond their ability to repay, led to the collapse of many banks and industries. Despite attempts to adjust federal financial policies, business did not revive until the early 1840s.

The Depression of 1856 came in the wake of a period of high prosperity and extensive industrial expansion. Railroad mileage had almost tripled since 1850; textile mills had also increased in number; and the supply of gold had gone up dramatically due to the strikes in California in the late 1840s. The panic, due primarily to overbuilding and overinvesting in all these areas, was less extreme than those of earlier years, primarily because the wealth of the country was greater overall, and the debts of businessmen much lower. The Civil War brought business back to life.

Post–Civil War Depressions. After the war and two brief recessions in the 1860s, major depressions took place from 1873 to about 1877 and from 1893 until 1896. The first came as a result once again of overspeculation in railroad expansion and was catalyzed in part by the collapse of the Jay Cooke Bank in Philadelphia, the primary financier for the Northern Pacific Railroad. In the 1880s an unprecedented boom in business foundings took place, only to be followed by another collapse in 1893.

In 1893 and thereafter, each economic downturn affected more people than previously. With a larger percentage of workers in industry and a declining percentage with family farms or other fallbacks for times of unemployment, depressions ceased being primarily an economic phenomenon and had more social implications. Furthermore, more middle-class people invested in stocks, such that in the recessions of 1903 and 1907, many individual investors lost their family savings. These changes, the decline of prosperity in rural industries such as mining and farming after World War I, and an unprecedented boom in consumer credit buying during the 1920s presaged the Wall Street stock market crash of Oct. 29, 1929, and the subsequent worldwide depression of the 1930s.

After the crash, the federal government reacted in its traditional historical role, making adjustments in its monetary policy to help business pull itself out of the slump. But stocks continued to fall, and by 1932 almost 25 percent of the American work force was unemployed. Franklin D. Roosevelt was elected president in 1932 and undertook a series of drastic actions, known collectively as the New Deal, to prevent banks and industries from closing their doors permanently and to provide government jobs for the unemployed. He initiated extensive regulations for financial transactions and in 1935 created a Social Security system that provided unemployment insurance and retirement pensions for workers. The Depression did not lift, however, until the United States began rearming for war in 1939.

While the United States has experienced several recessions since World War II, notably in the late 1970s, 1982, and 1992, no severe depression has occurred.

—SARAH H. GORDON

See Also: *Banks and Banking; Banks of the United States, First and Second; Great Depression; Industrial Revolution; Money and Currency.*

BIBLIOGRAPHY: Faulkner, Harold U., *American Economic History,* revised ed. (Harper 1976); Kirkland, Edward C., *History of American Economic Life* (Appleton-Century-Crofts 1969).

■ **DESEGREGATION,** removal of legal and social barriers that separate individuals on the basis of race. The U.S. Supreme Court's "separate but equal" doctrine enunciated in *Plessy* v. *Ferguson* (1896) encouraged racial segregation in virtually every form of social activity. In 1909 the newly founded National Association for the Advancement of Colored People (NAACP) began preparations to contest the legal foundations of segregation. Victories were won in cases such as *Buchanan* v. *Warley* (1917), which condemned housing segregation, and *Morgan* v. *Virginia* (1947), which outlawed racial seating arrangements on interstate buses. The NAACP and its Legal Defense Fund, headed by Thurgood Marshall, made steady progress that was capped in 1954 with victory in *Brown* v. *Board of Education of Topeka.* The *Brown* case attacked not only segregation but the *Plessy* doctrine that supported it. Meanwhile the armed services were desegregated by executive order in 1948, and the Congress of Racial Equality (CORE) had begun challenging segregation directly, through sit-ins and other demonstrations. Activism against segregation cascaded through the next two decades, including the Montgomery, Alabama, bus boycott, the sit-in movement, and the freedom rides. These early efforts culminated in the Civil Rights Act of 1964 and mark the first successes of the civil rights movement.

—JOHN R. NEFF

See Also: *African Americans; Civil Rights Movement; Desegregation of the Armed Forces; Marshall, Thurgood; National Association for the Advancement of Colored People (NAACP).*

DESEGREGATION OF THE ARMED FORCES,

policy ordered by Pres. Harry Truman in Executive Order 9981 (July 1948). Truman was motivated both by political considerations and concern about the quality of recruits. Many military leaders resisted, arguing that integration would impair combat efficiency, despite evidence to the contrary from World War II. While the debate continued, the Air Force, Marine Corps, and Army persisted in maintaining segregated units; the Navy typically made most of its African-American recruits into wardroom stewards. Not until 1954 did desegregation become even superficially complete.

See Also: African Americans.

DESERT INDIANS OF THE SOUTHWEST,

Indians who comprise roughly four groups: the Yuman Pima and Papago, Yuman, Pueblo, and Apache-Navaho. A hot, arid region of mountains, deserts, and basins, the Southwest comprises Arizona, New Mexico, and portions of adjoining states. Culturally and linguistically diverse, most of the Indians of the region were traditionally agriculturalists, although a few groups were foragers. The Yuman, Pima, and Papago peoples lived mainly in semiautonomous patrilineal villages, growing crops along river flood plains. The Pueblo inhabited numerous independent, spatially compact villages along the Rio Grande in northern New Mexico and northeast Arizona. The aggressive Apache-Navaho groups, who arrived in the Southwest less than 1,000 years ago, borrowed cultural practices from the region's older inhabitants.

After the mid-16th century, Spaniards attempted to control the Southwest. Many of the indigenous peoples, however, successfully resisted these attempts, in such actions as the 1680 Pueblo revolt and by the persistence of traditional cultural practices and religious beliefs. After the United States absorbed the lands of the Southwest from Mexico in the 1840s and 1850s, loss of Indian lands accelerated. Despite a heritage of dispossession, many of the Indians of the region have retained vital elements of their cultures. At the close of the 20th century, the Navaho were the largest Indian group in the country, while the Pueblo remained a growing and prominent force in the Southwest.

See Also: Apache; Indians of North America; Navaho; Pueblo Indians.

BIBLIOGRAPHY: Gutiérrez, Ramón A., *When Jesus Came, the Corn Mothers Went Away: Marriage, Sexuality, and Power in New Mexico, 1500-1846* (Stanford Univ. Press 1991); Spicer, Edward H., *Cycles of Conquest: The Impact of Spain, Mexico, and the United States on the Indians of the Southwest* (Univ. of Arizona Press 1962).

DESERT LAND ACT (1877),

extension of the Homestead Act of 1862. The Desert Land Act enabled settlers to buy a full section, 640 acres, if they could bring irrigation to the land. A boon to many farmers in arid areas, the act was widely abused by cattlemen and speculators.

See Also: Frontier in American History.

DE SOTO, HERNANDO (c. 1500-42),

Spanish explorer of North America. The first European to penetrate deeply into the interior of the North American continent, De Soto was born in Jerez de los Caballeros, Estremadura, Spain. At the age of 14, he sailed to Panama, probably with the fleet of Pedrarias Dávila. De Soto spent 17 years in Central America (1514-31), distinguishing himself in expeditions against local Indians. Between 1531 and 1535 he participated in Francisco Pizarro's conquest of the Inca empire and became perhaps the most outstanding figure of that conquest, except for Pizarro himself. Having gained fame, recognition, and enormous wealth, he triumphantly returned to Spain in 1536. Eager for new conquests, De Soto returned after having obtained (1538) a royal appointment as governor of Cuba and permission to conquer and govern the unexplored lands in North America. De Soto's expedition of about 600 men sailed from Cuba and landed in Florida on May 30, 1539, in search of a golden empire similar to that of the Incas. In three years (1539-42) he traveled across 4,000 square miles of territory of 10 future U.S. states. Instead of gold, however, the Spaniards found enormous hardships, disease, and hostile Indians. On May 21, 1542, De Soto died of fever on the Mississippi and was buried in the river. Of his men, 311 returned to Mexico in 1543. An expert cavalry officer and efficient commander, De Soto was ruthless, ambitious, hot-tempered, and often insubordinate.

See Also: Exploration and Discovery; Pizarro, Francisco; Spanish Colonies.

BIBLIOGRAPHY: Duncan, David E., *Hernando de Soto: A Savage Quest in the Americas* (Crown Publishers 1995); Swanton, John R., *Final Report of the United States De Soto Expedition Commission* (Smithsonian Institution Press 1985).

■ **DETECTIVES,** police or private investigators who use scientific methods to discover lawbreakers and evidence for civil actions. Since the 1830s they have used increasingly sophisticated forensic methods. Private detectives were often used as extralegal company police in the late 19th and early 20th centuries, guarding property and serving as strike breakers. The most famous agency was founded by Allan Pinkerton (1850).

See Also: Pinkerton, Allan.

■ **DEWEY, GEORGE (1837-1917),** naval officer and hero of the Battle of Manila Bay during the Spanish-American War. Dewey was born in Montpelier, Vermont. He secured an appointment to the Naval Academy and held various shipboard and bureaucratic positions in the Civil War and postwar period. By 1897 Dewey had attained the rank of commodore and was in command of the Asiatic Squadron. When war with Spain began in 1898, Dewey's squadron engaged the Spanish fleet in Manila Bay, the Philippines, on May 1. Every Spanish ship was sunk in the battle, with hundreds of Spanish casualties. The lopsided victory made Dewey a national hero. Congress promoted him to Admiral of the Navy, and public adulation was such that he considered a run for the White House in 1900. By then, however, his popularity had waned, and his political aspirations dissipated.

See Also: Manila Bay, Battle of; Spanish-American War.

BIBLIOGRAPHY: Dewey, George, *Autobiography of George Dewey: Admiral of the Navy* (reprint, Naval Institute Press 1987).

■ **DEWEY, JOHN (1859-1952),** educator and philosopher. Born and raised in Burlington, Vermont, Dewey graduated from the University of Vermont in 1879 and graduate school at Johns Hopkins University. Dewey spent 10 years at the University of Chicago (1894-1904), combining the study of psychology, education, and philosophy as the basis for individual and community development.

In 1904, Dewey became a professor of philosophy at Columbia University, where he taught for 26 years and achieved world renown for his voluminous writings on education and democracy. Dewey argued that the function of the intellect was to bring past experiences to bear on the present and future. Dewey advocated public awareness and discussion of problems afflicting society in order to avoid repeated mistakes. During the

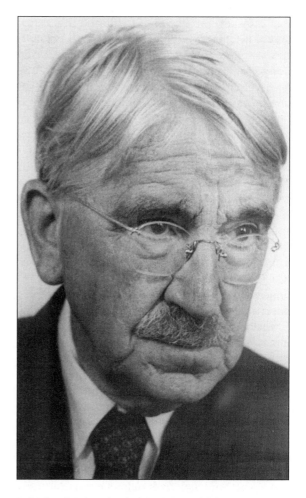

In his books *The School and Society* and *Democracy and Education,* philosopher and educator John Dewey challenged rigid and formal educational methods, advocating instead the cultivation of "creative intelligence" in schoolchildren.

1930s, Dewey became involved in political causes, such as the Civil Liberties Union, and was a founder of the New School for Social Research and the American Association of University Professors. Perhaps more successfully than any other American, Dewey made philosophy widely accessible and broadly applicable.

BIBLIOGRAPHY: Hook, Sidney, *John Dewey: An Intellectual Portrait 1939* (Prometheus Books 1995); Ryan, Alan, *John Dewey and the High Tide of American Liberalism* (Norton 1995).

■ **DEWEY, THOMAS E. (1902-71),** attorney and politician. Born in Owosso, Michigan, he practiced law and gained fame prosecuting mobsters as district attorney in New York City during the 1930s. Dewey ran for governor of New York as a Republican, serving three terms (1943-55). Twice his party's presidential nominee, he lost to Franklin D. Roosevelt in 1944 and to Harry S. Truman in 1948 after leading in most preelection polls.

See Also: Presidential Elections.

■ **DICKINSON, EMILY (1830-86),** poet, considered one of the greatest in American history; born in Amherst, Massachusetts, where she spent all but one year of her life. After a year at South Hadley Female Seminary (now Mt. Holyoke College), she began to withdraw from society, maintaining only a few close friendships through correspondence. Devoted to her family, she took advantage of the societal convention that approved of unmarried women who continued to live with their families. This allowed her to direct all of her energies toward her writing.

Dickinson and her work were not well known, much less acclaimed, during her lifetime. Only 10 of her poems were published, and those anonymously. After her death nearly 1,800 additional poems were discovered, many of which appeared in volumes published during the 1890s and first few decades of the 20th century. Not until 1955, however, did a complete collection of her work, *The Poems of Emily Dickinson,* appear.

The meter of hymns influenced Dickinson's spare, rhythmic style. Her religious consciousness often infused her poems with spiritual meaning and provided the tensions in her poetry between an inability to accept religious orthodoxy and a longing for spiritual comfort. Exploring the con-

Of the almost 2,000 poems Emily Dickinson wrote, fewer than a dozen were published in her lifetime, and these anonymously.

ventional poetic themes of love, nature, death, and a higher power, Dickinson used irregular rhymes, subtle metric variations, and a bold and startling imagery that anticipated 20th-century poetry.

—CATHERINE A. HAULMAN

See Also: Poetry; Women in American History.

BIBLIOGRAPHY: Cody, John, *After Great Pain: The Inner Life of Emily Dickinson* (Harvard Univ. Press 1971); Wolff, Cynthia Griffin, *Emily Dickinson* (Knopf 1986).

■ **DICKINSON, JOHN (1732-1808),** Revolutionary War statesman. Born in Talbot County, Maryland, Dickinson was a leading figure in the colonial American opposition to Britain. Between Dec. 2, 1767, and Feb. 15, 1768, Dickinson published his *Letters from a Farmer in Pennsylvania* in the *Pennsylvania Chronicle.* This influential series of letters protested the Townshend Acts, British taxes on imports designed to raise revenue. Despite his opposition to Parliamentary taxation, Dickinson opposed the decision to declare independence. By abstaining at the vote on July 2, 1776, however, he enabled the Pennsylvania delegation to vote in favor of independence.

See Also: Revolution, American; Townshend Acts.

■ **DIGGS, ANNIE (1848-1916),** populist organizer, writer, and politician born in London, Ontario, Canada. A proponent of Farmers' Alliances, workers' cooperatives, temperance, and women's suffrage, she was a major figure in the Populist movement of the 1890s, serving on the Populist National Committee in 1896.

■ **DIMAGGIO, JOE (1914-),** baseball player. A graceful, power-hitting center fielder for the New York Yankees (1936-51), he hit safely in a record 56 consecutive games in 1941. Known as the Yankee Clipper, DiMaggio led the Yankees to nine World Series titles and batted .325 for his career despite missing three seasons (1943-45) due to military service. Born in Martinez, California, he was one of three brothers who played major league baseball.

See Also: Sports.

■ **DIME NOVELS,** popular name for cheap paperback novels written in the United States during the latter half of the 19th century. Evolving from story papers and the novels of James Fenimore Cooper, the first dime novels appeared in 1860 and sold for either a nickel or dime. For the next four decades, publishers, such as Beadle and Adams, furiously printed this formulaic fiction.

In form and content dime novels were strikingly similar. They often emphasized democracy, individualism, and violence, set against a backdrop of melodramatic adventure and sentimental romance. Although not regarded for their literary merit, dime novels introduced such heroic cultural figures as Calamity Jane and Seth Jones. Often set on the frontier, this cheap fiction spawned the distinctly American genre of the Western. Among the most famous authors of dime novels were Prentiss Ingraham, Edward S. Ellis, and Edward L. Wheeler, the creator of the frontier tales of Deadwood Dick, the most popular series in the history of the genre.

Dime novels, first introduced in 1860, often featured heroic adventure tales set in the West.

The audiences for dime novels included both the middle and working classes. They consumed the product of a burgeoning publishing industry that commercialized fiction as never before. Although pulp magazines superseded dime novels as the most popular form of cheap fiction in about 1895, the legacy of the genre persists in the plots of television shows, movies, and popular fiction.

See Also: Novel.

BIBLIOGRAPHY: Jones, Daryl, *The Dime Novel* (Western Bowling Green State Univ. Press 1970); Smith, Henry Nash, *Virgin Land: The American West in Symbol and Myth* (Harvard Univ. Press 1950).

■ **DISARMAMENT, NUCLEAR,** process of reducing spending on and the production of nuclear weapons. Carried out primarily in diplomatic negotiations between the United States and the Soviet Union, nuclear arms control became a major initiative of Pres. Richard Nixon's administration (1969-74). With the assistance of National Security Adviser Henry A. Kissinger, President Nixon negotiated the Strategic Arms Limitations Treaty (SALT) with Soviet premier Leonid Brezhnev in 1972. This first, tentative move toward nuclear disarmament set limits on spending and on the growth of some nuclear weapons.

The second round of negotiations, SALT II, began in 1974 in Vladivostock between Brezhnev and Pres. Gerald R. Ford. Although they agreed to reduce the number of nuclear missiles, no treaty was signed. Early in his presidency, Jimmy Carter proposed even further reductions, but Brezhnev refused. Finally in Vienna in 1979, Carter and the Soviet premier signed SALT II, limiting strategic nuclear missiles to 2,400 per country. But when the Soviet Union invaded Afghanistan in 1979, the treaty failed to win confirmation in the Senate.

During the 1980s, Pres. Ronald Reagan generally opposed arms-control initiatives and oversaw the greatest military buildup in U.S. history. Between 1985 and 1988, however, Soviet leader Mikhail Gorbachev met with Reagan and forged a number of significant breakthroughs in disarmament and a thawing of Cold War tensions. Further progress was made after the collapse of the Soviet Union (1991) and the resulting lowering of tensions on the European continent. Nonetheless, nuclear arms were still being produced at the end of the century and disarmament remained a priority for countries around the world.

See Also: Carter, James Earl, Jr. (Jimmy); Cold War; Ford, Gerald Rudolph; Foreign Affairs; Kissinger, Henry A.; Nixon, Richard Milhous.

BIBLIOGRAPHY: Gaddis, John L., *Russia, the Soviet Union, and the United States: An Interpretive History* (Knopf 1978); LaFeber, Walter, *America, Russia, and the Cold War, 1945-1996,* 7th ed. (McGraw-Hill 1997).

▪ DISCIPLES OF CHRIST (CHRISTIAN CHURCHES),

Protestant religious denomination originating in the Restoration Movement of the early 19th century that aimed to restore evangelical Christianity and to unite all Christian churches. In 1831, Barton W. Stone's "Christians" and Alexander Campbell's "Dis-

ciples" merged to form the Christian Churches or Disciples of Christ. Today, Disciples have a national and regional structure and have generally maintained the practices of the Restoration churches—autonomy of congregations, plurality of elders, and Communion every Sunday—although most now accept nonimmersed believers into full membership.

See Also: Religion.

▪ DISEASE.

From its impact on the process of European settlement to its role in molding American society through the 20th century, disease has fundamentally shaped American culture.

The Columbian Exchange. With the rapid settlement that began in the 16th century after Columbus spread the word of the "new world," Europeans brought epidemic disease and death that led to the virtual destruction of the people who had lived on the American continents for 20,000 years or more. This spread of disease has been termed the "Columbian exchange." Smallpox has often been blamed for this devastation, although historical evidence suggests that swine influenza may have caused the population of more than 1 million natives in Hispaniola to drop to approximately 10,000 by the 1490s. In many cases, however, smallpox was almost definitely the cause of death, although other diseases, including typhus, diphtheria, yellow fever, dysentery, and influenza also took their toll on native populations.

These European diseases decimated the Indian population, in some cases clearing out entire villages that were then taken over by the new settlers. Some sources suggest that settlers intentionally spread disease in order to facilitate their territorial desires. However, settlers had limited knowledge of how diseases were spread and also were threatened, although far less severely, by the effects of disease. Syphilis is often thought to have been transmitted from Indians to the Europeans. The evidence for this contention is mixed, however, and scholars disagree about whether syphilis was part of the Columbian exchange at all, and if so, where it originated.

Disease in the Colonial Era. Settlers in the Chesapeake colonies from the 17th century on suffered from malaria and dysentery. These diseases helped to limit the early success of Jamestown and other villages until the new inhabitants found ways to control the causes of the diseases by improving their overall living conditions, especially their food and water supply. Disease was less endemic to the New England colonies in the early years; life expectancy in the North, therefore, was much higher than in the South.

Settlers were more successful fighting the European diseases because they had some natural immunity to them, protection that the natives lacked. They also were familiar with techniques for combating disease, initially focusing on the simple but effective quarantine, but also using early methods of inoculation that were sometimes beneficial.

Industrialization and Urbanization. With the rise of industry in the early 1800s came the growth of cities, and with cities came a greater concentration of filth and disease and a lack of reliable and clean water supplies. Yellow fever epidemics haunted the cities throughout the century, while the first major cholera outbreak took place in 1832. During the course of such outbreaks early health reformers, including Sylvester Graham and William Alcott, began to emphasize a greater need for cleanliness, as well as the traditional tool of quarantine. Their efforts were aided by the greater awareness that came with widespread disease among soldiers during the Civil War (1861-65). Far more soldiers died from disease, frequently caused by the squalor in army camps, than from the fighting. During the conflict, the federal government established the U.S. Sanitary Commission to help fight the spread of disease in the armed forces.

These efforts to reduce the growing impact of disease on American life were guided by the miasmatic theory of disease. Health reformers generally believed that filth and noxious fumes from garbage and other waste products in and of themselves caused disease. For this reason they focused on cleaning up city streets and individual homes, installing sewers to take away sewer gas, as well as promoting individual cleanliness, to cure disease. Sewers, running water, and regular garbage pickup were instituted as a part of public health efforts to control disease. These efforts helped to mold the public health measures and waste disposal infrastructure that characterize America today.

Modern Medicine and Modern America. These efforts changed slightly as the nature of disease became better understood with the germ theory and medical bacteriology in the 1880s, led by the Frenchman Louis Pasteur and the German Robert Koch. The understanding that germs caused disease caught on slowly in the United States, but it eventually led to efforts widely instituted in the early 20th century to guard the quality of milk, water, and food against harmful bacteria. These efforts were led by progressive reformers such as Alice Hamilton. Not filth but bacteria became the focus of efforts to prevent disease. In 1892, immigrants began being screened for disease at Ellis Island before they were allowed to enter the United States. The American population also developed the view that immigrants themselves were dirty and inherently carried with them a proclivity for disease.

Thus, Americans also worked hard to purify the people, efforts that were stepped up after the influenza epidemic of 1918-19 that killed more than 10 million people worldwide. Efforts to restrict immigration of groups that were considered undesirable for a variety of reasons, including the unfounded suspicion that they were carriers of disease, finally succeeded in 1921 and 1924. These restrictions placed greater limitations on the "new immigrants," namely groups from southern and eastern Europe.

Sexually transmitted diseases and hookworm also became targets of efforts to fight disease. The "social purity" movement worked to educate Americans about the prevention of sexually transmitted disease, primarily by counseling abstinence and urging young men to avoid prostitutes. Efforts to control hookworm, often called "the germ of laziness," were instituted in the south. Hookworm led to lethargy and fatigue in its victims, many of whom were poor African Americans in the south, contributing to stereotypes about blacks and poor whites.

The war against infectious and epidemic disease became more visible when the nation elected a victim of infantile paralysis (polio), Franklin Delano Roosevelt, to the presidency in 1932, although Roosevelt never discussed his handicap in public. By the 1950s, the country became aware of the role that vitamins could play in the prevention of disease and the ways in which vaccination could be widely employed to prevent diseases, especially after the invention of a vaccine to prevent the dreaded polio. Regular vaccination of infants for diseases, including smallpox, typhoid, diphtheria, and measles, became standard practice in the mid-20th century. Efforts against smallpox were so successful that by the late 20th century world health organizations announced the eradication of the disease, and infants are no longer vaccinated against it.

Late-20th-Century Disease. Perhaps the most significant diseases in late-20th-century America are cancer and acquired immune deficiency syndrome (AIDS). Cancer has been part of American society since the country's European settlement but received less attention because of the high mortality caused by epidemic diseases. While there is evidence that some cancers may be caused by viruses, in general they are not considered infectious disease and instead are caused by defective cell-replication processes in the body. In the latter half of the 20th century, however, rates of many cancers seemed to be on the rise, leading to some concern about cancer epidemic. Among women, breast cancer rates are particularly high, and the incidence of skin cancer is also increasing.

AIDS, caused by the human immunodeficiency virus (HIV), became prominent in the United States during the 1980s, and it has proven to be a particularly difficult disease to treat. At the beginning of the AIDS epidemic, many Americans associated AIDS mainly with nontraditional lifestyles, especially homosexuality or promiscuity, and as a result AIDS patients found themselves stigmatized. The stigma associated with AIDS, however, decreased somewhat as the disease has moved into the general population. Research into AIDS has increased greatly in the late 20th century. Despite the growth and prominence of cancer and AIDS, heart disease leads the list of disease killers in late-20th-century America.

As the understanding of heredity has increased during the 20th century, especially under the Human Genome Project, the relationship between genetics and disease has been explored. Scientists have discovered specific genetic mutations for many diseases traditionally considered genetic, including, for example, cystic fibrosis and Huntington's disease. Other conditions, including obesity and alcoholism, sometimes have been called "disease" as well. However, the causes are complex, and genes are frequently imperfect predictors of one's likelihood of developing certain diseases. Nonetheless, genetic screening of fetuses, children, and adults is on the rise as Americans try to understand and control diseases and conditions thought to be genetic.

—KATHY J. COOKE

See Also: Industrial Revolution; Medicine.

BIBLIOGRAPHY: Duffy, John, *The Sanitarians: A History of American Public Health* (Univ. of Illinois Press 1990); Kraut, Alan M., *Silent Travelers: Germs, Genes, and the "Immigrant Menace"* (Basic Books 1994); Leavitt, Judith Walzer, and Ronald L. Numbers, eds., *Sickness and Health in America: Readings in the History of Medicine and Public Health* (Univ. of Wisconsin Press 1978).

■ **DISFRANCHISEMENT,** depriving citizens of the right to vote. The 14th Amendment, ratified in 1868, guaranteed African Americans U.S. and state citizenship. But many states continued to prevent African Americans from voting. Consequently the 15th Amendment was adopted (1870). It states, "the right of citizens of the United States to vote shall not be denied or abridged by the United States or by any State on account of race, color, or previous condition of servitude."

Despite the 15th Amendment, however, white supremacist groups such as the Ku Klux Klan subjected politically active blacks to violence and terror. After the last federal troops were withdrawn from the South in 1877, southern states adopted strategies for limiting black suffrage, such as poll taxes, literacy tests, and the grandfather clause, which barred a person from voting if his grandfather had not voted. Not until the passage of civil rights legislation in the 1960s did African Americans in the South effectively gain the right to vote.

See Also: Civil Rights Movement; Ku Klux Klan; Reconstruction.

■ **DISNEY, WALT (1901-66),** filmmaker, producer, and entrepreneur. A purveyor of conservative ideas and utopian dreams, Disney left an indelible mark on American popular culture through his cartoon characters, animated films, and amusement parks. Disney, a native of

Walt Disney enjoys a ride at Disneyland with Mickey Mouse, his most famous and enduring character.

Chicago, began animating cartoons in Kansas City in 1920 and three years later relocated to Hollywood to make animated films with his brother Roy.

Disney first reached large audiences with his 1928 film, *Steamboat Willie*, the first appearance of Mickey Mouse. He followed this success by introducing other cartoon characters, including Donald Duck, Goofy, and the Three Little Pigs. Disney's fame burgeoned with the 1937 release of the first full-length animated film, *Snow White and the Seven Dwarfs*, followed by *Pinocchio* (1940), *Fantasia*, and *Bambi* (1942), and many others. During World War II, Disney featured many of his characters in government-sponsored military training films.

In the postwar years, Disney films, television ventures, and other products depicted a vision of cultural harmony. In 1955, the popular amusement park Disneyland opened in southern California, followed by Disney World in Florida in 1972. Disney's millions of fans worldwide were at-tracted by his utopian and conflict-free vision and helped make the Disney image one of the most recognizable and beloved icons in American popular culture. At the end of the 20th century, the Disney Corporation remains a powerful and influential giant in the entertainment industry.

See Also: *Motion Pictures.*
BIBLIOGRAPHY: Schickel, Richard, *The Disney Version: The Life, Times, Art, and Commerce of Walt Disney* (Simon & Schuster 1968).

■ **DISTILLING AND BREWING,** means of producing liquor and beer. In colonial America distilling rum became one important aspect of the "triangle trade" by which New England merchants traded in rum, slaves, and molasses between Massachusetts, Africa, and the West Indies. By 1750, more than 60 distilleries in Massachusetts Bay were exporting over 2 million gallons of rum. Farmers in the 18th century also distilled corn into whiskey, and an excise tax on strong drink levied in 1791 gave rise to the famous Whiskey Rebellion (1794). The "Whiskey Ring," which bribed tax collectors during the Grant years; the Pabst, Schlitz, Blatz, and Anheuser-Busch companies, which adopted vertical integration and national marketing networks; and the Distilling and Cattle Feeding Company, which controlled over 70 competing distilleries, were all evidence of the growth of the brewing and distilling industry during the late 19th century. When the 19th Amendment prohibited the manufacture, sale, and transportation of intoxicating liquors in 1920, the industry moved underground, and people made their own "bathtub gin." The 21st Amendment repealed Prohibition in 1933.

See Also: *Prohibition; Whiskey Rebellion.*

■ **DISTRICT OF COLUMBIA,** the seat of the federal government. With the same boundaries as the city of Washington, it is bounded by Maryland on the northwest, northeast, and southeast. The Potomac River separates it from Virginia to the west and south. Two-thirds of the District's residents are African Americans. About one-third of its workers are employees of the federal government. The District of Columbia became the nation's capital in 1800. In 1961, the 23rd Amendment to the Constitution gave residents the right to vote in presidential elections. In 1975, the District was granted home rule, with an elected mayor and city council.

Area: 68 square miles. Population (1995 est.): 559,000.

See Also: *Capitol; King, Martin Luther, Jr.; War of 1812; Washington, George.*

■ **DIVINE, FATHER (1877-1965),** religious leader. Born George Baker on Hutchison's Island, Georgia, he moved to New York City's Harlem around 1915. Father Divine created and headed the Peace Mission Movement, a religiously centered cooperative agency that provided low-cost food and housing for its followers. The movement was nonsectarian and interracial. At the height of the Depression, Divine's combination of communalism and religious enthusiasm was extremely popular among thousands who had little security or comfort.

See Also: *African Americans; New Deal.*

■ **DIVORCE,** the legal dissolution of a marriage. In the 17th and 18th centuries, divorce, rooted in patriarchal law, was almost as rare in America as it had been in Europe. The northern colonies, influenced by the Puritan conception of marriage as a civil contract, did allow some absolute divorce; the southern colonies, however, permitted only separations. Many couples bypassed the strict laws by using desertion to solve their marital difficulties.

After the American Revolution and through the 19th century, divorce restrictions began to loosen. Many states added "cruelty" to the list of grounds on which a divorce could be granted. Although they forfeited their property, lost their children, and bore social stigma, unhappily married women in the 19th century increasingly turned to the courts. The divorce rate rose dramatically: in 1880 only 1 in 21 marriages ended in divorce; by 1916 the figure had climbed to 1 in 9. By 1900 two-thirds of all divorce cases were brought by women. Women also began to gain custody of their children but not financial support.

In the 20th century, fueled by growing female economic independence and new romantic expectations, the divorce rate continued to outpace the divorce laws. As late as the 1950s divorce by mutual consent did not exist; South Carolina did not permit divorce at all. In 1969 California passed the first "no fault" divorce law, and other states soon followed. Although intended to eliminate the adversarial nature of divorce, "no fault" has proved financially devastating to women and children.

The social debate around divorce began in the late 19th century and continues today. Females and liberals regard the right to divorce as crucial to female independence, while conservatives view divorce as selfishness and a prelude to serious social disorder.

—Catherine Allgor

See Also: *Feminism; Marriage; Women in American History.*

BIBLIOGRAPHY: Blake, Nelson Manfred, *The Road to Reno: A History of Divorce in the United States* (Greenwood 1962); Griswold, Robert L., *Family and Divorce in California, 1850-1890: Victorian Illusions and Everyday Realities* (SUNY Press 1982).

■ **DIX, DOROTHEA (1802-87),** reformer, born in Hampden, Maine. In the 1840s and 1850s she tire-

Reformer Dorothea Dix launched a movement to establish hospitals for specialized treatment of the insane with her shocking report that mentally ill women were sent to prisons and locked up in "... cages, closets, stalls, [and] pens! Chained, naked, beaten with rods, and lashed into obedience!"

lessly investigated and documented the commonplace neglect and abuse of the mentally ill in prisons and hospitals around the country. Her findings, presented to state legislatures, earned her national recognition and inspired reforms in almost every state. From 1861 to 1866 she was the superintendent of female nurses for the Union Army.

See Also: Women in American History.

■ **DIXIE,** mythic name for the American South and the title of a popular 19th-century minstrel song. While the origin of the term is uncertain, Daniel D. Emmett's song "Dixie," composed in 1859 for Bryant's Minstrel Troupe of New York, widely popularized the term. A march version was performed at Jefferson Davis's inauguration as president of the Confederacy in 1861, and the Confederate army frequently marched to the tune. During and after the Civil War the former Confederate states became known as Dixie. The term also conjures up mythic notions of the Southern plantation system based on the white oppression of African Americans that existed before the Civil War. While slavery was overturned with the South's defeat in the Civil War, the white-controlled state legislatures implemented legal and economic measures after Reconstruction ended in 1877 to continue the subordination of African Americans. The 1939 movie *Gone With the Wind*, based on Margaret Mitchell's Pulitzer Prize–winning novel (1936), reflected and helped define the iconic image of Dixie in the modern American imagination.

■ **DIXIECRATS,** southern Democrats who walked out of the 1948 party convention to protest a civil rights plank and formed the States Rights party. They nominated Gov. Strom Thurmond of South Carolina for president and carried four Southern states.

See Also: Thurmond, Strom.

■ **DOLE, ROBERT (1923-),** politician and Republican presidential nominee in 1996. Born in Russell, Kansas, he was seriously wounded while with the U.S. Army in Italy (1945). Dole was elected to the U.S. House of Representatives (1960) and the Senate (1968), chaired the Republican National Committee (1971-73), and was his party's leader in the Senate (1985-96). He ran for

vice president with Pres. Gerald Ford in 1976 and sought the Republican presidential nomination in 1980, 1988, and 1996. He ran an ineffective campaign in 1996 and, with running mate Jack Kemp, was soundly defeated by incumbent Bill Clinton.

See Also: Presidential Elections.

■ **DOLE, SANFORD BALLARD (1844-1926),** politician and lawyer. He was born in Hawaii, the son of missionaries. A member of the Hawaiian legislature from 1884 to 1887, he took part in the passage of the Hawaiian Constitution in 1887 and the overthrow of Queen Liliuokalani in 1893. He was elected president of the Republic of Hawaii in 1894. In 1900, the United States annexed Hawaii, and Dole served as territorial governor until 1903, when he became a U.S. district court judge.

See Also: Gilded Age; Hawaii; Liliuokalani.

■ **DOLLAR DIPLOMACY,** foreign policy of Pres. William H. Taft's administration (1909-13) that used U.S. economic power to further American economic and political interests in Latin America and East Asia. Dollar diplomacy had its origins in Pres. Theodore Roosevelt's 1905 corollary to the Monroe Doctrine, establishing that the United States could intervene in the domestic affairs of any country in the Western Hemisphere that was vulnerable to European control.

After becoming president in 1909, Taft expanded this policy, stressing financial reform through loans and customs revenue as a means to political and economic stabilization in vulnerable nations. Directed primarily at Latin America, dollar diplomacy was used to justify American protection of the Panama Canal, direct intervention in Nicaragua, and refinancing of Haiti's national debt. Along with similar activities in other countries, these interventions stimulated American investment in the region and set precedents for future U.S. involvement. This policy was also pursued in China to thwart European, primarily Russian, development of railroads and encourage American trade.

Although justified as a more humane substitute to military intervention, which it by no means ruled out, the policy was attacked by some as a duplicitous effort to exploit Latin American and East Asian countries economically. After only four years as an official policy, dollar diplomacy was abandoned by Pres. Woodrow Wilson shortly after his inauguration in 1913. Conceptually, however, dollar diplomacy continued to influence American policy toward Latin America throughout the 20th century.

See Also: Nicaraguan Interventions; Panama Canal; Taft, William Howard.

BIBLIOGRAPHY: Gardner, Richard N., *Sterling-Dollar Diplomacy in Current Perspective* (Columbia Univ. Press 1980).

DOMINICANS, a religious order of Roman Catholic priests officially titled the Order of Preachers (OP). It was founded in 1215 by St. Dominic of Caleruega. There is an affiliated order of nuns and a third order of teachers. Traditionally, Dominicans, who wear white habits, were mendicant friars devoted to monastic observance and to preaching after long periods of study of scholastic theology and philosophy. The order was established in the United States early in the 19th century.

See Also: Religion; Roman Catholics.

DOMINION OF NEW ENGLAND, entity comprising all the colonies north and east of the Delaware River, created by James II in 1685. The decision to combine New England into one single provincial entity was part of a larger pattern of exerting greater royal control over the colonies that developed at the end of the 17th century. Creating the dominion centralized political power and placed it in the hands of the royal governor and council appointed by the king. Local assemblies of individual colonies ceased to operate. James II's removal and William and Mary's ascendance to the throne in 1688 ended the Dominion and reinstated colonial assemblies, but the economic and political autonomy of the earliest days of the colonies was not restored.

DONIPHAN'S EXPEDITION (1846-47), U.S. invasion of Mexico during the Mexican War. After U.S. troops took New Mexico in February, Alexander Doniphan led a force southward from Santa Fe. His army captured the city of Chihuahua, securing much of northern Mexico.

See Also: Mexican War.

DONNER PARTY, doomed emigrant company whose experience formed the basis for the most horrifying cautionary tale of the overland trek to the Pacific coast. In the spring of 1846 the brothers Jacob and George Donner led a company of 89 emigrants from their farmland of central Illinois bound for California. In an attempt to cut the time of their journey, they took the advice of the promoter Lansford Hastings and left the established trail near Fort Bridger for a new and untried "cutoff." But the new route actually took far more time, and the party did not begin the long climb over the Sierra Nevadas until late October. Before they had made it over the pass, an early onset of winter storms left them snowbound. After being stranded nearly two months, with supplies running dangerously low, a group of 15 volunteers set out to cross the mountains in mid-December. Caught in horrible storms, four died and their companions were forced to cannibalize their remains. Two Indian guides, who refused to touch human flesh, were killed for food. The survivors reached an Indian village after 32 days of suffering. A rescue party sent into the mountains did not find the stranded emigrants until mid-February; they too had resorted to cannibalism. In all, 44 people perished. The lesson of the Donner party was perhaps best summarized in the words of a 14-year-old survivor, Virginia Reed: "Never take no cutoffs and hurry along as fast as you can."

See Also: Frontier in American History; Overland Trail.

BIBLIOGRAPHY: Johnson, Kristin, ed., *Unfortunate Emigrants: Narratives of the Donner Party* (Utah State Univ. Press 1996); Stewart, George Rippey, *Ordeal by Hunger: The Story of the Donner Party* (Houghton Mifflin 1960).

DORR'S REBELLION (1842), movement against Rhode Island's charter. In the mid-19th century, the state of Rhode Island was still using the 1663 charter issued by King Charles II of England as its constitution. This charter limited suffrage to landholders and their eldest sons, effectively disfranchising the majority of the adult male population.

Thomas Dorr was a Rhode Islander who led a movement to extend the suffrage, and in 1841 Dorr and his followers drew up what they called the "People's Constitution." In response, a state Constitutional Convention was held and a new constitution approved, which extended the suffrage. In

December 1841, in an election in which all male citizens voted, the constitution was approved. The new constitution, however, was rejected by the qualified landholding voters, and Rhode Island's government remained under the old charter.

In the spring of 1842 Dorr and his supporters set up a new government under the People's Constitution and elected Dorr the governor. Rhode Island's sitting governor, Samuel King, appealed to Pres. John Tyler, but Tyler urged the two sides to settle their difference without federal intervention. King ignored the president's admonition and sent the state militia to attack the Dorrites at their armed headquarters in the northwestern part of the state. Dorr surrendered and was tried, convicted, and sentenced to life in prison, a sentence that was later rescinded. In the aftermath, the landholders revised the constitution to include male suffrage with slight restrictions.

—KATHRYN A. ABBOTT

See Also: Rhode Island.

BIBLIOGRAPHY: Gettleman, Marvin E., *A Study in American Radicalism, 1833-1849* (Random House 1973).

■ **DOS PASSOS, JOHN (1896-1970),** modernist novelist. A native of Chicago, Illinois, Dos Passos graduated from Harvard University in 1916. Dos Passos's early writings, published in journals such as *New Masses*, showed his radical beliefs about championing the working class and above all the individual. His masterpiece is the trilogy *U.S.A.*, comprising the novels *The 42nd Parallel* (1930), *Nineteen Nineteen* (1931), and *The Big Money* (1936). They incorporate experimental passages representing the profusion of communications media.

See Also: Novel.

■ **DOUGHBOYS,** nickname for U.S. Army infantrymen serving in the American Expeditionary Force in World War I. The term is thought to derive from the appearance of soldiers in the American West after being covered with dust.

See Also: American Expeditionary Force (AEF); World War I.

■ **DOUGLAS, STEPHEN ARNOLD (1813-61),** Democratic congressman, senator, and presidential candidate. Diminutive but pugnacious, Douglas, "the Little Giant," was born in Brandon, Vermont,

and educated at Canandaigua Academy in New York. At age 20, he immigrated to the rough-hewn Old Northwest town of Jacksonville, Illinois, where he taught school and read law.

Licensed to practice law in 1834, he began his long political career the next year. Douglas held a succession of state offices before entering the U.S. House of Representatives in 1843 for the first of two terms there

As a congressman, Douglas vigorously supported the expansionist policies of Pres. James K. Polk and the Mexican War. Elected in 1847 to the Senate, where he remained for the rest of his life, Douglas became chairman of the Committee on Territories. His parliamentary strategy was largely responsible for the passage of the Compromise of 1850. A powerful proponent of the so-called "popular sovereignty" doctrine, which allowed settlers in a territory to decide the fate of slavery themselves, Douglas grafted the concept onto the Utah

Having underestimated the degree of Northern hostility to the 1854 Kansas-Nebraska Act, Stephen Douglas, the "Little Giant" of Illinois, acknowledged his unpopularity and remarked, "I could travel from Boston to Chicago by the light of my own [burning] effigy."

and New Mexico territorial bills that formed part of the compromise. He also incorporated the principle into the fateful Kansas-Nebraska bill of 1854 that engendered fierce sectional strife.

More ominously, his denunciation in 1857 of the fraudulent Lecompton (Kansas) constitution, backed by the administration of Pres. James Buchanan and the proslavery wing of the Democratic party, caused a rift in the party that proved irreparable. Douglas won reelection to the Senate in 1858 after a series of famous debates with Republican candidate Abraham Lincoln.

Thwarted for the Democratic presidential nomination in 1852 and 1856, Douglas refused to bow to Southern pressure in 1860. The party then split, one wing nominating Douglas, the other John C. Breckinridge, a Southern rights supporter. The split sealed Lincoln's election and the ensuing breakup of the Union. Douglas continued to favor compromise during the secession crisis but firmly supported Lincoln once the war began.

—THOMAS E. SCHOTT

See Also: Bleeding Kansas; Civil War; Compromise of 1850; Kansas-Nebraska Act; Lincoln-Douglas Debates; Popular Sovereignty.

BIBLIOGRAPHY: Johannsen, Robert W., *Stephen A. Douglas* (Oxford Univ. Press 1973).

Associate justice of the U.S. Supreme Court from 1939 to 1975, William O. Douglas issued one of his most famous dissents in the 1951 case of *Dennis* v. *United States*, in which he eloquently defended free speech.

■ DOUGLAS, WILLIAM ORVILLE (1898-1980),

associate justice of the U.S. Supreme Court (1939-75). Born in Maine, Minnesota, Douglas led an enormously productive and unconventional life. A person of an active and keen intellect, he battled back from childhood polio and poverty to graduate from Columbia Law School, where he taught before moving to Yale Law School in 1928. He possessed a deep understanding of finance and served as chairman of the Securities and Exchange Commission (SEC) from 1936 to 1939.

In 1939, Pres. Franklin D. Roosevelt appointed Douglas, a staunch liberal and New Deal supporter, to the Supreme Court, where he served until 1975. During his years on the bench, Douglas passionately defended the First Amendment and individual rights of privacy, dissent, and political action. He believed strongly in equal access, for all people, to the economic and social benefits generally enjoyed by the few. With Justice Hugo Black, Douglas dissented from the

Court's McCarthy-era decisions that upheld anticommunist legislation. Douglas suppressed nascent political ambitions, when in 1948 he turned down President Truman's offer of the vice-presidential nomination.

Douglas, a prolific and controversial writer, angered many conservatives and faced an unsuccessful impeachment investigation in 1970 spearheaded by Rep. Gerald R. Ford of Michigan. He lectured widely on college campuses, pursued outdoor activities such as mountain climbing, and studied the science of ecology. As lively in mind as in body, Douglas was one of America's most colorful jurists.

See Also: Supreme Court.

BIBLIOGRAPHY: Ball, Howard, *Of Power and Right: Hugo Black, William O. Douglas, and America's Constitutional Revolution* (Oxford Univ. Press 1992); Simon, James F., *Independent Journey: The Life of William O. Douglas* (Harper & Row 1980).

■ DOUGLASS, FREDERICK (1818-95), antislavery and early civil rights leader. Frederick Augus-

tus Washington Bailey was born to Harriet Bailey on an outlying farm of his owner, Aaron Anthony, in Talbot County, Maryland. Douglass' early years were passed on this farm under the care of his grandmother, Betsy Bailey. His early years were spent working for Anthony, the wealthy Lloyd family, and the Auld family. After Anthony's death in 1827, Douglass ultimately was sent to Hugh Auld, the brother of Anthony's son-in-law. With the Aulds in Baltimore, Douglass was introduced to reading and writing and inaugurated a lifelong passion for learning. He was exposed to antislavery literature and debate and to diverse political opinions, and he underwent a religious conversion through a local African Methodist Episcopal (AME) church.

Sent in 1834 to work for a farmer in rural Talbot County who was a notorious "slave-breaker," Douglass endured much abuse, successfully confronted his tormentor, and vowed to allow no slaveholder to beat him again. Douglass began to focus on escaping slavery. After an 1836 attempt Douglass, once returned to Baltimore, was able in 1838 to borrow the clothing and papers of a local free black sailor and rode a train and a boat to freedom in New York City. He would never serve again as a slave. To signify this rebirth he abandoned the name "Bailey" and adopted "Douglass." He then sent for Anna Murray, a free black from Baltimore, and they married.

Antislavery Activities. By late 1838, the new couple settled in New Bedford, Massachusetts, where Douglass worked as a caulker but more often as a common laborer. He became active in the AME congregation and spoke out against slavery and the movement to remove free blacks to Africa. In August 1841 noted abolitionist William Lloyd Garrison heard Douglass's fervent oratory at an antislavery convention and immediately enlisted him as an antislavery lecturer. By 1843 he had become one of the most renowned orators on the circuit in the North, telling vividly the story of his life in the South as a slave. In 1844, encouraged by Garrison, Douglass began to write an autobiography in which he neither hid his identity nor the names of those who owned and hired him. In May 1845, *Narrative of the Life of Frederick Douglass* was published in Boston and sold thousands of copies. Yet, its very success jeopardized Doug-

Frederick Douglass escaped slavery in 1838 and published his autobiography, *Narrative of the Life of Frederick Douglass,* in 1845.

lass's freedom, and he undertook an extensive lecture tour in Britain. While there he became close friends with many British abolitionists, who raised enough funds to purchase his freedom and for him to start a newspaper. When he returned to America in 1847 he refused to abandon his plans for a newspaper despite Garrison's opposition. Indeed, he chose to move outside of Garrison's orbit to Rochester, New York, where on Dec. 3, 1847, he published the first issue of the *North Star.*

Over the coming years, Douglass's rift with Garrison widened. Douglass continued his antislavery lecturing throughout the 1850s as well as publishing the *North Star,* renamed *Frederick Douglass's Paper* in 1851, and his second autobiography, *My Bondage and My Freedom* (1855). After Congress passed a reinforced Fugitive Slave Act (1850), he assisted runaway slaves more vigorously and even began to endorse the use of violence to resist enslavement. In the late 1850s, Douglass supported his friend John Brown's plan to seize the federal armory at Harpers Ferry, Virginia, and use it as a base to spark a massive slave revolt but ultimately refused to join the mission. Implicated in the failed conspiracy, Douglass fled the country, not returning until early 1860, after charges were dropped.

In the 1860 presidential campaign Douglass endorsed Abraham Lincoln and then celebrated the South's secession. Douglass knew secession provided an unprecedented opportunity to end slavery, and he and his abolitionist allies increased their agitation for basing the war on an end to slavery and demanded further that African Americans be allowed to enlist in the army and fight. Under mounting military and political pressure, Lincoln decided in summer 1862 to issue the Emancipation Proclamation on Jan. 1, 1863, and to open the army to blacks. By the war's end, Douglass had become the most visible and powerful African American in the Republican party.

Postwar Career. Douglass quickly ran afoul of Andrew Johnson, Lincoln's successor, who he thought too conciliatory toward the Southern states and unsympathetic toward blacks. Douglass and numerous other black and white Republicans were appalled with these policies and blocked much of Johnson's program, replacing it with a plan for Radical Reconstruction. Douglass worked for this program and campaigned in 1868 for its defender, Ulysses S. Grant. By 1872, despite Grant's administration scandals and fading commitment to Radical Reconstruction, Douglass continued to campaign for him. His loyalty to the Republican party won him various official appointments from 1871, including consul general to Haiti (1889-91). Yet, Douglass never ceased speaking out against the persisting exploitation of African Americans and the failure to secure them full citizenship, especially as their social, political, and economic vulnerability worsened after 1876. In the early 1890s Douglass collaborated with Ida Barnett Wells to fight against the epidemic of lynchings then sweeping the South. He moved to Washington, D.C., in 1872 and, after the death of Anna in 1882, married (1884) his controversial white wife, Helen Pitts. Douglass revised his third and final autobiography, *The Life and Times of Frederick Douglass,* as late as 1892 and continued laboring vigorously until his death.

—PETER HINKS

See Also: African Americans; Antislavery Movement; Brown, John; Civil Rights Movement; Civil War; Garrison, William Lloyd; Reconstruction; Slavery.

BIBLIOGRAPHY: Blight, David, *Frederick Douglass' Civil War: Keeping Faith in Jubilee* (Louisiana State Univ. Press 1989); McFeely, William S., *Frederick Douglass* (Norton 1991); Preston, Dickson, *Young Frederick Douglass: The Maryland Years* (Johns Hopkins Univ. Press 1980).

■ **DOW, NEAL (1804-97),** American reformer and prohibitionist. Born in Portland, Maine, he became the city's mayor in 1851 and drafted a prohibition law that became known as the "Maine Law," the first statewide prohibition passed in the United States. Several other states soon followed suit. Dow is credited with cleaning up the liquor traffic in Portland, which earned him a national reputation. Dow was the Prohibition party's candidate for president in 1880.

See Also: Prohibition.

■ **DOWNING, ANDREW JACKSON (1815-52),** proponent of the picturesque in landscape and architecture. Born in Newburgh, New York, he had an avid interest in horticulture and ran his own nursery early in his career. In 1846, he began editing *The Horticulturist,* in which he presented his ideas on the value of a picturesque style of landscaping that made use of existing natural features. He published a series of books promoting his views, including *Cottage Residences* in 1842 and the influential *Architecture of Country Houses* in 1850. Downing completed such major commissions as landscaping the U.S. Capitol and the White House.

See Also: Architecture; White House.

■ **DRAFT RIOTS,** a wave of protest against the military draft that broke out in New York City in July 1863. Conscription was adopted by the Union in March 1863. The law allowed a draftee to hire a substitute or just to pay the government $300 to become exempt, an unaffordable price for the ordinary worker. In July 1863, a week-long riot took place in New York City. The riots broke out on Monday, July 13, and raged through July 17. The violence of the mob (many of whom were Irish workingmen) was directed against draft officers, wealthy individuals, proponents of war, and blacks. The latter were "the cause of war" and were also considered a threat to the whites' jobs. Besides, since the draft law pertained only to the citizens of the United States, blacks were not subject to conscription. Much of the violence was directed against famous abolitionists and their property. However, rioters met with stiff resistance from the police, the army, and, notably, from volunteer fire companies and many German Americans. Street clashes often grew into battles. By Thursday, July 16, the Union troops returning from Gettysburg started to clear the city, and on the next day order was basically restored. About 60,000 people were involved in the riots; and at least 400 were killed.

See Also: Civil War; Conscription Act.
BIBLIOGRAPHY: Bernstein, Iver, *The New York City Draft Riots* (Oxford Univ. Press 1990).

■ **DRAGGING CANOE (c. 1730-92),** Cherokee leader of the Chickamauga band. The son of chief Attakullakulla, Dragging Canoe led a force against settlers along the trans-Appalachian frontier in July 1776. In retaliation, colonial patriot forces under James Robertson and John Sevier laid waste to many Cherokee villages, destroying crops and crushing Cherokee military resistance. In the subsequent treaty, the Cherokees were forced to cede much of their territory. Dragging Canoe continued to resist the Americans until 1784.

See Also: Indians of North America; Revolution, American; Sevier, John.

■ **DRAKE, SIR FRANCIS (1543?-96),** English privateer, sea captain, and pirate. The most famous of the "Sea Dogs," Drake led early English efforts in the 1560s and 1570s to establish a slave-trading network and to profit from New World riches. As a member of John Hawkins's slave-trading expedition from the west African coast to the Gulf of Mexico in 1567, Drake first encountered Spanish hostility to English activity in the New World. He responded by launching a long series of devastating and lucrative raids against Spanish ports and ships in the Caribbean.

Under the employ of Queen Elizabeth I, Drake became the second man to circumnavigate the globe (1577-80). He followed Magellan's route until he reached the west coast of South America, when he proceeded northward. Drake was the first European to anchor in California and to encounter the region's natives. After returning to England via the Strait of Magellan with valuable cartographic information and spices, Drake was knighted by Queen Elizabeth.

During the 1580s, Drake resumed his raids on Spanish America. In 1588, King Philip II of Spain, outraged by English incursions into Spanish territory, sent the Spanish Armada, a fleet of 130 ships and 30,000 men, to invade England. Drake helped command the more maneuverable English ships in the defeat of the armada. He died of dysentery while sailing in the Gulf of Mexico.

See Also: Exploration and Discovery; Piracy.
BIBLIOGRAPHY: Cummins, John, *Francis Drake: The Lives of a Hero* (St. Martin's Press 1995); Sudgen, John, *Sir Francis Drake* (Barriet & Jenkins 1990).

■ ***DRED SCOTT V. SANDFORD* (1857),** case in which the Supreme Court ruled that African Americans, free or slave, had no rights under the

It took 11 years for *Dred Scott* v. *Sandford* to reach the Supreme Court and it took four long hours for 79-year-old Chief Justice Roger B. Taney to read his majority opinion, ruling against Scott in 1857.

Constitution and could not be citizens. One of the most important and controversial cases in American constitutional history, *Dred Scott* reflected the sectional conflict of the time and exacerbated tensions that led to the Civil War.

Dred Scott and his wife Harriet Robinson Scott, both slaves, sued their dead master's widow for freedom, but lost the case in a Missouri state court. After the widow's brother from New York, John Sanford (whose name was erroneously recorded as "Sandford" in the Supreme Court docket), assumed control of her affairs, including ownership of the slaves, Scott sued again, claiming that he had a right to be free under the Missouri Compromise because his master had taken him from Missouri (a slave state) to free northern territories. He lost the case and appealed to the U.S. Supreme Court.

The court divided along sectional and ideological lines, with two northern justices arguing for Scott's freedom under the Missouri Compromise. Seven justices, including five southerners, led by Chief Justice Roger B. Taney, declared that Congress had no authority to ban slavery in any of the territories and that the Missouri Compromise was therefore unconstitutional. Taney's infamous opinion for the Court declared Scott still a slave. Slaves, Taney wrote, could not be freed by traveling to northern territories.

Taney had hoped that the *Dred Scott* decision would settle the issue of slavery once and for all. Instead, it led to angry protests by antislavery supporters, divided northern and southern Democrats, and contributed greatly to the beginning of the Civil War four years later. Most historians and legal scholars consider *Dred Scott* and Taney's opinion to be among the worst Supreme Court decisions.

See Also: *Missouri Compromise; Supreme Court; Taney, Roger Brooke.*

BIBLIOGRAPHY: Ehrlich, Walter, *They Have No Rights: Dred Scott's Struggle for Freedom* (Greenwood Press 1979); Fehrenbacher, Don E., *The Dred Scott Case: Its Significance in American Law and Politics* (Oxford Univ. Press 1978).

■ **DREISER, THEODORE (1871-1945),** novelist. Born into a large, poor, and religious family in Terre Haute, Indiana, Dreiser satisfied his early appetite for reading with the works of Herbert

Theodore Dreiser wrote his controversial first novel, *Sister Carrie,* in 1900.

Spencer, Balzac, and Freud. These intellectual influences help to explain his disgust with organized religion and the naturalistic conviction in his writing. After a scant formal education, Dreiser began his career as a peripatetic newspaperman. He completed his first novel, *Sister Carrie,* in 1900, but the publisher suppressed it for over a decade because of its unconventional moral viewpoint. A period of personal and emotional turmoil followed, during which Dreiser ceased writing novels and worked as an editor.

In 1910 Dreiser resumed writing fiction and a year later completed *Jennie Gerhardt,* which, like *Sister Carrie,* focused on the female sexuality of a troubled heroine. During this prolific period he wrote a trilogy: *The Financier* (1912), *The Titan* (1914), and *The Stoic* (1947), based on the character Frank Cowperwood, a ruthless financial tycoon. Perhaps

Dreiser's finest novel is *An American Tragedy* (1925), a story about how the American success myth drives the protagonist to attempt a murder. During the 1920s and 1930s Dreiser became increasingly involved in socialism and left-wing politics.

Although attacked by many critics for his crude writing style, Dreiser has been acclaimed for his incisive depiction of the conflict in American society between basic human needs and the pursuit of wealth at any cost.

See Also: Novel.
BIBLIOGRAPHY: Lingman, Richard R., *Theodore Dreiser* (Putnam 1986-90); Swanberg, William A., *Dreiser* (Scribner 1965).

■ **DRESSLER, MARIE (1869?-1934),** stage and screen actress. Born in Coburg in Ontario, Canada, she was known before World War I for her portrayal of character roles in comic opera, vaudeville, and silent film. In her later years she became a major Hollywood star. In 1931 she was named best actress by the Academy of Motion Picture Arts and Sciences for her performance in *Min and Bill*.

■ **DRINKER, ELIZABETH SANDWITH (1736-1807),** colonial diarist born in Philadelphia, Pennsylvania. Her journal, written between 1758 and 1807, is one of the few historical documents recording a woman's perspective on 18th-century America. It is impressive for its length and insightful detail.

■ **DRUGS,** substances other than food taken for their effect on the body. Widespread abuse of drugs other than alcohol or nicotine began in the United States in the 19th century. Opium imports began to rise early in that century and reached a peak in the mid-1890s. When the adverse effects of uncontrolled distribution and consumption came to public attention, use of opiates began to decline. Gradually, the open market in drugs was restricted by a series of local and state laws, a process that culminated in passage of the federal Harrison Narcotics Act of 1914. This act limited the freedom of physicians to prescribe opiates and cocaine; although attacked as an unconstitutional invasion of the states' police power, it was upheld (5-4) by the U.S. Supreme Court in 1919.

Thereafter nonmedical opiate use in the United States declined until the 1950s, when it rose slightly. It surged between 1962 and 1974, roughly the period of U.S. involvement in the Vietnam War, then declined again and, in the form of heroin, taken intravenously, was concentrated in large cities.

Cocaine, refined from coca and ingested by smoking or sniffing, has largely supplanted heroin, perhaps owing to the role of needle sharing in spreading the deadly AIDS virus. Unlike opium, cocaine was not easily available in the United States until the 1880s. At first, it was perceived as a healthy tonic by some experts, but gradually such adverse effects of prolonged use as paranoia and compulsive drug-seeking radically changed its image. By the 1930s cocaine use had faded, not to reach significant levels again until about 1970. In the mid-1980s, "crack," a cheap, smokable form of cocaine, was introduced to the illicit market and rapidly gained a reputation as an unprecedented threat to public order, health, and morals. The cocaine-induced deaths of two young professional athletes in 1986 crystallized the public's fear of the drug, and casual use declined. A hard core of about a half-million regular cocaine users remained.

Marijuana became an issue in the United States in the 1920s and 1930s. As the Great Depression settled over the Southwest, unemployed field hands of Mexican origin were seen as a source of violence, which was blamed on the marijuana they were believed to consume. The Marijuana Tax Act of 1937 was meant to control that threat by requiring the documentation of all marijuana sales; registration and taxation of manufacturers, importers, dealers, and medical practitioners; and taxation of all transfers. Marijuana did not become widely used until the 1960s when young people began to experiment with it; by 1979 one out of 10 high-school seniors was a daily user. Marijuana use then declined.

Other controlled substances include LSD (lysergic acid diethylamide), a hallucinogenic; amphetamines, or "speed"; methamphetamines, stimulants with effects similar to cocaine; and barbiturates. Substances in glue and aerosol products are also abused, particularly by children, who inhale the vapors, which can result in irreparable brain damage or death.

The effectiveness of drug interdiction efforts was a subject of national debate at century's end.

Critics argued that drug-law enforcement—and its attendant vast increase in the nation's prison population—created more problems than it solved and advocated that drug possession for personal use be decriminalized. The vast majority of Americans, however, favored controls. At the same time, research, prevention, and treatment of addicts had failed to yield a solution to the abuse of illicit substances.

—DAVID F. MUSTO

See Also: *Medicine.*

BIBLIOGRAPHY: Bonnie, Richard J., and Charles H. Whitebread II, *The Marihuana Conviction: A History of Marihuana Prohibition in the United States* (Univ. of Virginia Press 1974); Courtwright, David T., *Dark Paradise: Opiate Addiction in America before 1940* (Harvard Univ. Press 1982); Morgan, H. Wayne, *Drugs in America: A Social History, 1800-1980* (Syracuse Univ. Press 1981); Musto, David F., *The American Disease: Origins of Narcotic Control* (Yale Univ. Press 1973, rev. ed. Oxford Univ. Press 1987); U.S. Public Health Service, *National Institutes of Health National Survey Results on Drug Use from the Monitoring the Future Study, 1975-1994* (U.S. Government Printing Office 1995).

■ **DUBINSKY, DAVID (1892-1982),** labor leader. He was born in Brest-Litovsk, Russia. Deported to Siberia for union activities in his homeland, he escaped to the United States in 1911 and became a naturalized citizen in 1916. Finding employment as a cloakmaker, Dubinsky joined the International Ladies' Garment Workers' Union (ILGWU). He was union president from 1932 to 1966. During his tenure the number of ILGWU members grew dramatically. He was also a founder of the American Labor party (1936), the Liberal party (1944), and the Americans for Democratic Action (1947).

See Also: *Labor Movement.*

■ **DU BOIS, W. E. B. (1868-1963),** African-American intellectual and human rights activist. Du Bois was born in Great Barrington, Massachusetts, on Feb. 23, 1868, and attended the local schools. In September 1885, Du Bois entered Fisk University, where he earned his B.A. in June 1888. While living in Nashville, he encountered racism and witnessed the subjugation of other African Americans. This experience had a profound effect on Du Bois; he spent the remainder of his life writing about African Americans. After graduating from Fisk, he entered Harvard College and earned his A.B., cum laude, in philosophy in June 1890. He won the Boylston Prize for Rhetoric, taking second place. Du Bois continued his education in Germany but returned to pursue a Ph.D. at Harvard. In 1895 he became the first African American to earn the doctoral degree.

Few universities, however, would hire him. The University of Pennsylvania hired him to write about the African-American community in Philadelphia but did not include his name in the university's catalog. He was not allowed an office. Most of his teaching was done at historically African-American colleges, such as Wilberforce and Atlanta Universities. As a public figure he was secretary of the Pan-African Conference, founder and general secretary of the Niagara Movement, and a founder of the National Association for the Advancement of Colored People (NAACP).

But Du Bois was a man of letters, and it is his writing for which he will be remembered. He edited the NAACP's magazine, *The Crisis,* from 1910 to 1934. He wrote more than 20 books, edited an-

"The problem of the twentieth century is the problem of the color line," declared scholar-reformer W.E.B. Du Bois, the first African American to receive a Ph.D. Du Bois challenged black Americans to fight for higher education and civic equality.

other 15, and published more than 100 pamphlets, essays, and articles. In his most famous work, *The Souls of Black Folk: Essays and Sketches* (1903), he writes persuasively about how the color line shapes and redefines the social status of African Americans in Georgia. Du Bois died on Aug. 27, 1963, in Accra, Ghana.

—DARRELL DONNELL DARRISAW

See Also: African Americans; Civil Rights Movement; National Association for the Advancement of Colored People (NAACP); Niagara Movement.

BIBLIOGRAPHY: Du Bois, W.E.B., *The Autobiography of W.E.B. Du Bois: A Soliloquy in Viewing My Life from the Last Decade of Its First Century* (International Publishers 1988); Lewis, David Levering, *W.E.B Du Bois: Biography of a Race, 1868-1919* (Henry Holt 1993).

■ **DUCHAMP, HENRI-ROBERT-MARCEL (1887-1968),** artist. Born in France, he spent much of his adult life in New York City, and America would become his adopted country. His *Nude Descending a Staircase* (1912) was the notorious sensation of the 1915 Armory Show and secured his reputation. Although he made no attempt to promote himself or his work, fame overtook him; his revolutionary beliefs, especially his idea that art is a "mental act," advanced the concept that art should be its own reality, not an imitation of something else.

See Also: Armory Show.

BIBLIOGRAPHY: Paz, Octavio, *Marcel Duchamp* (Viking 1978); Tomkins, Calvin, *Duchamp: A Biography* (John Macrae/Henry Holt 1996).

■ **DUELING,** social custom where two persons engage in prearranged, sometimes mortal, combat over personal disputes. Dueling occurred sporadically in New England prior to 1763 and rarely after the American Revolution. Dueling gained popularity in the antebellum South when it became linked with codes of personal conduct and honor among the planter classes. On July 11, 1804, Alexander Hamilton was fatally wounded in a notorious duel with Aaron Burr.

■ **DUE PROCESS OF LAW,** legal doctrine that seeks to avoid arbitrary government actions and to establish fair and predictable practices when the government places an obligation on a citizen.

Rooted in the Magna Carta (1215) and English common law, which insisted even the king was obligated to obey the laws of the land, due process is enshrined in the 5th and 14th Amendments to the U.S. Constitution. The 5th Amendment (1791) bars the federal government from depriving any citizen of "life, liberty or property without due process of law." The 14th Amendment (1868) applies the same requirement to state governments. The Court in the 1960s applied substantive due process to social issues by declaring fundamental rights to privacy in cases such as *Griswold* v. *Connecticut* (1965) and *Roe* v. *Wade* (1973). It also extended federal procedural due process protections to the states in *Mapp* v. *Ohio* (1961), *Gideon* v. *Wainwright* (1963), and other cases.

See Also: Gideon v. Wainwright; Griswold v. Connecticut; Mapp v. Ohio; Roe v. Wade.

■ **DUKE, JAMES B. (1856-1925),** industrialist. Born near Durham, North Carolina, he was raised on a leaf tobacco farm and became a partner in Washington Duke and Sons in 1878. When the firm entered the cigarette business in 1881, Duke introduced fast cigarette-rolling machines and generated a market for his product through innovative advertising and sales techniques. By 1889 his company produced half the cigarettes in the United States. In 1890, Duke combined the major tobacco producers into the American Tobacco Company and acquired other manufacturers. Although the Supreme Court ordered the dissolution of this "tobacco trust" in 1911, Duke presided over the reorganization, and the component companies conducted business more or less as they had before. Duke also created a $120 million endowment for his holdings, one-third of which he donated to what is now Duke University.

See Also: Antitrust Cases; Industrial Revolution.

■ **DULANY, DANIEL (1722-97),** Revolutionary War politician. Prominent in colonial Maryland politics and society, Dulany was born in Annapolis. During the Stamp Act crisis (1765) he wrote a best-selling pamphlet denouncing British policy. He was a Loyalist during the Revolution, and his influence waned.

See Also: Revolution, American.

John Foster Dulles served as Pres. Dwight D. Eisenhower's secretary of state from 1953 to 1959.

■ **DULLES, JOHN FOSTER (1888-1959),** U.S. statesman. He was born in Washington, D.C., received his B.A. from Princeton (1908), and subsequently studied at the Sorbonne (1908-09) and George Washington University, where he received (1911) his law degree. A specialist in international law, he served as counsel to the American Peace Commission (1918-19), after which he resumed his highly successful law practice. From 1946 to 1950, Dulles served as the U.S. delegate to the United Nations.

In 1953, he became President Eisenhower's secretary of state and held that post until his death in 1959. Dulles repudiated the "containment" of Soviet expansion, advocating instead the "liberation" of communist-dominated areas. He condemned the British-French aggression in Egypt (1956) and devised what came to be known as the Eisenhower Doctrine (1957), a policy favoring American economic and military aid to any Middle Eastern state that requested assistance against "overt armed aggression" of a communist-controlled country.

See Also: Cold War; Eisenhower, Dwight David.

■ **DUMBARTON OAKS CONFERENCE (1944),** a meeting of the representatives of the United

States, Soviet Union, Great Britain, and China at a private estate in Washington, D.C. The aim of the conference was to draft propositions for the constitution of the United Nations, an international organization devised to control peace preservation after World War II. The final "Proposals" of the conference (October 1944) set the principles and purposes of the United Nations, its membership, and its structure.

See Also: Cold War; United Nations (UN).

■ **DUNBAR, PAUL LAURENCE (1872-1906),** poet and novelist. Born in Dayton, Ohio, of former slaves, Dunbar published his first collection of poems in 1893 (*Oak and Ivy*). Numerous collections, including his hallmark work, *Lyrics of Lowly Life* (1896), and four novels followed. Dunbar's use of simple, direct verse and the innovation of black dialect in formal poetry made him extremely popular.

See Also: African Americans.

With bare feet and flowing scarves, Isadora Duncan challenged the formalism of dance in the United States in the early 20th century. Duncan introduced a system of modern dance that emphasized new techniques to interpret nature, music, and poetry.

■ **DUNCAN, ISADORA (1878-1927),** innovative dancer. She was born in San Francisco, California. She developed her own improvisational and emotive dance style, frequently finding inspiration for her movements in great sculptures and paintings. Although American audiences never developed a taste for her style and controversial personality, her solo performances, accompanied by the music of great classical composers, earned her considerable popularity in Europe.

See Also: Women in American History.

■ **DUNIWAY, ABIGAIL SCOTT (1834-1915),** suffrage leader. Born in Tazewell County, Illinois, she moved to Oregon in 1852 and was later politicized by the drudgery and injustice she experienced there as a pioneer woman. In 1871 she moved to Portland, Oregon, to publish a suffragist journal, *The New Northwest,* and also

Suffragist Abigail Scott Duniway used *The New Northwest,* a newspaper she founded in 1871, as a platform for woman's rights issues.

managed Susan B. Anthony's lecture tour of the Pacific Northwest. She founded the Oregon Equal Suffrage Association in 1873 and was made vice president of the National Woman Suffrage Association in 1884.

See Also: Anthony, Susan B.; Frontier in American History; Gilded Age; Woman Suffrage Movement; Women's Movement.

■ **DUNMORE, JOHN MURRAY, EARL OF (1732-1809),** royal governor of New York (1770-71) and Virginia (1771-75). Born in Scotland to an aristocratic family, Dunmore was appointed royal governor of New York in 1770, but he remained there only 11 months. In 1771, Dunmore became the governor of Virginia. A 1774 Virginia militia campaign against the Shawnee became known as Lord Dunmore's War and opened Kentucky to settlement. Initially popular, Dunmore's loyalist convictions put him at odds with the colonial assembly over its involvement in Revolutionary activities. Eventually, he fled the colony when his troops failed to subdue the Virginia patriots (1775).

See Also: Lord Dunmore's War.

■ ***DUPLEX PRINTING CO. V. DEERING (1921),*** U.S. Supreme Court case that struck down a law that protected labor unions from antitrust injunctions. The Sherman Act (1890) barred monopolies in restraint of trade. Courts used the antitrust law to attack labor union strikes and boycotts. In *Deering,* the Court ruled (6-3) that the Clayton Act (1914) did not exempt labor unions from antitrust laws. Congress in the Norris-LaGuardia Act (1932) again moved to exempt unions, and the Court upheld that law.

See Also: Clayton Antitrust Act; Supreme Court.

■ **DU PONT, ELEUTHÈRE I. (1771-1834),** manufacturer of gunpowder and business leader. Du Pont was born in Paris, France, where he worked at France's royal gunpowder works and with his father, publisher and economist Pierre Samuel du Pont de Nemours. Eleuthère and his family left France in the wake of the French Revolution, arriving at Newport, Rhode Island, in January 1800. When dreams of developing western land fell through, du Pont's father and brother established a trading company in New York, but it eventually failed. Noticing the relative inferiority of American gunpowder, Eleuthère and Peter Bauduy established a powder mill on Brandywine Creek near Wilmington, Delaware, in 1802. By 1804, the E. I. du Pont de Nemours and Co. had become the leading gunpowder producer in the nation, with a network of sales agents and a ready client in the U.S. government. The War of 1812 sealed the company's success. The woolens company du Pont formed with his brother and Bauduy fared less well, and du Pont was plagued with personal debt throughout his life. Nevertheless, he remained a leading business figure in America. He was a director of the Second Bank of the United States (1814-22), and he firmly established the du Pont family in the United States.

See Also: Industrial Revolution; Science.

■ **DURAND, ASHER B. (1796-1886),** painter and engraver. Born near Newark, New Jersey, Durand started his artistic career as an engraver, issuing editions of over 50 portraits of prominent citizens, as well as the *Signing of the Declaration of Independence*, adapted from John Trumbull's painting in 1823. After 1836 Durand turned to painting, focusing particularly on the landscape of upstate New York and New England. Durand is considered a leading member of the group of American landscape painters known as the Hudson River School.

See Also: Hudson River School; Painting; Trumbull, John.

■ **DUST BOWL,** the region of the Great Plains that was subject to severe drought and soil erosion from 1932 to 1940. Encompassing 97 million acres, the region includes southeastern Colorado, northeastern New Mexico, western Kansas, and the panhandles of Texas and Oklahoma.

Drought, together with friable soils and poor agricultural practices, made the region the victim of ferocious dust storms. These blew the topsoil from the land in black blizzards, carrying it as far as the Atlantic Ocean. The storms limited visibility, suffocated people and cattle, ruined property, and caused a high incidence of lung-related diseases.

At the beginning of the 20th century above-average rainfall and high crop prices led to an expansion of farming in the southern Great Plains. Farmers adopted new technology, including tractors, the one-way disk plow (which pulverized the soil, making it more vulnerable to erosion), and combine harvesters. These implements, bought on credit, forced farmers to bring more, often submarginal, land into cultivation to pay for them. The newly plowed fields reduced the amount of available pasturage for livestock, causing overgrazing on what was left. In the 1930s this overgrazing and overcultivation combined with drought, crop failure, and the traditional winds of the Great Plains to create the Dust Bowl conditions.

Dust Bowl farmers confronted disaster in the form of destroyed crops and starving livestock, in addition to the drastic fall in commodity prices brought on by the Great Depression. Yet most farmers remained on their land, receiving support from myriad New Deal agencies, most notably the Agricultural Adjustment Administration, the Resettlement Administration, and the Farm Security Administration. The Soil Conservation Service, the Works Progress Administration, and the Civilian Conservation Corps helped build farm ponds

In the mid-1930s, well over 100,000 square miles of the Great Plains suffered from drought. The resulting dust storms caused the worst environmental crisis in the nation's history.

and stock-watering dams, and planted trees as part of the Shelterbelt Program. Most of the Okies who migrated to California were not products of the Dust Bowl but rather of the collapsed cotton economy further to the east. The Soil Conservation Service also promoted better farming practices. It advocated conservation measures such as listing, contour plowing, and terracing together with cultivating more drought-resistant crops like sorghum, reseeding pasture with native grasses, and retiring submarginal land from cultivation. These practices helped stabilize wind-eroded lands in the region. But it was not until a more abundant rainfall cycle began in 1941 that prosperity returned to the agricultural life of the Dust Bowl.

—CLAIRE STROM

See Also: Great Depression.

BIBLIOGRAPHY: Bonnefield, Paul, *The Dust Bowl: Men, Dirt, and Depression* (Univ. of New Mexico Press 1979); Hurt, R. Douglas, *The Dust Bowl: An Agricultural and Social History* (Nelson-Hall 1981).

■ **DUSTIN, HANNAH (1657-1736?),** heroine of the colonial Indian wars. She was born in Haverhill, Massachusetts. After Indians murdered her newborn and took Hannah captive in a 1697 raid, she killed and scalped nine of her captors, including six children, rescuing herself and two other white colonists.

■ **DUTCH COLONIES,** colonies established in the Americas during the first half of the 17th century. Major leaders of European commerce, the Dutch were the greatest merchant and naval power of the Atlantic world at that time. Launching attacks on the Portuguese empire, Dutch warships succeeded in seizing a number of strategic locations and created a wide-flung empire consisting of trading posts in India, Indonesia, and China, as well as sugar plantations in Brazil. In one of their first American ventures, Dutch merchants sent the English explorer Henry Hudson in search of a northwest passage to Asia in 1609. While he failed in that elusive mission, he succeeded in locating the great river that was later named in his honor, a watercourse that emptied into a magnificent harbor and led deep into the interior homeland of the powerful Iroquois Confederacy. In 1624 the Dutch West India Company established the upriver outpost of Fort

Orange (later renamed Albany), and two years later a settlement at the river's mouth on Manhattan Island. Under the leadership of the first governor, Peter Minuit, the territory of New Netherland became a fur trading and farming colony.

The Dutch promoted settlement by offering large estates to men who would bring over 50 farming families. These grants, known as patroonships, were an attempt to export feudal property relations to America. Although the system was soon abandoned, the perpetual leases of the established patroons along the Hudson River were not abolished until the mid-19th century.

Attempting to expand their sphere of influence, in the 1630s the Dutch established a trading post on the Connecticut River, near the site of present-day Hartford. Conflict with the expanding settlements of Massachusetts Bay soon forced them to abandon that outpost. But in 1654 the Dutch captured the Swedish colonies on the Delaware River and incorporated those settlements into their territory.

New Netherland's heyday came during the tenure of governor Peter Stuyvesant, whose administration began in 1647 and lasted 17 years. During his term thousands of new settlers immigrated to the Hudson and Delaware valleys. The population of New Netherland differed significantly from those of other European colonies. It was a place of amazing ethnic and linguistic diversity; at least half the emigrants were non-Dutch, including large numbers of African slaves. Moreover, the colony included a large number of religious sects, including Protestants, Catholics, and Jews. In the mid-17th century New Netherland was the most heterogeneous colony in North America.

The economic foundation of the colony was the lucrative fur trade of the upper Hudson. The Dutch established an alliance with the Iroquois Confederacy, who backed by arms and ammunition began a series of military expeditions known as the Beaver Wars. In this conflict, the Iroquois attacked and dispersed the Hurons, allies of the French who had long controlled the flow of furs from the Great Lakes to the trading post at Montreal. The Indian nation that held this critical middleman position was assured enormous gains, since it received a percentage of the entire volume of the trade. Sitting in a strategic position between the coast and the interior, the Iroquois sought to channel all furs through their hands, extending the Dutch trading system deep into the continent. In the lower Hudson valley, however, the Dutch viewed Algonquian-speaking Indians as an obstacle to the growth of farming, and the persistent conflict erupted in a series of brutal wars during the 1650s. By the next decade most of these Indians had withdrawn into the interior.

The great success and profitability of New Netherland made it a lucrative prize. During the first of the Anglo-Dutch Wars in 1664 an English fleet forced Stuyvesant to surrender Manhattan, and the colony was renamed New York. The Dutch retook it during the last of the wars in 1673, but it was restored to the English by the treaty ending the conflict in 1674.

—JOHN MACK FARAGHER

See Also: Anglo-Dutch Wars; Beaver Wars; Exploration and Discovery; Patroonships; Stuyvesant, Peter; Swedish Colonies.

BIBLIOGRAPHY: Rink, Oliver A., *Holland on the Hudson: An Economic and Social History of Dutch New York* (Cornell Univ. Press 1986).

■ **DUTCH REFORMED CHURCH (REFORMED CHURCH IN AMERICA),** Calvinist denomination with a presbyterian system of governance. The first congregation was established on Manhattan Island in 1628 by Jonas Michaelius to serve Dutch settlers. The churches, mainly in New York and New Jersey, remained under the control of the mother church in the Netherlands until 1792. Separation came following debates, often led by the minister Theodore Freylinghuysen, over the Americanization of the Church, local education of ministers, and revivalism. Today, authority lies with the local consistory, a body of elders, deacons, and a pastor, who then send delegates to the classes and synods. In 1867, the Church dropped *Dutch* from its name and became the Reformed Church in America.

See Also: Religion.

■ **DUTCH WEST INDIA COMPANY,** a joint stock company with extensive commercial and political powers. Organized by Dutch merchants on June 3, 1621, the company planted settlements at Fort Orange (later named Albany) and Manhattan Island.

See Also: Dutch Colonies.

A Congregational minister and president of Yale College from 1795 to 1817, Timothy Dwight also was a leading member of the Connecticut Wits, a conservative group that opposed Jeffersonian democracy and hoped to establish a national literature.

■ **DUVALL, GABRIEL (1752-1844),** U.S. representative (1774-96) and associate justice of the U.S. Supreme Court (1811-35). A Prince Georges County, Maryland, native, Duvall frequently dissented from Chief Justice John Marshall's majority positions, most notably in the Dartmouth College decision (1819).

See Also: Dartmouth College Case; Marshall, John; Supreme Court.

■ **DWIGHT, TIMOTHY (1752-1817),** Congregational minister, educator, and author. He was born in Northampton, Massachusetts, and originally intended to study law at Yale College in New Haven, Connecticut, but abandoned that career for the ministry in 1774. A 1769 Yale graduate, he returned there as a tutor (1771-77), during which time he became the driving intellectual force behind the "Connecticut Wits." After serving as a chaplain in the Continental army (1777-79), he enjoyed great successes in his founding of two coeducational schools (in Massachusetts and Connecticut), his 12-year pastorship of a Connecticut church (1783-1795), and his presidency of Yale (1795-1817). After his cousin Aaron Burr killed Alexander Hamilton in a duel in 1804, Dwight preached a sermon, published in 1805 as *Folly, Guilt, and Mischiefs of Dueling*. He wrote numerous books, including *Greenfield Hill* (1794), a book of poetry; *Theology, Explained and Defended* (1818-19); and the highly acclaimed four-volume *Travels in New England and New York* (1821-22).

See Also: Congregationalists.

■ **DYER, MARY (d. 1660),** religious dissident in colonial Boston. Born in England, she moved to Massachusetts around 1635, where she became a follower of Anne Hutchinson in 1638. She converted to Quakerism on a 1654 trip to England. She was hanged in 1660 after returning to Boston to challenge a law that banished all Quakers from the colony on pain of death.

■ **DYLAN, BOB (1941-),** singer and songwriter whose transition from folk music to rock and roll introduced social protest to American popular music. Born Robert Zimmerman in Duluth, Minnesota, he adopted his stage name when he became a prominent participant in the folk music scene in New York City in the early 1960s, patterning himself on Woody Guthrie. After recording several important folk albums, he turned to rock in 1965 and became one of the most important performers of the 1960s.

See Also: Folk Music; Guthrie, Woody; Nineteen Sixties.

E

EADS, JAMES BUCHANAN (1820-87), engineer and inventor. Born in Lawrenceburg, Indiana, Eads educated himself and found work as a purser on a Mississippi River steamboat in 1838. With a diving bell Eads invented in 1842 he went into the salvage business, recovering cargo and machinery from sunken river boats. He was so successful that he earned a fortune and retired in 1857. Eads's experience led Pres. Abraham Lincoln to seek his advice on the military use of rivers in 1861, and in 100 days he built eight ironclad gunboats that helped Union forces take control of the Kentucky-Tennessee river systems. Eads went on to accomplish other challenging engineering feats, including building a bridge across the Mississippi River at St. Louis (1874), cutting a channel that deepened the mouth of the Mississippi, and building jetties at South Pass that opened the previously impassable delta to ships with over a 12-foot draft (1875-79). These daring projects all furthered the field of engineering and the success of St. Louis as a national urban center. Eads went on to design harbor improvements for Toronto, Canada; Veracruz, Mexico; and Liverpool, England. His *Addresses and Papers* were published in 1884.

See Also: Invention; Science.

EAKINS, THOMAS (1844-1916), renowned painter and portraitist. Born in Philadelphia, Eakins began studying art at the Pennsylvania Academy of Fine Arts (PAFA) in 1862. He also took anatomy classes at Jefferson Medical College, an indication of his lifelong concern with the accurate representation of the human body. In the early 1870s Eakins focused on the study of the human form in a series of pictures of rowers, the best-known of which is *Max Schmitt in a Single Scull* (1871). This fascination with the body and the sciences of studying it is also apparent in two of Eakins's best-known works, *The Gross Clinic* (1875) and *The Agnew Clinic* (1889), both of which

are portraits of doctors at work. Eakins taught at PAFA from 1876 to 1886, when he resigned because of controversy over his use of nude male models in classes attended by women. In addition to painting, Eakins also experimented with photography and sculpture; he completed 10 relief sculptures, including panels for the Trenton, New Jersey, Battle Monument (1893).

See Also: Painting.

EARL, RALPH (1751-1801), portrait painter. Born in Worcester, Massachusetts, Earl established himself as a painter in New Haven, Connecticut, in 1774, where he painted one of his best-known portraits, *Roger Sherman* (1775). He left soon after for England because of his Loyalist sympathies but returned to the United States in 1785 to resume his trade. His portraits are distinguished by their inclusion of details about the sitter, either revealed through the possessions shown or through the background landscape.

See Also: Painting.

EARP, WYATT (1848-1929), American marshal and frontiersman. He was born in Monmouth, Illinois, and moved with his family to California in 1864. From 1865 to 1867 he drove stagecoaches in California, Arizona, and Utah. Later, Earp worked for some time as a horse handler for railroads. He earned fame and repute as an expert sharpshooter and buffalo hunter. In 1870-71, he was a hunter for U.S. government surveyors in Kansas, Oklahoma, and Texas. He served as marshal in Ellsworth, Kansas (1873), and as deputy marshal in Wichita (1874-76) and Dodge City, Kansas (1876, 1877-79). He then moved to Arizona, where he served as deputy sheriff of Conchise County (1879-82) at Tombstone and became marshal in 1882. In 1881, Earp led his brothers Virgil and Morgan and Doc Holliday against Ike Clanton's band in the gunfight at the O.K. Corral in Tombstone. After he retired from law enforcement, he lived off income from real estate, oil, and mining investments and from gambling.

See Also: *Frontier in American History.*

■ **EASTMAN, CRYSTAL (1881-1928),** socialist reformer, feminist, and peace activist. She was born in Marlborough, Massachusetts. Her early sociological work, particularly *Work Accidents and the Law* (1910), influenced the creation of workman's compensation laws. She was active in the feminist and antimilitarist movements of the 1910s. Chairman of the Woman's Peace party, she wrote frequent articles on labor and women's issues for the *Nation* and the *New Republic* and edited the radical journal the *Liberator* with her brother, Max Eastman.

See Also: *Women's Movement.*

■ **EASTMAN, GEORGE (1854-1932),** inventor of photographic equipment, founder of Eastman Kodak Company, and philanthropist. Born in Waterville, New York, Eastman left school in the seventh grade to work in a bank. As a young man, he was fascinated with photography and invented a machine for coating dry photographic plates. Eastman gave up banking in 1880 to develop, manufacture, and sell photographic goods. In 1884, he invented a flexible, paper-backed film and sold it in 1888 together with the first Kodak box camera. "You press the button," he advertised, "we'll do the rest." His Eastman Dry Plate and Film Company (1884) became the Eastman Kodak Company (1901) and held patents to the inventions that he and chemist Henry Reichenbach made. The most important one was a flexible, transparent, self-supporting film (1889) that could be processed locally and used in the motion-picture camera that Thomas Edison had invented. Eastman controlled the market of photographic goods aggressively, advertising and expanding his company to an extent that led to an antitrust suit in 1921. During his lifetime, Eastman gave away more than $75 million, mainly to the Massachusetts Institute of Technology, the University of Rochester, and the Eastman School of Music.

See Also: *Edison, Thomas Alva; Industrial Revolution; Invention; Photography; Science.*

■ **EASTWOOD, CLINT (1930-),** film actor and director. Born in San Francisco, California, he was a journeyman film and television actor before starring in the Italian western *A Fistful of Dollars* (1967). As the cop with a powerful handgun and no patience for red tape in *Dirty Harry* (1972), he represented reaction to the social upheaval of the 1960s. Eastwood also directed and starred as an aging gunman in *Unforgiven* (1992).

■ **ECONOMIC OPPORTUNITY ACT (1964),** the cornerstone of Pres. Lyndon Johnson's Great Society plan. The $962 million legislation created the Office of Economic Opportunity, the Job Corps, and other education programs.

■ **ECONOMY.** *See: Banks and Banking; Banks of the United States, First and Second; Depressions and Recessions; Industrial Revolution; Manufacturing and Industry; Railroads; Shipping; Transportation.*

■ **EDDY, MARY BAKER (1821-1910),** founder of the Church of Christ, Scientist. She was born in Bow, New Hampshire. In 1875 she laid out the foundations of Christian Science in *Science and Health*, rejecting medicine and arguing that physi-

After making a remarkable recovery from a serious injury through "divine revelation, reason, and demonstration," Mary Baker Eddy of Massachusetts founded Christian Science in the late 1870s.

cal healing, like spiritual recovery, can only be attained through worship. She established the First Church of Christ, Scientist, known as the Mother Church, in Boston in 1892. In 1908, she founded a newspaper, the *Christian Science Monitor*.

See Also: Christian Science; Women in American History.

■ **EDISON, THOMAS ALVA (1847-1931),** the most prolific inventor in American history. Edison secured 1,093 patents, pioneered several major technologies, and, perhaps most significantly, developed the industrial research laboratory. Edison was born in Milan, Ohio, and educated primarily by his mother while growing up in Port Huron, Michigan. At the age of 12, he began selling newspapers and candy on a branch of the Grand Trunk Railroad. The teenager also printed a weekly newspaper and conducted chemical experiments in the train's baggage car. Learning telegraphy from the line's railway operators, he began working in the local telegraph office in 1862. Over the next several years he worked as an itinerant operator in the Midwest, studied and experimented with telegraph technology, and taught himself electrical science.

Edison began his career as an inventor after moving to Boston in 1868, and it took off the following year when he moved to New York and began working as a contract inventor for several major companies. With funds from his contracts he set up manufacturing shops in Newark, New Jersey, where he manufactured his inventions and also employed several experimental machinists to assist him in his invention work. There Edison invented a number of important telegraph improvements, most notably improved stock tickers and the quadruplex telegraph, which enabled two messages to be sent simultaneously in each direction on one wire.

The Great Inventions. Edison's most prolific period occurred during the years 1876 to 1880, when

Scientist-businessman Thomas Edison invited 3,000 people to Menlo Park, New Jersey, on Dec. 31, 1879, to marvel at his latest invention, vacuum bulbs that burned for 13 hours, the forerunner of electric lights.

he invented the carbon telephone transmitter, the phonograph, and the carbon-filament lamp and electric lighting system. But perhaps his most important invention during these years was his laboratory in Menlo Park, New Jersey. This was the first industrial research laboratory, which Edison created by separating the experimental machine shop from its traditional manufacturing environment and combining it with sophisticated electrical and chemical laboratories. The laboratory, with its large staff of experimental assistants and machinists all devoted to developing new technology conceived by Edison, enabled him to meet his goal of "a minor invention every ten days and a big thing every six months or so." Although the phonograph made Edison's reputation as the "Wizard of Menlo Park," it was his development of a process of research and development that enabled him to become the country's most prolific inventor.

Ironically, the very success of the Menlo Park laboratory caused Edison to abandon it. He moved back to New York in 1881 to oversee the commercialization of his electric lighting system, while continuing to develop the system at the new manufacturing shops he set up under the supervision of his Menlo Park assistants. Nonetheless, the laboratory became a model for other inventors, and Edison himself built an even larger laboratory in 1887 at West Orange, New Jersey, that would remain unsurpassed until the 20th century.

The West Orange laboratory served as the primary research facility for the Edison lighting companies until they merged into General Electric in 1892, but Edison maintained it as an independent institution and developed several other new technologies there. These included the wax-recording cylinder phonograph that became the industry standard, the motion picture camera and kinetoscope viewing system, and a system for concentrating low-grade ores. During the first decade of the 20th century he made improvements in cement manufacturing and devised a storage battery that became widely used in industry. During the last 20 years of his life Edison continued to work in his laboratory and to take an active part in the management of his businesses, which were combined into Thomas A. Edison, Inc., in 1911.

—PAUL ISRAEL

See Also: *Industrial Revolution; Invention; Science.*

BIBLIOGRAPHY: Dyer, Frank L., and Thomas C. Martin, *Edison: His Life and Inventions* (Harper 1929); Josephson, Matthew, *Edison: A Biography* (McGraw-Hill 1959); Millard, Andre, *Edison and the Business of Innovation* (Johns Hopkins Univ. Press 1990).

■ **EDUCATION.** *See: Adult Education; Chautauqua Movement; Education, Federal Aid to; Head Start; Literacy; Progressive Education; Women's Education.*

■ **EDUCATION, FEDERAL AID TO,** the subsidization of American education by the U.S. government. Congress established the U.S. Office of Education in 1867 and a cabinet-level Department of Education in 1979, but federal education programs remain controversial. Local control of public schools remains popular, and while federal financial aid is welcomed, federal controls are frequently resisted. By 1996 the Department of Education's budget exceeded $30 billion and billions of dollars more in other federal budgets were earmarked for education programs. Most education funding, however, continues to come from local or state treasuries. Since World War II the largest and most popular federal aid programs have been higher education loans and grants to individuals, under such legislation as the GI Bill (1944) and the 1972 Higher Education Act. Federal aid programs also help support programs for specific student groups such as the physically or mentally handicapped or subsidized construction programs.

BIBLIOGRAPHY: Williams, Mary F., ed., *Government in the Classroom: Dollars and Power in Education* (Capital City Press 1978).

■ **EDWARDS, JONATHAN (1703-58),** colonial Congregational preacher, theologian, and philosopher. Born in East Windsor, Connecticut, Edwards enrolled in Yale College at age 12, finished first in his class, and was head tutor by 1724. His wide range of interests is evident in his early papers, which cover such diverse topics as atoms, spiders, rainbows, being, and the mind. Edwards apprenticed for two years under his grandfather, Solomon Stoddard, a well-known Congregational minister in Northampton, Massachusetts, and in 1729 became the church's head preacher. His sermons (over 1,200) and treatises have influenced American religion to this day. In 1737, Edwards wrote *Faithful Narrative*, which describes the revivals in Northampton, on which many revivals worldwide were modeled. *Sinners in the Hands of an Angry God* (1741) is the most famous sermon of the Great Awakening. In *Some Thoughts concerning the Present Revival* (1743), he defends the Great Awakening, while *Religious Affections* (1746) is a psychological study of religion and is still used by evangelicals. In 1750, Edwards's congregation dismissed him in a conflict over standards for church membership. Edwards then accepted a post at an Indian mission in Stockbridge, Massachusetts, where he lived for seven years and spent less time preaching. At Stockbridge, he wrote his theological masterpiece, *Freedom of the Will* (1754). In 1758, Edwards became president of the College of New Jersey (Princeton) but died shortly after his arrival from a smallpox inoculation.

See Also: Religion.

BIBLIOGRAPHY: Miller, Perry, *Jonathan Edwards* (Sloane 1949); Winslow, Ola E., *Jonathan Edwards: A Biography* (Macmillan 1940).

■ *EDWARDS V. AGUILLARD* **(1987),** U.S. Supreme Court case that struck down a Louisiana law requiring public schools to teach "creation science" as an alternative to the theory of evolution. Creation science endorses the account of creation in the Book of Genesis and is supported by fundamentalist Protestant groups. The Court ruled (7-2) that the law, while never enforced, was an attempt to establish religion in violation of the First Amendment.

See Also: Supreme Court.

■ **EIGHT-HOUR DAY,** the establishment of maximum hours for a normal working day. The 8-hour day has been a primary goal of the American labor movement since the 1860s. Industrialization in the early 1800s lengthened the working day for many workers who had previously worked only in daylight hours with long and frequent breaks. Early labor unions fought to reduce their hours of toil and, although some artisans won an 8-hour day in the 1840s and 1850s, and President Van Buren mandated the 10-hour day for federal employees in 1840, by 1860 the average working day was 11 hours long.

In the years after the Civil War the 8-hour day became the rallying cry for American unions. Ira Steward, a Massachusetts machinist known as the "father of the 8-hour day," developed new economic arguments for the 8-hour day and built a coalition of workers and middle-class reformers that spread the 8-hour movement throughout America. Their slogan was "Eight hours for work, eight hours for rest, eight hours for what we will!" The Republican party responded by establishing the 8-hour day for federal employees by 1872, and laws establishing various maximum hours passed in six states. However, this proved a hollow victory as state laws were rarely enforced; consequently, labor leaders turned their attention to winning concessions from employers rather than from government. Trade unions set May 1, 1886, as the deadline for all employers to concede the 8-hour day, but the ensuing national wave of strikes and bloodshed, including Chicago's famous Haymarket Square Riot (May 4, 1886), failed to make 8 hours the industrial standard.

The Progressive movement revived the drive for legislative restrictions on working hours, especially for women and children. However, prior to the 1930s, the Supreme Court questioned the constitutionality of states regulating hours for men. By 1920, some 11 states had established an 8-hour day for women and, in 1916, Pres. Woodrow Wilson signed the Adamson Act mandating the 8-hour day for railroad workers. Labor protest during the Great Depression of the 1930s prompted a more sweeping federal regulation of the hours of labor, and in 1938 Congress passed the Fair Labor Standards Act making the 8-hour day the standard for most workers

—TIMOTHY MESSER-KRUSE

See Also: Adamson Act; Fair Labor Standards Act; Haymarket Incident; Labor Movement; Trade Unions; Work in America.

BIBLIOGRAPHY: Commons, John R., et al., *History of Labor in the United States* (1918-1935; Kelley); Roediger, David R., and Philip S. Foner, *Our Own Time: A History of American Labor and the Working Day* (Greenwood Press 1989).

■ **EINSTEIN, ALBERT (1879-1955),** theoretical physicist best known for the formulation of the relativity theory. His theories became the cornerstone of

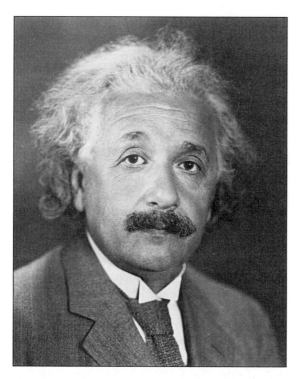

Hitler's rise to power in Germany prompted physicist Albert Einstein to move to the United States in 1933. Although a pacifist, Einstein urged that research be conducted on an atomic bomb in an August 1939 letter to Pres. Franklin D. Roosevelt.

20th-century physics. Born in Ulm, Germany, Einstein graduated from the Zürich Polytechnic Institute and, failing to attain a university position, took a job in the Swiss Patent Office in 1902. Einstein published three revolutionary papers in 1905 that set out the photon theory of light; the theory of Brownian motion, which explained the existence of atoms; and his special theory of relativity. This theory proposed a new understanding of time and space as relative and a new relationship between mass and energy that Einstein articulated in 1907 in his formula $E = mc^2$, meaning that energy in matter equals its mass multiplied by the square of the velocity of light. This formula anticipated the splitting of the atom and the release of atomic energy. When physicists started to recognize the importance of Einstein's theories, he was given a series of professorships, settling at the Kaiser Wilhelm Institute in Berlin (1914-33). He was awarded the Nobel Prize in Physics in 1921. Einstein became a vocal pacifist and Zionist after World War I and moved to the

United States in 1933 to escape Nazi Germany. He continued to work on his "unified field theory," which would unite gravitational and electromagnetic phenomena, at Princeton's Institute for Advanced Study. Although he wrote a letter to Pres. Franklin D. Roosevelt in 1939 advising him of the potential of atomic warfare, he played almost no role in developing nuclear weapons himself and later warned against nuclear war. Einstein never completed his unified field theory, but he profoundly altered prevailing conceptions of the nature of light, atomic phenomena, and space and time.

—ANNIE GILBERT COLEMAN

See Also: Science.

BIBLIOGRAPHY: Fösling, Albrecht, *Albert Einstein: A Biography* (Viking 1996); Frank, Philipp, *Einstein: The Life and Times* (Knopf 1947); Pais, Abraham, *Subtle Is the Lord* (Oxford Univ. Press 1982).

■ **EISENHOWER, DWIGHT DAVID (1890-1969),** 34th president of the United States (1953-61). Born in Denison, Texas, and reared in Abilene, Kansas, Eisenhower graduated from the U.S. Military Academy at West Point in the class of 1915. He married Mamie Doud in 1916 and reached the rank of temporary lieutenant colonel near the end of World War I. Between 1922 and 1924, he served in the Panama Canal Zone under Brig. Gen. Fox Conner, who directed Eisenhower's attention to military history. In the coming years, he would gain an academic reputation within the army. In 1940, Eisenhower returned to the United States from the Philippines, where he had been chief of staff to Gen. Douglas MacArthur, with whom he was not on good terms. By the time of Japan's attack on Pearl Harbor on Dec. 7, 1941, he had attained the rank of brigadier general.

Eisenhower had given 26 years of outstanding service prior to American involvement in World War II, and thereafter he rapidly rose to prominence. His first war duty found him in the War Plans (later Operations) Division shortly after the bombing of Pearl Harbor. A major general by the summer of 1942, Eisenhower led the Allied assault on North Africa beginning the following November and reached the rank of full general by its victorious conclusion (May 1943). At the end of 1943, he was appointed supreme commander of all Allied forces in Europe, and in 1944, he oversaw the Allied invasion of Normandy, known as Operation Overlord, his greatest military success. By the time Eisenhower secured the Allied victory in Europe in May 1945, he had achieved the rank of general of the army.

In peacetime, Eisenhower served first as chief of staff of the army (1945-48), then as president of Columbia University (1948-52), and also as the first supreme commander of the North Atlantic Treaty Organization (NATO, 1951-52). Eisenhower resigned the latter post in order to seek the Republican presidential nomination, which he won over the conservative Sen. Robert A. Taft of Ohio. In November 1952, Eisenhower and his vice-presidential candidate, Richard Nixon, went on to defeat his Democratic opponents, Gov. Adlai E. Stevenson of Illinois and Estes Kefauver.

Presidency. Eisenhower ended the Korean War within months of taking office in 1953, after which he reduced military spending and held the lid on it as long as he remained in office, a feat not matched, or in most cases even attempted, by his successors. Through careful crisis management, he avoided committing American forces to battle for the rest of his two terms. In addition, he balanced the budget three times in eight years (producing surpluses in 1956 and 1957) and eliminated the inflation that was raging when he took office, holding it thereafter to an average of 1.5 percent a year. Eisenhower pushed through legislation that funded the St. Lawrence Seaway (1954) and the interstate highway system that now bears

his name (1956). Enormously popular with the electorate, Eisenhower easily won reelection in 1956 despite serious illnesses in his first term.

Eager to preserve the position of leadership won by the United States during and after World War II, Eisenhower exhibited moderation, skillful management of foreign and domestic politics, and willingness to take on the powerful defense lobby, which he warned of as a "military-industrial complex" in his January 1961 farewell address, all making him one of the most successful postwar presidents. He was often underestimated in the matter of social reforms and was frequently criticized for failing to advance them, although he had never pretended to be a reformer. He was reluctant to deal with and speak out on the issue of civil rights, although in 1953 he appointed Earl Warren chief justice of the United States and later enforced the Supreme Court's school desegregation decision in *Brown v. Board of Education of Topeka* (1954). Eisenhower operated behind the scenes as much as possible, appearing less responsible for events, such as the fall of Joseph McCarthy, the demagogic senator from Wisconsin, than he actually was. With the passage of time, Eisenhower's accomplishments, especially his peacekeeping abilities, have become better appreciated.

—WILLIAM L. O'NEILL

See Also: *Cold War; Korean War; Nixon, Richard Milhous; Presidential Elections; President of the United States; World War II.*

Pres. Dwight D. Eisenhower (*front, center*) chats with Chief Justice Earl Warren (*second from right*) and Supreme Court associate justices and staff.

BIBLIOGRAPHY: Ambrose, Stephen E., *Eisenhower,* 2 vols. (Simon & Schuster 1983-84); Eisenhower, David, *Eisenhower at War 1943-1945* (Random House 1986); Eisenhower, Dwight D., *Crusade in Europe* (Doubleday 1948); Greenstein, Fred, *The Hidden Hand Presidency* (Basic Books 1982).

■ **ELECTORAL COLLEGE,** body of electors that selects the president and vice president. The electoral college was established under Article II, Section 1 of the U.S. Constitution, and modified by the 12th Amendment (1804). The intent was to have the selection of the president and vice president in the hands of electors who would presumably act in the national interest.

There are currently 538 electors with 270 votes needed for election. Each state has as many electors as it has senators and congressmen. California has the largest number with 54, while 7 states have the minimum of 3. The 23rd Amendment (1961) granted the right to vote and three presidential electors to the residents of the District of Columbia.

Electors are selected under state law and party practice. In presidential election years they assemble in their respective state capitals in mid-December to formalize the results of the previous month's popular vote. Each slate of electors is pledged to cast its ballot for the victorious candidate in its state. However, electors have on occasion voted for other eligible candidates because there is no constitutional or statutory requirement that they vote for the winning candidate in their state.

If no candidate receives the necessary majority, the House elects the president and the Senate the vice president. The House chooses from the top three candidates with each state having one vote. The Senate chooses from the top two candidates with each senator having one vote.

In 1888 Republican Pres. Benjamin Harrison was elected with a majority of electoral votes but with fewer popular votes than his opponent, the incumbent Democrat, Pres. Grover Cleveland. The elections of 1824 and 1876 were decided by the House because no candidate had a majority of votes in the electoral college.

Criticism of the electoral college has been expressed out of fear that either no candidate will receive a majority vote or that the events of 1888 might be repeated. The third-party candidacy of H. Ross Perot in 1992 focused renewed attention on the possibility of having an election decided by Congress. However, despite winning 19 percent of the vote, Perot failed to carry any states, and it appears unlikely that Congress will feel pressure to amend the Constitution.

—ALEXANDER WELLEK

See Also: *Constitution of the United States; Constitutional Amendments.*

BIBLIOGRAPHY: Flanigan, William, and Nancy Zingale, *Political Behavior of the American Electorate,* 8th ed. (Congressional Quarterly 1994); Peirce, Neal, and Lawrence Longley, *The Electoral College in American History and the Direct Vote Alternative* (Yale University Press 1981).

■ **ELIOT, CHARLES WILLIAM (1834-1926),** president of Harvard University (1869-1909). Born in Boston, he taught at Harvard (1858-63) and at the Massachusetts Institute of Technology (1865-69) before assuming the presidency of Harvard. Eliot was the most visible college president of his time, and he helped reshape U.S. higher education by introducing electives and the university system of distinct undergraduate, graduate, and professional schools at Harvard.

■ **ELIOT, JOHN (1604-90),** missionary to New England Indians. John Eliot arrived in the Massachusetts Bay Colony in 1631, settling in Roxbury. He began work among the Indians in 1646. In 1649 he founded the Company for Propagating the Gospel in New England and Parts Adjacent in North America, and in 1651 he established the "praying town" of Natick, where he hoped that through compassionate preaching the Indians would convert to Christianity. The praying towns, 14 in all at their height, were governed by strict codes that dictated dress, manners, and work habits. Many Indians in Massachusetts Bay Colony were forced into the "praying towns" to avoid extirpation at the hands of militant Puritans. Each village had a school that instructed in elementary subjects and doctrine, taught the English language, and trained the Indians in English handicrafts. Eliot produced the first Algonquian language catechism and, by 1663, had translated both the Old and New Testaments into Algonquian, the first Bible in any language to be printed in America.

See Also: *Indians of North America; Praying Indians.*

ELIOT, T. S. (THOMAS STEARNS) (1888-1965), poet. Born in St. Louis, Missouri, T.S. Eliot received his undergraduate and master's in literature degrees from Harvard by 1910 and then traveled to Paris for a year. He resumed graduate study at Harvard in 1911 and returned to Europe in 1914, remaining in England for the rest of his life. He soon met fellow expatriate Ezra Pound, with whose support he published "The Love Song of J. Alfred Prufrock" in the journal *Poetry* in 1915. *Prufrock and Other Observations* (1917) was followed by *Poems* (1919) and *Ara Vos Prec* (1920), which included "Gerontion." By this time, Eliot, though only just beginning to gain a reputation as a poet, was set to emerge as a prominent literary critic with the publication of his influential essays collected as *The Sacred Wood* (1920). The latter contained "Tradition and the Individual Talent" and his theories of the "objective correlative" and the "dissociation of sensibility."

In 1922, Eliot established himself as a leading modernist poet with the technically innovative "The Waste Land," which appeared in October in the first issue of his new quarterly, *Criterion*. In 1928, many of his readers felt betrayed upon reading, in his preface to *For Lancelot Andrewes*, of his joining the Church of England the previous year. In the future, Eliot would increasingly give expression to a conservative vision of a global Christian community. His criticism would seek to place poetry within a larger social context, as in *The Use of Poetry and the Use of Criticism* (1933), *After Strange Gods: A Primer of Modern Heresy* (1934), and *Notes Toward the Definition of Culture* (1948). Beginning in the mid-1930s, he turned to verse drama, hoping to reach more people through the theater, with such results as *Murder in the Cathedral* (1935), *The Cocktail Party* (1949), *The Confidential Clerk* (1953), and *The Elder Statesman* (1959), the last three of which appeared after Eliot had published *Four Quartets* (1943) and won the Nobel Prize for Literature (1948).

—JAMES KESSENIDES

See Also: Poetry.
BIBLIOGRAPHY: Moody, A. D., *Thomas Stearns Eliot: Poet* (Cambridge Univ. Press 1979).

ELKINS ACT (1903), federal legislation designed to strengthen the Interstate Commerce Act (1887). Passed by Congress at the urging of Pres. Theodore Roosevelt, the Elkins Act made illegal the practice of some railroads of offering secret rebates to their larger and more powerful shippers.

ELLERY, WILLIAM (1727-1820), merchant, lawyer, and politician during the American Revolution. Born in Newport, Rhode Island, Ellery served in the Second Continental Congress and signed the Declaration of Independence. After the war he was a member of Congress, chief justice of Rhode Island, and customs collector.

See Also: Declaration of Independence; Revolution, American.

ELLETT, ELIZABETH (1812?-77), poet, author, and historian. After an early career as a poet, translator, and essayist, she turned to history. In *The Women of the American Revolution* (1848-1850) and other works, she meticulously documented and popularized the previously ignored role of women in American history.

ELLINGTON, EDWARD KENNEDY ("DUKE") (1899-1974), pianist and bandleader. Born in Washington, D.C., Ellington took up the piano at age 7. As a young man, he played in a series of bands, finally forming his own in 1923. Soon Ellington moved to New York City, and in 1927 he and his band started playing at the Cotton Club in Harlem. Recordings of his music and radio performances earned him national and even international fame. Ellington's fertile musical imagination created tonal tapestries of great originality. He often wrote for particular performers, which made his sound unique and nearly impossible to duplicate. In addition to its original sonorities, Ellington's music had a rhythmic core that gave it an extremely appealing drive. For nearly five decades, Ellington and his band toured the globe, making some of the most popular music of the 20th century.

See Also: African Americans; Jazz.
BIBLIOGRAPHY: Ellington, Duke, *Music Is My Mistress* (Doubleday 1973).

ELLISON, RALPH (1914-94), novelist and essayist. Born in Oklahoma City, Oklahoma, he tried several things before finding his voice in literature. After working as a jazz musician and a photographer, he studied music for three years at the Tuskegee Institute before finding employment during the Depression with the Federal Writers Project. As a writer in New York City, Ellison contributed numerous short pieces, reviews, and essays to various periodicals. In 1952 he published his great work, *Invisible Man*, which was hailed as a masterpiece on the African-American experience in America. Ellison spent most of the rest of his life lecturing and teaching at various universities. Ellison published two collections of essays, *Shadow and Act* (1964) and *Going to the Territory* (1986), but never again returned to the novel, the form that had won him fame.

See Also: *African Americans; Novel.*

■ **ELLSWORTH, OLIVER (1745-1807),** political leader and 3rd chief justice of the United States (1796-1800). An active member of America's Revolutionary generation, Ellsworth was born in Windsor, Connecticut. He graduated from the College of New Jersey (now Princeton) in 1766 and after studying law passed the Connecticut state bar in 1771. His brief law practice was ended by his election in 1773 to the Connecticut state assembly. Both a politician and a revolutionary, Ellsworth served on a number of state and local committees and in the Continental Congress. After the Revolution, he became a judge of the Connecticut superior court and a delegate to the Constitutional Convention, where he supported the Connecticut Compromise that created a Senate based on equal representation and a House of Representatives based on proportional representation.

While serving as a U.S. senator (1789-96), Ellsworth's most lasting political contribution was his drafting of the bill to establish the federal judiciary, which led to the Judiciary Act of 1789. In 1796, Pres. George Washington appointed him chief justice of the United States. Three years later, Pres. John Adams called on Ellsworth to travel to Paris to assist in negotiating with France a commercial treaty. Soon after returning to the United States, Ellsworth resigned (1800) his seat on the Court because of poor health.

See Also: *Judiciary Act of 1789; Supreme Court.*

BIBLIOGRAPHY: Brown, William Garret, *The Life of Oliver Ellsworth* (1905; De Capo Press 1970); Casto, William R., *The Supreme Court of the Early Republic: The Chief Justiceships of John Jay and Oliver Ellsworth* (Univ. of South Carolina Press 1995).

A contemporary print of President Lincoln and his advisers shows them discussing the Emancipation Proclamation, which was announced after the Union success at the Battle of Antietam in September 1862 and took effect on Jan. 1, 1863.

■ **EMANCIPATION PROCLAMATION (1863),** one of the most important documents in American history, granting freedom to slaves in the Southern states. Pres. Abraham Lincoln came to the idea of emancipation gradually and reluctantly, insisting through the entire first year of the Civil War that the aim of the struggle was not the destruction of slavery but solely the preservation of the Union. Emancipation, however, was becoming more and more imperative; pressure came from all over Northern society, from abolitionist editors to the generals who freed Southern slaves in warfare zones. In July 1862 Lincoln read the draft of the proclamation to his Cabinet. Sec. of State William Seward persuaded Lincoln not to publish the document until the North won a major victory, so it would not appear like a desperate political measure of last resort. Lincoln issued the proclamation on Sept. 22, 1862, five days after the Battle of Antietam. The document stipulated that, starting Jan. 1, 1863, all slaves in the territories that were considered in rebellion against the United States, would be "then, thenceforward, and forever free." Slave owners loyal to the Union, however, kept their slaves, since nothing was said about slavery in lands under Northern control. The proclamation brought the Union forces into closer cohesion; led to the enlistment of thousands of blacks in the Union army; and substantially improved the international repute of the Lincoln administration.

See Also: Civil War; Lincoln, Abraham.
BIBLIOGRAPHY: Franklin, John Hope, *The Emancipation Proclamation* (Harlan Davidson 1995).

■ **EMBARGO ACT OF 1807,** act of Congress protesting British and French interference with American neutral shipping during the Napoleonic Wars. In an effort to use economic coercion to uphold American neutral trading rights following the *Chesapeake-Leopard* affair (1807) the act barred American vessels from European ports. The embargo failed, persuading neither Britain nor France to modify restrictions on U.S. commerce and injuring American agriculture and commerce. Smuggling flourished along the Canadian border, and New Englanders, whose manufactured exports were impeded, discussed secession from the Union. In March 1809 Congress repealed the law, replacing it with the Non-Intercourse Act.

See Also: Chesapeake and Leopard Affair; Non-Intercourse Act.
BIBLIOGRAPHY: Spivak, Burton, *Jefferson's English Crisis: Commerce, Embargo, and the Republican Revolution* (Univ. Press of Virginia 1979).

■ **EMERGENCY BANKING RELIEF ACT (1933),** federal legislation that granted sweeping fiscal powers to Pres. Franklin D. Roosevelt. It helped restore public confidence in the U.S. banking and currency systems.

See Also: New Deal.

■ **EMERSON, RALPH WALDO (1803-82),** essayist, lecturer, and poet. Born in Boston, Massachusetts, he graduated as his class poet from Harvard in 1821 and returned to attend its Unitarian Divinity School four years later. He began preaching in 1826 and became minister of Boston's Second Church before resigning in 1832. His refusal to administer Communion precipitated Emerson's break with the profession, after which his more fundamental reservations about the

In 1836, Ralph Waldo Emerson published his *Nature,* one of the key texts of the Transcendentalist movement.

Christian church took shape. A trip to Europe in 1832-33 proved highly significant, as Emerson met, among others, Thomas Carlyle, who funneled the thought of the German idealists into Emerson's eager mind.

Emerson returned to the United States to continue preaching for a few years but more importantly to begin lecturing, producing the material that, in the form of his two later collections of *Essays*, would earn him an international reputation. In 1836, Emerson published his first work, *Nature*, a key early text of the Transcendentalist strand of American Romanticism whose leading exponent he would become. In the same year, Emerson also helped bring such figures as Margaret Fuller, Amos Bronson Alcott, and Theodore Parker together as the Transcendental Club. In 1837, he delivered "The American Scholar" as Harvard's Phi Beta Kappa oration, judged by his contemporary Oliver Wendell Holmes to be the nation's "intellectual Declaration of Independence." Emerson followed with his indictment of organized Christianity, the "Divinity School Address," given before Harvard's graduating class of 1838, in which he urged, "dare to love God without mediator or veil." In 1841, Emerson proclaimed, in his lecture "Self-Reliance," that "Who so would be a man must be a nonconformist," and he also introduced his first volume of *Essays*. The appearance of a second volume of the latter in 1844 brought Emerson international prominence, and he would continue to influence the thought of his time in such later works as *Poems* (1847), *Addresses and Lectures* (1849), *Representative Men* (1850), and *The Conduct of Life* (1860).

—JAMES KESSENIDES

See Also: *New England Renaissance; Poetry; Transcendentalism.*

BIBLIOGRAPHY: Cayton, Mary Kupiec, *Emerson's Emergence: Self and Society in the Transformation of New England, 1800-1845* (Univ. of North Carolina Press 1989); Whicher, Stephen E., *Freedom and Fate: An Inner Life of Ralph Waldo Emerson,* 2nd ed. (Univ. of Pennsylvania Press 1971).

■ **EMMETT, DANIEL D. (1815-1904),** composer of "Dixie" (1859) and other songs. In 1842 he founded a blackface comedy troop, the Virginia Minstrels, the first of the traditional four-man minstrel shows. Emmett, who was born in Mount

Vernon, Ohio, joined Bryant's Minstrels in 1858 and wrote "Dixie" as a comic dance number. A Union supporter, he was greatly distressed when the tune was adopted as a Confederate marching song during the Civil War.

■ **ENERGY, DEPARTMENT OF,** cabinet department of the U.S. government established by Congress (1977) during Pres. Jimmy Carter's administration. The Energy Department oversees a variety of energy research, development, and conservation programs and regulates the nuclear power industry. The department was a response to the "energy crisis" of the 1970s, an aftermath of the 1973-74 oil embargo, which led to sharply higher petroleum prices.

■ **ENFORCEMENT ACTS (1870-71),** legislation to combat Ku Klux Klan violence in the South and election fraud throughout the United States. They were enacted specifically in response to the Ku Klux Klan's terrorist activities in the South. The 1870 law prohibited state officials from discriminating against voters on the basis of race. It also authorized the president to appoint supervisors for Southern elections and enable them to bring election fraud cases before a federal judge. The 1871 law was designed with Northern Democrats in mind and applied specifically to the election processes in cities. Both laws gave the federal government greater power against those who deliberately deprived African Americans and others of the right to vote, hold office, and enjoy civil liberties.

See Also: *Reconstruction.*

■ ***ENGLE V. VITALE* (1962),** U.S. Supreme Court case concerning the constitutionality of state-sponsored prayers in public schools. The Court ruled (7-1) that a prayer authorized by New York State school officials represented an establishment of religion and was banned by the First Amendment. *Engle* marked the height of legal efforts to build a wall separating church and state in the public schools on the grounds that any state support of religion is unconstitutional.

See Also: *Supreme Court.*

■ **ENGLISH IMMIGRANTS,** English settlers who first arrived in North America in the early 17th century and founded colonies in New England and the Chesapeake region. By 1700, English settlers composed the vast majority of Europeans in North America. Immigration continued unabated until the Revolution, when it was temporarily interrupted. In the 19th century immigrants from England accounted for about one-seventh of all immigrants. They migrated to America for a variety of reasons and settled throughout the eastern half of the United States, where they came to influence American manufacturing, mining, and technology.

The English influence on the United States and its institutions is indelible, especially in the nation's political culture. In addition, the close cultural and ethnic affiliation between English immigrants and most white Americans made adjustment and assimilation comparatively easy.

See Also: Ethnic Groups; Immigration.

■ **ENUMERATED GOODS,** American colonial products that under a 1660 law were designated for export to England or its provinces. They were intended to increase customs revenue and bolster English industry and by the 18th century included almost every profitable product.

See Also: Revolution, American.

■ *E PLURIBUS UNUM,* Latin phrase on the Great Seal of the United States and on every minted coin, meaning "out of many, one." Selected for the seal by John Adams, Benjamin Franklin, and Thomas Jefferson, the phrase emphasizes both national unity and the right of individual difference.

See Also: Revolution, American.

■ **EQUAL PROTECTION,** provision of the U.S. Constitution that required state governments to extend equal civil rights, such as the right to make contracts and own property, to the newly freed slaves. The 15th Amendment (1870) protected the right to vote. Not until the 1940s, however, did the U.S. Supreme Court begin to apply the equal protection clause to social issues and use it to overturn segregation laws and other forms of discrimination.

See Also: Supreme Court.

■ **EQUAL RIGHTS AMENDMENT (ERA),** constitutional amendment intended to prohibit legislation found to be discriminatory on the basis of sex. Drafted by Alice Paul and first submitted to Congress in 1923, the ERA was opposed by many feminists who favored special protective legislation for women. With the support of the National Organization for Women and the radicalized feminist movement of the 1960s, the ERA was approved by Congress in 1972 but was ratified by only 35 of the requisite 38 states and never became law.

See Also: Paul, Alice; National Organization for Women (NOW); Women in American History; Women's Movement.

■ **EQUIANO, OLAUDAH (c. 1750-97),** abolitionist and writer. Born in Benin, West Africa, Equiano was kidnapped and sold into slavery at the age of 11 and transported to the West Indies and then to Virginia. After a succession of owners, he eventually purchased his freedom in Philadelphia and immigrated to England. There Equiano wrote (1789) his autobiography, a vivid description and condemnation of the slave trade. He later petitioned Parliament directly for the abolition of slavery.

See Also: African Americans.

■ **EQUITY JURISDICTION,** legal remedies based in the English system of chancery law that seek to resolve disputes with fairness. Courts of equity oversee many areas of family law, such as custody and inheritance disputes, often operate with less formality than criminal courts, and rely on injunctions, declaratory judgments, and similar noncriminal sanctions to enforce their findings. In the United States, separate courts of law and equity have generally been replaced by a unified court system.

■ **ERA OF GOOD FEELINGS (1817-24),** name given to American politics during Pres. James Monroe's administration, originally coined by a Boston newspaper shortly after he became president. By 1816 the Federalist party had dwindled, and there was ostensibly only one political party—Monroe's Democratic-Republicans—in the United States. Thus, the president was able to get most legislation that he wanted passed by Congress. In the election of 1820 Monroe received all but one electoral vote. One of the last presidents to be nominated through the political caucus, Monroe himself thought that political parties were "not necessary to free government." While disdaining political parties, Monroe nonetheless pressed a political and economic agenda that served eastern interests. Westerners and back-country Americans saw little benefit in Monroe's policies, and they gravitated toward Tennessee politician Andrew Jackson. By the 1824 election the pretense of a unified polity had all but vanished.

See Also: Banks of the United States, First and Second; Monroe, James.

BIBLIOGRAPHY: Ammon, Harry, *James Monroe: The Quest for National Identity* (McGraw-Hill 1971); Sellers, Charles G., *The Market Revolution: Jacksonian America, 1815-1846* (Oxford Univ. Press 1991).

■ **ERICSSON, JOHN (1803-89),** engineer, inventor, and designer of the Civil War ironclad *Monitor*. Born in Värmland, Sweden, he trained as a cadet in the Swedish corps of mechanical engineers and worked in London, England (1826-38), where he perfected inventions that included a steam-fire en-

gine, a steam locomotive, and the screw propulsion system for steamships. Ericsson came to New York in 1839 to build a ship for the U.S. Navy and, despite his first intentions, ended up becoming a U.S. citizen in 1848. Ericsson designed and built the turreted, ironclad USS *Monitor*, which faced the CSS *Virginia* (formerly the USS *Merrimack*) during the Civil War in the first naval battle (1862) between ironclads. Ericsson continued to develop and build warships, launching one that could fire underwater torpedoes in 1878 and foreshadowing the development of modern destroyers.

See Also: Invention; Monitor and Merrimack; Science.

■ **ERIE CANAL (1825),** artificial waterway connecting Buffalo, New York, with Albany and the Hudson River. Gov. DeWitt Clinton dreamed of connecting New York City (on the lower Hudson) to the Great Lakes with a canal from Albany to Buffalo. He proposed the idea in 1817, when overland travel was prohibitively difficult and most natural water routes flowed in a north-south direction, and he convinced the New York legislature to

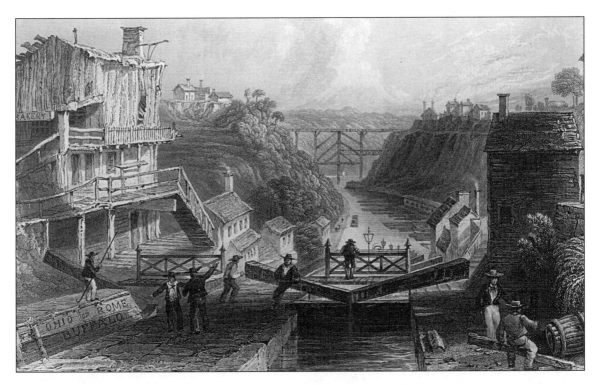

Constructed between 1817 and 1825, the Erie Canal extended from the Hudson River to Lake Erie and became the shipping route to the Great Lakes region. Its success spawned the building of thousands of miles of canals by mid-century.

support it with a $7-million bond issue. Built mostly by Irish contract laborers, the canal was 40 feet wide and 4 feet deep, ran 363 miles, and had 83 locks. It opened on Oct. 26, 1825. The Erie Canal drew settlers to farmland in Indiana, Illinois, and points west at the rate of 50,000 a year by 1830. Farmers in turn gained access to national and international markets via New York City. The canal encouraged the development of commercial agriculture and reduced the need for farm families to be self-sufficient and produce their own textiles. It also turned towns along the canal, including Utica, Rochester, and Buffalo, into cities and established the commercial and financial supremacy of New York City. The canal's great success sparked a canal-building boom from 1820 to 1840 that turned attention toward America's heartland.

See Also: Canals; Clinton, DeWitt.

■ **ERIKSSON, LEIF (c. 1000),** Norse explorer, son of the Greenland colonizer Erik the Red. Leif's exploits were recorded in 13th-century Icelandic sagas. One version suggests that Leif the Lucky, as he was sometimes called, converted to Christianity during a visit to Norway and attempted to return to Greenland to complete the island's Christian conversion. According to the sagas, Eriksson, blown off course, landed at Vinland (after 1000), somewhere on the northeast coast of North America. Others suggest that Eriksson sailed intentionally for the North American coast on a voyage of exploration. The explorer wintered at Vinland, variously identified by historians as Newfoundland, Nova Scotia, or New England. He then returned to Greenland. Eriksson's venture inspired another colonizing expedition that returned to Vinland. These settlements did not endure, and the conquest of North America would not begin until Columbus's voyages at the end of the 15th century.

See Also: Erik the Red; Exploration and Discovery; Vinland.

BIBLIOGRAPHY: Quinn, David, *North America from Earliest Discovery to First Settlements: The Norse Voyages* (Harper 1975).

■ **ERIK THE RED (c. mid-10th century),** Norse navigator. Born in Norway, Erik the Red journeyed with his father to Iceland as a child. In c. 982, he

led an expedition that discovered and explored a largely ice-bound island. Erik named the island Greenland to entice future settlers. Returning to Iceland, he organized a group of 500 colonists with whom in c. 986 he founded the settlement of Brattak-lid in southwestern Greenland. His son Leif Eriksson discovered Vinland, an unidentified region in northeastern North America.

See Also: Eriksson, Leif; Exploration and Discovery.

■ **ESCH-CUMMINS TRANSPORTATION ACT (1920),** federal legislation that terminated the federal control of the nation's rail system that had been imposed during World War I. It also provided amendments to the Interstate Commerce Act (1887) regarding rates and consolidation and created the Railroad Labor Board to assist in labor mediation.

See Also: Interstate Commerce Commission (ICC).

■ **ESPIONAGE ACT (1917),** federal law intended to quell antigovernment propaganda during World War I. It was followed in 1918 by the Sedition Act.

See Also: Sedition Act; World War I.

■ **ESTAUGH, ELIZABETH HADDON (1680-1762),** colonial pioneer and landowner born in Southwark, London, England. At 21, she took over her father's undeveloped tracts in western New Jersey, where she became a successful proprietor and the founder of Haddonfield, New Jersey. Henry Wadsworth Longfellow popularized the story of her courtship and marriage to Quaker preacher John Estaugh in *Tales of a Wayside Inn* (1863).

■ **ESTAVANICO (ALSO ESTEVANICO, ESTEVAN-ITO, ESTEBAN) (?-1539),** explorer. A Moroccan slave, Estavanico journeyed to Florida in 1527 as part of Pánfilo de Narváez's colonizing expedition. Its failure left Estavanico and his fellow survivors enslaved to Indians, from which condition they escaped to lives still, at times, as slaves, and as medicine men, along the coast of the Gulf of Mexico. After fleeing the coast several years later, Estavanico and three others, the only remaining survivors, including Álvar Núñez Cabeza de Vaca, reached the territory of New Spain in 1536. Cabeza de Vaca's report gave hope to those Spaniards who spoke of the Seven Golden Cities of Cíbola, and in 1539, Estavanico set out as guide for an expedition to Cíbola. He was killed when the expedition reached one of seven Zuni pueblos that had inspired the myth of Cíbola.

See Also: African Americans; Cabeza de Vaca, Álvar Núñez; Frontier in American History.

■ **ETHNIC GROUPS,** minority populations defined by such shared characteristics as language, national origin, historical legacy, religion, customs, cultural values, and physical features. Although ethnicity is sometimes construed as a subset of race, most scholars agree that culture, not biology, is the defining characteristic of the term.

Ethnic diversity has characterized American society from its beginnings. On the eve of European colonization there were more than 350 distinct native societies in North America, speaking nearly as many distinct languages. During the colonial period, large populations of western Europeans migrated to the British colonies; they included people of British, Dutch, and German descent, mostly adherents of Protestant faiths. In the South, African-American slaves created a culture based on the commonalities of their West African heritage. In the northern areas of the Spanish American empire that would become part of the United States, most colonists were of mixed Indian and Spanish descent, and Roman Catholic.

Immigration has been one of the most important social forces of American history, introducing dozens of new ethnic groups to the country. In the first half of the century hundreds of thousands of Irish, German, and Scandinavian immigrants arrived; after the Civil War the dominant immigrant groups included eastern and southern Europeans (Slavs, Jews, Magyars, Sicilians) and Asians (Chinese, Japanese, Filipinos, Koreans). During the first quarter of the 20th century there was a massive migration of Mexicans into the Southwest.

The dominant view during this period was the incompatibility of ethnic diversity with the social unity necessary for the development of a strong national state. In an American version of "ethnic cleansing," Indian communities were conquered and removed to distant and isolated locations ("reservations"), most infamously in the "Trail of Tears," the forced removal of the Cherokees and other Indian tribes from the southeastern region of the country. Most African Americans were kept in bondage before the Civil War and after emancipation were segregated in rural or urban enclaves, prohibited from mixing with other Americans, and denied any significant participation in civic affairs. There were also "nativist" movements that sought to restrict immigration, or the segregation of ethnic groups once they arrived in America. Thus further Chinese immigration was prohibited in 1882, Japanese immigration in 1908, and Asians were ruled ineligible for citizenship. Like African Americans, Asians and Mexicans were confined to their own ethnic ghettos.

There was also a great deal of residential clustering among European ethnic groups, and America's large cities had Irish, Italian, Polish, and Jewish neighborhoods. For the most part, however, European immigrants who sought integration into American society went through a process of assimilation (sometimes called "Americanization") in which their ethnic identity gradually dissolved and was replaced by a version of Anglo-American culture. The main agents in this process included mandatory public education, the spread of popular culture, and the unique opportunity the nation provided for social and economic mobility. Within two generations the descendants of most European immigrants spoke English as their primary language and thought of themselves as Americans. Nativist concerns, however, grew particularly strong after World War I, resulting in the passage of restrictive immigration laws that significantly reduced the volume of immigration.

After World War II several factors led to the increasing importance of ethnicity in American life. The civil rights struggles of African Americans, Mexican Americans, Indians, and other groups brought attention to the nation's record of racial and ethnic discrimination, leading to the development of "ethnic studies" curricula and new ethnic literatures, and fostered a positive view that ethnic identity could be a source of power for minority groups. Partly as a reaction to this trend and partly because of dissatisfactions with the perceived homogeneity of modern American culture, movements arose among the descendants of immigrants to reestablish connections with traditional ethnic ways. And perhaps most importantly, the immigration laws were dramatically liberalized in 1965, opening the door to millions of new immigrants, principally from Asia and Latin America.

Many political and cultural theorists continued to insist that assimilation and eventual dissolution of separate ethnic identities was necessary for the United States to remain a unified national society. But during the second half of the 20th century "Americanization" gradually gave way to "pluralism" as the preferred model for the operation of American society. Pluralists argued for the coexistence of a strong sense of national identity with correspondingly strong ethnic identities that provided a sense of cultural rootedness. Just as the federal political model argues that autonomous and independent states can contribute to a strong central government, the pluralist model of ethnic groups suggests that one of the most important things Americans have in common is the value they place on a society in which diversity is respected and valued.

—JOHN MACK FARAGHER

See Also: Acculturation; Americanization; Assimilation; Cultural Pluralism; Immigration; Melting Pot; individual groups.

BIBLIOGRAPHY: Fuchs, Lawrence H., *The American Kaleidoscope: Race, Ethnicity, and the Civic Culture* (Univ. Press of New England 1990); Seller, Maxine, *To Seek America: A History of Ethnic Life in the United States,* rev. ed. (Jerome S. Ozer 1988); Takaki, Ronald, *A Different Mirror: A History of Multicultural America* (Little, Brown 1993); Thernstrom, Stephan, et al., *Harvard Encyclopedia of American Ethnic Groups* (Belknap Press 1980).

■ **EVANS, GEORGE HENRY (1805-56),** reformer and editor of labor newspapers. Born in Bromyard, Herefordshire, England, Evans came to the United States in 1820. He apprenticed for a printer in Ithaca, New York. Evans edited *The Man at Ithaca* before moving to New York City, where he was involved with the publication of *The Working Man's Advocate,* the *Daily Sentinel,* and *Young America* in the 1830s and 1840s. In 1840 Evans issued *History of the Origin and Progress of the Working Men's Party.*

■ **EVANS, WALKER (1903-75),** dean of documentary photography. Born in St. Louis, Missouri, Evans began photographing in 1928. He documented rural life for the Resettlement Administration and the Farm Security Administration during the Great Depression of the 1930s. In 1936 he took a leave to travel with writer James Agee on a project that culminated in the 1941 publication of *Let Us Now Praise Famous Men,* a chronicle of Southern sharecropping that originally featured 31 of Evans's photographs.

See Also: Farm Security Administration (FSA); Great Depression; Photography; Resettlement Administration.

■ **EVARTS, WILLIAM MAXWELL (1818-1901),** lawyer and statesman. He was born in Boston, Massachusetts, and served on diplomatic missions to Great Britain during the Civil War (1863-64). Evarts was Pres. Andrew Johnson's defense counsel during Johnson's 1868 impeachment trial and U.S. attorney general (1868-69), and he represented the United States before the Geneva court of arbitration in the *Alabama* claims cases (1871-72). Later Evarts represented Rutherford B. Hayes before the 1877 electoral commission, served as U.S. secretary of state (1877-81), and was U.S. senator from New York (1885-91).

See Also: Alabama Claims; Hayes, Rutherford Birchard.

■ **EVERGLADES,** tropical marsh covering some 5,000 square miles of southern Florida. Stretching across the state's southern peninsula, the swampy region was home to Seminole Indians but remained largely uninhabited by whites until the 1880s. In 1947 Pres. Harry S. Truman dedicated the Everglades National Park, a 1.4 million-acre wildlife preserve that is the haven for a rich variety of flora and fauna and numerous endangered species.

■ **EVERS, MEDGAR WILEY (1925-63),** civil rights leader. Born in Decatur, Mississippi, Evers was at the forefront of one of the most volatile and dangerous arenas in the struggle for civil rights. In his capacity as field director (1954-63) of the Mississippi branch of the National Association for the Advancement of Colored People (NAACP), Evers worked to increase black voter registration and to desegregate the University of Mississippi in 1962. He was assassinated in 1963 at the front door of his home. It took three trials and more than 30 years before his assassin was finally convicted in 1994.

See Also: *Civil Rights Movement.*

■ **EXECUTIVE REORGANIZATION ACT (1939),** federal law that created the Executive Office of the President. Promoted as an efficiency measure, it allowed the subsequent expansion of the size and powers of the White House staff.

See Also: *New Deal.*

■ **EXETER COMPACT (1639),** agreement that served as a basis for social and legal institutions in the settlement of Exeter, New Hampshire. Written by Antinomian minister Rev. John Wheelwright and signed by his supporters, the compact was based upon the Mayflower Compact.

See Also: *Mayflower Compact.*

■ *EX PARTE MERRYMAN* **(1861),** U.S. Supreme Court case concerning both the president's authority to impose martial law and the operation of civilian courts under such an order. In the first months of the Civil War, Chief Justice Roger Taney had sent a writ of habeas corpus to military authorities in Baltimore, directing them either to try or to free John Merryman, who was being held on suspicion of disloyalty to the Union. After the military commander refused to comply, Taney challenged President Lincoln's authority to declare martial law and suspend habeas corpus. The issue remained unsettled until *Ex parte Milligan* (1866), when Taney's position was affirmed.

See Also: *Supreme Court; Taney, Roger Brooke.*

■ *EX PARTE MILLIGAN* **(1866),** U.S. Supreme Court case that considered the legality of martial law and the jurisdiction of military courts in areas where there was no open rebellion and where civilian courts were functioning. A military court had convicted and sentenced to death an Indiana man, Lambdin Milligan, for allegedly treasonous activities. Milligan appealed, arguing that an army panel had no constitutional authority to judge his case. Given that federal civilian courts were in operation in Indiana at the time, Milligan contended there was no reason

why he, a civilian, should be tried in a military court. The Supreme Court ruled unanimously that the military had improperly assumed jurisdiction in Milligan's case. The Court, however, split on the more general question of whether the federal government ever has the authority to subject civilians to martial law outside a theater of war. By a slim majority (5-4), the Court held that the federal government does not have such authority. Even so, the Court carefully worded its decision so as not to undermine the state of martial law then in force in the occupied Southern states.

See Also: *Supreme Court.*

■ *EX PARTE VALLANDIGHAM* **(1866),** U.S. Supreme Court case concerning the boundary between civilian and military legal jurisdictions. Clement L. Vallandigham, a leading Copperhead Democrat, had been convicted by a military tribunal for speaking out against the Union during the Civil War. He appealed his conviction to the Supreme Court, contending that the military court had overstepped its jurisdiction since he had always been a civilian. The Court (8-0) held that it had no jurisdiction in the case, one of several instances during the Civil War era when it declined to rule on the constitutionality of wartime restrictions on civil liberties.

See Also: *Copperheads; Supreme Court; Vallandigham, Clement L.*

■ **EXPLORATION AND DISCOVERY.** Neolithic migrants crossing the Bering Strait from Asia first explored and settled the Western Hemisphere. By the time the European exploration of North America began in the 16th century, the continent was laced with an elaborate network of trails that guided colonial conquerors, missionaries, traders, and settlers alike. There was relatively little long-range exchange of goods or information before the European era, however. Indian cultures were essentially local, and although groups often possessed a good deal of information about adjacent areas and peoples, for the most part they lacked a continental understanding of geography. The very fact of a colonial presence in the Western Hemisphere, on the other hand, suggests the importance of long-distance exchange in European culture. Imperial and commerce imperatives provided the incentive for the first systematic exploration of the continent

Sgt. Patrick Gass, a member of Lewis and Clark's "Corps of Discovery," included this drawing, entitled "Captain Clark and his men shooting Bears," in the 1807 edition of his journal of the expedition.

and its resources. Yet despite the steady accretion of geographic information, it took nearly three centuries of colonial experience to develop an accurate overall conception of the shape, size, and character of the continent.

European exploration rightfully begins with the voyages of the Portuguese, stimulated by Prince Henry the Navigator, although for the most part these expeditions were along the African coast. The exploration of the Caribbean began with the voyages of Christopher Columbus and Amerigo Vespucci for the Spanish. Ferdinand Magellan directed the first expedition to circumnavigate the globe, and Hernán Cortés and Francisco Pizarro led expeditions of conquest that first opened the wonders of Mexico and Peru to Europeans.

Spanish and French Exploration. But the first exploration of North America itself commenced when Juan Ponce de León, the conqueror of Puerto Rico, sighted and reconnoitered the coast of Florida in 1513. This coastal knowledge was extended by several Spanish expeditions along the Atlantic coast over the next 10 to 15 years, extending as far north as present Nova Scotia. The exploration of the interior proved to be far more difficult. Spanish conquistador Pánfilo de Narváez landed at Tampa Bay in 1528, but his expedition came to ruin along the Texas coast without finding any civilizations to plunder. One of the few survivors, Álvar Núñez Cabeza de Vaca, finally reached Mexico in 1536 after years of Indian captivity and a long overland march,

with tales of rich civilizations to plunder in the American Southwest.

Stimulated by this vision of a fabulous civilization, in 1539 Hernando de Soto inaugurated an expedition of conquest that began in Florida and moved north and west. By 1542, his troops had ravaged scores of Indian villages through much of the deep South, crossed the Mississippi River, and explored the lower reaches of the Arkansas River Valley, before returning to the great river in despair. When de Soto died, his retreating men became the first Europeans to float down the Mississippi to its mouth on the Gulf. Meanwhile, in 1540, Francisco Vasquez de Coronado and his lieutenants moved north from Mexico but found only the sedentary Pueblo and other even poorer Indian villages. Despite their failures these expeditions were the foundations of Spanish geographic knowledge of the southern continental tier and established the approximate northern limits of Spanish control.

French exploration began with the voyage of Giovanni di Verrazano along the Atlantic coast in 1524 and Jacques Cartier up the St. Lawrence River in 1535; it was not until the early 17th century, however, that France began a comprehensive program of imperial exploration. Samuel de Champlain entered the estuary of the St. Lawrence in 1603 and within a dozen years had explored a water route to Georgian Bay on Lake Huron via the Ottawa River. Champlain envisioned a northern empire based on the lucrative fur trade and linked by waterways, and this goal was largely realized by his successors.

By the 1650s French explorers had explored the Great Lakes, and in the wake (and sometimes in advance) of these explorations, Catholic missionaries and fur traders invaded the country, the first proselytizing, the second marrying Indian women and raising mixed-ancestry children who in turn entered the trade. In the process the French contributed to the creation of a new kind of society, one that was French and Indian at the same time. Learning of a great inland river system that could link the French empire of the north to the Gulf in the south, in 1673 Louis Jolliet and Père Jacques Marquette explored that connection, via Green Bay and the Wisconsin River, traveling down the Mississippi as far south as de Soto's crossing. Sieur de La Salle reached the Gulf via the Mississippi in 1682 and claimed the entire great valley, which he named Louisiana, for France. His work was extended by subsequent French explorers, who mapped other portages to the Mississippi system and pushed the fur trade up the Missouri River in the early 18th century. By the 1740s, the French had opened the Grand Portage from Lake Superior to Lake of the Woods, extended the water route to Lake Winnipeg, founded a post on the site of what would become Winnipeg, reached the Mandan villages on the upper Missouri River, and penetrated the grasslands as far west as the Black Hills of South Dakota.

English Exploration. One of the persistent aims of these explorations was the discovery of the fabled Northwest Passage to the Pacific or "South Sea." To this elusive goal the English devoted the most attention. John Cabot's voyage in 1497, like that of Columbus five years before, aimed to pioneer a new route to the Spice Islands. After Spanish and French expeditions had established the continuity of the coastline from Florida to New England, English efforts concentrated on the northern latitudes. Beginning in 1576, Martin Frobisher made three voyages in search of the Northwest Passage during which he charted the bay that bears his name. In 1607, Henry Hudson also explored those icy waters, and in 1610 sailed into the bay thereafter known as Hudson, providing the English with an accessible route to the continent's interior. In more temperate climes,

English explorers such as Humphrey Gilbert, Ferdinando Gorges, and John Smith sailed up numerous coastal rivers in the hope that they would lead to the riches of the Orient. However elusive, this search provided a powerful stimulus to Atlantic coastal mapping, essentially completed by the combined efforts of the European powers by the early 17th century.

After the first English colonies were planted along the Atlantic coast, the exploration of the fertile coastal plain began immediately, stimulated less by the desire for furs or plunder than by the hope for fertile lands on which to settle. The Appalachian chain, however, prevented further exploration of the interior. The settlement of the Shenandoah Valley did not begin until the second quarter of the 18th century, and it was not until Daniel Boone opened a road to Kentucky across Cumberland Gap in 1774 that the trans-Appalachian interior was made accessible to European agriculture.

The other important region of English inland exploration began on the shores of Hudson Bay. The Hudson's Bay Company, founded in 1670, established fur trade posts on the coastal waters of the bay, but not until goaded by the western penetrations of the French in the 1740s did the company send expeditions into the interior. Hudson's Bay men built Cumberland House, the company's first inland post in 1774. The greatest explorers of the Northwest, however, were the men of the North West Company, a Montreal fur trade combination put together in 1784 that carried on the tradition of the French trading system. Under the North West banner explorers such as Alexander Mackenzie opened the region north of Lake Athabasca to commercial exploitation.

Pacific Coast. Mackenzie's trip from Athabasca to the Pacific by way of the Fraser River in 1793 finally fulfilled the old vision of crossing the continent, some 300 years after Columbus. The Pacific coast had long been known to the Spanish, however. In 1513, Vasco Núñez de Balboa had claimed it for the Spanish Crown, and in 1542 the crew of Juan Cabrillo sailed as far north as the Oregon coast. Thirty-five years later the Englishman Francis Drake made a brief landing in California. Yet the coast had lain mostly undisturbed until the Russians began to extend their Siberian fur-trapping operations to the Alaskan coast. Vitus Bering's expedition of 1741 was followed by several other Russian expeditions, culminating in a landing on the Alaskan mainland by Pyotr Kuzinich Krenitsyn in 1768. In 1784, Gregor Shelekhov founded a Russian settlement on Kodiak Island. Compelled to counter these moves in order to protect their claim to California, in 1769 the Spanish sent Franciscan missionary Junipero Serra, in the company of military authorities, to establish missions and presidios up the California coast; California and Mexico were connected by an overland route explored, mapped, and marked by Juan Baptista de Anza from 1774 to 1776. At about the same time, the British admiral James Cook was exploring the coastline of the Pacific Northwest. Later it was comprehensively mapped by British naval cartographer George Vancouver.

Exploring the Interior. The mapping of the great interior of what would become the United States was largely the work of American explorers. In 1803 Pres. Thomas Jefferson appointed Meriwether Lewis and William Clark to conduct their famous expedition from the Mississippi to the Pacific coast. Their journey, from 1804 to 1806, provided the first detailed information on the northern Rockies and the Columbia River basin. Perhaps most important was the precedent the expedition established for a strong government role in the exploration of the West. In 1806, the year Lewis and Clark returned, Jefferson sent Lt. Zebulon Pike on an expedition to the headwaters of the Red and Arkansas rivers, during which Pike and his men spied on the Spanish settlements in New Mexico, were arrested, and were held prisoner for several months. The trip provided the new nation with valuable geographic and political knowledge. Pike was not impressed with the arid interior, an opinion seconded by Maj. Stephen Long, an army officer who explored the trans-Mississippi region in 1820, and on his map labeled the Great Plains the "Great American Desert."

The last of the great western explorations was conducted by John Charles Frémont for the Army Corps of Topographical Engineers. In 1838-41, he participated in an expedition to explore and map the upper Mississippi Country, and in 1843 he was commissioned to lead an expedition into the Rockies and the Oregon Country. The reports and maps from this journey stirred considerable interest in the Far West, and Frémont became known as the "Great Pathfinder." By 1850, the major features of the continent had become well known, and after the Civil War the detailed work of further mapping the country became the province of the professional staff of the Geological Survey.

—JOHN MACK FARAGHER

See Also: *Bering Strait Migration; Dutch Colonies; French Colonies; Frontier in American History; Fur Trade; Lewis and Clark Expedition; Norse Explorations and Settlements; Northwest Passage; Portuguese Exploration; Spanish Colonies; individual biographies.*

BIBLIOGRAPHY: De Voto, Bernard, *The Course of Empire* (Houghton Mifflin 1952); Goetzmann, William, ed., *The Atlas of North American Exploration* (Prentice-Hall 1992); Palmer, Stanley H., and Dennis Reinhartz, eds., *Essays on the History of North American Discovery and Exploration* (Texas A&M Univ. Press 1988).

F

FAIRBANKS, CHARLES WARREN (1852-1918), vice president of the United States (1905-09). He was born in Unionville Center, Ohio, and attended Ohio Wesleyan University. He became a prosperous railroad lawyer in Indiana and entered local Republican politics. Elected to the U.S. Senate in 1897, Fairbanks served there until 1905 when he was elected Theodore Roosevelt's vice president. He unsuccessfully ran again as vice president, under Charles Evans Hughes, in 1916.

See Also: Vice President of the United States.

FAIRBANKS, DOUGLAS (1883-1939), film actor. Born in Denver, Colorado, he combined physical grace and humor to become a silent screen idol in films such as *The Mark of Zorro* (1920) and *The Thief of Baghdad* (1925).

FAIR DEAL, economic reforms proposed by Pres. Harry S. Truman (1945-53). Announced in January 1949, the Fair Deal was an extension of New Deal reforms and was largely turned back by Republicans in control of Congress.

FAIR EMPLOYMENT PRACTICES COMMISSION (FEPC), federal government body established in 1941. Its mission was to promote the full use of all available manpower and to rid industry of discriminatory labor practices. Although its charter contained no provisions for enforcement, the FEPC helped increase the numbers of blacks employed in defense industries during World War II. The FEPC was eliminated in 1946 but was revived in a new form as the Equal Employment Opportunity Commission (EEOC) in 1964.

See Also: New Deal.

FAIRFAX RESOLVES (1774), resolutions passed in Virginia in response to Parliament's Intolerable Acts of 1774. Most likely drafted by George Mason, they called for unity among the American colonies, defense of their common rights, and the nonimportation of British goods.

See Also: Intolerable Acts; Revolution, American.

FAIR LABOR STANDARDS ACT (1938), the first permanent national minimum-wage law. Also known as the Wages and Hours Law, this New Deal legislation established minimum wages, maximum hours, and other conditions favorable to workers engaged in interstate commerce.

See Also: New Deal.

FAIR OAKS, BATTLE OF. *See: Seven Pines, Battle of.*

FAIRS AND EXPOSITIONS, spectacles that, after their transformation in the mid-19th century into world's fairs and international expositions, have inspired wonder, afforded entertainment, and helped shape the ways countless millions of Americans have thought about themselves and the rest of the world. The history of American world's fairs can be divided into Victorian-era, Depression-era, and Cold War-era expositions.

Technically the first world's fair held in the United States was the 1853 New York Crystal Palace Exhibition. But the American world's fair movement really began after the Civil War, as expositions became central vehicles for reconstructing America's national identity. Beginning with the 1876 Philadelphia Centennial Exhibition and continuing with the 1893 Chicago World's Columbian Exposition, the 1904 St. Louis Louisiana Purchase Exposition, and 1915-16 San Francisco Panama-Pacific International Exposition, America's Victorian-era fairs emphasized America's national progress toward utopia and America's growing role as an imperial power. At the St. Louis fair, for instance, the U.S. government put more than 1,000 Filipinos on display as part of its effort to win popular support for U.S. policies in the Philippine Islands.

The second generation of American world's fairs occurred during the Great Depression. Highlighting the fairs of this period were the 1933-34 Chicago Century of Progress Exposition and the 1939-40 New York World's Fair. These fairs, together with a host of smaller expositions in Dallas, San Diego, and Cleveland, emphasized science and technology as antidotes to the Depression and as guarantors of national progress.

The third generation of fairs included the 1962 Seattle Century 21 Exposition, the 1964 New York World's Fair, and smaller fairs in San Antonio, Spokane, Knoxville, and New Orleans. Forced to compete with new technologies of communications and the popularity of amusement parks that, ironically, traced their origins to America's Victorian-era fairs, the world's fairs of the Cold War period lost some of their overarching significance, but their influence on the American cultural landscape should not be minimized. The Century 21 Exposition, for example, played a leading role in boosting national support for science education and bequeathed the Space Needle to downtown Seattle.

America's fairs and expositions have not only mirrored technological, social, and cultural changes; they have instigated changes as well. Fairs have introduced Americans to scientific and technological innovations ranging from plastics to X rays. They have altered the way Americans have thought about architecture. They have also affected American political values. African Americans, for instance, seized upon the discriminatory policies of fairs to push forward a national civil rights agenda. Middle-class women reformers made use of women's buildings constructed at the fairs to win support for a variety of political causes, including suffrage and social welfare legislation.

World's fairs usually lasted about six months. But their legacies have been enduring. Chicago's Field Museum of Natural History as well as its Museum of Science and Industry were founded to house exhibits in the 1893 and 1933-34 fairs held in that city. To sum up, fairs and expositions lent both form and substance to American culture. For precisely this reason, they have been sites of happy memories about the past and bitter struggles over the future direction of the American republic.

—ROBERT W. RYDELL

See Also: Science.

BIBLIOGRAPHY: Benedict, Burton, *The Anthropology of World's Fairs* (Scolar Press 1983); Findling, John, and Kimberly Pelle, *Historical Dictionary of World's Fairs and Expositions, 1851-1988* (Greenwood Press 1990); Rydell, Robert W., *All the World's a Fair: Visions of Empire at America's International Expositions, 1876-1916* (Univ. of Chicago Press 1984); Rydell, Robert W., *World of Fairs: The Century of Progress Expositions* (Univ. of Chicago Press 1993).

■ **FALL, ALBERT BACON (1861-1944),** Republican politician and government official. Born in Frankfurt, Kentucky, he had established a lucrative law practice in New Mexico before being elected to the U.S. Senate in 1912. In 1921 he joined Pres. Warren G. Harding's cabinet as secretary of the interior. Fall resigned two years later when his involvement in the so-called Teapot Dome scandal became public. In 1924 he was indicted for conspiracy and charged with accepting a $100,000 bribe relating to the leasing of U.S. naval oil reserves in Teapot Dome, Wyoming, and Elk Hills, California. Cleared of the conspiracy charge in 1926, Fall was later found guilty of accepting the bribe and was sentenced to prison (1931-32).

See Also: Teapot Dome.

■ **FALLEN TIMBERS, BATTLE OF (Aug. 20, 1794),** battle fought between the United States and the Ohio Valley Confederacy. Led by the Miami war chief Little Turtle, the Indians of the Ohio Valley sought to halt American encroachment into their homelands following the American Revolution. After Little Turtle defeated Arthur St. Clair's army in 1791, Pres. George Washington committed over 80 percent of the federal government's operating budget to pressing a campaign against the confederacy, appointing Gen. Anthony Wayne to lead the American forces. On Aug. 20, 1794, Wayne and 3,000 American troops engaged Little Turtle's forces, which fell back, heading for the British Fort Miami (modern Toledo, Ohio). The British, however, refused to assist them. Wayne then attacked the fleeing Indians, routing them completely. The Battle of Fallen Timbers was an important victory for the United States and a decisive defeat for the Ohio confederacy. As a result of the defeat, in 1795 the representatives of 12 Indian nations signed the

Treaty of Greenville, which opened large parts of Indiana and Ohio to European settlement.

See Also: Greenville, Treaty of; Indians of North America; Little Turtle; Wayne, Anthony.

■ **FALL LINE,** boundary between an upland region and a coastal plain, over which rivers from the upland drop to the plain in falls. A fall line marks the limits of upstream navigability. In the eastern United States the line runs parallel to the Atlantic coast at the rise of the Piedmont Plateau. During colonial times the fall line represented the first American frontier. The cities of Trenton, Philadelphia, Baltimore, Washington, Richmond, and Augusta were all built along the eastern seaboard's fall line.

■ **FARM CREDIT ADMINISTRATION,** New Deal agency established by executive order of Pres. Franklin D. Roosevelt in 1933 to coordinate government farm credit programs. It sought to keep family farms out of bankruptcy during the Depression.

See Also: New Deal.

■ **FARMER, JAMES (1920-),** civil rights leader. Born in Marshall, Texas, Farmer was a founder of the Congress of Racial Equality (CORE), served as program director of the National Association for the Advancement of Colored People (NAACP) (1959-60), and assumed the national directorship of CORE (1961-66). From 1969 to 1970, he was an assistant secretary in the Department of Health, Education and Welfare.

See Also: Civil Rights Movement; Congress of Racial Equality (CORE).

■ **FARMER-LABOR PARTY,** third-party movement active in Minnesota between 1918 and 1944. Drawing upon a base of support that united the people in the state's rural grain-growing regions with the working class of Minneapolis-St. Paul, and the iron-mining centers to the north, the Farmer-Labor party advocated a progressive political agenda that included unemployment relief, a two-year moratorium on farm foreclosures, and old-age pensions. The peak of the party's power came in 1936, when it controlled Minnesota's governorship, the state house of representatives, both seats in the U.S. Senate, and 5 of the

state's 10 House seats. It merged with the Minnesota Democratic party in 1944.

See Also: Agriculture; Political Parties.

■ **FARM LEGISLATION,** laws setting and reflecting a social and economic agenda for farmers. Farm legislation has oscillated between strengthening agricultural economics and enhancing farming as the basis of civic life. While these two goals appear complementary, legislation for economic enhancement has always had the higher priority.

Republican Legislation. The American Revolution (1775-83) enhanced the concept of freehold tied to republican ideology. Advocates of freehold, like Thomas Jefferson, hoped to create civic virtue by allowing the widest possible ownership of land. The Continental Congress responded with the Ordinance of 1785, which established the rectangular land survey, and the Ordinance of 1787, which established a republican form of government for the territories. Congress continued this trend with land laws leading to the Preemption Act (1841), which allowed settlers to claim unsurveyed land; the Homestead Act (1862), which gave settlers 160 acres of land upon specified conditions; and the Morrill Land Grant Act (1862), which gave states land to fund agricultural colleges.

After 1850, economic and technological developments increased agricultural production costs, and consequently, farmers demanded legislation to increase the money supply and enlarge production and markets. They also asked for laws appropriate to settling the arid West. Congress responded by creating the Department of Agriculture in 1862 and elevating it to cabinet status in 1889. In 1887, the Hatch Act established agricultural experiment stations. The Desert Land Act (1877) and the Carey Act (1894) both encouraged, but poorly underwrote, irrigation.

Agricultural-Efficiency Legislation. Many farmers found congressional legislation inadequate to their needs. Members of farmers' organizations, such as the Grangers and the Farmers' Alliance, advocated railroad and money regulation, government crop subsidies, and cooperative communities as aids to agriculture. But, after 1900, a reform-minded Congress modeled its legislation on industrial standards of efficiency. The

Forest Reserve Act (1891) abetted federal planning of agricultural resources, and the Reclamation Act (1902) supported irrigation in the West. Through the Smith-Lever Act (1914), agriculturist Seaman A. Knapp directed county-extension agents who were scientifically trained in farming techniques.

During the next three decades, the congressional preoccupation with economics favored heavily capitalized farms. The McNary-Haugen bills, federal price-supports based on ratios fixed on prewar prices, failed during the 1920s, but Pres. Franklin D. Roosevelt's New Deal provided economic and production reforms. The Agricultural Adjustment Act (AAA) (1933) established price supports and production quotas. The Soil Conservation Service (1935) attacked soil erosion. The Resettlement Administration moved marginal farm families either to cities or to better lands. The U.S. Supreme Court declared the first AAA unconstitutional, but, in 1938, Congress responded with another that shaped policy for the next 60 years. This act included price subsidies and production controls, crop insurance, and conservation.

Corporate-Farm Legislation. World War II spurred the development of larger farms, greater mechanization, and rural depopulation while solidifying the relationship of the federal government to the agricultural economy. Corporate farming, whether in the form of family farms incorporated for tax purposes or subsidiaries owned by a parent company like Sunkist, came of age. In response, in the 1960s through the 1980s, environmentalists like Rachel Carson, James Hightower, Wendell Berry, and Wes Jackson lambasted corporate farming as destructive of land, communities, personal relations, and society.

Congress responded to demands for sustainable agriculture and environmental protection with the Food Security Act of 1985, which encouraged farmers to turn fragile crop lands into grasslands through the Conservation Reserve Program. Moreover, the act promoted soil conservation and protected wetlands, while keeping commodity supports at around $87,500 per farm. In 1996, a Republican-controlled Congress reacted with "free market" legislation that phased out crop subsidies and trimmed or reorganized environmental programs.

—JAMES E. SHEROW

See Also: *Agricultural Adjustment Act; Agriculture; Agriculture, Department of; Desert Land Act; Forest Reserve Act; Homestead Act; McNary-Haugen Bill; Morrill Land Grant Act; New Deal; Resettlement Administration.*

BIBLIOGRAPHY: Benedict, Murray R., *Farm Policies of the United States, 1790-1950: A Study of Their Origins and Development* (Octagon Books 1966); Opie, John, *The Law of the Land: Two Hundred Years of American Farmland Policy* (Univ. of Nebraska Press 1988).

■ **FARM LOAN ACT (1933),** federal law authorizing banks and the Commodity Credit Corporation to issue $2 billion in bonds to refinance farm loans. It was part of an ongoing federal effort to preserve family farms during the Depression.

See Also: *Commodity Credit Corporation; New Deal.*

■ **FARM SECURITY ADMINISTRATION (FSA),** government agency that implemented the Bankhead-Jones Farm Tenant Act (1937). The FSA sought to reduce rural poverty in the South and made mortgage loans to some 40,000 tenant farm families.

See Also: *Bankhead-Jones Farm Tenant Act; New Deal.*

■ **FARRAGUT, DAVID G. (1801-70),** U.S. naval officer famous for his naval victories during the Civil War. Born in Knoxville, Tennessee, he had his own command by age 23. As a Union naval commander, he played vital roles in the blockade of the South, the capture of New Orleans (April 1862), and the seizure of Vicksburg (July 1863). He is perhaps most famous, however, for his attack on Mobile Bay in 1864. When one of his flotilla hesitated for fear of mines, he admonished the captain, "Damn the torpedoes, full speed ahead."

See Also: *Civil War; Mobile Bay, Battle of; Vicksburg, Siege of.*

■ **FARRAKHAN, LOUIS (1933-),** founder of one of the groups known as the Nation of Islam. He was born to Jamaican parents in the Bronx borough of New York City and raised in Boston, Massachusetts. Active in the Episcopal Church and a bright student and star athlete, he dropped out of college to pursue a career as a singer and musician. In 1953, he became interested in the Black Muslims. After hearing Black Muslim leader Elijah Muhammad speak in 1955, he gave himself fully to the movement. Disappointed with changes, particularly white membership, in the movement after the leader's death in 1975, Farrakhan began his own Nation of Islam in 1978 and encouraged members to become involved in politics.

See Also: African Americans; Black Muslims (Nation of Islam); Religion.

■ **FAULKNER, WILLIAM CUTHBERT (1897-1962),** author. Born in New Albany, Mississippi, William Faulkner grew up primarily in Oxford, where he enrolled at the University of Mississippi in 1919. Although he withdrew the following year, Faulkner had begun writing steadily and published a number of poems. In 1924 he moved to New Orleans, whose more cosmopolitan setting included Sherwood Anderson, with whom Faulkner became friends. He turned to writing prose, and with Anderson's support, his first novel, *Soldier's Pay*, was published in 1926. Yet, for the next two decades, Faulkner would write short stories and Hollywood scripts to earn a living. Faulkner returned to Oxford in 1927 and introduced his imaginary Mississippi setting of Yoknapatawpha County, which reappeared in most of his work, in his third novel, *Sartoris* (1929). He then published such works as *The Sound and the Fury* (1929), *As I Lay Dying* (1930), *Sanctuary* (1931), *Absalom, Absalom!* (1936), and *The Unvanquished* (1938). Only in 1946, when critic Malcolm Cowley put together *The Portable Faulkner* for Viking Press, did Faulkner begin to gain popularity. *Intruder in the Dust* (1948) and *Knight's Gambit* (1949) appeared before he won the Nobel Prize in Literature in 1950. The success thus sparked enabled Faulkner to embark on lecture tours and, from 1957 to 1959, to assume a place as writer in residence at the University of Virginia, Charlottesville. He won two Pulitzer Prizes before suffering fatal injuries in a horse-riding accident in 1962. By the time of his death, Faulkner had established himself as one of the nation's greatest authors for having explored, as perhaps no other has, the transformations wringing a New South from the Old.

For 20 years after the publication of his first novel in 1926, William Faulkner earned a living writing magazine stories and Hollywood scripts. Only with the appearance of *The Portable Faulkner* (1946) did his novels begin to reach a large audience.

See Also: Novel.

BIBLIOGRAPHY: Blotner, Joseph, *Faulkner: A Biography*, 2 vols. (Random House 1974); Williamson, Joel, *William Faulkner and Southern History* (Oxford Univ. Press 1993).

■ **FEDERAL ARTS PROJECT,** New Deal jobs program for artists. Part of Pres. Franklin D. Roosevelt's Works Progress (later, Projects) Administration (1935-42), the Federal Arts Project hired hundreds of artists to decorate public buildings, conduct art appreciation classes, organize art exhibits, and collect and catalog

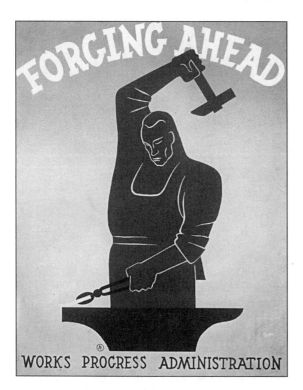

To relieve unemployment, Congress created the Works Progress Administration (WPA), one of whose agencies was the Federal Arts Project, which prepared this poster.

folk art and crafts. Its most visible projects were murals in post offices and other public buildings across the country, such as in San Francisco's Coit Tower. Many of the murals celebrated working people on farms and in factories in an often colorful, folk-influenced style known as "social realism." By acknowledging the nation's folk arts tradition, the project acknowledged the public's growing fascination with the nation's heritage and gave stature to crafts that had often been overlooked in the past. By using public funds to subsidize artists, the project also helped legitimize the creative arts as a valid profession and artists as contributing members of society.

See Also: New Deal; Works Projects Administration (WPA).

BIBLIOGRAPHY: Park, Marlene, *Democratic Vistas: Post Offices and Public Art in the New Deal* (Temple Univ. Press 1984).

■ **FEDERAL BUREAU OF INVESTIGATION (FBI),** the criminal investigation unit of the U.S. Department of Justice. Created in 1908 the FBI played an

important role in investigating alleged subversives and pacifists during World War I. Criticism of FBI operations led to a reorganization in 1924 and the appointment of J. Edgar Hoover (1895-1972) as director. Hoover professionalized the bureau and proved a masterful politician, bureaucrat, and publicist, turning the agency into a virtually autonomous empire. Thanks to the bureau's wide support in the media, FBI agents were seen by the public as crime-fighting "G-men" who protected the nation from gangsters and foreign agents. Hoover also directed agents to monitor political and social dissidents who he felt threatened the nation's stability. When evidence of illegal FBI activities surfaced in the 1970s after Hoover's death, the agency's public image was tarnished, and it was brought under tighter legislative and executive control.

See Also: Government; Hoover, J(ohn) Edgar.

BIBLIOGRAPHY: Theoharis, Athan G., and John Stuart Cox, *The Boss: J. Edgar Hoover and the Great American Inquisition* (Temple Univ. Press 1988).

■ **FEDERAL DEPOSIT INSURANCE CORPORATION (FDIC),** bank account insurance system created by the Glass-Steagall Act (1933), one of the first legislative measures of Pres. Franklin D. Roosevelt's New Deal. The FDIC guarantees deposits to a fixed amount in member banks of the Federal Reserve System.

A wave of bank failures in the early 1930s caused thousands of depositors across the country to lose their savings. With no assurance that depositors would get their money if a bank closed, rumors of a bank's financial trouble often caused large numbers of panicked depositors to withdraw all of their money. Such "runs" sometimes forced otherwise sound banks into bankruptcy. Because the FDIC created a government-backed insurance plan and extended membership only to banks that met Federal Reserve standards, public confidence was restored and the nation's financial system was stabilized.

See Also: New Deal.

BIBLIOGRAPHY: Seidman, L. William, *Full Faith and Credit: The Great S&L Debacle and Other Washington Sagas* (Times Books 1993).

■ **FEDERAL EMERGENCY RELIEF ADMINISTRATION (1933-35),** federal social welfare agency that operated as part of Pres. Franklin D. Roosevelt's New Deal. It distributed $3 billion in federal funds to state and local governments to aid the poor and unemployed during the Depression.

See Also: New Deal.

■ **FEDERALISM,** system of governance in which the national and state governments share power. The development of American federalism has corresponded closely to the major turning points in American history: the Revolution, the Civil War, and the Great Depression. The prevailing trend has been a shift from a decentralized governmental structure toward an increasing concentration of authority in the federal government.

Debates over the proper roles of the state and federal governments dominated the struggle to ratify the Constitution and the early years of the government under it. The future of federalism would be determined largely by the nation's courts and constitutional law, the economy, and the extent of representative democracy. During the period from 1789 to 1861 a system of dual federalism emerged, which held that national and state governments possessed their own separate and distinct spheres. The strongest assertions of federal power came from the federal judiciary, but local powerful political and economic interests challenged federal authority.

Federal authority, however, was greatly enhanced over states' rights by the Civil War and in the postwar period by the growth of the federal bureaucracy, a more assertive Court and Congress, and the government's response to big business. The New Deal of the 1930s introduced a new phase of federalism sometimes referred to as cooperative federalism. Under this system, the federal government appropriated much state and local authority, the Supreme Court worked to protect individual liberty as never before, the bureaucracy expanded to manage increased taxing and spending, and presidential power expanded. During the 1980s and 1990s the tide toward centralization began to reverse as Republican presidents and a Republican-controlled Congress attempted to return some social-welfare decision-making to the state level.

See Also: Constitution of the United States; Political Parties.

BIBLIOGRAPHY: Elazar, Daniel J., *American Federalism: A View from the States,* 3rd ed. (Harper & Row 1984); Kramnick, Isaac, ed., *The Federalist Papers* (Penguin 1987); Wildavsky, Aaron, ed., *American Federalism in Perspective* (Little, Brown 1967).

■ **FEDERALIST PAPERS, THE,** series of 85 essays published in New York City newspapers between Oct. 27, 1787, and May 28, 1788, then reprinted. The purpose of the series was to convince New Yorkers to elect delegates friendly to the Constitution to the forthcoming convention that would vote on its ratification. Judged on this basis alone, the essays were a failure because over two-thirds of the delegates elected to the New York convention initially opposed ratification without substantial amendments, although New York did in the end narrowly vote to ratify. However, the Federalist essays were recognized at the time to be the finest defense and explanation of the Constitution, and they have become the most frequently cited source for an understanding of the original intent of the founders.

The idea for the series began with Alexander Hamilton, who wrote at least 50 of the essays, and John Jay, whose illness allowed him to write only 5. James Madison was invited to join the project and contributed the remaining numbers. The authors, writing under the joint pseudonym "Publius," identified themselves only to a select few, and it was not until later that their authorship became widely known. Even now there is still dispute over whether Hamilton or Madison wrote some of the essays. Often the arguments put forth in the series differed from positions taken by the two in the Constitutional Convention.

In a temperate tone that eschewed partisan rancor, *The Federalist Papers* (1) stressed the importance of the union of the states; (2) demonstrated the weaknesses of the Articles of Confederation; (3) justified and clarified the provisions of the Constitution; and (4) explained the omission of provisions such as a bill of rights. In the introductory essay, Hamilton suggested that it was reserved for Americans "to decide the important questions, whether societies of men are really capable or not, of establishing good government from reflection and choice, or whether they are forever destined to depend, for their political constitutions, on accident and force." In defending the Constitution, Hamilton argued that the love of liberty too often gives rise to an "illiberal distrust" of government, but "that the vigour of government is essential to the security of liberty."

The arguments expressed by "Publius" were used by many others both in and out of ratifying conventions to champion the adoption of the Constitution. Thomas Jefferson wrote James Madison that *The Federalist Papers* were "the best commentary on the principles of government which ever was written." Writing to his son-in-law, Jefferson said that "descending from theory to practice there is no better book than *The Federalist.*"

—JOHN P. KAMINSKI

> **See Also:** *Constitution of the United States; Hamilton, Alexander; Jay, John; Madison, James.*

BIBLIOGRAPHY: Cooke, Jacob E., ed., *The Federalist* (Wesleyan Univ. Press 1961); Engman, Thomas S., et al., *The Federalist Concordance* (Univ. of Chicago Press 1988); Epstein, David F., *The Political Theory of The Federalist* (Univ. of Chicago Press 1984).

■ **FEDERAL RESERVE SYSTEM,** central banking system of the United States, established in 1913. Its most important function is to manage the country's money supply. Pres. Woodrow Wilson proposed the Federal Reserve Act largely in response to the Panic of 1907, which threatened widespread bank failures. The act created 12 regional banks under mixed public and private control. Each Federal Reserve Bank was owned by member banks in its district; all national banks became members and others could join if they wished. Reserve Banks issued currency (Federal Reserve notes, based 40 percent on government gold and 60 percent on promissory notes signed by borrowers) to private member banks, which would then loan the money out. This system made it possible to expand the money supply and bank credit during periods of high business activity, and it stabilized the banking system by requiring members to pool part of their reserves. A Federal Reserve Board appointed by the president helped name Reserve Bank board members and controlled the lending rate to member banks, tightening credit to fight inflation or lowering it to stimulate business through lending. This system established a new role for government in directing fiscal policy.

> **See Also:** *Banks and Banking.*

■ **FEDERAL THEATER PROJECT (1935-39),** jobs program for the theater. Directed by Hallie Flanagan and part of the Works Progress (later, Projects) Administration, it created experimental theaters emphasizing contemporary social issues.

> **See Also:** *New Deal; Works Projects Administration (WPA).*

■ **FEDERAL TRADE COMMISSION (FTC),** a five-member "watchdog" commission established in 1914 as part of Pres. Woodrow Wilson's progressive program to regulate big business. Its power to control competition by defining "unfair trade practices" and issuing "cease and desist" orders varied with commissioners.

> **See Also:** *Progressivism; Wilson, (Thomas) Woodrow.*

■ **FEDERAL WRITERS PROJECT,** federal employment program for writers created in 1935 as part of the Works Progress (later Projects) Administration (WPA). Harry Hopkins, a trusted adviser to Pres. Franklin D. Roosevelt, was named head of the WPA and was given the authority to create jobs programs for trades and professions hit by the Depression. The Writers Project employed hundreds of writers, both famous and unknown, to organize archives of public institutions, prepare newspaper and magazine indexes, and carry out historical or sociological research projects from 1935 to 1942. Its best-known project was a series of detailed travel guides to the United States, which often provided insightful and revealing glimpses into the histories and lives of American communities.

> **See Also:** *New Deal; Works Projects Administration (WPA).*

BIBLIOGRAPHY: Hobson, Archie, ed., *Remembering America: A Sampler of the WPA American Guide Series* (Columbia Univ. Press 1985).

■ **FEKE, ROBERT (c. 1705-c. 1750),** colonial era portrait painter. Born in Oyster Bay, New York, Feke traveled between Boston, Newport, Rhode Island, and Philadelphia garnering commissions for portraits. His 1741 group portrait, *Isaac Royall and His Family*, based on John Smibert's *The Bermuda Group* (1728-29), was his first success. He continued painting portraits throughout the 1740s, often incorporating into them a specific landscape associated with the sitter.

> **See Also:** *Painting; Smibert, John.*

FEMINISM, a consciousness of women's oppression and a commitment to equal rights and opportunity for women. The term "feminism" comes from *feminisme*, coined by a French advocate of women's political rights. In the 19th-century United States, reformers concerned with women's advancement (although not necessarily equality) called themselves the "woman movement," the singular "woman" implying a unity of sex.

In the 1910s the term "feminism" came into use in the United States. It indicated concern not only with the suffrage question but also with a wider range of issues, much as did the earlier "woman movement." Feminism in the early 20th century did not adopt the "equality" rhetoric of the suffrage movement, which was based on "natural rights" theories. Instead, it insisted on a recognition of female "difference," paradoxically combining a call to end sex specialization while positing female solidarity. This set of tensions— "equality" versus "difference"—still exists in feminist movements. Some historians have viewed the achievements of female suffrage in 1920 as the "decline of feminism." To others, however, 1920 marked the end of the suffrage movement and the beginning of modern feminism, which concerns itself with social as well as legal issues.

Although today "feminism" stands for all activities and issues concerning women's rights, society now recognizes many "feminisms," including "liberal" (or "mainstream") feminism, stressing equality; "social feminism," focusing on social justice; and "radical feminism," advocating "difference" and separation from men; as well as feminisms based on racial and ethnic categories. While feminist groups differ in their opinions about the causes of patriarchy and what process might end it, most feminists share a rejection of sexual hierarchy, an assumption that women's conditions are socially (rather than biologically) constructed, and a commitment to women as a group.

See Also: *National Organization for Women (NOW); Suffrage; Women in American History; Women's Movement.*

BIBLIOGRAPHY: Cott, Nancy F., *The Grounding of Modern Feminism* (Yale Univ. Press 1987); Lerner, Gerda, *The Creation of Feminist Consciousness: From the Middle Ages to Eighteen-Seventy* (Oxford Univ. Press 1993).

FENIAN UPRISING (1866-70), attempts by Irish American nationalists to invade Canada in hopes of forcing Great Britain to grant independence to Ireland. In 1858 Fenian organizations committed to Irish independence were formed in Ireland and America. The American group, known as the Fenian Brotherhood, was made up of Irish immigrants, many of whom had been active nationalists before emigration. Service in the U.S. Army during the American Civil War helped spread the movement as well as provide military training for the Fenians, who planned to invade Canada in June 1866. Most of the invasion force was captured before reaching the border, but one detachment did make it into Canada at the border near Buffalo, New York, only to be repelled by the Canadians and subsequently captured by American officials. Two more unsuccessful invasions of Canada were attempted in 1870 and 1871. Thereafter the Fenian movement languished but was revived in the early 1900s with the formation of another Irish nationalist group, the Sinn Fein.

BIBLIOGRAPHY: Neidhardt, Wilfred, *Fenianism in North America* (Pennsylvania State Univ. Press 1975).

FERBER, EDNA (1887-1968), author. She was born in Kalamazoo, Michigan. The acclaim won by her Pulitzer Prize–winning novel *So Big* (1924) and the extraordinary success of the stage and film versions of her novel *Show Boat* (1926) cemented her place in the American popular culture of the 1920s. *Giant* (1952) was also made into a movie. Ferber wrote for the theater as well, collaborating with George S. Kaufman on *The Royal Family* (1927), *Dinner at Eight* (1932), and *Stage Door* (1936).

See Also: *Novel; Women in American History.*

FERMI, ENRICO (1901-54), physicist, developer of the first nuclear reactor, and "father of the atomic bomb." Born in Rome, Italy, Fermi taught physics at the Universities of Florence and Rome (1924-38). His research led to the development of the Fermi-Dirac statistics (1926), which theoretically explained the behavior of electrons in solids. Fermi also produced more than 40 artificial radioactive substances by bombarding the nuclei of uranium atoms with neutrons (1930-32). For this pathbreaking work he was awarded the 1938 Nobel Prize in Physics. In response to Mussolini's fascist regime, Fermi left Italy to work at Columbia University (1939-42) and the University of Chicago (1942-54). He continued his work on nuclear fission there, constructing the first nuclear reactor and leading the research team that activated the first self-sustaining chain reaction on Dec. 2, 1942. He and other refugee scientists persuaded the U.S. government to fund the Manhattan Project, and Fermi joined J. Robert Oppenheimer at Los Alamos, New Mexico, to research and build the first atomic bomb, which was tested at Alamogordo, New Mexico, on July 16, 1945. After the war he took a position at the Institute of Nuclear Studies at Chicago, where he remained for the rest of his life.

See Also: Manhattan Project; Science.

■ **FERN, FANNY (1811-72),** pen name of author and journalist Sara Payson Willis Parton. She was born in Portland, Maine. After an 1852 divorce, she supported herself by writing short, witty essays for Boston magazines and newspapers. When these pieces were collected in *Fern Leaves from Fanny's Portfolio* (1853), the volume was an overnight bestseller. She moved to New York City, where she published other volumes and was, for two decades, a weekly columnist for the *New York Ledger*.

■ **FERRARO, GERALDINE (1935-),** politician, the first woman to run for vice president with the nomination of a major political party. She was born in New York City. She represented New York in the House of Representatives for three terms before becoming Walter Mondale's running mate in an unsuccessful Democratic bid for the White House in 1984. Suffering from accusations of tax fraud, she narrowly lost the 1992 New York State Democratic primary election for U.S. senator.

See Also: Democratic Party; Mondale, Walter; Women in American History; Women's Movement.

■ **FIELD, CYRUS WEST (1819-92),** businessman and financier. Born in Stockbridge, Massachusetts, he made his initial fortune as a paper mill owner in his native state and then in the paper wholesale business in New York City. In 1854, in collaboration with several other investors, Field organized the New York, Newfoundland, and

London Telegraph Company, which sought to construct a transatlantic cable. The U.S. and British governments also invested in the project, which failed several times until, in 1866, the two continents were finally linked by telegraph. This was heralded at the time as a tremendous accomplishment in communications for government and business as well as for personal use. With the fortune he made from this venture, Field went on in the 1870s to own a controlling interest in the New York Elevated Railroad Company and in two New York newspapers. He lost his control, and much of his fortune, after the collapse of the commodities market in 1887.

BIBLIOGRAPHY: Carter, Samuel, *Cyrus Field: Man of Two Worlds* (Putnam 1968).

■ **FIELD, DAVID DUDLEY (1805-94),** jurist. He was born in Haddam, Connecticut, and practiced law in New York City. An expert in legal codification, his *Field Code of Civil Procedure* was adopted in New York (1848) and later in many other states, the federal courts, and much of the British Empire. He also drafted a model penal code (1865) and a code of international law (1872). He was the brother of U.S. Supreme Court Justice Stephen Field and financier Cyrus Field.

See Also: Field, Cyrus West; Field, Stephen Johnson.

■ **FIELD, KATE (1838-96),** journalist and lyceum lecturer. Born in St. Louis, Missouri, she began her career by reporting from Italy and London for the *Boston Courier* and the *New York Tribune* in the 1860s and 1870s. She gained greater popularity for her opinionated, often satirical, essays on travel, literature, the arts, and social issues published weekly after 1890 in *Kate Field's Washington*. She also gave well-attended lectures on literary topics.

■ **FIELD, MARSHALL (1835-1906),** merchant. Born in Conway, Massachusetts, Field moved to Chicago in 1856 and worked his way up in the dry-goods business. He bought out his partner in Field, Leiter, and Company and opened Marshall Field and Company in 1881. Field went on to build a massive dry-goods business and promoted new merchandising trends. He reduced his prices by buying with cash, organized his store in departments, and offered money-back guarantees.

The volume of his business had risen to $68 million by 1905, founding a family fortune and establishing a Chicago institution.

See Also: Industrial Revolution.

■ **FIELD, STEPHEN JOHNSON (1816-99),** associate justice of the U.S. Supreme Court (1863-97); born in Haddam, Connecticut, to a distinguished family (brother David was a noted law reformer; brother Cyrus laid the first transatlantic telegraph cable; nephew David Brewer sat on the Supreme Court). Field graduated from Williams College in 1837 and was admitted to the New York bar in 1841. In 1849, during the gold rush, he moved to California, where he was elected a state legislator, helping to write the state codes of civil and criminal procedure. He became state supreme court justice (1857-63), adopting a rather pragmatic approach to the problems of creating order out of the chaos associated with the transition from Mexican to Anglo law. In 1863 President Lincoln appointed Field, a War Democrat, to the Supreme Court.

On the court, Field became a doctrinaire supporter of the limited nature of the Constitution's implied powers, eloquently opposing all government intervention in economic affairs and interpreting the 14th Amendment to protect private enterprise. His views, prominently stated in dissents to the Legal Tender Cases (1870-71), the Slaughterhouse Cases (1873), and *Munn* v. *Illinois* (1877), demonstrated his willingness to maintain his independence of other opinions on the court. Known as a pillar of laissez-faire, Field has been less acknowledged for his courageous decision striking down aspects of California's anti-Chinese legislation in *Ho Ah Kow* v. *Nunan* (1879).

Field upheld judicial immunity and became embroiled in a colorful incident that set an important precedent in this area. In 1888 he had charged lawyer David S. Terry with contempt, and Terry, a boisterous and passionate character, had threatened to murder Field if he appeared again in California. Field returned in 1889, accompanied by Deputy Marshal David Neagle, who shot and killed Terry as he approached them. In the resulting turmoil, both Neagle and Field were arrested, but the murder charge against Neagle was set aside in *In re Neagle* (1889), which ruled that federal officers may not be prosecuted for acts committed while on duty.

Field retired in 1897, having served on the Court longer than any previous justice. His conservative philosophy was extremely influential and dominated constitutional law for decades. Supreme Court decisions in the late 1930s finally eroded his interpretation of the 14th Amendment, and economic regulation gradually became more common.

—ROBERT C. KHAYAT

See Also: Field, Cyrus West; Field, David Dudley; Munn v. Illinois; Supreme Court.

BIBLIOGRAPHY: Swisher, Carl B., *Stephen J. Field: Craftsman of the Law* (1930; reprint, Univ. of Chicago Press 1969).

■ **FIELDS, W. C. (1880-1946),** stage and film comedian. Born in Philadelphia, he was a comic juggler skilled enough to be featured in the *Ziegfeld Follies* (1915-21). In a series of short comic films and features such as *The Bank Dick* (1940), Fields usually played misanthropic, often malicious, characters whose search for peace, quiet, and, frequently, a drink was constantly interrupted by bosses, wives, mothers-in-law, and cute children.

■ **FILIBUSTER,** attempt to block legislative action by refusing to end debate. In the U.S. Senate, debate can be ended only if three-fifths of the members vote to invoke cloture. If a three-fifths vote cannot be achieved, however, debate can continue indefinitely until the matter at issue is dropped. During debates on civil rights legislation in the 1950s and 1960s, the Senate was the scene of several round-the-clock filibusters led by southern Democrats opposed to civil rights laws. Members would hold the floor for hours, often speaking on matters with no relevance to the issue at hand. The spectacle of the nonstop filibuster largely disappeared with the arrival of television cameras in the Senate chamber. The threat of a filibuster remains, however, and is often a potent factor in the fate of controversial legislation. Supporters sometimes abandon proposals when threatened with a filibuster.

See Also: Cloture.

BIBLIOGRAPHY: Mann, Robert, *The Walls of Jericho: Lyndon Johnson, Hubert Humphrey, Richard Russell, and the Struggle for Civil Rights* (Harcourt Brace 1996).

■ **FILIBUSTERING EXPEDITIONS,** private military invasions of foreign countries or colonies with which the invader's own country is at peace. According to international law, a nation must prevent the use of its territory for organizing and initiating such invasions. However, such expeditions have occurred throughout the history of the modern nation-state.

Long before the term "filibustering" entered English usage (approximately in 1850) Americans and foreigners living in the United States invaded foreign domains in private expeditions of usually from several score to several hundred men, thus defying federal laws (the "Neutrality Acts") that had been drafted in part to deter such enterprises. Filibustering expeditions, however, peaked in frequency between 1848 and 1860, when the United States gained notoriety throughout Western Europe, Latin America, and even the Hawaiian kingdom as the world's center of filibustering activity. During this period filibustering schemes seriously complicated U.S. relations with Spain, France, and Britain and caused a significant rise of anti-American feeling throughout Latin America.

Most U.S. filibustering expeditions sought either the liberation of foreign peoples from rule by European colonial powers or the conquest of foreign territory, sometimes with the object of ultimately annexing such conquests to the United States. A number of expeditions were designed to facilitate the expansion of slavery. Some filibustering expeditions had more limited objectives, such as several pre–Civil War incursions into northern Mexico that sought the recovery of Texan fugitive slaves.

U.S. filibustering expeditions between 1789 and 1820 generally invaded Spanish colonial holdings in the Western Hemisphere. Between 1821 and the Civil War, U.S. filibusters primarily attacked Mexico, the Central American states, and the Spanish colony of Cuba. American filibusters were instrumental in the achievement of Texan independence from Mexico in 1836. Between late 1855 and early 1857 William Walker, probably the most famous filibusterer in American history, conquered and ruled Nicaragua. In addition to these attacks, a series of filibustering expeditions also crossed into Britain's Canadian provinces between 1837 and 1841.

Most late-19th-century U.S. filibustering expeditions invaded Canada, Cuba, and Mexican Baja California. The 1873 *"Virginius* Affair," a serious diplomatic crisis between the United States and Spain, revolved around a filibustering incident involving a ship carrying arms to Cuba, and filibustering played a role in the Cuban revolution of 1895-98. Filibustering episodes declined in frequency and magnitude during the 20th century.

Despite filibustering's illegal nature, a number of 19th-century U.S. presidents, most particularly James Madison, James Monroe, Franklin Pierce, and James Buchanan, were suspected by some contemporaries of sympathy with and even complicity in filibustering, in order to further their expansionist agendas. Some historians have echoed these charges, citing the ineffective nature of many federal efforts to interdict filibustering expeditions before their departure as evidence of this collaboration.

Filibuster participants generally paid a high price for participation in their adventures, even though relatively few filibusterers were prosecuted successfully by U.S. authorities for their infractions of federal law. Large numbers of filibusterers either died from battle wounds or from the disease and deprivations that were endemic to their military campaigns, or were executed or suffered long-term imprisonment in foreign countries following their capture.

—ROBERT E. MAY

See Also: *Frontier in American History.*
BIBLIOGRAPHY: Brown, Charles H., *Agents of Manifest Destiny: The Lives and Times of the Filibusters* (Univ. of North Carolina Press 1980); Harris Gaylord, Warren, *The Sword Was Their Passport: A History of American Filibustering in the Mexican Revolution* (Louisiana State Univ. Press 1943); May, Robert E., "Young American Males and Filibustering in the Age of Manifest Destiny: The United States Army as a Cultural Mirror," *Journal of American History* (Dec. 1991).

■ **FILIPINO IMMIGRANTS.** One of the largest Asian-American immigrant groups, Filipinos began arriving in the United States after the Spanish-American War (1898). When Spain ceded the Philippines to the United States in 1899, Hawaiian sugar plantation owners saw Filipinos as a valuable source of labor. Filipino males migrated to Hawaii in significant numbers starting in 1906 and shortly thereafter began moving to the mainland. By 1930 more than 50,000 Filipinos lived in the United States. During the height of the antiforeign sentiment in the 1920s and 1930s, Filipinos were encouraged and sometimes forced to repatriate. Their status in America improved during World War II, however, when many Filipinos fought courageously against the Japanese. When immigration restrictions loosened after 1965, Filipinos began arriving in the United States at an average of 30,000 per year.

Despite their various contributions to America, Filipinos have been discriminated against economically and socially. They have, however, formed labor and trade unions to advance their rights.

See Also: Ethnic Groups; Immigration.

■ **FILLMORE, MILLARD (1800-74),** 13th president of the United States (1850-53). Born in Cayuga County, New York, Fillmore served in the

Whig Millard Fillmore succeeded to the presidency upon the death of Zachary Taylor in 1850. Failing to win the endorsement of his party for a second term, Fillmore later ran for president as the candidate of the Know-Nothing party.

House (1833-35, 1837-43) as a Whig and was elected vice president in 1848. He succeeded to the presidency in 1850 when Pres. Zachary Taylor died. Fillmore signed the Compromise of 1850 and enforced the Fugitive Slave Act. He was also a champion of U.S. expansion and sent Adm. Matthew Perry to Japan in 1853. He lost his bid for the Whig presidential nomination in 1852 and later joined the Know-Nothing party. As that party's candidate he unsuccessfully ran for president in 1856.

See Also: Civil War; Compromise of 1850; Fugitive Slave Act; Know-Nothing Party; President of the United States; Whig Party.

■ **FILM NOIR,** film style of the immediate post–World War II period in which moody lighting and urban settings provided the context for anguished characters finding their way through complicated crime and psychological dramas. Classic film noir includes *Double Indemnity* (1944), *Out of the Past* (1947), and *The Third Man* (1949).

See Also: Motion Pictures.

■ **FINK, MIKE (1770?-1823),** legendary border hero. Born near Pittsburgh, Pennsylvania, Fink grew to folk hero status as a Mississippi Valley keelboat man after his death. Accompanying Gen. William Ashley's fur-trading expedition in 1822, Fink was slain in 1823 after killing a man while attempting to trick-shoot a cup from the victim's head. Fink's fame grew into legend by word of mouth on the Mississippi and later in J. M. Field's *Mike Fink: The Last of the Boatmen* (1847) and Emerson Bennett's *Mike Fink: Legend of Ohio* (1848).

See Also: Frontier in American History.

■ **FIRE-EATERS (1860-61),** Southern secessionists on the eve of the Civil War. The fire-eaters believed passionately in Southern nationalism and that the differences between North and South were irreconcilable. They always constituted a minority in the South, but their fiery oratory won them attention.

See Also: Civil War; Confederate States of America.

■ **FIRESIDE CHATS,** a series of radio talks on public policy issues broadcast by Pres. Franklin D. Roosevelt throughout his presidency (1933-45). A master of the still-young medium of radio, Roosevelt made his first chat, explaining his administration's banking reform plans, from a White House studio on Mar. 12, 1933, a week after taking office. Since most newspapers opposed his New Deal policies, he relied on radio throughout his administration to explain and win support for many of his proposals. The fireside chats, unlike more traditional platform speeches, were marked by Roosevelt's confident, relaxed delivery of plainly worded texts often featuring homey figures of speech. The president habitually addressed his radio audience as "my friends," and listeners by the thousands seemed to agree, flooding the White House with cards and letters that often included personal messages to the president and his family.

See Also: New Deal; Roosevelt, Franklin Delano.
BIBLIOGRAPHY: Yeilding, Kenneth D., and Paul H. Carlson, *Ah, That Voice: The Fireside Chats of Franklin Delano Roosevelt* (Shepperd Library of Presidents, Presidential Museum 1974).

■ **FIRST LADY,** term for the wife of a sitting American president. The phrase has occupied a place in the national vocabulary since the funeral of Dolley Madison in 1849, when Mrs. Madison was eulogized as "truly our First Lady." White House hostesses other than wives are not usually considered First Ladies.

The term itself may have originated in the custom of referring to elite women as "Lady," as in "Lady Washington," during the early days of the United States. Titles for males had been rejected as "unrepublican," so the regard for rank and desire for nobility focused on women. From the beginning of the republic to the modern era, the role of first lady has embodied tensions over the place of aristocratic practice in a republic, as the negative reactions to the influence and power of Nancy Davis Reagan (first lady 1981-89) demonstrated.

Even more than the presidency, the position of first lady, one not defined by any official document, has been shaped by its holders. Abigail Adams (first lady 1797-1801) discussed policy with her husband, John, bringing the element of "political partner" to the position. The White House refurbishing and social efforts of Dolley Madison (first lady 1809-17) set an important standard, adding responsibilities for granting access to the president, and serving as

curator of the president's house and as ceremonial figure. Eleanor Roosevelt's controversial and issue-oriented tenure (1933-45) offered the option of sponsoring social and political agendas. Recent first ladies have taken on duties as campaigners and communicators.

Scholars and historians have begun to use information about first ladies to measure expanding public roles for women as well as to illustrate the intersection of the public and private. Combining women's history and political science, "first ladies studies" has emerged as a distinct research area.

—CATHERINE ALLGOR

See Also: Adams, Abigail Smith; Clinton, Hillary Rodham; Madison, Dolley; Roosevelt, Eleanor (Anna); Women in American History.
BIBLIOGRAPHY: Anthony, Carl Sferrazza, *First Ladies: The Saga of the Presidents' Wives and Their Power, 1789-1961* (William Morrow 1990); Gould, Lewis L., ed., *American First Ladies: Their Lives and Their Legacy* (Garland 1996).

■ **FISH, HAMILTON (1808-93),** politician and diplomat. He was born in New York City, where he attended Columbia College. A Whig lawyer, he served in Congress (1843-45), as governor of New York (1849-51), and in the U.S. Senate (1851-57). Appointed secretary of state by Pres. Ulysses S. Grant (1869-77), he skillfully negotiated treaties with Great Britain, settling disputes related to the American Civil War, and pushed for U.S. recognition of the Cuban rebels in their fight against Spain.

See Also: Gilded Age.

■ **FISHERIES,** fishing areas of critical economic importance since colonial times. Fisheries off Newfoundland were fished by the French, Portuguese, Spanish, and English in the 16th century. Fishing became an economic mainstay for colonial New England, where waters were rich with cod, mackerel, and halibut. Boston merchants traded the best fish down the Atlantic coast for flour and tobacco; they sent the medium grade to Southern Europe in exchange for salt and wine; and they shipped the "refuse" to the sugar-producing islands to feed the slaves, encouraging the growth of shipbuilding and commerce in the process. New England fisheries reached their peak in 1807 before declining with the embargo and the War of 1812. On the Pacific coast and along the Columbia River salmon fishing sustained a large group of Indian societies including the Salish, Klamath, and Chinook, and by 1900 salmon, sardine, and tuna had turned San Francisco into a world fishing center.

Conflict over fishing rights raised problems on both sides of the continent. The American colonies received rights to fish along Newfoundland and Nova Scotia in the Treaty of Paris in 1783, but the British abrogated the treaty upon the outbreak of the War of 1812, and conflict between Canada and the United States was not finally settled until 1910. Implementation and enforcement of Indian tribal fishing rights continues to raise political, economic, cultural, and environmental controversies in the West and Alaska.

See Also: Treaty of Paris (1783); War of 1812.

BIBLIOGRAPHY: McEvoy, Arthur F., *The Fisherman's Problem* (Cambridge Univ. Press 1986); White, Richard, *The Organic Machine* (Hill & Wang 1995).

■ **FITZGERALD, F. SCOTT (1896-1940),** modernist novelist. Born in St. Paul, Minnesota, Fitzgerald attended Princeton University between 1913 and 1917 but left before graduation to serve in World War I. After the war Fitzgerald began

Having left Princeton without graduating, F. Scott Fitzgerald used it as the setting of his first novel, the best-selling *This Side of Paradise* (1920).

writing fiction while also working for an advertising agency. His first novel, *This Side of Paradise*, published in 1920, is an account of the extravagances of contemporary youth culture. Fitzgerald and his young wife, Zelda, publicly led a life similar to that of his characters. In 1922 Fitzgerald published both his second novel, *The Beautiful and the Damned*, and a collection of short stories entitled *Tales of the Jazz Age*. In 1925 he completed *The Great Gatsby*, considered one of his best works by critics but not as popular as his earlier novels. Fitzgerald moved to Hollywood in 1927 to try to earn his living by screenwriting. He wrote *Tender Is the Night* in 1934. It was ill-received in its day because it appeared to ignore the realities of life during the Great Depression. Fitzgerald died before finishing his last novel, *The Last Tycoon*.

See Also: Novel.

■ **FIVE CIVILIZED TRIBES,** five eastern tribes removed to Indian Territory between 1830 and 1842—the Cherokee, Creek, Chickasaw, Choctaw, and Seminole. So named because they adopted governing systems similar to that of the United States, these tribes had established the most successful settlement colonies in the American West by the 1850s. American policymakers pointed to the tribes as examples of Indian potential for "civilization." However, after the Civil War, all five tribes were forced to cede much of their land to the United States.

See Also: Indian Removal; Indians of North America.

■ **FIVE FORKS, BATTLE OF (1865),** Civil War engagement between the forces of Union Gen. Philip H. Sheridan and Confederate Gen. George Edward Pickett. Commanding Gen. Ulysses S. Grant sent Sheridan's cavalry to the rear of Petersburg, Virginia, under siege by Union forces, in order to cut the roads south of the Confederate capital, Richmond. On April 1, Sheridan's force united with a corps of infantry at Five Forks and successfully defeated Pickett's army, leaving Richmond and Petersburg at Grant's mercy. They were immediately evacuated.

See Also: Civil War; Sheridan, Philip Henry.

■ **FLAG,** a banner that often serves as a powerful political symbol. The "Stars and Stripes," the red, white, and blue U.S. flag, was created by resolution of the Second Continental Congress (June 14, 1777) during the Revolutionary War. Display and use of the flag are governed by traditions that have evolved over the years, and since 1895, June 14 has been designated as Flag Day. By displaying national and state flags, individuals and groups may demonstrate their allegiance to particular causes as well as political and cultural factions. The "Stars and Bars" battle flag flown by Confederate forces during the Civil War became a symbol of resistance to federal civil rights initiatives in the South during the 1950s and 1960s. The U.S. flag was a symbol of division during the Vietnam War era when supporters of U.S. military involvement and cultural conservatism embraced the flag as a symbol of patriotism, while opponents of the war saw it as a symbol of the war and oppression.

■ **FLAPPERS,** young women who dramatically changed women's fashion in the decade after World War I. Flappers cut their hair short and wore less restrictive, more revealing clothes, as well as rejecting traditional ladies' accessories such as hats, petticoats, and corsets. They also rejected social limitations earlier imposed on women. They played sports, smoked, drank, drove cars, and frequented movie houses and night clubs, all activities formerly reserved for males.

See Also: Roaring Twenties; Women in American History.

■ **FLATHEAD INDIANS.** *See: Great Basin and Rocky Mountain Indians.*

■ *FLETCHER V. PECK (1810),* U.S. Supreme Court case that for the first time reviewed the constitutionality of a state law. The case stemmed from a dispute over ownership of land along the Yazoo River in Georgia. A number of Georgia state legislators had been bribed by land speculators so the legislature would grant the speculators large tracts of land along the river at low prices. Only after some of the land had been resold at a profit did this scheme become known publicly. The next session of the state legislature moved quickly to repeal the original grant and void all titles stemming from it. The petitioner in this case, who held one such voided title, appealed to the U.S. Supreme Court to set aside a decision of the Georgia Supreme Court that had upheld the right of the legislature to void the Yazoo grant, regardless of resultant injuries to innocent third parties. In a unanimous ruling, the U.S. Supreme Court overturned the state court decision. Writing for the Court, Chief Justice John Marshall held that, instances of fraud notwithstanding, the contract clause of the Constitution explicitly barred states from any action that interfered with a contractual obligation. With this decision, the Court served notice that its right of judicial review was not limited to acts of Congress but included as well the authority to rule on the constitutionality of state statutes.

—MATTHEW E. BABCOCK

See Also: Marshall, John; Supreme Court; Yazoo Affair.

BIBLIOGRAPHY: Magrath, C. Peter, *Yazoo: Law and Politics in the New Republic* (Brown Univ. Press 1966).

■ **FLORIDA,** the southeasternmost state of the United States. A peninsula, it is bounded on the north by Alabama and Georgia, on the west by the Gulf of Mexico, on the south by the Straits of Florida, and on the east by the Atlantic Ocean. All of it is lowland, with a warm, sunny climate and abundant rainfall. Lake Okeechobee and the Everglades—the world's largest sawgrass swamp—are in the southern part of the state. The Florida Keys, a group of islands, fan to the southwest.

The Spanish were the first Europeans to explore and settle Florida. It became part of the United States in 1819 and became the 27th state in 1845. It joined the Confederacy in 1861 and was readmitted to the Union in 1868. The state's favorable climate fostered first citrus fruit farms and then the development of tourism. Population growth has been especially great since World War II. So many retirees have moved to Florida that the proportion of people 65 or older (18 percent in 1990) is higher than in any other state.

Capital: Tallahassee. Area: 58,680 square miles. Population (1995 est.): 14,166,000.

See Also: De Soto, Hernando; Everglades; Jackson, Andrew; Seminole.

■ **FLOYD, WILLIAM (1734-1821),** military leader and Revolutionary War politician. A signer of the

Declaration of Independence, Floyd was born in Brookhaven, Long Island. During the Revolution he served as a major general and in the Continental Congress.

See Also: Declaration of Independence; Revolution, American.

■ **FLYNN, ELIZABETH GURLEY (1890-1964),** labor organizer known as the "rebel girl." She was born in Concord, New Hampshire. A fiery orator for the International Workers of the World, she organized efforts in the West and in the 1912 Lawrence, Massachusetts, textile strike. In 1920, she helped found the American Civil Liberties Union and served on its board of directors for two decades. A leader of the Communist Party USA (CPUSA), she was convicted under the Smith, or Alien Registration, Act, designed to check subversive activities, during the McCarthy Era. In 1961 she became the first woman chairperson of the CPUSA.

See Also: American Civil Liberties Union (ACLU); Communist Party; Labor Movement; McCarthyism; Women in American History; Women's Movement.

■ **FOLK MUSIC.** Every group in American history has had its own music, song, and dance traditions, and these were refashioned by the impact of new neighbors or the adaptation to a new land. The Anglo-American tradition was thus only one among many, but the serious study of folk music has been preoccupied with it. The first scholarly work came in the late 19th century, when Harvard professor Francis James Child published his systematic compilation of traditional English ballads in the United States. Child's legacy was continued in the work of the next generation of Harvard-trained folklorists, including John A. Lomax and his son Alan Lomax, who not only studied ballads, but lyric songs, religious songs, and work songs. In the 1930s the Lomaxes pioneered the use of field recordings of folk performers, and their work for the Archive of Folk Song at the Library of Congress brought to light such folk artists as the African-Americans Huddie Ledbetter ("Leadbelly") and Muddy Waters.

This field work demonstrated the close connection between folk and commercial forms of music in America. Printed broadsides, often taking up the topical issues of the day in lyrics set to tradi-tional melodies, were very popular in the 19th century. Songsters, little pocket books of topical tunes, were widely sold. This music was not only part of the repertoire of ordinary folks, but of itinerant folk performers as well. During the 1920s, these performers made recordings that helped originate the commercial genres known as the blues and country and western music.

In the 20th century, commercial folk music has been the vehicle for political protest. The Industrial Workers of the World published a famous songster to "fan the flames of discontent." Woody Guthrie worked as a songwriter for the New Deal and wrote "This Land Is Your Land" as a counter to what he considered to be the reactionary sentiments of "God Bless America," written by Irving Berlin. In the 1950s, the Weavers carried a left-wing political message to large audiences while also recording nonpolitical "folk" hits such as "On Top of Old Smoky" and "Good Night, Irene." Although the Weavers became victims of the blacklist and fell from popular favor, they prepared the way for the emergence of the commercial folk genre, much of it protest music. This genre was at its most notable in the recordings and performances of Bob Dylan and Joan Baez, which were tied closely to the civil rights and antiwar movements of the 1960s.

See Also: Baez, Joan; Blues; Country and Western Music; Dylan, Bob; Guthrie, Woody; Ledbetter, Huddie ("Leadbelly"); Nineteen Sixties; Waters, Muddy (McKinley Morganfield).

BIBLIOGRAPHY: Lieberman, Robbie, *My Song Is My Weapon* (Univ. of Illinois Press 1989); Lomax, John A., and Alan Lomax, *Folk Song U.S.A.* (Duell, Sloan 1947); Malone, Bill C., *Country Music, U.S.A.* (Univ. of Texas Press 1985).

■ **FOLSOM CULTURE (12,000-8000 B.C.),** paleolithic culture of North America. As the large game that inhabited North America declined, indigenous hunters on the Great Plains began to hunt the American bison, more commonly called buffalo. To hunt more efficiently, the native peoples developed a new tool technology with more delicate and sharper points, known as Folsom points, than those previously used. Attached to lances, these points were probably used with wooden spear throwers that gave hunters the ability to launch their weapons with great accuracy and velocity over distances of a hundred yards. In one archaeological find, a Folsom point was discovered embedded between the fossilized ribs of a buffalo. Folsom culture became increasingly complex, with numbers of Indian communities cooperating in slaughtering and processing up to 200 buffalo at a time, an indication that they employed food-drying techniques and a division of labor.

See Also: Indians of North America.

■ **FOOD IN AMERICAN HISTORY.** The native peoples of the Americas developed a great variety of food crops. Potatoes (originating in the Peruvian Andes) and maize or Indian corn (from the highlands of Mexico) today contribute more to the world's supply of staple foods than do wheat and rice. Introduced into Europe in the 16th century, these "miracle crops" made possible a great expansion of human and livestock populations. Other indigenous American foods include squash, beans, tomatoes, peppers, cocoa (chocolate), and vanilla. Without these, and other New World crops such as tobacco, rubber, and American cotton—each of which became the basis for important new industries and markets—the history of the modern world would have been far different.

Europeans introduced livestock, which thrived in North America, particularly cattle and hogs. The American diet has, from its colonial beginnings, been rich in pork products. Colonists were less successful, however, in transplanting Old World wheat, which grew poorly in the first settled regions. (Wheat would later thrive in the continental interior.) Corn thus became the colonial staff of life, and it was prepared in numerous ways. It was ground and mixed with European grain to produce a loaf called "rye 'n' injun," cooked into "samp" or porridge, boiled with beans to make "succotash," soaked in lye to produce "hominy" (these Algonquian words testifying to the Indian origins of these dishes), or served simply as roasting ears.

The foundation of much of the American diet thus came from a mixing of the food traditions of Europeans and Indians. African styles of the culinary arts shaped the food traditions of the South.

Slaves played a prominent role in developing such Southern specialties as okra, black-eyed peas, boiled greens, and fried chicken; the liberal African use of red pepper, sesame seeds, and other sharp flavors established an early Southern preference for highly spiced foods. The American talent for culinary adaptation is perhaps best illustrated by the case of "barbecue." European colonists in the Caribbean learned this cooking technique from the Indians; the word itself comes from a native term for the framework of sticks on which meat was slowly cooked. Southerners typically barbecued pork fed on Indian corn and seasoned it with hot sauces influenced by African tastes. Thus, this ubiquitous American backyard ritual silently celebrates the heritage of diversity that went into making our common culture.

This tradition of culinary incorporation helps explain the unique American receptivity to immigrant foods over the past century: for example, German chopped meats (ancestors of hamburgers and hot dogs); Italian pasta (long known as "macaroni") and pizza; Jewish chicken soup and bagels; Chinese stir fry; and Mexican chili and tacos. The American table would be unrecognizable without them.

Good Diet. Another fundamental characteristic of the American diet was its neglect of fruit and vegetables. Vegetables entered the American diet in an important way as the result of several factors in the early 20th century: the creation of a large winter vegetable industry in California and Florida, the construction of an effective national transportation system, and the promotion of nutritional science through public schools and mass media. But it was only in the last half of the 20th century that Americans recognized the critical importance of the daily consumption of fresh fruits and vegetables. Ironically, this awareness accompanied the growth of the "fast food" phenomenon.

Over the long term the relative abundance of inexpensive food contributed to a generally healthier and longer span of life in the United States than was found elsewhere, although there were always groups such as slaves, reservation Indians, and the poor who suffered from inadequate nutrition. The history of American diet has been under-studied by historians, but it may be the key to understanding much of our past. In a famous essay on why there was no socialism in the United States, for example, German sociologist Werner Sombard once offered a five-word explanation: "roast beef and apple pie."

—JOHN MACK FARAGHER

See Also: Agriculture; New World Crops.

BIBLIOGRAPHY: Hooker, Richard J., *Food and Drink in America* (Bobbs-Merrill 1981); Levenstein, Harvey, *Paradox of Plenty: A Social History of Eating in Modern America* (Oxford Univ. Press 1993); Levenstein, Harvey, *Revolution at the Table* (Oxford Univ. Press 1988); Sokolov, Raymond, *Why We Eat What We Eat* (Summit Books 1991).

▓ **FOOTBALL,** popular spectator sport in the United States. The game, which became popular on college campuses in the 1870s, evolved from soccer and rugby. Walter Camp, who played for Yale University, devised rules that set the game apart from its ancestors: the line of scrimmage separating the offense and defense (1880) and the down and distance rule (1882), which originally required the offense to gain five yards in three plays or give up the ball. By the 1890s college football had become a major spectator sport. Critics charged that many schools overemphasized the game by hiring professional coaches and paying players. The game had also become too violent, and injuries and deaths were common.

The National Collegiate Athletic Association was founded (1906) to reform the sport, and rules changes, including the forward pass, opened up the game. By the 1920s games were played in huge stadiums, and stars such as Red Grange and teams such as coach Knute Rockne's Fighting Irish of Notre Dame were national heroes. Network television broadcasts of college games have flourished since the 1950s, bringing fame and fortune to the most successful schools and increasing the pressure to win. College football remains a spectacle, and the role of football on campus is still a subject of debate.

Professional teams were first formed in the 1890s, and the National Football League (NFL) was organized in 1920, but pro football did not equal the college game's appeal until the 1960s. At the urging of NFL commissioner Alvin (Pete) Rozelle, Congress in 1961 passed the Sports Broadcasting Act allowing NFL teams to pool television rights and sell them to the highest bidder. Television and pro football proved a perfect match. New technologies, such as videotape replays, made the game more exciting, and the sport attracted huge television audiences. The annual Super Bowl championship game, first played in 1967, regularly attracted the largest television audience of the year, and, by the 1990s, the NFL commanded hundreds of millions of dollars a year for the rights to broadcast its games.

—TIM ASHWELL

See Also: Sports.

BIBLIOGRAPHY: Danzig, Allison, *Oh, How They Played the Game: The Early Days of Football and the Heroes Who Made It Great* (Macmillan 1971).

▓ **FOOTE, MARY ANNA HALLOCK (1847-1938),** author and illustrator born a Quaker in Milton, New York. An established engraver in New York, she moved west with her husband, a mining engineer, in 1876. There through her drawings, articles, and novels serialized in *Century* magazine, she became an important interpreter of the mining frontier.

▓ **FORAKER ACT (1900),** federal legislation that allowed for the annexation of Puerto Rico as an "unincorporated" territory. This placed Puerto Rico and its people under direct control of the United States but omitted any provision regarding citizenship.

See Also: Puerto Rico.

▓ **FORCE ACTS.** *See: Enforcement Acts.*

▓ **FORCE BILL (1833),** federal act drafted in response to the so-called Nullification Crisis in which South Carolina sought to void federal tariff legislation. Pres. Andrew Jackson proposed the Force Bill in order to collect federally imposed tariff duties. The tariff was soon revised, and South Carolina repealed its nullification.

See Also: Nullification.

▓ **FORD, GERALD RUDOLPH, JR. (1913-),** 38th president of the United States (1974–77). Born July 14, 1913, in Omaha, Nebraska, as Leslie Lynch King (he would eventually take the name of his stepfather, Gerald R. Ford, Sr.), Ford grew up in Grand Rapids, Michigan. He was an all-star football player at the University of Michigan and then obtained a law degree from Yale Law School in 1941. During World War II, Ford served with distinction in the navy.

In 1948 he was elected as a Republican to the first of 12 consecutive terms in the House of Representatives. Specializing in financial and budgetary affairs, Ford earned a reputation as a member whose political word could be trusted. As a result, in 1965 he was elected House Minority Leader, a position he held until 1973, when Vice Pres. Spiro T. Agnew resigned in disgrace. Pres. Richard M. Nixon chose Ford as Agnew's successor because of Ford's popularity in the Congress, which had to confirm the choice.

Ford served only eight months as vice president; on Aug. 9, 1974, hounded by the Watergate revelations, Nixon resigned, and Ford acceded to the top office. Ford's brief presidency was a frustrating one. In an attempt to put Watergate behind him and to allow him to put forth his own agenda, on Sept. 9, 1974, Ford pardoned Nixon

Gerald Ford became the nation's president on Aug. 9, 1974, upon the resignation of Richard M. Nixon. Ford's popularity suffered after he granted Nixon an unconditional pardon.

for all illegal acts he may have committed while president. The protest that followed disrupted much of Ford's legislative program. His foreign policy, which was essentially a continuation of the détente begun under Nixon, was attacked by groups who argued for a harsher line, particularly with the Soviet Union.

Ford's greatest contribution to the presidency, restoring decency and honesty to the office after Watergate, was not enough to win him election in his own right. In 1976 he was defeated by Jimmy Carter of Georgia.

In 1980, in what would have been one of the most startling political comebacks of the modern era, Ford agreed to serve as Reagan's vice-presidential running mate and as a domestic policy "co-president" in the Reagan administration. Reagan terminated the deal when Ford prematurely announced it. This effectively ended Ford's political career.

—JOHN ROBERT GREENE

See Also: *Agnew, Spiro T.; Carter, James Earl, Jr. (Jimmy); Cold War; Nixon, Richard Milhous; Presidential Elections; President of the United States; Reagan, Ronald Wilson; Watergate.*

BIBLIOGRAPHY: Cannon, James, *Time and Chance: Gerald Ford's Appointment with Destiny* (Harper Collins 1994); Ford, Gerald R., *A Time to Heal: The Autobiography of Gerald R. Ford* (Harper & Row 1979); Greene, John Robert, *The Presidency of Gerald R. Ford* (Univ. Press of Kansas 1995).

■ **FORD, HENRY (1863-1947),** industrialist who perfected the mass production of the automobile and brought it within the reach of ordinary wage earners. Born on a farm near Dearborn, Michigan, Ford displayed a mechanical aptitude from an early age and delighted in working with machinery. At 16 he began working as a machinist in Detroit and 8 years later became an engineer with the local Edison Illuminating Company. In the evenings, in his own shop, he tinkered with internal combustion engines, and in 1896 he took his wife Clara and son Edsel for a ride in his first automobile. Over the next few years, Ford built a number of successful racing cars, but it was not until 1903 that he found financial backers and organized the Ford Motor Company. The company was plagued by patent difficulties for several years, but in 1908, Ford introduced the Model T and began his ascent to the top of American industry.

The Model T was immediately popular with the public. Inexpensive and reliable, it was at first built by hand. But in 1913, Ford introduced assembly-line production. Ford was able to drop the price of the Model T from $850 to $360 (about $5,000 in 1990 values), thereby creating enormous demand; production rose from 11,000 to 730,000 vehicles that first year. In 1914, when the average wage of industrial workers in the United States was just $11 per week, Ford attracted national attention by instituting a $5 minimum wage for an eight-hour day (the equivalent of a $17,000 annual income in 1990 values). His aim, he declared, was to create a work force that could afford to buy Ford automobiles. Ford retired in 1919, passing the presidency of the company to his son Edsel Bryant Ford, but the father actually remained in control behind the scenes. By this time Ford was sole owner of one of the world's largest industrial enterprises and had become one of the world's richest men.

During the 1920s, competing manufacturers such as General Motors introduced frequent model changes, options, and choices of colors to entice buyers, but Ford adamantly refused to alter the Model T. "You can have it in any color," he reportedly declared, "as long as it's black." His resistance cost his company the dominance of the market, and in 1927, after having manufactured 15 million of them, Ford retired the "Tin Lizzy" and introduced the flashier Model A.

Ford was a man of many contradictions. Horrified by the carnage of World War I, he chartered a ship in 1915 and with a group of pacifists and idealists sailed to Europe, hoping to put a stop to the fighting. At the same time, Ford was not afraid to use violence to prevent labor from organizing among his men and was a virulent anti-Semite. During the industrial union campaigns of the 1930s, he established a private paramilitary force and employed them against picketers and organizers. In the end, the Ford Motor Company was the last major automobile producer to be unionized.

Ford's introduction of assembly-line production techniques transformed American industry, but he himself became nostalgic for the simpler world into which he had been born. He collected 18th- and 19th-century artifacts and eventually installed them in "Greenfield Village," which he built in his hometown of Dearborn. A more enduring contribution was his creation in 1936 of the Ford Foundation, the world's largest philanthropic

Henry Ford sits in his first car, which dates from 1896. In 1908, Ford introduced his Model T, revolutionizing the automobile industry through mass production and selling more than 15 million of them over the course of nearly two decades.

endowment, which over subsequent decades directed hundreds of millions of dollars to scientific, educational, and charitable purposes.

See Also: Industrial Revolution; Science.

BIBLIOGRAPHY: Batchelor, Ray, *Henry Ford, Mass Production, Modernism, and Design* (St. Martin's Press 1994); Gelderman, Carol W., *Henry Ford: The Wayward Capitalist* (Dial Press 1981); Lacey, Robert, *Ford, The Men and the Machine* (Little, Brown 1986).

■ **FORD, JOHN (1895-1973),** motion picture director. Ford, born in Cape Elizabeth, Maine, made his first film in 1917 and his last in 1966. He drew on his Irish heritage for *The Informer* (1935) and *The Quiet Man* (1952) but is best known for Westerns such as *Stagecoach* (1939), *Fort Apache* (1948), and *The Searchers* (1952). Using Utah's Monument Valley as a setting and John Wayne as a hero, Ford's films helped shape the mythic West.

■ **FOREST RESERVE ACT,** part of the General Land Revision Act of 1891 under which Pres. Benjamin Harrison set aside some 16 million acres of forest reserves for preservation and protection from logging, overgrazing, and forest fires. Pres. Grover Cleveland placed an additional 21 million acres in the forest reserve in the 1890s.

See Also: Frontier in American History.

■ **FORREST, EDWIN (1806-72),** Shakespearean actor. Born in Philadelphia, he became America's leading star after appearing in *Othello* in New York (1826). Forrest's nationalistic supporters rioted with partisans of his great rival, the British actor William Macready, outside the Opera House in New York City's Astor Place on May 10, 1849. The militia was called, and more than 50 persons were killed or injured.

See Also: Astor Place Riot.

■ **FORTAS, ABE (1910-82),** associate justice of the U.S. Supreme Court (1965-69). Born in Memphis, Tennessee, he graduated from Yale Law School (1933), worked for several New Deal government agencies, and then entered private practice. Fortas was an adviser of political leaders and a defender of civil liberties in court. Named to the Supreme Court (1965) by Pres. Lyndon B. John-

son, he was nominated chief justice in 1968 but criticism of his relationship with Johnson, his liberal philosophy, and questionable financial dealings caused him to withdraw his name. He resigned from the Court the following year.

See Also: Supreme Court.

■ **FORTEN, CHARLOTTE (1837-1914),** educator and writer. Born in Philadelphia, she was the daughter of Robert Forten, an African-American businessman and backer of William Lloyd Garrison's American Anti-Slavery Society. In 1862 she went to Port Royal and Saint Helena, islands off the coast of South Carolina, where she worked to educate the children of the newly free African-American population, recording her experiences in several articles and a journal (published in 1953). In 1878 she married Francis James Grimké, brother of Sarah and Angelina Grimké.

See Also: Grimké, Sarah Moore and Grimké, Angelina Emily; Women in American History.

■ **FORTEN, JAMES (1766-1842),** entrepreneur and civic leader. Although he started as an errand boy in his native Philadelphia, Forten became one of the most influential members of that city's black community. Apprenticed to a sailmaker, he learned the trade so well that in 1798 he purchased the business from his master. Forten was adamantly opposed to the colonization of freed blacks in Africa and used his wealth and position to combat it and slavery.

See Also: African Americans.

■ **FORT LARAMIE TREATIES (1851, 1868),** treaties between the United States and the Indian peoples of the northern Great Plains. The first treaty, negotiated with more than 12,000 northern Plains tribespeople present, granted the United States the right to establish posts and roads across the plains in exchange for annuities in compensation for the loss of game. The native peoples also agreed to accept boundaries for each of the tribes. More importantly, the first Fort Laramie Treaty compromised the concept of permanent Indian country by creating an American corridor through the center of the plains. The second Fort Laramie Treaty, between the Lakota and Cheyenne and the United States, was negotiated after Lakota forces under Red Cloud routed the United States cavalry. The United States agreed to abandon forts along the Bozeman Trail, and, as the Americans left their forts, Lakota and Cheyenne warriors burned them. The Americans also granted the Lakota an enormous territory that extended westward from the Missouri River well into Montana and included the Black Hills.

See Also: Indians of North America; Red Cloud.

■ **FORT PILLOW, BATTLE OF (1864),** Civil War battle in which troops under Confederate Gen. Nathan Bedford Forrest on April 12 destroyed the Union garrison on the Mississippi River, 50 miles north of Memphis. In seizing the fort, the Confederates captured hundreds of African-American troops, whom they then summarily murdered. In reaction the Lincoln administration warned the Confederates that Southern officers would be set aside as hostages against further mistreatment of black prisoners.

■ **FORTS,** fortified outposts. Forts were first built in North America by the French and Spanish, and they often competed for the same sites. In Florida, French Huguenots, who were Protestant refugees, built Fort Caroline at the mouth of the St. Johns River in 1564. After the Spanish attacked and destroyed the site, the conquerors built Fort San Mateo. Later the Spanish garrisoned five different forts, including Fort San Marco, in the area of St. Augustine.

For the Spanish the mission may have been the preeminent frontier institution, but without the nearby fort or presidio, missions would never have been so effective. The presidio soldier, with his Indian or mestizo family raising crops for their support, was the settlement policeman as well as frontier guardian against Indians and rival colonial powers. Missionaries continually complained of the loose morals, lax discipline, poor equipment, and low morale of the presidio soldiers but knew they could not get along without them. In addition to those in Florida, important Spanish presidios included El Paso and Santa Fe in New Mexico, San Antonio in Texas, and San Diego and Monterey in California.

When the French expanded into the Great Lakes country and beyond, they undertook the greatest program of fort building in colonial America. Beginning in the 1660s, they established a great crescent of forts extending from Fort Mobile, protecting the approaches to the mouth of the Mississippi on the Gulf of Mexico, to Louisburg, the "Gibraltar of North America," guarding the Gulf of the St. Lawrence. Among the more important French forts were Fort Rosalie (Natchez) on the Mississippi, Fort Miami (Fort Wayne) in what would become Indiana, Fort La Baye (Green Bay), Fort Detroit, Fort Niagara, and Fort Toronto.

Fortifications were also one of the first preoccupations of the English settlers. What has become known as Fort Raleigh was built on Roanoke Island in the 1580s. In 1607 both Jamestown in Virginia and the Popham Colony in Maine included forts.

Upon landing in Massachusetts, the Pilgrims threw up a rough barricade of logs and branches and later fortified their meeting house on a dominant position above their village. Special forts of various kinds were built all along the English frontier of settlement, stretching from Fort Pownall on the Penobscot River in Maine to Fort St. George at the mouth of the St. Johns River in northern Florida. For the most part, however, the principal fortification was the garrison house, both dwelling and fort, found in virtually every settlement.

A great deal of fort building took place during the French and Indian War (1754-63), which began over French and British competition for control of the Ohio Valley. The French first built a series of forts linking the lakes to the sources of the Ohio, the most important of which was Fort Duquesne (later Fort Pitt and Pittsburgh). The English countered with a string of opposing forts. Many of them were reactivated during the American Revolution, although new locations also came into prominence, including Fort Moultrie in Charleston harbor and the forts at West Point, on the Hudson.

Western Forts. After the Revolution the United States came into possession of the French forts of the Mississippi Valley and, after Jay's Treaty in 1795, the British forts of the Great Lakes region. To counter the influence of British traders, the War Department began a program of fort construction in the West. Frequently these were no more than log palisades with blockhouses at the corners, but a few were imposing structures of brick or stone. Fort Snelling was established at the confluence of the Minnesota and Mississippi rivers in 1819 and Fort Leavenworth on the Missouri in 1826. In the Southwest, to counter the Indians and Spaniards, authorities built Fort Smith on the Arkansas River in 1817. These forts were provisioned and manned from Jefferson Barracks on the Mississippi, just south of St. Louis.

The cession of territory following the Mexican War (1846-48) brought fort building to the trans-Mississippi West. Forts were built to protect transportation routes, as central facilities in the Indian wars, and as administrative centers. Some of the more important far-western forts included Fort Kearney and Fort Laramie on the Platte River, protecting the Overland Trail; Fort Larned on the Santa Fe Trail; and Fort Defiance and Fort Union in the heart of Navaho and Apache country. By 1892 there were 96 forts within the limits of the United States, 63 of them west of the Mississippi. That represented the peak number in American history, for in that year the War Department declared that the Indian wars had come to a close.

—JOHN MACK FARAGHER

See Also: French and Indian War; French Colonies; Frontier in American History; Spanish Colonies.

BIBLIOGRAPHY: Frazer, Robert Walter, *Forts of the West: Military Forts and Presidios and Posts* (Univ. of Oklahoma Press 1965); Roberts, Robert B., *Encyclopedia of Historic Forts: The Military, Pioneer, and Trading Posts of the United States* (Macmillan 1988).

■ **FORT STANWIX TREATIES (1768, 1784),** agreements with the Iroquois Confederacy. In the first treaty, negotiated by the British, the Iroquois ceded lands claimed by right of conquest in the Ohio River Valley in exchange for guaranteed boundaries for the Iroquois. The later treaty with the newly formed United States forced acceptance of new boundaries and of American dominion by holding Iroquois hostages.

See Also: Indians of North America; Iroquois Confederacy.

■ **FORT SUMTER, BATTLE OF (1861),** first armed engagement of the Civil War. On Apr. 12, 1861, fearing a fleet would soon bring relief to the 76-man Union garrison at Fort Sumter in Charleston harbor, South Carolina, Confederate Gen. P. G. T. Beauregard initiated a bombardment of the fort that lasted 33 hours and expended 4,000 shells. The exhausted garrison could man only a fraction

of its guns in reply and surrendered the following day. On April 14 the Confederate flag was raised over the fort.

See Also: Beauregard, Pierre Gustave Toutant.

■ **FORT WAGNER, BATTLE OF (1863),** Civil War battle in which Union troops unsuccessfully attacked Fort Wagner, a Confederate earthwork defending the entrance to the Charleston, South Carolina's, harbor. The attack on July 18 was led by the 54th Massachusetts Infantry, an African-American regiment. Commanded by Col. Robert Gould Shaw, the regiment fought heroically and lost nearly half its men. Its performance did much to allay the prejudice against the use of black soldiers.

■ **FORTY-NINERS,** adventurers and gold seekers who went to California in 1849. The dream of overnight riches brought tens of thousands of would-be miners, called "Forty-Niners," to California after gold was discovered there by John A. Sutter in January 1848. Most Forty-Niners found hard work and poverty rather than wealth.

See Also: California Gold Rush; Frontier in American History.

■ **FOSTER, HANNAH WEBSTER (1758-1840),** early American author. She was born in Salisbury,

Military life at post-Civil War western forts was often tedious.

Massachusetts. In 1797 she anonymously published *The Coquette*, a sentimental novel about the seduction and desertion of a gentlewoman. Influenced heavily by the popular British novels of the day, *The Coquette* was reprinted eight times between 1824 and 1828. Her only other book, *The Boarding School* (1798), is a pedantic work about proper "female deportment."

■ **FOSTER, STEPHEN C. (1826-64),** self-taught composer whose minstrel show tunes were among the most popular songs of the 19th century and remain a part of U.S. folk culture. Born in Pittsburgh, Pennsylvania, he wrote simple, sentimental songs that romanticized life on slave plantations in the antebellum South. Among his best-known compositions were "Oh! Susannah" (1847), "Old Folks at Home (Way Down Upon the Swanee River)" (1851), "My Old Kentucky Home" (1853), and "Old Black Joe" (1857). While many of Foster's songs were intended to depict African Americans in the South to white minstrel show audiences in the North, his models were chiefly other minstrel performances. He is thought to have visited the South only once on a brief trip to New Orleans (1852). Foster suffered from alcoholism and received little financial benefit from his work. He died in poverty in a New York City rooming house.

See Also: *Folk Music; Minstrel Shows.*
BIBLIOGRAPHY: Emerson, Ken, *Doo-dah! Stephen Foster and the Rise of American Popular Culture* (Simon & Schuster 1997).

■ **FOUR FREEDOMS,** four principles devised by Pres. Franklin D. Roosevelt to prepare the American people for involvement in the war in Europe. They were introduced in his annual message to Congress on Jan. 6, 1941. Roosevelt had for some time been planning to involve the United States on the side of the British in World War II. Most Americans, however, had no enthusiasm for joining another war in Europe and remained firmly isolationist. Roosevelt made the case that the democracies were pledged to defend the "Four Freedoms": freedom of speech, freedom of worship, freedom from want, and freedom from fear. Four days after making this speech the president introduced the Lend-Lease bill in Congress to pro-

vide massive military aid to the British. Lend-Lease, in contravention of earlier neutrality acts, authorized the president to "lend" arms and supplies to any country he chose. Critics observed that Lend-Lease was a repetition of the arms trading policy that drew Americans into World War I and that incidents stemming from it would eventually draw the United States into the war. In August 1941 Roosevelt and British Prime Minister Winston Churchill met in Newfoundland to discuss war aims. As a result of their meeting, the principles of the Four Freedoms became the basis of a joint document known as the Atlantic Charter.
—STEVE O'BRIEN

See Also: *World War II.*
BIBLIOGRAPHY: Feis, Herbert, *Churchill, Roosevelt, Stalin* (Princeton Univ. Press 1957); Greenfield, Kent Roberts, *American Strategy in World War II* (Johns Hopkins Univ. Press 1963).

■ **FOURTEEN POINTS,** Pres. Woodrow Wilson's plan for a World War I peace settlement. He outlined the plan in an address to Congress on Jan. 8, 1918. Wilson formulated the Fourteen Points to end the war in Europe and also to create what he hoped would be a stable postwar world.

Point 1 called for "open convenants of peace, openly arrived at." Point 2 called for freedom of the seas. Point 3 and 4 sought the removal of artificial trade barriers among nations and reductions in national armaments. Point 5 promised a fair adjustment of colonial claims. Points 6 through 13 concerned the evacuation of countries and territories occupied by the Central Powers and also called for autonomy for the subject peoples living within the polyglot Ottoman and Hapsburg empires. Wilson's most cherished point was the 14th, which proposed the establishment of a League of Nations to guarantee world peace.

By promising the readjustment of borders along "recognizable lines of nationality," Wilson hoped to incite the subject populations of the Central Power nations to overthrow their governments. At the same time he indicated that should the Kaiser's government be overturned, peace terms for Germany would be lenient. While Wilson's plan seemed reasonable to most Americans, the European Allies sought reparations and revenge on Germany. Nevertheless the Fourteen

Points became the basis for the peace treaty talks convened in Paris in late 1918.

—STEVE O'BRIEN

See Also: *Versailles, Treaty of; Wilson, (Thomas) Woodrow; World War I.*

BIBLIOGRAPHY: Bailey, Thomas A., *Woodrow Wilson and the Lost Peace* (Macmillan 1944); Clements, Kenrick A., *Woodrow Wilson: World Statesman* (Twayne 1987).

■ **FOX INDIANS.** *See: Algonquian.*

■ **FRAME OF GOVERNMENT (1682, 1683),** a document created and approved in England by the first Pennsylvania colonists. The 24 articles established a provincial government with an appointed governor and council and an elected assembly.

See Also: *Pennsylvania.*

■ **FRANCISCANS,** a religious order of Roman Catholic priests officially titled the Order of Friars Minor (OFM). Founded in 1209 by St. Francis of Assisi, the order is divided into three distinct divisions: the Friars Minor, Friars Minor Conventual, and Friars Minor Capuchin. There is an affiliated order of nuns called Poor Clares. In the Americas the Franciscans were particularly influential as missionaries to the Indians during the period of Spanish exploration of the Southwest.

See Also: *Religion; Spanish Colonies.*

■ **FRANCO-AMERICAN ALLIANCE (1778),** an agreement under which France assisted America in its war of independence against Great Britain. Early in the American Revolution, the colonies sent the skilled diplomat Benjamin Franklin to France to establish a formal alliance. The French wanted to retaliate after their defeat at the hands of the British during the French and Indian War, but they were hesitant to recognize a colonial revolution against a monarchy. Their tacit support became overt, however, after the American victory at Saratoga in October 1777. This provided the French foreign minister, the Comte de Vergennes, with the necessary assurance of American might, and in February 1778 he signed the formal alliance. Effectively a French declaration of war against Britain, this alliance provided France with the chance to establish warm political and eco-

nomic relations with a potential overseas power. America's chances of victory and independence substantially increased with France's contribution of its naval fleet and some 12,000 soldiers.

See Also: *Franklin, Benjamin; French and Indian War; Revolution, American.*

BIBLIOGRAPHY: Morgan, Edmund S., *The Birth of the Republic: 1763-1789* (Univ. of Chicago Press 1992).

■ **FRANKFURTER, FELIX (1882-1965),** associate justice of the U.S. Supreme Court (1939-62). He was born in Vienna, Austria, and immigrated to the United States in 1894. A brilliant student, Frankfurter graduated from City College of New York and Harvard Law School. After serving as an assistant U.S. attorney in New York City, he joined the faculty of Harvard Law School (1913), where he instilled a generation of students with his ideal of respect for the law and the responsibility of public service. Frankfurter was a special labor adviser to Pres. Woodrow Wilson (1916-18) and maintained close ties with many political leaders. He was a member of Pres. Franklin D. Roosevelt's "brain trust" of advisers, and the president named many of Frankfurter's former students to important government positions. Even after joining the Court, Frankfurter continued advising the administration.

Politically a progressive, Frankfurter exercised restraint on the Court, frequently deferring to the actions of the elected branches. Accordingly, he was sometimes criticized for abandoning his progressive roots, as in *Minersville School District* v. *Gobitis* (1940), which upheld state law requiring public school students to salute the flag. Frankfurter saw the courts as an arena for balancing the needs of competing interests and believed that the Constitution established obligations of citizenship as well as rights. He believed it was vital to protect the integrity and independence of the judicial process.

See Also: *Supreme Court.*

BIBLIOGRAPHY: Kurland, Philip B., *Mr. Justice Frankfurter and the Constitution* (Univ. of Chicago Press 1971); Parrish, Michael E., *Felix Frankfurter and His Times* (Free Press 1982).

■ **FRANKLIN, ANN SMITH (1696-1763),** one of the first women printers in the British colonies and sister-in-law of Benjamin Franklin. She was born in Boston, Massachusetts. In 1735, when her husband James Franklin died, she took over his Newport, Rhode Island, press. As official printer of the Rhode Island General Assembly, she published the *Acts and Laws of 1745*.

■ **FRANKLIN, ARETHA (1942-)**, soul singer. Born in Memphis, Tennessee, the daughter of the well-known African-American minister Clarence L. Franklin, she began her career as a choir soloist in her father's church. Her first single, "I Never Loved a Man the Way that I Love You" (1967), and a string of other hit songs propelled her to the top ranks of American popular music. Other successful recordings include *Spirit in the Dark* (1970), *Young Gifted and Black* (1972), and her return to gospel music, *One Lord, One Faith, One Baptism* (1987).

See Also: African Americans; Gospel Music; Women in American History.

■ **FRANKLIN, BENJAMIN (1706-90)**, American printer, scientist, inventor, politician, diplomat, statesman, and author. He was born in Boston, Massachusetts. Franklin learned the printing trade on his brother's Boston paper, the weekly *New England Courant*, but the brothers quarreled and Benjamin left Boston before his apprenticeship expired.

Although Franklin attended formal school for less than three years, he read omnivorously and made magic squares of numbers for amusement. His self-study continued throughout life, resulting in erudition for which he was awarded honorary degrees by Yale, Harvard, William and Mary, St. Andrew's, and Oxford.

In Philadelphia Franklin worked as a journeyman printer. Hoping to set up his own business, he sailed to London with a promise of credit to buy equipment but found he had been hoodwinked. Easily finding employment in London, he found extravagance also, which plunged him into debt. A Quaker merchant, Thomas Denham, lent him the price of passage back to Philadelphia, where Franklin clerked in Denham's shop until the latter died and forgave Franklin's debt, which was larger than that in London.

Franklin pulled himself together and married Deborah Read by common law and adopted his illegitimate son, William. Saving money, he became a successful businessman, sold books, published the weekly *Pennsylvania Gazette*, clerked for the House of Representatives (Assembly), and promoted civic enterprises that still thrive.

Franklin courted patronage from Lord Thomas Penn and was rewarded with local offices. In alliance with Penn's secret agent William Smith, Franklin intrigued against German immigrants from the Rhineland whose large numbers seemed to threaten English sovereignty. Quakers had helped the Germans to come to Pennsylvania. In return, the Germans supported Quaker politicians, whom Penn tried to overthrow in order to seize personal rule.

Franklin was ambivalent toward the pacifist Quakers. He respected their toleration but hated their pacifism. During King George's War (1744-48), Franklin organized an extralegal military association that gained him much popular support and the enmity of Penn, who feared popular leaders. Meanwhile, in his spare time, Franklin experimented in the new science of electricity so successfully that London's Royal Society awarded him its Copley Gold Medal; and his international reputation rose along with his domestic one.

Appointed deputy postmaster (1753-74) of the mainland colonies, Franklin made the post office profitable. He also "franchised" several printers by supplying equipment on a profit-sharing basis, but his efforts to start German-language papers were defeated by the competition of independent Christopher Saur. In 1751 Franklin was elected to the Assembly, where he had to cooperate with the then-dominant Quakers. In 1755 he persuaded German farmers to rent their heavy wagons to Maj. Gen. Edward Braddock for the British general's doomed campaign against French Fort Duquesne (Pittsburgh).

The Seven Years' War (1756-63) traumatized Pennsylvania. As assemblyman, Franklin saw Quaker colleagues try to finance defense by euphemistic measures, only to encounter governors' vetoes directed by Lord Penn, while Penn refused to contribute a penny for defense or relief of "back settlers" fleeing from Indian raids. Franklin turned against Penn and became his bitter enemy even as he became master of the Assembly when Penn's conspiracies forced Quakers to resign.

Franklin helped authorize and organize a legal militia and was chosen its commanding colonel. He set up a ring of garrisoned forts for defense against raids by Indians, and he learned from those Indians that they were enraged by Penn's having swindled them out of their lands. He made a lobbying trip to England with little success. On his return, despite a political setback, he persuaded the Assembly to send him again with a mission to deprive the Penns of their lordship. But Quakers opposed, in fear of losing religious liberties guaranteed by William Penn's charter; so when Franklin's mission failed and he turned against the British Crown, he also turned against Quakers.

Revolutionary War Era. He became disgusted with the corruption everywhere evident in England. He suggested to turbulent Massachusetts to summon the First Continental Congress to unify protest by all the colonies. He left England just ahead of royal denunciation of him as a traitor, and he immediately moved into leadership of the Second Continental Congress and the American Revolution, helping (among other things) to compose the Declaration of Independence.

At the height of this glory, however, he behaved contemptibly toward his imprisoned Loyalist son, William, whose helpless wife was given small succor by Franklin; and he made no protest when Quakers and pietists were disfranchised by Revolutionary test oaths.

The Revolutionaries sent Franklin as ambassador to get French help, in which he was successful, and he later negotiated the 1783 Treaty of Paris for peace with Great Britain. In 1787 he helped write the U.S. Constitution.

Franklin's character was marred by his constant womanizing, his vengeful behavior toward Quakers with whom he had once teamed, and his meanness toward his Loyalist son's wife. His *Autobiography*, which omits these matters, is celebrated as avuncular wisdom, but it is wholly untrustworthy as biography. He was a master of public relations and politics; for history, one must read around him.

Despite these flaws, he was indisputably a genius and a hero who struggled successfully to end feudalism in what became the United States, who led the overthrow of the British Crown, and who made large contributions to government of the emerging nation. Almost casually, along the way, he was the single most influential founder of the science of electricity.

—Francis Jennings

See Also: Constitution of the United States; Declaration of Independence; Revolution, American.

BIBLIOGRAPHY: *The Autobiography of Benjamin Franklin* (Yale Univ. Press 1964); Jennings, Francis, *Benjamin Franklin, Politician* (Norton 1996); Labaree, Leonard W., et al., eds., *The Papers of Benjamin Franklin* (Yale Univ. Press 1959); Skemp, Shiela L., *Benjamin and William Franklin* (St. Martin's Press 1994); Van Doren, Carl, *Benjamin Franklin* (Viking Press 1938).

■ **FRANKLIN, STATE OF,** area in eastern Tennessee, formerly part of North Carolina, that organized itself as the "State of Franklin" between 1784 and 1788. The residents tried in vain to secure congressional recognition as a state, but they functioned as one for four years, writing a constitution, electing a governor, and collecting taxes. North Carolina regained control of the region in 1788 and ceded it to Tennessee in 1796.

See Also: Frontier in American History.

■ **FREDERICKSBURG, BATTLE OF (1862),** Civil War engagement between the forces of Union Gen. Ambrose Burnside and Confederate Gen. Robert E. Lee. On December 11, Union troops crossed the Rappahannock River on pontoon bridges and drove a rebel force out of Fredericksburg, Virginia. On December 13, the Union army staged furious assaults on the Confederate positions entrenched on the heights overlooking the town. The result was bloody disaster for the Union army. Burnside was removed from command soon thereafter.

See Also: Civil War.

■ **FREE BLACKS,** those African Americans who were not slaves. Prior to the era of the American Revolution, only a few thousand African Americans were free, a tiny fraction of the total African-American population of late colonial America. Yet by 1790 there were 60,000 free African Americans in the United States and by 1810 they would number almost 190,000, the fastest growing segment then of the population. The causes of this dramatic increase included abolition of slavery in Northern states, increasing manumission of slaves in the Upper South, and tens of thousands of slaves who freed themselves by running away during the Revolutionary War's great dislocations. Yet, despite the fact that upward of 30,000 slaves ran away in South Carolina alone during the war, the presence of free blacks in the Lower South where the commitment to slavery remained the most obdurate was comparatively small by the turn of the century. By 1810, most free blacks were in the Upper South states of Maryland, Virginia, Delaware, and North Carolina (95,000; 50 percent of the U.S. total). After 1810, the rate of free-black growth declined discernibly, and this trend continued until 1860 and the outbreak of the Civil War. This decline was in part due to the renewed tightening of laws against manumission and to the alarm of whites at the rapidly rising free black population. Nevertheless, by 1860 there were 488,000 free blacks, 90 percent of whom lived in the North or the Southern states along the Atlantic seaboard, with the largest numbers still concentrated in the Upper South.

While there were significant numbers of free blacks in the rural tidewater counties of Virginia and in the rural piedmont of North Carolina, antebellum free blacks settled largely in cities and towns where it was easier for them to create their own communities and find work. By the early 19th century, large free-black communities were coalescing in New York City, Philadelphia, Boston, Baltimore, Charleston, and New Orleans. Port towns offered many African-American men various kinds of work as laborers, while African-American women often labored as clothes washers, seamstresses, cooks, and domestic servants. While the overwhelming majority of free blacks were at the bottom of the urban economic ladder, some did rise on it and work was generally available for most African-American adults.

Black Institutions. Cities also afforded free blacks the opportunity to form their own enclaves and forge their own institutions. By the 1820s, free blacks in numerous cities and towns were congregating in their own discernible neighborhoods. While these neighborhoods tended to be among the poorest and the most commonly afflicted with social problems such as prostitution and alcoholism, they also provided security through numbers as well as a growing body of religious and mutual aid societies created by the local blacks themselves and intended to lift them above the poverty and discrimination.

But the most important of the indigenous free-black organizations was the black church. Free blacks in the North and South had been developing since the late 18th century semi-autonomous churches that retained connections with their counterpart white churches. But in 1816 in Philadelphia, Richard Allen and a number of associates broke from the local Methodist church supervising their black congregation and inaugurated the African Methodist Episcopal (AME) church, the first wholly autonomous black church in the nation. Branches soon spread elsewhere, and other autonomous black denominations formed, most notably the African Methodist Episcopal Zion (AMEZ) church in New York, which often competed with the AME. The AME, AMEZ, and the numerous semi-independent black churches became the centers of the young free-black communities, especially in the North, offering not only spiritual sustenance but also schools, self-improvement associations, and vehicles for limited political and antislavery activism.

These communities and the institutions undergirding them offered havens and safeguards against the routine racism free blacks encountered throughout the antebellum era. Free blacks faced employment discrimination everywhere, especially in the North; segregation in public conveyances, schools, restaurants, hotels, churches, and housing was the unwritten but pervasive rule, and by the 1820s, free blacks were barred from voting in almost all Northern states. While no state denied their basic right to legal protection and redress of grievances, many forbade black testimony in cases involving whites or jury service. Many of the new states in the Midwest also wrote laws intended to prevent free blacks from settling there. Everywhere antebellum free blacks turned, they confronted legal and customary discrimination.

Throughout the antebellum era, whites in the North and South commonly viewed free blacks as a nuisance and even as a menace, and by 1816 such leading white Americans as Francis Scott Key, Henry Clay, and John Randolph had organized the American Colonization Society (ACS) to promote the removal of the nation's free blacks to Africa. While the ACS contained some members who disliked slavery and were genuinely concerned for the welfare of free blacks, the vast majority of its supporters believed firmly in the inferiority of blacks and in their unfitness to participate in American political and social institutions. Throughout the 1820s and into the 1830s, many whites endorsed the ACS's plan for resolving the nation's racial problems and its strength while increasing pressure was brought to bear on free blacks to immigrate to its new colony in Liberia. Yet the rise of the ACS had the unintended effect of actually strengthening the young free-black communities by encouraging their members to organize to stand against this common enemy to their security and progress. As a result, by the mid-1830s, the ACS's influence was waning significantly.

Struggle Against Slavery. Riding this momentum, black communities in the North entered more assertively into an even more imposing struggle: that against slavery. Free blacks in the North had written and spoken against slavery since at least the 1790s. With the rise of the abolitionist movement in 1831 under William Lloyd Garrison and Arthur and Lewis Tappan, all influenced by blacks' attacks on the ACS and slavery, Northern free blacks finally found a vehicle for a much more public and aggressive assault on slavery. Thousands supported the American Anti-Slavery Society and Garrison's *The Liberator*, which were committed to challenging racism and fostering racial cooperation. Simultaneously, free blacks organized their own regional and local associations, such as the National Negro Convention Movement, dedicated to racial uplift and solidarity and to freeing the slaves. Black newspapers such as Frederick Douglass's *North Star* highlighted the events and concerns of black Americans generally ignored by white journals. All of these endeavors allowed for the rise of a much more prominent group of black leaders. The most notable was Frederick Douglass, a celebrity on the antislavery lecture circuit from the early 1840s. But many others, such as Henry Highland Garnet, Martin Delaney, Maria Stewart, and James McCune Smith, arose as well to lead the fight against slavery, racial discrimination, and

even the paternalistic guidance of white abolitionist patrons. This was unmistakably a new brand of black leadership.

The 1850s proved a grim decade for free blacks despite the vigor of their organizations and leaders. It opened with the passage of the Compromise of 1850, which reinvigorated an earlier fugitive slave law and imperiled thousands of free blacks in the North. The Kansas-Nebraska Act (1854) abolished the standard of the southern boundary of Missouri as the limit for how far north slavery could go and opened the possibility of slavery being legalized in new territories, while the *Dred Scott* decision (1857) established that the Constitution did not apply to blacks. By the late 1850s there was even a movement in the South to re-enslave all of the section's free blacks. While free blacks throughout the North never abandoned the struggle against slavery, the decade left many despairing of change in America, and some leaders seriously weighed encouraging African Americans to emigrate to some black-controlled site in the Caribbean or Africa.

The outbreak of Civil War reinstated the hopes of Northern free blacks who envisioned the war smashing slavery once and for all and with the assistance of black troops. But President Lincoln refused initially to base the war on ending slavery or to use black troops, whose presence he believed would only further alienate the South he still hoped to restore to the Union. Black leaders like Douglass and Delany applied pressure to Lincoln relentlessly to emancipate the slaves and to allow them to fight. In late 1862, Lincoln announced that the Emancipation Proclamation would be enforced by Jan. 1, 1863, if the South had not ceased hostilities. By summer 1863, the first Northern black regiments, such as the Massachusetts 54th, were seeing action in the South, and black leaders throughout the North were aggressively recruiting in black communities. Their force was absolutely central to the ultimate Union victory. By the end of the war 50,000 free blacks from the North—186,000 blacks altogether—would have fought in the conflict, with many casualties suffered. But the result would be a noble one: the designation of free black would be lost forever as all African Americans now became free.

—PETER HINKS

See Also: African Americans; American Coloniza-tion Society; Antislavery Movement; Emancipation Proclamation; Slavery.

BIBLIOGRAPHY: Berlin, Ira, *Slaves Without Master: The Free Negro in the Antebellum South* (Pantheon 1974); Curry, Leonard P., *The Free Black in Urban America, 1800-1850: The Shadow of the Dream* (Univ. of Chicago Press 1981); Horton, James, and Lois Horton, *In Hope of Liberty: Culture, Commu-nity, and Protest Among Northern Free Blacks, 1700-1860* (Oxford Univ. Press 1997); Litwack, Leon F., *North of Slavery: The Negro in the Free States, 1790-1860* (Univ. of Chicago Press 1961).

■ **FREEDMEN'S BUREAU,** organization created by Congress on Mar. 3, 1865, with Pres. Abraham Lin-coln's support, that counseled the former slaves in their transition to freedom. Officially the Bureau of Refugees, Freedmen, and Abandoned Lands, the bureau was an agency of the War Department. It was headed by a national commissioner, Oliver Otis Howard, and, in each Southern state where the bureau was established, an assistant commis-sioner who directed state bureau affairs. The heart of the agency, the local field agents, served as the vital link between the black and white communi-ties and local officials across the South.

The responsibilities of the Freedmen's Bureau included a vast array of duties. Perhaps the major role of its agents was to establish a free-labor phi-losophy among all classes and races, but they also performed numerous other activities, such as establishing schools; securing aid for the desti-tute, ill, and insane; and adjudicating disputes, especially over crop division. They served as mar-riage counselors, diplomats, educators, labor con-tract supervisors, sheriffs, judges, and juries.

Because it was officially linked with the mili-tary, the Freedmen's Bureau drew a majority of its agents from the U.S. Army. But it also employed civilians in several Southern states to perform the duties of a subassistant commissioner.

The bureau was controversial because it be-came involved in politics and was often an openly partisan promoter of the Republican party, as when agents assisted in establishing Union Leagues (the local wing of the Republi-cans) in black communities. But even when bu-reau agents were not sympathetic to the

Republican party, they faced daunting tasks, a hostile white community, local officials who de-tested their presence, and verbal and physical abuse. The Freedmen's Bureau ended its field op-erations in 1868 but continued an education de-partment until 1872.

Throughout its existence, the Freedmen's Bu-reau was racked by the conflict between Pres. An-drew Johnson and congressional Republicans. Johnson forced Commissioner Howard to remove assistant commissioners and even local agents who seemed to be overly sympathetic to the freed people. Although Howard has been charged with promoting a subtle form of racism and deflecting black aspirations, he maneuvered as best he could in an impossible situation. The local agents have also been criticized, but several recent publica-tions have suggested that the field personnel per-formed at an exceptional level.

—BARRY A. CROUCH

See Also: Du Bois, W. E. B.; Howard, Oliver Otis; Johnson, Andrew; Lincoln, Abraham; Reconstruction.

BIBLIOGRAPHY: Bentley, George R., *A History of the Freedmen's Bureau* (Univ. of Pennsylvania Press 1955); Carpenter, John A., *Sword and Olive Branch: Oliver Otis Howard* (Univ. of Pittsburgh Press 1964); Crouch, Barry A., *The Freedmen's Bureau and Black Texans* (Univ. of Texas Press 1992); McFeely, William S., *Yankee Stepfather: General O. O. Howard and the Freedmen* (Yale Univ. Press 1968).

■ **FREEDOM OF INFORMATION ACT (1967),** federal law limiting the ability of government agencies to classify information as secret and withhold it from the public. It reflected growing public distrust of government. Pres. Richard Nixon later issued an executive order reducing the number of agencies that could declare infor-mation "top secret" and requiring officials to state why information was being so classified. The related Privacy Act (1974) obliged federal agencies to furnish individuals any information relating to them in their files.

■ **FREEDOM RIDERS,** interracial groups of civil rights activists who traveled on interstate buses to challenge the segregation of public transporta-tion facilities. The first freedom rides were con-ducted by activists from the Congress of Racial

Equality (CORE) and the Fellowship of Reconciliation who, in 1947, rode buses through the Upper South to oppose segregated seating arrangements. This early effort expanded in 1961, when members of CORE and the Student Nonviolent Coordinating Committee (SNCC) rode buses into the Deep South to defy the segregation of bus station waiting rooms and lunch counters. Exercising nonviolence, activists entered white-only facilities and were jailed and assaulted. In Anniston, Alabama, a freedom rider bus was firebombed, and a second bus was the focus of mob violence in Montgomery, Alabama. But SNCC persisted, and the effort triumphed when the Interstate Commerce Commission ordered the desegregation of bus facilities on Nov. 1, 1961.

See Also: Civil Rights Movement.

■ **FREEHOLD,** prevailing system of land ownership in the English colonies, in which one held an estate for life as opposed to a set term of years. Most colonies restricted suffrage and public office to freeholders, whose estates were defined variously according to both size and value of the property. Excepting, for the most part, New England, quitrents, or fees in place of service, were levied on freeholders. Vast land resources in the colonies made such feudal models less practical, and after American independence they grew obsolete.

■ **FREEMAN, MARY ELEANOR WILKINS (1852-1930),** author. Born in Randolph, Massachusetts, she specialized in short stories about the quirky and outdated residents of small New England towns. She published much of her work in *Harper's* and in collections such as *A Humble Romance* (1887).

■ **FREEMASONS,** secret fraternal organization. The first "grand lodge" of Freemasons in America was founded in Boston in 1733, and by 1734 there were an estimated 6,000 Freemasons (or Masons) in America. Most of the American Revolutionary leaders were Freemasons, as were 50 of the 56 signers of the Declaration of Independence. In the early 19th century Freemasonry came under attack for its secrecy and elitism, but it continued and even gained in popularity by mid-century. Having recovered since the end of World War II from a tremendous decline in membership due to the Great Depression, the Freemasons today remain one of the nation's prominent fraternal societies.

■ **FREEPORT DOCTRINE,** Stephen A. Douglas's theory that territorial voters could effectively prohibit slavery by simply failing to pass the laws necessary to protect it. Enunciated during the Lincoln-Douglas debates (1858), it attempted to reconcile Douglas's popular sovereignty idea with the *Dred Scott* decision and cost Douglas support among Southerners.

See Also: Civil War; Douglas, Stephen Arnold; *Dred Scott* v. *Sandford*; Popular Sovereignty.

■ **FREE SILVER,** or the free and unlimited coinage of silver, a controversial issue in the late 19th century. It became a leading cause of the Populist party. During the 1870s, farmers suffered from a decline in prices and an increasing debt that became more difficult to pay off as crop prices fell. Many saw a solution in expanding the money supply to silver. Instead of only gold-backed currency, "free silver" would help inflate prices and relieve the farmers' suffering. The Coinage Act of 1873 had ended the coinage of silver just when silver production began to rise and owners would have sold it for coin. While the Bland-Allison Act (1878) and the Sherman Silver Purchase Act (1890) provided for some silver coinage, most farmers and silver miners pushed for the free and unlimited coinage of silver. This idea became part of the Populist party's platform in 1892 and a rallying cry for the American Bimetallic League. In 1894, William H. Harvey's best-selling book *Coin's Financial School* presented free silver as a panacea that would solve the nation's economic problems. The Populist party adopted the free-silver issue as their central platform in 1896, as did the Democrats when they chose William Jennings Bryan as their presidential candidate that same year. The election of William McKinley, however, ended the idea of free silver for good.

See Also: Populism.

■ **FREE SOIL PARTY,** political party organized in 1848 among those who opposed the extension of slavery into the territory conquered from Mexico during the Mexican War, precipitated by the congressional struggle over the Wilmot Proviso. Drawing antislavery supporters from both the Democrat and the Whig parties, the Free Soil party's slogan was "Free Soil, Free Speech, Free Labor, and Free Men." In the presidential election of 1848 the party nominated former president Martin Van Buren and received nearly 300,000 votes, drawing enough votes from Democrat Lewis Cass to swing the election to Whig candidate Zachary Taylor. The party disappeared in the early 1850s, but it was an early sign of the disintegration of the party system of Whigs and Democrats, and in 1856 its slogan was adopted and altered by the new Republican party, running John C. Frémont for president: "Free Soil, Free Speech, Free Men, Frémont."

See Also: Antislavery Movement; Political Parties; Presidential Elections; Republican Party; Van Buren, Martin; Wilmot Proviso.

■ **FREE-SPEECH MOVEMENT,** student movement at the University of California in Berkeley (1964-65). A precursor of campus protests across the country, the free-speech movement began in opposition to university rules barring student groups from handing out political literature on campus. It became a broader, sometimes disruptive, protest against bureaucratic higher education and in favor of student activism and freedoms.

■ **FREE TRADE,** economic concept articulated in Adam Smith's *Wealth of Nations* (1776), in which he argued that the market would regulate itself if left to its own designs. The British Parliament had restricted its colonies' trade according to the principles of mercantilism, and after the American Revolution the United States made new trade treaties with the Dutch (1787), Swedes (1783), Prussians (1785), and Moroccans (1787) and found new outlets for trade on their own in Europe, Africa, and Asia. Despite strong sentiment in favor of free trade, the U.S. government would not embrace Adam Smith's principles. Initiated in 1789 to raise revenue and advocated by Alexander Hamilton's *Report on Manufactures* (1791) to develop and protect American manufacturing, tariffs became such a tradition that protection has often been regarded as an American doctrine. In terms of passions aroused, revenue generated, and

industries affected, the tariff was the most important federal economic policy of the 19th century. After a period of early protectionism, the tariff was raised and extended between 1860 and 1933, reaching its peak with the Hawley-Smoot Tariff of 1930. Since then the General Agreement on Tariffs and Trade, formed to oversee international trade at the Bretton Woods Conference in 1944, has led to a reduction of trade restrictions. The North American Free Trade Agreement (NAFTA, 1993) allows goods and services to be sold freely among Mexico, the United States, and Canada, and represents President Clinton's advocacy of free trade.

See Also: Bretton Woods Conference; Hamilton, Alexander; Tariffs.

BIBLIOGRAPHY: Eckes, Alfred E., *Opening America's Market: U.S. Foreign Trade Policy Since 1776* (Univ. of North Carolina Press 1995).

■ **FRELINGHUYSEN, THEODORE JACOBUS (1691-1747),** Dutch Reformed minister. Frelinghuysen immigrated to America in 1720 and settled in New Jersey. As a minister, he demanded piety from fellow ministers and congregants. Frelinghuysen called for the exclusion of the unconverted from Communion, but his arbitrary enforcement of his standards drew suspicion and protest against him. His evangelicalism and itinerancy were forerunners of the Great Awakening in the middle colonies. In his later years, Frelinghuysen fought for greater autonomy of the Dutch Reformed Church in America.

See Also: Dutch Reformed Church (Reformed Church in America); Religion.

■ **FRÉMONT, JOHN CHARLES (1813-90),** explorer, soldier, and politician. He was born in Savannah, Georgia, the son of a French immigrant father and a Virginia mother. After studying science at the College of Charleston, Frémont worked during the early 1830s as a railroad surveyor. In 1838 a politically prominent family friend got him a commission in the U.S. Corps of Topographical Engineers. Frémont accompanied the scientist Joseph Nicollet on a reconnaissance of western Minnesota, then returned to Washington to help prepare the report. There he met and fell in love with 17-year-old Jessie Benton, the daughter of the powerful Sen. Thomas Hart Benton of Missouri. They eloped in 1841, and after

Benton had recovered from the shock, he became his son-in-law's patron and ensured that Frémont got the best assignments.

In 1842, Frémont was ordered on the first of several mapping expeditions of the American West, guided by mountain man Kit Carson and assisted by cartographer and artist Charles Preuss. The report of his second expedition in 1843, which took him across the Sierras and into California, was ghostwritten by his talented wife and illustrated with Preuss's drawings and detailed maps. It became a best-seller and made Frémont into a national hero. His third expedition took him back to California, where he learned that war had broken out with Mexico. Joining American settlers in the Bear Flag Revolt, he helped seize California from Mexico. But when Gen. Stephen Watts Kearny arrived to take command, Frémont refused to follow his orders. He was court-martialed, found guilty, and allowed to resign from the service.

Frémont retired to California, where he served as the state's first senator. In 1856, Frémont became the first presidential candidate of the Republican party, running unsuccessfully against Democrat James Buchanan on the campaign slogan "Free Soil, Free Speech, Free Men, Frémont." When the Civil War began, he was commissioned a major general and put in command of the Western Department, which was headquartered in St. Louis. Frémont's radical policy toward slavery led him to issue a proclamation freeing the slaves of Missouri rebels. Lincoln, angered by Frémont's unilateral proclamation, rescinded it and removed him from command. Reassigned to western Virginia, Frémont was outfought by Stonewall Jackson and in 1863 resigned. After the war Frémont invested in railroads. But he was never good at business and he was bankrupt by 1870. For the next several years he was supported by his wife's writing. In 1878, Frémont was appointed governor of Arizona Territory, but in 1883 he was forced to resign because of dereliction of duty. He lived out his remaining years in New York City.

See Also: *Exploration and Discovery; Mexican War.*
BIBLIOGRAPHY: Rolle, Andrew F., *John Charles Frémont: Character as Destiny* (Univ. of Oklahoma Press 1991); Nevins, Alan, *Frémont, Pathmarker of the West* (Appleton-Century 1939).

■ **FRENCH, DANIEL CHESTER (1850-1931),** sculptor of American historic figures. French was born in Exeter, New Hampshire, and studied art in Boston and Florence. He had studios in Washington, D.C. (1876-78), Boston and Concord, Massachusetts (1878-87), and New York City (from 1887). French won major commissions, including *The Minuteman* at Concord, Massachusetts (1874), the *Republic* at the World's Columbian Exposition in Chicago (1893), and Abraham Lincoln for the Lincoln Memorial in Washington, D.C. (1922).

■ **FRENCH AND INDIAN WAR (1754-63),** the last in a series of wars in which France and England vied for domination in North America. The term "French and Indian War" was coined to indicate that the French were allied with the Indi-

John C. Frémont's explorations of the West in the 1840s earned him the nickname "the Pathfinder." He was briefly U.S. senator from California, ran unsuccessfully for president in 1856, and served as a general for the Union during the Civil War.

In this engraving of the 1771 painting, *The Death of Wolfe,* Benjamin West depicts the final moments of British Gen. James Wolfe, killed in the French and Indian War in 1759.

ans in opposition to the British and their American colonists. Indian alliances in eastern North America were in fact much more complex. Indeed, the British themselves had Indian allies (the Iroquois, for example). In Europe, this war was first known as the Third Silesian War and then the Seven Years' War.

Bloodshed between Great Britain and France commenced in May 1754 with an encounter between colonial Virginians (led by 22-year-old George Washington) and a small contingent of French troops from Fort Duquesne. In the Allegheny Mountains of southwestern Pennsylvania the Virginians ambushed the French, killing Lt. Joseph-Coulon de Villiers de Jumonville, among others. Two months later, Washington was forced to surrender his hastily built Fort Necessity to Jumonville's half brother; Washington signed humiliating terms, acknowledging that his men had "assassinated" Frenchmen at a time when Great Britain and France were not at war. In June 1755 Washington returned to the area as guide to Gen. Edward Braddock, who with about 2,000 British regulars planned to seize Fort Duquesne. Again the British were humiliated when they were ambushed by a large party of French and Indians; Braddock himself was one of the many British soldiers killed.

British fortunes did not improve during the next two years. In 1756 the French seized Forts Ontario, George, Oswego, and Bull. The siege and "massacre" at Fort William, which novelist James

Fenimore Cooper immortalized in *The Last of the Mohicans,* dominated the action of 1757. This victory gave the French control of Lake George in New York, although the killing of several hundred prisoners by Indian allies of the French (who were reluctant to accept European rules of warfare) enraged public opinion in the British colonies and served to galvanize their war efforts. The next year, 1758, saw the tide turn slowly against the French. After being repulsed in an attack against Fort Carillon (at Ticonderoga), the British seized Fort Frontenac on Lake Ontario and Fort Duquesne at the fork of the Ohio; the latter was immediately rechristened Fort Pitt, eventually becoming Pittsburgh.

British Success. A war that had begun disastrously for Great Britain turned into a triumphal march during 1759. In July a party of Frenchmen (some militiamen from as far away as Illinois Country) and their Indian allies were decimated when they attempted to relieve the British siege of Fort Niagara, strategically located at the mouth of the Niagara River. The next day the British army, commanded by Sir William Johnson, occupied the fort. The same week another British army seized Fort Carillon, which then became the important stronghold Fort Ticonderoga. On September 13 one of the most famous Anglo-French confrontations in history occurred when Gen. Louis-Joseph de Montcalm imprudently led his French soldiers out of the citadel at Quebec to face the British army (led by Gen. James Wolfe), which had scaled the cliffs above the city. Both commanders were killed, Quebec City capitulated five days later, and the British rejoiced over a decisive victory.

The British victories of 1759 broke the back of French Canada. Montreal's fall a year later was virtually inevitable, and the entire province of New France surrendered in September 1760. French Louisiana was isolated and also doomed, although no military actions occurred there during the entire conflict. In the peace treaties of Fontainebleau in 1762 and Paris in 1763, France dispossessed itself of all its claimed territory in North America.

—CARL J. EKBERG

See Also: *French Colonies; Montcalm, Louis Joseph; Treaty of Paris (1763); Washington, George; Wolfe, James.*

BIBLIOGRAPHY: Eccles, W. J., *The Military Frontier, 1748-1760: The Canadian Frontier, 1534-1760* (Holt, Rinehart & Winston 1969; reprint Univ. of New Mexico Press 1986); Frégault, Guy, *Canada: The War of the Conquest,* tr. by Margaret M. Cameron (Oxford Univ. Press 1969); Steel, Ian K., *Warpaths: Invasions of North America* (Oxford Univ. Press 1994).

■ **FRENCH COLONIES,** settlements that began with the founding of Quebec by the French in 1608 (one year after the English settled Jamestown, Virginia) and which soon generated a bitter colonial rivalry in North America between England and France. From Quebec, French settlement proceeded slowly up the St. Lawrence River Valley, Trois Rivières being founded in 1636 and Montreal in 1642. This valley was the first axis of settlement in French North America, and it established the pattern of French colonies developing along major waterways, from the St. Lawrence River, to the Great Lakes, and down the Mississippi River to the Gulf of Mexico.

Although small-scale agriculture was practiced in New France (Canada), it was the fur trade and missionary zeal that propelled the French westward through the Great Lakes and eventually into the Mississippi Valley. With astonishing speed and audacity, Frenchmen pushed westward in birchbark canoes. By 1660 they had arrived at Michilmackinac, at the juncture of Lakes Michigan and Huron, and had explored the southern shore of Lake Superior and the western shore of Lake Michigan.

In 1673 Jesuit missionary Father Jacques Marquette and fur trader Louis Jolliet paddled up the Fox River from Green Bay, portaged their canoes over into the Wisconsin River, descended it to the Mississippi, and then proceeded as far south as the mouth of the Arkansas River. On their return voyage they ascended the Illinois River. Marquette began his missionary work with the Kaskaskia tribe of the Illinois nation, and the two explorers then portaged at "Checagou" back into Lake Michigan. This expedition effectively opened the Illinois and Mississippi valleys to the

French settlement of the St. Lawrence River Valley began in the early 17th century.

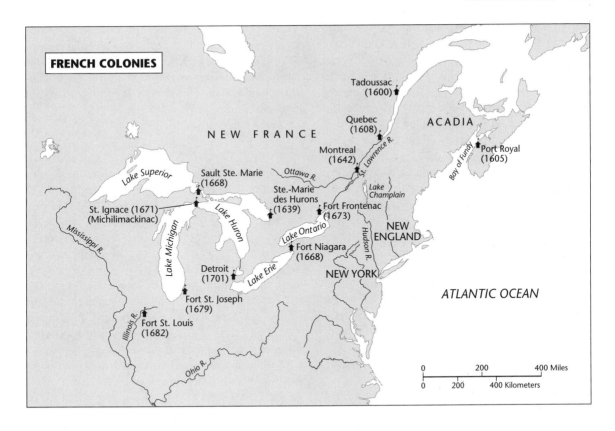

FRENCH COLONIES

Tadoussac (1600)

Quebec (1608)

ACADIA

NEW FRANCE

Montreal (1642)

Port Royal (1605)

Bay of Fundy

St. Lawrence R.

Lake Superior

Sault Ste. Marie (1668)

Ottawa R.

St. Ignace (1671) (Michilimackinac)

Ste.-Marie des Hurons (1639)

Fort Frontenac (1673)

Lake Champlain

Mississippi R.

Lake Michigan

Lake Huron

Lake Ontario

NEW ENGLAND

Fort Niagara (1668)

Hudson R.

Detroit (1701)

Lake Erie

NEW YORK

Fort St. Joseph (1679)

Illinois R.

Fort St. Louis (1682)

ATLANTIC OCEAN

Ohio R.

0   200   400 Miles
0   200   400 Kilometers

---

fur trade, to missionary work, and eventually to agriculture and permanent settlements.

In 1682 Robert Cavelier de La Salle and his lieutenant, Henri de Tonty, made their epic trip from Lake Michigan down the Mississippi River to the Gulf of Mexico. Claiming the entire Mississippi watershed for France, La Salle christened the territory "Louisiana" after King Louis XIV. Reascending the Mississippi, La Salle and Tonty erected Fort St. Louis at Starved Rock on the upper Illinois River. La Salle's untimely murder in east Texas in 1687 delayed his grand scheme of developing Louisiana into a province that could equal New France.

The Frenchmen at Fort St. Louis, led by Tonty, developed intimate relations—political, economic, and social—with the Kaskaskia tribe. In 1691 the fort was moved from Starved Rock to the lower end of Lake Peoria on the Illinois River, and the Kaskaskia resettled there with their French associates. This southward migration continued, probably because of pressure from other Indian tribes, especially the Mesquakie (Fox) and the Iroquois, and by 1703 the Kaskaskia, with their accompanying Jesuit missionaries, guides, and traders, had founded a new settlement, Kaskaskia, that was destined to become the metropolis of French Illinois.

18th Century. Meanwhile, in 1699, Seminarian priests had established a mission outpost at Cahokia with the Tamoroa and Cahokia tribes of the Illinois nation, and the next year Pierre Le Moyen d'Iberville implemented La Salle's plan and erected a fort on the Gulf coast at Biloxi, thereby founding the province of Louisiana. In 1701 Antoine de la Mothe Cadillac established a military outpost at the strategic *détroit* (straits) between Lakes Erie and Huron, christening the place, logically, "Détroit." Therefore, by the early 18th century, French settlements in North America swept in a wide arc from the St. Lawrence Valley, through the Great Lakes, proceeding down the Mississippi, and terminating at the Gulf of

Mexico. French North America was sparsely populated (estimated to be little over 15,000 in 1700), but its scope was breathtakingly vast and diverse.

In 1718 two new pillars of France's North American empire were established—Fortress Louisbourg on the northeast coast of Cape Breton Island and New Orleans on the lower Mississippi. By the time of the French and Indian War (1754-63), in which France opposed England, this empire, consisting of New France and Louisiana, had a total population of somewhat less than 70,000. Most of these French settlers were clustered in the St. Lawrence Valley, with secondary concentrations in New Orleans (approximately 5,000 persons, including African-American slaves) and Illinois Country (approximately 1,400, including slaves). At the same time, England's 13 colonies were populated by about 1.4 million persons. Outnumbered in North America by about 20 to 1, France entered into conflict with England at a decided disadvantage.

—CARL J. EKBERG

See Also: *Exploration and Discovery.*

BIBLIOGRAPHY: Conrad, Glenn R., *The French Experience in Louisiana* (Center for Louisiana Studies 1996); Eccles, W. J., *The Canadian Frontier, 1534-1760* (Holt, Rinehart & Winston 1969; reprint Univ. of New Mexico Press 1986); Ekberg, Carl J., *Colonial Ste. Genevieve: An Adventure on the Mississippi Frontier* (Patrice Press 1985); Harris, R. Cole, ed., *Historical Atlas of Canada: From the Beginning to 1800* (Univ. of Toronto Press 1987).

■ **FRENEAU, PHILIP (1752-1832),** editor and poet. Freneau was born in New York City and graduated from Princeton University in 1771. At the start of the Revolutionary era, he wrote satire against the British. He was captured by the British off the coast of the West Indies and held on a prison ship until exchanged in 1780; he recorded his experience in verse in *The British Prison-Ship, a Poem in Four Cantoes*, published in 1781. From 1781 to 1784 he worked in the Philadelphia post office, while contributing poems to the *Freeman's Journal*. Freneau began doing editorial work in 1789 and, appointed by Thomas Jefferson, served as a translating clerk in the U.S. State Department. In 1791 he founded the *National Gazette*, a newspaper that he edited until 1793. Throughout these

varied occupations, Freneau published collections of his poetry, including *The Poems of Philip Freneau* (1786) and *Poems Written and Published during the American Revolutionary War* (2 vols., 1809). Individual poems of note include "The Indian Burying Ground" and "The Wild Honeysuckle."

See Also: *Poetry.*

■ **FRICK, HENRY CLAY (1849-1919),** industrialist. Born in West Overton, Pennsylvania, Frick entered the coal business near Pittsburgh in 1871 and became a millionaire by age 30. He teamed up with Andrew Carnegie in 1882 and as chairman of Carnegie Steel (1889-1901) made operations more efficient, integrated the company from raw materials to finished goods, and drew criticism for his handling of the Homestead, Pennsylvania, strike (1892). Frick later became a director of the U.S. Steel Corporation under J. P. Morgan (1901). He left his art collection and New York mansion as a public museum.

See Also: *Carnegie, Andrew; Industrial Revolution.*

■ **FRIEDAN, BETTY (1921-),** feminist author and activist, born in Peoria, Illinois. In *The Feminine Mystique* (1963) she analyzed the disillusionment of middle-class housewives with the roles forced on them by American society. The best-selling book sparked the feminist movement of the 1960s and 1970s. Friedan founded the National Organization for Women and was its president from 1966 to 1970. *The Second Stage* (1981) asserted that feminism does not require women to reject all traditional feminine traits. In 1993 she wrote *The Fountain of Age*.

See Also: *National Organization for Women (NOW); Women in American History; Women's Movement.*

■ **FRIENDS, THE RELIGIOUS SOCIETY OF (QUAKERS),** religious group founded in 1652 by George Fox (1624-91) in England. Fox rejected clergymen and churches because he believed that every person had the Light of Christ within. The term "Quakers" was first used to describe the Friends in 1650 because many would tremble when they fell under the power of God. In their monthly meetings Friends gathered silently unless moved to prayer. They dressed plainly, addressed persons as thee and thou, refused to doff hats, and would not take oaths because a person's word should be his oath. They have refused to bear arms because of the commandment against murder, but they have contributed in wartime with noncombatant services.

The first Quakers arrived in the colonies in 1656. Mary Fisher and Ann Austin traveled from Barbados but were jailed because they were suspected of witchcraft. Later that year, eight Friends arrived in Boston but were also persecuted. As colonies passed laws against them, Friends found tolerance in Rhode Island. When in 1681 William Penn received a charter for Pennsylvania, his "Holy Experiment," the Friends had found a haven. Quakerism prospered throughout the 18th century. However, the Second Great Awakening in the early 19th century brought schisms that divided Friends into three groups: Hicksites, Gurneyites, and Wilburites. Gradually, Friends have adopted evangelical tendencies of revivalism and hymn singing, and congregations have added pastors.

The doctrine of the Inner Light in every human has led to democracy in church polity and to humanitarian activity. Women have shared in leadership since the movement's beginning. A significant number of women's rights leaders came from Quaker backgrounds, including Lucretia Mott, Abby Kelly, Susan B. Anthony, and Alice Paul. Humanitarian efforts of Friends have included abolitionism, Indian relations, prison reform, education, temperance, and care of the mentally ill.

—NANCY M. GODLESKI

See Also: Penn, William; Religion.
BIBLIOGRAPHY: Hamm, Thomas D., *The Transformation of American Quakerism: Orthodox Friends, 1800-1907* (Indiana Univ. Press 1988); Levy, Barry, *Quakers and the American Family: British Settlement in the Delaware Valley* (Oxford Univ. Press 1988); Nash, Gary, *Quakers and Politics: Pennsylvania, 1681-1726* new edition (Northeastern Univ. Press 1993).

■ **FRIENDS OF THE INDIANS,** white Christian associations in the late 19th and early 20th centuries devoted to "protecting" Indians from white avarice while at the same time abolishing tribal cultures, values, and land base. Friends of the Indians associations were composed mostly of eastern humanitarians hoping to change federal policy toward Indians. They advocated allotment, forced cultural modification (the prohibition of tribal religions and practices), education in non-Indian boarding and day schools, and turning Indians into citizens. The Indian Rights Association, perhaps the most noted of the organizations, was founded by Herbert Welsh in Philadelphia in the 1880s. It was instrumental in the passage of the 1887 General Allotment Act, which broke up tribal landholdings, and encouraged the introduction of civil service rules to the Bureau of Indian Affairs in the 1890s. The Friends of the Indians associations steadfastly supported assimilating Native Americans into American society, but this goal blinded them to the failures of the Dawes Act and to the increasing impoverishment of Native Americans under it. Beginning in 1883, Friends of the Indians associations met annually at Lake Mohonk in New Paltz, New York, where they shared ideas and coordinated agendas.

See Also: Allotment; General Allotment Act (Dawes Act); Indian Policy; Indians of North America; Wounded Knee, Occupation of.
BIBLIOGRAPHY: Hagan, William T., *The Indian Rights Association* (Univ. of Arizona Press 1985).

■ **FROBISHER, SIR MARTIN (c. 1535-1594),** English explorer. Frobisher sought a Northwest Passage to provide a sea route from England to Cathay (China). Securing the backing of Queen Elizabeth I, he sailed on a first voyage in 1576 into Arctic waters, reaching Frobisher Bay, a Baffin Island inlet. Subsequent expeditions in 1577 and 1578 failed to find the passage or the supposed gold the region held. Frobisher later sailed under Sir Francis Drake and fought to defeat the Spanish Armada in 1588.

See Also: Exploration and Discovery.

■ **FRONTENAC, LOUIS DE BUADE, COMTE DE (1622-98),** governor general of New France, military leader, and fur trader. Appointed governor general of New France by Louis XV, Frontenac served two terms (1672-82, 1689-98). A military leader, he commanded the colonial forces and frequently led them. A flamboyant man who lived far beyond his means, Frontenac vigorously supported western explorations, especially those of René-Robert Cavelier de La Salle (1679-82), for the potential profit of fur trade contacts and of the elusive Northwest Passage.

See Also: French Colonies.

■ **FRONTIER IN AMERICAN HISTORY,** topic that has attracted the attention of both the American public and scholars. The frontier generally refers to lightly populated regions at the edge of settled regions and that border on wilderness.

Popular Conceptions of the Frontier. Since the 1820s much of the American public has been fascinated with frontier history and has enshrouded both events and individuals associated with the frontier with considerable romanticism. During the 18th century Indian captivity accounts enjoyed a wide audience, and by 1825 frontiersmen such as Daniel Boone and Davy Crockett already had assumed legendary status. Meanwhile James Fenimore Cooper's fictional Leatherstocking Tales portrayed the history of the New England and trans-Appalachian frontiers in heroic terms. By mid-century Francis Parkman's account of the Oregon Trail and his multivolume history of the British-French struggle for control of North America (much of it focusing on the colonial frontier) also emphasized the frontier as a major theater of American history. In the decades following the Civil War, the public's focus shifted to the trans-Mississippi West. "Dime novels" by authors such as Ned Buntline portrayed the frontier as the scene of epic, if stereotyped, struggles between good and evil, or "savagism and civilization." By the early 20th century, Western novels, such as Owen Wister's *The Virginian* or the numerous works of Zane Grey, had replaced the earlier, less-sophisticated dime novels, but they still presented the historic frontier in romantic terms, a time and place inhabited by cowboys, Indians, lawmen, and gunslingers, creating scenarios in which women served only as foils in narratives inhabited primarily by heroic male figures.

In the 20th century the popular media continued to champion the romanticism of the American frontier, although the cast of heroes, heroines,

Fanny Palmer's "Across the Continent," an 1868 lithograph produced and distributed by Currier and Ives, idealized the process of western development, with Indians watching passively on the right.

and villains was enlarged and often transformed. During the 1940s and 1950s, movies portrayed a series of cowboy matinee idols who rode forever through an unchanging late-19th-century frontier, meting out justice in a two-dimensional world of good and evil. Wagon trains filled with sturdy pioneers crossed movie and television screens to tame a timeless wilderness. Yet in the 1960s, while the romantic image of the frontier continued, the heroic roles sometimes were reversed. Indians, who long had been pictured as proponents of frontier savagery, were recast as heroic figures, fighting to defend their homelands, while unscrupulous whites assumed the roles of villains. In addition, both movies and television enlarged their depiction of frontier women, acknowledging that women, like men, played major roles in a broad spectrum of economic and social activity. Depictions of these individuals and their societies remained romanticized, and most characters portrayed in the popular media retained their heroic qualities, but popular conceptions of the historic frontier were expanded, and the media's inclusion of women and ethnic minorities enlarged the public's understanding of the many forces that shaped frontier history.

The Turner Thesis. Scholars began a systematic examination of the frontier in American history during the 1890s, after historian Frederick Jackson Turner's essay "The Significance of the Frontier in American History" asserted that the existence of the frontier had a greater impact on the shaping of the American character, institutions, and history than any other factor or influence. According to Turner, the frontier, by offering relatively free land in the West, provided European settlers or Americans living in the East with a continued opportunity to improve their economic condition. Easterners only needed to migrate westward to the frontier where the availability of free or inexpensive land offered the opportunity for upward socioeconomic mobility and a fresh start. Moreover, Turner asserted that the frontier functioned as "a gate of escape" enabling Americans to flee west. It prevented the development of a stratified class system in more established parts of the United States. In addition he believed that the frontier experience shaped the American character, encouraging such traits as

individualism, self-reliance, democracy, energy, optimism, and materialism. Yet Turner's ideas also presented historians with several problems. His assertion that the frontier experience had ended in 1890 as a consequence of the relatively small remaining supply of free or inexpensive lands seemed to suggest that although the frontier had shaped the past, it had little or no meaning for a modern, industrialized, and urbanized America. In this view, frontier institutions and values were vestiges of the past; they had only limited application to the 20th century.

Turner's frontier thesis was a dominant force in American history during the first third of the 20th century, and many historians subscribed to his interpretation. Walter Webb, a historian from Texas, expanded Turner's ideas, arguing that from the 16th through the 19th centuries the entire Western Hemisphere, the United States included, served as a frontier or "treasure house" for western Europe. Webb stated that the "discovery" of the Western Hemisphere and the exploitation of its abundant natural resources markedly changed the ratio of material wealth to population, which promoted individualism. In politics individualism emerged as a belief in democracy and individual rights; in economics it was manifested in capitalism; and in religion individualism took the form of Protestantism. But Webb, like Turner, also believed that the frontier had ended in the late 19th century and predicted that American and Western European societies would be forced to place less reliance on individualism and the exploitation of abundant resources. In the future they would have to adopt more collective strategies of redistributing a limited amount of wealth or commodities.

Problems with Turner's Thesis. Both Turner and Webb attracted critics. Some historians argued that Turner's frontier thesis was applicable only to an agrarian Anglo-American frontier and failed to describe the frontier of New France, which expanded through the Great Lakes and into the Mississippi Valley. Turner's statement that the frontier represented a well-defined "meeting point between savagery and civilization" held little meaning for French fur traders and *coureurs de bois* who plied their trade among the Indian tribes of the Middle West, creating a cultural and genetic middle ground in which French and Indian ways were blended into lifestyles that reflected the values of both people. Free land was not the primary factor that attracted Frenchmen into the West, and the French frontier encompassed a vast region where cultures were blended, rather than a dividing line between the European and Indian worlds.

The Spanish frontier in the American Southwest also seemed anomalous to much of Turner's frontier thesis. Unlike the Anglo-American frontier, which kept progressing westward across the continent, the Spanish frontier in the Southwest marched northward from Mexico but stopped after reaching Texas, New Mexico, Arizona, and California. Instead of expanding, the Spanish frontier became defensive in nature, as Spain established a series of missions or presidios designed to protect Spanish possessions further south from European or American encroachment. Moreover, the northern provinces of New Spain remained sparsely populated, hardly gateways of opportunity that attracted settlers north from Mexico. Indeed, Spain's attempts to encourage migration into the region met with only limited success, as most inhabitants of colonial Mexico much preferred to remain south of the Rio Grande and Sonoran Desert. California was not settled until late in the 18th century, and the Spanish population of the province remained clustered around a series of missions and presidios closely tied to the seacoast. In addition, unlike the small pioneer farmers who flocked to Turner's frontier, the relatively few Spanish frontiersmen were lured north-

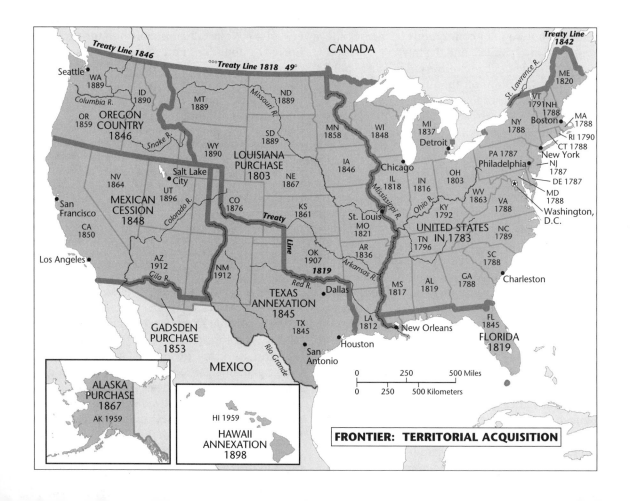

FRONTIER: TERRITORIAL ACQUISITION

ward only by the colonial government's promises of large land grants, which would become theirs only if they settled permanently in the northern frontier districts. And finally, in contrast to Turner's Anglo-American frontier, which emerged as the scene of a growing and evolving economy, much of New Spain's northern frontier region remained an economic backwater, whose ties to both Spain and Mexico were tenuous.

New Interpretations. During the 1960s and early 1970s scholarly interest in the history of the American frontier waned, but during the following two decades a new group of historians reexamined America's frontier experience. In contrast to Turner, they shifted their focus toward the trans-Mississippi West as a region, rather than concentrating their efforts on a "frontier process" that progressed from east to west across the United States. Often described as the "New Western historians," scholars such as Patricia Limerick and Richard White emphasized that the history of the American West has been, as the title of Limerick's book suggests, "the legacy of conquest." Unlike Turner's thesis, which emphasized that the frontier process had ended, the New Western historians see the history of the American West as an ongoing saga and argue that the contest for resources in the region continues. Consequently struggles between Indians and whites for control of western lands in the 19th century are being mirrored in the late 20th century in the competition between business interests, which want to utilize or exploit the region, and environmentalists, who wish to protect its natural resources. Moreover, legal battles between urban residents and agriculturalists over the use of the region's limited water supply are part of a persistent battle over water rights that emerged in the 19th century and most certainly will extend into the 21st.

Unlike Turner, who focused almost entirely on Anglo-American farmers, the New Western historians argue that Indians, Hispanics, Asians, and African Americans played major roles in the development of the West, and their interaction with Anglo-Americans and each other did much to shape the socioeconomic contours of the region. Rather than serving only as foils for Anglo-American expansion, ethnic minorities in the West contested the distribution of the region's resources, a

rivalry that continues today. Recent Indian challenges to government-negotiated, long-term mineral leases and water rights only reflect the latest phase of this competition. Furthermore, the competition for cultural dominance also continues. Current debates over immigration, bilingual education, and attempts to designate English as the "official" language of a state or the nation illustrate that these battles are far from over.

Although Turner and popular mythology both championed the frontier as the well-spring of rugged, self-reliant individualism, the New Western historians point out that the West always has been heavily dependent on the federal government and has especially benefited from federal largesse. Since the federal government controlled the distribution of federal lands and managed Indian affairs, federal officials always have played a significant role in western life. In fact while western states and territories have often boasted that their populations were comprised of "self-made, economic individualists," the populations have enjoyed more federal financial support proportionally than any other region of the United States save the District of Columbia. The Homestead, Desert Land, and Timber Culture acts provided western lands to settlers at minimal prices, while the Bureau of Land Management and the National Forest Service have continued to lease large parts of the public domain to western cattlemen and lumber interests at exceedingly low fees. In addition, federal officials subsidized the construction of western railroads through generous cash payments and the distribution of lands along the tracks to the railroad companies, while federal irrigation projects provided the water that has spurred the growth of western agriculture. Westerners may boast of their rugged individualism, but they have relied heavily on the federal government for their economic security.

Finally, the New Western historians argue that patterns and problems from the 19th-century West persist. Immigrants, both foreign and domestic, continue to flow into the region, and conflicts between long-term residents and newcomers present challenges for local, state, and federal governments. Indian communities still struggle to retain control over their resources and their sovereignty. Mining and oil field economies still follow boom-and-bust cycles that emerged in the late 19th century, and these cycles both reflect and shape larger economic patterns at the national level. Disputes continue over the proper use of western water, public lands, and wildlife. Indeed, social, economic, and political patterns once associated only with a "historic" frontier remain an important part of the modern West. Western history and "the frontier" continue.

—R. DAVID EDMUNDS

See Also: Cowboys; Forts; Indian Policy; Indians of North America; Land Policy; Log Cabin; Louisiana Purchase; Mining Rushes; Santa Fe Trail; Wagon Trains.

BIBLIOGRAPHY: Athearn, Robert G., *The Mythic West in Twentieth-Century America* (Univ. of Kansas Press 1986); Billington, Ray Allen, *America's Frontier Heritage* (Holt, Rinehart & Winston 1966); Billington, Ray Allen, *Westward Expansion: A History of the American Frontier* (Macmillan 1960); Limerick, Patricia Nelson, *The Legacy of Conquest: The Unbroken Past of the American West* (Norton 1987); Smith, Henry Nash, *Virgin Land: The American West as Symbol and Myth* (Harvard Univ. Press 1950); Webb, Walter Prescott, *The Great Frontier* (Houghton Mifflin 1952); Weber, David J., *The Spanish Frontier in North America* (Yale Univ. Press 1992); White, Richard, *"It's Your Misfortune and None of My Own": A New History of the American West* (Univ. of Oklahoma Press 1991).

■ **FRONTIERO V. RICHARDSON (1973),** U.S. Supreme Court case concerning the constitutionality of gender discrimination. The Court voided (8-1) a law granting married male members of the armed forces extra benefits automatically while allowing those benefits to married women only in certain circumstances. Four justices argued that gender, like race, was "suspect" and should always be subject to strict scrutiny; four agreed the law was unconstitutional but said gender divisions could be upheld if there was a rational basis for them.

See Also: Supreme Court.

■ **FROST, ROBERT LEE (1874-1963),** poet. Born in San Francisco, Robert Lee Frost entered Dartmouth (1892) and later Harvard (1897), withdrawing from both institutions without a degree. In 1894, his first published poem appeared, for which Frost received $15, suggesting to him a career as an author. Although he would write a number of remarkable poems over the next two decades, such as "An Old Man's Winter Night" and "The Death of the Hired Man," most remained unpublished, and in 1912, after a dozen years in New Hampshire, he moved his family to England. There he met such poets as T.S. Eliot, Ezra Pound, and William Butler Yeats and embarked upon a true literary career, publishing *A Boy's Will* (1913) and *North of Boston* (1914) in London. In 1915, Frost returned to the United States, now a major modern poet, and the following year, he gained membership to the National Institute of Arts and Letters and published *Mountain Interval*, which included "The Road Not Taken." He would accumulate numerous honors in the coming years, including Pulitzer Prizes for *New Hampshire* (1923), *Collected Poems* (1930), *A Further Range* (1936), and *A Witness Tree* (1942). At the inauguration of Pres. John F. Kennedy (1961),

Having published his first two collections of verse in England, Robert Frost returned to the United States in 1915, where he soon won recognition as one of the great modern American poets.

he read "The Gift Outright," and he won the Bollingen Prize for poetry shortly before his death, after which the appearance of publications detailing Frost's personal life destroyed the image the poet had cultivated of himself as a benevolent rural New Englander.

See Also: Poetry.

BIBLIOGRAPHY: Thompson, Lawrance, *Robert Frost: The Early Years, 1874-1915* (Holt, Rinehart & Winston 1966); Thompson, Lawrance, *Robert Frost: The Years of Triumph, 1915-1938* (Holt, Rinehart & Winston 1970); Thompson, Lawrance, and R. H. Winnick, *Robert Frost: The Later Years, 1938-1963* (Holt, Rinehart & Winston 1976).

■ **FUGITIVE SLAVE ACT (1850),** federal law concerning the forced return of fugitive slaves to their owners. It was the culmination of increasingly stringent legal protections of a slaveholder's right to human property, which had their origin in the Constitution. Article IV, section 2, states, in part, "No person held to service of labor in one State" shall be freed based on the laws of another state but shall be delivered upon claim of ownership. In 1793 Congress passed a fugitive slave law authorizing the return of runaway slaves to the states from which they had fled. Throughout the antebellum period abolitionists often flouted the laws, however, aiding fugitive slaves and publishing accounts of their ordeals. When California sought admission to the Union as a free state in 1849, Southern congressmen demanded a more rigorous fugitive slave law. Part of the Compromise of 1850, the resulting act made it easier for owners to capture fugitive slaves and also provided that Northern citizens could be compelled to assist in the slaves' detention and return. This compulsory clause made even those ambivalent or hostile toward slavery potential agents of slaveholders. The act's passage contributed greatly to the sectional tensions of the 1850s and hastened the crisis that resulted in the Civil War.

—JOHN R. NEFF

See Also: Compromise of 1850; Fugitive Slaves; Slavery.

■ **FUGITIVE SLAVES,** slaves who escaped from their bondage. Among the many strategies employed by slaves to resist the predations of slavery,

the most troublesome to slave owners was that used by those who, like Frederick Douglass, "stole themselves" and ran away from their captivity. Slave revolt may have been more feared, but runaway slaves were more common. Runaways encountered many hardships despite the efforts of sympathizers, which included the myth-shrouded Underground Railroad. If recaptured, reprisals were often brutal. Even if successful in reaching the "free" states of the North, fugitives rarely found much security and often were met with outright hostility. As a result many went on to seek final refuge in Canada. No reliable statistics exist concerning the number of fugitives from slavery. Yet even slaveholders not dismayed by the quantity of fugitives were perturbed by the belief that the problem was pervasive and that fugitives benefited from the complicity of Northern abolitionists. In no small part the efforts of fugitive slaves added to the sectional conflict that eventuated in the Civil War and thus to the abolition of slavery.

—JOHN R. NEFF

See Also: Antislavery Movement; Fugitive Slave Act; Slavery; Underground Railroad.

■ **FULBRIGHT, J. WILLIAM (1905-94),** U.S. senator and educator. Born in Sumner, Missouri, he was president of the University of Arkansas (1939-41) before being elected first to the U.S. House of Representatives (1942) and then to the Senate (1944) as a Democrat. He helped create the international programs for scholars that bear his name and in the late 1960s was a leading opponent of the Vietnam War. He was defeated in the 1974 Senate primary when he sought a sixth term.

See Also: Senate of the United States.

■ **FULLER, MARGARET (1810-50),** feminist, writer, and social critic. Born in Cambridgeport, Massachusetts, and her parents' eldest child, Fuller both benefited and suffered from her father's attention, spending her childhood in study. As a young girl she read Goethe (in German) and Shakespeare and could read Latin at age six. After her father died in 1835, she went to Boston to teach languages in a school run by Bronson Alcott.

From 1839 to 1844 Fuller conducted her famed "Conversations" in Boston, encouraging women to think aloud about such topics as art, ethics, educa-

In 1844, Margaret Fuller published her first book, *Summer on the Lakes, in 1843*, which caught the eye of New York editor Horace Greeley. He hired Fuller for his *New York Tribune*, making her the first female journalist to work for a major newspaper.

tion, and women's rights. In 1840 she and other transcendentalists founded and edited the literary journal *The Dial* and established a utopian community, Brook Farm, in West Roxbury, Massachusetts.

Fuller moved to New York City at Horace Greeley's invitation soon after the 1844 publication of her first book, *Summer on the Lakes, in 1843*. At Greeley's *New York Tribune*, she became the first professional book-review editor in America, using her position to promote new American literature. Fuller's *Woman in the Nineteenth Century* (1845), based on a *Dial* article, has remained a classic of feminist thought and served as the inspiration for the Seneca Falls Convention (1848).

In 1846 Fuller fulfilled her dream of European travel when Greeley sent her abroad as a foreign correspondent, a first for a woman. In 1847 she settled in Rome and fell in love with the Marchese Giovanni d'Ossoli, a leader of the Italian democratic movement. Fuller bore a son in 1848, and

the couple may have married a year later. Forced to flee at the fall of the Roman republic, Fuller and her family returned to America in 1850. Within sight of shore, the ship ran aground at Fire Island, and she perished. Her writings only hint at her enormous gifts, unfulfilled by her early death.

—CATHERINE ALLGOR

See Also: *Brook Farm; Seneca Falls Convention; Transcendentalism; Women in American History; Women's Movement.*

BIBLIOGRAPHY: Fuller, Margaret, *Woman in the Nineteenth Century*, (reprint, Norton 1971); Myerson, Joel, ed., *Critical Essays on Margaret Fuller* (Hall 1980).

■ **FULLER, MELVILLE WESTON (1833-1910),** chief justice of the United States (1888-1910). He was born in Augusta, Maine, and raised in the home of his grandfather, the chief justice of Maine's Supreme Judicial Court. Fuller read law, attended Harvard Law School, and was admitted to the bar (1855) but soon migrated to Illinois. An anti–Civil War Democrat, he practiced law in Chicago and was active in state politics. Following the war, he withdrew from the political arena, concentrated on the law and his investments, and prospered. Chosen as chief justice by Pres. Grover Cleveland, Fuller was a strict constructionist. He believed in limited governmental power, especially when economic regulation was at issue, and was often viewed as a defender of the propertied classes. Fuller wrote the majority opinions when the Court struck down a federal income tax in *Pollock* v. *Farmers' Loan & Trust Co.* (1895) and weakened antitrust law by supporting the sugar trust in *United States* v. *E. C. Knight Co.* (1895). Fuller also insisted the 14th Amendment did not provide a remedy for racial injustice and declined to invalidate state segregation laws in cases such as *Plessy* v. *Ferguson* (1896). Fuller served on the Venezuelan Boundary Commission (1897) and the Permanent Court of Arbitration in The Hague (1900-10).

See Also: *Supreme Court.*

BIBLIOGRAPHY: Furer, Howard B., *The Fuller Court, 1888-1910* (Associated Faculty Press 1986); King, Willard L., *Melville Weston Fuller, Chief Justice of the United States, 1888-1910* (Macmillan 1950).

■ ***FULLILOVE V. KLUTZNICK (1980),*** U.S. Supreme Court case that upheld minority set-asides in federal programs. The Court upheld (6-3) provisions of the Public Works Employment Act of 1977 that reserved 10 percent of the authorized contracts for minority-owned businesses. The Court ruled Congress acted to address a compelling governmental interest: correcting past discrimination against minority businesses. In *Richmond v. J. A. Croson Co.* (1989), the Court refused to allow state and local governments similar powers to adopt race-based quotas.

See Also: Supreme Court.

■ **FULTON, ROBERT (1765-1815),** inventor and artist. Born in Lancaster County, Pennsylvania, Fulton was a master at finding practical application for the ideas of others. This was especially true in the case of the steamboat, which he built using the theoretical work on steam power done by English and French engineers.

At an early age Fulton displayed an aptitude for art and mechanics. Following a short apprenticeship to a Philadelphia silversmith, he began work as an independent artist in 1785. Having amassed modest savings, Fulton sailed to England and studied art under Benjamin West. He eventu-

Returning to the United States in 1806 after nearly 20 years abroad, Robert Fulton designed the steamboat *Clermont,* which made the trip from New York City to Albany in only 32 hours in August 1807.

ally left his art career behind to pursue engineering full time and in 1796 received acclaim for his *Treatise on the Improvement of Canal Navigation.*

Before moving to France in 1797, Fulton tried unsuccessfully to interest the American and French governments in his canal projects. He built a submarine, the *Nautilus,* in 1800, but again could not find a buyer. Then, with the financial assistance from Robert R. Livingston, the U.S. minister to France, Fulton built an experimental steamboat in 1803. Both the French and British governments took little interest in the project, however, and Fulton was forced to return to the United States in 1806. On Aug. 17, 1807, Fulton's steamboat, the *Clermont,* made an impressive voyage from New York City to Albany. Although the *Clermont* was not the first steamboat invented, it was the first one that was commercially successful and inaugurated the age of steam-powered vessels that helped to transform the economy.

See Also: Industrial Revolution; Science; Steamboats.

BIBLIOGRAPHY: Philip, Cynthia Owen, *Robert Fulton: A Biography* (Franklin Watts 1985).

■ **FUNDAMENTALISM,** Protestant religious movements that emphasize literal interpretations of the Bible. American fundamentalism had its origins in the Great Awakening, the evangelical revivals of the 1730s and 1740s.

A divide over biblical inspiration arose within American Protestantism during the sectional crisis and after the Civil War (1861-65). During the late 19th century, some conservatives argued for inerrancy (infallibility) of the Bible and divine inspiration, while liberal theologians adopted a more flexible interpretation. Continued clashes between evangelicals and liberals in the first decades of the 20th century resulted in the formation of the fundamentalist movement. The publication of a series of pamphlets called *The Fundamentals* outlined fundamentalist orthodoxy while opposing liberal doctrine. The "five points of fundamentalism" included a belief in the authenticity of miracles, biblical inerrancy, and the virgin birth.

Fundamentalists experienced both their widest publicity and greatest defeat during the 1925 Scopes "monkey trial." Although they won the case against the teaching of evolutionary science in public schools, the fundamentalists were portrayed as uneducated, rural, and poor. In the decades after the trial, fundamentalists formed their own denominations, colleges, missionary societies, Bible camps, and publishing houses. A thriving Protestant subculture, fundamentalism resurfaced onto the national scene in the 1970s, influencing politics, society, and the place of religion in America. In the 1980s and 1990s, American fundamentalism found its loudest voice in preacher-activists and the political conservatism of the religious right.

See Also: *Religion; Scopes Trial.*

BIBLIOGRAPHY: Balmer, Randall H., *"Mine Eyes Have Seen the Glory": A Journey into the Evangelical Subculture in America* (Oxford Univ. Press 1989); Mardsen, George M., *Fundamentalism in American Culture: The Shaping of Twentieth-Century Evangelicalism, 1870-1925* (Oxford Univ. Press 1980).

■ ***FURMAN V. GEORGIA (1972),*** U.S. Supreme Court case that struck down the death penalty as cruel and unusual punishment banned by the Eighth Amendment. *Furman* combined three capital cases in Georgia and Texas. In each, juries had imposed the death penalty under laws granting wide sentencing discretion. While the majority of the divided Court (5-4) ruled that the death penalty was cruel and unusual punishment, only

Justices William Brennan and Thurgood Marshall said the death penalty was in and of itself unconstitutional. Three justices instead said state laws that did not include clear guidelines for imposing the death penalty resulted in an arbitrary and random application of capital punishment in similar cases. *Furman* suspended executions in the 39 states that imposed the death penalty. In *Gregg* v. *Georgia* (1976), the Supreme Court ruled that capital punishment was constitutional if states passed laws establishing guidelines for imposing the death penalty.

See Also: *Supreme Court.*

■ **FUR TRADE,** the exchange of European goods for beaver pelts, deerskins, buffalo robes, otter skins, and other commodities gathered and processed by native producers. The fur trade underwrote the colonization of New France, New Netherland, and Russian Alaska and stimulated the exploration and settlement of many regions of North America. On a local level, the trade could involve a seemingly simple barter transaction, but it is more accurate to view the trade as a vast import and export business that integrated the economies of many native communities with a European, even a global, system of exchange and network of markets. Moreover, the fur trade was,

Trading furs for European goods originated shortly after the first contact was established between Indians and the French in the 17th century. This image is taken from a Canadian map of 1777.

perhaps, the most important motive for and means of exchanging cultural information between Indian and European groups for more than two centuries. In this sense, the fur trade provided a practical foundation for a "middle ground" of social and political relationships that often did not exist in areas that simply became battlegrounds for the control of land.

The Nature of the Trade. The beaver was the central object of the fur trade from the 17th century until the 1830s, when it was supplanted by muskrat skins, raccoon pelts, and buffalo robes. The soft, barbed underfur of the beaver pelt was used in the manufacture of felt hats. Deerskins—the staple of the trade in the Carolinas, Georgia, and Louisiana—and moose hides were also sought, to be worked into leather for a variety of marketable items. Other animals such as otters, martens, and foxes were prized for their skins worn as furs.

Indian men hunted and trapped most of the animals, and Indian women processed the furs and hides through a series of operations including scraping, stretching, rubbing, and curing. Native people were not only essential as producers, they also constituted a key consumer market for European goods. Metal tools such as iron axes, kettles, knives, and fishhooks were more durable than the native items they replaced. Woolen blankets and calico shirts, liquor and even Chinese vermilion (used for body and face paint) became important articles of trade. Indian consumers could be quite discriminating about the prices, styles, and quality of the goods they bought. Although some Indian groups despised haggling over prices, others were good bargainers and quick to exploit competition between rival European traders.

For most native people, the exchange of goods carried with it the affirmation of social ties, even the implication of military alliance. Such relationships were eagerly sought by some European traders, especially the French in Canada, the Great Lakes region, and Louisiana, who depended on Indian allies to maintain their imperial claims against rival colonial powers.

The Colonial Fur Trade. Jacques Cartier inadvertently "discovered" the fur trade in 1534 when a group of Micmac Indians persuaded him to take in exchange their animal skins for knives, other metal goods, and a red hat. The fur trade was pursued throughout the 16th century as an adjunct to the North Atlantic fishing expeditions. In the 17th century, the French established posts at Quebec and later Montreal and the Dutch at Beverwijck (Albany) to pursue the fur trade. Both the French and the Dutch waited for their native trading partners, primarily the Huron and the Iroquois respectively, to bring furs to the posts. With the destruction of Huronia by the Iroquois in the 1640s, French traders left their posts and began to travel to the Great Lakes region and Illinois Country in search of new partners and sources of furs. Many French traders married into Indian communities, and a distinctive fur-trade society containing many métis or people of mixed blood began to emerge.

In New England, the fur trade had some importance until the late 17th century. It was, however, the rivalry between English and Dutch traders operating out of New York and Pennsylvania and the French in the Great Lakes country that fanned the flames of imperial warfare in the 18th century. A similar contest between British and French colonies emerged in the South, with both Charleston and New Orleans exporting more than 100,000 pounds of deerskins annually in the late 1750s. The other major trading system in this period revolved around the Hudson's Bay Company and the Cree and Assiniboine peoples who brought furs to such collection points as York Factory on the shores of the bay.

Monopolies and Mountain Men. At the time of the American Revolution, the two major fur trade networks were centered around Hudson Bay and the Great Lakes. The latter area was controlled by merchants from Montreal, mostly Scottish traders who had arrived after the fall of New France and eventually formed the Northwest Company. American efforts to profit from the trade were largely unsuccessful until, after the War of 1812, Congress moved to exclude foreigners from trading on American soil, and John Jacob Astor's American Fur Company became the dominant force in the Great Lakes region.

In the trans-Mississippi West, Creole merchants such as the Chouteau family operating out of St. Louis carefully expanded into the upper Missouri region in the 1820s. They were briefly challenged by William Henry Ashley, who boldly bypassed

Indian producers and gathered a group of American trappers to exploit the animal resources of the Rocky Mountains. Ashley's "rendezvous" system proved successful, but the mountain men could not match the output of the Indian-centered trade. The Chouteau company bought the Western Department of the American Fur Company in 1834 when Astor retired from the trade. With steamboats and trading posts in the West and lobbyists in Washington, Pierre Chouteau Jr. & Company dominated the fur trade of the American West until the Civil War. The fur trade had truly become a corporate enterprise.

In its final phase, the fur trade provided a means by which businessmen could profit from Indian annuity payments stipulated by treaties often influenced by those same businessmen. Debts owed to traders facilitated the making of treaties and the subsequent loss of tribal lands. Trading companies accumulated capital and diversified into land speculation, railroads, mining, and lumbering. Fur exports actually increased after the Civil War, but the nature of the trade had changed. It was no longer an activity that involved the meeting of people from very different cultures, no longer part of the drama of frontier geopolitics.

—JAY GITLIN

See Also: *Astor, John Jacob; Barter; French Colonies.*

BIBLIOGRAPHY: Gilman, Carolyn, et al., *Where Two Worlds Meet: The Great Lakes Fur Trade* (Minnesota Historical Society 1982); Phillips, Paul C., and J. W. Smurr, *The Fur Trade,* 2 vols. (Univ. of Oklahoma Press 1961); Wishart, David J., *The Fur Trade of the American West, 1807-1840* (Univ. of Nebraska Press 1979).

G

GABRIEL PLOT (1800), slave insurrection. On Aug. 30, 1800, Gabriel, an enslaved African-American blacksmith who lived near Richmond, Virginia, planned to mass with well over 100 of his supporters, march on the city, fire and seize it, and proclaim an end to slavery in Virginia. Gabriel was born on the plantation of Thomas Prosser in 1776 as the American Revolution was erupting in the colonies, and he would come of age steeped in the democratic rhetoric of liberty and equality. Yet, blacks' exclusion from these rights early fired in him a commitment to secure them for himself and for his fellow slaves. By late in his teens, Gabriel had also become a skilled blacksmith and was allowed to travel with near freedom in Richmond and the surrounding countryside selling his labor to plantation owners and shopkeepers and then returning most of his earnings to his owner. This system of hiring-out presented the slaves with unprecedented opportunities for mobility, covert communication, and individual initiative. By the spring of 1800, Gabriel discerned an excellent chance to strike against slavery, and organizing neared full swing. Gabriel especially recruited mobile slaves who managed to spread word of the plans as far south as Norfolk and as far west as Charlottesville. By summertime, he had surrounded himself with a core of associates including his two brothers and two artisans, Sam Byrd and Ben Woolfolk, and together they organized many covert barbecues, often occurring immediately after religious revivals that were heavily attended by slaves. At these meetings Gabriel and his lieutenants mixed scripture, republicanism, and intimidation to recruit many more slaves. By late August several hundred slaves had been exposed to the plot and enlisted in one form or another. Gabriel planned to so disrupt and terrify the state by the rebellion that its leading politicians and merchants would negotiate an end to slavery rather than continue the bloody mayhem. By August 30 the rebels were all coordinated but fate stole the moment from them: a torrential thunderstorm in the late afternoon washed out roads and bridges, making rebel movement impossible. Dispersed and informed upon, the leaders were soon apprehended, although Gabriel was not captured until late September. With the leaders executed or sold and transported from the region and with local militias patrolling vigilantly, the plot collapsed. Calm had been restored by the end of the year, but the networks and example Gabriel established contributed to renewed plotting and slave restlessness in Virginia and North Carolina in 1801 and 1802. White Virginians had been so seized with terror, however, by the scale of Gabriel's plot and how close it came to fruition that legislative debates occurred in the early years of the new century over the possibility of gradually ending slavery in the state.

—PETER HINKS

See Also: *Slave Revolts; Slavery.*

BIBLIOGRAPHY: Egerton, Douglas, *Gabriel's Rebellion: The Virginia Slave Conspiracies of 1800 and 1802* (Univ. of North Carolina Press 1993); Mullin, Gerald W., *Flight and Rebellion: Slave Resistance in Eighteenth Century Virginia* (Oxford Univ. Press 1972).

GADSDEN PURCHASE (1853), the acquisition by the United States of approximately 29,000 square miles of Mexican territory in present-day Arizona and New Mexico for $10 million, primarily to secure the best route for a southern transcontinental railroad. The purchase resulted from the failure of the Treaty of Guadalupe Hidalgo (1848) to delimit fully the boundary of the Mexican Cession, the U.S. desire to be released from enforcement of the treaty's Article XI that aimed to control Indian raids into Mexico, and renewed efforts, stimulated by the California Gold Rush, to gain transit rights across the Isthmus of Tehuantepec. Needing money to quell a revolt and fearful of war with the United States, the Mexican government accepted these modifications. The purchase completed the contiguous continental expansion of the United States.

See Also: Frontier in American History; Guadalupe Hidalgo, Treaty of; Mexican War.

BIBLIOGRAPHY: Garber, Paul N., *The Gadsden Treaty* (Press of the Univ. of Pennsylvania 1923); Martinez, Oscar J., *Troublesome Border* (Univ. of Arizona Press 1988).

■ **GAGE, THOMAS (1721-87),** British commander in chief in North America (1763-75) and governor of Massachusetts (1774-75). He hastened the outbreak of the American Revolution by ordering the seizure of colonial munitions and the arrests of Samuel Adams and John Hancock, thus precipitating the battles of Lexington and Concord (Apr. 19, 1775). After Britain's pyrrhic victory at the Battle of Bunker Hill (June 17, 1775), Sir William Howe replaced Gage as commander.

See Also: Bunker Hill, Battle of; Lexington and Concord; Revolution, American.

■ **GAG RULE,** rule that prevented debate about "slavery, or the abolition of slavery" in the House of Representatives. It was adopted at the insistence of southern representatives in 1836 and was not dropped until 1844.

See Also: Civil War.

■ **GALLATIN, ALBERT (1761-1849),** Swiss-American politician. Born Abraham Alfonse Albert Gallatin in Geneva, Switzerland, he immigrated to the newly formed United States in 1780, after refusing to fight with the Hessian army against the American rebels during the Revolution. Neither did he fight with the rebels but rather bought and sold tea, a scarce commodity in great demand. Settling in Pennsylvania, Gallatin was elected to the U.S. Senate in 1793, but he was not seated because he had not been a U.S. citizen for the required nine years. He was then elected to the House of Representatives, where he served from 1795 to 1801. As a congressman, he helped established the Finance Committee (later the Ways and Means Committee). He also served as secretary of the treasury (1801-14) and as minister to France (1816-23) and to Great Britain (1826-27) before retiring from political life in 1827. He had a lifelong interest in American Indian cul-

ture and in 1842 founded the American Ethnological Society, the first society devoted solely to the study of Indian tribes. In 1842 Gallatin wrote that all of his papers were of only "ephemeral" importance, except for his writing on Indians.

■ **GALLOWAY, JOSEPH (c. 1731-1803),** loyalist colonial statesman. Born in West River, Maryland, Galloway was elected to the Pennsylvania Assembly in 1756. As speaker of the Assembly from 1766 to 1775, he was an influential figure in colonial politics. During the imperial crisis he sympathized with colonial complaints about British policy but favored constitutional reform as the remedy. He hoped to achieve such reform through his plan of union, which he proposed to the Continental Congress in 1774. The Congress's rejection of this plan decisively alienated Galloway from the patriot cause. In 1778 he left America permanently for England.

See Also: Revolution, American.

■ **GAMBLING,** various forms of wagering and speculation, which in America have ranged from public lotteries to illegal betting on sporting events. During the colonial period, gambling most often took the form of private and public lotteries, which became an important source of municipal financing. A series of antilottery laws during the 1830s, however, led to the eventual proscription of lotteries between 1895 and 1963. Public lotteries returned when New Hampshire introduced a state lottery in 1964. During the next three decades other states, seeking funding for education and other public functions, followed suit.

Since the late 19th century the most popular forms of gambling have been the policy and numbers games, both related to the lottery. Betting on horse races and other sporting events became a large-volume business during the 20th century. Although legal in many states, these forms of gambling have been closely associated with illegal business and organized crime.

Popular gambling games, such as poker, roulette, and craps, all foreign in origin, entered the United States through New Orleans. From this port city these forms of gambling spread throughout America. Gambling houses proliferated in many cities and periodic crusades against gambling failed to curb their popularity. During the post–World War II years, Las Vegas, Nevada, became the center for high-stakes gambling and the multibillion dollar gambling business. In recent years gambling casinos have burgeoned on Indian reservations, stimulating many local economies.

See Also: Lotteries.

BIBLIOGRAPHY: Fabian, Ann, *Card Shops, Dream Books, & Bucket Shops: Gambling in 19th Century America* (Cornell Univ. Press 1990); Findlay, John M., *People of Chance: Gambling in American Society from Jamestown to Las Vegas* (Oxford Univ. Press 1986).

■ **GANGSTERS,** those who engage in criminal activities as part of an organized group, usually for profit. The term came into common usage during the 1920s when Prohibition encouraged the criminal sale of alcohol. Other activities commonly associated with gangsters are robbery, prostitution, and drug trafficking. Gangsters such as Al Capone came to be household names and symbolized the lawlessness of the period.

See Also: Capone, Al; Mafia; Prohibition; Rackets.

■ ***GARCIA V. SAN ANTONIO METROPOLITAN TRANSIT AUTHORITY (1985),*** U.S. Supreme Court case concerning the extension of federal regulatory authority over state and local government agencies. The Court ruled (5-4) that the commerce clause gave Congress the power to extend federal wage and hour laws to a municipal transit system. *Garcia* reversed *National League of Cities v. Usery* (1976) and marked a shift toward the federal government in the Court's continuing effort to balance state and federal powers.

See Also: Supreme Court.

■ **GARDNER, JOHN (1933-82),** novelist and professor of English literature. Gardner was born in Batavia, New York. He attended De Pauw University, Washington University, and Iowa State University. The upstate New York landscape in which Gardner grew up became the setting for several of his novels about issues of human responsibility, including *The Sunlight Dialogues* (1972) and *October Light* (1976). Gardner's scholarly works include *The Life and Times of Chaucer* (1977) and *On Moral Fiction* (1978).

See Also: Novel.

■ **GARFIELD, JAMES ABRAM (1831-81),** 20th president of the United States (1881). Born on Nov. 19, 1831, in Cuyahoga County, Ohio, Garfield was raised by his widowed and pious mother. A graduate of Williams College, he returned in 1856 to Ohio, where he found work as a teacher and served as a Disciples of Christ lay preacher. A skilled orator, he entered politics as a Republican in 1859 when elected to the Ohio state legislature. With the outbreak of the Civil War, Garfield recruited his own regiment and distinguished himself in battle. As a returning war hero, he was elected in 1863 to the U.S. House of Representatives where he stood out as a gifted negotiator.

Appointed Speaker of the House in 1876, Garfield emerged in 1880 as the "dark horse" or compromise presidential candidate at the deadlocked Republican national convention. He went on to win the presidency by a small margin and then entered into a running battle over civil service appointments with fellow Republican Roscoe Conkling, the powerful senator from New York. The dispute ended when Garfield was shot by unsuccessful office-seeker Charles J. Guiteau on July 2, 1881. Garfield died two months later, and Chester A. Arthur assumed the

The last U.S. president to be born in a log cabin, James Garfield became a major general in the Union army during the Civil War.

presidency. Public outrage over the death of a president resulted in the Pendleton Act (1883), the first significant step toward civil service reform.

See Also: Arthur, Chester Alan; Gilded Age; Pendleton Act; Presidential Elections; President of the United States.

BIBLIOGRAPHY: Peshin, Allan, *Garfield, A Biography* (Kansas State Univ. Press 1978); Taylor, John M., *Garfield of Ohio, the Available Man* (Norton 1970).

■ **GARLAND, JUDY (1922-69),** singer, actress, and movie star. Born Frances Ethel Gumm in Grand Rapids, Michigan, she won an Academy Award for her performance as Dorothy in *The Wizard of Oz* (1938). Her sweet voice and captivating screen personality contributed to many successful films for MGM, including *For Me and My Gal* (1942) and *Meet Me in St. Louis* (1944), but she lost her contract in 1950 after a string of suicide attempts. Married to director Vincente Minelli, she was the mother of actress Liza Minelli.

See Also: Women in American History.

■ **GARNER, JOHN NANCE (1868-1967),** vice president of the United States (1933-41). He was born in Red River County, Texas. A Democratic member of Congress from Texas (1903-33) and Speaker of the House (1931-33), he served as vice president during the first two terms of Pres. Franklin D. Roosevelt. Garner, nicknamed "Cactus Jack," had been the conservative choice to balance the more liberal Roosevelt on the ticket. He was replaced on the ticket in 1940 by Sec. of Agriculture Henry A. Wallace.

See Also: New Deal; Vice President of the United States.

■ **GARRISON, WILLIAM LLOYD (1805-79),** abolitionist and reformer. Garrison was born in Newburyport, Massachusetts, and raised in extreme poverty by his pious Baptist mother. At 13 Garrison found his calling while working as a printer's apprentice. He became a talented newspaperman and published his own paper at 21.

In 1829 Garrison went to Baltimore to assist the abolitionist newspaperman Benjamin Lundy. While there he embraced immediate abolition and began to abandon his earlier support for colonization of America's African Americans. After serving a jail term for libel, Garrison returned to

Upon his release from jail, where he had been imprisoned for libeling a slave trader, abolitionist William Lloyd Garrison began publishing the *Liberator* in Boston on Jan. 1, 1831.

Massachusetts. On Jan. 1, 1831, he began publishing the *Liberator*, vowing to be "as harsh as truth, and as uncompromising as justice" in the struggle against slavery. Garrison's vituperative language was quoted frequently in the Southern press as quintessential Northern antislavery "fanaticism." This gave him a notoriety, particularly among slaveholders, that exceeded his influence within the abolitionist movement.

Although Garrison was instrumental in founding the New England Anti-Slavery Society (1832) and the American Anti-Slavery Society (1833), his greatest talents were as an agitator, not an organizer. Largely self-educated in the cut-and-slash school of political journalism, Garrison allowed no shades of gray in his denunciations of colonizationists and slaveholders. In person, however, he was gracious and serene as well as highly courageous. In October 1835, when a Boston mob nearly lynched him, Garrison's composure in the face of violence converted many onlookers, including Wendell Phillips, to abolitionism.

Besides opposing slavery, Garrison tirelessly supported women's rights. He also came to embrace such causes as anti-sabbatarianism and universal peace. By the mid-1840s he opposed all governments as unjustly founded upon force. In 1854 he publicly burned the Constitution, branding it "a covenant with death and an agreement with Hell" because it sanctioned slavery. Garrison favored disunion until the Civil War broke out; once the war began, he worked to downplay abolitionists' differences with the Lincoln administration. After the Emancipation Proclamation, Garrison became a vocal supporter of the war. He ended the *Liberator* after the ratification of the 13th Amendment in 1865, considering the slavery issue settled. During his last years, Garrison traveled and wrote on various reforms.

—ROBERT P. FORBES

See Also: *Antislavery Movement; Civil War; Phillips, Wendell.*

BIBLIOGRAPHY: Garrison, William Lloyd, *The Letters of William Lloyd Garrison,* ed. by Walter Merrill and Louis Ruchames (Harvard Univ. Press 1971-81).

▪ GARVEY, MARCUS MOSIAH (1887-1940),

black nationalist, Pan-Africanist, African emigrationist, and exponent of black civil rights. The

In 1914, Marcus Garvey founded the Universal Negro Improvement Association in his native Jamaica. Arriving for the first time in the United States two years later, Garvey began attracting many African Americans to the group.

youngest of 11 children born to Marcus M. Sr. and Sarah Garvey in St. Ann's Bay, Jamaica, Garvey was exposed very early to both Roman Catholicism and the Wesleyan Methodist Church. From preachers in both traditions he learned elocution and platform decorum that would later contribute to his great success as a communicator and organizer.

Educated in an Anglican grammar school in Jamaica, Garvey became a printer's apprentice at 14 and the manager of a large printing company at 18. In 1907 he relinquished his job as a printer, became a full-time politician, and started a paper called *The Watchman,* through which he supported labor reforms. He left Jamaica for a brief time and worked in Costa Rica, Panama, and Ecuador, where he witnessed the oppression of blacks and Indians at all levels. From South America he traveled to London in 1912 and was briefly a student at Birkbeck College. Further exposure to Africans in London increased his knowledge of the economic exploitation and political tyranny in colonial Africa and stimulated his thinking concerning economics and black independence.

A reading of Booker T. Washington's *Up from Slavery* reinforced Garvey's view of black self-advancement and inspired him to organize the Universal Negro Improvement Association (UNIA) in Jamaica in 1914. He came to the United States and established the UNIA in New York City in 1916. From his headquarters in Harlem, Garvey vigorously pursued his vision of black solidarity, cooperative economic activity, and African emigrationism. With branches of the UNIA throughout the world, he organized the largest black mass movement in American history.

Garvey's dream of bringing together all African peoples of the world to establish their own government in Africa offered hope to millions of blacks who experienced economic depression, political disfranchisement, and social deprivation in post–World War I urban America. To implement this dream on a practical level, he started the Black Star Line, whose steamships were intended to make triangular voyages between the United States, the West Indies, and Africa. To publicize this scheme and to instill racial pride, a spirit of unity, and a sense of the richness of the African heritage, he started a weekly newspaper called *The Negro World* in 1918.

Armed with slogans, rituals, hymns, a catechism, and art that featured a black Christ, a black Madonna, and black saints, Garvey challenged the theology and symbolism of traditional black churches while attracting the support of many clergymen and lay persons in those institutions. In his religious and philosophical views, he influenced later developments among the black Jews, the African Orthodox Church, the Black Muslims, black Christian nationalism, and the black power and black theology movements.

Allegations of mail fraud against Garvey resulted in a fine and a five-year prison sentence in 1925. In 1927, the jail term commuted, he was deported to Jamaica. Attempts to sustain the UNIA from abroad failed, and Garvey died in London in 1940. Numerous monuments to his memory stand in the West Indies, Africa, and the United States.

—LEWIS V. BALDWIN

See Also: Black Muslims (Nation of Islam); Civil Rights Movement; Washington, Booker Taliaferro.

BIBLIOGRAPHY: Clarke, John H., ed., *Marcus Garvey and the Vision of Africa* (Vintage 1974); Cronon, E. David, *Black Moses: The Story of Marcus Garvey and the Universal Negro Improvement Association* (Univ. of Wisconsin Press 1972); Jacques-Garvey, Amy, ed., *Philosophy and Opinions of Marcus Garvey* (Atheneum 1973).

■ *GASPÉE* **INCIDENT (1772),** burning of a British vessel in Rhode Island by American colonists. During the spring of 1772 the schooner *Gaspée* strictly enforced the Navigation Acts along Rhode Island's coast. When the vessel ran aground on June 9, a group of colonists removed the crew and set it ablaze.

See Also: Navigation Acts; Revolution, American.

■ **GATES, WILLIAM (1955-),** computer industry entrepreneur. Gates was born in Seattle, Washington, and by the time he was 15 had built a device to control the city's traffic patterns. He dropped out of Harvard to write computer programs in 1975 and cofounded Microsoft Corporation to develop and produce DOS, his basic computer operating system, in 1977. International Business Machines (IBM) adopted DOS for all its personal computers in 1981, and by 1983 Gates had licensed it to more than 100 vendors. In the late 1990s he was the wealthiest person in the world by most estimates.

See Also: Invention.

■ **GEHRIG, LOU (1903-41),** baseball player. A first baseman for the New York Yankees (1923-39), he was born in New York City and played 2,130 consecutive games before contracting amythrophic lateral sclerosis, "Lou Gehrig's disease."

See Also: Baseball; Sports.

■ **GENERAL AGREEMENT ON TARIFFS AND TRADE (GATT),** an agreement on the basic rules and regime of international trade reached in Havana in 1948. Since 1995, the contents and organs of GATT have been incorporated in the World Trade Organization.

■ **GENERAL ALLOTMENT ACT (DAWES ACT) (1887),** federal act aimed at breaking up Indian tribal lands. The Dawes Act put into place provisions for allotment in severalty, an idea that had been contemplated by American policymakers since the early 1800s. After the Civil War, white pressure for lands in the West intensified. U.S. policymakers and Friends of the Indians associations argued that the division of tribal lands into individual farm plots and the opening up of surrounding territory to white settlement would "civilize" the Indians faster, eventually assimilating them into the mainstream of American society. The Dawes Act allowed the president of the United States (or his agent) to open a reservation for allotment without the approval of the people living there. Each head of household would receive 160 acres, single persons over 18 and orphans 80 acres, and other single persons 40 acres. The lands remaining after a reservation was allotted would be considered "surplus" and sold to white settlers. The allottee's land was held in trust for 25 years to prevent it from being sold. However, the 1906 Burke Act amended the Dawes Act allowing agents of the Bureau of Indian Affairs to release individual allotments from trust. By the time the allotment policy ended in 1934, 86 million of 138 million acres of land held by Indians in 1887 had passed out of Indian ownership and control.

See Also: *Allotment; Friends of the Indians; Indians of North America; Wounded Knee, Occupation of.*

BIBLIOGRAPHY: Hoxie, Frederick E., *A Final Promise: The Campaign to Assimilate the Indians, 1880-1920* (Univ. of Nebraska Press 1985).

■ GENERAL FEDERATION OF WOMEN'S CLUBS

(GFWC), a national umbrella for women's organizations, formed in 1889. While the earliest American women's groups had been charitable associations, the club movement of the second half of the 19th century shifted its focus to learning and social activism. Excluded from colleges and universities until after the Civil War, many older middle-class women educated themselves in their own reading and discussion societies. The most famous of these was Sorosis, founded by Jane Cunningham Croley in 1868. Croley called for the formation of the GFWC in 1889 to give the growing number of independent ladies' reading circles a formal structure. This initiative helped transform the self-education movement into a powerful force for civic involvement and social reform. By 1906 some 5,000 local clubs belonged to the GFWC. They successfully lobbied for the Pure Food and Drug Act, child labor laws, and the 8-hour day. In 1914 the GFWC formally endorsed the woman suffrage movement, though individually many club women were already active suffragists. In 1895 African-American women created a parallel organization called the National Association of Colored Women. While the GFWC received less public attention after World War II, it has continued to grow. In 1990 it included 11,000 clubs claiming more than 500,000 members.

See Also: *National Association of Colored Women; Women in American History.*

■ GENTLEMEN'S AGREEMENTS (1907-08), un-

derstandings reached between the United States and Japan on the immigration of Japanese workers to the United States. Japan agreed not to issue passports to laborers and to recognize the U.S. right to exclude Japanese immigrants with other foreign passports.

See Also: *Immigration; Japanese Immigration.*

■ GEORGE, HENRY (1839-97), economist. Born

in Philadelphia, he sailed as a foremast boy to Australia and India (1855-56) but later learned the printing business and was employed as a typesetter in San Francisco (1859). In 1866, he obtained an editorial position in San Francisco. The California land boom of the late 1860s and 1870s led him to think about the value of land in a capitalist economy. His first ideas on this subject appeared in the pamphlet *Our Land and Land Policy* (1871).

Later, George developed his reasoning in his classic work, *Poverty and Progress* (1879). He argued that the biggest drain on the workers' wages came not from industrial capital but from the land on which industrial enterprises were built. The growth of industrial production would more and more enhance the value of urban land, increasing land rent and leaving little for wages and interest. George suggested laying the entire government tax burden on land. The government would collect land rent through taxation, thus bringing land prices down and making land speculation unprofitable. This tax would alone be enough to cover all government needs, hence the term "single tax theory." Industry would be freed from taxation, monopoly advantage would disappear, and equal opportunity would be brought back. In the 1880s and 1890s, George lectured extensively and published several books on economics and social issues. He ran twice unsuccessfully for New York City mayor (1886, 1897) and died of apoplexy while campaigning.

—DENIS KOZLOV

See Also: *Labor Movement; Taxation.*

BIBLIOGRAPHY: Cord, Steven B., *Henry George: Dreamer or Realist?*, 2nd ed. (Robert Schalkenbach Foundation 1984).

■ GEORGIA, the state with the largest land area

east of the Mississippi River. It is bounded on the north by Tennessee and North Carolina, on the west by Alabama, on the west and south by Florida, and on the east by South Carolina and the Atlantic Ocean. The Sea Islands lie along the coast. The topography varies from the Appalachian Mountains in the far north to the southern and eastern plains. Georgia shares the Okefenokee Swamp with Florida.

Georgia's founder was James Oglethorpe, who established the first English settlement there in 1733. It was one of the original 13 colonies and

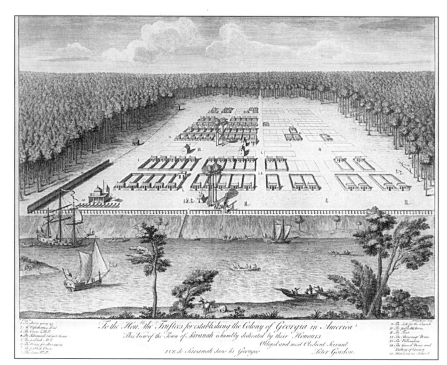

An early plan of Savannah, Georgia, shows it carved out of wilderness. Founded as the last of England's 13 colonies, Georgia was chartered to philanthropist James Oglethorpe and 20 other trustees in 1732.

states. During the Civil War a 60-mile-wide swath was devastated by Gen. William Tecumseh Sherman's march to the sea. Although the state economy, based on cotton planting, was slow to recover, there was sizable economic development after 1960, especially in the Atlanta area, which has thrived as a service-oriented financial, commercial, and transportation center.

Capital: Atlanta. Area: 58,930 square miles. Population (1995 est.): 7,201,000.

See Also: *Carter, James Earl, Jr. (Jimmy); Cherokee; Chickamauga, Battle of; Creek; De Soto, Hernando; King, Martin Luther, Jr.; Mitchell, Margaret; Oglethorpe, James E.; Sherman, William Tecumseh; Whitney, Eli.*

■ **GERMAIN, LORD GEORGE (1716-86),** British military leader and statesman. A native of London, Germain vehemently supported absolute British authority in the American colonies, as was seen in his opposition to the repeal of the Stamp Act. Germain has received much of the blame for the failure of British military moves during the American Revolution. His vagueness and poor strategic decisions subverted his effectiveness as a

leader, and he resigned when British efforts appeared futile in 1782.

See Also: *Revolution, American.*

■ **GERMAN IMMIGRANTS,** largest immigrant group in U.S. history, some 15 percent of all migrants to the United States between 1820 and 1980. A substantial exodus from the states that now make up Germany first began in the early 1700s, as peasants fleeing the wars of Louis XIV and famine in the Rhine region headed to the American colonies. By the time of the American Revolution (1776-83), there were already some 100,000 Germans living in the United States. Over the next century, upheavals in Europe connected to the Napoleonic Wars, crop failure, and rapid industrialization would propel roughly another 7 million Germans to the United States.

German immigrants were an extremely heterogeneous group, reflecting the many class, regional, and religious divisions of their homeland. Germans in America clustered both in urban centers and rural areas. In fact, supported by thriving German-language publications, schools, clubs, and churches, German remained perhaps the most commonly spoken foreign language in the United States until the early 20th century, when the anti-German sentiment surrounding the two world wars, combined with a tapering off in German immigration, pushed it into decline.

See Also: Ethnic Groups; Immigration.

■ **GERMAN REFORMED CHURCH,** Calvinist denomination originating in Switzerland and Germany. Most Reformed Germans did not emigrate as a religious group and were scattered throughout the Pennsylvania frontier. The first congregation gathered at Germantown in 1719 without a minister. Influenced by Michael Schlatter, who was sent by the Synod of South and North Holland and who petitioned for money and ministers, Germans remained under Dutch control until 1793, when the German Reformed Church was formed. In 1934, the church merged with another German Calvinist body, the Evangelical Synod of North America, to form the Evangelical and Reformed Church. In 1957, it adopted a presbyterian form of governance and joined with the Congregational and Christian Churches to form the United Church of Christ.

See Also: Religion.

■ **GERMANTOWN, BATTLE OF (1777),** American defeat in the Revolutionary War. A suburb of Philadelphia, the U.S. capital, Germantown served as the main encampment for British troops after they occupied the city. Gen. George Washington attacked the British fortifications on October 4, hoping for one last victory before winter. Although unsuccessful because poor visibility confused some units and Nathanael Greene's forces arrived late, Washington's Continental army acquitted itself well. It then moved to Valley Forge for the winter.

See Also: Revolution, American.

■ **GERONIMO (c. 1829-1909),** Apache leader. Geronimo, named Goyakla by his Chiricahua Apache band, was born near the Gila River in present-day Arizona. In 1858, Mexican soldiers attacked the Apache camp in Chihuahua, Mexico, killing Geronimo's mother, wife, and children. After this incident Geronimo carried a lifelong hatred of Mexicans, and he became a feared warrior in both Mexico and the United States. U.S. Indian agent John Clum first arrested Geronimo in 1877, but he and many other Apache escaped the reservation and began raiding the countryside of the American Southwest in 1881. Geronimo surrendered in 1884 but again escaped the reservation in 1885. The military forces sent to capture him included 42 companies of U.S. troops and 4,000 Mexican soldiers, while the Apache under Geronimo amounted to no more than 50 men and some women. In 1886 Geronimo surrendered. He was exiled and imprisoned in Florida and later transferred to Fort Sill, Oklahoma, where he earned money by selling signed mementos.

See Also: Apache; Frontier in American History; Gilded Age; Indians of North America.

Geronimo, a Chiricahua Apache, was an outstanding military leader of his people and became a legendary figure in his own lifetime.

■ **GERRY, ELBRIDGE (1744-1814),** merchant, Revolutionary War statesman, and vice president of the United States (1813–14). Born in Marblehead, Massachusetts, Gerry participated extensively in colonial politics, serving in the Second Continental Congress and the Constitutional Convention. While holding these positions, he signed the Declaration of Independence and the Articles of Confederation but initially opposed the Constitution because it failed to include a bill of rights. After serving in Congress and as a diplomat during the XYZ Affair (1797), he was elected governor of Massachusetts (1810) and later vice president (1813-14) under James Madison.

See Also: Declaration of Independence; Gerrymander; Vice President of the United States; XYZ Affair.

■ **GERRYMANDER,** creation of oddly shaped political districts to secure partisan advantage in future elections. The term originated during the 1812 election campaign for Congress in Massachusetts. Jeffersonians in the state legislature redrew district lines to divide the vote of the rival Federalists. A Federalist newspaper suggested one sprawling district in the northeastern portion of the state resembled a salamander and labeled a map of the district "the Gerry-mander" after Jeffersonian Gov. Elbridge Gerry (1744-1814). Although Gerry actually opposed the redistricting plan, the Federalists swept the state, and Gerry was defeated in his bid for a third term. The term persists to the present day in reference to a party's attempts to consolidate its power in state legislatures or Congress by dividing opposition voters among several districts to dilute their electoral strength.

See Also: Gerry, Elbridge.

BIBLIOGRAPHY: Rush, Mark E., *Does Redistricting Make a Difference?: Partisan Representation and Electoral Behavior* (Johns Hopkins Univ. Press 1993).

■ **GERSHWIN, GEORGE (1898-1937),** pianist and composer. A gifted writer of popular songs, he also composed symphonic music that drew on jazz and folk traditions. Born in Brooklyn, New York, Gershwin and his brother Ira, a creative lyricist, teamed to produce a series of Broadway hits including the *George White's Scandals* (1920-24), *Strike Up the Band* (1927), *Girl Crazy* (1930), and the Pulitzer Prize–winning *Of Thee I Sing* (1931). He also composed and performed orchestral works that combined popular jazz idioms with the romantic tradition. *Rhapsody in Blue* (1924), first performed by the Paul Whiteman Orchestra with Gershwin as piano soloist, was followed by *Concerto in F* (1925) and *An American in Paris* (1928). Gershwin's folk opera, *Porgy and Bess* (1935), opened on Broadway to mixed reviews but has become a popular classic thanks to frequent revivals and a film version (1959).

See Also: Folk Music; Jazz.

BIBLIOGRAPHY: Hyland, William G., *The Song Is Ended: Songwriters and American Music, 1900-1950* (Oxford Univ. Press 1995); Rosenberg, Deena, *Fascinating Rhythm: The Collaboration of George and Ira Gershwin* (Dutton 1991).

■ **GESELL, ARNOLD (1880-1961),** psychologist and pediatrician. Gesell was born in Alma, Wisconsin. He earned his Ph.D. in child psychology at Clark University. Gesell began teaching education at Yale University in 1911 and also entered the Yale Medical School, from which he graduated in 1915. Gesell founded the Yale Clinic of Child Development in 1911. In 1924 he began using photographic images to record child development, and he used these in *An Atlas of Infant Behavior* (1934) and *The First Five Years* (1940).

■ **GETTYSBURG, BATTLE OF (1863),** decisive Civil War battle between Confederates under Gen. Robert E. Lee and Union forces under Gen. George G. Meade, the climax of Lee's invasion of Pennsylvania. Fierce fighting around Gettysburg on July 1 drove the Union army back onto the high ground south of the town, where they dug in along a four-mile front. Rebel attacks, on the Union left and right on July 2 and on the center on July 3 (the famous "Pickett's Charge"), were repulsed with heavy loss. Lee was forced to retreat from Pennsylvania and never again assumed the strategic offensive.

See Also: Civil War; Lee, Robert Edward; Meade, George G.

■ **GETTYSBURG ADDRESS,** delivered by Pres. Abraham Lincoln at the dedication of a national cemetery on the site of the Pennsylvania battlefield where, July 1-3, 1863, there occurred the critical engagement between Union and Confederate troops that is considered the turning point of the Civil War. Lincoln's address consisted of only three paragraphs. He carefully composed it in Washington (not on the way to the occasion, as popular myth would have it) and delivered it following a two-hour oration by Edward Everett. The tired crowd showed little appreciation, but the address was immediately hailed by many who read it in the press as a poetic and noble expression of the issues at stake in the war. Although the address celebrated a military victory, it is not at all martial in spirit, but rather a moving tribute to those who made the ultimate sacrifice and to the ideals of American democracy.

The text of the address is as follows:

Four score and seven years ago our fathers brought forth on this continent, a new nation, conceived in Liberty, and dedicated to the proposition that all men are created equal.

Now we are engaged in a great civil war, testing whether that nation, or any nation so conceived and so dedicated, can long endure. We are met on a great battle-field of that war. We have come to dedicate a portion of that field, as a final resting place for those who here gave their lives that that nation might live. It is altogether fitting and proper that we should do this.

But, in a larger sense, we can not dedicate, we can not consecrate, we can not hallow this ground. The brave men, living and dead, who struggled here, have consecrated it, far above our poor power to add or detract. The world will little note, nor long remember what we say here, but I can never forget what they did here. It is for us the living, rather, to be dedicated here to the unfinished work which they who fought here have thus far so nobly advanced. It is rather for us to be here dedicated to the great task remaining before us, that from these honored dead we take increased devotion to that cause for which they gave the last full measure of devotion; that we here highly resolve that these dead shall not have died in vain; that this nation, under God, shall have a new birth of freedom; and that government of the people, by the people, for the people, shall not perish from the earth.

See Also: *Civil War.*

BIBLIOGRAPHY: Wills, Garry, *Lincoln at Gettysburg: The Words that Remade America* (Simon & Schuster 1992).

■ **GHENT, TREATY OF (Dec. 24, 1815),** treaty between Great Britain and the United States that ended the War of 1812. The military stalemate of the war led to terms based on prewar conditions, although the British made territorial concessions in the American Northwest and agreed to arbitration over Canadian boundary disputes.

See Also: *War of 1812.*

■ **GHOST DANCE,** central ritual of an American Indian messianic or religious movement of the late 19th century.

The first of the two Ghost Dance movements originated among the Northern Paiute Indians of Nevada's Walker River Reservation and was founded by the prophet Wodziwob. In 1869, a time of starvation and deprivation resulting from the loss of land to whites, Wodziwob prophesied supernatural events. He claimed that the world would end, that all white men would be killed, and that Indians would return and rebuild their world. He directed his followers to perform circular dances and sing. The movement spread to Indian peoples in Oregon and northern California but was abandoned when the prophecies were not realized.

A second Ghost Dance movement originated in the late 1880s with the Paiute prophet Wovoka and quickly spread to other Indian groups, including the Sioux and Cheyenne. After his visionary religious experience, Wovoka directed his followers to be good to one another and to live peacefully. This, he told them, would result in the restoration of their lands and a return to life of the Indian dead, and would occur if the Indians performed dances. The dance was performed over several days and was accompanied by hypnotic trances and shaking. As the Ghost Dance gained popularity across the West, whites became fearful. The military intervened in 1890 at Wounded Knee, South Dakota, killing almost 300 Sioux men, women, and children.

See Also: *Indians of North America; Wounded Knee Massacre; Sioux.*

BIBLIOGRAPHY: Thornton, Russell, *We Shall Live Again: The 1870 and 1890 Ghost Dance Movements as Demographic Revitalization* (Cambridge Univ. Press 1986).

■ **G.I.,** nickname for U.S. Army infantrymen in World War II. "G.I." stands for "government issue," a term normally applied to military equipment, but during the war it came to be applied to the soldiers themselves.

See Also: World War II.

■ **GIBBONS, JAMES (1834-1921),** cardinal of the Roman Catholic Church and the most influential U.S. Catholic prelate in the late 19th and early 20th centuries. Gibbons was born in Baltimore, Maryland, studied in Ireland, and returned to the United States to become a priest. After ordination he rose rapidly in the church hierarchy, becoming the cardinal of Baltimore in 1886. A powerful figure devoted to "social justice," Gibbons oversaw a period of tremendous growth in American Catholicism.

See Also: Religion; Roman Catholics.

■ *GIBBONS V. OGDEN* **(1824),** U.S. Supreme Court case that established the Constitution's commerce clause as the basis for broad federal regulatory power. The case originated in a dispute over the right to run a ferry service between New York and New Jersey. Aaron Ogden had purchased monopoly rights to run steamboats in the state of New York, including, or so he thought, a monopoly on ferry service between New York and New Jersey. After Thomas Gibbons, who had been licensed by the federal government to service coastal waterways, opened a competing interstate line, Ogden filed suit against his competitor. The case went to the Supreme Court, where Gibbons's right to his concession was unanimously upheld. Delivering the opinion of the Court, Chief Justice John Marshall used the case as a vehicle for introducing a broad construction of the Constitution's commerce clause. The Constitution reserved to Congress the power to regulate interstate commerce. In Marshall's view, that jurisdiction was truly vast, empowering the national government to intervene wherever the commerce in question was even remotely interstate. Congress's power to regulate, moreover, meant not just the power to *proscribe* unconstitutional commercial activity but also the power, whenever it saw fit, to *prescribe* positive laws bearing on interstate commerce. With this decision the Court, meaning mostly Marshall himself, had taken another, decisive step toward establishing the supremacy of the federal government over the states.

—MATTHEW E. BABCOCK

See Also: Marshall, John; Supreme Court.

BIBLIOGRAPHY: Baxter, Maurice G., *The Steamboat Monopoly: Gibbons v. Ogden* (Knopf 1972).

■ **GIBBS, JOSIAH WILLARD (1839-1903),** mathematician, physicist, and developer of physical chemistry. The son of Yale divinity professor Josiah Willard Gibbs, he was born in New Haven and earned his Ph.D. from Yale (1863). After studying in Europe, Gibbs was appointed professor of mathematical physics at Yale (1871-1903). His influence on science came mainly through his precise, elegant writing and his ability to draw connections between different disciplines. His earliest work melded principles of thermodynamics and statistical mechanics to arrive at a geometrical analysis of the thermodynamics of fluids and surfaces (1873). Gibbs's greatest achievement came with the publishing of his memoir, *On the Equilibrium of Heterogeneous Substances* (1876-78), in which he integrated chemical, physical, electrical, and electromagnetic phenomena into a cohesive system and laid the theoretical groundwork for the field of physical chemistry. Between 1880 and 1884, Gibbs developed a system of vector algebra from previous work done on quaternions and geometric algebra. He also formulated an electrical theory of optics (1882-89) and published *Elementary Principles in Statistical Mechanics* in 1902.

See Also: Science.

■ **G.I. BILL OF RIGHTS,** the Servicemen's Readjustment Act of 1944. Enacted near the end of World War II to ease the transition to peace, the G.I. Bill provided unemployment insurance, mortgages, business loans, and education subsidies to returning members of the military. The program allowed millions of men and women to obtain college degrees, leading to a boom in higher education and a subsequent democratization of the U.S. economy.

■ **GIBSON, ALTHEA (1927-),** tennis player. Born in Silver, South Carolina, she broke the color line at both the U.S. grass court championships at Forest Hills, New York (1950), and at Wimbledon, England. She earned the national African-American women's singles title 10 times and won the U.S. and English women's singles championships in 1957 and 1958.

See Also: Sports.

■ **GIBSON, JOSH (1911-47),** baseball legend. Born in Buena Vista, Georgia, Gibson became the home-run king of the Negro Leagues, hitting with power for a high average. A gifted catcher with one of the most powerful arms in baseball history, he hit more than 950 home runs in his career. Gibson played nearly year-round in the United States, Mexico, Puerto Rico, and the Dominican Republic. The strain of continual play along with emotional problems cut short a brilliant career. He was elected to the Baseball Hall of Fame in 1972.

See Also: African Americans; Baseball; Sports.

■ *GIDEON V. WAINWRIGHT (1963),* U.S. Supreme Court case that required states to provide legal counsel to indigent defendants in criminal cases. Earl Gideon was arrested for breaking into a Florida pool room. The local court refused to appoint a lawyer to assist in his defense, and Gideon was convicted. He appealed, claiming his constitutional rights had been violated. The Court ruled (9-0) that the Sixth Amendment's guarantee of assistance of counsel as applied to the states by the 14th Amendment required state courts to appoint attorneys for defendants unable to afford them. A new trial was ordered, and Gideon, represented by a court-appointed lawyer who located additional witnesses, was found not guilty.

Gideon overturned an earlier Court decision, *Betts v. Brady* (1942), which had held that counsel was required only in special circumstances such as capital cases. The decision in *Gideon* was widely anticipated. The Supreme Court appointed prominent Washington attorney and future associate justice Abe Fortas to represent Gideon, and 22 state attorneys general filed friend of the court briefs supporting Gideon's case. *Gideon* was an important step in the Supreme Court's "due process revolution" of the 1960s, which saw federal constitutional protections extended to state courts.

—TIM ASHWELL

See Also: Due Process of Law; Supreme Court.
BIBLIOGRAPHY: Lewis, Anthony, *Gideon's Trumpet* (Random House 1964).

■ **GILBERT, SIR HUMPHREY (c.1539-1583),** English soldier and explorer. Gilbert, half brother of Sir Walter Raleigh, spent his early military career colonizing Ireland. Intent on finding a Northwest Passage, he was granted a New World colonizing charter. In 1583 Gilbert landed at St. John's Bay, Newfoundland, and claimed it for Queen Elizabeth I. Gilbert and his ship were lost at sea during the return to England.

See Also: Exploration and Discovery.

■ **GILDED AGE,** a term applied to the late 19th-century United States. Taken from the title of a satirical novel by Mark Twain and Charles Dudley Warner, the term refers to the shallow and gaudy culture engaged in by the newly rich and the families of old wealth. Some historians interpret the ornate mansions of Newport and New York City, and the lavish parties held in them, as the expression of excess wealth earned through mindless greed.

See Also: Twain, Mark.

■ **GILLESPIE, DIZZY (1917-93),** jazz musician and composer. He was born in Cheraw, South Carolina. Recognized by his balloon cheeks and upswept trumpet, Gillespie, along with Charlie (Bird) Parker, is considered one of the leaders of the be-bop movement in modern jazz. Throughout his long career he played with every significant name in contemporary music and composed numerous innovative jazz standards, such as "Manteca" and "Night in Tunisia."

See Also: African Americans; Jazz.

■ **GILMAN, CHARLOTTE PERKINS (1860-1935),** socialist and feminist author and lecturer. A descendent of the Beecher family, she was born in Hartford, Connecticut. In *Women and Economics* (1898), her most important work, she argued that women should seek economic independence from men. She also wrote *Human Work* (1904), *Man-Made World* (1911), *His Religion and Hers* (1923), and a science fiction story called "Herland" about an all-female utopia.

See Also: Women's Movement.

■ **GILMAN, DANIEL COIT (1831-1908),** educator and college administrator. Born in Norwich, Connecticut, he graduated from Yale University in 1852 and helped organize Yale's Sheffield Scientific School (1861). He was president of the University of California (1872-75) before becoming the first president of Johns Hopkins University in Baltimore (1875-1901). Under his leadership, Johns Hopkins became a pioneering center of graduate education and scientific research. Gilman went on to become the first president of the Carnegie Institution in Washington, D.C. (1901-04), as well as the president of the National Civil Service Reform League (1901-07).

■ **GINGRICH, NEWT (1943-)**, Speaker of the U.S. House of Representatives (1995-). Born in Harrisburg, Pennsylvania, he earned a Ph.D. from Tulane (1971) and taught history before being elected to Congress as a Republican from Georgia (1978). Known as a fierce partisan, he mounted a campaign that led to the resignation of Democratic speaker Jim Wright (1989) and became speaker himself after his party gained control of the House in the 1994 elections.

See Also: House of Representatives; Republican Party.

■ **GINSBERG, ALLEN (1926-97)**, poet of the Beat Generation. Born in Newark, New Jersey, Ginsberg attended Columbia University. After diverse experiences undergoing psychiatric therapy, working as a market research consultant, and traveling in Mexico, Ginsberg settled in San Francisco. In 1956 Lawrence Ferlinghetti's City Lights Books published his *Howl and Other Poems* to great acclaim. Ginsberg's passionate expressions about American culture, in both his verse and readings, attracted a significant following.

See Also: Beats, The; Poetry.

■ **GINSBERG, RUTH BADER (1933-)**, Supreme Court justice. She was born in New York City. She was a professor at Columbia Law School (1972-80) and circuit judge for the U.S. Court of Appeals in Washington, D.C. (1980-93). In 1993 she was nominated to the Supreme Court by Pres. Bill Clinton, becoming the second woman to serve on the nation's highest court.

See Also: Supreme Court; Women in American History; Women's Movement.

■ **GISH, LILLIAN (1896-1993)**, stage and screen actress. Born in Springfield, Ohio, she is known for

After she met director D. W. Griffith, Lillian Gish established herself as a major movie star. Her career extended from silent movies to the Broadway stage and television shows.

her work with film director D. W. Griffith, including *Birth of a Nation* (1915). Her film career flourished through the 1920s after which she returned to the stage, where she earned critical acclaim for her portrayal of Ophelia in a 1948 version of *Hamlet*.

See Also: Griffith, D.W.; Motion Pictures.

■ **GITLOW V. NEW YORK (1925)**, U.S. Supreme Court case that began the process of extending First Amendment free speech protection to the states. Gitlow was convicted of violating New York's criminal anarchy law for advocating strikes and class action against the state. The Court upheld his conviction (7-2) but ruled that free speech was a fundamental right and that citizens could seek remedies in the federal courts.

See Also: Supreme Court.

■ **GLASGOW, ELLEN (1873-1945)**, novelist. She was born in Richmond, Virginia, and known for her southern realist style, she wrote novels about the conflict between the new middle class and the waning Southern aristocracy. Among her best are *The Voice of the People* (1900), *Barren Ground* (1925), *The Romantic Comedians* (1926), *Vein of Iron* (1935), and *In This Our Life* (1941). She was elected to the American Academy of Arts and Letters in 1938 and received the Pulitzer Prize for fiction in 1942.

See Also: Novel; Women in American History.

■ **GLASS-STEAGALL ACT (1933),** federal law regulating banking practices and creating the Federal Deposit Insurance Corporation. It helped restore public confidence in the banking system following a wave of bankruptcies.

See Also: New Deal.

■ **GLEASON, JACKIE (1916-87),** entertainer, born in New York City. His television variety and comedy shows, notably "The Honeymooners" (1955-56), were hits during the 1950s. He also starred in films, most memorably *The Hustler* (1961).

See Also: Television and Radio.

■ **GLORIOUS REVOLUTION IN AMERICA,** political unrest in the colonies connected with the Glorious Revolution in England (1688-89). Concerned with excessive autonomy of the American colonies, King Charles II prompted revocation of the Massachusetts charter in the Court of Chancery (Oct. 23, 1684). Having inherited the English throne on the death of Charles (1685), King James II then united all New England colonies into one Dominion of New England, with New York and New Jersey attached in 1688. Joseph Dudley was appointed governor, succeeded by the stern Edmund Andros (December 1686). The governor enjoyed the power to legislate, tax, and dispose of common and free land. Assemblies were abolished and town meetings restricted. Upon learning of James II's dethronement (1688), Bostonians rebelled (April 1689) and arrested Andros. The Dominion of New England collapsed and the colonies resumed their separate existences. In New York, a German-born merchant named Jacob Leisler seized power (June 1689), claiming he was acting on behalf of the new English sovereigns, William III and Mary II. Later, however, William and Mary appointed a royal governor, Henry Sloughter, whom Leisler imprudently resisted. When Sloughter arrived in New York, Leisler was tried and hanged as a traitor (May

1691). In Maryland, John Coode gained power (July 1689) and pledged allegiance to William and Mary, hoping to get rid of Lord Baltimore, the proprietor of the colony. The new monarchs indeed deprived Baltimore of political control over Maryland and appointed Lionel Copley governor (1690). Connecticut and Rhode Island, which had seen little unrest, got their charters back. Plymouth and Maine were incorporated into Massachusetts (September 1691), now a royal colony with a governor no longer elected but appointed by the Crown. New Hampshire remained separate but also became a royal colony.

See Also: Andros, Edmund; Dominion of New England; Leisler's Revolt.

BIBLIOGRAPHY: Lovejoy, David S., *The Glorious Revolution in America* (Harper & Row 1972); Webb, Stephen S., *Lord Churchill's Coup: The Anglo-American Empire and the Glorious Revolution Reconsidered* (Knopf 1995).

■ **GNADDENHUTTEN MASSACRE (1782),** American militia attack on a Moravian mission settlement of Indians. After the surrender of the British at Yorktown in 1781, Seneca, Delaware, and Shawnee warriors continued to raid western Pennsylvania settlements in hopes of retaining their homelands. In retaliation, a 300-man militia raided the Ohio Valley Gnaddenhutten mission killing some 90 peaceful converts, mostly women and children. Survivors fled to present-day Ontario, Canada.

See Also: Indians of North America.

■ **GODDARD, ROBERT H. (1882-1945),** physicist and rocket scientist. Born in Worcester, Massachusetts, Goddard dedicated his life to the goal of achieving high-altitude rocket flights. He earned his Ph.D. at Clark University (1911) and returned to teach there, with some interruptions, from 1914 to 1942. He won a grant from the Smithsonian Institution (1916) to work on solid-fuel rocketry, directed research that led to the recoilless rocket (ancestor to the bazooka) during World War I, and published his theory of rocket propulsion, *A Method of Reaching Extreme Altitudes*, in 1919. Goddard launched his first liquid-fueled rocket in 1926 and a more sophisticated model in 1929. With a grant from the Guggenheim Foundation, he continued his experiments near Roswell, New Mexico. There he discovered ways to ensure a continuous flow of power to rockets, devised gyroscopic steering mechanisms for their ascent and parachutes for their descent, and developed the theory of clustered and step rockets for reaching the moon. Goddard shot rockets across the New Mexico desert at speeds of more than 700 miles an hour and altitudes of 8,000 to 9,000 feet, but he fell short of his higher goals and before his death saw German V-2 rockets overtake his records.

See Also: Science.

■ **GODFREY, ARTHUR (1903-83),** radio and television personality known for his folksy manner. Born in New York City, he made his radio debut in 1930, and his television shows (1948-59) attracted huge audiences.

■ **GODKIN, E. L. (1831-1902),** editor and author. Godkin was born in Moyne, County Wicklow, Ireland, and immigrated to the United States in 1856. He was a founder and first editor of the *Nation*, a weekly periodical beginning in 1856. In 1881 the *Nation* was merged with the *New York Evening Post*, becoming its weekly edition. Two years later Godkin assumed the position of editor in chief of the *Evening Post*. Godkin's books include *Reflections and Comments, 1865-95* (1895) and *Problems of Democracy* (1896).

■ **GOETHALS, GEORGE (1858-1928),** engineer, soldier, and builder of the Panama Canal. Born in Brooklyn, New York, Goethals graduated from West Point (1880) and worked for the Army Corps of Engineers on canal, river, and harbor projects before being appointed by Pres. Theodore Roosevelt as chief engineer of the Panama Canal (1907-14). The Panama Canal opened in August 1914, and Goethals remained as governor of the Canal Zone until 1919, when he retired from the army.

See Also: Panama Canal; Science.

■ **GOLDBERG, ARTHUR JOSEPH (1908-90),** secretary of labor (1961-62), associate justice of the U.S. Supreme Court (1962-65), and ambassador to the United Nations (1965-68). Born in Chicago, Illinois, the youngest of eight children of Russian immigrant parents, he was a prominent labor

lawyer and counsel to the United Steelworkers union. Goldberg helped arrange the merger of the American Federation of Labor and the Congress of Industrial Organizations (1955). After serving in the cabinet, he was appointed by Pres. John F. Kennedy to the Supreme Court to replace Justice Felix Frankfurter. While Frankfurter had urged judicial restraint, Goldberg believed the Court should adopt a more active role to protect those excluded from political power. In 1965, Pres. Lyndon B. Johnson insisted Goldberg leave the Court and represent the United States at the United Nations (1965-68).

See Also: Supreme Court.

■ **GOLDEN HILL, BATTLE OF (1770),** violent incident between British soldiers and colonists in New York City. It occurred during a dispute over Parliament's Quartering Act. A street fight, the violence resulted in several injuries to both sides but no deaths.

■ **GOLDMAN, EMMA (1869-1940),** anarchist and feminist. Born in Kovno, Russia, she immigrated to the United States in 1885. She lectured and wrote on many subjects, including anarchism, the revolt of women, birth control, free speech, and the modern drama. With her lover Alexander Berkman, she edited the anarchist journal *Mother Earth*. Considering her a threat, the U.S. government deported Goldman in 1919. She became a critic of totalitarianism and spent her last years supporting the Republican cause in the Spanish Civil War. Her autobiography is titled *Living My Life* (1931).

See Also: Anarchism; Gilded Age; Labor Movement; Women in American History; Women's Movement.

■ **GOLD STANDARD,** monetary system in which the basic unit is defined by a fixed quantity of gold. The Coinage Act of 1792 authorized the free and unlimited coinage of silver and gold at a ratio of 15 to 1, but when gold's market value rose above this ratio owners ceased to present it for coinage. This phenomenon effectively put the country on a silver standard until 1837, when the government changed the ratio to 16 to 1, making silver more valuable in the market than in coinage and moving the country to a gold standard. The Coinage Act of 1873 ended the coinage of silver, infuriating free silverites and advocates of greenbacks who believed the nation needed a more flexible currency. The Sherman Silver Purchase Act of 1890 provided for some silver coinage but was repealed in 1893, and Republican William McKinley defeated William Jennings Bryan on a gold-standard platform in the election of 1896. The Gold Standard Act of 1900 declared that the gold dollar "shall be the standard unit of value" and lasted until 1933, when financial crisis prompted President Roosevelt to abandon the gold standard. The government then reduced the dollar's gold content by setting it equal to gold at $35 an ounce and discontinued the coinage and circulation of gold through the Gold Reserve Act of 1934. President Nixon dissolved the dollar's link to gold in 1971 when he declared that its value would be determined solely by its position on world currency exchanges.

See Also: Free Silver; Money and Currency.

BIBLIOGRAPHY: Timberlake, Richard H., *Monetary Policy in the United States: An Intellectual and Institutional History* (Univ. of Chicago Press 1993).

▨ GOLDTHWAITE, ANNE WILSON (1869-1944),

artist. Born in Montgomery, Alabama, she was influenced by the styles of French painters Edouard Manet and Paul Cézanne. She lived in Paris in the decade before World War I, where she helped to organize the Académie Moderne, a small group of young artists that met regularly and exhibited their work each spring. Her paintings hang in the Metropolitan Museum of Art in New York City and in the Library of Congress.

See Also: Painting.

▨ GOLDWATER, BARRY MORRIS (1909-98),

Republican U.S. senator from Arizona, presidential candidate (1964), and father of the modern conservative movement. He was born in Phoenix, to a prominent family. After a successful business career, he entered politics, winning election to the Phoenix City Council (1949, 1951) and then to a U.S. Senate seat (1952, 1958). With the publication of *The Conscience of a Conservative* (1960) and *Why Not Victory?* (1962), he emerged as America's leading political conservative. Goldwater called for the protection of individual rights, opposed the expansion of federal

authority at home, and advocated a rollback of communist gains abroad. Reflecting these positions, he voted against the Nuclear Test Ban Treaty (1963) and the Civil Rights Act (1964) while recommending a vigorous pursuit of the war in Vietnam.

Capturing the Republican party's presidential nomination in 1964, Goldwater pioneered a campaign strategy that sought to unite southern and western conservatives with ethnic voters in the eastern cities on a platform of anticommunism, military strength, fiscal conservatism, and law and order. Although he was defeated by Pres. Lyndon B. Johnson, the conservatives retained their grip on the Republican party. Reelected to the U.S. Senate (1968, 1974, 1980), he remained a critic of big government and a proponent of a strong military. Goldwater retired in 1986 but continued his defense of personal liberty against the encroachment of government, speaking in defense of gay rights and choice in abortion.

—ROBERT ALAN GOLDBERG

See Also: Cold War; Presidential Elections; Republican Party.

BIBLIOGRAPHY: Brennon, Mary C., *Turning Right in the Sixties: The Conservative Capture of the GOP* (Univ. of North Carolina Press 1995); Goldberg, Robert Alan, *Barry Goldwater* (Yale Univ. Press 1995); Goldwater, Barry, *Goldwater* (Doubleday 1988).

▨ GOMPERS, SAMUEL (1850-1924),

labor leader. A native of London, Gompers immigrated to New York City with his family in 1863. As a cigar maker, he became involved in a trade union and rapidly learned about the various strategies and ideologies of the labor movement. During the 1870s, Gompers developed a strong belief in centralized trade unionism and in economic, as opposed to political, action. Although never a Marxist, Gompers believed that trade unions could foster a sense of class identity among workers.

In 1877, Gompers became president of the Cigar Makers Union and four years later helped establish the Federation of Organized Trades and Labor Unions, which was restructured in 1886 as the American Federation of Labor (AFL).

As the founding president, Gompers directed the AFL for almost 40 years. During the first two decades, the AFL unionized skilled craft workers but intentionally neglected a growing, ethni-

Samuel Gompers cofounded the Federation of Organized Trades and Labor Unions in 1881, reorganized as the American Federation of Labor (AFL) in 1886.

cally diverse, and unskilled sector of the labor force. Seeking political alliances in a time of government regulation of big business, Gompers publicly supported Woodrow Wilson during the 1912 presidential election and helped mobilize labor support for the American effort during World War I.

Because of the AFL's decentralized structure, Gompers was ultimately unable to coalesce the autonomous unions into the massive, organized labor movement he envisioned. Dedicated and determined to the end, Gompers, in ill health, died on the return trip from his last AFL convention.

See Also: American Federation of Labor (AFL); Labor Movement.

BIBLIOGRAPHY: McKillien, Elizabeth, *Chicago Labor and the Quest for a Democratic Diplomacy, 1914-1924* (Cornell Univ. Press 1995); Mandel, Bernard, *Samuel Gompers: A Biography* (Antioch Press 1963).

■ **GOODMAN, BENNY (1909-86),** clarinetist and big band leader known as the "King of Swing." Born in Chicago, Illinois, he formed his own tour-

ing band (1934) and played a landmark concert at New York City's Carnegie Hall (1938). He favored arrangements influenced by African-American bands of the day and was among the first white band leaders to feature African-American musicians such as pianist Teddy Wilson and vibraphonist Lionel Hampton.

See Also: Big Bands.

■ **GOOD NEIGHBOR POLICY,** the Latin American policy of Pres. Franklin D. Roosevelt (FDR) that testified to the growing interdependence of the American republics. The Good Neighbor policy arose in response to concern about U.S. intervention in Latin America. At conferences held at Montevideo, Uruguay (1933), and Buenos Aires, Argentina (1936), the United States renounced the right to intervene as articulated by the 1904 Roosevelt Corollary to the Monroe Doctrine.

Early in 1933 even before FDR's inauguration, U.S. troops left Nicaragua. Then, in 1934 the United States abrogated the Platt Amendment of 1901, which had turned Cuba into a U.S. protec-

Benny Goodman debuted in Chicago in 1921 and became known as the "King of Swing" after forming his own popular jazz band in 1934.

torate. Yet, the Good Neighbor policy did not envision a truly equal partnership in the Western Hemisphere. The United States sought to maintain its political dominance, extend its economic reach, and expand its cultural influence. Roosevelt achieved the first goal by courting some of the region's most repressive leaders, including Cuba's Fulgencio Batista, Nicaragua's Anastasio Somoza, and the Dominican Republic's Raphael Trujillo. U.S. conflicts with Bolivia and Mexico over oil in the late 1930s were settled with economic leverage and forceful diplomacy.

In the depths of the Great Depression, the economic side of the Good Neighbor policy appealed to Latin America. The creation of the Export-Import Bank and the reciprocal trade program gave the United States advantages over commercial rivals. Central American countries and other nations that depended on U.S. markets quickly fell within the North American trade orbit. Brazil was contested territory. The start of World War II ended the contest and left Brazil a strong power as well as a friend of the United States in South America.

In the cultural realm, trade expansion permitted North American businessmen to develop close ties with their peers in the region. In August 1940, Roosevelt established the Office of the Coordinator of Inter-American Affairs, headed by Nelson A. Rockefeller, to foster cultural exchanges.

—WILLIAM O. WALKER III

See Also: New Deal; Platt Amendment; Roosevelt, Franklin Delano.

BIBLIOGRAPHY: Pike, Fredrick B., *FDR's Good Neighbor Policy: Sixty Years of Generally Gentle Chaos* (Austin 1995); Wood, Bryce, *The Making of the Good Neighbor Policy* (Columbia Univ. Press 1961).

■ **GOODYEAR, CHARLES (1800-60),** inventor of vulcanized rubber. After a period of great growth before 1830, the rubber industry collapsed because no one could find a way to prevent India rubber from melting, sticking, and decomposing in heat. Goodyear, who was born in New Haven, Connecticut, became obsessed with solving this problem. He continued his experiments on rubber despite extreme poverty, chronic illness, ignorance of the scientific principles involved, and repeated failures. Goodyear developed an "acid gas" process in 1837 that improved the texture of rubber but still left it af-

fected by summer heat. He also experimented with Nathaniel Hayward's sulfur-turpentine methods in 1838. Goodyear discovered the process of vulcanization in 1839 when he spilled a mass of sulfur and rubber mixture on a hot stove and it did not melt. After years more of experimentation he produced a uniform product and received his patent in 1844. By that time he was so deeply in debt that he sold licenses and set royalties for vulcanization at absurdly low prices. Goodyear saw many applications for vulcanized rubber (with the notable exception of tires) and won acclaim for his work at international exhibitions in 1851 and 1855, but he never escaped poverty during his lifetime.

See Also: Industrial Revolution; Invention; Science.

■ **GORE, ALBERT (1947-),** U.S. vice president (1993-). The son of Tennessee congressman and senator Albert Gore, he was born in Washington, D.C. After graduating from Harvard (1969) and military service in Vietnam, Gore worked as a newspaper reporter for the Nashville, Tennessee, *Tennessean.* He was elected to the U.S. House of Representatives in 1976 and the Senate in 1984. After seeking the Democratic nomination for president in 1988, he was chosen to run for vice president in 1992 with Gov. Bill Clinton of neighboring Arkansas. Running as moderate "new Democrats," the two Southerners were elected with 43.2 percent of the popular vote. Although he was the author of a best-selling book on the global environment, Gore devoted most of his energies as vice president to advocating efficiency reforms in the federal government and promoting the communications "information superhighway."

See Also: Vice President of the United States.

BIBLIOGRAPHY: Gore, Albert, *Earth in the Balance* (Houghton Mifflin 1992).

■ **GORGAS, WILLIAM CRAWFORD (1854-1920),** sanitary physician. Born near Mobile, Alabama, Gorgas earned a medical degree at Bellevue Hospital Medical College (1879) and joined the Army Medical Corps (1880). He survived an attack of yellow fever at Fort Brown, Texas, and so was placed because of his immunity in charge of a yellow fever camp in Cuba during the Spanish-American War (1898), soon becoming chief sanitary officer of Havana. Gorgas's efforts at ridding the city of disease failed until Walter Reed and his group proved that yellow fever was carried by mosquitoes; Gorgas then destroyed mosquito breeding grounds and cleaned up Havana. Gorgas and his staff were then transferred to the Panama Canal Zone in 1904. The American Canal Commission and the chief engineer, George Goethals, worried little about sanitation, but Pres. Theodore Roosevelt pledged his full support, and Gorgas lessened workers' health risks considerably. He went on to make the cities of Colón and Panama models of sanitation and came to be regarded as the foremost sanitary expert in the world. Gorgas was appointed surgeon general in 1914, retiring in 1918 after service in World War I.

See Also: Disease; Medicine; Panama Canal; Science.

■ **GORGES, SIR FERDINANDO (c. 1566-1647),** English promoter of New England colonization. Gorges received a royal charter in 1620 for the Council for New England. The Crown granted the council rights to issue land grants to North American territory between 40 and 48 degrees north latitude. Under Gorges's direction, the council helped to establish New England colonies. Gorges's land grants, however, overlapped with other charters. Gorges was granted the province of Maine in 1639 and later named its lord proprietor. He never set foot in New England.

See Also: Exploration and Discovery.

■ **GOSPEL MUSIC,** African-American religious art form. Slaves found salvation and spiritual uplift in religious beliefs based on literal interpretations of the Bible, specifically of the Gospels. These beliefs, along with the Nonconformist hymns of Englishman Thomas Watts and an African musical and cultural heritage, laid the foundation for gospel songs, or spirituals. The hopeful power of this music acquired even greater significance when, during the 19th century, Southern slaves escaped to the North and immortalized such songs as "Going to the Promised Land."

After emancipation, gospel music expanded to both non-African-American and non-American audiences through the help of the commercialized tours of the Fisk Jubilee Singers. True gospel music, however, was still the province of African-American churches and communities. During the 1930s

church recordings began to professionalize the genre, as performers such as Thomas A. Dorsey and Mahalia Jackson promoted gospel music as a form of secular entertainment as well as religious music.

Associated by some with jazz during the 1930s, gospel music earned its own prominence in the 1940s through the rise of radio programs and specialist groups. In the post–World War II years popular gospel artists, such as Aretha Franklin, emerged from religious backgrounds to broaden the appeal of their music, with the more commercialized brand developing into soul. Although gospel is a popular musical style performed by some white artists, its strong religious influence still emanates from African-American churches.

See Also: Franklin, Aretha; Jackson, Mahalia.

BIBLIOGRAPHY: Harris, Michael W., *The Rise of the Gospel Blues: The Music of Thomas Dorsey in the Urban Church* (Oxford Univ. Press 1992); Walker, Wyatt Tee, *"Somebody's Calling My Name": Black Sacred Music and Social Change* (Judson Press 1979).

■ **GOTTSCHALK, LOUIS (1829-69),** pianist and composer. A musical prodigy born in New Orleans, Louisiana, the handsome and sophisticated Gottschalk was the nation's first great concert artist. He studied in Europe under Frédéric Chopin and Hector Berlioz then toured the United States, Europe, and South America to great acclaim. He drew on popular tunes in his most successful piano compositions, such as "The Union" and "The Dying Poet."

■ **GOULD, JAY (1836-92),** railroad director and financier. He was born in Roxbury, New York. He opened a tannery in Pennsylvania in 1856, allegedly using his co-investor's profits as well as his own to buy a bankrupt railroad, which he then sold at a substantial profit. Several more similar buyouts enabled Gould to open his own New York brokerage house on the eve of the American Civil War. He entered into a successful stock war with Cornelius Vanderbilt for control of the Erie Railroad, becoming president of the line in 1868. A year later, he was part of an effort to corner the gold market that caused a severe, nationwide financial panic (Sept. 24, 1869). In the 1870s Gould gained control of several western railroads, including the Union Pacific, ruthlessly blocking the workers' efforts to unionize. He also owned a newspaper, the *New York World*, and the Western Union Telegraph Company. During his life, Gould was one of the nation's most vilified businessmen, a symbol of the speculative greed that many saw as endemic in the Gilded Age.

See Also: *Gilded Age; Railroads; Vanderbilt, Cornelius.*

BIBLIOGRAPHY: Klein, Maury, *The Life and Legend of Jay Gould* (Johns Hopkins Univ. Press 1986).

■ **GO WEST, YOUNG MAN,** phrase coined in the 1840s by newspaper editor Horace Greeley. The editor of the *New York Tribune*, Greeley wrote editorials espousing free western land for settlers. His advice was to "Go west, young man, and grow up with the country."

See Also: *Frontier in American History; Greeley, Horace.*

■ **GRAHAM, BILLY (WILLIAM FRANKLIN GRAHAM) (1918-),** evangelist. Born near Charlotte, North Carolina, Graham experienced a religious conversion during a revival in 1934 that shaped the rest of his life. He attended Bob Jones University and transferred to Florida Bible Institute, where he became a Southern Baptist and developed a persuasive preaching style. After graduation from Wheaton College, he became pastor of a small church in Chicago, began a weekly radio program, and in 1946 became an evangelist for Youth for Christ. Graham's Los Angeles crusade in 1949, with the aid of William Randolph Hearst, who told his newspapers to "puff Graham," brought him to national attention. In 1950 he founded the Billy Graham Evangelical Association, which provides a comprehensive program for converts, produces radio and television shows, operates a publishing enterprise, and oversees Graham's international crusades. Throughout his life, Graham has cooperated with mainstream Protestants and refused to be sectarian, which has caused many fundamentalists to label him a liberal even though he preaches the tenets of evangelicalism—the necessity of a spiritual rebirth and the imminent apocalypse. Graham's friendships with American presidents have placed him in the political arena, but he avoids taking stands on specific issues. Graham preaches a simple message: repent, accept Christ as your savior, and you will be saved.

See Also: *Religion.*

■ **GRAHAM, MARTHA (1895-1991),** dancer and choreographer, one of the most influential figures in modern dance. Born in Pittsburgh, Pennsylvania, she formed her own company in 1928 and began touring in 1939. Her stark and angular choreography was marked by technical precision and intense emotional expression. She developed historical, mythological, and psychoanalytic themes in dances such as *Primitive Mysteries* (1931), *Cave of the Heart* (1946), and *Archaic Hours* (1969).

See Also: *Women in American History.*

In 1928, Martha Graham founded in New York City what would become known a decade later as her School of Contemporary Dance.

■ **GRAND ARMY OF THE REPUBLIC,** organization of Union Civil War veterans. Founded in 1866 by Benjamin F. Stephenson, an Illinois former army surgeon, the Grand Army of the Republic became a powerful interest group closely tied to the Republican party. In the 1880s it had a membership of more than 800,000 and was influential in persuading Congress to pass the 1890 Disability Pension Act. Its last member died in 1956.

See Also: Civil War.

■ **GRAND BANKS,** broad shelf under the Atlantic Ocean southeast of Newfoundland, Canada. An extension of the North American continent, the 36,000-square-mile area attracts large numbers of fish because of the confluence of the cold Labrador Current and the warm Gulf Stream. Viking fishing expeditions ventured into the area as early as A.D. 1000. The Grand Banks were reported to Europeans by John Cabot in 1497. The French heavily fished the area in the 16th century.

■ **GRAND CANYON,** great gorge of the Colorado River in Arizona, a 217-mile-long chasm that is some 4 to 18 miles wide and 1 mile deep. Indians have lived for centuries in the area and more than 500 ancient pueblo sites have been identified along the lower canyon walls. John Wesley Powell provided detailed reports on the canyon during his 1869 boat trip down the Colorado River. In 1901 the Santa Fe Railroad built a line to the canyon and sought to capitalize on the scenery. In 1919 Congress created the 674,000-acre Grand Canyon National Park.

■ **GRANDFATHER CLAUSE,** a controversial loophole within the post-Reconstruction state constitutions of the South. Beginning in 1890 in Mississippi, southern states began passing state constitutions that effectively disfranchised most African-American males through such devices as poll taxes, literacy tests, and property requirements. Because many of these voting qualifications could potentially disfranchise poor whites as well, certain clauses were added to maintain the color line. The grandfather clause stated that only a man whose grandfather had been a registered voter could himself register to vote. Because in the 1890s the grandfathers of most southern blacks had been slaves, and therefore ineligible to vote, their grandsons also would be ineligible to vote. In 1898 the U.S. Supreme Court found that the grandfather clause was constitutional as it was not "on [its] face" discriminatory against blacks.

See Also: Reconstruction.

BIBLIOGRAPHY: Painter, Nell Irvin, *Standing at Armageddon: The United States, 1877-1919* (Norton 1987).

■ **GRANGE, RED (1903-91),** football player. A star halfback for the University of Illinois (1923-25) and the professional Chicago Bears (1925-33), he was the most famous football player of the 1920s. Born in Forkville, Pennsylvania, Grange was known as the Galloping Ghost for his speed and elusiveness. When he joined the Bears, thousands paid to see him play, and this helped establish the National Football League as a major sports attraction.

See Also: Football; Sports.

■ **GRANGER MOVEMENT,** organization for farmers, founded by Oliver Hudson Kelley in 1867 and officially known as the National Grange of the Patrons of Husbandry. Although the Grange began as a ritualistic, secret order that was focused on self-help and education, it became increasingly politicized in response to the difficulties faced by family farmers in the post–Civil War era. Seeing themselves as victimized by the undue economic influence wielded by railroads, merchants, and banks, Grangers persuaded the legislatures of Illinois, Iowa, Wisconsin, and Minnesota to pass the so-called Granger Laws. These statutes, enacted between 1869 and 1874, set the maximum rate that railroads and grain elevators within these states could charge. The affected companies bitterly contested the new laws, but in a series of decisions in 1877 (the best known being *Munn v. Illinois*) the U.S. Supreme Court ruled that such price regulation was constitutional, thus confirming one of the Grange's key assertions: that businesses of a public nature could be subjected to state oversight.

See Also: Agriculture; Munn v. Illinois.

■ **GRANT, ULYSSES SIMPSON (1822-85),** commanding general of the U.S. Army and 18th president of the United States (1869-77). He was born Hiram Ulysses Grant in Point Pleasant, Ohio, and

A weary Gen. Ulysses S. Grant rests after the Battle of Cold Harbor, Virginia, in 1864.

attended the U.S. Military Academy at West Point, graduating in 1843 (it was upon appointment to West Point that his name was mistakenly changed to include his mother's maiden name, Simpson). Lieutenant Grant earned a commendable record in the Mexican War (1846-48), gaining promotion to captain. Subsequently, heavy drinking forced him to resign from the army in 1854. Moving to St. Louis, Missouri, he tried several enterprises; none was successful. In 1860, he became a clerk in his father's leather-goods store in Galena, Illinois.

Civil War Leadership. Upon the outbreak of the Civil War in 1861, Grant received a volunteer colonel's commission. In a succession of assignments, he learned the responsibilities of command. Victories in northwestern Tennessee at Forts Henry and Donelson in February 1862 brought Grant promotion to major general of volunteers and propelled him to public attention when journalists matched his initials with his demand for the forts' "Unconditional Surrender." Grant conducted a campaign through Tennessee, winning a controversial battle at Shiloh on Apr. 6-7, 1862. He demonstrated the hallmarks of his generalship: determination, coolheadedness under pressure, and excellent use of all military resources under his control. When critics called for Grant's removal due to his missteps at Shiloh, Pres. Abraham Lincoln supported him, saying, "I can't spare this man; he fights."

Grant next moved to capture the Confederate fortified city of Vicksburg, Mississippi. After a grueling campaign, Grant obtained Vicksburg's surrender on July 4, 1863. The victory helped give the Union control of the Mississippi River, one of the North's strategic goals. Grant was promoted to major general in the regular army and directed a campaign that took the railroad center of Chattanooga, Tennessee, on Nov. 25, 1863.

President Lincoln called for Grant's promotion to lieutenant general and designated him to be commander of all Union armies. Formulating strategy for several offensives, Grant shifted to the east. In a series of hard battles in the spring and summer of 1864, Grant's Union forces hammered Gen. Robert E. Lee's Army of Northern Virginia mile by mile back to Richmond. At every turn, Grant sought a breakthrough. Union losses were heavy and controversial, but by autumn, Grant's armies began to ring Richmond, trapping Lee's Confederates. In April 1865, Lee broke out of the Richmond defenses, endeavoring to join a Confederate army in North Carolina. Grant's soldiers cut off Lee's line of escape and forced Lee to surrender at Appomattox Courthouse, Virginia, on April 9. Grant's strategic management of multiple armies and handling of logistics marked him as a great general.

Presidency. Nominated by the Republicans, Grant won the presidential election of 1868 over Democratic candidate Horatio Seymour. He was reelected in 1872 over Democrat Horace Greeley. President Grant faced several difficult issues: French intervention in Mexico, Indian wars in the West, the growing influence of big businesses, and federal

monetary policy. Most important was Reconstruction—rebuilding the war-damaged South and determining the role of African Americans in U.S. society. Grant's use of the army and federal marshals to assist African Americans and Republicans in the South generated more controversies. Several scandals rocked the government in Grant's second term. Despite the scandals, he still maintained remarkable personal popularity when he left office in 1877.

Later Years. Financially destitute by 1884, Grant agreed to write a magazine article about his Civil War experiences. So favorable was the response to this undertaking that his friend Mark Twain encouraged him to compile his memoirs into one significant work. The result, written during Grant's painful battle with throat cancer, was the two-volume *Personal Memoirs of U.S. Grant*, completed just days before his death on July 23, 1885, at Mount McGregor, New York. Published in 1885-86 by Twain, these memoirs not only bestowed financial security on Grant's heirs, they also earned a place among the most revered American autobiographies.

—JOSEPH G. DAWSON III

See Also: Appomattox Courthouse; Civil War; Presidential Elections; President of the United States; Reconstruction; Shiloh, Battle of.

BIBLIOGRAPHY: Catton, Bruce, *Grant Moves South* (Little, Brown 1960); Catton, Bruce, *Grant Takes Command* (Little, Brown 1968); McFeely, William, *Grant: A Biography* (Norton 1981).

■ **GRAU, SHIRLEY ANN (1929-),** novelist and short story writer. She was born in New Orleans, Louisiana. Her short stories, in collections such as *The Black Prince and Other Stories* (1955), have been described as "American gothic." Her novel *The Keepers of the House* (1965) won a Pulitzer Prize. Other works include *The Hard Blue Sky* (1958), *Evidence of Love* (1977), and *Nine Women* (1986).

See Also: Novel; Women in American History.

■ **GRAY, ASA (1810-88),** botanist. Born in Sauquoit, New York, Gray professionalized and popularized botany. He taught high school science and made botanical expeditions before joining friend and fellow botanist John Torrey in New York in 1836, the year he published *Elements of Botany*. Gray and Torrey were the first to replace the classic Linnaean system of plant classification with a more natural one, and together they wrote *The Flora of North America* (1838, 1843). In 1842, Gray accepted a professorship at Harvard (1843-73). Gray was a friend of Charles Darwin, who first outlined his theory of evolution in a letter to Gray (1857). Gray became one of Darwin's most ardent advocates. Although he argued with Harvard colleague Louis Agassiz, Gray maintained that Darwin's ideas could coexist with Protestant Christianity.

See Also: Agassiz, Louis; Science.

■ **GRAY, HORACE (1828-1902),** associate justice of the U.S. Supreme Court (1881-1902). Born in Boston, Gray frequently dissented and often clashed with Chief Justice Melville Fuller, as in *Bowman* v. *Chicago and North Western Railroad* (1888), where Gray argued for a broad interpretation of the states' police power.

See Also: Fuller, Melville Weston; Supreme Court.

■ **GREAT AMERICAN DESERT,** early-19th-century appellation given to the region of the central United States between the 95th meridian and the Rocky Mountains. Based on Zebulon Pike's (1806) and Stephen Long's (1820) explorations, pre–Civil War Americans understood the area to be an uninhabitable, dry wasteland to be quickly crossed on the way to Oregon or California. The Homestead Act of 1862 and land boosters encouraged American settlement of the area, which became more popularly known as the Great Plains. Ranchers and farmers soon moved onto the land. The severe drought of the 1930s forced many farmers out of the area. The migrations out of the so-called Dust Bowl are heroically fictionalized in John Steinbeck's *Grapes of Wrath* (1939).

See Also: Dust Bowl.

■ **GREAT AWAKENING,** revivalist waves of religious enthusiasm that spread over the American colonies in the 18th century. The excitement varied in intensity and duration from one area to another, the most concentrated expression of the movement being in New England in 1740-42.

In the middle and southern colonies the revivals did not have as clear a definition either in time or space as in New England. This indefinite character has led a few scholars to question whether the Great Awakening refers more to an "interpretive fiction" than to a historical reality. Whatever the case, revivalism occurred in all of the colonies, most of it identified, at least initially, with the name of George Whitefield.

Whitefield, a young Anglican orator at the time of his first visit from England to America in 1738, journeyed through literally all the colonies calling for repentance and a confession of faith in a newly appropriated savior, Jesus Christ. Soon crowds were pressing him, anxiously asking, "What must I do to be saved?" In his several missionary tours up and down the Atlantic coast, Whitefield drew enormous crowds, often so large that he had to preach out in the fields or on the commons.

Although an Anglican, Whitefield reached far beyond the Church of England; his eager listeners included Congregationalists, Presbyterians, Baptists, members of the Dutch and German Reformed churches, and others. He also appealed to both males and females, black and white, literate and illiterate. He affected those already pious as well as those who, like Benjamin Franklin, took their theology lightly.

Other itinerant, or traveling, revivalists preached in imitation of Whitefield wherever an audience could be found, often arousing considerable resentment among the local clergy. In fact, the Awakening, while promoting the cause of religion generally, sharply divided prorevivalists from antirevivalists, a division that had major consequences in politics, higher education, and denominational life.

—EDWIN S. GAUSTAD

See Also: Religion; Whitefield, George.

BIBLIOGRAPHY: Gaustad, Edwin S., *The Great Awakening in New England* (Harper 1957); Lovejoy, David S., *Religious Enthusiasm and the Great Awakening* (Prentice-Hall 1969); Whitefield, George, *Whitefield's Journals* (Banner of Truth Trust 1965).

■ **GREAT BASIN,** large arid swath of land in the western United States. Equally divided between mountains and valleys, the basin occupies nearly 200,000 square miles in Nevada, western Utah, and eastern California. For 19th-century travelers, the scarcity of fresh water and the hot weather impeded travel across the area to California. The Mormons, following Brigham Young, arrived in the Salt Lake valley in July 1847 and began irrigating the dry lands of the basin. In the 20th century the U.S. government has continued the irrigation of the area with numerous hydroelectric dams.

■ **GREAT BASIN AND ROCKY MOUNTAIN INDIANS,** inhabit one of the most difficult subsistence environments in North America. The Great Basin culture area includes all of Utah and Nevada and the bordering margins of Idaho, Oregon, California, Arizona, New Mexico, Colorado, and Wyoming. It is characterized by an arid basin and range topography with few rivers, interior drainage, and extremes in seasonal climates.

Archaeological evidence suggests continuous habitation of the region for more than 10,000 years, from the prehistoric Desert culture, to Fremont and Anasazi agriculturists (A.D. 400-1400), to the historic Numic (Shoshonean) speakers of the Uto-Aztecan language family. These include the Ute, Bannock, Northern and Eastern Shoshone, southern Paiute, Owens Valley Paiute, and Kawaiisu, as well as the Hokan-speaking Washoe.

Basin Indians traveled widely in small foraging groups—sometimes representing only a single family—rarely congregating for any length of time. Population densities as low as 1 person per 50 square miles reflect the seasonal scarcity and scattered nature of food sources. They utilized a wide variety of roots, berries, grass seeds, pine nuts, insects, reptiles, fish and waterfowl, rodents, rabbits, and the occasional antelope, deer, and desert sheep. Most groups constructed temporary brush shelters (wickiups), made fine baskets and leather bags, and wore little clothing beyond rabbit-skin blankets in winter.

Politically there was little or no tribal identity. Band recognition rested on shared language, custom, territorial use, and intermarriage, but even band-level activity was limited. Leadership was informal, based on consensus and recognized ability. There were few formal religious ceremonies beyond the belief in a supernatural puha or puwa ("power") that exists in all creation and can be focused for healing.

In the Rocky Mountain area, Indians adopted more Plains cultural features, including larger band congregations, more reliance on big game including bison for food and materials, and the horse. Ute and Shoshone became important bro-

kers in the horse trade connecting the Southwest with the northern Plains and Plateau.

Earliest Numic-European contact occurred in the mid-1700s as Spaniards searched for a land route between Santa Fe and California. In the eastern Basin, Ute became involved in a trading-raiding relationship with the Spanish, helping them fight Apache and Comanche and furnishing the Spanish with native slaves in exchange for horses. The Spanish made few settlement inroads, but trade goods and epidemic disease spread into the Great Basin.

By the 1810s free trappers out of New Mexico and companies of Northwest Fur Company trappers out of Montana opened up an active fur trade throughout the region. The pace of contact increased between 1840 and 1860, when westering American settlers and miners began competing with Numic Indians for scarce subsistence resources. Whites derogatorily called them "diggers" or "snakes," justifying Indian extermination. The U.S. government negotiated treaties and set aside small reservations for most Numic groups in the 1860s but failed to transform them into self-sufficient farmers. Allotment and federal withdrawal of lands from native control deepened their dependency. Out of this reservation situation emerged a Northern Paiute prophet named Wovoka, who disseminated the Ghost Dance religion, precipitating widespread Indian resistance culminating in the 1890 Wounded Knee massacre.

After a dismal beginning, the 20th century witnessed the political rebirth of Great Basin and Rocky Mountain Indians, from their reorganization as tribal entities in the 1930s to the claims case settlements of the 1950s-70s. While many social and economic problems remain, these tribes are taking charge of their resources and working to renew their group identity and sovereignty.

—DAVID RICH LEWIS

See Also: *Ghost Dance; Indians of North America; Wounded Knee Massacre.*

BIBLIOGRAPHY: Sturtevant, William C., ed., *Handbook of North American Indians,* vol. 11, *Great Basin,* ed. by Warren L. D'Azevedo (Smithsonian Inst. Press 1986).

■ **GREAT DEPRESSION,** economic downturn that began in 1929 and lasted until America entered

World War II (1941). The Great Depression was a transforming event in American history that altered society, politics, and culture. In the midst of a catastrophic economic collapse, Americans responded to the crisis in ways unique to a regulated market-economy, a federal political system, and a singular democratic culture. The Depression shook American confidence; led to a restructuring of the American economy; instituted new relations between government, business, and labor; and strengthened federal involvement in the economy and social welfare.

Roots of the Crisis. The immediate causes of the Great Depression in the United States are found in the stock market crash of 1929. During the 1920s, rampant stock speculation, fueled by low interest rates and by the widespread practice of buying on margin, shifted investment away from technology and capital improvements and into Wall Street. Stock prices rose to artificially high levels as huge investment companies issued more and more stock, further inflating security prices.

The world economy was already weakened by a surplus of agricultural products, by the withdrawal of British financial investment after World War I, and by the inability of primary producing nations to compete on the global market. Republican trade policy of high protective tariffs hindered nations from selling their goods in the large American market, thus further weakening their economies.

In the boom years of the 1920s, few worried that the bubble might burst as Americans enjoyed unrivaled prosperity. During the Harding-Coolidge years (1921-29), the gross domestic product rose 40 percent, per capita income rose 30 percent, and industrial production climbed 70 percent. Unemployment remained low and prices were stable. As a result, real earnings increased 22 percent for the average American worker. In these heady days, American consumers went on a buying binge. By 1929, 60 percent of all families owned a car. The extension of consumer credit allowed American families to buy new homes, automobiles, and appliances.

Few seemed to notice that not all was well. Many workers experienced sporadic unemployment because of seasonal layoffs. Agriculture did not prosper, nor did many "sick" industries, including cotton textiles, railroads, and coal mining. Although citrus farmers did well, most farmers faced declining prices for their crops because of declining European markets and new competition from abroad. By 1929, the average per capita income for farmers stood at approximately $220, compared to $879 for the nonfarm population.

Meanwhile, the stock market continued to boom despite a minor downturn in the early part of the decade. The Republican administration encouraged stock market speculation by maintaining low interest rates, which allowed speculators to borrow money to purchase stocks. This boom on Wall Street coincided with an intensive merger movement that brought even more stock issues

During the Great Depression, many farmers of the Oklahoma and Texas panhandles and the surrounding Dust Bowl areas were forced to abandon their farms.

on the market, especially in utilities, food processing, and retailing. The emergence of vast investment holding companies fueled an already explosive situation. By issuing millions of dollars worth of stock, investment houses built huge paper pyramids that appeared attractive from the outside but were structurally flimsy.

Collapse and Depression. The edifice collapsed in October 1929. Signs of trouble were evident earlier in the summer of 1929, when industrial production went into a slump, although the stock market appeared strong. By the fall, however, the market began to wobble. On Thursday, Oct. 24, the market fell into complete disorder with an unprecedented 12.9 million shares trading hands. Leading New York financiers stepped in to calm fears, but the following Tuesday, Oct. 29, 1929, the market collapsed. In what became known as "Black Tuesday," stock prices fell 43 points, more than 10 percent in a single day. Investment houses, brokers, and small investors were devastated, as tens of thousands of accounts were wiped out.

The most singular feature of the crash was that the economic decline continued. Industrial production fell to nearly half of what it had been. The Federal Reserve Bank's policy of shrinking the money supply, exactly at the moment when additional liquidity was needed, worsened the crisis. Declining consumer demand led to increased layoffs. By 1932, an estimated 13 million to 17 million workers, about one-quarter of the labor force, were unemployed. These layoffs particularly affected young, unskilled workers and older workers with uneven work histories or inadequate skills. Unable to find regular jobs, casual work, or even relief, the unemployed became desperate. Nearly 2 million young men (and a few women) took to the railroads and highways as tramps. The homeless gathered in makeshift camps that sprang up on the outskirts of towns. These rough settlements of primitive tar and paper shacks were sardonically called Hoovervilles, after the incumbent Republican president, Herbert Hoover.

To make matters worse, private and local government charities soon exhausted their relief funds under the weight of the large numbers of people seeking aid. More than half the families on unemployment relief were located in eight states,

and more than one-third were in four highly industrialized states: Pennsylvania, New York, Ohio, and Illinois. An estimated 40 percent of all people on relief were children. Still, overall exact numbers remained unknown because the federal government never tried to collect unemployment statistics. The Depression devastated the United States. Hamburgers sold two for 5 cents, but people could not afford to buy them; men and women worked for only 10 cents an hour, yet businesses seemed unable to make a profit; interest rates fell to below 1 percent, but few were willing to invest; farmers allowed their crops to rot in the field, while people went hungry.

Roosevelt and the New Deal. The election of Democrat Franklin D. Roosevelt as president in 1932 promised a return to prosperity through extensive agricultural and industrial recovery programs, as well as work and relief programs targeted at the unemployed. In the first hundred days of his administration, Roosevelt pushed through numerous legislative measures that sought to stimulate the economy. Along with strengthening the powers of the Federal Reserve Bank, the administration also took the United States off the domestic gold standard, a major shift in monetary policy.

During this time, the federal government entered directly into government ownership of public utilities through the Tennessee Valley Authority (TVA). The TVA experiment was unusual, however. The government policy toward concentrated power wavered between accommodation with corporate leaders in the interest of preserving capitalism through economic regulation and attempts by public officials to restore the market through antitrust activities. For a brief period, the economy looked like it was on the rebound. The gross national product rose from $56 billion in 1933 to $72 billion in 1935. Wholesale prices jumped a third.

At the same time, federal budget deficits funded work projects and relief efforts. For the first four years of the Roosevelt administration, the budget deficit was $3.6 billion in 1934, $2.8 billion in 1935, $4.4 billion in 1936, and $2.8 billion in 1937. During this same period the total deficit never exceeded $8.5 billion in any one year. As a result, budget deficits accounted for 46 percent of

Soup kitchens, such as this one in New York City's Bowery, provided relief to many during the Great Depression.

all federal expenditures during Roosevelt's first term. While unemployment continued to run high, many Americans felt that the worst was behind them.

Abroad, Roosevelt pursued a cautious policy of negotiating reciprocal trade agreements with trading partners while maintaining a protectionist policy toward trade rivals. In 1934, the Export-Import Bank was established to help stabilize the currencies of South American trading partners. This willingness to stabilize Latin American currencies, however, contrasted sharply with the administration's refusal to participate in European monetary stabilization. As a result, U.S. exports to Latin America rose more than 14 percent during this decade. The American economy appeared to be on a rebound by 1936.

Recession and War in the Late 1930s. Then, disaster struck in late 1937. Just as the federal budget appeared to be nearing balance, unemployment was falling, and industrial production rising, the economy went into another tailspin.

Later, critics blamed the administration's budget cuts, combined with increased tax hikes for the newly implemented Social Security system, but regional disparities in economic development also accounted for the weakness of the economy. Whatever the specific causes of the recession, the rapid decline in income and production in the nine months from September 1937 to June 1938 was without precedent in American history.

The federal government took the offensive once again. Rejecting fiscal conservatism, Roosevelt turned to a group of young economists (followers of English economist John Maynard Keynes) who urged the government to undertake a deliberate policy of deficit spending during economic slumps. Upon their advice, Roosevelt proposed a $4.5 million package to finance a public housing and highway construction program. A new farming bill, the Agricultural Adjustment Act (1937), allowed government not to plant crops in order to raise agricultural prices. Legislation was enacted to set minimum wages and maximum hours for the nation's workers.

The outbreak of World War II in Europe in 1939 further accelerated Roosevelt's efforts to bolster American industry. As the United States began to rearm and tacitly support England and its democratic allies, the economy slowly began to pull out of the economic doldrums that characterized the decade of the 1930s. The war, which the United States entered in 1941, and its aftermath ushered in a new prosperity and affluence unequaled in world history.

—DONALD T. CRITCHLOW

See Also: Coolidge, (John) Calvin; Federal Reserve System; Hoover, Herbert Clark; Keynes, John Maynard; New Deal; Roosevelt, Franklin Delano; Wall Street.

BIBLIOGRAPHY: Bernstein, Michael A., *The Great Depression: Delayed Recovery and Economic Change in America, 1929-1939* (Cambridge Univ. Press 1987); Brinkley, Alan, *The End of Reform: New Deal Liberalism in Recession and War* (Knopf 1995); Galbraith, John Kenneth, *The Great Crash* (Houghton Mifflin 1960); Gordon, Colin, *New Deals: Business, Labor and Politics in America, 1920-1935* (Cambridge Univ. Press 1994); Kindleberger, Charles, *The World in Depression, 1929-1939* (Univ. of California Press 1973); Nash, Gerald, *The Great Depression and World War II* (St. Martin's 1984); Stoneman, William E., *A History of Economic Analysis of the Great Depression in America* (Garland 1979).

■ **GREAT DISMAL SWAMP,** immense swamp in North Carolina and Virginia, some 400 square miles located between the Chesapeake Bay and Albemarle Sound. Known since earliest colonial times, it was surveyed and named by William Byrd in 1728. Colonial farmers fought to turn the swamp into productive farmland. George Washington, who owned 4,000 acres of the swamp, had his slaves build drainage canals in 1763 to transform the land. The Dismal Swamp Canal, begun in 1787 and finished in 1848, drained off significant amounts of water.

■ **GREAT LAKES,** five gigantic lakes in east-central North America. From west to east they are Lakes Superior, Michigan, Huron, Erie, and Ontario. The Great Lakes are the largest freshwater surface in the world and form a natural boundary between the United States and Canada. The Great Lakes region was inhabited primarily by Algonquian-speaking Indians on the west and Iroquois-speaking tribes on the east. In 1608 the French founded Quebec on the St. Lawrence River, which flows from Lake Ontario and is thus connected to the other lakes and to the Mississippi River. The lands of the region were transferred to the English in 1763, and in 1796 the Canada-United States boundary was nearly set. Under the Ordinance of 1787 the region around the Great Lakes north and west of the Ohio River was organized as the Northwest Territory, which was free of slavery. In 1825 Lake Erie was linked with the Hudson River by the 363-mile-long Erie Canal. During the 20th century transportation on the lakes has been key to the growth of industrialized cities like Detroit, Chicago, Buffalo, and Toledo.

■ **GREAT PLAINS,** North American grassland region roughly between the Rocky Mountains and the 95th meridian and running from Texas in the south to North Dakota in the north and into Canada. Also called the Great American Desert in the 19th century, this flat and gently rolling area covers roughly a third of the United States. The first explorers saw this vast area, which was occupied by Indians and buffalo, as unsuitable for cultivation or civilization. The term *Great Plains* first came into use in the 1860s, when railroad companies and town boosters wished to erase the persistent and popular "desert" image. In 1862 Congress passed the Homestead Act, which granted 160 acres to anyone who would settle the land for at least five years. This act, as well as the coming of the railroad, brought white settlers to the Plains. During the economic depression of the 1890s the People's party began in the Plains states, with William Jennings Bryan advocating the coinage of silver. During the Great Depression of the 1930s the Plains experienced severe drought and became popularly known as the Dust Bowl. Many Plains farmers went bankrupt and left their farms. In 1931 historian Walter Prescott Webb published his monumental work, *The Great Plains*, in which he argued that the region's unique environment forced settlers to adapt and perfect innovations such as barbed wire, the windmill, and the revolver.

■ **GREAT PLAINS INDIANS.** The Great Plains Indians are divided into two main groups, based on their way of life. First there were the farming peoples of the river valleys, the Arikaras, Mandans, and Hidatsas who built their earth-lodge villages along the upper Missouri in the present-day Dakotas, and the Pawnees, who lived on the Kansas and the Platte. It is probable that their history on the plains goes back many hundreds of years. Then there were the nomadic hunting peoples, the Assiniboines, Crees, Cheyennes, Arapahos, Crows, Sioux, Kiowas, and Comanches. All these tribes were relative newcomers to the Great Plains, arriving during the 18th and 19th centuries. It was the horse, which these peoples obtained from the Spanish settlements of northern New Spain, that permitted them to colonize the arid prairies and become mounted buffalo hunters. The first settlers of the Great Plains during the colonial era were Indians, rather than Europeans, and the mounted Plains Indian, so frequently used as the symbol of native America, was in fact a product of the colonial era.

These two groups—plains farmers and plains nomads—coexisted in an uneasy but essential relationship. The villages became the centers of trade on the plains, where nomads came to trade buffalo robes for corn, as well as for trade goods acquired from European traders. Nomadic hunters could not have existed without the villagers to provide them with these things, but the villages also became targets for raids, creating a long-standing hostility between the two groups. The Pawnees, for example, were inveterate opponents of the Sioux, and during the wars of the mid-19th-century Pawnee warriors served as scouts for American forces.

The nomadic peoples also came into conflict with each other as they colonized the plains. The Crows, formerly associated with groups of Siouan-speaking farming people on the Missouri, broke away from the mother group and took up the nomadic hunting way of life about 1700. Meanwhile the Algonquian-speaking Cheyennes left their farming villages in Minnesota and gradually pushed westward. In present South Dakota and Montana these two groups met headlong in the 18th century, and long before any European or American colonists reached the plains, they

had engaged in generations of warfare. The Cheyennes were being driven westward by a stronger and more populous people, the Lakota Sioux. The Lakota had practiced hunting, gathering, and a little farming in Minnesota, but as French traders pushed beyond the Great Lakes and onto the fringe of the plains, their allies the Crees and Ojibwas went to war against the Lakotas, pushing them out of their traditional homeland and westward. By the late 18th century the Lakotas had become the most powerful mounted group on the northern plains.

The masters of the southern plains were the Comanches. These people were cousins of the Shoshones and their original homeland was in the Great Basin. But adopting the horse they gradually migrated onto the plains, moving southeastward toward the area of present-day Kansas, Oklahoma, and Texas. The Comanches demonstrated the enormous range of these mounted nomads, circulating with a territory that was 500 to 700 miles in diameter, raiding village peoples from the Mississippi all the way to the Pueblo towns of the Rio Grande.

These nomadic hunting cultures shared some broad patterns in common. All of them used the portable teepee, housing that could be rolled up and transported easily. They all placed an enormous value on horses, and in what had formerly been egalitarian societies, men who were particularly successful at the hunt began to accumulate large herds of horses. There were wealthy men and poor men in plains culture—it was a world in which talent was rewarded with material plenty and accorded great status. Ironically, the plains peoples were playing out the very values being declared sacred by 18th-century Americans such as Benjamin Franklin. But unlike colonial Americans, the nomads worshiped deities residing in nature and strove for lives in balance with the natural world. The common practice throughout the plains of the Sun Dance ceremony—in which young men tested themselves with rituals of self-torture—symbolized the existence of a common nomadic culture of the plains.

The final decades of the 18th century were the golden age of plains culture. But in the 1780s and again in the 1830s the earth-lodge villagers would be devastated by smallpox epidemics. The nomads were protected somewhat from the spread of disease by the refusal to be concentrated in one spot, but in losing their village trading partners they were forced into dependence upon American traders. The American presence was firmly announced with the Fort Laramie Treaty of 1851, but soon the nomads were embroiled in warfare with the invaders. The worst fighting pitted the Comanches against the Texans; the Cheyennes, Arapahos, and Sioux against American cavalry. For all their mythic fame, the Plains Indian wars lasted for only a quarter-century. It ended with the destruction of the buffalo by hide-traders and the relocation of the nomads to reservations in the 1880s. Created by the reverberating effects of colonization, the colorful mounted culture of the plains had fallen victim to the very same forces.

—JOHN MACK FARAGHER

See Also: *Blackfeet; Crow Indians; Indian Policy; Indians of North America; Mandan; Pawnee; Sand Creek Massacre; Sioux.*

BIBLIOGRAPHY: Andrist, Ralph K., *The Last Days of the Plains Indians* (Collier Books 1993); Ewers, John C., *Plains Indian History and Culture* (Univ. of Oklahoma Press 1997); West, Elliott, *The Way to the West* (Univ. of New Mexico Press 1995).

■ **GREAT SALT LAKE,** largest saline lake in the Western Hemisphere, located in northern Utah. The lake's area fluctuates greatly in size as a result of climate changes and domestic and industrial use of the waters. In 1873 it covered about 2,400 square miles but a century later was only 940 square miles. The lake appeared on 18th-century European maps through reports from explorers and Indian sources. In 1843 and 1845 Capt. John Frémont provided the first descriptions of the lake. In 1847 Mormons, following Brigham Young, settled next to the lake and founded Salt Lake City.

■ **GREAT SMOKY MOUNTAINS,** range of southern Appalachian Mountains on the Tennessee-North Carolina border. They are named for the smoky haze that covers them much of the time. Most of the mountains were included in the Great Smoky Mountains National Park, created in 1926. The park preserves the last remaining southern hardwood forest in the United States. The mountains, noted for their lush vegetation, are a popular spot for tourists drawn by the national park, the Appalachian Trail, and the Blue Ridge Parkway.

See Also: *Appalachian Mountains.*

■ **GREAT SWAMP FIGHT (1675),** major battle in King Philip's War, fought in what is now South Kingstown, Rhode Island. An uneasy peace had prevailed between the Narragansett, the most powerful tribe in southern New England, and the colonists' New England Confederation for decades before the outbreak of conflict, and the Narragansett were not initially combatants in King Philip's War at all. However, when they refused to turn over Wampanoag warriors who sought refuge in their territory to the Confederation authorities, the Confederation on December 19 sent a force of more than 1,100 men to attack their fortified village in the Great Swamp. The initial assault was repulsed by musket fire, but soon the Confederation force prevailed, and soldiers began to set fire to the Indian wigwams inside the village perimeter. Somewhere between 500 and 1,000 Narragansett perished, many of them women and children. About 20 Confederation troops died in the fighting, and 200 were wounded, perhaps 60 fatally so. The Narragansetts fled their traditional territory and continued to fight sporadically, but they never regained their previous strength and power.

See Also: *King Philip's War.*

■ **GREELEY, HORACE (1811-72),** journalist and political leader. Greeley was born in Amherst, New Hampshire, and moved to New York City in 1831. He founded the first penny newspaper, the *New Yorker*, with Jonas Winchester in 1834 and wrote for a variety of Whig newspapers, such as the *Daily Whig*, the *Jeffersonian*, and the *Log Cabin*. He founded the *New York Tribune* in 1841. The *Tribune* in particular brought Greeley's editorial voice to Northern readers. Greeley was a supporter of trade unions and served as the first president of the New York Printers' Union in 1850. He advocated the free soil movement, abolitionism, and the sanctity of the Union but after the Civil War took the unpopular position of supporting Jefferson Davis's right to a fair trial and signed a bail bond to get him out of jail. Nonetheless Greeley was nominated for president in 1872, first by the Liberal Republicans and then by the Democrats. He lost to Pres. Ulysses S. Grant. Greeley is best remembered for his piece of advice to Josiah Bushnell Grinnell, "Go west, young man, and grow up with the country."

■ **GREENBACK LABOR PARTY,** a third party formed in 1878. Representing the interests of labor and farmers suffering from the continued effects of the depression of 1873, the party called for currency reform, a shorter work day, and restriction of Chinese immigration. It sent 14 representatives to Congress its first year but declined thereafter.

See Also: Labor Movement; Political Parties.

■ **GREENBACKS,** paper money issued by the federal government, so named because of its green color. The U.S. government first printed greenbacks in 1862 when Congress authorized $450 million of paper notes to help meet Union expenses during the Civil War. Unlike "hard" currency supported by gold or silver reserves, greenbacks gained their value only through confidence in the issuing institution. They saw the Union through its financial crisis without losing much value, but how to retire them after the war and to what extent became a contested issue. Many farmers and workers with heavy debts worried that this action would cause deflation and force them to repay their debts with more valuable money. In response, they formed the Greenback party, which became part of the Greenback Labor party in 1878.

■ **GREENE, NATHANAEL (1742-86),** Revolutionary War general. Greene was born in Warwick, Rhode Island, to a Quaker family. Despite his Quaker background, Greene did not hesitate to join American military forces in the armed conflict against Britain. In May 1775 the Rhode Island Assembly placed him in command of the state's Army of Observation at the siege of Boston. In June 1775 he was appointed a brigadier general in the Continental army, and he was promoted to major general in August 1776. From 1778 to 1780, Greene served as quartermaster general for the Continental army. Despite the improvements he made in this department, his relations with Congress became increasingly acrimonious. In defiance of Congress, Greene resigned this post in

During the American Revolution, Nathanael Greene served under George Washington before being given a separate command in the south, where he was very successful.

1780. In October 1780 he was appointed commander of the Southern Department of the Continental army, where he faced the task of regrouping American forces after their devastating defeat at Camden, South Carolina. Greene successfully pursued a policy of strategic retreats combined with quick, repeated attacks against the British, driving them out of most of Georgia and the Carolinas by 1781.

See Also: Guilford Court House, Battle of; Revolution, American.

BIBLIOGRAPHY: Thayer, Theodore, *Nathanael Greene: Strategist of the American Revolution* (Twayne 1960).

■ **GREEN MOUNTAIN BOYS,** armed groups of Vermont settlers formed in 1770 under Ethan Allen. Their purpose was to prevent the "New Hampshire Grants" (as Vermont was then called) from becoming part of New York, to which they had been awarded by the British. Allen, a land speculator, and the Vermont natives organized extralegal militia companies to protect their holdings. They terrorized settlers who accepted New York grants and threatened New York officials who ventured into the region. During the American Revolution, the Green Mountain Boys fought

In defense of their land claims in what is now Vermont, the Green Mountain Boys, with Ethan Allen as their commander, used threats, intimidation, and violence to keep free of New York control. On May 10, 1775, the Green Mountain Boys captured Fort Ticonderoga from the British.

for the patriot cause and helped the colonists capture Fort Ticonderoga (1775) and claim victory at the Battle of Bennington (1777). In the same year, a group of Green Mountain Boys declared Vermont an independent republic. Vermont remained a separate political entity until 1791, when it entered the Union.

See Also: Allen, Ethan; Bennington, Battle of; Revolution, American.

BIBLIOGRAPHY: Bellesiles, Michael A., *Revolutionary Outlaws: Ethan Allen and the Struggle for Independence on the Early American Frontier* (Univ. of Virginia Press 1993).

■ **GREEN MOUNTAINS,** principal mountain range in Vermont and a northern extension of the Appalachian Mountains. They were a barrier to early settlement but attracted emigrants from New Hampshire in the late 1700s. The resources of the area, especially marble, granite, and timber, were utilized throughout the 19th century. The Green Mountain National Forest was established in 1932 to protect the surviving maple, beech, and birch trees.

See Also: Appalachian Mountains.

■ **GREENOUGH, HORATIO (1805-52),** sculptor. Born in Boston, Massachusetts, Greenough graduated from Harvard University in 1825 and then studied art in Italy. Although he maintained a studio in Florence from 1828 until the year before

his death, he worked on American subjects. In 1832 Greenough was commissioned by the U.S. Congress to cast a statue of George Washington for the rotunda of the Capitol. He also did *The Rescue* for the exterior of the Capitol in 1837.

See Also: Sculpture.

■ **GREENVILLE, TREATY OF (Aug. 3, 1795),** agreement between the United States and the Ohio Valley Confederacy led by the Miami Little Turtle after his defeat at Fallen Timbers. In the treaty, the Indians gave up two-thirds of Ohio and part of Indiana to the United States.

See Also: Fallen Timbers, Battle of; Indians of North America; Little Turtle.

■ **GRENADA INVASION (1983),** intervention ordered by Pres. Ronald Reagan to defend U.S. citizens (mostly medical students) on the Caribbean island, restore order, and halt construction of a new airport. It was called Operation Urgent Fury. As Grenadian Marxist Prime Minister Maurice Bishop's government leaned leftward, the United States feared a network of Soviet-dominated states in the region, including Cuba, Grenada, and Nicaragua. Neighboring governments, including Jamaica and the Dominican Republic, expressed concern over the lack of order on Grenada. Shortly after Bishop was assassinated by party rivals, several Caribbean governments formally asked the United States to intervene and restore order. The invasion, begun on

October 25, arrayed elite American forces and overwhelming firepower against 650 Cuban military construction workers and a tiny and demoralized Grenadian army. The operation suffered from poor interservice communications, and critics faulted the military's obvious desire to throw off the "Vietnam syndrome" and the closely controlled press coverage. From a political-military viewpoint, however, it was a clear success.

BIBLIOGRAPHY: Payne, Anthony, Paul Sutton, and Tony Thorndike, *Grenada: Revolution and Invasion* (St. Martin's Press 1984).

■ **GRENVILLE, GEORGE (1712-70),** British politician. As first lord of the treasury, chancellor of the exchequer, and prime minister, Grenville sought to relieve Britain's financial woes through a series of colonial taxes. Upon introducing the Sugar Act in 1764 and the Stamp Act in 1765, he argued that the colonies should pay for the cost of stationing British troops in America. He was vilified in the colonies and left office during the Stamp Act crisis after quarreling with King George III.

See Also: Revolution, American; Stamp Act.

■ **GRIER, ROBERT COOPER (1794-70),** associate justice of the U.S. Supreme Court (1846-70). A Cumberland County, Pennsylvania, native, Grier joined the majority in the *Dred Scott* case (1857), whose outcome he leaked in advance to Pres.-elect James Buchanan. Grier often objected to the Reconstruction era's expansion of federal authority.

See Also: Dred Scott v. Sandford; Supreme Court.

■ *GRIFFIN V. ILLINOIS* **(1956),** U.S. Supreme Court case that ordered the state of Illinois to provide trial transcripts to indigent defendants and helped establish that poverty could not prevent accused criminals from appealing lower court convictions. *Griffin* was among the first of a series of cases that made up the Supreme Court's "due process revolution" in which it extended federal civil protections to the state courts.

The case involved two convicted armed robbers who asked Illinois authorities to give their court-appointed attorneys transcripts so they could prepare an appeal. The state court refused. The Supreme Court ruled (5-4) that by refusing to provide the transcripts necessary to prepare an adequate appeal Illinois was denying the poor due process and equal protection under the law. States are not constitutionally required to establish a criminal appeals system, Justice Hugo Black wrote, but if such a system exists, the state cannot limit access to appeals to those who can pay for lawyers and transcripts or the Constitution's assurance of a fair trial would be worthless. In *Mayer v. Chicago* (1971) the Court expanded *Griffin* to encompass misdemeanor appeals. In *United States v. MacCollum* (1976), however, the Court ruled requests could be turned down if the appeal was judged to be frivolous.

See Also: Supreme Court.

BIBLIOGRAPHY: Bodenhamer, David J., *Fair Trial: Rights of the Accused in American History* (Oxford Univ. Press 1992).

■ **GRIFFITH, D. W. (1875-1948),** film director. Born in Floydsfork, Kentucky, David Wark Griffith began making films in 1908. He liberated film from stage conventions through the use of closeups and, in *The Birth of a Nation* (1915) and *Intolerance* (1916), created epic sagas that shaped modern

D. W. Griffith, a pioneer in the early history of motion pictures, brought all his talents to the making of his most famous movie, *Birth of a Nation* (1914), a racist defense of white supremacy.

moviemaking. *The Birth of a Nation*, with its bias in favor of the South in the Civil War, triggered protests across the country and helped set the stage for the revival of the Ku Klux Klan in the 1920s.

See Also: *Motion Pictures.*

■ **GRIMKÉ, SARAH MOORE (1792-1873)** and **GRIMKÉ, ANGELINA EMILY (1805-79),** abolitionists and women's rights advocates. Born into the slaveholding Charleston, South Carolina, aristocracy, both sisters questioned the morality of slavery from an early age. Sarah also resented the male-dominated world that prohibited her from pursuing a professional career. In 1821 she joined the Society of Friends and moved to Philadelphia. Angelina became a Quaker seven years later and also journeyed north. By 1835 Angelina openly embraced the abolitionist cause. She wrote a letter of support to the abolitionist crusader William Lloyd Garrison, which he published, without her consent, in his newspaper, the *Liberator*. In 1836, despite pressure from Sarah and Quaker friends who equivocated on the slavery issue, Angelina authored a pam-

A decade before the Seneca Falls Convention, Sarah Grimké published her *Letters on the Equality of the Sexes and the Condition of Woman* (1838). The work established Grimké as one of the nation's pioneer feminists.

In 1838, Angelina Grimké became the first U.S. woman to testify before a legislative body. She presented the Massachusetts state legislature with tens of thousands of antislavery petitions gathered by women.

phlet, *Appeal to the Christian Women of the South*, which encouraged southern women to oppose slavery on moral grounds. Later that year Sarah too joined the antislavery movement, and the sisters commenced a series of lectures throughout the Northeast. Their appearances before audiences of both sexes marked a departure from prescribed gender roles and aroused strong protests from male traditionalists. Sarah responded with a statement of women's rights and responsibilities, *Letters on the Equality of the Sexes and the Condition of Woman* (1838). In May 1838 Angelina married the prominent abolitionist Theodore Dwight Weld. Both sisters contributed research and documentation to Weld's *American Slavery As It Is* (1839). In later years they became less active publicly as their activities were subsumed by Weld's career in education.

—MARTHA J. KING

See Also: *Women in American History; Women's Movement.*

BIBLIOGRAPHY: Birney, Catherine H., *The Grimké Sisters: Sarah and Angelina Grimké* (Lee & Shepard

1885); Lerner, Gerda, *The Grimké Sisters from South Carolina* (Houghton Mifflin 1967); Lumpkin, Katherine De Pre, *The Emancipation of Angelina Grimké* (Univ. of North Carolina Press 1974).

■ **GRISWOLD V. CONNECTICUT (1965),** U.S. Supreme Court case that invalidated a state ban on birth control as violating an implied constitutional right of privacy. A rarely enforced 1879 Connecticut law made it a crime to use any device or medication to prevent conception. When Planned Parenthood of Connecticut challenged the law, two members of the group were convicted for operating a birth control counseling center. The Supreme Court reversed (7-2) the decision on appeal.

The majority held that the 14th Amendment extended fundamental constitutional rights to the states and that those rights extended beyond the ones explicitly listed in the Constitution and Bill of Rights. These "unenumerated" rights included a right to privacy. Justice William O. Douglas suggested that unenumerated rights are logical extensions of the Bill of Rights. Privacy, for example, was implicit in the Fourth Amendment's protection against unreasonable search and seizure. Justice Arthur Goldberg argued more broadly that unenumerated rights evolved from history and tradition and could be incorporated as constitutional protections. Justice Hugo Black warned in dissent that *Griswold*'s creation of a new right was an improper extension of judicial power.

Privacy rights established in *Griswold* were applied in *Roe* v. *Wade* (1973) and have remained a source of continuing controversy as Congress and the courts seek a balance between individual rights and social order.

—TIM ASHWELL

See Also: Birth Control; Due Process of Law; Supreme Court.
BIBLIOGRAPHY: Wawrose, Susan C., *Griswold v. Connecticut: Contraception and the Right of Privacy,* (Franklin Watts 1996).

■ **GROUP THEATER,** a 1930s New York City stage troupe that introduced the Stanislavsky Method to American audiences and specialized in political and social dramas such as Clifford Odets's *Waiting For Lefty* (1935).
See Also: Theater.

■ **GROVE CITY V. BELL (1984),** U.S. Supreme Court case that weakened laws against gender discrimination in education. The Court ruled (6-3) that while Title IX of the Education Act amendments of 1972 barred gender discrimination in schools and colleges receiving federal funds, funding could be denied only to those specific programs that discriminated. The Civil Rights Restoration Act of 1987 overturned *Grove City* and specified that gender discrimination in any school program could lead to a suspension of all federal funding to the school.
See Also: Supreme Court.

■ **GUADALCANAL OFFENSIVE (1942),** first significant World War II U.S. offensive in the Pacific to retake territory conquered by the Japanese. To prevent the Japanese from completing an airfield on Guadalcanal in the Solomon Islands, the U.S. 1st Marine Division was landed on August 7 with little resistance. The Japanese attempted to retake the islands, and a series of fierce land and sea battles continued until February 1943, when the Japanese evacuated their remaining troops.
See Also: World War II.

■ **GUADALUPE HIDALGO, TREATY OF (1848),** treaty that ended the Mexican War. In the treaty, negotiated for the United States by Nicholas Trist, Mexico ceded about 1 million square miles of its northern provinces and accepted the Rio Grande as the U.S.-Mexican border. Mexico received $15 million in compensation. President Polk was outraged that the United States did not receive more land, while Mexicans seethed with resentment at losing almost half of their territory.
See Also: Polk, James Knox; Mexican War.

■ **GUAM,** island (c. 200 square miles) in the west central Pacific Ocean, an unincorporated territory of the United States and the southernmost of the Marianas. Spain formally claimed Guam in 1565, and it remained a Spanish colonial outpost for the next two centuries. The United States seized the island during the Spanish-American War (1898). In 1941, at the outset of World War II in the Pacific, the Japanese occupied the island, which was retaken by the United States in 1944. The indigenous people of Guam are Chamorros (mixed Spanish, Filipino, and Indonesian descent), but more than half of the current population was born elsewhere (mainly Asia or the United States).

■ **GUERRILLA WARFARE,** brutal hit-and-run hostilities that emerged during the Civil War (1861-65). In 1861, large numbers of Southern sympathizers lived behind Union lines, while communities of Unionists resided within areas of Confederate military control. This was a recipe for guerrilla warfare, which indeed broke out in terrible ways from Appalachia to Missouri. Historians are just beginning to analyze this widespread irregular warfare, which lacked the honor and glory attributed to conventional battles such as Gettysburg.

Missouri was the theater of the best-known guerrilla struggle, in this instance conducted by young Southern raiders who could blur into the surrounding rural population when they were not raiding the small Union units that garrisoned towns and supply routes. In part, the bitterness in Missouri grew from a previous guerrilla war in 1856, when Missourian proslavery "Border Ruffians" contested antislavery Northern settlers over the new Kansas Territory. The conflict, which resumed in 1861, has traditionally been depicted as the work of Kansas Unionist raiders into Missouri, "Jayhawkers," and of William C. Quantrill and his company of perhaps 200 Southern bushwhackers, which climaxed in Quantrill's raid on Lawrence, Kansas, on Aug. 21, 1863, where they slaughtered 150 civilian men and boys. In response, Union authorities issued General Order No. 11, creating camps for the 20,000 rural citizens of northwestern Missouri and then burned every dwelling in the area, the most extreme Union counterinsurgency measure taken in a Union state.

Dreadful as they were, these events were but dramatic examples of a far wider process of destruction by both sides across the state, including looting, arson, lying, deceit, cold-blooded killing of civilian men and boys, and mutilation of corpses, which also led to vast streams of war refugees. Women became engaged in the conflict, both as victims and as suppliers and informers for both sides. In order to fight guerrillas, Union forces adopted guerrilla tactics, which multiplied the horrors. Although there are no firm statistics,

perhaps 10,000 Missourians were killed in this conflict, while 300,000 (of 1 million) more fled their homes for Union outposts or distant states.

Missouri guerrillas were far to the north of Southern armies and hence out of any effective Confederate control for most of the war, but Southern authorities recognized their usefulness in keeping Union forces tied down, thus depleting Northern armies. And yet, out of their honor-bound Christian gentry values, as well as from their fear of social disorganization, Confederate leaders refrained from generally adopting guerrilla tactics, which might have made them unbeatable. In East Tennessee, the forces were reversed, as Unionists took to the hills in a running struggle with Confederate forces, leading to much the same chaos Missouri experienced. In western Virginia and North Carolina, northern Georgia, Alabama, Mississippi, and Arkansas, and most notably in Kentucky, the pattern true in East Tennessee was repeated countless times in inglorious and inconclusive conflict.

After the South lost the war and the Union imposed Reconstruction, thousands of former Confederates again took to guerrilla warfare throughout the South in the Ku Klux Klan and other irregular units. Through intimidation and violence, including lynching, directed against African Americans and against whites involved in Reconstruction, ex-Confederates "redeemed" the South for a hundred years of white racial dominance, which would be maintained by segregation and widespread violence: the stuff of guerrilla warfare.

—MICHAEL FELLMAN

See Also: *Civil War; Lynching; Quantrill, William.*
BIBLIOGRAPHY: Fellman, Michael, *Inside War: The Guerrilla Conflict in Missouri During the American Civil War* (Oxford Univ. Press 1989); Paludan, Philip Shaw, *Victims: A True Story of the Civil War* (Univ. of Tennessee Press 1981).

■ **GUGGENHEIM, DANIEL (1856-1930),** industrialist. Born in Philadelphia, Pennsylvania, Daniel Guggenheim was one of seven sons who extended their father's mining and smelting businesses. The family always sought expert advice and made group decisions, but Daniel supervised all the operations of M. Guggenheim's Sons and became the family leader as they acquired ore deposits and built smelting plants in Mexico in 1891 to complement those they owned in Colorado. They gained control of their competitors by taking over the American Smelting and Refining Company (ASARCO) in 1901. As director and chairman, Daniel integrated mining, smelting, and refining processes with control over sources of supply and came to embody American industrial imperialism. He developed Bolivian tin mines; Yukon gold mines; copper mines in Alaska, Utah, and Chile; and rubber plantations and diamond mines in the Congo and Angola. As a philanthropist, Guggenheim sponsored free concerts in New York City's Central Park and established the Daniel and Florence Guggenheim Foundation and the Daniel Guggenheim Fund for the Promotion of Aeronautics.

See Also: Industrial Revolution.

■ **GUILFORD COURT HOUSE, BATTLE OF (1781),** battle in the American Revolution fought in North Carolina. After two months of skirmishes in the South, Gen. Nathanael Greene's American force in March engaged General Cornwallis's British troops in a major confrontation. Although Cornwallis's soldiers narrowly defeated the Americans, they paid a heavy toll. The decimated and haggard British troops had to retreat to Wilmington for supplies before marching to Virginia, where they were eventually defeated at Yorktown in October 1781.

See Also: Greene, Nathanael; Revolution, American.

■ **GULF OF TONKIN RESOLUTION,** congressional resolution in the Vietnam War. Reports of North Vietnamese torpedo attacks on U.S. ships in the Gulf of Tonkin led Congress on Aug. 7, 1964, to authorize Pres. Lyndon B. Johnson to repel such attacks and aid U.S. allies in Southeast Asia. Johnson used the measure to justify escalation of the war. Congress repealed the resolution in 1970.

See Also: Vietnam War.

■ **GUTHRIE, WOODY (1912-67),** songwriter and balladeer. Born in Okemah, Oklahoma, Guthrie traveled the country with his guitar and wrote more than a thousand songs that helped shape American folk music traditions, including "This Land Is Your Land," "So Long (It's Been Good to Know Ya)," and "Union Maid." His recordings, beginning with *Dust Bowl Ballads* (1940), and his progressive politics influenced the folk revival of the 1960s.

See Also: Folk Music.

Singer-songwriter Woody Guthrie, here performing in 1940 at McSorley's saloon in New York City, greatly influenced folk music with such songs as "This Land Is Your Land."

■ **GWINNETT, BUTTON (1735-77),** statesman and Revolutionary War leader. Born in Gloucestershire, England, Gwinnett immigrated to Georgia in 1765 and embarked on a turbulent political career. He held provincial offices and a seat in the Second Continental Congress, where he signed the Declaration of Independence. Gwinnett was killed in a duel.

See Also: Declaration of Independence.

H

HABEAS CORPUS, WRIT OF, the "Great Writ," which allows judges to review any loss of personal liberty. Based in English common law and Magna Carta (1215), habeas corpus, Latin for "you may have the body," is most often utilized by individuals appealing criminal convictions. The writ requires the person in charge of the petitioner, usually a law enforcement official, to bring the petitioner to court so the judge can decide whether the confinement is legal.

HAGUE PEACE CONFERENCES, two international conferences held at The Hague, Netherlands, one in 1899 and the other in 1907. Called by Russia, the conferences were supposed to reduce armaments, set up a court of international arbitration, and discuss ways to arbitrate disputes between countries without recourse to war.

HAKLUYT, RICHARD (1553-1616), author, geographer, and associate of Sir Walter Raleigh. Educated at Oxford, Hakluyt eventually became a lecturer and was the first to teach the use of globes. As a friend of Raleigh and member of the company of adventurers promoting the colonization of Virginia, Hakluyt wrote several treatises advocating English colonization in the New World. He argued that England needed colonies to protect itself against Spain's imperial power. Determined to promote English colonization, Hakluyt gathered all of the information available on the New World and began to publish a variety of collections. His most famous, *Principal Navigations, Voyages, Traffics, and Discoveries of the English Nation* (1589-1600), circulated widely in England.

See Also: Raleigh, Sir Walter.

HALAS, GEORGE (1895-1983), professional football team owner and coach. Born in Chicago, "Papa Bear" Halas founded the Decatur (Illinois) Staleys (1920) and moved the team to Chicago (1921), renaming it the Bears. He coached the Bears through 1967.

HALE, NATHAN (1755-76), soldier and Revolutionary War hero. Born in Coventry, Connecticut, Hale fought in the siege of Boston and helped the unsuccessful defense of New York City. He penetrated enemy lines on Long Island in August 1776 to gather information but was captured while returning. Ordered hanged the following day, he is immortalized by his last words: "I only regret that I have but one life to lose for my country."

See Also: Revolution, American.

HALE, SARAH JOSEPHA BUELL (1788-1879), magazine editor and author. She was born in Newport, New Hampshire. In 1830 she published "Mary Had a Little Lamb" in *Poems for Our Children*. In 1837 she became editor of *Godey's Lady's Book*. A cautious editorialist, silent on the matter of slavery and opposed to equal rights for women, she nevertheless championed such causes as improved educational and professional opportunities for women and the kindergarten movement.

See Also: Women in American History.

HALE, SUSAN (1833-1910), author and artist born in Boston, Massachusetts. She published a number of travel books and several works of literary criticism, including *Men and Manners of the Eighteenth Century* (1885). She also gained renown for her literary readings and for her watercolor sketches.

HALF-WAY COVENANT (1662), means of extending partial membership in New England Congregational churches. It granted membership to adult offspring of full members but withheld the Lord's Supper and voting privileges in the church until they offered acceptable proof of personal conversion, or "regeneration." Most important, "half-way" members' children could be baptized.

See Also: Congregationalists; Religion.

■ **HALL, ANNE (1792-1863),** painter of miniatures and commercially successful portraitist, born in Pomfret, Connecticut. Her work is compared with that of the great miniaturist Edward Green Malbone. In 1827, she became the first woman to be elected to the National Academy of Design.

■ **HALL, G. STANLEY (1846-1924),** psychologist and educator. Born in Ashfield, Massachusetts, he taught psychology at Johns Hopkins University in Baltimore between 1883 and 1888, during which time he started the *American Journal of Psychology*. In 1889 he assumed the position of president of Clark University. Two years later Hall became the first president of the American Psychological Association. Among his many writings is *The Contents of Children's Minds* (1883).

■ **HALL, LYMAN (1724-90),** minister, physician, and politician. Born in Wallingford, Connecticut, Hall moved to Georgia in 1758, where he became an early advocate for the patriot cause during the American Revolution. Elected as a member of the Second Continental Congress, he signed the Declaration of Independence.

See Also: Declaration of Independence.

■ **HALSEY, WILLIAM FREDERICK (1882-1959),** World War II admiral, born in Elizabeth, New Jersey. He commanded fleet forces in the South Pacific theater, leading spectacular carrier raids in the Marshall and Gilbert islands. A popular and respected personality, Halsey commanded the Third Fleet at the Battle of Leyte Gulf in the Philippines (October 1944).

See Also: Leyte Gulf, Battle of; World War II.

■ **HAMILTON, ALEXANDER (1755-1804),** soldier, political leader, and statesman. Hamilton was born out of wedlock in the West Indies. He moved to the American mainland in 1772, attending King's (Columbia) College the next year, where he associated with the founding members of the King's Literary Society. He quickly became part of the patriot movement, giving speeches, pamphleteering, and serving as a soldier and aide-de-camp to Gen. George Washington (1777-81), with whom he had a close relationship.

Alexander Hamilton was a Federalist leader and the first secretary of the treasury (1789-95). After using his influence to keep Aaron Burr out of the presidency and the New York governorship, Hamilton accepted Burr's challenge to a duel in which he was fatally shot.

In 1780, Hamilton cemented his rising position by marrying Elizabeth Schuyler, member of a powerful Hudson River Valley family. An aristocratic idealist, he argued for strengthening the powers of the federal government in *The Continentalist* essays (1781-82), the two *Letters from Phocion* (1784), and *The Federalist Papers* (1787-88), coauthored with James Madison and John Jay. Although critical of the Constitution he helped to draft in 1787, Hamilton nevertheless fought hard for its ratification.

Hamilton's true genius lay in his vision of the new nation's future and in his abilities as an administrator. Appointed by President Washington as secretary of the treasury in 1789, Hamilton reversed the financial chaos of the postwar era by having the federal government assume the states' debts, funding the federal debt at face value, and creating the First Bank of the United States. Hamilton's ideas were often ahead of his time. Although most Americans feared standing armies, he argued for the development of a professional military as early as 1783. In his *Report on Manufactures* (1791), Hamilton advocated a "mixed economy," arguing that the U.S. government should take an active role in developing the nation's commercial potential.

This vision of a commercial nation and a strong federal government, along with Hamilton's pro-British bias, alarmed Thomas Jefferson, James Madison, and their "Republican" followers. The Federalists led by Hamilton and the Republicans led by Jefferson and Madison soon divided the country. Hamilton left the Treasury in 1795 to practice law but remained an important political figure, helping to fund a Federalist newspaper, the *New York Evening Post*. Pres. John Adams and Hamilton actively disliked each other, but Adams bowed to Washington's wishes and made Hamilton inspector general of the army during the quasi-war with France in 1798.

Hamilton and Aaron Burr were rivals in New York politics. After Hamilton supported Jefferson for the presidency over Burr in 1800 and then supposedly slandered Burr, Burr challenged Hamilton to a duel. Although Hamilton had lost a son in 1801 to dueling, they fought in Weehawken, New Jersey, on July 11, 1804, and Burr fatally shot him. Hamilton was buried at Trinity Church on Wall Street in Manhattan.

A proud, ambitious man of intense energy, the proponent of unpopular and prophetic ideas about government, Hamilton remains the least understood member of the founding generation. But his efforts secured the future of the new nation, making the ideals of the Constitution tangible and real.

—Catherine Allgor

See Also: *Banks of the United States, First and Second; Burr, Aaron; Constitution of the United States; Federalist Papers, The; Revolution, American.*

BIBLIOGRAPHY: McDonald, Forrest, *Alexander Hamilton: A Biography* (Norton 1979); Stourzh, Gerald, *Alexander Hamilton and the Idea of Republican Government* (Stanford Univ. Press 1970).

■ **HAMILTON, HENRY (1734-96),** British soldier and politican. Born in Ireland, Hamilton assumed the lieutenant governorship of Detroit in 1775 and surrendered to American forces at Vincennes in 1779. After his imprisonment in Virginia, he served as a British official in Quebec, Barbados, and Dominica.

See Also: *Revolution, American.*

■ **HAMLIN, HAMILTON (1809-91),** vice president of the United States (1861-65) during Abraham Lincoln's first term. Born in Paris Hill, Maine, Hamlin was a Radical Republican. Believing Andrew Johnson would improve his reelection chances, Lincoln replaced Hamlin with Johnson on the 1864 ticket.

See Also: *Civil War; Vice President of the United States.*

■ **HAMMERSTEIN, OSCAR, II (1895-1960),** lyricist. The grandson of theater impresario Oscar Hammerstein (1846-1919), he was born in New York City and teamed with composer Jerome Kern for a series of Broadway hits including *Show Boat* (1927). He later joined Richard Rodgers to create a series of musical theater classics including *Oklahoma* (1943), *Carousel* (1945), *South Pacific* (1949), *The King and I* (1951), and *The Sound of Music* (1959).

See Also: *Theater.*

■ ***HAMMER V. DAGENHART (1918),*** U.S. Supreme Court case that invalidated the Keating-Owen Child Labor Act (1916), which barred goods manufactured by child labor from interstate commerce. The Court ruled (5-4) that Congress had overstepped its powers. The Constitution, wrote Justice William Rufus Day, granted Congress the power to regulate interstate commerce, but the regulation of manufacturing was a state responsibility.

Justice Oliver Wendell Holmes dissented, writing that the majority's endorsement of classic laissez-faire economic doctrine reflected its own prejudices and did not take into account either the law or the nation's growing revulsion with child labor. He also argued that the Keating-Owen law clearly regulated commerce as the Constitution allowed. Child labor could still be used to manufacture goods; the products simply could not be traded across state lines. Congress responded by passing a new anti-child labor law that relied on federal tax policies to regulate manufacturing. That law was also voided by the Court in *Bailey* v. *Drexel Furniture* (1922). Holmes's position was finally upheld in 1941, when a unanimous Court upheld Congress's right to regulate child labor and commerce in *United States* v. *Darby Lumber Co.*

See Also: *Keating-Owen Act; Supreme Court; United States* v. *Darby Lumber Co.*

BIBLIOGRAPHY: Wood, Stephen B., *Constitutional Politics in the Progressive Era: Child Labor and the Law* (Univ. of Chicago Press 1968).

■ **HAMMETT, DASHIELL (1894-1961),** mystery novelist. Born in St. Mary's County, Maryland, Hammett created the hard-boiled detective Sam Spade in *The Maltese Falcon* (1930) and the debonair crime-solving couple Nick and Nora Charles in *The Thin Man* (1932). Active in left-wing causes, he served six months in jail in 1951 for refusing to identify contributors to a defense fund for suspected Communist party members.

See Also: Novel.

■ **HAMPTON, WADE (1818-1902),** Confederate general and political leader. Born in Charleston, South Carolina, Hampton initially opposed secession, but at the outbreak of the Civil War he joined the Confederate army. He distinguished himself at the first Battle of Bull Run (1861) and was promoted to brigadier general (1862). He became J.E.B. Stuart's second in command in the Army of Northern Virginia. After the war, Hampton served as governor of South Carolina (1876-79) and U.S. senator (1879-90).

See Also: Bull Run, Battles of; Civil War.

■ **HAMPTON ROADS CONFERENCE (1865),** meeting between Union and Confederate officials to discuss ending the Civil War. Representing the Confederacy were Vice Pres. Alexander H. Stephens, Senate Pres. Robert Hunter, and Asst. Sec. of War John Campbell. The Union delegation was headed by Pres. Abraham Lincoln and Sec. of State William H. Seward. The meeting took place on February 3 aboard the Union steamer *River Queen* in Hampton Roads, off the Virginia coast. Lincoln insisted that the Confederate states rejoin the Union and abolish slavery. The Confederate leaders refused, and the war continued.

See Also: Civil War; Seward, William Henry; Stephens, Alexander H.

■ **HANCOCK, JOHN (1737-93),** American patriot leader. Born in Braintree, Massachusetts, Hancock inherited a Boston mercantile business. Angered by parliamentary restrictions on trade, he joined the Sons of Liberty and became one of its leaders. British Gen. Thomas Gage's attempt to arrest him and Samuel Adams as rebels and seize colonial munitions led to the Battles of Lexington and Concord (Apr. 19, 1775) and precipitated the American Revolution. As president of the Second Continental Congress (1775-77), Hancock was the first to sign the Declaration of Independence (July 4, 1776) and did so with such a bold flourish that his name has become synonymous with the word "signature." He later served as governor of Massachusetts (1780-85, 1787-93) and was instrumental in persuading his state to ratify the U.S. Constitution (1788). A sincere patriot but of limited ability and oversized ego, Hancock remained the idol of the Massachusetts masses until his death.

See Also: Continental Congresses; Declaration of Independence; Revolution, American.

BIBLIOGRAPHY: Fowler, William M., Jr., *The Baron of Beacon Hill: A Biography of John Hancock* (Houghton Mifflin 1980).

■ **HAND, (BILLINGS) LEARNED (1872-1961),** federal judge. Born in Albany, New York, and educated at Harvard Law School, he was appointed to the U.S. District Court in New York (1909) and the Court of Appeals for the Second Circuit (1924). Hand was chief judge of the Second Circuit from 1939 to 1951 and remained active as a senior judge until his death. An advocate of judicial restraint, he believed judges should respect precedent and show deference to the elected branches.

■ **HANDSOME LAKE (c. 1735-1815),** Seneca founder of the Longhouse religion. Handsome Lake was born in present-day New York State and, as a young man, fought for the British during the French and Indian War and the American Revolution. Following the American Revolution, the Seneca lost most of their homelands and were left with only small reservations. Handsome Lake became dissolute. On recovering from an alcohol-induced coma in 1799, he told of a journey he had taken with four messengers who told him of the "Good Word" and of the evils of alcohol, abortion, and witchcraft. Handsome Lake advocated transforming Seneca society by restructuring the matrilineal clan into the nuclear family and shifting to European-style farming. At the same time, Handsome Lake preached the value of reciprocity and seasonal rituals as traditionally practiced by the Seneca. The Longhouse religion, as it became known, was thus a syncretic revitalization, incorporating elements of Seneca beliefs with Protestant Quakerism.

See Also: Indians of North America.

■ **HANDY, W. C. (WILLIAM CHRISTOPHER) (1873-1958),** musician and band leader, one of the great figures in the history of the blues. Born in Florence, Alabama, Handy began his career playing the cornet in a minstrel show. Known as the "Father of the Blues," Handy was among the first to put the blues down in written form. He is remembered for such classic compositions as "St. Louis Blues" (1914) and "Beale Street Blues" (1917). Handy published most of his work himself and helped popularize the blues in the United States and around the world.

See Also: African Americans; Blues.

■ **HANNA, MARCUS ALONZO (MARK) (1837-1904),** Republican politician and businessman. Born in New Lisbon, Ohio, the son of a wholesale grocer, he became involved in a variety of suc-

W. C. Handy led in the popularization of blues music with his compositions of "Memphis Blues" (1912) and "St. Louis Blues" (1914).

cessful and lucrative business interests. After 1880, Hanna became active in the Republican party. In 1888 he led the unsuccessful campaign of Sen. John Sherman for the party's presidential nomination. Eight years later, as chairman of the Republican National Committee, Hanna ran the successful presidential campaign of Gov. William McKinley. Appointed to the U.S. Senate in 1897, he was elected in his own right the following year. In the Senate, Hanna remained one of McKinley's most trusted advisers while cementing the close relationship between corporate interests and the Republican party. Even after Theodore Roosevelt became president on McKinley's assassination in 1901, Hanna remained an important presidential adviser, playing a key role in settling the 1902 anthracite coal strike.

See Also: Gilded Age; McKinley, William.

BIBLIOGRAPHY: Croly, Herbert D., *Marcus Alonzo Hanna, His Life and Work* (Archon Books 1965).

■ **HARDING, WARREN GAMALIEL (1865-1923),** 29th president of the United States (1921-23). He was born on Nov. 2, 1865, in Corsica, Ohio, attended Ohio Central College, and later studied law. While editor and publisher of the *Marion Star*, he entered local politics as a Republican, eventually serving in the Ohio state senate and as the state's lieutenant governor. In 1914, he was elected to the U.S. Senate, serving one term before he won a landslide victory in the 1920 presidential campaign by promising the nation a return to normalcy after the tumultuous World War I era.

The Harding administration was marked by its pro-business stance and its lax cronyism. Never quite comfortable with his presidential responsibilities, the congenial Harding surrounded himself with old friends and relatives, known as the "Ohio Gang," appointing several of them to key posts. As the news of potential corruption spread among those closest to the president, Harding became ill while on tour of the West. He died, possibly from a cerebral embolism, on Aug. 2, 1923, before the worst of the scandals led to the indictments of Atty. Gen. Harry M. Daugherty, Sec. of the Interior Albert B. Fall, and director of the Veteran's Bureau Col. Charles R. Forbes.

See Also: Fall, Albert Bacon; Presidential Elections; President of the United States.

Promising a "return to normalcy" Republican Warren G. Harding decisively defeated Democrat James M. Cox in the presidential election of 1920.

BIBLIOGRAPHY: Murray, Robert K., *The Politics of Normalcy: Governmental Theory and Practice in the Harding-Coolidge Era* (Norton 1973); Trani, Eugene P., and David Wilson, *The Presidency of Warren G. Harding* (Regents Press of Kansas 1977).

■ **HARD LABOR, TREATY OF (1768),** agreement between representatives of the Cherokee and the British, establishing a boundary between tribal hunting lands and the colony of Virginia. In the Proclamation of 1763, Great Britain established the principle of a dividing line between colonial lands and "Indian Country" to run along the crest of the Appalachians. But because colonial settlers had already breeched that divide, this treaty (as well as the Fort Stanwix Treaty with the Iroquois Confederacy of the same year) moved the boundary westward and established it with more specificity. Even then, however, it was discovered that the Hard Labor line cut off Virginians who had established settlements west of the Kanawha River, and the boundary was pushed further westward in the subsequent Treaty of Lochaber (1770).

See Also: Fort Stanwix Treaties; Indians of North America; Proclamation of 1763.

BIBLIOGRAPHY: De Vorsey, Louis, *The Indian Boundary in the Southern Colonies, 1763-1775* (Univ. of North Carolina Press 1966).

■ **HARIOT, THOMAS (1560-1621),** scientist and explorer, participant in the initial attempt to settle a colony at Roanoke, Virginia (1585). Hariot and John White, an artist, went to Roanoke to record the flora, fauna, and natural resources of the area around Roanoke as well as the life of the local natives. He prepared for the adventure by learning the Algonquian language from two Indian men brought to England the year before. Although the settlement at Roanoke failed, Hariot and White produced an impressive study of America's natural history and of native life in the colonial period.

See Also: Roanoke, Lost Colony of; Science.

■ **HARLAN, JOHN MARSHALL (1833-1911),** associate justice of the U.S. Supreme Court (1877-1911). Born to a slaveholding family in Boyle County, Kentucky, Harlan came of age during the turbulent years before the Civil War. He supported the Know-Nothing party in the 1850s and served as a county judge in Kentucky in 1858. Harlan sided with the Union at the outbreak of the Civil War and saw action as a colonel. He nonetheless opposed both the 13th Amendment abolishing slavery and Pres. Abraham Lincoln's bid for reelection in 1864.

In a remarkable reversal of social and racial ideology, Harlan accepted and then supported civil rights for African Americans after the war. As a newly converted Republican, he garnered support for Rutherford B. Hayes's presidential nomination in 1876. President Hayes reciprocated by appointing Harlan to the Supreme Court in 1877. During his 34 years on the bench, Harlan staunchly opposed the conservative Court, offering numerous, passionate dissents.

Harlan believed strongly in government regulation of industry, especially the railroads and trusts. His most significant contribution, however, came in the civil rights controversies. While the Court's majority favored a policy of retrenchment on many civil rights amendments and statutes, Harlan held to his moral views. His dissent in *Plessy* v. *Ferguson* (1896), which legalized racial segregation in public accommodations, was characteristic of his efforts. He wrote that "In respect to civil rights, all citizens are equal before the law."

See Also: Plessy v. *Ferguson; Supreme Court.*

BIBLIOGRAPHY: Beth, Loran P., *John Marshall Harlan: The Last Whig Justice* (Univ. of Kentucky Press 1992); Yarbrough, Tinley E., *Judicial Enigma: The First Justice Harlan* (Oxford Univ. Press 1995).

▪ **HARLAN, JOHN MARSHALL (1899-1971),** associate justice of the U.S. Supreme Court (1955-71). Born in Chicago, Illinois, Harlan was the grandson of Justice John Marshall Harlan, who served on the Court from 1877 to 1911. He was an advocate of judicial restraint, arguing that while the Court must defend individual liberties and the judicial process, judges should defer to the wisdom of elected authorities. Harlan became the leading conservative voice on the Court with the retirement of Felix Frankfurter (1962).

See Also: Supreme Court.

▪ **HARLEM,** neighborhood in New York City. Originally a Dutch settlement, Nieuw Haarlem, founded in 1658 on upper Manhattan Island, it became in the 20th century an important focus of African-American life and culture. Beginning about 1904, many of the great influx of southern blacks migrating to New York began to move into Harlem, which until then had been a predominantly white community. An explosion of artistic and intellectual expression in the 1920s, known as the Harlem Renaissance or New Negro Movement, made Harlem the capital of African-American culture and a national center of popular music. Clubs and nightspots like the Cotton Club and the Apollo Theater showcased the best of African-American performers. Harlemites have, at times, been captivated by dynamic black leaders,

most notably Marcus Garvey, Father Divine, and Adam Clayton Powell, Jr., although the sources of their appeal varied as widely as their individual temperaments. In addition to serving as inspiration for America's finest artistic and intellectual minds, Harlem was the site of some of the first civil rights activism and boycotts, even in the midst of the 1930s Depression. It has also been scarred by race riots and has suffered from economic decline, crime, and drugs, although recent years have brought both economic and social revitalization to the area. Throughout its ebullient, turbulent history, black Harlem has often been as important as an idea and symbol as it has been as a community. After World War II many Hispanic Americans settled in east Harlem, which became known as Spanish Harlem.

See Also: African Americans; New Negro Movement.

▪ **HARLEM RENAISSANCE,** an African-American, primarily literary, movement of the 1920s centered in the New York City neighborhood known as Harlem, in upper Manhattan. Members of the Harlem Renaissance exerted a major and lasting influence upon American culture as they joined in a self-consciously collective African-American artistic outpouring. In the early 1920s, a trio of journals set the stage for the renaissance. Although *Crisis*, the *Messenger*, and *Opportunity* served as organs for the broad concerns of, respectively, the National Association for the Advancement of Colored People (NAACP), labor leaders A. Philip Randolph and Chandler Owen, and the National Urban League, these magazines printed the work of such literary talents as Langston Hughes and Claude McKay, helping win African Americans contracts with leading New York publishers. The movement then took its cue from Alain Locke's edited anthology, *The New Negro: An Interpretation*, whose appearance in 1925 did much to foster a collective identity both African-American and artistic among those who had begun to contribute to what Locke termed the "Negro Renaissance."

Hughes, the movement's preeminent poet, issued a clarion call to his fellow young African-American writers in 1926 with his "The Negro Artist and the Racial Mountain," published in the *Nation*. Among those who came, with Hughes, to shape the renaissance were McKay, Arna Bontemps, Countee Cullen, Jessie Fauset, Zora Neale Hurston, Nella Larsen, and Jean Toomer. These and other renaissance authors by no means constituted a monolithic movement or elicited uniform praise. Still, many African-American contemporaries assured the movement's success through their strong support, even while others were reserved in theirs, and a number of whites, whose patronage had as one of its motivators the exotic appeal of African-American culture, also played an important role in the Harlem Renaissance. Its writers' explorations of African-American identity and history led to a common concern for African-American folk traditions and a shared effort to figure the latter into new visions of African-American culture.

—JAMES KESSENIDES

See Also: African Americans; Cullen, Countee; Hughes, (James) Langston; Hurston, Zora Neale.
BIBLIOGRAPHY: Baker, Houston A., Jr., *Modernism and the Harlem Renaissance* (Univ. of Chicago Press 1987); Huggins, Nathan, *Harlem Renaissance* (Oxford Univ. Press 1971).

■ **HARLOW, JEAN (1911-37),** movie actress. Born in Kansas City, Missouri, she was known as "the Blonde Bombshell" for her stunning good looks and platinum blonde hair. She appeared in *Bombshell* (1933) and *Dinner at Eight* (1933) and was a top box-office attraction until her illness and death at 26.

■ **HARPER, IDA HUSTED (1851-1931),** journalist, woman suffragist, and historian. She was born in Fairfield, Indiana. She worked as publicity coordinator for the national suffrage movement in the California campaign of 1896 and again from 1916 to 1918. Her most important contributions were her three-volume *Life and Work of Susan B. Anthony* (1898, 1903) and her collaboration with Anthony on the *History of Woman Suffrage* (Harper wrote volumes IV-VI, 1900-22).

See Also: Anthony, Susan B.; Woman Suffrage Movement; Women's Movement.

■ **HARPER, WILLIAM RAINEY (1856-1906),** first president of the University of Chicago (1891-1906). Born in New Concord, Ohio, he was a He-

braic scholar and professor at Baptist Union Theological Seminary in Chicago (1876-86) and at Yale University (1886-91) before moving to the new University of Chicago. His administrative skills and financial backing from the Rockefeller family soon made Chicago the leading academic center in the Midwest.

See Also: Rockefeller Family.

■ **HARPERS FERRY RAID (1859),** attack on federal arsenal at Harpers Ferry, Virginia. Abolitionist John Brown led the raid, hoping to incite a slave revolt. Brown seized the arsenal, but the revolt did not materialize. Brown was captured and later executed. Southern fears of Northern abolitionists increased because of the attack.

See Also: Brown, John; Civil War.

■ **HARRIMAN, WILLIAM AVERELL (1891-1986),** financier and diplomat. The heir of railroad magnate Edward Henry Harriman, he was born in New York City. Harriman moved through the world of railroads and finance and then into the world of government and diplomacy. After working at the Union Pacific Railroad (1915-17), he headed a shipyard (1917-25), started a bank (1920), and became chairman of the board of the Union Pacific (1932-46). Pres. Franklin D. Roosevelt appointed Harriman to the National Recovery Administration in 1934, after which they became friends. Turning to diplomacy, Harriman became ambassador to the Soviet Union (1943-46) and Great Britain (1946) and secretary of commerce (1946-48). He later directed economic aid to Europe through the Marshall Plan (1948-50). Harriman was elected governor of New York in 1954 and served one term. As an elder statesman he held various posts, including ambassador at large under Presidents Kennedy and Johnson, and headed the U.S. delegation at the Paris peace talks on Vietnam. Harriman donated $10 million for the study of the Soviet Union to what is now Columbia University's W. Averell Harriman Institute.

See Also: Industrial Revolution.

■ **HARRIS, JOEL CHANDLER (1848-1908),** local color writer. A native of Putnam County, Georgia, Harris worked on the staff of the *Savannah Morning News* and the *Atlanta Constitution* in the 1870s and 1880s. At the *Constitution* he began writing down the tales that he had heard from African Americans while growing up on a plantation, trying to capture the local dialect. He created the characters of Uncle Remus, Br'er Rabbit, and Br'er Fox in his many books, among them *Uncle Remus, His Songs and His Sayings* (1880) and *Nights with Uncle Remus* (1883).

■ **HARRISON, BENJAMIN (1833-1901),** 23rd president of the United States (1889-93). He was born on Aug. 20, 1833, in North Bend, Ohio, the son of Rep. John Scott Harrison and grandson of Pres. William Henry Harrison. A graduate of Miami University, he entered an Indianapolis law firm in 1853 and soon became active in the newly formed Republican party, holding a variety of local and state offices in Indiana. He served hon-

In 1888, Benjamin Harrison won the presidency with fewer popular, but more electoral college, votes than his opponent, the incumbent Grover Cleveland.

orably as commander of Indiana's 70th Infantry during the Civil War. After the war, Harrison practiced law again and remained active in Indiana Republican state politics until his election for one term to the U.S. Senate in 1881.

In 1888, he was the compromise presidential candidate of the faction-ridden Republican party. Although the incumbent, Pres. Grover Cleveland, received more popular votes, Harrison handily carried the electoral college. During 1890 he supported and signed into law the Sherman Antitrust Act, the Sherman Silver Purchase Act, the McKinley Tariff Act, and the Dependent (Veterans) Pension Act. An expansionist, Harrison supported increased trade with Latin America and Asia as well as expansion of the U.S. Navy. Growing national financial woes and his failure to annex Hawaii led to his defeat in 1892 by the man he had defeated in 1888, Grover Cleveland. Harrison spent his final years as a respected elder spokesman of the Republican party.

See Also: Presidential Elections; President of the United States.

BIBLIOGRAPHY: Sokolofsky, Homer E., *The Presidency of Benjamin Harrison* (Univ. of Kansas Press 1987).

■ **HARRISON, PETER (1716-75),** colonial era architect. Harrison was born in York, England, and emigrated in 1740, settling in Newport, Rhode Island, where he started his architectural practice. He is one of the first American architects known to have created designs for others to build. Harrison designed the Redwood Library in Newport (1750), King's Chapel in Boston, Massachusetts (1754), the Lady Pepperell House in Kittery Point, Maine (1760), and the Touro Synagogue in Newport (1763).

See Also: Architecture.

■ **HARRISON, WILLIAM HENRY (1773-1841),** military leader and ninth president of the United States (1841). Born in Charles City County, Virginia, he studied medicine with Dr. Benjamin Rush but enlisted in the military after his father's death in 1791. Serving in the army until 1798, Harrison was aide-de-camp to Gen. "Mad" Anthony Wayne during the Battle of Fallen Timbers (1794). Harrison was appointed governor of Indiana Territory (1800-12) and in that capacity ne-

The Whig party styled their 1840 presidential nominee, William Henry Harrison, as the "Log Cabin" candidate, a common man of the West. In fact, Harrison came from a privileged background.

gotiated treaties with the Indians of the Old Northwest to obtain land in the Ohio Valley, which by 1809 brought him into conflict with the Shawnee leader Tecumseh. In October 1811 Harrison led troops in a raid against Prophetstown, a settlement of Tecumseh's followers. The Battle of Tippecanoe in November sealed Harrison's reputation as an "Indian fighter," though it was less important than his subsequent leadership at the Battle of the Thames, which broke the power of the Indians. In 1840, in his run for president, Harrison's "Log Cabin" campaign portrayed him as "Old Tippecanoe." Although elected, Harrison contracted pneumonia at his inauguration (Mar. 4, 1841) and died a month later (April 4), the first U.S. president to die in office. He served the shortest term of any president in U.S. history.

See Also: Presidential Elections; President of the United States; Tippecanoe, Battle of.

BIBLIOGRAPHY: Cleaves, Freeman, *Old Tippecanoe: William Henry Harrison and His Time* (Scribner's 1939); Peterson, Norma Lois, *The Presidencies of William Henry Harrison and John Tyler* (Univ. of Kansas Press 1989).

■ **HART, JOHN (c. 1711-79),** statesman and Revolutionary War leader. Hart, a signer of the Declaration of Independence, was born in Stonington, Connecticut. After moving to New Jersey he entered local and provincial politics and later became vice president of the Second Continental Congress.

See Also: Declaration of Independence.

■ **HART, WILLIAM S. (1870-1946),** hero of silent Westerns who came to film after a stage career, which included playing the lead role of *The Virginian* on Broadway. His most important films include *Hell's Hinges* (1917) and *Tumbleweeds* (1925).

■ **HARTE, BRET (1836-1902),** short story writer. Born in Albany, New York, Harte relocated to San Francisco in 1854 and began working as a typesetter for *Golden Era,* a journal for which he started to write poems and sketches. He contributed to the *Californian* and in 1868 became an editor of *Overland Monthly,* in which he published some of his best-known stories, such as "The Luck of the Roaring Camp" (1868) and "The Outcasts of Poker Flat" (1869). Harte lived the latter half of his life abroad.

See Also: Short Story.

■ **HARTFORD CONVENTION (1814-15),** meeting of Federalists protesting U.S. policy during the War of 1812. Originally called by the Massachusetts legislature, acting at the urging of New England commercial interests, the Hartford Convention included 26 representatives from Massachusetts, Connecticut, and Rhode Island. The New England states of Vermont and New Hampshire sent no representatives to the secret meetings, which were held between Dec. 15, 1814, and Jan. 5, 1815. Led by Bostonian Harrison Gray Otis, the group debated whether to call for a general convention to revise the U.S. Constitution. Affected by restrictions against New England shipping and concerned about the defense of the New England coast, the convention adopted measures recommending the use of federal troops for state defense and supporting constitutional amendments to limit southern political power by eliminating the "three-fifths clause," which gave slave states the right to claim a slave as three-fifths of a person for purposes of congressional representation. The convention itself was an expression of northern states' rights sentiments and was condemned for its secrecy and seen by opponents as treasonous.

See Also: War of 1812.

BIBLIOGRAPHY: Dwight, Theodore, *History of the Hartford Convention 1833* (reprint, Da Capo 1970); Morison, Samuel Eliot, *Harrison Gray Otis, 1765-1848: The Urbane Federalist* (Houghton Mifflin 1969).

■ **HASSAM, CHILDE (1859-1935),** impressionist painter. Born in Boston, Massachusetts, Hassam received his early training there, while also working for the publisher Little, Brown & Company. From 1886 to 1889 Hassam studied in Paris, where he became entranced by the work of the French Impressionists. In paintings such as *Flag Day* (1919), he blended Impressionist techniques with the American realist tradition. Hassam helped found an association of Impressionist painters known as the Ten American Painters.

See Also: Painting.

■ **HAT ACT (1732),** British legislation, one of the Navigation Acts, that prohibited the export of American-made beaver hats from the colonies. It included a ban on craftsmen lacking appropriate apprenticeships and confined bona fide hatmakers to two apprentices.

See Also: Navigation Acts.

■ **HATCH ACT (1939),** U.S. law barring most federal employees from active participation in partisan political campaigns. A 1940 amendment to the act included the first tentative limits on campaign spending and contributions.

See Also: New Deal.

■ **HATFIELDS AND MCCOYS,** feuding families that fought each other in the mountains of southern West Virginia and northeastern Kentucky during the 19th century. Although legend attributes hundreds of deaths over a century to the feud, it actually resulted in only 12 during the years 1878-90. Anderson "Devil Anse" Hatfield (1839-1921) and Randolph "Old Ranel" McCoy (1825-1913) became entangled in a feud over ownership of land and logging rights. On election day in 1882 three sons of McCoy attacked and killed a brother of "Anse" Hatfield, who fought back by ritually executing the three sons. There were no further incidents, however, until six years later (1888), when a relative of McCoy's, a lawyer named Perry Cline (1849-1891), persuaded Gov. Simon Buckner of Kentucky to authorize a posse to cross the state boundary into West Virginia and arrest the Hatfields. Because extradition procedures had been violated, the case went to the Supreme Court of the United States, where Kentucky's right to try the Hatfields was upheld. All eight were tried; seven spent time in the penitentiary and one was hanged.

—ALTINA L. WALLER

BIBLIOGRAPHY: Waller, Altina L., *Feud: Hatfields, McCoys and Social Change in Appalachia 1860-1900* (Univ. of North Carolina Press 1988).

■ **HAVANA CONFERENCE (1928),** a forum of the Organization of American States held shortly after the 1926 U.S. intervention in Nicaragua. A resolution criticizing U.S. interventionism was proposed, but Charles E. Hughes, heading the U.S. delegation, managed to block its passage.

See Also: Nicaraguan Interventions; Organization of American States (OAS).

■ **HAWAII,** the nation's only island state, consisting of 8 islands and 124 islets in the Pacific Ocean, about 2,400 miles southwest of San Francisco. The islands are the tips of volcanic mountains descending to the ocean floor. Mauna Loa, on Hawaii Island, is the world's largest active volcano. The state's tropical climate, beaches, and scenic beauty attract millions of visitors each year and provide a vital support to the state's economy. Also vital are its military bases; the Pacific Command, stationed here, is responsible for all U.S. forces in the Pacific and Indian oceans and southern Asia.

Hawaii was settled by Polynesians more than 1,000 years ago. Europeans discovered it in 1778. Hawaii was annexed by the United States in 1898 and became a state in 1959. Its racial balance is unique with large minorities of people of Japanese and native Hawaiian ancestry.

Capital: Honolulu. Area: 6,459 square miles. Population (1995 est.): 1,187,000.

See Also: Dole, Sanford Ballard; Liliuokalani; Pearl Harbor; Whaling.

■ **HAWKINS, SIR JOHN (1532-95),** English privateer, adventurer, and trader. Hawkins participated in the African slave trade (1562-67) and in privateering expeditions to take Spanish treasure galleons off the coast of the Carolinas. He held various posts in the British Royal Navy, such as treasurer and controller, and also participated in a series of naval exploits with the British Commanders Sir Martin Frobisher (Portuguese coast, 1590) and Sir Francis Drake (West Indies, 1595).

See Also: Slave Trade.

■ **HAWKS AND DOVES,** term used to denote pro- and antiwar advocates, respectively, during the Vietnam era (1960s-70s). Those who sought military victory were designated *hawks*, while those who called for negotiations or immediate withdrawal from Vietnam were categorized as *doves*.

■ **HAWTHORNE, NATHANIEL (1804-64),** short story writer and novelist. Born in Salem, Massachusetts, Hawthorne graduated from Bowdoin College in 1825, a classmate of Henry Wadsworth Longfellow. His first success came with the publication of *Twice-Told Tales* in 1837. Hawthorne invoked the Puritan origins of colonial New England in several of his works, including the stories "Young Goodman Brown" (1835) and "The Minister's Black Veil" (1836). In 1841 he lived at the utopian community of Brook Farm and then settled in Concord, Massachusetts. At Concord Hawthorne wrote *The Scarlet Letter* (1850), one of the masterpieces of American literature, which was published to great acclaim and financial success. It was followed by *The House of Seven Gables* (1851) and a thinly veiled account of his experience at Brook Farm, *The Blithedale Romance* (1852). Hawthorne spent the 1850s living in England as a U.S. consul and traveling in Italy. After returning to Concord he finished his last novel, *The Marble Faun* (1860). Hawthorne's greatest works probe deeply into the psychology of human character and deal with themes of evil and guilt.

See Also: Brook Farm; Novel; Utopian Communities.

■ **HAY, JOHN MILTON (1838-1905),** American diplomat. He was born in Salem, Indiana, and graduated from Brown University in 1858. He studied law in Springfield, Illinois, at the same time that Abraham Lincoln practiced there. When he became president, Lincoln took Hay with him to Washington, D.C., as his assistant private secretary. After Lincoln's assassination, Hay pursued a diplomatic career and served as assistant secretary of state (1878-81).

In 1897, President McKinley appointed him ambassador to Great Britain, but recalled him in 1898 to become secretary of state. Hay retained this post until his death. He was the author of the Open Door Policy (1899), a diplomatic course favoring equal access for American and foreign entrepreneurs to markets in China. Hay also initiated several international agreements with Great Britain, Colombia, and Panama (1900-03) that facilitated the construction of the Panama Canal. Besides his career as a statesman, Hay was also a writer and poet.

See Also: Hay-Bunau-Varilla Treaty; Hay-Pauncefote Treaty; Open Door Policy.

■ **HAY-BUNAU-VARILLA TREATY (1903),** a U.S.-Panama accord signed between U.S. Sec. of State

Nathaniel Hawthorne, whose most famous novel, *The Scarlet Letter* (1850), explored 17th-century New England Puritanism, was himself of Puritan ancestry. His forebears included a judge who presided at the Salem witch trials of 1692.

John M. Hay and the Panamanian envoy to Washington, Philippe Bunau-Varilla. The United States guaranteed the independence of Panama, while the latter gave the United States sovereign rights over the proposed Panama Canal Zone.

See Also: Hay, John Milton; Panama Canal.

■ **HAYDEN, THOMAS (1939-),** political activist. Born in Royal Oak, Michigan, he was a founder of Students for a Democratic Society (1961) and author of the Port Huron Statement (1962), SDS's manifesto, which called for a set of social democratic reforms to expand the welfare state at the expense of the warfare state. He was active in the civil rights and antiwar movements and was one of the "Chicago 7" arrested and tried for conspiracy to riot after the 1968 Democratic convention in Chicago. Hayden was elected to the California state legislature (1982) and has remained active in California politics.

See Also: Students for a Democratic Society (SDS).

■ **HAYES, HELEN (1900-93),** stage and screen actress. Hayes was born in Washington, D.C., and, in an extraordinary career spanning eight decades, earned acclaim for numerous stage performances including her roles in *Caesar and Cleopatra* (1925) and *Harvey* (1970). She also won Academy Awards for her performances in the films *The Sin of Madelon Claudet* (1932) and *Airport* (1969).

■ **HAYES, RUTHERFORD BIRCHARD (1822-93),** 19th president of the United States (1877-81). He was born on Oct. 4, 1822, in Delaware, Ohio, and educated at Kenyon College and Harvard Law School. Hayes settled in Cincinnati and was active in local politics until the outbreak of the Civil War. He served with bravery as a major in the 23rd Ohio Regiment until 1864, when he resumed his political career with election as a Republican to the U.S. House of Representatives. After one term in Washington, Hayes returned to Ohio, where he served as governor (1868-72). In 1876, he was chosen as the Republican presidential candidate. In the election, Hayes appeared to have been defeated by the Democratic candidate, Samuel J. Tilden, but Republicans challenged the returns of four states. After several months of debate, much of which focused on the continued northern presence in the Recon-

struction South, the so-called Compromise of 1877 was reached in the U.S. Senate: Hayes was named president, and the last of the federal troops were soon removed from the South, marking the end of Reconstruction. The remainder of Hayes's one term as president was shaped by the national issues—civil service and currency reforms and the labor question—that the country would address in the post-Reconstruction era. Hayes took steps toward civil service reform, passing an executive order that prohibited federal employees' involvement in political campaigns. Since he backed the gold standard, the Bland-Allison Silver Act of 1878 had to be passed over his veto. In 1877, he set a precedent by sending in federal troops to smash the great railroad strikes of that year.

See Also: Gilded Age; Presidential Elections; President of the United States.

BIBLIOGRAPHY: Hoogenboom, Ari, *The Presidency of Rutherford B. Hayes* (Univ. of Kansas Press 1988).

After volunteering for the Union army in 1861, Republican Rutherford B. Hayes distinguished himself in battle and rose to the rank of major general. At the beginning of his presidency (1877-81), Reconstruction in the South was ended with the final withdrawal of federal troops.

■ **HAYMARKET INCIDENT,** violence at a May 4, 1886, labor rally, which killed eight Chicago police. The rally in Haymarket Square, Chicago, like those in many cities around the nation, grew out of the intense struggle of workers for the eight-hour workday. Labor unions, social reformers, political groups, and sympathizers of all kinds had campaigned since the 1830s to reduce the hours of the industrial workday from 12 to 10 and 10 to 8. After laws passed by some state legislatures (including Illinois) were ignored in practice, organizations of working people declared that by their own peaceful actions on May Day (May 1), 1886, they would compel employers to accede to their demands.

Intense fears and wildly exaggerated rumors of a "communist uprising" led by "foreigners" filled newspapers for weeks before May Day. In Chicago a strike of 80,000 took place, with workers from many trades participating. Two days later lumber workers appealing for a shorter workday joined strikers at the huge McCormick Harvest Works who were involved in a separate conflict. Police fired shots into the crowd, killing at least two strikers and wounding many. Chicago anarchists thereupon called a meeting to protest police violence.

The resulting demonstration at Haymarket Square, held in heavy rain and sparsely attended, was altogether peaceful. Police, however, rushed the demonstrators. Just at that moment, a bomb went off, provoking a veritable police riot. For weeks thereafter, police in many cities raided the offices of labor newspapers, fraternal halls, and the headquarters of local socialist movements. The person or persons actually responsible for the bomb were never found. The nation's first "red scare" culminated in the arrest of eight Chicago anarchists, however, none associated with the bombing incident itself but deemed guilty for their expression of radical ideas. In November 1887, after the eight were convicted in a trial rife with prejudicial treatment, four were executed by hanging. Gov. John Peter Altgeld released the surviving three in 1893, claiming their civil liberties had been violated in the unjust trial.

—PAUL BUHLE

See Also: Altgeld, John Peter; Labor Movement.
BIBLIOGRAPHY: Avrich, Paul, *The Haymarket Tragedy* (Princeton Univ. Press 1984); Nelson, Bruce D., *Beyond the Martyrs: A Social History of Chicago Anarchism, 1870-1900* (Rutgers Univ. Press 1988).

■ **HAY-PAUNCEFOTE TREATY (1901),** a U.S.-British accord that enabled the United States to construct the Panama Canal. Britain disclaimed its rights to a joint protectorate with the United States over a trans-isthmian canal (as agreed between the two nations in 1850). The United States received virtual sovereignty over the canal zone.
See Also: Panama Canal.

■ **HAYS, MARY LUDWIG. See:** Pitcher, Molly.

■ **HAYWOOD, WILLIAM DUDLEY (1869-1928),** labor leader. Born in Salt Lake City, Utah, he was known as "Big Bill" Haywood, both for his height and for his towering presence on the speaker's platform. He went to work as a miner's helper at the age of 15 and by 1901 was national secretary-treasurer of the Western Federation of Miners (WFM). A radical socialist, Haywood was also a founding member of the Industrial Workers of the World (IWW) in 1905. A year later, he was charged with killing former Idaho Gov. Frank Steunenberg but was acquitted in 1907. Haywood then became one of the most popular Socialist party speakers. After 1912, he concentrated on organizing for the IWW, participating in some of the largest strikes of the pre–World War I era. Removed from the Socialist party national committee because he refused to disavow the use of violence, Haywood became secretary-treasurer of the IWW, overseeing its successful union drives among migrant laborers, copper miners, and loggers in the American West. In 1917 Haywood was indicted, along with scores of other American radicals, under the Sedition Act. He escaped to the former Soviet Union in 1921, dying there in 1928.
See Also: Industrial Workers of the World; Labor Movement; Sedition Act.

■ **HEAD START,** federal early education program in the United States for the children of low-income families. Created in 1965 as part of the U.S. Office of Economic Opportunity, Project Head Start was one element of Pres. Lyndon B. Johnson's "war on poverty." Its goal was to break the "cycle of poverty" by giving low-income children a "head start" toward the cultural, educational, and social skills they need to succeed in school. Head Start's preschool program teaches readiness skills at local centers in both urban and rural areas across the country. Head Start centers also act as clearinghouses for various government and private nutrition, medical, and social service support programs. Although centers are staffed by professional teachers, the program relies heavily on volunteers and teachers' aides. The parents of participating children often fill those roles, giving Head Start a training and jobs component.

BIBLIOGRAPHY: Zigler, Edward, and Jeanette Valentine, eds., *Project Head Start: A Legacy of the War on Poverty* (Free Press 1979).

■ **HEALTH AND HUMAN SERVICES**, cabinet department of the U.S. government established by Congress (1979) during Pres. Jimmy Carter's administration to oversee a variety of federal health and welfare programs. It was created when the duties of the Department of Health, Education and Welfare, which had been established (1953) during Pres. Dwight D. Eisenhower's administration, were divided between Health and Human Services and a new cabinet-level Department of Education.

■ **HEARST, WILLIAM RANDOLPH (1863-1951)**, newspaper publisher. Hearst was born in San Francisco, California, an heir to a fortune built on mining. After attending Harvard University, Hearst put together a chain of newspapers that included the *San Francisco Daily Examiner*, the *Chicago American*, the *Boston American*, the *New York American*, and the *New York Mirror*. Hearst's holdings were the largest combination of newspapers in the nation. His papers are often described as examples of "yellow journalism," which emphasized the sensational aspects of news to entice readers. Hearst and publisher Joseph Pulitzer competed in this way to sell more newspapers. Hearst also owned the widely circulated magazines *Hearst's International-Cosmopolitan*, *Good Housekeeping*, and *Harper's Bazaar*. He won a seat in the U.S. House of Representatives in 1903 and served there until 1907. Hearst also ran for mayor of New York City in 1905 and 1909 and for governor of New York State in 1906 but lost each time.

See Also: Pulitzer, Joseph; Yellow Journalism.

■ **HEART OF ATLANTA MOTEL V. UNITED STATES (1964)**, U.S. Supreme Court case that upheld federal law banning racial discrimination in public accommodations. The owner of a small Georgia motel refused to accommodate African-American customers as required by Title II of the Civil Rights Act of 1964. The owner said his business primarily catered to in-state transients rather than interstate travelers, so it should not be subject to federal legislation based on Congress's constitutional authority to regulate interstate commerce. The Court, citing precedents dating back to *Gibbons* v. *Ogden* (1824), ruled (9-0) that the commerce clause allowed Congress to regulate both interstate commerce and activities within a state that affected interstate commerce. In a companion case, *Katzenbach* v. *McClung* (1964), the Court used the same reasoning to rule (9-0) that restaurants could not discriminate because of race.

See Also: Gibbons v. Ogden; Supreme Court.

■ **HEBARD, GRACE RAYMOND (1861-1936)**, educator and author born in Clinton, Ohio. A trustee, professor of political economy, and university librarian at the University of Wyoming at Laramie, she wrote several books on local history and championed the preservation of historical sites in Wyoming.

■ **HECKWELDER, JOHN GOTTLIEB (1743-1823)**, author and pioneer Moravian Church missionary to Indians in the Ohio region. Born in Bedford, England, Heckwelder came to Pennsylvania as a young boy. Although apprenticed to a cooper, his interest lay in preaching, especially to Indians. He eventually spent 15 years (1771-86) with the Delaware people, assisting them in their move to the West. Heckwelder recorded his experiences and knowledge of Indian culture in a series of published works.

■ **HELLMAN, LILLIAN (1905-84)**, playwright. Hellman spent much of her childhood moving with her family between her native New Orleans and New York City. Her early experiences in the South and the people she met there influenced her plays. After attending New York University for two years, she left to work as an editor and reviewer. Among the numerous literary figures she met during this period were the playwright Arthur Kober, whom she married and divorced, and novelist Dashiell Hammett, who later became Hellman's mentor and lover.

Hellman published her extremely successful first play, *The Children's Hour* (1934), through the encouragement of Hammett. Her plays are often melodramatic but are also marked by craftsmanship and a strong interest in moral issues. Indeed, morality stands at the center of Hellman's two most popular plays, *The Little Foxes* (1939) and *Watch on the Rhine* (1941).

During her lifetime, Hellman was renowned as America's greatest female playwright, but she also received notoriety because of her politics. During the 1930s she was a fervent antifascist, and in 1952 her support for left-wing causes resulted in her being summoned, along with Hammett, before the House Un-American Activities Committee. Blacklisted in Hollywood, she and Hammett were forced to sell their prized New York State farm. Hellman's life and work are testimony to her moral conviction that evil and injustice must be confronted in one's private and public affairs.

See Also: Hammett, Dashiell; Theater; Un-American Activities, House Committee on (HUAC); Women in American History.

BIBLIOGRAPHY: Moody, Richard, *Lillian Hellman: Playwright* (Pegasus 1972); Wright, William, *Lillian Hellman: The Image, the Woman* (Simon & Schuster 1986).

▪ HELPER, HINTON ROWAN (1829-1909),

southern antislavery advocate. Born in western North Carolina, Helper was an outspoken opponent of slavery. He claimed that slavery degraded the labor of white men in the South and left the South unable to compete economically with the North because plantation farming ruined the soil and inefficiently exploited the South's natural resources. In 1857, Helper published *The Impending Crisis*, outlining his ideas. The book sold 130,000 copies in the North, but most southern states outlawed it. When the Civil War began, Helper went to the North. He served as U.S. consul to Buenos Aires (1861-66).

See Also: Civil War.

▪ HEMINGWAY, ERNEST MILLER (1899-1961),

author. Born outside Chicago in Oak Park, Illinois, he embarked upon his literary career in Paris in the early 1920s. He had volunteered for the American Red Cross in Italy during World War I, been seriously injured, and spent six months recovering in Milan before returning to the United States in 1919. However, like several other Americans who had served in the war and would later become leading writers, Hemingway's disillusionment with U.S. life prompted his move to the seemingly more cultured continent of Europe in late 1921. After arriving in Paris, he met Gertrude Stein, who would dub him and his fellow literary expatriates a "lost generation."

Hemingway established himself as one of its leading spokesmen with the publication of his widely praised first novel, *The Sun Also Rises* (1926), whose concise prose marked Hemingway's writing style for the rest of his life. His wartime experiences in Italy provided the material for his next novel, *A Farewell to Arms* (1929). A lover of the outdoors who valued courage perhaps more than anything else, Hemingway had become a bullfighting aficionado since his first trip, in 1923, to the annual festival at

Ernest Hemingway's first novel, *The Sun Also Rises* (1926), helped establish him as the leading spokesman of the American expatriates in Paris, dubbed the "lost generation" by Gertrude Stein.

Pamplona, Spain. In 1932, he published his exploration of the sport, *Death in the Afternoon*. He reported on the Spanish civil war of 1936-39, in which struggle he supported the Loyalists and which inspired the novel, *For Whom the Bell Tolls* (1940). Although Hemingway's *Across the River and into the Trees* (1950), his first novel after covering and serving in World War II, did not do well, he won the 1953 Pulitzer Prize in fiction for *The Old Man and the Sea* (1953) and was awarded the 1954 Nobel Prize for Literature. In 1957-58, he composed a memoir of his life in Paris, published as *A Moveable Feast* (1964), after which Hemingway, suffering from depression and a number of other illnesses, committed suicide with one of his shotguns.

See Also: Novel; Short Story.

BIBLIOGRAPHY: Baker, Carlos, *Ernest Hemingway: A Life Story* (Charles Scribner's Sons 1969).

■ **HENDERSON, JAMES FLETCHER ("SMACK") (1897-1952),** band leader and arranger. Born in Cuthbert, Georgia, Henderson was a pioneer of jazz in a big band format. His band, with arrangements by Don Redman and Henderson, played with such renowned musicians as Louis Armstrong and Coleman Hawkins. Arranging for himself or for others, Henderson in the 1920s created the swing sound that influenced so many musicians, most notably Benny Goodman.

See Also: African Americans; Big Bands; Jazz.

■ **HENDRICK (c. 1680-1755),** Mohawk leader. Born a Mahican, Hendrick was adopted by the Mohawks. A spokesman for the Iroquois Confederacy, Hendrick was one of the four Indian "kings" who visited Queen Anne's court in London in 1710. Hendrick renounced the British at the 1754 Albany Congress because they had failed to prevent settlers from invading the Iroquois frontier. Hendrick nonetheless led Mohawk troops against the French during the Seven Years' War, during which he was killed in battle.

See Also: Albany Congress; Indians of North America; Iroquois Confederacy.

■ **HENDRICKS, THOMAS ANDREW (1819-85),** senator and vice president (1885). Born in Ohio, Hendricks entered politics as a Democratic state representative in the Indiana legislature. He went on to serve in the U.S. Congress (1851-55) and the U.S. Senate (1863-69) before being elected governor of Indiana (1872-77). He was defeated in his vice-presidential bid on the Democratic Tilden ticket in 1876 but was elected vice president with Pres. Grover Cleveland in 1884, only to die in office less than a year later.

See Also: Gilded Age; Vice President of the United States.

■ **HENRI, ROBERT (1865-1929),** painter and art teacher. Born in Cincinnati, Ohio, Henri enrolled at the Pennsylvania Academy of Fine Arts in 1886. He opened his first studio in Philadelphia in 1891 and moved to New York in 1899. Henri's lasting artistic influence is the result not only of his own paintings, such as *Spanish Gypsy* (1906) and *Laughing Boy* (1907), but also of his teachings. First in Philadelphia and then in New York, Henri taught younger American realists such as John French Sloan and George Bellows. In 1923 he published his views on art in *The Art Spirit*. Although a member of such mainstream organizations as the National Academy of Design, Henri was concerned with giving younger artists opportunities to exhibit. In 1908 at the Macbeth Gallery, Henri organized an exhibition of eight artists who, although they differed stylistically, all sought to depict daily life in the United States accurately. Originally dubbed The Eight, some members of the group were also nicknamed "the ashcan school" for their realistic portrayals of the urban environment.

See Also: Bellows, George; Painting; Sloan, John French.

■ **HENRY, JOSEPH (1797-1878),** scientist, the first secretary of the Smithsonian Institution. Born in Albany, New York, Henry was the son of a day laborer and had a variety of jobs before becoming a professor at Albany Academy (1826-31). There, he began the first sustained experimental research by a scientist in America. He invented an improved electromagnet with layers of insulated coils around an iron core (1829-30) that has been put into wide use, discovered the principle of induction independently of Englishman Michael Faraday (1830), and was the first to build an electromagnetic motor (1832). The modern unit of induction is called the "henry" in his honor. Henry became a professor at Princeton (1832-46), where he continued his experiments and developed the principles behind modern transformers (1838-42). His study of inductive discharges of electricity (1842) influenced the later development of radio. Henry left Princeton to become the first secretary and director of the Smithsonian Institution (1846-78), where he emphasized its support of original research. He also helped organize the American Association for the Advancement of Science, helped found the National Academy of Sciences, and served as its president (1868-78).

See Also: *Science; Smithsonian Institution.*

■ **HENRY, PATRICK (1736-99),** orator and statesman during the Revolutionary War era. Born at Studley plantation in Hanover County, Virginia, Henry was raised in a frontier environment in a refined household, where he was inspired by the sermons of Samuel Davis. At the age of 15 he became a store clerk and later opened his own store with his brother William as partner. Henry eventually turned to the study of law and obtained a license in the spring of 1760, thereby commencing a successful legal career. Although few authentic versions of his speeches are extant, his persuasive, anti-British oratory earned him a reputation and influenced the actions of his listeners. Henry became a member of the Virginia House of Burgesses, where he championed backcountry interests. While in the Burgesses he proposed seven resolutions in reaction to the Stamp Act (1765), including the strong claim that Virginia exercise complete legislative autonomy. Henry's resolutions, known as the Virginia Resolves, prompted widespread agitation throughout the colonies and secured his renown.

When Lord Dunmore dissolved the Virginia Assembly in May 1774, Henry organized the disbanded delegates to meet at the Raleigh Tavern in Williamsburg. In March 1775, Henry advocated armed resistance against the British in a rousing speech in which he declared, "I know not what course others may take; but as for me, give me liberty or give me death!" Although a delegate to the Continental Congress from 1774 to 1776, Henry opposed complete separation from Britain, thereby costing him a role as a national leader and limiting his future political activities to Virginia.

At the beginning of the American Revolution

Henry became colonel of the first regiment formed in Virginia. Denied advancement by political opponents, he resigned his commission in protest in February 1776 and returned home. Yet he reappeared in the political arena when he was elected to the third revolutionary convention, helped to draft the Virginia constitution, and, in June 1776, was elected governor of Virginia. During his term, he authorized George Rogers Clark's expedition to the Northwest Territory.

Henry served again as governor from 1784 to 1786. As a delegate to the 1788 Virginia Convention, he opposed ratification of the Constitution because he believed it gave too much power to the national government.

After his retirement as governor Henry remained active in politics and law. At George Washington's request, he campaigned for election as a Federalist to the Virginia House of Delegates in January 1799, thereby opposing nearly all of his former political allies in an unexplained shift of political ideology. Henry defeated John Randolph for the contested seat but died, on June 6, 1799, before he could take office.

—MARTHA J. KING

See Also: *Revolution, American; Stamp Act; Virginia Resolves.*

BIBLIOGRAPHY: Mayer, Henry A., *Son of Thunder: Patrick Henry and the American Republic* (Franklin Watts 1986); Wirt, William, *Sketches of the Life and Character of Patrick Henry* (Derby & Jackson 1817).

■ **HENRY AND DONELSON, BATTLES OF FORTS (1862),** strategically important Civil War engagements that opened up the Tennessee and Cumberland rivers to navigation by the Union navy. On February 6, Union gunboats under Commodore Andrew Foote bombarded Fort Henry on the Tennessee. Fort Henry surrendered soon after its Confederate commander evacuated most of his garrison to Fort Donelson, 12 miles away on the Cumberland. At Donelson, an attempted Confederate breakout was beaten back by Union Gen. Ulysses S. Grant, who accepted the fort's unconditional surrender on February 16.

See Also: *Civil War.*

■ **HENRY THE NAVIGATOR, PRINCE (1394-1460),** Portuguese sponsor of exploration. Prince Henry, son of King John I of Portugal, earned the title of Henry the Navigator through his enthusiastic support of his nation's sea exploration. Muslim control of the land routes to the profitable Asian markets provided the spur for his work. Convinced that the key to Portuguese commercial success required the discovery of an alternate sea route to the Asian trade centers, Prince Henry established a school for navigators and cartographers. Beginning in 1418, the prince sent out expeditions that greatly expanded Portuguese knowledge. In 1427 the Portuguese discovered the Azores, Atlantic islands lying 900 miles west of Portugal. Later voyages explored south along the African coast as far as Sierra Leone by the time of the Prince's death. These ventures helped Portugal establish a profitable trade in slaves and gold. Prince Henry set the stage for Portugal's early colonial expansion into the Indian Ocean and across the Atlantic.

See Also: Exploration and Discovery.

■ **HENSON, JIM (1936-90),** puppeteer. Born in Greenville, Mississippi, he created the whimsical Muppets, described as half marionettes and half puppets, in the 1960s. The ever-expanding cast of characters appeared in numerous films and television shows including the award-winning children's program *Sesame Street* (1969-). Henson himself voiced and manipulated the best known of the Muppets, Kermit the Frog.

■ **HEPBURN, KATHARINE (1907-),** movie actress who frequently portrayed witty and dominating characters. Born in Hartford, Connecticut, Hepburn is best known for her work beside leading man Spencer Tracy, with whom she collaborated on nine films. She won her first of four Academy Awards for her role in *Morning Glory* (1933).

■ **HEPBURN ACT (1906),** law passed by Congress as part of Pres. Theodore Roosevelt's efforts to regulate the railroads. The act empowered the Interstate Commerce Commission (ICC) to set and oversee maximum shipping rates, at the same time granting the courts the right to review any ICC rate decisions.

See Also: Interstate Commerce Commission (ICC).

■ **HERBERT, VICTOR (1859-1924),** composer and conductor. Born in Dublin, Ireland, he immigrated to the United States in 1886. Herbert composed symphonic music and grand operas and conducted the Pittsburgh Symphony (1898-1904), but he gained his greatest success with popular operettas including *Babes in Toyland* (1903) and *Naughty Marietta* (1910). He founded the American Society of Composers and Publishers (1914) to protect musical copyrights.

■ **HERNDON V. LOWRY (1937),** U.S. Supreme Court case that revived the "clear and present danger" test first expressed in *Schenck v. United States* (1919) to determine the limits of political speech. Herndon, a Communist party organizer, was convicted of breaking a Georgia sedition law by recruiting African Americans with promises of an independent black government. The Court reversed his conviction (5-4), finding his efforts posed no immediate threat of insurrection. The minority urged the Court to continue to apply the "bad tendency" test adopted in *Gitlow v. New York* (1925).

See Also: Schenck v. United States; Supreme Court.

■ **HESSIANS,** German mercenaries who fought for Britain during the American Revolution. Following the initial battles of the Revolution, King George III searched abroad to bolster his depleted army. His ministers first attempted to negotiate for 20,000 Russian mercenaries, but Empress Catherine the Great refused to hire out her subjects. The king then turned for support to the lord of the German state of Hesse-Cassel, whose first wife was the daughter of King George II. Hesse-Cassel obliged and offered 17,000 troops, along with another 12,000 Prussian-trained German soldiers. This large contingent accounted for about one-third of the entire British force in America. The Hessians contributed significantly to the decisive British victories at Long Island in 1776 and at Brandywine in 1777. They suffered a crucial defeat at Trenton, however, late in 1776, giving the American forces a much-needed boost in morale. After the war many Hessians settled in the United States and Canada.

See Also: Revolution, American.

■ **HEWES, JOSEPH (1750-79),** merchant and Revolutionary War leader. Hewes, born in Kingston, New Jersey, moved to North Carolina to continue his successful trading business. There he entered politics, eventually serving in the Second Continental Congress and signing the Declaration of Independence.

See Also: Declaration of Independence.

■ **HEYWARD, THOMAS (1746-1809),** lawyer and Revolutionary War leader. A signer of the Declaration of Independence, Heyward was born in St. Luke's Parish, South Carolina. During the Revolution he participated in his colony's legislature and militia and served in the Second Continental Congress.

See Also: Declaration of Independence.

■ **HIAWATHA (c. 1500s),** legendary cofounder of the Iroquois Five Nations Confederacy. According to one story, Hiawatha, a Mohawk, was living in isolation as a cannibal after the brutal murder of his family when the god Dekanawidah appeared to him and urged him to form the confederacy to stop the feuding among the Five Nations. In another version, Dekanawidah is depicted as a Huron visionary, who required Hiawatha as his spokesman because of a speech impediment.

See Also: Dekanawidah; Indians of North America; Iroquois Confederacy.

■ **HICKOK, WILD BILL (JAMES BUTLER) (1837-76),** frontier marshal. Born on an Illinois farm, Hickok shot and killed three men at the Rock Creek, Nebraska, stage station in 1861, a number that grew to 10 to 30 slain in dime Western novels shortly after. After serving in the Union army, Hickok's stint as marshal of Abilene, Kansas, in 1871 ensured his immortality. Hickok rode in Buffalo Bill's Wild West Show in the early 1870s before marrying circus owner Mrs. Agnes Lake Thatcher in 1876. Hickok was shot in a Deadwood, Dakota Territory, saloon on Aug. 2, 1876. His killer was tried and hanged.

See Also: Frontier in American History.

■ **HICKS, EDWARD (1780-1849),** painter of *The Peaceable Kingdom.* Born in Bucks County, Pennsylvania, Hicks worked as a coach maker in Langhorne. He also did coach, sign, and ornamental painting as part of his trade. Hicks began painting landscapes and religious scenes, al-

though not commercially. He painted over 100 versions of *The Peaceable Kingdom,* a serene vision of nature and its animal inhabitants, often with a scene in the distance of William Penn signing a treaty with Indians.

■ **HIDATSA INDIANS.** *See: Mandan.*

■ **HIGGINSON, THOMAS WENTWORTH (1823-1911),** abolitionist and women's rights advocate. Born in Cambridge, Massachusetts, Higginson was a Unitarian minister. In 1854 he tried to rescue runaway slave Anthony Burns, who had been arrested in Boston under the Fugitive Slave Act. He was indicted for inciting a riot, but the charges were dismissed. Later, Higginson was one of a group of northern abolitionists known as the Secret Six who supported John Brown's raid on Harpers Ferry. Higginson served as a colonel during the Civil War and led the first African-American regiment in the Union army.

See Also: Civil War; Fugitive Slave Act.

■ **HIGHWAY BEAUTIFICATION ACT (1965),** law limiting billboards and junkyards along interstate highways. The bill, a favorite of First Lady Claudia (Lady Bird) Johnson, set aside $240 million for roadside landscaping.

■ **HILL, JAMES JEROME (1838-1916),** founder and builder of the Great Northern Railway. The son of a farmer, Hill was born near Guelph, Ontario, Canada. He left home at 14 and traveled in America, finally working on the wharves in St. Paul, Minnesota.

In 1878, having made a considerable amount of money in the shipping business, Hill with four other investors purchased the bankrupt St. Paul and Pacific Railroad. Within a year the line stretched to the Canadian border. Hill continued to extend the line, now called the Great Northern Railway, without the benefit of land grants, and it reached Puget Sound in 1893.

Hill's railroad was profitable and well run, surviving the Panic of 1893 that destroyed so many businesses. In 1894, with the help of banker J. P. Morgan, Hill was able to acquire the bankrupt Northern Pacific. Despite the Sherman Antitrust Act (1890), Hill proceeded to consolidate his and other lines into the Northern Securities Company. In 1904 the Supreme Court broke up this holding company in the Northern Securities case. Hill's ownership of the lines continued; they were finally amalgamated into the Burlington Northern in 1970.

Hill had many other interests. He was involved in coal mining in Iowa, trans-world shipping, agricultural development, and townsite planning. Three months after his retirement from railroad management in 1912, he purchased two St. Paul banks (the First National and the Second National). Hill married Mary Mehegan in 1867, and they had ten children, nine of whom survived infancy.

—CLAIRE STROM

See Also: Industrial Revolution; Morgan, J. P. (John Pierpont); Railroads.
BIBLIOGRAPHY: Malone, Michael, *James J. Hill: Empire Builder of the Northwest* (Univ. of Oklahoma Press 1996).

■ **HILL-BURTON ACT (1946),** federal health care law. The act approved $1.125 billion for hospital construction and required hospitals receiving federal funds to set aside a share of their budgets to care for the poor.

■ **HILLMAN, SIDNEY (1887-1946),** labor leader. Born in Zagere, Lithuania, he immigrated to the United States in 1907 after participating in the Russian Revolution of 1905. He found work in Chicago's garment industry and served as business agent for Local 39, United Garment Workers of America. In 1914 unhappy locals, including Hillman's, broke away and formed the Amalgamated Clothing Workers of America (ACW). He was elected the first national president of ACW, a position he held until his death.

During the 1920s Hillman led the efforts to establish a "new unionism" based on the organization of industrial workers and the implementation of union-based social programs, many of which would be put into place on a national level during the New Deal. Under Hillman, the ACW was a pioneer in labor banking, consumer cooperatives, and unemployment insurance.

In 1935 Hillman joined with several other more radical labor leaders, breaking away from the American Federation of Labor to form the Committee for (later Congress of) Industrial Organizations, eventually becoming vice president of the new federation. A staunch New Dealer, he and John L. Lewis launched Labor's Non-Partisan League in 1936, a vehicle to enlist labor in the reelection campaign of Pres. Franklin D. Roosevelt.

See Also: AFL-CIO; Congress of Industrial Organizations (CIO); Labor Movement; Lewis, John L.; Roosevelt, Franklin Delano.

■ **HIROSHIMA AND NAGASAKI,** Japanese cities destroyed during World War II (August 1945) in the first use of atomic bombs on populated targets. A government-financed program to harness the explosive power of nuclear fission had been in progress in the United States since 1940 and eventually grew into the $2 billion Manhattan Project. By the summer of 1945 Germany had already been defeated, but the Japanese appeared to be willing to fight to the last man. American strategists, therefore, were forced to consider the prospects of a bloody and protracted invasion of the home islands. On July 15 Pres. Harry S. Truman, who at the time was attending an Allied conference at Potsdam, Germany, approved the use of an atomic bomb if Japan had not surrendered by August 2. After considering the many factors for and against use, Truman decided that any weapon that might shorten the war would be preferable to a full-scale invasion of Japan. On Aug. 6, 1945, a B-29 bomber named the *Enola Gay* dropped a bomb over Hiroshima, an important industrial center in southern Japan. The blast leveled most of the city and killed or injured some 130,000 people. Many of those injured died later of radiation sickness. On August 9, when the Japanese had still not surrendered, a second bomb (and the last one in America's arsenal) was dropped on the port city of Nagasaki, killing or wounding approximately 75,000 people. The Japanese were finally forced to capitulate, formally signing documents of surrender on September 2 aboard the battleship *Missouri*.

—STEVE O'BRIEN

See Also: Manhattan Project; World War II.
BIBLIOGRAPHY: Butow, Robert, *Japan's Decision to Surrender* (Stanford Univ. Press 1954); Giovannitti, Len, and Fred Freed, *The Decision to Drop the*

This photo illustrates the devastating destruction caused by the atomic bomb dropped by the United States on the Japanese city of Hiroshima on Aug. 6, 1945.

Bomb (Coward-McCann 1965); Sherwin, Martin J., *A World Destroyed: The Atomic Bomb and the Grand Alliance* (Knopf 1975).

■ **HISS-CHAMBERS CASE,** legal battle arising from concerns over the influence of international Communism on the U.S. government. In 1948, journalist and former Communist Whittaker Chambers accused Alger Hiss, a former State Department official and president of the Carnegie Endowment for World Peace, of having passed secrets to him for transmission to the Soviet Union. Hiss sued unsuccessfully for libel and, after denying that he had ever known Chambers, was convicted of perjury in 1950 and sentenced to five years in jail. The case became a symbol of Cold War concerns over subversive activities in government.

See Also: Cold War.

■ **HISTORY,** form of American letters that began with the writings of Puritans such as William Bradford and John Winthrop, who interpreted their settlement of the New World as a demonstration of God's "wonder working providence." The title of Cotton Mather's 1702 historical magnum opus spelled it out plainly: *Magnalia Christi Americana* ("Great Achievements of Christ in America"). The Puritan view of American history inspired the principal historians of the Revolutionary generation, writers such as David Ramsay and Mercy Otis Warren, who substituted "natural law" for divine authority. "America's purpose," Ramsay wrote in his history of the Revolution, "is to prove the virtues of republicanism, to assert the Rights of Man."

History in Early America. The practice of history flourished in the early republic. It became a patriotic duty to record the nation's history. To "diffuse the principles of virtue and patriotism," Noah Webster in 1790 produced the first historical primer for schoolchildren, a compilation of important dates and events beginning with Columbus's voyage and ending with the British surrender at Yorktown. In 1800, Mason Locke Weems published his famously influential (albeit fictionalized) biography of George Washington. Abraham Lincoln later remembered how profoundly impressed he had been as a child reading Weems's account of "the struggles for the liberties of the country."

The enthusiasm for patriotic history led the federal government and many of the states to establish archives for the preservation of historical documents and to publish the official papers, proceedings, and writings of the founding fathers.

During the early 19th century, civic-minded individuals organized dozens of historical societies and mounted campaigns to preserve historic buildings (among them Independence Hall, Fort Ticonderoga, and Mount Vernon). The first college course in American history was taught at William and Mary in 1821, and in 1839, Jared Sparks of Harvard was appointed the nation's first professor of history.

Most historians of the 19th century, however, were independent gentlemen of wealth and leisure. The most prominent of them was George Bancroft, often considered "the father of American history." He studied in Germany, where in 1820 he became the first American to earn a Ph.D. Bancroft and his generation were much influenced by German "historicism," an intellectual offspring of the romantic movement. Historians were to envelop themselves in the past in order to discover the essence of national cultures. In the celebrated first volume of his multivolume *History of the United States of America* (1834), Bancroft argued that America's essence was its mission to establish liberty in the world. Other important gentleman historians included William Prescott and Francis Parkman, both great stylists who believed that historical truth was best approached by writing stirring narratives. The importance of historical storytelling was part of the romantic tradition as well. Historians of the 19th century were greatly influenced by the Scottish historical romances of Sir Walter Scott as well as by Scott's American counterparts, James Fenimore Cooper, Washington Irving, and William Gilmore Simms. For romantic historians, history was a variety of literature, closely related to fiction and poetry.

The Professionalization of History. In the late 19th century, the idea of history as literature was gradually replaced by the practice of history as science. A new generation of historians devoted themselves to the "empirical" method of doing history, the inductive process of arriving at conclusions only after sifting through great masses of evidence. Close studies of particular events and periods ("monographs") replaced sweeping narratives. Much influenced by the intellectual furor over Darwinism, young historians rejected the search for essence in favor of an analysis of causation. These trends were consolidated by the professionalization of historical practice. After receiving a German doctorate in 1876, Herbert Baxter Adams opened the first American graduate program at Johns Hopkins, and other universities soon followed suit. Colleges began hiring newly minted American Ph.D.s to staff new departments of history. An important sign of the advance of professionalization was the organization of the American Historical Association (AHA) in 1884.

Among the most prominent or the first generation of professional historians were Charles McLean Andrews of Yale, William Archibald Dunning of Columbia, John Bach McMaster of the University of Pennsylvania, and Frederick Jackson Turner of Wisconsin, later Harvard. Turner would have the most enduring influence. In 1893, he delivered a paper at a meeting of the AHA entitled "The Significance of the Frontier in American History," in which he argued that the frontier had been the greatest determinant of American civilization. This "frontier thesis" would become the most influential interpretation of American history during the first half of the 20th century. Turner also made one of the earliest expressions of the "presentist" sensibility of 20th-century historians, when he argued that "each age writes the history of the past anew with reference to the conditions uppermost in its own time."

This idea would become the hallmark of a new group of historians, among them James Harvey Robinson of Columbia, whose manifesto, *The New History* (1912), called for studies illuminating the historical development of the political and cultural controversies of the day. Robinson's call was most famously answered by his Columbia colleague Charles A. Beard in *An Economic Interpretation of the Constitution* (1913), which outraged conservatives with an argument that the founding fathers had been motivated by personal economic interests. Beard's interpretation of American history as an epic struggle between conflicting classes (presented in the best-selling *The Rise of American Civilization* [1927], written with his wife Mary Ritter Beard) dovetailed nicely with the progressive politics of liberalism between the wars.

History in the Postwar Era. Beard's views fell from favor following World War II. Historians such as Perry Miller of Harvard and Richard Hofstadter of Columbia argued that ideological consensus rather than conflict characterized the American past. The so-called "consensus history" of the 1950s fit the intellectual climate of Cold War anticommunism and illustrated Turner's prescient point that historical writing is always shaped by contemporary interests. Similarly, the growing opposition to the Vietnam War produced yet another interpretive turn that reflected the growing political conflict of the 1960s. The most influential historian among these "New Left" revisionists was William Appleman Williams of the University of Wisconsin, who traced the roots of American "imperialism" back to the earliest years of the American republic.

The most important trend of the last quarter of the 20th century was the "new social history," a movement to research and write history "from the bottom up," emphasizing the experience of ordinary people and everyday life. Historians began writing books on the history of sexuality, childhood, and the family, and on the history of communities and workplaces. Many historians took their inspiration from the civil rights movements of African Americans, minorities, and women. Historians rewrote the story of African Americans, following the work of the civil rights leader W. E. B. Du Bois, whose *Black Reconstruction in America* (1935) had documented the political activism of freed slaves after the Civil War. There was a similar florescence of American Indian history, pioneered by historians such as D'Arcy McNickle, an activist of the Flathead nation, whose *They Came Here First* (1949) was an early example of what would become known as "ethnohistory." One of the first proponents of women's history was Mary Ritter Beard, who published *Women as a Force in History* (1946). The most enduring historical work of the last two decades of the 20th century detailed the complex history of this diverse nation.

—JOHN MACK FARAGHER

See Also: *Bancroft, George; Beard, Charles Austin; Bradford, William; Du Bois, W. E. B.; Irving, Washington; Mather, Cotton; Parkman, Francis; Prescott, William H.; Turner, Frederick Jackson; Webster, Noah; Winthrop, John.*

BIBLIOGRAPHY: Callcott, George H., *History in the United States, 1800-1860* (Johns Hopkins Univ. Press 1970); Foner, Eric, *The New American History* (Temple Univ. Press 1997); Higham, John, *History: Professional Scholarship in America* (Johns Hopkins Univ. Press 1983); Novick, Peter, *That Noble Dream: The "Objectivity Question" and the American Historical Profession* (Cambridge Univ. Press 1988).

▓ **HOBART, GARRET AUGUSTUS (1844-99),** vice president of the United States (1897-99). He was born in Long Branch, New Jersey, and was admitted to the New Jersey bar in 1869. A lawyer in Paterson, New Jersey, he also served as city counsel. Active in Republican state politics, he was elected to the New Jersey Assembly and the state senate. In 1896 he was elected vice president on the ticket of Republican Pres. William McKinley. He died before completing his first term.

See Also: *Gilded Age; McKinley, William; Vice President of the United States.*

▓ **HOE, RICHARD M. (1812-86),** inventor and industrialist. Son of Robert Hoe, a printing press manufacturer, Richard Hoe was born in New York City and joined his father's company at age 15. He invented a rotary press that printed on a cylinder instead of a flat plate. This invention and his type-revolving press (1847) revolutionized newspaper printing. A competitor developed a rotary press that printed on a continuous roll of newsprint by 1865, but Hoe produced (1871) an improved design, the web press, that incorporated all the main features of his rival's machine. Hoe left the company to his nephew Robert in 1886, under whose leadership the business continued to succeed.

See Also: *Invention; Science.*

▓ **HOFFA, JAMES RIDDLE (JIMMY) (1913-1975?),** labor leader. Born in Brazil, Indiana, he became active in the Teamsters Union in Detroit, rising to international vice president by 1952. In 1957 Hoffa was elected international president and for the next 10 years led an organizing drive that resulted in a membership of over 2 million. Long suspected of ties to organized crime, Hoffa was convicted of pension fund fraud in 1967. He mysteriously disappeared on July 30, 1975, and was officially declared dead in 1983.

See Also: *Labor Movement.*

▓ **HOFFMAN, ABBIE (1936-89),** radical activist. Born in Worcester, Massachusetts, he became a leading figure of the youth rebellion of the 1960s. Educated at Brandeis and the University of California, Hoffman was active in the civil rights movement in the South in the mid-1960s before moving to New York City and taking a leading role in a variety of antiwar and social movements. A brilliant publicist who knew how to play to the media, he showered the trading floor of the New York Stock Exchange with dollar bills and proposed running a pig for president in 1968 under the Youth International Party (Yippie) banner. Hoffman was indicted for conspiracy to riot after the 1968 Democratic convention in Chicago and helped turn the trial into a media circus. Facing drug charges, he went underground in 1973, surrendered to authorities in 1980, and soon returned to drumming up protests and publicity on campus and in the community. He committed suicide in 1989.

BIBLIOGRAPHY: Hoffman, Abbie, ed. by Dan Simon, *Selections '89: The Best of Abbie Hoffman* (Four Walls Eight Windows 1989).

■ **HOFFMAN, MALVINA (1887-1966),** sculptor. Born in New York City, she studied with French sculptor Auguste Rodin from 1910 to 1917 and spent several years, in the 1930s, traveling the world to produce more than 100 anthropological portraits of "racial types." Her portrait of John Muir is displayed at the American Museum of Natural History in New York City.

See Also: *Muir, John.*

■ **HOLDING COMPANIES,** corporations that hold enough shares of other companies to control their operations. Products of late-19th-century industrialization, holding companies allowed large corporations to reduce competition through means other than pools or trusts, which had proved vulnerable to prosecution under laws against monopoly or restraint of trade. Because stock is scattered among many small holders, one holding company could control an entire industry with just 10 or 20 percent of company stock. The Pennsylvania Railroad adopted this organizational device as early as 1870; American Bell did so a decade later. New Jersey had laws favoring holding companies, so when Standard Oil's structure was challenged under the Sherman Antitrust Act in 1892, John D. Rockefeller reorganized his empire under the hold-

ing company Standard Oil of New Jersey. J. P. Morgan's U.S. Steel (1901), capitalized at $1.4 billion, was the largest holding company in the nation for years.

Holding companies grew so large that the Supreme Court ordered the dissolution of the Northern Securities Company (1904), the American Tobacco Company (1911), and the Standard Oil Company (1911). The Wheeler-Rayburn Holding Company Act (1935) ended the pyramiding of public utility companies, and in 1961 the Supreme Court, in an effort to dissolve monopoly devices in big business, ruled that the du Pont Company had to divest itself of its General Motors Corporation holdings.

See Also: *Antitrust Cases; Industrial Revolution; Monopoly; Morgan, J. P. (John Pierpont); Rockefeller, John Davison; Sherman Antitrust Act.*

■ **HOLIDAY, BILLIE ("LADY DAY") (1915-59),** jazz singer. Holiday's success as a jazz soloist in the big band era is testimony to her talent as a

Jazz singer Billie Holiday made her first recordings in New York City in 1933.

great innovator. Although she never achieved the widespread popularity during her lifetime that was enjoyed by contemporaries such as Ella Fitzgerald and Mildred Bailey, Holiday won renown among later critics as the greatest jazz vocalist ever recorded.

Holiday was born Eleanora Fagan in Philadelphia. During her difficult and economically unstable childhood in Baltimore, she assumed her father's surname and that of her screen idol, Billie Dove. As a teenager, she moved to New York City with her mother and embarked on her singing career, which accelerated quickly. After being discovered in a club, she recorded her first album in 1933. Over the next two decades Holiday continued performing in such visible New York clubs as Café Society and recorded both solo and with other artists such as Count Basie, Benny Goodman, Lester Young, and Artie Shaw.

Despite her success, Holiday was plagued by a long-term drug addiction, for which she spent nine months in a West Virginia jail in 1947 and from which she eventually died at the age of 44. Nonetheless, her life resounded with achievements. In 1939, for example, she became one of the first African-American performers to integrate an all-white band. Perhaps more significantly, she left an enduring legacy of innovative music.

See Also: African Americans; Jazz; Women in American History.

BIBLIOGRAPHY: Clarke, Donald, *Wishing on the Moon: The Life and Times of Billie Holiday* (Viking 1994); Nicholson, Stuart, *Billie Holiday* (Northeastern University Press 1995).

■ **HOLLYWOOD,** section of the city of Los Angeles, California, that is home to the U.S. motion picture industry. The term *Hollywood* has also come to signify the U.S. film industry in general. First settled in 1853, the city of Hollywood was incorporated in 1903 and later became a district of Los Angeles (1910).

Motion picture technology developed in Europe during the 1890s, and by the second decade of the 20th century, American-made films began to attract sizable audiences at home and abroad. After the 1913 release of *The Squaw Man,* the first feature produced in Hollywood, other filmmakers flocked to southern California. The mix of writers, celebri-

ties, and money gave Hollywood a reputation for experimentation and excess that lingers today. By the 1930s, the industry had shifted from silent to talking pictures. Large and powerful studios controlled every aspect of the process, from the scripts and actors to the theaters. During World War II, movies enjoyed record attendance as Hollywood maintained a virtual monopoly on popular entertainment and a strong hold on the public imagination. With the introduction of television and an antitrust suit in the 1950s, the studios declined in power and prestige. Hollywood reached its nadir in the 1970s, as many studio-produced films failed at the box office. During the last few decades a new generation of filmmakers replaced the men who had dominated the industry since its inception, and the 1980s and 1990s witnessed a resurgence of interest in movies, particularly independent films.

—CATHERINE A. HAULMAN

See Also: Motion Pictures.

BIBLIOGRAPHY: Charyn, Jerome, *Movieland: Hollywood and the Great American Dream Culture* (Putnam 1989); Davis, Ronald, *The Glamour Factory* (Southern Methodist Univ. Press 1995).

■ **HOLMES, OLIVER WENDELL (1809-94),** doctor and literary figure. A native of Cambridge, Massachusetts, Holmes graduated from Harvard University in 1829 and received his medical degree there in 1836. He practiced medicine in Boston and then became a professor of anatomy at Dartmouth College (1838-40) and Harvard Medical School (1847-82). Holmes's first writings were in the medical field; he wrote *The Contagiousness of Puerperal Fever* in 1842. In 1857 he began contributing poems and literary sketches to the *Atlantic Monthly.* The next year he published *The Autocrat of the Breakfast-Table* (1858), followed by *The Professor at the Breakfast-Table* (1860) and *The Poet at the Breakfast-Table* (1872). Holmes also wrote novels, such as *Elsie Venner* (1861) and *The Guardian Angel* (1867). Later he turned to the genre of biography; his acclaimed biography of his friend Ralph Waldo Emerson was published in 1885. Holmes is remembered for such poems as "Old Ironsides," "The Chambered Nautilus," and "Dorothy Q." He was the father of the jurist Oliver Wendell Holmes, Jr.

See Also: Holmes, Oliver Wendell, Jr.

■ **HOLMES, OLIVER WENDELL, JR. (1841-1935),** associate justice (1902-32) of the Supreme Court. Born in Boston, the son of a physician noted for his literary talents, Holmes graduated from Harvard in 1861 and then fought in the Civil War, during which he was wounded three times, before entering Harvard Law School, graduating in 1866. He enjoyed studying law more than its actual practice and worked to combine his writing talents with legal study. He became a lecturer at Harvard Law School and, after the publication of his *The Common Law* (1881), a professor there, which in turn helped lead to his appointment to the Massachusetts Supreme Judicial Court as associate (1882-99) and chief (1899-1902) justice.

Supreme Court Years. In 1902, Holmes was appointed to succeed Horace Gray on the U.S. Supreme Court. While on the Court, he became known as the "Great Dissenter" and as a justice who wrote penetrating opinions that simplified the complexities of the issues under considera-

An associate justice of the U.S. Supreme Court from 1902 to 1932, Oliver Wendell Holmes, Jr., influenced many liberals, including future associate justice Felix Frankfurter, and wrote several of his most important opinions as dissents.

tion. In *Lochner* v. *New York* (1905), which challenged a New York law limiting the hours bakers could work, Holmes disagreed with the Court majority, which struck down the law, stating that the Court did not have the authority to invalidate the state legislature's socioeconomic approach or to promote its own conservative economic beliefs. In *Schenck* v. *United States* (1919), Holmes stated his "clear and present danger" theory, holding that the effort by Socialists to disrupt the draft in World War I threatened the U.S. military effort and could be outlawed constitutionally.

After Associate Justice Louis Brandeis joined the Court in 1916, Holmes found a philosophical ally, and the two men became friends. In *Abrams* v. *United States* (1919), Holmes and Brandeis dissented, holding that there was no clear and present danger in the distribution of leaflets promoting a general strike in protest against U.S. military activities in Russia. As a result of his clear and reasoned thinking, several later Supreme Court opinions upheld the views of Holmes by overturning earlier decisions in which he had dissented. His influence on constitutional law remained important long after his retirement from the Court in 1932.

—ROBERT C. KHAYAT

See Also: Abrams v. United States; Brandeis, Louis Dembitz; Lochner v. New York; Schenck v. United States; Supreme Court.

BIBLIOGRAPHY: Aichele, Gary, *Oliver Wendell Holmes, Jr.: Soldier, Scholar, Judge* (G.K. Hall 1989); Pohlman, H.L., *Justice Oliver Holmes and Utilitarian Jurisprudence* (Harvard Univ. Press 1984).

■ **HOME OWNERS REFINANCING ACT (1933),** federal law authorizing subsidized government loans to homeowners who had fallen behind on mortgage payments. About one million loans were issued before the law expired in 1936.

See Also: New Deal.

■ **HOMER, WINSLOW (1836-1910),** leading 19th-century naturalist painter. Born in Boston, Massachusetts, Homer was apprenticed to a lithographer from 1855 to 1857, when he opened his first studio in Boston, followed by one in New York two years later. He started his career as an illustrator for *Ballou's Pictorial* in Boston and *Harper's Weekly* in New York. Homer did drawings of the Virginia battle front for *Harper's* during the Civil War, and his first paintings were of army life. Following the war, he turned to rural scenes, as in *Snap the Whip* (1872); the industrializing countryside, as in *Morning Bell* (c. 1870); and recreation, as in *Croquet Scene* (1866). In 1883, after discovering an affinity for seascapes while traveling in England, Homer moved permanently to Prout's Neck, Maine. In watercolors and etchings, as well as oil paintings, he began depicting the naturalistic seascapes for which he is best remembered, such as *Fog Warning* (1885), *Eight Bells* (1886), and *Northeaster* (1895).

See Also: *Painting.*

■ **HOMESTEAD ACT (1862),** federal law giving 160 acres of land free to any settler who cultivated a claim for five years and who pledged to take U.S. citizenship. Such a measure had been advocated as early as the 1830s by those who hoped to transform the vast public domain in the West into a landscape of independent yeoman farmers. But opposition had come from Southern leaders, worried that the Western territories would be peopled with antislavery settlers. Some Easterners were also opposed, fearing that the opening up of lands in the West would undermine their land values. Southern secession during the Civil War broke this deadlock, and on May 20, 1862, Pres. Abraham Lincoln (whose Republican party had made the measure part of its 1860 platform) signed the act into law.

Ironically, the passage of the Homestead Act came just as the Civil War was helping to undermine the social and economic position of the independent farmer. Even though the number of American farms increased by some 4.4 million between 1860 and 1920, speculators acquired large portions of the public lands by filing dummy claims. Thus, the number of propertyless tenant farmers and urban laborers did not decline as predicted.

See Also: *Agriculture; Civil War.*

■ **HOMESTEAD STRIKE (1892),** labor dispute. The Amalgamated Association of Iron, Steel, and Tin Workers had won a strike at the Carnegie Steel Mill in Homestead, Pennsylvania, in 1889, but when that contract expired in June 1892, steel magnate Andrew Carnegie gave orders to his plant manager, Henry Clay Frick, to break the union. While Carnegie vacationed in his Scottish castle, Frick refused to negotiate with the union, locked out the workers before he officially discharged them, and erected an eight-foot fence around the plant. When 300 Pinkerton agents arrived on July 6 to protect nonunion workers, fighting broke out between the Pinkertons and the discharged workers. Nine steelworkers and seven Pinkertons died. By mid-July the governor of Pennsylvania sent in the state militia, and the mill reopened with nonunion workers. The union workers were not hired back; several of them were indicted for murder, rioting, and conspiracy but were eventually found not guilty. Steelworkers would be without union representation until the 1930s.

See Also: *Labor Movement; Lockout.*

■ **HOOKER, THOMAS (1586-1647),** Puritan minister, theologian, and political theorist. A Puritan leader in England, he fled in 1633 to Boston. After a dispute, Hooker led his congregation in an exodus to the Connecticut River and founded the town of Hartford in 1636, where he was pastor until his death. His political theories were reflected in the Fundamental Orders of Connecticut (1639), which did not require church membership for the franchise, as was the rule in Massachusetts. In his *Survey of the Summe of Church Discipline* (1648), he expressed his views on church government: authority rests with the competent—the people may choose, but the chosen shall rule.

See Also: *Connecticut; Puritanism; Religion.*

■ **HOOPER, WILLIAM (1742-90),** lawyer and Revolutionary War leader. After beginning his career as a lawyer in his native Boston, Hooper moved to North Carolina in 1764. He served in the First and Second Continental Congresses and signed the Declaration of Independence.

See Also: *Declaration of Independence.*

■ **HOOVER, HERBERT CLARK (1874-1964),** 31st president of the United States (1929-33). Born in West Branch, Iowa, Hoover was sent to live with a series of uncles after his parents died when he was nine years old. A member of the first graduating class of Stanford University (1895), Hoover earned a degree in geology and began a successful career as a mining engineer. Before he was 40 years old he was a multimillionaire, with offices of his mining engineering firm on three continents.

In 1914, immediately following the onset of World War I, Hoover became head of the program to coordinate food relief for war-torn areas of Belgium and northern France. His success in this endeavor led Pres. Woodrow Wilson to name him the nation's food administrator when the United States entered the war in 1917. After the war Hoover was called upon to help both the European allies and Germany get through the winter of 1918-19, one of the coldest on record.

By 1920 Hoover was a household name, revered for his humanitarian efforts and sought after by both political parties. He threw his lot in with the Republicans and in 1921 was named secretary of commerce by Pres. Warren G. Harding. Hoover stayed on through Harding's presidency and that of his successor, Calvin Coolidge, reaping much of the credit for the business boom of the 1920s. In 1927, when Coolidge announced that he would not seek reelection, Hoover was the overwhelming favorite of the Republican party. The following year he was nomi-

nated and went on to defeat Democrat Al Smith of New York, winning 58 percent of the popular vote.

Hoover's presidency was dominated by economic calamity. Although he was clearly not responsible for the stock market crash of October 1929, which devastated the world economy and led to the Great Depression of the 1930s, Hoover was unwilling to use the full power of government to intervene. An unabashed individualist, Hoover believed that the economy would eventually right itself if left alone. Furthermore, he believed that any federal aid given to the destitute would only take away their self-respect; as a result, he supported no government relief efforts.

Hoover's philosophy may have contributed to the severity of the Great Depression, although at the end of his term he proposed a number of government-sponsored initiatives to stimulate business. Given the situation, Hoover's landslide defeat at the hands of Franklin D. Roosevelt in the fall of 1932 was inevitable.

Hoover spent the entirety of the Roosevelt years speaking out publicly against the New Deal. He was called back to public life in the Tru-

Born into a Quaker family and trained as an engineer, Herbert Hoover became a millionaire by the age of 40. In 1928, Republican Hoover won the presidency, only to have the stock market crash hit during his first year in office.

man and Eisenhower administrations, when he chaired several committees that studied the makeup of the executive office and helped create food relief programs in post–World War II Europe.

—JOHN ROBERT GREENE

See Also: Great Depression; President of the United States.

BIBLIOGRAPHY: Degler, Carl, "The Ordeal of Herbert Hoover," *Yale Review* 52 (Summer 1963: 563-83); Nash, George, *The Life of Herbert Hoover*, 3 vols. (W. W. Norton 1983-96).

■ **HOOVER, J(OHN) EDGAR (1895-1972),** the first and longest-serving director of the Federal Bureau of Investigation (FBI). The son and grandson of minor U.S. government officials, he was born and lived his entire life as a bachelor in Washington, D.C.

Hoover was educated in public schools and began his career as a file clerk at the Library of Congress after high school. He attended night law school at George Washington University, and in 1917, after securing his law degree and following the U.S. entry into World War I, he joined the Justice Department's newly formed alien enemy registration section. The section's mission was to pursue enemy agents in the country for purposes of deportation, but after the Russian Revolution in 1917 and Germany's surrender in 1918 Hoover and his colleagues used their vague authority to pursue "Bolsheviks," as they said, and other radicals.

In 1919, Hoover was empowered to establish under his own direction a General Intelligence Division (GID) within the unchartered and little-known Bureau of Investigation. The ensuing, largely manufactured, "red scare" brought the bureau brief celebrity and subsequent notoriety, but Hoover himself escaped adverse publicity. In 1921, following a purge of the bureau's top executives for corruption and overreaching their authority, Hoover was named its assistant director.

The bureau's unauthorized antiradical activities during the Harding administration brought the agency into disrepute again, and a second purge followed, but again Hoover escaped blame. In 1924, at 29, he was named acting director of the bureau and, later that year, director. He was a superb administrator, but he disobeyed orders by continuing to maintain secret files on radicals and unsuspecting notables, practices that came

to light only many years later. In the 1930s he promoted the renamed Federal Bureau of Investigation into a crime-fighting legend.

After World War II, Hoover mounted another red scare using allies in Congress to whom he leaked FBI files. However, the enthusiasm for so-called McCarthyism waned in the later 1950s, and Hoover and his bureau came under increasing scrutiny. Still, no president dared to dismiss him—Nixon tried and failed—and Hoover died in office, leaving a legacy of secrecy and distrust.

—JOHN STUART COX

See Also: Cold War; Red Scare.

BIBLIOGRAPHY: Power, R. G., *Secrecy and Power* (The Free Press 1987); Theoharis, A. G., and J. S. Cox, *The Boss* (Temple Univ. Press 1988).

■ **HOPE, BOB (1903-),** radio, television, and film comedian. Born Leslie Townes Hope in Eltham, England, but raised in Cleveland, Ohio, his rapid-fire comedy monologues made him a hit on radio from 1935 and television after 1952. He starred in many films, most notably a series of six *Road* comedies costarring Bing Crosby (1940-52). Hope also traveled around the world entertaining U.S. troops overseas from 1940 to 1991.

■ **HOPI,** Pueblo Indian tribe of the Southwest. Located in the plateau country of northern Arizona, the 10 Hopi settlements are surrounded by the Navaho Reservation. Most of the Hopi towns have existed since at least the 16th century, and the village of Oraibi, established in the 13th century, is thought to be the oldest continuously inhabited town in the United States. During the Spanish and Mexican occupation, Catholic missionaries attempted to convert the Hopis to Christianity, but most Hopis continue to practice their traditional religion. The Hopis were farmers who irrigated terraced fields in the arid terrain and who lived in multistoried adobe houses. After the acquisition of the Southwest by the United States in 1848, the Hopis remained isolated in their mesa-top settlements and took no part in warfare against non-Indians. In 1882 the United States set aside the Hopi Indian Reservation. Most of the more than 6,000 Hopi people are involved in farming, cattle-raising, or off-reservation wage labor. The Hopis have a high percentage of college graduates, and many are engaged in professional occupations.

See Also: Indians of North America; Pueblo.

■ **HOPKINS, HARRY L. (1890-1946),** government official, an intimate and influential adviser to Pres. Franklin D. Roosevelt. Born in Sioux City, Iowa, he became a social worker in New York City, where he witnessed massive poverty. His work in New York won him praise in Washington, and in 1933, Roosevelt appointed Hopkins the first chief administrator of the Federal Emergency Relief Administration.

Over the next seven years Hopkins also directed the Civil Works Administration and the Works Progress (later Projects) Administration, and served as secretary of commerce. Hopkins strenuously advocated relief for the poor and underemployed through increased work opportunities, instead of direct monetary relief. These efforts were most visible in the WPA, which employed millions of Americans in the years after 1935. Although these programs proved popular with the public, they came under political attack. Hopkins and Roosevelt were accused of creating a politically motivated, self-perpetuating process of taxing and spending to support relief programs. Nonetheless, the legacy of these relief programs were evident in the domestic policies of Presidents Kennedy, Johnson, and Nixon.

In the wake of these controversies, Roosevelt moved Hopkins into the White House to act as a personal adviser in domestic and foreign affairs. During World War II, Hopkins represented the United States at many of the major international military conferences.

See Also: New Deal; Works Projects Administration (WPA).

BIBLIOGRAPHY: McJimsey, George T., *Harry Hopkins: Ally of the Poor and Defender of Democracy* (Harvard Univ. Press 1987).

■ **HOPKINS, STEPHEN (1707-85),** statesman and Revolutionary War leader. A member of the Second Continental Congress and signer of the Declaration of Independence, Hopkins was born in Scituate, Rhode Island. During his long career, he was a jurist, pamphleteer, and governor of Rhode Island.

See Also: Declaration of Indepedence.

■ **HOPKINSON, FRANCIS (1737-91),** statesman, artist, and musician. Born and educated in Philadelphia, Pennsylvania, Hopkinson was an eminent lawyer and judge who represented New Jersey in the Second Continental Congress and signed the Declaration of Independence. During the Revolutionary War he held several government posts, wrote patriotic essays, and designed the "Stars and Stripes" national flag. His *Seven Songs* (1788) was the first secular music published in the United States.

See Also: Declaration of Independence.

■ **HOPPER, EDWARD (1882-1967),** realist painter. Hopper was born in Nyack, New York. He began his career as an illustrator and in 1915 started studying etching. For about a decade he devoted his prints to outdoor scenes such as that depicted in *The Railroad and the American Landscape* (1923), which reflected his personal desires for escape and freedom, winning prizes for his work at the International Printmakers Exhibition and the Chicago Society of Etchers in the early 1920s. He had his first show of watercolors in New York in 1924, followed five years later by his first exhibition of oil paintings. In addition to contemporary urban scenes, New York and New England landscapes became his major subjects, as in *Lighthouse at Two Lights* (1929) and *New York, New Haven, and Hartford* (1931). Hopper's paintings are often devoid of human figures, or depict a solitary person, and can evoke a sense of isolation and loneliness. Increasingly popular in the 1930s and 1940s, Hopper won acclaim for such paintings as *Early Sunday Morning* (1930) and *Night Hawks* (1942).

See Also: Painting.

■ **HORSE,** hoofed mammal, extinct in the Americas until reintroduced by Europeans in the 16th century. The horse's advantages to European settlers were many. Not only did mounted-horse soldiers prove especially effective in battles against Indians, but once the horse was hitched to a plow or cart, colonists could harness the animal's energy for tasks ranging from the planting of crops to the transporting of goods to market.

The horse was a fickle ally, however, and soon strayed from the European settlements where it had initially been located. By 1720 escaped Spanish horses had reached the Great Plains, and a decade later their range extended all the way into northern Canada. While many of these animals remained feral (as do some of their descendants today), others came into contact with Indian peoples, precipitating during the late 1700s and early 1800s the rise of a nomadic, buffalo-hunting culture that has become perhaps the most enduring symbol of the Indians' America.

The development of the gasoline-powered internal combustion engine in the late 1890s displaced the horse from its once preeminent position in American life. The introduction of Henry Ford's Model T in 1908 made the automobile an affordable alternative to horse-drawn transportation. By the 1920s, gas-powered tractors had begun to replace horses and mules on many farms. As a result, the population of horses and mules in the United States declined sharply, from close to 20 million in the early 1900s to less than 4 million by 1960, and the horse's use became increasingly limited to the ceremonial occasions where it is most commonly seen today: parades, races, rodeos, and similar events.

—KARL JACOBY

See Also: Agriculture.
BIBLIOGRAPHY: Nowak, Ronald, *Walker's Mammals of the World,* 5th ed. (Johns Hopkins Univ. Press 1991).

■ **HORSE RACING,** a popular sport since colonial times. Wealthy planters in Virginia began raising English thoroughbreds in the late 16th century and often staged high stakes contests. Race courses spread across the country in the 19th century featuring thoroughbreds, quarter horse sprinters, and standard bred pacers and trotters. In recent years the number of tracks has declined and pari-mutuel betting has become the sport's major attraction.

■ **HORSESHOE BEND, BATTLE OF (Mar. 27, 1814),** fought between U.S. and American Indian troops under Gen. Andrew Jackson and the Creek Red Sticks. The Red Stick faction of Creeks were followers of the militant resistance movement of Tecumseh, which sought to halt U.S. incursions into lands held by Indians between the Appalachian Mountains and the Mississippi River. In 1813 and 1814 the Red Sticks attacked American settlements in western Georgia and Alabama, culminating in the capture of Fort Mims

on the Alabama River, an attack that killed more than 500 people. In March 1814 Jackson and 5,000 American militiamen combined with regiments of Creeks, Cherokees, Choctaws, and Chickasaws to attack the Red Stick town of Tohopeka on the Tallapoosa River in Alabama, killing more than 800 Creeks in the decisive Battle of Horseshoe Bend. At the subsequent treaty (Aug. 9, 1814), Jackson forced the Creek nation to cede more than 22 million acres of land in southern Georgia and central Alabama.

See Also: Indians of North America; Jackson, Andrew; Tecumseh.

■ *HORTON V. CALIFORNIA* **(1990),** U.S. Supreme Court case that allowed police to seize items in plain view during a legal search. Police, with a warrant to search Horton's home for stolen goods, found and seized weapons that, they admitted in court, were not specified in the warrant but that they had hoped to find. The Court ruled (7-2) to uphold the search and conviction, saying the Fourth Amendment protects privacy but gives police some latitude.

See Also: Supreme Court.

■ **HOUSE OF REPRESENTATIVES.** The House of Representatives was established as a coequal legislative branch by the framers of the Constitution. Members are elected to a two-year term and may be reelected without limits. They must be 25 years of age and citizens of the United States for at least 7 years. Representatives are elected from individual districts and, consequently, are faced with the difficulty of simultaneously representing the needs of their constituents and those of the nation as a whole.

Legislation passed in 1929 fixed the size of the House at 435 members. However, every state has at least one representative. States may be required to reapportion their districts after the national census that is taken every 10 years. House districts were often unequal in size until a Supreme Court decision in 1964 forced states to draw proportionally equal district boundaries to ensure the principle of "one man, one vote."

The large size of the House has necessitated reliance on committees and more restrictive procedural flexibility than in the Senate. The powerful House Rules Committee is responsible for establishing the rules of debate. However, a procedure does exist to bring to the full House a bill that is stalled in committee. A "discharge petition" may be signed by an absolute majority of House members (218) to remove a bill from committee for consideration by the full House. The Rules Committee along with Appropriations and Ways and Means are the most important of the 19 standing or permanent committees and almost 100 subcommittees. Appropriations is important because the House has the constitutional right to originate revenue raising measures (Article I, Section 7). The majority party organizes the House and has the majority of seats on the committees and also a majority of the House staff. Although the seniority rule has been weakened over the last quarter century, most committee chairs are still held by members who have served the longest.

The Speaker of the House is elected by the majority party and has considerable influence over the legislative process. He has the power to assign bills to a particular committee and also plays a major role in the assignment of members to committees. He is assisted by the House majority leader and various party "whips." The minority party elects similar leadership positions. The Speaker occupies a prominent position in American political life. He is also the first in line to succeed to the presidency after the vice president. In addition, with the adoption of the 25th Amendment in 1967, the Speaker plays a role in the process of determining presidential disability.

When the House passes legislation, it goes to the Senate for consideration. Because House and Senate versions of legislation are never identical, the bill goes to a conference committee to work out the differences. The final version of the legislation is sent to the president for his action. The House, like the Senate, can conduct investigations and compel witnesses to testify. The Constitution gives the House the sole power of impeachment (Article I, Section 3). If the House votes for impeachment, the trial is conducted by the Senate. The House, along with the Senate, must give two-thirds approval before any proposed constitutional amendment can be sent to the states for their consideration. Despite frustrations over campaigning and fund-raising, representatives exercise considerable influence shaping American public life.

—ALEXANDER WELLEK

See Also: *Constitution of the United States.*

BIBLIOGRAPHY: Currie, James, *The United States House of Representatives* (Krieger 1988); Israel, Fred, ed., *The House of Representatives* (Chelsea House 1987); Redmon, Eric, *The Dance of Legislation* (Simon & Schuster 1973); Sinclair, Barbara, *Majority Leadership in the United States House of Representatives* (Johns Hopkins Univ. Press 1983).

■ **HOUSING ACT (1954),** law shifting federal housing efforts toward home ownership rather than apartments. It lowered down payments for federally insured mortgages and strengthened the Federal National Mortgage Association.

■ **HOUSING AND URBAN DEVELOPMENT,** cabinet department of the U.S. government that oversees federal urban renewal and housing programs. Created by Congress (1965) as part of Pres. Lyndon B. Johnson's Great Society reforms, the department controls billions of dollars in government grants and loans. An investigation of corrupt practices in the department during the administration of Pres. Ronald Reagan (1981-89) led to the conviction of several administration officials.

■ **HOUSTON, SAM (1793-1863),** soldier and political leader. Born in Rockbridge County, Virginia, he lived as a youth intermittently among the Cherokees of East Tennessee. A skillful and decorated soldier, he fought in the War of 1812, attracting the attention of Andrew Jackson. After serving two terms in Congress, Houston was elected governor of Tennessee in 1827 but left office two years later to live again among the Cherokees.

In 1832, Houston ventured to Texas, where he quickly became involved in Anglo settlers' growing political protest against Mexican rule. As commander of the Texan army during the Texas Rebellion, Houston led his troops to a decisive victory at San Jacinto in 1836. He figured prominently in the new republic, serving two terms as president. After U.S. annexation, Houston served 13 years in the U.S. Senate (1846-59). Although a slaveholder, he became a leading opponent of sectionalism, advocating preservation of the Union.

See Also: *Frontier in American History; Texas Rebellion.*

■ **HOWARD, OLIVER OTIS (1830-1909),** Civil War general and Reconstruction administrator.

When his wife abruptly left him in 1829, Sam Houston resigned as governor of Tennessee and moved west, finally settling in Texas. He was a leader of the Texas Rebellion and later served as governor of the state.

Born in Leeds, Maine, Howard graduated from West Point in 1854. In the Civil War he was defeated by Stonewall Jackson at Chancellorsville (May 1863) and also commanded without distinction at Gettysburg (July 1863). Howard headed the Freedmen's Bureau (1865-72) and was a founder and the first president (1869-74) of Howard University. He fought the Nez Perce Indians (1877) and was head of West Point (1881-82).

See Also: Civil War; Freedmen's Bureau; Reconstruction.

■ **HOWE, ELIAS (1819-67),** inventor who patented the sewing machine. Born in Spencer, Massachusetts, Howe apprenticed in a cotton mill and then worked in machine shops, where he built a sewing machine that he patented in 1846. This machine had an eye-pointed needle that worked in conjunction with a lower thread-loaded shuttle, which was thrown through loops of thread made by the upper needle and could sew 250 stitches a minute. In the 1860s Howe received royalties that reached $4,000 a week and became a millionaire before he died. He established the Howe Machine Company in 1865, and his name became a house-

hold word. The degree to which Howe was responsible for the invention itself, however, remains in question. Walter Hunt had designed a similar machine by 1834 but did not patent it.

See Also: Invention; Science.

■ **HOWE, JULIA WARD (1819-1910),** woman suffrage leader and poet. She was born in New York City. She is remembered primarily for her poem "The Battle Hymn of the Republic," which became a popular anthem for Northerners during the American Civil War. After the war, Howe joined Lucy Stone in the leadership of the American Woman Suffrage Association. Her lectures against the antiquated ideals of high society were collected in *Is Polite Society Polite?* (1895) and other volumes.

See Also: American Woman Suffrage Association; Civil War; Stone, Lucy; Women in American History; Women's Movement.

■ **HOWE, SIR WILLIAM (1729-1814),** British general in the American Revolution. Commander of the British army in America from 1775 to 1778,

Author and social reformer Julia Ward Howe wrote the lyrics for "The Battle Hymn of the Republic," which was enormously popular in the North during the Civil War.

Howe engaged the Americans in such famous battles as Bunker Hill and Brandywine. He failed to win any decisive victories and eventually resigned his command.

See Also: Bunker Hill, Battle of; Revolution, American.

■ **HOWELLS, WILLIAM DEAN (1837-1920),** writer, editor, and proponent of realism. Howells was born in Martin's Ferry, Ohio. He joined the staff of the *Ohio State Journal* in 1856, working in Columbus until 1861. In 1860 Howells published *Life of Lincoln*, a campaign-year biography. He served as the U.S. consul in Venice, Italy, from 1861 to 1865. Upon his return to the United States, Howells became assistant editor of the *Atlantic Monthly*, a literary journal to which he had been contributing. He became editor in 1871, a position he held for 10 years. Howells also worked on the editorial staffs of *Harper's Magazine* (1886-91) and *Cosmopolitan Magazine* (1891-92). Howells wrote in a variety of literary genres, advocating realism both in his criticism and through the example of his own novels. His novels captured the social world of the Gilded Age, primarily in Boston and New York City. *The Rise of Silas Lapham* (1885) and *A Hazard of New Fortunes* (1890) are particularly sharp portrayals of shifting status designations in an industrial economy.

See Also: Gilded Age.

■ **HUDSON, HENRY (d. 1611),** English explorer. Financed by the Dutch, Hudson sailed in the vessel *Half Moon* from Amsterdam in 1609 in search of a route to India and China. Crossing the Atlantic, Hudson explored the river that bears his name as far as Albany, New York. This visit served as the basis for Dutch claims in North America. In 1610, sailing for the English, Hudson again crossed the Atlantic, in pursuit of his dream of finding a Northwest Passage. In the ship *Discovery* he crossed Hudson Bay in August of 1610 but could not find a route to the Pacific. Trapped by the onset of winter, Hudson and his crew were forced to wait until the spring thaw. Tensions mounted, and by spring much of the crew mutinied, setting Hudson, his son, and seven others adrift in a small boat. With Hudson's fate sealed, the mutineers set sail for England. The leaders of the mutiny, however, died during the return trip.

See Also: Exploration and Discovery; Northwest Passage.

BIBLIOGRAPHY: Morison, Samuel Eliot, *The Great Explorers: The European Discovery of America* (Oxford Univ. Press 1978).

■ **HUDSON RIVER,** mighty and majestic river in New York State. Beginning in the Adirondack Mountains at Lake Tear of the Clouds, the Hudson flows south 316 miles into Upper New York Bay at New York City. Before Europeans came upon the Hudson, the Iroquois tribes lived in palisaded villages along parts of the river. The Englishman Henry Hudson first sailed up the river in 1609 in the service of the Dutch East India Company. The Dutch then began settling the Hudson at New Amsterdam on Manhattan and at Fort Orange (present-day Albany). In 1664 the English seized New Amsterdam from the Dutch and renamed it New York. The completion of the Erie Canal across central New York in 1825 allowed grain and other agricultural products to pass from the Great Lakes to the Hudson River and down to the New York City harbor. Nineteenth-century artists and writers, including Washington Irving, Thomas Cole, and Frederick Church, were inspired by the Hudson's stunning landscapes and remnants of Dutch colonial culture. During the 20th century industrial pollution damaged much of the Hudson's fish, bird, and plant life. Since the 1970s, however, attempts have been made to control the river's pollution levels.

See Also: Hudson, Henry.

■ **HUDSON RIVER SCHOOL,** collective name for the American artists, mostly New York–based, who specialized in landscape scenes in the middle years of the 19th century. First used in an exhibition review, the label was meant to poke fun at these painters, who, traveling into the Hudson River Valley in search of wild vistas, proclaimed themselves students of nature, not art academies. The artists and their supporters thought of themselves as abandoning old, exhausted art traditions associated with a morally bankrupt Europe in favor of new aesthetic and geographic horizons associated with the westward-expanding United States.

The preeminent Hudson River School painter was Thomas Cole (1801-48), who stirred the New York art world in the late 1820s with his dramatic views of the Catskill Mountains. When Cole embarked on a painting expedition to Italy, his greatest champion, the nature poet and newspaper editor William Cullen Bryant, urged him not to forsake New World spontaneity for Old World conventionality. Asher B. Durand (1796-1886), who issued an influential series of essay-letters equating artistic scrutiny of the wilderness with devotion to the Almighty, painted a memorial tribute to Cole that stands as the canonical work of the Hudson River School: *Kindred Spirits* (1849) depicts Cole and his friend Bryant communing on a Catskill promontory, peering reverently at the lofty sights spread before them. In the second generation of Hudson River School artists, Cole's only pupil, Frederick Church (1826-1900), won international acclaim as a painter of minutely detailed and dramatically scaled panoramas of the Andes Mountains.

—DAVID M. LUBIN

See Also: Cole, Thomas; Durand, Asher B.; Painting.
BIBLIOGRAPHY: Flexner, James Thomas, *That Wilder Image* (Little, Brown 1962); Howat, John K., et al., *American Paradise: The World of the Hudson River School* (exhib. cat., Metropolitan Museum of Art 1987); Truettner, William H., and Alan Wallach, *Thomas Cole* (exhib. cat., Yale Univ. Press 1994).

■ **HUDSON'S BAY COMPANY,** corporation chartered by King Charles II of England in 1670 for the purpose of trade and settlement of the Hudson Bay region of North America. The company, which continues to operate department stores in Canada, had its origins in European explorations of the western Great Lakes region during the mid-17th century. The charter granted the company mineral and proprietary rights and a monopoly on trade in Rupert's Land, an extensive region west and north of the Great Lakes. Within a few years of the charter, the company had established several profitable posts on the Hudson and James bays and had developed lucrative trading ties with the region's natives, the Crees. French attacks and competition in trade did little to threaten the company, and in 1713, England's gains in the Treaty of Utrecht solidified the company's position. Despite the trading success and establishment of posts, however, the Hudson's Bay Company's almost exclusive business approach precluded the development of an English society in the region.

Competition from independent traders during the mid-18th century was followed by concerted opposition from the North West Company in the 1780s. After decades of intermittent conflict, the two companies merged in 1821. Schemes of annexation, both on the part of the United States and the region's discontented settlers, led to an end to the company's trading monopoly in 1859 and to the selling of its lands to Canada in 1870.

See Also: French Colonies; Frontier in American History; Fur Trade.
BIBLIOGRAPHY: Rich, E. E., *History of the Hudson's Bay Company, 1670-1870*, 3 vols. (Macmillan 1961).

■ **HUGHES, CHARLES EVANS (1862-1948),** political leader, diplomat, associate justice (1910-16) of the U.S. Supreme Court, and chief justice (1930-41) of the United States. Born in Glens Falls, New York, he entered Madison College (now Colgate University) at age 14; transferred to Brown University, from which he graduated in 1881; and then taught school before becoming a lawyer in 1884. After successfully helping to expose utility and gas company abuses in New York, he was elected the state's Republican governor in 1906, serving until 1910, when President Taft appointed him to the Supreme Court to succeed Associate Justice David Brewer. During his tenure as an associate justice, he was considered a liberal, primarily in the areas of civil rights, the power of Congress under the Constitution's commerce clause, and states' rights.

Hughes resigned from the Supreme Court to run for president as a Republican against incumbent Woodrow Wilson. After narrowly losing the election, he returned to private law practice until 1921, when he was appointed secretary of state by Pres. Warren G. Harding. As secretary Hughes helped convene the Washington Armament Conference (1922) on limiting the world's major navies. He resigned in 1926 to take a seat on the Permanent Court of Arbitration and then also became a judge on the Permanent Court of International Justice (1928).

Chief Justice. In 1930, Hughes was nominated by Pres. Herbert Hoover to succeed William Howard Taft as chief justice of the United States. While chief justice, his most significant opinions were in the areas of civil liberties and civil rights, especially First Amendment rights, such as freedom of the press in *Near v. Minnesota*. Hughes voted with the majority in upholding early New Deal legislation and in overturning later legislation such as the National Industrial Recovery Act in *Schechter Poultry Corp.* v. *United States* (1935).

After Pres. Franklin Roosevelt's court packing plan had been turned back, Hughes voted to sustain New Deal legislation in *National Labor Relations Board* v. *Jones and Laughlin Steel Corp.* (1937), which upheld the National Labor Relations Act, and *Steward Machine Co.* v. *Davis* (1937), which upheld federal unemployment compensation. Hughes retired from the Court in 1941.

—ROBERT C. KHAYAT

See Also: *Court Packing; Near v. Minnesota; New Deal; Presidential Elections; Schechter Poultry Co. v. United States; Supreme Court; Washington Armament Conference.*

BIBLIOGRAPHY: Perkins, Dexter, *Charles Evans Hughes and American Democratic Statesmanship* (1956; reprint Greenwood 1978).

■ HUGHES, (JAMES) LANGSTON (1902-67),

author. Born in Joplin, Missouri, and class poet in Cleveland, Ohio, he had decided by the time of his 1920 high school graduation that he would become a writer. Soon after, riding on a train to visit his father in Mexico, Hughes composed the poem, "The Negro Speaks of Rivers," first printed in *Crisis*, the organ of the National Association for the Advancement of Colored People (NAACP), in June 1921. "The Weary Blues" revealed early in his life Hughes's desire and extraordinary ability to incorporate aspects of African-American popular culture, in this case blues music, into his work, and it won him first prize in a poetry contest sponsored by the National Urban League's journal, *Opportunity*, in 1925. He soon met critic and writer Carl Van Vechten, whose support helped convince Alfred A. Knopf to publish Hughes's first collection of verse, *The Weary Blues*, in 1926, in which year also appeared his essay for the *Nation*, "The Negro Artist and the Racial Mountain."

With these, as well as his second book of poetry, *Fine Clothes to the Jew* (1927), Hughes emerged at the forefront of the Harlem Renaissance and certainly as its most prominent poet.

His first novel, *Not Without Laughter*, followed in 1930 and trips to the Caribbean and the Soviet Union over the next few years turned Hughes toward Marxism, whose influence upon him would wane in later years. In the 1930s, he completed a number of plays, including *Mulatto*, which was given a Broadway production in 1935, and he founded the Harlem Suitcase Theatre in 1938. While working in Hollywood late in the decade, Hughes produced his first autobiography, *The Big Sea* (1940). In 1942, he moved to the Harlem section of New York City, where he remained for the rest of his life writing prodigiously, often to condemn racial segregation. Among this period's publications are the extended poem, *Montage of a Dream Deferred* (1951), the second autobiography, *I Wonder As I Wander* (1956), and the play, *Jericho-Jim Crow* (1964). In 1961, Hughes was elected to the National Institute of Arts and Letters, although he had already long assured his lasting place in American literature.

—JAMES KESSENIDES

See Also: *African Americans; Harlem Renaissance; New Deal; Poetry.*

In the 1920s and 1930s, the writings of Langston Hughes established him as a leader of the Harlem Renaissance. Later Hughes bought a house in Harlem, where he lived and worked until his death.

BIBLIOGRAPHY: Rampersad, Arnold, *The Life of Langston Hughes,* 2 vols. (Oxford Univ. Press 1986, 1988).

■ **HUGUENOTS,** French Protestants, the first major Continental European immigrants to British America. About 2,000 Huguenot refugees arrived in the British colonies in the 1690s following King Louis XIV's 1685 revocation of the Edict of Nantes, which had guaranteed Protestant rights.

Many Huguenots prospered quickly, having arrived just as the British colonies began 80 years of unprecedented growth. Boston's Faneuils, South Carolina's Manigaults, and New York's Delanceys were among the wealthiest Americans on the eve of the Revolution. Others intermarried quickly; by 1710 more than half of Huguenot brides and grooms in New York and Boston regularly took English or Dutch spouses. Huguenots often became Anglicans or Presbyterians, and by 1750 most separate Huguenot churches had closed. When the American Revolution began, Huguenots had simply disappeared as a separate ethnic or national group, a remarkable, if perhaps aberrant, example of the melting pot at work in colonial society.

—JON BUTLER

See Also: Religion.

BIBLIOGRAPHY: Baird, Charles W., *History of the Huguenot Emigration to America* (Dodd, Mead 1885); Butler, Jon, *The Huguenots in America: A Refugee People in New World Society* (Harvard Univ. Press 1983).

■ **HULL, CORDELL (1871-1955),** political leader and secretary of state (1933-45). Born in Overton County, Tennessee, he left his law practice in 1907 to serve in the House of Representatives (1907-31), where he drafted such progressive legislation as the Federal Income Tax Act (1913) and the Federal Inheritance Tax Act (1916). He served in the U.S. Senate for two years before being appointed secretary of state by Pres. Franklin D. Roosevelt.

Hull's appointment was due in large part to his support for rebuilding the world economy through reciprocal trade agreements. During his first year in office Hull pushed through Congress the Reciprocal Trade Agreements Act (1934). This act became the focus of Roosevelt's foreign economic policy, giving the president broad powers in negotiating trade and tariff agreements. Hull successfully negotiated trade agreements with European powers and Latin American countries.

As a result of these and other successes, Hull enjoyed widespread popularity. He did, however, experience difficulties in the State Department when he was denied a leading role in developing policy toward Europe and Germany. Hull also experienced a bitter rivalry with Under Sec. of State Sumner Welles. More importantly, however, Hull received the Nobel Peace Prize in 1945 for his contribution to the creation of the United Nations.

See Also: New Deal; Roosevelt, Franklin Delano; United Nations (UN).

BIBLIOGRAPHY: Pratt, Julius, *Cordell Hull* (Cooper Square Pub. 1964).

■ **HULL HOUSE,** settlement house opened in 1889 by Jane Addams and Ellen Gates Starr in an immigrant, working-class neighborhood in Chicago. Inspired by the English settlement house Toynbee Hall, Addams and the other settlement workers (many of whom were women who lived in the house as well as worked there) sought to provide much-needed services to their neighbors. English-language classes were offered as well as instruction in infant hygiene. A nursery was established for working parents, and boys and girls clubs were a staple of Hull House, which served as a model for similar settlements across the country. Funded through private donations, Hull House residents' investigatory efforts resulted in many local and state progressive reforms such as the Illinois Factory Act of 1893. These activities played a major role in the eventual professionalization of social work.

See Also: Addams, Jane.

BIBLIOGRAPHY: Addams, Jane, *Twenty Years at Hull House* (Univ. of Illinois Press 1990); Lissak, Rivka S., *Pluralism and Progressivism: Hull House and the New Immigrants* (Univ. of Chicago Press 1989).

■ **HULL-NOMURA DISCUSSIONS (1941),** series of fruitless diplomatic negotiations between U.S. Sec. of State Cordell Hull and Japanese Ambassador Kichisaburo Nomura in November and early December. The surprise Japanese attack on Pearl Harbor, Hawaii, on December 7 cut off the discussions and precipitated war.

See Also: Hull, Cordell; Pearl Harbor; World War II.

■ **HUMPHREY, HUBERT H. (1911-78),** vice president of the United States (1965-69). Born in Wallace, South Dakota, he worked as a pharmacist (1933-37) before becoming a political science professor, political activist, and mayor of Minneapolis, Minnesota (1945-48). He was elected to the U.S. Senate (1948) and became a leader of the liberal, anticommunist wing of the Democratic party. A gregarious advocate of "the politics of joy" and a believer in activist government, Humphrey unsuccessfully sought his party's nomination for president in 1960 and was elected vice president in 1964 with Pres. Lyndon B. Johnson. In 1968, he ran for president after Johnson withdrew and won the nomination after a divisive campaign that saw the party shatter over Johnson administration policies in Vietnam. He was narrowly defeated by Richard M. Nixon in the general election and was twice reelected to the Senate (1970, 1976).

See Also: Vice President of the United States.
BIBLIOGRAPHY: Humphrey, Hubert H., *The Education of a Public Man* (Doubleday 1977).

■ **HUNDRED DAYS,** name given to the special congressional session from March to June 1933, during the opening months of Pres. Franklin D. Roosevelt's first administration. In an effort to relieve the effects of depression that had gripped the nation since 1929, Roosevelt pushed through Congress an extraordinary numbers of acts. The Hundred Days, which became the foundation of the New Deal, did not result in a unified program but a series of relief and reform efforts.

Five programs proved particularly important. On Mar. 31, Congress established the Civilian Conservation Corps (CCC) to provide unemployed young men with work constructing roads and bridges and helping to protect natural resources. The creation of the Federal Emergency Relief Administration (FERA) on May 12 authorized $500 million for state and local relief efforts. On the same day, Congress passed the Agricultural Administration Act (AAA) to assist farmers through a program of subsidies and price regulation for seven farm commodities. On May 18, Congress established the Tennessee Valley Authority (TVA). This ambitious and controversial project developed the Tennessee Valley through the construction of dams and power plants. Finally, on June 16, Congress passed the National Recovery Act, a plan for economic recovery that established the Public Works Administration (PWA) and the National Recovery Administration (NRA).

The legislation of the hundred days helped transform the federal government into the primary facilitator of social and economic change.

See Also: Civilian Conservation Corps (CCC); Federal Emergency Relief Administration; Great Depression; National Recovery Administration (NRA); New Deal; Roosevelt, Franklin Delano; Tennessee Valley Authority.
BIBLIOGRAPHY: Sargent, James E., *Roosevelt and the Hundred Days: Struggle for the Early New Deal* (Garland 1981).

■ **HUNT, WARD (1810-82),** associate justice of the U.S. Supreme Court (1873-82). He was a Utica, New York, native. Hunt's tenure on the Court was cut short by a stroke.

See Also: Supreme Court.

■ **HUNTINGTON, COLLIS POTTER (1821-1900),** railroad magnate. Born in Harwinton, Connecticut, Huntington, as part of the "Big Four" with Charles Crocker, Mark Hopkins, and Leland Stanford, built the Central Pacific and Southern Pacific railroads. Having spent years in the South as a peddler, Huntington went to the California Gold Rush in 1849 and made more money supplying miners than mining. Huntington saw the economic potential of an overland transportation route and helped finance Theodore D. Judah's transcontinental survey project. Having learned congressional lobbying from Judah, Huntington was instrumental in the passage of the 1864 Pacific Railroad Act. The eastern agent for the Central Pacific and Southern Pacific railroads, Huntington and his associates built and purchased lines from Sacramento to San Francisco, Los Angeles, San Diego, and El Paso, Texas, eventually pushing their Southern Pacific line to New Orleans. Huntington's management skills were essential to the Central and Pacific's economic rise in the 1880s and 1890s, especially after taking over presidency of the company in 1890. Rarely philanthropic, Huntington retired to New York's Adirondacks.

See Also: Frontier in American History; Railroads.

■ **HUNTINGTON, SAMUEL (1731-96),** jurist and Revolutionary War statesman. President of the Second Continental Congress and signer of the Declaration of Independence, Huntington was born in Windham, Connecticut. While governor of his native state (1786-96) he strongly supported ratification of the Constitution.

See Also: Declaration of Independence.

■ **HURON (WYANDOT),** Indian tribe originally in northeastern North America. The Iroquoian-speaking Hurons lived in a small area east of Lake Huron in present-day southern Ontario. Huron women were able farmers, producing corn, beans, squash, and sunflowers in a short growing season. Huron men fished and hunted communally. At the time of European contact the Hurons numbered some 30,000 people. Reciprocity and gift-giving were highly valued. In the early years of the French trade the Hurons were active middlemen between the French and the interior tribes. Between 1630 and 1649 a series of smallpox epidemics combined with conflicts with the Iroquois Confederacy to spell doom for the Hurons. In several wars known as the Beaver Wars the Iroquois killed or captured many Hurons. The tribe splintered, with one group moving west to present-day Michigan and Wisconsin and another group remaining on small reserves near present-day Quebec.

See Also: Beaver Wars; Indians of North America; Iroquois Confederacy.

■ **HURSTON, ZORA NEALE (1891-1960),** author associated with the Harlem Renaissance, a movement of African-American artists and intellectuals in post–World War I New York City. Born in Eatonville, Florida, she studied with anthropologist Franz Boas, publishing several works on Afro-Caribbean folklore, including *Mules and Men* (1935). She also wrote numerous works of fiction, celebrating the lives of African-American characters living in a segregated society. The greatest of these is *Their Eyes Were Watching God* (1937). In the 1970s, Hurston's novels were rediscovered, providing inspiration to a new generation of African-American women writers.

See Also: Boas, Franz; Harlem Renaissance; Women in American History.

■ **HUTCHINSON, ANNE MARBURY (1591-1643),** religious leader. Born in Lincolnshire, England, Anne Marbury Hutchinson, the pious and intelligent daughter of a Church of England clergyman, persuaded her husband, William, to emigrate from England to the new Massachusetts Bay Colony in 1634. Hutchinson, a Puritan, emphasized the Covenant of Grace, that is, the notion that unworthy sinners could do nothing to influence their salvation. The idea that good works could earn one's way into heaven (the Covenant of Works) was anathema to her.

A skilled medical practitioner, she began explicating her religious ideas in Boston in the context of childbed gatherings, where women regularly faced death surrounded solely by other women. Soon she had developed a devoted following, and she initiated religious meetings in her home to explain sermons and expound her own beliefs. Yet her doctrines frontally challenged Massachusetts orthodoxy by undermining the authority of the clergy (who she claimed preached the Covenant of Works), by threatening the unity of the state (some of her male followers refused to fight in the Pequot War of 1637), and by subverting familial hierarchies.

Accordingly, she was twice tried and convicted—in November 1637, in a secular court, for libeling the colony's ministers; and in March 1638, in the Boston church, for heresy. Banished, she moved first to Rhode Island and then to New Netherland, where she and some members of her family were killed by Indians in 1643.

—MARY BETH NORTON

See Also: Puritanism; Religion; Women in American History.

BIBLIOGRAPHY: Battis, Emery, *Saints and Sectaries: Anne Hutchinson and the Antinomian Controversy in the Massachusetts Bay Colony* (Univ. of North Carolina Press 1962).

■ **HUTCHINSON, THOMAS (1711-80),** royal governor of Massachusetts. He was born in Boston to a prominent merchant family. Hutchinson's political ascent began in 1737, when he was elected to the Massachusetts House of Representatives. In 1760 he became chief justice of the Massachusetts superior court, two years after his appointment as lieutenant governor. Throughout his career Hutchinson sincerely desired to promote the welfare of his native province. At the same time, he firmly maintained the supremacy of Parliament and rigorously enforced British policy during the imperial crisis. Thus, he opposed the Stamp Act (1765) by appealing to considerations of expediency rather than principle. Hutchinson served as acting governor from 1769 to 1771, when he was officially appointed royal governor of Massachusetts. In 1773, his refusal to allow tea cargoes arriving in Boston to return to England precipitated the Boston Tea Party. Through such actions Hutchinson came to symbolize for Americans the forces of corruption and tyranny that threatened their liberty. In 1774 Gen. Sir Thomas Gage replaced Hutchinson as governor. In 1775 Hutchinson departed for England, where he died in exile.

See Also: Boston Tea Party; Gage, Thomas; Revolution, American; Stamp Act.

BIBLIOGRAPHY: Bailyn, Bernard, *The Ordeal of Thomas Hutchinson* (Harvard Univ. Press 1974).

HUTTERITES (HUTTERIAN BRETHREN), an Anabaptist sect originating in Moravia under the leadership of Jakob Hutter (died 1536). During the Counter-Reformation, many fled to Hungary and Romania, and later to the Ukraine. Three groups immigrated to America from 1874 to 1877. Most Hutterites moved to Canada during World War I, but many later returned to the United States. They believe in adult baptism, pacifism, and separation of church and state. They dress distinctively and live communally. Today there are over 300 communities in the United States and Canada.

See Also: Religion.

I

■ **IBERVILLE, PIERRE LEMOYNE, SIEUR D' (1661-1706),** French Canadian explorer and naval commander. Born in Montreal, Quebec, to a wealthy provincial family, Iberville became a military leader early in his career. He participated in a series of expeditions against English settlements as well as in attacks on the English fur trade outposts on Hudson Bay (1686-97). Charged by the French Crown in 1698 to establish a French presence in Louisiana, Iberville founded the first permanent French settlement in the Louisiana territory at Biloxi in present-day Mississippi (1700).

    See Also: *Exploration and Discovery.*

■ **ICE HOCKEY,** introduced at McGill University in Montreal, Quebec (1879), was originally played with nine players to a side and now uses five skaters and a goaltender. In 1893 Lord Stanley of Preston, governor-general of Canada, donated a cup to the national championship team. The Stanley Cup now goes to the annual champion of the professional National Hockey League (founded 1917). Ice hockey has been an Olympic sport since 1920.

    See Also: *Sports.*

■ **ICKES, HAROLD L. (1874-1952),** secretary of the interior (1933-46). One of the most influential officials in the administration of Franklin D. Roosevelt, Ickes was born in Frankstown, Pennsylvania. He began his career as a reporter in Chicago, where he developed strong progressive political beliefs. He detested political graft and influence of business on politics. During the 1920s he practiced law and served as president of the Chicago chapter of the National Association for the Advancement of Colored People (NAACP). Ickes became known in political circles for his promotion of African-American rights and commitment to progressive government.

    After his inauguration in 1933, President Roosevelt appointed Ickes secretary of the interior and shortly thereafter director of the Public Works Administration (PWA). Ickes quickly established himself as a tireless promoter of national conservation planning. His continued interest in civil rights made him one of the New Deal's greatest advocates of equality for African Americans in the federal government. Because Ickes directed the PWA with almost obsessive integrity, it was one of the few New Deal agencies to escape the criticism of conservative officials. Intolerant of conservative Democrats who did not fully support

As secretary of the interior between 1933 and 1946, Harold Ickes outspokenly supported conservation and was one of the New Deal's leading advocates of civil rights.

the New Deal, Ickes helped orchestrate the "purge of 1938," during which Roosevelt attempted unsuccessfully to defeat adversarial Democrats in the primaries. Despite Ickes's effective leadership, he did not enjoy public support. He retired in 1946 after having had difficulty adjusting to working in the new Truman administration.

See Also: African Americans; New Deal; Public Works Administration (PWA).

BIBLIOGRAPHY: Clarke, Jeanne N., *Roosevelt's Warrior: Harold L. Ickes and the New Deal* (Johns Hopkins Univ. Press 1996); Watkins, T. H., *Righteous Pilgrim: The Life and Times of Harold L. Ickes, 1874-1952* (Henry Holt 1990).

■ **IDAHO,** the smallest of the eight Rocky Mountain states. It is bounded on the north by British Columbia, on the west by Washington and Oregon, on the south by Nevada and Utah, and on the east by Montana and Wyoming. It is extremely mountainous, except for the Snake River Valley in the south. Idaho leads all states in silver and potato production and is among the leaders in lumber output.

Exploration of what is now Idaho did not begin until the 19th century. This area became part of the United States in 1846. Idaho became a state in 1890.

Capital: Boise. Area: 83,574 square miles. Population (1995 est.): 1,163,000.

See Also: Nez Percé; Lewis and Clark Expedition.

■ **ILLINOIS,** the most populous and wealthiest state in the Midwest. It is bounded on the north by Wisconsin, on the west by Iowa, on the west and south by Missouri, on the south and east by Kentucky, and on the east by Indiana and Lake Michigan. The Mississippi River forms its western border and the Ohio River its southern border. Most of the northern two-thirds of the state is flat prairie, ideal for farming. Illinois vies with Iowa for first place in corn and soybean production.

Illinois became a state in 1818. It grew rapidly because of its rich soil and its location in the heart of the Midwest, with river, lake, and canal links to the East and South. Pres. Abraham Lincoln is the state's most famous figure. By 1900, Chicago had become one of the world's great cities. The Chicago area still dominates the state, but its economy rests more on services, finance, and trade and less on manufacturing than in the past.

Capital: Springfield. Area: 56,343 square miles. Population (1995 est.): 11,830,000.

See Also: Black Hawk War; Cahokia; Chicago; Clark, George Rogers; Haymarket Incident; Jolliet, Louis; Lincoln, Abraham; Lincoln-Douglas Debates; Marquette, Pere Jacques; Northwest Territory; St. Lawrence River and Seaway.

■ **IMMIGRATION,** to the colonies and the United States, the largest population movement in recorded history. Substantial English migration began in the 1630s, and by 1700 the colonies included 250,000 people. Over the next century the population increased by more than a factor of 10, and although most of this was due to natural increase in the relatively disease-free American environment, immigration was a significant factor. More than 100,000 Germans and 250,000 Scots-Irish came before the Revolution. It is often forgotten, however, that the largest immigrant group was half a million Africans. Slavery and bound labor were extremely important in the recruitment of colonial population. Although historians disagree about the exact proportions, it is probable that over half the Europeans came to the colonies as indentured servants or convict laborers. In 1790 the first federal census

West Coast immigration officials administer an intelligence test to a prospective immigrant, one way in which immigrants might be refused entry to the United States through the early 20th century.

After a crowded passage and impersonal examinations by the immigration bureaucracy on Ellis Island, new arrivals made the short trip to New York City.

enumerated a population whose origins were about 50 percent English, 20 percent African and African American, 15 percent Scots and Irish, and 7 percent German, with smaller groups of Dutch, French, and Scandinavian ancestry.

Since the American Revolution, more than 50 million immigrants have entered the United States. Before the 1830s some 350,000 persons arrived, a substantial number that continued the colonial pattern, but relatively modest compared to the subsequent flood. English, Irish, German, and Scandinavian immigration increased greatly in the 1830s, and for the next 50 years formed the bulk of what later would be known as the "old immigration." More than 9 million people came to the United States during this period. Included among them were more than 200,000 Chinese, mostly men, who settled and labored in the American West. Historians have directed most of their attention to the immigrant populations of northeastern cities, but others have called attention to the fact that the West was the most ethnically diverse section of the country by 1880.

The New Immigration. The 1880s to the beginning of World War I was the period of the "new im-migration," dominated by southern and eastern Europeans, especially Italians, Russians, Hungarians, Poles, and Jews. In little more than 30 years nearly 25 million people arrived in the United States. This unparalleled migration peaked during the decade 1905-14, when newcomers numbered more than 10 million, 75 percent of whom had come from southern and eastern Europe. There is little doubt that many immigrants thought of America as their new home; this was, for example, especially true of Jews. But a number of historians have pointed out that surprisingly large numbers came as temporary workers, always intending to return. In 1903-13, for example, approximately 2 million Italians arrived, but another 1.2 million returned home. Overall, a third of the "new immigrants" may have repatriated.

Also part of this phase were the Japanese immigrants, who between 1890 and 1920 totaled more than 200,000. An important and often unacknowledged group of new residents were Canadians, more than 2 million of whom relocated in the United States before 1930. The first important wave of Mexican immigration began in the early 1900s, and nearly 700,000 Mexicans arrived before the Great Depression of the 1930s.

Immigration Restrictions. Usually viewed as the product of the conservative 1920s, efforts to curb the flow of immigration in fact began much earlier. Before the Civil War the American or Know-Nothing party proposed a ban on Catholic immigrants. Anti-Chinese sentiment resulted in passage of the Chinese Exclusion Act in 1882. Japanese immigration was curtailed by the Gentleman's Agreement between Pres. Theodore Roosevelt and the Japanese government in 1907, causing great resentment within Japan. Only presidential vetoes, in 1896, 1913, and 1915, prevented Congress from enacting literacy tests designed to restrict immigration, but in 1917 such legislation was finally passed over President Wilson's veto. It was during the 1920s, however, that Congress first enacted a comprehensive series of quota laws, the most important of which was the Immigration Act of 1924, which set limits by a national origins quota based on the census of 1890, in a successful attempt to exclude "new immigrants." This law was widely supported by politicians, labor leaders, and intellectuals. Immigration fell to its lowest level since before the 1840s.

The quota policy was reaffirmed in the McCarran-Walter Act of 1952. Major exceptions were made, however, for refugees displaced by warfare, and these persons constituted the major class of immigrants for the 20 years following World War II. In 1965, however, Congress, with the encouragement of President Johnson, repealed the quota system and established an annual maximum with "preferential" selection, in which certain classes of immigrants were given priority. More than 16 million persons entered the country legally from 1945 through the end of the 1980s. Over this period, immigrants increasingly came from Latin America (principally Mexicans, Cubans, and West Indians), the Pacific basin (Chinese, Filipinos, Koreans, Vietnamese, and other Southeast Asians), India, and Pakistan. By the 1980s, nearly half of all immigrants were Asian. Compared to other periods, the 1980s comprised the third highest decade in the history of immigration to the United States.

These statistics do not include millions of illegal immigrants who entered the country during the decade, most of them from Mexico. This has generally been understood as a recent problem, but Mexico has in fact formed an essential part of the labor market of the Southwest and California since the late 19th century, supplying workers for the railroads, mines, and farms. Mexicans were exempted from the quota law because of their importance. Under the "Bracero" program, from 1942 to 1964, Congress allowed the admission of temporary Mexican contract workers. Yet even then, because of the proximity of the border, many crossed for work while maintaining residence in Mexico, a variety of the immigration pattern that also characterized many Europeans. The economic crisis of Mexico during the late 1970s and 1980s propelled millions more north to find jobs. After years of unsuccessfully trying to police the border, Congress in 1986 passed a new immigration law that prohibited the hiring of illegal aliens but provided amnesty and potential naturalization for certain categories of them. These new rules, however, failed to stem the flow of people streaming across the border illegally.

Push and Pull. Immigration responds to both "push and pull" factors. In Europe, the breakup of feudal land systems and, in countries such as Ireland and southern Germany, famine caused by crop failures such as the potato blight "pushed" people to America. East European Jews fled religious persecution and violent pogroms before World War I, Mexicans escaped the violent revolutionary turmoil of the 1910s, and Vietnamese and Cubans in the 1970s and 1980s abandoned repressive governments. When hard times ended, as during the German prosperity of the late 19th century or the consolidation of the Mexican revolution during the 1930s, migration frequently fell off.

Among important "pull" factors, the Homestead Act of 1862 served as a beacon to farmers from Scandinavia, Northern Pacific Railroad agents in northern Europe tempted potential emigrants with land bargains along its right of way, and even the low wages paid for industrial or agricultural labor looked good to the impoverished Irish and Mexicans. Overall, it was American economic development that most stimulated the human tides. The rate of immigration corresponds rather well to the cycles of economic prosperity in the United States.

The Role of Immigration. The contribution of the foreign-born to economic development has been crucial. The Chinese built the western railroads and the Japanese introduced the intensive farming techniques that enabled California to become the most agriculturally productive state in the union. In 1907, 75 percent of the workers in the garment industry were immigrants, and the heavy industries of the northeast were long dominated by ethnic groups from eastern Europe. Immigration influenced every aspect of American life. Religion, politics, labor organization, urbanization, industry, commerce, the arts, education, and cuisine all bear its stamp.

There has been, however, great controversy over the influence of immigration on America. Many feared that foreigners would reduce the quality of American life and emphasize their alien customs, religions, languages, and ideologies, forgetting that a polyethnic heritage goes back to the colonial period. Also, such critics have attributed many of America's problems—a fluctuating economy, labor unrest, crime, political corruption, overcrowding, and deterioration of neighborhoods in cities from Boston to Chicago, New York to Los Angeles—to the foreign-born. Proponents of unrestricted immigration, on the other hand, have ranged from employers motivated by self-interest to those who maintained that America's strength derived precisely from its multicultural population.

—JOHN MACK FARAGHER

See Also: Acculturation; Americanization; Assimilation; Cultural Pluralism; Ethnic Groups; Melting Pot; Nativism.

BIBLIOGRAPHY: Handlin, Oscar, ed., *Immigration as a Factor in American History* (Harvard Univ. Press 1959); Hansen, Marcus L., *The Atlantic Migration, 1607-1860* (reprint, Ayer 1940); Reimers, David, *Still the Golden Door: The Third World Comes to America* (Columbia Univ. Press 1985).

■ **IMMIGRATION AND NATIONALITY ACT (1965),** law abolishing national origins quotas as a criteria for admission to the United States. The act gave priority to the reunification of families, to the need for certain categories of labor, and to refugees, leading to greater immigration from Asia and Latin America.

See Also: Immigration.

■ ***IMMIGRATION AND NATURALIZATION SERVICE (INS) V. CARDOZA-FONSECA (1987),*** U.S. Supreme Court case that eased standards for political asy-

lum. A Nicaraguan woman sought asylum in the United States because she feared her family's political views would make her a target of government retaliation if she returned to Nicaragua. The INS ruled she demonstrated no clear probability of persecution. The Court voted (6-3) that the INS standard was too strict and that asylum could be granted if a refugee demonstrated a well-founded fear of persecution.

See Also: Supreme Court.

■ ***IMMIGRATION AND NATURALIZATION SERVICE (INS) V. CHADHA (1983),*** U.S. Supreme Court case that eliminated the "legislative veto" as a check on executive power. From the 1930s Congress had sought to limit the power of the presidency by retaining authority to approve or reject certain actions by executive agencies. In *Chada* the U.S. House of Representatives intervened in an immigration case, and opponents of the legislative veto seized the opportunity to bring suit. The Court ruled (7-2) that legislative vetoes subverted the separation of powers and were unconstitutional.

See Also: Separation of Powers; Supreme Court.

■ **IMMIGRATION REFORM AND CONTROL ACT (1986),** law designed to curb the flow of illegal immigration from Mexico and Central America into the United States. It was inspired partly by a backlash against the social and economic costs created by immigration.

See Also: Immigration.

■ **IMPEACHMENT,** legal process by which federal officials are accused and tried for misconduct and, if convicted, removed from office. As outlined in the Constitution, officials may be impeached for "Treason, Bribery, or other high Crimes and Misdemeanors." The meaning of exactly which crimes and misdemeanors warrant impeachable offenses is ambiguous and has been a source of unresolved controversy since the 18th century. Only a majority vote in the House of Representatives has the authority to bring charges of impeachment. Once charges are brought, the case is presented to the Senate, where a two-thirds vote is needed for conviction. Convictions result only in removal from office and disqualification from ever holding another federal post.

This group of congressmen—led by Rep. Thadeus Stevens (with cane)—managed the impeachment of Pres. Andrew Johnson before the Senate in March 1868. The Senate failed to convict by one vote.

The impeachment clauses of the Constitution originated from English constitutional law. Under the English system, for example, impeachment was used at times during the 16th and 17th centuries to threaten political opponents of the Crown. This system was transferred to the colonial legislatures before it became part of the American political system.

Since 1789, the House of Representatives has impeached 15 officials, 7 of whom were convicted and removed by the Senate. Although most of those impeached were federal judges, two presidents, Andrew Johnson and Richard Nixon, have been charged with impeachable offenses. Johnson was acquitted in 1868 by the Senate, while Nixon's resignation in 1974 stopped the impeachment process.

See Also: Johnson, Andrew; Nixon, Richard Milhous; President of the United States.

BIBLIOGRAPHY: Busnell, Eleanore, *Crimes, Follies, and Misfortunes: The Federal Impeachment Trials* (Univ. of Illinois Press 1992); Labovitz, John R., *Presidential Impeachment* (Yale Univ. Press 1978).

▪ IMPRESSMENT, seizure of seamen from American ships by the British Royal Navy during the early 19th century. Between 1790 and 1815, some 20,000 men, including some deserters from the Royal Navy, enlisted as seamen on American ships. The impressment crisis was part of a larger crisis in which Britain claimed that its subjects could not change loyalties, whereas Americans claimed that individuals had the right to change allegiance to a particular country. The issue came to a head during Britain's wars with Napoleonic France. The British claimed that they had the right to board neutral ships on the high seas and remove any seamen that they deemed to be "British." The problem, which began around 1790, reached a breaking point in the years leading up to and including the War of 1812 between the United States and Great Britain. British impressment of American sailors was a critical part of its sea war against France. The British boarding parties were given the power by their commanders to determine who was and was not a British subject. The main criterion used was whether a seaman spoke English. Hence, it is estimated that only about one-tenth of the 10,000 people impressed from American ships were in fact British subjects. The United States first lodged protests against impressment in 1787, but to no avail, and by the early 19th century, impressment had escalated. In 1807, the British boarded the American vessel *Chesapeake* off the Virginia coast and seized four American seamen. The impressment of American seamen by the British was a leading cause of the War of 1812.

See Also: War of 1812.

BIBLIOGRAPHY: Horsman, Reginald, *The Causes of the War of 1812* (Univ. of Pennsylvania Press 1962).

■ **INCOME TAX,** tax first imposed by Congress in 1861 to raise money for the Union war effort. Set at 3 percent of incomes over $800 and increased in 1864, these taxes met only 21 percent of wartime expenditures and were ended in 1870. Efforts to authorize a federal income tax to improve the government's revenue base and secure more tax support from corporations and the wealthy raised the questions of whether the federal government could levy direct taxes on individuals. The Supreme Court thought not and struck down the income tax provision in the Wilson-Gorman Tariff Act of 1894 the next year. Demands for income taxes grew along with the Progressive movement, leading to the first state income tax (Wisconsin, 1911) and culminating in 1913 with the ratification of the 16th Amendment authorizing a federal income tax.

The Underwood-Simmons Tariff of 1913 implemented a 1 percent tax on incomes over $3,000 and a graduated surtax on incomes over $20,000. The Revenue Act of 1916 doubled the basic tax from 1 to 2 percent, raised the surtax from a maximum of 6 percent to 13 percent, added a graduated estate tax of up to 10 percent, instituted a new tax on corporation capital, surplus, and excess profits, and represented the clearest victory for radical Progressives in the Wilson period. Individual income tax receipts have steadily increased in importance as a source of revenue for the federal government and for the states.

See Also: Progressivism; Taxation.

BIBLIOGRAPHY: Witte, John F., *The Politics and Development of the Federal Income Tax* (Univ. of Wisconsin Press 1985).

■ **INCOME TAX CASES (1895),** also known as *Pollock* v. *Farmers Loan and Trust Company*, U.S.

Supreme Court case in which the Income Tax Act of 1894 was found unconstitutional. The question of law before the Court was straightforward: did the act impose a "direct tax"? The Constitution was clear that any direct tax had to be apportioned among the states in a manner comparable to the apportionment of congressional representatives. Once the Court determined that the income tax was in fact a direct tax, the act's constitutional infirmity was inescapable, since the law mandated a tax on the basis of individual income and nowhere considered apportionment by state population. The sharp division in the Court, reflected in a narrow majority (5-4) that came only after reargument, was itself a reflection of deep divisions within the country over clashing visions of a national political economy. Opponents of the act saw in the income tax the specter of European communism; supporters of the act, the legitimate exercise of the federal government's authority.

See Also: Supreme Court.

■ **INDENTURED SERVITUDE,** common form of bound labor in colonial America, originated as a means of defraying the cost of transportation to the English colonies. In exchange for passage, immigrants committed their labor services for a period of years. The term derived from the contract, written on a large sheet of paper that was divided along a jagged or indented edge. Although its origins are obscure, indentured servitude was common as early as the 1620s, when it was used by the Virginia Company to transport workers to its colony. At least three-quarters of the English immigrants to the Chesapeake came as indentured servants. Most were young, unskilled males who served from two to seven years, but indentured servants also included skilled craftsmen, women, and even children, who were expected to serve until they reached the age of 21.

In the 18th century thousands of Germans, Irish, and Scots immigrated to the colonies as indentured laborers, with most of them arriving in Pennsylvania. At least half of the immigrants to British America, probably more, arrived as bound laborers. Labor in Pennsylvania "is performed chiefly by indentured servants," wrote Benjamin Franklin, "because the high price it bears cannot be performed in any other way." One historian, accounting for the cost of passage and upkeep, estimates that bound laborers earned their masters, on average, about £50 sterling over their terms of service.

Reliance on indentured labor was unique to the English colonies. The economy of New France was based on the fur trade and had little need for a systematic resort to servitude, while the Spanish depended upon the labor of American Indians or enslaved Africans. Africans were first introduced to the Chesapeake Bay area in 1619, but slaves were more expensive than servants, and as late as 1680 they made up less than 7 percent of the population of Virginia and Maryland. For many indentured servants, however, the distinction between slavery and servitude may have seemed academic. Extremely high rates of mortality, the result of malaria, influenza, typhoid fever, and dysentery, meant that approximately two of every five servants failed to survive their terms. In the hard-driving climate of the 17th-century tobacco colonies, many masters treated servants cruelly, and women especially were vulnerable to sexual exploitation.

There were other similarities with slavery. The ocean crossing was frequently traumatic. One German immigrant described a passage from Rotterdam to Philadelphia in which several hundred people were packed like sardines in the ship's hold, with "smells, fumes, horrors, vomiting, [and] various kinds of sea sickness, . . ." In 1750 Pennsylvania finally passed a law to prevent the overcrowding of immigrant ships. Bound laborers remained on board ship after arrival in America, awaiting inspection by potential buyers, who poked muscles, peered into open mouths, and pinched women.

Moreover, the period of service was often filled with harsh and grueling labor, especially in the Chesapeake. Servants enjoyed little personal freedom: They could not travel, marry, or own property. Women who bore illegitimate children had their term lengthened to compensate for time lost in childbirth and infant care. Many servants tried to escape, but capture could mean a doubling of their terms.

Conditions of Freedom. For those servants who endured, however, freedom beckoned. "Freedom dues" might include a suit of clothes, tools, money, and sometimes land. But the social mo-

bility of former servants was limited. Of the thousands of men who came to the British colonies as indentured servants during the 17th and 18th centuries, only about 20 percent achieved positions of moderate comfort. The majority died before their terms were completed, returned to England, or continued in miserable poverty. But opportunities for advancement increased somewhat as the 18th century progressed. By 1750 the chances of moderate success for former servants was probably better than fifty-fifty.

—JOHN MACK FARAGHER

See Also: Immigration; Slavery.

BIBLIOGRAPHY: Galenson, David W. White, *Servitude in Colonial America: An Economic Analysis* (Cambridge Univ. Press 1981); Meaders, Daniel, ed., *Eighteenth-Century White Slaves: Fugitive Notices* (Greenwood Press 1993); Van de Zee, John, *Bound Over: Indentured Servitude and American Conscience* (Simon & Schuster 1985).

■ **INDEPENDENCE ROCK,** graffiti-covered rock in central Wyoming. Beginning in the 1840s travelers on the Overland Trail who were following the Sweetwater River northwest to South Pass called this rock "the register of the desert." They left their imprints by scratching names and dates into the rock's soft surface.

See Also: Overland Trail.

■ **INDEPENDENT TREASURY ACT (1846),** congressional legislation to establish independent federal depositories. The U.S. Congress originally passed a bill in 1840 setting up a treasury system independent of private business and state banks, but it was vetoed in 1841 by Pres. William Henry Harrison and his successor, John Tyler. During the presidency of James Knox Polk (1845-49), however, the bill was revived and in 1846 was passed, giving the U.S. government autonomous care of its own funds.

See Also: Banks and Banking.

■ **INDIANA,** the smallest state in the Midwest. It is bounded on the west by Illinois, on the south and east by Kentucky, on the east by Ohio, on the east and north by Michigan, and on the north by Lake Michigan. The Ohio River forms its southern border and the Wabash River the southern part of its western border. The terrain is mostly flat in the north and hilly in the south. Although somewhat overshadowed by its larger and more populous midwestern neighbors, Indiana is an important farming and manufacturing state. The northwestern part, adjoining Chicago, has a great concentration of heavy industries, especially steel mills and oil refineries. Indiana leads the nation in steel production and was its automaking center before Michigan.

Indiana was part of the Northwest Territory created after Great Britain ceded the area to the new United States at the close of the Revolutionary War. It became a state in 1816.

Capital: Indianapolis. Area: 36,185 square miles. Population (1995 est.): 5,803,000.

See Also: Clark, George Rogers; French and Indian War; Harrison, Benjamin; Harrison, William Henry; Ku Klux Klan (KKK); La Salle, René-Robert Cavalier, Sieur de; Northwest Territory; Shawnee; Tippecanoe, Battle of.

■ **INDIAN AFFAIRS, BUREAU OF (BIA),** agency of the federal government charged with overseeing the relationship with Indian tribes. Founded in 1824 as part of the War Department, the bureau was transferred to the newly created Department of the Interior in 1849. Throughout the 19th and early 20th centuries the BIA functioned as an administrative bureaucracy carrying out the policies of U.S. presidents and Congress, but beginning with the administration of John Collier in 1934 the bureau took a more active role in determining policy. The BIA has moved toward a policy of self-determination in recent years.

See Also: Collier, John; Indians of North America.

■ **INDIAN CLAIMS COMMISSION (ICC) (1946-78),** agency set up to settle American Indian claims against the United States. The ICC was established at the urging of the National Congress of American Indians to hear claims arising from broken treaties dating back to the 18th century. Initially, it was hoped that the ICC's work would be completed in 10 years, but it ended up taking more than 30. The ICC could not return lands taken illegally and could make cash reparations only on the basis of the value of land when it was taken. By the time the ICC was dissolved, it had considered nearly 400 cases and awarded more than $670 million in claims. The studies undertaken by the staff of the ICC to evaluate the claims of treaty violations encompass hundreds of volumes detailing the history of dozens of Indian tribes. Hence, the ICC's investigations were the first comprehensive attempt to reinterpret the history of the colonization of North America from the perspective of the American Indians.

See Also: Indians of North America; National Congress of American Indians (NCAI).

■ **INDIAN COUNTRY OR TERRITORY,** lands set aside for the various American Indian tribes, mostly in the western United States. *Indian Country* and *Indian Territory* are terms whose definition has changed over the past 500 years. The original idea of Indian Territory in the United States developed in the 19th century as the eastern tribes of the southern United States were removed to lands west of the Mississippi in present-day Oklahoma. Indian Territory lands were guaranteed to these removed tribes, but this guarantee proved as elusive as earlier promises made in treaties. Residence in Indian Territory was complicated by the presence of indigenous peoples already living there. Today, Indian Country is used more generally to refer to lands within reservation boundaries, whether that land is held by Indians or by others. Indian reservations have limited jurisdiction over civil and legal matters within their borders.

See Also: Indian Removal; Indians of North America.

■ **INDIAN INTERCOURSE ACTS (1790-1834),** early laws regulating the relationship of the United States with the American Indians. The thrust of early policy toward Indians was to eliminate open conflict with those closest to the territorial limits of the United States. The first Indian Intercourse Act was enacted "to regulate trade and intercourse with the Indian tribes." The Intercourse Acts created a legal distinction between the territorial jurisdictions of the states and the regions where Indians lived. Indian nations were not permitted to have "state-to-state" relations with any other countries. This exclusion also applied to state governments, since, under the terms of the Intercourse Act, the power to establish relations with Indian nations was reserved to the U.S. president in his capacity as the head of state. The Intercourse Acts also created a licensing system for the Indians and established subsidized federal trading houses, or "factories," where Indians could obtain goods at reasonable prices.

See Also: *Indians of North America.*

■ **INDIAN LANGUAGES.** Linguists estimate that before the era of European colonization the native peoples of the Western Hemisphere spoke more than 2,000 different languages, a number demonstrating the great diversity of culture among American Indians. North of Mexico alone there were 200 to 300 distinct languages, with more than 100 still spoken today. Approximately a third of all Indians remain fluent in a native language, with the highest rates of native-speakers among the Navahos, Iroquois, Eskimos, Papagos and Pimas, Apaches, and Sioux.

The first attempt to classify Indian languages was published in 1891. Since then, this system has been revised and refined, and the most current classification groups the indigenous languages of North America into some 66 "families" and "isolates," organized further into seven "phyla" (with several families in an eighth "undetermined" phylum). Eight of these language families account for approximately 70 percent of the preconquest population north of Mexico. In order of their numerical strength the language families were: Algonquian (the language of Pocahontas, Squanto, Tecumseh, and Black Hawk), Eskimo-Aleutian, Siouan (Lakota, Mandan, Crow, Winnebago), Iroquoian (Iroquois Confederacy, Huron, and Cherokee), Muskogean (Choctaw, Chickasaw, Creek, and Seminole), Uto-Aztecan (Shoshoni, Paiute, Hopi, and Aztec), Athapaskan or Na-Dene (including Navaho and Apache), and Salishan (Flathead, Spokane, and other peoples of the Northwest).

The study of Indian languages has demonstrated that languages change very slowly, even when speakers migrate great distances and experience vast change. Language is much more stable than other features of culture. Most authorities believe that in an earlier period there was an even greater number of languages, each confined to a small population and a limited area. The wide distribution of a few major language families, the pattern most characteristic of the eastern half of the continent, is thought to be a development of comparatively recent times. This distribution may reflect the great cultural changes associated with the diffusion of horticulture north from Mexico during the first millennium A.D. Along the Pacific coast, by contrast, subsistence living remained relatively constant over a considerable period, and linguistic change was much more conservative. Preconquest California—with no fewer than 64, and possibly as many as 80, mutually unintelligible tongues and hundreds of dialects—was perhaps the most complex linguistic tangle in the world, rivaling such similarly heterogeneous regions as West Africa, New Guinea, and the territory encompassing upper Burma, Thailand, and southwest China.

BIBLIOGRAPHY: Greenberg, Joseph H., *Language in the Americas* (Stanford Univ. Press 1987).

■ **INDIAN POLICY,** designed by the U.S. government to regulate formal relations between the government and American Indian tribes and also to provide broad guidelines for the integration of Indian people into American society. Until the mid-20th century most federal Indian policies were based on the assumption that the Indians would lose their unique identity as they eventually assimilated into the American "melting pot."

Early Federal Policy: "Civilization" and "Removal." During the 1790s, Congress passed the Indian Intercourse Acts, which attempted to regulate trade between Indians and whites, provide for "an impartial dispensation of justice" when crimes were committed by whites against Indians and vice-versa, and prohibit the purchase of tribal lands by any individual or agency other than the federal government. The acts also endeavored to control the traffic in alcohol ("ardent spirits") to the tribes and to promote federally sponsored programs designed to introduce Indian people to the "blessings of civilization," such as Christianity, yeoman agriculture, and other white cultural values. In addition they provided for federally managed "Indian factories," or trading houses, to be established along the western frontier, which would provide the tribes with durable trade goods at equitable prices. Unfortunately, these laws proved difficult to enforce, as federal agents had only limited authority and were forced to rely on local officials or court systems more responsive to white settlers than to the altruism of federal legislation.

In 1824 the War Department established a Bureau of Indian Affairs specifically assigned to oversee relations between the government and the tribes. Thomas McKenney, the former superintendent of Indian trade, became the first "superintendent of Indian affairs," a title changed to "commissioner of Indian affairs" in 1832. By the 1820s many federal officials believed that the government's "civilization" program had failed and that tribal people were not embracing the more desirable tenets of American culture. Moreover, new states in the trans-Applachian West pressed the federal government to remove the tribes from within their boundaries. In consequence, in 1830 Congress passed the Indian Removal Act, which authorized officials to purchase tribal lands east of the Mississippi and to remove the Indians to tracts of lands assigned to them on the eastern periphery of the Great Plains, primarily in Kansas and Oklahoma. The government promised to reimburse the tribes for any "improvements" (buildings) on their lands in the East, pay for their journeys to the West, and support them for one year in their new homes or until they had an opportunity to plant and harvest crops. Federal officials argued that removal would protect the tribes from the negative influence of frontier whites and enable them to acculturate at their own pace until they could be integrated into American society. More realistically, however, the policy masked U.S. attempts to obtain valuable Indian land east of the Mississippi. Many of the removals were poorly planned and administered, and the tribes suffered many hardships during the removal process. The "Trail of Tears" was the name given to the horrendous removal of the Cherokee and other southeastern tribes.

Warfare, Reservations, and Allotments. During the middle decades of the 19th century, as settlers crossed the plains en route to California and Oregon, federal officials adopted a policy of "concentration" toward the tribes on the Great Plains. Attempting to minimize contacts between the Plains tribes and the emigrants, officials concluded treaties at Ft. Laramie (1851 and 1868),

Medicine Lodge Creek (1867), and other places in which the Sioux, Cheyenne, Kiowa, Comanche, and other tribes agreed to stay away from the emigrant routes in return for annuity goods and federal guarantees of their lands in more remote regions. Yet during the 1860s these agreements were violated by both sides, and warfare erupted. In response Pres. Ulysses S. Grant's administration initiated a formal "peace policy" that assigned tribes to reservations and appointed missionaries as Indian agents. Federal officials hoped that a policy of benevolence would finally transform Indians into yeoman farmers, but often the reservations were ill-suited for agriculture, and many Indians resisted the government's effort. In addition, the Bureau of Indian Affairs often failed to provide promised equipment and technical assistance. For all these reasons the policy generally failed.

By the 1880s white settlement had progressed onto the plains and into the more fertile regions of the Far West. Local and state officials pressured the federal government to "open" many of the remaining Indian reservations to white settlement. Meanwhile eastern white reformers argued that Indians had failed to embrace white agricultural patterns because they continued to hold reservation lands communally and still resided in villages rather than on small individual homesteads. In response Congress in 1887 passed the Dawes Severalty Act, which stated that at the discretion of the president reservation lands would be divided into small plots (usually 160 acres) that would be awarded to individual Indians. To prevent individuals from selling or "losing" their allotments, Congress stipulated that they would be held "in trust" by the federal government for 25 years, after which they would be handed over "in fee simple" to the individual. Congress hoped that during the 25-year period Indians would settle on their allotments, become educated, and establish small family farms similar to those of whites in the East or Midwest.

Most tribes were opposed to the Dawes Act, but those reservations that possessed good farmland were immediately targeted for allotment. The Five Civilized Tribes (Cherokee, Choctaw, Chickasaw, Creek, and Seminole) in Oklahoma initially were exempted from allotment, but in 1898 the Curtis Act extended the process to their lands. During the 1890s, from Nebraska to Oklahoma, former reservations were divided, and the remaining lands opened to white settlers. Not surprisingly, those reservations poorly suited for agriculture (among them Pine Ridge, Fort Belknap, and Navaho) were not allotted because few whites wished to farm in those regions.

Although the individual allotments originally were to be held in trust for 25 years, the Burke Act of 1906 empowered the president, on the recommendation of local Indian agents, to declare certain individuals "competent" prior to that period. Accordingly, those Indians were given title to their allotments and allowed to utilize, rent, or sell their lands as they wished. Many of these allotments passed from Indian possession at a rapid pace, and coupled with inexperience, bureaucratic bungling, and outright fraud, more than 80 million acres changed from Indian to non-Indian hands in the four decades between 1890 and 1933, when the federal government ended the allotment policy. These decades also witnessed the nadir of Indian population, which was recorded as 237,196 in 1900. In 1924, however, Congress in the Citizenship Act granted American citizenship to all Indians who previously had been denied such status.

Tribalism, Termination, and Relocation. The passage of the Indian Reorganization Act (Wheeler-Howard Act) in 1934 marked a dramatic change in federal policy. Convinced that previous attempts to facilitate the assimilation of Indians into the melting pot had failed, reformers led by Commissioner of Indian Affairs John Collier championed new policies that strengthened both tribalism and Indian identity. The Indian Reorganization Act terminated the allotment process and provided that any remaining surplus lands would be restored to tribal ownership. It also furnished funds for tribal governments to purchase lands to add to tribal estates. In addition, the act strengthened tribal governments and enabled them to exercise more control over tribal affairs. The tribes were encouraged to establish business committees and form tribal corporations, which had access to federal funds for investment and development. Other provisions promoted the retention of Indian art forms and encouraged tribal educational programs through

which tribal languages were taught to children. Although some very traditional American Indian communities, particularly in the Southwest, rejected the Indian Reorganization Act, most Indians welcomed these policies and actively participated in the new federal programs. Acreages were purchased and added to tribally held lands, and agricultural production on native land increased. The Indian birthrate, which had declined for half a century, increased, and a new pride in American Indian identity emerged within the tribal communities.

During World War II many Indians served in the armed forces. Following the war, federal officials temporarily reverted to the assimilationist policies of the past. Collier resigned from his post in 1945, and his successors again sought to extinguish ties between the tribes and the federal government and to open reservation lands to non-Indian settlement. Heavily influenced by western politicians who wanted access to tribal lands and their resources, Congress in 1953 passed House Resolution 108, providing for the "termination" of selected tribes. The resolution dissolved tribal governments and suggested that any services previously provided by the federal government should be assumed by state or local agencies. Tribal assets would be divided among enrolled tribe members. Several tribes, including the Menominee and Klamath (whose tribal lands contained valuable timber resources) were pressured by federal officials to accept termination. Both tribes, relatively prosperous prior to termination, soon slipped into economic decline.

Increased American Indian Sovereignty. In the 1960s the government returned to a policy of supporting the reservation communities, and termination was discontinued. Championing self-determination, officials in the Johnson administration extended to the reservation communities federal programs such as the Job Corps, Head Start, Upward Bound, and Community Action Programs under the Office of Economic Opportunity. Continuing many of Johnson's policies, the Nixon administration championed the return of Blue Lake, a sacred religious site, to Taos Pueblo and supported the passage of the Indian Education Act (1972). Yet by 1970 Indian activists in the American Indian Movement had seized the initiative, and federal officials found themselves reacting to the "Trail of

Broken Treaties" (1972), activist-led events that included the occupation of Bureau of Indian Affairs offices in Washington (1972) and the seizure and occupation of Wounded Knee, South Dakota, in 1973. Indian militancy subsided in the mid-1970s, but in 1975, Congress established the American Indian Policy Review Commission (AIPRC), led by Sen. James Abourezk, which investigated a broad spectrum of Indian issues and recommended increased sovereignty for tribal governments.

Since the late 1970s, Indian sovereignty over tribal affairs has increased. During the decade of the 1970s, as the energy crisis heightened, many western tribal governments formed the Council of Energy Resources Tribes (CERT) as a protest against previously negotiated long-term leases that paid little to the tribes whose lands held valuable energy resources. By the early 1980s, as the energy crisis lessened, CERT's influence declined, but the federal government did intervene to force a renegotiation of the leases. Attempts to expand tribal sovereignty over reservation water rights have been less successful, but the Reagan administration's policy of negotiating with tribes on a "government to government" basis spurred the growth of tribal sovereignty over taxation, local services, hunting and fishing, and gaming. Indeed, the expansion of gaming on tribal lands, while often controversial, has markedly increased both employment and per capita income for some tribal communities and has provided tribal governments with funds for expanded education and social services. Meanwhile, attempts by Indians to assert their sovereignty over taxation, gaming, and hunting and fishing rights has triggered a backlash from many non-Indians who feel threatened by these activities.

More recently, the passage of the Native American Graves Protection and Repatriation Act (1990) has expanded Indian control over the excavation, display, and retention of Indian skeletal remains, grave goods, and sacred objects. Although some archaeologists and museums seem threatened by this legislation, others have been willing to cooperate with tribal officials to ensure that tribal skeletal remains and sacred objects are either returned to tribal communities or are protected and displayed in accordance with tribal religious beliefs and traditions.

—R. DAVID EDMUNDS

See Also: *Allotment; Indian Removal; Indians of North America; Indian Treaties; Relocation; Termination.*

BIBLIOGRAPHY: Fixico, Donald L., *Termination and Relocation: Federal Indian Policy, 1945-1960* (Univ. of New Mexico Press 1986); Hoxie, Frederick, *A Final Promise: The Campaign to Assimilate the Indians, 1880-1920* (Univ. of Nebraska Press 1984); Prucha, Francis Paul, *The Great Father: The United States Government and the American Indians* (Univ. of Nebraska Press 1984); Satz, Ronald, *American Indian Policy in the Jacksonian Era* (Univ. of Nebraska Press 1975); Sheehan, Bernard, *Seeds of Extinction: Jeffersonian Philanthropy and the American Indian* (Univ. of North Carolina Press 1973).

■ **INDIAN REMOVAL,** process by which whites removed Indians from their homelands, often by force or legal coercion. Indian removal first became an official U.S. government policy during Thomas Jefferson's administration (1801-09). Jefferson advocated the removal of Indians to settled areas west of the Mississippi River, where they could receive instruction in becoming "civilized." By the 1820s, however, many Indian groups remained in the east, and many whites in the south grew increasingly determined to remove the Five Civilized Tribes—the Choctaw, Cherokee, Chickasaw, Creek, and Seminole.

By 1830, under constant pressure from white settlers, the five tribes had ceded most of their land, yet they retained large tracts in Florida, Georgia, Alabama, and Mississippi. Advocates of removal found a champion in Pres. Andrew Jackson. A famous Indian fighter, Jackson supported state action for removal and in 1830 pushed the Removal Act through Congress. The Cherokee contested the law in *Cherokee Nation v. Georgia* (1831) and in *Worcester v. Georgia* (1832). Although the Supreme Court upheld the Cherokee's right to remain on their land, Jackson ignored the decision and proceeded with plans for removal to Oklahoma.

The Choctaw moved west in 1830 and, after resisting, the Creek, Chickasaw, and Seminole were forcibly removed by the U.S. military. In 1838 some 7,000 soldiers led 16,000 Cherokee to Oklahoma along the "Trail of Tears." An estimated 4,000 Cherokee died on the march.

See Also: Cherokee Nation Cases; Jackson, Andrew; Trail of Tears.

BIBLIOGRAPHY: Wallace, Anthony F. C., *The Long, Bitter Trail: Andrew Jackson and the Indians* (Hill & Wang 1993); Weeks, Philip, *Farewell, My Nation: The American Indian and the United States, 1820-1890* (Harlan Davidson 1990).

■ **INDIAN REORGANIZATION ACT (IRA) (1934),** key legislation of the "Indian New Deal" whereby Commissioner of Indian Affairs John Collier sought to restore the American Indians' land base and to allow for tribal self-government. The IRA authorized tribes to reorganize under tribal constitutions and to develop reservation resources. It provided for federal training programs for tribal members and funds for the development of courses in tribal culture. Ending the policy of the General Allotment Act (Dawes Act), the IRA allowed for the voluntary consolidation of allotted lands for communal use. It also set up a revolving credit fund for developing reservation resources. However, the Bureau of Indian Affairs retained veto power over the decisions of tribal councils and continued to supervise the fiscal affairs of Indian tribes. Although reorganization worked to undermine the political and economic systems of tribal cultures, it marked a shift in government policy and ended the disastrous allotment program.

See Also: Collier, John; General Allotment Act (Dawes Act); Indians of North America.

■ **INDIAN RESERVATIONS,** lands set aside by the U.S. government (or, in a few cases, by state governments) for occupancy and use by American Indians. Official separation of Indian territories from lands occupied by whites has a long history, in which Indian and white purposes have frequently been at odds. At first, there was a north-south line dividing white and Indian lands. The line moved westward as tribes ceded lands east of the Mississippi River, but eventually the line crumbled. After the United States gained what became Oregon Territory in 1846 and substantial lands from Mexico in 1848 as a result of the Mexican War, white miners and settlers swarmed into the newly acquired regions and crossed other Indian lands to get there.

Government Reservation Policies. In the 1850s, the United States adopted a policy of forcing Indians onto limited "reservations." Some of these were sections "reserved" for the Indians when they ceded the bulk of their homelands. Others were designated for occupancy by tribes removed from the East or moved from one part of the West to another to get them out of the way of whites. Until 1871, the reservation boundaries were usually defined by treaties. Then congressional statutes, sometimes approving negotiated "agreements" with the tribes, served the purpose. And, from 1855 to 1919, the president established other reservations by executive order. Most of the reservations are west of the Mississippi.

The federal government created the reservations in order to prevent destructive conflicts between Indians and whites, and as the pressures to assimilate Indians into mainstream white society increased, it used the reservations to promote the assimilation process. The hoped-for transformation of the Indians, however, did not take place, and the reservations themselves were blamed for the failure. The reservation boundaries, officials and reformers argued, kept the Indians closed off from wholesome contact with white citizens, whom they needed to imitate.

Allotment of Reservation Lands. In 1887, the General Allotment Act (Dawes Act) directed the president of the United States to survey the reservations, divide the land into small parcels (generally 160 acres), and allot these plots to individual Indians. The unallotted lands remaining within the reservation boundaries were purchased by the federal government and opened to white settlement.

The allotted reservations were radically altered by the change in land tenure. The reservations became checkerboarded, with sections of land owned by Indians mixed in with sections owned by others. In 1934, the Indian Reorganization Act stopped the allotment process. The law provided also for a revival of tribal governments, which assumed jurisdiction over the reservations, but the intermixture of Indians and white landowners caused serious jurisdictional conflicts between tribal and state governments.

Indian Reservations Today. Not counting the numerous villages of Alaska Natives, there are

Chiricahua Apache leader Geronimo finally surrendered in 1886 and was imprisoned before being sent to an Oklahoma reservation.

currently about 300 reservations, ranging in size from the Navaho Reservation of 14 million acres to small rancherias in California of only a few acres. The Indian tribal lands and allotments are held in trust by the federal government.

Although some reservations are rich in mineral resources, in general reservations are areas of sparse resources and high unemployment. Many Indians have left them for urban areas, so that today fewer than half the Indians are reservation-based.

American Indians view the land base that the reservations provide as essential for cultural survival. And the tribal governments' jurisdiction over the reservations supports the Indian tribes' inherent, but now restricted, sovereignty.

—FRANCIS PAUL PRUCHA

See Also: *Indians of North America.*

BIBLIOGRAPHY: *Indian Reservations: A State and Federal Handbook* (McFarland 1986); *Indian Land Areas Map* (U.S. Department of the Interior, Bureau of Indian Affairs 1989).

■ **INDIAN SELF-DETERMINATION,** the policy of having American Indians "become independent of Federal control without being cut off from Federal concern and Federal support." Self-determination became the official U.S. policy of the United States toward Indians in the 1970s during the administration of Pres. Richard M. Nixon. With the 1975 passage of the Indian Self-Determination and Education Assistance Act, the implementation of self-determination began. Self-determination essentially means that Indians have the right of self-rule within the parameters laid out by the Bureau of Indian Affairs (BIA). Indian nations had long fought for the right to practice this internal sovereignty.

Self-determination was a radical shift from the termination policy of the 1950s and 1960s. The termination era had seen the abolition of Indian governments and curtailment of federal assistance of health, housing, education, and other social services. In 1965 Pres. Lyndon B. Johnson declared termination a mistake, but it was another decade before its replacement, self-determination, was made into law.

Beginning in 1970, a series of events paved the way for self-determination. In 1970 Nixon urged

Congress to return 48,000 acres, including the sacred Blue Lake site, to the Taos Pueblo. This land had been taken by the United States in 1906 and was the first seized land ever returned to an Indian group. Increasingly in the 1960s and 1970s, activists and tribal leaders called for a greater voice in determining their futures, demanding real decision-making powers and the power to control tribal resources without the interference of the BIA. Many tribal councils took over educational and social programs on reservations to emphasize tribal culture and values.

In 1975 Congress established the American Indian Policy Review Commission, which determined that "Indian tribes are sovereign political bodies." The commission further found that the "trust" relationship between the U.S. government and the American Indian nations was "continually evolving." Other acts bolstering self-determination were the Indian Child Welfare Act (1978), which gave tribes the right to decide placement and custody of their children, the 1978 American Indian Religious Freedom Act (and the more significant 1993 Native American Free Exercise of Religion Act), which guaranteed freedom of religion, and the Tribally Controlled Community College Assistant Act (1978), which provided financial support to tribally controlled colleges. The era of self-determination has seen the federal recognition of new tribes (especially in the East) as well as the reconstitution of tribal governments. Many Indians are using the U.S. legal system more forcefully to advocate for their societies and reservations.

There are drawbacks to the policy of self-determination. Despite the Indian Self-Determination and Education Assistance Act, the BIA retains the power to veto tribal contracts, including financial allocations for tribal programs. Programs for the Indian nations are most often designed by the BIA or the Indian Health Service and then executed by the tribes. The problems of a central administration determining implementation programs are particularly acute for Indians because of the diversities of Indian peoples within the United States. In addition, a central bureaucracy ensures a mountain of red tape for the tribal governments.

—KATHRYN A. ABBOTT

See Also: *American Indian Policy Review Commission; American Indian Religious Freedom Act; Indian Affairs, Bureau of (BIA); Indians of North America; Termination; Wounded Knee, Occupation of.*

BIBLIOGRAPHY: Vine, Deloria, Jr., and Clifford Lytle, *The Nations Within: The Past and Future of American Indian Sovereignty* (Pantheon 1984).

■ **INDIANS OF NORTH AMERICA,** the aboriginal inhabitants of the continent, who have played a significant role in American history. Indian people occupied the North American continent for at least 18,000 years prior to the coming of the Europeans, and during that period they participated in a process of cultural change similar to ones found in Africa or Eurasia. Although some Indians resided in small communities whose economies were sustained by hunting and gathering, others developed complex societies and urban centers that rivaled those of the Old World. The Mississippian culture that spread across the Southeast encompassed ceremonial centers and incipient city-states, such as Cahokia, opposite modern St. Louis, while the Hohokam and Anasazi cultures of the Southwest also supported large populations with extensive agriculture and elaborate religious ceremonialism.

Societies After European Arrival. By 1500 most of these sophisticated American Indian cultures were declining. Just at that time the introduction of Old World epidemics for which they had no natural immunities precipitated a catastrophic population decline, particularly among the tribes in the eastern half of the continent. Consequently, by the early 17th century, when Europeans began to settle along the eastern seaboard, the Indians they encountered were the survivors of a biological holocaust. Because the initial European settlers were few in number and at first seemed inept, Indians did not envision the newcomers as a threat and generally welcomed them. Indians in Virginia and Massachusetts supplied English settlers with food, while Algonquian tribespeople in the St. Lawrence Valley assisted French traders in their penetration of the Great Lakes region. With some exceptions the relationship between the French and Indians became very close, as the two peoples intermarried and blended their cultures and way of life.

During the colonial period many Indians actively participated in the fur trade, exchanging pelts or deerskins for European manufactured goods. Many of them became somewhat dependent on these trade goods, but they adapted them for their own use and continued to follow their traditional ways of life. In the 18th century Indian warriors participated in the colonial contests for control of the North American continent, and although the European powers enlisted their aid in the intermittent warfare during this period, the tribespeople also used the contests to their own advantage, often playing the British against the French, and vice-versa. The natives' ability to "tip the scales" in this political balance of power enabled them to demand and receive material benefits from the colonial powers. It also enabled them to remain relatively independent of European control throughout the period.

In the American Southwest, Indians maintained an ambiguous relationship with the Spaniards. During the 17th century, as Spanish forces occupied New Mexico some Pueblo villages such as Acoma initially resisted them, but after Spanish soldiers defeated and killed or enslaved many Pueblo people, most of the Pueblos quietly, if begrudgingly, accepted Spanish hegemony. Yet, Franciscan priests accompanying the Spanish officials attempted to suppress Indian religious ceremonies, and the Pueblo people deeply resented this oppression. In 1680 the Pueblos rose in revolt

An Indian scout fights with the U.S. Army forces during California's Modoc Wars in 1873.

and forced the Spanish to retreat to El Paso, where they remained for almost two decades before reoccupying New Mexico. The new Spanish occupation was less oppressive, and the Catholic Church integrated considerable Indian ritual and beliefs into its ceremonies. Meanwhile Spanish and Pueblo populations intermarried and produced the unique Spanish-Indian culture that dominated the region prior to the Mexican War (1846-48).

Although the pueblo-dwelling people eventually were integrated into the Spanish colonial system, nomadic tribes remained outside Spanish control. Navaho and Apache tribesmen remained with the Spaniards and their Pueblo allies but also raided their ranches and settlements. Similar patterns also developed in Texas and California. In Texas, Spanish officials were able to integrate the small subsistence hunting and gathering tribes of south Texas into the mission system but remained unable to control mounted buffalo hunters such as the Wichita and Comanche, who remained north of the Spanish missions and presidios. In California, Indians remained completely outside Spanish hegemony until the late 18th century, when Catholic priests established a series of missions along the coastal region, from San Diego to Santa Rosa, north of San Francisco. Historians disagree whether the California coastal tribes were coerced into or willingly joined the mission system, but they concur that the tribes of the interior valley and the more isolated mountainous regions remained independent of Spanish authority.

Relations with the United States. During the American Revolution the eastern tribes generally supported the British, and in the decades following the conflict they were hard pressed to protect their lands from onrushing American settlement. In response many of the tribes of the trans-Appalachian region formed pantribal alliances, and supported by the British, they engaged in a series of military conflicts with U.S. forces. During the early 1790s the northwestern tribes crushed American armies led by Joseph Harmar (1790) and Arthur St. Clair (1791) before they were beaten at the Battle of Fallen Timbers and forced to sign the Treaty of Greenville (1795), which ceded much of Ohio to the United States.

Two decades later, led by Tecumseh and the Shawnee Prophet, the tribes rose again. Another pantribal movement united Indians from Alabama to Wisconsin, and when the War of 1812 erupted, Tecumseh's confederacy fought with the British against the Americans. Abandoned by their British allies, the tribes in the aftermath of the war again were forced to surrender lands to the Americans.

The second quarter of the 19th century was a disastrous period for the tribes east of the Mississippi. Although many tribespeople attempted to subscribe to the government's "civilization" programs, pressure mounted for their remaining lands. In 1830, during Andrew Jackson's presidency, Congress passed the Indian Removal Act, which provided for the removal of the eastern tribes to the West. War chiefs, such as Osceola of the Seminole and Black Hawk of the Sac and Fox, fought to defend their homelands, but other tribes, such as the Cherokee, resisted removal through political action and the federal court system. Although the Supreme Court ruled in their favor, Jackson refused to honor the Court's decisions, and the Cherokee and other "civilized tribes" were removed to the West. Ironically, during the mid-19th century the Cherokee, Creek, Choctaw, and Chickasaw formed new communities in eastern Oklahoma that remained models of "civilization" on the American frontier until the late 19th century. The literacy rate of the Cherokee Nation, for example, remained higher than that of the white South until the 1870s.

While the eastern tribes established new homes in the West, the western tribes defended their homelands. Popular culture often depicts mounted warriors attacking wagon trains, but such activity rarely occurred, and the Plains tribes more regularly traded with white emigrants than fought with them. But as miners spread across the West, they trespassed on Indian lands, and violence resulted. Meanwhile, white buffalo hunters slaughtered the bison herds, and in response the Plains tribes and desert nomads (Apache and Navaho) struck back with a vengeance. Warfare flared in Colorado during the late 1850s and 1860s, then spread to Montana, Wyoming, and the Dakotas. The Sioux, Northern Cheyenne, and Arapaho fought the government to a standstill in the late 1860s but were eventually defeated a decade later, although they annihilated George Custer's command at the Little Bighorn (1876). On the southern plains Comanche and Kiowa warriors fought to retain control of the buffalo range in west Texas and New Mexico but also were forced onto reservations in the late 1870s. Meanwhile Apache resistance continued intermittently in the desert Southwest until Geronimo and his followers were forced to surrender (1886) and were exiled first to Florida, then to Oklahoma.

The final two decades of the 19th century and the first decade of the 20th century were a bleak period for American Indians. Settled on reservations and encouraged to farm lands often unfit for agriculture, the Indian population reached its nadir in 1900, when the census reported only 237,196 indigenous people residing in the United States. Associated with the population decline was the image of "vanishing Americans" personified by James Earle Fraser's sculpture *The End of the Trail* (1915), which features a downcast, mounted warrior slumped over a bedraggled pony. No longer envisioning Indians as a military threat, much of the American public believed that Indians finally would either be absorbed into the general population or simply become extinct.

But in fact during the 20th century the Indian population has increased. Although some of the reservations were divided and Indians were forced to accept individual allotments, the tribal communities have continued. During the 1930s, after the passage of the Indian Reorganization Act, tribal governments were revitalized and Indians assumed more control over their lives. During World War II many modern warriors served in the armed forces, and following the conflict Indians migrated to urban areas in growing numbers. In the 1960s urban Indian communities became the seedbed for the American Indian Movement, which served as the Indian voice in the protest politics of the period. More recently Indian leaders have championed the growth of tribal sovereignty and have endeavored to assert increased tribal hegemony over natural resources, hunting and fishing rights, and other economic activities on tribally held lands. The most widely publicized component of this activity has been the growth of Indian gaming.

White Conceptions of the Indians. Since 1492 both Europeans and Americans have used Indian people and their cultures as foils to measure their own progress or failures. In the early colonial period European explorers and newly arrived settlers often emphasized Indian cultural traits that they associated with primitivism to demonstrate that Europeans had attained a more advanced stage of civilization. In New England, Puritan leaders described Indians in terms of their "paganism" and depicted their raids as God's punishment for Puritan shortcomings. In contrast, Puritan military campaigns against Indians were depicted as holy wars against the forces of Satan. In either case, Indians and their "place" in the world were manipulated by Europeans to fit their own prescribed concepts of order.

During the 19th century American politicians used Indians as counterpoints to rationalize their doctrine of progress. In contrast to indigenous cultures, which they erroneously described as "static," Americans took pride in emphasizing the technological advances of the industrial revolution, which seemed to assure increased material prosperity. If Indians refused to embrace such "progress," they were doomed to be left behind as part of the past. Indian military resistance to American expansion therefore was both futile and regressive but often was glamorized by whites, since by emphasizing the military skill of Indians, they could enhance their own image as the victors over such warriors.

On the other hand, some Europeans have continually attempted to romanticize Indian people. Discouraged by the pretentiousness and corruption of their own societies, these Europeans depicted Indians as "noble savages" living in an Eden free of artificial restraints. For these Europeans and their American heirs, Indian people and their communities represented the more idyllic natural societies from which mankind had descended. American Indians were romanticized as part of the past when men and women lived simpler but happier and more wholesome lives.

In the 20th century these stereotypes persisted. Many Americans continue to envision Indians as part of America's romantic past and believe that "real Indians" still follow the lifestyles of their great-grandfathers in the 19th century. Since the 1960s the image of Indians also has been closely associated with the environment, and although tribal people traditionally have maintained a respectful relationship with the natural world, their adherence to modern concepts of environmentalism is rather tenuous. As the stereotyped image of Indians has become more popular, increasing numbers of Americans have claimed Indian ancestry. Unquestionably, Indians have often intermarried with other ethnic groups, but census returns indicate that the Indian population has more than doubled since 1970, and much of this increase has been the result of individuals of mixed-lineage identifying themselves as Indians for the first time.

Indians have always played an important part in American history. Looking ahead, that role will no doubt continue.

—R. DAVID EDMUNDS

See Also: Frontier in American History; Indian Languages; Indian Policy; Indian Removal; Indian Reservations; Trail of Tears; Virgin Soil Epidemics; individual biographies and tribes.

BIBLIOGRAPHY: Berkhofer, Robert F., *The White Man's Indian: Images of the American Indian from Columbus to the Present* (Knopf 1978); Deloria, Vine, Jr., *Custer Died for Your Sins: An Indian Manifesto* (Macmillan 1969); Gibson, Arrell M., *The American Indian: Prehistory to the Present* (D.C. Heath 1980); Hagan, William T., *American Indians*, 3rd ed. (Univ. of Chicago 1993); Josephy, Alvin M., ed., *The Native Americans: An Illustrated History* (Turner Publishing Inc. 1993); Josephy, Alvin M., ed., *America in 1492: The World of the Indian Peoples Before the Arrival of Columbus* (Knopf 1992).

■ **INDIAN TREATIES,** formal signed agreements between commissioners of the United States and chiefs and warriors of Indian tribes or bands, ratified by the U.S. Senate according to the provisions of the Constitution. There are about 370 such treaties, the first with the Delaware in 1778, the last with the Nez Percé in 1868. In 1871, Congress declared that no more treaties were to be made with Indian tribes. At the same time, however, it reaffirmed the validity of treaties already ratified.

Historic Uses of Treaties. Treaties were a major instrument in the government's dealings with Indian tribes. They were the means by which

Indians ceded land to the United States; in return for the land, the Indians received annuities or other payments in goods or money, upon which they came to rely for their existence. Treaties were also used to bring frontier tribes into the political orbit of the United States, make peace with hostile tribes, regulate trade between whites and Indians, provide for punishment of criminals, and pay debts owed by Indians to traders and other citizens. In addition, the treaties specifically promoted the government's drive to assimilate American Indians into white society, with their provisions for schools, agricultural implements, blacksmiths, and mills, and in the 1850s and 1860s, for allotment of reservation land to individual Indians.

Present-day Reliance on Treaties. The end of treaty making in 1871 and the subsequent drive to detribalize the Indians introduced a long period in which treaties were ignored or condemned by government officials and the public. In recent years, however, the treaties have regained a new prominence. They are the basis for Indian claims to land and other rights, and present-day arguments for Indian sovereignty, in many cases, rest on treaties.

The treaties bear witness to the anomalous political status of the American Indian tribes, which in some ways are considered sovereign nations, but which are also restricted in their external relations and in many ways are dependent upon the U.S. government under its trust responsibility for Indians.

—FRANCIS PAUL PRUCHA

See Also: Indians of North America.
BIBLIOGRAPHY: Prucha, Francis Paul, *American Indian Treaties: The History of a Political Anomaly* (Univ. of California Press 1994); Rappler, Charles J., comp., *Indian Affairs: Laws and Treaties,* vol. 2: *Treaties* (Gov. Printing Office 1904; reprint Interland 1972).

■ **INDIGO,** member of the pea family, which when boiled and dried produces a rich blue dye. First grown in the Americas in 1739, indigo may have been introduced by slaves from Africa, where the plant had long been cultivated. Indigo's acceptance as a staple crop in the American colonies was encouraged by the British, who, needing the dye for textiles, paid a bounty to indigo producers. The American Revolution ended this bounty in the 1770s, however, and advances in chemistry soon led to the introduction of chemical dyes and reduced indigo to a minor crop.

See Also: Slavery.

■ **INDUSTRIAL REVOLUTION.** The industrial revolution first took place in England and the United States, with scientific and theoretical beginnings in the 18th century resulting in the rapid expansion of industry throughout the 19th and early 20th centuries. A series of basic changes in the way products were manufactured made possible the mass production of goods through mechanization, so that as many goods as possible could be made in an efficient and inexpensive way. This expansion of production meant that large quantities of goods were manufactured for markets all over the world, not just for local markets.

The Enlightenment, an explosion of scientific discovery in the 18th century, encouraged the inventions that made industrialization possible. During this period, scientists in England and the colonies, in universities, scientific societies, and in small shops of their own, experimented with electricity (Ben Franklin), steam power (James Watt), agricultural production (Ezra Stiles, Jared Elliot, and others), chemistry (Humphrey Davey and others), and many other fields, finding ways of applying logic, mathematics, and scientific findings to practical problems of 18th-century life.

In the preindustrial societies of 18th-century England and America, the most pressing practical problems were the production of sufficient food, clothing, and shelter. Hand spinning and weaving in the home by women and children turned flax, cotton, wool, and other materials into cloth. In New England, indigent women and children had been put to work in spinning shops, designed to produce the needed textiles for clothing. Local water-powered mills served to grind grains for bread and cut trees for lumber.

Textile Production. Shortly before 1800, inventors in Europe and the United States sought to develop machinery and factories that would increase output and diminish the need for manual labor. By 1820, the production of clothing, food, and lumber in the United States had begun to be revolutionized. In 1790, Samuel Slater introduced machinery that carded wool or cotton by steam power, rather than by the manual labor of women and children. An expatriot Englishman named Richard Arkwright secreted the plans for a power loom out of England and saw them reach fruition with Slater in Rhode Island.

Eli Whitney of Connecticut contributed to the transformation of textile production when in 1793 he demonstrated the value of the cotton engine, or 'gin, for removing seeds from raw cotton. This, like carding and all the other steps in cloth production, had formerly been done by hand. His 'gin encouraged the spread of cotton farming in the American South, and bales of Southern cotton were shipped to New England textile mills for spinning and weaving. And in his New Haven, Connecticut, workshop, Whitney developed the idea of mass producing guns by molding the parts rather than shaping them individually. This not only sped up the pace of production, but each part he molded was interchangeable and identical with others. In 1820, Francis Lowell founded textile mills in Lowell, Massachusetts, to mass produce cloth. The large sheds he constructed to house the machinery and the large numbers of women he hired to run the machinery have given his mills the reputation as among the earliest factories, which shipped cloth to markets all over the world. Soon New Englanders began mechanized production of other products as well. Oliver Evans of Delaware designed a grist mill that automated the processes from grinding to packing. Throughout the 19th century steam power gradually displaced water power in most mills and factories.

Transportation. As the technique of mass production spread to other industries, it led to the need for improved transportation to send a greater volume of products to markets farther and farther away from the factories themselves. In 1807, Robert Livingston and Robert Fulton successfully demonstrated that steam power could move a boat when their *Clermont* navigated from New York City upstream to Albany on the Hudson River. This increased the value of rivers for transportation in both directions since the old river boats could move upstream only a few miles an hour. The change led to steam navigation on the Ohio and Mississippi rivers too, a key devel-

opment in the opening of the American West. Steamboats carried manufactured goods from cities to the rural frontier, and cotton, lumber, and food from rural areas to factories and ports in the United States. Improved ocean-going boats, especially James McKay's American clipper ship, took products to seaports in Europe, Asia, and South America.

With the success of steamboats, states began raising money to build canals to connect major bodies of water and thus extend trade routes further into the interior of North America. The Erie Canal, completed in 1825, connected the Hudson River and Lake Erie, while canals dug across the state of Ohio connected Lake Erie with the Ohio and Mississippi rivers.

Railroads. This effort to develop internal water routes was cut short, however, by the successful introduction of railroads during the last years of the 1820s. The Mohawk and Hudson Railroad connected the two rivers of the same names. The Baltimore and Ohio Railroad sought to connect the port of Baltimore with the Ohio River; and the South Carolina Railroad sought to bring cotton and other agricultural products into the port of Charleston. Thereafter, railroads were constructed in cities all along the eastern seaboard to connect ports with interior markets and the West by rail.

After the mid-1840s, the digging of new canal mileage all but ceased, and a surge in railroad construction led to the construction of shops and factories for track, railroad car parts, and locomotives made of iron. Iron mining became of national interest, and as the natural supply of wood rapidly diminished as a source for fuel, coal mining took on a new importance as a source of fuel. When it became clear that iron track wore out quickly, the search for a way to mass produce steel, a much harder metal, resulted in the successful importation of the Bessemer process, first developed in Europe.

In 1846, the electrical telegraph, perfected by Samuel F. B. Morse, became popular as a way to schedule and dispatch trains. Copper telegraph wires followed railroad routes throughout the country, and mining for copper became another lucrative pursuit. In 1850, the Singer factory produced a sewing machine adopted in both the family and factory settings where clothes as well as textiles were then mass produced.

Economy. The 1850s saw an unprecedented expansion of business in the United States, based on the demand for these innovations. The railroads stretched from the Atlantic to the Mississippi River, and midwestern cities, particularly Cincinnati, Chicago, and St. Louis, had developed into industrial centers, providing manufactured goods for new settlers, as well as markets for goods coming from the East. While the Civil War slowed development in the West and stopped it in the South, many Northern entrepreneurs became wealthy mass producing clothes, boots, guns, ammunition, and the other equipment of war for the U.S. government.

In the later decades of the 19th century, American cities became increasingly crowded with immigrants seeking opportunity in the new industrial economy, and inventors found ways of accommodating the enormous crowds that resulted. Architects developed the steel frame building that could be many stories taller than any traditionally designed building, and James Otis's elevator made it possible to travel vertically in these new skyscrapers. Electric trolleys and then subways made street level transit faster than ever before.

The construction of factories, steamboats and railroads, and skyscrapers all required large sums of money beyond the means of only one or two people. Each such enterprise was therefore organized as a corporation, soliciting money through the sale of stocks and bonds, to be repaid from future profits. Thus the rise of the corporation became an integral part of industrialization. Laws regarding the founding of corporations were liberalized by state governments so that more people could participate, resulting in a more competitive and more democratic business environment. This was intended to speed up the settlement of the frontier by allowing more people to take part in the establishment of institutions and businesses.

Capitalism. To some measure, the liberalization of business practices also led to periodic financial panics, which resulted in great part from overzealous speculation for quick returns and from largely unregulated markets. Financial panics took place in 1819, 1837, 1857, and periodically thereafter. Nevertheless, the speed of American industrial growth had outstripped all other nations before the end of the century, and the volume of production created a new class of monied capitalists in this country. Capitalism also increased the influence of American banks, which bought and sold shares in American investments such as railroads and offered loans to growing business and industry.

Paralleling the trend toward mechanization in industry was a search for ways to increase production in agriculture. In 1840 Cyrus McCormick demonstrated the value of a mechanical reaper, which cut wheat, thereby drastically reducing the manual labor needed to harvest grains. Widespread scientific experimentation with fertilizers, more varied crops, and hybrid seeds increased crop yields. Agricultural fairs, held annually throughout rural areas of the country, exhibited the new time- and labor-saving reaper and gave prizes for the best farm stock and produce. Even before the Civil War, state and federal governments began issuing educational circulars to farmers, advising them of ways to raise crops on proven scientific principles in order to increase yield.

Industrialists. The Northern victory led to the domination of American leadership by industrial and business interests, who sought a completely free hand for investment and trade without any legal restraint. Against a rising tide of protest from the general public, industrialists such as John D. Rockefeller of Standard Oil, the Vanderbilt family of the New York Central Railroad, Jay Gould of the Erie Railroad and Western Union Telegraph, Andrew Carnegie of the steel industry, and John Pierpont Morgan in banking moved ever closer to achieving monopoly control of their respective businesses, driving out competition by highly illegal means, and set their own terms for doing business with their employees and with their customers.

New inventions, such as Alexander Graham Bell's telephone in 1876 and Thomas A. Edison's electric light bulb of the 1870s, were quickly bought up and developed through corporations organized by bankers and captains of industry. New fortunes were created as well, with the introduction of Henry Ford's assembly-line approach to production by which he produced Model T cars with internal combustion engines in 1908. Seeing the potential for profits, entrepreneurs flooded the new field of automobile manufacturing.

Workers. While profits continued to mount for business owners, many laborers worked 16-hour, 7-day weeks for less than 25 cents an hour. They lived in crowded and unsanitary urban tenement houses and worked in dangerous industrial environments. Therefore, even as the country pushed ahead of England in becoming the richest nation in the world, the free market system, which had allowed the country to expand with unprecedented speed, became discredited as contrary to the spirit of American equality. Henry Ford was one of the very few capitalists who paid his workers enough to allow them to buy his own product. Local, state, and federal regulations began to increase the margin of safety and prosperity for workers. Limited work hours, minimum wage, and safety requirements in the workplace became more common.

Other workers took a more radical route in opposing the enormous wealth of the few. Labor unions, such as the Knights of Labor, and trade unions, such as the American Federation of Labor, organized to represent their membership in negotiations with business. However, this right did not become firm until 1936. Concurrently, the Socialist party organized in the United States, seeking the redistribution of wealth, based on the belief that labor was entitled to a much greater share of the wealth than they had received.

Despite bitter struggles over regulation of business, unionization of the laborers, and inequities of wealth, the United States entered the 20th century as the undisputed industrial leader of the world. Not until the Great Depression of the 1930s did the United States begin to question its industrial strength.

—SARAH H. GORDON

See Also: Automation; Cotton Gin; Mass Production; Monopoly; Water Power; individual biographies.

BIBLIOGRAPHY: Faulkner, Harold U., *American Economic History* (rev. ed., Harper 1976); Kirkland, Edward C., *History of American Economic Life* (Appleton-Century-Crofts 1969).

■ **INDUSTRIAL UNIONS,** the organizational form of labor encompassing all employees in an industry, skilled and unskilled, rather than in a single trade or craft alone.

Industrial unionism had its origins in the efforts of 19th-century labor activists to create forms of self-defense suitable to the emerging patterns of production and in the notion of labor "solidarity" proclaimed by visionaries. Brewery workers, for instance, had been successfully organized by socialists in Germany and brought their methods to the New World. Coal miners, working in conditions of great danger and socially close-knit within geographically isolated communities, learned from experience that only a unified movement could protect the miner during the various stages of his work life.

But most efforts at industrial unionism, notably in textiles but also in steel, rubber, shoes, automobiles, electrical parts, and sections of the garment industry, were markedly unsuccessful until the 1910s and even the 1930s and 1940s. Employers' bitter resistance was joined with that of the American Federation of Labor (AFL), whose leaders regarded unskilled workers as undeserving and incapable of organization.

The task of creating industrial unions fell largely to the anticapitalist, radical end of the labor spectrum. The Knights of Labor, aiming to improve labor's status and eventually to supplant the wage system with cooperative production, formed "assemblies" formally based on geographical location but often coinciding with a factory work force. During the Knights' high point of 1885-87, a large portion of their half-million members were, in fact, industrial unionists. The defeat of the Knights threw the initiative toward smaller movements in the East and West.

The Industrial Workers of the World (IWW), organized in 1905, made industrial unionism its *raison d'être* and the replacement of the existing political system with a functional industrial democracy its goal. However, despite a series of spectacular strike victories during 1909-12 and ardent support among migratory western workers, the IWW could not put down roots. During World War I the Amalgamated Clothing Workers (ACW) set the pace. Other unions that sought to duplicate the ACW success were, however, quashed by employers after the war.

For more than a decade industrial unionism became the watchword of communists, mostly unorganized immigrant workers. Although largely unsuccessful in their own efforts, radicals of various kinds spurred formation of the Committee and then the Congress of Industrial Organizations (CIO) during the middle and later 1930s. By the early 1940s more than 60 percent of industrial workers belonged to unions.

After 1945 the more conservative political climate turned the tables on labor. New measures, especially the Taft-Hartley Act, prompted the labor movement to abandon visions of solidarity in favor of conservative, AFL-style unionism. Plans to organize industry in the South and the rapidly growing clerical, largely female, work force were abandoned.

The merger of the AFL and the CIO in 1955 consolidated the hold of craft unions on labor's destiny. Only a dramatic leadership change in 1995, bringing an end to decades of falling memberships and extraordinary bureaucratic corruption, reset organized labor's aim once more on industrial unionism for American workers at large.

—PAUL BUHLE

See Also: *American Federation of Labor (AFL); Congress of Industrial Organizations (CIO); Industrial Workers of the World; Knights of Labor; Taft-Hartley Act.*

BIBLIOGRAPHY: Lipsitz, George, *"A Rainbow at Midnight": Labor and Culture in Cold War America* (Univ. of Illinois Press 1994); Montgomery, David, *The Fall of the House of Labor* (Cambridge Univ. Press 1987); Preis, Art, *Labor's Giant Step* (Pathfinder Press 1965).

■ **INDUSTRIAL WORKERS OF THE WORLD,** known as the "IWW" or "Wobblies," the most democratic and influential labor organization agitating among unskilled workers from the early 1900s to the mid-1920s.

Founded in Chicago by Bill Haywood and others at a historic labor convention in 1905, the Industrial Workers of the World arose in response to the failures of the conservative and exclusionary American Federation of Labor. The IWW's main predecessor, the Knights of Labor, had for a few years during the 1880s organized a half-million workers for improved conditions and for a future "industrial republic" of cooperative workshops.

After the sharp decline of the Knights, only the Western Federation of Miners and a small Socialist Trade and Labor Alliance carried on radical ideals. Meanwhile, unions suffered repeated defeats during the severe depression of the 1890s, and changes in production outmoded many crafts historically represented by unions of skilled tradesmen.

The IWW set out to organize the bottom-most layers of labor: unskilled operatives, recent immigrants, agricultural workers, women, and non-whites, among others. By 1909-13, they attained real success. A series of spectacular strikes highlighted by the Lawrence, Massachusetts, textile conflict of 1912 seemed to promise a future industrial democracy. The combined opposition of employers, press, and craft unions proved too great, however.

By the middle 1910s the IWW held on mainly in western lumber camps and among migratory labor. Its opposition to World War I brought ferocious repression, frequent beatings, occasional lynchings, and long jail sentences for IWW activists. Nearly destroyed, the IWW continued to propagandize for industrial unionism and cast a long shadow across the formation of such unions in the 1930s.

—PAUL BUHLE

See Also: *Haywood, William Dudley; Knights of Labor.*

BIBLIOGRAPHY: Foner, Philip S., *The Industrial Workers of the World, 1905-1917* (International Publishers 1965); Kornbluh, Joyce L., ed., *Rebel Voices—An IWW Anthology* (Charles H. Kerr 1988).

■ **INEQUALITY OF WEALTH,** the disparity in wealth between the prosperous and the poor, one of the least studied important topics in American history. In part this is because of insufficient data; in part because the whole idea runs against the myth of classlessness in American society. But scattered statistics drawn from tax records and probate records before the 20th century, as well as useful data on wealth concentration in the 20th century, provide enough evidence for an outline history.

The British colonies in North America experienced a steady growth rate, and most middle- and upper-class British Americans enjoyed living conditions that improved within their lifetimes. Yet, this growth also produced increasing concentrations of wealth. In Boston in 1687 the wealthiest 10 percent of households owned 42 percent of the taxable property; by 1771 their share had risen to 65 percent. In the commercial farming region of Chester County, Pennsylvania, the share of taxable property held by the wealthiest tenth rose from 24 percent in 1693, to 30 percent in 1760, to 38 percent in 1802; meanwhile, the share owned by the poorest six-tenths fell from 39 percent, to 27 percent, to 18 percent. These figures are typical for 18th-century cities and commercial farming areas, whether slave or free. The general standard of living may have been rising, but the rich were getting richer and the poor poorer.

An even greater advance in inequality took place during the period from the Revolution to the Civil War. The statistics from Boston are instructive. The share of wealth owned by the city's top tenth grew from 75 percent to 82 percent from 1833 to 1848, while the share held by the lowest 80 percent fell from 14 percent to only 4 percent. These were the transformative decades of the industrial revolution, characterized by explosive economic growth. They were also the decades when large numbers of rural Americans as well as rural Irish and Germans became factory workers. Recent studies of national wealth have estimated that in 1774 the top 1 percent of wealth holders owned 13 percent of all assets. By 1860 the share of the top 1 percent had risen to 29 percent. There are few available statistics for the late 19th and early 20th centuries. But after World War I the federal government began tracking wealth holdings. The share of total American assets held by the wealthiest 1 percent was 32 percent in 1922, 36 percent in 1929.

The trend toward the increasing concentration of wealth was reversed by the combined effect of the Great Depression, the New Deal, and World War II. In 1933 the proportion held by the wealthiest 1 percent had declined to 28 percent, which illustrates the result of the stock market crash. The "progressive" (or "confiscatory") tax rates of the New Deal further reduced the holdings of the super rich. The share of the top 1 percent was measured at 31 percent in 1939, 22 percent in 1945, and reached a low of 21 percent in 1949. Some reconcentration took place during the 1950s and 1960s, with the share of the top 1 percent increasing to 26 percent in 1962 and leveling off at 24 percent in 1972.

The 1980s and 1990s, however, witnessed what one economist termed "a big unprecedented jump in inequality to Great Gatsby levels." The share of wealth owned by the top 1 percent jumped to 31 percent in 1983 and had soared to 37 percent by 1989, while the holdings of most Americans remained flat or declined. At the end of the century inequality is greater than any time since the great leveling of wealth that took place during the New Deal.

—JOHN MACK FARAGHER

See Also: *New Deal.*

BIBLIOGRAPHY: Williamson, Jeffrey G., and Peter H. Lindert, *American Inequality: A Macroeconomic History* (Academic Press 1980).

■ **INFLATION,** condition of rapidly rising prices. It can be caused by a shortage in the supply of goods, an increase in the demand for goods, or an oversupply of credit or money. Periods of war often brought all these forces together, producing inflation. During the American Revolution the states printed abundant supplies of paper currency, and the Continental Congress issued unsecured currency of its own. "Continental" dollars traded against Spanish dollars at the rate of 3 to 1 in 1777, 40 to 1 in 1779, and 146 to 1 in 1781—thus the phrase, "not worth a continental." Wartime inflation ended suddenly with the postwar economic depression. The government issue of "greenbacks" during the Civil War helped produce an inflation rate of 96 percent between 1860 and 1865. The demand for goods during World War I drove up prices in the United States by 118 percent from 1914 to 1920. Learning the lesson, during World War II the federal government enacted wage and price controls that kept inflation down to only 22 percent from 1941 to 1945.

Using published information about commodities in newspapers and other sources, economic historians have assembled a Composite Consumer Price Index (CCPI) that extends from the last century to the present. These data demonstrate that despite the inflation of the Civil War period, as well as other short-term fluctuations, the 19th century was a period of relatively stable or falling prices. In the 20th century, by contrast, prices have taken a long upward swing. The prolonged inflation of the century has been a worldwide phe-

Inflation

The Composite Consumer Price Index (in which the year 1860 is arbitrarily assigned the value of 100, and all other years are expressed as partibles or multiples of that number) is useful in converting historical dollar values to contemporary "real dollars." In order to convert the values of one year to those of another, simply divide the index number for the year for which the value is known into the index for the year in question, then multiply this result by the dollar value. Using the index numbers for 1990 and 1950, for example, one can establish that, if housing prices had changed over the years to the same extent as all commodity prices, a house that cost $10,000 in 1950 would be valued at $54,000 in 1990 dollars. But since, over those thirty years, housing costs outran the average inflation rate for all prices, the house that cost $10,000 in 1950 would typically have increased in value to $70,000 by 1990, $16,000 more than the figure predicted by the use of the CCPI, which tracks the average change in prices of a mix of goods and services.

Composite Consumer Price Index
(1860=100)

year	index	year	index	year	index	year	index
1790	110	1870	157	1920	240	1960	354
1800	151	1880	123	1925	210	1965	377
1810	148	1890	109	1930	200	1970	464
1820	141	1895	101	1935	164	1975	643
1830	111	1900	101	1940	168	1980	985
1840	104	1905	106	1945	215	1985	1287
1850	94	1910	114	1950	288	1990	1563
1860	100	1915	121	1955	320	1995	1823

The following table examines the differential rise or fall of the value of selected goods over the period 1962–1992. Using average hourly wage rates for 1962, 1972, 1982, and 1992, it shows how long the typical American had to work to buy a particular item. Many lower cost goods have actually become less expensive over this period: the cost of a long-distance telephone call or a roll of color film, for example. But many high cost goods have become more expensive, in some cases much more expensive: the cost of a college education, a house, or medical care.

Value of Selected Goods

	1962	1972	1982	1992
small items	hours of work			
postage (first class stamp)	1.1	1.6	1.7	1.6
newspaper (New York Times, daily)	1.4	2.4	2.3	2.8
long-distance call (3 minutes, NY to LA)	60.8	23.5	13.4	4.3
gasoline	7.5	5.2	9.1	6.4
milk (1/2 gallon)	12.5	9.6	8.8	7.8
ground beef (chuck, 1 lb.)	15.3	13.9	13.0	11.1
film (Kodak, 35mm, color prints)	60.0	37.9	27.7	27.2
medium items	hours of work			
record album (cd, 1992)	1.8	2.2	1.2	1.6
electricity (500 kwh)	4.6	3.3	4.2	3.9
theater ticket (Broadway, best seat)	3.4	4.1	5.2	5.7
television (RCA, 19 inch)	85.1	121.6	42.6	21.7
dishwasher (GE, midpriced)	112.2	64.9	55.3	35.5
washing machine (Sears, midpriced)	92.3	52.7	58.3	37.8
refrigerator (Frigidaire, top-freezer)	168.0	99.2	83.7	59.8
large items	hours of work			
auto insurance (national average)	7.1	7.8	7.3	11.3
income taxes (federal)	50.0	48.3	63.8	49.0
child delivery (normal)	15.5	37.2	33.3	62.2
college, public (U Michigan: tuition, room & board)	61.7	64.1	68.9	99.2
car (average, new)	203.1	131.0	161.0	197.8
college, private (Colgate: tuition, room & board)	129.5	140.4	144.0	251.4
house (3 bedroom ranch, Matawan, NJ)	1125.5	1330.7	1530.0	1777.3

nomenon, something historians characterize as a "price revolution." The cause of this revolution is little understood, but it is surely related to the growth of world population relative to the available supply of land and resources. After the deflation of the Depression and the price controls of World War II, inflation became a fact of life in post–World War II America. It was most notable during the 1970s, when the increase in the CCPI was the highest in American history.

See Also: Federal Reserve System; Greenbacks; Money and Currency.

BIBLIOGRAPHY: Fisher, David Hackett, *Great Wave: Price Revolutions and the Rhythm of History* (Oxford Univ. Press 1996).

■ **INITIATIVE,** method of allowing laws to be enacted directly by voters. First adopted by South Dakota (1898) as a way to enact reform laws opposed by a majority of the state legislature, the initiative requires supporters to gather signatures to place a proposed law on the ballot for a referendum.

See Also: Referendum.

■ **INNESS, GEORGE (1825-94),** 19th-century landscape painter. Born near Newburgh, New York, Inness apprenticed for two years at the New York engraving firm of Sherman and Smith. At 19, he first exhibited a landscape painting at the National Academy of Design. Inness's early work shows the influence of the waning Hudson River School, but after traveling in Europe in the 1850s and again in the 1870s, he moved toward the French Barbizon school. His late paintings have a greater emphasis on color, light, and the horizon line than the literal depictions of his earlier work. Inness's work gained a more abstract quality over time, with foreground objects becoming less important than the overall atmosphere of the scene. Inness's late paintings are infused with a sense of spirituality, revealing the influence of Swedenborgianism at this period. Among his best-known works are *Golden Sunset* (1862), *Peace and Plenty* (1865), *The Monk* (1873), and *Home of the Heron* (1893).

See Also: Hudson River School; Painting.

■ **IN RE DEBS (1895),** U.S. Supreme Court case that concerned the federal government's authority to settle industrial conflicts through use of

court injunctions. Out of sympathy for striking workers at the Pullman Car Company, the American Railway Union (ARU) had directed its members to stop working on all railroad lines that used Pullman coaches. As the boycott spread, train traffic around the country ground to a halt. Union leader Eugene V. Debs, who had opposed the sympathy strike only to be overruled by the membership of his own union, soon found himself named in a federal court injunction ordering ARU members back to work. After Debs ignored the court's order, he was arrested and convicted of contempt of court. Represented by Clarence Darrow, Debs appealed his conviction to the Supreme Court. The Court unanimously rejected Debs's petition. It held that the union's boycott amounted to an illegal conspiracy to hinder interstate commerce, a violation of the Sherman Antitrust Act. Until passage of the 1932 federal law outlawing its use in such cases, the injunction remained a potent legal club for suppressing labor unrest.

See Also: Darrow, Clarence; Debs, Eugene V.; Sherman Antitrust Act; Supreme Court.

■ **IN RE GAULT (1967),** U.S. Supreme Court case concerning the application of many legal "due process" requirements to the nation's juvenile courts. Acting in an Arizona case, the Court ruled (8-1) that traditionally informal juvenile court proceedings must still comply with such basic constitutional guarantees as the rights to counsel and to confront witnesses. *In re Gault* was part of the Court's efforts in the 1960s to extend constitutional protections throughout the judicial system.

See Also: Supreme Court.

■ **INSULAR CASES (1901-04),** a group of 14 cases decided by the U.S. Supreme Court following the Spanish-American War (1898) that dealt with the application of constitutional law to newly acquired overseas possessions. The decisions reflected the ongoing political debate over U.S. expansion and, historians believe, acknowledged the results of the 1900 election, in which Pres. William McKinley and the expansionist Republicans scored a clear victory over the anti-imperial Democrats and their candidate William Jennings Bryan.

Several key points were at issue in the Insular Cases. Did the federal government have the authority to acquire territory by treaty? Did existing federal laws apply to new territories? Did the Bill of Rights apply? The Court's deliberations were colored by the debate over the future of the territories. Many people believed the inhabitants of the new possessions were unfit to become citizens, making statehood impossible. Others pointed to the policy first proclaimed in the Northwest Ordinances (1784-87) that new territories would join the Union as equal partners.

In *DeLima* v. *Bidwell* (1901) the Court ruled the federal government through long tradition had the right to obtain new territory. The issue of how to apply existing law to the new territory was, however, more difficult to settle. In several cases culminating in *Dorr* v. *United States* (1904) the Court gradually adopted the position that the term "the United States" meant the states themselves. Constitutional protections, therefore, would not apply to the territories until they were incorporated as states of the Union.

—TIM ASHWELL

See Also: Northwest Ordinance; Supreme Court.
BIBLIOGRAPHY: Foner, Philip S., *The Spanish-Cuban-American War and the Birth of American Imperialism 1895-1902* (Monthly Review Press 1972).

■ **INSURANCE,** means of reducing risk by requiring a small premium to cover an uncertain but potentially large loss. Insurance in the United States developed from the model of Great Britain, where a group of underwriters would agree to insure a marine vessel or cargo through an association like Lloyd's Coffee House in London. The first such colonial office formed in Philadelphia (1721). The Insurance Company of North America (1794) was the first chartered corporation that backed their policies with capital instead of underwriters' reputations, and it became a model for dozens of similar marine insurance companies. Charleston, South Carolina, residents formed a mutual fire insurance society (1735), and the first life insurance company appeared in Philadelphia (1759). By 1800, more than 30 companies issued policies on a number of risks. A growing merchant marine, big urban fires, and changes in life insurance policies caused huge growth in the industry by 1900. Corrupt practices uncovered in the early 1900s revealed a need for better regulation, but the industry continued to grow in the range of risks it covers (including health, property, unemployment, and malpractice) and the financial power of its assets.

■ **INTERIOR, DEPARTMENT OF,** cabinet department of the U.S. government in charge of both the development of natural resources and public lands and of conservation. Created in 1849, the department includes such agencies as the National Park Service, the Bureau of Land Management, and the Bureau of Mines. The department's dual mandate has led to friction between developers and conservationists. Pres. Warren G. Harding's interior secretary, Albert Fall (1921-23), was convicted of fraud in 1929 in connection with oil leases at Teapot Dome, Wyoming, and Elk Hill, California.

See Also: National Parks; Teapot Dome.

■ **INTERNAL SECURITY ACT (1950),** Cold War law requiring U.S. communists to register with the government. Known as the McCarran Act after its sponsor, Sen. Pat McCarran of Nevada, it restricted travel and allowed the government to arrest suspected subversives.

See Also: Cold War.

■ **INTERNATIONAL COURT OF JUSTICE,** sometimes called the Hague Court or World Court, a body designed to settle disputes between nations. The court was established under the United Nations charter in 1946. It is composed of 15 members, no 2 of the same nationality.

See Also: United Nations (UN).

■ **INTERNATIONAL MONETARY FUND (IMF),** an organization created at the Bretton Woods Conference in 1944 with the aim of providing member nations with assistance whenever their balance of payments was in deficit. The IMF is currently a major regulator of world economy.

See Also: Bretton Woods Conference.

■ **INTERNET,** sometimes called the Information Superhighway, a system of networks that allows direct communication between connected computers through telephone lines or satellite hookup. Although the Internet itself is not the property of any one individual or corporation, it is governed by a volunteer organization, the Internet Society. During the early 1990s the number of Internet users exploded. It has been estimated that in 1995, anywhere from 20 to 30 million people worldwide used the system to do research, pay their bills, make consumer purchases, or simply "chat" through E-mail.

While most academic and government institutions were already hooked up, business and home use has expanded with the proliferation of commercial services such as America On-line and CompuServe. Moreover, many public libraries have installed public access computers (PACs). The revolution in communications and increased public access to information spawned by the Internet has raised serious questions regarding copyright issues as well as concerns about privacy rights.

See Also: Computers.

■ **INTERSTATE COMMERCE COMMISSION (ICC) (1887),** federal agency established by the Interstate Commerce Act to regulate interstate transportation and monitor railroad rates. During the 1870s railroad companies often adopted unfair rate practices. State Granger Laws set maximum rates for freight, but the Supreme Court ruled in *Wabash* v. *Illinois* (1886) that states could not regulate interstate rates. In response, Congress established the five-member Interstate Commerce Commission in 1887 to ensure that railroads did not grant rebates, enter pools, or set discriminatory rates. The Supreme Court weakened its power, however, by ruling for the railroads in 15 or 16 cases before 1905. The Hepburn Act (1906) strengthened the ICC by allowing it to set maximum rates, examine financial records, and enforce its decisions without going to court. It expanded the ICC's regulation to pipelines, express companies, sleeping-car companies, bridges, and ferries; the Mann-Elkins Act (1910) extended it further to telephone and telegraph companies. Like other regulatory agencies, the ICC could still come under the influence of those it was supposed to regulate. Presidents Wilson and Harding received criticism for appointing conservative businessmen to the ICC. At the end of 1995, the ICC was abolished by Congress, and its functions were taken over by the Department of Transportation.

■ **INTOLERABLE ACTS (1774),** laws passed by Parliament in response to the American colonies' defiance of the tea tax and the Boston Tea Party. In the spring of 1774 the Crown decided that Massachusetts should be punished for its recalcitrance and imposed the Intolerable, or Coercive, Acts. The first of the five measures effectively closed the ports of Boston harbor until the town compensated the East India Company and the customs commission for the destroyed tea. The second act annulled the colonial charter, replacing colonial officials with royally appointed ones and banning town meetings. The third act protected royal officials from being tried in colonial courts. The fourth measure legalized the quartering of troops in public buildings and private homes. The final act established a government in Quebec and awarded it territory claimed by the colonists north of the Ohio River. The Intolerable Acts were designed to isolate Massachusetts and force it to acquiesce. The plan backfired, however, and prompted the calling of the First Continental Congress (September 1774).

See Also: Boston Tea Party; Revolution, American.

■ **INUITS (ESKIMOS),** indigenous peoples of Alaska and the Arctic region of North America known for their creative adaptation to the harsh northern climate. Before European contact, most Inuits lived north of the treeline in the Arctic tundra, subsisting as fishers and hunters of caribou and sea animals. Their spiritual life was based on the hunting tradition, which emphasized the relationship between hunter and prey. The Inuit's primary residence was the igloo. The first Europeans to colonize Inuit lands in present-day Alaska and Canada were the Russians, who arrived in the early 1700s. After the sale of Alaska to the United States in 1868, material conditions worsened for the Inuits as miners and settlers moved in. The 1971 Alaska Native Claims Settlement Act attempted to resolve Inuit claims to lands in Alaska, but, for many, life has not improved. Today, there are numerous village corporations involved in Arctic investment, but the balance between traditional lifeways and modern development, which they seek, is often difficult to maintain.

See Also: Alaska Native Claims Settlement Act; Indians of North America.

■ **INVENTION,** emerged as a significant activity in American society between 1790 and 1850. Those years marked the formative period of American ideas about invention as well as the organization of inventive activity within the society and its integration into the nation's economic system. During this period cultural beliefs regarding the nature of invention and its relationship to social progress were embodied in the patent clause of the Constitution (Article I, Section 8). The patent system reflected widely held political and economic philosophies that equated social progress with a democratic but limited government designed primarily to protect private property rights and guarantee equal opportunity for each individual to strive for personal advancement. The most important change in the patent system came in 1836, when Congress instituted a process for examining patent applications for novelty, originality, and practicality. Patent activity greatly increased following this reform, as inventors found their intellectual property rights better protected and thus easier to sell. While the patent system was perceived as the most important incentive for invention, the growth of manufacturing and the introduction of new production methods provided the greatest economic inducement for inventors as well as an institutional setting for their work.

A Setting for Invention. At the center of inventive activity were machine shops and their skilled operators. The increased use of machinery in manufacturing placed great value on the skills of machinists, who were usually proficient in the operation of all the machines in the shop and capable of making, repairing, and often designing a variety of machinery. Machinists experienced significant geographic and occupational mobility, and as they moved to improve their situation, they transmitted new techniques and tools to different regions and industries.

While traditional craft practice consisted of specialized knowledge invested in individuals who carefully guarded their techniques, the rise of machinery and mechanical technology fostered a new openness in the transmission of techniques. The extensive use of metalworking machinery meant that similar processes were common to a broad range of industries and that machinists and machine tool companies were able to apply their skills and techniques to problems affecting many industries. In this way technological knowledge became more open and more widely diffused. Design became an interactive process in which machinists collaborated with those who used machinery in their factories and workshops. As a result, machine shops became experimental laboratories for new industrial processes and machinery.

The Social Process of Invention. Working in a tradition of cooperative shop invention, the individual inventor of the 19th century was not the lone inventor of mythology. Invention involved an interactive process of construction, experimentation, and redesign that required not only materials and mechanisms but also the talents of skilled mechanics. Although the literature of invention has long recognized the need for such experimentation, it has failed to give credit to the skilled craftsman who constructed devices and whose own design ideas, growing out of familiarity with materials and mechanisms, often modified an inventor's design in subtle ways that helped to make it successful.

Because the patent system rewarded only the original inventor, it encouraged inventors to present their own work in terms of an initial inventive insight, with the rest of the process a mere working out of the idea. The process of inventive work also encouraged this view, as a new design usually did start with a creative insight that combined component parts into a new pattern. Public descriptions of their work offered by inventors seeking recognition and reward identified such an insight as the crucial moment of "eureka." Yet the act of turning such insights into practical inventions encompassed much more.

Even before beginning to design an invention, inventors acquired knowledge through both practical experience and reading in scientific and technical literature. Although 19th-century invention is usually regarded as highly empirical, technical journals constantly emphasized how important it was for inventors to grasp the underlying scientific principles of mechanisms and processes and thus avoid wasting time and money on inadequate designs.

Those involved in developing new technology recognized that the laws of mechanics and other scientific principles provided only one source of knowledge and inspiration to inventors. More significant, particularly for the majority of inventors whose designs improved on existing machines and techniques, was awareness of the state of the art in a particular industry. It was for this reason that drawings and models of machinery were considered a crucial aid and inspiration to inventors, who also exchanged information and studied working apparatus in an industry's operating rooms and machine shops.

Industrial settings provided nascent inventors with practical experience through the operation and manufacture of machines, experience that they supplemented by reading books and journals produced by leading members of the technical community. Through participation in technical communities, inventors gained crucial resources of knowledge and skill and often found a source of employment and financing as well. Access to such resources was uneven, and most inventors were men; the inventive contributions of women and African Americans often reflected their exclusion from or limited participation in such groups.

The Emergence of Industrial Research. An important shift in the organization of inventive activity occurred in 1876 when Thomas Edison established his laboratory in Menlo Park, New Jersey. The Menlo Park laboratory did not mark a sharp break with the shop tradition of invention. Now, however, the skilled workmen and tools that had formerly been found in manufacturing shops were adapted solely to inventive work. This allowed Edison rapidly to construct, test, and alter experimental devices, thus significantly increasing the rate at which he could develop new inventions. But Menlo Park also looked forward to a new model of research as Edison merged the shop tradition with sophisticated electrical and chemical laboratories. Such laboratories could be found on a smaller scale in some manufacturing enterprises, but what set Edison's effort apart from those of his contemporaries was its scale and

scope. The laboratory he built in Menlo Park was the largest private laboratory in the United States and certainly the largest devoted to invention.

The creation of the laboratory was made possible by the growing importance of large-scale, technology-based corporations in the American economy. Western Union Telegraph Company, the first corporation to dominate its industry on a truly national scale, was also one of the first to learn that greater control over the inventive process through direct support of inventors could produce competitive advantages. Edison was one of these inventors and his contracts with Western Union provided him with the funds to build and operate his laboratory. Western Union officials, although constrained by 19th-century beliefs in the unpredictability of inventive genius, nonetheless recognized that the laboratory enabled Edison to make invention a more regular and predictable process. They were therefore willing to invest personally in Edison's subsequent research on electric lighting, which enabled him to expand further the scale of his laboratory and to elaborate on his system of research and development.

Edison's Menlo Park laboratory and the larger one he built in West Orange, New Jersey, became models for other inventors, while demonstrating how invention, when properly organized, could become an industrial process with significant long-term benefits to the corporation. During the 1880s and 1890s independent inventors and leading companies in the electrical industry, such as General Electric and Bell Telephone, established similar laboratories. At the same time, firms in other industries hired chemists and established laboratories to standardize and improve materials used in their products. Increasingly, however, corporate technical staffs received their primary education in university science and engineering programs, as the sources of technological knowledge began to shift away from the shop floor.

By the first decade of the 20th century a number of large corporations were supporting industrial research in some form. While such research often included testing and standardization, most laboratories were involved in improving technology through minor and major improvements in products and process. Most firms refined their strategies toward invention and industrial research by a process of trial and error. A few companies such as General Electric, AT&T, Eastman Kodak, and Du Pont established sophisticated strategies that set them apart from their contemporaries. The nature of the technical problems they faced convinced managers in these corporations that deeper scientific understanding of materials and processes could lead to radical technological change. They established laboratories employing Ph.D. scientists and developed long-term research programs to secure or enhance the competitive positions of their companies and were rewarded with important new technologies, such as transistors and synthetic fabrics. Nonetheless, even at these companies a significant component of industrial research resulting in new inventions continues to take place in engineering or manufacturing laboratories, while innovative new technology is still produced by independent inventors working outside of major corporations.

—PAUL ISRAEL

See Also: Edison, Thomas Alva; Science.
BIBLIOGRAPHY: Israel, Paul, *From Machine Shop to Industrial Laboratory: Telegraphy and the Changing Contest of American Invention* (Johns Hopkins Univ. Press 1992); Macdonald, Anne L., *Feminine Ingenuity: Women and Invention in America* (Ballantine Books 1992); Reich, Leonard S., *The Making of American Industrial Research: Science and Business at GE and Bell 1876-1926* (Cambridge Univ. Press 1985).

■ **IOWA,** the leading agricultural state in the Midwest, ranking second only to California in income from farming. It is bounded on the north by Minnesota, on the west by South Dakota and Nebraska, on the south by Missouri, and on the east by Illinois and Wisconsin. The Mississippi River forms its eastern border and the Missouri River most of its western border. Iowa's land is characterized by rich prairie soil. The state ranks first in hog production. It is usually first in corn and occasionally first in soybeans, edging out Illinois. Food processing dominates its industries.

Iowa became a state in 1846. There have been few major events to mar its tranquillity since Indians were cleared from the area in the decades before the Civil War. Many rural areas are losing population, however, as big operations increasingly dominate farming.

Capital: Des Moines. Area: 56,276 square miles. Population (1995 est.): 2,842,000.
See Also: Black Hawk War; Hoover, Herbert Clark; Jolliet, Louis; Louisiana Purchase; Marquette, Pere Jacques; Sioux.

■ **IRAN-CONTRA AFFAIR,** series of covert actions carried out by officials of President Reagan's administration that were designed to free American-held hostages in Lebanon and to circumvent a congressional ban on funding the Contra movement in Nicaragua. Operations began in 1985, when Israeli contacts alerted administration officials in the Middle East that Iranian moderates could secure the release of hostages if the United States would sell arms to Iran. Marine Lt. Col. Oliver North, working for the National Security Council (NSC), directed arms shipments to Iran via Israel from mid-1985 through late 1986. Beginning in the spring of 1986, the excess profits garnered from the sales were diverted to the Contras, who were attempting to overthrow the Marxist Sandinista government of Nicaragua.

In October 1986, the affair surfaced after a Lebanese newspaper published a story that resulted in a flood of information and allegations about the illegal activities. President Reagan, as he did throughout, denied any involvement and appointed a special investigating committee to explore the role of the NSC. More than two years of congressional and prosecutorial investigations followed, during which a tangled web of secret activities was uncovered. This largest and most damaging scandal of the Reagan administration resulted in the criminal indictments of four officials and initiated a debate about the relationship between the president and Congress in the making of foreign policy.

See Also: North, Oliver; Reagan, Ronald Wilson.
BIBLIOGRAPHY: David, Charles Philippe, *Foreign Policy Failure in the White House: Reappraising the Fall of the Shah and the Iran-Contra Affair* (Univ. Press of America 1993); Draper, Theodore, *A Very Thin Line: The Iran Contra Affairs* (Hill & Wang 1991).

■ **IRAN HOSTAGE CRISIS,** diplomatic conflict between the United States and Iran (1979-81). In October 1979, Shah Muhammad Reza Pahlevi, who had been forced to leave Iran in January

1979, was admitted to a hospital in New York City. By that time, the exiled Shah had been formally deposed and sentenced to death in Iran. During his reign (1941-79), he had enjoyed substantial U.S. support, provoking severe anti-American feelings among extreme Muslim leaders, notably Ayatollah Khomeini.

On Nov. 4, 1979, the long-ripening crisis broke out. A mob of Iranian students stormed the American Embassy in Teheran and seized 52 staff members as hostages in an attempt to force the U.S. government to send the Shah back to Iran. Pres. Jimmy Carter rejected this as blackmail. However, in December 1979 the Shah left the United States and eventually flew to Egypt, where he died in 1980. President Carter froze all Iranian assets in the United States to try to force the release of hostages, but this had no effect. In April 1980, an American military helicopter rescue operation was launched but failed disastrously, causing much political trouble for Carter's administration and contributing to his defeat by Ronald Reagan in the presidential election in November. After behind-the-scenes negotiations, the hostages were finally released after 444 days of captivity on Jan. 20, 1981, the day of Reagan's inauguration.

See Also: Carter, James Earl, Jr. (Jimmy); Reagan, Ronald Wilson.

BIBLIOGRAPHY: Moses, Russell L., *Freeing the Hostages: Reexamining U.S.-Iranian Negotiations and Soviet Policy, 1979-81* (Univ. of Pittsburgh Press 1996); Sick, Gary, *October Surprise: America's Hostages in Iran and the Election of Ronald Reagan* (Times Books 1991).

■ **IREDELL, JAMES (1751-99),** associate justice of the U.S. Supreme Court (1790-99). Born in England, Iredell was an outspoken Federalist. He distinguished himself on the Court as an early guardian of the sovereign, independent federal judiciary, a principle evident in his opinion in *Calder v. Bull* (1798).

See Also: Supreme Court.

■ **IRISH IMMIGRANTS.** One of the largest immigrant groups in American history, the Irish began arriving in America in the 17th century. They came for a variety of reasons. Oppressed by the English, many Irish who migrated during the colonial period were poor, indentured servants. The period most associated with Irish immigration,

however, is the late 1840s, when about 1.5 million fled Ireland to avoid starvation caused by the potato famine. In the postfamine years immigration to the United States became a routine part of Irish life, touching families at all levels of society.

Most Irish immigrants were Catholic and, although from rural Ireland, settled in cities along the east coast. Throughout their history in the United States, Irish immigrants have experienced exploitation and prejudice. They were often scorned for being Catholic, anti-British, and poor. Nonetheless, Irish immigrants have heavily influenced U.S. politics, religious life, and labor movements. Many Irish Americans have also remained active in Irish politics, especially in the independence movement and in the conflict in Northern Ireland. By 1980 more than 40 million people of Irish ancestry lived in the United States.

See Also: Immigration; Roman Catholics.

■ **IRON ACTS (1750, 1757),** British legislation that encouraged the production of American bar and pig iron. By exempting bar and pig iron from English import duties, the acts encouraged their export to England's iron and steel factories while banning the manufacture of refined metal goods in the colonies.

■ **IRON CURTAIN,** a term coined by British Prime Minister Winston Churchill in his Fulton, Missouri, speech in March 1946. The Soviets, Churchill said, had drawn an "iron curtain" across Europe, forcefully separating the areas they controlled from the rest of the continent.

See Also: Cold War.

■ **IROQUOIS CONFEDERACY,** the largest and most influential association of Indian peoples in colonial North America. It was in the 16th century, prior to the onset of European settlement, that the five Iroquois "nations" formed a confederacy pledging not to war against one another. From east to west across the Mohawk Valley and Finger Lakes region in what is now upstate New York, these nations were the Mohawk, the Oneida, the Onondaga, the Cayuga, and the Seneca. They performed the Condolence Council ritual at Onondaga, and they subscribed to what was known as the "Great Law," which was remembered in oral tradition until the 19th century when it was written in several versions.

Iroquois polities were local "kinship states," each village of which governed itself. The rituals central to the Iroquois association were attended by the village sachems, the gathering of which was long assumed to be a political league of Iroquois leaders. Recent thought, however, stresses the religious significance of such gatherings and ascribes political functions to ad hoc alliances of two or more nations within the league cooperating in particular projects.

Iroquois locations between New France and New Netherland (later New York) made the Iroquois strategically important in imperial power struggles. They sided as clients of the Dutch and then of the British against the French and were badly beaten in the 17th century by French troops and France's Indian allies, after which the Iroquois were required to be "neutrals," avoiding overt hostilities against New France. Nevertheless, the French permitted them to keep tribal territories in order to act as buffers between New France's Indian clients and the seductive bargains of trade in New York's Albany.

Myth has the Iroquois conquering "a great savage empire" when they were actually at the bottom of their fortunes. British diplomats invented this "empire," arguing that the Iroquois were recognized as subjects of the British Crown (although the Iroquois denied it) and therefore their purported conquests belonged to Britain. Having invented the logic, the British invented conquests to substantiate it. The Iroquois happily accepted this mythic reputation and made it part of their "tradition." French diplomats laughed at the flimsy pretexts, but Anglophile scholars perpetuated the myth with much credibility.

The reality was a system of tribal alliances called the Covenant Chain. It was formed by treaties and presided over by the Iroquois with British authority and support. It fell apart, along with the basic Iroquois League, during the American Revolution of 1775-83.

The league was revived in two versions, in Canada as well as New York, but Iroquois peoples today have split up among traditional communities and others with written constitutions and elected officials.

—FRANCIS JENNINGS

See Also: *Indians of North America.*

BIBLIOGRAPHY: Aquila, Richard, *The Iroquois Restoration: Iroquois Diplomacy on the Colonial Frontier, 1701-1754* (Wayne State Univ. Press 1983); Jennings, Francis, *The Ambiguous Iroquois Empire* (Norton 1984); Jennings, Francis, et al., eds., *The History and Culture of Iroquois Diplomacy* (Syracuse Univ. Press 1985); Richter, Daniel K., *The Ordeal of the Longhouse: The Peoples of the Iroquois League in the Era of European Colonization* (Univ. of North Carolina Press 1992).

IRRIGATION, the use of water for agriculture. Knowledge of irrigation techniques allowed people to inhabit the arid West from about 300 B.C. The Hohokam built the first irrigation system in America along the Gila River in Arizona, and the Anasazi people, who lived in the region where New Mexico, Colorado, Arizona, and Utah meet, used irrigation during the height of their culture from about 900 to 1150. The Pueblo of the Southwest had incorporated irrigation into their culture by the time of European contact in the 16th century. Water equaled power in the Hispanic Southwest, and irrigation systems became tools for colonization and sources of conflict from then to today. The Mormons' well-planned irrigation system helped them settle in Salt Lake City; the Newlands Reclamation Act (1902) helped the settlement of the entire West. The act set up the Bureau of Reclamation, which oversaw huge projects including the Hoover Dam and the California Central Valley projects in the 1930s, the Columbia Basin Project in the 1930s and 1940s, Glen Canyon Dam in the 1950s, and the Central Arizona and Utah Projects in the 1960s and 1970s. The initial goal of providing 160 acres of irrigated land to every farmer quickly gave way to supporting large-scale agribusiness and urbanization. Indian rights to irrigation water, granted by the Supreme Court through the Winters Doctrine in 1908, were largely ignored.

See Also: *Agriculture.*

BIBLIOGRAPHY: Meyer, Michael C., *Water in the Hispanic Southwest: A Social and Legal History, 1550-1850* (Univ. of Arizona Press 1984); Worster, Donald, *Rivers of Empire: Water, Aridity, and the Growth of the American West* (Pantheon 1985).

IRVING, WASHINGTON (1783-1859), author. Born in New York City, he studied law and passed the bar examination (1806) but engaged in writing early on. His first work was *Letters of Jonathan Oldstyle* (1802-03), a series of nostalgic correspondences about the manners of the past, that Irving sent to New York's *Morning Chronicle*, a newspaper his brother William published. In 1807-08, together with his brother William and James K. Paulding, he published 20 satirical pamphlets called "Salmagundi." In 1809, Irving published *A History of New York*, a mock portrayal of the Dutch times in the city on behalf of an eccentric 25-year-old scholar Diedrich Knickerbocker. Irving also used Knickerbocker as narrator in "Rip Van Winkle," probably the most famous of his short stories, and "The Legend of Sleepy Hollow," published in *The Sketch Book* (1819-20). His *Bracebridge Hall*, another collection of satiric, nostalgic, and whimsical

From 1815 to 1832, Washington Irving lived in Europe, where he wrote "Rip Van Winkle" and "The Legend of Sleepy Hollow." Upon returning to the United States, he was heralded as the country's leading man of letters.

sketches, appeared in 1822 as a follow-up to *The Sketch Book*. In 1826, Irving accepted an invitation to join the American diplomatic mission in Spain. There he served until 1829, publishing *History of... Christopher Columbus* (1828) and *A Chronicle of the Conquest of Granada* (1829). In 1829-32 he was secretary of the U.S. legation in London. In 1832, Irving published *Alhambra*. After serving as U.S. minister to Spain (1842-46), he returned to America to reside at "Sunnyside," his country house near Tarrytown, New York. During his later years, he published *Oliver Goldsmith* (1849), *Mahomet and His Successors* (1849-50), and the five-volume *Life of Washington* (1855-59).

See Also: *Short Story.*

BIBLIOGRAPHY: Brooks, Van Wyck, *The World of Washington Irving* (Dutton 1944); Johnston, Johanna, *The Heart That Would Not Hold: A Biography of Washington Irving* (Evans 1971).

■ **ISHI (c. 1862-1916),** Indian known as "the last Yahi." During his childhood, Ishi witnessed the systematic massacre of his small tribe by scalp hunters in California's Sierra Mountains. After 1868, the Yahi consisted of no more than a dozen survivors, all of whom but Ishi had died shortly after a group of surveyors stole their possessions as souvenirs in 1908. Three years later, Ishi came out of hiding, creating a sensation throughout the country. Anthropologist Alfred Kroeber used Ishi as an informant, housing him at the Anthropological Museum of the University of California in San Francisco, where he became a "living exhibit" for the museum on Sundays. Ishi's story was later told in a famous book by Theodora Kroeber, Kroeber's wife.

See Also: *Indians of North America.*

■ **ISOLATIONISM,** term used to describe America's policy of avoiding political or economic involvement with other nations. Its roots were in the colonial period, when settlers hoped to create a society whose politics and values were superior to those they had left behind in Europe.

During the 17th and 18th centuries, America, in relation to Europe, was geographically distant and militarily and economically weak—it was literally isolated. Isolationism as a philosophy and a policy was advocated by leading political figures, including Washington and Jefferson. Despite American economic and territorial expansion during the 19th century, most politicians and other Americans continued to advocate isolation from the whims of European affairs. Technological, economic, and political changes, however, increasingly drew Europe and America together.

American participation in World War I (1917-18) marked a significant departure from traditional isolationism. Opposition to U.S. involvement, however, persisted in the interwar years among many western politicians, rural Americans, and European immigrants. A significant reversal of these policies and views occurred in 1940, when America's sovereignty and security seemed threatened by a potential Axis victory. American participation in World War II (1941-45) succeeded in creating a generation of internationalists. Beginning with World War II and Pres. Franklin D. Roosevelt, isolationism as a practical policy was dead. Nevertheless, isolationist voices were heard in the post–Cold War era as some political leaders questioned whether America could afford to play the role of "policeman of the world."

See Also: World War I; World War II.

BIBLIOGRAPHY: Guinsburg, Thomas N., *The Pursuit of Isolationism in the United States Senate from Versailles to Pearl Harbor* (Garland 1982); Williams, William Appleman, *The Tragedy of American Diplomacy* (World Publishing 1957).

■ **ITALIAN IMMIGRANTS.** With a long history in America, Italian immigrants have included people from a wide variety of backgrounds. Christopher Columbus was an Italian, as were many other early explorers. In general, the Italians who arrived in the United States before 1880 were professionals or skilled workers and hailed from northern Italy. More prosperous than later arrivals, these Italians were generally accepted by other Americans.

Italian immigration after 1880 was a mass movement of poor workers and peasants from southern Italy, mainly Sicily. These immigrants were often not readily accepted by most Americans, including northern Italian immigrants. Many of the post-1880 immigrants, most of them single men and Catholics, settled in cities along the east coast and formed the core of "Little Italys," Italian neighborhoods in large urban centers. In these communities Italians adapted to American life but also retained much of their culture, including the Catholic religion, their cuisine, and their language. Many Italian immigrants have attained prominence in America, from high-ranking politicians to influential artists.

See Also: Ethnic Groups; Immigration; Roman Catholics.

■ **IVES, CHARLES (1874-1954),** a New England composer of daunting complexity who was also a successful insurance man. Born in Danbury, Connecticut, he learned music from his bandmaster father and was educated at Yale, where he studied composition. Ives wrote music that combined 19th-century band music and New England transcendentalism with the tonalities and rhythms of European modernism. Many of his songs, chamber pieces, and orchestral works included fragments of familiar march tunes or old hymns and were intended to evoke the people and places of New England. Although his *Third Symphony* (1904) won a Pulitzer Prize in 1947, his demanding music was rarely performed during his lifetime, and Ives was little involved with the musical community. Instead, he ran an insurance brokerage (1898-1930) and occasionally published booklets extolling self-reliance, free enterprise, and democracy.

BIBLIOGRAPHY: Perlis, Vivian, *Charles Ives Remembered: An Oral History* (Norton 1976).

■ **IWO JIMA, BATTLE OF (1945),** a costly World War II battle between three U.S. Marine divisions and entrenched Japanese defenders on the tiny volcanic island of Iwo Jima in the Bonin group. The island was desired as a base where disabled B-29 bombers could land after raiding Japan. The invasion began on February 19, and four days later a stunning photograph showed the marines raising the American flag on Mount Suribachi. The island was declared secured on March 26.

See Also: World War II.

J

■ **JACKSON, ANDREW (1767-1845),** seventh president of the United States (1829-37). Born in Waxhaw, South Carolina, Jackson fought in the American Revolution at the age of 13 and was captured and beaten by the British, an experience that turned him into a lifelong Anglophobe. Orphaned the following year by the death of his mother, he was forced to make his own way in the world. He studied law, was admitted to the bar at the age of 20, and in 1788 was appointed solicitor for western North Carolina. He eventually moved to Nashville and became a successful attorney, participated in the constitutional convention that created the state of Tennessee (1796), and was elected to be the state's first congressman (1796-97), then U.S. senator (1797), and then a justice of the state's supreme court (1798-1804).

In 1791, Jackson married Rachel Donelson, who mistakenly believed she had been divorced from her first husband. The incident provided his critics with scandal enough for a lifetime of criticism. A man with a fierce temper and a refined sense of honor, Jackson engaged in several duels and once killed an opponent. He also engaged in political feuds, which drove him to announce his retirement from politics in 1804. In addition to having a highly successful law practice, Jackson became a cotton planter, managing a plantation with dozens of slaves from his elegant mansion, "The Hermitage," on the banks of the Cumberland River.

Jackson achieved national fame during the War of 1812. As major general of the Tennessee militia, he defeated the Creeks in 1813-14, was commissioned major general in the U.S. Army, and decisively defeated a British invasion at the Battle of New Orleans in 1815. His brilliant, tough generalship earned him the acclaim of the nation and the nickname of "Old Hickory." As commanding officer during the Seminole War of 1818, Jackson invaded Florida, where his execution of two British subjects whom he accused of inciting the war led to an international incident. But his actions also led to the Spanish cession of Florida to the United States the next year. In 1821, Jackson served as the military governor of Florida.

Returning to national politics in 1823 as senator from Tennessee, Jackson soon announced his intention to seek the presidency. In the election of 1824, he ran against three other candidates and received the largest number of popular votes. Since he failed to win a majority in the electoral college, however, the election went to the House of Representatives, where what Jackson supporters called a "corrupt bargain" resulted in the election of John Quincy Adams. Four years later, however, Jackson defeated Adams and was swept into office in one of the most decisive elections in American history. He was reelected in 1832, defeating Henry Clay.

This, the only extant photograph of Andrew Jackson, was taken in 1845, his last year.

Presidency. Jackson's victory inaugurated an era of party politics in the United States. He began his term by turning out of office those who had supported his opponent and rewarding the loyalists who had backed him. As one of them put it, "to the victor belong the spoils"; thus, granting government positions to the party faithful became known as the "spoils system." It prevailed for 50 years, until the civil service reform begun by the Pendleton Act of 1883. Under Jackson's leadership, the Democratic party became a disciplined political machine that was able to deliver the votes in Congress. When Jackson failed to get his way he had none of the reluctance of earlier presidents about using his veto power. Under Jackson the presidency became the commanding branch of the federal government for the first time. From the administration of George Washington, presidents had relied on "cabinet government," putting all major decisions before the cabinet as a whole. Jackson, instead, relied on a small set of loyal party activists for advice, a group that became known as the "Kitchen Cabinet."

Jackson demonstrated his authority in the first major struggle of his presidency, the Indian removal policy. Always an opponent of American Indians, Jackson pressed Congress into passing the Removal Act in 1830, which provided funds for moving all Indian communities residing in the states to new homes west of the Mississippi. The Cherokee put up the most resistance, in 1832 winning a favorable ruling against removal from the U.S. Supreme Court. Jackson simply ignored the Court, and the Cherokee were removed.

A firm believer in laissez-faire economics, Jackson quashed the idea of federal support for canal and road building ("internal improvements") and went to war against the Bank of the United States. His economic ineptitude, however, led to the Panic of 1837, the worst depression the nation had yet experienced. But Jackson was also a strong nationalist, stoutly defending the authority of the federal government during the "nullification" crisis with South Carolina in 1833. Jackson's legacy was ambiguous. He was an aristocratic and authoritarian slave master who made his reputation killing Indians, but he was also acclaimed as the president who brought democracy to Washington and governed in the name of the "common man."

His contradictions embodied those of the United States itself.

—JOHN MACK FARAGHER

See Also: *Bank War; Corrupt Bargain; Democratic Party; Indian Removal; Kitchen Cabinet; Nullification; President of the United States; Spoils System.*

BIBLIOGRAPHY: Remini, Robert V., *The Life of Andrew Jackson* (Harper & Row 1988); Rogin, Michael Paul, *Fathers and Children: Andrew Jackson and the Subjugation of the American Indian* (Knopf 1975); Sellers, Charles, ed., *Andrew Jackson: A Profile* (Hill & Wang 1971).

■ **JACKSON, HELEN HUNT (1830-85),** author and Indian rights activist. Born in Amherst, Massachusetts, she was a friend of poet Emily Dickinson. Jackson's poetry was highly regarded by her mentor Thomas Wentworth Higginson and by such luminaries as Ralph Waldo Emerson. She is best remembered as the author of *A Century of Dishonor* (1884), a history of the U.S. government's unjust and brutal Indian policies, and for *Ramona* (1884), a romantic novel that illustrated the plight of American Indians.

See Also: *Dickinson, Emily; Emerson, Ralph Waldo; Frontier in American History; Higginson, Thomas Wentworth; Women's Movement.*

■ **JACKSON, HOWELL EDMUNDS (1832-95),** associate justice of the U.S. Supreme Court (1893-95). A Paris, Tennessee, native, Jackson served on the Court after a long career in public life. He dissented in *Pollock* v. *Farmers Loan and Trust Company* (1895), contending that a federal income tax was constitutional. However, he believed the salaries of Supreme Court justices should be tax exempt.

See Also: *Supreme Court.*

■ **JACKSON, JESSE LOUIS (1941-),** minister and civil rights leader. Born in Greenville, South Carolina, Jackson left his training at the Chicago Theological Seminary to join (1965) Martin Luther King, Jr., and the Southern Christian Leadership Conference (SCLC) in the struggle for civil rights. His captivating, rhythmic voice helped his rise to leadership, first of the economic arm of SCLC, Operation Breadbasket, and then as founder and national president of People United to Serve Humanity (PUSH). In 1984 Jackson reached out again, first to found the National Rainbow Coalition and then in an unsuccessful bid for the Democratic presidential nomination. In 1988 he tried for the nomination again. Although his studies were interrupted, the Chicago Seminary awarded Jackson an honorary doctor of divinity degree. In 1968 he was ordained in the Baptist Church. Jackson remains a strong moral and religious force for social and political reform.

See Also: African Americans; Civil Rights Movement.

■ **JACKSON, MAHALIA (1911-72),** gospel singer known as "the Queen of the Gospel," born in New Orleans, Louisiana. Much influenced by secular blues singers such as Bessie Smith, she brought gospel music to a wider audience than ever before, selling more than one million copies of her 1945 recording "Move on Up a Little Higher." After 1954, she had a weekly show on the CBS radio network. During the 1960s, her voice was emblematic of the civil rights movement.

See Also: African Americans; Civil Rights Movement; Gospel Music.

For holding off the Union offensive at the first battle of Bull Run in July 1861, Thomas J. Jackson earned the nickname "Stonewall."

■ **JACKSON, ROBERT HOUGHWOUT (1892-1954),** associate justice of the U.S. Supreme Court (1941-54). He was born in Spring Creek, Pennsylvania, and was the last justice to become a member of the bar (1913) without graduating from law school. Jackson, often considered a judicial conservative, was solicitor general (1938-40) and later attorney general (1940-41) before he was named to the Court. He served as the chief U.S. prosecutor at the Nuremberg War Trials (1945-46).

See Also: Supreme Court.

■ **JACKSON, THOMAS J. "STONEWALL" (1824-63),** Confederate general. Born in Clarksburg, Virginia, Jackson graduated from West Point (1846) and served in the Mexican War (1846-48). He then became a professor at Virginia Military Institute (1851). When the Civil War broke out (1861), he was made a brigadier general. Jackson was Gen. Robert E. Lee's most valued subordinate. He was given his nickname because at a critical point in the First Battle of Bull Run (Manassas) (June 1861) his troops declared that their commander was standing "like a stone wall" in the face of the battle. Jackson's brilliant generalship in the Shenan-

doah Valley (1861-62) is still studied in military schools today. He was instrumental in the Confederate victories at the Second Battle of Bull Run (August 1862) and Chancellorsville (May 1863). At Chancellorsville, however, he was accidentally shot by his own men and died a few days later.

See Also: Bull Run, Battles of; Chancellorsville, Battle of; Civil War; Fredericksburg, Battle of.

■ **JAMES, ALICE (1848-92),** writer. The sister of philosopher William James and novelist Henry James, she was born in New York City. She is remembered for the powerful journal she wrote in the last few months before her premature death. First published in 1934 as *Alice James: Her Brothers, Her Journal,* it is an insightful memoir of a talented sister overshadowed by her brilliant brothers.

See Also: James, Henry; James, William.

■ **JAMES, HENRY (1843-1916),** author. Reared until the age of 12 in his birthplace, New York City, and in Albany, New York, Henry James, younger brother of William, then traveled to Europe with his family for a three-year stay. After a number of return visits, he settled in London in

1876 and proceeded to write, among other books, *Roderick Hudson* (1876), *The American* (1877), *The Europeans* (1878), and *The Portrait of a Lady* (1881). With the exception of *Daisy Miller* (1879), popularity largely eluded James's novels and short stories, a condition he believed would be remedied in 1886 with the publication that year of *The Bostonians* and *The Princess Casamassima*. Although James erred in the latter judgment, he had succeeded in establishing himself as an essayist and literary critic with such works as *French Poets and Novelists* (1878), *Hawthorne* (1879), and *Portraits of Places* (1883). Regardless of the extent of his readership, James continued to create first-rate novels and stories, including *The Aspern Papers* (1888), "The Turn of the Screw" (1898), *The Wings of the Dove* (1902), *The Ambassadors* (1903), and *The Golden Bowl* (1904). James toured the United States in 1904-05, resulting in *The American Scene* (1907). Frustrated by the seeming inaction of the United States upon the outbreak of World War I, James obtained British citizenship in 1915. A prodigious author, James once had written of himself, "I want to leave a multitude of pictures of my time," and he did.

 See Also: *Novel.*

BIBLIOGRAPHY: Edel, Leon, *Henry James: A Life* (Harper & Row 1985).

After fighting for the Confederacy in the Civil War, Jesse James and his brother Frank led a gang of outlaws that robbed banks and held up trains throughout the midwestern states.

■ **JAMES, JESSE (WOODSON) (1847-82),** bank and train robber who, with his brother, Franklin Alexander James (1843-1915), became an outlaw legend. Born to a minister in Clay County, Missouri, Jesse joined "Bloody Bill" Anderson's guerrillas in 1864 during the Civil War and participated in the Centralia massacre of 24 unarmed Union soldiers. Frank and Jesse robbed their first bank together in Liberty, Missouri, killing an innocent bystander, on Feb. 13, 1866. Joining with the Younger brothers, the James gang robbed numerous banks, stages, and trains from Iowa to Alabama in the late 1860s and early 1870s. As their popularity increased in the press as legendary Robin Hoods, redistributing wealth to the poor, their crimes became more and more audacious. Their train robberies set Pinkerton Detectives on their trail and on Jan. 5, 1875, their half-brother was killed and their mother maimed in a Pinkerton raid on their home, furthering their public sympathy. A raid on the Northfield,

Minnesota, bank in 1876 ended in disaster with the Youngers captured, three of the gang killed, and the James boys narrowly escaping, moving to Nashville and living under assumed names. After they murdered two men in 1881, a $5,000 reward was put on their heads by the state of Missouri. One of their own gang, Robert Ford, shot Jesse James in the back on Apr. 3, 1882. Frank eventually surrendered but despite three separate trials was not convicted, and he lived out his life in peace.

 See Also: *Frontier in American History.*

■ **JAMES, WILLIAM (1842-1910),** psychologist and philosopher. James was born in New York City, the older brother of the novelist Henry James. He graduated from Harvard Medical School in 1869 and began teaching anatomy, physiology, and hygiene there in 1872. He was named professor of philosophy in 1881 and continued teaching until 1907. James was a prolific writer in both of his chosen fields. In 1890 he wrote the two-volume *The Principles of Psychology*, in which he explored the importance of the senses. The work was later abridged and commonly used as a textbook. In *The Varieties of Religious Experience* (1902), James advocated abandoning abstract absolutes. James was one of the leaders of the philosophical movement pragmatism, which he introduced by that name in lectures at the Lowell Institute and Columbia University, although he credited Charles Peirce with the original conception. In the books *Pragmatism* (1907) and *The Meaning of Truth* (1909), James advanced the ideals of concrete actions based on factual knowledge.

See Also: Peirce, Charles S.; James, Henry.

■ **JAMES RIVER,** broad shallow river in Virginia running 340 miles east into the Chesapeake Bay. In 1607 the English founded their first permanent settlement in America at Jamestown, on the river's lower course. During the 18th century tobacco, worked primarily by slaves, was the principal crop grown on James River plantations. The towns of Williamsburg, Richmond, Newport, and Lynchburg were all founded on the river as trading centers for Virginia tobacco and English manufactured goods.

■ **JAMESTOWN SETTLEMENT,** the first (1607) permanent English settlement in North America. Established near the mouth of Chesapeake Bay, it was known to be a risky venture. The Spanish had earlier attempted to found a mission there, but the undertaking had fallen victim to an Indian massacre. In 1606 the British Crown, challenging Spanish dominance in North America, chartered the London Company of private adventurers, which in 1607 sent about 100 men into Chesapeake Bay.

Met by Indian hostility, the colonizers chose a defensible site on a peninsula (now Jamestown Island) at the mouth of the James River. There their members were decimated by Indian attacks and rampant disease. Led by ineffectual commanders and composed of too many "gentlemen," Jamestown suffered casualties worse than those of most combat organizations. Food was insufficient, and the settlers resisted performing the work of planting. Those who survived the first winter lived on corn and fish purchased or pillaged from the Indians. Revived the

next year under the leadership of Capt. John Smith only to endure renewed famine in the severe winter of 1609-10 (the "starving time"), Jamestown's settlers were preparing to abandon the colony when the royal governor, Lord De La Warr, arrived in June 1610 with reinforcements.

To rescue the colony from anarchy, De La Warr laid down a fiercely dictatorial and punitive set of laws. Conditions improved, and planting became more attractive when tobacco was introduced in 1612 as a cash crop. However, the tobacco trade alone could not rescue the foundering colony. By 1622 the London Company had sent out between 6,000 and 10,000 settlers and only 2,000 were left alive.

Powhatan, the paramount chief of the surrounding Indians, presided over an "empire" of between 14,000 and 21,000 tribesmen, who, if united, might have pushed the English into the sea. Diplomatically, Capt. Christopher Newport, the colonists' leader, proposed to make Powhatan a vassal of England's kings, and Capt. John Smith overawed the Indians by aggressive military tactics. When Smith went too far and was captured, Powhatan tried reverse diplomacy by making Smith a subchief "vassal" of himself. Neither device worked for long, although diplomacy included even the exchange by Smith to Powhatan in 1609 of Henry Spelman, an English boy who later became a captain in the colony, for an Indian village.

Despite propaganda about saving savage souls, the London Company confidentially told the colonists, "you cannot carry yourselves so towards them [the Indians] but they will grow discontented with your habitation." Pretense of a mission enabled the company to collect contributions from churches throughout England, but the fund was spent on other than conversion. Mismanagement and the loss of 347 lives in a 1622 Indian massacre led the British authorities in 1624 to revoke the company's charter and bring the colony under royal control.

—FRANCIS JENNINGS

See Also: James River; Powhatan; Smith, John.
BIBLIOGRAPHY: Barbour, Philip L., ed., *The Complete Works of Captain John Smith*, 3 vols. (Univ. of North Carolina Press 1986); Feest, Christian, "Virginia Algonquians," *Handbook of North American Indians*, vol. 15, ed. by William C. Sturtevant (Smithsonian Inst. Press 1978); Jennings, Francis, *The*

Invasion of America (Univ. of North Carolina Press 1975); Morgan, Edmund S., *American Slavery: American Freedom* (Norton 1975).

■ JAPANESE-AMERICAN INTERNMENT (1942-45),

the relocation of Japanese Americans by the U.S. government during World War II. Following the Japanese bombing of Pearl Harbor on Dec. 7, 1941, the U.S. War Department believed that Japanese Americans posed a threat of sabotage. In February 1942 the War Department received authorization from Pres. Franklin D. Roosevelt to establish the War Relocation Authority (WRA) in order to exclude persons considered "risky" from any "military zone," which, by War Department definition, included essentially the whole West Coast. Because most Americans of Japanese her-

itage lived on the West Coast, the evacuation by the WRA was massive. After being rounded up and detained briefly in 15 "assembly centers" and four Department of Justice internment camps, approximately 110,000 Japanese Americans were interned in 10 inland concentration camps.

How Japanese Americans experienced internment varied, according to camp administrative policies, local conditions, personal and demographic factors, and political persuasion. However, in most cases they endured tragic consequences. Most of them suffered both material losses in property and wages in addition to restrictions on their religious, political, and civic freedoms.

After the war the plight of the interned Japanese Americans continued. Having been stripped of their homes and jobs in 1942, many found them-

A Japanese-American girl sits with her family's belongings, en route to an internment camp. Early in 1942, Pres. Franklin D. Roosevelt issued an executive order that ultimately interned more than 100,000 Japanese Americans.

selves driven out of the camps in 1945 when administrators simply cut off essential services. Once outside, some faced severe resistance to their return to the West Coast, resulting in drive-by shooting incidents, litigation cases depriving them of their pre-internment property, and even deportation cases. Further compounding their tragedy, Japan turned its back on them too, leaving them with little choice but to live among people who only recently had interned them, who had stolen their property, and who had deprived them of the rights they had cherished as American citizens.

The racial inequity associated with the internment has long been an issue of controversy. At the time, politicians and military officials justified the forced evacuation of Japanese Americans on grounds of "military necessity," despite the remote possibility of a Japanese invasion. Yet, although the United States was also at war with Germany and Italy, Americans of German and Italian descent were not interned.

—BRIAN MASARU HAYASHI

BIBLIOGRAPHY: Daniels, Roger, *Concentration Camps, North America: Japanese in the United States and Canada During World War II* (Robert E. Krieger 1981); Girdner, Audrie, and Anne Loftis, *The Great Betrayal* (Macmillan 1969); Weglyn, Michi, *Years of Infamy: The Untold Story of America's Concentration Camps* (Morrow 1976).

■ **JAPANESE-AMERICAN RELOCATION CASES (1943-44),** four U.S. Supreme Court cases in which the legality of Japanese-American internment by the War Relocation Authority was challenged. Reasoning that wartime exigencies justified the mass detention, the Supreme Court initially upheld the legality of internment in three cases against the United States filed separately by Masuo Yasui, Gordon Hirabayashi, and Fred Korematsu. In December 1944, however, in the case of *Mitsuye Endo* v. *United States*, the Court finally overturned the relocation order in a unanimous decision. Endo, who was an employee at the California Department of Motor Vehicles, was born in the United States, had never visited Japan, could not speak Japanese, and had a brother serving in the U.S. Army. Although the Court avoided passing judgment on the question of the constitutionality of relocation, it concluded nonetheless that "whatever power the War

Relocation Authority may have to detain other classes of citizens, it has no authority to subject citizens who are concededly loyal."

In 1981, a law historian named Peter Irons discovered archival documents recording complaints from government lawyers in the Yasui, Hirabayashi, and Korematsu cases charging that evidence had been suppressed. In 1983, writs of error were filed on behalf of all three supplicants. Although Yasui died before the writ of error could be granted, both Hirabayashi's and Korematsu's convictions were eventually reversed, and in 1988 the Civil Liberties Act granted $20,000 to surviving internees as a form of redress.

—BRIAN MASARU HAYASHI

See Also: *Supreme Court.*

BIBLIOGRAPHY: Hatamiya, Leslie T., *Righting a Wrong: Japanese Americans and the Passage of the Civil Liberties Act of 1988* (Stanford Univ. Press 1993); Irons, Peter, *Justice at War: The Story of the Japanese American Internment Cases* (Oxford Univ. Press 1983); Irons, Peter, ed., *Justice Delayed: The Record of the Japanese American Internment Cases* (Wesleyan Univ. Press 1989).

■ **JAPANESE IMMIGRATION,** the arrival of immigrants from Japan to the United States, which occurred largely in the late 19th and early 20th centuries. Japanese first settled in the United States in 1868, after the Meiji Restoration in Japan. Japanese immigration reached its peak in the wake of the Chinese exclusion laws (1882), which cut off the supply of cheap agricultural labor to the Pacific states. Between 1890 and 1924 some 300,000 Japanese migrated to the United States, mostly to California and Hawaii. These numbers would have been considerably greater had not Japan, in 1908, after signing the Gentlemen's Agreements with the United States, voluntarily undertaken to reduce immigration to America by one-third. As a further deterrent to would-be Japanese immigrants, California passed the Alien Land Act in 1913, which barred "aliens ineligible for citizenship" from owning agricultural property.

In 1990 the U.S. census counted about 850,000 Americans of Japanese descent, of whom 116,000 were foreign born.

See Also: *Ethnic Groups; Gentlemen's Agreements.*

A Japanese family in San Francisco poses for a formal portrait. About 50,000 Japanese immigrated to the United States in the first decade of the 20th century, most settling in California.

BIBLIOGRAPHY: Ichihashi, Yamato, *Japanese in the United States: A Critical Study of the Problems of the Japanese Immigrants and Their Children* (Stanford Univ. Press 1932); Ichioka, Yuji, *The Issei: The World of the First Generation Japanese Immigrants, 1885-1924* (Free Press 1988).

■ **JAY, JOHN (1745-1829),** political leader, jurist, and diplomat. Born and raised in New York City, Jay graduated from King's College in 1764. He read law and was admitted to the bar in 1768. In 1774 he married Sarah Livingston, daughter of William Livingston. Although an opponent of independence, Jay became a member of New York's Committee of Correspondence and served in the First and Second Continental Congresses. He was the primary author of the New York constitution of 1777 and became the state's first chief justice (1777-79). He returned to Congress in December 1778 and was elected president of that body.

Jay's diplomatic career began when Congress selected him on Sept. 27, 1779, as U.S. minister to Spain. After more than two frustrating years trying to get Spain to recognize the new nation, to provide loans and supplies, and to enter into treaties of alliance and commerce, Jay was sent to Paris as one of America's peace commissioners to negotiate with Great Britain. He arrived in Paris on June 23, 1782, and played a leading role in negotiating the extremely favorable Treaty of Paris of 1783.

Jay returned to New York in July 1784 to find that Congress had selected him to be secretary for foreign affairs. He accepted the appointment in December 1784 and became the most powerful national figure in public office, serving, in essence, as prime minister. Virtually all matters—domestic as well as diplomatic—came to his attention. His abortive negotiations with Spanish agent Don Diego de Gardoqui in the mid-1780s made southerners suspicious of his motives, as he recommended that Congress give up the American right to navigate the Mississippi River for 25 years in exchange for a commercial treaty with Spain that would benefit the north.

As secretary for foreign affairs, Jay saw the need to strengthen Congress. He became a supporter of the Constitution of 1787 and was a coauthor of *The Federalist Papers*, although illness prevented him from writing more than five essays. He also wrote an extremely influential pamphlet advocating the ratification of the Constitution and served as the key Federalist member of the New York ratifying convention in June and July 1788.

Appointed by Pres. George Washington the first chief justice of the United States, Jay established many of the procedural precedents of the Court. His decision in *Chisholm* v. *Georgia* in 1793 gave rise to the 11th Amendment to the Constitution (1795), which established the sovereign immunity of the states. In 1792 Jay ran for governor of New York against the incumbent George Clinton. Although he received a majority of the votes, a partisan board of canvassers disallowed the vote of four counties, which cost him the election. While serving as chief justice, Jay was sent by Washington to negotiate with Great Britain. The Jay Treaty (1794) was extremely controversial but received Washington's support and was ratified by the Senate. When Jay returned from Great Britain, he found that he had been elected governor of New York. After serving two three-year terms (1795-1801) uneventfully, he retired from public life, turning down an offer from Pres. John Adams to be nominated again as chief justice.

—JOHN P. KAMINSKI

See Also: *Committees of Correspondence; Constitution of the United States; Federalist Papers, The; Jay's Treaty; Livingston, William; Treaty of Paris (1783); Supreme Court.*

BIBLIOGRAPHY: Johnston, Henry P., ed., *The Correspondence and Public Papers of John Jay*, 4 vols. (G.P. Putnam's Sons 1890-93); Morris, Richard B., *The Peacemakers: The Great Powers and American Independence* (Harper & Row 1965); Morris, Richard B., *Witnesses at the Creation: Hamilton, Madison, Jay, and the Constitution* (Holt, Rinehart & Winston 1985).

■ **JAY'S TREATY (1794),** U.S. agreement with Great Britain that addressed differences over the Treaty of Paris (1783), neutral rights, and commerce. In response to British seizures of American ships carrying French trade in the West Indies, President Washington sent Chief Justice John Jay to London to seek the withdrawal of British troops from U.S. territory in the Northwest, reparations for American ships seized under the British Order-in-Council of November 1793, an end to British impressment of U.S. sailors, compensation for slaves abducted during the Revolution, and free trade in the West Indies. Aware of the Federalists' desire for settlement, the British government agreed only to evacuate the northwestern posts by 1796, pay $10 million in reparations, and open the British West Indies to U.S. vessels on a very limited basis. In return Jay agreed to establishment of commissions to settle prerevolution debts owed to British creditors and allowed British subjects to continue their fur trade on American soil. The treaty's terms set off a furious debate in the United States and crystallized the development of national political parties. The Senate narrowly approved the treaty, after removing the West Indies trade clause, and Washington reluctantly signed it. French fears that the treaty contained a secret Anglo-American alliance contributed to the quasi-war with France (1798-1800). But Jay's Treaty brought a much-needed period of peace with England that lasted until 1812.

—DEAN FAFOUTIS

See Also: *Frontier in American History; Jay, John; Revolution, American.*

BIBLIOGRAPHY: Bemis, Samuel Flagg, *Jay's Treaty: A Study in Commerce and Diplomacy* (Yale Univ. Press 1962); Combs, Jerald A., *The Jay Treaty: Political Background of the Founding Fathers* (Univ. of California Press 1970).

■ **JAZZ,** America's distinctive contribution to the world's music. Jazz emerged at the beginning of the 20th century, the result of the blending of African and European musical traditions. Characterized by rhythmic enthusiasm, improvisation, and self-expression, jazz was the basic source for the great outpouring of commercially popular music in modern America. All of its great innovators have been African Americans.

Ragtime music, developed in the 1890s by pianists such as Scott Joplin of St. Louis and Ferdinand "Jelly Roll" Morton of New Orleans, was the first notable form of jazz. "Ragging" a tune referred to a style in which the pianist played a melody line with the right hand syncopated

Duke Ellington (*conducting*) achieved national renown as a jazz composer before he and his orchestra started touring widely in the 1930s.

against a left-hand 2/4 ground beat. This kind of cross-rhythm—which derived from the poly-rhythmic tradition of African music—was one of the fundamental characteristics of jazz. Ragtime quickly developed into a national craze, not only for the music but for a distinctive style of social dancing as well. Ensemble playing in a similarly cross-rhythmic style developed in New Orleans at about the same time, when black brass bands began ragging or "swinging" their melodies.

Ragtime became popular through the sale of sheet music, but the New Orleans style swept the country through the medium of phonograph records, first produced during World War I. In 1917, the Original Dixieland Jazz Band, a group of white musicians in New York City, made the first jazz record, a fact that testifies to the diffusion of the music from south to north and from black to white performers. The first true artists of jazz, however, were African American, notably the King Oliver Band, featuring the young trumpeter Louis Armstrong. The band became a popular sensation in Chicago in the early 1920s. Like ragtime, the popularity of ensemble jazz was driven

by a craze for dances such as the Charleston and the Black Bottom. Armstrong soon organized groups of his own and broke away from the ensemble style with inspired flights of improvised solo playing. Jazz performers of the 1920s were deeply influenced by the recorded blues of Bessie Smith and Gertrude "Ma" Rainey. The 12-bar blues form quickly became the standard for jazz composition.

In the early 1930s, performers such as Fletcher Henderson, Duke Ellington, and Count Basie formed the first jazz big bands and pioneered intricate compositions featuring harmonic instrumentation and improvised solos, played against a strong 4/4 dance beat. Radio played a key role in the popularization of this music, known as "swing." In 1935 clarinetist Benny Goodman became known as "the King of Swing" when his band was featured on national radio broadcasts. The music inspired yet another craze for dances such as the "jitterbug" and the "Lindy hop." Big band jazz—featuring performers such as saxophonist Lester Young and vocalists Billie Holiday and Frank Sinatra—continued to be the country's most popular musical form through the end of World War II.

Although African-American musicians had created jazz and swing music, white bandleaders and musicians reaped most of the recognition and profit. In reaction, during the 1940s some of the most creative talents in jazz—performers such as Dizzy Gillespie, Thelonius Monk, Charlie Parker, and Miles Davis—invented a new form of playing, known as be-bop, requiring a sophisticated knowledge of harmony and featuring more complex rhythms and extended improvisation. Over the next two decades players such as John Coltrane experimented with new musical forms, including the use of modal scales and eventually the elimination of melody, something called "free jazz." The jazz of the postwar era was musically challenging and intellectually exciting, but it was not dance music, and it failed to find a wide popular audience.

In recent years, jazz has been hailed as "America's classical music." The reissue of great recordings on compact disc has sparked revivals of older styles, and the compositions of the great jazz masters have become standards in the repertoire of most players.

—JOHN MACK FARAGHER

See Also: Be-Bop; Big Bands; Blues.

BIBLIOGRAPHY: Collier, James Lincoln, *The Making of Jazz* (Houghton Mifflin 1978); Hentoff, Nat, *Hear Me Talkin' To Ya* (Dover 1955).

■ **JEFFERS, ROBINSON (1887-1962),** poet. Jeffers was born in Pittsburgh, Pennsylvania. He studied a variety of fields, including literature, medicine, forestry, and the law, but when he inherited enough money to live on, he settled in Monterey, California, to write poetry. Jeffers's poems are usually considered pessimistic accounts of modern culture, which is portrayed as pursuing material gain at any expense. His works include *Californians* (1916), *Tamar and Other Poems* (1924), and *The Double Axe* (1948).

See Also: Poetry.

■ **JEFFERSON, THOMAS (1743-1826),** principal author of the Declaration of Independence, third president of the United States (1801-09), and chief symbol of the democratic legacies of the American Revolution. An unquestioned leader of America's most famous generation of statesmen, Jefferson has been the subject of more books than any other figure in American history except Abraham Lincoln. He is also one of the most controversial and contested figures in American history.

Born in the foothills of the Blue Ridge Mountains of central Virginia on Apr. 13, 1743, Jefferson was the son of Peter Jefferson, a moderately successful planter and surveyor. His mother, Jane Randolph Jefferson, descended from one of Virginia's most prominent families. After graduating from the College of William and Mary in 1762, Jefferson read law with George Wythe in Williamsburg for three years, then embarked on his own legal career.

National Prominence. He immediately became involved in the protest movement against the Stamp Act (1765) and gained national recognition for a pamphlet denying the British Parlia-

In addition to serving as the nation's third president (1801-09), Thomas Jefferson was a scientist, architect, and philosopher-statesman, with deep interest in education, literature, and the arts.

ment's authority over the American colonies. His reputation for writing against British imperial policies with uncommon elegance was perhaps matched only by his reputation as a handsome, wealthy landowner with a remarkable knowledge of such diverse subjects as agriculture, architecture, and music. By the time of his marriage to Martha Wayles Skelton (1772), his Virginia estate ("Monticello") included more than 10,000 acres of land and almost 200 slaves.

A member of the Second Continental Congress (1775-76), Jefferson was asked to draft the Declaration of Independence, a task he most reluctantly accepted. His fellow delegates revised and excised about 20 percent of Jefferson's original text, but left the early section on natural rights almost unchanged. The quintessential words of American history—"We hold these truths to be self-evident..."—are his alone. During the American Revolution, Jefferson served a term as governor of Virginia (1779-81) and revised its legal code. In 1782, the year of his wife's death, he wrote *Notes on Virginia,* a pioneering natural history of Virginia, in which he advocated the gradual abolition of slavery. It was the only book he ever published.

From 1785 to 1789, Jefferson served as American minister to France and observed the coming of the French Revolution. He returned to the United States to become America's first secretary of state, under Pres. George Washington. By 1793, Jefferson and James Madison had established the early version of an opposition party, the Democratic-Republicans, to counter the economic policies of Alexander Hamilton and the Federalists. In 1797, Jefferson became vice president, having lost his bid for the presidency to John Adams. He then defeated Adams in the election of 1800 and served two terms as president.

Presidency. Jefferson's greatest presidential success was the Louisiana Purchase (1803), which nearly doubled the size of the nation. His greatest failure was the Embargo Act of 1807. Designed to protect American neutrality and to prevent British impressment of American citizens at sea, the Embargo Act imposed trade restrictions devastating to the American economy and actually helped draw the United States closer to war with England.

Jefferson retired to his beloved Monticello in 1809 and devoted his remaining years to prolific correspondence (about 18,000 letters survive), to

opposing what he called "consolidation" (meaning the expansion of federal power at the expense of the states), and to the establishment and design of the University of Virginia (1819). Both he and John Adams died on July 4, 1826, the 50th anniversary of the signing of the Declaration of Independence.

It has been said of Jefferson that no man wrote so much and revealed so little of himself. Part of the interpretive problem derives from his multiple interests, which stretched across architecture, education, politics, and science. Even more daunting, however, are the paradoxes and contradictions at the core of his character. Slavery provides the most dramatic example. The author of the most eloquent statement about human equality in American history was a lifelong slave owner. Despite his clear conviction that slavery violated the founding principles of the American republic, Jefferson never freed the vast bulk of his own slaves and never believed that blacks and whites could live together in harmony after emancipation. His fear of racial mixing has added additional intrigue to the charges, first made in 1802, that he fathered several children by Sally Hemings, a mulatto slave at Monticello. Although most scholars who have studied the charges have concluded that they are probably not true, the evidence is insufficient for a clear verdict for or against.

Jefferson's political legacy is equally ambiguous. Although enshrined in Washington's Jefferson Memorial as the primary symbol of individual rights, Jefferson has been appropriated by all camps: states' righters and New Dealers; segregationists and civil rights advocates; isolationists and imperialists; student radicals of the 1960s and conservative disciples of Ronald Reagan. Jefferson is America's preeminent man for all seasons. His abiding genius, it would seem, derives from his unique ability to articulate elemental truths at a sufficient level of abstraction to conceal their contradictions.

—JOSEPH J. ELLIS

See Also: *Constitution of the United States; Continental Congresses; Declaration of Independence; Embargo Act of 1807; Louisiana Purchase; Revolution, American.*

BIBLIOGRAPHY: Ellis, Joseph J., *American Sphinx* (Knopf 1997); Malone, Dumas, *Jefferson and His Time,* 6 vols. (Little, Brown 1948-81); Onuf, Peter, ed., *Jeffersonian Legacies* (Univ. Press of Virginia 1993).

■ **JEHOVAH'S WITNESSES,** a religious body founded in 1870 by Charles Taze Russell. He studied the Bible privately and came to adventist beliefs. Witnesses believe Satan's rule of the world will soon end with Christ's return to Earth. The movement grew from a Bible study led by Russell in Pittsburgh. In 1876 he and the group began publishing *Zion's Watchtower*, a small magazine. Eventually it became today's *Watchtower*, of which more than 18 million copies are published bimonthly in 106 languages. In 1884 the organization became the Zion's Watch Tower Tract Society and moved its headquarters to Brooklyn, New York. The group's theology is based on Russell's seven-volume *Studies in the Scriptures* (1886-1917), whose last volume led to a schism in the organization. Most of the members joined J. F. Rutherford and formed the Millennial Dawnists, who became the Jehovah's Witnesses in 1931. Others formed the Dawn Bible Student's Association. Jehovah's Witnesses have roughly 3 million members worldwide. In the 1930s and 1940s the Witnesses fought and won many cases in the courts regarding religious freedom.

See Also: Religion.

■ **JEHOVAH'S WITNESSES CASES (1938-43),** a series of U.S. Supreme Court cases concerning the clash between the right of free expression of a religious group and mandatory patriotic exercises in public school. In the 1930s several states passed laws requiring schoolchildren to start the day by pledging allegiance to the U.S. flag. Members of Jehovah's Witnesses believed saluting the flag and reciting the pledge violated their ban against worshiping false gods. In *Minersville School District* v. *Gobitis* (1940), the Supreme Court ruled (8-1) that Jehovah's Witnesses could be expelled from school for refusing to salute the flag. Promoting national unity, the Court said, was an important government function, and patriotic ceremonies could be made mandatory. But in *West Virginia State Board of Education* v. *Barnette* (1943), the Court reversed itself and ruled (6-3) that refusing to salute the flag was free expression protected by the First Amendment to the Constitution.

See Also: Constitution of the United States; Jehovah's Witnesses; Supreme Court.

■ **JEMISON, MARY (1743-1833),** Shawnee captive. Jemison was born on shipboard in passage from Northern Ireland to Philadelphia. In 1758, she was captured by the Shawnee during the French and Indian War. At 14, she was adopted by a Seneca family, with whom she chose to remain after the war. In 1760, she married a Delaware warrior, Sheinjee, and moved to a tribal grant near the Genesee River. Her story, published by Dr. James E. Seaver in 1824 as *A Narrative of the Life of Mrs. Mary Jemison*, is considered a classic example of the captivity narrative.

See Also: Captivity, Indian.

■ **JENKINS'S EAR, WAR OF (1739-43),** hostilities in the New World between Britain and Spain. Commercial rivalry and tensions between the two countries over their colonial possessions led to a naval battle off the coast of Florida, during which British sailor Robert Jenkins lost an ear. Britain soon declared war and began a naval campaign in the Caribbean and land attacks on the Florida-Georgia border. Invasion and counterinvasion along the border persisted into 1743, and the conflict then merged into King George's War (1744-48).

See Also: King George's War.

■ **JENNEY, WILLIAM LE BARON (1832-1907),** innovative architect. Born in Fairhaven, Massachusetts, Jenney studied engineering at Harvard University and in Paris. He then established an architectural firm in Chicago; he employed many of the architects who would later be known as the Chicago School, including Louis Sullivan and Daniel H. Burnham. Jenney designed the Home Insurance Company office building in Chicago (1884), using a skeleton construction that is considered a precursor to skyscrapers.

See Also: Burnham, Daniel; Skyscrapers; Sullivan, Louis.

■ **JESUITS,** a religious order of Roman Catholic priests officially titled the Society of Jesus (SJ). It was founded in 1534 by Ignatius Loyola, a Basque soldier. Jesuits swear an oath of fealty to the pope and work primarily as missionaries and educators. In the Americas the Jesuits did much missionary work among the Indians and were active in the founding of Maryland. In the United States they founded and continue to administer a number of high schools and universities.

See Also: Religion.

■ **JEWETT, SARAH ORNE (1849-1909),** author. She was born in South Berwick, Maine. Famous for her sympathetic portraits of life in the New England countryside, she published many collections of stories and sketches, including *Deephaven* (1877) and her masterpiece, *The Country of the Pointed Firs* (1896). Her novels include *A Country Doctor* (1884), *A Marsh Island* (1885), and *The Tory Lover* (1901).

See Also: Novel.

■ **JEWISH IMMIGRANTS.** A diverse population, Jewish immigrants, often seeking refuge from religious or ethnic persecution, arrived in North America in three distinct waves. The initial period of immigration began during the 17th century, when Sephardic Jews fled Portuguese Brazil. Forbidden to worship publicly, the Sephardic community in early America remained small. The second wave of immigration was made up of German Jews. Between 1820 and 1880 about 250,000 arrived in the United States, and many became leaders in business and the professions. Fleeing European anti-Semitism, these 19th-century immigrants took advantage of U.S. religious tolerance and created a new branch of Judaism known as the Reform Movement. The final great wave of Jewish immigration began in about 1880 and come from eastern Europe, especially Russia, the Austro-Hungarian Empire, and Romania. Like previous Jewish immigrants, these newcomers adapted to American life and made significant contributions to the development of the American economy. An estimated 150,000 Jews also arrived from Europe during the early stages of the Nazi persecution in Germany in the 1930s.

See Also: Ethnic Groups; Immigration; Jews.

■ **JEWS,** followers of Judaism. With their origins in biblical times, Jews have long been a persecuted minority who have sought refuge in numerous countries, including America.

Jews first arrived in America in the Dutch colony of New Netherland in 1654. The first large-scale immigration occurred in the 1830s, when German Jews fled a hostile and economically stagnant eastern Europe. Settling in large East Coast cities, many became successful merchants and bankers and maintained strong familial and community relations. Jewish emigration from eastern Europe accelerated during the late 19th and early 20th centuries, and by 1920 there were some 3.5 million Jews in America. In the 1930s, some middle-class professionals escaped Nazi Germany, but most European Jews perished in the Holocaust. By 1996, the Jewish population of the United States numbered 4.3 million.

Jews have adapted to life in America in ways as numerous as their countries of origin. During the 19th century, for example, many German Jews reformed their religious practices and assimilated more into secular society, in the process creating a wealthy, vibrant, and socially active religious community. Conversely, many turn-of-the-century immigrants remained closer to their orthodox roots, communicating in Yiddish and identifying as laborers with socialism.

In the postwar years the American Jewish community has been the largest and most active in the world. American Jews have left their mark on virtually every aspect of life in the United States, especially in science, the economy, law, and literature.

See Also: Religion.

BIBLIOGRAPHY: Sorin, Gerald, *Tradition Transformed: The Jewish Experience in America* (Johns Hopkins Univ. Press 1997); Sachar, Howard Morley, *A History of the Jews in America* (Knopf 1992).

■ **JIM CROW LAWS,** term for the statutes and regulations that enforced racial segregation after 1877. Segregation had been common in Northern states throughout the 19th century but, ironically, rather uncommon in the slaveholding South. But after the collapse of Reconstruction in 1877, state governments in the South enacted laws prohibiting the mingling of whites and blacks. Virtually every aspect of social life was covered, from transportation to restaurants, theaters, housing, churches, hospitals, and cemeteries. The principle of segregation received the approval of the U.S. Supreme Court in the 1896 *Plessy* v. *Ferguson* case, which found that "separate but equal" accommodations satisfied the 14th Amendment. In practice Jim Crow laws ensured the separation but not the equality of Southern institutions. The term "Jim Crow" was derived from a minstrel song, "Jump Jim Crow."

See Also: Plessy v. Ferguson.

■ **JOHN BIRCH SOCIETY,** ultraconservative political organization. Founded in 1958 by Robert

Welch, a candy manufacturer, its members believed the United States was being undermined by a communist conspiracy that had reached the highest levels of government. The organization, named after a Baptist missionary who had been killed by communists in China in 1945, had about 100,000 members in the mid-1960s.

See Also: Cold War.

■ **JOHNS, JASPER (1930-)**, avant-garde painter. Johns was born in Augusta, Georgia. He moved to New York in 1952, where he worked as a commercial artist and designer of window displays along with fellow artist Robert Rauschenberg. Johns's first one-man show at the Leo Castelli Gallery in New York was a success, selling every painting. Using the familiarity of subjects, such as numbers, letters, and targets, as an opportunity to experiment with painting technique and color, Johns quickly became well known for these representations, although his appropriation of the American flag caused some controversy. Johns worked with encaustic, a mixture of beeswax and pigment, in his paintings and also created lithographs and sculptures; later, he worked with Sculpmetal to create metallic reliefs on canvas. Johns had connections to both the abstract expressionist and pop art painters but was not associated wholly with either group. He formed lasting ties to avant-garde practitioners of other art forms; for example Johns, like Rauschenberg, designed costumes for choreographer Merce Cunningham.

See Also: Painting.

■ **JOHNSON, ANDREW (1808-1875)**, 17th president of the United States (1865-69) and the only president to be impeached. Born in Raleigh, North Carolina, on Dec. 28, 1808, Johnson settled in Tennessee, where as a Jackson Democrat he served as state legislator, U.S. representative (1843-53), governor (1853-57), and U.S. senator (1857-62). During the secession crisis he was the most prominent Southern Unionist, remaining in his Senate seat after Tennessee had joined the Confederacy. In 1862, Pres. Abraham Lincoln appointed him military governor of Tennessee, and in 1864 the National Union Convention nominated him as Lincoln's running mate. After Lincoln's assassination, newly inaugurated President Johnson announced that he would retain

Representing Tennessee, Andrew Johnson was the only Southern senator to support the Union throughout the Civil War and was rewarded by being selected as Abraham Lincoln's vice-presidential running mate in 1864.

the cabinet and continue the Reconstruction policies of his predecessor.

Presidency. Essentially that is what he did, issuing a general proclamation of amnesty for Confederates and proclamations establishing loyal governments in the seceded states. The Radical Republican leaders of Congress, however, formulated harsher plans and argued that Johnson's version of Reconstruction betrayed the former slaves. In 1866, Johnson vetoed the Freedman's Bureau bill and the Civil Rights Act, which alienated moderate Republicans; his vetoes were overridden. Radical Republican victories in the 1866 congressional elections further weakened the president's position. The confrontation reached a crisis when Johnson dismissed Sec. of War Edwin M. Stanton in 1868, violating the Tenure of Office Act, which Congress had passed to bait the president. The House impeached Johnson, but by a one-vote margin the Senate failed to convict him. At the expiration of his term he returned to Tennessee and in 1874 was once again elected to the U.S. Senate but died soon after taking his seat.

See Also: Civil War; Impeachment; President of the United States; Reconstruction; Secession; Stanton, Edwin McMasters; Tenure of Office Act.

BIBLIOGRAPHY: McKitrick, Eric L., *Andrew Johnson and Reconstruction* (Univ. of Chicago Press 1960); Trefousse, Hans L., *Andrew Johnson: A Biography* (Norton 1989).

■ **JOHNSON, EARVIN, JR. ("MAGIC") (1959-),** basketball player. Born and reared in Lansing, Michigan, he led his Michigan State University team to the National Collegiate Athletic Association (NCAA) championship in 1979. He then joined the National Basketball Association (NBA) Los Angeles Lakers, leading the team to the championship in 1980, its first of five with Johnson at guard. His brilliant passing and unselfish play renewed the guard's role in the game and helped earn him the league's Most Valuable Player (MVP) award three times. Announcing that he had tested positive for the AIDS virus in November 1991, Johnson retired. In 1992, Johnson played on the gold-medal U.S. Olympic team in Barcelona, Spain. He briefly attempted a return to the NBA before retiring with the NBA record for career assists, 9,921.

See Also: African Americans; Basketball; Sports.

■ **JOHNSON, JACK (ARTHUR JOHN) (1878-1946),** heavyweight boxer. He was born in Galveston, Texas. After nine years on the heavyweight circuit, mostly as a sparring partner, Johnson defeated Tommy Burns in 1908 to become the first African American to win the world heavyweight championship. Resentment among whites induced former champion Jim Jeffries to come out of retirement and fight for the title. Johnson, however, defeated him in 1910. Two years later, Johnson was charged with taking a white woman across state lines for "immoral purposes," a violation of the Mann Act. Waiting to appeal his conviction, Johnson fled to Canada and then Europe. He defended his title four times in Paris and once in Buenos Aires, Argentina, before losing to Jess Willard in Havana, Cuba, in 1915. Johnson later claimed he had thrown the fight. He then fought in Mexico and Spain until returning to the United States in 1920. Arrested at the border, he spent less

than a year in prison, after which he fought until his retirement in 1933. Johnson's career record stands at 107 wins and 6 losses.

See Also: African Americans; Boxing; Sports.

■ **JOHNSON, JAMES (WILLIAM) WELDON (1871-1938),** poet and author. Born in Jacksonville, Florida, Johnson worked as a high school principal after graduation from Atlanta University. At the same time he started a newspaper, the *Daily American*, and studied law. Although he was admitted to the bar, he earned financial success not as a lawyer but as a writer of musical variety and comic songs. A member of the Colored Republican Club of New York, he was appointed the consul in Venezuela (1906) and Nicaragua (1909). In 1912, Johnson published his most famous work, *The Autobiography of an Ex-Colored Man*, a novel about race perception and identity. On his return to the United States in 1914, Johnson became an editor for the *New York Age* and first a field secretary and then the first black secretary of the National Association for the Advancement of Colored People (NAACP). His book of free verse poetry, *God's Trombones*, was published in 1927.

See Also: African Americans; Poetry.

■ **JOHNSON, LYNDON BAINES (1908-73),** 36th president of the United States (1963-69). He was born on Aug. 28, 1908, in Stonewall, Texas, and graduated from Southwest Texas State Teachers College. After a brief career as a high school teacher, he took a job (1932) as the secretary to a U.S. congressman. Johnson was appointed (1935) Texas director of the National Youth Administration and in 1937 was elected to the House of Representatives. His first attempt to win a seat in the U.S. Senate (1941) was unsuccessful, but he was elected in 1948 after a controversial victory by 87 votes in the Democratic primary. In 1955, Johnson was elected Senate majority leader, a role in which he was highly effective because of his mastery of the legislative process and a powerful personality that was not afraid to manipulate, persuade, and bully.

LBJ, as Johnson became known, sought the Democratic presidential nomination in 1960 but was defeated by John F. Kennedy, who offered him the vice-presidential spot on the ticket. With Johnson's help, Kennedy carried Texas and won the election. Johnson, however, was not a member of the White House inner circle, and his vice presidency was an unhappy one. Everything changed on Nov. 22, 1963, when Kennedy was assassinated in Dallas, Texas, and Johnson was catapulted into the presidency.

National Leader. Johnson plunged into his presidential responsibilities with gusto. He secured passage of the landmark Civil Rights Act of 1964, a feat that had eluded Kennedy, and the following year pushed through the Voting Rights Act. He had gotten off to a good start and enjoyed high popularity ratings in his first year in office. In 1964, the Republican presidential nominee, Sen. Barry Goldwater of Arizona, was seen as an extreme conservative who frightened people with loose talk about nuclear warfare. LBJ was easily elected in his own right. In addition, he swept into Congress an unusually large number of liberal Democrats.

With their help, Johnson was able to overcome the resistance of conservative Southern Democratic leaders and enact the most impressive body of domestic legislation since Franklin D. Roosevelt's New Deal in the 1930s. In addition to the civil rights legislation, his Great Society programs included Medicare, Medicaid, and numerous other bills.

Johnson's downfall was the war in Vietnam. American troops were already in combat there when Johnson became president, but the scale of the fighting was still small. Determined to win the war, Johnson increased U.S. involvement enormously but did so without asking Congress for a declaration of war. By 1968 there were nearly 500,000 U.S. troops in South Vietnam, and at the end of the year the bulk of the more than 58,000 Americans who would be killed in Vietnam had already perished.

With every escalation of the war, domestic opposition to it rose proportionately. Most demonstrations involved college students, but the opponents of the war eventually came from all walks of life and included many political and busi-

Democrat Lyndon B. Johnson is sworn in as president on-board Air Force One shortly after the assassination of John F. Kennedy. The president's widow, Jacqueline Kennedy, stands at Johnson's left; his wife, Lady Bird, on his right.

ness leaders. Johnson was reduced to speaking publicly only before friendly audiences, such as military bases, a far cry from 1964, when huge, admiring crowds had surrounded him everywhere.

In spring 1968, Johnson was challenged in the New Hampshire primary by Sen. Eugene McCarthy of Minnesota, who, running on a peace platform, nearly beat him. That close call, coupled with the communist Tet Offensive earlier in 1968 during which the enemy briefly took control of parts of many cities in South Vietnam, was the turning point for Johnson and the war. He announced that he would not stand for reelection in 1968 and began peace talks with North Vietnam that would long outlast his presidency. Although 1968 was the bloodiest year of the Vietnam War, Johnson began the process of de-escalation that would eventually bring an end to the fighting and, well before that, to a massive reduction in American casualty rates.

Vietnam blighted Johnson's presidency. But he should be remembered, too, for the Great Society, which changed America for the better.

—WILLIAM L. O'NEILL

See Also: Civil Rights Acts; Cold War; President of the United States; Vietnam War.

BIBLIOGRAPHY: Bernstein, Irving, *Guns or Butter: The Presidency of Lyndon Johnson* (Oxford Univ. Press 1996); Caro, Robert A., *The Years of Lyndon Johnson: The Path to Power* (Knopf 1982); Caro, Robert A., *The Years of Lyndon Johnson: Means of Ascent* (Knopf 1990); Dallek, Robert, *Lone Star Rising: Lyndon Johnson and His Times, 1908-1960* (Oxford Univ. Press 1990); *Flawed Giant: Lyndon Johnson and His Times, 1961-1973* (Oxford Univ. Press 1998); Johnson, Lyndon B., *The Vantage Point* (Holt, Rinehart & Winston 1971).

■ **JOHNSON, PHILIP CORTELYOU (1906-)**, influential 20th-century architect. Born in Cleveland, Ohio, Johnson interspersed study at Harvard University with travel in Europe. Graduating in 1930, he became the first director of the Department of Architecture and Design at the Museum of Modern Art in New York City. In 1932 he and Henry-Russell Hitchcock wrote *The International Style*, the defining text of modernism in architecture. He is remembered for such buildings as the Glass House in New Canaan, Connecticut (1949).

See Also: Architecture.

■ **JOHNSON, RICHARD MENTOR (1780-1850)**, American soldier and vice president of the United States (1837-41). Born near present-day Louisville, Kentucky, he served as a Democrat in the U.S. House of Representatives (1807-19; 1829-37) and in the U.S. Senate (1819-29). In 1813, during the War of 1812, he reportedly killed the Shawnee leader Tecumseh at the Battle of the Thames. Johnson ran against three others for U.S. vice president in 1836, but because no candidate received an electoral majority, the electoral decision was passed to the U.S. Senate. The Senate's choice was Johnson, making him the only U.S. vice president to be thus elected.

See Also: Vice President of the United States.

■ **JOHNSON, THOMAS (1732-1819)**, associate justice of the U.S. Supreme Court (1791-93). A Calvert County, Maryland, native, Johnson concluded after only two years on the Court that the job, especially its circuit responsibilities, was too taxing, and he resigned.

See Also: Supreme Court.

■ **JOHNSON, WILLIAM (1771-1834)**, associate justice of the U.S. Supreme Court (1804-34). A Charleston, South Carolina, native, Justice Johnson frequently disagreed with Chief Justice John Marshall. Nevertheless, he usually backed Marshall's efforts to strengthen the authority of the national government, as in *Gibbons v. Ogden* (1824). There Johnson agreed with the majority that final regulatory authority over navigation rested with the federal government. Not afraid of unpopular stands, Johnson insisted that interstate commerce, specifically the slave trade, fell squarely under federal jurisdiction, a position that made him highly unpopular in his home state.

See Also: Gibbons v. Ogden; Supreme Court.

■ **JOHNSTON, HENRIETTA (1670-1728 or 1729)**, painter, possibly the first woman artist in British North America. Born in England, she emigrated to Charleston, South Carolina, in 1705. Thought to have little formal training, she painted portraits to supplement her family's meager income. Her works are very early examples of pastel painting.

See Also: Painting; Women in American History.

■ **JOHNSTON, JOSEPH E. (1807-91),** Confederate general. Born in Prince Edward County, Virginia, Johnston graduated from West Point in 1829. He served in the Black Hawk War (1832), as Gen. Winfield Scott's aide-de-camp during the second Seminole War (1835-42), and in the Mexican War (1848-48). In 1860 he became quartermaster general for the United States, but he resigned in April 1861 to organize the Virginia Volunteers for the Confederacy. He led the Army of Northern Virginia until replaced in 1862 by Robert E. Lee. In 1865 Johnston surrendered the last major Confederate army to Gen. William T. Sherman in North Carolina. Johnston served as a U.S. congressman (1879-81) and as a U.S. railroad commissioner (1885-91).

See Also: *Civil War.*

■ **JOHNSTOWN FLOOD (1889),** flood that destroyed Johnstown, Pennsylvania, 78 miles southwest of Pittsburgh. On May 31, 1889, the South Fork Dam burst, releasing a wall of water more than 40 feet high and half a mile wide. The city was demolished within eight minutes and suffered millions of dollars in property damage. Upwards of 2,000 people died, and survivors were faced with the horror of a river clogged with corpses and debris for days.

■ **JOINT STOCK COMPANY,** organization of a group of stockholders, governed by a president and board of assistants, who pooled their capital to invest in trading and colonial ventures. In general, company associates met and voted democratically on proposed ventures and administration of colonial possessions. The interest and wealth of the various joint stock companies formed at the end of the Elizabethan period made the exploration and planting of British colonies possible in North America.

■ **JOLLIET, LOUIS (1645-1700),** French Canadian explorer. Born in Quebec, Jolliet joined Jesuit Father Jacques Marquette in opening the upper Mississippi Valley to French traders and missionaries. In May 1673 the pair, accompanied by five voyageurs, left the fur-trade post Michilimackinac in canoes. They paddled along Green Bay, up the Fox River, portaged to the Wisconsin River, and then paddled down it to the Mississippi River. The small band of experienced woodsmen reached the great river on June 17 and proceeded down to the present site of Arkansas City, Arkansas. Jolliet and Marquette returned via the Illinois River and Lake Michigan, charting a vast new territory for the French. Jolliet's explorations continued with subsequent trips to Labrador and Hudson Bay. Based on his extensive explorations, Jolliet was appointed royal hydrographer for New France in 1697.

See Also: *Exploration and Discovery; Marquette, Pere Jacques.*

■ **JOLSON, AL (1886-1950),** stage, film, and radio entertainer. He emigrated from Srednike, Russia, to New York City in 1893 and became a vaudeville and Broadway star. In 1927 Jolson starred in *The Jazz Singer,* the first synchronized-sound "talking picture," in which he re-created several of his most famous numbers, including a blackface rendition of "Mammy." He launched a popular and long-running radio series in 1932.

See Also: *Motion Pictures.*

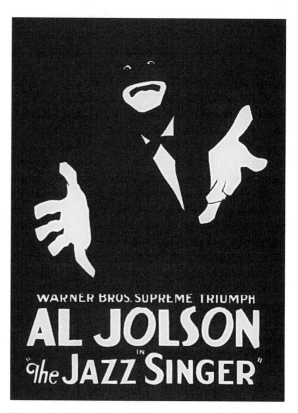

Warner Brothers released *The Jazz Singer,* starring Al Jolson, in 1927, inaugurating the sound era in film.

■ **JONES, CASEY (1864-1900),** locomotive engineer immortalized in song, was born John Luther Jones in Fulton County, Kentucky. When running the *Cannon Ball* express from Memphis, Tennessee, to Canton, Mississippi, he sacrificed his own life to save those of his passengers in a wreck outside Vaughan, Mississippi.

■ **JONES, JOHN PAUL (1747-92),** naval commander and hero of the American Revolution. Born in Scotland as John Paul, he had a distinguished yet tempestuous career as a seaman in the Atlantic, becoming a merchant captain at the age of 22. While commanding a ship in the Caribbean, he killed the leader of a mutiny and fled to Virginia to avoid trial. There he assumed Jones as his surname and sided with the patriot cause during the Revolution. In 1775 Congress commissioned him a lieutenant in the navy, and a year later he became captain of the *Providence*, seizing many prizes while in command. His greatest victories occurred in European waters. Aboard the *Ranger* in 1778 he raided British ports and captured his first British ship. The following year, aboard the *Bonhomme Richard*, Jones captured the British flagship, *Serapis*, three hours after defying an order to surrender with the words "I have not yet begun to fight." During his lifetime Jones received little recognition in the United States for his exploits. He spent his final years living in France. Jones's remains were interred at Annapolis, Maryland, in 1913.

See Also: Revolution, American.

■ **JONES, MARY HARRIS (MOTHER) (1830-1930),** labor organizer. Born in Cork, Ireland, she immigrated to the United States as a child. After an epidemic killed her husband and their four children in 1867, she devoted herself to the radical labor movement as an effective organizer for the United Mine Workers of America, leading the fight against child labor, and as a founder of the Industrial Workers of the World.

See Also: Industrial Workers of the World; Labor Movement.

■ **JOPLIN, SCOTT (1868-1917),** African-American composer and pianist, known as "The King of Ragtime." He was born into a musical family in Texarkana, Texas. Joplin was playing in honkytonks by his teens and received formal training at George Smith College in Sedalia, Missouri, where he learned to transcribe the syncopated or "ragged" sound of his compositions. His "Maple Leaf Rag" (1899) was an immediate popular success and spawned the ragtime craze. He considered his many compositions "serious" music and was distressed by their almost exclusively popular audience. In New York City he tried to reach a more critical audience, but his opera *Treemonisha* (1915) was performed only once during his lifetime and was considered a failure. He died embittered. A popular revival and deeper appreciation of his music occurred during the 1970s.

See Also: African Americans; Ragtime.

BIBLIOGRAPHY: Haskins, James, *Scott Joplin* (Doubleday 1978); Gammond, Peter, *Scott Joplin and the Ragtime Era* (St. Martin's 1975).

■ **JORDAN, LOUIS (1908-75),** singer, saxophonist, and songwriter. Born in Arkansas, he began his career as a minstrel performer, worked with the big band of Chick Webb in New York City, then founded his own "jump band," the Tympany Five. A series of hit songs after World War II—including "Ain't Nobody Here But Us Chickens" and "Choo Choo Ch'boogie"—made him one of the first African-American performers to "cross over" to success on the white pop chart. He was widely influential on the next generation of rock and roll performers, notably Chuck Berry.

See Also: Berry, Chuck.

■ **JORDAN, MICHAEL (1963-),** basketball player, often acclaimed as the best to play the game. Born in Wilmington, North Carolina, he attended the University of North Carolina at Chapel Hill and was twice chosen collegiate player of the year. He turned professional in 1984 after his junior year and then played on the winning U.S. Olympic basketball team before joining the Chicago Bulls of the National Basketball Association (NBA). A perennial NBA offensive and defensive all-star and scoring leader, he is noted for his acrobatic moves on the court. He retired from basketball after the 1993 season to play professional baseball but returned to the Bulls late in the 1994-95 season. He led the Bulls to five NBA titles between 1991 and 1997 and in 1997 became the third highest scorer in NBA history. His popularity and visibility are enhanced by his many product endorsements.

In 1877, at the end of the Nez Percé War, Chief Joseph spoke one of the most famous lines of American Indian history when he declared, "I will fight no more forever."

■ **JOSEPH, CHIEF (c. 1840-1904),** Nez Percé leader. Born in the Wallowa Valley of present-day Oregon, he took the name of his father, known as Old Joseph, who was a Christian and had been friendly to whites. In the 1860s, Old Joseph opposed attempts to reduce the Nez Percé Reservation from 10,000 to 1,000 square miles. He became a leader of the Nontreaty Nez Percé, who refused to accept the fraudulently obtained treaty of 1863, and his leadership passed to his son when he died in 1871. Chief Joseph was a civil chief, not a war chief, but in June 1877, frustrated over continuing white encroachment into the Wallowa Valley, which had been granted to the Nez Percé in 1873, he led a group of warriors against the white settlers. The Nez Percé War continued throughout the summer, but in September 1877, Chief Joseph and his band were stopped while trying to escape to Canada. Chief Joseph was credited with the victories in the brief war because of his oratorical skill, including his famous "I will fight no more forever" speech, delivered on Oct. 5, 1877, at his surrender.

See Also: Indians of North America; Nez Percé.

■ **JUDICIAL REVIEW,** the power of the U.S. Supreme Court to determine whether laws passed by Congress and the states are constitutional. Although not explicitly mentioned in the Constitution, judicial review is rooted in English common law and tradition. During the debates over ratifying the Constitution, many political leaders argued in support of its system of checks and balances that the courts would serve as a safeguard against a runaway legislature. The Court's use of judicial review has ebbed and flowed over time, with periods of activism alternating with eras of deference to legislative action.

Chief Justice John Marshall helped establish the Court's power to review federal law in *Marbury v. Madison* (1803) and to strike down state laws when they conflicted with the Constitution in *McCulloch v. Maryland* (1819) and *Gibbons v. Ogden* (1824). In the late 1800s the Court expanded its use of judicial review by relying on constitutional guarantees of freedom of contract and substantive due process to strike down state and federal regulatory laws in cases such as *Allgeyer v. Louisiana* (1897) and *Lochner v. New York* (1905).

The Court's use of judicial review reflects the political temper of the times. When it invalidated several important pieces of New Deal economic legislation, Pres. Franklin D. Roosevelt proposed expanding the size of the Court (1937). While this "court-packing" plan failed, the Court quickly proved more responsive to New Deal initiatives.

See Also: Gibbons v. Ogden; Lochner v. New York; McCulloch v. Maryland; Marbury v. Madison; Marshall, John; Supreme Court.

BIBLIOGRAPHY: Antieau, Chester James, *Adjudicating Constitutional Issues* (Oceana Publications 1985); Nino, Carlos S., *The Constitution of Deliberative Democracy* (Yale Univ. Press 1996).

■ **JUDICIARY ACT OF 1789,** the statute creating the federal court system. The law created a three-level federal judiciary, composed of district and circuit courts as well as a six-member Supreme Court. Under the act, the Supreme Court exercised appellate jurisdiction over both the lower federal courts and the state courts when a question of federal law arose.

See Also: Supreme Court.

■ **JUDICIARY ACTS (1801-02),** two laws responsible for the brief existence of an independent federal circuit court system. The act of 1801, an effort by the lame-duck Federalist Congress to pack the bench with sympathetic judges, replaced the old system, in which two justices and a district court judge sat as the circuit court, with a new system of separate circuit court judges. When the Jeffersonians came to power, they enacted the act of 1802, abolishing the new circuit system and returning to the original one.

See Also: Supreme Court.

■ **JURY TRIAL,** legal process for determining issues of fact in common law. With its origins in medieval England, the jury trial became a central component of English common law, serving to protect individual rights. Transplanted from England to the American colonies, the jury trial has ever since been essential in most criminal and civil common law cases.

In the United States, the right to a jury trial is guaranteed by Article III of the Constitution and by the 6th, 7th, and 14th Amendments. Although Article III, Section 2, provided that "The Trial of all Crimes . . . shall be by Jury," it did not include civil cases. The omission spurred debate that was not quelled until the passage of the Bill of Rights, which extended the provision for jury trials to civil cases.

The procedure of the jury trial has evolved since the adoption of the Constitution and has varied among state and federal courts. The federal court system has adhered strictly to the Constitution, in that it requires unanimous verdicts from juries of 12 persons in criminal trials. Some states, on the other hand, have varied the number of jury members and do not demand unanimous verdicts in all criminal cases.

The power of the jury lies in its ability to interpret the facts of a case. Some critics in the 20th century, however, have assailed juries for their legal inexperience and their occasional unrepresentative racial and gender composition.

See Also: Bill of Rights; Constitution of the United States.

BIBLIOGRAPHY: Constable, Marianne, *The Law of the Other: The Mixed Jury and Changing Conceptions of Citizenship, Law, and Knowledge* (Univ. of Chicago Press 1994); Kalver, Harry, Jr., and Hans Zeisel, *The American Jury* (Little, Brown 1966).

■ **JUSTICE, DEPARTMENT OF,** cabinet department of the U.S. government that oversees federal legal affairs. It is headed by the attorney general. The office of attorney general was created by Congress in 1789, but the Department of Justice was not established until 1870. The attorney general at first served as legal adviser to the president and also argued government cases before the U.S. Supreme Court. In 1861, at the start of the Civil War, the attorney general was placed in charge of U.S. attorneys and marshals across the country. When the Department of Justice was formed, the attorney general became its administrative head, and a solicitor general was appointed to argue cases before the Supreme Court. Today assistant attorneys general head divisions overseeing civil rights, antitrust actions, immigration issues, and other functions. The Federal Bureau of Investigation was created as an arm of the department in 1908.

BIBLIOGRAPHY: Clayton, Cornell W., *The Politics of Justice: The Attorney General and the Making of Legal Policy* (M. E. Sharpe 1992).

■ **JUSTICE OF THE PEACE,** title of local judges who often handle minor criminal offenses, such as traffic violations, and civil matters, such as wedding ceremonies. Justices of the peace have been part of the English system of common law since the Middle Ages. In the United States they served as the first level of the justice system in sparsely populated rural areas, where distances and poor transportation made travel to regional courthouses difficult. In the South and West in the 19th century, justices of the peace were often the only manifestation of the legal system and exercised considerable authority to detain and punish accused criminals. Often associated with informal, opinionated, and sometimes erratic proceedings, they remained an important part of the U.S. criminal system until the 1950s. By then most states had established district court systems, and better transportation made travel easier. Justices of the peace are most often part-time judges whose income is derived from fees and fines. This often leads critics to complain that rural justices are quick to impose hefty fines on visitors while ignoring violations by their local neighbors. In states such as Nevada that have less restrictive marriage laws, justices of the peace promote their legal power to conduct marriage services and create profitable wedding businesses.

K

KAHN, LOUIS ISADORE (1901-74), modernist architect and educator. Kahn was born in Oesel, Estonia; he immigrated to the United States and settled with his parents in Philadelphia, becoming an American citizen in 1915. He graduated in 1924 from the School of Fine Arts at the University of Pennsylvania and worked for a variety of Philadelphia architecture firms until 1932. During the Great Depression he organized the Architectural Research Group to do studies of housing and city planning and was employed by the Works Progress (later Projects) Administration doing similar work, including a design for the Jersey Homesteads Cooperative Development in Hightstown, New Jersey (1935-39). In later private practice, Kahn designed the Art Gallery and British Art Center at Yale University (1951-53; 1969-74) and the Richards Medical Research Building at the University of Pennsylvania (1957-64). Kahn also influenced the architectural community as a critic for architecture programs, including those at the University of Pennsylvania and Yale University.

See Also: Architecture; Great Depression; Works Projects Administration (WPA).

KALTENBORN, H. V. (1878-1965), radio commentator. A native of Milwaukee, Wisconsin, Kaltenborn was editor of the *Brooklyn Eagle* from 1910 to 1930. He first went on the air in 1922 and broadcast erudite news and comment for the Columbia Broadcasting System (1929-40) and National Broadcasting Company (1940-55). Kaltenborn's distinctive clipped delivery became famous when he aired reports during the Munich crisis (September 1938).

See Also: Television and Radio.

KANAGAWA, TREATY OF (1854), agreement between the United States and Japan. Although Japan had a policy of strict isolation, Pres. Franklin Pierce sent Commodore Matthew Perry with eight well-armed ships (a quarter of the American navy) to convince the Japanese shogunate to sign this treaty, which opened the Japanese ports of Shimoda and Hokadate to limited trade. Japan was favorably convinced and further agreed to treat shipwrecked Americans well and to allow an American minister at Shimoda.

See Also: Perry, Matthew.

KANSAS, the second largest Midwest state, located at the geographic center of the 48 contiguous states. It is bounded by Nebraska on the north, Colorado on the west, Oklahoma on the south, and Missouri to the east. The Missouri River forms the northern part of its eastern border. Kansas is a prairie state, but only the western part belongs to the Great Plains proper. An important farming state, Kansas usually leads the nation in wheat production and ranks third in cattle. It is also a significant oil producer and is home to firms manufacturing most of the world's general-aviation aircraft.

Kansas was fiercely contested by pro- and antislavery forces. In 1861, just before the Civil War, it entered the Union as a free state. Boom towns like Abilene and Dodge City flourished after the war as cowboys drove cattle to market. The railroads brought settlers, many of them from Europe. Less colorful in the 20th century, Kansas is predominantly rural in character.

Capital: Topeka. Area: 82,282 square miles. Population (1995 est.): 2,565,000.

See Also: Bleeding Kansas; Coronado, Francisco Vásquez de; Indian Country or Territory; Kansas-Nebraska Act; Louisiana Purchase; Santa Fe Trail.

KANSAS CITY, city located at the junction of the Missouri and Kansas rivers in the northwestern part of Missouri and near the geographic center of the country. The Kansas tribe lived in the region until forced to relocate by the U.S. government in the 1820s. A fur-trading post was established on the site in 1821, and a permanent settlement, named Westport, was founded in 1838. Westward travelers on the Oregon and Santa Fe trails used the city as their main departure point. In the 1840s as many as 900 wagons passed through the town annually. It was incorporated as Kansas City in 1850. Prior to the Civil War Kansas City became a base for Southerners terrorizing abolitionist settlers in Kansas. The city continued growing after 1900 as a center for Midwestern grain and livestock. At the beginning of the 20th century Kansas City undertook an extensive city renewal program, building parks, broad boulevards, and civic buildings. Kansas City is adjacent to Kansas City, Kansas, and together they form a large commercial and industrial center of the Midwest. Population (1994): 443,878.

See Also: *City in American History; Midwest, The.*

■ **KANSAS-NEBRASKA ACT (1854),** legislation permitting the residents of Kansas and Nebraska territory to decide for themselves whether they would permit slavery. Introduced by Sen. Stephen A. Douglas, Democrat of Illinois, the measure enacted the doctrine of "popular sovereignty," which Democrats hoped would defuse the national debate over the expansion of slavery by shifting the controversy to localities. The legislation essentially repealed the Missouri Compromise of 1820, in which Congress had agreed to exclude slavery from western territories north of 36°30', and was denounced by opponents of slavery as a violation of a "sacred pledge." Following the passage of the act a surge of pro- and antislavery forces into Kansas territory sparked a border war ("Bleeding Kansas") and incited more national controversy, thus subverting the aims of Douglas. The resulting political imbroglio was a major cause of the breakup of the old party system and the rise of the Republicans as a sectional northern party.

See Also: *Bleeding Kansas; Civil War; Douglas, Stephen Arnold; Missouri Compromise; Popular Sovereignty.*

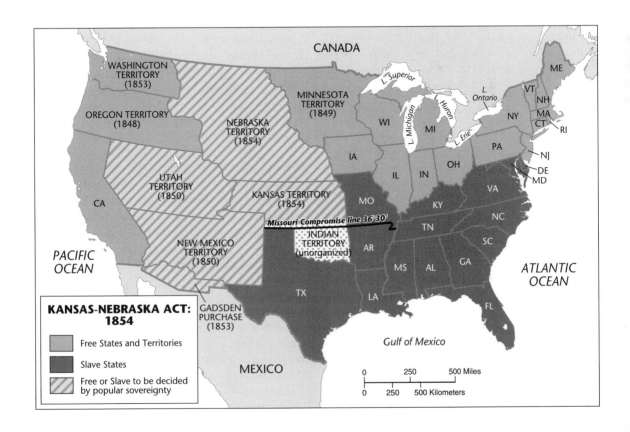

BIBLIOGRAPHY: Johannsen, Robert W., *The Frontier, the Union, and Stephen A. Douglas* (Univ. of Illinois Press 1989); Morrison, Michael A., *Slavery and the American West: The Eclipse of Manifest Destiny and the Coming of the Civil War* (Univ. of North Carolina Press 1997).

■ **KASSERINE PASS, BATTLE OF (1943),** World War II battle in which Axis forces under German Field Marshal Erwin Rommel nearly overwhelmed a combined American-Anglo army under U.S. Gen. Dwight D. Eisenhower in Tunisia. On February 14, Rommel sent his powerful Afrika Korps to smash an inexperienced American force at the Kasserine Pass. It appeared that the Allies might be completely routed, but Rommel called off the attack because of his own unwilling allies and a major reinforcement of American artillery.

See Also: World War II.

■ *KATZ V. UNITED STATES* **(1967),** U.S. Supreme Court case that limited the government's ability to eavesdrop on citizens. Katz was convicted of running an illegal betting business on the basis of evidence secretly recorded by a listening device attached to the outside of a public telephone booth. An appeals court said the recording was not an illegal search banned by the Fourth Amendment because the wall of the phone booth had not been physically penetrated.

The Court reversed (7-1) the conviction. Writing for the majority, Justice John M. Harlan said the government acted improperly because Katz, who routinely made telephone calls about betting information, had an expectation of privacy when he used the public phone booth, and most members of the public would think that Katz's expectation of privacy was reasonable. The Court has subsequently wavered in its interpretation of what constitutes a reasonable expectation of privacy as it has attempted to balance the Fourth Amendment prohibition against unreasonable searches with the public's demand for aggressive law enforcement. In *California v. Ciraolo* (1986) the Court ruled building a high fence around a property did not give the owner an expectation of privacy if police made an aerial search. Because any airplane could look down from above, the Court ruled, law enforcement officials could, too.

See Also: Supreme Court.
BIBLIOGRAPHY: Regan, Priscilla M., *Legislating Privacy: Technology, Social Values and Public Policy* (Univ. of North Carolina Press 1995).

■ **KAZAN, ELIA (1909-),** stage and film director. Born in Istanbul, Turkey, he specialized in stories with social messages, encouraging emotional performances from his actors. Kazan directed *A Streetcar Named Desire* (1947) on Broadway. He then began making movies and directed the film version of *Streetcar* (1951) and *On the Waterfront* (1954), both starring Marlon Brando, and *East of Eden* (1955) with James Dean.

See Also: Motion Pictures.

■ **KEARNY, STEPHEN WATTS (1794-1848),** general in the Mexican War. Born in Newark, New Jersey, Kearny served as an officer with the 13th Infantry in the War of 1812 before exploring the West with the 2nd Infantry. In the Mexican War, Kearny and 1,600 troops formed a provisional government in Santa Fe, New Mexico, after invading and declaring it a U.S. territory in 1846. Pushing on to California, Kearny captured Los Angeles with Commodore Robert Field Stockton in 1847. Kearny opposed John Frémont's appointment as governor of California, ousting Frémont through court-martial. Kearny died of yellow fever in St. Louis in 1848. Fort Kearney is named after him, but the name is misspelled.

See Also: Frontier in American History; Mexican War.

■ **KEATING-OWEN ACT (1916),** the first federal act outlawing child labor. Long a demand of Progressive reformers and organized labor, the act finally gained the support of Pres. Woodrow Wilson who until the election year of 1916 thought such a law to be unconstitutional. The U.S. Supreme Court found the act unconstitutional in 1918.

See Also: Progressivism.

■ **KEATON, BUSTER (1895-1966),** motion picture director and comedian. An inventive director, the Piqua, Kansas, native is best known as an unflappable comic presence in dozens of silent films. His stony visage in the face of imminent disaster was demonstrated in *Sherlock Jr.* (1924), *The General* (1926), and *Steamboat Bill Jr.* (1927)

and was reprised a generation later in comedies such as *It's a Mad, Mad, Mad, Mad World* (1963).

See Also: Motion Pictures.

■ **KEENE, LAURA (1820?-73),** stage actress and theatrical manager. She was one of the first women successfully to manage an American theater. Born in England, she moved to the United States in 1852, where she operated Laura Keene's Theater in New York City and played the female lead in every production from 1856 to 1863.

■ **KEFAUVER, (CAREY) ESTES (1903-63),** U.S. senator (1949-63). Born in Martinsville, Tennessee, he was elected to the U.S. House as a Democrat from Tennessee in 1938 and was elected to the Senate in 1948. He chaired a subcommittee probing organized crime in a series of televised hearings (1950-52) and sought his party's nomination for president in 1952 and 1956. He ran for vice president with Adlai E. Stevenson in 1956.

See Also: Senate of the United States.

■ **KELLEY, FLORENCE FINCH (1859-1932),** social reformer. Born in Philadelphia, the daughter of Republican congressman William Daragh Kelley, she studied in Zurich, Switzerland, where she became a committed socialist. From 1891 she operated from Hull House, the settlement house in Chicago, to conduct investigations of working conditions in the city's tenements. A friend and colleague of reformers Jane Addams, Lillian D. Wald, and Eugene V. Debs, she wrote the influential *Some Ethical Gains Through Legislation* (1905) and was active in the National Child Labor Committee, the National Association for the Advancement of Colored People, the National Woman Suffrage Association, and the Socialist Party of America.

See Also: Addams, Jane; Debs, Eugene V.; Hull House; Wald, Lillian; Women's Movement.

■ **KELLOGG, FRANK BILLINGS (1856-1937),** American lawyer, politician, and diplomat. He was born in Potsdam, New York, and as a child moved to Minnesota, where he eventually practiced law and was elected to the U.S. Senate (1917-23). Appointed Pres. Calvin Coolidge's secretary of state (1925-29), Kellogg is best remembered for negotiating the Kellogg-Briand Pact

(1928), for which he was awarded the Nobel Peace Prize in 1929.

See Also: Kellogg-Briand Pact.

■ **KELLOGG-BRIAND PACT,** international peace agreement formally known as the Treaty for the Renunciation of War. It was signed in Paris in 1928 by 15 nations and was soon accepted almost worldwide. The brainchild of U.S. Sec. of State Frank B. Kellogg and the French foreign minister, Aristide Briand, the pact declared war to be unacceptable as a means of national policy. It was, however, completely ineffective in preventing the actual outbreak of war, as evidenced by the Japanese invasion of Manchuria (1931), the Italian invasion of Ethiopia (1935), and, most dramatically, World War II (1939-45).

See Also: Kellogg, Frank Billings.

■ **KELLY, GENE (1912-96),** dancer, singer, film director, and choreographer. Born in Pittsburgh, Pennsylvania, he was known for his athletic and exuberant dances in Hollywood musicals such as *On the Town* (1949), *An American in Paris* (1951), and the classic *Singin' in the Rain* (1952), which featured Kelly's performance of the title song. He directed many of his own dance sequences and films such as *Hello, Dolly* (1969).

■ **KEMBLE, FRANCES ANNE (1809-93),** actress and author, better known as Fanny Kemble. Born in London, Kemble made her professional debut as Juliet in 1829 at her father's Covent Garden Theatre. Her performance was an overwhelming success and she soon joined her parents, uncle, and aunt as one of the most celebrated performers in London. In 1832, on the brink of financial ruin, the family company embarked on an American tour with Fanny as leading lady. She was received with enthusiasm by American audiences but she did not like America, finding the cities dirty and the people "impudent and vulgar." Though she was particularly appalled by the practice of slavery, she married Pierce Butler, a plantation owner, in 1834. Butler convinced her to omit her views on slavery from the *Journal* in which she published her first impressions of America. But during the Civil War she published *Journal of Residence on a Georgian Plantation*

(1863), an important antislavery book that helped reshape public opinion in predominantly pro-Confederate England. In her later years she left the stage but continued to give public readings. She also wrote essays for the *Atlantic Monthly* and published a critical work titled *Notes upon Some of Shakespeare's Plays* (1882).

See Also: Civil War; Women in American History.

BIBLIOGRAPHY: Furnas, J. C., *Fanny Kemble: Leading Lady of the Nineteenth-Century Stage: A Biography* (Dial Press 1982).

■ **KENDALL, EDWARD (1886-1972),** biochemist. Born in South Norwalk, Connecticut, Kendall graduated from Columbia (Ph.D., 1910) and became a research chemist for Parke, Davis and Company in Detroit (1910-11) and then a hormone biochemist at St. Luke's Hospital in New York City (1911-14) before working at the Mayo Clinic (1914-51). There he isolated and named thyroxin, the principal thyroid hormone, and isolated six hormones from the adrenal cortex including cortisone. Kendall won a Nobel Prize in Physiology and Medicine in 1950 for his work in endocrinology. He continued his research while professor of chemistry at Princeton University from 1951 to 1972.

See Also: Science.

■ **KENNAN, GEORGE FROST (1904-96),** diplomat, historian, and statesman. Often accorded authorship of the doctrine of containment, Kennan was born in Milwaukee, Wisconsin, and attended Princeton University. He joined the fledgling Foreign Service in 1926 and served in various diplomatic posts over the next two decades while developing expertise as a Soviet specialist. The dispatch of his Long Telegram from Moscow in February 1946 brought him to the attention of key American policymakers. His 1947 "X" article, "The Sources of Soviet Conduct," in *Foreign Affairs,* brought him wider public attention. In it he advocated containment as the appropriate American strategy to meet the postwar Soviet challenge.

As director of the policy planning staff in the State Department from 1947 to 1950, Kennan primarily advocated political and economic steps, such as the Marshall Plan, to implement containment. He unsuccessfully opposed more military

measures such as the North Atlantic Treaty Organization and left the State Department in 1950 in disagreement with the forceful approach to containment pursued by Sec. of State Dean Acheson. While Kennan served briefly as ambassador to the Soviet Union in 1952 and to Yugoslavia in 1961-63, he never again exercised significant direct influence over policy formulation.

In 1953, Kennan joined the Institute for Advanced Study at Princeton, from where he pursued a distinguished career as both historian and foreign policy critic. He won scholarly acclaim for his historical works and provoked serious discussion with his critiques of American foreign relations. His concern to root foreign policy in calculations of national interest led him to emphasize the limits of American power. He emerged as an eloquent opponent of U.S. involvement in Vietnam and passionately objected to the nuclear arms race. The end of the Cold War endowed him with the status of revered elder statesman.

—WILSON D. MISCAMBLE

See Also: Cold War; Containment.

BIBLIOGRAPHY: Mayers, David, *George Kennan and the Dilemmas of U.S. Foreign Policy* (Oxford Univ. Press 1988); Miscamble, Wilson D., D.S.C., *George F. Kennan and the Making of American Foreign Policy, 1947-1950* (Princeton Univ. Press 1992).

■ **KENNEDY, ANTHONY (1936-),** associate justice of the U.S. Supreme Court (1988-). He was born in Sacramento, California. After graduating from Harvard Law School (1961), Kennedy practiced in San Francisco and taught constitutional law at the University of the Pacific's McGeorge School of Law. He was appointed to the Ninth Circuit U.S. Court of Appeals (1975). Kennedy was appointed by Pres. Ronald Reagan to the Supreme Court after the Senate rejected the nominations of former solicitor general Robert Bork and Harvard law professor Douglas Ginsburg.

See Also: Supreme Court.

■ **KENNEDY, JOHN FITZGERALD (1917-63),** 35th president of the United States (1961-63). He was born in Brookline, Massachusetts, and graduated from Harvard in 1940. Although many Irish-Catholics of his day were culturally and socially discriminated against, the Irish-Catholic Kennedy

In 1960, John F. Kennedy defeated Richard M. Nixon to become the nation's youngest, and first Roman Catholic, president. His vibrant style and young family—wife Jacqueline, daughter Caroline (*left*), and son John in a 1963 photograph—marked the emergence of a new generation of political leadership.

inherited all of the privileges of aristocracy because his father, Joseph P. Kennedy, was a successful entrepreneur and U.S. ambassador to Great Britain, and his mother, Rose, was the daughter of the wealthy John F. Fitzgerald, former mayor of Boston.

Wealth and influence, along with intelligence, charisma, and ambition, contributed to Kennedy's publication of *Why England Slept* (1940) and the Pulitzer Prize–winning *Profiles in Courage* (1956) as well as to his political rise from the U.S. House of Representatives (1947-53) and Senate (1953-61) to the White House in 1961. Another political asset for Kennedy was his marriage in 1953 to Jacqueline Bouvier, a woman whose intelligence, beauty, and elegance captivated the nation and eventually the world. The youth and charm of this couple (and later, their two children) made them media favorites.

Yet Kennedy also surmounted several handicaps that would have destroyed lesser men. He suffered from a severe chronic back problem; Addison's disease, a malfunction of the adrenal glands; and other serious ailments. His poor health failed to prevent him from emerging from World War II as an authentic war hero. Nor did it deflate

his buoyant personality, his vigor, and his genuine love of people. Kennedy also successfully distanced himself politically from his unpopular father and defied the so-called stigma of his Roman Catholicism to win the 1960 presidential election.

Presidency. Kennedy's abbreviated presidency, which he started by proclaiming his vision of a "New Frontier," left many promises unfulfilled. He did, however, strengthen the country militarily, enabling it to withstand Soviet leader Nikita Khrushchev's menacing moves in Berlin in 1961. He also abated the crisis in Laos by agreeing to support a coalition government headed by a neutralist. Even though scholars rightly recognize that Kennedy contributed to an unnecessary missile crisis in Cuba, his response to Soviet nuclear weaponry there was measured, prudent, and courageous. By the fall of 1962 he seemed a much more effective leader than during the Bay of Pigs debacle of 1961, unquestionably his greatest foreign policy failure. Still, Vietnam remained his most serious challenge at the time of his death.

Domestically, due to his narrow election victory, a recalcitrant Congress, and his own weaknesses as a legislative leader, Kennedy failed to accomplish most of his major objectives such as Medicare, federal aid to education, and civil rights. Nevertheless, no president up to his time had embraced the African-American cause to the same extent as Kennedy. His economic policies, culminating with the tax cut of 1964, ended economic stagnation and reduced unemployment and the balance of payments deficit.

His presidency ended abruptly at approximately 1:00 P.M. on Nov. 22, 1963, as a result of fatal gunshot wounds in Dallas, Texas. Later that day, he was succeeded by Vice Pres. Lyndon B. Johnson, who continued to sponsor many of the reforms initiated by Kennedy.

—JAMES N. GIGLIO

See Also: Cold War; Cuban Missile Crisis; Johnson, Lyndon Baines; Kennedy Family; President of the United States.

BIBLIOGRAPHY: Giglio, James N., *The Presidency of John F. Kennedy* (Univ. Press of Kansas 1991); Parmet, Herbert S., *JFK: the Presidency of John F. Kennedy* (Dial Press 1983); Reeves, Richard, *President Kennedy: Profile of Power* (Simon & Schuster 1993); Reeves, Thomas, *A Question of Character: A Life of John F. Kennedy* (Macmillan 1991); Schlesinger, Arthur M., Jr., *A Thousand Days, John F. Kennedy in the White House* (Houghton Mifflin 1995); Sorensen, Theodore, *Kennedy* (Harper & Row 1965).

■ **KENNEDY, ROBERT (1925-68),** U.S. attorney general and senator. Born in Brookline, Massachusetts, he was a younger brother of Pres. John F. Kennedy (1917-63) and served as chief political adviser to his brother, managing his election to the Senate (1952) and the presidency (1960). As a congressional staff attorney (1953-60), he was known for leading investigations of the Teamsters Union (1957-59) and for his devotion to his brother's career. Appointed attorney general by his brother (1961), he served until 1964 when he resigned and was elected to the Senate from New York. He opposed escalation of the Vietnam War and became closely associated with the civil rights and antipoverty movements. He ran for the Democratic nomination for president as an antiwar candidate in 1968. Kennedy was assassinated in Los Angeles (June 6, 1968)

just after winning the California presidential primary.

See Also: Kennedy, John Fitzgerald; Kennedy Family.

BIBLIOGRAPHY: Newfield, Jack, *Robert F. Kennedy: A Memoir* (Berkley Publishing 1978); Schlesinger, Arthur M., Jr., *Robert Kennedy and His Times* (Houghton Mifflin 1978).

■ **KENNEDY FAMILY,** American political dynasty that produced a president, three U.S. senators, and numerous other politicians. They were descended from Patrick Kennedy (1823-58) and Bridget Murphy (1822-88), both from County Wexford, Ireland, who immigrated to Boston in 1849. One of their sons, Patrick Joseph (P. J.) (1857-1929), a saloonkeeper, entered Democratic politics and served in the Massachusetts senate. He and his wife, Mary Augusta Hickey (1857-1923) had three children, including Joseph Patrick (1888-1969). Entrepreneur, part-time movie mogul, and financier, Joseph P. Kennedy was a millionaire before he was 40 years old. In 1914 he married Rose Elizabeth Fitzgerald (1890-1993) the daughter of John F. ("Honey Fitz") Fitzgerald, a mayor of Boston. Their eldest son, Joseph P., Jr. (1915-44), died in World War II. The second son, John F. (1917-63), became the nation's 35th president and was assassinated in Dallas, Texas. Robert F. (1925-68) served as attorney general in his brother's administration and was later elected senator from New York. He was assassinated in Los Angeles, California, while campaigning for the 1968 Democratic presidential nomination. Edward M. ("Ted") (1932-) continues to serve as a senator from Massachusetts, a post he has held since 1962.

Several of Joseph and Rose Kennedy's grandchildren have continued the family's tradition of public service. The two eldest of Robert's 11 children are presently serving in government: Kathleen Kennedy Townsend (1951-) is the first female lieutenant governor of Maryland, and Joseph P. Kennedy II (1952-) is a member of Congress representing Massachusetts's 8th district. John's two children (one son, Patrick, died hours after his birth in 1963) are both lawyers who have moved into literary ventures: Caroline Kennedy Schlossburg (1957-) has written several books and speaks widely on the issue of the constitutional right to privacy; John F., Jr. (1960-) is the editor in chief of *George* magazine. Edward's youngest child (of three) represents the 1st district of Rhode Island in Congress.

—JOHN ROBERT GREENE

See Also: *Kennedy, John Fitzgerald; Kennedy, Robert.*
BIBLIOGRAPHY: Collier, Peter, and David Horowitz, *The Kennedys: An American Drama* (Summit Books 1984); Wills, Garry, *The Kennedy Imprisonment* (Little, Brown 1982).

■ **KENT, JAMES (1763-1847),** jurist. He was born in Fredricksburgh, New York, practiced law (1785-93), and taught law at Columbia College (1793-98) before joining the New York Supreme Court (1798). Kent was chief judge (1804-23) and also chancellor of the New York Court of Chancery (1814-23) before returning to Columbia (1923-26). Kent's chancery decisions helped shape the U.S. system of equity jurisdiction, and his four-volume *Commentaries on American Law* (1826-30) is an early classic of U.S. legal theory.

■ **KENTUCKY,** one of the border states that has historically straddled the North and South. It is bounded on the north and east by Ohio, on the east by West Virginia, on the east and south by Virginia, on the south by Tennessee, on the west by Missouri, and on the west and north by Indiana and Illinois. The Ohio River forms its northern border and the Mississippi River its western border. Kentucky slopes from the fringes of the Appalachian Mountains in the east to the coastal plains of the Mississippi in the west. The fertile Bluegrass region is in east-central Kentucky.

Migrants from the Middle Atlantic colonies came down the Ohio River or through the Cumberland Gap to settle Kentucky. It became a state in 1792. Kentucky was deeply divided during the Civil War; Pres. Abraham Lincoln and Confederate Pres. Jefferson Davis both were born in the state. The turbulence of these years continued well into the postwar era. By the end of World War II, Kentucky had shifted from a principally agricultural economy to a mainly industrial one.

Capital: Frankfort. Area: 40,411 square miles. Population (1995 est.): 3,860,000.

See Also: *Appalachian Mountains; Davis, Jefferson; Lincoln, Abraham; Perryville, Battle of.*

■ **KERN, JEROME (1885-1945),** composer. Born in New York City, Kern studied classical composition in Europe. He composed operettas such as *Sunny* (1925) and *Roberta* (1933) and, with lyricist Oscar Hammerstein II, the landmark *Show Boat* (1927), which featured "Ol' Man River" and "Only Make Believe" and was the first musical to integrate song and story in the plot. Among Kern's other songs were "Smoke Gets in Your Eyes" and "The Song Is You."

See Also: *Theater.*

■ **KEROUAC, JACK (1922-69),** novelist of the Beat Generation. Kerouac was born in Lowell, Massachusetts, and attended Columbia University on a football scholarship. His first novel, *The Town and the City*, was published in 1950, but it was not until the 1957 publication of *On the Road* that Kerouac became well known as an author. He conceived of his 19 novels as one great work, *The Legend of Duluoz*. In his novels Kerouac tried to use "spontaneous prose" to depict the experiences of postwar American life.

See Also: *Beats, The; Novel.*

■ **KETTERING, CHARLES (1876-1958),** engineer who invented products used in automobiles. Born near Loudonville, Ohio, Kettering graduated from Ohio State (1904) and worked for the National Cash Register Company until he and a partner, Edward A. Deeds, founded the Dayton Engineering Laboratories Company (Delco) in 1909. There, Kettering developed the first electrical ignition system (adopted by Cadillac in 1910) and the first self-starter for automobiles (1911), devices that established the primacy of gasoline engines over electric and steam power, made driving easier, and won him fame as an inventor. In 1916, he sold Delco to United Motors, which was absorbed by General Motors (GM) in 1918 and evolved into General Motors Research Laboratories. Kettering became head of the laboratories and vice president of General Motors. He led research over the next 30 years that produced motor fuels that prevented engine knock; a light, fast, diesel engine; shock absorbers; variable speed transmissions; safety glass; fast-drying automobile paint; and the refrigerant Freon. Kettering retired from General Motors in 1947 and used his wealth to establish, with his friend and past General Motors chairman

Alfred P. Sloan, the Sloan-Kettering Institute for Cancer Research in New York City.

See Also: *Invention; Science.*

■ **KEYNES, JOHN MAYNARD (1883-1946),** British economist who theorized that compensatory government spending could be used to balance the economy and ensure full employment. Born in Cambridge, England, Keynes combined an academic career with government service while at the same time becoming wealthy through astute stock investments. He served in the British Treasury during World War I and was an adviser to the British delegation to the 1919 Versailles peace conference. He predicted in *The Economic Consequences of Peace* (1919) that the Versailles Treaty would cause political turmoil in Germany. He was created Baron Keynes of Tilton in 1942 and led the British delegation to the 1944 Bretton Woods Conference, which created the International Monetary Fund.

Keynes's most influential work, *The General Theory of Employment, Interest, and Money* (1935), had a profound impact on government policies in Britain and the United States. By arguing that government spending could compensate for shortfalls in private investment, Keynes held out hope that the boom-and-bust business cycle could be controlled and that the state could moderate the excesses of modern industrial capitalism without resorting to public ownership or detailed central planning. In the United States, in response to the 1937-38 recession, Keynesian economists recommended government spending programs. These proved to be the New Deal's solution to the recession by the time the nation entered World War II in late 1941. Keynesian thought continued to influence American policy throughout the war and in the 1960s attained the status of, as one Keynesian put it, "conventional wisdom."

See Also: *New Deal.*
BIBLIOGRAPHY: Felix, David, *Biography of an Idea: John Maynard Keynes and The General Theory of Employment, Interest, and Money* (Transaction Publ. 1995).

■ **KICKAPOO INDIANS. See:** *Algonquian.*

■ **KIDD, WILLIAM (CAPTAIN) (1654-1701),** American privateer hanged for piracy on May 23, 1701. Born in Scotland, Kidd settled in New York, where he commanded a privateering vessel owned by American investor Robert Livingston as well as several English peers. On a voyage into the Indian Ocean (1696-1700), Kidd turned from privateering to pirating, and the East India Company demanded royal intervention. Eventually, Kidd was captured and brought to trial in England.

See Also: *Piracy.*

■ **KING, BILLIE JEAN (1943-),** professional tennis player and women's rights activist. The top player in the game in the late 1960s and early 1970s, she won a record 20 Wimbledon titles and four U.S. Lawn Tennis women's singles titles. She used her celebrity to promote the cause of equal rights for women. In 1973, in a much publicized "battle of the sexes," she defeated tennis star Bobby Riggs in a match, thus legitimizing women's athletics to the American public.

See Also: *Sports; Women in American History.*

Billie Jean King, a champion player, was instrumental in making women's professional tennis a popular sport.

KING, CLARENCE (1842-1901), geologist and first head of the U.S. Geological Survey. King was born in Newport, Rhode Island, and after graduating from Yale (1862) he rode horseback across the country to survey in Nevada and California (1863-66). King then took charge of surveying an area of about 100 miles in width from eastern Colorado to California (1867-77) and wrote the seven-volume *Report of the Geological Exploration of the Fortieth Parallel* (1870-80). King introduced the method of using contour lines to describe topography and used the laboratory to solve geophysical problems. In 1878, Congress combined all western surveys into the U.S. Geological Survey, and King became its first head. He retired in 1881. After his death it was discovered that under the name of John Todd, he had established a family with an African-American woman named Ada Copeland in Brooklyn, New York.

See Also: Science.

Martin Luther King, Jr., delivered his famous "I Have a Dream" speech during the March on Washington in 1963, which prompted Pres. John F. Kennedy to advocate a civil rights law.

KING, MARTIN LUTHER, JR. (1929-68), African-American civil rights leader and Baptist clergyman. The second of three children born to Martin Luther King, Sr., and Alberta Williams King in Atlanta, Georgia. King was a descendant of three generations of Baptist preachers who challenged racial injustice. He very early demonstrated a concern for human community that was shaped by his exposure to the African-American church, an extended family, and segregation in the South.

Early Life. Educated in the public schools for blacks in Atlanta, King enrolled in Morehouse College in that city in 1944 at the age of 15. There he studied under Benjamin E. Mays, George D. Kelsey, and other African-American clergymen-educators who combined social analysis and activism with biblical piety and theological liberalism. Such exposure figured in King's decision in 1948 to become an ordained minister. After receiving a B.A. in sociology from Morehouse, he entered Crozer Theological Seminary in Chester, Pennsylvania, and graduated with a B.D. in 1951. While at Crozer King was introduced to the Christian ethics of George W. Davis, the social gospelism of Walter Rauschenbusch, and the nonviolent philosophy and methods of Mohandas K. Gandhi. His interest in these sources continued at Boston University, where he also studied personalism and the Christian realism of Reinhold

Niebuhr and where he received a Ph.D. in philosophical theology in 1955. King's power and genius blossomed as he fashioned from his studies and from the old-fashioned religiosity of the southern African-American church a philosophy and method to eliminate racism, economic exploitation, violence, and human destruction.

Civil Rights Leadership. King married Coretta Scott on June 18, 1953, and the couple had four children. King's family and his deep-rooted spirituality became his most important sources of support as he led nonviolent demonstrations against injustice in the segregated South and later throughout the United States. His leadership of the Montgomery bus boycott (1955-56), while serving as pastor of the Dexter Avenue Baptist Church, catapulted him to national and international fame. To coordinate these and other activities, King led in the founding (1957) of the Southern Christian Leadership Conference (SCLC) in Atlanta, which he served as president. He led major civil rights campaigns in Albany, Georgia (1962), in Birmingham, Alabama, and Washington, D.C. (1963), in Selma, Alabama (1965), in Chicago, Illinois (1966-67), and in Memphis, Tennessee (1968). Such efforts contributed to the passage of the Civil Rights Act (1964) and the Voting Rights Act (1965) and to federal government initiatives toward affirmative action. In time King's concerns embraced racism, poverty, and violence on a national and international scale. He sought to achieve what he termed "the beloved community," a completely integrated society based on love and justice as ethical norms.

A gifted thinker and prolific writer, King wrote six books and hundreds of articles on social justice issues. In addition he spoke at numerous colleges and universities throughout the world, thus combining his interests as an intellectual with his civil rights activities and his work as a co-pastor with his father at Atlanta's Ebenezer Baptist Church.

Last Years. King's sense of the relationship between the African-American struggle and the struggles of the oppressed worldwide broadened in the last three years of his life as he denounced South African apartheid, U.S. involvement in Vietnam, and the economic impact of colonialism and neocolonialism on the so-called Third World. He was awarded the Nobel Peace Prize in 1964. King was assassinated on Apr. 4, 1968, in Memphis, where he had gone to support a sanitation workers' strike. The assassin was James Earl Ray; debate continues as to whether Ray acted alone. The murder occurred only weeks before King was to start a massive Poor Peoples' Campaign with demonstrations in Washington, D.C., on behalf of and involving people of different racial and ethnic backgrounds. In 1983, Congress declared his birthday a national holiday.

—LEWIS V. BALDWIN

See Also: African Americans; Civil Rights Acts; Civil Rights Movement; Southern Christian Leadership Conference (SCLC); Voting Rights Act.

BIBLIOGRAPHY: Ansbro, John J., *Martin Luther King, Jr.: The Making of a Mind* (Orbis Books 1982); Baldwin, Lewis V., *To Make the Wounded Whole: The Cultural Legacy of Martin Luther King, Jr.* (Fortress Press 1992); Branch, Taylor, *Parting the Waters: America in the King Years* (Simon & Schuster 1988); King, Martin Luther, Jr., *Stride Toward Freedom: The Montgomery Story* (Harper & Brothers 1958).

KING, WILLIAM RUFUS DE VANE (1786-1853),

American politician and diplomat. Born in Sampson County, North Carolina, King was elected to the House of Representatives in 1810, serving until 1816. In 1818 he settled in Alabama and became one of that state's first U.S. senators. In 1844 Pres. John Tyler appointed King minister to France, hoping he could avert French interference in Texas. King ran again for the Senate in 1846, but his pro-Union stance led to his defeat by proponents of states' rights. In 1852 he was elected as Franklin Pierce's vice president but was unable to serve. King died from tuberculosis just six weeks after the inauguration.

KING GEORGE'S WAR (1744-48), war in North America between Britain and France. Called in Europe the War of the Austrian Succession, the conflict ended three decades of peace between Britain and France and ushered in the final phase of imperial conflicts in North America. After a pair of French victories in Nova Scotia, British and colonial troops captured Louisburg in 1744. Neither side achieved a decisive victory, and the tenuous Treaty of Aix-la-Chapelle ended the war in 1748.

KING PHILIP'S WAR (1675-76), New England's most devastating war with American Indians. "King Philip" was actually Metacomet, a Wampanoag sachem whose tribal lands were coveted by the English settlement of New Plymouth.

Origins. Lacking a royal charter, New Plymouth's legitimacy rested on its dubious "treaty" with Wampanoag sachem Massasoit. When Massasoit died, his heir, Wamsutta (known to the English as Alexander), sold land to Rhode Islanders, thus diminishing Plymouth's territorial claims. Alarmed, Plymouth threatened Alexander. When Alexander died, his brother Metacomet (Philip) became the Wampanoag sachem, inheriting the unstable relationship between his tribe and the Plymouth Colony. Reluctantly, Philip agreed to sell land only to Plymouth, but when Plymouth's town of Swansea formed next to Philip's homeland at Sowams (Pokanoket, Bristol), friction resulted in the death of a Wampanoag and the retaliatory deaths of six colonists. Eager to settle the score, Plymouth mobilized for war. Massachusetts sent a troop of mercenary buccaneers but sent them to the much coveted lands of the Narragansett Indians in Rhode Island's jurisdiction. In defiance of Rhode Islanders' protests, Narragansett lands were to be seized by "rights of conquest." Connecticut invaded with the same intention.

In this 18th-century engraving of King Philip's War of 1675-76, Wampanoag chief Metacomet (King Philip) led a war of Indian resistance to the English settlement of southern New England.

Open Hostility. Philip was trapped at Sowams, but he escaped to raid towns in Plymouth and Massachusetts. The Narragansett tried desperately to avoid fighting, even seizing Wampanoag captives and turning them over to Connecticut, but Massachusetts' buccaneers had been promised plunder, so they promptly attacked the Narragansett. Others were killed in the Great Swamp Fight organized by Puritan governments. Furious warriors escaped and joined Philip and his other allies the Nipmuck, who had been "converted" to Puritan Christianity at gunpoint. Others of John Eliot's "praying Indians" sided with Massachusetts, as also did the Wampanoag on Cape Cod and Martha's Vineyard. The Mohegan sided with Connecticut. Raids and massacres were standard for both sides. Philip was defeated decisively when New York's governor, Edmund Andros, armed his allied Mohawk and sent them against Philip's warriors. When demoralized fighters broke up and tried to return to familiar homelands, many were massacred by Connecticut's cavalry. Philip returned covertly to his "throne," where an angry dissident betrayed him and he was shot to death.

Aftermath. Besides widespread destruction to property, New England lost a greater percentage of its population than in any war since that time. In October 1676, a royal emissary reported losses of 600 men and "upward of three thousand Indians, men, women and children destroyed." Tribal independence ended in southern New England except for the dependably subservient Mohegan. The Wampanoag lost to New Plymouth, which, in turn, was swallowed up by Massachusetts to become the counties of the "Old Colony." Narragansett lands reverted to nonbelligerent Rhode Island. Many Indians fled to refuge in Canada, Pennsylvania, and New York. When a Puritan embassy demanded death for refugees at New York's refuge of Schagticoke on the Hudson River, Governor Andros permitted them only to make a peace treaty embracing them and the Iroquois tribes allied to New York. The Iroquois role of spokesmen for the refugees became a precedent in the so-called Covenant Chain then founded as a perpetual alliance between English colonies and tribes accepting Iroquois leadership.

Traditional mythology has made King Philip's War into a war of "civilized" and righteous Puritans against bloodthirsty and evil savages, from which accounts the issues of land seizures and intercolonial competition disappear. Much falsification and fabrication of sources have been performed to preserve the myth.

—FRANCIS JENNINGS

See Also: *Great Swamp Fight; Indians of North American; Massachusetts; Massasoit; Metacomet; Puritanism; Rhode Island.*

BIBLIOGRAPHY: Jennings, Francis, *The Invasion of America: Indians, Colonialism, and the Cant of Conquest* (Norton 1976); Leach, Douglas Edward, *Flintlock and Tomahawk: New England in King Philip's War* (Macmillan 1958); Vaughan, Alden T., *New England Frontier: Puritans and Indians, 1620-1675,* 3rd ed. (Univ. of Oklahoma Press 1995).

■ **KING'S MOUNTAIN, BATTLE OF (1780),** American victory in North Carolina during the American Revolution. After the British victory at Camden, South Carolina (1780), Britain's General Cornwallis attempted to reclaim control of the South by invading North Carolina. Cornwallis divided his army, leaving Patrick Ferguson in command of Loyalist forces that encountered American frontiersmen at King's Mountain in October. The Americans decimated Ferguson's troops, ending the British invasion of North Carolina.

See Also: *Revolution, American.*

■ **KINGSTON, MAXINE HONG (1940-),** Chinese-American writer, born in Stockton, California. *The Woman Warrior* (1976) and *China Men* (1981) deal with a young Chinese American girl's perceptions of Chinese folk traditions. Her other books include *Hawi'i One Summer* (1987) and *Tripmaster Monkey and His Fake Book* (1989). She became Chancellor's Distinguished Professor of English at the University of California at Berkeley in 1990.

See Also: *Novel; Women in American History.*

■ **KING WILLIAM'S WAR (1689-97),** first of Britain's wars with France in North America. Known as the War of the League of Augsburg in Europe, King William's War grew out of the commercial rivalry between Britain and France. The conflict began with English-Iroquois attacks on Montreal. The French retaliated by raiding western settlements in New York, New Hampshire, and Maine. Ultimately inconclusive, the war was ended by the Treaty of Ryswick in 1697.

■ **KINO, EUSEBIO FRANCISCO (1645-1711),** author, cartographer, and missionary to Indians of the Southwest. Kino was born in Segno, Italy, and became a Jesuit in 1665. In 1681, he traveled to northern Mexico, where he established several missions and explored the Southwest as far as the Pacific coast. With his firsthand knowledge, Kino produced finely detailed maps of lower California and also wrote a detailed memoir, *Favores Celestiales* (1708).

■ **KINSEY, ALFRED C. (1894-1956),** researcher on human sexuality. Kinsey was born in Hoboken, New Jersey, and attended Bowdoin College and Harvard University, specializing in entomology. He taught biology at Harvard and then zoology at Indiana University, where he became a full professor in 1929. Kinsey's research on human sexual behavior began after he was assigned to teach a new course on marriage offered at Indiana. In 1947 Kinsey formed the Institute for Sex Research to act as a repository for the confidential survey information. The results of his study were published in two reports, *Sexual Behavior in the Human Male* in 1948 and *Sexual Behavior in the Human Female* in 1953.

See Also: *Science.*

■ **KIOWA INDIANS. *See:*** *Great Plains Indians.*

■ **KIRKLAND, CAROLINE (1801-64),** author, born in New York City. In her *A New Home—Who'll Follow? or Glimpses of Western Life* (1839), she broke with the traditional romantic accounts of the West. Her accurate and uncompromising style is the earliest example of frontier realism.

■ **KIRKLAND, LANE (1922-),** labor leader. Born in Camden, South Carolina, he attended the U.S. Merchant Marine Academy and served on merchant marine ships during World War II. In 1948 he went to work as a pensions specialist for the American Federation of Labor (now the AFL-CIO). In 1960 he became executive assistant to AFL-CIO president George Meany. In 1969 Kirkland was elected secretary-treasurer and became president on Meany's retirement in 1979, serving during a period of general decline in the labor movement. He retired in 1995.

See Also: *AFL-CIO; Labor Movement; Meany, George.*

KISSINGER, HENRY A. (1923-), U.S. secretary of state (1973-77) and foreign policy consultant. Born in Fuerth, Germany, Kissinger and his family immigrated to the United States in 1938 to escape Nazism. He began to study at City College of New York, but World War II intervened. During the war Kissinger first worked as an intelligence officer and then for the military government of occupied Germany. In 1947 he entered Harvard, where he earned his undergraduate degree in 1950 and his Ph.D. in 1954. After graduating, Kissinger worked as a consultant to Nelson Rockefeller until 1958, when he accepted a position as a professor at Harvard. Kissinger quickly positioned himself as a political consultant on foreign policy, dispensing information to both Democratic and Republican leaders alike. Brought to the attention of James Allen, Richard Nixon's foreign policy adviser, Kissinger was named special assistant for national security affairs after Nixon's 1968 presidential victory.

During his five-year tenure as national security adviser and his three-year service as secretary of state to both Nixon and Pres. Gerald R. Ford, Kissinger was at the center of all major foreign policy initiatives. His own best press agent, he planted information, wooed reporters, and was even dubbed "Super-K" by one pundit. The foreign policy of the Nixon administration was developed by Nixon, who never fully trusted Kissinger and was openly disdainful of both his academic contacts and his propensity for the nightlife. Nixon, however, clearly valued Kissinger's extraordinary skills as a negotiator and was content to let his adviser take a large share of the public credit for both détente with the Soviets and Communist China, and for the peace treaty (1973) that ended American troop involvement in the war in Vietnam.

Ford placed more personal trust in Kissinger than had Nixon, largely because of Ford's lack of background in foreign policy. But despite an improved private relationship with the president, by 1976 Kissinger's influence within government had considerably waned. Not only had his role in negotiating détente made him vulnerable to attacks from the growing right wing of the Republican party, but public reports of his involvement in the scandals of the Nixon administration, most notably his ordering of wiretaps on several of his own underlings at the National Security Council

and his role in the overthrow of the Chilean government, lessened his credibility in the press.

After Ford's defeat in 1976 Kissinger returned to the private sector, forming his own consulting firm in New York City. Yet his has been far from an anonymous departure from politics. In 1980, for example, Kissinger tried to broker a deal that would have had Ford sign on as Ronald Reagan's running mate in the presidential election, an agreement that disintegrated when Reagan reneged. Kissinger continued to speak, consult, and maintain a high profile in the national media.

—JOHN ROBERT GREENE

See Also: Cold War; Ford, Gerald Rudolph; Nixon, Richard Milhous; Vietnam War.

BIBLIOGRAPHY: Isaacson, Walter, *Kissinger* (Simon & Schuster 1992); Schulzinger, Robert D., *Henry Kissinger: Doctor of Diplomacy* (Columbia Univ. Press 1989); Shawcross, William, *Sideshow: Kissinger, Nixon, and the Destruction of Cambodia* (Simon & Schuster 1979).

KITCHEN CABINET (1829-31), name derisively given to Pres. Andrew Jackson's first cabinet and his unofficial advisers. When he took office in 1829, Jackson appointed obscure men to most of his official cabinet posts. Only Martin Van Buren, secretary of state, commanded much national respect. Jackson's cabinet appointments reflected his attempts to reconcile the factions and regions that had given him the most support in his run for the presidency, but many of his choices were suspect. His choice for secretary of war was fellow Tennessean John H. Eaton, an undistinguished protégé of Jackson. Other personal friends of Jackson, including William Lewis, Amos Kendall, and Isaac Hill, were given subcabinet posts. These men, along with other cronies of Jackson, determined policy more than some of his actual appointments. By putting his friends and political supporters in the cabinet, Jackson was able to thwart the political power of his South Carolina opponents who sought to take a strong stand against the national tariff. Jackson's cabinet was reorganized along more conventional lines in 1831.

See Also: Jackson, Andrew; Van Buren, Martin.

BIBLIOGRAPHY: Schlesinger, Arthur M., Jr., *The Age of Jackson* (Little, Brown 1945); Sellers, Charles G.,

The Market Revolution: Jacksonian America, 1815-1846 (Oxford Univ. Press 1991).

■ **KLONDIKE,** region in northwest Canada bordering on the Klondike and Yukon rivers and lying east of Alaska. In 1897 rumors of gold finds in the area reached San Francisco and Seattle. Thousands of prospectors swarmed into the region during the next couple of years, making the name Klondike synonymous with gold rush. Several years later, when the accessible placer mines had been played out, the population plummeted.

See Also: Mining Rushes.

■ **KNICKERBOCKER SCHOOL,** early 19th-century literary circle. The Knickerbocker School was a loosely affiliated cohort of writers in antebellum New York City. Their aim was not a specific style of writing or a particular philosophical viewpoint but rather the promotion of a national literature with their native New York at the center of it. Much of the activity of the group centered on the *Knickerbocker Magazine*, a literary journal published between 1832 and 1865. Although the journal initially floundered, after 1834, when Lewis Gaylord Clark became editor, it grew into a well-respected venue for American literature from all regions. Washington Irving, one of the better known of the group's writers, had used the name Diedrich Knickerbocker as a pseudonym for his early and successful book, *A History of New York* (1809). Irving was a contributing editor to the magazine from 1839 to 1841. Other authors of the Knickerbocker School included James Fenimore Cooper, William Cullen Bryant, James K. Paulding, Clement Moore, and Lydia Maria Child.

See Also: Bryant, William Cullen; Child, Lydia Maria; Cooper, James Fenimore; Irving, Washington.

■ **KNIGHT, SARAH KEMBLE (1666-1727),** diarist. She was born in Boston, Massachusetts, and is remembered for the witty and insightful journal she kept on her travels from Boston to New Haven, Connecticut, and New York City in 1704. The diary was published in 1825 as *The Journal of Madame Knight*.

■ **KNIGHTS OF LABOR,** officially known as the "Noble and Holy Order of the Knights of Labor" (KOL), a national labor federation that uniquely straddled the worlds of the antebellum artisan and the modern worker. Organized by a group of Philadelphia garment workers in 1869, the KOL was initially a secret labor fraternity. Its meetings were steeped in pomp and ritual, and its members were sworn to secrecy. The KOL spread gradually throughout the Northeast under the able leadership of its "Grand Master Workman," Uriah Stephens. In 1882, the Knights abandoned their secrecy and soon became the largest and most diverse labor federation of the time. Barring only lawyers, bankers, gamblers, speculators, and liquor dealers (as well as workers of Chinese descent) from membership, the Knights attracted a diverse membership including many women and a sizable number of African Americans. With the surprising victory of KOL workers over the railroad tycoon Jay Gould in the Southwestern Railway strike of 1885, hundreds of thousands of workers across the country flooded into the KOL. But the conservative leadership of Terence V. Powderly, who denounced strikes and resisted giving them financial support, and the loss of a number of dramatic labor struggles in 1886 resulted in a sharp membership decline. In the same year, large constituencies of skilled workers shifted their allegiance to the newly formed American Federation of Labor, and by the early 20th century, the KOL had passed into history.

See Also: American Federation of Labor (AFL); Gould, Jay; Labor Movement; Powderly, Terence Vincent.

BIBLIOGRAPHY: Fink, Leon, *Workingmen's Democracy: The Knights of Labor and American Politics* (Univ. of Illinois Press 1983); Weir, Robert E., *Beyond Labor's Veil: The Culture of the Knights of Labor* (Pennsylvania State Univ. Press 1996).

■ **KNOW-NOTHING PARTY,** nativist political organization, officially known as the American party. It emerged in 1852 from the consolidation of several secret anti-Catholic societies of the late 1840s. The curious name originated from the vow members took, to answer "I know nothing" when asked about the organization. The Know-Nothings rose in reaction to the great increase in Irish and German Roman Catholic immigration. They proposed to rewrite the naturalization law, requiring a 21-year waiting period for citizenship, and pledged never to vote for Catholic candidates for public office on the grounds that Catholics took their orders straight from the Pope in Rome. Most Know-Nothings were urban workers or small farmers who felt threatened by the cheap labor and unfamiliar culture of the new immigrants.

The Know-Nothings scored impressive victories in local and state elections in 1854, winning control of the Massachusetts legislature and polling 40 percent of the vote in Pennsylvania. But in 1855 the party divided over the question of slavery, splitting into southern (proslavery) and northern (antislavery) wings. In the presidential election of 1856 the Know-Nothings ran ex-President Millard Fillmore as their candidate. Fillmore attracted strong support in the South but succeeded in carrying only the state of Maryland. In the North most Know-Nothings voted for John C. Frémont, the candidate of the newly formed Republican party. In the aftermath of the election, nativist politics were submerged in the growing political debate over slavery.

See Also: Fillmore, Millard; Political Parties; Presidential Elections.

BIBLIOGRAPHY: Billington, Ray Allen, *The Protestant Crusade, 1800-1860: A Study of the Origins of American Nativism* (1938; Rinehart 1952); Anbinder, Tyler Gregory, *Nativism and Slavery: The Northern Know Nothings and the Politics of the 1850s* (Oxford Univ. Press 1992).

■ **KNOX, HENRY (1750-1806),** military leader of the Revolutionary War and the first U.S. secretary of war. Born in Boston, Knox served as a close adviser to Gen. George Washington during the American Revolution. In 1776, Knox captured the British artillery from Fort Ticonderoga, which formed the basis of the rebels' artillery for the war. In December 1783 he succeeded Washington as commander of the army, but he retired to private life just several weeks later. Knox was the founder of the Society of Cincinnati, a group of Revolutionary War veterans. He became the secretary of war in 1785, under the Articles of Confederation, a position he retained when Washington became the first U.S. president. He retired in 1794. The gold vault at Fort Knox is named for him, but Knox himself was a profli-

gate businessman, speculating in land and borrowing heavily to finance his business ventures. As a result, he was involved in many lawsuits with his creditors.

See Also: Cincinnati, Society of; Revolution, American.

■ **KOREAN IMMIGRANTS,** immigrant group with U.S. roots that date back to the early 20th century. The first Korean immigrants to what is now the United States arrived in 1903-04, when sugar planters in Hawaii recruited 7,200 Koreans as field hands for their plantations. The following year, however, further migration from Korea was prohibited by the Japanese, who had taken over Korea as a colonial "protectorate."

Many of the Koreans in Hawaii eventually remigrated to the U.S. West Coast, where they opened small-scale businesses such as groceries, laundries, and barber shops—one of the few avenues open to a people locked out of the labor market because of frequent racial discrimination. Koreans residing in the United States also established organizations that were to play a prominent role in the struggle for Korean independence from Japanese colonialism.

The number of Koreans in the United States remained small until the end (1945) of World War II, when the U.S. occupation of Korea triggered renewed migration (many of the first immigrants being brides of American servicemen). With the removal of racial restrictions on immigration in 1965, the U.S. Korean population grew rapidly. The 1990 census recorded some 800,000 people of Korean descent living in the United States, a quarter of them in Los Angeles.

See Also: Ethnic Groups; Immigration.

BIBLIOGRAPHY: Kim, Elaine, and Eui-Young Yu, *East to America: Korean American Life Stories* (New Press 1996); Takaki, Ronald, *Strangers from a Different Shore: A History of Asian Americans* (Little, Brown 1989).

■ **KOREAN WAR (1950-53),** the first major conflict involving the United States after World War II, starting on June 25, 1950, and ending with an armistice on July 27, 1953. With United Nations (UN) approval, the United States intervened militarily after communist North Korea invaded South Korea and waged a limited war to prevent communist conquest of the peninsula. The Korean War was a key turning point in U.S. foreign policy in the Cold War. As a consequence of it, the United States expanded its commitments in East Asia to block communist seizures of power, vastly increased defense spending, strengthened NATO, and campaigned to rearm West Germany.

Origins of the Two Koreas. The United States and the Soviet Union intruded on a civil war in Korea at the end of World War II. The United States proposed Korea's division into Soviet and U.S. zones of military occupation. Stalin's acceptance of this plan saved Korea south of the 38th parallel from communist rule but froze both sides in the civil war. Hoping to resolve its dilemma, Washington persuaded a reluctant UN to pass a resolution calling for supervised national elections to unite Korea.

Following Moscow's anticipated refusal to cooperate with the UN, U.S. policy shifted to the creation of a separate government in South Korea, capable of self-defense. The UN, bowing to American pressure, supervised and certified elections in the South alone during May 1948, resulting in the formation of the Republic of Korea (ROK). Responding in kind, the Soviets sponsored formation in the North of the Democratic People's Republic of Korea (DPRK) in September. In the South Pres. Syngman Rhee formed a repressive, authoritarian, anticommunist regime, while in the North, Kim Il Sung followed Moscow's model of political, economic, and social development. Soviet troops pulled out of the North late in 1948, underscoring the need for U.S. withdrawal. But a major uprising in October 1948 against the Rhee regime persuaded Truman to postpone military disengagement until June 1949.

Truman believed South Korea could survive and prosper without U.S. military protection because he assumed that Moscow would not allow North Korea to attack. Sec. of State Dean Acheson's exclusion of South Korea from the U.S. "defensive perimeter" in 1950 later prompted charges that he had given the communists a "green light" to invade.

Invasion of the South. On the morning of June 25, 1950, North Korea invaded South Korea. Revisionists later accused South Korea of provoking the conflict, but Soviet and Chinese documents

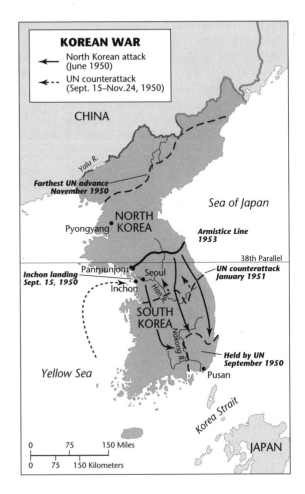

KOREAN WAR

← North Korean attack (June 1950)

←-- UN counterattack (Sept. 15–Nov. 24, 1950)

CHINA

Yalu R.

Farthest UN advance November 1950

NORTH KOREA

Pyongyang

Sea of Japan

Armistice Line 1953

38th Parallel

Inchon landing Sept. 15, 1950

Panmunjom

Seoul

Han R.

UN counterattack January 1951

Inchon

SOUTH KOREA

Naktong R.

Held by UN September 1950

Yellow Sea

Pusan

Korea Strait

JAPAN

0   75   150 Miles

0   75   150 Kilometers

have confirmed that North Korea planned and initiated the war with Stalin's assent. Had Kim Il Sung not been bent on reuniting Korea, however, it appears there would have been no war.

Truman announced on June 27 that the United States was sending aid to the ROK, while strengthening local defenses against communist expansion elsewhere in Asia. Yet Washington did not commit ground troops in Korea for almost a week, referring the matter instead to the UN and banking on South Korea's ability to defend itself. After North Korea ignored a UN resolution calling upon the DPRK to cease hostilities and withdraw, the Security Council passed a second resolution urging members to help defend South Korea. Moscow was unable to veto these measures because it was boycotting the Security Council to protest its refusal to seat the People's Republic of China (PRC). The United States was able to portray its actions as an example of collective security, although it contributed far more men and material than the other 15 nations who fought on the UN side.

Truman committed ground combat forces on June 30 after Gen. Douglas MacArthur, the U.S. commander in East Asia, advised that, without them, communist conquest of South Korea was certain. The president never asked Congress to declare war, endorsing a newsman's description of Korea as a "police action." North Korea's advance continued until UN forces retreated to the Pusan Perimeter, a rectangular area in the southeast corner of the peninsula. But despite this seemingly desperate situation, Truman's advisers, certain that battlefield victory was inevitable, debated throughout July whether to seek forcible reunification once the communist army had been thrown out of the South. State Department officials argued persuasively that the United States should destroy North Korea's army and then hold elections for a government to rule a united Korea. U.S. military leaders opposed this change in war aims until July 31, when UN defensive lines finally stabilized.

Invasion of the North. MacArthur launched his first counterattack on August 7. By then Tru-

man had decided to authorize an attempt at forcible reunification. MacArthur already had devised plans for a counteroffensive, which included an amphibious landing behind enemy lines. The Joint Chiefs of Staff (JCS) had serious concerns about MacArthur's intention to land at the port of Inchon, 35 miles west of Seoul, because of high tides and narrow access. But the Inchon landing on September 15 succeeded brilliantly and two weeks later, after liberating Seoul, UN forces were poised for an advance across the parallel. Truman's plan for the conquest of North Korea provided for only Korean forces in the most northern provinces, reflecting fears of provoking Soviet or Chinese entry and igniting global war. After the DPRK refused to surrender, the UN on October 7 passed a resolution instructing MacArthur to "ensure conditions of stability throughout Korea."

The PRC perceived the UN offensive as a grave threat to China's security. Chinese Premier Zhou Enlai tried to avoid war, telling the Indian ambassador on October 2 that China would intervene if U.S. forces crossed the 38th parallel. U.S. leaders thought the Chinese were bluffing. On October 15, MacArthur, at a personal meeting with Truman at Wake Island, stated that "if the Chinese tried to get down to Pyongyang [the DPRK capital] there would be the greatest slaughter." Even after the first clash

American and North Korean negotiators sign a cease-fire agreement during peace talks ending the Korean War in 1953.

between the UN and Chinese "volunteers" later that month, MacArthur remained supremely confident, despite Truman's refusal on November 8 to approve bombing of Chinese positions in Manchuria because Britain objected. On November 24 MacArthur launched his "Home by Christmas Offensive" with U.S. troops in the vanguard. Two days later China counterattacked in force, sending the UN into a massive retreat. Panic gripped Washington as Truman declared a state of national emergency.

Military Stalemate. After Communist China intervened, Truman decided to fight a "limited war" in Korea to restore the prewar status quo. MacArthur opposed this strategy, insisting that escalation or evacuation were the only options. By March 1951 Gen. Matthew B. Ridgway, the U.S. Eighth Army commander, the commander in the field, had driven the Chinese forces back into North Korea. Truman then planned to propose a cease-fire, but MacArthur scuttled the peace initiative when he issued a humiliating ultimatum to the communists that demanded immediate surrender. Truman ignited a firestorm of criticism when he recalled MacArthur on April 11, but MacArthur had been insubordinate, and Truman did not want the general to control atomic weapons recently deployed for possible use in Korea. On returning home, MacArthur, in a televised address to Congress, said that there was "no substitute for victory." During Senate hearings, the testimony of JCS Chairman Gen. Omar N. Bradley effectively rebutted MacArthur's views. By then most Americans just wanted an end to "Mr. Truman's War."

Meanwhile UN forces had repulsed two Chinese communist offensives, establishing a defensive position just north of the parallel. Battlefield stalemate apparently persuaded the belligerents to seek a truce. After the Soviet ambassador to the UN publicly advocated a cease-fire, truce talks opened in July in Korea at Kaesong. A nasty initial exchange over the U.S. proposal for a demilitarized zone deep in North Korea created an acrimonious tone. After violations of the neutral zone caused a two-month suspension, the talks moved to Panmunjom, where haggling began on inspection procedures to enforce the truce. Agreements emerged that the demilitarized zone would follow the line of battle and a postwar conference would discuss withdrawal of foreign troops and reunification. But then the talks deadlocked on the issue of repatriation of the prisoners of war (POWs). Not all the communist prisoners wished to return home. While Truman insisted on nonforcible repatriation, the communists demanded, as the Geneva Convention required, return of all POWs. This issue led the UN to suspend the talks in October 1952.

Armistice and Aftermath. Angry American voters elected Dwight D. Eisenhower president in November 1952 largely because they expected him to end the very unpopular war in Korea. His policy was to signal that the alternative to a cease-fire was an expanded war employing atomic weapons. These threats may have influenced the PRC, but internal economic problems might have been more important incentives. Stalin's death on March 5 added to China's sense of political vulnerability, causing the communists to break the logjam at Panmunjom. After accepting a UN proposal for exchanging sick and wounded POWs late in March, the two sides agreed in June to turn over those POWs resisting repatriation to a committee of neutral nations. But Rhee, who opposed any armistice that left Korea divided, almost torpedoed the pending cease-fire when he released 27,000 Korean POWs. Eisenhower bought Rhee's acceptance of the armistice in July 1953 with promises of money and a security pact.

From 1941 to 1953 the United States paid a steadily rising price for its involvement in Korea, as it later did in Vietnam. The Korean War cost the United States 33,000 dead and 105,000 wounded. Because of it Congress approved a costly rearmament program. Truman ended his term as the most unpopular president in U.S. history despite his courage in defending the national security and the Constitution. U.S. relations with China were poisoned for 20 years, especially after Washington persuaded the UN to condemn the PRC for aggression in Korea. U.S. leaders spoke about collective security, but the Korean War severely strained relations between Washington and its allies. And the United States was now more closely tied to odious regimes in Taiwan and South Korea. Worse, the Korean War convinced U.S. leaders that use of direct military power alone could contain what they now saw as a far more dangerous Soviet threat to the entire world.

—JAMES I. MATRAY

See Also: *MacArthur, Douglas; Truman, Harry S.*

BIBLIOGRAPHY: Cumings, Bruce, *The Origins of the Korean War,* 2 vols. (Princeton Univ. Press 1981, 1990); MacDonald, Callum A., *Korea: The War before Vietnam* (The Free Press 1986); Matray, James I., *The Reluctant Crusade: American Foreign Policy in Korea, 1941-1950* (Univ. of Hawaii Press 1985); Stueck, William, *The Korean War: An International History* (Princeton Univ. Press 1995).

■ **KRENITSYN, PETR KUZ'MICH (?-1770),** Russian naval officer and explorer. Leading a Russian expedition, the second such venture since Vitus Bering's voyage of 1741, Krenitsyn surveyed the Aleutian Island chain beginning in 1768. After wintering on Unimak Island, he returned to the Kamchatka Peninsula in Siberia on July 30, 1769. Krenitsyn drowned a year later. His second-in-command, M. D. Levashev, returned to St. Petersburg and in 1777 completed a map of the Aleutian Islands based on the expedition's discoveries.

See Also: Exploration and Discovery.

■ **KRUTCH, JOSEPH WOOD (1893-1970),** literary critic. A native of Knoxville, Tennessee, Krutch was a professor of English literature at Columbia University from 1937 to 1952. During this time he also served as drama critic for *The Nation* magazine. His works of literary criticism include *Comedy and Conscience after the Restoration* (1924), *Edgar Allan Poe—A Study in Genius* (1926), and *Henry David Thoreau* (1948). Krutch also wrote analyses of modern culture, including *The Modern Temper* (1929) and *The Measure of Man* (1954).

■ **KU KLUX KLAN (KKK),** name of several secret societies. The first was a white supremacist organization founded in 1866 by Confederate veterans to terrorize blacks and their white allies in the South during Reconstruction. Using elaborate rituals, hooded costumes, and midnight rides as well as outright violence, it aimed to keep blacks from voting and aid the return to power of conservative white Democrats.

The second Klan was a national organization founded in 1915 by William J. Simmons. It was anti-Catholic, anti-Semitic, and anti-immigrant as well as antiblack. After achieving considerable success as a social club in the 1920s, it declined when several leaders were convicted of serious crimes and members could no longer pay dues during the Depression.

Since the 1950s terrorist groups calling themselves the KKK have used violence to intimidate civil rights workers. Eventually law enforcement agencies effectively suppressed most of this activity.

See Also: Race and Racism; Reconstruction.

Large rallies in the 1920s revived the Ku Klux Klan in both the North and South. Preaching its doctrine of "100 percent Americanism," the new Klan not only advocated hatred of African Americans, but immigrants as well.

■ **KU KLUX KLAN CASES,** Supreme Court decisions that affected Ku Klux Klan activities. Through the Civil Rights Enforcement Act of 1870-71, the Radical Republican–controlled Congress was responding to the spread of violence against recently freed slaves who attempted to exercise their right to vote. The laws criminalized any coercive activity that intended to restrict or prevent blacks' political participation. In the first KKK case, *United States* v. *Harris* (1883), the Court found unconstitutional the Civil Rights Enforcement Act of 1871. Writing for the Court, Justice William Burnham Woods held that the 14th Amendment did not extend to individuals but only to the states. Thus Congress had acted unconstitutionally by creating a class of federal crimes under the 14th Amendment. In *Ex parte Yarbrough* (1884), however, the Court upheld the Enforcement Act of 1870 and broadened its interpretation of the 15th Amendment. The Court let stand the conviction of Georgia Ku Klux Klan member Jasper Yarbrough for preventing a black from voting. Writing for a unanimous Court, Justice Samuel Miller stated that the federal government had the right to bar racial discrimination in voting in order to uphold the 15th Amendment.

See Also: *Ku Klux Klan (KKK); Supreme Court.*

■ **KUNIYOSHI, YASAO (1893-1953),** painter and promoter of American artists. Born in Okayama, Japan, Kuniyoshi was trained as a weaver and textile dyer. He came to the United States to study industrial production in 1906. Kuniyoshi, whose work shows both East Asian and European influences, painted both human figures, as in *Child* (1923), and landscapes, as in *Nevadaville* (1942). The founder and first president of Artists' Equity Association, Kuniyoshi also supported other organizations dedicated to furthering the cause of American artists, such as the Artists' Congress and the American Society of Painters, Sculptors, and Engravers.

See Also: *Painting.*

■ **KWAKIUTL INDIANS.** *See:* *Northwest Coast Indians.*

■ **KWAME TOURÉ.** *See:* *Carmichael, Stokely (Kwame Touré).*

L

■ **LABOR, DEPARTMENT OF,** cabinet department of the U.S. government that oversees many federal workplace regulations and employment programs. First established as the Bureau of Labor within the Interior Department (1884), it became an independent agency (1888) and was elevated to cabinet status as part of the Department of Commerce and Labor (1903). The separate Department of Labor was created (1913) during Pres. Woodrow Wilson's administration.

■ **LABOR MOVEMENT,** diverse social and political movement in American history designed to improve the conditions of wage earners. The American labor movement has adopted a variety of forms and objectives over the last 200 years as working men and women have sought to improve their lot in life by concerted action under changing circumstances. Although the term labor movement has usually been identified simply with labor unions since World War II, it had previously encompassed a wider variety of institutions.

Between 1827 and 1832 working men's political parties contested elections in 35 towns. Although the parties had little success in electing workers to public office, they cultivated a sense of common interest among craftsmen of diverse occupations and stimulated discussion about poverty, schooling, the hours of labor, and popular liberties.

That discussion bore fruit in the rapid spread of trade unions after 1834 and in a number of labor actions. A general strike for a 10-hour day in Philadelphia (1835) and the organization of strikes by female wage earners in Lowell and Lynn, Massachusetts, were early examples of concerted labor activities. A struggle in Rhode Island to enfranchise working men culminated in armed confrontation with the state authorities (1843).

Although the crippling of trade unions by the depression of 1837-43 and the subsequent upsurge of anti-Catholic movements undercut these early efforts by labor, the New York Industrial Congress of 1850 signaled a vigorous revival of the movement in large cities. In New England conventions of women textile workers and reformers petitioned for state laws restricting the workday in mills to 10 hours. This environment also stimulated a proliferation of utopian writings and communities, each offering various formulas for a society without exploitation and want.

Before 1850, however, there were more slaves than wage earners in the United States, and slaves had no opportunity to assemble and petition. Free African Americans of northern cities often appealed to the public on behalf of the slaves through conventions and publications and also assisted individual slaves to escape from bondage. Although many white wage earners supported the abolitionist movement, labor organizations (with the exception of the New England conventions) shunned the question of slavery, and virtually all antebellum trade unions restricted their membership to whites.

Labor in the Gilded Age. The rapid growth of manufacturing between 1843 and 1873 and the demise of slavery in 1865 generated a new and different labor movement. Trade unions enrolled more than 300,000 members and demanded that state legislatures establish an eight-hour day. When such laws enacted by eight states proved ineffectual, workers in Chicago (1867), the Pennsylvania mines (1868), and New York City (1872) struck to enforce them. The National Labor Union, created in 1866, declared the eight-hour day, the cultivation of trade unions, cooperative manufacturing, and a labor party as its primary objectives. Unlike the pre–Civil War labor movement, it also summoned white and African-American workers to join in the common cause.

Between the 1870s and the 1890s the United States became the world's leading industrial producer, while a growing urban working class produced a movement in which trade unionists,

Knights of Labor, and socialists contended for influence. Trade unions strove for a gradual improvement of life for their members through improved earnings and mutual protection. In 1886, major national unions joined together to form the American Federation of Labor (AFL) in order to lend each other support in dealing with employers and the government.

Another labor organization, the Knights of Labor (1869-1921), sought to gather "into one fold all branches of honorable toil, without regard to nationality, sex, creed or color." The Chinese, however, were excluded, and the Knights fought to exclude them from the country. Functioning as a union, fraternal order, political organization, and promoter of cooperatives, the Knights were at times both a rival and an ally to trade unions. By 1886 they had grown quickly to between 750,000 and 1,000,000 members. Effective employer opposition, internal dissension, and the defection of important segments to the new AFL, however, undermined the Knights' influence after that point.

The movement for social ownership of the means of production found expression in the U.S. sections of the International Workingmen's Association (IWA) after 1868. By 1880 the movement had developed two main branches: the Socialist Labor Party (SLP), which sought to reach its goal through power in government, and the International Working People's Association (IWPA), which preached the abolition of government. The IWPA exerted great influence in Chicago and Milwaukee during the great strikes of May 1, 1886, for the eight-hour day. After a bloody confrontation in Chicago's Haymarket Square eight of its members were tried for conspiracy to murder a policeman, and four of them were hanged on Nov. 11, 1887.

The American Railway Union (ARU), another influential labor organization, enrolled all grades of workers and endorsed government ownership of railroads and mines. The ARU grew rapidly to 150,000 members before it was crushed by the government during the Pullman boycott of 1894. The Socialist Party of America fused the remnants of the ARU with defecting segments of the SLP in 1901 to form the country's most influential socialist organization.

Although socialist delegates remained an important force in the early AFL, the AFL president,

Samuel Gompers, and other dominant leaders grew increasingly antagonistic to their proposals. A successful strike of midwestern coal miners in 1897 stimulated unprecedented union growth and made the negotiation of trade agreements with employers the AFL's primary objective. Widespread use of court injunctions against unions by hostile business groups, however, drove the AFL into open alliance with the Democratic party, which opposed such injunctions by 1908.

The founding of the Industrial Workers of the World (IWW) in 1905 challenged the basic practices of the AFL. The IWW solicited the support of all workers—regardless of occupation, race, or sex—and spurned contracts, strike funds, and electoral involvement. Its proclaimed goal was to "take possession of the earth and the machinery of production, and abolish the wages system."

Labor from the New Era to the New Deal. The booming economy of World War I (1914-18) enabled unions to enroll 20 percent of potential members. It led to a tightening of governmental regulation and the appearance of dissident currents within the AFL. The depression of the early 1920s, however, enabled employers to drive unions out of most heavy industry and encouraged the remaining unions to collaborate with the small, local-market firms. The main legacy of wartime militancy for labor was on the political front: the success of Minnesota's Farmer-Labor party and the independent campaign of the pro-labor Robert M. La Follette for president in 1924.

The New Deal of the 1930s both resuscitated union growth and drew the labor movement into tight alliance with the dominant Democratic party. Legislation assisting unions culminated in the Wagner Act (1935), which declared that "encouraging the practice and procedure of collective bargaining" was "the policy of the United States." The impatience of activists in heavy industry with the AFL's cautious legacy of the 1920s led to the formation (1938) of the rival Congress of Industrial Organizations (CIO).

Tactics and goals underwent changes during the 1930s. Sit-down strikes brought union bargaining into the nation's largest corporations. The new unions supported a welfare state but sought their goals through the Democrats, rather than through farmer-labor or socialist parties. By 1944 the CIO had become a central element of a dominant urban-liberal coalition in national politics.

Labor During the Cold War. The postwar years saw unions expand to their all-time peak of 33 percent of potential members (1953). Living standards were also bolstered through industry-wide bargaining. But anticommunism became a centerpiece of government policy in the late 1940s, leading to the expulsion of nine unions from the CIO on charges of "communist-domination" (1949) and the marginalization of left-wing influences in national life. The AFL and CIO merged in 1955 as their leaders agreed that rising productivity coupled with union contracts was the key to improved living standards. Late in the 1950s, labor came under congressional scrutiny, as the power of racketeers in several major unions provided a target for investigations. The Landrum-Griffin Act regulating internal practices of unions (1959) was one outcome of the hearings.

The 1960s were a stormy decade for the AFL-CIO. While membership declined steadily in the traditional manufacturing sectors of unionism, public employees and especially school teachers flocked into unions to the point where they outnumbered private-sector production workers. The civil rights movement of the 1960s evoked support from union leaders but also unleashed criticism of the racial practices of the unions themselves. In foreign affairs, the AFL-CIO loyally championed Pres. Lyndon B. Johnson's war in Vietnam against its critics.

In response to inflation both government and management undertook to roll back union gains during the 1970s. The deindustrialization of historic manufacturing centers and the international mobility of business made strike-breaking and concession bargaining commonplace after 1978 and ground down total union membership to less than 15 percent of potential members. However, union officials committed to a more aggressive response and to revitalized alliances with other liberal constituencies won elections in major unions during the 1990s and in the AFL-CIO itself in 1995.

—DAVID MONTGOMERY

See Also: AFL-CIO; American Federation of Labor (AFL); Congress of Industrial Organizations (CIO); Industrial Revolution; Industrial Unions; Trade Unions; Work; individual biographies.

BIBLIOGRAPHY: Dubofsky, Melvyn, *The State and Labor in Modern America* (Univ. of North Carolina Press 1994); Lichtenstein, Nelson, *The Most Dangerous Man in Detroit: Walter Reuther and the Fate of American Labor* (Basic Books 1995); Montgomery, David, *Fall of the House of Labor: The Workplace, the State, and American Labor Activism, 1865-1925* (Cambridge Univ. Press 1987); Wilentz, Sean, *Chants Democratic: New York City and the Rise of the American Working Class, 1788-1850* (Oxford Univ. Press 1984).

■ **LACROSSE,** field sport derived from baggataway, an American Indian ritual game originated by the Algonquians and played in what is now the eastern United States and Canada. Players carry and toss a ball with a netted stick resembling a bishop's *crosier,* whence the name. The game was first played by whites in Canada in 1844, and rules were codified in the 1860s calling for nine field players and a goalkeeper on each team. An indoor version of the game, box lacrosse, is played with six on a team. Lacrosse is the national sport of Canada, and since the late 19th century, it has been popular at U.S. schools and colleges in the Northeast. The game is now played internationally and has long been popular as a women's sport.

See Also: Sports.

BIBLIOGRAPHY: Scott, Bob, *Lacrosse: Technique and Tradition* (Johns Hopkins Univ. Press 1976).

■ **LA FARGE, JOHN (1835-1910),** painter and stained glass artist. La Farge was born in New York City. After attending St. Mary's College in Maryland and briefly studying law, he went to Paris in 1856. Upon his return, he studied with William Morris Hunt in Newport, Rhode Island. From 1860 to 1876, La Farge painted primarily landscape paintings; he then began executing murals and large panel paintings for public buildings. His first large-scale commission was a series of murals in Trinity Church, Boston (1876-77). La Farge also designed murals for the Church of the Incarnation (1885) and the Church of the Ascension (1888), both in New York City, as well as lunettes for the Supreme Court Room at the Minnesota State Capitol in St. Paul (1904). He began experimenting with stained glass in the mid-1870s and developed opalescent glass (glass clouded by fissures and bubbles). In 1893 he wrote a pamphlet entitled *The American Art of Stained Glass.* His work in stained glass includes the Columbia University Chapel (1879) and William Vanderbilt House (1881), both in New York City.

See Also: Painting.

■ LAFAYETTE, MARIE JOSEPH PAUL YVES ROCH GILBERT DU MOTIER, MARQUIS DE (1757-1834),

French army officer and American Revolutionary War general. Lafayette was born at the family chateau of Chavaniac in Auvergne, France. A wealthy French nobleman who was orphaned at the age of 13, he began a military career at 14 and married the well-to-do Marie Adrienne Françoise de Noailles at the age of 16. Moved by America's struggle for independence, Lafayette traveled to America at his own expense in 1777. Although he was only 19, Congress somewhat reluctantly commissioned him a major general without a command.

George Washington was impressed with the eager young Frenchman who spoke little English and befriended him. The marquis fought at Brandywine in September 1777, where he received a slight wound in the left thigh. In early December 1777, Lafayette assumed command of a division of Virginia light troops. The marquis proved his loyalty to Washington during the hardships of the winter at Valley Forge. He also participated in actions at Barren Hill and distinguished himself as well during the Monmouth campaign. In 1778 Washington gave him command of two veteran brigades at Newport. Lafayette's activities helped lay the groundwork for the Comte Rochambeau's expeditionary force, which was sent by France to America in 1780 to serve under Washington.

Perhaps Lafayette's renown as a soldier was best shown at Green Spring in 1781, when he rescued Anthony Wayne's Pennsylvania troops from a trap set by Lord Cornwallis. Lafayette later also participated in the subsequent siege at Yorktown, which ensured American victory over the British. The marquis returned to France in December 1781.

Lafayette revisited the United States in 1784 at Washington's invitation, and over the next five years assisted Thomas Jefferson as a minister to France on various political and economic matters. Lafayette's popularity in France reached its height in 1790, just one year after the French Revolution. Two years later, however, with the rise of the fiercely antiroyalist Jacobins, he fled to Belgium and was subsequently imprisoned by the Austrians and Prussians. Napoleon Bonaparte released him in September 1797, but on his return to France, the marquis found his fortunes destroyed. Declining Jefferson's offers of office, including the governorship of Louisiana, Lafayette kept out of politics and cultivated his estate at La Grange, 43 miles outside Paris.

In 1824 he accepted Pres. James Monroe's invitation to revisit America. Hailed as the symbol of French support for the American Revolution, Lafayette represented the integrity and idealism that formed the bond between the United States and France.

—MARTHA J. KING

See Also: Monmouth, Battle of; Revolution, American; Yorktown, Siege of.

BIBLIOGRAPHY: Bernier, Olivier, *Lafayette: Hero of Two Worlds* (Dutton 1983); Gottshalk, Louis R., *Lafayette and the Close of the American Revolution* (Univ. of Chicago Press 1942); Idzerda, Stanley J., ed., *Lafayette in the Age of the American Revolution: Selected Letters and Papers, 1776-1790,* 6 vols. (Cornell Univ. Press 1977).

■ LAFITTE, JEAN (1780-1821),

French adventurer who directed a profitable smuggling operation near New Orleans. During the War of 1812, British officers approached Lafitte and offered him lucrative compensation to help in a planned attack on New Orleans. After delaying the British, he informed Louisiana officials about the whole affair. Although U.S. officials dismantled his smuggling operation, Lafitte and his men fought with the Americans in the Battle of New Orleans and earned pardons.

See Also: New Orleans, Battle of; War of 1812.

■ LA FOLLETTE, ROBERT (1855-1925),

progressive political leader and U.S. senator. Born into a farming family in Primrose, Wisconsin, La Follette attended the University of Wisconsin in Madison and there drew inspiration from its crusading president, John Bascom. An ambitious lawyer and originally a faithful McKinley Republican, La Follette increasingly viewed the corporate "special interests" and the political "bosses" as allied against the "people."

La Follette's campaign oratory and political energy brought him the Wisconsin governorship in 1900. He had run on a platform of fair taxation, open primaries, state regulation of the trusts, and protection of natural resources. Closely associated with the "Wisconsin Idea" of clean, nonpartisan administration, La Follette quickly became a nationally admired reform figure.

La Follette was elected to the U.S. Senate in 1905 and remained there until his death, a scourge of conservatives and corruption. Considered a leading potential candidate for the new Progressive party in 1912, he was beaten out by Theodore Roosevelt, whom he thought a militarist and a bully. In 1917 La Follette distinguished himself as one of only two senators to vote against U.S. entry into World War I.

Repudiated by his Republican base, La Follette quickly recast himself as the leader of Wisconsin's Progressive party, a farmer- and worker-based movement. In 1924 he ran for president as the Progressive party candidate, winning only Wisconsin but polling almost 6 million votes out of 30 million cast.

See Also: Progressive Party; Progressivism.
BIBLIOGRAPHY: Kaye, Harvey, "Robert La Follette," in Buhle, Mari Jo, et al., eds., *The American Radical* (Routledge 1994); Thelen, David, *Robert La Follette and the Insurgent Spirit* (Univ. of Wisconsin Press 1976).

■ LA GUARDIA, FIORELLO HENRY (1882-1947),

colorful mayor of New York City (1934-45). Born in New York City of immigrant parents, La Guardia, a progressive, reform-minded Republican who frequently voted across party lines, was first elected to the U.S. House of Representatives in 1916. He left Congress to serve as an army major in World War I. He was reelected in 1920 and served until 1933, when he was elected mayor of New York on a fusion ticket backed by both Republican and Democratic reform elements. La Guardia's administration was marked both by his efforts to curb vice and corruption and by his sheer zest for the office. He rode fire trucks, helped smash slot machines seized from illegal gambling operations, and never tired of the spotlight. During a newspaper strike, he went on the radio to read the Sunday comics to the city's children. At the outbreak of World War II he served as head of the U.S. Office of Civil Defense (1941-42). He held the office of mayor until 1945, and in 1946 served as director general of the United Nations Relief and Rehabilitation Administration.

See Also: New Deal.
BIBLIOGRAPHY: Kessner, Thomas, *Fiorello H. La Guardia and the Making of Modern New York* (McGraw-Hill 1989).

■ LAISSEZ-FAIRE,

theory that an economic system functions best when free from governmental interference, first articulated by Adam Smith in *The Wealth of Nations* (1776). Smith argued that if one left the market alone and let economic players act in their own self-interest and compete against each other, the system would achieve a natural rate of progress. Democratic-Republicans adopted the philosophy of laissez-faire and free trade, while the Federalists and Hamiltonians supported government protection of industry through tariffs and a government-sponsored national bank. President Jackson opposed any such coalition between government and business, ironically turning the laissez-faire rationale for republican simplicity into a justification for the growth of unregulated centers of economic power far greater than that of the "monster" national bank.

Powerful businessmen in the late 19th century combined Darwin's ideas with laissez-faire theories, arguing that government interference through the regulation of business and the graduated income tax impeded progress by helping the unfit survive. Because monopolistic corporations were capable of subverting competition, reformers began to demand government regulation and rejected their earlier support for laissez-faire. Although Progressive reforms, the New Deal, and social programs of the 1950s and 1960s moved the United States ever farther away from laissez-faire, limiting government intervention has gained increasing support in recent years.

See Also: Free Trade; Progressivism; Tariffs.
BIBLIOGRAPHY: Fine, Sidney, *Laissez-Faire and the General Welfare State* (Univ. of Michigan Press 1956).

■ **LAKE CHAMPLAIN, BATTLE OF (1814),** American victory in the War of 1812. U.S. Capt. Thomas MacDonough, given charge of a small, ramshackle fleet on this lake between Vermont and New York, defeated his British counterpart, Capt. George Downie, on September 11. MacDonough's flagship, *Saratoga*, had only 26 guns to the British *Confiance*'s 37. MacDonough's victory ruined British plans for a joint land and water offensive requiring control of the lake, and it also provided a needed morale boost to the American public.

See Also: War of 1812.

■ **LAKE ERIE, BATTLE OF (1813),** U.S. victory in the War of 1812. U.S. Commodore Oliver Hazard Perry raced to construct a fleet on the lake to counter a British force under Commodore Robert Barclay. In the September 10 battle, Barclay lacked adequate supplies, and Perry's tactics were superior. Perry's legendary report to Gen. William Henry Harrison—"We have met the enemy and they are ours"—spurred the general to pursue and demolish a British-Indian force at the Battle of the Thames River.

See Also: Perry, Oliver Hazard; War of 1812.

■ **LAMAR, JOSEPH RUCKER (1857-1916),** associate justice of the U.S. Supreme Court (1911-16). Born in Elbert County, Georgia, he practiced law and sat on the Georgia Supreme Court before being named to the U.S. Supreme Court by Pres. William Howard Taft.

See Also: Supreme Court.

■ **LAMAR, LUCIUS QUINTUS CINCINNATUS (1825-93),** U.S. representative (1857-60, 1873-77), U.S. senator (1877-85), and associate justice of the U.S. Supreme Court (1888-93). A Putnam County, Georgia, native and a loyal Southerner, Lamar's tenure in Congress was interrupted by his service to the Confederacy during the Civil War. During Reconstruction Lamar earned widespread respect for his reasonableness. On the Court he distinguished himself as a staunch defender of states' rights. Consistent with these views was his dissent in *United States* v. *Texas* (1892), where he disputed the assumption that the federal courts automatically have original jurisdiction when the United States is a litigant.

See Also: Supreme Court.

■ **LAND, EDWIN (1909-91),** scientist who invented the Polaroid instant camera. Born in Bridgeport, Connecticut, Land entered Harvard in 1930 but left as a freshman to conduct research on his own. In 1932, he invented Polaroid, a substance that allowed objects to be seen without glare. He developed optical systems for military use during World War II and announced his most famous invention in 1947: the "instant camera" that could produce a complete photograph in 60 seconds. This camera netted over $5 million in 1948. Teaching at Massachusetts Institute of Technology (1956), holding 533 patents, and building a commercial empire, Land successfully combined the roles of scientist, inventor, and businessman.

See Also: Invention; Photography; Science.

■ **LAND COMPANIES,** private investment companies that played a significant role in the development of the North American frontier, particularly in the late 18th and early 19th centuries. In the 1750s and 1760s several groups of investors, including the Ohio Company of Virginia and the "suffering traders" of Pennsylvania, schemed unsuccessfully to get Great Britain to grant them control of large tracts of land in the Ohio Valley.

After the American Revolution the number of land companies mushroomed. The Ohio Company of Associates purchased millions of acres from the U.S. government in 1787. Other companies, including the Holland Land Company, which acquired more than 3 million acres in western New York in the 1790s, bought tracts from individuals. Finally some companies acquired land from states. In 1795 Georgia sold 35 million acres—most of what is now Mississippi and Alabama—to four land companies for $500,000. Later revoked by the legislature, this "Yazoo" land sale became a source of great political and judicial controversy.

Historians have understandably focused on the greed and deception that characterized much of the activity of land companies. Their purpose, after all, was to make money for their investors. Typically company agents lobbied governments for the right to purchase a huge tract of land at the cheapest possible price. In return the company promised to secure, settle, and develop the land it acquired. While this arrangement smacks of corruption, it was a common practice for financially strapped, premodern governments to contract many of their responsibilities to private groups. In many ways American land companies continued a practice begun by English joint-stock corporations such as the Massachusetts Bay Company and the Virginia Company in initially settling North America.

In theory the sale of land to companies benefited both public and private interests. Investors could not make the profits they wanted until they had improved their holdings enough to attract customers. Development meant ensuring the safety and property of settlers, as well as providing some kind of basic infrastructure to facilitate transportation and commerce. While speculators might make a financial killing, they also relieved governments of some of the costs—and risks—of securing their borders.

In practice speculators (many of whom never moved to the frontier) usually overestimated the expense and time involved in the development of distant lands. They also underestimated the tenacity of both Indians and European American frontierspeople in resisting their plans for orderly development. Most land companies were thus economic failures, although the imprint of their ambitious designs often remained on the landscapes they tried to develop.

In the 19th century, with a growing legal insistence on a clear-cut separation of private and public interests, land companies began to function more like private corporations. Governments continued to rely on land grants to companies as a way of developing the frontier, as in the ceding of public land along the rights-of-way of the Union Pacific and Central Pacific railroads to encourage the construction of a transcontinental railroad in the 1860s. But in general the blurred line between private and public interests was clarified and the commingling of government and corporate interests came to be seen as simple corruption.

—ANDREW CAYTON

See Also: Frontier in American History; Yazoo Affair.
BIBLIOGRAPHY: Abernethy, Thomas P., *Western Lands and the American Revolution* (Appleton-Century 1937); Shaw, Livermore, *Early American Land Companies* (Commonwealth Fund 1939).

■ **LAND POLICY,** governmental policies on the disposition of land, among the most contested and crucial arenas of government action from the beginning of European settlement in North America. Throughout the colonial era and the first century of American independence, policymakers debated how to shift public lands into private hands. Beginning at the end of the 19th century, however, the federal government broke from this principle, and during the 20th century, national policy turned toward the preservation of the public domain.

Extinguishing Indian claims and establishing private property rights was the cornerstone of colonial land policy. To encourage immigration to North America, British colonial officials offered grants of various sizes. Headrights, which provided a set amount of acreage to emigrants (or to those who paid the cost of transportation for Europeans to go to North America), were a common inducement. To increase populations and extend the area of European settlement, policymakers also recognized what were called "corn" and "cabin" rights, whereby occupants were given ownership of specific tracts on the basis of their having cultivated a minimum number of acres and having made other required improvements.

These promotional schemes, which typically involved small amounts of land, were overshadowed by the enormous grants that were made to the wealthy and the well-connected. Individuals and companies favored with such grants, which sometimes ran into the hundreds of thousands of acres, were in turn expected to settle their lands with tenants or buyers. But more than increasing population, vast grants motivated speculation on a grand scale and prompted unrest among the growing ranks of landless American colonists.

Federal Period. After the American Revolution the U.S. government inherited responsibility for the disposition of the public domain. By the 1783 Treaty of Paris with the British and the 1803 Louisiana Purchase from the French, the United States gained sovereignty over millions of acres. But these lands were occupied by Indians too powerful to be removed. Disinclined to wage expensive wars against the Indians of the Northwest Territory, yet determined to assert federal control over western territories, the administration of Pres.

George Washington (1789-97) attempted to restrain the rate of frontier expansion and to raise substantial revenues from the sale of lands. As in the colonial era, the land policy of the new nation generated discontent among western settlers.

By contrast, the election of Thomas Jefferson to the presidency in 1800 and the era that followed boosted the hopes of homesteaders (at the expense especially of Indian occupants). Following Jeffersonian principles, Congress made it easier for settlers to become landowners by bringing down the price of the public domain, reducing minimum purchase requirements, and easing terms of payment. The enactment of a preemption statute in 1841 extended preferences to squatters who desired to purchase the lands they occupied. The Homestead Act of 1862 completed the trend, offering 160 acres free (or with only a modest fee) to any person who would inhabit and develop the tract for five years.

Old controversies did not disappear, however, because new legislation left agrarian promises unfulfilled. Federal policy did not eliminate tenancy. Nor did it inhibit large-scale engrossment, as was exemplified by the bequest of 174 million acres to railroad companies. Most of the land still available for would-be homesteaders lay in arid and semiarid territories in which 160 acres was insufficient to support a family farm.

Late 19th Century-Present. During the last third of the 19th century, a series of acts attempted to address the problems of aridity by permitting settlers to augment the size of homesteads if they planted trees or irrigated fields. The same years, however, witnessed the gathering of support for the conservation of natural resources, including land. A growing awareness of limits led to the passage of laws that reserved portions of the public domain from private ownership.

In the early decades of the 20th century, the drift toward permanent public management resulted in the creation of scores of national forests and national parks and culminated with the passage of the Taylor Grazing Act of 1934. Yet, while that act effectively closed off the era of homesteading, it did not end the pursuit of private advantage on public lands. Nor has any subsequent legislation settled the questions of private rights versus public interest and profit versus preservation that have long concerned the shapers of American land policy.

—STEPHEN ARON

See Also: Frontier in American History.

BIBLIOGRAPHY: Gates, Paul, *History of Public Land Law Development* (U.S. Public Land Law Review Commission 1968); Robbins, Roy, *Out Landed Heritage: The Public Domain, 1776-1936* (Princeton Univ. Press 1942); Rohrbough, Malcolm, *The Land Office Business: The Settlement and Administration of American Public Lands, 1789-1837* (Oxford Univ. Press 1968).

■ **LANGE, DOROTHEA (1895-1965),** photographer, born in Hoboken, New Jersey. During the 1920s and 1930s she photographed workers in San Francisco and collaborated with her husband, economist Paul Taylor, to produce *American Exodus* (1939), a report on the conditions of migrant laborers in California. Her photographs, such as "White Angel Breadline" (1933), hauntingly documented the social ills of the Great Depression. She later worked for the Farm Security Administration (1935-42) and as a photojournalist for *Life* magazine.

See Also: Great Depression; New Deal; Photography; Women in American History.

■ **LANGDELL, CHRISTOPHER C. (1826-1906),** legal educator. He was born in New Boston, New Hampshire, and practiced law in New York City (1854-70). As dean of Harvard Law School (1870-95), Langdell is credited with introducing the case method of study to U.S. law schools. The author of several case study texts, Langdell stepped down as dean in 1895 and retired from the Harvard faculty in 1900.

■ **LANGLEY, SAMUEL (1834-1906),** astronomer and aviation pioneer. Born in Roxbury, Massachusetts, he became director of the Allegheny Observatory (1867-87) and used astronomical measurements to tell accurate time for the railroads (1869). Langley designed a delicate electrical thermometer (the bolometer, 1878), made spectral measurements of solar radiation, and so earned an international reputation. He became secretary of the Smithsonian Institution (1887-

1906) and laid experimental groundwork in the then-ridiculed field of aviation. His model aircraft flew in 1896, but tests with a pilot in 1903 failed.

See Also: *Science.*

■ **LANGMUIR, IRVING (1881-1957),** chemist and physicist. Born in Brooklyn, New York, Langmuir conducted a wide range of research at the General Electric Laboratory in Schenectady, New York (1909-50). He invented gas-filled light bulbs and vacuum radio tubes, developed concepts fundamental to thermonuclear fusion, experimented with ionized gases he named plasmas, discovered and studied electron temperature, and clarified the nature of surface adsorption. Langmuir won the Nobel Prize in Chemistry in 1932 for his work in surface chemistry. After World War II, he expanded his research to cloud seeding.

See Also: *Science.*

■ **LARCOM, LUCY (1824-93),** poet, teacher, and magazine editor, best known for her memoir *A New England Girlhood* (1889). Born in Beverly, Massachusetts, she grew up working in a textile mill in nearby Lowell, an experience described in "Among Lowell Mill-Girls: A Reminiscence," which appeared in the *Atlantic Monthly* in 1881. She also published poetry about rural New England in the *Atlantic Monthly*, *Youth's Companion*, and *St. Nicholas*; was an editor for *Our Young Folks* from 1865 to 1873; and taught at Wheaton Seminary.

See Also: *Poetry; Women in American History.*

■ **LA SALLE, RENÉ-ROBERT CAVELIER, SIEUR DE (1643-1687),** French explorer, whose expeditions contributed to the southward expansion of France's North American empire. Born in Rouen, France, to an upper-middle-class family, La Salle was educated in theology by the Jesuits but forsook a career in the church to pursue his fortune in the New World. La Salle was politically connected to Louis de Buade, Comte de Frontenac, who served two terms as governor of New France (1672-82, 1689-98). Frontenac conveyed to La Salle jurisdiction of Fort Frontenac on the eastern end of Lake Ontario, as well as the right to establish fur-trading outposts in the far west.

Turning his ambitions westward, La Salle hoped to find a water route through North Amer-

The French explorer Sieur de La Salle descended the Mississippi, reaching its mouth in April 1682 and claiming possession of the entire region for France. This 18th-century engraving is more fanciful than factual.

ica. When a northwest passage to the Orient proved fanciful, he directed his efforts southward through Lake Michigan, down the Illinois River, and into the Mississippi Valley. Fort Crevecoeur (on the east side of the Illinois River near present-day Peoria) was built in the spring of 1680 but was occupied only briefly.

Mississippi Explorations. Starting at Lake Michigan in late December 1681, La Salle and his loyal lieutenant, Henri de Tonti, made their epic voyage down the Illinois and Mississippi rivers to the Gulf of Mexico. Arriving at the Gulf in April 1682, La Salle claimed the entire Mississippi watershed on behalf of King Louis XIV, naming the immense territory "Louisiana." Retracing their route, La Salle helped Tonti construct Fort St. Louis (on the south side of the Illinois River at present-day Starved Rock State Park) during the winter of 1682-83; this became the first substantial European outpost in the region. La Salle then returned to France, where he sought royal support to explore Louisiana via the Gulf of Mexico.

Wishing to create a vast commercial empire in the heart of North America, La Salle sailed into the Gulf of Mexico in 1686. Inadvertently missing the mouths of the Mississippi, he landed on the coast of Texas and was planning to proceed overland to Illinois when disgruntled associates murdered him on Mar. 19, 1687. Although La Salle did not live to see his ambitions for France fully realized, by the early 18th century, France's expansive North American holdings indeed included all of the territories that La Salle had traversed.

—CARL J. EKBERG

See Also: Exploration and Discovery; French Colonies; Frontenac, Louis de Buade, Comte de.

BIBLIOGRAPHY: Eccles, W. J., *Frontenac: The Courtier Governor* (Univ. of Toronto Press 1959); Galloway, Patricia, ed., *La Salle and His Legacy* (Univ. of Mississippi Press 1982); Parkman, Francis, *La Salle and the Discovery of the Great West* (Little, Brown 1897).

■ **LAS CASAS, BARTOLOMÉ DE (1474-1566),** critic of Spanish exploitation of Indians and author of pamphlets describing Spanish atrocities in the Americas. A Franciscan priest, he came to the Americas with Governor Ovando of Hispaniola (1502). For 10 years Las Casas participated in the *encomienda*, the Spanish system of slave labor imposed on the indigenous peoples. Shortly after he moved to Cuba in 1512, Las Casas experienced an epiphany; he realized he had shared in a terrible injustice. Renouncing his property, he preached against the forced labor system. Summoned to Spain in 1519, he lobbied the Spanish monarchy to end the practice. By 1542 King Charles V responded by enacting the New Laws, which freed the Indians and brought them under the law. Within a year, however, the New Laws were abrogated. Resolute, Las Casas turned to historical writing to make his case. He published a series of pamphlets describing the Spanish conquest of the Americas in the most graphic terms. These writings became the basis for the "Black Legend." Although Las Casas intended to save the Indians, in the end his efforts to protect them secured their welfare at the expense of black Africans who were imported to the New World as slaves in their place.

See Also: Black Legend of Spanish Colonization.

BIBLIOGRAPHY: Wagner, Henry Raup, *The Life and Writings of Bartolome de Las Casas* (Univ. of New Mexico Press 1967).

■ **LAS VEGAS,** largest and most glittering city in Nevada. It is located in southeastern Nevada 30 miles from the Colorado River in a desert that was once inhabited by the Paiute tribe. A group of Salt Lake City Mormons arrived in the region to build a fort in 1855, but the small colony abandoned the site in 1858. In 1864 the federal government established Fort Baker in the area. In 1905 the Union Pacific railroad declared the site a major railroad division point and began to auction off town lots. The town grew slowly as a center for mining and ranching until Nevada legalized gambling in 1931. That same year the federal government undertook the monumental construction project of Boulder Dam across the Colorado River. This hydroelectric dam provided Las Vegas with electricity and water and allowed it to grow as a thriving gambling oasis in the desert. Since World War II Las Vegas has become a tourist destination in a class by itself, with gigantic gambling casinos, spectacular performances, and the always-sparkling neon signs. Population (1994): 327,878.

See Also: City in American History.

■ **LATROBE, BENJAMIN (1764-1820),** engineer and Greek-revival architect. Born in Fulneck, England, Latrobe immigrated to the United States in 1796. His first building in the United States was the Penitentiary building in Richmond, Virginia (1797-98). Latrobe moved to Philadelphia in 1798 and in that year designed the Bank of Pennsylvania. In Philadelphia he also achieved an engineering feat in designing the first water supply system in the United States, partly housed in the Greek-revival Waterworks buildings (1799). In 1803 Pres. Thomas Jefferson offered Latrobe a position as surveyor of public buildings in Washington, D.C. In this post Latrobe designed the South Wing of the Capitol, remodeled the Patent Office, and oversaw renovations to the White House. After the Capitol was burned by the British in the War of 1812 Latrobe worked on its rebuilding (1815-17). He also had private commissions in Washington, including St. John's Episcopal Church (1817). Latrobe was working on a waterworks system for the city of New Orleans when he died.

See Also: Architecture; Jefferson, Thomas; White House.

■ **LAUREL AND HARDY,** film comedy team. Slender Stan Laurel (1890-1965) and rotund Oliver Hardy (1892-1957) first teamed in silent films in 1927 and easily made the transition to sound. Laurel, a native of Ulverston, England, who immigrated to the United States in 1910, played the innocent who frustrated the Atlanta-born Hardy's schemes. Known for their physical comedy, they made their final film together in 1951.

See Also: Motion Pictures.

■ **LAURENT, ROBERT (1890-1970),** wood carver and sculptor. Laurent was born in Concarneau, France. He met the American painter Hamilton Easter Field in Brittany in 1902 and returned with him to the United States to study. After apprenticing with a wood carver on one of his study trips to Europe, Laurent took up this art form. His early work represented plant forms; over time, he was influenced by a variety of artistic styles, among them African sculpture, keeping himself in the forefront of modern sculpture.

See Also: Sculpture.

■ **LAW.** *See:* Civil Liberties; Common Law; Due Process of Law; Habeus Corpus, Writ of; Martial Law; Supreme Court; individual biographies.

■ **LAWRENCE, ERNEST (1901-58),** nuclear physicist who invented the cyclotron. Born in Canton, South Dakota, Lawrence taught at Yale (1925-28) before becoming a professor at the University of California at Berkeley (1928-58). In 1929, Lawrence developed the idea of the cyclotron, a device using an electromagnetic field to hold nuclear particles in a circular orbit and accelerate them within a vacuum chamber. He built the first experimental cyclotron in 1930 with M. Stanley Livingston and continued to improve on it through World War II. This work let physicists study the atom by producing artificially created radioisotopes and new manmade elements heavier than uranium. It also led to the discovery of the neutron (1932), the establishment of the Radiation Laboratory at the University of California (1932), Lawrence's appointment as di-

rector there (1932), and his winning of the Nobel Prize in Physics (1939). During World War II, Lawrence played a major role in the Manhattan Project and made most of the uranium 235 for the Hiroshima bomb. After the war, scientists at his laboratory built new kinds of accelerators, such as McMillan's synchrotron. Lawrence became an adviser to the Atomic Energy Commission and the Department of Defense and made his laboratory the world center for nuclear physics.

See Also: Manhattan Project; Science.

■ **LAWRENCE, JACOB (1917-),** painter. Born in Atlantic City, New Jersey, he studied at the Harlem Art Workshop of the Works Progress (later Projects) Administration (WPA) in the 1930s, becoming one of the most notable African-American painters of the 20th century. His best-known works are in his series on historical themes, such as "And the Migrants Kept Coming" (1940).

See Also: African Americans; Painting.

■ **LAZARUS, EMMA (1849-87),** poet and author. Born in New York City, she was an outspoken advocate for Jewish immigrants. She is best known for the last stanza of her 1883 sonnet "The New Colossus," which is inscribed on the pedestal of the Statue of Liberty: "Give me your tired, your poor, Your huddled masses, yearning to breathe free, The wretched refuse of your teeming shore. Send these, the homeless, tempest-tost to me, I lift my lamp beside the golden door!"

See Also: Immigration; Poetry.

■ **LEAGUE OF NATIONS,** international association of countries formed in the wake of World War I and dedicated to the preservation of peace. Pres. Woodrow Wilson arrived at the peace conference at Versailles, France, in January 1919 with an ambitious plan for world order that reflected his liberal progressivism. Articulated in his Fourteen Points, this plan offered a series of proposals for maintaining peace and prosperity in Europe. The central but most controversial part of Wilson's plan proved to be the League of Nations, which the president designed to implement his proposals and mediate future international disputes.

Wilson's optimism was soon diminished by secret deals between various countries and the continued compromising of his ideals. Despite the harsh realities of power politics at Versailles and months of debate, the final treaty was signed on June 28, 1919, with a commitment to the League of Nations. When Wilson brought the treaty home for Senate ratification, he confronted resolute opposition, especially over Article 10 of the League covenant, which called for collective security. Opponents, led by Sen. Henry Cabot Lodge, criticized Article 10 as a surrender of America's sovereignty and independence. Intransigent and in ill health, Wilson campaigned tirelessly for the treaty and League. In the end, neither Wilson nor Lodge's version of the treaty was ratified, and the United States never joined the League. Although the League of Nations existed from 1920 to 1946, the absence of the United States weakened its structure and effectiveness. It was replaced after World War II by the United Nations.

See Also: Fourteen Points; Lodge, Henry Cabot; United Nations (UN); Versailles, Treaty of; Wilson, (Thomas) Woodrow.

BIBLIOGRAPHY: Knock, Thomas J., *To End All Wars: Woodrow Wilson and the Quest for a New World Order* (Oxford Univ. Press 1992); Northege, F. S., *The League of Nations: Its Life and Times, 1920-1946* (Holmes & Meier 1986).

■ **LEAGUE OF WOMEN VOTERS,** a nonpartisan lobbying group founded in 1920. It grew out of the National American Woman Suffrage Association in the months before passage of the 19th Amendment and originally aimed to educate women in how to use their new political rights. In the 1920s the League successfully lobbied for legislation that would assist women, such as the 1922 Cable Act, which granted U.S. citizenship to married women independent of their husbands' status, and the 1921 Sheppard-Towner Act, which authorized federal funding of state aid to maternity and infant health care. However, the League has focused mainly on providing nonpartisan information to voters.

See Also: Women in American History.

■ **LEAHY, WILLIAM (1875-1959),** U.S. naval officer. Born in Hampton, Iowa, Leahy had a distinguished career serving in the Spanish-Ameri-

For many years, the League of Women Voters sponsored debates among presidential candidates in election years. Here, Ronald Reagan debates Walter Mondale in the campaign of 1984.

can War, the Philippines, and World War I before being named chief of naval operations (1937). He became governor of Puerto Rico two years later and then ambassador to France (1940). His friend Pres. Franklin D. Roosevelt appointed Leahy chief of staff (1942) and made him admiral of the navy (1944). Leahy remained chief of staff until 1949.

See Also: World War II.

■ **LEASE, MARY ELIZABETH (1850-1933),** lecturer and populist leader. She was born in Ridgway, Pennsylvania. From 1885 to 1894 her captivating oratory and fiery personality were fixtures of the western labor movement and the Populist party. She reportedly told Kansas farmers to "raise less corn and more hell."

See Also: Frontier in American History; Gilded Age; Populism; Women in American History.

■ **LECOMPTON CONSTITUTION (1857),** proslavery constitution of Kansas. Pushed through by proslavery men from Missouri, the Lecompton Constitution legalized and protected slavery despite the fact that antislavery forces were a majority in Kansas. Congress rejected the Lecompton Constitution.

See Also: Civil War; Kansas; Slavery.

■ **LEDBETTER, HUDDIE ("LEADBELLY") (1888-1949),** folk singer. Born in Mooringsport, Louisiana, of Cherokee and black descent, he earned his living as an itinerant guitar player. Ledbetter's life was marred by frequent imprisonments. While in prison he was "discovered" by the folklorist John A. Lomax, who wrote (1936) a book about Ledbetter's songs and blues style. Ledbetter became a professional entertainer and toured France in 1949. He recorded his music for the Library of Congress and helped spark a general revival of interest in the folk song as an art form in the 1940s.

See Also: African Americans; Folk Music.

■ **LEDERBERG, JOSHUA (1925-),** geneticist. Born in Montclair, New Jersey, Lederberg taught at the University of Wisconsin (1947-58) and Stanford (1958-78) before becoming president of Rockefeller University (1978-90). He shared the 1958 Nobel Prize in Physiology and Medicine for his work on the genetics of bacteria. By demonstrat-

ing that bacteria can reproduce sexually and discovering how to artificially introduce new genes into bacteria, Lederberg made the study of heredity easier and raised the issue of genetic engineering. He also wrote a column in the *Washington Post* and served as a government consultant.

See Also: Science.

■ **LEE, FRANCIS LIGHTFOOT (1734-97),** Revolutionary-period statesman, brother of Richard Henry Lee, born in Westmoreland County, Virginia. He was an active and influential champion of revolutionary resistance to Britain. He helped form the Virginia Committee of Correspondence in 1773 and was a member of the Virginia Convention of August 1774. As a member of the Continental Congress from 1775 to 1779, he signed the Declaration of Independence and called for the right to free navigation of the Mississippi River by American citizens.

See Also: Declaration of Independence; Lee, Richard Henry.

■ **LEE, MOTHER ANN (1736-84),** religious leader. Born in Manchester, England, in 1758, Lee joined the "Shakers," or "shaking Quakers," so-called because they danced, shook, and spoke in tongues during worship. In 1770 Lee became leader of the group. Her visions helped refine the Shaker belief that the second coming of Christ was imminent. Confession, chastity, and simplicity of life, she preached, were the keys to salvation. She also argued for sexual and racial equality. In 1774 Lee moved the Shakers to America. They settled in Niskeyuna, New York.

See Also: Religion; Shakers; Women in American History.

■ **LEE, RICHARD HENRY (1732-94),** Revolutionary War statesman. Lee was born in Westmoreland County, Virginia, and was a leading opponent of British taxation. He prompted the formation of committees of correspondence and proposed to Congress in June 1776 that America declare independence. He served in both Continental Congresses and signed the Declaration of Independence. Although a member of Congress through 1792, he opposed ratification of the Constitution because, in his view, it diminished states' rights.

See Also: *Declaration of Independence; Lee Family; Revolution, American.*

■ **LEE, ROBERT EDWARD (1807-70),** Confederate general and one of the premier figures in American military history. The son of Revolutionary War hero Henry "Light-Horse Harry" Lee, he was born in Westmoreland County, Virginia, and graduated from the U.S. Military Academy at West Point in 1829. He married Mary Ann Randolph Custis (great-granddaughter of Martha Washington) in 1831 and fathered seven children. During the Mexican War (1846-48), he served with great distinction on the staff of Gen. Winfield Scott. Lee's subsequent assignments included important engineering projects, the superintendency of the Military Academy (1852-55), and a short stint with the Second Cavalry in Texas.

When the Civil War began in 1861, Lee resigned his commission and entered the Confederate service. Although he held a number of positions, his fame rests on his command of the Army of Northern Virginia from June 1862 to April 1865, and his campaigns of unparalleled audacity in the face of great odds. He initially won impressive victories at Second Manassas (Aug. 29-30, 1862), Fredericksburg (Dec. 13, 1862), and Chancellorsville (May 2-4, 1863) and suffered only one significant defeat, at Sharpsburg (Sept. 17, 1862). By seizing the initiative, Lee disrupted Union military operations for a year. But his subsequent invasion of Pennsylvania, which ended disastrously at Gettysburg (July 1-3, 1863), underscored the high cost in manpower of his aggressive strategy. This and the cumulative loss of competent junior officers reduced the army to a more defensive role thereafter. Although Lee continued to win victories, or at least achieve stalemates, as at the Wilderness (May 5-6, 1864), Spottsylvania (May 8-19, 1864), and Cold Harbor (June 1-3, 1864), the increasingly frequent, prolonged combat finally reduced him to defending a series of trenches protecting Richmond and Petersburg. Driven from these after a siege of more than eight months, he surrendered at Appomattox Courthouse on Apr. 9, 1865.

Some historians argue that Lee's aggressive tactics consumed disproportionate resources that might have been better utilized elsewhere. Others contend that his dazzling victories and stalwart defense of the Confederacy's capital boosted Southern morale, contributed to Northern war weariness, and provided the South's best hope of winning foreign recognition. Following the war Lee served as president of Washington College in Lexington, Virginia, and on his death the school was renamed Washington and Lee.

—WILLIAM GARRETT PISTON

See Also: *Appomattox Courthouse; Civil War; Confederate States of America; Lee Family; Grant, Ulysses Simpson.*

BIBLIOGRAPHY: Connelly, Thomas L., *The Marble Man: Robert E. Lee and His Image in American Society* (Knopf 1977); Freeman, Douglas Southall, *R. E. Lee,* 4 vols. (Charles Scribner's Sons 1934-35); Thomas, Emory M., *Robert E. Lee* (Norton 1995).

Upon the outbreak of the Civil War, Robert E. Lee declined an offer of field command in the U.S. Army, choosing instead to lead Virginia's military forces. After the Confederacy's defeat, he became president of what is now Washington and Lee University.

■ **LEE, SHELTON JACKSON ("SPIKE") (1957-),** film director and actor. He was born in Atlanta, Georgia, and attended Morehouse College. From his first film release, *She's Gotta Have It* (1986), Lee has deftly explored race relations in America. Later films such as *Do the Right Thing* (1989), *Mo' Better Blues* (1990), and *Jungle Fever* (1991) have treated themes that include black anger, interracial marriage, and middle-class black values and attitudes. Among Lee's recent films are biographies of Malcolm X and Jackie Robinson.

See Also: *African Americans; Motion Pictures.*

■ **LEE FAMILY,** prominent American family beginning with Richard Lee (d. 1664). Lee, an Englishman, established the Virginia-based dynasty when he emigrated there in 1641, acquired land, and established himself as a wealthy planter. Richard's great-grandson, Richard Henry Lee (1732-94), was a member of the Virginia House of Burgesses and a delegate from that state to the Continental Congress. After the Revolutionary War Richard Henry Lee served in the Virginia legislature and the U.S. Senate. Another descendant of Richard Lee, Henry (Light-Horse Harry) Lee (1756-1818), served in the Continental army as well as the U.S. Congress. A son of Light-Horse Harry, Robert Edward Lee (1807-70), is best known for his role as the commander in chief of the Confederate army during the Civil War. Robert Edward Lee's two sons, William H. Fitzhugh Lee (1837-91) and George Washington Custis Lee (1832-1913), both served as officers in the Confederate army.

See Also: *Lee, Francis Lightfoot; Lee, Richard Henry; Lee, Robert Edward.*

■ **LEGAL TENDER CASES (1870-71),** sequence of U.S. Supreme Court cases that ultimately upheld the Legal Tender Acts and the right of the federal government to issue paper money. In *Hepburn* v. *Griswold* (1870), the Court had held (4-3) that the "original intent" of the framers had been to prevent the circulation of paper currency, and thus the Legal Tender Acts were unconstitutional. Only a year later, the Court revisited the question, but this time the newly enlarged Court had nine justices not seven, William Strong and Joseph Bradley having been appointed that year by Pres. Ulysses S. Grant. Whether or not Grant, a supporter of the government's power to print greenbacks, "packed" the Court with the intention of reversing the *Hepburn* decision, such was the result. In the 1871 Legal Tender Cases the Court discarded its "original-intent" reasoning of the year before and found the Legal Tender Acts constitutional.

See Also: *Supreme Court.*

■ **LEISLER'S REVOLT (1689-91),** an insurrection in colonial New York. In the spring of 1689 news of England's Glorious Revolution elicited a violent reaction in New York. Jacob Leisler, a German merchant and militia captain, seized control of Fort James in New York City. Allied with the Dutch colonial elite, Leisler sought to snatch political and economic power from the prominent Anglo-Dutch faction. To solidify his position, he called on the surrounding counties and towns to join with him in the name of the new English monarchs, William and Mary. Suffolk, Queens, and Westchester counties threw out their appointed officials and elected new ones in their place, but the popular support Leisler expected did not materialize. Instead, the deepened ethnic and religious divisions bred disaster. When a hostile force of French and Indians attacked the frontier outpost at Schenectady, the anti- and pro-Leisler factions were so contentious that they left the town's gates unguarded. Within hours Schenectady was in ruins, and its surviving inhabitants were marched off into captivity. In 1691 Henry Sloughter, the new governor commissioned by William III, arrived to take control of New York. Accompanied by an English regiment, Sloughter demanded that Fort James be relinquished to him. When Leisler hesitated, Sloughter quickly declared Leisler a traitor, jailed him, and then tried him for treason. Although a pardon eventually arrived from England, the court had already moved quickly to execute Leisler and Jacob Milbourne, his chief lieutenant.

See Also: *Glorious Revolution in America.*

BIBLIOGRAPHY: Voorhees, David William, "In behalf of the true Protestants religion: The Glorious Revolution in New York" (Ph.D. dissertation, New York Univ. 1988).

■ **LEMAY, CURTIS E. (1906-90),** U.S. Air Force officer and leading theorist and tactician of strategic bombing. Born in Columbus, Ohio, he served during World War II in both Europe and Asia (where he developed controversial incendiary-bombing tactics), commanded postwar U.S. air forces in Europe, and, after 1948, headed the U.S. Strategic Air Command.

See Also: World War II.

■ **LEND-LEASE,** U.S. policy during World War II of furnishing material aid to nations fighting the Axis powers. In March 1941, Congress passed the Lend-Lease Act, authorizing the president to sell, transfer, exchange, or lease arms or other materials to any country whose defense was deemed vital to American security. The program was administered by Harry Hopkins and later by Edward Stettinius. The first beneficiary of lend-lease law was Great Britain, but by May 1941 China started to receive American goods as well. After Germany attacked the Soviet Union in June 1941, the USSR also became a recipient of U.S. lend-lease shipments. Once the United States entered World War II in December 1941, lend-lease became a major part of the U.S. war effort. By the end of the war, about $50 billion in goods had gone to 38 nations.

See Also: Roosevelt, Franklin Delano; World War II.

■ **L'ENFANT, PIERRE CHARLES (1754-1825),** soldier, engineer, and original planner of Washington, D.C. Born in Paris, L'Enfant came to the United States in 1777 to serve in the Continental army. After his retirement from the army in 1784, he remodeled a building to be used as the temporary headquarters of the new federal government in New York City. In 1791, L'Enfant was appointed by George Washington to plan Washington, D.C. His plan for that city included the urban gridiron that underlies the city's structure.

■ **LENNI-LENAPE INDIANS.** *See: Delaware Indians.*

■ **LESLIE, FRANK (1821-80),** journalist and magazine publisher. Leslie was born in Ipswich, England, and came to the United States in 1848. He worked for *Gleason's Pictorial and Illustrated News* in the early 1850s. Leslie started his own periodical, *Frank Leslie's Ladies' Gazette of Paris, London, and New York Fashions,* in 1854. The next year he began publishing the immensely popular *Frank Leslie's Illustrated Newspaper.* Leslie targeted a variety of age and class groups with his different journals.

■ **LEWIS, FRANCIS (1713-1802),** merchant and Revolutionary War politician. Born in Wales, Lewis immigrated to New York in 1738 and established a trading business. Siding with the colonists during the Revolution, he served in the Second Continental Congress and signed the Declaration of Independence.

See Also: Declaration of Independence.

■ **LEWIS, GILBERT (1875-1946),** physical chemist. Born in Weymouth, Massachusetts, Lewis taught chemistry at Harvard and studied abroad before joining a research laboratory led by Arthur A. Noyes at Massachusetts Institute of Technology (1905-11). He later became a professor at the University of California at Berkeley and dean of the College of Chemistry there (1912-46). Lewis ranged widely in his work, publishing several papers on Einstein's theory of relativity (1908), discovering the tretratomic oxygen molecule (1919), and, perhaps most significantly, developing the valence theory of chemical bonds (1916-23) whereby two atoms are held together by shared electrons. In 1933, Lewis discovered and made "heavy" water (deuterium oxide) with his student Harold Urey and collaborated with Ernest O. Lawrence in the first use of the deuteron, accelerated in the cyclotron, as a means for studying atomic nuclei. Lewis went on to study the symmetry of time in physics, the biology of heavy water, neutron optics, a generalized theory of acids and bases, and the color of organic substances. In his retirement, he devoted time to the study of prehistoric America.

See Also: Science; Urey, Harold.

■ **LEWIS, (HARRY) SINCLAIR (1885-1951),** author. Born in Sauk Centre, Minnesota, he graduated from Yale University in 1908, having become an editor of its *Literary Magazine.* He published his critically successful novel, *Our Mr. Wren,* in 1914 and began to write short stories for *The Saturday Evening Post* the following year. Yet not until 1920, with the appearance of *Main Street,* did Lewis gain literary prominence, both nationally and internationally. Controversial in its depiction of small-town America, *Main Street* was followed by the similarly provocative *Babbitt* (1922) and *Arrowsmith* (1925). The latter earned Lewis a 1926 Pulitzer Prize in fiction, which he rejected, denouncing such awards as constraints upon creative freedom. Lewis completed four more novels before the decade was out: *Mantrap* (1926), *Elmer Gantry* (1927), *The Man Who Knew Coolidge* (1928), and *Dodsworth* (1929). In 1930, he became the first American ever awarded the Nobel Prize in Literature, an honor he accepted.

Over the next two decades, Lewis produced 10 more novels, a pair of which, reminiscent of his work in the 1920s, enjoyed popular success and sparked controversy: *It Can't Happen Here* (1935) and *Kingsblood Royal* (1947). In the 1930s, *Dodsworth* and *It Can't Happen Here* were dramatized, as Lewis pursued an interest in theater earlier revealed in his 1919 play, *Hobohemia*. But Lewis's novels remain his lasting contribution to American literature.

See Also: Novel.

BIBLIOGRAPHY: Schorer, Mark, *Sinclair Lewis: An American Life* (McGraw-Hill 1961).

The son of a Welsh miner, United Mine Workers' leader John L. Lewis resigned as vice president of the American Federation of Labor (AFL) in 1935 to establish what would become the Congress of Industrial Organizations (CIO).

■ **LEWIS, JOHN (1940-)**, civil rights leader and politician. Born in Troy, Alabama, Lewis was among the students at the center of the sit-ins and freedom rides of the 1960s. He chaired the Student Nonviolent Coordinating Committee (SNCC) (1963-66) and in 1970 became director of the Voter Education Project. After service in the domestic program ACTION under Pres. Jimmy Carter in the late 1970s, Lewis went to Atlanta, Georgia, and entered politics. He first won a place on the Atlanta city council and was elected to the U.S. Congress in 1986.

See Also: Civil Rights Movement.

■ **LEWIS, JOHN L. (1880-1969)**, labor leader. Born in Iowa, Lewis joined his Welsh father in the local coal mines at the age of 16 and later worked as a miner in Colorado, Montana, and Illinois. Active in the United Mine Workers, he was elected president of a local chapter in Illinois in 1909 and later that year took a position as a state legislative agent for the union. Over the next 11 years, Lewis rose through the ranks. He was elected president in 1920 and served for 40 years. Leading his union through several highly publicized and suc-

cessful strikes in the anti-union climate of the 1920s, Lewis became one of the most powerful of the inner circle of the American Federation of Labor (AFL).

His determined commitment to the strategy of industrial unionism—organizing into one union all the workers of an industry regardless of their craft specialty—brought him into conflict with the craft-based AFL. When the AFL leadership balked at supporting a massive campaign of industrial organizing during the early New Deal era, Lewis pulled the UMW out of the federation and in 1935 took the first steps that resulted in the formation of the rival Congress of Industrial Organizations (CIO). He was a prominent supporter of Pres. Franklin D. Roosevelt's reelection in 1936 and helped lead aggressive unionization drives among workers in the steel, automobile, and textile industries. Lewis broke with Roosevelt in 1940 and then, in 1942, refusing to accept the no-strike pledge to which other labor leaders agreed for the duration of World War II, took the UMW out of the CIO. The miners struck and won their demands. Another strike in 1946 led to federal seizure of the coal mines and to the passage of the Taft-Hartley Act (1947). Except for a brief period of affiliation with the AFL in 1946-47, Lewis kept the UMW independent for the rest of his life. (The union finally joined the AFL-CIO in 1989.) Lewis was one of the most determined and effective labor leaders of the 20th century. Under his helm, UMW members became the best-paid and best-insured miners in the world.

See Also: Labor Movement.

BIBLIOGRAPHY: Dubofsky, Melvyn, and Warren Van Tine, *John L. Lewis: A Biography* (Univ. of Illinois Press 1986).

■ **LEWIS, MERIWETHER (1774-1809),** military officer and explorer. Born in Albemarle County, Virginia, Lewis joined the Virginia militia in 1794, became a captain in the army in 1800, and served as personal secretary to Pres. Thomas Jefferson a year later. In 1803, Jefferson commissioned Lewis, along with William Clark, to explore the American northwest. With heightened urgency after the Louisiana Purchase, the Lewis and Clark party set out from St. Louis in the spring of 1804. After wintering at a site near present-day Bismarck, North Dakota, they resumed their journey in the spring of 1805, crossed the Rockies, and eventually reached the Pacific Ocean. The party returned to St. Louis in September 1806.

The expedition furnished influential and voluminous notes and drawings of the region's Indians, geography, flora, and fauna and helped initiate an era of American continental expansion. Following the expedition, Lewis served as governor of the Louisiana territory. Always a man of mercurial temperament, he fell into a profound depression in 1809 and committed suicide.

See Also: Clark, William; Exploration and Discovery; Louisiana Purchase.

BIBLIOGRAPHY: Ambrose, Stephen E., *Undaunted Courage: Meriwether Lewis, Thomas Jefferson, and the Opening of the American West* (Simon & Schuster 1996); Bergon, Frank, ed., *The Journals of Lewis and Clark* (Penguin 1989); Lavender, David, *The Way to the Western Sea: Lewis and Clark Across the Continent* (Harper & Row 1988).

■ **LEWIS AND CLARK EXPEDITION.** In 1803, the year the United States purchased rights to the vast Louisiana territory from France, Pres. Thomas Jefferson appointed Meriwether Lewis, a 29-year-old army captain, to lead an expedition of exploration to mark a trade route from the Mississippi River to the Pacific coast. Jefferson had read the account of Alexander Mackenzie's discovery of a river route to the coast in 1793 and was familiar with the British expeditions of exploration under James Cook and George Vancouver. Young Lewis received a cram course in natural science to prepare him for his duties and selected 33-year-old William Clark, another Virginia-born army officer, to be his co-captain.

The two captains, leading 25 men, left in the spring of 1804, and spent the summer and fall traveling up the Missouri River to the Mandan villages in present North Dakota, where they made their first winter encampment. With guidance from Indians (including Sacajewea, wife of a French fur trapper), they traveled the following spring to the sources of the Missouri, crossed the Rocky Mountains, then followed tributaries of the Columbia River to the Pacific. After wintering at the mouth of the Columbia, they made their return to St. Louis, completing their historic journey in the early fall of 1806. The journey had taken a total of 28 months.

The explorers brought back the preserved remains of dozens of animal specimens and even live birds and prairie dogs. Their journals fill many published volumes, detailing an incredible amount of scientific information, including descriptions of hundreds of species of fish, reptiles, mammals, birds, plants, and trees. They document their encounter with dozens of Indian tribes who were anxious for trade connections with the new republic. But at best, the commercial objectives of the expedition were only partly realized. Lewis and Clark failed to find what Jefferson had declared to be the most important object of the mission, a commercial route linking the waters of the Atlantic and the Pacific. In the long run, the most important accomplishment of the expedition was locking Louisiana Territory securely into the minds and plans of the young nation and associating the distant Pacific Northwest so closely with it that Americans thereafter assumed that it was their own preserve. In the words of historian Bernard De Voto, the mission "satisfied desire and it created desire: the desire of a westering nation."

See Also: Clark, William; Exploration and Discovery; Lewis, Meriwether; Louisiana Purchase.

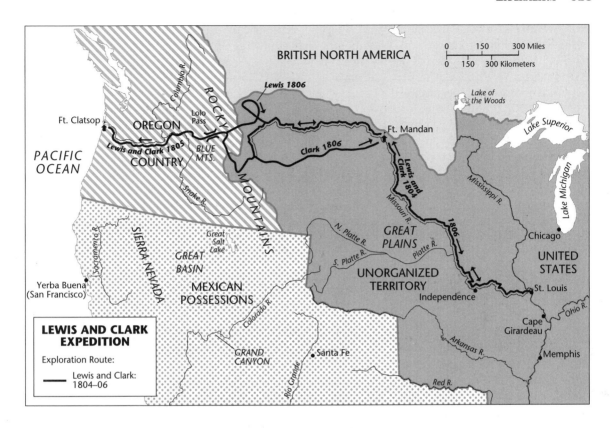

LEWIS AND CLARK EXPEDITION

Exploration Route:

—— Lewis and Clark: 1804–06

BIBLIOGRAPHY: Ambrose, Stephen E., *Undaunted Courage: Meriwether Lewis, Thomas Jefferson, and the Opening of the American West* (Simon & Schuster 1996); Bakeless, John, ed., *The Journals of Lewis and Clark: A New Selection* (New American Library 1964); Moulton, Gary E., ed., *The Journals of the Lewis and Clark Expedition,* 11 vols. (Univ. of Nebraska Press 1983-97); Ronda, James, *Lewis and Clark Among the Indians* (Univ. of Nebraska Press 1984).

■ **LEXINGTON AND CONCORD,** Massachusetts towns where the initial skirmishes of the American Revolution were fought between American militiamen and British troops on Apr. 19, 1775. Marching from Boston to seize a stockpile of arms, a large British force was met at Lexington Green by the local "minutemen," who had been alerted by Paul Revere. These militiamen were repulsed, but at Concord and on the road back to Boston fighting resulted in heavy British casualties.

See Also: Minutemen; Revere, Paul; Revolution, American.

■ **LEYTE GULF, BATTLE OF (1944),** World War II naval battle, the largest in history, which resulted in Japanese seapower being decisively smashed by the U.S. fleet. In October 1944 U.S. forces had begun to retake the Philippines, but the Japanese staged a complex attack to decoy Adm. William F. Halsey's carrier group and then destroy a defenseless transport group. Halsey was outmaneuvered, but on October 25 other American units decimated the Japanese in Leyte Gulf.

See Also: Halsey, William Frederick; World War II.

■ **LIBERALISM,** political philosophy that has had changing meanings in different historical periods. American liberalism originated in the 18th-century Enlightenment, whose ideals of individual freedom and liberty formed the philosophical basis of the American Revolution. Englishman John Locke (1632-1704) was the first philosopher to offer a comprehensive liberal theory. Locke argued that society was originally composed of free and atomistic individuals who created community and limited government through a social contract. Property rights, religious toleration, and consent of the governed were natural rights and not bestowed on individuals by government. Therefore, the government that governs the least governs the best.

By the 19th century, writers such as Adam Smith (1723-90) and John Stuart Mills (1806-73) had called for minor government regulation of a market economy, frequent elections, fewer restrictions on speech and the press, and political equality for women and minorities.

The American political philosopher Louis Hartz wrote that a "liberal consensus" existed between the left and the right in America because unlike Europe, the United States lacked an aristocratic tradition and hence also lacked a radical socialist tradition to oppose it. Nevertheless, liberal consensus has made the term *liberalism* thoroughly confusing as a label in U.S. political rhetoric. Modern American liberalism emerged from the late 19th century progressive movement to expand government regulation of the market and to provide for the general welfare of the population. Pres. Franklin D. Roosevelt's New Deal programs during the 1930s institutionalized the progressive agenda and added poverty relief as an entitlement of citizens. In response to the New Deal, traditional "conservatism" more and more advocated free market economics and an individualistic self-help philosophy: the original tenets of classical liberalism.

Although the welfare state achieved legitimacy after the 1930s, the debate then shifted to whether or not to expand it. Pres. Lyndon B. Johnson's Great Society programs in the mid-1960s called not merely for temporary poverty relief but for a "war on poverty." Johnson's failed Vietnam policy, however, divided social liberals and opened the door for a conservative revival. Pres. Ronald Reagan swept into office in 1980 and 1984 on a conservative program of tax cuts, deregulation, anticommunist defense spending, and attacks on welfare-state liberalism. Reagan's rhetorical legacy made "liberalism" politically difficult for leaders to advocate, and his legacy of budget deficits made liberalism fiscally impossible to implement. Even Democratic Pres. Bill Clinton said in his 1995 State of the Union address that "the era of big government is over."

—SCOTT L. MCLEAN

See Also: Political Parties.

BIBLIOGRAPHY: Goldman, Eric F., *Rendezvous with Destiny* (Knopf 1952); Hartz, Louis, *The Liberal Tradition in America* (Harcourt Brace Jovanovich 1955); Hofstadter, Richard, *The American Political Tradition* (Knopf 1948); Young, James P., *Reconsidering American Liberalism* (Greenwood Press 1996).

■ **LIBERIA,** country in West Africa. In 1822 the American Colonization Society began settling former American slaves in the region. Although Liberia became an independent nation in 1847, it long remained a quasi-dependency of the United States. Years of grappling with European colonial interests destabilized its economy and led to American financial intervention in 1909. Liberia's production of rubber and its location made it a strategic American ally during World War II.

See Also: Antislavery Movement; Slavery.

■ **LIBERTARIANISM,** political philosophy that gives primacy to individual rights and the exercise of free will. Like the classical liberalism of English political philosophers such as John Locke, libertarian doctrine contends that rights rest with individuals and government exists only with the consent of the governed. Modern libertarians see government as a threat to individual freedom. They advocate a minimal role for government at all levels and argue that the federal government should limit itself to duties explicitly stated in the Constitution, such as defending the nation's borders. Libertarian candidates for political office call for lower taxes and fewer government programs but part company with conservatives, who espouse similar goals, by also favoring an end to laws that attempt to regulate personal morality. Libertarians see measures that, for example, ban certain sexual acts and recreational drug use as restrictions of personal freedom.

■ **LIBERTY, STATUE OF,** colossal statue in New York City harbor. Built in 1886 as a gift from France, it was the collaborative effort of sculptor Frederic Auguste Bartholdi, engineer Gustave Eiffel, and architect Richard Morris Hunt.

■ **LIBERTY BELL,** historic relic of the American Revolution and a symbol of American independence. Housed in Philadelphia's Independence

Hall, the Liberty Bell rang to declare American independence on July 8, 1776. It was hidden from the British during the Revolution. The bell's famous crack developed during the 1830s and 1840s.

See Also: *Revolution, American.*

■ **LIBERTY LEAGUE,** organization of business leaders and conservative Democrats founded in 1934 to oppose the New Deal policies of Pres. Franklin D. Roosevelt. Supporters included former New York governor and Roosevelt ally Alfred E. Smith.

See Also: *New Deal.*

■ **LIBERTY LOANS (1917-19),** federal bond program instituted to help finance America's involvement in World War I. It helped raise almost two-thirds of the $33 billion spent during the war. Citizens were encouraged by celebrities and politicians to show their patriotism through the purchase of Liberty Loans.

See Also: *World War I.*

■ **LIBERTY PARTY,** antislavery political party. The party ran James G. Birney for president in 1844. By splitting the Whig vote, it helped elect Democrat James K. Polk. In 1848 the party merged with the Free Soil party.

See Also: *Civil War; Free Soil Party; Political Parties.*

■ **LIBRARIES** were relatively scarce in colonial America. The first library was created with John Harvard's 1638 bequest of his personal collection of books to the Massachusetts college that bore his name. By the early 18th century there were also college libraries at William and Mary in Virginia and Yale in Connecticut. These collections concentrated on religious books. In 1700, clergyman Thomas Bray, sent to the colonies by the Anglican Church to invigorate its operations in America, established a series of small religious libraries for each of the 30 parishes of Maryland, as well as for the Anglican communities in Boston, New York, and Charleston. The first secular library in the colonies was the Library Company of Philadelphia, a subscription library organized by Benjamin Franklin. Similar libraries were established in Newport, Rhode Island (1747), Charleston, South Carolina (1748), and New York (1754).

The first free public libraries date from the mid-19th century. The first to be publicly funded was established in Peterborough, New Hampshire, in 1833. The Boston Public Library (1852) was the first to be supported by a general town tax. The New York Public Library was formed from the consolidation of the private libraries of the Lenox, Tilden, and Astor families in 1895. But the spread of public libraries to small towns and rural communities did not begin until late in the 19th century. In 1893, New Hampshire became the first state to mandate public libraries in all townships; other states eventually followed this example. The founding of local public libraries was greatly advanced by the offer of industrialist Andrew Carnegie in 1881 to construct a building for any municipality willing to pledge public funds for the purchase of books and ongoing operations. By 1900, there were approximately 1,700 free public libraries in the country, by 1950 more than 7,000, by the end of the 20th century around 7,500.

One of the pioneers of professional librarianship in America was Melvin Dewey, who first formulated the widely used "decimal classification" for library collections in 1873 and published it in 1876, the same year that the American Library Association held its first meeting. In 1887, Dewey founded the New York State Library School, the first in the nation. In the mid-20th century, Dewey's system of classification was replaced with one of more comprehensive scope devised by the Library of Congress, which had been founded in 1800. Through its classification service for subscribing libraries, as well as its printed (and now electronic) catalog, the Library of Congress has had a decisive impact on modern librarianship.

See Also: *Library of Congress.*

BIBLIOGRAPHY: Carpenter, Kenneth E., *Readers and Libraries: Toward a History of Libraries and Culture in America* (Library of Congress 1996); Rosenberg, Jane Aikin, *The Nation's Great Library: Herbert Putnam and the Library of Congress, 1899-1939* (Univ. of Illinois Press 1993); Van Slyck, Abigail A., *Free to All: Carnegie Libraries and American Culture, 1890-1920* (Univ. of Chicago Press 1995).

■ **LIBRARY OF CONGRESS,** national library of the United States and one of the world's leading research centers. Created by Congress in 1800, the library was destroyed when the British invaded Washington, D.C., during the War of 1812. It began rebuilding its collection by purchasing the 6,000-volume personal library of former president Thomas Jefferson in 1815. By 1996 the collection had grown to nearly 100 million items. Housed in three buildings on Capitol Hill in Washington, the Library of Congress is both a reference resource for Congress and a center for the study and celebration of American culture. Its holdings include millions of maps, drawings, photographs, films, sound recordings, and the personal papers of famous Americans as well as books and magazines. The Library of Congress has also played a leading role in information science, promoting a cataloging system that has become the standard in major libraries and pioneering in the digital distribution of information by computer.

See Also: Libraries.

■ **LICENSE CASES (1847),** common name for three U.S. Supreme Court cases, *Thurlow v. Massachusetts, Pierce v. New Hampshire,* and *Fletcher v. Rhode Island,* concerning the right of the states to regulate internal commerce. In dispute was the authority of state governments to control the traffic in alcoholic beverages across their borders. The Supreme Court ruled unanimously that such regulations came squarely within the states' police power. The Court's apparent unanimity notwithstanding, six justices wrote concurring opinions.

See Also: Supreme Court.

■ **LICHTENSTEIN, ROY (1923-97),** pop art painter. Born in New York City, Lichtenstein studied art at Ohio State University. He taught art in the late 1950s and early 1960s, while developing the new realist painting style he is best known for. Lichtenstein enlarged the Benday pointillist process used to print comic strips, a screen of tiny colored dots enclosed within heavy outlines, and applied it to enamel-on-steel paintings, such as *The Engagement Ring* (1961) and *Whaam!* (1963).

See Also: Painting.

■ **LIFE EXPECTANCY,** statistical determination of the probable length of a person's life. In America this has increased from about 40 years in 1800 to about 77 years in 1990. Until 1870 or so, however, average American life expectancy, while on the rise, did not change very much. Only in the 20th century have Americans seen dramatic increases in their life expectancy. This dramatic increase in the life expectancy of Americans was due to the public health movements of the late 19th and early 20th centuries, which did much to prevent disease; improvements in medical care, which began the conquest of disease; a rising standard of living, which meant better nutrition; and even a declining birthrate, which may have allowed families and society to devote more care and attention to their infants and children. In fact, perhaps the major reason why American life expectancy increased so dramatically in the 20th century is that infant mortality rates declined precipitously. In 1900, 190 of every 1,000 babies born in America died before their first birthday; by 1990, fewer than 10 of every 1,000 babies born in America died before their first birthday.

Although this rise in life expectancy in America is paralleled by a similar rise in Western Europe, colonial Americans seemed to have a greater life expectancy than did preindustrial Europeans. This discrepancy may have been due to colonial America's more dispersed population as well as to its freedom from the ravages of the bubonic plague. America, however, always had its share of epidemic disease, which did much to keep the average life expectancy contained. (These same diseases—both tropical and European—also did much to decimate American Indian populations and accordingly lower their average life expectancy dramatically.) Because of these epidemic diseases, some areas of America were less healthy than others. New England colonists saw a death rate of about 15 to 25 per every 1,000 people, but those in the Chesapeake saw a death rate of about 50 per every 1,000 people because of malaria. Rural areas saw fewer deaths than urban areas, even with their infant mortality rates running as high as 25 percent.

Although the story of American demography is one of increasing life expectancy over time, there are many discrepancies. As America industrialized and urbanized, life expectancy rates for children actually declined somewhat between 1789 and 1850. African Americans have always had lower life expectancy rates than European Americans. For instance, in 1900 the average life expectancy for white males was 47 years and for white females it was 49, but for African Americans as a whole, it was only 33 years. In 1920, while white males had an average life expectancy of 54 years and white females had one of 56, African-American life expectancy was only 45 years. In the 1960s average white life expectancy was about 70 years, but average African-American life expectancy was only 60. And African-American infant mortality rates are higher than those for other American ethnic groups. Racism and poverty undoubtedly play roles in these discrepancies.

—Louis Haas

See Also: *African Americans; Disease; Medicine; Science.*

BIBLIOGRAPHY: Nugent, Walter, *Structures of American Social History* (Indiana Univ. Press 1981); Wells, Robert, *Revolutions in Americans' Lives* (Greenwood 1982); Wells, Robert, *Uncle Sam's Family* (State Univ. of New York Press 1985).

■ **LILIUOKALANI (1838-1917),** the last sovereign of Hawaii. Born in Honolulu, she ascended to the throne after the death of her childless brother, King Kalakaua, in 1891. Her reign was marked by frustrated attempts to restore the power of the Hawaiian monarchy. Perceiving her as a threat, a committee of American colonists, supported by U.S. troops, deposed her in 1893. When her supporters revolted, she was imprisoned. In 1898 the United States annexed Hawaii, permanently abolishing the monarchy.

See Also: *Frontier in American History; Gilded Age; Hawaii; Women in American History.*

■ **LINCOLN, ABRAHAM (1809-65),** 16th president of the United States (1861-65). He was born in Hardin County, Kentucky. His father, Thomas, was a pioneering farmer; his mother, Nancy Hanks, who married Thomas on June 12, 1806, was of uncertain ancestry and birth date. In December 1816, the family moved to present-day Spencer County, Indiana. Nancy died in October 1818, and the next year Thomas married Sarah Bush Johnston, who encouraged Abraham to get an education.

Born in a Kentucky log cabin to a struggling family, Abraham Lincoln became a successful attorney and national political figure before gaining the Republican presidential nomination and winning the election in 1860, when this photograph was taken.

Lincoln had an enormous capacity for self-education, reading the Bible, Parson Weems's *Life of Washington*, and Shakespeare, all of which became formative influences. His self-education, with occasional advice from others, embraced grammar, Euclid, surveying, law, and warfare.

In 1828 and 1830, he made flatboat trips to New Orleans, affording him views of the lower South. The family moved to Illinois in 1830, and in 1831 Lincoln left farm life and moved to New Salem, Illinois, where he performed a variety of jobs, winning recognition for his physical strength and debating skill. When the Black Hawk War broke out (1832), he was unanimously elected captain in the militia, although he saw no fighting. In 1834, he was elected to the state legislature, where he served four consecutive terms. He learned lawmaking, politics, and leadership. An ardent Whig, he admired Sen. Henry Clay and together with a colleague formally declared that slavery was based "on both injustice and bad policy."

Licensed as an attorney in 1836, he began legal practice, gaining influence among an elite group. A romance with Ann Rutledge, the depth of which is controversial, ended with her death. In 1837, he moved to Springfield, the new state capital, which offered a wider scope for law, politics, and society. His courtship of Mary Todd, a Kentuckian of genteel family, resulted in marriage in 1842. The Lincolns had four sons, only one of whom lived to maturity.

In 1846, Lincoln was elected to the U.S. House of Representatives. In Congress he notably opposed President Polk's inaugurating the Mexican War, supported the Wilmot Proviso to ban slavery from any territorial conquest by the war, and proposed gradual, compensated abolition of slavery in the District of Columbia. After serving one term, Lincoln resumed his law practice, which flourished and thrust him forward to become one of the foremost lawyers in the state.

National Prominence. "Thunderstruck" by Sen. Stephen A. Douglas's Kansas-Nebraska bill that opened the Louisiana Purchase territory to slavery, Lincoln reentered politics. Speaking in 1854 with greater maturity and skill than he had heretofore shown, he denounced the immorality of slavery and the disgrace it dealt to a republican form of government resting on the Declaration of Independence. These ideas animated him during the remainder of his life. Defeated as the Whig candidate for U.S. senator in 1855, Lincoln joined the new Republican party in 1856. At the party's nominating convention that year, he garnered 110 votes for the vice presidency.

Two years later, the Illinois Republican convention unanimously nominated him to run for the Senate against Douglas. His acceptance speech announced, "A house divided against itself cannot stand; I believe this government cannot endure, permanently half slave and half *free.*" In the 1858 campaign, Lincoln and Douglas held a series of debates by which Lincoln won widespread attention but not the office. Lincoln succeeded in pointing up the discrepancy between Douglas's notion of popular sovereignty and the Supreme Court's *Dred Scott* decision prohibiting Congress from banning slavery in the territories. Lincoln also applied the Declaration of Independence to African Americans, expanding on the implication of its principles. In the final debate, he ringingly asserted, the issue is whether slavery is right or wrong.

A speech at Cooper Union in New York City in early 1860 enhanced his reputation. The Republican national convention in May nominated him for the presidency over better-known candidates. The Democratic party divided over the territorial issue, and a fourth party, the Constitutional Union, assumed a neutral stance. Lincoln was elected by less than 40 percent of the popular vote, almost entirely from the free states.

As the lower South seceded, Lincoln maintained a public silence while privately refusing to sanction the territorial expansion of slavery. He was resolved to perpetuate the Union and to employ force if necessary; in his cabinet he incorporated the leading elements of his party. His inaugural address stressed national unity and gave assurance he did not intend to interfere with slavery in the states.

Early War Years. He was immediately confronted with a crisis, whether Fort Sumter in South Carolina should be evacuated or held by the federal government. After hearing divided counsels, Lincoln determined to maintain the fort. Confederate forces captured it (Apr. 12-14, 1861), and Lincoln promptly demonstrated his capacity for leadership.

Beginning on April 15, in a series of executive acts without authorization by Congress, Lincoln called forth the militia, in effect declaring war; suspended the privilege of the writ of habeas corpus; appropriated money; and blockaded the Confederate coast. When Congress met on July 4, 1861, at his summons, he claimed the president had the duty of employing what he called "the war power." Under this justification, invoking his oath to defend the Constitution and his role as commander in chief, Lincoln during the war curbed civil liberties in the North, emancipated rebels' slaves, and began to reconstruct the Union.

Congress speedily ratified the president's actions except for suspension of habeas corpus. Meanwhile a federal circuit court had ruled that Congress, not the president, had the right to suspend habeas corpus. Lincoln ignored the ruling, even though Congress did not sanction executive suspension until March 1863. In the same month the

Supreme Court in a divided opinion declared the president was "bound to accept the challenge without waiting for any special legislative authority."

Waging war to restore national unity soon demanded Lincoln's attention as Confederate forces gathered near the nation's capital. The 90-day enlistment of militia was about to expire; politicians, press, and popular sentiment clamored for action. Setting aside military advice, Lincoln ordered the fighting that culminated in the Union reversal at the First Battle of Bull Run in Virginia (July 21, 1861).

Although Lincoln left diplomacy largely to Sec. of State William H. Seward, he made Seward understand that authority resided in the president and early in the war altered a dispatch Seward drafted to the U.S. minister in England that could have ruptured relations between the two countries. During the Trent Affair—a diplomatic crisis between the United States and Great Britain (1861)—Lincoln kept a public silence while resolved to withstand popular clamor and avoid war with England.

Lincoln's appointment of Gen. George B. McClellan to command the Division of the Potomac after First Bull Run began a prolonged search for a general who would aggressively fight, pursue, and conquer rebel forces. Not until Gen. U. S. Grant took charge in 1864 did he find a general who shared his grasp of what was needed.

Although he believed slavery caused the war, Lincoln moved slowly to uproot the institution. Early in 1862, he urged a policy of gradual state emancipation, encouraged by federal compensation and accompanied by voluntary colonization. The failure of the border states to embrace the policy, reverses in military efforts to end the war, rising Northern sentiment for emancipation, and concern that Europe might intervene in the war prompted Lincoln to take executive action.

After the Union victory at Antietam (September 1862), Lincoln issued a preliminary Emancipation Proclamation, stressing restoration of the Union as the war's purpose and giving the seceded states 100 days in which to return to the Union, thus sparing themselves from emancipation. No state availed itself of this opportunity and on Jan. 1, 1863, Lincoln issued his final proclamation. Invoking his authority as commander in chief in wartime, he declared free those slaves in rebel areas and said freedmen would be received in the armed services. Thereafter, his vigorous recruitment of African Americans for the military resulted in the enlistment of nearly 190,000 African Americans. Concerned about the legality of his proclamation, Lincoln pushed through Congress the 13th Amendment to the Constitution abolishing involuntary servitude.

Later War Years. Although vexed by importunate office seekers, Lincoln was a consummate politician in distributing patronage, civil and military. His appointments helped unify the North and the Republican party and ensured his renomination in 1864. In the election of that year, he prevailed against rival Republicans S. P. Chase and J. C. Frémont, Democrat General McClellan, a peace movement, and—until early September—war weariness and defeatism. Sherman's capture of Atlanta and other military successes gained his reelection with an electoral vote of 212 to 21 and 400,000 more popular votes than McClellan.

Lincoln had announced his plan to reconstruct the Union in December 1863. He offered pardon and amnesty to rebels who would take an oath of future loyalty. Moreover, in each state, when 10 percent of the 1860 voting population had taken the oath and had formed a republican form of government that recognized freedom for slaves, he would recognize that state.

Congress rejected his plan and proposed its own, which Lincoln vetoed, leaving the matter in midair when he died. In his last public address, he disclosed his preference to give the vote to African Americans who were "very intelligent" and soldiers. Peace came upon his terms of reunion and emancipation. He had tried to set the tone of Reconstruction in his second inaugural address when he pleaded for a government "With malice toward none; with charity for all." His assassination by John Wilkes Booth in Ford's Theater in Washington on Apr. 14, 1865, cut short his administration of reconstruction and rights for African Americans. Historians have consistently rated him the greatest American president.

—JAMES A. RAWLEY

See Also: *Booth, John Wilkes; Civil War; Emancipation Proclamation; Gettysburg Address; Lincoln-Douglas Debates; McClellan, George C.; Pesidential Elections; President of the United States; Reconstruction; Republican Party; Seward, William Henry; Slavery.*

BIBLIOGRAPHY: Basler, Roy P., ed., *The Collected Works of Abraham Lincoln,* 9 vols., 2 supplements (Rutgers Univ. Press 1953-90); Beveridge, Albert J., *Abraham Lincoln, 1809-1858,* 2 vols. (1928; Reprint Service 1992); Donald, David Herbert, *Lincoln* (Simon & Schuster 1995); Neeley, Mark E., Jr., ed., *The Abraham Lincoln Encyclopedia* (1982; Da Capo 1984).

■ **LINCOLN, MARY TODD (1818-82),** first lady of the United States. Born in Lexington, Kentucky, she married Abraham Lincoln in 1842. Mrs. Lincoln was caught in the regional tensions of the Civil War era and was widely unpopular. After the death of their son Willie in 1862 and her husband's assassination in 1865, her emotional and physical health declined. She traveled to Europe and spent time in a sanitarium before her death.

See Also: Civil War; Women in American History.

■ **LINCOLN-DOUGLAS DEBATES (1858),** a series of seven public confrontations between incumbent Democrat Stephen A. Douglas and Republican challenger Abraham Lincoln during the campaign for senator from Illinois. Since senators were not popularly elected but chosen by a vote of the state assembly, the candidates were not seeking votes for themselves but for legislative candidates. Attended by crowds of 10,000 or more, the debates were grand political events, covered by the national press. The dominant issue was slavery and its extension to the territories, which had preoccupied the country since the passage of the Kansas-Nebraska Act that had resulted in the border fighting in "Bleeding Kansas." Prior to the debates Douglas had joined Republicans in the Senate in opposing the Lecompton Constitution, put forward by Kansas pro-slavery forces, arguing that it had been approved by fraud and was thus a mockery of "popular sovereignty," the doctrine by which citizens could vote slavery up or down. As a result, many Republicans urged his reelection. This forced Lincoln to emphasize the morality of the slavery issue. He demanded that Douglas reconcile his support of popular sovereignty with the Supreme Court's decision in the *Dred Scott* case, which implied that any prohibition of slavery in the states was unconstitutional. Douglas responded with what became known as the "Freeport Doctrine," the argument that territories could prohibit slavery simply by refusing to pass the laws necessary to protect it.

The Democrats won a majority in the assembly and reelected Douglas. But his "Freeport Doctrine" lost him the support of Southern Democrats and split the party in the 1860 presidential election. The debates brought Lincoln to national attention and, despite his loss of the campaign, made possible his nomination as Republican candidate for president in 1860. While they included a good deal of political hot air, the debates featured a serious examination of political differences and are worth reading today for their illumination of the divisions that led to the Civil War.

See Also: Bleeding Kansas; Civil War; Dred Scott v. Sandford; Douglas, Stephen Arnold; Kansas-Nebraska Act; Lincoln, Abraham; Popular Sovereignty.

BIBLIOGRAPHY: Holzer, Harold, ed., *The Lincoln-Douglas Debates: The First Complete, Unexpurgated Text* (HarperCollins 1993); Zarefsky, David, *Lincoln, Douglas, and Slavery: In the Crucible of Public Debate* (Univ. of Chicago Press 1990).

■ **LIND, JENNY (1820-87),** opera singer known as the "Swedish nightingale." She was born in Sweden. After a successful career in European opera houses, she toured the United States from 1850 to 1852 under the management of P. T. Barnum. In 1852 she married Otto Goldenschmidt and moved to Dresden where she taught at the Royal College of Music.

See Also: Opera; Women in American History.

■ **LINDBERGH, CHARLES AUGUSTUS (1902-74),** aviator. Born in Detroit, Lindbergh learned to fly at the age of 20. While working as an airmail service pilot, he began making plans for the first transatlantic flight in the hope of winning a $25,000 prize. Taking off from Long Island, New York, on May 20, 1927, in his new monoplane, the *Spirit of St. Louis,* he flew 33½ hours nonstop to Paris. The flight made Lindbergh an instant international hero and helped attain public acceptance of aviation. Also in 1927, Lindbergh made the first nonstop flight from Washington, D.C., to Mexico City, where he met his future wife, Anne Morrow, daughter of the U.S. ambassador to Mexico. Over the next several years the couple traveled widely together, making many pioneering flights. In the late 1920s, Lindbergh entered commercial aviation as a technical consultant to Transcontinental Air Transport Company and Pan American Airways.

In 1932, the Lindberghs' two-year-old son was kidnapped and murdered. Always a bit reclusive and uncomfortable with fame, Lindbergh reeled at the public fascination with the case and furtively moved to England with his wife in 1935. A year later Lindbergh visited Nazi Germany and became impressed with that country's military might. Shortly thereafter, he became an outspoken advocate of American isolationism. These views as well as his defense of Nazi Germany damaged his reputation in later years. Lindbergh eventually settled in Hawaii, where he became interested in environmental issues.

See Also: Isolationism.

BIBLIOGRAPHY: Davis, Kenneth S., *The Hero: Charles A. Lindbergh and the American Dream* (Doubleday 1959); Milton, Joyce, *Loss of Eden: A Biography of Charles and Anne Lindbergh* (HarperCollins 1993).

■ **LINDSAY, VACHEL (1879-1931),** poet and public speaker. Originally from Springfield, Illinois, Lindsay attended Hiram College between 1897 and 1900. After studying art in Chicago and New York, he traveled through the southern and western United States, presenting his poetry to local audiences. His first volume of poems, *General William Booth Enters into Heaven and Other Poems*, was published in 1913. Lindsay is remembered for poems such as "A Gospel of Beauty" and "Abraham Lincoln Walks at Midnight."

See Also: Poetry.

■ **LIPMANN, FRITZ ALBERT (1899-1986),** biochemist. Born in Koenigsberg, Germany, Lipmann studied cell metabolism (M.D., 1922; Ph.D., 1927). He immigrated (1939) to the United States after the rise of Nazism in Germany and taught at Cornell and Harvard. At Massachusetts General Hospital in Boston (1941-57), he continued his research into carbohydrate-fueled energy systems, discovered coenzyme A (necessary for cellular energy generation), and clarified the Krebs citric acid energy cycle. He shared the 1953 Nobel Prize in Physiology and Medicine with English biochemist H. A. Krebs and in 1957 went to Rock-

efeller Institute (now University) to research bodily energy systems.

See Also: Science.

■ **LIPPMANN, WALTER (1889-1974),** writer, editor, and public intellectual. A native of New York City, Lippmann graduated from Harvard University in 1910. Lippmann's first book, *A Preface to Politics* (1913), analyzed the problems he saw in contemporary society and considered socialism as a possible solution, but his second book, *Drift and Mastery* (1914), questioned socialism and Marxism. Lippmann's early writings brought him to the attention of Herbert Croly, who hired him to work on the *New Republic* in 1914. In 1917 Lippmann served as assistant to U.S. Sec. of War Newton Baker, and at the close of World War I he worked for Col. E. M. House, preparing data for the Paris Peace Conference of 1918-19. Lippmann then returned to the *New Republic* as associate editor. Between 1921 and 1931 Lippmann was on the editorial staff of the *New York World*, where he was editor the last two years. From 1931 on Lippmann wrote for the *New York Herald-Tribune*, where he began the column "Today and Tomorrow," which was later syndicated widely and became highly influential.

■ **LITERACY ACTS (1917),** laws that imposed literacy requirements on immigrants. During the nationalistic fervor of the World War I era Congress passed these bills over Pres. Woodrow Wilson's veto. Designed to restrict immigration and to Americanize immigrants, the literacy tests required anyone over 16 wishing to enter the country to be able to read.

See Also: Immigration.

■ **LITERATURE.** *See: History; Novel; Poetry; Science Fiction; Short Story; individual biographies.*

■ **LITTLE BIGHORN, BATTLE OF (June 25, 1876),** popularly known as Custer's Last Stand, most notable defeat of U.S. forces by Indians. In 1874-76, a gold rush brought a flood of white miners into Sioux territory in the Black Hills. In 1876, American agents called for the Sioux to come into the reservation headquarters, and all who refused were considered "hostiles." A large group of Sioux went out as usual for the annual buffalo hunt, assembling in a huge village containing Sioux, Cheyennes, and Arapahos at a place in Montana called the Greasy Grass and known to the Americans as Little Bighorn. A few days later, the village was attacked shortly after noon by the Seventh Cavalry's Lt. Col. George Custer and 600 American soldiers. The 2,000 Indian warriors thoroughly defeated him, killing almost all the Americans, including Custer. The Cheyenne Wooden Leg later recalled the reaction to the victory at the Indian camp: "There was no dancing nor celebrating of any kind. . . .Too many people were in mourning." Custer had disobeyed orders and refused to wait for reinforcements, but he represented historical forces of immense magnitude, and in his death he achieved an apotheosis that, for a time, outranked most American heroes.

See Also: Custer, George Armstrong; Indians of North America.

■ **LITTLE CROW (c. 1810-63),** Dakota leader, born Taheton Wakawa Mini. A chief of the Mdewakanton Santees in present-day Minnesota, Little Crow was friendly to whites for most of his life. However, as white settlement increased in the 1850s, he became wary. In 1862, when the Indian agent refused to deliver the Dakota's rations without a "kickback," Little Crow led a group of Dakotas against him and nearby white settlers in the Sioux Uprising of 1862. The rebellion was quashed, and Little Crow was killed by white bounty hunters in 1863.

See Also: Indians of North America; Sioux.

■ **LITTLE TURTLE (1752-1812),** Miami leader. Little Turtle was born in present-day Indiana in the Ohio River Valley and fought with the British during the American Revolution. Until the British surrendered in 1783, Little Turtle and his warriors had successfully defended their homelands, but after the Revolution, thousands of Americans swarmed into the Ohio Valley. In response, Little Turtle led raids against American towns and settlements. Gen. Josiah Harmar's troops, sent in 1790 by Pres. George Washington to subdue the uprising, were pounded in several engagements by Little Turtle's forces using guerrilla-style tactics. His greatest victory came in November 1791 when his warriors utterly routed 2,000 men under Gen. Arthur St. Clair,

the single greatest defeat of an American force in a war against Indians. Afterward, Washington strengthened the American army, putting it under the command of Gen. Anthony Wayne, who defeated Little Turtle at the Battle of Fallen Timbers in August 1794. A year later, at the Treaty of Greenville, Little Turtle was signatory to an agreement ceding most of present-day Ohio and much of Indiana. After his defeat Little Turtle became an accommodationist, encouraging peace and acculturation among his people.

See Also: Fallen Timbers, Battle of; Frontier in American History; Greenville, Treaty of; Indians of North America; St. Clair, Arthur; Wayne, Anthony.

■ **LIVERMORE, MARY ASHTON RICE (1820-1905),** journalist and leader of the suffrage and temperance movements. She was born in Boston, Massachusetts. In 1857, she and her husband, Universalist minister Daniel Parker Livermore, moved to Chicago, where they edited *The Covenant*, a Universalist magazine. During the American Civil War she and Jane Hoge ran the Northwestern Sanitary Commission. Livermore moved to Boston in 1869 to edit the *Woman's Journal* and served as president of the National American Woman Suffrage Association from 1893 to 1903. In 1872, she started lecturing, giving an average of 150 lectures a year for the rest of her life.

See Also: American Woman Suffrage Association (AWSA); Sanitary Commission; Suffrage; Women in American History.

■ **LIVINGSTON, HENRY BROCKHOLST (1757-1823),** associate justice of the U.S. Supreme Court (1806-23). A New York City native and a Democratic-Republican, while on the Court Livingston increasingly tilted toward the nationalism and federalism of Chief Justice John Marshall and away from his earlier Jeffersonian belief in limited and local government.

See Also: Marshall, John; Supreme Court.

■ **LIVINGSTON, PHILIP (1716-78),** merchant, philanthropist, and Revolutionary War politician. Livingston, who earned a fortune in his trading business and contributed large sums to civil projects, was born in New York to an influential family. During the Revolution he served in the First and Second Continental Congresses and signed the Declaration of Independence.

See Also: Declaration of Independence; Livingston Family.

■ **LIVINGSTON, ROBERT R. (1746-1813),** American lawyer and politician. He was born in New York City to a prominent political family. He served in the Continental Congress (1775-77; 1779-81) and was one of five men who drew up the Declaration of Independence. He was the first U.S. secretary of foreign affairs (1781-83) and in 1789 he administered the oath of office to Pres. George Washington. Livingston became Pres. Thomas Jefferson's minister to France (1801-04), a position he held at the time of the Louisiana Purchase (1801). He later aided Robert Fulton in building the steamboat and attempted to help Fulton secure a monopoly (which was later broken) on the steam engine.

See Also: Fulton, Robert; Livingston Family.

■ **LIVINGSTON, WILLIAM (1723-90),** attorney, essayist, and first governor of the state of New Jersey. A graduate of Yale College, Livingston became involved in New York politics, was leader of the so-called Presbyterian party, and advocated the separation of religion and politics. In 1772, he retired to New Jersey but was drawn into Revolutionary War politics again and was the state's governor from 1776 until 1790.

See Also: Livingston Family; Religion.

■ **LIVINGSTON FAMILY,** politically prominent early American family. Robert Livingston (1654-1728) immigrated to America in 1673 from Scotland, establishing a 160,000-acre estate at Albany, New York. He served as a member of the New York provincial assembly (1709-11; 1716-25). Grandson Philip (1716-78), born in Albany, became a successful New York merchant, was a member of the Continental Congress (1774-78), and was a signer of the Declaration of Independence. Philip's brother William (1723-90), also born in Albany, was governor of New Jersey (1776-90) and a signer of the U.S. Constitution. William's son Henry Brockholst (1757-1823) was born in New York City and served as an associate justice of the U.S. Supreme Court (1806-23).

Robert's great-grandson Robert R. (1746-1813), born in New York City, was one of the committee who drew up the Declaration of Independence, and he administered the nation's first presidential oath of office to George Washington in 1789. Robert R.'s brother Edward (1764-1836) served in the U.S. House of Representatives (1823-29), in the U.S. Senate (1829-31), and as Pres. Andrew Jackson's secretary of state (1831-35).

See Also: Livingston, Henry Brockholst; Livingston, Philip; Livingston, Robert R.; Livingston, William.

■ **LLOYD, HENRY DEMAREST (1847-1903),** writer and reformer. Born in New York City, he was briefly involved in reform politics there before he moved to Chicago in 1873, joining the editorial staff of the *Chicago Tribune*. He wrote numerous articles critical of the growing power of monopolies. In 1885, he left the *Tribune* to concentrate on social reform, publishing several books that emphasized the need for industrial justice as well as consumer protection. His most famous work, *Wealth Against Commonwealth*(1894), exposed the exploitative business practices of the Standard Oil company.

See Also: Gilded Age; Monopoly; Standard Oil Trust.

■ **LOBBYING,** urging a legislator to support or oppose a position. The term originated in the fact that, first in the British Parliament and subsequently in U.S. legislatures, one-on-one advocacy occurred in the lobby off the meeting floor. Lobbying has come to have a largely negative connotation in U.S. politics.

Individuals and groups seek to influence government to act in their favor. Many organizations maintain full-time lobbying operations with offices in Washington, D.C., and state capitals to provide lawmakers with information favorable to their interests. Often the information is accompanied by promises of support in future political campaigns. National business groups, labor unions, organizations of the elderly, and the National Rifle Association have been among the most effective lobbyists. Given the nation's traditional mistrust of "factions" and "interests," virtually any organized lobbying is viewed with suspicion by many people. Reformers contend lobbyists buy access and favorable government action with campaign contributions, and various laws have been enacted at all levels of government to regulate lobbying.

BIBLIOGRAPHY: Birnbaum, Jeffrey H., *The Lobbyists: How Influence Peddlers Get Their Way in Washington* (Times Books 1992).

■ *LOCHNER V. NEW YORK* **(1905),** controversial U.S. Supreme Court decision involving New York State's 1895 Bakeshop Act limiting bakers' work hours. New York courts upheld the law, but the U.S. Supreme Court declared it unconstitutional in a pivotal decision. Justice Rufus W. Peckham ruled for a five-to-four majority both that the bakeshop law was an excessive use of the state's police powers because it was not a legitimate health measure and that it violated the bakers' right to "liberty of contract" in negotiating employment conditions, a right he argued was implied by the 14th Amendment's due process clause. In notable dissents Justice John Marshall Harlan condemned the ruling as unwarranted judicial meddling in legislation, while Justice Oliver Wendell Holmes, Jr., attacked it for reading laissez-faire economics and Social Darwinism into the Constitution.

Numerous contemporaries, including Pres. Theodore Roosevelt, denounced the decision as an effort by reactionary judges to block social legislation. Nonetheless, during the "*Lochner* era" (1905-37), the Supreme Court continued to apply *Lochner's* reasoning to nullify state minimum wage, child labor, banking, and insurance statutes. The Court finally abandoned *Lochner's* jurisprudence in *West Coast Hotel* v. *Parrish* (1937), but "*Lochnerism*" continues to symbolize the misuse of judicial power.

—DONALD W. ROGERS

See Also: *Holmes, Oliver Wendell, Jr.; Peckham, Rufus Wheeler, Jr.; Supreme Court.*

BIBLIOGRAPHY: Gillman, Howard, *The Constitution Besieged: The Rise and Demise of Lochner Era Police Powers Jurisprudence* (Duke Univ. Press 1993); Kens, Paul, *Judicial Power and Reform Politics: The Anatomy of Lochner v. New York* (Univ. Press of Kansas 1990).

■ **LOCKE, ALAIN LEROY (1886-1954),** educator and critic. Born in Philadelphia, Pennsylvania, Locke attended Harvard and was the first African-American Rhodes scholar. From 1917 to 1953 he was professor of philosophy at Howard University. His avocation, and his passion, was heralding New Negro Movement (Harlem Renaissance) artists. His many books, such as *The New Negro* (1925) and *Negro Art: Past and Present* (1936), highlighted the contributions of black artists.

See Also: *African Americans.*

■ **LOCKE, JOHN (1632-1702),** English philosopher. Throughout the 18th century, Locke's philosophy and political theories remained influential in Europe and America. A prominent figure in the Enlightenment, Locke was perhaps most renowned in America for his *Two Treatises on Civil Government* (1690), which influenced Thomas Jefferson's drafting of the Declaration of Independence.

Born in Wrington, Somerset, Locke was educated at Oxford, where he later taught philosophy, rhetoric, and Greek. He became secretary for the future Earl of Shaftesbury, who served as one of the proprietors of the young Carolina colony. In 1669, at Shaftesbury's behest, Locke drafted the Carolina constitution, a document that called for a balance of interests between the landed aristocracy and the independent land-holding common planters. Locke fled to the Netherlands in 1683 when Shaftesbury was suspected in plots against the government. There he wrote the *Two Treatises* and *An Essay Concerning Human Understanding* (1690).

Among his contributions to Revolutionary thought in America was his insistence, in the *Second Treatise*, that government had an obligation to protect people's property and possessions. Accordingly, citizens must submit willingly to civil law and obey the ruler. Ultimately, however, the people, not the executive, were sovereign. Indeed, Locke contended that government rests on popular consent and rebellion is permissible to protect rights and liberties. His *Essay on Toleration* (1689) also influenced Jefferson's and James Madison's views on religious freedom.

See Also: *Revolution, American.*

BIBLIOGRAPHY: Ashcraft, Richard, *Revolutionary Politics and Locke's Two Treatises on Government* (Princeton Univ. Press 1986); Dunn, J., *The Political Thought of John Locke* (Cambridge Univ. Press 1969); May, Henry F., *The Enlightenment in America* (Oxford Univ. Press 1976).

■ **LOCKOUT,** the closing of a place of employment by the employer to prevent the workers' entry, usually as a result of the refusal of those workers to meet employer demands. In contrast, a strike is a stoppage of labor initiated by workers.

See Also: Labor Movement.

■ **LOCOFOCOS,** faction of the Democratic party during the 1830s. The name Locofoco originated during a Democratic party meeting at New York's Tammany Hall on Oct. 29, 1835, when the Jacksonian wing of the Democrats seized control of the meeting from the conservatives. In response, their opponents turned off the gas, leaving the hall in darkness. The Jacksonians then lit candles with matches (called "locofocos") and continued their meeting. The program of the Locofocos centered on strict Democratic orthodoxy. They objected to paper money and the Bank of the United States, and they opposed Democrats within New York who chartered banks and endorsed government spending for internal improvements. The Locofocos supported labor unions and welcomed labor leaders into their fold. They sought to rid the Democratic party of the taint of privilege and to instill the democratic ideal of equality. Locofocoism spread throughout the eastern cities of the United States, as radical Democratic factions sprang up in Philadelphia and Boston.

Locofocoism was regional, however, as western Democrats favored the printing of paper money and bank credit in order to promote expansion there. Thus, the scope of the Locofocos was always limited. Andrew Jackson held some of the Locofocos' views, and he waged an unremitting and hostile war against the Bank of the United States and against paper money, leading to the economic depression of 1837. The Locofocos kept the debate about political participation and equality for men in the national limelight.

—Kathryn A. Abbott

See Also: Banks of the United States, First and Second; Democratic Party; Jackson, Andrew; Political Parties.
BIBLIOGRAPHY: Fox, Dixon Ryan, *The Decline of Aristocracy in the Politics of New York, 1801-1840* (Harper & Row 1965); Schlesinger, Arthur M., Jr., *The Age of Jackson* (Little, Brown 1945).

■ **LODGE, HENRY CABOT (1850-1924),** political leader, noted for his opposition to the League of Nations. Born in Boston and a member of a powerful Massachusetts family, he graduated from Harvard (1871) and Harvard Law School (1874) and wrote several historical works before entering politics as a Republican. After serving in the U.S. House of Representatives (1887-93), he entered the Senate in 1893 and remained there until his death. He rose to become majority leader and chairman of the Foreign Relations Committee (1918-24). A believer in U.S. leadership in world affairs and in a strong American military, Lodge greatly influenced his friend Theodore Roosevelt. Lodge supported America's entry into World War I but opposed the Treaty of Versailles and the Covenant of the League of Nations, which led to their rejection by the Senate.

■ *LOEWE* V. *LAWLOR* **(1908),** U.S. Supreme Court case in which labor unions were held liable to prosecution under antitrust laws. Often called "the Danbury Hatters' case," *Loewe* involved a suit by the owner of a Connecticut hat company against the hatters' union and its local agent. The union was attempting to organize workers at the hat factory, and the American Federation of Labor was urging a boycott of the hat company's products. The Court ruled (9-0) that union strikes and boycotts could be considered illegal combinations in restraint of trade under the Sherman Antitrust Act (1890) and that union members could be held personally liable for economic damages suffered by a business. The decision marked a major setback for the labor movement and was not fully reversed until Congress passed the Wagner National Labor Relations Act (1935), which guaranteed workers the right to form labor unions.

See Also: Supreme Court.

■ **LOGAN, JAMES (1674-1751),** colonial administrator and jurist. Born in Ireland, Logan came to Pennsylvania as a secretary to William Penn in 1699. He later served on the provincial council (1703-47) and as mayor of Philadelphia (1722) and chief justice of the Pennsylvania Supreme Court (1731-39). An amateur botanist, Logan corresponded and exchanged plant specimens with Swedish botanist Carolus Linnaeus.

■ **LOG CABINS,** ubiquitous symbol of pioneer America. They first appeared in the Delaware

Valley in the 17th century, where they were built by settlers from Sweden and Finland who came with a tradition of using axes to build in wood. The technique was quickly picked up by other settlers, for with a few tools and a little training, several men could erect a rough shelter in a day and a solid house in a week. Indians also quickly learned these construction techniques and probably did as much as colonists to spread the practice of building in wood across the frontiers of North America. Descriptions of Indian towns in Pennsylvania and Ohio frequently remark on their resemblance to the pioneer settlements of whites. Indeed, the Delaware Valley was what cultural geographers call a "cultural hearth," the originating place for a unique woodland material culture that combined traits from both the Old and New Worlds. Indians, for example, learned European log construction while Europeans copied Indian subsistence and survival techniques. In the 19th century the log cabin came to stand for the rising importance of the West in the economic and political life of the nation, especially after 1840, when William Henry Harrison won the presidency by appealing to voters as the "log cabin" candidate from Ohio.

See Also: Frontier in American History.

BIBLIOGRAPHY: Jordan, Terry G., and Matti Kaups, *The American Backwoods Frontier: An Ethnic and Ecological Interpretation* (Johns Hopkins Univ. Press 1989); Shurtleff, Harold R., *The Log Cabin Myth* (Harvard Univ. Press 1939).

■ **LOMBARD, CAROLE (1908-42),** top movie actress of the 1930s. Born June Alice Peters in Fort Wayne, Indiana, she starred in "screwball" comedies such as *Nothing Sacred* (1937) and *To Be or Not To Be* (1942) and married leading man Clark Gable in 1939. She died in an airplane crash.

See Also: Motion Pictures.

■ **LOMBARDI, VINCE (1913-70),** football coach. Born in Brooklyn, New York, he was a star lineman at Fordham University and became an assistant coach at the college and professional levels. He later coached the National Football League's Green Bay Packers (1959-68) and Washington Redskins (1969). Lombardi led the Packers to five league championships and two Super Bowl titles (1967-68) with a trademark style based on solid fundamentals and crisp execution.

See Also: Football, Sports.

■ **LONDON, JACK (1876-1916),** naturalist author and journalist. London was born in San Francisco, California, and spent the earlier years of his life in the waterfront communities of the West Coast. He became politically active as a socialist in the 1890s. London traveled to the Klondike gold region in 1897-98 and upon his return began submitting his writings to magazines. His work was published in *Overland Monthly* in December 1898 and *Atlantic Monthly* in 1899. He published his first collection of stories in 1900. The Klondike expedition also provided the fodder for two early novels, *The Call of the Wild* (1903) and *White Fang* (1906). Considered a naturalist for his portrayals of characters gravely affected by their physical and emotional surroundings, London wrote *The Sea Wolf* (1904), *The Road* (1907), the autobiographical *Martin Eden* (1909), *John Barleycorn* (1913), and *The Strength of the Strong* (1914). He served as a war correspondent in Vera Cruz, Mexico, in 1914. London was a prolific author, writing over 50 books between 1900 and his death at the age of 40.

See Also: Novel.

■ **LONDON ECONOMIC CONFERENCE (1933),** international conference on trade, economic, and monetary policy issues. Convened in June 1933 as the United States and Europe were gripped by the Great Depression, the conference was widely seen as an opportunity for the major powers to reverse the worldwide economic decline. The delegations included many eminent political leaders and economic theorists, but the nations were unsure of what actions to take. Pres. Franklin D. Roosevelt's administration was divided over whether international cooperation or righting the domestic economy would be the most effective first measure to end the Depression. Many of Roosevelt's advisers feared the Europeans wanted to force the United States to again link the value of the dollar to the price of gold. Roosevelt on July 3 attacked the conference for focusing on monetary issues and ignoring the root causes of the Depression. With the United States on the sidelines, the conference soon adjourned.

See Also: New Deal.

BIBLIOGRAPHY: Schlesinger, Arthur M., Jr., *The Age of Roosevelt: The Coming of the New Deal* (Houghton Mifflin 1959).

■ **LONDON NAVAL CONFERENCE (1930),** international peace conference aimed at limiting new construction of warships. The conference resulted in a treaty allowing Japan to operate three heavy cruisers for every five in the U.S. and British fleets. Britain negotiated an escape clause in the treaty that allowed the Royal Navy to build additional cruisers if either France or Italy increased the size of its navy. The "5-5-3" ratio actually allowed Japan to increase the relative size of its battle fleet in the Pacific, but it was seen by the Japanese military as acceptance of second-class naval status by the civilian government in Tokyo and a threat to Japanese hopes to achieve military superiority in the eastern Pacific. When the military gained control of the Japanese government in 1934, the new cabinet immediately repudiated the London treaty and launched a major naval building program to catch up with the United States and Britain.

See Also: Navy; New Deal.

BIBLIOGRAPHY: O'Connor, Raymond G., *Perilous Equilibrium: The United States and the London Naval Conference of 1930* (Greenwood Press 1969).

As governor and U.S. senator, Huey Long amassed much power within the state of Louisiana and brandished significant influence in national politics by the time of his assassination in 1935.

■ **LONG, HUEY (1893-1935),** governor of Louisiana and U.S. senator. One of the most extraordinary politicians in 20th-century America, Long was born and raised in Winnfield, a town in the poor hill country of Louisiana. He became a successful lawyer and railroad commissioner before his election as governor in 1928. During the campaign, Long tapped into statewide discontent with conservative rule by advocating tax-the-rich programs. While in office, the "Kingfish," as he was called, constructed a powerful political machine, through which he controlled nearly every level of government in Louisiana. Apart from implementing tax reforms, Long expanded social services and developed the state's infrastructure. Long was impeached for misconduct in 1929 but never convicted. In 1930 he was elected to the U.S. Senate, but he did not take his seat until 1932, after he had assured the succession of the governorship to a political ally.

Although he initially supported Pres. Franklin D. Roosevelt, Long began publicly to criticize the president in 1933 for allegedly succumbing to con-

servative constituencies. For the next two years Long's populist shadow stretched far beyond the Senate floor. Now a national figure, he proposed a radical redistribution of personal wealth, which would assure every American a certain standard of living and access to the same benefits and services enjoyed by the few. With his popularity soaring, Long began in 1935 to discuss a possible run for the presidency. This ambition was ended, however, by Long's assassination at the hands of the son-in-law of a defeated political opponent.

See Also: New Deal; Populism; Share-Our-Wealth.

BIBLIOGRAPHY: Hair, William Ivy, *The Kingfish and His Realm: The Life and Times of Huey P. Long* (Louisiana State Univ. Press 1991); Williams, T. Harry, *Huey Long* (Knopf 1969).

■ **LONG, STEPHEN HARRIMAN (1784-1864),** American army engineer and explorer. Born in Hopkinton, New Hampshire, Long pioneered the use of steamboat travel while exploring the upper Mississippi

River in 1819. In 1820 he extended his survey overland, crossing the Great Plains to the Colorado Rockies. His party made the first ascent of Pike's Peak, and Long's Peak was named for him. Long's published maps of the region, which labeled the plains east of the mountains the Great American Desert, helped to perpetuate Zebulon Pike's earlier conclusion (1806) that the area was unfit for cultivation and settlement. These descriptions influenced American expansion in the region for several decades. His reconnaissance, sponsored by the government, served as a model for future western exploration. In 1823 Long led an expedition along the plains border with British Canada. For most of the rest of his life, Long acted as a consulting engineer to railroad development, finally retiring at the age of 78.

See Also: *Exploration and Discovery; Pike, Zebulon.*
BIBLIOGRAPHY: Goetzmann, William H., *Exploration and Empire: The Explorer and the Scientist in the Winning of the American West* (Norton 1966).

■ **LONGFELLOW, HENRY WADSWORTH (1807-82),** poet. Longfellow was born in Portland, Maine,

The most popular American poet by the time of his death in 1882, Henry Wadsworth Longfellow authored such American classics as *Evangeline*, *Hiawatha*, and "Paul Revere's Ride."

and graduated from Bowdoin College in 1825, a classmate of Nathaniel Hawthorne. He returned to Bowdoin as a professor of modern languages (1829-35) and then taught at Harvard University. Longfellow's first volume of poetry, *Voices of the Night*, was published in 1839 and included the poem "A Psalm of Life," which became one of the most popular poems of the era. In 1841 he published a collection entitled *Ballads*, which contained "The Village Blacksmith," and then in 1847 wrote the famous *Evangeline: A Tale of Arcadie* (1847). Longfellow retired from teaching in 1854 and devoted himself to poetry. He was concerned with creating a national literature, and many of his best-known poems narrate either a specific event or re-create the atmosphere of America in the colonial era. *The Song of Hiawatha* (1855), *The Courtship of Miles Standish* (1858), and *Tales of a Wayside Inn* (1863) all were great successes.

See Also: *Poetry.*

■ **LONG ISLAND,** 120-mile-long island in southeastern New York, the fourth largest (1,723 square miles) island in the United States. Long Island is densely populated, and two of its four counties (Queens and Kings) are part of New York City. The island was originally inhabited by Algonquian tribes. In the 17th century the Massachusetts Bay Colony and the Dutch East India Company founded settlements there. Industrial and residential growth accelerated rapidly after World War II. The south shore of the island is a popular recreational area.

■ **LONG ISLAND, BATTLE OF (1776),** American defeat in the Revolutionary War. Seeking to defend New York City from British forces based on Staten Island, Gen. George Washington in August took up positions on Brooklyn Heights, on the western edge of Long Island. Sir William Howe led a British attack, supported by naval forces under his brother Richard. Fearful of being trapped and anticipating defeat, Washington pulled his men out on the night of August 29 and withdrew to Manhattan.

See Also: *Revolution, American.*

■ **LONGSTREET, JAMES (1821-1904),** Confederate general. Born in Edgefield District, South Carolina, Longstreet was a career officer in the U.S. Army, serving under Zachary Taylor and Winfield

Scott. He resigned in June 1861 to join the Confederate army and was appointed brigadier general. In 1862 he became commander of the First Corps of the Army of Northern Virginia. At Gettysburg (July 1863), Longstreet commanded the right wing. Later he was accused of losing the battle by delaying an attack on the second day. He was with Robert E. Lee at the surrender at Appomattox. In the postwar years Longstreet joined the Republican party and was appointed U.S. minister to Turkey in 1880.

See Also: Civil War; Gettysburg, Battle of.

■ LOOKOUT MOUNTAIN, BATTLE OF (1863),

Civil War battle for control of the city of Chattanooga and, ultimately, eastern Tennessee. On November 24, Union troops scaled the mountain in the face of little Confederate resistance. The next day other Union troops, without orders, negotiated a steep hill called Missionary Ridge under the Confederate guns, but the guns could not be lowered enough to be effective. This stunning and heroic victory soon gained the mythical-sounding name of the "Battle Above the Clouds."

See Also: Civil War; Missionary Ridge, Battle of.

■ LORD DUNMORE'S WAR (1764), war between

the Shawnees and American colonists. In the spring of 1774, Virginia Gov. John Dunmore helped provoke war by circulating a proclamation that the Shawnees and colonists were already engaged in a war. Although Shawnee leader Cornstalk assured British authorities of his good intentions, American colonists had already begun killing Shawnees, and by mid-May, Shawnee warriors had retaliated in attacks along the frontier. Fighting continued throughout the summer, and on October 10 Cornstalk and 300 Shawnee and Delaware warriors fought a battle with militia under the command of Daniel Boone at Point Pleasant on the Ohio River. Following the battle the army of Virginia surrounded Shawnee towns on the Scioto River, forcing their surrender. In the Treaty of Camp Charlotte, Cornstalk and other chiefs yielded Shawnee hunting rights south of the Ohio River in exchange for American promises to keep colonists out of the northern Ohio Valley.

See Also: Boone, Daniel; Cornstalk; Indians of North America; Revolution, American.

■ LOS ANGELES, largest city in California and

second largest in the United States, encompassing 463.9 square miles on the Pacific Ocean coast in the southern part of the state. The site of the "City of Angels" was visited in 1769 by Franciscan fathers traveling with the Spanish explorer Gaspar de Portolá. A town was established there in 1781 to supply the Spanish presidios with fresh produce. Los Angeles grew under Spanish and Mexican rule as a cattle-ranching center. After the Mexican War, California became a United States territory in 1848. Steady population growth began with railway connections to San Francisco and Santa Fe in the 1870s. Los Angeles boomed in the early 20th century with the discovery of oil and the beginnings of the motion picture industry. As world headquarters for the movie industry Los Angeles was the location of "Hollywood," a mythic, iconic place, with movie stars, movie sets, and an eternally sunny climate. During World War II Los Angeles grew with an influx of population to work in the war industry plants. After World War II, the surrounding area exploded with suburban development in Orange County and San Bernardino County. More recently Los Angeles has come to represent the ultimate modern ethnic mix in the United States. In addition to its white and African-American populations, the city has acquired a vast influx of Hispanics (mostly Mexicans) and Asians seeking to resettle and work in California. The strains of this diversity and growth have occasionally exploded into urban violence, as in the rioting following the verdict in the Rodney King case in 1992. Population (1994): 3,448,613.

See Also: City in American History; Ethnic Groups; Hollywood.

■ LOS ANGELES RIOTS (1992), one of the most

violent episodes of urban unrest and ethnic conflict in 20th-century America. On March 3, 1991, a bystander videotaped four white Los Angeles police officers brutally beating Rodney King, an African-American motorist, after having stopped him for a traffic violation. Televised across the country, the incident shocked the public and outraged African Americans. Because of the widespread publicity of the case, the trial of the four police officers charged with the beating was moved to Simi Valley, a predominantly white suburb north of Los Angeles. On Apr. 30, 1992, the jury composed of 10 whites, one Hispanic, and one Asian American acquitted the four officers.

Shortly after the verdict was announced, rioting and arson erupted in the African-American community of South Central Los Angeles. Although many of the participants directed their outrage at whites, they also attacked Korean-American shopkeepers, who were seen in the community as obstacles to the economic freedom of African Americans. Hispanics also participated widely in the riots, causing an anti-immigrant backlash among some white Angelenos.

By the time the police and National Guard had restored a tenuous order, more than 50 people were dead, over 2,000 injured, and some 12,000 arrested. Widespread looting and vandalism resulted in property damage of almost $3 billion. Although the outcome of the Rodney King trial precipitated the riots, the escalating poverty and neglect of South Central Los Angeles fostered resentment among many African Americans that found its outlet in the violence.

See Also: Ethnic Groups; Race and Racism.
BIBLIOGRAPHY: Chang, Edward T., and Russell C. Leong, eds., *Los Angeles—Struggles Toward Multiethnic Community: Asian American, African American, and Latino Perspectives* (Univ. of Washington Press 1994); Gooding-Williams, Robert, ed., *Reading Rodney King/Reading Urban Uprising* (Routledge 1993).

■ **LOST CAUSE,** sentimental, mythical conception of the Confederate States of America. *The Lost Cause* was the title of Edward A. Pollard's history of the Confederacy, first published in 1866, but the term came to signify the mourning of Southerners over the loss of the Southern way of life based on plantation slavery. By the 1880s, the Lost Cause ideal had become a celebration of the Confederacy. Numerous monuments and statues were built commemorating Confederate generals and battles. Southern veterans formed the United Confederate Veterans. Children of the veterans formed the Sons of Confederate Veterans and the United Daughters of the Confederacy. The idea of the Lost Cause kept alive a sense of Southern pride and honor, along with less lofty ideals such as white supremacy.

See Also: Confederate States of America; Reconstruction; Slavery.

■ **LOST GENERATION,** early 20th-century circle of expatriate authors. The coining of the term "The Lost Generation" to refer to a group of American authors living in Europe, particularly Paris, between the two world wars is credited to Gertrude Stein. In the preface to *The Sun Also Rises* (1926), Ernest Hemingway quotes Stein as having said to him, "You are all a lost generation." The term was taken up by literary critic Malcolm Cowley in his accounts of the group, *The Lost Generation* (1931) and *Exile's Return* (1934). Cowley was also involved with the magazines *Secession* and *Broom*, which, along with *Transition*, *Exile*, and others, published the circle. Traveling or settled abroad were such noted figures as Hemingway, F. Scott Fitzgerald, Hart Crane, John Dos Passos, Ezra Pound, and Cowley himself. Hemingway's *A Moveable Feast*, posthumously published in 1964, was a memoir of the community in Paris during the 1920s. Additional works that describe the circle include Robert McAlmon's *Being Geniuses Together* (1938) and Morley Callaghan's *That Summer in Paris* (1963).

See Also: Hemingway, Ernest Miller; Stein, Gertrude.

■ **LOTTERIES,** popular alternative to taxes in most states. Federal, state, and local governments routinely sponsored lotteries throughout the early 19th century to finance public projects. But in the 1830s reformers attacked state lotteries as immoral because they encouraged gambling, and by the Civil War most government lotteries had been abolished. The Louisiana Lottery, a state-chartered monopoly, flourished until 1895, when Congress banned interstate lotteries. The first modern state lottery was introduced in New Hampshire in 1963 as an alternative to a state sales or income tax. Lotteries spread across the country in the 1970s and 1980s as state legislatures turned to legalized gambling as a new source of revenue that did not require new taxes. Critics of state lotteries contend lottery games, which are widely accessible and inexpensive to play, tend to exploit people with lower incomes, who may see them as a means of escaping poverty. In many states casino gambling, which promises better odds and more frequent payoffs, has become a competitor of the state lottery.

■ **LOTTERY CASE.** *See: Champion v. Ames.*

■ **LOUDOUN, 4TH EARL OF.** *See: Campbell, John, 4th Earl of Loudoun.*

■ **LOUIS, JOE (1914-81),** champion boxer. Born Joseph Louis Barrow in Lafayette, Alabama, he began his professional career in 1934. Over the

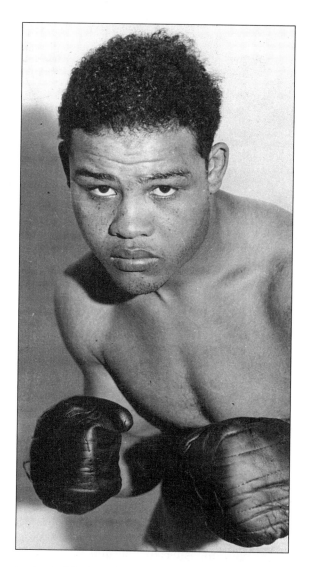

Joe Louis, "the Brown Bomber," defended his title 24 times, more than any other heavyweight champion.

next 15 years Louis was defeated only once, by the German Max Schmeling in 1936. A year later Louis devastated James Braddock, taking the heavyweight championship and earning the nickname "the Brown Bomber." In a 1938 rematch Louis convincingly knocked out Schmeling in a little over two minutes, winning both the bout and a profound moral victory over the state-sponsored racism of Nazi Germany. Louis remained champion longer than any other heavyweight, winning a record 25 title defenses. He retired undefeated in 1949 with a career record of 68 victories and 1 loss. Two brief comeback attempts in 1950 and 1951 failed against younger fighters.

See Also: African Americans; Boxing; Sports.

■ **LOUISIANA,** state named for the territory that once covered more than 800,000 square miles of the North American continent. It is bounded by Arkansas on the north, Texas on the west, the Gulf of Mexico on the south, and Mississippi on the north and east. The Mississippi River forms part of its eastern border and passes through New Orleans, one of the nation's leading ports. Louisiana ranks fourth in oil production and second in natural gas; both commodities are found along the Gulf coast and also offshore. Louisiana is also second in commercial fishing. Oil refineries and petrochemical plants are by far the dominant industrial facilities.

Louisiana was ruled by the French and Spanish before being purchased by the United States in 1803. It became a state in 1812. Plantations worked by slaves dominated the economy before the Civil War. Following the Civil War, the state was slow to recover until oil was discovered in 1901. Huey P. Long, governor and U.S. senator from Louisiana, was the state's leading 20th-century political figure.

Capital: Baton Rouge. Area: 53,803 square miles. Population (1995 est.): 4,342,000.

See Also: Acadians; Cajuns; Farragut, David G.; Jazz; La Salle, René-Robert Cavalier, Sieur de; Long, Huey; Louisiana Purchase; Mississippi River; New Orleans; New Orleans, Battle of.

■ **LOUISIANA PURCHASE (1803),** the purchase by the United States of the French claims to some 820,000 square miles of North American territory. By 1800, the United States spanned nearly 1 mil-

OREGON
COUNTRY

Columbia R.

Snake R.

BRITISH NORTH AMERICA

ME
(to MA)

VT

NH　MA

NY

RI

CT

Mississippi R.

ILLINOIS
TERR.
1809

MICH.
TERR.
1805

Missouri R.

PA

NJ

INDIANA
TERR.
1809

OH

MD

DE

Platte R.

LOUISIANA
PURCHASE

Ohio R.

KY

VA

Colorado R.

Arkansas R.

TN

NC

SPANISH
TERRITORY

SC

MISS. TERR.
1804

GA

ATLANTIC
OCEAN

PACIFIC
OCEAN

Rio Grande

SPANISH
FLORIDA

Gulf of Mexico

0　　　250　　　500 Miles

0　　250　　500 Kilometers

LOUISIANA PURCHASE: 1803

lion square miles, extending west to the Mississippi River, whose trade had assumed a significant place in the nation's economy. The port of New Orleans provided the linchpin of this trade. Louisiana comprised the Spanish possessions not only of the Mississippi and New Orleans but also of the majority of the territory west of the river to the Rocky Mountains and extending from the Gulf of Mexico in the south to British North America. In 1801, Pres. Thomas Jefferson learned of Spain's intent to cede Louisiana to France, and by 1802 he had authorized the ambassador to France, Robert Livingston, to negotiate a U.S. purchase of New Orleans if possible. On Apr. 11, 1803, Livingston was surprised to receive France's offer to sell its rights to all of Louisiana, including New Orleans. For $15 million the United States doubled the size of territory it claimed.

France's unexpected move resulted from the failure of Emperor Napoleon's colonial designs in the Caribbean. France had lost St. Domingue (modern-day Haiti) following a slave rebellion led by Pierre Dominique Toussaint L'Ouverture and hoped to regain it, an initiative supported by Jefferson, who was eager to prevent the spread of such rebellion to the American south. As long as Napoleon thought that victory in St. Domingue was possible, he refused to entertain the idea of selling North American territory. The French army was devastated in St. Domingue, however, and Napoleon surrendered his colonial dream, deciding to sell the vast Louisiana territory to the United States.

The purchase launched American expansion across the continent, and as 19th-century American historian Henry Adams observed, the nation owed its transformation from a weak confederation on the Atlantic Ocean to an empire to "the desperate courage of five hundred thousand Haitian negroes who would not be enslaved." Prior to the acquisition, Jefferson had authorized Meriwether Lewis, his private secretary, and William Clark, a former army officer, to explore the northwestern territory between the Mississippi and the Pacific Ocean. With the purchase, the expedition took on added significance for the nation. Between May 1804 and September 1806, as they journeyed from St. Louis to the Pacific and back, Lewis and Clark paved the way for the later incorporation of the territory lying beyond the Mississippi with the rest of the nation. In 1812, Louisiana would become the first of 13 states to emerge from the territory bought nearly a decade earlier.

—DOREN BEN-ATAR

See Also: Frontier in American History; Jefferson, Thomas; Lewis and Clark Expedition.
BIBLIOGRAPHY: Deconde, Alexander, *This Affair of Louisiana* (Scribner 1976); Tucker, Robert W., and David C. Hendrickson, *Empire of Liberty: The Statecraft of Thomas Jefferson* (Oxford Univ. Press 1990).

■ **LOVEJOY, ELIJAH P. (1802-37),** abolitionist. Born in Albion, Maine, Lovejoy was a Presbyterian minister. As editor of the *St. Louis Observer*, he supported temperance and abolitionist causes. Harassed because of his abolitionist views, he moved to Albion, Illinois, in 1836, but he continued to be harassed, and three of his printing presses were destroyed. In November 1837, while trying to save a fourth press, Lovejoy was shot and killed by a mob. John Quincy Adams wrote that his murder sent a shock as of an earthquake throughout the country.

See Also: Slavery.

■ *LOVING V. VIRGINIA* **(1967),** U.S. Supreme Court case that struck down Virginia's antimiscegenation law barring marriages between blacks and whites. Loving, a white man married to a black woman, challenged his conviction under the law. The Court ruled (9-0) that such laws represented an improper government infringement on individual liberty.

In *Pace* v. *Alabama* (1893) the Supreme Court had allowed states to punish interracial fornication. The so-called equal discrimination exception to the 14th Amendment's equal protection clause created in *Pace* was in clear conflict with *Brown* v. *Board of Education* (1954) and subsequent civil rights cases that insisted on legal equality among the races.

The Court, however, had been reluctant to act against miscegenation laws, realizing such a decision would increase white resistance to the civil rights movement in the South. It also perhaps hoped that an ongoing campaign to repeal such laws would in time succeed. Fifteen states had repealed miscegenation laws since 1950, but Virginia was one of 16 southern states that continued to carry such a law on the books.

See Also: Civil Rights Movement; Supreme Court.
BIBLIOGRAPHY: Washington, Joseph R., *Marriage in Black and White* (Beacon Press 1972; reprint Univ. Press of America 1993).

■ **LOWELL, AMY (1874-1925),** poet and intellectual, leading figure in the Imagist literary movement. Born in Boston, Massachusetts, into a well-established family of industrialists, intellectuals, and poets that included such notables as Abbot Lawrence Lowell, Percival Lowell, Robert Lowell, and James Russell Lowell, Amy grew up as a bright, well-bred, but unattractive member of Boston society. She occupied her time with social functions and extensive travel until 1908, when she published her first sonnets in the *Atlantic*

Amy Lowell won the Pulitzer Prize in poetry in 1926 for her collection *What's O'Clock*.

Monthly. Thereafter poetry was her primary activity. In 1912 she published her first collection, *A Dome of Many-Coloured Glass* (1912), and in 1913 she moved to England where, with Ezra Pound, she became the leader of the emerging Imagist movement. She edited three anthologies called *Some Imagist Poets* (1915, 1916, 1917). During the next decade Lowell's commanding personality and excellent poetry earned her a central place in the literary world. She continued to publish poems in magazines and journals and several more collections, including *What's O'Clock* (1925, Pulitzer Prize). She also wrote influential criticism in *Six French Poets* (1915) and *Tendencies in Modern American Poetry* (1917) and a two-volume biography of John Keats in 1925.

See Also: Lowell, James Russell; Poetry; Women in American History.

■ **LOWELL, JAMES RUSSELL (1819-91),** poet, essay writer, and public figure. Lowell was born in Cambridge, Massachusetts. He graduated from Harvard University in 1838 as class poet and received his law degree there in 1840. The next year Lowell published his first volume of poetry, *A Year's Life*. In 1848 he published four volumes: *Poems: Second Series, A Fable for Critics, The Biglow Papers*, and *The Vision of Sir Launfal*. Together they showed the range and promise of his literary career. Lowell succeeded Henry Wadsworth Longfellow as a literature professor at Harvard in 1855. He was the first editor of the *Atlantic Monthly* (1857-61) and with Charles Eliot Norton edited the *North American Review* as well. Lowell served as the U.S. ambassador to Spain from 1877 to 1880 and then to England from 1880 to 1885. Throughout these years as an editor and public servant, Lowell also published extensively in the genres of poetry and the essay. His work includes satirical verses about his fellow literary lights, political addresses, and moralizing writings on the culture of his day.

See Also: Poetry.

■ **LOYALISTS,** American colonists opposed to separation from Great Britain during the American Revolution, called "Tories" by the Revolutionaries. Perhaps a fifth of the population, as many as half a million people, remained loyal to the British Crown. Loyalism was strongest in the lower south and weakest in New England. Americans who served as colonial officials were almost always Loyalists, as were most Anglican clergymen and large numbers of lawyers who had worked with colonial administrators. Loyalists also included members of ethnic minorities who had been persecuted by the dominant majority, such as the Highland Scots of the Carolinas and western New York. Moreover, many slaves and most Indians, the latter fearing aggressive expansion by independent American states, identified with the Loyalists. Some Loyalists were conservatives who were fearful of political or social upheaval. Others were people temperamentally opposed to resistance to established authority.

To suppress loyalism, patriots passed state treason acts that prohibited speaking or writing against the Revolution. They also punished Loyalists with bills of attainder, a legal process by which persons were deprived, without trial, of their civil rights and property (something later made illegal in the U.S. Constitution). In some areas, notably New York, South Carolina, Massachusetts, and Pennsylvania, Loyalists faced mob violence. A favorite punishment was the "grand Tory ride," in which a crowd hauled victims through the streets astride a sharp fence rail. Another was tarring and feathering, in which men were stripped to "buff and breeches" and their naked flesh coated liberally with heated tar and then feathers.

The British strategy for suppressing the Revolution depended upon mobilizing the Loyalists, but in most areas this proved impossible. The Loyalists were not a monolithic group and were often divided in their opinions. Many were sympathetic to patriot arguments, but the force of tradition simply made them unwilling to be disloyal to the Crown. Others believed in British invincibility and were apathetic. Still others were enthusiastic and committed supporters of continued membership in the British Empire. As many as 50,000 of these Loyalists fought for the king during the Revolution. Many joined Loyalist militias or engaged in irregular warfare, especially in the lower south. In 1780, when Gen. George Washington's Continental army numbered about 9,000 men, there were 8,000 American Loyalists serving in the British army in America.

As many as 80,000 Loyalists fled the country after the Revolution, taking up residence in England, the

British West Indies, or Canada. Their property was confiscated by the states and sold at public auction. Although the British government compensated many for their losses, most of the Loyalists were reluctant and unhappy exiles. Former governor Thomas Hutchinson of Massachusetts wrote that he "had rather die in a little country farm-house in New England than in the best nobleman's seat in old England." Despite their disagreement with the patriots on essential political questions, most Loyalists remained Americans. Their melancholy reflected the realization that they had lost their country.

See Also: Revolution, American.

BIBLIOGRAPHY: Calhoon, Robert M., *The Loyalists in Revolutionary America, 1760-1781* (Harcourt Brace Jovanovich 1973); Magee, Joan, *Loyalist Mosaic: A Multi-Ethnic Heritage* (Dundurn Press 1984); Moore, Christopher, *The Loyalists: Revolution, Exile, Settlement* (Macmillan of Canada 1984); Norton, Mary Beth, *The British-Americans: The Loyalist Exiles in England, 1774-1789* (Little, Brown 1972).

■ **LUCE, CLARE BOOTH (1903-87),** playwright, politician, and diplomat, born in New York City. She was the managing editor of *Vanity Fair* in the early 1930s. In 1935 she married publisher Henry R. Luce. She wrote the hit plays *The Women* (1936), *Kiss the Boys Goodbye* (1938), and *Margin for Error* (1939). In 1943, she won a seat in the U.S. House of Representatives as a Republican from Connecticut and served two terms. From 1953 to 1956 she was ambassador to Italy for the Eisenhower administration.

See Also: Luce, Henry; Women in American History.

■ **LUCE, HENRY (1898-1967),** journalist, editor, and publisher. The son of a Presbyterian missionary, he was born in Tengchow, China. In 1913, Luce arrived at the Hotchkiss School in Lakeville, Connecticut, where he met Briton Hadden. Both attended Yale, and then together they founded the weekly *Time*, the first issue appearing in February 1923. The magazine's originality lay in its offering a concise summary and evaluation of the week's news. Hadden's death in 1929 left Luce in control of Time Incorporated. He hired Hadden's cousin, John S. Martin, to edit the magazine, which Hadden had done, and *Time*'s circulation began to increase noticeably. In 1930, Luce initiated publication of the monthly *Fortune*, and he introduced his photo magazine *Life* in 1936. *Life* sold extraordinarily well from the start, attaining a circulation greater than half a million within its first month. Luce wrote the introduction to John F. Kennedy's 1940 *Why England Slept*, but *Life* would endorse Republican presidential candidate Richard M. Nixon in his 1960 race against the Democratic Kennedy. During World War II, Luce came to view the Soviet Union as a great threat to the role of the United States as he had envisioned it in his 1941 article for *Life*, "The American Century." Luce brought out *Sports Illustrated* in 1954, which required several years to begin to turn a profit, and retired a decade later, having shaped the nation's news media in a lasting fashion. He was married (1935) to editor and author Clare Boothe Luce.

—JAMES KESSENIDES

See Also: Magazines.

BIBLIOGRAPHY: Elson, Robert T., *Time Inc.: The Intimate History of a Publishing Enterprise, 1923-1941* (Atheneum 1968); Elson, Robert T., *The World of Time Inc.: The Intimate History of a Publishing Enterprise, 1941-1960* (Atheneum 1973).

■ **LUMBERING,** for most of American history, a frontier industry. By the time of the American Revolution, most of the East Coast had been denuded of local timber, and builders were increasingly relying on lumber from the pine forests of northern New England, where the first great logging and milling companies developed. By the mid-19th century, production had shifted to western Pennsylvania, upper New York State, and then to the forests of the western Great Lakes states. Western timber made possible the settlement of the Great Plains, where wood was scarce. Northern forests also supplied the insatiable demand of the railroads; it is estimated that half of all the timber cut after the Civil War was milled into railroad ties. By the end of the 19th century the center of the industry had moved to the piney woods of the Southeast and the great redwood forests of the Pacific Northwest.

Concern for the dwindling supply of forest land led to conservation efforts in the early 20th century. Under the agency of the Forest Service, the federal government assumed management of millions of acres of land, and timber companies began to adopt principles of "sustained yield," which involved selective cutting and replanting. Heavy demand after World War II, however, led to overcutting and public controversies over the loss of old-growth forests and the destruction of habitat for woodland creatures such as the spotted owl of the Northwest. Even in the 20th century, the lumbering industry has had a difficult time overcoming the mentality of its frontier origins.

See Also: Frontier in American History.

BIBLIOGRAPHY: Fries, Robert F., *Empire in Pine: The Story of Lumbering in Wisconsin, 1830-1900* (Wm. Caxton 1989); Langston, Nancy, *Forest Dreams, Forest Nightmares: The Paradox of Old Growth in the Inland West* (Univ. of Washington Press 1995); Shepherd, Jack, *The Forest Killers: The Destruction of the American Wilderness* (Weybright & Talley 1975).

■ **LUNDY, BENJAMIN (1789-1839),** abolitionist. Born in Hardwick, New Jersey, Lundy organized one of the first antislavery societies in the United States, the Union Humane Society, in Ohio in 1815. He edited several antislavery newspapers, including *The Genius of Universal Emancipation*, published from 1821 until his death, and the *National Enquirer* (later the Pennsylvania *Freeman*) from 1836 to 1838. Lundy supported emancipation combined with colonization projects, hoping to settle freedmen in other nations. Lundy represents a conservative trend in abolitionist activity, the movement to free slaves while physically removing them from the United States.

See Also: Slavery.

■ **LUNDY'S LANE, BATTLE OF (1813),** battle during the War of 1812. It occurred in late July, three weeks after American forces led by Generals Jacob Brown and Winfield Scott defeated the British at Chippewa. At Lundy's Lane in Canada, along the Niagara River, American troops and British regulars fought to a costly stalemate in a two-day battle. The engagement proved to be the final battle along the Canadian border, as the British shifted their attention to New York and New Orleans.

See Also: War of 1812.

■ **LURTON, HORACE HARMON (1844-1914),** jurist. Born in Newport, Kentucky, he practiced law in Tennessee and served on the state's supreme court (1886-93) before becoming an associate justice of the U.S. Supreme Court (1910-14).

See Also: Supreme Court.

■ ***LUSITANIA, SINKING OF THE (1915),*** incident that helped lead to U.S. intervention in World War I. On Feb. 8, 1915, Germany declared the seas around Britain a war zone and started attacking neutral shipping. On May 15 a German submarine sank the liner *Lusitania*, killing 1,100 people, including 100 Americans. The incident swayed American public opinion sharply against Germany and provided interventionists with valuable propaganda. Although it also spurred government action to increase U.S. military readiness, two years passed before the United States entered the war.

See Also: World War I.

■ **LUTHERANS,** Protestant denominational family, followers of German theologian and reformation leader Martin Luther (1483-1546). Luther opposed the wealth and corruption of the papacy and believed that salvation would be granted on the basis of faith alone rather than by works. The first Lutheran congregations in America were formed by the Dutch in New York and the Swedes on the Delaware. The larger German immigration in the 18th century was a greater influence. Their congregations began in 1703. Henry Melchior Muhlenberg, perhaps the outstanding personality in American Lutheranism, came to America in 1742 to gather Lutherans and establish the church. Today most Lutherans in America are members of one of three bodies: the Evangelical Lutheran Church in America, the Lutheran Church–Missouri Synod, or the Wisconsin Evangelical Lutheran Synod. Many small independent churches remain. Lutherans in America are noted for their diversity, which is due mainly to emigrating from many different areas of northern Europe and to differing doctrines.

See Also: Religion.

■ **LYNCH, THOMAS (1749-79),** politician. Born in Winyaw, South Carolina, Lynch participated widely in that colony's war efforts against the British during the American Revolution. Apart from his many local political appointments, he was a member of the First and Second Continental Congresses and signed the Declaration of Independence.

See Also: Declaration of Independence.

■ **LYNCHING,** term applied to various methods of summary punishment inflicted without regard to legal procedures. Although not uniquely American, lynching has been conspicuous throughout American history and figures prominently in the regional identities of the South and West.

The origin of the word "lynching" remains obscure. The term probably entered the American lexicon during the Revolution when Charles Lynch (1736-96) of Bedford County, Virginia, waged a vigilante campaign against suspected Loyalists. In subsequent decades popular tribunals throughout the nation periodically punished transgressors of community standards.

Only after roughly 1830 did lynching become synonymous with death at the hands of a mob. Regional distinctions in lynching also emerged. In the North courts and police increasingly suppressed lynch mobs. In the West lynchings occurred more frequently. They were condoned as a necessary form of spontaneous frontier justice that persisted until formal institutions emerged. In the South both slavery and Southern notions of honor encouraged white men to respond to challenges to their authority and honor through extralegal means. Abolitionists and slaves charged with insurrection became targets of increasingly deadly Southern mobs.

After the Civil War lynching became pervasive in the South. Southern mobs continued to execute victims long after lynching had become a rarity elsewhere. For African Americans lynching became one of the most glaring symbols of their oppression. Between 1880 and 1930 Southern mobs lynched approximately 3,220 African Americans and some 723 whites. After 1930 lynching diminished rapidly, until it virtually ceased as a regular occurrence during the 1950s.

Various explanations have been offered for the prevalence of lynching in American history. Apologists contended that lynchings occurred where legal institutions were distant. White Southerners defended lynchings as their justifiable response to African-American criminality. Little evidence substantiates either justification. Lynchings routinely occurred where courts operated and law officers were present. Southern mobs regularly executed victims for noncapital offenses or for no crime whatsoever. A more convincing explanation for lynching is that it reflected racism, xenophobia, and antiradicalism; the ritual of lynching warned African Americans and other minority groups that their lives were never secure. Traditions of popular justice, localism, suspicion of government, and contempt for legal procedures also sustained the practice. Lynching only diminished with the strengthening of civil authority and the weakening of traditional racial domination in the South during the 20th century.

—W. FITZHUGH BRUNDAGE

See Also: African Americans; Civil Rights Movement; Race and Racism.

BIBLIOGRAPHY: Brown, Richard Maxwell, *Strain of Violence: Historical Studies of American Violence and Vigilantism* (Oxford Univ. Press 1975); Tolnay, Stewart E., and E. M. Beck, *A Festival of Violence: An Analysis of Southern Lynchings, 1882-1930* (Univ. of Illinois Press 1995).

LYON, MARY (1797-1849), educator. She was born in Buckland, Massachusetts, and during the 1820s she collaborated with her friend Zilpah Grant on several unsuccessful attempts to create permanent seminaries for the education of young women. In 1837 Lyon founded the Mount Holyoke Female Seminary in South Hadley, Massachusetts (now Mount Holyoke College). She convened a board of trustees and single-handedly raised an endowment then taught classes and served as principal for 10 years.

See Also: Women's Movement.

In 1837, Mary Lyon founded the Mount Holyoke Seminary, the nation's first women's college, in South Hadley, Massachusetts.

M

■ MACARTHUR, DOUGLAS (1880-1964), U.S. Army general and one of the most controversial figures of the 20th century. Born on Jan. 26, 1880, in Little Rock Barracks, Arkansas, MacArthur was the son of Gen. Arthur MacArthur, Jr., Civil War hero and later commander of U.S. forces in the Philippines after the Spanish-American War, and Mary Hardy MacArthur. MacArthur graduated first in his class from the U.S. Military Academy at West Point in 1903. His first tour of duty was in the Philippines. After service in Mexico and with the Rainbow Division in France during World War I, he served twice again in the Philippines in the 1920s. In 1932 he

In 1941, on the eve of U.S. entry into World War II, Douglas MacArthur came out of retirement from the U.S. Army to command the nation's forces in the Far East and then all Allied forces in the Southwest Pacific.

led the troops that dispersed the Bonus Army in Washington, D.C. In the late 1930s, he became field marshal in the Philippine army after his retirement as U.S. Army chief of staff.

In July 1941, he was recalled as commanding general of the U.S. Army forces in the Far East, and in April 1942, he was named supreme commander of the Southwest Pacific Area, from which post he achieved fame as one of the most significant military leaders in World War II despite the fall of the Philippines early in the war. As supreme commander, he was chosen to receive the Japanese surrender on Sept. 2, 1945, and thereafter to serve as the supreme commander for the Allied powers during the occupation of Japan.

In the Korean War, MacArthur was named commander in chief of the United Nations forces. In September 1950, he initiated the Inchon Landing, arguably the strategic decision upon which his fame will ultimately rest. After his relief from duty due to disagreements with Pres. Harry S. Truman, he retired from the army. Thereafter, he served as chairman of the board of Sperry Rand Corporation and as an unofficial adviser to Presidents Dwight D. Eisenhower and John F. Kennedy, while living quietly with his second wife, Jean Faircloth MacArthur, and his son, Arthur MacArthur IV.

—CAROL MORRIS PETILLO

See Also: Korean War; Truman, Harry S.; World War II.

BIBLIOGRAPHY: James, D. Clayton, *The Years of MacArthur*, 3 vols. (Houghton Mifflin, 1970-85).

■ MCCARREN ACT. *See: Internal Security Act.*

■ MCCARRAN-WALTER ACT (1952), immigration law passed at the beginning of the Cold War. Although it barred racial barriers to immigration, the law retained national-origin quotas and severely limited immigration from Asian countries. The act also required screening of immigrants to eliminate security risks.

See Also: Immigration.

■ **MCCARTHY, JOSEPH (1908-57),** U.S. senator associated with the anticommunist crusade of the early 1950s. Born in Grand Chute, Wisconsin, McCarthy was a minor Republican officeholder when he was elected to the U.S. Senate from Wisconsin in 1946. On Feb. 9, 1950, he gave a speech in Wheeling, West Virginia, alleging that 205 State Department employees were known communists. He parlayed the accusations into national publicity and, for the next four years, was the most feared man in Washington. McCarthy, encouraged by the leaders of his party, attacked members of the Democratic administration of Pres. Harry S. Truman for being soft on communism. Following the election of Republican Pres. Dwight D. Eisenhower in 1952, he continued his assault but went too far in 1954 when he held hearings on subversion in the U.S. Army. On Dec. 2, 1954, a discredited McCarthy was censured by the Senate.

See Also: Cold War; McCarthyism.

BIBLIOGRAPHY: Griffith, Robert, *The Politics of Fear: Joseph R. McCarthy and the Senate* (Univ. of Kentucky Press 1970).

■ **MCCARTHYISM,** term for the search for communists in government in the United States in the early 1950s. On Feb. 9, 1950, Joseph R. McCarthy, an obscure Republican senator from Wisconsin, charged that 205 communists were working in the State Department. The claim was preposterous. McCarthy knew nothing about communists in government or anywhere else. His aim was publicity, and his timing was right. Americans were frightened by Soviet aggression in Europe since the end of World War II. In recent months, China had fallen to Communist rule, Alger Hiss had been convicted of perjury, and Russia had successfully tested an atomic bomb. What made McCarthy so popular was his ability to provide a simple explanation for these alarming events. The communists were "winning" the Cold War, he insisted, because traitors within the U.S. government were aiding their cause. The real enemy wasn't in Moscow; it was in Washington, D.C.

McCarthy became an instant celebrity. His face adorned the covers of *Time* and *Newsweek*, and the cartoonist Herblock coined a new word, "McCarthyism," to describe the reckless charges. When the Korean War erupted in June 1950, McCarthy's message took on special force. With American troops battling communist soldiers in Asia, the fight against domestic subversion gained fresh momentum. Indiana forced professional wrestlers to sign a loyalty oath; Tennessee ordered the death penalty for those seeking to overthrow the state government. Congress, not to be outdone, passed the Internal Security Act over President Truman's veto, requiring the registration of "Communist action groups," whose members could then be placed in internment camps during "national emergencies."

McCarthy, meanwhile, became the nation's leading "Red-hunter." Easily reelected in the Republican landslide of 1952, he became chairman of the committee on government operations and its powerful subcommittee on investigations. Filling key staff positions with ex-FBI agents and former prosecutors such as Roy M. Cohn from New York, McCarthy set out to investigate "communist influence" in the federal government. His targets included the Voice of America, the Government Printing Office, and the Foreign Service. At the same time, the House Un-American Activities Committee (HUAC) and the Senate Internal Security Subcommittee (SISS), searched for "reds" in the nation's schools, churches, and labor unions.

McCarthy's hearings did not uncover any communists. They did, however, ruin numerous careers, undermine government morale, and make the United States look ridiculous in the eyes of the world. The senator's personal downfall began with his 1954 investigation of "subversive activity" in the U.S. military. The public got to see him up close in the televised army-McCarthy hearings. The cumulative impression of McCarthy—his windy speeches, frightening outbursts, and crude personal attacks—was devastating. The highlight of the hearings came after McCarthy questioned the loyalty of a young lawyer who worked for army counsel Joseph Welch. "Have you no sense of decency?" Welch responded. "At long last, senator, have you no sense of decency?" The spectators burst into applause.

In November 1954, the Senate censured McCarthy for bringing that body "into dishonor and disrepute." Many believed that his censure was linked to an easing of Cold War tensions. The Korean War was over, Joseph Stalin was dead, and the radical right was in disarray. Depressed and no longer able to get his message across, McCarthy spent his final months railing against those who had deserted his cause. He died of alcoholism in 1957, virtually alone, but the word McCarthyism lives on as a pejorative, a reminder of the worst times of the early Cold War.

—DAVID M. OSHINSKY

See Also: Army-McCarthy Hearings; Cold War; Eisenhower, Dwight David; Internal Security Act; McCarthy, Joseph.

BIBLIOGRAPHY: Navasky, Victor S., *Naming Names* (Penguin 1981); Oshinsky, David M., *A Conspiracy So Immense: The World of Joe McCarthy* (Collier Macmillan 1983); Schrecker, Ellen, *The Age of McCarthyism: A Brief History With Documents* (St. Martin's 1994).

■ **MCCLELLAN, GEORGE BRINTON (1826-85),** U.S. Army officer. Born in Philadelphia, this most cantankerous of Civil War generals graduated near the top of his West Point class in 1846 and saw service in the Mexican War (1846-48). He left the army in 1850, returning to the service on the eve of the Civil War in 1860 as a general of Ohio volunteers. He caught President Lincoln's eye, who gave him overall command of the Union army. Chided for his seeming reluctance to engage the enemy, McClellan tried in September 1861 to take Richmond via the Yorktown peninsula. The Peninsular Campaign faltered because he refused to attack an enemy he erroneously believed outnumbered him. Lincoln removed him in favor of Maj. Gen. John Pope but returned McClellan to command after Pope's failure at Second Bull Run (August 1862). In the Antietam campaign (September 1862), McClellan could have destroyed the Army of Northern Virginia, but he failed to press Confederate commander Gen. Robert E. Lee hard. Lincoln then permanently removed him from command. McClellan unsuccessfully ran against Lincoln in the presidential election of 1864.

See Also: Antietam (or Sharpsburg), Battle of; Civil War; Lincoln, Abraham; Peninsular Campaign.

BIBLIOGRAPHY: Sears, Stephen W., *George B. McClellan: The Young Napoleon* (Ticknor & Fields 1988).

Mr. and Mrs. George McClellan pose for a *carte de visite* in the early years of the Civil War.

■ **MCCLINTOCK, BARBARA (1902-92),** botanist and geneticist, born in Hartford, Connecticut, she earned a doctorate at Cornell University. Through studying the genetics of corn in the 1940s and 1950s, she discovered the existence of "transposable elements" of DNA. In 1970 she was awarded the National Medal of Science, and, in 1983, she received the Nobel Prize in Physiology for Medicine.

See Also: Science.

■ **MCCORMICK, CYRUS (1809-84),** inventor and manufacturer of a mechanical reaper. Born in Rockbridge County, Virginia, McCormick worked on the family farm and took over his father's abandoned efforts to build a mechanical reaper. He exhibited his reaper in 1831 and patented it in 1834, a year after Obed Hussey had patented a similar one. McCormick focused on manufacturing his reaper after 1843, touring the Midwest with his invention in 1844 and starting a factory in Chicago in 1847. Despite competition from rival manufacturers, McCormick dominated the production and sale of reapers. He organized a mass-production system at his factory and invested in labor-saving machinery, introduced deferred payments, employed testimonials and money-back guarantees in extensive advertising, gave demonstrations, and established a research department to help him continually improve his product. McCormick won international acclaim and made over $1 million by 1856. Crop failures in Europe and the Civil War (1861-65) at home increased his profits. McCormick ran unsuccessfully for Congress as a Democrat in 1864, promoted southern trade, and contributed to the Presbyterian Church and the Union Theological Seminary of Virginia.

See Also: Invention; Science.

■ MCCULLERS, CARSON (1917-67),

novelist, born Lula Carson Smith in Columbus, Georgia. In her late teens, she moved to New York City, where she worked and studied creative writing at Columbia University. In 1936 McCullers published her first story, "Wunderkind," in *Story* magazine. At only 22 she published *The Heart is a Lonely Hunter*, a remarkable novel about a deaf man who befriends an odd assortment of social misfits in a small southern town. She followed with the novel *Reflections in a Golden Eye* (1941) and several prize-winning short stories. "A Tree, A Rock, A Cloud" was published in the *O. Henry Memorial Award Prize Stories* (1942), and "The Ballad of the Sad Cafe" appeared in *Best American Short Stories* (1944). She then added her most famous novel *The Member of the Wedding* (1946), which appeared as a stage play in 1950, winning the Drama Critic's Circle Award (1951). The great promise of McCullers's early career was overshadowed by ill health and a tumultuous relationship with her husband, Reeves McCullers. She was left partially paralyzed by two strokes in 1947. Despite her disability and the emotional strain of Reeves's suicide in 1953, she produced the play *The Square Root of Wonderful* (1958) and a final novel *Clock Without Hands* (1961). Often compared to Eudora Welty and Flannery O'Connor, she explored themes of loneliness and alienation, writing about eccentric and sometimes grotesque characters in remote corners of the South.

See Also: Novel; Women in American History.
BIBLIOGRAPHY: Carr, Virginia Spencer, *The Lonely Hunter: A Biography of Carson McCullers* (Doubleday 1975).

■ MCCULLOCH V. MARYLAND (1819),

U.S. Supreme Court case in which the implied powers doctrine was first invoked, establishing the constitutional supremacy of the federal government over the states. The case grew out of a dispute between the state of Maryland and the Bank of the United States. James William McCulloch, the cashier at the Baltimore branch of the Bank of the United States, had been arrested and convicted for not paying a state tax on the federal banknotes he had dispensed. The case worked its way up to the Supreme Court, where the constitutional issue before the justices was clear: could a state regulate the power of the federal government, as Maryland had intended in this instance, by attempting to impose a tax on a federal agency? In a unanimous decision, the Court held that the Maryland tax violated the principle of federal supremacy. Writing for the Court, Chief Justice John Marshall grounded his opinion in the necessary-and-proper clause of Article I, Section 8, of the Constitution. It accords Congress the power "to make all laws which shall be necessary and proper for carrying into execution the foregoing powers, and all other powers vested by this Constitution in the government of the United States." Thomas Jefferson and Alexander Hamilton long had quarreled over the meaning of this language: Jefferson arguing for a narrow reading; Hamilton for a broad one. Marshall aligned himself squarely with the Hamiltonian view, asserting that "necessary and proper" *implied* powers other than those explicitly enumerated in the Constitution, including the power of the federal government to operate a national bank, exempt from any and all state regulation or taxation.

—MATTHEW E. BABCOCK

See Also: Banks of the United States, First and Second; Marshall, John; Supreme Court.
BIBLIOGRAPHY: Gunther, Gerald, ed., *John Marshall's Defense of McCulloch v. Maryland* (Stanford Univ. Press 1969).

■ MCDANIEL, HATTIE (1898-1952),

vaudeville performer and movie actress. Born in Wichita, Kansas, McDaniel is best remembered for her role opposite Paul Robeson in *Show Boat*. She was named best supporting actress for *Gone With the Wind* (1939), the first African-American woman to win an Academy Award.

See Also: African Americans; Motion Pictures.

■ **MACDOWELL, EDWARD (1860-1908),** pianist and composer. Born in New York City and trained in Europe, he taught music at Columbia University (1896-1904) in New York and composed orchestral works, piano pieces, and songs in the romantic tradition, often inspired by New England settings. His widow established the MacDowell Colony for composers, artists, and writers in his memory at their summer home in Peterborough, New Hampshire (1910).

■ **MCGILLIVRAY, ALEXANDER (1759-93),** Creek leader. The son of a Scottish father and mixed-blood mother, McGillivray was born in present-day Alabama and educated in South Carolina. He became an important Creek chief, supporting the British during the American Revolution by leading the Creeks in attacks on settlers in Georgia and Tennessee. After the war, McGillivray became a successful trader and leader. In 1790, he was one of the signers of the Treaty of New York, which established boundaries for the Creek Nation.

See Also: Creek; Indians of North America.

■ **MCGINLEY, PHYLLIS (1905-71),** poet, born in Ontario, Oregon. The author of humorous and sometimes irreverent verse, she was awarded the 1960 Pulitzer Prize for her *Times Three*. Other collections of her verse are *A Pocketful of Wry* (1940) and *The Love Letters of Phyllis McGinley* (1950).

■ **MCGOVERN, GEORGE (1922-),** U.S. senator (1965-81) and Democratic presidential candidate (1972). Born in Avon, South Dakota, he was a bomber pilot in World War II and a history teacher at Dakota Wesleyan University (1949-53) before becoming active in politics. He was a member of the U.S. Congress from South Dakota (1957-63) and, after a failed run for the Senate (1960), was director of the Food for Peace foreign aid program (1961-64) during the Kennedy administration. McGovern was elected to the Senate in 1964 and soon became an outspoken critic of the Vietnam War. He sought the 1968 nomination as an antiwar candidate, entering the race

after the assassination of presidential candidate Sen. Robert Kennedy. In 1972, taking advantage of new Democratic party primary rules, he won the nomination but carried only Massachusetts and the District of Columbia as he was defeated by Pres. Richard Nixon. A liberal champion, McGovern was defeated in a primary during his campaign for reelection to the Senate in 1980.

See Also: Cold War; Presidential Elections.

BIBLIOGRAPHY: McGovern, George S., *Grassroots: The Autobiography of George McGovern* (Random House 1977); White, Theodore S., *The Making of the President 1972* (Atheneum 1973).

■ **MCGUFFEY, WILLIAM HOLMES (1800-73),** educator and author of a series of influential reading texts. Born near Claysville, Pennsylvania, he was a Presbyterian minister and president of Cincinnati College (1836-39) and Ohio University (1839-43) before becoming professor of moral philosophy at the University of Virginia (1845-73). McGuffey compiled a series of six *Eclectic Readers* (1836-57), which sold 120 million copies and helped shape U.S. education and literary tastes throughout the 19th century. Written as texts for community schools, they were widely used throughout the country and were especially popular in the Midwest. McGuffey's *Readers* included British and American poetry and prose selections that reflected his stern Calvinist morality. Subsequent editions published after his death moderated McGuffey's content, reflecting the views of the emerging middle classes of the time.

BIBLIOGRAPHY: Sullivan, Delores P., *William Holmes McGuffey: Schoolmaster to the Nation* (Fairleigh Dickinson Univ. Press 1994).

■ **MCKEAN, THOMAS (1734-1817),** jurist and Revolutionary War statesman. McKean, born in Chester County, Pennsylvania, served in the First and Second Continental Congresses and signed the Declaration of Independence. Although he held many political offices in Delaware, he was most prominent in Pennsylvania, where he was governor (1799-1808).

See Also: Declaration of Independence.

■ **MCKENNA, JOSEPH (1843-1926),** politician and jurist. Born in Philadelphia, Pennsylvania, he practiced law in California, served in the U.S. House of Representatives (1885-92), and was U.S. attorney general (1897-98) before becoming an associate justice of the U.S. Supreme Court (1898-1925).

See Also: Supreme Court.

■ **MCKENNEY, THOMAS (1785-1859)**, first U.S. commissioner of Indian affairs. McKenney was an administrator of policy toward Indians under four presidents from James Madison to Andrew Jackson. In 1816, he was appointed superintendent of the Indian trade, administering the unsuccessful "factory" system developed by the United States in the early 19th century. In 1824, when the Bureau of Indian Affairs was created as part of the War Department, McKenney was its first director. He focused on "civilizing" Indians through education and missionary efforts.

See Also: Indian Affairs, Bureau of (BIA); Indians of North America.

■ **MACKENZIE, ALEXANDER (1764-1820)**, fur trader and explorer in far northwestern North America. Born in Scotland, he immigrated with his father to New York in 1774 but was sent to school in Montreal after the outbreak of the American Revolution. Entering the Canadian fur trade in 1779, he became a wintering partner of the North West Company in 1787. In 1789, Mackenzie explored the river running from Great Slave Lake to the Arctic Ocean; it was named in his honor. In 1793, in the company of Indian guides, he became the first European to reach the Pacific from the interior by way of the northern river system, preceding the expedition of Lewis and Clark by more than a decade. His journals were published in England in 1801. Mackenzie was knighted the next year, returned to Canada, and later retired to Scotland.

See Also: Exploration and Discovery.

■ **MCKIM, MEAD, AND WHITE**, Gilded Age architecture firm. In 1879 Charles Follen McKim (1847-1909), William Rutherford Mead (1846-1928), and Stanford White (1853-1906) formed a partnership that became one of the best-known architecture firms of the late 19th century, distinguished particularly by its elegant classical style. Among their many projects were the Boston Pub-

lic Library (1887-95), Madison Square Garden (1891), the restoration of the White House in Washington, D.C. (1902), and the Pennsylvania Railroad Terminal in New York (1904).

See Also: Architecture; White House.

■ **MCKINLEY, JOHN (1780-1852)**, U.S. representative (1833-35), U.S. senator (1826-31, 1837), and associate justice of the U.S. Supreme Court (1837-52). He was born in Culpeper County, Virginia. McKinley's dissent in *Groves* v. *Slaughter* (1841) stands as his most significant opinion.

See Also: Supreme Court.

■ **MCKINLEY, WILLIAM (1843-1901)**, 25th president of the United States (1897-1901). Born in Niles, Ohio, McKinley attended Allegheny College and joined the Union army at the outbreak of the Civil War. In 1865, having attained the rank of major, he returned to civilian life, studied law, and in 1867 was admitted to the Ohio bar. McKinley began practicing law but soon turned his attention to politics, becoming a Republican member of the U.S. House of Representatives in 1877. In a time of rapid industrial expansion, McKinley was a staunch protectionist of American markets and primary author of the McKinley Tariff of 1890.

After serving as governor of Ohio (1892-96), McKinley won the Republican presidential nomination in 1896. His Democratic opponent, William Jennings Bryan, strongly endorsed the inflation of the currency by silver coinage, while McKinley underscored his commitment to the gold standard and high tariffs. The Republicans and McKinley triumphed in a highly sectional vote.

Shortly after taking office, McKinley approved the Dingley Tariff (1897) and used his shrewd tact and amiable personality to win over Congress. Domestic concerns, however, soon became subsumed by pressing foreign policy issues. Reluctantly, McKinley gave into public pressure for U.S. involvement in Cuba's rebellion against Spain and in 1898 declared war against the declining Iberian power. Victory in the Spanish-American War transformed the U.S. into a major power and increased its colonial territories throughout the world. After winning reelection in 1900, McKinley was assassinated in September 1901 by anarchist Leon Czolgosz. He was succeeded by Theodore Roosevelt.

The last veteran of the Civil War to be elected president, William McKinley was assassinated in September 1901.

See Also: *Gilded Age; Presidential Elections; President of the United States; Roosevelt, Theodore; Spanish-American War.*

BIBLIOGRAPHY: Gould, Lewis L., *The Presidency of William McKinley* (Univ. of Kansas Press 1970); Morgan, H. Wayne, *William McKinley and His America* (Syracuse Univ. Press 1963).

■ **MCLEAN, JOHN (1785-1865),** U.S. representative (1813-16) and associate justice of the U.S. Supreme Court (1829-61). A Morris County, New Jersey, native and a blunt critic of slavery, McLean dissented in the *Dred Scott* case (1857). He invoked moral as well as constitutional authority in condemning slavery and state slave codes.

See Also: *Dred Scott* v. *Sandford; Supreme Court.*

■ **MACLEISH, ARCHIBALD (1892-1982),** playwright, poet, and public servant. MacLeish was born in Glencoe, Illinois, educated at Yale University and Harvard Law School, and served in World War I. As an editor at *Fortune*, MacLeish publicly supported the New Deal. He was librarian of Congress from 1939 to 1944, when he became assistant secretary of state. MacLeish won Pulitzer Prizes for his two collections of poetry, *Conquistador* (1932) and *Collected Poems, 1917-1952*, and for a play, *J.B.* (1958).

See Also: *Poetry.*

■ **MCLUHAN, MARSHALL (1911-80),** influential communication theorist and literary critic who argued that new technologies fundamentally change the structure of society. Born in Edmonton, Alberta, he studied to be an engineer before turning to literature and teaching. A master of sometimes contradictory aphorisms that caught the public's ear, McLuhan argued that the medium is the message and that electronic technology would shrink the world to a global village. Hot media such as film, packed with information and requiring little involvement, were contrasted with cool media such as television, which required users to become actively involved in filling in the blanks. McLuhan's most influential books, *The Gutenberg Galaxy* (1962) and *Understanding Media* (1964), and his insistence that television mattered helped make him a popular figure in the 1960s.

BIBLIOGRAPHY: McLuhan, Marshall, *Understanding Media: The Extensions of Man* (McGraw-Hill 1964); Marchand, Philip, *Marshall McLuhan: The Medium and the Messenger* (Ticknor & Fields 1989).

■ **MCMILLAN, EDWIN (1907-91),** physicist. Born in Redondo Beach, California, McMillan worked at the Lawrence Radiation Laboratory at the University of California, Berkeley (1934-73). With Glenn Seaborg, he discovered (1941) plutonium as well as other transuranium elements. While at Los Alamos (1942-45) during World War II, McMillan improved the design of the cyclotron. His synchrotron (1946) accelerated a beam of particles faster than ever before by using an alternating electric field whose frequency could be adjusted for relativistic mass changes.

McMillan shared a Nobel Prize in Chemistry with Seaborg in 1951.

See Also: Science.

■ **MCNAMARA, ROBERT S. (1916-)**, business executive and U.S. secretary of defense (1961-67). Born in San Francisco, California, he was president of Ford Motor Company and a registered Republican when Pres. John F. Kennedy named him secretary of defense. McNamara intended to bring rational, modern business practices to the military but became embroiled instead in the Vietnam War. He administered the growing U.S. forces in Vietnam under Kennedy and Pres. Lyndon B. Johnson, but by 1965 he was arguing privately that the war was lost. He resigned in 1967 and then served as president of the World Bank (1968-81), where McNamara concentrated on economic growth and government reforms in developing nations. He created a furor in 1995 when he published his memoirs, in which he admitted that the U.S. involvement in Vietnam was a mistake that had been allowed to continue far too long.

See Also: Cold War; Vietnam War.
BIBLIOGRAPHY: McNamara, Robert S., *In Retrospect* (Times Books 1995).

■ **MCNARY-HAUGEN BILL (1925-28)**, congressional attempt to address declining prices for agricultural products through the establishment of federal price supports based on the notion of "fair exchange value." The measure was vetoed by Pres. Calvin Coolidge in 1927 and again in 1928.

■ **MCPHERSON, AIMEE SEMPLE (1890-1944)**, pentecostal preacher, born near Ingersoll, Ontario, Canada. After the death of her first husband and an unsuccessful second marriage, she toured the country holding evangelical religious revivals. Her fundamentalist message attracted tens of thousands of worshipers and earned her an official endorsement from the Ku Klux Klan. In 1923 she built the Angelus Temple in Los Angeles, and in 1927 she founded the Church of the Four Square Gospel.

See Also: Religion; Women in American History.

■ **MCREYNOLDS, JAMES CLARK (1862-1946)**, associate justice of the U.S. Supreme Court (1914-41).

An Elkton, Tennessee, native and judicial conservative, McReynolds consistently objected to expansions of federal regulatory power, a view evident in his opposition to most New Deal legislation.

See Also: Supreme Court.

■ **MADISON, DOLLEY (1768-1849)**, first lady of the United States. Born in New Garden, North Carolina, she married James Madison, her second husband, in 1794. She was also White House hostess for Thomas Jefferson, a widower. When the British burned the White House in 1814, Mrs. Madison salvaged important documents and works of art.

See Also: First Lady; Madison, James; Women in American History.

■ **MADISON, JAMES (1751-1836)**, political leader, statesman, fourth president of the United States (1809-17). Born in Port Conway, Virginia, Madison graduated from the College of New Jersey (Princeton) in 1771 and embarked on a 50-year commitment to public life. Although poor health prevented service in the Continental army, Madison was a radical patriot from the beginning of the American Revolution, serving its cause in a variety of governmental posts.

Madison made his most lasting contribution to the nation during the Constitutional Convention of 1787. Hoping to overcome the confusion and disorder of the postrevolutionary period, he was one of the leaders in calling for the convention and contributed more than any other single delegate to the drafting of the Constitution. Madison proposed the preliminary resolutions that provided the framework for the new document; coauthored (with Alexander Hamilton and John Jay) *The Federalist Papers* (1787-88), a collection of essays explaining the new system; and outdebated the formidable Patrick Henry to ensure the Constitution's passage in his home state.

The first Congresses during the Washington and Adams administrations found Madison engaged in shaping and refining the newly ratified Constitution by drafting laws, setting precedents, and adding a Bill of Rights. Although he had been a nationalist and proponent of strong government, Madison soon joined Thomas Jefferson in forming the Republican party to combat Hamilton's financial policies and the Federalists'

James Madison served as Thomas Jefferson's secretary of state (1801-09) and then succeeded Jefferson as president (1809-17).

pro-British bias as well as the Adams administration's encroachment on individual liberties. In 1794 the 43-year-old Madison married Dolley Payne Todd, a 26-year-old widow with a son. The seemingly unlikely marriage of the shy, slight Madison and the gregarious, charismatic Dolley was a happy one.

National Leader. Madison served as secretary of state for Jefferson's two terms as president (1801-09) and succeeded Jefferson as president in 1809. Historians have often characterized Madison's performance as chief executive and commander in chief during the War of 1812 as inept, but the nation emerged from the war intact, and when Madison left office in 1817, Americans enjoyed a new sense of optimism, a commitment to the Union, and a stable economy.

In retirement Madison keenly followed public affairs, advising Pres. James Monroe, speaking out against nullification, and serving as a delegate to the 1829 Virginia Constitutional Convention. He was a trustee and later the rector of the University of Virginia. As part of his concern for what he considered America's greatest evil, slavery, Madison headed the American Colonization Society. Although not as colorful as other leaders of the founding generation, Madison played a crucial role in the creation of the new nation's political system.

—CATHERINE ALLGOR

See Also: *American Colonization Society; Bill of Rights; Constitutional Convention; Constitution of the United States; Presidential Elections; President of the United States; War of 1812.*

BIBLIOGRAPHY: Ketcham, Ralph, *James Madison: A Biography* (Macmillan 1971); Rutland, Robert Alan, *The Presidency of James Madison* (Univ. of Kansas Press 1990).

■ **MAFIA,** a criminal organization that originated in Sicily and came to the United States during the late 19th century when Italian immigration was at its peak. Operating in most major American cities, the Mafia was particularly active in handling illegal alcohol during the Prohibition era of the 1920s. Later, the Mafia expanded into prostitution, gambling, narcotics, and labor racketeering. To this day, the traditional Mafia code of silence, combined with the sheer depth of the organization, defy law enforcement efforts to eradicate it.

See Also: *Organized Crime; Prohibition.*

■ **MAGAZINES,** in America began with Andrew Bradford's *American Magazine* and Benjamin Franklin's *General Magazine*, both of which began publication at Philadelphia in 1741 and ended within a few months. Over the next several decades several dozen magazines began and ended their lives with only a few issues, including Thomas Paine's *Pennsylvania Magazine* (1775-76) and Matthew Carey's *American Museum* (1787-92). All these were high-toned publications for an elite audience, as were the early-19th-century periodicals *Port Folio* (Philadelphia, 1801-27) and *Monthly Anthology* (Boston, 1803-11), forerunners of the intellectual *North American Review* (1815-1939).

The first general interest, popular magazines appeared in the early 19th century. Among the most important were *Knickerbocker Magazine* (1833-65), *Saturday Evening Post* (1821-1969), and *Frank Leslie's Illustrated Weekly* (1855-1922). Slightly more intellectual were *Harper's Magazine* (1850-present), which had a circulation of 200,000 by 1860, and *Atlantic Monthly* (1857-present). Women's magazines began to be published early in the 19th century and have been among the most popular ever since. The first, *Godey's Lady's Book* (1830-98), was for 40 years edited by Sarah Josephia Hale. Its success stimulated competition from *Harper's Bazaar* (1867-present), *Vanity Fair* (1868-1936), *Woman's Home Companion* (1873-present), and *Ladies Home Journal* (1883-present).

The so-called "muckraking" magazines, crusading against corporate and governmental corruption, appeared at the end of the century. *Munsey's* (1889-1929) was the first; *McClure's* (1893-1929) published Lincoln Steffens on city corruption and Ida Tarbell on Standard Oil; *Collier's* (1888-1957) published Upton Sinclair's series on Chicago meat packing; Steffens, Tarbell, and other crusading journalists bought *American Magazine* (1906-56) and turned it into an outlet for their exposés. The early 20th century saw the founding of several magazines aimed at the intelligentsia: *The Smart Set* (1914-23), H. L. Mencken's *American Mercury* (1924-33), and *The New Yorker* (1925-present). Diametrically opposed was the lowbrow *Reader's Digest* (1922-present), which popularized condensations of generally conservative magazine articles and books.

The oldest continuously published magazine of political opinion is *The Nation* (1865-present), which began with a libertarian editorial policy (conservative by today's standards) but by the 1930s had moved to the left. *The New Republic* (1914-present) has consistently taken a liberal point of view. More recently, these two were joined by conservative *National Review* (1952-present). Henry Luce founded *Time* (1923-present), the first of the weekly news magazines (soon followed by *Newsweek* [1933-present] and *U.S. News* [1933-present]), and built his success into a publishing empire, including the photo journal *Life* (1936-1971), the business-oriented *Fortune* (1930-present), *Sports Illustrated* (1952-present), and the celebrity-obsessed *People* (1974-present).

The demise of the *Saturday Evening Post, Life,* and a number of other perennials in 1969-72 was the cause of notable lamentations about modern American culture. But the magazine business has always been volatile and risky, and the fact was that more magazines were being published at the end of the 20th century than at any time in American history. In 1995 alone, 838 new magazines began publication; it was estimated that of those, only three in ten would survive three years of publication.

The most important trend of the late 20th century was the development of what were known as "niche magazines," publications with relatively low circulation (fewer than 250,000) designed to appeal to special interest groups, with titles such as *Civil War Times, Old House Journal,* and *Cigar Aficionado.*

See Also: *Luce, Henry; Mencken, H. L.; Muckrakers.*
BIBLIOGRAPHY: Abrahamson, David, *Magazine-Made America: The Cultural Transformation of the Postwar Periodical* (Hampton Press 1996); Tebbel, John, and Mary Ellen Zuckerman, *The Magazine in America: 1741-1990* (Oxford Univ. Press 1991).

■ MAGELLAN, FERDINAND (c. 1480-1521),

Portuguese leader of the first expedition to circumnavigate the globe. Magellan sailed and fought for Portugal in that country's efforts to secure a trade route to the Spice Islands (Moluccas) of the East Indies. Following Balboa's discovery of what would later be named the Pacific Ocean (1513), Magellan, then in the service of Charles I of Spain, proposed to sail westward into it and open a new route to the Indies. Magellan left Seville on Sept. 20, 1519, with five ships, crossed the Atlantic, and wintered in Patagonia. Passing through a strait at the southern tip of South America, later named for him, Magellan in November 1520 entered the "new" ocean and named it the Pacific. Crossing the open sea, the expedition, by then reduced to three ships, reached Guam and later the Philippines. Magellan died in a fight with Philippine natives on Apr. 27, 1521. Seventeen Europeans survived the voyage, however, and returned to Spain on Sept. 8, 1522. The expedition conclusively established the Americas to be a new continent.

See Also: *Exploration and Discovery.*
BIBLIOGRAPHY: Morison, Samuel Eliot, *The European Discovery of America: The Southern Voyages,* A.D. *1492-1616* (Oxford Univ. Press 1974).

■ **MAHAN, ALFRED THAYER (1840-1914),** naval officer and influential theorist of the political implications of naval power. Born at West Point, Mahan entered the Naval Academy at 16 and spent most of the Civil War on tedious blockade duty. In the postwar period Mahan spent years in various bureaucratic assignments. His hitherto pedestrian career skyrocketed in 1886 when he was appointed to lecture at the Naval War College in Newport, Rhode Island. In 1890, Mahan published his lecture notes as *The Influence of Sea Power Upon History 1660-1783*; his premise being that to be a great power, a nation must control the seas. Mahan's book fit perfectly the expansionist and imperialist policies of the European nations of his day and, more ominously, those of Japan. In later years he continued to write naval history and lived to see his theories invoked by his acolyte Theodore Roosevelt and others to justify the Spanish-American War.

See Also: Navy; Roosevelt, Theodore.
BIBLIOGRAPHY: Puleston, Captain W. D., *Mahan: The Life and Work of Captain Alfred Thayer Mahan, U.S.N.* (Yale Univ. Press 1939).

■ **MAHICAN INDIANS.** *See: Algonquian.*

■ **MAILER, NORMAN (1923-),** novelist and essayist. Mailer was born in Long Branch, New Jersey. He studied engineering at Harvard University but also began writing there; he won a prize for the best college fiction of 1941 from *Story* magazine. Mailer was drafted into the army and served during World War II. He drew on his military experiences for his acclaimed first novel, *The Naked and the Dead* (1948), the story of American troops invading a Pacific island. In 1955 he started writing columns for the New York City weekly newspaper *Village Voice* that were later collected in *Advertisements for Myself* (1959) and *The Presidential Papers* (1963). Mailer's later works interpret what he perceived to be critical events in American history: *Armies of the Night* (1968) explores a 1966 protest march at the Pentagon; *Miami and the Siege of Chicago* (1968) and *St. George and the Godfather* (1972) recount political conventions; and *The Prisoner of Sex* (1972) examines the women's liberation struggle. In these works Mailer expresses an increasingly pessimistic view of his culture.

See Also: Novel.

■ **MAINE,** the easternmost U.S. state and the largest state in New England. It is bounded on the north, west, and east by Canada, on the west by New Hampshire, and on the south and east by the Atlantic Ocean. Maine has a rugged, rocky coastline and a thickly wooded interior through which run the Appalachian Mountains. The economy depends on its natural resources, fisheries and lumber, and tourism. The manufacture of paper-mill products is Maine's chief industry. Maine was part of Massachusetts before becoming a state in 1820.

Capital: Augusta. Area: 33,128 square miles. Population (1995 est.): 1,241,000.

See Also: Aroostook War; Webster-Ashburton Treaty.

■ ***MAINE*,** **SINKING OF THE (1898),** incident that sparked the Spanish-American War. The battlecruiser USS *Maine* blew up in Havana harbor on February 15. An inquiry fixed the blame on an underwater mine and by implication, the Spanish, who controlled Cuba. Although the Spanish were almost surely not to blame, the American "yellow press" and warlike "jingoes" used the incident to pressure Pres. William McKinley to ask for a declaration of war.

See Also: Spanish-American War.

■ **MALAMUD, BERNARD (1914-86),** novelist and short story writer. A native of Brooklyn, New York, Malamud graduated from New York's City College in 1936 and earned an M.A. from Columbia University in 1942. From 1949 to 1961 he taught at Oregon State University while beginning his career as a novelist. His first novel, *The Natural* (1952), about the national love of baseball, was followed by *The Assistant* (1957). In 1958 Malamud won the National Book Award for his short story collection, *The Magic Barrel*.

See Also: Novel; Short Story.

■ **MALCOLM X (1925-65),** African-American leader, Muslim minister, and proponent of black nationalism and Pan-Africanism. Born Malcolm Little in Omaha, Nebraska, he was the fourth of eight children of Louise and Earl Little, a Baptist preacher. Malcolm's parents were followers of the philosophy of the African emigrationist Marcus Garvey. After Malcolm's birth the family settled near Lansing, Michigan. When he was six his father was murdered by white terrorists, a tragedy that later contributed to his mother's mental breakdown and to the family's disintegration.

Malcolm was educated in the public schools of Lansing and Mason, Michigan, where he was exposed to racial discrimination despite his solid academic performance. Discouraged by the racism of a white teacher, who destroyed his dream of becoming a lawyer, he completed eighth grade and moved to Boston to live with his sister Ella. His formal education ended, he now learned about life on the streets. Shuttling between Boston and New York while still in his teens, Malcolm trafficked in numbers, narcotics, prostitution, and petty crime. In 1946 he was convicted in Massachusetts of robbery and sentenced to 10 years in prison.

An avid reader in prison, Malcolm was introduced to Elijah Muhammad's Black Muslim movement by his brother Reginald. The doctrines of this movement, formally known as the Nation of Islam, transformed his thinking and compelled him to choose a new course in life. On his release from prison in 1952 Malcolm joined the Nation of Islam and became Muhammad's most dynamic and successful minister. He served temples in Detroit, Boston, and Philadelphia before accepting an appointment to Temple Number Seven in Harlem in 1954. There he associated with Betty X, later known as Beth Shabazz, a Muslim whom he married in 1958. The couple had six children.

As the national representative of Muhammad, Malcolm advocated black supremacy, racial separatism, black self-defense, and black self-help as an alternative to the universal love ethic, integrationism, and nonviolent tactics of Martin Luther King, Jr., and other moderate civil rights leaders. Malcolm was frequently featured on radio and television and in newspapers and magazines, and he lectured at numerous colleges and universities. He achieved national and international prominence before a dispute with Muhammad forced him out of the Nation of Islam in December 1963.

In March 1964 Malcolm founded the Muslim Mosque, Inc., to provide a spiritual base for his continuing efforts to free African Americans. He traveled widely in Africa and the Middle East, seeking support for his plan to take the United States before

Malcolm X, a compelling public speaker, was assassinated in 1965, two years after he broke away from the Nation of Islam.

the United Nations for violating the human rights of African Americans. During his pilgrimage to Mecca in April 1964 he abandoned racial thinking and embraced orthodox Islam, as well as a more enlightened and explicit internationalism. He then adopted the name El-Hazz Malik El-Shabazz.

As a way of appealing to a broader segment of the African-American community, Malcolm founded the Organization of Afro-American Unity on June 18, 1964. As president of the organization, he consistently linked the African-American struggle with the struggles of Africans and of the oppressed worldwide. Malcolm was assassinated in New York City on Feb. 21, 1965, while addressing his followers. Disputes about the killing persist, although many believe the Nation of Islam was responsible.

—LEWIS V. BALDWIN

See Also: *African Americans; Black Muslims (Nation of Islam); Civil Rights Movement; Garvey, Marcus Mosiah.*

BIBLIOGRAPHY: Baldwin, Lewis V., "A Reassessment of the Relationship Between Malcolm X and Martin Luther King, Jr." *The Western Journal of Black Studies* Vol. 13 (1989); Decaro, Louis A., *On the Side of My People: A Religious Life of Malcolm X* (New York Univ. Press 1996); Malcolm X with Alex Haley, *The Autobiography of Malcolm X* (Grove Press 1965); Malcolm X, *Malcolm X Speaks*, ed. by George Breitman (Pathfinder 1965).

■ **MALINCHE (c. 1500-c. 1550),** consort of and translator for Cortés in the conquest of Mexico. The daughter of an Aztec chief, Malinche was sold into slavery on her mother's remarriage. In 1519, she was given to the Spanish conquistador Hernán Cortés, who made her his mistress and translator. She bore him a child and eventually married another Spaniard. A gifted linguist, Malinche was instrumental in the Spanish conquest of the Aztec empire, leading to her reputation as a "traitor" despite the limited options available to her.

See Also: Aztecs; Cortés, Hernán; Frontier in American History; Indians of North America; Women in American History.

■ **MAMMOTH CAVE,** one of the largest caves in the world, located in southern Kentucky. An extensive system of limestone caverns, Mammoth Cave consists of more than 300 miles of passageways and the underground Echo River. The cave was formed by a tributary of the Green River, which carved out underground spaces, and then by ground water seeping down and slowly depositing minerals. When Congress authorized the Mammoth Cave National Park in 1926, much of the area was in private hands, and the park was not fully established until 1941.

See Also: National Parks.

■ **MANDAN,** Siouan-speaking tribes. The Mandan originated along the Ohio River and migrated to the northern Great Plains in the 15th century, where they lived in permanent villages as farmers and hunters. They were active in the fur trade in the late 18th and early 19th centuries and acted as intermediaries between nomadic hunting groups and the American trading companies. However, a series of smallpox epidemics and attacks by Lakota warriors in the 1830s decimated the Mandan, leaving only a few hundred survivors.

See Also: Indians of North America.

■ **MANHATTAN,** island in southeast New York, a borough of New York City. Although only one of the city's five boroughs, Manhattan, with its famous skyline, has come to symbolize New York. Flanked by the Hudson River to the west and the East River on the east, Manhattan is only two and a half miles wide and some 12 miles long. The island was first inhabited by Algonquian Indians, who exchanged the land to the Dutch for 60 gilders. In 1626 the Dutch West Indies Company founded the settlement of New Amsterdam on the southern tip of the island and made it a trading point for manufactured goods and tobacco. The British captured the Dutch colony in 1664 and renamed it New York. Throughout the 19th century Manhattan was a commercial center for the Hudson River Valley crops. The stupendous economic growth of New York in the 19th century was largely the result of immigration and the city's near monopoly on transportation to the west through the Erie Canal (1825) and its railroads extending outward from the city. In the 20th century Manhattan has come to represent the extremes of wealth and poverty as well as some of the world's most celebrated urban monuments, including the Empire State Building, Rockefeller Center, the World Trade Center, and the recent AT&T (later Sony) Building. The list of Manhattan's American icons seems endless and includes Harlem, the Statue of Liberty, Ellis Island, Central Park, Broadway, Times Square, Wall Street, and the Brooklyn Bridge.

■ **MANHATTAN PROJECT,** government-sponsored program during World War II to develop the atomic bomb. After two German scientists achieved atomic fission in uranium in 1939, a group of physicists in the United States, including Albert Einstein, convinced Pres. Franklin D. Roosevelt to fund a research project. Known as the Manhattan Project, this top-secret program joined together teams of scientists under the direction of Gen. Leslie Groves of the army to coordinate research and production.

From 1942 to 1945, the government spent $2 billion in a race against time to build the first bomb. Various aspects of production were carried out at laboratories in Tennessee, Washington, and at Los Alamos, New Mexico, where J. Robert Oppenheimer, a brilliant physicist, directed the entire project. At Alamogordo, New Mexico, on July 16, 1945, the first atomic bomb was detonated. Less than a month later, on August 6, Pres. Harry S. Truman ordered an atomic bomb dropped on Hiroshima, Japan, followed three days later by a second on Nagasaki. Five days after the Nagasaki bombing, Japan surrendered, thus ending World War II.

See Also: Oppenheimer, J. Robert; Science.

BIBLIOGRAPHY: Feis, Herbert, *The Atomic Bomb and the End of World War II* (Princeton Univ. Press 1966).

■ **MANIFEST DESTINY,** argument used by 19th-century American expansionists to justify the conquest of the continent by the United States. The ideology of Manifest Destiny proclaimed that American expansion westward, southward, and even northward was inevitable, destined by Providence, and thus justified in the name of progress. Of course, those who stood in the way—Indians, Mexicans, Canadians, and officials of the remnant British and Spanish North American empires — did not view American expansion in the same terms. Although the sentiment was present in American thought from the beginning of the national period, the phrase did not appear in print until July 1845, when John L. O'Sullivan, a Democratic journalist, argued for the justice of the acquisition of Texas by insisting on "our manifest destiny to overspread the continent allotted by Providence for the free development of our yearly multiplying millions." The slogan quickly became popular among nationalist orators and writers.

The most important proponent of Manifest Destiny was Pres. James K. Polk (1845-49), who seized a third of Mexico in the Mexican War and arranged a compromise with Great Britain that resulted in the acquisition of Oregon, thus making the United States a continental nation. After the Civil War, Sec. of State William Seward used the idea to promote American acquisitions and dominance of the Pacific; he bought Alaska (1867) from the Russians and had dreams of further territorial expansion. Manifest Destiny later reappeared as an argument for the colonization of Cuba and the Philippines during the Spanish-American War of 1898.

See Also: Frontier in American History; Mexican War; Polk, James Knox.

BIBLIOGRAPHY: Merk, Frederick, *Manifest Destiny and Mission in American History: A Reinterpretation* (1963, repr. Harvard Univ. Press 1995); Stephanson, Anders, *Manifest Destiny: American Expansionism and the Empire of Right* (Hill & Wang 1995); Weinberg, Albert K., *Manifest Destiny: A Study of Nationalist Expansionism in American History* (Johns Hopkins Univ. Press 1935).

■ **MANILA BAY, BATTLE OF (1898),** naval battle at the beginning of the Spanish-American war. The April 30 battle resulted in the utter destruction of the antiquated Spanish fleet by U.S. Commodore George Dewey's Asiatic Squadron, which was ordered to the Philippines by Asst. Sec. of the Navy Theodore Roosevelt. The mismatched battle left Dewey in control of Manila Bay. Without a landing contingent he was forced to delay entering Manila until August 13, after reinforcements arrived.

See Also: Dewey, George; Spanish-American War.

■ **MANKILLER, WILMA (1945-),** Cherokee leader. Born at the Cherokee capital of Talequah of a Cherokee father and Dutch-Irish mother, Mankiller moved at age 10 with her family to San Francisco. She became an activist in the late 1960s and participated in the symbolic occupation of Alcatraz Island by Indians in 1969. In 1976, Mankiller moved back to Oklahoma, where she was elected deputy chief of the Cherokee Nation in 1983. She became principal chief in 1985 but resigned in 1995 to accept a position at Dartmouth College.

See Also: Indians of North America.

■ **MANN, HORACE (1796-1859),** educator and reformer. The founder of the public common school in America, Mann was born in Franklin, Massachusetts. After receiving a scant education as a child, he graduated from Brown University in 1819, studied law, and was admitted to the bar in 1823. Following a brief time in a law practice, Mann served in the Massachusetts state legislature until 1837, when he became secretary of the Massachusetts Board of Education.

With a singleness of purpose, Mann effected change in the school system and influenced the philosophy of education in America. He launched a bi-weekly *Common School Journal* for teachers in 1838, served as an advocate for education reform in the state legislature, and published scores of articles on education. When he left office in 1848, state appropriations for public education had more than doubled, teacher salaries had risen more than 50 percent, some 50 new public schools had been established in Massachusetts, the school year had been extended, and the first teacher-training program had been created.

Mann carried his program of reform into the U.S. House of Representatives after the election of 1848. An antislavery Whig, he supported the temperance movement and lobbied for a hospital for the insane in Massachusetts. After he was defeated as a Free Soil party candidate in the race for governor in 1852, Mann assumed the presidency of Antioch College in Ohio.

BIBLIOGRAPHY: Messerli, Jonathan, *Horace Mann: A Biography* (Knopf 1972).

■ **MANN ACT (1910),** federal legislation also known as the White Slave Traffic Act. It was prompted by concerns over the allegedly growing practice of luring young women into prostitution. The act made it a federal crime to transport a woman across state lines for "immoral purposes."

■ **MANN-ELKINS ACT (1910),** congressional measure to increase the authority of the Interstate Commerce Commission (ICC). Passed with the support of Pres. William Howard Taft, the act was much stronger than the previous, related Hepburn Act (1906). The Mann-Elkins Act empowered the ICC to regulate further railroad and telegraph companies, including the power to initiate rate changes.

See Also: *Hepburn Act.*

■ **MANTLE, MICKEY (1931-95),** Hall of Fame baseball player who played center field for the New York Yankees (1951-68). Born in Spavinaw, Oklahoma, he led the Yankees to 12 World Series and hit 536 home runs.

See Also: *Baseball; Sports.*

■ **MANUMISSION,** voluntary release of slaves from their bondage by their owners. In early and antebellum America, servitude was defined by a contract for a finite period, but there were no such limits on slavery. One of the ways slaves could gain their free-

dom was through manumission. The wills of slave owners often contained clauses freeing slaves upon the owners' deaths or upon the slaves' reaching a certain age in the service of their heirs. At his death, for example, John Randolph freed more than 400 slaves in 1833. Meritorious service might also win manumission. Hundreds of slaves won their freedom through military service in the Revolutionary War. Following the Revolution, and perhaps inspired by its ideals, most Northern states passed laws that encouraged manumission. Virginia passed such a law in 1782 (later, however, Virginia revised the law to make manumission more difficult). Other Southern states passed laws forbidding manumission except in extraordinary cases.

See Also: *Antislavery Movement; Slavery.*

BIBLIOGRAPHY: Davis, David Brion, *The Problem of Slavery in the Age of Revolution, 1770-1823* (Cornell Univ. Press 1975).

■ **MAPLE SUGAR,** sweetener produced by rendering the sap of the sugar maple, a deciduous tree native to the northeastern United States. The production of maple sugar originated with Indians. In early spring, Indian women would collect maple sap in wooden troughs, reducing it to crystallized sugar by adding heated rocks. The introduction of brass and copper kettles after the arrival of Europeans greatly facilitated this process of boiling down the sap, and by the early 1700s many European colonists used maple sugar as a substitute for expensive, imported sugar from the Caribbean. Abolitionists favored maple sugar because, unlike most cane sugar, it was not produced using slave labor.

See Also: *Agriculture.*

BIBLIOGRAPHY: Nearing, Helen, and Scott Nearing, *The Maple Sugar Book* (John Day, 1950).

■ ***MAPP V. OHIO (1961),*** U.S. Supreme Court case that extended the Fourth Amendment's protection against unreasonable searches to state courts. Ohio police obtained a search warrant to enter Dolly Mapp's home to look for a fugitive from justice and for gambling equipment they believed was stored inside. They found neither but discovered allegedly obscene publications. Mapp was arrested and convicted of possession of obscene literature. The Court reversed (5-3) the conviction, ruling the search was illegal.

With *Mapp* the Court partially clarified an earlier case, *Wolf* v. *Colorado* (1949), and began the so-called due process revolution of the 1960s. In *Wolf* the justices had ruled that the 14th Amendment's due process clause extended the Bill of Rights' protections to the states, but they did not set explicit limits on state police searches. In *Elkins* v. *United States* (1960) the Court ruled that the 14th Amendment "incorporated" the 4th Amendment's safeguards against improper searches, but because the case did not involve a state criminal prosecution, it did not provide a proper vehicle for overturning *Wolf*. In *Mapp* the divided Court said the "exclusionary rule" that bars police from using improperly seized evidence in a trial must be applied to state as well as federal courts.

See Also: *Due Process of Law; Supreme Court.*
BIBLIOGRAPHY: Stevens, Leonard A., *Trespass!: The People's Privacy vs. The Power of the Police* (Coward, McCann & Geohegan 1977).

▌ **MAPS,** efficiently organized, conveniently compact representations of much larger landscapes. Maps have had varied roles in the enactment and writing of American history, serving as fundamental tools of navigation, exploration, territorial expansion, nation building, military defense, settlement, economic development, commerce, legislative apportionment, natural science, land management, and (more recently) environmental protection and growth management.

As a highly generalized, inherently selective portrait of land and people, a map is often a rhetorical statement influenced by its author's knowledge and viewpoint and should therefore be read critically. For example, the late-18th-century map that shows only the few European settlements and place names beyond the Appalachians denies the presence of native peoples there and endorses the territorial claims of westward-trending national and state boundary lines. Although few historical maps contain blatant propaganda, many are social constructions of a reality that scholars with divergent experiences and agendas might portray differently.

For entrepreneurs trying to satisfy widespread public demand for geographic information, making a living was a stronger motive than shaping opinion. Mapmakers like Mathew Carey, who in 1795 published the first atlas of the United States, and John Melish, who produced numerous school atlases and travel books in 1812 and 1826, were successful businessmen who understood both technology and marketing. Among the private surveyors and mapmakers who served state and local governments as well as private citizens was Jason (Jay) Gould, who published several county maps in eastern New York between 1850 and 1856 before moving on to more lucrative ventures in railways and finance. At cartographic centers in Baltimore, Boston, Chicago, New York, and Philadelphia the most profitable product was the county atlas, a rapidly prepared collection of detailed lithographed maps showing individual farms, residences, and businesses. In addition to mapping roads and buildings, field surveyors sold the atlas by advance subscription to local residents, who often paid extra to include a flattering engraving of their home.

In addressing needs neglected by commercial mapmakers, government assumed an increasingly larger share of the growing cartographic enterprise. Gen. George Washington established a Military Cartographic Headquarters at Ringwood, New Jersey, in 1777, and for the next hundred years federal mapping efforts focused on defense and marine navigation. In 1882, the U.S. Geological Survey (USGS) undertook the massive task of producing a nationwide series of detailed, systematic base maps—the nation's "mother maps," according to Henry Gannett, first chief topographer at the USGS, who recognized their contribution to a variety of derivative "geographic" maps. In the 1930s, the Department of Agriculture undertook another kind of mother map: the county-level soils map, which became the foundation for a variety of maps used widely in soil conservation, real-estate assessment, landfill siting, and wetlands preservation. Among other federal agencies with an active cartography program, the Bureau of the Census not only supported its decennial head count with highly detailed maps of built-up areas but also fostered a wider understanding of demography and agriculture through innovative statistical maps and atlases. In addition, state and local governments make and use maps for purposes ranging from urban and regional planning to tourism and law enforcement.

Mapmakers have been especially resourceful in adapting surveillance and data processing technology. In the 1920s, for instance, cartographers began compiling topographic and land use maps from aerial photography, and experiments initiated in the 1950s led to successful adaptations of camouflage-detection (false-color) imagery and satellite remote sensing. Software for the automated storage, retrieval, analysis, and display of geography data has kept pace with improvements in electronic computing, and electronic atlases and dynamic cartography support customized, interactive, and animated maps especially relevant to historical data.

—MARK MONMONIER

See Also: *Census; Gould, Jay.*

BIBLIOGRAPHY: Buisseret, David, ed., *From Sea Charts to Satellite Images: Interpreting North American History through Maps* (Univ. of Chicago Press 1990); Monmonier, Mark, *Technological Transition in Cartography* (Univ. of Wisconsin Press 1985); National Geographic Society, *Historical Atlas of the United States* (1988); Ristow, Walter W., *American Maps and Mapmakers: Commercial Cartography in the Nineteenth Century* (Wayne State Univ. Press 1985); Schwartz, Seymour J., and Ralph E. Ehrenberg, *The Mapping of America* (Harry N. Abrams 1980); Thrower, Norman J. W., *Maps and Civilization: Cartography in Culture and Society* (Univ. of Chicago Press 1996).

■ *MARBURY V. MADISON* **(1803),** U.S. Supreme Court case that established the principle that the Court had the authority to declare acts of Congress unconstitutional. William Marbury was appointed justice of the peace for the District of Columbia at the end of Pres. John Adams's administration. Marbury's commission was mislaid during the presidential transition and was then withheld by James Madison, President Jefferson's secretary of state. Marbury filed suit for a writ of mandamus ordering Madison to deliver the commission. Chief Justice John Marshall held for a unanimous Court that Marbury's commission was legal and that a writ of mandamus could be ordered. However, since the Constitution had not specifically authorized the Supreme Court to issue such a writ, the justices were without the power to do so. Moreover, Marshall ruled that the Judiciary Act of 1798, which granted the Court this power, had been unconstitutional. The decision thus established the exclusive constitutional jurisdiction of the Supreme Court, while affirming the Court's right to review the constitutionality of acts of Congress.

See Also: *Judiciary Acts; Marshall, John; Supreme Court.*

■ **MARCH ON WASHINGTON (1963),** in full, March on Washington for Jobs and Freedom, mass demonstration for racial justice. Prompted by revulsion at the harsh suppression of African-American civil rights demonstrators in Birmingham, Alabama, in spring 1963 Pres. John F. Kennedy proposed sweeping civil rights legislation to Congress. In support of the bill, hundreds of thousands of marchers from all over the nation assembled in Washington, D.C., on August 28. Every major civil rights group and many labor and church organizations supported the march. In orderly fashion the integrated throng moved from the Washington Monument to the Lincoln Memorial. Orators of the day included A. Philip Randolph, John Lewis, and Martin Luther King, Jr., whose famous "I Have a Dream" address encapsulated the ideals and emotions of the march and, in a sense, of the entire civil rights movement. Even though the optimism generated by the march was dimmed by Kennedy's assassination the following November, Pres. Lyndon B. Johnson secured passage of the Civil Rights Act in 1964.

See Also: *Civil Rights Acts; Civil Rights Movement; King, Martin Luther, Jr.; Randolph, Asa Philip.*

■ **MARCIANO, ROCKY (1923-69),** heavyweight boxing champion. Known as "the Hard Rock from Brockton" after his Massachusetts birthplace, he was famed during his professional ring career (1947-56) for his brawling, aggressive style. The child of Italian immigrants, Marciano knocked out Jersey Joe Walcott to win the championship (1952) and retired undefeated (1956) with a career record of 49 victories.

See Also: *Boxing; Sports.*

■ **MARIN, JOHN (1870-1953),** painter. Born in Rutherford, New Jersey, Marin worked as an architect in the 1890s but his attention shifted to painting. He first exhibited his paintings in 1909

The emotional high point of the March on Washington of Aug. 28, 1963, was the "I Have a Dream" speech of Martin Luther King, Jr.

at Alfred Stieglitz's 291 Gallery. His watercolors of the Woolworth Building in New York City were included in the American section of the Armory Show, an exhibition of modern art held in New York City in 1913. In addition to these urban architectural views, his primary subjects included seascapes and landscapes of Maine and New York, as in *Sun, Sea, Land, Maine* (1923).

See Also: Armory Show; Painting; Stieglitz, Alfred.

■ **MARINE CORPS,** branch of the U.S. armed forces, created Nov. 10, 1775. In the American Revolution the Continental marines provided shipboard detachments that enforced discipline, swept enemy decks with small-arms fire, and led boarding parties. Marines joined landing parties at New Providence (1776) and Whitehaven (1778) and assisted the Continental army in the attack on Princeton (1776). At war's end Congress disbanded the marines until 1794, when marine detachments were formed for the ships of the new U.S. Navy. On July 11, 1798, the U.S. Marine Corps was established within the Department of the Navy. Marines served creditably aboard ships during the undeclared war with France

(1798-1800). They captured Derna during the Tripolitan War (1805) and in the War of 1812 fought at Bladensburg (1814) and New Orleans (1815).

Seeking roles to demonstrate their continued value in the postwar world, marines helped put down Nat Turner's Rebellion (1831), fought the Seminole Indians in Florida (1836-37), assaulted Chapultepec (1847) during the Mexican War, and helped capture John Brown (1859).

Civil War marines filled traditional shipboard duties and guarded naval bases but contributed little to the Union victory. Between 1866 and 1889 marines landed to protect U.S. citizens and their property 24 times, including operations in Korea (1871), Egypt (1882), and Panama (1885). During the Spanish-American War they captured Guantanamo Bay, Cuba, and in the following decades became colonial policemen protecting U.S. interests in China and the Caribbean. During World War I marines fought (1917-18) in France at Belleau Wood, Soissons, St. Mihiel, and in the Meuse-Argonne. Although returned to colonial police duties after the war, the corps also prepared to conduct amphibious warfare.

Ready for World War II in the Pacific, marines seized (1942-45) Guadalcanal, conducted the Solomon Islands campaign, and spearheaded the Central Pacific drive through the Gilbert, Marshall, and Mariana islands, Iwo Jima, and Okinawa. Attempts to alter or abolish the corps inspired by postwar defense unification ideas ended with the Korean War (1950-53) when marines stiffened the Pusan Perimeter, landed at Inchon, and fought at the Chosen Reservoir.

During the next half century marines developed new techniques to respond rapidly to crises worldwide and employed them during interventions in Lebanon (1958, 1982), the Dominican Republic (1965), and Grenada (1983). Vietnam became the marines' most costly war. They were assigned primary responsibility for the conduct of operations in the northern portion of South Vietnam and suffered 103,255 casualties, more even than the 90,709 of World War II. In 1990 the marines rushed units to Saudi Arabia to counter Iraq's invasion of Kuwait. During the ensuing Gulf War, marine units invaded Kuwait and tied down Iraqi troops by threatening an amphibious landing northward.

—JAMES C. BRADFORD

See Also: *Civil War; Revolution, American; War of 1812; World War I; World War II.*

BIBLIOGRAPHY: Millett, Allan R., *Semper Fidelis: The History of the United States Marine Corps* (Macmillan 1980); Moskin, J. Robert, *The U.S. Marine Corps Story* (McGraw-Hill 1977).

■ **MARION, FRANCIS (1732-95),** American Revolutionary War general. Born in Berkeley County, South Carolina, Marion earned his legendary reputation as a military leader when the focus of the Revolution turned to the South in 1780. His ability to coordinate his plans with those of Nathanael Greene's Continental forces brought him deserved praise and decisive victories. Marion's effective use of guerilla tactics against the British earned him the moniker "Swamp Fox."

See Also: *Greene, Nathanael; Revolution, American.*

■ **MARNE, SECOND BATTLE OF THE (July 1918),** major World War I battle in north central France in which American troops played a key role. The Second Battle of the Marne (the first was fought in 1914) began with the launching on July 15 of the

Known as the "Swamp Fox," Francis Marion of South Carolina's militia played an important role in the American Revolution's success in the South, using guerrilla tactics against the British.

fifth major German offensive of 1918, designed to drive a wedge between the British and the French lines. The attack came between Chateau-Thierry and Massiges, a distance of more than 50 miles. About 85,000 Americans attached to the French armies fought valiantly throughout the engagement. The U.S. Third Division halted the German attack at the River Marne, and one of its regiments, the 38th Infantry, earned the nom de guerre "the Rock of the Marne" for its steadfastness. On July 18 the U.S. First and Second Divisions spearheaded a counteroffensive, overrunning German positions near Soissons despite heavy resistance and cutting the enemy off from its supply lines. The battle is generally recognized as a critical turning point in the war: Gen. Erich Ludendorff on July 22 ordered his troops to fall back from the Marne salient, and the initiative passed to the Allies for the remainder of the war.

See Also: *World War I.*

■ **MARQUETTE, PERE JACQUES (1637-75),** French missionary and explorer. Born in Laon, France, Marquette arrived in Quebec in 1666. After studying Indian languages for two years, he established a mission at present-day Sault Ste. Marie, Michigan, in 1668. In 1670 he founded another mission at St. Ignace, Michigan. When Louis Jolliet arrived while on his journey searching for the Mississippi River, Marquette joined him. In May 1673, together with five voyageurs, they crossed Wisconsin by canoe, portaged between the Fox and Wisconsin rivers, and arrived at the Mississippi on June 17, 1673. They followed the Mississippi to its confluence with the Arkansas River. Convinced that the river led to the Gulf of Mexico, they returned via the Illinois River and Lake Michigan. Marquette resumed his work converting the Indians to Christianity but died soon after. The journal of his travels with Jolliet was published in 1681.

See Also: Exploration and Discovery; Jolliet, Louis.

▨ **MARRIAGE.** Marriage has had a complicated history in America. There were a great variety of marriage systems among American Indians, but in general marriage did not play the central organizing role that it did for Europeans; other groupings, such as same-sex societies and extended kinship relations, were more significant. For most Indian peoples, the bonds of marriage were weak compared to European patterns, and divorce was a relatively simple matter. Colonists were frequently critical of Indian marriage, because it did not conform to the European patriarchal ideal.

New England colonists stressed the importance of "well-ordered" marriages. The husband and father was to be the head of the household, required to support his wife and children just as they were required to obey him. Throughout the colonies, homes were the primary workplace in society, and marriage was thus first and foremost a relationship of work. Men tended to delay marriage until they were in their late twenties, by which time they had acquired the skills or the property necessary to support a family. Women married at a median age of 22 or 23. Women's labor was critical to the family economy, but upon their marriage women became "femme covert" in the eyes of the law, "covered" by the civil identity of their husbands. They could not sign contracts, had no right to their own earnings, could not own property, could not vote in civil or church elections. "A true wife accounts her subjection her honor and freedom," declared the Puritan leader John Winthrop, and his sister, Lucy Winthrop Downing, wrote, "I am but a wife, and therefore it is sufficient for me to follow my husband." The Puritans considered marriage a civil contract, not a religious sacrament, and in New England divorce was possible, if extremely rare. Elsewhere in the colonies, marriage was sanctified by the church and divorce was outlawed (authorities sometimes allowed legal separations, but without the possibility of remarriage).

African-American slaves in the South seldom sought or were granted legal sanctions for their marriages. Owners sometimes officiated at slave weddings, but it was more common for marriages to be celebrated secretly by the slave community. Some masters attempted to arrange slave marriages, but it appears that slaves usually picked their own mates. Historical studies of slave marriage have compiled evidence suggesting that they were frequently broken by sale; one estimate puts the rate at one in five. Perhaps because of the fragility of the marriage bond, slaves emphasized "fictive" kinship; children were taught to think of all their elders as "aunts" and "uncles" and their age peers as "brothers" and "sisters." Yet, the commitment of slaves to their mates was demonstrated by the number of divided spouses who searched each other out after the Civil War. "In their eyes the work of emancipation was incomplete until the families which had been dispersed by slavery were reunited," observed one official of the Freedmen's Bureau.

19th and 20th Centuries. During the 19th century, as more people left farming for work in the cities, marriage ceased to be a relationship of productive work and was increasingly understood as a private refuge from stress of the public world. The husband, wrote the author of one early-19th-century advice book, should regard the home as "an elysium to which he can flee and find rest from the stormy strife of a selfish world." Practical concerns gave way to romantic love as the major determinant in mate selection. "Companionate marriage" became the new ideal. Wives should be "companions, equals, and helpers," wrote the reformer Sarah Grimké. There were legislative moves to terminate some of the old patriarchal supports. Most states passed "Married Women's Property

Acts," providing women with more economic autonomy within marriage, and many liberalized their divorce laws. But there were also signs that men were uncomfortable with the weakening of their authority. For example, as the birthrate fell (one of the most important signs of the changing nature of marriage), state legislators reacted by limiting women's access to contraception and abortion. One important aspect of the change was the increasing proportion of American women who never married, which in the course of the 19th century doubled, from about 5 percent in the early decades to more than 10 percent in 1900.

But this trend turned around in subsequent years, and by the mid-20th century some 95 percent of American women were marrying, one of the highest rates of marriage in the world. People also began marrying at earlier ages; by the 1950s the median age of first marriages for men was only 22, for women only 20. What accounts for this change? It was, almost surely, linked to the increasing popularity of divorce. Although historians lack good evidence for the late 19th century, there was much clamor about the increasing frequency of divorce. By the 1920s, when reliable statistics began being collected, the divorce rate stood at 10 for every thousand women, which was probably double the rate of 50 years before. From 1960 to 1980 the increase in the rate of divorce was explosive, climbing to a high of 22.6 in 1980. While rates leveled off a bit in the final two decades of the century, by the mid-1990s nearly one American marriage in two was terminating in divorce. An equally important statistic, however, is the extremely high rate of remarriage; in the 1990s nearly 95 percent of divorced men and women remarried. Americans had learned to use divorce as a marriage safety-valve, giving them a way out and an opportunity to try again.

—JOHN MACK FARAGHER

See Also: *Birth Control; Divorce; Sexual Revolution; Women in American History.*

BIBLIOGRAPHY: Degler, Carl, *At Odds: Women and the Family in America from the Revolution to the Present* (Oxford Univ. Press 1980); Demos, John, *Past, Present, and Personal: The Family and the Life Course in American History* (Oxford Univ. Press 1986); Mintz, Steven, and Susan Kellogg, *Domestic Revolutions: A Social History of American Family Life* (Free Press 1988).

■ **MARRIED WOMEN'S PROPERTY ACTS,** legislation passed by most states between 1848 and 1870, and by Congress in 1875, that for the first time gave married women the right to own property. Previously the legal convention known as coverture had given all economic rights of married women to their husbands. After the Seneca Falls Convention of 1848, Elizabeth Cady Stanton, Susan B. Anthony, and other leading feminists attacked this economic imprisonment in articles and speeches. The passage of Married Women's Property acts in state legislatures was one of the first great victories of the women's movement.

See Also: *Anthony, Susan B.; Coverture; Stanton, Elizabeth Cady; Women's Movement.*

■ **MARSH, REGINALD (1898-1954),** illustrator and painter of the urban scene. Marsh was born in Paris, but his family returned to the United States two years after his birth. After graduating from Yale University in 1920, Marsh began drawing illustrations and cartoons for magazines, such as *Vanity Fair* and *Harper's Bazaar*, and newspapers, such as the *New York Daily News*. He won the commission for murals at the United States Post Office in Washington, D.C., in 1935 and at the Customs House in New York City in 1937.

■ **MARSHALL, GEORGE C., JR. (1880-1959),** military leader and statesman, who served as army chief of staff (1939-45), secretary of state (1947-49), and secretary of defense (1950-51). Born in Uniontown, Pennsylvania, Marshall graduated from the Virginia Military Institute in 1901 and was commissioned as a 2nd lieutenant in 1902. He served with distinction as a staff officer in France during World War I. Named army chief of staff on Sept. 1, 1939, he reorganized the army's structure and training methods. After the United States entered World War II, he became the most trusted military adviser of Presidents Franklin D. Roosevelt and Harry S. Truman, as well as the most influential member of the Joint Chiefs of Staff.

Shortly after Marshall retired as five-star general of the army, Truman sent him to China (December 1945-January 1947) to mediate between warring factions. Marshall next became secretary of state (January 1947-January 1949). Persuaded that Europe was on the verge of economic collapse, he had subordinates draw up what would become known as the "Marshall Plan." Instituted in 1948, it greatly stimulated European recovery. Marshall resigned in early 1949 following major surgery.

Truman appointed Marshall president of the American Red Cross in September 1949 and, after the Korean War began, made him secretary of defense. A firm believer in civilian control of the military, he supported Truman's dismissal of Gen. Douglas MacArthur for insubordination. Marshall had agreed to be secretary of defense for only six months but stayed a year before his final retirement from government service.

During the 1952 presidential election, Sen. Joseph McCarthy accused Marshall of disloyalty. Republican candidate Dwight D. Eisenhower, whom Marshall had elevated from obscurity, failed to defend his mentor.

England's Winston Churchill named George C. Marshall "the true organizer of victory" for his role in World War II. In 1947, while secretary of state, Marshall introduced his plan for Europe's recovery from the war.

Marshall received the Nobel Peace Prize in 1953 for his part in European recovery. He was one of the most respected Americans of the 20th century. His intelligence and strength of character impressed those who knew him. Winston Churchill, with whom he had clashed several times during World War II, called him "the noblest Roman of them all."

—ROBERT JAMES MADDOX

See Also: *Cold War; MacArthur, Douglas; Mc-Carthy, Joseph; Marshall Plan; Roosevelt, Franklin Delano; Truman, Harry S.; World War II.*

BIBLIOGRAPHY: Pogue, Forrest C., *George C. Marshall,* 4 vols. (Viking 1963-87).

■ **MARSHALL, JOHN (1755-1835),** fourth chief justice of the United States (1801-35), often considered the most distinguished justice to sit on the Supreme Court and the one who shaped its place in American government. Born in rural Prince William (later Fauquier) County, Virginia, he received little education as a youth. He served in the Revolutionary War, studied law briefly at the College of William and Mary before being admitted to the bar in 1780, and became active in state politics, often serving in the Virginia House of Delegates through 1796. A prominent Virginia Federalist, Marshall was made minister to France in 1797, which stabilized his precarious finances, and was appointed secretary of state by Pres. John Adams in 1800. When Chief Justice Oliver Ellsworth decided to resign, Adams in January 1801 nominated Marshall to replace him. Marshall served as both secretary of state and chief justice for the last six weeks of the Adams administration.

Chief Justice. Marshall soon put his stamp on the Court, establishing the principle of judicial review by the Supreme Court in *Marbury* v. *Madison* (1803), in which the Court invalidated a section of an act of Congress. He also helped to affirm the Court's independence from politics while presiding at the treason trial of Aaron Burr (1807). Marshall's opinion in *Fletcher* v. *Peck* (1810) was a landmark decision in establishing the supremacy of the national government in conflicts with state authorities and the importance of the contract clause of the Constitution. The contract clause was upheld again and expanded several years later in *Dartmouth College* v. *Woodward* (1819).

Marshall also strongly supported an active role for the federal government. In *McCulloch v. Maryland* (1819) and *Gibbons v. Ogden* (1824), Marshall's opinions expanded the powers of the federal government. In *McCulloch* he broadened the interpretation of the Constitution's "necessary and proper" clause, while in *Gibbons* he extended the commerce clause. In other key decisions, such as *Cohens v. Virginia* (1821), Marshall upheld the authority of the federal courts to review state court decisions.

In his later years as chief justice, Marshall's opinions often modified the broad sweep of earlier landmark decisions, and he suffered some defeats. In *Cherokee Nation v. Georgia* (1831), Marshall stated that the Cherokee and other tribes were under the protection of the federal government and in *Worcester v. Georgia* (1832) held that the Cherokee were entitled to hold their lands in Georgia. However, the state of Georgia did not abide by the decision, and Pres. Andrew Jackson would not enforce it, leading to the removal of the Cherokee west of the Mississippi River. His advanced age and changes in the composition of the Court made Marshall less powerful in his last years as chief justice. He died from injuries sustained in a stage coach accident after the 1835 Supreme Court term ended.

—ROBERT C. KHAYAT

See Also: *Cherokee Nation* Cases; *Constitution of the United States; Dartmouth College* Case; *Fletcher v. Peck; Marbury v. Madison; Supreme Court.*

BIBLIOGRAPHY: Loth, David G., *Chief Justice John Marshall and the Growth of the Republic* (1949; Greenwood Press 1970); Rudko, Frances H., *John Marshall and International Law: Statesman and Chief Justice* (Greenwood Press 1991); White, G. Edward, *The Marshall Court and Cultural Change, 1815-1835* (Oxford Univ. Press 1991).

■ **MARSHALL, THOMAS RILEY (1854-1925),** vice president of the United States. He was born in North Manchester, Indiana. A graduate of Wabash College, he went on to practice law in Columbia City, Indiana. Running as a Democrat, he was elected governor of Indiana in 1909. He served until 1912, when he was elected to the first of two terms as Woodrow Wilson's vice president. Marshall was an extremely popular vice president, regarded highly both at home and abroad for his warmth, tolerance, and sense of humor. During a Senate debate he made the statement for which he is probably best known: "What this country needs is a good five-cent cigar."

See Also: Vice President of the United States.

■ **MARSHALL, THURGOOD (1908-93),** associate justice of the U.S. Supreme Court (1967-91). Appointed by Pres. Lyndon B. Johnson, he was the first African American to sit on the Court.

Marshall was a champion of civil liberties both as a lawyer and later as a Supreme Court justice who often dissented on issues involving racial and economic justice as well as personal liberty. But his fame as one of the great lawyers in the history of the American legal system is a result of his role as the man who shaped and led the struggle to destroy the constitutional basis for racial segregation. That struggle culminated in his argument in the landmark *Brown v. Board of Education of Topeka* (1954), the case in which a unanimous Supreme Court declared that "segregation is inherently unequal" and thus unconstitutional.

The great-grandson of a slave named "Thoroughgood," for whom he was named (a name he later shortened), Marshall grew up in a Baltimore that was rigidly segregated. He was legally barred because of his race from attending the University of Maryland and thus had to commute to Howard University Law School in Washington, D.C., the college from which he graduated in 1933. Marshall was the most renowned student of the legendary Howard dean, Charles Hamilton Houston, and he continued and developed Houston's desegregation strategy of making the "separate but equal" doctrine too costly to implement by demanding equality in fact.

Marshall joined the legal staff of the National Association for the Advancement of Colored People (NAACP) in New York in 1936. In 1940 he became director-counsel of the NAACP Legal Defense and Educational fund, the legal arm of the NAACP, and led it to victory in 27 of 30 cases before the U.S. Supreme Court. Among the cases were decisions that voided all-white voting primaries, private covenants that prohibited sales of real property to people of color, segregated seating in interstate transport, and exclusion of African Americans

In 1954, Thurgood Marshall argued the landmark case of *Brown v. Board of Education of Topeka* before the Supreme Court. In 1967 Pres. Lyndon Johnson appointed him as the first African American to serve on the high court.

from graduate and professional schools. In 1961 Pres. John F. Kennedy appointed Marshall as a judge of the U.S. Court of Appeals, a position he held until 1965, when President Johnson appointed him solicitor general, the lawyer who represents the U.S. government before the Supreme Court.

In the struggle against racial oppression and racism, Marshall's faith in the transformative power of the legal system was often contrasted with the civil disobedience and "direct action" of civil rights leaders such as Martin Luther King, Jr. Both approaches have proven to be essential in the ongoing eradication of legally sanctioned racial prejudice.

—HENRY W. MCGEE, JR.

See Also: *African Americans; Brown v. Board of Education of Topeka; Civil Rights Movement; Supreme Court.*

BIBLIOGRAPHY: Davis, Michael D., and Hunter R. Clark, *Thurgood Marshall: Warrior at the Bar, Rebel on the Bench* (Birch Lane Press 1992); Kluger, Richard, *Simple Justice: The History of Brown v. Board of Education and Black America's Struggle for Equality* (Knopf 1975); Rowan, Carl, *Dream Makers, Dream Breakers: The World of Justice Thurgood Marshall* (Little, Brown 1993); Tushnet, Mark V., *Marking Civil Rights Law: Thurgood Marshall and the Supreme Court, 1936-1961* (Oxford Univ. Press 1994).

■ **MARSHALL PLAN,** U.S.-funded program for the economic reconstruction of Europe after World War II. In his commencement address at Harvard University on June 5, 1947, Sec. of State George C. Marshall announced that the United States would provide financial assistance to European nations still recovering from the devastation and dislocation of the war. Three months earlier Pres. Harry S. Truman had requested $400 million from Congress for aid to Greece and Turkey and pledged similar assistance to other countries fighting communist insurgencies. Now, in keeping with the desire of U.S. leaders to foster a global marketplace as the foundation of postwar peace and prosperity, the Truman administration aimed to help the economies of Europe and to reduce the possibility of Soviet-backed revolution. To that end the administration requested an appropriation of $17 billion from Congress, to be spent over a four-year period (1948-52).

Although some congressional leaders opposed this "New Deal" for Europe, President Truman was aided by the communist takeover of Czechoslovakia in February 1948 in securing legislative approval of the request. European leaders themselves, meanwhile, had determined how the funds would be used, and in April 1948 they formed the Organization for European Economic Cooperation (later the Organization for Economic Cooperation and Development). The United States had extended an invitation to the Soviet Union and other communist countries to participate, but the Soviet and Polish delegations withdrew from early talks. The resulting European Recovery Program ultimately used only $13.3 billion of the appropriated funds. The Marshall Plan was not solely responsible for the economic "miracles" that made Western Europe so prosperous in the postwar period, but a dramatic 33 percent increase in per capita income in Europe between

1947 and 1951 contributed to the plan's reputation as an extraordinary success.

In the postwar rivalry developing between the United States and the Soviet Union, the Soviets would prove to be competitive militarily, but they could never match U.S. financial largesse. The Marshall Plan's role in fostering transatlantic cooperation was equally important to the United States during the Cold War. Sixteen nations participated in the European Recovery Program: Austria, Belgium, Britain, Denmark, France, West Germany, Greece, Iceland, Ireland, Italy, Luxembourg, the Netherlands, Norway, Portugal, Sweden, and Turkey. Thirteen of these countries would join the North Atlantic Treaty Organization, while the other three (Austria, Ireland, and Sweden) remained neutral.

—MAARTEN L. PEREBOOM

See Also: Cold War; Marshall, George C., Jr.; North Atlantic Treaty Organization (NATO); Truman Doctrine.

BIBLIOGRAPHY: Hogan, Michael J., *The Marshall Plan* (Cambridge Univ. Press 1987); Milward, Alan S., *The Reconstruction of Western Europe, 1945-1951* (Univ. of California Press 1984).

■ **MARTIAL LAW,** legal procedure allowing military authorities to exercise control over civilians when civil authority is inadequate. Martial law was imposed by Rhode Island authorities when an opposition faction established a rival state government in Dorr's Rebellion (1842). During Reconstruction (1865-77) after the Civil War, Union forces exercised martial law for various periods over the defeated Confederate states until new governments were established.

See Also: Dorr's Rebellion; Reconstruction.

■ *MARTIN V. HUNTER'S LESSEE* **(1816),** U.S. Supreme Court case that established the Court's power to review state court decisions. In dispute was the ownership of a Virginia estate property that had belonged to a British loyalist, Lord Fairfax, but which, after seizure during the Revolutionary War, had been granted to Hunter. The treaty ending the war provided for the return of confiscated property to Loyalists, so Martin, Fairfax's heir, sued in Virginia to recover the property. After the state court rejected his claim, Martin petitioned the Supreme Court to intervene. When the Supreme Court overruled

(1813) the state court and affirmed Martin's right to the property, Virginia again brought the issue to the Supreme Court, arguing that the Court had acted outside its jurisdiction in reviewing a state court decision. Writing for the Court, Justice Joseph Story rejected Virginia's position, holding that under the 1789 Judiciary Act the Supreme Court had appellate jurisdiction to review state court decisions that involved the federal government.

See Also: Story, Joseph; Supreme Court.

■ *MARTIN V. MOTT* **(1827),** U.S. Supreme Court case addressing the authority of the federal courts to review a presidential muster order for the militia. In a unanimous decision, the Court ruled that states had to obey such an order. The opinion written by Justice Joseph Story found that the president had received from Congress the sole authority to call up the militia and moreover such presidential authority was not even subject to judicial review.

See Also: Story, Joseph; Supreme Court.

■ **MARTINEAU, HARRIET (1802-76),** author. Born in Norwich, England, she was deaf from childhood and troubled by ill health throughout her life. A popular nonfiction writer, she was a fierce opponent of slavery. After visiting the United States in 1834, she wrote *Society in America* (1837) and *Retrospect of Western Travel* (1838), both highly critical of American culture. Her other books include *Illustrations of Political Economy* (1832-34) and *The Playfellow* (1841).

■ **MARX BROTHERS,** New York–born stage and film comedians known for their anarchic, slapstick routines. A film version of their vaudeville hit *Cocoanuts* (1929) launched the screen careers of these vaudevillians. The wise-cracking Groucho (1890-1977), who later starred on radio and television, Chico (1891-1961), who portrayed a piano-playing Italian sharpster, and the mute and maniacal Harpo (1893-1964) were featured. Gummo (1894-1977) and Zeppo (1901-79) appeared briefly as straight men.

See Also: Vaudeville.

■ **MARYLAND,** one of the smallest states. Located on the eastern seaboard, it is bounded on

Capping a quarter-century in vaudeville and on Broadway, the Marx Brothers (*clockwise from top left*: Zeppo, Groucho, Harpo, Chico) made a series of popular, irreverent, and zany comedies that had a lasting impact upon the nation's popular culture.

the north by Pennsylvania, on the north and east by Delaware, on the east by the Atlantic Ocean, and on the south and west by Virginia, the District of Columbia, and West Virginia. The Chesapeake Bay divides the state; the Potomac River forms much of its southern and western border. Baltimore, on the bay, is one of the nation's busiest ports. Once chiefly an industrial state, Maryland now depends more on services. The federal government is its chief employer, partly because so many Marylanders live in suburbs of the nation's capital.

Although Maryland was founded as a haven for Roman Catholics, Protestants soon were in the ascendancy, as in the other English colonies. (It began as a proprietary province of the Lords Baltimore but became a royal colony in 1692. Maryland was one of the 13 original states.) A slaveholding border state, it was quickly occupied by Union troops in the Civil War because of its strategic position. More than half the population now lives in the Baltimore metropolitan area or the suburbs of Washington, D.C.

Capital: Annapolis. Area: 10,455 square miles. Population (1995 est.): 5,042,000.

See Also: Antietam (or Sharpsburg), Battle of; Baltimore, Lords; Gettysburg, Battle of; Naval Academy; Star-Spangled Banner, The.

■ **MASON, GEORGE (1725-92)**, Revolutionary War statesman. A wealthy planter in his native Virginia, Mason influenced Revolutionary politics with his prolific pen. He authored both the Fairfax Resolves, accepted by the First Continental Congress in 1774, and his state's Declaration of Rights in 1776. This latter document influenced Thomas Jefferson's Declaration of Independence and served as the basis for the Bill of Rights of 1789. As a member of the Constitutional Convention he opposed ratification because the document initially lacked a bill of rights, and his pressure for such a bill proved instrumental in its adoption.

See Also: Constitution of the United States; Fairfax Resolves; Revolution, American.

■ **MASON-DIXON LINE**, boundary line begun in 1763 to mark the official borders of Pennsylvania, Maryland, and Virginia in response to Lord Baltimore's proprietary claim to the entire Potomac River. The survey was completed in 1767 by

Charles Mason and Jeremiah Dixon. In 1784, the line was extended westward and became the established boundary between free and slave soil.

■ **MASSACHUSET INDIANS.** *See: Algonquian.*

■ **MASSACHUSETTS,** the most populous New England state. It is bounded on the north by Vermont and New Hampshire, on the west by New York, on the west and south by Rhode Island, on the south by Connecticut, and on the east by the Atlantic Ocean. Cape Cod is a peninsula jutting into the Atlantic, and Nantucket and Martha's Vineyard are important islands. The Connecticut River runs through western Massachusetts. Boston is the largest city and busiest port in New England.

The history of Massachusetts has been central to the American experience ever since the Pilgrims landed on Plymouth Rock in 1620. The American Revolution began there, the nation's first large-scale factories were built there, and the state bred a host of eminent writers, scientists, philosophers, and social reformers. Although no longer the nation's cultural capital, the Boston area is home to many universities (including Harvard) and thrives in the fields of high technology and banking and finance.

Capital: Boston. Area: 8,262 square miles. Population (1995 est.): 6,074,000.

See Also: Adams, John; Boston; Boston Massacre; Boston Tea Party; Embargo Act of 1807; Garrison, William Lloyd; Kennedy, John Fitzgerald; King Philip's War; Lexington and Concord; Minutemen; Plymouth Settlement; Sacco-Vanzetti Case; Whaling; Witchcraft.

■ **MASSACHUSETTS SCHOOL ACT (1647),** law that initiated public education in America. Puritans deemed education essential so that every person could read the Bible and understand laws. The act called for towns to employ a schoolmaster or found a school.

■ **MASSASOIT (c. 1580-1661),** Wampanoag leader. Grand sachem of the Wampanoag Confederacy when the Pilgrims landed in 1620, Massasoit sought an alliance with the English settlers to bolster his position against the neighboring Narragansett. He traded for goods and firearms with the English and had his people teach them native farming methods. He sent his sons Alexander and Philip (Metacomet) to be educated by the English. As settlement by the English expanded, however, Massasoit came to resent their presence.

See Also: Indians of North America; Metacomet.

■ **MASS PRODUCTION,** manufacturing system, developed in the 19th century and refined in the 20th-century automobile industry. Firearms manufacturers such as Eli Whitney took the first step toward mass production. In 1799, after failing to profit from his cotton gin, Whitney made muskets for the government with interchangeable parts. This system depended upon making standardized parts rather than crafting a unique finished product, and from it grew highly precise machine tools capable of making identical parts such as the milling machine, as well as drilling jigs, taps and gauges, and die-forging techniques. Increasingly efficient machinery and factory organization spurred the mass production of petroleum, sugar, vegetable oil, beer, and whiskey by the 1870s and of cigarettes, matches, flour, oatmeal, canned goods, soap, and photographic film by the 1880s.

The automobile industry integrated techniques of mass production from these and the metalworking industries with the use of overhead conveyors of 1910; innovations to reduce the time and cost of final assembly came soon after; and by 1913 Henry Ford was using a continuous, motor-driven conveyor to produce Model T automobiles. The efficiency of his Highland Park plant was not equaled elsewhere until the 1920s. Mass production sparked a new era of advertising and consumption. It also prompted the growth of the Industrial Workers of the World (1905-18) and the Congress of Industrial Organizations (1935), the last of which had unionized the automobile, steel, rubber, oil, and electronics industries by the 1940s.

See Also: Industrial Revolution; Labor Movement.
BIBLIOGRAPHY: Hounshell, David A., *From the American System to Mass Production, 1800-1932* (Johns Hopkins Univ. Press 1984).

■ **MASTERS, EDGAR LEE (1869-1950),** regional poet and biographer. Masters was born in Garnett, Kansas, but grew up in Illinois near the Spoon River that would be central to his work. Although he worked as a lawyer, his avocation was writing, and he published both poetry and prose. He is best remembered for *Spoon River Anthology* of 1915, a collection of character portraits. Masters also completed biographies of Abraham Lincoln (1931), Vachel Lindsay (1935), Walt Whitman (1937), and Mark Twain (1938).

See Also: Lincoln, Abraham; Lindsay, Vachel; Poetry; Twain, Mark; Whitman, Walt(er).

■ **MATHER, COTTON (1663-1728),** Puritan minister and theologian. The precocious and learned son of Increase Mather, he was born in Boston. Cotton began preaching in 1680 and was elected pastor of Old North Church in 1683, where his father was the teacher. An enlightened scholar, he published 469 works on ethics, religion, natural history, medicine, and science and helped make New England a cultural center. He was an early supporter of the highly controversial smallpox vaccination. His most important work is *Magnalia Christi Americana* (1702), a history of the church in New England. Despite his wide interests, he is best known for his defense of witchcraft persecutions in *Wonders of the Invisible World* (1693).

See Also: Mather, Increase; Puritanism; Religion; Witchcraft.

■ **MATHER, INCREASE (1639-1723),** Puritan minister, theologian, and president of Harvard College. The son of Richard Mather, he was born in Dorchester, Massachusetts, and educated at Harvard and at Trinity College in Dublin, Ireland. As president of Harvard, he supported the study of science but concentrated on his church and the political welfare of the colony. Involved in early American diplomacy, he secured a new charter for Massachusetts. Mather wrote 130 books and pamphlets on the concerns of the day, including the King Philip's War, the Salem witch trials, and smallpox vaccinations.

See Also: Mather, Cotton; Puritanism; Religion; Witchcraft.

■ **MATTHEWS, STANLEY (1824-89),** U.S. senator (1877-79) and associate justice of the U.S. Supreme Court (1881-89). A Cincinnati, Ohio, native, Matthews made his most significant contribution to constitutional jurisprudence in *Hurtado* v. *California* (1888), which concerned criminal due process.

See Also: Supreme Court.

■ **MAURY, MATTHEW FONTAINE (1806-73),** oceanographer known as "Pathfinder of the Seas." Born near Fredericksburg, Virginia, Maury entered the U.S. Navy in 1825 and spent nine years at sea studying navigation. He became superintendent of the Depot of Charts and Instruments (later the U.S. Naval Observatory and Hydrographical Office) in 1842, where he researched old logs and collected enough data on winds and currents to chart new sea lanes that cut weeks off long voyages. While mapping the North Atlantic Ocean floor (1852) he found a plateau for laying the first telegraph cable.

See Also: Science.

■ **MAYFLOWER COMPACT (Nov. 11, 1620),** an agreement signed by the Pilgrims on board the *Mayflower* establishing civil government, rule of law, and government by mutual consent. After a calamitous nine weeks at sea, the desperate passengers on the *Mayflower* sighted Massachusetts rather than their original destination in Virginia. Making landfall off northern Cape Cod, Pilgrim leaders knew the decision to land and settle there left them in a tenuous position. To be sure, they carried a charter granting them rights to occupy the land and to establish a civil government, but not in New England, which was not under the Virginia Company. The compact, composed by the leadership and ratified by the group, resolved their uncertainty. Written in the style of contemporary English church covenants, the compact bound the entire community together by mutual consent, even those who were less committed to the enterprise or objected to the relocation of their settlement. Under the compact, only those settlers who were full members of the congregation or "saints" could elect governing officials and a representative assembly; no one else could legally hold public office or vote.

See Also: Massachusetts; Pilgrims; Plymouth Settlement.

BIBLIOGRAPHY: Morison, Samuel Eliot, *History of Plymouth Plantation* (Knopf 1952).

■ **MAYO, WILLIAM J. (1861-1939),** physician. Born in Le Sueur, Minnesota, he joined his father (William) and his brother (Charles) as a surgeon at St. Mary's Hospital in Rochester, Minnesota, and with them founded in 1889 what would become the internationally famous Mayo Clinic in 1903. He and his brother traveled widely to bring back surgical techniques that they subsequently synthesized and refined. The clinic included more than 200 specialists practicing medicine cooperatively, an arrangement that allowed doctors time to travel and study. William acted as chief and with his brother founded the Mayo Foundation for Medical Education and Research in 1915.

See Also: Medicine.

■ **MAYS, WILLIE (1931-)**, baseball player. Born in Westfield, Alabama, Mays played center field for the Giants (both in New York and San Francisco) from 1951 to 1972. An outstanding hitter, his total of 660 home runs is third only to Hank Aaron's and Babe Ruth's records. Mays was elected to the Baseball Hall of Fame in 1979.

See Also: Baseball; Sports.

■ **MEAD, MARGARET (1901-78)**, anthropologist. A pioneer in her discipline, Mead was born in Philadelphia. She received a B.A. from Barnard College in 1923 and an M.A. in psychology (1924) and a Ph.D. (1929) from Columbia, where she studied under Franz Boas and Ruth Benedict. While working on her doctorate, in 1925-26, Mead researched the indigenous peoples of the Samoan Islands. From her field work she produced her first book, *Coming of Age in Samoa* (1928), which not only enjoyed popularity but established her as an authority in her discipline. Throughout her career, Mead asserted that socialization, rather than biology, influenced behavior. Further works studied peoples in New Guinea and Bali.

In 1926, Mead was appointed assistant curator of ethnology at the American Museum of Natural History in New York and by 1964 was promoted to curator. In the interim, she lectured at Vassar College and in 1954 became adjunct professor of anthropology at Columbia. She also served as president of the American Anthropological Association and chaired Fordham University's department of social sciences.

Mead was a founder of psychological anthropology, which examined the influences of culture on personality. Although her interpretations were not always well received within the academy or by popular audiences, Mead was an innovator in

Willie Mays, noted for his exuberance, was a great hitter and center fielder for the New York and San Francisco Giants. Mays returned to New York to end his baseball career with the Mets.

methodology and remains perhaps the most widely known anthropologist in history.

See Also: Benedict, Ruth Fulton; Boas, Franz; Science; Women in American History.

BIBLIOGRAPHY: Grosskurth, Phyllis, *Margaret Mead* (Penguin 1988); Mead, Margaret, *Blackberry Winter: My Earlier Years* (Morrow 1972).

■ **MEADE, GEORGE G. (1815-72)**, Union general. Born in Cadiz, Spain, the son of a U.S. naval agent, Meade graduated from West Point in 1835. He was promoted from captain to brigadier general in the Union army at the outbreak of the Civil War. On June 28, 1863, Meade was named commander of the Army of the Potomac, just days before the Battle of Gettysburg. At Gettysburg Meade defeated Confederate Gen. Robert E. Lee but did not vigorously pursue the Confederate army. Meade later led the Army of the Potomac in the Virginia campaigns of the Wilderness, Spotsylvania, Cold Harbor, Petersburg, and Appomattox.

See Also: Civil War; Gettysburg, Battle of.

■ **MEANY, GEORGE (1894-1980)**, labor leader. Meany was born in New York City where he eventu-

Anthropologist Margaret Mead's research on the cultures of the South Pacific focused on the issues of child rearing, personality, and culture.

ally became active in the Plumbers Union, serving as business agent for Local 463 in New York City from 1922 to 1934, when he was elected president of the New York State Federation of Labor, a post he held for five years. In 1939 Meany became secretary-treasurer of the American Federation of Labor (AFL), also serving on the National Labor Relations Board during World War II. He became president of the AFL in 1952 after the death of William Green. Meany oversaw the merger of the AFL with the Congress of Industrial Organizations (CIO) in 1955 and served as AFL-CIO president until 1979. He was a vocal anticommunist, an effective stance for organized labor during the Cold War. A supporter of the Vietnam War, Meany encouraged fellow labor leaders to remain neutral during the presidential election of 1972 despite labor's long support of the Democratic party. A year later, however, he joined with many in calling for Pres. Richard M. Nixon's impeachment in reaction to the Watergate scandal. He died a year after stepping down from the AFL-CIO presidency, just as the organization he helped build went into decline.

See Also: *AFL-CIO; American Federation of Labor; Labor Movement.*

BIBLIOGRAPHY: Robinson, Archie, *George Meany and His Times: A Biography* (Simon & Schuster 1981).

■ **MEAT INSPECTION ACT (1906),** federal legislation passed in response to growing consumer concern over the conditions under which meat was processed for sale. Public awareness and anxiety about this issue had been effectively stirred by Upton Sinclair's novel *The Jungle* (1906). The resulting program of federal inspection was hailed by progressives as a crowning achievement of social reform.

See Also: *Pure Food and Drug Act; Sinclair, Upton.*

■ **MEATPACKING,** processing beef and pork for mass consumption. It developed as an industry in the second half of the 19th century and was heavily influenced by the growth of railroads. Railroads enabled livestock to be shipped to urban stockyards, where they could be processed in large numbers and more completely, economically, and efficiently than by local butchers. The meatpacking centers of Cincinnati and St. Louis gave way to Chicago after 1860, as meatpacking magnates such as Gustavus Swift and Philip Armour established plants near the giant Union stockyards. Their plants became models of efficiency, using modern assembly lines to butcher beef and hogs and incorporating "everything but the squeal" in numerous by-products ranging from buttons and glue to sausage. Huge amounts of waste were also spilled into the Chicago River. The refrigerated railroad car (1868) allowed Swift and Armour to establish national distribution centers and ship dressed carcasses to eastern cities. As their industrial reach expanded, Chicago eventually declined as a meatpacking center. Progressives called for reform of the meatpacking industry after the publication of muckraker Upton Sinclair's *The Jungle* in 1906. Later that year, Congress passed a new Meat Inspection Act.

See Also: *Sinclair, Upton.*

■ **MEDICARE,** U.S. government health insurance program for people 65 and over and for those under 65 with certain disabling conditions. The plan was implemented in 1965 by amending the Social Security Act. Benefits are divided into two parts. Hospital insurance (Part A) covers the costs of hospital care, limited nursing home stays, and home health services, but it does not include prescription drugs, eyeglasses, and dental care. Part A is funded by payroll taxes and is an automatic entitlement under the Social Security program. Part B is voluntary and covers services like physicians' visits and outpatient services. In 1996 participants paid a $42.50 per-month premium. Since the premium provides only a quarter of the money needed, the remaining three-quarters comes from general government revenues.

In the 1990s politicians disagreed about how to cut Medicare costs in light of predictions from the Congressional Budget Office and the trustees of the Medicare system that the Part A fund would go bankrupt as early as 2001. The Clinton administration and the Republican Congress were divided over how to achieve spending reductions to forestall the projected bankruptcy of the Part A trust fund.

The issue of Medicare reform is tied to the larger debate over how much America can afford for health care and who will pay as the population ages and lives longer. As the end of the century arrives, pressures will continue for a comprehensive national health-insurance program.

See Also: *Clinton, William Jefferson (Bill); Social Security Act.*

BIBLIOGRAPHY: Blumenthal, David, et al., *Renewing the Promise: Medicare and its Reform* (Oxford Univ. Press 1988); Jehle, Faustina, *The Complete and Easy Guide to Social Security and Medicare* (Williamson Publishing 1995); Mazo, Judith, et al., *Providing Health Care Benefits in Retirement* (Univ. of Pennsylvania Press and Pension Research Council 1994); *Medicare Handbook* (Gordon Press 1994).

■ **MEDICINE,** theory and practice of healing the body. Within the United States, medicine arguably ranks as one of the most powerful influences in terms of its combined social, economic, and political effect. In discussing how medicine has grown, it is necessary to distinguish between medicine as a practical set of techniques for healing the body and medicine as a set of professional and institutional bodies. In the former sense, medicine has been in existence since the beginnings of civilization, but it is only during the past century that it has become truly efficacious. In the latter sense, medicine has grown from relative insignificance into a massive economic and social presence in American culture.

Medicine as a Healing Art. Every society has its healers, and the practice of the art of healing in America closely mirrors the development of American society. Among American Indians, a wide variety of healing practices existed. Some of these traditions are preserved among surviving Indian cultures, although many such practices were lost during the devastation of indigenous populations that occurred as part of the Columbian exchange. Europeans brought with them Western medical traditions along with a host of diseases previously unknown in the New World.

The medical practice of these earliest settlers was limited, as was their understanding of the body. It was not until around the time of the founding of the American republic in the late 18th century that real progress in medical practice began to occur in Europe. The career of Benjamin Rush, a signer of the Declaration of Independence, illustrates the manner in which the medical practices of the early republic followed closely the advances in medicine that were taking place in France, England, and Germany at the time. This was the era when modern scientific medicine was born. Rush, a medical doctor trained at one of the leading European medical schools at Edinburgh, Scotland, brought back with him from Europe the latest medical knowledge. He became a member of the faculty of the first medical school in the colonies, at the College of Philadelphia, and helped to pass this knowledge to newly trained American physicians.

America would continue to depend on European medical training and knowledge well into the 19th century. Not all Americans were satisfied, however, with the limited effectiveness of European medical knowledge. As a result, various uniquely American medical ideas also sprang up during this period. These included homeopathy, osteopathy, chiropractic, and even Christian Science, all of which provided alternative means of healing that were sometimes just as effective as the remedies prescribed by conventional doctors.

Only during the 20th century has scientific medicine been able to offer really effective therapeutics. The American medical and research establishment has emerged as the world leader in this movement. The advent of antibiotics such as penicillin was the first big step forward. Since the 1930s, a host of new drugs have been developed that specifically target various disease-causing agents. While these advances have certainly been significant, it could be argued that a greater influence on health in America has actually been achieved through public-health measures, especially improvements in sanitation and diet. These changes have contributed to the dramatic increase in life expectancy and overall health that has taken place in the last century.

The Medical Profession and Corporate Medicine. As a profession, doctors have capitalized both on the increase in knowledge of health and disease over the past two centuries, and on the broad social concern with health that has gripped the country in the last 50 years. Organized through the American Medical Association (AMA), doctors made their field into one of the most powerful, prestigious, and well-compensated professions. This social position has been almost entirely the product of developments during the 20th century, as increased medical expertise allowed doctors to lay claim to power in the form of specialized knowledge. Going hand in

hand with this rise to prominence of the medical profession was the development of massive corporate entities surrounding medicine, including insurance and drug companies, private hospitals, and research institutes. These organizations have helped draw massive sums of money into medicine, a process that spurred an inflationary spiral in medical costs that culminated in the 1980s. This process, the product of the success of institutional and corporate medicine, may ironically also have been its downfall. During the 1980s, a significant backlash developed against the economic excesses of medicine. As a result, a corporate restructuring began in the early 1990s, and it continues to the present. The outcome of this structural change in medicine is yet to be seen. Whatever finally evolves, it will help determine the social role and economic status of medicine in the next century.

—DAVID A. VALONE

See Also: *Disease; Rush, Benjamin.*

BIBLIOGRAPHY: Cravens, Hamilton, Alan I. Marcus, and David M. Katzman, eds., *Technical Knowledge in American Culture: Science, Technology, and Medicine since the Early 1800s* (Alabama University Press 1996); Shryock, Richard Harrison, *Medicine and Society in America, 1660-1860* (New York Univ. Press 1960); Starr, Paul, *The Social Transformation of American Medicine* (Basic Books 1982).

■ **MEDICINE SHOW,** traveling entertainment used to sell cure-all remedies in 19th-century rural America. Featuring song-and-dance or circus acts, the shows attracted crowds that would then listen to the sales pitch.

■ **MELTING POT,** metaphor representing the idea of a composite American identity, the result of cultural blending. The phrase was first popularized by Israel Zangwill, a Jewish immigrant playwright, in his drama *The Melting Pot* (1908) in which he has a character declare, "America is God's crucible, the great Melting Pot, where all the races of Europe are melting and reforming!" The idea, however, is much older. J. Hector St. John de Crèvecoeur, in *Letters from an American Farmer* (1782), asked the famous question, "What is the American, this new man?" His answer: A "strange mixture of blood, which you will find in no other country. . . . Here individuals of all nations are melted into a new race of men, whose labours and posterity will one day cause great changes in the world." The product of the melting pot would be a distinct American identity.

In the early 20th century the idea of the melting pot was presented as an alternative to the notion of Americanization, conceived as a necessary process in which immigrants (as well as Indians and perhaps African Americans) would give up their languages and distinct customs and adopt Anglo-American cultural standards. The image of the melting pot, while agreeing on the importance of a process of cultural assimilation, suggested that minority cultures had something positive to contribute to America.

For the most part, the melting pot was simply a figure of speech, although among European immigrants there has been a good deal of actual mixture through the process of intermarriage. But important cultural distinctions were preserved. Sociologists have sometimes described the process as a "triple melting pot," in which the primary categories of mate selection were religious. In the mid-20th century, 80 to 90 percent of Protestants were marrying Protestants, Catholics were marrying Catholics, and Jews were marrying Jews, although by the late 20th century there were signs that these religious distinctions in mate selection were breaking down. But intermarriage and blending between the so-called races was much less common. While rates of interracial marriage have increased somewhat in recent years, to an extraordinary degree European Americans, African Americans, Asian Americans, and Latinos have continued to choose mates within these customary ethnic/racial categories.

See Also: *Acculturation; Assimilation; Crèvecoeur, J. Hector St. John de; Cultural Pluralism; Ethnic Groups; Immigration.*

BIBLIOGRAPHY: Gordon, Milton M., *Assimilation in American Life* (Oxford Univ. Press 1964); Glazer, Nathan, and Daniel Patrick Moynihan, *Beyond the Melting Pot* (M.I.T. Press 1963).

■ **MELVILLE, HERMAN (1819-91),** author. By the time of Melville's birth in New York City, his father's financial troubles had begun to distin-

In the early 1840s, Herman Melville traveled the South Seas on an American whaling vessel, amassing the experiences he drew upon for several novels, including his masterpiece, *Moby-Dick*, published in 1851.

guish the family from its aristocratic forebears. Melville left home in 1837 to ship to Liverpool, England, as a cabin boy. His appetite for the sea was not satisfied, however, and Melville embarked for the South Seas in January 1841, finally returning to Boston in October 1844. Melville had now gathered four years' experience at sea that would provide him with literary subject matter for the rest of his life. He published *Typee* in 1846 and then *Omoo* (1847), *Mardi* (1849), *Redburn* (1849), and *White-Jacket* (1850). Melville's next work, *Moby-Dick* (1851), was a critical and public failure in his own time but has since come to be acknowledged as his masterpiece. *Pierre: Or, the Ambiguities* (1852), *Israel Potter* (1855), and *The Confidence Man* (1857) followed. Melville wrote a number of short stories between 1853 and 1856, collected as *The Piazza Tales*, and he also turned to poetry, beginning with *Battle-Pieces and Aspects of the War* (1866). Three more volumes of verse appeared in the next quarter century, and Melville completed the manuscript of his final novel, *Billy Budd*, shortly before his death in 1891. Only in 1924 was the latter published, as Melville came posthumously to earn recognition as one of the 19th century's greatest authors.

See Also: Novel.

BIBLIOGRAPHY: Rogin, Michael Paul, *Subversive Genealogy: The Politics and Art of Herman Melville* (Knopf 1983).

■ **MENCKEN, H. L. (1880-1956),** editor, literary critic, and commentator. A native of Baltimore, Maryland, Mencken began his career on the staff of that city's *Morning Herald* in 1899. In 1905 he became editor of the *Baltimore Evening Herald* and later worked on the *Sun* (1906-10) and *Evening Sun* (1910-16, 1918-36). During this same period Mencken worked on several journals; he was a literary critic and coeditor of *Smart Set* (1908-23), a contributing editor of the *Nation* (1921-32), and cofounder and coeditor of the *American Mercury* (1924-33). From these literary pulpits, as well as in his own collections of essays such as the six-volume *Prejudices* (1919-27), Mencken preached a revolt against such hallowed American traditions as the virtues of small-town living and organized religion; he supported new writers such as Theodore Dreiser and Sinclair Lewis. In 1918 he issued *The American Language*, an acclaimed lexicographic study. Mencken also contributed several volumes of autobiography: *Happy Days 1880-92* (1940), *Newspaper Days 1899-1906* (1941), and *Heathen Days 1890-1936* (1943).

See Also: Dreiser, Theodore; Lewis, (Harry) Sinclair.

■ **MENNONITES,** followers of Dutch reformer Menno Simons (1496-1561), a quiet, pacifistic Anabaptist. There are basically two Mennonite cultures in America. Those of the Swiss-American tradition escaped persecution and immigrated to Germantown, Pennsylvania, in 1683. They believed in a strict church-world dualism. The Amish separated from this group. The Dutch-Russian Mennonites, who were more likely to become involved in local social and political matters, immigrated to Kansas and Manitoba. "Old Order" groups, those who maintain simple and separatist lifestyles, may be found in either tradition.

See Also: Amish; Religion.

■ **MENOMINEE INDIANS.** *See: Algonquian.*

■ **MENOTTI, GIAN-CARLO (1911-),** composer and founder of the Spoleto Arts Festivals. Born in Cadegliano, Italy, he immigrated to the United States in 1928. Although he composed many chamber and orchestral works, he is best known for two operas, *The Medium* (1946) and the Christmas favorite *Amahl and the Night Visitors* (1951). Menotti founded two arts festivals, the Spoleto, Italy, festival (1948) and Spoleto U.S. in Charleston, South Carolina (1988).

See Also: Opera.

■ **MERCANTILISM,** economic theory and government policy dominant in most European nations in the 16th-18th centuries. The term was coined by the Scottish economist Adam Smith (1723-90). Mercantilism held that the wealth of a nation was based on the accumulation of precious metals, especially gold and silver. The best instrument to acquire such metals was foreign trade, in which the goal for the state was to achieve a surplus of exports over imports and thus gain a net profit of bullion. To ensure that gold and silver would flow only *into* the nation but not out of it, extensive government protection of domestic merchants was necessary. Import and export duties were imposed, and monopolies were entrusted to merchant companies. Similar protection applied to manufacturing, agriculture, and mining: The government legally promoted and sometimes subsidized national industries, justly believing that it was much more profitable to export finished products than raw material. In a mercantilist economy, colonies also played a great role. They were primarily a source of raw materials. Colonies freed the state from having to buy timber, tobacco, or foodstuffs from foreign merchants and allowed it to preserve its bullion within national boundaries. Colonies were also a stable market for the goods produced within the mother country. Trade with colonies was regulated by strict laws to ensure maximum profit for the nation.

BIBLIOGRAPHY: Heckscher, Eli F., *Mercantilism,* 2 vols. (Allen & Unwin; Macmillan 1955); Horrocks, J. W., *A Short History of Mercantilism* (Methuen & Co. 1925); Minchinton, Walter E., ed., *Mercantilism: System or Expediency?* (D. C. Heath 1969); Rutman,

Darrett B., *The Morning of America, 1603-1789* (Houghton Mifflin 1971).

■ MERCHANT MARINE ACTS (1920, 1928, 1936),

federal legislation designed to create and develop a strong peacetime (yet war-ready) merchant marine fleet. The act of 1920 repealed the emergency legislation related to World War I, including the disposition of the wartime fleet. In 1928 the act was further clarified, establishing a federal subsidy for ocean mail contracts and a construction loan program to encourage repair or replacement of the increasingly aging wartime fleet. The act of 1936 enabled the previous objectives to be met by authorizing adequate federal subsidies.

■ MERGANTHALER, OTTMAR (1854-99), inventor.

Born in Hachtel, Germany, he was a watch- and clock-making apprentice before immigrating to the United States in 1872. In America, he worked in a scientific instrument shop in Washington, D.C., and in Baltimore until he started his own shop in 1883. The next year, Merganthaler built the first linotype machine, an invention that cast type directly from metal matrices and so reduced the cost of printing and sped up newspaper production. His National Typographic Company manufactured the machines, which he continued to improve for the rest of his life.

See Also: Invention.

■ MERGERS, business tactic

that was a crucial factor in the rise of corporate capitalism from the 1880s, concentrating industrial structure by creating one business from two and appealing to businessmen seeking profits through monopoly, integration, and economies of scale. A period of intense merger activity occurred in almost every industry from 1895 to 1904, enabling the 100 largest corporations to increase their size by a factor of 4 and gain control of 40 percent of the nation's industrial capital. Mergers declined when the Supreme Court ruled that J. P. Morgan had to dissolve some of his railroad consolidations in the *Northern Securities* case (1904), after which corporations including Standard Oil and American Tobacco were forced to split.

During the 1920s a more relaxed public policy toward mergers combined with changes in the market and rising stock prices to produce another wave of activity. Affecting similar industries as the first, this period of mergers expanded such companies as Union Carbide, Kraft-Phoenix, General Mills, United Aircraft, and Caterpillar Tractor, and ended with the stock market crash of 1929-30. During the 1950s and 1960s high merger activity was characterized by conglomerates such as Ling-Temco-Vought (LTV) joining unrelated industries. A series of anti-merger court cases in the 1960s resulted in rulings against Pabst Brewing, Borden, and Proctor and Gamble, but it was falling stock prices after 1970 that ended this period of consolidation. In the late 1990s, numerous mergers of unprecedented size took place while the stock market boomed.

See Also: Antitrust Cases; Holding Companies.
BIBLIOGRAPHY: Fligstein, Neil, *The Transformation of Corporate Control* (Harvard Univ. Press 1990).

■ MESABI RANGE, Minnesota hills

containing one of the largest and most accessible iron deposits in the world. Mesabi is an Ojibwa Indian name meaning *giant*. Iron mining was begun by white settlers in 1890. The iron ore was shipped from Duluth, on Lake Superior, to eastern markets.

■ METACOMET (KING PHILIP) (c. 1639-76),

Wampanoag leader. Born in present-day Rhode Island, Metacomet, the son of Massasoit, became the grand sachem of the Massachusetts Wampanoag in 1662. Metacomet became increasingly disaffected with the Puritan colonists, especially when they attempted to extend English law over the Indians. In January 1675 three Wampanoag were arrested for the death of a Christian Indian ally of the English. In June the Wampanoag rose in rebellion, known as King Philip's War, waging a guerrilla war throughout New England, attacking 52 out of 92 English settlements and completely destroying a dozen. By the beginning of 1676, however, the uprising was in collapse. Encountering hostility rather than assistance from the Mohawks, Metacomet retreated to his homeland, where an English colonial army burned villages and killed hundreds of Indians. In April 1676, the English defeated Metacomet's army near modern-day Kingston, Rhode Island, in a battle known as the Great Swamp Fight.

Known as "King Philip" to the English, Metacomet (shown here in an 18th-century engraving) succeeded his brother as Wampanoag sachem in 1662 and fought the colonists in King Philip's War (1675-76).

Metacomet was killed, and the English marched his head on a pike through their towns.

See Also: *Great Swamp Fight; Indians of North America; King Philip's War.*

■ **METHODIST CHURCH,** evangelical Protestant denomination founded in England on the teachings of John Wesley (1703-1791) and his brother Charles Wesley (1707-1788). While students at Oxford University, the Wesleys, George Whitefield, and others formed a "Holy Club" with the purpose of achieving greater methodical discipline; hence, the name "Methodists," given them by fellow students. The Wesleys believed that salvation came not by work alone but by faith. With continuing discipline and faith, one would be freed from sin and love God completely, referred to as Christian perfection or perfect love.

In 1735 the Wesleys visited Georgia, but Methodism did not spread throughout the colonies until the Methodist itinerant George Whitefield began touring and preaching. In 1771, John Wesley sent missionary Francis Asbury to America, where he ordained many circuit riders.

During the Revolution, Methodism was associated with Toryism because John Wesley openly supported King George III. Following the war, at a conference in Baltimore in 1784, the Methodist Episcopal Church was formed and Asbury and Thomas Coke were elected bishops.

During the 19th century, Methodists prospered but split into varying groups. They were major participants in the Second Great Awakening with their corps of circuit riders, and by 1840 they constituted the largest denomination in America. But two controversies split the Methodists. The first schism was over the power of the bishops, while the second was over slavery. The three main bodies reunited in 1939 to form the Methodist Church. In 1968 it joined with the Evangelical United Brethren Church to create the United Methodist Church, today the second largest Protestant body in the United States.

—Nancy M. Godleski

See Also: *Religion; Second Great Awakening; Whitefield, George.*

BIBLIOGRAPHY: Bucke, Emory S., ed., *History of American Methodism* (Abingdon 1964); Richey, Russell E., *Early American Methodism* (Indiana Univ. Press 1991).

■ **METRO BROADCASTING V. FEDERAL COMMU-NICATIONS COMMISSION (1990),** U.S. Supreme Court case concerning the constitutionality of a government program to increase the number of radio and television licenses granted to members of racial and ethnic minorities. The Court ruled (5-4) that the federal government could exercise greater discretion than state or local governments in using affirmative action programs to advance social policies. The Court also held that such programs are more acceptable when used to distribute licenses and other privileges.

See Also: *Supreme Court.*

■ **MEUSE-ARGONNE OFFENSIVE (1918),** the last major American offensive of World War I. Under Gen. John J. Pershing, 600,000 U.S. troops in three corps attacked the German line between the Meuse River and the Argonne Forest on September 26. By early October the offensive had stalled. American advances remained piecemeal for the rest of the month. A new series of attacks beginning on November 1 threw back the demoralized Germans and ended only with the armistice on November 11.

See Also: *Pershing, John Joseph; World War I.*

■ **MEXICAN AMERICANS,** multiracial ethnic group, rather than a racial group, 90 percent of whom reside in the southwestern United States, the territory seized during the Mexican War of 1846-48. By the terms of the Treaty of Guadalupe Hidalgo, some 80,000 Mexicans became citizens of the United States in 1848; their numbers had increased to approximately 500,000 by 1900, but with the enormous influx of Americans from the east, they had become a minority. From Texas to California, Mexican Americans were victims of residential and occupational segregation, Jim Crow laws in public and private accommodations, and the focus of white hostility.

At the beginning of the 20th century, emigration from Mexico soared. Migrants were attracted by the industrial development of the Southwest, especially the expansion of commercial agriculture, which required a large labor force. During the 1910s they were also fleeing the violence of the Mexican Revolution. Official government statistics record the entry of more than 700,000 Mexicans between 1900 and 1930, but historians estimate that perhaps as many more crossed the border illegally, which would place the total immigration at about 10 percent of the entire population of Mexico. Immigration fell during the Depression of the 1930s. Indeed, repatriation programs in various states and localities assisted the return to Mexico of as many as a million Mexican aliens, as well as tens of thousands of children who were U.S.-born citizens. Immigration began to soar again during the 1950s, and official statistics record the entry of more than 2 million Mexicans before 1990, again with perhaps that many more entering illegally. But throughout the post–World War II period immigrants have never composed more than 20 percent of the Mexican-American population.

Mexican-American labor activist César Chávez leads a demonstration of the United Farm Workers in Los Angeles in the mid-1960s.

Before the war, farm labor was the major livelihood of the majority of Mexican Americans. In 1940, they were the most rural of all American ethnic groups. But a federally sponsored *bracero* or guest-worker program begun during the war encouraged the shift of Mexican Americans to industrial employment and to the cities. By 1990, Mexican Americans had become the most urban of American ethnic groups, with approximately 90 percent residing in cities. At the end of the century, Mexican Americans were the fastest growing ethnic group in the country.

See Also: *Ethnic Groups; Immigration; Mexican War.*
BIBLIOGRAPHY: Gutiérrez, David G., *Walls and Mirrors: Mexican Americans, Mexican Immigrants, and the Politics of Ethnicity* (Univ. of California Press 1995); Meier, Matt S., and Feliciano Ribera, *Mexican Americans, American Mexicans: From Conquistadors to Chicanos* (Hill & Wang 1993); Sánchez, George J., *Becoming Mexican American* (Oxford Univ. Press 1993).

■ **MEXICAN BORDER CAMPAIGN (1916-17),** U.S. military operation against the Mexican revolutionary movement of Pancho Villa. In early 1916, Villa conducted two deadly raids on U.S. territory. His intent was to provoke a war with the United States, which he expected would discredit the government of Venustiano Carranza, upon which he might seize power. In response, Pres. Woodrow Wilson organized in March a punitive expedition under Gen. John J. Pershing to pursue and capture Villa. Wilson had already used, and was embarrassed by, military intervention at Veracruz in 1914. The punitive expedition brought similarly barren results.

Pershing, with 6,675 men, chased Villa through northern Mexico for 11 months. He never caught up with Villa himself, although Pershing nearly captured him at Guerrero on March 28. Mexican authorities did not welcome the expedition and dispatched their army to keep watch over Pershing's "invasion." A skirmish at Parral on April 12 between American and Mexican forces nearly brought on the war Villa had hoped to provoke, prompting Wilson to end the active pursuit of Villa in the interest of cordial relations between the United States and Mexico. With Wilson's approval, however, Pershing occupied the

Brig. Gen. John Pershing leads cavalry during the Mexican Border Campaign in March 1916, in pursuit of Mexican revolutionary Pancho Villa.

province of Chihuahua into 1917, hoping to force Villa into the hands of Mexican authorities.

For the U.S. Army, the punitive expedition provided an opportunity to use new military technology—automobiles, airplanes, and field telegraphy—in a combat situation. Pershing's truck convoys acquitted themselves well in keeping the expedition supplied, and the telegraph allowed rapid communication to Pershing's base of operations in Columbus, New Mexico. Frequent crashes and mechanical problems prevented the airplanes from making a significant contribution.

By the time Wilson withdrew Pershing in February 1917, he had gained the enmity of the Mexican people and government. Pershing's failure to capture Villa and the subsequent occupation of Chihuahua was another Mexican-relations embarrassment to Wilson. Only the likelihood of war with Germany enabled the U.S. president to extricate himself somewhat gracefully from this misadventure.

—T. R. BRERETON

See Also: Pershing, John Joseph.
BIBLIOGRAPHY: Eisenhower, John S. D., *Intervention: the United States and the Mexican Revolution, 1913-1917* (Norton 1993); Molloy, Herbert Mason, *The Great Pursuit* (Random House 1970).

■ **MEXICAN WAR (1846-48),** war of territorial expansion, in which the United States sought control of a vast expanse of northern Mexico, including what is now California, New Mexico, Arizona, Utah, Nevada, and Colorado. In 1845 Pres. James K. Polk offered to buy California and other Mexican lands, but Mexican leaders had no interest in selling half of their nation. Complicating the situation was the status of Texas, a former Mexican province that had won its independence in 1836. Because Mexico had never recognized Texan independence, when the United States annexed Texas in 1845 and sent soldiers there in 1846, Mexico declared war, claiming that its territory had been violated. Mexican soldiers won the war's first skirmish (Apr. 24, 1846) on the north side of the Rio Grande, which the United States claimed as the international boundary. President Polk called for Congress to acknowledge that a state of war existed, making the resounding

claim that "American blood had been shed on American soil." On May 13 Congress overwhelmingly endorsed Polk's call for war.

Several critics opposed the war. Northern Whigs contended that the war was prosecuted to gain territory for new slave states, but Sen. John C. Calhoun, slavery's greatest defender, also criticized the war. Other opponents included former president John Quincy Adams, who called the war "unconstitutional," and essayist Henry David Thoreau, who termed it "unjust." Ulysses S. Grant, who as a young lieutenant fought in Mexico, described the war as "one of the most unjust ever waged by a stronger against a weaker nation."

Undaunted by critics, Polk aggressively moved to take territory that Mexico had refused to sell. Devising an ambitious strategy, Polk ordered small U.S. military expeditions to invade New Mexico and California, knowing that Mexico stationed

Ulysses S. Grant, who was a second lieutenant at the beginning of the Mexican War, served with distinction, as did his Civil War adversary, Robert E. Lee.

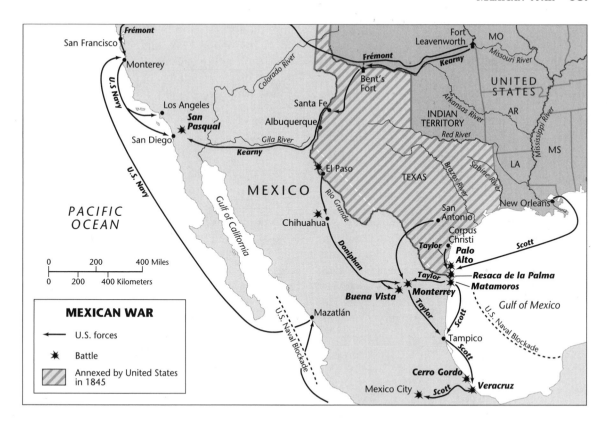

MEXICAN WAR

→ U.S. forces

★ Battle

▨ Annexed by United States in 1845

few soldiers in those provinces. Meanwhile, Gen. Zachary Taylor, with almost half of the U.S. Army, was ordered to push Mexican forces south of the Rio Grande. Polk reckoned that if U.S. forces occupied New Mexico and California and patrolled the Rio Grande, Mexico would have to concede defeat.

Military Campaigns. Invading northern Mexico and California, the U.S. military implemented Polk's strategy. Taylor's army won victories at Palo Alto and Resaca de la Palma (May 8-9) north of the Rio Grande, occupied Matamoros and Camargo, and then captured Monterrey (September 23). At Buena Vista, near Saltillo, Taylor gained a hard-won victory (Feb. 22-23, 1847) to end his campaigning. Meanwhile, an expedition under Brig. Gen. Stephen W. Kearny captured Santa Fe, New Mexico, and then proceeded to California. Assisted by a navy squadron, the U.S. Army fought skirmishes with Mexican defenders and secured California by mid-January 1847. However, Mexico refused to

negotiate a treaty that would officially recognize the U.S. conquests.

Accordingly, Polk assigned Maj. Gen. Winfield Scott to lead another invasion of Mexico, intended to take Mexico City itself, in order to demand an end to the war. Scott assembled an army of 14,000 soldiers that included Taylor's best troops supplemented by thousands of new volunteers and a few marines. Scott launched his invasion in March 1847, captured the port of Veracruz, and marched into the interior. Opposing Scott was a patriotic Mexican army of about 25,000, led by Gen. Antonio López de Santa Anna, Mexico's volatile, talented, and nationalistic president. Santa Anna hoped to defeat Scott's army or force it to retreat. In a major battle at Cerro Gordo (April 18), Scott pushed back Santa Anna's units and, after receiving reinforcements, continued toward Mexico City. In a series of bitter battles around the capital, the U.S. Army breached the Mexican defenses. Scott's army entered Mexico City on September 14 and occupied it until June 1848 while diplomats negotiated the war's end.

Effects of War. By the Treaty of Guadalupe Hidalgo (named after the suburb of Mexico City where discussions took place), the United States gained a vast stretch of territory, taking about 50 percent of Mexico's land and about 1 percent of its population. The Rio Grande would be the boundary between the two nations. In return, the United States agreed to pay Mexico $15 million and paid another $3 million to U.S. citizens who had claims against the Mexican government.

Winning the war against Mexico made the United States a continental power stretching from the Atlantic to the Pacific. General Taylor became a national hero and won the presidency in 1848. U.S. politicians argued over the status of slavery in the lands taken from Mexico, intensifying debates over issues relating to slavery and contributing to the sectional crisis of 1860 and the Civil War of 1861-65.

—JOSEPH G. DAWSON III

See Also: Frontier in American History; Gadsden Purchase; Manifest Destiny; Southwest, The; individual battles and biographies.

BIBLIOGRAPHY: Bauer, K. Jack, *The Mexican War* (Macmillan 1974); Pletcher, David M., *The Diplomacy of Annexation: Texas, Oregon, and the Mexican War* (Univ. of Missouri Press 1973); Robinson, Cecil, ed., *The View from Chapultepec: Mexican Writers and the Mexican-American War* (Univ. of Arizona Press 1989); Singletary, Otis A., *The Mexican War* (Univ. of Chicago Press 1960).

■ **MIAMI,** city on the southeastern end of the Florida peninsula. Located on Biscayne Bay, an inlet of the Atlantic Ocean, Miami is the commercial and tourist center of south Florida. A failed Spanish mission was founded there in 1567 and again in 1743. During the second Seminole War in 1836 the first permanent settlement, named Ft. Dallas, was established. Significant development of the town did not occur until 1895, when it was made a railroad terminus. Miami experienced spectacular growth during the Florida land boom of the 1920s, and by 1940 its population was around 400,000. Long one of America's favorite resort centers, with hotels, beaches, horseracing, and sunshine, Miami attracts millions of visitors annually

from all over the world. With Fidel Castro's rise to power in Cuba in 1959, Miami became home to a large community of Cuban expatriates. They were the first of a large number of Latin American immigrants who give the city its distinctive Hispanic character. Population (1994): 373,024.

■ **MIAMI INDIANS.** *See: Algonquian.*

■ **MIANTONOMO (c. 1600-43),** Narragansett leader. Friendly to Rhode Island founder Roger Williams, in 1636-37, Miantonomo supported the colonial troops in the Pequot War, assisting in the attack on the Pequot village at present-day Mystic, Connecticut. In 1643, when war broke out between the Narragansett and the Mohegan, the Mohegan leader Uncas turned Miantonomo over to the colonists, allegedly for plotting against them. Tried and found guilty by the colonists, Miantonomo was executed by Uncas's Mohegans.

See Also: Indians of North America; Pequot War; Uncas; Williams, Roger.

■ **MICHELSON, ALBERT (1852-1931),** physicist. Born in Strelno, Prussia, he moved to the United States in 1854 and graduated from Annapolis in 1873. Michelson measured the speed of light in 1879, 1887, and 1927. If light waves moved through ether, as scientists believed, then the earth's rotation would affect their speed. Michelson found no evidence of such interference. His results questioned current laws of physics and supported Einstein's later theories of relativity. Michelson also measured stars, set the wavelength of cadmium light as the standard unit of measure, and was the first American scientist to win a Nobel Prize in Physics (1907).

See Also: Science.

■ **MICHIGAN,** state that consists of two peninsulas and borders four Great Lakes. The lower peninsula is bounded by the Straits of Mackinac to the north, Lake Michigan to the west, lakes Huron and Erie to the east, and Indiana and Ohio to the south. The upper peninsula juts northeast from Wisconsin and separates Lake Superior from lakes Michigan and Huron. Rivers, lakes, and bays separate the state from Ontario.

The French and British established forts and trading posts in Michigan. Even after the area was awarded to the new United States in 1783, the British were slow to leave. Michigan became a state in 1837. Detroit became the world's motor-vehicle capital in the early 20th century. Michigan was still producing about one-quarter of the nation's automobiles and trucks in the 1990s.

Capital: Lansing. Area: 58,513 square miles. Population (1995 est.): 9,549,000.

See Also: Cadillac, Antoine de la Mothe; Ford, Gerald Rudolph; Great Depression; Great Lakes; Marquette, Pere Jacques; Treaty of Paris (1783); Pontiac's Rebellion; Rogers, Robert; War of 1812.

■ **MICHILIMACKINAC,** Algonquian name for an island in the Straits of Mackinac, Michigan. In the 17th century the Chippewa established their chief village on the island. In 1671 the French explorer Jacques Marquette established a mission at Michilimackinac, and in 1817 the fur trader John Jacob Astor established a trading post. Michigan designated most of the island a state park in 1895, and it has been a popular tourist spot since. Automobiles are not allowed on the island.

■ **MICMAC INDIANS.** *See: Algonquian.*

■ **MIDDLE PASSAGE,** term that refers to the Atlantic Ocean voyage of Africans captured and bound for enslavement in the Americas. From various locations all along the west and west-central African coasts, and extending eastward to the shores of what is now Mozambique, Tanzania, and Kenya and southward to Angola, Africans of diverse background were collected and placed aboard slave ships, often referred to as "slavers" in the literature, and taken away. Before boarding, captives had usually spent significant time in coastal holding areas, or barracoons, convalescing from forced marches of varying distances from points in the interior. The barracoon phase could last a few days or a few years, depending upon local circumstances. The average duration of the Middle Passage is difficult to determine. Some scholars believe it lasted two or three months, but this figure is complicated by the fact that slavers often had to journey from place to place along African coasts to fill their quota of captives, which necessarily added to the total time that a captive spent on board a ship.

It had become standard practice by the end of the 18th century to chain males together at the wrists and ankles as they entered the slaver. Women and girls were usually unfettered and separated from the enslaved males. These precautions were necessary to guard against mutinies, which were frequent enough throughout the period of the slave trade. Ostensibly to promote hygiene, both males and females were stripped of all, or most, clothing. Many were branded with the slaver company's coat of arms or name prior to embarkation for the New World. In the case of the Portuguese in West Central Africa, Angola, and Mozambique, for example, captives were also baptized (often without the slightest bit of information as to the rite's significance). After such preparation, the voyage began in earnest.

Shipboard Conditions. Aboard the ship, captives were fed twice a day. During such times, they were brought on deck and supplied with a diet that could include horse beans, yams, rice, and palm oil. Water was the main drink, which was rationed along with the food very carefully. In order to monitor the health of the captives, the English began to require the presence of medical technicians, called surgeons, on board every slaver. Of dubious ability, these surgeons were as busy concealing disease (with a view to marketing the captives) as they were treating it. As such, malnutrition and unsanitary conditions characterized the captive experience. Their sufferings included dysentery (the "bloody flux"), measles, smallpox, scurvy, and yaws.

The captives spent most of their time below, in the hold of the slaver. There they tried to calm their fear that their captors were in fact cannibals who would soon eat them, an apprehension consistently expressed throughout the primary sources on the passage. Generally speaking, the captives were terrified by their difficult present and uncertain future. It was in the hold of the ship that they experienced "tight packing," where they had very little room in which to lie. Scholars differ on the question of tight packing, with some arguing that it was the exception rather than the rule, and others claiming that it had little to do with issues of mortality and disease. Whatever the scholarly position, few contest the estimate that some 15 to 20 percent of all captives who entered the Atlantic on the African side never made it to the American side. Disease, cruelty, and to a lesser extent suicide account for the enormous loss of life. It was through circumstances such as these that the involuntary immigration of millions of Africans into the New World was achieved.

—MICHAEL A. GOMEZ

See Also: Slavery.

BIBLIOGRAPHY: Galenson, David W., *Traders, Planters, and Slaves: Market Behavior in Early English America* (Cambridge Univ. Press 1986); Kleig, Herbert S., *The Middle Passage* (Princeton Univ. Press 1978).

■ **MIDDLETON, ARTHUR (1742-87),** lawyer and Revolutionary War politician. A delegate to the Second Continental Congress and a signer of the Declaration of Independence, Middleton was born on his family's estate in South Carolina. As a member of the gentry, he was an influential figure in his home state.

See Also: Declaration of Independence.

■ **MIDNIGHT JUDGES (1800-01),** somewhat derisive name given to the 16 Federalists granted judgeships by the Judiciary Act of 1801. After the election of Thomas Jefferson, but before he took office, the defeated Federalist Congress passed a Judiciary Act that created 16 new federal judgeships as well as other judicial offices. Outgoing Pres. John Adams made appointments to the new posts until 9:00 P.M. on his last day in office. The new Republican Congress repealed the Judiciary Act and abolished the 16 judgeships. Jefferson, however, was disappointed in his attempt to rid the U.S. Supreme Court of the last-minute Federalist appointee, Chief Justice John Marshall.

See Also: Judiciary Acts.

■ **MIDWAY, BATTLE OF (1942),** World War II battle between U.S. and Japanese fleets that proved to be the turning point in the Pacific theater. The Japanese invaded the Aleutian Islands and launched a carrier-based attack on Midway Island on June 3 and 4, but American code specialists had already detected the plan and Adm. Chester Nimitz positioned his ships to intercept the Japanese fleet. A number of American planes were lost, but U.S. aircraft sank four Japanese carriers, seriously weakening Japan's offensive capability.

See Also: Navy; World War II.

The Allies gained their first major naval victory over Japan at the Battle of Midway (June 3-6, 1942), the turning point in World War II in the Pacific theater.

■ **MIDWEST, THE,** north-central region of the United States. The word *Midwest* is a vague regional term that is usually considered to apply to Illinois, Indiana, Michigan, Ohio, and Wisconsin on the eastern side of the Mississippi River, and to Iowa, Kansas, Minnesota, Missouri, Nebraska, North Dakota, and South Dakota on the western side. The eastern portion of the Midwest was the first area of European settlement beyond the natural ridge of the Appalachian Mountains. The region was divided and allotted according to the Land Ordinance of 1785, which established the grid form of surveying as the national standard. Using this form of surveying, new states were created from the long horizontal bands of land that originally belonged to some of the original 13 states. The survey grid was well suited to the flat prairie landscape of much of the region. The Midwest is rich agricultural land and produces a variety of grain, a fact that earned it the nickname "Bread Basket of the United States." Although agriculture is still important to the region, the Midwest also is home to the major cities of Chicago, St. Louis, and Kansas City.

■ **MIES VAN DER ROHE, LUDWIG (1886-1969),** leader in modern architecture. Born in Aachen, Germany, Mies learned masonry from his father and also apprenticed in architecture. In the years after World War I Mies won acclaim for his work in Germany, ranging from steel skyscrapers sheathed in glass to houses with zones but no distinct rooms. This second idea was typified by his design for the 1929 Barcelona International Exposition German Pavilion, in which interior and exterior spaces seemed to merge. He also designed furniture for the pavilion, such as the "Barcelona chair" made of steel and leather. From 1930 to 1933 he was the last director of the influential Bauhaus School of Design in Dessau, Germany. Mies came to the United States in 1937, where he joined the faculty of the Armour Institute of Technology in Chicago, later to become the Illinois Institute of Technology, for which he designed the campus. Mies's famous phrase, "Less is more," became one of the tenets of modernism.

See Also: Architecture; Modernism; Skyscrapers.

■ **MILITARY ACADEMIES,** U.S. government colleges established to create an elite, educated offi-cer corps. Students receive both academic and military training and are commissioned as officers upon graduation. The oldest, the U.S. Military Academy at West Point, New York, was founded in 1802 as an engineering school. Sylvanus Thayer, the superintendent of West Point from 1817 to 1833, turned the school into a military academy modeled after European institutions. In 1845 the U.S. Naval Academy was founded in Annapolis, Maryland, to train naval officers. A shipboard U.S. Coast Guard Academy was established in 1876 and relocated to Baltimore, Maryland, in 1900. This academy moved to its current site in New London, Connecticut, in 1910. U.S. Air Force Academy, the newest American military academy, was established in Colorado Springs, Colorado, in 1955. Additionally, the U.S. Department of Transportation operates a military-style Merchant Marine Academy in Kings Point, New York. The previously all-male service academies were opened to women in 1976.

See Also: Air Force Academy; Education; Naval Academy; West Point.

■ **MILITARY-INDUSTRIAL COMPLEX,** a term describing the character and reach of the modern American defense industry. The growth of a civilian military enterprise dates from the 1950 issuance of a National Security Council report, known as NSC-68, by the administration of Pres. Harry S. Truman. In this top-secret document, written months before the start of the Korean War and couched in anticommunist hyperbole, the administration called for a tripling of the defense department budget. Thus was created an industry whose yearly output was soon measured in the tens of billions of dollars.

Based initially on the aircraft and space industries, and by the 1960s on the high-technology industries as well, the defense conglomerates quickly began to influence American politics. Through their lobbyists, they brought pressure to bear on Congress, individual members of which were only too happy to oblige with support for public investment in their districts. The potential for conflicts of interest was irresistible.

Few in American political life ventured to criticize so popular a venture. One who did, and in so doing defined the growing industry, was Pres.

Dwight D. Eisenhower. In his 1961 Farewell Address as he left the presidency, Eisenhower warned the nation to "guard against the acquisition of unwarranted influence, whether sought or unsought, by the military-industrial complex . . . ." The issue of the relationship between lobbyists, politicians, and defense contractors, known in Washington as the "Iron Triangle," remains a problem of political life.

—JOHN ROBERT GREENE

See Also: Cold War; Defense, Department of; Eisenhower, Dwight David; Korean War.

BIBLIOGRAPHY: Martin, Andrew Kirby, ed., The Pentagon and the Cities (Sage 1991).

■ **MILITIA AND NATIONAL GUARD,** American states' armed forces, first formed in colonial times for local defense. Equipment and membership varied with slaves, students, and clergy serving in some but excluded from others. Militiamen fought in Indian and colonial wars (1622-1763) and in the American Revolution, regionally and on expeditions. Suspicion of standing armies influenced the U.S. Constitution's militia articles and subsequent laws, such as the 1792 Militia Act. In the 1790s, federalized militiamen quashed several rebellions. Some 80,000 were alerted during the Quasi-War with France, but militia performed unevenly in the War of 1812. By the 1820s states funded only first-line militia units.

Expandable Army. In the major U.S. wars between 1848 and 1901, regulars commanded armies composed mainly of volunteer units, with most militias staying close to home. From 1815 to 1861, militiamen served in Indian wars and in ethnic and labor troubles. They enforced the Fugitive Slave Laws and, in the South, augmented the slave patrol. Federal military governors relied heavily on African-American militias during Reconstruction. As Reconstruction ended in 1877, the Posse Comitatus Act forbade the policing of civilians by regular troops, placing the main burden of dealing with labor problems on the militia. From the 1880s militias increasingly were brought under regular army standards, culminating in the 1903 Dick Act, which made all state militias "the National Guard of the United States."

World War to Cold War. Many guardsmen were on Southwest border duty as World War I mo-

bilization began in 1917, scrambling guardsmen, regulars, and draftees as military professionals filled many key guard division command slots. Between World War I (1914-18) and World War II (1939-45), guardsmen frequently engaged in disaster relief and strikebreaking. Although many of the 250,000 young guardsmen mobilized in 1940 became officers and noncommissioned officers, guard divisions were again fragmented with regulars in most senior positions. In 1948 Cold War crises rejuvenated a shrunken guard threatened by Universal Military Training (UMT) proposals. Army and air guardsmen deployed to Europe. Four divisions and air units served in Korea (1951-53), but in the following slump, guard leaders fended off a "home front constabulary" role and charges of obsolescence while supporting the 1955 Reserve Forces Act, which stimulated recruiting. In 1957, Arkansas guardsmen were federalized by Pres. Dwight D. Eisenhower during school integration riots. Guard units were called in during the 1961 Berlin Crisis, a tense diplomatic standoff between the Soviet Union and the United States, Britain, and France over the West's refusal to recognize the German Democratic Republic, but the units had difficulties attaining combat readiness. In 1965, Pres. Lyndon B. Johnson refused to mobilize guardsmen and reservists for Vietnam, but called some units later. Many Vietnam-era guardsmen saw campus and ghetto riot service, most notably the Watts riots of 1965 and the Kent State tragedy of 1970.

Total Force. After Vietnam, Pentagon planners, fearing another Vietnam, assigned guard and reserve units the key mobilization roles that became visible in the Gulf War (1991). In 1981, Congress eased Posse Comitatus restrictions to increase military antidrug efforts. In the mid-1990s, new reserve-guard merger schemes were proposed as self-proclaimed "militias" appeared, and the "downsized" army guard stood at 400,000 and the air guard at 100,000.

—ROGER BEAUMONT

BIBLIOGRAPHY: Cooper, Jerry, ed., The Militia and National Guard in America Since Colonial Times: A Research Guide (Greenwood Press 1993); Hill, Jim Dan, The Minute Man in Peace and War: A History of the National Guard (Stackpole 1964); Mahon, John K., History of the Militia and National Guard (Macmillan 1983).

MILLAY, EDNA ST. VINCENT (1892-1950), poet known for her excellent sonnets. She was born in Rockland, Maine, and graduated from Vassar. In 1917 she moved to Greenwich Village in New York City, where she acquired a reputation as a bohemian. Her unconventional love poetry in *A Few Figs from Thistles* (1920) and *Second April* (1921) and her satirical essays reinforced this image and earned her great popularity. She won a Pulitzer Prize for *The Harp Weaver* (1923). *Two Slatterns and a King* (1921) and two other plays were produced by the Provincetown Players.
See Also: Poetry.

MILLER, ALFRED JACOB (1810-75), painter of the American West. Born in Baltimore, Maryland, Miller studied painting in Philadelphia in 1831-32 and then in Europe, including time in Paris at the Ecole des Beaux-Arts. In 1837 Miller joined a Scottish traveler, William Stewart, on an expedition to the Rocky Mountains, where he completed about 200 watercolor sketches of the ways of life of Indians and mountain men. For much of his career Miller continued to base oil paintings on these sketches.
See Also: Painting.

MILLER, ARTHUR (1916-), playwright. A native of New York City, Miller attended the University of Michigan. Graduating from college in the midst of the Great Depression, Miller worked for the Federal Theater Project and later wrote radio plays. His first play produced on Broadway was *The Man Who Had All the Luck*, which opened to an indifferent audience in 1944. Miller had his first success in 1947 with *All My Sons*, which won the Drama Critics' Circle Award that year. In 1949 Miller completed *Death of a Salesman*, which garnered both critical and commercial success and remains one of his best-known works. Miller's liberal views were represented in *The Crucible* of 1953, a play set in Puritan New England. The plot deals with the Salem witchcraft trials and seemed to parallel closely the contemporary actions of the House Committee on Un-American Activities, which subpoenaed Miller in 1956. He was fined for contempt of Congress but later exonerated. Miller was married (1956-60) to Marilyn Monroe and wrote the film script for *The Misfits* (1960), in which she starred.

See Also: Federal Theater Project; Monroe, Marilyn; Theater; Un-American Activities, House Committee on (HUAC).

MILLER, GLENN (1904-44), band leader. Born in Clarinda, Iowa, he played trombone in bands led by the Dorsey brothers, Ray Noble, and others before forming his own wildly successful big band. Its smooth arrangements featuring the reed section included "Moonlight Serenade" and "String of Pearls." Miller enlisted and formed the Army Air Force Band in 1943. He was lost in a plane accident over the English Channel in December 1944.
See Also: Big Bands.

MILLER, HENRY (1891-1980), writer and novelist. Miller was born in New York City and brought up in Brooklyn, where most of his works are set. He left the City College of New York after two months to travel and work at places ranging from his father's tailor shop to a speakeasy. Between 1930 and 1940 Miller lived in Paris, where he published his first books, including *Tropic of Cancer* (1934), *Black Spring* (1936), and *Tropic of Capricorn* (1939). All three were autobiographical and drew on his experiences from his Brooklyn boyhood through his Paris sojourn. These early works, for which he is best known today, were deemed obscene and remained largely unavailable in the United States until the early 1960s. Miller's experience with censorship led him to write *The Plight of the Creative Artist in the United States* (1944) and *Obscenity and the Law of Reflection* (1945) in addition to his many novels. He is also remembered for his correspondence with other literary figures, such as Lawrence Durrell and Anais Nin.
See Also: Censorship; Novel.

MILLER, SAMUEL FREEMAN (1816-90), associate justice of the U.S. Supreme Court (1862-90). A Richmond, Kentucky, native, Miller left the practice of medicine to join the legal profession in his early 30s. On the Court, Miller earned the respect of his colleagues, especially for his powers of persuasion. Despite his concern for individual rights, Miller consistently defended the expansion of federal authority during the Reconstruction era.

The highlight of Miller's tenure on the Court came with the Slaughterhouse Cases (1873). Miller's majority opinion held that the 14th Amendment did not ban state-created monopolies.

See Also: Slaughterhouse Cases; Supreme Court.

■ **MILLER-TYDINGS ENABLING ACT (1937),** federal "fair trade" law that allowed manufacturers to set retail prices. Fair trade laws were backed by small retailers who feared competition from discount chain stores and mail-order houses.

See Also: New Deal.

■ **MILLIKAN, ROBERT (1868-1953),** physicist, educator, and founder of California Institute of Technology (Caltech). Born in Morrison, Illinois, Millikan studied physics at Columbia (Ph.D., 1895) and in Berlin and Göttingen. He then joined the faculty at the University of Chicago (1896-1921), where he isolated the electron and determined that each one had an identical charge and mass. This finding became one of the most important constants in atomic physics. From 1912 to 1916, Millikan experimentally confirmed Albert Einstein's photoelectric equation and evaluated Planck's constant, h, the elementary quantum of action. For this work he won the Nobel Prize in Physics in 1923. Millikan headed the U.S. Signal Corps science and research division during World War I. In 1921, he became head of Throop College and transformed the school into one of the world's leading technical institutions, the California Institute of Technology. At Caltech he studied the ionization of air at high altitudes, determined that it was caused by radiation from outer space, and named them "cosmic rays." During World War II, Millikan supervised Caltech research projects in jet propulsion, artillery rockets, and antisubmarine warfare.

See Also: Science.

■ **MILLING,** process by which grain is ground into flour. Flour milling was first widespread in the middle colonies, where wheat grew more successfully than elsewhere, and expanded after the American Revolution. By about 1790, flour was the nation's most valuable export. Oliver Evans's mill designs (1783-1808) saved labor and cut costs by the use of grain elevators and conveyor belts. After the Civil War, the focus of flour milling moved. Settlement and technological improvements including the steel plow, McCormick's reaper, and spring wheat opened new grain fields to the west. New mills with steel rollers made appealing white flour, and the railroads connected producers and millers to national markets. In the late 19th century, flour mills became the center of a large wheat industry centered in Minneapolis and St. Paul. Access to Canadian wheat and proximity to eastern facilities later made Buffalo an important milling center.

See Also: Agriculture.

■ **MILLION MAN MARCH,** mass demonstration of African Americans in Washington, D.C., held on Oct. 16, 1995. The march was organized by Louis Farrakhan of the Nation of Islam and Benjamin Chavis, Jr., of the National Association for the Advancement of Colored People. On that "Day of Atonement and Reconciliation," orators, including Rosa Parks, Betty Shabazz, and Jesse Jackson, stressed themes of renewal and familial responsibility and criticized the social policies of the Republican-dominated U.S. Congress.

See Also: African Americans; Farrakhan, Louis.

■ **MILLS, ROBERT (1781-1855),** architect of public buildings. Born in Charleston, South Carolina, Mills moved his practice to Washington, D.C., in 1830. From 1836 to 1851 he designed many of the federal government's buildings, including the Patent Office (1837), the Treasury Building (1836), and the General Post Office (1839). Mills won the 1833 design competition for the Washington Monument, which was started in 1848 but not completed until 1884.

See Also: Washington Monument.

■ **MINING RUSHES,** rush by many people to exploit an area's minerals. California is traditionally counted as the first of the great mining rushes of the 19th-century West, but the little-known Georgia gold rush of 1829 actually prefigured it. Thousands of miners clamored into the foothills of the southern Appalachians, extracting as much as $10 million in gold and pushing the Cherokee off their homelands. Shockingly disorderly mining towns appeared overnight. Yet, within a few years mining companies had consolidated the majority of individual claims, and the men who remained

The discovery of gold in California's lower Sacramento River Valley in January 1848 set the stage for a half-century of mining rushes in the American West.

in the diggings toiled for wages. What happened on a smaller scale in Georgia was repeated in the Golden State as well as dozens of other mining strikes throughout the West.

The California Gold Rush, however, was the lodestone for the exploitation of the Far West during the second half of the 19th century. Gold was discovered at the sawmill of John Sutter in early 1848, and by May the town of San Francisco had been emptied of able-bodied men. Pres. James K. Polk announced the discovery to the nation in his State of the Union address in December, igniting the frenzy of '49. The news hit a continent still awash with thousands of dislocated and unsettled veterans of the Mexican War (1846-48), not only in the United States but in Mexico itself. Thousands of American men headed west by wagon and by foot, while thousands more booked passage on clipper ships; they were joined on the coast by thousands of Mexicans, Peruvians, Chileans, Australians, and Chinese, all bound for "the diggings" in the foothills of the Sierra Nevadas.

Characteristics of Mining Rushes. Over the next few years two things happened that would be repeated in all the gold and silver rushes in the West. First, the easily obtained surface supply of ore was quickly exhausted and the miner's take drastically reduced; and second, "placer" mining with pick and pan gave way to "quartz" mining,

requiring the application of industrial processes to extract the gold from the surrounding rock. These operations required large capital investments as well as a large labor force. Thus, the men who had hoped to "strike it rich" were forced to go to work for wages. As a result, when word came of strikes elsewhere, thousands of men were ready to "rush" to the new site. There were seemingly endless rounds of rushes: to the Fraser River in British Columbia in 1858; to the Colorado Rockies west of the emerging city of Denver, as well as to the Washoe country of Nevada in 1859; to Idaho and Montana in 1860 and 1862; to the Black Hills of the Dakotas in 1876; to Leadville, Colorado, and Tombstone, Arizona, in 1877; to the Coeur d'Alene region of Idaho in 1883; and in 1896-97, to the northern Yukon country of Canada, a rush that quickly spread to Nome and Fairbanks, Alaska.

Each rush created new population centers and also presented the familiar kaleidoscope of lonely prospectors with their mules and pans, crowds of jostling men of every conceivable nationality, jerry-built stores along muddy streets, mirrored saloons, prostitutes and dancing girls, outlaws, claim jumpers, and vigilance committees—all soon supplanted by smelters and mills, slag heaps and underground burrows, company towns, Pinkerton detectives, and labor unions, leading finally to strikes with the fist instead of the shovel. Mining added a significant dimension to the social, economic, and imaginative development of the West.

—JOHN MACK FARAGHER

See Also: *California Gold Rush; Frontier in American History.*

BIBLIOGRAPHY: Marks, Paula Mitchell, *Precious Dust: The American Gold Rush Era, 1848-1900* (W. Morrow 1994); Williams, David, *The Georgia Gold Rush: Twenty-Niners, Cherokees, and Gold Fever* (Univ. Of South Carolina Press 1993).

■ **MINNESOTA,** the largest of the Midwest states. It is bounded by Ontario and Manitoba to the north, North Dakota and South Dakota to the west, Iowa to the south, and Wisconsin and Lake Superior to the east. The Mississippi River, which rises in Minnesota and flows past the twin cities of Minneapolis and St. Paul, forms part of its eastern border. The Red River of the North forms most of the western border. Southern Minnesota is prime farming country; the north is rugged and heavily forested. The state has over 15,000 lakes.

French missionaries and French and British fur traders explored what is now Minnesota before it became part of the United States between 1783 and 1803. It became a state in 1858. Farming, mining, lumbering, and food processing long dominated the economy, but after World War II other industries, such as electronics, computers, and chemicals, also became important.

Capital: St. Paul. Area: 84,397 square miles. Population (1995 est.): 4,610,000.

See Also: *Farmer-Labor Party; Louisiana Purchase; Mississippi River; Ojibwa (Chippewa); Sioux; St. Lawrence River and Seaway.*

■ *MINOR V. HAPPERSETT* **(1875),** U.S. Supreme Court case pivotal for the direction of the woman suffrage movement. In 1872 Virginia Minor had attempted to vote in Missouri elections but was barred from the polls by a registrar, Reese Happersett. Minor sued under the 14th Amendment, contending that her rights as a citizen had been violated. The Supreme Court disagreed, holding that the citizenship rights protected by the 14th Amendment did not include the right to vote. This decision convinced most advocates of woman suf-

frage that nothing short of a constitutional amendment would guarantee women the right to vote.

See Also: *Constitution of the United States; Supreme Court; Woman Suffrage Movement.*

■ **MINSTREL SHOWS,** stage productions in which white men in blackface performed Negro songs, were a major form of American stage entertainment in the years before the Civil War. Daniel Rice, composer of "Jump Jim Crow" (1830); Dan Emmett, who wrote "Dixie" (1859); and E. P. Christy, of "Christy's Minstrels" and popularizer of Stephen Foster's songs, were the most famous minstrel artists of the antebellum period. Although racist in its conception of African Americans, historians now recognize that minstrels later provided African-American performers with an entrance into show business, became an important vehicle for the dissemination of African-American music and humor, and was one of the foundations of vaudeville.

See Also: *Emmett, Daniel D.; Rice, Daniel McLaren; Vaudeville.*

BIBLIOGRAPHY: Toll, Robert C., *Blacking Up: The Minstrel Show in Nineteenth Century America* (Oxford Univ. Press 1974).

■ **MINT ACT (1792),** legislation creating the federal mint in order to produce U.S. currency. Not passed until three years after the United States adopted its Constitution, the act enabled the Philadelphia mint, established in 1793, to begin making coins in 1794.

See Also: *Money and Currency.*

■ **MINTING,** production of monetary coins. Congress established the first national mint in Philadelphia in 1793 to produce gold, silver, and copper coins. Until 1871, when the U.S. Supreme Court upheld paper currency as legal tender, coins were the preferred form of cash, and foreign, domestic, and privately struck gold and silver coins circulated freely. In 1873 the Coinage Act placed the United States on the gold standard, and all minting in the United States was brought under the control of the Treasury Department. The production of gold coins ended in 1934 when Congress approved the Gold Reserve Act. The Bureau of the Mint continues to operate mints in Philadelphia, Denver, and San Francisco and also operates assay offices, which certify the purity of gold, and gold bullion depositories, including the most famous at Fort Knox, Kentucky. Paper money is produced by the Bureau of Engraving and Printing in Washington, D.C., another division of the Treasury Department.

See Also: Gold Standard; Money and Currency.

■ **MINTON, SHERMAN (1890-1965),** associate justice of the U.S. Supreme Court (1949-56). Born in Georgetown, Indiana, he was a Democratic U.S. senator from Indiana (1935-41) and loyal supporter of Pres. Franklin D. Roosevelt's New Deal. Minton was named to the Seventh Circuit U.S. Court of Appeals (1941) by Pres. Harry S. Truman, a former Senate colleague. Minton believed the courts should generally defer to executive and legislative decisions.

See Also: Supreme Court.

■ **MINUIT, PETER (1580-1638),** director general of New Netherland (1626-31) and governor of New Sweden (1638). A native of Prussia, Minuit arrived in New Netherland (1625) and served as intermediary with the Indians, from whom he purchased Manhattan Island in 1626. That year he was appointed the first director general of the colony by the Council of New Netherland. Under his administration, New Amsterdam became the center of political and military might in the colony. In 1631, however, the Amsterdam Council recalled Minuit. By 1637, a disgruntled Minuit was working for a Swedish trading company. Installed as their new governor, Minuit led the Swedish colonists to an area along the east bank of the Delaware River and negotiated its purchase from the local Indians. Soon after the completion of a small fortification, Minuit left with a cargo of trade goods for the Caribbean and was lost in a hurricane.

See Also: Dutch Colonies.

■ **MINUTEMEN,** members of militia regiments during the American Revolution who were prepared to fight the British at a minute's notice. As tensions mounted after Parliament passed the Intolerable Acts (1774), Massachusetts' colonial leaders moved to establish an organized military. In October 1774 the First Massachusetts Provincial Congress required all towns to organize militias and minutemen regi-

ments. Minutemen proved decisive on Apr. 19, 1775, when British troops marched toward Concord to seize military stores. Minutemen responded first at Lexington and later at Concord to thwart the Redcoat advance. This initial military confrontation of the Revolution resulted in a British retreat back to Boston. Following the victory, minutemen regiments were absorbed into the Continental army. The Continental Congress, however, encouraged other colonies to follow the Massachusetts model, and minutemen participated throughout the Revolution in regions that were not protected by the regular army.

See Also: Lexington and Concord; Revolution, American.

BIBLIOGRAPHY: Gross, Robert A., *The Minutemen and Their World* (Hill & Wang 1976).

■ *MIRANDA V. ARIZONA* **(1966),** U.S. Supreme Court decision that determined that the Fifth Amendment provision against self-incrimination extended to an individual in police custody. The *Miranda* case signaled a high point in the Court's defense of individual civil rights. Conservative detractors criticized the decision as undermining the powers of law enforcement.

Ernesto Miranda, a poorly educated and indigent 23-year-old, was found guilty of rape and kidnapping. The prosecution had based its case on Miranda's confession, signed after two hours of police interrogation. At no point, however, had the officers advised Miranda of his right to consult with an attorney or to remain silent.

In light of the facts of the case, the Court's review of police interrogation procedures, many of which were codified in law enforcement manuals, formed the basis for the decision. The Court found that the fact of "custodial interrogation" encourages intimidation and violates individual rights.

In order to protect individual rights the Court ruled that four "Miranda warnings" must be given to suspects before being questioned. Suspects must be informed of their right to remain silent, that anything they say can be used against them in court, that they have the right to have a lawyer present, and that if they cannot afford a lawyer one can be provided. Statements taken without compliance with these warnings are not admissible in court.

See Also: Bill of Rights; Civil Rights Movement; Supreme Court.

BIBLIOGRAPHY: Baker, Live, *Miranda: Crime, Law, and Politics* (Antheum 1983).

■ **MISCEGENATION,** a term introduced as a neologism in a racist political tract of 1866, refers to the sexual intermixing of what are presumed to be separate races of people. In North America sexual relations began shortly after the first contact between Indians and Europeans. It continued when the first Africans arrived in Virginia in 1619. The term "miscegenation" is most often used to refer to sexual relations between African Americans and whites. Sex across the color line violated the norm of accepted social interactions, but that did not prevent widespread intermixing between all the races on the continent. Most significant were sexual relations between white slave owners and African-American slave women, who, of course, had little choice about the matter. Estimates are that at the time of the Civil War some 12 percent of all southerners were mulattos, that is, of mixed European and African origin. After the Civil War jurisdictions in the South and elsewhere enacted legal proscriptions against sexual mixing and marriage between whites and nonwhites. They lasted for a century. Not until *Loving* v. *Virginia* (1967) did the Supreme Court rule that such laws against interracial marriage were unconstitutional.

See Also: Loving v. Virginia; Reconstruction.

■ **MISSIONARY RIDGE, BATTLE OF (1863),** Civil War engagement during the Chattanooga campaign (August-November 1863). Chattanooga, Tennessee, a key communications center for the Confederacy, had long been an objective of Union Gen. Ulysses S. Grant. Missionary Ridge, which lies to the east of the city, was the last Confederate stronghold in the area after Gen. Joseph Hooker's forces drove the Confederates from Lookout Mountain on November 24. The fighting for Missionary Ridge commenced when Gen. William T. Sherman's troops attacked the defenders from the north after a mid-morning artillery barrage. The Southern force, under Braxton Bragg, repulsed Sherman's troops several times. In mid-afternoon Grant ordered Gen. George Thomas to attack the ridge from the west. Displaying both audacity and great courage, Union forces led by Thomas's subordinates Thomas J. Wood and Philip Sheridan had by day's end pushed the Confederates off the ridge and into a disorganized retreat. Casualties were heavy on both sides. After the battle Grant was promoted to lieutenant general, and Bragg was relieved of command at his own request.

See Also: Civil War; Grant, Ulysses Simpson; Sherman, William Tecumseh.

■ **MISSIONS AND MISSIONARIES,** the propagation of religious faith and the people who carry it out. One way or another the American people have been involved with missionary work since the 17th century.

The Promise of the New World. Even before the first permanent English settlers arrived in North America in 1607, propagandists in England had spoken of the New World as a mission opportunity. Whatever the motives underlying missionary activity on behalf of the Indians, missionary zeal did stimulate English colonization. It also led certain individuals already in the colonies to pursue the promise: John Eliot in Massachusetts, with his famous Indian Bible (1663); John Campanius of Delaware, with his lesser-known Lutheran catechism; and David Brainerd of New York and New Jersey, whose short life was made famous by Jonathan Edwards's *Life of the Late Reverend Mr. David Brainerd* (1749). Despite successes here and there, perhaps most notably on Martha's Vineyard and among the Moravians, Protestant missionary labors in colonial America did not meet with conspicuous success.

Roman Catholics left a more permanent mark on the territory that ultimately became the United States. Missionaries dispatched by the influential orders of Dominicans (Bartolomé de Las Casas), Jesuits (Eusebio Kino), and Franciscans (Junipero Serra) left an impressive heritage. While Las Casas never ventured north of the Rio Grande, his reputation as "defender of the Indians" did. That defense, along with the papal *Sublimus Deus* of 1537, mitigated the worst horrors inflicted on indigenous populations.

In the 18th century a growing African-American population presented another missionary challenge. Notwithstanding the brutalities of slavery,

African Americans turned in overwhelming numbers to the religion of their captors. In the biblical stories of slavery in Egypt and the Exodus, blacks found both legitimacy and hope. When African Americans assumed leadership of their own churches, both before and after emancipation, membership grew at a greatly accelerated pace.

In the new nation of the 19th century, missionaries turned their attention to the demands that a rapidly expanding population and a rapidly moving frontier presented. As early as 1802 Presbyterians and Congregationalists banded together in a Plan of Union that pooled resources to meet the sudden demographic and geographic demands. Baptists and Methodists sent missionaries out West but even more effectively became missionaries on the frontier themselves. Denominations created on the frontier, such as the Disciples of Christ, likewise strengthened the effort to keep the West solidly Christian. This whole effort, often called "home missions," also resulted in the founding of an enormous number of religious colleges in the Midwest and Far West. At the same time, voluntary agencies such as the American Bible Society and the American Tract Society made publishing the strong arm of missions.

American Missions Abroad. Amazingly, American Protestant missionaries simultaneously spread out around the world. They sailed around Cape Horn to the Sandwich, or Hawaiian, Islands, to the Philippines, Japan, China, Burma, and India; and across the Atlantic to Africa, Palestine, and Turkey. This was "the great century" of Protestant missions.

Roman Catholic missions at this time developed more slowly because the Vatican regarded the United States itself as a mission field until 1908. Moreover the Catholic Church in 19th-century America had the burden of trying to meet the needs of millions of immigrants arriving in the crowded seaport cities of the East. In 1911 the Catholic Foreign Missionary Society of America was formed in Maryknoll, New York. From that ever more active and imaginative center, missionaries moved out, proving themselves to be especially effective in Central and South America.

By the mid-20th century mainline Protestant denominations pulled back from their earlier evangelism to give more attention to relief agencies like Church World Service, Lutheran World Relief, and Meals for Millions. More conservative evangelical denominations such as the Holiness and Pentecostal churches moved into the vacuum left by the departing "mainliners." Meanwhile, the Maryknoll fathers and sisters continued their ministries in Latin America, occasionally falling victim to periodic revolutionary and counterrevolutionary violence.

—EDWIN S. GAUSTAD

See Also: Baptist Church; Methodist Church; Mormons; Religion; Roman Catholics; Serra, Junipero.

BIBLIOGRAPHY: Bowden, Henry W., *American Indians and Christian Missions: Studies in Cultural Conflict* (Univ. of Chicago Press 1981); Carpenter, Joel A., and Wilbert R. Shenk, eds., *Earthen Vessels: American Evangelicals and Foreign Missions, 1880-1980* (Eerdmans 1990); Hocking, William E., et al., *Re-Thinking Missions: A Laymen's Inquiry After One Hundred Years* (Harper & Brothers 1932); Hutchison, William R., *Errand to the World: American Protestant Thought and Foreign Missions* (Univ. of Chicago Press 1987); Latourette, Kenneth Scott, *A History of the Expansion of Christianity*, esp. Vol. 4 (Harper 1937-1945); Nevins, Albert J., *The Meaning of Maryknoll* (McMullen 1954).

■ **MISSISSIPPI,** southeastern state. With Alabama, it forms the heartland of the Deep South. Mississippi is bounded on the north by Tennessee, on the west by Arkansas, on the west and south by Louisiana, on the south by the Gulf of Mexico, and on the east by Alabama. The Mississippi River forms most of its western border. The entire state is lowland plain, although hilly in parts.

Ruled by France and Spain before becoming part of the United States, Mississippi became a state in 1817. Its economy, based on plantation cotton growing, was destroyed in the Civil War. The state has struggled since to develop its industries, with considerable success since World War II. However, Mississippi still has the lowest per capita personal income of any state. The legacy of slavery remained strong, and the state resisted desegregation, sometimes violently. It has the highest proportion of African Americans (36 percent) of any state.

Capital: Jackson. Area: 47,695 square miles. Population (1995 est.): 2,697,000.

See Also: *De Soto, Hernando; Faulkner, William Cuthbert; Mississippi River; Prohibition; Vicksburg, Siege of.*

■ **MISSISSIPPIAN CULTURE (c. 900-1550),** precontact North American culture so-named because its influence was greatest along the Mississippi River and its tributaries. The Mississippians were maize farmers and mound builders who lived in permanent villages that, in some places, grew into large urban areas. The most important Mississippian city was Cahokia, on the east side of the river across from present-day St. Louis. By the mid-13th century Cahokia was a vast urban cluster of some 30,000 people stretching 6 miles along the river. Other regional centers were located at present-day Spiro, Oklahoma; Moundville, Alabama; Hiwassee Island on the Tennessee River; and along the Etowah and Ocmulgee rivers in Georgia. All these centers were linked by a vast, waterborne transportation system. Mississippian culture had a social division of labor that included craftsmen, priests, and an elite class of rulers. The culture began to decline in the late 14th century, in part because of a long-term drought. In 1540, when Hernando de Soto marched through the Southeast, most of the major urban sites had been abandoned. The Spanish army left behind epidemic diseases, leading to the further decline of Mississippian culture and the rise of smaller village-based groups such as the Caddos, Chickasaws, Choctaws, and Creeks.

See Also: *Cahokia; De Soto, Hernando; Indians of North America; Mississippi River.*

■ **MISSISSIPPI BUBBLE (1720),** name given to an investment scheme devised by John Law, a Scottish speculator, to promote French colonization in Louisiana. To finance the effort, Law established a bank, the Compagnie D'Occident, which secured a royal monopoly on Mississippi River trade. Using the monopoly and money invested by French stockholders, Law set out to attract settlers to the region, but overleveraged paper notes ruined the bank, although settlers came to the area.

■ **MISSISSIPPI RIVER,** longest north-south river in North America. The Mississippi River rises above Minneapolis and St. Paul in Lake Itasca and runs south for some 2,350 miles past St. Louis, Memphis, Natchez, and New Orleans, where it empties into the Gulf of Mexico. With its 250 tributaries, the vast Mississippi drainage system touches 31 states and two Canadian provinces. Hernando de Soto's expedition for Spain in 1541 is credited with being the first group of Europeans to sight the river. In 1673 the French explorers Louis Jolliet and Father Jacques Marquette traveled south on the Mississippi as far as the Arkansas River. Then, in 1681, Father Louis Hennepin explored the northern Mississippi and traveled south to the Gulf of Mexico. The French soon established settlements on the Mississippi in order to profit from the western fur trade. But the encounter with Europeans proved disastrous for the Indian tribes of the river valley, who were severely reduced in number by smallpox and cholera. During the 18th century English fur traders and later farmers pushed over the Appalachian Mountains and into the Mississippi Valley. The United States acquired the Mississippi in 1803, when France exchanged the vast Louisiana Purchase for $15 million. With fertile land, easy transportation, and cheap slave labor, large plantations thrived along the river's banks from New Orleans to Memphis until the Civil War (1861-65). In the 19th century American farmers living in the Ohio River Valley used the Mississippi as the main transportation route for their products.

■ **MISSOURI,** state strategically located in the nation's heartland. The site of the U.S. center of population, it is bounded on the north by Iowa, on the west by Nebraska, Kansas, and Oklahoma, on the west and south by Arkansas, and on the east by Illinois, Kentucky, and Tennessee. The Missouri River enters the state at Kansas City and empties into the Mississippi River, which forms the state's eastern border, near St. Louis. The Ozark Plateau occupies most of southern Missouri.

Missouri was ruled by France and Spain before passing to the United States in the Louisiana Purchase (1803). St. Louis was the gateway to the West in the early 19th century. It became a state in 1820. A slaveholding border state, Missouri remained loyal to the Union but was a battleground during the Civil War. It became a heavily industrialized state in the 20th century.

Capital: Jefferson City. Area: 69,709 square miles. Population (1995 est.): 5,324,000.

See Also: James, Jesse (Woodson); Kansas City; Louisiana Purchase; Missouri Compromise; St. Louis; Truman, Harry S.

■ **MISSOURI COMPROMISE (1820-21),** a set of congressional measures that temporarily settled the sectional crisis triggered by Missouri's application for admission to the Union as a slave state. Although the Northwest Ordinance of 1787 had barred slavery from the area north of the Ohio River, no policy applied to the vast lands west of the Mississippi. In February 1819, New York's Rep. James Tallmadge introduced an amendment to the Missouri Statehood bill that would have barred entry to new slaves and emancipated at adulthood those already there. Tallmadge's amendment launched an intense debate over the future of slavery in the territories and forced Americans to take stock of the growing extent and power of the institution.

Congress remained deadlocked over the amendment for a year, with the House of Representatives in favor and the Senate opposed. In January 1820 Southerners linked statehood for Maine to Missouri's admission with slavery, a move that outraged Northerners, but pointed to a compromise, proposed by Indiana's Sen. Jesse Thomas, by which Maine would be admitted together with Missouri, with slavery to be barred from the Louisiana Territory north of 36° 30' N (the southern border of Missouri). While few found the plan satisfactory, fears of sectional strife resulted in its narrow passage (Mar. 3, 1820).

Many Northerners continued to oppose Missouri's statehood, however, and the territory's draft constitution (July 1820), which barred free African Americans from the state, gave them the grounds they needed to reopen the controversy. After another long stalemate, the House adopted (Feb. 26, 1821) Henry Clay's ambiguous language declaring that the antiblack clause in Missouri's constitution should never be construed as violating the constitutional rights of any citizen—a precedent that, in practice, weakened the citizenship rights of free African Americans. A week later the House voted to admit Missouri to statehood.

Although contemporaries regarded the Missouri Compromise as a Southern victory, it in fact restricted the expansion of slave states and seemed to ensure an early Free State majority in the Senate. The repeal of the Compromise by the Kansas-Nebraska Act in 1854 galvanized antislavery sentiment, and spurred the formation of the Republican party.

—ROBERT P. FORBES

See Also: Clay, Henry; Kansas-Nebraska Act.

BIBLIOGRAPHY: Brown, Richard H., "The Missouri Crisis, Slavery, and the Politics of Jacksonianism," *South Atlantic Quarterly* (Winter 1966); Dangerfield, George, *The Era of Good Feelings* (Harcourt, Brace 1952); Moore, Glover, *The Missouri Controversy, 1819-1821* (Univ. of Kentucky Press 1953).

■ **MISSOURI RIVER,** longest river in the United States (2,714 miles) and principal tributary of the Mississippi River. With headwaters in the Rocky Mountains of southwestern Montana, the Missouri flows southeast across the Great Plains states of North Dakota, South Dakota, Nebraska, Kansas, and Iowa. Seventeen miles upstream from St. Louis it converges with the Mississippi River. The river drains nearly 600,000 square miles of land and is nicknamed the "Big Muddy" for the heavy load of soil carried in its stream. Numerous Plains Indian tribes, including the Missouri, Osage, Kaw, Omaha, Crow, and Blackfeet, lived around the Missouri. During the 18th century the Sioux moved into the middle Missouri basin. After the acquisition of Upper Louisiana by the United States, the Lewis and Clark expedition followed the river west in 1804. Subsequently fur trappers and traders came into the territory for beavers and otters. During the 20th century six large dams have been completed on the Missouri in order to control the river's floods and provide hydroelectric power for municipalities.

■ **MITCHELL, MARGARET (1900-49),** author. She was born in Atlanta, Georgia. She wrote feature stories for the *Atlanta Journal Sunday Magazine* from 1922 to 1926 but is remembered for her one novel, *Gone with the Wind* (1936). An exhaustively detailed and deeply nostalgic historical romance about a Southern family during the Civil War, it won the 1937 Pulitzer Prize and became one of the best-selling novels of all time. A film version, starring Vivian Leigh and Clark Gable, appeared in 1939.

See Also: Novel; Women in American History.

■ **MITCHELL, MARIA (1818-89),** astronomer. She was born in Nantucket, Massachusetts. A librarian, she spent her free hours reading about stellar navigation and assisting her father, William Mitchell, in his astronomical observations for the United States Coastal Survey. On Oct. 1, 1847, she discovered a comet and became a national celebrity. In 1848 she became the first woman elected to the American Academy of Arts and Sciences, and in 1865 she became a professor at the newly founded Vassar College, where she uncovered much about the nature of sunspots.

■ **MITCHELL, WILLIAM (BILLY) (1879-1936),** American army officer and advocate of air power. Born in Nice, France, to American parents, he began a long military career by joining the U.S. Army in 1898. After serving in Cuba, the Philippines, and Mexico, Mitchell learned to fly in 1915. A talented and highly decorated World War I combat pilot over France, he rose rapidly in rank to brigadier general in 1918. After the war, he became a champion for air-power theory, arguing that the airplane would make land warfare obsolete. He also argued that the navy had become an anachronism in the age of air power, a claim he demonstrated in 1921 by sinking several captured German battleships from the air. The refusal of the Navy and War Departments to endorse his views led him to denounce the conduct of both in 1925, for which he was court-martialed. Mitchell had hoped to use the trial as a public forum and vindication of his views, but he was instead forced to contradict himself by an aggressive prosecution. Convicted of insubordination, he resigned in February 1926.

See Also: Air Force.
BIBLIOGRAPHY: Hurley, Alfred F., *Billy Mitchell: Crusader for Air Power* (Watts 1964).

■ **MIXED-BLOODS AND MESTIZOS,** people of mixed-Indian and European or African ancestry. Such people have played major roles in American history, but their contributions often have been ignored. Negatively portrayed as "half-breeds," caught between two cultures and alienated from

both, they traditionally have been depicted as misfits with little influence in either Indian or non-Indian communities.

In contrast, historians now argue that mixed-bloods often played pivotal roles in defining the relationship between Indian communities and European or American societies. In the Great Lakes region, merchants of mixed Indian-French ancestry rose to positions of prominence, serving as middlemen in the exchange of furs and trade goods between Indian and European communities. Many mixed-blood merchants retained their prominence well into the 19th century, dominating the Indian trade and leading many of the Great Lakes tribes through the removal period.

Mixed-blood populations also emerged in the South. In the late 18th and early 19th centuries,

Brig. Gen. Billy Mitchell, a highly decorated veteran of World War I, advocated greater military use of air power in the 1920s.

Seminole tribespeople in Florida provided refuge and sometimes intermarried with African Americans fleeing slavery. Meanwhile, among the Cherokee, Creek, and Choctaw, tribal leaders of Indian and Irish or Scots-Irish lineage emerged who championed the adoption of American cultural patterns, including plantation agriculture, chattel slavery, and Protestant Christianity. They also established formal tribal governments modeled after the United States. Many unsuccessfully attempted to retain tribal lands in the Southeast, but after these tribes were removed to Indian Territory, the mixed-bloods reemerged and again dominated tribal politics until Oklahoma was admitted to statehood (1907).

In the Southwest, mestizo people of Indian-Spanish descent emerged behind the Spanish frontier, where they formed the majority of the population and functioned within the Spanish or Mexican political and socioeconomic systems. Although they were subjected to considerable discrimination, particularly after these lands became part of the United States, their influence markedly shaped the culture in this region. In the late 20th century their population and their cultural and political influence in this region have increased.

—R. DAVID EDMUNDS

See Also: *Ethnic Groups; Frontier in American History.*
BIBLIOGRAPHY: Szasz, Margaret, ed., *Between Indian and White Worlds: The Cultural Broker* (Univ. of Oklahoma Press 1994); Weber, David J., *The Spanish Frontier in North America* (Yale Univ. Press 1992).

▓ **MOBILE BAY, BATTLE OF (1864),** Civil War engagement that formed part of a combined Union naval and land effort to reduce the Confederate port of Mobile, Alabama. On August 5, Adm. David G. Farragut led 4 monitors and 12 wooden ships into Mobile harbor, where they defeated a Confederate flotilla that included the C.S.S. *Tennessee.* Faced with the danger of mines (known as "torpedoes"), Farragut was reported to have said: "Damn the torpedoes, full speed ahead." Mobile itself would hold out until war's end.

See Also: *Civil War; Farragut, David G.*

▓ **MODERNISM,** literary and artistic movement of the early 20th century. Modernism is characterized not so much by a specific form or style as by the belief that cultural works should express the vitality of the present day. Modernist writers and artists saw themselves not as the preservers of a past cultural heritage but rather those who forged new and forward-looking styles. In literature modernism often implied experimental use of language, a spareness in form, and a break from traditional narratives. Poetry by Ezra Pound, E. E. Cummings, Hart Crane, Wallace Stevens, and William Carlos Williams and fiction by Ernest Hemingway, F. Scott Fitzgerald, William Faulkner, and John Dos Passos exemplify modernist literature. In the fine arts the introduction of modernism to the United States is often traced to the Armory Show, an exhibition of American and European art held in New York in 1913. One prominent circle of American modernist artists centered on the photographer and gallery owner Alfred Stieglitz, who championed the work of painters such as Georgia O'Keeffe, Marsden Hartley, and John Marin. In architecture modernism was carried to the United States by Europeans such as Walter Gropius and Ludwig Mies van der Rohe, the first and last directors, respectively, of the German Bauhaus School. Philip Johnson and Henry-Russell Hitchcock helped to define architectural modernism in their 1932 book, *The International Style.* Architects Louis Kahn, I. M. Pei, and Eero Saarinen took up the modernist mantle.

—MARINA MOSKOWITZ

See Also: *Architecture; Armory Show; Novel; Poetry.*
BIBLIOGRAPHY: Hoffman, Michael J., and Patrick D. Murphy, eds., *Critical Essays on American Modernism* (Maxwell Macmillan 1992); Milroy, Elizabeth, *Painters of a New Century: The Eight and American Art* (Milwaukee Art Museum 1991).

▓ **MODJESKA (MODRZEJEWSKA), HELENA (1840-1909),** Polish-born stage actress. She appeared in 284 roles at the Imperial Theater in Warsaw before immigrating to California in 1876. Modjeska earned much attention in New York for her portrayal of the title role in *Camille* in 1877 and toured the United States and Europe to wide acclaim for two decades.

▓ **MODOC INDIANS.** *See: California Indians.*

▓ **MOHEGAN INDIANS.** *See: Algonquian.*

■ **MOJAVE INDIANS.** *See: Desert Indians of the Southwest.*

■ **MOLASSES ACT (1733),** British legislation, one of the Navigation Acts meant to encourage trade with the British West Indies, limit trade with the French West Indies, and stifle the competition between French and English planters for New England provisions. Aware the law could devastate the New England economy, New Englanders virtually ignored it.

See Also: Navigation Acts.

■ **MOLEY, RAYMOND (1886-1975),** American educator, journalist, and adviser to Pres. Franklin D. Roosevelt. Born in Berea, Ohio, he became a professor of government (1923-28) and public law (1928-54) at Columbia University in New York City. Moley was the original leader of the "brain trust," an informal collection of academics who helped shape many of Roosevelt's New Deal policies. Named assistant secretary of state in 1933, Moley helped write several economic policy laws, including the National Industrial Recovery Act (1933). Sympathetic to the needs of business, he advocated a cooperative planning process involving both private industry and government. He became disenchanted with what he saw as the growing antibusiness tilt of the Roosevelt administration and broke with the president in 1936. Moley founded and edited *Today* magazine (1933-37) and was a contributing editor and regular columnist for *Newsweek* (1937-68).

See Also: New Deal.

BIBLIOGRAPHY: Moley, Raymond, *The First New Deal* (Harcourt, Brace & World 1966).

■ **MOLINO DEL REY, BATTLE OF (1847),** a battle in Mexico City during the Mexican War. The bloodiest single encounter of the war, it took place on September 8, after an armistice expired during which Mexican Pres. Antonio López de Santa Anna shored up his defenses in Mexico City. U.S. Gen. Winfield Scott's forces overwhelmed the Mexican positions at Molino Del Rey, but not before 700 Americans and some 2,000 Mexicans died. The American victory led to the final battle of the war at Chapultepec.

See Also: Mexican War; Scott, Winfield.

■ **MOLLY MAGUIRES,** a secret society established in the United States by Irish immigrants working in the Pennsylvania coal mines during the 1860s and 1870s. It was modeled after an Irish society that used violence to protest the abuses of tyrannical landlords during the potato famine of the

A secret organization of coal miners in northeastern Pennsylvania during the 1860s and 1870s, the Molly Maguires initiated a violent campaign to resist the conditions in which they lived and worked.

1840s. The Irish coal miners in Pennsylvania also faced oppressive conditions, exploited at work by mine owners who also owned the miners' housing and controlled local government, including the police. In 1875 the miners went out on strike, and Molly Maguires increased their violent attacks on the mine owners and their superintendents. In retaliation, Franklin B. Gowen, owner of the Philadelphia and Reading Coal and Iron Company, hired a Pinkerton Detective Agency operative by the name of James McParlan, who joined the Molly Maguires as a spy and later presented evidence in court that resulted in the murder conviction and eventual execution of 20 of the organization's members. At the time few questioned the appropriateness of the trials, at which the mine owner, Gowen, served as one of the prosecutors. Thereafter, the Molly Maguires effectively ceased to exist but came to represent for many the apparent futility of fighting the oppression of industrial capital.

—KATHLEEN BANKS NUTTER

See Also: Labor Movement.

BIBLIOGRAPHY: Coleman, James W., *The Molly Maguire Riots* (Arno Press 1969); Lewis, Arthur H., *Lament for the Molly Maguires* (Harcourt Brace 1964).

■ **MOMADAY, N. SCOTT (1934-),** author. Born in Lawton, Oklahoma, and raised on reservations in the Southwest, Momaday is a member of the Kiowa tribe. He attended the University of New Mexico and Stanford University. Momaday's first novel, *House Made of Dawn* (1968), won the Pulitzer Prize for its portrayal of an Indian youth trying to mediate between his own heritage and the larger cultural world. Momaday next published *The Way to Rainy Mountain* (1969), which incorporated his own memories of childhood and Kiowa tales. In addition to these novels, Momaday has written collections of poetry, including *Angle of Geese* (1973) and *The Gourd Dancer* (1976). *The Names* (1976) returned to a prose form and makes use of stories about Momaday's ancestors. In *The Ancient Child* (1989) he again explores a central character's experience coming to terms with an Indian heritage. Momaday has taught literature at the University of California, Stanford University, and the University of Arizona.

See Also: Novel.

■ **MONDALE, WALTER (1928-),** U.S. vice president (1977-81). Born in Ceylon, Minnesota, he practiced law and was elected attorney general of Minnesota in 1960. He was appointed to the U.S. Senate in 1964 when his fellow Democrat Hubert Humphrey was elected vice president and was elected in his own right in 1966 and 1972. A leading Senate liberal, he was elected vice president with Gov. Jimmy Carter of Georgia in 1976. They were defeated in a bid for a second term in 1980. Mondale captured the Democratic presidential nomination in 1984 and selected New York congresswoman Geraldine Ferraro as his running mate. Facing Pres. Ronald Reagan, a well-liked conservative incumbent, and a reviving economy, they won only 41 percent of the popular vote, the lowest Democratic percentage since 1928, and carried only Mondale's home state and the District of Columbia. Mondale later served as U.S. ambassador to Japan (1993-96).

See Also: Ferraro, Geraldine.

BIBLIOGRAPHY: Gillon, Steven M., *The Democrats' Dilemma: Walter F. Mondale and the Liberal Legacy* (Columbia Univ. Press 1992).

■ **MONEY AND CURRENCY,** generally accepted mediums of exchange. Throughout the colonial period, various forms of money were used, including wampum, tobacco, English specie, and Spanish coins. During the American Revolution, the Continental Congress attempted to bring order to the monetary system and to raise revenue by issuing bills of credit, which depreciated rapidly. In 1791, Congress established a bimetallic standard of gold and silver, but the valuation of currency remained in flux. Two national Banks of the United States (1791-1811 and 1816-36) helped to stabilize the money supply by issuing U.S. notes and coins and devaluing state currencies. By the 1830s, silver ceased to circulate because it was devalued at the mint, making the system monometallic.

To finance the Civil War, Congress issued $450 million in paper money, popularly known as greenbacks. The National Bank Act of 1863 both reconfirmed national paper money as the standard currency and chartered national banks. In the closing decades of the 19th century, a political debate raged between supporters of the free coinage of silver and adherents to a gold standard. The issue was settled in 1900 by the Gold Standard Act, which established an official monometallic gold standard.

In 1933, during the Hundred Days of the New Deal, Pres. Franklin D. Roosevelt effectively took the United States off the gold standard. The government ceased producing silver dollars for circulation in 1965 and three years later eliminated the gold reserves against federal deposits. Thereafter, U.S. currency was fiat money—money backed only by the credit of the government.

See Also: Banks of the United States, First and Second; Free Silver; Treasury, Department of.

BIBLIOGRAPHY: Friedman, Milton, and Anna Jacobsen Schwartz, *A Monetary History of the United States, 1867-1960* (Princeton Univ. Press 1963); Studenski, Paul, and Herman E. Kross, *Financial History of the United States* (McGraw-Hill 1963).

■ ***MONITOR* AND *MERRIMACK*,** the most famous ironclad warships of the Civil War. The Confederate *Merrimack* (renamed the C.S.S. *Virginia*) was a huge reconditioned frigate; the Union *Monitor* a smaller, more maneuverable vessel. The two ships met off Norfolk, Virginia, on Mar. 9, 1862, in a duel that left both battered. Following this stalemate, the *Merrimack* steamed back to Norfolk, where it was blown up by its crew on May 9, after Union forces seized the city.

See Also: Civil War; Navy.

■ **MONK, THELONIOUS SPHERE (1917-82),** jazz pianist and composer, born in Rocky Mount, North Carolina. Along with Dizzy Gillespie and Charlie Parker, Monk created the be-bop movement in jazz during the 1940s and 1950s. Usually directing his own small groups, Monk composed in an astringent, dissonant style. His most famous compositions, such as "'Round Midnight," were marked by harmonic and rhythmic subtlety and have become standards of the art form.

See Also: African Americans; Jazz.

■ **MONMOUTH, BATTLE OF (1778),** battle in the American Revolution. Fought near the town of Freehold in Monmouth County, New Jersey, it was the first confrontation for American troops after their winter at Valley Forge and was the last major battle of the Revolution in the North. British troops led by Henry Clinton and American forces commanded by Charles Lee fought to a tactical draw, but their skill and effectiveness imbued the American troops with confidence.

See Also: Revolution, American.

■ **MONOPOLY,** exclusive control over the production or supply of some commodity. European governments granted monopolies to encourage economic ventures in the New World, and some colonial governments issued them to encourage

On Mar. 9, 1862, the Confederate ship *Virginia,* formerly the U.S.S. *Merrimack,* and the U.S.S. *Monitor* engaged in the first naval battle between ironclads. It lasted less than five hours and ended in a draw.

local enterprises such as the production of salt. Postal service has been a federal monopoly since colonial times, and states still grant monopolies for transport or communication facilities in which competition would be inefficient.

In the late 19th century business leaders sought monopolies through pools, trusts, and holding companies in order to maximize their profits. Andrew Carnegie and J. P. Morgan bought out competitors, for instance, until their companies controlled the steel and railroad industries respectively. Companies including U.S. Steel, Standard Oil, and American Tobacco became powerful enough to convince reformers and the government that monopolies could be dangerous. The Sherman Antitrust Act (1890) forbade contracts, combinations, or conspiracies in restraint of trade or in the effort to establish monopolies in interstate or foreign commerce. Progressive muckrakers exposed the power of monopolistic corporations to corrupt if not control government in newspapers and books such as *Wealth Against Commonwealth* (1894). The Supreme Court ordered the dissolution of the Northern Securities Company (1904), the American Tobacco Company (1911), and the Standard Oil Company (1911), and it has continued to regulate monopolistic consolidation.

See Also: Antitrust Cases; Holding Companies; Industrial Revolution; Morgan, J. P. (John Pierpont).
BIBLIOGRAPHY: Himmelberg, Robert F., ed., *The Monopoly Issue and Antitrust, 1900-1917* (Garland 1994).

■ **MONROE, JAMES (1758-1831),** fifth president of the United States (1817-25). He was born in Westmoreland County, Virginia. In 1776 he left William and Mary College to fight in the American Revolution, later studying law under Thomas Jefferson. Elected to the Virginia legislature in 1782, he served in the Continental Congress (1783-86) and the U.S. Senate (1790-94), actively opposing the administration of Pres. George Washington. In 1794 Washington sent Monroe as minister to revolutionary France but recalled him two years later. From 1799 to 1802 Monroe was governor of Virginia. In 1803, as envoy to France, he helped to negotiate the purchase of Louisiana; diplomatic assignments in London and Madrid were less successful. On his return to the United States, Monroe flirted with challenging James Madison for the presidency, but Jefferson effected a reconciliation between the two men, and in 1811 Monroe accepted the position of secretary of state in Madison's cabinet. Monroe's effective and courageous service during the War of 1812 made him a logical choice for the presidency, which he won decisively in 1816.

While the least brilliant president of the "Virginia dynasty," Monroe was the most cosmopolitan. His efforts to heal the breach between Republicans and Federalists caused his administration to be known as the "Era of Good Feelings." Monroe's talented cabinet included John C. Calhoun and John Quincy Adams, who, as secretary of state, acquired Florida from Spain, extended the nation's border to the Pacific, and drafted the Monroe Doctrine (1823), which barred European intervention in the New World.

Domestically, Monroe's achievements were more mixed. His ambitious nationalist goals were hamstrung by economic downturn and sectional

James Monroe served as James Madison's secretary of state (1811-17) and then succeeded his fellow Virginian as president (1817-25). His administration was known as the Era of Good Feelings.

dissension. His quiet influence helped pass the Missouri Compromise (1820), which restricted the spread of slavery beyond the Mississippi, but he failed in his efforts to achieve an anti-slave-trade treaty with Britain. Although, in 1819, he vetoed the Cumberland Road bill, which sought federal funds for the first road so financed, he came to support federal internal improvements. Reelected with only one dissenting electoral vote, Monroe enjoyed broad but shallow support, and his second term was plagued by factional strife among his would-be successors. He died in New York City on July 4, 1831.

—ROBERT P. FORBES

See Also: President of the United States.

BIBLIOGRAPHY: Ammon, Harry, *James Monroe: The Quest for National Identity* (McGraw-Hill 1971); Cunningham, Noble E., Jr., *The Presidency of James Monroe* (Univ. Press of Kansas 1996); Dangerfield, George, *The Era of Good Feelings* (Harcourt, Brace 1952); Monroe, James, *Autobiography*, ed. by Stuart Jerry Brown (Syracuse Univ. Press 1959).

Marilyn Monroe became a sexual icon after starring in such films as *Gentlemen Prefer Blondes* (1953).

■ **MONROE, MARILYN (1926-62),** movie actress. She was born Norma Jean Baker in Los Angeles, California. Her voluptuous good looks and breathless screen personality propelled her to the status of national sex symbol in movies such as *Niagara* (1952), *The Seven Year Itch* (1955), *Bus Stop* (1956), *Some Like It Hot* (1959), and *The Misfits* (1960). Her suicide at age 36 only increased Americans' fascination with her. Among her three husbands were baseball great Joe DiMaggio and playwright Arthur Miller.

See Also: DiMaggio, Joe; Miller, Arthur; Women in American History.

■ **MONROE DOCTRINE (1823),** a declaration of U.S. foreign policy, which stated that European intervention in the Americas would not be tolerated and that the United States would not interfere with European affairs in Europe. The collapse of the Spanish empire in Latin America during the second decade of the 19th century was followed by an internal crisis in Spain. In 1820 a rebellion forced Ferdinand VII to approve a liberal constitution. Two years later, over British objections, the European powers decided to intervene. France appointed itself executive power of the European order, invaded Spain in April, entered Madrid in May, crushed the republican forces, and restored Ferdinand to his absolute powers.

Rumors spread that France intended to help Ferdinand regain his overseas empire. Britain's foreign secretary, George Canning, approached the United States and proposed a joint Anglo-American declaration recognizing de facto the separation between Spain and its colonies and opposing international intervention. Pres. James Monroe turned to his presidential predecessors, Thomas Jefferson and James Madison, for advice. Both urged accepting Canning's initiative. Sec. of State John Quincy Adams, however, doubted that France would send troops across the Atlantic and persuaded President Monroe to use his 1823 annual address to Congress to make a unilateral policy statement outlining the principles of American foreign policy.

"The American continents," Adams had written, "are henceforth not to be considered as subjects for future colonization by any European powers." The noncolonization principle addressed the conflict with Russia and Britain over the Pacific coast. Russia had claimed the northwest from Alaska to San Francisco and in 1821 sealed the coast to all non-Russian vessels. The Russian decree excluded the United States from territory obtained from Spain in the Adams-Onis Treaty of 1819 and also challenged British sovereignty in western Canada. The Monroe Doctrine was issued while the three powers were negotiating the issue in St. Petersburg. Alexander I, who was more concerned with British power than with the United States, accepted the principle, while Canning withdrew his representative from the negotiations over the northwest. Noncolonization played one European power against another to the advantage of the United States.

Next, Adams turned to the two-spheres principle. The occasion was provided by a Greek rebellion against Turkish rule, which excited widespread support in the United States. Thousands of dollars were sent to the rebels, and many Americans, including President Monroe, opposed entangling the young republic in faraway conflicts. "In the wars of the European powers," he stated, "we have never taken any part, nor does it comport with our policy so to do."

Finally, Adams established the nonintervention principle in relation to the Latin American question. He stated his belief that Spain's efforts to subdue its colonies were hopeless and declared that the United States would consider any attempt to intervene in Latin America as "dangerous to our peace and safety." What deterred European intervention, however, was not the American stand, but the strong British opposition. While Canning was waiting for the American response, he informed the French government that any intervention would trigger British recognition of the rebels. Unwilling to challenge Britain, France backed down.

In the Monroe Doctrine, the United States proclaimed itself the master, protector, and spokesman of the hemisphere. American leaders, beginning with Pres. James K. Polk in 1845, invoked Monroe's words to establish an exclusive sphere of influence for the United States in Latin America. In 1895 Pres. Grover Cleveland's secretary of state, Richard Olney, forced Britain to submit its boundary dispute with Venezuela to arbitration and declared: "The United States is practically sovereign on this continent." In

1904, in an effort to block Europeans from seizing control of Caribbean nations that defaulted on their foreign debts, Pres. Theodore Roosevelt issued a corollary to the doctrine, explaining that the backwardness of nations in the Western Hemisphere might "ultimately require intervention" by the United States "to the exercise of an international police power." The United States soon took over the collection of customs in the Dominican Republic and later used Roosevelt's corollary to justify its intervention in Haiti and Nicaragua. Ultimately, the Monroe Doctrine came to stand not for the protection of the hemisphere from European meddling, but for American condescension and imperialism.

—DORON BEN-ATAR

See Also: Adams, John Quincy; Adams-Onis Treaty; Monroe, James; Roosevelt, Theodore.

BIBLIOGRAPHY: May, Ernest R., *The Coming of the Monroe Doctrine* (Belknap Press 1975); Perkins, Dexter, *A History of the Monroe Doctrine* (Little, Brown 1941); Smith, Gaddis, *The Last Years of the Monroe Doctrine* (Hill & Wang 1994).

MONTANA, the largest Rocky Mountain state. It is bounded on the north by three Canadian provinces, on the west and south by Idaho, on the south and east by Wyoming, and on the east by North Dakota and South Dakota. The Great Plains occupy the eastern 60 percent of the state; the Rocky Mountains the remainder. The source of the Missouri River is in southwestern Montana.

Fur trappers and traders were the first Europeans to visit what is now Montana, most of which passed to the United States from France in the 1803 Louisiana Purchase. Montana did not become a state until 1889.

Capital: Helena. Area: 147,046 square miles. Population (1995 est.): 870,000.

See Also: Custer, George Armstrong; Joseph, Chief; Lewis and Clark Expedition; Little Bighorn; Louisiana Purchase; Missouri River; Rankin, Jeanette; Rocky Mountains.

MONTCALM, LOUIS-JOSEPH, MARQUIS DE (1712-59), French general. A native of France, Montcalm became a major general in 1756 and assumed command of French forces in Canada during the French and Indian War. With poorly supplied and outnumbered troops, he still managed to defeat the British in early battles and was named a lieutenant general in 1758. While defending Quebec in 1759, Montcalm was defeated by British forces under Gen. James Wolfe on the Plains of Abraham and died in the battle. The defeat led the French to surrender Canada to the British.

See Also: *French and Indian War; French Colonies; Plains of Abraham.*

■ **MONTEVIDEO CONFERENCE (1933),** international conference of American states held in Montevideo, Uruguay, in December 1933. The goal of Pres. Franklin D. Roosevelt and his administration was to advertise the principle of U.S. nonintervention in Latin American affairs that came to be known as the Good Neighbor Policy. At the conference, U.S. Sec. of State Cordell Hull declared that "no state has the right to intervene in the internal or external affairs of another." To put the principle into practice, the government abrogated the Platt Amendment of 1901, through which the United States had previously retained the right of intervention in Cuba. In 1934 the United States withdrew its troops from Haiti, where they had served since 1916. As a result, U.S. forces in the Panama Canal Zone became the only remaining U.S. military presence in the Western Hemisphere outside the United States.

See Also: *Good Neighbor Policy; Platt Amendment.*

■ **MONTEZ, LOLA (1818-61),** dancer, actress, and celebrity. Born in Ireland, she forged her great beauty and exotic reputation into a legendary career as a performer, adventurer, and provocative public figure. Before coming to America in 1851, she had been the consort and suspected lover of Ludwig I, King of Bavaria.

■ **MONTEZUMA, CARLOS (1867-1923),** Yavapai Indian reformer and physician. Montezuma was born Wassaja in present-day Arizona and, as a young child, was kidnapped by Pimas. He was later sold for $30 to photographer Carlos Gentile who took the boy east and abandoned him in Chicago. Montezuma was taken in by a Baptist minister and received private tutoring for two years before enrolling at the University of Illinois. He graduated in 1884 and then attended Chicago Medical College, graduating in 1889. Montezuma went into the federal Indian Service, in which he worked at the Fort Stevenson Indian School in North Dakota, the Western Shoshone Agency in Nevada, and the Colville Agency in Washington. In 1894, frustrated over the conditions on Indian reservations, Montezuma went to work as a physician for the Carlisle Indian School.

Returning to Chicago two years later, Montezuma became an active critic of the Bureau of Indian Affairs (BIA) and the reservation system. He advocated citizenship and acculturation for Indians. Like many educated Indians, Montezuma embraced a "progressive" view that encouraged the adoption of the values and lifestyle of white Americans. Offered the position of commissioner of Indian affairs by both presidents Theodore Roosevelt and Woodrow Wilson, Montezuma turned it down because he favored abolition of the BIA. At the same time, he continued his political advocacy. Stubborn, Montezuma was convinced that his vision was the only hope for Indian survival. Although one of the founding members of the Society of American Indians in 1911, he quit that organization because he thought it was being manipulated by the BIA. Montezuma published three books in support of his plans for Indian liberation from U.S. wardship. When his health failed in 1922, he returned to the land of the Yavapais in Arizona.

—KATHRYN A. ABBOTT

See Also: *Carlisle Indian School; Indian Affairs, Bureau of (BIA); Indians of North America; Society of American Indians (SAI).*

BIBLIOGRAPHY: Iverson, Peter, *Carlos Montezuma and the Changing World of American Indians* (Univ. of New Mexico Press 1982).

■ **MONTICELLO,** Thomas Jefferson's home in Charlottesville, Virginia. Monticello was Jefferson's first work of architectural design. In the Georgian style with its aristocratic dome and bricked exterior, it was built from 1769 to 1775 and remodeled over time. Monticello appears on the U.S. nickel.

■ **MONUMENT VALLEY,** vast valley with large red sandstone formations, located in northeastern Arizona and southern Utah. The valley is completely within the Navaho Indian Reservation. The "monuments" are actually red sandstone monoliths that rise 1,000 feet from the valley floor. The Navaho first occupied the region in the 1860s, when a large part of the tribe moved into the area. William Henry Jackson, the pioneer photographer of the West, photographed the rock formations in the 1880s. John Ford then immortalized the landscape in his films, especially *Stagecoach* (1939) and *The Searchers* (1956).

■ **MOODY, DWIGHT LYMAN (1837-99),** evangelist. Born in Northfield, Massachusetts, Moody was self-taught and never ordained. While a shoe salesman in 1858, he began a Sunday school in the Chicago slums. During the Civil War (1861-65), he worked with the U.S. Christian Commission, speaking to soldiers and distributing gospel tracts. In the 1870s, he joined forces with Ira David Sankey, a singer and organist, and the two undertook evangelistic campaigns in Europe and America. Moody became an international urban revivalist. His interest in religious training prompted him to found many educational institutions.

See Also: Religion.

■ **MOODY, WILLIAM HENRY (1853-1917),** jurist and politician. Born in Newbury, Massachusetts, he was special prosecutor in the Lizzie Borden murder trial (1893), congressman (1895-1902), secretary of the navy (1902-04), and attorney general (1904-06) before serving as an associate justice of the U.S. Supreme Court (1906-10).

See Also: Supreme Court.

■ **MOORE, ALFRED (1755-1810),** associate justice of the U.S. Supreme Court (1799-1804). A New Hanover County, North Carolina, native, Moore delivered his most significant opinion in *Bas* v. *Tingy* (1800). Speaking for the Court, he held that during wartime, government interests override private commercial rights.

See Also: Supreme Court.

■ **MOORE, MARIANNE (1887-1972),** Pulitzer Prize–winning poet, born in St. Louis, Missouri. Moore graduated from Bryn Mawr College in 1909. She taught business courses at the Carlisle Indian School (1911-15) and worked as a librarian in New York City (1921-25). In New York she

In 1952, Marianne Moore won both the National Book Award and the Pulitzer Prize in poetry for her *Collected Poems* (1951).

began writing and became part of the Greenwich Village literary circle, winning a prize from *Dial* magazine in 1924. On the reputation of her first two collections of poetry, *Poems* (1921) and *Observations* (1924), in 1926 she became *Dial*'s editor in chief. Her poems, usually about animals, birds, or fish, are tightly organized, highly intellectual, and often satirical. In the next years she added *What Are Years* (1941), *O to Be a Dragon* (1959), and *Complete Poems* (1967). She was awarded the 1951 Pulitzer Prize and the 1952 National Book Award for her *Collected Poems* (1951). She also translated the animal fables of French author Jean La Fontaine as *The Fables of Fontaine* (1954).

See Also: Poetry; Women in American History.

■ **MORAVIANS,** common name for the Unity of the Brethren in the United States. The movement originated in 1457 with the followers of John Huss in Moravia. Under the leadership of Augustus G.

Spangenberg, the missionary group came to Savannah, Georgia, in 1735. They then moved to Bethlehem, Pennsylvania, in 1741. Early ministers traveled among the German settlers and conducted mission work with the Indians. Moravians built the Pennsylvania towns of Nazareth and Lititz and a settlement in Salem, North Carolina. Moravians stress Christian unity and personal service. Their worship services are noted for their congregational singing.

See Also: Religion.

■ **MORGAN, DANIEL (1736-1802),** military leader. Born in Hunterdon County, New Jersey, Morgan began his long military career during the French and Indian War (1756-63). He ascended the ranks during the American Revolution, becoming a brigadier general in the Continental army. Morgan proved himself first in the attempted invasion of Canada in 1775 and later at Saratoga in 1777. His greatest victory came at Cowpens in South Carolina in 1781. After the Revolution he commanded U.S. forces against the rebels in Pennsylvania's Whiskey Rebellion (1794).

See Also: Cowpens, Battle of; Revolution, American; Whiskey Rebellion.

■ **MORGAN, HENRY (1635-88),** English pirate and British official in Jamaica. Born in Wales, Morgan went to sea early and participated in various naval adventures including a British expedition to Jamaica (1655). A privateer in the Caribbean by 1668, Morgan launched a series of raids against Spanish targets that became outright pirating. Reprimanded for his conduct, but knighted in 1674, Morgan eventually returned to Jamaica, first as lieutenant governor (1675) and then commander in chief, remaining until his death.

See Also: Piracy.

■ **MORGAN, LEWIS HENRY (1818-81),** ethnologist, known as the "Father of American Anthropology." Morgan was born near Aurora, New York, and graduated from Union College in 1840. He started practicing law in 1844 and served in the New York State Assembly and State Senate while also studying American Indian cultures. In 1851 Morgan published *League of the Ho-dé-no-sau-nee, or Iroquois,* the first ethnographic study of an Indian

tribe. He continued this exploration in *Systems of Consanguinity and Affinity of the Human Family* (1871), in which he argued that Iroquois family structure was not unique but was paralleled by other tribes. Other works included *The American Beaver and His Works* (1868), *Ancient Society; or Researches in the Lines of Human Progress* (1877), and *Houses and House-Life of the American Aborigines* (1881). Morgan became the first chairman of the Section of Anthropology of the American Association for the Advancement of Science in 1875 and in 1879 was elected president of the parent group as well.

See Also: Anthropology and Ethnology.

■ **MORGAN, J. P. (JOHN PIERPONT) (1837-1913),** financier. Morgan, a legendary figure during his lifetime, was born to a wealthy family in Hartford, Connecticut, and was educated in Germany. Following in his father's footsteps, he began a career in the finance industry on Wall Street in 1857 and established his own firm in 1862. After merging with

J. P. Morgan built a colossal financial and industrial empire, including the U.S. Steel Corporation (1901), the world's first billion-dollar corporation.

Anthony Drexel's firm in 1872, Morgan emerged as a leading broker in federal securities.

After the Civil War, railroads expanded rapidly, although many suffered from poor management, overbuilding, and brutal competition. During the 1880s, Morgan began to reorganize major railroads, resulting in enormous financial earnings for the financier and a stabilized industry. In 1890, Morgan took over his recently deceased father's company, renaming it J. P. Morgan and Company.

During the economically turbulent 1890s, Morgan's company benefited from shrewd maneuvers in investment banking. Perhaps more significant was his financing and reorganization of large industrial corporations, including General Electric, International Harvester, and U.S. Steel. By 1907 his wealth, prestige, and influence were so large that he single-handedly restored confidence in the nation's banks and stock market when a panic threatened the financial industry.

A confident and forceful figure, Morgan came to epitomize the successful financier. He was legendary for conducting business on a personal level, for he insisted on knowing all his debtors. During the last 20 years of his life, Morgan began to acquire a massive art collection that he donated to museums.

See Also: *Banks and Banking; Industrial Revolution; Stock Exchange.*
BIBLIOGRAPHY: Carosso, Vincent P., *The Morgans: Private International Bankers, 1854-1913* (Harvard Univ. Press 1987); Sinclair, Andrew, *Corsairs: The Life of J. Pierpoint Morgan* (Little, Brown 1981).

◼ **MORGAN, THOMAS HUNT (1866-1945),** geneticist. Born in Lexington, Kentucky, Morgan taught at Columbia University (1904-28) and began his revolutionary genetic experiments with the fruit fly *Drosophila* in 1908. He discovered that genes were discrete chromosomal units of heredity, and he developed the concept of sex linkage through the study of mutation. Morgan also mapped the genes of *Drosophila* chromosomes and wrote *The Mechanism of Mendelian Heredity* (1915). He went to the California Institute of Technology in 1928, continued to research and write, and won the 1933 Nobel Prize in Physiology and Medicine for his work in heredity.
See Also: *Science.*

◼ **MORGENTHAU, HENRY, JR. (1891-1967),** secretary of the treasury (1934-45) under Pres. Franklin D. Roosevelt. Born in New York City, the son and namesake of a prominent banker who served as U.S. ambassador to Turkey, Morgenthau served as the government's chief financial officer during most of the New Deal, a time of unprecedented budget growth. An expert on the economics of agriculture, he published *American Agriculturist* magazine (1922-33) before joining Roosevelt's administration in 1933 as undersecretary of the treasury and governor of the Farm Credit Administration.

As treasury secretary from 1934, Morgenthau administered New Deal tax programs and oversaw the sales of billions of dollars of government bonds, initially for new domestic programs and then for the costs of World War II. He proposed the Morgenthau Plan (1944), which would have prevented Germany from rebuilding its industrial base and military strength by forcing it to adopt an agricultural economy.

See Also: *New Deal; Roosevelt, Franklin Delano.*
BIBLIOGRAPHY: Blum, John Morton, *Roosevelt and Morgenthau* (Houghton Mifflin 1970).

◼ **MORISON, SAMUEL ELIOT (1887-1976),** historian. A Boston, Massachusetts, native, Morison won Pulitzer Prizes for biographies of Christopher Columbus (1942) and John Paul Jones (1959) and wrote a 25-volume U.S. naval history of World War II and other works. The author of the *Oxford History of the American People* (1965), late in his career he published a definitive two-volume study of the voyages of Early American exploration.
See Also: *History.*

◼ **MORMONS,** people connected by membership or heritage to the Church of Jesus Christ of Latter-day Saints (the Mormon church), organized in 1830 in western New York under the leadership of Joseph Smith, Jr. Regarding their church as the restoration of the New Testament body, the members recognized their leader as a prophet, believed that through him the ancient priesthood was restored, and accepted the *Book of Mormon*—a work Smith said he translated from engravings on golden plates—as a supplement to the Bible. Revelation decreed that the body's official name would be the Church of Jesus Christ of Latter-day Saints. Often called Mormons, its members are also called Latter-day Saints. Of the original church's many institutional progeny, the Latter-day Saints church headquartered in Salt Lake City, Utah, and the Reorganized church (RLDS) headquartered in Independence, Missouri, are the most important.

Because they were subjected to ridicule and persecution, the Mormons left New York in 1831. While small congregations were organized in the Northeast and Midwest, revelation told them to live as a gathered people. In compliance with this command, they established Mormon enclaves in Ohio and Missouri. Smith and many of his followers settled in Kirtland, Ohio, near Cleveland; Mormons also flocked to Independence, Missouri, the place revelation identified as the site of Christ's Second Coming.

The local inhabitants' fear that they would be overwhelmed by Mormons led to intense hostility between the new arrivals and their neighbors. During the 1830s violence drove the Mormons from both areas. They fled to northwestern Missouri, but formation of a new Mormon enclave there led to the Missouri Mormon War. Driven from the state, they fled back to Illinois, where they settled in a town they renamed Nauvoo. For a brief period, Nauvoo was the largest city in the state. But renewed violence led to Smith's murder, a scattering of the gathering, and a fracturing of the movement.

While many Mormons abandoned the enclave concept, settling in the Midwest and elsewhere in the nation, the largest group went with Brigham Young to the intermountain West. There they created the gathered community that, after an extended struggle with the federal government, would enter the union as the state of Utah. Mormonism is a proselytizing faith, sending thousands of missionaries around the world. As a result of their efforts, Mormonism has become one of the world's most rapidly growing religions. While Salt Lake City remains the movement's center, by 1996 more Mormons lived outside than inside the United States.

—JAN SHIPPS

See Also: Religion; Smith, Joseph; Utah; Young, Brigham.

BIBLIOGRAPHY: Arrington, Leonard J., and Davis Bitton, *The Mormon Experience: A History of the Latter-day Saints* (Knopf 1979).

■ **MORRILL LAND GRANT ACT (1862),** federal law, passed during the Civil War, giving each state that remained loyal to the Union land to endow public agricultural and mechanical colleges. Proposed by Rep. (later Sen.) Justin Morrill of Vermont, each eligible state received an allotment of 30,000 acres of federal land for each of its members of Congress. If there were not enough empty federal lands within a state, the state received land in the Western territories. Land sales raised more than $8 million and resulted in the founding of more than 70 colleges, primarily in the East and Midwest. A second Morrill Act in 1890 extended the program to southern states. The so-called "land grant" colleges created by the act form the backbone of today's U.S. system of public higher education. A provision of the original act requiring that military training be available at land grant colleges later led to the creation of the Reserve Officers Training Corps (ROTC) program.

■ **MORRIS, GOUVERNEUR (1752-1816),** lawyer and Revolutionary-era statesman. Born to a prominent family in Morrisania, New York, Morris urged reconciliation with Britain in 1775 as a member of New York's provincial congress. Because of this unpopular view he was promptly voted out of office but returned in 1776 and supported the cause for independence. In 1778 he was elected as a delegate to the Second Continental Congress, where he influenced many important pieces of legislation. After being ousted from office again, Morris moved to Philadelphia, where in 1781 he was appointed assistant to Robert Morris (no relation), the superintendent of finance in the new government. A member of the Constitutional Convention, Morris advocated a powerful executive and a strong central government composed of elite men. He served on the Style Committee and contributed heavily to the wording of the final document. After the Revolution, Morris served as minister to France (1792-94) and as a Federalist in Congress (1800-03).

See Also: Revolution, American.

■ **MORRIS, LEWIS (1726-98),** military leader and Revolutionary War politican. Morris was born into a prominent family in Westchester County, New York, and became an active participant in the Revolution. He commanded troops in the militia, served in the Second Continental Congress, and signed the Declaration of Independence.

See Also: Declaration of Independence.

■ **MORRIS, ROBERT (1734-1806),** merchant, political leader, and financier. Morris, a native of Liverpool, England, immigrated to America in 1747. Beginning as an apprentice, he became a partner in a Philadelphia shipping firm in 1754. A prosperous and ambitious entrepreneur, Morris supported colonial protests against British policies in the 1760s but did not advocate independence. Despite his moderate stance, Morris served as a delegate to the Continental Congress (1776-78), signed the Declaration of Independence, and successfully obtained munitions and other needed supplies from abroad. He became respected by other leaders for his administrative abilities but was defeated in a bid for reelection to Congress in 1778.

Morris reentered politics in 1781 as superintendent of finance under the Articles of Confederation. Over the next three years he implemented a series of financial reforms, through which he funded the debt, secured a loan from France, and obtained funds from the states. Morris also helped to finance the victorious Yorktown campaign in 1781 and established the Bank of North America in 1783. The revenue plan fell short of Morris's hopes, however, as many provincial politicians and merchants succeeded in altering his vigorous national financial system.

After the Revolution, Morris supported ratification of the Constitution and served as a Federalist in the U.S. Senate (1789-95). During the mid-1790s, massive land speculations brought him financial ruin, and he spent three years in a debtor's prison. He died in poverty in 1806.

See Also: Constitution of the United States; Declaration of Independence; Revolution, American.

BIBLIOGRAPHY: Ver Steeg, Clarence L., *Robert Morris: Revolutionary Financier* (Univ. of Pennsylvania Press 1954).

■ **MORRISON, TONI (1931-),** novelist and critic who had a major impact on the American literary scene. Morrison was born Chloe Anthony Wofford in Lorain, Ohio, and after graduating from Howard University (1953) and earning an M.A. at Cornell University (1955), she taught English at Texas Southern and Howard universities. In 1965, she assumed the position of literary editor at Random House and became senior editor by 1969.

Writing in the tradition of African-American women novelists, Morrison's works focus on black women. In stunning prose, she contends with contemporary issues of race and gender as well as timeless questions of identity, community, and good versus evil.

The Bluest Eye, her first novel, published in 1970 at the height of black cultural nationalism, received notice and established Morrison as a literary figure. Her second work, *Sula*, was nominated for the National Book Critics' Circle Award in 1975. Other novels include *The Song of Solomon* (1977), *Tar Baby* (1981), *Beloved* (1987), *Jazz* (1992), and *Paradise* (1998). Morrison's achievements earned her the 1993 Nobel Prize for Literature, of which she was the first African-American recipient.

Morrison has held academic appointments at Yale, the State University of New York at Albany, Rutgers, Berkeley, and Princeton. Although her novels have always been infused with social criticism, her most recent books are works of social commentary as she continues her career as a prominent writer and public intellectual.

See Also: African Americans; Novel; Women in American History.

BIBLIOGRAPHY: Rigney, Barbara Hill, *The Voices of Toni Morrison* (Ohio State Univ. Press 1991); Peach, Linden, *Toni Morrison* (St. Martin's Press 1995); Morrison, Toni, *Playing in the Dark: Whiteness and the Literary Imagination* (Harvard Univ. Press 1992).

■ *MORRISON V. OLSON* **(1988),** U.S. Supreme Court case concerning the Ethics of Government Act (1978). The law authorized the appointment of an independent counsel to investigate alleged wrongdoing by high-ranking government officials. The Court ruled (7-1) that the law, which was passed after the Watergate scandals and allows a special judicial panel to appoint a prosecutor at the request of the U.S. attorney general, did not violate the Constitution's separation of powers.

See Also: *Separation of Powers.*

■ MORSE, SAMUEL FINLEY BREESE (1791-1872),

American painter and inventor, known as the "father of telegraphy." Born in Charlestown, Massachusetts, he was the first of three sons of the Reverend Jedidiah Morse, a prominent Calvinist minister and geographer, and Elizabeth Ann Breese, the granddaughter of Dr. Samuel Finley, a president of the College of New Jersey in Princeton. While at Yale College (class of 1810), Morse painted amateur portaits, landscapes, and historical subjects.

Encouraged by American Romantic artist Washington Allston to pursue a career as a professional painter, Morse traveled to London, attended formal art classes at the Royal Academy, and was privately mentored by Allston and American artist Benjamin West. Morse's colleagues, as well as the British press, acclaimed his academic picture *The Dying Hercules* (1812-13). Upon his return to the United States in 1815, Morse painted portraits itinerantly in New England, New York City, and South Carolina. *The House of Representatives* (1822-23) was his first American effort to return to the historical subjects advocated by his teachers at the Royal Academy. But the painting, like his later *The Gallery of the Louvre* (1832-33), was not popular with a mass audience that preferred to think of art more as entertainment than as intellectual matter. However, his portraits, such as the *Marquis de Lafayette* (1825-26), and his involvement with New York's social and intellectual elite established his central position in the arts and letters of New York City.

In 1826, Morse organized many of the professional artists of New York into the National Academy of Design, over which he presided until 1845 and again from 1861 to 1862. With its teaching and exhibition programs and Morse's aggressive public lecturing, the National Academy of Design became the most influential art academy in antebellum America. By the mid-1830s, however, he had become convinced that the United States was incapable of supporting high culture. He painted his last picture in 1837.

In the mid-1830s he began his first experiments at New York University on the electromagnetic

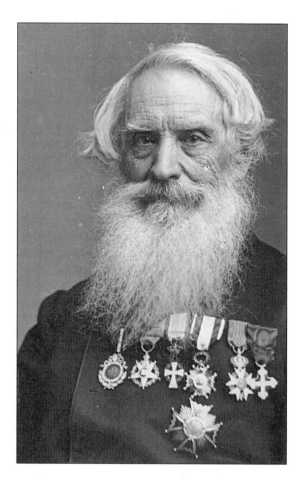

In 1844, Samuel F. B. Morse, previously noted as a painter, received a patent for the telegraph after transmitting the message, "What hath God wrought!" over a line between Baltimore and Washington, D.C.

telegraph. Morse sent his first short-distance message in December 1837, using a mechanical language of dots and dashes known as the Morse code. In 1844, he demonstrated his telegraph before Congress by sending the words "What hath God wrought" from Washington, D.C., to Baltimore. In securing American patents and licensing others to use the machine and erect telegraph poles that came to cover the continent, Morse became the most famous inventor of the antebellum period. The electromagnetic telegraph revolutionized culture by separating for the first time communications from transportation. Although it would be largely replaced by the telephone in the early 20th century, the binary language of the

Morse code became the conceptual basis for computer languages in the late 20th century.

—PAUL STAITI

See Also: Industrial Revolution; Invention; Painting; Science.

BIBLIOGRAPHY: Larkin, Oliver, *Samuel F. B. Morse and American Democratic Art* (Little, Brown 1954); Mabee, Carleton, *The American Leonardo: A Life of Samuel F. B. Morse* (Knopf 1943); Morse, Edward Lind, ed., *Samuel F. B. Morse: His Letters and Journals,* 2 vols. (Houghton Mifflin 1914); Staiti, Paul J., *Samuel F. B. Morse* (Cambridge Univ. Press 1990).

■ **MORTON, FERDINAND ("JELLY ROLL") (1885-1941),** jazz composer and pianist. Born in Gulfport, Louisiana, Morton was one of the most influential of the early jazz pioneers. During the 1920s, he and his group, Red Hot Peppers, made a series of recordings of his most popular works, including "New Orleans Blues," "King Porter Stomp," and "Jelly Roll Blues."

See Also: African Americans; Jazz.

■ **MORTON, JOHN (1724-77),** statesman and Revolutionary War figure. He was born in Ridely, Pennsylvania. After holding provincial offices, Morton served in the Stamp Act Congress and the First and Second Continental Congresses and signed the Declaration of Independence.

See Also: Declaration of Independence.

■ **MORTON, LEVI PARSONS (1824-1920),** vice president of the United States (1889-93) and financier. Born in Shoreham, Vermont, he entered business in Hanover, New Hampshire, before moving to Boston and then New York, where he opened an investment bank. He served in Congress (1879-81) and as U.S. minister to France (1881-85). He served one term as vice president under Republican Pres. Benjamin Harrison (1889-93) and as governor of New York (1895-97) before returning to the financial world in 1899.

See Also: Gilded Age; Harrison, Benjamin; Vice President of the United States.

■ **MORTON, WILLIAM (1819-68),** dentist and anesthetist. Born in Charlestown, Massachusetts, Morton practiced dentistry in Boston, where he

and his partner experimented with nitrous oxide as anesthesia. After experimenting with ether on chickens, his dog, and himself, he used it successfully for a tooth extraction in 1846. Morton used it with an inhalator on surgical patients at Massachusetts General Hospital that same year and spent the rest of his life fighting for the profits from its use and for credit as its discoverer.

See Also: Science.

■ **MOSES, ANNA MARY ROBINSON (GRANDMA) (1860-1961),** painter of American farm life. Born in Washington, New York, she was a farm wife for over half a century before she began painting in her late 70s when she could no longer manage hard physical labor. Her paintings of simple farm life, such as *Oaken Bucket, Thanksgiving Turkey,* and *Sugaring Off,* were popular as the subjects of greeting cards and prints. In 1960 she illustrated Clement Moore's "'Twas the Night Before Christmas."

See Also: Painting.

■ **MOSES, GRANDMA.** *See: Moses, Anna Mary Robinson.*

■ **MOSES, PHOEBE ANN.** *See: Oakley, Annie.*

■ **MOSES, ROBERT PARRIS (1935-),** civil rights activist. Born in New York City, Moses in 1959 met Bayard Rustin, who encouraged him to join the Southern Christian Leadership Conference (SCLC). Moses worked at voter registration in McComb, Mississippi, and as a member of the Student Nonviolent Coordinating Committee (SNCC) helped create the Mississippi Freedom Democratic party. Moses was largely responsible for creating the Mississippi Summer Project of 1964 but left SNCC in 1965 over disputes within the project over the issues of nonviolence and white participation.

See Also: Civil Rights Movement.

■ **MOTION PICTURES,** first exhibited in the United States in 1896 using a variant of a projector designed by Thomas Edison. Edison's studio in New Jersey was the largest producer of early films, most of which were short clips of ordinary scenes noted for the simple fact of motion. The first film to tell a story, *The Great Train Robbery* (1903), turned the motion picture business from a fad into a phenomenon. By 1910, there were more than 10,000 movie houses in operation. Edison, in association with two other studios, attempted to enforce a monopoly of the technology, but in 1909 that was broken by the suit of independent producer William Fox, who formed Fox Studios in Hollywood.

The most important of the early Hollywood studios was Paramount, founded by Adolph Zukor in 1912. Zukor introduced vertical integration into the film business, combining production and exhibition through a chain of theaters owned by the company. This control was the backbone of the "studio system," and it provided the studios with the financial clout to sign directors and actors to exclusive contracts.

By the late 1920s the industry was dominated by five studios: Fox, Paramount, MGM (Metro-Goldwyn-Mayer), Warner Brothers, and RKO (Radio-Keith-Orpheum). Under the auspices of the studios, motion pictures became more sophisticated, the product of the joint effort of directors, writers, photographers, editors, and actors. The director D. W. Griffith developed many techniques, including "montage" (the assemblage of many different images in rapid succession) and the "close-up," while Mack Sennett originated slapstick comedy, and Cecil B. De Mille adapted plays from the stage. The studios quickly developed what became known as the "star system," the promotion of films less for their stories than for their performers. The leading silent stars included Douglas Fairbanks (action films), Mary Pickford, Lillian Gish, and Rudolf Valentino (sentimental romances), Charlie Chaplin, Buster Keaton, Marie Dressler, and the team of Laurel and Hardy (comedies), Pearl White (serials), and William S. Hart (Westerns).

The Studio System. The studios made the switch from silent films to sound in 1927, the same year the American Academy of Motion Picture Arts and Sciences began handing out the Academy Awards. The first "talking picture" with audible dialogue was *The Jazz Singer*, starring Al Jolson. Production costs were much lower for silent films. Indeed, film historians estimate that the number of silent films produced from 1903 to 1927 was equal to or greater than the number of pictures made since. But since silent films were printed on film stock made from cellulose nitrate, a highly unstable material (safety acetate film was not available until 1952), most of them have been lost. The high capital costs of making films on soundproof stages increased the dominance of the studios, which controlled 95 percent of American film output by 1938.

The dominance of the studios brought conformity to film production. In 1915, the U.S. Supreme Court had ruled that movies were not covered by the First Amendment, and the studios had tried to police themselves to avoid censorship. During the silent era, however, it was relatively simple for independent filmmakers to make and distribute controversial pictures or even pornography. In the early 1930s, several studios released a number of risky and risqué pictures—including films featuring comedic "sex goddess" Mae West—which led to cries for censorship. In 1934, the studios adopted a production code that severely restricted what they might show on screen.

But the studio system of the 1930s also excelled in producing high-quality motion pictures with what became known as solid "production values." Warner Brothers became known for its gritty crime melodramas, MGM for costume pictures and (a little later) for musicals, Fox for solid drama. It was the golden age of Hollywood, with great directors such as Frank Capra and John Ford; musical entertainers like Fred Astaire, Gene Kelly, Judy Garland, and Bill "Bojangles" Robinson (one of the few African Americans able to avoid playing racist stereotypes); hard-boiled actors like Humphrey Bogart and James Cagney; Western stars like John Wayne and Gary Cooper; and comedic geniuses like W. C. Fields and the Marx Brothers. Walt Disney developed the largest Hollywood animation workshop, which eventually grew into an operation that rivaled the size of the other studios.

Film Industry Since World War II. The rise of television after World War II fundamentally changed the motion picture industry. Innovations such as drive-ins, wide screens, and 3-D failed to keep up ticket sales. The studios' troubles mounted in 1947 when the Supreme Court declared that the control of both production and distribution was a combination in restraint of trade. The most important development of the postwar era was the rise of independent filmmakers. In the 1940s independent-minded filmmakers such as Orson Welles were prevented from working within the system, but by the 1960s it was commonplace for good producers, directors, and actors to seek and value artistic freedom.

Postwar films were considerably more varied, ranging from serious art films (many inspired by the new wave of innovative filmmaking in Europe and Japan) to standard studio fare to cheap exploitation pictures. In 1966, the Hollywood studios relaxed their production code, replacing it with a rating system. The films of this era became increasingly loaded with obscenity, violence, and soft-core sexuality.

In the last decades of the 20th century the film industry was also affected by the introduction of cable television and the video cassette player. Feature films moved quickly from theater to pay cable channels such as Home Box Office (HBO), then into rental stores on video cassette, while vast portions of the film catalog of the studios were also transferred to cassette, an enormous boon for film buffs. The remaining studios consolidated in a series of mergers that made Paramount a part of a huge media conglomerate called Viacom and Warner Brothers a subsidiary of Time-Life. To give viewers a reason to pay $9 for tickets at the multiplex theaters, Hollywood devoted itself to producing blockbuster hits with digital "surround sound" and 70mm projection.

—JOHN MACK FARAGHER

See Also: *Academy Awards; Censorship; Comedy; Film Noir; Hollywood; Westerns; individual biographies.*

BIBLIOGRAPHY: Halliwell, Leslie, *Halliwell's Filmgoer's Companion,* 8th ed. (Scribner 1984); Sklar, Robert, *Film: An International History of the Medium* (Abrams 1993); Sklar, Robert, *Movie-Made America: A Cultural History of American Movies* (Vintage 1975).

■ **MOTT, LUCRETIA COFFIN (1793-1880),** Quaker minister, feminist, and abolitionist. She was born in Nantucket, Massachusetts. A progressive Quaker, she aided fugitive slaves and was an active member of abolitionist William Lloyd Garrison's American Anti-Slavery Society. She was excluded as a delegate from the 1840 World Anti-Slavery Convention in

A tireless worker for reform, particularly the abolition of slavery, Lucretia Mott, with Elizabeth Cady Stanton, organized the first women's rights convention at Seneca Falls, New York, in 1848.

London because she was a woman. This led to her collaborating with Elizabeth Cady Stanton to organize the Seneca Falls women's rights convention in 1848. She was president of the American Equal Rights Association (1866-69) and wrote *Discourse on Woman* (1850). With her husband, James Mott, she helped to found Swarthmore College (1864).

See Also: *American Anti-Slavery Society; American Equal Rights Association (AERA); Garrison, William Lloyd; Seneca Falls Convention; Stanton, Elizabeth Cady; Women in American History; Women's Movement.*

■ **MOUND BUILDERS (c. 400 B.C.-A.D. 1500),** name given to Indian peoples who constructed earthen mounds at different times in different locations, mainly in eastern North America. Some groups built burial mounds, while other mounds were ceremonial temples or residences of important chiefs. Important mound-building cultures included the Hopewell, Adena, and Mississippian. Early European settlers doubted whether indigenous Americans could have built such elaborate structures.

See Also: Adena; Indians of North America; Mississipian Culture.

■ **MOUNTAIN MEN,** name given to the fur traders and trappers of the Rocky Mountains during the heyday of the American fur trade, the 30 years or so following the conclusion of the War of 1812. These men contrasted with earlier participants in the fur trade, for rather than relying on the Indians to do their hunting and trapping, they did their own. Unlike earlier fur traders, the mountain men did not work out of fixed posts, as did the employees of the Hudson's Bay Company. Instead, they were supplied by pack and wagon train at the annual summer "rendezvous," a prodigal celebration matched in color and excitement by few other assemblies in American history, perhaps excepting the New Orleans Mardi Gras.

The ranks of the mountain men included some of the most notable characters in the history of the American West, men such as Mike Fink, Kit Carson, James Beckwourth, and James Bridger. They went west for adventure, some seeking asylum from a rapidly developing civilization, others in search of profits. Many of the mountain men adopted the styles and many of the values of western Indians, and most of them married Indian women and raised families of mixed ancestry children. When the fur trade declined in the 1840s because of a shift of fashion from beaver to silk hats, many mountain men turned to such careers as scouts or guides.

See Also: Bridger, Jim (James); Carson, Kit; Frontier in American History; Fur Trade.

BIBLIOGRAPHY: De Voto, Bernard, *Across the Wide Missouri* (Houghton Mifflin 1947); Hafen, Leroy R., ed., *The Mountain Men and the Fur Trade of the Far West,* 10 vols. (Arthur H. Clark 1965-72); Van Kirk, Sylvia, *"Many Tender Ties": Women in Fur-Trade Society in Western Canada, 1670-1870* (Watson & Dwyer 1980).

■ **MOUNT RUSHMORE NATIONAL MEMORIAL,** mountainside monument in South Dakota. The memorial was conceived in 1923 by Doane Robinson, head of the South Dakota Historical Society, and eventually funded by the state and the U.S. Congress. Sculptor Gutzon Borglum carved the monumental busts of U.S. presidents George Washington, Thomas Jefferson, Abraham Lincoln, and Theodore Roosevelt. Each head is roughly 60 feet high. The project, carried out from 1927 to 1941, cost approximately $1 million, $836,000 of which came from the federal government.

■ **MOUNT VERNON,** home of George Washington in Virginia. Washington inherited the 500-acre estate on the Potomac River in 1762. In 1853 Ann Pamela Cunningham organized one of the first preservation efforts, creating a national shrine at Mount Vernon.

■ **MUCKRAKERS,** a group of writers, working primarily in journalism in roughly the first decade of the 20th century, who publicized the ills of American life. In an off-the-record talk in early 1906, Pres. Theodore Roosevelt invoked the man with the muckrake of John Bunyan's *Pilgrim's Progress* to describe those writers who had, since 1902 or so, been revealing the nation's flaws in critical and occasionally sensationalistic accounts, mostly about politics and industry. Shortly afterward, he offered the same analogy in a public speech, reminding his audience of Bunyan's "man who could look no way but downward, with a muckrake in his hands; who was offered a celestial crown for his muckrake, . . . but continued to rake to himself the filth of the floor." Yet figures such as Lincoln Steffens, Ida M. Tarbell, and Upton Sinclair persisted in producing their "literature of exposure," as contemporaries knew it.

In the very first years of the 20th century, major changes in journalism, such as the emergence of a national news market in the latter half of the prior century, had converged with the emergence of progressivism to produce muckraking efforts like Steffens's *The Shame of the Cities* (1904), Tarbell's *The History of the Standard Oil Company* (1904), and Sinclair's novel *The Jungle* (1906), each initially published as a series of magazine articles. In their work, these and other muckrakers

Who Said Muck Rake?
(The Smile That Won't Come Off.)

Pres. Theodore Roosevelt coined the nickname "muckrakers" in 1906 for journalists like Ida Tarbell who were dedicated to exposing the corporate and political shortcomings of the nation.

did not prescribe solutions but rather issued a call for reform that reached millions of Americans, particularly middle-class ones, helping assure the passage of such measures as the Pure Food and Drug Act (1906). Although muckraking, along with progressivism, declined in the second decade of the 20th century, its insistent belief in the objective reporting of American life left a permanent mark upon the nation's news media.

—JAMES KESSENIDES

See Also: Sinclair, Upton; Steffens, Lincoln; Tarbell, Ida Minerva.

BIBLIOGRAPHY: Weinberg, Arthur, and Lila Weinberg, eds., *The Muckrakers: The Era in Journalism That Moved America to Reform—The Most Significant Magazine Art* (Simon & Schuster 1961).

■ **MUGWUMPS,** the Algonquian word for chief, a term applied to reform-minded Republicans in the 1880s. In 1884, disturbed by their party's nomination of the allegedly corrupt party boss, James G. Blaine, several leading Republicans, including Carl Schurz, Charles Francis Adams, Jr., and Edwin L. Godkin, bolted from the party and threw their support to the Democratic nominee, Grover Cleveland, who went on to win the presidential election. The term "mugwump," as first used by the *New York Sun*, referred to these reformers, who appeared to some as self-important and pompous. Primarily from Massachusetts and New York, Mugwumps sought not social but political reform, arguing that the powerful machine system put in jeopardy America's political values while at the same time threatening their traditional role as political leaders. Good Government Associations sprang up across the country, targeting especially those local machines associated with ethnic voters. Their most lasting achievement was the adoption during the early 1890s of the Australian Ballot, which by listing all candidates on a single ballot and assuring a secret vote, ended party control of the voting process.

See Also: Political Parties.

BIBLIOGRAPHY: McFarland, Gerald W., *Mugwumps: Morals and Politics, 1884-1920* (Univ. of Massachusetts Press 1975).

■ **MUIR, JOHN (1838-1914),** Scottish-American naturalist. He was born in Dunbar, Scotland, and immigrated to America as a young man, arriving in California in 1868. There, he was immediately taken with the beauty of the Yosemite Valley, which in 1864 the federal government had designated a public space for "pleasuring, resort, and recreation." Muir dedicated the rest of his life to preserving America's wilderness. He was a member of the U.S. Geodetic Survey team, which mapped out the Great Basin (1876-79). In 1890 he and other conservationists convinced Pres. Benjamin Harrison to declare some of California's vast forest lands off-limits to loggers. Thus, Yosemite, King's Canyon, and Sequoia national parks were established. In 1892 Muir was one of the founding members of the Sierra Club. In 1908 Muir Woods National Monument was established near San Francisco, acknowledging his 40 years of conservation work.

See Also: Conservation and Environmental Movements.

BIBLIOGRAPHY: Cohen, Michael P., *The Pathless Way: John Muir and the American Wilderness* (Univ. of Wisconsin Press 1984); Fox, Stephen R., *John Muir and His Legacy: The American Conservation Movement* (Little, Brown 1981).

■ **MULATTOS,** term used to describe peoples of mixed Caucasian and African ancestry. Pejorative in its original, historical context, the term *mulatto* has taken on various meanings for different peoples.

Black and white racial mixing began during the earliest contacts in the 17th century between white servants and African slaves. As they have been throughout American history, mulattos were legally characterized as people who possessed any amount, however small, of African ancestry. Beginning in the 1660s, colonial officials imposed statutes proscribing interracial sex. Liaisons between white women and black men were especially subject to the most severe punishments. Sexual exploitation of black women by white masters, however, was commonplace. Although black women resisted, sometimes successfully, these violations led to the birth of many mulattos, who were still considered slaves by white society.

After emancipation, white Southerners sought to retain the system of racial hierarchy by making interracial marriages illegal. Both black and white women, however, still gave birth to mulatto children. Despite the social stigmas, the number of black-white couples continued to grow throughout the 20th century. By 1990, black-white couples comprised 396 of every 100,000 marriages. Not until *Loving* v. *Virginia* (1967), however, were laws prohibiting such marriages found unconstitutional.

Mulattos have never been considered a separate "race" but have at times been ostracized by both white and African-American communities.

See Also: African Americans; Loving v. Virginia; Marriage.

BIBLIOGRAPHY: Spikard, Paul R., *Mixed Blood: Intermarriage and Ethnic Identity in Twentieth-Century America* (Univ. of Wisconsin Press 1989); Williamson, Joel, *New People: Miscegenation and Mulattos in the United States* (Free Press 1980).

■ **MULLER, HERMAN (1890-1967),** geneticist. Born in New York City, Muller studied with Thomas Hunt Morgan at Columbia and used the fruit fly *Drosophila* to discover that X rays can produce mutations. He taught at the University of Texas (1920-32), the University of Edinburgh (1937-40), Amherst College (1940-45), and the University of Indiana (1945-64) and did research in Moscow (1933-37). Muller used X rays to speed up the natural rate of mutation, transmute genes and create new ones, and thereby artificially speed up the evolutionary process. He won the 1946 Nobel Prize in Physiology and Medicine for his work in radiation genetics.

See Also: Science.

◼ *MULLER* **V.** *OREGON* **(1908),** milestone U.S. Supreme Court decision regarding women's work hours. The Supreme Court's 1905 *Lochner* v. *New York* decision had questioned the validity of protective work laws by nullifying New York's maximum-hours law for bakers on the grounds that it violated the employers' "liberty of contract."

In *Muller* v. *Oregon*, Portland laundry owner Curt Muller challenged Oregon's 1903 statute limiting women's work hours before the Supreme Court, but Boston attorney Louis Brandeis defended the law with an innovative "Brandeis brief" filled with sociological data assembled by National Consumers' League researchers, especially Josephine Goldmark. Stressing women's "special physical organization" and showing that long work hours harmed their health, the brief argued that women deserved exemption from *Lochner*'s rule. Expanding this, Justice David Brewer sustained Oregon's law for a unanimous Court, ruling that state legislation could give women special protection because of their "obvious" physical weakness and childbearing capacity.

Muller was pivotal. It popularized Brandeis briefs, signaled judicial acceptance of much protective labor legislation, and temporarily legitimized female difference as a rationale for women's protective laws. In the 1960s, however, rising opposition to sex discrimination generated by the women's movement and civil rights laws challenged *Muller* and women's protective legislation. Since then, court decisions and statutes have eliminated sex-based employment restrictions.

—DONALD W. ROGERS

See Also: *Brandeis, Louis Dembitz; Brewer, David Josiah; Supreme Court.*

BIBLIOGRAPHY: Woloch, Nancy, *Muller v. Oregon: A Brief History with Documents* (Bedford Books 1996).

◼ **MULTICULTURALISM.** *See:* *Cultural Pluralism.*

◼ *MUNN* **V.** *ILLINOIS* **(1877),** U.S. Supreme Court case, the best known of the so-called Granger Cases, which addressed the regulatory authority of the states. The case centered on an 1871 Illinois law enacted under pressure from the Granger Movement that fixed the maximum prices grain elevator operators could charge farmers. A suit by some operators against Illinois eventually reached the Supreme Court, where the justices upheld (7-2) the Illinois statute. Writing for the Court, Chief Justice Morrison Waite held that when a business's property served an important public purpose, the interests of the public in that property overrode certain rights of the owner, even those, such as due process, that might otherwise be guaranteed under the 14th Amendment. Waite's reading of the Constitution permitted Illinois to regulate the elevator prices because the state was legitimately exercising its police power in the public interest. Waite's opinion was remarkable for its expansiveness, seeming to leave the regulation of no business outside the potential police power of the states. The opinion was largely forgotten, however, until it was recovered from precedential memory during the 1930s. Since the New Deal the Granger precedent has been the constitutional basis for most business regulations.

See Also: *Granger Movement; Supreme Court.*

◼ **MURFREESBORO (STONES RIVER), BATTLE OF (1862-63),** Civil War engagement between the forces of Union Gen. William Rosecrans and Confederate Gen. Braxton Bragg just to the west of the Stones River, Tennessee. Early on December 31 the Confederates attacked the Union right, forcing it back nearly to the river. The Union line barely held at a right angle to its original position. After an uneventful January 1 a Confederate attack east of the river on January 2 was repulsed. The Confederates were forced to retreat.

See Also: *Civil War.*

◼ **MURPHY, WILLIAM FRANCIS (FRANK) (1890-1949),** associate justice of the U.S. Supreme Court (1940-49). Born in Harbor Beach, Michigan, he was a progressive mayor of Detroit (1930-33), the governor general and high commissioner of the Philippines (1933-36), and governor of Michigan (1937-38). Never a legal theorist, Murphy saw the Court as a protector of the powerless and oppressed and was an outspoken advocate of human rights and expanded civil liberties.

See Also: *Supreme Court.*

◼ **MURRAY, JUDITH SARGENT (1751-1820),** early American feminist and author who wrote under the pen name Constantia. She was born in Gloucester, Massachusetts. In a 1784 essay she argued that women are the intellectual equals of men. She also wrote poetry and an important series of essays on political and social topics, titled *The Gleaner* (1793). In 1788 she married her second husband, John Murray, considered the founder of Universalism in America.

■ **MURRIETA (MURIETA), JOAQUIN (c. 1830-1853?),** bandit. "The Ghost of Sonora," Murrieta was born in Sonora, Mexico, and moved to California after his marriage in 1848. Arrested for robbery in 1850, Murrieta raised a group of bandits who raided gold miners and wealthy settlers in the San Joaquin Valley. It is unclear if Murrieta was beheaded by California Rangers in July 1853, or if he escaped to retire in Sonora, Mexico. Murrieta was resurrected as a symbol of ethnic resistance and pride in the 1960s Chicano movement.

See Also: Frontier in American History.

■ **MURROW, EDWARD R. (1908-65),** broadcast journalist. Born in Greensboro, North Carolina, he joined the Columbia Broadcasting System (CBS) in 1935 and became the network's European director in 1937. Famed for his reports on the bombing of London (1940-41), Murrow became the leading radio war correspondent. He hosted several television news programs, such as *See It Now* (1951-58), and became a critic of television's superficial news coverage. He resigned from CBS (1961) to become director of the U.S. Information Agency.

See Also: Television and Radio.

■ **MUSEUMS,** an integral part of American cultural life from the founding days of the nation. Besides being repositories of artistic, historical, or scientific achievement and knowledge, museums are institutions by which social groups disseminate, through careful selection and display, a public sense of their own identity and worth. The nation's first museum was founded by the artist Charles Willson Peale (1741-1827) in 1786 in Philadelphia, then the national capital. Devoted to natural history, Peale's museum, depicted in his self-portrait, *The Artist in His Museum* (1822), contained shelf upon shelf of natural artifacts, including a mastodon bone exhumed in New Jersey. Arranged in double rows above the artifacts were portraits of the republic's leading soldiers, statesmen, and diplomats. Thus in this first American museum, the natural and the national were gathered together under a single roof, and after a transfer of location in 1802, the roof was that of Independence Hall, an architectural symbolism not lost on Peale and his contemporaries. Since then, museums in America, whatever their focus, have tended to carry a freight of nationalistic purpose, most manifestly so in the temporary museums erected for the two great "world's fairs" of the late 19th century held in Philadelphia in the Centennial year, 1876, and Chicago in 1893. New York's Metropolitan Museum of Art, today the world's most comprehensive art museum, was founded in 1870 as a testament to the country's cultural coming of age but also, in an era of remarkable conspicuous consumption, as proof of New York's financial preeminence. In Washington, D.C., the Smithsonian Institution, established in 1846 for scientific research, eventually swelled into the largest U.S. collection of museums, "the nation's attic," storehousing virtually everything produced in America from art to airplanes, fashions to Frisbees.

—DAVID M. LUBIN

After raising radio news reporting to a new level with his broadcasts from London during World War II, Edward R. Murrow pioneered several successful television news shows for CBS.

BIBLIOGRAPHY: Karp, Ivan, and Steven D. Lavine, *Exhibiting Cultures: The Poetics and Politics of Museum Display* (Smithsonian 1991); Sherman, Daniel J., and

Irit Rogoff, eds., *Museum Culture: Histories, Discourses, Spectacles* (Univ. of Minnesota Press 1994); Vergo, Peter, ed., *The New Museology* (Reaktion 1989).

■ **MUSIC. *See:*** *Be-Bop; Big Bands; Blues; Country and Western Music; Folk Music; Gospel Music; Jazz; Opera; Ragtime; Religious Music; Rhythm and Blues; Rock and Roll; Spirituals; Symphony Orchestras; Tin Pan Alley; individual biographies.*

■ **MUSICAL EDUCATION,** part of a broader movement to define a unique national culture after World War I. Schools such as Eastman in Rochester, New York (1918), Curtis in Philadelphia, Pennsylvania (1924), and Juilliard in New York City (1926) offered formal training in performance and composition to students who had previously been forced to seek private instruction in Europe. Elementary and secondary educators saw music as an important group activity that created a common culture and maintained standards. The folk movement of the 1920s and 1930s helped schools discover a national musical culture, while the study of classical music was seen by elites as a counterweight to the growing influence of popular music. Radio and television concerts by conductors such as Walter Damrosch (1862-1950) and Leonard Bernstein (1918-90) promoted "music appreciation" to elevate the public's taste.

See Also: Bernstein, Leonard.

BIBLIOGRAPHY: Consortium of National Arts Education Associations, *Dance, Music, Theatre, Visual Arts: What Every Young American Should Know and Be Able To Do in the Arts* (Music Education National Conference 1994).

■ **MUSLIMS,** people who practice Islam. Slaves brought from West Africa introduced Islam to North America, but the faith did not survive into the next generation. Islam reappeared in America in the late 19th century when the Ottoman Empire was deteriorating, and Muslims sought economic opportunities in America. The first outspoken advocate of Islam was Alexander Russell Webb, the American consul in the Philippines. He resigned his position and lectured on his faith. In the early 20th century, Muslims from Syria began to settle in the industrial areas of the Midwest, primarily northern Indiana and Detroit, Michigan. At the same time, several movements within the African-American community drew from Islamic themes, among them the Nation of Islam. Islam is not only a religion but a way of life. First, God has sent a series of messengers, including Abraham, Moses, and Jesus, all of whom carried the same message. It is found in the Koran as transmitted to Muhammad, God's final messenger. The Koran explains the five pillars of life, or the basic duties of the Muslim: *shahawda* ("witness" that there is only one God, Allah), *salat* ("ritual prayer" said five times a day), *zakat* ("giving alms"), *siyam* ("fasting" during the month of Ramadan), and *hajj* ("pilgrimage" to Mecca at least once in a lifetime, if possible).

See Also: Religion.

N

■ **NABOKOV, VLADIMIR (1899-1977),** poet and novelist. Nabokov was born in St. Petersburg, Russia, where he published his first volume of poetry at age 17. His family left the country in 1919 after the Russian Revolution; Nabokov went to Cambridge University in England to study. He then lived in Berlin and later Paris until the beginning of World War II, when he moved to the United States. Even before this move, Nabokov had started translating his works into English. *The Real Life of Sebastian Knight* (1941) was his first novel written in English, the language in which he continued to work. Nabokov is best known for the novel *Lolita* (1955), an exploration of the character of Humbert Humbert, who is obsessively attached to the young Dolores Haze. Originally turned down by American publishers as too controversial, *Lolita* was first published in Paris. Nabokov taught at Cornell University from 1948 to 1959, when he settled in Montreaux, Switzerland. Nabokov was a virtuoso of language; thematically his works often focus on an individual's struggle between desire and moral responsibilities and deal with the nature of time.

See Also: Novel.

■ **NADER, RALPH (1934-),** reformer and consumer advocate, born in Winsted, Connecticut. After graduating from Harvard Law School in 1958, he campaigned for auto safety reform both at the state and national levels. He left government in 1965 to write a book, *Unsafe at Any Speed*. A best-seller, the book condemned the auto industry, especially General Motors, for emphasizing style and profits instead of safety. Largely through Nader's influence, Congress passed the National Traffic and Motor Vehicle Safety Act of 1966.

Nader then embarked on campaigns for improved meat-packing standards, safer natural gas pipelines, and restricted use of pesticides, all of which resulted in the passage of federal reform legislation during the 1960s. Growing awareness of consumer rights and Nader's rising popularity led to the formation of "Nader's Raiders," a group of volunteers and students who fought for consumer protection. During the 1970s and 1980s Nader established a number of influential consumer and public interest groups. He launched two unsuccessful bids for the presidency: in 1992 as an independent write-in candidate and in 1996 as the candidate for the Green party.

Throughout his career, Nader's reform efforts have been driven by his crusade against the abuses of big business and distrust of government as a protector of the public interest.

BIBLIOGRAPHY: McCarry, Charles, *Citizen Nader* (Saturday Review Press 1972).

■ **NAFTA.** *See: North American Free Trade Agreement.*

■ **NAPOLEONIC CODE (1804),** the codification of French civil law under Napoleon I. Civil law, a derivative of Roman law, applied throughout much of Latin North America including the French Empire. When French Louisiana was acquired by the United States (1803), it became, in the words of one historian, "a civil law island in a sea of common law." In 1808 the United States recognized many of the code's procedures and rules, particularly concerning property and family law, to be controlling in Louisiana. Jury trial, however, an English-law import, was readily accepted by Louisianans.

■ **NARRAGANSETT INDIANS.** *See: Algonquian.*

■ **NAST, THOMAS (1840-1902),** political cartoonist. A native of Landau, Germany, who immigrated to New York City in 1846, he drew cartoons satirizing politics for *Harper's Weekly* and other publications. Nast created the Democratic donkey and Republican elephant as symbols of the political parties and openly attacked the corruption of New York Democratic party boss William Marcy Tweed (1823-78) and his Tammany Hall allies.

See Also: Tammany Hall; Tweed, William Marcy.

■ **NATCHEZ,** native tribe of the Southeast in the Mississippian tradition. The Natchez lived east of the Mississippi River in present-day Mississippi. Agriculturalists who settled in permanent villages, they supplemented their farming through hunting, fishing, and gathering wild foods. The Natchez lived in a stratified society, with a leader known as the Great Sun. The laborers who occupied the bottom of the social scale were known as stinkers. During the colonial era, the Natchez became trading partners with the English in South Carolina. Opposing French attempts to control the Mississippi Valley trade, they revolted against the French in 1729 and were brutally repressed by the Choctaw allies of the French. In February 1730 the Natchez surrendered, and most of the remaining people were sold into slavery. A few joined the Chickasaw, and their culture became extinct.

See Also: Indians of North America.

■ **NATION, CARRY AMELIA (1846-1911),** militant temperance crusader. She was born in Gerrard County, Kentucky. Convinced that God had chosen her to rid the country of saloons, she led prayer meetings at bars around the Midwest, singing hymns and then smashing bottles and furniture with her hatchet. This strategy of "hatchetation" made her a popular icon of the temperance movement, although more respectable leaders took pains to distance themselves from her. She supported her activities by giving lectures and eventually performed in the vaudeville circuit, recreating scenes of saloon smashing.

See Also: Gilded Age; Temperance Movements; Women in American History; Women's Movement.

■ **NATIONAL AERONAUTICS AND SPACE ADMINISTRATION (NASA),** U.S. government agency in charge of space exploration. NASA was created (1958) during Pres. Dwight D. Eisenhower's administration, one year after the Soviet Union launched the first man-made earth satellite. The so-called space race was part of the Cold War competition between the United States and the U.S.S.R. When in 1961 Pres. John F. Kennedy pledged to land Americans on the moon before the end of the decade, NASA was given the assignment. On July 20, 1969, Neil Armstrong and Edwin Aldrin walked on the moon. NASA's next

Carry Nation was one of the most vehement leaders of the prohibition movement in the early 20th century.

major project was the space shuttle program, designed to make space travel routine and relatively inexpensive; the first shuttle flight took place in 1981. The worst tragedy of the program occurred on Jan. 28, 1986, when the shuttle *Challenger* exploded shortly after take-off, killing its crew. In the 1990s, without a new mission that excited the public imagination, NASA's activities were substantially reduced.

See Also: Space Exploration.

BIBLIOGRAPHY: Wolfe, Tom, *The Right Stuff* (Farrar, Straus, & Giroux 1979).

■ **NATIONAL ARCHIVES,** U.S. government agency created in 1934 to take charge of government records. Previously each department was in charge of its own files. The National Archives and Records Administration operates central repositories in the Washington, D.C., area, regional archives across the country, and presidential libraries. Originals of both the Declaration of Independence (1776) and the Constitution (1787) are displayed at the archives headquarters in Washington, D.C.

■ NATIONAL ASSOCIATION FOR THE ADVANCEMENT OF COLORED PEOPLE (NAACP),

organization committed to achieving political, educational, and civil equality for African Americans. The NAACP was founded in New York City in 1909-10 by a group of white and African-American intellectuals who opposed the gradualist integration policies of Booker T. Washington. Among its many programs to promote racial equality was its official magazine, *Crisis*, edited by W. E. B. Du Bois.

The NAACP also began a campaign for equality and desegregation through the courts. It won important victories before the U.S. Supreme Court, including *Guinn v. United States* (1915), which struck down the grandfather clause. During the 1920s and 1930s the NAACP focused on anti-lynching legislation. Through the efforts of organization leaders such as James Weldon Johnson and Walter White, the NAACP saw its membership in the South burgeon as it became the country's most influential civil rights group.

In 1950, the NAACP began its campaign to overturn the legal doctrine of racial segregation in schools. Attacking *Plessy v. Ferguson* (1896), the organization's lawyers won a historic victory in *Brown v. Board of Education of Topeka* (1954), which declared segregation in schools unconstitutional.

Although rivalries between civil rights groups during the 1960s threatened the movement, the NAACP helped organize such mass actions as the March on Washington in 1963. The NAACP remains one of the most visible forces confronting racial injustice in modern America.

See Also: African Americans; Brown v. Board of Education of Topeka; Civil Rights Movement; Du Bois, W. E. B.; Washington, Booker Taliaferro.

■ *NATIONAL ASSOCIATION FOR THE ADVANCEMENT OF COLORED PEOPLE (NAACP) V. ALABAMA EX. REL PATT* (1958),

U.S. Supreme Court case that established freedom of association as part of the First Amendment's protections of free speech and assembly. The case reached the Supreme Court after an Alabama state court held the

NAACP in contempt and fined the organization $100,000 for violating the state's corporate filing laws. Alabama officials had sought to bar the NAACP from operating in the state on the grounds that the organization's desegregation campaigns threatened the rights of Alabama citizens. The state court demanded a list of all NAACP members. The NAACP said such a list could be used to harass and intimidate members, effectively denying them their First Amendment rights.

The Court agreed (9-0) that a right to free association, while not explicitly stated, was implicit in the First Amendment. The Court ruled that any requirement that members of the NAACP announce their intention to associate would have a chilling effect on both that right and the organization. It found that Alabama had shown no overriding need to obtain the names and set aside the lower court judgment. The decision was a major victory for the civil rights movement in the South as well as another example of the Supreme Court's tendency in the 1950s and 1960s to expand individual civil liberties.

See Also: National Association for the Advancement of Colored People (NAACP); Supreme Court.

BIBLIOGRAPHY: Hughes, Langston, *Fight for Freedom: The Story of the NAACP* (Norton 1962); Raines, Howell, *My Soul Is Rested: Movement Days in the Deep South Remembered* (Putnam 1977).

■ NATIONAL ASSOCIATION OF COLORED WOMEN,

voluntary benevolent organization of African-American women committed to social activism. Chartered in 1895, the association's chapters devoted themselves to the social, economic, religious, and moral welfare of women and children. Following their motto, "Lifting As We Climb," the organization has sought to improve community life through the creation of hospitals, girls' homes, and other social work.

See Also: Civil Rights Movement.

■ NATIONAL ASSOCIATION OF MANUFACTURERS (NAM),

organization formed in 1895 to address issues of national concern to manufacturers in the United States. It advocated specific policies and sent representatives to Washington to lobby for favorable legislation such as uniform commercial codes and a canal through Nicaragua.

After 1902, the NAM became a militant opponent of organized labor. When the National Labor Relations Act (Wagner Act) of 1935 guaranteed labor the right to organize, the NAM set out to dissolve union power through legislation such as the Taft-Hartley Act of 1947.

See Also: Industrial Revolution; National Labor Relations Act; Taft-Hartley Act.

■ **NATIONAL BANKING SYSTEM,** monetary and banking system set up by the Lincoln administration and Congress during the Civil War. Controlling the federal government, the Republican party took effective action to provide for the financial demands of the war, establish a stable currency, and stimulate economic growth. The Legal Tender Act of 1862 authorized the issuance of $150 million in Treasury notes ("greenbacks"), creating the first national paper currency in American history. The National Banking Act of 1863 granted federal charters to state banks that met certain standards. The charters required them to buy federal bonds and allowed them to issue banknotes equal to 90 percent of the value of the bonds. A tax levied on state banknotes in 1865 drove most out of circulation and forced state banks to convert to the federal charters. These measures established the basis for a banking system that lasted until the creation of the Federal Reserve System in 1913.

See Also: Greenbacks.

■ **NATIONAL COLORED FARMERS' ALLIANCE,** collective of southern African-American farmers organized by Charles W. Macune. More than 1 million farmers joined the alliance by 1889 in an effort to exert political and economic power.

See Also: African Americans; Civil Rights Movement.

■ **NATIONAL CONGRESS OF AMERICAN INDIANS (NCAI),** pan-tribal group founded in 1944 to advocate for American Indian causes. The original organization contained leaders from 50 tribes nationwide who stated as their goals protection of Indian civil rights, improvement of education, protection of cultural values, and settlement of Indian claims against the U.S. government. The NCAI lobbied for legislation establishing the Indian Claims Commission in 1946 and fought against the termination policy (which ended support and programs for several tribes) and relocation in the 1950s.

See Also: Indian Claims Commission (ICC); Indians of North America; Relocation; Termination.

■ **NATIONAL DEFENSE ACT (1916),** legislation to strengthen the U.S. military establishment. Passed while World War I raged in Europe but before the United States entered the conflict, it provided for an expanded army and more training facilities.

See Also: World War I.

■ **NATIONAL EDUCATION ASSOCIATION,** American teachers' organization. Founded in 1857 and chartered by Congress in 1906, it represents elementary, high school, and college teachers across the country. The organization claimed 2.2 million members in 13,000 communities in 1996.

■ **NATIONAL FARMERS' ALLIANCE,** agrarian reform movement of the late 19th century. There were, in fact, three organizations that went by the name National Farmers' Alliance during the 1880s: the Northern Farmers' Alliance; the Southern Farmers' Alliance and Industrial Union; and the National Colored Farmers' Alliance, a primarily African-American movement. Each shared many of the same concerns about the increasingly unstable position of the American farmer. Much like the Granger Movement before it, the Farmers' Alliance experimented with self-help and collective enterprises, but its limited success in these ventures propelled the alliance into politics. In 1892, representatives from the various branches of the National Farmers' Alliance met in Omaha, Nebraska, to launch the People's (Populist) party.

See Also: Agriculture; Granger Movement; Populism.

■ **NATIONAL LABOR RELATIONS ACT (1935),** law that created the National Labor Relations Board (NLRB) and guaranteed workers the right to unionize and bargain collectively. Despite the unprecedented social and economic reforms of the early New Deal measures of 1933, many Americans continued to need relief and felt unsatisfied with the pace of reform. Discontent manifested itself among laborers in the widespread strikes of the spring and summer of 1934. Recognizing the persisting inequities, Pres. Franklin D. Roosevelt initiated new measures in 1935 in an effort to expand progressive lawmaking. The National Labor Relations Act (known also as the Wagner Act for its chief sponsor, Sen. Robert F. Wagner of New York) was passed during this period.

The act established the right of workers to seek improved wages, benefits, and working conditions through unions and collective bargaining. The NLRB was to serve as the official body to protect these rights. Its two primary functions were to supervise secret-ballot elections for workers to determine union representation and to stop unfair labor practices by employers. The act stimulated union growth, especially in the steel, automobile, and textile industries, and broadened support for Roosevelt and the New Deal. The Wagner Act had an adverse effect on labor, however, as the NLRB's role as mediator between unions and employers weakened the effectiveness of strikes.

—GUY NELSON

See Also: Hundred Days; Labor Movement; New Deal; Wagner, Robert Ferdinand.

BIBLIOGRAPHY: Conkin, Paul K., *The New Deal* (Harlan Davidson 1975).

■ **NATIONAL ORGANIZATION FOR WOMEN (NOW),** the largest and most influential U.S. women's organization. On June 30, 1966, feminists founded NOW in response to the Equal Employment Opportunity Commission's refusal to recognize sexual as well as racial discrimination. With author Betty Friedan as its first president, NOW released the 1967 Bill of Rights, demanding equal employment and educational opportunities, child care, legalized abortion, passage of the Equal Rights Amendment (ERA), and other reforms. In 1970 NOW founded the NOW Legal Defense and Education Fund to concentrate on workplace and family issues.

With its philosophy of "full equality for women in truly equal partnership with men" in all areas of society, NOW defined 1970s feminism. The 1970s and 1980s saw the founding of other organizations, many by former NOW officers, devoted to NOW's mission. The fight to pass the ERA and to secure legal abortion occupied NOW in the 1970s. The failure to win ratification of the ERA and the rise of the right-to-life movement in the 1980s were setbacks, but NOW's influence has grown steadily.

NOW's pragmatic strategy concentrates on legal reform and attitudinal and behavior changes to transform a sexist society. In addition to more traditional activities—marching, lobbying, and disseminating information—it has focused on issues of housework-sharing, representations of women in the media, and the use of the term *Ms.*

Although often characterized as a forum for white middle-class women, NOW has struggled, sometimes against itself, to include the elderly, women of color, poor women, lesbians, and radical feminists and to address the issues of these groups. NOW's commitment to egalitarianism has allowed local chapters the freedom to address local needs. In the mid-1990s NOW had 260,000 members and 600 chapters and was active in all 50 states.

—CATHERINE ALLGOR

See Also: Abortion; Equal Rights Amendment (ERA); Friedan, Betty; Women in American History; Women's Movement.

BIBLIOGRAPHY: Carden, Maren Lockwood, *The New Feminist Movement* (Russell Sage 1974); Frost-Knappman, Elizabeth, *Women's Progress in America* (ABC-CLIO 1994).

■ **NATIONAL ORIGINS ACT (1924),** immigration law designed to limit entries to the United States from southeastern Europe and Japan. The act mandated that the number of immigrants admitted annually from a given country could not exceed 2 percent of that nationality's population in the United States in 1890, a time when most immigrants were of western European origin.

See Also: Immigration.

■ **NATIONAL PARKS,** first established to protect the "natural curiosities" of the landscape of the American West. In 1864, at the request of a group of citizens including prominent landscape architect Frederick Law Olmsted, designer of New York's Central Park, Congress granted the spectacular Yosemite Valley to the state of California "for public use, resort and recreation." A few years later, Congress moved to protect the geothermal wonders of the Yellowstone region as a "pleasuring ground for the benefit and enjoyment of the people," but since no state had yet been created for this western territory, the legislation passed in 1872 placed Yellowstone under federal protection as a "national park." The United States thus became the world's first nation to create such a preserve.

Yellowstone remained unique until 1890, when Congress applied the same designation to the wilderness areas surrounding the Yosemite Valley (which the state of California voluntarily returned to federal control in 1906) and likewise marked off the region of soaring sequoia redwoods in the southern Sierra Nevada mountains of California as Sequoia National Park. Over the next 25 years, Congress created several additional western parks, including Mount Rainier (1899) in the state of Washington, Crater Lake (1902) in Oregon, Glacier (1910) in Montana, and Hawaii Volcanoes (1916) on the island of Hawaii. These facilities were administered by the army until 1916, when Congress established the National Park Service as part of the Department of Interior.

National parks are often confused with national forests, but they are quite different. The mandate of the U.S. Forest Service (established in 1905 within the Agriculture Department), which oversees hundreds of millions of acres, involves the conservation of forest resources and their use by means of lumbering, mining, and grazing. No such uses are permitted in the areas supervised by the National Park Service. Pursuing the sometimes contradictory goals of both "pleasure" and "preservation," the Park Service has built highways and trails to facilitate public access, erected interpretive facilities, and laid out tourist villages within national parks. Controversy has accompanied these operations since the 1920s, when concerned scientists first complained that the development of public recreational facilities was compromising the well-being of natural landscapes and their wildlife. These controversies have grown more intense over the 20th century and are not likely to go away.

Most of the parks administered by the Park Service are in the West, not only because of the spectacular landscape there, but because the extensive federal land holdings in the West made the generation of parks there a matter of simply

Mount Fairweather rises in Glacier Bay National Park in Alaska, where many of the largest parks are located. Yellowstone, the first national park, was established in 1872.

transferring authority from one federal department to another. The creation of national parks in the East was more difficult, for it required the acquisition of land. The first eastern example, Acadia National Park in Maine, was established in 1919 after wealthy residents of the Bar Harbor area donated Mount Desert Island to the federal government. Great Smoky Mountains National Park (1930) in North Carolina and Shenandoah National Park (1935) in Virginia were created from lands donated by the Rockefeller family.

Monuments and Historic Sites. In 1933 the Park Service was given the additional responsibility of administering the system of "National Monuments." The Antiquities Act of 1906 had given the president the authority to declare such preserves where he determined there were threats to sites of cultural or natural significance. Pres. Theodore Roosevelt acted immediately, proclaiming the spectacular cliff dwellings of Mesa Verde in Colorado and Devil's Tower in Wyoming as national monuments. Presidents have frequently used this designation to protect sites prior to their establishment as national parks by Congress. Thus Grand Canyon, declared a monument by Roosevelt in 1908, became a national park by congressional action in 1919; and 56 million acres of public lands in Alaska, designated national monuments by Pres. Jimmy Carter in 1978, were made into national parks by Congress a decade later.

Congress passed the Historic Sites Act in 1935, placing under the jurisdiction of the Park Service the responsibility for sites of national historic significance, places such as Fort Sumter in South Carolina, the Statue of Liberty in New York City, and Gettysburg Cemetery in Pennsylvania. This mandate was further expanded under the terms of the National Historic Preservation Act (1966). The Park Service keeps the National Register of Historic Places, the nation's official list of historic properties worthy of preservation. It has also created a number of "National Historical Parks," such as the one established at Lowell, Massachusetts, in 1978, which illustrates the early industrial heritage of the country.

—JOHN MACK FARAGHER

See Also: *Frontier in American History; Grand Canyon; Yellowstone; Yosemite.*

BIBLIOGRAPHY: Bartlett, Richard A., *Nature's Yellowstone* (Univ. of New Mexico Press 1974); Bartlett, Richard A., *Yellowstone: A Wilderness Besieged* (Univ. of Arizona Press 1985); Murtagh, William J., *Keeping Time: The History and Theory of Preservation in America* (Main Street Press 1988); Runte, Alfred, *National Parks: The American Experience*, 3rd ed. (Univ. of Nebraska Press 1997).

■ **NATIONAL PROHIBITION ENFORCEMENT ACT (1919),** law passed by Congress to enforce the recently adopted 18th Amendment, which made illegal the manufacture, transportation, or sale of intoxicating liquors after Jan. 20, 1920. The act became best known as the Volstead Act, for its author, Rep. Andrew Joseph Volstead of Minnesota. Because little money was appropriated, however, enforcement was generally lax, at best.

See Also: *Prohibition.*

■ **NATIONAL RECLAMATION ACT (1902),** federal legislation passed as part of Pres. Theodore Roosevelt's program of conservation, an attempt to preserve and protect the natural environment. The act expanded government reserves to almost 200 million acres.

■ **NATIONAL RECOVERY ADMINISTRATION (NRA),** New Deal agency (1933-35) that sought to stabilize the economy by creating industrial codes. Created by Pres. Franklin Roosevelt's National Industrial Recovery Act (1933), the NRA helped industries write codes dictating wages, production, prices, and manufacturing processes. Led by the flamboyant Gen. Hugh Johnson, the NRA launched a nationwide publicity campaign to restore consumer confidence in the economy. Businesses displayed the NRA's blue eagle symbol and "We Do Our Part" motto. The NRA codes attracted criticism from both liberals, who felt the codes unfairly benefited big business, and conservatives, who claimed the codes gave government too much influence over business. Important elements of the NRA were ruled unconstitutional by the Supreme Court in *Schecter Poultry Co. v. U.S.* (1935), which NRA critics dubbed "the dead chicken case" as a slurring parody of the blue eagle symbol.

See Also: *New Deal; Schecter Poultry Co. v. United States.*

BIBLIOGRAPHY: Brand, Donald R., *Corporatism and the Rule of Law: A Study of the National Recovery Administration* (Cornell Univ. Press 1988).

■ **NATIONAL REPUBLICAN PARTY,** American political party that emerged as an alternative to the Republican party that supported Andrew Jackson. After the election of John Quincy Adams by the U.S. House of Representatives in 1824, the (Jeffersonian) Republican party split in two. The name given to the supporters of President Adams and Sec. of State Henry Clay was "National Republicans," and the name applied to the supporters of Jackson was "Democratic-Republicans." The National Republicans supported Northern economic interests and an active capitalist state, arguing that free enterprise is the cornerstone of equality. They argued for a strong national economy based on a national currency, the promotion of manufacturing, and the extension of America's national market through internal improvements. Jacksonian Democrats opposed national currency, high tariffs, and internal improvements. Jacksonians denounced the National Republicans as "stingy undemocratic" aristocrats bent on controlling the nation's wealth. The National Republicans were absorbed by the Whig party in 1834.

See Also: *Adams, John Quincy; Political Parties; Whig Party.*

■ **NATIONAL ROAD,** federally funded road from the Atlantic coast to Ohio and beyond, symbolizing the nation's commitment to westward expansion and a period of nationalistic internal improvements. Construction began in 1811, and by 1838 the road was open from Cumberland, Maryland, to Vandalia, Illinois.

See Also: Transportation.

■ **NATIONAL SECURITY ACTS (1947, 1949),** laws revamping the U.S. military establishment after World War II by creating a unified Department of Defense. The 1947 act created an independent U.S. Air Force and the National Military Establishment to oversee all armed forces. It also established the Central Intelligence Agency and the National Security Council to advise the president. The 1949 act brought the services together under a single cabinet-level Department of Defense.

See Also: Central Intelligence Agency (CIA); Cold War; Defense, Department of.

■ **NATIONAL YOUTH ADMINISTRATION,** program established in 1935 as part of the federal Works Progress (later Projects) Administration. It provided part-time jobs to high school and college students, including many African Americans, through its Office of Minority Affairs.

See Also: New Deal; Works Projects Administration (WPA).

■ **NATIVE AMERICAN CHURCH (chartered 1918),** pan-tribal church also known as the Peyote religion. The Native American Church began informally in the 1880s as a Christian movement that stressed family, self-help, reciprocity, frugality, and the avoidance of alcohol. Although it contained many elements of evangelical Christianity, the central ritual of the Native American Church was the ingestion of the hallucinogen peyote in an elaborate ceremony during which the participants sought knowledge and healing. The Peyote religion spread throughout Indian Country and, in some communities, worked to counteract the devastating effects of cultural disintegration by providing Indians with a distinctive religion. Although the use of peyote brought U.S. attempts to suppress the religion and its ceremonies, those attempts failed. Peyote use is strictly controlled,

however, and non-Indians are prohibited from participation.

See Also: Indians of North America.

■ **NATIVISM,** the attitude or policy of favoring native Americans over immigrants, has been a persistent feature of American life since the mid-19th century. Nativist sentiment first arose during the wave of German and Irish immigration in the late 1840s and 1850s. Most of these immigrants moved into urban neighborhoods where they retained their native language and customs, including their Roman Catholicism; frequently they affiliated with the Democratic party, which during the Jacksonian period had organized urban political machines in the large cities of the northeast. Anti-Jackson forces thus also tended to be nativist in their outlook. They built a nativist political movement in the American party, known as the Know-Nothings. But nativist politics soon were submerged in the growing political debate over slavery.

Nativism reemerged after the Civil War, first in the West, where there was a vigorous anti-Chinese campaign. Between 1850 and 1880 more than 300,000 Chinese entered the country, and especially during the depression years of the 1870s, many white workers viewed them as competitors for scarce jobs. There were anti-Chinese riots throughout the West, most notably in San Francisco in 1877, where Chinese homes and businesses were burned, and in Rock Springs, Wyoming, in 1885, where mobs burned Chinatown and 28 Chinese died in the flames. In 1882, Congress passed the Chinese Exclusion Act, which suspended Chinese immigration, limited the civil rights of resident Chinese, and forbade their naturalization. Similar sentiments were applied to the Japanese who settled on the Pacific Coast; their immigration was restricted by the so-called Gentleman's Agreement that Pres. Theodore Roosevelt made with the Japanese government in 1908, and in 1921 the Supreme Court ruled them ineligible for naturalization.

The huge wave of immigration from eastern and southern Europe that began in the 1890s was a cause for the revival of nativism in the East. The American Protective Association and the Immigration Restriction League were two organizations of the 1890s that lobbied Congress for limits on immigration. A spate of books appeared decrying the negative effects of foreign influence; in *The Passing of the Great Race* (1916), Madison Grant argued that inferior southern and eastern European and Jewish stock threatened the superior "Aryan" American race. These sentiments were fueled by the "100 percent Americanism" campaign of World War I then aggravated by the postwar depression. In the early 1920s the Ku Klux Klan reemerged from obscurity as a nativist organization. Organizing around the slogan "Native, White, Protestant Supremacy," the KKK counted 3 million members by 1924.

The Immigration Act of that year fundamentally revised American immigration policy, setting the maximum level at 164,000 persons per year and establishing quotas for national groups based on their representation in the census of 1890, before the great wave of "new immigration" had begun. Congressman Albert Johnson, cosponsor of the legislation, declared that it would prevent America from being "diluted by a stream of alien blood." This quota system lasted for 41 years, not repealed until the Immigration Act of 1965. In the 30 subsequent years some 14 million new immigrants have entered the country legally, the majority from Asia and Latin America; in addition, authorities estimate that 5 to 10 million people (most from Mexico) entered illegally. This new wave of immigration has likewise spawned a new nativist movement, much of it focusing on demands that English be made the official language of the country.

—JOHN MACK FARAGHER

See Also: *Chinese Exclusion Act; Immigration; Know-Nothing Party.*

BIBLIOGRAPHY: Bennett, David H., *The Party of Fear* (Univ. of North Carolina Press 1988); Higham, John, *Strangers in the Land: Patterns of American Nativism* (Rutgers Univ. Press 1988); Knobel, Dale T., *America for the Americans: The Nativist Movement in the United States* (Twayne 1996); Tatalovich, Raymond, *Nativism Reborn? The Official English Language Movement and the American States* (Univ. Press of Kentucky 1995).

■ **NAT TURNER'S INSURRECTION (1831),** loosely organized slave uprising led by the charismatic Nat Turner in Southampton County, Virginia. Nat Turner was born the slave of Benjamin Turner in Southampton County. From a very early age, Nat's mother, father, and African grandmother inculcated in him a belief that he was marked for some great purpose. Religion early preoccupied him, and he often spent long periods of time by himself in the woods, fasting and praying. During one of these devotions Nat believed God ordained him to accomplish great things in the world. By 1825 he had concluded that he was appointed to lead a dramatic battle between whites and blacks. By the late 1820s he was becoming a celebrated preacher at revivals. Nat recognized his great power over his fellow slaves and as early as 1825 "began to prepare them for my purpose."

From the late 1820s, Nat perceived natural signs that reinforced his belief in an impending racial conflagration. After an eclipse in February 1831, Nat concluded the time had come to begin organizing others, and he revealed his mission to four trusted friends. They had planned to commence "the work of death" on the fourth of July but Nat became sick, perhaps with anxiety, and the action had to be postponed. On August 20, Nat and his trusted cohorts met one last time and planned a barbeque for the rebels for the next night, just prior to beginning the uprising. At about 2:00 A.M. on August 22, the party of seven men stealthily entered the house of Joseph Travis, where Nat currently worked. Their plan was fairly simple: move quickly and quietly through their rural area, killing all the whites they encountered whether in houses or outside, seizing their horses and weapons, and rallying their slaves to follow them, thus steadily expanding the rebels' numbers. At the Travis house, all five occupants were killed with ax blows to the head, guns and powder seized, and several more slaves recruited. From there they moved on to another house where they murdered more residents. This pattern continued until well after daybreak; as the number of rebels grew, the murdered mounted, and the rebels had encountered only light resistance. By noon they were at their greatest strength, with up to 60 armed and mounted slaves and close to 60 white men, women, and children killed. Nat now decided to march toward Jerusalem, the county seat.

But by then the surrounding countryside had been alerted, and whites had either fled their homes or armed themselves in defense while local militias were summoned and readied. When a number of Nat's soldiers approached another house soon after noon, they were repulsed by a small militia there. While they suffered no losses, his troops began becoming disorganized and started deserting. Soon he discovered that the main road to Jerusalem was guarded and that a secondary route was also blocked. Other attempted assaults were repulsed, and some of Nat's principal associates were captured or killed. By the evening of August 23, the rebels were totally dispersed, and Nat fled alone. He hid in various places around the Travis farm until he was discovered and captured on October 30. He was tried and executed by hanging on November 11. Prior to his apprehension, more than 50 implicated slaves and a few free blacks had been tried. About 15 were acquitted while 17 were hanged and the balance convicted and transported.

Repercussions. The repercussions from the uprising were immediate and dramatic. Whites in Virginia and the rest of the South were horrified by the slaughter and by the betrayal of slaves they imagined loyal. Violent reprisals against blacks, free and slave, fell swiftly. Some have estimated that well over 100 innocent blacks were killed in these actions. Panics over further slave uprisings swept Virginia and North Carolina in Turner's wake. While not definitely established, some evidence suggests that Turner may have laid plans with other rebels in Virginia and North Carolina for a much larger insurrection but that they moved one week too soon and foiled the plot. Throughout Virginia and the South, laws restricting slave religious worship were reinforced, especially those pertaining to slave preachers. The uprising contributed significantly to deepening doubts in Virginia about slavery's viability, and while Virginia finally recommitted itself to slavery, Nat's legacy haunted the South for the balance of the antebellum years.

—PETER HINKS

See Also: African Americans; Slave Revolts.
BIBLIOGRAPHY: Oates, Stephen B., *The Fires of Jubilee: Nat Turner's Fierce Rebellion* (Harper & Row 1975); Tragle, Henry Irving, *The Southampton Slave Revolt of 1831: A Compilation of Source Material* (Univ. of Massachusetts Press 1971).

■ **NATURALISM,** turn-of-the-century literary and artistic movement. Naturalism shared with realism a commitment to the accurate representation of everyday life but allowed for a deeper exploration of the role of external forces on its characters. Naturalists were influenced by Charles Darwin's theories of evolution and natural selection, which they tried to adapt to social situations. They believed in historical determinism, especially as explained by Karl Marx. Life was seen as a product of chance as much as intention. Interior influences and emotions did feature prominently in the lives of characters in naturalist novels, but these were presented as animalistic and uncontrollable, such as the drives of fear and hunger. Influenced by the French novelists Emile Zola and the Goncourt brothers, American naturalist authors explored the influence of heredity and environment on human development, particularly in urban and working-class settings and characters. Stephen Crane's *Maggie: A Girl of the Streets* (1893), Frank Norris's *McTeague* (1899), and Theodore Dreiser's *Sister Carrie* (1900) established their authors as leaders of literary naturalism. Naturalist writing could be taken to the point of propaganda, as in Upton Sinclair's *The Jungle* (1906). In painting naturalism tended to focus more on the power of nature over people or on a particular environment. Winslow Homer and Albert Pinkham Ryder were the leading naturalist painters of the late 19th and early 20th centuries.

See Also: Realism.
BIBLIOGRAPHY: Pizer, Donald, *The Theory and Practice of American Literary Naturalism* (Southern Illinois Univ. Press 1993).

■ **NATURALIZATION ACT (1798),** law that extended the period of residence for U.S. citizenship from 5 to 14 years. This act was passed by the Federalist majority in Congress, which feared that immigrants were introducing dangerous democratic and republican ideals.

See Also: Immigration.

■ **NAVAHO,** the largest Indian tribe in the United States, with over 100,000 members. The Navahos (or Navajos) also occupy the largest reservation in the United States, an area of more than 28,000 square miles that includes parts of Arizona, New Mexico, and Utah. The reservation encompasses much of the Navahos' traditional land, which is defined by four sacred mountains. The area is made up primarily of desert grasslands and sage brush areas. The higher elevations, above 7,500 feet, are forested with Ponderosa pine, Douglas fir, and aspen.

The Navahos belong to the Na-Dene language family. Their arrival in the Southwest from Canada has been dated to the 15th century by studying Navaho architecture. Hogans, round houses of forked poles and brush covered with earth, are distinctive to the Navahos. They practiced hunting, gathering, and limited agriculture. The Pueblo cultures in the vicinity influenced the Navahos, who learned weaving and agricultural techniques that led them to a less nomadic lifestyle. The Navahos, however, incorporated Pueblo traits into their own distinctive values, continuing to live in small scattered camps rather than towns as the Pueblo did. In religious rituals the Navahos emphasized individual rather than community goals. They acquired sheep and goats from the Spanish, and livestock became a vital part of their cultural life and economy. Over time Navaho silverwork and weaving became highly prized.

Resistance by the Navahos to Spanish and later American incursions into their territory lasted until the late 1860s, when they were finally able to secure a 3.5-million-acre reservation where they could raise their livestock. During World War II, Navaho recruits became renowned for their language abilities. The Navaho language was used as a code and was never broken by the Axis powers. Navaho "code talkers" are recognized in annual celebrations. In recent years the extraction of oil, gas, coal, and uranium from reservation lands has made some Navaho wealthy. But many still earn modest livings from sheepherding and artwork.

—RYAN MADDEN

See Also: Indians of North America; Pueblo.
BIBLIOGRAPHY: Downs, James, *The Navajo* (Holt 1972); Weaver, Thomas, ed., *Indians of Arizona* (Univ. of Arizona Press 1974).

■ **NAVAL ACADEMY,** U.S. military school. It was established in 1845 when Sec. of the Navy George

Bancroft set aside Fort Severn in Annapolis, Maryland, for educational purposes and ordered midshipmen to report there after finishing their sea tours. Like West Point, Annapolis represented a large step forward in military professionalism. The academy moved to Newport, Rhode Island, for the duration of the Civil War (1861-65). Its example helped create the Naval War College in Newport, Rhode Island, and the Naval Postgraduate School in Monterey, California. The academy's annual enrollment is about 3,400. Most of the students are selected by the president, vice president, and members of Congress and from among the children of naval personnel.

■ **NAVAL STORES ACT (1705),** one of the Acts of Trade and Navigation (1651-1767), which placed the regulation of colonial commerce within the scope of England's mercantilist policies. The act added naval stores (such as pitch, tar, resin, turpentine, lumber) to a list of enumerated colonial articles that could only be shipped to England and its colonies and sought to foster their production by offering bounties on them.
See Also: Navigation Acts.

■ **NAVIGATION ACTS (1651-1767),** series of English commercial laws designed to regulate colonial trade for the economic benefit of England and to ensure colonial dependence. Throughout the colonial period, new statutes were passed and enforcement of old ones made stricter, as English administration developed and as colonials sought ways to circumvent the legislation.

In the face of a burgeoning Dutch trade in the Atlantic, Parliament passed the Navigation Act of 1651. Three of its provisions, which formed the basis for colonial commerce, assured strict English control of trade, limiting intercolonial commerce and economic independence. In 1660, new legislation expanded previous statutes by requiring certain "enumerated goods" of colonial growth or manufacture to be shipped first to England. In 1663, Parliament passed a new statute designed to impose a monopoly on colonial ports, primarily through high duties.

Ineffective administration and colonial evasion of the laws resulted in modified legislation in 1673 and 1696. Although the 1673 law imposed a tax on departure of goods from colonial ports, its purpose was not revenue but regulation. The 1696 statute outlined a series of changes in colonial administration of commerce.

During the 18th century, Parliament only passed supplementary legislation. In the colonies, officials often looked away while colonial merchants continued to trade relatively freely. After 1760, however, English officials began to rigorously enforce the Navigation Acts, thus causing increased colonial resistance and resentment that led to the American Revolution.

See Also: Revolution, American.

BIBLIOGRAPHY: Harper, Lawrence A., *The English Navigation Laws: A Seventeenth-Century Experiment in Social Engineering* (Octagon Books 1964).

■ **NAVY,** military sea power of the U.S. government. Long coastlines and extensive seaborne commerce make a navy vital to the United States. During the Revolutionary War (1775-83), the Continental navy was established to ferry diplomats and munitions, capture supplies, provide coastal defense, and pressure Britons by attacking their coasts and commerce. Although minuscule compared to Britain's Royal Navy, American naval forces accomplished all these things and also won a strategic victory at Lake Champlain's Valcour Island (1776).

Growth of the Navy. Nearly bankrupt, the United States was without a navy from 1785 to 1794, when attacks on its merchant shipping led to the establishment of the U.S. Navy. The fledgling service won single-ship actions against France during the Quasi-War (1798-1800), against the Barbary corsairs during the war with Tripoli (1801-05), and against Britain during the War of 1812 (1812-15), as well as decisive squadron victories against the British on Lakes Erie (1813) and Champlain (1814).

When the United States extended its commerce around the world, the navy was reorganized under the Board of Navy Commissioners (1815), and its ships were divided into squadrons stationed in the Mediterranean, Caribbean, East Indies, South Atlantic, and Pacific. The 1840s and 1850s saw the establishment of the bureau system (1842), which divided administrative responsibilities, and Naval Academy (1845); the seizure

of California and the defeat of Mexico (1845-48); the collection of wind and ocean current data and the exploring expeditions to the South Seas (1838-42), Dead Sea (1848), and North Pacific (1853-55); the adoption of steam-powered, iron-hulled vessels with innovative ordnance; and diplomatic initiatives such as the "opening" of Japan (1853-54).

During the Civil War, the navy grew from 50 to 600 vessels and contributed to the Union victory by blockading the South, supporting army operations on the Mississippi River, and capturing Confederate ports, including New Orleans (1862) and Mobile (1864). The first engagement between ironclad ships, the battle between the *Monitor* and the *Merrimack*, took place during the war. Postwar retrenchment ended in the 1880s when Americans, looking outward, began constructing a "New Navy" of steel cruisers and battleships. Establishment of the Naval Institute (1873), Office of Naval Intelligence (1882), and Naval War College (1884) heralded a new professionalism. At century's end, naval historian Alfred T. Mahan's writings provided an intellectual rationale for naval expansion while rallying support for the navy.

Seeking Command of the Sea. Victories at Manila Bay and Santiago during the Spanish-American War (1898) shattered Spanish power and marked the emergence of the United States as a world power with the acquisition of the Philippines, Puerto Rico, and Hawaii. The navy replaced its traditional strategy of coastal defense and commerce raids with a strategy of seeking battle with enemy fleets to obtain command of the sea. In 1916, Pres. Woodrow Wilson vowed to build "a navy second to none," and although it played little role in World War I, the navy emerged by 1920 able to claim parity with Britain's at the Washington Naval Conference (1921-22). Starved for funds during the 1920s and 1930s, the navy nevertheless continued both its tradition of exploration by sending expeditions to polar regions and its technological leadership by creating an air arm. The rise of totalitarian regimes and a desire to create jobs during the Depression of the 1930s led to programs that provided most of the ships that fought World War II.

Japan's 1941 attack on Pearl Harbor propelled the United States into global war. Commanded by

Ernest Joseph King and Chester Nimitz, naval forces protected Allied shipping and supported amphibious assaults on North Africa, Italy, and Normandy in the war against Germany and won crushing victories against Japan at Midway (1942), the Philippine Sea (1944), and Leyte Gulf (1944) in the Pacific. It supported the Army's drive from New Guinea to the Philippines while conducting its own campaign in the Solomon Islands and driving across the Central Pacific in its assault on the Gilbert, Marshall, and Marianas Islands, Iwo Jima, and Okinawa.

Late 20th Century. In 1950, the U.S. Navy stood unchallenged at sea but was vulnerable to cost-cutters and air power advocates at home until the Korean War demonstrated the need for sea transport, carrier aviation, and amphibious forces. During the Cold War, the United States used its navy to counter Soviet influence around the world. New destroyers and weapons systems were developed to protect sea lines of communications, and Adm. Hyman Rickover spearheaded the design and construction of nuclear-powered submarines capable of destroying enemy submarines and firing ballistic and cruise missiles as part of America's strategic deterrent forces.

Operations in the Vietnam War forced postponement of fleet modernization and gave the U.S.S.R. a chance to mount a challenge at sea. Post-Vietnam reductions in defense spending and the adoption of the "volunteer" military weakened the navy during the 1970s, but it rebounded during the 1980s with new classes of ships and an aggressive "maritime strategy." Greatly reduced following the implosion of the Soviet Union, the navy still performed well in support of interventions in Panama (1989-90) and Haiti (1995), in the Gulf War (1991), and in evacuating Americans from Liberia (1990) and Somalia (1991). As it begins its third century, the U.S. Navy is undergoing many changes: in doctrine, to allow it to operate jointly with other services; in missions, by adding humanitarian relief and peacekeeping to traditional forms of intervention; in personnel, as women enter combat positions; and in technology, should it adopt the arsenal ship, arguably the first new type of ship since the aircraft carriers and nuclear-powered submarine.

—JAMES C. BRADFORD

See Also: Civil War; Korean War; Naval Academy; Spanish-American War; Vietnam War; War of 1812; World War II.

BIBLIOGRAPHY: Hagan, Kenneth J., *This People's Navy* (The Free Press 1991); Love, Robert W., Jr., *History of the U.S. Navy,* 2 vols. (Stackpole Books 1992).

■ **NEAR V. MINNESOTA (1931),** U.S. Supreme Court case concerning freedom of the press. The Court struck down (5-4) a Minnesota "gag law" that allowed a judge to halt the publication of "scandalous" or otherwise offensive newspaper articles. In a test case involving the weekly *Saturday Press* of Minneapolis, the Court ruled such prior restraint violates 1st Amendment protections incorporated in the 14th Amendment's due process clause and applicable to the states.

See Also: Supreme Court.

■ **NEBBIA V. NEW YORK (1934),** U.S. Supreme Court case that upheld a state's right to regulate the economy for the welfare of the public. In response to the economic crisis of the Depression, New York State adopted emergency milk price controls (1933) that capped the retail price of milk at nine cents a quart. Leo Nebbia, a Rochester grocer, sold milk at a higher price and was convicted of breaking the law. He appealed, and a divided Court (5-4) upheld his conviction, finding the state law constitutional. *Nebbia* marked a retreat from the Court's longstanding support for free market economics and limited state business regulation. In his majority opinion Justice Owen Roberts wrote that when the public welfare is at stake, states may properly regulate all aspects of business, including prices.

See Also: Supreme Court.

■ **NEBRASKA,** a state in the western part of the Midwest. It is bounded on the north by South Dakota, on the west by Wyoming, on the west and south by Colorado, on the south by Kansas, and on the east by Missouri and Iowa. More than two-thirds of Nebraska lies within the Great Plains. The Platte River enters the state from the west and empties into the Missouri River, which forms its eastern and northeastern boundary. Nebraska's economy depends on agriculture and food processing. It was opened to white settlement in 1854 and became a state in 1867.

Capital: Lincoln. Area: 77,359 square miles. Population (1995 est.): 1,637,000.

See Also: Frémont, John C.; Kansas-Nebraska Act; Missouri River; Platte River.

■ **NELSON, SAMUEL (1792-1873),** associate justice of the U.S. Supreme Court (1845-72). A Hebron, New York, native, Nelson drafted an opinion in the *Dred Scott* case (1857) that would have denied the Supreme Court's jurisdiction in the matter. Initially accepted, his draft was ultimately rejected by the majority.

See Also: Dred Scott v. Sandford; Supreme Court.

■ **NELSON, THOMAS, JR. (1738-89),** general and Revolutionary War statesman. A member of Virginia's gentry educated at Cambridge University, Nelson served in the Second Continental Congress and signed the Declaration of Independence. He commanded Virginia troops throughout the Revolution and became that state's governor in 1781.

See Also: Declaration of Independence.

■ **NEOLIN (DELAWARE PROPHET) (c. 1700s),** spiritual leader of Pontiac's Rebellion (1763). After the defeat of the French in North America in the French and Indian War, many Ohio Valley Indians were demoralized by the loss of their ally. They became the followers of the visionary Neolin (meaning "the enlightened one"), who urged an uprising. A former despondent drunk, Neolin claimed to have received a message from the Master of Life telling Indians to avoid alcohol and internecine fighting and to reject all things European, including guns, cloth, food, and alcohol. Neolin's message was substantially reinterpreted by the Ottawa Chief Pontiac and others to be more specifically anti-English.

See Also: Indians of North America; Pontiac's Rebellion.

■ **NEUTRALITY ACTS (1935-39),** acts of Congress aimed at shielding the United States from entanglement in crises engulfing Europe and Asia by restricting U.S. trade with warring countries. Isolationist legislators, demonstrating a resurgent congressional initiative in the formation of foreign policy and believing that U.S. involvement in World War I had been a mistake, attempted to define neutrality in terms far stricter than those that had prevailed during the period 1914-17. However, the wars of the 1930s—involving Italy and Ethiopia, Spain, China, and Japan, and finally all Europe—eroded the legislation. Neutrality proved to be impossible for the United States, then by far the world's leading economic power, as major shifts in the global balance of power threatened its interests.

In 1934 and 1935 a congressional committee chaired by Sen. Gerald P. Nye, Republican of North Dakota, examined the origins of U.S. involvement in World War I and concluded that bankers and arms manufacturers—vilified as "merchants of death"—had pushed the United States into the war for their own material profit, a view consonant with Depression-era public contempt for business leaders. The Neutrality Act of 1935, a temporary measure set to expire the following year, stated in the event of war between two or more foreign countries, following a presidential proclamation of the existence of that war, U.S. export of arms or ammunition to any port of any belligerent would be illegal. It also warned U.S. citizens against travel on ships of belligerent countries. The Neutrality Act of 1936 continued the 1935 restrictions and forbade U.S. loans and credits to belligerents. Pres. Franklin D. Roosevelt initially had favored the passage of neutrality legislation, believing it would grant him discretionary power to apply principles of neutrality as he saw fit; instead, the 1935 and 1936 laws in effect forced the president to impose mandatory arms embargoes on all warring powers.

The push for more permanent legislation led to the "cash-and-carry" compromise at the center of the 1937 Neutrality Act: Restrictions on loans continued but excluded short-term credits, and belligerent powers could purchase certain strategic goods in the United States with cash and ship them back on non-U.S. carriers. The outbreak of European war in September 1939 led to further erosion of the trade restrictions: In November 1939 a new neutrality act allowed the purchase of arms by Britain and France, although on a "cash-and-carry" basis. The new policy suited a public that favored Britain and France over Nazi Germany but did not wish to intervene in the war. However, lack of U.S. assistance contributed to the British and French disasters of May and June 1940. British withdrawal from the continent and the fall of France demonstrated to many that the United States could no longer afford neutrality.

—MAARTEN L. PEREBOOM

See Also: Nye Committee; World War II.
BIBLIOGRAPHY: Cole, Wayne S., *Roosevelt and the Isolationists* (Univ. of Nebraska Press 1983); Divine, Robert A., *The Illusion of Neutrality* (Univ. of Chicago Press 1962).

■ **NEUTRALITY PROCLAMATION (Apr. 22, 1793),** U.S. proclamation issued by Pres. George Washington in which he declared American neutrality during the war between France and Great Britain. Following the Jacobins' rise to power in France during the second phase of the French Revolution, Great Britain declared war on France. While many Americans (including Sec. of State Thomas Jefferson) felt sympathy for the French cause, some (such as Sec. of the Treasury Alexander Hamilton) were more sympathetic to Britain, but most (like Washington) wished to remain neutral. France encouraged this neutrality, as the United States could continue to provide food and naval stores to France without fear of attack. The Neutrality Proclamation, drawn up by Att. Gen. Edmund Randolph and signed by Jefferson, was a landmark in international law and neutrality rights. The proclamation warned U.S. citizens against joining either side in the conflict, under penalty of "punishment or forfeiture under the law of nations." The proclamation itself did not use the word "neutrality" but was accepted by the combatant powers as an assertion of such. The policy in the proclamation was studiously carried out and set an American precedent for neutrality.

■ **NEVADA,** Rocky Mountain state, the wealthiest per person. It is bounded on the north by Oregon and Idaho, on the west and south by California, on the south and east by Arizona, and on the east by Utah. The Colorado River forms part of its southern and eastern border. Nevada is the driest state, averaging less than four inches of precipitation a year. The 1859 discovery of the Comstock Lode, a huge deposit of gold and silver, led to statehood in 1864. After World War II,

Nevada struck it rich again, this time on the hotel-casinos of Las Vegas and Reno.

Capital: Carson City. Area: 110,567 square miles. Population (1995 est.): 1,530,000.

See Also: Colorado River; Comstock Lode.

■ **NEVELSON, LOUISE (1900-88),** modernist sculptor. She was born in Kiev, Russia, and immigrated with her family to Maine in 1905. Examples of her work, large abstract constructions made from found objects, cast metal, and scraps of wood, entirely painted in a single color, are displayed in New York City at the Museum of Modern Art and at the Whitney Museum of American Art.

■ **NEVINS, ALAN (1890-1971),** historian. Born in Camp Springs, Illinois, Nevins taught at Columbia University. He won Pulitzer Prizes for biographies of Grover Cleveland (1932) and Hamilton Fish (1936) and wrote a multivolume history of the Civil War. Nevins was a leader of his profession at the midpoint of the 20th century and, as a former journalist, was a promoter of history as good writing.

■ **NEW DEAL,** program of domestic reform launched by Pres. Franklin D. Roosevelt shortly after he assumed office in 1933. The New Deal was a historic departure in American history in that it attempted to modify democratic capitalism by conferring new government responsibilities for the protection of labor, the poor, the elderly, and the public interest in general.

From 1933 through America's entrance in World War II (1941), the Roosevelt administration undertook a pragmatic approach to solving the economic crisis that began with the crash on Wall Street in the fall of 1929. Confronted by the early 1930s with the worst depression in history, Roosevelt experimented with a variety of programs and policies, often contradictory in nature, to aid economic recovery and provide relief to a society devastated by the crisis. The New Deal provided work for the unemployed, security for the elderly, legal rights to organized labor, and subsidies to farmers. It also offered relief to artists, actors, writers, and historians; granted work-study opportunities to college students; offered loans to homeowners; and introduced reforms to the banking, security, and utilities industry.

In the process, American political life underwent a profound transformation as Roosevelt shaped the Democratic party into a majority coalition built around ethnic and racial minorities, organized labor, blue-collar workers, and large segments of urban dwellers and farmers. This New Deal coalition became the foundation for Democratic party power well into the 1970s.

The First Hundred Days. In his speech accepting the presidential nomination in 1932, Roosevelt called for "a new deal for the American people." The term became an umbrella label for his administration's reform efforts. In his first hundred days in office, Roosevelt targeted industrial and agricultural recovery through legislation that granted federal powers to control agricultural production and to set industrial prices and wages. These measures challenged fundamental American assumptions about the government's role in society and drew intense criticism from conservatives. Confronted with a banking crisis that brought the financial system close to collapse, Roosevelt, on his first day in office, declared a "bank holiday" that closed all banks until Congress had enacted the Emergency Banking Act to provided federal loans to distressed banks. Later banking legislation separated commercial banks that provided checking and savings accounts from investment banks handling stocks and bonds. Congress also established the Federal Deposit Insurance Corporation (FDIC) to insure deposits in individual banks.

In the first hectic hundred days of the New Deal, Congress enacted other legislation that affected Wall Street, unemployment relief, and home mortgages, and endorsed a constitutional amendment ending Prohibition. What emerged was neither planned nor comprehensive, but a series of practical responses generally informed by progressive concerns.

"Alphabet" Agencies. At the heart of this first legislative program were two programs: the Agricultural Adjustment Act (AAA) and the National Industrial Recovery Act (NIRA). With the AAA, federal farm policy was transformed by a program that controlled the supply of agricultural goods placed on the market. Through a tax on food-processing plants, farmers received subsidies not to plant certain crops. Shortly after the enactment of the AAA, Sec. of Agriculture Henry Wallace ordered farmers to slaughter 6 million pigs and plow under 100 million acres of cotton—one-fourth of the entire 1933 crop.

The second keystone of the early New Deal was the NIRA, which called upon business and labor to meet to set wage-and-price controls through cooperative codes overseen by a federal board. These codes determined production quotas, working hours, business practices, standards of quality, and methods of competition. Moreover, section 7A of the act gave employees the right to form labor unions and set minimum wages and maximum hours for all employees. This section received the support of the American Federation of Labor (AFL) and offered organized labor an opportunity to enroll new members into its ranks. The NIRA also appropriated $3.3 billion for the Public Works Administration (PWA), to be placed under Sec. of the Interior Harold Ickes, a former progressive Republican from Chicago.

At the same time, Roosevelt undertook more direct relief for the unemployed with the Federal Relief Act that provided $500 million to states for relief through the Federal Emergency Relief Administration (FERA), headed by a flamboyant New York social worker named Harry Hopkins. More than 4.7 million Americans were on relief by 1933. To confront this unemployment problem of historic magnitude, Hopkins disbursed within a month over $51 million in matching grants to states. Nonetheless, federal relief only slightly dented the unemployment problem. Worried that 12.5 million Americans were still unable to find work, Hopkins convinced Roosevelt to establish a temporary Civil Works Administration (CWA) to put another 4 million people to work. In its brief span during the winter of 1933-34, the CWA built roads, schools, playgrounds, and airports.

Other efforts to address unemployment came with the Civilian Conservation Corps (CCC) established in 1933 to put the nation's unemployed youth to work in camps in national parks and forests. The CCC proved to be one of the New Deal's greatest successes.

The creation of the Home Owners Loan Corporation provided refinancing for middle-class homeowners facing foreclosure on mortgages, and the Tennessee Valley Authority (TVA), sponsored in Congress by progressive Republican Sen.

George Norris of Nebraska, brought the federal government's entry into public utilities. Conservative Republicans denounced the TVA as socialism, but they were further dismayed when Roosevelt announced he was taking America off the domestic gold standard.

The greatest achievement of the New Deal's first hundred days was that it offered relief and hope to a demoralized nation. Eventually, the gross national product rose from $56 billion in 1933 to $72 billion in 1935. People began to speak of an "NRA recovery." The Democrats swept the mid-term congressional elections of 1934, electing 322 congressmen, a gain of 13 seats for Roosevelt's party.

Early Opposition to the New Deal. In early 1935, however, the economy began to falter, and political opponents on the right and the left began to criticize the New Deal. Matters worsened when the NRA ran into problems under its huge bureaucratic apparatus, which drew criticism from organized labor when corporations formed their own company unions to skirt section 7A. Other NRA opponents included small businesses that felt the codes benefited the larger companies, and African Americans who perceived the codes as discriminatory. African-American leaders denounced the NRA as standing for the "Negro Run Around," the "Negro Removal Act," and "Negro Rarely Allowed." Finally, much to Roosevelt's public embarrassment and frustration, the NRA was ruled unconstitutional by the Supreme Court in *Schecter* v. *United States* (1935).

The AAA also drew fire from opponents, many of whom were African-American tenant farmers who were thrown off their farms as a result of the act. In early 1936, in *United States* v. *Butler*, the Supreme Court ruled the AAA unconstitutional because of its tax on food processors.

Demagogues, Leftists, and the Right. In these circumstances, political opposition to Roosevelt's New Deal emerged from across the political spectrum and from assorted demagogues. Some critics found the New Deal a little too tame and too pragmatic. In California, the socialist novelist Upton Sinclair won the Democratic party nomination for governor in 1934 on a decidedly socialist platform he called "End Poverty in California"(EPIC). Sinclair was soundly defeated in

the general election by his Republican opponent in a vicious media campaign financed by Louis B. Mayer of Metro-Goldwyn-Mayer.

Also in California, Francis Townsend, a retired dentist from South Dakota, attracted a large following with his scheme that called for a federally funded monthly payment of $200 to any unemployed person over the age of 60. By 1935, the Townsend movement claimed 3.5 million supporters and had enough strength to win seats in Congress. Another radical, a Roman Catholic priest named Charles Coughlin, gained a national following though his inflammatory radio broadcasts that featured vitriolic denunciations of the New Deal and anti-Semitic overtones.

The most serious threat, however, came from Sen. Huey P. Long of Louisiana, who called for a "soak the rich" tax program that promised a guaranteed income to every American. Long's Share-Our-Wealth Clubs swept the nation and gained a following of, he claimed, 7.5 million supporters. Townsend, Coughlin, and Long seemed to threaten the prospects of Roosevelt's bid for reelection in 1936. Long's assassination in late 1935, however, removed one thorn from Roosevelt's side and eased his way toward a second term.

Further to the left, the Communist party experienced a modest revival during the New Deal. By 1935, the party adopted the slogan, "Communism Is Twentieth Century Americanism" and formed coalitions through "popular fronts" with liberal groups. The party attracted support from a number of distinguished writers during this time, including John Dos Passos, Theodore Dreiser, James T. Farrell, Richard Wright, and Ernest Hemingway. Although critically supportive of the New Deal, party members played important roles in organizing the Congress of Industrial Organizations (CIO) and won some support with the African-American community with their call for forming a separate black nation in the South.

The right proved far less well organized than the left. Conservatives and corporate business organized the Liberty League, which denounced the New Deal as socialist. Further to the right, the American Bund, a fascist organization, found support among a small group of German Americans, but in large part the far right proved ineffectual during the New Deal period.

The "Second New Deal." In order to counter the attacks from the left and the right, Roosevelt pushed for another round of legislation, a "second New Deal." One of the most important pieces of legislation of this period transformed the nature of the American welfare state: the Social Security Act of 1935 marked a decisive turning point in the history of social policy in the United States by extending federal responsibility for care to the elderly, the poor, and the disabled. In addition, it established a federal-state system of unemployed insurance and workers' compensation.

Roosevelt also moved in 1935 to secure a new public works program (the Works Progress [later Projects] Administration) and new legislation protecting labor and unions (the Wagner Act). The Wagner Act came at a time when workers were increasingly restless. Strikes by taxi drivers in Philadelphia and New York, a communist-led farm worker strike in California, a nationwide textile strike, a Trotskyist-led truckers strike in Minneapolis, and a general strike in San Francisco in support of dock workers, led by Harry Bridges, a Communist party follower, were all signs of the tense labor unrest of the mid-1930s. Shortly after the passage of the act, John L. Lewis, who believed in organizing unskilled workers, helped found the Congress of Industrial Organizations (CIO).

In 1935, Congress also passed the Holding Company Act, which broke up many utility holding companies, while the Federal Power Act regulated interstate electric and natural gas rates. The Rural Electrification Act brought electricity to the nation's farms, especially in the South.

In the 1936 election, Roosevelt easily defeated his Republican opponent Alf Landon, by carrying every state except Vermont and Maine. His victory solidified a new Democratic coalition that added urban white ethnic groups in the industrial Northeast, organized labor, and African Americans to the party's traditional white southern base.

The New Deal in Decline. With this mandate, Roosevelt attempted to change the composition of the Supreme Court by adding new members for any justices over the age of 70. Critics charged that the plan was a "court-packing" scheme. Roosevelt had been frustrated by the Court's striking down of early New Deal laws, and he was genuinely afraid that Social Security would be the next to go. The plan, however, was a major political miscalculation on his part, and it led to a furious attack, not only by Republicans, but also by some Democrats. In the end, Roosevelt's proposed reform of the Court was defeated by his own Democratic-controlled Congress.

Another major mistake of his second term came when Roosevelt attempted to balance the budget by curtailing government expenditures. Because the economy still remained weak and dependent on government expenditures it went into another downward spiral. The rapid decline in income and production in the nine months from Sept. 1937 to June 1938 was disastrous. Reacting to this crisis, Roosevelt once again took the offensive. He rejected fiscal conservatism by undertaking a deliberate policy of deficit spending through a $4.5 million package to finance public housing, highway construction, and bolstering relief agencies. A new farming bill, the Agricultural Adjustment Act of 1938 was enacted that allowed the federal government to pay farmers not to plant crops.

Roosevelt also revitalized the antitrust division in the Justice Department, imposed new corporate taxes, and increased taxes on the wealthy. The Fair Labor Standards Act (1938) set minimum wages and maximum hours.

Despite these later reforms, however, most of the momentum behind the New Deal had waned by the time World War II erupted in Europe on Sept. 1, 1939. Roosevelt began to increase defense spending even before America entered the conflict in 1941, and common wisdom said that the war eventually brought America out of the Depression. But what was really meant was that spending on the war effort finally ended the economic depression.

The New Deal: An Assessment. The New Deal had accomplished much. The role of the federal government had been extended into new areas of the economy and the states. A social security system had been created that became the basis of the modern welfare state. New legislation provided a place for organized labor and farmers at the table. Although the New Deal's record on behalf of ethnic minorities was mixed, African Americans were integrated into work and relief programs. The New Deal reorganized the Bureau of Indian Affairs to allow tribal government and tribal ownership of Indian lands. Aided by government work-study programs, more women entered college during the 1930s, reaching a quarter of those attending university. Moreover, Roosevelt appointed many women and African Americans to key positions in his administration.

Despite the grave threat of the Depression, the nation did not experience an economic revolution, nor did it take the road to socialism. To many, the New Deal had preserved American democracy, and capitalism had survived.

—DONALD T. CRITCHLOW

See Also: Alphabet Agencies; Court Packing; Fireside Chats; Good Neighbor Policy; Great Depression; Hundred Days; Neutrality Acts; Share-Our-Wealth; Social Security Act; individual biographies.

BIBLIOGRAPHY: Brinkley, Alan, *The End of Reform: New Deal Liberalism in Recession and War* (Knopf 1995); Brinkley, Alan, *Voices of Protest: Huey Long, Father Coughlin, and the Great Depression* (Knopf 1982); Burns, James MacGregor, *Roosevelt: The Lion and the Fox* (Harcourt, Brace 1956); Freidel, Frank, *Franklin D. Roosevelt*, 4 vols. (Little, Brown 1952-76); Gordon, Colin, *New Deals: Business, Labor and Politics in America, 1920-1935* (Cambridge Univ. Press 1994); Kirby, John B., *Black Americans in the Roosevelt Era: Liberalism and Race* (Univ. of Tennessee Press 1980).

■ **NEW DEAL CASES,** series of Supreme Court decisions that either upheld or overturned New Deal programs and legislation during the 1930s. The Supreme Court had a great impact on the New Deal, Pres. Franklin D. Roosevelt's domestic program of reform during his first two terms (1933-41). Roosevelt, believing that constitutional power existed to confront the economic and social difficulties of the Depression, effectively pushed through Congress a series of reform and relief measures.

Initially, the Supreme Court accepted state regulatory measures and federal legislation, including the upholding of private contracts in the Gold Clause Cases of 1935 and the creation of the Tennessee Valley Authority in *Ashwander* v. *Tennessee Valley Authority* of 1936. The conservative bloc, however, led by five justices, overturned a number of important New Deal programs. The Court, for example, voided both the National Industrial Recovery Act in *Schecter* v. *United States* (1935)

and the Agricultural Adjustment Act in *United States* v. *Butler* (1936). By the end of 1936, the Court had effectively adopted a stance of obstructing government efforts to relieve Americans of the travails of the Depression on the general grounds that the federal government lacked authority in these areas.

Roosevelt responded in 1937 with a plan to neutralize the Court's conservatives by adding more justices. Although his "court-packing" plan failed, it probably moved the Supreme Court to adopt a less conservative posture. The reversal began with *West Coast Hotel Company* v. *Parrish* (1937) and solidified with the retirement of members of the conservative bloc in the late 1930s.

See Also: Court Packing; New Deal; Supreme Court.

BIBLIOGRAPHY: Conklin, Paul K., *The New Deal* (Harlan Davidson 1975); McCloskey, Robert, *The American Supreme Court* (Univ. of Chicago Press 1960).

■ **NEW ENGLAND,** northeast region of the United States, extending along the Atlantic Coast northward from Connecticut to Rhode Island, Massachusetts, New Hampshire, Maine, and including land-locked Vermont. The area was said to be named by Captain John Smith in 1614 when he explored the coastline for London merchants. New England was soon after settled by English Puritans seeking religious freedom. In the 17th century the influential towns of Plymouth, Boston, Providence, New Haven, and Hartford were all founded. During the 18th century New England wealth came primarily from trade, fishing, and shipbuilding. Because of its dependence on trade, New England was severely affected by the passage of detrimental British trade and taxation laws. The region agitated for independence from Great Britain and was a hotbed of the American Revolution, largely because of taxation issues. During the 19th century New England was the first part of the United States to industrialize, mainly through the use of waterpower to run textile and leather plants in Lowell, Lynn, and Worcester, Massachusetts, and Manchester, New Hampshire. In the years following World War II, however, New England has experienced a steady decline in its manufacturing industries, many of which have relocated to the South or abroad.

New England is still mythologized as a traditional place of small towns with white clapboard churches, moss-covered houses, practical inventors, and Mayflower descendants.

■ **NEW ENGLAND ANTI-SLAVERY SOCIETY,** organization dedicated to the immediate elimination of slavery. Founded in 1831 by William Lloyd Garrison and 14 others, the society proved the model for other antislavery groups. Garrison's uncompromising stand, as well as the prominent role of women in his society, made the New England group the most vocal and radical within the abolitionist movement.

See Also: Antislavery Movement.

■ **NEW ENGLAND CONFEDERATION (1643-84),** union formed for the common defense of the colonies of Massachusetts, Plymouth, Connecticut, and Rhode Island. In the aftermath of the Pequot War (1637), the four colonies realized they needed to combine forces to provide for a more effective defense. In May 1643, an assembly met to draw up an agreement that outlined their goals. The 12 articles of confederation guaranteed the territorial integrity of the four colonies but allowed for confederation representatives to act as a body when declaring and engaging in war. The cost of confederation military activity would be underwritten by individual colonies, based upon the proportion of male inhabitants in each colony. Moreover, the union held jurisdiction over intercolonial quarrels, fugitives, and Indian affairs. The assembly met annually, except in time of war, until 1684.

■ **NEW ENGLAND PRIMER,** colonial-era reading textbook. The primer contained a rhyming alphabet and readings that taught Puritan values. Although its origin is unknown, one version of the primer was produced by Boston printer Benjamin Harris by 1690.

■ **NEW ENGLAND RENAISSANCE,** flowering of literary activity between 1835 and 1855, often referred to as the American Renaissance. It culminated in a five-year period of the most imaginative, literary activity of the century and it included the major writers of the Romantic period. Between 1850 and 1855, the following works appeared: Emerson's *Representative Men* (1850); Hawthorne's *The Scarlet Letter* (1850), *The House of Seven Gables* (1851), *The Snow Image and Other Twice-Told Tales* (1851), and *The Blithedale Romance* (1852); Melville's *Moby-Dick* (1851), *Pierre* (1852), and memorable short stories; Thoreau's *Walden* (1854); and Whitman's *Leaves of*

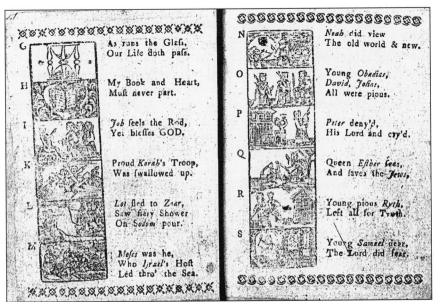

First published by Benjamin Harris in 1690, the *New England Primer* served as the region's sole grammar school textbook for half a century.

Grass (1855). All these writers, except Whitman, had written important works before 1850, but the amazing burst of creative energy during this short period of time truly was a "literary rebirth."

As different as these five writers were from each other, there were common elements in their work. The Jacksonian period (1828-36) had brought about a spirit of optimism that the ideals of the American Revolution would finally be realized. Although all five writers were deeply concerned about the role of democracy, Emerson, Thoreau, and especially Whitman were more positive and hopeful about its future, while Hawthorne and Melville had their doubts, often expressed in pessimistic tones. These writers were concerned about exploring the nature of good and evil and about nature and its relationship to the individual and society. They all experimented artistically, especially in integrating form and theme, and although they only received modest recognition during their own century, by the middle of the 20th, they were hailed as founding fathers and their works as cornerstones of American literature.

See Also: Emerson, Ralph Waldo; Hawthorne, Nathaniel; Melville, Herman; Thoreau, Henry David; Whitman, Walt(er).

BIBLIOGRAPHY: Matthiessen, F. O., *American Renaissance: Art and Expression in the Age of Emerson and Melville* (Oxford Univ. Press 1941); Myerson, Joel, ed., *The American Renaissance in New England* (Gale Research 1978); Reynolds, David S., *Beneath the American Renaissance* (Knopf 1988).

▨ **NEW FREEDOM,** term for the domestic policies and programs that guided the first years of Pres. Woodrow Wilson's administration. During the election campaign of 1912 Progressive party candidate Theodore Roosevelt proposed a set of economic and social reforms called the New Nationalism. Wilson, the Democratic candidate, countered with the New Freedom, a group of reform ideas based largely on the ideas of the progressive lawyer Louis Brandeis.

Roosevelt's call for the regulation of large industrial corporations, according to Wilson, was the wrong response to the social, political, and economic inequities caused by monopolies. Instead, the New Freedom favored federal antitrust action to dismantle such corporations. In addi-

tion, Wilson assailed Roosevelt's strong regulatory policies as inhibitors, rather than promoters, of economic growth. Wilson, agreed, however, that laissez-faire economics did not serve the public interest, for under his plan strong government authority was required to protect Americans from the vagaries of the market.

Despite the campaign rhetoric that gave rise to the New Nationalism and the New Freedom, Wilson and Roosevelt remained close philosophically. Indeed, after only two years in office, Wilson realized that the New Freedom was an insufficient program for the times. By 1915 he had adopted the central tenets of Roosevelt's New Nationalism, as he began to use regulation as the principal mode of the federal government's approach toward business.

See Also: Wilson, (Thomas) Woodrow.
BIBLIOGRAPHY: Cooper, John Milton, Jr., *The Warrior and the Priest: Woodrow Wilson and Theodore Roosevelt* (Harvard Univ. Press 1983); Link, Arthur S., *Woodrow Wilson and the Progressive Era* (Harper & Row 1954).

▨ **NEW FRONTIER,** the label chosen by Pres. John F. Kennedy for his short-lived administration (1961-63). The phrase sought to project the vigor of the "new generation" that Kennedy represented, while recalling the traditional challenge of the frontier in American history.

See Also: Cold War; Kennedy, John Fitzgerald.

▨ **NEW HAMPSHIRE,** a New England state. It is bounded on the north and west by Quebec, on the west by Vermont, on the south by Massachusetts, and on the east by Maine and the Atlantic Ocean. The Connecticut River forms its border with Vermont. The White Mountains are in the north. An industrial, low-tax state, it has many electronics firms that have moved north from Massachusetts, of which it was once part. New Hampshire was one of the original 13 states and the first to declare its independence.

Capital: Concord. Area: 9,283 square miles. Population (1995 est.): 1,148,000.

See Also: Connecticut River; Pierce, Franklin; Primaries; Wheelock, Eleazar; White Mountains.

▨ **NEW HARMONY,** utopian town founded in 1825 in Indiana. The brainchild of Welsh manufacturer and social reformer Robert Owen, New Harmony's brief existence from 1825 to 1828 on 30,000 acres was a model of industrial utopian socialism. Based on Owen's successful factory community, New Lanark, in Great Britain, New Harmony promoted communal housing, eating, child rearing, and education, along with fair wages, good working conditions, and company stores with fair prices. New Harmony failed because of infighting, but many of its ideals eventually found their way into the American workplace.

See Also: Frontier in American History; Utopian Communities.

■ **NEW JERSEY,** one of the Middle Atlantic states, the most densely populated state and the only one whose population lives entirely within metropolitan areas. It is bounded on the north and west by Pennsylvania, the north and east by New York, and the east and south by the Atlantic Ocean. The Delaware River and Delaware Bay separate it from Delaware to the west and south. The Delaware River also forms its border with Pennsylvania. The Hudson River forms part of its eastern border. New Jersey is an industrial state that faces in two directions: southwest to Philadelphia and northeast to New York City. It ranks first among states in pharmaceuticals. Many big corporations moved their headquarters to New Jersey from New York City after 1960.

The future state was part of the Dutch colony of New Netherland before 1664, when it passed to the English. Five major Revolutionary War battles were fought in New Jersey. It was one of the original 13 states and the first to ratify the Bill of Rights.

Capital: Trenton. Area: 7,790 square miles. Population (1995 est.): 7,945,000.

See Also: Bill of Rights; Delaware River; Edison, Thomas Alva; Stuyvesant, Peter; Washington, George; Wilson, (Thomas) Woodrow.

■ **NEW JERSEY PLAN (1787),** proposal written by William Paterson to the Constitutional Convention. A response to the Virginia Plan, the New Jersey Plan favored smaller states by advocating a one-house legislature in which the states were equally represented.

See Also: Constitution of the United States.

■ **NEWLANDS RECLAMATION ACT (1902),** federal legislation, named for Rep. Francis G. Newlands of Nevada, authorizing the construction of federal irrigation projects in the West. Thought at the time to be a new Homestead Act, providing small irrigated farms for ordinary Americans, over time it was used principally for the benefit of large agribusiness.

See Also: Agriculture; Frontier in American History.

■ **NEW LEFT,** grew out of a disillusionment with the social apathy and political conservatism of the 1950s, accompanied by disgust with the ineffectiveness of the "Old Left," the largely Democratic, big-government holdovers from the New and Fair Deals. Thinkers such as C. Wright Mills and Staughton Lynd called for young radicals to ignore the older, establishment liberals and jump forward out of what Mills called the "Age of Complacency" into a new world of activism.

This call engaged young thinkers on college campuses who had been mired in the repression of McCarthyism and were primed for an intellectual explosion. In response, two such students, Thomas (Tom) Hayden and Al Haber, organized the Students for a Democratic Society (SDS). Hayden's "Port Huron Statement," with its demand for "participatory democracy," became the New Left's manifesto.

The New Left was both strengthened and ultimately compromised by the movement for social justice and international peace, which it supported and which came to symbolize the 1960s. Thus, the New Left applauded both the work of civil rights leader Martin Luther King and his supporters in the 1956 Montgomery Bus Boycott and the later efforts of groups like the Student Nonviolent Coordinating Committee (SNCC) to take the black movement to a new, more radical phase. But it had difficulty supporting the emerging militarism of the Black Power movement.

While the writings of New Left thinkers such as Hayden spurred the student movement and led to the formation of SDS, this early intellectualism was ultimately buried by an anti–Vietnam War movement, which became more violent and less intellectual as the 1960s drew to a close. Ironically, then, the New Left was superseded by many of the same forces it had helped to create,

The New Left reached the apex of its influence in the March on the Pentagon, in October 1967.

and by the 1970s the intellectuals of the New Left—largely abandoned by both the Black Power and the antiwar movements—found that their pleas for a radical utopia had quickly fallen out of date.

—JOHN ROBERT GREENE

BIBLIOGRAPHY: Mills, C. Wright, "Letter to the New Left," *New Left Review* (1961); Unger, Irwin, *The Movement: A History of the American New Left, 1959-1972* (Dodd, Mead 1974).

■ **NEW MEXICO,** one of the Rocky Mountain states of the American Southwest. It is bounded on the north by Colorado, on the west by Arizona, on the east and south by Mexico and Texas, and on the east by Oklahoma. The Rio Grande runs south through the state. Mountain ranges separate the center of the state from the eastern third, which is part of the Great Plains. New Mexico has a higher proportion of Hispanics (39 percent in 1990) than any other state and also many Indians (9 percent). The state is a leader in copper, potash, and oil and gas production. The manufacture of electronic equipment is its chief industry.

New Mexico was a center of Indian settlement before the Spanish arrived at the end of the 16th century. It was part of the area ceded to the United States in 1848, at the end of the Mexican War. New Mexico did not become a state until 1912.

Capital: Santa Fe. Area: 121,598 square miles. Population (1995 est.): 1,685,000.

   See Also: *Billy the Kid; Coronado, Francisco Vásquez de; Gadsden Purchase; Great Plains; Kearny, Stephen Watts; Mexican War; Pueblo; Rio Grande; Rocky Mountains; Santa Fe Trail.*

■ **NEW NEGRO MOVEMENT,** flowering of African-American cultural expression. Commonly referred to as the Harlem Renaissance, the New Negro Movement was hardly contained within Harlem. A national movement, it was partly a function of changing demographics as a result of the Great Migration of southern blacks to northern cities and partly a response to civil rights advocates like W. E. B. Du Bois, who called on black artists to make their unique contributions to American civilization. Every field of cultural endeavor was touched by the ferment. From the close of World War I to 1934, novelists such as James Weldon Johnson and Claude McKay, and poets such as Langston Hughes and Countee Cullen, and essayists including Jesse Fauset expanded literature in new and exciting ways. Zora Neal Hurston, Sterling Brown, and Arna Bontemps incorporated folktales into their writing. Painters Aaron Douglas, Archibald Motley, Jr., and Laura Wheeling Waring and sculptors like Meta Warrick Fuller exhibited striking talent. Music was also an important aspect of the movement and ranged from the spirituals of Marion Anderson and Paul Robeson to the blues of Bessie Smith and Ma Rainey and the jazz of Louis Armstrong and Duke Ellington. These were but a few bright stars in the brilliant firmament of cultural expression that was the New Negro Movement.

—JOHN R. NEFF

See Also: Civil Rights Movement.

BIBLIOGRAPHY: Bontemps, Arna, *The Harlem Renaissance Remembered* (Dodd, Mead 1972); Lewis, David L., *When Harlem Was in Vogue* (Random House 1981).

■ **NEW ORLEANS,** southern port city near the mouth of the Mississippi River. New Orleans was founded in 1718 by the French explorer and colonizer Jean Baptiste Le Moyne, Sieur de Bienville, in order to fortify France's holdings in the Mississippi Valley. The original town was laid out on a wide bend in the Mississippi River in a gridiron pattern. This area, known as the Vieux Carré or French Quarter, formed the limits of the town until the 19th century. New Orleans, which was ceded to Spain in 1763 and then back to France in 1800, was acquired by the United States from France in 1803 as part of the Louisiana Purchase, and French and Creole influences are still evident today. During the 1830s and 1840s steamboat traffic bringing agricultural and manufactured goods up and down the Mississippi River established New Orleans as one of the leading ports in America. As the primary port of the Confederacy, New Orleans was an early Union objective. It fell to Adm. David Farragut in April 1862 and was occupied by Union troops for the rest of the war. After the Civil War New Orleans experienced one of the most violent race riots of the Reconstruction period, when whites killed more than 35 blacks in July 1866. During the 20th century New

Orleans has remained an important Mississippi port and has become increasingly dependent on the oil production of the Gulf Coast region. Tourism is also vital to the city's economy. Population (1994): 484,149.

See Also: City in American History.

■ **NEW ORLEANS, BATTLE OF (1815),** last battle of the War of 1812, a crushing U.S. victory. On Dec. 13, 1814, a British army under Gen. Sir Edward Pakenham landed and moved on New Orleans. The U.S. commander, Gen. Andrew Jackson, positioned his motley but gritty force behind a strong breastwork at Rodriguez Canal. After probing U.S. defenses, Pakenham launched his main attack on January 8. It was repulsed with heavy British losses, including Pakenham himself. Neither side was aware that peace had been signed two weeks earlier at Ghent in Belgium.

See Also: Ghent, Treaty of; Jackson, Andrew; War of 1812.

■ **NEWSPAPERS,** publications that were conspicuous by their absence in 17th-century America and came to have a major influence on American life. The first publication approximating a newspaper was *Publick Occurrences, Both Foreign and Domestic* by Benjamin Harris of Boston, in which the conduct of King William's War (1689-97) was criticized. Authorities promptly suppressed it. Some years later, the *Boston News-Letter* (1704-76) and the *Boston Gazette* (1719-41) were published as the mouthpieces of officialdom and were used to print proclamations and convey acceptable news from London. The next truly independent paper to appear was the work of James Franklin of Boston. His *New England Courant* (1721-26) offered lively and critical commentary but landed him in jail in 1723 for criticizing colonial authorities. Franklin's brother Benjamin moved to more liberal Philadelphia where, in the 1720s, he worked for the *American Mercury* (1719-41) before purchasing the *Philadelphia Gazette* (1728-1815), which he edited from 1729 to 1766. In New York, William Bradford published the *New York Gazette* (1724-44), which enjoyed official sanction. The heavy hand of the censor continued to hang over these efforts, however, until 1735, when New York editor John Peter Zenger was indicted for seditious libel after printing articles critical of colonial authorities in his *New York Weekly Journal* (1733-52). His acquittal established the principal that truth is a defense against libel and is considered the foundation of American freedom of the press.

On the eve of the American Revolution there were 37 newspapers in the American colonies, including three that are still publishing: Portsmouth's *New Hampshire Gazette* (founded 1756), the *Newport Mercury* (1758), and Connecticut's *Hartford Courant* (1764). By 1790 the number had grown to 92, including eight dailies, the first being the *Pennsylvania Evening Post* (1783).

Most papers took a highly partisan political stance. The Democratic-Republicans were supported by the *National Gazette* (1791-93) and the *Philadelphia Aurora* (1794-1835), while the Federalists made their case in the *American Minerva* (1793-1803) and the *New York Evening Post* (1801), later edited by William Cullen Bryant. The First Amendment had guaranteed the freedom of speech or of the press, but the Federalist Alien and Sedition Acts (1797-98) attempted to curb the media, and in their opposition to these measures the Democratic-Republicans played an important role in establishing the working principle of a free press. As Jefferson proclaimed in his first inaugural address, "error of opinion may be tolerated where reason is left free to combat it."

19th Century. The number of newspapers greatly expanded in the 19th century as the nation planted thousands of new cities and towns across the continent. At mid-century there were more than 500 newspapers, a number that grew to nearly 2,000 by 1900. Meanwhile, the invention of the steam press (1814), the cylindrical rotary press (1865), and the linotype machine (1886) lowered the unit cost of news publishing and turned journalism into a mass-circulation business.

The story of competitive journalism has typically focused on New York, beginning with the rise of the "penny press." *The Sun* (1833), the first of the penny dailies, flourished with a mix of crime, scandal, and "human interest." James Gordon Bennett's *Herald* (1835) combined brief news reports with opinion in what became the prototype of the modern American newspaper. If Bennett was primarily an entertainer, his competitor Horace Greeley was a crusader, and his

Tribune (1841) attacked slavery, promoted moral reform, and encouraged western expansion ("Go West, Young Man!"). In 1847, Greeley hired Charles Anderson Dana to edit the *Tribune*; Dana later moved to the *Sun*, which became known as the "newspaperman's newspaper," the most distinguished daily in the country. By the 1850s, these New York papers were printing hundreds of thousands of copies each day.

In the late 19th century, the struggle for mass circulation in New York spawned what became known as "yellow journalism." In 1883, St. Louis publisher Joseph Pulitzer purchased the failing *New York World* and through the use of illustrations, color comics, and stunts turned it into the biggest paper in the city, with a circulation of 250,000. In 1895, William Randolph Hearst of San Francisco took over the *New York Journal* and began a circulation war with Pulitzer, which he won by whipping up popular enthusiasm in 1898 for the American war with Spain. When an illustrator whom Hearst had sent to Cuba complained that he could not find any battles to sketch, Hearst famously telegraphed back, "You furnish the pictures and I'll furnish the war."

The next episode was the "war of the tabs," or tabloids, the half-size, heavily photo-illustrated papers that included the *Daily News* (1919), *Daily Mirror* (1924), and *Daily Graphic* (1924), each seeking to scoop the others with ever more sensational stories of sex, crime, and corruption, a combination that would be taken up by local television news in the late 20th century. By World War II, the *Daily News* had achieved the highest circulation of any paper in American history, reaching a peak of 4 million with its Sunday edition. It was in reaction to sensationalism that in 1896 Adolph S. Ochs acquired the *New York Times*, pledging to make it into the national "newspaper of record" by providing coverage of "neglected non-sensational news."

20th Century. But it was the Hearsts of the business who were most successful. Hearst built the first newspaper chain, which at its peak during World War II included 42 daily papers. Other press barons with large chains included Edward Scripps (Scripps-Howard) and Frank Munsey, of whom the Kansas editor William Allen White wrote that he possessed "the talent of a meat packer, the morals of a money changer, and the manners of an undertaker." The "industrialization" of journalism included the growth of large new agencies that distributed news stories, columns, and comics to subscribing papers. The first, the Associated Press, was formed by a combination of several New York papers in 1827; by 1860 it had absorbed dozens of local press bureaus to become the first national agency. Scripps and Hearst built news agencies of their own, which combined in 1958 to form United Press International.

In the second half of the 20th century, as Americans turned to television for an increasing portion of their news, newspaper circulation fell and the number of papers dropped to fewer than 1,500 nationally. Total daily circulation remained relatively steady (53 million in 1949, 59 million in 1965, 57 million in 1995), but with an overall increase in population of about 90 percent, this meant that far fewer people were subscribing to and reading newspapers. The automation of production resulted in a wave of strikes by union pressmen that added to the woes of publishers, and there were many mergers and bankruptcies. By late century most cities had been reduced to only one daily paper.

In the early 1980s, the Gannett chain began publication of the first national daily paper, *USA Today*, whose combination of color, innovative graphics, and short articles made it a popular success. The *Wall Street Journal* and the *New York Times* soon followed with national editions of their own, using satellite transmission of digital information to print the papers regionally, making it possible to get home delivery in most metropolitan areas of the country. In 1995, the 10 papers with the largest circulation were, in order: *Wall Street Journal* (1.8 million), *USA Today* (1.7 million), *New York Times* (1.1 million), *Los Angeles Times* (1.1 million), *Washington Post* (820,000), *New York Daily News* (730,000), *Chicago Tribune* (660,000), *Chicago Sun-Times* (490,000), *Boston Globe* (460,000), and *Philadelphia Inquirer* (420,000).

—JOHN MACK FARAGHER

See Also: Bennett, James Gordon; Bryant, William Cullen; Dana, Charles A.; Greeley, Horace; Hearst, William Randolph; Ochs, Adolph; Pulitzer, Joseph; White, William Allen.

BIBLIOGRAPHY: Hench, John B., ed., *Three Hundred Years of the American Newspaper* (American Antiquarian Society 1991); Squires, James D., *Read All About It! The Corporate Takeover of America's Newspapers* (Times Books 1993); Stevens, John D., *Sensationalism and the New York Press* (Columbia Univ. Press 1991).

■ **NEW WOMAN,** term describing the social role of women who assert economic and civic autonomy by educating themselves, pursuing careers, marrying only by choice, and controlling their own fertility. The concept of the new woman was first used by journalists in the early 20th century, to describe a generation of young women who benefited from the social transformations wrought by the club women and feminist reformers of the late 19th century. Better educated than their predecessors, these women worked, participated in public debate, lived on their own before marriage, and sometimes remained single by choice. The revival of feminism in the 1960s brought a renewed emphasis on this "new" role for women in society, and the succeeding decades brought unprecedented gains in social and economic autonomy for American women. Nonetheless, a competing conception of femininity known as the "cult of true womanhood" persists. According to this view, women have little place in the masculine sphere of business and public affairs because of clear, natural differences between the sexes. Their natural role is in the private sphere, as caregivers, wives, mothers, and moral guardians.

See Also: Women in American History; Women's Movement.

BIBLIOGRAPHY: Sochen, June, *The New Woman* (Quadrangle 1972).

■ **NEW WORLD CROPS,** crops native to the Americas and unknown in the rest of the world before the explorations that began with Columbus in 1492. Many of them constitute an important part of the "Columbian Exchange" that profoundly altered the world's ecology. On his first voyage Columbus and members of his landing parties observed the cultivation on Caribbean islands by native Taino farmers of maize, or "Indian corn"; tobacco; and cassava, or manioc. He brought back to Spain ears of Indian corn as curiosities.

Food Crops. The adoption of certain domesticated Native-American plants enabled European, African, and Asian farmers to cultivate new soils and extend growing seasons, which led to greater food supplies. This, in turn, contributed to a four-fold increase in the world's population between 1650 and 1950. About one-third of today's global food and feed crops originated in the Americas.

New World farmers, who had no beasts of burden and no metal tools, domesticated hearty, productive, and easily grown plants. Their staples were maize (*Zea mays*), first domesticated about 5,000 B.C. by natives of Mexico or Central America; the white potato (*Solanum tuberosum*), first domesticated between 5,000 and 2,000 B.C. by inhabitants of the Andes Mountains; the sweet potato (*Ipomoea batatas*), whose earliest archaeological remains, between 10,000 and 12,000 years old, have been discovered in Peru; and cassava, or manioc (*Manihot esculenta*), a tropical shrub first domesticated around 3,000 or 2,000 B.C. by Central or South Americans who learned to grate, pound, and squeeze its roots to remove their excessive levels of prussic acid and to bake the resulting flour into bread in earthenware pottery. These crops were easily and widely adopted by New World settlers, Europeans, Africans, and Asians. Maize has provided for more human needs than any other single crop. Other American food plants that have proved very valuable are certain beans and squashes, pumpkins, peanuts, tomatoes, avocadoes, guavas, papayas, pineapples, cocoa beans, and chile peppers.

Nonfood Crops. The indigenous New World nonfood crops of tobacco (*Nicotiana tabacum*) and upland cotton (*Gossypium hirsutum*) have also had a major impact on American and world history. Cultivation of tobacco, the leaves of which were probably first smoked in Mexico before A.D. 432, provided the first profitable export of England's Virginia Company and led to the settlement and development of Virginia and the other southern colonies of British North America in the 1600s and 1700s. The plantation system that evolved in the South was primarily responsible for the forced migration of African slaves beginning in 1619. Over 6 million metric tons of tobacco are cultivated throughout the world today. Upland cotton, which was probably first domesticated along the Gulf coast of Mexico and the Caribbean coast of Colombia no later than 3,500 B.C., was grown primarily for home production of cloth until 1793. After the invention of the cotton gin in that

year upland cotton became a major agricultural commodity that reinvigorated the Southern slave system and supported the economies of the Confederate States of America and the reconstructed South until the Mexican boll weevil devastated southern cotton fields in the early 1900s.

—MARK A. MASTROMARINO

See Also: Agriculture; Cotton Gin; Plantation System.

BIBLIOGRAPHY: Brooks, Jerome E., *The Mighty Leaf: Tobacco through the Centuries* (Little, Brown 1952); Brown, Harry Bates, and Jacob Osborn Ware, *Cotton*, 3rd ed. (McGraw-Hill 1958); Crosby, Alfred W., Jr., *The Columbian Exchange: Biological and Cultural Consequences of 1492* (Greenwood Press 1972); Hobhouse, Henry, *Seeds of Change: Five Plants that Transformed Mankind* (Sidgwick & Jackson 1985); Salaman, Redcliff N., and W. G. Burton, *The History and Social Influence of the Potato*, rev. ed. (Cambridge Univ. Press 1985); Wallace, Henry A., and William L. Brown, *Corn and Its Early Fathers*, rev. ed. (Iowa State Univ. Press 1988).

■ **NEW YORK,** a Middle Atlantic state and the most populous state east of the Mississippi River. It is bounded on the north by Quebec, on the north and west by Ontario and Lakes Ontario and Erie, on the west and south by Pennsylvania and New Jersey, on the south by the Atlantic Ocean, and on the east by Connecticut, Massachusetts, and Vermont. The St. Lawrence River forms part of its northern border, and the Hudson River part of its eastern border. Long Island is the largest U.S. island east of the Mississippi. Dominating the state is New York City, the nation's largest city and its financial, communications, and cultural capital

New York was settled by the Dutch as New Netherland in 1624 and passed to the English in 1664. It was one of the original 13 states and the site of many Revolutionary War battles. Completion of the Erie Canal in 1825 made it a gateway to the West. Its rapid industrial development after the Civil War made New York truly the "Empire State."

Capital: Albany. Area: 49,112 square miles. Population (1995 est.): 18,136,000.

See Also: Erie Canal; Hudson, Henry; Hudson River; Iroquois Confederacy; Liberty, Statue of; Long Island; New York City; Roosevelt, Franklin Delano; Saratoga, Battles of; Seneca Falls Convention; United Nations (UN); West Point.

■ **NEW YORK CITY,** spectacular port city located on the Atlantic seaboard, the most populous and in many ways the foremost, although atypical, city in the United States. Since Dutch settlement in the early 1600s, New York has been a thriving port, with the Hudson River, East River, and Upper and Lower New York Bays all emptying into the Atlantic Ocean. The Dutch established New Amsterdam in 1624 on the tip of Manhattan island and controlled it until the British seized the colony in 1664. With the opening of the Erie Canal (1825) New York City experienced extraordinary growth. Since 1898 New York City has been composed of the five boroughs of Manhattan, Queens, Staten Island, Brooklyn, and the Bronx. During the late 19th and early 20th centuries the city's population became increasingly diverse. Immigrants from Ireland and Italy, African Americans from the South, whites from rural New England, European Jews, and Chinese were among the many who flocked into New York and created their distinctive neighborhoods. New York has been the country's financial, artistic, theatrical, and publishing center for the last 150 years. During the 20th century the city, dubbed the "Big Apple" by jazz artists, became the cultural capital of the nation. Its ethnic mix changed once again as immigrants from the Caribbean and Latin America, Korea, Vietnam, and India moved to New York City. Population (1994): 7,333,253.

See Also: *City in American History; Erie Canal; Manhattan; Skyscrapers.*

■ **NEW YORK CONSPIRACY (1741),** alleged grand plot on the part of slaves and some whites to destroy New York City through arson and violence. While investigating a robbery, city officials learned of heated slave discontent voiced at a local tavern. After several African Americans were arrested, numerous fires were set in the city over several days. While some were retaliatory, others were unconnected to the arrests. But interpreting the outbreaks as evidence of a widespread conspiracy, city authorities arrested dozens of slaves. Eventually 72 slaves were shipped out of New York, 17 hanged, and 13 burned at the stake. Four whites, including 2 women, were also hanged. Trial records indicate that the prosecutors were as afraid of French and Spanish Catholicism as they were of a slave revolt, and the only thing uniting the slaves was a shared hatred of their bondage.

BIBLIOGRAPHY: Davis, Thomas J., *A Rumor of Revolt* (Free Press 1985).

■ ***NEW YORK TIMES* V. *SULLIVAN* (1964),** U.S. Supreme Court case that reshaped libel law and made it more difficult for public figures to win libel judgments. Sullivan, a city official in Montgomery, Alabama, sued the *New York Times* and four African-American clergymen, claiming he had been libeled in an advertisement published in the newspaper. All parties agreed the advertisement contained several errors of fact, and Sullivan received a $2.5 million judgment in an Alabama court.

The Supreme Court reversed (9-0) the state court verdict. Justice William Brennan wrote for the Court that the First Amendment was meant to ensure robust public debate on important issues and inevitably such debate will include incorrect statements. To avoid a chilling effect on future public debate, Brennan wrote, public officials should not be allowed to recover damages because of false statements concerning their official actions unless they could demonstrate the statements were made with actual malice and those who made the statements either knew they were false or demonstrated reckless disregard for whether the statements were accurate or not.

New York Times v. *Sullivan* marked a significant change in legal thinking on libel. The focus shifted from the individual's right to fair treatment to the public's right to full debate of important issues. In 1967 the Court in *Curtis Publishing* v. *Butts* and *Associated Press* v. *Walker* extended *New York Times* v. *Sullivan*'s "reckless disregard" standard to well-known public figures who were not public officials.

—TIM ASHWELL

See Also: *Supreme Court.*

BIBLIOGRAPHY: Lewis, Anthony, *Make No Law: The Sullivan Case and the First Amendment* (Random House 1991).

■ **NEZ PERCÉ,** North American Indians centered primarily in present-day Idaho, Washington, and

Oregon. Nez Percé means "pierced nose" in French, a term that is somewhat mistaken since most members of the tribe never pierced their noses. The Nez Percé lived at the time of European contact along the Snake River, subsisting primarily on salmon and other fish as well as on wild vegetables. The Nez Percé adopted the horse around 1730 and became well known for their horse-breeding skills. When they began to participate in large hunting expeditions onto the Great Plains, they came into conflict with other horse-bound tribes. In the first half of the 19th century the Nez Percé traded actively with the Americans, but they were pressured into moving onto several reservations and ceding most of their lands by mid-century. After the 1860s, when gold was discovered near their main reservation, the United States reduced their land base by 75 percent. In 1877 increasing tensions led to a brief war led by Chief Joseph, who resisted attempts to force the Nez Percé onto the small reservation. At the close of the 20th century, many Nez Percé were living on a small reservation in Idaho.

See Also: Indians of North America; Joseph, Chief.

■ **NIAGARA FALLS,** world-renowned falls located on the United States–Canadian border in northwestern New York. The Niagara River connects Lakes Ontario and Erie and forms the spectacular 2,500-foot-wide and 176-foot-high Horseshoe Falls. The French Father Louis Hennepin first described the falls for Europeans in 1683. By the mid-19th century the falls had become an immensely popular tourist destination. Daredevils capitalized on the falls' popularity with stunts like tightrope walking or riding a wooden barrel over the falls. New York made the land near the falls its first state park in 1885 and during the 20th century the falls became a legendary honeymoon destination.

■ **NIAGARA MOVEMENT,** civil rights organization. In 1905, chaffing under Booker T. Washington's philosophy of accommodation and self-improvement, W. E. B. Du Bois and 28 other African-American professionals and intellectuals met in Niagara, Canada, to promote a more vigorous social activism. Through litigation, public meetings, and conventions, the Niagara Movement sought to mount vigorous opposition to those who denied political and social equality

to African Americans. In their annual conventions Niagara Movement members consciously echoed the efforts of abolitionists. Their convention sites—Harpers Ferry in 1906, Boston in 1907, and Oberlin, Ohio, in 1908, chosen for their resonance with the cause of emancipation—highlighted the lack of progress in race relations since the Civil War. The Niagara Movement, plagued by internal disputes and lack of outside support, was short lived, but it served as a catalyst for the creation of the National Association for the Advancement of Colored People (NAACP) in 1909.

See Also: Civil Rights Movement; National Association for the Advancement of Colored People (NAACP).

■ **NICARAGUAN INTERVENTIONS,** symbol of U.S. influence in Central America. The United States has intervened in Nicaragua three times since 1900 on the pretext of protecting vital economic, strategic, and security interests. U.S. troops first arrived in Nicaragua in mid-1912 to quell a revolt against the Conservative government of Adolfo Díaz. Díaz, in power since May 1911, accepted U.S. control of his nation's customs house, welcomed multimillion-dollar loans from New York banks, and agreed not to allow any nation other than the United States to construct an interoceanic canal across Nicaragua. U.S. marines crushed the revolt and guaranteed Nicaragua's status as a U.S. protectorate. The 1916 Bryan-Chamorro Treaty formalized Nicaragua's dependent status.

A Search for Order. Conflict continued into the 1920s. A fraudulent election in 1924 entrenched Conservative rule, leading to a brief withdrawal of U.S. troops. A Liberal rebellion in 1926, aided by Mexico and guided by Juan B. Sacasa, returned Díaz to power and brought back the marines. Their mission was to establish a Liberal-Conservative coalition government as arranged by former secretary of war and corporation lawyer Henry L. Stimson.

Some Nicaraguans rejected the U.S.-supervised elections, scheduled for 1928. César Augusto Sandino, an uncompromising anticolonialist, organized resistance against the marines. Guerrilla war ensued, which the United States countered from the air and with ground forces. Stimson, while Pres. Herbert Hoover's secretary of state, saw the irony in a

U.S. military presence in Nicaragua as he condemned Japanese aggression in Manchuria in 1931.

President Hoover decided to remove the troops. Left behind to guarantee order were the U.S.-trained National Guard forces of Anastasio Somoza, who cemented his hold on power after the marines departed in 1933. Somoza used the ruse of an amnesty to seize Sandino and have him executed.

The Modern Sandinistas. Almost 50 years later another crisis engulfed the two nations. A successful revolution in July 1979 ended the harsh rule of the Somoza dynasty. The Sandinistas, as they called themselves, admired Cuba's Fidel Castro but did not create a pure Marxist state. Over half of the economy remained in private hands and criticism of Sandinista rule, notably by the Catholic Church, persisted.

The Sandinistas posed a challenge to U.S. dominance in the hemisphere. For this they would pay dearly. Opposition forces, some patriotic, some opportunistic, formed a loosely knit group called the Contras, whose leaders Pres. Ronald Reagan likened to the U.S. founding fathers. Reagan committed himself to toppling the Sandinistas.

Using Honduras as its principal base of operations, the Central Intelligence Agency (CIA) tried to turn the Contras into a tough, counterrevolutionary outfit. The effort failed and sparked fears of "another Vietnam" among administration foes. Reagan pressed on, as Congress sought to block Contra aid with the 1984 Boland amendment in response to CIA mining of Nicaraguan harbors and destruction of oil storage facilities. Relatively fair elections in 1984, denounced in Washington, validated the Sandinistas' hold on power.

The Reagan White House still sought their ouster. A covert operation, which became known as the Iran-Contra Affair when exposed, used revenues obtained from secret arms sales to Iran to fund Contra activities. Public exposure of the enterprise embarrassed the president and aided a regional peace effort led by Pres. Oscar Arias Sánchez of Costa Rica. Reagan's successor, George Bush, wearied of the conflict with Nicaragua and, as the Cold War was ending, accepted the Arias initiative. U.S. intervention ceased. In an unexpected development, the Sandinistas lost the election in February 1990.

—WILLIAM O. WALKER III

See Also: Cold War; Gentlemen's Agreement; Iran-Contra Affair; Platt Amendment.

BIBLIOGRAPHY: Kagan, Robert, *A Twilight Struggle: American Power and Nicaragua, 1977-1990* (Free Press 1996); Macauley, Neill, *The Sandino Affair* (Quadrangle Books 1967).

■ **NICKLAUS, JACK (1940-),** golfer. Born in Columbus, Ohio, he turned professional in 1961 and dominated the sport for the next two decades, winning 17 major championships. He later became a leading golf course designer.

See Also: Sports.

■ **NIEBUHR, KARL PAUL REINHOLD (1892-1971),** Protestant theologian and ethicist. Born in Wright City, Missouri, Niebuhr was a pastor in Detroit from 1915 to 1928 and involved with issues of racial conflict, economic justice, and international relations. He then taught at Union Theological Seminary in New York City until 1960. As a democratic-socialist thinker, he wanted to reform the Socialist party but supported Franklin D. Roosevelt for the presidency in 1940. He later worked for the Americans for Democratic Action and was a leader in the Liberal party. In his most important work, *The Nature and Destiny of Man* (1941-43), Niebuhr established the school of "Christian realism."

See Also: Religion.

■ **NIMITZ, CHESTER W. (1885-1966),** World War II admiral who commanded the U.S. Pacific Fleet and was commander in chief of the huge Pacific Ocean Area. Nimitz entered the Naval Academy in 1901 and moved steadily up the ranks. When war broke out after the surprise Japanese attack on Pearl Harbor (Dec. 7, 1941), he was ordered to rebuild the decimated fleet. Nimitz masterminded victories at the Coral Sea (May 1942) and Midway (June 1942) and subsequently led his fleet to the ultimate victory over Japan.

See Also: Coral Sea, Battle of the; Midway, Battle of; World War II.

■ **NINETEEN SIXTIES,** the most turbulent decade of the second half of the 20th century. By 1965 it was clear that great changes, often accompanied by violence, were remaking the country. The fight for civil rights led the way. In February 1960 four African-American students sat down at a whites-only lunch counter in Greensboro, North Carolina. At that time virtually all facilities in the South were segregated, and few African Americans were allowed to vote. The "sit-in" movement swept across the South and was followed by "freedom rides" in buses, desegregation campaigns in cities such as Birmingham and Selma, Alabama, Dr. Martin Luther King's great March on Washington in 1963, and the "freedom summer" in Mississippi the following year. Many activists were killed, 15 during the freedom summer alone, and thousands more were beaten and arrested. But within five years the movement had forced passage of the Civil Rights Act of 1964 and the Voting Rights Act of 1965 that together destroyed racial segregation.

However, beginning in Watts, an area of Los Angeles, in August 1965, the tide of violence began to turn. Instead of white mobs attacking African-American activists, African-American mobs began rioting in the inner cities. After Watts, riots took place in Newark, New Jersey, Detroit, Washington, D.C., and elsewhere. The civil rights movement became divided, as young militants abandoned the nonviolent ethic of Dr. King and advocated, if they did not practice, violence. The rise of the Black Panthers was the ultimate expression of this tendency. By the end of the 1960s, the civil rights movement was divided and seemed to have lost much of its momentum.

The assassinations of Pres. John F. Kennedy in 1963, Malcolm X in 1965, and Dr. King and Sen. Robert F. Kennedy in 1968 further scarred the era. By that time many inner cities lay in ruins, and many college campuses had become scenes of violence, as anti–Vietnam War demonstrations turned into fights between students and police. Most of these were led by members of a "New Left" who hoped to use the peace issue to overthrow capitalism. But the antiwar movement was too big to manipulate and included leaders from all walks of life. In 1968 it had helped drive Pres. Lyndon B. Johnson from office. That year, Richard M. Nixon was elected president, and he eventually took America out of Vietnam.

Cultural Changes. At the same time a sexual and moral revolution was taking place that would have far-reaching consequences. Many forms of censorship were relaxed, "free love" was proclaimed, and the pornography industry emerged from underground. Colleges gave up playing the role of parent substitute, allowing students to live where and with whom they pleased and to keep any kind of hours. All aspects of the mass media were influenced by these changes, and also by the growing popularity of narcotics, especially marijuana and LSD. These were mainstays of the counterculture that emphasized self-indulgence and personal pleasure. Counterculturists were urged by gurus like Dr. Timothy Leary to "turn on, tune in, and drop out" of society.

Unlike the New Left, which quickly burned itself out, the counterculture lived on, not as an establishment movement but as a code of conduct mandating that each person do his or her "own thing." A great increase in the rates of divorce, adoption, and illegitimacy were among its inevitable outcomes. To some extent the increase in personal and sexual freedom was partly the natural culmination of trends that had been growing since the 1920s. Then, too, the enormous prosperity of the era made it seem that there would be no personal or social cost for doing what previously had been forbidden.

The United States today is a country formed, to a large extent, by what happened in the 1960s. African Americans are free, and the South is a two-party region, because of the civil rights movement, the era's most enduring legacy. But the sexual revolution and its consequences and widespread drug use are also legacies of the 1960s.

—WILLIAM L. O'NEILL

See Also: Civil Rights Movement; Vietnam War.

BIBLIOGRAPHY: Gitlin, Todd, *The Sixties: Years of Hope, Days of Rage* (Bantam 1987); O'Neill, William L., *Coming Apart: An Informal History of the 1960s* (Quadrangle Brooks 1971).

■ **NINETEENTH AMENDMENT,** amendment to the U.S. Constitution that guarantees American women the right to vote. The amendment was passed by Congress in 1919 and ratified by the states in 1920. While the Constitution ostensibly guarantees universal suffrage for all citizens, women were denied the vote until the woman suffrage movement forced the passage of the 19th Amendment. By the end of the 19th century, the powerful writing and oratory of the older generation of suffrage leaders, such as Susan B. Anthony, Lucy Stone, and Elizabeth Cady Stanton, had already achieved substantial gains through the efforts of the National American Woman Suffrage Association (NAWSA). Laws were passed protecting the property rights of married women and securing full voting rights for women in 12 states.

In the early 20th century, however, the movement stagnated. Carrie Chapman Catt, president of NASWA, took advantage of the atmosphere of relative openness that followed the start of World War I to launch a skillfully orchestrated campaign for a federal suffrage amendment. Catt appealed to younger, more militant suffragists to build up the membership of the NASWA, while she raised funds, secured the support of Pres. Woodrow Wilson, and presented millions of signatures to Congress. As a result of the amendment's ratification, 8 million women voted for president for the first time in 1920.

See Also: *Constitution of the United States; Suffrage; Woman Suffrage Movement; Women's Movement.*

■ **NIXON, RICHARD MILHOUS (1913-94),** 37th President of the United States (1969-74), who also served as a U.S. representative (1947-51), senator (1951-53), and vice president (1953-61). He resigned as president after his role in the Watergate cover-up was discovered and congressional impeachment proceedings were begun against him.

Born in Yorba Linda, California, on Jan. 9, 1913, and raised in nearby Whittier, Nixon grew up in modest circumstances. His Quaker parents, Francis (Frank) and Hannah Milhous Nixon, ran a small grocery store, where Richard and his four brothers worked after school. After graduating from Whittier College (1934) and Duke University Law School (1937), Nixon returned to California to practice law. His marriage to Thelma Catherine (Pat) Ryan in 1940 produced two daughters, Tricia and Julie.

Nixon served as a naval officer in the South Pacific during World War II. In 1946 he ran for Congress as a Republican and defeated the Democratic incumbent, Jerry Voorhis, in a bitter campaign. As a member of the House Un-American Activities

Republican Richard M. Nixon, vice president under President Eisenhower, was elected president in 1968 and reelected in 1972. In 1974, facing impeachment for his cover-up of the Watergate Affair, he became the first president to resign from office.

Committee, Nixon developed a reputation as a staunch anticommunist. In 1950, he won a Senate seat after accusing his opponent, Rep. Helen Gahagan Douglas, of being "soft on communism."

In 1952 the Republican party nominated Gen. Dwight D. Eisenhower for president and Nixon for vice president. Nixon faced trouble, however, when a newspaper report accused him of accepting secret contributions. In response, Nixon delivered a televised defense of his finances that included a folksy reference to the family dog, Checkers. The so-called "Checkers speech" saved his political career. As vice president, Nixon kept a high profile. On one foreign trip, he confronted angry demonstrators in Caracas, Venezuela; on another, he engaged Soviet leader Nikita Khrushchev in the famous "kitchen debate." Above all, Nixon filled in capably for President Eisenhower, who suffered a heart attack in 1955 and a stroke two years later.

After winning the Republican presidential nomination in 1960, Nixon waged a vigorous fight against his Democratic opponent, Sen. John F. Kennedy of Massachusetts. The two men squared off in a series of televised debates that marked the beginning of modern presidential campaigns. Kennedy won the election with 303 electoral votes to Nixon's 219. Yet, the popular vote was the closest since 1888, with Kennedy getting 49.7 percent and Nixon 49.6 percent.

In 1962, Nixon lost another bruising election, this time for governor of California. Moving to New York City, he launched a political comeback that brought him the Republican presidential nomination in 1968. With his running mate, Gov. Spiro Agnew of Maryland, Nixon campaigned as the spokesman for America's "silent majority," the people who worked hard, went to church, and obeyed the law. Against a backdrop of urban riots and campus demonstrations, Nixon narrowly defeated his Democratic opponent, Vice Pres. Hubert H. Humphrey.

Presidency. As president, Nixon charted a moderate course in domestic affairs. Facing Democratic majorities in Congress, he tried unsuccessfully to change the welfare system by instituting a guaranteed family income and requiring able-bodied recipients to work. Yet, Nixon and Congress joined together on legislation that created the Environmental Protection Agency, strengthened the Equal Employment Opportunities Commission, and implemented a federal revenue-sharing plan with states and localities.

Nixon's primary interest, however, lay in foreign affairs. Working with Henry Kissinger, his national security adviser and then his secretary of state, Nixon opened relations with the People's Republic of China, established détente with the Soviet Union, and achieved serious arms control through the Strategic Arms Limitation Treaty, or SALT I. Using covert methods, the Nixon administration helped to overthrow the leftist government of Salvador Allende in Chile. Using massive aid, it helped to protect Israel in the 1973 Yom Kippur War.

Most controversial, however, was Nixon's plan to withdraw U.S. troops from Vietnam during the Vietnam War. Know as Vietnamization, the plan to replace U.S. soldiers with local forces involved further bombing of North Vietnam and a widening of the war into neighboring Cambodia. Although American troop levels dropped slowly in Vietnam, antiwar protests grew dramatically at home, infuriating President Nixon and his advisers.

On June 17, 1972, less than five months before the presidential election, police arrested five men for breaking into the Democratic National Committee headquarters at the Watergate complex in Washington, D.C. Reporters quickly discovered a link between the burglars and the Nixon White House. While Nixon easily won reelection in 1972, trouncing Democratic Sen. George McGovern, the Watergate probe uncovered a mountain of sordid activity, including other break-ins, illegal campaign contributions, and a White House "enemies" list.

In 1973 a Senate committee chaired by Democrat Sam Ervin of North Carolina investigated the Watergate affair. When its hearings uncovered the existence of a taping system inside the Oval Office, the committee demanded the recordings of conversations related to Watergate, but Nixon refused to turn them over, claiming executive privilege. As the House of Representatives began impeachment proceedings, the Supreme Court ruled that Nixon must relinquish the tapes to a special prosecutor. Their release offered clear proof of his involvement in plans to cover up the Watergate burglary. With impeachment now a certainty, he resigned on Aug. 8, 1974. A month later his successor, Pres. Gerald Ford, pardoned Nixon for any federal crimes that he may have committed while in office.

Last Years. Nixon spent the remaining years of his life trying to salvage his reputation. He wrote books on foreign affairs, met with world leaders in foreign capitals, and offered political advice to those in trouble. After he died in New York City on Apr. 2, 1994, the obituaries noted his accomplishments as well as his disgrace over Watergate. All of them described Nixon as the most commanding and controversial political figure of his generation.

—DAVID M. OSHINSKY

See Also: *Eisenhower, Dwight David; Ford, Gerald Rudolph; Kissinger, Henry; Presidential Elections; President of the United States; Vietnam War; Watergate.*
BIBLIOGRAPHY: Ambrose, Stephen E., *Nixon: The Education of a Politician, 1913-1962* (Simon & Schuster 1987); Ambrose, Stephen E., *Nixon: The Triumph of a Politician, 1962-1972* (Simon & Schuster 1989); Bernstein, Carl, and Bob Woodward, *The Final Days* (Simon & Schuster 1976); Nixon, Richard M., *The Real War* (Warner 1980); Nixon, Richard M., *RN: The Memoirs of Richard Nixon* (Grosset 1978).

■ **NOGUCHI, ISAMU (1904-88),** modern sculptor. Born in Los Angeles, California, Noguchi lived in Japan from age 2 to 11, but his parents sent him back to the United States for school. After high school, Noguchi worked for sculptor Gutzon Borglum, the creator of Mount Rushmore. He then studied at Columbia University (1923). At 22, he won a Guggenheim Award to go to Paris to study sculpture with Constantin Brancusi. Noguchi alternated in his work between abstract forms and portrait heads, the latter providing his income early in his career. He worked in a variety of media, including cement, ceramic, stone, and steel. In 1940, he completed a large-scale stainless steel plaque for the Associated Press Building at Rockefeller Center in New York City. The plaque, which depicted symbolic figures of an editor, reporter, photographer, and teletype and telephone operators, was the largest stainless steel casting done at that time. Noguchi was interned at Poston, Arizona, during World War II.

■ **NONIMPORTATION,** form of protest that called for the suspension of imports from Britain on the part of the American colonists against a punitive British policy. First implemented effectively in Boston during the Stamp Act Crisis in 1765-66 and revived in 1767 after the Townshend Acts, nonimportation became a common colonial action in the years before the American Revolution. In addition to Boston, other port cities such as New York, Providence, and Newport participated in the boycotting of British goods. Artisans commonly led support of nonimportation associations, but some merchants felt that boycotts threatened their livelihood. Nonimportation helped coalesce anti-British sentiment

in rural districts, as the associations urged the curtailment of luxury and encouraged local industry. Women's efforts in nonimportation burgeoned in 1768-69. Groups, some calling themselves Daughters of Liberty, organized such activities as spinning bees, which symbolized female frugality and industry. These local and individual efforts received support from colonial legislators who voted to establish associations that officially prohibited British imports.

See Also: *Revolution, American; Sons and Daughters of Liberty; Stamp Act.*

■ **NONIMPORTATION ACT (1806),** federal legislation prohibiting the importation of English goods that could be produced domestically or bought elsewhere. The U.S. Congress passed the Nonimportation Act in response to British seizures of American shipping and the impressment of American seamen into the British military.

See Also: *Impressment.*

■ **NON-INTERCOURSE ACT (1809),** federal trade legislation signed by Pres. Thomas Jefferson just three days before the end of his presidency. In 1807 the Jefferson administration had pushed through the disastrous Embargo Act, forbidding American ships from sailing to foreign ports. The Non-Intercourse Act replaced the Embargo Act and reopened trade with all nations except England and France.

See Also: *Embargo Act of 1807.*

■ **NOOTKA SOUND CONTROVERSY (1789),** conflict precipitated by the Spanish and English expeditions that coincidently reached Nootka Sound on Vancouver Island on the northwest coast of North America. The Spaniards seized the arriving British seamen and ships and sent them to Mexico. As the controversy heightened, the two nations prepared for war. While Britain received assurances of support from its allies, revolutionary France demurred from supporting Spain. In October 1790 Spain was forced to concede most of its claims in the Northwest.

See Also: *Spanish Colonies.*

■ **NORDICA, LILLIAN (1857-1914),** opera singer. Born in Farmington, Maine, she is remembered more for her hard work and versatility than for her virtuosity. She excelled in Wagnerian soprano parts and performed regularly at New York City's Metropolitan Opera from 1893 to 1907.

■ **NORMALCY,** a word coined by Republican presidential candidate Warren G. Harding when he misread the word "normality" during a campaign speech in May 1920. Harding was elected and the term "normalcy" caught on, referring to Harding's promise to restore tranquillity and prosperity to America after the horror of World War I and the national division over the proposed League of Nations, the "red scare," the prolonged labor unrest, and the postwar inflation and subsequent high unemployment. Normalcy implied a return to an America that would be probusiness domestically yet at the same time isolated from international conflicts and concerns. Harding's administration (1921-23) and that of his successor, Calvin Coolidge, sought to do just that.

See Also: Harding, Warren Gamaliel.
BIBLIOGRAPHY: Murray, Robert K., *The Politics of Normalcy: Government Theory and Practice in the Harding-Coolidge Era* (Norton 1973).

■ **NORMAND, MABEL (1893?-1930),** actress in silent films. Born in Boston, Massachusetts, she was a gifted stage comedienne and premier silent film actress. She appeared in 11 films with Charlie Chaplin and was his mentor. Her most enduring film is *Micky* (1918).

See Also: Chaplin, Charlie.

■ **NORRIS, FRANK (1870-1902),** novelist in the naturalist tradition. Norris was born in Chicago but moved to San Francisco as a boy. He attended the University of California and Harvard University, where he began working on some of the novels that he would publish several years later. He worked for the *San Francisco Chronicle* as a war correspondent in South Africa in 1895-96. On his return Norris published his first novel, *Moran of the Lady Letty* (1898), in serial form. Norris was a correspondent for *McClure's Magazine* in Cuba in 1898-99. In 1899 he began working for the publishing company of Doubleday, Page and Company, which published his well-known novel *McTeague.* At that time Norris planned a trilogy of

novels that would focus on the growth and distribution of wheat to give perspective on the larger progress of the American West. He published *The Octopus* (1901), about railroad owners' influence on the wheat trade in Chicago, and *The Pit* (1903), about the marketing of wheat in San Francisco, but died before completing the third novel.

See Also: Naturalism.

■ **NORRIS, GEORGE WILLIAM (1861-1944),** U.S. senator. He was born in Sandusky County, Ohio, and attended Baldwin College and the Northern Indiana Normal School. After a brief career as a Nebraska lawyer and judge, he was elected to the U.S. House of Representatives as a Republican in 1902. He served five terms and was active in reform, including the successful efforts to curb the power of House Speaker Joseph G. Cannon. In 1912 Norris went to the Senate, where, as one of the Midwestern Progressive "insurgents," he opposed U.S. entry into World War I and later spoke out against the Treaty of Versailles. Long an advocate of public regulation of utilities, Norris finally achieved that in the passage of the Tennessee Valley Authority Act in 1933. Also a friend to labor, he cowrote the Norris-LaGuardia Act of 1932, which limited the use of the injunction during strikes. His support of the New Deal cost him his standing within the Republican party, and he was denied reelection in 1942.

See Also: Cannon, Joseph Gurney; Progressivism; Tennessee Valley Authority.
BIBLIOGRAPHY: Lowitt, Richard, *George W. Norris: The Making of a Progressive, 1861-1912* (Syracuse Univ. Press 1963); Lowitt, Richard, *George W. Norris: The Persistence of a Progressive, 1913-1933* (Univ. of Illinois Press 1971); Lowitt, Richard, *George W. Norris: The Triumph of a Progressive* (Univ. of Illinois Press 1978).

■ **NORSE EXPLORATIONS AND SETTLEMENTS.** At the end of the first millennium A.D., the Norse were the greatest sailors, navigators, and colonists in Europe. In the last years of the 8th century, Danes and Norwegians settled the northern Atlantic Shetland and Orkney islands, and from this base they raided and colonized the Hebrides, the Irish and English coasts, Normandy, and even the Mediterranean coast of southern France. This intense expansionist drive was also evident in Norse island-hopping across the Atlantic, which by the year 1000 had taken them to the shores of North America. Norse expansion in the north Atlantic, unlike 16th-century transatlantic European expansion, was not directed by royal or merchant design but was a folk movement. Modern knowledge of this expansion comes from oral sagas, written down generations later, providing only a broad outline of Norse achievements.

The Norse discovery of Iceland, about 850 A.D., was a result of their sail-driven ships being blown off course in the fierce and unpredictable weather of the north Atlantic. By the end of the century the Icelandic coast was dotted with permanent settlements based upon a pastoral economy. Greenland was similarly discovered at the end of the 10th century by Eric the Red and then colonized. The encounter with the coast of North America was a logical extension of this process of accidental discovery.

About 985 the ships of Bjarni Herjulfson, sailing from Iceland to Greenland, were blown off course and, struggling to return, encountered three distinct coastlines, thought now to be those of Newfoundland, Labrador, and Baffin Island. Leif Eriksson followed this discovery with a voyage of exploration in 1001. At the southernmost of his landfalls Herjulfson built dwellings and wintered before returning to Greenland, where he named his encampment Vinland (from the Norse *vin*, meaning "meadow"). Thorvald Eriksson and Thornfinn Karlsefni made several later attempts to colonize the site, but because of the uncertainty of the supply lines to Greenland and conflicts with the aboriginal inhabitants, these were unsuccessful, and by 1014 the site was abandoned.

Historians have proposed a multitude of locations for the site of Vinland. Artifacts from an archaeological site at the fishing village of L'Anse aux Meadows in Newfoundland are similar to those found in the Shetlands, Iceland, and Greenland and clearly document a Norse presence in North America. But carbon-14 tests indicate an occupation as early as the 9th century, a hundred years or more before the dating provided for Eriksson's Vinland in the oral sagas, suggesting that there may have been several Norse landfalls, of which only Herjulfson's and Eriksson's were long remembered. Other possible sites of Norse settlements exist at Pamiok Island and Ungava Bay in northern Quebec.

Common knowledge of these Norse discoveries was evident in the literature of medieval Europe. English fishermen were in Iceland as early as 1410, and what they learned there may have helped inform John Cabot in Bristol. One tradition relates a trip made by Christopher Columbus to Iceland before his famous voyage, but even in mainland western Europe he could have learned of the Norse demonstration of the feasibility of transatlantic navigation and of the possibility of western lands.

—JOHN MACK FARAGHER

See Also: *Erik the Red; Eriksson, Leif; Exploration and Discovery.*

BIBLIOGRAPHY: Magnusson, Magnus, and Herman Palsson, eds., *The Vineland Sagas: The Norse Discovery of America* (Penguin 1965); Morison, Samuel Eliot, *The European Discovery of America: The Northern Voyages, AD 500-1600* (Oxford Univ. Press 1971); Seaver, Kirsten A., *The Frozen Echo: Greenland and the Exploration of North America* (Stanford Univ. Press 1996).

■ **NORTH, LORD FREDERICK (1732-92),** British prime minister (1770-82) during the American Revolution. He provoked the colonists by pushing the Tea Act (1773) and Intolerable Acts (1774) through Parliament. During the war, North developed no coherent strategy and suffered incompetent ministers and excessively cautious generals. He resigned after the British surrender at Yorktown (Oct. 19, 1781).

See Also: *Boston Tea Party; Intolerable Acts; Revolution, American.*

■ **NORTH, OLIVER (1943-),** White House aide during the Reagan presidency. Born in San Antonio, Texas, he was implicated in the Iran-Contra scandal in which the National Security Council became involved in secret weapons transactions and other activities prohibited by the U.S. Congress. He testified before Congress (1987), was convicted of perjury but freed on appeal, and ran unsuccessfully for the U.S. Senate from Virginia in 1992.

■ **NORTH, THE,** term used to designate the northeastern region of the United States north of the Mason-Dixon line, the boundary line between

Maryland and Pennsylvania fixed in 1767 and extending westward as far as Ohio. This region includes the New England states of Connecticut, Maine, Massachusetts, New Hampshire, Rhode Island, and Vermont, as well as Delaware, Maryland, New Jersey, New York, and Pennsylvania, this latter group also referred to as the Mid-Atlantic states. In the 19th century the term *the North* referred to the states that maintained their allegiance to the Union during the Civil War, including the states of the old Northwest Territory.

See Also: *Mason-Dixon Line.*

■ **NORTH AFRICAN INVASION (1942),** World War II landings that marked the first combat for U.S. soldiers in the Western theater. Under Gen. Dwight D. Eisenhower, a joint British-American amphibious force made three landings on the North African coast near Casablanca in Morocco and at Oran and Algiers in Algeria. Resistance by Vichy French forces was strongest at Casablanca, but by November 11 all three cities had capitulated. In the next two weeks Eisenhower moved forces overland toward Tunis, the capital of Tunisia, but German forces counterattacked and stopped the Allied advance 20 miles short of the city.

See Also: *Eisenhower, Dwight David; World War II.*

■ **NORTH AMERICAN FREE TRADE AGREEMENT (NAFTA),** agreement to eliminate tariffs and other trade barriers among Canada, Mexico, and the United States, signed in 1992 and effective from Jan. 1, 1994. The agreement targeted trade restrictions in such areas as manufactured goods, services, and agriculture. Many tariffs were eliminated immediately, while others were lowered over periods of up to 15 years.

■ **NORTH ATLANTIC TREATY ORGANIZATION (NATO) (1949),** collective security agreement among the United States, Canada, and noncommunist countries of Europe. On Apr. 4, 1949, the foreign ministers of Belgium, Britain, Canada, Denmark, France, Iceland, Italy, the Netherlands, Norway, Portugal, and the United States signed the North Atlantic Treaty in Washington, D.C. The treaty called for assistance from all signatories to any member attacked. Prompted by growing hostility between the Western wartime allies and the Soviet Union, the treaty established the North Atlantic Treaty Organization, a framework for international political and military cooperation among member countries.

As Britain, France, and the United States moved toward merging their occupation zones in Germany, the United States encouraged the formation of a regional collective security pact in Europe. Britain and France already had formed an alliance in 1947, and on Mar. 17, 1948, they joined Belgium, the Netherlands, and Luxembourg in the Brussels Treaty, pledging to provide military and other forms of aid to one another in case of attack against any one of them. On June 11, 1948, the U.S. Senate passed the Vandenberg Resolution, approving U.S. membership in regional security pacts as long as they did not violate the United Nations Charter.

For the United States, which had never formed an alliance during peacetime, NATO reflected a new perception of how the country should conduct itself internationally to protect and promote its interests. Seeking to cultivate and maintain a global marketplace, the United States needed to fend off threats to the new world order it aimed to establish. The Truman Doctrine and Marshall Plan of 1947 demonstrated a commitment to containing communism and nurturing European recovery; NATO represented a firm U.S. commitment to the defense of Western Europe.

NATO has expanded since 1949: Greece and Turkey joined in 1952; West Germany in 1955, prompting the Soviet Union and its satellites to form the Warsaw Pact that same year; Spain became a member in 1982. The end of the Cold War led to a reassessment of NATO's role, but the desire of former Warsaw Pact members to join during the 1990s suggested the organization's continuing importance to European security.

—MAARTEN L. PEREBOOM

See Also: *Cold War; Marshall Plan; Truman Doctrine.*
BIBLIOGRAPHY: Diefendorf, Jeffry, et al., eds., *American Policy and the Reconstruction of West Germany, 1945-1955* (German Hist. Inst. 1993); Kaplan, Lawrence, *NATO and the United States,* rev. ed. (Twayne 1994).

■ **NORTH CAROLINA,** a South Atlantic state. It is bounded on the north by Virginia, on the north and west by Tennessee, on the west and south by South Carolina, on the south by Georgia, and on the east by the Atlantic Ocean. Forty-three peaks of the Great Smoky Mountains, in the far west of the state, rise higher than 6,000 feet. The elevation slopes downward to the coastal plain and the Outer Banks, narrow islands of shifting sandbars. North Carolina leads the nation in tobacco and turkey farming. It also leads all states in the production of textiles, cigarettes, and furniture.

North Carolina was one of the original 13 states. It was the last state to join the Confederacy but provided more troops to the cause than any other state. Industrialization grew dramatically after World War II; a notable development was Research Triangle Park, near Raleigh, a home for industrial and scientific laboratories.

Capital: Raleigh. Area: 52,672 square miles. Population (1995 est.): 7,195,000.

See Also: Great Smoky Mountains; Johnston, Joseph E.; Roanoke, Lost Colony of; Sit-Ins; Wright, Wilbur and Wright, Orville.

▦ **NORTH DAKOTA,** a western Midwest state. It is bounded on the north by Saskatchewan and Manitoba, on the west by Montana, on the south by South Dakota, and on the east by Minnesota. The Missouri River flows through much of the western part of the state, and the Red River of the North forms its eastern border. The eastern part of the state belongs to the Central Plains; the western part to the Great Plains. In some years, North Dakota leads the nation in wheat production, but it has the lowest per-capita income of any Midwest state. North Dakota became a state in 1889.

Capital: Bismarck. Area: 70,704 square miles. Population (1995 est.): 641,000.

See Also: Great Plains; Louisiana Purchase; Missouri River.

▦ **NORTHWEST COAST INDIANS,** the American Indian people of present-day Oregon, Washington, British Columbia, and southeastern Alaska: the Tlingit, Haida, Tsimshian, Kwakiutl, Bella Colla, Nootka, Makah, Quinault, and Chinook of the lower Columbia River.

These Indian peoples were dependent primarily on salmon and sea mammals for subsistence. They used the cedars and firs of the coastal rain forest for houses, canoes, and crafts. A wide variety of languages were spoken, along with special languages designed for trade. The basic settlement pattern of the Northwest Coast was large, permanent winter villages in protected coves near shellfish beds and summer camps at fishing stations. This pattern persisted from c. 3000 B.C. until the mid-19th century.

Ceremonies were a significant part of daily life, especially during the winter months. The salmon ceremony is a good example of the many rituals practiced. The Indian peoples of the Northwest Coast believed that salmon represented a race of supernatural beings who dwelled in a great house beneath the sea. When a salmon died, its spirit returned to its place of origin, and thus humans should not offend the salmon people by careless use. If the salmon bones were properly returned to the water, the being resumed humanlike form and could repeat its trip upstream the next season. All Northwest Coast peoples had a long list of taboos and prohibitions designed to maintain good relations with the salmon people and revealing a profound ecological wisdom.

At various times starting in the 16th century, Spanish, Russian, and English explorers visited the Northwest Coast and documented the Indians' huge, decorated plank houses, the distinctions based on class, the abundance of food, and the great sophistication in dealing with traders. White settlers after 1846 permitted the Indians to practice some commercial fishing and logging and allowed some upper-class Northwest Coast families to retain their traditional leadership and ceremonies, such as the potlatch feast, a gift-giving ceremony. But epidemic diseases decimated the population, unfair treaties reduced tribal lands, and missionary antagonism to Indian rituals created friction.

—RYAN MADDEN

See Also: Indians of North America.

BIBLIOGRAPHY: Boxberger, Daniel, *Native Americans: An Ethnohistorical Approach* (Kendal/Hunt 1990); Drucker, Philip, *Cultures of the North Pacific Coast* (Chandler 1965).

▦ **NORTHWEST ORDINANCE (1787, 1789),** congressional act that established a blueprint for the political development of the territory northwest of the Ohio River. First enacted by the Congress of the Confederation on July 13, 1787, the ordinance laid out the procedures for federal administration of the "Northwest Territory" and provided a framework for the admission of new states. While the U.S. Constitution was being framed, the Northwest Ordinance was reenacted by the U.S. Congress in 1789. It was thus enshrined as the basic charter for the governance of the national domain.

The problem of governing the "western country" was among the most serious challenges facing American leaders. By the Treaty of Paris (1783), the United States acquired sovereignty over the entire Ohio Valley. Land cessions from various states confirmed the national government's authority over these western lands. But treaty transfers and state cessions did not translate into effective control. During the 1780s, Indians determinedly rejected the rule of the United States over their Ohio Valley homelands. Defiance arose as well among American citizens, some of whom sought to circumvent the U.S. authority by concluding private land purchases with Indians. At the same time, hundreds of other pioneer settlers disdained both Indians and the Congress of the Confederation by moving to lands north of the Ohio River. The trespasses of these squatters provoked hostility with Indian occupants and exposed the weakness of the Confederation's hold.

Ordinance Provisions. Its framers intended the Northwest Ordinance as a mechanism to regulate better the colonization of western lands and to secure the territory's political connection to the new nation. Promising "justice and humanity" toward indigenous inhabitants, the ordinance sought to slow and order the movement of Anglo-Americans into the Old Northwest. National authority was augmented by the provisions for territorial government. These gave the U.S. president power to select the territorial governor, who in turn appointed all other officials. The governor also retained an absolute veto over the acts of the territorial assembly.

In addition to guaranteeing certain civil rights to territorial inhabitants, the ordinance plotted the phased transfer of power to locally elected officials and mapped out the stages that would culminate in the creation of new states. Once a district's population reached 5,000 adult males, what the ordinance called "second stage" government commenced. During this period, qualified voters gained the right to elect the lower house of the territorial assembly, although the appointed governor kept his absolute veto. When the census showed 60,000 inhabitants, the territory became eligible for statehood, with all the rights of previously existing states. According to the 1787 plan, three to five states would emerge from the Northwest Territory. The states of Ohio, Indiana, Illinois, Michigan, and Wisconsin were those established.

The most contentious plank of the Northwest Ordinance was its prohibition of slavery. Article VI of the ordinance explicitly stated that "there shall be neither Slavery nor involuntary Servitude" in the territory. Yet this barrier proved permeable, and efforts to legalize slavery continued through the 1820s.

—STEPHEN ARON

See Also: *Frontier in American History; Northwest Territory; Treaty of Paris (1783).*

BIBLIOGRAPHY: Jensen, Merrill, *The New Nation: A History of the United States during the Confederation, 1781-1789* (Knopf 1950); Onuf, Peter, *Statehood and Union: A History of the Northwest Ordinance* (Indiana Univ. Press 1987).

■ **NORTHWEST PASSAGE,** sea route from the Atlantic Ocean to the Pacific, cutting through and around northern North America. It was the object of an intensive European search for over 300 years before its existence was verified in the mid-19th century. The search began as soon as navigators and geographers agreed that Christopher Columbus's landfall was, as Amerigo Vespucci declared, a new continent. After the earliest explorers for the passage, Giovanni de Verrazano in the 1520s and Jacques Cartier in the 1530s, established the continuity of the North American coast to the latitudes of Labrador and eliminated the possibility of a passage at the St. Lawrence River, attention shifted to the far north. The Spanish and Portuguese, who had developed southern empires and trade routes, left the field to the northern Europeans.

The English, who first attempted to locate a northeast passage through the Arctic waters north of Asia in the 1550s but could get no farther than

Novaya Zemlya, inaugurated a long series of explorations of the northwest Atlantic with the voyages of Martin Frobisher in the 1570s. But it was Henry Hudson, in 1610, who first passed through the strait and into the great bay that thereafter took his name; he assumed that Hudson Bay was the Pacific and died before other explorers proved otherwise. The continuing explorations of Hudson Bay finally demonstrated conclusively the lack of an outlet to the Pacific from the bay.

Vitus Bering pointed toward the possibility of a western approach to the passage with his discovery in 1741 of the strait between Asia and North America. James Cook was on such a search in the 1770s. George Vancouver surveyed the area of the Strait of Juan de Fuca for the inlet to a passage in the 1790s. These various explorations established the continuity of the Pacific coast of North America from Oregon to northern Alaska and ruled out any but the most northerly passage.

This northernmost passage, through the straits and channels of the Arctic Ocean, was shown to exist in the 1850s, but the first European to pilot through them was Roald Amundsen in 1906. Even today the Northwest Passage is impractical as a commercial seaway because of the severe ice and weather.

See Also: *Exploration and Discovery.*

BIBLIOGRAPHY: Struzik, Edward, *Northwest Passage: The Quest for an Arctic Route to the East* (Blandford 1991).

■ **NORTHWEST TERRITORY,** also known as the Old Northwest, the northwestern quadrant of the early American republic. More specifically, the term denotes the territory "northwest of the Ohio River"—an area of nearly 250,000 square miles bounded by the Ohio River, the Great Lakes, and the Mississippi River—which was created by the Northwest Ordinance, enacted by the U.S. Congress on July 13, 1787. Along with the Land Ordinance of 1785, the Northwest Ordinance of 1787 established the procedures for transferring this vast national domain to private owners and for turning the Northwest Territory into the present states of Ohio, Indiana, Illinois, Michigan, and Wisconsin, as well as a portion of Minnesota.

According to the Northwest Ordinance of 1787, a population of at least 60,000 persons was required before any part of the Northwest Territory could graduate to statehood, yet in that year, the whole territory contained fewer than that number. Some 45,000 Indians then shared the region with approximately 2,000 French villagers. Only a handful of Anglo-American pioneers had settled north of the Ohio, and these had done so at considerable risk. While the United States asserted sovereignty, Northwest Indians, with support from the British, maintained their possession. Only after an American army under the command of Gen. Anthony Wayne defeated an Indian confederacy at the Battle of Fallen Timbers (1794) were pioneers able to occupy more safely the southern and eastern portions of what is now Ohio. Within 10 years Ohio's census qualified it for statehood. Further north and west, however, Indian resistance continued to impede U.S. settlement for another two decades.

As Indians were dispossessed, the U.S. population increased and spread across the Northwest Territory. These newcomers hailed from both northern and southern states, lending diversity to the cultural geography of the Old Northwest. It also thrust the question of slavery onto the political agenda. While Article VI of the Northwest Ordinance of 1787 prohibited slavery from the Northwest Territory, hundreds of slaves were brought across the Ohio River under the guise of being "indentured servants." In Indiana and Illinois proslavery politicians occupied important territorial offices, from which they led the fight to overturn Article VI. They failed to get slavery sanctioned in either state's constitution, however, and in 1824, after Illinois voters narrowly rejected a call for a new convention, the "free state" future of the Northwest Territory was secured.

—STEPHEN ARON

See Also: *Frontier in American History; Northwest Ordinance.*

BIBLIOGRAPHY: Barnhart, John D., *Valley of Democracy: The Frontier Versus the Plantation in Ohio Valley, 1775-1818* (Indiana Univ. Press 1953); Cayton, Andrew R. L., and Peter S. Onuf, *The Midwest and the Nation: Rethinking the History of an American Region* (Indiana Univ. Press 1990); Rohrbough, Malcolm J., *The Trans-Appalachian Frontier: People, Societies, and Institutions, 1775-1850* (Oxford Univ. Press 1978).

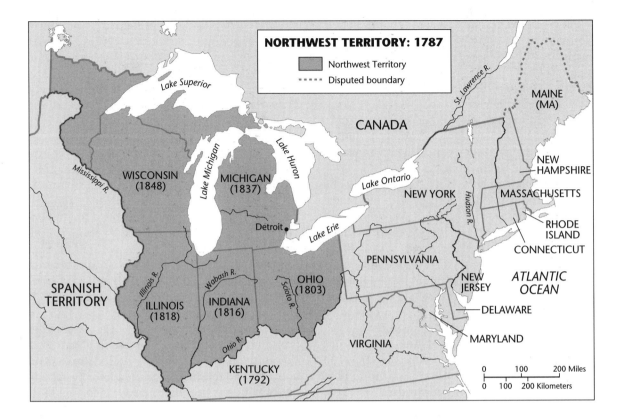

NORTHWEST TERRITORY: 1787

Northwest Territory
Disputed boundary

■ **NOVEL,** from humble beginnings, the American novel has developed into a vital and complex narrative form; its growth has been rich and varied. Fiction was not read much in the colonies. After the Revolutionary War, however, novels imitating English and Continental traditions became popular. William Hill Brown's *The Power of Sympathy* (1789) borrows Samuel Richardson's epistolary style and theme of seduction, while Susannah Rowson's *Charlotte Temple* (1794) and Hannah Foster's *The Coquette* (1797) repeat the same theme. In addition, Hugh Henry Brackenridge's *Modern Chivalry* (published serially between 1792-1815) imitates Cervantes's *Don Quixote* in satirizing human foibles in the new democracy.

Charles Brockden Brown, America's first major novelist, treats character and setting in imaginative ways. In *Edgar Huntly* (1799) and *Arthur Mervyn* (1800), Brown's use of the enclosure device (a cave, attic, cellar, various small chambers) is particularly significant in these coming-of-age narratives. Although written hastily and without much editing or revision, Brown's novels provide an important transition between the sentimental, didactic

tales of the late 18th century and the symbolic works that characterize the Romantic period.

The Romantic Period. Between 1820 and the beginning of the Civil War (1861), the novel in America came to fruition, culminating in two of the century's greatest works, *The Scarlet Letter* (1850) and *Moby-Dick* (1851). Two earlier contributors to the genre's development, however, are important. Edgar Allan Poe in *The Narrative of Arthur Gordon Pym* (1838) shows the influence of Brown, the Gothic tradition, and scientific exploration (which Poe turns into pseudoscience). *Pym* chronicles its protagonist's sea adventures in highly creative, enclosure imagery that foreshadows the sea romances of James Fenimore Cooper and Herman Melville.

While swashbuckling and romantic, Cooper's sea stories are not his best work, and although he wrote historical novels and novels of social criticism, his most important contribution to the genre is the Leatherstocking Series. In depicting his main character's (Natty Bumppo is the name most frequently used) trek across the continent and into the wilderness, Cooper renders a mythic version of the advance of the frontier, later popularized in dime novels and stories and films of the West. The traits of independence, resourcefulness, and rugged individualism Cooper celebrates in his hero have been hailed as the basic ingredients of our westward movement and even echoed by the noted historian Frederick Jackson Turner in his famous essay of 1893, "The Significance of the Frontier in American History." The mythic suggestiveness in Cooper's character marks a new development in the novel's growth.

Annoyed by critics who failed to understand *The Scarlet Letter* (they read it as a novel), Nathaniel Hawthorne, in the "Preface" to *The House of Seven Gables* (1851), distinguishes between the "novel" and the "romance." The novel, he writes, must "aim at a very minute fidelity," but the romance while not swerving from "truth of the human heart has fairly a right to present that truth under circumstances . . . of the writer's own choosing." The writer of romances may "mingle the Marvellous" with the "ordinary," and may create complex levels of meaning, which demand careful scrutiny and imaginative interpretation. While not recognized as such at the time, *The Scarlet Letter* is a major contribution to the genre. Hawthorne was ahead of his time; the themes of sin, guilt, obsession, communal isolation, and psychological alienation speak more directly to the 20th century than to the 19th.

The most remarkable novel of this period, and probably the whole century, Herman Melville's *Moby-Dick*, is greatly influenced by Hawthorne's themes and symbolism. Beginning as Poe does in *Pym* with a young person's search for self, Melville expands his narrator's sea journey to a metaphysical quest. In Ahab, Melville has depicted a dark, disturbing, complex character, unrivaled in American literature.

Realism and Naturalism. During the period following the Civil War and until the end of World War I (1918), the novel turned away from grand themes and metaphysical quests and focused on "the texture of ordinary life," describing common characters struggling to survive their routine lives. This depiction was accomplished with humor and light satire in the "smiling realism" of William Dean Howells, who advised young writers to "hold

a mirror up to life." However, the novels of Mark Twain, Frank Norris, Stephen Crane, Jack London, and Theodore Dreiser are more cynical in satirizing societal conventions. In *The Adventures of Huckleberry Finn* (1884), Twain uses the journey motif (the Mississippi River) to enhance his protagonist's coming-of-age in a slave society filled with hypocrisy and corruption. *Huck Finn* has captured the imaginations of American readers, especially in the 20th century, in a way few novels have, becoming one of our most popular novels. Less popular but no less significant are the naturalistic novels of Crane, Norris, London, and Dreiser. Most popular literature of the day celebrates freedom, not the diminution, of the will and rugged individualism. The most important naturalistic novels include Dreiser's *Sister Carrie* (1900) and *An American Tragedy* (1925).

During the period of realism and naturalism, most writers did not spend much time developing the inner lives of their characters. The environment acts, the characters react, sometimes without much forethought. Henry James is a major exception to this "pessimism on a narrow basis" (his definition of naturalism). James produced a body of novels focusing on what critics have called his international theme. These works generally feature wealthy, young Americans "affronting . . . [their] destiny"; James tests these naifs in sophisticated, often corrupt, European settings. Europe appears to win in these "contests" between Old World and New, but the Americans manage to rise, sometimes tragically, above their surroundings and achieve a new sense of freedom. James renders these journeys in detailed, carefully constructed descriptions of his characters' conscious life. He does not use interior monologue of the kind James Joyce or William Faulkner would develop; rather, he provides complex description of a character's inner life not depicted in other novels of the time.

Although influenced by naturalism, Edith Wharton wrote some compelling novels that, like those of James, depict characters who are capable of growth and change. Her major works include *The House of Mirth* (1905), *The Custom of the Country* (1913), and *The Age of Innocence* (1920).

The Modern Period. After World War I, the novel, like most other forms of modern art, experienced new creativity and artistic energy. Some experiments did not stand the test of time, for example, John Dos Passos's *U.S.A.*, but many novels of the 1920s and 1930s have been considered the most important America has produced. The work of F. Scott Fitzgerald, Ernest Hemingway, and Thomas Wolfe, among others, captures the spirit of postwar alienation and existential ennui. Fitzgerald's *The Great Gatsby* (1925), while depicting the superficiality of the Roaring Twenties, tragically dramatizes conflicts (for example, materialism vs. idealism) in the American Dream. Hemingway focuses on disillusionment and expatriotism in *The Sun Also Rises* (1926) and *Farewell to Arms* (1929). Wolfe, trying to articulate the essence of American experience, tackles the theme of search for self in *Look Homeward, Angel* (1929).

William Faulkner's fiction has had the most significant impact on the development of the novel in the 20th century. Influenced by James Joyce and T. S. Eliot, Faulkner uses stream of consciousness, interior monologue, shifting narrative voice, and abrupt time changes to create his fictional Yoknapatawpha County. Although set in the deep South and often dealing with issues surrounding the Old South and the New, his books are not at all regional or provincial but universal. "Man will not merely endure: he will prevail," Faulkner stated in his Nobel Prize Address (1950), and the writer's duty is to help him endure "by lifting his heart." His more notable works include *The Sound and the Fury* (1929), *As I Lay Dying* (1930), *Light in August* (1932), and *Absalom, Absalom!* (1936).

The subject matter and theme in much of Faulkner's work run counter to the literary temper of the 1930s, which tends to focus on political and social consciousness rather than on individual struggle. The dominant fictional form is the proletariat novel, depicting a young person's radicalization, exemplified by a work like James T. Farrell's *Studs Lonigan* (1935). Two of the most powerful and disturbing novels of this type are John Steinbeck's *The Grapes of Wrath* (1939) and Richard Wright's *Native Son* (1940).

After World War II, the genre takes an introspective turn, with a spate of novels by authors like Ralph Ellison, Joseph Heller, Norman Mailer, Philip Roth, William Styron, Bernard Malamud, Saul Bellow, James Baldwin, John Barth, Truman Capote, and John Updike. In a confessional style that combines autobiography and fiction, these writers explore their characters' pasts, specifically their racial and ethnic roots, in precise and exhaustive detail. Purporting to document history, but clearly blurring the line between history and fiction, Truman Capote's *In Cold Blood* (1966) is a good example. During this period, the novel seems unsure of itself, uncertain of its meaning or the direction. It often imitates film, attempting to create scenes and characters through visual rather than verbal logic. Nevertheless, the postwar novel is an important link, especially in its experiments with deconstructing meaning, to the postmodern novel.

Postmodernism. The multiplicity of meaning found in some modern novels leads to a serious questioning of meaning in many works from the 1960s on. The postmodern novel deconstructs meaning, calls logic and history into question, and undermines modernist themes and techniques. The journey/quest motif, when it is used, is often hallucinatory, resulting in a surrealistic narrative depicting a directionless journey where the purpose and outcome of the quest are unclear or unknown. Thomas Pynchon's novels *V* (1963), *The Crying of Lot 49* (1966), and *Gravity's Rainbow* (1973) are good examples.

In the last two decades the American novel has been graced with a remarkable suffusion of energy. Coming from various cultural, ethnic, and racial storytellers, this exciting new trend tends to define or redefine identity while deconstructing a previous false identity. For example, Indian authors N. Scott Momaday, Leslie Silko, and Louise Erdrich dramatize the difficulty of a character's attempt to discover his native identity while living in a society that has gone to great lengths to eliminate the identity.

If these latest efforts are any indication of the future of the novel in America, the genre is vital and alive, responding vigorously and creatively to the issues and passions of people, dramatizing their hopes and dreams, but most of all telling a good story.

—LEONARD W. ENGEL

See Also: *Baldwin, James; Bellow, Saul; Capote, Truman; Cooper, James Fenimore; Faulkner, William Cuthbert; Fitzgerald, F. Scott; Hawthorne, Nathaniel; Hemingway, Ernest Miller; James,*

Henry; Mailer, Norman; Melville, Herman; Poe, Edgar Allan; Steinbeck, John; Twain, Mark; Wharton, Edith; Wolfe, Thomas; Wright, Richard Nathaniel.

BIBLIOGRAPHY: Bewley, Marius, *The Eccentric Design: Form in the Classic American Novel* (Chatto & Windus 1959); Fisher, Philip, *Hard Facts: Setting and Form in the American Novel* (Oxford 1985); Rubin, Louis D., Jr., and John Rees Moore, eds., *The Idea of an American Novel* (Crowell 1961); Wagenknecht, Edward, *Cavalcade of the American Novel* (Holt 1952); Woodress, James, ed., *American Literary Scholarship: An Annual/1963* (Duke Univ. Press 1965 and annually).

■ **NUCLEAR TEST BAN TREATY (1963),** first agreement to limit development of nuclear weapons. The initial proposal for a treaty to ban testing nuclear weapons came in 1955 at a meeting of the U.N. General Assembly. The proposal was tabled, however, as discussions deadlocked over inspection difficulties and an atmosphere of mutual suspicion between the United States and the Soviet Union. Pres. John F. Kennedy renewed the quest for a test ban treaty in 1963, after the two superpowers had stood on the brink of nuclear war during the Cuban Missile Crisis the previous year. The Soviets responded favorably to Kennedy's plea for a treaty but limited the talks to nuclear tests that contaminated the atmosphere. The U.S. joint chiefs of staff initially demanded a ban on underground testing but relented after Sec. of Defense Robert McNamara pointed out the research and defense benefits of continued subterranean testing. In July 1963, the United States, the Soviet Union, and Great Britain signed the treaty, which proscribed tests in the atmosphere, underwater, and in outer space. The Senate ratified the treaty in September by a vote of 80 to 19.

The failure to achieve a comprehensive test ban led to the research and development of more destructive nuclear weapons in both the United States and the Soviet Union. By the 1980s, over 100 countries had adhered to the treaty, although two nuclear powers, China and France, had declined to sign it.

See Also: Cold War; Cuban Missile Crisis; Disarmament, Nuclear; United Nations (UN).

BIBLIOGRAPHY: Gaddis, John L., *Russia, the Soviet Union, and the United States: An Interpretive History* (Knopf 1978); LaFeber, Walter, *America, Russia, and the Cold War, 1945-1996* (McGraw-Hill 1997).

■ **NULLIFICATION,** doctrine that states have the right to overrule federal legislation within the bounds of their own sovereignty. An early expression of this view was found in the Virginia and Kentucky Resolutions (1798), drafted by Thomas Jefferson and James Madison, but the doctrine was most famously argued after Congress passed the tariff of 1828, which raised the tax on imported goods so high that it became known as the "Tariff of Abominations." As exporters of agricultural commodities and importers of manufactured goods, legislators in the Southern states felt especially aggrieved. South Carolina adopted a set of resolutions declaring the tariff unconstitutional and accompanied them with an unsigned essay, written by Sen. John C. Calhoun, expounding the doctrine of "nullification." At the insistence of Pres. Andrew Jackson, Congress lowered the tariff in 1832, but the next year the South Carolina legislature adopted an Ordinance of Nullification, declaring the tariff "null and void" and threatening secession and armed resistance if the federal government attempted to collect the tariff at the port of Charleston. Jackson then issued a proclamation declaring "disunion by armed force is treason" and asked Congress for military authority to uphold the revenue laws. The so-called Force Act was passed in 1833, coupled with an even lower set of tariff duties, a compromise engineered by Sen. Henry Clay. The South Carolina legislature voted to rescind its ordinance, although the legislators coupled it with a bill "nullifying" the Force Act, a gesture of bravado Jackson chose to ignore. Thus the crisis passed, but nullification and the associated doctrine of secession would return during the crisis created by the election of Abraham Lincoln as president in 1860.

See Also: Jackson, Andrew; Secession.

BIBLIOGRAPHY: Ellis, Richard E., *The Union at Risk: Jacksonian Democracy, States' Rights, and the Nullification Crisis* (Oxford Univ. Press 1987).

■ **NYE COMMITTEE,** U.S. Senate subcommittee (1934-36). Chaired by isolationist Republican Sen. Gerald Nye of South Dakota, the panel concluded that munitions makers and international bankers had drawn the United States into World War I.

O

OAKLEY, ANNIE (1860-1926), sharpshooter and Western legend. She was born Phoebe Ann Moses in Darke County, Ohio. An extraordinary marks-woman, she performed with Buffalo Bill's Wild West Show for 17 years, touring the United States and Europe. She also performed in the melodramas *Dead-wood Dick* (1887-88) and *The Western Girl* (1902-03). She became a Western heroine of numerous exag-gerating books, movies, television shows, and an Irving Berlin musical, *Annie Get Your Gun.*

> **See Also:** Cody, William ("Buffalo Bill"); Women in American History.

OCCUM, SAMSON (1723-92), Mohegan leader. Born in New London, Connecticut, Occum was an English-educated, Christian leader who brought In-dian children into Moor's Indian Charity School, founded by Eleazar Wheelock. Among his recruits was Mohawk leader Joseph Brant. Occum traveled to England in 1765 to raise funds for Wheelock's missionary and educational ventures in the Ameri-can colonies. In later life, Occum became disen-chanted with Wheelock's paternalism and began preaching among the New England tribes as an in-dependent missionary.

> **See Also:** Brant, Joseph; Indians of North America; Wheelock, Eleazar.

OCCUPATIONAL SAFETY LAWS, laws govern-ing worker safety and providing compensation for on-the-job injury or death. These laws origi-nated in the mid-1800s, when state courts began requiring employers both to exercise "due care" in providing safe workplaces and to pay damages to injured workers and survivors when they did not. Yet, to promote business, courts also recog-nized "defenses" such as that provided by the "fellow-servant" rule, which exempts from liabil-ity employers who could show that injury resulted from the negligence of a fellow employee.

Beginning with Massachusetts in 1877, worker pressure caused states to enact machine safety, sanitation, and factory inspection measures. By 1900, most northern industrial states had such laws, but loopholes, state-to-state variations, and overworked and sometimes corrupt factory in-spectors weakened them.

Around 1911, accident exposés, labor unrest, busi-ness enlightenment, and Progressive reform sentiment persuaded New York, Wisconsin, and other states to replace work-injury litigation with workers' compen-sation. Simultaneously, Wisconsin inaugurated the first industrial commission modeled after public utility regulation to formulate administrative safety codes. By 1920, most states had adopted compensation, al-though the commission idea spread more slowly. Many states expanded compensation to cover occu-pational disease after World War I, when munitions plants introduced toxic chemicals, and in the 1930s, when tunnel and quarry workers contracted silicosis.

Federal occupational safety law grew slowly. Congress enacted the Safety Appliance Act in 1893 to protect installers of railroad couplers and air brakes; in 1908, it required workmen's com-pensation for federal employees, and in 1919, during the Progressive era, it created the Bureau of Mines, a research and education-oriented orga-nization. During Pres. Franklin D. Roosevelt's New Deal years (1933-41), Sec. of Labor Frances Perkins directed the Bureau of Labor Standards to assist state safety administrators, the Social Secu-rity Act (1935) authorized state-run industrial health clinics, and the Walsh-Healey Act (1936) promoted safety in federal contract work.

In the late 1960s, environmental conscious-ness and union activism finally produced the first comprehensive federal programs: the 1969 Coal Mine Health and Safety Act and, more impor-tantly, the 1970 Occupational Safety and Health Act (OSHA), established to make and enforce fed-eral occupational safety and health standards.

—DONALD W. ROGERS

> **See Also:** Industrial Revolution; Labor Movement; Social Security Act.

BIBLIOGRAPHY: Aldrich, Mark, *Safety First: Technology, Labor, and Business in the Building of American Work Safety, 1870-1939* (Johns Hopkins Univ. Press 1997); Graebner, William, *Coal-Mining Safety in the Progressive Era: The Political Economy of Reform* (Univ. of Kansas Press 1976); Rosner, David, and Gerald Markowitz, *Deadly Dust: Silicosis and the Politics of Occupational Disease in Twentieth Century America* (Princeton Univ. Press 1991); Rosner, David, and Gerald Markowitz, eds., *Dying for Work: Workers' Safety and Health in Twentieth-Century America* (Indiana Univ. Press 1987).

■ **OCHS, ADOLPH (1858-1935),** newspaper publisher. Ochs's first newspaper venture was a boyhood job as a carrier in his native Cincinnati, Ohio; he later worked as a printer and compositor. In 1878 he bought his first newspaper, the *Chattanooga Times*, which he served as proprietor and publisher (1878-1935). Under Ochs the *Times* grew, and with it came recognition for him in the community. He was chairman of the Southern Associated Press from 1891 to 1894. Ochs purchased what would become his flagship paper, the *New York Times*, in 1896. He wanted a paper devoted strictly to "the news," with minimal editorial comment and as unbiased a perspective as possible. From 1900 until his death, Ochs served as director of the executive committee of the newly reorganized Associated Press. Ochs was concerned with disseminating information not only through his newspapers; he also supported the initial publication of the *Dictionary of American Biography* with a donation of $500,000.

See Also: Newspapers.

■ **O'CONNOR, FLANNERY (1925-64),** novelist and short story writer. Born Mary Flannery O'Connor in Savannah, Georgia. She graduated from the Women's College of Georgia in 1945 and then attended the Writer's Workshop at the University of Iowa, where she developed a morbid comic style, sometimes described as Southern Gothic. O'Connor published several chapters of her first novel, *Wise Blood* (1952), before falling ill with disseminated lupus in 1950. An experimental treatment saved her life but left her disabled. She returned to her family's farm and continued writing fiction that deals with the intense spiritual conflicts of Southern characters. She lived on grants and fellowships and support from her mother. O'Connor published a collection of stories, *A Good Man Is Hard to Find*, in 1955, and a second novel, *The Violent Bear It Away*, in 1960. Her short stories won O'Henry prizes in 1957, 1963, and 1964. O'Connor's illness returned after 1960, but despite her waning health, she completed a second collection of stories, *Everything that Rises Must Converge* (1965).

See Also: Women in American History.

BIBLIOGRAPHY: Hendin, Josephine, *The World of Flannery O'Connor* (Indiana Univ. Press 1970).

■ **O'CONNOR, SANDRA DAY (1930-),** first woman justice of the U.S. Supreme Court. Born in El Paso, Texas, she received her law degree from Stanford University (1952), then served in Arizona as assistant attorney general (1965-69) and as a Republican state senator (1969-74). She was an Arizona judge and an appeals court judge until 1981, when Pres. Ronald Reagan nominated her for the Supreme Court. Generally considered a conservative at the time of her appointment, she became part of a centrist bloc on the Court in the early 1990s, helping to moderate the Court's positions on abortion and civil rights.

See Also: Supreme Court; Women in American History.

Nominated to the U.S. Supreme Court by Pres. Ronald Reagan in 1981, Sandra Day O'Connor was sworn in by Chief Justice Warren Burger.

■ **OCONOSTOTA (died 1785),** Cherokee leader. In the 1730s, Oconostota was a principal war chief, resisting English advances into Cherokee territory. In 1760, during the Seven Years' War, he led a party of Cherokees against Fort Prince George, South Carolina. Oconostota's Cherokees attacked English colonial settlements along the Cherokee border for several months, but in 1761, an attack by colonial militia and British regulars forced the Cherokees to cede large portions of their eastern lands to British colonial settlers.

See Also: Cherokee; Indians of North America.

■ **OGLESBY, CARL (1935-),** political activist and author. Born in Akron, Ohio, he became president of Students for a Democratic Society (1965), a national student organization known for its involvement in the civil rights movement and activism against the Vietnam War.

■ **OGLETHORPE, JAMES E. (1696-1785),** English philanthropist, founder of Georgia Colony, and member of the British Parliament (1722-54). Born in London, Oglethorpe became interested in America when he developed a plan to resettle there men freed from debtor's prison. He received a charter to establish a colony in Georgia in 1732. Oglethorpe accompanied the first contingent of colonists to Georgia and remained to administer the colony until 1734.

See Also: Georgia.

■ **OHIO,** the easternmost of the Midwestern states. It is bounded on the north by Michigan and Lake Erie, on the west by Indiana, on the west and south by Kentucky, on the south and east by West Virginia, and on the east by Pennsylvania. The Ohio River forms its southern and part of its eastern boundary. Ohio's auto factories, steel mills, and rubber plants have made it an important industrial state since about 1850. Inventors Thomas A. Edison and Orville Wright were Ohio natives.

The land that became Ohio was a much-coveted frontier area when the United States became a nation. Made a state in 1803, it was the third most populous state by 1850. The Union's two leading Civil War generals, Ulysses S. Grant and William Tecumseh Sherman, were born in Ohio. Also among its natives have been seven presidents (including Grant), all Republicans.

Capital: Columbus. Area: 41,329 square miles. Population (1995 est.): 11,151,000.

See Also: Clark, George Rogers; Edison, Thomas Alva; Fallen Timbers, Battle of; Grant, Ulysses Simpson; Mound Builders; Ohio River; Perry, Oliver Hazard; Rockefeller, John Davison; Sherman, William Tecumseh; Stokes, Carl B.; Wayne, Anthony.

■ **OHIO RIVER,** principal eastern tributary of the Mississippi River. Formed by the confluence of the Allegheny and Monongahela rivers in western Pennsylvania, at Pittsburgh, the Ohio circuitously runs some 980 miles southwest to the Mississippi River at Cairo, Illinois. The river drops 460 feet between Pittsburgh and the Mississippi and is navigable all year round. The Ohio, which is Iroquois for "fine river," was long navigated by Indians. French fur traders used the river before the 18th century, calling it La Belle Riviere. The French and British began to struggle for control of the Ohio Valley during the 1750s, with the British gaining victory after the French and Indian War. After the American Revolution, however, the English ceded (1783) the lands west of the Ohio as far as the Mississippi River to the new United States. With the opening of the Erie Canal (1825) in New York, the Ohio became the major route to the West. During the 20th century a complex system of 50 locks and dams was installed on the Ohio to facilitate the movement of commodities up and down the river.

■ *OHIO V. AKRON CENTER FOR REPRODUCTIVE HEALTH* **(1990),** U.S. Supreme Court case concerning the constitutionality of some state regulations limiting a woman's access to abortion services. The Court ruled (6-3) that an Ohio law requiring minors seeking abortions to notify a parent or receive court permission was not so burdensome that it compromised the right to abortion outlined in *Roe* v. *Wade* (1973).

See Also: Abortion; Roe v. Wade; Supreme Court.

■ **OJIBWA (CHIPPEWA),** Algonquian-speaking tribe in Canada and the United States around the Great Lakes. During the 17th century, proto-Ojibwa migrated to the hunting grounds of the western Great Lakes, where they engaged in hunting for the French fur trade until the 19th century. After the French left North America, many Ojibwas moved west and north, settling in present-day Wisconsin, Minnesota, and North Dakota, as well as Ontario, Canada. The Ojibwas, with 100,000 people in 1990, are one of the most populous Indian groups in the United States.

See Also: Indians of North America.

■ **O'KEEFFE, GEORGIA (1887-1986),** one of the most popular American painters of the 20th century, known for her watercolors of flowers and her desert landscapes. Born in Sun Prairie, Wisconsin, O'Keeffe studied at the Art Institute of Chicago and at the Art Students League in New York. Alfred Stieglitz, a photographer and art dealer whom she married in 1924, organized her first exhibition in 1916. She quickly gained attention for her detailed, brightly colored, and sensual renderings of flowers and as the subject of many of Stieglitz's portraits. In 1946, O'Keeffe joined a growing community of artists and authors living near Taos, New Mexico. At her ranch in nearby Abiquiu, she painted her well-known landscapes of the scorched desert, with the sun-bleached remains of cattle. A classic example of her Southwestern landscapes is *Cow's Skull Red, White, and Blue* (1931 Metropolitan Museum). O'Keeffe was elected to the American Academy of Arts and Letters in 1969.

See Also: Painting; Stieglitz, Alfred; Women in American History.

BIBLIOGRAPHY: Cowart, Jack, and Juan Hamilton, *Georgia O'Keeffe: Arts and Letters* (Little, Brown 1989).

■ **OKLAHOMA,** a west south-central state. It is bounded on the north by Colorado and Kansas, on the west by New Mexico, on the west and south by Texas, and on the east by Arkansas and Missouri. The Red River forms much of its southern border. Most of Oklahoma is a gently rolling plain, but the western panhandle is part of the Great Plains. Oklahoma generally ranks fifth among states in oil, third in natural gas, and fifth in cattle and wheat production.

What later became eastern Oklahoma was set aside in 1830 as Indian Country for the Five Civilized Tribes of the Southeast: the Cherokee, Chickasaw, Creek, Choctaw, and Seminole. Western Oklahoma, although also reserved to Indians, was opened to homesteaders in 1889. Both parts were united when Oklahoma became a state in 1907. Oklahoma has more Indians (252,000 in 1990) than any other state.

Capital: Oklahoma City. Area: 69,903 square miles. Population (1995 est.): 3,278,000.

See Also: Coronado, Francisco Vásquez de; Dust Bowl; Five Civilized Tribes; Great Plains; Indian Country or Territory; Louisiana Purchase; Oklahoma City Bombing; Trail of Tears.

■ **OKLAHOMA CITY BOMBING (Apr. 19, 1994),** attack on the Murrah federal office building in Oklahoma City, Oklahoma. A rented truck filled with fertilizer and diesel fuel was detonated outside the building. The explosion killed 169 persons, injured more than 1,000, and damaged more than 300 businesses. The federal building, damaged beyond repair, was razed. Timothy McVeigh and Terry L. Nichols, fanatics of the far right, were later arrested and charged with the crime. In a 1997 trial, McVeigh was convicted and sentenced to death. Nichols was convicted later in a separate trial.

■ **OLDENBURG, CLAES (1929-),** avant-garde artist. Born in Stockholm, Sweden, Oldenburg came to the United States with his family in 1937. After graduating from Yale University in 1950, he was drawn to the art world, moving to New York in 1956. Oldenburg's work evolved from paintings to soft sculptural forms representing large-scale versions of everyday objects, such as a giant hamburger or fan. He created total environments as works of art, for example *The Street* in 1960 and *The Store* in 1960-61.

See Also: Painting.

■ **OLD SOUTHWEST,** the standard designation for the southwestern quadrant of the early American republic. Stretching from the Appalachian Mountains to the Mississippi River and from the Gulf of Mexico to the Ohio River, the borders of the Old Southwest, although never precisely defined, basically mirrored those of the Old Northwest.

Indeed, in the struggles that accompanied their occupation by American pioneers, these frontiers shared many similarities. Beginning with the 1775 settlement of Kentucky, Anglo-Americans gradually scattered their farmsteads across both sides of the Ohio Valley. North and south of the Ohio, Indian peoples struggled for decades to preserve their homeland—some militarily, and others by the adaptation of Anglo-American ways. The latter tactic earned the Choctaw, Chickasaw, Creek, Seminole, and especially Cherokee the somewhat dubious distinction of being classified as "civilized tribes." But during the 1830s federally mandated removal swept away the claims of these Indians, opening the whole of the Old Southwest to Anglo-American land seekers and their African-American slaves.

It was this expansion of slavery that decisively distinguished the Old Southwest from its counterpart north of the Ohio River. Unlike in the Old Northwest, no congressional ordinance banned slavery in the territory south of the Ohio. As important, the climate and soil of the Old Southwest was favorable to the cultivation of cotton and the propagation of slave labor. Transformed into the "cotton kingdom," the Old Southwest eventually became the heart of the Confederate States of America.

—STEPHEN ARON

See Also: Confederate States of America; Frontier in American History; Slavery.

BIBLIOGRAPHY: Clark, Thomas D., and John D. Guice, *Frontiers in Conflict: The Old Southwest, 1795-1830* (Univ. of New Mexico Press 1989); Rohrbough, Malcolm J., *The Trans-Appalachian Frontier: People, Societies, and Institutions, 1775-1850* (Oxford Univ. Press 1978).

■ **OLIVE BRANCH PETITION (1775),** final attempt by the American colonies for a peaceful resolution of differences with Britain. Adopted by the Second Continental Congress after the initial battles of the American Revolution, this unanswered letter urged King George III to end all military actions against the colonists.

See Also: Revolution, American.

■ **OLMSTED, FREDERICK LAW (1822-1903),** leader of American landscape architecture. Born in Hartford, Connecticut, Olmsted ran his own farm on Staten Island in New York from 1848 to 1854 and wrote essays for Andrew Jackson Downing's *The Horticulturist.* In 1857 Olmsted received an appointment as superintendent of New York's Central Park. The next year he joined forces with landscape designer Calvert Vaux to submit the winning entry for the design of the park. Their design was innovative in its application of a picturesque style, with winding paths, broad lawns, and a variety of plantings, to a public space. During the Civil War Olmsted served as secretary to the U.S. Sanitary Commission, but he returned to his landscape practice after the war. Olmsted and Vaux designed Prospect Park in Brooklyn in 1865 and Riverside, a residential subdivision in Chicago, in 1869. Working on his own after 1872, Olmsted took on such ambitious projects as the grounds of the U.S. Capitol (1880) and the Stanford University Campus in Palo Alto, California (1888).

See Also: Downing, Andrew Jackson; Sanitary Commission.

■ **OLNEY, RICHARD (1835-1917),** U.S. attorney general (1893-95) and secretary of state (1895-97). During the U.S.-British conflict over Venezuela in 1895, Olney declared the United States "practically sovereign on this continent," thus proclaiming U.S. hegemony in the Western Hemisphere.

■ **OLYMPIC MOUNTAINS,** mountains in northwestern Washington, part of the Coast Range. Dominated by Mount Olympus (7,965 feet), the mountains contain dense rain forests of Douglas fir, western red cedar, and western hemlock. After an intense battle between the Department of the Interior, which wanted the area preserved, and the Forest Service, which argued for commercial development of the wood and minerals, Olympic National Park was established in 1938. Alpine meadows, lakes, streams, rugged mountains, and glaciers are characteristics of the park.

■ **OÑATE, JUAN DE (c. 1550-1630),** Spanish explorer. Born in New Spain (present-day Mexico) and appointed governor of New Mexico in 1595, Oñate claimed the territory (near present-day El Paso) for Spain in April 1598. Proceeding to Albuquerque, he proclaimed Spain's dominion over the Puebloan villages and then occupied a Tewa pueblo, renaming the site San Juan, near present-day Santa Fe. While he was not the first Spaniard to venture into this region, Oñate initiated the permanent settlement of northern New Spain. Interested in more than just colonizing, he searched for the fabled gold of Quivira, exploring the eastern plains of Kansas (1601), then down the Colorado River to the Gulf of California (1605). Relieved as governor in 1609, Oñate was convicted in 1614 on charges of misconduct but later pardoned.

See Also: *Exploration and Discovery; Spanish Colonies.*

BIBLIOGRAPHY: Weber, David J., *The Spanish Frontier in North America* (Yale Univ. Press 1992).

■ **O'NEILL, EUGENE (1888-1953),** playwright. Born in New York City, he had attempted suicide by the age of 24 and then contracted tuberculosis. While recovering from the illness, O'Neill started to write drama. His parents' troubled relationship and his own torturous personal life would forever mark his work with a deep tragic sense. In 1916, he joined the Provincetown Players, who had staged many of his one-act plays by the end of the decade. *Beyond the Horizon*, O'Neill's first full-length drama, appeared on Broadway in 1920 and won him that year's Pulitzer Prize. O'Neill was now at the top of his profession, and he received a second Pulitzer for *Anna Christie* in 1922. He turned to writing very long plays, whose performances ran several hours, such as *Strange Interlude*, winner of the 1928 Pulitzer. Awarded the 1936 Nobel Prize for Literature, O'Neill had not yet completed any of the dramas thought by many to be his best. O'Neill struggled with illness to finish these plays before having to retire, a decade before his death. Only one of these, *The Iceman Cometh* (1946), was produced in his lifetime. Published in 1952, *A Moon for the Misbegotten* appeared before the staging of *A Long Day's Journey Into Night* (1956), which won the 1957 Pulitzer, and *A Touch of the Poet* (1957).

See Also: *Theater.*

BIBLIOGRAPHY: Gelb, Arthur, and Barbara Gelb, *O'Neill* (Harper 1962); Sheaffer, Louis, *O'Neill: Son and Artist* (Little, Brown 1973); Sheaffer, Louis, *O'Neill: Son and Playwright* (Little, Brown 1968).

■ **O'NEILL, THOMAS P. (TIP) (1912-94),** Speaker of the U.S. House of Representatives (1977-87). Born in North Cambridge, Massachusetts, he was first elected to the Massachusetts legislature as a Democrat in 1936, became Speaker of the state House in 1947, and was elected to Congress in 1952. O'Neill was elected Speaker in 1977 and served until his retirement, often opposing the policies of Republican Pres. Ronald Reagan in the 1980s.

■ **OPECHANCANOUGH (c. 1545-1644),** Pamunkey leader. When his brother Powhatan died in 1618, Opechancanough assumed the leadership for the Powhatan Confederacy. Inspired by the prophet Nemattanew's revitalization message, Opechancanough launched a surprise attack on the Jamestown settlement in 1622, killing 377 of the more than 1,200 English colonists. A full-scale war, in which the English burned crops and destroyed villages, continued for almost a decade before both sides agreed to peace. Opechancanough led another effort against the English in 1644, but he failed and was executed.

See Also: *Indians of North America; Jamestown Settlement; Powhatan Confederacy.*

■ **OPEN DOOR POLICY,** U.S. diplomatic principle that attempted to give all nations equal trading rights and access to development in China. Toward the end of the 19th century European powers and Japan had divided China into spheres of influence, giving each nation an area of economic dominance. Recognizing the potential economic benefits for the United States, Sec. of State John Hay sought a way to assure equal recognition for American commercial interests in China. In 1899 he devised the Open Door policy, and a year later it became the official American policy toward China.

Although Japan opposed the policy, France, Italy, Russia, Germany, and Britain recognized it, establishing a tenuous balance between the imperial powers. The outbreak of the Russo-Japanese War in 1904, however, threatened both stability and American interests in the region. Pres. Theodore Roosevelt mediated a settlement that established a Japanese protectorate over Korea. This initiated three decades of diplomatic tension between the United States and Japan over China. Although the Open Door policy was periodically invoked by American officials, neither Japan nor many of the other powers paid it much heed. When Japan invaded Manchuria in 1932, the United States was the only nation to protest. By the outbreak of World War II the Open Door policy was obsolete. Nonetheless some historians believe the Open Door policy was the foundation of American foreign policy in the 20th century.

See Also: Hay, John Milton.

BIBLIOGRAPHY: Williams, William Appleman, *The Tragedy of American Diplomacy* (World Publishing Co. 1959).

■ **OPEN SHOP,** a term applied to a place of work in which employees are not required (as they would be in a closed shop) to be members of a trade union, even in cases where union representation is available.

See Also: Closed Shop; Labor Movement.

■ **OPERA,** work combining music, drama, and spectacle. Opera originated in Italy around 1600. In early-18th-century America, English ballad operas such as John Gay's *The Beggar's Opera* were performed regularly, but during the American Revolution operatic activity declined because of increasing mistrust of luxury and extravagance. After the war, a new form of American opera emerged, examples of which included James Hewitt's *Tammany, or The Indian Chief* (New York 1794) and John Bray's *The Indian Princess* (Philadelphia 1808).

Throughout the 19th century, operas of European and American creation found audiences in the United States, particularly among elites. Opera also began to disseminate from the northern seaport cities to western urban areas. Comic English-language operas, such as those composed by the Britons W. S. Gilbert and Sir Arthur Sullivan, gained popularity. Late in the century, operatic institutions opened in many large cities, although most did not enjoy the levels of financial and cultural success of the Metropolitan Opera in New York.

At the beginning of the 20th century, American composers produced romantic European-style operas, but immediately before and after World War I, indigenous American musical and dramatic themes resurfaced in American opera. Public apathy, along with the rise of the motion picture industry in the 1920s and 1930s, threat-

ened the very existence of opera in the United States. From the 1960s, however, opera experienced a renaissance that reestablished its prominence within the American cultural scene.

BIBLIOGRAPHY: Dizikes, John, *Opera in America: A Cultural History* (Yale Univ. Press 1993); Ottenberg, June C., *Opera Odyssey: Toward a History of Opera in Nineteenth-Century America* (Greenwood Press 1994).

■ **OPERATION DESERT STORM,** name given to the combat phase, lasting from January 17 to the ceasefire established on Feb. 28, 1991, of the Persian Gulf War. *See: Persian Gulf War.*

■ **OPPENHEIMER, J. ROBERT (1904-67),** physicist. Embroiled in the problems of the nuclear age, Oppenheimer presided over the development of the atomic bomb as director of the Manhattan Project but later advocated arms control. A native of New York City, Oppenheimer graduated from Harvard

J. Robert Oppenheimer, appointed director of the Los Alamos Scientific Laboratory in 1942, came to be known as the "father of the atomic bomb."

in 1925 and received his Ph.D. in theoretical physics in Germany in 1927. By 1929, his brilliant research in theoretical physics earned him a joint appointment at the University of California at Berkeley and California Institute of Technology. An equally adroit teacher, Oppenheimer made Berkeley an international center for research in physics.

During the 1930s, he began to seek application of his research for military use of atomic energy. In 1942, he was named director of the Los Alamos Scientific Laboratory—the central research facility of the Manhattan Project. Under Oppenheimer's leadership, scientists designed and built the atomic bombs that destroyed Hiroshima and Nagasaki in August 1945.

After directing the world into the nuclear age, Oppenheimer became director of Princeton's Institute for Advanced Study and served on numerous government committees, including the Atomic Energy Commission (AEC). As concern mounted during the Truman administration about Soviet nuclear capabilities, Oppenheimer supported an arms-control agreement and opposed development of the hydrogen bomb. His opposition to arms buildup and his previous communist associations brought a barrage of McCarthy-era accusations of disloyalty. In 1954, an AEC security hearing led to the loss of his security clearance. He returned to Princeton and continued his work in theoretical physics.

—GUY NELSON

See Also: Manhattan Project; Science.

BIBLIOGRAPHY: David, Nuel Pharr, *Lawrence and Oppenheimer* (Simon & Schuster 1968); Goodchild, Peter, *J. Robert Oppenheimer: Shatterer of Worlds* (Houghton Mifflin 1980).

■ **ORDER IN COUNCIL (1807),** British measures that hampered American commerce and heightened tensions between Britain and the United States. In an attempt to undermine the economy of France, England issued two orders in council, one placing French commerce under blockade and the other preventing American ships from sailing into British ports. These orders only deepened the British-American animosity that would lead to the War of 1812.

■ **OREGON,** a Pacific Northwest state. It is bounded on the north by Washington, on the north and east by Idaho, on the south by California and Nevada, and on the west by the Pacific Ocean. The Snake River forms part of its eastern border and the Columbia River part of its western border. Two-thirds of the state, east of the Cascade Range, is an arid plateau. The fertile Willamette River Valley lies between the Coast and Cascade ranges. Oregon leads the nation in timber production, and lumber, wood, and paper products are its chief manufactured goods.

British and American fur trappers vied for control of Oregon before an 1846 treaty set a boundary line between British and American territories. By then settlers had begun migrating from Missouri on the Oregon Trail. Oregon became a state in 1859.

Capital: Salem. Area: 87,052 square miles. Population (1995 est.): 3,141,000.

See Also: Astor, John Jacob; Columbia River; Lewis and Clark Expedition; Snake River.

■ **OREGON QUESTION,** dispute between the United States and Great Britain over the disposition of Oregon. After 57 years of controversy, the 49th parallel was defined as Oregon's northern boundary on June 15, 1846, in a treaty between the two countries under which Oregon was ceded to the United States.

See Also: Frontier in American History.

■ **ORGANIZATION OF AMERICAN STATES (OAS),** the major consultative body in the Western Hemisphere, created in 1947 by the United States and Latin American governments. The impetus for the OAS originated at the 1826 Congress of Panama. In the 1880s, U.S. Sec. of State James G. Blaine revived the idea when he sought support for an agency to promote economic development and resolve disputes.

After World War II the United States wanted to restrict foreign influence in the Americas. Latin Americans hoped to strengthen U.S. pledges of nonintervention that characterized the Good Neighbor policy. The OAS could presumably serve both needs.

The OAS and the Cold War. In the age of global Cold War, however, the United States tried to determine OAS actions. In 1954, with plans under way to oust Pres. Jacobo Arbenz Guzman of Guatemala, the Eisenhower administration courted

OAS members. An OAS resolution only promised consultation concerning "dangers originating outside the hemisphere." In the early 1960s, though, the OAS joined the United States in isolating Fidel Castro from regional affairs through Cuba's expulsion from the OAS and by an economic blockade. During the Cuban Missile Crisis in October 1962, the United States obtained OAS backing for a quarantine of Cuba after promising economic assistance. The OAS then supported U.S. intervention in the Dominican Republic in April 1965, an action that impaired OAS credibility among opponents of U.S. policy. Acceptance of U.S. intervention detracted from joint OAS–Alliance for Progress projects to promote economic growth.

Human Rights. Support for human rights moved the OAS out of Washington's shadow in the mid-1970s. The OAS had shown concern for human rights since the late 1950s when it urged members to break relations with Raphael Trujillo's Dominican Republic. At Santiago, Chile, in 1976, the OAS advocated attention to human rights. Business associations like the Council of the Americas resisted the effort, as did U.S. Sec. of State Henry Kissinger, who valued stability more highly. He had once insisted that the U.S. ambassador to Chile "cut out the political science lectures" about human rights.

Pres. Jimmy Carter supported the activities of the Inter-American Commission on Human Rights (IACHR), an OAS agency. In June 1977 he signed the American Convention on Human Rights and Sec. of State Cyrus Vance linked U.S. foreign aid to respect for human rights. The OAS itself could not actually help the cause of human rights because Latin American states viewed the matter as one of internal politics.

The OAS therefore remained dependent upon the United States to give substance to human rights concerns. Still, the Pinochet regime in Chile and Argentina's "dirty war" in the 1970s received IACHR scrutiny. The Argentine junta weathered a public relations storm in 1980 by threatening to resign from the OAS if it criticized Argentina by name. The OAS and the United States also differed over policy toward Nicaragua. The Carter administration asked the OAS in 1979 to send a peacekeeping force to Nicaragua to prevent the Sandinistas from taking complete power. As they

began their final offensive that June, the OAS issued a scathing report on human rights violations under the Somoza regime and concluded that the Somozas had forfeited all claims to political legitimacy. All prospects for a coalition Sandinistas-moderates regime vanished.

New Directions. The Central American crisis of the 1980s helped the OAS play a role less linked to U.S. goals. The 1982 Falklands/Malvinas War had shown both the limits of OAS influence and the importance of a multilateral approach to the resolution of disputes. The OAS could therefore support peace efforts in Central America despite reservations about its role.

The OAS also monitored progress toward democracy in troubled nations. Condemning human rights abuses by Gen. Manuel Noriega of Panama in the late 1980s, denouncing the 1991 coup against Haiti's Jean-Bertrand Aristide, and arbitrating other disputes in the region gave the OAS newfound respectability. Nations' claims to sovereignty still limited overall OAS effectiveness, however.

—WILLIAM O. WALKER III

See Also: *Cold War; Cuban Missile Crisis; Good Neighbor Policy; Kennedy, John Fitzgerald.*

BIBLIOGRAPHY: Ball, M. Margaret, *The OAS in Transition* (Duke Univ. Press 1969); Farer, Tom, ed., *Beyond Sovereignty: Collectively Defending Democracy in the Americas* (Johns Hopkins Univ. Press 1996).

■ **ORGANIZED CRIME,** operation of criminal activities as major industries. It first took shape in the United States during Prohibition (1920-33), when there were enormous profits to be made from "bootlegging" (producing, distributing, and selling illegal alcoholic beverages). Criminal gangs, most of them organized along ethnic lines, had operated in the working-class neighborhoods of America's cities since the mid-19th century. But during the 1920s, Italian gangsters, refining tactics used by the Mafia in Sicily, effectively employed kinship networks to form insulated, disciplined, and deadly organizations that crushed rival Irish and Jewish gangs. Successful criminal leaders—Al Capone of Chicago was the most infamous—became celebrities. "Everybody calls me a racketeer," Capone declared. "I call myself a businessman."

Indeed, criminal overlords like Capone acted in the manner of classic capitalist robber barons, using money and violence to consolidate their operations into larger and more complex enterprises. In New York City in 1931, for example, Italian gang leaders Giuseppe Masseria, Vito Genovese, Joseph Profaci, and Lucky Luciano, among others, organized the infamous Five Families, criminal organizations that included several thousand "made" (or inducted) members. These organizations are known today by the names of their former bosses: Bonanno, Colombo, Gambino, Genovese, and Lucchese. In other cities, criminal gangs organized similar syndicates. Eventually, in an attempt to prevent warfare among regional organizations, the bosses from a number of cities organized a national "commission," a loose board of directors charged with dividing up territory. An important element in their success was their ability to work with the political machines of numerous eastern and midwestern cities, bribing and corrupting politicians, judges, prosecutors, police officers, and even newspaper reporters.

When the 18th Amendment was repealed in 1933, these Mafia families had the administrative expertise to expand into a wide range of illegal activities, for example, prostitution, gambling, extortion, and loan-sharking (loaning money at exorbitantly high rates of interest). Organized criminals also found work as "goons," men hired by both management and unions during the labor wars of the 1930s. In the process, another lucrative enterprise, labor racketeering, was opened to criminal activity. In New York City, the five families eventually became a controlling force in the garment industry, trucking, shipping, construction, and garbage hauling.

Decline of the Mafia. For more than 40 years, Mafia families controlled organized criminal activity in the United States. For reasons yet unclear, J. Edgar Hoover, director of the Federal Bureau of Investigation, barely acknowledged their existence, despite congressional hearings in the 1950s and the investigation of organized crime figures and corrupt union leaders by Atty. Gen. Robert F. Kennedy in the early 1960s. (Indeed, before his own assassination, Kennedy told a colleague that the assassination in 1963 of his brother, Pres. John F. Kennedy, might have been organized by mobsters. Such allegations remain unproven.) In the 1980s and 1990s, however, federal prosecutors successfully used the provisions of the Racketeer Influenced and Corrupt Organizations Act (RICO) to wage war on the bosses of organized crime, prosecuting and jailing dozens of local and regional leaders.

By 1995, authorities were claiming that the Mafia had been beaten in most U.S. cities (New York and Chicago remained exceptions). In addition to the results of aggressive prosecution, the deterioration of these criminal syndicates was attributed to the dispersal of whites from urban neighborhoods to the suburbs and the decline of urban political machines. Most important, however, was the rise of rival criminal organizations controlled by African Americans, Asians, Russians, and Colombians, groups dominating the illegal drug trade. Chinese international gangs known as "Triads" moved into bookmaking, loan-sharking, and labor racketeering. At the end of the century, organized crime had become far more international than it had been in the past.

—John Mack Faragher

See Also: *Bootlegging; Capone, Al; Drugs; Gangsters; Mafia; Prohibition; Rackets.*

BIBLIOGRAPHY: Block, Alan, *East Side, West Side: Organizing Crime in New York, 1930-1950* (Transaction Books 1983); Fox, Stephen R., *Blood and Power* (Morrow 1989); Woodiwiss, Michael, *Crime, Crusades, and Corruption* (Barnes & Noble 1988).

■ **ORISKANY, BATTLE OF (1777),** battle in the American Revolution. In the summer of 1777 British Col. Barry St. Ledger left Montreal to attack American positions along the Mohawk River and meet up with Generals Burgoyne and Howe at Albany. St. Ledger's role in the plan failed when American troops led by Gen. Nicholas Herkimer stopped him at Oriskany, New York, near Fort Stanwix. The British effort at Oriskany was undermined when their Indian allies left the battlefield.

See Also: *Revolution, American.*

■ **OSCEOLA (c. 1803-38),** Seminole leader during the Second Seminole War in Florida (1835-42). After the Indian Removal Act of 1830 called for the relocation of the southeastern Indians to west of the Mississippi, Osceola waged a guerrilla war against the U.S. Army in the Florida swamps. For two years, the Seminole completely thwarted attempts to remove them. In 1837, U.S. Gen. Thomas Jesup called for peace talks with the Seminoles as a pretense for seizing Osceola and other leaders. Osceola died in prison in January 1838.

See Also: Indian Removal; Indians of North America; Seminole.

■ **OSTEND MANIFESTO (1854),** U.S. diplomatic statement to pressure Spain into selling Cuba. On Feb. 28, 1854, Cuban authorities in Havana seized the American merchant ship *Black Warrior* in error. Pierre Soulé, U.S. minister to Spain, demanded that Spain pay indemnities. Soulé, along with other members of Pres. Franklin Pierce's administration, hoped to provoke Spain into war as a pretext for annexing Cuba. However, Spain apologized and agreed to pay the reparations. Taking a different approach, on Oct. 18, 1854, Soulé met with John Mason and James Buchanan, the U.S. ministers to France and Britain, respectively, at Ostend, Belgium, and drew up a manifesto declaring that Cuba was essential to U.S. security and the protection of slavery and offering to buy it from Spain for $130 million. Spain refused, and the Ostend Manifesto became an embarrassment for the Pierce administration, resulting in Soulé's resignation.

■ **OTIS, ELISHA GRAVES (1811-61),** mechanic who invented the safety elevator. Born in Halifax, Vermont, Otis manufactured wagons and carriages in Vermont (1938-45), invented a turbine water wheel in Albany, and became a master mechanic (1851) at a bedstead factory in New Jersey. When the factory moved to Yonkers, New York, Otis was in charge of installing the machinery and developed a system to hoist workers and equipment from one floor to the next. His elevator incorporated some new and unique features, including a safety device that prevented the elevator from falling if the lifting chain or cable broke. Otis opened his own manufacturing shop in Yonkers, took orders for freight and passenger elevators, and demonstrated his safety elevator at a fair in New York (1854). His business was not a success, however, until Otis invented and patented the steam elevator and established the Otis Elevator Company in 1861. His sons carried on his work and expanded the business with

great success. In addition to the safety elevator, Otis also developed and patented railroad car trucks and brakes (1852), a steam plow (1857), and a baking oven (1858).

See Also: Invention; Science.

■ **OTIS, JAMES, JR. (1725-83),** Revolutionary-era statesman. Otis was born in West Barnstaple, Massachusetts. In 1761, he made himself a leading figure in the Revolutionary opposition to Britain through his argument against the use of writs of assistance, which authorized customs officials to search for smuggled goods. He contributed several influential pamphlets to the patriot cause, including *The Rights of the British Colonies Asserted and Proved* (1764). Otis both defended colonial rights and upheld Parliamentary sovereignty. Such ambiguities, together with his erratic behavior, increasingly alienated contestants on both sides. After incurring head injuries during a fight with Crown officer John Robinson in 1769, Otis gradually lost his sanity, and his Revolutionary activities effectively came to an end.

See Also: Revolution, American.

■ **OTTAWA INDIANS.** *See:* Subarctic Indians.

■ **OVERLAND MAIL,** transcontinental mail service mandated by Congress in 1857. The contract was awarded to the Overland Mail Company. The first trip began in September 1858 and took 20 days on a route from St. Louis and Memphis to El Paso, Texas, and Tucson, Arizona, and terminated in Los Angeles and San Francisco. Passengers could also ride the Concord Coach for about $200. Financially troubled, the service was transferred to the Wells, Fargo, & Company in 1866. Completion of the transcontinental railroad on May 10, 1869, rendered the overland mail route obsolete.

See Also: Frontier in American History.

■ **OVERLAND TRAIL,** wagon route across the Great Plains and Rocky Mountains to Oregon and California, used by western emigrants from the 1840s to the 1860s. Travelers traversed the approximately 2,000-mile distance at the rate of just 12 to 15 miles per day, the speed of oxen and wagons. They departed in the spring, as soon as the grass was high enough for the stock to graze, and

A small family moving West pauses for a cold meal in Colorado. Their farm wagon is typical of the vehicles used by pioneers on the Overland Trail.

prayed they would make it over the mountains before the first winter storms. May and June were spent following the Platte River across the plains to Fort Laramie, Wyoming, a lingering landmark of the fur trade refitted as a military post by the federal government. Heading up the Sweetwater River, they then traveled over the broad saddle in the Rockies known as South Pass. Soon thereafter, in early August, came the parting of the ways to California and Oregon. Emigrants had traveled two-thirds of the distance, but their journey was only about half completed. The heartbreaking reality about the trail was that the closer the destination, the tougher and slower the going. The Oregon route clung to torturous cliff ledges along the Snake River and then the dreaded Blue Mountains, surmounted only with the aid of ropes, pulleys, and quickly made winches. The California trail led across burning deserts and over the steep ascent of the Sierra Nevadas, where in 1846 the Donner Party met its tragic fate. If all went well, travelers reached their destinations in October.

The Overland Trail was used by an estimated 300,000 emigrants from the first appearance of "Oregon fever" in 1843 to the completion of the transcontinental railroad in 1869. It was most heavily traveled in 1849 and the half dozen years thereafter, when tens of thousands headed for the gold fields of California.

See Also: Donner Party; Frontier in American History; Wagon Trains.

BIBLIOGRAPHY: Faragher, John Mack, *Women and Men on the Overland Trail* (Yale Univ. Press 1979); Unruh, John D., Jr., *The Plains Across: The Overland Emigrants and the Trans-Mississippi West, 1840-1860* (Univ. of Illinois Press 1979).

■ **OWEN, ROBERT (1771-1858),** Welsh socialist and reformer. After buying the New Lanark textile mill in Manchester, England, in 1799, he initiated programs to alleviate poor conditions in the factories. In conjunction with his partners, Quaker philanthropist William Allen and English jurist Jeremy Bentham, he created and implemented several landmark labor policies, including the establishment of sickness and old-age insurance, the prohibition of child labor, and the operation of educational and recreational facilities for employees. Owen argued in *A New View of Society* (1813) that character is the product of environment. He envisioned a communistic society of small towns that combined industry and agriculture with good schools and healthy work for all.

He later founded several utopian communities in the United States and Great Britain, which became known as "Owenite" communities. The community in New Harmony, Indiana, was quite unharmonious, however, as the 1,000 community members argued among themselves and often refused to work. In 1829 Owen sold his interest in the New Lanark mill and spent his money investing in social improvement and in spreading his ideas about education, morality, and socialism.

■ **OWEN-GLASS ACT (1913),** federal legislation that created the Federal Reserve System, 12 regional banks administered by a central board. The law was the first reorganization of the U.S. banking system since the Civil War.

See Also: *Federal Reserve System; New Deal.*

■ **OWENS, JESSE (1913-80),** track and field athlete. He was born in Danville, Alabama. Owens broke five world records in 1935 and earned a place on the U.S. team at the 1936 Olympics in Berlin, Germany. During those games, Owens won four gold medals, tying or breaking records in the 100- and 200-meter dashes, the long jump, and the 400-meter relay. These successes by a black athlete so upset Adolf Hitler that the German dictator refused to congratulate Owens.

See Also: *African Americans; Sports.*

■ **OZARK MOUNTAINS,** hilly upland plateau (50,000 square miles) primarily in Missouri and Arkansas. The Ozarks are locally referred to as "mountains." The area was settled during the early 19th century by Scots-Irish farmers. After the Civil War (1861-65), mining and lumber corporations became the largest landholders and employers in the region. During the Depression of the 1930s, the region's rural whites became a kind of image of contemporary American poverty. The forests, streams, and mineral springs of the Ozarks have made it a popular tourist attraction.

P

■ **PACA, WILLIAM (1740-99),** statesman and Revolutionary War leader. A signer of the Declaration of Independence, Paca was born in Maryland. During the Revolution he served in the Continental Congress and afterward as a judge and governor of Maryland (1782-85).

See Also: Declaration of Independence.

■ **PACIFIC NORTHWEST,** term that designates the northwestern region of the United States. This heavily wooded and mountainous area includes Washington, Oregon, and the western portion of Idaho. Large numbers of Indian tribes, including the Salish, Klamath, Chinook, and Kwakiutl, lived in the region. The English explorers Francis Drake in 1579 and then Captain James Cook in 1778 claimed the land for England. In 1805-06 Lewis and Clark's American expedition explored the region and followed the Columbia River to the Pacific coast. In 1811 the American John Jacob Astor established his fur-trading post along the Columbia River. During the mid-1830s Christian missionaries established posts in the area, and by the 1840s American settlers were traveling the Oregon Trail from the Mississippi River area to settle in the Willamette River Valley's rich agricultural lands. Britain finally ceded the Pacific Northwest to the United States with the Oregon Treaty of 1846.

See Also: Astor, John Jacob; Fur Trade.

■ **PACIFIC RAILROAD ACT (1862),** law providing for the construction of a transcontinental railroad. The act gave two corporations—the Union Pacific and the Central Pacific—the right to construct "a continuous railroad" roughly along the 42nd parallel, following from the east the Platte River route of the Overland Trail. The companies received, free of charge, a 400-foot right-of-way through public land, grants of 10 five-square-mile sections of land per mile of track, timber mineral rights on adjacent public lands, and government bond subsidies. After construction of the railroad,

the companies were free to dispose of their surplus land in any way they wished. The legislation also authorized federal loans to the companies for construction costs, $16,000 per linear mile for tracks on level ground and $48,000 per linear mile through the mountains. The two corporations received some 45 million acres of the public domain, giving them tremendous power in the West.

See Also: Railroads.

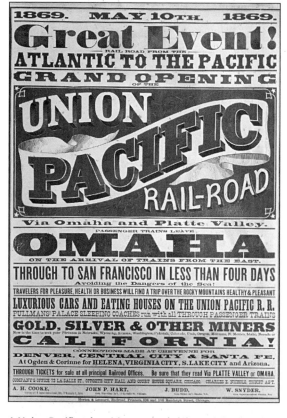

A Union Pacific advertising poster celebrated the opening in 1869 of the transcontinental railroad, authorized by the Pacific Railroad Act. The completed line was a major factor in opening the West to settlement.

PACIFISM, principled opposition to armed conflict of any kind and also the movement to establish and preserve peace among nations through the creation of international laws and organizations. Pacifism has been a persistent force in America since colonial times, when such groups as the Society of Friends, the Mennonites, and the Moravians lived by a religiously based ethic of nonresistance to violence. In the 19th century a number of societies dedicated to the preservation of peace among nations were established in the United States. The first of these was the New York Peace Society (1815), but the most influential was probably the American Peace Society (1828), which sought not only to establish world peace but to encourage greater awareness of international affairs and problems among Americans. Its influence, like that of other such groups, declined for a time because of conflicting beliefs and strategies among members concerning slavery and the Civil War (1861-65). After that conflict, however, the peace movement gathered new momentum, often linking the cause of world peace with the extension of American laws and moral values to the world community. Peace societies and institutions played a key role in the antiwar movement that accompanied the Spanish-American War (1898), and peace-minded Americans were active at the first Universal Peace Congress (1898) held in Paris. Peace activists during both 20th-century world wars were greeted with skepticism and derision by Americans generally, and the number of true conscientious objectors—those who refused to bear arms for reasons of conscience—in both conflicts was rather small. Many who advocated pacifist principles during the Cold War, including members of the antiwar movement during the Vietnam War, were often attacked as communist sympathizers. The level of visibility of pacifism in the United States, and its impact on U.S. foreign policy, has waxed and waned over time as peace societies, religious groups, and other reformers have struggled to create and maintain coalitions to meet the challenges posed by various wars and causes.

—JAMES A. WARREN

BIBLIOGRAPHY: Chatfield, Charles, ed., *Peace Movements in America* (Schocken 1973).

PAIGE, ROBERT LEROY ("SATCHEL") (1906-82), baseball player. Born in Mobile, Alabama, Paige was a legendary pitcher in the Negro Leagues (1924-47). In 1948, at the age of 42, he became the first black pitcher in the American League, joining the Cleveland Indians. Paige's fastball was renowned for its speed and pinpoint accuracy. He played in the majors for six years and pitched a career total of 2,500 games. In 1971, Paige became the first player from the Negro Leagues to be inducted into the Baseball Hall of Fame.

See Also: Sports.

PAINE, ROBERT TREAT (1731-1814), minister, jurist, and Revolutionary War statesman. Born in Boston, Paine was a member of the Second Continental Congress and signer of the Declaration of Independence. He also served as a prosecutor in the trial of the British soldiers involved in the Boston Massacre.

See Also: Boston Massacre; Declaration of Independence.

PAINE, THOMAS (1737-1809), Revolutionary pamphleteer who had a profound effect on European and American politics in the last quarter of the 18th century. Paine was born in Thetford, England, where he attended grammar school for only five years. At the age of 12 he began a 7-year apprenticeship with his father as a maker of stays for women's corsets. For the next 20 years he unsuccessfully held a succession of jobs.

Paine arrived in Philadelphia in November 1774. He soon became editor of the *Pennsylvania Magazine* and a staunch opponent of British imperial policy toward America. In January 1776 he published *Common Sense*, a 47-page pamphlet that urged Americans to declare their independence and to replace the monarchy with a republic. Written, as were all of his subsequent works, in a lively, appealing style easily understood by the masses, the pamphlet became an instant success, selling 120,000 copies in three months, and three times that amount over the next few years.

Throughout the American Revolution Paine wrote many essays to bolster the war effort. His most popular series, the *American Crisis*, started with the words, "These are the times that try men's souls" (December 1776). As clerk of the Pennsylvania Assembly in 1780, Paine wrote the preamble to the first bill emancipating slaves enacted by an American legislature.

After the war, in the mid-1780s, Paine designed and promoted an iron bridge and wrote political tracts against paper money and in support of banks. In April 1787 he returned to Europe to obtain the scientific community's endorsements of his bridge. From 1787 to 1790 he traveled between England and France, welcomed by liberals in both countries. In 1791, Paine responded to Edmund Burke's criticism of the French Revolution with the first part of the *Rights of Man*, which he hoped would be an English version of *Common Sense*. The second part followed in February 1792. More than 200,000 copies were sold by 1793. Indicted for treason and tried in absentia in England for his seditious writing, Paine was convicted in December 1792.

In August 1792 Paine was made a French citizen. Despite his inability to speak French, he was elected to the French National Convention in September 1792, where he allied with the moderate Gironde group. When the Jacobins seized power, they revoked his French citizenship and imprisoned him from December 1793 until November 1794, during which time Paine wrote the first part of the *Age of Reason*—an articulation of Deism in which he denounced formal religion, especially Christianity. The second part appeared in 1796.

Paine's assault on religion and his bitter attack in a "Letter to George Washington" (1796) assured him a cool reception in America when he returned in 1802. The last seven years of Paine's life were marked by poverty, sickness, reclusiveness, and excessive drinking as he was abandoned by many of his old friends.

—JOHN P. KAMINSKI

See Also: *Revolution, American.*

BIBLIOGRAPHY: Foner, Eric, *Tom Paine and Revolutionary America* (Oxford Univ. Press 1976); Keane, John, *Tom Paine* (Little, Brown 1995).

Thomas Paine's pamphlet *Common Sense*, published anonymously in 1776, advocated an immediate declaration of American independence from Great Britain. His *Rights of Man* (1791) supported the French Revolution.

■ **PAINTED DESERT,** arid region of north-central Arizona. It extends from the Grand Canyon National Park in the west to the Little Colorado River in the east and is about 20 miles wide and some 200 miles long. The irregularly eroded layers of sediment and clay in the area create striking combinations of yellow, red, mauve, and purple throughout the mesas and valleys. Parts of the Navaho and Hopi Indian reservations are located in the center of the Painted Desert. Joseph Ives and John Newberry's government exploration in 1858 first named the region.

■ **PAINTING,** an important aspect of American culture since the 17th century. At that time itinerant artists offered their skills to rural folk and town-dwellers alike who paid to see themselves and their family members recorded for posterity. Either self-taught or only informally instructed by their immediate predecessors, these artists were for the most part crude and repetitive in technique, but of some 400 surviving American portraits from the late 17th century, an occasional one such as the anonymously painted *Mrs. Elizabeth Freake and Baby Mary* (c. 1674) dazzles the eye with its intricate composition, vibrant color, and flat, ornamental design.

Eighteenth-Century Painting. Painting in 18th-century America was primarily British in origin, though derived from Continental sources. Scottish-born John Smibert (1688-1751) raised the technical standard of American painting and demonstrated the ability of art to be ideological with his *Bermuda Group* (c. 1729), a group portrait of missionary educators rendered in the baroque style, with a romantic glimpse of New World wilderness in the background. By making his personal collection of Old Master prints, copies, and sculptures readily available to those who were interested, Smibert provided an invaluable education to young American artists who had never been to Europe.

The most brilliant of these was John Singleton Copley (1738-1815), the finest portraitist produced by the colonies. In dramatically lit, psychologically concentrated depictions of individual Bostonians, among them the silversmith and patriot Paul Revere (1768), Copley blended his knack for conveying tactile phenomena such as crisp cotton shirts and polished mahogany tables with his gift for creating the illusion of a sitter's characteristic physical expression. On the eve of the Revolution Copley expatriated to England, where he joined America's other leading painter of the era, the Pennsylvanian Benjamin West (1738-1820), who had already taken up residence in London. Official history painter to King George III and a founder of the Royal Academy of Arts, West won fame for his depictions of key events in Anglo-American history, such as *The Death of Wolfe* (1770) and *Penn's Treaty with the Indians* (1771), which he innovatively rendered in the neoclassical style but with modern dress.

At one time or another during West's distinguished career, numerous young American artists studied with him in London. Two of the best known were Gilbert Stuart (1755-1828), creator of the famous portrait head of George Washington (1796), and Col. John Trumbull (1756-1843), celebrated for tableaux, such as *The Battle of Bunker Hill* (1786) and *The Signing of the Declaration of Independence* (1786-94), which defined ever after how Americans pictured the heroes of the Revolution.

Nineteenth-Century Painting. Art lore has it that it was the aged Colonel Trumbull who first recognized the rough and raw talent of the young English-born landscape painter Thomas Cole (1801-48). Cole and his fellow romantic portrayers of the great outdoors were dubbed the "Hudson River School" in droll recognition of their predilection for traveling north of New York City into the Catskills or the White Mountains in search of stirring natural vistas. Cole's masterwork, commonly called *The Oxbow* (1836), shows the intersection of wilderness and cultivated nature in the Connecticut River Valley and suggests, symbolically, that America's purpose is to spread civilization westward (a popular concept of the time captured in the phrase "Manifest Destiny"). Other eminent Hudson River School artists were Asher B. Durand (1796-1886), who taught that faithfully depicting nature was a means of communing with the Almighty, and Frederick Church (1826-1900), whose minutely detailed panoramas of the Andes Mountains dazzled throngs of exhibition-goers.

Contemporary with these artists were the popular painters of genre scenes, or scenes of everyday life. The Long Islander William Sydney Mount (1807-68) showed rural folk engaged in activities such as dancing, fiddling, bargaining for a horse, relaxing from strenuous labor in a hay field, or, in the memorable *Eel Spearing at Setauket* (1845), gliding a skiff across a glassy smooth surface on a summer's day. The Missouri painter George Caleb Bingham (1811-79) depicted godlike river men dancing on barges and hayseed yokels patiently standing in line at the polling place. Lilly Martin Spencer (1822-1901) made lighthearted fun of bourgeois husbands and showed plucky maids and feisty cooks taking a break from their labors in the kitchen.

After the Civil War, the nativism implicitly or explicitly espoused by the landscape and genre painters appeared lamentably old-fashioned to a younger generation of artists who embraced internationalism and hastened abroad, largely to Paris and Munich, in search of training and inspiration. The most notable of these were James Mac-Neill Whistler (1834-1903), an acid-tongued wit and flamboyant advocate of "art for art's sake," who championed harmonic unity of color and design, as in his celebrated portrait of his mother, *Arrangement in Gray and Black* (1872); Mary Cassatt (1845-1926), a painter of mother-and-child scenes who learned from and exhibited with the French Impressionists; John Singer Sargent (1856-1925), a stylish high-society portraitist whose brushwork in oil and watercolor alike was unsurpassed; and Henry Ossawa Tanner (1859-1937), an African-American expatriate to Paris who applied Symbolist techniques to biblical subjects.

Continuing to live in America during this period and concentrating on American settings and themes, Winslow Homer (1836-1910), a self-taught Civil War graphic illustrator, matured into a brilliant watercolorist and strikingly dramatic oil painter. Especially notable are his scenes of solitary individuals confronting the elements, as in *The Fog Warning* (1885) and *The Gulf Stream* (1899). Homer's younger contemporary Thomas Eakins (1844-1916), a realist based in Philadelphia, painted dour, almost aesthetically brutal portraits of local singers, scientists, sportsmen, and physicians, as in the mammoth *Anatomy Clinic of Dr. Samuel Gross* (1875), which was publicly derided for its candor in highlighting the blood on the hands of the famous surgeon it depicted.

Twentieth-Century Painting. The heirs to Homer and Eakins were the turn-of-the-century urban realists such as Robert Henri (1865-1929), whose greatest impact was as an inspirational art teacher; George Bellows (1882-1925), whose brushwork in paintings such as *Stag at Sharkey's* (1907) conveyed the juicy, muscular pulse of the city; and John Sloan (1871-1951), famous for his gritty paintings of urban rituals and locales, as in *McSorley's Bar* (1912). Known jokingly as the "Ashcan School," the urban realists were thought daringly progressive painters until the Armory Show exhibition of 1913, which introduced European modernism to the United States, suddenly made them seem provincial, even backward. They were superseded as America's avant-garde

by semi-abstractionists such as Marsden Hartley (1877-1943), one of the first and boldest practitioners of Cubism; Georgia O'Keeffe (1887-1986), who envisioned skyscrapers at night as hulking otherworldly forms and transformed delicate flowers into powerful, sexually charged abstractions; and Stuart Davis (1894-1964), whose Jazz Age syncopations in color and composition trampolined off the energies of modern commercial advertising and industrial design.

With the advent of the Great Depression, abstraction lost credibility even with many of its sympathizers as being too brazenly detached from real-world concerns. Three leading artists of the 1930s were Edward Hopper (1882-1967), a student of Henri, who was a poet of quiet desperation and urban alienation, as in his portrayal of an isolated theater usher in *New York Movie* (1939); Thomas Hart Benton (1889-1975), a midwestern regionalist who painted curving, organic, crowded-with-life murals of the American scene; and Ben Shahn (1898-1969), a Lithuanian-born artist who employed a semirealist style aimed at calling attention to social and political inequities, as in his viciously satirical series of paintings (1931-32) on the Sacco-Vanzetti case.

Benton's pupil Jackson Pollock (1912-56) emerged in the late 1940s as the leader of the Abstract Expressionist movement and was popularly known as "Jack the Dripper" because of his unique method of pouring paint directly from cans to canvas in spontaneously random and intricate networks of lines. Pollock's Dutch-born colleague Willem De Kooning (1904-97) was, like Sargent several generations earlier, unrivaled as a brushmaster. He applied thick, throbbing swatches of pigment to canvas in dazzling abstract compositions that were sometimes grounded in representational imagery, as in *Woman I* (1952), the first in a series of turbulent paintings controversially dedicated to the female as subject.

As Abstract Expressionism ran its course by the mid-1950s, younger artists such as Robert Rauschenberg (1925-), Jaspar Johns (1930-), and Andy Warhol (1930-87) developed a cool, ironic style that borrowed from painterly abstraction but reinvented it in a playful, mocking mode, as in Johns's series of paintings of the American flag or Warhol's slick depictions of brand-name commodities such as soup cans and cola bottles. They were leaders of an international movement known as "Pop Art," which sought to break down, or at least scramble, the traditional high/low hierarchy in Western culture.

In the final quarter of the 20th century so many art movements flourished in painting (Minimalism, Op-Art, Photo-Realism, Post-Painterly Abstraction) that it became difficult even for experts to keep track of all the comings and goings. American painting seemed jeopardized both by the erosion of the formerly rigorous emphasis in art schools on teaching traditional painting techniques and by the hypercommercialization of the art market, in which celebrity artists could make a fortune while new artists or not-well-known older artists could barely make a living. Meanwhile the growing prestige of photography, video, and computer technologies as art media marginalized painting all the more.

—DAVID M. LUBIN

See Also: Armory Show; Hudson River School; Museums; individual biographies.

BIBLIOGRAPHY: Baigel, Matthew, A Concise History of American Painting and Sculpture (Icon Editions 1996); Calo, Mary Ann, ed., Critical Issues in American Art: A Book of Readings (Westview Press/Icon Editions 1997); Hughes, Robert, American Visions: The Epic History of Art in America (Knopf 1997); Prown, Jules David, American Painting: From Its Beginnings to the Armory Show (Skira 1969); Rose, Barbara, American Art: The Twentieth Century (Skira 1969).

■ **PALMER, ARNOLD (1929-),** golfer. Born in Youngstown, Pennsylvania, he turned professional in 1954 and won seven major championships. His skill and personality helped launch a golf boom in the 1960s.

See Also: Sports.

■ **PALMER RAIDS (1919-20),** series of government-sanctioned mass arrests of alleged political agitators instigated by U.S. attorney general A. Mitchell Palmer. Thousands of American citizens and legal resident aliens were rounded up between November 1919 and Jan. 1, 1920, as suspected anarchists and revolutionaries. In part of the national "red scare," hundreds of aliens were quickly deported, including anarchists Emma Goldman and Alexander Berkman.

See Also: Anarchism; Goldman, Emma; Red Scare.

■ **PANAMA CANAL,** across the Isthmus of Panama, constructed by the United States between 1904 and 1914. Such a canal had been high in the priorities of the United States, Great Britain, and France in the last half of the 19th century. In 1850 the United States and Britain signed the Clayton-Bulwer Treaty, pledging that neither party would seek independent rights over a Central American canal. In 1881 a French company secured permission from Colombia, which included the Panamanian Isthmus within its boundaries, and began construction, but the company quickly went bankrupt. After the Spanish-American War (1898) the canal became a priority for the United States; in the Hay-Pauncefote Treaty of 1901 Britain agreed to relinquish its claim, and the next year the United States purchased the right to construct the canal from the New Panama Canal Company, the successor to the bankrupt French company.

The United States negotiated with Colombia, but the country's legislature refused to ratify the agreement, holding out for better terms. With the encouragement of the Americans, canal supporters in the isthmus led a bloodless uprising against the authority of Colombia and declared independence. The Republic of Panama was quickly recognized by the United States, and the two countries signed a treaty with the terms rejected by Colombia: a lease of the "Canal Zone" for 99 years, a cash payment to Panama of $10 million, and an annual rent of $250,000 per year. This treaty was ratified by the U.S. Senate in 1904.

The construction of the canal, under the direction of Col. George W. Goethals of the Army Corps of Engineers, took 10 years, required the excavation of 240 million cubic yards of earth, and cost $720 million. The canal was opened to shipping in August 1914. In 1921, the United States paid Colombia $25 million in recognition of its loss of territory.

After World War II, resentment in Panama grew over U.S. control of the canal and the American zone that extended five miles on either side. In 1963 violent protests led to Panama suspend-

The ship *Ancon* steams through the Panama Canal on opening day, Aug. 15, 1914.

ing diplomatic relations with the United States, which were resumed in 1964 with the promise of negotiations over sovereignty. These talks had dragged on for more than a decade when presidential candidate Jimmy Carter declared his support for turning the canal over to Panama. After Carter's election (1976), his administration concluded the negotiations, and in 1977 he signed a treaty promising Panamanian control in 1999. After an acrimonious and bitter national debate, the Senate ratified the treaty in 1978.

See Also: *Clayton-Bulwer Treaty; Goethals, George; Hay-Pauncefote Treaty.*

BIBLIOGRAPHY: LaFeber, Walter, *The Panama Canal* (Oxford Univ. Press 1989); McCullough, David, *The Path Between the Seas: The Creation of the Panama Canal, 1870-1914* (Simon & Schuster 1977).

■ **PANAMA INVASION (1989),** U.S. military operation known as "Operation Just Cause." Pres. George Bush ordered the strike to remove Panamanian dictator Gen. Manuel Noriega—accused

of international drug smuggling, betraying U.S. intelligence information, and endangering U.S. citizens in Panama—and to set the stage for a democratic government in the Central American country. Noriega achieved power during the 1980s through a series of political and military maneuvers, including an alliance with earlier dictator Omar Torrijos. Noriega's personal reputation for brutality aside, his value to U.S. intelligence agencies seemed high during the Reagan administration, in particular because of his willingness to help funnel support to the Contra rebels in Nicaragua. However, after relations deteriorated, and the United States feared Noriega might threaten the strategic Panama Canal, Gen. Colin Powell arrayed huge U.S. land and air forces (many already based inside the country) against the Panama Defense Force and civilian street thugs called "Dignity Batallions." The operation ran from December 17 to 27. Noriega fled to the Vatican embassy in Panama City before emerging after several days of negotiation and siege. He was transported to the United States, where he was convicted and sentenced to prison for drug trafficking and racketeering, and new elections were held in Panama in 1990.

See Also: Powell, Colin Luther, Jr.

BIBLIOGRAPHY: Flanagan, Edward M., *Battle for Panama* (Brassey's 1993).

■ **PAN-AMERICAN UNION,** an international organization of the republics of North and South America, founded in 1890 at the first Pan-American Conference at Washington, D.C. Its original name was the International Bureau for American Republics. The union provided for commercial, technical, and cultural exchange among its member nations. Under the auspices of the union, many agreements on trade, migration, coastal neutrality zones, telegraph and railway communications, health care, and education were concluded among its members. In May 1915, the first Pan-American financial conference met in Washington. In May 1923, members of the union signed the Pan-American Treaty for the peaceful settlement of disputes. During Pres. Franklin D. Roosevelt's administration, the United States made considerable efforts to remove persistent distrust of the United States among Latin American governments. In 1933, Roosevelt publicly repudiated the policy of U.S. intervention in Latin America. In October 1939, the Pan-American conference in Panama issued a general declaration of neutrality of the American republics toward the hostilities in Europe. However, at the meeting in Havana in July 1940, the member nations agreed that the American republics, jointly or individually, should act as their defense interests required. The Pan-American Union became part of the newly formed Organization of American States (OAS) in 1948 and is currently part of the OAS administrative machinery. It has four departments—economics and social affairs; international law; cultural affairs; and administrative services.

See Also: Organization of American States (OAS).

■ **PANICS, FINANCIAL,** part of a recurring business cycle, usually following an overextension of resources. The Panic of 1819 ensued largely because state banks overextended credit to land speculators, and when the Second Bank of the United States called in its debts, hundreds of banks closed down. Pres. Andrew Jackson fueled the financial expansion, canal and railroad construction, and land speculation of the early 1830s by funding "pet" state banks. He issued his Specie Circular to suppress the speculation that led to the Panic of 1837. The overextension of banks to fund railroad construction enabled the failure of one company to kick off the Panic of 1857. In 1873, railroad speculation, unregulated business practices, and a shaky financial structure led to the failure of Jay Cooke's banking house and the worst depression the nation had seen. In 1893 a member of the debt-ridden railroad industry declared bankruptcy. As a result, the stock market collapsed, setting off a crisis that caused over 16,000 businesses to fail and commodity prices to plummet. J. P. Morgan and Company helped finance the revival from the Panic of 1907, but an unregulated stock market and a series of other factors culminated in the Panic of 1929, which ushered in the Great Depression.

■ **PARIS, TREATY OF.** *See: Treaty of Paris* for treaties of 1763, 1783, and 1898.

■ **PARKER, ARTHUR C. (1881-1955),** Seneca anthropologist. Parker was born on the Cattaraugus Indian Reservation in New York. In 1904, Parker became the archaeologist for the New York State Museum, where he studied Iroquois culture extensively. A founding member of the Society of American Indians in 1911, Parker advocated pan-Indianism and Indian citizenship. Although committed to acculturation into U.S. mainstream society, Parker emphasized the importance of regaining aspects of Indian culture and identity.

See Also: Indians of North America; Society of American Indians.

■ **PARKER, CHARLES CHRISTOPHER, JR. (CHARLIE) (1920-55),** jazz saxophonist. Born in Kansas City, Kansas, Parker was given a saxophone by his mother at the age of 11 and soon began his all too brief but brilliant career in jazz. Parker's early work was quickly marked by a genius improvisation, but drug addiction often interrupted his career and ultimately cut short his life. Around 1941, "Bird," as he came to be called, met Dizzy Gillespie in New York City. Both on the upward curves of heroic careers, they bonded personally even as their highly individual styles found resonance in each other's music. Together they altered the jazz landscape by introducing be-bop. Parker was a truly gifted instrumentalist and composer-arranger, writing such songs as "Now's the Time," "The Yardbird Suite," and "Confirmation." Parker's legacy of spirited and blues-colored jazz has touched every jazz musician since.

See Also: Jazz.

■ **PARKER, ELY S. (c. 1828-95),** Seneca, first Indian commissioner of Indian Affairs. Born on the Tonawanda Reservation, Parker collaborated with Lewis Henry Morgan, an early ethnographer, on a book about the Iroquois. In 1861, Parker was refused as an enlistee in the Union army because of his race, but in May 1863, his friend Gen. Ulysses S. Grant commissioned him as a captain and his aide-de-camp. In 1869, Grant, then president, appointed Parker commissioner of

Seneca chief Ely Parker served in the Civil War with Ulysses S. Grant, who, as president, appointed Parker as the first Indian to serve as commissioner of Indian Affairs.

Indian Affairs. He resigned in 1871 amid charges that he defrauded the federal government by sending supplies to starving western Indians without congressional approval.

See Also: Indian Affairs, Bureau of (BIA); Indians of North America; Morgan, Lewis Henry.

■ **PARKER, QUANAH (c. 1845-1911),** Comanche leader born at Cedar Lake, Texas. In the 1870s, as the U.S. Army attempted to force the Southern Plains tribes into submission, Parker led the Quahada band of Comanche in raids against white settlements in northern Texas and Oklahoma. In 1874, the United States launched an offensive against the raiders, forcing their surrender in December 1874. After his defeat, Parker became a member of the Native American Church.

See Also: Indians of North America; Native American Church.

■ **PARKER, THEODORE (1810-60),** Unitarian minister and transcendentalist theologian. Born in Lexington, Massachusetts, he was the pastor of the Unitarian Church at Roxbury from 1837 to 1846. After the publication of *Discourse of Matters Pertaining to Religion* (1842), however, he was ostracized by orthodox Unitarians as a radical liberal. In 1846, he became pastor of a church in Boston. Parker led a grueling life lecturing across the country in support of nearly every reform in antebellum America, especially the antislavery movement.

See Also: Antislavery Movement; Religion; Unitarians.

■ **PARKMAN, FRANCIS (1823-93),** historian. Born in Boston to a distinguished New England family, he attended Harvard, where as an undergraduate he first entertained the notion of writing history. After receiving his degree in 1844, Parkman stayed on at Harvard's Law School, fulfilling its requirements by 1846. Still, Parkman had been taken by colonial American history, and, eager to learn more of Indian culture, he set off for the Oregon Trail, returning to Boston six months later. In 1847, Parkman's account of the journey appeared first in serial form and then in 1849 as a book, *The California and Oregon Trail*. In 1848, Parkman began to research and write his first historical work, *The History of the Conspiracy of Pon-*

tiac. His work was interrupted by an array of mental and physical illnesses that affected him from his college days. Nevertheless, *Pontiac* was published in 1851.

Parkman gained his reputation as a historian with the appearance of the popular *Pioneers of France in the New World* (1865). It was the first of his nine-volume series, *France and England in North America*, which included *The Jesuits in North America* (1867), *La Salle and the Discovery of the Great West* (1879), and *Montcalm and Wolfe* (1884). As one of the 19th century's most prominent historians, Parkman brought a novelistic quality to his craft, emphasized the importance of searching out and thoroughly researching original historical documents, and exhibited a romantic sensibility, though not in his representation of Indians as the "savage" inferiors to Anglo-American Protestants. His biases also devalued those of a different class and gender than his own, as revealed, for example, in his *Some Reasons Against Woman Suffrage* (1887). In the century after Parkman's death, such prejudices would contribute to the increasing decline in popularity of his work.

—JAMES KESSENIDES

See Also: History.

BIBLIOGRAPHY: Jacobs, Wilbur R., *Francis Parkman, Historian as Hero: The Formative Years* (Univ. of Texas Press 1991); Levin, David, *History as Romantic Art: Bancroft, Prescott, Motley, and Parkman* (Stanford Univ. Press 1959).

■ **PARKS, GORDON (1912-),** photographer, author, composer, and film director. Born in modest circumstances in Fort Scott, Kansas, Parks possesses an unusually diverse talent. Starting out as a freelance photographer, he shot fashion photos for *Vogue* and spent 20 years working for *Life*. In addition he wrote 12 works of poetry, nonfiction, and fiction and composed concertos, a ballet (*Martin*, 1990), and works for piano. Parks also directed films, adapted his own book *The Learning Tree* (1969) for the screen, and directed *Shaft* (1972) and *Leadbelly* (1976). In 1970, Parks founded *Essence* magazine. He was awarded the Spingarn Medal in 1972.

See Also: African Americans.

BIBLIOGRAPHY: Parks, Gordon, *Voices in the Mirror* (Doubleday 1990).

■ **PARSONS, ELSIE CLEWS (1875-1941),** sociologist and anthropologist. Born in New York City, she was educated at Columbia University. She began her career writing theoretical critiques of social limitations imposed on women. Her later work on folklore and ethnography, influenced by her friend Franz Boas, dealt largely with Indians of the Southwest, as in *The Social Organization of the Tewa of New Mexico* (1929), *Hopi and Zuni Ceremonialism* (1933), and *Pueblo Indian Religion* (1939).

See Also: Boas, Franz.

■ **PASTORIUS, FRANCIS DANIEL (1651-1720),** colonial lawyer and land agent. Pastorius was born in Sommerhausen, Germany. As a young lawyer, he became interested in immigrating to America when a Quaker sect hired him to be their land agent (1683). He traveled to Pennsylvania on their behalf and made arrangements to secure a tract of land that became the Quaker settlement of Germantown.

■ **PATENT OFFICE,** U.S. government agency that issues patents to inventors, granting them exclusive use of new products or processes for a period of years. The Patent Office is authorized by Article I, Section 8, of the Constitution and was established by Congress in 1790 as part of the State Department. It was transferred to the Interior Department in 1849 and to the Department of Commerce in 1925. The patent system was considered vital for encouraging and protecting industry in the United States. By allowing an inventor to enjoy a limited monopoly on the proceeds of a new idea, the system, it was believed, encouraged innovation that would lead to new industries and economic growth. Millions of patents have been issued since the Patent Office was created, nearly 110,000 in 1993 alone. The Patent Office also administers the government's trademark registration system, which allows companies to protect brand names and symbols.

■ **PATERSON, WILLIAM (1745-1806),** U.S. senator (1789-90), governor of New Jersey (1790-93), and associate justice of the U.S. Supreme Court (1793-1806). A native of County Antrim, Ireland, Paterson grew up in New Jersey. As a Federalist senator, he helped draft the Judiciary Act of 1789.

After joining the Court, Paterson distinguished himself as a supporter of a strong national government, as in upholding *Vanhorne's Lessee v. Dorrance* (1794), a circuit-court decision asserting the right of federal courts to rule on the constitutionality of state laws.

See Also: Constitution of the United States; Judiciary Act of 1789; Supreme Court.

■ **PATROONSHIPS,** form of feudal landholding in New Netherland (present-day New York and New Jersey). To promote settlement on tracts claimed by the Dutch West India Company, the Dutch States General confirmed the Charter of Freedoms and Exemptions (1629) granting the company the right to endow certain settlers with patroonships. Under the terms of the charter, the prospective patroons had to transport at least 50 settlers to their particular grant. In exchange, the patroons were given estates fronting 16 miles and as far inland as settlement would permit on navigable rivers with exclusive rights to trade and exemption from any kind of taxation for at least eight years. The patroons also retained the right to hold courts and settle disputes between their tenants. By 1630 at least five patroonships were granted and three were settled. The most successful of these was the patroonship of Rensselaerswyck.

See Also: Dutch Colonies.

■ **PATTON, GEORGE SMITH, JR. (1885-1945),** U.S. Army officer. One of the most flamboyant soldiers in army history, Patton was born in San Gabriel, California. A West Point graduate trained in the horse cavalry, he turned to the mechanized variety in World War I and tirelessly advocated armored doctrine thereafter.

During World War II's Operation Torch in North Africa in 1942, his stern discipline and keen understanding of the art of war enabled him to reverse American misfortunes against the German *Afrika Korps.* Patton later conquered Sicily (1943) with limited support but nearly ruined his career by slapping an American soldier. This cost him a role in the D-Day landings scheduled for June 1944. When the invasion bogged down in Normandy, he was brought out of exile to command the newly formed Third Army, with which he organized an American blitzkrieg across

In World War II, George S. Patton, Jr., recognized as one of the nation's greatest military tacticians, held key commands in North Africa and Europe.

France. He was instrumental in the relief of Bastogne in December 1944 and then drove on through Bavaria. Patton died in a German hospital in December 1945 from injuries sustained in a car accident.

See Also: World War II.

BIBLIOGRAPHY: Blumenson, Martin, *Patton, the Man Behind the Legend, 1885-1945* (Morrow 1985).

■ **PAUL, ALICE (1885-1977),** feminist leader and author of the Equal Rights Amendment (1923). She was born in Moorestown, New Jersey. Paul worked with radical suffragists while studying in England (1907-10). Committed to militant tactics, she was expelled from the National American Woman Suffrage Association and in 1913 formed the more radical National Women's party.

See Also: Equal Rights Amendment (ERA); Women's Movement.

■ **PAULING, LINUS (1901-94),** structural chemist and peace advocate. Born in Portland, Oregon, Pauling taught at the California Institute of Technology for most of his career (1927-63). He used X-ray crystallography to study the nature of chemical bonding and developed a theory of bonding (1928) that applied the quantum mechanical concept of resonance to classical structural chemistry. His work on molecular structure broadened the scope of modern chemistry and won him a Nobel Prize in Chemistry (1954). Pauling applied his theories to biology starting in the 1930s, studying the structure of proteins and discovering that sickle-cell anemia results from a hereditary defect in blood hemoglobin. During the 1950s, Pauling led a group of U.S. scientists concerned over nuclear fallout in opposing atomic weapons testing. He won the Nobel Peace Prize in 1962 for his efforts and joined the Center for the Study of Democratic Institutions in 1963. Pauling then taught at the University of California, San Diego (1967), and Stanford (1969), causing some controversy in 1970 when he claimed that large doses of vitamin C would prevent or cure the common cold.

See Also: Science.

■ **PAWNEE,** Caddoan-speaking tribe of the Great Plains. In the early 17th century, the Pawnees settled in present-day Nebraska, where they farmed and hunted buffalo. At times in conflict with neighboring Siouan tribes, the Pawnees also acted as intermediaries between the nomadic Sioux and French and English fur traders. In the 19th century, increasing white American pressure for the fertile Plains land made the Sioux and Pawnee bitter enemies in the territorial struggle. Although many Pawnee men became scouts for the U.S. Army, in 1874 the U.S. government moved the Pawnee south into western Indian Territory

See Also: Fur Trade; Indians of North America.

■ **PAXTON BOYS,** mob that killed Indians in Pennsylvania in land dispute in 1763. Outraged by the ceding of western Pennsylvania lands to Indians by the British Proclamation of 1763, an angry mob known as the Paxton Boys slaughtered over 20 Indian men, women, and children in December of that same year near Conestoga

on the Susquehanna River. Protesting the impending arrest of the Paxton Boys, some 600 backwoods frontiersmen marched on Philadelphia, where Benjamin Franklin's skillful negotiations barely averted a riot.

See Also: Frontier in American History.

■ **PAYNE-ALDRICH TARIFF ACT (1909),** controversial congressional legislation supported by Pres. William Howard Taft. The act was written so as to protect eastern-made industrial products at the expense of midwestern producers, angering many progressive Republicans.

■ **PAYTON, WALTER (1954-),** Hall of Fame football player. A running back born in Columbia, Mississippi, he ran for a National Football League record 16,726 yards during his career with the Chicago Bears (1975-87).

■ **PEABODY, ELIZABETH PALMER (1804-94),** transcendentalist, intellectual, and educational reformer. Born in Billerica, Massachusetts, she was a charter member of the Transcendentalist Club and the first independent woman publisher in Boston. She used her considerable energies and talents to refine and popularize the work of her friends William Ellery Channing, Bronson Alcott, Ralph Waldo Emerson, Henry David Thoreau, and Nathaniel Hawthorne. Also a champion of educational reform and a disciple of German educator Friedrich W. A. Froebel, she founded the first English-speaking kindergarten in the United States in 1860 and in 1873 wrote *Kindergarten Messenger.*

■ **PEACE CORPS,** U.S. government agency that sends volunteer aid workers to developing countries. Founded in 1961 during Pres. John F. Kennedy's administration and first headed by Kennedy's brother-in-law R. Sargent Shriver, the Peace Corps originally attracted idealistic young people who worked in various community service projects in Africa, Asia, and South America. The Peace Corps reflected both the Kennedy administration's desire to involve young people with their government and the conviction that the U.S. foreign policy of opposition to Soviet expansion in developing nations could be advanced by promoting economic development. Frequently the

Established by the Kennedy administration in 1961, the Peace Corps sent most of its volunteers to Africa, Asia, and Latin America.

target of attacks in Congress, it was merged with its domestic counterpart, Volunteers in Service to America (VISTA), in 1970. The Peace Corps subsequently tried to recruit volunteers who brought with them specific practical skills.

See Also: Cold War.

BIBLIOGRAPHY: Schwarz, Karen, *What You Can Do for Your Country: An Oral History of the Peace Corps* (Morrow 1991).

■ **PEALE, CHARLES WILLSON (1741-1827),** patriarch of a family of early American painters. Peale was originally from Queen Anne County, Maryland. He studied painting under John Hesselius and visited John Smibert and John Singleton Copley in Boston. Funded by his neighbors in Maryland, Peale traveled to London, where he worked in the studio of Benjamin West. He returned to Maryland in 1769 and established a studio; his portraits of George Washington brought Peale attention and further commissions. He also executed numerous portraits of his family; several of his children, including Raphaelle,

Rembrandt, and Rubens Peale, went on to become artists in their own right. An avid naturalist, Peale established a natural history museum in Baltimore in 1786. He encouraged the burgeoning artistic tradition in the United States by helping to found the Pennsylvania Academy of Fine Arts in 1805. Peale's self-portrait (1822) shows him drawing open a curtain to his natural history museum while holding a palette, a depiction of his two main interests.

See Also: Copley, John Singleton; Painting; Peale Sisters; Smibert, John; West, Benjamin.

■ **PEALE, NORMAN VINCENT (1898-1993),** minister and author. The son of a Methodist circuit rider, Peale flourished as a pastor, drawing large audiences. In 1932 he accepted a call to Marble Collegiate Church in New York City and joined the Reformed Church in America. There he recognized the need to combine psychiatry and the ministry and opened a religio-psychiatric clinic. He wrote several self-help books and pamphlets, the most popular of which was *The Power of Positive Thinking* (1952). His other enterprises included a radio program and the monthly inspirational magazine *Guideposts*.

See Also: Religion.

■ **PEALE SISTERS,** Anna Claypoole (1791-1878), Margaretta Angelica (1795-1882), and Sarah Miriam (1800-85), painters of portraits and still lifes, the first American women to achieve full status as professional artists. Their father, miniaturist James Peale, and their uncle, portrait artist Charles Willson Peale, trained the girls. Sarah was the most successful, moving first to Baltimore (1831) and then to St. Louis (1846) and soon becoming the most popular portrait artist in each city.

See Also: Peale, Charles Willson.

■ **PEARL HARBOR,** U.S. naval base on the Pacific island of Oahu in the Hawaiian archipelago. The surprise attack by Japanese carrier-based warplanes on the American fleet in the harbor on Sunday, Dec. 7, 1941, triggered the U.S. declaration of war against Japan. Pres. Franklin D. Roosevelt described the event as "a date that will live in infamy." The Japanese killed 2,335 sailors, soldiers, and marines, destroyed approximately 240

On Dec. 7, 1941, the ammunition magazine of the U.S. destroyer *Shaw* explodes during Japan's surprise attack on Pearl Harbor, which resulted in the nation's entrance into World War II.

aircraft, and sank or damaged 18 warships. The devastation included the battleship *Arizona*, which blew up and sank taking 1,000 of its crew to their deaths.

Some have attributed the defeat to a conspiracy. One theory holds that President Roosevelt knew of the enemy plans in advance but did not warn the local commanders. He hoped, some assert, that the Japanese would strike and thereby unite Americans in support of his goal of full intervention in the developing war against Adolf Hitler as well as Japan. No real proof exists. The reasons for the defeat lie in the failures of American command and intelligence and, more importantly, in Japanese initiative, technical skill, and audacity.

The Japanese planned to destroy the fleet and force the United States to negotiate a settlement that would leave Japan the great power of Asia.

Instead, the attack aroused the American people to a fury of revenge that ultimately defeated the Japanese Empire.

—FRANK J. WETTA

See Also: Roosevelt, Franklin Delano; World War II.
BIBLIOGRAPHY: Prange, Gordon W., et al., *At Dawn We Slept: The Untold Story of Pearl Harbor* (Mc-Graw-Hill 1981); Prange, Gordon, Donald M. Goldstein, and Katherine V. Dillon, *Pearl Harbor: The Verdict of History* (McGraw-Hill 1986); Wohlsetter, Roberta, *Pearl Harbor: Warning and Decision* (Stanford Univ. Press 1962).

■ **PEARY, ROBERT EDWIN (1856-1920),** American Arctic explorer, born in Cresson, Pennsylvania, credited as the first person to reach the North Pole. Relying on Eskimo survival skills learned during his extensive Arctic travels, Peary and his

African-American assistant, Matthew Henson, reached the Pole on Apr. 6, 1909. Explorer Frederick Cook claimed to have reached the Pole a year earlier. In 1911 the U.S. Congress recognized Peary's claim, although debate continues.

See Also: Exploration and Discovery.

■ **PECKHAM, RUFUS WHEELER, JR. (1838-1909),** associate justice of the U.S. Supreme Court (1895-1909). An Albany, New York, native and judicial conservative, Peckham spoke for the Court in *Lochner* v. *New York* (1905), which struck down a law that had set a 10-hour-maximum workday for bakers.

See Also: Lochner v. New York; Supreme Court.

■ **PEI, IEOH MING (1917-),** prominent modern architect. Born in Canton, China, I. M. Pei came to the United States to study architecture in 1935. Pei's early work was typified by large-scale urban complexes of the urban-renewal era, such as Mile High Center in Denver, Colorado (1955). He later won commissions for monumental buildings such as his East Building of the National Gallery in Washington, D.C. (1978), and the John F. Kennedy Library in Boston, Massachusetts (1979). The designs for these are based on geometric forms.

■ **PEIRCE, CHARLES S. (1839-1914),** mathematician, logician, and philosopher. Peirce was born in Cambridge, Massachusetts, and attended Harvard University. Between 1861 and 1891 he served on the staff of the U.S. Coast Survey. While with the survey, Peirce studied again at Harvard under Louis Agassiz and lectured on philosophy there. In the 1870s he was a member of the Cambridge Metaphysical Club and associated with other noted thinkers of his day, notably William James and Chauncy Wright. Between 1879 and 1884 Peirce taught logic at Johns Hopkins University. He was a prolific author of reports and papers on logic, probability, and the scientific method. Peirce was one of the founders of the philosophy of pragmatism; in an 1878 essay in *Popular Science Monthly*, entitled "How to Make Our Ideas Clear," he outlined several of the concepts later taken up and named by James. Peirce called his own work pragmaticism and included notions of absolutes

and universal experiences later rejected by James and other philosophers.

See Also: Agassiz, Louis; James, William.

■ **PENDLETON ACT (1883),** congressional reform that sought to regulate civil service positions through open examinations. Introduced after the assassination of Pres. James A. Garfield in 1881, the act, which initially covered only 10 percent of government jobs, was later expanded by Pres. Theodore Roosevelt.

■ **PENINSULAR CAMPAIGN (March-July 1862),** Civil War campaign in Virginia. Gen. George B. McClellan landed his large Union army on the peninsula between the York and George rivers, intending to march on the Confederate capital, Richmond. McClellan exaggerated his force's weaknesses and his opponent's strengths; the Confederate army, under Gen. Joseph E. Johnston, was forced to fall back to within six miles of Richmond, where it turned to fight at the Battle of Seven Pines (May 31-June 1, 1862).

See Also: Civil War; Johnston, Joseph E.; McClellan, George Brinton; Seven Pines (Fair Oaks), Battle of.

■ **PENN, JOHN (1740-88),** lawyer and Revolutionary War statesman. A native of Caroline County, Virginia, Penn moved in 1744 to North Carolina, where he entered politics. He served in the Second Continental Congress and signed the Declaration of Independence.

See Also: Declaration of Independence.

■ **PENN, WILLIAM (1644-1718),** Quaker leader and founder of Pennsylvania. Son of a successful admiral, Penn was born in London. In his early 20s, while overseeing his father's estates in Ireland, he was converted to the pacifist religion of the Society of Friends (Quakers). Penn soon became a prominent Quaker activist, for which he was jailed several times. On one occasion he insisted on a right against self-incrimination, which became precedent for the Fifth Amendment of the U.S. Constitution.

Penn was a lifelong courtier. Friendly with aristocrats in exile before the 1660 Restoration of Charles II, he cultivated these friendships after the Restoration in order to get tolerance for Quak-

This engraving of Benjamin West's *Penn's Treaty with the Indians* depicts the negotiations between the Quakers and the Delaware Indians in 1682. William Penn stands at the center of the painting.

ers and to support the court party of James II. In 1681, Charles II acknowledged a debt to Penn's admiral father, who had died in 1670, by granting Penn the charter to Pennsylvania (named in honor of Admiral Penn), an American feudal estate larger than Ireland. Penn organized large-scale sale of lands there to settlers from England and Germany. Besides the "soil," he had been granted ownership of the government, limited only by a representative assembly of freemen. He gave his own charter of government to the settlers, most notable for its guarantee of full freedom of religion extending even to Roman Catholics and tribalist Indians. Penn's energy and policies created the fastest-growing colony in British North America and, in Philadelphia, the largest, most prosperous city.

Penn is noted for his fair treatment of the Delaware and Conestoga Indians, with whom he negotiated and never fought and whose lands he purchased by treaty. He was careless of accounts, however, and his lavish spending landed him in debtors' prison in England in 1701, from which he was freed after several months by Quakers who took a mortgage on his estate and who named James Logan (secretary of Pennsylvania's provincial council) as their agent.

A debilitating stroke in 1712 made it impossible for Penn to return to America. His second wife, Hannah, managed his provincial affairs until her death in 1717. Penn's oldest son, William, by his first marriage, made a legal bid for the rights to Pennsylvania, but ultimately the entire proprietorship was awarded to John, Thomas, and Richard, Penn's sons by Hannah. Thomas Penn became the estate's dominant lord.

—FRANCIS JENNINGS

See Also: *Pennsylvania.*

BIBLIOGRAPHY: Dunn, Mary Maples, *William Penn: Politics and Conscience* (Princeton Univ. Press 1967); Dunn, Richard S., and Mary Maples Dunn, eds., *The World of William Penn* (Univ. of Pennsylvania Press 1986); Illick, Joseph E., *William Penn the Politician* (Cornell Univ. Press 1965); Jennings, Francis, *The Ambiguous Iroquois Empire* (Norton 1984); Nash, Gary B., *Quakers and Politics: Pennsylvania, 1681-1726* (Princeton Univ. Press 1968).

■ **PENNSYLVANIA,** a Middle Atlantic state. It is bounded on the north by Lake Erie, on the north and east by New York, on the east and south by New Jersey, on the south by Delaware and Maryland, on the south and west by West Virginia, and on the west by Ohio. The Delaware River forms its eastern border. Ridges and valleys of the Appalachian Mountains run through the western half of Pennsylvania. More than half the people live in the Philadelphia or Pittsburgh metropolitan areas. The state has long been a leader in industrial output, but coal and steel are not as important to its economy as in the past.

Founded by Quaker William Penn in 1682 as a refuge for the persecuted, Pennsylvania quickly prospered. Philadelphia grew to be the largest city in the 13 colonies, and the Declaration of Independence was proclaimed here. The biggest battle of the Civil War was fought at Gettysburg. A "Rust Belt" state, Pennsylvania has reduced its dependence on declining heavy industries.

Capital: Harrisburg. Area: 45,759 square miles. Population (1995 est.): 12,072,000.

See Also: Buchanan, James; Charter of Privileges; Declaration of Independence; Frame of Government; Gettysburg, Battle of; Homestead Strike; Johnstown Flood; Penn, William; Philadelphia; Pittsburgh; Valley Forge, Pennsylvania; Whiskey Rebellion.

■ **PENNSYLVANIA DUTCH,** German immigrants who settled in Pennsylvania in colonial times. As the largest population of German immigrants in the United States, these settlers resisted assimilation, retained much of their culture, and developed their own German dialect, known as Pennsylvania Dutch.

See Also: Ethnic Groups.

■ **PENTAGON PAPERS CASE (1971),** U.S. Supreme Court case that was the culmination of a legal battle over the right of newspapers to publish classified government documents. On June 13, 1970, the *New York Times* published the first of a series of articles based on the so-called Pentagon Papers, a classified government study of U.S. policy during the Vietnam War. The study had been leaked to the *New York Times* by Daniel Ellsberg, a one-time Pentagon analyst turned antiwar activist. On June 15 the government obtained a restraining order barring further publication. The *New York Times* appealed. The Supreme Court heard arguments in *New York Times* v. *United States* on June 26 and voted (6-3) on June 27 to deny the government's request for a permanent restraining order.

The Court was divided over the issue of prior restraint. Three justices argued it was never permissible to halt publication in advance; three others agreed in this instance that prior restraint was wrong but reserved to the courts the right to stop publication in some circumstances. The three dissenters objected in large part to the haste with which the case was rushed through the courts. Ellsberg himself was ultimately tried for leaking the documents, but his case ended in a mistrial. The Pentagon Papers themselves and the government's attempt to suppress them heightened public mistrust of government and emboldened the media in its bid to serve as a public watchdog.

See Also: Supreme Court.

BIBLIOGRAPHY: Ungar, Sanford J., *The Papers and the Papers: An Account of the Legal and Political Battle over the Pentagon Papers* (Columbia Univ. Press 1989).

■ **PENTECOSTALISM,** name given to various Christian congregations whose members seek to be filled with the Holy Spirit. Roots of Pentecostalism are in the Holiness movement of the late 19th and early 20th centuries, a protest against the formalism, modernism, and middle-class character of the large denominations. Emphasis is placed on the emotional, nonrational, mystical, and supernatural: miracles, wonders, and "gifts of the Spirit." Classical Pentecostals believe that the conversion to Christ should be followed by a Spirit baptism, which is often evidenced by speaking in tongues.

See Also: Religion.

■ **PEQUOT WAR (1637),** brutal conflict in which the Pequot nation was decimated by English colonials. In 1637 the Puritan colonies of Massachusetts Bay and Connecticut competed for "rights of conquest" over the territory of the Pequot inhabiting the Atlantic Coast along the Pequot (now Thames) River. Both colonies organized for war. Massachusetts accused the Pequot of treaty violations and demanded their surrender as tributaries to the colony.

Pequot rejection of these demands made an offensive war legally "just," but political disputes delayed action by Massachusetts. Unchartered Connecticut seized the opportunity to launch its own troops under Capt. John Mason. Other soldiers intruded under Capt. John Underhill, whose patrons were a group of vaguely chartered lords in England.

Narragansett allies informed the combined troops of two stockaded villages of Pequot, one held by warriors, the other set aside as a refuge for children, women, and old men. Captains Mason and Underhill marched against the noncombatants' refuge and massacred its inhabitants, disregarding protests from the Narragansett. Massachusetts's men arrived late on the scene and were rebuffed.

Pequot warriors in the other stockade heard the gunshots and rushed to the scene. Demoralized by the slaughter, they fought briefly, then scattered and were defeated in a series of follow-up campaigns. Surviving Pequot were assigned as captives, mostly to Connecticut's Mohegan allies under Chief Uncas, and some to Massachusetts's Narragansett allies under Chief Miantonomo.

The Puritan colonies squabbled over which had gained rights of conquest, but Connecticut seized control, and Pequot lands eventually were included in Connecticut's charter. For years, histories consisted of false hate propaganda against the Pequot and equally false excuses for their attackers.

A band of Mashantucket Pequot still survives on a reservation near Ledyard, Connecticut, where it now enjoys hefty revenues from its highly popular casino. The financial success of this enterprise has enabled the Pequot to enlarge its reservation through several significant land purchases.

—FRANCIS JENNINGS

See Also: Indians of North America.

BIBLIOGRAPHY: Jennings, Francis, *The Invasion of America: Indians, Colonialism and the Cant of Conquest* (Univ. of North Carolina Press 1975); Salisbury, Neal E., *Manitou and Providence: Indians,* Europeans, and the Making of New England, 1500-1643 (Oxford Univ. Press 1982).

■ **PERKINS, FRANCES (1882-1965),** social reformer and secretary of labor. She was born in Boston, Massachusetts. She worked in settlement houses and was active in the movement to reform labor laws in New York State. In 1929 Gov. Franklin D. Roosevelt appointed her industrial commissioner of New York State to enforce laws concerning factory safety, working conditions, and maximum hours. As labor secretary (1933-45) and the first woman ever to hold a cabinet position in the U.S. government, she helped with the passage of the Social Security Act (1935) and other New Deal legislation.

See Also: Labor Movement; New Deal; Roosevelt, Franklin Delano; Social Security Act; Women's Movement.

■ **PERRY, MATTHEW CALBRAITH (1794-1858),** U.S. naval officer and brother of Oliver Hazard Perry. He was born in South Kingstown, Rhode Island. In 1847 Perry helped capture the Mexican city of Veracruz during the Mexican War. Commodore Perry's best-known accomplishment resulted from his assignment to force contact with Japan (implicitly without starting a war). In 1853, Perry steamed into Tokyo Bay with four ships. Refusing to detour to the southern port of Nagasaki, the only one then open to foreigners, Perry presented several petitions to the emperor asking for the right to buy coal, protection for shipwrecked U.S. sailors, and the opening of a new port to U.S. trade. He then left for the China coast and returned the following year with even greater ceremony and force. The Tokugawa shogunate responded favorably to this impressive show, concluding a treaty that opened the cities of Shimoda and Hakodate to American ships and merchants. Congress paid Perry a handsome $20,000 stipend and published his account of the affair.

BIBLIOGRAPHY: Perry, Matthew C., *The Japan Expedition,* ed. by Roger Pineau (Smithsonian Institution Press 1968).

■ **PERRY, OLIVER HAZARD (1785-1819),** U.S. naval officer and brother of Matthew C. Perry. Born in South Kingstown, Rhode Island, he was commissioned by the navy in 1813 during the

Oliver Hazard Perry defeated the British in the Battle of Lake Erie on Sept. 10, 1813, sending the victory message, "We have met the enemy and they are ours."

War of 1812 to build a fleet on Lake Erie. Racing against time, Perry completed his vessels and engaged a British flotilla under Robert Barclay. After transferring from his burning flagship, *Lawrence*, to *Niagara*, Perry defeated his opponent and sent the famous message to his superior: "We have met the enemy and they are ours."

See Also: *Lake Erie, Battle of; War of 1812.*

■ **PERRYVILLE, BATTLE OF (1862),** climactic battle of the Confederate invasion of Kentucky. On October 8 two divisions of the Confederate force of Gen. Braxton Bragg attacked the left of the Union army of Gen. Don Carlos Buell, driving his raw troops back over a mile. These gains were neutralized by Union advances in the center. This confused engagement ended when Bragg recognized he was outnumbered, gathered his scattered forces, and led a retreat out of Kentucky through the Cumberland Gap.

See Also: *Civil War.*

■ **PERSHING, JOHN JOSEPH (1860-1948),** U.S. Army officer, nicknamed "Black Jack." Born in Laclede, Missouri, he became the most famous soldier of his day, earning a rank worn by no other American general since George Washington. A West Point graduate, he began his military career in 1886, served on the western frontier (1886-98), taught tactics at West Point (1897-98), and participated in the Spanish-American War (1898). During the Philippine insurrection, which began in 1899, he subdued the Moros on Mindanao, an action he would repeat in 1913. His friendship with Pres. Theodore Roosevelt won him a promotion from captain to brigadier general in 1906, an advancement that placed him ahead of 862 officers senior to him in rank. In 1916-17, Pershing commanded the ill-fated Mexican Border Campaign against Pancho Villa.

Pershing is best remembered for his command of the American Expeditionary Force (AEF) in World War I. He was given the difficult task of assembling, training, and committing to battle an anticipated one million American soldiers. In the process, he antagonized the French and British armies by declaring that trench warfare had sapped the fighting spirit of their troops. He claimed instead that only American enthusiasm, morale, and maneuver warfare could break the deadlock of the Western Front. He also insisted, over the heated objections of the Allies, that he command an independent American army.

Pershing's high hopes for the AEF were undone by the 1918 German spring offensives, which curtailed training and forced him to send raw soldiers to the front. The Allied offensive that followed gave him no reprieve. The AEF did well at St. Mihiel in northeastern France in September, but it failed to live up to Pershing's expectations in the Meuse-Argonne campaign that followed. American casualties mounted quickly in clumsy frontal assaults against German machine guns. By November, Pershing's army was fighting much better, but further improvement was halted by the November 11 armistice. Despite the AEF's mixed record, Pershing was lauded as a hero on his stateside return and in 1919 was promoted to "General of the Armies of the United States," a title previously conferred only on Washington. Pershing served as army chief of staff until 1924.

—T. R. Brereton

As a brigadier general John J. Pershing led U.S. troops in the Mexican Border Campaign (1916-17) before successfully commanding the 2-million-strong American Expeditionary Force (AEF) in France in World War I.

See Also: *American Expeditionary Force; Mexican Border Campaign; World War I.*

BIBLIOGRAPHY: Smythe, Donald, *Pershing: General of the Armies* (Indiana Univ. Press 1986); Vandiver, Frank E., *Black Jack: The Life and Times of John J. Pershing* (Texas A&M Univ. Press 1977).

■ **PERSIAN GULF WAR,** conflict between an international coalition of forces led by the United States and the Iraqi army of Saddam Hussein. Aggravated by disagreements over their boundaries and oil policies, Iraq invaded neighboring Kuwait on Aug. 2, 1990. By invading Kuwait, Iraq also threatened Saudi Arabia, which possesses the world's largest oil reserves—oil that was vital for the well-being of the American, European, and Japanese economies.

Shortly after the invasion, Pres. George Bush announced that the United States would not tolerate either Iraq's aggression or its threat to Saudi Arabia. Bush persuaded the Saudi king to allow U.S. forces to deploy to the Arabian peninsula and defend Saudi Arabia from Saddam, who commanded the world's fourth-largest army. Bush then asked the United Nations to condemn Iraq's aggression. The UN General Assembly passed resolutions demanding that Iraq withdraw from Kuwait.

To enforce the UN resolutions, Bush obtained pledges of military support from Great Britain, France, Canada, and Australia as well as financial support from Japan. Appearing unimpressed, Saddam stationed more than 4,000 tanks, 3,000 artillery pieces, and 350,000 soldiers in Kuwait, where they looted the emirate and brutally crushed any opposition. Saddam also possessed biological and chemical weapons and, many feared in the West, would have no hesitation using them.

In response to Iraq's actions, 34 nations formed an international coalition to oppose Saddam. The United States contributed the most forces to the coalition, eventually deploying 530,000 military personnel to Saudi Arabia and the Persian Gulf, including thousands of reservists, along with 120 ships (including 4 aircraft carriers), hundreds of airplanes, and hundreds of tanks. Other coalition members, including Islamic nations such as Saudi Arabia, Egypt, and Syria, contributed 200,000 military personnel,

After Iraq's invasion of Kuwait in August 1990, the United States initiated Operation Desert Shield, sending troops to Saudi Arabia, along whose borders Iraqi forces had gathered, and to other bases in the Middle East.

along with tanks, ships, and airplanes. The American general, H. Norman Schwarzkopf, commanded the coalition's forces. Among its first actions, the coalition imposed a naval blockade and prepared for the greater use of force.

Meanwhile, some skeptical American politicians, professors, ministers, and journalists criticized Bush's military policy against Iraq. After sending forces overseas, Bush laid the issues before Congress. On Jan. 12, 1991, the House of Representatives voted 250 to 183 and the Senate voted 52 to 47 in favor of a resolution calling for U.S. force to expel Iraq from Kuwait. Even before Congress voted, Saddam tried to fuel antiwar sentiment and undermine the coalition. Sending mixed messages, he promised to withdraw from Kuwait but at the same time gestured belligerently toward Israel, threatened hostages held in Iraq, and built massive fortifications in Kuwait. By mid-January Iraq had not fulfilled the UN resolutions.

On the morning of Jan. 17, 1991, the coalition initiated Operation Desert Storm to expel Iraq from Kuwait. The opening military move was a 38-day air campaign that involved cruise missiles and about 2,500 airplanes, of which America provided almost 2,000. Round-the-clock air bombardment crippled Iraq's antiaircraft defenses, decimated its air force, damaged its transportation network, knocked out much of its electric power, and inflicted serious casualties among Iraqi units in Kuwait. Trying to bring Israel into the war (thereby undermining Arab support within the coalition), Iraq launched Scud missiles

into the Jewish nation, but the Israelis, under pressure from the United States, did not retaliate. Still, Iraq would not withdraw from Kuwait.

On February 24 the coalition launched the next phase of the military operation, a ground attack into Iraq and Kuwait. In 100 hours, the coalition divisions pushed Saddam's army out of Kuwait and also struck deep inside Iraq. In a masterful strategic stroke, some coalition units outflanked Saddam's forces in Iraq and advanced as far as the Euphrates River. Other coalition divisions battled Iraqis in the desert and inside Kuwait. Coalition aircraft destroyed hundreds of Iraqi tanks and artillery pieces. Iraqi casualties were staggering. Estimates vary, but Iraq probably lost more than 10,000 soldiers killed and 30,000 wounded, and 80,000 were taken prisoner. Thousands of Iraq's armored vehicles were destroyed. American casualties totaled around 500, of whom 294 were killed in action or died from accidents. Losses among other coalition forces totaled 400 killed and wounded. On February 27 the fighting came to an end when President Bush ordered a cease-fire.

The Persian Gulf War produced mixed results. Although the coalition expelled Iraq's army from Kuwait, the emirate was devastated, and Saddam Hussein still controlled Iraq. UN resolutions required Iraq to reveal all of its chemical, biological, and nuclear facilities, but UN officials suspected that Saddam hid some stockpiles. The United Nations had forged a workable coalition that held together despite ethnic, religious, and political differences. The war displayed the tremendous military power of the United States and its willingness to project that power. President Bush demonstrated notable capabilities as commander in chief and enjoyed high public opinion ratings. But his popularity plummeted when the American economy turned sour, and he lost the presidential election of 1992.

—JOSEPH G. DAWSON III

See Also: Bush, George H. W. ; Schwarzkopf, H. Norman.

BIBLIOGRAPHY: Gordon, Michael R., and Bernard E. Trainor, *The Generals' War: The Inside Story of the Gulf Conflict* (Little, Brown 1995); Hallion, Richard P., *Storm over Iraq: Air Power and the Gulf War* (Smithsonian Press 1992).

■ **PERSONAL LIBERTY LAWS,** laws passed by most Northern states to inhibit the enforcement of the 1793 and 1850 federal slave laws. The personal liberty laws were based on the premise that all individuals are inherently free.

■ **PETERSBURG, BATTLE OF (1864),** Civil War battle and siege. After the disaster at Cold Harbor (June 1-3, 1864), Gen. Ulysses S. Grant swung his Union force across the James River to threaten the important railroad junction of Petersburg, Virginia. In mid-June the Union army missed opportunities to take the city, then lightly defended. On June 30 Union engineers opened a large gap in the Confederate defenses with a mine, but, in the ensuing Battle of the Crater, Union forces failed to break through. The two armies then settled into a siege that lasted until Petersburg fell on Apr. 3, 1865, a week before war's end.

See Also: Civil War; Cold Harbor, Battle of; Crater, Battle of the; Grant, Ulysses Simpson.

Union troops rest in the trenches during the siege of Petersburg, Virginia. Gen. Ulysses S. Grant lost approximately 8,000 men during the 1864 siege but was unable to take the city until the next year, when Lee's resistance was finally broken.

On Aug. 27, 1859, near Titusville, Pennsylvania, drilling operations struck oil at a depth of 69 feet. Learning of the discovery, John D. Rockefeller entered the emerging petroleum industry and became the nation's leading oilman.

■ **PETROLEUM,** natural resource that has helped transform American technology, business practices, and the environment. The petroleum industry had its origins in the discovery of oil in 1859 near Titusville, Pennsylvania. Among the most successful to take advantage of the discovery was John D. Rockefeller, founder of the Standard Oil Company. Railroads assisted the rapid growth of Standard and other oil companies, as petroleum products were transported to the East Coast and abroad by 1866.

In 1901, one of the largest and most significant oil strikes occurred in U.S. history near Beaumont, Texas. This gusher, called Spindletop, flooded the market with oil. Ten years later, a 1911 Supreme Court antitrust decision effectively ended a possible Standard monopoly.

Demand kept pace with supply in the first decades of the 20th century, as the automobile industry required larger volumes of petroleum and more refined gasoline. It was World War II, however, that revolutionized the oil industry. Research and development led to a broader array of petroleum products, while the domestic economy and foreign policy became increasingly influenced by the supply of oil. During the postwar years oil lay at the center of many major crises—the 1956 Suez crisis, the oil shortage of the early 1970s related to Middle East politics and the Organization of Petroleum Exporting Countries (OPEC), and the Persian Gulf War of 1991. As domestic reserves diminished and demand increased, the United States became increasingly dependent on Middle Eastern oil. By the 1990s the United States consumed nearly two-thirds of the world's oil supply but had done relatively little to develop alternative energy sources.

See Also: Rockefeller, John Davison.

BIBLIOGRAPHY: Painter, David S., *Oil and the American Century* (Johns Hopkins Univ. Press 1986).

■ **PHILADELPHIA,** historic city in Pennsylvania, located at the confluence of the Schuylkill and Delaware rivers. In 1682 William Penn and a group of Quakers founded Philadelphia, meaning "city of brotherly love" in Greek, as a "holy experiment" in religious tolerance and as a business investment. Throughout the 18th century English, Welsh, German, and Swiss immigrants moved to the port city. By the late 1700s Philadelphia was the most populous city in America. It was the site of important events of the American Revolution and the founding of the new nation. The Continental Congress was held there (beginning in 1774) and the Declaration of Independence (1776) and the Constitution (1787) were written in the city. Philadelphia served as the nation's first capital from 1777 to 1788 and then from 1790 to 1800 under the new Constitution. During the 19th century, Philadelphia remained the financial center of America until it was eclipsed by New York City. In 1876 the city staged the Centennial Exposition to honor the United States' first hundred years as a nation. After World War II Philadelphia undertook a massive downtown urban renewal and highway building program. Population (1994): 1,524,249.

See Also: City in American History.

■ **PHILANTHROPY,** charitable giving and works of beneficence. From the founding of the British colonies in the early 17th century, philanthropy has always been a prominent aspect of American social action. Encouraged by the religious and social ethic of Protestantism, many wealthy colonists donated funds to support the establishment of colleges, hospitals, and institutions to aid the poor.

The traditional conception of philanthropy as charity and love of humanity, however, changed in the late 19th century. Women progressive reformers used philanthropy to socially reform immigrants and the poor and to teach others the merits of giving. At the same time, increasingly wealthy American businessmen, such as Andrew Carnegie, donated large sums of money to a variety of charitable causes. Some Americans, namely religious leaders and women reformers, however, viewed this "gospel of wealth" with suspicion.

During the early 20th century two significant developments in philanthropy altered the character of charitable giving in America. The first was the rise of philanthropic foundations, which managed and donated large sums on a consistent basis to certain institutions. The other was the growth of federated funds, such as the Red Cross, which raised money from numerous donors to support local and national institutions. Nevertheless, the private giving remained the most significant source of philanthropic benevolence and was even given a boost when income tax laws encouraged such giving. Beginning in the 1960s, in keeping with the changing nature of philanthropy, much private and institutional philanthropy advocated social action by minority groups.

BIBLIOGRAPHY: Bremner, Robert H., *American Philanthropy,* 2nd ed. (Univ. of Chicago Press 1988).

■ **PHILIPPINES,** republic in the southwest Pacific, consisting of some 7,100 islands 500 miles off the southeast coast of Asia. The largest islands are Luzon, with the capital of Manila, and Mindanao to the south. The native Filipinos arrived on the islands from the Asian mainland. In 1521 the Portuguese navigator Ferdinand Magellan visited the islands and was killed there in a dispute between two groups of natives. The first permanent European settlement was established at Cebu in 1565 by the Spanish. During the 18th century Manila became a center for trade in precious metals and Chinese silks. During the 19th century the growing of coffee, hemp, and sugar became important to the economy. After the Spanish-American War the Philippines were ceded to the United States in 1898. In 1916 the U.S. Congress passed the Jones Act, which granted the Philippines independence contingent on the establishment of a stable government. As preparation for full independence a Philippine commonwealth was formed in 1935. However, in 1942, at the outset of American participation in World War II, the Japanese invaded and occupied the Philippines. After the war the Philippines finally achieved independence on July 4, 1946. Philippine politics have gone through periods of instability since independence. In 1965 Ferdinand

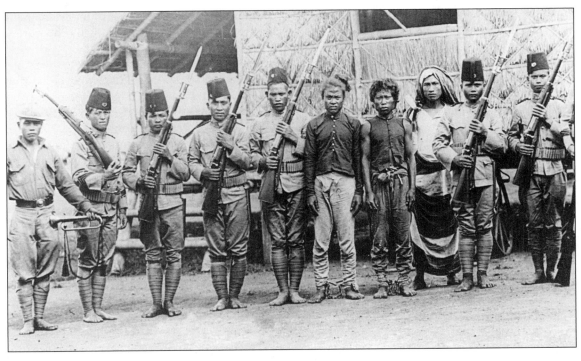

After the Spanish-American War, the United States annexed the Philippines, sparking a rebellion, especially among the Moro people. Two captured Moro rebels were photographed in chains.

Marcos was elected president and in 1972 he declared martial law. After much protest and violence, Corazon Aquino, the widow of a murdered opposition leader, was elected to the presidency in 1986, and Marcos was forced into exile.

See Also: Spanish-American War.

■ **PHILIPPINE WAR (1899-1902),** conflict following the U.S. acquisition of the Philippines after the Spanish-American War (1898). Led by Emilio Aguinaldo, Filipino nationalists rejected U.S. sovereignty and proclaimed the Philippine Republic. Fighting broke out on Feb. 4, 1899, and an American army under Gen. Elwell S. Otis drove back Aguinaldo's army but lacked sufficient manpower to hold more than a limited perimeter around Manila. In November, Otis's troops dispersed Aguinaldo's army, and by early 1900, U.S. troops occupied towns throughout the archipelago. Otis and his successor, Gen. Arthur MacArthur, executed Pres. William McKinley's policy of "benevolent assimilation." Garrison officers established governments in the occupied towns and implemented social reform projects to conciliate the Filipinos to U.S. rule.

Aguinaldo's supporters struck back, establishing clandestine governments in the towns and relying on a mixture of patriotic appeals and intimidation to secure recruits, supplies, intelligence, and shelter from the population. Officered by local elites and composed largely of part-time irregulars, they employed hit-and-run guerrilla tactics. Their goal was less military victory than to inflict casualties, create war weariness in the United States, and prevent collaboration. The war became a variety of regional struggles, forcing U.S. soldiers to devise counterinsurgency techniques to overcome the local opposition in their areas. They were assisted by U.S. Navy gunboats and by Filipino collaborators who opposed the guerrillas for a variety of motives.

In December 1900, MacArthur implemented policies designed to break up the clandestine organizations in the occupied towns and to punish guerrillas and their supporters. He mobilized military forces against the remaining centers of resistance and made more efficient use of Filipino auxiliaries. Together with increased military operations, the rapid transition from military to civil rule in the pacified provinces, and the rewards heaped on collaborators made resistance increasingly futile. By late 1901, the American army had forced the surrender of the top guerrilla leaders, including Aguinaldo, and pacified most of the archipelago, but continued fighting in a few provinces delayed the declaration of peace until July 4, 1902.

—BRIAN McALLISTER LINN

BIBLIOGRAPHY: Gates, John M., *Schoolbooks and Krags: The United States Army in the Philippines, 1898-1902* (Greenwood Press 1973); Linn, Brian M., *The U.S. Army and Counterinsurgency in the Philippine War, 1899-1902* (Univ. of North Carolina Press 1989); Welch, Richard E., *Response to Imperialism: The United States and the Philippine-American War, 1899-1902* (Univ. of North Carolina Press 1979).

■ **PHILLIPS, WENDELL (1811-84),** lecturer and abolitionist. Born in Boston, Massachusetts, Phillips graduated from Harvard Law School but abandoned the study of law to join the abolitionist work of William Lloyd Garrison and Elijah Lovejoy. In the antebellum period Phillips lectured throughout the North as a member of the American Anti-Slavery Society and denounced the Fugitive Slave Act of 1850. He opposed the Republican party in 1860 because he thought it too moderate on the slavery question. During the Civil War and immediately after, Phillips was an advocate of African-American civil and political rights and Radical Reconstruction. He also supported John C. Frémont for the Republican presidential nomination in 1864 because he thought Lincoln's amnesty and reconstruction plan too lenient.

See Also: Slavery.

■ **PHONOGRAPH,** device to record and reproduce sound from tracings on flat disks or cylinders. The progenitor of the phonograph was designed in 1857 in Paris by Leon Scott. Charles Cros, utilizing Scott's innovations, designed a phonograph in France in April 1877. Following closely, Thomas Edison applied for a British patent in July 1877 and a U.S. patent in December for his version. These early phonographs were primitive machines that played unintelligible sounds on fragile tinfoil records.

Breakthroughs in research and development occurred at Alexander Graham Bell's laboratory in Washington, D.C., during the 1880s and 1890s. By the beginning of the 20th century, sounds could be reproduced on wax-coated zinc disks, and companies such as the Victor Talking Machine Company competed for louder and better-quality sound. Despite the rapid growth in urban markets, the phonograph experienced increasing competition from radio during the 1920s. With the development of more durable records during World War II, phonograph companies produced longer-playing records at lower prices. The record industry helped solidify its place in American consumer markets with the introduction of the stereo in 1958 and the development of quadraphonic sound in the 1970s.

See Also: Edison, Thomas Alva; Invention.

BIBLIOGRAPHY: Millard, A. J., *America on Record: A History of Recorded Sound* (Cambridge Univ. Press 1995).

■ **PHOTOGRAPHY,** introduced in the United States in 1839 with the daguerreotype, the forerunner of modern photography. The artist-inventor Samuel F. B. Morse was himself an enthusiastic daguerreotypist, and he taught the process to the young Mathew Brady, who went on to become America's leading photographer, daguerreotyping many notables, including Abraham Lincoln.

During the Civil War, Brady outfitted 20 teams of photographers with elaborate photographic equipment for recording all the key military engagements. This epic undertaking, producing some 3,500 documentary images, led to his bankruptcy. One member of the team, Alexander Gardner, later published a two-volume *Photographic Sketchbook of the War* (1866) that is eerie in its grisly but calm account of human mortality. Another Brady photographer, Timothy O'Sullivan, operated his camera in the midst of raging bombardments on the South Carolina front, and his record of the Battle of Gettysburg reveals, in Gardner's words, "the blank horror and reality of war, in opposition to its pageantry."

After the war O'Sullivan worked as an expeditionary photographer, accompanying a three-year-long geological survey of the Nevada Territory. His landscape photographs from this and other remote locations are stunning in their otherworldliness.

The photographs that his colleague William Henry Jackson brought back from the Yellowstone region in 1872 were shown to both houses of Congress and were instrumental in having that area declared the nation's first national park.

Another photographer of the West, Eadweard Muybridge, is best known for his experiments in multiple exposure "stop-action" photography, which he began in 1872 in order to determine if a galloping horse ever lifts all four feet off the ground (it does not). His subsequent work in stop-action photography influenced contemporary artists including Thomas Eakins, the Philadelphia realist who was himself a photographer, employing the medium to assist him in his efforts at painting modern life with the utmost accuracy.

Early 20th Century. At the turn of the century a new generation of photographers became self-consciously artistic in their endeavors, showing more interest in the aesthetic potential of the photograph than its documentary capabilities. The foremost figure here was Alfred Stieglitz, who not only set an extraordinarily high standard with his dynamically composed photographs of urban street life but also edited influential journals of photography, championed the work of other innovative photographers, and established a prestigious avant-garde gallery that treated photographs, along with modern sculpture and painting, as works of art. Stieglitz's colleague Edward Steichen, equally committed to photography as a medium of personal expression, made a series of dark, moody, and soft-focused photographs that resembled the watery nocturnes of the painter James Whistler.

Other turn-of-the-century photographers preferred to emphasize photography's documentary capabilities. The Danish-born journalist and social reformer Jacob Riis investigated New York's slums with his camera in order to show middle-class viewers, as in the title of his book of photographs, *How the Other Half Lives*. With a similar dedication to social reform, as well as a university degree in sociology, Lewis Hine provided hard-edged photographic studies of newly arrived immigrants at Ellis Island, child laborers in sweat shops, coal miners in Pittsburgh, and construction workers balancing themselves precariously on the steel girders of Manhattan skyscrapers. Hine's student Paul Strand began his career by making powerful documentary images of modern urban life, with an emphasis on the loneliness and alienation.

Taken under wing by the avant-garde Stieglitz group and influenced by theories of cubism, Strand set aside his documentary concerns and refashioned himself as a brilliant photographer of geometric forms in nature, machinery, and the built environment. Others who led photography in this direction were Strand's friend Charles Sheeler, a semiabstract painter who photographed barns, staircases, and automobile factories for their intricate geometric patterns; Edward Weston, who emphasized the pure formal beauty of sand dunes, still lifes, and human nudes; and Ansel Adams, whose breathtaking views of Western skies, mountains, and forests were photographed with extreme depth-of-focus and printed in a "straight" (unmanipulated) manner.

Documentary photography was reinvigorated in the 1930s when the pressures of the Great Depression compelled Americans to examine the harsh realities affecting millions of their fellow citizens. The federal government's Farm Security Administration (FSA) hired leading photojournalists to fan out into the countryside and show the public the dire living conditions of migrant workers and poor farmers. Walker Evans lived with rural families in order to depict their plight with honesty and rigor. Dorothea Lange similarly balanced her sympathy for her subjects with cool-eyed objectivity, and probably no single image of the Great Depression is more deeply engraved in public memory than her photograph of a gaunt and anxious migrant mother huddling with her children in a camp tent.

Late 20th Century. American photography flourished in the postwar era, with photographers supported in their endeavors as never before by foundation grants, university fellowships, book-publishing contracts, glossy magazine assignments, and a healthy national economy. Both of the major and often divergent directions of American photography—social documentation and artistic self-expression—were vigorously pursued. Traveling across the United States in the mid-1950s, Robert Frank bore witness to a Cold War America painfully divided along lines of class, race, and gender. Other insightful recorders of the daily scene included Diane Arbus, Bruce Davidson, and Lee Friedlander. Nature photographers Wynn Bullock and Minor White continued Edward Weston's pioneering investigations into natural form. Meanwhile, photographers such as Aaron Siskind and Jerry Uelsmann made imaginative use of unusual film stocks, multiple exposures, and darkroom manipulations in order to explore the formal properties of the medium itself.

Fashion and portrait photography, previously disdained for its commercial bent, has recently acquired critical cache. Richard Avedon and Irving Penn, both of whom began working for fashion magazines in the late 1940s, are known for the pungency and inventiveness of their photographs—Avedon for his harshly lit closeups of famous people and Penn for his whimsical, almost surreal fashion set-ups. Robert Mapplethorpe, a controversial but undeniably talented photographer, produced superbly printed images of artists, celebrities, and male homosexuals in poses that ranged from gravely serious to witty to pornographic. Cindy Sherman is a self-portraitist who photographs herself in elaborate disguises that allow her the opportunity to play out a multitude of female—and sometimes male—personae borrowed from art history, advertising, and the movies.

American photography appears to be thriving, but precisely because of its unprecedented commercial success in recent years it runs the risk of falling into complacency, thus losing the acute social consciousness and artistic integrity that have characterized it from the start.

—DAVID M. LUBIN

See Also: Adams, Ansel; Brady, Mathew B.; Evans, Walker; Lange, Dorothea; Steichen, Edward; Stieglitz, Alfred.

BIBLIOGRAPHY: Doty, Robert M., ed., *Photography in America* (Whitney Museum of American Art 1974); Green, Jonathan, *American Photography* (Harry N. Abrams 1984); Newhall, Beaumont, *The History of Photography from 1839 to the Present Day* (Museum of Modern Art 1982); Rosenblum, Naomi, *A World History of Photography* (Abbeville Press 1997).

■ **PICKETING,** the practice engaged in by union members during a labor dispute when workers post themselves adjacent to their workplace, carrying signs as a way of making their demands known and encouraging other workers also affected to join in the labor action.

See Also: Labor Movement.

■ **PICKFORD, MARY (1893-1979),** movie actress and producer. She was born in Toronto, Ontario. A talented actress, she won an Academy Award for her performance in *Coquette* (1929). In 1919, with Charlie Chaplin, D. W. Griffith, and her husband, Douglas Fairbanks, she founded United Artists, a film distribution firm.

See Also: Motion Pictures.

■ **PIERCE, FRANKLIN (1804-69),** 14th president of the United States (1853-57). Born in Hillsborough, New Hampshire, Pierce, a Democrat, served in the U.S. House of Representatives (1833-37) and in the Senate (1837-42). He also fought in the Mexican

In the presidential election of 1852, Franklin Pierce, the Democratic party's compromise presidential nominee, defeated Winfield Scott, under whom he had served in the Mexican War.

War (1846-48). In 1852 Pierce was elected president after being nominated by the Democrats as a compromise candidate in the slavery controversy. As president he signed the disastrous Kansas-Nebraska Act (1854), which gave settlers in the territory the right to vote on the slavery issue, and he actively enforced the Fugitive Slave Act. In foreign affairs he negotiated the Gadsden Purchase (1853) with Mexico and the Treaty of Kanagawa (1854), which opened several of Japan's ports to U.S. trade. Unpopular, Pierce was ignored at the 1856 Democratic convention. During the Civil War he publicly opposed Pres. Abraham Lincoln's policies.

See Also: Bleeding Kansas; Civil War; Gadsden Purchase; Presidential Elections; President of the United States.

PIKE, ZEBULON (1779-1813), American soldier and explorer born in Lamberton, New Jersey. After years of military service in the Old North-

Zebulon Pike explored the Louisiana Purchase in expeditions of 1805-06 and 1806-07. During the second trip, near Santa Fe, New Mexico, he and his men were arrested by Spanish soldiers and held prisoner in Mexico for several months.

west, Pike was ordered to make a military reconnaissance of the Upper Mississippi in August 1805. Returning the following spring, Pike and his small party prepared the first serious map of the region extending into Minnesota. By summer 1806 Pike was on the trail again, exploring westward from St. Louis across present-day Kansas and up the Arkansas River into Colorado. He discovered the Colorado peak later named in his honor. Crossing the Sangre de Cristo Range, Pike reached the headwaters of the Rio Grande, mistaking the river for the Red River. Treading deeply into Spanish territory, Pike was arrested by New Mexican authorities and taken to Sante Fe and Chihuahua. He was returned to American authorities in Louisiana in June 1807. Pike's report on Sante Fe spurred American expansion into Texas. Promoted to brigadier general, Pike died during the assault on York (Toronto) during the War of 1812 with Britain.

See Also: Exploration and Discovery.

PILGRIMS, English Separatists who colonized Plymouth. The Pilgrims were Puritans who originated in Scrooby, England. In 1608 the congregation fled to Holland to avoid persecution after refusing to conform to the established Church of England. In 1620, after obtaining a grant from the Virginia Company and financing from London merchants to establish a trading post in America, the *Mayflower* was hired. In September 1620 some 100 men, women, and children sailed from Plymouth. They arrived at the tip of Cape Cod on November 21. There they signed the Mayflower Compact and soon thereafter elected John Carver as governor. In December they discovered Plymouth harbor and anchored the *Mayflower* there. By April, 44 people had perished. Following Carver's death in April 1621, William Bradford was elected governor. Under his leadership and the ministry of William Brewster, the Pilgrims built a town and began a new life. Not until November 1621, with the arrival of the *Fortune* with provisions and more people, did they receive a charter for Plymouth Colony.

See Also: Bradford, William; Mayflower Compact; Plymouth Settlement; Religion.

BIBLIOGRAPHY: Bradford, William, *Of Plymouth Plantation, 1620-1647* (1856; Knopf 1989).

■ **PINCHOT, GIFFORD (1865-1946),** American conservationist. He was born in Simsbury, Connecticut, graduated from Yale University in 1889, and served 12 years (1898-1910) in the U.S. Agriculture Department as chief forester. During the presidency of Theodore Roosevelt (1901-09), Pinchot received great support for his program to protect and preserve the country's natural resources. In 1910 he was fired by Pres. William Howard Taft for insubordination for his part in the Ballinger-Pinchot Controversy. He went on to be governor of Pennsylvania (1923-27, 1931-35) and from 1903 to 1936 was a professor in the School of Forestry he helped establish at Yale.

See Also: *Ballinger-Pinchot Controversy.*

■ **PINCKNEY FAMILY,** South Carolina family prominent in the 18th and 19th centuries. The most famous Pinckneys of the Revolutionary era were second cousins, Charles Pinckney (1757-1824) and Charles Cotesworth Pinckney (1746-1825), and Charles Cotesworth's brother Thomas (1750-1828). The mother of the latter two was Elizabeth (Eliza) Lucas Pinckney (c. 1722-93), who is credited with the development of indigo as a staple crop in colonial South Carolina. Charles Cotesworth served in the South Carolina militia during the American Revolution and was a delegate to the Constitutional Convention in 1787, where he opposed a religious test for political office. He also introduced the clause calling for a ban on the international slave trade in 1808. Thomas, also a Revolutionary-era soldier, served as South Carolina's governor (1787-89) and was an active member of South Carolina's Society of Cincinnati, a group of Revolutionary War veterans.

Cousin Charles also served in the Revolutionary army and, as a member of Congress from South Carolina in 1787, called for a constitutional convention to revise the Articles of Confederation. He authored a series of amendments to the Articles of Confederation, called the "Pinckney draft" of the Constitution. His original plan, however, is no longer extant. He lobbied extensively in South Carolina for passage of the Constitution.

■ **PINCKNEY'S TREATY (1795). *See:*** *San Lorenzo, Treaty of.*

■ **PINCUS, GREGORY GOODWIN (1903-67),** biologist who is sometimes referred to as the "father of the pill." Born in Woodbine, New Jersey, Pincus became influenced by the ideas of Jacques Loeb, a proponent of biological engineering, and devoted his professional life to developing ways to control mammalian physiology. He studied the effects of pH on mammalian sperm with his mentor, William Crozier, at Harvard, taught there from 1930 to 1937, and studied in-vitro fertilization and artificial parthenogenesis in mammals. Denied tenure at Harvard for his controversial work (and for what Pincus considered anti-Semitism), he cofounded the Worcester Foundation for Experimental Biology with Hudson Hoagland and continued his research. He became a pioneer in biotechnology, developing the first oral contraceptive with the financial and moral support of Margaret Sanger's birth control movement and the scientific work of Carl Djerassi, who had synthesized orally active analogs of progesterone. Pincus developed a pill that would induce a reversible state of "pseudopregnancy" in fertile women and thus suppress ovulation. It was marketed in 1960, and Pincus became known as "the father of the pill." As a result of his work, he achieved international fame and was elected to the National Academy of Science in 1965.

See Also: *Science.*

■ **PINKERTON, ALLAN (1819-94),** detective. He was born in Glasgow, Scotland, and immigrated to the United States as a young man. After exposing a counterfeiting ring, he was appointed sheriff of Cook County, Illinois, and, in 1850, became the only detective on the Chicago police force. At the same time, he organized Pinkerton's National Detective Agency, which worked primarily for the railroad industry. While his agency solved several robbery cases, it was the 1861 discovery of an assassination plot against president-elect Abraham Lincoln that earned Pinkerton national fame. After the American Civil War, he expanded his agency, specializing in anti-union protection. Pinkerton agents often resorted to violence in their efforts, most notably during the great railroad strikes of 1877, in their campaign against the Molly Maguires in the coal industry during the 1870s, and in the Homestead steel strike of 1892. Pinkerton authored 18 books on the art of detection.

See Also: Detectives; Homestead Strike; Molly Maguires.
BIBLIOGRAPHY: Horan, James D., *The Pinkertons* (Crown 1968); Morn, Frank, *"The Eye That Never Sleeps": A History of the Pinkerton National Detective Agency* (Indiana Univ. Press 1982).

■ **PIRACY,** robbery at sea. The legends of the buccaneers have made piracy more than mere theft. The Spanish considered the English a nation of pirates, mainly because English voyages of discovery commonly turned to raids on Spanish Caribbean colonies as a means of paying for the costs of the expedition. Piracy was widespread in the 17th-century Caribbean, and raids became even greater in size and frequency. Henry Morgan's raid on Panama in 1671, with nearly 2,000 men, represented the height of buccaneering power.

Piracy was familiar in the Atlantic port towns of the North American colonies; not because the colonists were victims, but because they were participants. The colonies welcomed pirate ships because of their valuable contraband. There was also the business of outfitting pirate ships, which enriched merchants in Boston, Newport, Manhattan, Philadelphia, and Charleston. New York in particular was associated with notorious pirates such as William "Captain" Kidd.

By the 1680s, the buccaneers began expanding out of the Caribbean to Africa, the Indian Ocean, and into and across the Pacific. Their increased activity eventually raised the anger of states and merchants who had grown accustomed to the profits of legal trading (including slave trading, which itself could be considered a form of human piracy). Eventually, governments (particularly the English) refused to tolerate pirate activities, and at the end of Queen Anne's War in 1713 the Royal Navy was sent against them.

In the struggle against the British navy the odds were against the pirates. In addition, as the colonial ports grew stronger with the prosperity of the Atlantic trade, pirates were cut off from their traditional suppliers. The pirates were not easily defeated, however. They continued to recruit men willing to abandon their homes to go to sea with the raiders. They could terrify whole communities as Robert Teach (Blackbeard) and Stede Bonnet did to Charleston in 1717 and 1718. But by 1730,

large-scale piracy, so prevalent in the 17th century, was at an end. Piracy continued into the early 19th century, but never on the same scale of importance.

See Also: Kidd, William (Captain); Privateering.
BIBLIOGRAPHY: Rediker, Marcus Buford, *Between the Devil and the Deep Blue Sea* (Cambridge Univ. Press 1987); Ritchie, Robert C., *Captain Kidd and the War Against the Pirates* (Harvard Univ. Press 1986).

■ **PISTON, WALTER (1894-1976),** composer, writer, and teacher. A composer of numerous chamber and symphonic works, Piston was awarded Pulitzer Prizes for his third (1938) and seventh (1961) symphonies. A native of Rockland, Maine, he taught music composition at Harvard University (1926-59), where Leonard Bernstein was among his students. He also wrote several texts on musical composition, notably *Harmony* (1941).

■ **PITCHER, MOLLY (1754?-1832),** heroine of the Revolutionary War. Born Mary McCauley near Trenton, New Jersey, she earned her nickname by carrying water to wounded soldiers in the scorching heat of the Battle of Monmouth (1778). When her husband fell, overcome by heat, legend has it that she took his place loading the cannon until the fighting was over.

See Also: Women in American History.

■ **PITNEY, MAHLON (1858-1924),** associate justice of the U.S. Supreme Court (1912-22). Born in Morristown, New Jersey, he practiced law, served in the U.S. House of Representatives (1895-99), and was chancellor of New Jersey (1908-12) before joining the high court.

See Also: Supreme Court.

■ **PITTSBURGH,** major industrial city, located in the western part of Pennsylvania, at the point where the Allegheny and Monongahela rivers form the Ohio River. Pittsburgh began when the Iroquois town of Shannopin became a fur-trading post in the late 17th century. The French established Fort Duquesne there in 1750, only to have the British capture it eight years later and rename it Fort Pitt. Because of the river's location and mineral deposits in the area, heavy industry, especially glass, iron, coal, and steel production, expanded rapidly during the first half of the 19th century. Boats traveled down the Ohio to the Mississippi River carrying Pittsburgh's industrial products to the Gulf of Mexico. The city was a major supplier of Union munitions during the Civil War (1861-65). Industrial development continued throughout the early 20th century earning Pittsburgh the nickname "Smoky City." The decline in domestic steel manufacture during the 1970s, however, brought severe economic problems to the once-prosperous city. A massive urban revitalization program in the 1970s and 1980s induced corporations to relocate in Pittsburgh's downtown, and today the city enjoys a prosperous and diverse economy. Population (1994): 358,883.

See Also: *City in American History.*

■ **PIZARRO, FRANCISCO (c. 1475-1541),** Spanish explorer, conqueror of the Inca empire in Peru. Born in Trujillo, Spain, Pizarro gained experience in New Spain serving under Hernán Cortés in Hispaniola and acting as second-in-command on Balboa's Pacific Ocean discovery expedition in 1513. On two expeditions into what is today Colombia and Peru, Pizarro found gold. When Panama's Spanish governor refused to allow Pizarro to continue his forays into this region, Pizarro appealed to Spain and received permission to renew his New World ventures. In 1530 Pizarro reconnoitered the Pacific coasts of Ecuador and Peru. By 1532 the conquistador had penetrated inland. After meeting Atahualpa, the Inca emperor, Pizarro feigned friendship, seized the emperor, demanded an enormous ransom, and then executed him in August 1533. Within a year the Spaniards captured in brutal fashion Cuzco, the Inca capital. They established their own capital of Lima in 1535. A counterattack by an Inca army led by Manco Cupac was suppressed in 1536-37. Pizarro's ruthless ambition earned him immense wealth and secured Peru for Spain.

See Also: *Exploration and Discovery; Spanish Colonies.*

■ **PLAINS OF ABRAHAM,** plateau near Quebec City and site of a decisive battle in the French and Indian War. In a final effort to save Quebec, French General Montcalm led his troops against British forces commanded by Gen. James Wolfe. The ensuing battle in September 1759, won by the British, was epic and bloody. More than 2,000 soldiers lost their lives, including both Wolfe and Montcalm. The British victory led to the fall of Quebec and ultimately to the French defeat in the war.

See Also: *French and Indian War; Montcalm, Louis-Joseph, Marquis de.*

■ **PLANTATION DUTY ACT (1673),** British legislation designed to keep intercolonial trade in the hands of British merchants. The act assessed custom duties at the point of shipment on enumerated goods (defined in the Navigation Acts) shipped between colonies.

■ **PLANTATION SYSTEM,** dominant mode of economic organization in the South from the 17th through the 20th centuries. Enduring in various forms, the plantation system was premised on the efficient running of a centralized agricultural unit that produced mainly agricultural staples for export markets as well as some subsistence crops for plantation consumption. At its height in the last 30 years prior to the Civil War, the plantation linked white planter with black slave in complicated ways while simultaneously braiding the South's plantation economy into an international system that traded Southern cotton for Northern and European manufactures.

Plantations had been long established in Ireland, Brazil, the West Indies, and elsewhere. The southern plantation system, located originally in Virginia and spreading quickly to the Tidewater region of the Carolinas and Maryland, at first grew tobacco. From the outset these plantations, because they served European demands for a staple, found themselves tied to an international market system. The day-to-day agricultural operation and management of tobacco plantations became increasingly systematized, and the growing scarcity of white indentured servants at the end of the 17th century led Chesapeake planters to experiment with slave laborers. Resulting increases in production persuaded tobacco planters that African slave labor was profitable as well as racially desirable. Other planters, notably in South Carolina and Georgia, soon followed suit and by the opening decades of the 18th century used slave labor to cultivate rice and indigo.

The System at Its Peak. The plantation system's halcyon days occurred between 1790 and 1860, when it spread westward into the rich lands of Alabama, Mississippi, and east Texas. Spurred on by the invention (1793) and subsequent duplication of Eli Whitney's cotton gin, the westward expansion of the plantation system was contingent primarily on the cultivation of short staple cotton. Although southern plantations also grew Sea Island cotton in South Carolina and Georgia, hemp in Kentucky, tobacco in Virginia and North Carolina, and sugar in parts of Louisiana, short staple cotton typified the plantation system not least because its market was external and stimulated primarily by textile manufacturing in industrializing New England and Britain.

Masters and Slaves. Efforts to modernize the plantation system in the three decades preceding the Civil War had the ostensibly paradoxical effect of systematizing the internal workings of southern plantations while rendering relations between master and slave increasingly paternalistic. Aware that sufficiently high yields to satisfy international orders for cotton relied not only on good land but also on economies of scale and the efficient management of slave labor, late antebellum planters concluded that working 20 or more slaves was optimal to support efficient and productive plantations. While acknowledging that this is a somewhat arbitrary number, historians agree that ownership of at least 20 slaves was the defining characteristic of the antebellum planter and of the plantation system. Although wielding great economic, social, and political influence, planters constituted a small class. In the 15 slave states in 1850, only about 5 percent of whites owned any slaves, and of these roughly 12 percent possessed 20 or more bondsmen. While larger holdings were rarer still, it should be remembered that about half of all southern slaves worked on plantations.

The invention of the cotton gin in 1793 led to the expansion of the plantation system into the new states of Alabama, Mississippi, and Louisiana.

Recent work has reaffirmed the idea that southern plantations were profitable and efficient enterprises. Linked intimately to international demands for cotton via coastal factors and inland merchants, antebellum planters were able to regulate plantation production not simply to satisfy this demand but also to make the most of their slaves' labor. During slack seasons when cotton required little tending, planters employed their slaves in the cultivation of subsistence crops. Not only did this system prove to be an efficient reallocation of potentially idle labor but it also enabled planters to attain a degree of self-sufficiency by producing vegetables, corn, and other nonexport crops for consumption by their large labor force. Efforts to rationalize the internal workings of the southern plantation from the 1830s on also rendered the production of staple crops more efficient and orderly. Relying primarily on the gang system, antebellum masters instituted a precise and sophisticated division of labor on their plantations. Specialized gangs of slaves performed specialized jobs, and these gangs were in turn supervised by slave drivers, overseers, and, ultimately, by the plantation owner. An involved system of incentives and punishments enabled planters to make their slaves work intensively and, by some accounts, proficiently. Slaves who worked diligently could expect promotion and small rewards; the less assiduous were punished in a variety of ways, whipping being among the most common. These labor practices, combined with a gradual shift toward more scientific agricultural practices that utilized the benefits of mechanization and fertilization, made the antebellum plantation system a profitable, efficient, and orderly one whose products were of sufficiently high quality and quantity to help power northern and European industrialization.

Profit-minded though antebellum planters undoubtedly were, the behavior of their bondsmen sometimes forced masters to forgo the ideal of absolute plantation efficiency. The closing of the foreign slave trade in 1808 forced antebellum planters to come to terms with the fact that the future of their slave society was dependent on the natural reproduction of their work force rather than on its importation. This economic reality, combined with planters' cultural need to see their slaves as acquiescent human beings, afforded slaves opportunities to exploit the paternalist ethos that masters tried to impose on their relations with bondsmen. As a result slaves demanded rights from their masters, and planters ultimately found themselves embroiled in negotiations with slaves concerning the forming of kin networks, the use of their free time, and the practice of religion. Because their identity was dependent on the cultural hegemony they tried to impose on their slaves and because their economic livelihood depended on the productive capacity of their plantation work force, planters became involved in complex, subtle relationships with their chattel that sometimes served to curtail plantation profits.

After the Civil War. The Civil War and the attendant emancipation of slaves, while altering the plantation system, did not destroy it. Perhaps as many as half of all southern plantations, it has been estimated, were still in the hands of the same families in 1880 as before the war. To be sure, the social and economic relations of production changed: Freedmen were nominally free laborers in the postbellum era and had ostensible rights to sell their labor to former masters. But the plantation, in modified and fragmented form, remained the physical and intellectual space in which planter and freed laborer met and negotiated. Still with an eye to staple production and the social control of black people, postbellum plantation owners continued their attempts to control and exploit labor. But former slaves refused to be subjected to such close supervision. Instead they rejected the gang system of plantation labor, exercised their freedom of movement, and negotiated hard about their working rights. One product of these competing visions between freedmen and planters was sharecropping. Instead of selling land to former slaves, planters, under threat of freedmen withdrawing their labor altogether, allowed them to farm independent units of land and paid them a share of the crop or, occasionally, wages, at the end of the year. This more fragmented plantation system proved onerous for freedmen, who were often cheated, heavily indebted, and, without access to land and tools, in peonage to the postbellum planter. Sharecropping and the tenant system, which provided laborers with a greater degree of autonomy, entrapped both former slaves and, increasingly, poor whites.

The Disintegration of the System. Between the 1880s and 1930s, the fragmented plantation system endured even as the composition of its work force changed. With southern blacks migrating from the countryside, southern whites increasingly joined the ranks of sharecroppers and tenants. This fragmented plantation system, however, disintegrated over the following three decades. New Deal subsidy programs, which allowed planters to evict sharecroppers, and the devastation wrought by the boll weevil conspired to erode fragmented plantation agriculture. Capital-intensive, mechanized farming took its place, and provided the basis for modern agribusiness outside the South. The labor component of the plantation system was all but gone by the 1950s. Neoplantations resembled antebellum plantations only insofar as the plantation was centralized under the power of the owner and the staples were still intended primarily for export from the plantation.

—MARK M. SMITH

See Also: Cotton Gin; Slavery; Slave Trade.
BIBLIOGRAPHY: Courtenay, P. P., *Plantation Agriculture*, revised (Bell & Hyman 1980); Fogel, Robert William, *Without Consent or Contract: The Rise and Fall of American Slavery* (W. W. Norton 1989); Wright, Gavin, *Old South, New South: Revolutions in the Southern Economy Since the Civil War* (Basic Books 1986).

■ **PLATH, SYLVIA (1932-63),** poet and novelist. Born in Boston and a precociously talented writer, Plath focused much of her work on her experiences and troubled life. Her stable, middle-class childhood was shattered when her father died suddenly in 1940. Writing poetry became a means of expressing her profound sense of loss. With encouragement from her mother, Plath published numerous poems before she won a scholarship to Smith College. Her college years proved even more productive but were interrupted by a year-long absence after a suicide attempt and subsequent depression. On a Fulbright grant at Cambridge University in England, she met and married the poet Ted Hughes. Her married life in Devon, England, appeared outwardly idyllic, with two children, a successful writing career, and a country home. But she suffered from recurring depressions and her marriage ended in 1962. The following year she committed suicide.

Plath's best-known collection of poetry, *Ariel*, was composed furiously in the final months of her life. Despite the tormented state in which she wrote them, the poems demonstrate her control over form and emotion and ability to make personal experiences universal. *The Bell Jar* (1963), an autobiographical novel about a mental breakdown she suffered while in college, depicts the stereotyping of women's roles in the 1950s and the turmoil of a young woman writer.

See Also: Poetry; Women in American History.
BIBLIOGRAPHY: Alexander, Paul, *Rough Magic: A Biography of Sylvia Plath* (Viking 1991); Wagner-Martin, Linda, *Sylvia Plath: A Biography* (Simon & Schuster 1987).

■ **PLATT AMENDMENT,** U.S. legislative provision introduced after the Spanish-American War (1898), limiting the sovereignty of the young Cuban republic. The amendment received its name after Connecticut Sen. Orville Platt and was initially added to the 1901 army appropriations bill. According to the amendment, Cuba was forbidden to make any treaty limiting the island's independence or to incur excessive foreign debt. The paternalistic attitude of the U.S. government toward Cuba went so far as to grant the United States naval-base rights in Cuba, together with the right to intervene, if necessary, "for the preservation of Cuban independence." On June 12, 1901, in order to end American military occupation of the island, the Cuban constitutional convention incorporated the amendment into the constitution that came into force in 1902. The United States used its right to intervene in Cuba in 1906, 1912, and 1920. In 1934, Cuba abrogated the conditions of the Platt Amendment. Nevertheless, American economic domination over the island did not cease. In military terms, the U.S. retained its lease of the naval base at Guantanamo Bay. It has been argued that the Bay of Pigs military invasion of 1961 was an extension of the American tradition of attitude toward Cuba laid by the Platt Amendment.

See Also: Cuban Missile Crisis.
BIBLIOGRAPHY: Morgan, H. Wayne, *America's Road to Empire: The War with Spain and Overseas Expansion*

(Wiley 1967); Williams, William A., *The Tragedy of American Diplomacy,* 2nd ed. (Dell 1972).

■ **PLATTE RIVER,** wide, winding river primarily in Nebraska. Formed by the confluence of the North and South Platte rivers, the Platte flows east for some 300 miles from the Rocky Mountains to the Missouri River. In the 1840s settlers traveling on the Oregon Trail followed the river west to the North Platte, then to the Sweetwater River and onto South Pass through the Rocky Mountains.

■ **PLATTSBURGH BAY, BATTLE OF (1814),** battle in the War of 1812. Invading New York in September, British Gen. George Prevost confronted Gen. Alexander Macomb's U.S. troops at Plattsburgh, New York, on Lake Champlain's western shore. Prevost ordered Capt. George Downie to send his fleet against the American flotilla in Plattsburgh Bay. With excellent tactical decisions by Commander Thomas Macdonough, the Americans destroyed the British fleet in a bloody battle. Prevost was then defeated and retreated to Canada.

See Also: War of 1812.

■ **PLATTSBURGH IDEA,** federal program of voluntary summer military training camps for college students, in existence from 1911 until 1916. Founded and administered by Gen. Leonard Wood and named after one of the camps located at Plattsburgh Barracks, New York, the program was designed to provide a cadre of men trained as officers for emergency duty in wartime. Catering primarily to the elite of eastern colleges, the Plattsburgh idea was part of the "preparedness" movement that presaged American involvement in World War I (1917-18).

See Also: Preparedness Movement.

■ *PLESSY V. FERGUSON* **(1896),** U.S. Supreme Court case that established the constitutionality of the "separate but equal" doctrine, the legal basis for racial segregation in the South for the first half of the 20th century. Homer Plessy, who was one-eighth black, had been arrested in Louisiana after refusing to leave a whites-only train car. Plessy filed suit, claiming that his 14th Amendment right to equal protection had been violated. By an 8-1 vote, the Supreme Court upheld the Louisiana law, which legalized the racial segregation of public accommodations. The case actually raised two related but distinct questions. First, the Court held that separation on the basis of race, even legally prescribed separation, did not imply that one race was inferior to another. Writing for the Court, Justice Henry Brown declared that the protections accorded by the 14th Amendment applied only to political equality. Thus states were free to enforce racial segregation in other spheres of life as they saw fit. The second question before the Court dealt with whether the states had the authority to classify people on the basis of race. Justice Brown affirmed the authority of the states to determine racial status, concluding that the power to enforce racial segregation plainly implied the power to first define who belonged to which race. The majority opinion in this case provoked a blistering dissent from Justice John Harlan. He castigated his colleagues for retreating from the principle of racial equality. Impassioned dissents notwithstanding, *Plessy* stood for more than 50 years.

—MATTHEW E. BABCOCK

See Also: Supreme Court.

BIBLIOGRAPHY: Lofgren, Charles A., *The Plessy Case: A Legal-Historical Interpretation* (Oxford Univ. Press 1987); Medley, Keith Weldon, "The Sad Story of How 'Separate But Equal' Was Born," *Smithsonian* (Feb. 24, 1994).

■ **PLYMOUTH SETTLEMENT,** first English settlement in New England. In 1619, a group of English religious dissenters known as Separatists, who had fled to Holland (1608), obtained a patent from the Virginia Company of London for establishing a colony in North America. The total of 101 migrants (later called the Pilgrims) sailed from England on the *Mayflower* on Sept. 16, 1620, bound for Virginia. Storms drove their ship to the north, however, and they reached Cape Cod in what is now Massachusetts on November 21 and landed at Plymouth harbor on December 21. Lacking the jurisdiction of their original patent, 41 adult males of the expedition signed a compact before landing that bound the settlers together into a body politic for the purpose of enacting and enforcing laws (the Mayflower Compact). John Carver was chosen governor.

The colonists settled on the site of Pawtuxet, an Indian village depopulated in a recent epidemic. Although half of the settlers died during the winter of 1620-21, Plymouth survived. Economically, it became a subsistence farming community, with the cold climate not allowing the growth of a staple commodity like tobacco in Virginia and with no prospect of enrichment through agriculture. Politically, the colony was at first quite democratic. Since almost every male head of a household was a shareholder in the company, he could vote to elect the governor. Important questions were resolved by majority vote. Plymouth gave little profit to its English investors, and in 1627 they agreed to sell their shares in the company to the settlers. The initial settlement gave its name to the colony, which spread through present-day southeastern Massachusetts. Plymouth existed as a separate commonwealth until 1691, when it merged with Massachusetts Bay Colony.

See Also: *Frontier in American History; Massachusetts Bay Colony; Pilgrims; Women in American History.*

BIBLIOGRAPHY: Bradford, William, *History of Plymouth Settlement, 1608-1650* (Dutton 1920); Lord, Arthur, *Plymouth and the Pilgrims* (Houghton Mifflin 1920); Rutman, Darrett B., *Husbandmen of Plymouth: Farms and Villages in the Old Colony, 1620-1692* (Beacon Press 1967).

■ **POCAHONTAS (c. 1595-1617),** legendary Indian woman who saved the life of Captain John Smith. Daughter of Chief Powhatan of the Algonquian tribes in eastern Virginia, her real Indian name was said to be Matoaka. Perhaps a nickname, Pocahontas translates as "the playful one." She gained fame because of John Smith's description, in his *Generall Historie of Virginia, New England, and the Summer Isles* (1624), of how she had saved him from being clubbed to death by Powhatan's men in 1607. According to Smith, Pocahontas held his head in her arms and thus prevented him from being beaten. In 1612 Captain Samuel Argall abducted Pocahontas and took her to Jamestown as a hostage for English prisoners in Powhatan's hands. While at Jamestown she converted to Christianity and was baptized with the name Rebecca (1613). In April 1614 she married John Rolfe (1585-1622), a planter who introduced tobacco cultivation to Virginia. In 1615 their son Thomas was born. Pocahontas accompanied John Rolfe to England (1616), where she was presented to King James I and Queen Anne and had great success. While in London she sat for the Simon Van de Passe engraving of her, the only depiction of her from life. Pocahontas died in Gravesend, England, while preparing to leave for America. Her life inspired generations of American writers, poets, and artists, who created multiple versions of her story.

See Also: *Frontier in American History; Powhatan; Rolfe, John; Smith, John; Women in American History.*

BIBLIOGRAPHY: Tilton, Robert S., *Pocahontas: The Evolution of an American Narrative* (Cambridge Univ. Press 1994).

■ **POE, EDGAR ALLAN (1809-49),** short story writer, poet, and essayist. Born in Boston, Poe took his middle name from his foster parents, with whom he lived from about the age of three, by which time his birth parents had died. As a youth in Richmond, Virginia, Poe absorbed much from the books and journals his merchant father, John

Although his poem "The Raven" brought him fame, Edgar Allan Poe continued to live a life of poverty until his death.

Allan, imported. Although Allan came into a major inheritance in 1825, it was roughly at this point that his and Poe's relationship began to grow increasingly troubled, so that Poe would see very little of his father's wealth before Allan's death in 1834, and none of it after. In 1827, Poe managed to find a publisher in Boston for his first work, *Tamerlane and Other Poems*. After nearly two years in the U.S. Army, he introduced his second collection of verse, *Al Aaraaf, Tamerlane, and Minor Poems* (1829), followed by *Poems by Edgar A. Poe* (1831).

He first won attention with the short story, "A MS. Found in a Bottle," in 1833, gaining him a connection to the editor of Richmond's *Southern Literary Messenger*, to which he started to contribute in 1835, also becoming its assistant editor. Poe published *The Narrative of Arthur Gordon Pym* in 1838, in which year he moved from New York City to Philadelphia, and coedited *Burton's Gentleman's Magazine* between 1839 and 1840, printing his own story, "The Fall of the House of Usher," in that time. *Tales of the Grotesque and Arabesque*, Poe's first book of short stories, came out in 1839. While he was literary editor of *Graham's Lady's and Gentleman's Magazine* in 1841-42, Poe's reputation grew significantly, and "The Gold Bug" (1843), an outstanding example of his contribution to the detective story, furthered his popularity. His return to New York City in 1844 was followed the next year by the publication of his poem "The Raven," which brought him national prominence, and by his *The Raven and Other Poems*. Even fame, however, could not alter the condition of poverty with which Poe had had to contend since first going in pursuit of a literary career almost two decades earlier. Having struggled with illness, most notably alcoholism, his whole adult life, he died just a few years after the appearance of "The Raven."

See Also: Poetry; Short Story.
BIBLIOGRAPHY: Symons, Julian, *The Tell-Tale Heart: The Life and Works of Edgar Allan Poe* (Harper & Row 1978).

■ **POETRY.** The history of American poetry parallels that of other American cultural entities, particularly fiction and music. An originally imitative and derivative art ripens to a characteristic national identity in the 19th century; then, by absorbing and combining diverse historical and aesthetic influences, it achieves a kind of worldwide primacy, embodied, in the case of poetry, in the work of the major modernist poets. Afterward, the tendency is toward an almost bewildering expansiveness, variety, and inclusiveness.

The development of American poetry during the colonial and federalist periods (roughly 1650-1800) reflects the general historical dependency upon, and later emancipation from, British culture. Whether divine or secular in its subjects and themes, the poetry of this period relies heavily upon British models and verse forms (sonnets, odes, epistles, satires, occasional poems, and so forth). At its best, as in the work of Anne Bradstreet and Edward Taylor, it can almost stand up to favorable comparison with the work of contemporaneous British poets. Much of the poetry of the later 18th century, understandably, took on a political cast, as in the work of Philip Freneau, as America forged its independence from Great Britain.

Romanticism and Realism. A second period (roughly 1800-65) roughly corresponds to and extends the period of British romanticism. The work of the so-called "Fireside Poets" such as Henry Wadsworth Longfellow, William Cullen Bryant, and John Greenleaf Whittier shows an increased assimilation of British and continental models, with an application to characteristically American scenes, places, characters, and historical figures. In the work of Ralph Waldo Emerson, and particularly Walt Whitman and Emily Dickinson, the national poetry attains a quality and distinctiveness of form that shows a true emancipation from foreign influence. In the innovative free verse of Whitman and in the idiosyncratic New England hymnal stanzas of Dickinson, American poetry truly comes of age.

In the years between the Civil War and World War I, American poetry, like the fiction of the time, veers toward an increased realism tinged with social concerns and a naturalism that acknowledges scientific and technological developments while emphasizing the importance of heredity and environment as determinants of human character. Novelist Herman Melville turned almost exclusively to writing poetry during this period. Of greater influence was the work of New Englander Edward Arlington Robinson, who prepared the way for Robert Frost, arguably America's first modernist poet. American poetry after World War I becomes increasingly difficult to characterize. The poetry of Frost, Ezra Pound, T. S. Eliot, W. H. Auden, Wallace Stevens, and William Carlos Williams tends to be difficult, symbolic, ironic, highly allusive, and skeptical or pessimistic. Whether in free verse, like much of the poetry of Pound and Eliot, or in the rhythmical and often rhymed verse preferred by Frost and Auden, American modernist poetry, which perhaps reaches its zenith in the playful, generally atheistic, and formally complex work of Stevens, is of extraordinarily high quality, is broadly influential, and is reflective of the special, political, and religious turbulence of the first half of the century. In the work of these modernist poets, American poetry achieves a kind of worldwide importance that it has probably not yet relinquished.

After 1960, American poetry explodes in a welter of voices, styles, and tendencies. Inclusiveness and variety are the only certainties. A generation of poets trained in college creative writing courses and workshops cultivated a noteworthy sophistication and attention to form. The later work of Robert Lowell, perhaps the most representative poet of the century's third quarter, spawned an interest in personal confession that also characterizes the work of Sylvia Plath and Anne Sexton. Poets of the Beat movement, such as Allen Ginsberg and Lawrence Ferlinghetti, strike a countercultural, more popular, and politically engaged note in free verse reminiscent of Whitman's "barbaric yawp." In recent years, the burgeoning interest in American multiculturalism has tended to generate work by, and to promote interest in, poetry by African-American, Indian, and Latino/Latina poets. Gay and lesbian writers have also produced a significant body of work. Writers as diverse as James Merrill, Adrienne Rich, Robert Pinsky, Jorie Graham, Gary Soto, and Yusef Komunyakaa capture the vitality and richness of American poetry at century's end.

—MARK JOHNSTON

See Also: *Beats, The; Bradstreet, Anne; Bryant, William Cullen; Dickinson, Emily; Eliot, T.S. (Thomas Stearns); Emerson, Ralph Waldo; Frost, Robert Lee; Ginsberg, Allen; Longfellow, Henry Wadsworth; New England Renaissance; Plath, Sylvia; Pound, Ezra; Robinson, Edward Arlington; Stevens, Wallace; Whitman, Walt(er); Whittier, John Greenleaf.*

BIBLIOGRAPHY: Gioia, Dana, *Can Poetry Matter?: Essays on Poetry and American Culture* (Graywolf Press 1992); Pearce, Roy Harvey, *The Continuity of American Poetry* (Princeton Univ. Press 1961).

■ **POINT FOUR PROGRAM (1949),** plan for economic aid to Third World nations proposed by Pres. Harry S. Truman. The program, run by the State Department's Technical Cooperation Administration, included improvement of food availability, basic health, and housing.

See Also: *Cold War.*

■ **POITIER, SIDNEY (1924-),** actor and director. Born in Miami, Florida, Poitier is among the most renowned actors of film and stage. He began acting with the American Negro Theater in New York before moving into films. In 1963, Poitier became the first black male actor to win an Academy Award for his performance in *Lilies of the Field.*

See Also: *African Americans; Motion Pictures.*

■ **POLISH IMMIGRANTS.** The first Polish immigrants to America arrived as early as 1608 in Jamestown. During the colonial period the few Poles who immigrated were prompted by personal or religious, rather than economic or political, reasons. Several Poles ventured to America during the 1770s to fight against the British during the Revolution. The first major influx of Polish immigrants began in 1795, after Poland was partitioned by neighboring nations. These political refugees settled mainly in cities in the northeast. In the 1870s Polish migration to the United States increased dramatically as economic conditions for rural workers hit desperate lows. The hundreds of thousands of Poles who immigrated between 1870 and 1920 formed a large segment of the U.S. industrial labor force. In urban areas Polish immigrants formed ethnic communities, where they retained their culture in newspapers, businesses, and social organizations. Most importantly, however, the Roman Catholic Church became the center of such communities.

See Also: *Ethnic Groups; Immigration.*

■ **POLITICAL MACHINE,** tightly knit organizations that controlled local politics and were largely centered on the influence of political parties. While strong party leaders had long been a fixture of American politics, the frenetic pace of immigration between 1870 and 1890 made the power of the local machine leader—the "boss"—rival that of elective national politicians. Immigrants unfamiliar with the ways of their new home were more than willing to pledge their loyalty to a boss in return for help in finding a job and a place to live, particularly as national leaders seemed to be unable to cope with the growing urban problems of America. The political machines in a sense filled a void. Men like William Marcy Tweed of New York's Tammany Hall, George Cox of Cincinnati, and Daniel O'Connell of Albany, all of whom provided basic necessities for their constituents when state and national governments either could not or would not, grew in influence and power, some achieving national notoriety.

However, with the turn of the 20th century, the bosses came upon hard times. Progressive reformers attacked the bosses as the epitome of everything that was wrong with American politics. More important for the progressives was their belief that the mere presence of bosses was an indication that urban politics had become undemocratic. Progressives were aided in their crusade to clean up city politics by journalists such as Lincoln Steffens, who in a series of magazine articles later published as *The Shame of the Cities* (1904) effectively described the corruption in six of the nation's largest cities. By the end of the progressive era, the power bosses had effectively been circumscribed. While they still were influential in several of the nation's largest surviving machines, they were soon under attack from either zealous prosecutors or reform-minded politicians.

Yet the final blow to the urban bosses may well have come from a new kind of "machine." The New Deal reforms of Pres. Franklin D. Roosevelt created a vast federal machinery of programs. No longer did Americans turn to the local machines when looking for answers to the Great Depression. This growth in central-government power, along with the rise of suburbanization that, in the 1950s, effectively lessened the influence of the cities, all but negated the need for

tight control of urban politics. Most historians believe that the death of Chicago's Mayor Richard Daley in 1976 effectively ended the era of urban machine politics in the United States.

—JOHN ROBERT GREENE

See Also: *City in American History; Political Parties; Progressivism.*

BIBLIOGRAPHY: Stave, Bruce M., and Sondra Stave, *Urban Bosses, Machines, and Progressive Reformers,* 2nd ed. (Krieger 1984).

■ **POLITICAL PARTIES,** durable political organizations with significant popular following and participation that seek governmental power by running candidates for elective office. The American norm has been a competitive political system in which only two parties have had a significant chance of winning the preponderance of government offices.

U.S. political history has passed through a series of phases that some political scientists have called "party systems." Party systems tend to take shape during periods of turmoil; political controversy shatters old alliances and leads to "critical elections" that signal a realignment of popular sentiment and party organizations. Following such elections the new party formations settle into a new period of pragmatic competition. By such reckoning, it is possible to discern six distinct party systems in American history.

The First Party System. The First Party System began to take form during Pres. George Washington's term when the leaders of the young republic faced the difficult task of making a postcolonial political environment. The great debates of the day centered on the role of the federal government versus the states and the place of the United States in the Atlantic world. Political alignments in the early republic formed around the group known as the Federalists (led by Alexander Hamilton), which favored a strong central government and cooperation with Great Britain, and another group that became known as the Democratic-Republicans (led by Thomas Jefferson), which feared central authority, wanted power vested in the states, and tended to be anti-British and pro-French.

Underlying these issues, however, were more fundamental questions. Republican government was still considered an experiment, and it was unknown the extent to which political stability depended on the continued deference of the public to ruling elites. Beyond this, partisan political conflict had very little legitimacy. President Washington condemned the "spirit of party and faction." There was a sense that republican government could survive only by political consensus. In such a political environment there was very little understanding of the idea of a "loyal opposition."

During the presidency of John Adams, the Federalists overplayed their hand. They sent troops into Pennsylvania to support federal tax collectors. They threatened to begin an unpopular war with France. They attempted to outlaw dissent through passage of the Alien and Sedition Acts. And they lambasted their Jeffersonian opponents as "godless" and "Jacobins." In the presidential election of 1800 the Democratic-Republicans triumphed, electing Thomas Jefferson president. Without question what was critical about this election was the peaceful transition from the Federalists to the Jeffersonians. It marked the consolidation of what some call the First American Party System. A better label might be the "preparty system," for what Federalist decline suggested was the continuing uncertainty about the compatibility of partisan politics and republican government. At the level of national politics, political opposition was contained within the congressional caucus system, increasingly dominated by the Jeffersonians. In 1820 the presidential election was uncontested. Sometimes this period is called the "Era of Good Feelings." It was the only time in American history when the political system could be characterized as a one-party state.

That system broke down in the 1820s over the political question of elitism. It broke down also because of the immense popularity of the first democratic political hero in American history—Andrew Jackson. When Jackson ran for president in 1824 he played by the rules of the party system. He was a member of the Senate. He was nominated by a caucus of his peers. He won a large plurality of the popular vote. But because the vote had been split among four candidates, none of whom achieved a majority in the electoral college, the decision was thrown to the House of Representatives, where Henry Clay and John Quincy Adams forged their "corrupt bargain" to make Adams president and Clay his secretary of state and heir-apparent.

Jackson and his popular followers were outraged. Over the next four years his supporters organized intensely throughout the nation, the first time such a thing had taken place. Over the previous two decades the states had gradually extended suffrage to include most white male voters, but rates of political participation had remained low. Now suddenly, like an earthquake, the era of mass politics arrived. More than three times as many voters cast their ballots in 1828 as had in 1824; Jackson won a landslide victory. The election of 1828—surely one of the most critical in American history—-proclaimed the democratization of the presidency and ushered in the Second American Party System.

The Second Party System. This period, which lasted until the late 1850s, was the most politically creative in American history. The political convention, adopted in the early 1830s, took the nominating process from the Congress and placed it in the hands of the party apparatus. Jackson, who considered himself the incarnate voice of the people, warred with the other branches of government, wielding party discipline over the Congress and ignoring, if he chose, the rulings of the Supreme Court. He dismantled the economic system that had been first outlined by Hamilton then agreed to by the Jeffersonians by blocking federal funding for internal improvements and declared war on the national bank. He insisted on the removal of the Indians of the eastern United States to new homelands west of the Mississippi, a program hugely popular with white farmers who hungered after land. By 1834, Jackson had provoked a strong organized party opposition—the Whigs—who learned their lessons from Jackson and the Democrats and eventually used the same mass political methods to win the presidential elections of 1840 and 1848. The Democrats were the dominant party, but the Whigs made a respectable showing; on average, in the presidential, congressional, and gubernatorial elections from 1834 to 1853, the Democrats won approximately 56 percent of the vote, the Whigs 43 percent, with minor parties capturing the remainder.

Sectionalism was the Achilles heel of the Second Party System. One historian has described the Senate during this period as a "congress of ambassadors" from North, South, and West, whose main work was the attempt to negotiate intersectional compromises. After the Mexican War (1846-48) an intense sectional debate arose over the question of whether slavery would be permitted in the conquered territory. It now became increasingly difficult for the major parties to keep their sectional coalitions intact. The debate over slavery and the place of African Americans in the life of the nation made the 1850s one of the most tumultuous periods in American political history.

This becomes evident in the number of "third parties" running for national office from 1848 to 1856. By the mid-1850s one of those third parties—the Republicans—had displaced the Whigs to become the major party of opposition to the Democrats. Running in 1856 on a platform that declared slavery to be a "pillar of barbarism," it became clear that a Republican victory would mean either the dismantling of slavery, and the social and political regime based upon it, or disunion.

The Third Party System. The contest of 1860 was clearly a critical election marking the beginning of the Third Party System. The Republicans and Abraham Lincoln carried the entire North, the Midwest, and the Far West. The Democrats, fracturing into sectional factions that each ran different candidates, carried the South and border states. Sectionalism had destroyed the previous party system. Now a purely sectional party based in the North would take power and make a social revolution in America. Not only did the Civil War destroy slavery and the Southern social system, but the Republicans in Congress enacted an integrated federal program of economic development: banking and currency reform, high protective tariffs, liberal immigration laws, subsidies for a transcontinental railroad, and land grants for homesteaders. After the war Republican radicals hoped that by enfranchising freed African Americans and disenfranchising former Confederates they could build a political machine in the South.

But by 1870 the popular enthusiasm for social revolution had run its course. The reentry of "redeemed" and unreconstructed Southern states into national politics in the mid-1870s deadlocked the Third Party System for the next 20 years. This is evident from a comparison of party strength before and after 1873. From 1856 to 1873, Republican strength in presidential, congressional, and gubernatorial elections averaged 66 percent, Democrats 30 percent (with the remainder to minor parties); from 1873 to 1894 Republicans averaged 49 percent, Democrats 51 percent.

These decades of political stalemate—which produced a crop of largely faceless presidents—was the age of massive industrialization in the United States. Industrialization produced two large groups of discontented citizens: farmers and urban workers, neither of whom found a home in the major political parties. The great depression of 1893 threw American politics into turmoil. The national Democratic party, with its base in the white, rural politics of the South, was able to mount an appeal to western farmers but unable to organize effectively among workers in northeastern cities. In the critical election of 1896, the "free-silver" platform of the Democrats scared off urban voters, who feared higher prices. Catholics, uncomfortable with the Protestant pieties of Democratic candidate William Jennings Bryan, deserted the party, while German immigrants voted in large numbers for William McKinley. Discontented workers turned to one of the socialist or Marxist parties of the day or abandoned politics altogether.

The Fourth Party System. The subsequent Fourth Party System was extremely sectional. The South and the border states were dominated by the Democrats; African Americans were disenfranchised by intimidation or outright campaigns of lynching, and segregation was institutionalized as the prevailing social order. It is worth noting that segregation was brought to Washington, D.C., by the administration of Woodrow Wilson, the only Democrat to be elected to the presidency during this period. Wilson's victory was made possible by the split between incumbent William Howard Taft and former president Theodore Roosevelt, who ran on a third-party ticket. With the exception of this election of 1912, Republican candidates dominated the North and the West almost to the same extent as Democrats did the South. Only in the Midwest was there a truly competitive political system.

Change was bubbling beneath the surface, however. Political discontent was evident in a number of impressive third-party challenges. The Socialist party candidate for president, Eugene V. Debs, regularly polled hundreds of thousands of votes—nearly a million in 1920, when he conducted his campaign from a prison cell. In 1924, Sen. Robert M. La Follette, candidate of the Progressive party who proposed state ownership of railroads and utilities, claimed 17 percent of the vote. In the cities of the northeast, Democrats had begun organizing around the politics of "urban liberalism," a moderate version of social democracy. In the campaign of 1928, Democrat Al Smith, the governor of New York, ran better in the big cities of the northeast than any nominee of his party since the Civil War.

The Fifth Party System. But it was the Great Depression of the 1930s that destroyed the Fourth Party System. The overwhelming victory of Franklin D. Roosevelt in 1932, and his even more decisive reelection in 1936, forged the New Deal coalition of the Democratic party: Southerners, big-city political machines, industrial workers of all ethnic groups and races, trade unionists, and many depression-ravaged farmers. African Americans, long affiliated with the party of Lincoln, abandoned the Republicans for Roosevelt. The Democrats enacted a program of state regulation of the economy, began constructing what became known as the "social safety net" of social security and unemployment insurance, and offered encouragement to unionizing workers.

During this Fifth Party System, which lasted until the late 1960s, the Republicans succeeded only with the candidacy of war hero Dwight D. Eisenhower in 1952 and 1956. The political tenor and limits of this period are suggested by the fact that Eisenhower never contemplated rolling back most of the policies and institutions of the New Deal. Democrat Lyndon B. Johnson added to the New Deal safety net with his Great Society programs, and civil rights legislation of the 1960s extended to African Americans the same integration into the political process that the New Deal has offered immigrants and workers. The federal government also supported efforts to dismantle the system of segregation in the South.

The struggles of the civil rights movement and the opposition to Johnson's Cold War adventure in Vietnam, however, made the 1960s another of those tumultuous decades of political transformation. The lasting political legacy of the decade, however, was signaled in Republican Barry Goldwater's losing campaign against Johnson in 1964. Goldwater succeeded in carrying the deep South, a historic first for a Republican. In 1968, an election won by Republican presidential candidate Richard M. Nixon, those same states were carried by third-party candidate George Wallace, who as governor of Alabama had promised "segregation forever." In 1972, in what his advisers called "the southern strategy," Nixon used many of the same buzz words and slogans as Wallace, appealing to those fearful about crime, drugs, and social change.

The Sixth Party System. The New Deal coalition was in the process of disintegration. Not only had the South abandoned the Democrats for the Republicans, but the ethnic working-class coalition shattered along lines of values and generations. The elections of 1968 and 1972 marked a decisive political shift. But the Democrats continued to control Congress. Moreover, Nixon's humiliation in the Watergate scandal of 1972-74, and the reactive presidential victory of Democrat Jimmy Carter in 1976, obscured what the Republicans accomplished in those years. It took the election of Ronald Reagan in 1980 and 1984, and the Republican seizure of both houses of Congress in 1994, to finally fulfill the promise of Nixon's southern strategy. During this Sixth Party System, Republicans have demonstrated none of Eisenhower's reluctance to dismantle the accomplishments of the New Deal. Bill Clinton's Democratic administration that began in 1993 may go down as the exception that proves the rule, akin perhaps to Wilson's interregnum of 1913-21. It was Clinton himself who stated what was perhaps the best summary of political trends during this period when he said, "The era of big government is over."

—John Mack Faragher

See Also: *Communist Party; Conservatism; Democratic Party; Liberalism; Primaries; Republican Party; Socialism; Third Parties.*

BIBLIOGRAPHY: Aldrich, John H., *Why Parties? The Origin and Transformation of Political Parties in America* (Univ. of Chicago Press 1995); Chambers, William Nisbet, and Walter Dean Burnham, eds., *The American Party Systems* (Oxford Univ. Press 1975).

■ **POLK, JAMES KNOX (1795-1849),** 11th president of the United States (1845-49). Born in Mecklenburg County, North Carolina, Polk graduated from the University of North Carolina and was admitted to the bar in 1820. In 1824 he married Sarah Childress, a well-educated woman, who proved a valuable asset to his career. In 1825 Polk, a Jacksonian Democrat, entered the House of Representatives. He served in Congress for 14 years, including 4 as Speaker of the House (1835-39), and was governor of Tennessee (1839-41). In 1844 a deadlocked Democratic party convention nominated the dark horse Polk for the presidency, and he narrowly defeated the Whig party's Henry Clay and the Liberty party's James G. Birney.

A conscientious but uninspiring leader, Polk nevertheless proved an effective executive. He achieved all his major goals, including a lower tariff and restoration of the independent treasury. His most enduring accomplishment, however, lay in the arena of westward expansion. During his administration the United States gained 522 million acres by diplomacy and war. Polk negotiated with Great Britain to establish the Oregon boundary on the 49th parallel (1846) and obtained California and the New Mexico Territory through war with Mexico (1846-48). The war fanned the flames of sectionalism and brought the issue of slavery in the new territories to public debate.

Polk was a one-term president by choice. When his term ended, he retired to his home in Tennessee and died only three months later.

See Also: *Mexican War; Oregon Question; Presidential Elections; President of the United States.*

BIBLIOGRAPHY: Bergeron, Paul H., *The Presidency of James K. Polk* (Univ. Press of Kansas 1987); McCormac, Eugene I., *James K. Polk: A Political Biography* (Russell & Russell 1922).

■ **POLLOCK, (PAUL) JACKSON (1912-56),** abstract expressionist painter. Born in Cody, Wyoming, and raised on the West Coast, Pollock left high school to study art in New York City at 17. He took classes with John French Sloan and Thomas Hart Benton at the Art Students League, and his early work reflects the influence of the American Scene painters who depicted landscape and everyday life in America, often incorporating social criticism in their renderings. After working for the Federal Arts Project in New York City during the Great Depression, Pollock moved toward abstraction in the mid-1940s. In the late 1940s he stopped painting on an easel and began using the technique for which he is best remembered. He would spread his large canvases on the floor of his studio and drip fluid paint, one color at a time, onto the surface. Starting this style with bright colors, he later used black and browns and eventually began creating slightly more representational forms by concentrating paint in certain areas of the canvas. Although his approach to painting was questioned by some art critics, Pollock became a central figure in the abstract expressionist movement. He died in an automobile accident on Long Island.

See Also: *Benton, Thomas Hart; Federal Arts Project; Painting; Sloan, John French.*

Democrat James K. Polk defeated Whig Henry Clay in the presidential election of 1844. Polk led the country to war with Mexico, seizing the northern third of that nation's territory.

■ **POLL TAX,** head tax levied on citizens as a requirement for voting. A staple of colonial governments prior to the American Revolution, the poll tax was later used to limit the franchise, especially in Southern states where it was one of several measures employed to deny the vote to African Americans. The 24th Amendment to the U.S. Constitution (1964) barred states from using the poll tax requirement to determine who could or could not vote in federal elections.

■ **PONCE DE LEÓN, JUAN (1460-1521),** Spanish explorer and European discoverer of Florida. Ponce de León sailed with Columbus's second expedition in 1493 and in 1508 conquered the island of Puerto Rico. He landed near the future site of St. Augustine, Florida, in 1513, reputedly searching for the Fountain of Youth, in fact, raiding for slaves. In 1521, attempting to colonize Florida, Ponce de León was wounded in an Indian attack near Tampa Bay. He died later in Havana, Cuba.

See Also: Exploration and Discovery.

■ **PONTIAC'S REBELLION (1763),** a series of sieges against British military posts in the upper Great Lakes and surrounding areas by a confederation of Indians that had been organized by Chief Pontiac of the Ottawa. When northeastern Indians realized at the end of the Seven Years' War (1756-63) that British troops would stay in their territories, many tribes conspired against the British. The Seneca circulated an appeal for united war, and the Delaware prophet Neolin taught rejection of European power and culture.

Pontiac, an influential Ottawa chief, coordinated a strategy to besiege Fort Detroit, which he hoped to capture by a ruse, but Detroit's commandant, Maj. Henry Gladwin, was warned of the plan. Gladwin closed the fort's gates against an unsuccessful six-month siege that began on May 9, 1763.

European forts were generally defensible against Indian attack, but a number succumbed to subterfuges, the most important being Fort Michilimackinac (present-day Mackinac, Michigan) on June 2, 1763, which was taken by Ojibwa warriors who threw a lacrosse ball over its wall and rushed after it. Other captured forts in the upper lakes region included Sandusky, St. Joseph, Miami, and Ouiatenon. Farther east, Indians overcame Forts Venango, Le Boeuf, and Presque Isle.

Forts Detroit, Niagara (at the mouth of the Niagara River in New York), and Pitt (present-day Pittsburgh) held out as the "principal theater" of the war. Detroit was attacked by Ottawas, Wyandots, Potawatomis, Eries, Ojibwas, Missisauga-Ojibwas, and some Hurons. Niagara was besieged by Seneca, Pitt by Delaware and Shawnee. At Fort Pitt, Capt. Simeon Ecuyer broke the siege by parleying with Delaware chiefs, to whom he presented blankets from the smallpox hospital. As Ecuyer had intended, a deadly smallpox epidemic spread among Indians throughout the area.

The Indians were unable to sustain these key sieges, largely because of ammunition shortages, so they had to negotiate when relief forces were sent to Fort Pitt in August under Cols. Henry Bouquet and John Bradstreet. En route to Pitt, Bouquet defeated the Indians in battle at Bushy Run (in what is now Greensburg, Pennsylvania), an action hailed as a great victory because it stopped further Delaware advances. In contrast, Bradstreet's treaties at Presque Isle and Detroit are usually denounced as insufficiently punitive, but Bouquet's "victory" was a dead end, and Bradstreet did get to Detroit.

Negotiating with Indians there (without Pontiac), Bradstreet made them accept England's king as their sovereign "father" rather than an allied "brother." Ultimately, despite military rivalries, Bradstreet's treaties were upheld by higher authority.

The Indians' hope of French support died when they realized that New France ended with the 1763 Treaty of Paris. Without French assistance, Pontiac's confederation was forced to submit to British terms of peace. Pontiac and his allies concluded formal peace at Fort Ontario in 1766.

—FRANCIS JENNINGS

See Also: Indians of North America.

BIBLIOGRAPHY: Godfrey, William G., *Pursuit of Profit and Preferment in Colonial North America* (Wilfred Laurier Univ. Press 1982); Jennings, Francis, *Empire of Fortune* (Norton 1988); Peckham, Howard H., *Pontiac and the Indian Uprising* (Univ. of Chicago Press 1961); Tanner, Helen Hornbeck, *Atlas of Great Lakes Indian History* (Univ. of Oklahoma Press 1987).

■ **PONY EXPRESS (Apr. 3, 1860-October 1861),** transcontinental mail service. Perhaps more important in myth than in the reality of its brief 18-month existence, the Pony Express made its first delivery between St. Joseph, Missouri, and Sacramento, California, on Apr. 3, 1860. Formed by Russell, Majors, and Waddell to compete with the Overland Mail Company, the Pony Express promised to deliver letters from Missouri to California at a cost of $5 an ounce, in less than 10 days, half the time the Overland Mail Route took. A system of more than 190 stations was established, 10-15 miles apart, the distance a horse could be galloped or loped at a fast pace. The mail was passed to the next rider, dashing on down the line. The trip was a test of the stamina of both horses and men. The route was particularly important between the ends of the telegraph lines at Fort Kearney, Nebraska, and Fort Churchill, Nevada, where horseback was the only way for information to move. The Pony Express was a huge publicity success, but a financial failure, costing Russell, Majors, and Waddell some $100,000 to $200,000 in losses, a fortune at the time. The U.S. government subsidized the final six months of operation, but the completion of the transcontinental telegraph rendered the Pony Express obsolete in October 1861. The Pony Express, despite its brief history, became an essential image of the West.

See Also: Frontier in American History.

■ **POOLS,** informal business organization used during the 1870s and 1880s in which companies agreed to establish production quotas and set prices to limit competition. The Sherman Antitrust Act (1890) hurt small companies by outlawing pools and encouraging corporate consolidation.

See Also: Sherman Antitrust Act.

■ **POPÉ (?-1690),** San Juan Pueblo medicine man and leader. In the 1670s, the Pueblo in present-day New Mexico experienced a revitalization of traditional religions, and the Spanish reacted with repression. In August 1680, Popé led a pan-Pueblo revolt, seizing the capital of Santa Fe and driving the Spanish back to El Paso. However, by 1690, the Pueblo Confederation under Popé fell apart and he was deposed.

See Also: Indians of North America; Pueblo Revolt.

■ **POPULAR CULTURE. See:** *Broadway; Burlesque; Circuses; Gambling; Motion Pictures; Newspapers; Television and Radio; Theater; Vaudeville; individual biographies.*

■ **POPULAR SOVEREIGNTY,** a political solution crafted to resolve the controversy over slavery in the U.S. territories of the mid-19th century. Proposed in 1847 by Sen. Lewis Cass of Michigan during debate over the Wilmot Proviso, popular sovereignty would delegate to the citizens of a territory the decision whether or not to allow slavery. Cass introduced the rule to quiet Southern partisans who argued that the Fifth Amendment forbade Congress to prohibit slave ownership in the territories. His proposal elegantly finessed the debate by exempting Congress from making any blanket decision regarding slavery in the territories. Southerners accordingly assumed that popular sovereignty meant that the territories were open to slavery and might remain that way should their citizens wish. Alternately, Northerners assured themselves that slavery could likewise be proscribed. Subsequent events proved the doctrine's downfall, for it only exacerbated sectional enmity. Partisans of both sides used it as a means of advancing their own agendas. Stephen Douglas further complicated the issue with his 1857 Freeport Doctrine, which stipulated that popular sovereignty would allow territorial citizens tacitly to exclude slavery, despite its federal sanction, by simply refusing to enforce laws that protected it.

See Also: Douglas, Stephen Arnold; Wilmot Proviso.

BIBLIOGRAPHY: Potter, David, *The Impending Crisis, 1848-1861* (Harper & Row 1976); Stampp, Kenneth M., *America in 1857: A Nation on the Brink* (Oxford Univ. Press 1990).

■ **POPULATION.** The growth and redistribution of the American population is best understood as a complex interaction among three basic processes—fertility, migration, and mortality. Demographic historians study the changes in these essential mechanisms of population redistribution; the primary source for their study of past populations is the decennial census. Historians supplement the national census with state censuses, birth and death registries, genealogies, church records, immigrant lists, and city directories. In addition, they look to the archaeological record to understand the demographics of America prior to European arrival.

The Tragedy of Conquest. Current estimates for the pre-Columbian population in the area north of the Rio Grande range between 5 and 10 million people. Some of these people were nomadic hunters but many others were agriculturalists residing in towns and villages.

The impact of the European and African migrations to the New World was far reaching and tragic. Isolated from the diseases of Europe, Asia, and Africa, Indians lacked even the most limited immunities necessary to protect against smallpox, measles, plague, and malaria. With first contact, Indians died by the thousands. Adding the deaths due to war, starvation, and enslavement, the toll was extraordinarily high. Some tribes were extinct within decades of first contact, while others suffered to a point where little resistance to white advance was possible. By 1900 the Indian population had fallen by 90 percent. In the years since, however, the Indian population has rebounded, growing by 150 percent.

The Colonial Period. In the century after the settlement of Jamestown and Plymouth more than 500,000 Europeans migrated to America. Initially, the English dominated the stream of migrants to North America, with scatterings of Dutch, French, and Spanish settlers. Black Africans were first brought to Virginia as slaves in 1619. Initially, their numbers increased slowly, but in the 18th century the slave trade accelerated, with as many as 350,000 Africans arriving by the 1770s. In the mid-18th century, emigration from Scotland, Ireland, and Germany swelled, equaling migration from England. The growing diversity of the population had important social and political consequences, and by the American Revolution fewer than half the colonials could trace their ancestry to England.

Although migration from abroad was the major impetus for population growth, slowly a remarkable transformation occurred. Mortality rates fell and fertility rose as the colonies experienced a modest "baby boom" in the 18th century. Where the sex ratio was favorable, marriage rates were high. With divorce an exceptional event, death was the primary reason that a marriage ended. Despite the likelihood that one spouse would die before middle age, colonial families were large, averaging between six and eight children, higher than most European communities. This surge in fertility was relatively short lived.

Health and mortality conditions in the colonies varied widely. In the late 17th century, life expectancy at birth for white males in New England was better than 50 years, but less than 30 for Southerners. The death rates for women were higher than those of men. In all cases the greatest chances of death came in childhood. Some diseases such as plague, malaria, and smallpox declined in frequency as the centuries passed. Others, such as cholera and tuberculosis, would emerge with greater virulence as America's cities grew larger.

By the American Revolution the colonial population of British North America was nearly 3 million. It was still growing rapidly, averaging a startling 3.5 percent annually. It was a young population with a median age of about 15. Land pressures on the coast promoted internal migration, and by the late 18th century settlement of the trans-Appalachian west had begun in earnest. America's cities grew rapidly as well, with nearly 5 percent living in settlements of more than 2,500 inhabitants.

Steady Growth: 1780-1860. In the decades following the Revolution, European immigration ebbed, and fertility rates in many areas began to fall. Nonetheless, even in this period of international conflict and economic instability, the new republic maintained impressive average annual growth rates over 3 percent. Much of the growth is attributable to the large percentage of young people starting families. Fertility was still quite high, and with declining mortality, their offspring were much more likely to survive and have children. The total fertility rate was about 7 children per woman in 1800. It continued to fall steadily, but it was still above 5 children at mid-century.

From the 1770s through the 1840s, immigration to the United States was relatively low and was a relatively small component of overall population growth. Then, famine and political turmoil forced nearly 4 million Europeans to migrate to America in the 15 years prior to the

Civil War. Many of these immigrants settled in the growing cities of the northeast or the fertile midwest farmland.

The real story of demographic change in this period was in the internal migration and redistribution of the American population. In 1790, the first national census showed that fewer than 5 percent of the nation's 4 million people resided west of the Appalachians. With the Louisiana Purchase (1803), the normalization of relations with Great Britain (post-1815), and the suppression of Indian resistance, a flood of settlers crossed the mountains into the Ohio and Mississippi watershed. More than 10 million people had moved west by mid-century. By the Civil War, roughly half the nation's total population and nearly 30 percent of the urban residents resided in the trans-Appalachian west.

Equally important was the development of an integrated national economy marked by a growing regional differentiation and an evolution toward a modern urban system centered on the northeast. Except for 1811-20, the growth of America's urban population ranged from 60 to 99 percent in every decade from 1790 to 1860. The United States had nine cities of more than 100,000 in 1860, where it had none in 1800. Starting in New England and Middle Atlantic states, then spreading into the Ohio/Erie corridor, the central core of American manufacturing was established. Urban industrial development would serve as a demographic magnet for migrants from both the American hinterland and Europe.

At the same time, the demographic structure of the South increasingly departed from the rest of the country. In response to the expansion of plantation crops, especially cotton, the number of slaves in the South grew from roughly 700,000 in 1800 to nearly 4 million at the start of the Civil War. Most of the increase was due to the internal growth of the slave population. Not only was the racial mix of the South decidedly different, the Southern states remained relatively nonurbanized with little manufacturing. Therefore, the region was largely unaffected by the rising European immigration of this period.

Migration and Economic Growth: 1860-1920. By the Civil War the broad contours of American demographics were well established.

There would be continued decline in fertility and mortality rates in most groups and across all regions. While these changing differentials between fertility and mortality shaped long-term growth, immigration, urbanization, and inter-regional migration shaped the U.S. demographic map until World War I.

U.S. fertility rates declined steadily in the 19th century. Women of the 17th century could expect on average 7.4 children; by 1860, on average 4.9 children. The rate plummeted still further to 2.8 children in the late 19th century. The population growth rate continued to increase in large part because of rising immigration. Although many immigrant groups had higher fertility rates when they arrived, they soon joined the native-born trend to control family size.

The health of most Americans continued to improve. At mid-century white male Americans could expect to live about 40 years if they survived birth; by 1920 it reached 56.3 years; for white women, the increase was from 43 years in 1850 to 58.5 in 1920. For African Americans life expectancy at birth ranged from 32 to 36 years as late as 1900. Mortality rates among Indians continued to rise until 1900. However, many women died during childbirth, and infant mortality remained high.

Throughout the 19th century, therefore, regional and urban-rural differentials in population growth were partly the result of differences in fertility and mortality. Migration, however, had a more immediate impact. The great migration west continued to century's end. California and the Pacific Northwest were the destinations for settlers from the 1840s and into the 20th century. After the 1880s much of the settlement in the western territories was a "filling-in" process, helped by railroad expansion. Roughly 2.25 million Americans moved to the Pacific Coast and Rocky Mountain regions between 1870 and 1910. The westward migration of the late 19th century came at the expense of areas settled before the Civil War. Those who left the Middle West were replaced in turn by immigrants from Europe.

The settlement of the West also brought with it urbanization. St. Louis, Omaha, and Kansas City on the eastern side of the great prairies; San Francisco, Portland, and Spokane on the west; and

Denver at the edge of the Rockies all served as "gateway" cities to the region. In 1870, two years after the completion of the transcontinental railroad, only 3 cities in the West had populations over 50,000; by 1910, there were 14.

Although the rate of urbanization declined steadily into the early 20th century, the absolute numbers were so very much larger that the demographic magnetism of America's cities hardly waned. The urbanized population rose from roughly 10 million in 1870 to nearly 55 million in 1920.

U.S. immigration in the 19th century followed a pronounced cyclical pattern, reflecting economic and political conditions in both the countries of origin and the United States. More than 33 million immigrants came to America between 1820 and 1920. Although opposition to unrestricted immigration dated back to the 1830s, in the closing decades of the century the native-born elite viewed this shift in ethnicity with growing alarm. The first targets of restriction were Asian immigrants. Then, in 1921, Congress restricted immigration to 3 percent of the numbers reported in the 1910 census. Much more aggressive, however, was the National Origins Act (1924), which established quotas favoring the "old" immigration (pre-1890) over the "new" immigration dominated by southern and eastern Europeans. The results were immediate. Only 164,000 immigrants arrived in 1924, and the era of unrestricted immigration was over forever.

Growth and Redistribution: 1920-2000. Immigration restriction was not the only important factor that highlighted the 1920s as a benchmark period in American demographic history. The 1920 census was the first to report that the majority of Americans resided in towns and cities, with 51.2 percent residing in settlements of more than 2,500 people.

The process of urbanization took on a new complexity after 1920. The manufacturing centers of the Northeast and the Ohio–Great Lakes industrial corridor reached the height of their economic power in the 1920s, but the long-run trend was toward the rise of "sunbelt" cities in Florida, Texas, California, and the Southwest. The rapid growth of Los Angeles was a harbinger of things to come. It grew from slightly more than 100,000 inhabitants in 1900 to 1.25 million in 1930 and then to 2.5 million by 1960.

Although by 1990 more than half the U.S. population lived in the largest 39 metropolitan areas, the urbanization process was not dominated solely by the growth of the largest cities. Between the 1920s and 1980s the number of communities in the 2,500 to 10,000 range roughly tripled; cities between 25,000 and 100,000 inhabitants attracted migrants in about equal proportion to the largest urban centers, due in large part to suburbanization. The fall of America's farming population continued through the 1980s.

The racial mix of America's urban population has changed profoundly since 1900. The great African-American migration really involved two redistribution processes that were not completely distinguishable. It was, in part, a migration to America's major cities. But the migration of African Americans to cities often reflected a rejection of life in the South as well. The attraction of employment opportunities during World War I began the modern movement out of the South in earnest. It accelerated in the 1940s and 1950s, with black Americans rapidly moving to cities in the North and West. In 1900 more than 90 percent of the African-American population resided in the South. By the 1970s more than 40 percent of black Americans lived either in the Northeast or North Central region, and slightly more than 50 percent remained in the South.

Over the 20th century, the population's decennial growth rate averaged about 14 percent, with the highest periods of growth coming in 1901-10 and in 1945-60. The surge in demographic growth in the post-1945 period was internally generated, primarily the result of a significant deviation from the long-term trends in declining fertility, lower marriage rates, and rising divorce. By the 1960s, these new trends slowed, but not before generating the most significant demographic phenomenon of the late 20th century—the "baby boom." The Depression and World War II had led many American couples to postpone having children, but in 1947 more than 3.8 million babies were born, nearly a million more than in 1945. The total number of children born would reach 4.3 million in 1957.

Even at the height of the baby boom, however, American couples did not return to the very large families. A lower average age of marriage, higher overall rates of marriage, and lower divorce rates all contributed further to the surge in fertility in the 1950s. After 1958, the birthrate dropped steadily until the mid-1970s when the number of births (3.6 million) equaled that of 1943. Because the nation's total population had grown sharply, the 1970s birthrate was only 14.8 per 1,000, the lowest in American history. Recently, the birthrate has risen slightly to 15.0 per 1,000 women.

The decline in fertility is but one of a number of revolutionary changes in the American household and family. More Americans live alone than ever before—more than a fifth of all households. Between 1870 and 1970 the percentage of marriages ended by divorce jumped from just over 5 to 44 percent. The number of unmarried couples residing together is at an all-time high, nearing 3 million. Nearly a third of all households are headed by women, double the percentage of 1950. These trends have led many observers to conclude that the family is facing a crisis of major proportions.

Another important aspect of America's changing demography is the general aging of the population. Perhaps most important are the implications on Social Security, health care, and consumption. The long-term trends of declining fertility and declining mortality also tend to propel America toward a more aged population. In 1920, only 4.7 percent of the population was over 65; presently the over-65 group is about 13 percent. Without a major change in fertility behavior, the trend toward an aging population is only likely to be offset by immigration. There are nearly 22 million foreign-born in America, by far the largest number in history, and many of them arrived after 1970, including millions of illegal immigrants, mostly from Latin America. The total numbers (both legal and illegal) rose slowly from about a million in the 1940s to 4.5 million (legal) arrivals in the 1970s. Starting in the late 1970s, however, arrivals accelerated rapidly; more than 7 million immigrants arrived in the 1980s, a number only rivaled by the 8.8 million who arrived in 1900-09.

Without exaggeration it can be said that the history of population change in America provides the essential canvas over which political, eco-nomic, and cultural histories are layered. The extraordinary changes that have occurred in the distribution and mix of the American population are truly impressive. If current immigration rates hold for the next decade, the U.S. population will grow to roughly 325 million by the year 2020. All evidence suggests that Americans will remain a highly mobile population and will overwhelmingly choose cities as the place of residence. Finally, the wide variation in household living patterns will persist well into the nation's future.

—JOHN SHARPLESS

See Also: African Americans; City in American History; Disease; Frontier in American History; Immigration; Slavery.

BIBLIOGRAPHY: Anderson, Margo J., *The American Census: A Social History* (Yale Univ. Press 1988); Thornton, Russell, *American Indian Holocaust and Survival: A Population History Since 1492* (Univ. of Oklahoma Press 1987); Wells, Robert V., *Uncle Sam's Family: Issues in and Perspectives on American Demographic History* (State Univ. of New York Press 1985); Wright, Russell O., *A Twentieth-Century History of United States Population* (Scarecrow Press 1996).

POPULISM, refers both to the People's party of the 1890s and a style of protest found throughout American history. The People's party was a movement of farmers, workers, and middle-class reformers who protested the growing inequality of wealth and political corruption in the Gilded Age. Several factors explain the rise of the People's party. The industrializing economy of the late 19th century expanded markets and allowed farmers access to new land. However, commodity prices declined during this period, which generally had a negative impact on farmers, especially those with debts. Falling prices for wheat, cotton, and livestock required indebted farmers to devote a greater percentage of the product of their labor to repaying fixed loans. As a result, many farmers throughout the country felt as though they were trapped in a vise. Conditions were especially bad for tenant farmers, white and black, in the South. To obtain the credit necessary to purchase seed and implements, tenant farmers turned to merchants, who lent money at high interest rates and secured their loans through liens on tenants' crops. Under the crop lien system, tenant farmers were unable to escape a vicious cycle of escalating indebtedness and misery. Farmers throughout the country complained of other economic problems such as excessive railroad rates, land monopoly, and middlemen.

By the late 1880s farmers' alliances had sprung up in thousands of rural communities throughout the United States. Through these alliances farm women and men articulated their economic grievances, and they discussed their belief that democracy was in grave danger. Alliance members criticized the monopolization of political office by the wealthy, arguing that legislation benefited the privileged classes. They contended that the "plain people" had been shut out of the political process.

As a result of mounting economic and political discontent, farmers' alliances in Kansas and Nebraska fielded their own candidates in the 1890 state elections. This led to the organization of the People's party and the nomination on July 4, 1892, of James B. Weaver of Iowa for president. The preamble to the party's "Omaha platform," written by Ignatius Donnelly, proclaimed a crisis in the nation's affairs and called on the common people to reclaim American democracy. The platform called for the nationalization of railroads, a system of government-funded credit, free coinage of silver, a graduated income tax, the direct election of senators, and the initiative and referendum. Farmers were the core constituency of the People's party, but labor leaders, wage workers, and middle-class reformers also supported the party. Weaver won 22 electoral votes.

Over the next four years, the People's party struggled to remain a viable political party. However, while the Populists had some electoral successes, they were unable to increase their momentum. Election laws made it difficult for third parties to do well in the United States. In addition, Populists were hampered by internal divisions about issues and strategies. By 1895 Populists had divided into two camps. The first group, known as "fusionists," advocated reducing the Omaha platform to the free coinage of silver and cooperating with the Democratic party. The second group, known as "mid-roaders," favored retaining the entire Omaha platform and regarded fusion as political suicide. In 1896 the De-

mocratic party nominated William Jennings Bryan for president, and the fusionists endorsed him. Using the fiery language of Populism, Bryan denounced monopolists, bankers, and corrupt politicians and called for "free silver" to restore prosperity. His Republican opponent, William McKinley, solemnly warned of the disastrous economic and moral consequences of a Bryan victory. McKinley outspent Bryan by a ratio of 20 to 1 and won the most intense battle for the White House since 1860.

In the 20th century the term "populist" has been applied to figures as diverse as Huey Long, George Wallace, and Ronald Reagan. What these and other "populists" share is a style of rhetoric that speaks in the name of the common people against a small minority that has illegitimately gained economic or political power. Some 20th-century populists have shared the People's party's emphasis on using the federal government to break up concentrations of wealth and political power. More often, however, modern populists have regarded the federal government with suspicion or disdain. Many 20th-century populists have advocated white supremacy and various conspiracy theories, some of which have been anti-Semitic. For the most part these styles of thought were muted or absent in the Populist movement of the 1890s.

—JEFFREY OSTLER

See Also: *Free Silver; Gilded Age; Political Parties.*
BIBLIOGRAPHY: Kazin, Michael, *The Populist Persuasion: An American History* (Basic Books 1995); McMath, Robert C., Jr., *American Populism: A Social History, 1877-1898* (Hill & Wang 1993).

■ **PORTER, KATHERINE ANNE, (1890-1980),** author known for her short stories. She was born in Indian Creek, Texas. Her collections, *Flowering Judas* (1930), *Pale Horse, Pale Rider* (1939), and *The Leaning Tower* (1944), earned her great popularity and critical acclaim. She also wrote several novels including *Ship of Fools* (1962). Her *Collected Stories* (1965) won the National Book Award and the Pulitzer Prize.

See Also: *Short Story.*

■ **PORT ROYAL EXPERIMENT,** Civil War program in which former slaves successfully worked land abandoned by white owners. Early in the war (1861), Union troops liberated the Sea Islands off the coast of South Carolina and their main harbor, Port Royal. The whites on the islands fled, leaving behind 10,000 African-American slaves. Several private Northern charities stepped in to help the African Americans become self-sufficient. The result was a model of what Reconstruction could have been. The African Americans demonstrated their ability to work the land efficiently and live independently of white control. They assigned themselves daily tasks for cotton growing and spent their extra time cultivating their own crops, hunting, fishing, and enjoying life as they saw fit. By selling their surplus crops, the African Americans acquired small amounts of property. The Port Royal Experiment offered clear proof that African Americans could handle freedom responsibly. Unfortunately, at war's end (1865) Pres. Andrew Johnson ended the experiment, returning the land to its previous white owners.

See Also: Reconstruction.

■ **PORTSMOUTH PEACE CONFERENCE (1905),** peace talks held in Portsmouth, New Hampshire, to bring about an end to the Russo-Japanese War. Organized by Pres. Theodore Roosevelt, the conference attempted to restore a balance of power in Asia between Imperial Russia and Japan yet heavily favored Japanese interests. After four weeks of deliberation, the Treaty of Portsmouth was signed on Sept. 5, 1905. For his part in the conference, Roosevelt received the Nobel Peace Prize in 1906.

See Also: Roosevelt, Theodore.

■ **POSTAL SYSTEM,** arrangement for transmitting mail. In colonial America postal service began in Massachusetts (1639) and was rapidly expanded under royal control. Benjamin Franklin served as postmaster general under British rule and then became America's first postmaster general (1775-76). The United States Post Office was created by Congress in 1789 under Article I, Section 8, of the U.S. Constitution. Jobs were often given out by the president and constituted a major source of political patronage until the late 19th century.

Improvements in service reflected developments in technology. For example, the postage stamp was invented by an English bureaucrat, Rowland Hill, in 1840 as a means of reducing fraud by requiring prepayment. The British post office also hoped to lower rates, increase usage, and make more money. American stamps were first used in 1847.

The Pony Express was introduced in 1860 to carry mail on horseback from Missouri to California in 10 days. However, it lasted only 18 months because of the Civil War and the completion of a transcontinental telegraph. The railroad and the introduction of airmail in 1918 brought revolutionary changes in the speed of delivery.

The Post Office Department was replaced in 1971 by a nonprofit corporation subsidized by Congress but designed to become self-sufficient. The United States Postal Service is an independent agency of the United States Government administered by a board of governors, a majority of whom are nominated by the president. The U.S. Postal Service has experienced considerable competition from commercial services. However, it has become competitive through automation (the ZIP code system was introduced in 1963) and the introduction of new services such as overnight and priority mail. Despite frequent increases in the cost of first class mail (32 cents in 1996), rates in the United States are less expensive than those found in most parts of the world.

See Also: Franklin, Benjamin; Pony Express.
BIBLIOGRAPHY: Browne, Christopher, *Getting the Message: The Story of the Post Office* (Sutton 1993); Cushing, Marshall, *The Story of Our Post Office,* 2 vols. (Gordon Press 1993); Graham, Richard, *United States Postal History* (Linn's Stamp News 1990).

■ **POSTMODERNISM,** post–World War II cultural movement, especially in literature, criticism, and architecture. As the name implies, postmodernism is often defined in relation to the tenets of modernism, particularly as a reaction against the concentration on spare form and unadorned technique practiced by many modernists. Postmodernism was brought before the public eye by French literary and social critics such as Jean-Francois Lyotard and Jean Baudrillard. Postmodern theorists accept the multiplicity of meanings that appears characteristic of late 20th-century culture and encourages the attempt to express this breadth of perspective and experience. These perspectives may include the references to the past that the modernists eschewed in their own works, but such references are often used in an eclectic way. American fiction writers such as Kurt Vonnegut, Thomas Pynchon, John Barth, Grace Paley, and Ishmael Reed often employ a fragmented and open-ended narrative to capture the unresolved quality of contemporary life; this focus on narrative as a means of both understanding and constructing society and culture is central to postmodern thought. In *Complexity and Contradiction in Architecture* (1966), architect Robert Venturi questioned whether the austere emphasis on form of the modernists adequately expressed the complex culture of the late 20th century. Postmodern architects such as Michael Graves and Robert A. M. Stern quote both historical academic styles and the vernacular of the contemporary scene in their designs.

See Also: Modernism.

BIBLIOGRAPHY: Jameson, Frederic, *Postmodernism, or, The Cultural Logic of Late Capitalism* (Duke Univ. Press 1991); Jencks, Charles, *Post-modernism: The New Classicism in Art and Architecture* (Rizzoli 1987).

■ **POTATOES,** one of the most important of the food crops indigenous to the Americas. Several thousand varieties were domesticated by the Indian peoples of the Andes, from where they spread northward. Columbus noted the cultivation of the "batata" by the Tainos of Hispaniola, and he carried home yellow or "sweet" potatoes. "White" potatoes were first introduced into Europe by veterans of Pizarro's conquest of Peru in the 1530s. Within a few decades, potatoes were being grown by European farmers as feed for livestock. Walter Raleigh introduced white potatoes to Ireland in the late 1500s, and they became the staple crop of the Irish peasantry. Likewise, potatoes provided the margin between famine and subsistence for poor farmers throughout northern Eurasia. They also provided the raw material for the production of vodka.

Several varieties of sweet potatoes were cultivated by Indians in North America and were quickly adopted by southern colonists, but white potatoes were unknown until introduced by Irish immigrants in the 18th century. By the time of the American Revolution they were a common field crop but still considered fit only for livestock and the lower classes. Potatoes entered the American diet in the 19th century, particularly after scientist Luther Burbank developed the starchy "Idaho" potato in the 1870s. Today potato cultivation is commercially important in northern agricultural regions such as Maine, Idaho, and Alaska.

See Also: Agriculture; Food in American History; New World Crops.

BIBLIOGRAPHY: Salaman, Redcliffe N., *The History and Social Influence of the Potato* (Cambridge Univ. Press 1985).

■ **POTOMAC RIVER,** 290-mile–long river flowing southeast from western Maryland to the Chesapeake Bay. As it nears the Chesapeake it forms the border between Washington, D.C., and Virginia. In 1608 English colonist John Smith recorded the river's Powhatan name as Patawomeck. During the 17th and 18th centuries English colonists established tobacco plantations below the river's falls, which are located upstream from Washington. In 1828 the Chesapeake and Ohio Canal permitted navigation as far upstream as Cumberland, Maryland. In 1929 the George Washington Memorial Parkway was begun along the river's bank, which continues to serve as a recreational area and wildlife refuge.

■ **POTSDAM CONFERENCE (1945),** meeting near Berlin, Germany, between U.S. Pres. Harry Truman, Soviet leader Joseph Stalin, and British Prime Minister Winston Churchill (replaced by Clement Attlee) from July 16 to August 2, after the defeat of Germany in World War II. They decided that Germany would be divided into four zones, but Stalin's demands for huge reparations were rebuffed. Britain and the United States, which had just then successfully tested the atomic bomb, issued the "Potsdam Declaration" to Japan, demanding unconditional surrender.

See Also: Truman, Harry S.; World War II.

■ **POUND, EZRA (1885-1972),** poet. Pound was born in Hailey, Idaho, and graduated from Hamilton College in 1905. After receiving an M.A. from the University of Pennsylvania in 1906, he traveled through Spain, Italy, and France before settling in London. His first volumes of poetry were published during this time, including *A Lume Spento* (1908), *Personae* (1909), *Exultations* (1909), *Provença* (1910), and *Canzoni* (1911). In 1912 *Ripostes* was published, one of the earliest collections of poetry in which each entire poem describes a single image. Pound also edited a volume of imagist poetry, *Des Imagistes*, in 1914. Pound wrote *Hugh Selwyn Mauberly* (1920), in which he expressed his disillusionment with World War I. In 1920 Pound moved to Paris and in 1924 to Rapallo, Italy. He became intrigued with Mussolini's fascism and during World War II gave propaganda broadcasts over Italian radio. After the war he was charged with treason and committed to a sanitarium. His *Pisan Cantos* from this period were awarded the Bollingen Prize in 1948.

See Also: Poetry.

■ **POWDERLY, TERENCE VINCENT (1849-1924),** labor leader. Born in Carbondale, Pennsylvania, he went to work as a railroad laborer at 13. In 1866 Powderly became an apprentice machinist, a trade he would follow until 1877. He joined the Machinists and Blacksmiths Union in 1871 and was inducted into the Noble Order of the Knights of Labor (K of L) five years later. He rose up through the ranks of the K of L until, in 1879, he was elected grand worthy foreman, a position he held until 1893. A man of many contradictions, Powderly discouraged political movements within the K of L but was elected mayor of Scranton, Pennsylvania, on the Greenback Labor ticket, serving three two-year terms (1878-84). Powderly was head of the K of L during its peak years in the early 1880s. The organization was greatly influenced by his vision of a "cooperative commonwealth," but, when it later went into decline and was divided by factionalism, Powderly was ousted from its leadership (1893). He went on to serve as U.S. commissioner of immigration (1897-1902) and held several appointments within the U.S. Department of Labor.

See Also: Greenback Labor Party; Knights of Labor; Labor Movement.

BIBLIOGRAPHY: Falzone, Vincent J., *Terence V. Powderly, Middle Class Reformer* (Univ. Press of America 1978).

■ **POWELL, ADAM CLAYTON, JR. (1908-72),** pastor and political leader. Born in New Haven, Connecticut, he was early influenced by Marcus Garvey and, like Garvey, made Harlem his own. Stylish, formidably charismatic, and persuasive, Powell in 1931 succeeded his father as minister of a Harlem church. In the midst of the Depression, Powell organized demonstrations against businesses that did not hire African-American workers, and he started a soup kitchen and other relief efforts. In 1941 he was elected to the New York City Council and in 1945 became a U.S. representative, an office he held until being defeated in 1970. Powell chaired the House Committee on Education and Labor from 1960 to 1967 and, despite one of the highest absentee records in Congress, authored more than 50 pieces of social legislation. His later career was marked by legal embroilments, including criminal contempt of court in New York and congressional charges of misuse of public funds that led to his expulsion from the House for a time. Powell nevertheless remained popular among his constituents.

See Also: African Americans; Civil Rights Movement.

■ **POWELL, COLIN LUTHER, JR. (1937-),** military leader. Born in New York City, Powell entered the military through a ROTC commission as a sec-

Gen. Colin L. Powell, chairman of the Joint Chiefs of Staff, tours an American installation in 1991 during the Persian Gulf War.

ond lieutenant in the army. He advanced steadily through the ranks, serving with distinction in Vietnam and in the 1970s becoming a top U.S. commander in Europe. From 1982 to 1989 he served in the Reagan administration, first as military assistant to the deputy secretary of defense and then as deputy assistant for national security affairs to the president. Pres. George Bush made Powell a four-star general and appointed him chairman of the Joint Chiefs of Staff for two terms (1989-93) at which time Powell achieved national recognition during the Persian Gulf War. After retiring from the military, Powell was frequently mentioned as a possible candidate for a high elective office.

See Also: African Americans; Persian Gulf War.

■ **POWELL, JOHN WESLEY (1834-1902),** American explorer, geologist, and ethnologist. Born in Mount Morris, New York, Powell fought for the Union forces during the Civil War, losing his right arm at the battle of Shiloh and earning promotion to the rank of major. After the war he turned his interest in natural history into a full-time pursuit, gaining government sponsorship for expeditions down the Green River and the Grand Canyon of the Colorado River in 1869 and 1871. A self-taught geologist and ethnologist, Powell conducted the official survey of the Colorado Plateau region. Powell was a noted public lands reformer and in his 1878 *Arid Lands Report* he argued for the scientific and ordered disposal of western lands. He helped organize the U.S. Geological Survey in 1879 and headed the agency from 1881 to 1894. Powell also directed the Bureau of American Ethnography. Committed to the rational use of resources, Powell's ideas led to the passage of the Newlands Reclamation Act in 1902, which set the course for federal irrigation development.

See Also: Exploration and Discovery.

BIBLIOGRAPHY: Stegner, Wallace, *Beyond the 100th Meridian: John Wesley Powell and the Second Opening of the West* (Houghton Mifflin 1954).

■ **POWELL, LEWIS FRANKLIN, JR. (1907-),** associate justice of the U.S. Supreme Court (1972-87). He was born in Suffolk, Virginia, and educated at Washington and Lee and Harvard. Powell became an important figure in Richmond, Virginia, legal and civic circles, leading efforts to desegregate the

John Wesley Powell (right) led exploration trips of the Colorado River and in 1879 became director of the Smithsonian Institution's Bureau of Ethnology.

city's schools as chairman of the Richmond school board (1952-61). Appointed to the Supreme Court by Pres. Richard M. Nixon, Powell was a moderate and nonideological justice well-liked by his colleagues. He occupied the center of the Court and frequently provided the decisive vote in closely divided cases.

See Also: Supreme Court.

■ **POWELL V. ALABAMA (1932),** the first of the "Scottsboro Boys" cases decided by the U.S. Supreme Court. In a 1931 case that drew national publicity and became a symbol of racial injustice in the South, nine African-American youths were charged with raping two white women. The defendants were represented in court by two local lawyers appointed by the judge on the day their trials began. Eight were convicted after brief trials, and seven convictions were upheld by the Alabama Supreme Court. The U.S. Supreme Court ruled (7-2) that the 14th Amendment's due process clause required the states to guarantee defendants a fair trial, and the lack of adequate counsel denied the defendants that right in this case. The Court did not rule that all criminal defendants must be represented by counsel; it determined that an attorney must be provided if lack of counsel would result in an unfair trial.

See Also: Due Process of Law; Supreme Court.

■ **POWERS, HIRAM (1805-73),** sculptor. Born in Woodstock, Vermont, Powers moved to Washington, D.C., in 1834. In 1835, he sculpted the likeness of Pres. Andrew Jackson, and this led to other commissions. Despite his success, Powers moved permanently to Italy in 1837. Powers's best-known work is *The Greek Slave* (1843), which toured the United States in 1847. He won commissions for the statues of Benjamin Franklin (1862) and Thomas Jefferson (1863) in the U.S. Capitol building in Washington, D.C.

See Also: Sculpture.

■ **POWHATAN CONFEDERACY,** related Indian tribes that inhabited tidewater Virginia when English colonization began. For centuries before the founding of Jamestown in 1607 most of these Algonquian-speaking people (including the Appamattuck, Pamunkey, Rappahannock, Mattaponi, Nansemond, Chickahominy, and others) lived in scores of towns south of the Potomac River, within the coastal plain. Each primary town along the Rappahannock, York, and James rivers was controlled by a chief, or *weroance*. In the late 16th century, a Pamunkey named Powhatan emerged as a paramount chief, inheriting control of six chiefdoms and conquering others. When English settlers reached Jamestown, Powhatan sought to draw them into his expanding empire, at one point holding hostage their leader, John Smith. (Much later, after Powhatan's daughter Pocahontas had married Englishman John Rolfe and created a stir in England, Smith would claim she had saved his life, but she was a young girl at the time and the tale is almost certainly false.)

After Powhatan's death in 1618 his paramount chiefdom was soon controlled by his younger brother, Opechancanough, who hoped to remove European planters encroaching on Indian farmland. On Mar. 22, 1622, his warriors attacked the English homesteads, killing 377 settlers, a quarter of the colonial population. Survivors of the sudden uprising, reinforced from England, waged a long and successful war of reprisal. Outnumbered, Opechancanough agreed to peace in 1632, but on Apr. 18, 1644, he launched another major attack, killing about 400. The old leader was captured and killed by the English (who forced a treaty in 1646 demanding symbolic annual tribute). One of Opechancanough's descendants, Pamunkey queen Cockacoeske, tried to renew the paramount chiefdom in the next generation, but epidemics and warfare had decimated the smaller groups. Descendants of the larger groups still live in the tidewater area. A few Pamunkey and Mattaponi families continue to reside on the remnants of two reservations set aside in colonial times.

—PETER H. WOOD

See Also: Indians of North America; Jamestown Settlement; Pocahontas; Smith, John.

BIBLIOGRAPHY: Rountree, Helen C., *Pocahontas's People: The Powhatan Indians of Virginia Through Four Centuries* (Univ. of Oklahoma Press 1990); Rountree, Helen C., *The Powhatan Indians of Virginia: Their Traditional Culture* (Univ. of Oklahoma Press 1989).

■ **PRAYING INDIANS (1651-76),** term given to Christian Indians in early New England. Puritan missionary John Eliot began preaching to New England's Indians in 1646, and, in 1651, he established the first "praying town" at Natick, Massachusetts. Eliot believed that Indians could be saved spiritually only by "reducing them to civility." The Indian converts were governed by a strict code that required them to adopt English manners and customs. As Puritan settlement advanced, many Indians in Massachusetts Bay were forced into the "praying towns" to avoid the militant Puritans. Each village had a school that instructed in elementary subjects and doctrine, taught the English language, and trained the Indians in English handicrafts. By 1674 there were

14 villages containing more than 4,000 converts in Massachusetts. During King Philip's War (1675-76) colonists took out their anger toward the rebelling Narragansetts and Wampanoags by attacking their Christian Indian neighbors.

See Also: Eliot, John; Indians of North America; King Philip's War.

■ **PREPAREDNESS MOVEMENT (1913-16),** peacetime campaign to establish a volunteer army reserve program. Concerned about the state of U.S. military readiness, Army Chief of Staff Leonard Wood initiated a series of summer camp programs designed to encourage public awareness of and involvement in national preparedness for war. Wood's principal aim was to enlist support for a genuine army reserve, rather than relying solely on the National Guard, from which the army could draw a cadre of trained officer candidates. Also known as the Plattsburgh Idea, by 1916 Wood's camps had attracted more than 10,000 volunteers across the country, which encouraged Congress to study army proposals for universal military training. Although this was not adopted, the movement did prompt Congress to enact the National Defense Act of 1916, which gave the army more control over the National Guard and provided for a system of national mobilization.

See Also: Plattsburgh Idea.

BIBLIOGRAPHY: Kriedberg, Marvin A., and Merton G. Henry, *History of Military Mobilization in the United States Army, 1775-1945* (Dept. of the Army 1955).

■ **PRESBYTERIAN CHURCH,** Protestant church governed by presbyters and committed to Calvinist doctrine. As a system of representative church government, authority lies with the presbyter, a court comprised of clergy and elders who have equal status. French Huguenots brought the system to America in the 17th century, but it did not succeed until the arrival of the Scots-Irish.

Presbyterian missionary Francis Makemie (1658-1708), considered the father of American Presbyterianism, came to Maryland in 1683. He appealed for additional missionaries, and by 1706 he formed the Philadelphia Presbytery. As Scots-Irish immigration increased so did the Presbyterian numbers. The Great Awakening in the 1730s and 1740s caused a temporary schism between Old Side (those who opposed evangelicalism) and New Side (those who advocated it). Gilbert Tennent espoused evangelicalism but later worked to unite the two sides. The College of New Jersey (Princeton) was founded in 1746 by New Siders to train ministers. By the time of the Revolution, Presbyterianism was second only to Congregationalism in numbers.

During the 19th century, Presbyterians proved successful on the frontier, but their strict doctrine and polity and high educational standards for the clergy hindered them in comparison to the Baptists and Methodists. In 1801, Presbyterians and Congregationalists agreed to a Plan of Union for cooperation on the frontier. The plan favored the former as many Congregational churches became Presbyterian. However, this caused a schism between the Old School and New School. Then, before the Civil War, issues over slavery, theology, and relations with other Christian denominations further divided Presbyterians. During the 20th century, major Presbyterian bodies have consolidated and become tightly organized, the largest being the Presbyterian Church (U.S.A.).

—NANCY M. GODLESKI

See Also: Great Awakening; Religion.

BIBLIOGRAPHY: Schmidt, Leigh Eric, *Holy Fairs: Scottish Communions and American Revivals in the Early Modern Period* (Princeton Univ. Press 1989); Trinterud, Leonard J., *Forming of an American Tradition* (Westminster 1949).

■ **PRESCOTT, WILLIAM H. (1796-1859),** historian of Spain. Born in Salem, Massachusetts, Prescott attended Harvard University between 1811 and 1814. Despite an accident that left him almost blind, Prescott persisted in his study of Spanish history. He worked for 12 years to complete his first work, the three-volume *History of the Reign of Ferdinand and Isabella the Catholic* (1838). He then wrote his masterpiece, the *History of the Conquest of Mexico* (1843), and the *History of the Reign of Philip II* (1855-58).

See Also: History.

■ **PRESIDENTIAL ELECTIONS.** Presidential elections and their procedures are established by Article II of the Constitution. The president is elected to a four-year term by an indirect process: the selection in the separate states of slates of "presidential electors" equal to the number of the state's senators and representatives; the chosen electors, known collectively as the electoral college, in turn cast ballots that are tallied by a joint session of Congress.

The authors of the Constitution devised this system in order to provide a check on the popular will, allowing states to determine the manner in which presidential electors were selected. Originally, many states authorized selection by elected representatives, but since 1824 all the states have utilized popular election by the people. Thirteen times in American history (1844, 1856, 1860, 1880, 1884, 1892, 1912, 1916, 1948, 1960, 1968, 1992, 1996) the electoral college has delivered majorities for candidates who received only a plurality of the popular vote; in one election (1888) the incumbent president won the popular vote but lost in the electoral college.

In three elections (1800, 1824, 1876), no candidate received a majority vote in the electoral college, and following constitutional procedures the election was decided in the House of Representatives. In the first instance the problem resulted from the constitutional provision that the candidate receiving the majority of votes became president, and the runner-up became vice president; but since the electors who supported Thomas Jefferson cast all their ballots for Jefferson and his running mate Aaron Burr they unintentionally created a tie and forced the election into the House. The 12th Amendment, establishing separate ballots for president and vice president, was ratified in time for the next election. In the other two cases (John Quincy Adams in 1825, Rutherford B. Hayes in 1877) the House voted in favor of a candidate who had lost the popular vote.

Historians have identified a relatively small number of presidential elections that signaled the realignment of popular sentiment and party organization. Such "critical elections" took place in 1800, which established the precedent of a peaceful and orderly transition from one political party to another; in 1828, which heralded the democratization of the electoral process and ushered in the Jacksonian party competition between Democrats and Whigs; in 1860, which marked the collapse of the old parties and the rise of the Re-

publicans as the party of industrializing America; in 1896, when the Democrats failed to put together a farm-labor coalition and shrank to the status of a regional party based in the South; in 1932, when the Democrats succeeded in building what became known as the "New Deal coalition," which dominated national politics for the subsequent three decades; and in 1968, when the Republicans broke the Democratic lock on the "solid South" and became the majority party in presidential politics.

1789. George Washington was unanimously elected the first president of the United States by the electors of the 10 states participating (New York could not agree on electoral procedures; North Carolina and Rhode Island had not yet ratified the Constitution). Washington's 69 electoral votes far outdistanced John Adams, who became vice president.

1792. Washington was unanimously reelected, but an opposition had coalesced around Thomas Jefferson, later to be known as the Democratic-Republican party.

1796. Washington declined to run for a third term, setting a precedent that lasted until Franklin D. Roosevelt's run in 1940. Federalist Vice Pres. John Adams defeated Democratic-Republican Thomas Jefferson, but Jefferson became vice president, the first and only time that the president and vice president have been from different political parties.

1800. Democratic-Republican Jefferson won over Adams, plagued by ideological splits among the Federalists; votes for Jefferson and his running mate Aaron Burr were tied in the electoral college, throwing the election to the House of Representatives, where Federalists attempted to win Burr's election; Jefferson was finally elected on the 36th ballot. The 12th Amendment, requiring separate ballots for president and vice president, took effect before the next election.

1804. Jefferson, benefiting from national prosperity and expansion (Louisiana Purchase, 1803), overwhelmingly defeated Federalist Charles C. Pinckney.

1808. Democratic-Republican James Madison, a fellow Virginian tapped by Jefferson, won over dissident party member James Monroe and Federalist Pinckney.

1812. The War of 1812 with Britain dominated the election campaign, which the renominated Madison won over Monroe, nominated by antiwar Democratic-Republicans and endorsed by antiwar Federalists.

1816. With the endorsement of Madison, James Monroe won easily and continued the hold of Virginians on the presidency; Federalist-supported Rufus King finished a distant second.

1820. Monroe was easily reelected in the only uncontested presidential contest in American history; one electoral vote went to John Quincy Adams.

1824. John Quincy Adams and Andrew Jackson were the main candidates in a crowded presidential field; Jackson led Adams in the popular vote, but because no candidate had an electoral majority the election was decided in the House of Representatives. Henry Clay, the third-leading candidate, switched his support to Adams, assuring his victory. Jackson claimed a "corrupt bargain" when Clay subsequently became secretary of state.

1828. Democratic-Republicans split into two factions; the National Republicans nominated Adams; Democrats nominated Andrew Jackson, who ran the first populist campaign in American history and won the election handily.

1832. Jackson ran for a second term against his old opponent Henry Clay in which the major issue was Jackson's opposition and Clay's support for the recharter of the Bank of the United States; Jackson was overwhelmingly reelected.

1836. The newly organized Whig party failed to approve a national nominee, splitting their votes ineffectually among several regional candidates, and the election was won by Democrat Vice Pres. Martin Van Buren.

1840. Having learned their lesson, Whigs united behind war hero William Henry Harrison who opposed incumbent Van Buren. Although the popular vote was close, Harrison won easily in the electoral college but died shortly after his inauguration and was succeeded in office by John Tyler.

1844. Democrats turned away from Van Buren and nominated little-known James K. Polk, while Whigs chose Henry Clay rather than President Tyler, who became the first president not to be renominated. Polk won narrowly and led the nation into the Mexican War.

1848. Mexican War hero Zachary Taylor received the Whig nomination; Polk chose not to run, and Democrats nominated Lewis Cass. Dissident antislavery Democrats and Whigs backed Martin Van Buren as Free Soil candidate; Van Buren divided the Democratic vote and Taylor won the election.

1852. Whigs turned from Millard Fillmore, who became president after Taylor's death in 1850, and nominated Gen. Winfield Scott, another Mexican War hero, to run against Democrat Franklin Pierce, a New Hampshire senator who endorsed the Compromise of 1850 and won the election.

1856. As the slavery question became more intense, the Democrats nominated the uncontroversial James Buchanan, while the new Republican party chose western explorer John C. Frémont and the Know-Nothings nominated former President Fillmore. Sweeping the South and winning some other key states, Buchanan took the election.

1860. The election campaign reflected the growing divisions in the country over slavery. The Republicans nominated Abraham Lincoln, while

Republican Pres. Abraham Lincoln led the Union throughout the Civil War.

the Democrats put up Stephen A. Douglas, who had alienated the South by rejecting a proslavery constitution for Kansas. Southern Democrats nominated John C. Breckinridge while border state Democrats ran John Bell. Although Lincoln received substantially less than a majority, he swept the North and dominated the electoral college vote. The election led directly to Southern secession.

1864. The three-year Civil War dominated the election. Democrats nominated former Union Gen. George B. McClellan who pledged to stop the war, but a string of victories helped Lincoln win easily. He was assassinated less than two months into his second term.

1868. Republicans abandoned incumbent Andrew Johnson, just acquitted of impeachment charges, and nominated war hero Ulysses S. Grant; Democrats nominated lackluster Horatio Seymour. Grant won convincingly, bolstered by African-American votes in the South.

1872. Despite administration corruption scandals, Republicans renominated incumbent Grant, who defeated newspaper editor Horace Greeley, the candidate of both Democrats and reformist Liberal Republicans.

1876. Democrat Samuel Tilden received more popular votes than Republican nominee Rutherford B. Hayes, but the Republican-controlled Congress challenged electoral votes from three southern states, and Tilden failed to win an electoral majority. A congressional Electoral Commission (eight Republicans, seven Democrats) voted along party lines to award the election to Hayes. Democrats protested but finally accepted when Republicans pledged noninterference in the South. After his inauguration Hayes ordered federal troops from the South, effectively ending Reconstruction.

1880. Hayes declined to run for a second term and Republicans nominated (on the 36th ballot) James A. Garfield, who narrowly defeated Democratic challenger Winfield Hancock and two minor-party candidates.

1884. In a campaign noted for personal invective, Democrat Grover Cleveland, backed by Republican "Mugwump" reformers, defeated Republican James G. Blaine and candidates of the Prohibition and Greenback Labor parties.

1888. Easily renominated, Cleveland supported a lower tariff and won the popular vote by a thin margin but lost in the electoral college to Republican Benjamin Harrison, strongly backed by business interests favoring higher tariffs.

1892. In a rematch, Republican President Harrison squared off against Democrat Cleveland, with the tariff again the primary campaign issue. The People's party (Populists) fielded a surprisingly strong candidate, James B. Weaver, who received more than a million votes. Cleveland won the electoral vote easily.

1896. With the nation mired in depression, the economy dominated the campaign. Republican William McKinley defeated Democrat William Jennings Bryan, who failed to unite the northern and southern wings of the party.

1900. In the wake of a revived economy and the stunning U.S. success in the Spanish-American War, the Republicans renominated McKinley, who defeated Bryan in a rematch.

1904. Theodore Roosevelt, who succeeded to the presidency when McKinley was assassinated in 1901, was nominated by Republicans; winning the support of both conservatives and progressives, he triumphed over Democrat Alton B. Parker and Socialist Eugene V. Debs.

1908. Roosevelt declined to run and Republicans nominated his hand-picked choice, Sec. of War William H. Taft, who turned back the challenges of Democrat Bryan (his third run) and Socialist Debs (his second).

1912. Republicans split into conservative and progressive factions, the first renominating incumbent Taft, the second (known as the Progressive or Bull Moose ticket) Theodore Roosevelt. Republican disarray allowed Democrat Woodrow Wilson to win the election handily with nearly five times as many electoral votes as Taft. Socialist Debs, in his third run, tallied nearly a million votes.

1916. Democrat Wilson, reminding voters he had kept the country out of the European war, won reelection by a thin margin over Republican candidate Charles Evans Hughes, a Supreme Court justice supported by Theodore Roosevelt.

1920. Republican Warren G. Harding, promising the war-weary nation a "return to normalcy," won a landslide victory over Democrat James M. Cox in the first election in which women were allowed to vote.

1924. Democrats, split between urban northeastern and rural southern and western interests, nominated John W. Davis after a long convention fight. Republican Calvin Coolidge, who succeeded to the presidency when Harding died in 1923, carried the banner for Republicans and won easily over Davis and Progressive party candidate Robert M. La Follette, who accumulated the largest third-party vote to that time.

1928. Riding an economic boom, Republicans nominated Herbert Hoover after Coolidge declined to run. Democrat Alfred E. Smith, a Roman Catholic, lost overwhelmingly in the electoral college after a campaign notable for its anti-Catholic campaigning.

1932. Three years into the Great Depression the Republicans renominated Hoover. With no agenda for economic recovery he was outpolled nearly three to two by Franklin D. Roosevelt, who put together a winning national coalition for the Democrats.

1936. With the economy showing signs of recovery, Roosevelt campaigned for New Deal measures against Republican nominee Alfred M. Landon, who pledged to balance the budget. FDR won all the states except Vermont and New Hampshire, producing the most lopsided electoral vote since 1820.

1940. With European war looming, Roosevelt broke with tradition and ran for a third term; Republicans nominated New Yorker Wendell L. Wilkie, who campaigned vigorously but unsuccessfully on a program similar to Roosevelt's.

1944. Republican Thomas E. Dewey charged Roosevelt with errors in war policy, but with Allied victories and the hope of a quick end to the war, voters returned the incumbent for a fourth term.

1948. Democrat Harry Truman, who became president when FDR died in 1945, was opposed by Republican Dewey as well as progressive Democrat Henry Wallace and segregationist Strom Thurmond. Despite the Democrat division, Truman won in an upset.

1952. Preoccupied with the Korean War, Truman declined to run again and Democrats nominated Adlai E. Stevenson. Republicans chose World War II hero Dwight D. Eisenhower, who won the election with a pledge to end the war.

1956. In a rematch Eisenhower, benefiting from the end of the Korean War and a robust economy, beat Stevenson even more convincingly.

1960. Vice Pres. Richard M. Nixon received the Republican nomination, while Democrats chose charismatic John F. Kennedy. The campaign featured the first televised debates between presidential candidates, which boosted Kennedy, who became the first Roman Catholic president.

1964. Democrat Lyndon B. Johnson, having succeeded to the presidency after Kennedy's assassination in 1963, was opposed by Republican conservative Barry Goldwater. Portraying his opponent as an extremist, and promoting his Great Society programs, Johnson won in a landslide, carrying all but six southern and western states.

1968. Growing opposition to the Vietnam War forced Johnson to withdraw, and Democrats nominated Vice Pres. Hubert H. Humphrey to run against Republican Richard M. Nixon, who won a narrow victory over Humphrey and American Independent party nominee George Wallace of Alabama, who carried the deep South.

1972. Nixon, running for reelection against liberal Democrat George McGovern, won the election in a landslide after a campaign that featured the Watergate break-in, which Nixon attempted to cover up, ultimately forcing his resignation in 1974.

1976. Republicans nominated Gerald Ford, who had assumed the presidency when Nixon resigned. Democrats chose former Georgia governor Jimmy Carter, who ran as an honest outsider and won a close election.

1980. Incumbent Carter was saddled with economic problems and the continuing hostage crisis in Iran. He was crushed in the electoral vote by telegenic Republican conservative Ronald Reagan.

1984. Reagan, with a booming economy (despite record budget deficits), won a landslide victory over Democrat Walter Mondale and running mate Geraldine Ferraro, the first woman nominated for vice president by a major party.

1988. Republican Vice Pres. George Bush won easily over Massachusetts Democrat Michael Dukakis, who failed to capture the imagination of voters.

1992. Democrats nominated Bill Clinton, personable and telegenic governor of Arkansas. Despite alleged personal scandals, he defeated incumbent Bush, crippled by the third-party candidacy of H. Ross Perot, who attracted 19 percent of the popular vote, the largest in American history for a third party.

1996. Clinton, riding the wave of a booming economy and brushing aside continued allegations of scandal, won decisively over Republican nominee Robert Dole and third-party candidate Perot, whose vote total dropped drastically.

See Also: *Democratic Party; President of the United States; Republican Party; Third Parties.*

BIBLIOGRAPHY: Congressional Quarterly, *Presidential Elections* (Congressional Quarterly 1995); Dover, E. D., *Presidential Elections in the Television Age: 1960-1992* (Praeger 1994); Schlesinger, Arthur M., Jr., ed., *History of American Presidential Elections, 1789-1968,* 4 vols. (Chelsea House 1971); Wright, Russell O., *Presidential Elections in the United States: A Statistical History, 1860-1992* (McFarland 1995).

■ **PRESIDENTIAL SUCCESSION,** procedure specified by law for selecting a new president when the incumbent dies, resigns, is impeached, or becomes disabled. Article II, Section 1, of the Constitution states the vice president will assume the duties of president if a vacancy occurs, and eight vice presidents have become chief executive in this way. Article II also directs Congress to create a further line of succession. The first succession act (1792) placed the president pro tempore of the Senate and the Speaker of the House in line after the vice president. Congress amended the law in 1886 to place the cabinet secretaries in line after the vice president in order of the creation of their departments. The law was amended again in 1947 to favor elected officials by making the Speaker of the House third in line and the president pro tempore fourth. The 25th Amendment (1967) allows for a new president to appoint a new vice president subject to confirmation by Congress and authorizes the vice president to become acting president should the president become temporarily disabled.

■ **PRESIDENT OF THE UNITED STATES,** the head of state and chief executive officer of the federal government. He or she must be a natural-born citizen of the United States, must have resided in the country for at least 14 years prior to his or her election, and must be at least 35 years old. The 22nd Amendment to the Constitution (1951) prohibits any person from being elected president more than two times. The president may be removed from office for "treason, bribery, or other high crimes and misdemeanors" by a majority vote of impeachment in the House of Representatives and a two-thirds vote of conviction in the Senate. In 1868, Pres. Andrew Johnson was impeached by vote of the House, but by a one-vote margin he was acquitted by the Senate. In 1974 the House Judiciary Committee voted to recommend the impeachment of Pres. Richard M. Nixon, but he resigned from office before the full House had the opportunity to vote.

Article II of the Constitution explicitly lays out the powers of the presidency. It makes the president commander in chief of the nation's armed forces, an embodiment of the principle of civil authority over the military. It provides the power to grant reprieves and pardons for federal offenses (except in case of impeachment). It confers the power to make treaties and appoint ambassadors to foreign governments (both with the "advice and consent" of the Senate), thus giving the president the major responsibility for the nation's foreign policy and making him the ultimate spokesman for the United States in world affairs. It provides the authority to nominate judges for appointment to the Supreme Court, as well as other high officers of the executive branch of government (again, with the confirmation of the Senate). Finally, the Constitution gives the president the broad responsibility to "take care that the laws be faithfully executed," a sweeping grant of executive authority.

Influences on the Presidency. Beyond the explicit definition of the presidency in the Constitution, the office has been shaped by the men who have filled it. George Washington presided over a "cabinet government," appointing strong personalities to direct the agencies of the executive branch and consulting them on all important decisions. Reserved and solemn, he did a great deal to establish the important ceremonial function of the president as head of state, delivering his addresses to Congress, personally seeking the "advice and consent" of the Senate, and in his "Farewell Address" speaking directly to the American people.

One of the most important evolving powers of the presidency has been as party leader. Thomas Jefferson was the first president considered the leader of an organized political faction, but it was

Andrew Jackson who most dramatically made the presidency into a political office. By the time of his election in 1828, most states had introduced forms of universal manhood suffrage, and Jackson's Democratic party popularized the convention system for the nomination of candidates and the "spoils system" for awarding patronage jobs to political supporters. Jackson was the first president who presumed to speak in the name of "the people," and on their behalf (or his perception of the same) he used the veto power liberally, which made the president for the first time a primary actor in the legislative process.

Times of national crisis or disaster have also dramatically affected the presidency. During the Civil War, Abraham Lincoln acted with extraordinary dispatch and authority (some later found to be unconstitutional), greatly expanding the powers of the office. His use of the president's power as commander in chief to abolish effectively the institution of slavery with the Emancipation Proclamation was without doubt the most decisive act in the history of the presidency. He also was a president who best used the office to provide aid and inspiration to the American people, notably in his elegant speeches and addresses. Other presidents since Lincoln have effectively used the presidency as what Theodore Roosevelt termed the "bully pulpit."

Roosevelt was the first president to preside over an enormous expansion in the role of the federal government as a regulator of the environment, the economy, and to a certain extent the relations between labor and capital. Congress passed legislation that greatly increased the president's statutory power by providing him with the power to appoint regulatory commissioners. These functions were enlarged by Woodrow Wilson, then expanded beyond all precedent by the New Deal programs of Franklin D. Roosevelt during the Great Depression.

Finally, the rise of the United States as a major world power in the 20th century greatly enhanced the president's power as commander in chief, as chief of state, and as spokesman for the nation in world affairs. Wilson's dominating role as the nation's leader during World War I was repeated by FDR during World War II, then institutionalized during the Cold War by the creation of what has come to be called the "imperial presidency" during the administrations of Lyndon B. Johnson and Richard M. Nixon, who directed the intervention of the United States in world affairs with little attention to congressional approval, a problem ineffectively addressed by the War Powers Act. President Nixon's downfall with the Watergate scandal was indication of presidential power run amok. The authority and dignity of the office was partially restored during the administration of Ronald Reagan, although Reagan himself was more of a symbolic and ceremonial figure, delegating authority to cabinet officers and lieutenants, which resulted in the Iran-Contra affair.

—JOHN MACK FARAGHER

See Also: Cabinet; Electoral College; Impeachment; Presidential Elections; Presidential Succession; Secret Service; Veto; Vice President of the United States.

BIBLIOGRAPHY: Abbott, Philip, *Strong Presidents: A Theory of Leadership* (Univ. of Tennessee Press 1996); Dallek, Robert, *Hail to the Chief: The Making and Unmaking of American Presidents* (Hyperion 1996); McDonald, Forrest, *The American Presidency: An Intellectual History* (Univ. Press of Kansas 1994); Schlesinger, Arthur M., Jr., *The Imperial Presidency* (Houghton Mifflin 1973).

■ **PRESLEY, ELVIS (1935–77),** rock singer. Presley, the "king of rock 'n' roll," was born to poor sharecroppers in Tupelo, Mississippi. In 1948 the family moved to Memphis, where Presley later began his singing career. In 1954 Sam Phillips, the president of Sun Records, recognized Presley's immense talent as a white performer with an intense, electric stage presence and an intoxicating black sound. His early Sun records from 1954 to 1955 are considered by many critics as his best work, displaying an innovative blues tempo with a raw and powerful voice.

In 1956 Presley's manager, Col. Tom Parker, wrested the singer away from Sun and sold his contract to RCA. This began a three-year period during which Presley dominated the pop music industry with songs such as "Don't Be Cruel" and "Hound Dog." Suggestive dancing that included wild pelvic gyrations, even on television appearances, drove a generation of parents to distraction but enshrined Presley as the embodiment of youthful rebellion.

Presley's two-year stint in the army (1958-60) did little to diminish his stardom, but his work was trivialized by the increasing pop character of his music and his prolific acting career. Although he made a comeback in 1968, Presley never recaptured his original passion and ingenuity. When he died from an apparent drug overdose, millions not only grieved the tragic end to an American success story but promptly elevated Presley to the status of cultural icon. Graceland, his Memphis home, remains a well-visited shrine to one of the most revolutionary figures in the history of pop music.

See Also: Rock and Roll.

BIBLIOGRAPHY: Goldman, Albert Harry, *Elvis* (McGraw-Hill 1981).

■ **PRICE, LEONTYNE (1927-)**, opera singer. A powerful soprano with an extraordinary range, she was born in Laurel, Mississippi. In 1966 she was featured in the first of New York City's Metro-

The first African American to gain international fame as an opera singer, Leontyne Price concluded her career with a 1985 performance at New York City's Metropolitan Opera House.

politan Opera performances at Lincoln Center. She is especially well regarded for her performances in the title roles of Giuseppe Verdi's *Aida* and Giacomo Puccini's *Madama Butterfly*.

■ **PRIESTLEY, JOSEPH (1733-1804)**, scientist, educator, and Unitarian minister. Born in Leeds, England, Priestley developed many interests and became famous as a scientist, teacher, and dissident minister. He published *The History and Present State of Electricity* (1767), in which he set out the inverse-square law of electrostatics, explained the formation of the rings occurring as a result of electrical discharges on metallic surfaces, and tried to measure electrical resistance and impedance. Priestley isolated oxygen (1771) and described its basic properties (1774), along with eight other gases, including ammonia and carbon monoxide. Priestley was the first to teach modern history and introduce science to the secondary school curriculum. Despite his prominence, however, Priestley's republican leanings caused him great difficulties. His views destroyed a friendship with Edmund Burke, and his sympathy for the French Revolution led to the burning of his house, his books, and all his possessions in 1791. He immigrated to the United States in 1794. Priestley continued his scientific experiments and wrote most of his theological works in America, where he became the chief protagonist of the Unitarian movement and developed a friendly relationship with Thomas Jefferson.

See Also: Science.

■ **PRIMARIES**, means of nominating candidates for government office by popular vote. The primary system emerged at the start of the 20th century. Candidates had previously been selected by caucuses of elected officeholders or conventions dominated by party regulars. Primaries were seen as a democratic reform that allowed the rank and file to play the decisive role in the nominating process. Primary systems vary from state to state and office to office. In most states potential candidates must collect a predetermined number of signatures of registered voters to qualify for the primary ballot. Some primaries are open only to enrolled party members. Other states allow independent voters to participate in party primaries. A few states hold "open" primaries in which any voter can cast a ballot. Primaries became increasingly important in the presidential nominating process in the 1950s and 1960s but did not become the rule until 1972.

See Also: Conventions, Political; Political Parties; Presidential Elections.

■ **PRIMOGENITURE AND ENTAIL,** social and legal customs concerning the devolution of property on family members. Under primogeniture, the eldest son inherited all or most of the estate of the parents. New Englanders tended to modify primogeniture and divide assets more equally among children, while New Yorkers and most Southerners observed a more strict primogeniture before the American Revolution. Entail limited property inheritance to a specific unalterable succession of heirs. Again, this practice was more prevalent in New York and the South than New England until the Revolution.

■ **PRINCETON, BATTLE OF (1777),** battle in the American Revolution. Shortly after the crucial American victory at Trenton, Gen. George Washington's Continental army clashed again with British forces at Princeton, New Jersey, on Jan. 3, 1777. Inflicting heavy losses on the British, Washington's troops forced the enemy back to New York. Although the victory had little strategic importance, it provided a much-needed morale boost to the American army.

See Also: Revolution, American; Trenton, Battle of; Washington, George.

■ **PRIVATEERING,** piracy against enemy ships commissioned by sovereign powers. During the period of the Spanish conquest of Central and South America, treasure ships conveying wealth from the Aztec and Incan empires regularly sailed for Spain in large convoys. English and Dutch sailors saw this as an opportunity for wealth, and investors regularly outfitted ships to capture treasure galleons. Although nearly indistinguishable from pirating, English privateering, masked as nationalism, became a patriotic act; every ship taken lessened the wealth of Spain, the enemy. The first attempts at English colonization often included privateering, as prize ships could help finance colony-planting. During the American

Revolution and the War of 1812 American privateers regularly assaulted English ships, again using nationalist logic to justify their actions.

See Also: Piracy.

■ **PROCLAMATION OF 1763 (Oct. 7, 1763),** edict of the British Crown commanding its American colonists to stop expanding westward into "lands reserved" to the Indians "as their hunting grounds." Royal superintendents of Indian affairs were ordered to meet with tribal chiefs to determine what boundaries would be recognized between tribal lands and the Crown's direct jurisdiction.

Superintendents John Stuart and Sir William Johnson negotiated with the chiefs and told them that they were surveying boundaries between Crown land and Indian lands. Using maps, they marked these boundaries with lines, which were joined to make a single "Proclamation Line"—the demarcation that subsequently inspired an imagined theory of a line "between civilization and savagery."

During the French and Indian War (1754-63) northeastern tribes had demanded an end to colonial expansion. In October 1758 they were promised by the British a boundary in the Treaty of Easton (Pennsylvania), by which they were detached from the French at Fort Duquesne (now Pittsburgh). But when the French were themselves forced to abandon the fort in November, the British abandoned their promise. Fort Duquesne became the British garrison Fort Pitt, which was administered as an army occupying native territories. The British were reminded of their promise by Pontiac's Rebellion (1763-65), an allied tribal uprising that included Indians who had participated at Easton. Besides the British military defense, Crown bureaucrats devised a political response in the royal proclamation, which had for them the special advantage of holding colonial settlers within a range where royal government could be effective.

Issued by authority of royal prerogative, the Proclamation of 1763 bypassed possible opposition in Parliament but enraged colonial opponents by canceling western territorial jurisdictions in colonial charters and thus frustrating plans of land speculators. However, many such speculators read the fine print and understood that the proclamation was "for the present." They intensified lobbying in London until Parliament's Quebec Act of 1774 made such activities useless. The royal Proclamation of 1763 is still regarded as judicial precedent in Canada and Australia.

—FRANCIS JENNINGS

See Also: Indian Policy.

BIBLIOGRAPHY: De Vorsey, Louis, Jr., *The Indian Boundary in the Southern Colonies, 1763-1775* (Univ. of North Carolina Press 1961); Jennings, Francis, *Empire of Fortune* (Norton 1988); Short, Adam, and Arthur G. Doughty, eds., *Documents Related to the Constitutional History of Canada, 1759-1791* (Canadian Archives Sessional Paper 18, 1907); Sosin, Jack M., *Whitehall and the Wilderness* (Univ. of Nebraska Press 1961).

■ **PROGRESSIVE PARTY,** founded in 1924, actually the second of three Progressive parties formed in the United States during the 20th century. The first, also known as the Bull Moose party, was organized in 1912. The third Progressive party would take shape in 1948. The origins of the 1924 movement lay in the failure of the first Progressive party, whose former national treasurer, J. A. H. Hopkins, organized the Committee of Forty-eight in 1917-18. The committee aimed to reestablish a Progressive party and helped found the Conference for Progressive Political Action (CPPA) in 1922. The CPPA held a national convention on July 4, 1924, in Cleveland, nominating the veteran progressive standard bearer Sen. Robert M. La Follette of Wisconsin for president.

The La Follette campaign had the support of midwestern farmers as well as of organized labor. Even American socialists supported his presidential bid, among still others. This coalition of diverse interests resulted in a platform that included demands for farm credit, public ownership of utilities, nationalization of the railroads, abolition of labor injunctions, direct election of the president without the mechanics of the electoral college, popular election of federal judges for limited terms, and ratification of a child-labor amendment. But this was no match for the support for and the financial backing of the Republican nominee, incumbent Pres. Calvin Coolidge, who handily defeated both La Follette and Democratic nominee John W. Davis. La Follette, however, received almost 17 percent of the popular vote, an impressive showing for a third-party candidate.

—KATHLEEN BANKS NUTTER

See Also: Political Parties; Progressivism; Third Parties.

BIBLIOGRAPHY: MacKay, Kenneth C., *The Progressive Movement of 1924* (Columbia Univ. Press 1947); Thelan, David P., *Robert M. La Follette and the Insurgent Spirit* (Little, Brown 1976).

■ **PROGRESSIVISM,** a turn-of-the-20th-century reform movement, spawned by young intellectuals who wanted to respond to what they saw as the excesses of the Gilded Age. The Progressives were more moderate in their demands than late-19th century reformers who had called for radical changes. Indeed these young, middle-class, old-money stock, college-educated men (and, with but few exceptions, the progressive reformers were white males) called for a temperate reform of an industrial America from which they had personally profited but with which they were beginning to become disillusioned. These young activists had been exposed to the seamier side of the Gilded Age—urban slums, mistreatment of immigrant populations, and the destructive effects of the factory system—through the exposés of the new journalists. Such conditions troubled these young men, who were clearly of a more activist bent than had been their fathers. But the Progressives were never galvanized to the point where they wanted to destroy the industrial system. Nor did they join the Populists and the suffragists in their call for substantial reform of machine politics—most Progressives owed their career to a machine. Rather, the Progressives tended to see the cause of reform as a political opportunity; they proposed reforms with the caution of a politician rather than the zeal of a crusader.

The archetypical Progressive was Theodore Roosevelt. Young, blustery to a fault, gifted, and articulate, Roosevelt gave the distinct impression from his "bully pulpit" that he was out to bust the trusts and discipline industrial America. In reality, Roosevelt often avoided crossing swords with big business. Roosevelt avoided tinkering with the tariff and invoked the Sherman Antitrust Law against three times fewer monopolies than his successor. Causes such as the Pure Food and Drug Act were, in fact, supported by most Americans, thanks to the influence of the press and Upton Sinclair's exposé of the meat-packing industry, *The Jungle* (1906).

Robert La Follette of Wisconsin personified the Progressive reform movement, crusading for comprehensive changes in his state's political system. Although La Follette was able to get his ideas passed in Wisconsin, few politicians elsewhere in the nation supported his call for restrictions on lobbying and campaign spending, a child-labor law, and major tax reforms. Indeed, many of the excesses of the Gilded Age went untouched by the Progressives. Most notable was the lot of women. Although the Supreme Court ruled in 1908 in favor of a law limiting women laundry workers to 10 hours a day (*Muller* v. *Oregon*), little was done to improve conditions for women factory workers. Most Progressives avoided the issue of women's suffrage, which was not achieved until 1919.

Society was, then, changed by the Progressives. But those changes, while not merely cosmetic, were far from radical or even liberal in nature. Rather, the Progressives succeeded in moving toward a more balanced society, redressing some ills while leaving the basic structure of industrial America—with all its assets and ills—still firmly in place. Progressivism as a movement dissipated as the United States approached World War I and did not regenerate after the war.

—JOHN ROBERT GREENE

See Also: Meat Inspection Act; Normalcy; Political Machine; Progressive Party; Pure Food and Drug Act; Square Deal; individual biographies.

BIBLIOGRAPHY: Colburn, David R., and George Pozzetta, eds., *Reform and Reformers in the Progressive Era* (Greenwood Press 1983).

■ **PROHIBITION,** term for the period 1920 to 1933 when a constitutional amendment forbade the manufacture and sale in the United States of alcoholic beverages. The prohibition movement began with the temperance campaigns of the pre–Civil War era. Many Americans, especially white middle-class women, viewed drinking as the source of many social ills, including unemployment, domestic violence, and poverty. By the end of the 19th century the Woman's Christian Temperance Union, the Anti-Saloon League, middle-class progressives, and rural Protestants led the fight to ban alcohol. These diverse groups coalesced around shared anti-immigrant sentiments and their relatively homogeneous ethnic, class, and religious

characteristics. In 1917 a congressional coalition of urban progressives and rural fundamentalists pushed through a constitutional amendment to ban alcohol. Ratified in 1919, the 18th Amendment (known also as the Volstead Act) became law in January 1920.

While many Americans viewed Prohibition as a worthy moral reform, it proved impossible to enforce. Understaffed federal and state agencies faced a hearty demand for alcohol that spurred widespread bootlegging. In towns and cities across the country, speakeasies provided alcohol and entertainment. Although Prohibition decreased the annual per capita consumption of alcohol (probably due to increased prices on the illegal market), it fostered a rapid growth in violent organized crime. With large profits from alcohol to be garnered, organized crime infiltrated government, law enforcement, and legitimate business. Seen as a failed law by many, Prohibition was repealed with the ratification of the 21st Amendment in 1933.

—GUY NELSON

See Also: Constitution of the United States; "Roaring Twenties"; Temperance Movements.

BIBLIOGRAPHY: Clarke, Norman H., *Deliver Us From Evil: An Interpretation of American Prohibition* (Norton 1976); Rumbarger, John J., *Profits, Power, and Prohibition: Alcohol Reform and the Industrializing of America, 1800-1930* (State Univ. of New York Press 1989).

■ **PROSLAVERY IDEOLOGY,** body of thought that sought to rationalize and defend slavery as an institution. As long as slavery existed in America, there were those who argued in its favor. In seeking authority for human bondage, slaveholders relied on theories of natural law, economic necessity, and Scripture ("Servants obey in all things your masters," Col. 3:22) as sources of justification. Most proslavery thought centered upon the presumed inferiority of African Americans, who were asserted to be unsuited for any other socioeconomic position because of their ignorance, passivity, and animalistic sensibility. The proslavery argument took on a new, more militant, cast after 1830, no doubt in response to abolitionist agitation. John C. Calhoun in 1837 was one of the first prominent proponents of slavery as a

THE SMASHER'S MAIL

PRICE 5 CTS.

VOL. I.   TOPEKA, KANSAS, NOVEMBER, 1901.   NO. 12.

SUB. 50¢ PER YEAR.

"Peace On Earth, Good Will Toward Men."

COPYRIGHTED 1901
NICHOLS AND
DAVIDSON

Carrie Nation, Your Loving Home Defender.

Carry Nation, with her trademark hatchet in one hand and a Bible in the other, became a symbol of the Prohibition movement.

"positive good," claiming it provided needed labor services while favoring an inferior race with the benefits of American civilization. Slave owners also often boasted that slavery compared favorably with wage labor in Northern cities, an early nonsocialistic critique of capitalism. Proponents of slavery received scientific support with the development of the American school of anthropology and the writings of Josiah Nott. Measurements of cranial capacity and other spurious evidence were used to "prove" the inherent inferiority of Africans and their descendants.

See Also: *Calhoun, John Caldwell; Slavery.*
BIBLIOGRAPHY: Faust, Drew Gilpin, *The Ideology of Slavery* (Louisiana State Univ. Press 1981); McKitrick, Eric, ed., *Slavery Defended* (Prentice-Hall 1963).

■ **PROTESTANT EPISCOPAL CHURCH,** also called the Episcopal Church, the American body of the Anglican Communion. Before the American Revolution, it was an extension of the Church of England. Robert Hunt organized the first colonial Anglican church in Jamestown, Virginia, in 1607. Throughout the colonial period, America lacked a bishop, which meant that many responsibilities, including the selection of ministers, were neglected or fell to the laity, thus creating a sense of autonomy for many lay people.

The American Revolution brought a crisis to the Episcopal Church. Many of the clergy in the North remained loyal to England and fled or closed churches rather than change the liturgy by removing prayers for royalty. The laity generally supported the Revolution. In fact, most of the signers of the Declaration of Independence were Episcopalian. Following the war, the task was to create a denomination. The first general convention met in Philadelphia in September 1785 and took on a democratic character. The church adopted an episcopal system of governance in which bishops would oversee a diocese of clergy and parishes, and a general convention composed of two houses—the House of Bishops and the House of Deputies (four priests and four laypersons from each diocese)—would meet every three years.

During the 19th century, the Episcopal Church grew from its missionary work. Surprisingly, the issues of the Civil War caused only temporary factions, not permanent schisms. Later and throughout the 20th century, the Episcopal Church has been involved in the ecumenical movement.

Episcopalians uphold ancient creeds, the Apostles' Creed and Nicene Creed. Historically, the church has been very tolerant, as the presence of evangelicals, charismatics, liberals, and Anglo-Catholics within the Church confirms; and the worship, as articulated in The Book of Common Prayer, unifies the Church.

—NANCY M. GODLESKI

See Also: Religion.
BIBLIOGRAPHY: Albright, Raymond Wolf, *A History of the Protestant Episcopal Church* (Macmillan 1964); Reid, Daniel G., ed., *Dictionary of Christianity in America* (InterVarsity 1990).

PUBLIC BROADCASTING, noncommercial television and radio programming. From its inception in the 1920s, radio broadcasting received no financial assistance from the federal government. The unregulated radio industry thus spawned competitive broadcasting companies driven by commercial advertising. Although colleges and universities were among the most active radio broadcasters in the 1920s, they languished in the following two decades. The growth of television broadcasting in the 1940s and 1950s reflected these established patterns of commercial advertising. Public television broadcasting received its first governmental sanction in 1952, when the Federal Communications Commission (FCC) helped to set aside 242 channels for educational programming. As with all public broadcasting, these channels struggled financially, receiving funding from private foundations and individuals, but little from the government.

Prompted by the abandonment of noncommercial and public-service programming by the three networks, Congress passed the Public Broadcasting Act in 1967. Competing local stations and two bureaucracies, the Public Broadcasting Service (PBS) and the Corporation for Public Broadcasting (CPB), were given authority to run the public radio and television stations. The strongest area of public television broadcasting is cultural programming, especially children's shows, concerts, plays, and documentaries. National Public Radio and American Public Radio have received public radio's largest and most dedicated audiences.

See Also: Television and Radio.
BIBLIOGRAPHY: Gibson, George H., *Public Broadcasting: The Role of the Federal Government, 1912-76* (Praeger 1977); Sterling, Christopher H., and John M. Kittross, *Stay Tuned: A Concise History of American Broadcasting* (Wadsworth 1990).

PUBLIC DEBT, sum of all the obligations of the federal government to pay its creditors. Due to the costly American Revolution, the American nation was born with a public debt. After Congress failed to solve the debt problem during the 1780s, Alexander Hamilton offered a masterful plan in 1790 to fund all national and state debts (a combined $75 million) at face value. Despite a vigorous debate, Congress passed Hamilton's plan, which restored faith in the government and public credit, attracted foreign investment, and stimulated the economy.

The fiscal frugality of presidential administrations and a booming economy resulted in the debt being cut almost in half between 1804 and 1811 and eliminated completely in 1835-36. The history of the public debt during the 19th century can be characterized by rapid increases in wartime and gradual reductions in peacetime. The largest expansion occurred during the Civil War.

The Great Depression marked a watershed in the history of the public debt, as it soared to more than $22 million in 1933 due to falling government revenues and increasing expenditures. The debt reached a record high of 128 percent of the gross national product in 1946. The trend from 1946 to 1980 was toward a lower public debt, only to rise rapidly and exceed $1 trillion during the administration of Ronald Reagan (1981-89). A constant issue of political debate, the public debt grew steadily through the final years of the 20th century.

BIBLIOGRAPHY: Heilbroner, Robert, and Peter Bernstein, *The Debt and the Deficit* (Norton 1989).

■ **PUBLIC DOMAIN,** land owned by the U.S. government. Seven of the original 13 states ceded their western holdings to the new federal government (1781-1802). The acquisitions of Louisiana (1803), Florida (1819), Oregon (1846), Texas (1848), the Gadsden Purchase territory (1853), and Alaska (1867) later added vast areas of unorganized land to the nation. In hopes of encouraging white settlement and economic development of the West, the government sold public lands and awarded land grants to homesteaders, miners, loggers, and railroads. The seemingly endless expanse of public land led to wasteful exploitation of natural resources. The Desert Land Act (1877), the Forest Reserve Act (1891), and the Cary Land Act (1894) sought to control abuses, and the creation of a network of national parks, forests, and wilderness areas and the formation of the Bureau of Land Management (1946) brought remaining territories under stricter control. Resistance to federal restrictions on land use led to the "sagebrush rebellion" in the western states in the 1980s.

See Also: Conservation and Environmental Movements; Frontier in American History.
BIBLIOGRAPHY: Dick, Everett, *The Lure of the Land: A Social History of the Public Lands from the Articles of Confederation to the New Deal* (Univ. of Nebraska Press 1970).

■ **PUBLIC WORKS ADMINISTRATION (PWA),** a $4.25 billion federal-aid program created by the National Industrial Recovery Act (1933) as part of the New Deal's attempt to relieve the Great Depression. It funded 34,000 projects such as roads and public buildings and created millions of jobs from 1933 to 1939.

See Also: New Deal.

■ **PUEBLO,** Indian groups of the Southwest who are descended from the Anasazi peoples. Geographically, linguistically, and culturally diverse, the Pueblo derive their name from the Spanish word for "village."

The recorded history of the Pueblo began with the expedition of Francisco de Coronado in 1540-42. During the following 150 years, the Pueblo experienced often brutal repression at the hands of the Spanish, as Franciscans attempted to convert them to Christianity. Led by the religious leader Popé, the Pueblo revolted, forcing all Spaniards to abandon the region. Although the Spanish reestablished control over many villages after 1692, the Pueblo retained vital aspects of their cultures. Like many other Indian groups, the Pueblo experienced a new set of problems during the American period. Nonetheless, many Pueblo groups were able to remain on their lands, adapt to new circumstances, and retain their cultures.

Among the distinguishing characteristics of the Pueblo are permanent villages, underground ceremonial chambers (kivas), a subsistence economy based on cultivated staple crops, and distinctive adobe architecture. Despite centuries of influence by Europeans, the Pueblo have maintained distinct identities, as is seen in their material culture and Kachina cults. Their success is also due in part to pan-Pueblo organizations, such as the All Pueblo Council.

See Also: Indians of North America; Popé.
BIBLIOGRAPHY: Gutiérrez, Ramón A., *When Jesus Came the Corn Mothers Went Away: Marriage, Sexuality, and Power in New Mexico, 1500-1846* (Stanford Univ. Press 1991); Ward, Alan Minge, *Acoma: Pueblo in the Sky* (Univ. of New Mexico Press 1991).

■ **PUEBLO REVOLT (1680),** Indian revolt against the Spanish. The Spanish settled in the northern

Taos Pueblo, in northern New Mexico, constructed in the 14th century, was at least 200 years old before the arrival of the Europeans. It is one of the oldest, continuously occupied communities in the United States.

Rio Grande Valley in present-day New Mexico in 1610. From their capital at Santa Fe, they forced a labor tribute from the many Pueblo villages to the north and sent out missionaries to teach the Roman Catholic religion. Some Pueblo people adopted Catholicism but usually only as an appendage to their own complex religious systems. Beginning in the 1660s, a drought intensified Spanish demands on Pueblo lands and led the Pueblos to doubt the value of Christianity. In 1675, in response to a flourishing revival of the Pueblo religions, the Spanish brutally executed some Indian priests and publicly flogged others, including the San Juan leader, Popé. Following his release, Popé organized a secret pan-Pueblo rebellion that began on August 10. On August 14 the Pueblo forces attacked Santa Fe, and on August 21 the Spanish fled to El Paso. It was the first successful Indian revolt in North America.

See Also: Indians of North America; Popé.

■ **PUERTO RICAN IMMIGRANTS.** Puerto Ricans, unlike other Hispanic groups, are U.S. citizens by birth. Their status is a result of Puerto Rico's position as a commonwealth of the United States. After Puerto Rico became a territory at the end of

the Spanish-American War in 1898, immigration to the mainland became—and has remained—relatively easy, although large-scale movements did not occur until after World War II. Most Puerto Rican immigration has been affected by the relative strength of the mainland and island economies during the postwar era. Generally, the strong U.S. economy has provided more job opportunities for Puerto Ricans.

Most Puerto Rican immigrants settled in New York City, where by 1970 they made up more than 10 percent of the city's population. Although many Puerto Ricans chose to remain permanently in the United States, return migration has always been a feature of Puerto Rican immigration. The political status of Puerto Rico has long been a volatile issue, with factions favoring commonwealth status, statehood, or independence.

See Also: Ethnic Groups; Immigration.

■ **PUERTO RICO,** a commonwealth of the United States. An island about 1,000 miles southeast of Miami, it is bounded on the north by the Atlantic Ocean, on the south by the Caribbean Sea, and on the west and east by straits that separate it from the Dominican Republic and Virgin Islands, respectively. The commonwealth also includes several smaller islands. It is more densely populated than any U.S. state. Manufacturing is the main source of income. Settled by Spain in 1508, Puerto Rico was occupied by U.S. troops during the Spanish-American War and ceded to the U.S. at war's end. Puerto Ricans were made U.S. citizens in 1917, and the island chose its first elected governor in 1949. The island became a commonwealth of the United States in 1952, a status reconfirmed in an election of 1993.

Capital: San Juan. Area: 3,492 square miles. Population (1995 est.): 3,700,000.

See Also: Columbus, Christopher; Ponce de León, Juan; Spanish-American War.

■ **PULASKI, CASIMIR (1747-79),** Polish-American Revolutionary War general. Pulaski, while in exile from Poland in Paris, was recruited into military service for the United States by Benjamin Franklin. Upon arrival in America in 1777 he was appointed brigadier general by Gen. George Washington. After a year of ineffective leadership and inability to take orders, Pulaski resigned, only to form his own cavalry. Congress then assigned him a post in the southern campaign. He was mortally wounded in the siege of Savannah.

See Also: Revolution, American.

■ **PULITZER, JOSEPH (1847-1911),** newspaper publisher and philanthropist. Pulitzer was born in Macó, Hungary, and came to the United States in 1864. He enlisted in the Union army and fought in the Civil War. Pulitzer's first job in journalism was as a reporter for the *Westliche Post*, a German-language daily paper in St. Louis, Missouri. He became a naturalized U.S. citizen in 1867 and was elected to the Missouri state legislature in 1869. In 1878 Pulitzer bought the *St. Louis Dispatch* and merged it with the *Post* to form the *Post-Dispatch*. In 1883 he moved to New York City, where he bought the *World* and later founded the *Evening World*. Pulitzer and William Randolph Hearst were rivals in New York's newspaper business and competed for readers with "yellow journalism." He was elected to the U.S. House of Representatives in 1884 and served one term. In 1903 Pulitzer founded and endowed a journalism school at Columbia University. He also established the Pulitzer Prizes for public service and literary and journalistic achievement.

See Also: Hearst, William Randolph; Pulitzer Prizes; Yellow Journalism.

■ **PULITZER PRIZES,** annual awards in letters, journalism, and music. Joseph Pulitzer, a Hungarian-born American journalist and newspaper proprietor, bequeathed over $2 million to Columbia University both to found its School of Journalism and establish the annual prizes that bear his name. After his death (1911), Pulitzer's will empowered an advisory board, renamed the Pulitzer Prize Board in 1979, to alter the original categories and create new ones. Annually appointed juries in each category make nominations to the board, which accepts, rejects, or substitutes the choices.

The number of categories has increased since the first Pulitzers were awarded in 1917. In letters, awards are given to authors for distinguished work in the fields of U.S. history and biography, general nonfiction, drama, fiction, and poetry. The 14 journalism awards are given to newspapers for public service and to individuals for excellence in feature and editorial writing, explanatory journalism, commentary, criticism, editorial cartooning, spot news photography, feature photography, and spot news, investigative, beat, national, and international reporting. A Pulitzer Prize is also awarded for a larger musical work.

Although Pulitzer Prizes include a modest cash award, the real value comes from the recognition of distinction by the recipients' peers and the larger public. Many of the most talented and influential historians, poets, novelists, journalists, and other writers have received Pulitzer Prizes.

BIBLIOGRAPHY: Hohenberg, John, *The Pulitzer Prizes: A History of the Awards in Books, Drama, Music, and Journalism* (Columbia Univ. Press 1974).

■ **PULLMAN STRIKE (1894),** one of the largest strikes in American history. When sales for the Pullman Palace Car Company dipped with the depression of 1893, George M. Pullman, who owned the Illinois company town he named for himself, cut workers' pay by a third but maintained their rents unchanged. When Pullman fired three of the members of a committee sent to negotiate with him, 4,000 workers walked off the job (May 11, 1894).

A contemporary drawing illustrated the violence of the Pullman Strike, which was broken when Pres. Grover Cleveland sent in regular army troops.

Pullman workers were members of the American Railway Union (ARU), a brash young union that challenged the conservative craft-based Railway Brotherhoods by organizing all railroad workers into one industrial union. Delegates to an ARU convention voted to enforce a national boycott of Pullman's sleeping cars, and railroad owners turned the boycott into a strike by firing workers who refused to handle Pullman cars. By the end of June, over a quarter million railroad workers were on strike on a dozen different railroads.

Using the excuse that the federal mails were obstructed, Pres. Grover Cleveland sent federal troops into Chicago, the center of the strike, killing dozens of workers in the ensuing riots, while federal courts issued the most sweeping labor injunction in history, thus crushing the strike. The leaders of the ARU were jailed, and union organizer Eugene V. Debs himself spent six months in federal prison, a sentence the U.S. Supreme Court upheld in 1895, thereby unleashing the widespread use of injunctions against unions.

—TIMOTHY MESSER-KRUSE

See Also: Cleveland, Grover; Debs, Eugene V.; Labor Movement.

BIBLIOGRAPHY: Brecher, Jeremy, *Strike!* (South End Press 1972); Lindsey, Almont, *The Pullman Strike* (Univ. of Chicago Press 1942); Salvatore, Nick, *Eugene V. Debs: Citizen and Socialist* (Univ. of Illinois Press 1982).

■ **PUPIN, MICHAEL (1858-1935),** physicist. Born in Idvor, Hungary, to Serbian parents, he came to New York in 1874 as a penniless teenager and graduated from Columbia in 1883. After more study at Cambridge and Berlin (Ph.D., 1889), he returned to Columbia to teach electromechanics. His inventions include an electrical resonator to reduce distortions in alternating current, inductance coils along telephone wires to increase efficiency and clarity, and the fluoroscope, with which he took the first X-ray photographs. Pupin wrote on science and religion, and his autobiography won a Pulitzer Prize in 1924.

See Also: Science.

■ **PURE FOOD AND DRUG ACT (1906),** federal legislation passed in conjunction with the Meat Inspection Act. It was the congressional response to consumer concerns over the production of medicinal and food products after muckraking journalists exposed the potential hazards of the uncontrolled patent-medicine industry. Also, central to public awareness was Upton Sinclair's novel *The Jungle* (1906), which graphically detailed the unsanitary conditions of the meat industry.

See Also: Meat Inspection Act; Sinclair, Upton.

■ **PURITANISM,** a reform movement within the Church of England that had its greatest impact in colonial New England. During the long reign of Queen Elizabeth I (1558-1603), many Anglicans, both clerical and lay, worked to complete the reform of their national church by moving it toward a more consistent embrace of Protestantism, especially of the Calvinist stripe. A few Puritans advocated a complete break with the Church of England, thus becoming known as separatists. Most continued to press for reform from within, but they received little encouragement from Elizabeth's successor, James I, and even less from his son, Charles I, who came to the throne in 1625. In fact, Charles along with his archbishop of Canterbury, William Laud, prompted in the 1630s the mass migration of Puritans to America.

Puritans in America. Leaders of both the separatist and the reformist groups who came to Massachusetts were able and literate men. William Bradford (1590-1657) of Plymouth Plantation wrote a history that has become a classic of simplicity and conviction. His description of life aboard the *Mayflower* and of the landfall within the shelter of Cape Cod meshes with the driving purpose of "propagating and advancing the gospel of the kingdom of Christ in those remote parts of the world." John Winthrop (1588-1649), layman and lawyer, as governor directed for nearly two decades the fortunes of the Massachusetts Bay Colony that developed around Boston. Like Bradford, he saw these religious migrations as comparable to the Israelites' moving under God's direction into the promised land. And like the ancient state of Israel, the Bay Colony would be blessed if it maintained obedience to the Lord's commands. But if these zealous believers turned from their high spiritual purposes to seek "great things for ourselves and our posterity, the Lord will surely break out in wrath against us, be revenged of such a perjured people, and make us know the price of the breach of such a covenant."

The Boston settlement, much the larger of the two, grew steadily from the 1630s on and before the end of the 17th century had absorbed the smaller Plymouth colony. From Boston, Puritan practices and ideas radiated throughout New England. The white-spired meetinghouses still standing on many village greens symbolize this pervasive Puritanism that eventually took the denominational title of Congregationalism.

The Puritan Legacy. That Puritan hold did not go unchallenged, even in the earliest years, as people such as Roger Williams and Anne

Hutchinson led dissident groups. Denominational challenges came as well from Baptists, Quakers, and Anglicans (or Episcopalians). A subterranean popular religion mixing divination, magic, astrology, and unofficial rituals likewise competed with Puritanism for the loyalty of the laity. In its determination to survive all challenges, Puritanism—at some cost to its reputation—became rigid and punitive. The witchcraft hysteria associated with Salem, Massachusetts, in the early 1690s damaged its reputation even more.

Nevertheless Puritanism attained a level of intellectual and theological sophistication, conspicuously so in the person of Jonathan Edwards, that guaranteed its prominence in America's history. Puritanism, often dismissed or derided, endured with long-lasting effects in literature, education, and religion.

—EDWIN S. GAUSTAD

See Also: *Congregationalists; Edwards, Jonathan; Hutchinson, Anne Marbury; Pilgrims; Religion; Williams, Roger; Winthrop, John.*

BIBLIOGRAPHY: Foster, Stephen, *The Long Argument: English Puritanism and the Shaping of New England Culture, 1570-1700* (Univ. of North Carolina Press 1991); Heimert, Alan, and Andrew Delbanco, *The Puritans in America: A Narrative Anthology* (Harvard Univ. Press 1985); Middlekauf, Robert, *The Mathers: Three Generations of Puritan Intellectuals, 1596-1728* (Oxford Univ. Press 1971); Morgan, Edmund S., *The Puritan Dilemma: The Story of John Winthrop* (Little, Brown 1958).

■ **PURPLE HEART,** America's oldest military decoration. The purple heart was established by George Washington in 1782 but fell into disuse after the American Revolution. Reinstated in 1932, it is awarded for wounds received in action.

■ **PYNCHON, WILLIAM (c. 1590-1662),** colonist, author, and entrepreneur. Pynchon arrived in Massachusetts Bay with the fleet of John Winthrop (1630). One of the original proprietors of Springfield, Massachusetts, Pynchon developed an extensive plantation and frontier trading post on the Connecticut River. Denounced as a heretic for his liberal views on the atonement expressed in *The Meritorious Price of our Redemption* (1650), Pynchon left the colony, returning to England in 1652.

Q

■ **QUAKERS.** *See: Friends, The Religious Society of (Quakers).*

■ **QUANTRILL, WILLIAM (1837-65),** Confederate bushwacker. Born in Canal Dover, Ohio, Quantrill was a petty criminal who became a guerrilla fighter in Missouri during the Civil War. Commissioned a Confederate captain, he led the 1863 sacking of Lawrence, Kansas, that killed 150 men. In 1865 Quantrill planned to assassinate Abraham Lincoln but was killed in Kentucky by federal troops.

■ **QUAYLE, J. DANFORTH (1947-),** vice president of the United States (1989-93). Born in Indianapolis, Indiana, he was elected to the U.S. House of Representatives from Indiana in 1976 and won a Senate seat in 1980. Quayle, a conservative with little national recognition, was Republican nominee George Bush's surprise choice for vice president in 1988. They served one term and were defeated for reelection in 1992.
See Also: Vice President of the United States.

■ **QUEEN ANNE'S WAR (1702-13),** a conflict in North America and the Caribbean between Britain on one side and France and Spain on the other. Part of the War of the Spanish Succession in Europe, Queen Anne's War was an extension of the unsettled conflict over territorial possessions. The hostilities began in America in 1704 when British colonists attacked Spanish St. Augustine, Florida. The war affected South Carolina and frontier settlements in New England. It was ended by the Treaty of Utrecht in 1713.
See Also: Spanish Colonies.

■ **QUITRENT,** a feudal tax levied on freeholders by land grant proprietors. Early colonial charters included quitrent interests, but New Englanders generally gained property title quickly. Free tenure quickly expanded to other English colonies.

R

RABI, ISIDOR ISAAC (1898-1988), physicist. Born in Rymanow, Austria, Rabi studied at Cornell and in Europe. At Columbia (1929-67) he developed an atomic and molecular beam resonance method of measuring the magnetic properties of atoms, molecules, and atomic nuclei (1937), which led to the invention of the laser, the atomic clock, and the magnetic resonance imaging (MRI) device used in hospitals. He won a Nobel Prize in Physics in 1944. Instead of working on the Manhattan Project, he studied microwave radar during World War II and later became a strong advocate of nuclear arms control.

See Also: Science.

RACE AND RACISM. In the United States the issues of race and racism have often been identified with white supremacy, the systematic beliefs and practices of certain whites attempting to hold onto unequal levels of power and resources, resulting in a racial pyramid topped by whites. Although fossil and DNA evidence indicates that all humans belong to the same racial family, there is little agreement about the sources, causes, or definition of racism. It is based primarily on outward physical and cultural distinctions although supported by no biological reality.

In English North America, 17th-century colonial contacts between Indians and European settlers degenerated into wars lasting into the late 19th century. In the Declaration of Independence, Thomas Jefferson labeled Native Americans "merciless Indian savages. . . ." By 1889 future president Theodore Roosevelt confessed, "I don't go so far as to think that the only good Indians are the dead Indians, but I believe nine out of every ten are, and I shouldn't inquire too closely into the case of the tenth." Indeed most Indians were denied U.S. citizenship until 1924. Africans, first brought to the colonies in 1619, were enslaved by the millions by 1860.

Racial intermarriages were prohibited by law in most colonies before the American Revolution and barred in most states after that time. However, this did not stop rising numbers of sexual contacts, forced and voluntary, between racial groups and growing numbers of mixed-blood children in the American population. As late as 1967, 16 states outlawed racial intermarriage, laws struck down by the U.S. Supreme Court in *Loving* v. *Virginia* (1967).

In 1790 immigration law defined the new nation as a "white" (Anglo-Saxon-Celtic) country open to white immigrants, and by 1860 the United States was the world's fourth-most-populous white nation. However, as French traveler Alexis de Tocqueville observed in the 1830s in *Democracy in America*: "The most formidable evil threatening the future of the United States is the presence of the blacks on their soil."

It was a threat Americans tried to avoid by controlling Africans and their offspring. In the Supreme Court's *Dred Scott* v. *Sandford* (1857) decision, Chief Justice Roger B. Taney summarized traditions of the nation's white majority when he stated blacks were ". . . altogether unfit to associate with the white race . . . had no rights which the white man was bound to respect: and . . . might justly and lawfully be reduced to slavery for his benefit." The statement remains one of the purest expressions of white supremacy in the American record.

Late-19th-Century Developments. The Civil War ended slavery with the 13th Amendment (1865), conferred citizenship upon blacks, promised "equal protection" under law (14th Amendment), and granted suffrage to all adult males (15th Amendment). But these rights were exercised at great risk. White supremacy groups such as the Ku Klux Klan (KKK) lynched and terrorized many who pursued freedom.

Asians faced similar problems. In 1882 Congress denied Chinese immigrants U.S. citizenship and barred their future immigration, an exclusion later extended to other groups by the Immigration Act of 1924.

In *Plessy* v. *Ferguson* (1896), the Supreme Court, noting that separation of the races was widely practiced, ruled it a lawful exercise of legislative and policing powers.

Genetic Theories and Responses. English scientist Charles Darwin's theory of evolution inspired many racial theorists. Some suggested that nature had poorly prepared blacks and other members of the colored races for the advances of civilization. These Social Darwinists viewed Darwinism as justification for a race-stratified society.

Reflecting on harsh realities of community life among people of color, W. E. B. Du Bois observed in 1903, "The problem of the twentieth century is the problem of the color-line—the relation of the darker to the lighter races of men in Asia and Africa, in America and the islands of the sea." Concern over racism prompted interracial alliances to form the National Association for the Advancement of Colored People (NAACP, 1909) and the National Urban League (1910).

Increasingly, America was being entered by European immigrants dissimilar from its Anglo-Saxon-Celtic origins: Jews, Eastern Europeans, and Italians. They quickly became subject to nativism, anti-Semitism, racial stereotyping, and abuse from what in 1964 sociologist E. Digby Baltzell labeled America's ruling White-Anglo-Saxon-Protestant (WASP) establishment.

In the late 19th and early 20th centuries, American followers of eugenicist Sir Francis Galton and racial purity theorized that heredity sharply influenced social conditions such as criminality, poverty, retardation, and immorality. These social ills might be corrected by carefully monitored human breeding. Since good breeding was lacking among many of the new immigrants (blacks, Asians, and Hispanics) their reproductive efforts might be carefully controlled and in some instances prevented altogether.

During World War I a team of psychologists probed intellectual abilities among immigrant, native white, and black U.S. Army recruits. Bypassing conflicting evidence, team leader Robert M. Yerkes claimed immigrants, including a majority of Mediterranean ethnics, ". . . are markedly inferior in mental alertness to the native-born American . . . almost as great as the intellectual difference between negro and white . . . are the differences between white racial groups . . . ."

Linking supposed genetic and hereditary deficiencies to societal shortcomings has been basic to justifications of unequal treatment of racial and ethnic minorities in the public mind. In the late 1960s a noted educational psychologist and a Nobel physics laureate lectured nationwide about heritable genetic and racial inferiority and its social consequences. In the 1990s others argued that perceived racial differences in intelligence created social and economic inequalities as a by-product of limited genetic gifts that could not be blamed on social injustice.

Media Racism. Racial stereotyping and bias gained wide airing with the coming of radio, motion pictures, and television. Distorted images of blacks and other racial minorities spread widely. In the 1915 movie *Birth of a Nation* white actors in blackface portrayed black brutes lusting after white women. Movie roles for black actors and Hispanics were until recently largely limited to those of servants, as well as pimps, prostitutes, gang members, or drug dealers living outside the law.

World War II Era. World War II stimulated widespread reflection about race matters. A few months after the Japanese attack on Pearl Harbor on Dec. 7, 1941, Pres. Franklin Roosevelt issued Executive Order 9066 leading to the relocation of 120,000 individuals of Japanese ancestry in isolated camps. Most were American citizens, not guilty of crimes, but detained on average two-to-three years by reason of race. In 1988, Congress agreed to pay limited reparations to Japanese internment survivors and relatives. American soldiers in turn fought the enemy in racially segregated units. Army policy segregated blood, regardless of type, by race, and some white Americans indicated they would prefer that their wounded sons die on the battlefield before having the blood of blacks transfused to their veins.

Others saw the moment differently. Ashley Montagu in *Man's Most Dangerous Myth: The Fallacy of Race* (1942), Ruth Benedict and Gene Weltfish in *The Races of Mankind* (1943), and Gunnar Myrdal in *American Dilemma: The Negro Problem and Modern Democracy* (1944) urged Americans to support racial understanding and equality.

Racist extermination of millions by Nazi Germany awakened many to the dangers of structuring any society upon doctrines of racial supremacy.

Pressured by black Americans and various egalitarian-minded associations, practices and laws based on race were systematically assaulted. In 1947 President Truman began desegregation of the military. That same year black baseball player Jackie Robinson, despite death threats and racial slurs, began desegregation of professional sports, symbolizing for some Americans the competition of blacks on an equal footing with whites.

Progress and Problems. Worldwide changes, including perceived threats from communism and African liberation struggles, persuaded American leaders to support racial progress. In *Brown* v. *Board of Education of Topeka* (1954) the Supreme Court struck down the racial doctrine of separate but equal. Indicating that there had never been racial equality in America, the decision noted that racial segregation and discrimination had a detrimental impact on all society and should be eliminated, not overnight but "with all deliberate speed."

Additional court rulings and congressional civil rights legislation in the 1950s, 1960s, and 1970s were stimulated by agitation from civil rights groups and their leaders, including Dr. Martin Luther King, Jr., Rosa Parks, Malcolm X, and numerous others. While meeting with resistance from some local, state, and national officials, the civil rights movement expanded blacks' rights in public accommodations and voting. A massive demonstration of their determination was the 1963 March on Washington.

Still, following years of civil and racial unrest, the Kerner Commission, a presidential commission on civil disorders, in 1968 states: "This is our basic conclusion: Our nation is moving toward two societies, one black, one white—separate and unequal. . . . It is time to make good the promises of American democracy to all citizens. . . ." The Kerner Commission considered defeating racism "the major unfinished business of the nation."

To achieve this goal new policies and programs were initiated. Among the most controversial has been affirmative action, an attempt to adjust levels of racial discrimination by remodeling society to aid qualified minorities gain footing in areas of American life previously largely closed to them—medical schools, law schools, graduate schools, and corporations.

But concerned advocates for and against resolving racial inequalities have criticized affirmative action for continuing preferential treatment of one group over another. Some whites labeled it a form of reverse discrimination. In *Bakke* v. *The University of California* (1978) the Supreme Court appeared to lend limited endorsement of this view in education.

Recent discussions of race and racism in America have been both encouraging and troublesome. Laws that discriminate against individuals based on race have largely disappeared, and publicly most organizations and institutions have adopted the words "equal opportunity" on logos and pronouncements. But at the same time many individuals and private and public institutions continue traditions of racial discrimination.

—LESLIE HOWARD OWENS

See Also: *African Americans; Brown* v. *Board of Education of Topeka; Civil Rights Movement; Desegregation; Dred Scott* v. *Sandford; Du Bois, W. E. B.; Immigration; Japanese-American Internment; March on Washington; Plessy* v. *Ferguson; Slavery.*

BIBLIOGRAPHY: Farley, Reynolds, and Walter R. Allen, *The Color Line and the Quality of Life in America* (Oxford Univ. Press 1989); Higginbotham, A. Leon, Jr., *In the Matter of Color—Race and the American Legal Process: The Colonial Period* (Oxford Univ. Press 1978); Takaki, Ronald, *A Different Mirror: A History of Multicultural America* (Little, Brown 1993).

RACKETS, organized criminal activities such as loan-sharking, bribery, extortion, or the obstruction of justice to ensure the continuation of illegal business practices. In 1970 Congress passed the Racketeer Influenced and Corrupt Organizations Act (RICO) to combat these activities. Under this law, both Mafia leaders and Wall Street traders have been prosecuted in recent years.

See Also: *Mafia; Organized Crime.*

RADICAL REPUBLICANS, faction of the Republican party during the Civil War (1861-65) and Reconstruction (1865-77). Initially the Radical Republicans were those members of the party who were most adamantly abolitionist. Led by Charles Sumner and Thaddeus Stevens among others, the Radical Republicans became dominant after the secession of the Southern states (1861) and the onset of the Civil War. They advocated the immediate emancipation of the slaves and a punitive policy toward the South. They opposed the so-called 10 percent Reconstruction plan of Pres. Abraham Lincoln and supported instead the Wade-Davis bill, which was tougher on the South and would put Congress in control of Reconstruction. The Radicals opposed the mild Reconstruction plans of Pres. Andrew Johnson and led the fight for his impeachment. In 1867 they successfully pushed for passage of the Reconstruction Act and the 14th Amendment, with which they hoped to reform the South and guarantee political and civil rights for African Americans.

See Also: Reconstruction; Republican Party; Wade-Davis Bill.

■ **RAGTIME,** American musical form. First appearing in the 1890s, ragtime combined American and European elements in a unique, syncopated style that emanated from the same African-American source as jazz and the blues, as well as from European classical music. Its origins in America can be detected in the music of African-American entertainers from the mid-19th century. At first, only slightly syncopated "rags" appeared in the form of "cakewalks" and other popular dances. Essentially piano music, these pieces were somewhat akin to European-style waltzes and marches. They consisted of a brief, flowery introduction followed by contrasting sections. African-American musician Scott Joplin, the best and most well-known ragtime composer, perfected the form with pieces like "Maple Leaf Rag" and "The Entertainer." His works, along with those of lesser-known composers, enjoyed extremely popular success very quickly. With commercialization and the appropriation of ragtime by Tin Pan Alley, the music became more rhythmically smooth and comic, losing its more distinctive and subtle elements. It was eventually absorbed into early jazz traditions and largely forgotten. Not until the 1970s were the works of Joplin and others republished and ragtime rediscovered as a valued, uniquely American art form.

See Also: Joplin, Scott.
BIBLIOGRAPHY: Jasen, David A., and Trebor Jay Tichenor, *Rags and Ragtime: A Musical History* (Seabury Press 1978).

■ **RAILROAD LEGISLATION,** state and federal laws regulating U.S. railroads. With the advent of the Railway Age in the 1830s and 1840s, regulatory restrictions began to emerge. State legislatures mostly controlled carriers, usually supervising service matters rather than the setting of rates. In the post–Civil War decades, however, consumer demands for rate controls grew. Spearheaded during the 1870s by the Grangers, a coalition of farmers and merchants, precedent-making legislation was enacted in the states of the upper Mississippi Valley, particularly Iowa and Wisconsin, regulating carriers in the "public interest." New state railroad commissions, modeled after pioneer ones in New England, appeared, and long-haul versus short-haul rate discriminations were addressed.

In 1887 a major event in public control occurred. A combination of consumer agitation and an 1886 U.S. Supreme Court decision (the *Wabash* case), which invalidated major provisions of the Granger laws, prompted Congress to pass the Interstate Commerce Act. This measure forbade rebates, pools, and related discriminations, decreed that more money could not be charged for a shorter distance than for a longer one over the same line, and created the Interstate Commerce Commission (ICC).

But federal regulatory machinery did not end consumer complaints. In 1906 the Hepburn Act made the ICC a stronger body, giving it greater authority in rate enforcement and extending its power to bridge and ferry, express, pipeline, and sleeping-car companies. This Progressive Era triumph contained other important provisions, most notably allowing the ICC to prescribe a uniform system of bookkeeping. Four years later progressive reformers also pushed through the Mann-Elkins Act, which placed on railroads the burden of proving the "justice of contemplated charges" and permitted the ICC to suspend new rates for 10 months pending investigation.

Although the Transportation Acts of 1920, 1940, and 1958 modified the core federal regulations, the next landmark event did not take place until 1980, when Congress brought about the partial deregulation of the railroad industry. The key provisions allowed carriers to negotiate rates with shippers and offer rebates for guaranteed traffic volumes. At last industry complaints of "enterprise denied" largely ended. Railroads took advantage of this favorable regulatory environment, dramatically improving their physical plant and rolling stock and increasing their profitability.

—H. ROGER GRANT

See Also: *Granger Movement; Interstate Commerce Commission (ICC); Railroads; Transportation Act.*

BIBLIOGRAPHY: Buck, Solon Justus, *The Granger Movement, 1870-1880* (Harvard Univ. Press 1913); Hoogenboom, Ari, and Olive Hoogenboom, *A History of the ICC: From Panacea to Palliative* (Norton 1976); Martin, Albro, *Railroads Triumphant* (Oxford Univ. Press 1992).

■ **RAILROADS,** first built in the United States in the early 1830s. Since their inception railroads increased transportation options for Americans. Although the initial lines often connected only a few communities, usually linking them to a waterway—lake, river, or canal—the railway map of the nation dramatically changed by the Civil War. In 1860 rail mileage reached 30,626. Construction continued in several bursts until the 1920s. The 1880s witnessed the heyday of railroad building. As the decade dawned, the American rail network stood at 93,267 miles; 10 years later it had soared to 163,597, a spectacular 43 percent gain. Mileage finally peaked in 1916, when 254,251 miles of steel rails laced the republic. Not only did much of the national railroad map resemble a plate of wet spaghetti, but the number of large companies increased. After the Civil War, "system building" had swept the industry, and railroads became the country's first big business. Companies like the Boston & Maine, Chicago & North Western, and Pennsylvania expanded greatly by absorbing independent firms, at times becoming interregional in scope.

The Impact of Railroads. The "iron horse" changed America. For one thing the physical appearance of the countryside was altered. The "railroad corridor" with its graded right-of-way,

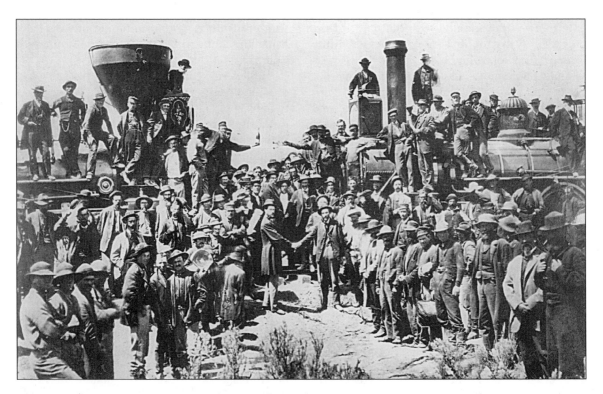

Railroad workers and dignitaries of the Central Pacific and Union Pacific lines celebrate at Promontory Point, Utah, as the first transcontinental railroad is completed in 1869.

A Union Pacific camp, known as "Hell-on-Wheels," at the "end-of-track" in 1868. More workers died from exposure, violence, and disease in these tent-towns than in many industrial accidents during construction.

track, bridges, stations, and support facilities created a new look. A variety of industries sprang up at trackside, including elevators, factories, mills, and other businesses. Rails also hastened the country's industrial takeoff: flanged wheels greatly stimulated commercial agriculture and diversified manufacturing. Pockets of isolation within regions were greatly reduced. "Railroads will make the state [Ohio] into a truly productive Eden," opined a Cleveland businessman in the 1850s. "There is no better way to move goods and people. . . . The locomotive is a heaven-sent invention." Few disagreed.

With railroads came depots. These structures, which initially were often hotels or some other adaptable building and later were often constructed from standard plans, served as literal "front doors" to hundreds of cities, towns, and villages. The depot facilitated regular contact with the outside world. Visitors and residents, newspapers and mail, merchandise and carload freight passed through the facility. The station's chattering telegraph machine offered the sole source of fast information. Understandably during the Railway Age virtually everyone knew the location of the depot or depots, the name of the agent or

agents, and the arrival and departure times of passenger trains, perhaps even of pokey freights. By the early years of the 20th century, the nation possessed from 75,000 to 80,000 depot buildings. And larger communities had separate freight stations through which vast amounts of goods passed.

Railroads in the 20th Century. Few Americans, including industry leaders, believed that any other form of transportation would ever challenge the dominance of railroads. By the 1920s the new motor era was firmly established; automobiles and buses captured much of the short-distance intercity passenger business, and trucks took increasing amounts of less-than-carload freight. Then with the introduction of larger aircraft in the 1930s, most notably the DC-3, railroads began losing their long-distance monopoly on passenger travel. The Great Depression of the 1930s, however, damaged the financial health of railroads more than did modal competition, and World War II seemingly brought the industry back to a robust condition.

Indeed the wartime era marked a time of greatness for railroads. As the only viable alternative to land and water transportation, carriers managed to handle 83 percent of the increase in *all* traffic between 1941 and 1944. And they moved 91 percent of all military freight and 98 percent of all military personnel. Freight traffic, measured in ton miles, soared from 373 billion in 1940 to 737 billion in 1944 (the industry would not again equal the latter figure until 1966). Passenger volume, expressed in revenue passenger miles, soared from 23 billion in 1940 to 95 billion in 1944, a peak figure never again attained.

By the 1950s, however, conditions had changed. Railroad executives felt the sting of highway competition after turnpikes and interstate "super" roads opened. Yet officials benefited from the replacement of steam locomotives with diesel-electric ones. After these savings had run their course, railroads became keenly interested in mergers, which were designed for savings and efficiency. In the 1960s "merger madness" swept the industry and continued through the 1990s, producing giant "mega" carriers. As a result rail lines, particularly feeders, were abandoned or sold to short-line operators, a process made easier by partial federal deregulation in 1980. By the 1990s the railroad industry, which benefited from computer technology, liberalization of union work rules, and congested roadways, had become a growth business. Even the quasi-public National Railroad Passenger Corporation, Amtrak, which started in 1971, exhibited strength in several markets. Perhaps a new Railway Age was at hand.

—H. ROGER GRANT

See Also: *Railroad Legislation; Transportation.*
BIBLIOGRAPHY: Barriger, John W., *Super-Railroads for a Dynamic American Economy* (Simmons-Boardman 1956); Grant, H. Roger, *Erie Lackawanna: Death of an American Railroad, 1938-1992* (Stanford Univ. Press 1994); Klein, Maury, *Unfinished Business: The Railroad in American Life* (Univ. Press of New England 1994); Martin, Albro, *Railroads Triumphant* (Oxford Univ. Press 1992); Saunders, Richard, *The Railroad Mergers and the Coming of Conrail* (Greenwood 1978); Stover, John F., *The Life and Decline of the American Railroad* (Oxford Univ. Press 1970).

■ **RAILWAY LABOR ACT (1934),** federal legislation ensuring American rail workers collective bargaining rights. The act, one of several New Deal laws aimed at stabilizing the railroad industry during the Depression, also created joint labor-management mediation and adjustment boards to settle strikes.

See Also: *New Deal; Railroads.*

■ **RAINEY, GERTRUDE (MA) (1886-1939),** blues singer often called "the mother of the blues." Born in Columbus, Georgia, the daughter of minstrel performers, she grew up immersed in the fertile African-American folk traditions of the South. She married William (Pa) Rainey in 1904, and the two formed a traveling vaudeville show. She developed what became known as the "classic blues" style. From 1923 to 1928 Rainey recorded 94 songs, at least 47 of which were her own compositions.

See Also: *Blues.*

■ **RAIN-IN-THE-FACE (c. 1835-1905),** Hunkpapa Sioux leader. Named as a teenager when rain spread his warpaint down his face, Rain-in-the-Face became a war leader because of his bravery in battle, leading the Sioux during the wars with the United States in the 1860s and 1870s and fighting with Sitting Bull during the Black Hills War of 1876-77. After his surrender in 1880, he lived at the Standing Rock Reservation in South Dakota.

See Also: *Indians of North America; Sioux; Sitting Bull.*

■ **RALEIGH, SIR WALTER (1554-1618),** English soldier and early sponsor of North American settlement. Raleigh enjoyed the favor of Queen Elizabeth I. In 1584, inspired by the colonizing efforts of his half brother, Sir Humphrey Gilbert, Raleigh gained a charter to found a colony in the New World. A reconnaissance expedition located a likely site south of Chesapeake Bay. Raleigh named the new land Virginia in honor of Queen Elizabeth and sent an expedition to settle Roanoke Island in 1585. The settlers, more interested in gold than colonizing, abandoned the project within a year. In 1587 Raleigh sent a second group of 120 settlers to the Roanoke site. War with Spain in 1588 prevented the colony's resupply. When a ship finally returned to Roanoke in 1590, the colonists had vanished. Raleigh turned his attention in 1595 to exploring the Orinoco River in present-day Venezuela for gold. With the accession of James I to the throne, Raleigh fell into disfavor and was executed in 1618.

See Also: *Roanoke, Lost Colony of.*

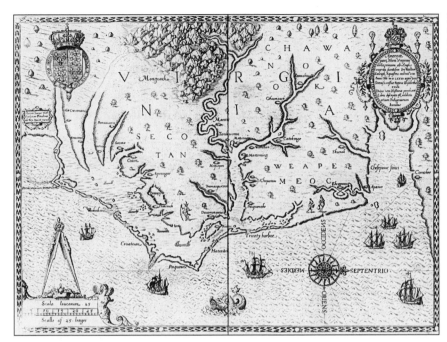

In 1584, Sir Walter Raleigh organized the expedition that explored Roanoke Island, which was colonized the following year. This map is from the official report of the expedition.

■ **RAND, ELLEN (1875-1941),** portrait artist and cousin of Henry James. Well regarded by contemporaries for her empathy and her technical expertise, she was elected to the National Academy of Design in 1934. Her rendering of Franklin Delano Roosevelt has endured as his official portrait.

See Also: *Painting.*

■ **RANDOLPH, ASA PHILIP (1889-1979),** labor activist and civil rights leader. Born in Crescent City, Florida, Randolph in 1917, with Chandler Owen, started and edited the *Messenger.* From this forum Randolph advocated a program of class solidarity among white and black workers. He organized the Brotherhood of Sleeping Car Porters and Maids in 1925 and served as its president until 1968. In 1941, Randolph threatened a march on Washington to protest discriminatory labor practices in defense-related industries. Largely as a result of pressure from Randolph, President Roosevelt banned discrimination in defense-related employment and created the Fair Employment Practices Commission. When the American Federation of Labor and Congress of Industrial Organizations merged in 1955, Randolph was made a vice president of the new organization. And repeating some of his tactics of 20 years before, he served as director of the celebrated March on Washington in August 1963.

See Also: *African Americans; Civil Rights Movement; Labor Movement; March on Washington.*

■ **RANDOLPH, EDMUND (1753-1813),** lawyer and statesman. Born to a wealthy Virginia family in Williamsburg, Randolph practiced law briefly before becoming George Washington's aide-de-camp in 1775. He rose quickly through the political ranks, serving in the Virginia Convention in 1776 and as attorney general of Virginia from 1776 to 1786. He was elected as a delegate to the Second Continental Congress in 1779 and became governor of Virginia in 1786. A delegate to the Constitutional Convention, Randolph proposed the Virginia Plan, which advocated a strong central government. He played an important role in Washington's administration, first as U.S. attorney general from 1789 to 1794 and later as secretary of state (1794-95). Randolph was forced to resign by Washington after he was falsely accused of being partial to the French and interested in receiving a bribe. His name was cleared in later years.

See Also: *Constitution of the United States; Revolution, American; Virginia Plan.*

Labor and civil rights leader A. Philip Randolph applied the pressure that resulted in the presidential orders banning racial discrimination in defense industries (1941) and desegregating the military (1948).

■ **RANKIN, JEANETTE (1880-1973),** pacifist and the first woman to serve in the U.S. Congress. She was born in Missoula, Montana. As a Republican member of Congress (1917-19, 1941-43), she voted against U.S. involvement in both world wars. In 1968 she led the Jeanette Rankin Brigade to Washington, D.C., to protest the Vietnam War.

See Also: Pacifism.

■ **RAPP, GEORGE (1757-1847),** German-American religious leader. Born Johann Georg Rapp in Wurttemberg, Germany, Rapp founded the Harmony Society, a religious sect also known as the Harmonites and the Rappites. Faced with persecution in Europe, Rapp and his followers immigrated to Butler County, Pennsylvania, in 1803. They relocated to the Wabash River Valley in Indiana in 1814, then to Beaver County, Pennsylvania, in 1825. The Harmony Society adopted a written constitution with Rapp as its supreme leader. Millennial in outlook and pietistic in temperament, the celibate Harmonites produced wines, whisky, woolens, and other manufactures and became relatively wealthy, using much of their revenues for charitable ventures.

See Also: Religion.

■ **RAUSCHENBERG, ROBERT (1925-),** avant-garde artist. Born in Port Arthur, Texas, Rauschenberg began his artistic training at the Kansas City Art Institute in 1946-47. His early work on large white canvases was a forerunner of minimalism, but his later works used a variety of media and incorporated objects into their surfaces. Rauschenberg was committed to collaborative art projects, as in his work as costume and stage designer with choreographer Merce Cunningham and composer John Cage (1955-64).

See Also: Cage, John; Cunningham, Merce; Painting.

■ **RAUSCHENBUSCH, WALTER (1861-1918),** religious leader and theologian of the Social Gospel. Born in Rochester, New York, Rauschenbusch was educated in Germany and at the University of Rochester. After graduating from Rochester Theological Seminary in 1886, he was the pastor at the Second German Baptist Church in New York City. Located near "Hell's Kitchen," he saw firsthand the conditions of poverty, unemployment, malnutrition, disease, and crime. Rauschenbusch became active in social reform and sought spiritual teachings to counter the plight he was witnessing. In 1891 he studied in Berlin and England and became interested in Fabian Socialism, which called for the gradual change to governmental control of industry. He assisted with the founding of the Brotherhood of the Kingdom in 1892, an organization of social Christianity. Prompted by the depression of 1893, Rauschenbusch struggled for a way to make Christianity an instrument of social reform. While a professor of church history at Rochester Seminary, he explained his beliefs in *Christianity and the Social Crisis* (1907), which became a bestseller and was translated into several languages. Its popularity placed him in high demand as a speaker and author until his death from cancer.

His other writings include *Prayers of the Social Awakening* (1910), *Christianizing the Social Order* (1912), *The Social Principles of Jesus* (1916), and *A Theology for the Social Gospel* (1917).

See Also: Religion.

■ **RAWLINGS, MARJORIE KINNAN (1896-1953),** journalist and author. She was born in Washington, D.C. Her masterpiece, *The Yearling* (1938), won a Pulitzer Prize. Her other novels about life in rural Florida include *South Moon Under* (1933), *Golden Apples* (1935), and *The Sojourner* (1953). She also wrote an autobiography titled *Cross Creek* (1942).

See Also: Novel.

■ **RAYBURN, SAM (1882-1961),** Democratic legislator and Speaker of the U.S. House of Representatives (1940-49, 1951-53, 1955-61). Born in Roane County, Tennessee, he practiced law and served in the Texas state legislature (1907-13) before winning election to the U.S. House (1912), where he served for the rest of his life. A superb legislative tactician, Rayburn became majority leader (1937) and Speaker three years later.

See Also: House of Representatives.

■ **READ, GEORGE (1733-98),** judge and Revolutionary War statesman. Read was born in Cecil County, Maryland, and later moved to Delaware. He was a signer of the Declaration of Independence and member of the Second Continental Congress. After the Revolution Read served as a U.S. senator and state chief justice.

See Also: Declaration of Independence.

■ **REAGAN, RONALD WILSON (1911-),** 40th president of the United States (1981-89). Born in Tampico, Illinois, Reagan graduated from Eureka College in Illinois in 1932. After a brief stint as a play-by-play sports announcer on a local radio station in Iowa, Reagan went to Hollywood and began a film career, making 51 full-length movies in all. During World War II, he was assigned to a special unit that made training films. In 1940 Reagan married the actress Jane Wyman. They were divorced in 1948, and in 1952 he married the actress Nancy Davis.

Early Political Career. Reagan's political career began when he joined the Screen Actors Guild and eventually served as its president (1947-52, 1959-60). Originally a Democrat, Reagan evolved into a philosophical conservative and militant anticommunist. He was one of the lone bright spots for the Republican party in 1964; Reagan's impassioned speech in favor of presidential candidate Barry Goldwater brought him national attention as a spokesman for conservatism. Two years later, Reagan won the first of two terms (1967-75) as governor of California. He ran for the Republican presidential nomination in 1968 and 1976 (narrowly losing in the latter year to incumbent Pres. Gerald R. Ford) and finally captured the nomination in 1980, with George Bush as his running mate. Reagan's gentle confidence more than overshadowed incumbent Pres. Jimmy Carter's tense preoccupation with the Iranian hostage crisis. His campaign slogan "Are you better off now than you were four years ago?" struck a chord with an America depressed with foreign and economic troubles. Reagan handily defeated Carter as well as third-party challenger John Anderson, winning 489 electoral votes to Carter's 49.

First Presidential Term. Reagan's first term began on a note of optimism, as the Iranian hostages were freed moments before his inaugu-

Ronald Reagan won the presidential elections of 1980 and 1984, leading a resurgence of conservative political power in the nation.

ration on Jan. 20, 1981. The president's economic package, however, which called for immediate and deep tax cuts, appeared to be stalled in the Democratic-controlled Congress. Then, on Mar. 30, 1981, a lone assassin made an attempt on Reagan's life. Although seriously wounded, Reagan eventually recovered. His soothing poise during the ordeal only increased public affection toward him and gave him additional political clout. By the end of the year, Reagan had engineered a 5 percent tax cut, and the term "trickle-down economics" (referring to the savings that would supposedly "trickle down" to consumers after they had benefited from the tax cut) became a part of the American vocabulary.

Yet, in the same session of Congress, the administration cut $35 billion from domestic programs such as Medicaid, Medicare, and food stamps. Budget cuts continued throughout Reagan's first term, and when coupled with additional 10 percent tax cuts in 1982 and 1983, each of which favored wealthier Americans, "Reaganomics" was branded by many liberals as a policy that had little benefit for less-fortunate Americans.

Although Reagan cut taxes and some domestic programs, he increased defense spending in an intentional effort to undermine the Soviet Union. As a result, the budget deficit ballooned to more than $200 billion a year by 1988, the highest in American history. Reagan's fiscal conservatism, plus his invasion of Marxist Grenada (1982) and his uncompromising stand toward the tottering Soviet Union, which he branded an "evil empire" in a 1983 speech, endeared him to the American electorate. Reagan sailed to reelection in 1984, easily defeating Democrat Walter Mondale.

Second Presidential Term. One of the most notable developments of Reagan's second term was the softening of his rhetoric toward the Soviet Union in the wake of the succession to power of the more moderate Mikhail Gorbachev. Impressed with Gorbachev's attempts to reform the Soviet economy (*perestroika*) and introduce more political openness (*glasnost*), Reagan helped engineer a treaty (1988) limiting medium-range nuclear missiles. Although he never abandoned his hope to gain an antiballistic missile system that could destroy incoming missiles—a system called the Strategic Defense Initiative (SDI) and nicknamed

"Star Wars"—Reagan succeeded in vastly improving American relations with the Soviet Union.

Reagan's legacy was compromised by the involvement of his administration in what became known as the Iran-Contra Affair. Reagan was obsessed with overthrowing Nicaragua's Marxist-leaning Sandinista government. His administration backed an anti-Sandinista insurgent group known as the Contras. But in October 1984, worried about entering a long-term military commitment in Latin America, Congress outlawed any aid to the Contras. Despite this prohibition, Lt. Col. Oliver North of the National Security Council arranged to have about $12 million of the profits from a secret arms sale (1986) to Iran sent to the Contras. By selling arms to Iran, the administration had hoped that the Iranians would use their influence to obtain the release of U.S. hostages in Lebanon.

The story was revealed in 1987, and the resulting investigations led to several resignations and indictments. Whether Reagan knew about the diversion of funds remains at issue. When he left the White House in January 1989, Reagan's personal popularity was at the greatest peak of any president since Dwight Eisenhower. In 1994, Reagan announced that he was suffering from Alzheimer's Disease and thereafter effectively dropped out of public view.

—JOHN ROBERT GREENE

See Also: Bush, George H. W.; Cold War; Iran-Contra Affair; Presidential Elections; President of the United States.

BIBLIOGRAPHY: Cannon, Lou, *President Reagan: The Role of a Lifetime* (Simon & Schuster 1991); Schaller, Michael, *Reckoning with Reagan: America and Its President in the 1980s* (Oxford Univ. Press 1992); Schieffer, Bob, and Gary Paul Gates, *The Acting President* (Dutton 1989).

■ **REALISM,** late-19th-century cultural movement. Realism was a response to romanticism and became prominent in the United States in the second half of the 19th century. Realist writers and painters set as their aim the accurate and truthful representation of everyday life in their own era, with an emphasis on the ordinary. Realist writers used a limited narrative perspective in the third person but steered away from the idea of the omniscient narrator. Henry James, Mark Twain, and William Dean Howells led the realist movement in American literature. Howells was its major proponent, not only in the examples of his own fiction but also in his role as literary critic and editor of the *Atlantic Monthly* and *Harper's*, major journals of the late 19th century. In painting a group of artists known as "The Eight," or the "Ashcan School," shared the aim of accurate depiction of contemporary culture, though in a slightly later period than the literary movement. Painters such as Robert Henri, John Sloan, and George Bellows were prominent in the early decades of the 20th century.

See Also: Bellows, George; Henri, Robert; Howells, William Dean; James, Henry; Painting; Romanticism; Sloan, John French; Twain, Mark.

■ **RECALL,** procedure for removing an elected official from office before the end of a term. First enacted for municipal officials in Los Angeles (1903), recall laws usually require a public referendum to oust an officeholder.

■ **RECONSTRUCTION,** term used both for the period (1865-77) following the Civil War and for the reintegration into the Union of the states of the defeated Confederacy during that period. Reconstruction has been almost as controversial among historians as it was among contemporaries. Once construed as a depraved and spiteful era mismanaged by ignorant freedmen—the freed slaves—and corrupt politicians, historians have reinterpreted it in a more positive light. The legacy of the changes wrought by Reconstruction lasted well into the 20th century.

Efforts to reconstruct the nation were contemplated even before the end of the Civil War. As slaves fled to the freedom of Union lines and as the military benefits of the Emancipation Proclamation (1863) became increasingly apparent, Pres. Abraham Lincoln announced his Proclamation of Amnesty and Reconstruction on Dec. 8, 1863. Defining the terms on which the Confederacy could be reunited with the Union, Lincoln's plan pardoned all southerners, except Confederate leaders, who affirmed an oath of loyalty to the Union and supported emancipation. When 10 percent of a state's population had taken such an oath, they could establish a new state government. Resistance by Radical Republicans in Congress, who wanted reconstructed states to guarantee African Americans equal rights, effectively aborted Lincoln's plans for reconstruction.

Presidential Reconstruction. Because Lincoln had taken the initiative to begin Reconstruction, his successor, Pres. Andrew Johnson, argued that responsibility for its implementation lay with the president, not Congress. Johnson ushered in the period of Presidential Reconstruction, which lasted from 1865 to 1867. If some Republicans considered Lincoln's Reconstruction policy too lenient, many were outraged at Johnson's, which pardoned increasing numbers of southerners, ex-Confederate officials included, and set few limits on how new southern state governments were to be formed. Although Johnson insisted that state governments repudiate secession and abolish slavery, he gave them considerable scope in running their affairs. These governments took advantage of such leniency not only by electing former Confederates to public office but also by instituting a series of Black Codes designed to limit the liberties of the freedmen.

Presidential Reconstruction was characterized by a bitter political struggle between Johnson and Radical Republicans like Charles Sumner and Thaddeus Stevens, who sponsored legislation to protect the civil liberties of the freedmen. Johnson's commitment to state sovereignty and his patent disregard for blacks' voting rights led many Republicans to the conclusion that Reconstruction had to be implemented by a Republican Congress. Johnson was weakened by congressional elections in 1866, by impeachment proceedings, and by the South's almost unanimous rejection of the 14th Amendment, which prohibited states from depriving citizens of equal protection before the law. The election of Republican Ulysses S. Grant as president in 1868 ensured that responsibility for Reconstruction would rest with Congress.

Congressional Reconstruction. Lasting until 1877, Congressional, or Radical, Reconstruction began with the Reconstruction Acts of 1867, which divided the South into five military districts and mandated how southern governments were to be established and administered. By 1870 all the former Confederate states had been readmitted to the Union, and the majority of these were controlled by Republicans.

Southern Republicanism was very much a biracial alliance. Former Union soldiers, Freedmen's Bureau agents, northern businessmen, teachers, and other whites, many of whom had come South during Presidential Reconstruction, formed one component of the alliance. In addition to these so-called carpetbaggers, native whites, or scalawags, comprised another strand made up mostly of staunch Unionists who had despaired of secession. This most reviled group of southern traitors, as former Confederates liked to cast them, was anxious to modernize the South and recognize black civil rights but retain control over the mechanics of state government, primarily to stay any attempts by former rebels to regain political power.

For their part African-American Republicans proved honest, competent, and effective politicians who were probably less corrupt than most public officials in what was widely recognized as a corrupt era. Although only South Carolina and Louisiana had African-American legislative majorities, hundreds of African Americans served in state legislatures and local offices, and 16 made it to Congress. The achievements of Republican states, once portrayed as vengeful and self-serving, were in fact impressive. To be sure, class interests sometimes divided southern African-American legislators. Nevertheless southern Republicans worked together to promote publicly funded schools and asylums, legislate equitable taxation policies, protect plantation workers from excessive exploitation, and adopt economic policies designed to elevate the region as a whole.

The last of these policies was of particular importance. While northern industry and agriculture benefited from the Civil War, the South's economy was decimated by it. In the postbellum period, northern capital was invested in southern industries in an effort not only to provide healthy returns for northern entrepreneurs but also revitalize the southern economy. The results were often mixed, and southern economic progress was hampered, particularly in agriculture, by planters' reluctance to deal with former slaves on equitable terms. Attempts to tie blacks to the land

through debt peonage, sharecropping, and restrictive tenancy arrangements were thinly veiled efforts by planters to reassert their mastery in a free-wage labor context. The economic consequences of such schemes proved debilitating for blacks, poor whites, cash-starved planters and farmers, and the southern economy as a whole. Lacking any substantive base for sustained economic growth, the South fared worse than the North in the years following 1873, when depression halved the price of cotton and put an even tighter squeeze on credit.

These very real problems notwithstanding, freedmen made the most of the freedom they won and the political freedoms Congressional Reconstruction tried to grant them. As soon as they were emancipated, former slaves exercised their new right to move about, locate family members who had been sold during slavery, and learn how to read and write. With the help of Freedmen's Bureau agents, they negotiated with erstwhile masters for fairer working conditions and pay. Freedmen also instigated a variety of fraternal and religious networks by establishing black churches and benevolent societies that remained outside white control. These institutions proved remarkably enduring and were important for affording southern African Americans protection from Jim Crow after Reconstruction had ended. In short, much of Reconstruction was spent by former slaves trying to define what freedom meant and testing its limits.

The Undoing of Reconstruction. For many southern whites, Radical Reconstruction was just that: radical. Not only had slavery ended, not only had the cornerstone of southern economic and social relations disintegrated under Reconstruction, but whites' political world had also been turned upside down. The sight of former slaves exercising their right to vote and hold political office outraged many southern whites. Recognizing that African Americans' right to vote was protected under the 15th Amendment (1870), southern whites devised extralegal means to keep African Americans from the polls and thereby end Reconstruction. Attempts to "redeem" the South for white Democrats took many forms. The Ku Klux Klan terrorized local Republican leaders and intimidated African Americans who refused to work under oppressive labor arrangements. Not until Congress passed the Enforcement Acts in 1871 was the Klan brought under control and political and racial violence stemmed. But local elections in the South continued to erupt into violence during the 1870s, and African-American voters found themselves increasingly intimidated at the polls. Southern efforts to end Radical Reconstruction were aided by a worsening economy in 1873 and congressional elections in 1874, when Democrats won control of the House of Representatives and it became clear that other issues were beginning to eclipse Reconstruction. By 1876 only three southern states remained under Republican control.

Reconstruction ended with a political compromise between Democrats and Republicans in 1877. In return for a variety of sweeteners that served to strengthen Democratic control of the South, including the withdrawal of federal troops from the region, Republican Rutherford B. Hayes brokered a deal for the presidency with Democratic nominee Samuel J. Tilden. Distracted by economic concerns in the North and West, Republicans formally ended their experiment to reconstruct the South and thereafter turned a blind eye to the dismantling of African Americans' political rights and the gradual institution of Jim Crow.

But Reconstruction was not a complete failure. A unique experiment, it gave southern African Americans a glimpse of freedom and afforded them the opportunity to establish social and institutional networks that would help sustain them until the Second Reconstruction in the 1960s.

—Mark M. Smith

See Also: Carpetbaggers; Civil War; Disfranchisement; Freedmen's Bureau; Ku Klux Klan (KKK); Radical Republicans; Reconstruction Acts; Scalawags.

BIBLIOGRAPHY: Foner, Eric, *Reconstruction: America's Unfinished Revolution 1863-1877* (Harper & Row 1988); Franklin, John Hope, *Reconstruction after the Civil War* (Univ. of Chicago Press 1994); Saville, Julie, *The Work of Reconstruction: From Slave to Wage Laborer in South Carolina, 1860-1870* (Cambridge Univ. Press 1994).

■ **RECONSTRUCTION ACTS (1867-68),** a series of four laws passed by Congress between March 1867 and March 1868 that imposed terms and conditions on the Southern states for readmission to the Union. The legislation, which passed over Pres. Andrew Johnson's veto, embodied the Radical Republican plan for reconstruction: It asserted congressional rather than executive control over the process.

The first and most significant Reconstruction Act, passed on Mar. 2, 1867, divided the South into five military districts each under the command of an army general and subject to martial law. To be restored to the Union, 10 former Confederate states (Tennessee had been readmitted in July 1866) were required to call constitutional conventions elected by universal manhood suffrage. These conventions had to establish state governments guaranteeing the franchise to Negroes and then ratify the 14th Amendment. Ex-Confederates were specifically excluded from this process. Congress reserved to itself the power to decide whether states had met these requirements, to end military government, and to seat representatives.

Subsequent acts passed on Mar. 23 and July 19, 1867, granted sweeping enforcement powers to the military regimes when the South proved recalcitrant in complying with the original act. The final Reconstruction Act of Mar. 11, 1868, declared a majority of the votes cast rather than a majority of registered voters sufficient to put new state constitutions into effect.

—Thomas E. Schott

See Also: Reconstruction.

■ **RED BIRD (c. 1788-1828),** Winnebago leader. Born near Prairie du Chien, Wisconsin, he became a war chief during the 1827 Winnebago Uprising, a series of sporadic raids over the course of a month that resulted from the arrest of two Winnebago men for attacking a family of French Canadian settlers. Red Bird surrendered and was later pardoned for his part in the incident. In August 1829, Winnebago leaders ceded all tribal lands in Illinois and Wisconsin south of the Fox and Wisconsin rivers.

See Also: Indians of North America.

■ **RED CLOUD (1822-1909),** Oglala Sioux chief. Red Cloud was born on the Platte River in what is now Nebraska. Legend has it that a meteorite

In 1868, Red Cloud concluded a peace treaty with the federal government at Fort Laramie, Wyoming, preserving Sioux hunting rights in the Powder River region.

flashed across the sky that night and inspired his name. As he grew to be a leader of his people, his main concern was the overland migration of thousands of whites heading to Oregon or California on the Bozeman Trail. Unable to negotiate a settlement with the U.S. government, Red Cloud's warriors closed down parts of the trail. Skirmishes followed until the government, realizing the high cost of maintaining its Bozeman forts, eventually backed down and yielded to Red Cloud. In the Fort Laramie Treaty (1868), the United States agreed to abandon the posts in exchange for the cessation of Indian raids. The treaty created the Great Sioux Reservation, which occupied half of the present-day state of South Dakota and parts of Wyoming and Nebraska.

The peace was short-lived, however. Lt. Col. George Custer broke the agreement by leading (1875) mining experts into the Black Hills, sacred to the Sioux. There they discovered gold, and a new round of warfare was forced upon the Sioux to protect their lands. Red Cloud summed up the agreements with the United States in this fashion: "They made us many promises, more than I can remember, but they never kept but one. They promised to take our land, and they took it."

In 1870 Red Cloud headed a delegation of Sioux to Washington, D.C., to meet with Pres. Ulysses S. Grant. Red Cloud became the main negotiator between the Sioux and the U.S. government. He advocated a peace policy, even after the defeat of Custer in 1876, but he slowly began to lose his power within the tribe and was deposed as chief in 1881. Red Cloud died in 1909 on the Pine Ridge, South Dakota, reservation.

—RYAN MADDEN

See Also: Custer, George Armstrong; Indians of North America; Sioux.

BIBLIOGRAPHY: Utley, Robert, *The Last Days of the Sioux Nation* (Yale Univ. Press 1963); Weeks, Philip, *Farewell, My Nation: The American Indian and the United States, 1829-1890* (Harlan Davidson 1990).

■ **RED CROSS, AMERICAN NATIONAL,** organization founded in 1881 as a private agency by American Civil War nurse Clara Barton, who, while visiting Europe in 1870, had been impressed by the relief provided by the International Red Cross during the Franco-Prussian war. Congress granted the American Red Cross an official charter that was revised in 1905. It remains a semigovernment agency primarily dependent on private funding. The functions of the Red Cross, then as now, were to assist in communication between members of the military and their families and to provide disaster relief. The American Red Cross played a key role in providing medical services during every military conflict of the 20th century. Beginning with relief provided to victims of massive forest fires in Michigan in 1881, the agency has also assisted victims of earthquakes, hurricanes, and other natural disasters.

See Also: Barton, Clarissa Harlowe (Clara); Sanitary Commission.

BIBLIOGRAPHY: Gilbo, Patrick, *The American Red Cross* (Chelsea House 1987).

■ **REDEMPTION,** movement of conservative southern whites during Reconstruction. Founded in the immediate aftermath of the Civil War and gaining strength with the Panic of 1873, the Redemption movement sought to restore white southern control of land and politics. The Redemption movement excluded blacks. Members of the movement, called "Redeemers," hoped to build a New South based on modern business methods while thwarting the Reconstruction reforms supported by Republicans. By 1876, Redeemers had gained control of all the southern states except South Carolina, Louisiana, and Florida.

See Also: Reconstruction.

■ **RED JACKET (c. 1758-1830),** Seneca leader. Red Jacket fought for the British during the American Revolution. After the war, as members of the Iroquois Confederacy were forced to cede much of their homelands, Red Jacket spoke out against his uncle Cornplanter's accommodationist position and advocated a return to traditional Iroquois values and a ban on missionaries in Seneca territory. He also opposed the Longhouse religion of his uncle Handsome Lake. He was deposed in 1827. Ironically, he was buried in a Christian ceremony.

See Also: Cornplanter; Handsome Lake; Indians of North America.

■ **RED SCARE,** term connoting the hysteria and denial of civil liberties that occurred during and just after World War I and again in the later 1940s and 1950s during the Cold War. The Palmer Raids of 1919, named after Attorney Gen. A. Mitchell Palmer, marked the worst suppression of civil liberties in U.S. history. Opposition to World War I initially provoked the government's harsh actions, and fear of radicalism after the 1917 Bolshevik Revolution in Russia gave the repression added impetus. The Espionage Act (1917) identified any effort to oppose the nation's military operations with disloyalty or treason. The Sedition Act (1918) established punishments for a range of activities previously considered merely unpatriotic. Other laws provided for the deportation of aliens guilty of certain beliefs or of association with others deemed guilty.

In large part the red scare was directed at the Socialist party and the Industrial Workers of the World (IWW). Socialist newspapers were denied use of mailing permits and their public meetings canceled, while IWW headquarters were raided, local leaders taken to jail without charges, and their strikes broken by federal troops. Meanwhile the new Bureau of Investigation (later known as the Federal Bureau of Investigation) instigated spy procedures, sending hundreds of agents into radical organizations, and preparing a dragnet for 10,000 arrests. The Immigration Act of 1920, closing gaps in previous acts, made aliens punishable merely for possessing literature or indicating sympathy for radical beliefs, rather than carrying out radical teachings in some specific fashion. State "criminal syndicalism" acts and the organization of the National Guard on a peacetime basis gave states the procedures they required for continued repression of "unrest."

The post–World War II Cold War with the Soviet Union and the fear, not totally unfounded, of Soviet espionage revived the repression of dissent. Pres. Harry S. Truman's loyalty-security program, announced in 1947, led to a purge of the labor movement and to widespread "blacklisting" in films and television. Although fewer individuals were imprisoned than in the earlier red scare, FBI harassment and the monitoring of private life abused civil liberties. Outdoing Truman's program, congressional investigating committees, notably the one led by Sen. Joseph McCarthy, Republican of Wisconsin, cruelly ruined many innocent people's careers.

—PAUL BUHLE

See Also: Federal Bureau of Investigation (FBI); Industrial Workers of the World; McCarthy, Joseph; McCarthyism.

BIBLIOGRAPHY: Murray, Robert K., *Red Scare: A Study in National Hysteria, 1919-1920* (Univ. of Minnesota 1955); Preston, William, Jr., *Aliens and Dissenters: Federal Suppression of Radicals, 1903-1933* (Harvard Univ. Press 1963).

■ **RED SHOES (c. 1700-46),** Choctaw leader. In his early years, Red Shoes favored alliance with the French, but after a Frenchman raped his wife in the 1730s, Red Shoes changed his support to the British.

As a result, the French governor of Louisiana ordered his death, which occurred at the hands of pro-French Choctaw in 1746. The incident led to a civil war known as the Choctaw Revolt.

See Also: Choctaw Indians; Indians of North America.

■ **REED, STANLEY FOREMAN (1884-1980),** associate justice of the U.S. Supreme Court (1938-57). Born in Maysville, Kentucky, he also served as general counsel of the Federal Farm Board (1929-32) and the Reconstruction Finance Corporation (1932-35) and as solicitor general (1935-38).

See Also: Supreme Court.

■ **REED, WALTER (1851-1902),** physician and head of the U.S. Army Yellow Fever Commission. Born in Belroi, Virginia, Reed earned medical degrees from the University of Virginia (1869) and Bellevue Hospital Medical College (1870) before being commissioned in the U.S. Army Medical Corps (1875). He spent a number of years on frontier garrison duty, pursuing graduate work in bacteriology in 1890 and becoming, in 1893, a professor of bacteriology and microscopy at the Army Medical School. Reed was appointed head of a commission to study typhoid fever (1898), which had broken out among American troops fighting the Spanish-American War, and helped prove the disease was spread by dust and flies. Reed then became head of a commission to study yellow fever in Cuba in 1900. With bacteriologist James Carroll and entomologist Jesse Laear, he experimented on human subjects to discover that the disease was carried by the mosquito *Aëdes aegypti*. Their work allowed sanitary engineer William Gorgas to eradicate yellow fever from Cuba and the Panama Canal Zone.

See Also: Disease; Medicine; Science.

■ **REFERENDUM,** requirement that certain laws or state constitutional amendments be approved by the voters after being passed by the legislature. First enacted in South Dakota (1898), the referendum is seen as a democratic check on the power of government.

■ **REFUGEE RELIEF ACT (1953),** law that provided for entry into the United States of 186,000 immigrants who sought to avoid communist persecution. An additional 214,000 immigrants were admitted into the United States under this emergency law.

See Also: Immigration.

■ **REGENTS OF THE UNIVERSITY OF CALIFORNIA V. BAKKE (1978),** U.S. Supreme Court case that limited racial preferences at state universities. Alan Bakke, a white man, was one of 2,664 candidates for 100 openings at the University of California Medical School at Davis in 1972. The medical school, hoping to train more minority physicians, set aside 16 spots for African-American, Hispanic, Asian-American, and Indian applicants even if they did not boast the academic credentials of white candidates. After being rejected, Bakke sued, claiming the separate admissions procedures for minorities denied him equal protection under the law. A sharply divided Court voted (5-4) to strike down the racial quota admissions system.

The Court ruled that public universities could consider racial factors, such as the overall composition of an incoming class, when making admissions decisions but could not establish fixed racial quotas. The justices were, however, split on their reasons and filed six separate and sometimes contradictory opinions. One faction argued any racial separation of applicants was improper. Another argued that race-conscious remedies were proper if necessary to redress past injuries and achieve an important state purpose.

Bakke ultimately had little practical effect on admissions at public universities. The case, however, signaled that affirmative action and racial preferences would become a major political battleground in the 1980s.

See Also: Affirmative Action; Equal Protection; Supreme Court.

BIBLIOGRAPHY: Schwartz, Bernard, *Behind Bakke: Affirmative Action and the Supreme Court* (New York Univ. Press 1988).

■ **REGIONALISM,** the recognition that culture varies over space. It includes both the study of spatial variations within a culture and a people's sense of belonging to the portion of the globe they inhabit. Regionalism recognizes the irrepressible diversities of culture and nature, and it traces how people and places interact to create an ever-changing mosaic of cultural landscapes. A regional view of American history sees the nation as a fabric of interconnected parts and analyzes the shifting relationships between New England, for example, and the Deep South, or between the Midwest, the Southwest, the Pacific Northwest, and any other cultural areas larger than the face-to-face neighborhood and smaller than the faceless nation-state.

In contrast to sectionalism, which stresses political tensions between geographical pieces of the nation, regionalism emphasizes their cultural contributions to the larger whole. Emerging as a formal concept after the Civil War, regionalism came to signify an organic harmony of loyalties—to community, region, nation, and eventually the world—while sectionalism indicates a narrower, often divisive allegiance to a particular place. Perceived both as native ground and groundwork for wider loyalties, regionalism is especially compelling in a continent-sized country bristling with natural and cultural diversity, and it is a force that continues to engage Americans as an analytical concept, a social cause, and a source of identity.

Regionalism as an Analytical Concept. America's sprawling complexity often confounds even the most cautious generalizations, and it can be argued that the United States is best seen as a composite of regions; without them, it slides out of focus and becomes a blank abstraction. Beyond being a lens for sharper historical vision, regionalism can also be visualized as the basic framework and building block of American life. Pre-Columbian America was a complex tapestry of native cultural areas, and beginning in the 15th century, waves of willing and unwilling immigrants from Europe, Africa, Latin America, and Asia affected the new land and each other to create a fabric of regional cultures that would eventually constitute a nation-state.

Geographers and historians have devoted much energy to defining regions and tracing their changes over time. From Jedidiah Morse's tripartite division of the United States into northern, middle, and southern regions at the end of the 18th century to Donald Meinig's magisterial analysis of the growth of regional cores, domains, and spheres two centuries later, myriad scholars have sketched the nation's changing spatial con-

figuration. Recently, urban historians and world systems theorists have applied regional principles to understanding the human ecology of the city and the structure of the new global order.

Regionalism as a Social Cause. American regionalism has waxed and waned as a social cause, with calls for regional renewal peaking during the 1890s, 1930s, and 1990s. The first self-conscious regional movement emerged in France in the 1850s as an offshoot of romantic nationalism and spread to the United States several generations later. Building upon romantic theories of the land and folk, haunted by the Civil War, and troubled by the end of the frontier and rise of corporate capitalism, a first generation of American regionalists, including explorer John Wesley Powell, philosopher Josiah Royce, writer Hamlin Garland, architect Frank Lloyd Wright, and historian Frederick Jackson Turner, promoted regionalism as a balance between fractious sectionalism and the centralized state.

Economic and environmental dislocations stirred up a host of regionalists in the 1930s: southern agrarians railed against technology, New Deal planners reshaped the Tennessee Valley, midwestern painters and footloose writers rediscovered the land and folk, and intellectuals as varied as Lewis Mumford, Howard Odum, and Walter Prescott Webb ardently championed regional renewal. Regionalism faded after World War II as Americans fixed upon simplistic visions of national unity. Such notions were shattered by the social protests and multicultural movements of the 1960s that in turn paved the way for a regional resurgence by the 1980s. Increasingly aware of the race, gender, class, religious, and age-based segments of American culture, and skeptical of sweeping platitudes about such a variegated society, a spectrum of bioregionalists, economists, and self-proclaimed new western historians, including Patricia Limerick, Donald Worster, and Richard White, have reclaimed regionalism as the spatial dimension of American cultural pluralism.

Regionalism as a Source of Identity. People have predicted the death of regionalism ever since settlers subdued the wilderness, machines entered the American garden, and the North won the Civil War. Transcontinental railroads, interstate freeways, and the Internet, for example, seem to erase regions and produce increasingly placeless national and global societies. Yet, the prospect of placelessness evokes a desire for rootedness. The sheer immensity of national and world orders engenders a need for more intimate places of belonging, and regionalism thrives in many forms—from bioregional ideals to ethno-regional sensibility—as a necessary balance to the emptiness of globalism and the nation-state. Far from being a lost cause doomed by the forces of modernity, regionalism remains a powerful source of identity in the United States and throughout the world at the end of the 20th century.

—MICHAEL C. STEINER

BIBLIOGRAPHY: Jensen, Merrill, ed., *Regionalism in America* (Univ. of Wisconsin Press 1951); Meinig, D. W., *The Shaping of America: A Geographical Perspective on 500 Years of History*, 2 vols. (Yale Univ. Press 1986, 1993); Mumford, Lewis, *The Culture of Cities* (Harcourt Brace 1938); Odum, Howard W., and Harry Estill Moore, *American Regionalism: A Cultural-Historical Approach to National Integration* (Henry Holt 1938); Zelinsky, Wilbur, *The Cultural Geography of the United States* (Prentice-Hall 1973).

▪ REGULATION OF LOBBYING ACT (1946),

reform law requiring individuals and groups lobbying Congress to register. The law did not affect the executive branch and was tied to a pay raise for members of Congress.

▪ REGULATORS,

movements of North and South Carolina frontiersmen during the 1760s against arbitrary taxation, local corruption, lawlessness, and an unfair judicial system. The movement in North Carolina started in Anson, Orange, and Granville counties in 1764 as a protest against taxation and official corruption. The Regulators won control of the provincial assembly in 1769 but failed to influence the courts or the governor. In September 1770, under the leadership of Henry Husband (1724-95), they rioted on the premises of the Hillsboro Court. Acts of violence ensued, and Gov. William Tryon called out the militia. On March 16, 1771, with 1,400 militiamen from eastern counties, he defeated 2,000 Regulators at Alamance. Thereafter, the movement in North Carolina was suppressed. In South Carolina, the Regulators arose to protest lawlessness and the lack of officials and courts in their counties. Many of their grievances were redressed when the colonial assembly passed the Circuit Court Act, establishing courts in the interior of the province. The Regulator movement in South Carolina then subsided.

See Also: North Carolina; South Carolina.

BIBLIOGRAPHY: Brown, Richard M., *The South Carolina Regulators* (The Belknap Press of Harvard Univ. Press 1963); Middleton, Lamar, *Revolt U.S.A.* (1938; reprint, Books for Libraries Press 1968).

▪ REGULATORY COMMISSIONS,

government agencies designed to regulate certain industries and portions of the economy and to safeguard the public's civil rights, health, and safety. The era of the regulatory commission began in 1887 when Congress established the Interstate Commerce Commission (ICC) to regulate the expanding railroad industry. Since then regulatory agencies have grown in three successive stages.

The first stage occurred in the first two decades of the 20th century. Congress expanded the jurisdiction of the ICC, established the Federal Reserve Board to stabilize the nation's banking system, and created the Federal Trade Commission (FTC) to regulate big business. The second stage was triggered by the economic crisis of the Great Depression. In response New Deal agencies included the National Recovery Administration to assist weakened industries, the Securities and Exchange Commission to regulate the stock market and securities industry, and the Federal Deposit Insurance Corporation to stabilize the banking system. New Dealers in Congress also helped to establish other regulatory commissions to govern industries from aviation to electrical power.

Unlike the first two stages, which solely provided economic regulation, the final stage established various forms of social regulation. These 1960s and 1970s commissions include the Environmental Protection Agency, the Equal Employment Opportunity Commission, and the Consumer Product Safety Commission. Since the late 1970s regulatory commissions have been at the center of partisan political conflicts, with congressional Republicans seeking deregulation.

See Also: Federal Reserve System; Federal Trade Commission (FTC); Interstate Commerce Commission (ICC).

BIBLIOGRAPHY: Mitnick, Barry M., *The Political Economy of Regulation: Creating, Designing, and Removing Regulatory Forms* (Columbia Univ. Press *1980*).

■ **REHNQUIST, WILLIAM HUBBS (1924-)**, 16th chief justice of the United States (1986-). Born in Milwaukee, Wisconsin, Rehnquist graduated from Stanford University in 1949, received an M.A. from Harvard University a year later, and graduated from Stanford Law School in 1952. Following a clerkship under Supreme Court Associate Justice Robert H. Jackson, Rehnquist, a conservative, entered private practice in Phoenix, Arizona, in 1953. In 1969 he became assistant attorney general for the Office of Legal Council, where he opposed civil rights legislation while supporting vigorous anti-crime programs.

Seeking to name conservatives and strict constructionists to the Supreme Court, Pres. Richard M. Nixon appointed Rehnquist an associate justice in 1971. In his first years on the Court, Rehnquist was a voice of conservative dissent. He opposed loose and implied interpretations of the Constitution, dissented in *Roe* v. *Wade* (1973), and followed a restrictive interpretation of individual rights under the First Amendment. Throughout his time on the bench, Rehnquist challenged centralized authority in the federal government, favoring increased state autonomy. He interpreted the 14th Amendment as limiting equal protection to cases of racial discrimination. His opposition to affirmative action rested in part on the 14th Amendment's statement of racial neutrality.

In 1986, Pres. Ronald Reagan appointed Rehnquist chief justice. Although many thought his ascendancy would initiate a conservative era, the Court has not diverged significantly from precedents established in the Warren and Burger courts.

See Also: *Roe v. Wade; Supreme Court.*

BIBLIOGRAPHY: Davis, Sue, *Justice Rehnquist and the Constitution* (Princeton Univ. Press 1989); Irons, Peter H., *Brennan v. Rehnquist: The Battle for the Constitution* (Knopf 1994).

■ **RELIGION,** spiritual belief, which in America has had manifold aspects. Much of American religion, and most of its variety, resulted from importation—initially from Europe, then from the Middle and Far East. However, the discoverers found religion already in place when they arrived; in addition later Americans created new-faith communities of their own, adding further to the rich patterns of American religious heterogeneity.

American Indians. Both before and after European conquest Indian religious rituals varied widely, depending on where each tribe lived, what language it spoke, and when it migrated across the Siberian land bridge. The beliefs (or myths) lying behind the rituals manifested similar variety. Like most peoples around the world, American Indians had sacred places and sacred times, as well as rituals that centered on the major transitions of life: birth, puberty, marriage, and death.

Since the arrival of the Europeans, Indian religions have struggled to maintain their legitimacy and survival. Even the Native American Church, largely assimilated to Christianity, has been obliged, because of its ritual use of peyote, to fight for its freedom of worship. In the 20th century American Indians have repeatedly resorted to the courts to maintain (or regain) control of their sacred spaces. Because the First Amendment to the Constitution, ratified in 1791, guaranteed religious liberty to all American citizens, a special guarantee to Indians (who did not become citizens until 1924) would have seemed unnecessary. But that was not the case. In 1978, therefore, Congress passed the Indian Religious Freedom Act, which settled some, but by no means all, of the American Indians' struggles for full freedom of religious expression.

European Religion in America. In the 17th and 18th centuries the American colonies received the prevailing, and in some cases the upstart, denominations of Britain and continental Europe. Only in Virginia and South Carolina did an official establishment of Anglicanism take place, and even there it was challenged. The other, and more effective, established or state-supported religion in America, Congregationalism, dominated New England.

Otherwise, denominations scrambled for bits and pieces of sacred space. Baptists found liberty in the tiny colony of Rhode Island but often were persecuted elsewhere. Quakers—fined, jailed, pilloried, and hanged—sought sanctuary in Pennsylvania, whose founder, William Penn, was himself a Quaker. English Roman Catholics, penalized at home, made Maryland their own—for a time. Presbyterians from both England and Scotland flourished in the mid-Atlantic colonies. Lutherans and the German Reformed Church took advantage of Pennsylvania's guarantees of religious freedom, especially from the 1730s on. The Dutch Reformed Church put down its roots in New York and New Jersey while New York was still New Amsterdam. Methodism came into its own about the same time the United States did; both institutions did very well together in the decades that followed.

Trends in the 19th Century. The immigration resulting from Ireland's potato famine in the 1840s permanently changed the face of American religion. By 1850 Roman Catholicism, negligible in the colonial period, had become the largest single denomination in America. Later immigrations from the Austro-Hungarian Empire, Germany, and Italy added new recruits to the Catholic population. Also in the 19th century and continuing in the 20th, Jewish immigration, initially from Germany and later from eastern Europe, established Judaism as a major American religion.

Meanwhile new sects and denominations were proliferating, all of them 19th-century innovations. The frontier Disciples of Christ, or Campbellites, became not one but three new denominations. Likewise the Mormons, or Latter-Day Saints, split, although only into two major branches: the Utah Church and the much smaller Reorganized Church (later united). Another American innovation, the Seventh-Day Adventists, survived the millennial disappointment of an erroneous prophecy in 1843 to establish itself as a continuing institution. Jehovah's Witnesses, also millennialists, established in the 1870s, have carried their message far beyond the nation's borders. Christian Science, which arose in New England, ultimately became a national presence—although not on the scale of any of those just mentioned. Finally a host of utopian experiments enjoyed transitory existences: Oneida, Amana, New Harmony, and Shakers (English in origin but American in importance).

Middle Eastern and Far Eastern Religions. America in the 19th century saw samplings of religions from Asia and the Middle East (for example, at the World's Parliament of Religions in Chicago in 1893), only the 20th century saw major infusions from these regions of the world. Buddhists and Muslims have had the greatest impact, while Hindus, Sikhs, Taoists, and others have had lesser ones.

Colonial America was a religiously diverse society, although not always tolerant of its different faiths. Persecuted Quakers, shown in an early meeting, sought refuge in the colony established in 1681 by their co-religionist William Penn.

Clearly the older formula of "Protestant, Catholic, and Jew" no longer served by the end of the 20th century as a fair description of religion in America.

Pluralism and Its Problems. Pluralism has resulted not only from the multiplicity of denominations imported or spawned in America but also from theological fissures and increasing secularism. In the first quarter of the 20th century, liberals and conservatives fought for sway in their religious communities, usually under the labels of "modernists" and "fundamentalists." Many churches split, as did several religious colleges and seminaries. While the press followed with eager interest accounts of heresy trials and scuttled careers, the social order for the most part sailed on smoothly.

A revival of a politically active fundamentalism in the 1980s and 1990s rocked the political structures more severely. The much-touted "rise of the religious right" received press, radio, and television coverage because fundamentalism now chose to enter the political fray rather than retreat from it. Coalitions of quite conservative evangelicals endorsed or vetoed candidates, or even put forward their own candidates for political office, including the office of U.S. president.

Liberal theologians, meanwhile, felt power slipping away as their numbers declined and their position as an elite deteriorated. At the height of the Social Gospel movement in the early 20th century, the names of Washington Gladden, Walter Rauschenbusch, and John A. Ryan—liberals all—commanded headlines and reordered priorities. Later the names of Reinhold Niebuhr and Paul Tillich had weight in the halls of learning and of power, although not always on behalf of liberalism.

Secularism also made significant strides in the second half of the 20th century. Although Americans, in comparison with Europeans, remained a "religious people," large segments of American life moved out from under the "sacred canopy" of the churches and their denominational headquarters. With some exceptions (such as Baptists in the Southeast, Lutherans in the Upper Midwest, Catholics in the Northeast, and Mormons in the West), religion no longer dominated culture.

Pluralism's problems are most evident in the arena of litigation and political controversy.

Since the 1940s the U.S. Supreme Court, along with most other courts, has been called on to solve problems that a more homogenous society would not have posed. The thorniest issues concern education: in public education, the question of what may be taught or religiously observed; in private education, the question of the application of tax monies to religious or parochial schools.

In some sense religion remains at the core of American culture, but the nature of that religion and the depth of that core are in steady flux.

—EDWIN S. GAUSTAD

See Also: *African-American Religion; Camp Meetings; Fundamentalism; Great Awakening; Missions and Missionaries; Revivals; Second Great Awakening; individual denominations and biographies.*

BIBLIOGRAPHY: Albanese, Catherine L., *America: Religions and Religion,* 2nd ed. (Wadsworth 1992); Gaustad, Edwin S., *A Religious History of America* (Harper 1990); Glazer, Nathan, *American Judaism,* 2nd ed. (Univ. of Chicago Press 1972); Haddad, Yvonne Y., ed., *The Muslims of America* (Oxford Univ. Press 1991); Handy, Robert T., *A History of the Churches in the United States and Canada* (Oxford Univ. Press 1984); Hennesey, James J., *American Catholics: A History of the Roman Catholic Community in the United States* (Oxford Univ. Press 1981); Lincoln, C. Eric, and Lawrence H. Mamiya, *The Black Church in the African American Experience* (Duke Univ. Press 1990).

■ **RELOCATION,** the government-sponsored moving of Indian peoples to urban areas. Relocation began as an experiment by the U.S. government to alleviate starving conditions among Indians in the Southwest. During the winter of 1947-48, when blizzards endangered the Navajo, the government relocated Navajo families to Denver, Salt Lake City, and Los Angeles and found them jobs and housing. In 1952 the Bureau of Indian Affairs offered relocation to Indians living on reservations and in rural areas, a program that continued until the early 1970s.

Relocation offices opened up in cities, and Indian agencies on reservations encouraged Indians to apply for relocation. Applicants were required to be at least 18 years old and have relatively good health. Limited education or job skills were a concern but were not sufficient reasons for rejection. During the 1950s and 1960s Indians were relocated to major western cities such as Denver, San Francisco, Oakland, Seattle, Salt Lake City, Phoenix, Albuquerque, and Los Angeles, which became the largest urban Indian area. Eastern relocation sites included Chicago, Cleveland, Detroit, and Minneapolis-St. Paul.

In these cities Indian centers were established in order to provide counseling for the relocated people who were finding that such issues as alcoholism and job training ranked high among their urban problems. Frustration in adjusting to a strange urban culture while encountering prejudice, discrimination, and racism caused many relocatees to go home. But many remained, and today—three generations since relocation began—just over two-thirds of the total Indian population live in urban areas.

—DONALD L. FIXICO

See Also: Indian Policy; Indians of North America.
BIBLIOGRAPHY: Fixico, Donald L., *Termination and Relocation: Federal Indian Policy, 1945-1960* (Univ. of New Mexico Press 1986); Weibel-Orlando, Joan, *Indian Country, L.A.: Maintaining Ethnic Community in Complex Society* (Univ. of Illinois Press 1991).

■ **REMINGTON, FREDERIC (1861-1909),** artist of the American West. Born in Canton, New York, Remington attended the Yale School of Fine Arts from 1878 to 1880, when he began his extensive travels in the American West. Working in the West, in 1882 he began selling drawings to *Harper's Weekly*; in 1887 Remington began exhibiting regularly at the National Academy of Design. In 1898 he was a correspondent covering Cuba during the Spanish-American War. Remington worked in a variety of media, such as painting, drawing, and bronze sculpture. He helped to promote a mythic image of the American West, particularly in representations of Indians and cowboys. He did illustrations for *Pony Tracks* (1895), *Crooked Trails* (1898), and *The Way of an Indian* (1906). Remington's sculptures include *Bronco Buster* (1895) and *Wounded Bunkie* (1896), and his paintings include *A Cavalryman's Breakfast on the Plains* (1890), *The Fight for the Waterhole* (1895-1900), and *Cavalry Charge on the Southern Plains* (1907).

See Also: Painting; Sculpture.

■ **RENWICK, JAMES (1818-95),** architect. Born in New York City, Renwick graduated from Columbia University in 1836 and worked as an engineer for the Erie Railroad. In 1843, Renwick won the competition for the design of Grace Church in New York City, bringing him acclaim and additional commissions, such as that for Saint Patrick's Cathedral, New York (1858-79). His other public buildings include the original Smithsonian Institution (1846-55) and the original Corcoran Gallery (1873), both in Washington, D.C.

See Also: Smithsonian Institution.

■ **REPARATIONS,** payments made by defeated nations to the victors for damages incurred during war. As dictated by the Treaty of Versailles (1919) at the end of World War I, Germany was obliged to pay reparations to the victorious Allies. Along with the "war guilt" clause, reparations were justified as a public show of German guilt and created a national wound that festered until the Nazis came to power in 1933. The amount of the reparations Germany was ordered to pay totaled 132 billion gold marks. Given the devastation of the war, the loss of key industrial centers, and the high postwar inflation, Germany found it difficult to make the payments as scheduled. In 1924 the Reparations Commission under Charles G. Dawes, set up a new payment schedule. After the Great Depression started in 1929, meeting reparation payments became nearly impossible for the beleaguered Germany. In 1931 Pres. Herbert Hoover urged the French, to whom the bulk of the reparations was due, to permit a one-year moratorium on payments. A year later, as the world economy collapsed, all payments basically ceased.

See Also: Dawes, Charles Gates.
BIBLIOGRAPHY: Kent, Bruce, *The Spoils of War: The Politics, Economics and Diplomacy of Reparations* (Oxford Univ. Press 1989).

■ **REPUBLICANISM,** the belief that a society needs only authority that is derived from within itself. "Classical" republicanism suffused early American political language so completely that mere allusions could convey whole systems of meaning. Republicanism undermined American adherence to the British Crown and offered a script for a different order. But pure classical republicanism proved unsuited to the needs of the American republic.

The vision of republicanism reached back to ancient Rome, as the Latin root *res publica* ("public good") demonstrates. Filtered through experience in Renaissance Italy and Cromwellian England; developed by thinkers like Machiavelli, James Harrington, and Montesquieu; and popularized by publicists in Georgian England, republican thought criticized the direction of 18th-century events. As they viewed social complexity, powerful central governments, and a money economy, republican thinkers saw corruption at every level, from individuals to whole societies.

The perfect republic was a Swiss canton, or the city-state of Venice, or Harrington's fictional "Oceana." In these, citizens put their common interest ahead of individual pursuits and displayed a hardy, independent manhood that scorned domination. Citizens' "civic virtue" expressed their personal qualities and the principle on which their society cohered. Yet a problem instantly appeared: such a people was likely to prosper by its energy or to conquer others by the force of its arms. With prosperity or conquest, virtue would fail, public spirit would give way to self-seeking turmoil, and a tyrant's takeover would grow likely. Seemingly, a republic could work only under specific social conditions and among special people.

Republican citizenship implied mastery of one's appetites, of the economic and martial skills that independence required, of property so that nobody could give the citizen orders, and, in all probability, mastery over family members, servants, and even slaves. There was no presumption that being a denizen within a republic also meant being a citizen of it.

In colonial America the vision enjoyed particular power in Virginia, where the shared "public interest" of white men consisted of growing tobacco and controlling slaves. It was also strong in Massachusetts, where small-community economics and the communal heritage of Puritanism possessed great power. Both states still call themselves "commonwealths" even now. Virginians like George Washington and Yankees like Samuel Adams prided themselves on the stiff rectitude and spartan self-denial and simplicity that repub-

lican citizenship seemed to require. Yet in 1776, it was Pennsylvania, the most complex of all the states, that went furthest toward turning republican thought into working political reality. With annual elections, broad suffrage and eligibility for office, a one-house legislature, and virtually no executive power, Pennsylvania's revolutionary constitution assumed that a virtuous people could know its will and act upon it. Vermont copied the document directly, and only five states (Massachusetts, Connecticut, Rhode Island, New York, and Maryland) wholly rejected its vision.

It did not work, perhaps because of human failures, perhaps because American society was already too complex for simple institutions to resolve its problems. In what James Madison called "a republican remedy for the vices of republican government," the federal Constitution abandoned the idea of small, coherent, single-interest states and the idea of simple government. Madison also abandoned the notion that his fellows were inherently virtuous, retreating to the idea that if virtue could be found, it would be among the elite. Nonetheless, the republican vision, or the mood that underpins it, has never entirely faded.

—EDWARD COUNTRYMAN

See Also: *Revolution, American.*

BIBLIOGRAPHY: Appleby, Joyce, *Liberalism and Republicanism in the Historical Imagination* (Harvard Univ. Press 1992); Rodgers, Daniel T., "Republicanism: The Career of a Concept," *Journal of American History* (June 1992); Wood, Gordon S., *The Radicalism of the American Revolution* (Knopf 1992).

■ **REPUBLICAN PARTY,** one of the two major 20th-century political parties in the United States, tracing its origins to the debate over slavery in the decade before the Civil War. In 1854 every northern Whig in both houses of Congress voted against the Kansas-Nebraska Act; every southern Whig voted for it. This division destroyed the Whig party. In the aftermath of this vote, a group of congressmen announced their intention of forming a new party and declared themselves the "Republicans," a name that had last been claimed by the followers of John Quincy Adams and Henry Clay in the early 1830s. The new party was a coalition of forces previously known as

Abraham Lincoln was the first Republican candidate to win the presidency, establishing a Republican dynasty that lasted until the New Deal.

Free-Soilers, Conscience Whigs, Know-Nothings, Barnburners, and abolitionists.

In the presidential election of 1856 the party unsuccessfully ran John C. Frémont, who had been elected by California to the Senate in 1850 as a Democrat. Indeed, half the delegates who nominated Abraham Lincoln in 1860 were former Democrats. In the 1860 election the Democrats split into sectional factions, and Lincoln won an electoral majority with less than 40 percent of the popular vote. Republicans took control of Congress when the southern states seceded from the Union. The party passed an integrated program of federal support for economic development, fought and won the Civil War, abolished slavery, and extended suffrage to former male slaves. It was the closest thing to a social revolution in American history. The Republicans hoped to become a national party, supported in the South by African Americans, but by 1870 popular enthusiasm for social revolution had waned. The reentry of unreconstructed southern states into national politics—all of them dominated by the Democrats—ended this Republican hope. But the party had the edge in national politics from the Civil War to the Great Depression, losing the White House only to Democrats Grover Cleveland and Woodrow Wilson. The most important Republican president after Lincoln was Theodore Roosevelt, a strong nationalist and the first president to commit the federal government to a program of economic regulation of modern capitalism.

The Great Depression reshaped American politics, and the Republicans became the party of opposition. From the election of 1932 to that of 1968, Dwight Eisenhower was the only Republican candidate to capture the White House, and Republicans controlled both houses of Congress for only four years (1947-49, 1953-55). The era of Democratic dominance, however, ended in the late 1960s. The key to the Republican resurgence was its rise to power in the formerly Democratic "Solid South." The first indication of this came in 1964, when Republican candidate Barry Goldwater won the deep South. In 1968 those same states were carried by third-party candidate George Wallace. That election had been won by Republican Richard Nixon, and in his reelection campaign of 1972 his "southern strategy" built a new coalition of conservatives, Roman Catholics, and former southern Democrats. Nixon's victories marked the end of the New Deal era and the beginning of the modern period of Republican dominance. That achievement was obscured by Nixon's humiliation in the Watergate scandal and the victory of Jimmy Carter in 1976. But the triumph of Ronald Reagan in 1980 and 1984, and the Republican seizure of both houses of Congress in 1994, continued in 1996, were powerful confirmations.

—JOHN MACK FARAGHER

See Also: Conventions, Political; Political Parties; Presidential Elections.

BIBLIOGRAPHY: Batchelor, John Calvin, *Ain't You Glad You Joined the Republicans? A Short History of the GOP* (Henry Holt 1996); Rutland, Robert Allen, *The Republicans: From Lincoln to Bush* (Univ. of Missouri Press 1996).

■ **RESETTLEMENT ADMINISTRATION (1935-37),** federal agency concerned with rural poverty during the Depression. It offered loans and technical advice to tenant farmers who wanted to buy land. It was replaced by the Farm Security Administration.

See Also: Farm Security Administration (FSA); New Deal.

■ **RESORTS,** health and recreational facilities that first appeared in the United States in the early 19th century. These resorts attracted wealthy people who sought healing springs and cool weather to escape dangerous summer climates. Places like Saratoga Springs and the Catskill Mountains in New York provided luxurious havens in the 1820s. Spectacular hotels housed the sick and the socially anxious, who saw such places as essential for meeting the right kind of people.

Later in the 19th century, as leisure became an expectation of middle-class people, places like Martha's Vineyard and the beaches of New Jersey and Long Island became popular resorts. Cheap, convenient railroad travel and a new emphasis on the importance of American scenery and history made resorts boom after the Civil War. These changes also drove tourism west, where grand hotels in Colorado Springs, Colorado, and Monterey, California, lured an exclusively upper-class clientele.

In the 20th century, resorts revolved around activities and spectacles that allowed people a complete escape from their everyday lives. Americans became cowboys on dude ranches in the Rockies after World War I. They flocked to ski resorts after 1936, when the Union Pacific Railroad opened Sun Valley, Idaho, the first nationally known ski area. The gambling meccas of Las Vegas opened to great success in the 1940s, and Atlantic City, rejuvenated in the 1970s, represented another resort type. When Disneyland opened in 1955, it introduced fantasy resorts that have made tourism central to the world economy.
—ANNE F. HYDE

BIBLIOGRAPHY: Dulles, Foster Rhea, *America Learns to Play: A History of Popular Recreation* (Appleton 1940); Findlay, John, *Magic Lands: Western Cityscapes and American Culture After 1940* (Univ. of California 1992); Sears, John, *Sacred Places: American Tourist Attractions in the Nineteenth Century* (Oxford Univ. Press 1989).

■ **REUTHER, WALTER P. (1907-70),** labor leader. Born in Wheeling, West Virginia, Reuther left school in 1922 to work as a tool-and-die maker. In 1926, he moved to Detroit, where he became a foreman at the Ford motor plant, but he was fired for union activities in 1933. After a three-year trip around the world, Reuther returned to Detroit in 1935. An ambitious and skillful labor organizer, he worked for the United Auto Workers (UAW), becoming a member of the executive board in 1936. He continued his swift rise in union leadership, becoming vice president of the UAW in 1942 and president in 1946.

Politically adept, Reuther garnered the support of world leaders as he continued his ascent. He was elected vice president of the Congress of Industrial Organizations (CIO) in 1946 and president six years later. In 1968, Reuther, disgruntled with complacent and rigid policies, broke with the AFL-CIO, taking the UAW with him.

One of the most influential labor leaders of the 20th century, Reuther was a lifelong civil rights activist and social reformer. Reuther's legacy can be seen in the continued strength of the UAW and its commitment to broad social reform. Reuther died in an airplane crash.

See Also: AFL-CIO; Congress of Industrial Organizations (CIO); Labor Movement.

BIBLIOGRAPHY: Lichtenstein, Nelson, *The Most Dangerous Man in Detroit: Walter Reuther and the Fate of American Labor* (Basic Books 1995).

■ **REVENUE ACT (1935),** federal law, backed by Pres. Franklin D. Roosevelt, raising taxes on some businesses and the wealthy. Intended to appeal to followers of Sen. Huey P. Long of Louisiana, it was part of the progressive "Second" New Deal.

See Also: Long, Huey; New Deal.

■ **REVERE, PAUL (1735-1818),** Revolutionary War hero. He was immortalized in Henry Wadsworth Longfellow's poem (1863) for his "midnight ride" to warn his fellow Americans of an impending British attack. Much folklore still surrounds the life of Paul Revere. The Boston-born silversmith learned his trade from his Huguenot father, Apollos Rivoire, and was self-taught in copper engraving. He also developed talents in other crafts, including portrait engraving, political cartoons, and the manufacture of dental devices. Young Revere later served as an officer during the French and Indian War. He became an early leader in the Boston Sons of Liberty and as a fervent anti-British propagandist helped popularize the protest to the Stamp Act and Boston Massacre through his widely circulated engravings. Revere also participated in the planning and actions of the Boston Tea Party in December 1773. He served as a courier for several patriot organizations and carried the Suffolk Resolves to Philadelphia during one of his many courier journeys from Massachusetts. Revere's most notable service in this capacity came on April 18-19, 1775, when he rode on horseback from Boston to Lexington to warn patriot leaders John Hancock and Samuel Adams that the British were marching to capture them and seize colonial arms and munitions. After delivering his message in Lexington, he continued on to Concord with his fellow messengers, William Dawes and Samuel Prescott. A British patrol stopped the trio and captured Revere. Later released without his horse, he returned to Lexington on foot.

During the Revolution, Revere helped to manufacture gunpowder and became an engraver for Congress. He printed the first issue of Continental currency and made the first official seal for the colonies. Revere's military career was not successful. He briefly served as a lieutenant colonel in the militia and was involved in the disastrous Penobscot expedition in 1779. Cleared of charges of cowardice, disobedience, and unsoldierly conduct by a court-martial in 1782, Revere returned to silversmithing and copper manufacturing. His foundry cast bells and cannon and supplied the copper accessories for the frigate U.S.S. *Constitution* (*Old Ironsides*).

—MARTHA J. KING

See Also: *Boston Massacre; Boston Tea Party; French and Indian War; Lexington and Concord; Stamp Act.*

BIBLIOGRAPHY: Fischer, David Hackett, *Paul Revere's Ride* (Oxford Univ. Press 1994); Forbes, Esther, *Paul Revere and the World He Made* (Houghton Mifflin 1942).

■ **REVIVALS,** religious awakenings. Revivals have occurred throughout the history of Christianity. Revivals are meetings or series of meetings marked by spiritual intensity. The unconverted surrender to Christ, and the converted are reawakened. Revivalism is a chief feature of American religious life. It cuts across regions, class lines, gender, and ethnicity. It is both rational and emotional. All denominations have been affected by revivalism, although it has been the strongest in Baptist, Methodist, Holiness, and Pentecostal groups. Within the revivals there is an emphasis on preaching and noticeable conversion experiences. The Great Awakening of the 1730s to the 1760s—led by Jonathan Edwards, William and Gilbert Tennent, Theodore Frelinghuysen, and George Whitefield—was the first outburst of American religious fervor and left a legacy within Protestantism. The Second Great Awakening of the 1820s and 1830s, led by Charles G. Finney, introduced the camp meeting, an outdoor revival meeting. Accompanying each of these revivals were great social and moral reform activities. In the 1850s, sometimes called the Prayer Meeting Revival or Laymen's Revival, meetings moved to urban settings. After the Civil War, it is difficult to pinpoint a general awakening, but revivalism has continued sporadically, notably with people such as Dwight L. Moody, Billy Sunday, Oral Roberts, and Billy Graham.

See Also: *Camp Meetings; Edwards, Jonathan; Great Awakening; Religion; Whitefield, George.*

■ **REVOLUTION, AMERICAN (1775-83),** America's successful war of independence from the colonial rule of Great Britain. The Revolution began as a protest against unwanted change and ended changing nearly all aspects of American life. Revolutionary America stood still in only one way. Between 1763, when France evacuated Canada at the conclusion of the French and Indian War, and 1803, when the French emperor Napoleon sold Louisiana (which he had acquired from Spain) to the United States, American space was defined by the Atlantic Ocean, the Florida boundary and Gulf Coast, the Mississippi River, the Great Lakes, and the upper St. Lawrence Valley. Within those bounds, everything else was altered.

Causes. The triumphant British faced many problems in 1763. Their national debt was huge.

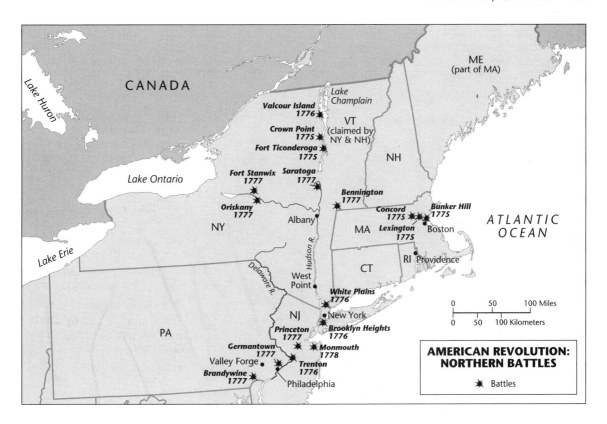

AMERICAN REVOLUTION: NORTHERN BATTLES

✴ Battles

They had to defend their empire against enemies and disintegration. They needed to sort out relations between American Indians who accepted the British Crown as a protector and white colonials who acknowledged the Crown as their sovereign. The white colonials were fractious and disorderly and less than enthusiastic toward the Crown. Economically, the northern colonies rivaled Britain while tobacco-growing Virginia, rice-growing South Carolina, and the sugar-growing West Indies complemented it.

Somehow, the Crown's officials thought, British power could resolve those problems. Britain would tighten existing administration. It would block white expansion into Indian country by a "proclamation line" and later by putting the Ohio Valley under the administration of Quebec. It would raise money from white colonials by direct parliamentary act and use it to pay governors, judges, customs men, and, if necessary, garrisons. It would hamper colonial manufactures, ban the paper money on which the northern colonies depended, and allow direct British competition with colonial merchants.

These policies assumed that white colonials were British in the same sense that the English, Welsh, and Scottish were. All Britons, according to this reasoning, were equally subject to the "king-in-parliament." Parliament's House of Lords and House of Commons distinguished the British monarchy from its absolutist European counterparts and guaranteed "British freedom." Taken together, however, the monarch, the lords, and the commons were as powerful as any dynastic Bourbon or Hapsburg. Colonial institutions like Virginia's House of Burgesses were mere conveniences, to be overridden, altered, or even abolished if the king and Parliament saw fit.

White colonials had a different understanding. Before the crisis their position was just as incoherent as that of ministers in London, but the two already differed sharply. To these colonials, being

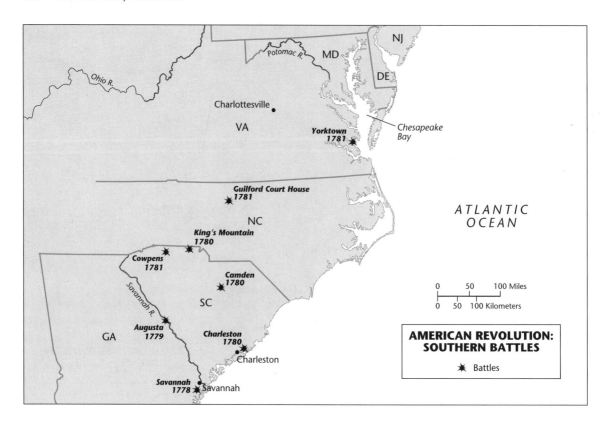

AMERICAN REVOLUTION: SOUTHERN BATTLES

★ Battles

British meant being subject on their own terms to the British king and following local customs, albeit of British derivation. It meant running their societies through institutions that honored Parliament by imitating it but that existed in their own right. Monarchies throughout early-modern Europe had operated on the understanding that a single king might reign over many polities. Now this notion of "composite monarchy" was almost dead in Britain, with Wales, Scotland, and even Ireland subordinated to Westminster. To British officials, colonials ought to be subordinated as well, especially as Parliament's function was to represent Britons everywhere, in the name of a common identity and interest.

This half-articulated problem of imperial theory, not "taxation without representation," was what drove America's white colonials and Britain apart. Responding to administrative reforms in 1763, the Revenue (or "Sugar") Act of 1764, the Stamp Act of 1765, the Townshend duties in 1767,

and the Tea Act in 1773, colonial spokesmen insisted that their charter rights, local customs, and traditional "liberties" could defeat Parliament's will. For Parliament's part, the matter turned from individual policies to asserting that it could bind colonials "in all cases whatsoever." So said the Declaratory Act, passed as a sop to Parliament's self-image when it retreated in 1766 from its attempt with the Stamp Act to reach directly into the colonial economies. Parliament retreated again in 1770, repealing the Townshend duties, which had taxed colonial imports. But it continued one duty, on tea, to assert what it could do.

In 1773 Bostonians dumped East India Company tea into their harbor rather than pay the tax, even though the company could undercut colonial competitors who smuggled Dutch tea "honestly." This time Parliament did not stop at words or gestures but moved toward suppression of what seemed outright rebellion. Gen. Thomas Gage, the commander in chief of British forces in

America, became governor of Massachusetts. In April 1775 Gage sent troops to the town of Concord to capture colonial supplies that he knew were hidden there. What broke out was a revolution that would last until a formal peace was signed in 1783.

Consolidating the Rebellion. Even after Concord, colonials did not think they were rebelling against legitimate authority. They were merely in quasi-legitimate revolt against illicit change. Revolt became rebellion and then revolution for many reasons. One was the body of ideas that had long been corroding the whole rationale of monarchy. All colonials knew how Parliament had replaced King James II with William and Mary in 1688, when it decided that James had overstepped his powers. New Englanders revered old England's earlier Puritan revolution, which had overthrown and beheaded King Charles I, abolished the House of Lords, and brought into being an English republic under "Lord Protector" Oliver Cromwell for a time. Literate colonials were steeped in a republican tradition that reached back through Cromwellian England to Renaissance Italy and ancient Rome and Greece.

Revolt also became revolution because all sorts of colonials got involved. An astute but frightened New Yorker named Gouverneur Morris watched "the mob begin to think and to reason" during a mass meeting in 1774 to elect a revolutionary committee. Despite his alarm, Morris chose the Revolution. About 60,000 whites, elite and plebian alike, rejected it so strongly that they emigrated rather than accept its victory. How many more held their doubts quiet and tried to stay neutral will never be known. Loyalists and neutrals endured crowd hostility, legal discrimination, the loss of property, and midnight arrests by political police like New York's "Commissioners for Detecting and Defeating Conspiracies." In the southern backcountry, the Mohawk Valley, and the area around New York City that the British seized in 1776 and held until 1783, the loyalist quarrel with the Revolution became outright civil war.

Britain's resort to force against Massachusetts in 1774 stirred the province's countryside deeply. Country people who had stayed out of the dispute until the "Tea Party" closed the Crown's courts late that summer, rather than allow Britain's new punitive laws to be administered. With that, royal government died throughout Massachusetts except in Boston, which was under military occupation. By May 1776 royal government was gone everywhere, with a ramshackle structure of Continental and provincial congresses and local committees of safety to take its place.

Forging a National Identity. As old institutions disintegrated, political and institutional dispute about British identity turned into a general crisis of belonging and belief. Both sides warned American Indians to stay out of this dispute among white brothers, but Iroquois, Cherokee, and Algonquian all understood that the argument was bound to affect them. They knew the land hunger of East Coast whites. They also knew that their survival long had hinged on playing whites against one another: French, British, Spanish, and East Coast colonists alike. In 1776 the French were gone, but the Spanish and the British still counted. As the colonists moved toward a separate identity and political independence, only their closest allies among the Indians had any reason to side with them. Some pro-British Indians, most notably Mohawk, chose exile when Britain surrendered. Most had no sense that Britain could give away their land when it conceded American victory in 1783. It took almost five decades for the republic's triumph to become complete east of the Mississippi. But whatever side the Indians chose, the Revolution did them very little good.

"How is it," asked an exasperated Dr. Samuel Johnson of London in 1776, "that we hear the loudest *yelps* for liberty among the drivers of Negroes?" The question would not have stung in 1765, because the liberties that white colonials had set out to protect were no more than their specific privileges, which might even include holding slaves. By 1776 the question did sting. One reason is that specific British liberties gave way to general human liberty in American understanding and rhetoric. Thomas Jefferson and Thomas Paine led the change, the former in his "Summary View" (1774) and in the Declaration of Independence (1776), the latter with *Common Sense* (1776). However imperfectly white Americans lived up to what they began now to say, the change in their terms made a difference.

CAMBRIDGE, 21st August, 1775.

WANTED for the CONTINENTAL ARMY.

One Million of Bricks.
Three Thousand Cords of Fire Wood.
Two Hundred Thousand Feet of Pine Boards and Scantling.
Five Hundred Bushels of Charcoal.
One Hundred and Fifty Tons of English Hay.
Twelve Hundred Bushels of Indian Corn.
Twelve Hundred Bushels of Oats.
Three Hundred Shovels.
Three Hundred Spades.
Fifty Pick Axes.
One Hundred and Fifty Hand-Saws.
Five Thousand Bushels of Lime.
One Hundred and Fifty Tons of Rye Straw.

Those Persons who are willing to supply the Army with the Articles above-mentioned, may apply to the Quarter-Master-General, in Cambridge.

During the Revolution, necessities from food to guns and ammunition were often difficult to obtain, and military commanders made appeals to civilians for supplies.

The logical culmination was Vermont's decision when it cut free of New York in 1777 to abolish slavery completely and immediately. Only a very few slaves actually gained freedom there, but Pennsylvania started gradual emancipation of its much larger slave force in 1780. In 1783 a court decision killed slavery in Massachusetts. Being black in America was ceasing to mean that a person was almost certainly a slave. Even in the Chesapeake Bay area, where slavery lasted until the Civil War, the free African-American population was five times larger in 1810 than in 1770.

The problem of slavery had come alive, but that was not just white Americans' doing. Since enslavement had begun, captured African Americans had shown a "fondness for freedom." With war, thousands responded to invitations from Lord Dunmore, the last royal governor of Virginia, and Sir Henry Clinton of the British army to win freedom by opposing patriot masters. Many left with the British at the war's end, going to New-

foundland, Britain, and even Sierra Leone, which became a refuge for former slaves. On the patriot side, African Americans gave military service and brought lawsuits for freedom. As slavery started to crumble, former slaves could form families without the fear that a spouse or child would be sold. African-American churches could assemble. Free African-American neighborhoods, businesses, schools, and associations could appear. Against great odds, African Americans could forge their own freedom.

"Male and female are the distinctions of nature," wrote Paine in *Common Sense*, as if there were no more to say. Within a few years a great deal was being said, as the social and political meaning of gender turned into one of the most pressing items on the American agenda. The great English feminist Mary Wollstonecraft drew directly on Paine in her *Vindication of the Rights of Woman* (1792), which was rapidly reprinted in America. Meanwhile, the Massachusetts writer

Judith Sargent Murray was making the most of Wollstonecraft's points in her "Constantia" essays. Revolutionary feminism culminated in 1848, when a women's rights convention in Seneca Falls, New York, published a "Declaration of Sentiments" that directly echoed the Declaration of Independence.

Creating a Sovereign Nation. Institutional uncertainty began to resolve with the state constitutions that appeared between 1776 and 1780. It ended when the U.S. Constitution took effect in 1789. That document's authors were the national elite who had come to know one another during the war as generals, ambassadors, high officials, congressmen, and supply officers. Their project included national salvation in the face of undoubted foreign intimidation and what seemed like disintegration at home. It also included safeguarding their sense that they alone were fit to rule, without denying the equality of white men. But what they produced proved larger than themselves. The Constitution assumed a life of its own, asserting as it did that "the People of the United States" exists and can act in its own interests. The document laid down the rule of law rather than the rule of man, thereby making an evolving body of constitutional law. The Constitution protected a national economy that had only begun to exist and that now could flourish. The document was sociology, establishing the terms of race, class, and regional relations, and safeguarding slavery without ever directly mentioning it, along with "the blessings of liberty." Together with the Northwest Ordinances of 1784, 1785, and 1787, it set the terms of expanding the American empire.

The changes were enormous. By 1790 an American people had come into being, replacing an earlier identity that had combined British subject status with identification with one's own town, county, and province. White Americans were republicans, locating sovereignty in themselves rather than submitting to authority that descended from above. They possessed the instruments of their power in the state and federal governments. They could use those instruments to defend and govern themselves and to assert imperial authority over anybody west of them. They had a public agenda that turned on American citizenship, rather than on British subjection.

Everybody involved, including white American citizens, African-American people both free and enslaved, and Indians whom whites were coming to think of as their own subjects, had to live under the national polity and within the national economy that the Revolution had forged. Both polity and economy were vastly stronger than the institutions of British dominion had been. They operated in different ways, and the people who lived under them thought differently, too. Whatever protesting colonials had first intended, the United States had lived through a revolution that left everyone within it fundamentally changed.

—EDWARD COUNTRYMAN

See Also: Committes of Correspondence; Declaration of Independence; Franco-American Alliance; Intolerable Acts; Loyalists; Minutemen; Stamp Act; Townshend Acts; individual battles and biographies.

BIBLIOGRAPHY: Bailyn, Bernard, *The Ideological Origins of the American Revolution* (Harvard Univ. Press 1967); Countryman, Edward, *The American Revolution* (Hill & Wang 1985); Countryman, Edward, "Indians, the Colonial Order, and the Social Significance of the American Revolution," *William and Mary Quarterly* (April 1996); Davis, David Brion, *The Problem of Slavery in the Age of Revolution, 1770-1823* (Cornell Univ. Press 1976); Nash, Gary B., *Forging Freedom: The Formation of Philadelphia's Black Community, 1720-1840* (Harvard Univ. Press 1986); Norton, Mary Beth, *Liberty's Daughters: The Revolutionary Experience of American Women, 1750-1800* (Little, Brown 1980); Wood, Gordon S., *The Creation of the American Republic, 1776-1787* (Univ. of North Carolina Press 1969); Wood, Gordon S., *The Radicalism of the American Revolution* (Knopf 1992).

RHODE ISLAND, a New England state, the smallest of the 50 U.S. states. It is bounded on the north and east by Massachusetts, on the south by the Atlantic Ocean, and on the west by Connecticut. Narragansett Bay cuts deeply into the state and holds within it three large islands. Services have replaced manufacturing as Rhode Island's chief economic sector. Founded in 1636, Rhode Island was the last of the original 13 states to ratify the Constitution and join the Union.

Capital: Providence. Area: 1,213 square miles. Population (1995 est.): 990,000.

See Also: Dorr's Rebellion; Hutchinson, Anne Marbury; Williams, Roger.

■ **RHYTHM AND BLUES,** name given to African-American popular music in the years immediately following World War II. "Rhythm" referred to the stripped-down "jump bands" that evolved after the decline of the big bands. Performers such as Louis Jordan combined a driving rhythm section (drums, bass, and piano) with electric guitar, saxophone, and ironic or comic vocals, often with double-entendre lyrics. "Blues" designated the raw, powerful "urban blues" performed by the likes of Muddy Waters. The term was invented by *Billboard* magazine, when in 1949 it decided to drop the term "Race Records," the previous label for its black popular music chart, in favor of a more neutral name.

The music was produced by dozens of independent record labels that sprang up in the postwar period: King in Cincinnati, Chess in Chicago, Specialty in Los Angeles, as well as the black-owned Duke/Peacock in Houston and VJ in Chicago. The popularity of rhythm and blues music among white audiences in the early 1950s—both because of its danceability and its "hip" sensibility—was one of the originating forces in the development of rock and roll. But much of what is considered rock and roll music, especially the contributions of African-American performers, was actually part of the continuing tradition of African-American popular music. During the 1960s the most important sources of the music came from African-American-owned Motown records of Detroit and Stac records in Memphis. As rock and roll transmuted into stadium "rock," this new gospel-inspired music retained its dance audience and became known as "Soul," the name *Billboard* adopted for its African-American pop music chart in 1969. But however it was labeled, African-American popular music continued as one of the most dynamic forces in American commercial music.

See Also: Blues; Gospel Music; Jordan, Louis; Rock and Roll; Waters, Muddy (McKinley Morganfield).

BIBLIOGRAPHY: Deffaa, Chip, *Blue Rhythms: Six Lives in Rhythm and Blues* (Univ. of Illinois Press 1996); Guralnick, Peter, *Sweet Soul Music* (Harper 1986).

■ **RICE, DANIEL MCLAREN (1823-1900),** circus performer and manager. Born in New York City, he was a clown and acrobat in P. T. Barnum's troupe who later managed his own traveling circus. In his later years Rice was a popular homespun humorist who created and wore the traditional red, white, and blue "Uncle Sam" costume while performing. As a clown, Rice often lampooned Shakespearean tales and characters in his routines.

See Also: Barnum, Phineas T.

■ **RICE, ELMER (1892-1967),** playwright. Rice was born in New York City. He first worked as a lawyer, and issues and images of the legal profession figure in several of his dramatic works. Rice's first play, *On Trial* (1914), was noted for its use of cinematic techniques adapted to the stage. In 1929 Rice won a Pulitzer Prize for the play *Street Scene*, which realistically portrayed conditions of urban decline. Rice's later works were increasingly political, commenting on the conditions of the Cold War.

■ **RICE, THOMAS (JIM CROW) (1808-60),** pioneer performer in the popular stage entertainments known as minstrel shows. Born in New York City, he created "Jim Crow," a blackface caricature of an African-American slave, for a minstrel show in Louisville, Kentucky (c. 1828). Known as the father of American minstrelsy, Rice performed the song-and-dance act on stages across the United States and Europe, where it became both a hit and a long-lived racial stereotype.

See Also: Jim Crow Laws; Minstrel Shows.

■ **RICE,** cereal grass of southeastern Asian origin, most commonly grown in temperate climates. The earliest center of rice cultivation in the American colonies was South Carolina, where by the early 1700s rice had become the leading cash crop. The plant's cultivation depended on African slaves, who also introduced many varieties of rice and agricultural techniques, rice having long been a West African staple crop. Following the Civil War, rice cultivation moved westward to the coastal prairies of Texas and Louisiana (and, eventually, California), where it became a highly mechanized, capital-intensive industry.

BIBLIOGRAPHY: Grist, D. H., *Rice*, 5th ed. (Longman 1975).

■ **RICHARDSON, HENRY HOBSON (1838-86),** architect. Richardson was born in St. James Parish, Louisiana; he graduated from Harvard University in 1859 and studied at the Ecole des Beaux-Arts in Paris. After the Civil War, Richardson returned to the United States, settling first in New York City and then, after 1878, establishing his own practice in Brookline, Massachusetts, a suburb of Boston. Several of his early commissions were churches, including Church of the Unity in Springfield, Massachusetts (1860), Episcopal Church in West Medford, Massachusetts (1866), and Brattle Street Church in Boston (1870). He also designed Sever Hall (1878) and Austin Hall (1881) at Harvard University. He is well remembered for the Marshall Field Building in Chicago (1885) as well as for domestic designs, such as the Glessner House in Chicago (1887). Richardson designed masonry buildings distinguished by arches, an adaptation of the Romanesque style called the "Richardsonian" style.

See Also: Architecture.

■ **RIDGWAY, MATTHEW B. (1895-1993),** U.S. Army officer. Born in Fort Monroe, Virginia, Ridgway graduated in the West Point class of 1917. In World War II, he was a division commander in several European theaters. He led a number of airborne assaults and parachuted with his troops in the Normandy invasion. During the Korean War he initially led the U.S. 8th Army and then succeeded Gen. Douglas MacArthur as Allied commander in Asia. In 1952 Ridgway became supreme commander of Allied troops in Europe and, in 1953, U.S. Army chief of staff. He retired in 1955.

See Also: World War II.

■ **RIGHT-TO-WORK LAWS,** legislative acts that outlaw the closed shop. Passed on the state level, as allowed by Section 14b of the Taft-Hartley Act (1947, 1951), right-to-work laws guaranteeing employment regardless of union membership had been enacted by 21 states by 1996. Organized labor views such laws as anti-union, arguing that even when employees decline to join the appropriate union for their occupation, they receive the benefits negotiated by that union and thus should be required to pay union dues. In some cases unions have successfully lobbied for legislation allowing so-called "agency fees" to be collected from nonunion employees. However, many right-to-work laws have banned even agency fees. Although in 1996 such laws had been enacted only on the state level, primarily in the South and the West, there was also some effort to secure a national right-to-work act.

See Also: Closed Shop; Labor Movement; Taft-Hartley Act.

■ **RIMMER, WILLIAM (1816-79),** sculptor. Rimmer was born in Liverpool, England, but his family immigrated to the United States in 1818. He began his career as a stonecutter, sculptor, and painter in East Milton, Massachusetts, and started a studio in Boston late in his life (1870). Rimmer cast sculptures with a broad range of subjects in both granite and bronze, from *St. Stephen* (1860) and the *Falling Gladiator* (1861) to Boston's *Alexander Hamilton* (1864), Rimmer's only public commission.

See Also: Sculpture.

■ **RIO CONFERENCE,** World War II diplomatic meeting held in Rio de Janeiro, Brazil, in 1942. At the conference the United States attempted to persuade the Latin American nations either to declare war on the Axis nations or to sever all diplomatic relations with them. Only pro-German Argentina strongly opposed the initiative.

See Also: World War II.

■ **RIO GRANDE,** river forming part of the U.S.-Mexican border. It begins in the San Juan Mountains of Colorado, runs 1,885 miles south past Albuquerque and Las Cruces, New Mexico, El Paso, Texas, and then east as the U.S.-Mexican border to the Gulf of Mexico. In 1519 the Spanish Capt. Alonso Alvarez de Pineda sailed into the lower Rio Grande while mapping the Gulf coast. After the Pueblo Revolt of 1680, when Indians along the upper Rio Grande attacked Spanish missions, the Spanish maintained their colonial capital at El Paso for 13 years until they had reconquered the northern territory. The American explorer Zebulon Pike was captured by the Spanish while he was exploring the upper Rio Grande area in 1806. During the 1820s and 1830s, Anglo-Americans were recruited by Mexico, which was eager to separate Texas from Spanish control, to settle in the Spanish lands of Texas. The Americans, however, wanted Texas to be a part of the United States. When the United States annexed the Texas Republic in 1845, the disputed lands between the Nueces and Rio Grande rivers were a factor in the outbreak of the Mexican-American War (1846-48). The Treaty of Guadalupe Hidalgo in 1848 transferred the disputed land to the United States. During the 20th century large agricultural companies moved into the Rio Grande Valley to make use of low-paid Mexican labor, inexpensive water, and the long growing season.

■ **RIPLEY, GEORGE (1802-80),** American editor, reformer, and writer. Born in Greenfield, Massachusetts, he vowed early in life to "make a dictionary," a task that eventually led him to make an encyclopedia. Trained as a Unitarian minister, Ripley embraced a liberal, often utopian, view of Christianity and humanity. Beginning in 1838, he helped translate and edit the works of European philosophers in the 14-volume *Specimens of Foreign Standard Literature,* which became the foundation for many of the American transcendentalists' ideas. Continuing controversy within the Unitarian Church led Ripley to resign his ministry in 1841. He attended the first meeting of the "Transcendental Club" in Boston in 1836 and was active in the 1840 founding of the transcendental magazine *Dial.* He cofounded and was leader of a utopian community, Brook Farm (1841-47), in Concord, Massachusetts, which sought to balance physical labor with intellectual camaraderie. Ripley was a literary critic for the *New York Tribune* (1849-80) and in 1850 founded *Harper's New Monthly Magazine.*

    See Also: Brook Farm; Transcendentalism.

■ **RITTENHOUSE, DAVID (1732-96),** scientist. Noted for his extraordinary abilities in astronomy, physics, and instrument making, Rittenhouse was born in Germantown, Pennsylvania. His precise workmanship in producing instruments from clocks to compasses aided his masterful surveying. His own instruments for observing astronomical phenomena and his contributions in mathematics and physics earned him renown throughout America and Europe. He served as first director of the U.S. Mint in 1792 and president of the American Philosophical Society (1791-96).

    See Also: Revolution, American; Science.

■ **ROANOKE, LOST COLONY OF,** England's first, and unsuccessful, colonization attempt in the New World. What has been called "England's first Virginia" began its brief, mysterious life in 1584 when English adventurer Sir Walter Raleigh sent two small ships to scout the Outer Bank islands of North Carolina. They brought back two Algonquian Indians, Manteo and Wanchese, whose information persuaded Raleigh to send a fleet of seven vessels in 1585 with about 600 intended colonizers, but storms and piracy diverted most of them. Commander Sir Richard Grenville left 100 men on Roanoke Island for the winter while he returned to England for reinforcements.

    Under Capt. Ralph Lane, transferred from colonizing in Ireland, the Roanoke settlers built and explored, but Lane antagonized local Indians under Chief Wingina, whom Lane eventually killed. Scientist Thomas Harriott and artist John White made invaluable records of Southern Algonquian culture, but the colony's supplies ran out. When English navigator Sir Francis Drake stopped by after plundering West Indian Spaniards, he picked up the colonists for return to England. Thus ended the first Roanoke colony.

    Grenville was late with supplies. Finding the place abandoned, he left fewer than 20 men in occupation. After conflict with the Indians, this second colony vanished.

    A third attempt was made in 1587 under White, who had made friends with Manteo, a chief of Croatoan Island. White settled 110 persons, including his married daughter, who gave birth to Virginia Dare, the first native-born English American. White, too, returned for help, but it was denied because of preparations for defense against the Spanish Armada of 1588. White could not return to Roanoke until 1590, when he found that his colonists had abandoned the place, apparently in peaceful circumstances. A sign indicated that they had gone southward for refuge to Manteo's Croatoan, but White could not pursue them because of dangerous weather and opposition from his ship's crew.

    Writers have speculated that the colonists wandered inland and were killed by Indians. It is more likely that Manteo's people adopted them to replace losses from epidemic sickness, a common practice among American Indians. North Carolina's Lumbee tribe preserves a tradition of English ancestors. If true, the most successful promoter of Roanoke colony was Manteo. The thought is irresistible: was Virginia Dare a Lumbee ancestor?

—FRANCIS JENNINGS

See Also: Raleigh, Sir Walter.

BIBLIOGRAPHY: Hulton, Paul, ed., *America 1585: The Complete Drawings of John White* (Univ. of North Carolina Press 1984); Quinn, David B., *North America from Earliest Discovery to First Settlements* (Harper & Row 1977); Quinn, David B., *The Roanoke Voyages, 1584-1590,* 2 vols. (Hakluyt Soc. 1955).

■ **ROARING TWENTIES,** phrase used to describe the 1920s, a decade in American history that has clearly been oversimplified by most historians. Rather than being, in the words of one contemporary observer, simply a "long, lost drunken weekend" in U.S. history, the 1920s was a complex mix of social progressivism, economic expansion, and civil repression.

The fundamental factor in the shaping of the 1920s was World War I. As America emerged from the horrors of war, it attempted to close out the world. A prominent example of American isolationism in the 1920s was immigration restriction. Prior to the 1920s, legislation had been passed to exclude Chinese workers, but in the mid-1920s, a quota system was established for the first time. Its purpose was to limit the overall number of immigrants who did not come from the Western Hemisphere.

This same desire to insulate the nation from all that was foreign or "decadent" led to a civil repression that was quite pronounced. The trial of Nicola Sacco and Bartolomeo Vanzetti, two Italian anarchists charged with murder, was so overtly nativistic that many continue to believe in their innocence. Another sign of repression was the growth of the Ku Klux Klan. By mid-decade, the Klan had been fully reestablished and had initiated over 5 million new members.

Isolationism also shaped the popular culture of the period, as Americans searched for an entertainment that was peculiarly their own. They found it in sports, which grew to such proportions that it became one of the nation's biggest businesses. The nation's first commercialized sports figures emerged: baseball's Babe Ruth, boxing's Jack Dempsey, football's Red Grange, and tennis's "Big Bill" Tilden.

Yet the 1920s did, indeed, "roar" with the sound of a nation that was breaking loose from the shackles of Victorianism. Women, in particular, broke free: "flappers" dressed in short skirts, had bobbed hair, and in many cases developed a fondness for bootlegged liquor and cigarettes. In many respects, their emancipation was aided by Prohibition, which made the purchase of alcohol illegal but provided for many Americans a quest: if they could obtain alcohol, it was the ultimate act of protest against the government, which they equated with repression and war.

The decade also roared with the sounds of big business reasserting itself for the first time since the Gilded Age. In a decade that followed both economic calamity (the Panic of 1907 was still a bitter memory) and the deprivation of wartime, Americans idolized the businessman and all he stood for. It was not a coincidence that Henry Ford, then the owner of the nation's largest business, was chosen overwhelmingly in a 1927 poll as being the nation's number one choice for president.

The business boom of the Roaring Twenties, however, came to an abrupt halt on Oct. 24, 1929, with the first phase of the stock market crash. Americans would not enjoy another such period of consumer wildness until the 1950s.

—JOHN ROBERT GREENE

See Also: Immigration; Ku Klux Klan (KKK); Progressivism; Prohibition.

BIBLIOGRAPHY: Allen, Frederick Lewis, *Only Yesterday* (reprint, Telegraph Bks. 1986); Leuchtenburg, William, *The Perils of Prosperity* (Univ. of Chicago Press 1958); Shannon, David A., *Between the Wars: America, 1919-1941* (Houghton Mifflin 1979).

■ **ROBBINS, JEROME (1918-),** stage and screen director and choreographer who helped popularize modern dance. Born in New York City, he created memorable dances for the New York City Ballet and the musical theater. Robbins choreographed composer Leonard Bernstein's *Fancy Free* (1944) and *On the Town* (1945), as well as the musical comedy based on the latter, and later directed and choreographed Bernstein's *West Side Story* on stage (1957) and screen (1960).

See Also: Bernstein, Leonard.

■ **ROBERTS, OWEN JOSEPHUS (1875-1955),** associate justice of the U.S. Supreme Court (1930-45). He was born in Germantown, Pennsylvania, and was a special U.S. prosecutor in the Teapot Dome scandal (1924). Named to the Court by Pres. Herbert Hoover, Roberts was a conservative who resisted government intervention in the economy and opposed many of Pres. Franklin D. Roosevelt's New Deal initiatives. He chaired the government's inquiry (1942) into the Japanese attack on Pearl Harbor (1941).

See Also: Supreme Court; Teapot Dome.

■ **ROBESON, PAUL LEROY (1898-1976),** actor, singer, and activist, born in Princeton, New Jersey. He was the son of Rev. William D. Robeson, who had escaped from slavery in North Carolina, and Maria L. Bustill, a member of a noted abolitionist family.

At Rutgers College, which he entered in 1915 as the sole African-American student, Robeson gained national fame as a football star (twice All American) and was a brilliant scholar. He married Eslanda Goode in 1921. Their only child, Paul, Jr., was born in 1927. After finishing Columbia University Law School in 1923, Robeson pursued a career as an actor.

Robeson won fame as a performing artist, first as a starring actor in plays by Eugene O'Neill in 1924 and then as a concert singer the following year. His dual talents won him international renown in London productions of *Show Boat* (1928) and *Othello* (1930) and starring roles in British and U.S. movies. His New York appearance in *Othello* (1943) had a run of 296 performances, a record for a Shakespearean play on Broadway.

At the height of his popularity Robeson became involved in militant antifascist activity. He supported the socialist experiment in the Soviet Union and other left-wing causes. As founder of the Council on African Affairs and the Harlem newspaper *Freedom*, he campaigned for African liberation and equal rights for African Americans.

Hailed by some as a forerunner of the civil rights movement, Robeson was denounced by others and blacklisted during the McCarthy period as "un-American." His passport was canceled by the State Department in 1950. Robeson's book *Here I Stand* was published in 1958, and that year he won back his right to travel.

After a long illness, Paul Robeson died on Jan. 21, 1976, and was buried at Ferncliff Cemetery, Hartsdale, New York. Words from a 1937 speech are his epitaph there: "The artist must elect to fight for freedom or slavery. I have made my choice. I had no alternative."

—LLOYD L. BROWN

See Also: African Americans; Civil Rights Movement; Cold War.

BIBLIOGRAPHY: Brown, Lloyd L., *The Young Paul Robeson: "On My Journey Now"* (Westview Press 1997); Duberman, Martin Bauml, *Paul Robeson* (Knopf 1988); Robeson, Paul, *Here I Stand* (reprint, Beacon Press 1971).

■ **ROBINSON, BILL ("BOJANGLES") (1878-1949),** entertainer. Born in Richmond, Virginia, Robinson first tap-danced in minstrel shows and vaudeville. He was known as "Mr. Bojangles" and his tap dance up and down staircases became his signature piece. Robinson also starred on Broadway and made 14 films.

See Also: Minstrel Shows; Vaudeville.

■ **ROBINSON, EDWIN ARLINGTON (1869-1935),** poet. Robinson was born in Head Tide, Maine, and grew up in Gardiner, Maine, which inspired many of the characters and settings of his poetry. Pres. Theodore Roosevelt championed his work. Robinson won the Pulitzer Prize for poetry three times, for *Collected Poems* (1921), *The Man Who Died Twice* (1924), and *Tristram* (1927). The latter is a dramatic poem set in the time of King Arthur, but Robinson is best known today for his shorter poems depicting varieties of human character.

See Also: Poetry.

■ **ROBINSON, HARRIET HANSON (1825-1911),** leader of the woman suffrage movement. Born in Boston, Massachusetts, she worked in the mills as a youth. Robinson became a leading abolitionist and one of suffragist Susan B. Anthony's few allies in New England. She wrote *Massachusetts in the Woman Suffrage Movement* (1881).

See Also: Anthony, Susan B.; Woman Suffrage.

■ **ROBINSON, JACKIE (JACK ROOSEVELT) (1919-72),** baseball player. Born in Pasadena, California, Robinson began his sports career in football, playing in college at UCLA and professionally with the Los Angeles Bulldogs. After returning from military service in World War II, Robinson turned to baseball and played in the Negro Leagues for the Kansas City Monarchs. He was talented enough to draw the attention of the Brooklyn Dodgers, who signed him to their farm team. In April 1947 he began playing in the major leagues for the Dodgers, shattering the racial barrier that had stigmatized professional baseball. While Robinson will always be remembered for his integration of the game, his play in the field, at bat, and on the bases earned him the respect of millions. He hit .311 lifetime, played on six pennant-winning teams, and was the National League's Most Valuable Player in 1949.

A superb hitter, Jackie Robinson became the first African American to play major league baseball when he joined the Brooklyn Dodgers on Apr. 15, 1947.

Robinson retired after the 1956 season. He was elected to baseball's Hall of Fame in 1962.

See Also: *African Americans; Baseball; Sports.*

■ **ROBINSON-PATMAN ACT (1935),** an amendment to the Clayton Antitrust Act (1914). A "fair trade" law to protect small retailers, the Robinson-Patman Act (also known as the Anti-Price Discrimination Act) banned discount price-fixing by nationwide chain stores.

See Also: *Clayton Antitrust Act; New Deal.*

■ **ROCK AND ROLL,** the most important popular musical genre of the second half of the 20th century. Rock music took shape in the early 1950s when white musicians began emulating the styles of African-American performers. With the decline of big band swing music and the be-bop experimentations of jazz artists, the tastes of many young listeners began to turn toward more danceable rhythm and blues music. As the audience for this style broadened, white producers began to re-record (or "cover") the work of African-American musicians, while disc jockies on mainstream radio stations—such as Alan Freed of Cleveland—began playing the original music. In order to avoid the racial connotations of "rhythm and blues" (which had been known as "race music" until 1949), Freed coined the name "rock and roll" (a sexual euphemism in the African-American community) to describe the music.

The important creative breakthrough came in 1954 with the recordings of Elvis Presley, a white performer who never failed to acknowledge the deep influence of blues and gospel, as well as country and western music, on his style. "The colored folks been singing and playing it just like I'm doing now," he told an interviewer, "for more years than I know." Under the direction of producer Sam Phillips of Memphis, who had previously recorded many African-American blues artists on his Sun Records label, Presley creatively fused these traditions into an immensely popular musical form. His wild and sensual performance style—hips gyrating, knees bending, long hair tossing—delighted teenagers and frightened their parents.

Elvis soon signed a contract with RCA, one of the giants of the recording industry, and rock and roll swept the country. For the first time, African-American performers "crossed over" to join white rock and roll artists on the pop music chart, breaking the code of commercial segregation that had kept African-American and white music separate throughout the first half of the century. Classic rock and roll was interracial, another reason for the panic it produced among conservative Americans.

Generally taking the form of 12-bar blues-based music with a dominating, danceable back beat in the tradition of ragtime and big band music, rock and roll was driven by an enthusiasm for social dancing among young people. The lyrics frequently focused on youth culture. The African-American performer Chuck Berry—the greatest songwriter and most influential guitarist among rock and roll artists—captured teenage concerns with humor, irony, and passion in compositions about school ("School Days"), cars ("Maybellene"), love ("Memphis"), and the music itself ("Rock and Roll Music"). The phenomenon suggested the increasing importance of the market created by the large generation of baby boomers born after World War II.

The rise of rock and roll was also connected with changes in the entertainment industry. Television replaced radio as the center of family entertainment, while radio became an accompaniment to other activities; now there were clock radios, car radios, and hand-held transistor radios. Network radio programs gave way to disc jockeys with "Top Forty" formats. Ample broadcast opportunities stimulated the growth of hundreds of independent record labels, fostering an exciting diversity in the new music. The many styles of rock and roll's first decade included group harmonies ("doo-wop"), country sounds ("rockabilly"), beach music ("surf"), as well as African-American music with wide popular appeal ("soul").

Later Stages. The sudden popularity of the British group the Beatles in 1964 marked an important transition. In addition to their consummate musical ability, the Beatles introduced young Americans to an intoxicating mix of humorous irreverence and mild social protest. They were the leading edge of the connection between rock and roll music (or "rock," as it came to be known) and the youth "counterculture" that developed in the 1960s. Folk music had already gained popularity as the voice of the civil rights movement. In 1965, folk singer-songwriter Bob Dylan traded his acoustic guitar for an electric model and added social protest as an important dimension of rock music. Rock groups became a symbol of the counterculture, especially after 400,000 young fans gathered at the music festival of "peace and love" at Woodstock in August 1969.

But the rise of "stadium rock," heralded by Woodstock and other music festivals, was accompanied by a decline in the danceability of the music. During the 1970s rock lost its dance energy, which was taken up by other genres, notably "disco" and later "rap" music, both of which emerged from urban dance clubs. By the last decade of the century rock and roll, like jazz, had been overtaken by nostalgia, ceding its creative energies to other emergent musics.

—JOHN MACK FARAGHER

See Also: Be-Bop; Berry, Charles Edward Anderson ("Chuck"); Big Bands; Blues; Country and Western Music; Dylan, Bob; Folk Music; Gospel Music; Nineteen Sixties; Presley, Elvis; Ragtime; Rhythm and Blues; Television and Radio; Woodstock.

BIBLIOGRAPHY: Gillett, Charlie, *The Sound of the City* (Pantheon 1983); Chapple, Steve, and Reebee Garofalo, *Rock and Roll Is Here to Pay* (Nelson Hall 1977); Ward, Ed, Geoffrey Stokes, and Ken Tucker, *Rock of Ages: The Rolling Stone History of Rock and Roll* (Summit Books 1986).

■ **ROCKEFELLER, JOHN DAVISON (1839-1937),** industrialist and philanthropist. A founder of the Standard Oil Company and the American petroleum industry, Rockefeller was born in Richford, New York, and raised in Cleveland. He began his business career in 1855 in a commission house as a bookkeeper-clerk. An astute and visionary businessman, Rockefeller built his first oil refinery in 1863, soon after the first drilling of oil in Pennsylvania. Disturbed by the chaotic nature of the early oil industry, he worked diligently to keep his company stable and profitable. In 1870, Rockefeller, with a few others, formed the Standard Oil Company. Through price cutting, the buying out of competitors, railroad rebates, and other predatory practices, Standard Oil gained control of 90 percent of the market by 1880.

In 1882, Rockefeller and the other partners reorganized the expanding and unwieldy enterprise

In 1870, John D. Rockefeller cofounded the Standard Oil Company, which quickly rose to dominance of the nation's petroleum industry.

into one of the first and largest trusts. Profits soared, but reformers and other critics assailed Standard and Rockefeller for unfair, even illegal, practices. Rockefeller, however, operated within the law.

In 1897, Rockefeller retired as president of Standard Oil to devote himself full time to charitable giving. A devout Baptist, Rockefeller became one of America's greatest philanthropists, giving away some $550 million by the end of his life. He helped establish such institutions as the University of Chicago, the Rockefeller Foundation, the General Education Board, and the Rockefeller Institute.

See Also: Industrial Revolution; Petroleum; Rockefeller Family; Trusts.

BIBLIOGRAPHY: Hawke, David Freeman, *John D.: The Founding Father of the Rockefellers* (Harper & Row 1980); Nevins, Allan, *Study in Power: John D. Rockefeller, Industrialist and Philanthropist* (Scribner 1953).

■ **ROCKEFELLER, NELSON (1908-79),** governor of New York (1959-73) and U.S. vice president (1974-77). Born in Bar Harbor, Maine, he was a grandson of Standard Oil founder John D. Rockefeller. He led the liberal wing of the Republican party in the 1960s and made several unsuccessful runs for the presidency. He was appointed vice president by Pres. Gerald Ford, who had become president following Richard Nixon's resignation in 1974.

See Also: Rockefeller Family.

■ **ROCKEFELLER FAMILY,** prominent, wealthy, and philanthropic family whose members were the relatives and descendants of John D. Rockefeller (1839-1937). The Rockefeller family fortune emanates from the Standard Oil Company, which became the first and largest of the trusts and which controlled 90 percent of the oil industry by 1880. Although attacked by reformers, John D. Rockefeller never engaged in illegal business practices. During his life he donated over $550 million to charitable causes and with his wife, Laura, lived a devoutly religious life as a member of the Baptist church. The Rockefellers had four children: Bessie, Alta, Edith, and John D., Jr. Among the noted members of the family were the following:

William (1841-1922), brother of John, built the great export division of Standard Oil and a large personal fortune but never made any charitable bequests. He married his wife, Almira, in 1864 and left almost $200 million to his four children.

John, Jr. (1874-1960), worked for Standard Oil but after 1911 primarily managed his father's philanthropic ventures. During the next five decades, this work resulted in the reconstruction of colonial Williamsburg (Virginia) and a large number of prominent Manhattan construction projects, including Rockefeller Center. Married twice, John, Jr., had six children.

David (1915-), son of John, Jr., has been a prominent banker since the 1950s. His older brother, Nelson (1908-79), was governor of New York (1959-73) and vice president of the United States (1974-77). His nephew John D. (Jay) Rockefeller IV (1937-) was Democratic governor of West Virginia (1977-85) and U.S. senator from West Virginia (1985-). The Rockefeller family has produced some of the most successful entrepreneurs, bankers, and philanthropists in American history.

See Also: Rockefeller, John Davison; Rockefeller, Nelson.

BIBLIOGRAPHY: Harr, John Ensor, and Peter J. Johnson, *The Rockefeller Century* (Scribner 1988); Harr,

John Ensor, and Peter J. Johnson, *The Rockefeller Conscience: An American Family in Public and Private* (Scribner 1991); Stasz, Clarice, *The Rockefeller Women: Dynasty of Piety, Privacy, and Service* (St. Martin's 1995).

■ **ROCKINGHAM, LORD (1730-82),** British statesman. As a prominent Whig leader in England during the American Revolution, Rockingham led a faction that opposed the Stamp Act (1765). He worked for reconciliation with America and was prime minister after the fall of Lord North (1782), but he died before a peace settlement was reached.

See Also: Revolution, American; Stamp Act.

■ **ROCKWELL, NORMAN (1894-1978),** painter and illustrator. Rockwell was born in New York City and studied art there at the National Academy of Design and the Art Students League. At 17, he started his career as an illustrator; his first salaried job was for *Boys' Life*, the magazine of the Boy Scouts. In 1916, he started working for the *Saturday Evening Post*. His cover paintings of American small-town and rural life were immensely popular. Rockwell illustrated special editions of Mark Twain's *Tom Sawyer* and *Huckleberry Finn* in the 1930s and continued to illustrate the annual Boy Scouts' calendar until 1976. *The Four Freedoms*, paintings done for the *Saturday Evening Post*, were published as posters by the United States Office of War Information during World War II and became some of his most popular images. Rockwell won the Presidential Medal of Freedom in 1977, a tribute to his career spent representing American life.

See Also: Painting.

■ **ROCKY MOUNTAINS,** the major mountain system of North America, running some 3,000 miles from Alaska through Canada and into the western United States. The highest point is Mt. Elbert (14,431 feet) in Colorado. The Southern Rockies, the highest part of the system, are located in New Mexico, Colorado, and southern Wyoming. The Middle Rockies lie to the north and cover northeastern Utah and western Wyoming. The Northern Rockies extend from northwestern Wyoming through Idaho and northeastern Washington. The western slopes of the Rockies rise slowly from a series of plateaus and basins to the west. The eastern slopes, however, rise abruptly from the Great Plains. The explorer Meriwether Lewis passed through the Rockies in 1803 and recognized what a formidable barrier they presented to westward expansion. Fur trappers were the first group of people to explore the mountains extensively. Nineteenth-century travelers avoided the most dangerous parts of the mountains by following the Oregon Trail through South Pass in Wyoming or by taking the Santa Fe Trail around the mountains to the south. Among the ever-popular tourist sites in the Rockies are Yellowstone National Park, Rocky Mountain National Park, and Mesa Verde National Park.

■ **RODEO,** central aspect of open-range ranching that later became a sporting and entertainment event. The practice of cattle ranching in the United States had its origins in Iberian, English, African, and Latin American traditions. The term *rodeo* derives from the Spanish word *rodear*, meaning to surround or go around.

Nineteenth-century open-range rodeos, or roundups, brought together riders and stockmen from across the American West and Mexico. Directed by general roundup bosses, they selected cattle for slaughter, broke in young horses, and branded calves, colts, and unbranded cattle. During the latter half of the 19th century, roundups grew to include up to 300 riders and dozens of wagons and covered hundreds of square miles of range. These open-range rodeos sometimes became festival-like gatherings.

With changes in the cattle industry during the late 19th century, especially the fencing of open ranges into private ranches, rodeos developed into shows where cowboys could demonstrate their skills in competitions and exhibitions. Buffalo Bill's Wild West Show helped to popularize the traveling exhibition, while rodeos developed independently as well. Some rodeos, such as the 101 Ranch, traveled around the West, while others became annual festivals, such as Frontier Days in Cheyenne, Wyoming. Professional and local riders alike participated in steer and bronco riding, calf roping, bulldogging, and other rodeo activities. During the 20th century, the rodeo developed into a popular spectator and highly professionalized sport.

See Also: Sports.

BIBLIOGRAPHY: Wooden, Wayne S., and Gavin Ehringer, *Rodeo in America: Wranglers, Roughstock, & Paydirt* (Univ. of Kansas Press 1996).

■ **RODGERS, RICHARD (1902-79),** composer. Born in New York City, he launched his Broadway career with lyricist Lorenz Hart with *The Garrick Gaieties* (1925). They produced songs such as "Manhattan," "My Funny Valentine," and "Bewitched" in hit shows including *Babes in Arms* (1937) and *Pal Joey* (1940). After Hart's death, Rodgers joined Oscar Hammerstein II to compose a string of classic musicals including *Oklahoma* (1943), *South Pacific* (1947), and *The Sound of Music* (1959).

See Also: Hammerstein, Oscar, II.

■ **RODNEY, CAESAR (1728-84),** military leader and Revolutionary War politician. A native of Dover, Delaware, Rodney sat in the First and Second Continental Congresses and signed the Declaration of Independence. During the Revolution he also served as a general in the militia.

See Also: Declaration of Independence.

■ **ROEBLING, JOHN (1806-69),** civil engineer who made wire rope and built suspension bridges. Born in Mühlhausen, Germany, Roebling was educated in Berlin and immigrated to the United States in 1831. After a stint as a farmer near Pittsburgh, he worked on canal projects for the state of Pennsylvania. There, he invented a cable made from twisted strands of wire that was much smaller and stronger than the hemp rope in use, and he began to manufacture it in 1841. His cables proved strong enough to haul canal boats and to support an aqueduct across the Allegheny River (1845). The next year, Roebling built his first suspension bridge, across the Monongahela River at Pittsburgh. He moved his factory to Trenton, New Jersey, in the late 1840s and continued to build bridges, among them the first railroad cable suspension bridge, across Niagara Falls (1851-55). In 1857, Roebling proposed to link Manhattan with Brooklyn by building a bridge over the East River. He was appointed chief engineer of the project in 1867, perfected his plans, and started work

in 1869. While inspecting the site in June, however, a tug crushed his foot, and he died of tetanus a few days later. His son, Washington A. Roebling, succeeded him as chief engineer and saw the Brooklyn Bridge completed in 1883.

See Also: Science.

■ **ROE V. WADE (1973),** landmark Supreme Court case that established a woman's unrestricted right to an abortion within the first trimester of pregnancy. The plaintiff "Jane Roe" (Norma McCorvey) could not under restrictive Texas law receive a legal abortion to terminate her unwanted pregnancy. In response, McCorvey sued the state. Her case, a challenge to all state abortion laws, eventually appeared before the Supreme Court.

The Court, led by Chief Justice Warren Burger, ruled 7-2 in favor of Roe. The decision extended the right to personal privacy in sexual matters that originally resulted from the decision in *Grisworld* v. *Connecticut*, which in 1965 held that severe restrictions on the availability of contraceptives was a violation of the implied constitutional right to privacy.

Justice Harry Blackmun wrote the majority opinion in *Roe* v. *Wade*, with Justices William Rehnquist and Byron White dissenting. The decision in this controversial case continues to stimulate debate. The "right-to-life" movement, supported by the Christian Coalition, the Roman Catholic Church, and many conservative politicians, continues to lobby for a constitutional amendment that will with a few exceptions prohibit abortion. "Pro-choice" activists and groups such as the National Organization for Women (NOW) support the decision as establishing a woman's right to reproductive control, even though the Court's opinion did not explicitly deal with issues of women's rights and gender equality.

See Also: Abortion; Supreme Court; Women's Movement.

BIBLIOGRAPHY: Darrow, David J., *Liberty and Sexuality: The Right to Privacy and the Making of Roe v. Wade* (Oxford Univ. Press 1978); Faux, Marian, *Roe v. Wade: The Untold Story of the Landmark Supreme Court Decision That Made Abortion Legal* (Macmillan 1994).

■ **ROGERS, JOHN (1829-1904),** popular genre sculptor. Rogers was born in Salem, Massachusetts. In 1859-60, he won attention with the New York exhibition of the group *The Slave Auction*, but he is best known for small-scale works, which he reproduced and distributed successfully through a mail-order catalog. He cast plaster statuette groups of various genre vignettes of American rural life, such as *The Checker Players* (1859), Civil War scenes, such as *"Wounded to the Rear"—One More Shot* (1864), and scenes from literature and drama.

■ **ROGERS, ROBERT (1731-95),** frontier settler and military leader. Born on the frontier in Methuen, Massachusetts, Rogers early developed a reputation for recklessness and bravery. In the French and Indian War he fought in several major military expeditions, including that against Crown Point in 1755. Commissioned in a ranger unit, by 1758 he was a major in charge of nine units (known as Rogers' Rangers), but peacetime brought misfortune since Rogers was a poor, sometimes dishonest, administrator. A loyalist, he immigrated to England after the American Revolution and died in debtor's prison.

■ **ROGERS, WILL (1879-1935),** humorist. Born William Penn Adair in Oologah, Oklahoma, of Cherokee ancestry, he was a working cowboy and joined the Ziegfeld Follies in 1915 as a rope-twirler who spiced his routine with humorous comments on the current scene. His syndicated newspaper column (1922-35), books, and frequent radio and film appearances made him the nation's favorite homespun philosopher. An ardent promoter of aviation, Rogers died in an airplane crash in Alaska.

■ **ROLFE, JOHN (1585-1622),** English colonist and entrepreneur. Born in Norfolk, England, Rolfe settled in Virginia in 1610. Part of the contingent of settlers who established a successful colony at Jamestown, Rolfe also made the colony viable by developing a method for curing tobacco, which made it commercially valuable. He married Pocahontas, daughter of Powhatan, in 1614. After their marriage Rolfe took Pocahontas to England, where she died (1617).

See Also: Jamestown Settlement; Pocahontas.

■ **ROMAN CATHOLICS,** practitioners of Catholicism and members of the Christian church headed by the pope. Numbering some 60 million in 1995, American Roman Catholics have developed into an influential group in society. During the colonial period, the few Roman Catholics settled primarily in Maryland and in the French and Spanish colonies. Although Protestants predominated in British America, the heritage of French and Spanish Catholicism can still be seen in New Orleans and the Southwest, respectively.

Between the early 19th and the mid-20th centuries, successive waves of foreign immigration shaped American Catholicism. The church's rapid growth began in the mid-19th century with emigration from Germany and Ireland, continued with an influx from Italy and Poland between 1880 and 1920, and ended with emigration from Latin America in the 1920s.

Before gaining national prominence as a humorist in the 1920s, Will Rogers performed deftly with a lariat on the vaudeville stage.

Protestants and nativists, often harboring anti-Catholic sentiments, regularly attempted to "Americanize" the newcomers. But despite occasional religious and ethnic strife, Catholics did not renounce their religion. Instead, they formed their own institutions, namely churches and schools. Priests, who held dominant positions in Catholic communities, created parishes where the church and school together assumed a variety of societal roles. As Catholics grew stronger, they became more active in the larger American society. After the mid-20th century, Catholics were no longer primarily immigrants but established and influential Americans. In the post–World War II years, the laity participated more actively in the church but was still subject to the authority of the Vatican.

See Also: *Religion.*

BIBLIOGRAPHY: Dolan, Jay P., *The American Catholic Experience: A History from Colonial Times to the Present* (Doubleday 1985); Hennesey, James J., *American Catholics: A History of the Roman Catholic Community in the United States* (Oxford Univ. Press 1981).

■ **ROMANTICISM,** 19th-century literary and artistic mode of expression. Romanticism had its roots in the late 18th and early 19th centuries in England and other European nations but took hold as a dominant style in the United States in the early and mid-19th century. Romanticism was a reaction against an earlier emphasis on rationalism and instead advocated the expression of emotion and the roles of intuition and the senses. Romantic writers and artists championed the individual and the value of direct experience. Many romantic writings and paintings explored nature, and particularly wilderness, as a parallel to human society and culture. These romantic ideals were often expressed through the themes of nostalgia for past ways of life and interest in folk cultures, sublime landscapes, and heroic figures, often artists. In the United States romanticism was introduced in the poems of William Cullen Bryant and the fiction of Washington Irving, Nathaniel Hawthorne, James Fenimore Cooper, Herman Melville, and Edgar Allan Poe. Walt Whitman, Ralph Waldo Emerson, and Henry David Thoreau carried the romantic movement toward the American expression of transcendentalism. In painting American romanticism was seen most clearly in the Hudson River School painters, who explored the Hudson Valley's landscape in search of beauty and the sublime. Thomas Cole, Asher Durand, and George Inness led this loose association of artists. The romantic fascination with nature led directly to the movement to protect spectacular landscapes—such as Yosemite or Yellowstone—in national parks.

—MARINA MOSKOWITZ

See Also: *Bryant, William Cullen; Hudson River School; Irving, Washington; Novel; Painting; Poetry; Transcendentalism.*

BIBLIOGRAPHY: Wolf, Bryan Jay, *Romantic Re-Vision: Culture and Consciousness in Nineteenth-Century American Painting and Literature* (Univ. of Chicago Press 1982).

■ **ROMBERG, SIGMUND (1887-1951),** composer. A native of Nagykanizsa, Hungary, he immigrated to the United States in 1909, led a popular orchestra, and became a leading composer of popular operettas known for their lilting melodies and romantic, often exotic, settings. His first success, *Maytime* (1917), was followed by *The Student Prince* (1924) and *The Desert Song* (1926). Romberg also composed film scores and toured with his orchestra.

■ **ROOSEVELT, (ANNA) ELEANOR (1884-1962),** reformer, Democratic party activist, and first lady (1933-45). A member of the elite Roosevelt clan, she was born in New York City and had a lonely and sheltered childhood. A lifelong reformer, Roosevelt used her position as an elite white woman to challenge prevailing attitudes about women, the poor, and African Americans. She married her cousin, Franklin Delano Roosevelt, in 1905, and they raised six children.

Roosevelt's political education accelerated in 1911, when her husband entered the New York state senate. Although their marriage lacked intimacy, she and Franklin Roosevelt formed an effective political partnership. He relied on her advice and her moral vision throughout his career, and she used her position to foster her own independent political action, influencing the course of Democratic politics from the 1920s to the 1960s. After Franklin was struck by polio in 1921, her activities kept the Roosevelt name alive in political circles.

Married in 1905, Franklin D. and Eleanor Roosevelt served the nation as president and first lady from 1933 to 1945, with Eleanor playing a more active role in public affairs than any previous first lady.

Although elevation to first lady curtailed Eleanor Roosevelt's involvement with her own social and political causes, she continued to travel, lecture, and write. She published a daily newspaper column, "My Day." Stimulated by the idea that the federal government could be a force for good in people's lives, she advocated many of the humane and radical aspects of the New Deal. Criticized by some for her active role, especially on behalf of unions and civil rights, she was admired by many Americans as a woman of conviction.

After her husband's death in 1945 Roosevelt worked for international cooperation and world peace. As a member of the U.S. delegation to the United Nations, she drafted and lobbied for the Declaration of Human Rights (1948), which passed unanimously. Considered one of the most influential women of the 20th century, her reputation has grown as historians have uncovered her political legacy.

—CATHERINE ALLGOR

See Also: New Deal; Roosevelt, Franklin Delano; Women in American History; Women's Movement.

BIBLIOGRAPHY: Black, Allida M., *Casting Her Own Shadow: Eleanor Roosevelt and the Shaping of Postwar Liberalism* (Columbia Univ. Press 1996); Cook, Blanche Wiesen, *Eleanor Roosevelt*, vol. 1 (Viking 1992).

■ ROOSEVELT, FRANKLIN DELANO (1882-1945),

32nd president of the United States (1933-45). He was born to a distinguished New York family on an estate in Hyde Park, New York. There was little in Franklin Roosevelt's early life that suggested that he would become one of the great world leaders of the 20th century and a symbol of the common man in America.

Early Life. Raised in affluence by an older father, James Roosevelt, and an indulgent, dominant mother, Sara Delano, Roosevelt grew up as a sheltered only child, taught at home by a Swiss governess until the age of 14, when he was sent to Groton. From Groton, Roosevelt went on to Harvard, where he was an average but popular student. Following his graduation from Harvard, he entered Columbia Law School, which he attended until his third year, when he passed his bar examinations but left the school before completing his degree.

An important turning point in Roosevelt's life came in 1905 when he married Anna Eleanor Roosevelt, a distant cousin and the niece of Pres. Theodore Roosevelt. Thin, shy, and earnest, Eleanor Roosevelt was in many ways the opposite of her outgoing, fun-loving husband. For the first years of their marriage, Roosevelt seemed little more than another young New York socialite and lawyer. He had, however, powerful political ambitions, even at this young age.

Early Political Career. In 1910, Roosevelt accepted the Democratic party nomination for the New York state senate representing Dutchess

County. Running in a heavily Republican district, Roosevelt undertook a vigorous campaign that attacked political bosses and corruption in both parties. In a Democratic landslide, the 28-year-old Roosevelt won the election, making him suddenly one of the best-known political figures in the state.

In 1912, Roosevelt sought reelection, but he also hurled himself into the presidential campaign by supporting the Democratic nominee, Woodrow Wilson (even though cousin Theodore Roosevelt was running against Wilson on a third-party ticket). Using the Roosevelt name, he became a leading spokesman on the campaign trail for the Democratic ticket. After Wilson's election, Roosevelt was appointed assistant secretary of the navy, a post he had coveted because Theodore Roosevelt had launched his national political career in the 1890s from that position.

Roosevelt spent the next seven years in Washington working under Josephus Daniels, the secretary of the navy, where he made lasting political connections that were critical to his later political career. His marriage, however, entered a crisis period during these years after Eleanor discovered that Franklin was having an affair with her social secretary, Lucy Mercer. Realizing that a divorce would ruin any prospects for a future political career, Roosevelt gave up the affair, although his relationship with Eleanor was damaged.

Years of Crisis. Following the war, Roosevelt became a leading supporter of Wilson's League of Nations. That support helped win him the Democratic party's nomination for vice president in 1920 on the ticket headed by Gov. James M. Cox, an Ohio progressive. Although the Republican candidate, Warren G. Harding, won the presidency in a landslide election, the 39-year-old Roosevelt had run an enthusiastic campaign and received favorable national attention.

Following the campaign, Roosevelt returned to private life in New York. He had every reason to believe, however, that he would one day reenter politics. But his world crashed suddenly in August 1921, when, while vacationing at his mother's summer home in Campobello, New Brunswick, he contracted polio. He survived the disease but was left a permanent paraplegic. Unable to walk and deeply depressed, Roosevelt seemed destined to be a house-bound invalid for the rest of his life.

After years of painful adjustment to his paralysis, Roosevelt gradually reentered politics over the objections of his mother but with the strong encouragement of Eleanor, who had faithfully helped maintain his political connections during the most difficult years of his illness. A retiring woman in her early life, Eleanor emerged in the 1920s in her own right as an effective public speaker and political force in state Democratic politics with close associations with progressive causes.

As part of his return to political life, Roosevelt allied himself with the popular New York governor, Alfred E. Smith, and managed his unsuccessful campaign to win the presidential nomination in 1924. In 1928, Smith won the presidential nomination (only to be defeated by Republican Herbert Hoover in the election). That same year, Roosevelt surprised many by accepting Smith's proposal to run as his successor for governor of New York. Roosevelt eked out a narrow victory in a year when other Democrats were buried in the Republican landslide.

Governor of New York. As governor, Roosevelt established himself as a progressive and an activist. His administration undertook public development of hydroelectric power on the St. Lawrence and Niagara rivers, regulation of telephone and utility rates, judicial and prison reform (including a controversial new parole system), and tax cuts for farmers. When the nation went into a severe economic depression in the early 1930s, Roosevelt established a Temporary Emergency Relief Administration under Harry Hopkins that later became a model for relief in the nation. Roosevelt easily won reelection in 1930, thereby making him a leading candidate for the Democratic presidential nomination in 1932.

In a well-orchestrated campaign, he won the nomination and went on to defeat Hoover easily, who appeared inept and disdainful of the plight of ordinary people. With the Democrats sweeping both the House and the Senate, Roosevelt was prepared to enact his recovery program.

First Term as President: The New Deal. Where Roosevelt actually stood on most issues was unclear. During the campaign he came out for the repeal of Prohibition, and he appeared to be a fiscal conservative, but on many other key issues he had carefully waffled. Nonetheless, in his first hundred days in office he proposed an extensive legislative agenda that came to be known as the New Deal. His programs targeted industrial and agricultural recovery through legislation that granted federal powers to control agricultural production and to set industrial prices and wages. He also backed regulatory legislation that brought banking and financial markets under stricter federal control.

Direct relief for the unemployed was offered through legislation that created the Federal Emergency Relief Administration (FERA), headed by Harry Hopkins, while the Public Works Administration, under Harold Ickes, secretary of the interior, provided work on large projects such as highways, bridges, and dams. He also established the Civilian Conservation Corps (CCC), which recruited a quarter-million young Americans to work in national parks and forests. The New Deal challenged fundamental assumptions about the government's proper role in society and drew intense criticism from conservatives. The economy recovered somewhat, but only temporarily.

Although the Democrats swept the midterm congressional elections in 1934, the inability of the Roosevelt administration to restore full prosperity aroused political opposition on both the right and the left. Countering his opponents, Roosevelt aggressively pursued new welfare measures, including the Social Security Act (1935) that became the centerpiece of what became known as the second New Deal. Roosevelt also moved to secure new farm, public works, and labor legislation that included the Works Progress (later Projects) Administration (WPA) and the Wagner Act, which offered new protections for labor.

The Second Term: Domestic and Foreign Problems. The opposition that seemed so threatening in 1935 melted away by 1936, when the popular president won a landslide reelection over Republican Alf Landon, the governor of Kansas. But Roosevelt soon found his administration embattled over his scheme to add more members to the Supreme Court and his failure to address another downturn in the economy. Once again Roosevelt took the offensive. He undertook a deliberate policy of deficit spending and passed new farming legislation (the Agricultural Adjustment Act of

1937), new labor legislation (the Fair Labor Standards Act of 1938), and antimonopoly legislation.

In his second term, Roosevelt confronted increasingly ominous foreign policy problems as ruthless dictatorships in Europe—Hitler in Germany and Mussolini in Italy—and Japan threatened the world order. Congress, reflecting general public sentiment, sought to isolate the United States from international events. The outbreak of World War II in Europe in 1939 led Roosevelt, a consistent internationalist, to support England and its democratic allies against the wishes of a well-organized isolationist movement.

After winning an unprecedented third term in 1940 against Republican Wendell Wilkie, Roosevelt increased aid to England through a lend-lease program in 1941. Japan's attack on the U.S. Pacific fleet in Pearl Harbor, Hawaii, in 1941 brought the United States into the war in full force.

War Leader. Once the United States entered the war, it went all out to win. Roosevelt created myriad federal agencies to manage the war, and as war production boomed, so did the economy. In leading the American people in this global war fought on many fronts, Roosevelt revealed his exceptional abilities to manage both the home front and the massive war effort as commander in chief. He also emerged as an international statesman by designing an alliance between Great Britain under Winston Churchill and the Soviet Union under Joseph Stalin. These three leaders, Roosevelt, Churchill, and Stalin, coordinated strategy for ending the war and shaped the postwar world order.

Roosevelt held fast to his overriding priority for the postwar world: the creation of a new international organization, the United Nations. He began preparing for the postwar world even before the United States entered the war. In August 1941, Roosevelt and Churchill met off the coast of Newfoundland, where they issued a joint declaration called the Atlantic Charter. This proclamation affirmed democracy's adherence to the Four Freedoms: freedom from want, freedom from fear, freedom of speech, and freedom of religion. Soon after the attack on Pearl Harbor, Roosevelt announced the formation of the United Nations alliance, composed of nations opposed to the Axis powers.

The most difficult relationship within the alliance was with the Soviet Union, which was controlled by its ruthless dictator, Stalin, who continued to remain fiercely nationalistic and suspicious of the Western democracies. Nevertheless, the necessity of war forced Stalin to cooperate with the Western powers. A series of wartime meetings dealt with relations between the Western democracies and the Soviet Union. The Teheran meeting in November 1943 marked the height of Allied cooperation by reaching an agreement on a number of matters, including a date for an invasion of France. Major issues concerning recognition of the London-based Polish government in exile and a commitment to a new international organization remained unresolved.

Shortly after his inauguration for a fourth term in early 1945, Roosevelt traveled to Yalta in the Russian Crimea where he met once again with Churchill and Stalin. Roosevelt, clearly ill, came to Yalta with one primary goal: the creation of the United Nations. Later critics charged that Roosevelt had underestimated Stalin and had made too many concessions to Russia in Eastern Europe.

Shortly after the Yalta meeting, on Apr. 12, 1945, Roosevelt died of a massive cerebral hemorrhage. Before his death, however, he had started to become disillusioned with Stalin and had sent warnings about the situation in Poland. Roosevelt died without witnessing the end of the war or the formal establishment of the United Nations.

At the time of his death, Roosevelt was eulogized as one of the outstanding leaders of the 20th century. While some contemporaries and later historians considered Roosevelt a leader who often pursued pragmatism and political opportunity over principle, his reputation as a major figure in modern American history remains, for the most part, undiminished. His unprecedented 12 years as president marked major changes in American society and in the place of the United States in the world. Historians are likely to continue to rank Roosevelt as one of the most influential presidents of this century, the man who led the nation through great depression and global war.

—DONALD T. CRITCHLOW

See Also: *Fireside Chats; Great Depression; Hundred Days; New Deal; Presidential Elections; President of the United States; Roosevelt, (Anna) Eleanor; World War II.*

BIBLIOGRAPHY: Blum, John Morton, *V Was for Victory: Politics and American Culture During World War II* (Harcourt Brace Jovanovich 1976); Brinkley, Alan, *The End of Reform: New Deal Liberalism in Recession and War* (Knopf 1995); Burns, James MacGregor, *Roosevelt: The Lion and the Fox* (Harcourt, Brace 1956); Burns, James MacGregor, *Roosevelt: The Soldier of Freedom* (Harcourt, Brace 1970); Freidel, Frank, *Franklin D. Roosevelt,* 4 vols. (Little, Brown 1952-76); Schlesinger, Arthur M., Jr., *The Age of Roosevelt,* 3 vols. (Houghton Mifflin 1957-60); Schwartz, Jordan, *The New Dealers: Power Politics in the Age of Roosevelt* (Knopf 1993).

■ **ROOSEVELT, THEODORE (1858-1919),** 26th president of the United States. Born on Oct. 27, 1858, in New York City, Roosevelt was a sickly child. He was urged, however, by his father to take control of his health and build up his body. As a result, Roosevelt developed into a rambunctious young adult, with a love of both athletics and the outdoors. He attended eastern prep schools, graduated from Harvard in 1880, and began to study

Theodore Roosevelt, operating a steam shovel during the construction of the Panama Canal.

law. Not finding that discipline to his liking, he entered Republican party politics and was elected to the New York state legislature in 1882. Two years later his wife and mother died on the same day, leaving Roosevelt despondent and temporarily disinterested in politics. He spent two years on a ranch in the Dakotas before returning east to remarry (1886) and reenter the political arena.

Roosevelt served as a civil service commissioner in Washington (1889–95) and as a member of the New York City board of police commissioners (1895–96). He was then appointed (1897) assistant secretary of the navy in the administration of Pres. William McKinley and from this post became actively involved in preparing the United States for war with Spain. In order to participate in the Spanish-American War (1898), Roosevelt resigned his post at the Navy Department and helped form a volunteer cavalry regiment known as the Rough Riders. After their dramatic exploits at the battle of San Juan Hill in Cuba, Roosevelt parlayed his veteran's status to political advantage. He was elected governor of New York in 1898, where he quickly earned a reputation as a reformer and a maverick. To ease him out of Albany, Republican party bosses in New York engineered his nomination as McKinley's running mate in 1900. The ticket easily won, and when McKinley was assassinated in September 1901, Roosevelt was catapulted into the presidency at the age of 42. One political boss griped, "Now that damned cowboy is president!"

Presidency and Later Life. Roosevelt's presidency has often been characterized as one of relentless trust busting. In reality, his tenure was far more moderate. While he did prosecute several trusts, Roosevelt made it clear that he was out to regulate, not destroy monopolies. His successor in the White House, William Howard Taft, prosecuted more than twice as many trusts during his four-year term as Roosevelt did in seven years. In dealings with labor, Roosevelt took pains to see to it that both sides were satisfied (what he called the "Square Deal"), and during the financial panic of 1907 he called upon banker J. P. Morgan to help prop up the sagging financial markets.

On the world scene, Roosevelt was far more forceful. He bullied Colombia into allowing the United States to build a canal through the isthmus of one of its protectorates, Panama. He also forced

During the Spanish-American War, future president Theodore Roosevelt served as lieutenant colonel of the First U.S. Volunteer Cavalry, known as the "Rough Riders."

the Germans to back down in Africa and Latin America and yanked the Japanese and Russians to the peace table in 1905 after the breakout of war (for his efforts, he won the 1906 Nobel Peace Prize). Roosevelt's famous maxim "Speak softly and carry a big stick" was only a partial reflection of reality. He often used bluster and bravado as a diplomatic tool and thus avoided using his "big stick." In fact, Roosevelt never once had to commit American troops into combat during his administration.

Honoring a pledge he made in 1904, Roosevelt did not run for a third term in 1908. Instead, he supported his protégé, William Howard Taft, who won election. Roosevelt, however, eventually became disenchanted with Taft. He attempted to wrest the Republican nomination from Taft in 1912, and when that effort failed Roosevelt entered the presidential fray at the head of a third party, the Progressive ("Bull Moose") party. The Republican split threw the election to the Democratic candidate, Woodrow Wilson. For the last seven years of his life, Roosevelt was an outspoken critic of Wilson's foreign policy, warning first of the president's cavalier attitude toward Germany's military buildup, and, once World War I broke out in Europe, criticizing Wilson's policy of official neutrality. When the United States entered the war in 1917, Roosevelt asked for a military command, but Wilson refused. His health broken by expeditions to Africa and Brazil, Roosevelt died prematurely on Jan. 6, 1919.

—JOHN ROBERT GREENE

See Also: Panama Canal; Presidential Elections; President of the United States; Progressive Party; Rough Riders; Spanish-American War.

BIBLIOGRAPHY: Blum, John, *The Republican Roosevelt* (Harvard Univ. Press 1954); Gould, Lewis L., *The Presidency of Theodore Roosevelt* (Univ. Press of Kansas 1991); Morris, Edmund, *The Rise of Theodore Roosevelt* (Putnam 1979).

■ **ROOT, ELIHU (1845-1937),** American lawyer and statesman. He was born in Clinton, New York, graduated from Hamilton College in 1864, and received his law degree from New York University in 1867. After a distinguished legal career, he was appointed secretary of war (1899-1904) by Pres. William McKinley and secretary of state (1905-09) by Pres. Theodore Roosevelt, paying great attention to U.S.–Latin American relations. As a U.S. senator from New York (1909-15), Root concentrated on problems of international security. In 1912, he was awarded the Nobel Peace Prize. In 1917, he headed a special U.S. diplomatic mission to Russia. In 1921-22, Root served as U.S. delegate to the Washington Armament Conference.

See Also: McKinley, William; Roosevelt, Theodore.

■ **ROOT, JOHN W. (1850-91),** Chicago architect. Root was born in Lumpkin, Georgia, and trained in New York City with James Renwick but made

Chicago his home and professional base. In 1873 he formed a partnership with Daniel H. Burnham that lasted until Root's death. Root designed the Chicago Academy of Fine Arts (1882) and Chicago's Union Station (1888). He was a consulting architect for the 1893 World's Columbian Exposition in Chicago but died while construction was in progress.

See Also: Burnham, Daniel; Renwick, James.

■ **ROOT-TAKAHIRA AGREEMENT (1908),** agreement between the United States and Japan, negotiated by Sec. of State Elihu Root as part of Pres. Theodore Roosevelt's continued efforts to legitimize the American presence in Asia. This pact maintained the status quo in Asia and specifically reaffirmed an open trade policy (usually referred to as the "Open Door Policy") in China.

Throughout his presidency (1901-09), Roosevelt sought to equalize American relations with the Japanese, excluding when possible Russia and Great Britain and usually overlooking the sovereignty of Korea and China, two nations over which all the others wished to have greater influence. At the same time, the United States wanted to maintain friendly relations with the Japanese, who were increasingly bothered by the racist treatment of Japanese immigrants in America.

See Also: Open Door Policy; Roosevelt, Theodore; Root, Elihu.

BIBLIOGRAPHY: Esthus, Raymond A., *Theodore Roosevelt and Japan* (Univ. of Washington Press 1967); Leopold, Richard W., *Elihu Root and the Conservative Tradition* (Little, Brown 1954).

■ **ROSE, PETE (1941-),** baseball player and manager. An infielder born in Anderson Ferry, Ohio, he collected a record 4,256 hits in his playing career (1963-86) but was banned from baseball in 1989 for betting on games.

See Also: Sports.

■ **ROSS, BETSY (1752-1836),** legendary maker of the first American flag. Born in Philadelphia, she was twice widowed by the American Revolution and supported her family as a seamstress. According to legend, she was secretly visited by George Washington, in 1776 or 1777, and commissioned to produce the first Stars and Stripes.

See Also: Flag; Women in American History.

■ **ROSS, GEORGE (1730-79)**, lawyer and Revolutionary War statesman. Born in Delaware, Ross moved to Pennsylvania to establish a law practice before the Revolution. During the war he served in the First and Second Continental Congresses and signed the Declaration of Independence.

See Also: Declaration of Independence.

■ **ROSS, JOHN (1790-1866)**, principal chief of the Cherokees. A descendant of Scottish traders who married Cherokee women, Ross was born in the Cherokee Nation near present-day Center, Alabama, on Oct. 3, 1790. He gradually became involved in Cherokee politics, inclining to his maternal heritage. He gained the support of the full-blooded majority of the Cherokees, who admired his commitment to maintaining the native homeland. After helping to write the nation's constitution in the late 1820s, he became the first elected principal chief, an office he held until his death nearly 40 years later.

In the 1830s a series of crises beset the Cherokees. Gold was discovered on Cherokee lands and non-Indian settlers poured in. Surrounding states, particularly Georgia, pressured the federal government to oust the tribe. Pres. Andrew Jackson secured an Indian removal bill from Congress and sent federal commissioners to demand that Indians move west. Supreme Court cases, such as *Cherokee Nation v. Georgia*, failed to gain the Cherokees security against unlawful intrusions. With no apparent alternative available, a small group signed a removal treaty in 1835, but Ross and his party protested the pact, resisting it until federal troops began forcibly removing the tribe. The chief then took over and led his people across the infamous Trail of Tears to Indian Territory (now Oklahoma) in 1838. There vendettas were carried out against treaty signers, and near-civil war ensued before peace was established in the mid-1840s.

The Civil War renewed internal dissensions over the issues of slavery and political power. Ross, although a slaveholder himself, led the nonslaveholding, full-blooded majority of the Cherokees, who remained loyal to the Union, while a mixed-blood minority wanted to side with the Confederacy to gain power. Ross finally gave in under pressure, fearing a Confederate invasion and a split in the tribe. He fled north and sought to enlist the sympathy of Pres. Abraham Lincoln's administration. At war's end, he returned home and, in his final days, tried once more to reunite his people. He died on Aug. 1, 1866, with the knowledge that a new treaty that he had crafted would guarantee tribal unity.

—GARY E. MOULTON

See Also: Cherokee; Cherokee Nation Cases; Indian Removal; Indians of North America; Jackson, Andrew; Lincoln, Abraham; Trail of Tears.

BIBLIOGRAPHY: Moulton, Gary E., *John Ross, Cherokee Chief* (Univ. of Georgia Press 1978); Moulton, Gary E., *The Papers of Chief John Ross*, 2 vols. (Univ. of Oklahoma Press 1985); Wilkins, Thurman, *Cherokee Tragedy* (Univ. of Oklahoma Press 1986).

■ **ROTHKO, MARK (1903-70)**, abstract expressionist painter. Born in Dvinsk, Russia, Rothko immigrated to the United States with his family at the age of 10. In 1925 he settled in New York City, studying art at the Art Students League. He began exhibiting in New York City in 1929 and worked for the Federal Arts Project during the Great Depression. He is known for large-scale abstract paintings of brightly colored rectangles, with diffuse edges that appear to float in the picture plane, as seen in *Red, Brown and Black* (1958).

See Also: Federal Arts Project; Painting.

■ **ROTH V. UNITED STATES (1957)**, U.S. Supreme Court case that decided obscenity was not protected by the First Amendment and that therefore state and federal obscenity laws were, if carefully drafted to respect free speech, constitutional.

Obscene speech, like slander or perjury, had long been held to be beyond the protection of the Constitution. In *Roth* and a companion case, *Alberts v. California*, the Supreme Court upheld that view. The Court, however, also limited the definition of obscenity. Justice William Brennan wrote in the majority (6-3) opinion that only material that was "utterly without redeeming social importance" could be considered obscene. In the past, courts had often held works of acknowledged literary value obscene if portions of them were considered offensive to sensitive readers. Brennan proposed a new standard: material could be found obscene only if "taken as a whole," it appealed to the "prurient interest" of "the average person."

Roth, on the one hand, empowered authorities to prosecute obscenity but, on the other, established a higher threshold for court action. The decision made it clear that obscenity law must defer to First Amendment free speech protections. Left unclear was how exactly the new standard for determining obscenity would be applied.

—TIM ASHWELL

See Also: Supreme Court.
BIBLIOGRAPHY: Hawkins, Gordon, *Pornography in a Free Society* (Cambridge Univ. Press 1988).

■ **ROUGH RIDERS,** a unit organized during the Spanish-American War by Theodore Roosevelt, officially titled the First U.S. Volunteer Cavalry. Roosevelt assembled a diverse group of Ivy League horsemen, western cowboys, and others for service in Cuba and led them in an attack on Kettle Hill (erroneously thought to be San Juan Hill). Because of logistical problems few of the Rough Riders had horses, and most fought dismounted instead.

See Also: Roosevelt, Theodore; San Juan Hill, Battle of; Spanish-American War.

■ **ROURKE, CONSTANCE MAYFIELD (1885-1941),** author. Born in Cleveland, Ohio, she taught English literature at Vassar College (1910-15) and wrote articles for the *New Republic* and *Freeman*. Her greatest contribution was *American Humor: A Study of the National Character* (1931). In it she analyzed the traditions of Yankee, backwoods, and African-American humor, showing how popular comic lore found its way into the work of Herman Melville, Nathaniel Hawthorne, Edgar Allan Poe, and Mark Twain.

See Also: Hawthorne, Nathaniel; Melville, Herman; Poe, Edgar Allan; Twain, Mark.

■ **ROWLAND, HENRY (1848-1901),** physicist. Born in Honesdale, Pennsylvania, Rowland studied the magnetic properties of iron, steel, and nickel (1873), expressed the concept of magnetic force lines mathematically (1875), which led to the development of transformers and dynamos, and improved the understanding of the electron by studying static electricity (1875). As the first professor of physics at Johns Hopkins (1876) he measured the ohm (1878) and the mechanical equivalent of heat (1880) and designed a superior diffraction grating (1882), with which he studied spectra.

See Also: Science.

■ **ROWLANDSON, MARY WHITE (1635?-82?),** captive of American Indians and author. She was born in England. In February 1676, during King Philip's War, she and three of her children were captured in a raid on the frontier town of Lancaster, Massachusetts. She endured captivity for three months before she could be ransomed by her husband, Joseph Rowlandson. Her account of her miserable life among the Indians, *The Sovereignty and Goodness of God* (1682) became one of the most widely read books in colonial America.

See Also: Captivity, Indian; Frontier in American History; Women in American History.

■ **ROWSON, SUSANNA HASWELL (1762?-1824),** author, performer, and educator. Born in Portsmouth, England, she moved to Boston, Massachusetts, with her family in 1768 but returned to Europe after the American Revolution. Between 1792 and 1797, she acted—first in England and then in the United States—in over a hundred plays, many of which she also wrote. She also wrote novels. In 1797 she opened a Young Ladies Academy in Boston, one of the first schools in the United States to offer secondary education to girls.

■ **ROYALL, ANNE NEWPORT (1869-1954),** eccentric author and newspaperwoman. Born near Baltimore, Maryland, she had a brief career as a travel writer in the 1920s, then settled in 1930 in Washington, D.C., where she became a well-known curmudgeon and editorialist, publishing muckraking newspapers well into her 80s.

See Also: Muckrakers.

■ **ROYCE, JOSIAH (1855-1916),** philosopher. Born in Grass Valley, California, Royce taught philosophy at Harvard University from 1882 to 1916. Royce advocated an approach to idealism that stressed individual will rather than innate ability. Among his philosophical works are *The Religious Aspects of Philosophy* (1885), *The Spirit of Modern Philosophy* (1892), *The World and the Indi-*

vidual (1900), and *The Hope of the Great Community* (1916). He also wrote a history of his native state, *California, A Study of American Character* (1886), that was highly critical of the violence of the pioneers.

■ **RUBBER,** elastic substance produced by coagulating the juices of certain tropical plants. Rubber was imported and eventually produced synthetically in the United States. Imported India rubber sparked interest in the early 19th century, but no one could prevent it from melting, sticking, and decomposing in heat. Charles Goodyear discovered the process of vulcanization in 1839, which prevented rubber from melting. This discovery established a rubber industry that boomed with the rise of automobiles in the 1920s. The largest consumer of imported rubber, the automobile industry created a huge market and supported an import trade that survived the worldwide economic crisis of the late 1920s. In 1940, Goodyear, Firestone, B. F. Goodrich, General Tire, and United States Rubber formed the Rubber Reserve Company as a subsidiary of the Reconstruction Finance Corporation in order to end U.S. dependence upon Japanese-controlled supplies in Indochina. During World War II the demand for rubber skyrocketed. The government took over the company's 630,356-ton stockpile. Tires became the first rationed item, and since the war had cut off trade in natural rubber, the government announced a $4 billion program to produce it synthetically. By 1945, the Rubber Reserve Company was producing 760,000 tons of synthetic rubber a year, reaching 1 million tons a year by 1960.

■ **RUFFIN, EDMUND (1794-1865),** agriculturalist and Southern nationalist. A native of Prince George's County, Virginia, Ruffin was the first to use marl as a fertilizer to replenish exhausted soil. This revolutionary development brought him fame as a leading agriculturalist. In the antebellum period, Ruffin voiced his strenuous defense of slavery. He fired the first shot on Fort Sumter in 1861 and joined the Charleston Palmetto Guard. Despondent over the South's defeat in the Civil War, he committed suicide.

See Also: Fort Sumter, Battle of.

■ **RUKEYSER, MURIEL (1913-80),** poet born in New York City. Her poems deal with the struggle of individuals to cope with a complex and changing society. She published a number of collections, including *Theory of Flight* (1935) and *Speed of Darkness* (1968).

■ **RURAL ELECTRIFICATION ADMINISTRATION (REA),** New Deal agency that helped bring electric power to rural areas. Created by Pres. Franklin D. Roosevelt in 1935, the REA was established as an independent agency by Congress in 1936 and incorporated in the Department of Agriculture in 1939. It provided subsidized loans to power cooperatives organized to build electric distribution systems in sparsely populated farming regions. By 1941, the REA had distributed $434 million in loans, and 40 percent of the nation's farms had electricity. By the end of the 1950s electricity was available in virtually every corner of the country. Private power companies opposed the REA as socialism, but the threat of competition from REA-backed cooperatives sometimes spurred local power monopolies to extend lines into rural areas they had previously ignored and often led to lower electric rates.

See Also: New Deal.

BIBLIOGRAPHY: Brown, D. Clayton, *Electricity for Rural America: The Fight for the REA* (Greenwood Press 1980).

■ **RURAL FREE DELIVERY,** service of free mail delivery to rural regions. Mandated by Congress (1896) after lobbying from farm groups, rural free delivery (RFD) helped end the isolation of farm life and proved a boon to the mail-order catalog business.

■ **RURAL LIFE,** defining aspect of the history of the United States, whose central transformation has been the change from an agrarian society to an urban and industrial one. During the colonial period and throughout most of the 19th century, American society was predominantly agricultural. In 1820, some 92.7 percent of Americans lived in rural areas and 71.8 percent of the labor force farmed. In 1920, however, for the first time the majority of the population lived in urban areas. By the late 1990s only about one-fourth of

Pennsylvania farmers make apple butter in a 19th-century photograph. The United States remained a primarily rural society before the 20th century, with the majority of Americans producing much of their own food.

Americans lived in rural areas, and only 2.4 percent of workers were in agriculture.

Initially, rural life in the United States was characterized by self-contained communities that consisted mainly of family farms. Farmers raised a variety of crops to provide for family needs and sold or bartered locally whatever was left over. All members of the family contributed to the work of the farm, and farmers regularly exchanged help with their neighbors during peak periods of harvesting and haying. Occasionally, they hired outside help, typically a young man from the community who would eventually own his own farm. Such a society gave rise to a widespread sense of independence and egalitarianism among the yeomen farmers, even though inequalities between men and women, rich and poor, and old and young existed. That independence, in turn, was celebrated by Thomas Jefferson and others who espoused the superiority of agrarian life and its centrality to republican ideology. Plantation slavery was the great exception to the agrarian ideal because southern planters relied on black slave labor and specialized in cash crops for sale in distant markets. In spite of this, southerners also subscribed to an agrarian ethos, even though their own independence and

equality ultimately depended on the servitude and subordination of others.

The increasing commercialization of agriculture during the 19th century represented an important change for family farmers. To supply food for the growing industrial population in northern cities, they began specializing in cash crops for these outside markets instead of practicing mixed agriculture for local consumption. Consequently, farmers became more dependent on the market and vulnerable to price fluctuations and other conditions beyond their control. They also began to invest in expensive farm machinery and hire more outside labor, sharpening the social distinctions between those who owned farms and those who did not. And women's traditional tasks on the farm, which typically did not result in market sales and were not mechanized, came to be seen as less important. Despite these changes, however, the family farm remained the basic unit in rural society, and the local community continued as its primary frame of reference.

20th Century. The first part of the 20th century posed new challenges for rural Americans that lessened the primacy of the local community. Government centralized political authority in the state at the expense of local control and the increasing power of large corporations led farmers to form their own organizations, which also transcended the local community. Inventions such as the automobile, the radio, and motion pictures lessened the importance of the immediate community, narrowed the differences between city and countryside, and brought rural Americans into the orbit of a new consumer culture that emanated from the city. At the same time, new agricultural technologies such as the gasoline tractor facilitated the consolidation of larger farming operations, which contributed to migration away from the farm and declining population in many rural areas.

Those trends continued after World War II and were exacerbated by the emergence of agribusiness and the policies of the federal government, which encouraged the development of larger and larger farming operations and the decline of smaller family farms. Today, the farmers who produce the nation's food make up only 10 percent of those who live in rural areas, while the vast majority work in nonagricultural jobs in nearby towns or cities. In spite of these changes, American culture continues to express great nostalgia for rural life and deep-seated ambivalence about the city.

—HAL S. BARRON

See Also: Agriculture.

BIBLIOGRAPHY: Barron, Hal S., *Mixed Harvest: The Second Great Transformation in the Rural North, 1870-1930* (Univ. of North Carolina Press 1997); Danbom, David B., *Born in the Country: a History of Rural America* (Johns Hopkins Univ. Press 1995).

■ **RUSH, BENJAMIN (1746-1813),** physician and statesman. One of the most influential doctors in 18th-century America, Rush was a vocal supporter of American independence. He was born in Byberry, Pennsylvania, and began his medical practice and teaching career in Philadelphia in 1769. A noted patriot, he was elected to the Second Continental Congress and signed the Declaration of Independence. In 1777 the Continental army called on his medical abilities, appointing him surgeon general. He was forced to resign, however, after he openly criticized Washington's and other leaders' abilities. After returning to teaching and private practice, Rush engaged in numerous humanitarian endeavors, including antislavery, education, penal reform, and temperance movements. He also entered the most prolific writing period of his life, and much of his work was published as *Essays, Literary, Moral, and Philosophical* in 1798. As a member of the state ratifying convention he supported the Constitution. He also served as treasurer of the U.S. Mint from 1797 to 1813.

See Also: Declaration of Independence; Medicine; Revolution, American.

■ **RUSH-BAGOT AGREEMENT (1817),** exchange of notes between acting U.S. Sec. of State Richard Rush and British Minister Charles Bagot in Washington, D.C., on Apr. 28-29, 1817. The two nations agreed to demilitarize the Great Lakes and Lake Champlain, greatly diminishing the number and size of naval ships on the lakes. This was the first example of reciprocal naval disarmament. The agreement was approved by the Senate in 1818. It remains in force, providing for a peaceful U.S.-Canadian border.

See Also: Frontier in American History.

■ **RUSK, DEAN (1909-94),** U.S. secretary of state (1961-69). Born in Cherokee County, Georgia, and educated at Oxford and Berlin, he served in the army (1940-47). From 1947, he worked at the Department of State. As secretary of state under Presidents Kennedy and Johnson, Rusk generally resisted forceful U.S. demonstrations against the Soviet bloc. In Vietnam, however, fearing Soviet and Chinese expansion, he supported American involvement in the war.

See Also: Cold War; Johnson, Lyndon Baines; Vietnam War.

■ **RUSSELL, WILLIAM FELTON ("BILL") (1934-),** basketball player, born in Monroe, Louisiana. Russell's unparalleled defensive play spurred his Boston Celtics to 11 National Basketball Association (NBA) championships in 13 seasons (1957-69). He later coached in the NBA.

See Also: Sports.

■ **RUSSIAN IMMIGRANTS.** Russian settlers arrived in North America via the Bering Strait during the 18th century and established hunting and trapping posts from Alaska to present-day San Francisco. Although many had returned by 1867, when Alaska was sold by Russia to the United States, the few who remained established a vibrant community in San Francisco.

Large numbers of Russians did not arrive in the United States until the first two decades of the 20th century. A heterogeneous group of an estimated 90,000, these immigrants represented various ethnicities and regions of Russia. At least 85 percent male, they worked as unskilled laborers in mining, steel and iron manufacturing, and meat packing in northeastern and midwestern cities. Their community, however, was torn apart by intraethnic conflict within the Russian Orthodox Church, a central institution of immigrant life. Russian immigrants were viewed with extreme suspicion after the Bolshevik Revolution (1917) and during the red scare of the 1920s and the Cold War after World War II.

See Also: Alaska; Ethnic Groups; Immigration.

▓ **RUSTIN, BAYARD (1910-87),** civil rights leader. Born in West Chester, Pennsylvania, Rustin was inculcated early with a commitment to nonviolence. A conscientious objector during World War II, his passion and his organizational skills later carried him into the heart of the civil rights movement. He worked with A. Philip Randolph, joined the Fellowship of Reconciliation, and pioneered the freedom rides with the Congress of Racial Equality. In 1955, Rustin joined the Southern Christian Leadership Conference (SCLC) as Martin Luther King, Jr.'s special assistant, taking on the logistical coordination of the March on Washington (1963). In 1964 he accepted the executive directorship of the A. Philip Randolph Institute and influenced national policy for many years thereafter.

See Also: African Americans; Civil Rights Movement; March on Washington.

▓ **RUTH, GEORGE HERMAN (BABE) (1895-1948),** baseball player. A record-setting home run hitter, Ruth was the biggest baseball star of the 1920s. Born in Baltimore, he was a star left-handed pitcher for the Boston Red Sox (1914-19) before being sold to the New York Yankees (1920-34). His 714 career home runs, including 60 in 1927, led the

Home run king Babe Ruth transformed baseball into an offensive game through the sheer power of his bat.

Yankees to seven World Series. His mighty homers and winning personality helped fans forget the 1919 World Series gambling scandal.

See Also: Baseball; Sports.

▓ **RUTLEDGE, EDWARD (1749-1800),** lawyer and Revolutionary War politician. A native of Charleston, South Carolina, Rutledge served his state in many capacities during the Revolution. He fought in the Battle of Charleston, sat in the First and Second Continental Congresses, and signed the Declaration of Independence.

See Also: Declaration of Independence; Revolution, American.

▓ **RUTLEDGE, JOHN (1739-1800),** associate justice of the U.S. Supreme Court (1789-91) and unconfirmed chief justice of the United States (1795).

He was born in Charleston, South Carolina, and, after studying law in London, became a successful lawyer and politician. Rutledge represented South Carolina in the Continental Congress (1774-76, 1782-83) and served as president of the South Carolina Assembly (1776-82) and delegate to the convention that wrote the U.S. Constitution (1787). Pres. George Washington appointed him to the Supreme Court, but Rutledge, who reportedly believed he had been slighted by not being named chief justice, resigned in 1791 to become chief justice of the South Carolina Court of Common Pleas. In 1795, when John Jay resigned as chief justice to become governor of New York, Washington named Rutledge chief justice. Rutledge presided over a brief special session of the Court in August, but his confirmation ran into difficulty when Federalist senators learned he had led a Charleston meeting protesting ratification of Jay's Treaty with Great Britain (1794). Angered at his opposition to their party's foreign policy, Federalists opposed him, and the Senate defeated his nomination 14-10. Shortly afterward Rutledge attempted suicide by leaping into Charleston Bay. He spent the rest of his life in seclusion.

See Also: Supreme Court.

BIBLIOGRAPHY: Barry, Richard, *Mr. Rutledge of South Carolina* (Duell, Sloan & Pearce 1942).

■ **RUTLEDGE, WILEY BLOUNT, JR. (1894-1949),** associate justice of the U.S. Supreme Court (1943-49).

Born in Cloverport, Kentucky, he taught law at the University of Colorado (1924-26) and then served as dean of the law schools at Washington University (1926-35) and Iowa State University (1935-39). He was a judge on the U.S. Court of Appeals (1939-43) before serving on the Supreme Court.

See Also: Supreme Court.

■ **RYDER, ALBERT PINKHAM (1847-1917),** naturalist painter. Ryder was born in New Bedford, Massachusetts. He began painting the landscape near his home but did not receive formal training until the late 1860s when he moved to New York City and attended classes at the National Academy of Design. In the 1870s Ryder was one of 22 young artists who founded the Society of American Artists as an alternative to the more academic National Academy of Design. Early in his career Ryder took his subjects from biblical and literary characters and settings, as in *The Flying Dutchman* (1880s) and *Siegfried and the Rhine* (1888-91), but even in these works he sought to depict the force of nature inherent in the scene. Ryder is also known for his seascapes; works such as *Moonlight* (1885) and *Moonlight Marine* (1870-90) show the sea, sky, and clouds as alternating tonal bands punctuated by a solitary boat. Ryder's work, which had a slightly abstract quality that pointed toward the modern movement in painting, was included in the Armory Show of 1913.

See Also: Armory Show; Painting.

S

■ **SAARINEN, EERO (1910-61),** modernist architect. Born in Finland, Saarinen became an architect like his father Eliel Saarinen, in association with whom he designed the Berkshire Music Center in Tanglewood, Massachusetts (1938). The younger Saarinen designed the Trans World Airlines Terminal at Kennedy International Airport in New York (1962) and the Jefferson National Expansion Memorial, known popularly as the Arch, in St. Louis, Missouri (1964).

See Also: Architecture; Saarinen, Eliel.

■ **SAARINEN, ELIEL (1873-1950),** architect and educator. Born in Helsinki, Finland, Saarinen was a successful architect and city planner in his native country. He gained praise in the United States when he won second prize in the *Chicago Tribune* building competition (1922) and moved permanently to the United States in 1923. Saarinen designed the campus for—and became the first head of—the Cranbrook School of Design in Michigan. From 1936 to his death, he practiced in partnership with his son, Eero Saarinen.

See Also: Architecture; Saarinen, Eero.

■ **SACAJEWEA (c. 1784-1884),** Indian guide and interpreter. A Shoshone, Sacajewea was born in present-day Idaho. As a girl, she was kidnapped by Hidatsa; in 1804, she was bought by a French-Canadian trader, Toussaint Charbonneau, whom she married. Meriwether Lewis and William Clark hired Charbonneau and Sacajewea as interpreters for their 1804 expedition. Sacajewea spoke many Indian dialects and could also communicate through sign language. In addition, she helped the explorers negotiate the unfamiliar terrain of the West. As a woman, she was a sign of peace to the tribes the expedition encountered. In 1805, when Sacajewea was reunited with her Shoshone family, she and her husband left the expedition. Some accounts claim that Sacajewea died from disease in 1812, while others say she lived to be an old woman, settling on the Wind River Reservation in Wyoming, where she was buried.

See Also: Frontier in American History; Indians of North America; Lewis and Clark Expedition.

■ **SACCO-VANZETTI CASE,** trial, conviction, and execution in 1927 in Massachusetts of two Italian immigrants and self-proclaimed anarchists, Nicola Sacco and Bartolomeo Vanzetti. In the wake of the "red scare" of 1919 anti-immigrant sentiments and fear of foreign radicalism persisted. The most notorious manifestation of this hysteria occurred in 1920, when Sacco, a shoemaker, and Vanzetti, a fish vendor, were arrested and charged with murdering a guard and paymaster during the robbery of a shoe company in South Braintree, Massachusetts.

Despite weak circumstantial evidence, the two men were found guilty in 1921. The trial was a mockery of justice, as the defendants' political radicalism and Italian origins became the main issues. Motions by defense attorneys fell on the deaf ears of Judge Webster Thayer, who openly sided with the prosecution. After Thayer sentenced Sacco and Vanzetti to death in 1927, public appeals and demonstrations fueled widespread support for the defendants but to no avail. The Massachusetts Supreme Court upheld their convictions, and they were executed by electric chair on Aug. 23, 1927.

The controversy surrounding the trial mirrored larger debates across the nation, which pitted middle-class and wealthy white Protestants against lower-class immigrants and other minorities. Outrage over the Sacco-Vanzetti case continued into the 1930s among American socialists and other critics of American society.

See Also: Red Scare.

BIBLIOGRAPHY: Avrich, Paul, *Sacco and Vanzetti: The Anarchist Background* (Princeton Univ. Press 1991); Russell, Francis, *Sacco & Vanzetti: The Case Resolved* (Harper & Row 1986).

After much controversy surrounding their murder conviction six years earlier, Nicola Sacco and Bartolomeo Vanzetti (*center*) were executed in 1927.

■ **SACRAMENTO RIVER,** longest river in California, running some 380 miles from the Sierra Nevada Mountains to the San Francisco Bay. In 1817 Spanish soldiers were the first Europeans to explore the river. Gold was discovered on the Sacramento at Sutter's Mill in 1848 by James Marshall, and by 1850 thousands of prospectors had descended on the area. Large-scale hydraulic mining activities diverted the river's flow and dredged its sand. In 1945 the Bureau of Reclamation erected Shasta Dam (part of the Central Valley Project) for flood control, water conservation, and electric power.

■ **ST. CLAIR, ARTHUR (1736-1818),** American military leader. Born in Thurso, Scotland, he immigrated to Pennsylvania in 1762. At the onset of the Revolutionary War, St. Clair was commissioned a colonel to aid in the American retreat from Canada (1775). As brigadier general, he then joined in George Washington's New Jersey campaigns and then received command of Fort Ticonderoga on Lake Champlain in 1777, as a major general. In July, however, with the British severely threatening the fort, St. Clair evacuated, for which he was court-martialed but acquitted the following year. He became the first governor of the Northwest Territory in 1787 and in November 1791 led an unprepared U.S. force against the Ohio Valley Confederacy headed by the Miami tribal leader Little Turtle. St. Clair's forces were defeated and more than 900 of his men killed at the battle known as St. Clair's Defeat, the worst defeat of an army by Indians in North American history. In the aftermath, St. Clair resigned his military command.

See Also: *Revolution, American.*

■ **ST. DENIS, RUTH (1877-1968),** dancer. She was born Ruth Dennis in Newark, New Jersey. She danced with a troupe led by David Belasco until 1906, when she began touring with her own company. Her choreography in dances such as *Radha* and *Insence* was heavily influenced by Eastern traditions. She and her husband, Ted Shawn, started the Denishawn dance schools in Los Angeles (1914) and New York City (1920).

See Also: Shawn, Ted; Women in American History.

■ **SAINT-GAUDENS, AUGUSTUS (1848-1907),** renowned sculptor. Saint-Gaudens was born in Dublin, Ireland, but moved with his family to New York City as an infant. He studied art at the Cooper Union and the National Academy of Design; in 1867, he went to Paris and then Italy. In his first major commission—a monument to Adm. David G. Farragut for New York City's Central Park completed in 1881—he incorporated the techniques of naturalism into monumental sculpture. After this commission, Saint-Gaudens established studios in both New York and Cornish, New Hampshire. In 1884, Saint-Gaudens won the commission for what would become one of his best-known works, the bronze relief in Boston Common that serves as a memorial to Col. Robert Gould Shaw (1884-96). In addition to portrait reliefs, Saint-Gaudens continued to sculpt three-dimensional figures, such as his 1892 statue, *Diana*, for the top of Madison Square Garden in New York City. One of Saint-Gaudens's masterpieces is the Adams Memorial in Rock Creek Cemetery, Washington, D.C. (1886-91).

See Also: Sculpture.

■ **ST. LAWRENCE RIVER AND SEAWAY,** one of the major rivers of North America, flowing 744 miles from the northeast end of Lake Ontario along the U.S.-Canadian border, then into Quebec and the Gulf of St. Lawrence. The French explorer Jacques Cartier discovered the river in 1535. In 1608 Samuel de Champlain established a trading post at Quebec to obtain furs from the native Algonquian. In 1763 the British gained control of the area, and after the end of the American Revolution (1783), Britain rewarded loyalists with lands in Nova Scotia, thus marking the beginning of an English-speaking Canadian population. In response to the opening of the Erie Canal in New York in 1825, Montreal merchants dug eight canals to circumnavigate the St. Lawrence

rapids. In 1959 the St. Lawrence Seaway, a joint Canadian-American project, was opened. This international waterway is a series of locks, canals, and dams that allows ocean-going vessels to connect with the Great Lakes and the Atlantic Ocean. With the urban centers of Montreal and Quebec, the St. Lawrence Valley remains Canada's most important economic and cultural area.

■ **ST. LOUIS,** city in Missouri, located 17 miles south of the confluence of the Missouri and Mississippi rivers. In 1764 Pierre LaClede established a French fur-trading post named in honor of St. Louis, the patron saint of King Louis XV, on the site of the present city. The town eventually became known as the "Gateway to the West" for settlers beginning their trek to the Pacific Coast. Lewis and Clark launched their 1804 expedition from St. Louis. After 1817 steamboats traveled up and down the Mississippi River, making the city a commercial and transportation hub for the Midwest. Later in the 19th century immigrants from Ireland and Germany arrived in large numbers, transforming the city. By 1870 St. Louis was the third largest city in America after New York and Philadelphia. In 1904 city boosters staged the Louisiana Purchase Exposition. After 1950 the city government began a major urban renewal program designed to restore the central city. Union Station was converted into a shopping mall, public-housing skyscrapers were built, and the 630-foot-high Gateway Arch, designed by Eero Saarinen, was constructed. Population (1994): 368,215.

See Also: City in American History.

■ **ST. MIHIEL SALIENT,** World War I German defensive zone. In preparation for a general Allied offensive on the Western front, the U.S. First Army was to seize a 16-mile-deep salient around the French town of St. Mihiel. On Sept. 12, 1918, seven U.S. divisions pitched into the salient in two pincer movements. Since the German defenders had already begun a withdrawal, the attackers quickly seized their objectives. By the 14th, the entire salient was in Allied hands, but most of the German force had avoided capture.

See Also: World War I.

■ **SALARY GRAB ACT (1873),** an act that increased congressional salaries by 50 percent and

American infantrymen fire on enemy positions during the successful Allied offensive against the St. Mihiel salient in September 1918.

doubled the salaries of the president and Supreme Court justices. Public reaction was so negative that Congress repealed its share of the raises in early 1874.

See Also: Gilded Age.

■ **SALISH INDIANS.** *See: Northwest Coast Indians.*

■ **SALK, JONAS (1914-95),** immunologist who developed the first polio vaccine. Born in New York City, Salk earned his medical degree from New York University (1939) and worked with virologist Thomas Francis, Jr., at the University of Michigan (1942-47), where he helped develop commercial vaccines for influenza. At the University of Pittsburgh (1947-63), Salk became director of virus research and focused his attention on creating a poliomyelitis vaccine. This disease mostly attacked small children, leaving them dead or paralyzed and often dependent on an iron lung for life. Efforts to produce a polio vaccine during the war had failed; in 1952 the disease struck more than 50,000 people in the United States and killed some 3,300. Salk conducted field tests on a killed-virus vaccine in 1952 and released it for use in the United States in 1955, at which point he became a hero. A live virus oral vaccine developed by Albert Sabin in 1960 has now largely sup-

planted Salk's vaccine, but there is still debate over their relative merits. Salk went on to establish the Institute for Biological Sciences (now the Salk Institute) in San Diego (1963) and continue his research, developing an improved flu vaccine and turning before his death to the problem of AIDS.

See Also: Disease; Medicine; Science.

■ **SALUTARY NEGLECT,** lack of imperial management of the British colonies in North America in the period between the planting of the first successful settlements and the Restoration of Charles II (1660). The policy allowed American colonial society to expand and mature into an independent, distinct society.

■ **SAMPSON, DEBORAH (1760-1827),** American Revolutionary War soldier. She was born in Plympton, Massachusetts. Dressed in men's clothing, she fought with the Continental army under the name of Robert Shurtleff. Discovered and discharged in 1783, she later lectured about her military experience and was eventually granted a soldier's pension.

■ **SANDBURG, CARL (1878-1967),** poet, biographer, and promoter of America's cultural heritage. Sandburg was born in Galesburg, Illinois.

He served in Puerto Rico during the Spanish-American War. Sandburg worked on the staffs of the magazine *System* and the *Chicago Daily News* while starting to write poetry. In 1914 he won a prize from the magazine *Poetry* and in 1919 and 1921 won prizes from the Poetry Society of America. Sandburg was concerned with the development of a uniquely American culture, and in addition to writing he collected ballads and folk songs. His poetry in the volumes *Chicago Poems* (1915), *Corn Huskers* (1918), *Smoke and Steel* (1920), and *Slabs of the Sunburnt West* (1922) cap-

Carl Sandburg received the Pulitzer Prize in history for his biography of Abraham Lincoln, *The War Years*, and in poetry for his *Collected Poems*.

tured in free verse the essence of midwestern life, both rural and urban. Sandburg also wrote biographies that complemented his poetry by exploring examples of the American character. His biographies of Abraham Lincoln (1926, 1939) are perhaps best known, but he also wrote a biography of his good friend and brother-in-law, the photographer Edward Steichen (1929).

See Also: *Lincoln, Abraham; Poetry; Steichen, Edward.*

■ **SAND CREEK MASSACRE (1804),** the slaughter of Cheyenne and Arapaho Indians by Colorado militia. When the Colorado territorial governor, seeking to end Indian raids, ordered all tribes within his jurisdiction to collect at military forts, a Cheyenne chief named Black Kettle sought to comply. He led his band of Cheyennes and Arapahos to Sand Creek in eastern Colorado, some 30 miles from the nearest military post, where they made camp and awaited instructions. On Nov. 29, 1864, Colorado troops under Col. John M. Chivington arrived. Black Kettle raised both the American flag and a white flag but to no avail. Most of the young Indian men were miles away in Kansas that morning, hunting for food. First the militia ran off all the horses, so that escape was impossible. Next they riddled the camp with cannon and rifle fire, followed by a frontal assault. Then the camp was encircled, and troops fired point-blank at any Indian they saw. Men were castrated, and their genitals saved as souvenirs. Men, women, and children were slaughtered for over two hours. Some few Cheyennes managed to escape, Black Kettle among them.

More than 150 Cheyennes and Arapahos died at Sand Creek, and the massacre instigated more raids and counterattacks. A U.S. Joint Committee on the "Conduct of War" investigated the incident and found that Chivington and his men had committed a "foul and dastardly massacre."

The Cheyennes and Arapahos kept on the move after the massacre. Some wandered the plains, avoiding contact with whites. Some moved north into Sioux territory. Others organized war parties. In October 1865 the Cheyennes and Arapahos signed a new treaty that required them to relinquish all claims to their Colorado lands, including the Sand Creek reserve. In return the U.S. government promised a new reserve on the Arkansas River. Only a minority of chiefs signed the document, but the government took it as law and forced the others to comply. None of the tribes actually received the new reserve lands, as the government later amended the treaty. Reparations for the Sand Creek massacre have never been made.

—RYAN MADDEN

See Also: *Black Kettle; Indians of North America.*
BIBLIOGRAPHY: Hoebel, Adamson, *The Cheyennes* (Holt 1978); Weeks, Philip, *Farewell, My Nation: The American Indian and the United States, 1829-1890* (Harlan Davidson 1990).

■ **SANFORD, EDWARD TERRY (1865-1930),** associate justice of the U.S. Supreme Court (1923-30). Born in Knoxville, Tennessee, he practiced law and served as a U.S. District Court judge before joining the Supreme Court.

See Also: *Supreme Court.*

■ **SAN FRANCISCO,** port city in northwestern California, noted for its hills, cable cars, and bracing, foggy weather and located on a peninsula between the Pacific Ocean and San Francisco Bay. In 1776 Spanish Franciscans established a mission there to convert the local Costanoan Indians to Catholicism. The village of Yerba Buena grew alongside the mission. In 1847 the name of the settlement was changed to San Francisco, and shortly thereafter the United States occupied the city during the Mexican War. Mexico ceded the area to the United States in 1848. In the same year the discovery of gold at Sutter's Mill in the Sierra Nevada Mountains, northeast of the city, attracted thousands of prospectors; in 1849 alone more than 40,000 arrived. Construction of the transcontinental railroad in the 1860s employed thousands of Chinese laborers, almost all of whom had settled in San Francisco. The population of the city climbed quickly, from a mere 56,000 in 1860 to 342,000 by 1900. The great earthquake of Apr. 18, 1906, and the ensuing fire destroyed much of the city, but it was quickly rebuilt and hosted the Panama-Pacific Exposition in 1915. Population (1994): 734,676.

■ **SAN FRANCISCO CONFERENCE ON INTERNATIONAL ORGANIZATION,** planning meeting for the United Nations. Delegates from 50 nations met (April-June 1945) to organize a post–World War II international peacekeeping alliance.

See Also: *United Nations (UN).*

■ **SANGER, MARGARET (1879-1966),** social activist and early advocate of birth control. One of 11 children born to Irish-American parents in Corning, New York, Sanger came to regard her family's size as the cause of their financial struggles and her mother's death at age 49. After attending Claverack College and nursing school, Sanger married William Sanger, an artist and architect, and spent a few years as a suburban homemaker. She later moved with her husband to Manhattan, where she worked as a nurse and became active in radical politics. Sanger joined the Socialist party and supported the Industrial Workers of the World. Her participation in this network, coupled with her experiences in nursing, led Sanger to believe that women should control their own reproductive lives.

In 1916, Margaret Sanger established the nation's first birth-control clinic. Five years later, she founded the American Birth Control League, later renamed the Planned Parenthood Federation of America.

Sanger began to speak out about birth control and women's health. In 1914, she published a feminist newspaper entitled *Woman Rebel* and an instructive pamphlet on contraception, *Family Limitation*. After authorities issued a warrant for her arrest, she fled to Europe, returning the following year to find a national birth-control movement under way. In 1921, she founded the American Birth Control League, which became Planned Parenthood in 1942. Her activism and leadership pushed many states to legalize contraception. She died in 1966 but remains a controversial figure in the debate over women's reproductive freedom.

See Also: *Birth Control; Women in American History; Women's Movement.*

BIBLIOGRAPHY: Chesler, Ellen, *Woman of Valor: Margaret Sanger and the Birth Control Movement in America* (Simon & Schuster 1992); Kennedy, David M., *Birth Control in America: The Career of Margaret Sanger* (Yale Univ. Press 1970).

■ **SANITARY COMMISSION,** private relief organization created in 1861. Modeled on the British Sanitary Commission established during the Crimean War (1853-56), the U.S. Sanitary Commission grew out of the Women's Central Association of Relief in New York City. Its goals included raising the standards of hygiene in the Civil War Union army camps, improving the soldiers' diets, sending food and supplies, and caring for the wounded. Largely staffed by women, the Sanitary Commission was hampered in its mission at times by opposition to women caring for soldiers on the front lines. The commission's professionalization of nursing and raising of standards of care helped to save lives during the war, when most deaths were the result of disease, and set the stage for the expansion of relief and hospital services after the war. The commission was superseded by the American Red Cross.

See Also: *Civil War; Red Cross, American National.*

■ **SAN JACINTO, BATTLE OF (1836),** decisive battle in the Texas Rebellion. After the fall of the Alamo and Texas's declaration of independence, Texan commander Sam Houston led his troops in an attack on Pres. Antonio López de Santa Anna's Mexican army near the San Jacinto River. During the 18-minute battle on April 21 the Texans destroyed the Mexican force. The following day Santa Anna was captured, and he later agreed to withdraw all Mexican troops from Texas, thus ending the conflict.

See Also: *Houston, Sam; Texas Rebellion.*

■ **SAN JUAN HILL, BATTLE OF (1898),** engagement during the Spanish-American War in which U.S. troops captured both San Juan and Kettle hills on July 1. Although the Spanish occupied a strong position near the crest of San Juan Hill, withering fire from a battery of Gatling guns enabled American troops to scale the heights and drive off the Spanish defenders. The Americans won their objectives, but at the heavy cost of 1,700 casualties.

See Also: *Rough Riders; Spanish-American War.*

■ **SAN LORENZO, TREATY OF (1795),** treaty between the United States and Spain. Known also as Pinckney's Treaty, it recognized the 31st parallel as the southern boundary of the United States and gave the United States navigation rights to the Mississippi and the right of deposit at the port of New Orleans. The treaty, negotiated by Thomas Pinckney, helped solidify U.S. sovereignty over lands west of the Appalachians and created a vast market that stretched from New Orleans to Boston

See Also: *Pinckney Family.*

■ **SANTA ANNA, ANTONIO LÓPEZ DE (1794-1876),** Mexican general and president. Born in the state of Veracruz, Santa Anna earned his military reputation in the War for Mexican Independence (1810-21). A man of great political ambition, although without ideological conviction, he became president 11 separate times between 1833 and 1855. While he was president, Mexico suffered defeats at the hands of Americans in the Texas Rebellion (1835-36) and the Mexican War (1846-48).

See Also: *Alamo; Mexican War; Texas Rebellion.*

■ ***SANTA CLARA COUNTY V. SOUTHERN PACIFIC RAILROAD CO. (1886),*** U.S. Supreme Court case that confirmed that corporations, like individual citizens, are protected by the due process clause of the 14th Amendment to the U.S. Constitution. As the economic power of the railroads grew in the late 19th century, railroads and governments frequently found themselves in court as state and local authorities sought to regulate and tax the lines. Santa Clara County and other California jurisdictions sued the Southern Pacific and Central Pacific Railroads to collect property taxes on fences adjoining the lines' tracks. Although the Court held (9-0) that such fences could not be defined as taxable property under California law, the Court used the case to reaffirm its belief that corporations were protected by the 14th Amendment. In the 1880s and 1890s the courts frequently invoked the 14th Amendment to shield corporations from state and local government regulation and taxation.

See Also: *Supreme Court.*

■ **SANTA FE TRAIL,** trail between Missouri and Santa Fe, in present-day New Mexico. William Becknell, an Indian trader from Missouri, stumbled across a band of Mexican soldiers in the fall of 1821 on the Southern Plains and found that Mexican independence had eased trade restrictions between New Mexico and the United States. Becknell also found that the trade was highly profitable and hastened back to Franklin, Missouri, from where he embarked along the trail to Santa Fe with three heavily loaded wagons in the summer of 1822. Others joined Becknell, and by 1824, American traders grossed some $190,000 annually on the Santa Fe Trail. Hostilities with the Kiowa and Comanche led Missouri's Sen. Thomas Hart Benton to persuade Congress to authorize an official survey of the route and begin treaty negotiations with Indians along the trail. By 1830, the trailhead had moved to Independence, Missouri. Most of the journey was well-watered from Pawnee Rock to the Arkansas River, although the shorter Cimarron cutoff crosses some 60 dry miles before hitting the Cimarron River. Wagons passed the Rabbit Ears and Wagon Mound before reaching Miguel del Vado and continuing on to Santa Fe. The longer Mountain Branch had less risk of Indian attack and had no dry desert to cross but was more rugged as wagons continued past the Cimarron cutoff to Bent's Fort before crossing Raton Pass and rejoining the route to Santa Fe.

Large Conestoga wagons, pulled by teams of mules or oxen, traveled some 10 to 15 miles a day on the 800-mile journey, which took nearly three months on average. And although the risk of natural disaster, as well as attack by Indians or bandits was high, profits were substantial and well worth the gamble. The arrival of the wagon trains in Santa Fe was greeted with a celebration, as citizens were eager to see the new goods and acquire manufactured items. Many of the trade items continued south, through other traders, into northern Mexico, along the much older Chihuahua Trail. Pack trains would venture up from Zacatecas and Chihuahua to acquire the American goods, purchased with silver from Mexican mines. Many New Mexicans entered the trade as well, sending wagons of their own to Independence as well as on the Chihuahua Trail.

Problems with arbitrary tariffs and exploitive taxation of goods were frequent. Traders seeking business with Chihuahua often bypassed Santa Fe by sticking to the Eastern Plains of New Mexico. There were custom houses at Miguel del Vado and also at Taos, but Santa Fe was the main point of entry for the trail. Gov. Manuel Armijo enacted a tariff of $500 a wagon for a while, regardless of the vehicle's size, which encouraged larger and larger wagons to be built. Many of the taxes collected found their way into personal fortunes rather than civic coffers.

With the end of the Mexican War in 1848, American merchants entered Santa Fe behind Gen. Stephen Watts Kearny and the Mexican tariffs disappeared. Business increased steadily and profitably, with trade volumes near $5 million annually by 1855 as teamsters tried to keep the American government supplied over the trail. The Santa Fe Trail was the significant route for trade with New Mexico until the railroad finally arrived at Lamy, near Santa Fe, in 1880.

—J.C. MUTCHLER

See Also: *Frontier in American History.*
BIBLIOGRAPHY: Conner, Seymour V., and Jimmy M. Skaggs, *Broadcloth and Britches: The Santa Fe Trade* (Texas A&M Univ. Press 1977); Simmons, Marc, *The Old Trail to Santa Fe* (Univ. of New Mexico Press 1996); Vestal, Stanley, *The Old Santa Fe Trail* (Houghton Mifflin 1939).

■ **SARATOGA, BATTLES OF (Sept. 19 and Oct. 7, 1777),** two related battles that constituted the first significant American victory of the Revolutionary War. In September 1777, British Gen. John Burgoyne's army of 9,000 men slowly advanced south from Montreal toward its objective, Albany, New York. Facing him were equal numbers under American generals Horatio Gates and Benedict Arnold, entrenched and blocking Burgoyne's route at Bemis Heights near the village of Saratoga (now Schuylerville), some 30 miles north of Albany. Arnold attacked one of Burgoyne's divisions at nearby Freeman's Farm on September 19, causing heavy English casualties. Burgoyne, running short on food, considered withdrawing, but not before he made a final attempt to dislodge the Americans. On October 7, he advanced on Bemis Heights with 1,500 men. The attack was a disaster, after which Burgoyne began his retreat. Gates and Arnold caught up with him and surrounded his army, forcing Burgoyne's surrender on October 17. The American victory altered the course of the war, for it secured French support for the rebellion and proved that the colonists could indeed mobilize the force of their scattered militia.

See Also: Arnold, Benedict; Revolution, American.
BIBLIOGRAPHY: Higginbotham, Don, *The War of American Independence* (Macmillan 1971); Ketchum, Richard M., *Saratoga* (Henry Holt 1998).

■ **SARGENT, JOHN SINGER (1856-1925),** renowned portrait painter of the Gilded Age. Sargent was born in Florence, Italy, to American parents. With them he traveled in Europe throughout his youth, studying art in Rome, Florence, and Paris. He was influenced by the French impressionists, incorporating their techniques into a distinctive style of portraiture. Sargent gained notice with paintings such as *The Daughters of Edward Darley Boit* (1882), *El Jaleo* (1882), *The Breakfast Table* (1883-84), and *Madame X* (1884). The last of these caused a stir when exhibited in Paris because of the notorious character of his sitter, Sargent's cousin, Virginie Avegno. At the end of the 19th century Sargent traveled extensively between Europe and the United States; in 1903 he established a studio in Boston. In addition to his portraits, Sargent was commissioned to paint mural decorations for the Boston Public Library (1890), for which he did a series on the development of religion, and the Boston Museum of Fine Arts (1916), for which he depicted classical figures.

See Also: Painting.

■ **SARNOFF, DAVID (1891-1971),** broadcasting industry executive. Born in Minsk, Russia, he immigrated to New York City in 1900 and in 1919 became commercial manager of the Radio Corporation of America (RCA). Sarnoff organized the National Broadcasting Company as the radio (1926) and television (1939) broadcasting subsidiary of RCA. As president and chairman of the broadcasting and manufacturing firm, he was the most powerful individual in the industry.

See Also: Television and Radio.

■ **SASSACUS (c. 1560-1637),** Pequot sachem and leader. Born near present-day Groton, Connecticut, in the 1630s Sassacus ruled over some 26 villages and fought against English colonists in present-day Connecticut. After the English fomented the Pequot War (1636-37), Sassacus attacked the English Fort Saybrook. The colonists then attacked Sassacus's village on the Mystic River early on May 25, 1637, burning the Pequots as they slept. Sassacus and some 20 followers escaped, only to be killed by Mohawk in July 1637.

See Also: Indians of North America; Pequot War.

■ **SAUK INDIANS.** *See: Algonquian.*

■ **SCALAWAGS,** derogatory term for Southern whites in the Republican party after the Civil War. It referred to the inbred livestock of the Scottish island of Scalaway. Southern Democrats used the term to convey an image of corrupt poor whites who profited from the South's defeat.

See Also: Reconstruction.

■ **SCALIA, ANTONIN (1936-),** associate justice of the U.S. Supreme Court (1986-). He was born in Trenton, New Jersey, and educated at Georgetown University and Harvard Law School. After teaching at the universities of Virginia (1967-71) and Chicago (1977-82) and holding various governmental posts, Scalia was named to the U.S.

Court of Appeals in 1982 and elevated to the Supreme Court in 1986, when William Rehnquist advanced to chief justice. Scalia became the Court's most conservative justice, known for his incisive and sometimes acerbic opinions.

See Also: Supreme Court.

■ **SCALPING,** act of removing the scalp or hair of an enemy. Practiced primarily by certain Indian groups, scalping was an act of both warfare and heroism that often took on ceremonial or ritual significance. It derived from the taking of enemy heads, a practice perhaps more common during the pre-Columbian era. The scalp, viewed as representing the slain enemy, was taken by various techniques and dried, decorated, and displayed as a trophy. Stereotypically associated by many whites with savage, whooping Indians on horseback, scalping was initially practiced mainly by the Muskogean and Tunica peoples of the Southeast and by the Algonquian and Iroquoian peoples of the East. After Indian contact with whites, scalping began to spread across North America. Dispossession and dislocation of Indian groups often increased the frequency of intertribal warfare and thus scalping. The practice spread, however, primarily as a result of scalp bounties paid by European and American governments, which encouraged the destruction of hostile Indian groups. By the 19th century, virtually all Plains groups honored scalping as a heroic warrior trait.

Although whites have long viewed scalping disparagingly solely as an Indian practice, some whites took the scalps of their Indian enemies. Like other forms of cultural exchange, scalping was adopted by both Indians and whites as a warfare strategy.

—GUY NELSON

See Also: Indians of North America.
BIBLIOGRAPHY: Axtell, James, "Who Invented Scalping?" *American Heritage* (8: 1977); Hoxie, Frederick E., ed., *Indians in American History* (Harlan Davidson 1988).

■ **SCANDINAVIAN IMMIGRANTS.** Immigrants from the Scandinavian countries of Norway, Sweden, Denmark, and Finland share as many similarities as differences in their experiences in the United States. For each group, major waves of im-

migration occurred during the second half of the 19th century and the first few decades of the 20th. Swedish immigration was the strongest during this period, with some 1.3 million people moving to the United States. Finns experienced the latest and slowest rate of immigration, when about 350,000 arrived, most after 1900.

Much like the other Scandinavian groups, Norwegian immigrants initially settled in the farming regions of the Midwest and the Pacific Northwest. By the end of the 19th century, however, most Scandinavian immigrants were settling in urban, industrial centers. Danes had the widest array of reasons for emigrating, largely because of the political, religious, and economic upheavals in their country. In general Scandinavian immigrants assimilated readily into American society.

See Also: Ethnic Groups; Immigration.

■ **SCENIC RIVERS ACT (1968),** environmental law. Eight rivers were initially designated wild, scenic, or recreational areas subject to development restrictions. Parts of 27 other rivers were identified for future inclusion.

■ *SCHECTER POULTRY CO. V. UNITED STATES* **(1935),** U.S. Supreme Court case that invalidated the National Industrial Recovery Act (NIRA) (1933), a key element of Pres. Franklin D. Roosevelt's New Deal economic recovery program. NIRA called on major industries to draft codes of conduct to regularize competition and stabilize the economy. Schecter Poultry was a small Brooklyn, New York, slaughterhouse that allegedly violated industrywide wage and hour rules established by the code. The Supreme Court ruled (9-0) that NIRA's declaration of an economic emergency did not permit the government to exercise new authority; that Congress had extended its reach beyond interstate commerce into local business; and that the law improperly delegated government powers to private industry. *Schecter* was one of the decisions of the conservative Court that led President Roosevelt to propose his court-packing plan.

See Also: New Deal; Supreme Court.

■ *SCHENCK V. UNITED STATES* **(1919),** U.S. Supreme Court case that limited the right of free speech. During World War I public opinion was divided over U.S. participation in the conflict, and the administration of Pres. Woodrow Wilson launched a concerted campaign to build support for the war effort. Charles Schenck, a socialist, was convicted of violating the Espionage Act (1917) by mailing anticonscription leaflets to young men. The Court upheld (9-0) Schenck's conviction. Justice Oliver Wendell Holmes, writing for the Court, stated Schenck's actions were not political speech protected by the First Amendment because they posed a clear and present danger to military preparations that had been duly approved by Congress. Holmes drew a distinction between dissent in peacetime and during war and began what would become an ongoing effort by the Supreme Court to interpret the First Amendment and distinguish between protected and unprotected speech.

See Also: Espionage Act; Gilded Age; Supreme Court.

■ **SCHENECTADY RAID (1690),** an attack by French soldiers and Indians on Schenectady, New York, during King William's War (1689-97). French Gov. Louis Frontenac sent three raiding parties into New York, one of which attacked the frontier town of Schenectady. Many inhabitants were captured or killed, and some 60 houses and churches destroyed. The survivors fled to Albany, but many returned to rebuild the town.

See Also: King William's War.

■ **SCHOENBERG, ARNOLD (1874-1951),** composer and pianist. He developed the 12-tone, or serial, system that revolutionized musical composition. Schoenberg's challenging, atonal piano, orchestral, and vocal works, which often drew on Jewish traditions, were widely criticized by audiences and some musicians for their dissonance, but the technique was hugely influential. Born in Vienna, Austria, he immigrated to the United States in 1933 to escape fascism.

■ **SCHURZ, CARL (1829-1906),** journalist and U.S. senator. Born near Cologne, Germany, Schurz came to the United States after the failed German revolution of 1848. Admitted to the bar in 1859, he became active in the Republican party and the antislavery movement. His good friend Pres. Abraham Lincoln appointed him minister to Spain in 1861, a post he gave up to join the Union army during the American Civil War. After the war he turned to writing and politics. He served one term (1869-75) as a senator from Missouri and then was appointed secretary of the interior (1877-81) by Pres. Rutherford B. Hayes. Schurz later moved to New York City, where he started a daily newspaper, the *New York Evening Post.* An inspired speaker and prolific writer, he supported civil service reform through his leadership in the National Civil Service Reform League (1892-1900) and in the Civil Service Reform Association of New York (1893-1906). A committed anti-imperialist, he broke with the Republican party in 1900 to support the presidential candidacy of the Democrat, William Jennings Bryan.

See Also: Bryan, William Jennings; Gilded Age; Lincoln, Abraham.

BIBLIOGRAPHY: Trefousse, Hans Louis, *Carl Schurz, A Biography* (Univ. of Tennessee Press 1982).

■ **SCHWARZKOPF, H. NORMAN (1934-),** U.S. Army officer who commanded Allied forces during the Persian Gulf War in 1991. He was born in Trenton, New Jersey. Schwarzkopf had been responsible for drawing up contingency plans for war in the Middle East and was chosen to lead the coalition of American and Allied troops in Operation Desert Storm to dislodge the Iraqi army from Kuwait. After a six-week air bombardment and a ground campaign of only 100 hours, Iraq capitulated, and Schwarzkopf emerged as a popular hero.

See Also: Persian Gulf War.

■ **SCIENCE,** systematic study of the natural world and the organized body of knowledge resulting from it. Science has been a leading contributor to America's rise to dominance in world affairs. During the 20th century, the United States became a world leader in scientific research, aiding in its preeminence in both military and economic terms. While U.S. science has enjoyed unparalleled prestige, especially in the second half of the 20th century, America has not always been at the forefront of science. Indeed, during the first hundred or more years of the republic's existence, America was a scientific backwater. The transformation into the dominant player in the world of science is one of the most significant

In January and February 1991, Gen. H. Norman Schwarzkopf commanded Operation Desert Storm, a multinational counterattack that successfully ended Iraq's occupation of Kuwait.

changes in America's fortunes during the entire period of its history.

The Natural History of the New World. The period of early exploration and colonization of the New World coincided with the rapid transformation of knowledge of the natural world, a change often called the Scientific Revolution. During this era, roughly encompassing the 17th century, medieval ideas about the natural world, based on the remnants of classical knowledge, underwent a fundamental reorientation. The exploration of the New World was, in many respects, both a sign of and a contributor to this process. Improvements in shipbuilding techniques, navigational technology, cartography, and chronometry during the late Middle Ages and Renaissance made voyages of exploration and discovery possible. In turn, such voyages revealed new lands with a bewildering diversity of animal and plant life, as well as previously unimagined civilizations. All of these cried out for further investigation and explanation.

One of the earliest of these descriptions was commissioned by Sir Walter Raleigh and undertaken by Thomas Harriot. Raleigh wanted a systematic survey of the new territory of Virginia to help to determine its value. Harriot, an Oxford-trained mathematician and natural philosopher, joined in a voyage to the New World in 1585 to map the region and to undertake a catalog of its mineral, plant, and animal resources. The account of his discoveries, entitled *A Briefe and True Report of the New Found land of Virginia*, along with some of the natural wonders that he brought back with him to England, helped to make the New World a focus of research among natural philosophers. For the next century, the territories of the New World continued to be of particular interest among the growing class of European men of science.

The Beginnings of American Science and Inventiveness. The establishment of institutions of higher learning in the colonies during the 17th century made possible indigenously American science. Puritan minister Increase Mather made a modest effort to found a society of men interested in advancing the study of natural history in the colonies in 1681, but his effort was short-lived. It was not until the early 18th century that a native of the American colonies, Benjamin Franklin (1706-90), became a leading figure in the world of natural philosophy. In particular, he began to explore the phenomenon of electrical charges. Through a series of experiments, he began to unravel some of the fundamental mysteries of the nature of what he called "the electric fire," most notably first describing the idea of positive and negative poles, determining the electrical nature of lightning, and inventing the lightning rod.

While Franklin's impressive series of experiments and his prominence as both a scientific and political figure gave visibility to American science, he stands alone as the only great figure to emerge in the field of American science during the 18th and early 19th centuries. As America established itself as a nation and focused on expanding its domain westward, there seems to have been little incentive to undertake basic scientific work. Instead, America became a breeding ground of technological innovation that sometimes used the experimental method of science but focused on finding ways of improving existing knowledge and techniques rather than on making fundamental discoveries.

The epitome of this model of American inventiveness is Thomas Edison (1847-1931). Edison used the experimental methods of science as a bludgeon to hammer through problems rather than as an elegant and precise instrument to test scientific hypotheses. His numerous inventions, including the light bulb and the phonograph, helped to show how experimental techniques could be used to make great industrial and consumer innovations and be highly profitable as well. Edison was not truly a scientist, nor were other great American inventors, such as Eli Whitney, William Morgan, Samuel Morse, or the Wright brothers. But their practical innovations, the cotton gin, anesthesia, the telegraph, and the airplane, respectively, contributed greatly to the rise of science in this country through the creation of an American myth linking practical knowledge, hard work, and progress.

American Science as a World Power. It was not until the second half of the 19th century that America emerged from the scientific shadow cast by England, France, and Germany. At the newly founded Smithsonian Institution in Washington, D.C., Joseph Henry took the lead in promoting scientific endeavors in the United States during this era. Henry's vision was to make the Smithsonian into a national leader in scientific endeavors; he sought to promote scientific work that was both theoretically advanced and useful. It was during this time period as well that American universities, like the newly founded Johns Hopkins University, finally began to undertake the development of their own scientific programs including graduate training in the sciences. By the late 19th century, it was no longer necessary for young American scientists to travel to Europe to complete their studies, although many continued to do so through the first few decades of the 20th century.

It was during this period as well that the first truly great American scientist, J. Willard Gibbs (1839-1903), began his work in theoretical physics at Yale University. While Gibbs's explorations of thermodynamics were too abstract to capture the attention of many within the United States, they earned for him a place of honor among the great minds of Europe. Gibbs uncovered some of the most fundamental principles of matter and provided an invaluable set of analytical tools for solving complex problems in chemistry and physics. His work was instrumental in the development of the modern chemical industry, and it was rapidly put to use in the manufacturing of military and agricultural chemicals.

Gibbs was the harbinger of the emergence of American physics. Gibbs was followed by A. A. Michelson (1852-1931), who would win the first Noble Prize in Physics awarded to an American (1907) for his work on the speed of light. During the 1920s and 1930s, the rise of American physics was confirmed by the awarding of four more Noble prizes to Americans for work predominately in the emerging field of atomic physics. Robert Millikan (1868-1953), the first in this string of awardees, would leverage this honor to become America's most well-known man of science during the first half of the 20th century. As the leader of the California Institute of Technology, he would also help to build one of the nation's greatest scientific institutions of higher learning.

America emerged as the true world leader in science during World War II. In many ways the building of the atomic bomb (1945) is emblematic of the way that American excellence in science became merged with industrial and military applications of science to provide the foundation for American world power. The bomb project, carried out by a team of elite theoretical physicists headed by J. Robert Oppenheimer (1904-67), demonstrated how far America had progressed in the development of its scientific community during the early 20th century. It also provided a legacy of funding by the U.S. government for basic and applied scientific research, much of it military in nature, during the era of the Cold War.

Since the 1960s, enormous scientific and economic resources have also been poured into research in the biomedical sciences in the United States. Beginning with the "war on cancer," an increasing share of the federal budget has been committed to health care, both clinical and experimental. The late 20th century has seen the emergence of the biotechnological revolution and the development of a host of private biotech companies. These, together with the technology driving the computer revolution of the 1960s and 1970s, have reaffirmed America's leadership in science entering the 21st century.

—DAVID A. VALONE

See Also: Computers; Darwinism; Fairs and Expositions; Inventions; Manhattan Project; Scopes Trial; Space Exploration; Surveying; individual biographies.

BIBLIOGRAPHY: Jaffe, Bernard, *Men of Science in America* (Simon & Schuster 1958); Reingold, Nathan, *Science American Style* (Rutgers Univ. Press 1991); Van Tassel, David D., and Michael G. Hall, eds., *Science and Society in the United States* (The Dorey Press 1966).

■ **SCIENCE FICTION,** body of literature often exploring the effect of scientific innovation upon human possibility, emerging in the United States as a self-conscious literary genre in the early 20th century. Its global pedigree and diverse forms and themes have produced an assortment of definitions for science fiction and preclude easy generalizations regarding it. Although examples of science fiction can be found in 19th-century American writing, not until the 1920s did publications devoted exclusively to the subject matter appear. After publishing science fiction pieces in his *Modern Electrics,* Hugo Gernsback introduced his magazines *Amazing Stories* (1926) and *Science Wonder Stories* (1929). Science fiction periodicals provided the primary market for this growing field through World War II. Comic strips and radio, and later television and film, also proved outlets for science fiction, the most prominent example in broadcasting from this time being Orson Welles's 1938 radio adaptation of the

novel *War of the Worlds* by British author H. G. Wells, which aroused panic in many credulous listeners. The appearance of science fiction paperbacks helped account for the genre's increasing effect upon postwar American culture, and the publication of such works as Isaac Asimov's enormously influential *Foundation* trilogy (1951-53) inaugurated a transformation of its "pulp" status. In the 1960s, science fiction began to enter the nation's literary mainstream, and with the establishment of the Science Fiction Research Association in 1970 and a number of professional journals, the introduction of new creative talent, and the expansion of an interested reading public, science fiction has continued to gain importance in the late 20th century.

See Also: Novel.

BIBLIOGRAPHY: Ben-Tov, Sharona, *The Artificial Paradise: Science Fiction and American Reality* (Univ. of Michigan Press 1995); Lerner, Frederick A., *Modern Science Fiction and the American Literary Community* (Scarecrow 1985).

■ **SCOPES TRIAL,** famous Tennessee court case also known as the "Scopes Monkey Trial." The defendant, John T. Scopes, taught high school biology in the small mining town of Dayton, Tennessee. He was arrested in 1925 for teaching Charles Darwin's theory of evolution, thereby violating Tennessee's Butler Act, which forbade the instruction of any theory about the origins of human life contrary to the biblical story of creation.

William Jennings Bryan, a prominent lawyer and former Democratic presidential candidate and cabinet member, argued the state's case. He asserted the right of citizens to decide what their children would study in school. Clarence Darrow, also an eminent attorney, defended John Scopes. Darrow requested that scientific testimony regarding evolution be allowed as evidence, but Judge John Raulston refused on the grounds that the issue was whether Scopes broke the law, not whether that law was appropriate.

Darrow's only witness was his adversary Bryan. He challenged Bryan's fundamentalist, literal interpretation of the Bible, effectively discrediting and publicly humiliating him. Bryan died shortly thereafter. Despite Darrow's courtroom performance, the jury found Scopes guilty and fined him $100. He returned to teaching, while Darrow continued his successful career in law. Scopes's conviction was later overturned by the state supreme court, but not until 1968 did the U.S. Supreme Court resolve the constitutional issue, overturning an Arkansas law similar to the Butler Act.

See Also: *Bryan, William Jennings; Darrow, Clarence; Science.*

BIBLIOGRAPHY: de Camp, L. Sprague, *The Great Monkey Trial* (Doubleday 1968); Larsen, Edward J., *Summer for the Gods: The Scopes Trial and America's Continuing Debate over Science and Religion* (Basic Books 1997).

■ **SCOTS-IRISH.** The term Scots-Irish refers to people of Scottish ancestry who immigrated to America from northern Ireland. During the first half of the 17th century, many Scottish Presbyterians fled religious persecution in Scotland for Ireland. Between about 1717 and 1775 an estimated 200,000 to 250,000 of these Scottish residents of Ireland immigrated to the American mainland colonies. Driven from Ireland by restrictive English economic and religious policies, many Scots-Irish immigrants arrived as indentured servants. Those who had freedom of movement settled in the religiously tolerant colony of Pennsylvania. Open lands in the back country attracted many Scots-Irish, who established communities along the foothills of the Appalachians. During and after the Revolution these Scots-Irish settlers moved westward into Kentucky and Tennessee. Although Scots-Irish developed a strong sense of ethnic identity while in Ireland, the sparse immigration to the United States after 1800 led to an eventual erosion of ethnic consciousness.

See Also: *Ethnic Groups; Immigration.*

■ **SCOTT, WINFIELD (1786-1866),** soldier, known as "Old Fuss and Feathers." He was born on his family's farm, Laurel Branch, near Petersburg, Virginia, on June 13, 1786. He entered William and Mary College in 1805 but left within the year to read law in Petersburg.

During the War of 1812 Scott distinguished himself at the battles of Queenston Heights (Oct. 13, 1812), Fort George (May 27, 1813), Chrysler's Farm (Nov. 11, 1813), Chippewa (July 5, 1814), and

In the Mexican War, Gen. Winfield Scott, known as "Old Fuss and Feathers," commanded the capture of Vera Cruz and Mexico City.

Lundy's Lane (July 25, 1814). Three times wounded, he was breveted to the rank of major general.

In 1832, he was assigned to command U.S. forces in the Black Hawk War; later that year he went to South Carolina to counter the Nullifiers, who threatened to use force against the federal government to defend the right of South Carolina to declare the federal tariff acts null and void within its state borders. In 1836 he took command of the forces engaged against the Seminoles in Florida and afterward was transferred to Georgia to deal with an uprising of the Creeks. In 1838 he was engaged in diplomatic missions to the British, Canadians, and Cherokees.

On July 5, 1841, Scott was elevated to the command of the U.S. Army with the permanent rank of major general. Owing, however, to a partisan disagreement between Scott and Pres. James K. Polk at the outbreak of the Mexican War in 1846,

Maj. Gen. Zachary Taylor received the command of the principal U.S. field army. In November 1846 Polk nevertheless approved Scott's plan to lead an amphibious assault on Mexico's Gulf Coast and to capture Mexico City. Scott took Vera Cruz on March 27 and then led his army inland, routing the forces of Antonio López de Santa Anna at Cerro Gordo on April 18. Advancing toward the enemy's capital, Scott won major victories at Contreras, Churubusco, Molino del Rey, and Chapultepec. Mexico City fell to Scott's army on September 14.

Scott's success made him such a threat to the Democratic administration that President Polk relieved him of his command and convened a court of inquiry to investigate the Whig general's alleged misconduct during the campaign. Although cleared of all charges, Scott lost the Whig presidential nomination to Taylor in 1848 and in 1852, as the Whig candidate, was overwhelmingly defeated by Franklin Pierce. As a consolation, Scott was breveted lieutenant general on Feb. 22, 1855, the only U.S. Army officer to hold that grade between George Washington and Ulysses S. Grant.

With the coming of the Civil War, Scott formulated his "Anaconda Plan" (1861), a proposal to disrupt the economies of the seceded states by blockade. An impatient American people demanded immediate action, however, and four years of brutal warfare ensued. Although forced by age and illness to pass the field command of the Union army to Brig. Gen. Irvin McDowell, Scott bore the blame for the Union debacle at First Manassas (July 21, 1861), and when Gen. George B. McClellan was named commander of the Army of the Potomac, Scott resigned from the army on Oct. 31, 1862. He died at his home at West Point on May 29, 1866, and is buried there at the Post Cemetery.

—THOMAS W. CUTRER

See Also: *Anaconda Plan; Civil War; Lundy's Lane, Battle of; McClellan, George Brinton; Mexican War; Pierce, Franklin; Polk, James Knox; Santa Anna, Antonio López de; Taylor, Zachary; War of 1812.*

BIBLIOGRAPHY: Elliot, Charles Wilson, *Winfield Scott: The Soldier and the Man* (Macmillan 1937); Scott, Winfield, *Memoirs of Lieut.-General Winfield Scott, LL.D.* (Sheldon 1864).

■ **SCOTTSBORO CASE.** *See: Powell v. Alabama*

■ **SCULPTURE.** Sculpture began in America as the most permanent way to honor the dead and to make life more pleasant. The immigrant and native craftsmen who carved the nation's gravestones and furniture prepared the New World for the monuments and public art that would follow. The artisan carvers in colonial America brought their designs with them from Europe or copied them from pattern books, prints, and imported goods. As economic conditions in the colonies improved, so did the quality of the carving and decoration, and more costly things were imported, including finely carved funerary reliefs in marble. A higher standard of living attracted in evergreater numbers itinerant European carvers, and indigenous carvers joined these ranks.

After the Revolution, there was a flurry of activity to produce likenesses of its new leaders and monuments to its heroes. New York City's first public monument to a Revolutionary hero, the Montgomery memorial, still stands in St. Paul's Chapel in Manhattan. America attracted such outstanding European artists as France's leading sculptor, Jean-Antoine Houdon. His portraits of Benjamin Franklin, George Washington, and other founding fathers were important models for both patrons and sculptors and helped to establish standards of excellence.

19th and 20th Centuries. With the dawn of the 19th century, appropriate sculpture was required for the nation's new capital in Washington, D.C., and Italian sculptors, followers of Antonio Canova, were imported to work in the Neoclassical style. Academies of art were formed, particularly in New York and Philadelphia, and had great influence in establishing the European tradition in the United States.

By the 1820s and 1830s, the first wave of American expatriate sculptors, Horatio Greenough, Hiram Powers, and Thomas Crawford, had settled in Italy to be close to its ancient models, marble quarries, and artisan tradition of marble carvers and to an international community of artists. They were followed by a second generation of American sculptors, including a group of women, who worked primarily in marble, which inspired Henry James to dub them whimsically the "White Marmorean Flock." Already, however, the Americans had shown their independence. Instead of copying Greek gods and goddesses, which had no meaning for their age, they used the ancient models for Old and New Testament figures as well as for contemporary historical and literary subjects to produce a Yankee Classicism.

The art center in Europe shifted from Italy to Paris around mid-century, and the expatriates went to the Ecole des Beaux-Arts to learn a blend of ancient, Renaissance, and Baroque called the Beaux-Arts tradition. Bronze replaced marble as the popular medium, providing American sculptors with new flexibility in producing the great outdoor monuments to its heroes and leaders in the post–Civil War period. Augustus Saint-Gaudens, whose superlative blend of naturalism and idealism opened a new era in American sculpture, established a standard of excellence yet to be equaled.

Foundries in America that had been originally engaged in military and domestic production were now making sculpture—even such monuments as the equestrian statue of George Washington in Union Square Park in New York City. Advances in bronze-casting techniques in European foundries made it possible to reproduce subtleties in modeling never before achieved. The quality of American casting also improved, as evidenced in the minute detail of Frederic Remington's Indian and cowboy pieces.

The grand age of the Beaux-Arts tradition was between the Philadelphia Centennial of 1876 and World War I. The National Sculpture Society, founded in 1893, institutionalized the Beaux-Arts tradition, which dominated American sculpture until the early 20th century. With the advent of direct carving in the first decade of the 20th century, the preference for simplified form and abstraction replaced the Beaux-Arts naturalism and idealism.

Through the European artists who settled in America and the American artists who studied abroad, foundations were laid for the emergence of the two major post–World War II movements of American sculpture: Abstract Expressionism, with its spontaneous assertion of the individual, and Constructivism with its assertion of sculptural space rather than sculptural mass. The principles underlying those two movements found expression in an enormous variety of works by some of America's major masters of modern sculpture—from the soft sculptures of Claes Oldenburg to the intimate and magical box constructions of Joseph Cornell. Those boxes are no less nostalgic than Louise Nevelson's large wooden walls, honeycombs of found objects from old houses, strikingly personal compared to her later indoor and outdoor environments.

Industrial materials and new technologies helped to shape the sensibilities of a large contingent of abstract sculptors. The most original and most influential American constructivist sculptor was David Smith, while George Rickey emphasized the abstract foundations of constructivism.

Two quite different yet truly international masters of the 20th century were Alexander Calder and Isamu Noguchi. Noguchi married the traditions of the East and the West, from his early academic portraits to his later gardens, playgrounds, and landscapes. Moreover, he looked ahead to the later experiments in earth sculpture. Calder's stabiles, mobiles, and miscellaneous constructions, whether whimsical or scientific, range from portraits and caricatures to full-fledged activated environments for all ages, all people, and all times.

—DONALD MARTIN REYNOLDS

See Also: Architecture; Calder, Alexander; Greenough, Horatio; Nevelson, Louise; Noguchi, Isamu; Oldenburg, Claes; Powers, Hiram; Remington, Frederic; Saint-Gaudens, Augustus; Smith, David.

BIBLIOGRAPHY: Craven, Wayne, *Sculpture in America*, new and rev. ed. (Univ. of Delaware Press 1984); Reynolds, Donald Martin, *Masters of American Sculpture, the Figurative Tradition, from the American Renaissance to the Millennium* (Abbeville 1993).

■ **SEABORG, GLENN (1912-)**, physical chemist who discovered plutonium. Born in Ishpeming, Michigan, Seaborg worked his way through college and received his Ph.D. from Berkeley (1937). He researched radioactive isotopes with Gilbert Lewis at Berkeley and discovered some that are now used in medical therapy and scientific research. In 1939, Seaborg turned to transuranium elements (those with nuclei heavier than uranium) and, with the help of Edwin McMillan and the cyclotron, produced the synthetic element plutonium in 1940. In a year they had created the fissionable isotopes plutonium 239 and U-233, adding to the supply of nuclear fuel and making Seaborg's laboratory the leader in heavy-element research. He and McMillan shared the Nobel Prize in Chemistry for their discoveries (1951). During World War II, Seaborg moved to the University of Chicago to work on the Manhattan Project and produced the plutonium for the atomic bombs that destroyed Hiroshima and Nagasaki in 1945. Returning to Berkeley after the war, he and his team discovered eight more transuranium elements. He went on to be chancellor of the University of California (1958-61) and chairman of the Atomic Energy Commission (1961-71).

See Also: Lewis, Gilbert; Manhattan Project; Science.

■ **SEAMAN, ELIZABETH COCHRANE (1865?-1922),** journalist and reformer. She was born in Cochrane Mills, Pennsylvania. In 1887, to research an article about the brutally neglectful mental health system, she pretended to be mentally ill and was admitted to a public asylum. This type of research became her specialty. She similarly went under cover to expose injustice and corruption in prisons, sweatshops, and political lobbies.

■ **SECESSION,** the act by which a state breaks its ties with the Union, an act for which the U.S. Constitution includes no provision. Secession was theoretical and interpreted as the ultimate act of "states' rights." The secession crisis of 1860-61 was one of the immediate causes of the Civil War.

Secession had roots in the early national period. The Virginia and Kentucky Resolutions (1798) referred to the Constitution as merely a "compact" among the states, which implied that states could break their association with the Union. Opponents of the War of 1812 met in a convention at Hartford, Connecticut, airing their grievances against the federal government and discussing disunion. During the Nullification controversy (1832-33), South Carolina's legislature passed an ordinance nullifying federal tariffs and contended that if the military enforced the tariffs, South Carolina would secede. Texas, a Mexican state, rebelled and seceded from Mexico in 1836, establishing an independent republic that joined the United States in 1845.

Before 1860, the issue of slavery in the national territories sparked disagreement between Northerners and Southerners. Provoking worries among Southerners, Northern abolitionists called for an end to slavery. Some abolitionists became leaders in the new Republican party, which intended to block slavery's expansion into the territories. By 1860 many Southern politicians believed that the federal government might take action against slavery in states where it was legally established.

In the 1860 presidential election, controversies over slavery intensified. Republicans also proposed social and economic programs involving federal action, such as land grant colleges, a transcontinental railroad, a homestead bill for western settlers, and higher tariffs. Democrats opposed the Republican proposals but divided over slavery. Northern Democrats nominated Sen. Stephen A. Douglas of Illinois, a nationalist who equivocated on slavery. Southern Democrats nominated a Kentuckian, Vice Pres. John C. Breckinridge, a strong advocate of slavery's expansion. A Southern Unionist, John Bell of Tennessee, ran as the candidate of the short-lived Constitutional Union party. Abraham Lincoln, Republican party nominee from Illinois, won a majority in the electoral college, and his election provided the catalyst for secession.

Formation of the Confederacy. South Carolina led the way, calling a special convention that unanimously voted for an ordinance of secession (Dec. 20, 1860), contending that the United States was only a "compact between the states" and that states could secede. South Carolina's ordinance charged that the "nonslaveholding states" refused to uphold the Fugitive Slave Act of 1850, "denounced as sinful the institution of slavery," "assisted thousands of our slaves to leave their homes," and intended to deny the property rights of slaveowners in the national territories. In conclusion, South Carolinians asserted that the election of Lincoln had brought "a man to the high office of President of the United States whose opinions and purposes are hostile to slavery."

Citing similar reasons and using similar conventions in 1861, other Deep South states claimed to secede, including Mississippi (Jan. 9), Florida (Jan. 10), Alabama (Jan. 11), Georgia (Jan. 19),

Louisiana (Jan. 26), and Texas (Feb. 1). In February, delegates from the seceded states met in Montgomery, Alabama, to form the Confederate States of America. President Lincoln never recognized the process of secession, saying only that some states were out of their "proper relationship" with the Union. After Confederate forces fired on Fort Sumter, in Charleston, South Carolina, Lincoln announced he would suppress the insurrection, prompting claims of secession by Virginia (Apr. 17), Arkansas (May 6), Tennessee (May 7), and North Carolina (May 20). Although they never passed secession ordinances, Missouri and Kentucky received seats in the Confederate Congress and stars on the Confederate flag. The Union victory in the Civil War made secession a dead letter in American politics.

—JOSEPH G. DAWSON III

See Also: Civil War; Fugitive Slave Act; Hartford Convention; Nullification.

BIBLIOGRAPHY: Holden-Reid, Brian, *The Origins of the American Civil War* (Longman 1996); Potter, David, *The Impending Crisis, 1848-1861* (Harper & Row 1976).

■ **SECOND GREAT AWAKENING,** a series of religious revivals that swept the United States in the 1820s and 1830s and had lasting influences on American religion and reform. In the highly emotional revivals the unconverted were awakened, while the converted were reawakened. Preachers offered a practical evangelical message that countered the Calvinist approach of the Great Awakening of the 1730s and 1740s. According to the great revivalist Charles Grandison Finney, a lawyer turned itinerant preacher whose greatest success was in the "burned-over district" of New York State, people could be "free moral agents" and earn salvation through their own efforts. To entertain and appeal to the average person, preachers developed new techniques—sustained meetings, campaigns, and the "anxious bench" for those about to convert.

On the western frontier, camp meetings were early signs of the coming revivalism. The first camp meeting was held in 1800 by James McGready in Logan County, Kentucky. In August 1801, Barton Stone led a famous camp meeting in Cane Ridge, Kentucky, that lasted nearly a week. At this meeting many participants reacted physically to their conversions. Some fell to the ground and others began to shake, called the "jerks." Methodist and Baptist circuit riders thrived in this energetic environment and built hundreds of new churches in the South and Southwest frontier regions.

The Second Great Awakening had lasting effects on American culture. Some historians argue that the revival movement instilled discipline by calling people to work diligently and avoid sin. And by spreading the belief that heaven on earth was obtainable, the Second Great Awakening ignited many reform movements, including temperance, abolition, anti-dueling, and public education. The fervor also led to the founding of new denominations and utopian movements.

—NANCY M. GODLESKI

See Also: Camp Meetings; Great Awakening; Religion.

BIBLIOGRAPHY: Conkin, Paul Keith, *Cane Ridge: America's Pentecost* (Univ. of Wisconsin Press 1990); Hatch, Nathan O., *The Democratization of American Religion* (Yale Univ. Press 1989).

■ **SECRET SERVICE,** security branch of the U.S. Treasury Department. Best known for protecting the president, the Secret Service is also responsible for guarding the integrity of the nation's money supply. Formed (1864) during the Civil War, the service took charge of protecting presidents and providing security for the rest of the executive branch of government following the assassination of Pres. Abraham Lincoln (1865). The Secret Service is also responsible for investigating foreign and domestic counterfeiting of U.S. currency, forgery, illegal currency shipments, and other federal crimes that could jeopardize the financial stability of the nation by undermining public confidence in the money supply. During World Wars I and II, the Secret Service also provided security at defense plants and oversaw the transportation of munitions and war materials around the country.

BIBLIOGRAPHY: Melanson, Philip H., *The Politics of Protection: The U.S. Secret Service in the Terrorist Age* (Praeger 1984).

■ **SECTIONALISM,** term used to describe political and economic tensions between geographical parts of a nation. It derives from the word "section," whose Latin root "secarc" means "a piece cut out," and in its earliest American usage a section referred to any faction of people as well as to any portion of land carved out for settlement. Officially employed as the basic mile-square unit of Thomas Jefferson's rectangular survey system in 1785, "section" gained larger, more discordant meanings during the decades leading to the Civil War. By the 1820s, large areas of the country that seemed at odds with each other were called sections, and politicians fulminated against sectional animosity. By the 1850s, the word sectionalism was coined to characterize the growing antipathy between North and South that would soon erupt in war.

Sectionalism remains a conflict-laden concept, referring both to the divisive dynamics of the Civil War and to ongoing differences between rival sections of the nation. Emphasizing political and economic differences, sectionalism considers the uneven distribution of power and wealth over space and the fervent emotions sparked by these disparities. A sectional view of American history sees the nation as an uneasy confederation, or loose patchwork, of self-serving parts, and it traces their competitive, often contentious relationship over time.

Sectionalism is most clearly understood when matched with its sister concept of regionalism. Underscoring differences between increasingly self-conscious entities, section and sectionalism filled American discourse through most of the 19th century, while the more integrative terms region and regionalism have enriched and dominated the discussion ever since. Like twin stars, attracting and repelling each other in a reciprocal relationship, regionalism knits groups of people together within a complex whole, while sectionalism divides them into self-determining entities. Paradoxically, sectionalism often duplicates the bellicose extremes of nationalism: in its prideful desire to secede from or impose its will on other places, the section behaves like a smaller, concentrated form of the nation. The Civil War, then, can be seen as the collision of sections striving to become nations rather than a tragic manifestation of regionalism.

Although irrevocably linked to the South and the Civil War, sectionalism has cropped up else-where in other forms. In the 1770s, Frenchman Hector St. John de Crèvecoeur was astonished by the volatile differences between New Englanders, Pennsylvanians, and Virginians, while in his 1796 Farewell Address, George Washington warned that the new nation was endangered by the "jealousies and heart burnings" of diverging sections. Tensions between southern-rooted Jeffersonians and northern-based Hamiltonians plagued the early republic, and New England bitterly protested the War of 1812 by threatening to break from the Union in 1814, ironically setting a precedent for Southern secession.

Post–Civil War Sectionalism. After 1865, sectionalism assumed new forms. During the 1890s, for example, Southern and Western Populists like Thomas Watson and Mary Elizabeth Lease were denounced by Northern capitalists as "new sectionalists" and "calamity howlers" bent upon dismembering the nation. Sectionalism resurfaced in the 1930s as unreconstructed Southerners like Donald Davidson and John Crowe Ransom rejected the industrial state and as angry Westerners like Bernard DeVoto and Walter Prescott Webb analyzed their native lands as a plundered province. A scattering of voices at the end of the 20th century echo sectional themes: Sage Brush Rebels repudiate federal land control; Earth First! Environmentalists sabotage power projects; radical economists build sustainable communities; and members of various minority groups promote geographically separate societies. Although these and other efforts are unlikely to splinter, fragment, or balkanize the United States, they indicate that centrifugal forces of sectionalism continue to complicate American culture.

—MICHAEL C. STEINER

See Also: Regionalism.

BIBLIOGRAPHY: Bensel, Richard Franklin, *Sectionalism and American Political Development* (Univ. of Wisconsin Press 1984); Potter, David M., *The South and the Sectional Conflict* (Louisiana State Univ. Press 1968); Turner, Frederick Jackson, *The Significance of Sections in American History* (Henry Holt 1932); Webb, Walter Prescott, *Divided We Stand: The Crisis of a Frontierless Democracy* (Acorn Press 1937); Webb, Walter Prescott, *Twelve Southerners, I'll Take My Stand: The South and the Agrarian Tradition* (Harper 1930).

■ **SECURITIES AND EXCHANGE COMMISSION (SEC),** independent U.S government agency that regulates stock and bond markets. Created (1934) during Pres. Franklin D. Roosevelt's administration, the SEC enforced new legislation designed to regulate and restore public confidence in financial markets in the wake of the 1929 stock market crash. The five-member commission licenses and monitors stock exchanges and requires both corporations and traders to file financial disclosure forms.

See Also: Stock Exchange.

■ **SECURITIES EXCHANGE ACT (1934),** federal law passed to regulate the securities industry. Many scholars and politicians in the 1930s attributed the stock market crash of 1929 to the rampant extension of credit for stock speculation and the unethical behavior of those dealing in stocks. Conversely, the crash was blamed for the collapse of banks and the credit system and the subsequent depression of the 1930s. When Pres. Franklin D. Roosevelt and the New Dealers came to power in 1933, they vowed to overhaul the system and prevent further abuses in the securities industry.

The Securities Act of 1933, the first piece of legislation intended to rectify the system, imposed a series of regulations on the trading of securities. A year later the more expansive Securities Exchange Act was passed, establishing the Securities and Exchange Commission (SEC), an independent agency with a chairman appointed by the president. Opponents argued that the SEC would inhibit investment, while some New Dealers were skeptical of a self-regulating trade association. In the end, the law allowed for a revival of an orderly investment market.

Early SEC officials established a pattern of efficiency and integrity, giving it a positive reputation among financial leaders. Some New Dealers, however, lamented that the Securities Exchange Act and the resulting SEC did not achieve a complete overhaul of the securities industry.

See Also: New Deal; Securities and Exchange Commission (SEC).

BIBLIOGRAPHY: Parrish, Michael E., *Securities Regulation and the New Deal* (Yale Univ. Press 1970).

■ **SEDITION ACT (1918),** federal law passed during World War I. It aimed to punish speech that interfered with the war effort, stimulated dissent, or gave comfort to the enemy. Vaguely worded, the law resulted in about 2,000 prosecutions, mostly of radicals.

See Also: World War I.

■ **SEGREGATION.** *See:* African Americans; Desegregation; Race and Racism.

■ **SELECTIVE DRAFT LAW CASES (1918),** U.S. Supreme Court cases concerning the constitutionality of the World War I military draft. Draft opponents argued that conscription authorized by the Selective Service Act of 1917 violated 13th Amendment protections against involuntary servitude and First Amendment religious protections. But the Court ruled (9-0) that since history and tradition showed that citizenship included obligations as well as privileges, Congress had the authority to raise armies through a draft.

■ **SELECTIVE SERVICE ACT (1917),** first nationwide conscription in American history, passed at the beginning of America's entry into World War I. The act required all men aged 18 to 45 to register for military service. Eventually, nearly 3 million men were drafted and 2 million of those served overseas during the remainder of the war (1917-18).

See Also: World War I.

■ **SELECTIVE SERVICE ACT (1940),** first peacetime conscription in American history. The act was engineered by Pres. Franklin D. Roosevelt to enlarge the army in anticipation of eventual U.S. involvement in World War II. It required all men aged 21 to 35 to register for military service.

See Also: World War II.

■ **SELECTIVE SERVICE SYSTEM,** government organization established to register men for military service in the world wars and in subsequent wars. The actual decision of who would serve was left up to local draft boards, which had great leeway in granting or denying deferments.

■ **SEMINOLE,** Indian people of Florida, originally Muskogees (or Creeks) who migrated into the Florida peninsula in the 18th century in the wake of the destruction of the indigenous peoples who had been missionized by the Spanish, then destroyed in raids by the British and their Indian allies. The name derives from the Spanish *cimarrón* (meaning "wild"), pronounced in the distinctive Muskogee way. The Seminoles also included thousands of escaped slaves from South Carolina and Georgia, who established independent communities among the Indians and gradually adopted a Seminole ethnic identity. Like their Creek cousins, the Seminoles were a village people, and they had little tribal unity.

Seminole warriors sided with the British during the American Revolution and again during the War of 1812, and the group was especially hated by slaveholders along the sea island coast, who saw their presence in Florida as encouragement to slave revolt and fugitivism. In 1818 the United States sent an expeditionary force under the command of Andrew Jackson into Spanish East Florida; Jackson's mission was as much to capture slaves as to make war against the Indians. The First Seminole War occasioned an international incident when Jackson executed two British traders whom he claimed had armed and incited the Seminoles. Sec. of State John Quincy Adams skillfully used the incident to convince the Spanish that they should cede Florida to the United States, which they did in 1821. Two years later, in the Treaty of Moultrie Creek, the Seminoles agreed to relocate further south into the Florida interior; there they formed a centralized tribal leadership.

During the removal period the United States pressed the Seminoles to relocate to the trans-Mississippi West along with the other tribes of the Southeast. In 1832 a few Seminole chiefs agreed to removal in the Treaty of Payne's Landing, but the majority of the people refused to abide by it. When the army moved into central Florida to enforce the removal order in 1836, the Seminoles struck back and defeated them. This Second Seminole War, the longest and costliest Indian war in American history, lasted six years and claimed the lives of 1,500 American troops and an unknown number of Indians. By 1842 approximately 3,000 Seminoles had been forcibly removed to Indian Territory. Another thousand remained hidden in the swamps and the Everglades, but the United States finally called off the campaign, which had become extremely unpopular.

Like the other tribes in Indian Territory, the Seminoles were torn apart by the Civil War. Despite the fact that as many fought for the Union as against it, after the war federal authorities treated the tribe as a defeated enemy, reducing its land base to a mere tenth of its former size. A period of relative prosperity and peace followed the war, but that ended in 1898 when the tribe agreed to allotment. The land base was divided among families, and tribal government was formally dissolved. In the aftermath of allotment many of both the red and black towns broke up, and many Seminoles left the area. Following the Indian Reorganization Act, in 1935 tribal government was reestablished. Today there are some 10,000 Seminole people living in Oklahoma.

Those Seminoles who remained behind in Florida were granted three reservations. In 1957 the residents of those reservations organized the Seminole Tribe of Florida. Today's population of about 1,200 includes traditional people who make their livings by hunting and fishing, as well as others who work at the high-stakes bingo parlor in Hollywood, Florida.

—JOHN MACK FARAGHER

See Also: *Creek; Indian Reorganization Act; Indians of North America.*

BIBLIOGRAPHY: Covington, James W., *The Seminoles of Florida* (Univ. Press of Florida 1993); McReynolds, Edwin C., *The Seminoles* (Univ. of Oklahoma Press 1957); Wright, J. Leitch, Jr., *Creeks and Seminoles: The Destruction and Regeneration of the Muscogulge People* (Univ. of Nebraska Press 1986).

■ **SENATE OF THE UNITED STATES.** The Senate was established by the framers of the Constitution as the upper legislative branch of Congress as part of a compromise over the issue of equality of representation. Each state, regardless of population, has two senators. They are elected for six years and can be reelected without term limits. A senator must be at least 30 years of age and have been a citizen of the United States for 9 years. One-third of the Senate is up for election every two years. Members of the Senate were elected by their state legislatures until direct election was provided by the 17th Amendment to the Constitution, which was adopted in 1913. The vice president of the United States is the president of the

Senate (Article I, Section 3), but it is a largely ceremonial role. However, in the event of a tie vote, the vice president casts the deciding ballot. The Senate also elects a president pro tempore, usually the senior member of the majority party, who presides in the absence of the vice president. Junior members of the Senate also take turns presiding over sessions.

Senators have a high degree of political visibility on the national level, in part because of their unique constitutional role. The Senate is responsible for providing "advice and consent" for presidential nominations of ambassadors, federal judges, and other public officials such as members of the president's cabinet (Article II, Section 2). In recent years, the Senate has rejected a number of nominees to the Supreme Court because their judicial philosophy was not shared by a majority of senators. The Senate is also responsible for ratifying treaties, which require a two-thirds vote to become law. In addition, the Senate has the sole power, upon recommendation from the House of Representatives, to try all impeachments. Conviction and removal from office requires a two-thirds majority of the members present (Article I, Section 3).

The Senate operates under more flexible rules of procedure than does the House. The most visible example is the filibuster. One senator seeking to prevent a vote on legislation can hold the floor by continually speaking and blocking all other legislative business. Currently, three-fifths of the entire membership must vote for a cloture motion to end a filibuster. The Senate, like the House, relies on committees and subcommittees to process the large flow of proposed legislation. There are 16 standing or permanent committees and almost 100 subcommittees. In the modern era the Senate has come to rely increasingly on its rapidly growing staff. Moreover, since senators serve on so many committees, the chairs develop expertise, seniority, and, consequently, a great deal of influence over the legislative process.

Leadership in the Senate is largely the responsibility of the majority leader, who is elected by the members of his or her party. The majority leader is the most visible member of the body and often develops a close relationship with the Speaker of the House and the president. In addi-

tion, the Senate has majority and minority "whips," who are supposed to ensure that members understand the issues and vote according to the wishes of the party leadership.

—ALEXANDER WELLEK

See Also: *Constitution of the United States.*

BIBLIOGRAPHY: Harris, Fred, *Deadlock or Decision: The United States Senate and the Rise of National Politics* (Oxford Univ. Press 1992); Matthews, Donald, *United States Senators and Their World* (Greenwood Press 1980); Redmon, Eric, *The Dance of Legislation* (Simon & Schuster 1987); Sinclair, Barbara, *The Transformation of the United States Senate* (Johns Hopkins Univ. Press 1989).

■ **SENECA FALLS CONVENTION (1848),** the first public women's rights meeting, held in Seneca Falls, New York, on July 19-20, 1848. It was organized by Lucretia Mott and Elizabeth Cady Stanton, who met in 1840 when they were excluded from an international antislavery meeting in London because of their sex. Educated by their public efforts on behalf of abolition, Mott and Stanton decided to create a place for women's rights in public discourse. Working from Stanton's home, Mott, Stanton, and three other women sent out a call for the discussion of the "social, civil and religious rights of women" to be held a week later in the Wesleyan Chapel in nearby Seneca Falls.

The size of the turnout daunted the women; nearly 300 people participated, 40 of them men, including the abolitionist Frederick Douglass, and they asked Mott's husband, James, to chair the meeting. The convention issued the "Declaration of Sentiments," modeled on the Declaration of Independence, which detailed the oppression of women by men and their deprivation of the full rights and privileges of citizens. The accompanying resolutions, which called for equal rights in religion, education, employment, and political life, were unanimously approved, except for the demand for suffrage. Some participants believed that women should hold themselves above the dirty business of politics, but eventually, with the support of Douglass, the suffrage resolution passed narrowly.

Two weeks later, in Rochester, New York, an even larger meeting convened, and thereafter women's meetings were held annually. The Seneca Falls Convention marked a milestone in establishing a major aspect of the women's movement—that women must rely on themselves for their emancipation—and demonstrated the close connection between the movements to free slaves and to grant white women equal status with white men.

—CATHERINE ALLGOR

See Also: Mott, Lucretia Coffin; Stanton, Elizabeth Cady; Women in American History; Women's Movement.

BIBLIOGRAPHY: Dubois, Ellen Carol, *Feminism and Suffrage: The Emergence of an Independent Women's Movement in America, 1848-1869* (Cornell Univ. Press 1978); Hewitt, Nancy, *Women's Activism and Social Change, Rochester, New York, 1822-1872* (Cornell Univ. Press 1984).

■ **SENNETT, MACK (1880-1960),** film director and producer. The king of silent film slapstick comedy was born in Richmond, Quebec, Canada. After working under the director D. W. Griffith in Hollywood, Sennett formed the Keystone studio (1912) and churned out hundreds of low-budget, popular short films featuring broad, physical comedy, bathing beauties, pie fights, car chases, and the hilariously inept Keystone Kops. Charlie Chaplin and Roscoe "Fatty" Arbuckle were among his early stars.

See Also: Hollywood; Motion Pictures.

■ **SEPARATION OF POWERS,** division of power and authority within the federal government among three branches—the legislature, the executive, and the judiciary. In the U.S. Constitution the separation of powers was intended to prevent a concentration of power in government. Properly speaking, it is a system of separate institutions sharing powers, not a "separation of powers."

There was no true separation of powers in the Articles of Confederation adopted in 1777, which gave Congress executive power and weak judicial powers. Shays's Rebellion against Massachusetts in 1786-87 became a rallying point for those advocating a strong federal government and influenced Massachusetts's decision to ratify the new U.S. Constitution.

The framers created a system where representatives in the House would be selected on the basis of population, senators selected by state legislatures, the president selected by the electoral college, and the Supreme Court selected by the president and ratified by the Senate. This system would create independent power bases for each branch. James Madison wrote in *The Federalist* Number 51 that separation of powers creates a system of opposite and rival interests that fragments majorities and makes ambition counteract ambition.

Nevertheless, Madison, along with Thomas Jefferson, envisioned strong presidential leadership and modern mass parties as a means of overcoming the separation of powers and empowering national majorities. Eventually, democratizing tendencies tended to blur the separation of powers as envisioned by the framers. The electoral college has never operated as the framers envisioned, as the election of the president evolved into a democratic mandate. The selection of senators was moved from state legislatures and put in the hands of voters. The creation of the Interstate Commerce Commission in 1887 opened the way for another layer of government power—independent regulatory agencies with quasi-legislative and quasi-judicial powers.

Despite these developments to democratize the government, the separation of powers is still quite effective in preventing excessive concentrations of power and abuse of the majority will. A president elected with a huge majority cannot be certain that Congress will cooperate with him even if it is controlled by the same political party. Ticket splitting and "independent" voters are increasingly common, while tensions exist between congressional protection of local interests and the president's national agenda. Although separation of powers prevents abuse by the majority, it also contributes to governmental "gridlock," a phenomenon that enrages the very population that has voted to divide the government.

—SCOTT L. McLEAN

See Also: Checks and Balances; Constitution of the United States; Electoral College; Federalist Papers, The.

BIBLIOGRAPHY: Beard, Charles, *An Economic Interpretation of the Constitution of the United States* (Macmillan 1913); Hamilton, Alexander, John Jay, and James Madison, *The Federalist Papers* (Bantam 1982); Hudson, William E., *American Democracy in Peril* (Chatham House 1996).

■ **SEQUOYAH (c. 1770-1843),** inventor of the Cherokee syllabary. Also known as George Guess, Sequoyah was born in present-day Tennessee and fought in the Creek War of 1813-14 under Gen. Andrew Jackson. In 1818 he moved to present-day Arkansas with a group of Cherokee traditionalists under Chief John Jolly. In 1809 Sequoyah began work on a Cherokee syllabary, eventually using characters from the Greek and Roman alphabets so that the Cherokee language could be set in type. He finished his project in 1821, the first person to invent an entire syllabary on his own. The Cherokee language was the first written Indian language north of Mexico, and the syllabary became popular among the Cherokees, who quickly adopted a written constitution and a bilingual newspaper, *The Cherokee Phoenix*. Many Cherokees in Arkansas and Georgia used the syllabary to write to their relatives; by the late 1820s, the Cherokees had a very high literacy rate. Sequoyah later became a leader of the re-united Cherokees in Indian Territory.

See Also: Cherokee; Indians of North America; Jackson, Andrew.

■ **SERPENT MOUND (c. 300 B.C.-A.D. 400),** one of the first evidences of complex social organization in North America north of Mexico, this ritual earthwork was constructed by the Adena culture in southern Ohio and is the largest effigy earthwork in the world.

See Also: Adena; Indians of North America.

■ **SERRA, JUNIPERO (1713-84),** founding Roman Catholic missionary of California's Spanish era. Born in Petra, Majorca, Spain, Serra entered the Franciscan order in 1730 and gained a reputation as a great theologian and philosopher before being ordained a priest. Although likely to rise in the church's hierarchy, Serra instead chose the arduous life of a missionary to the Indians in the New World. He labored for some years in Mexico and Texas before being chosen as *presidente* of a new missionary effort in California. On July 16, 1769, Serra's San Diego mission was founded, and over the next 15 years he founded 8 more. These missionary settlements and the 12 founded after his death became some of California's early cities. Serra's motto, "always forward, never back," sum-

marized his life, but he often clashed with the military authorities over the treatment of the Indians. Despite poor health, he walked thousands of miles across California to visit his far-flung missions. Serra died near Monterey on Aug. 28, 1784.

See Also: California; Exploration and Discovery; Missions and Missionaries; Religion; Spanish Colonies.

BIBLIOGRAPHY: Englebert, Omer, *The Last of the Conquistadors: Junipero Serra* (Harcourt 1956).

■ **SESSIONS, ROGER (1896-1985),** composer known for his technically demanding neoclassical and 12-tone works. A modernist influenced by composers Igor Stravinsky and Arnold Schoenberg, Sessions was awarded Pulitzer Prizes for his body of work in 1974 and for Concerto for Orchestra in 1981. Born in Brooklyn, New York, he taught composition at Princeton University (1935-45, 1953-65) and the Juilliard School of Music (1965-85).

■ **SETON, ELIZABETH ANN BAYLEY (1774-1821),** Roman Catholic leader, first American-born saint. Born in New York City, she converted to Catholicism in 1805. She helped lay the foundations of parochial education in the United States and became Mother Superior to the first American sisterhood. She was canonized in 1974.

■ **SEVEN DAYS' BATTLES (June 25-July 1, 1862),** series of Civil War battles between the forces of Union Gen. George McClellan and Confederate Gen. Robert E. Lee. With Union forces threatening Richmond, Virginia, the Confederate capital, engagements at Mechanicsville (June 26), Gaines Mill (June 27), Savage Station (June 29), and White Oak Swamp (June 30) drove McClellan south to Malvern Hill, where his forces entrenched. On July 1 Confederate frontal assaults were repulsed by Union artillery. Despite the victory, McClellan fell back to Harrison's Landing on the James River.

See Also: Civil War; Lee, Robert Edward; McClellan, George Brinton.

■ **SEVEN PINES (FAIR OAKS), BATTLE OF (1862),** Civil War engagement between the forces of Union Gen. George McClellan and Confederate Gen. Joseph E. Johnston. As McClellan prepared to besiege the Confederate capital, Richmond, Virginia, on May 31, Johnston struck at the Union left south of the Chickahominy River with the corps of Gen. James Longstreet. The Union left was driven back a mile, but Union Gen. Edwin Sumner led a division, half-wading over rickety bridges, across the Chickahominy and stopped Longstreet's advance. The wounded Johnston was replaced with Gen. Robert E. Lee.

See Also: Civil War; Johnston, Joseph E.; Longstreet, James; McClellan, George Brinton.

■ **SEVEN YEARS' WAR (1756-63),** European conflict that incorporated what the North American colonists called the French and Indian War (1754-63). This complex series of hostilities involved every major state on the European continent, as well as featuring global rivalry for overseas colonies between Great Britain and France.

See Also: French and Indian War.

■ **SEVIER, JOHN (1745-1815),** American soldier and politician. Born near New Market, Virginia, he settled in Tennessee in 1772. During the American Revolution, he led a rebel force across the Smoky Mountains, engaging the British at the Battle of King's Mountain (Oct. 7, 1780). Sevier served as the governor of Franklin, a temporary state (1784-88) that had been part of western North Carolina and that is now part of eastern Tennessee. His interest in the somewhat renegade statehood movement of Franklin was land speculation, a pursuit for which his scheming nature seemed well suited. After the Franklin enterprise failed, he went on to represent North Carolina in the U.S. House of Representatives (1789-91), served as Tennessee's first governor (1796-1801, 1803-09), and returned to the House as a Tennessee congressman (1811-15). He was known for his harsh policies toward Indians living within Tennessee.

See Also: Franklin, State of; King's Mountain, Battle of.

■ **SEWARD, WILLIAM HENRY (1801-72),** political leader and secretary of state (1861-69). Born in Florida, New York, he entered state politics under the tutelage of newspaper editor Thurlow Weed. After two terms as an Anti-Mason state senator (1830-34), Seward served as Whig governor (1839-43), when he gained a reputation as a social reformer and humanitarian. As a U.S. senator (1849-61), Seward emerged as a leader first of the Whig and then of the Republican parties. His unequivocal condemnation of slavery may have cost him the Republican presidential nomination in 1860, but Lincoln appointed him secretary of state. Seward's success in preventing foreign recognition of the Confederacy and his telling use of the Monroe Doctrine against French intervention in Mexico together with his purchase of Alaska and efforts to increase trade with Asia rank him among the greatest secretaries of state.

See Also: Alaska; Lincoln, Abraham; Seward's Folly.
BIBLIOGRAPHY: Taylor, John M., *William Henry Seward: Lincoln's Right Hand* (HarperCollins 1991).

■ **SEWARD'S FOLLY (1867),** the U.S. purchase of what is now the state of Alaska, also referred to as "Seward's Icebox" and "Johnson's Polar Bear Garden" by those critical of it. In 1867, Pres. Andrew Johnson's secretary of state, William Henry Seward, negotiated with Imperial Russia for the $7.2 million acquisition. An enormous territory, the purchase price broke down to about two cents an acre. Secretary Seward's goal was to block any advance by Asian or European powers, especially Great Britain, in North America. Criticism was also countered by what turned out to be the relatively low congressional estimates of revenue from fur, fishing, lumber, and mineral resources. Seward's Folly, or Alaska, remained a U.S. territory until 1959, when it became the 49th state.

See Also: Alaska; Gilded Age; Seward, William Henry.
BIBLIOGRAPHY: Hoblo, Paul S., *Tarnished Expansion: The Alaska Scandal, The Press, and Congress, 1867-1871* (Univ. of Tennessee Press 1983); Paolino, Ernest N., *The Foundations of the American Empire: William Henry Seward and U.S. Foreign Policy* (Cornell Univ. Press 1973).

■ **SEWING MACHINE,** invention patented by Elias Howe in 1846. Howe's machine had an eye-pointed needle that worked in conjunction with a lower thread-loaded shuttle and could sew 250 stitches a minute. Unable to find support in the United States, he went to England and returned to find that his machine had become popular and that others had manufactured it. Howe instituted patent infringement lawsuits in 1849 and won final judgment in 1854. In the meantime, Allen B. Wilson and Isaac M. Singer had made important improvements on Howe's machine. Singer opened the Singer Manufacturing Company in New York City in 1853. Sewing machine manufacturers sold 1.5 million machines from 1856 to 1859, and 4.8 million between 1869 and 1878. Howe became a millionaire from royalties, and the name Singer became a household word. The sewing machine enabled clothing to be mass produced, which in turn had widespread ramifications. The boot and shoe, garment, bookbinding, awning, tent, sails, and saddlery manufacturing industries reorganized to incorporate this machine, some hiring women for the first time. The sewing machine also made the home production of clothing easier and thus altered women's domestic roles. Singer developed an electric sewing machine in 1889.

See Also: Howe, Elias; Invention.

■ **SEXTON, ANNE (1928-74),** poet. She was born in Newton, Massachusetts. In her poems, marked by irony and intense introspection, she often dealt with the struggle to maintain her sanity. She published several collections and, in 1966, won a Pulitzer Prize for *Live or Die*.

See Also: Poetry.

■ **SEXUALLY TRANSMITTED DISEASES,** known also as venereal diseases, have existed in North America since before Columbus's first voyage. According to recent archaeological evidence, syphilis was present in pre-Columbian America and spread to Europe shortly after first contact. Venereal diseases existed throughout the colonial period, and little progress was made in reducing them.

Shortly after the Civil War, J. H. Salisbury produced the first scientific work on the germ theory and its causal relationship to syphilis and gonorrhea. Public aversion to discussions related to sex and the disregard by the medical community effectively tabled his findings. The first federally supported venereal disease clinics opened during World War I (1914-18) but were closed at its conclusion. Public and scientific awareness of sexually transmitted diseases became general during the 1930s. The discovery of penicillin in 1943 marked the greatest breakthrough in treatment. The sexual revolution of the 1960s and 1970s signaled the reemergence of sexually transmitted diseases as a national problem. Several new diseases appeared, including genital herpes and AIDS (acquired immune deficiency syndrome), a mortal disease for which there is no known cure.

See Also: AIDS; Medicine.

BIBLIOGRAPHY: Brandt, Allan M., *No Magic Bullet: A Social History of Venereal Diseases in the United States since 1880* (Oxford Univ. Press 1985); Spongberg, Mary, *Feminizing Venereal Disease: The Body of the Prostitute of Nineteenth-Century Medical Discourse* (New York Univ. Press 1997).

■ **SEXUAL REVOLUTION,** term used to describe a wide-ranging change in the attitudes and actions of Americans toward sex. A sexual revolution occurred in the 1960s as Americans came to accept artificial contraception, premarital sexual relations, promiscuity, and a series of new attitudes toward sex in general.

The 1950s. This change in public attitudes about sex came in the midst of a social, technological, and cultural transformation in America. The 1950s were a flourishing period for the traditional family as Americans married more readily and at younger ages and, as a result, produced more children than ever before in modern history. The United States in this decade had one of the highest marriage rates in the world. By 1950, almost 70 percent of males and 67 percent of females over the age of 15 were married. Furthermore, the divorce rate dropped to only 10 percent in 1950. The rising birthrate reflected economic prosperity. People could afford children, and the middle class wanted more children. Surveys showed that most Americans thought that the ideal family should have three or four children.

Also during the 1950s, public officials on the federal, state, and local levels launched campaigns to suppress pornography. Beginning in 1952, Congress launched investigations of paperbacks, magazines, and comic books to expose the extent of "obscene" sexual material distributed in America. These congressional investigations encouraged citizens' campaigns and local law-enforcement drives. In Houston, Minneapolis, and

New York City, for example, law-enforcement officials responded with major raids. Local citizens formed Citizens for Decent Literature, with chapters located throughout the country.

Behind this apparent stability and social conservatism regarding sex, however, changes in people's attitudes were becoming apparent, leading to talk by the early 1960s of a "sexual revolution" among American youth. How much sexual practices had in fact changed remained unclear. Alfred Kinsey's *Sexual Behavior in the Human Male*, published in 1948, introduced to the public for the first time a broad portrait of American sexual behavior that suggested that people were more promiscuous and sexually experimental than previously imagined. Although Kinsey's survey methods were later disputed, his study, crammed full of charts, tables, and graphs, gave every appearance of being dry and scientific. Nonetheless, Kinsey's report quickly reached a larger public audience, selling eventually 250,000 copies, placing it on the *New York Times* best-seller list for 27 weeks.

Five years later, in 1953, Kinsey followed up his study of the human male with a report on female sexual behavior that reinforced what was to become a stereotypical image—that many Americans led secret sexual lives. Other evidence of changing attitudes toward sex became evident with the publication in December 1953 of the first issue of Hugh Hefner's *Playboy* magazine, which offered readers revealing photographs of bare-breasted women.

Changes in the 1960s. By the early 1960s, widespread discussion of a sexual revolution had many Americans feeling quite uncomfortable. Methodist bishop Gerald Kennedy of Los Angeles worried that sexual promiscuity had become acceptable. *Time* magazine, observing this "second sexual revolution" (the first having occurred in the 1920s), scolded that the "cult of pop hedonism and phony sexual sophistication" had become prevalent.

But others welcomed this revolution with open arms. The publication of Helen Gurley Brown's *Sex and the Single Girl* in 1962 encouraged sexual experimentation among younger, single women. In this runaway best-seller, Brown urged young women to put aside their feelings of guilt and enjoy sex and the single life. She told her readers

that she had yet to encounter a happy virgin. Lawrence Lipton, author of *The Erotic Revolution: An Affirmative View of the New Morality* (1965), declared that the "old morality" did not fit the new, affluent, urban America.

The popular press, social psychologists, and theologians weighed in to comment on this sexual revolution. In the spring of 1964, *Newsweek* magazine ran a six-page feature story on "The Moral Revolution on the U.S. Campus." What they found was mostly talk and little action. Traditionalists were reassured when the magazine reported that 75 percent of female college students were still virgins. Harvard University sociologist David Riesman, however, insisted that those who thought sexual revolution was "all talk" should realize there had been a real change. Later social science surveys in the late 1960s revealed that the proportion of college females having premarital sex in a dating relationship had increased to 23 percent in 1968. These studies indicated an increased tolerance toward premarital sexual relations, an increased number of sexual partners, and a substantial decline of guilt feelings after the first sexual experience. Social scientists reported that oral contraception ("the pill"), introduced in 1961, had largely removed the fear of pregnancy and feelings of guilt from young teenagers and college coeds, who now increasingly engaged in premarital sex, even without the prospect of marriage from their partners.

Indicative of this change in cultural attitudes toward sexual relations was the Supreme Court's decision to legalize the sale of contraceptives in *Griswold* v. *Connecticut* in 1965. The *Griswold* decision garnered little opposition, either from Catholic bishops or other religious leaders. A new sense of privacy fit well into the new singles' culture that emerged in the postwar period. After World War II, the single working woman became an important feature of economic life. The rapid expansion of the retail and service sector of the postwar economy drew single as well as married women into the work force. In the 1960s, young, unmarried professionals gained enormous discretionary buying power, comprising a $60 billion market for business.

Youth Rebellion and Gay Activism. Coinciding with the emergence of this single, professional culture came the youth rebellion of the 1960s. As college students joined the civil rights and anti-Vietnam War protest movements, they also called for the end to restrictive campus regulations. Students called for the distribution of oral contraceptives at university health services, for coed dorms, for an end to restrictions on visiting hours in dormitories, and for the right to live off campus without being married. Along with antiwar buttons, students wore buttons proclaiming "take it off" and "I'm willing if you are."

Along with cultural radicalism and political protest, the "counterculture" of the late 1960s further challenged traditional sexual mores. The hippie movement attracted attention first in early 1967 with their "Human Be-in" in Golden Gate Park in San Francisco. The guru of this movement, Timothy Leary, a Harvard University research psychologist, urged America's youth to abandon middle-class values for a drug-oriented, sexually free, and antimaterialistic lifestyle. In the summer of 1969, hundreds of thousands of youth gathered near Woodstock, New York, for a three-day rock festival in which they indulged in drugs, nudity, and sexual encounters. This defiance of sexual taboos found its way onto Broadway, where musicals such as *Hair* and *Oh! Calcutta* displayed nudity and explicit sexual language.

While attitudes toward heterosexual relations were changing, so were attitudes toward homosexuality. World War II brought many homosexuals together for the first time as they served in the armed forces. In the 1940s, the first openly gay bars were established in such diverse places as San Jose, California; Denver; Kansas City; Buffalo, New York; and Worcester, Massachusetts. By the 1950s, Boston had more than two dozen gay bars. While homosexuals were subjected to arrest and police raids in the 1950s, the following decade brought homosexuality out into the open. The gay liberation movement traced its beginning to a riot that occurred on June 27, 1969, in New York City, when the police raided a gay bar, the Stonewall Inn in Greenwich Village, and attempted to arrest some patrons. Politically aware gays, under the slogan of "gay power," called for the end of repression of homosexuals.

The sexual revolution was a cultural phenomenon that signaled a radical shift in sexual attitudes and practices that became prevalent among married couples, single heterosexuals, and gays. As a result of this upheaval, many Americans were left uncertain about the future role of the traditional American family and American culture as a whole.

—DONALD T. CRITCHLOW

See Also: *Birth Control; Kinsey, Alfred C.; Nineteen Sixties; Women's Movement.*

BIBLIOGRAPHY: Bell, Robert R., *Premarital Sex in a Changing Society* (Prentice-Hall 1976); Brown, Helen Gurley, *Sex and the Single Girl* (Bernard Geis Assoc. 1962); Christenson, Cornelia V., *Kinsey: A Biography* (Indiana Univ. Press 1971); Degler, Carl, *At Odds: Women and the Family in America from the Revolution to the Present* (Oxford Univ. Press 1980); Friedman, D'Emilio, and Estelle Friedman, *Intimate Matters: A History of Sexuality in America* (Harper & Row 1988); Pomeroy, Wendell B., *Dr. Kinsey and the Institute for Research* (Harper & Row 1972).

■ SHAKERS (UNITED SOCIETY OF BELIEVERS IN CHRIST'S SECOND APPEARING),

millenarian communal sect. The Shakers originated in Manchester, England, under the leadership of Jane and James Wardly. After having a vision that revealed that the sex act, original sin, was the root of all evil and that celibacy was the ideal, Ann Lee led a group of followers to an area near Albany, New York, in 1774. At first, the group was under suspicion because of their English backgrounds, pacifism, and celibacy. But soon they established a community and gained members through missionary efforts. After Lee's death, the community moved to New Lebanon, New York. Leadership passed first to James Whittaker and then in 1787 to Joseph Meacham, who appointed Lucy Wright (1760-1821) as co-leader, which began the parallel lines of male and female leadership. By the 19th century there were 11 Shaker villages with a total of about 2,000 Shakers. The Shaker population reached its peak around 1840 with 4,500 members in 19 communities as far west as Indiana. Shakers lived a communal lifestyle, organized in "families" where male and female members worshiped together, but contact was restricted and living arrangements were fully segregated. Shakers believed that Christ had come again and that God was of a dual nature, male and female—some believed that Ann Lee was the daughter of God. Shakers had a distinctive worship life that regulated behavior and required confessions of sins. Their lively worship services, which included original hymns and dances, attracted audiences. Remembered for their simple, functional furniture, the Shakers were also pioneers in selling garden seeds in packets.

See Also: Lee, Mother Ann; Religion.

BIBLIOGRAPHY: Stein, Stephen J., *The Shaker Experience in America: A History of the United Society of Believers* (Yale Univ. Press 1992).

■ **SHARECROPPING.** *See:* Tenant Farming.

■ **SHARE-OUR-WEALTH,** catchphrase for various populist political movements of the 1930s advocating redistribution of wealth. Share-Our-Wealth clubs created by Sen. Huey P. Long of Louisiana backed higher taxes on the rich and income subsidies for the poor. Dr. Francis Townsend of California advocated senior citizen pensions to help the elderly and stimulate retail sales. The EPIC ("End Poverty in California") campaign, which culminated in writer Upton Sinclair's unsuccessful run for governor of California (1934), and the National Union of Social Justice founded by Rev. Charles Coughlin (1935), which backed Rep. William Lemke of North Dakota for president in 1936, expressed similar beliefs that the Depression would end if the nation's wealth were more fairly divided. While none of the Share-Our-Wealth movements offered a coherent plan for economic recovery and stability, passage of the Social Security Act (1935) and higher taxes on businesses, inherited wealth, and the rich reflect their political influence.

See Also: Coughlin, Charles; Long, Huey P.; New Deal; Sinclair, Upton.

BIBLIOGRAPHY: Brinkley, Alan, *Voices of Protest: Huey Long, Father Coughlin, and the Great Depression* (Knopf 1982).

■ **SHARPSBURG, BATTLE OF.** *See:* Antietam (or Sharpsburg), Battle of.

■ **SHAW, ANNA HOWARD (1847-1919),** reformer, preacher, and doctor. Born in Newcastle-on-Tyne, England, she grew up in a homestead on the Michigan frontier. Later, struggling to sup-

port herself as a substitute preacher, she attended Boston University, where she earned a degree in divinity in 1878. Rejected by the Methodist Episcopal Church because she was a woman, she was finally ordained by the Methodist Protestant Church (1880). She returned to Boston University to study medicine, taking her M.D. in 1887. In 1888 she formed a friendship with suffragist Susan B. Anthony and thereafter devoted herself to lecturing in favor of temperance and woman suffrage. She was vice president (1894-1904) and president (1904-15) of the National American Woman Suffrage Association.

See Also: Anthony, Susan B.; Religion; Temperance Movements; Woman Suffrage Movement; Women in American History; Women's Movement.

■ **SHAW, LEMUEL (1781-1861),** jurist. He was born in Barnstable, Massachusetts, and practiced law in Boston. Shaw drafted the first Boston City charter (1822), which remained the city's form of government until 1913. He served as chief justice of the Massachusetts Supreme Judicial Court (1830-60) and was the father-in-law of Herman Melville, author of *Moby-Dick*.

See Also: Melville, Herman.

■ **SHAW, ROBERT GOULD (1837-63),** Union general. Born in Boston, Massachusetts, Shaw was the son of abolitionists. At the outbreak of the Civil War, he dropped out of Harvard College and joined the Massachusetts militia. In June 1863 Shaw became the commander of the Union 54th Massachusetts Infantry, the first unit of African-American soldiers. He led the regiment in the successful battle on James Island, South Carolina, on July 16, 1863, and in the unsuccessful but heroic attack on Fort Wagner, the main approach to Charleston. Shaw was killed in the attack.

See Also: Civil War.

■ **SHAWN, TED (1891-1972),** dancer and choreographer. A pioneer of interpretive modern dance, Shawn was born in Kansas City, Missouri. With his dancing partner and wife Ruth St. Denis, he cofounded the influential Denishawn dance school (1915). Their style emphasized expressive body movement and rejected the formalized movements of classical ballet. In 1941 Shawn founded the Jacob's Pillow summer dance festival in Becket, Massachusetts.

See Also: *St. Denis, Ruth.*

■ **SHAWNEE,** Algonquian-speaking Indian tribe that played an important role in American history during the late 18th and early 19th centuries. The Shawnees originally lived in the Ohio Valley but dispersed in the late 17th century to form scattered villages in Illinois, Alabama, and Pennsylvania. By 1750 they had reassembled in central and western Ohio, where some assisted the French during the French and Indian War or joined in Pontiac's Rebellion (1763), but most remained tied to the British, trading extensively with colonial merchants from Pennsylvania. They opposed colonial expansion into the Ohio Valley and staunchly supported the British against the Kentuckians during the American Revolution. In the postwar period the Shawnees were leading proponents in the multitribal coalition that fought in defense of Indian lands in Ohio. They participated in both Harmar's (1790) and St. Clair's (1791) defeats, and fought at the Battle of Fallen Timbers (1794), before being forced to cede much of their Ohio homeland at the Treaty of Greenville in 1795.

During the American Revolution some Shawnees fled to Missouri, but the majority remained in Ohio and Indiana where they attempted to live peacefully with the Americans. Led by Black Hoof, most of the Ohio Shawnees welcomed missionaries and Indian agents, but socioeconomic conditions among the tribe deteriorated, and in 1805 Tenskwatawa, the Shawnee Prophet, emerged as the leader of a new religious revitalization movement. By 1809, Tecumseh, the Prophet's older brother, had transformed the religious fervor into a pan-Indian political movement intent upon centralizing Indian political power and preventing the further cession of Indian lands to the Americans. Black Hoof and many other Shawnees opposed Tecumseh, and during the War of 1812 part of the tribe allied with the British, while others fought with the Americans.

During the 1820s and 1830s most of the Ohio Shawnees were also removed to Missouri and Kansas, where they eventually split into three bands. The "Absentee Shawnee" became associated with the Cherokees and Delawares, first moving to Texas, then back to Oklahoma, where they established villages along the Canadian River, east of modern Oklahoma City. Today they maintain a tribal office near the town of Shawnee, Oklahoma.

In 1825, following the government's purchase of Shawnee lands in Missouri, those Shawnees who did not join the Cherokees and Delawares were consolidated on a reservation in eastern Kansas. Some eventually fled to the Absentee Shawnee villages, but the others split into two communities, and in 1854, when the Shawnee reservation in Kansas was allotted, one of these communities sought refuge among the Cherokee in Oklahoma and became known as the "Eastern Shawnees." The remainder of the Shawnees from Kansas joined with a Seneca group on a separate reservation in modern Ottawa County, Oklahoma, and since they supported the Union during the Civil War they were known as the "Loyal Shawnees."

Today these three communities of relatively acculturated Shawnee people remain as federally recognized tribes. Other small communities of Shawnees, while not "officially" recognized by the federal government, still reside in Kansas, Missouri, and Ohio.

—R. David Edmunds

See Also: *Fallen Timbers, Battle of; Greenville, Treaty of; Indians of North America; Tecumseh; Tenskwatawa.*

BIBLIOGRAPHY: Edmunds, R. David, *Tecumseh and the Quest for Indian Leadership* (Little, Brown 1984); Howard, James H., *Shawnee: The Ceremonialism of a Native Indian Tribe and Its Cultural Background* (Ohio Univ. Press 1981).

■ **SHAYS'S REBELLION (1786-87),** one of several violent episodes that occurred as a reaction to the economic depression that struck America in the mid-1780s. This depression resulted in falling commodity and land prices. Farmers who could not pay their debts or taxes were losing their land or being imprisoned for debt. In several states there were violent protests, the best known of which was Shays's Rebellion in Massachusetts in the fall and winter of 1786-87.

In July and August 1786 conventions met to demand relief measures in the eastern counties of Bristol and Middlesex and in the western counties of Worcester, Hampshire, and Berkshire. In August and September armed farmers forcibly closed the courts in five counties to prevent farm foreclosures.

In January and February 1787 about 7,000 militia under the commands of Benjamin Lincoln and William Shepard routed the armed farmers near Springfield, the site of a federal arsenal, at Petersham, and at Stockbridge. Although casualties were light, the insurgents (numbering perhaps 3,000 at their highest), under the leadership of former Continental army officers Daniel Shays, Luke Day, Eli Parsons, and Adam Wheeler, were scattered.

Although the insurgents were defeated, there was sympathy in Massachusetts for their cause and against harsh punishment. In 1787 elections, incumbent governor James Bowdoin was defeated by John Hancock, who, along with the newly elected majority in the General Court, was more sympathetic toward the farmers. Hancock eventually pardoned all of the rebels.

Some historians believe that Shays's Rebellion persuaded many political leaders throughout America that a radical reform of government was required to prevent the country from sinking into anarchy. It gave impetus to the movement for a constitutional convention that eventually led to the Philadelphia Convention in the spring of 1787. Indeed, George Washington wrote to James Madison in November 1786 that "We are fast verging to anarchy and confusion." And in March 1787 he told Madison that he hoped the Philadelphia Convention would "provide radical cures," which is precisely what it did.

—RICHARD LEFFLER

See Also: Constitutional Convention.

BIBLIOGRAPHY: Gross, Robert A., ed., *In Debt to Shays: The Bicentennial of an Agrarian Rebellion* (Univ. Press of Virginia 1993); Gross, Robert A., "White Hats and Hemlocks: Daniel Shays and the Legacy of the Revolution," in Ronald Hoffman and Peter J. Albert, eds., *The Transforming Hand of Revolution: Reconsidering the American Revolution as a Social Movement* (Univ. Press of Virginia 1995); Szatmary, David P., *Shays' Rebellion: The Making of an Agrarian Insurrection* (Univ. of Massachusetts Press 1980).

■ **SHELEKHOV, GRIGORY IVANOVICH (1748-1795),** Russian-American fur merchant. Shelekhov established a fur-trade post on Kodiak Island in August 1784 that was the first permanent European settlement on the Alaskan coast. From this base, the Russians expanded their fur trading to the Alaskan mainland and the Aleutian Islands, establishing additional colonies. Depending on Aleutian Islanders' hunting expertise, the Russians subjugated the coastal native peoples and forced them to aid in the Russians' pursuit of the valuable sea otter and fur seal trade. Shelekhov's firm received a monopoly charter in 1799. Known as the Russian-American Company, the venture endured until the United States' purchase of Alaska from Russia in 1867. Shelekhov, sometimes dubbed the "Russian Columbus," imagined Russian settlement as far south as California. The Russian company did establish Fort Ross, just north of San Francisco Bay in 1812. The Russian settlements in America, intent on pursuing the profitable maritime fur trade, always remained small in population.

See Also: Alaska; Exploration and Discovery.

BIBLIOGRAPHY: Gibson, James R., *Imperial Russia in Frontier America: The Changing Geography of Supply of Russian America, 1784-1867* (Oxford Univ. Press 1976).

■ ***SHELLEY V. KRAEMER* (1948),** one of four U.S. Supreme Court cases that prohibited state or federal court enforcement of restrictive racial real estate covenants. In *Shelley* the Court ruled (6-0) that, while the creation of covenants barring the sale of property to nonwhites is private activity beyond the reach of the courts, judicial enforcement of such covenants is state action and thus banned by the 14th Amendment's guarantees of equal protection of the law.

See Also: Equal Protection; Supreme Court.

■ **SHENANDOAH VALLEY CAMPAIGN (1863),** Civil War campaign in western Virginia in which the army of Confederate Gen. Thomas J. (Stonewall) Jackson repeatedly outmaneuvered three separate Union armies that, combined, totaled more than twice his force. In five weeks in May and June, Jackson's army marched over 350 miles and won five battles, diverting 60,000 Union troops from operations around Richmond,

Virginia, and in Tennessee. With his success, Jackson acquired a reputation for invincibility.

See Also: *Civil War; Jackson, Thomas J. "Stonewall."*

■ **SHERIDAN, PHILIP HENRY (1831-88),** U.S. military leader. A tough, outspoken soldier, Sheridan became the Union's foremost cavalry officer during the Civil War (1861-65). His parents, Irish immigrants, raised Philip and their four other children in the large Roman Catholic community of Somerset, Ohio. Three years after quitting school, Sheridan, 17 years old, entered West Point Military Academy. An infantryman by choice, he was assigned to a cavalry unit in mid-1862. Between October 1862 and January 1863, he distinguished himself in battle at Perryville, Kentucky, and at Murfreesboro, Tennessee, and rose to the rank of major general. At Chattanooga, Tennessee, in November 1863 soldiers under his command charged up Missionary Ridge with such a relentless advance that what was intended to be a diversionary tactic turned into a stunning Union victory. Sheridan was credited with the success of the attack and gained the favorable attention of

Philip H. Sheridan, who graduated from West Point in 1853, commanded the Union's Army of the Shenandoah in the Civil War and served as general in chief of the army from 1883 to 1888.

Gen. Ulysses S. Grant, who brought him east for his 1864 Virginia campaign. Sheridan's cavalry raids on Richmond and the Shenandoah Valley brought him great acclaim and did serious damage to the Confederacy. In the spring of 1865 at Petersburg, Virginia, he was instrumental in forcing the Confederate army under Gen. Robert E. Lee to abandon the city. By cutting off Lee's escape at Appomattox, Sheridan helped make Lee's April 9 surrender inevitable.

After the war Sheridan served briefly as a Reconstruction military governor. In 1868 he campaigned against Indians in Kansas and Indian Territory (now part of Oklahoma), during which he allegedly claimed that "the only good Indians I ever saw were dead." Promoted to lieutenant general in 1869, he conceived the 1876 campaign that resulted in Col. George A. Custer's death at Little Bighorn and the eventual destruction of the Sioux nation. Sheridan reached the pinnacle of his career in 1883 by succeeding William T. Sherman as general in chief of the U.S. Army.

—T. R. Brereton

See Also: *Civil War; Grant, Ulysses Simpson.*
BIBLIOGRAPHY: Hutton, Paul Andrew, *Phil Sheridan and his Army* (Univ. of Nebraska Press 1985); Morris, Roy, *Sheridan: The Life and Wars of General Philip Sheridan* (Crown 1992).

■ **SHERMAN, JAMES SCHOOLCRAFT (1855-1912),** vice president (1909-12) of the United States. He was born outside Utica, New York. Educated at Hamilton College, he practiced law and served as the mayor of Utica (1884-85). In 1887 Sherman was elected to the U.S. House of Representatives as a Republican. He served 10 terms (1887-91 and 1893-1909) before his election as vice president under William Howard Taft in 1908.

See Also: *Vice President of the United States.*

■ **SHERMAN, ROGER (1721-93),** Revolutionary War statesman. A signer of the Declaration of Independence, the Articles of Confederation, and the Constitution, Sherman was born in Newtown, Massachusetts, and settled in New Milford, Connecticut. As a member of the Second Continental Congress he helped draft the Declaration. Perhaps his greatest contribution to American politics, however, was his introduction of the Connecticut

Compromise at the Constitutional Convention, which established a two-house Congress consisting of a House of Representatives and a Senate.

See Also: Connecticut Compromise; Declaration of Independence; Revolution, American.

■ **SHERMAN, WILLIAM TECUMSEH (1820-91),** Civil War general and commander of the Union army in the West (1864-65). Born in Lancaster, Ohio, he was devastated at age nine by the loss of his father. This, along with an undistinguished prewar career (first in the peacetime army and later as a banker), left him low in self-esteem. Sherman failed in his first command in Kentucky in 1861, suffering a clinical depression. Rescued by his wife, Ellen Ewing Sherman, and by fellow officers and his excellent political connections, Sherman's reputation and spirits rose dramatically through his stubborn and effective command of a division at the Battle of Shiloh in April 1862. Shiloh also cemented his bond with Gen. Ulysses S. Grant, whom he served loyally and effectively until March 1864, when Grant moved east to assume overall command of the Union forces and Sherman replaced him in the west.

After a long and conventional campaign against Gen. Joseph E. Johnston's (and later, Gen. John Bell Hood's) Confederates, Sherman's army captured Atlanta on Sept. 2, 1864, a victory that, particularly given the demoralizing stalemate of the eastern armies, proved crucial to the reelection of Pres. Abraham Lincoln that fall. Somewhat against the wishes of Grant and Lincoln, after sending Gen. George M. Thomas northward with a blocking force to stop Hood's advance, Sherman cut his lines of communication and embarked on his famous "March to the Sea," a giant raid against Southern civilians and supplies, which he recognized as a war of terror meant to demoralize the Confederacy. Sherman was able to tap his considerable martial fury in the sinister and effective propaganda effort that accompanied his march to Savannah, which fell on December 21, and his subsequent and even more destructive campaign up through the Carolinas as the war ground to a close.

After the war Sherman planned the destruction of the Plains Indians and later served as commanding general of the army, a largely ceremonial post, while he pursued fame, attacked the

Renowned for his exploits in the South during the Civil War, Sherman continued serving and became commander of the army (1869-83).

reputations of other generals in the press, wrote his insightful (if self-serving) memoirs, refused to run for president on the Republican ticket, and wooed a variety of elegant women.

—Michael Fellman

See Also: Civil War; Grant, Ulysses Simpson; Shiloh, Battle of.

BIBLIOGRAPHY: Fellman, Michael, *Citizen Sherman: A Life of William Tecumseh Sherman* (Random House 1995); Lewis, Lloyd, *Sherman: Fighting Prophet* (Harcourt, Brace 1932); Sherman, William T., *Memoirs* (Appleton 1875).

■ **SHERMAN ANTITRUST ACT (1890),** legislation passed during Pres. Benjamin Harrison's administration to prevent restraint of trade. The law outlawed trusts and any other contracts, combinations, or conspiracies in restraint of trade, but it failed to define its terms clearly and thus allowed the Supreme Court to interpret it in ways sympathetic to big business. Small companies could not form pools under this law, but it allowed corporate mergers and consolidation and was even used to bring suit against labor unions. The law's symbolic message thus outweighed its practical application.

See Also: Antitrust Cases; Trusts.

■ **SHERMAN SILVER PURCHASE ACT (1890),** legislation that required the Treasury Department to purchase 4.5 million ounces of silver each month and issue payment in Treasury notes redeemable in silver or gold. This act set farmers seeking inflation and silver miners against eastern businessmen but had little effect on the economy.

See Also: Free Silver.

■ **SHIKELLAMY (?-1748),** Oneida leader. Born a Cayuga, Shikellamy was adopted into the Oneida tribe of the Iroquois Confederacy and picked to become the representative for Iroquois holdings in Pennsylvania. In 1736, he arranged for the Iroquois to become responsible for the Indians in Pennsylvania. In 1737, Shikellamy worked in collaboration with Pennsylvania colonial authorities in dispossessing the Delaware Indians.

See Also: Indians of North America.

■ **SHILOH, BATTLE OF (1862),** Civil War engagement, also known as Pittsburg Landing, in which Confederate Gen. Albert Sidney Johnston's army moved north from Corinth, Mississippi, to Pittsburg Landing, on the Tennessee River, to confront the army of Union Gen. Ulysses S. Grant before reinforcements arrived from Nashville. On April 6, a Confederate advance drove back two miles the Union troops, many of whom were untested. The following day, Grant, reinforced by the divisions of Gens. Don Carlos Buell and Lew Wallace, retook the lost ground and forced the Confederates, now under Gen. P.G.T. Beauregard (Johnston had been killed) to retreat as far as Corinth, a key rail center. Battle losses of both sides were extremely heavy.

See Also: Beauregard, Pierre Gustave Toutant; Civil War; Grant, Ulysses Simpson.

■ **SHIPBUILDING,** vital industry that developed in colonial times. It was fostered by the Navigation Act of 1660 and prospered in New England because of abundant, high-quality timber, skilled shipbuilders, low building costs (20 to 50 percent below European costs), and ready foreign markets. The first schooner ever was built at Gloucester, Massachusetts, in 1713. By 1760, one-third of the total British tonnage was built in the colonies, and ships were America's chief manufacture for export. American-made clipper ships (1830-60) set numerous long-distance speed records. U.S. shipbuilding flourished as long as wooden vessels prevailed on the seas, but Americans were reluctant to shift to steam, and the development of the metal steamship put British shipbuilders at an advantage. The U.S. proportion of trade-vessel tonnage slipped from 90 percent in 1821 to 71 percent by 1860. Steamboats appeared on American rivers after Robert Fulton built the first successful one in 1807. By 1900, the shipbuilding industry was healthy owing to the huge growth of internal commerce, although American vessels only carried 9.3 percent of U.S. foreign-trade goods. Production boomed during World War I and again after the Depression during World War II, but by the 1960s the American shipbuilding industry was in decline.

■ **SHIPPING,** the trade in goods by ships at sea, a central aspect of the American economy from the colonial period to the present. Colonial merchants earned great fortunes from shipping slaves, manufactured goods, raw materials, and commodities produced on slave plantations. The transatlantic trade had a profound multiplier effect, giving rise to New York, Boston, Philadelphia, and Charleston, the four original American seaports and centers of colonial society. In the 1760s and 1770s colonials rebelled, in part, against restricted trade that subordinated their needs to those of the mother country. The period from 1790 to 1807 marked an international shipping boom and reinforced the importance of the Atlantic trading system to the American national economy. Controversies over the rights of neutrals, however, drove the United States to establish embargoes restricting trade between 1807 and 1815.

The establishment of the first transatlantic steamship service in 1838 strengthened the shipping industry. In the 1870s the compound engine allowed steamships to operate more cheaply and eventually to carry heavier and more costly cargoes faster and farther. The 1920s saw the oil tanker become widespread as it sustained the growing petroleum industry. During the postwar years, shipping has made possible the growth of multinational corporations and increased the interconnectedness of once distant markets.

See Also: Industrial Revolution.

BIBLIOGRAPHY: Bauer, K. Jack, *A Maritime History of the United States: The Role of America's Seas and Waterways* (Univ. of South Carolina Press 1988); Shepherd, James F., and Gary H. Walton, *Shipping, Maritime Trade, and the Economic Development of Colonial North America* (Cambridge Univ. Press 1972).

■ **SHIRAS, GEORGE, JR. (1832-1924),** associate justice of the U.S. Supreme Court (1892-1903). A Pittsburgh, Pennsylvania, native, Shiras was the swing vote in *Pollock v. Farmers Loan and Trust Company* (1895), the decision that found the federal income tax unconstitutional.

See Also: Supreme Court.

■ **SHIRLEY, WILLIAM (1694-1771),** colonial governor of Massachusetts (1741-56). Born in Sussex, England, Shirley decided to immigrate to Massachusetts and, in 1731, acquired a post as Admiralty Court judge in Boston. As an imperialist, he regularly came into conflict with Gov. Jonathan Belcher over cases involving the Navigation Acts, and when Belcher was removed in 1741, Shirley was appointed his replacement. In 1745 Shirley advocated and launched Britain's only successful maneuver of King George's War (1740-48), the attack on the French fortress at Louisbourg, Cape Breton Island. When his inadequacies as a military leader became evident in the opening hostilities of the Seven Years' War, Shirley was himself replaced (1756).

■ **SHOCKLEY, WILLIAM (1910-89),** physicist. Born in London, England, Shockley went to Bell Telephone Laboratories in 1936 and experimented with solid-state amplifiers. In 1948, his group at Bell invented the transistor, a tiny but highly efficient replacement for vacuum tubes in electrical devices, including radios, hearing aids, and computers. Shockley shared a Nobel Prize in Physics with his collaborators in 1956, became president of the Shockley Transistor Corporation in 1958, and began teaching at Stanford. His adamant belief in dysgenics led him to be criticized for conduct unbecoming a Nobel laureate.

See Also: Science.

■ **SHORT STORY,** a literary genre that emerged in the United States in the early 19th century. Short prose fiction had existed for centuries prior to 1783, the year in which the American Revolution ended and the nation's first short story writer, Washington Irving, was born. Yet Irving and, in the generation after him, Nathaniel Hawthorne and Edgar Allan Poe were to fashion a kind of literature distinct from earlier short narratives in creating the American short story. In 1819, Irving published *The Sketch Book of Geoffrey Crayon, Gent.*, which included the short stories "Rip Van Winkle" and "The Legend of Sleepy Hollow." More than two decades later, in an 1842 review of a new edition of Hawthorne's *Twice-Told Tales*, which had first appeared in 1837, Poe suggested that the "skilful literary artist" composes a "prose tale" intending "a certain unique or single effect to be wrought out" of it. The work of Irving, Hawthorne, and Poe exhibited an incipient realism that later writers would further develop in their efforts to achieve verisimilitude in the short story. The second half of the 19th century saw such authors as Herman Melville, in *The Piazza Tales* (1856), Mark Twain, in *The Celebrated Jumping Frog of Calaveras County, and Other Sketches* (1867), and Ambrose Bierce, in *Tales of Soldiers and Civilians* (1891), contribute to the genre's growth. In the 1890s, Stephen Crane produced some of the nation's greatest short prose, including the title piece in *The Open Boat and Other Stories* (1898), and in the early 20th century, the prolific William Sydney Porter, under the pseudonym O. Henry, popularized the genre as no one else until then had. The publication in 1919 of Sherwood Anderson's short story collection, *Winesburg, Ohio*, has conventionally been thought to have revivified the genre creatively, and indeed such writers as William Faulkner, F. Scott Fitzgerald, Ernest Hemingway, Katherine

Anne Porter, and John Steinbeck added much to the form in the following decades. By the late 20th century, the genre's importance in American literature has spawned an extensive academic network of specialized study devoted to the short story.

See Also: *Crane, Stephen; Faulkner, William Cuthbert; Fitzgerald, F. Scott; Hawthorne, Nathaniel; Hemingway, Ernest Miller; Irving, Washington; Poe, Edgar Allan; Steinbeck, John; Twain, Mark.*

BIBLIOGRAPHY: May, Charles E., ed., *Short Story Theories* (Ohio Univ. Press 1976).

■ **SHOSHONI INDIANS.** *See:* *Great Basin and Rocky Mountain Indians.*

■ **SHOWBOATS,** floating theaters that plied the Ohio and Mississippi rivers from the 1830s until the early 20th century. In the late 1800s elegant showboats presented circuses, dramas, and minstrel and variety shows.

See Also: *Circuses; Minstrel Shows.*

■ **SICILY CAMPAIGN (1943),** invasion that marked the Allies' reentry into Western Europe in World War II. Following the conquest of North Africa, Anglo-American forces landed at several points on Sicily's south and east coasts, supported by drops from two airborne divisions, on July 10. By that evening all the beachheads were secure. Over the next month, U.S. Gen. George S. Patton's Seventh Army and Britain's Field Marshal Bernard Montgomery's Eighth Army cleared the island, Patton's Second Division reaching Messina on August 17. Although marred by disputes between British and American commanders, the Allied campaign led to the resignation of the Italian fascist premier, Benito Mussolini, on July 25.

See Also: *Patton, George Smith, Jr.; World War II.*

■ **SIERRA NEVADA MOUNTAINS,** granite mountains extending from south-central California some 400 miles northward to Oregon. They contain the highest peak in the coterminous United States: Mt. Whitney (14,495 feet). The Sierra Nevadas are the southern extension of the Cascade Mountains and separate the wet Pacific Coast from the arid interior of the Great Basin.

The mountains trap moisture drifting eastward from the Pacific Ocean and thus remain quite wet year round. Long deep canyons drain the western slope of the mountains, watering the rich agricultural lands of California's Central Valley. In the 19th century westward settlers passed over the Sierra Nevadas at what is now called Donner Pass, the site of one of the best-known tragedies of westward migration. Since World War II hundreds of motels, hotels, and resorts have been established in the mountains, especially near Reno, Nevada, and Lake Tahoe, California, to cater to the tourist trade in skiing and outdoor activities.

See Also: *Donner Party.*

■ **SIGOURNEY, LYDIA HOWARD HUNTLY (1791-1865),** author, nicknamed the "Sweet Singer of Hartford." She was born in Norwich, Connecticut. After a brief career as a schoolteacher, she became one of the first successful American female writers. She wrote numerous poems and short works of poetic prose, published in newspapers and magazines and then collected in books, such as *Moral Pieces, in Prose and Verse* (1815) and *Traits of the Aborigines of America* (1922). Her autobiography is titled *Letters of Life* (1866).

See Also: *Women in American History.*

■ **SILVER,** metal that was the center of a 19th-century western mining industry and a national monetary debate. Visions of silver led Spanish explorers to the Southwest in the 16th century, but silver mining did not begin on a large scale until 1859, with the opening of the Comstock Lode in Virginia City, Nevada. Other western boom towns such as Leadville, Colorado, flourished as a result of silver mining, encouraging western settlement and the expansion of railroads. Production in the United States rose from $2 million in 1861 to $38 million in 1880, and reached a height of $82 million in 1892. This value was intimately tied to how much silver the government was willing to coin. The Coinage Act of 1792 provided for the legal coinage of silver, but a law in 1873 outlawed it. Silver mining interests and farmers who wanted the free coinage of silver argued against eastern financiers and those who believed currency should be backed only by gold. They compromised in the Sherman Silver Purchase Act of 1890, but its repeal in 1893 and the Currency

Act of 1900 broke the back of the silver mining industry and ended all coinage of silver. The Silver Purchase Act of 1934 and the Silver Act of 1963 revived the issues, although much less controversially.

See Also: Comstock Lode; Mining Rushes.

■ **SIMMS, WILLIAM GILMORE (1806-70),** novelist and historian. Simms was born in Charleston, South Carolina. He wrote in a variety of genres but was best known for his works of historical fiction. Simms traveled as a young man among the Creek, Choctaw, and Cherokee nations and often depicted Indians in his novels, such as *The Yemassee* (1835). He also set seven novels in the Revolutionary War—era south. His historical works include *Slavery in America* (1838) and *A History of South Carolina* (1840).

■ **SIMON, NEIL (1927-),** prolific comic playwright. Born in New York City, Simon wrote for several television comedians, notably Sid Caesar (1956-57), before turning to Broadway with almost annual success. Many of his joke-filled hits depicting life in New York—including *Barefoot in the Park* (1963), *The Odd Couple* (1965), and *Brighton Beach Memoirs* (1983)—were subsequently made into successful films.

■ **SIMPSON, ORENTHAL JAMES ("O.J.") (1947-),** athlete, sportscaster, and actor. Born in San Francisco, Simpson was an outstanding football running back. After stellar play at the University of Southern California that won him the Heisman Trophy, Simpson played professionally, first for the Buffalo Bills and then for his hometown San Francisco 49ers, setting numerous running and scoring records. His involvement in the 1994 murder of his ex-wife and her friend, however, has overshadowed his sports fame.

See Also: African Americans; Sports.

■ **SINATRA, FRANK (1915-98),** singer and actor. Born in Hoboken, New Jersey, he became a teen idol in the 1940s with the Harry James and Tommy Dorsey bands and later as a soloist. He became a brilliant and best-selling interpreter of jazz-tinged popular songs by the 1950s but often described himself as a saloon singer. He has also starred in many films, winning an Academy Award for his performance in *From Here to Eternity* (1953).

■ **SINCLAIR, UPTON (1878-1968),** writer and political activist. Sinclair was born in Baltimore, Maryland, and attended New York's City College, graduating in 1897. He unsuccessfully ran as a Socialist for a New Jersey seat in the U.S. House of Representatives in 1906, the same year his best-known novel, *The Jungle*, was published. *The Jungle* won vast attention for its indictment of the meat-packing industry in Chicago and garnered support for the passage of the Pure Food and Drug Act the same year. Sinclair moved to California and ran, again as a Socialist and again unsuccessfully, for the U.S. House in 1920, for the Senate in 1922, and for governor of California in 1926 and 1930. In 1934 he won the Democratic nomination for governor and, running on a platform promising to end poverty, was narrowly defeated. Sinclair also founded the California chapter of the American Civil Liberties Union. Throughout the years of his political activity, Sinclair continued to write novels. In the 1940s he began an 11-volume series about the character Lanny Budd that included *World's End* (1940) and the Pulitzer Prize–winning *Dragon's Teeth* (1942).

See Also: Meat Inspection Act; Novel; Pure Food and Drug Act.

■ **SIOUX.** The Sioux Indians refer to themselves as *Ocheti Sakowin* ("seven council fires") or by a variation of the term *dahkota* ("alliance of friends"). The word "Sioux" is a French corruption of a derogatory Ojibwa name meaning "snakes" or "enemy." From their homeland near the headwaters of the Mississippi, the Sioux were pushed west in the 16th century by the Ojibwa, armed by French traders. The three principal divisions of the Sioux settled in different areas: the Dakotas (or Santees) on the Minnesota River, in what is today southern Minnesota; the Nakotas (or Yanktons) along the Missouri, near the present Nebraska–South Dakota border; and the Lakotas (or Tetons—including the noted bands known as the Brulé, the Hunkpapa, and the Oglala) in the Badlands and Black Hills of South Dakota.

The Santees and Yanktons, making up about half the Sioux, were sedentary village farmers and had a long history of amicable relations with the French and the Americans, who nevertheless in the early 19th century pressed them to cede most of their lands. By 1860 they were confined to a series of small reservations. Corrupt administration led to starvation, and in 1862 there was an uprising among the Santees in which more than 700 whites and an uncounted number of Indians died. After a brutal campaign of reprisal, American authorities hanged 38 Santee warriors in the town of Mankato; it was the largest mass execution in American history. Most of the Santees were assigned to reservations in Nebraska and the Dakotas, and they avoided participation in the later wars between the Tetons and the federal government. By the early 20th century most Yanktons and Santees had acquired individual land allotments and American citizenship.

Most historical attention has been focused on the militant Tetons, who moved to the northern plains, adopted the horse, and became expert buffalo hunters and mounted warriors. They fought wars of expansion against neighboring tribes and in turn defended their hard-won territory from the expanding Americans. Their first official connection with the United States was the Treaty of Fort Laramie (1851), in which they agreed not to disturb American traffic on the Overland Trail. Major conflict did not break out until the mid-1860s, when the federal government developed the Bozeman Trail through Teton territory to the mining district of Montana and sought to defend that trail with a string of forts. Led by the Oglala war leader Red Cloud, the Tetons fought the Americans to a draw and in the second Treaty of Fort Laramie (1868) won the privilege to hunt in the western country that would later become Montana and Wyoming, as well as a huge reservation in the western half of present South Dakota, including the Black Hills, which the Tetons considered their most sacred site.

In 1874 gold was discovered in the Black Hills and miners rushed into the region, angering the Tetons. Fearing trouble, the next year the army demanded that all the Tetons remain on their reservations, but militant leaders such as Sitting Bull and Crazy Horse refused to bring in their followers, who were hunting buffalo to the west. The campaign to round up the Tetons in 1876 included the overwhelming Indian victory against Lt. Col. George Armstrong Custer and the Seventh Cavalry at the Little Bighorn River in June of 1876 but ended with the defeat of the Sioux. Although Sitting Bull and Crazy Horse and their supporters remained at large for a few more years, eventually they surrendered. The federal government forced the tribe to cede the Black Hills, and the Tetons were ensconced on several barren reservations. In the late 1880s many of the people turned to the Ghost Dance religion, and the attempt by Indian agents and the army to suppress this movement led to the tragic Wounded Knee Massacre in 1890. In contrast to success of the Santees and Yanktons, the Tetons found it difficult to make the transition from hunting to reservation life.

The Tetons have never ceased to agitate for the return of the Black Hills. Finally, in *United States* v. *Sioux Nation* (1980) the Supreme Court recognized the legitimacy of their claim, although the decision authorized a monetary settlement that the tribe refused. Today more than 100,000 enrolled members of the three principal divisions of the Sioux live on reservations in North and South Dakota, Nebraska, and Minnesota.

—JOHN MACK FARAGHER

See Also: *Crazy Horse; Fort Laramie Treaties; Ghost Dance; Indian Policy; Indians of North America; Little Bighorn, Battle of; Red Cloud; Sitting Bull; United States* v. *Sioux Nation; Wounded Knee Massacre.*

BIBLIOGRAPHY: Hoover, Herbert T., *The Sioux and Other Native American Cultures of the Dakotas* (Greenwood Press 1993); Meyer, Roy W., *History of the Santee Sioux* (Univ. of Nebraska Press 1968); Utley, Robert, *The Last Days of the Sioux Nation* (Yale Univ. Press 1963).

■ **SIT-INS,** form of protest in which demonstrators physically occupy a space. In the 1930s automobile workers seeking better working conditions and recognition of their union sat-in at their plants in Detroit. Sit-ins were first employed in the struggle for civil rights by the Congress of Racial Equality (CORE) in the 1940s. Then, on Feb. 1, 1960, four college students began a sit-in at the Woolworth's lunch counter in Greensboro, North Carolina, in an attempt to desegregate the eating place. Without any experience or organizational assistance, this small protest cascaded over the next several months into dozens of similar sit-ins throughout the South and even into Ohio. Although they faced harassment and violence, the protesters remained steadfastly dedicated to the principles of nonviolence. Beginning in April 1960, many targeted restaurants, hotels, and theaters began to offer integrated services. The student leadership of these movements gravitated together to form the Student Nonviolent Coordinating Committee (SNCC). Subsequently sit-ins were used by protesters for other causes, as in the student protests of the late 1960s, when school administrative offices were often occupied.

See Also: Civil Rights Movement; Congress of Racial Equality (CORE); Student Nonviolent Coordinating Committee (SNCC).

■ **SITTING BULL (c. 1834-90),** Sioux Indian leader. Known also by his Sioux name, Tatanka Iyotake, Sitting Bull was born near the Grand

Sitting Bull was a leader of the Sioux at the Battle of the Little Bighorn, where Lt. Col. George Armstrong Custer died and the Seventh Cavalry was destroyed.

River, South Dakota. Early in life, he earned a reputation as a courageous warrior and skillful leader in battle. During the 1860s he first participated in skirmishes with U.S. forces, developing an even greater enmity toward whites. Through these experiences, Sitting Bull, a resolute protector of Sioux lands and traditions, became a respected and influential political and military leader.

Angered by white mining in the Black Hills, the Sioux, led by Sitting Bull, organized a military resistance in 1875. The U.S. Army sent Lt. Col. George A. Custer to launch a campaign against the Indian forces, which included Sioux, Cheyenne, and Arapaho. Underestimating the size of their encampment (approximately 11,000), Custer, with only 264 troops, attacked at the Little Bighorn in southern Montana. Under the leadership of Sitting Bull, Crazy Horse, and Rain-in-the-Face, the Indians routed Custer and his men on June 25 and 26, 1876.

Sitting Bull fled to Canada, only to return and, facing starvation, surrender to U.S. troops in 1881. He was sent to the Standing Rock reservation, where he continued to urge the Sioux to resist giving up their land. In 1885, he traveled with Buffalo Bill Cody's Wild West Show then returned to his reservation home. During the Ghost Dance crisis in 1890, he was killed by Sioux reservation police attempting to arrest him on orders from the Indian agent. Sitting Bull was a practical leader who fought against enormous odds to defend Sioux lands and traditional values and customs.

See Also: Custer, George Armstrong; Frontier in American History; Indians of North America; Little Bighorn, Battle of; Sioux.

BIBLIOGRAPHY: Utley, Robert M., *The Lance and the Shield: The Life and Times of Sitting Bull* (John Macrae/Henry Holt 1993).

■ **SKENANDOA (?-1816),** Oneida leader. Skenandoa supported the English during the French and Indian War and the American colonists during the American Revolution, providing the patriots with warriors and information on pro-British Iroquois activity. His support did not help the Onedia cause. Although they were promised protection after the war, the Oneidas were among the first Indian groups to experience the effects of American expansion in the 1780s and 1790s.

See Also: Indians of North America.

■ **SKIDMORE, OWINGS, AND MERRILL,** prominent architectural firm formed in 1939 as a partnership between Louis Skidmore (1897-1962), Alexander Owings (1903-), and John Ogden Merrill (1896-1975). In 1942 the firm planned the town of Oak Ridge, Tennessee, for the U.S. government's Manhattan Project. The firm is best known for large office buildings, such as the landmark Lever House in New York City (1952), and campuses, such as the U.S. Air Force Academy in Colorado Springs, Colorado (1962).

See Also: Architecture.

■ **SKINNER, B. F. (1904-90),** behavioral psychologist. Born in Susquehanna, Pennsylvania, Skinner graduated from Hamilton College with a degree in English. His interest in literature turned into an even greater fascination with human behavior, and he enrolled in graduate school in psychology at Harvard University, graduating in 1931. Skinner was most interested in experimental work, and he developed the "Skinner box," in which animals performed simple tasks, as an alternative research strategy to the mazes commonly used to study animal behavior. Skinner remained at Harvard until 1936, when he began teaching at the University of Minnesota. During World War II Skinner began working with pigeons and gained a government contract to develop homing pigeons that could guide missiles. In 1948 Skinner wrote the controversial novel *Walden Two*, about a community based on behaviorist theories. His scientific writings include the textbook *Science and Human Behavior* (1953), *Schedules of Reinforcement* (1957), *Verbal Behavior* (1957), and *About Behaviorism* (1974).

■ **SKINNER, CONSTANCE LINDSAY (1877-1939),** writer and historian. She was born in Quesnel, British Columbia, and raised at a frontier trading post. Like her friend Fredrick Jackson Turner, she believed that the frontier played a vital role in the formation of America's national identity. She wrote excellent children's books and poetry about frontier life, such as *Songs of the Shore Dwellers* (1930), but her scholarly works, including *Pioneers of the Old Southwest* (1919) and *Adventures of Oregon* (1920), are generally considered weak.

See Also: Turner, Fredrick Jackson; Women in America History.

■ **SKYSCRAPERS,** modern buildings of great heights, a technological achievement in architecture. In the 1880s architects in Chicago pioneered the use of an iron or steel skeleton to frame buildings. Several of the architects who made up the Chicago School, such as Daniel H. Burnham and Louis Sullivan, originally worked for engineer William Le Baron Jenney, who designed the Home Insurance Company Building in Chicago in 1884. Although the new buildings were as little as eight stories high, they towered over their neighbors. Elevators, electricity, and other modern technologies allowed for efficient use of the increased interior spaces. The ability to rent office, and later residential, space on multiple levels made urban land lots more valuable. Most early skyscrapers were ornamented, particularly at ground level and at their rooflines and with ornate entrances and windows. In the 1920s and 1930s, architects began to narrow the top segments of buildings, letting more light reach the street level, and resulting in New York City's distinctive skyline, characterized by such buildings as William Van Alen's Chrysler Building (1930) and Shreve, Lamb, and Harmon's Empire State Building (1931). After World War II, architects designed in the modernist style, which stressed the visible expression of construction and function. This style led to buildings such as Lever House by Skidmore, Owings, and Merrill (1949-52), and the Seagram Building by Ludwig Mies van der Rohe with Philip Johnson (1958), which used austere walls of glass and metal to cover the steel skeleton.

See Also: Architecture; Burnham, Daniel; Jenney, William Le Baron; Johnson, Philip Courtelyou; Mies van der Rohe, Ludwig; Skidmore, Owings, and Merrill; Sullivan, Louis.

BIBLIOGRAPHY: Bluestone, Daniel, *Constructing Chicago* (Yale Univ. Press 1991); Goldberger, Paul, *The Skyscraper* (Knopf 1981); Landau, Sarah Bradford, and Carl W. Condit, *Rise of the New York Skyscraper, 1865-1913* (Yale Univ. Press 1996).

■ **SLATER, SAMUEL (1768-1835),** manufacturer, founder of the American cotton-spinning industry. Born in Belper, England, Slater was apprenticed in 1783 to Jedidiah Strutt, who, with partner Richard Arkwright, developed cotton manufacturing machinery. Slater demonstrated unusual aptitude and grew attracted to the opportunities for textiles in America. He familiarized himself thoroughly with English cotton machinery, learned all aspects of the business, and left for America in 1789. Since the British government forbade the export of textile machinery and the emigration of textile workers, Slater memorized blueprints and traveled in disguise as a farm laborer. After a stint working for New York Manufacturing Company, he met Moses Brown in Providence, Rhode Island, and agreed to reproduce Arkwright's machinery for Almy & Brown in 1790. The next year they opened the country's first cotton-spinning mill in Pawtucket, Rhode Island. As Almy, Brown, & Slater they built a bigger factory in 1793. Slater formed Samuel Slater & Co. in 1798 to manufacture his own machinery, opened his first plant near Pawtucket (1799), and added spinning mills in Smithfield (later Slaterville), Rhode Island (1806); East Webster, Massachusetts (1812); and Amoskeg Falls, New Hampshire. Slater imported the technical knowledge that enabled the country to mechanize and train machinists, managers, and skilled operatives who helped transform manufacturing methods and speed the industrial revolution.

See Also: Industrial Revolution; Textile Industry.
BIBLIOGRAPHY: Tucker, Barbara M., *Samuel Slater and the Origins of the American Textile Industry, 1790-1860* (Cornell Univ. Press 1984).

■ **SLAUGHTERHOUSE CASES (1873),** U.S. Supreme Court cases in which the Court first interpreted the 14th Amendment. In 1869 Louisiana had enacted a law incorporating the Crescent City Live Stock Landing and Slaughterhouse Company and awarding the new concern a monopoly over the New Orleans slaughterhouse industry. Their economic lives at stake, a group of local independent butchers sued, claiming that the monopoly was a violation of their 14th Amendment right not to be deprived of their "privileges or immunities" as citizens without "due process of law." By a slim margin (5-4), the Court rejected the claims of the independent butchers. The opinion, delivered by Justice Samuel Miller, held that the protections guaranteed by the 14th Amendment, in particular that of due process, were intended to apply to recently freed slaves and did not extend to questions of economic regulation, such as those at

issue in this case. Among the dissenters were Justices Stephen Field and Joseph Bradley, who argued for a broader definition of due process. While the immediate effect of the decision was to narrow the scope of the 14th Amendment, the dissents of Justices Field and Bradley anticipated in large measure the future direction of the Court. Over the next 20 years a broader, or "substantive," reading of the 14th Amendment's due process protections gradually supplanted Justice Miller's earlier narrow construction.

See Also: Due Process of Law.

■ **SLAVE CODES,** body of ordinances enacted from the late 17th century until the early 19th century. Their purpose was to control and punish enslaved blacks. An evolving body of law, the slave codes varied from state to state and were often the product of reactions to slave insurrections.

See Also: Slavery.

■ **SLAVE REVOLTS,** violent resistance to slavery. Africans and later African Americans resisted their enslavement throughout their centuries of subjugation yet no slave revolt was ever implemented that fundamentally jeopardized the institution's viability in America. As early as 1526, long before English settlement in North America, a short-lived Spanish colony near present-day Charleston, South Carolina, was plagued with problems including a rebellion by their African slaves. Slave resistance, however, was fairly sparse in 17th-century British North America because the slave presence in the colonies was very small. As their population grew after 1680 in colonies such as Virginia, Maryland, South Carolina, New York, New Jersey, and Massachusetts, so also did the incidence of rebellion. Many of these Africans commonly resisted their predicament by running away in groups—often along tribal lines—and attempting to re-create African communities in the wilderness. But a handful actually plotted to rise up directly against their white overlords and kill them. Such alarming conspiracies were uncovered in South Carolina in the early 1710s and in New York City in 1712. As the number of Africans in colonial America grew dramatically between 1700 and 1740, further plots followed. In South Carolina where slaves outnumbered free whites 2:1 by the 1730s, more

Nat Turner, the leader of the largest and most violent slave revolt in American history, was captured on Oct. 30, 1831. After confessing his role in the revolt, he was hanged along with 20 other slaves.

than 100 slaves, many from Angola, raided a small armory at Stono in September 1739 and seized weapons but were soon subdued by the militia. In spring 1741 in New York City, a plot to fire the city and aid the Spanish was discovered. After a lengthy trial, 31 slaves were burned or hanged, along with 4 whites. While innumerable incidences of petty resistance also occurred during this era, the swift and brutal retribution of the slaveholders and their constant vigilance prevented any of these actions from threatening their control over their colonies.

The dislocations during the era of the American Revolution offered unprecedented opportunities for African Americans to act against their enslavement. Well over 50,000 slaves in the South alone ran away from their owners over the course of the war. Powerful planters in the Deep South colonies of Georgia and South Carolina where slaves greatly outnumbered whites were also very cautious about supporting the patriot cause initially for fear that their slaves would rebel once hostilities broke out.

19th-Century Revolts. But slavery would grow enormously in the United States after its independence, especially after the invention of the cotton gin, and this paradox would fuel mounting discontent among the slaves. The period from the 1790s through the early 1830s embodied some of the most turbulent decades in the history of American slavery and witnessed the most organized and widest challenges to the institution. By August 1800, an enslaved blacksmith in Richmond, Virginia, named Gabriel had been orchestrating a slave revolt for many months. Gabriel and his associates rallied perhaps several hundred slaves over a number of counties to descend upon Richmond late on the night of August 31, but a torrential storm that afternoon washed out bridges and roads, making mobilization impossible and soon the rebels were discovered and stopped by the militia. Ensuing trials led to the execution of at least 35 rebels. In Charleston, South Carolina, in 1822, Denmark Vesey, a free black carpenter, labored secretly for perhaps as long as five years with an inner circle of conspirators to raise a slave revolt in the town. By early June 1822, the leaders had successfully recruited many slaves on the large rice plantations nearby. But as happened with so many American slave conspiracies, the plot was revealed by a slave to authorities at the last moment, troops were raised, and the local jail was soon swollen with the arrested. Once again many were hanged, but ripples of resistance persisted in the South Carolina low country for years to come.

Vesey may well have inspired a free black man, David Walker, who had lived for some time in Charleston before settling in Boston by 1825. Walker like Vesey was an ardent republican who believed the Bible proclaimed an essential equality among all humans. In late 1829, he completed a passionate booklet entitled *Appeal . . . to the Colored Citizens of the World* that indicted American slaveholders and summoned the slaves to resist. With the help of sailors, he distributed the booklet covertly in several Southern ports, hoping that it would then be carried into the surrounding countryside and rally the multitude of slaves there. Once alarmed southern authorities learned of its circulation, they quickly recovered most of the copies.

Walker terrified the white South with his bold calls for slave empowerment, but no one represented black rebellion as dramatically as Nat Turner. A charismatic slave preacher admired by both blacks and whites in Southampton County, Virginia, Turner concluded by the late 1820s that God had designated him to lead a conflagration against slavery. Possibly in league with slaves in neighboring counties of Virginia and North Carolina, Turner and a cohort of slaves planned to strike against local whites very early on Aug. 22, 1831, and recruit further rebels as they marched. By daybreak, they had raised close to 50 slaves and killed as many whites. Alarms throughout the county had been signaled, however, and the rebels soon found their passage blocked at all routes. While all the key participants were

hanged and no further uprisings occurred, Nat Turner embodied for the popular imagination over the balance of the antebellum era the reality of slaves' willingness to revolt.

Yet, in all the years following 1831 to the Civil War (1861-65), no insurrection or conspiracy on the scale of Gabriel, Vesey, or Turner would surface again. By no means did this indicate that hatred for slavery and the willingness to resist it had faded among African Americans or that they failed to marshal any further actions against it. But the opportunities for the slaves to orchestrate an attack truly capable of threatening the viability of slavery in the South were very rare after 1800 and virtually nonexistent after 1831. Slaveholders throughout the South augmented their already vaunted vigilance and everywhere maintained regular patrols and militias. Despite a black demographic predominance in some areas of the antebellum South such as the Carolina low country and the Black Belt of Alabama, Mississippi, and Louisiana, whites usually outnumbered blacks, and this fact, coupled with their weapons, gave them an overwhelming advantage against any revolt. Demographic, geographic, and military realities made the organizing of slave rebellion in America extremely difficult and its execution if realized likely suicidal. Localized resistance against slavery by individuals and groups was always being taken, but such very restricted actions were to slaveholders only the unavoidable irritants of managing an otherwise usually profitable labor force. They in no way posed the far more dangerous threat of a general social uprising.

—PETER HINKS

See Also: *African Americans; Gabriel Plot; Nat Turner's Insurrection; Slavery; Stono Rebellion; Vesey Conspiracy; Walker, David.*

BIBLIOGRAPHY: Aptheker, Herbert, *American Negro Slave Revolts*, 5th ed. (International Publishers 1987); Dillon, Merton, *Slavery Attacked: Southern Slaves and Their Allies, 1619-1865* (Louisiana State Univ. Press 1990); Egerton, Douglas, *Gabriel's Rebellion: The Virginia Slave Conspiracies of 1800 and 1802* (Univ. of North Carolina Press 1993); Hinks, Peter, *To Awaken My Afflicted Brethren: David Walker and the Problem of Antebellum Slave Resistance* (Pennsylvania State Univ. Press 1997).

■ **SLAVERY,** in the Americas, the owning as property of one person—African and sometimes Indian—for life by another, usually European. Slavery is not the same as indentured servitude, in which a person was legally bound to work for another for a specified period of time, frequently seven years. Slavery is one of the oldest human institutions and existed before the keeping of written records.

Scholars generally agree that although owning slaves has been a practice in many areas of the world, only five societies in world history can accurately be labeled slave societies because of the numbers of individuals they enslaved and their dependence on slave labor: ancient Greece, ancient Rome, Brazil, the Caribbean colonies, and the British North American colonies that became the United States. The last three were established after the explorations launched by Christopher Columbus in 1492.

Slavery in America. Modern slavery was African slavery and left a legacy of racial tensions for the contemporary United States. In North America the history of slavery was increasingly intertwined with the growth of democracy after 1776. American Revolutionary pamphleteers sometimes compared colonists to enslaved Africans. This view is clearly expressed in the Declaration of Independence. Yet such comparisons neglected the thousands of actual slaves, whose lack of freedom was little considered. Many American masters also believed that Christianity sanctioned slavery and cited biblical explanations to justify its practice. Followers of the Quakers and Methodism, however, disputed this reading of the Bible.

The first Africans in the American colonies were brought by Dutch traders in August 1619 to Jamestown, Virginia, and sold to Virginia planters. By the 1660s colonial legislation had fixed the future status of new African arrivals as slaves. By 1750 slavery was a fact of law in every North American colony. Precisely how many enslaved Africans were brought into the colonies before the American Revolution is not known, but reliable estimates suggest more than 300,000. In the history of the Atlantic slave trade, 5 percent of more than 10 million Africans who survived the "Middle Passage" across the Atlantic to the Western Hemisphere were imported to the United States. According to the first U.S. Census (1790), there were 697,624 enslaved Africans in the United States. They belonged to many ethnic tribal groups taken mostly from Angola, the Gold Coast, the Bight of Biafra, and Senegambia in West Africa. By 1830 the enslaved numbered 2,009,043, and by 1860, 3,993,760. The southern colonists quickly saw that slaves were vital to the mass cultivation of tobacco, rice, and sugar and, following the invention of the cotton gin in 1793, to cotton. The labor of women and children was particularly useful in raising cotton, and their work in cotton fields greatly expanded slavery's economic importance in the 19th century. The New England and middle colonies (north of Maryland) prospered from slavery too, through substantial trade in fish, corn, wheat, flour, lumber, and animals with the West Indies slave economies in exchange for rum, molasses, sugar, ginger, and related products. This trade sustained a thriving shipbuilding and rum industry.

Following the American Revolution, however, the United States agreed with Britain that its citizens should be prohibited from participating in the international slave trade no later than 1807. By 1804 all the northern states had abolished slavery or had passed laws calling for gradual emancipation. An illegal trade in African slaves continued, however, into the final year (1865) of the Civil War. It lasted until the 1880s in Brazil.

Life under Slavery. The treatment received by the enslaved has been a central issue in the historiography of slavery. The quality of slaves' diets and their physical punishments—especially whipping—have been subjects of great interest in the present-day United States to the descendants of both the enslaved and the masters. Testimony on these matters was long dominated by the records kept by masters, but more recently what the enslaved thought about the conditions of their enslavement and about those who enslaved them has gained the attention of researchers concerned with creating a more accurate view of slavery. It was illegal to teach the enslaved to read, although some masters ignored this prohibition, and the limited number of written sources created by former slaves limits historical research. Oral and archaeological sources, however, have helped considerably.

The slave's diet was basic and monotonous, often consisting of one to two pounds of corn and one-half pound of salt pork daily for an adult worker. Unbalanced diets and disease contributed to illness and high death rates among adults and children. Also terribly harmful to the slave population was the breakup of slave families through sales, often at public auctions. The practice of slave breeding to sustain a domestic slave trade was similarly damaging.

Controlling the behavior of the enslaved was a primary concern of masters. They worried about rebellions and resistance to authority. Daily resistance, such as refusing to obey orders or burning crops, was not uncommon, but the number of reported slave insurrections was relatively small. Important rebellions included those in Stono, South Carolina, and New York in 1739; in Louisiana in 1811; in Charleston, South Carolina, in 1822; and the Nat Turner rebellion in Southhampton, Virginia, in 1831. Turner, a religiously motivated field hand who learned to read, led an uprising that ended in the deaths of 50 to 60 masters, mistresses, and their children. A comparable number of slaves were killed or executed. One consequence was that in the three decades following the Turner insurrection slave discipline perhaps became even harsher as masters determined never to endure an uprising like Turner's again. During the same period abolitionist attacks on slavery, spearheaded by the American Anti-Slavery Society, also reached a peak.

Slavery and the U.S. Government. Slavery's economic and political hold on Americans was powerful. Four of the first five presidents of the United States came from Virginia, the most influential state in the nation, whose tobacco economy was dependent on slave labor. All four of these Virginian presidents—George Washington, Thomas Jefferson, James Madison, and James Monroe—were slaveholders, as were Andrew Jackson, William Henry Harrison, and James K. Polk.

The Constitution of the United States, although it did not include the actual word "slave" or "slavery" in its text, protected slavery until its abolition by the 13th Amendment in 1865. Initially the Constitution allowed three-fifths of the total number of slaves to be counted as part of the general population for purposes of determining the number of representatives a state had in the House of Representatives (Article I, Section 2). It prohibited Con-

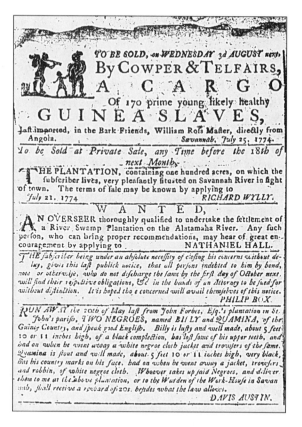

By the late 18th century, the Southern economy revolved around slavery, with the purchase of slaves and operating plantations paramount.

gress from interfering with the Atlantic slave trade until 1808 (Article I, Section 9). It also contained a clause providing for the return of fugitive slaves to their masters (Article IV, Section 2). Many influential people saw the ownership of slaves as important to personal and national welfare and as consistent with private property rights and freedom in a democratic society.

The rights of slaveholders were further protected in law by the Missouri Compromise of 1820, the Fugitive Slave Act of 1850, and the Kansas-Nebraska Act of 1854. Each sought to reduce political conflict between Northern and Southern interests over the issue of slavery by clarifying property rights in enslaved human beings outside the Southern states. In each instance tensions were temporarily reduced, but the institution of slavery created new issues that eventually brought on the Civil War (1861-65). In 1857 the U.S. Supreme Court ruled in the *Dred Scott* decision that people of African heritage had no rights under the Constitution and could not be citizens of the United States.

A key document in the history of U.S. slavery is the Emancipation Proclamation issued by Pres. Abraham Lincoln on Jan. 1, 1863. It proclaimed, in part, "All persons held as slaves within any State or designated part of a State, the people whereof shall then be in rebellion against the United States, shall be then, thenceforward, and forever free." Issued as a war measure, the Emancipation Proclamation applied, however, only to areas not in fact then subject to the authority of the federal government. It was intended to encourage slaves in the Confederacy to rebel and flee to Union lines. Not until the 13th Amendment was ratified in late 1865 was slavery formally and irrevocably ended everywhere in the United States.

—LESLIE HOWARD OWENS

See Also: *African Americans; Antislavery Movement; Cotton; Fugitive Slaves; Manumission; Middle Passage; Plantation System; Proslavery Ideology; Slave Codes; Slave Revolts; Slave Trade.*

BIBLIOGRAPHY: Douglass, Frederick, *A Narrative of the Life of Frederick Douglass* (Antislavery Office 1845); Gaspar, David Barry, and Darlene Clark Hine, eds., *More than Chattel: Black Women and Slavery in the Americas* (Indiana Univ. Press 1996); Wright, Gavin, *The Political Economy of the Cotton South: Households, Markets and Wealth in the Nineteenth Century* (Norton 1978).

■ **SLAVE TRADE,** intercontinental commercial exchanges through which African captives were brought across the Atlantic Ocean to provide slave labor in the New World. The transatlantic slave trade spanned the period from the end of the 15th century to the mid-19th century. Estimates for the total number of captives exported from Africa range from 11.9 million to 15.4 million. The volume of the trade reached its highest level between 1700 and 1810, when approximately 6.5 million Africans were exported. Some 60 percent of all those exported were shipped between 1721 and 1820, evidence that the slave trade came under increasing criticism in the 19th century.

African slaves were distributed widely throughout the Americas. South America received 49.1 percent, while 42.2 percent were sent to the Caribbean. North America (including Central America) got 6.8 percent, and the Old World, 1.8 percent. The percentage of Africans imported into what would become the United States is somewhere around 5 percent of the total.

The origins of the transatlantic slave trade lie in the Mediterranean world of the 13th and 14th cen-

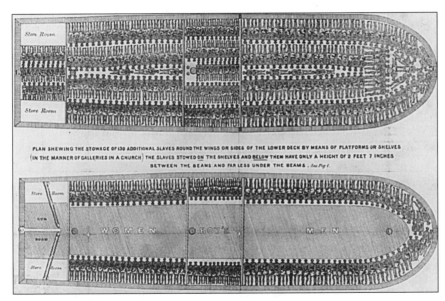

Although some nations imposed regulations on the slave trade, conditions on board ships were severely overcrowded, resulting in many deaths during the transatlantic voyage.

PLAN SHEWING THE STOWAGE OF 130 ADDITIONAL SLAVES ROUND THE WINGS OR SIDES OF THE LOWER DECK BY MEANS OF PLATFORMS OR SHELVES (IN THE MANNER OF GALLERIES IN A CHURCH) THE SLAVES STOWED ON THE SHELVES AND BELOW THEM HAVE ONLY A HEIGHT OF 2 FEET 7 INCHES BETWEEN THE BEAMS AND FAR LESS UNDER THE BEAMS.

turies, where the previous discovery by Crusaders of sugarcane in the Middle East subsequently led to the transplantation of the crop to suitable climates in southern Iberia, Sicily, Crete, and Cyprus. A number of factors, including the Black Death's decimation of European populations in the 14th century, led to increased reliance upon servile labor to cultivate sugarcane, labor that was initially Greek and Iberian/Arabo-Berber but became increasingly Slavic from the Black Sea area. With the Christian reconquest in 14th-century Iberia (along with Christian-Muslim pacts) and as a result of the Muslim conquest of Constantinople in 1453, the supply of war captives from the Black Sea and within Spain-Portugal dramatically declined. Mediterranean planters, therefore, increasingly turned to subsaharan African servile labor. By the end of the 15th century slaves in Sicily and Naples were largely African and male. By the time of the European discovery of the New World around the same time, the association of African servile labor and plantation agriculture had been well established. The decimation of Indian populations as a result of the introduction of Old World diseases only reinforced the association of Africans and slavery.

Beginning with the Portuguese and the Spanish, a number of European nations participated in the transatlantic slave trade, including Holland, England, and France. Maritime innovations such as the compass, the astrolabe, the technique of tacking, and the adoption of the lateen sail (from the Indian Ocean *dhow*) gave Europe a decided technological advantage vis-à-vis Africa. Beginning with Senegambia, slave traders began to purchase captives from various regions or supply zones. In addition to Senegambia, these regions included Sierra Leone (also called the Windward Coast), the Gold Coast, the Bight of Benin, the Bight of Biafra, West Central Africa, and Mozambique-Madagascar.

While the French and the English supplied their own New World colonies with captives, Portugal and Spain contracted slavers from other countries to supply their colonies by way of the *asiento*, a special license of authorization. U.S. slavers also traded along the West African coast for captives, but for the most part the United States relied upon English slavers and others for its supply of servile labor. The United States was exceptional in that it imported more or less equivalent numbers of males and females, whereas elsewhere in the Americas approximately twice as many males as females were imported. It was also the case that the United States imported a considerable percentage of prepubescent children, somewhere between 25 and 33 percent. The gender and age of shipments of slaves were determined by both the preferences of New World planters and their suppliers.

Slavers in Africa. Africans themselves played a role in the slave trade. While there can be no doubt that Europeans were the principal agents in the trade, having initiated, financed, and created market conditions requiring it, there is also no question that indigenous agents were indispensable to the trade's success. The primary means by which Africans were procured for export was warfare and raiding, or kidnapping, which in certain contexts became indistinguishable. Some African polities were entirely predatory in their approach to slave trading. But it is equally true that a number of African states were opposed to the slave trade and fought to at least prevent their own people from becoming casualties of it. Nevertheless, the reality was that by the 19th century much of Africa from Senegambia south to the Cape and north to Kenya (with the notable exception of what became South Africa, a net importer of slaves) was directly affected by the transatlantic trade. East Africa was also involved in the Red Sea and Indian Ocean slave trades, whereas West Africa from Senegambia to Lake Chad and beyond were simultaneously heavily invested in the trans-Saharan exchange in captives.

Scholars debate the effect of the slave trade on Africa, with some arguing that the trade was the principal vehicle of African underdevelopment. There is also the question of the trade's impact on Europe. Some insist that the rise of Europe was predicated on the trade in African slaves.

—MICHAEL A. GOMEZ

See Also: *Slavery.*

BIBLIOGRAPHY: Curtin, Philip D., *The Atlantic Slave Trade: A Census* (Univ. of Wisconsin Press 1969); Inikori, J. E., *Forced Migration: The Impact of the Export Trade on African Societies* (Africana 1982); Manning, Patrick, *Slavery and African Life: Occidental, Oriental, and African Slave Trades* (Cambridge

Univ. Press 1990); Williams, Eric, *Capitalism and Slavery* (Univ. of North Carolina Press 1994).

■ **SLIDELL, JOHN (1793-1871),** Confederate diplomat. Born in New York City, Slidell moved to New Orleans in 1819 and practiced commercial law. He served in the U.S. House of Representatives (1843-45) and in the Senate (1853-61), resigning during the secession crisis. Confederate Pres. Jefferson Davis appointed Slidell ambassador to France. He failed to gain French recognition of the Confederacy but did negotiate a key loan. Slidell remained in Europe and died in England.

See Also: Civil War.

■ **SLOAN, JOHN FRENCH (1871-1951),** realist painter. Born in Lock Haven, Pennsylvania, Sloan studied at the Pennsylvania Academy of Fine Arts and later with Robert Henri. He began his career as an illustrator, working for periodicals such as *Harper's, Collier's,* and *Scribner's.* Moving to New York in 1904, Sloan associated with a group of artists often known as "the ashcan school" for their realistic depictions of the urban scene. Sloan was among the more political of these artists, serving as an editor of *The Masses.*

See Also: Henri, Robert; Painting.

■ **SMALLPOX,** a highly contagious disease transmitted by airborne virus and contracted either by inhalation or contact with contaminated objects. From the 15th to the 18th century, smallpox epidemics were endemic to Europe. The Spanish introduced smallpox to the New World early in the 16th century, and within decades, the disease produced extreme mortality among the indigenous peoples. By 1600, 9 out of 10 South American natives succumbed to European diseases, many of them to smallpox. In North America, a 1618 pandemic began in New England and spread to Virginia, reducing the native populations by nearly 90 percent. In New England, outbreaks occurred with such regularity that acres of fields previously cultivated by Indians were left vacant. English settlers became convinced the disease-related loss of life among Indians was the result of divine intervention. Smallpox claimed nearly 50 percent of the total populations of Huron and Iroquois peoples in the 17th century, with similar death rates among tribes in the southeastern interior. Throughout North and South America, smallpox continued to periodically flare up among the indigenous as well as the immigrant populations until the use of vaccines stopped the cycle in the mid- to late-19th century.

See Also: Disease; Medicine.

BIBLIOGRAPHY: Crosby, Alfred W., *Ecological Imperialism* (Cambridge Univ. Press, 1986).

■ **SMEDLEY, AGNES (1892?-1950),** journalist. Born to a working-class family in Osgood, Missouri, she lived in California during the 1910s, where her friend novelist Upton Sinclair introduced her to socialism. She went to China in 1928 as a correspondent for the *Frankfurter Zeitung.* For over a decade she traveled with the Red Army covering the war against Japan and the Chinese revolution. Among her books are *Chinese Destinies* (1933), *Battle Hymn of China* (1943), and *Daughter of Earth* (1929), an autobiographical novel.

See Also: Cold War; Sinclair, Upton; Women in American History; Women's Movement.

■ **SMIBERT, JOHN (1688-1751),** colonial-era painter. Smibert was born in Edinburgh, Scotland, and immigrated to the British colonies in 1728, accompanying the philosopher George Berkeley, who planned to establish a college in the Bermudas. Smibert's best-known painting is *The Bermuda Group,* a group portrait of his traveling companions finished in 1729. Having established his reputation with this painting, Smibert opened a studio in Boston in 1730 and won commissions from the colonial elite for portraits such as *Francis Brinley* (1730) and *Sir William Pepperell* (1747).

See Also: Berkeley, George; Painting.

■ **SMITH, ALFRED EMANUEL (1873-1944),** American politician. Born and educated in New York City, he was elected to the New York State Assembly, where he served 12 years (1903-15), including the distinction of being its Democratic leader (1911) and its speaker (1913). Smith was elected governor of New York in 1919, serving a total of four terms (1919-21, 1923-29). Throughout his political career he was a champion of social reform, including increased state expenditures for the mentally ill, protective labor legislation for women and minors, and equal pay for women public-school teachers.

He sought his party's presidential nomination in 1920 and 1924 before finally being chosen the Democratic nominee in 1928. Smith lost by a landslide to the Republican Herbert Hoover, whose bid for the White House was helped by Smith's unpopular stance against Prohibition and his long association with Tammany Hall, a Democratic party organization in New York City much marred by scandal and corruption. But perhaps most damaging to the Smith presidential campaign was his religion. He was the first Roman Catholic to run for president of the United States. This discriminatory barrier would remain unbroken until the 1960 candidacy of John F. Kennedy.

See Also: *Presidential Elections; Tammany Hall.*
BIBLIOGRAPHY: Handlin, Oscar, *Al Smith and His America* (Northeastern Univ. Press 1987); Smith, Alfred E., *Up to Now: An Autobiography* (Viking Press 1929).

■ **SMITH, BESSIE (1894-1937),** blues singer nicknamed "the Empress of the Blues." She was born in Chattanooga, Tennessee. Discovered around 1910 by Gertrude (Ma) Rainey, she became her protégée. Among the first blues artists to record her music, she recorded more than 160 songs between 1923 and 1930, gaining popularity for songs such as "Nobody's Blues But Mine" and "St. Louis Blues." Her full-throated blues style influenced a generation of jazz singers, including Billie Holiday and Louis Armstrong.

See Also: *Armstrong, Louis; Blues; Holiday, Billie; Jazz; Rainey, Gertrude (Ma); Women in American History.*

■ **SMITH-CONNALLY ANTI-STRIKE ACT (1943),** legislation establishing a mandatory 30-day cooling-off period before a strike could be called and banning strikes in defense-related industries. It was passed over Pres. Franklin D. Roosevelt's veto.

See Also: *Labor Movement.*

■ **SMITH, DAVID (1906-65),** major 20th-century sculptor. Smith was born in Decatur, Indiana; his first artistic training was a correspondence course from the Cleveland Art School. In the summer of 1925 he worked for the Studebaker automobile plant in South Bend, Indiana, where he learned the metalworking that would later be central to his artwork. He moved to New York City in 1926 and took courses at the Art Students League; Smith also worked for the Federal Arts Project during the Great Depression. Keeping abreast of European developments in modern art, Smith was influenced by cubist, surrealist, and constructivist art, but he wove these strands together into a personal style. Smith was the first American sculptor to experiment with welding techniques, which he began using in the 1930s. Smith often created groups or series of sculptures, ranging from his early *Medals of Dishonor* (1937-40), which incorporated recognizable forms, to *Agricola* (early 1950s), which featured found objects, to the more abstract *Cubi* (1963-65), which used circular and rectangular forms as its basis.

See Also: *Federal Arts Project; Sculpture.*

■ **SMITH, JAMES (c. 1719-1806),** lawyer, general, and Revolutionary War statesman. Born in Northern Ireland, Smith and his family immigrated to Pennsylvania in 1729. A staunch opponent of British rule, he served in the Second Continental Congress and signed the Declaration of Independence.

See Also: *Declaration of Independence.*

■ **SMITH, JOHN (1580-1631),** explorer and colonizer. Born in Lincolnshire, England, Smith ventured as a teenager to the European continent, where he traveled widely and fought with a European army in Hungary against the Turks. Upon returning to England in 1604, Smith was well prepared for a military career and life in foreign lands. Promoters of the Virginia Company recognized these attributes and appointed Smith a captain in the garrison for the Virginia colony.

After arriving with the first group of settlers in 1607, Smith helped found Jamestown and began to explore the Chesapeake region. According to legend, during one exploration, Indians of the Powhatan Confederacy captured Smith but spared his life at the urging of the chief's daughter, Pocahontas. When he returned to Jamestown, personal enemies in the governing council sentenced him to death for losing men in his party. Smith received a reprieve when new colonists arrived, and he was named president of the colony

John Smith was a leader of the Jamestown colony and author of the settlement's first history (1608). His *Description of New England* (1616) coined the name given to that region and created the interest that led to the Pilgrim settlement in 1620.

in 1608. He ruled vigorously, commanding every person to work equally for the common good, instilling discipline in the struggling colony, and dealing ruthlessly with the region's Indians. Under pressure from dissenters and injured from a gunpowder explosion, Smith returned to England in 1609. He made a final journey to North America in 1614 and designated the northern coast "New" England.

Perhaps Smith's most lasting contributions were his prodigious writings. During the last two decades of his life, he chronicled his explorations, while championing North America as the locus for England's imperial future.

See Also: *Exploration and Discovery; Jamestown Settlement; Pocahontas.*

BIBLIOGRAPHY: Barbour, Philip L., *The Three Worlds of Captain John Smith* (Houghton Mifflin 1964); Emerson, Everett H., *Captain John Smith* (Twayne 1993).

■ **SMITH, JOSEPH (1805-44),** founder of the Church of Jesus Christ of Latter-Day Saints (Mormons). Born in Sharon, Vermont, Smith came from a poor farming family. In 1816 the family moved to Palmyra, New York, located in the "burned-over district" where revivals were popular and many religious movements began. In 1820, while praying in the woods, Smith had a vision in which God forgave him his sins and instructed him to keep a pure heart. Three years later during an evening prayer, he was visited by an angel named Moroni who told him of an ancient book that gave the history of earlier inhabitants of the Western Hemisphere who had come from the Near East. After obtaining the plates, Smith dictated the contents to his wife and other scribes. In 1830 he published the *Book of Mormon*. In 1830, he founded the Church of Christ (later renamed the Church of Jesus Christ of Latter-Day Saints) in Fayette, New York.

Smith was a skilled organizer. He ordained people to various positions in the Church and assigned each appropriate tasks. He also organized cities, farms, industries, temples, a university, and a woman's auxiliary. Controversy surrounded him and his community, which had relocated to Kirtland, Ohio, in 1832 and then in 1838 to Nauvoo, Illinois, where they prospered. But the success of the community provoked fears among their neighbors, who saw themselves being overwhelmed. Throughout his life Smith was persecuted, enduring kidnappings, tarrings and featherings, and lawsuits. In 1844 Smith and his brother Hyrum were murdered by a mob while being held in a Carthage, Illinois, jail, accused of inciting a riot. After his death, Brigham Young became the leader of the main body of Mormons.

See Also: *Mormons; Religion; Young, Brigham.*

BIBLIOGRAPHY: Bushman, Richard L., *Joseph Smith and the Beginnings of Mormonism* (Univ. of Illinois Press 1984).

■ **SMITH, MARGARET CHASE (1897-1995),** Republican politician from Maine. Born in Skowhegan, Maine, she filled the vacant congressional seat of her husband, Clyde Smith, after his death in 1940 and was then elected to four terms in Congress. In 1948, she was elected to the Senate, where she served until 1973.

SMITH, THEOBALD (1859-1934), pathologist. Born in Albany, New York, Smith organized the department of bacteriology at George Washington University (1886-95), taught at Harvard Medical School, and directed the pathology laboratory at the Massachusetts Board of Health (1895-1915). He later directed animal pathology at Rockefeller Institute (1915-29). Smith's work on swine plague, hog cholera, and Texas cattle fever (1891-93) showed how parasites carry disease. He also studied tuberculosis (1898), worked on a smallpox vaccine and diphtheria and tetanus antitoxins, and did research on allergic reactions.

See Also: Science.

SMITHSONIAN INSTITUTION, museums and research facilities headquartered in Washington, D.C. James Smithson (1765-1829), an English chemist who never visited the United States, left a bequest of £100,000 to the nation for the creation of "an establishment for the increase and diffusion of knowledge." After nearly a decade of debate, Congress accepted the gift and chartered the Smithsonian in 1838. The first building opened in 1846 and the Smithsonian has since expanded to become a network of museums in Washington, a zoo, a museum in New York City, and related properties. The Smithsonian's museums on the Mall in Washington have become the capital's leading tourist attraction. Sometimes called "the nation's attic" because of its vast and diverse holdings, the Smithsonian must balance its dual roles of celebrating and critically examining the nation's past.

See Also: Museums.

BIBLIOGRAPHY: Conaway, James, *The Smithsonian: 150 Years of Adventure, Discovery, and Wonder* (Smithsonian Books 1995).

SMUGGLING, secret and unlawful importing and exporting. Smuggling was most significant during the 17th and 18th centuries. The British government controlled the trade of its American colonies according to the concept of mercantilism and through a series of Navigation Acts. The colonists, accustomed to managing on their own, paid little attention to early acts limiting their trade to England or its colonies. Colonial merchants learned to conform to the machinery of mercantilism over time, with some exceptions. Most notable was the smuggling of sugar, molasses, and rum from the non-English Caribbean. New England distilleries regularly obtained molasses from the French sugar islands, since they used more than the British West Indies could supply. Although not strictly enforced, the Molasses Act of 1733 threatened New England's prosperity, and few merchants obeyed it. New England's dependence on trade for its economy also led colonial merchants to trade illegally with the French during King George's War and the Seven Years' War. Smuggled tea became an important symbol of independence after the Townshend Acts (1767). Smuggling, however, played less of a role in colonial trade than traditional narratives have implied. It did nonetheless contribute to conflict between England and its colonies.

SNAKE RIVER, principal tributary of the Columbia River. Beginning in Wyoming's Yellowstone National Park, the Snake stretches westward for 1,038 miles through Idaho, Oregon, and Washington. In 1805 Lewis and Clark's expedition followed the Snake westward to the Columbia River. Numerous trading posts were erected along the Snake during the first decades of the 19th century as the river became a major thoroughfare to the Pacific Northwest. The most significant of these, Ft. Hall, became a meeting place for trappers, traders, and, later, Oregon Trail travelers. The control of the Snake through federally funded dams has provided inexpensive electricity for surrounding towns and has put at least 4.5 million acres under irrigation.

SOCIAL DARWINISM, a theory of the late 19th century, which claimed that an individual's place in society was determined by a process akin to the theory of evolution in nature as developed by Charles Darwin. As applied to human society, Social Darwinism argued that humans, like other forms of life, competed for survival and that the "fittest" were those who were rich and powerful while the poor were the unfit.

First developed by the British philosopher Herbert Spencer, Social Darwinism was popularized in the United States through the work of William Graham Sumner, a professor of sociology at Yale

University. Sumner and others argued that social progress must be allowed to follow its natural course without intervention from the social or economic reforms of government. Even the efforts of private charities were criticized since, according to the dictates of Social Darwinism, those who lived in poverty were meant to suffer and so eventually die off. Left alone, the "fit" would prosper, with or without assistance. From the late 19th and into the early 20th century, Social Darwinism served as a theoretical basis for racism, imperialism, and unchecked capitalism.

See Also: *Gilded Age.*

BIBLIOGRAPHY: Hofstadter, Richard, *Social Darwinism in American Thought* (1944; Beacon Press 1994).

■ **SOCIALISM,** philosophies, programs, and movements that seek to "socialize" the ownership and operation of the means of production, abolishing private productive property.

The earliest socialist movements in America were religious in nature and grew with the rise of a market economy at the end of the 18th century. The most successful of these, the "Shakers," a strict religious order descended from the English Quakers, had by 1794 succeeded in planting over a dozen communal settlements throughout New England and New York. But religious socialism proved to have limited appeal; the secular enlightenment of the 18th century, rather than Christianity, laid the groundwork for modern socialism. Artisans, hard pressed by growing competition and the subdivision of their craft into unskilled tasks, developed a native critique of capitalism by combining the free thought of political theorist Thomas Paine and the popular ideology of republicanism with their observation that all wealth was created by labor. At the same time, the elaborate utopian visions of French philosophers Saint-Simon and Charles Fourier, popularized in America by Robert Owen (1801-77) and Albert Brisbane (1809-90), inspired many reformers who, realizing that America's expansive frontier and liberal state afforded opportunities for communal experimentation, founded scores of ephemeral socialist settlements in the 1840s.

By the early 1870s the quickening pace of industrialization, a rising labor movement, and an increasing public disillusionment with corrupt politics created a receptive climate for the ideas of Karl Marx and united many American radicals under the banner of the London-based International Workingmen's Association (IWA). In a pattern often repeated, the IWA's Marxists, convinced of the need for ideological discipline, purged the party of native reformers who championed the causes of women's equality and civil rights that were unpopular with immigrant workingmen. As a result, in spite of the immense popularity of some socialist ideas and visions—Edward Bellamy's utopian socialist novel *Looking Backward* sold over a million copies in the 1880s—socialism remained a primarily immigrant movement for the remainder of the 19th century. The IWA's successor, the Socialist Labor party, was no more successful at spreading socialism than its charismatic leader, Daniel De Leon, who also chose ideological purity over building a socialist coalition.

20th Century. Socialism in America reached its peak with the founding of the Socialist party (SP) in 1901 and the Industrial Workers of the World (IWW) in 1905. The two movements espoused widely divergent tactics; the IWW held a "syndicalist" theory that socialism would be gained by workers' struggles in the shop, while the SP believed that socialism could be won at the ballot box. By 1912 the SP's candidate for president, Eugene V. Debs, polled nearly a million votes and SP mayors governed 73 American cities and towns. However, both movements were cut short by the political repression unleashed by World War I and the internal ideological divisions sparked by the Bolshevik Revolution in Russia.

After 1917, American socialism was largely defined by events in the Soviet Union; the new Communist party's (CP) conversion to the revolutionary ideas of Lenin drew American socialism once again into a cycle of doctrinal purification and sectarian splintering. The CP grew during the Great Depression and the unifying crusade against fascism in the 1930s and 1940s and played a central role in building the industrial labor movement, pressuring passage of New Deal reforms, and advancing the cause of civil rights. Such gains proved short-lived as the onset of the Cold War brought federal prosecution, pervasive blacklisting, and the abandonment of the CP by many of its followers. In the 1960s a "New Left" arose whose concern for democratic principles, opposition to war, and cultural rebelliousness had more in common with the American radicals of the 19th century than the "Old Left" they had supplanted.

—TIMOTHY MESSER-KRUSE

See Also: Bellamy, Edward; Debs, Eugene V.; Industrial Workers of the World; Labor Movement; New Left; Owen, Robert; Paine, Thomas; Political Parties; Shakers; Socialist Party.

BIBLIOGRAPHY: Buhle, Paul, *Marxism in the USA: From 1870 to the Present Day* (Verso 1987); Egbert, Donald, and Stow Persons, eds., *Socialism and American Life* (Princeton Univ. Press 1952); Quint, Howard H., *The Forging of American Socialism: Origins of the Modern Movement* (Bobbs-Merrill 1953).

■ **SOCIALIST PARTY,** founded in 1901, attained its maximum influence during the 1910s. The Socialist party impressed its reform ideas on the mainstream of the Progressive Era, expounded a popular vision of socialism, and waged the most important struggle against war until the Vietnam conflict.

The origins of the Socialist party can be traced to the industrial conflicts and agrarian discontent of the post–Civil War era. Future members passed through Greenback and Populist movements, hard-pressed labor unions, and utopian experiments to "colonize" the West cooperatively. Eugene V. Debs, leader and imprisoned martyr of the Pullman Strike of 1894, brought competing socialist groups together and in 1900 ran for president for the first of five times.

The Socialist party's main strength lay in its educational campaigns and above all its press. *The Appeal for Reason,* its newspaper published in Girard, Kansas, alone circulated more than three-quarters of a million copies each week. Dozens of daily, weekly, and monthly papers in more than a dozen languages touched lower-class Americans almost everywhere but the Deep South.

Socialists reached their maximum influence in 1912, when Debs won almost 1 million votes and hundreds of Socialists were elected to local or state office. After regaining wide popularity in 1917-19 through opposition to American participation in World War I, the party was crushed by Attorney

Gen. A. Mitchell Palmer during the "red scare." Its newspapers suppressed and Debs and fellow activists jailed, it fell into disarray with the rise of American communism. The Socialist party revived once more under the leadership of Norman Thomas during the 1930s, but the New Deal dealt it a final blow by offering the reform-minded an alternative within the dominant political system.

—PAUL BUHLE

See Also: Debs, Eugene V.; Labor Movement; Political Parties; Red Scare; Thomas, Norman Mattoon.

BIBLIOGRAPHY: Judd, Richard, *Socialist Cities: Explorations into the Grass Roots of American Socialism* (SUNY Press 1990).

■ **SOCIAL SCIENCES,** in the United States, a set of academic disciplines emerging in the late 19th and early 20th centuries. Beginning roughly in the final decade of the 19th century, the academic disciplines known as the social sciences took their place between the natural sciences (such as physics and biology), on the one hand, and the humanities (such as English literature and history), on the other. Consisting primarily of anthropology, economics, political science, and sociology, the social sciences have produced diverse, indeed often conflicting, bodies of knowledge. They grew, in good measure, out of the conditions generated by the nation's increasing industrialization in the late 19th century, as many reformers hoped to address modernity's shortcomings by developing a class of experts, working in various fields, who would directly influence, and perhaps even administer, public policy.

By the early 20th century, the social sciences had appeared as independent, professionalized academic disciplines based in college and university departments, with their corresponding organizations (such as the American Political Science Association, 1903) and journals (*American Political Science Review*). They have grown increasingly specialized, so that each discipline has come to possess a number of subdisciplines, the practitioners of which often know very little about currents in the rest of their field. Beginning in the 1960s, the social sciences' founding belief in their ability to achieve full objectivity has been seriously challenged, and in the late 20th century, they have begun to look to philosophers, historians, and literary critics, among others, in renewing their academic province.

BIBLIOGRAPHY: Haskell, Thomas L., *The Emergence of Professional Social Science* (Univ. of Illinois Press 1977); Ross, Dorothy, *The Origins of American Social Science* (Cambridge Univ. Press 1991).

■ **SOCIAL SECURITY ACT (1935),** law that provided for unemployment compensation and old-age pensions through a combination of federal and state-administered programs. The first experiments in social security were sporadic state-sponsored programs in the early 20th century. The move for a federal program grew out of the Great Depression, when demands for unemployment and old-age relief intensified. In 1934, Pres. Franklin D. Roosevelt appointed a commission to study the issue, and in 1935 legislation was passed by Congress and signed into law by Roosevelt. The act created the Social Security Board to administer the system. Federal taxes on workers and their employees funded retirees, who received monthly pensions after the age of 65. Initially, the benefits ranged from $10 to $85 a month, depending on how many years employees and employers contributed to the plan. The unemployment compensation program, administered by the states, established a limited number of weeks of cash payments to the unemployed, funded by a federal tax on employers.

The original law had many flaws. It failed to cover farm and domestic workers and casual laborers, many of whom were Hispanics and African Americans. In addition, the initial old-age pensions were insufficient for many recipients. In 1939 a series of amendments created the modern social security program, rectifying many of these deficiencies. Although the law was attacked from its inception by conservatives and liberals alike, it nevertheless established a system of federal responsibility for America's most vulnerable citizens.

See Also: *Great Depression; New Deal.*

BIBLIOGRAPHY: Witte, Edwin E., *The Development of the Social Security Act* (Univ. of Wisconsin Press 1962).

■ **SOCIAL WELFARE,** the means by which the United States has provided for its poor and dis-

abled residents. Colonial Americans relied on local authorities to administer relief to the poor. Although public in character, this aid often took the form of placing poor or disabled persons in the care of a more fortunate relative. In this manner relief depended not so much on specialized institutions, such as jails or insane asylums, but rather on the generosity of the community itself.

19th-Century Approaches. In the 19th century this system started to change, and communities began to depend more on such entities as insane asylums, schools for the blind and deaf, and, above all, poorhouses. Rhode Island towns in 1851, for example, had a number of options, including auctioning the poor to the lowest bidder or placing them in a poorhouse. These poorhouses were intended both to maintain people already poor and to deter others from seeking relief. Their purposes reflected an optimistic 19th-century belief that poverty in America could be eradicated. In reality the poorhouses failed to have the transforming effects that their advocates intended. Mid-19th-century observers condemned poorhouses as uncomfortable places whose existence did little to lower the rate of poverty.

Nonetheless many middle-class 19th-century Americans worried about the demoralizing effects of "outdoor relief" on the poor, fearing aid that allowed recipients to remain at home would make them permanently dependent on welfare or, in the expression of the day, "pauperize" them. In the 1870s, in the midst of America's worst depression to date, a concerted campaign began against the provision of outdoor relief. Large cities such as Brooklyn, New York, and Baltimore, Maryland, took steps to abolish such aid. Increasingly these cities relied on private organizations, known as Charity Organization Societies, such as the one started in Buffalo, New York, in 1877, to coordinate the efforts of public and private charities. The goal of these societies was to provide, in the contemporary expression, "not alms, but a friend," a reference to the practice of "friendly visiting," in which genteel women visited the poor in their homes and made efforts to put them in touch with individuals or organizations that might help them. In the early 20th century, therefore, poor relief remained a local responsibility and continued to depend on a hodgepodge of public and private agencies to dispense aid that came in a wide variety of forms.

Progressive Era Changes. In the Progressive Era states began to pass laws that altered the traditional poor law system. In 1911 Wisconsin created a workers' compensation program for workers injured in the course of employment. The new program, which replaced part of the injured worker's salary and paid the worker's medical bills, reflected the belief that accidents were an inevitable result of industrial employment. Rather than requiring a worker to sue his employer to recover damages or forcing the worker to apply for aid to local poor law or Charity Organization Society authorities, workers' compensation advocates in Wisconsin and elsewhere reasoned that the state would be better served by simply making the compensation of industrial accidents the responsibility of employers. The state therefore asked employers to buy insurance against the risk of an accident occurring in their plant. It was the first example in America of a social insurance approach to social welfare. No longer would social welfare be organized solely by where a person lived; it now mattered where the person worked. Between 1911 and 1919, 43 states created workers' compensation laws.

Other important Progressive Era social welfare innovations included mothers pension laws, begun in 1911 and extended by 1931 to every state except Georgia and South Carolina, and the creation in 11 states in the 1920s of special monetary grants to the indigent elderly. The first of these new laws provided monetary aid, outside of the poorhouse, to widows who had children under their care. The reasoning was that the deterrent features of the poor law should not be applied to such individuals and that instead they should be given sufficient monetary aid to enable them to stay home and raise their children. To be sure, state and local authorities scrutinized the widows who came to them for aid. The result was that only 250,000 children received money through the pension laws in 1931, and nearly all of the recipients conformed to the prevailing stereotypes about the sorts of families who were worthy of aid. That meant that few black families received a mothers pension. Similar considerations applied to elderly citizens who sought aid. All the state

laws contained stringent restrictions about who could be aided, and most permitted a great deal of discretion to local government authorities. In Ohio, for example, if an elderly couple receiving aid owned a house worth more than $500, they had to turn the house over to the state. When they died, the state had the legal right to sell the house.

The Social Security Act and Its Consequences. The Great Depression of the 1930s strained local systems of social provision to their limits. States experimented with special programs that supplemented their traditional poor relief with what came to be called unemployment relief. When Franklin Roosevelt became president (1933), he asked his acquaintance Harry Hopkins, a prominent social worker, to begin a national program of emergency relief that combined federal and state funds. At the same time the president contemplated an end to this sort of aid, which he called the "dole." He sought to substitute a social insurance program that would provide permanent, rather than emergency, protection against the major hazards of industrial life, such as unemployment and the economic insecurity that often accompanied old age.

The result of the president's initiative was the passage of the Social Security Act in the summer of 1935. The new law consolidated old programs, such as an infant and maternal health program that had been created in 1921, and established at least three important new programs: a state-run unemployment compensation program; federally aided but state-run public assistance programs that allowed the states to grant payments—"welfare"—to dependent children, the indigent elderly, and the blind; and a new program of old-age insurance that came to be known as Social Security.

Old-age insurance turned out to be the most important of the programs established by the Social Security Act. It started slowly. Beginning in January 1937, workers in industrial and commercial employment discovered that 1 percent of their paychecks had been deducted to pay for Social Security. Since no one had ever received a Social Security benefit and most workers felt they could spare little from their paychecks, many questioned the new deductions. For workers who were unemployed or already retired, Social Security lacked any sort of relevance. Many of these people favored the plan that had been devised by Dr. Francis Townsend that would have paid $200 to each elderly citizen each month, on the condition that the recipient spend all of the money received that month. Workers also noticed that the elderly receiving welfare from the states had paid nothing for it, in contrast to those who were being asked not only to pay taxes for those on welfare but also to provide for their own retirement. As late as 1950 more than twice as many people were on the state welfare rolls receiving old-age assistance than were receiving retirement benefits from the federal government under Social Security. The average monthly welfare payment was $42 in 1949, compared with an average Social Security benefit of $25.

In time these flaws in Social Security were corrected. Beginning in 1940, the program paid survivor benefits to the widows and children of workers who died before retirement age. In 1950 Social Security coverage was extended to self-employed workers, and benefit levels were raised substantially. Between 1950 and 1972 the program experienced many coverage extensions and benefit increases, often legislated to coincide with congressional elections. The result of these various changes was that about 142 million persons made contributions to the program in 1996 totaling about $380 billion. Forty-four percent of the elderly's income came from Social Security in 1987, and 47.5 percent of the elderly would have fallen below the poverty line in 1986 were it not for Social Security and other welfare benefits.

Not only did Social Security benefits become more adequate, they also expanded in scope. In 1956, benefits were widened to include disability coverage for those who suffered from an impairment that forced them to retire before the normal retirement age. In 1965 Congress added Medicare coverage to Social Security. It provided payments to cover the hospital and doctor visits of the elderly.

The Welfare Problem. The public assistance programs developed in a different manner. So long as welfare went mainly to the elderly, as it did between 1935 and 1957, concerns about welfare leading to pauperization receded to the background. In 1957, however, for the first time more people received aid to families of dependent children (AFDC), the successor to Progressive Era mothers

pension laws, than received aid to the elderly. During the 1950s the AFDC caseload rose by nearly 800,000 people. Such a rise in a time of prosperity prompted a public discussion about how to reform welfare so as to lower the rolls, decrease the rate of babies born out of wedlock, and increase the productivity of potential welfare recipients.

Between 1958 and 1996, this discussion took many twists and turns. At first, policymakers emphasized providing welfare recipients with skills. Then in the late 1960s the discussion turned to the creation of economic incentives that would encourage welfare beneficiaries to work. During the 1970s welfare once again became a hotly contested topic, as experts debated the fine points of program design and the public questioned the utility of paying welfare mothers not to work. Both the deterioration of the national economy and changes in the black family—in 1980, 43 percent of black families were headed by women—influenced the discussion. After repeated failures to pass comprehensive welfare reform, Congress enacted the Family Support Act in 1988. It established comprehensive state education and training programs and mandated transitional child care and medical assistance. In 1996 a new law gave state and local governments additional responsibilities for the provision of welfare.

By the end of the 20th century some Americans wanted in effect to reinvigorate the local tradition of the colonial poor laws. In the intervening years, however, an enduring program of social insurance had permanently altered the old poor-law system, even as Americans continued to debate the proper balance between public and private responsibility.

—EDWARD BERKOWITZ

See Also: Charitable Associations; Hopkins, Harry L.; Progressivism.

BIBLIOGRAPHY: Berkowitz, Edward D., *America's Welfare State From Roosevelt to Reagan* (Johns Hopkins Univ. Press 1991); Katz, Michael B., *In the Shadow of the Poorhouse: A Social History of Welfare in America* (Free Press 1996); Trattner, Walter I., *From Poor Law to Welfare State: A History of Social Welfare in America* (Free Press 1984).

■ SOCIETY OF AMERICAN INDIANS (SAI) (1911-24), formed to advocate for education, "progres-

sive" social advancement, and civil rights, was the first major pan-tribal Indian organization in the United States. In 1911, when it first met in Columbus, Ohio, the SAI declared "that the time has come when the American Indian race should contribute, in a more united way, its influence and exertion with the rest of the citizens of the United States in all lines of progress and reform, for the welfare of the Indian race in particular, and humanity in general." Initially, the SAI had the support of many "Friends of the Indians," white associations devoted to the assimilation of Indians, but when it became clear that many SAI members did not advocate a total break with tribal traditions, these groups dissociated themselves from the SAI. Some SAI leaders, such as Carlos Montezuma, condemned the Bureau of Indian Affairs and also those Society members who sought to preserve any elements of traditional Indian culture. Other SAI members, however, were proud of tribal values and wanted Americans to recognize the accomplishments of Indians. Finally, some members, especially Charles A. Eastman, worried that the SAI did not reflect the interests of the majority of Indians but only those of a highly educated, acculturated minority.

See Also: Friends of the Indians; Indians of North America; Montezuma, Carlos.

BIBLIOGRAPHY: Olson, James Stuart, and Raymond Wilson, *Native Americans in the Twentieth Century* (Univ. of Illinois Press 1984).

■ **SOLDIERS BONUS ACT (1924),** federal legislation authorizing a $1,000 bonus for veterans of World War I, to be paid in 1945. During the height of the Great Depression, unemployed veterans demanded early payment, sparking the Bonus Army controversy of 1932.

See Also: Bonus Army.

■ **SOMALIA INTERVENTION (1992-95),** joint U.S.-UN mission begun to safeguard the delivery of food and other humanitarian aid to Somalia. Called Operation Restore Hope, it failed for several reasons: continued vicious fighting among Somali clans, declining support in Congress after the October 1993 ambush and death of several U.S. troops, and "mission creep"—the expansion from the original security role to a wider, nation-

building objective. U.S. military forces left Somalia on Mar. 30, 1994. The following year the United States helped evacuate the remaining United Nations troops.

■ **SOMME OFFENSIVE (1918),** World War I confrontation in France between the Allies and Germans. On March 21, after an influx of manpower released by the collapse of the eastern front, the Germans launched a massive offensive on a 50-mile front north and south of the Somme River. Using poison gas and new infiltration tactics, the Germans advanced 40 miles in two weeks until exhaustion stopped them just short of Amiens. The offensive spurred the U.S. commander, John J. Pershing, to pledge immediately all ready and available American troops to the war effort.

See Also: Pershing, John Joseph; World War I.

■ **SONS AND DAUGHTERS OF LIBERTY,** colonial organizations in America created in response to repressive British policies. The Sons of Liberty originated in Boston after Parliament passed the Stamp Act in 1765 and eventually expanded to other colonies. They participated in the events that led up to the Boston Massacre in 1770 and instigated the Boston Tea Party in 1773. The Sons of Liberty circulated petitions, published polemical anti-British articles, held public demonstrations, tarred and feathered Loyalists, and attacked the homes of British officials. Equally influential as their male counterparts, the Daughters of Liberty assembled in communities throughout the colonies to support nonimportation and the patriot cause in general. Their primary function was to hold spinning bees at which women would gather at the homes of sympathizers to produce homespun for local consumption. The Daughters of Liberty received praise in newspapers for their hard work, but what resounded loudest was the political character of the activities and the symbolic message of female virtue.

See Also: Boston Massacre; Boston Tea Party; Revolution, American; Stamp Act.

■ **SOUSA, JOHN PHILIP (1854-1932),** band master and composer. Known as "The March King," the Washington, D.C., native led the U.S. Marine

Corps Band (1880-92), then formed his own touring brass band. Composer of more than 100 patriotic marches including "Semper Fidelis" (1888) and "Stars and Stripes Forever" (1897), he also organized military bands for the U.S. Army during both the Spanish-American War and World War I.

◼ **SOUTER, DAVID (1939-),** associate justice of the U.S. Supreme Court (1990-). He was born in Melrose, Massachusetts, and was a relatively obscure federal appeals court judge and former New Hampshire state attorney general when he was nominated by Pres. George Bush to replace Justice William Brennan on the Court. Although his appointment was hailed by political conservatives, Souter proved to be a moderate swing voter on the Court.

See Also: Supreme Court.

◼ **SOUTH, THE,** term used to designate the southeastern region of the United States, specifically the former slave states south of the Mason-Dixon line. The South is usually taken to mean the states of Virginia, North Carolina, South Carolina, Kentucky, Tennessee, Georgia, Alabama, Mississippi, Arkansas, Louisiana, and, by some accounts, Texas and Florida. The climate of the Southern states is milder than that of the North. Its warm, humid summers and temperate winters were especially conducive to the original agricultural crops of tobacco, cotton, and rice. The term *the South* is also used as the designation for the states that seceded from the Union in 1860-61 to create the Confederate States of America during the Civil War (1861-65). The port city of Charleston, South Carolina, was an early urban center in the region, but industry has favored towns such as Birmingham, Alabama, and Atlanta, Georgia, now the major metropolises of the South.

◼ **SOUTH CAROLINA,** the smallest of the South Atlantic states. It is bounded on the north and east by North Carolina, on the south and west by Georgia, and on the south and east by the Atlantic Ocean. The Savannah River forms most of its border with Georgia. The southeastern half of the state is a coastal plain; the northwestern part consists of rolling hills. Chemicals, metalworking, and textiles are the state's chief industries.

South Carolina was one of the 13 colonies that formed the United States. Heavily dependent on slave labor, it was the first state to secede from the Union and the site of the opening battle of the Civil War. It suffered widespread devastation by the end of the Civil War. Foreign investment contributed noticeably to an economic upsurge in the 1970s and 1980s, although the state remained one of the nation's poorest.

Capital: Columbia. Area: 31,117 square miles. Population (1995 est.): 3,673,000.

See Also: Charleston; Sherman, William Tecumseh; Vesey Conspiracy.

◼ **SOUTH DAKOTA,** a western Midwest state. It is bounded on the north by North Dakota, on the west by Montana and Wyoming, on the south by Nebraska, and on the east by Minnesota and Iowa. The Missouri River runs south through the center of the state before forming the eastern part of its southern border. The eastern two-fifths of South Dakota is prairie, the western three-fifths part of the Great Plains. The Black Hills, in the southwest, are an extension of the Rocky Mountains. South Dakota's economy relies heavily on agriculture and food processing plants. It became a state in 1889.

Capital: Pierre. Area: 77,121 square miles. Population (1995 est.): 729,000.

See Also: Black Hills; Great Plains; Lewis and Clark Expedition; Missouri River; Mount Rushmore; Sioux; Wounded Knee, Occupation of; Wounded Knee Massacre.

◼ **SOUTHERN CHRISTIAN LEADERSHIP CONFERENCE (SCLC),** civil rights organization. The successful Montgomery, Alabama, bus boycott (1955-56) identified two important elements in the struggle for racial equality: the power of the black church and the leadership abilities of Rev. Martin Luther King, Jr. In January 1957, King and others, including Bayard Rustin, Fred Shuttlesworth, and Ralph Abernathy, formed the SCLC to provide aid and direction to the efforts of local church and civic groups working for racial justice throughout the South. King's charismatic leadership thrust the SCLC into a position of public prominence among civil rights organizations. After some setbacks, SCLC's campaigns to desegregate Birmingham and

Selma, Alabama, drew national attention to the problem of racial justice in the South and the cause of civil rights. Building on the achievements of the passage of the Civil Rights Act of 1964, SCLC turned to the issue of voting rights and equality of economic opportunity. A SCLC campaign in 1966 in Chicago showed that the South held no monopoly on racial inequality. SCLC then made plans for a national "Poor People's Campaign." Following King's assassination in April 1968, the SCLC continued under the leadership of Ralph Abernathy, but the radicalization of social protest after 1968 and the absence of King's magnetic leadership cast long shadows over subsequent SCLC activities.

—JOHN R. NEFF

See Also: Abernathy, Ralph David; Civil Rights Movement; King, Martin Luther, Jr.

BIBLIOGRAPHY: Raines, Howell, *My Soul Is Rested* (Penguin 1977).

■ **SOUTH PASS,** wide pass through the Rocky Mountains in central Wyoming. In the 1840s settlers traveling west on the Oregon Trail followed the Sweetwater River to South Pass. The 7,550-foot-high pass provided the ideal passageway over the Continental Divide because it was wide and the grades to and from it were accessible to wagons. South Pass's importance as a transit point was enhanced because the headwaters of the Platte, Missouri, Arkansas, Rio Grande, Snake, and Colorado rivers all rise relatively nearby.

See Also: Continental Divide.

■ **SOUTHWEST,** term used to designate the southwestern region of the United States. The Southwest is both the oldest and the youngest part of the United States, with ancient Indian settlements and major 20th-century urban centers. After the War of 1812 the term *Southwest* meant Missouri, Arkansas, and Louisiana. After the Mexican War ended in 1848, however, the term came to embrace parts of the newly acquired regions of Texas, New Mexico, Arizona, Utah, Colorado, and Nevada. The designation frequently overlapped with the meaning of the West, although California was excluded. One of the defining characteristics of the region is its aridity, and the conservation of water resources has long been the Southwest's chief concern. The Southwest has few

natural lakes, but federally built hydroelectric dams on the area's rivers have created huge artificial lakes, among them Lake Havasu, Lake Powell, Lake Texoma, and Lake Mead. Until the early 20th century the Southwest's economic mainstays were agriculture and livestock. The discovery of oil—at Bartlesville, Oklahoma, in 1897 and Beaumont, Texas, in 1901—transformed the region's economy turning Tulsa, Oklahoma City, Dallas, Houston, and San Antonio into the area's metropolitan centers. More recently Phoenix and Tucson have experienced rapid urban growth as the region's economy shifted to high-tech industries.

See Also: Mexican War.

■ **SOUTHWORTH, EMMA (1819-99),** popular writer of sentimental novels about the antebellum South, born in Washington, D.C. In *The Hidden Hand* (1859) and other works, she created strong women characters who overcome adversity without the aid of male heroes.

■ **SOYBEANS,** a legume of northeast Asian origin. First introduced to the United States in 1804, the soybean remained a novelty crop that was used primarily for animal feed for much of the 19th century. Not until German chemists developed a technique for removing the unpalatable flavor from soybean oil in the 1930s did soybeans become widely accepted in America for human consumption. Following World War II, soybean cultivation spread into the Midwest and the South, often replacing cotton as the leading cash crop.

■ **SPACE EXPLORATION,** investigation of outer space through the use of manned and unmanned spacecraft. While human beings have been exploring space visually since the earliest civilization began to contemplate the heavens, the modern space age is commonly associated with the launching of the Sputnik satellite by the Soviet Union on Oct. 4, 1957. The first man-made object to orbit the earth, Sputnik touched off a furor in the United States as Americans came face to face with the Soviet superiority in rocket technology. During the height of the Cold War in the 1950s, this Soviet advantage was perceived to have implications not only for space exploration, but for matters of national security as well.

In response to this crisis, the Eisenhower administration undertook a major effort to bridge the gap between U.S. and Soviet space technology. In an effort to catch up with the Soviets, Eisenhower pushed through major funding for science education, arguing that more U.S. scientists were needed to compete technologically with the Soviets. In 1958, the National Aeronautics and Space Administration (NASA) was founded to spearhead efforts to beat the Soviets in the space race. Early in that year, the United States had launched its own first satellite, Explorer I.

From the very beginning, both the U.S. and the Soviet programs focused on manned exploration. In 1961, the Soviets once again achieved a milestone when Yuri Gagarin became the first man in space, orbiting the earth a single time in his Vostok 1 spacecraft. Less than a month later, the

The space shuttle has become the workhorse of the National Aeronautics and Space Administration (NASA).

United States followed with a suborbital flight by Alan Shepard, Jr., the first U.S. astronaut in space. Immediately after this, Pres. John F. Kennedy announced America's commitment to being first to land on the Moon, a goal he believed could be achieved by the end of the decade. This was the origin of the Apollo space program that fulfilled Kennedy's promise on July 20, 1969, when Neil Armstrong and Edwin Aldrin, Jr., became the first men to set foot on the Moon.

While the attention of the nation was largely focused on manned space exploration, other space programs were also under way that ultimately may have been more significant in terms of understanding our universe and in changing the daily life of Americans. The earliest U.S. space mission, Explorer I, for example, had carried scientific instruments designed by James Van Allen that had discovered radiation belts surrounding the earth. In 1960, the first U.S. weather satellite was launched, initiating the revolution in our understanding of global weather that took place beginning in the 1960s. By the mid-1960s, communication satellites were facilitating contact with the farthest reaches of the globe and allowing for vast increases in intercontinental communications. Advances in ground-based observations allowed astronomers to probe more deeply into the recesses of the universe and to begin to unravel its origins. A series of unmanned probes also was launched to investigate the properties of other regions of the solar system, especially our neighboring planets and the Sun. The landing of Viking 2 on Mars in 1976 drew wide public attention because of its search for Martian life, although its experiments detected no organisms at that time. In 1997, however, an unmanned vehicle successfully landed on Mars and began sending photographs and geological data back to earth. The landing was a major milestone in the space program.

Since the achievements of the 1960s and the 1970s, the space program has been struggling to define its role and has faced increasing public scrutiny. Skylab, a manned space exploration station launched in 1973, failed to capture the public's imagination or pave the way for a more permanent manned space station. During the early 1980s, a space shuttle was developed as a reusable orbiter making space missions safer, more affordable, and more cost efficient. Tragically, the explosion of the space shuttle *Challenger* in January 1986, and the subsequent investigation into its causes, exposed a number of failures within the shuttle program. NASA and the U.S. space exploration program recovered their credibility and prestige. By the late 1990s, the shuttle was flying on a fairly regular basis. During the 1990s, an era of cost cutting and budgetary crisis, the space program sought to redefine its role in a time of shrinking funds and public disinterest.

—DAVID A. VALONE

See Also: Science.

BIBLIOGRAPHY: McCurdy, Howard E., *Inside NASA: High Technology and Organizational Change in the U.S. Space Program* (Johns Hopkins Univ. Press 1993); McDougall, Walter A., *The Heavens and the Earth: A Political History of the Space Age* (Basic Books 1985); Shelton, William Roy, *American Space Exploration: The First Decade* (Little, Brown 1967).

■ **SPANISH-AMERICAN WAR (1898-99),** conflict that ended Spain's overseas empire and secured for the United States a de facto protectorate over Cuba and possession of Puerto Rico, Guam, and the Philippines. Begun in 1895, the Cuban guerrilla war for independence devastated the island and threatened American strategic and economic interests. Spanish atrocities, publicized in the American newspapers, notably the "yellow journals," aroused widespread humanitarian indignation. Presidents Grover Cleveland and William McKinley failed to secure a diplomatic settlement of the war because of Spain's unwillingness to grant Cuban independence. The explosion of the U.S.S. *Maine* in Havana harbor on Feb. 15, 1898, further inflamed American public opinion. On April 19 Congress authorized armed American intervention to end the Spanish-Cuban conflict. On April 21 McKinley ordered a naval blockade of Cuban ports; and by the end of the month the United States and Spain had exchanged declarations of war. Adm. George Dewey decimated the Spanish fleet in the Philippines at the Battle of Manila Bay on May 1.

The Course of the War. Following a previously developed war plan, the newly modernized U.S. fleet under Rear Adm. William T. Sampson blockaded Cuba to cut off supplies to Spain's 150,000 troops on the island. In the Pacific, as part of the same plan, the Asiatic Squadron under Commodore George Dewey on May 1 destroyed a Spanish flotilla in the Battle of Manila Bay. Following up this success, McKinley directed the U.S. Army, which was struggling to expand from its peacetime strength of 25,000 men into a war force of nearly 300,000 regulars and volunteers, to launch immediate expeditions against Manila and Havana. The 10,000-man Philippine expedition departed from San Francisco between May 25 and June 29 and by August 1 was ashore and ready to attack Manila.

The Havana expedition never sailed. Spain late in April dispatched four armored cruisers and three torpedo boat destroyers under Adm. Pascual Cervera to the Caribbean. This squadron, formidable on paper but actually ill-prepared for combat, arrived in the harbor of Santiago de Cuba on May 19. In response the United States shifted Sampson's fleet from Havana to blockade Santiago and dispatched a 15,000-man army expedition to help the navy destroy Cervera's ships and take the city, Cuba's second largest. Postponing the Havana assault, McKinley ordered preparation of a second expedition to seize Puerto Rico after Santiago fell.

The Santiago expedition—all regular army troops except for three volunteer regiments, including the famous Rough Riders—left Tampa, Florida, on June 14 and disembarked east of Santiago on June 22. Moving inland toward the city, the army, led by Maj. Gen. William R. Shafter, fought a skirmish with a Spanish rear guard at Las Guasimas on June 24. On July 1, in the war's only major land engagement, Shafter's troops overran the outer defenses of Santiago at San Juan Hill and El Caney at a cost of about 1,500 American dead and wounded. The Spanish lost perhaps 700 killed, wounded, and captured. This victory brought Santiago under close siege. With capture of the city certain, Cervera on July 3 took his ships out of the harbor in a vain attempt to run the American blockade. Sampson's fleet, which lost only one man killed in the action, destroyed Cervera's entire squadron in a few hours. The Santiago garrison, short of food and ammunition, capitulated on July 17, leaving the Americans in control of the entire eastern end of Cuba.

The remaining military operations of the war

American troops occupy the Philippines during the Spanish-American War of 1898. The United States emerged from the war with its own overseas empire, including the Philippines and Puerto Rico.

went easily for the Americans. Maj. Gen. Nelson A. Miles landed at Ponce, Puerto Rico, with 17,000 troops on July 25 and rapidly overran most of the island against weak resistance. In the Philippines, American land and naval forces on August 14 captured Manila after only a token Spanish defense.

The Peace Settlement. With Santiago and Cervera's fleet lost, Spain sued for peace. Through French mediation, the United States and Spain on August 12 agreed to preliminary terms: an immediate cease-fire (news of which reached Manila only after the city's fall); Spanish withdrawal from Cuba; cession of Puerto Rico and Guam to the United States; and American occupation of Manila pending a final peace treaty. That treaty, signed at Paris on December 10, repeated the terms of the preliminary protocol and transferred ownership of the Philippines to the United States in return for a payment to Spain of $20 million. The United States had acquired an overseas empire and entered the ranks of the Great Powers.

—GRAHAM A. COSMAS

See Also: Dewey, George; Gilded Age; Maine, Sinking of the; Rough Riders.

BIBLIOGRAPHY: Cosmas, Graham A., *An Army for Empire,* 2d ed. (White Mane 1994); Trask, David F., *The War with Spain in 1898* (Macmillan 1981).

■ **SPANISH COLONIES,** possessions of Spain from California to Florida in what is today the United States. Spain planted permanent colonies in North America before its European rivals and held onto those on the mainland until 1821. Built largely for defense on the northern periphery of the empire, the Spanish colonies in North America drained the royal exchequer, offered little opportunity for individual profit, and remained sparsely populated.

In the half-century after Columbus's discovery, a small number of Spanish explorers scoured North America by land and by sea. They reported that the lands north of Mexico lacked precious metals or a strait to Asia. Nonetheless, Spain established bases in North America to secure its coasts from other European powers.

In order to protect the route that homeward-bound, treasure-laden Spanish vessels had to follow as the Gulf Stream carried them out of the Caribbean through the Bahama channel, King

Philip II authorized Pedro Menéndez de Avilés to occupy Florida. Menéndez established several outposts, one as far away as Virginia, but only his initial settlement, at St. Augustine, endured. It became the capital of Spanish Florida and the oldest permanent European settlement in what is today the United States.

Spanish Texas came into being as Spain sought to check the French from pushing the borders of Louisiana westward toward northern Mexico and its rich mines. In 1716 Spain established a permanent presence in Texas on the edge of Louisiana. The small fort of Los Adaes, built in 1721 near the Red River just 12 miles from the French post of Nachitoches, became the capital of Texas. Meanwhile, soldiers and their families founded San Antonio in 1718 as a way station along the 600-mile trail from the Rio Grande to the Red River.

In 1762 defensive considerations prompted Spain to acquire Louisiana from France in the secret Treaty of Fontainbleau at the end of the Seven Years' War. Until 1800, when it secretly ceded Louisiana back to France, Spain hoped that the colony would serve as a buffer against the westward expansion of Britain and, after 1783, the United States.

On the Pacific coast, Spain's perception that Great Britain and Russia might occupy what is today California led it to expand to San Diego (1769), Monterey (1770), San Francisco (1776), and points in-between. Although Russians established Fort Ross to the north of San Francisco Bay in 1812, California remained securely Spanish. Farther north on the Pacific coast, Spain tried to block Britain with settlements on Vancouver Island (1789) and on the Washington state side of the Straits of Juan de Fuca (1792), but they proved short-lived.

New Mexico and Sonora (which extended into today's Arizona) were established without strategic objectives in mind. Juan de Oñate, who gambled his family's fortune to settle among the Pueblo on the Rio Grande in New Mexico in 1598, hoped to find silver or gold or a strait through the continent that would connect the Pacific to the Atlantic. He found neither. Jesuits moving northward to bring their god and their culture to Pima Indians began working in today's southern Arizona in 1700.

Spain sought to incorporate Indians into its colonies. Many of the Hispanics who settled in North America were themselves mestizos, descended from unions of Spaniards and Indians. On its frontiers Spain relied heavily on missionaries to Hispanicize as well as Christianize Indians. European diseases swept away appalling numbers of Indians in and out of the missions, but many of the survivors learned Spanish ways and found niches in Spanish society. So, too, did Indians captured by Spanish slave hunters or ransomed by Spaniards from other tribes. Indians who remained independent of Spaniards found their cultures altered by Spanish horses and trade goods, particularly metal weapons and tools. Old World flora and fauna introduced by Spaniards altered the land as well as its peoples.

However sparsely populated, the Spanish colonies reshaped the physical and human geography of North America from California to Florida. They left an enduring Hispanic imprint on all aspects of life in the Sunbelt states, from the patterns of rural and urban settlement to laws, architecture, and techniques for ranching and farming in dry country. Hispanics themselves, incorporated into the expanding United States, transmitted that culture to the newcomers.

—DAVID J. WEBER

See Also: Exploration and Discovery.
BIBLIOGRAPHY: Bushnell, Amy Turner, *Situado and Sabana: Spain's Support System for the Presidio and Mission Provinces of Florida* (American Museum of Natural History 1994); Weber, David J., *The Spanish Frontier in North America* (Yale Univ. Press 1992).

■ **SPANISH MAIN,** region of South America on the Caribbean Sea from the Isthmus of Panama east to the mouth of the Orinoco River in Venezuela. During colonial times the term probably referred to the holdings of the Spanish on the South American mainland. "Spanish Main" came to symbolize the supposed romance of English pirates who attacked Spanish fleets carrying silver and gold back to Europe.
See Also: Piracy.

■ **SPEAKEASIES,** illegal saloons that sprang up across the country following passage of the 18th Amendment (1919), which began the 14-year era of federal Prohibition. In New York City alone, there were an estimated 30,000 speakeasies, which ranged from elegant nightclubs to shabby back rooms. Subject to periodic police raids, most speakeasies operated with the tacit approval of local law enforcement officials.

See Also: Prohibition.

■ **SPECIE CIRCULAR (July 11, 1836),** executive order issued by Sec. of the Treasury Levi Woodbury, ordering U.S. land offices to accept only gold or silver coin as payment. At a time when inflation threatened to run rampant, many speculators were using credit, often from foreign banks, to finance land purchases and other investments. Other people used "wildcat" money printed by local banks. By midsummer 1836 it had become clear that the influx of questionable capital had stimulated more production than labor could afford to consume, and the Bank of England raised interest rates for Americans. Interest rates in New York rose to 24 percent, and in July Pres. Andrew Jackson directed Woodbury to issue the Specie Circular. Panicked investors rushed to change paper money into species, and U.S. banks began to call in loans, resulting in the Panic of 1837. Numerous businesses went under, and the United States was in the throes of a deep economic depression for the next seven years.

See Also: Bank War.

BIBLIOGRAPHY: Sellers, Charles G., *The Market Revolution: Jacksonian America, 1815-1846* (Oxford Univ. Press 1991).

■ **SPENCER, LILLY MARTIN (1822-1902),** realist painter of portraits and family scenes. Born in Exeter, England, she immigrated to the United States in 1830. She enjoyed commercial success through commissions and lithograph reproductions. In 1850, she illustrated Elizabeth Ellet's *Women in the American Revolution.*

■ **SPIELBERG, STEVEN (1947-),** film director and producer. Born in Cincinnati, Ohio, he began working in television in the late 1960s and then directed a series of popular and profitable box office hits including *Jaws* (1975), *E.T.* (1982), and *Jurassic Park* (1993). Criticized for avoiding serious issues in these works, Spielberg later won an Academy Award for *Schindler's List* (1994), an account of the Jewish Holocaust during World War II, and won plaudits for *Amistad* (1997).

See Also: Motion Pictures.

■ **SPIRITUALS,** religious folk songs. Spirituals originated in American revivalist activity between the mid-18th century and the end of the 19th. African Americans and whites each developed a distinct but related category of spirituals.

African-American spirituals constitute the largest and perhaps most recognizable body of American folksongs. Closely associated with gospel music, African-American spirituals grew out of the Southern slave experience and emphasize hope and salvation. There are also strong influences of white religious music and African elements in the songs. Their original contexts include religious meetings and work; many of them are structured on a call-and-response pattern. The Fisk University Jubilee Singers first brought these spirituals to large white audiences in the United States and in Europe in 1871. As their popularity grew, however, their appeal in African-American churches waned, and they were often replaced by gospel music.

The less well-known white spirituals originated during the important religious awakenings of the 18th and 19th centuries. This type is composed of folk hymns, religious ballads, and camp-meeting revivals, as well as secular folksongs.

—GUY NELSON

See Also: Gospel; Music.

BIBLIOGRAPHY: Lovell, John, Jr., *Black Song: The Forge and Flame—The Story of How the Afro-American Spiritual was Hammered Out* (Macmillan 1972); Walker, Wyatt Tee, *"Somebody's Calling My Name": Black Sacred Music and Social Change* (Judson Press 1979).

■ **SPOILS SYSTEM,** the derogatory label affixed to Pres. Andrew Jackson's attempt to reform the political patronage system in the 1830s. The phrase refers to the practice of using government jobs to reward followers. American politicians had initially rejected this Old World custom, but leaders soon discovered the wisdom of filling administrative posts with friends and family. Democratic politicians, with a vision of politics controlled by parties, insisted that party loyalty be put above personal allegiance.

Although this spoils system had long existed in American politics, it became most associated with Jackson's presidency (1829-37), which made office removal an official policy. Jackson believed that long tenures in government office led to moral and financial corruption as well as the growth of an official aristocracy. He championed "office rotation"—regular replacements that would make government more democratic.

Jackson's critics saw the president's policy as an excuse for patronage, an impression reinforced by New York's Sen. William L. Marcy, a Jackson supporter who declared, "To the victor goes the spoils." According to his enemies, Jackson abused his power by replacing numbers of men of the better classes with uneducated political cronies. Recent research has demonstrated that he actually replaced fewer than 10 percent of incumbents, generally with men of similar education and experience but of more modest backgrounds.

Although Jackson's removal policy initially uncovered dramatic abuses of the public trust and opened government service more widely, it provided a bad precedent for subsequent administrations and was carried to new heights of abuse by his critics, the Whigs. Congress finally reformed the system with the Pendleton Act (1883), which established the Civil Service Commission.

—CATHERINE ALLGOR

See Also: Civil Service; Jackson, Andrew; Pendleton Act.

BIBLIOGRAPHY: Cole, Donald B., *The Presidency of Andrew Jackson* (Univ. Press of Kansas 1933); Remini, Robert V., *Andrew Jackson and the Course of American Freedom, 1822-1832* (Harper & Row 1981).

■ **SPOKANE INDIANS.** *See: Great Basin and Rocky Mountain Indians.*

■ **SPORTS,** major American leisure-time activities that reflect the diversity of the United States. Spectator sports and organized physical activities have evolved in response to economic, social, and cultural changes throughout the nation's history.

European settlers brought traditional sports with them to America. Horse racing, frequently accompanied by heavy gambling, was popular among wealthy planters in Virginia and Maryland. Local taverns became sporting centers for the working class. Sporting activities were often viewed with suspicion by the moralistic middle class. Violent sports such as boxing and wrestling were seen as antithetical to social stability and were frequently associated with gambling and drinking. Despite organized opposition, spectator sports, including professional foot racing (pedestrianism), horse racing, and boxing became increasingly popular in the early 1800s.

In the years following the Civil War (1861-65), a new sport, baseball, became the national pastime. Based on such traditional stick and ball games as town ball and rounders, modern baseball rules were codified in 1845 by Alexander Cartwright, a member of the New York Knickerbockers club. Ball teams blossomed across the country, representing ethnic and political organizations, social clubs, and companies. The growth of the game reflected the nation's development as an industrial economy. Rules were standardized, and the sport became organized and professionalized. The first avowedly professional team, the Cincinnati Red Stockings, debuted in 1869 and in 1876 the National League of Professional Baseball Clubs was organized.

In the late 1800s, the therapeutic and educational values of sports were also promoted by reformers concerned with the threat of urbanization and immigration. Groups such as the Young Men's Christian Association saw sports as a means to instill discipline, order, and morality on urban youth, and educators began incorporating sports and physical education in their curricula. Sports and physical activity were also promoted as an antidote to the comforts of modern life. College sports provided manly activities for upper-class youth.

Intercollegiate sports had begun in the 1850s and became widely popular in the 1870s. By the 1890s, college football had become a major spectator sport. The uniquely American system of intercollegiate sports as commercial entertainment was firmly in place by World War I (1914-18). Upper-class youth also participated in club sports such as golf and tennis, sports that quickly spread to the middle class as well. Baseball remained the nation's favorite sport at the turn of the century, but the professional game was segregated. African-American athletes were barred from organized baseball.

20th-Century Trends. The 1920s were a Golden Age of sport. Economic prosperity and new media such as radio and newsreels lifted spectator sports to new popularity. Star performers such as baseball's Babe Ruth, boxing's Jack Dempsey, and golf's Bobby Jones became celebrities idolized by the public. Women athletes such as swimmer Gertrude Ederle and tennis star Helen Wills shared the limelight, but sports were still seen as a man's world. In schools, while boys played organized team sports, girls often participated in noncompetitive play days. Excessive physical activity was feared to be unhealthy for girls, and competition was seen as unfeminine.

Sports provided an important distraction for the nation during the Depression of the 1930s and World War II (1941-45). The postwar era proved a new Golden Age. Jackie Robinson broke the color line in baseball (1947), and during the next decade African Americans entered the major leagues in substantial numbers. Television turned sports such as professional football and basketball as well as old standbys such as baseball and boxing into mass entertainment. Professional sports followed the population West and South, and both spectator and participant sports flourished.

While spectator sports became mass entertainment, and professional sports stars rivaled show business celebrities in fame and fortune, participant sports also reached new heights. Commercial fitness and recreation became multibillion dollar businesses as adults became increasingly health conscious. Youngsters, both boys and girls, took part in organized sports in record numbers as their parents hoped sports would provide wholesome activity and future financial rewards such as college scholarships. Sports in America continue to provide mass entertainment, recreation, and social structure to an increasingly diverse nation.

—TIM ASHWELL

See Also: Baseball; Basketball; Boxing; Football; Lacrosse; Rodeo; individual biographies.

BIBLIOGRAPHY: Gorn, Elliott J., and Warren Goldstein, *A Brief History of American Sports* (Hill & Wang 1993); Guttman, Allen, *From Ritual to Record: The Nature of Modern Sports* (Oxford Univ. Press 1978).

■ **SPOTSYLVANIA, BATTLE OF (1864),** Civil War battle. With Gen. Robert E. Lee's Confederate army entrenched around Spotsylvania Courthouse in Virginia, Union Gen. Ulysses S. Grant attempted flanking and frontal assaults on May 9 and 10, but the Confederate line held firm. On May 11 a local attack by Gen. Winfield Hancock threatened to split Lee's army in two, but a fierce Confederate counterattack and ferocious trench fighting in the infamous "Bloody Angle" resulted in stalemate. Grant gave up on Spotsylvania and marched his army to the south to threaten Richmond.

See Also: Civil War.

■ **SPRUANCE, RAYMOND AMES (1886-1969),** World War II admiral, born in Baltimore, Maryland. Spruance emerged as the victor in the pivotal Battle of Midway (June 3-6, 1942). Spruance's fleet repulsed a huge Japanese invasion force and sank three Japanese carriers, thus turning the tide of the war in the Pacific.

See Also: Midway, Battle of; World War II.

■ **SQUANTO (c. 1580-1622),** Wampanoag Indian. Squanto was kidnapped around 1605 by an English sea captain and sold into slavery. Later, he was ransomed and taken to England. He returned to his New England homeland around 1619, where he found that his entire village of Patuxet had been wiped out by an epidemic of bubonic plague. Squanto subsequently stayed with Massasoit's Wampanoag and, when the English Pilgrims landed at the site of Patuxet in 1620, Squanto acted as Massasoit's interpreter.

See Also: Frontier in American History; Indians of North America; Massasoit.

■ **SQUARE DEAL,** Pres. Theodore Roosevelt's term for the basis of his domestic policies. During his first term (1901-05), Roosevelt viewed progressive reform only as a means to head off potential class war. Thus when he spoke of the "square deal" in 1903, he was still essentially a conservative. Under this vague conception, the president would exercise regulatory responsibility to see that each group of economic participants behaved fairly, or square. Roosevelt asserted that this would contribute to the economic well-being of the entire nation. Although persuasive in principle, the conception lacked detail. The only specific proposal of the square deal was for establishing a bureau of corporations to monitor and regulate interstate business and large corporations.

After Roosevelt's reelection in 1904, his domestic policies became increasingly more progressive. His square deal came to include more direct business regulation and greater economic redistribution. Among his lasting policy changes were federal workers' unemployment compensation and veterans' pension programs. By the end of his second term, Roosevelt had introduced the most wide-reaching economic and social programs ever proposed in America. Despite his steady shift from conservative to progressive, Roosevelt continued to advocate a domestic policy based on the original "square deal"—one in which the president would be an impartial mediator between various economic interests.

—GUY NELSON

See Also: Progressivism; Roosevelt, Theodore.
BIBLIOGRAPHY: Blum, John Morton, *The Republican Roosevelt* (Harvard Univ. Press 1952); Gould, Lewis L., *The Presidency of Theodore Roosevelt* (Univ. of Kansas Press 1991).

■ **STALWARTS AND HALF-BREEDS,** terms used to describe factions within the Republican party of the 1870s and 1880s. The primary issue was that of civil service reform. Stalwarts, such as Roscoe Conkling of New York, opposed regulation because their power rested on the ability to hand out government jobs. Such patronage—or the spoils system, as it was then called—angered those who felt that government appointments should be made on the basis of merit. Ardent supporters of civil service reform were known as Mugwumps, while those who fell between the two extremes were called Half-Breeds. These two groups united in 1880 in support of James A. Garfield's presidential candidacy. Republican Stalwarts were appeased with having one of their own, Chester A. Arthur, as vice-presidential candidate. Four months after taking office, Garfield was shot by a recently fired government clerk. While the Stalwarts were not behind the assassination, Garfield's death amplified the cry for civil service reform, resulting in passage of the 1883 Pendleton Act.

See Also: Arthur, Chester Alan; Conkling, Roscoe; Garfield, James Abram; Gilded Age; Mugwumps; Pendleton Act; Republican Party; Spoils System.

■ **STAMP ACT (1765),** act of the British Parliament that imposed taxes on a wide variety of public documents used in the American colonies. Its purpose was to help pay for a standing army in America. This tax provoked widespread resistance from Americans, who considered it a violation of their right to representative taxation, and Parliament repealed it in 1766.

See Also: Revolution, American.

■ **STAMP ACT CONGRESS (1765),** convention composed of delegates from nine American colonies who gathered in New York City to respond to Parliament's imposition of the Stamp Act. The congress declared that English citizens could not be taxed without their consent.

See Also: Revolution, American; Stamp Act.

■ **STANDARD OIL TRUST (1882),** organization formed by John D. Rockefeller to control the petroleum industry. Rockefeller formed the Standard Oil Company in 1870 and developed every aspect of the industry, from transporting crude oil to marketing the final product. He cut deals with the railroads, used pools to crush rivals, and controlled 90 percent of the country's oil-refining capacity by 1879. To consolidate his business interests more efficiently, he established the Standard Oil Trust in 1882. More effective and permanent than pools, the trust legally centralized control over different companies by setting up one board of trustees to run them. Rockefeller's stockholders exchanged their stock for trust certificates, which allowed Standard Oil Trust to integrate the petroleum industry vertically by controlling everything from production to local retailing, and horizontally by merging competing oil companies into one giant system. The company became a model of corporate consolidation and an object of social criticism. In 1892, the Supreme Court of Ohio ordered Standard Oil Trust dissolved because it restrained trade. Rockefeller reorganized it as a holding company, Standard Oil of New Jersey, which broke up after an antitrust suit in 1911.

See Also: Antitrust Legislation; Industrial Revolution; Rockefeller, John Davison.

■ **STANDING BEAR (c. 1829-1908),** Ponca leader. Standing Bear and his peaceful tribe lived on the Great Plains in northern Nebraska. In 1868, the federal government gave the treaty-guaranteed homelands of the Ponca to the Sioux. In 1877, when the Ponca were forcibly removed to southern Indian Territory, Standing Bear led a group of Ponca on a journey back to their homeland. They were arrested, but Standing Bear's case aroused public sympathy. He was allowed to return to the Great Plains, where the Ponca were eventually granted a small reservation.

See Also: Indians of North America.

■ **STANDISH, MILES (1584-1656),** military leader and early pioneer at Plymouth colony. Born in Lancashire, England, Standish became acquainted with the Puritans living in Leyden when campaigning in the Low Countries. In 1620 the Pilgrims hired Standish to sail with them to America. At Plymouth he served variously as chief explorer, military adviser, negotiator with the Indians, and defense architect. Initially, Standish was an employee of the Pilgrim group, but eventually he became a full member of the community, holding public office and amassing a considerable estate.

See Also: Plymouth Settlement.

■ **STANFORD, LELAND (1824-93),** railroad builder, governor of California, U.S. senator, and philanthropist. Born in Watervliet, New York, Stanford first pursued a career as a lawyer. He left the law in 1855 to join his brothers' wholesaling business in California. Stanford ran for governor in 1859 and lost but tried again in 1861 and won. During his term he approved grants of public lands to the Central Pacific Railroad, of which he was president and director.

Ground was broken for the Central Pacific in 1863, and the last spike driven in 1869. The railroad benefited from federal land grants and through the diversion of government funds. The partners of the Central Pacific formed the Contract and Finance Company, which then built the line at hugely inflated costs. Stanford was dead when the scandal erupted in 1894 and the U.S. government filed suit against his estate for $15 million. The case was resolved in his widow's favor in 1896.

In 1885 Stanford was elected to the U.S. Senate, where he served until his death. He also spent time developing his country estates. There he bred racehorses, experimented with photography, and established an extensive vineyard.

In 1850 Stanford married Jane Elizabeth Lathrop. Their only son, Leland, Jr., died in 1884 at 15. In his memory the Stanfords founded Stanford University, which became the primary occupation of Jane after her husband's death.

—CLAIRE STROM

See Also: Industrial Revolution; Railroads.

BIBLIOGRAPHY: Tutorow, Norman E., *Leland Stanford: Man of Many Careers* (Pacific Coast Publishers 1971).

■ **STANLEY, WENDELL (1904-71),** biochemist. Born in Ridgeville, Indiana, he worked at the Rockefeller Institute (1931-48), where he was the first to isolate a virus as a pure, crystalline chemical compound (1935). His isolation of the tobacco mosaic disease virus revealed a thin crystal to be the causative agent of disease, a discovery that opened up a new field of biochemical and medical study and earned him a share of the 1946 Nobel Prize in Chemistry. He established the virus lab at the University of California, Berkeley, in 1948 and crystallized the polio virus in 1955.

See Also: Science.

■ **STANTON, EDWIN MCMASTERS (1814-69),** U.S. attorney general and secretary of war. Born in Steubenville, Ohio, Stanton practiced law and held minor public offices before becoming Pres. James Buchanan's attorney general in 1860. A Democrat, Stanton was a supporter of states' rights who nevertheless adamantly opposed slavery. In 1862 he was appointed secretary of war by Pres. Abraham Lincoln and, although he had no military experience and often disagreed with Lincoln, he served very efficiently. Stanton was present at Lincoln's deathbed (1865). Continuing in office under Lincoln's successor, Andrew Johnson, Stanton sharply disagreed with Johnson's lenient Reconstruction policy. The president's attempt to fire him (1867) in defiance of the Tenure of Office Act precipitated Congress's impeachment of Johnson. Stanton resigned when Johnson was acquitted. Pres. Ulysses S. Grant appointed Stanton to the Supreme Court (1869), but Stanton died before actually sitting on the Court.

See Also: Civil War; Johnson, Andrew; Tenure of Office Act.

■ **STANTON, ELIZABETH CADY (1815-1902),** women's rights leader, social critic, and reformer. Born in Johnstown, New York, into an elite family, Elizabeth Cady received the finest education available to women. An active abolitionist, she fell in love with fellow reformer Harry B. Stanton. They married in 1840 and traveled to London to attend the World's Antislavery Convention. There Cady Stanton met Quaker activist Lucretia Mott when they were both denied a seat in the convention because of their sex.

In 1848, a young mother in rural New York, Cady Stanton was the moving spirit and organizer of the first public forum on women's rights, the Seneca Falls Convention. She adapted the Declaration of Independence as a women's rights manifesto and, over the objections of Stanton and Mott, included a suffrage resolution.

In 1851, Cady Stanton began her lifelong collaboration and friendship with Susan B. Anthony. Anthony was the organizer, and Cady Stanton the visionary. Cady Stanton always preferred to stay home and write, partly because of her family duties—she bore 7 children in 17 years. Anthony, however, always urged her into more public roles. During the Civil War the two founded the National Women's Loyalty League; after the war, when the 14th and 15th Amendments failed to grant universal adult suffrage, Cady Stanton and Anthony formed the National Woman Suffrage Association (1869). Testing the Constitution's gender-neutral language on candidate eligibility, Cady Stanton ran for Congress in 1866, garnering just 24 votes out of 12,000. She cofounded a periodical with Anthony, *The Revolution* (1868-70), and traveled west to campaign for suffrage.

As Anthony increasingly narrowed her focus to the issue of female suffrage, Cady Stanton took a larger, more radical view of women's condition. Her most famous speech, "The Solitude of the Self" (1892), stressed human individuality over gender solidarity. She was the first American publicly to advocate a woman's right to divorce and speak about sexual issues, including a woman's right to refuse marital sex and to prevent pregnancy. Although she continued a proponent of suffrage, Cady Stanton saw political equality as a means to the larger end of changing culture.

In 1869, Elizabeth Cady Stanton cofounded the National Woman Suffrage Association with her lifelong friend and partner in feminism, Susan B. Anthony.

Cady Stanton's atheism, however, brought about her marginalization in the increasingly Christian reform and suffrage movements. She argued that organized religion inculcated submission to authority and conservatism; moreover, she viewed Christianity as essentially antiwoman. She offended many by publishing *The Woman's Bible* (1898), which offered a feminist interpretation.

Although Cady Stanton's contribution to suffrage in particular (the language of the 19th Amendment differs little from her 1878 version) and women's rights in general was immense, historians and the public have long ignored her role.

—CATHERINE ALLGOR

See Also: *Anthony, Susan B.; Gilded Age; Mott, Lucretia Coffin; Seneca Falls Convention; Women in American History; Women's Movement.*

BIBLIOGRAPHY: DuBois, Ellen Carol, ed., *Elizabeth Cady Stanton, Susan B. Anthony: Correspondence, Writings, Speeches* (Schocken 1981); Stanton, Elizabeth Cady, *Eighty Years and More, Reminiscences, 1815-1897* (reprint; Schocken 1971).

■ **STAPLE ACT (1663),** British legislation requiring that all European goods bound for the colonies first pass through English ports. This promoted British merchants' interests over those of colonial merchants and consumers by forcing them to pay handling charges and resale costs.

■ **STARR, BELLE (1848-89),** legendary southwestern outlaw. Born near Carthage, Missouri, she was a convicted horse thief and consort of outlaws such as the James brothers. After her death, she was immortalized by the largely invented account of her life published in Richard K. Fox's *Bella Starr, the Bandit Queen; or, the Female Jesse James* (1889).

    See Also: Frontier in American History.

■ **STAR ROUTE FRAUDS,** gross overcharging for services by the privately contracted mail delivery systems for remote areas in the American West. After the frauds were exposed in 1881, second assistant postmaster general Thomas J. Brady was charged with but later acquitted of receiving bribes in exchange for allowing contractors to overcharge.

    See Also: Gilded Age.

■ **STAR-SPANGLED BANNER, THE,** designated the U.S. national anthem in 1931. Francis Scott Key's lyrics recount the British attack on Fort McHenry, Baltimore (Sept. 13-14, 1814), and were set to the tune of "Anacreon in Heaven," a tavern song.

■ **STATE, DEPARTMENT OF,** cabinet department of the U.S. government responsible for administering foreign policy. The State Department was the first executive agency created (1789) by Congress under the new Constitution and assumed administration of foreign policy from the Department of Foreign Affairs that had been established under the Articles of Confederation (1781). Pres. George Washington appointed Thomas Jefferson the first secretary of state. From 1800 through 1824 the State Department was the traditional stepping stone to the presidency; each president from Jefferson to John Quincy Adams had previously served as secretary of state. The importance of the department grew in the 20th century as the United States expanded its role in world affairs. Following World War II, three strong secretaries of state—George C. Marshall (1947-49), Dean Acheson (1949-53), and John Foster Dulles (1953-59)—helped create the U.S. policy of containment of the Soviet Union during the Cold War.

    See Also: Acheson, Dean; Dulles, John Foster; Marshall, George C., Jr.

BIBLIOGRAPHY: Acheson, Dean, *Present at the Creation: My Years in the State Department* (Norton 1969).

■ **STEAMBOATS,** as a major transportation system date from Robert Fulton's demonstration of his paddle wheeler *North River* (later renamed the *Clermont*) on the Hudson River in 1807. The boat made the trip from New York City to Albany in only 32 hours, far faster than a sailing vessel. But contrary to myth, Fulton did not invent the steamboat. In the 1780s American inventors John Fitch (on the Delaware River) and James Rumsey (on the Potomac) separately and independently demonstrated steamboats of their own design, and in 1806 John Stevens, who held an American patent for a steam boiler, sailed the first successful seagoing steamship. It was Fulton's design, however, that proved commercially viable and opened American rivers to steam power. The steamboat was the first American invention to have worldwide impact.

    The first steamboat to operate on the Mississippi River was the side-wheeler *New Orleans*, its maiden voyage between New Orleans and Natchez in 1811. Five years later Henry M. Shreve launched the *Washington*, a double-deck, shallow-hull side-wheeler with light yet powerful high-pressure boilers. Shreve's design allowed boats to carry large cargoes on relatively shallow waters, and soon hundreds of boats were plying the inland waters. Steamboats transformed commerce on the country's great inland river system, and cities such as Pittsburgh, Cincinnati, and St. Louis experienced a surge of economic growth. They were especially important in the transport of cotton along the lower Mississippi. By the 1840s steamboats on western waters were annually hauling 10 million tons of freight.

    As the number of steamboats grew, steamboat accidents increased. Boilers exploded, and deadly fires often claimed the lives of dozens and destroyed freight valued in the millions. In 1838, Congress passed the Steamboat Act (strengthened in 1852), which set standards for the construction and operation of boilers, required measures to prevent fires and collisions, and established an inspection system to ensure that the regulations were enforced.

In the 1830s steamboats began to suffer from the competition of inland canals, which drained much commercial traffic eastward, away from the north-south Mississippi system. The eastward flow of goods then surged with the construction of railroads, which connected the Ohio Valley to eastern markets by the 1850s. But the most serious decline in steamboat transportation came after the Civil War, with the completion of the national rail system. Steamboat companies lobbied Congress for federally funded river improvements, and government responded with millions of dollars to deepen channels, remove snags, and construct locks and dams to ensure year-round navigation. River commerce remained important, but by the end of the century steamboats had given way to boats powered by internal combustion engines.

—JOHN MACK FARAGHER

See Also: Fulton, Robert; Transportation.

BIBLIOGRAPHY: Gandy, Joan W., and Thomas H. Gandy, *The Mississippi Steamboat Era in Historic Photographs* (Dover 1987); Hunter, Louis C., *Steamboats on the Western Rivers* (Harvard Univ. Press 1949); Owens, Harry P., *Steamboats and the Cotton Economy* (Univ. Press of Mississippi 1990); Taylor, George Rogers, *The Transportation Revolution, 1815-1860* (Rinehart 1951).

■ **STEFFENS, LINCOLN (1866-1936),** editor and journalist. He was a leading advocate of muckraking, the Progressive Era school of journalism, that exposed political and corporate corruption during the first decade of the 20th century. Born in San Francisco, California, Steffens wrote for *McClure's Magazine* (1902-11). His articles on municipal government were published as *The Shame of the Cities* (1904), and his *Autobiography* (1931) remains a classic account of American journalism.

■ **STEICHEN, EDWARD (1879-1973),** influential photographer and curator. Steichen was born in Luxembourg, but his family moved to the United States when he was three. At the age of 15, Steichen was apprenticed to a lithographer, who also taught

him photography. Stopping in New York City on his way to study in Paris, Steichen met the photographer Alfred Stieglitz, who bought a few of his prints; later Steichen worked with Stieglitz on the opening of the 291 Gallery. After serving in World War I as a photographer, Steichen became chief photographer for Condé Nast magazines, including *Vanity Fair* and *Vogue* (1923-36), and also took advertising photographs for the J. Walter Thompson Advertising Agency. Steichen again served the United States in World War II, leading the U.S. Navy's photographic department. He then became head of the photography department at the Museum of Modern Art in New York City, a position he filled from 1947 to 1962. There, in 1955, he curated The Family of Man, a renowned exhibition of international photography.

See Also: Photography; Stieglitz, Alfred.

In 1903, author Gertrude Stein moved to Paris, where she wrote and greatly influenced a group of American expatriate writers of the 1920s.

■ **STEIN, GERTRUDE (1874-1946)**, modernist author and poet. Born in Allegheny, Pennsylvania, Stein moved to Europe in 1903, where she befriended and patronized Pablo Picasso, Henri Matisse, Juan Gris, and other modernist painters. Between the world wars, she was the leader of "the lost generation," a group of expatriate American writers including Ernest Hemingway and F. Scott Fitzgerald. In her own work, such as *Three Lives* (1909), *The Making of Americans* (1925), and *The Autobiography of Alice B. Toklas* (1933), she experimented with syntax, often repeating the same words, or using words rhythmically rather than for meaning.

See Also: Fitzgerald, F. Scott; Hemingway, Ernest Miller; Women in American History.

■ **STEINBECK, JOHN (1902-68)**, novelist. Steinbeck was born in Salinas, California; the landscape of his native Monterey County was a setting for many of his works. Steinbeck briefly at-

John Steinbeck's *The Grapes of Wrath* (1939) gained national attention, won the Pulitzer Prize for literature, and was made into a popular film by director John Ford.

tended Stanford University but spent time working at a variety of laboring jobs on the West Coast. His experience with fishermen, fruit pickers, and other workers led to a concern for their working conditions evident in much of his fiction. For example, the novel *Tortilla Flat* (1935), one of Steinbeck's first successes, focuses on the lives of Mexican-American workers in Monterey. In 1937 Steinbeck published *Of Mice and Men*, the dramatic version of which won the Drama Critics' Circle Award. Steinbeck published his Pulitzer Prize–winning masterpiece, *The Grapes of Wrath*, in 1939; the story of the Joad family's journey from the Dust Bowl of Oklahoma to California seemed to capture the national experience of the Great Depression. Later works include *The Pearl* (1947) and *East of Eden* (1952). Steinbeck won the Nobel Prize for Literature in 1962.

See Also: Great Depression; Novel.

■ **STEINEM, GLORIA (1936-)**, journalist and leader of the women's movement. She was born in Toledo, Ohio. An outspoken activist for women's rights, in 1971 she helped to found the national Women's Political Caucus and the Women's Action Alliance. She served as editor of *Ms.* magazine, which she founded in 1972. Her books include *Outrageous Acts and Everyday Rebellions* (1983), *Revolution from Within* (1992), and *Moving Beyond Words* (1994).

See Also: Women in American History; Women's Movement.

■ **STEINMETZ, CHARLES PROTEUS (1865-1923)**, electrical engineer. Born in Breslau, Germany, he immigrated to the United States in 1889. Steinmetz showed how magnets lose power while generating alternating current, deriving the law of hysteresis and analyzing its application in 1892. While working at General Electric (1893-1923), he developed a now-standard method of calculating alternating current mathematically (1897) and used an equation to produce lightning in his lab (1921). He wrote several books, did consulting work at General Electric, and taught at Union College (1903-23).

See Also: Science.

■ **STELLA, FRANK PHILIP (1936-)**, artist. Born in Malden, Massachusetts, Stella broke into the

New York art scene in his early 20s. His early paintings were series of black pinstripes, a style that he later modified with metallic paints and by shaping his canvases to echo the configurations of the lines he painted. Stella moved away from his early minimalist style, using collage techniques, bright colors, and a disruption of the picture plane as in his *Exotic Bird Series* of the late 1970s.

See Also: *Painting.*

■ **STEPHENS, ALEXANDER H. (1812-83),** vice president of the Confederate States of America (1861-65). Born in Crawfordsville, Georgia, Stephens became a lawyer and was elected to the Georgia legislature (1836). Initially a Whig, Stephens served in the U.S. House of Representatives (1843-59). Stephens initially opposed Southern secession but eventually signed Georgia's Ordinance of Secession. He was elected vice president of the Confederacy in February 1861 and was instrumental in persuading Virginia to join the Confederacy. During the war Stephens clashed with Confederate Pres. Jefferson Davis over the issue of states' rights and supported the obstructionist Georgia government of Gov. Joseph E. Brown. Stephens was a Confederate delegate to the unsuccessful Hampton Roads Conference with Union leaders in February 1865. After the war he was jailed in Boston for six months. A vehement foe of Reconstruction, Stephens wrote a defense of the Confederacy (1868-70) and bought (1871) the Atlanta *Southern Sun*, in which he assailed local and national politics. He served again in the U.S. House (1873-82) and was elected governor of Georgia (1882) shortly before he died.

See Also: *Civil War; Confederate States of America.*

■ **STEPHENS, ANN SOPHIA (1810-86),** author and primary figure in New York's mid-19th-century literary circles. Born in Derby, Connecticut, she was a contributing editor to *Peterson's Magazine* and wrote numerous books, including a bestselling dime novel, *Maleska: The Indian Wife of the White Hunter* (1860).

See Also: *Women in American History.*

■ **STETTHEIMER, FLORINE (1871-1944),** modernist painter and hostess to the New York aesthetic elite. She was born in Rochester, New York. She helped create the important Stettheimer art salon but refused to exhibit or sell her own paintings. Her work was shown posthumously in a retrospective at New York City's Museum of Modern Art in 1946.

See Also: *Painting.*

■ **STEVENS, JOHN PAUL (1920-),** associate justice of the U.S. Supreme Court (1975-). Born in Chicago, Illinois, he studied law at Northwestern University and clerked for Supreme Court Justice Wiley Rutledge. Stevens was a prominent antitrust attorney and law professor in Chicago when he was appointed (1970) to the U.S. Court of Appeals for the Seventh Circuit. Nominated to the Supreme Court by Pres. Gerald Ford, he quickly developed a reputation as an independent swing vote among the justices and would frequently issue individual concurrences and dissents. Stevens is known for his concise and well-crafted opinions and has paid particular attention to issues of procedural due process, such as separation of powers and election laws.

See Also: *Supreme Court.*

■ **STEVENS, THADDEUS (1792-1868),** Radical Republican congressman. Born in Danville, Vermont, Stevens graduated from Dartmouth College and then practiced law in Pennsylvania, where he served in the state legislature (1833-41). In the U.S. House of Representatives (1849-53, 1859-68), Stevens was a leader of abolitionist Republicans before the Civil War and a major architect of Radical Reconstruction after it. He advocated seizing 400 million acres of land in the South from Confederate owners for distribution among the freed slaves and for resale to pay for the war debt. Stevens's plans for far-reaching social reforms failed to gain the needed support in Congress. He also supported civil and political rights for African Americans and harsh penalties against Confederate officers and politicians. Stevens was a leader in the fight for Andrew Johnson's impeachment and was instrumental in writing the 14th Amendment to the Constitution.

See Also: *Civil War; Radical Republicans.*

■ **STEVENS, WALLACE (1879-1955),** modernist poet. Originally from Reading, Pennsylvania, Stevens attended Harvard University (1897-1900).

He published poems and short stories in the *Harvard Monthly* and the *Harvard Advocate*, the literary magazine on which he worked. Stevens then went to New York Law School and was admitted to the bar in 1904. He worked in New York City until 1916, while he read and learned about various avant-garde literary movements, ranging from French symbolism to orientalist influences. In 1916 Stevens started working as a lawyer for an insurance company in Hartford, Connecticut, a position he held for the rest of his life even as he became an acclaimed poet. In 1923 Stevens published *Harmonium*, his first collection of poetry, which includes "Sunday Morning," "The Emperor of Ice-Cream," and "Thirteen Ways of Looking at a Blackbird," among others. Stevens was awarded the Bollingen Prize in 1949, the National Book Award in 1951 and 1955, and the Pulitzer Prize in 1955.

See Also: Poetry.

■ **STEVENSON, ADLAI EWING (1835-1914),** vice president of the United States (1893-97). Born in Christian County, Kentucky, he was a lawyer and active in Illinois Democratic politics. He served two terms in the U.S. House of Representatives (1875-77, 1879-81) before serving as first assistant postmaster general during Pres. Grover Cleveland's first administration (1885-89). He then served as vice president during Cleveland's second administration (1893-97).

See Also: Cleveland, Grover; Vice President of the United States.

■ **STEVENSON, ADLAI EWING (1900-65),** governor of Illinois (1949-53) and two-time Democratic presidential candidate (1952, 1956). The grandson of Vice Pres. Adlai Stevenson (1835-1914), he was born in Los Angeles, California, and later practiced law in Chicago. During the administrations of Presidents Franklin D. Roosevelt and Harry S. Truman, he worked in the Agriculture Adjustment Administration (1933-35), the Navy Department (1941-44), and State Department (1945-47). Elected governor of Illinois in 1948, he was praised for his liberal policies and graceful wit, but he was twice defeated for president by Republican Dwight D. Eisenhower. Stevenson was named ambassador to the United Nations by Pres. John F. Kennedy (1961)

but played no significant role in the administration's foreign policy decisions. His attempts to initiate peace talks with North Vietnam were blocked by Pres. Lyndon B. Johnson.

See Also: Cold War.

BIBLIOGRAPHY: Davis, Kenneth S., *The Politics of Honor: A Biography of Adlai Stevenson* (Putnam 1967).

■ **STEWART, POTTER (1915-85),** associate justice of the U.S. Supreme Court (1958-81). He was born in Cincinnati, Ohio, attended Yale Law School, and after naval service in World War II practiced in New York and Cincinnati, where he participated in local politics. On the U.S. Sixth Circuit Court of Appeals (1954-58) and later on the Supreme Court, Stewart established himself as a moderate voice that cannot be easily categorized.

See Also: Supreme Court.

■ **STIEGLITZ, ALFRED (1864-1946),** photographer and champion of modern art. Stieglitz was born in Hoboken, New Jersey. In 1881 he set out for Berlin, Germany, to study mechanical engineering, but he ended up becoming fascinated with photography. Returning to the United States in 1890, Stieglitz undertook to promote photography as a fine art. In 1902 he founded the photo-secession movement in support of art photography and in 1903 began publishing the journal *Camera Work*. With Edward Steichen, he opened the Little Galleries of the Photo-Secession, also known as "291," in 1905. He stressed the evocative, as opposed to documentary, potential of photography, as exemplified in his own works, such as *Steerage* (1907). Stieglitz is celebrated for the bold honesty and arresting sensuality that characterized the portraits of his wife, the painter Georgia O'Keeffe. At 291, Stieglitz showed both photography and art by contemporary American and European artists, including John Marin, O'Keeffe, Pablo Picasso, and Henri Matisse; the gallery was the first American venue for many modern artists, who had no other place to exhibit until the Armory Show of 1913. Although he closed 291 in 1917, Stieglitz continued to exhibit modern artists at the Intimate Gallery (1925-29) and An American Place (1929-46).

See Also: Armory Show; O'Keeffe, Georgia; Photography.

■ **STIMSON, HENRY LEWIS (1867-1950),** presidential adviser, regarded as the dean of the U.S. foreign policy establishment during the first half of the 20th century. His career coincided with the emergence of the United States as a global power. Born in New York City and educated at Yale, Stimson was appointed a U.S. attorney by Pres. Theodore Roosevelt in 1908. He served as Pres. William Howard Taft's secretary of war (1911-13) and fought in World War I. Stimson served as governor-general of the Philippines (1927-29) and secretary of state under Pres. Herbert Hoover (1929-33). Franklin D. Roosevelt's election as president in 1932 sent Stimson, a Republican, back into private law practice, but in 1940, after Stimson broke with the majority of Republicans to call for assistance to Britain, Roosevelt appointed him secretary of war, a position he held until fall 1945.

Stimson became secretary of state with an impressive diplomatic record, having helped to mediate conflict in Nicaragua and smooth U.S. relations with the Filipinos during the 1920s. However, confronted with Japan's conquest of Manchuria in 1931, he faced the consequences of America's unwillingness to back its global economic ambitions with political and military power. While the League of Nations' Lytton Commission struggled over its response to the aggression, Stimson declared the United States' refusal to recognize territorial changes brought about by force. He wished to go further and have the world's major naval powers join to threaten military force against Japan, although he understood that this would be mere bluff. The Stimson Doctrine of nonrecognition did nothing to curb Japanese aggression against China; only Allied victory against Japan in 1945 expelled Japan from the Asian mainland.

As secretary of war Stimson coordinated U.S. military preparations prior to entry into World War II, favoring enactment of the draft and weighing British requests for military assistance against eventual U.S. needs. During the war he advocated a direct assault on Nazi Europe, criticized Britain's strategy aimed at preserving its empire, and opposed plans to dismember Germany at the end of the war. His management of the U.S. military effort included approval of the internment of Japanese Americans and the continued segregation of African-American troops. Stimson also oversaw the Manhattan Project that built the atom bomb and strongly advocated the bomb's use against Japan in 1945.

—MAARTEN L. PEREBOOM

See Also: *Cold War; Manhattan Project; Stimson Doctrine; World War II.*

BIBLIOGRAPHY: Current, Richard N., *Secretary Stimson: A Study in Statecraft* (Rutgers Univ. Press 1954); Hodgson, Godfrey, *The Colonel: The Life and Wars of Henry Stimson* (Knopf 1990).

■ **STIMSON DOCTRINE,** rationale for U.S. policy toward China and Japan, devised in 1932 by Sec. of State Henry Stimson as a response to the Japanese occupation of Manchuria. Stimson made a desperate effort to restore the status quo or at least to put the process of Chinese-Japanese dispute resolution under international control, even expressing an uncharacteristic willingness to cooperate with the League of Nations. When the Japanese army completed the conquest of southern Manchuria (January 1932), Secretary Stimson issued a rather defensive statement declaring that the United States would not recognize any agreement between China and Japan that would impair the principles of the Open Door policy or the rights of the United States or its citizens in China. Stimson also vaguely protested against the Japanese infringement upon "the sovereignty, the independence, or the territorial administrative integrity of the Republic of China."

See Also: *Cold War; Open Door Policy; Stimson, Henry Lewis.*

■ **STOCK EXCHANGE,** organized marketplace where securities, such as stocks and bonds, are bought and sold. Stock exchanges had their origins in Amsterdam and London during the 16th century. Closely mirroring the European model, the first stock exchange in America opened in 1790 in Philadelphia. Two years later, after Sec. of the Treasury Alexander Hamilton began issuing government securities to fund the national debt, the New York Stock Exchange was established by a group of wealthy merchants. It quickly became the largest in the United States. During the 19th century, regional stock exchanges emerged in Boston, Philadelphia,

Chicago, Buffalo, San Francisco, and Los Angeles to provide a marketplace for local corporate securities. In the fall of 1929, prices on the New York Stock Exchange tumbled, causing the worst stock market crash in U.S. history and contributing greatly to the ensuing economic depression. In 1933, Congress passed the Securities Act, and in 1934, it created the Securities and Exchange Commission in an attempt to regulate the market. Since then the Federal Reserve Board has regulated the nine American stock exchanges. Despite regulation, however, the market still fluctuates widely. In 1987, it dropped precipitously, losing some 40 percent of its value.

See Also: Federal Reserve System; Industrial Revolution; Securities Exchange Act; Securities and Exchange Commission (SEC).

BIBLIOGRAPHY: Bruchey, Stuart W., *Modernization of the American Stock Exchange, 1971-1989* (Garland Publishers 1991); Sobel, Robert, *The Curbstone Brokers: The Origins of the American Stock Exchange* (Macmillan 1970).

■ **STOCKTON, RICHARD (1730-81),** lawyer and Revolutionary War politician. Born in Princeton, New Jersey, he was a signer of the Declaration of Independence and a member of the Second Continental Congress. Stockton became a renowned lawyer before the Revolution and was captured and imprisoned by the British from 1776 to 1777.

See Also: Declaration of Independence.

■ **STOCKYARDS,** areas that concentrated livestock for sale and slaughter. First located in eastern cities, stockyards moved westward with settlement, and by the 1850s all but the smallest had rail connections to eastern cities. Appearing in Chicago as early as 1837, stockyards collected cattle from Texas, Missouri, Kansas, Illinois, Iowa, Wisconsin, and Minnesota and sent them, live and as packed meat, to the East. Chicago's railroads and its meat-packing industry attracted so much business during the 1850s and the Civil War that in 1865 the city's nine largest railroads, in conjunction with members of the Chicago Pork Packer's Association, developed the Union stockyards to consolidate the city's livestock business. By 1868, the Union stockyards covered 100 acres of ground with 2,300 pens capable of handling

21,000 head of cattle, 75,000 hogs, 22,000 sheep, and 200 horses, all at the same time. Sewage and offal, however, drained into the Chicago River, giving the city a distinct smell visitors could not forget. Refrigerated railroad cars enabled meat packers to build stockyards and packing plants closer to western cattle at Kansas City, St. Louis, Omaha, and Denver during the 1880s and 1890s, leading to Chicago's decline as a stockyard center.

See Also: Meatpacking.

■ **STOKES, CARL B. (1927-96),** political leader, judge, and diplomat. Born in Cleveland, Ohio, Stokes was elected mayor of the city in 1967, making him America's first African-American mayor of a major city. After serving two terms (1967-71) he moved to New York City, becoming that city's first African-American television anchorman. Back in Cleveland Stokes became a judge (1983-94) and in 1995 was appointed U.S. ambassador to the Seychelles. He is remembered for the grace with which he dismantled racial barriers.

See Also: African Americans; Civil Rights Movement.

■ **STONE, HARLAN FISKE (1872-1946),** 12th chief justice of the United States (1941-46). Born in Chesterfield, New Hampshire, Stone attended Amherst College and graduated from Columbia University Law School in 1898. For the next 25 years Stone engaged in private practice and taught law at Columbia, where he also served as dean of the law school from 1910 to 1923. In 1924, Pres. Calvin Coolidge named Stone attorney general and a year later appointed him an associate justice on the Supreme Court. Although an advocate of judicial restraint, Stone generally aligned himself with the Court's liberal members.

In the controversies over New Deal legislation, Stone staunchly supported congressional actions that sought to improve the economy. He frequently dissented from the conservative majority, and in perhaps his greatest contribution to constitutional law, Stone ruled in *United States* v. *Carolene Products Company* (1938) that the Court would abandon close scrutiny of economic legislation but would examine more carefully statutes affecting individual rights. In 1941, Pres. Franklin D. Roosevelt, in a bipartisan gesture, named Stone, a

Republican, chief justice. Although he had an active and astute legal mind, Stone proved to be an ineffective administrator of one of the most divided Courts in American history.

See Also: New Deal Cases; Supreme Court.

BIBLIOGRAPHY: Mason, Thomas A., *Harlan Fiske Stone's Pillar of the Law* (Viking Press 1956); Urofsky, Melvin I., *Division and Discord: The Supreme Court under Stone and Vinson, 1941-1953* (Univ. of South Carolina Press 1997).

■ **STONE, LUCY (1818-93),** feminist leader, orator, and journalist. Born in West Brookfield, Massachusetts, Stone was educated at Mount Holyoke Female Seminary and Oberlin College. A captivating speaker, Stone lectured for Garrison's American Anti-Slavery Society in the late 1840s and throughout the 1850s lectured and organized for the American Equal Rights Association and the New England Woman Suffrage Association. In 1869 the woman suffrage movement fractured in two, partly because of differences in ideology but

A leader of the National American Woman Suffrage Association, Lucy Stone was the founder of its *The Woman's Journal* in 1872.

also because of personal animosity between Stone and rival leaders Susan B. Anthony and Elizabeth Cady Stanton. Along with Julia Ward Howe, Stone became the leader of the more genteel American Woman Suffrage Association. Stone and her husband, Henry Blackwell, founded in Boston in 1872 *The Woman's Journal*, which quickly became the leading journalistic voice of the women's movement. In 1890 the schism between Stone and her rivals was mended, leading to the creation of the unified National American Woman Suffrage Association (NAWSA). Stone was chairman of the executive committee of NAWSA until her death.

See Also: Anthony, Susan B.; Blackwell Family; Stanton, Elizabeth Cady; Woman Suffrage Movement; Women in American History; Women's Movement.

BIBLIOGRAPHY: Kerr, Andrea Moore, *Lucy Stone: Speaking Out for Equality* (Rutgers Univ. Press, 1992).

■ **STONE, THOMAS (1743-87),** lawyer and Revolutionary War politician. Born in Charles County, Maryland, Stone was politically active in every phase of the Revolution. He served in the Second Continental Congress, signed the Declaration of Independence, and served briefly in the U.S. Congress.

See Also: Declaration of Independence.

■ **STONO REBELLION (1739),** slave insurrection. On September 9, 20 slaves from Angola gathered in rebellion near Charleston, South Carolina. Gaining arms and using drums to rouse other slaves, they sought to escape southward toward Spanish Florida. A skirmish with the militia scattered the rebels, but it was three years before the last slave was recaptured. Thirty whites and 44 blacks were killed in the course of the rebellion and its suppression.

■ **STORY, JOSEPH (1779-1845),** U.S. representative (1808-09) and associate justice of the U.S. Supreme Court (1811-45). Born in Marblehead, Massachusetts, Story was one of the greatest legal minds of his time. His influence on the direction of the Supreme Court and the shape of American jurisprudence was second only to that of Chief Justice John Marshall. After a brief career in politics, Story began his tenure on the Supreme Court inauspiciously, as Pres. James Madison's fourth choice to fill a vacancy. Chosen at age 32, Story remains the youngest person to be appointed to the Court. He aligned himself with Chief Justice Marshall, consistently concurring with Marshall's landmark opinions that consolidated federal supremacy over the states. In *Martin* v. *Hunter's Lessee* (1816) Story wrote one such "nationalist" opinion himself, holding that state court decisions could be subject to Supreme Court review. With Marshall's death and the installation of Roger Taney as chief justice (1836), Story increasingly found himself in the minority. Story dissented, for instance, in the *Charles River Bridge* (1837) case. His influence on American law, however, was never limited to his role on the Court. His legacy includes a collection of *Commentaries* that were regarded, well into the second half of the 19th century, as the leading authority on American jurisprudence.

See Also: Charles River Bridge v. Warren Bridge; Supreme Court.

▨ STOWE, HARRIET BEECHER (1811-96), writer

and social critic. She was born in Litchfield, Connecticut, the seventh child of Roxana Foote and famed Congregational minister Lyman Beecher. Harriet enjoyed an excellent education, attending the Pierce Academy and the Hartford Female Seminary, founded by her sister Catharine. She taught for her sister, first in Connecticut and then in Ohio, where the whole family had moved in 1832. Living across the Ohio River from Kentucky, she first observed chattel slavery.

In 1836 Harriet Beecher married Calvin Ellis Stowe, a professor of biblical literature. They raised seven children, and as her writing became a source of family support, Stowe struggled with the demands of home and work. Stowe wrote in an antebellum context of "parlor literature"—domestic literary productions meant to entertain and instruct. In 1850, Stowe wrote *Uncle Tom's Cabin* in response to the Fugitive Slave Act. The novel became the most widely read book of its time as well as a marketing phenomenon. *Uncle Tom's Cabin* explored the effects of slavery on the characters, souls, and families of both enslaved and enslavers. In the course of making antislavery an emotional and religious issue rather than a political one, she asserted women's right to discuss the subject and went far in creating a role for women in public discourse.

Stowe's works include another antislavery novel, *Dred: A Tale of the Great Dismal Swamp* (1856), and *A Minister's Wooing* (1859), a historical novel that attacked the rigid Calvinism in which she was raised. An energetic, optimistic Christian, she played a significant role in creating a national culture by speaking across the deep racial, regional, class, and gender divides of 19th-century America.

—Catherine Allgor

See Also: Civil War; Fugitive Slave Act; Women in American History; Women's Movement.

BIBLIOGRAPHY: Hedrick, Joan D., *Harriet Beecher Stowe: A Life* (Oxford Univ. Press 1994); Sklar,

Author of many works, Harriet Beecher Stowe was best known for *Uncle Tom's Cabin,* which first appeared as a serial in the antislavery paper *National Era* in 1851-52.

Kathryn Kish, *Catharine Beecher: A Study in American Domesticity* (Norton 1976).

■ **STRAVINSKY, IGOR F. (1882-1971),** composer. Born in Oranienbaum, Russia, he immigrated to Paris, where he composed *The Firebird* (1910), *Petrushka* (1911), and *The Rite of Spring* (1913) for Sergei Diaghilev's Ballets Russes. Modernist works rooted in Russian tradition, the ballets created a sensation and established Stravinsky's international reputation. In 1940 he moved to the United States, where he eventually abandoned neoclassical traditions to experiment with serial composition into the late 1960s.

■ **STREISAND, BARBRA (1942-),** singer, actor, and film director. Born in Brooklyn, New York, she took Broadway and the recording industry by storm in the mid-1960s as a young talent who embraced the popular song tradition rather than rock and roll. She starred in *Funny Girl* on stage (1964-65) and screen (1968) and later directed several films, including *Yentl* (1983). She also continued to give rare, but always well-received, concert appearances.

■ **STRICKLAND, WILLIAM (1787-1854),** leader of the Greek revival in American architecture. Strickland was born in Philadelphia and became an engraver, engineer, and architect, training with Benjamin Latrobe. He designed several Greek-revival structures in his native city, including the Masonic Temple (1810) and the Merchant's Exchange (1832-36). Strickland also is known for the Tennessee State Capitol at Nashville (1845-53) and the marble sarcophagus of Pres. George Washington at Mount Vernon, Virginia.

See Also: Architecture; Latrobe, Benjamin.

■ **STRICT CONSTRUCTION,** standard of constitutional interpretation based on a close reading of the U.S. Constitution and the presumed intent of its authors. In the early republic, strict construction was advocated by the Jeffersonians to defend states' rights and limit the federal government. More recently conservative politicians and some jurists have embraced strict construction as a reaction to the judicial activism of the Supreme Court, especially during the tenure of Chief Justice Earl Warren

(1953-69). Critics of decisions such as *Brown v. Board of Education of Topeka* (1954), which struck down racial segregation in public schools, *Griswold v. Connecticut* (1965), which invoked the Ninth Amendment to expand personal privacy rights, and *Roe v. Wade* (1973), which legalized abortion, argued the courts were using their power to further political ends that were not addressed by the Constitution and should best be decided by Congress and state legislatures. Ironically progressive critics of the Supreme Court had used the same line of argument to criticize conservative justices who struck down state and federal reforms on the grounds that they were not explicitly authorized by the Constitution. Such criticisms were especially sharp in the early 1900s and the mid-1930s, when the Supreme Court struck down much social reform legislation and many early New Deal reforms.

See Also: Constitution of the United States.

BIBLIOGRAPHY: Pohlman, H. L., ed., *Political Thought and the American Judiciary* (Univ. of Massachusetts Press 1993).

■ **STRIKES,** work stoppages by employees to pressure employers to comply with demands. Workers have walked off the job usually to persuade employers to improve wages or other terms of employment but have also struck to protest some action by government. The term was probably first applied to a 1768 decision of sailors in the port of London to haul down ("strike") the sails of their vessels in objection to their working conditions.

Between 1790 and 1840 occasional U.S. strikes occurred by craftsmen in eastern cities, female textile workers, and canal laborers. This labor unrest preceded a surge of urban strikes between 1835 and 1837 that sparked conspiracy trials, declarations of support from political candidates, and the first legislative investigation into working conditions (Pennsylvania, 1837). Between 1845 and 1875 strikes spread to the coal mines, foundries, and factories of inland towns, and they were increasingly organized by trade unions. Some actions involved tens of thousands of workers, as in New York City in 1872 and Pennsylvania's anthracite coal fields in 1875. After the Civil War, unions and employers' associations experimented with plans to resolve disputes through arbitration, but strikes still occurred. During the last two weeks of July 1877, a furious wave of strikes against wage reductions spread along the major railroad lines from coast to coast.

Trends in Strikes. In the aftermath of that upheaval, systematic efforts were made to collect data on strikes by the U.S. commissioner of labor. Data were collected between 1881 and 1905, and after a hiatus from 1905 to 1916, the Department of Labor regularly published information on the nation's strikes. This evidence reveals that between 1882 and 1922 strikes became more frequent and larger; were concentrated especially in the coal mining, building construction, and clothing manufacturing industries; were increasingly coordinated by unions; and were successful more often than not. During recessions, wage reductions by employers provoked major strikes, while in boom times workers acted to improve their earnings and shorten hours. Large companies and employers' associations often retaliated by locking out their employees, that is, dismissing them en masse until they agreed to work on the companies' terms.

Women who did not work in the skilled crafts that then constituted the core of union membership assumed special prominence in strikers' ranks. Strike waves in the aftermaths of the two world wars (1919-22, 1945-46) involved workers in numbers that dwarfed all other periods of the country's history. In contrast, the lowest recorded strike activity came between 1923 and 1932 and between 1985 and 1995.

By far the largest number of strikes in America have occurred over wages or the unwillingness of employers to deal with unions and accept union standards on the job. Strikes with explicitly political objectives have been much less common in the United States than in Europe but are not unknown. Sympathetic strikes, undertaken by some workers to assist others in winning their demands, became especially widespread in the early 1890s (culminating in the Pullman boycott of 1894) and on later occasions developed into citywide general strikes, for example in Philadelphia (1910); Kansas City (1918); Seattle (1919); and Stamford, Connecticut; Rochester, New York; Lancaster, Pennsylvania; Pittsburgh; and Oakland (all in 1946).

Legal restraints on strikes in the 19th century took the form of prosecutions for criminal conspiracy, court orders enjoining union actions, and

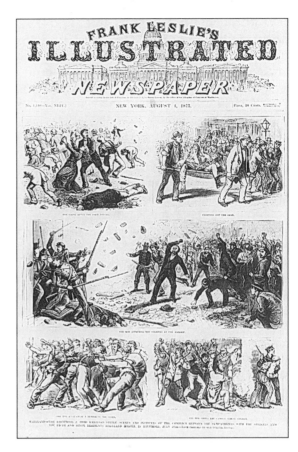

During the 1870s the United States experienced an unprecedented series of strikes, including the first nationwide railroad strike in 1877. Newspapers and magazines were generally unsympathetic to the strikers.

military intervention. Since the 1930s the law has allowed employers to replace strikers while also upholding workers' right to strike, with exceptions for some government employees. Some laws, however, have prohibited sympathetic strikes and strikes in violation of contracts and have mandated a return to work during a cooling-off period ordered by the president.

—DAVID MONTGOMERY

See Also: *Labor Movement; Trade Unions; Work in America.*

BIBLIOGRAPHY: Edwards, P. K., *Strikes in the United States, 1881-1974* (Basil Blackwell 1981); Griffin, J. H., *Strikes: A Study in Quantitative Economics* (Columbia Univ. Press 1939); Montgomery, David, "Strikes in Nineteenth-Century America" (*Social Science History* Feb. 1980).

■ **STRONG, GEORGE TEMPLETON (1820-75),** diarist and treasurer of the U.S. Sanitary Commission. Born in New York City, Strong became a lawyer. His diary, kept from 1835 until his death, is a vivid account of life in 19th-century New York. A political conservative, Strong nevertheless supported the presidential candidacy of Abraham Lincoln in 1860. Strong was a staunch unionist. During the Civil War he became treasurer of the newly formed U.S. Sanitary Commission, which aimed to improve the hygiene of the Union army. Much to Strong's dismay, his wife Ellen Ruggles Strong joined the 3,000 Northern women who worked for the sanitary service as nurses and aides at the front lines.

See Also: Civil War.

■ **STRONG, WILLIAM (1808-95),** U.S. representative (1847-51) and associate justice of the U.S. Supreme Court (1870-80). A Somers, Connecticut, native, Strong wrote the Court's opinion in *Knox v. Lee* (1871), upholding the federal government's authority to print paper currency.

See Also: Supreme Court.

■ **STUART, GILBERT CHARLES (1755-1828),** leading portrait painter of the Revolutionary era. Stuart was born in North Kingstown, Rhode Island, and received early artistic training both in Newport and traveling with an itinerant Scottish painter, Cosmo Alexander. At the time of the American Revolution, Stuart moved to London, eventually painting in the studio of Benjamin West. By assisting West with history paintings and state portraits, Stuart developed a high technical proficiency, especially for portraiture. With the acclaim won by his portraits of West (1780-81) and William Grant in *The Skater* (1782), Stuart developed a very successful business in London. After time in Dublin, he returned in 1792 to the United States, where he had a succession of studios in New York City, Philadelphia, Washington, D.C., and Boston. He painted the eminent personages of his day, most notably in his five full-length portraits of Pres. George Washington, as well as those of presidents John Adams (1800-15), Thomas Jefferson (1805-07), James Madison (1805-07), and James Monroe (1812-20).

See Also: Painting; West, Benjamin.

James Ewell Brown ("Jeb") Stuart, noted as a daring cavalry leader for the Confederacy during the Civil War, was fatally wounded in battle in 1864.

■ **STUART, JAMES EWELL BROWN (1833-64),** Confederate general and the foremost cavalry officer in American military history. Born in Patrick County, Virginia, "Jeb" Stuart graduated from the U.S. Military Academy in 1854 and served in the West prior to resigning his commission at the outbreak of the Civil War. Initially colonel of the First Virginia Cavalry, he rose to the rank of major general and commanded the cavalry corps of the Army of Northern Virginia. In his use of cavalry to collect vital intelligence about the enemy he was without peer, and the information he collected contributed significantly to the successes of Gen. Robert E. Lee. Stuart conducted two major raids in 1862, won the battle of Brandy Station (June 9, 1863), and triumphed in numerous smaller engagements. His tardiness during the Gettysburg campaign, however, contributed to the Confederate failure. He was mortally wounded at Yellow Tavern, Virginia, on May 11, 1864.

—William Garrett Piston

See Also: Civil War; Gettysburg, Battle of.

BIBLIOGRAPHY: Thomas, Emory M., *Bold Dragoon: The Life of J.E.B. Stuart* (Harper & Row 1986).

■ **STUDENT NONVIOLENT COORDINATING COMMITTEE (SNCC),** civil rights organization. In April 1960 Ella Baker of the Southern Christian Leadership Conference (SCLC) sponsored an organizational meeting for student leaders of the sit-in movements throughout the South. The meeting led to the formation of SNCC. Committed to nonviolent protest, SNCC became the focus of youth activism in behalf of civil rights. Its leadership was centered less in a single charismatic leader (like Martin Luther King, Jr.) and more in a coterie of dedicated activists that included Marion Barry, Bob Moses, Diane Nash, and John Lewis. After the sit-ins, SNCC members joined with the Congress of Racial Equality (CORE) in organizing the "freedom rides," which challenged the segregation of interstate travel. Concentrating its efforts on the Deep South, SNCC then proceeded on two fronts: direct action, as in protest marches and boycotts, and voter registration drives to remedy the racial imbalance of southern politics. As victories became more fleeting and as frustrations grew at the slow pace of racial progress, some members at SNCC began to question their commitment to nonviolence and the role of white students in the cause of black liberty. SNCC took on a more radical edge after the election of Stokely Carmichael as its chairman in 1966. Carmichael and SNCC became associated with the controversial "black power" slogan, which caused the organization to lose much of its support.

—JOHN R. NEFF

See Also: Baker, Ella Josephine; Carmichael, Stokely; Civil Rights Movement; Freedom Riders.
BIBLIOGRAPHY: Carson, Clayborne, *In Struggle* (Harvard Univ. Press 1981); Stoper, Emily, *The Student Nonviolent Coordinating Committee* (reprint; Carlson 1989).

■ **STUDENTS FOR A DEMOCRATIC SOCIETY (SDS),** organization of college students that advocated the social and political agenda of the New Left during the 1960s. In June 1962 founding members of the SDS met in Port Huron, Michigan, to draft a political platform. The statement, composed mainly by a young activist named Tom Hayden, condemned widespread social injustice, racism, poverty, American materialism, and political alienation. With its roots in the American socialist movement, the SDS envisioned itself a new kind of political movement that would relocate political power from institutions to individuals and communities.

During the mid-1960s, the SDS practiced participatory democracy by creating the Economic Research and Action Project (ERAP). Under this program, members were sent to poor districts in cities across the nation to encourage neighborhood residents to improve their own communities and demand government assistance. Through ERAP and actions such as numerous campus protests, the SDS experienced modest success in achieving its goals as outlined at Port Huron.

As American involvement in Vietnam escalated, the SDS turned its attention from domestic concerns to foreign policy issues. By 1967 it had adopted a largely antiwar agenda, leaving domestic projects to wither. At its height in 1968, the SDS had grown to some 350 chapters and almost 100,000 members. Within a few short years, however, the SDS had effectively collapsed, discredited by the increasing violence of its confrontational tactics and out of favor with a student body growing increasingly conservative.

—GUY NELSON

See Also: Hayden, Thomas.
BIBLIOGRAPHY: Miller, Jim, *Democracy in the Streets: From Port Huron to the Siege of Chicago* (Simon & Schuster 1987); Sale, Kirkpatrick, *SDS* (Random House 1973).

■ **STUYVESANT, PETER (1592-1672),** Dutch director general of New Netherland (1646-64). Born in Friesland, Netherland, Stuyvesant became a mercenary for the Dutch West India Company as a young man. His military career ended in 1646 in the Caribbean when he lost his right leg. After his recovery, Stuyvesant petitioned to be placed in administrative service and was appointed director general of New Netherland. As such, Stuyvesant developed stable economic relations with New England, drove the Swedish colony of New Sweden from the Delaware River area (1655), and opposed a movement to install an independent assembly in New Amsterdam. In 1664 Stuyvesant failed to repel the conquering

Peter Stuyvesant served as director of the Dutch colony of New Netherland from 1646 until 1664, when he was forced to surrender it to the English, after which it became New York.

English forces and, subsequently, was recalled to the Netherlands to account for his failure. He returned to New York (formerly New Amsterdam) in 1665 and remained a private citizen there until his death.

See Also: Dutch Colonies.

■ **SUBARCTIC INDIANS,** Indians who live in a vast territory including much of Alaska and Canada. The subarctic region's weather is harsh and requires supreme adaptive skills to survive. Rainy summers and long, snowy winters are the norm. The landscape contains many chains of lakes, rivers, and bogs. For centuries canoeing in the summer and snowshoeing in the winter have provided means to travel in this large area. There were literally hundreds of local groups throughout the subarctic; however, they can be divided into two main stocks by language.

The Athabascan speakers of western Canada and Alaska include the Carriers, Ingaliks, Dogribs, Hans, Hares, Koyukons, Kutchins, Slaves, Tananias, and Yellowknives, among others. The Algonquian speakers of eastern Canada include the Crees, Micmacs, Ojibwas, and Montagnais. Key to these groups' survival in the harsh environment were the vast herds of caribou, which could be taken in large numbers during their annual migrations and which provided much-needed protein as well as fur for clothing and bones for tools and weapons. Housing was in small groups, usually in hide- or bark-covered teepees that could be easily moved. Religion was a crucial part of everyday life for subarctic peoples. They believed in guardian spirits with whom they maintained a proper relationship through correct living and ceremony. Many groups also believed that the forest harbored "windigos," giant monsters who followed unsuspecting hunters in the forests, causing them to panic and run and go mad. The windigo legend is still powerful, and even experienced woodsmen of today tell of feeling the presence of the windigo behind them, always just out of sight.

The eastern subarctic, especially the Great Lakes region, was interfered with by the fur trade in the 16th and 17th centuries. European diseases and trade goods wiped out much of the population of the area and brought new conflicts. In western Canada and Alaska many groups remained outside the area of Euro-American conquest until well into the 19th century, but disease, trading posts, missions, and miners eventually made their way into these territories as well, causing population loss and cultural dissolution. Yet these groups have persisted through these hardships, using spiritual and legal methods to retain their culture and land.

—RYAN MADDEN

See Also: Indians of North America.
BIBLIOGRAPHY: Erdoes, Richard, and Alfonso Ortiz, eds., *American Indian Myths and Legends* (Pantheon 1984); Kehoe, Alice, *North American Indians* (Prentice-Hall 1981).

■ **SUBURBANIZATION,** technological, cultural, and political changes in history that have produced a landscape and a form of community that emphasize a pastoral setting dominated by private residences with convenient access to urban workplaces and services. The suburbs of medieval and early modern Europe were literally places outside the walls of the city. Such suburbs often contained noxious businesses such as tanneries and slaughterhouses. The residents of such districts were too poor to afford the security, status, and convenience of the urban center. The modern notion of suburbia, however, has its roots in the mid-18th-century English practice of wealthy city dwellers buying country homes and farms as second residences. This ideal of the country villa or cottage as a source of status, natural simplicity, and moral vitality became popular in the United States, a nation already accustomed to land speculation and mobility. Even as the cities of the young republic increased in size and population during the pre–Civil War period, the urban elite—eager to escape immigrants, periodic epidemics, and pollution—cast their eyes on the highlands, shores, and farms beyond the city.

Commuting. Americans embraced a variety of new transportation modes in the 19th century, each one providing more and more citizens with the means to separate the workplace from the home. For example, by 1860, ferries between Brooklyn and Manhattan averaged 100,000 passengers per working day. Railroads opened up new suburban vistas to those who could afford the relatively high cost of commuting. The greatest period of growth of these relatively well-to-do suburbs came after the Civil War, with the development of Philadelphia's Main Line and Chicago's North Shore. Grand Central Station opened in New York City in 1871, and Westchester County's population doubled every two decades from 1850 to 1910.

The development of the electric streetcar in the 1880s freed cities from their dependence on horse power—a sanitation nightmare—and made affordable homes on the fringes of the city available to those of moderate means. The promise of access to urban services—schools, street lights, paved roads, water delivery systems, and sewers—eased the sale of suburban lots and spurred the municipal annexation movement of the late 19th century. The growth of new residential areas along trolley lines connected at the hub also led to the growth—usually skyward—and transfor-

mation of the urban center. Central business districts now became meccas of shopping and entertainment serving office workers and suburban consumers. However, the potential for decentralization had already been established with the spread of electricity and telephone lines. The eventual triumph of the automobile would confirm this potential and significantly alter the urban landscape.

To Levittown and Edge City. The growing importance of trucking by the 1920s led to the relocation of many factories and warehouses to the urban periphery. The city had begun to unravel. Auto-friendly commercial establishments such as drive-in filling stations (the first gas stations featured curbside pumps) and motels began to proliferate in the 1920s. Country Club Plaza in Kansas City (1923) popularized the idea of the integrated shopping facility with off-street parking on the outskirts of town, although suburban shopping centers would not become commonplace until after World War II. (The first enclosed mall, Southdale, opened near Minneapolis in 1956.)

The idea of functionally segregated street systems and land-use zones became popular in the 1920s as builders, real-estate brokers, and bankers attempted to control the suburban development of areas made more accessible by the automobile. When the Depression of the 1930s short-circuited the housing industry, various government initiatives promoted zoning and residential neighborhoods. Federal legislation addressed the housing crisis created by foreclosures, a depressed private sector, and rising marriage and birthrates during and after World War II primarily by insuring long-term mortgage loans made by private lenders. By making borrowing easier, the federal government created the preconditions for a democratization of home ownership. By 1951, a new type of community builder, Levitt and Sons, had erected 17,500 low-cost single-family homes on Long Island using new materials and mass-production techniques. The suburban population of the United States more than doubled from 1950 to 1970, the census of the latter year marking the emergence of a suburban majority nationwide. Since the 1970s, the suburbanization of office space and retailing has resulted in new multicentered regions referred to variously as edge cities, technoburbs, and postsuburbia. A host of 20th-century technological innovations has decreased the need for face-to-face interaction in cities and suburbs alike. Within this new landscape, people connect themselves to significant places in their lives in a new way, abandoning the idea of a shared grid for a set of personal destinations.

—JAY GITLIN

See Also: City in American History.

BIBLIOGRAPHY: Garreau, Joel, *Edge City* (Doubleday 1991); Jackson, Kenneth T., *Crabgrass Frontier* (Oxford Univ. Press 1985); Stilgoe, John R., *Borderland: Origins of the American Suburb, 1820-1939* (Yale Univ. Press 1988).

■ **SUBVERSIVE ACTIVITIES CONTROL ACT,** Cold War federal law. Passed by Congress in 1950 over Pres. Harry S. Truman's veto, it created a Subversive Activities Control Board to monitor the activities of communists and other "subversives." It remained in place until 1973.

See Also: Cold War.

■ **SUFFOLK RESOLVES (1775),** a statement drawn up by delegates from Boston's Suffolk County to protest the Intolerable Acts (1774). The resolves, sent to the First Continental Congress, also called for rapid preparation for war by the colonies.

See Also: Intolerable Acts; Revolution, American.

■ **SUFFRAGE,** the right to vote. Suffrage has expanded throughout American history. Colonial voting rights rested on property ownership, often a "freehold" of land. This enfranchised most white men, but laws still excluded some religions, most free African Americans and women, slaves, propertyless men, and indentured servants.

American Revolution. Revolutionary ideology and politics liberalized voting rights but most states kept property tests. All states dropped religious tests, some adopted taxpaying qualifications, most permitted free African Americans to vote. New Jersey allowed female voting, and Kentucky lifted all property standards. The U.S. Constitution (1787) left the question of voting rights to the states.

The "Age of Democracy." From 1790 to 1850 commercial growth, Romantic ideas, partisan competition, and European suffrage debates generated successive waves of state reform ending property tests and founding "universal" white manhood suffrage. By Andrew Jackson's presidency (1829-37), these reforms had vastly expanded the active electorate.

Suffrage expansion did not help everyone. States now disfranchised free African Americans, New Jersey banned women voters after 1807, and "nativist" politicians tried—unsuccessfully—to curb naturalized Irish and German immigrant voting rights. The first women's rights convention (1848) in Seneca Falls, New York, issued a resolution for woman suffrage, but to no avail.

Civil War Era. Post–Civil War reconstruction raised the issue of suffrage to constitutional status. To empower freedmen and broaden southern support, congressional Republicans legalized African-American men's votes through Reconstruction laws; the 14th Amendment (1868), which, by declaring that all persons born or naturalized in the United States were American citizens, established the citizenship of blacks; and the 15th Amendment's (1870) ban against race-based voting discrimination. Although these measures fostered southern African-American voting and officeholding, southern white terrorism soon stifled it, and subsequent election laws nearly ended it.

Meanwhile, the 14th and 15th Amendments still excluded woman suffrage. In 1890, when suffragists formed the National American Woman Suffrage Association (NAWSA), public hostility persisted.

Age of Reform. Late-19th-century agrarian unrest and urbanization introduced voting restrictions. Populist protest led white southern Democrats to implement poll taxes and literacy tests, allegedly to end election fraud, but effectively to disfranchise African Americans and poor whites. Northern urban reformers instituted secret ballots and registration to curtail machine influence, thereby suppressing immigrant voting.

After 1900, however, the social climate improved for woman suffrage. Despite opposition, new NAWSA leaders, helped by protests by the militant Congressional Union for Woman Suffrage led by Alice Paul, skillfully lobbied for the 19th Amendment's 1920 ratification and then founded the League of Women Voters.

Modern Era. After World War II, civil rights activists tried to restore southern African-American voting rights through federal civil rights litigation and voter registration. Turning next to public protest, activists met violence at the 1965 Selma, Alabama, civil rights march, causing Pres. Lyndon B. Johnson to seek the 1965 Voting Rights Act. This established federal control over southern elections and thus increased minority registration, voting, and officeholding. Suffrage expanded again when the 26th Amendment (1971) lowered the national voting age to 18 to accommodate youthful anti–Vietnam War protesters.

Simultaneously, the U.S. Supreme Court advanced equality of representation by invalidating malapportioned state legislative districts under the "one man, one vote" doctrine. Later Voting Rights Act decisions annulled racially gerrymandered and multimember districts "diluting" minority votes, but the Court continued to reject "race-based" districts.

Recent reforms have eased registration to boost voter turnout. The 1993 federal National Voter Registration ("motor-voter") Act directs states to permit voter registration with driver licensing.

—DONALD W. ROGERS

See Also: *Civil Rights Movement; Constitutional Amendments; League of Women Voters; Voting Rights Acts; Woman Suffrage Movement.*

BIBLIOGRAPHY: Elliott, Ward E. Y., *The Rise of Guardian Democracy: The Supreme Court's Role in Voting Rights Disputes, 1845-1969* (Harvard Univ. Press 1974); Parker, Frank R., *Blacks Votes Count: Political Empowerment in Mississippi after 1965* (Univ. of North Carolina Press 1990); Rogers, Donald W., ed., *Voting and the Spirit of American Democ-*

In 1913, long-time suffrage leader Abigail Scott Duniway cast her vote in Oregon, which had passed a woman suffrage law the previous year.

racy (Univ. of Illinois Press 1992); Scott, Anne Firor, and Andrew MacKay Scott, *One Half the People: The Fight for Woman Suffrage* (Univ. of Illinois Press 1982); Williamson, Chilton, *American Suffrage from Property to Democracy* (Princeton Univ. Press 1960).

■ **SUFFRAGISTS,** participants in the woman suffrage movement, active from the mid-19th century until passage of the 19th Amendment in 1920. Led by such notables as Susan B. Anthony, Lucy Stone, Lucretia Mott, and Elizabeth Cady Stanton, these women, many of whom were also leading abolitionists before the Civil War, fought for and won the right to vote for American women. Because they were a powerful opposition movement, the term suffragist is preferred to the commonly used diminutive, suffragette.

See Also: Nineteenth Amendment; Suffrage; Women's Movement.

■ **SUGAR ACT (1764),** law passed by Parliament to stop illegal trade in molasses in the British colonies and to raise money to support the costs of British troops in America. The colonists bitterly resented the act, which became an underlying grievance leading to the American Revolution.

See Also: Revolution, American.

■ **SUGARCANE,** primary source of sucrose in the American diet and one of the first crops grown in the New World with slave labor. Most sugar production was first centered on Caribbean islands such as Barbados, Jamaica, and Haiti, where as early as 1650 vast numbers of enslaved Africans were used to cultivate the crop. Sugar plantations—semi-industrial institutions that not only grew sugarcane but processed it into brown sugar and molasses—also developed in the American south, particularly among the French in Louisiana. Not until the early 1900s, when sugar planting expanded into Florida and the new American possessions of Puerto Rico and Hawaii, did Louisiana lose its status as the chief U.S. sugar-growing region. Today, with the average citizen ingesting some 125 pounds of sugar per year, the United States consumes far more sugar than it produces.

See Also: Agriculture; Slavery.

BIBLIOGRAPHY: Mintz, Sidney, *Sweetness and Power: The Place of Sugar in Modern History* (Viking 1985);

Wilkinson, Alec, *Big Sugar: Seasons in the Cane Fields of Florida* (Knopf 1989).

■ **SULLIVAN, HARRY STACK (1892-1949),** psychiatrist. Born in Norwich, New York, Sullivan worked at the Sheppard and Enoch Pratt Hospital in Baltimore (1923-31), where he developed his concept that personality characteristics and psychiatric disorders were interpersonal phenomena. By treating schizophrenics through group therapy, Sullivan removed schizophrenia from the list of incurable disorders, offered psychotherapy as an option to shock treatment, and validated the growing emphasis on social factors in science. He opened his own practice in 1931 but continued to teach and write.

■ **SULLIVAN, LOUIS (1856-1924),** leading Chicago School architect. Sullivan was born in Boston, Massachusetts; after studying briefly at the Massachusetts Institute of Technology, he began working for William Le Baron Jenney in Chicago. In 1874 Sullivan went to Paris and studied at the Ecole des Beaux-Arts. On his return to Chicago, he began a partnership with Dankmar Adler, becoming a full partner of Adler and Sullivan in 1881. Sullivan, following in the engineering footsteps of Jenney, made use of the skeleton construction that allowed for tall buildings, applying to it his unique sense of naturalistic ornamentation. His contributions to Chicago's urban landscape included the Auditorium building (1889), the transportation building at the World's Columbian Exposition (1893), the Chicago Stock Exchange (1894), and the Gage building (1898). His acclaimed National Farmers' Bank at Owatonna, Minnesota (1908), was followed by a series of midwestern bank buildings toward the end of his career.

See Also: Architecture; Jenney, William Le Baron; Skyscrapers.

■ **SUMMIT CONFERENCES,** diplomatic meetings between the president of the United States and the heads of state of other powers, notably the Soviet Union during the Cold War. The term was first used by Winston Churchill in 1950, when he advocated a "parley at the summit," meaning among himself, Pres. Harry S. Truman, and Stalin. Newswriters picked up the term. But it has been applied by historians back in time to the meetings among the "Big Three" at the Casablanca (1943), Yalta (1945), and Potsdam (1945) conferences. The first Cold War meeting among the heads of state of the Western powers and the U.S.S.R. took place at Geneva in 1955, when Pres. Dwight D. Eisenhower met with the head of the Soviet Communist party, Nikita Khrushchev. The "spirit of Geneva" was supposed to signal an era of "peaceful coexistence." It was broken in 1960 by the U2 incident, which canceled the scheduled summit between Eisenhower and Khrushchev in Paris. In 1961 Khrushchev met with Pres. John F. Kennedy in Vienna with no noticeable lessening of international tensions. The next summit did not take place until Pres. Lyndon B. Johnson met Soviet Premier Alexsei Kosygin in 1967 at Glassboro College in New Jersey, but again there was little to show for the session.

There were notable achievements in the summit conferences of Pres. Richard M. Nixon, however, who pursued a policy of "détente." In 1972 he met with Communist boss Leonid Brezhnev in Moscow, where they pledged to freeze their nuclear arsenals. The next year Brezhnev came to Washington where the two made progress on a strategic arms limitation treaty (SALT). In June 1974 Nixon returned to Moscow once again but, weakened by the Watergate scandal, was unable to make further progress. That was left to his successor, Pres. Gerald Ford, who met with Brezhnev at Vladivostok in November where they signed a temporary agreement limiting offensive nuclear weapons. In 1979 Pres. Jimmy Carter met with Brezhnev in Vienna where they signed the SALT II agreement limiting long-range nuclear missiles and bombers.

The final round of important Cold War summit meetings took place between Soviet leader Mikhail Gorbachev and Pres. Ronald Reagan. In meetings at Geneva (1985) and Reykjavik, Iceland (1986), Reagan and Gorbachev achieved a remarkable reduction in arms, and at Washington in 1987 they signed a historical treaty limiting intermediate nuclear forces (INF).

During the Cold War these summits had an air of drama, as two world leaders met person to person to avert war. In the post–Cold War era, summits have become routine state visits, with most of the negotiations left to diplomats.

See Also: Cold War.

BIBLIOGRAPHY: Eubank, Keith, *The Summit Conferences, 1919-1960* (Univ. of Oklahoma Press 1966); LaFeber, Walter, *America, Russia, and the Cold War, 1945-1996* (McGraw-Hill 1997).

■ **SUMNER, CHARLES (1811-74),** U.S. senator. Born in Boston, Massachusetts, Sumner graduated from Harvard (1830) and taught law there. He lectured against the Mexican War and was elected to the U.S. Senate as an opponent of slavery's extension (1851). Sumner became a Republican and abolitionist in the 1850s. In his famous "Crime against Kansas" speech (1856), he assailed Sen. Andrew Butler of South Carolina. Two days later Rep. Preston Brooks of South Carolina, a relative of Butler, attacked Sumner in the Senate chamber with a cane, beating him repeatedly. Sumner was seriously injured and did not recover for three years. A Radical Republican, Sumner argued for emancipation during the Civil War (1861-65) and Radical Reconstruction after it. He was one of the leaders of the impeachment fight against Pres. Andrew Johnson (1867).

See Also: Bleeding Kansas; Civil War; Radical Republicans; Reconstruction.

■ **SUMNER, WILLIAM GRAHAM (1840-1910),** economist and sociologist. Born in Paterson, New Jersey, Sumner became a deacon in the Protestant Episcopal Church in 1867 and two years later was ordained as a priest. Beginning in 1872, Sumner taught political and social science at Yale University. His earlier writings dealt with political economy and espoused laissez-faire capitalism, attempting to apply Darwinian theories to human affairs. These works include *A History of the American Currency* (1874), *American Finance* (1875), and *What Social Classes Owe to Each Other* (1883). Sumner also wrote biographies of American historical figures, including Andrew Jackson (1882), Alexander Hamilton (1890), and Robert Morris (1892). After the turn of the century, Sumner turned more toward the discipline of sociology and attempts to characterize social groups and their interactions. He published *Folkways* in 1907 and at the time of his death was at work on *The Science of Society*, later completed by A. G. Keller and published in 1927.

See Also: Social Sciences.

■ **SUNDAY, WILLIAM (BILLY) ASHLEY (1862-1935),** evangelist. Born into a farming family near Ames, Iowa, Sunday was known as "the baseball evangelist." With a modest education, Sunday began a professional baseball career in 1883. At Chicago's Pacific Garden Rescue Mission in 1886 he gave his life to Christ. Five years later he left baseball to become a full-time Christian minister. He worked for the YMCA and two traveling evangelists until he was invited to conduct a revival in Garner, Iowa. After that, he never lacked preaching engagements. The Presbyterian Church licensed him in 1898 and ordained him in 1903. He began preaching in small midwestern towns, but by World War I his revivals were in big cities, including Chicago, Boston, and New York City. Sunday's success was due to his unorthodox, flamboyant style and the organizational skills of his wife, Helen Amelia Thompson, who selected the cities and arranged the campaigns.

Sunday had both admirers and enemies. Common people enjoyed his energy and down-home style, while other clergy disliked his theatrics. Conservatives disapproved of his support of women's rights and his outreach to African Americans, just as others opposed his fight for prohibition. Sunday raised millions of dollars for the U.S. effort in World War I. Until Billy Graham, no American preacher reached as many people as Billy Sunday.

See Also: Religion.

■ **SUPREME COURT,** highest court in the United States. Article III of the Constitution establishes one Supreme Court and grants Congress the power to establish lower courts. The Supreme Court is the only court specified in the Constitution. The number of justices sitting on the Court is determined by Congress. Justices, who are nominated by the president, must be approved by the Senate and serve for life or until resignation. They may be removed only by impeachment by Congress. The judiciary is the only nonelected branch of the federal government.

Jurisdiction. The Constitution establishes jurisdiction of the federal court system. Generally, the jurisdiction extends to cases and controversies. The Supreme Court can only decide an issue that comes before it in an adversarial context and cannot give advisory opinions. Specifically, jurisdiction extends to cases arising under the Constitution, laws and treaties of the United States, cases affecting ambassadors and public ministers, cases of maritime and admiralty issues, controversies where a state or the United States is a party, and cases between citizens of different states.

The Supreme Court is given both original and appellate jurisdiction. Original jurisdiction means that the case will originate in the Supreme Court—that the Supreme Court will be the first court to hear it. Original jurisdiction extends to all cases affecting ambassadors, other public ministers and consuls, and those in which a state is a party. In its appellate jurisdiction the Supreme Court hears the case on appeal from lower federal courts or in some cases from the highest state courts. The Supreme Court has appellate jurisdiction in all other cases and controversies mentioned above.

Other Federal Courts. Congress created lower federal courts under the Judiciary Act of 1789. The U.S. district courts are courts of original jurisdiction and serve as the trial courts of the federal system. The court of appeals is the first level appellate court and hears appeals from the district courts. Cases may be appealed from the court of appeals to the Supreme Court.

Most cases come to the Supreme Court by writ of certiorari (Latin for "to be informed of"). Certiorari (or "cert") is the discretionary power of the Court to hear a case from a lower court. The Supreme Court receives thousands of cert petitions every year but accepts only between 100 and 150. A cert petition needs four votes by the justices in order to be accepted for argument. The Court tends to accept cases in which different circuit courts of appeal have decided a similar issue differently.

The Supreme Court generally follows the doctrine of stare decision (Latin for "let the decision stand"). If the Court had previously decided a case with similar facts, the decision of the previous case will be followed by the Court and not overturned. The system of honoring precedent assures fairness as similar cases are decided the same way.

Justices. The Court as originally established in 1789 had 6 justices, including a chief justice. The number of justices has changed over the years, to

7, then 10, and finally to 9, which is the current number. When Franklin D. Roosevelt was president, he suggested (1937) increasing the number of justices using a formula of one new justice for every sitting justice over the age of 70. The plan would have increased the Court to 15 justices and allowed Roosevelt to nominate 6 new justices. This "court-packing" idea was exceedingly unpopular, and Roosevelt abandoned the idea.

The chief justice is the administrative leader of the Court. He presides over case conferences and assigns the writing of opinions. At times, the chief justice has been the intellectual leader of the Court, setting the tone for the jurisprudence followed while he is chief. The successful performance of this role depends a great deal on the personality of the chief and of the other justices. The chief justice has the same one vote as do the other justices.

The Marshall Court. The Constitution was unclear about the role of the Supreme Court in relation to the other branches of government. Under the early chief justices, John Jay (1789-95), John Rutledge (1795), and Oliver Ellsworth (1796-1800), the Court had a poor public reputation. While serving as chief justice, Jay also accepted an appointment as ambassador to England, and Ellsworth became a special envoy to France. Their

acceptance of other government positions diminished the productivity and prestige of the Court during these early years.

It was the fourth chief justice of the United States, John Marshall (1801-35), who largely created the role of the current Supreme Court and shaped the interpretation of the Constitution. The case of *Marbury* v. *Madison* (1803) set forth the doctrine of judicial review and established the Supreme Court's power to rule on the constitutionality of acts of Congress. Marshall stated, "It is emphatically the province and duty of the judicial department to say what the law is. . . ." The Court in *Marbury* found that a section of the Judiciary Act of 1789, increasing the Court's original jurisdiction, was unconstitutional because it granted the Court powers not in the Constitution. In *Fletcher* v. *Peck* (1810), the Supreme Court exercised its power to declare a state law unconstitutional. And in *Martin* v. *Hunter's Lessee* (1816), the Supreme Court declared a decision by a state supreme court to be unconstitutional.

During Marshall's tenure as chief justice, the Supreme Court strengthened its authority to define the law and helped create a national government through the pivotal case of *McCulloch* v. *Maryland* (1819). The issues before the Supreme Court were whether Congress had the power to es-

Under Chief Justice Salmon P. Chase (*seated center*), the Supreme Court in several decisions, such as *Mississippi* v. *Johnson* (1867), upheld federal government actions in the states of the defeated Confederacy.

tablish a bank and whether a state could tax the national government. The Marshall Court gave the necessary and proper clause of the Constitution a broad construction and found that Congress had the power to establish a bank. But it also found that a state could not tax the national bank because the national government was supreme. The assertion of the supremacy clause further expanded the role of the national government.

The Taney Court. Marshall's successor as chief justice, Roger Brooke Taney (1836-64), led a Court already established and accepted by the public. Taney placed greater emphasis on states' rights and wrote the majority opinion in *Dred Scott v. Sandford* (1857). This landmark case raised the issue of whether a slave, taken by his owner from Missouri into free territory, became free in the process. The issue arose in the context of the larger issue of whether Congress could prohibit slavery in new territories. The Supreme Court could have decided the case on the bare grounds that Missouri law applied. Instead, the Taney Court tried to use its influence to settle the slavery issue. The Court found that Congress could not limit slavery in the territories because it interfered with the rights of property under the Fifth Amendment's due process clause. Rather than settling the slavery controversy, the *Dred Scott* case inflamed it by giving slavery constitutional protection. *Dred Scott* resulted in a weakening of the Court's power and prestige.

The Court in the Post–Civil War Era. One of the most important post–Civil War decisions involved the Slaughterhouse Cases (1873). Butchers in New Orleans challenged a state statute that gave a monopoly to certain slaughterhouses in the city. They claimed they were being denied the privileges and immunities of citizens as set forth in the 14th Amendment. The Court decided that the privileges and immunities clause did not give state citizens any national rights that could be enforced in federal courts. This decision had the effect of limiting the ability of former slaves to challenge state laws in federal court.

From this case, until about 1937, the Supreme Court generally found in favor of the freedom to contract and supported this freedom as part of the liberty and property protected under the substantive due process clauses. The case of *Lochner* v. *New York* (1905) is another in which the Court refused to interfere with private contractual obligations. New York had passed a law prohibiting bakers from working more than 10 hours per day. The Court found this law unconstitutional and an example of a paternalistic government interfering in a person's right to contract. The Court accepted the underlying theory of laissez-faire economics, allowing the private market to operate freely without government regulation.

Another major case of this era was *Plessy* v. *Ferguson* (1896). Homer Plessy, a man who was seven-eighths Caucasian and one-eighth African American, refused to move into a segregated car on a railroad in Louisiana and sued. The Court found that separate but equal accommodations satisfied the equal protection clause of the 14th Amendment. John Harlan's dissent argued that segregation was in itself discriminatory, but the majority opinion established the law for another 58 years.

It was during the latter part of this era that William Howard Taft became chief justice (1921-30). Taft is the only person to have served as both president of the United States (1909-13) and chief justice. Taft continued the conservatism of the prior Courts.

Oliver Wendell Holmes served on the Court from 1902 to 1932 and advocated the doctrine of judicial restraint. He believed that if a law was reasonable and not against the spirit of the Constitution, the Court should defer to the legislature. Louis D. Brandeis (1916-39) was the first Jewish justice appointed. He emphasized that the justices must also consider the social and economic facts and conditions surrounding a case and must examine how a law actually affected people.

The Roosevelt Era Court. Charles Evans Hughes became chief justice in 1930 and served until 1940. From 1930 to 1937, the Hughes Court continued laissez-faire jurisprudence and struck down much New Deal regulatory legislation, restricting power of the federal government to regulate public health, safety, and welfare. As one New Deal act after another was struck down, President Roosevelt offered his "court-packing" plan. The Senate rejected the plan, but the Court soon started reversing itself on regulatory issues. With the same justices sitting on the Court, the Court in 1937 held constitutional a minimum-wage law and overturned a similar case that had rejected a minimum-wage law only nine months earlier. Roosevelt soon was able to fill a number of vacancies on the Court, and the anti–New Deal atmosphere disappeared.

Pragmatism is what guided the Court in the wartime case of *Korematsu* v. *United States* (1944). The Court found constitutional the evacuation of Japanese-American citizens from California to inland relocation centers. The Court recognized that discrimination based on race was suspect but upheld the law as a valid wartime measure.

The Warren Court. When he was attorney general of California, Earl Warren had supported the evacuation of Japanese Americans. Yet, the Warren Court (1953-69) became known for its

Earl Warren served as chief justice of the United States from 1953 to 1969. Under his leadership, the Court unanimously ruled against the segregation of public schools in *Brown v. Board of Education of Topeka.*

protection of individual and civil rights. Warren himself wrote the unanimous opinion of *Brown* v. *Board of Education of Topeka* (1954). In this case, the Court unanimously found that segregated schools were inherently unequal, in violation of the equal protection clause of the 14th Amendment, and therefore unconstitutional. The ruling overturned the *Plessy* decision of 1896. The *Brown* case was followed by other cases finding segregation in public parks, public buildings, and public transportation unconstitutional. The attorney who argued the *Brown* case on behalf of the plaintiffs, Thurgood Marshall, later became the first African American appointed to the Supreme Court (1967).

The Warren Court also found that many of the rights in the Bill of Rights had to be followed by the states. Three major decisions affecting the rights of criminal defendants were decided during the Warren era. *Mapp* v. *Ohio* (1961) held that the Fourth Amendment exclusionary rule (by which evidence obtained by an illegal search and seizure is excluded in a trial) applied to state proceedings as well. *Gideon* v. *Wainwright* (1963) declared that counsel must be appointed for indigent defendants in state felony cases. And in *Miranda* v. *Arizona* (1966) the Court held that criminal defendants must be informed of their right to counsel and right against self-incrimination before police can question them. These cases limited the power of the state against individuals in criminal proceedings.

During the same period the Court also decided two major cases concerning voting rights. *Baker* v. *Carr* (1962) and *Reynolds* v. *Simms* (1964) held that legislative apportionment must be based on population. This application of "one man, one vote" forced most states to reapportion their legislative districts.

The Burger Court. The Supreme Court under the leadership of Warren Burger (1969-86) was a more conservative court than Warren's. Most significantly, it narrowed decisions regarding the rights of criminal defendants. Perhaps its most controversial case, however, was *Roe* v. *Wade* (1973). This case considered whether the right to an abortion was a liberty protected by the Constitution. The Court found that the right to privacy applied to the decision to have an abortion and placed no limits on this right during the first trimester of pregnancy. Thereafter, however, it ruled that a state could regulate abortion because of a compelling interest in the health of the mother and the protection of potential life. During the Burger era, the first female justice, Sandra Day O'Connor, was appointed (1981).

The Rehnquist Court. Associate Justice William Rehnquist was appointed chief justice in 1986. The majority of the justices on the Court have changed since 1986 as a result of resignations, and the Rehnquist Court is still evolving. It remains, however, a generally conservative court. On the issue of abortion, for example, the Rehnquist Court has narrowed the scope of *Roe* but at the same time has consistently refused to overturn the decision. Similarly, the rights of criminal defendants that were so broadly laid out in the Warren era have continued to be redefined in a narrower, more conservative fashion.

Nevertheless, by the mid-1990s the Rehnquist Court was still considered more of a pragmatic than doctrinally conservative institution and one that was not necessarily predictable in its direction on all issues.

—JILL E. MARTIN

See Also: *Bill of Rights; Clear and Present Danger; Constitution of the United States; Equal Protection; Judicial Review; Judiciary Acts; Separation of Powers; Strict Construction; individual biographies and cases.*

BIBLIOGRAPHY: Abraham, Henry J., and Barbara A. Perry, *Freedom and the Court,* 6th ed. (Oxford Univ. Press 1994); Choper, Jesse H., ed., *The Supreme Court and Its Justices* (American Bar Association 1987); Currie, David P., *The Constitution of the United States* (Univ. of Chicago Press 1988); Schwartz, Bernard, *A History of the Supreme Court* (Oxford Univ. Press 1993).

■ **SURVEYING,** the technology of measuring and describing land or its location, or sea and its physical features. It has had a profound impact on America's settlement patterns and scientific knowledge. Boundary surveys that marked and fixed borders described imprecisely (if not erroneously or ambiguously) in land grants provided the necessary framework for land subdivision. In addition, exploratory surveys stimulated settlement, and topographic surveys provided an accurate base map for economic development and a variety of special-purpose maps.

Perhaps the most famous colonial boundary was the line surveyed between 1764 and 1767 by English astronomers Charles Mason and Jeremiah Dixon. Widely cited as the cultural divide between North and South, the Mason-Dixon Line settled a controversy that arose from a grossly inaccurate estimate of latitude. William Penn's patent, issued in 1681, established Pennsylvania's southern boundary at 40N. But Maryland's northern boundary, based on the 40th parallel portrayed on a less accurate 1608 map of Virginia by John Smith, would have made Philadelphia, in the words of one partisan, "the finest city in Maryland." In 1750, an English judge anchored the border at a point 15 miles south of Philadelphia, but this compromise meant little until surveyors had marked the line with stone monuments one mile apart.

The first official survey of the United States was the Survey of the Coast, established in 1807. In addition to recording the shoreline, submerged hazards, and important marine features, federal surveyors mapped the landscape three miles inland. The duties of the present-day National Ocean Survey include not only coastal and marine mapping but also the higher-order geodetic and control surveys that determine a place's precise latitude and longitude and tie local topographic and property maps to the worldwide grid of parallels and meridians.

The U.S. Public Land Survey, devised by Thomas Jefferson and endorsed by Congress in the Land Ordinance of 1785, subdivided land according to a rectangular grid with a far-reaching imprint on the trans-Appalachian landscape. Grid lines six miles apart divided the land into east-west rows identified by *township* number and north-south columns referenced by *range* number. A finer grid divided each six mile by six mile square (called a *township*) into 36 square-mile *sections*, which were divided further into half-mile by half-mile quarter sections, each containing 160 acres—the basic parcel in the settlement of the Midwest and Great Plains. The rectangular land survey's legacy is a systematic pattern of roads and fields aligned with section boundaries. By contrast, in states east of the Ohio River, from Maine through Georgia, comparatively chaotic networks of roads and local political boundaries reflect metes-and-bounds descriptions of the perimeters of irregular land parcels partitioned before the government established an official land survey.

Exploratory surveys, often conducted by the military, identified routes and resources in the largely unmapped territory west of the Mississippi. Beginning with the expedition of Meriwether Lewis and William Clark (1804-06), Congress authorized numerous surveys that informed later efforts to resolve international boundaries, subdue indigenous peoples, extend railways, and settle the land. In the decade following the Civil War, four federal surveys, each named after its leader (Clarence King, F. V. Hayden, John Wesley Powell, and Lt. George M. Wheeler), addressed the growing demand for information about the West's forests, minerals, and agricultural potential. Staffed by geologists and other natural scientists as well as surveyors, these expeditions published their observations in numerous volumes and maps issued during the 1870s and 1880s.

In 1879, Congress recognized the limitations of rival surveys driven by personal initiative and established the U.S. Geological Survey (USGS). In 1882, the USGS initiated a topographic survey (now called the National Mapping Program). Although the USGS has surveyed and mapped densely settled parts of the country many times, it did not complete detailed, large-scale cartographic coverage of the contiguous 48 states until 1990.

—MARK MONMONIER

See Also: Lewis and Clark Expedition; Mason-Dixon Line; Science.

BIBLIOGRAPHY: Bartlett, Richard A., *Great Surveys of the American West* (Univ. of Oklahoma Press 1962); McEntyre, John G., *Land Survey Systems* (John Wiley & Sons 1978); National Geographic Society, *Historical Atlas of the United States* (1988); Thrower, Norman J. W., *Original Survey and Land Subdivision: A Comparative Study of the Form and Effect of Contrasting Cadastral Surveys* (Assn. of American Geographers 1966).

■ **SUSQUEHANNA RIVER,** largest river on the eastern seaboard, flowing 444 miles from central New York state in a southerly direction through Pennsylvania to the Chesapeake Bay in Maryland. Rising in Otsego Lake near Cooperstown, New York, the Susquehanna runs through lands that were a constant battleground between the Iroquois and the European settlers. During the American Revolution the Iroquois aligned themselves with the British, and after the conflict they were removed from the land and replaced by American settlers. Farming prevailed along the Susquehanna until the 1840s, when anthracite was discovered in the area. In addition to coal mining, the land also supported lumbering and industrial developments.

■ **SUSQUEHANNOCK INDIANS.** *See: Algonquian.*

■ **SUTHERLAND, GEORGE (1862-1942),** politician and associate justice of the Supreme Court. Born in Buckinghamshire, England, he came to the United States in 1864 and later represented Utah in the U.S. House (1901-03) and Senate (1905-17) before serving on the Supreme Court (1922-38).

See Also: Supreme Court.

■ **SUTTER, JOHN AUGUSTUS (1803-80),** pioneer who settled in California. A German by birth, Sutter fled debt and an unhappy marriage, arriving in Mexican California in July 1839. Gov. Juan Bautista Alvarado granted Sutter nearly 50,000 acres to found New Helvetia, near what is now Sacramento. Sutter's Fort was a major trading post from 1841 to 1848, when gold was discovered near Sutter's mill. Ironically, the gold rush ruined Sutter financially as his workers fled and squatters destroyed his property. He eventually fled California for Pennsylvania and spent his later years unsuccessfully petitioning the U.S. government for reimbursement of his losses.

See Also: California Gold Rush; Frontier in American History.

■ **SWAYNE, NOAH HAYNES (1804-84),** associate justice of the U.S. Supreme Court (1862-81). A Frederick County, Virginia, native, Swayne is remembered for his balanced opinions. He consistently applied a test of reasonableness when considering a case, especially when individual and government rights clashed.

See Also: Supreme Court.

■ **SWEATSHOPS,** places of employment where employees work long hours for less than minimum wage, often under hazardous conditions, as a way of reducing the employers' overhead and production costs. Most often associated with the garment industry, the practice of sweating historically involves a middleman, or "sweater," who distributed the necessary materials to workers who then assembled the products, often in a personal residence. During the 1890s sweatshops proliferated in most American cities, employing millions of recent immigrants from southern and eastern Europe, young and old alike, who sewed clothes, made artificial flowers, or pasted costume jewelry. Paid for piecework, sweatshop workers often worked upward of 14 hours a day and yet earned less than a living wage. The system also encouraged the widespread use of child labor. Trade unions agitated against sweatshops, arguing that the exploitative conditions hurt all wage labor. Social reformers lobbied against sweated labor on the grounds that poor work conditions led to goods being produced in unsanitary surroundings. By the late 1930s with the passage of the Fair Labor Standards Act, the use of sweatshops declined. However, in the 1990s, the practice flourished again in several major U.S. cities, employing, as before, recent immigrants, this time from Asia and Central America, again primarily in the garment industry.

See Also: *Fair Labor Standards Act; Labor Movement.*

■ **SWEDISH COLONIES,** Delaware Valley settlements founded between 1638 and 1655. During the 1630s, Swedish officials and merchants began discussing possible locations for an Atlantic colony. In 1636, a Dutchman, Peter Minuit, convinced Swedish officials to establish a colony along the coast of North America.

With support from Dutch and Swedish investors and a Swedish royal charter in hand, Minuit, the former director of New Netherland, guided a small group of Swedes and Finns to settle along the Delaware River in 1638. The strategically placed settlement, Fort Christina, on land purchased from local Indians, became the center of the only Swedish colony in the Americas. In 1642, the New Sweden Company bought all shares of the colony held by Dutch investors, bringing the colony under the Swedish Crown.

The once-peaceful relations with the Dutch turned sour in 1647 as the new director of New Netherland, Peter Stuyvesant, sought to reclaim the fur-trading supremacy once enjoyed by the Dutch. On the brink of dissolution, New Sweden was saved in 1654 when a Swedish ship carrying more than 300 settlers defeated a defenseless Dutch fort and recaptured control over the Delaware River. A year later the Dutch struck back, forcing the surrender of all Swedish possessions and ending the 17-year history of the colony. Swedish presence on the Delaware, however, persisted as the majority of colonists remained to live under Dutch and, after 1664, English rule.

—GUY NELSON

See Also: *Delaware; Minuit, Peter; Stuyvesant, Peter.*

BIBLIOGRAPHY: Aberg, Alf, *The People of New Sweden: Our Colony on the Delaware River, 1638-1655* (Natur Och Kultur 1988); Weslager, C. A., *New Sweden on the Delaware, 1638-1655* (Middle Atlantic Press 1988).

■ **SWISSHELM, JANE GREY (1815-84),** journalist, abolitionist, and feminist, born in Pittsburgh, Pennsylvania. In the 1840s, she began writing sharply worded newspaper articles attacking slavery and advocating the rights of women. In 1848 she founded her own newspaper, *The Visitor*, which she edited until 1857. In 1863 she toured the East Coast, lecturing in favor of suffrage and arguing for harsh retribution against the Sioux for their 1862 uprising. A close friend of Mary Todd Lincoln, she lived in Washington, D.C., during the Civil War, working as a secretary in the War Department.

See Also: *Frontier in American History; Lincoln, Mary Todd; Women in American History; Women's Movement.*

■ **SYMPHONY ORCHESTRAS,** music ensembles of strings with wind, brass, and percussion instruments. In the 17th century, the American colonies did not produce any large, permanent, European-style instrumental ensembles, but by the early 18th century, instrumental and vocal concerts were given in cities like New York and Boston.

Established in 1799, the New York Philharmonic, the most permanent and successful of its kind, performed several types of concerts. Like New York, other large cities began to recruit players who would form the core of the 19th-century orchestra, which was influenced heavily by German institutions, composers, and conductors as the appetite for European art music increased. In the 1830s, a group of 30 players was considered a reasonable size for an orchestra, yet larger ones were not uncommon. These ensembles were funded mainly through subscriptions, which offered a stable financial base and provided a degree of respectability not enjoyed by the theater. Orchestras were established in East Coast cities as well as the new urban centers of the Midwest, such as Chicago and St. Louis.

During the period of the world wars, demand for the German music that was once so popular plummeted, and many orchestras struggled financially. In the postwar era, orchestras have received some government funding and have tested new markets in order to stay afloat. The American Symphony Orchestra League lists 1,400 ensembles of varying sizes that not only perform subscription concerts but also tour and provide educational programs.

—Catherine A. Haulman

BIBLIOGRAPHY: Hart, Philip, *Orpheus in the New World: The Symphony Orchestra as an American Cultural Institution* (Norton 1973); Mueller, John Henry, *The American Symphony Orchestra: A Social History of Musical Tastes* (Indiana Univ. Press 1951).

SYPHILIS, an infectious venereal disease, usually passed through sexual contact. Originally called "Bubas" by the Spanish, the disease was renamed "syphilis" around 1530 by Girolamo Fracastoro, an Italian physician. Because the earliest evidence of syphilis is found in the skeletal remains of pre-Columbian South Americans, historians believe it was a New World disease that traveled back to Europe with the first Spanish explorers (c. 1494).

See Also: *Disease; Sexually Transmitted Diseases.*

T

TAFT, ROBERT ALPHONSO (1889-1953), U.S. senator (1939-53) and conservative Republican stalwart. The son of Pres. William Howard Taft (1857-1930), he was born in Cincinnati, Ohio. A graduate of Yale University (1910), he worked for the U.S. Food Administration during World War I and served in the Ohio state legislature (1921-26). Elected to the U.S. Senate in 1938, he consistently opposed the policies of Democratic presidents Franklin D. Roosevelt and Harry S. Truman. Taft resisted U.S. involvement in World War II, supported Sen. Joseph McCarthy's anticommunist investigations (1950-54), and cosponsored the Taft-Hartley Act (1947), which banned closed union shops and permitted the government to ban strikes temporarily. Known as "Mr. Republican," he remained suspicious of activist government and internationalism. Taft unsuccessfully sought his party's presidential nomination in 1940, 1948, and 1952.

See Also: Republican Party; Taft-Hartley Act (1947, 1951).

BIBLIOGRAPHY: Patterson, James T., *Mr. Republican: A Biography of Robert A. Taft* (Houghton Mifflin 1972).

TAFT, WILLIAM HOWARD (1857-1930), 27th president of the United States (1909-13) and 10th chief justice of the United States (1921-30). Born to a wealthy Cincinnati family, Taft graduated from Yale Law School and practiced for a time in his hometown. His first love was always the law. Taft served as a state judge, U.S. solicitor general, and a federal circuit judge. From the judiciary, he accepted Pres. Theodore Roosevelt's clarion call and moved into public administration, serving as governor of the Philippines after the Aguinaldo insurrection and as Roosevelt's secretary of war (overseeing the building of the Panama Canal). When Roosevelt decided to retire from the presidency at the end of his term in 1909, he threw his support to his friend Taft, and this support was more than enough to guarantee Taft's election in 1908.

Taft was as poor a politician as he was a strong judge. In the White House, he succeeded in quickly alienating both major wings of the Republican party. He alienated the conservatives by supporting a federal income tax and by utilizing the Sherman Antitrust Act against monopolies. Taft, in fact, prosecuted trusts at a far greater rate than did Roosevelt. He also alienated progressives by dismissing Gifford Pinchot, Roosevelt's hand-picked head of the Interior Department's forestry division, and by supporting an upward revision of the tariff. By 1912, Roosevelt was in open opposition to Taft. Yet, despite Roosevelt's enormous

After serving as the nation's president (1909-13), William Howard Taft joined Yale's law faculty until appointed chief justice of the United States by Pres. Warren G. Harding (1921).

popularity, Taft's control of the national patronage won him the nomination. Roosevelt stormed out of the party and formed the Progressive ("Bull Moose") party. Stung by what he perceived to be Roosevelt's disloyalty, Taft campaigned hard in 1912 (as he told a reporter, "even a rat in a corner will fight"). It was this feud that paved the way for the victory of Woodrow Wilson and the Democrats and the return of Taft to private life.

His retirement, however, was relatively brief. After a stint as a professor of law at Yale, Taft was named chief justice of the United States by Pres. Warren Harding in 1921. He thus became the only man in history to hold the highest executive and judicial posts in the U.S. government. Taft reveled in his tenure on the Court, telling a colleague that being chief justice was the one "position which I would rather have than any other in the whole world." He brought a needed stability to the Court's conferences, streamlining the decision-making process. Ill health forced Taft to resign from the court in February 1930; he died one month later.

—JOHN ROBERT GREENE

See Also: *President of the United States; Progressive Party; Roosevelt, Theodore; Supreme Court.*
BIBLIOGRAPHY: Coletta, Paolo E., *The Presidency of William Howard Taft* (Univ. Press of Kansas 1973).

■ **TAFT-HARTLEY ACT (1947, 1951),** officially known as the Labor-Management Relations Act, a series of amendments to the National Labor Relations Act (NLRA) of 1935. By 1947, the pro-labor sentiments of Congress had waned, and the Taft-Hartley Act was an attempt to roll back some of the sweeping pro-union guarantees put in place by the NLRA. Most objectionable to organized labor was Section 14b, which allowed states to pass right-to-work laws, effectively outlawing the closed shop. Passed in the early years of the Cold War, the Taft-Hartley Act also required union officers to sign loyalty oaths, certifying that they were not members of the Communist party. The act was amended to expand slightly the 1947 restrictions regarding the establishment of the union shop and in 1957 to prohibit secondary boycotting by unions during a labor dispute and to restrict the use of picketing.

See Also: *Closed Shop; Labor Movement; National Labor Relations Act (NLRA); Picketing; Right-to-Work Laws.*

■ **TAMMANY (c. 1625-1701),** Delaware leader. Tammany was living along the Delaware River in present-day Pennsylvania when William Penn arrived in 1682. Tammany negotiated two treaties with Penn that allowed Penn to establish his colony. An advocate of peaceful accommodation with European colonists, Tammany became a symbol of American resistance to the British during the American Revolution. In 1789, New York City's Society of St. Tammany was named for him. It later became known as Tammany Hall, the center of the Democratic party organization in New York City.

See Also: *Indians of North America; Penn, William; Tammany Hall.*

■ **TAMMANY HALL,** the meeting place of the Tammany Society and the name of the New York City–based political machine that for more than a century controlled Democratic politics in the state and at times even enjoyed national influence. Originally formed in 1789 as an antifederalist organization, Tammany was named for a legendary Delaware Indian chief. In 1798, Aaron Burr gained control, turning Tammany into a political machine that assisted in the 1800 election of Thomas Jefferson as president with Burr as his running mate. Martin Van Buren launched his successful bid for the presidency in 1836 with the backing of Tammany, of which he was then the acknowledged leader or "sachem." Thereafter, Tammany Hall had its greatest influence in local and state politics. A series of Tammany sachems, including William Marcy (Boss) Tweed, maintained the society as a powerful political machine, influencing local and state government and engaging in widespread corruption despite the frequent attacks of various reformers.

Well into the 20th century, Tammany maintained its influence. Only after a state investigation into the administration of New York City Mayor Jimmy Walker, which led to Walker's resignation in 1932, did the power of Tammany seem to wane. During Democratic reformer Fiorello H. La Guardia's several terms as mayor (1933-45), Tammany was out of power although it did manage to field candidates successfully again in the late 1940s. By the early 1960s, with the increase of reform within the Democratic party and a changing municipal electorate, Tammany Hall finally faded from the political scene.

—Kathleen Banks Nutter

See Also: Democratic Party; Tweed, William Marcy (Boss).

BIBLIOGRAPHY: Allen, Oliver E., *The Tiger: The Rise and Fall of Tammany Hall* (Addison-Wesley 1993).

■ **TANEY, ROGER BROOKE (1777-1864),** fifth chief justice (1836-64) of the United States. Born to a wealthy slaveholding family in Calvert County, Maryland, Taney graduated from Dickinson College in 1795 and four years later was admitted to the bar. An early Federalist, he sat in the state legislature from 1799 to 1800 and managed local banks until 1823. Taney supported Andrew Jackson, becoming the president's attorney general and later secretary of the treasury. After Taney assisted Jackson in his opposition to the national bank, the president appointed him (1836) chief justice to succeed John Marshall.

An advocate of judicial restraint, Taney ruled in *Charles River Bridge* v. *Warren Bridge* (1837) that

Chief Justice Roger B. Taney, who served from 1836 to 1864, voted with the majority against Dred Scott's appeal for freedom in 1857.

contracts must be construed narrowly and ambiguous clauses must favor private rights.

In other cases, he argued strenuously for the Court's support of state powers while also helping to expand the role of the federal judiciary. Although he made significant contributions to constitutional law, Taney is best known for his role in the controversies over slavery.

During the 1850s and early 1860s, Taney attempted to use the Court to preserve slavery and support the South, hoping in the process to end the debate over slavery once and for all. In his opinion in *Dred Scott* v. *Sandford* (1857), he ruled that African Americans, even if freed, were not and could never be citizens, and he denied Congress's authority to outlaw slavery in the territories. After the outbreak of the Civil War (1861), Taney objected to Pres. Abraham Lincoln's suspension of the writ of habeas corpus, but Lincoln ignored the aging chief justice, who died in 1864 and was replaced by Salmon Chase.

—Guy Nelson

See Also: Charles River Bridge v. Warren Bridge; Dred Scott v. Sandford; Jackson, Andrew; Supreme Court.

BIBLIOGRAPHY: Lewis, H. H. Walker, *Without Fear or Favor: A Biography of Chief Justice Roger Brooke Taney* (Houghton Mifflin 1965).

■ **TAPPAN, ARTHUR (1786-1865)** and **TAPPAN, LEWIS (1788-1873),** brothers and businessmen active in the antislavery movement. The Tappans were silk merchants. Arthur Tappan was born in Northampton, Massachusetts, and became associated with the radical abolitionist William Lloyd Garrison in the 1830s, providing financial support for his work. He was cofounder and first president of the American Anti-Slavery Society and organized the American and Foreign Anti-Slavery Society in 1840, which promoted church-oriented abolitionism. Lewis Tappan, also born in Northampton, founded the American Missionary Association (1846) to carry Christian abolitionism into the South. He also helped found the *National Era*, an abolitionist newspaper. Lewis became a supporter of the Liberty party in the 1840s, arguing that the U.S. government had the constitutional right to abolish slavery in the South.

See Also: Antislavery Movement; Garrison, William Lloyd; Liberty Party; Slavery.

Journalist Ida M. Tarbell's history (1904) of the Standard Oil Company was one of the most popular muckraking series and sparked a series of antitrust reforms.

■ **TARBELL, IDA MINERVA (1857-1944),** muckraking author, born in Erie County, Pennsylvania. From 1892 she worked for *McClure's* magazine. Her criticisms of Standard Oil and its director, John D. Rockefeller, published in *McClure's* and then as *The History of the Standard Oil Company* (1904), created a sensation. Regretful that her feminist youth had robbed her of the experiences of marriage and motherhood, she wrote *The Business of Being a Woman* (1914). Her autobiography is titled *All in a Day's Work* (1939).

See Also: Muckrakers; Rockefeller, John Davison; Women in American History.

■ **TARIFFS,** taxes placed on goods imported into the country. The nation's first tariff, passed in 1789, was designed to produce revenue. Indeed, until the imposition of corporate and income taxes in the early 20th century, tariff revenues provided the bulk of federal revenues. But tariff policy was also used to "protect" domestic industries by setting prohibitively high rates that made imported goods very expensive. Alexander Hamilton, the nation's first secretary of the treasury, argued for such protective rates in his famous *Report on Manufactures* (1791), and in 1792 he succeeded in persuading Congress to raise rates to protective levels on certain key commodities. The debate over tariff protection quickly became one of the defining political controversies of American history, with industrialists and their workers, based mostly in the Northeast, in favor, while farmers and southern planters, who depended on international markets for the sale of their agricultural commodities, mostly opposed.

Congress adopted the first truly protective rates with the tariff of 1828, which the South condemned as the "Tariff of Abominations." A slight reduction in 1832 failed to mollify the planters, and led the next year to the controversy between Pres. Andrew Jackson and the state of South Carolina over "nullification." In 1833, Congress adopted a schedule for regular reductions, and rates continued to trend downward until, by 1857, the United States had essentially adopted a free-trade policy.

The Civil War inaugurated a fundamental change in tariff policy. With the secession of the South, the Republican Congress adopted the Morrill Tariff of 1861, raising rates to an average of 20 percent and generating revenue to help pay for the war. In the 1880s, with economic hard times for farmers, the tariff again became a contentious political issue. Congress created a tariff commission, which recommended slashing the duties. But the business interests in control of the Republican party would not consider cutting rates. The Democrats, on the other hand, pledged themselves to tariff reduction. Pres. Grover Cleveland struggled with Congress to enact lower rates, but the Republicans kept them high. By the time of the Dingley Tariff Act of 1897, average tariff rates had climbed to 57 percent.

20th-Century Tariffs. The next Democratic administration, that of Pres. Woodrow Wilson (1913-21), persuaded Congress to reduce rates to an average of 27 percent in the Underwood Tariff of 1913, but the return to Republican control after World War I resulted in the reassertion of protectionism.

The United States had emerged from the war as the world's most powerful economy, and the giant corporations of the early 1920s hardly appeared like "infant industries" in need of protection; yet, the Fordney-McCumber Tariff of 1922 established the highest protective tariffs to that date. After the onset of the Great Depression of the 1930s, Congress raised rates to an average of over 65 percent with the infamous Smoot-Hawley Tariff of 1930. Universally condemned by economists, the tariff created a rate war with America's trading partners and contributed to a worsening of the Depression by suppressing international trade.

The era of protectionism ended in 1934 when the New Deal Congress passed the Trade Agreements Act. This law empowered the president to negotiate free-trade "most-favored-nation" agreements with individual countries. By 1937, the Roosevelt administration had made 30 such agreements. The act was renewed in 1937 and has remained a permanent feature of U.S. trade policy since.

In 1948, the United States was a leader in the negotiations that led to the signing of the General Agreement on Tariffs and Trade (GATT), a multilateral treaty setting forth rules for the conduct of international trade. GATT played a major role in the massive expansion of world trade in the second half of the 20th century. In a series of international trade conferences, the United States led the way in reducing the world average of tariffs on industrial goods from 40 percent in 1947 to less than 5 percent in 1993. GATT went out of existence in 1994, replaced by the World Trade Organization, with 125 participating nations accounting for 90 percent of world trade.

By the end of World War II most Republicans had been converted from protectionism to free trade. Free trade, in fact, was the official position of both major political parties through the second half of the 20th century. The great controversy in the United States over the 1993 North American Free Trade Agreement (NAFTA), which aimed to make the continent into a huge free-trade zone, demonstrated the changed political alignment. While both parties officially supported the agreement, there was considerable dissent, with some conservatives, many leftists, and most labor leaders arguing that Americans still needed protection from the unfair competition of foreign industry.

—JOHN MACK FARAGHER

See Also: Free Trade; General Agreement on Tariffs and Trade (GATT).

BIBLIOGRAPHY: Goldstein, Judith, *Ideas, Interests, and American Trade Policy* (Cornell Univ. Press 1993); Ratner, Sidney, *The Tariff in American History* (Van Nostrand 1972); Taussig, Frank William, *The Tariff History of the United States* (Putnam 1923).

■ **TAXATION,** has taken various forms in American history. Colonial governments at the level of province, county, parish, or town relied on a combination of property taxes, poll taxes, excise taxes, and fees on particular commodities such as beer or distilled spirits. These taxes tended to be regressive, favoring the wealthy and hitting the poor the hardest, but the burden of taxation fell relatively lightly on all, especially compared with taxes in Great Britain. The British had imposed duties on certain commodities, but these were intended not to raise revenue but to regulate colonial trade. The understaffed and corrupt customs service in North America, however, was unable to enforce the provisions effectively. But in the 1760s, the British enacted measures to raise colonial revenues and beefed up the customs service. Protests against the Sugar Act (1764) and the Stamp Act (1765) sparked a tax revolt that led to the American Revolution.

Fresh from this experience, the framers of the Articles of Confederation denied Congress the right to levy any taxes at all, forcing it instead to meet the expenses of the general government by assessments on the states. This system proved unworkable, and in the Constitution that went into effect in 1789, Congress was empowered to levy and collect taxes. But the politics of taxation remained controversial. In 1791, Congress imposed a tax on whiskey, a measure that led three years later to the Whiskey Rebellion. And the nearly continuous 19th-century debate over the tariff led to such dramatic confrontations as the crisis over "nullification." With the exception of the Civil War, however, when Congress enacted an income and inheritance tax that remained in effect until 1872, the federal government continued to rely on tariff duties and excise taxes for most of its revenue. Democrats opposed the high protective tariff rates kept in effect by the Republican majority after the Civil War, arguing that an income tax would be a fairer method of raising revenues. Democrats controlled Congress only once during the late 19th century (1893-95) and at that time took advantage of their majority to pass legislation imposing a tax of 2 percent on annual incomes above $4,000. The law, however, was overturned by a ruling of the Supreme Court in 1895.

20th-Century Taxation. By the early 20th century—with the federal government undertaking a variety of new regulatory programs—customs and excise revenues were failing to keep up with expenditures. In 1909, Congress levied the first tax on corporate profits and in the same year passed an amendment to the Constitution permitting the taxation of personal income. Approval of the 16th Amendment in 1913 was followed by the enactment of the first graduated income tax by the Democratic Congress swept in with the election of Pres. Woodrow Wilson the year before. During World War I, the tax rates for the highest income brackets were as steep as 70 percent, but during the Republican ascendancy of the 1920s, these rates were cut back drastically. Tax rates were adjusted upward during the New Deal of the 1930s, reaching their highest levels in American history during World War II (1941-45), when the minimum rate was 23 percent and the maximum 94 percent.

The most important adjustment in tax policy in the postwar period came during the presidency of Ronald Reagan (1981-89). In 1981, Congress agreed to his proposal for a massive cut in income and corporate taxes amounting to $747 billion over five years. According to the "supply-side" economic doctrine of the administration, revenues lost through lower tax rates would be more than made up by new economic growth. By the 1990s, tax rates in the United States were the lowest of all the industrial democracies, but the cuts had contributed to chronic budget deficits and a mushrooming federal debt.

—JOHN MACK FARAGHER
See Also: Income Tax; Tariffs.
BIBLIOGRAPHY: Becker, Robert A., *Revolution, Reform, and the Politics of American Taxation, 1763-1783* (Louisiana State Univ. Press 1980); Browlee, W. Elliot, *Federal Taxation in America: A Short History* (Cambridge Univ. Press 1996); Pollack, Sheldon D., *The Failure of U.S. Tax Policy: Revenue and Politics* (Pennsylvania State Univ. Press 1996).

■ **TAXATION WITHOUT REPRESENTATION,** slogan used in the American colonies to challenge Parliament's power to tax. Coined in 1637 by British orator James Hampden and used first in the colonies by James Otis in 1761 ("No taxation without representation"), it signified the strong colonial opposition to British taxes.
See Also: Revolution, American.

■ **TAYLOR, ELIZABETH (1932-),** film actress. Born in London, England, she became an international celebrity known as much for her tumultuous private life as her screen roles. Taylor debuted in *National Velvet* (1944) and subsequently starred in *Cleopatra* (1963) and *Who's Afraid of Virginia Woolf?* (1966) with Welsh actor Richard Burton, to whom she was twice married (1964-74, 1975-76). She founded an AIDS research foundation in 1991.
See Also: Motion Pictures.

■ **TAYLOR, FREDERICK W. (1856-1915),** engineer, inventor, and efficiency expert. Born in Germantown, Pennsylvania, Taylor worked his way up through the Midvale Steel Company (1878-90) and studied engineering at the Stevens Institute of Technology. When Midvale introduced piece work, Taylor grew interested in the most efficient way to perform specific tasks. He measured workers' procedures and output closely, designed new methods and equipment to maximize the efficiency of each operation, and determined who best fit each job, thereby improving labor relations (he hoped) and increasing profits. At Midvale he raised output by 300 percent and pay by 25 to 100 percent. In 1893, Taylor became the first scientific management consultant, signing on with the Bethlehem Steel Company, where he and Maunsel White developed a process for treating steel that increased metal-cutting capacities by 200 to 300 percent. He received over 100 patents for machines he designed. After Taylor left Bethlehem Steel in 1901, he developed his ideas further and wrote *The Principles of Scientific Management* (1911). Known as "Taylorism," his ideas were adopted widely in shops, offices, and factories after 1900 and proved inseparable from the development of mass production and industrial management.
See Also: Industrial Revolution.

■ **TAYLOR, GEORGE (1716-81),** metallurgist and Revolutionary War statesman. A native of Northern Ireland, Taylor immigrated to Pennsylvania in 1736 and later established an ironworks. Active during the Revolution, he was a member of the Second Continental Congress and signed the Declaration of Independence.

See Also: Declaration of Independence.

■ **TAYLOR, PAUL (1930-),** dancer and choreographer. Born in Allegheny County, Pennsylvania, he performed with Martha Graham's modern dance company (1953-61) and then formed his own influential troupe (1961). Known for the emotional content of his dances, Taylor stressed collaborative development of new works, and many of his dancers, notably Twyla Tharp, later became important choreographers themselves.

■ **TAYLOR, ZACHARY (1794-1850),** 12th president of the United States (1849-50). Born in Montebello, Virginia, Taylor was raised on his family's slave-worked farm in Kentucky. Barred from the professions by his sketchy formal education, he chose the army as a career. Taylor rose slowly through the officer ranks, making a name for himself in the War of 1812 and the Second Seminole War (1835-42). Disdain for sartorial polish and physical hardship earned him the nickname "Old Rough and Ready" among his men. In 1846 General Taylor commanded an army during the Mexican War, leading it to four decisive victories.

Taylor's status as both a slave owner and a war hero gave him appeal to all regions and led the Whig party to nominate him for president in 1848. He won, defeating candidates from the Democratic, Free Soil, and Liberty parties. Taylor proved an ineffective executive leader. His military style—conservative, inflexible, and short-sighted—did not serve him well in the world of politics. Much to his Southern supporters' dismay, Taylor championed nationalist over proslavery sentiments. He opposed the extension of slavery into the new territory acquired from Mexico and threatened to use force to prevent Southern secession. He also resisted the Compromise of 1850, which sought to bring a peaceful solution to the issues between North and South, in favor of admitting California and New Mexico directly as free states. Although the hero of an expansionist war,

Zachary Taylor gained national attention for his generalship during the Mexican War, which helped him to win the presidential election of 1848 as the nominee of the Whigs. He died after only a year and a half in office.

Taylor rejected the idea of "Manifest Destiny" and the Monroe Doctrine in his foreign policy decisions.

Honest and well-intentioned, Taylor underestimated the power of sectionalism and the passion around the slavery issue. He died of gastroenteritis on July 9, after only one year and four months in office.

—CATHERINE ALLGOR

See Also: Compromise of 1850; Mexican War.
BIBLIOGRAPHY: Bauer, K. Jack, *Zachary Taylor: Soldier, Planter, Statesman of the Old Southwest* (Louisiana State Univ. Press 1985); Smith, Elbert B., *The Presidencies of Zachary Taylor and Millard Fillmore* (Univ. Press of Kansas 1988).

■ **TEA ACT (1773),** British law that lowered prices on tea imported to the American colonies by the faltering British East India Company. Parliament designed the act to bolster the company and bring in revenue by undercutting the prices of the American merchants. It enraged many colonists and precipitated the Boston Tea Party (Dec. 16, 1773).

See Also: Boston Tea Party; Revolution, American.

■ **TEAPOT DOME,** political scandal during the administration of Pres. Warren G. Harding (1921-23). In 1912 Pres. William Howard Taft set aside some 70,000 acres of oil land in the Elk Hills of California as the Naval Oil Reserves. Two years later Pres. Woodrow Wilson added 10,000 acres at Teapot Dome, Wyoming, to the reserves, which were to be maintained by the government until the navy needed the oil. The General Leasing Act of 1920 empowered the secretary of the navy to "use, store, exchange or sell" the oil for the benefit of the United States.

After Harding became president in 1921, his secretary of the interior, Albert Fall, persuaded the president to issue a secret executive order transferring control of the Elk Hills and Teapot Dome oil reserves from the Department of the Navy to the Department of the Interior. This was done with the consent of Edwin Denby, then secretary of the navy. The following year Fall leased the reserves to two powerful oil operators. Teapot Dome was leased to Harry F. Sinclair, and Elk Hills to Edward L. Doheny. Fall's argument to the president was that the oil was leaking onto private sites, and that Doheny and Sinclair would drill before all the oil leaked away and thus save it for the government. In reality, Fall received large financial payments from both men ($100,000 from Doheny and $250,000 from Sinclair) in return for his allowing them to drill on public lands and sell the oil for their own personal profit.

Harding learned of this chicanery just before his death in August 1923, but it was left to his successor, Calvin Coolidge, to live with the political fallout of the scandal. Once the scandal was made public, a congressional committee, headed by Sen. Thomas J. Walsh of Montana, investigated the allegations. As a result, Denby was forced to resign from Coolidge's cabinet in March 1924. Fall also resigned and, after undergoing criminal prosecutions, was sentenced in June 1924 to one year in prison and fined $100,000. For their part, Doheny served only a few months of his jail term, and Sinclair was cleared of all charges. In December 1927 the U.S. Supreme Court invalidated the leases to Doheny and Sinclair, noting that they had been obtained by fraud and corruption.

—JOHN ROBERT GREENE

See Also: *Harding, Warren Gamaliel.*

BIBLIOGRAPHY: Murray, Robert K., *The Harding Era: Warren G. Harding and His Administration* (Univ. of Minnesota Press 1969); Werner, Morris, and John Starr, *Teapot Dome* (Viking Press 1959).

■ **TECUMSEH (1768-1813),** Shawnee war chief who attempted to form a pan-tribal confederacy to resist American expansion onto Indian lands in the Ohio and Mississippi valleys. Tecumseh was born to a Shawnee father and a Creek mother at Old Piqua, a Shawnee village in Ohio. His father was killed fighting the Virginians in 1774, and he was raised by an older sister. He grew to manhood amid the warfare of the American Revolution. In 1791, Tecumseh served as a scout at St. Clair's Defeat, and he also fought at the Battle of Fallen Timbers (1794), but he refused to sign the subsequent Treaty of Greenville, which surrendered most of the Indian lands in Ohio.

In 1798 he established a small Shawnee village on the Whitewater River in Indiana, where in 1805 Lalawethika, his younger brother, experienced a

Shawnee chief Tecumseh worked to unite Indians to defend their lands from encroachment by whites. He fought with the British against the United States in the War of 1812 and was killed at the Battle of the Thames (1813).

series of visions that transformed this former alcoholic into a powerful religious leader known as Tenskwatawa, or the Shawnee Prophet. After the Prophet successfully predicted an eclipse of the Sun, tribespeople flocked to Tecumseh's village and American authorities became alarmed about the Shawnee holy man's growing influence. In 1808 the Shawnee brothers established Prophetstown, a new village near the juncture of the Tippecanoe and Wabash rivers in western Indiana. From Prophetstown, Tecumseh visited many midwestern tribes, transforming his brother's religious following into a political movement and urging all tribespeople to unite under his leadership and to cede no more lands to the Americans.

In 1811, while Tecumseh recruited followers among the southern tribes, William Henry Harrison attacked Prophetstown, defeated the Prophet at the Battle of Tippecanoe, and destroyed the Shawnee village. In 1812, after returning from the South, Tecumseh journeyed to Canada where he allied his movement with the British. During the War of 1812 he fought with the British on the Detroit-Maumee frontier, participating in the capture of Detroit and the unsuccessful British attacks upon Fort Meigs and Fort Stephenson. In 1813, when American forces invaded Canada, Tecumseh forced the British to make a stand, but he was killed on Oct. 5, 1813, at the Battle of the Thames, when the British army fled and the Americans overwhelmed the Indians.

During his lifetime Tecumseh was highly respected by both friends and foes, and after his death he became a legendary figure. He remains one of America's most honored Indian leaders.

—R. DAVID EDMUNDS

See Also: *Frontier in American History; Harrison, William Henry; Indians of North America; Shawnee; Tenskwatawa; Thames, Battle of the; Tippecanoe, Battle of.*

BIBLIOGRAPHY: Dowd, Gregory, *A Spirited Resistance: The Native American Struggle for Unity, 1745-1815* (Johns Hopkins Univ. Press 1992); Edmunds, R. David, *Tecumseh and the Quest for Indian Leadership* (Little, Brown 1984); Sugden, David, *Tecumseh: A Life* (John Macrae/Henry Holt 1998).

■ **TEEDYUSCUNG (1700-63),** Delaware leader. In 1737, Teedyuscung accused the British of fraud after the Delawares were dispossessed from their lands in present-day Pennsylvania. At the outbreak of the French and Indian War, Teedyuscung joined with Shawnee and Mahican leaders in attacking English colonial settlements, but after negotiations with the British Indian agent, Teedyuscung agreed to fight with the British. He died in a house fire believed to have been set by a group trying to open western Pennsylvania for white settlement.

See Also: *Indians of North America.*

■ **TEHERAN CONFERENCE (1943),** World War II meeting in Iran between U.S. Pres. Franklin Roosevelt, British Prime Minister Winston Churchill, and Soviet leader Joseph Stalin from November 28 to December 1. They decided that a cross-channel invasion of France, entitled "Overlord," would go forward as soon as possible, and that the Russians would enter the Pacific War after the defeat of Germany. In addition, an international planning organization would be established to decide the fate of Germany.

See Also: *World War II.*

■ **TELEGRAPH,** form of electrical communication. By the mid-1830s, several electrical scientists had developed much of the technology necessary for the telegraph. Recognizing its social utility, Samuel Morse, a professor of art at New York University, developed the first functioning system in 1838. Through an electrical line, messages were sent by "Morse Code," a system by which the alphabet is transmitted by various combinations of audible "dots" and "dashes." In 1843, Congress awarded Morse $30,000 to establish the first intercity line between Baltimore and Washington, D.C.

The telegraph industry grew rapidly, as dozens of companies sprang up, laying some 15,000 miles of line by 1852. In 1861, the first transcontinental line was completed, and five years later a permanent link between Europe and America was established. In the decades after the Civil War, the Western Union Company became the dominant provider as technological innovations such as the wireless telegraphy system proliferated. By the end of the 19th century, however, the telegraph had been supplanted by the telephone as the standard mode of distance communication.

—GUY NELSON

See Also: *Morse, Samuel Finley Breese.*

BIBLIOGRAPHY: Blondheim, Manehem, *News Over the Wires: The Telegraph and the Flow of Public Information in America, 1844-1897* (Harvard Univ. Press 1994); Israel, Paul, *From Machine Shop to Industrial Laboratory: Telegraphy and the Changing Context of American Invention* (Johns Hopkins Univ. Press 1992).

◼ **TELEPHONE,** world's most widely used communication device, invented by speech researcher Alexander Graham Bell in 1875. Bell was only one of a number of inventors attempting to transmit speech vibrations as electrical impulses over conducting wire, but he was the one granted (1876) a U.S. patent, often described as the most valuable ever issued. The Bell Company's patent was challenged by a number of competitors, including Western Union, which had initially turned down Bell's offer of all rights to the device. Soon thereafter, Western Union became painfully aware of the threat the telephone posed to its control of telecommunications. The two parties settled in 1879, when the Bell Company promised to stay out of telegraphy.

By that time Bell himself had sold out to a group of investors. Over the next 20 years company researchers perfected the telephone's original design, invented the rotary dialer, built the first switchboards and central exchanges, and introduced regional long-distance service. The Bell subsidiary, American Telephone and Telegraph (AT&T), founded in 1885 to build a national long-distance system, was made parent company of the Bell system in 1899.

Through its control of long-distance, AT&T built itself into the greatest monoply in American corporate history, as it acquired independent local telephone companies and consolidated them into a series of regional systems. Long-distance connections were extended from New York to Denver in 1911 and to the Pacific Coast in 1915. In 1910, the corporation gained control of Western Union, thus achieving monopoly control over all telecommunications in the United States. In the Graham-Willis Act of 1921, AT&T was declared a "natural monopoly" and granted immunities from antitrust laws. In turn the corporation agreed to provide long-distance service to the few remaining independent phone companies. Over the next 50 years,

AT&T built the world's largest, most advanced, and most efficient telecommunications network.

AT&T initially marketed the telephone as a business tool. Local companies worried that subscribers were using "the wires as they pleased" and condemned the "large numbers of communications of the most trivial character." But telephones were immediately popular among residential users, who used the device to cultivate existing local relationships. It was not until the 1920s that Bell System managers got the message and began to respond to the considerable demands for expanded residential service. The uses of the telephone were not determined by makers and marketers but emerged instead through a complex process of consumption and innovation.

By the 1970s, AT&T had nearly a million employees and was the largest company in the world. Declaring that AT&T had become a monopoly in restraint of trade, the U.S. Department of Justice instituted (1974) an antitrust suit, and in 1982 the parties reached a settlement in which AT&T agreed to get out of the local telephone business, spinning off seven regional companies ("Baby Bells"). AT&T retained its long-distance service but was required to compete against a new set of players. By the end of the century, telephone service had become enormously complicated, with many corporations competing for expanded service that included data and video delivery transmitted over high efficiency fiber-optic networks.

—JOHN MACK FARAGHER

See Also: Bell, Alexander Graham.
BIBLIOGRAPHY: Fischer, Claude S., *America Calling* (Univ. of California Press 1992); Young, Peter, *Person to Person* (Granta 1991).

◼ **TELSTAR,** the first satellite to relay television broadcasts. Equipped with transponders that received, amplified, and transmitted signals, it was launched July 10, 1962, from Cape Canaveral, Florida.

◼ **TELEVISION AND RADIO,** in the United States began about 1906 with transmissions by developers and amateurs using "wireless" equipment, the product of experiments by Guglielmo Marconi in England, and in the United States by Lee De Forest, Irving Langmuir, Edwin H. Armstrong, and Ernst F. W. Alexanderson.

The Growth of Radio. In 1912, Congress passed the Radio Act, establishing the principal of government regulation by requiring operators to obtain licenses from the Commerce Department. Marconi saw radio as a substitute for the telephone, but it was David Sarnoff, working for Marconi's U.S. affiliate, who in 1915 proposed a "radio music box" for receiving transmissions of concerts, sports, and news broadcasts from central locations or "stations."

The federal government assumed control of radio during World War I, but in 1919 the Commerce Department brought together several huge corporations to form the Radio Corporation of America (RCA). Sarnoff became general manager and later president and chairman of the board. Sarnoff's principal interest was in the sale of radio receivers.

The first regular broadcast station, KDKA in Pittsburgh, went on the air in November 1920 with the returns of the presidential election. The federal government had licensed eight stations by the end of 1921; a year later, 564 had been licensed. Advertisers began using the medium immediately, and although there were proposals for broadcasting to be controlled by a government corporation (as it was in England with the British Broadcasting Corporation [BBC]), or by a non-profit organization, by 1923, the year the National Association of Broadcasters was formed, broadcasting had become a thoroughly commercial operation. The Radio Act of 1927 established the principal of public ownership of the airwaves but licensing of broadcasting stations as profit-making entities. The Communications Act of 1934 created the Federal Communications Commission (FCC) to license and regulate commercial broadcasting in the public interest.

In November 1924, the American Telephone and Telegraph Company (AT&T) linked stations around the country via long-distance telephone lines in order to broadcast the election returns from a central location. This was the beginning of network broadcasting. The National Broadcasting Company (NBC), a subsidiary of RCA, went on the air in 1926. The Columbia Broadcasting System (CBS) followed in 1927 and the American Broadcasting Corporation (ABC) in 1943. Early programming included the broadcast of news (H. V. Kaltenborn was the first radio correspondent), concerts, and dramas. The success of the "Amos 'n' Andy Show" in 1928 led to dozens of radio se-

Since the early 1960s, American presidents have used television effectively to present their programs directly to the American people. Here, Pres. Lyndon B. Johnson delivers an address in 1967.

ries, including comedy, crime and mystery, daytime serials (called "soap operas" because of sponsorship by detergent brands), and variety programs. Pres. Franklin D. Roosevelt spoke to the nation in 1933 in the first of his "fireside chats," the first demonstration of radio as a medium of political persuasion. A few years later right-wing "radio priest" Father Charles E. Coughlin originated what became known as "hate radio." But the power of the medium was most clearly shown by the panic produced by the broadcast of a dramatization of a Martian invasion in "War of the Worlds" by the actor and director Orson Welles in 1938. By that time there were radios in some 90 percent of American households and annual radio advertising totaled $171 million.

The broadcast of real warfare began that same year with the reports of Edward R. Murrow on the Munich crisis and later the German invasion of

Poland and bombing of London. On Dec. 7, 1941, most Americans heard of the attack on Pearl Harbor on the radio and listened the next day to live broadcasts of President Roosevelt speaking to Congress requesting a declaration of war against Japan. Radio correspondents broadcast from the European and Pacific theaters during World War II but accepted voluntary censorship of their reports. During the war Americans came to rely on radio as their prime source of news.

The Development of Television. Television in the United States was developed in the laboratories of RCA by scientists such as Vladimir Zworykin. The first television broadcast in the United States was NBC's coverage of President Roosevelt's address opening the New York World's Fair in 1939. By 1940, 23 TV stations had been licensed, and commercial broadcasting began in 1941. But the production of receivers was curtailed by the war, and the first mass-produced sets did not go on the market until 1947. The three broadcast networks moved into TV after the war, programming the same assortment of shows developed for radio. Among the most important early TV performers were Milton Berle, Lucille Ball, Jackie Gleason, and Arthur Godfrey. There were 108 television stations in 1948, and 2,051 by 1952. By 1962, television could be found in more than 90 percent of American households. That year, FCC chairman Newton Minow famously described television programming as a "vast wasteland."

The most important innovation of early television was the live broadcast of news events. In 1951, Sen. Estes Kefauver captivated millions of Americans with his hearings on organized crime, and in 1954 the Army-McCarthy hearings turned the public against right-wing Sen. Joseph McCarthy. The 1952 conventions and elections were the first to be broadcast live, and that year Richard Nixon delivered his famous "Checkers" speech defending himself against charges of corruption. Edward R. Murrow created the innovative public affairs program "See It Now."

The event that demonstrated the enormous power of the medium in public affairs was the assassination of Pres. John F. Kennedy in November 1963; all three networks suspended regular programming and put their news staffs on the air. Millions of Americans were watching two days

Radio pioneer David Sarnoff stayed at his post for 72 hours in 1912 in order to report on the *Titanic* disaster.

later when Jack Ruby shot and killed Lee Harvey Oswald on live television. That same year, CBS began regular one-half-hour evening news broadcasts by correspondent Walter Cronkite, who had apprenticed with Edward R. Murrow during World War II.

The first educational station went on the air in 1953, and by the mid-1960s there were several hundred. In 1967, Congress passed the Public Broadcasting Act, providing federal funding for the creation of a network, PBS. In 1969, the Corporation for Public Broadcasting was created as a joint public-private effort to support educational production. The greatest early success for PBS was the children's program "Sesame Street," created by puppeteer Jim Henson.

Radio and TV in the Modern Era. The success of television had dramatic effects on radio. Network dominance faded quickly after World War II and, increasingly, radio programs were produced locally. By the 1950s the most common format was the broadcast of recorded music by disc jockeys, something local stations could do very inexpensively. In 1956, 70 percent of the broadcast time of the country's 2,700 AM stations had been given over to music. Disc jockeys were responsible for the rising popularity of country and western, rhythm and blues, and rock and roll music. Radio developed several new formats in the 1960s: all-news and talk radio on AM, and on FM "easy-listening" and educational broadcasting (National Public Radio, 1969).

Meanwhile, in the last decades of the 20th century, television was being transformed by new technology. Cable systems first began operating in 1947 as a way of bringing television signals to remote locations. In the late 1960s, however, cable operators began to expand their systems, providing clearer signals. By 1974, 12 percent of American homes had been wired, but by 1990, 67 percent had cable. Cable dovetailed with another development, the use of satellites for the transmission of television signals.

The first TV satellite was Telstar, which made possible national live broadcasts when it was placed in orbit in 1962. Telstar 2, launched the following year, provided live transatlantic broadcasts, first used for the summer Olympics of 1964. Commercial use of satellite technology began in the 1970s, making it possible for cable operators to download signals and place them on their systems. Among the first of these cable channels were MTV (Music Television) and CNN (Cable News Network), both of which began operations in 1981. "Narrowcasting" allowed for the creation of dozens of new channels, leading to a decline in the dominance of the broadcast networks and the promise of greater variety for viewers, although at the end of the century many Americans found themselves in agreement with the rock artist Bruce Springsteen, who sang: "I can see by your eyes friend you're just about gone/Fifty-seven channels and nothin' on."

—JOHN MACK FARAGHER

See Also: *Alexanderson, Ernst; Amos 'n' Andy; Armstrong, Edwin; Ball, Lucille; Berle, Milton; Communications Act of 1934; Coughlin, Charles Edward; Cronkite, Walter; De Forest, Lee; Gleason, Jackie; Godfrey, Arthur; Kaltenborn, H. V.; Langmuir, Irving; Murrow, Edward R.; Public Broadcasting; Sarnoff, David; Welles, Orson; Zworykin, Vladimir.*

BIBLIOGRAPHY: Barfield, Ray, *Listening to Radio, 1920-1950* (Praeger 1996); Barnouw, Erik, *Tube of Plenty: The Evolution of American Television* (Oxford Univ. Press 1990); Douglas, Susan J., *Inventing American Broadcasting, 1899-1922* (Johns Hopkins Univ. Press 1987); Kisseloff, Jeff, *The Box: An Oral History of Television, 1929-1961* (Viking 1995); Marc, David, *Demographic Vistas: Television in American Culture* (Univ. of Pennsylvania Press 1996).

■ **TELLER, EDWARD (1908-)**, physicist who helped develop atomic and hydrogen bombs and a proponent of maintaining a strong nuclear arsenal. Born in Budapest, Hungary, Teller studied physics in Germany. He immigrated to the United States in 1935 and became a professor at George Washington University (1935-41), where he and George Gamow studied beta decay and thermonuclear reactions. Teller supported the creation of the atomic bomb and went to Columbia to work with Enrico Fermi in 1941. He later moved to the University of Chicago and to the Los Alamos, New Mexico, laboratory that produced the first atomic bomb in 1945. He helped speed the development of the first H-bomb and its testing in the Marshall Islands in 1952. He then went to the University of California at Berkeley and directed the Lawrence Radiation Laboratory, retiring in 1975. A believer in using technology to maintain superiority in the Cold War, Teller testified against the nuclear test ban treaty (1963), promoted the antiballistic missile system (1969), and was a supporter of the Strategic Defense Initiative ("Star Wars") project.

See Also: Manhattan Project; Science.

■ **TELLER RESOLUTION,** amendment to U.S. declaration of war against Spain (1898). Sponsored by Sen. Henry Teller of Colorado, it opposed annexation of Spanish territory such as the Philippines or Puerto Rico.

See Also: Spanish-American War.

■ **TEMPERANCE MOVEMENTS,** social and political organizations that urged abstention from the consumption of alcohol. In 1830, the per capita consumption of hard liquor was more than twice today's rate. In response, white, middle-class Americans formed associations like the American Temperance Society, while artisans and workers joined the reform cause as well. A movement also grew out of the women's rights convention at Seneca Falls (1848), and women continued to play a prominent role in the temperance movement.

Alcohol came to symbolize moral depravity and the antithesis of white, middle-class respectability. Religious impulses in particular led people to oppose the consumption of spirits. In the 1870s, women emerged from church meetings to protest in the streets, singing and praying in front of saloons. The women held that these establishments threatened the safety and sanctity of domestic and family life. Frances Willard, the first president of the Women's Christian Temperance Union (WCTU), positioned women as the defenders of the home against drunkenness. She and her followers demanded only "home protection," not the franchise. In 1888, Republicans incorporated temperance into their platform.

The Anti-Saloon League spearheaded the prohibition cause into the 20th century, sponsoring "dry" political candidates who promoted reform. Increasing agitation, pressure, and research into the social and physical consequences of drink eventually led to the 18th Amendment (repealed in 1933 by the 21st Amendment), which in 1919 banned the manufacture, sale, and transport of alcohol in the United States.

—CATHERINE A. HAULMAN

See Also: Alcohol; Prohibition; Willard, Frances.
BIBLIOGRAPHY: Blocker, Jack S., *American Temperance Movements: Cycles of Reform* (Twayne Publishers 1989); Epstein, Barbara Leslie, *The Politics of Domesticity: Women, Evangelism, and Temperance in Nineteenth-Century America* (Wesleyan Univ. Press 1981).

■ **TEMPLE, SHIRLEY (1928-),** child film star and later diplomat (as Shirley Temple Black). Born in Santa Monica, California, she became one of the biggest box office stars of the 1930s, playing cheerful moppets in films such as *The Littlest Rebel* (1936). Her film career faded as she matured, and she became active in Republican politics. She was a member of the U.S. delegation to the UN General Assembly (1969-70), U.S. ambassador to Ghana (1974-76), chief of protocol for Pres. Gerald Ford (1976-77), and a member of the U.S. delegation on African Refugee Problems in 1982.

See Also: Motion Pictures.

■ **TENANT FARMING,** arrangement under which a propertyless farmer cultivates another person's land, compensating the landowner with either a cash rent or a share of the crop. Although most commonly linked with the cotton plantations of the post–Civil War South, tenant farming was a common feature of many agrarian landscapes, especially those areas where property owning was highly concentrated or where a sizable landless class lived. Colonial Virginia, for example, possessed a significant number of tenant farmers as early as the mid-1600s, and by the 1830s even Illinois possessed a tenant farmer class. By 1890, in fact, 39 percent of the farmers in Illinois were tenants, as were 26 percent of the farmers in Pennsylvania and 23 percent of the farmers in California.

Although tenant farming had existed in the South during the antebellum period, it became particularly widespread in the region in the 1860s, following the dislocations brought about by the Civil War. Under the southern system, recently freed slaves or propertyless whites would farm a 20-40 acre section of a plantation, sometimes as cash renters but more commonly as sharecroppers, who contributed a certain portion of the crop at year-end to the landlord. Depending on whether the tenant supplied his own mule or tools, the rate was usually one-quarter to one-half of the crop. The landlord would charge his sharecroppers for any "furnish" that they had purchased at the plantation commissary during the year, leaving many impoverished "croppers" with little to show for a year's worth of labor.

Tenant farming expanded steadily in the South during the late 19th and early 20th centuries as an increasing number of once-independent farmers slid into tenant status. The system reached its high point in 1930, when there were close to 2 million tenant farmers in the South, two-thirds of them white (although among the low-status sharecroppers the percentages of white and black were about equal). Tenant farming collapsed not long afterward, as the mechanization of first the planting and then the picking of cotton in the 1930s and 1940s pushed many of these tenants off the land and into the great migrations to the cities of the World War II and postwar eras.

—KARL JACOBY

See Also: *Agriculture; Reconstruction.*

BIBLIOGRAPHY: Faragher, John, *Sugar Creek: Life on the Illinois Prairie* (Yale Univ. Press 1986); Jones, Jacqueline, *The Dispossessed: America's Underclass from the Civil War to the Present* (Basic Books 1992); Morgan, Edmund, *American Slavery, American Freedom: The Ordeal of Colonial Virginia* (Norton 1975).

◼ **TEN-HOUR DAY,** the effort to reduce the working day to 10 hours. Beginning in the 1820s in the United States, industrial workers in the nation's major cities began demanding a 10-hour day and in certain skilled trades were granted that guarantee, especially in New York City and Philadelphia. In 1840 Pres. Martin Van Buren signed an executive order mandating a 10-hour day for all federal employees, including those working on government contracts. In Massachusetts the movement spread during the 1840s, much of the agitation led by the so-called Yankee mill girls, who worked in the giant factories of Lowell and Lawrence or in other, smaller towns

for upward of 12 to 14 hours a day. Legislation enforcing the 10-hour day for women and children in the textile industry was finally passed by the Massachusetts legislature in 1874 but was inconsistently enforced for several years. By the start of the 20th century, many American industrial workers did work a 10-hour day on average. Notable exceptions remained, especially within the garment and steel industries, as well as within whole regions, such as the South.

◼ **TENNENT, WILLIAM (1673-1746)** and **TENNENT, GILBERT (1703-64),** Presbyterian ministers. Born in Ireland, William Tennent earned an M.A. at the University of Edinburgh (1693) and in 1704 took orders in the Church of England. In 1718, he and his family immigrated to Pennsylvania, where he joined the Presbyterian Church. He served pastorates in New York and Neshaminy, Pennsylvania, where he began tutoring young men, including his four sons, who were preparing for the ministry. In 1735 he built a log building for his school, known as the Log College.

Gilbert Tennent, William's eldest son, received his M.A. from Yale in 1725 and was licensed by the presbytery of Philadelphia the same year. He served a pastorate in New Brunswick, New Jersey, where he met Dutch Reformed minister Theodore Frelinghuysen whose evangelicalism dramatically influenced the young minister. Tennent became the principal supporter of the Great Awakening in the middle colonies, which caused the schism of the Presbyterians into Old Side and New Side believers. In his sermon "The Danger of an Unconverted Ministry," Tennent attacked the Old Side, opponents of the Awakening, and contributed to the dispute. After accepting a pastorate in Philadelphia in 1743, Tennent worked to reunite the church. He was ultimately successful, and the two sides reunited in 1758, with the New Side dominant.

See Also: *Great Awakening; Religion.*

◼ **TENNESSEE,** the wealthiest and most populous of the four east south-central states. It is bounded on the north by Kentucky and Virginia, on the east by North Carolina, on the south by Georgia, Alabama, and Mississippi, and on the west by Arkansas and Missouri. The Mississippi River forms its western border. Tennessee slopes downward from the Appalachian Mountains in its extreme east to the Mississippi coastal plain.

Settled by pioneers spilling over the Appalachians through the Cumberland Gap, Tennessee became a state in 1796. It was the home of three forceful and controversial presidents. The last state to secede from the Union and join the Confederacy, it was the scene of many critical Civil War battles. In the 20th century, Tennessee became one of the most industrialized states in the South.

Capital: Nashville. Area: 42,145 square miles. Population (1995 est.): 5,256,000.

See Also: Appalachian Mountains; Cherokee; Chickasaw; Cumberland Gap; Franklin, State of; Handy, W. C. (William Christopher); Jackson, Andrew; Johnson, Andrew; King, Martin Luther, Jr.; Polk, James Knox; Scopes Trial; Shiloh, Battle of; Tennessee Valley Authority.

TENNESSEE VALLEY AUTHORITY, agency designed to develop, use, and conserve the resources of the Tennessee River Valley. The Tennessee Valley Authority (TVA) had its origins in government efforts during World War I to build a large hydroelectric power complex on the Tennessee River. Construction of a series of dams and plants at government-owned Muscle Shoals, Alabama, was halted, however, at the conclusion of the war. Sen. George W. Norris of Nebraska led an unsuccessful fight to retain government ownership of the Muscle Shoals properties.

Elected in 1932, Pres. Franklin D. Roosevelt supported government ownership of the properties, and the TVA was established in May 1933. One of the most controversial programs of the New Deal era, the TVA was an independent agency financed by federal funds. Throughout the Tennessee Valley, it built dams and power plants, produced chemical fertilizers for farmers, created jobs for underemployed rural residents, and provided cheap electricity for the first time to thousands of people.

The TVA encountered opposition from conservatives, who denounced it as a socialist agency, and by power companies, who feared the competition of inexpensive electricity. Although it surmounted this opposition to become the largest producer of electric power in the United States by 1940, its projects had destructive environmental effects. Nonetheless, the TVA demonstrated how government planning could improve the standard of living of thousands of Americans.

—GUY NELSON

See Also: New Deal.

BIBLIOGRAPHY: Creese, Walter L., *TVA's Public Planning: The Vision, The Reality* (Univ. of Tennessee Press 1990); Hubbard, Preston J., *Origins of the TVA: The Muscle Shoals Controversy, 1920-1932* (Vanderbilt Univ. Press 1961).

TENSKWATAWA (c. 1778-1837), Shawnee leader also known as the Shawnee Prophet. The younger brother of Tecumseh, Tenskwatawa was a poor warrior and led a dissolute life until 1805 when he underwent a conversion while in an alcohol-induced coma. When he awoke, Tenskwatawa told of meeting the Master of Life, who told him to reject white religion, customs, and material culture and to return to traditional ways. After the Shawnee defeat at Tippecanoe (1811), he had little influence.

See Also: Indians of North America; Tecumseh.

TENURE OF OFFICE ACT, law enacted (1867) to limit the power of Pres. Andrew Johnson. It was passed as part of the struggle between Johnson and Congress, led by the Radical Republicans, over Reconstruction. Johnson's efforts to undermine Congressional Reconstruction by removing federal officials in the South led Congress to pass the Tenure of Office Act in a special session on March 2. The law prohibited a president from removing officials, including cabinet secretaries, whose appointments he had made with Senate approval without first obtaining the Senate's consent. When Johnson attempted to fire Sec. of War Edwin Stanton, who had been appointed by Pres. Abraham Lincoln, the Radical Republicans proceeded with their plans to impeach Johnson. Violating the Tenure of Office Act was one of the 11 charges against Johnson. Congress repealed the law in 1887 and the Supreme Court declared it unconstitutional in 1926.

See Also: Johnson, Andrew; Radical Republicans; Reconstruction.

TERMINATION, policy of the federal government calling for "getting the government out of the Indian business," in the words of one of its supporters. In the congressional elections of 1946 the Republicans captured control of Congress; men who had considered New Deal Indian policy to be a "communist experiment" now sat in control of the congressional committees that oversaw Indian affairs. In 1947 Congress requested William Zimmerman, associate commissioner of Indian Affairs, to compile a list of tribes that could get along without continued federal assistance.

Congress passed separate legislation for each termination case. The first involved the Menominee people of Wisconsin. Over the previous century the Menominees had succeeded in retaining their tribal land base, some 230,000 acres of bountiful northern timberland. They operated their own prosperous sawmilling operation, providing jobs and modest incomes for 3,200 tribal members. In the 1940s the tribe sued the federal government for the mismanagement of its trust fund, and in the early 1950s won a settlement of nearly $8 million. Congress had to appropriate the funds to pay the settlement, and when it did so it also required the Menominees to agree to the termination of their trust relationship with the federal government, which meant the end of Menominee sovereignty on their reservation. Despite Menominee objections termination went forward. The Menominee tribe of Indians was abolished, along with treaty rights and protections and federal services. Menominee enterprises were now taxed by federal and state governments; unable to pay these taxes, the Menominees were forced to begin selling off their land to raise revenues. With fewer acres, timber production fell, and Indians were thrown out of work. By the mid-1960s over half the people were on some form of federal welfare. Meanwhile reservation health clinics, hospitals, and schools were closed. Menominees lost their treaty-guaranteed rights to hunt and fish in the traditional manner. It required years of costly litigation—going all the way to the Supreme Court—before those rights were reconfirmed.

Other termination cases followed—the Klamaths of Oregon, the Alabama-Coushattas of Texas, the Ourays and Utes of Utah, and the Paiutes of Nevada. From 1954 to 1960 there were some 109 terminations, involving tribes, communities, bands, or individuals who held allotments in trust with the United States.

The failure of the policy, evident among other tribes as well as the Menominees, led to Sec. of the Interior Stewart Udall (1961-69) calling a halt. The government restored "recognition" to the Menominees in 1973, and federal recognition of Indian tribes, under the watchword of "self-determination," has been the trend in Indian affairs since that time.

—DONALD L. FIXICO

See Also: Indian Policy; Indians of North America.

BIBLIOGRAPHY: Burt, Larry, *Tribalism in Crisis* (Univ. of New Mexico Press 1984); Fixico, Donald L., *Termination and Relocation: Federal Indian Policy, 1945-1960* (Univ. of New Mexico Press 1986); Peroff, Nicholas, *Menominee Drums: Tribal Termination and Restoration, 1954-1974* (Univ. of Oklahoma Press 1982).

■ **TERRELL, MARY CHURCH (1863-1954),** educator, civil rights leader. Born into a newly emancipated African American family in Memphis, Tennessee, she graduated from Oberlin College in 1884. Terrell became the first president of the National Association of Colored Women in 1896 and in 1898 was the first African-American woman appointed to the Washington, D.C., Board of Education. She was a founding member of the National Association for the Advancement of Colored People and authored such important works as "Lynching from a Negro's Point of View" (1904) and *Autobiography of a Colored Woman in a White World* (1940).

See Also: Race and Racism.

■ **TERRITORIES AND POSSESSIONS,** areas other than the states of the Union that are or were governed by the United States. Early American territorial policy focused on the organization and expansion of western lands, beginning with passage of the Northwest Ordinances. They were enacted (1784-87) by the Congress under the Articles of Confederation and were designed to provide an orderly process for the settlement of lands north of the Ohio River. The nation then doubled in size with the Louisiana Purchase from France in 1803. The United States also harbored territorial ambitions at the expense of the British in Canada, the

Spanish in Florida, and in Oregon Country, which was claimed by the United States, Spain, and Britain. While the War of 1812 with Britain did not lead to the acquisition of Canadian territory, the United States subsequently negotiated a treaty with Spain (1819) by which it received Florida and Spain renounced its claims in Oregon.

Expansion to the Pacific. Many Americans believed that the idea of "Manifest Destiny" gave the country a God-given right to expand to the limits of the continent. Claims of ownership of Texas and other western territories led to war with Mexico in 1846. With the defeat of Mexico (1848), the United States acquired the huge expanse of the "Mexican Cession": the territories of California and New Mexico, which comprise all or part of seven present-day states. It also won recognition of the Rio Grande as the boundary between Texas and Mexico. Continuing differences with Great Britain over Oregon Country were also resolved in 1846. An agreement was negotiated by which the territory was divided at the 49th parallel of latitude, in close proximity to the current boundary between the United States and Canada. An additional acquisition from Mexico was the Gadsden Purchase (1853), a strip of land along Mexico's northern border west of the Rio Grande. It was anticipated that the newly proposed transcontinental railroad would follow a southerly route through the area.

Sec. of State William Seward, who served presidents Abraham Lincoln and Andrew Johnson, was a confirmed nationalist and eager to buy Alaska from Russia. The $7.2 million purchase (1867) was controversial and led critics to refer to the area as "Seward's folly." The purchase of Alaska presented the government with the dilemma of deciding the legal status of the residents of the territory and any others that may be acquired. The question was not resolved until 1901, when the Supreme Court made a distinction between incorporated and unincorporated territories. Constitutional rights applied only in incorporated territories; Congress possessed the right to make and apply the distinction. Unincorporated territories were not destined for statehood; however, the residents of unincorporated territories were considered to be U.S. nationals with limited constitutional rights. Alaska became an incorporated

territory by an act of Congress in 1912, and then on Jan. 3, 1959, it became the 49th state.

Securing strategic port facilities lay behind the annexation of Midway Island in 1867. These coral atolls lie some 1,300 miles west of Hawaii and have been continuously administered by the U.S. military. (The Battle of Midway was one of the most important naval engagements and a turning point in World War II.) Port facilities were further enhanced in 1878 by the acquisition of the port of Pago Pago in the Samoan Islands, some 2,300 miles south of Hawaii. The United States eventually gained control of all the Samoan islands, which are still governed today as an unincorporated territory.

American interest in overseas expansion, particularly in Asia, grew in the latter part of the 19th century. The U.S. Navy desired port facilities in the Pacific, and Pearl Harbor on the Hawaiian island of Oahu presented an attractive site. American commercial interests supported a rebellion against the Hawaiian monarchy in 1893 and asked for U.S. military protection. Annexation was delayed because of American political differences until 1898, when Hawaii became an incorporated territory. It was admitted to the Union as the 50th state on Aug. 21, 1959.

Territories Acquired from Spain. The Spanish-American War brought new possessions, challenges, and controversies with the acquisition of the Philippine Islands, Puerto Rico, and Guam under the terms of the 1898 Treaty of Paris and a de facto protectorate over Cuba. The acquisitions provoked controversy between proponents of expansion ("New Manifest Destiny") and those who were reluctant to have the country acquire overseas responsibilities and assume the role of a world power.

The Philippines rebelled against American rule and were only subdued in 1902 after a bloody and bitter conflict. Although the islands were governed by an American governor (the first governor was William Howard Taft, the future president), Congress proclaimed that Philippine independence was the ultimate goal. Independence was scheduled for 1946. During World War II, Japan occupied the islands (1942-45). Following the defeat of Japan, the islands were granted full independence on July 4, 1946. The United

States continued to maintain military facilities and supported the rule of Ferdinand Marcos (1965-86). After the overthrow of Marcos, Philippine opposition to the U.S. military presence led to a complete pullout by 1994.

Initially Puerto Rico was administered by Congress. Puerto Ricans were granted citizenship in 1917. Commonwealth status was granted in 1952, allowing the island greater local autonomy. Puerto Rico has its own constitution, elected governor, and nonvoting congressional representative. Elections have focused on divisions between factions supporting statehood, continued commonwealth status, and complete independence.

Guam, which was also annexed after the Spanish-American War, is the largest unincorporated U.S. territory. The island is located in the southern part of the Mariana Island chain, some 1,500 miles east of the Philippines. Guam was initially administered by the U.S. Navy and was a principal Pacific naval base. It was attacked and occupied for more than two years by the Japanese during World War II. The United States declared Guam a territory in 1950 and granted citizenship to the residents. The Department of the Interior was given responsibility for administration. Executive power currently rests with an elected governor and a territorial legislature. Like other territories, Guam sends a nonvoting delegate to Congress.

Other Pacific Territories. The United States also exercises control over a variety of uninhabited Pacific islands, atolls, and reefs. Several were claimed under the Guano Act of 1856, which authorizes the United States to take possession of uninhabited areas to mine guano deposits for fertilizer production.

During World War II, the United States occupied a number of islands in the western Pacific that had been administered by Japan under the mandate system established by the League of Nations. The islands are located in Micronesia and include the Caroline, Mariana (except for Guam), and Marshall Islands. When the United Nations was established, the Security Council authorized the United States to administer the islands in "trust" for the UN and made it responsible for reporting on social and economic progress to the United Nation's Trusteeship Council. As a consequence of criticism of the slow pace of social and

economic progress in the islands, the United States divided the trust into four internally self-governing groups. The Northern Marianas voted in 1975 for commonwealth status, and the residents became U.S. citizens. In 1983 the Marshall Islands and the Federated States of Micronesia (the eastern Caroline Islands) voted for compacts of free association with the United States. These agreements provided for self-government, with the United States retaining responsibility for the defense of the islands. The United States then notified the United Nations in 1986 that it had completed its trust responsibilities. Four years later the Security Council gave its approval. The situation in the trust territory of Palau in the Carolines was complicated when the islanders refused to approve changes in their constitution that would permit visits by U.S. nuclear vessels. It took eight attempts before the islanders finally voted in 1993 to approve self-rule and establish political, economic, and military ties with the United States. Palau was the last remaining trust territory under UN supervision.

The Panama Canal Zone and Virgin Islands. When the United States acquired the right to construct the Panama Canal (1903), it received a "perpetual lease" on a 10-mile-wide section of Panamanian territory through which the canal was built. The Canal Zone was administered by the president, who appointed the governor. Panamanian agitation for termination of U.S. control led to the signing of a treaty (1977) during the presidency of Jimmy Carter. Under the treaty administration of the Canal Zone was turned over to Panama in October 1979, and all U.S. involvement in the operation of the canal was to end by the year 2000.

After the outbreak of World War I (1914), concerns over protecting the sea lanes leading to the newly opened Panama Canal led the United States to purchase the Danish West Indies for $25 million. The transaction was completed in 1917, shortly before America entered the war. The three islands (St. Croix, St. John, and St. Thomas) known as the Virgin Islands, lie approximately 50 miles east of Puerto Rico and are administered as an unincorporated territory by the U.S. Department of the Interior but with an elected governor and a territorial legislature. The residents are U.S. citizens and send a nonvoting delegate to Congress. The islands no longer provide a strategic function and today derive most of their income from tourism.

—ALEXANDER WELLEK

See Also: Alaska; Frontier in American History; Hawaii; Louisiana Purchase; Manifest Destiny; Northwest Ordinance; Oregon; Panama Canal; Philippines; Spanish-American War.

BIBLIOGRAPHY: Dobson, John, *America's Ascent: The United States Becomes a World Power, 1890-1914* (Northern Illinois Univ. Press 1978); Karnow, Stanley, *In Our Image: America's Empire in the Philippines* (Random House 1989); McCullough, David, *Path between the Seas: Creation of the Panama Canal* (American Society of Civil Engineers 1977); Munro, Dana, *Intervention and Dollar Diplomacy in the Caribbean, 1900-21* (Greenwood Press 1980); Toussant, Charmian, *The Trusteeship System of the United Nations* (Greenwood Press 1976).

■ **TESLA, NIKOLA (1856-1943),** electrical engineer and inventor. Born in Smiljan, Austria (now Croatia), Tesla was a genius with a difficult personality. He worked as an electrical engineer before coming to the United States in 1884 and taking a job with Thomas A. Edison. He left Edison a year later to open his own laboratory. Soon forced out of his own company, Tesla formed the Tesla Electric Company in 1887, where he invented an electromagnetic motor that established the basis for alternating-current machinery. His work on arc lights and high-frequency currents produced the Tesla coil, a resonant air-core transformer, and gained him an international reputation. Tesla's polyphase alternating-current system illuminated the 1893 Chicago World's Fair. He also designed the world's first hydroelectric plant, which opened at Niagara Falls in 1896, and built a model radio-controlled ship in 1898. Tesla continued to invent in his later years, but few of his ideas succeeded, and he grew increasingly eccentric, reclusive, and poor. He forecast the use of solar power and wireless radio but refused a Nobel Prize in 1912 on the grounds that his co-recipient, Thomas Edison, was not a true scientist.

See Also: Edison, Thomas Alva; Invention; Science.

■ **TEST OATH CASES (1867),** two U.S. Supreme Court cases, *Ex Parte Garland* and *Cummings* v. *Missouri*, that addressed the constitutionality of loyalty oaths required by the federal and certain state governments. Soon after the outbreak of the Civil War, Congress enacted a series of laws requiring that a loyalty oath be administered to employees of the federal government, a group that was understood to include anyone who worked for the government, even private contractors. The oath required a pledge of loyalty and fealty to the Union, the so-called Ironclad Oath. Whether or not the oath actually enforced loyalty, it became a popular mechanism among Union officials after the war for justifying the denial of basic civil rights when politically or militarily expedient. In 1867 in *Ex Parte Garland*, a case initiated by a former employee of the Confederacy who had been obliged earlier to take an oath of loyalty to the Union, the Supreme Court struck down the oath statutes as unconstitutional on ex post facto grounds. Unimpressed by the Court's negative ruling, Congress the same year instituted yet another oath, this time for citizens of the defeated Southern states as a condition for regaining the right to vote.

■ **TET OFFENSIVE (1968),** surprise Communist attack in the Vietnam War during the Vietnamese holiday Tet. Nearly 200 villages and cities in South Vietnam were assaulted. Media pictures of U.S. forces fighting vicious street battles with Vietcong and North Vietnamese troops deeply affected Pres. Lyndon B. Johnson and the American public. Tet was an unquestionable tactical defeat for the Communists, who lost nearly half their forces. But it was a political triumph. Johnson announced he would not run for reelection, limited the bombing of North Vietnam, and agreed to begin talks to end the war.

See Also: Vietnam War.

■ **TEXAS,** a south west-central state as big as France, second among states in both area and population. It is bounded on the west and north by New Mexico, on the north by Oklahoma, on the north and east by Arkansas, on the east by Louisiana, on the east and south by the Gulf of Mexico, and on the south by Mexico. The Rio Grande forms its southern border and the Red River part of its northern border. Culturally, well-watered East Texas belongs to the South, while the rest of the state is more arid and belongs to the West. Texas leads all states in the production of oil and natural gas. It also leads in cattle, cotton, and petroleum and petrochemical products.

Texas was part of Mexico before migrants from the United States established an independent republic in 1836. It joined the United States in 1845 but seceded from the Union in 1861 to enter the Confederacy. The state's oil resources transformed its economy, which became increasingly industrialized in the 20th century.

Capital: Austin. Area: 266,873 square miles. Population (1995 est.): 18,724,000.

See Also: Alamo; Austin, Stephen Fuller; Bush, George H. W.; Johnson, Lyndon Baines; La Salle, René-Robert Cavalier, Sieur de; Mexican War; Rio Grande; San Jacinto, Battle of.

■ **TEXAS RANGERS,** noted law-enforcement agency in Texas. In 1826, representatives meeting with Stephen F. Austin in Texas agreed to raise a body of rangers to protect their colonies from Indians and bandits. At an 1835 meeting called the Consultation, 58 Texans met to decide on action to be undertaken regarding Mexico and General Santa Anna and resolved to create a ranger detail to patrol the frontier between the Brazos and Trinity rivers and protect settlements against Indians as far west as the Guadeloupe River. An irregular unit, providing their own horses and arms, the Rangers were as well known for their victories over the Comanches at the Council House and Plum Creek as they were for terrorizing Mexicans living in Texas. Defending the Republic of Texas from 1836 to 1845, a regiment of rangers served with Generals Winfield Scott and Zachary Taylor in the Mexican War. Such Ranger leaders as Ben McCulloch, W. A. A. "Bigfoot" Wallace, and John Coffee Hays are still legends in Texas. After the post–Civil War Reconstruction era, there was a reformation of the Texas Rangers to combat lawlessness from 1874 to 1890 and leaders like Leander McNelly brought outlaws like Sam Bass, King Fisher, and John Wesley Hardin to justice. Still a sanctioned law enforcement unit in Texas today, the legend of the Texas Rangers has undergone revision from heroes of the West to men who both kept the law and broke it, often oppressing Mexicans and Mexican Americans.

—J.C. MUTCHLER

See Also: Frontier in American History; Texas Rebellion.

■ **TEXAS REBELLION,** successful revolt against the Mexican government by Anglo Americans and some Mexican Texans (Tejanos) in 1835-36. In the years following Mexican independence from Spain in 1821, liberal Mexican land laws attracted some 25,000 Anglo-American immigrants to Texas. Settling mainly in East Texas, they became Mexican citizens but retained their American identity. Antislavery laws in Mexico passed after 1824 failed to stop the immigration of slaveholders. After Mexico passed an anti-immigration law in 1830, differences between Mexicans and American immigrants grew.

Fearful of the authoritarian government of Gen. Antonio López de Santa Anna and encouraged by the Anglo leader Stephen F. Austin, East Texas Anglos began a separatist independence movement in the summer of 1835. After a Mexican defeat in the fall, General Santa Anna led 6,000 ill-trained troops on a grueling march from Mexico City to San Antonio. Two decisive victories in March 1836 at the Alamo and Goliad gave Santa Anna the advantage over Sam Houston's retreating Texan forces. But at San Jacinto in late April, Houston's men launched an attack on the unprepared Mexican troops, defeating them quickly and capturing Santa Anna. The defeat ended Mexico's attempt to subdue Texas and marked the beginning of the short history of the Texas republic.

See Also: Alamo; Austin, Stephen Fuller; Houston, Sam; San Jacinto, Battle of; Santa Anna, Antonio López de.

BIBLIOGRAPHY: Lack, Paul D., *The Texas Revolutionary Experience: A Political and Social History, 1835-1836* (Texas A&M Univ. Press 1992).

■ ***TEXAS V. JOHNSON* (1989),** U.S. Supreme Court case that decided the First Amendment protects flag-burning as symbolic speech. Texas police had arrested a man for burning a flag at a political rally in Dallas during the 1984 Republican convention. The Court's controversial 5-4 decision led Congress to pass the Flag Protection Act (1989) banning flag desecration. The Supreme Court struck down that law in *United States* v. *Eichman* (1990).

See Also: Supreme Court.

■ **TEXAS V. WHITE (1869)**, U.S. Supreme Court case dealing with the post–Civil War legal status of the Confederate states. The Court held (6-3) that states do not have a constitutional right to remove themselves from the Union and that Texas, therefore, legally had never ceased to be a state.

See Also: *Supreme Court.*

■ **TEXTILE INDUSTRY**, historic industry in America that affected organized labor, big business, social and gender relations, and technology. The American textile industry was essentially imported from England by Samuel Slater in the 1790s. Slater established a modified cotton-spinning mill in Rhode Island to meet the demands of New England society. This resulted in a rapidly growing system that featured small-scale production, partnerships and individual ownership, and the employment of family labor.

In 1813, Francis Cabot Lowell, a wealthy Boston merchant, developed a competing system that used power looms to weave cotton as well as to spin yarn. Dependent on the labor of girls and women, the Lowell system introduced large-scale and professionally managed factories. In the 1830s, the female workers, many of whom lived in company boarding houses, went on strike in one of the first demonstrations of collective action taken by industrial laborers.

By the mid-19th century, the textile industry had developed into a highly profitable corporate enterprise, but one that often exploited its workers. Volatile labor disputes in Philadelphia during the 1840s not only pitted laborers against management but divided workers along ethnic, national, gender, and age lines. The Northeast remained the center of the textile industry until the 1880s, when small, Slater-like mills moved to the South. During the early 20th century, labor organizations fought to improve wages and conditions in the mills but with only moderate success. Constantly forced to adapt to changing technology and markets, the American textile industry lost ground in the post–World War II era to firms in Asia and Latin America.

—GUY NELSON

See Also: *Industrial Revolution; Labor Movement; Slater, Samuel.*

BIBLIOGRAPHY: Dublin, Thomas, *Women at Work: The Transformation of Work and Community in Lowell, Massachusetts, 1826-1860* (Columbia Univ. Press 1979); Tucker, Barbara M., *Samuel Slater and the Origins of the American Textile Industry, 1790-1860* (Cornell Univ. Press 1984).

■ **THAMES, BATTLE OF THE (1813)**, battle during the War of 1812. After the British captured Detroit and the Northwest, Gen. William Henry Harrison led a U.S. force to recover the territory. With Harrison in pursuit, a British army under Gen. Henry A. Proctor and its allied Indian force led by Tecumseh made a stand at the Thames River, east of Detroit. The Americans defeated the enemy with superior tactics and recaptured the Northwest.

See Also: *Harrison, William Henry; War of 1812.*

■ **THEATER.** Thought to be a breeding ground of immorality and vice, theater was outlawed in most of the colonies in the 17th century. By the 18th century, however, there were functioning theaters in Williamsburg, Charleston, Philadelphia, and New York City, and country people were sometimes entertained by strolling players or touring troupes of actors. Yet during the American Revolution, the Continental Congress banned all "exhibitions of shews, plays, and other expensive diversion and entertainments." Not until after the Revolution was the theater finally accorded social approval by the attendance of such public figures as George Washington, who loved dramas.

Recognizable American characters first appeared in Royal Tyler's comedy *The Contrast* (1787), which depicted a favorite American theme, the triumph of native American honesty over foreign affectation. Brownson Howard skewered high society in *Saratoga*, a comedy of manners (1870). But aside from such isolated examples, American playwrights of the 19th century failed to create an indigenous tradition, and the popularity of theater derived from performances of the classics or contemporary English comedy and drama by British actors or Americans such as Edwin Forrest, Charlotte Cushman, Laura Keene, and the Booth family. By the end of the 19th century the theater district on Broadway in New York had developed into a thriving commercial industry, sending touring productions throughout the country. Imported dramas featured actors such as the distinguished Barrymore family, but Broadway's greatest innovation was the musical comedy, pioneered by playwrights and producers such as George M. Cohan. In the 20th century the American musical would reach its apogee in the work of Oscar Hammerstein II, Richard Rodgers, and Jerome Kern.

The first American dramas with authentic American roles did not originate from this Broadway tradition, however, but from a number of "little theater" companies, such as the Washington Square Players and the Provincetown Players, which produced the first plays of Eugene O'Neill. "Art theater," so called, was sponsored by the Theater Guild (1918), which encouraged the production of plays by O'Neill and other dramatists on Broadway. The influence of the Russian director Konstantin Stanislavsky encouraged the development of a new psychological style of acting by actors such as Alfred Lunt, Lynn Fontanne, Helen Hayes, and John Barrymore.

In 1931 a group of actors inspired by Stanislavsky formed the Group Theater to help develop new writers and actors working on American themes. Their work dovetailed with the creation in 1935 of the WPA Federal Theater Project, which provided employment for out-of-work actors and produced hundreds of plays, providing ample opportunity for playwrights to develop their craft. Out of these efforts came a new generation of American drama, including the work of Arthur Miller and Tennessee Williams. After World War II two graduates of these groups, director Lee Strasberg and playwright Elia Kazan, organized the Actors Studio, which would train a new generation of actors such as Marlon Brando and become the single most influential force in American theater. Other innovative developments took place "off Broadway," with new plays candidly examining racial issues by African Americans such as James Baldwin and a new permissiveness about the display of nudity and sexuality on stage pioneered by companies such as the Living Theater.

—JOHN MACK FARAGHER

See Also: *Actors Studio; Albee, Edward; Barrymore Family; Booth Family; Broadway; Cohan, George M.; Cushman, Charlotte; Federal Theater Project;* *Forrest, Edwin; Group Theater; Hammerstein, Oscar, II; Hayes, Helen; Kazan, Elia; Keene, Laura; Kern, Jerome; Miller, Arthur; O'Neill, Eugene; Rodgers, Richard; Simon, Neil; Williams, Tennessee.*

BIBLIOGRAPHY: Bigsby, C. W. E., *Modern American Drama, 1945-1990* (Cambridge Univ. Press 1992); Henderson, Mary C., *Theater in America: 200 Years of Plays, Players, and Productions* (Abrams 1986); Kislan, Richard, *The Musical* (Applause Theater Book Publishers 1995); Wainscott, Ronald H., *The Emergence of the Modern American Theater, 1914-1929* (Yale Univ. Press 1997).

■ **THIRD PARTIES,** political parties that have played an important role in American politics since the early 19th century. The modern Republican party, which was formed in 1854 as an outgrowth of protest over fears that slavery might be expanded, represents the only example of a minority party that later achieved majority status. Third parties have not enjoyed much success at the presidential level because our political system is based on the principle of "winner takes all." Candidates almost never have received any votes in the electoral college unless they have a majority of the states' popular vote. This phenomenon was clearly demonstrated in the 1992 presidential election, when Ross Perot captured 19 percent of the national vote but did not receive any electoral votes.

Third parties have not fit any particular ideological pattern. The least successful have focused on a single cause (for example, free silver in the late 19th century) to the exclusion of all others. These groups then disappear once their particular concern is no longer an issue or has been taken up by one of the major parties. Ideological parties have enjoyed greater success as catalysts for social protest. The Populist party, for example, played a leading role during the 1890s as a proponent of social and economic reform. During the early 20th century, Socialist party candidates such as Eugene V. Debs ran for the presidency advocating widespread and radical reforms, some of which were later achieved, but they never won electoral votes.

Factional parties have also formed as offshoots of the major parties. When former Republican Pres. Theodore Roosevelt became dissatisfied with the direction of the party, he ran as a Progressive candidate in the election of 1912. Roosevelt won more popular and electoral votes than the incumbent Republican, Pres. William Howard Taft. The Republican split ensured the victory of the Democratic candidate, Woodrow Wilson.

The Democratic party has also experienced its share of factionalism. President Truman's reelection bid in 1948 was hurt by the formation of a States' Rights party whose candidate, Strom Thurmond, won 39 electoral votes in the South as a protest over Truman's civil rights policies. Other Democrats, disgruntled with Truman's Cold War policies toward the Soviet Union, organized around Henry Wallace, who received over a million votes as a Progressive candidate.

The 1968 presidential campaign featured the candidacy of George Wallace, the former governor of Alabama, who founded the American Independent party as a protest against the civil rights policies of the Kennedy-Johnson administrations. Wallace received close to 10 million popular votes and 46 electoral votes in the South. His intended strategy was to deny either of the two major party candidates a majority in the electoral college. In that event, the House of Representatives would choose the president and the Senate the vice president.

Many other candidates have run for president without any party label or affiliation. In some instances, the candidate was running to protest against his party's nominee. John Anderson, for example, continued to run as an independent in 1980 after losing the Republican nomination to Ronald Reagan. Anderson won 7 percent of the vote nationally but no electoral votes. Generally, most protest candidates fail to attract more than a smattering of support. However, Americans would probably be surprised to discover that in any given presidential election there are often dozens of candidates. Third parties and candidates are hurt by the public perception that a vote for them is a vote wasted. In addition, public financing laws were enacted that favor the established parties by awarding federal money only to those whose total vote exceeds 5 percent.

—ALEXANDER WELLEK

See Also: Political Parties; Presidential Elections.
BIBLIOGRAPHY: Mazmanian, Daniel, *Third Parties in Presidential Elections* (Brookings Institution 1984); Rosenstone, Steven, et al., *Third Parties in America* (Princeton Univ. Press 1984); Smallwood, Frank, *The Other Candidates: Third Parties in Presidential Elections* (Univ. Press of New England 1983).

■ **THIRTEEN COLONIES,** the British North American colonies that revolted, established independence, and formed the United States. Stretching along the eastern seaboard, the original 13 colonies included Massachusetts, New Hampshire, Rhode Island, Connecticut, New York, Pennsylvania, New Jersey, Delaware, Maryland, Virginia, North Carolina, South Carolina, and Georgia. There were other British colonies that did not join the revolt. The Continental Congress made overtures to Canada, but when the Canadians failed to respond positively and immediately the congress authorized a military expedition to conquer the province. Most of the other British colonies were sympathetic. But in Nova Scotia the British had established a naval stronghold at Halifax, and the province remained secure within the empire. The British army was able to suppress support for the revolt in Florida. Popular assemblies in Jamaica, Grenada, and Barbados all formally declared their sympathy with the Continental Congress, but the British navy prevented them from sending delegates. Bermuda actually sent representatives to Philadelphia, but they were ignored. Thus it became 13 colonies against the British Empire.

See Also: Colonial Government; Revolution, American.

BIBLIOGRAPHY: Fischer, David Hackett, *Albion's Seed: Four British Folkways in America* (Oxford Univ. Press 1989); Middleton, Richard, *Colonial America: A History, 1585-1776*, 2nd ed. (Blackwell 1996).

■ **THOMAS, CLARENCE (1948-),** associate justice of the U.S. Supreme Court (1991-). He was born in Savannah, Georgia, and served in the administration of Pres. Ronald Reagan before being appointed to the U.S. Court of Appeals for the District of Columbia (1990). A leading African-American conservative, he was named to the Court when Justice Thurgood Marshall retired. Thomas's nomination was nearly derailed when Anita Hill, a former colleague, accused him of unwanted, offensive sexual advances. After televised Senate hearings, he was confirmed by a 52-48 vote, the narrowest margin in more than 100 years.

See Also: Supreme Court.

■ **THOMAS, GEORGE H. (1816-70),** Union general. Despite having been born in Virginia, Thomas, a West Point graduate, stayed with the Union army at the outbreak of the Civil War. At the Battle of Chickamauga (September 1863), his stubborn defense of Snodgrass Hill earned him the nickname "Rock of Chickamauga." Later Thomas led the Army of the Cumberland to victory in the Battle of Chattanooga (November 1863). In May 1864 Thomas took part in the fiercest battles for Atlanta, and in December 1864 his division completely routed Confederate Gen. John Bell Hood at the Battle of Nashville.

See Also: Chickamauga, Battle of; Civil War.

■ **THOMAS, ISAIAH (1750-1831),** Revolutionary-era printer. Thomas was born in Boston. He founded the *Massachusetts Spy*, a newspaper, and printed it in Boston (1770-75) and Worcester (1775-1802). In Worcester he expanded his trade to books, magazines, and sheet music. Among his masterworks were a folio edition of the Bible and *Perry's Dictionary*. Thomas wrote *The History of Printing in America* (1810). He was also the founding president of the American Antiquarian Society in 1812.

■ **THOMAS, MARTHA CARY (1857-1935),** educator and feminist. Born in Baltimore, Maryland, she earned a doctorate from the University of Zurich in 1882. In 1885 she was appointed dean and professor of English at the newly established Bryn Mawr College for women. As president of Bryn Mawr from 1894 to 1922, she demanded high standards and worked tirelessly to improve educational opportunities for women. She was president of the National College Women's Equal Suffrage League from 1906 to 1913 and was active in the National Women's party.

See Also: Suffrage.

■ **THOMAS, NORMAN MATTOON (1884-1968),** Socialist party leader and U.S. presidential candidate (1928-48). He was born in Marion, Ohio, attended Princeton University and Union Theological Seminary, and was ordained a Presbyterian minister (1911; resigned, 1931). A pacifist opposed to World War I, Thomas joined the Socialist party in 1918 and succeeded Eugene V. Debs as party leader in 1926. An outspoken critic of the excesses of industrial capitalism and a defender of civil liberties, he was a leader of the anticommunist left for four decades. He presented a cultured, moderate image that made him an acceptable participant in political debate. Thomas was a founder of the American Civil Liberties Union (1920), codirector of the League for Industrial Democracy (1922-37), and a leader of the World Federalism movement following World War II. Thomas's, and the party's, influence waned in the 1950s as the Cold War isolated all leftist critics of the status quo.

See Also: American Civil Liberties Union (ACLU); New Deal; Socialist Party.

BIBLIOGRAPHY: Swanberg, W. A., *Norman Thomas: The Last Idealist* (Scribner 1976).

■ **THOMAS, THEODORE (1835-1905),** violinist and conductor. Born in Esens, Germany, he immigrated to the United States in 1845 and performed widely with his chamber quintet (1855) and orchestra (1862). His success inspired the founding of many U.S. orchestras in the late 19th century. Thomas became conductor of the Chicago Symphony (1891), where he championed German Romantic works by Brahms, Bruckner, Wagner, and others.

■ **THOMPSON, DOROTHY (1893-1961),** journalist and political analyst. She was born in Lancaster, New York. In 1928 she married Sinclair Lewis. She was a European correspondent between the world wars. After 1936 she wrote a regular column in the *New York Herald Tribune* and a syndicated column read by more than 8 million people. Vehemently anti-Nazi, she was known for her support of Zionism but was critical of Israel's treatment of the Palestinians.

See Also: Lewis, (Harry) Sinclair.

■ **THOMPSON, SMITH (1768-1843),** associate justice of the U.S. Supreme Court (1823-43). An Amenia, New York, native, Thompson stood out on the Court as a defender of states' rights. In 1828 his unsuccessful bid for governor of New

York generated considerable public anger when he refused to step down from the Court before running.

See Also: Supreme Court.

■ **THOMSON, VIRGIL (1896-1989),** composer and influential music critic for the *New York Herald Tribune* (1940-54). He was born in Kansas City, Missouri. His work often celebrated American themes. Thomson's film scores included *The River* (1937) and *Louisiana Story* (1948), and he collaborated with author Gertrude Stein on two operas including *The Mother of Us All* (1947), based on the life of suffragist Susan B. Anthony.

See Also: Stein, Gertrude.

■ **THOREAU, HENRY DAVID (1817-62),** essayist and poet. Born in Concord, Massachusetts, he was early infused with a love of nature that would mark him for the rest of his life. Having graduated from Harvard in 1837, Thoreau began teaching school with his brother in their parents' home the following year, doing so until 1841, when he began a two-year residence in the house of Ralph Waldo Emerson, who had moved to Concord in 1834. Emerson introduced Thoreau to the Transcendental Club, in whose journal, the *Dial*, he published several articles, and provided him with the land upon which to build his retreat at Concord's Walden Pond, where Thoreau lived between July 1845 and September 1847. Refusing to pay the Massachusetts poll tax in the summer of 1846 because of his opposition to the nation's war against Mexico, which he viewed as the expansionist work of proslavery interests, Thoreau spent a night in jail, an experience later recollected as part of his very influential essay of 1849, "Resistance to Civil Government." In it, he offered his act as a model of "peaceable revolution." A trip to Concord, New Hampshire, in 1839 provided Thoreau with the material for his first book, *A Week on the Concord and Merrimack Rivers* (1849). In 1853, he completed *Walden*, published the following year, after which he increasingly took up the abolitionist cause, defending John Brown's raid at Harpers Ferry in 1859 in a series of lectures. Thoreau died of tuberculosis in 1862, having published only two books, and leaving the majority of his writing, drawn primarily from his

Henry David Thoreau's antislavery sentiments prompted his refusal to pay the Massachusetts poll tax during the Mexican War, which he argued was being waged in the interest of the expansion of slavery.

journals, letters, and poems, to be published posthumously.

—JAMES KESSENIDES

See Also: New England Renaissance; Transcendentalism.

BIBLIOGRAPHY: Richardson, Robert D., Jr., *Henry Thoreau: A Life of the Mind* (Univ. of California Press 1986).

■ **THORNDIKE, EDWARD LEE (1874-1949),** educational psychologist. Born in Williamsburg, Massachusetts, he earned his doctorate from Columbia University in New York City (1898) and then taught (1899-1940) and directed the psychology division at Columbia's Institute of Educational Research (1922-40). Thorndike pioneered the use of scientific experiments and quantitative measurement to determine how humans learn.

■ **THORNTON, MATTHEW (1714-1803)**, physician, judge, and Revolutionary War politician. A member of the Second Continental Congress and signer of the Declaration of Independence, Thornton was born in Ireland. He immigrated to Massachusetts and later moved to New Hampshire, where he was active in the Revolution.

See Also: Declaration of Independence.

■ **THORPE, JAMES FRANCIS (JIM) (1888-1953)**, American Indian athlete. The great-grandson of the Sauk chief Black Hawk, Thorpe was born near Prague, Oklahoma, of Sauk, Fox, Potawatomi, and Ojibwa stock. At a time when Indians were being urged to give up their culture and their heritage, Thorpe was proud of his ancestry. From 1903 to 1912 he attended the Carlisle Indian School in Carlisle, Pennsylvania, known for its program of assimilation into white society. Thorpe was an all-around athlete, one of the greatest in American history. While at Carlisle, he played several sports, including football and baseball, and he played two seasons of semiprofessional baseball. At the 1912 Summer Olympic Games in

Jim Thorpe puts the shot during the decathlon at the 1912 Summer Olympics in Stockholm. The winner of both the pentathlon and the decathlon, Thorpe was later stripped of his medals because he had played semiprofessional baseball one summer.

Sweden, Thorpe won gold medals in the pentathlon and the decathlon, awards later rescinded because of his prior professional career in baseball. After the games, Thorpe went on to careers in professional football and baseball, retiring in 1929. The Olympic medals were returned to his descendants in 1982.

See Also: Indians of North America; Sports.

■ **THURMOND, STROM (1902-)**, U.S. senator (1955-). Born in Edgefield, South Carolina, he was a local officeholder when elected governor of South Carolina (1946). He ran for president on the States' Rights ("Dixiecrat") ticket in 1948 and carried four southern states. Defeated in a bid for the U.S. Senate in 1950, he was elected as a write-in candidate in 1954 and in 1964 became a Republican and supported Barry Goldwater for president.

See Also: Dixiecrats.

■ **TILDEN, SAMUEL JONES (1814-86)**, lawyer and Democratic politician. Born in New Lebanon, New York, he was admitted to the bar in 1841. He served as corporate counsel for several railroads and amassed a sizable personal fortune through wise investments. Active in the New York State Democratic party, he chaired it for eight years (1866-74). Initially a supporter of political boss William Marcy Tweed, Tilden broke with him in 1870 and thereafter worked to expose Tweed's various illegal activities. That effort gained Tilden the New York governorship in 1874. He lost his 1876 bid for the presidency to Republican Rutherford B. Hayes in a controversial election that was decided in 1877 by an electoral commission appointed by Congress. He died 10 years later, leaving much of his $5 million fortune for the establishment of the New York City Public Library.

See Also: Hayes, Rutherford Birchard; Tweed, William Marcy (Boss).

BIBLIOGRAPHY: Flick, Alexander C., *Samuel J. Tilden* (Kennikat Press 1963); Severn, Bill, *Samuel J. Tilden and the Stolen Election* (I. Washburn 1968).

■ **TIN PAN ALLEY**, New York City music district originally around 14th Street. The term, coined around 1900 from the sounds of composers playing their songs on out-of-tune pianos, came to stand for the popular music industry.

■ **TIPPECANOE, BATTLE OF (1811),** War of 1812–era engagement between American forces, led by William Henry Harrison, and a multitribal Indian force led by the Shawnee Prophet near Prophetstown, at the juncture of the Tippecanoe and Wabash rivers in Indiana. Established in 1808, Prophetstown was the center for the pan-tribal religious and political movement led by the Shawnee Prophet and Tecumseh that arose in opposition to American expansion into Indian lands in the Ohio Valley.

In the fall of 1811, after Tecumseh left Indiana to visit the southern tribes, Harrison led more than 1,000 regulars, militia, and volunteers up the Wabash Valley from Vincennes and on November 6 met with the Shawnee Prophet near the mouth of the Tippecanoe. Negotiations failed, and at 4:00 A.M. on November 7, the Prophet's warriors (primarily Winnebago, Kickapoo, and Potawatomi) attacked Harrison's camp. The battle raged until about 7:00 A.M. when the tribesmen withdrew and abandoned nearby Prophetstown. Harrison then burned the Indian village and captured or destroyed large quantities of Indian food and ammunition.

The Americans suffered 188 casualties; at least 62 were fatal. Indian losses were much the same, although fewer than 700 warriors fought in the battle. More serious for Tecumseh and the Prophet were the loss of food and ammunition and the destruction of their village, which greatly diminished the influence of the Shawnee Prophet.

—R. DAVID EDMUNDS

See Also: Harrison, William Henry; Indians of North America; Shawnee; Tecumseh; Tenskwatawa.
BIBLIOGRAPHY: Edmunds, R. David, *The Shawnee Prophet* (Univ. of Nebraska Press 1983).

■ **TITLE IX,** legislation passed in 1972 to end discrimination against women in school athletics. Title IX blocks federal funding to educational institutions that practice sexual discrimination.

See Also: Women in American History.

■ **TLINGIT,** Indian tribe of the Northwest coast of North America. At the time of first contact with the Russians in the 1740s, the Tlingit population numbered around 10,000. A hunting and fishing people, they utilized the great abundance of resources in the Northwest. Tlingit religion emphasizes the relationship between people and the animal spirits. They also practice the potlatch ceremony, in which important men in the tribe redistribute goods and often ritually destroy material possessions. Tlingit society is matrilineal, descent passing through the mother. The Tlingit produce beautiful wood carvings and basketry. About 14,000 Tlingit live in the United States.

See Also: Indians of North America.

■ **TOBACCO,** one of the most powerful natural stimulants known and one of the most addictive and toxic. Indian peoples throughout the Americas used it in religious and medical rituals. Columbus observed the Tainos of Hispaniola smoking "taboca," which caused them "to become benumbed and almost drunk." After it was introduced in Europe, tobacco was prescribed by doctors as an antidote for plague and, ironically, as a cure for cancer. In 1604, King James I of England condemned smoking, but he also enjoyed a royal tax on tobacco that tied the state's fortunes to the growth of the habit. Similarly, Napoleon III once promised a ban on the vice as soon as his ministers could "name a virtue that brings in as much revenue." This dilemma continues to haunt government today.

Virginia's first plantations prospered supplying tobacco to European smokers. The spread of tobacco production spurred rapid expansion onto new lands in the interior. Because tobacco cultivation requires intense labor, it also stimulated the growth of African slavery. Tobacco and slaves eventually spread into the Mississippi Valley. Chewing and pipe smoking continued to drive consumption relentlessly upward, but in the late 19th century demand exploded with the creation of brand-name cigarettes. By combining industrial methods of production with modern advertising, James Duke and other magnates created the modern tobacco industry.

Domestic consumption declined after the 1960s public health campaigns began linking smoking with lung cancer and heart disease in the late 20th century. But the powerful tobacco industry continued to prosper by opening huge new markets in the underdeveloped world. Gross revenues in 1990 topped $100 billion, an all-time high. Tobacco remains one of the most important commercial crops in American history.

See Also: Agriculture; Drugs; New World Crops.

BIBLIOGRAPHY: Goodman, Jordan, *Tobacco in History* (Routledge 1993).

■ **TOCQUEVILLE, ALEXIS DE (1805-59),** French political writer and chronicler of America. Born in Paris of an aristocratic family, he arrived in New York in May 1831 with Gustave de Beaumont to begin a nine-month journey around the United States. Seeking to escape the unstable political situation in France, the two proposed to undertake an examination of the American prison system.

But Tocqueville had actually come to America to observe democracy in action. In 1835 he released the first volume of his *Democracy in America*, which covered the origins and character of American laws, constitutions, and politics. Its publication brought him fame, wealth, and the attention of figures like John Stuart Mill. Tocqueville's political career as a significant liberal voice in France delayed for five years the publication of the second volume, which discussed the influence of political equality on social, intellectual, and artistic life.

In 1841 Tocqueville received membership as an "immortal" in the Academie Française. He continued to write, producing, most notably, a classic of antislavery literature, "Report on the Abolition of Slavery" (1839), and *The Old Regime and the French Revolution* (1856).

In *Democracy in America*, Tocqueville praised the results of equality that he saw in America, while warning of the mediocrity that can result from the "tyranny of the majority." For him the antidote to such danger lay in "individualism," a word he coined. *Democracy in America* remains a classic examination of the American character and is still studied today. Unlike more anecdotal observers, Tocqueville saw the significance of the new American experiment in democracy, and many of his observations have a prophetic quality that continues to provoke discussion.

—CATHERINE ALLGOR

BIBLIOGRAPHY: Mancini, Matthew, *Alexis de Tocqueville* (Twayne 1994); Pierson, George Wilson, *Tocqueville and Beaumont in America* (Oxford Univ. Press 1938).

■ **TODD, THOMAS (1765-1826),** associate justice of the U.S. Supreme Court (1807-26). A King and Queen County, Virginia, native who lived in Kentucky, Todd was the first justice to rise to the Court via the new "western" circuit. His circuit responsibilities kept him in the trans-Appalachian West much of the year, often forcing him to miss Supreme Court sessions.

See Also: Supreme Court.

■ **TOMOCHICHI (c. 1650-1739),** Creek leader. He was born in present-day Alabama. Tomochichi signed a trade agreement with the British colonists from South Carolina in 1733. In 1734, he traveled with a delegation to England, where he was presented to King George II.

See Also: Indians of North America.

■ **TOMPKINS, DANIEL D. (1774-1825),** governor of New York (1807-17) and vice president of the United States (1817-25). He was born in Scarsdale, New York, and entered state politics in 1801, eventually becoming a justice on the New York Supreme Court (1804-07). His gentle manner and humanism earned him the nickname "farmer's boy." He became New York's governor in 1807, and, although elected with the support of DeWitt Clinton, he became Clinton's political enemy. Tompkins opposed slavery and was in favor of raising the taxes of the propertied elite. He was elected James Monroe's vice president for both of Monroe's terms.

See Also: Clinton, DeWitt; Monroe, James; Vice President of the United States.

■ **TORDESILLAS, TREATY OF (1494),** covenant negotiated between Spain and Portugal to avoid conflict over colonial possessions. The treaty emerged as a compromise over two papal bulls issued by Pope Alexander VI in 1493. At the request of Ferdinand and Isabella of Spain, Alexander VI had in these two bulls designated Spain the lawful claimant to all lands not under Christian rule and 100 leagues west of the Azore Islands. Under the treaty, the demarcation line was relocated 1,100 miles west of the Cape Verde Islands, reconfirming Spanish claims to any new lands discovered to its west and granting the new lands east of it—thought to consist of the west coast of Africa—to Portugal. Only after the discovery and exploration of the coast of South America was it realized that the line drawn by the treaty gave Portugal control over Brazil.

See Also: Exploration and Discovery.

■ **TORNADOES,** funnel-shaped, violently swirling masses of wind. These small, intense whirlwinds are created in the unstable atmospheric conditions of severe thunderstorms. If a tornado touches the ground, its high-speed winds (some as high as 200-300 miles per hour) destroy nearly everything in its path. Tornadoes occur most frequently during the spring and summer and are most prevalent in the region of the United States nicknamed "Tornado Alley," a broad path stretching across the central Plains states of Texas, Oklahoma, Kansas, Nebraska, Illinois, South Dakota, and North Dakota. In these areas people frequently use storm cellars in order to avoid tornadoes. One of the worst tornadoes in the United States occurred on Mar. 18, 1925. Called the "Tri-State Tornado," it whipped 219 miles from Missouri to Illinois and into Indiana. The tornado killed 689 people in a little more than three hours on the ground. Tornadoes were immortalized in the 1939 movie *The Wizard of Oz*, in which Dorothy, played by Judy Garland, is whisked away from Kansas to the land of Oz by a tornado. Tornadoes appeared again in movies in the 1996 film *Twister*, which was about tornado trackers.

■ **TOSCANINI, ARTURO (1867-1957),** conductor, known for his commanding presence on the podium and his prodigious musical memory. The Italian-born Toscanini was music director at Milan's La Scala (1898-1907, 1921-31) and New York's Metropolitan Opera (1908-21) and also conducted the New York Philharmonic Symphony (1926-36) and the National Broadcasting Company (NBC) Symphony (1937-54). His radio and television broadcasts on NBC made him a celebrity.

■ **TOURGEE, ALBION W. (1838-1905),** U.S. judge in North Carolina during Reconstruction. Born in Williamsfield, Ohio, Tourgee served in the U.S. Army during the Civil War, spending some four months as a prisoner of war. After the war Tourgee, a lawyer, moved to Greensboro, North Carolina. In April 1868 he was elected judge in the 17th district of North Carolina. During his tenure central North Carolina saw some of the worst excesses of Ku Klux Klan violence. Although actually a moderate on Reconstruction issues, Tourgee was to southerners

the quintessential carpetbagger. He later published several legal tracts, essays, and novels.

See Also: *Reconstruction.*

■ **TOWN MEETING,** assembly of local voters that functions as the municipal legislature in many New England communities. The town meeting system is an exercise in direct democracy rooted in the Congregational Church of the 17th century, which emphasized equality among members rather than a hierarchical structure. As town governments evolved in New England, male residents met each year to elect town officials, apportion taxes, and appropriate funds. In communities with open town meetings today, every registered voter is eligible to attend and cast votes deciding government policies for the coming year. Since the 1930s many larger New England communities have adopted the representative town meeting, in which voters elect representatives to serve as the local legislature. Because "town meeting" evokes images of citizen control of government, the phrase is often used to describe any public forum for discussion of policy issues.

See Also: *Congregationalists.*

BIBLIOGRAPHY: Bresler, Kenneth, *Citizen's Primer on Town Meeting* (Secretary of the Commonwealth [of Massachusetts] 1996).

■ **TOWNSHEND ACTS (1767),** laws passed by Parliament that imposed import duties on certain goods in the American colonies. Named after their author, Chancellor of the Exchequer Charles Townshend, the measures led to a colonial boycott of British goods and were withdrawn in 1770.

See Also: *Revolution, American.*

■ **TRADE ACTS (late 17th–early 18th century),** restrictive series of laws promoted by the Board of Trade (1696-1782), a British agency for governing the colonies. The acts sought to extract colonial resources while restraining competition with British manufactures.

■ **TRADE UNIONS,** organizations formed by wage earners to improve their terms of employment. Throughout the 19th century, most unions sought to enroll people who engaged in the same occupation, regardless of who employed them.

Such craft-based unions appeared, disappeared, and reappeared frequently among printers, shoemakers, carpenters, iron molders, and other skilled workers, but dock workers and certain other unskilled laborers also banded together, as did coal miners, who were also prominent union supporters.

The first mission undertaken by craft unions was to establish a minimum wage below which no member of the group would accept employment. As early as the 1810s, trades like printers had adopted elaborate scales of wages for various types of work. By the last half of the century, most unions had also prescribed rules to guide their members' conduct on the job, seeking to minimize abuse and overwork. After the 1860s, unilateral union enactment and enforcement of wages and work rules was gradually replaced by negotiation between employers and unions, a process that became known as collective bargaining. During the same period many unions also developed their own funds to insure members in case of death, unemployment, injury, or travel needs. Such benefits were especially characteristic of the brotherhoods of railroad engineers, firemen, and trainmen.

Local unions combined their forces on two levels. In the 1830s they developed citywide councils to lend each other support in battles for a 10-hour day and for better wages. Although these early institutions soon disappeared, similar bodies subsequently reappeared under various names, and they assumed special importance during the 1880s as mobilizers of boycotts against hostile employers, struggles for an 8-hour day, and political action.

National Unions. Between the 1860s and the 1880s, unions in various localities also formed national unions of their trades (called "international unions" when Canadian locals were included). On the national level, the National Labor Union (1866-75) held annual congresses of delegates from national unions, although it also welcomed local unions and reform clubs. The American Federation of Labor (AFL) (1886-1955) was constituted by representatives of national and international unions after an earlier effort to create such a national institution under the name Federation of Organized Trade and Labor Unions (1881-86). AFL membership grew rapidly between 1897 and 1904, when trade unions enrolled 12 percent of America's nonagricultural workers.

During the 19th century, the craft union form of organization was challenged by universalist principles of the Knights of Labor (1869) and the Industrial Workers of the World (1905). Unions tended to expand their jurisdictions and "amalgamate" related trades over the course of the 20th century, but the craft form of organization proved resilient in the construction, printing, and culinary occupations. After 1935 the rapid expansion of industrial unions was advanced by the Congress of Industrial Organizations (CIO), which organized workers on the basis of the industry in which they worked rather than the nature of their jobs. The CIO also repudiated the racial and gender exclusiveness widely associated with craft unionism and inspired major AFL unions to compete for the adherence of all manufacturing employees.

The bitter rivalry between the AFL and the CIO ended with their merger as the AFL-CIO in 1955. Many constituent unions subsequently merged with each other or absorbed groups not a part of their earlier jurisdictions. Unions representing only a homogeneous occupational group have become rare in the post–World War II era.

—DAVID MONTGOMERY

See Also: Labor Movement; Work in America.

BIBLIOGRAPHY: Commons, John R., et al., *History of Labour in the United States,* vols. 1-4 (Macmillan 1918-35); Laurie, Bruce, *Artisans into Workers: Labor in Nineteenth-Century America* (Hill & Wang 1989); Lorwin, Louis L., *The American Federation of Labor: History, Policies, and Prospects* (Brookings Institution 1933); Tomlins, Christopher L., *The State and the Unions: Labor Relations, Law, and the Organized Labor Movement in America, 1880-1960* (Cambridge Univ. Press 1985).

■ **TRAIL OF TEARS,** the phrase referring to and characterizing the forced migrations during the 1830s of the Southeast's "civilized" Indians from their homelands to the so-called Indian Territory west of the Mississippi River. These tribes held thousands of square miles of land within the borders of Georgia, Alabama, Mississippi, and Tennessee, and the exploding American population of these states demanded the tribes' dispossession. Thomas Jefferson had suggested that such tribal dispossession would solve the "Indian problem" and benefit the Indians themselves. The Indians disagreed. Aggressive settlers watched with dismay as Cherokees, Creeks, Chickasaws, and Choctaws adopted "civilization" in refutation of propaganda about their supposed savagery.

The Chickasaws saw the handwriting on the wall and began moving west in the 1820s. In 1830 the administration of Pres. Andrew Jackson supported the passage of the Indian Removal Act, following it immediately with an ultimatum to the Choctaws in the Treaty of Dancing Rabbit Creek. The U.S. Army evicted the Choctaws in 1831. French political analyst Alexis de Tocqueville described the Choctaws' crossing of the Mississippi in the dead of winter: "They brought in their train the wounded and the sick, with children newly born and old men upon the verge of death. They possessed neither tents nor wagons, but only their arms and some provisions."

The Cherokees refused to cede more land and turned to the U.S. Supreme Court, which ruled in their favor in 1832 in *Worcester* v. *Georgia*. According to legend, President Jackson remarked, "John Marshall has made his decision; now let him enforce it." The Treaty of New Echota followed in 1835, and the army forced the Cherokees west in 1838. Of the 13,000 making that trek, 4,000 died of privation and exposure.

The Creeks lost their leaders when 85 of their chiefs, including Osceola, were seized at treaty negotiations in 1837 and imprisoned. Osceola died in prison four months later. Nevertheless, the Seminoles (of the Creek confederacy) fought on in the longest American war before Vietnam. In 1857 most of the Seminoles moved west after being given a cash settlement.

Under pressure of removal, many issues arose to divide the tribes. Some, recognizing the odds against them, formed "treaty parties" to negotiate the best terms possible. Opposing them were fiercely resistant groups determined never to abandon their homelands. Economic and racial issues emerged to divide treaty advocates, who were mostly prosperous and of mixed ancestry, from "full blood" Indians, typically lacking property. The latter hid in the eastern mountains and asserted "true" tribal identity against the emigrants. The Civil War (1861-65) caused more trouble as Indians divided their loyalties between the Union and the Confederacy.

—FRANCIS JENNINGS

See Also: Indian Policy; Indian Removal; Indians of North America; Jackson, Andrew.

BIBLIOGRAPHY: DeRosier, Arthur H., Jr., *The Removal of the Choctaw Indians* (Univ. of Tennessee Press 1970); Foreman, Grant, *Indian Removal* (Univ. of Oklahoma Press 1972); Gibson, Arrell Morgan, *The Chickasaws* (Univ. of Oklahoma Press 1971); Green, Michael D., *The Politics of Indian Removal: Creek Government and Society in Crisis* (Univ. of Nebraska Press); Perdue, Theda, and Michael D. Green, eds., *The Cherokee Removal: A Brief History with Documents* (St. Martin's Press 1995); Wilkins, Thurman, *Cherokee Tragedy: The Ridge Family and the Decimation of a People* (Univ. of Oklahoma Press 1988).

■ **TRANSCENDENTALISM,** a loose intellectual movement in New England dating roughly from the early 1830s to the onset of the Civil War in 1861. A very influential strand of American romanticism, transcendentalism emerged as a challenge to Unitarianism, in which many of its members had been trained, though its reach extended far beyond the religious. Although a diverse group, the transcendentalists found common ground in their elevation of the individual, their belief in his or her intuition, rather than organized religion's doctrines, as the source of truth, and their desire for an unmediated relationship between the individual and God. The publication of Ralph Waldo Emerson's *Nature* in September 1836 served to crystallize the transcendentalist ferment already brought about by the likes of Orestes A. Brownson, Frederic Henry Hedge, and George Ripley. A week after *Nature* appeared, Emerson, along with Hedge and Ripley, orchestrated the first gathering of what would come to be known as the Transcendental Club, with Brownson, Convers Francis, James Freeman Clarke, and Amos Bronson Alcott also in attendance. Among others who would regularly join in the meetings, which lasted until 1843, were William Henry Channing, Margaret Fuller, and Theodore Parker.

Profoundly influenced by such German authors as Goethe and a number of English writers, including Goethe's translator, Thomas Carlyle, Samuel Taylor Coleridge, and William Wordsworth, the transcendentalists offered a romantic critique of American culture that at times accommodated the nation's increasing materialism and at others contested it, as in later transcendentalist Henry David Thoreau's *Walden*, based upon his two-year retreat to Walden Pond. The movement's pronounced emphasis upon the individual did not preclude transcendentalist efforts at social reform, as with, for example, Brownson's democratic advocacy for working-class Americans, Fuller's pioneering feminist writing, and Parker's abolitionism. Nor did it prevent a six-year experiment in collective living among several transcendentalists themselves, outside of Boston at Brook Farm (1841-47). Yet by the time of Abraham Lincoln's election as president, transcendentalism's collective energy had been sapped; its members' commitments for some time had been too changing and dispersed to support a movement faced with the Civil War. Still, the transcendentalists had left a permanent mark upon the nation's literary history.

—JAMES KESSENIDES

See Also: Alcott, Amos Bronson; Brook Farm; Emerson, Ralph Waldo; Fuller, Margaret; New England Renaissance; Parker, Theodore; Thoreau, Henry David; Unitarians.

BIBLIOGRAPHY: Miller, Perry, *The Transcendentalists: An Anthology* (Harvard Univ. Press 1950); Rose, Anne C., *Transcendentalism as a Social Movement, 1830-1850* (Yale Univ. Press 1981).

■ **TRANSPORTATION,** the means and modes of travel. The United States has been favored with the means to develop an exceptional transportation network. Early settlers quickly exploited coastal waterways and their principal tributaries, including the Delaware, Hudson, and James rivers. In time the Ohio-Mississippi-Missouri drainage systems and the Great Lakes offered viable, albeit seasonal transport routes. With the introduction of steamboats in the first and second decades of the 19th century, travel times dropped, load limits increased, and safety conditions improved.

Yet natural waterways did not fully meet public needs. In the formative years of the republic, turnpikes linked principal cities and tapped nearby areas; indeed, the commercial success of the Lancaster Turnpike between Philadelphia and Lancaster, Pennsylvania, triggered a short-lived turnpike craze. But popular excitement for canals soon overtook it. The astonishing success of the Erie Canal, which connected the Hudson River and Lake Erie and opened in 1825, served as the harbinger for the construction of several thousand miles of "ditches." These man-made waterways tied coastal ports with interior points and with the streams and lakes of the trans-Appalachian West. Several canals also linked the Great Lakes with the Ohio-Mississippi river system.

New Means of Travel. The "iron horse," however, revolutionized intercity travel. The national railroad network quickly began to take shape before the Civil War and then burgeoned after the conflict. A highlight was the completion in May 1869 of the nation's first transcontinental artery, built by the Union Pacific and Central Pacific companies. Americans, with few exceptions, considered railroads to be the magic carpets for swift and dependable commerce.

Events in the 20th century greatly altered the Railway Age. First electricity, specifically the electric interurban railways, effectively competed with steam carriers on short-distance passenger runs and for less-than-carload (LCL) freight. By 1916 nearly 16,000 miles of interurbans laced the nation and served hundreds of communities. Somewhat later automobiles, buses, and trucks, aided by technological advancements and stunning gains made by "Good Roads" movements, damaged the profitability of both steam and electric railroads.

Although the exceptional transportation needs created by World War II provided a resurgence of railroad usage—in part because of rubber and fuel rationing and federal mandates—modal competition, most of all from automobiles and trucks, caused the demise of nearly all the surviving electric interurbans and most of the short-haul railroad passenger, carload freight, and LCL traffic, as well as a sizable part of the intercity bus business. Railroads also faced stiff competition for long-distance passengers. Private automobiles, operating on ever improved roads, including the approximately 40,000 miles of interstate highways by 1970, siphoned off riders.

Late 20th–Century Developments. Those individuals who wished to use commercial transportation turned with increasing frequency to airplanes. Although air mail contracts sparked the development of commercial aviation in the mid-1920s, dramatically better and larger equipment, most notably introduction of the DC-3 aircraft about a decade later, made airlines increasingly popular with business travelers and financially viable. In the late 1950s a revolution of sorts took place with the introduction of jet-powered planes. The Jet Age so damaged the intercity rail passenger business that Congress was forced in 1971 to take over most of these operations, doing so under the aegis of the National Railroad Passenger Corporation, commonly known as Amtrak. Jets, too, virtually destroyed regularly scheduled transoceanic steamship service, just as railroads had done with stage coaches, steamboats, and canal packets a century or more earlier.

Although some transportation writers in the 1970s contemplated writing the obituary for the railroad industry, this durable form of transportation did not wither away. Rather, partial deregulation in 1980, better management, altered work rules that reduced worker "featherbedding," and constantly improving technologies energized the enterprise. By the 1990s, Americans enjoyed a balanced transportation network of trains, trucks, and airplanes, in addition to the ubiquitous automobile.

—H. ROGER GRANT

See Also: Canals; Railroads.
BIBLIOGRAPHY: Childs, William R., *Trucking and the Public Interest* (Univ. of Tennessee Press 1985); Corn, Joseph J., *The Winged Gospel: America's Romance with Aviation, 1900-1950* (Oxford Univ. Press 1983); Hilton, George W., and John F. Due, *The Electric Interurban Railways in America* (Stanford Univ. Press 1960); Shaw, Ronald E., *Canals for a Nation: The Canal Era in the United States, 1790-1860* (Univ. of Kentucky Press 1990); Stover, John F., *American Railroads* (Univ. of Chicago Press 1961); Taylor, George Rogers, *The Transportation Revolution, 1815-1860* (Holt, Rinehart & Winston 1951).

■ **TRANSPORTATION, DEPARTMENT OF,** cabinet department of the U.S. government responsible for overseeing federal transportation policy. Established (1966) during the administration of Pres. Lyndon B. Johnson, the department's divisions include the Federal Aviation Administration, the Federal Highway Administration, the Urban Mass Transit Administration, and other agencies that regulate, promote, and administer federal aid to transportation.

See Also: Transportation.

■ **TRANSPORTATION ACT. See:** *Esch-Cummings Act.*

■ **TREASON,** crime in which a citizen attempts to subvert the state to which he or she owes allegiance or overthrow its government by force. In many countries in the 18th century, any public opposition to the monarch could be considered treason. The U.S. Constitution sought to balance freedom to dissent with the nation's need to defend itself and explicitly defined treason (Article III, Section 3) as "levying war" against the United States "or in adhering to their enemies, giving them aid and comfort." The Constitution also imposes a heavy burden of proof for conviction: Two witnesses must testify to the same overt act, or the accused must confess in open court.

The federal government has prosecuted fewer than 40 treason cases in its history and did not charge Confederates with treason after the Civil War. The nation's most notorious treason case involved former vice president (1801-05) Aaron Burr, who in 1807 was tried and acquitted of charges of raising an army to create an independent state in the Louisiana Territory. Several states also have treason laws that have been even more rarely invoked. Abolitionist John Brown was tried and executed under Virginia's treason law, following his raid on the federal arsenal at Harpers Ferry (1859).

See Also: Brown, John; Burr, Aaron.
BIBLIOGRAPHY: Abernethy, Thomas P., *The Burr Conspiracy* (Oxford Univ. Press 1954).

■ **TREASURY, DEPARTMENT OF,** cabinet department of the U.S. government created by Congress (1789) to collect and distribute federal revenues. The department now includes the Customs Service, which collects tariffs and duties, the Internal Revenue Service, which collects taxes, and the Mint and the Bureau of Engraving and Printing, which manufacture coins and currency. The department also oversees the U.S. Secret Service and, in peacetime, the U.S. Coast Guard.

See Also: Coast Guard; Minting.

■ **TREATY OF PARIS (1763),** one of the three major treaties that concluded the great European and colonial wars of the mid-18th century. To curtail British territorial expansion, France's King Louis XV and his foreign minister, Etienne-François Choiseul, decided in November 1762 to convey to Carlos III of Spain (Louis XV's first cousin), by the secret Treaty of Fontainebleau, all French-claimed territory in North America west of the Mississippi, in addition to New Orleans on the east bank of the river.

In February 1763 the Treaty of Hubertusburg ended the European war; in the same month the Treaty of Paris concluded the colonial war. Victorious Britain spurned acquisition of the rich French sugar islands of Martinique and Guadeloupe in favor of acquiring New France (Canada) and all French-claimed land east of the Mississippi and south of the Great Lakes (except New Orleans). France retained fishing rights on Newfoundland's banks and possession of two neighboring islands, Miquelon and St. Pierre. Spain retained Cuba, in return for which Britain acquired East and West Florida.

At the conclusion of the three treaties of 1762-63, Britain possessed one of the largest empires the world had ever seen. On the other hand, France and the French monarchy had been badly humiliated, and thirst for revenge ultimately helped persuade France to assist the Americans in their revolution against Britain.

—CARL J. EKBERG

BIBLIOGRAPHY: Dorn, Walter L., "The Seven Years' War," *The Competition for Empire, 1740-1763* (Harper & Brothers 1940); Lindsay, J. O., ed., *The New Cambridge Modern History: The Old Regime 1713-1763* (Cambridge Univ. Press 1966); Rashed, Z. E., *The Peace of Paris, 1763* (Univ. of Liverpool Press 1951).

■ **TREATY OF PARIS (1783),** peace accord between Britain and the United States ending the American Revolution and recognizing American independence. The talks, which began in April 1782 in Paris after the British defeat at Yorktown, involved Britain, America, France, Spain, and the Netherlands. In the treaty, Britain recognized the Mississippi as America's western boundary and permitted American fishing in waters off New-

foundland. America in turn agreed to stop persecution of Loyalists and to return their property.

See Also: Revolution, American.

■ **TREATY OF PARIS (1898),** peace treaty between Spain and the United States signed on December 10, formally ending the Spanish-American War. The United States acquired Puerto Rico and Guam and agreed to pay $20 million for the Philippines. Anti-imperialists in America opposed the annexation of these lands, fearing rightly that the Philippines would prove to be an Achilles heel in time of war. However, the Senate ratified the treaty on Feb. 6, 1899.

See Also: Spanish-American War.

■ **TRENT AFFAIR (1861),** U.S.-British diplomatic crisis during the Civil War. The *Trent*, a British mail steamer, was stopped on Nov. 8, 1861, by the U.S.S. *San Jacinto*. On board the *Trent* were two Confederate commissioners, John Mason and John Slidell, on their way to England. Capt. Charles Wilkes, commanding the *San Jacinto*, had them removed and taken to Boston, where they were held until January 1862. Wilkes's action violated international law, provoked sympathy for the Confederacy in Britain, and threatened to cause war between the United States and Britain. Recognizing that the United States was in the wrong, Sec. of State William H. Seward ordered the release of Mason and Slidell.

See Also: Slidell, John; Wilkes, Charles.

■ **TRENTON, BATTLE OF (1776),** battle in the American Revolution. After a series of setbacks in fall 1776, Gen. George Washington's Continental army experienced low morale and large-scale desertions. Faced with ultimate defeat, Washington rallied his troops, crossed the Delaware River on Christmas night, and surprised the Hessian garrison stationed at British headquarters in Trenton, New Jersey, on Dec. 26, 1776. The Americans routed the Hessians, giving Washington and his troops a much-needed morale boost.

See Also: Revolution, American; Washington, George.

■ **TRIANGULAR TRADE,** pattern of colonial commerce that involved exchanges between Europe, Africa, and the Americas. These continents were the three points of the most important of the "triangular trades," of which the African slave trade was the best known. Rum and trade goods were sent to Africa and exchanged for slaves, who were taken to the West Indies or to America's southern colonies (the Middle Passage), where they were exchanged for sugar or tobacco that was then shipped back to Europe.

Another triangular route involved the shipment of fish, grain, lumber, and provisions from the northern colonies to the West Indies, where it was exchanged for sugar, molasses, or fruit, which was then shipped on to England. An exchange in England occurred for manufactured products to take back to the port of origin. American fish, lumber, and wheat were also shipped to Spain and Portugal, where they were traded for salt and wine, which was then taken to England and exchanged for manufactures that eventually ended up in America.

The idea of a triangular trade was a concept created by 19th-century historians. But modern historical studies have demonstrated that true triangular trading voyages were a relatively unimportant part of colonial commerce. Less than 1 percent of the annual average tonnage clearing New England between 1768 and 1772, for example, was destined for Africa, and relatively few vessels departed the northern colonies headed for the West Indies and then England. Although some commerce followed the triangular pattern, the majority of trading voyages involved just two ports on either side of the Atlantic.

—JOHN MACK FARAGHER

See Also: Slave Trade.

BIBLIOGRAPHY: Hugill, Peter J., *World Trade Since 1431: Geography, Technology, and Capitalism* (Johns Hopkins Univ. Press 1993); Smith, Alan K., *Creating a World Economy: Merchant Capital, Colonialism, and World Trade, 1400-1825* (Westview Press 1991); Tracey, James D., ed., *The Rise of Merchant Empires: Long-Distance Trade in the Early Modern World, 1350-1750* (Cambridge Univ. Press 1990).

TRIMBLE, ROBERT (1776-1828), associate justice of the U.S. Supreme Court (1826-28). An Augusta County, Virginia, native who grew up in Kentucky, Trimble was the second occupant of the "western" seat on the Supreme Court, succeeding Thomas Todd. During his brief tenure, Trimble was a consistent supporter of Chief Justice John Marshall's judicial nationalism.

See Also: Supreme Court.

TRUMAN, HARRY S. (1884-1972), 33rd president of the United States (1945-53). Born in Lamar, Missouri, he moved at age six with his family to Independence. After high school, he worked in a bank, later managed the family farm, and saw action as an army captain in World War I. He married Elizabeth Virginia "Bess" Wallace in 1919 and opened a men's clothing store. When the shop failed in 1923, he entered politics and served several terms as county judge. He was elected to the U.S. Senate in 1934 and reelected in 1940. Chosen by Pres. Franklin D. Roosevelt as his running mate in 1944, Truman was elected vice president. He became president when Roosevelt died on Apr. 12, 1945.

Presidency. The most pressing problem Truman inherited as president was the growing friction with the then Soviet Union. He met with Soviet leader Joseph Stalin at the Potsdam Conference (July 17–Aug. 2, 1945), where they, along with the British, reached several agreements that appeared to provide the basis for cooperation.

Truman at Potsdam called upon the Japanese to surrender. When they refused, atomic bombs were dropped on Hiroshima and Nagasaki. Truman said he acted to end the war without a costly invasion. Some critics claim that he knew Japan was near surrender but used the bombs to awe the Soviets. This charge has attained popularity despite being baseless. Truman had rough going at home after the war. He was blamed for not bringing the boys home quickly enough and for not lifting price and wage controls. On Sept. 6, 1945, he sent to Congress a 21-point program for broad economic and social welfare reforms. Little of what he later would call the "Fair Deal" was passed.

Relations with the Soviets worsened from late 1945 through 1946. In March 1947, Truman asked Congress for funds to help Greece and Turkey resist Soviet pressures. In 1948, the Marshall Plan began to provide massive aid to European nations to stave off collapse and possible

Harry S. Truman takes the oath of office as president after the death of Franklin D. Roosevelt in April 1945.

communist takeovers. It stands as one of Truman's greatest achievements.

Despite his domestic problems, Truman won reelection in 1948 over Thomas E. Dewey, the favored Republican candidate. Truman tried again in 1949 to implement the Fair Deal but with small success. His second administration was plagued by events such as the "fall" of Nationalist China in 1949 and the outbreak of war in Korea in 1950. Sen. Joseph R. McCarthy and others began accusing Truman of being "soft" on communism at home and abroad. His dismissal of Gen. Douglas MacArthur from his Far Eastern commands caused more trouble.

Truman's last two years in office were dismal. The Korean war ground on; "McCarthyism," unfounded accusations of procommunist activities, was rampant; and a series of minor scandals within the administration reflected badly on Truman's competence. A poll of November 1951 showed an approval rating of only 23 percent. By then in his late 60s, Truman was tired and had no

wish to seek reelection. He spent the first few years of his retirement working on his memoirs and the creation of his presidential library in Independence.

History has been kinder to Truman than were his contemporaries. Most scholars give him high grades for his foreign policies and for domestic achievements such as integration of the armed forces (1948). Although he failed to get his Fair Deal enacted, it helped set the national agenda for the future.

—ROBERT JAMES MADDOX

See Also: *Cold War; Dewey, Thomas E.; Fair Deal; MacArthur, Douglas; McCarthyism; Marshall Plan; Potsdam Conference; Presidential Elections; President of the United States; Roosevelt, Franklin Delano.*

BIBLIOGRAPHY: Ferrell, Robert H., *Harry S. Truman: A Life* (Univ. of Missouri Press 1994); Hamby, Alonzo L., *Man of the People: A Life of Harry S. Truman* (Oxford Univ. Press 1995); McCullough, David, *Truman* (Simon & Schuster 1992).

■ **TRUMAN DOCTRINE,** U.S. foreign policy first formulated by Pres. Harry S. Truman in March 1947. The United States would provide aid to free nations in order to help them preserve free government and contain communism within its already existing territorial limits.

See Also: *Cold War; Truman, Harry S.*

■ **TRUMBULL, JOHN (1756-1843),** history painter of the Revolutionary era. Trumbull was born in Lebanon, Connecticut, and graduated from Harvard College in 1773. Son of the governor of Connecticut, Trumbull served in the Continental army during the Revolutionary War, but he resigned in 1777 to study art in Boston. As the war drew to a close, he moved to London and worked in the studio of Benjamin West. There, in 1785, he began a series of paintings depicting the recently ended war, including *Death of General Warren at the Battle of Bunker's Hill* and *Death of General Montgomery in the Attack on Quebec*, both of 1786. Trumbull returned to the United States in 1789; he painted portraits and had his history paintings engraved for wider distribution. In 1817 he was commissioned by Congress to paint four murals for the rotunda of the Capitol in Washington, D.C. These paintings, *Declaration of Independence, Surrender of General Burgoyne at Saratoga, Surrender of Lord Cornwallis at Yorktown,* and *Resignation of General Washington at Annapolis*, were completed in 1824.

See Also: *Painting; West, Benjamin.*

■ **TRUSTS,** combinations of companies formed to dominate markets and to reduce or eliminate competition. Trusts came into existence after the Civil War (1861-65). Fierce competition, economic recessions, and more complex and costly technology encouraged many businesses to attain higher yields on investments and increase maximum outputs. While some companies chose to increase demand by seeking out additional customers, others decided to negotiate agreements to eliminate competitors by setting quotas, limiting production, and fixing prices.

The first trust was the Standard Oil Trust, established in 1882. Led by John D. Rockefeller, Standard, like many other trusts, consolidated the stock of numerous firms and controlled over 90 percent of the industry. Despite ruthless business practices, Rockefeller boasted that trusts brought stability to previously chaotic markets. Others, especially politicians and middle-class reformers, however, viewed trusts as undermining free and fair competition. Agitation against trusts resulted in the Sherman Antitrust Act of 1890, the first effort at governmental regulation of industrial trusts. Nonetheless, trusts, such as U.S. Steel Corporation, continued to corner markets.

Several 20th-century presidents have taken on trusts with varying degrees of success. Theodore Roosevelt's "trust busting," Woodrow Wilson's New Freedom, and Franklin D. Roosevelt's New Deal policies all targeted trusts. Presidential, congressional, and Supreme Court actions have limited the scope of trusts but have not eliminated them from the American economy.

—GUY NELSON

See Also: *Antitrust Legislation; Rockefeller, John Davison; Sherman Antitrust Act.*

BIBLIOGRAPHY: Dewey, Donald J., *The Antitrust Experiment in America* (Columbia University Press 1990); Rozwenc, Edwin Charles, ed., *Roosevelt, Wilson, and the Trusts* (Heath 1950).

■ **TRUTH, SOJOURNER (1797?-1883),** pseudonym taken by a female abolitionist, an unusually tall woman named Isabella. She was born a slave

Sojourner Truth, noted for her oratorical power, earned an important place in both the fight for the abolition of slavery and for women's rights.

in Ulster County, New York, and was freed under the New York State emancipation law (1827). While working in New York City as a house servant, she stayed for a brief time at the famous "Kingdom of Matthias," a cooperative religious community near New York. In 1834, a newspaper reporter accused her of the murder of Lev Pierson, a leader of the community. She sued the reporter for libel and won the case. In 1843, she left New York and, having taken the name "Sojourner Truth," started to travel around the country, attending religious meetings and preaching. From late 1843 she lived in Northampton, Massachusetts, where she met Frederick Douglass and William Lloyd Garrison. In 1850, with Garrison's help, she published her autobiography, *Narrative of Sojourner Truth*. Being illiterate, she had dictated it to Olive Gilbert, a Connecticut abolitionist. Soon after, Truth began her career as an antislavery and women's rights orator, lecturing around New England and the West. A powerful speaker, she possessed outstanding ability to captivate her audience. She had developed a conspicuous image of herself—always in a white Quaker bonnet and a shawl, with a carpet bag. Although illiterate, she had extraordinary memory and knew much of the Bible by heart. She also composed her own songs and performed them at the meetings.

—DENIS KOZLOV

See Also: *African Americans; Antislavery Movement; Douglass, Frederick; Garrison, William Lloyd; Women in American History; Women's Movement.*

BIBLIOGRAPHY: Bernard, Jacqueline, *Journey toward Freedom: The Story of Sojourner Truth;* (reprint, Feminist Press 1990).

■ **TUBMAN, HARRIET (1820?-1913),** abolitionist, born in Dorchester County, Maryland. After escaping from slavery in 1849, she returned to Maryland in 1850 to help her sister and nieces escape. Over the following decade she made 19 more trips to the South, guiding as many as 300 slaves to freedom. She became well known among leading abolitionists, including Frederick Douglass and John Brown. During the American Civil War she served as a spy, scout, and army nurse in South Carolina.

See Also: *Antislavery Movement; Brown, John; Douglass, Frederick; Women in American History; Women's Movement.*

■ **TUCHMAN, BARBARA (1912-89),** historian. Born in New York City, she won two Pulitzer Prizes for her scholarly works, *The Guns of August* (1962) and *Stillwell and the American Experience in China, 1911-45* (1971). Known for readable narratives and rich description, she also wrote several best-selling popular histories, including *A Distant Mirror* (1978).

■ **TUCKER, SOPHIE (1884-1966),** entertainer. Born in Russia, she was a touring vaudeville performer but also appeared on Broadway and in several films. Her energetic style and strong singing voice earned her the nickname "the last of the red hot mamas."

■ **TUGWELL, REXFORD GUY (1891-1979),** American economist and adviser to Pres. Franklin D. Roosevelt. He was born in Sinclairville, New York, and became professor of economics at Columbia University (1920-37). Tugwell was an advocate of centralized national economic planning because, he believed, modern corporations had grown too large to be controlled by free-market forces. In keeping with this philosophy, he became a member of Roosevelt's "Brain Trust," an informal group of academics who helped shape New Deal policies. As a policy adviser and later undersecretary of agriculture (1934-37), he helped draft and implement the Agricultural Adjustment Act (1933), which sought to stabilize prices by controlling farm production. To critics of the New Deal, Tugwell became a symbol of intrusive big government bureaucracy. He was governor of Puerto Rico (1941-46) before becoming a professor of political science at the University of Chicago (1946-57).

See Also: *Brain Trust; New Deal.*

BIBLIOGRAPHY: Tugwell, Rexford G., *The Brains Trust* (Viking 1968).

■ **TURNER, FREDERICK JACKSON (1861-1932),** historian, proponent of the "frontier thesis" of American history, which maintained that American distinctiveness was attributable to the legacy of "westering." Born in Portage, Wisconsin, Turner, who was among the first Americans to receive professional historical training, was awarded a doctorate in 1891 from Johns Hopkins University. He taught at the University of Wisconsin until 1910, then at Harvard University until 1924, when he retired to a position as senior research associate at the Huntington Library in southern California.

Turner first detailed his interpretation of American history in a famous paper, "The Significance of the Frontier in American History," delivered in 1893 and published many times thereafter. Rebelling against the views of his mentor, Herbert Baxter Adams, that all significant American institutions derived from German and English antecedents, Turner argued instead that Europeans had been transformed by the process of settling the American continent and that what was unique about the United States was its frontier history. Turner's thesis became the dominant interpretation of American history for the next half century and more. Historians today, however, tend to reject such sweeping theories and emphasize the importance of a variety of factors in their interpretation of the past.

Although Turner published relatively few books, he was a brilliant essayist, and through his work he promoted new methods in historical research, including the techniques of the newly founded social sciences. In addition, he urged his colleagues to study such new topics as immigration, urbanization, economic development, and social and cultural history. Turner was one of the "progressive historians" who understood history as part of a dialogue between the past and the present rather than a fixed record of events. He trained a new generation of historians in this spirit and helped build two of the century's great history departments. Turner was a leader of the American Historical Association, serving as its president in 1910.

—JOHN MACK FARAGHER

See Also: History.

BIBLIOGRAPHY: Billington, Ray Allen, *Frederick Jackson Turner: Historian, Scholar, Teacher* (Oxford Univ. Press 1973); Hofstadter, Richard, *The Progressive Historians: Turner, Beard, Parrington* (Knopf 1968).

■ **TURNER, NAT (1800-31),** leader of a slave rebellion. Born a slave in Southampton County, Virginia, and possessed of a strong religious sensibility, Turner had a vision he interpreted as a divine message to lead a slave revolt. After planning and postponement, on Aug. 21, 1831, Turner led the uprising. In the ensuing violence about 60 whites were killed. Turner eluded capture until October 30, and he was hanged on Nov. 11, 1831.

See Also: African Americans; Nat Turner's Insurrection; Slave Revolts.

■ **TURNPIKES,** toll roads constructed and maintained by private corporations. Built from about 1790 to 1830, turnpikes eased overland travel and helped farmers ship produce to market. The most famous turnpike, the 62-mile stone and gravel Lancaster Pike in Pennsylvania, was completed in 1794. By 1810, more than 300 turnpike corporations had been chartered, building roads across New England, New York, and Pennsylvania, developing the corporation system in America, and ushering in the transportation revolution.

By 1840, canals and railroads had rendered turnpikes obsolete.

See Also: Transportation.

■ **TUSCARORA,** Iroquoian-speaking tribe. At the time of European contact, the Tuscarora were based in present-day North Carolina. Their society was matrilineal (descent reckoned through the mother), and they lived in longhouses headed by a clan mother. The women of the tribe farmed, producing an abundance of corn, hemp, beans, squash, and other foods. The men were primarily hunters. Beginning in the early 1700s, English colonists began encroaching on Tuscarora lands, often capturing Tuscaroras and selling them into slavery. For their part, the Tuscarora often welcomed runaway African slaves into their society. The tension between the colonists and the Tuscarora led to the Tuscarora War of 1711-13, in which the South Carolinians and their Indian allies routed the Tus-

Dismissed as a writer of "boys' stories" in his own day, Samuel Clemens (Mark Twain) is today considered one of the greatest of American writers.

carora, killing 1,000 and capturing 700. The remaining 1,500 Tuscarora then migrated north with the help of the Iroquois Five Nations Confederacy, situated in present-day upstate New York and southern Canada. In 1722, the Tuscarora became the Sixth Nation of the Confederacy. Today, there are close to 3,000 Tuscarora living in the United States and an estimated 1,200 living in Canada.

See Also: Indians of North America; Iroquois Confederacy.

■ **TWAIN, MARK (1835-1910),** author and lecturer. Born in Florida, Missouri, as Samuel Langhorne Clemens, he worked as a printer, journalist, river pilot, Confederate volunteer, and western prospector before establishing himself as a writer and lecturer under the pseudonym Mark Twain. In 1865, Twain first received notice as a talented humorist with the publication of his story "The Celebrated Jumping Frog of Calaveras County." He started to lecture the following year, a career tack Twain would come to despise as he grew more bitter, although one that would enable him to pay off his debts in the 1890s. A trip to the Mediterranean and the Holy Land furnished Twain with the material for *The Innocents Abroad* (1869), which won him national recognition. In confronting such serious issues as class and race throughout his career, Twain nonetheless secured his place as one of the nation's great humorists. Among his prominent works are *Roughing It* (1872), *The Gilded Age* (coauthored with Charles Dudley Warner, 1873), *The Adventures of Tom Sawyer* (1876), *Life on the Mississippi* (1883), and *The Adventures of Huckleberry Finn* (1884). Examples of Twain's increasing cynicism can be found in *A Connecticut Yankee in King Arthur's Court* (1889) and *The Tragedy of Pudd'nhead Wilson and the Comedy, Those Extraordinary Twins* (1894), as well as in his later attacks upon Western imperialism. By the time of his death, Twain had become the nation's leading man of letters.

—JAMES KESSENIDES

See Also: Novel.

BIBLIOGRAPHY: Emerson, Everett, *The Authentic Mark Twain: A Literary Biography of Samuel L. Clemens* (Univ. of Pennsylvania Press 1984).

■ **TWEED, WILLIAM MARCY (BOSS) (1823-78),** politician. Born in New York City, he entered politics as a Democrat, serving as city alderman (1851) and in the U.S. Congress (1853-55). Returning to a position as alderman, he effectively controlled the New York City Democratic party as leader of the Tammany Hall machine, over which he maintained power through a small group of henchmen, known as the "Tweed Ring." By 1868 he had gained control of the party on the state level as well. The Tweed Ring bought votes, extorted bribes from potential contractors, and corrupted the judicial system. In the process, Tweed became a millionaire and cost the city of New York millions in inflated costs of municipal projects. In 1871 the *New York Times* published a series of articles detailing the corruption.

In 1871, the "ring" that Tammany Hall's Boss Tweed had formed around himself began to unravel when his corrupt activities were revealed in a series of newspaper articles. Seven years later Tweed died in jail.

Charged with embezzlement, Tweed was eventually sentenced in 1874 and served one year. Rearrested on other charges, he escaped to Cuba, only to be returned by Spanish authorities in 1876. He died in his cell in New York City's Ludlow Street jail.

See Also: Tammany Hall.

BIBLIOGRAPHY: Bales, William A., *Tiger in the Streets* (Dodd, Mead 1962); Hershkowitz, Leo, *Tweed's New York* (Anchor Press 1977).

■ **TYLER, JOHN (1790-1862),** 10th president of the United States (1841-45). Born in Charles City County, Virginia, he entered politics early and was a supporter of Pres. James Madison and the War of 1812. In 1816 Tyler was elected to the U.S. House of Representatives, where he served until 1821. In Congress he was a strict constructionist who opposed the Bank of the United States on constitutional grounds. He opposed Pres. Andrew Jackson during the Nullification Crisis of 1832 for the same reason. In the 1830s Tyler joined the newly formed Whig party as a states' rights advocate. In 1840, he was successful in his bid for the vice presidency as William Henry Harrison's running mate. When President Harrison died in April 1841, after less than a month in office, Tyler became the first vice president to replace a deceased president in office. As president, Tyler opposed plans to recharter the Bank of the United States, a move that brought him disfavor within his own party, which generally supported the bank. He lost his party's nomination for president in 1844. Tyler attempted to get a treaty annexing the Republic of Texas to the United States in 1844 but failed to win the required two-thirds majority in the Senate. However, in

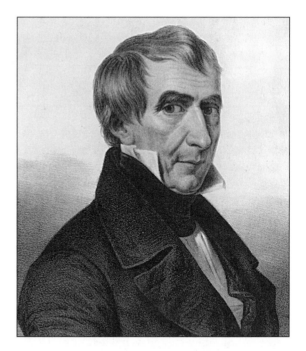

Whig John Tyler assumed the office of president in 1841 upon the death of William Henry Harrison, who had served just one month.

March 1845, just days before leaving office, he pushed through a joint resolution annexing Texas, which led to the Mexican War.

See Also: Banks of the United States, First and Second; Mexican War; Nullification; Presidential Elections; President of the United States.

BIBLIOGRAPHY: Peterson, Norma Lois, *The Presidencies of William Henry Harrison and John Tyler* (Univ. of Kansas Press 1989).

U

UN-AMERICAN ACTIVITIES, HOUSE COMMITTEE ON (HUAC), committee of the House of Representatives charged with investigating alleged subversive activities. HUAC was formed in 1938 to investigate alleged fascists and communists in American government. Chairman Martin Dies, a Republican from Texas, largely ignored this charge, concentrating instead on harassing New Deal agencies. In 1945 the committee was made permanent, and it quickly became part of the postwar "red scare" that accompanied the expanding Cold War. Led by Republican Rep. Richard M. Nixon of California, the committee began what many viewed as a witch hunt. HUAC investigated not only domestic communists but any group of social critics with a liberal past. The most infamous examples of this were HUAC's 1947 investigation of the movie industry, leading to the blacklisting of many Hollywood actors, writers, and producers, and the 1948 investigation of former State Department official Alger Hiss, which led to his 1949 conviction for perjury. HUAC was the springboard for Nixon's national career and it remained a force throughout the 1950s. Despite the protests of the 1960s, HUAC continued investigations, particularly of suspected communist influences in the civil rights movement. Renamed the House Internal Security Committee in 1969, it was abolished in 1975.

—JOHN ROBERT GREENE

See Also: Civil Rights Movement; Cold War; Hiss-Chambers Case; Nixon, Richard M.

BIBLIOGRAPHY: Ceplair, Larry, and Steven England, *The Inquisition in Hollywood* (Anchor Press/Doubleday 1983); Goodman, Walter, *Committee: The Extraordinary Career of the House Committee on Un-American Activities* (Farrar, Straus, & Giroux 1968).

UNCAS (c. 1606-c. 1682), Mohegan leader. Originally a member of the Pequot tribe in present-day Connecticut, Uncas became the founder of the Mohegan, an offshoot advocating friendly relations with the English Puritans. Uncas provided military support to the Puritans during the Pequot War (1636-37), in which many of his former tribesmen were burned alive as they slept. After the war, the English named him leader of the surviving Pequots. Later, he supported the English during King Philip's War (1675-76).

See Also: Indians of North America; King Philip's War; Pequot War.

UNCLE SAM, nickname for the government of the United States, first developed as a term of derision during the War of 1812, derived probably from the initials "U. S." on government-issued goods. By the mid-19th century the term was widespread and had lost its negative connotations. Uncle Sam's distinctive red, white, and blue costume was taken from the stage dress of the American minstrel performer Daniel Rice.

See Also: Rice, Daniel McLaren.

UNCONDITIONAL SURRENDER, controversial policy enunciated by Pres. Franklin D. Roosevelt at the Casablanca Conference in January 1943 demanding that the Axis nations surrender unequivocally and without prior negotiating terms. Some critics felt that the policy would only prolong the war by forcing the Axis nations to fight on long after they had lost the conflict. The policy, however, remained in place, and Germany and Japan surrendered unconditionally in 1945.

See Also: Casablanca Conference; World War II.

UNDERGROUND RAILROAD, network of anti-slavery sympathizers who supported and aided fugitives in their escape from slavery. A slaveholder whose slaves eluded him in Ohio is said to have originated the name. Shrouded in mystery and myth, the exact nature of the network is now difficult to assess. But while the scope of the Underground Railroad's activities can be overestimated, there is no doubt that numerous figures, such as the white Quaker Levi Coffin and the black ex-slave Harriet Tubman, earnestly worked to assist slaves in their liberation. Pathways to freedom were as varied as the slaves who traveled them, but most roads led north, often into Canada, although many slaves also escaped into Mexico. Although the true extent of the Underground Railroad will never be fully determined, it is clear that the existence of such a "network" of support to runaway slaves contributed greatly to the anxiety of slaveholders, who chafed under the flaunting of the fugitive slave laws. Their anxiety unquestionably contributed to the coming of the Civil War.

See Also: Fugitive Slaves; Slavery; Tubman, Harriet.
BIBLIOGRAPHY: Gara, Larry, *The Liberty Line: The Legend of the Underground Railroad* (reprint, Univ. Press of Kentucky 1996).

■ **UNEMPLOYMENT,** condition in which people who seek work for income are unable to obtain it. In colonial times most adults either provided their own basic needs or were slaves dependent on provisions furnished by masters. Destitution, therefore, was most commonly associated with physical incapacity, widowhood, or wars. With industrial development, periodic joblessness became part of the normal workings of a market economy and a recurrent cause of working-class protests. Since the 1930s, the quest for possible remedies for unemployment has been a central issue in public policy debates.

Few wage earners in the growing industrial economy of the 19th century experienced steady employment, year in and year out. The time workers spent between jobs (called by economists "frictional unemployment") regularly tested the ingenuity of families and encouraged fraternal organizations and trade unions to provide some benefits for members temporarily without income.

Winter was a season in which the cost of living rose, while available work declined sharply as construction halted, shipping dwindled, and water to power mills froze. After the mid-1800s, the growing influence of fashion on sales and the mechanization of production served to concentrate work in clothing manufacture to specific times of the year. Other than domestic service,

urban jobs for women were so unsteady that many women became occasionally dependent on municipal poor relief or private charities.

The economic growth from the 1840s through the 1920s that transformed the United States into the manufacturing colossus of the world was punctuated by frequent recessions and such periodic major depressions as those that began in 1857, 1873, 1893, 1904, 1908, 1914, and 1921. The large numbers of men and women who were dismissed from their jobs, reduced to part-time work, or suffered wage reductions during those crises stimulated debate over the causes of the distress and appropriate public policies.

Labor organizations demanded that city governments employ jobless men (especially) on public works. They were usually met with the irate response from public officials and economic theorists that free people should take care of themselves and not expect to be maintained at taxpayers' expense. During the depression of the 1890s organizations of the unemployed demanded federal policies to stimulate the economy and a constitutional amendment to affirm the right of everyone to have work.

Modern Unemployment Issues. The Great Depression that began in 1929 left one-quarter of the nation's workers without jobs and 27 million people dependent on federal relief or works projects by 1934. Because of improvements in productivity, more than 14 percent of the labor force was still unemployed in 1937, when manufacturing output surpassed that of the prosperous year 1928. The ability of companies to select among many applicants made the work force increasingly well educated, experienced, white, and between 25 and 45 years of age. Other categories of would-be workers formed a large pool of people who were often without jobs for a year or more.

After the United States entered World War II in 1941, war production expanded the labor force. The numbers employed went from 53 million (with 7 million unemployed) in 1940 to 68 million (including 19 million women) in 1944. The war also initiated a period of protracted upswing in job creation that lasted until the late 1960s; marginalized groups, however, were left dependent on welfare. Postwar labor demands for government guarantees of full employment were unsuccessful, and by the 1970s government policy aimed at training people for available jobs while hoping to keep unemployment not lower than 6 percent in order to combat inflation.

—DAVID MONTGOMERY

See Also: Labor Movement; Strikes; Trade Unions; Work in America.

BIBLIOGRAPHY: Garraty, John A., *Unemployment in History: Economic Thought and Public Policy* (Harper & Row 1978); Jensen, Richard J., "The Causes and Cures of Unemployment in the Great Depression," *Journal of Interdisciplinary History* (Spring 1989); Keyssar, Alexander, *Out of Work: The First Century of Unemployment in Massachusetts* (Cambridge Univ. Press 1986).

■ **UNION LEAGUE CLUBS,** organizations of pro-Republican Northern supporters of the Civil War. Following the Republican party's poor showing in the 1862 elections, the clubs were founded to combat the influence of the antiwar Copperheads.

See Also: Copperheads; Reconstruction.

■ **UNITARIANS,** those who believe that God is one Person rather than a Trinity. Unitarianism originated with the followers of Michael Servetus (1511-53) in Geneva, Switzerland, and Faustus Socinus (1539-1604) in Poland. In America, Unitarianism roots are with a group of Boston Arminians—led by Charles Chauncey, Ebenezer Gay, and Jonathan Mayhew—who grew cautious of the revivalism of the Great Awakening and traditional Puritan Calvinism. The first sign of their rejection of the Trinity was when King's Chapel, an Episcopal church in Boston, removed Trinitarian references from its services and became Unitarian in 1785. In Philadelphia, Joseph Priestley founded a Unitarian church in 1796. Gradually, a liberal Congregational faction in New England formed a denomination. After William Ellery Channing delivered his sermon "Unitarian Christianity" (1819) in Baltimore, the establishment was complete. Unitarians were closely associated with Transcendentalism. Unitarianism does not require professional clergy nor does it have a creed. The Unitarians and Universalists merged in 1961 and formed the Unitarian Universalist Association (UUA). The UUA continues the liberal tradition of Unitarianism and is committed to progressive social issues such as environmentalism, feminism, and gay rights.

See Also: Channing, William Ellery; Great Awakening; Religion; Transcendentalism; Universalists.

■ **UNITED NATIONS (UN),** international organization established in 1945, at the conclusion of World War II, to maintain world peace and security. The UN was founded by joint effort of the five principal Allied powers—the United States, the Soviet Union, Great Britain, France, and China—who became the permanent members of the Security Council, each with veto power. A total of 51 charter member states joined the UN, with all members meeting in the General Assembly. The UN was the successor to the League of Nations (founded in the wake of World War I) and in 1946 absorbed the former organization's physical and administrative apparatus, including the International Court of Justice (also known as the World Court). In 1952 the UN moved into permanent headquarters in New York City.

The Cold War between the United States and the Soviet Union dominated the UN's security functions during the organization's first 50 years. The rivalry between the two superpowers infused many regional disputes, making it difficult if not impossible for the Security Council to reach agreement on conflict resolution. A notable exception came early in the Cold War, when in 1950 the Soviet Union staged a boycott of the Security Council that coincided with the outbreak of war between North and South Korea. With the Soviet delegate absent, the council voted to assist South Korea, allowing the United States to argue that the Korean War was a "police action." Thereafter, both the United States and its allies as well as the Soviet Union made liberal use of their veto power, frustrating the ability of the UN to act effectively.

The primary challenge for the organization in the postwar world was the decolonization of Africa, Asia, and the Middle East, a task that presented a daunting array of political, economic, and social challenges. Dozens of new nations in the Third World (those nations, especially less-developed countries, that were outside the two contending Cold War camps) dramatically increased the membership of the organization. By 1965, the UN had 117 members; by 1990 the number had risen to 159. The United States began the postwar period by appealing to its European allies to dismantle their empires, but found it expedient to equivocate in the context of the Cold War, thus allowing the Soviet Union and the People's Republic of China to claim the mantle of "anti-imperialism." Perhaps the most tragic example of the way such politics blocked the UN's mission was the decolonization crisis in the Congo. When Belgium hastily pulled out in 1960, tribal and regional antagonisms resulted in widespread violence. The nationalist prime minister, Patrice Lumumba, requested and received UN assistance, but the Western powers would not agree to use these forces to suppress a revolt in resource-rich Katanga province, a revolt underwritten by the Belgians. Lumumba felt compelled to appeal to the Soviet Union for military aid, which so alarmed the United States that it helped stage a coup by Mobutu Sese Seko, an army officer. Lumumba was murdered, Mobutu proclaimed himself dictator of Zaire (his name for the country) and then operated one of the world's most corrupt regimes for the next 30 years. It was a cautionary tale of how a divided UN could work for ill.

The end of the Cold War in the late 1980s and the effective response to the Iraqi invasion of Kuwait in the Persian Gulf War (1991) suggested that the UN had entered a new era. The UN peacekeeping forces were awarded the Nobel Peace Prize in 1988 for their contributions in many parts of the world. But at the same time, the organization was nearly bankrupt. By the late 1990s member states owed the UN more than $4 billion, and the United States was the single most delinquent country.

—JOHN MACK FARAGHER

See Also: Cold War; World War II.

BIBLIOGRAPHY: Bennett, A. LeRoy, *Historical Dictionary of the United Nations* (Scarecrow Press 1995); Brinkley, Douglas, *FDR and the Creation of the UN* (Yale Univ. Press 1997); Maxwell, Seymour, *American Ambassadors at the UN: People, Politics, and Bureaucracy in Making Foreign Policy* (Holmes & Meier 1988).

■ **UNITED STATES OF AMERICA,** republic of North America. The contiguous 48 states are bounded by Canada to the north, Mexico to the south, and the Atlantic and Pacific oceans to the east and west, respectively. Alaska is to the north, bounded by Canada to the east and south and the Arctic Ocean to the west and north. Hawaii lies in the Pacific Ocean, about 2,000 miles west of California. Area: 3,675,000 square miles. Population (1996 est.): 265,000,000.

The conviction that the Western Hemisphere was in fact Asia, or "the Indies," persisted in Europe long after the death of Christopher Columbus in 1506. This cartographic notion informed Hernan Cortes's conception of Mexico in the 1520s and even Jean Nicolet's exploration of the Great Lakes in the 1630s. Yet, after his second voyage across the Atlantic in 1501, the Florentine navigator Amerigo Vespucci published a widely disseminated account of his expedition, calling into question the prevailing Columbian geography. Vespucci's contention that the northern coast of South America was a "Mundus Novus" made him the first to recognize the Americas as the New World. In 1507 a group of scholastic monks christened the New World "America" in Vespucci's honor in a revised edition of Waldseemüller's world map. The German cartographer Gerhardus Mercator also used "America" in his ubiquitous 1538 world map.

America came to refer to both North and South America until the British colonies proclaimed themselves, in the Declaration of Independence (1776), the United States of America. Under the Articles of Confederation (1776-77), the 13 original states were considered sovereign and only loosely connected. Unsatisfactory to some Americans, this conception of the United States was altered in the Constitution to connote a federation of states brought together under a central government. This federalist notion of the United States of America contributed heavily to the creation of the nation-state and to the idea of a unified American people.

See Also: Frontier in American History.

BIBLIOGRAPHY: Arciniegas, German, *Amerigo and the New World: The Life and Times of Amerigo Vespucci* (Knopf 1955); Wood, Gordon S., *The Creation of the American Republic, 1776-1787* (Univ. of North Carolina Press 1969).

■ ***UNITED STATES* V. *CLASSIC* (1941),** U.S. Supreme Court case concerning Congress's power to regulate primary elections. The Court voted (5-3) that Louisiana officials violated federal civil rights laws by miscounting primary ballots to manipulate re-

UNITED STATES OF AMERICA

sults. In so deciding, the Court reversed an earlier decision, *Newberry v. United States* (1921), and ruled that Congress's authority to regulate the election of its members extended to primaries that limit the field of candidates.

See Also: Supreme Court.

■ **UNITED STATES V. DARBY LUMBER CO. (1941),** U.S. Supreme Court case that upheld minimum wage and maximum hour laws enacted by Congress prior to World War II. In ruling (9-0) that the Fair Labor Standards Act (1938) was constitutional, the Court overturned *Hammer v. Dagenhart* (1918), which had overturned a law banning the products of child labor from interstate commerce. In *Darby* the Court endorsed a broader interpretation of Congress's powers under the commerce clause to regulate working conditions in businesses across the country.

See Also: Fair Labor Standards Act; Hammer v. Dagenhart; Supreme Court.

■ **UNITED STATES V. GOUVEIA (1984),** U.S. Supreme Court case that clarified prison inmates' right to legal counsel. Four federal prison inmates were placed in administrative detention for 19 months while prison officials investigated the killing of another inmate. When authorities charged the four with murder, they were provided counsel who sued to dismiss the charges. The Court ruled (8-1) that inmates are not entitled to legal counsel until judicial proceedings begin.

See Also: Supreme Court.

■ **UNITED STATES V. NIXON (1974),** U.S. Supreme Court case concerning the limits of executive privilege. The decision led to the resignation of Pres.

Richard M. Nixon. The Court ruled (8-0) on July 24, 1974, that while the judiciary should show deference to the chief executive, the president enjoyed only conditional legal immunity and was not above the law.

The case helped conclude the Watergate affair (1972-74), the scandal that drove Nixon from office. Investigations revealed that Nixon had installed an audio tape recording system in the White House. Special prosecutor Archibald Cox sought tapes of certain meetings between Nixon and his aides that, he believed, would settle conflicting accounts of what had occurred. Nixon refused to surrender the tapes and ordered Cox dismissed. The resulting public outcry led to the appointment of a new special prosecutor, Leon Jaworski, who also sought the tapes. U.S. District Court Judge John Sirica issued a subpoena for them.

Writing for the Court, Chief Justice Warren Burger, a Nixon appointee, ordered the president to comply with the subpoena. He rejected White House arguments that the courts had no authority over a dispute within the executive branch and stated that the president did not enjoy absolute immunity. The tapes revealed Nixon had taken part in discussions about how to block investigations of alleged criminal activity. The president resigned on Aug. 9, 1974, rather than face impeachment.

—TIM ASHWELL

See Also: Nixon, Richard Milhous; Supreme Court; Watergate.

BIBLIOGRAPHY: Schudson, Michael, *Watergate in American Memory: How We Remember, Forget, and Reconstruct the Past* (Basic Books 1992); Woodward, Bob, and Carl Bernstein, *The Final Days* (Simon & Schuster 1976).

■ *UNITED STATES V. SIOUX NATION* **(1980),** U.S. Supreme Court case that decided the Sioux Indian tribe should be compensated by the United States for the loss of the Black Hills region of South Dakota. The U.S. government had pledged in the Fort Laramie Treaty (1868) that the Black Hills would remain in the hands of the Sioux forever unless three-fourths of the tribe's adult males agreed to give up the land. After the U.S. Army defeated the Sioux (1876), the government forced the tribe to accept a new treaty and give up the

Black Hills in exchange for a new and smaller reservation and promises of food and shelter in the future. Because only 10 percent of the tribe's men signed the new treaty, Congress in 1877 abrogated the 1868 Fort Laramie Treaty and imposed the new one.

For a century the Sioux Nation sought without success to overturn the 1877 treaty. In 1978, after Congress passed legislation authorizing the courts to revisit the issue, the U.S. Court of Claims ruled the treaty was a "taking" of property by the government and the Sioux deserved fair compensation. The Supreme Court agreed (8-1) that Congress had not improperly interfered with the court system by allowing a new hearing and that the 1877 treaty was a taking of private property for public use. Under the Fifth Amendment to the U.S. Constitution, such an action required just compensation.

—TIM ASHWELL

See Also: Sioux; Supreme Court.

BIBLIOGRAPHY: Robinson, Charles M., *A Good Year to Die: The Story of the Great Sioux War* (Random House 1995).

■ *UNITED STATES V. WONG KIM ARK* **(1898),** U.S. Supreme Court case that upheld the birthright to U.S. citizenship. The Court ruled (6-2) that a man born in California to Chinese parents was a U.S. citizen despite a law denying citizenship to Chinese immigrants. The decision, based on the 14th Amendment's provision that all persons born in the United States are citizens, was a major victory for Asian Americans, who were subject to frequent racist attacks.

See Also: Chinese Immigration; Supreme Court.

■ **UNIVERSALISTS,** those who believe that God will save all individuals. Universalists argue that eternal punishment for sin is inconsistent with the belief in a loving, merciful God. Universalism first came to America with various pietistic and mystical groups from Germany. Jonathan Mayhew and Charles Chauncey, who wrote *The Salvation of All Men* (1784), were proponents of an early form of universalism. In Gloucester, Massachusetts, John Murray, an English-born preacher, established Universalism in America. He was, hence, excommunicated by the Methodists. Internally, Universalists debated over the status of the soul after death. Some argued that the soul went through a period of punishment, while ultra-Universalists believed that the soul went immediately to heaven after death. Abner Kneeland, a Universalist clergyman, was an editor of liberal magazines and served a brief time in jail in 1838 for expressing his views as a free thinker.

The Universalists and Unitarians merged in 1961 and formed the Unitarian Universalist Association (UUA). The UUA continues the liberal tradition of Unitarianism and is committed to progressive social issues such as environmentalism, feminism, and gay rights.

See Also: Religion; Unitarians.

■ **UNIVERSAL NEGRO IMPROVEMENT ASSOCIATION (UNIA),** organization created in 1914 by the black nationalist leader Marcus Garvey. It was chartered to further his philosophy of racial pride and solidarity among black peoples throughout the world.

See Also: Civil Rights Movement; Garvey, Marcus Mosiah.

■ **URBAN LEAGUE,** social service and civil rights organization. Founded (1911) to improve urban African Americans' social and economic well-being, the league steadily broadened its efforts to become, by the 1960s, one of the leading civil rights organizations in America.

See Also: Civil Rights Movement.

■ **UREY, HAROLD (1893-1981),** physical chemist. Born in Walkerton, Indiana, Urey worked as a research chemist and instructor at Montana State University before earning his Ph.D. at the University of California, Berkeley (1923). He studied atomic structure with Niels Bohr in Copenhagen (1923-24), taught at Johns Hopkins (1924-29), and joined the faculty of Columbia University (1929-45). While at Columbia, Urey discovered deuterium, a hydrogen isotope called heavy hydrogen. The discovery had a significant impact on the scientific world and won him a Nobel Prize in Chemistry in 1934. Urey also developed new ways to separate isotopes, and during World War II he directed the search to separate uranium 235 from uranium 238 for the Manhattan Project. After the

war, he spoke out on the ethical problems involved in the use of atomic weapons. Urey joined the Institute for Nuclear Studies at the University of Chicago (1945-58), where he applied his isotope research to problems of geology and paleontology and developed an oxygen thermometer used to study ancient climactic temperatures. Urey also studied the origin and development of the planets and analyzed lunar rocks from the Apollo missions while at the University of California (1958-81).

See Also: Manhattan Project; Science.

■ **UTAH,** a Rocky Mountain state. It is bounded on the north by Idaho, on the north and east by Wyoming, on the east by Colorado, on the south by Arizona, and on the west by Nevada. Most of Utah is arid, especially the Great Basin in the western third of the state. The Great Salt Lake and Utah Lake are remnants of an ancient, much larger inland body of water. Utah's diversified economy rests on minerals, manufacturing, and irrigated agriculture, as well as on services and government.

Beginning in 1847, Utah was settled by persecuted members of the Church of Jesus Christ of Latter-Day Saints (Mormons). The United States would not admit the territory to the Union as a state until 1896, after the Mormon church had forsworn plural marriage. Mormons accounted for 72 percent of the state population in 1990.

Capital: Salt Lake City. Area: 84,904 square miles. Population (1995 est.): 1,951,000.

See Also: Bridger, James (Jim); Frémont, John C.; Great Basin; Great Salt Lake; Mormons; Young, Brigham.

■ **UTE INDIANS.** *See: Great Basin and Rocky Mountain Indians.*

■ **UTOPIAN COMMUNITIES,** attempts by individuals and groups to create ideal societies. Such communities have flourished in the United States because of the availability of land for settlements and the existence of religious and political freedom. The first significant utopian community in America was a German Pietist colony founded in 1732 by the mystic Conrad Beissel at Ephrata, Pennsylvania. Another religious group, the

United Society of Believers in Christ's Second Appearing, popularly known as the Shakers, migrated to the United States in 1774 after suffering persecution in England. This celibate sect was led by "Mother" Ann Lee, who had visions and believed that sexual intercourse was the root of all sin. The Shakers prospered in America and by 1860 had established 26 colonies as far west as Indiana with 4,000 members.

During the first half of the 19th century several secular ideologies, most notably Owenism and Fourierism, generated colonies such as New Harmony (1825-27) and Brook Farm (1841-47), an educational cooperative in Massachusetts that attracted writers and thinkers like Nathaniel Hawthorne, Charles Dana, and Isaac Hecker. Colonies were organized with specific reforms in mind. Nashoba (1826-29), founded by the Scottish reformer and feminist Frances Wright, was dedicated to social emancipation for freed slaves. The religious community of Oneida (1848-80) was one of the most innovative and long-lived. Led by John H. Noyes, it developed as a controlled free love colony, practiced a unique birth control system (male continence), and in 1869 instituted the only eugenics experiment (stirpiculture) ever tried in the United States. Oneida was an economic success, producing fine silk products, traps, and silverware.

The utopian tradition continued during and after the Civil War as communities were established in response to urbanization and industrialization. Colonies were established in the West to promote vegetarianism (Harmonial Vegetarian Society, 1860-64), the cultivation of silk (by French workers in the Kansas Cooperative Farm, 1870-84), the care of orphaned children (Shalam in New Mexico, 1884-1901), and the settlement of immigrant Russian Jews on the land (numerous sites in Louisiana, Kansas, and Oregon).

20th-Century Communities. In the 20th century colonies were organized around particular charismatic leaders, such as Alexander Dowie's faith healing planned town at Zion, Illinois (1901-06); around progressive social agendas, such as Upton Sinclair's Helicon Hall (1906-07); or around countercultural ideas, such as the decentralist and back-to-the-land communities of Ralph Borsodi in the 1930s.

The 1960s saw a great resurgence of interest in utopian colonies as part of an alternative lifestyle movement. Some were "hippie" communes like Drop City (1965-73), started by a group of artists who built and lived in geodesic domes in southern Colorado. They embraced Eastern mysticism, drugs, and avant-garde art. Other groups, like Ananda Cooperative Village, 1967, embraced American Indian philosophies.

Two communities—Jonestown (1963-78) and the Branch Davidians (1979-93)—erupted in death and destruction. Jonestown was led by Jim Jones, an ordained evangelical minister, who moved from Indiana to northern California to establish a colony, then to San Francisco, and finally to Guyana, where in 1978 he and his members committed mass suicide. The Branch Davidians, led by David Koresh, belonged to a dissident Seventh Day Adventist sect. Koresh took over leadership of the colony at Mt. Carmel, Texas, in 1979. A confrontation with federal authorities (1993) led to the death of 74 members.

During the 1980s evangelical and charismatic groups dominated the utopian settlement pattern, although "New Age" and Eastern-oriented communities like the Hare Krishna community in West Virginia continued to attract members.

—ROBERT S. FOGARTY

See Also: *Brook Farm; Owen, Robert; Sinclair, Upton; Wright, Frances Fanny.*

BIBLIOGRAPHY: Bestor, Arthur, Jr., *Backwoods Utopias* (Univ. of Pennsylvania Press 1950); Fogarty, Robert S., *All Things New* (Univ. of Chicago Press 1990); Fogarty, Robert S., *Dictionary of American Communal and Utopian History* (Greenwood Press 1980); Veysey, Lawrence, *The Communal Experience* (reprint, Univ. of Chicago Press 1973).

■ **U-2 INCIDENT,** diplomatic crisis. The Soviet Union claimed it shot down a U.S. Central Intelligence Agency U-2 spy plane on May 1, 1960. Pres. Dwight Eisenhower initially denied the report, but the U.S.S.R. produced the pilot, Francis Gary Powers, and canceled a planned conference between Eisenhower and Soviet leader Nikita Khrushchev. Powers was convicted of espionage and exchanged for senior Soviet agent Rudolph Abel in 1962.

See Also: *Cold War.*

V

VALENTINO, RUDOLF (1895-1926), silent film star. Born in Castellaneta, Italy, he immigrated to the United States in 1913 and made his film debut in 1918. Valentino used his exotic good looks, physical grace, and sensual screen presence to become a romantic screen idol in *The Four Horsemen of the Apocalypse* (1921), *The Sheik* (1921), and *Blood and Sand* (1922). His sudden death at 31 triggered an outpouring of grief from his female fans.

See Also: Motion Pictures.

VALLANDIGHAM, CLEMENT L. (1820-71), politician. Born in New Lisbon, Ohio, Vallandigham was elected to Congress as a Democrat in 1856. During the Civil War, Vallandigham was a leading Copperhead, opposing the Lincoln administration's arbitrary arrests, emancipation measures, use of African Americans in battle, and military draft. He was defeated for reelection in 1862. In May 1863 a military court convicted him of treason, and President Lincoln banished him. From Windsor, Canada, Vallandigham campaigned unsuccessfully for the governorship of Ohio in 1863. Returning in 1864, he helped to write the "peace plank" of Democratic nominee George B. McClellan at the Democratic National Convention in Chicago.

See Also: Copperheads.

VALLEY FORGE, PENNSYLVANIA, site (1777-78) of the Continental army's winter quarters following the British occupation of Philadelphia. After suffering defeat in three battles at the hands of the British, the 11,000 soldiers led by Gen. George Washington dug in for the bitter winter in December 1777. A place of suffering and endurance, the camp at Valley Forge was located in an easily defensible position on the Schuylkill River about 20 miles from Philadelphia. By the time camp was broken in June 1778, some 2,500 soldiers had died of exposure, malnutrition, and disease. Because the Continental Congress would not pay the exorbitant prices for provisions charged by contractors, the army suffered severe shortages. A harrowing experience, Valley Forge helped develop a strong sense of brotherhood among the soldiers. This common struggle brought together men and women from different localities and various ethnic backgrounds. Forming a sense of American identity, the Valley Forge experience provided the army with momentum and confidence.

See Also: Revolution, American.

VAN BUREN, MARTIN (1782-1862), eighth president of the United States (1837-41). He was born at Kinderhook, New York, the son of a farmer and tavern keeper. From his earliest years he was enthralled by politics, playing an influen-

Democrat Martin Van Buren won the presidential election of 1836 and soon faced major economic problems with the Panic of 1837.

tial role in a congressional nominating caucus at age 17. Admitted to the bar in 1803, Van Buren served as Columbia County surrogate (1808-13), state senator (1813-20), and attorney general (1816-19). After his removal by Gov. DeWitt Clinton, Van Buren successfully welded the anti-Clinton opposition into one of the most effective political machines in American history, the "Albany Regency," which he directed while a U.S. senator (1821-28). Having managed an unsuccessful presidential campaign for William M. Crawford in 1824, Van Buren served as principal architect of the Democratic party, mobilizing the opponents of John Quincy Adams in Andrew Jackson's victorious campaign in 1828.

As Jackson's secretary of state, Van Buren quickly overshadowed Vice Pres. John C. Calhoun as Jackson's closest confidant. In 1831, Van Buren resigned. This brought about the resignation of the rest of the Cabinet, giving Jackson the opportunity to eliminate Calhoun's supporters there. Calhoun's tie-breaking Senate vote against Van Buren's confirmation as minister to Great Britain provoked a backlash of sympathy and ensured his election as vice president in 1832. As vice president, Van Buren supported Jackson's bank war and, more tepidly, his battle against South Carolina's nullifiers. In the presidential campaign of 1836, Van Buren defeated three regional Whig candidates on a platform of continuing Jackson's policies and suppressing abolitionism.

Just days after Van Buren's inauguration, the nation plunged into a serious economic depression. His subtreasury plan failed to reverse the slide. Van Buren presided over Cherokee removal in 1838 (the "Trail of Tears") and prosecuted the Seminole War. He defused a confrontation with Canada and declined to annex Texas. Soundly defeated by William Henry Harrison in the "log cabin and hard cider" campaign of 1840, Van Buren lost the 1844 Democratic nomination due to his Texas stance. In 1848, he ran for president as a Free Soiler, dividing the Democrats and helping to ensure the election of the Whig Gen. Zachary Taylor. Van Buren died in Kinderhook on July 24, 1862.

—ROBERT P. FORBES

See Also: *Nullification; Trail of Tears.*

BIBLIOGRAPHY: Cole, Donald B., *Martin Van Buren and the American Political System* (Princeton Univ. Press 1984); Niven, John, *Martin Van Buren: The Romantic Age of American Politics* (Oxford Univ. Press 1983); Remini, Robert V., *Martin Van Buren and the Making of the Democratic Party* (Columbia Univ. Press 1959.); Van Buren, Martin, *Autobiography of Martin Van Buren,* ed. by John C. Fitzpatrick (Annual Report of the American Hist. Assoc. 1918, vol. 2. Government Printing Office 1920).

■ **VANCOUVER, GEORGE (1758-98),** English explorer and cartographer. In the wake of the explorations of James Cook, the British navy sent him in 1791 on a mission to map the northwest coast of North America, a task he took four years to complete. His report, published in 1798, provided a set of remarkably detailed and accurate maps of the Pacific coast that were used well into the 20th century.

See Also: *Exploration and Discovery.*

■ **VANDERBILT, CORNELIUS (1794-1877),** steamship and railroad promoter. A major economic figure and folk hero in the 19th century, Vanderbilt was born in Staten Island, New York. He left school at the age of 11 to work along the waterfront and at age 16 purchased a small boat to begin a ferry service in New York harbor. He expanded the service until he sold it in 1818 to become a steam ferry captain.

In 1829, with $3,000 in hand, Vanderbilt established his own steamship company, which operated numerous lines out of New York City. With fast ships and competitive prices, his business prospered. After 1849, during the California Gold Rush, Vanderbilt built faster ships to service his route from New York to San Francisco via Nicaragua. Entering the Atlantic trade in 1854, he found it difficult to compete with the highly subsidized British Cunard Line.

Worth more than $10 million, Vanderbilt began to invest in railroads in 1857. His shrewd and often ruthless business acumen again served him well, as he purchased and consolidated several rail systems into one that stretched from New York to Buffalo. Despite competition, Vanderbilt's railroad empire fortune exceeded $100 million. Although he donated $1 million to found Vanderbilt University in Nashville, Tennessee, Vanderbilt bequeathed his entire estate to his son William.

—GUY NELSON

See Also: *Industrial Revolution; Railroads.*

At the age of 16, Cornelius Vanderbilt began a ferry service between Manhattan and Staten Island. He made a fortune in steamships and railroads.

■ **VANDERLYN, JOHN (1775-1852),** American romantic painter. Born in Kingston, New York, Vanderlyn was apprenticed to an art dealer in New York City. There he came to the attention of Sen. Aaron Burr, who arranged for Vanderlyn to work in portrait painter Gilbert Charles Stuart's studio and then, in 1796, sent him to Paris to study. Vanderlyn aspired to history painting and executed canvases with both American subjects, as in *Death of Jane McCrea* (1804), and classical ones, as in *Marius Amid the Ruins of Carthage* (1807).

See Also: Burr, Aaron; Painting; Stuart, Gilbert Charles.

■ **VAN DEVANTER, WILLIS (1859-1941),** associate justice of the U.S. Supreme Court (1910-37). Born in Marion, Indiana, he moved to Wyoming (1884) and became a leading figure in territorial politics. On the Eighth Circuit U.S. Court of Appeals (1903-10) and the Supreme Court, Van Devanter was devoted to limited government and also the most important of the "Four Horsemen," the conservative justices who opposed Pres. Franklin D. Roosevelt's New Deal.

See Also: Supreme Court.

■ **VAUDEVILLE,** type of live variety show that became extremely popular in the United States during the second half of the 19th century. Vaudeville shows had their roots in both British music hall performances and American minstrelsy. The French term vaudeville came to describe the singers, dancers, musicians, acrobats, jugglers, and comedians that typically converged in revue-style performances. Composed of a series of unconnected acts, vaudeville shows had no plot and usually drew from popular forms, themes, and music.

Vaudeville was often associated with bawdy, working-class establishments until Tony Pastor in 1881 opened a theater in New York dedicated to what he referred to as clean, family, variety entertainment. Pastor is sometimes considered the "father" of vaudeville, but others like B. F. Keith contributed greatly to the genre's success. By 1915, Keith's booking company controlled 1,500 theaters across the county. The shows were almost entirely run by booking agencies. A separate organization, the Theater Owners Booking Association, scheduled African-American acts for black audiences.

Vaudeville reached its zenith with the opening of New York's Palace Theater in 1913, which featured such performers as Sarah Bernhardt and Maurice Barrymore. By the 1920s, the variety shows were supplanted by musical theater, radio, and films, yet vaudeville continued in some theaters well into the 20th century.

—CATHERINE A. HAULMAN

BIBLIOGRAPHY: DiMeglio, John E., *Vaudeville, U.S.A.* (Bowling Green Univ. Press 1973); Snyder, Robert W., *The Voice of the City: Vaudeville and Popular Culture in New York* (Oxford Univ. Press 1989).

■ **VEBLEN, THORSTEIN (1857-1929),** economist and social critic. Veblen was born in Cato, Wisconsin. He taught social science at the University of Chicago (1892-1906), Stanford University (1906-

09), the University of Missouri (1911-18), and the New School for Social Research in New York City (1919). Veblen is perhaps best known for *The Theory of the Leisure Class* (1899), in which he coined the phrase "conspicuous consumption" to describe the concept of social status based on the ability to purchase. Veblen critiqued the growing industrial and corporate forms of mass production in *The Theory of Business Enterprise* (1904) and *The Instinct of Workmanship* (1914). In his later books, such as *The Engineers and the Price System* (1921) and *Absentee Ownership and Business Enterprise in Recent Times* (1923), he advocated replacing a sole concentration on business competition with a concern for the public good in the management of industrial production. Veblen's work provided rigorous backing to reformers and activists in the Progressive Era.

See Also: Progressivism.

■ **VENTURI, ROBERT (1925-),** architect and theorist. Born in Philadelphia, Venturi was educated at Princeton University and worked for architects Eero Saarinen and Louis Kahn. Venturi called into question the austerity of modernism and championed the vernacular both in designs, such as the 1963 house for his mother at Chestnut Hill, Pennsylvania, and in writings, such as *Learning from Las Vegas* (1972), which he coauthored with his wife and colleague, Denise Scott Brown, and their associate, Steven Izenour.

See Also: Architecture; Kahn, Louis Isadore; Saarinen, Eero.

■ **VERACRUZ, BATTLE OF (1847),** battle in the Mexican War. Leading the main U.S. invasion of Mexico, Gen. Winfield Scott landed his 10,000 troops near the fortified coastal city of Veracruz in early March. Scott ordered his soldiers to surround the city and attack from the rear. After cutting off supply lines, the Americans relentlessly bombarded the city and refused to allow women, children, and other civilians to leave. With more than 1,000 dead, the Mexicans surrendered Veracruz on March 27.

See Also: Mexican War; Scott, Winfield.

■ **VERMONT,** the least populous of the New England states. It is bounded on the north by Quebec, on the west by New York, on the south by Massachu-

setts, and on the east by New Hampshire. The Connecticut River forms its boundary with New Hampshire, and it shares Lake Champlain with New York. The Green Mountains extend north-south through the state. Vermont is two-thirds rural, a higher proportion than any other state. Vermont joined the United States in 1791, the first state to do so after the original 13.

Capital: Montpelier. Area: 9,615 square miles. Population (1995 est.): 585,000.

See Also: Allen, Ethan; Champlain, Samuel de; Champlain, Lake; Connecticut River; Coolidge, (John) Calvin; Green Mountain Boys; Green Mountains; Lake Champlain, Battle of.

■ **VERRAZANO, GIOVANNI DA (c. 1485- c. 1528),** Florentine explorer. Sailing for the French king, Francis I, in 1524, Verrazano explored the Atlantic coast of North America from present-day North Carolina to Newfoundland. Searching for a passage to the Pacific Ocean and the markets of China and the East Indies, he discovered the mouth of the Hudson River and Narragansett Bay. He anchored in New York Bay between Staten Island and Manhattan, a body of water now known as the Verrazano Narrows and spanned by the bridge of the same name. In a letter to the French king, Verrazano asserted that his coastal reconnaissance proved that North America represented an independent continent. During a second crossing of the Atlantic in 1528, he again searched for a western passage to Cathay (China). Landing on a Caribbean island, en route to Central America, Verrazano was killed by West Indian natives.

See Also: Exploration and Discovery; Northwest Passage.

BIBLIOGRAPHY: Morison, Samuel Eliot, *The Great Explorers: The European Discovery of America* (Oxford Univ. Press 1978).

■ **VERSAILLES, TREATY OF (1919),** treaty signed at Versailles, France, on June 28 that officially ended World War I. The Paris Conference convened from December 1918 to May 1919, with Pres. Woodrow Wilson's Fourteen Points used as a basis for the talks. The Allies, however, were less interested in creating what Wilson termed a "just peace" than in exacting reparations and territory from the Germans, who were allowed no part in the negotiations and forced to accept a "war guilt clause" and agree to pay the astronomical sum of $33 billion to the European victors. Russia also was not represented. Wilson's Fourteen Points called for the establishment of a League of Nations, and that proposal was adopted, although Wilson had to bargain away much of the rest of his plan to appease the Allies. The U.S. Senate was prepared to ratify the treaty with several reservations having to do with the League, but the intransigent Wilson refused to accept some of them, and so the treaty was ultimately rejected by the United States.

See Also: Fourteen Points; Wilson, (Thomas) Woodrow; World War I.

BIBLIOGRAPHY: Mee, Charles L., Jr., *The End of Order: Versailles 1919* (E. P. Dutton 1980).

■ **VESEY CONSPIRACY (1822),** plan for a slave rebellion in Charleston, South Carolina, in June 1822, led by a free black carpenter, Denmark Vesey. Originally a slave, Vesey purchased his freedom after winning $1,500 in a local lottery in 1800. Vesey's hatred of slavery and of white domination appears only to have grown after he purchased himself. He also became a leader in a local branch of the African Methodist Episcopal Church from 1817.

The most active phase of organizing for the rebellion occurred between January and June 1822. Vesey gathered about him a core of committed conspirators, all also devoted members of the church. All of these slaves were highly trusted by their masters and allowed to hire their own time, so they could move about freely in Charleston and the surrounding rice plantations without arousing suspicion. They were instrumental in recruiting hundreds more slaves for the revolt. While the original date for the uprising was set for July 15, the date was advanced to Sunday, June 16. Sunday was an opportune day, for slaves poured into Charleston from the surrounding countryside to sell and buy in the black-dominated marketplace. By early June well over 100 were actively involved in the plot, and a Vesey cohort claimed that he had more than 6,000 slaves ready in the countryside. The leaders planned to situate armed columns of slaves at various points around the city and attack it. As surprised whites emerged from their houses, they

were to be killed. Vesey inspired the conspirators with the example of the successful slave revolt in Haiti in the 1790s and claimed that Haiti's president, Jean-Pierre Boyer, would send ships to evacuate them if the rebellion failed. The suspicions of officials were raised on June 8 when a lesser conspirator confessed. By the planned evening of attack, the militia was out in full force and any massing of the rebels was impossible. Postponing the attack, Vesey and his principal associates were soon arrested and summarily tried and were hanged on July 2. By the end of the trials and hangings in August, 35 of the rebels had been executed and 43 deported. While no uprising occurred, significant repercussions from the conspiracy followed closely: the African church was razed and a reinforced slave code placed new restrictions on blacks. The scale and viability of the conspiracy deeply shook the white populace.

—PETER HINKS

See Also: Slave Revolts.

BIBLIOGRAPHY: Freehling, William, *Prelude to Civil War: The Nullification Controversy in South Carolina, 1816-1836* (Harper & Row 1966).

■ **VESPUCCI, AMERIGO (1454-1512),** Italian navigator and explorer, for whom the Americas are named. The Florence-born Vespucci, sailing for Spain, discovered the mouth of the Amazon River during a 1499 expedition that also visited the West Indies. During a 1501 voyage for the Portuguese, he traced the coast of South America as far south as the Rio de la Plata. Vespucci's system for computing longitude and his three transatlantic voyages established the extent of the South American mainland, leading to a more accurate understanding of the globe. His false claim of having made a 1497 voyage to South America led to his being credited initially with the discovery of the New World mainland. This confusion led to his name being affixed to early maps of the *Mundus Novus* by Martin Waldseemüller in 1507. In 1508 Vespucci was appointed Spain's pilot major, responsible for training mariners and charting advances in New World mapping.

See Also: Exploration and Discovery.

BIBLIOGRAPHY: Morison, Samuel Eliot, *The Great Explorers: The European Discovery of America* (Oxford Univ. Press 1978).

■ **VETERANS ADMINISTRATION ACT (1930),** federal law creating the Veterans Administration (VA) to supervise all federal programs for military veterans. The VA administers a network of hospitals as well as pension, insurance, and education programs.

See Also: New Deal.

■ **VETO,** *(Latin: I Forbid)* executive power to reject legislative bills. When the president vetoes a bill passed by the House and Senate, the measure is returned to the branch of Congress in which it originated. The U.S. Constitution requires that the president provide reasons for his veto (Article I, Section 7). If both houses then approve the legislation by a two-thirds vote, the bill becomes law, and the veto is overridden. The president may also refuse either to sign or veto the bill. Then, it becomes law after 10 congressional working days. If Congress adjourns during those 10 days, the bill is "dead," and the president has exercised what is known as a "pocket veto." Most presidential vetoes are not overridden because it is difficult to secure a two-thirds majority in both branches of Congress.

State constitutions also provide veto powers to their governors. However, the majority needed to override varies by state. In addition, some states allow the governor to veto portions of a bill. This practice, called a line-item veto, has been supported by presidents from both parties.

In 1996, the Republican-controlled 104th Congress passed a bill that grants the president limited line-item veto power. Pres. Bill Clinton signed the measure, which took effect in 1997. However, most constitutional scholars and members of Congress believe an unrestricted line-item veto would require a constitutional amendment.

—ALEXANDER WELLEK

See Also: Clinton, William Jefferson (Bill); Constitution of the United States; President of the United States.

BIBLIOGRAPHY: Jackson, Carlton, *Presidential Vetoes, 1792-1945* (Univ. of Georgia Press 1976); Watson, Richard, *Presidential Vetoes and Public Policy* (Univ. Press of Kansas 1993).

■ **VICE PRESIDENT OF THE UNITED STATES,** the nation's second highest elected official. Article I,

Section 3, of the U.S. Constitution stipulates that the vice president must meet the same qualifications as the president, although the powers of his office are limited to serving as the presiding officer of the U.S. Senate and casting the tie-breaking ballot if the Senate is equally divided. The vice president can be removed by the impeachment process set out in Article II, Section 4, of the Constitution.

The Constitution specifies (Article II, Section 1) that in the event of the death, resignation, or inability of the president to discharge his duties, those duties shall "devolve upon" the vice president. Vice presidents have succeeded to the presidency following the deaths of Presidents William Henry Harrison in 1841, Zachary Taylor in 1850, Abraham Lincoln in 1865, James Garfield in 1881, William McKinley in 1901, Warren G. Harding in 1923, Franklin D. Roosevelt in 1945, John F. Kennedy in 1963, and with the resignation of Pres. Richard M. Nixon in 1974. Pres. Theodore Roosevelt became the first vice president to succeed to the presidency and subsequently win the position by election.

In early American political history, the presidential candidate with the second highest number of electoral votes became the vice president. The 12th Amendment to the Constitution (1804) provided separate electoral ballots for president and vice president. Since the 20th Amendment (1933), the president and vice president have taken the oath of office at the same ceremony on January 20. If the election is not decided in the electoral college, the vice president is chosen by the Senate from the two top candidates. A two-thirds quorum is necessary with a majority of the entire Senate needed for election.

Vice presidents were generally selected to balance the ticket by providing candidates of different regional, age, and even philosophical backgrounds. They had few responsibilities, and the job was generally considered a "dead-end" position, particularly for anyone with political ambitions.

The office was strengthened in the 20th century as the vice president began to attend cabinet meetings, serve on the National Security Council by act of Congress (1949), and generally receive and assume greater responsibilities from the president. Moreover, in recent years a number of vice presidents have either become president (Harry S. Truman, Richard M. Nixon, Lyndon B. Johnson, Gerald R. Ford, George H. W. Bush) or unsuccessfully run for the office.

The position and role of the vice president was clarified and strengthened by the 25th Amendment (1967). It specifies that, if the office of vice president becomes vacant, the president shall nominate a replacement who must be confirmed by the Senate. Prior to 1967, if the vice president became president or did not finish his term, the office remained vacant until the next election. The amendment also establishes procedures whereby the vice president can temporarily assume the duties of president if the latter is incapacitated.

The 25th Amendment was employed when Vice Pres. Spiro T. Agnew was forced to resign in 1973 over charges that he had accepted illegal payments while governor of Maryland and vice president. President Nixon nominated the House Minority Leader, Gerald Ford, who became president with the resignation of Nixon. Ford, using the 25th Amendment, nominated former New York Gov. Nelson A. Rockefeller as his replacement.

In the modern electronic era, the high visibility enjoyed by the vice president is likely to make the position attractive. If prospective candidates believe they will be offered major responsibilities by the president, the position will become increasingly prestigious and the main path to the presidency.

—ALEXANDER WELLEK

See Also: Constitution of the United States; President of the United States.

BIBLIOGRAPHY: Dunlap, Leslie, *Our Vice Presidents and Second Ladies* (Scarecrow Press 1988); Goldstein, Joel, *The Modern American Vice Presidency: The Transformation of a Political Institution* (Princeton Univ. Press 1981); Light, Paul, *Vice Presidential Power* (Johns Hopkins Univ. Press 1984); Natoli, Marie, *American Prince, American Pauper: The Contemporary Vice President in Perspective* (Greenwood Press 1985); Sindler, Allan, *Unchosen Presidents: The Vice President and Other Frustrations of Presidential Succession* (Univ. of California Press 1976).

■ **VICKSBURG, SIEGE OF (1863),** decisive Civil War confrontation. Gen. Ulysses S. Grant had been trying since the autumn of 1862 to take Vicksburg, the Confederate "Gibraltar of the West" on the Mississippi River. In April, Grant sent cavalry to tear up Vicksburg's supply lines while his army crossed the Mississippi below the city, uniting with a Union flotilla that had blasted its way past Vicksburg's batteries. After winning a series of engagements in mid-May, the Union force placed the city under siege. Its garrison and civilians starving, Vicksburg surrendered on July 4, cutting the Confederacy in two.

See Also: Civil War; Grant, Ulysses Simpson.

■ **VICTOR, FRANCES AURETTA (1826-1902),** historian, author of dime novels, stories about pioneer women, and romantic poetry. Born in Rome, New York, she contributed greatly to the local history of Oregon and Washington, writing at least five volumes of Hubert Howe Bancroft's *History of the Pacific States* (1890). Her sister was author Metta Fuller Victor.

■ **VICTOR, METTA FULLER (1831-85),** author of popular literature, born in Rome, New York. She surpassed her older sister, Frances Auretta Victor, in popularity, editing the *Cosmopolitan Art Journal* and publishing more than 100 dime novels. Her top seller was a "slave romance" titled *Maum Guinea and Her Plantation "Children"* (1861).

See Also: Novel.

■ **VICTORY LOANS,** government-sponsored drives to help defray the costs of World War II through the sale of "victory bonds." Approximately $150 billion worth of bonds were sold through the war years, often at large rallies attended by celebrities.

See Also: World War II.

■ **VIETNAM WAR.** American involvement in Vietnam is surrounded in controversy. Some believed that the war represented a noble crusade that delayed the spread of communism in Indochina for 20 years. Others pictured an arrogant America squandering its power in a regional civil war.

Prelude to American Combat. During the Korean War, Pres. Harry S. Truman reiterated the "containment" policy to block Communist expansion and provided munitions to French colonial troops fighting Communist guerrillas in Indochina. Noting that Ho Chi Minh, a Vietnamese Communist, led Indochinese nationalists

American soldiers rush a wounded comrade to a waiting medical evacuation helicopter during the Vietnam War.

against the French, some Americans contended that the Soviet Union directed Communist actions in several countries.

Also supporting containment, Pres. Dwight D. Eisenhower followed Truman in office and approved more assistance to the French but refused to dispatch U.S. forces to Indochina. Defeated at the battle of Dien Bien Phu, the French withdrew from Vietnam in 1954. The Geneva Accords temporarily divided Vietnam at the 17th parallel, pending national elections that were never held. Ho Chi Minh governed from Hanoi in North Vietnam, and in Saigon Ngo Dinh Diem administered South Vietnam. Buddhists and other opponents maintained that Diem, a Catholic, was oppressive and corrupt. Diem attacked his adversaries, including Communist guerrillas, whom he derogatorily labeled "Viet Cong" (VC). Determined to unite Vietnam and combining

communism with nationalism, Ho Chi Minh mobilized for war against Diem's regime. Eight hundred American advisers trained the South's Army of the Republic of Vietnam (ARVN) in conventional warfare, but factionalism and corruption undercut its effectiveness. By contrast, the North's People's Army of Vietnam (PAVN) was skillful and impressive.

In 1961, Pres. John F. Kennedy promised that America would "pay any price" to aid allies against communism. Antagonistically, Soviet Premier Nikita Khrushchev pledged Communist support for "wars of national liberation." To sustain South Vietnam, Kennedy sent more than 15,000 military personnel by 1963, including "Green Beret" Special Forces units. Kennedy's critics asserted that America had replaced France as a colonial power in Indochina. Finding Diem intractable, Kennedy approved a coup to topple him on Nov. 1, 1963. Three weeks later Kennedy was assassinated. The new president, Lyndon B. Johnson, kept Kennedy's advisers, including the influential secretary of defense, Robert S. McNamara.

American Buildup. In the summer of 1964 a controversial incident drew America further into the Vietnam conflict. According to President Johnson, North Vietnamese patrol boats attacked U.S. Navy ships in international waters of the Tonkin Gulf. Johnson sought support in Congress. Passed overwhelmingly on Aug. 7, 1964, the Gulf of Tonkin Resolution authorized Johnson to block North Vietnamese aggression. Soon, the Viet Cong attacked American bases in South Vietnam. PAVN regiments entered the South through Laos and Cambodia along the "Ho Chi Minh Trail," thus widening the war. Johnson ordered marine and army divisions to South Vietnam.

Johnson's choice of strategy and decisions as commander in chief were debatable. To fulfill his goal of preventing South Vietnam from falling under communist control, Johnson employed the strategy of limited war. Concerned about spreading the war, he would not use nuclear weapons or invade North Vietnam. Johnson tried to balance Vietnam with his ambitious domestic programs, the Great Society. Critics believed that Johnson was never comfortable making military decisions or conferring with the joint chiefs of staff. The president was skeptical of reports from the military and the Central Intelligence Agency. Relying mostly on civilians for advice, Johnson and McNamara underestimated the North Vietnamese and miscalculated the demands of the war.

Despite the Green Berets' veneer of counterinsurgency, the U.S. Army was a conventional force of mechanized infantry, tanks, and artillery designed to defeat Russia. Around 1960, the army developed the concept of having hundreds of helicopters transport large units in Europe and transferred the technique to Vietnam. To support U.S. troops, bases were built throughout South Vietnam. To manage personnel assignments, the Pentagon set combat tours at one year.

Rejecting mobilization of military reserves, Johnson prosecuted the war by increasing draft calls, sparking protests against conscription. By December 1965, there were 180,000 troops stationed in Vietnam. From ships offshore and bases in nearby countries, the navy and air force contributed to the war effort. By December 1966, almost 400,000 soldiers and marines were in South Vietnam; later the total reached 543,000.

Johnson's employment of airpower caused contention. After the VC attacked the American base at Pleiku, South Vietnam, on Feb. 6, 1965, Johnson and McNamara prioritized targets in North Vietnam. Rather than striking many targets in a few weeks, an air bombardment campaign, called "Rolling Thunder," gradually increased over many months. Squadrons, including B-52 bombers, blasted most strategic targets. But North Vietnam established an excellent air defense system, shot down many U.S. planes, and took many pilots prisoner. Johnson mistakenly believed that incre-

VIETNAM WAR

■ U.S bases

0 ——— 150 ——— 300 Miles

0 ——— 150 ——— 300 Kilometers

mental bombing would show his restraint and persuade North Vietnam to halt the war.

Undeterred by America's buildup, Ho Chi Minh and his chief strategist, Gen. Vo Nguyen Giap, remained dedicated to unifying Vietnam. They may have interpreted Johnson's gradual application of American force as a lack of resolve and believed a protracted war was to their advantage. Integrating strategy, logistics, tactics, diplomacy, terrorism, deception, and propaganda, the Communist leaders fought a total war.

Trying to categorize the war raises debates. Combat intensity varied across Vietnam in jungles, mountains, coastal plains, rice paddies, and cities, combining elements of conventional and guerrilla warfare. Obviously, it was a civil war: Vietnamese of different ideologies and regions fought to control the nation. But international rivalries overlay the civil war: Russian and Chinese Communists poured military aid into North Vietnam. Johnson decided that stopping those supplies might bring China or Russia into the war. Covertly, China sent thousands of military engineers and other advisers to North Vietnam. South Vietnam received modest help from South Korea, Australia, New Zealand, Thailand, and the Philippines.

American Strategy and Tactics. As commander of American forces in Vietnam, Gen. William C. Westmoreland designed "search and destroy" operations to achieve high levels of Communist attrition. When battles or firefights occurred, Americans, supported by artillery and air strikes, inflicted serious casualties on the enemy, but attrition was unsuccessful. If their losses prevented conventional operations, the PAVN consolidated elsewhere or left a province to VC guerrillas. For three years the Americans claimed victory in major campaigns, such as that in the Ia Drang Valley (October-November 1965). In late 1967, General Westmoreland announced that he could see "light at the end of the tunnel"—the war was being won.

Contradicting Westmoreland's announcement, the VC and the PAVN launched a surprise offensive on Jan. 30, 1968, attacking major cities and American bases in the South and violating the cease-fire for Tet, the annual Vietnamese new year's holiday. Displaying careful North Vietnamese planning, the Tet Offensive marked a turning point in the war. Americans counterattacked, inflicting heavy losses on the VC; PAVN regulars replaced them. Tactically, Tet was a communist defeat, but the offensive's ferocity, high U.S. casualties, and controversial media coverage, especially of the battles at Hué and Khe Sanh, turned many Americans against the war, giving the Communists a strategic victory. Johnson's war policy had failed; he declined to run for reelection.

Saying he had a secret plan to end the war, Richard M. Nixon won the 1968 presidential election. Nixon ended the draft and implemented "Vietnamization": ARVN would be enlarged, resupplied, and take over combat operations while U.S. forces withdrew. As Gen. Creighton Abrams supervised the phased withdrawal, U.S. losses mounted. American soldiers' morale declined; some defied orders or indulged heavily in alcohol or drugs. American airpower supported the withdrawal by heavy bombing of North Vietnam and Cambodia and mining the North's seaport of Haiphong. An American and ARVN incursion into Cambodia (April-May 1970) to destroy PAVN sanctuaries also covered the withdrawal. Many Americans protested against Nixon's bombing, the Cambodian incursion, and the slow withdrawal of U.S. military units, completed by November 1972. The last American military advisers left in March 1973, following a negotiated cease-fire in Indochina in which Henry Kissinger played a major role. Beginning in December 1974, the PAVN conducted a massive conventional invasion and won the war on Apr. 30, 1975, when Saigon fell.

America suffered 58,000 dead (killed in action or died from disease or accident) and 313,000 wounded in Vietnam. There were untold thousands of Indochinese casualties. Controversies lingered over U.S. prisoners of war and missing in action. During the 1980s, an all-volunteer American military reformed and in 1990-91 won the Persian Gulf War. Vietnam stained the image of presidents, made allies question U.S. foreign policies, caused politicians to explain why they did not serve in the military, and produced widespread cynicism among Americans. Disputes continued over the war's causes, conduct, and meaning, making Vietnam a perpetually contentious subject.

—JOSEPH G. DAWSON III

See Also: *Abrams, Creighton; Gulf of Tonkin Resolution; Johnson, Lyndon Baines; Kissinger, Henry A.; McNamara, Robert S.; Nixon, Richard Milhous; Tet Offensive; Westmoreland, William Childs.*

BIBLIOGRAPHY: Clodfelter, Mark, *The Limits of Airpower* (Free Press 1989); Herring, George, *America's Longest War* (revised, McGraw-Hill 1992); Krepinevich, Andrew, *The Army and Vietnam* (Johns Hopkins Univ. Press 1986); Palmer, Bruce, *The Twenty-five Year War: America's Military Role in Vietnam* (Univ. of Kentucky Press 1984).

■ **VIGILANTES,** members of extralegal citizens organizations who police and administer justice. Usually associated with the western frontier, vigilantes have existed in America since the colonial period. Vigilantes, who throughout U.S. history have had such names as Regulators, Moderators, Militiamen, and White Caps, performed various functions. Some acted as socializing forces in the absence of official law enforcement and legitimate legal systems, while others, like the Ku Klux Klan, attempted to rid their communities of different racial, ethnic, or religious groups.

The first large-scale vigilante movement arose in the back country of South Carolina during the 1760s. Frontier farmers, known as Regulators, protesting against eastern domination of government, resorted to armed force to claim control of the political and legal systems of western counties. Similar organizations emerged during the 19th century, the most extensive ones in East Texas (1840-44), Missouri (1842-44), and southern Illinois (1846-50). Many of these Regulator movements gave rise to countermovements, often called Moderators.

Apart from rebelling against unpopular laws and local governments, vigilante movements arose across the West during the mid and late 19th century in response to lawlessness. Many of the hundreds of local organizations often administered justice by lynch law in order to deal swiftly with criminals. Accused transgressors were given hasty trials and, if found guilty, banished, flogged, or hanged. Although vigilantism ceased on a large scale at the close of the 19th century, it continued sporadically in the West and South in the 1900s.

See Also: Frontier in American History; Ku Klux Klan (KKK); Regulators.

BIBLIOGRAPHY: Brown, Richard Maxwell, *Strain of Violence: Historical Studies of American Violence and Vigilantism* (Oxford Univ. Press 1975); Culberson, William C., *Vigilantism: Political History of Private Power in America* (Greenwood Press 1990).

■ **VINLAND,** 10th-century Viking settlement on the coast of modern-day Newfoundland, Canada. More than 500 years before Columbus sailed for the Caribbean, Scandinavian explorers, also known as Vikings, explored the North Atlantic region including Greenland, Labrador, and Newfoundland. Eric the Red sailed west from Iceland in 984 to a large island in the North Atlantic he named Greenland. During the next decade Vikings created small settlements on the southern coastlines of Greenland as well as along the coast of Labrador. Leif Eriksson, son of Eric the Red, established the settlement of Vinland in northern Newfoundland near present-day L'Anse aux Meadows. Although the Vikings were determined to establish themselves in this region, their settlements were short-lived owing to the distance from Iceland, hostile Indians, and political turmoil in Scandinavia.

■ **VINSON, FREDERICK MOORE (1890-1953),** chief justice of the United States (1946-53). Born in Louisa, Kentucky, he attended Centre College, where he achieved highest academic honors and subsequently earned his law degree. A Democrat, Vinson was elected district attorney (1921) and then elected to Congress (1925-29, 1931-37), where he was a strong supporter of Pres. Franklin D. Roosevelt's New Deal policies. Vinson was appointed to the U.S. Court of Appeals (1937) but resigned (1943) to become director of economic stabilization. He held several other executive branch posts and in 1945 was named secretary of the treasury by Pres. Harry S. Truman. He was appointed chief justice the next year.

Not highly regarded as a legal theorist or scholar, Vinson was a politician whose skills were needed to administer a Court that was split along ideological lines. Vinson usually voted with the conservative wing headed by Justices Robert Jackson and Felix Frankfurter. He generally backed the actions of the executive branch, joining the minority that supported Truman's seizure of the steel industry in *Youngstown Sheet & Tube Co. v.*

Sawyer (1952) and supporting government suppression of the Communist party in *Dennis v. United States* (1951). But Vinson was a liberal on civil rights, upholding several challenges to state racial segregation laws.

—TIM ASHWELL

See Also: *Supreme Court; Youngstown Sheet & Tube Co. v. Sawyer.*

BIBLIOGRAPHY: Palmer, Jan, *The Vinson Court Era: The Supreme Court's Conference Votes* (AMS Press 1990).

■ **VIRGINIA,** a South Atlantic state. It is bounded on the north and west by West Virginia and Kentucky, on the south by Tennessee and North Carolina, on the east by Chesapeake Bay and the Atlantic Ocean, on the east and north by Maryland, and on the northeast by the District of Columbia. The Potomac River forms part of its northeast border. Virginia slopes eastward from Appalachian Mountain ranges to the coastal plain. Because of Virginia's many military installations and its proximity to Washington, D.C., the federal government plays a larger role in its economy than in any other state but Hawaii. Hampton Roads is one of the nation's busiest ports.

Virginia was the first English colony in the New World, one of the original 13 colonies, the seat of the Confederacy, and the birthplace of eight U.S. presidents, more than any other state. Famous Virginians include presidents George Washington and Thomas Jefferson and Confederate Gen. Robert E. Lee. The state was the principal theater of the Civil War.

Capital: Richmond. Area: 40,598 square miles. Population (1995 est.): 6,618,000.

See Also: *Appalachian Mountains; Bacon's Rebellion; Berkeley, Sir William; Jamestown Settlement; Jefferson, Thomas; Lee, Robert Edward; Potomac River; Turner, Nat; Washington, George; Williamsburg; Yorktown, Siege of.*

■ **VIRGINIA AND KENTUCKY RESOLUTIONS (1798-99),** protest against the Alien and Sedition Acts of 1798 and the administration of Pres. John Adams. The first resolution was passed by the Kentucky legislature on Nov. 16, 1798, the second by the Virginia legislature on December 24 of the same year. The following year, on November 22, Kentucky reiterated its resolution, this time including the word "nullification"—the idea that a state's legislature can negate a federal law that it does not support. The Virginia and Kentucky Resolutions took the position that Congress had overstepped the constitutional authority of the federal government in signing the Alien and Sedition Acts. The Alien Act allowed the U.S. president to deport undesirable foreigners even in time of peace. The Sedition Act called for the imprisonment of anyone who spoke out against the U.S. government or its officials.

Thomas Jefferson wrote the resolution passed by the Kentucky legislature, while James Madison wrote the Virginia resolution. Both resolutions expressed the view that the federal government was a "compact" between the national government and the states, and that, as such, the states had the power to judge if the national government had broken its part of the "compact." Other states failed to endorse similar resolutions, much to Jefferson's dismay. The Virginia and Kentucky Resolutions were the articulation of a radical states'-rights view of the Union and were later used by the Southern states to support first nullification of the national tariff and later secession from the Union.

—KATHRYN A. ABBOTT

See Also: *Adams, John; Alien and Sedition Acts; Nullification.*

BIBLIOGRAPHY: Levy, Leonard, *Legacy of Suppression: Freedom of Speech in Early American History* (Belknap 1960); Smith, James M., *Freedom's Fetters: The Alien and Sedition Laws and American Civil Liberties* (Cornell Univ. Press 1966).

■ **VIRGINIA PLAN (1787),** proposal presented to the Constitutional Convention by James Madison calling for a national legislative branch with representation based on population. Portions of the plan were incorporated into the Connecticut Compromise.

See Also: *Connecticut Compromise; Constitution of the United States.*

■ **VIRGINIA RESOLVES (1765),** series of resolutions passed in the Virginia House of Burgesses against the Stamp Act. Drafted by Patrick Henry, the resolves helped set the tone for the colonial denunciation of the Stamp Act and other taxes.

See Also: Henry, Patrick; Revolution, American; Stamp Act.

■ **VIRGINIA STATUTE FOR RELIGIOUS FREE-DOM (1786),** one of the first official American mandates of absolute religious liberty. Drafted by Thomas Jefferson, this statute outlawed mandatory church attendance and discrimination based on religious belief. Jefferson considered it one of his three greatest achievements.

See Also: Revolution, American.

■ **VIRGIN ISLANDS,** group of about 100 islands in the West Indies, in the eastern Caribbean east of Puerto Rico. They are divided politically into an unincorporated territory of the United States and a British colony. In 1672 Danes founded the first permanent European settlement on St. Thomas. The following year African slaves were brought to work the island's sugar plantations. Slave rebellions occurred throughout the 19th century until slavery was abolished in 1848. The United States purchased the Danish Virgin Islands in 1916.

■ **VIRGIN SOIL EPIDEMICS,** diseases, previously unknown in the Americas, that devastated American Indian communities. The arrival of Europeans in North America created havoc among Indians, often even before they saw a white face. The introduction of lethal diseases caused more death among the Indians than any warfare the whites waged against them. The diseases that Europeans brought to North America depopulated vast areas of their indigenous inhabitants, who had no immunity to them.

Except for parasites, occasional malnutrition, and minor diseases, American Indians were quite healthy. They used herbal remedies and medications and practiced cleanliness in sweat baths. This proved sufficient to deal with most illness until the European arrival. The virgin soil epidemics—smallpox, measles, and perhaps the plague—spread quickly across the continent, and Indians had no way to stop their advance. Only innovative and adaptable communities were able to preserve enough of their character to survive one of these microbiological attacks. But outlasting a single epidemic was often only the overture to a series of epidemic assaults that assailed an increasingly weakened population. For example, in the 1630s and 1640s smallpox killed half the population of the Huron and Iroquois in the St. Lawrence-Great Lakes region. Two hundred years later it took two-thirds of the Blackfeet in the Montana area. Around the same time the Mandan population fell from 1,600 to fewer than 150 from the same cause.

Currently there is heated scholarly debate as to the extent of these virgin soil epidemics and the size of the pre-epidemic Indian population. Estimates vary widely from a conservative 1 million inhabitants in North America to 50 to 100 million inhabitants before the Europeans' arrival, with most historians accepting a figure of 10 to 15 million. Whatever the original number, there is little doubt as to the devastation the virgin soil epidemics wrought.

—RYAN MADDEN

See Also: Disease; Indians of North America.
BIBLIOGRAPHY: Ballantine, Betty, and Ian Ballantine, eds., *The Native Americans* (Turner 1993); Boxberger, Daniel, *Native Americans: An Ethnohistorical Approach* (Kendall/Hunt 1990).

■ **VOLSTEAD ACT.** *See: National Prohibition Enforcement Act.*

■ **VON NEUMANN, JOHN (1903-57),** mathematician. Born in Budapest, Hungary, Von Neumann earned his Ph.D. in mathematics at the University of Budapest (1926), taught in Berlin and Hamburg, and came to the United States to be a lecturer at Princeton in 1930. After teaching there he joined Princeton's new Institute for Advanced Study (1933-57). Equally at home in pure and applied mathematics, he formulated the principles of quantum mechanics, contributed to the abstract fields of logic and set theory, and developed game theory, which he and coauthor Oskar Morgenstern applied to economic behavior, social organization, and military strategy in *Theory of Games and Economic Behavior* (1944). He helped develop the atomic and hydrogen bombs and became a member of the Atomic Energy Commission (AEC) in 1955. Von Neumann played a leading role in the development of high-speed computers, introducing the idea of a stored program and working on UNIVAC, ENIAC, and ORDVAC computers. His NORC (naval ordinance research computer) predicted weather and tidal changes and solved logistical problems for the navy. Von Neumann won the AEC's Enrico Fermi award in 1956 along with the Presidential Medal of Freedom.

See Also: Computers; Science.

VOTING RIGHTS ACT, 1965 statute and later extensions mandating federal supervision of state elections, notably in the South. The acts originated in the modern civil rights crusade against voter discrimination in southern states where literacy tests, poll taxes, and all-white primaries had disfranchised African Americans for decades. After both litigation under the 1950s Civil Rights Acts and voter registration drives proved futile, civil rights groups protested. When marchers met violence in Selma, Alabama, Pres. Lyndon B. Johnson sought the 1965 Voting Rights Act.

The unprecedented 1965 act imposed direct federal control over mainly southern state and local elections, banned literacy tests and other devices restricting African-American voting, authorized federal marshals to register minority voters, and ordered states to get "preclearance" for election law changes. Enlarged in 1970 and 1975, the 1965 law became the most successful modern civil rights measure. It vastly increased minority voting and officeholding.

A pivotal 1982 extension to the act shifted policy from ending voter discrimination to securing "meaningful" ballots. Initially opposed by Pres. Ronald Reagan, it banned electoral systems that had the result, if not the intent, of reducing minority opportunity to participate in elections and elect chosen candidates. Subsequent lawsuits challenged gerrymandered and multimember districts that "diluted" minority votes. After the 1990 census, states redrew electoral district lines in compliance with the law, but Supreme Court decisions annulled some new districts as unconstitutionally "race-based." Voting Rights Act enforcement at the end of the 20th century remained contentious.

—DONALD W. ROGERS

See Also: Civil Rights Movement; Johnson, Lyndon Baines.

BIBLIOGRAPHY: Ball, Howard, Dale Krane, and Thomas P. Lauth, *Compromised Compliance: Implementation of the 1965 Voting Rights Act* (Greenwood Press 1982); Lawson, Stephen F., *Black Ballots: Voting Rights in the South, 1944-1969* (Columbia Univ. Press 1976); Parker, Frank R., *Black Votes Count: Political Empowerment in Mississippi after 1965* (Univ. of North Carolina Press 1990).

W

■ **WADE-DAVIS BILL (1864),** Radical Republican Reconstruction plan. Offered in opposition to President Lincoln's more lenient plan, the bill called for restoration of state government in the South only after half of the white male citizens swore loyalty to the Union. It also guaranteed civil rights for freed slaves but not voting rights. Lincoln vetoed the bill.

See Also: Reconstruction.

■ **WAGE AND PRICE CONTROLS,** government techniques to address the problem of wage/price inflation or to help mobilize economic resources during wartime. In a modern economy the process of wage and price inflation can normally be stopped only through a recession or depression. The government can restrain such inflation directly through wage and price controls, a process that conflicts with laissez-faire economic policy but is viewed by some as a necessary choice. In 17th-century New England and briefly during the American Revolution, colonies set maximum wages in some building trades as a response to labor shortages. Later, effective price and wage control required a visibly large administrative apparatus and often invoked some suspicion of government intervention and bureaucracy. During World War II the Office of Price Administration (1942) fixed price ceilings on all commodities except farm products, controlled rents in defense areas, rationed scarce commodities such as automobile tires, and held wartime price increases to a low 31 percent. President Truman used the Office of Economic Stabilization to stabilize wages and prices between 1950 and 1953. Between 1971 and 1973 President Nixon was the first to use general controls during peacetime, in an effort to suppress wage/price inflation and give fiscal support for employment. This move worked temporarily and helped him win the election of 1972 but fell apart in 1973 and left President Ford with galloping inflation and a steep recession.

—Annie Gilbert Coleman

See Also: Depressions and Recessions; Inflation; Laissez-faire.
BIBLIOGRAPHY: Rockoff, H., *Drastic Measures: A History of Wage and Price Controls in the United States* (Cambridge Univ. Press 1984).

■ **WAGNER, ROBERT FERDINAND (1877-1953),** Democratic politician and social reformer. He was born in Germany and came to the United States as a child. He was educated at the City College of New York and briefly worked as a lawyer before election to the New York State Assembly in 1904. In 1908 Wagner was elected to the state senate, where he served for 10 years, until being appointed a justice of the New York Supreme Court. In 1926 he was elected to the U.S. Senate, where he continued to fight for social reform until retiring in 1949.

Wagner pushed through Congress much of the New Deal legislation that Pres. Franklin D. Roosevelt, his former political associate from New York, sought as a way of addressing the economic collapse known as the Great Depression. Wagner oversaw passage of the National Industrial Recovery Act (1933), the Social Security Act (1935), and the National Labor Relations Act, commonly known as the Wagner Act (1935).

See Also: National Labor Relations Act; New Deal.
BIBLIOGRAPHY: Huthmacher, Joseph J., *Senator Robert F. Wagner and the Rise of Urban Liberalism* (Atheneum 1968).

■ **WAGNER-STEAGALL ACT (1937),** federal law creating the U.S. Housing Authority. An early urban renewal program, this New Deal legislation authorized low-interest federal loans for slum clearance and low-income housing to local governments.

See Also: New Deal.

■ **WAGON TRAINS,** important means of transporting emigrants and goods in the American

West during the decades before the construction of railroads. The best known are the wagon trains of the Overland Trail, the central route over the Great Plains and Rocky Mountains to the Pacific Coast. In reality, only a minority of the several hundred thousand immigrants to Oregon and California from the 1840s to the 1860s traveled in organized wagon trains. During the first years, when the route was unfamiliar, or during times of danger from Indians, people would come together for protection in trains of several dozen wagons. But at other times the preference was to travel in small companies, for that made grazing, camping, and sanitation easier to manage, and drivers could spread their small farm wagons out over the plain to avoid eating each other's dust.

The most impressive wagon trains of western history were those devoted to commerce. The heavily loaded Conestoga wagons of the Santa Fe Trail usually moved in large formations, often under a self-imposed military discipline, because they made such a tempting target for bandits and Indian raiders. Far less well known are the large trains of the *Métis*, the people of mixed Indian and European ancestry who lived on the northern plains. Whole communities, often including hundreds of people, would move out onto the plains once or twice annually for great communal buffalo hunts. The *Métis* traveled in distinctive two-wheeled carts, with ungreased axles (for grease quickly clogged with dust) that made an awful screeching one observer compared to "the scraping of a thousand finger nails on a thousand panes of glass," a sound that could be heard for miles. *Métis* freighters created a lucrative trade with the town of St. Paul that in value rivaled the trade with Santa Fe, but somehow the cart trains failed to find a place in the lore of western America, perhaps because they were driven by mixed-bloods rather than Missourians.

See Also: Frontier in American History; Mixed-Bloods and Mestizos; Overland Trail; Santa Fe Trail.

BIBLIOGRAPHY: Conner, Seymour V., and Jimmy M. Skaggs, *Broadcloth and Britches: The Santa Fe Trade* (Texas A&M Univ. Press 1977); Harrison, Julia D., *Métis: People Between Two Worlds* (Douglas & McIntyre 1985); Unruh, John D., Jr., *The Plains Across: The Overland Emigrants and the Trans-Mississippi West, 1840-1860* (Univ. of Illinois Press 1979).

■ **WAITE, MORRISON REMICK (1816-88),** chief justice of the United States (1874-88). The son of a lawyer who became chief justice of the Connecticut Supreme Court, Waite was born in Lyme, Connecticut, attended Yale University, read law with his father, and then migrated to Ohio, where he was admitted to the bar in 1839. A successful lawyer who was active in the state Whig and later Republican parties, Waite remained little known nationally until he was named a U.S. counsel in the *Alabama* claims arbitration cases before the Geneva tribunal (1871). After returning in triumph with a $15 million verdict, he was named chief justice by Pres. Ulysses S. Grant in 1873.

Waite proved an effective administrator and leader of the Court. Neither an innovative legal theorist nor a writer of memorable judicial opinions, he believed the states, rather than the federal government, should take the leading role in economic regulation and civil rights. Waite limited federal protection for newly freed slaves in *United States* v. *Cruikshank* (1876). He upheld state regulations, angering the railroad industry, in *Munn* v. *Illinois* (1877). In *Reynolds* v. *United States* (1879), Waite upheld the conviction in federal court of a Mormon for polygamy.

—TIM ASHWELL

See Also: Alabama Claims; Supreme Court.

BIBLIOGRAPHY: Magrath, C. Peter, *Morrison R. Waite: The Triumph of Character* (Macmillan 1963).

■ **WAKSMAN, SELMAN A. (1888-1973),** soil microbiologist who discovered the antibiotic streptomycin. Born in Priluka, Ukraine, Waksman immigrated to the United States in 1910, earned his master's degree from Rutgers under Jacob Lipman (1916), and became a naturalized citizen. He received a Ph.D. from the University of California, Berkeley, then returned to Rutgers to pursue his interest in soil microbiology for the rest of his career (1918-58). Waksman studied the roles microbes and fungi play in soils and composts, the nature of humus, and the distribution of soil microbe populations, opening up the new field of soil microbiology in the process. Research on the antibiotic properties of the mold *Penicillium* led Waksman to search for other antibiotics among microbes. His discovery of streptomycin (1943), which proved effective against the tuberculosis bacillus and penicillin-resistant bacteria, won him a Nobel Prize for Physiology and Medicine (1952). Waksman distributed over half of his patent income among the many students and associates who had researched antibiotics with him. He also founded the Institute for Microbiology (now the Waksman Institute for Microbiology) at Rutgers.

See Also: Medicine; Science.

■ **WALCOTT, MARY MORRIS (1860-1940),** naturalist and painter of wildflowers born in Philadelphia, Pennsylvania. The Smithsonian Institution published *North American Wildflowers* (1925), a five-volume collection of her watercolers. In 1933 she became president of the Society of Women Geographers.

See Also: Women in American History.

■ **WALD, LILLIAN (1867-1940),** pioneer of public health nursing and social reformer. She was born in Cincinnati, Ohio. In 1895 she founded the Henry Street Settlement to provide basic health care in the tenements of New York's Lower East Side, inventing the new field of public health nursing. She was also a leader in the child welfare movement. Her work inspired the formation, in 1913, of the National Children's Bureau.

See Also: Women in American History.

■ **WALKER, ALICE (1944-),** author. She was born in Eatonton, Georgia. While working for the Mississippi Department of Welfare, she wrote her first book, *The Third Life of Grange Copeland* (1970). She went on to produce numerous collections of short stories, poetry, essays, and novels. She won a Pulitzer Prize for *The Color Purple* (1983). In the 1970s and 1980s her scholarship was central to a revival of interest in the post-World War I movement of African-American artists in New York City known as the Harlem Renaissance.

See Also: African Americans; Harlem Renaissance; Women in American History.

■ **WALKER, DAVID (1796?-1830),** author of *An Appeal to the Colored Citizens of the World* and a leader of Boston's free black community. Walker was probably born in or near Wilmington, North Carolina, to a free woman of color. Wilmington

was the commercial center of a region rich in naval stores, lumber, and rice. Black slaves predominated there demographically 2:1 over whites and were the foundation of the region's key enterprises. They also contributed largely to the formation of the Methodist church in the town. These examples of black strength and resourcefulness likely deeply impressed Walker.

Free blacks amounted to just a handful of African Americans in the region and almost all labor—skilled and unskilled—was reserved for slaves. These realities probably led Walker to move to Charleston, South Carolina, between 1815 and 1820 where the free black population was much larger and much more economic opportunity existed for them. While in Charleston, Walker had two significant and related experiences. In 1817, a branch of the newly formed African Methodist Episcopal (AME) Church was organized in the town and immediately became a center for black religious and social life. Yet its relative independence from white control threatened local authorities who harassed it steadily and many of its members were implicated in the Vesey Slave Plot. The church was razed by the authorities in 1822. Walker, a devoted Methodist, had his thinking on the use of religion to empower and mobilize blacks likely influenced significantly by Vesey and his followers.

Walker soon left Charleston, settling by 1825 in Boston, where he opened a used-clothing shop near the wharves. He quickly became an active and leading member of Boston's energetic black community; married a local woman, Eliza Butler, in 1826; and in 1827 became Boston's principal agent of *Freedom's Journal*, the nation's first black newspaper, and was one of the founders of the Massachusetts General Colored Association, one of the first avowedly political organizations for blacks in the country. By early 1829, Walker had moved from focusing largely on organizing local blacks to conceiving bold new ways of rousing and orchestrating them nationally to fight their subjugation—North and South.

In September 1829, Walker made his greatest and most enduring contribution to this effort, publishing his *Appeal to the Colored Citizens of the World*, one of the most significant black political documents of the 19th century. In unprecedented terms of outrage and vividness, Walker excoriated the uniquely savage and un-Christian treatment blacks suffered in the United States, especially as slaves. The *Appeal* trumpeted the worth of blacks as individuals, their noble history in Africa, and God's special love for them and summoned them to refuse to submit further to enslavement and degradation.

In late 1829, Walker commenced a bold and innovative plan to circulate the work covertly throughout the South. Relying on black and white sailors to introduce the book into key southern ports and sometimes using the mail, Walker envisioned it moving from the ports far into the hinterlands and rallying large numbers of slaves to its message. While finally no serious repercussions issued from its circulation and officials seized many of the books, its presence alarmed white southerners who responded by strengthening laws against slave literacy, the circulation of antislavery matter, and contact between black sailors and local blacks. Walker's analysis and forthrightness heralded a new, more assertive activism among African Americans. He died of a lung disease in August 1830.

—Peter Hinks

See Also: African Americans; Civil Rights Movement.
BIBLIOGRAPHY: Hinks, Peter, *"To Awaken My Afflicted Brethren": David Walker and the Problem of Antebellum Slave Resistance* (Pennsylvania State Univ. Press 1997); Stuckey, Sterling, *Slave Culture: Nationalist Theory and the Foundations of Black America* (Oxford Univ. Press 1987).

■ **WALLACE, GEORGE C. (1919-),** four-term governor of Alabama (1963-67, 1971-79, 1983-87). Born in Clio, Alabama, he served in the Alabama state legislature (1947-53) and as an elected judge (1953-59), when he blocked federal civil rights regulations with decisions upholding state segregation laws. Pledging "segregation forever," Wallace was elected governor in 1962 and in 1963 stood in the doorway of a University of Alabama administration building to prevent two African-American students from enrolling, forcing the federal government to mobilize the National Guard. He ran for president as an independent in 1968 and carried five southern states by emphasizing limited federal government, states' rights, and traditional values.

In his 1963 inaugural speech as governor of Alabama, George C. Wallace famously declared, "Segregation now! Segregation tomorrow! Segregation forever!"

He sought the Democratic nomination in 1972, but his campaign was cut short when he was shot and wounded during a campaign rally in Laurel, Maryland. Partially paralyzed, he served three more terms as governor.

See Also: Civil Rights Movement.
BIBLIOGRAPHY: Carter, Dan T., *The Politics of Rage* (Simon & Schuster 1995).

■ **WALLACE, HENRY A. (1888-1965),** vice president of the United States (1941-45). After serving as secretary of agriculture under Pres. Franklin D. Roosevelt (1933-40), Wallace was elected vice president with Roosevelt in 1940 but replaced in 1944 because of his liberal views. He was commerce secretary in Pres. Harry S. Truman's cabinet (1945-46) and ran for president on the Progressive ticket in 1948, advocating cooperation with the Soviet Union.

See Also: Cold War; Vice President of the United States.

■ **WALL STREET,** financial center of the United States. Home of the New York Stock Exchange (NYSE), the American Stock Exchange, and the largest brokerages and investment banking firms in the country, Wall Street has been synonymous with high finance since the 19th century and, with the ascendance of the American economy and the stock exchange during World War I, the financial capital of the world. Wall Street, near the tip of Manhattan, got its name from the palisades built by Dutch colonists in the 17th century to protect themselves from the Indians.

See Also: Industrial Revolution; Stock Exchange.

■ **WALTER, THOMAS USTICK (1804-87),** neoclassical architect. Walter was born in Philadelphia and trained with William Strickland. He designed Girard College in his native city (1833-40). He was appointed by Pres. Millard Fillmore to succeed Robert Mills as architect of the U.S. Capitol in 1851. In this position, he designed the wings added to the central building, as well as the larger cast-iron dome, and oversaw construction of these additions.

See Also: Architecture; Mills, Robert; Strickland, William.

■ **WALTHAM SYSTEM,** also known as the Lowell System, manufacturing system developed by Francis Cabot Lowell and the Boston Associates. Lowell smuggled home plans from British power looms in 1811 and brought every aspect of textile manufacture together at the Boston Associates' textile mill in Waltham, Massachusetts (1814). This mill revolutionized the industry by depending on large capital investments to finance water- or steam-powered machinery and to concentrate textile manufacturing on one site under unified management. This system proved so successful for the Boston Associates that they built an entire industrial community named Lowell on the Merrimack River in 1823. They recruited young New England farm women as workers. Supervised dormitories, lectures, and compulsory church attendance reassured parents that these women would not become an oppressed working class and further distinguished the Lowell system. Attracted by the pay and the chance to escape farm life, the "Lowell mill girls" worked 12-hour days within a rigid schedule. Wage cuts and speed-ups led to strikes during the 1830s and reform movements in the 1840s. During the next decades Irish workers replaced the local girls, and Lowell became just another mill town.

See Also: Boston Associates; Industrial Revolution; Textile Industry.

■ **WALTON, GEORGE (1741-1804),** lawyer and Revolutionary War leader. Born in Virginia, Walton moved to Georgia, where he became a prominent figure in the Revolution. He fought in the war, served in the Second Continental Congress, signed the Declaration of Independence, and was elected governor of Georgia in 1778.

See Also: Declaration of Independence.

■ **WAMPUM,** tubular beads laboriously made by drilling clam shells and regarded by Indians in the Northeast as highly valuable. Wampum had religious, commercial, political, and archival functions according to associated rituals. In 17th-century New England wampum served as hard currency with fixed values for various quantities. Counterfeit glass beads called "bugles" were easily recognized by Indians and discounted.

"Strings" or "belts" of wampum were often required as political devices during treaty negotiations. Protocol seems to have been invented by the Iroquois, who taught it to other Indians as well as to Europeans. Without wampum, a proposition was just talk, not serious. The size of belts indicated the importance of propositions. Procedure demanded presentation of a string or belt "across the fire" and acceptance for consideration. A belt dropped to the ground signified instant rejection. Otherwise, response came in a counterpart belt a day or more later.

White belts generally proposed peace; black or purple belts meant war, but there was no code for emblems woven into belts. Sending parties "read into" a belt their intended messages. Its carrier merely spoke it; the message was incarnated in the belt. Belts of agreement were preserved carefully and annually "read" to the leading young men who were required to memorize them. Thus, archives were kept viable. Historians have learned that they were remarkably accurate, often more so than written records.

—FRANCIS JENNINGS

See Also: Indians of North America.

BIBLIOGRAPHY: Jennings, Francis, et al., eds., *History and Culture of Iroquois Diplomacy* (Syracuse Univ. Press 1985); Weeden, William B., *Indian Money as a Factor in New England Civilization* (Johns Hopkins Univ. Press 1884).

■ **WAR, DEPARTMENT OF,** cabinet department of the U.S. government, established by Congress on

Aug. 7, 1789, to administer the U.S. Army under the command of the president and the secretary of war. President Washington appointed Henry Knox the first secretary of war. Sec. John C. Calhoun undertook a reorganization of the department after the War of 1812. Responsibility for various army functions was divided among different bureaus, each with a civilian chief and a commanding general. In the wake of the Spanish-American War (1898), Sec. Elihu Root sought to gain more control over the bureaus by appointing both a general staff for planning and a chief of staff, who served as the overarching administrator. The National Defense Act (1916) granted more independence to the individual bureaus, but when competition among them for scarce munitions and other supplies almost paralyzed American industrial preparation for World War I, Sec. Newton D. Baker again centralized authority. In 1939 Gen. George C. Marshall became the department's chief of staff. He and Sec. Henry L. Stimson split the department into three commands: Army Ground Forces, Army Air Forces, and the Army Service Forces, which provided logistical and administrative support to the other two commands. In 1947 the National Security Act converted the War Department into the Department of the Army, part of the new Defense Department.

See Also: *Defense, Department of.*

■ **WAR CRIMES,** violations of rules and codes governing the conduct of war. People have long attempted to mitigate the barbarity of war by rules, but only in recent centuries have international conventions been accepted as legally binding on all signatories. Among the international agreements to regulate and discourage—although not outlaw—international warfare are the Geneva Conventions (1864, 1906), the Hague Resolutions (1907), the Kellogg-Briand Pact (1928), the Anti-War Treaty on Non-Aggression and Conciliation (1933), and the Act of Chapultepec (1945).

War Crimes before World War II. Nations in antiquity observed some conventions in warfare, particularly those regarding the treatment of prisoners of war. From the Middle Ages, European nations gradually adopted some general rules of war, at least for combat among themselves. There was no concerted attempt to codify these rules until the mid-19th century. After the Civil War, Confederate

Capt. Henry Wirz was executed for crimes committed against Union prisoners of war in the Andersonville Prison, which he commanded. The Allies, victorious in World War I, compiled a list of 901 Germans accused of violating the laws of war during the war. But German courts either refused to indict or acquitted 888 of them.

World War II and After. To avoid a repetition of this miscarriage, the Allies in World War II decided to hold their own trials. The most important were held in Nuremberg, Germany. Major German indictees were accused of actions having no particular locality and dealing with no specific crime in the ordinary sense of the word: conspiracy, crimes against peace, war crimes, and crimes against humanity. Death sentences were handed down in 12 cases, life imprisonment in 3, lesser prison sentences in 4, and acquittals in 3. The United Nations War Crimes Commission (UNWCC) reported in 1946 that a total of 1,108 accused war criminals had been tried in Europe. Of these 413 were sentenced to death, 485 imprisoned, and 210 acquitted.

The International Military Tribunal for the Far East (IMTFE) tried and convicted 28 Japanese in Tokyo. Other trials of Japanese were held by the American Eighth Army and by Britain, Australia, the Netherlands, France, and China. Of 1,350 men tried for war crimes in the Far East, 384 were sentenced to death, 704 imprisoned, and 262 acquitted.

Before it was phased out in March 1948, the UNWCC reported the total number of war crimes trials held in Europe, excepting those in the U.S.S.R. and some nations under its control, as: American 809; British 524; Austrian 256; French 254; Dutch 30; Polish 24; Norwegian 9; and Canadian 4.

By 1963 the United States had tried 1,814 people for war crimes in Europe, the United Kingdom 1,085, the U.S.S.R. about 10,000, and West Germany 12,846. Between 1945 and 1983, nearly 88,000 war crimes cases were opened in West Germany. Almost 80,000 resulted in acquittals.

Controversies. Some critics of war crimes trials acknowledge the need for them but argue that the tribunals should include members from neutral and vanquished nations as well from the victors. Others deny the legal right of any nation to try the soldiers or leaders of a defeated nation for what amounts to violation of ex post facto or even nonexistent laws. Still others insist that the laws of a civilized nation would not permit the execution of criminals for capital cases with a jury divided three-to-one, as was the case at Nuremberg, or six-to-five, as at the IMTFE. Opponents of war crimes trials generally agree that the trials lower legal standards and reduce the victors to the level of the criminals. In the late 1990s war crimes trials were in process for atrocities committed in the civil strife in Bosnia and Rwanda.

—NORMAN E. TUTOROW

BIBLIOGRAPHY: Canot, Robert E., *Justice at Nuremberg* (Carroll & Graf 1983); Minear, Richard H., *Victors' Justice: The Tokyo War Crimes Trial* (Princeton Univ. Press 1971); Tusa, Ann, and John Tusa, *The Nuremberg Trial* (Atheneum 1984); Tutorow, Norman E., *War Crimes, War Criminals, and War Crimes Trials: An Annotated Bibliography and Source Book* (Greenwood Press 1986).

■ **WARD, AARON MONTGOMERY (1843-1913),** mail-order merchant. Born in Chatham, New Jersey, Ward worked in retail and became a traveling salesman out of St. Louis (1870), where he saw that rural people were paid low prices for their produce but still had to buy expensive retail goods. In response, Ward decided he could buy dry goods from the manufacturer and sell them at lower cost by mail. He and partner G. R. Thorn put out a single price sheet in 1872, guaranteed customer satisfaction, and enjoyed instant success. By 1876, the Montgomery Ward catalog had more than 150 pages, and by 1888 sales had reached $1 million.

See Also: Industrial Revolution.

■ **WARD, ARTEMUS (1834-67),** humorist. Artemus Ward was the pen name of Charles Farrar Browne. He was born near Waterford, Maine. Ward trained as a printer before beginning to submit humorous articles to newspapers and magazines. He joined the staff of *Vanity Fair* in 1859. In 1861 Ward embarked on travels across the United States giving lectures. He collected stories of his experiences in *Artemus Ward, His Book* (1862) and *Artemus Ward, His Travels* (1865). Ward died of tuberculosis while lecturing in England.

■ **WARD, LESTER FRANK (1841-1913),** sociologist. Ward was born in Joliet, Illinois. He worked

for the U.S. Treasury Department (1865-81) and then as a geologist and paleontologist for the U.S. Geological Survey (1881-1905). Interest in the conflict between science and religion turned him in the direction of sociology. Ward contributed to the birth of the field in the United States with books such as *Dynamic Sociology* (1883) and *Outlines of Sociology* (1898). He taught sociology at Brown University from 1906 until his death.

See Also: Social Sciences.

■ **WARD, NANCY (c. 1738-1822),** Cherokee leader sometimes called "the Pocahontas of the West." Raised in Great Echota, Tennessee, she used her influence to aid colonists during the American Revolution by warning them against Cherokee uprisings in 1776 and 1780. The legend of her friendship for the colonists was popularized in Pres. Theodore Roosevelt's *The Winning of the West* (1905).

See Also: Indians of North America.

■ **WAR HAWKS,** term applied to a group of western and southern nationalist congressmen who called for war against England in 1812. Among them were Speaker of the House Henry Clay of Kentucky and John C. Calhoun of South Carolina.

See Also: Calhoun, John Caldwell; Clay, Henry.

■ **WARHOL, ANDY (1930-87),** foremost pop art practitioner. Warhol was born in Pittsburgh, Pennsylvania, and studied at the Carnegie Institute of Technology. He moved to New York in 1952, where his work in commercial art—for example, a series of large-scale paintings of Dick Tracy comic strips used in a Lord and Taylor department store window in 1961—evolved into his signature style. Warhol's best-known work, which he began in the early 1960s, is characterized by repeated images of either commercial icons, as in *Green Coca-Cola Bottles* (1962) or *Campbell's Soup Can* (1965), or celebrities such as Marilyn Monroe or Jacqueline Kennedy. Warhol made use of silkscreen techniques to create these patterns of identical images, in one sense removing his own imprint as the artist, but at the same time creating a distinctive look. Warhol also made three-dimensional works, again often borrowing from the commercial culture around him for inspiration.

With these art works, as well as with his series of underground films, Warhol was at the center of the pop art movement.

See Also: Painting.

■ **WAR IN AMERICAN HISTORY.** *See: Air Force; Army; Coast Guard; Marine Corps; Militia and National Guard; Navy; War Crimes; Women in the Armed Forces; specific wars.*

■ **WAR INDUSTRIES BOARD (WIB),** government agency established in July 1917 to control war production. As head of the WIB, the financier Bernard Baruch was given autocratic powers to determine what would be manufactured and to allocate raw materials and fix prices.

See Also: World War I.

■ **WAR OF 1812 (1812-15),** war between the United States and Great Britain. The conflict was an outgrowth of the French Revolutionary and Napoleonic Wars (1792-1815). During this era of sustained warfare in Europe, Britain and France repeatedly encroached on American neutral rights. Unable to win any concessions from the belligerents by employing trade restrictions, the United States declared war on Britain on June 18, 1812.

The United States went to war to force the British to give up their Orders in Council, which regulated American trade with the European continent, and impressment, the forcible removal of seamen from American merchant vessels. Pres. James Madison and other Republican leaders in Washington also saw war as a means of unifying their party and silencing the Federalists, who had long opposed the anti-British thrust of American foreign policy. The vote on the declaration of the war was the closest on any such measure in American history—79 to 49 in the House and 19 to 13 in the Senate. All the Federalists voted against the bill, and so too did about 20 percent of the Republicans.

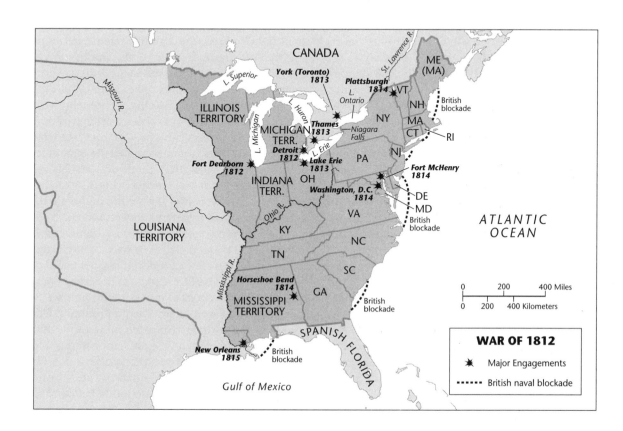

In 1814, during the War of 1812, British forces invaded Washington, D.C., burning both the Capitol and the White House.

The United States launched a three-pronged invasion of Canada in 1812, but the campaign ended in disaster. One army, under Gen. William Hull, surrendered at Detroit; a second, under Gen. Stephen Van Rensselaer, was defeated on the Niagara River frontier; and a third, under Gen. Henry Dearborn, retreated from the St. Lawrence River frontier after making little more than a demonstration. The United States launched another three-pronged attack in 1813, and this campaign fared somewhat better but only in the West. Cmdr. Oliver H. Perry's spectacular triumph on Lake Erie led to the burning of York (Toronto), the capital of Upper Canada (Ontario), and to Gen. William Henry Harrison's victory over the British in the Battle of the Thames, which secured the whole Northwest for the United States. In the more important eastern theaters, however, the United States continued to suffer defeat.

1814–15. In the spring of 1814 Napoleon's defeat and exile from Europe brought peace to the European continent for the first time in a decade. Freed from the demands of the European war, Britain shifted military and naval assets to the American war and took the offensive. Although the British succeeded in burning Washington, D.C. (in retaliation for the destruction of York), and occupying eastern Maine, they were rebuffed at Plattsburgh (largely because of Thomas Macdo-

nough's victory on Lake Champlain), forced to retreat from Baltimore, and suffered at the hands of Gen. Andrew Jackson at New Orleans one of the most lopsided defeats in British military history.

Throughout the war the Madison administration in Washington had trouble recruiting troops and raising money. As a result, the army frequently operated short-handed, and the government teetered on the verge of bankruptcy.

The administration also had to contend with determined Federalist opposition, which was particularly fierce in New England. Control of the New England state governments enabled the Federalists to obstruct the war effort there by withholding their militia from federal service. They also feuded with federal officials over the control of those militia units that were called into service. Federalist opposition climaxed at the Hartford Convention (Dec. 15, 1814–Jan. 5, 1815), a New England conference held to protest Republican policies and provide for the defense of the region. The convention recommended a series of amendments to the U.S. Constitution as well as state sequestration of federal tax money to pay for defense measures. But the war ended before any significant action could be taken to implement these proposals.

Representatives from the United States and Britain met at Ghent (in modern-day Belgium) in August 1814 to try to end the war. After much haggling, both sides retreated from their initial demands—the British had asked for territorial concessions—and on Dec. 24, 1814, signed the Treaty of Ghent, which restored the antebellum status quo. The war ended when instruments of ratification were exchanged in Washington on Feb. 17, 1815. Although the United States had failed to win any concessions on the maritime issues in dispute or to conquer Canada, Republican leaders seized on the great victory at New Orleans (which was actually fought two weeks after the peace treaty was signed) to portray the war as a great success. Thus the War of 1812 passed into history not as a futile and costly struggle in which the United States had barely escaped military and financial disaster but as a glorious triumph in which the young republic had single-handedly defeated the conqueror of Napoleon and mistress of the seas.

—DONALD R. HICKEY

See Also: *Ghent, Treaty of; Impressment; Madison, James; Orders in Council; Thames, Battle of the.*

BIBLIOGRAPHY: Hickey, Donald R., *The War of 1812: A Forgotten Conflict* (Univ. of Illinois Press 1989); Mahon, John K., *The War of 1812* (Univ. of Florida Press 1972); Stagg, J. C. A., *Mr. Madison's War: Politics, Diplomacy, and Warfare in the Early American Republic, 1783-1830* (Princeton Univ. Press 1983).

■ **WAR POWERS ACT,** name of two federal laws. The first (1942) gave Pres. Franklin D. Roosevelt the ability to centralize the country's economic war-making potential during World War II. The second (1973) reflected widespread dissatisfaction with the Vietnam War in Congress and among the American public. It required the president to obtain congressional approval within 60 days of deploying troops in combat situations. Passed over Pres. Richard Nixon's veto, the measure was an attempt to make more clear the distinction between executive decision making and congressional oversight and budget control.

■ **WAR PRODUCTION BOARD,** government agency established at the beginning of U.S. involvement in World War II (Jan. 1942) to oversee the allocation of scarce resources to industries. By 1943 the board was largely superseded by the more powerful Office of War Mobilization.

See Also: World War I.

In 1963-64, Chief Justice Earl Warren headed the presidential commission's investigation of Pres. John F. Kennedy's assassination.

■ **WARREN, EARL (1891-1974),** Republican political leader, governor of California (1943-53), chief justice of the United States (1953-69), noted especially for the desegregation decisions made while he led the Court. Born in Los Angeles, Warren received his undergraduate and law degrees from the University of California at Berkeley. He practiced law privately, served in World War I, and returned to California to enter public life as a city and county district attorney. Active in Republican politics, he was elected California attorney general in 1938, in which position he earned a reputation as a conservative concerned about subversive elements in society. In 1942 he won the first of three terms as governor of California and became a national figure. In the 1948 presidential election he was the vice-presidential running mate of Republican Thomas Dewey, who lost the election to Pres. Harry Truman. As governor, Warren initially remained conservative, supporting the internment of Japanese Americans, but gradually became more liberal.

He later expressed regret about his strong backing of internment. In 1953, after failing to win the Republican nomination for president in 1952, Warren announced that he would not run for a fourth term as governor. The same year President Eisenhower nominated Warren to succeed Chief Justice Fred Vinson; Warren was easily confirmed early in 1954.

Chief Justice. Although Warren had not served as a judge, he had extensive political experience in achieving consensus, a talent that he exercised with great skill as chief justice. Almost immediately, Warren was called upon to use this talent, in the landmark desegregation decision *Brown* v. *Board of Education of Topeka*. In the *Brown* case, Warren was able to mold a unanimous decision in overturning *Plessy* v. *Ferguson* (1896), the legal precedent upon which segregation had depended. The first *Brown* decision held that segregation in schools was unconstitutional; a second *Brown* decision, in 1955, ruled that desegregation should proceed "with all deliberate speed." Again, Warren was able to convince the Court to issue a unanimous decision. The Warren Court in 1967 issued another important desegregation ruling in *Loving* v. *Virginia*, in which a Virginia statute barring interracial marriages was held unconstitutional.

A number of other decisions of the Warren Court led to seeking changes in U.S. social and political practices. In *Baker* v. *Carr* (1962), Warren voted with the majority in deciding that voter reapportionment was within federal-court jurisdiction. A subsequent decision, *Reynolds* v. *Sims* (1964), held that legislative districts should be apportioned on a population basis. Warren was also in the majority in two controversial decisions that outlawed Bible reading and prayer in schools, *Engel* v. *Vitale* (1962) and *School District of Abington Township* v. *Schempp* (1963). Other key Warren Court decisions gradually extended the rights of criminal defendants and reined in some common law enforcement practices. *Griffin* v. *Illinois* (1956) invalidated state laws requiring appeals fees from indigent defendants, while *Mapp* v. *Ohio* held that illegally seized evidence could not be used, and *Gideon* v. *Wainwright* guaranteed a defendant's right to legal representation. Warren voted with the majority in *Escobedo* v. *Illinois* (1964), which overturned a conviction because the accused had been denied access to his lawyer, and wrote the majority opinion in *Miranda* v. *Arizona* (1966), in which the Court held that a person in police custody must be warned of his right to remain silent and to consult an attorney before being questioned.

In 1963, Warren was appointed by Pres. Lyndon B. Johnson to head a commission investigating the assassination of Pres. John F. Kennedy. Known as the Warren Commission, the group issued a report that concluded that Kennedy had been killed by a single assassin, Lee Harvey Oswald. The report and Warren were attacked for ruling out the widespread belief that Oswald had been part of a broader conspiracy.

In 1969, Warren retired from the Court after 15 years as chief justice. Under his pragmatic leadership, the Court had taken a more active role than ever before in defending civil liberties and civil rights. Warren was succeeded as chief justice by Warren Burger, and the Court soon became more conservative.

—ROBERT C. KHAYAT

See Also: *Baker v. Carr; Brown v. Board of Education of Topeka; Japanese-American Internment; Loving v. Virginia; Miranda v. Arizona; Supreme Court.*

BIBLIOGRAPHY: Schwartz, Bernard, *Super Chief: Earl Warren and His Supreme Court—A Judicial Biography* (New York Univ. Press 1983); White, G. Edward, *Earl Warren: A Public Life* (Oxford Univ. Press 1987).

■ **WARREN, MERCY (1728-1814),** poet and historian. She was born in Barnstable, Massachusetts. She wrote two satirical plays poking fun at Tory leaders, *The Adulateur* (1772) and *The Group* (1775). After the American Revolution, she was attacked by conservative Bostonians for supporting the French Revolution and opposing ratification of the new U.S. Constitution in *Observations on the New Constitution* (1788). Her *History of the Rise, Progress and Termination of the American Revolution* (1805) is a vigorous study of Revolutionary leaders.

See Also: *Constitution of the United States.*

■ **WARREN, ROBERT PENN (1905-89),** poet, novelist, and educator. Warren was born in Guthrie, Kentucky, and attended Vanderbilt University, where he coedited a short-lived literary journal, the *Fugitive* (1922-25). Warren went on to graduate work at the University of California and Yale University. He was a Rhodes scholar at Oxford University in 1929-30. From 1934 to 1942 Warren taught at Louisiana State University. While there he began working with Cleanth Brooks on a series of textbooks, including *Understanding Poetry* (1938) and *Understanding Fiction* (1943), that advocated analysis based on close reading. Warren and Brooks were also founders of the *Southern Review*. Warren taught at the University of Minnesota from 1942 to 1950, when he joined the faculty at Yale. Throughout his career as a professor, Warren was a prolific author of novels, and he returned to his early love of poetry. His novel *All the King's Men* won the Pulitzer Prize for fiction in 1947, and he also won the prize for poetry in 1958, among other honors. Warren was appointed the first Poet Laureate of the United States in 1986.

See Also: Poetry.

■ **WASHAKIE (c. 1804-1900),** Shoshone-Flathead chief. Raised among his father's Flathead people in present-day Montana, Washakie moved with his Shoshone mother to the Wind River Reservation in Wyoming after his father's death. As leader of the Eastern Shoshone, Washakie became a trading partner of Kit Carson and Jim Bridger and helped American settlers along the Oregon Trail. During the Indian wars in the late 1860s, Washakie and his followers were scouts and fighters for the U.S. Army against the Sioux, Cheyenne, and Arapaho.

See Also: Bridger, Jim (James); Carson, Kit; Indians of North America.

■ **WASHINGTON, BOOKER TALIAFERRO (c. 1856-1915),** African-American educator and political leader. Washington was born into slavery near Hale's Ford, Virginia. Upon Emancipation in 1865, he moved with his family to Malden, West Virginia. While working in the salt mines in Malden, Washington began to thirst for an education. He attended classes at the public school and then made the 500-mile trip to the Hampton Normal and Agricultural Institute in Virginia. He completed the three-year program at Hampton, working as a janitor to pay his expenses. While at

Hampton he was greatly influenced by Gen. Samuel Chapman Armstrong, the Institute's founder. Armstrong emphasized learning by doing, hard work, and thrift, all ideals Washington would later incorporate in his own work.

After briefly teaching school in Malden, Washington returned to Hampton for further training and in 1881 accepted a position as principal of an African-American teacher-training school in Tuskegee, Alabama. He arrived to find that the school had not yet been organized. Washington decided to start a manual training program such as that at Hampton to help establish Tuskegee Institute. He put his students to work cleaning and repairing the existing buildings and clearing land to plant a cotton crop as a source of income. Within the first year he won the respect of the local citizens and began a series of speaking tours in the North to raise funds, gaining national attention.

The turning point in Washington's public career came in 1895 with a speech he gave before the Cotton States and International Exposition in Atlanta. In this speech he expounded his political conservatism, stressing the need for economic advancement rather than political rights. He advised African Americans to "cast down your

In 1881, Booker T. Washington founded the Normal and Industrial Institute for Negroes at Tuskegee, Alabama, modeling it after the Hampton Institute, which he had attended as a student.

buckets where you are" rather than migrating to the North in search of a better life. Emphasizing the dignity of honest labor, he advised his audience that "socially we can be as separate as the fingers, but as one as the hand in all things essential to mutual progress." With this one speech Washington rose to the status of leader of his race. His prestige depended on his ability to forge a compromise between African Americans, northern white philanthropists, and conservative southern politicians.

Despite its enthusiastic reception the speech brought criticism from many northern African Americans, who called it the "Atlanta Compromise." They believed that Washington was compromising African Americans' chances of achieving equal status by deemphasizing political rights. In truth when Washington tried to move beyond a conservative public position, he found himself rebuffed by the white supporters on whom he relied for funds and political favors. Privately he initiated lawsuits to challenge segregation laws and voting restrictions, but his failure to make his opposition known brought him rebuffs from African-American supporters. While publicly disparaging political agitation, Washington worked behind the scenes to obtain appointments for African Americans to influential political positions.

In 1900 Washington founded the National Negro Business League. This organization served as a clearinghouse for information for small businesses and emphasized African-American capitalism and educated businessmen as the key to racial uplift.

Washington achieved the height of his political influence during the administration of Pres. Theodore Roosevelt. Roosevelt continually sought Washington's advice on racial matters and African-American political appointments. Washington used this influence to secure support from the northern African-American professional community and to stifle public opposition to his leadership. On Oct. 16, 1901, Roosevelt symbolically confirmed Washington's leadership status in the black community by inviting him to dine at the White House.

After Roosevelt left office in 1909, Washington still wielded considerable power among northern businessmen and Republican politicians. When Woodrow Wilson became president in 1913 and Democrats took control of appointments, however, Washington lost much of his patronage power.

On Nov. 13, 1915, Washington died at his home in Tuskegee, after suffering serious stress-related illnesses. He is buried next to the chapel at Tuskegee Institute.

—JACQUELINE MOORE

See Also: African Americans; Civil Rights Movement; Niagara Movement.

BIBLIOGRAPHY: Harlan, Louis R., *Booker T. Washington: The Making of a Black Leader, 1856-1901* (Oxford Univ. Press 1972); Harlan, Louis R., *Booker T. Washington: The Wizard of Tuskegee, 1901-1915* (Oxford Univ. Press 1983); Meier, August, *Negro Thought in America, 1880-1915* (Univ. of Michigan 1963); Washington, Booker T., *Up From Slavery* (Doubleday 1902).

■ **WASHINGTON, BUSHROD (1762-1829)**, associate justice of the U.S. Supreme Court (1798-1829). A Westmoreland County, Virginia, native and nephew of George Washington, Bushrod Washington studied law under James Wilson and many years later filled the vacancy on the Court created by Wilson's death. On the Court Washington allied himself closely with Chief Justice John Marshall. His notable opinion in *Green* v. *Biddle* (1823) affirmed the right of the Supreme Court to overturn a state statute if it violated the Constitution's contract clause.

See Also: Supreme Court.

■ **WASHINGTON, GEORGE (1732-99)**, commander of the Continental army and first president of the United States. Popularly regarded as the "father of his country," Washington rendered indispensable service to the United States.

Early Life. Washington was born on Feb. 22, 1732, at Pope's Creek in Westmoreland County, Virginia, the eldest child of Augustine and Mary Ball Washington. His father died in 1743, leaving his best properties to George's older half-brothers: Lawrence inherited Little Hunting Creek plantation, which he later named Mount Vernon, after his former British commander, Adm. Edward Vernon; and Augustine, Jr., inherited the Westmoreland County plantation. George inherited only the modest farm near Fredericksburg on which

John Trumbull's portrait of George Washington portrays him as a robust leader of men. Washington dominated the American scene from the beginning of the Revolution to his death.

his family lived. He taught himself surveying in order to maintain his gentry status.

Washington's early career benefited from Lawrence's connection with his in-laws, the wealthy Fairfax family of Belvoir. Lord Fairfax made Washington a surveyor of his Northern Neck property and supported his 1748 appointment as Culpeper County surveyor. The boy developed methodical habits of mind and wilderness survival skills as a surveyor of Virginia's unsettled western lands, earned substantial fees, acquired lands of his own for cultivation

and speculation, and impressed officials with his fairness, honesty, and dependability. By 1751, when he visited Barbados with Lawrence, young Washington had accumulated almost as many acres in the Shenandoah Valley as his half-brother had on the Potomac River. Lawrence died in 1752, and in 1754 Washington leased Mount Vernon from his widow, who held a life title to it.

The French and Indian War. A burning ambition for personal distinction compelled Washington to leave the tobacco field for the battlefield. He persuaded Virginia's governor to appoint him to Lawrence's position as adjutant in 1752, responsible for training the colony's militia. In October 1753 Washington volunteered to investigate French encroachments on Virginia's western frontier. His wilderness journal, published in Williamsburg in 1754, earned him widespread recognition, and in May he became commander of a regiment raised to oppose the French in the Ohio Valley.

French retaliation for an attack on a party across the Alleghenies provided the young colonel his first military defeat: the surrender of Fort Necessity in July 1754. Washington learned much in the resulting French and Indian War, especially from the British generals under whom he served, Edward Braddock and John Forbes. He earned a reputation as an able, courageous commander and efficient administrator but resented never receiving a regular army commission.

Master of Mount Vernon. With his prestige enhanced by his military career and his land holdings increased by bounties granted to the Virginia Regiment (he owned 45,000 western acres at his death), Washington returned to private life a very eligible bachelor. On Jan. 6, 1759, he married Martha Dandridge Custis, the wealthy widow of Daniel Parke Custis, and soon became the guardian of her two children, John Parke and Martha Parke Custis, devoting much time and attention to managing their estate. As his brother's residual heir, Washington became the outright owner of Mount Vernon when Lawrence's widow died in 1761.

Washington was now one of Virginia's wealthiest planters, and his life was happy and full. He had no children of his own but raised Martha's children and later two of her grandchildren,

Eleanor and George Washington Parke Custis. Washington also devoted much time to his many plantation responsibilities. He began to shift Mount Vernon's farms from traditional tobacco to wheat cultivation, built a gristmill, and experimented with various crops and livestock breeds. He supervised the management of an enslaved labor force (at the end of his life about 275 slaves worked Mount Vernon's 7,300 acres), provided and cared for the entire plantation community, and maintained the lavish lifestyle required of Virginia's planter elite.

The American Revolution. Washington also sacrificed leisure time for public service. He was first elected to the Virginia House of Burgesses in 1758 and served 16 years there, as well as 14 on the Fairfax County court. In the deepening crisis with Britain in the 1760s and 1770s Washington advocated the patriot cause and was a Virginia delegate to the First Continental Congress in 1774. In May 1775 he again traveled to Philadelphia to sit in the Second Continental Congress, which appointed him the following month commander of all the militia besieging the British army in Boston.

The new general arrived in Cambridge, Massachusetts, on July 2, 1775. Washington's first challenge was to mold an inexperienced group of patriotic volunteers into a real army. He did so by emphasizing discipline, cleanliness, and colonial unity and by instilling a professional ethic in the officers. He also had to obtain dependable, long-term enlisted men without arousing Americans' inherent fear of a standing army.

After forcing the British to abandon Boston in March 1776, Washington immediately marched to New York City, correctly guessing it would be the enemy's next target. Well aware of military geography, he also sent troops to Canada in an unsuccessful attempt to secure the other end of the Hudson River–Lake Champlain corridor, by which the British could isolate New England. Although driven from New York in the fall, he learned from his errors, saved the Continental army from annihilation, and brilliantly counterattacked at Trenton and Princeton in the winter of 1776-77.

Washington's greatest achievement was to hold the army together over the next several years despite public apathy. Marginal state support and inadequate congressional assistance led to the winter of privation at Valley Forge (1777-78), and his subsequent attempt to destroy the British army as it moved from Philadelphia to New York ended in frustration. Only French assistance enabled Washington finally to mount a strategic offensive, which ended in his capture of Lord Cornwallis's entire army at Yorktown, Virginia, in 1781 and a favorable peace in 1783. Then, like the Roman hero Cincinnatus, Washington resigned his commission and retired to private life.

National Political Leader. Washington's return to Mount Vernon was not permanent, however, for he soon realized that America's hard-won independence was threatened anew. In a 1783 circular letter to the states, he stated that respectable national existence required an indissoluble federal union, sacred regard for public justice, adoption of proper measures for national defense, and suppression of local prejudices. Shays's Rebellion convinced him that the Articles of Confederation could not ensure domestic tranquillity, and he lent his prestige to the formation of a more perfect union.

When the Constitutional Convention was called to meet in Philadelphia in 1787 to revise the articles, Virginia sent Washington as part of its delegation. Against his wishes he was elected presiding officer. The Constitution written by the convention bore little of his handiwork but depended on his reputation for its success. After it was ratified in 1788, he was unanimously elected president of the new government. John Adams was chosen vice president.

First President of the United States. The same sense of duty that saw Washington through the Revolution compelled him to take the oath of office on Apr. 30, 1789, in the temporary federal capital of New York City. Dignity, common sense, political acumen, and a keen judgment of men were Washington's chief assets in establishing general precedents, relating to the new Congress, and making appointments. The heads of his executive departments—Sec. of State Thomas Jefferson, Sec. of the Treasury Alexander Hamilton, and Sec. of War Henry Knox, as well as Attorney Gen. Edmund Randolph—were men of talent, integrity, and even brilliance.

Washington supported Hamilton's fiscal programs, which chiefly benefited the moneyed classes, as the only way the United States could restore its national credit and assume its proper rank among the nations. Hamilton's policies also sought close commercial ties with Britain. Even before the end of Washington's first administration, during which he laid the groundwork for the new federal city on the Potomac River that would later bear his name, opposition to Hamilton had coalesced around Sec. of State Jefferson and Congressman James Madison. They supported a stricter interpretation of the Constitution based on states' rights, domestic policies favoring agricultural interests, and a foreign policy less favorable to Britain.

With the growing polarization between Hamilton's Federalists and Jefferson's Democratic-Republicans, Washington's sense of duty prevented him from retiring after a single term, and he was again unanimously elected president. The United States was then caught between warring European powers as the French Revolution entered an international phase. Differences over John Jay's 1794 treaty with Britain, ratified in 1795, sparked Democratic-Republican criticisms that Washington had become the head of a party instead of the nation. In America there was trouble with the Indians in the Northwest, and Washington had to call out the militia to suppress frontier protests against a new excise tax on whiskey. He was subjected to fierce newspaper attacks, which he tended to take personally.

Washington refused pleas that he serve a third term as president and happily handed the reins of government over to his successor, John Adams, in March 1797. Washington was aware that the very success of his leadership made it no longer indispensable to the nation's survival. His final political testament to the American people was the Farewell Address, drafted by Hamilton and widely printed in September 1796.

Last Years. As war with France threatened in 1798, President Adams named Washington commander in chief of the newly enlarged army. The crisis soon passed, but not before Washington almost precipitated another by insisting on Hamilton as his second-in-command. Washington devoted his nearly full attention to private affairs in the final two years of his life but never suc-ceeded in making Mount Vernon a profitable agricultural venture. Despite discomfort from ill-fitting dentures (made of human teeth and ivory, not wood), he did, however, continue to enjoy generally good health until the very end.

But on Dec. 13, 1799, Washington became ill after a long ride around his plantation in a snowstorm. Early the next day doctors were sent for when an extremely sore throat made breathing and speaking difficult. At 10:30 that night, after repeated blood-lettings and blisterings, the 67-year-old national patriarch died of what was probably a streptococcus infection, aggravated by his ill-advised medical treatment. Calm and patient to the end, he uttered his final words, "'Tis well." By providing in his will for the freeing of his slaves after his wife's death, Washington added a final admirable private statement to his invaluable public career.

—MARK A. MATROMARINO

See Also: Constitution of the United States; French and Indian War; Hamilton, Alexander; Jay's Treaty; Jefferson, Thomas; President of the United States; Revolution, American.

BIBLIOGRAPHY: Abbott, W. W., et al, eds., *The Papers of George Washington, 1748-1799* (28 vols. to date, Univ. Press of Virginia 1983-); Ferling, John E., *The First of Men: A Life of George Washington* (Univ. of Tennessee Press 1988); Freeman, Douglas Southall, *George Washington: A Biography*, 6 vols. (Scribner's 1948); Jackson, Donald, and Dorothy Twohig, eds., *The Diaries of George Washington, 1748-1799* (Univ. Press of Virginia 1976-79).

■ **WASHINGTON,** a Pacific Northwest state. It is bounded on the north by British Columbia, on the west by the Pacific Ocean, on the south by Oregon, and on the east by Idaho. The Columbia River forms most of its southern border. Three straits link the Pacific to Puget Sound, one of the world's great natural harbors. The Coast and Cascade ranges run north-south through humid western Washington, while the eastern half of the state is an arid plateau. Washington's economy is dominated by the aerospace giant Boeing Corporation.

The Pacific Northwest was only thinly settled when the United States gained sovereignty over what is now Washington in 1848. It grew rapidly after completion of a transcontinental rail line linked it to the East in 1887, and it became a state in 1889.

Capital: Olympia. Area: 68,126 square miles. Population (1995 est.): 5,431,000.

See Also: Columbia River; Lewis and Clark Expedition; Pacific Northwest; Whitman, Marcus and Whitman, Narcissa.

■ **WASHINGTON, D.C.** *See: District of Columbia.*

■ **WASHINGTON ARMAMENT CONFERENCE,** international forum initiated by the United States and held in Washington, D.C., in 1921-22 for the main purpose of naval disarmament of the United States, Britain, Japan, France, and Italy. According to the final treaty (1922), the United States would reduce its capital-ship tonnage (warships with more than 10,000 tons of water displacement and equipped with eight-inch guns) to 525,000 tons, destroying 30 of its 48 capital ships. Britain was also entitled to 525,000 tons and obliged to destroy 25 of its 45 ships. Japan would destroy 17 of its 27 capital ships, bringing its tonnage down to 315,000 tons. Thus, the proportion of 5:5:3 was reached among the three largest world navies. France and Italy were entitled to 175,000 tons each. Additionally, a pact was signed by the United States, Britain, France, and Japan, providing for mutual consultation in the Pacific region. Several agreements were signed establishing the principle of consultation and cooperation in China and respect for its sovereignty.

See Also: Navy; World War II.

■ **WASHINGTON MONUMENT,** memorial in Washington, D.C. Architect Robert Mills's obelisk won the 1833 design competition for the memorial held by the Washington National Monument Association. Construction began in 1848 but was not completed until 1884.

■ **WASHINGTON'S FAREWELL ADDRESS (1796),** statement by Pres. George Washington published several months before the end of his term. It appealed for national unity, warned against the dangers of political parties, and urged neutrality in European affairs.

See Also: Revolution, American; Washington, George.

■ **WASHINGTON TREATY (1871),** U.S.-British accord that settled American claims against Britain for providing the Confederacy with warships during the Civil War. The treaty included a British expression of regret and created a commission to determine by arbitration the size of British payments.

■ **WATERGATE,** a political scandal during the administration of Pres. Richard M. Nixon (1969-74). "Watergate" refers to a series of abuses of power, of which the June 1972 burglary at Washington's Watergate apartment and office building and the subsequent attempted cover-up were the final acts. Taken together, these abuses of power destroyed the Nixon presidency.

The Nixon White House operated for much of its tenure with a political bunker mentality. Convinced that political opponents were personal enemies and that social critics were unpatriotic and dangerous, Nixon and his staff set out to destroy both groups. From the first weeks of the administration, the White House wiretapped reporters' telephones and obtained their files from the Federal Bureau of Investigation (FBI) in order to leak embarrassing tidbits. To more easily identify administration opponents, a sophisticated "political enemies project" was developed, leading to the compilation of an "enemies list." With the help of the Central Intelligence Agency (CIA), the White House illegally infiltrated both the anti–Vietnam War movement and the Black Panthers, a militant black organization. They investigated the personal life of Sen. Edward M. (Ted) Kennedy and disrupted the campaigns of virtually every Nixon opponent in the 1972 elections.

These acts would probably have remained secret had it not been for the publication in the *New York Times* of the Pentagon Papers—a top-secret collection of memoranda and analyses, commissioned by the Pentagon in 1966, which proved that each of the presidents since Harry S. Truman had played a covert role in escalating the war in Vietnam. Although Nixon's administration was not mentioned in the report, he stormed that its publication violated national security. When the Supreme Court ruled that the *Times* was within its rights in publishing the report, Nixon agreed to the creation of "the plumbers"—a group of operatives under the control of domestic adviser John Ehrlichman who were charged with plugging leaks to the press from within the White House. When the plumbers broke into the Los Angeles office of the psychiatrist treating the man who leaked the Pentagon Papers, they were almost caught but were nevertheless promoted by Ehrlichman.

Several of the plumbers joined the intelligence effort of the Nixon reelection team, headed by former CIA agent G. Gordon Liddy. Liddy's plan to gain political information from the Democratic National Committee headquarters at the Watergate was a fiasco from the start. On June 17, 1972, while attempting to repair listening devices that had been placed during an earlier break-in at the Watergate, Liddy's team was arrested.

Cover-Up and Aftermath. The White House immediately shifted into crisis mode but not out of any desire to save the burglars. The cover-up, engineered by White House Counsel John Dean with the full cooperation of Nixon, was intended to prevent the burglars from talking about the earlier abuses of power with which several of them had been intimately connected, but it failed miserably. Attempts to pay off the burglars, orders to stop the FBI investigation, and threats of governmental retaliation went for naught as the incarcerated burglars began to speak about what they knew.

Ultimately, their word might not have held against that of the president of the United States had it not been revealed in the spring of 1973 that Nixon had recorded virtually all of his conversations in the Oval Office since the first year of his presidency. Each of the several investigations into the Watergate burglary subpoenaed the tapes. At first, Nixon, arguing that he had a constitutional right to keep private any presidential material, refused to give them up. However, political pressures forced him to release a highly sanitized set of transcripts in April 1973, and in July 1974 the Supreme Court compelled him to release all the subpoenaed tapes.

The tapes, now available in the National Archives, make clear that Nixon planned and ordered his staff to carry out the cover-up. In the famous "smoking gun" conversation of June 23, 1972, Nixon ordered his chief of staff, H. R. Haldeman, to put pressure on the FBI to abandon its investigation of the burglary. This was a clear obstruction of justice, but on Aug. 9, 1974, before Nixon could be either indicted in a criminal court or impeached in the Congress, he resigned the presidency. Exactly one month later, Gerald R. Ford pardoned Nixon for any illegalities that he may have been involved in during his presidency.

—JOHN ROBERT GREENE

See Also: *Black Panthers; Cold War; Ford, Gerald Rudolph; Nixon, Richard Milhous; Pentagon Papers Case; Vietnam War.*

BIBLIOGRAPHY: Greene, John Robert, *The Limits of Power: The Nixon and Ford Administrations* (Indiana Univ. Press 1992); Kutler, Stanley I., *The Wars of Watergate: The Last Crisis of Richard Nixon* (Knopf 1990).

■ **WATER POWER,** harnessing of water to create power for industry. Water power first developed on the Blackstone River at Pawtucket, Rhode Island, where Samuel Slater established an industrial center in the 1790s. Over the next 50 years, water power enabled the development of similar sites on the Passaic River in New Jersey and the Merrimack River in Massachusetts, and canal corporations sold power produced at their locks. Selling hydroelectricity, however, was difficult before George Westinghouse developed alternating-current electrical systems (1886). His company opened a hydroelectric plant at Niagara Falls in 1894. During World War I, the federal government built a huge plant at Muscle Shoals on the Tennessee River, and after 1920 the development of water power on navigable streams was controlled by the Federal Power Commission. The start of construction on Hoover Dam in 1929 ushered in an era of government dam building beginning a phase that culminated in huge hydroelectric plants along the Colorado, Columbia, and Missouri rivers. The New Deal's Tennessee Valley Authority (TVA) provided broad-based regional development and supplied power for the manufacture of World War II munitions. Massive development of these rivers, however, has led many to question the environmental costs of cheap electricity.

See Also: *Industrial Revolution; Tennessee Valley Authority.*

■ **WATERS, ETHEL (1896-1977),** actress, dancer, and singer, also known as "Sweet Mama Stringbean," born in Chester, Pennsylvania. The first African-American actress to star in a dramatic role on Broadway, she also appeared in films and was nominated for an Academy Award for her role in *Member of the Wedding* (1953), in which she repeated her Broadway role. As a singer she is best remembered for her interpretations of "Dinah" and "Stormy Weather" and for the recordings she made with Duke Ellington and other top jazz artists. After 1957 she performed regularly at revivals and on television with evangelist Billy Graham.

See Also: Ellington, Edward Kennedy (Duke); Jazz.

■ **WATERS, MUDDY (MCKINLEY MORGAN-FIELD) (1915-83),** singer, guitarist, and songwriter, African-American pioneer of the "urban blues." Discovered and recorded by the folklorist Alan Lomax at his home in Clarksdale, Mississippi, in 1941, Waters moved to Chicago in 1943, where he formed a band and became one of the first bluesmen to adopt the electric guitar. His compositions, including "Rolling Stone" and "Mannish Boy," are blues classics. During the 1960s he was rediscovered by artists such as the Rolling Stones and enjoyed a revival of his career.

■ **WATIE, STAND (1806-71),** Cherokee leader. Watie was a member of the pro-removal party of Cherokees in the 1830s and was one of the signers of the resettlement treaty who escaped assassination by irate tribesmen. He became a foe of the anti-removal leader, John Ross. At the outbreak of the Civil War, Watie lost a bitter fight for a formal alliance of the Cherokee with the Confederacy. During the war, he nevertheless commanded a regiment of Cherokee soldiers for the South. In June 1865, Watie was the last Confederate general to surrender to the Union.

See Also: Cherokee; Indian Removal; Indians of North America; Ross, John.

■ **WATSON, THOMAS EDWARD (1856-1922),** populist politician and writer. He was born near Thomson, Georgia. In 1876 he began work as an attorney, representing small southern farmers exploited by the railroads and banks. Watson won a seat in the Georgia state legislature in 1882. He became a leader of the Southern Alliance, a farmers' movement strong in the South,

and was elected to Congress in 1890. In his effort to address the concerns of poor farmers, he stressed the need for interracial cooperation, a politically dangerous position in the segregated Jim Crow South. In 1892 Watson was among those who organized the People's or Populist party, but violence and election fraud limited the party's success in the South. In 1896 he was nominated by the Populists to run as William Jennings Bryan's vice-presidential candidate. After Bryan's defeat Watson turned to writing and published his own journal, *Watson's Magazine*, which gave voice to his new-found racism and ever-constant anti-Catholicism and anti-Semitism. He returned to Georgia politics in 1908, serving in both the U.S. Congress and the Senate until his death in 1922.

See Also: Bryan, William Jennings; National Farmers' Alliance; Populism.

BIBLIOGRAPHY: Bryan, Gerald J., *Henry Grady or Tom Watson? The Rhetorical Struggle for the New South, 1880-1890* (Mercer Univ. Press 1994); Woodward, C. Vann, *Tom Watson, Agrarian Rebel* (Macmillan 1938).

■ **WAYNE, ANTHONY (1745-96),** Revolutionary War general and Indian fighter. Born in Waynesboro, Pennsylvania, Wayne assumed command of the Fourth Pennsylvania Battalion early in the war as a colonel. In 1776 he led the force that covered the American retreat from Quebec. After joining Washington's army as a brigadier general in 1777, he fought in the battles near Philadelphia (fall 1777). Wayne was court-martialed for negligence in the defeat of American troops at Paoli but was exonerated. Called "Mad Anthony" for his bravado and penchant for vituperative outbursts, Wayne maneuvered adeptly in the Battle of Monmouth (1778), giving Washington's troops time to reform their defensive lines and preventing an American loss from degenerating into a rout. On the night of July 15-16, 1779, Wayne led a brilliantly successful assault against the British garrison at Stony Point on the Hudson River. The battle gave a much-needed boost to American morale and secured Wayne's reputation as a superb general. He went on to fight with Nathanael Greene in the South and in the triumphant Yorktown campaign (1781). After the war Wayne dabbled in pol-

Daniel Webster, the most renowned orator of antebellum America, was best known for the final sentence of his speech in the Senate in 1830, which became a Union rallying cry during the Civil War: "Liberty and Union, now and forever, one and inseparable."

itics and business, but he returned to soldiering in 1792, leading an expedition into Ohio country to fight the Delawares and Shawnees, whom he defeated at the Battle of Fallen Timbers (1794). He secured the Treaty of Greenville (1795), in which the Indian tribes ceded some 28,000 square miles of land to the United States.

See Also: Revolution, American.

BIBLIOGRAPHY: Nelson, Paul D., *Anthony Wayne: Soldier of the Early Republic* (Indiana Univ. Press 1985).

■ **WAYNE, JAMES MOORE (1790-1867),** associate justice of the U.S. Supreme Court (1835-67). He was born in Savannah, Georgia, practiced law in Georgia, and was elected to the U.S. House of Representatives (1828). Wayne was a defender of slavery but remained on the Court when the Civil War broke out.

See Also: Supreme Court.

■ **WAYNE, JOHN (1907-79),** film actor. Born in Winterset, Iowa, he began working as a screen extra while playing football at the University of Southern California. His rugged good looks and physical presence led to roles in low-budget Westerns and a featured role in director John Ford's *Stagecoach* (1939), which established him as the prototypical strong, silent cowboy hero. He frequently played Western or military roles, often to best advantage in Ford's films.

See Also: Ford, John; Motion Pictures.

■ **WEBB-KENYON ACT (1913),** federal legislation championed by the Anti-Saloon League. The act was an attempt to reinforce state prohibition laws by making it a federal crime to transport alcohol into any state in violation of that state's law.

See Also: Prohibition.

■ **WEBSTER, DANIEL (1782-1852),** lawyer, political leader, and statesman. He was born in Salisbury, New Hampshire, and graduated from Dartmouth College in 1801. As a young congressman from New Hampshire (1813-17), Webster opposed the War of 1812 and hinted at nullification, but he spent most of his congressional (1823-27) and senatorial (1827-41, 1845-50) career advocating economic growth through federal action. With Henry Clay of Kentucky and John C. Calhoun of South Carolina, he formed the "Great Triumvirate" that attempted to thwart Pres. Andrew Jackson. Webster opposed the annexation of Texas and the Mexican War because he feared slavery's extension. To preserve the Union, however, he supported the Compromise of 1850, which permitted some territories to decide the slavery question for themselves.

An outstanding secretary of state (1841-43, 1850-52), Webster negotiated the Webster-Ashburton Treaty, which resolved a long-standing boundary dispute with Great Britain. As a lawyer he influenced the development of constitutional law, strengthening commercial interests, the judiciary, and federal authority. Although the highest paid attorney of his time, Webster lived and died in heavy debt.

Nicknamed "Black Dan," both for his dark complexion and one side of his personality, Webster was a charismatic figure. His physical presence—a barrel chest, leonine head, and heavy black eyes and brows—contributed to his lasting fame as an orator. His words moved judges and juries in court, crowds of ordinary folk at patriotic occasions, and his colleagues in Congress, as in his attack on nullification in the famed Webster-Hayne Debate (1830).

See Also: Calhoun, John Caldwell; Clay, Henry; Compromise of 1850; Webster-Ashburton Treaty; Webster-Hayne Debate.

BIBLIOGRAPHY: Bartlett, Irving H., *Daniel Webster* (Norton 1978); Peterson, Merrill D., *The Great Triumvirate: Webster, Clay, and Calhoun* (Oxford Univ. Press 1987).

■ **WEBSTER, NOAH (1758-1843),** lexicographer and journalist. Born in West Hartford, Connecticut, Webster served in the Revolutionary War. After graduating from Yale College in 1778, he taught school and studied for the bar, to which he was admitted in 1781. In 1783 Webster published the first section of his *Grammatical Institute of the English Language,* which eventually consisted of a spelling book, grammar book, and reader. Politically Webster was a Federalist and he outlined his ideas about a strong central government in *Sketches of American Policy* (1785) and in two newspapers, the *Minerva* and the *Herald,* which he published in the 1790s. Webster published *A Compendious Dictionary of the English Language* in 1806. He moved to Amherst, Massachusetts, in 1812 and served in the Massachusetts state legislature and as one of the founders of Amherst College. In 1828, after moving back to his college town of New Haven, Connecticut, Webster issued the two-volume *American Dictionary of the English Language.* A second edition followed in 1840.

■ **WEBSTER-ASHBURTON TREATY (1842),** U.S. agreement settling several disputes with Great Britain that threatened a third Anglo-American war. The dispute over the Maine–New Brunswick border, an area rich in timber and important to Canada's defense, had brought both nations to the brink of hostilities during the Aroostook War (1839). U.S. Sec. of State Daniel Webster and British Foreign Minister Lord Ashburton reached a settlement giving Britain 5,000 of the 12,000 square miles of contested territory. In return the United States acquired control of the Aroostook

Valley and navigation rights to the St. John's River through New Brunswick. Britain accepted American claims elsewhere along the U.S.-Canadian border and yielded some 6,500 square miles between Lake Superior and Lake of the Woods, a part of the iron-rich Mesabi Range. Other disputes were also settled in the treaty. Britain agreed not to interfere in slave revolts aboard American vessels landing at British ports and pledged cooperation in suppressing the slave trade. Webster resolved the *Caroline* Affair (1837) by admitting that the ship had engaged in illegal activities. By maintaining Anglo-American peace through compromise, the treaty facilitated the settlement of the Oregon and Central American controversies in the late 1840s and 1850s.

—DEAN FAFOUTIS

See Also: Aroostook War; Caroline *Affair*; Frontier in American History; Webster, Daniel.

BIBLIOGRAPHY: Corey, Albert B., *The Crisis of 1830-1842 in Canadian-American Relations* (Russell & Russell 1970); Jones, Howard, *To the Webster-Ashburton Treaty: A Study in Anglo-American Relations, 1783-1843* (Univ. of North Carolina Press 1977).

■ **WEBSTER-HAYNE DEBATE (1830),** U.S. Senate debate. Initially over public lands and tariff policies, the debate turned into a historic discussion of theories of states' rights, nullification, and the nature of the Union. In January Sen. Robert Y. Hayne of South Carolina proposed an amendment to a public land bill. Opposing protective tariffs, Hayne argued they were unconstitutional and dismissive of states' rights. His arguments drew largely on the "Exposition of 1828," an essay by Vice Pres. John C. Calhoun. They expounded Calhoun's theory of nullification, the idea that an individual state could reject a law passed by Congress. Sen. Daniel Webster of Massachusetts responded to Hayne by arguing that the Supreme Court, not the states, had the power to pass on federal laws and that nullification would wreck the Union. Webster ended with his famous vision of "Liberty and Union, now and forever, one and inseparable."

See Also: Calhoun, John Caldwell; Nullification; Webster, Daniel.

■ *WEBSTER V. REPRODUCTIVE HEALTH SERVICES* **(1989),** U.S. Supreme Court case that upheld the constitutionality of a Missouri law limiting the use of public funds, facilities, and personnel for abortions. A divided Court ruled (5-4) that states could discourage but not ban abortions permitted under *Roe* v. *Wade* (1973). Four justices also endorsed a preamble to the law that declared life begins at conception, thereby indicating their willingness to revise *Roe* and further restrict access to legal abortion.

See Also: Roe v. Wade; Supreme Court.

■ **WEISER, JOHANN CONRAD (1696-1760),** Indian agent. Born in Württemberg, Germany, Weiser immigrated with his family to New York in 1710. As a young man, he became fluent in the Mohawk language and, after moving to Pennsylvania, was instrumental in negotiating good relations with the Indians there (1730-48). Later in life, he served in a number of public offices, including justice of the peace, judge, and commissioner of Reading, Pennsylvania.

■ **WELD, THEODORE DWIGHT (1803-95),** American reformer, abolitionist, minister, and writer. Born in Hampton, Connecticut, Weld became a Protestant preacher and was greatly influenced by the Second Great Awakening and the preaching of Charles G. Finney. He persuaded businessmen Arthur and Lewis Tappan, politician Edwin Stanton, preacher Lyman Beecher, and others to support the abolitionist cause. Weld delivered antislavery lectures at the Lane Theological Seminary in Oberlin, Ohio. Eventually dismissed from Lane, he took much of the Lane student body with him to Oberlin College in 1834. Weld was one of the organizers of the American and Foreign Anti-Slavery Society. In 1838 he married the southern abolitionist Angelina Grimké and became active in supporting women's rights. Weld anonymously published *The Bible against Slavery* (1837) and *American Slavery As It Is* (1839), which influenced Harriet Beecher Stowe in her *Uncle Tom's Cabin*.

See Also: Antislavery Movement; Stowe, Harriet Beecher.

■ **WELLES, GIDEON (1802-78),** editor and politician. Born in Glastonbury, Connecticut, Welles was editor and part owner of the *Hartford Times* from 1826 to 1836. He was Hartford's postmaster from 1836 to 1841 and in 1854 helped organize the Republican party. He was secretary of the navy during and immediately after the Civil War and oversaw the navy's expansion. A supporter of both Presidents Abraham Lincoln and Andrew Johnson, Welles opposed the Radical Republicans' plan for Reconstruction.

■ **WELLES, ORSON (1916-85),** stage, radio, and film actor and director. Born in Kenosha, Wisconsin, he joined John Houseman to form the Mercury Theatre (1937). They produced stage and radio plays, notably the historic 1938 broadcast of "The War of the Worlds," and films including the classic *Citizen Kane* (1941). Welles's later career was marked by failed projects interspersed with memorable acting roles in films such as *The Third Man* (1947).

See Also: Hollywood; Motion Pictures.

■ **WELLS BARNETT, IDA BELL (1862-1931),** prominent feminist. She was born in Holly Springs, Mississippi. Having studied briefly at Shaw University, she became a schoolteacher and moved to Memphis, Tennessee, where in 1884 she brought suit against the Chesapeake, Ohio and Southwestern Railroad for having racially discriminated against her while she was on a train. She won the suit before the circuit court, but the Tennessee Supreme Court overturned the decision. In 1884, Wells Barnett had a journalism career, writing about discrimination against African Americans. In 1889 she became coeditor and then editor of the *Free Speech and Headlight* newspaper in Memphis. After the lynching of three African Americans in the city in 1892, she wrote a fiery antilynching editorial in her newspaper, particularly denying the general characterization of African Americans as rapists of white women. An outraged mob destroyed the newspaper office. Wells moved to New York (1892) and then to Chicago (1895), where she married Ferdinand L. Barnett, an African-American lawyer and editor of the *Chicago Conservator*. She succeeded him as editor in July 1895. Together, they became prominent figures in Chicago's African-American community. Wells Barnett was the pioneer of the antilynching crusade in the United States. She lectured, participated in several African-American organizations, and published numerous articles and pamphlets on the rights of

African Americans. She also introduced African-American women's clubs in Chicago. Strongly denying the accommodationist ideas of Booker T. Washington, Wells Barnett favored active protest by African Americans against lynching, segregation, and disfranchisement.

—DENIS KOZLOV

See Also: African Americans; Civil Rights Movement; Women in American History; Women's Movement.

BIBLIOGRAPHY: Thompson, Mildred I., *Ida B. Wells-Barnett: An Exploratory Study of an American Black Woman, 1893-1930* (Carlson 1990); Wells, Ida B., *Crusade for Justice: The Autobiography of Ida B. Wells* (Univ. of Chicago Press 1970).

WELTY, EUDORA (1909-), author. She was born in Jackson, Mississippi. Known for her skillful use of local dialects and the colorful, sometimes bizarre, characters of her novels and short fiction, she won the Pulitzer Prize for *The Optimist's Daughter* (1972). Her autobiography is titled *One Writer's Beginnings* (1984). She was awarded the National Book Foundation Medal in 1991.

See Also: Women in American History.

WEST, BENJAMIN (1738-1820), painter of the Revolutionary War era. West was born near Springfield, Pennsylvania. After briefly having studios in Philadelphia and New York City, he left the colonies, first for travel and study in Italy, and then to settle in London in 1763. He opened a studio for portraiture but also was successful with his innovative history paintings. In works such as *The Death of Wolfe* (1770), West is credited with creating the first "modern history paintings," with subjects portrayed in modern dress and setting, a style adopted by John Singleton Copley and John Trumbull. Engravings of *The Death of Wolfe* brought West not only acclaim but fortune. West did commissions for King George III but also depicted American subjects, such as his well-known *William Penn's Treaty with the Indians* (1772). Although West did not return to the United States, he remained an important influence on American art; his studio became the training ground for American artists studying abroad, including Trumbull and Gilbert Charles Stuart.

See Also: Copley, John Singleton; Stuart, Gilbert Charles; Painting; Trumbull, John.

WEST, MAE (1892-1980), actress. Born in Brooklyn, New York, she first performed in burlesque stage shows and in theater productions of *Sex* (1926) and *Diamond Lil* (1928). In the 1930s, she became a film comedienne, thrilling movie audiences with overt sexual references and stretching the limits of Hollywood's censorship code in films such as *She Done Him Wrong* (1933) and *Go West Young Man* (1936).

See Also: Women in American History.

WEST, THE, term that designates the western region of North America. According to the federal government's definition, the West includes the states of Alaska, Arizona, California, Hawaii, Idaho, Montana, Nevada, New Mexico, Oregon, Utah, Washington, and Wyoming. The West, however, is as much an elusive term of the American imagination as it is a geographic entity. Nearly every part of the present United States has been understood as "the West" at some point in American history. But in current parlance, the West is usually meant to be the last frontier of white American settlement during the late 19th century. Geographically, the West is located west of the Mississippi River extending as far as the Pacific Ocean and includes the Great Plains, the Rocky Mountains, the desert Southwest, the Sierra Nevadas, and the Pacific Coast. While arguments will continue over the exact geographic definition of the West, romantic images of cattle drives, cowboys, gunfights, Indians, outlaws, prospectors, and frontier towns, derived often from Western novels and movies, have created the West of the imagination. During the 20th century the West has experienced phenomenal rates of urban growth, especially in such cities as Los Angeles, Phoenix, Denver, San Antonio, Dallas, Houston, Las Vegas, and Tucson.

WESTERNS, formulaic types of popular fiction and film set in the American West, depicting a conflict between civilization and wilderness, in which barbaric and anarchic elements of wild nature (Indians, outlaws, the hostile landscape or environment) threaten to annihilate a tenuous, unstable, frontier family or community, with the hero caught between these forces. Although part of the old life, the hero usually fights on the side of the community, and by defending civilization, he is necessarily aiding in the destruction of the old order (himself included) and helping to establish the new. Although this formula has changed over the years to reflect changing attitudes and values, the basic ingredients have remained the same, thus mythologizing westward movement and the West.

The Fictional Western. Both fictional and film Westerns owe a debt to James Fenimore Cooper's novel featuring the frontier hero Natty Bumppo and the dime novel Western of the 1860s. Dime novels embellished the lives of real people like Billy the Kid, exploiting the wild landscape and glamorizing outlaw life. Literary naturalism provides another direction in Western writing. In the late 19th century, writers like Bret Harte, Stephen Crane, Jack London, Frank Norris, among others, began to use the environment as a major influence on their characters, situations, and actions. Later practitioners, like Ernest Haycox, Max Brand, Clay Fisher, Walter Van Tilburg Clark, and Jack Schaefer, continued to dramatize the alienating effects of the vast empty spaces on their characters.

Owen Wister's *The Virginian* (1902), often regarded as the first important Western novel, deals with issues of frontier violence and vigilantism, major concerns in the settlement of the West. Wister's cowboy hero is a prototype for many fictions and films coming later, and his marriage to Molly, the feisty schoolmarm from the East, foreshadows one of the conventions in the genre. Zane Grey, a prominent imitator of Wister, reached a wide audience with his epic confrontations. In *Riders of the Purple Sage* (1912), Grey used the landscape in a symbolic way to heighten the conflict. Another vastly popular writer of Westerns featuring epic confrontations, Louis L'Amour is perhaps best known for his novel *Hondo* (1953) and for his highly charged chronicles of pioneer families.

While L'Amour, Grey, and others mythologize the West—its landscape and characters—most modern Western writers engage in deconstructing myths. Larry McMurtry does both. In *Lonesome Dove* (1985), he mythologizes the cowboy hero and describes the trail drive in epic terms, but in other fiction he shows a modern, empty, wasted West filled with characters who have lost touch with them-

selves and the land. This latter view of the West has been dramatized with special urgency by recent American Indian writers, such as N. Scott Momaday, Leslie Silko, Louise Erdrich, and Gerald Vizenor.

The Film Western. The spectacular western landscape has been a visual paradise for filmmakers. Beginning in 1903 with *The Great Train Robbery*, the film Western was an immediate success, reaching the height of its popularity in the 1940s and 1950s. However, by the early 1970s, the genre seemed to have reached an impasse, and a new, anti-mythic version emerged, undermining themes earlier Westerns had celebrated, using landscape imagery to emphasize the antiheroic and the estranged and deconstructing elements of the formula in other ways. Ironically, these "new Westerns," while undermining older myths, created new ones of their own, artistically reshaping the formula, and producing some aesthetically compelling works of art. Sam Peckinpah's *The Wild Bunch* (1969) is a landmark in this new trend that has continued into the 1990s with Clint Eastwood's disturbing, anti-heroic *Unforgiven* (1992) and Kevin Costner's postmodern *Dances with Wolves* (1993). These provocative Westerns indicate that the genre, far from dead, still reminds us of the power of our myths, while creatively reimagining them in new ways and providing us with exciting entertainment.

—LEONARD W. ENGEL

See Also: Dime Novel; Motion Pictures; Novel.

BIBLIOGRAPHY: Buscombe, Edward, ed., *The BFI Companion to the Western* (Atheneum 1988); Cawelti, John, *Adventure, Mystery, and Romance: Formula Stories as Art and Popular Culture* (Univ. of Chicago Press 1976); Kitses, John, *Horizons West* (Indiana Univ. Press 1970); Tuska, John, *The American West in Film* (Greenwood Press 1985).

■ **WESTINGHOUSE, GEORGE (1846-1914),** inventor and manufacturer. Born in Central Bridge, New York, Westinghouse served in the Union army and navy during the Civil War and then worked in his father's farm implement factory. He obtained his first patent for a rotary steam engine in 1865 and invented an air brake for railroad cars in 1869. His Westinghouse Air Brake Company revolutionized the railroad industry by making high-speed travel safe. Studying European devices for ideas, Westinghouse also developed and manufactured electrically controlled railroad switch and signal systems (1882). He invented a system for transmitting natural gas over long distances (1883) and developed alternating-current electrical systems that used transformers to allow local distribution (1886). The Westinghouse Electric Company (1886) flourished despite competition from Thomas A. Edison, winning the contract to light the Chicago World's Columbian Exposition (1893) and to develop the power of Niagara Falls. The company fell into bankruptcy during the panic of 1907, however, and Westinghouse was unable to revive it to its previous prosperity. After he retired in 1911 he continued to conduct experiments with steam turbines and automobile air springs. He is credited with more than 400 patents throughout his lifetime.

See Also: Invention; Science.

■ **WESTMORELAND, WILLIAM CHILDS (1914-),** commander of U.S. forces in Vietnam (1964-68), and U.S. Army chief of staff (1968-72). Born in Spartenburg, South Carolina, Westmoreland graduated from West Point (1936) as first captain of the Cadet Corps. He served with distinction in combat in Europe in World War II and went on to hold many important posts in the army, including commandant of West Point. In June 1964 Westmoreland was promoted to head Military Assistance Command, Vietnam (MACV), having served six months as deputy commander. It was on his watch that American forces in Vietnam increased from fewer than 20,000 advisers to 500,000 troops (1968), and Westmoreland played an important role in the shaping of U.S. strategy in this period. He deemphasized American involvement in the pacification of villages and was an ardent believer in large-scale "search and destroy" missions, where superior American mobility and firepower could be brought to bear on communist troops. In 1966 and 1967, U.S. units inflicted heavy casualties on the Viet Cong, and an optimistic Westmoreland returned to the United States briefly in November 1967 to announce that "the end was beginning to come into view." But in January 1968 Hanoi unleashed the massive Tet Offensive, severely damaging Westmoreland's (and the entire Johnson administration's) credibility. While the offensive proved a military disaster for the

communists, it turned American public opinion against the war effort and thus was the conflict's turning point. Soon after Tet, Westmoreland advocated expanding the scope of military activity in Vietnam, but Washington rejected that option and brought him home to serve as army chief of staff. In 1982 Westmoreland filed a highly publicized libel suit against CBS News after that organization aired a report claiming he had falsified casualty reports. An out-of-court settlement was reached. Westmoreland's strategy and his overarching view of the Vietnam War have been widely criticized, but a number of historians have argued persuasively that America's failed crusade in Southeast Asia was more the result of wrongheaded political decisions made in Washington than military ones made in Vietnam.

—JAMES A. WARREN

See Also: Tet Offensive; Vietnam War.

BIBLIOGRAPHY: Karnow, Stanley, *Vietnam: A History* (Viking 1983); Westmoreland, William C., *A Soldier Reports* (Doubleday 1976).

■ **WEST POINT,** U.S. military academy. Initially a fort on the Hudson River, it was nearly betrayed to the British (1780) by Benedict Arnold in the American Revolution. The academy was established at the fort in 1802 and represented a major step forward in the professionalism of American arms. The academy's role expanded as the War of 1812 underscored the lack of talent and training in U.S. military leadership. Sylvanus Thayer, "father of the academy," made significant changes to the institution's structure (1817-33). Many West Point graduates served in the Mexican and Civil Wars. Gen. Douglas MacArthur modernized the curriculum after World War I. Today the academy is run by the Department of the Army. The student body consists of about 4,000 male and female cadets, who must be nominated by public officials and other dignitaries. The cadets receive a college education as well as military training.

See Also: Army.

■ **WEST VIRGINIA,** a state bordered on the north and east by Pennsylvania and Maryland, on the south, east, and west by Virginia, on the south and west by Kentucky, and on the north and west by Ohio. The Ohio River forms its northwest border. It is wholly within the Appalachian Moun-

A West Point graduating class around 1900 listens to graduation speeches. An act of Congress established the U.S. Military Academy at West Point in 1802.

the law on religious grounds, the majority ruled (6-3) the reason students declined to salute the flag was unimportant. Instead the Court invoked the First Amendment's broad free speech protections to strike down the law.

See Also: *Supreme Court.*

■ **WHALING,** industry that began on Long Island, Cape Cod, and Nantucket as early as the mid-17th century, when small boats hunted along the northern coast. New Bedford, Massachusetts, became the center of the whaling industry after 1755. British colonists sought whale oil for lamps, spermaceti for candles, ambergris for perfumes, and whalebone for corsets and stays. Between 1768 and 1772 whale products made up the fourth largest export commodity from New England; in 1774 a fleet of 360 ships collected 45,000 barrels of whale oil and 75,000 pounds of bone. Initially hunting only right whales, whalers sought sperm whales in increasingly distant waters after 1712. New England ships hunted whales from Baffin Bay to Antarctica, and after the first one rounded Cape Horn in 1791 they plied the Pacific as well, leaving home for years at a time. In 1830 whalers brought in 115,000 barrels of whale oil and 120,000 pounds of bone. Although the explosive harpoon head lessened the risk of whaling in the 1850s, petroleum replaced whale oil as an illuminant, and the whaling industry declined. In modern times concerns over whale populations have far outweighed demand for whale products and have almost ended whaling.

■ **WHARTON, EDITH (1862-1937),** author. Born in New York City, she was raised among the wealthy elite living there. Her novels—the best of which are *House of Mirth* (1905) and *The Age of Innocence* (1920), which won the Pulitzer Prize—depict passionate and imaginative characters suffocated by the rigid moral confines of polite society. Her style is often compared with that of her close friend Henry James. She was honored by the governments of Belgium and France for her work with refugees and orphans during World War I.

See Also: *James, Henry; Novel.*

tain region. Rugged terrain has left it one of the poorest states, although its economy is heavily industrial. During the Civil War this part of Virginia remained loyal to the Union and was granted statehood in 1863.

Capital: Charleston. Area: 24,232 square miles. Population (1995 est.): 1,828,000.

See Also: *Appalachian Mountains; Brown, John; Harpers Ferry Raid; Ohio River.*

■ *WEST VIRGINIA STATE BOARD OF EDUCATION V. BARNETTE (1943),* U.S. Supreme Court case that overturned a state law requiring schoolchildren to salute the flag. Although the parents challenging the statute were Jehovah's Witnesses who opposed

■ **WHEAT,** cereal grain of Old World origin, commonly used for making bread. Wheat was an early import to the American colonies, arriving with the English in 1607, but because of disease and the difficulties of planting and processing, it was slow to come into widespread use. By the 19th century, however, wheat had become for many farmers (particularly those on the midwestern prairies) their principal cash crop, for wheat brought a higher price in relation to its weight than other grains. The cultivation of wheat demanded intensive human labor, though, leading many to experiment with technological alternatives—most famously Cyrus McCormick, whose horse-drawn reaper, mass-produced in Chicago from 1847 onward, greatly accelerated the task of harvesting wheat. Automated harrows, grain drills, and threshers soon followed, so that by the 1880s, the average wheat farmer was dependent on mechanization in order to produce his crop.

See Also: *Agriculture.*

BIBLIOGRAPHY: Cronon, William, *Nature's Metropolis: Chicago and the Great West* (Norton 1991); Kahn, E. J., *The Staffs of Life* (Little, Brown 1985).

■ **WHEATLEY, PHILLIS (c. 1754-84),** poet. Born in West Africa, she was kidnapped and sold into slavery in 1761. A family of Philadelphia Quakers bought her, tutored her in English, and allowed her freedom to develop her considerable intellectual gifts. In 1770 she published her first of many poems. Her achievements and short-lived celebrity challenged the commonly held notion that African Americans were mentally inferior to Europeans. After the death of her mistress and an unsuccessful marriage, Wheatley and her child died of exposure.

See Also: *African Americans; Poetry.*

■ **WHEELER, WILLIAM ALMON (1819-87),** vice president of the United States (1877-81). Born in Malone, New York, he was admitted to the New York bar in 1845. He served in the New York State Assembly (1850-59) and in the U.S. Congress (1861-63, 1869-77). As a Republican congressman, he engineered the settlement of the 1874 election dispute in Louisiana known as the Wheeler Compromise. In 1877 a special electoral commission designated Rutherford B. Hayes and his running mate, Wheeler, the winners of the disputed 1876 presidential election.

See Also: *Hayes, Rutherford Birchard; Vice President of the United States.*

■ **WHEELER-LEA ACT (1938),** a federal "truth in advertising" law. The act gave the Federal Trade Commission new powers to regulate false and misleading advertising. First proposed in 1933, the law was opposed by many business interests.

See Also: *Federal Trade Commission; New Deal.*

■ **WHEELOCK, ELEAZAR (1711-79),** missionary to the American Indians. Born in Windham, Connecticut, Wheelock was among the earliest Europeans to advocate the assimilation of Indians through the boarding school experience. A Congregational minister in Lebanon, Connecticut, in

Edith Wharton won the Pulitzer Prize for *The Age of Innocence* (1920), which is considered her most important novel.

the 1740s, Wheelock began educating Indian students at the Moor's Indian Charity School, which eventually became a boarding school for educating them as missionaries. Among his students were Samson Occum and Joseph Brant. In 1770, he moved to Hanover, New Hampshire, where he established Dartmouth College, which included Indians in its student body.

See Also: Brant, Joseph; Indians of North America; Occum, Samson.

■ **WHIG PARTY,** political party that developed in opposition to the Democratic party of Pres. Andrew Jackson (1829-37), incorporating factions from the defunct Federalist party. The first appearance of the Whigs came during the presidential campaign of Henry Clay in 1832. The party, which formally organized in 1834, supported Clay's conservative "American System," a program of protective tariffs to stimulate industry, a national bank to facilitate credit and exchange, and federally funded internal improvements (roads and canals) to aid trade and commerce.

The Whigs' first major success came in 1840 when—taking their political cues from the Democrats—the Whigs waged an aggressive presidential campaign using mass rallies, political propaganda, and the winning slogan "Tippecanoe and Tyler too." But "Old Tippecanoe," Whig Pres. William Henry Harrison, died just weeks into his term (Apr. 4, 1841) and was succeeded by his vice-presidential running mate, John Tyler, who soon reverted to his Democratic origins. After Clay lost his last campaign for the presidency to James K. Polk in 1844, the Whigs successfully ran another war hero in 1848, Gen. Zachary Taylor of Mexican War fame. By that point, however, the party was being torn apart by anti- and proslavery factions, who were dubbed the "Conscience Whigs" and the "Cotton Whigs," respectively. In 1852, the party ran another general, Winfield Scott, but he was badly beaten by Democrat Franklin Pierce. It proved to be the final appearance of the Whigs on the national political stage.

See Also: Clay, Henry; Harrison, William Henry; Political Parties.

BIBLIOGRAPHY: Brown, Thomas, *Politics and Statesmanship: Essays on the American Whig Party* (Columbia Univ. Press 1985); Howe, Daniel Walker, *The Political Culture of the American Whigs* (Univ. of Chicago Press 1979); Poage, George Rawlings, *Henry Clay and the Whig Party* (Univ. of North Carolina Press 1936).

■ **WHIPPLE, WILLIAM (1730-85),** businessman and Revolutionary War politician. Whipple was born in Kittery, Maine, where he began his career as a sea captain. He later moved to New Hampshire and entered politics as a member of the Second Continental Congress and signer of the Declaration of Independence.

See Also: Declaration of Independence.

■ **WHISKEY REBELLION,** the first major insurrection against the authority of the federal government. The excise tax on distilled spirits passed by Congress in 1791 met with fervent opposition in the region of Trans-Appalachia. During the years 1793 and 1794 this opposition touched off an open rebellion in more than 20 counties in Pennsylvania, Maryland, Virginia, Kentucky, Ohio, and North Carolina.

The rebellion in western Pennsylvania reflected tensions that had been building for decades. The region's inhabitants resented their underrepresentation in state legislatures. Most settlers rented or squatted on land owned by absentee landlords and speculators. Consequently, many lived in extreme poverty amid some of the richest farmland in the country. In frustration, some frontiersmen had even discussed the possible secession of the back country with British and Spanish authorities in the years leading up to 1791.

Opposition to the whiskey excise flourished among back country farmers who distilled their grain into whiskey before transporting it to market. Comparing the excise to the Stamp Act of 1765, frontiersmen argued that the distant national government in Washington was no more representative of their interests than Parliament had been. They also saw the excise as an aristocratic conspiracy to deprive poor yeomen of their property by taxing their only source of cash income.

In the fall of 1791 crowds in western Pennsylvania began to assault and harass excise collectors, still inspectors, and their supporters. By 1794 poor frontiersmen had organized quasi-political militias, such as the Mingo Creek Society.

That summer federal authorities in Pennsylvania began to enforce the excise. When the Mingo Creek militia marched in protest on excise inspector John Neville's farm on July 16, 1794, Neville and his slaves opened fire, killing one of the militia men. The people of western Pennsylvania were enraged. On Aug. 1, 1794, some 7,000 armed insurgents gathered outside Pittsburgh to demonstrate their defiance of the law. The rebels brandished a six-striped flag signifying the independence of six western counties in Pennsylvania and Virginia.

By late summer the rebels had dispersed, some 2,000 fleeing west into the Ohio Valley. A national army of 13,000 men, initially commanded by Pres. George Washington, found no resistance when it arrived in the area. The army detained over 150 suspects, but the rebel leaders had escaped. Two poor farmers whose participation had been minor were convicted of treason. President Washington subsequently pardoned both men.

Although the rebellion did not produce political independence for the back country, it did deepen the ideological divide between advocates of a strong national government and advocates of liberty and decentralized government. Out of this division, the Federalist and Republican parties emerged in the years after 1794. The Republicans repealed the whiskey excise after coming to power in 1800.

—ROBERT H. CHURCHILL

BIBLIOGRAPHY: Crow, Jeffrey J., "The Whiskey Rebellion in North Carolina," *North Carolina Historical Review* (1989); Slaughter, Thomas P., *The Whiskey Rebellion: Frontier Epilogue to the American Revolution* (Oxford Univ. Press 1986).

■ **WHISTLER, JAMES (1834-1903)**, painter. Born in Lowell, Massachusetts, Whistler was a cadet at the U.S. Military Academy at West Point but did not complete school. He worked for about a year for the U.S. Coast and Geodetic Survey, learning drawing and etching, before going to Paris in 1855 to study art. In Paris, he associated with bohemian circles, particularly avant-garde artists and writers; he moved to London in 1859. Whistler's work was controversial for its abstract qualities and emphasis on variations in tone. The criticism of British art critic John Ruskin of Whistler's 1874 *Nocturne in Black and Gold: The Falling Rocket* resulted in a famous slander trial, which Whistler won but with only a token financial reward. Whistler still achieved success; his *Arrangement in Gray and Black No. 1: The Artist's Mother* (1872) was eventually acquired by the Louvre in Paris, and both his paintings and interior settings, such as the *Peacock Room* (1876-77), influenced the next generation of artists in America and Europe.

See Also: Painting.

■ **WHITE, ANDREW DICKSON (1832-1918)**, educator and diplomat. Born in Homer, New York, he was a professor at the University of Michigan (1857-62) before helping financier Ezra Cornell found Cornell University in Ithaca, New York. White was the first president of Cornell (1868-85) and served as U.S. minister to Germany (1879-81, 1897-1902) and Russia (1892-94). He also chaired the U.S. delegation to the Hague Peace Conference (1899).

See Also: Hague Peace Conferences.

■ **WHITE, BYRON RAYMOND (1917-)**, associate justice of the U.S. Supreme Court (1962-93). Born in Fort Collins, Colorado, he was a football star at the University of Colorado and in the National Football League, a Rhodes scholar at Oxford University, and a naval officer in the Pacific during World War II. While practicing law in Colorado, White played an active role in John F. Kennedy's presidential election campaign (1960). Kennedy then nominated him to the Supreme Court. White's tenure on the Court was marked by a pragmatic view of the law, but he tended to ally with conservative colleagues on many issues. While White often cast liberal votes in civil rights cases, he sided with conservatives on many abortion, free speech, obscenity, and criminal cases. White dissented in *Roe* v. *Wade* (1973), which established abortion rights, and in *Miranda* v. *Arizona* (1966), which required police to advise criminal suspects of their rights.

See Also: Supreme Court.

■ **WHITE, EDWARD DOUGLASS (1845-1921)**, associate justice of the U.S. Supreme Court (1894-1910) and chief justice of the United States (1910-21). The son of a wealthy sugar planter who served as governor of Louisiana and a member of

Congress, White was born in LaFourche Parish, Louisiana. He read law in New Orleans following the Civil War, served on the Louisiana Supreme Court (1878-80), and was briefly a U.S. senator (1891-94). An advocate of protective tariffs, especially tariffs protecting Louisiana sugar, White delayed accepting his appointment to the Supreme Court until the Senate completed work on a new and higher sugar tariff.

Conservative by temperament, White on the Court believed the courts should be able to exercise discretion. Although the Sherman Antitrust Act (1890) barred all combinations in restraint of trade, White instead advocated a "rule of reason," saying only "unreasonable" restraints should be unlawful. He also advocated the doctrine of "incorporation," extending constitutional protections to residents of territories annexed after the Spanish-American War (1898). When Chief Justice Melville Fuller died (1910), Pres. William Howard Taft, at the urging of White's colleagues, made White the first associate justice to be elevated to chief justice.

See Also: Supreme Court.

BIBLIOGRAPHY: Highsaw, Robert B., *Edward Douglass White, Defender of the Conservative Faith* (Louisiana State Univ. Press 1981).

■ **WHITE, JOHN (fl. 1577-93),** artist and colonist. In 1585 White accompanied (with scientist Thomas Harriot) the colonizing expedition organized by Sir Walter Raleigh that landed on Roanoke Island off the Virginia coast. White's watercolors of the flora, fauna, and native life he observed were copied by engraver Théodore de Bry. Not until the 20th century were the original watercolors rediscovered. They are perhaps the most accurate and sensitive images of North American Indians made at the moment of their contact with Europeans. White came to Roanoke Island again in 1587 as governor of the first English attempt at a self-sustaining and reproducing settlement. The next year he left his followers, including his daughter and granddaughter (Virginia Dare), to go to England for supplies. His return was delayed by the war with Spain, and when he again stepped ashore on Roanoke in 1591, the colony had disappeared. Nothing is known of his later years.

See Also: Dare, Virginia; Painting; Roanoke, Lost Colony of.

BIBLIOGRAPHY: Hulton, Paul, ed., *America 1585: The Complete Drawings of John White* (Univ. of North Carolina Press 1984); Quinn, David B., *Set Fair for Roanoke: Voyages and Colonies, 1584-1606* (Univ. of North Carolina Press 1985).

■ **WHITE, PEARL (1889-1938),** silent movie actress. Born in Green Ridge, Missouri, she was one of the most popular stars of early serial films, also known as "cliff-hangers." She is best remembered for her title role in *The Perils of Pauline* (1914).

See Also: Motion Pictures.

■ **WHITE, STANFORD (1853-1906),** architect. White was born in New York City and trained in the architectural practice of Henry Hobson Richardson. As a partner of the firm of McKim, Mead, and White, which he formed in 1879, he designed the Metropolitan Club (1894) and Washington Memorial Arch (1889), both in New York City. White met his infamous end when he was murdered on the roof of Madison Square Garden, which he had also designed, by Harry K. Thaw, the jealous husband of a former mistress of White, Evelyn Nesbit.

See Also: McKim, Mead, and White; Richardson, Henry Hobson.

■ **WHITE, WILLIAM ALLEN (1868-1944),** journalist and midwestern regional writer. A native of Emporia, Kansas, White attended the University of Kansas. Beginning in 1895, White was the proprietor and editor of the *Emporia Gazette*, a small newspaper that he made famous through his vibrant editorials. Throughout his career as editor, White also published stories and novels, including *The Real Issue and Other Stories* (1896), *In Our Town* (1906*)*, *In the Heart of a Fool* (1918), and *A Puritan in Babylon* (1938).

■ **WHITEFIELD, GEORGE (1714-70),** English itinerant preacher of the Great Awakening. Born in Gloucester, England, Whitefield graduated from Oxford University, where he met John and Charles Wesley, the founders of Methodism. Their teachings on piety and the necessity of spiritual regeneration greatly influenced Whitefield. In 1737 he was ordained a deacon in the Church of England and began preaching immediately. His emotional, powerful delivery was better suited for the open air than the Anglican pulpit, so he made a career of traveling place to place preaching a message of free grace to all who would listen.

Between 1738 and 1770, Whitefield made seven trips to America, five of which were speaking tours. He was popular from Georgia to New England. Extemporaneous preaching as well as intinerancy were identified with Whitefield's ministry. His oratory generated such excitement that crowds seemed out of control as they pushed and shoved to hear Whitefield's words. In Philadelphia, he preached to a crowd of 20,000. Even the skeptic Benjamin Franklin was impressed, and the two became lifelong friends. Whitefield's greatest success was in Massachusetts and Connecticut, where during a 45-day tour in 1740 he delivered 175 sermons to thousands of people. By the time of his death in 1770 in Newburyport, Massachusetts, he was probably the best-known individual in the American colonies.

See Also: *Great Awakening; Religion.*
BIBLIOGRAPHY: Stout, Harry S., *The Divine Dramatist: George Whitefield and the Rise of Modern Evangelicalism* (Eerdmans 1991).

■ **WHITE HOUSE,** U.S. president's residence in Washington, D.C. Architect James Hoban designed the building and oversaw its original construction, which started in 1792. Additions were designed by Benjamin Latrobe in 1807 and McKim, Mead, and White in 1902.

See Also: *Latrobe, Benjamin; McKim, Mead, and White.*

■ **WHITE MOUNTAINS,** principal mountain range of the northern Appalachian Mountains in New Hampshire. Its highest point is Mt. Washington (6,288 feet). With some of the highest peaks in the eastern United States, the White Mountains were sparsely settled during colonial times. During the 19th century the area became a popular vacation spot, with grand hotels for Boston and New York's wealthy. In 1925 Congress created the White Mountain National Forest. The Appalachian Trail was constructed through the area in the 1920s and 1930s.

See Also: *Appalachian Mountains.*

■ **WHITE PLAINS, BATTLE OF (1776),** battle in the American Revolution. During the campaign

for New York City, Gen. George Washington's Continental army dug in around the town of White Plains, New York. On October 28 British forces led by Gen. William Howe attacked, taking the town and driving the Americans back to North Castle. Although the battle was a victory for the British, Howe's decision not to pursue Washington's army gave the Americans a chance to regroup.

See Also: *Revolution, American; Washington, George.*

■ **WHITMAN, MARCUS (1802-47)** and **WHITMAN, NARCISSA (died 1847),** Oregon pioneers born in Rushfield, New York. After receiving his medical degree in 1832, Marcus spent four years as a doctor in Canada. On his return to New York, Marcus resumed medical practice and became an elder in the Presbyterian Church. After an 1835 tour of the Pacific Northwest looking for a mission site, Marcus returned east and married Narcissa Prentiss, who had been raised in an evangelical household and agreed to join him in his missionary work. In February 1836, Marcus was sent to Oregon as a lay missionary for the American Board of Commissioners for Foreign Missions, accompanied by Henry Spalding and his wife, William Gray, and Narcissa. The Oregon missionaries quarreled bitterly among themselves and, in 1842, the commissioners decided to close the Oregon missions. Marcus traveled east and pleaded with the board, which relented, and he returned west in 1843 with a large group of Oregon settlers. The Whitmans' mission in the Walla Walla Valley at Waiilatpu was an important stop for Oregon Trail travelers, especially for medical attention. The Whitmans' missionary efforts included trying to eradicate Indian cultural practices, and finally, in 1847, outraged Cayuse Indians massacred Marcus, Narcissa, and 12 others.

See Also: *Frontier in American History; Overland Trail.*

■ **WHITMAN, WALT(ER) (1819-92),** poet. Born in Huntington, New York, Whitman supported himself for roughly 30 years, beginning in the early 1830s, by working for New York newspapers and magazines in various capacities. From 1841 to 1845, he wrote stories for the *Democratic Review,* advice, for the third edition (1860) Whitman added 45 new poems exploring male homosexuality in a section entitled "Calamus." The Civil War provided the subject matter for Whitman's *Drum Taps*, which appeared in 1865, after he had volunteered as a nurse for both Northern and Southern soldiers in and near Washington. The collection contained "When Lilacs Last in the Dooryard Bloom'd," inspired by Pres. Abraham Lincoln's death. Whitman left Washington in 1873, moving to Camden, New Jersey, where he remained the rest of his life. Although best known for *Leaves of Grass*, Whitman also produced important works of prose, such as *Democratic Vistas* (1871), *Memoranda during the War* (1875), and *Specimen Days and Collect* (1882).

—JAMES KESSENIDES

See Also: Poetry.

BIBLIOGRAPHY: Reynolds, David S., *Walt Whitman's America: A Cultural Biography* (Knopf 1995).

■ **WHITNEY, ELI (1765-1825),** manufacturer and inventor. Known for the cotton gin and for manufacturing with interchangeable parts, Whitney, born in Westborough, Massachusetts, began his career by helping his father operate a shop that manufactured nails during the American Revolution. After graduating from Yale College in 1793, Whitney traveled south as a tutor. In Georgia, he visited his friend Phineas Miller, manager of Mulberry Grove Plantation, and began to design a machine that would separate cotton from the seeds. Supported financially by Miller, Whitney created a cotton gin for which he secured a patent in 1794, although others copied his device. The gin failed to bring him prosperity but rendered the growing of cotton much more profitable because it could be processed so much faster.

Returning north and purchasing a factory in Mill Rock near New Haven, Connecticut, Whitney manufactured 10,000 muskets for the federal government using the interchangeable-parts system, which came to be known as the "American system." Whitney popularized the process and revolutionized mass production, and his contracts with the government during the War of 1812 made him wealthy. A consummate businessman, Whitney was attuned to social and political issues only insofar as they affected his industry. He died the owner of a prosperous business that was

Walt Whitman's *Leaves of Grass* (1855) greatly influenced later poets. His experiences as a volunteer nurse ministering to both camps during the Civil War found expression in *Drum Taps* (1865).

whose other contributors included Nathaniel Hawthorne and Edgar Allan Poe, and between 1846 and 1848, he edited a Brooklyn newspaper, the *Democratic Eagle*, from which position he was fired because of what would soon be called his Free Soil sensibilities. After a few months in New Orleans, Whitman returned to Brooklyn in 1848, where he continued to make a living in journalism and to pursue the creative interest in poetry he had taken up a decade earlier. In 1855, *Leaves of Grass* appeared, in which Whitman offered a lengthy preface to 12 untitled poems, including the one that would come to be called "Song of Myself." Mixed critical reviews and a generally unbuying public greeted this first of 10 editions, although Ralph Waldo Emerson wrote to Whitman, "I find it the most extraordinary piece of wit and wisdom that America has yet contributed." Its often frank treatment of the human body and exploration of sexuality proved provocative, yet against Emerson's handed down to his son and grandson before it was sold to the Winchester Arms Company.

—CATHERINE A. HAULMAN

See Also: Cotton Gin; Industrial Revolution; Invention; Science.

BIBLIOGRAPHY: Green, Constance McLaughlin, *Eli Whitney and the Birth of American Technology* (Little, Brown 1956).

■ *WHITNEY V. CALIFORNIA* **(1927),** U.S. Supreme Court case that upheld a California criminal syndicalism law targeting the Industrial Workers of the World, a radical labor organization. Although the Court upheld (9-0) the law on the grounds that the state could protect itself from violent attack, Justices Louis Brandeis and Oliver Wendell Holmes argued that the courts must take care to protect freedom of speech and assembly unless a clear and present danger exists.

See Also: Industrial Workers of the World.

■ **WHITTAKER, CHARLES EVANS (1901-73),** associate justice of the U.S. Supreme Court (1957-62). Born in Troy, Kansas, he enrolled in law school before graduating from high school and was admitted to the bar in 1923. He practiced in Kansas City, Missouri, until he was appointed to the U.S. District Court (1954).

See Also: Supreme Court.

■ **WHITTIER, JOHN GREENLEAF (1807-92),** poet. Whittier was born in Haverhill, Massachusetts. He was largely self-educated and strongly influenced by his Quaker heritage. Through his writings Whittier became a noted abolitionist. A prolific poet, Whittier is best remembered today for poems such as "Snow-Bound," "Barbara Fritchie," and "Maud Muller." His volumes of poetry and prose include *Legends of New England in Prose and Verse* (1831), *Songs of Labor* (1850), *In War Time and Other Poems* (1864), and *At Sundown* (1890).

See Also: Poetry.

■ **WIENER, NORBERT (1894-1964),** mathematician. Born in Columbus, Ohio, he worked as an editor and taught philosophy and engineering at Massachusetts Institute of Technology before settling into its mathematics department (1919-64). His work on differential space, harmonic analysis,

Fourier transforms, and Tauberian theorems established him as a mathematician of the first rank. During World War II, he helped develop high-speed electronic radar, and he published *Cybernetics* in 1948. This book made him famous and popularized important aspects of communication theory.

See Also: Science.

■ **WILDER, THORNTON (1897-1975),** novelist and playwright. Wilder was born in Madison, Wisconsin, and graduated from Yale University in 1920. He taught at the Lawrenceville Academy in New Jersey (1921-28) and the University of Chicago (1930-36). Wilder won the Pulitzer Prize three times, for the novel *The Bridge of San Luis Rey* (1927) and for the plays *Our Town* (1938) and *The Skin of Our Teeth* (1942). Other works include *The Cabala* (1925), *Heaven's My Destination* (1938), and *Theophilis North* (1973).

■ **WILDERNESS, BATTLE OF THE (1864),** Civil War battle. On May 4, 1864, the Union Army of the Potomac, under Gen. Ulysses S. Grant, moved across the Rapidan River in northern Virginia and into the dense woods known as the "Wilderness." An encounter with two corps of Confederate Gen. Robert E. Lee's army there initiated the battle on the 5th. On May 6 Grant tested the Confederate right flank, but initial gains were soon reversed. The Union line then just barely withstood attacks to both its flanks. Rather than retreat, however, on May 7 Grant ordered a march around Lee's right to Spotsylvania, where the two armies redeployed.

See Also: Civil War; Grant, Ulysses Simpson; Lee, Robert Edward; Spotsylvania, Battle of.

■ **WILDERNESS PRESERVATION ACT (1964),** environmental law setting aside 9.1 million acres of federal land as wilderness areas. It also created a conservation fund financed by recreation fees to maintain wilderness areas.

■ **WILDERNESS ROAD,** trail through the Appalachians followed by Daniel Boone. In 1775, Boone followed Indian hunting trails to blaze a path from Cumberland Gap to the Kentucky River at Boonesboro. Still in use, this road became a major emigration route for hundreds of thousands of settlers passing into Kentucky and the Ohio Valley.

See Also: Boone, Daniel; Frontier in American History.

■ **WILD WEST SHOWS,** popular entertainment spectacles of the late 19th and early 20th centuries. Capitalizing on the public's fascination with the American West as an exotic land of cowboys and Indians, touring troupes presented circus-like performances featuring trick riding and roping, sharpshooting exhibitions, and reenactments of battles between Indians and the cavalry. The leading Wild West show was organized by William F. "Buffalo Bill" Cody (1846-1917), a former guide and buffalo hunter. Cody's show debuted in 1883 and toured the United States and Europe for 30 years. Cody helped build the legend of "Custer's Last Stand" by re-creating the June 25, 1876, battle at the Little Bighorn River. Sitting Bull, the leader of the Sioux against Custer, toured in Cody's show in 1885. Wild West shows solidified popular images of heroic soldiers and settlers subduing hostile Indians to tame the frontier.

See Also: Cody, William ("Buffalo Bill"); Indians of North America.

BIBLIOGRAPHY: Blackstone, Sarah J., *Buckskins, Bullets, and Business: A History of Buffalo Bill's Wild West* (Greenwood Press 1986).

■ **WILKES, CHARLES (1798-1877),** U.S. naval officer and explorer, born in New York City. Wilkes commanded the U.S. Exploring Expedition, which circumnavigated the globe between 1838 and 1842. With a number of prominent scientists, the expedition proceeded westward around the tip of South America. Wilkes's expedition charted some 1,500 miles of the Antarctic coastline, establishing its existence as a separate continent. During the nearly four-year expedition, the government-sponsored flotilla managed to chart numerous Pacific islands and much of the northwest coast of North America. Wilkes determined that Puget Sound might serve as an ideal port. He advocated that the United States claim possession as far north as latitude 54°40'. President Polk would later use this line—"54°40' or fight"—as a rallying cry for American claims to the region. During the Civil War Wilkes arrested two Confederate officials traveling aboard the British vessel *Trent* (1861). The Trent

Affair, which nearly brought Britain into the Civil War on the side of the Confederacy, and later violations of neutral rights led to his suspension from duty in 1864, although he was reappointed as rear admiral in 1866.

See Also: Exploration and Discovery; Oregon; Trent Affair.

■ **WILKINS, ROY (1901-81),** civil rights leader. Born in St. Louis, Missouri, Wilkins majored in sociology and minored in journalism at the University of Minnesota. He began his professional career as a journalist, editing the weekly Kansas City, Missouri, *Call* from 1923 to 1931. In 1931 he joined the staff of the National Association for the Advancement of Colored People (NAACP). Wilkins succeeded W. E. B. Du Bois as editor of the NAACP journal, the *Crisis*, a position he held for 15 years. An articulate and dedicated member, Wilkins long served as the organization's executive secretary (1955-64) and executive director (1965-77). He became one of the best-known moderate civil rights leaders in America. Wilkins's quiet yet determined leadership helped shape the role of the NAACP in the civil rights movement for nearly three decades. He was awarded the Spingarn Medal in 1964.

See Also: African Americans; Civil Rights Movement; National Association for the Advancement of Colored People (NAACP).

■ **WILKINSON, JAMES (1757-1825),** American military leader. Born in Calvert County, Maryland, Wilkinson was a captain in the Continental army during the American Revolution and was with Gen. Benedict Arnold during the retreat from Montreal to Albany (1776). In 1796 Wilkinson became the ranking officer in the U.S. Army. During the 1807 trial of former vice president Aaron Burr on treason charges, Wilkinson was the chief prosecution witness. Wilkinson was also tried for conspiracy against the U.S. government but was acquitted in 1811. During the War of 1812 he commanded the American forces in Canada. He retired from the army with an honorable discharge in 1815.

See Also: War of 1812.

■ **WILLARD, EMMA (1787-1870),** pioneer in women's education. Born in Berlin, Connecticut, she departed from the normal pattern of New England farm girls by seeking a formal education at the Berlin Academy in 1802. She spent several years teaching in various schools for girls and, in 1819, delivered "An Address to the Public . . . Proposing a Plan to Improve Female Education" to the New York state legislature. Her greatest accomplishment was the creation in 1821 of the Troy Female Seminary (now the Emma Willard School).

See Also: Women in American History; Women's Movement.

■ **WILLARD, FRANCES (1839-98),** temperance leader and suffragist, born in Churchville, New York. As dean of women, she presided over the introduction of coeducation to Northwestern University in 1873. She helped to found the Women's Christian Temperance Union in 1874 and served as president of the organization from 1879 to 1898. She used her influence to broaden the goals of the temperance movement, lobbying for suffrage and other progressive reforms.

See Also: Temperance Movements; Women's Christian Temperance Union (WCTU).

■ **WILLIAMS, HANK (1923-53),** country and western singer and songwriter. Born near Georgiana, Alabama, he enjoyed a meteoric career that helped make country and western music popular from coast to coast but was marred by drug abuse and violence. Williams was best known for what he called "lonesome songs" such as "I'm So Lonesome I Could Cry" and "Your Cheatin' Heart" but also wrote the joyful, up-tempo "Jambalya."

See Also: Country Music.

■ **WILLIAMS, ROGER (1603-83),** minister, religious dissenter, and founder of Rhode Island. Like thousands of other Puritans, Williams grew discontented with the Anglican Church and in 1630 departed his native London for the Massachusetts Bay Colony. Once in America, he condemned New England Puritanism for its moderate theology and relocated to Plymouth, where he found a more acceptable religious environment. Embracing the radical tenets of separatism, Williams constantly sought a closer, more personal relationship with God and rejected those who did not

share such aspirations.

Apart from attacking religious orthodoxy, Williams assailed the English Crown. After meeting Indians and becoming familiar with their culture, he concluded that America rightfully belonged to them and that England could not give away their land. He also openly advocated a separation of church and state and the toleration of various religious sects. These religious and political convictions ran counter to Puritan ideology and resulted in his banishment from Massachusetts in 1636.

Williams traveled south and established a settlement at Providence, Rhode Island, on land purchased from local Indians. He and his fellow colonists framed a government that tolerated individual religious views. Williams secured a colonial charter in 1644 and remained active in Rhode Island affairs for the remainder of his life. His amicable relationship with the Narragansett deteriorated with the onset of King Philip's War in 1675.

—GUY NELSON

See Also: King Philip's War; Puritanism; Rhode Island.

BIBLIOGRAPHY: Gaustad, Edwin S., *Liberty of Conscience: Roger Williams in America* (Eerdman's 1991); Morgan, Edmund S., *Roger Williams: The Church and the State* (Harcourt, Brace & World 1967).

■ **WILLIAMS, TED (1918-),** baseball player for the Boston Red Sox (1939-60). Born in San Diego, California, the left fielder was the finest hitter of his time, batting .406 in 1941 and .344 for his career with 521 home runs.

See Also: Sports.

■ **WILLIAMS, TENNESSEE (1911-83),** playwright. Williams was born in Mississippi but as a boy moved with his family to St. Louis. After spending time at the University of Missouri and Washington University, Williams eventually graduated from the University of Iowa in 1938 with a degree from the playwriting program. Among his early literary influences were the plays of August Strindberg and the poems of Hart Crane. Williams had his first success with the 1945 Broadway production of *The Glass Menagerie*, about the wistful interaction between four characters in a St. Louis apartment, which established him as one of the important playwrights of his era. He won the New York Drama Critics' Cir-

A Streetcar Named Desire (1947) won Tennessee Williams a Pulitzer Prize for drama and offered audiences the memorable characters Blanche DuBois and Stanley Kowalski. He won a second Pulitzer for *Cat on a Hot Tin Roof* (1955).

cle Award for this work and subsequently for *A Streetcar Named Desire* (1947), *Cat on a Hot Tin Roof* (1955), and *The Night of the Iguana* (1961). Williams struggled with alcohol and drug addiction but continued to write prolifically, completing more than 60 plays, as well as two volumes of poetry, four books of short stories, essays, and two novels.

See Also: *Theater.*

■ **WILLIAMS, WILLIAM (1731-1811),** statesman and Revolutionary War leader. A native of Lebanon, Connecticut, Williams was a member of the Second Continental Congress and signed the Declaration of Independence. In addition to his extensive political activity, he worked to provision the Continental army.

See Also: *Declaration of Independence.*

■ **WILLIAMSBURG,** capital of Virginia from 1699 to 1779. A palisaded outpost established between the James and York rivers in 1633, the town was named Williamsburg in 1699. The College of William and Mary in Virginia was founded there in 1693.

See Also: *Virginia.*

■ ***WILLIAMS V. LEE* (1959),** U.S. Supreme Court case that reaffirmed the jurisdiction of tribal courts on Indian reservations. Lee, the white operator of a federally licensed general store on a Navaho reservation in Arizona, sued Williams, a Navaho, and his wife over a disputed sale. Lee wanted the civil matter settled in the Arizona state court; Williams claimed that since the store was on the reservation, the tribal court had jurisdiction. The Court noted Arizona had not taken advantage of a 1953 federal law allowing states to absorb Indian reservations and ruled (9-0) that the reservation was a distinct legal entity established by federal authority. The fact that Lee was not a Navaho, the Court decreed, was immaterial. He did business on the reservation and weakening the power of the tribal court would be an assault on the established right of reservation Indians to govern themselves.

See Also: *Supreme Court.*

■ **WILMOT PROVISO (1846),** amendment to a House of Representatives appropriation bill prohibiting the extension of slavery into any new territory acquired by the United States as a result of the Mexican War. Introduced by David C. Wilmot, a Pennsylvania Democrat, the proviso spurred rancorous debate and placed the slavery question firmly on the national stage for the duration of the antebellum period.

Wilmot, a disgruntled former supporter of Pres. James K. Polk, introduced his amendment to embarrass the president rather than from any moral or ideological motive. Attached to an otherwise unremarkable bill to provide $2 million to facilitate negotiations with Mexico for territorial cessions, the proviso passed the House on Aug. 8, 1846, but died during discussion in the Senate on August 10, when the first session of the 29th Congress closed. Reintroduced by Wilmot in February 1847 with a stronger slavery exclusion clause and attached to a similar appropriation bill for $3 million, the proviso again passed the House. But the Senate voted down an attempt to attach it to its own bill. This Senate bill, lacking the proviso, eventually passed both houses of Congress in early March 1847.

The core principle of the Wilmot proviso, congressional exclusion of slavery from the territories, continued to appear in congressional debates and became the main plank in the platforms of the Free Soil and Republican parties.

—THOMAS E. SCHOTT

See Also: Free Soil Party; Republican Party.

BIBLIOGRAPHY: Fehrenbacher, Don E., *Sectional Crisis and Southern Constitutionalism* (Louisiana State Univ. Press 1995); McPherson, James M., *Battle Cry of Freedom: The Civil War Era* (Ballantine 1988); Morrison, Chaplain W., *Democratic Politics and Sectionalism: The Wilmot Proviso Controversy* (Univ. of North Carolina Press 1967).

■ **WILSON, EDMUND (1895-1972),** literary and social critic. Originally from Red Bank, New Jersey, Wilson graduated from Princeton University in 1916. After serving in World War I, Wilson worked as managing editor of *Vanity Fair* and book review editor for the *New Republic.* He also wrote book reviews for the *New Yorker* (1944-48). Wilson's works of criticism include *Axel's Castle* (1931) on symbolism; *To the Finland Station* (1940) on the European revolutionary tradition; and *Patriotic Gore* (1962) on the literature of the American Civil War era. He also wrote short stories and plays.

■ **WILSON, HENRY (1812-75),** vice president of the United States (1873-75). Born Jeremiah Jones Colbath in Farmington, New Hampshire, he spent his youth as an indentured farm worker and later became a successful shoe manufacturer in Natick, Massachusetts. He served in the Massachusetts state legislature in the 1840s and was elected (1855-73) to the U.S. Senate as a Republican. He was Pres. Ulysses S. Grant's running mate when Grant ran for his second term in 1872. He died while in office.

See Also: Grant, Ulysses Simpson; Vice President of the United States.

■ **WILSON, JAMES (1742-98),** political leader and associate justice of the U.S. Supreme Court (1789-

98). Born in Carskerdo, Scotland, Wilson immigrated to Pennsylvania in 1765 and became one of the colony's preeminent attorneys. In 1774 he published a pamphlet arguing that Parliament had no authority over the American colonies. As a member (1774-77) of the Continental Congresses, Wilson rather reluctantly voted for independence. He assumed a leading role in the Constitutional Convention of 1787, advocating a strong executive and judiciary to balance the power of Congress. Appointed to the Supreme Court (1789), Wilson served until his death. His opinion in *Chisholm v. Georgia* (1793), arguing that the United States comprised a nation of citizens rather than a confederation of states, exerted considerable influence on later constitutional theory. Financially ruined because of failed land speculations, Wilson fled to North Carolina just before his death. He remains one of the most undeservedly neglected founding fathers.

See Also: Chisholm v. Georgia; Constitutional Convention; Continental Congresses; Declaration of Independence; Supreme Court.

BIBLIOGRAPHY: Hall, Mark David, *The Political and Legal Philosophy of James Wilson, 1742-1798* (Univ. of Missouri Press 1997).

■ **WILSON, (THOMAS) WOODROW (1856-1924),** 28th president of the United States (1913-21). Born in Staunton, Virginia, young Wilson combined ambition with a sense of moralism inherited from his father, a Presbyterian minister. Wilson tried the law but found it too confining, and he reentered college to study history and political science. In 1885, he graduated from Johns Hopkins University with a Ph.D., and his dissertation, published that same year as *Congressional Government*, quickly became a classic critique of American government.

Wilson taught college until 1902, when he became president of Princeton University, his undergraduate alma mater. There, he oversaw a highly successful modernization of the curriculum. In 1910, the Democratic machine of New Jersey convinced Wilson to run for governor; in the two years he served in that office Wilson challenged the authority of the very machine that placed him in office and became one of the nation's first state executives to support the primary election system. In 1912, with the help of an admiring William Jen-

Pres. Woodrow Wilson, a Democrat, served as a college professor, president of Princeton University, and governor of New Jersey before running successfully for president in 1912. He was the only president in American history to hold a Ph.D.

nings Bryan, Wilson was nominated by the Democratic party for the presidency. Thanks to Theodore Roosevelt's third party candidacy that fall, which split the Republican party, Wilson won.

Presidency. During that election, Wilson argued for an approach to government that came to be called the "New Freedom." Wilson called for government to provide the means by which business could set itself completely free of monopoly and special privilege. His idealism, however, did not consistently find its way into practice during his first term. While he worked Congress masterfully to win a downward revision of the tariff and create the Federal Reserve System, which stabilized the nation's banking system, he also compromised on an antitrust act that essentially left the nation's larger monopolies alone, despite the creation of the Federal Trade Commission.

In foreign policy, Wilson's idealism was even more compromised. Dubbed "Wilsonian idealism" by historians, Wilson's diplomacy was a brand of moral imperialism that in certain situations desired to transplant ideals and forms of government to foreign shores—by force, if necessary. In practice, his foreign policy was more often realpolitik than moralism. In Mexico, for example, Wilson found himself first refusing to support a government that had overthrown the legitimate government, but after being pressured by the British to change his mind, he reversed himself and recognized the new regime. Indeed, it was Wilson's pro-British sentiments that dominated his foreign policies, especially after 1914, the year when Europe stumbled into World War I. Wilson demanded that Americans be neutral in thought and action. He himself, however, clearly was not neutral. Wilson's private letters made his position clear well before he went to Congress in April 1917 to ask for a declaration of war against Germany.

Once committed to the war, Wilson positioned it as a great crusade to save the world from the imperial folly of all the European nations. Thus, he demanded that the war be one that offered no spoils of victory to any of the participants. His "Fourteen Points" included a provision for an international organization called the League of Nations.

Wilson's worldview was met with open contempt by his allies, all of whom were versed in old-fashioned politics and eager for revenge against Germany. When, after the armistice was declared in November 1918, Wilson went to France to participate in treaty negotiations, he found his idealistic beliefs shattered by nations that wanted harsh terms against the enemy. In the final Treaty of Versailles, only the League remained of Wilson's Fourteen Points.

Back in the United States, the Republican-controlled Senate had grave reservations about the treaty, especially the terms for U.S. membership in the League. Nevertheless, ratification was not out of the question, especially if Wilson had been willing to compromise on the wording of a number of clauses in the treaty.

Wilson, however, refused to agree to any changes in the document and embarked on a whirlwind cross-country journey in the fall of 1919 to take his case directly to the American people. His powers of persuasion were considerable, and the tactic had worked in the early years of his presidency, but he suffered a paralyzing stroke in the midst of the trip. Seriously ill for the remainder of his term, he steadfastly refused all attempts at compromise, and in the end, the treaty and American membership in the League were defeated.

Wilson left the presidency in 1921, an embittered and ailing man. His final years were spent in Washington, where he died in 1924.

—JOHN ROBERT GREENE

See Also: Fourteen Points; League of Nations; President of the United States; Versailles, Treaty of; World War I.

BIBLIOGRAPHY: Blum, John Morton, *Woodrow Wilson and the Politics of Morality* (Little, Brown 1956; reprint 1962); Link, Arthur, *Wilson: The Road to the White House* (Princeton Univ. Press 1947); Link, Arthur, *Wilson: The Struggle for Neutrality 1914-1915* (Princeton Univ. Press 1960).

■ **WINFREY, OPRAH (1954-),** actress, television personality, and producer, born in Koscuisko, Mississippi. Winfrey won a Golden Globe Award and was nominated for an Academy Award for her portrayal of Sophie in the film *The Color Purple* (1986). In 1988 her own company took over the production of her Chicago-based talk show, the "Oprah Winfrey Show", by then the most watched talk show on national television. This made Winfrey the first African-American woman to own and host her own television show. One of the wealthiest and most powerful people in show business during the 1990s, she used her influence to improve opportunities for people of color and women in the entertainment industry.

See Also: African Americans; Television and Radio.

■ **WINNAMUCCA, SARAH (c. 1844-91),** Paiute leader. She was born Thoc-me-tony (Shell-flower) in the Humbolt Sink, in what is now Nevada. She was an interpreter and scout for the American army during the 1860s. In 1880, Winnamucca and her father, Chief Winnamucca II, traveled to Washington, D.C., to report the mistreatment of Indians by Indian agents and white settlers to Pres. Rutherford B. Hayes. This visit and her subsequent lecture tour of the Northeast inspired educator Elizabeth Palmer Peabody and other reformers but could not force government action.

See Also: Peabody, Elizabeth Palmer.

■ **WINNEBAGO INDIANS. See:** Algonquian.

Founding governor of the Massachusetts Bay Colony, John Winthrop penned his famous sermon, "The Modell of Christian Charity," during the voyage to New England in 1630.

■ **WINTHROP, JOHN (1587-1649),** first governor of Massachusetts, born in Suffolk, England. Winthrop's Puritan convictions led him to give up a thriving law practice and valuable assets to immigrate with his family to New England with the Company of the Massachusetts Bay (1630). He was elected governor of the colony before his departure, and his "The Modell of Christian Charity"—written while he was still on board ship—advanced the goal of the Massachusetts Bay settlers to establish a model Puritan community for others to emulate. By promoting group discipline and individual responsibility, Winthrop implemented this social experiment during his 12 terms as governor (1631-45).

See Also: Puritanism.

■ **WIRETAPPING CASES (1967-72),** a series of related U.S. Supreme Court cases that limited government's right to eavesdrop on citizens. The Fourth Amendment promises the people security in their persons, papers, houses, and effects against unreasonable search and seizure. The Court had ruled in *Olmstead v. United States* (1928) and *Silverman v. United States* (1961) that wiretapping did not constitute a search as defined by the Fourth Amendment because there was no physical entry into a protected space. In *Katz v. United States* (1967) the Court changed course and ruled (7-1) that federal agents had indeed conducted a "search" by attaching a listening device to a public telephone booth used by Katz. The Court said Katz had a reasonable expectation of privacy when he spoke into a telephone. Congress passed legislation (1968) barring federal government agencies from wiretapping in domestic criminal cases unless they obtained a warrant from a federal judge.

See Also: Supreme Court.

■ **WISCONSIN,** a midwestern state. It is bounded on the north by Lake Superior, on the north and east by Michigan and Lake Michigan, on the south by Illinois, and on the south and west by Iowa and Minnesota. The Mississippi River forms its southwestern border. Wisconsin's terrain ranges from prairie to rolling hills, densely wooded in the north. There are more than 8,000 lakes. Industry dominates the economy, with machinery and food processing the main manufacturing sectors. It is also the nation's leading dairying state.

Wisconsin was part of the Northwest Territory established by the newly created United States after this area was ceded by Great Britain in 1783. It became a state in 1848 and drew many immigrants from northern Europe in subsequent decades.

Capital: Madison. Area: 54,314 square miles. Population (1995 est.): 5,123,000.

See Also: Black Hawk War; Jolliet, Louis; La Follette, Robert; McCarthy, Joseph; Marquette, Pere Jacques; Northwest Territory; Progressive Party; Treaty of Paris (1783).

■ **WITCHCRAFT,** use of sorcery or magic. Witchcraft was greatly feared by Americans of the early colonial period. Indians, African slaves, and Europeans all believed in the dangers of black magic, although the content of their beliefs varied by culture.

Cafes of Confcience
Concerning evil
SPIRITS

Perfonating Men, Witchcrafts, infallible Proofs of Guilt in fuch as are accufed with that Crime.

All Confidered according to the Scriptures, Hiftory, Experience, and the Judgment of many Learned men.

By **Increafe Mather,** Prefident of **Harvard College** at **Cambridge,** and Teacher of a Church at BOSTON in New-England.

Prov. 22. 21. ---- *That thou mighteft Anfwer the words of Truth, to them that fend unto thee.*

Efficiunt Dæmones, ut quæ non funt, fic tamen, quafi fint, confpicienda hominibus exhibeant. Lactantius Lib. 2. Inftit. Cap. 15. *Diabolus Cenfulitur, cum ijs medijs utimur aliquid Cognofcendi, quæ a Diabolo funt introducta.* Ames. Caf. Confc. L. 4. Cap. 23.

BOSTON Printed, and Sold by *Benjamin Harris* at the London Coffee-Houfe. 1693.

In 1693, Increase Mather's *Cases of Conscience Concerning Evil Spirits* helped persuade Massachusetts governor William Phipps to end the Salem witch trials.

Historians have generally focused their attention on witchcraft beliefs among the colonists. In 1484, Pope Innocent VIII warned that the evils of the world were the work of satanic forces that often employed the talents of female witches. During the next two centuries thousands of victims, most of them women, were hanged or burned in Europe. A belief in the danger of witchcraft, held both by Catholics and Protestants, was notably strong among the Puritan settlers of 17th-century New England, where over several decades more than 300 residents were accused of practicing black magic, and at least 36 were hanged. Again, most of the victims were women.

The majority of accused women were childless or widowed, or had reputations among their neighbors for assertiveness and independence. Other than the declarations of the "bewitched" and the forced confessions of the "witches," there is no evidence suggesting that any colonists actually practiced witchcraft. Charges commonly grew out of local disputes, with accusers attributing personal misfortune to the hostility of a neighbor. In the vast majority of cases these accusations were dismissed by local authorities.

The most infamous example of witchcraft obsession occurred in Salem, Massachusetts, in 1692-93, when a group of girls claimed that they had been bewitched by a number of old widows. The accusations threw the whole community into a panic of recrimination. Before the colonial governor finally called a halt to the persecutions, 14 women and 6 men had been tried, condemned, and executed. The best explanation of the episode points to social tensions within the community. Salem was a booming port, but while some of the residents were prospering, others were not. Most of the victims came from the eastern, more commercial, section, while the majority of their accusers lived on the economically stagnant western side of town. Most of the accused also came from families whose religious sympathies were with sects of Anglicans, Quakers, or Baptists, not Puritans. A majority were old women, suspect because they lived alone, without men. The shame and self-criticism of Puritan colonists in the aftermath of the Salem executions, notable in Increase Mather's *Cases of Conscience* (1693), put an end to the "witchcraft delusion" in New England.

—JOHN MACK FARAGHER

See Also: Mather, Increase.

BIBLIOGRAPHY: Boyer, Paul, and Stephen Nissenbaum, *Salem Possessed: The Social Origins of Witchcraft* (Harvard Univ. Press 1974); Karlsen, Carol F., *The Devil in the Shape of a Woman* (Norton 1987); Starkey, Marion, *The Devil in Massachusetts* (Knopf 1950); Weisman, Richard, *Witchcraft, Magic, and Religion in 17th-Century Massachusetts* (Univ. of Massachusetts Press 1984).

■ **WITHERSPOON, JOHN (1723-94),** minister, educator, and Revolutionary War politician. A native of Scotland, Witherspoon, a Presbyterian minister, immigrated to America in 1768 to become president of the College of New Jersey (Princeton University). During his 26-year tenure, he helped unite the fractured Presbyterian church in America. He also fomented radical, anti-British sentiments in New Jersey through his advocacy of personal rights. Witherspoon served in the Second Continental Congress and signed the Declaration of Independence.

See Also: Declaration of Independence.

■ **WOLCOTT, OLIVER (1726-97),** military leader and Revolutionary War statesman. Born in Windsor, Connecticut, Wolcott served in the Second Continental Congress and signed the Declaration of Independence. During the Revolution he commanded American troops against the British and later served as governor of Connecticut (1796-97).

See Also: Declaration of Independence.

■ **WOLFE, THOMAS (1900-38),** novelist and short story writer. Wolfe was born in Asheville, North Carolina; he graduated from the University of North Carolina in 1920 and received his M.A. from Harvard University in 1922. He taught English at New York University between 1924 and 1930. Wolfe wrote four huge autobiographical novels: *Look Homeward, Angel* (1929), *Of Time and the River* (1935), *The Web and the Rock* (1939), and *You Can't Go Home Again* (1940). The last two were issued by editor Edward Aswell after Wolfe's death.

See Also: Novel.

■ **WOMAN SUFFRAGE MOVEMENT,** campaign for women's voting rights leading to the 19th Amendment. Despite exceptions, custom and law kept most American women from voting until the 1900s. In the 1840s, however, social ferment, the antislavery crusade, and the widening of white men's political rights inspired America's first women's movement, culminating with the 1848 Seneca Falls Convention, where Elizabeth Cady Stanton first formally demanded women's "inalienable right to the elective franchise."

Ensuing years brought women legal gains, but the post–Civil War 14th and 15th Amendments excluded woman suffrage and split the movement. Suffragists like Stanton and Susan B. Anthony tried new tactics, but the Supreme Court's decision in *Minor* v. *Happersett* (1875) denied that the citizenship ensured by the 14th Amendment entitled women to suffrage, a constitutional amendment proposed in 1878 failed, and only a few western states gave women votes. In 1890, when the National American Woman Suffrage Association (NAWSA) reunited suffragists, social hostility persisted.

After 1900 industrial growth and Progressive reform improved public attitudes, while new NAWSA leaders stressed woman suffrage's social benefits. After 1910, despite strong opposition, NAWSA's Carrie Chapman Catt promoted a "winning plan" for a constitutional amendment, while Alice Paul's Congressional Union for Woman Suffrage militantly pressured politicians. With Pres. Woodrow Wilson's blessing, the 19th Amendment was ratified in August 1920. NAWSA leaders then founded the League of Women Voters. Although suffragists narrowed demands to get the amendment, it has vastly expanded women's political opportunities, especially since the 1960s.

—DONALD W. ROGERS

See Also: Anthony, Susan B.; Catt, Carrie Chapman; Constitutional Amendments; Minor v. Happersett; Paul, Alice; Seneca Falls Convention; Stanton, Elizabeth Cady; Women in American History; Women's Movement.

BIBLIOGRAPHY: Dubois, Ellen Carol, *Feminism and Suffrage: The Emergence of an Independent Women's Movement in America, 1848-1869* (Cornell Univ. Press 1978); Kraditor, Aileen S., *The Ideas of the Woman Suffrage Movement, 1890-1920* (Doubleday 1971); Scott, Anne Firor, and Andrew MacKay Scott, *One Half the People: The Fight for Woman Suffrage* (Univ. of Illinois Press 1982).

■ **WOMEN IN AMERICAN HISTORY.** Women have been an integral part of the economic, political, social, and cultural history of all Americans. Not always recognized for their contributions and achievements, women have, nevertheless, helped to shape the history of every community in numerous ways.

Women and Work. American women have always worked. Among Indians who began to settle in North America more than 10,000 years ago, women were not only childbearers; they were also primary agriculturalists, domesticating corn into one of the world's most important food grains and

disseminating its culture throughout the continent. Indian women were responsible for all stages of food production and gathering; they also accompanied hunting and fishing expeditions. In some tribes, like the Hopi, women owned the land and organized the agricultural process with the help of men who married into their communities. In many tribes, such as the Iroquois, women managed commercial transactions, bargaining and bartering for goods while men were off on long-distance trading or hunting expeditions. Indian women also wove baskets or made pottery (for carrying and storage), made clothing (from deerskin or fibers), helped build and move the homes that provided summer and winter shelter, and did the nursing and child rearing without which no community could survive.

Among European colonists, women were equally important. Preindustrial and early industrial production was a function of the household rather than of individuals. Thus, a house was frequently recorded in a man's name, causing widespread misperceptions about the significance of women's work and economic contributions.

Colonial housewives, and women in frontier or rural America even up to modern times, were truly "Janes-of-all-trades." For example, the first settlers brought their own flax seeds to plant and grow for making linen—a complex, labor-intensive process of preparation, bleaching, and weaving for which women's labor was indispensable. Then and later, women bartered sheepskins, carded, spun and wove wool for family clothing, and learned to knit and sew for warmth and survival. Women carried out the backbreaking labor of carrying heavy pails of water, doing the family laundry by hand, managing large gardens, and producing a variety of items to sell for added income. They also ran wayside taverns or village shops. Women with midwifing skills, like Boston's indomitable Ann Hutchinson, became indispensable health-care providers for far-flung communities.

By the mid-19th century, the medical profession began to restrict and exclude women, as did other professions, but women began to be prolific writers. Anne Bradstreet in the 17th century was America's first great poet, while the 19th century produced the reclusive Emily Dickinson. Many

Susan B. Anthony played a leading role in the public issues that concerned many women in the 19th century: the abolition of slavery, temperance reform, and woman suffrage.

other women novelists and essayists wrote for widespread audiences, achieving both popularity and lucrative incomes.

Thousands of 19th-century women became the main labor force of newly established factories. Treasury Sec. Alexander Hamilton told Congress in 1791 that manufacturing should be encouraged as a way to make use of "idle women and children" and thus improve the national economy. The labor of African-American women—during and after slavery—in cotton, tobacco, and cane sugar production was also a major source of American wealth. As new immigrants poured into the United States in the decades after the Civil War, women were involved in the Gilded Age economy, not only through factory labor but also by keeping boardinghouses, being servants for the well-to-do, and becoming secretaries, department-store salesgirls, and telephone operators—the latter an exclusively women's job until the 1980s. During World War I, 25 percent of defense industry workers were women, and even more during World War II, when "Rosie the Riv-

eter" became a national symbol of patriotism.

As the public school system developed in the 19th century, women were welcomed into the teaching profession as cheap labor, often at one-third of the cost of a man's salary. (Pay rates began to equalize when men returned to teaching during the post–World War II era.) Gradually, more kinds of nondomestic work began to open to women, replacing or adding to the household work they had always done. After the 1964 Civil Rights Act established the Equal Employment Opportunities Commission, discrimination based on gender (as well as race) became illegal. Today women work as astronauts, engineers, and in all other professions (many previously closed to them), even as they also make up a large proportion of lower-paid service workers. Through their continuing work in child rearing and home management, as well as in marketplace employment, women contribute substantially to the national economy.

Women and Political Power. Women exercised political power even when they were officially denied public participation or voting rights. They were both community builders and community reformers throughout American history.

Indian women were often de facto rulers even though Europeans did not recognize them as such. Hernando de Soto forged his disastrous way throughout the Southeast in the 1540s, taking the hospitable Cacica of Cutifachiqui captive in order to gain control of her subjects over thousands of square miles of territory. French voyageurs and later fur traders of every sort quickly discovered that alliances—marital or otherwise—with Indian women were a necessity for doing business. English explorers were rescued and feasted by the unnamed "wife of Granga-nimo" and her warriors on Roanoke Island in 1584. (Unfortunately, the English were as destructive as the Spanish; her village was burned by English colonists three years later.) Numerous Indian women acted as diplomats, peacemakers, and leaders of their people, but Euro-American ideologies about women's lesser status created policies that ignored their contributions and deprived them of many traditional rights.

European women settlers, whether Spanish, French, or English, had few political rights. Nor did most ordinary men of the colonial era. The law defined women as subjects of their fathers or brothers, and then of their husbands, with freedom to manage their own property or businesses only if they were single or widowed. A few wealthy English women, such as Long Island's Deborah Moody or Maryland's Margaret Brent, were granted their own land in the colonies, but this fact did not allow them the voting rights of male landowners, as Margaret Brent discovered when she tried to vote in the 1647 Maryland assembly.

Although women were deeply involved in the American Revolution, they gained few of the freedoms that the war brought to men. Sarah Updike Goddard's *Providence Journal* was influential in the anti–Stamp Act protests of 1765. Her daughter, Mary Katherine Goddard, edited the patriotic *Maryland Gazette* during the war, and the Continental Congress named her official printer of the Declaration of Independence. But her brother was the legal owner who took over the business in 1784. She later died in poverty.

Women organized Revolutionary War boycotts of English goods, making the wearing of homespun cloth a patriotic duty and turning the nation into a coffee- rather than tea-drinking society. Esther deBerdt Reed organized fund-raising for the army in Philadelphia. Deborah Champion carried the Continental army payroll on horseback through British lines from Lebanon, Connecticut, to Boston in 1775—an accomplishment that may have saved General Washington's army from early disbandment. But only New Jersey made women voters in the new nation, and it rescinded that right in 1807.

During the Civil War, women were the primary organizers of the Sanitary Commission, which gathered and delivered medical and food supplies from every town and village to the Union army. Southern women were similarly engaged. Clara Barton organized women as behind-the-battlefield nurses, laying the foundations for what eventually became the International Red Cross. Catholic nuns also nursed at battlefield tent hospitals and ran the government's designated Satterlee Military Hospital in Philadelphia, serving more than 80,000 wounded men between 1862 and 1865.

Women's work as army nurses and as civilian organizers of relief supplies during World War I was one of many factors that convinced Congress to pass the 19th Amendment (1919) granting women the right to vote. It was ratified in 1920, 50 years after the amendment was first introduced in Congress and 72 years after the 1848 Seneca Falls Convention. At Seneca Falls, 300 women, led by Elizabeth Cady Stanton and Lucretia Mott, first publicly demanded the right to economic and political freedom. It had been a long and painfully fought campaign.

Women were active in various reform movements long before they could vote. Throughout the 19th century they established local organizations with national affiliations to promote charitable aid societies, oppose prostitution, encourage temperance and alcohol prohibition, improve education, fight for women's rights and suffrage, and, above all, abolish slavery. Women throughout the country gathered so many signatures on petitions to abolish slavery in the 1830s that the southern-dominated Congress passed an infamous "gag rule" to avoid reading the mountains of documents. Harriet Beecher Stowe's novel *Uncle Tom's Cabin* (1852) popularized antislavery sentiment and helped set the stage for the Civil War.

After 1920, women still found it difficult to obtain full equality. An equal rights amendment introduced in 1923 was finally passed by Congress in 1972, but it was bitterly contested and never ratified. Through the League of Women Voters (founded 1920), the National Organization for Women (NOW, founded 1964), and many other groups, women participated in political action on many issues. Numerous women held public offices on local, state, and federal levels. Eleanor Roosevelt, the activist wife of Pres. Franklin D. Roosevelt, in her role as first U.S. ambassador to the United Nations after World War II, chaired the committee that produced the Universal Declaration of Human Rights, unanimously adopted in 1948.

Women formed the phalanx of the African-American civil rights movement in modern America. Ida B. Wells and Mary Church Terrell were among many women who fought both privately and publicly against lynching and for better education. When Rosa Parks refused to give up her seat on a Montgomery, Alabama, bus in 1955, the Women's Political Council of which she was a member had been organizing for nine years to plan for such action. That organization made possible a successful 18-month boycott that ended bus segregation in Montgomery. Women such as Ella Baker were crucial civil rights leaders for a generation of Americans, along with the many young African-American girls who braved jeering crowds in order to integrate southern schools and colleges.

A tremendous increase in research, writing, and knowledge about women in history has occurred during the last 30 years. These studies reveal the diversity of women's accomplishments, the impossibility of generalizing about gender roles under changing cultural circumstances, and the importance of recognizing many forms of political and social power in any society. Today's American women have achieved greater freedom and more equality with respect to education, political, and legal rights. They have more autonomy in matters of fertility, marriage and divorce, and even health and athletic prowess. But violence against women abounds, and women still face economic disparity; the proportion of women and children living in poverty increased significantly in the 1980s and 1990s.

—RUTH BARNES MOYNIHAN

See Also: Equal Rights Amendment (ERA); Feminism; National Organization for Women (NOW); Woman Suffrage Movement; Women in the Armed Forces; Women's Movement; individual biographies.

BIBLIOGRAPHY: Evans, Sara M., *Born for Liberty: A History of Women in America* (Free Press 1989); Moynihan, Ruth Barnes, et al., eds., *Second to None: A Documentary History of American Women,* 2 vols. (Univ. of Nebraska Press 1993); Woloch, Nancy, *Women and the American Experience* (Knopf 1984).

■ **WOMEN IN THE ARMED FORCES,** women on active duty in the U.S. Army, Navy, Marines, and Air Force. Women began entering the services in large numbers during World War II. By the mid-1990s women made up 13 percent of the armed forces. Although traditionally excluded from combat positions, women in the armed forces are eligible for 80 percent of all military jobs.

See Also: Women in American History.

■ **WOMEN'S AUXILIARY ARMY CORPS (WAAC),** special U.S. army unit created in 1942, during World War II, to enlist women in the army for noncombatant jobs. After 1943 it was known as the Women's Army Corps (WAC). More than 100,000

First admitted into the armed forces during World War I, women served in much greater numbers during World War II in such noncombat units as the Women's Auxiliary Army Corps (WAAC). By the time of the Persian Gulf War, women were serving in substantial numbers.

WACs served as clerks, typists, medical technicians, and in other positions during the war.

See Also: World War II.

■ **WOMEN'S CHRISTIAN TEMPERANCE UNION (WCTU),** reform society. Founded in 1874, the WTCU grew out of informal meetings and protests but became a sophisticated political organization with more than 800,000 members. Conservative and Protestant, much of its rhetoric was colored by anti-Catholic and anti-immigrant prejudices. Frances Willard, WCTU president from 1879 to 1898, broadened its goals to include woman suffrage, the moral reform of prostitutes, and prison reform. In 1920, the WCTU successfully forced the passage of the 18th Amendment, establishing Prohibition.

See Also: Prohibition; Temperance Movements; Willard, Frances; Woman Suffrage Movement; Women's Movement.

■ **WOMEN'S MOVEMENT.** The women's movement has historically involved many themes, all with roots in American history. In the 1770s, Abigail Adams instructed her husband, John, to "remember the ladies" in the Declaration of Independence. Massachusetts writer Judith Sargent Murray continued to assert that the American Revolution's ideas about liberty and education should apply to women as well as men in her *Gleaner* essays in the 1790s, and many future leaders of the women's movement read British writer Mary Wollstonecraft's *Vindication of the Rights of Women* at the turn of the century. During the Second Great Awakening (1830-50), religious women gained self-esteem, learned organizing tactics in their moral reform societies, and developed strong feelings of sisterhood.

Trends in the 19th Century. The antislavery movement was, however, the most significant source of an organized movement for women's rights. Early leaders of female antislavery activities included Angelina and Sarah Grimké, Quakers from a South Carolina slaveholding family, and Lucretia Mott, who led the Philadelphia Female Anti-Slavery Society in the 1830s. The first American woman to speak in public was an African-American antislavery activist, Maria Stewart. The Grimké sisters became the first female antislavery agents, and Sarah Grimké, in a series of letters, "On the Equality of the Sexes"(1838), drew parallels between the enslaved condition of Africans and the lack of liberty of all American women.

At the same time, the women's labor movement, led by Sarah Bagley and Harriet Hanson Robinson, agitated for better conditions and a 10-hour day for factory workers in Lowell, Massachusetts. Improved education at the early seminaries of Emma Willard and Catharine Beecher and at Mary Lyon's Mt. Holyoke also contributed to women's advancement. These strands came together when Lucretia Mott and Elizabeth Cady Stanton met at the World Anti-Slavery Convention in London in 1840 and envisioned a women's rights convention; this vision came true eight years later in Seneca Falls, New York. The Seneca Falls Convention produced a "Declaration of Sentiments" that discussed discrimination against women in the family, employment, inheritance, and education. This document also demanded women's right to vote for the first time in U.S. history.

Organizers of the many antislavery and women's rights conventions of the 1850s were Stanton and her life-time collaborator, Quaker schoolteacher Susan B. Anthony, as well as Lucretia Mott, Lucy Stone, Julia Ward Howe, and Louisa May Alcott. At an Akron, Ohio, convention in 1854, former slave Sojourner Truth demanded recognition for African-American women in her famous speech asking, "And ain't I a Woman?"

During the Civil War, both Union and Confederate women organized nursing brigades and in other ways supported their fighting forces. After the war, the disappointment of Stanton and Anthony over the 14th Amendment's provision of equal rights only for African-American men caused them to split off from Lucy Stone's American Woman Suffrage Association (which had supported the amendment) and form the National Woman Suffrage Association. The two groups continued agitating for the vote for women and for women's education and property rights, but their effectiveness was limited until they merged in 1890 as the National American Woman Suffrage Association (NAWSA). Frances Willard's enormous Women's Christian Temperance Union threw its support behind woman suffrage in the 1880s. Other important women's movements of the late 19th century included the antilynching movement organized by African-American leader Ida B. Wells Barnett and the powerful National Association of Colored Women, led by Barnett and Mary Church Terrell.

By 1915, the NAWSA, under Carrie Chapman Catt, had 2 million members and was competing with the smaller but more militant National Women's Party (NWP), led by Alice Paul. Huge prosuffrage marches took place in New York, Washington, Chicago, and other cities. Members of the NWP gained notoriety by chaining themselves to the White House fence, going to jail, and engaging in hunger strikes. The 19th Amendment, granting women the vote, was ratified in 1920, and with this victory the NAWSA became the League of Women Voters. The NWP first introduced an equal rights amendment (ERA) in 1923, bringing them into open conflict with feminists from the social settlement movement such as Jane Addams and Florence Kelley, who feared that if women were considered entirely equal to men, they might lose hard-won protective legislative reforms. This conflict continued into the 1950s when these groups finally reunited to work for an ERA.

The Women's International League for Peace and Freedom, founded by Jane Addams, arose in

Women of the National Women's Party applaud suffrage leader Alice Paul in 1920, after the 19th Amendment, giving women throughout the nation the right to vote, was ratified by the states.

response to World War I, and the 1920s and 1930s also brought organized activism in the birth control movement under the leadership of Margaret Sanger. Although there was no organized women's movement during the Great Depression of the 1930s, first lady Eleanor Roosevelt, Democratic National Committee Chair Molly Dewson, African-American educator Mary McLeod Bethune, and Sec. of Labor Frances Perkins were influential in bringing about social reforms that benefited women.

During World War II (1941-45), women proved their mettle as war-industry workers ("Rosie the Riveter") and noncombatant members of the armed forces. Their participation in the work force increased dramatically, altering permanently the public's consciousness of women's capabilities and laying the groundwork for the re-emergence of organized feminism in the decades ahead.

Late 20th Century. Early in the 1960s, a new women's peace movement, Women Strike for Peace, called for a work stoppage in 1961, and an

estimated 50,000 women walked out of kitchens and offices; this group also confronted the House Un-American Activities Committee in 1962. In 1958, NAACP member Rosa Parks refused to move to the back of a Birmingham bus, the designated area for African Americans, and thus triggered the civil rights movement that spawned new thinking about equal rights not only for African Americans but also for all women. In 1960, President Kennedy appointed a Commission on the Status of Women, chaired by Eleanor Roosevelt, that published a report in 1963, establishing state commissions and calling for yearly meetings. The same year, Betty Friedan's influential book, *The Feminine Mystique*, became an instant best-seller. The Civil Rights Act of 1964 included Title VII, which banned employment discrimination based on race and sex, and established the Equal Employment Opportunities Commission (EEOC), but lack of enforcement of the sex-discrimination guidelines led Betty Friedan and others to form the National Organization for Women (NOW) in 1966.

The founding of NOW signaled the beginning of a new era of organized feminism that saw the publication of *Ms* magazine by Gloria Steinem and Letty Cottin Pogrebin in 1971 and the founding of the National Women's Political Caucus by Friedan, Steinem, and Congresswomen Bella Abzug and Shirley Chisolm in the same year. The late 1960s and early 1970s were characterized by frequent large demonstrations for equal rights that culminated in congressional passage of the ERA in 1972. Clerical workers organized the Nine to Five Union, and other working women banded together in CLUW (Congress of Labor Union Women).

At the same time, emerging from the antiwar movement were more radical women's organizations such as New York Redstockings, WITCH (Women's Terrorist Conspiracy from Hell), Boston's Bread and Roses Collective, the NWRO (National Welfare Rights Organization), the African-American women's Combahee River Collective, the Radicalesbians, and the Furies. These are only a few of the organizations whose radical publications, such as the newspaper *Off Our Backs* (1968), the health handbook *Our Bodies Ourselves* (1971), and *Quest* (1973), the journal of radical feminist theory, called for revolutionary change instead of the reforms that occupied organizations like NOW.

The early 1970s also saw the emergence of hundreds of collegiate women's studies programs; and they spawned a new wave of feminist scholarship that has transformed the way we think about gender and politics. In the early 1970s, both Planned Parenthood and the National Abortion Rights Action League (NARAL) were educating the public about women's reproductive rights. In 1973, the Supreme Court's *Roe* v. *Wade* decision made abortion safe and legal in the United States, and this right has held, in spite of threats and abridgments, to the present.

The 1980s and 1990s were characterized by the continuing strength of NOW, with other women's movements springing up as circumstances demanded. One progressive event was Geraldine Ferrarro's unsuccessful run for the vice presidency on the Democratic ticket. In spite of some successes, the 1980s can also be seen as an era of "backlash" against women's gains of the 1960s and 1970s. For example, the ERA failed to be ratified by the 1982 deadline; the Supreme Court's

Webster decision (1989) curtailed some abortion rights; violent demonstrators murdered abortion providers and tried repeatedly to prevent access to abortion clinics; and the Reagan and Bush administrations rolled back civil rights legislation and affirmative action.

In the 1990s, the Clinton administration failed to improve the situation for gays in the military, permitted the silencing of Hillary Rodham Clinton, and approved welfare legislation that could be especially damaging to women and children. Still, Clinton's Parental Leave Act was an important first step in providing necessary reforms for working women; Title IX of the Education Act of 1972 brought increased access for women in sports, providing female role models in a wide variety of sports; and Janet Reno was appointed the first female attorney general and Madeleine Albright the first female secretary of state. Maya Angelou was the poet of Clinton's second inauguration, and television has made heroes out of characters such as policewomen Cagney and Lacy, news anchor Murphy Brown, chief of surgery Kate Austin, and working-class waitress and mother Roseanne. The future is not totally clear; but what is clear is that because of the women's movements of the 19th and 20th centuries, American women's sense of empowerment has increased, and their lives have improved. Things will never be the same.

—LAURIE CRUMPACKER

See Also: *Equal Rights Amendment (ERA); Feminism; National Organization for Women (NOW); Nineteenth Amendment; Suffragists; Woman Suffrage Movement; Women in American History; individual biographies.*

BIBLIOGRAPHY: Davis, Flora, *Moving the Mountain: The Women's Movement in America since 1960* (Simon & Schuster 1991); Flexner, Eleanor, *Century of Struggle: The Women's Rights Movement in the United States* (Atheneum Press 1968); Kerber, Linda, and Jane Sherron DeHart, *Women's America: Refocusing the Past* (Oxford Univ. Press 1991); Moynihan, Ruth, Cynthia Russett, and Laurie Crumpacker, *Second to None: A Documentary History of American Women, from the Sixteenth Century to the Present* (Univ. of Nebraska Press 1993).

■ **WOOD, GRANT (1892-1942),** painter of American rural and small-town life. Born in Anamosa,

Iowa, Wood taught art in the Cedar Rapids, Iowa, public schools from 1919 to 1924. He is best remembered for *American Gothic* (1930) and other paintings of agrarian scenes, but he also commented on American history and myths in paintings such as *The Midnight Ride of Paul Revere* (1931) and *Parson Weems's Fable* (1939), a comment on the myth of George Washington and the cherry tree.

See Also: **Painting.**

■ **WOODBURY, LEVI (1789-1851),** governor of New Hampshire (1823-24), U.S. senator (1825-31, 1841-45), and associate justice of the U.S. Supreme Court (1846-51). A Francetown, New Hampshire, native, Woodbury wrote several important opinions during his brief tenure on the Court, including one upholding the Fugitive Slave Act of 1793.

See Also: **Supreme Court.**

■ **WOODHULL, VICTORIA CLAFLIN (1838-1927),** spiritualist, stockbroker, and radical journalist. She was born in Homer, Ohio. From 1853 to 1866, she and her sister, Tennessee Celeste Claflin, traveled the Midwest giving spiritual advice, conducting seances, and selling patent medicine. Then, with the support of financier Cornelius Vanderbilt, the sisters moved to New York, where they established a brokerage firm and became known for their eccentricity and radical opinion. In 1870 they began publishing *Woodhull and Claflin's Weekly*, which printed the first American edition of Marx's *Communist Manifesto* in 1872.

See Also: **Claflin, Tennessee Celeste; Women's Movement.**

■ **WOODS, WILLIAM BURNHAM (1824-87),** associate justice of the U.S. Supreme Court (1880-87). Although a Newark, Ohio, native, Woods was governor of Alabama during Reconstruction, which explains his appointment as a "Southern" justice. Formerly an ardent Unionist, Woods wrote several opinions, including the majority opinion in *United States* v. *Harris* (1883), that weakened federal civil rights laws.

See Also: **Supreme Court.**

■ **WOODSTOCK,** a landmark outdoor rock-and-roll concert held Aug. 15-17, 1969. Billed as "An Aquarian Exposition: Three Days of Peace and Music," the festival was to be held in Walkill, New York, more than 20 miles from the Catskill Mountains arts community of Woodstock. After townspeople protested, the event was moved to a 600-acre dairy farm owned by Max Yasgur in Bethel, New York. More than 400,000 fans arrived to hear the music, overwhelming all preparations. Despite the lack of food, water, and sanitary facilities and a surplus of marijuana and rainy weather, the concert became in retrospect a symbol of the 1960s youth movement. Featured acts included Joe Cocker, Richie Havens, Jimi Hendrix, Janis Joplin, and The Who. Their performances were included in two subsequent films and record albums that gave millions more an opportunity to participate in the event and the concert producers the chance to recoup a reported $1 million loss.

See Also: **Rock and Roll; Nineteen Sixties.**

BIBLIOGRAPHY: Curry, Jack, *Woodstock: The Summer of Our Lives* (Weidenfeld & Nicholson 1989); Miller, Jim, ed., *The Rolling Stone Illustrated History of Rock and Roll* (Rolling Stone Press 1976).

■ **WOODWARD, ROBERT BURNS (1917-79),** biochemist. Born in Boston, Massachusetts, he attended Massachusetts Institute of Technology (Ph.D., 1937) and worked at Harvard (1938-79) and as a consultant. During World War II, he achieved the first synthesis of quinine. Woodward became world famous for his synthesis of other organic compounds, including steroids, alkaloids, chlorophyll, cortisone, tetracycline, and vitamin B-12. He also joined amino acids into polypeptide chains, which aided the manufacture of plastics and artificial antibiotics. Woodward won the Nobel Prize in Chemistry in 1965.

See Also: **Science.**

■ **WOOL ACT (1699),** British legislation that prohibited the export of wool fabric from the American colonies. While the act did not forbid the production of domestic woolens, it moved to prevent their circulation beyond local markets.

■ **WOOLLEY, MARY EMMA (1863-1947),** educator and reformer. Born in South Norwalk, Connecticut, she attended Wheaton Seminary and was the first woman to graduate from Brown University (1894). She was professor of biblical studies at Wellesley College and president of Mount Holyoke College (1901-37). A feminist and a progressive, she was also vice chairman of the American Civil Liberties Union and president (1927-33) of the American Association of College Women.

See Also: American Civil Liberties Union (ACLU).

■ **WOOLMAN, JOHN (1720-72),** Quaker leader, author, and early abolitionist. Born in Rancocas, New Jersey, into a Quaker family, Woolman attended a Quaker common school. As a young man, he began to travel and preach at Quaker meetings all over the Eastern Seaboard from New Hampshire to North Carolina. Although he sometimes preached within mainstream Quaker teachings, opposing conscription and taxation for military activity, he most often addressed slavery in his public sermons. During his years as an active preacher, he also wrote and published a variety of abolitionist tracts, arguing that slavery was the greatest contradiction to Christian as well as to republican principles in America.

See Also: Friends, the Religious Society of (Quakers).

■ **WORK IN AMERICA,** a central theme of national discourse and national identity since colonial times. Puritans believed that everyday toil bestowed upon human beings their dignity and "the regard of Heaven." Their poet John Milton had made Adam reply to the curse placed upon him when God expelled him from Eden: "with labour must I earn/My Bread; what harm? Idleness had been worse. . . ."

But the Puritan ethic was replete with contradictions, which were brought to the surface by the growth of commerce and inequality. It justified seizure of land that Indians had not cultivated in the colonists' style, but it also generated persistent fears that Europeans living amid abundant game and remote from market incentives would sink into "dissolute" life. Although Puritans contended that society needed the exchange of goods and services to bind people together and that prosperity came to those who labored faithfully, both farmers and the clergy warned against displays of wealth and "vanity," and they summoned magistrates to guard against "oppression in wages and prices."

While wealth could be a sign of God's grace, the wealthy were particularly vulnerable to the temptations of sin. Mercantile activity, especially overseas commerce and moneylending, were the most common sources of large fortunes by the 18th century, although even the busiest of Boston merchants rarely spent three hours a day in the counting house and mixed their business with the male sociability of coffee houses and judicial chambers. Their pursuit of profit was championed by mercantilist theorists like Benjamin Franklin, who celebrated "the Hope of one day being able to purchase and enjoy Luxuries" as "a great Spur to Labour and Industry."

Farmers and artisans, who regarded themselves as "upright, manly, and independent citizens," alternated bouts of intense productive activity (as during harvests) with conviviality, public gatherings, and innumerable funerals. Women's tasks of child care (about half the population was younger than 16), preparation of food and clothing, and interminable spinning left them much less idle time, but those tasks were also immersed in social networks.

The "mechanical arts," or fabrication of goods, occupied more than half the urban adult male population in early America. The immutable and predictable ways in which wood, iron, and other materials responded to cutting, heating, and pounding taught artisans not only that their exertions added to society's wealth but also that their efforts would accomplish the desired results only if they conformed to the "natural laws" that governed the physical world. Their societies proudly proclaimed, "By Hammer in Hand All Arts Do Stand."

The image of the mechanic and farmer whose independence and virtue were underwritten by knowledge of their trades, self-employment, and daily engagement with fellow citizens in the marketplace and in public debate dominated American literary and political discourse until the end of the 19th century, long after it had become anachronistic in regions of rapid economic development. The style of work represented by the farmer and mechanic stood in sharp contrast to both chattel slavery and industrial wage labor.

Commerce, Slavery, and Industry. It was on the slave plantations of early America that large numbers of workers were first assembled for large-scale commodity production under a regime of work discipline imposed by others. Slaves constituted more than 30 percent of the labor force in 1810 and 1820. The cotton, tobacco, rice, and sugar they raised generated the lion's share of the new country's foreign exchange and investment capital. Although the rhythms of agricultural production allowed various seasons of the year when slaves might pursue their own needs, large plantations had sufficiently diversified their production by the second quarter of the 19th century that little remained of such slack seasons for the slaves, except at Christmas time. Horns announced the beginning and end of the day's toil, and whips enforced the required working pace.

The development of modern industry also transformed the meaning of work for many free men and women. Factory production assigned a specialized task to each individual within an enterprise. Although some of those jobs required highly skilled laborers, most were repetitive of the same mechanized operation. All employees were subject to the supervision of overseers with power to hire and fire. Work began and ended at times announced by company clocks and whistles, and company rules, enforced by dismissal or fines, governed everyone's conduct during the long hours of work.

For factory operatives and laborers, who had often migrated from distant parts of the globe in search of income, work offered little dignity or independence. Although the material standards of living improved between 1850 and 1900, everyday experience made work seem unavoidable, unpredictable, and unrewarding. Labor leader George McNeill complained that the worker "when at work" was "continually under surveillance," but "when out of work" was "the pariah of society."

Many people pursued their own purposes through industrial life, but those who had mastered some skilled occupation enjoyed the greatest chance of realizing their goals. Skilled workers were at home in the machine age, identified strongly with their crafts, and often expressed disdain for rural life. They sought to impose their own pace on their jobs, to buy a house, to get sons into a good trade, and to prepare their daughters to be teachers or secretaries. To combat the scourge of unemployment, and to enjoy more of life outside the factory, they sustained a pro-

tracted struggle to establish the eight-hour day. By 1921 the average work week was 48 hours.

Middle-class life nurtured a success ethic for men, which celebrated the "self-made man" as the archetypal American. Long hours of effort in the office promised the dream of ownership of one's own firm, a respectable station in society, and a comfortable home removed from the bustle of industrial neighborhoods. A special status was reserved for middle-class women who devoted themselves to the management of the home and the nurturing of children. Many such women, however, repudiated what they considered their confinement as "the pets of society" and challenged obstacles to their participation in professions.

The low income of working-class women, however, hindered their pursuit of options. Most of them earned wages in industry or in other people's households until they married and bore children, after which they sought to augment their husbands' incomes by bringing work into the home and by sending their children out to work.

Corporate America. After 1890 a wave of business mergers transformed the national economy, with important consequences for the nature of work. By 1909, 4.8 percent of the firms in manufacturing employed 62.2 percent of the country's industrial wage earners. The elaborate managerial staffs of the new enterprises changed the career options open to young men of the middle and upper classes, the very people to whom the individualistic success ethic of the previous century had been most meaningful. Their advancement came to depend on educational credentials and teamwork. Loyalty to the company characterized "the organization man."

During the 20th century, farming lost its dominant position in both the work experience and the values of the country. The exodus from the farm, noteworthy in the 1920s, became a torrent after 1940. By 1990 agriculture employed scarcely 2 percent of the labor force.

Mass production guided by the teachings of scientific management subjected manufacturing workers to stopwatch regulation and removed skilled work from the production floor. The surge in productivity made consumer goods accessible as never before, but it also provoked fears of "technological unemployment" between the world wars and of "automation" in the 1950s. Roughly 45 percent of males in the labor force were production workers in 1970, however, just as they had been in 1920.

The work of women changed dramatically during the first half of the 20th century. The proportion of women earning wages drew abreast of that of men, but it was clerical, sales, and service occupations, not manufacturing, that provided the new jobs. By the mid-1950s the number of all workers who produced goods fell below 50 percent of the work force. That trend accelerated in the 1970s, when the increase in employment in food service alone surpassed total employment in the automobile and steel industries combined.

In offices and factories alike, computer control of information displaced the historic ways humans had manipulated raw materials to create useful goods. That development has both increased the authority of experts and encouraged new forms of teamwork. It has also helped make stress the most common workplace disease.

—DAVID MONTGOMERY

See Also: Labor Movement; Unemployment.
BIBLIOGRAPHY: Crowley, J. E., *This Sheba, Self: The Conceptualization of Economic Life in Eighteenth-Century America* (Johns Hopkins Univ. Press 1974); Rogers, Daniel T., *The Work Ethic in Industrial America, 1850-1920* (Univ. of Chicago Press 1978); Terkel, Studs, *Working* (Avon Books 1972); Zuboff, Shoshana, *In the Age of the Smart Machine: The Future of Work and Power* (Basic Books 1988).

■ **WORKS PROJECTS ADMINISTRATION (WPA),** New Deal agency created to provide jobs to unemployed Americans. Established in 1935 as the Works Progress Administration, the WPA was designed as a permanent program to replace the emergency relief projects. Under the initial leadership of Harry L. Hopkins, the WPA employed millions of Americans in a wide variety of work. Building projects resulted in the construction of hospitals, dams, roads, schools, airports, and parks. Perhaps the most innovative of the WPA programs were the service projects that employed jobless writers, musicians, and artists.

Although the WPA was one of the New Deal's most extensive and successful programs, it had flaws. Ineligibility left some of the most destitute without work or relief. Moreover, some local officials discriminated against minorities and women, leaving many unemployed. Attacks from without threatened the WPA. Conservative officials, for example, assailed the usefulness and political motives of WPA artists, writers, and musicians. In light of such attacks, Congress passed the Reorganization Act of 1939, renaming the WPA and placing it under the control of the Federal Works Agency. With a new director, Francis C. Harrington, the new WPA reduced its emphasis on women's and service programs and increased the funding for construction projects. With employment opportunities soaring in the preparation for war, the WPA dissolved in 1943. The WPA left an enduring legacy with its building and cultural projects.

—GUY NELSON

See Also: Hopkins, Harry L.; New Deal.
BIBLIOGRAPHY: Conkin, Paul K., *The New Deal*, 2nd ed. (Harlan Davidson 1975).

■ **WORLD COURT,** popular term for the International Court of Justice at The Hague, Netherlands, which succeeded a League of Nations body when the United Nations was formed in 1945. The judicial branch of the United Nations, the World Court arbitrates treaty and international law violations.

■ **WORLD WAR I (1914-1918),** global war entered by the United States in 1917. In August 1914, general war began in Europe for the first time in a century. American leaders understood from the beginning of hostilities that the conflict might threaten U.S. security, and Pres. Woodrow Wilson sought grounds for a negotiated peace before unforeseen events drew the United States into the conflict. Many historians have argued that geopolitical and economic issues influenced Wilson's decision for war, but the most current interpretations indicate that traditional questions of neutral rights precipitated by German submarine warfare actually brought him, on Apr. 5, 1917, to lead the nation into the battle.

The Home Front: 1917-18. During the Progressive Era, Americans had been engaged in reforming and reorganizing their decentralized 19th-century political system to meet the demands of a 20th-century urban-industrial state. Political leaders hoped to rationalize and formalize a new "cooperative commonwealth" by combining, through voluntary means, traditional private institutions with federal authority. Such arrangements would establish efficiency and order without the threats to liberty posed by centralized bureaucratic authority. The war gave reformers a chance to test their theories. At first, they worked through newly created state and local councils of national defense, but within a year, decentralized, voluntary cooperation gave way to central direction from emergency war agencies under presidential control. William G. MacAdoo handled finance and the railroads; Herbert Hoover concentrated on food; Vance McCormick oversaw trade and economic warfare; Bernard Baruch and his War Industries Board acted as the president's "eye" on industrial mobilization; and Alfred Hurley allocated shipping. By mid-1918—joined by Sec. of War Newton D. Baker, Army Chief of Staff Peyton C. March, Sec. of the Navy Josephus Daniels, and Sec. of State Robert Lansing in a War Cabinet—these men constituted a primitive national security council. The introduction of Selective Service was an example of the rapid movement from voluntarism to compulsion. Wilson had opposed even the mention of conscription before the war. In April 1917, in part to prevent former president Theodore Roosevelt from raising a volunteer division, the Wilson administration executed a complete change in direction. The country had volunteered en masse for the war, the president announced, and people, like any other resource, were going to be allocated efficiently and systematically through the draft. Such references to volunteering continued until the spring of 1918, when Wilson announced in his "Force to the Utmost" speech that all the country's resources must be mobilized for the war effort. Ultimately, the government seized railroads and shipping and went into business building war materials on a mammoth scale. It even attempted, through George Creel's Committee on Public Information, to conscript public opinion.

The war catalyzed other forces as well. Women entered the work force in unprecedented numbers, and, temporarily at least, opportunities in war industry emerged for African Americans. Many of the most significant changes in postwar American society evolved from wartime movements on the home front. In 1919 and 1920, respectively, the 18th (Prohibition) and 19th (woman suffrage) Amendments to the Constitution were approved.

Pres. Woodrow Wilson's effective leadership on the home front in 1917 helped to rally public opinion to support the war effort.

But no amount of idealism, no presidential proclamation or administrative scheme, could buy the time to expand military production. On Armistice Day (Nov. 11, 1918), the home front was in disarray. Aside from small arms, production programs had never reached fruition, and in Europe, the U.S. Army had fought with French and British airplanes, artillery, and tanks.

Wilson the Diplomat: 1914-18. Like the Russian revolutionary leader V. I. Lenin, President Wilson believed that the war offered an opportunity to reshape the world. Wilson sought to create a new American international system to replace the balance of power. In December 1916, the president offered U.S. mediation and participation in a postwar community of nations. On Jan. 22, 1917, in his famous "Peace without Victory" speech to Congress, Wilson proposed a peace of reconciliation in Europe, self-determination of peoples, freedom of the seas, arms limitation, and some sort of league for peace that might replace traditional balance of power politics with collective security. Once at war, he did not change his basic objectives. In his "Fourteen Points" of Jan. 8, 1918, he proposed a new world order including open diplomacy, self-determination of peoples, freedom of the seas, arms limitation, general reconciliation, collective security, and international cooperation.

Inter-Allied Relations: 1917-18. World War I was a coalition war. The Allies feared Wilson almost as much as they feared the Germans. Eng-

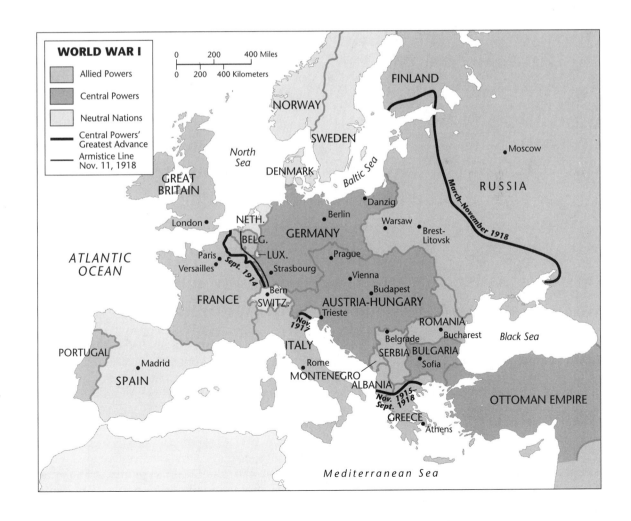

WORLD WAR I

- Allied Powers
- Central Powers
- Neutral Nations
- Central Powers' Greatest Advance
- Armistice Line Nov. 11, 1918

0   200   400 Miles
0   200   400 Kilometers

African-American infantrymen of the 369th Infantry defend a trench in May 1918, during World War I.

land's Prime Minister David Lloyd George and France's Premier Georges Clemenceau feared an American peace would rob their countries of the fruits of victory and sought to reduce American political participation while maximizing their own control of U.S. military and economic resources.

Wilson insisted on a separate and independent American army to give him a strong hand at the peace table and pressed for a Supreme War Council and military unity of command to assure the Americans, who chose the title Associated Power, equality in policymaking. In late 1917, a war council was created to coordinate grand strategy, and during the summer of 1918, similar councils were established to coordinate economic affairs. Wilson insisted on U.S. participation in all those

organizations. The coordination of the military and political sphere, where the Americans were gaining strength, and the financial sphere, where they were powerful from the very beginning of the war, created the first transnational politico-economic organization of modern times.

The United States in Battle: 1917-18. When the United States joined the war, conditions on the western front had reached a critical juncture. The war had degenerated into nightmarish battles of attrition, which had reached a climax at Verdun and the Somme in 1916 and at Passchendaele in 1917. Only on the eastern front—where the vast spaces of Poland and western Russia and the inadequacies of Russian administration created favorable conditions for conventional military exploitation—had the Central Powers achieved victory. And there, by late 1917, war had become revolution. In November 1917, the Russians left the war, and the Italians suffered defeat at Caporetto. In Germany, military leaders believed that the moment had come to crown success in the east with victory in the west. In March 1918, Gen. Eric Ludendorff opened Operation Michael to win the war before the Americans could arrive in strength. The German offensive failed in part because of the timely intervention of U.S. forces.

The planning of the American reinforcement was a classic example of strategic overkill. The original Thirty Division Project of July 1917 was an appropriate response to conditions on the western front, but the Eighty Division Program of July 1918 was disconnected from military realities, and the Wilson administration developed an army twice the size it needed to meet the emergency.

The American buildup began in May 1917, when Gen. John J. Pershing was ordered to France with broad power to construct an American striking force. In the next 16 months, the U.S. Navy, ably assisted by the British, convoyed almost 2 million American soldiers across the ocean, making it possible for Pershing to create the American Expeditionary Force (AEF). The troops were inadequately organized, segregated in Jim Crow units, badly trained, British- and French-equipped, and at times poorly led, but when they joined the fighting in strength in June and July 1918, they helped block the final German push, and in September at the Meuse-Argonne they provided the Allies a margin sufficient for victory.

The Treaty of Versailles. Between December 1918 and June 1919, President Wilson hammered out the Treaty of Versailles with its League of Nations Covenant. It was not a peace of reconciliation, but it was not a complete victor's peace either. He then moved to win Americans over to the new Wilsonian internationalism and to carry the treaty through the U.S. Senate. There, Wilson was on shaky ground. During the war, his support had come from the forces of political reform. But radical reformers had opposed the war and had suffered from government surveillance and suppression. Some liberals were alienated by compromises Wilson made at Paris, and the president had already offended traditionalists and Re-

publicans like Theodore Roosevelt. In the Senate, Henry Cabot Lodge, chairman of the Foreign Relations Committee, proposed certain reservations to the treaty, which Wilson found unacceptable. Ultimately, Wilson's means were inadequate to secure his objectives. Once the American people understood the implications of the treaty Wilson advocated, they rejected them. The treaty failed, and the country settled for limited internationalism. It would take another crisis before Americans would accept Wilson's view that 19th-century policies must be abandoned.

—DANIEL R. BEAVER

See Also: *American Expeditionary Force (AEF); Dawes Plan; Fourteen Points; Lusitania, Sinking of the; Selective Service Act (1917); Versailles, Treaty of; individual battles and biographies.*

BIBLIOGRAPHY: Coffman, Edward M., *The War To End All Wars: The American Military Experience in World War I* (Oxford Univ. Press 1968); Ferrell, Robert H., *Woodrow Wilson and World War I 1917-1921* (Harper & Row 1985); Kennedy, David M., *Over Here: The First World War and American Society* (Oxford Univ. Press 1980); Schaffer, Ronald, *America in the Great War* (Oxford Univ. Press 1991); Trask, David F., *The AEF and Coalition Warmaking 1917-1918* (Univ. Press of Kansas 1993).

■ **WORLD WAR II,** global conflict that permanently changed patterns in U.S. history. It started on Sept. 3, 1939, when Britain and France declared war on Germany in response to the Nazi invasion of Poland, and ended with Japan's formal surrender on Sept. 2, 1945. At the war's outset, Pres. Franklin D. Roosevelt declared U.S. neutrality, but he did not ask Americans to "remain neutral in thought as well." He saw the potential Axis conquest of Europe as a huge threat but knew that most Americans thought the U.S. entry into World War I had been a mistake. On Dec. 7, 1941, Japan's attack on Pearl Harbor forced the United States to enter World War II.

Aid to the Allies. Roosevelt wanted to aid the European nations fighting against Germany and Italy, but three neutrality laws Congress passed during the 1930s limited his freedom to act. Prohibiting loans and the sale of arms to belligerents, isolationists believed, would prevent Britain, France, or American munitions makers from maneuvering the United States into another war. In November 1939, Congress passed a fourth neutrality act, restoring a loophole permitting arms sales on a "cash and carry" basis. Few thought the United States needed to do more, since no fighting had taken place in Europe in what was known as the "Phony War."

Germany's Adolf Hitler placed U.S. isolationists on the defensive in spring 1940 when Nazi forces conquered Norway, Denmark, Holland, and Belgium. Germany invaded France in June, and Roosevelt pledged open access for all victims of aggression to economic resources in a U.S. "Arsenal for Democracy." After Paris fell on June 13, Britain fought Hitler alone. Prime Minister Winston Churchill appealed for more arms, planes, and ships, but Roosevelt doubted that Congress would lift the embargo. Outflanking isolationists, he used an executive agreement in September to exchange 50 U.S. destroyers to combat Nazi submarines in return for leases on British bases in the Atlantic and Caribbean.

In November 1940, Roosevelt's election to a third term indicated that most voters agreed that aiding the Allies would make intervention unnecessary. But Britain could not pay for the vast increase of military equipment needed to halt a Nazi invasion. Skirting neutrality laws again, Roosevelt persuaded Congress to pass the Lend Lease Act in March 1941, allowing him to transfer defense assets to nations deemed vital to U.S. security. Nazi submarines sank a growing number of ships carrying Lend Lease aid, causing Roosevelt to extend the security zone. Now U.S. naval patrols helped Britain locate submarines, provoking an attack on the U.S.S. *Greer* in September 1941. Orders to "shoot on sight" and convoy ships into British ports led to the sinking of the U.S.S. *Reuben James* on November 1. Roosevelt did not ask a divided Congress to declare war because he wanted to lead a united nation into World War II.

Road to Pearl Harbor. Although U.S. policy tried to oppose Japan's drive for hegemony in Asia, it failed to deter the Japanese occupation of Manchuria in 1931. Japan and Germany signed the Anti-Comintern Pact in 1936 then added Italy to form the Tripartite Pact. Japan provoked a war to conquer China in July 1937, prompting Roo-

sevelt's call to "quarantine" aggressors. Japan then proclaimed a "New Order" in Asia in 1938, ignoring American demands for respect of its treaty commitments.

To halt Japanese expansion, Roosevelt increased economic and military aid to China. He also imposed economic sanctions, exploiting Japan's dependence on U.S. aircraft parts, scrap iron, and oil. In July 1939, the U.S. Pacific Fleet redeployed to Pearl Harbor, Hawaii.

War in Europe encouraged Japan to occupy northern French Indochina in June 1940 in pursuit of its Greater East Asia Co-Prosperity Sphere. In September, Japan, Germany, and Italy formed an Axis Alliance, conveying frightening images of a united fascist steamroller moving toward world conquest. Roosevelt now broadened the embargo on metals, causing Japan in April 1941 to open talks for a settlement. Tense negotiations could not reconcile Japan's imperial ambition with inflexible U.S. demands for withdrawal from all occupied areas. After Japan seized southern Indochina in July 1941, Roosevelt froze Japanese assets and embargoed oil. Japanese militants secured the emperor's consent for war after one last failed stab at compromise. U.S. leaders knew an attack was at hand, having broken Japan's secret code, but thought the Philippines was the probable target.

The Grand Alliance. British and American military planners already had agreed in secret strategy sessions before Pearl Harbor that if the United States joined the fighting, the defeat of Germany would be the first priority. Help would come from the Soviet Union, which entered the war after Germany invaded Russia in June 1941. Roosevelt and Churchill had agreed on Allied war aims in August 1941, issuing the Atlantic Charter. To maintain Lend Lease aid, Soviet leader Joseph Stalin signed this policy statement but demanded land concessions for a postwar defensive buffer zone in East Europe. Stalin deferred an agreement on territorial issues in return for Roosevelt's pledge to open a second front in France in 1942. Churchill opposed an early invasion across the English Channel, and the Anglo-American landing came in North Africa in November.

Hitler's plans for global conquest met defeat in Russia in the carnage at Stalingrad during the

American infantrymen move ashore on Normandy's beaches on D-Day, June 6, 1944.

winter of 1942-43. Stalin's anger over delays in opening a front in France grew when Anglo-American forces invaded Sicily in July 1943 and then landed in mainland Italy that fall. U.S. and British strategic bombing against Germany began in May 1942 and became a ceaseless daily barrage by 1944 but failed to reduce greatly enemy morale or production. At last, on June 6, 1944 (D-Day), Anglo-American forces staged the vast and elaborately planned cross-channel invasion at Normandy. Meanwhile, the Red Army moved through East Europe, occupying Warsaw in August 1944 as Allied forces liberated Paris. In December, a setback at the Battle of the Bulge merely delayed Hitler's defeat.

The Pacific Theater. After its spectacular success at Pearl Harbor, Japan quickly seized Guam, Wake Island, and Hong Kong. Early in 1942, Malaya, Singapore, Burma, the Dutch East Indies, and New Guinea fell. The Philippines then surrendered. But at Coral Sea and Midway in May and June 1942, U.S. carriers won decisive victories, saving New Zealand and Australia. Japan lost men and material in the China-Burma-India theater, but the Chinese Nationalists focused more on fighting the Communists than the Japanese. Just two months after the first American bombing raid on Tokyo in April 1942, Japan was on the defensive.

Limited Allied counteroffensives in the summer of 1942 saw implementation of the "island hopping strategy." Allied forces would strike at weak Pacific installations, bypassing and severing the supply lines to more fortified positions. The capture of Guadalcanal in August initiated a series of amphibious landings with air support that won control of the Solomons in February 1943. In the central Pacific, Adm. Chester W. Nimitz moved through the Gilbert Islands to the Marshalls, capturing the Eniwetok Atoll in February 1944. He now urged assaulting Taiwan and linking with the Chinese for an invasion of Japan. This meant bypassing the Philippines, and Gen. Douglas MacArthur objected. After Roosevelt backed MacArthur, Japan's remaining naval forces met destruction at Leyte Gulf in October 1944. Liberation of the Philippines early in 1945 left Japan open to invasion.

Domestic Mobilization. Roosevelt persuaded Congress to raise defense spending immediately after World War II began. He pressed business and industry to expand productivity to provide unlimited aid to the Allies, and Congress passed in September 1940 the first peacetime draft in U.S. history. The Japanese attack on Pearl Harbor silenced voices of opposition. A War Production Board allocated all resources and coordinated military procurement, while a War Manpower Commission secured workers for the defense industry. A National War Labor Board set wages, hours, and working conditions to prevent strikes; and a War Food Administration provided incentives to boost output in agriculture.

Wartime prosperity ended the Depression, as purchasing power and gross national product more than doubled. Wartime government spending and indebtedness dwarfed New Deal expenditures and borrowing. Corporate profits skyrocketed. To check inflation, Roosevelt froze wages, rents, and prices in 1943. A rationing system worked because of popular cooperation that extended to saving tin cans and growing food in "liberty gardens." Women and African Americans joined a labor force that had increased its production levels by 1944 to twice that of the Axis nations combined.

Americans paid a price for victory on the home front. Under the War Labor Disputes Act, Roosevelt could seize factories to block work stoppages, while imposing fines and jail terms on strikers. Alleged subversives, dissenters, and radicals faced prison sentences under the Smith Act. In 1942, Roosevelt authorized the internment of Japanese Americans, despite the lack of any evidence of disloyalty. That the Supreme Court upheld this action reflected the reactionary mood of a fearful and increasingly conservative public. Roosevelt dropped reformer Henry Wallace as vice president in favor of moderate Sen. Harry S. Truman to ensure reelection in 1944. Roosevelt's deteriorating health worsened, and on Apr. 12, 1945, he died while recuperating in Warm Springs, Georgia.

Preparations for Peace. Suspicion mounted in the Grand Alliance because of divergent war aims. Tension increased when Stalin would not attend the Casablanca Conference in January 1943. To reassure the Soviets, Roosevelt and Churchill announced an unconditional surrender doctrine, but a conditional peace with Italy in September revived Stalin's distrust. Also, Britain and the United States, while rejecting return of Russian land lost

after World War I, courted Vichy France and Franco Spain. Poland tested prospects for the postwar cooperation. When Poland's prewar government in 1943 called for investigation of the Katyn Forest massacre of Polish officers by Russians, Stalin broke relations and picked loyal Communists for a new government.

Building postwar cooperation was the goal at the Teheran Conference set for late 1943 in Iran, the first meeting of the "Big Three" of Roosevelt, Churchill, and Stalin. Optimism soared in October, following a foreign ministers' meeting in Moscow at which Stalin said that the Soviets would join a postwar security organization and enter the war against Japan. At Teheran, Roosevelt agreed that the Soviet Union would gain land in eastern Poland with compensation coming from Germany. Accords were reached on three occupation zones in Germany and postwar withdrawal from Iran. Discussion of Roosevelt's concept of "Four Policemen" to preserve postwar peace provided guidance for negotiators at the Dumbarton Oaks Conference in August 1944, where an outline for the future United Nations (UN) was drafted. Earlier that summer, the Bretton Woods Conference made the dollar the basis for currency convertibility and created the World Bank and International Monetary Fund to promote economic recovery.

Triumph in Europe. The final Allied offensives into Germany began early in 1945 as Roosevelt, Churchill, and Stalin met for a second time in southern Russia at Yalta. Compromise resolved differences about the UN, while Stalin agreed to reorganize Poland's government. Concessions to Stalin in Asia for promising to join the Pacific war within three months following Hitler's defeat were condemned later. The extent of reform and the amount of reparations from Germany were left unanswered, but free elections for new governments were guaranteed. The Soviet imposition after Yalta of Communist rule in Poland, Romania, and Bulgaria alarmed Roosevelt and convinced Truman that "Sovietization" was an intolerable threat. On April 24, Soviet forces entered Berlin and Hitler's successors surrendered on May 7.

Listening to his anti-Soviet advisers, Truman sharply criticized Stalin's violation of the Yalta accords. He also abruptly ended Lend Lease to Russia in May 1945, while China and Britain still received aid. But that same month, Truman's concessions on Poland showed a desire to preserve Allied harmony. During the spring of 1945, formal creation of the UN at the San Francisco Conference was encouraging, but the Potsdam Conference in July exposed the depth of Soviet-American animosity. Joining Truman and Stalin for acrimonious negotiations was Britain's new prime minister, Clement Attlee. Allied leaders would refer contentious issues ranging from composition of governments in East Europe to reconstruction of Germany to their foreign ministers for later unproductive meetings.

Atomic Victory in Asia. While en route to the Teheran Conference in 1943, Roosevelt and Churchill stopped in Cairo, Egypt, for discussions with Nationalist Chinese leader Chiang Kai-shek about military strategy and Asia's future. On Dec. 1, 1943, the Cairo Declaration pledged to demilitarize Japan and strip it of its imperial holdings after achieving unconditional surrender. Extremely bloody military operations followed early in 1945. On Iwo Jima in February, U.S. losses reached 26,000, exceeding Japanese casualties. In April, the capture of Okinawa was even more costly. U.S. leaders expected an invasion of Japan to result in horrific losses. Then, on July 16, 1945, Truman learned of the successful test in New Mexico of an atomic device capable of destroying an entire city.

At Potsdam, the Allies had threatened Japan with utter destruction if it did not surrender immediately. After the Japanese rejected this ulti-

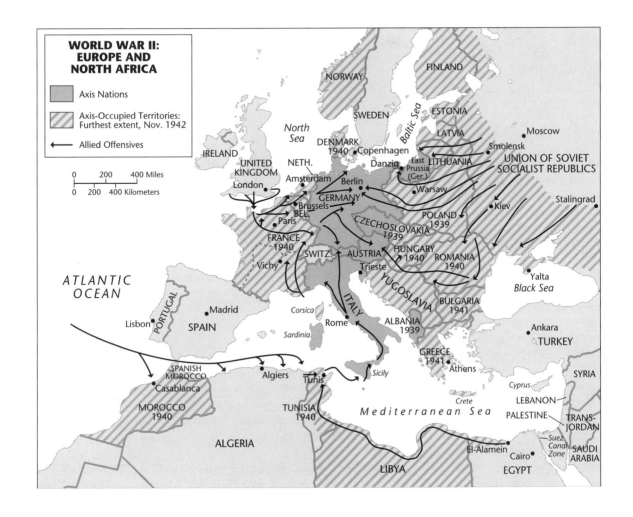

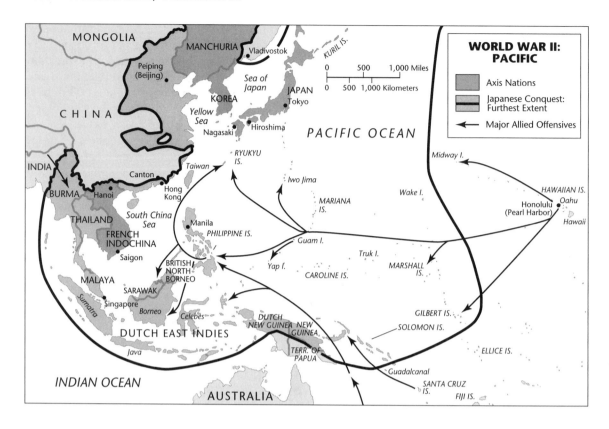

WORLD WAR II: PACIFIC

Axis Nations

Japanese Conquest: Furthest Extent

Major Allied Offensives

matum, Truman authorized the dropping of one atomic bomb on Hiroshima on August 6 and a second on Nagasaki three days later. The Soviet Union declared war on August 8 and its troops swiftly moved into Manchuria and Korea. On August 14, Japan accepted terms allowing retention of the emperor, and the fighting stopped. Three weeks later, aboard the U.S.S. *Missouri*, Japan's surrender formally ended World War II.

Angry and emotional debate about the necessity of using atomic weapons to achieve peace has persisted. Merciless air bombing and naval shelling in July had caused staggering civilian losses and left Japan in ruins. Truman wanted to save lives, but he also hoped to limit Soviet expansion in Asia.

Aftermath and Impact. News of victory in World War II ignited wild celebrations, and later conflicts in Korea and Vietnam reinforced the belief that World War II was a "good war." But Americans soon were wrestling with the twin challenges of determining the fate of New Deal reform and defining a new U.S. world role. An elusive search for answers would frustrate the nation for the remainder of the 20th century.

—JAMES I. MATRAY

See Also: Casablanca Conference; Hiroshima and Nagasaki; Isolationism; Lend-Lease; Potsdam Conference; War Production Board; Yalta Conference; individual battles and biographies.

BIBLIOGRAPHY: Blum, John Morton, *V Was for Victory: Politics and American Culture during World War II* (Harcourt Brace 1976); Divine, Robert A., *The Reluctant Belligerent: American Entry into World War II* (Wiley 1967); Millett, Allan R., and Peter Maslowski, *For the Common Defense: A Military History of the United States* (Free Press 1984); Smith, Gaddis, *American Diplomacy during the Second World War, 1941-1945* (Wiley 1985).

■ **WOUNDED KNEE, OCCUPATION OF (Feb. 27–May 9, 1973).** In 1972 traditional Oglala Sioux at the Pine Ridge Reservation asked the American Indian Movement (AIM) for protection against the tribal government of Richard Wilson. The traditionals and AIM were also concerned with whites' abuse of Indians when off the reservation. In February 1973 some 200 Pine Ridge residents and AIM supporters occupied the Wounded Knee trading post, the site of an 1890 massacre by the U.S. Cavalry. The occupation resolved little, and in the three years following it, some people believe that at least 100 traditionals and AIM activists were murdered by reservation police at Pine Ridge.

See Also: American Indian Movement (AIM); Indians of North America.

■ **WOUNDED KNEE MASSACRE,** site in South Dakota where the U.S. Army killed (1890) a large community of Sioux Indians. The Indian wars in the continental United States were all but over in the late 1880s, but the pointless slaughter at Wounded Knee, one of the last outbreaks of violence, has come to symbolize the many massacres of Indians and misunderstandings of their culture throughout American history.

The events at Wounded Knee had their origin in a new Indian religion. In 1888 a Paiute named Wovoka started the Ghost Dance religion. He claimed that the world would soon end and then come alive again. All the Indian dead in past ages would inherit the new earth. To earn this new life, Indians had to live in harmony and avoid the ways of whites, especially alcohol.

Indians of the Plains and Far West quickly began practicing the Ghost Dance religion. As the religion spread among the various tribes, each adapted Wovoka's original vision to its own situation. The Sioux claimed that special Ghost Shirts could stop bullets and that in the new life the buffalo would soon return. White officials were alarmed by the new religion and banned the Ghost Dance on Sioux reservations. One of the Sioux chiefs, Big Foot, wishing to avoid conflict, led a band of 350 Indians, 230 of them women and children, to the Catholic mission of Wounded Knee on the Pine Ridge, South Dakota, reservation, as ordered by the U.S. military. On Dec. 29, 1890, troops were ordered to collect all Indian firearms at Wounded Knee. When the soldiers tried to confiscate the weapons, a rifle discharged and hand-to-hand combat erupted. The troops then fired their heavy artillery, cutting down men, women, and children alike. At least 150 and possibly as many as 300 Indians died at Wounded Knee, with still more injured. The Ghost Dance, however, was not stamped out. It moved underground and contin-

Chief Big Foot lies dead and frozen in a macabre position in the aftermath of the massacre at Wounded Knee in late December 1890.

ued to be performed in secret.

The date of the Wounded Knee massacre is conventionally used to mark the end of Indian military resistance on the Plains. Wounded Knee would again be the subject of national attention when representatives of the American Indian Movement (AIM) occupied the site in 1973 to protest conditions and corruption on the Pine Ridge Reservation.

—RYAN MADDEN

See Also: Ghost Dance; Indians of North America; Sioux.

BIBLIOGRAPHY: Utley, Robert, *The Last Days of the Sioux Nation* (Yale Univ. Press 1963); Weeks, Philip, *Farewell, My Nation: The American Indian and the United States, 1829-1890* (Harlan Davidson 1990).

■ **WOVOKA (c. 1856-1932),** prophet of the Ghost Dance religion. A Paiute, Wovoka was born in present-day Nevada. For part of his childhood, he lived with a white family named Wilson, and his English name became Jack Wilson. In 1889, while gravely ill, Wovoka experienced a vision and claimed that he had been taken to the spirit world. At a time when Indians were coming to terms with their loss of sovereignty and land, Wovoka preached that if the Indians prayed and danced, the world would be destroyed and replaced by a new Indian world, in which the dead would rejoin the living and the rapidly diminishing buffalo herds would return. Hence, his religion became known as the Ghost Dance religion. This new revitalization religion caught on among many western tribes, including the Cheyenne, the Arapaho, and the Sioux and led to the Wounded Knee Massacre at the Pine Ridge Reservation in 1890. Wovoka married and had four children. He died in 1932 at the Walker River Reservation in Nevada.

See Also: Frontier in American History; Ghost Dance; Indians of North America; Wounded Knee Massacre.

■ **WRIGHT, FRANCES FANNY (1795-1852),** author and reformer, born in Dundee, Scotland. Her enthusiastic accounts of her travels in the United States (1818-20) were published as *Views of Society and Manners in America* (1821), one of the earliest books on travel in the United States. In 1824 she moved to the United States and in 1825 founded Nashoba, a short-lived colony for freed slaves. In later writings she argued for equal rights for women, desegregation, free love, and birth control.

See Also: Women's Movement.

■ **WRIGHT, FRANK LLOYD (1869-1959),** prominent American architect. Born in Richland Center, Wisconsin, Wright moved to Chicago in 1887. Until 1893, he worked under Louis Sullivan at the firm of Adler and Sullivan, where he did primarily residential work. In his designs for houses, such as his own home in Oak Park, Illinois (1889), Wright developed the characteristics that made him the originator of "the prairie school" of architecture—an emphasis on horizontality, low profiles, and wide-eaved, hipped rooflines. Wright continued designing both residential and institutional buildings, seeming never to run out of architectural innova-

Frank Lloyd Wright, shown in his late 50s, continued to practice his art into his 80s and became the most influential architect in American history.

tions—ranging from the Imperial Hotel in Tokyo (1922), with earthquake-proof curtain walls, to his residential masterpiece, Falling Water, in Bear Run, Pennsylvania (1936), which cantilevered out over a waterfall, to the Guggenheim Museum in New York City (1956). Wright was also concerned with large-scale housing, and in the 1930s and 1940s created prototypes for "Usonian" houses, compact units designed for mass production.

See Also: Architecture.

BIBLIOGRAPHY: Bolson, Carol R., et al., eds., *The Nature of Frank Lloyd Wright* (Univ. of Chicago Press 1987).

■ **WRIGHT, PATIENCE LOVELL (1725-86),** among the earliest of American sculptors. Born in Bordentown, New Jersey, she lived among the political and social elite in Philadelphia, New York, and London,

modeling many of her well-known contemporaries in wax. Her portrait of William Pitt stands in London's Westminster Abbey.

See Also: Sculpture.

■ **WRIGHT, RICHARD NATHANIEL (1908-60),** novelist. Born in Roxie, Mississippi, Wright moved to Chicago in 1927 and supported himself doing menial labor. Socially conscious, Wright found the Communist party's championing of the working class appealing, and he joined the party in 1932. During the Depression he worked for the Federal Writers Project (1935-37) and edited the Communist paper, *Daily Worker.* Wright's social concerns found artistic expression in his novel *Native Son* (1940), about an African-American boy growing up in Chicago's slums. Around this time

Wilbur and Orville Wright completed construction of the world's first powered airplane at Kitty Hawk, North Carolina, where the brothers made four flights on Dec. 17, 1903.

Wright grew disenchanted with the Communists, and he resigned from the party in 1944. He wrote the autobiographical *Black Boy* in 1945. In 1946, Wright left the United States for self-exile in Paris, where the racism that provided the themes of his writing was less pervasive. Other notable works followed, including *The Outsider* (1953) and *Lawd Today* (1963). Wright remains one of America's and the world's most powerful literary voices of the 20th century.

See Also: *African Americans; Novel.*

■ **WRIGHT, WILBUR (1867-1912)** and **WRIGHT, ORVILLE (1871-1948),** inventors and aviators. Born in Millville, Indiana, and Dayton, Ohio, respectively, the brothers grew up in a tightly knit and religious family. Although neither graduated from high school, they both possessed keen intellects and a talent for mechanics. Always entrepreneurs, they opened a print shop in 1889 and began manufacturing bicycles on a small scale in 1895.

Wilbur and Orville became interested in flying after reading about the aeronautical experiments of Otto Lilienthal and his death in a glider accident in 1896. After familiarizing themselves with the previous experiments and efforts to fly, the Wright brothers built a series of gliders and powered airplanes between 1899 and 1905. In 1901, they designed and built their own wind tunnel, where they conducted hundreds of tests on different wing and biplane surfaces. Their dogged experimentation paid off on Dec. 17, 1903, at Kitty Hawk, North Carolina, when they made the first flights in a piloted, heavier-than-air, powered plane.

Returning to Dayton, they continued their experiments in the face of public skepticism about flying and legal battles over patents. By the end of 1905, they had developed the first practical flying machine and three years later won international fame with their public demonstrations. The brothers founded the Wright Company to build and sell aircraft, but Orville sold out in 1915, three years after his brother's sudden death.

—GUY NELSON

See Also: *Science.*

BIBLIOGRAPHY: Crouch, Tom D., *The Bishop's Boys: A Life of Wilbur and Orville Wright* (Norton 1989); Howard, Fred, *Wilbur and Orville: A Biography of the Wright Brothers* (Knopf 1987).

■ **WYOMING,** a Rocky Mountain state. It has fewer people than any other state. A perfect rectangle (like Colorado), it is bounded on the north and west by Montana, on the west by Idaho, on the west and south by Utah, on the south by Colorado, and on the east by Nebraska and South Dakota. The eastern third of Wyoming is part of the Great Plains. Oil, gas, and coal now fuel the state economy, but ranching is still important. Wyoming became a state in 1890.

Capital: Cheyenne. Area: 97,819 square miles. Population (1995 est.): 480,000.

See Also: *Bridger, Jim (James); Great Plains; Yellowstone.*

■ **WYTHE, GEORGE (1726-1806),** Revolutionary-era lawyer and political leader. Born in Virginia, Wythe served in the Second Continental Congress and was a signer of the Declaration of Independence. He is regarded as one of the great legal thinkers in early America.

See Also: *Declaration of Independence.*

XYZ

XYZ AFFAIR (1798), diplomatic controversy that heightened existing tension between France and the United States. French seizures and confiscations of American shipping in the West Indies in the latter half of the 1790s threw Franco-American relations into crisis. Pres. John Adams dispatched John Marshall, Elbridge Gerry, and Charles C. Pinckney to Paris to negotiate an end to the raids and compensation to American merchants. French foreign minister Talleyrand, however, refused to meet the delegation. Instead, four of his agents approached the Americans and demanded that the United States assume the vast American claims against the French government, finance a loan to the French government, and provide a personal bribe of £50,000 sterling to Talleyrand.

When President Adams learned of the debacle, he announced that he had lost hope in the negotiations. Congress demanded to see the correspondence that Adams had received. Sec. of State Timothy Pickering replaced the names of the French agents with the letters X, Y, and Z, and on Apr. 3, 1798, Adams submitted the dispatches. Within days newspapers throughout the country reprinted the humiliating accounts and the episode came to be known as the "XYZ Affair."

The news temporarily reversed the decline of the Federalist party, and in the 1798 elections, the party gained control of both houses. Federalists proceeded to use the crisis to attack the pro-French Jeffersonian opposition, passing the Alien and Sedition Acts and spurring a movement to crush their political rivals. Meanwhile, Talleyrand, realizing that his actions were driving the United States into the anti-French coalition, finally halted the seizures. The Convention of Mortefontaine, signed on Sept. 30, 1800, officially terminated the Franco-American alliance of 1778, which had been crucial to the success of the American Revolution.

—DORON BEN-ATAR

See Also: Revolution, American.

BIBLIOGRAPHY: Elkins, Stanley, and Eric McKitrick, *The Age of Federalism: The Early American Republic, 1788-1800* (Oxford Univ. Press 1993); Sharp, James Roger, *American Politics in the Early Republic: The New Nation in Crisis* (Yale Univ. Press 1993); Stinchcombe, William, *The XYZ Affair* (Greenwood Press 1980).

YAKIMA INDIANS. *See:* Northwest Coast Indians.

YALOW, ROSALYN SUSSMAN (1921-), medical physicist, born in New York City. With Dr. Solomon A. Berson, she developed the radioimmunoassay (RIA) test, using radioisotopes to measure small amounts of hormones and enzymes in the body. She was awarded the Nobel Prize for Physiology or Medicine in 1977.

See Also: Science.

YALTA CONFERENCE (1945), World War II meeting of Pres. Franklin D. Roosevelt, British Prime Minister Winston Churchill, and Soviet Premier Joseph Stalin. The three leaders met at the resort town of Yalta in the Soviet Crimea from February 4 to February 11.

The three Allied leaders agreed to divide Germany into four zones of occupation, one under each of their countries and another under France. They determined that the Great Powers would possess vetoes over important matters in the United Nations. Moreover, Stalin agreed that the Soviet Union would join the fight against Japan within three months of the end of the war in Europe in exchange for territorial and other concessions.

Agreement on the fate of Poland was not so easily reached. Stalin insisted that Poland's postwar government be dominated by a pro-Communist group based in Lublin. Churchill and Roosevelt called for the inclusion of anti-Communist Polish exiles who had spent the war in London. The three leaders failed to bridge the gap between Lublin and

In February 1945, Pres. Franklin D. Roosevelt met with British Prime Minister Winston Churchill (*left*) and Soviet Premier Joseph Stalin at the Yalta Conference. Behind them are their foreign ministers, respectively, Edward Stettinius (*middle*), Anthony Eden (*left*), and V. M. Molotov (*right*).

London, instead papering it over. Stalin consented vaguely to allow democratic elections and broaden the Lublin regime by including some Londoners, and Churchill and Roosevelt took him at his word.

Nearly every issue discussed at Yalta became a source of controversy as the world war segued into the Cold War. The peace conference that was to have determined Germany's future fizzled, leaving Germany divided and occupied. Great Power vetoes in the United Nations prevented that body from fulfilling its promise as an antidote to international anarchy. The completion of the atomic bomb and its use against Japan rendered Soviet entry into the Pacific war largely unnecessary; the concessions Stalin received, some of which touched on Chinese interests, were blasted as a sellout of China to the Communists. Stalin's promises regarding Poland proved as illusory as they were vague; the occupying Red Army quickly enforced a pro-Moscow orthodoxy on the country, prompting additional charges of a Roosevelt sellout.

—H. W. BRANDS

See Also: *Cold War; Roosevelt, Franklin Delano; United Nations (UN); World War II.*

BIBLIOGRAPHY: Yergin, Daniel, *Shattered Peace* (Houghton Mifflin 1977).

■ **YAMASEE WAR (1715-28),** war between South Carolina Indians and the colonists. A tribe in present-day South Carolina, the Yamasees traded with the English on their arrival in the 1680s, exchanging deerskins and Indian slaves for English goods. The Yamasees fought with the Carolina colonists in the Tuscarora War of 1711-13, but after the war the Yamasees were no longer able to maintain a balance of trade with the English, and they fell into debt. They were also concerned about continuing English encroachment onto their lands. Allying with the Creeks and the Catawbas, the Yamasees waged a war against South Carolina, attacking English traders and settlements beginning in 1715. The Carolinians used African slaves to fight the Yamasees, driving them into exile in Florida. From there, the Yamasees continued a guerrilla war against South Carolina, but in 1728, the South Carolinians waged a final assault against the Yamasees, exterminating them as a distinct tribe.

See Also: *Catawba; Creek; Indians of North America; Tuscarora.*

■ **YANKEE,** term possibly derived from the Hudson Dutch "jankee" ("little John"). It was pejoratively applied by the English to New Englanders, particularly sailors, in the early 18th century. The song "Yankee Doodle," apparently first sung by derisive British troops during the American Revolution, was quickly picked up by Americans as a celebration of their distinctive nationality, giving the term wide currency. Royall Tyler's 1787 comedic play *The Contrast* first suggested the stereotype of the Yankee traits of cynical wit, caution, and shrewdness in business that has become commonplace. During the Civil War, "Yankee" became a contemptuous term for Northern soldiers among Confederates. In the modern United States the term is generally applied to natives of the Northeast or New England, but abroad it stands for all Americans and has taken on both positive and negative connotations. "The Yanks Are Coming" was a cheer to the Allies during World War I, while the less friendly graffiti "Yanqui Go Home" has been scrawled on the walls of Latin American countries.
BIBLIOGRAPHY: Botkin, B. A., *A Treasury of New England Folklore* (1957; reprint, Crown Publishers 1984).

■ **YANKEE DOODLE,** song popular among the patriots of the American Revolution. Americans soon picked it up as a celebration of their distinctive nationality. The earliest manuscript lyric dates from 1775 and the earliest printed version from 1778, although the music and lyrics were not published in the United States before 1794.

■ **YAZOO AFFAIR,** lengthy controversy regarding land speculation in Georgia. In the 1790s four land-speculation companies bid for Georgia's western holdings, known as the Yazoo Tract. In return for their support, several Georgia legislators were given large grants of land in eastern Georgia. Many people protested the fraudulent sale, which culminated in the U.S. Supreme Court case *Fletcher* v. *Peck*. In 1810 the Supreme Court ruled that the contract in the Yazoo case was the "supreme law of the land" under the U.S. Constitution, and despite the bribery, the contract selling the land was forever binding.
See Also: Fletcher v. *Peck.*

■ **YELLOW JOURNALISM,** term applied to sensationalistic news reporting in the late 19th century. James Gordon Bennett, founder of the *New York Morning Herald*, introduced sensationalism in print in the 1830s. But in the late 19th century, the development of inexpensive pulp paper and expanding advertising revenues brought newspaper prices down and increased readership. Advertising rates were based on circulation, making it important to win readers with more and more elaborate "news." Joseph Pulitzer's paper, the *New York World*, published a Sunday edition complete with feature articles and comics. One of the comic strips contained a character known as the "Yellow Kid," from which originated the term "yellow journalism." In 1895, William Randolph Hearst, publisher of the *San Francisco Examiner*, bought the *New York Journal*. Hearst's paper competed for readers with Pulitzer's *World*, initiating a paper war in which the use of sensationalistic reporting escalated. The issue of U.S. intervention in Cuba's rebellion against Spanish rule in 1898 provided ample material for propagandistic news in both papers and helped provoke the Spanish-American War. Although not all newspapers adopted yellow journalism's strategy, by the turn of the century certain elements, such as bold headlines and Sunday features, were absorbed by the mainstream press. The roots of today's tabloids can be found in the sensational papers of the late 19th century.

—CATHERINE A. HAULMAN

See Also: Hearst, William Randolph; Newspapers; Pulitzer, Joseph.
BIBLIOGRAPHY: Baldasty, Gerald J., *The Commercialization of News in the Nineteenth Century* (Univ. of Wisconsin Press 1992); Milton, Joyce, *The Yellow Kids: Foreign Correspondents in the Heyday of Yellow Journalism* (Harper & Row 1989).

■ **YELLOWSTONE,** the nation's first national park, located principally in northwestern Wyoming and covering more than 2.2 million acres. The area was visited by numerous western explorers, but the Hayden expedition in 1871 prompted the public's interest, mainly because of William Henry Jackson's monumental photographs. On Mar. 1, 1872, Congress established the park as a public "pleasuring-ground." Most of Yellowstone lies on a plateau formed of once-molten lava. Containing geysers (the most famous being Old Faithful), hot springs, and lava formations as well as wolves, grizzly bears, elk, moose, and stunning scenery, the park has long been a celebrated tourist spot of the West. Yellowstone is the largest national park in the United States.

See Also: National Parks.

■ **YORKTOWN, SIEGE OF (1781),** decisive American victory in the Revolutionary War. Coordinating with a French fleet under Comte de Grasse, Gen. George Washington led about 9,000 American and French troops from New York to Virginia. There he joined a smaller force under the Marquis de Lafayette and trapped British Gen. Charles Cornwallis's army at Yorktown on Chesapeake Bay. The French fleet blocked an attempt to reinforce Cornwallis, who surrendered on October 19. Yorktown was the last major engagement of the war.

See Also: Lafayette, Marie Joseph Paul Yves Roch Gilbert du Motier, Marquis de; Revolution, American; Washington, George.

■ **YOSEMITE,** western part of Sierra Nevada mountains in California, site of the 760,000-acre Yosemite National Park. James Hutchings led the first tourists into the Yosemite Valley in 1855. The naturalist John Muir took Ralph Waldo Emerson to Yosemite in the early 1870s and then wrote eloquently about Yosemite's grandeur. Muir's efforts eventually led Congress to declare the area a national park in 1890. Yosemite contains cliffs and pinnacles, lakes, streams, and more than 1,000 varieties of flowering plants. It is the site of the highest falls in the United States.

See Also: Muir, John; National Parks.

■ **YOUNG, ANDREW (1932-),** civil rights and political leader. Born in New Orleans, Young enrolled in the Hartford Theological Seminary after graduating from Howard University. While serving as pastor of the United Church of Christ (1955-57), he was drawn to social activism. In 1961 Young joined Martin Luther King, Jr., in the Southern Christian Leadership Conference (SCLC). He was executive director of SCLC from 1964 to 1970. After two terms as a U.S. representative from Georgia (1973-77)—the first black to represent the state in Congress since Reconstruction—Young served as U.S. ambassador to the United Nations (1977-79). He then returned to Atlanta, where he was mayor (1982-90) and co-chair of the 1996 Atlanta Committee for the Olympic Games. In 1978, Young was awarded the Spingarn Medal and, in 1980, the Medal of Freedom for his life of public service.

See Also: African Americans; Civil Rights Movement; Southern Christian Leadership Conference (SCLC).

Gen. Charles Cornwallis offers his sword in surrender at Yorktown on Oct. 19, 1781. An allied force of more than 16,000 American and French troops began the siege of Yorktown in late September.

■ **YOUNG, BRIGHAM (1801-77),** pioneer leader and colonizer, territorial governor, and second president of the Mormon church. Born in Whitingham, Vermont, Young grew up in New York state, where he became a carpenter and cabinet maker. Reading the *Book of Mormon* in 1830 started him on a religious journey that carried him from Methodism to Mormonism.

Young joined the Mormon church in 1832 and immediately started preaching the Mormon gospel full time. The next year he moved to Kirtland, Ohio, which brought him into intimate contact with Joseph Smith, the founder of the Mormon faith, known as the "Prophet." Young's appointment to the original Quorum of the Twelve Apostles (1835), plus his evident administrative gifts, thrust him into a leadership role that became ever more central as the movement struggled to find a secure place on the religious landscape.

Repeated episodes of violence against the Mormons and propaganda campaigns that pictured them as mad, criminal, and heretical were preludes to the murder of Smith in 1844. His killing opened up a breach between those Mormons who saw themselves primarily as church members and those who viewed themselves both as church members and as members of a chosen race engaged in the literal construction of God's kingdom. Brigham Young became the leader of the latter party.

Renewed threats of violence caused him to lead the Mormons from Illinois to the valley of the Great Salt Lake. In the 30 years between their arrival and his death, Young presided over the creation of an intermountain kingdom that incorporated the whole of the theocratic and religious program—including the practice of plural marriage—that had been put forth in Joseph Smith's revelations. As governor, church president, and patriarch (with more than 30 wives), he directed the affairs of the territory; supervised the settlement of Mormon colonies throughout the area; built up the church; and was responsible for reconstitution of a patriarchal order within Mormonism. While forced to engage in unceasing struggle with the federal government, Young was primarily responsible for preserving Mormonism in a form that would allow it to become a distinctive religious tradition.

—JAN SHIPPS

Brigham Young succeeded as president of the Mormon Church upon Joseph Smith's assassination in 1844. Two years later, Young initiated the successful migration of thousands of Mormons to Utah.

See Also: *Frontier in American History; Mormons; Religion; Smith, Joseph.*

BIBLIOGRAPHY: Arrington, Leonard J., *Brigham Young: American Moses* (Knopf 1985).

■ **YOUNG, CY (1867-1955),** Hall of Fame baseball pitcher. A right-hander born in Gilmore, Ohio, he won a record 511 games during his career (1890-1911). Baseball's annual outstanding pitching award is named for him.

See Also: *Sports.*

■ **YOUNG, LESTER WILLIS (PREZ) (1909-59),** jazz musician. Born to a musical family in Woodville, Mississippi, Young became adept at several instruments but especially the tenor saxophone. He played with many groups but is most remembered for his work with Count Basie and with Billie Holiday. Young was a key figure in the shift to the "cool" style of jazz, emphasizing a lyrical, floating sound. His music strongly influenced all subsequent jazz saxophonists.

See Also: Jazz.

■ **YOUNG AMERICA,** phrase used to denote the enterprise and potential of mid-19th century America. The concept of Young America connected the ideas of capitalism, romantic individualism, and strident nationalism. As democratic revolutions spread across Europe in 1848, Americans saw them as evidence that America was destined to spread democracy, capitalism, and individualism throughout the world. Supporters of the Young America ideal enthusiastically embraced the Mexican War and American expansionism in the 1840s and 1850s. There was a Young America faction within the Democratic party in the 1850s, and some historians believe that it was an attempt to combat the friction caused by the slavery question, although the vision of Young America certainly included the spread of slavery. The Young America faction of the Democratic party sought to unite the sections of the country on a platform of free trade, open markets, southern expansion into Latin America, and the spread of American-style republicanism abroad. One Philadelphia newspaper espousing the Young American view described the United States as a country bound on the "East by sunrise, West by sunset, North by the Arctic Expedition, and South as far as we darn please." Young Americanism was thus an arrogant expression of American nationalism and presumed superiority. It was impossible for the Young America movement to separate its ideas from the escalating sectional tensions created by the slavery issue, however, and by the late 1850s, Young Americanism had disappeared.

BIBLIOGRAPHY: Riegel, Robert Edgar, *Young America, 1830-1840* (Univ. of Oklahoma Press 1949).

■ *YOUNGSTOWN SHEET & TUBE CO. V. SAWYER* **(1952),** U.S. Supreme Court case that rejected the president's claim to have constitutional authority to seize private steel companies in the name of national security. Fearing a threatened steel strike would harm U.S. military efforts in the Korean conflict, Pres. Harry S. Truman directed Sec. of Commerce Charles Sawyer to operate the nation's steel mills. While Truman informed Congress of his action, no legislative action to approve or disapprove of the step was taken. The steel industry sued, maintaining that the Taft-Hartley Act (1947) gave Congress, not the president, authority to become involved in labor disputes. The Court voted (6-3) that only Congress had the power to seize private property and, given the constitutional separation of powers, the president had overstepped his authority. Justice Robert Jackson, in a concurring decision, stated that the failure of Congress to authorize the takeover was the decisive factor.

See Also: Supreme Court; Taft-Hartley Act.

■ **YUMA INDIANS.** *See:* Desert Indians of the Southwest.

■ **ZAHARIAS, MILDRED DIDRICKSON (BABE) (1913-56),** one of the greatest female athletes of the 20th century. Born in Port Arthur, Texas, she won two gold medals in track and field in the 1932 Olympics. She also won 33 tournaments after she became a professional golfer in 1947. In 1938 she married wrestler George Zaharias.

See Also: Sports.

■ **ZENGER, JOHN PETER (1697-1746),** printer and American journalist. Born in Germany, Zenger immigrated to New York with his family as a young man (1710). Shortly after his arrival he became an apprentice to William Bradford, a New York printer. After a brief interlude in Maryland at the end of his indenture, Zenger returned to New York, set up, and, by 1733, was printing an antiestablishment newspaper. Most of the articles attacked the dismissal of the chief justice by political rivals in the assembly. Assembly members, angered by Zenger's continued criticism of their decision, ordered him arrested and imprisoned for his editorials. During the trial, Zenger's attorney argued that he had the right to print his opinion, and although the judge attempted to disallow the argument, the jury acquitted Zenger. This case is generally viewed as a landmark in American jurisprudence for protecting freedom of the press.

See Also: Newspapers.

■ **ZIMMERMANN NOTE,** a telegram sent on Jan. 16, 1917, by German Foreign Minister Arthur

Zimmermann to the German ambassador to the United States. It proposed that if the United States entered World War I against Germany, Mexico should aid Germany and receive territory ceded to the United States in 1848 in return. Intercepted and published by the British, it increased U.S. anti-German sentiment.

■ **ZWORYKIN, VLADIMIR (1889-1982),** physicist and electrical engineer, sometimes called the "father of television." Born in Mourom, Russia, Zworykin earned a degree from St. Petersburg Institute of Technology in 1912 and immigrated to the United States in 1919. While helping develop radio tubes and photoelectric cells for the Westinghouse Company (1920-29), he earned a Ph.D. from the University of Pittsburgh (1926).

Zworykin spent much of his time pursuing his interest in television, developing the ionoscope transmitting tube and the kinescope, or cathode-ray tube, receiver. He demonstrated this television system successfully in 1929 and became the director of the Radio Corporation of America (RCA) research laboratory (1929-54). At RCA, Zworykin invented the infrared image tube, which allowed humans to see in the dark, and an electron tube that made infrared and ultraviolet rays visible. In 1937, he started applying these tubes to microscopy and invented the electron microscope, which, by 1949, could magnify up to 200,000 times. During World War II, Zworykin directed research for the air force and went on to develop, among other electrical devices, color television.

See Also: *Invention; Science; Television and Radio.*

■ APPENDIX

The Declaration of Independence

When in the course of human events it becomes necessary for one people to dissolve the political bands which have connected them with another and to assume, among the powers of the earth, the separate and equal station to which the laws of nature and of nature's God entitle them, a decent respect to the opinions of mankind requires that they should declare the causes which impel them to the separation.

We hold these truths to be self-evident, that all men are created equal; that they are endowed by their Creator with certain unalienable rights; that among these are life, liberty, and the pursuit of happiness. That, to secure these rights, governments are instituted among men, deriving their just powers from the consent of the governed; that, whenever any form of government becomes destructive of these ends, it is the right of the people to alter or to abolish it, and to institute a new government, laying its foundation on such principles, and organizing its powers in such form, as to them shall seem most likely to effect their safety and happiness. Prudence, indeed, will dictate that governments long established should not be changed for light and transient causes; and, accordingly, all experience hath shown that mankind are more disposed to suffer, while evils are sufferable, than to right themselves by abolishing the forms to which they are accustomed. But when a long train of abuses and usurpations, pursuing invariably the same object, evinces a design to reduce them under absolute despotism, it is their right, it is their duty, to throw off such government and to provide new guards for their future security. Such has been the patient sufferance of these colonies, and such is now the necessity which constrains them to alter their former systems of government. The history of the present King of Great Britain is a history of repeated injuries and usurpations, all having, in direct object, the establishment of an absolute tyranny over these States. To prove this, let facts be submitted to a candid world:

He has refused his assent to laws the most wholesome and necessary for the public good.

He has forbidden his governors to pass laws of immediate and pressing importance, unless suspended in their operation till his assent should be obtained; and, when so suspended, he has utterly neglected to attend to them.

He has refused to pass other laws for the accommodation of large districts of people, unless those people would relinquish the right of representation in the legislature; a right inestimable to them and formidable to tyrants only.

He has called together legislative bodies at places unusual, uncomfortable, and distant from the depository of their public records, for the sole purpose of fatiguing them into compliance with his measures.

He has dissolved representative houses, repeatedly for opposing, with manly firmness, his invasions on the rights of the people.

He has refused, for a long time after such dissolutions, to cause others to be elected; whereby the legislative powers, incapable of annihilation, have returned to the people at large for their exercise; the state remaining, in the meantime, exposed to all the danger of invasion from without and convulsions within.

He has endeavored to prevent the population of these States; for that purpose, obstructing the laws for naturalization of foreigners, refusing to pass others to encourage their migration hither, and raising the conditions of new appropriations of lands.

He has obstructed the administration of justice by refusing his assent to laws for establishing judiciary powers.

He has made judges dependent on his will alone for the tenure of their offices and the amount and payment of their salaries.

He has erected a multitude of new offices and sent hither swarms of officers to harass our people and eat out their substance.

He has kept among us, in time of peace, standing armies, without the consent of our legislatures.

He has affected to render the military independent of, and superior to, the civil power.

He has combined with others to subject us to a jurisdiction foreign to our Constitution and unacknowledged by our laws, giving his assent to their acts of pretended legislation—

For quartering large bodies of armed troops among us;

For protecting them by a mock trial from punishment for any murders which they should commit on the inhabitants of these States;

For cutting off our trade with all parts of the world;

For imposing taxes on us without our consent;

For depriving us, in many cases, of the benefit of trial by jury;

For transporting us beyond seas to be tried for pretended offences;

For abolishing the free system of English laws in a neighboring province, establishing therein an arbitrary government, and enlarging its boundaries, so as to render it at once an example and fit instrument for introducing the same absolute rule into these colonies;

For taking away our charters, abolishing our most valuable laws, and altering, fundamentally, the powers of our governments;

For suspending our own legislatures and declaring themselves invested with power to legislate for us in all cases whatsoever.

He has abdicated government here by declaring us out of his protection and waging war against us.

He has plundered our seas, ravaged our coasts, burnt our towns, and destroyed the lives of our people.

He is, at this time, transporting large armies of foreign mercenaries to complete the works of death, desolation, and tyranny already begun with circumstances of cruelty and perfidy scarcely paralleled in the most barbarous ages, and totally unworthy the head of a civilized nation.

He has constrained our fellow citizens, taken captive on the high seas, to bear arms against their country, to become the executioners of their friends and brethren, or to fall themselves by their hands.

He has excited domestic insurrections amongst us and has endeavored to bring on the inhabitants of our frontiers, the merciless Indian savages, whose known rule of warfare is an undistinguished destruction of all ages, sexes, and conditions.

In every stage of these oppressions, we have petitioned for redress in the most humble terms; our repeated petitions have been answered only by repeated injury. A prince whose character is thus marked by every act which may define a tyrant is unfit to be the ruler of a free people.

Nor have we been wanting in attention to our British brethren. We have warned them, from time to time, of attempts made by their legislature to extend an unwarrantable jurisdiction over us. We have reminded them of the circumstances of our emigration and settlement here. We have appealed to their native justice and magnanimity, and we have conjured them, by the ties of our common kindred, to disavow these usurpations, which would inevitably interrupt our connections and correspondence. They, too, have been deaf to the voice of justice and consanguinity. We must, therefore, acquiesce in the necessity which denounces our separation, and hold them, as we hold the rest of mankind, enemies in war, in peace, friends.

We, therefore, the representatives of the United States of America, in general Congress assembled, appealing to the Supreme Judge of the world for the rectitude of our intentions, do, in the name and by the authority of the good people of these colonies, solemnly publish and declare, that these united colonies are, and of right ought to be, free and independent states: that they are absolved from all allegiance to the British Crown, and that all political connection between them and the state of Great Britain is, and ought to be, totally dissolved; and that, as free and independent states, they have full power to levy war, conclude peace, contract alliances, establish commerce, and to do all other acts and things which independent states may of right do. And, for the support of this declaration, with a firm reliance on the protection of Divine Providence, we mutually pledge to each other our lives, our fortunes, and our sacred honor.

The Constitution of the United States of America

We the people of the United States, in order to form a more perfect union, establish justice, insure domestic tranquillity, provide for the common defense, promote the general welfare, and secure the blessings of liberty to ourselves and our posterity, do ordain and establish this Constitution for the United States of America.

ARTICLE I

Section 1.

All legislative powers herein granted shall be vested in a Congress of the United States, which shall consist of a Senate and House of Representatives.

Section 2.

1. The House of Representatives shall be composed of members chosen every second year by the people of the several States, and the electors in each State shall have the qualifications requisite for electors of the most numerous branch of the State legislature.

2. No person shall be a representative who shall not have attained to the age of twenty-five years, and been seven years a citizen of the United States, and who shall not, when elected, be an inhabitant of that State in which he shall be chosen.

3. Representatives and direct taxes shall be apportioned among the several States which may be included within this Union, according to their respective numbers, which shall be determined by adding to the whole number of free persons, including those bound to service for a term of years, and excluding Indians not taxed, three fifths of all other persons. The actual enumeration shall be made within three years after the first meeting of the Congress of the United States, and within every subsequent term of ten years, in such manner as they shall by law direct. The number of representatives shall not exceed one for every thirty thousand, but each State shall have at least one representative; and until such enumeration shall be made, the State of New Hampshire shall be entitled to choose three, Massachusetts eight, Rhode Island and Providence Plantations one, Connecticut five, New York six, New Jersey four, Pennsylvania eight, Delaware one, Maryland six, Virginia ten, North Carolina five, South Carolina five, and Georgia three.

4. When vacancies happen in the representation from any State, the executive authority thereof shall issue writs of election to fill such vacancies.

5. The House of Representatives shall choose their speaker and other officers; and shall have the sole power of impeachment.

Section 3.

1. The Senate of the United States shall be composed of two senators from each State, chosen by the legislature thereof, for six years; and each senator shall have one vote.

2. Immediately after they shall be assembled in consequence of the first election, they shall be divided as equally as may be into three classes. The seats of the senators of the first class shall be vacated at the expiration of the second year, of the second class at the expiration of the fourth year, and of the third class at the expiration of the sixth year, so that one third may be chosen every second year; and if vacancies happen by resignation, or otherwise, during the recess of the legislature of any State, the executive thereof may make temporary appointments until the next meeting of the legislature, which shall then fill such vacancies.

3. No person shall be a senator who shall not have attained to the age of thirty years, and been nine years a citizen of the United States, and who shall not, when elected, be an inhabitant of that State for which he shall be chosen.

4. The Vice President of the United States shall be President of the Senate, but shall have no vote, unless they be equally divided.

5. The Senate shall choose their other officers, and also a president pro tempore, in the absence of the Vice President, or when he shall exercise the office of the President of the United States.

6. The Senate shall have the sole power to try all impeachments. When sitting for that purpose, they shall be on oath or affirmation. When the President of the United States is tried, the chief justice shall preside: and no person shall be convicted without the concurrence of two thirds of the members present.

7. Judgment in cases of impeachment shall not extend further than to removal from office, and disqualification to hold and enjoy any office of honor, trust or profit under the United States: but the party convicted shall nevertheless be liable and subject to indictment, trial, judgment and punishment, according to law.

Section 4.

1. The times, places, and manner of holding elections for senators and representatives, shall be prescribed in each State by the legislature thereof; but the Congress may at any time by law make or alter such regulations, except as to the places of choosing senators.

2. The Congress shall assemble at least once in every year, and such meeting shall be on the first Monday in December, unless they shall by law appoint a different day.

Section 5.

1. Each House shall be the judge of the elections, returns and qualifications of its own members, and a majority of each shall constitute a quorum to do business; but a smaller number may adjourn from day to day, and may be authorized to compel the attendance of absent members, in such manner, and under such penalties as each House may provide.

2. Each House may determine the rules of its proceedings, punish its members for disorderly behavior, and, with the concurrence of two thirds, expel a member.

3. Each House shall keep a journal of its proceedings, and from time to time publish the same, excepting such parts as may in their judgment require secrecy; and the yeas and nays of the members of either House on any question shall, at the desire of one fifth of those present, be entered on the journal.

4. Neither House, during the session of Congress, shall, without the consent of the other, adjourn for more than three days, nor to any other place than that in which the two Houses shall be sitting.

Section 6.

1. The senators and representatives shall receive a compensation for their services, to be ascertained by law, and paid out of the Treasury of the United States. They shall in all cases, except treason, felony, and breach of the peace, be privileged from arrest during their attendance at the session of their respective Houses, and in going to and returning from the same; and for any speech or debate in either House, they shall not be questioned in any other place.

2. No senator or representative shall, during the time for which he was elected, be appointed to any civil office under the authority of the United States, which shall have been created, or the emoluments whereof shall have been increased, during such time; and no person holding any office under the United States shall be a member of either House during his continuance in office.

Section 7.

1. All bills for raising revenue shall originate in the House of Representatives; but the Senate may propose or concur with amendments as on other bills.

2. Every bill which shall have passed the House of Representatives and the Senate, shall, before it become a law, be presented to the President of the United States; If he approves he shall sign it, but if not he shall return it, with his objections, to that House in which it shall have originated, who shall enter the objections at large on their journal, and proceed to reconsider it. If after such reconsideration two thirds of that House shall agree to pass the bill, it shall be sent, together with the objections, to the other House, by which it shall likewise be reconsidered, and if approved by two thirds of that House, it shall become a law. But in all such cases the votes of both Houses shall be determined by yeas and nays, and the names of the persons voting for and against the bill shall be entered on the journal of each House respectively. If any bill shall not be returned by the President within ten days (Sundays excepted) after it shall have been presented to him, the same shall be a law, in like manner as if he had signed it, unless the Congress by their adjournment prevent its return, in which case it shall not be a law.

3. Every order, resolution, or vote to which the concurrence of the Senate and the House of Representatives may be necessary (except on a question of adjournment) shall be presented to the President of the United States; and before the same shall take effect, shall be approved by him, or being disapproved by him, shall be repassed by two thirds of the Senate and House of Representatives, according to the rules and limitations prescribed in the case of a bill.

Section 8.

The Congress shall have the power

1. To lay and collect taxes, duties, imposts, and excises, to pay the debts and provide for the common defense and general welfare of the United States; but all duties, imposts, and excises shall be uniform throughout the United States;

2. To borrow money on the credit of the United States;

3. To regulate commerce with foreign nations, and among the several States, and with the Indian tribes;

4. To establish a uniform rule of naturalization, and uniform laws on the subject of bankruptcies throughout the United States;

5. To coin money, regulate the value thereof, and of foreign coin, and fix the standard of weights and measures;

6. To provide for the punishment of counterfeiting the securities and current coin of the United States;

7. To establish post offices and post roads;

8. To promote the progress of science and useful arts, by securing for limited times to authors and inventors the exclusive right to their respective writings and discoveries;

9. To constitute tribunals inferior to the Supreme Court;

10. To define and punish piracies and felonies committed on the high seas, and offenses against the law of nations;

11. To declare war, grant letters of marque and reprisal, and make rules concerning captures on land and water;

12. To raise and support armies, but no appropriation of money to that use shall be for a longer term than two years;

13. To provide and maintain a navy;

14. To make rules for the government and regulation of the land and naval forces;

15. To provide for calling forth the militia to execute the laws of the Union, suppress insurrections and repel invasions;

16. To provide for organizing, arming, and disciplining the militia, and for governing such part of them as may be employed in the service of the United States, reserving to the States respectively, the appointment of the officers, and the authority of training the militia according to the discipline prescribed by Congress;

17. To exercise exclusive legislation in all cases whatsoever, over such district (not exceeding ten miles square) as may, by cession of particular States, and the acceptance of Congress, become the seat of the government of the United States, and to exercise like authority over all places purchased by the consent of the legislature of the State in which the same shall be, for the erection of forts, magazines, arsenals, dockyards, and other needful buildings; and

18. To make all laws which shall be necessary and proper for carrying into execution the foregoing powers, and all other powers vested by this Constitution in the government of the United States, or any department or officer thereof.

Section 9.

1. The migration or importation of such persons as any of the States now existing shall think proper to admit, shall not be prohibited by the Congress prior to the year one thousand eight hundred and eight, but a tax or duty may be imposed on such importation, not exceeding ten dollars for each person.

2. The privilege of the writ of habeas corpus shall not be suspended, unless when in cases of rebellion or invasion the public safety may require it.

3. No bill of attainder or ex post facto law shall be passed.

4. No capitation, or other direct, tax shall be laid, unless in proportion to the census or enumeration hereinbefore directed to be taken.

5. No tax or duty shall be laid on articles exported from any State.

6. No preference shall be given by any regulation of commerce or revenue to the ports of one State over those of another: nor shall vessels bound to, or from, one State be obliged to enter, clear, or pay duties in another.

7. No money shall be drawn from the treasury, but in consequence of appropriations made by law; and a regular statement and account of the receipts and expenditures of all public money shall be published from time to time.

8. No title of nobility shall be granted by the United States: and no person holding any office of profit or trust under them, shall, without the consent of the Congress, accept of any present, emolument, office, or title, of any kind whatever, from any king, prince, or foreign State.

Section 10.

1. No State shall enter into any treaty, alliance, or confederation; grant letters of marque and reprisal; coin money; emit bills of credit; make any thing but gold and silver coin a tender in payment of debts; pass any bill of attainder, ex post facto law, or law impairing the obligation of contracts, or grant any title of nobility.

2. No State shall, without the consent of the Congress, lay any imposts or duties on imports or exports, except what may be absolutely necessary for executing its inspection laws: and the net produce of all duties and imposts laid by any State on imports or exports, shall be for the use of the treasury of the United States; and all such laws shall be subject to the revision and control of the Congress.

3. No State shall, without the consent of the Congress, lay any duty of tonnage, keep troops, or ships of war in time of peace, enter into any agreement or compact with another State, or with a foreign power, or engage in war, unless actually invaded, or in such imminent danger as will not admit of delay.

ARTICLE II

Section 1.

1. The executive power shall be vested in a President of the United States of America. He shall hold his office during the term of four years, and, together with the Vice President, chosen for the same term, be elected, as follows:

2. Each State shall appoint, in such manner as the legislature thereof may direct, a number of electors, equal to the whole number of senators and representatives to which the State may be entitled in the Congress: but no senator or representative, or person holding any office of trust or profit under the United States, shall be appointed an elector.

The electors shall meet in their respective States, and vote by ballot for two persons, of whom one at least shall not be an inhabitant of the same State with themselves. And they shall make a list of all the persons voted for, and of the number of votes for each; which list they shall sign and certify, and transmit sealed to the seat of the government of the United States, directed to the president of the Senate. The president of the Senate shall, in the presence of the Senate and House of Representatives, open all the certificates, and the votes shall then be counted. The person having the greatest number of votes shall be the President, if such number be a majority of the whole number of electors appointed; and if there be more than one who have such majority, and have an equal number of votes, then the House of Representatives shall immediately choose by ballot one of them for President; and if no person have a majority, then from the five highest on the list the said House shall in like manner choose the President. But in choosing the President, the votes shall be taken by States, the representation from each State having one vote; a quorum for this purpose shall consist of a member or members from two thirds of the States, and a majority of all the States shall be necessary to a choice. In every case after the choice of the President, the person having the greatest number of votes of the electors shall be the Vice President. But if there should remain two or more who have equal votes, the Senate shall chose from them by ballot the Vice President.

3. The Congress may determine the time of choosing the electors, and the day on which they shall give their votes; which day shall be the same throughout the United States.

4. No person except a natural born citizen, or a citizen of the United States, at the time of the adoption of this Constitution, shall be eligible to the office of President; neither shall any person be eligible to the office who shall not have attained to the age of thirty-five years, and been fourteen years a resident within the United States.

5. In case of the removal of the President from office, or of his death, resignation, or inability to discharge the powers and duties of the said office, the same shall devolve on the Vice President, and the Congress may by law provide for the case of removal, death, resignation or inability, both of the President and Vice President, declaring what officer shall then act as President, and such officer shall act accordingly until the disability be removed, or a President shall be elected.

6. The President shall, at stated times, receive for his services a compensation which shall neither be increased nor diminished during the period for which he shall have been elected, and he shall not receive within that period any other emolument from the United States, or any of them.

7. Before he enter on the execution of his office, he shall take the following oath or affirmation:—``I do solemnly swear (or affirm) that I will faithfully execute the office of President of the United States, and will to the best of my ability, preserve, protect and defend the Constitution of the United States.''

Section 2.

1. The President shall be commander in chief of the army and navy of the United States, and of the militia of the several States, when called into the actual service of the United States; he may require the opinion in writing, of the principal officer in each of the executive departments, upon any subject relating to the duties of their respective offices, and he shall have power to grant reprieves and pardons for offenses against the United States, except in cases of impeachment.

2. He shall have power, by and with the advice and consent of the Senate, to make treaties, provided two thirds of the senators present concur; and he shall nominate, and by and with the advice and consent of the Senate, shall appoint ambassadors, other public ministers and consuls,

judges of the Supreme Court, and all other officers of the United States, whose appointments are not herein otherwise provided for, and which shall be established by law; but the Congress may by law vest the appointment of such inferior officers, as they think proper, in the President alone, in the courts of laws, or in the heads of departments.

3. The President shall have power to fill up all vacancies that may happen during the recess of the Senate, by granting commissions which shall expire at the end of their next session.

Section 3.

He shall from time to time give to the Congress information of the state of the Union, and recommend to their consideration such measures as he shall judge necessary and expedient; he may, on extraordinary occasions, convene both Houses, or either of them, and in case of disagreement between them with respect to the time of adjournment, he may adjourn them to such time as he shall think proper; he shall receive ambassadors and other public ministers; he shall take care that the laws be faithfully executed, and shall commission all the officers of the United States.

Section 4.

The President, Vice President, and all civil officers of the United States, shall be removed from office on impeachment for, and conviction of, treason, bribery, or other high crimes and misdemeanors.

ARTICLE III

Section 1.

The judicial power of the United States shall be vested in one Supreme Court, and in such inferior courts as the Congress may from time to time ordain and establish. The judges, both of the Supreme and inferior courts, shall hold their offices during good behavior, and shall, at stated times, receive for their services, a compensation, which shall not be diminished during their continuance in office.

Section 2.

1. The judicial power shall extend to all cases, in law and equity, arising under this Constitution, the laws of the United States, and treaties made, or which shall be made, under their authority;—to all cases affecting ambassadors, other public ministers and consuls;—to all cases of admiralty and maritime jurisdiction;—to controversies to which the United States shall be a party;—to controversies between two or more States;—between a State and citizens of another State;—between citizens of different States;—between citizens of the same State claiming lands under grants of different States, and between a State, or the citizens thereof, and foreign States, citizens or subjects.

2. In all cases affecting ambassadors, other public ministers and consuls, and those in which a State shall be party, the

Supreme Court shall have original jurisdiction. In all the other cases before mentioned, the Supreme Court shall have appellate jurisdiction, both as to law and fact, with such exceptions, and under such regulations as the Congress shall make.

3. The trial of all crimes, except in cases of impeachment, shall be by jury; and such trial shall be held in the State where the said crimes shall have been committed; but when not committed within any State, the trial shall be at such place or places as the Congress may by law have directed.

Section 3.

1. Treason against the United States shall consist only in levying war against them, or in adhering to their enemies, giving them aid and comfort. No person shall be convicted of treason unless on the testimony of two witnesses to the same overt act, or on confession in open court.

2. The Congress shall have power to declare the punishment of treason, but no attainder of treason shall work corruption of blood, or forfeiture except during the life of the person attainted.

ARTICLE IV

Section 1.

Full faith and credit shall be given in each State to the public acts, records, and judicial proceedings of every other State. And the Congress may by general laws prescribe the manner in which such acts, records and proceedings shall be proved, and the effect thereof.

Section 2.

1. The citizens of each State shall be entitled to all privileges and immunities of citizens in the several States.

2. A person charged in any State with treason, felony, or other crime, who shall flee from justice, and be found in another State, shall on demand of the executive authority of the State from which he fled, be delivered up to be removed to the State having jurisdiction of the crime.

3. No person held to service or labor in one State under the laws thereof, escaping into another, shall, in consequence of any law or regulation therein, be discharged from such service or labor, but shall be delivered up on claim of the party to whom such service or labor may be due.

Section 3.

1. New States may be admitted by the Congress into this Union; but no new State shall be formed or erected within the jurisdiction of any other State; nor any State be formed by the junction of two or more States, or parts of States, without the consent of the legislatures of the States concerned as well as of the Congress.

2. The Congress shall have power to dispose of and make all needful rules and regulations respecting the territory or other property belonging to the United States; and nothing in this Constitution shall be so construed as to prejudice any claims of the United States, or of any particular State.

Section 4.

The United States shall guarantee to every State in this Union a republican form of government, and shall protect each of them against invasion; and on application of the legislature, or of the executive (when the legislature cannot be convened) against domestic violence.

ARTICLE V

The Congress, whenever two thirds of both Houses shall deem it necessary, shall propose amendments to this Constitution, or, on the application of the legislatures of two thirds of the several States, shall call a convention for proposing amendments, which in either case, shall be valid to all intents and purposes, as part of this Constitution, when ratified by the legislatures of three fourths of the several States, or by conventions in three fourths thereof, as the one or the other mode of ratification may be proposed by the Congress; Provided that no amendment which may be made prior to the year one thousand eight hundred and eight shall in any manner affect the first and fourth clauses in the ninth section of the first article; and that no State, without its consent, shall be deprived of its equal suffrage in the Senate.

ARTICLE VI

1. All debts contracted and engagements entered into, before the adoption of this Constitution, shall be as valid against the United States under this Constitution, as under the Confederation.

2. This Constitution, and the laws of the United States which shall be made in pursuance thereof; and all treaties made, or which shall be made, under the authority of the United States, shall be the supreme law of the land; and the judges in every State shall be bound thereby, any thing in the Constitution or laws of any State to the contrary notwithstanding.

3. The senators and representatives before mentioned, and the members of the several State legislatures, and all executive and judicial officers, both of the United States and of the several States, shall be bound by oath or affirmation to support this Constitution; but no religious test shall ever be required as a qualification to any office or public trust under the United States.

ARTICLE VII

The ratification of the conventions of nine States shall be sufficient for the establishment of this Constitution between the States so ratifying the same.

Done in Convention by the unanimous consent of the States present the seventeenth day of September in the year of our Lord one thousand seven hundred and eighty-seven, and of the independence of the United States of America the twelfth. In witness whereof we have hereunto subscribed our names.

* * * Articles in addition to, and amendment of, the Constitution of the United States of America, proposed by Congress, and ratified by the legislatures of the several States, pursuant to the fifth article of the original Constitution.

Amendment I [First ten amendments ratified December 15, 1791]

Congress shall make no law respecting an establishment of religion, or prohibiting the free exercise thereof; or abridging the freedom of speech, or of the press; or the right of the people peaceably to assemble, and to petition the government for a redress of grievances.

Amendment II

A well regulated militia, being necessary to the security of a free State, the right of the people to keep and bear arms, shall not be infringed.

Amendment III

No soldier shall, in time of peace be quartered in any house, without the consent of the owner, nor in time of war, but in a manner to be prescribed by law.

Amendment IV

The right of the people to be secure in their persons, houses, papers, and effects, against unreasonable searches and seizures, shall not be violated, and no warrants shall issue, but upon probable cause, supported by oath or affirmation, and particularly describing the place to be searched, and the persons or things to be seized.

Amendment V

No person shall be held to answer for a capital or otherwise infamous crime, unless on a presentment or indictment of a grand jury, except in cases arising in the land or naval forces, or in the militia, when in actual service in time of war or public danger; nor shall any person be subject for the same offense to be twice put in jeopardy of life or limb; nor shall be compelled in any criminal case to be a witness against himself, nor be deprived of life, liberty, or property, without due process of law; nor shall private property be taken for public use, without just compensation.

Amendment VI

In all criminal prosecutions, the accused shall enjoy the right to a speedy and public trial, by an impartial jury of the State and district wherein the crime shall have been committed, which district shall have been previously ascertained by law, and to be informed of the nature and cause of the accusation; to be confronted with the witnesses against him; to have compulsory process for obtaining wit-

nesses in his favor, and to have the assistance of counsel for his defense.

Amendment VII

In suits at common law, where the value in controversy shall exceed twenty dollars, the right of trial by jury shall be preserved, and no fact tried by a jury shall be otherwise re-examined in any court of the United States, than according to the rules of the common law.

Amendment VIII

Excessive bail shall not be required, nor excessive fines imposed, nor cruel and unusual punishments inflicted.

Amendment IX

The enumeration in the Constitution of certain rights shall not be construed to deny or disparage others retained by the people.

Amendment X

The powers not delegated to the United States by the Constitution, nor prohibited by it to the States, are reserved to the States respectively, or to the people.

Amendment XI [January 8, 1798]

The judicial power of the United States shall not be construed to extend to any suit in law or equity, commenced or prosecuted against one of the United States by citizens of another State, or by citizens or subjects of any foreign State.

Amendment XII [September 25, 1804]

The electors shall meet in their respective States, and vote by ballot for President and Vice President, one of whom, at least, shall not be an inhabitant of the same State with themselves; they shall name in their ballots the person voted for as President, and in distinct ballots, the person voted for as Vice President, and they shall make distinct lists of all persons voted for as President and of all persons voted for as Vice President, and of the number of votes for each, which lists they shall sign and certify, and transmit sealed to the seat of the government of the United States, directed to the President of the Senate;—The President of the Senate shall, in the presence of the Senate and House of Representatives, open all the certificates and the votes shall then be counted;—The person having the greatest number of votes for President, shall be the President, if such number be a majority of the whole number of electors appointed; and if no person have such majority, then from the persons having the highest numbers not exceeding three on the list of those voted for as President, the House of Representatives shall choose immediately, by ballot, the President. But in choosing the President, the votes shall be taken by States, the representation from each State having one vote; a quorum for this purpose shall consist of a member or members from two thirds of the States, and a majority of all the States shall be necessary to a choice. And if the

House of Representatives shall not choose a President whenever the right of choice shall devolve upon them, before the fourth day of March next following, then the Vice President shall act as President, as in the case of the death or other constitutional disability of the President. The person having the greatest number of votes as Vice President shall be the Vice President, if such number be a majority of the whole number of electors appointed, and if no person have a majority, then from the two highest numbers on the list, the Senate shall choose the Vice President;a quorum for the purpose shall consist of two thirds of the whole number of Senators, and a majority of the whole number shall be necessary to a choice. But no person constitutionally ineligible to the office of President shall be eligible to that of Vice President of the United States.

Amendment XIII [December 18, 1865]

Section 1.

Neither slavery nor involuntary servitude, except as a punishment for crime whereof the party shall have been duly convicted, shall exist within the United States, or any place subject to their jurisdiction.

Section 2.

Congress shall have power to enforce this article by appropriate legislation.

Amendment XIV [July 28, 1868]

Section 1.

All persons born or naturalized in the United States, and subject to the jurisdiction thereof, are citizens of the United States and of the State wherein they reside. No State shall make or enforce any law which shall abridge the privileges or immunities of citizens of the United States; nor shall any State deprive any person of life, liberty, or property, without due process of law; nor deny to any person within its jurisdiction the equal protection of the laws.

Section 2.

Representatives shall be apportioned among the several States according to their respective numbers, counting the whole number of persons in each State, excluding Indians not taxed. But when the right to vote at any election for the choice of electors for President and Vice President of the United States, representatives in Congress, the executive and judicial officers of a State, or the members of the legislature thereof, is denied to any of the male inhabitants of such State, being twenty-one years of age, and citizens of the United States, or in any way abridged, except for participating in rebellion, or other crime, the basis of representation therein shall be reduced in the proportion which the number of such male citizens shall bear to the whole number of male citizens twenty-one years of age in such State.

Section 3.

No person shall be a senator or representative in Congress, or elector of President and Vice President, or hold any office, civil or military, under the United States, or under any State, who having previously taken an oath, as a member of Congress, or as an officer of the United States, or as a member of any State legislature, or as an executive or judicial officer of any State, to support the Constitution of the United States, shall have engaged in insurrection or rebellion against the same, or given aid or comfort to the enemies thereof. But Congress may by a vote of two thirds of each House, remove such disability.

Section 4.

The validity of the public debt of the United States, authorized by law, including debts incurred for payment of pensions and bounties for services in suppressing insurrection or rebellion; shall not be questioned. But neither the United States nor any State shall assume or pay any debt or obligation incurred in aid of insurrection or rebellion against the United States, or any claim for the loss or emancipation of any slave; but all such debts, obligations, and claims shall be held illegal and void.

Section 5.

The Congress shall have the power to enforce, by appropriate legislation, the provisions of this artic

Amendment XV [March 30, 1870]

Section 1.

The right of citizens of the United States to vote shall not be denied or abridged by the United States or by any State on account of race, color, or previous condition of servitude.

Section 2.

The Congress shall have power to enforce this article by appropriate legislation.

Amendment XVI [February 25, 1913]

The Congress shall have power to lay and collect taxes on incomes, from whatever source derived, without apportionment among the several States, and without regard to any census or enumeration.

Amendment XVII [May 31, 1913]

The Senate of the United States shall be composed of two senators from each State, elected by the people thereof, for six years; and each senator shall have one vote. The electors in each State shall have the qualifications requisite for electors of the most numerous branch of the State legislature.

When vacancies happen in the representation of any State in the Senate, the executive authority of such State shall issue writs of election to fill such vacancies: Provided, That the legislature of any State may empower the executive thereof to make temporary appointments until the people fill the vacancies by election as the legislature may direct.

This amendment shall not be so construed as to affect the election or term of any senator chosen before it becomes valid as part of the Constitution.

Amendment XVIII [January 29, 1919]

After one year from the ratification of this article, the manufacture, sale, or transportation of intoxicating liquors within, the importation thereof into, or the exportation thereof from the United States and all territory subject to the jurisdiction thereof for beverage purposes is hereby prohibited.

The Congress and the several States shall have concurrent power to enforce this article by appropriate legislation.

This article shall be inoperative unless it shall have been ratified as an amendment to the Constitution by the legislatures of the several States, as provided in the Constitution, within seven years from the date of the submission hereof to the States by Congress.

Amendment XIX [August 26, 1920]

The right of citizens of the United States to vote shall not be denied or abridged by the United States or by any State on account of sex.

Congress shall have the power to enforce this article by appropriate legislation.

Amendment XX [January 23, 1933]

Section 1.

The terms of the President and Vice President shall end at noon on the 20th day of January and the terms of Senators and Representatives at noon on the 3d day of January, of the years in which such terms would have ended if this article had not been ratified; and the terms of their successors shall then begin.

Section 2.

The Congress shall assemble at least once in every year, and such meeting shall begin at noon on the 3d day of January, unless they shall by law appoint a different day.

Section 3.

If, at the time fixed for the beginning of the term of President, the President-elect shall have died, the Vice President-elect shall become President. If a President shall not have been chosen before the time fixed for the beginning of his term, or if the President-elect shall have failed to qualify, then the Vice President-elect shall act as President until a President shall have qualified; and the Congress may by law provide for the case wherein neither a President-elect nor a Vice President-elect shall have qualified, declaring who shall then act as President, or the manner in which one who is to act shall be selected, and such person shall act accordingly until a President or Vice President shall have qualified.

Section 4.

The Congress may by law provide for the case of the death of any of the persons from whom the House of Representatives may choose a President whenever the right of choice shall have devolved upon them, and for the case of the death of any of the persons from whom the Senate may choose a Vice President whenever the right of choice shall have devolved upon them.

Section 5.

Sections 1 and 2 shall take effect on the 15th day of October following the ratification of this article.

Section 6.

This article shall be inoperative unless it shall have been ratified as an amendment to the Constitution by the legislatures of three-fourths of the several States within seven years from the date of its submission.

Amendment XXI [December 5, 1933]

Section 1.

The Eighteenth Article of amendment to the Constitution of the United States is hereby repealed.

Section 2.

The transportation or importation into any State, Territory, or possession of the United States for delivery or use therein of intoxicating liquors in violation of the laws thereof, is hereby prohibited.

Section 3.

This article shall be inoperative unless it shall have been ratified as an amendment to the Constitution by conventions in the several States, as provided in the Constitution, within seven years from the date of the submission thereof to the States by the Congress.

Amendment XXII [March 1, 1951]

No person shall be elected to the office of the President more than twice, and no person who has held the office of President, or acted as President, for more than two years of a term to which some other person was elected President shall be elected to the office of the President more than once.

But this article shall not apply to any person holding the office of President when this article was proposed by the Congress, and shall not prevent any person who may be holding the office of President, or acting as President, during the term within which this article becomes operative from holding the office of President or acting as President during the remainder of such term.

This article shall be inoperative unless it shall have been ratified as an amendment to the Constitution by the legislatures of three-fourths of the several States within seven years from the date of its submission to the States by the Congress.

Amendment XXIII [March 29, 1961]

Section 1.

The District constituting the seat of Government of the United States shall appoint in such manner as the Congress may direct.

A number of electors of President and Vice President equal to the whole number of Senators and Representatives in Congress to which the District would be entitled if it were a State, but in no event more than the least populous State; they shall be in addition to those appointed by the States, but they shall be considered, for the purposes of the election of President and Vice President, to be electors appointed by a State; and they shall meet in the District and perform such duties as provided by the twelfth article of amendment.

Section 2.

The Congress shall have power to enforce this article by appropriate legislation.

Amendment XXIV [January 23, 1964]

Section 1.

The right of citizens of the United States to vote in any primary or other election for President or Vice President, for electors for President or Vice President, or for Senator or Representative in Congress, shall not be denied or abridged by the United States or any State by reason of failure to pay any poll tax or other tax.

Section 2.

The Congress shall have power to enforce this article by appropriate legislation.

Amendment XXV [February 10, 1967]

Section 1.

In case of the removal of the President from office or of his death or resignation, the Vice President shall become President.

Section 2.

Whenever there is a vacancy in the office of the Vice President, the President shall nominate a Vice President who shall take office upon confirmation by a majority of both Houses of Congress.

Section 3.

Whenever the President transmits to the President pro tempore of the Senate and the Speaker of the House of Representatives his written declaration that he is unable to discharge the powers and duties of his office, and until he transmits to them a written declaration to the contrary, such powers and duties shall be discharged by the Vice President as Acting President.

Section 4.

Whenever the Vice President and a majority of either the principal officers of the executive departments or of such other body as Congress may by law provide, transmit to the President pro tempore of the Senate and the Speaker of the House of Representatives their written declaration that the President is unable to discharge the powers and duties of his office, the Vice President shall immediately assume the powers and duties of the office as Acting President.

Thereafter, when the President transmits to the President pro tempore of the Senate and the Speaker of the House of Representatives his written declaration that no inability exists, he shall resume the powers and duties of his office unless the Vice President and a majority of either the principal officers of the executive departments or of such other body as Congress may by law provide, transmit within four days to the President pro tempore of the Senate and the Speaker of the House of Representatives their written declaration that the President is unable to discharge the powers and duties of his office. Thereupon Congress shall decide the issue, assembling within forty-eight hours for that purpose if not in session. If the Congress, within twenty-one days after receipt of the latter written declaration, or, if Congress is not in session, within twenty-one days after Congress is required to assemble, determines by two-thirds vote of both Houses that the President is unable to discharge the powers and duties of his office, the Vice President shall continue to discharge the same as Acting President; otherwise, the President shall resume the powers and duties of his office.

Amendment XXVI [June 30, 1971]

Section 1.

The right of citizens of the United States who are eighteen years of age or older to vote shall not be denied or abridged by the United States or by any State on account of age.

Section 2.

The Congress shall have power to enforce this article by appropriate legislation.

Presidents of the United States

Name	Party	Birth Date	Birthplace
George Washington	Federalist	Feb. 22, 1732	Pope's Creek, VA
John Adams	Federalist	Oct. 30, 1735	Braintree (now Quincy), MA
Thomas Jefferson	Democratic-Republican	Apr. 13, 1743	Shadwell, VA
James Madison	Democratic-Republican	Mar. 16, 1751	Port Conway, VA
James Monroe	Democratic-Republican	Apr. 28, 1758	Westmoreland County, VA
John Quincy Adams	Democratic-Republican	Jul. 11, 1767	Braintree (now Quincy), MA
Andrew Jackson	Democratic	Mar. 15, 1767	Waxhaw, SC
Martin Van Buren	Democratic	Dec. 5, 1782	Kinderhook, NY
William Henry Harrison	Whig	Feb. 9, 1773	Berkeley, VA
John Tyler	Whig	Mar. 29, 1790	Charles City County, VA
James Knox Polk	Democratic	Nov. 2, 1795	Mecklenburg County, NC
Zachary Taylor	Whig	Nov. 24, 1784	Montebello, VA
Millard Fillmore	Whig	Jan. 7, 1800	Summerhill, NY
Franklin Pierce	Democratic	Nov. 23, 1804	Hillsborough, NH
James Buchanan	Democratic	Apr. 23, 1791	Cove Gap, PA
Abraham Lincoln	Republican	Feb. 12, 1809	Hodgenville, KY
Andrew Johnson	Union	Dec. 29, 1808	Raleigh, NC
Ulysses Simpson Grant	Republican	Apr. 27, 1822	Point Pleasant, OH
Rutherford Birchard Hayes	Republican	Oct. 4, 1822	Delaware, OH
James Abram Garfield	Republican	Nov. 19, 1831	Orange, OH
Chester Alan Arthur	Republican	Oct. 5, 1829	Fairfield, VT
Stephen Grover Cleveland	Democratic	Mar. 18, 1837	Caldwell, NJ
Benjamin Harrison	Republican	Aug. 20, 1833	North Bend, OH
Stephen Grover Cleveland	Democratic	Mar. 18, 1837	Caldwell, NJ
William McKinley	Republican	Jan. 29, 1843	Niles, OH
Theodore Roosevelt	Republican	Oct. 27, 1858	New York, NY
William Howard Taft	Republican	Sept. 15, 1857	Cincinnati, OH
Thomas Woodrow Wilson	Democratic	Dec. 28, 1856	Staunton, VA
Warren Gamaliel Harding	Republican	Nov. 2, 1865	Corsica, OH
John Calvin Coolidge	Republican	Jul. 4, 1872	Plymouth, VT
Herbert Clark Hoover	Republican	Aug. 10, 1874	West Branch, IA
Franklin Delano Roosevelt	Democratic	Jan. 30, 1882	Hyde Park, NY
Harry S. Truman	Democratic	May 8, 1884	near Lamar, MO
Dwight David Eisenhower	Republican	Oct. 14, 1890	Denison, TX
John Fitzgerald Kennedy	Democratic	May 29, 1917	Brookline, MA
Lyndon Baines Johnson	Democratic	Aug. 27, 1908	Stonewall, TX
Richard Milhous Nixon	Republican	Jan. 9, 1913	Yorba Linda, CA
Gerald Rudolph Ford	Republican	Jul. 14, 1913	Omaha, NE
James Earl Carter, Jr.	Democratic	Oct. 1, 1924	Plains, GA
Ronald Wilson Reagan	Republican	Feb. 6, 1911	Tampico, IL
George Herbert Walker Bush	Republican	Jun. 12, 1924	Milton, MA
William Jefferson Clinton	Democratic	Aug. 19, 1946	Hope, AR

Death Date	Place of Death	Term of Office	Vice President
Dec. 14, 1799	Mt. Vernon, VA	1789–97	John Adams
Jul. 4, 1826	Quincy, MA	1797–1801	Thomas Jefferson
Jul. 4, 1826	Charlottesville, MA	1801–09	Aaron Burr (1801–05); George Clinton (1805–09)
Jun. 28, 1836	Montpelier, VA	1809–17	George Clinton (1809–12); Elbridge Gerry (1813–14)
Jul. 4, 1831	New York, NY	1817–25	Daniel D. Tompkins
Feb. 23, 1848	Washington, DC	1825–29	John C. Calhoun
Jun. 8, 1845	Nashville, TN	1829–37	John C. Calhoun (1825–32); Martin Van Buren (1833–37)
Jul. 24, 1862	Kinderhook, NY	1837–41	Richard M. Johnson
Apr. 4, 1841	Washington, DC	1841	John Tyler
Jan. 18, 1862	Richmond, VA	1841–45	
Jun. 15, 1849	Nashville, TN	1845–49	George M. Dallas
Jul. 9, 1850	Washington, DC	1849–50	Millard Fillmore
Mar. 8, 1874	Buffalo, NY	1850–53	
Oct. 8, 1869	Concord, NH	1853–57	William R. King
Jun. 1, 1868	Lancaster, PA	1857–61	John C. Breckinridge
Apr. 15, 1865	Washington, DC	1861–65	Hannibal Hamlin (1861–65); Andrew Johnson (1865)
Jul. 31, 1875	Carter Station, TN	1865–69	
Jul. 23, 1885	Mt. McGregor, near Saratoga, NY	1869–77	Schuyler Colfax (1869–73); Henry Wilson (1873–1875)
Jan. 17, 1893	Fremont, OH	1877–81	William A. Wheeler
Sept. 19, 1881	Elberon, NJ	1881	Chester A. Arthur
Nov. 18, 1886	New York, NY	1881–85	
Jun. 24, 1908	Princeton, NJ	1885–89	Thomas A. Hendricks
Mar. 13, 1901	Indianapolis, IN	1889–93	Levi P. Morton
Jun. 24, 1908	Princeton, NJ	1893–97	Adlai E. Stevenson
Sept. 14, 1901	Buffalo, NY	1897–1901	Garret A. Hobart (1897–99); Theodore Roosevelt (1901)
Jan. 6, 1919	Oyster Bay, NY	1901–09	Charles W. Fairbanks (1905–09)
Mar. 8, 1930	Washington, DC	1909–13	James S. Sherman
Feb. 3, 1924	Washington, DC	1913–21	Thomas R. Marshall
Aug. 2, 1923	San Francisco, CA	1921–23	Calvin Coolidge
Jan. 5, 1933	Northampton, MA	1923–29	Charles G. Dawes (1925–29)
Oct. 20, 1964	New York, NY	1929–33	Charles Curtis
Apr. 12, 1945	Warm Springs, GA	1933–45	John N. Garner (1933–41); Henry A. Wallace (1941–45); Harry S. Truman (1945)
Dec. 26, 1972	Kansas City, MO	1945–53	Alben W. Barkley (1949–53)
Mar. 28, 1969	Washington, DC	1953–61	Richard M. Nixon
Nov. 22, 1963	Dallas, TX	1961–63	Lyndon B. Johnson
Jan. 22, 1973	San Antonio, TX	1963–69	Hubert H. Humphrey (1965–69)
Apr. 22, 1994	New York, NY	1969–74	Spiro T. Agnew (1969–1973); Gerald R. Ford (1973–74)
		1974–77	Nelson A. Rockefeller
		1977–81	Walter F. Mondale
		1981–89	George Bush
		1989–93	J. Danforth Quayle
		1993–	Albert A. Gore, Jr.

Vice Presidents of the United States

Name	Party	Birth Date	Birthplace
John Adams	Federalist	Oct. 30, 1735	Braintree (now Quincy), MA
Thomas Jefferson	Democratic-Republican	Apr. 13, 1743	Shadwell, VA
Aaron Burr	Democratic-Republican	Feb. 6, 1756	Newark, NJ
George Clinton	Democratic- Republican	Jul. 26, 1739	Little Britain, NY
Elbridge Gerry	Democratic-Republican	Jul. 17, 1744	Marblehead, MA
Daniel D. Tompkins	Democratic-Republican	Jun. 21, 1774	Fox Meadows, NY
John Caldwell Calhoun	Democratic-Republican	Mar. 18, 1782	Abbeville District, SC
Martin Van Buren	Democratic	Dec. 5, 1782	Kinderhook, NY
Richard Mentor Johnson	Democratic	Oct. 17, 1780	Floyd's Station, KY
John Tyler	Whig	Mar. 29, 1790	Charles City County, VA
George Mifflin Dallas	Democratic	Jul. 10, 1792	Philadelphia, PA
Millard Fillmore	Whig	Jan. 7, 1800	Summerhill, NY
William Rufus DeVane King	Democratic	Apr. 7, 1786	Sampson County, NC
John Cabell Breckinridge	Democratic	Jan. 21, 1821	near Lexington, KY
Hannibal Hamlin	Republican	Aug. 27, 1809	Paris, ME
Andrew Johnson	Union	Dec. 29, 1808	Raleigh, NC
Schuyler Colfax	Republican	Mar. 23, 1823	New York, NY
Henry Wilson	Republican	Feb. 16, 1812	Farmington, NH
William Almon Wheeler	Republican	Jun. 30, 1819	Malone, NY
Chester Alan Arthur	Republican	Oct. 5, 1829	Fairfield, VT
Thomas Andrews Hendricks	Democratic	Sept. 7, 1819	Muskingum County, OH
Levi Parsons Morton	Republican	May 16, 1824	Shoreham, VT
Adlai Ewing Stevenson	Democratic	Oct. 23, 1835	Christian County, KY
Garret Augustus Hobart	Republican	Jun. 3, 1844	Long Branch, NJ
Theodore Roosevelt	Republican	Oct. 27, 1858	New York, NY
Charles Warren Fairbanks	Republican	May 11, 1852	Unionville Center, OH
James Schoolcraft Sherman	Republican	Oct. 24, 1855	Utica, NY
Thomas Riley Marshall	Democratic	Mar. 14, 1854	North Manchester, IN
Calvin Coolidge	Republican	Jul. 4, 1872	Plymouth, VT
Charles Gates Dawes	Republican	Aug. 27, 1865	Marietta, OH
Charles Curtis	Republican	Jan. 25, 1860	Topeka, KS
John Nance Garner	Democratic	Nov. 22, 1868	Red River County, TX
Henry Agard Wallace	Democratic	Oct. 7, 1888	Adair County, IA
Harry S. Truman	Democratic	May 8, 1884	Lamar, MO
Alben William Barkley	Democratic	Nov. 24, 1877	Lowes, KY
Richard Milhous Nixon	Republican	Jan. 9, 1913	Yorba Linda, CA
Lyndon Baines Johnson	Democratic	Aug. 27, 1908	Stonewall, TX
Hubert Horatio Humphrey	Democratic	May 27, 1911	Wallace, SD
Spiro Theodore Agnew	Republican	Nov. 9, 1918	Baltimore, MD
Gerald Rudolph Ford	Republican	Jul. 14, 1913	Omaha, NE
Nelson Aldrich Rockefeller	Republican	Jul. 8, 1908	Bar Harbor, ME
Walter Frederick Mondale	Democratic	Jan. 5, 1928	Ceylon, MN
George Herbert Walker Bush	Republican	Jun. 12, 1924	Milton, MA
James Danforth Quayle	Republican	Feb. 4, 1947	Indianapolis, IN
Albert Arnold Gore, Jr.	Democratic	Mar. 31, 1948	Washington, DC

Death Date	Place of Death	Term of Office	President
Jul. 4, 1826	Quincy, MA	1789–97	George Washington
Jul. 4, 1826	Charlottesville, VA	1797–1801	John Adams
Sept. 14, 1836	Staten Island, NY	1801–05	Thomas Jefferson
Apr. 20, 1812	Washington, DC	1805–12	Thomas Jefferson (1805–09); James Madison (1809–12)
Nov. 23, 1814	Washington, DC	1813–14	James Madison
Jun. 11, 1825	Tompkinsville, Staten Island, NY	1817–25	James Monroe
Mar. 31, 1850	Washington, DC	1825–32	John Quincy Adams (1825–29); Andrew Jackson (1829–32)
Jul. 24, 1862	Kinderhook, NY	1833–37	Andrew Jackson
Nov. 19, 1850	Frankfort, KY	1837–41	Martin Van Buren
Jan. 18, 1862	Richmond, VA	1841	William Henry Harrison
Dec. 31, 1864	Philadelphia, PA	1845–49	James K. Polk
Mar. 8, 1874	Buffalo, NY	1849–50	Zachary Taylor
Apr. 18, 1853	Cahaba, AL	1853	Franklin Pierce
May 17, 1875	Lexington, KY	1857–61	James Buchanan
Jul. 4, 1891	Bangor, ME	1861–65	Abraham Lincoln
Jul. 31, 1875	Carter's Station, TN	1865	Abraham Lincoln
Jan. 13, 1885	Mankato, MN	1869–73	Ulysses S. Grant
Nov. 22, 1875	Washington, DC	1873–75	Ulysses S. Grant
Jun. 4, 1887	Malone, NY	1877–81	Rutherford B. Hayes
Nov. 18, 1886	New York, NY	1881	James Garfield
Nov. 25, 1885	Indianapolis, IN	1885	Grover Cleveland
May 16, 1920	Rhinebeck, NY	1889–93	Benjamin Harrison
Jun. 14, 1914	Chicago, IL	1893–97	Grover Cleveland
Nov. 21, 1899	Paterson, NJ	1897–99	William McKinley
Jan. 6, 1919	Oyster Bay, NY	1901	William McKinley
Jun. 4, 1918	Indianapolis, IN	1905–09	Theodore Roosevelt
Oct. 30, 1912	Utica, NY	1909–12	William H. Taft
Jun. 1, 1925	Washington, DC	1913–21	Woodrow Wilson
Jan. 5, 1933	Northampton, MA	1921–23	Warren Harding
Apr. 23, 1951	Evanston, IL	1925–29	Calvin Coolidge
Feb. 8, 1936	Washington, DC	1929–33	Herbert Hoover
Nov. 7, 1967	Uvalde, TX	1933–41	Franklin D. Roosevelt
Nov. 18, 1965	Danbury, CT	1941–45	Franklin D. Roosevelt
Dec. 26, 1972	Kansas City, MO	1945	Franklin D. Roosevelt
Apr. 30, 1956	Lexington, VA	1949–53	Harry S. Truman
Apr. 22, 1994	New York, NY	1953–61	Dwight D. Eisenhower
Jan. 22, 1973	San Antonio, TX	1961–63	John F. Kennedy
Jan. 13, 1978	Waverly, MN	1965–69	Lyndon B. Johnson
Sept. 17, 1996	Berlin, MD	1969–73	Richard M. Nixon
		1973–74	Richard M. Nixon
Jan. 26, 1979	New York, NY	1974–77	Gerald R. Ford
		1977–81	James E. Carter, Jr.
		1981–89	Ronald W. Reagan
		1989–93	George Bush
		1993–	William J. Clinton

Chief Justices of the United States

Name	Chief Justice
Burger, Warren E.	1969–86
Chase, Salmon P.	1864–73
Ellsworth, Oliver	1796–1800
Fuller, Melville W.	1888–1910
Hughes, Charles Evans	*1930–41
Jay, John	1789–95
Marshall, John	1801–35
Rehnquist, William Hubbs	*1986–
Rutledge, John	*pro tem 1795
Stone, Harlan Fiske	*1941–46
Taft, William Howard	1921–30
Taney, Roger Brooke	1836–64
Vinson, Frederick M.	1946–53
Waite, Morrison R.	1874–88
Warren, Earl	1954–69
White, Edward D.	*1910–21

* also served as Associate Justice

Associate Justices of the Supreme Court

Name	Supreme Court Service	Name	Supreme Court Service
Baldwin, Henry	1830–44	Livingston, Henry Brockholst	1806–23)
Barbour, Philip Pendleton	1836–41	Lurton, Horace Harmon	1909–14
Black, Hugo Lafayette	1937–71	McKenna, Joseph	1898–1925
Blackmun, Harry Andrew	1970–94	McKinley, John	1837–52
Blair, John	1789–96	McLean, John	1829–61
Blatchford, Samuel Milford	1882–93	McReynolds, James Clark	1914–41
Bradley, Joseph P.	1870–92	Marshall, Thurgood	1967–91
Brandeis, Louis Dembitz	1916–39	Matthews, Stanley	1881–89
Brennan, William Joseph, Jr.	1957–90	Miller, Samuel Freeman	1862–90
Brewer, David Josiah	1889–1910	Minton, Sherman	1949–56
Breyer, Stephen Gerald	1994–	Moody, William Henry	1906–10
Brown, Henry Billings	1890–1906	Moore, Alfred	1799–1804
Burton, Harold Hitz	1945–58	Murphy, Frank	1940–49
Butler, Pierce	1922–39	Nelson, Samuel	1845–72
Byrnes, James Francis	1941–42	O'Connor, Sandra Day	1981–
Campbell, John Archibald	1853–61	Paterson, William	1793–1806
Cardozo, Benjamin Nathan	1932–38	Peckham, Rufus Wheeler, Jr.	1895–1909
Catron, John	1837–65	Pitney, Mahlon	1912–22
Chase, Samuel	1796–1811	Powell, Lewis Franklin, Jr.	1971–87
Clark, Tom Campbell	1949–67	Reed, Stanley Forman	1938–57
Clarke, John Hessin	1916–22	Rehnquist, William Hubbs	*1971–86
Clifford, Nathan	1858–81	Roberts, Owen Josephus	1930–45
Curtis, Benjamin Robbins	1851–57	Rutledge, John	*1789–91
Cushing, William	1789–1810	Rutledge, Wiley Blout, Jr.	1943–49
Daniel, Peter Vivian	1841–60	Sanford, Edward Terry	1923–30
Davis, David	1862–77	Scalia, Antonin	1986–
Day, William Rufus	1903–22	Shiras, George, Jr.	1892–1903
Douglas, William Orville	1939–75	Stevens, John Paul	1975–
Duvall, Gabriel	1811–35	Souter, David H.	1990–
Field, Stephen Johnson	1863–97	Stewart, Potter	1959–81
Fortas, Abe	1965–69	Stone, Harlan Fiske	*1925–41
Frankfurter, Felix	1939–62	Story, Joseph	1811–45
Ginsburg, Ruth Bader	1993–	Strong, William	1870–80
Goldberg, Arthur Joseph	1962–65	Sutherland, George	1922–38
Gray, Horace	1881–1902	Swayne, Noah Haynes	1862–81
Grier, Robert Cooper	1846–70	Thomas, Clarence	1991–
Harlan, John Marshall	1877–1911	Thompson, Smith	1823–43
Harlan, John Marshall	1955–71	Todd, Thomas	1807–26
Holmes, Oliver Wendell, Jr.	1902–32	Trimble, Robert	1826–28
Hughes, Charles Evans	*1910–16	Van Devanter, Willis	1910–37
Hunt, Ward	1873–82	Washington, Bushrod	1798–1829
Iredell, James	1790–99	Wayne, James Moore	1835–67
Jackson, Howell Edmunds	1893–95	White, Byron Raymond	1962–93
Jackson, Robert Houghwout	1941–54	White, Edward D.	*1894–1910
Johnson, Thomas	1791–93	Whittaker, Charles Evans	1957–62
Johnson, William	1804–34	Wilson, James	1789–98
Kennedy, Anthony McLeod	1988–	Woodbury, Levi	1846–51
Lamar, Joseph Rucker	1911–16	Woods, William Burnham	1880–87
Lamar, Lucius Quintus Cincinnatus	1888–93		

* also served as Chief Justice

States of the United States

Name	Date Admitted (rank)	Capital	Population, 1995 Est. (rank)	Area (rank)	Nickname
Alabama	Dec. 14, 1819 (22)	Montgomery	4,253,000 (22)	51,718 sq mi (30)	Heart of Dixie
Alaska	Jan. 3, 1959 (49)	Juneau	604,000 (48)	587,875 sq mi (1)	The Last Frontier
Arizona	Feb. 14, 1912 (48)	Phoenix	4,218,000 (23)	114,006 sq mi (6)	Grand Canyon State
Arkansas	Jun. 15, 1836 (25)	Little Rock	2,484,000 (33)	53,182 sq mi (28)	Land of Opportunity
California	Sept. 9, 1850 (31)	Sacramento	31,589,000 (1)	158,647 sq mi (3)	Golden State
Colorado	Aug. 1, 1876 (38)	Denver	3,747,000 (25)	104,100 sq mi (8)	Centennial State
Connecticut	Jan. 9, 1788 (5)	Hartford	3,275,000 (28)	5,026 sq mi (48)	Nutmeg State
Delaware	Dec. 7, 1787 (1)	Dover	717,000 (46)	2,026 sq mi (49)	Diamond State
Florida	Mar. 3, 1845 (27)	Tallahassee	14,166,000 (4)	58,680 sq mi (22)	Sunshine State
Georgia	Jan. 2, 1788 (4)	Atlanta	7,201,000 (10)	58,930 sq mi (21)	Peach State
Hawaii	Aug. 21, 1959 (50)	Honolulu	1,187,000 (40)	6,459 sq mi (47)	Aloha State
Idaho	July 3, 1890 (43)	Boise	1,163,000 (41)	83,574 sq mi (13)	Gem State
Illinois	Dec. 3, 1818 (21)	Springfield	11,830,000(6)	56,343 sq mi (24)	Prairie State
Indiana	Dec. 11, 1816 (19)	Indianapolis	5,803,000 (14)	36,185 sq mi (38)	Hoosier State
Iowa	Dec. 28, 1846 (29)	Des Moines	2,842,000 (30)	56,276 sq mi (25)	Hawkeye State
Kansas	Jan. 29, 1861 (34)	Topeka	2,565,000 (32)	82,282 sq mi (14)	Sunflower State
Kentucky	Jun. 1, 1792 (15)	Frankfort	3,860,000 (24)	40,411 sq mi (37)	Blue Grass State
Louisiana	Apr. 30, 1812 (18)	Baton Rouge	4,342,000 (21)	53,803 sq mi (27)	Pelican State
Maine	Mar. 15, 1820 (23)	Augusta	1,241,000 (39)	33,128 sq mi (39)	Pine Tree State
Maryland	Apr. 28, 1788 (7)	Annapolis	5,042,000 (19)	10,455 sq mi (42)	Old Line State
Massachusetts	Feb. 6, 1788 (6)	Boston	6,074,000 (13)	8,262 sq mi (45)	Bay State
Michigan	Jan. 26, 1837 (26)	Lansing	9,549,000 (8)	58,513 sq mi (23)	Wolverine State
Minnesota	May 11, 1858 (32)	St. Paul	4,610,000 (20)	84,397 sq mi (12)	Gopher State
Mississippi	Dec. 10, 1817 (20)	Jackson	2,697,000 (31)	47,695 sq mi (32)	Magnolia State
Missouri	Aug. 10, 1821 (24)	Jefferson City	5,324,000 (16)	69,709 sq mi (19)	Show Me State
Montana	Nov. 8, 1889 (41)	Helena	870,000 (44)	147,046 sq mi (4)	Treasure State
Nebraska	Mar. 1, 1867 (37)	Lincoln	1,637,000 (37)	77,359 sq mi (15)	Cornhusker State
Nevada	Oct. 31, 1864 (36)	Carson City	1,530,000 (38)	110,569 sq mi (7)	Silver State
New Hampshire	Jun. 21, 1788 (9)	Concord	1,148,000 (42)	9,283 sq mi (44)	Granite State
New Jersey	Dec. 18, 1787 (3)	Trenton	7,945,000 (9)	7,790 sq mi (46)	Garden State
New Mexico	Jan. 6, 1912 (47)	Santa Fe	1,685,000 (36)	121,598 sq mi (5)	Land of Enchantment
New York	Jul. 26, 1788 (11)	Albany	18,136,000 (3)	49,112 sq mi (31)	Empire State
North Carolina	Nov. 21, 1789 (12)	Raleigh	7,195,000 (11)	52,672 sq mi (29)	Tar Heel State
North Dakota	Nov. 2, 1889 (39)	Bismarck	641,000 (47)	70,704 sq mi (17)	Peace Garden State
Ohio	Mar. 1, 1803 (17)	Columbus	11,151,000 (7)	41,329 sq mi (35)	Buckeye State
Oklahoma	Nov. 16, 1907 (46)	Oklahoma City	3,278,000 (27)	69,903 sq mi (18)	Sooner State
Oregon	Feb. 14, 1859 (33)	Salem	3,141,000 (29)	87,052 sq mi (10)	Beaver State
Pennsylvania	Dec. 12, 1787 (2)	Harrisburg	12,072,000 (5)	45,759 sq mi (33)	Keystone State
Rhode Island	May 29, 1790 (13)	Providence	990,000 (43)	1,213 sq mi (50)	Ocean State
South Carolina	May 23, 1788 (8)	Columbia	3,673,000 (26)	31,117 sq mi (40)	Palmetto State

States of the United States

Name	Date Admitted (rank)	Capital	Population, 1995 Est. (rank)	Area (rank)	Nickname
South Dakota	Nov. 2, 1889 (40)	Pierre	729,000 (45)	77,121 sq mi (16)	Mount Rushmore State
Tennessee	Jun. 1, 1796 (16)	Nashville	5,256,000 (17)	42,145 sq mi (34)	Volunteer State
Texas	Dec. 29, 1845 (28)	Austin	18,724,000 (2)	266,873 sq mi (2)	Lone Star State
Utah	Jan. 4, 1896 (45)	Salt Lake City	1,951,000 (34)	84,904 sq mi (11)	Beehive State
Vermont	Mar. 4, 1791 (14)	Montpelier	585,000 (49)	9,615 sq mi (43)	Green Mountain State
Virginia	Jun. 25, 1788 (10)	Richmond	6,618,000 (12)	40,598 sq mi (36)	Old Dominion
Washington	Nov. 11, 1889 (42)	Olympia	5,431,000 (15)	68,126 sq mi (20)	Evergreen State
West Virginia	Jun. 20, 1863 (35)	Charleston	1,828,000 (35)	24,232 sq mi (41)	Mountain State
Wisconsin	May 29, 1848 (30)	Madison	5,123,000 (18)	54,314 sq mi (26)	Badger State
Wyoming	Jul. 10, 1890 (44)	Cheyenne	480,000 (50)	97,819 sq mi (9)	Equality State

Opening of the New World: To 1699

	World	Western Hemisphere	
	World Events	**Politics and War**	**Migration, Exploration, and Settlement**
to 1399	**10,000 B.C.** Near Eastern peoples harvesting grain with sickles, flint blades, and bone handles **c.3000 B.C.** Stonehenge built in England **c.1193 B.C.** Trojan War **431-404 B.C.** Peloponnesian War **A.D. 100** New Testament is composed **1066** Battle of Hastings (Norman conquest of England) **1096** First Crusade **1215** Magna Carta is sealed by King John of England		**25,000 B.C.** Date of the earliest human fossil evidence in the Americas **c.5000 B.C.** Beginning of Athapaskan migration **c.3000 B.C.** Beginning of Inupiat and Aleut migrations **1000 B.C.** Leif Eriksson reaches Newfoundland **A.D. 1150** Foundation of Hopi village, Oraibi (oldest town in the United States still occupied) **1300** Athapaskans arrive in the Southwest **1325** Aztec city Tenochititlán founded
1400 to 1499	**1431** Joan of Arc is burned at the stake in Rouen, France **1479** Spain is created when Aragon and Castile unite under Ferdinand the Catholic and Isabella	**1438** Pachacutec establishes Inca rule in Peru **1451** Founding of the Iroquois Confederacy	**1492** Christopher Columbus lands in the Caribbean **1494** Treaty of Tordesillas divides islands and mainland of the New World between Spain and Portugal **1497** John Cabot explores east coast of North America **1499** Amerigo Vespucci explores South America's northern and eastern coasts
1500 to 1549	**1503** Casa Contratacción (colonial office) is established in Madrid to handle American Affairs **1507** Niccolo Machiavelli publishes *The Prince* **1517** Martin Luther protests the sale of indulgences, beginning the Reformation	**1519** Hernán Cortés imprisons the Aztec emperor, Montezuma, who later dies in battle	**1513** Juan Ponce de León lands in Florida **1516** Smallpox introduced to the Americas **1519-22** Ferdinand Magellan circumnavigates the world **1519** Hernán Cortés arrives in Mexico **1535** Jacques Cartier begins exploring the St. Lawrence **1539-40** Expeditions of Hernán de Soto and Francisco Vásquez de Coronado
1550 to 1599	**1577-80** Sir Francis Drake circumnavigates the globe **1594** William Shakespeare completes *Romeo and Juliet*	**1565** French Huguenot colony of Ft. Caroline is destroyed by Spain's Pedro Menéndez de Avilés **1586** Sir Francis Drake destroys Spanish settlements in Florida and the West Indies	**1564** French Huguenot colony of Ft. Caroline established near the mouth of the St. John's River in Florida **1565** The Spanish found St. Augustine **1584-87** Sir Walter Raleigh establishes "lost" colony on Roanoke Island **1598** Juan de Oñate explores New Mexico
1600 to 1649	**1603** Sir Walter Raleigh is imprisoned for conspiring to dethrone James I of England **1616** Miguel de Cervantes completes part II of *Don Quixote* **1648** Oliver Cromwell demands the end of allegiance to the king of England	**1621** Plymouth Colony concludes treaty with Massasoit, Wampanoag chief **1637** Pequot War **1643** Massachusetts Bay, Plymouth, Connecticut, and New Haven colonies form the New England Confederation **1644** Opechancanough and the Pamunkeys revolt in Virginia	**1607** Settlement of Jamestown, Virginia **1608** Quebec founded. **1609** Henry Hudson discovers the Hudson River; Spanish found Santa Fé (first Spanish settlement in New Mexico) **1619** First Africans are sold as slaves in Virginia **1620** Pilgrims settle Plymouth **1625** Puritans settle Massachusetts Bay
1650 to 1699	**1660** Parliament invites Charles II to return to England **1665** Isaac Newton experiments on gravitation **1695** John Locke publishes *The Reasonableness of Christianity*	**1650-96** Parliament enacts the Navigation Acts **1669** South Carolina founded **1675** King Philip's War **1676** Bacon's Rebellion **1680** Pueblo Revolt **1689** Leisler's Rebellion	**1664** English conquer New Amsterdam **1665** New Jersey colony is founded **1670s** British and French begin the fur trade in western Canada **1681** Settlement of Philadelphia **1681-82** Exploration of the Mississippi by Sieur de La Salle

Agriculture, Science, and Technology	Society and Culture	Religion
c.9000 B.C. Extinction of big-game animals **c.7000 B.C.** Earliest cultivation of plants in Mexican highlands **A.D. 650** Earliest evidence of bow and arrow, flint hoes, and Northern Flint corn in the Northeast **1000** Cultivation of tobacco throughout North America **1276** Beginning of brutal drought in the Southwest	**10,000 B.C.** Clovis Culture/Technology **8000 B.C.** Folsom Culture/Technology **2500 B.C.** Date of the Serpent Mound located in the Ohio Valley **A.D. c.500** Height of Mayan Culture (in Mexico) **1050-1250** Peak of Cahokia Culture (in Illinois) **c. 1200** High point of Mississippian and Anasazi cultures	
1496 Spaniards bring sugarcane, cattle, and cotton to Santo Domingo		
	1542 Alvar Núñez Cabeza de Vaca publishes *Relación*	
1567 Typhoid kills estimated 2 million in South America	**1552** Bartolomé Las Casas publishes *Destruction of the Indies* **1582** Richard Hakluyt publishes *Divers Voyages*, his book about American discoveries	**1565** Spanish missions introduce Catholicism to Florida **1598** Spanish missions are established in New Mexico
1612 Introduction of tobacco cultivation in Virginia	**1608** John Smith publishes *A True Relation of Occurrences in Virginia* **1630-47** William Bradford writes *History of Plimouth Plantation*	**1609** Church of England is established by law in Virginia **1625** Jesuit missionaries arrive in New France **1628** Dutch Reformed Church organized in New Amsterdam
1696 Introduction of rice cultivation in South Carolina	**1677** Increase Mather publishes *The Troubles That Have Happened in New England* **1682** Mary Rowlandson publishes *Sovereignty and Goodness of God* **1692** Salem witch trials	**1654** First group of Jews arrive in New Amsterdam from Curaçao **1656** First Quakers arrive in Boston **1661** Algonquian New Testament becomes the first Bible printed in North America **1683** Earliest Mennonites settle in Pennsylvania

The Colonial Experience: 1700–1799

	World	North America	
	World Events	**Politics and War**	**Exploration and Expansion**
1700 to 1724	**1701-1714** War of Spanish Succession **1713** Quadruple Alliance formed among France, England, Holland, and the Empire **1721** J.S. Bach composes *The Brandenburg Concertos*	**1702** St. Augustine burned by South Carolinians **1705** Virginia Slave Code is established **1713** France cedes Acadia to Britain	**1720-22** Spain occupies Texas
1725 to 1749	**1730** John and Charles Wesley found their Methodist sect at Oxford University **1740** Frederick II (the Great) becomes king of Prussia **1745** British take Louisburg, Canada, from France	**1730s** French slaughter the Natchez and defeat the Fox Indians **1733** Molasses Act **1739** Stono Rebellion; War of Jenkins's Ear **1740** Naturalization Act	**1733** Settlement of Georgia **1741** Vitus Bering explores Alaska
1750 to 1774	**1754** Jean-Jacques Rousseau publishes *Discourse on the Origin of Inequality* **1756** Beginning of the Seven Years War **1768** England appoints a secretary of state for colonies **1773** Edmund Burke publishes *On American Taxation*	**1754-63** French and Indian War **1763** Pontiac's Rebellion; Paxton Boys Massacre **1764** Sugar Act **1765** Stamp Act **1767** Townshend Acts **1770** Boston Massacre **1773** Tea Act (leads to Boston Tea Party) **1772** Gaspee Incident **1774** First Continental Congress meets	**1763** Proclamation of 1763 designates "Indian Country" **1767-68** Daniel Boone explores Kentucky **1768** Treaty of Fort Stanwix **1769** Beginning of Spanish settlement in California
1775 to 1799	**1776** F.M. von Klinger's drama "Sturm und Drang" launches the "storm and stress" movement in German literature; Adam Smith publishes "An Inquiry into the Nature and Causes of the Wealth of Nations" **1784** Russians settle the Aleutian Islands in the North Pacific **1780-81** Serfdom is abolished in Bohemia, Hungary, and Austria **1789** Storming of Paris Bastille (beginning of French revolution) **1791** Black slave revolt in Santo Domingo **1793** Louis XVI of France is executed; Reign of Terror begins	**1775** Battles of Lexington and Concord; George Washington named commander-in-chief of the Continental Army; Battle of Bunker Hill **1776** Declaration of Independence; Washington occupies Boston; Battle of Long Island; Battle of Trenton; slavery abolished in Vermont **1777** Battle of Saratoga (secures alliance with France) **1777-78** Continental Army spends the winter in Valley Forge **1778** British capture Savannah and Charleston **1779** Spain enters the war **1781** Ratification of the Articles of Confederation; General Cornwallis surrenders at Yorktown **1783** Treaty of Paris; Britain recognizes U.S. independence **1785** Land Ordinance of 1785 **1787** Shays's Rebellion in Massachusetts; Constitutional Convention **1789** Washington inaugurated as president; Annapolis Convention; Bill of Rights **1791** Bank of the United States is chartered **1794** Whiskey Rebellion **1795** Ratification of Jay's Treaty **1798** XYZ Affair; Alien and Sedition Acts are passed	**1775** Daniel Boone is sent to Cumberland Gap by the Transylvania Co. to begin development of Kentucky's bluegrass region **1776** San Francisco is founded **1780s** New England ships enter the sea otter trade in the Pacific NW **1781** Los Angeles is founded **1787** Northwest Ordinance **1790** First American ship reaches Hawaii

Society and Culture	Religion	Agriculture, Science, and Technology
1710 Cotton Mather publishes *Essays to Do Good*	**1706** First presbytery organized in Philadelphia **1716** Spanish build missions in Texas **1723** German Baptists organize	**1700s** Plains Indians begin using horses **1721** First smallpox inoculations are administered by Zabdiel Boylston
1732 Benjamin Franklin begins the publication of *Poor Richard's Almanac*	**1735** Moravians arrive in Georgia **1738** George Whitefield begins preaching in the colonies	**1739-44** Eliza Lucas (Pinckney) of South Carolina succeeds in producing indigo profitably with slave labor
1752 Jonathan Edwards publishes *Misrepresentations Corrected and Truth Vindicated* **1774** Thomas Jefferson publishes *View of the Rights of British America*	**1760s** Height of the Great Awakening in the South **1766** Methodism begins in America **1773** First black Baptist church in Georgia founded **1774** First Shakers arrive in colonies	**1752** Benjamin Franklin performs his kite experiment and discovers the nature of lightning **1759** John Winthrop publishes *Two Lectures on Comets* **1769** David Rittenhouse observes the transit of Venus across the sun
1776 Thomas Paine publishes *Common Sense* **1782** J. Hector St. John Crevecoeur publishes *Letters from an American Farmer* **1784** Thomas Jefferson publishes *Notes on Virginia* **1791** Founding of Philip Freneau's *National Gazette* **1793** Gilbert Stuart paints *Mrs. Richard Yates*; Noah Webster establishes *The American Minerva,* pro-Federalist newspaper	**1780** First Universalist church founded **1790s** Beginning of Second Great Awakening **1792** Russian Orthodox Church begins missionary activity in Alaska **1794** Deism becomes popular after Thomas Paine's *Age of Reason*	**1784** Benjamin Franklin invents the first bifocal eyeglasses **1787** The first American steamboat is launched on the Delaware River by John Fitch **1790** Samuel Slater's first mill opens in Rhode Island **1793** Eli Whitney invents the cotton gin **1799** Nathaniel Bowditch publishes the *Practical Navigator*

Expansion and War: 1800–1899

World	United States	
World Events	**Politics and War**	**Exploration and Expansion**
1800 to 1824 **1801** Hegel and Schelling publish the *Critical Journal of Philosophy* **1806** End of the Holy Roman Empire **1815** Decatur's Algerian Expedition **1817** Rush-Bagot Agreement with Great Britain **1821** Mexico achieves independence from Spain **1823** Mexico becomes a republic	**1800** Thomas Jefferson elected President **1803** Battle of Sitka (Alaska) between Russians and Tlingits **1808** Congress bans further importation of slaves **1809** James Madison elected president **1811** Battle of Tippecanoe **1812** War of 1812 **1815** Battle of New Orleans **1817-25** Pres. James Monroe's "Era of Good Feelings" **1818** First Seminole War **1822** Denmark Vesey's slave revolt	**1803** Louisiana Purchase **1804** Beginning of Louis and Clark Expedition **1806** Zebulon Pike explores the Great Plains to the Rocky Mountains **1820** Missouri Compromise **1823** Monroe Doctrine **1824** Hudson's Bay Co. establishes Ft. Vancouver in Oregon Country
1825 to 1849 **1825** Russian Decembrist Revolt is crushed **1835** Texas Revolt against Mexico **1845** Beginning of the Irish Potato Famine spurs wave of immigration to the United States	**1831** Nat Turner's slave uprising **1836** Battles of Alamo and San Jacinto **1841** Amistad Case **1846** Beginning of Mexican War; Wilmot Proviso **1848** Women's Rights Convention at Seneca Falls; Treaty of Guadalupe Hidalgo ends Mexican War	**1830** Indian Removal Act **1843-44** John C. Frémont maps trails to Oregon and California **1845** Texas annexed to the United States as a slave state **1846** Oregon Treaty **1849** California Gold Rush
1850 to 1874 **1850** Britain agrees to recognize the neutrality of the Isthmus canal project (Clayton-Bulwer Treaty) **1853** Commodore Matthew Perry opens Japan to U.S. trade **1853-56** Crimean War begins **1855** William Walker leads filibustering expedition to Nicaragua **1859** Karl Marx publishes *Critique of Political Economy* **1868** Burlingame Treaty encourages Chinese emigration to the U.S. West **1871** Bismarck unites Germany	**1854** Gadsden Purchase **1856** John Brown's Raid; Caning of Sen. Charles Sumner **1857** Dred Scott Case **1858** Lincoln-Douglas debates **1860** Lincoln elected president **1861** Civil War begins; First Battle of Bull Run **1862** Battles of Monitor and Merrimack, Shiloh, Antietam, and Fredericksburg **1863** Emancipation Proclamation; Battles of Chancellorsville, Gettysburg, and Vicksburg; New York City Draft Riots **1864** Atlanta falls; Sand Creek Massacre **1865** Lee surrenders at Appomattox; Lincoln assassinated **1865-66** Freedmen's Bureau established; Black Codes enacted in South **1865-67** Great Sioux War **1867** Reconstruction Acts passed despite Johnson's veto **1868** House of Representatives impeaches Johnson; Senate acquits him by one vote **1871-86** Apache Wars in New Mexico	**1850** Compromise of 1850; California admitted as a free state **1853** Organization of Washington Territory **1854** Kansas-Nebraska Act **1856-58** Bleeding Kansas **1860** Pony Express established **1862** Pacific Railway Act; Homestead Act **1863** Montana gold rush **1864** Montana Territory formed from part of the Idaho Territory **1865-69** 4 million cattle transported north on the "Long Drive" **1867** U.S. purchases Alaska from Russia; Oklahoma Reservation established for the Five Civilized Tribes; Black Hills Reservation established for the Sioux
1875 to 1900 **1880** Chinese treaty enables the United States. to "regulate, limit or suspend" the entry of Chinese laborers **1889** First pan-American conference (creation of the Pan-American Union) **1898** *Maine* explodes in Havana harbor, triggering Spanish-American War	**1876** Battle of Little Bighorn; Rutherford B. Hayes wins disputed presidential election **1881** President Garfield assassinated **1882** Chinese Exclusion Act **1884** Ku Klux Klan cases **1890** Wounded Knee Massacre **1896** *Plessy v. Ferguson* upholds "separate but equal"; William Jennings Bryan's "Cross of Gold" speech **1898** Spanish-American War	**1879** Major John W. Powell publishes *Report on the Lands of the Arid Region* **1887** Dawes Severalty (Allotment) Act **1893** Overthrow of Hawaii's Queen Liliuokalani **1898** United States acquires overseas territories from Spain; annexes Hawaii

Society, Culture, and Religion	Labor, Industry, and Economy	Science and Technology
1805 Rappists (German pietists) found New Harmony, Ind.; Shawnee Indian, Tenskawatawa, "The Prophet," begins preaching Indian revitalization **1814** Francis Scott Key writes "The Star Spangled Banner" during the British bombardment of Ft. McHenry **1816** African Methodist Episcopal Church formed in Philadelphia **1817** American Colonization Society founded **1819** Unitarian Church founded **1820s** Growth of Shaker colonies	**1813** Boston Manufacturing Co. introduces the "Waltham System" of converting cotton into cloth by power **1819** Panic of 1819	**1805** Robert Fulton builds the first marine torpedo **1810** First steamboat on the Ohio River
1830s Second Great Awakening **1830** Joseph Smith founds the Mormon Church **1831** William Lloyd Garrison begins the *Liberator* **1837** Sarah Grimké publishes *Letters on the Equality of the Sexes and the Condition of Women*	**1825** Baltimore and Ohio railroad begins operation; Erie Canal opens **1837** Financial panic begins 7-year recession **1842** *Commonwealth* v. *Hunt* authorizes union organization	**1839** John Deere begins manufacturing steel plows **1844** First successful telegraph transmission **1846** Elias Howe invents the sewing machine
1851 Publication of Harriet Beecher Stowe's *Uncle Tom's Cabin* **1854** Henry David Thoreau publishes *Walden* **1855-92** Walt Whitman publishes various editions of *Leaves of Grass* **1855** Henry Wadsworth Longfellow publishes *Hiawatha* **1861** Mathew Brady begins his photographic record of the Civil War **1862** Julia Ward Howe composes the "Battle Hymn of the Republic" **1863** Stephen Foster composes "Beautiful Dreamer," Samuel Clemens adopts "Mark Twain" as his penname **1865** Last issue of Garrison's *Liberator* is distributed, Whitman publishes *Drum Taps* (collection of Civil War poetry) **1868** Louisa May Alcott's *Little Women* becomes a best seller **1871** Chicago fire **1874** Thomas Nast's cartoon in *Harper's Weekly* establishes the elephant as a Republican Party symbol	**1857** Panic of 1857 **1863** National Bank Act establishes national banking system **1867** Foundation of the Patrons of Husbandry (Granger Movement) **1868** Formation of the Carnegie Steel Co. **1869** Knights of Labor founded **1870** John D. Rockefeller forms Standard Oil Co. **1873** Congress suspends the coining of silver	**1852** Elisha Otis invents the first passenger elevator **1861** George Washington Carver experiments with crop rotation **1864** George Pullman invents the sleeping car for trains **1868-72** George Westinghouse invents the air brake **1874** Invention of barbed wire
1879 Carlisle Indian School founded **1881** Tuskegee Institute founded **1888** Wovoka, Paiute Indian, begins the Ghost Dance movement **1889** Jane Addams founds Hull House **1890** National American Woman Suffrage Assoc. founded	**1886** American Federation of Labor founded; Haymarket bombing **1887** Interstate Commerce Act **1890** Sherman Antitrust Act **1893** Panic of 1893 **1894** Pullman Strike; Coxey's Army marches to Washington	**1876** Alexander Graham Bell invents the telephone **1879** Thomas Edison invents the light bulb **1883** The Brooklyn Bridge, designed by John Roebling, is completed **1886** Ottmar Mergenthaler invents the linotype machine

America on the World Stage: 1900–1949

World	United States
World Events and Foreign Wars	**Politics**

1900 to 1909

World	United States
1903 U.S. secures canal rights in Panama **1905** Portsmouth Conference (Roosevelt mediates peace treaty between Japan and Russia) **1907** "Gentlemen's Agreement" with Japan **1908** Root-Takahira Agreement	**1900** Robert LaFollette becomes governor of Wisconsin **1901** President McKinley is assassinated; Theodore Roosevelt becomes president **1909** W.E.B. DuBois helps found National Association for the Advancement of Colored People (NAACP)

1910 to 1919

World	United States
1911 Beginning of the Mexican revolution; first U.S. intervention in Nicaragua **1914** Beginning of World War I; opening of the Panama Canal **1915** German U-Boat sinks the *Lusitania* **1916** Denmark cedes the U.S. Virgin Islands **1916-17** Mexican Border Campaign **1917** Germany declares unrestricted submarine warfare; Zimmerman Telegram; U.S. declares war on the Central Powers; beginning of Russia's Bolshevik revolution **1918** U.S. troops fight in France; armistice ends WWI; Wilson announces his Fourteen Points **1919** The U.S. Senate rejects the Treaty of Versailles	**1912** Woodrow Wilson defeats Taft, Theodore Roosevelt, and Eugene Debs for the presidency **1916** Wilson, promising to keep the United States out of the war, wins second term; National Park Service is established **1917** 18th Amendment passes, prohibiting the manufacturing and sale of alcoholic beverages **1918** Sedition Act; Eugene Debs is imprisoned **1919** Red Scare and Palmer Raids begin; Chicago race riot

1920 to 1929

World	United States
1921-22 Washington Armament Conference **1922** Mussolini takes power in Italy **1924** Dawes Plan rearranges German reparations payments **1928** Kellogg-Briand Treaty outlaws war as an instrument of national policy	**1920** Warren Harding is elected president; 19th Amendment guarantees women's right to vote **1921** Congress establishes first immigration quotas **1923** President Harding dies; exposure of Teapot Dome and other scandals involving Harding **1924** Congress extends citizenship to all Indians **1925** Scopes Monkey trial in Dayton, Tennessee **1927** Execution of Sacco and Vanzetti

1930 to 1939

World	United States
1931 Japan invades Manchuria **1933** Hitler seizes power in Germany **1935** Italy invades Ethiopia **1937** Japan invades China **1939** Germany annexes the rest of Czechoslovakia and invades Poland; beginning of WWI	**1932** Franklin D. Roosevelt elected president **1933** First New Deal **1934** Indian Reorganization Act **1937** Roosevelt's Court Packing plan thwarted

1940 to 1949

World	United States
1941 Germany invades Soviet Union; Japan attacks Pearl Harbor; United States enters WWII **1942** Pacific Battles of Coral Sea and Midway; beginning of Operation Torch in North Africa **1943** Soviets defeat the Germans in Stalingrad; German Afrika Korps surrenders in Tunisia; allied invasion of Italy; Teheran Conference **1944** Liberation of Paris **1945** Yalta Conference; surrender of Germany; Potsdam Conference; U.S. drops atomic bombs on Hiroshima and Nagasaki; Japan surrenders **1946** Churchill's Iron Curtain speech **1948** State of Israel is founded; Berlin Crisis **1948-49** Berlin Airlift **1949** NATO forms; Communists assume power in China	**1940** Franklin Roosevelt elected to third term; Selective Service and Training Act passed **1941** A. Philip Randolph organizes the March on Washington movement **1942** Internment of Japanese Americans; Congress of Racial Equality (CORE) established **1943** Race riots in Detroit and Los Angeles **1944** Roosevelt elected to fourth term **1945** Roosevelt dies in office; Truman becomes president **1947** Marshall Plan proposed; Truman Doctrine; HUAC hearings in Hollywood **1948** Whittaker Chambers names Alger Hiss as fellow Soviet spy; Truman desegregates the military **1949** Truman announces Fair Deal

Society, Culture, and Religion	Labor, Industry, and Economy	Science and Technology
1900 Theodore Dreiser publishes *Sister Carrie* **1902** Lincoln Steffans publishes *The Shame of the Cities* **1903** Jack London publishes *The Call of the Wild*, W.E.B. DuBois publishes *The Souls of Black Folk*	**1900** U.S. commits to gold standard with the Currency Act **1902** National coal strike **1906** Upton Sinclair's *The Jungle* exposes working conditions at the Chicago stockyards **1907** Panic of 1907	**1903** Wright brothers launch the first successful manned flight in Kittyhawk, N.C. **1905** Albert Einstein develops his special theory of relativity $E=mc^2$ **1908** Henry Ford produces the first Model T automobile
1915 Release of D.W. Griffith's *Birth of a Nation* **1916** Norman Rockwell first illustrates the cover of *The Saturday Evening Post* **1917** Race riot in East St. Louis, Illinois **1919-30** Harlem Renaissance	**1912** "Bread and Roses" strike in Lawrence, Massachusetts **1914** Clayton Anti-Trust Act, Ford establishes $5 workday **1916** Adamson Act establishes 8-hour day for railroad workers; Keating-Owen Act bars products of child labor from interstate commerce **1918** National War Labor Board is established **1919** Steel strike begins	**1911** Robert Millikan measures the electrical charge of an electron **1913** Margaret Sanger begins advocating for birth control
1925 F. Scott Fitzgerald publishes *The Great Gatsby* **1926** Ernest Hemingway publishes *The Sun Also Rises* **1927** Babe Ruth hits his 60th home run, Willa Cather publishes *Death Comes for the Archbishop*	**1923** Supreme Court overturns the law limiting women's working hours **1929** New York Stock Exchange crashes	**1925** Albert Michelson measures the speed of light **1927** Charles Lindbergh's solo flight from New York to Paris
1930 Edward Hopper paints "Early Sunday Morning" **1933** Gertrude Stein publishes *The Autobiography of Alice B. Toklas* **1934** Shirley Temple stars in *Bright Eyes*	**1930s** Great Depression **1932** Bonus March on Washington **1934** General strike in San Francisco **1935** Social Security Act passed **1938** Formation of Congress of Industrial Organizations; Fair Labor Standards Act	**1933** Aldo Leopold publishes *Game Management* **1935** Anthropologist Ruth Benedict publishes *Patterns of Culture*
1941 Henry Luce forecasts the dawn of the "American Century" **1943** Rodgers and Hammerstein produce *Oklahoma!* **1944** Aaron Copland composes the ballet; *Appalachian Spring* **1945** Igor Stravinsky composes *Symphony in Three Movements* **1947** Jackie Robinson becomes the first African-American major league baseball player **1949** William Faulkner wins the Nobel Prize for Literature	**1941** Roosevelt forms the Fair Employment Practices Committee **1943** Coal miners strike **1945** Union membership reaches an all-time high of 14.8 million **1946** United Mine Workers' strike **1947** Taft-Hartley (Labor-Management Relations) Act **1948** General Motors agrees to the first sliding-wage-scale contract	**1942** Beginning of the Manhattan Project to create the atomic bomb **1943** Selman Waksman discovers streptomycin, an antibiotic that cures tuberculosis **1944** Robert B. Woodward synthesizes quinine **1945** First atomic bomb is detonated at Alamogordo, N.M. **1946** Richard Evelyn Byrd leads an expedition to the South Pole **1947** Edwin Land invents the Polaroid instant camera

Era of the Superpowers: 1950–1998

World	United States
World Events and Foreign Wars	**Politics**

	World Events and Foreign Wars	Politics
1950 to 1959	**1950** Beginning of the Korean War **1953** Armistice agreement in Korea **1954** Siege of Dien Bien Phu; French withdraw from Vietnam; the CIA overthrows the Guatemalan government **1956** Fidel Castro leads guerrilla forces into Cuba to overthrow the dictatorship of Fulgencio Batista **1957** Israel withdraws its forces from the Gaza Strip and Sinai Peninsula	**1950** Sen. Joseph McCarthy begins his crusade against communists **1951** General MacArthur is dismissed by President Truman **1952** Dwight D. Eisenhower becomes president **1954** Brown v. Board of Education (Supreme Court orders school desegregation); United States explodes first hydrogen bomb; Army-McCarthy hearings **1956** Foundation of the Southern Christian Leadership Conference (SCLC); Montgomery, Alabama, bus boycott ends successfully **1957** President Eisenhower sends the National Guard to desegregate Little Rock High School
1960 to 1969	**1960** U2 Incident **1962** Cuban Missile Crisis **1964** Gulf of Tonkin Resolution escalates the Vietnam War **1965** Mobutu Sese Seko assumes power in Zaire (the Congo); India and Pakistan fight for control of Kashmir **1966-69** Cultural Revolution in China **1968** Tet Offensive in South Vietnam **1969** Yasir Arafat becomes leader of the Palestine Liberation Organization	**1960** John F. Kennedy elected president; foundation of the Student Nonviolent Coordinating Committee (SNCC) **1963** Assassination of President Kennedy **1964** Civil Rights Act **1965** Malcolm X is assassinated **1966** Formation of the Black Panthers; National Organization for Women (NOW) is established **1968** Lyndon B. Johnson withdraws his candidacy for president; Martin Luther King and Robert Kennedy are assassinated
1970 to 1979	**1970** U.S. incursion into Cambodia **1972** President Nixon visits the Soviet Union and China **1973** Signing of the Vietnam cease-fire; OPEC forms **1975** Khmer Rouge seize control of Cambodia **1979** Iran Hostage Crisis	**1970** Shooting of Kent State student protesters **1971** Alaska Native Claims Settlement Act **1973** Roe v. Wade, AIM (American Indian Movement) occupies Wounded Knee; Watergate congressional hearings **1974** House Judiciary Committee votes to impeach Nixon; Nixon resigns; Ford pardons Nixon **1975** Indian Self-Determination Act **1976** Jimmy Carter elected president
1980 to 1989	**1981** Egyptian president Anwar Sadat assassinated **1982** Great Britain defeats Argentina in war over Falkland Islands **1983** U.S.-led international force invades Grenada to halt Cuban influence **1985** Mikhail Gorbachev begins glasnost and perestroika in the U.S.S.R. **1986** Corazon Aquino defeats Philippine President Ferdinand Marcos in popular elections **1989** United States invades Panama, overthrows regime of General Noriega; Communism collapses in Eastern Europe	**1982** The Equal Rights Amendment (ERA) dies, three votes short of passage **1983** Congressional committee condemns WWII internment of Japanese Americans and recommends compensation **1985** Ake v. Oklahoma **1987** Iran-Contra hearings
1990-1997	**1990-91** Persian Gulf War **1991** Croatia and Slovenia declare independence (Yugoslavia disintegrates) **1994** Rwandan refugees flee to Zaire; Mexican peasant revolt in Chiapas; Russian Army invades Chechnya **1995** UN Fourth World Conference on Women in Beijing **1997** Hong Kong reverts to Chinese rule	**1992** Rodney King verdict incites race riots in Los Angeles; Democrat Bill Clinton defeats George Bush for president **1993** Clinton introduces controversial policy permitting homosexuals to serve in military **1995** Million Man March **1996** Clinton reelected, defeating Robert Dole **1997** Congress and President Clinton agree on five-year plan to balance the budget

Society, Culture, and Religion	Labor, Industry, and Economy	Science and Technology
1951 Willem de Kooning paints *Night Square* **1952** Flannery O'Connor publishes *Wise Blood* **1953** Arthur Miller publishes *The Crucible* **1955** Marian Anderson becomes first black person to sing at Metropolitan Opera **1956** Allen Ginsberg publishes *Howl* **1957** Debut of Jerome Robbins's *West Side Story*	**1952** AFL and CIO endorse Adlai Stevenson for president **1955** Merger of AFL and CIO **1957** Teamsters vice president James Hoffa charged with misappropriation of funds	**1953** Alfred Kinsey publishes *Sexual Behavior in the Human Female* **1954** The USS *Nautilus*, the first atomic-powered ship, is launched **1955** Gregory Pincus develops a successful birth control pill; Jonas Salk creates a vaccine for polio
1961 John Steinbeck publishes *The Winter of Our Discontent* **1962** Andy Warhol paints *Green Coca Cola Bottles;* Students for a Democratic Society's (SDS) Port Huron Statement **1963** Martin Luther King, Jr. writes "Letter from Birmingham Jail"; Betty Friedan publishes *The Feminine Mystique* **1964** Cassius Clay (Muhammed Ali) wins the heavyweight boxing title **1969** Woodstock rock festival	**1962-63** Longshoremen's strike ties up shipping at East Coast and Gulf Coast ports **1964** Economic Opportunity Act **1965** César Chavez leads the farm workers strike in San Joaquin Valley **1966** First New York City transit strike	**1962** Rachel Carson publishes *Silent Spring* **1963** Robert B. Woodward synthesizes colchicine, a pain reliever for gout sufferers **1965** Edward White becomes the first man to walk in space **1969** American Neil Armstrong is the first man on the moon
1971 *Pentagon Papers* case; Neil Simon writes *The Prisoner of Second Avenue* **1972** Gloria Steinem founds *Ms.* magazine **1974** Hank Aaron hits his 715th home run, breaking Babe Ruth's record **1976** Writer and cultural critic Thomas Wolfe announces the "Me Decade" **1979** Norman Mailer publishes *The Executioner's Song*	**1973** Alaska oil pipeline construction begins **1975** 2,000 interns and residents strike at 21 New York City metropolitan hospitals **1978** New York newspaper strike shuts down *The New York Times, New York Daily News,* and *New York Post*	**1970** Linus Pauling suggests that Vitamin C might prevent the common cold and the flu **1972** Underground nuclear test on the Alaska island of Amchitka **1976** First Concorde supersonic jet service between the United States and Europe
1981 MTV and CNN start broadcasting **1982** Alice Walker publishes *The Color Purple* **1987** Jim Bakker leaves TV evangelism amid financial and sexual scandals **1989** Director Spike Lee releases *Do the Right Thing*	**1986** Hormel meat workers in Minnesota end a year-long strike **1987** Stock market crashes **1988** End of a 22-week strike by movie and television writers	**1981** First space shuttle *Columbia* is launched **1986** Space shuttle *Challenger* explodes **1988** Aspirin is found to reduce the risk of heart attacks **1989** The tanker *Exxon Valdez* causes the largest oil spill in U.S. history in the Gulf of Alaska
1993 Toni Morrison wins the Nobel Prize for Literature; film producer Steven Spielberg releases *Jurassic Park* and *Schindler's List* **1994** Richard Herrnstein and Charles Murray publish controversial book, *The Bell Curve* **1995** Oklahoma City bombing kills 168 **1997** *Titanic* establishes new movie box-office record	**1990** Coal miners in Virginia end a strike and agree to a new contract after the Department of Labor intervenes **1993** Congress approves NAFTA **1994** United Airlines employees buy controlling interest in the company; Teamsters end bitter strike **1998** Booming economy pushes Dow-Jones average above 9,000	**1991** Hewlett-Packard introduces a hand-held lightweight computer **1993** The internet links close to 30 million people in 137 countries through computers; George Washington University Medical Center reports cloning of human embryos **1998** India resumes nuclear testing

Illustration Credits

1 Courtesy of Atlanta Braves
3 Library of Congress
4 National Portrait Gallery, Smithsonian Institution
5, 6, 7 Library of Congress
8 Wallace Kirkland
10 New York State Department of Commerce
11 Merkle Press
13 U.S. Army Military History Institute
23 U.S. Air Force Academy
24, 26, 29, 37 Library of Congress
38 U.S. Army Military History Institute
40, 42 Library of Congress
47 U.S. Army Military History Institute
49, 54, 56 Library of Congress
65 New York City Ballet; Library of Congress
66 Bob Adelman
68 Wells Fargo Bank
71 Library of Congress
74 U.S. Information Agency
75 Courtesy of The American National Red Cross
76 National Archives
79 U.S. Army Military History Institute
81, 86, 89 Library of Congress
97 Kansas State Historical Society, Topeka
99 Columbia University
101, 103 Library of Congress
106 Boy Scouts of America
108 Library of Congress
111 U.S. Army Military History Institute
113, 114 Library of Congress
115 National Film Board of Canada
116 U.S. Army Military History Institute
117, 119 Library of Congress
120 The White House
127, 128 Library of Congress
129 Wells Fargo Bank
136 Library of Congress
137 Associated Photographers
139 Library of Congress; The White House
141, 145, 147, 152 Library of Congress
154 American HeritageóHarpers Weekly
157 Library of Congress
162 United Press International
163 Culver Pictures
166, 167, 169, 171, 173, 174 Library of Congress
175 The White House
178 The Buffalo Bill Historical Center, Cody, Wyoming
187, 193 Library of Congress
209 CBS News Photo
210, 211, 217, 218, 223 Library of Congress
225 U.S. Air Force
228, 229, 232 Library of Congress
234 U.S. Air Force
235 U.S. Army Military History Institute
237, 238 Library of Congress
250 Columbia University

251 Harper & Row
252 American Heritage
256 Walt Disney Productions
257, 260 Library of Congress
261 National Archives
262, 264 Library of Congress
265 National Archives
267 Library of Congress
269 National Archives; NYPL Lincoln Center
270 Courtesy of David C. Duniway
271, 273, 276, 277, 280 Library of Congress
281 National Archives
284 U.S. Army Military History Institute
285, 288 Library of Congress
293 Rare Books Room, NY Public Library
301 University of Mississippi
302, 309, 311, 316, 317, 320, 330 Library of Congress
331 U.S. Army Center of Military History
332, 336, 340, 342, 343, 344, 349, 350 Library of Congress
351 Wide World Photos
354, 355, 360, 364 Library of Congress
367 National Archives
370 Library of Congress
373 U.S. Department of Agriculture
375 Culver Pictures
379, 380 Library of Congress
381 Museum of Modern Art/Film Stills Archive
382 Library of Congress
385 Courtesy of Marjorie Guthrie
388 Library of Congress
391 Bibliothèque Nationale (Paris)
392, 395 Library of Congress
396 U.S. Army Military History Institute
398, 399 Library of Congress
402 Helen Breaker, Paris
408 Atomic Energy Commission
411 Culver Pictures
413 Library of Congress
415 Herbert Hoover Presidential Library
420 Library of Congress; Underwood-Bettmann
423, 429 Library of Congress
430 National Archives
431, 434, 443 Library of Congress
445 U.S. Army Military History Institute
462, 465 Library of Congress
467 National Archives
468 Library of Congress
470 National Archives
472 Los Angeles County Museum of Natural History
474 Duke Ellington, Inc.
475 New York City Art Commission
479 Library of Congress
481 The White House
483 The Kobal Collection
485 Smithsonian Institution National Anthropological Archives
492 John F. Kennedy Library

495 World Team Tennis
496 AP/Wide World Photos
498 Library of Congress
504 United Nations
506, 517 Library of Congress
520 League of Women Voters Education Fund
522 Library of Congress
525 National Archives
531 Library of Congress
541 World Wide Photos
542 Library of Congress
545 International News Photos
547 National Archives
551 Mount Holyoke College
553 U.S. Army
555, 559, 561 Library of Congress
564 United Press International
570 National Archives
571, 574 Library of Congress
576, 578 National Archives
581 New York National League Baseball Club
582 The American Museum of Natural History
585, 588 Library of Congress
589 United Farm Workers of America
590, 591 U.S. Military Academy Archives
595 U.S. Navy
600 Library of Congress
607 U.S. Army
609, 611, 612 Library of Congress
613 United Artists
616 Viking Press
617 Morgan Bank
621, 624 Library of Congress
626 Drake Well Museum
629 CBS News
632 Library of Congress
636 National Park Service
650 Library of Congress
653 National Archives
662 Library of Congress
676 The White House
681 Courtesy of the Institute for Advanced Study
686 Culver Pictures
689 Union Pacific Railroad Museum Collection
691 Library of Congress
695 U.S. Signal Corps
697 U.S. Army Military History Institute
699 U.S. Military Academy Archives
701 Peace Corps
702 U.S. Navy
704, 707 Library of Congress
708 National Archives
709 U.S. Army
710 Library of Congress
711 Drake Museum
713 U.S. Army Military History Institute
716 Library of Congress
717 Independence Hall
721 Library of Congress
725 Courtesy of the American Antiquarian Society
732 Library of Congress
742 U.S. Navy

743 U.S. Geological Survey
747 Library of Congress
752 National Archives
756 The Kansas State Historical Society, Topeka
759 New Mexico Department of Development
761 Library of Congress
769, 770 Union Pacific Railroad Museum Collection
772, 773 Library of Congress
774 Karl Schumacher, The White House
779 Smithsonian Institution National Anthropological Archives
785 Library of Congress
789 U.S. Army Military History Institute
795 Library of Congress
802 Courtesy of the Brooklyn Dodgers
804 Library of Congress
807 Will Rogers Memorial Commission, Claremore, Oklahoma
809, 812, 813 Library of Congress
818 Massillon Museum
820 National Archives
824 Library of Congress
826 U.S. Army Signal Corps
827, 828 Library of Congress
834, 837 U.S. Army
855 U.S. Army Military History Institute
856, 862, 867, 868, 869, 873 Library of Congress
883 National Aeronautics and Space Administration
885, 892, 894 Library of Congress
895 Viking Press
900, 901 Library of Congress
903 B & O Railroad Museum
904, 906 Library of Congress
909 Oregon Historical Society
913 Library of Congress
915 National Archives
921, 923, 924, 927, 928 Library of Congress
931 CBS News
932 RCA News
946 Library of Congress
947 Cumberland County Historical Society
957 National Archives
958 Sophia Smith Collection, Smith College
960, 961, 962 Library of Congress
971 National Portrait Gallery, Smithsonian Institution
973 Library of Congress
978 National Archives
988, 993 Library of Congress
994 National Archives
996, 998 Library of Congress
1004 Library of Congress
1010 U.S. Military Academy Archives
1011, 1016 Library of Congress
1020 Sam Shaw, courtesy of New Directions Publishing Corporation
1022, 1023, 1024, 1027 Library of Congress
1029 U.S. Navy
1031, 1037 Library of Congress
1039 U.S. Army Signal Corps
1042 U.S. Coast Guard
1046 Smithsonian Institution, Bureau of American Ethnology
1047, 1048 Library of Congress
1053 Franklin D. Roosevelt Library
1055, 1056 Library of Congress

■ INDEX

Page numbers that appear in boldface type
   indicate the main entry for the subject.